20°E 40°E 60°E 80°E 100°E 120°E 140°E 160°E 180°

ARCTIC OCEAN

80°N

60°N

URAL MTS.

Ob

Volga

40°N

EUROPE

ALPS

ASIA

GOBI DESERT

HINDU KUSH

HIMALAYA MTS.

Indus

Ganges

Yangtze

SYRIAN
DESERT

AHARA

Nile

AFRICA

DECCAN
PLATEAU

Tropic of Cancer

20°N

PACIFIC OCEAN

Equator   0°

INDIAN OCEAN

NAMIB DESERT

KALAHARI
DESERT

GREAT
SANDY
DESERT

20°S

Tropic of Capricorn

AUSTRALIA

Cape of
Good Hope

0   1000   2000   3000 Km.

0   1000   2000   3000 Mi.

60°S

Antarctic Circle

ANTARCTICA

80°S

180°

A HISTORY OF WORLD SOCIETIES

Senior Sponsoring Editor: Patricia A. Coryell
Senior Associate Editor: Jeffrey Greene
Manufacturing Manager: Florence Cadran
Marketing Manager: Clint Crockett

Printed in the U.S.A.
Library of Congress Catalog Card Number: 95-76958
ISBN Student Text: 0-395-75377-5
ISBN Examination Copy: 0-395-76588-9
  23456789-VH-99 98 97 96

FOURTH EDITION

A HISTORY OF WORLD SOCIETIES

John P. McKay

University of Illinois at Urbana-Champaign

Bennett D. Hill

Georgetown University

John Buckler

University of Illinois at Urbana-Champaign

HOUGHTON MIFFLIN COMPANY

Boston   Toronto
Geneva, Illinois   Palo Alto
Princeton, New Jersey

❖ About the Authors

John P. McKay Born in St. Louis, Missouri, John P. McKay received his B.A. from Wesleyan University (1961), his M.A. from the Fletcher School of Law and Diplomacy (1962), and his Ph.D. from the University of California, Berkeley (1968). He began teaching history at the University of Illinois in 1966 and became a professor there in 1976. John won the Herbert Baxter Adams Prize for his book *Pioneers for Profit: Foreign Entrepreneurship and Russian Industrialization, 1885–1913* (1970). He has also written *Tramways and Trolleys: The Rise of Urban Mass Transit in Europe* (1976) and has translated Jules Michelet's *The People* (1973). His research has been supported by fellowships from the Ford Foundation, the Guggenheim Foundation, the National Endowment for the Humanities, and IREX. His articles and reviews have appeared in numerous journals, including *The American Historical Review, Business History Review, The Journal of Economic History,* and *Slavic Review.* He edits *Industrial Development and the Social Fabric: An International Series of Historical Monographs.*

Bennett D. Hill A native of Philadelphia, Bennett D. Hill earned an A.B. at Princeton (1956) and advanced degrees from Harvard (A.M., 1958) and Princeton (Ph.D., 1963). He taught history at the University of Illinois at Urbana, where he was department chairman from 1978 to 1981. He has published *English Cistercian Monasteries and Their Patrons in the Twelfth Century* (1968) and *Church and State in the Middle Ages* (1970); and articles in *Analecta Cisterciensia, The New Catholic Encyclopaedia, The American Benedictine Review,* and *The Dictionary of the Middle Ages.* His reviews have appeared in *The American Historical Review, Speculum, The Historian, The Catholic Historical Review,* and *Library Journal.* He has been a fellow of the American Council of Learned Societies and has served on committees for the National Endowment for the Humanities. Now a Benedictine monk of St. Anselm's Abbey, Washington, D.C., he is also a Visiting Professor at Georgetown University.

John Buckler Born in Louisville, Kentucky, John Buckler received his B.A. (*summa cum laude*) from the University of Louisville in 1967. Harvard University awarded him the Ph.D. in 1973. From 1984 to 1986 he was an Alexander von Humboldt Fellow at the Institut für Alte Geschichte, University of Munich. He has lectured at the Fondation Hardt at the University of Geneva, and has participated in numerous international conferences. He is currently the professor of Greek history at the University of Illinois. In 1980 Harvard University Press published his *The Theban Hegemony, 371–362 B.C.* He has also published *Philip II and the Sacred War* (Leiden 1989), and co-edited *BOIOTIKA: Vorträge vom 5. International Böotien-Kolloquium* (Munich 1989). He has assisted the National Endowment for the Humanities, and reviews articles for journals in the United States and Europe. He has published substantially on Plutarch in *Aufstieg und Niedergang der römischen Welt* (Berlin, New York. 1992). His articles have appeared in journals both here and abroad, including the *American Journal of History, Classical Philology, Rheinisches Museum für Philologie, Classical Quarterly, Wiener Studien, Symbolae Osloenses,* and many others.

Contents in Brief

Contents

❋ CHAPTER 1

❋ CHAPTER 2

Maps

Timelines/Genealogies

* The comparative timeline, *A History of World Societies: A Brief Overview,* begins on page 1232.

Listening to the Past

Preface

A History of World Societies has grown out of our desire to infuse new life into the study of world civilization. We know full well that historians are using imaginative questions and innovative research to open up vast new areas of historical interest and knowledge. We recognize that these advances have dramatically affected economic, intellectual, and, especially, social history, and that new research and fresh interpretations are revitalizing the study of traditional, mainstream political, diplomatic, and religious developments. Despite history's vitality as a discipline, however, it seems to us that both the broad public and the intelligentsia have been losing interest in the past.

It is our conviction, based on considerable experience in introducing large numbers of students to the broad sweep of civilization, that a book reflecting current trends can excite readers and inspire a renewed interest in history and the human experience. Our strategy has been twofold.

First, we have made social history the core element of our work. We not only incorporate recent research by social historians but also seek to re-create the life of ordinary people in appealing human terms. A strong social element seems especially appropriate in a world history, for identification with ordinary people of the past allows today's reader to reach an empathetic understanding of different cultures and civilizations. At the same time we have been mindful of the need to give great economic, political, intellectual, and cultural developments the attention they deserve. We want to give individual students and instructors a balanced, integrated perspective so that they can pursue on their own or in the classroom those themes and questions that they find particularly exciting and significant.

Second, we have made every effort to strike an effective global balance. We are acutely aware of the great drama of our times—the passing of the era of Western dominance and the simultaneous rise of Asian and African peoples in world affairs. Increasingly, the whole world interacts, and to understand that interaction and what it means for today's citizens, we must study the whole world's history. Thus we have adopted a comprehensive yet manageable global perspective. We study all geographical areas and the world's main civilizations, conscious of their separate identities and unique contributions. We also stress the links between civilizations, for it is these links that have been transforming multicentered world history into the complex interactive process of different continents, peoples, and cultures that we see today.

CHANGES IN THE FOURTH EDITION

In preparing the fourth edition, we worked hard to keep *A History of World Societies* up-to-date and to strengthen our distinctive yet balanced approach. Six goals shaped our plan for this new edition.

More Concise Treatment of Western History

To achieve the optimal length, we shortened the text by approximately 10 percent overall. We accomplished this reduction primarily through cuts in Western-oriented material while adding important new information to our non-Western coverage. Thus the proportion of non-Western material has grown, but the overall length of the book has decreased. For this edition, two chapters on Rome were combined into one (Chapter 7), three chapters on medieval Europe were combined into two (Chapters 12 and 13), and three chapters on nineteenth-century Europe were combined into two (Chapters 25 and 26).

Updated Approach to Social History

In a thorough revision of our coverage of social developments we give greater attention to cultural and intellectual life and somewhat less to quantitative and demographic aspects. Increased emphasis on culture and attitudes invigorates our social history core and accurately reflects current scholarship and changing interests within the historical profession. Accordingly, this edition has expanded discussions of religious life, including the spread of Buddhism in ancient India (Chapter 3); popular religion in Mesopotamia (Chapter 1), in classical Greece (Chapter 5), in Aztec and Inca society (Chapter 14), and in revolutionary France (Chapter 23); the evolution of Jewish religion (Chapter 2), of Eastern monasticism (Chapter 8), and of Calvin's Geneva (Chapter 15); and the resurgence of Christianity (Chapter 31) and of Islam (Chapter 34) in the twentieth century.

Consistently greater attention to popular culture includes new sections on the experiences of Jews under Islam and Christianity (Chapter 9); on the cult of the royal mummies in Inca society (Chapter 14); on troubadour poets and recreation in the Middle Ages (Chapters 12 and 13); on community values in eighteenth-century Europe (Chapter 19); on Chinese attitudes toward wealth and consumption (Chapter 22); and on the counterculture in the 1960s (Chapter 33). New material on health and health care features recent research on medieval European practices and early hospitals (Chapter 12), on eighteenth-century practitioners in Europe (Chapter 19) and the Ottoman Empire (Chapter 21), and on declining birthrates in Asia and Latin America (Chapter 36).

Interactions between cultures are also highlighted: the relations between Egyptians and Nubians (Chapter 1), pagans and Christians (Chapter 7), Muslims and Jews (Chapter 9), European educated elites and popular classes (Chapters 18 and 19), Europeans and Africans in the slave trade (Chapter 20), Chinese and foreigners in the eighteenth century (Chapter 22), and rich and poor nations since 1945 (Chapter 36).

We also carefully revised sections on the life of the people to set social developments consistently in their broad historical context.

Incorporation of Recent Scholarship

We carefully revised every chapter to reflect recent scholarship. Because we are committed to a balanced approach, we once again incorporated important new findings on political, economic, and intellectual developments. Revisions of this nature include material on the Babylonian Captivity (Chapter 2), the spread of Buddhism in India (Chapter 3), living patterns in neolithic China (Chapter 4), democratic ideology in Athens and the political background of Plato and Aristotle's thought (Chapter 5), and Roman commerce and frontier relations between Romans and Germans (Chapter 7). Similar revisions in Chapter 8 through 17 incorporate new material on Islamic education in world perspective (Chapter 9), African geography (Chapter 10), the origins of European feudalism (Chapter 12), the Aztec practice of human sacrifice (Chapter 14), the political uses of pornography in early modern Europe (Chapter 15), and Louis XIV's relations with the nobility (Chapter 17).

There is important new material reflecting recent scholarship on the cultural impact of the Enlightenment (Chapters 18 and 19); the Swahili states and transatlantic slave trade (Chapter 20); the institutions of the Mughal state under Akbar (Chapter 21); Chinese foreign policy under the Qing (Chapter 22); banks in continental industrialization and the early labor movement (Chapter 24); the role of class conflict in nineteenth-century domestic politics, imperialism, and the origins of World War I (Chapters 26, 27, and 29); educational reforms and political culture in republican France (Chapter 26); the idea of race in the United States (Chapter 28); Nietzsche and his influence (Chapter 31); the Nazi state and the origins of Italian fascism (Chapter 32); and the growing diversity of life in the Third World (Chapter 35). Recent developments in Europe and the Western Hemisphere (Chapter 33) and in Asia and Africa, especially in China and South Africa (Chapter 34), are examined from an updated post–cold war perspective.

In short, recent research keeps the broad sweep of our history fresh and up-to-date.

Integrated Treatment of Women and Gender

We broadened our treatment of women's history and gender issues and integrated it into the main narrative rather than reserving it for separate sections. This approach reflects current scholarly thinking. Our updated discussion of Hellenistic women is integrated in the central narrative (Chapter 5). Gender roles and attitudes toward divorce are considered in the context of early Islam (Chapter 9). New material on European women in agriculture and commerce during the Middle Ages (Chapters 12 and 13), on gender roles in Aztec society (Chapter 14) and in early European arts and letters (Chapter 16), on women in the Ottoman Empire (Chapter 21), and on Japanese women in agriculture and family relations (Chapter 22) are appropriately positioned. Elite women and peasant women in village communities are reconsidered in the context of the Enlightenment (Chapters 18 and 19) and the French Revolution (Chapter 23). Women in twentieth-century European dictatorships are compared systematically (Chapter 32), and the place of women in Third World economic development and population growth is stressed (Chapter 35).

New "Problems of Historical Interpretation"

The addition of more "problems of historical interpretation" in the third edition was well received, so we increased their number in the fourth. We believe that the problematic element helps students develop the critical-thinking skills that are among the most precious benefits of studying history. New examples of this more open-ended, interpretive approach include the debate over the origins of Rome (Chapter 7), the impact of the Renaissance on the lives of ordinary and elite women (Chapter 15), the motives and legacy of Christopher Columbus (Chapter 16), popular reading habits in eighteenth-century Europe and their significance (Chapter 19), the question of racial identity in the United States and how it developed (Chapter 28), European social tensions and the origins of World War I (Chapter 29), the nature of twentieth-century dictatorships (Chapter 32), the validity of *Third World* as an analytical concept (Chapter 35), and prospects for the United Nations and world government (Chapter 36).

Revised Full-Color Art and Map Programs

Because the past can speak in pictures as well as in words, artwork remains an integral part of our book, and the illustrative component of our work was carefully revised. We added many new illustrations—our art program includes nearly two hundred color reproductions—letting great art and important events come alive. As in earlier editions, all illustrations were carefully selected to complement the text, and all carry captions that enhance their value. The use of full color throughout this edition clarifies the maps and graphs and enriches the textual material. The maps and their captions have been updated.

DISTINCTIVE FEATURES

Distinctive features, both new and revised, guide the reader in the process of historical understanding. Many of these features also show how historians sift through and evaluate evidence. Our goal is to suggest how historians actually work and think. We want the reader to think critically and to realize that history is neither a list of cut-and-dried facts nor a senseless jumble of conflicting opinions.

New Primary-Source Chapter Feature

One of our goals is to show how historians sift through and evaluate evidence—to suggest how historians actually work and think. We want to encourage students to think critically and to realize that history is neither a list of cut-and-dried facts nor a senseless jumble of conflicting opinions. To help students come to this realization, at the end of each chapter in the fourth edition we added a two-page passage from a primary source. This important new feature, entitled "Listening to the Past," extends and illuminates a major historical issue considered in the chapter. For example, in Chapter 3, a selection from the *Mahabharta* tells an ancient Indian creation story; and in Chapter 6, a selection from *Plutarch's Lives* recounts the sacrifice of a famous queen for her people. Chapter 12 presents a mind-opening Arab account of the First Crusade, and the German traveler Olearius provides a fascinating and influential picture of the Russian state and society in Chapter 17. A report on discussions with Africans concerning the abolition of the slave trade is found in Chapter 20, and a Jesuit priest's report on a trip to the Mughal court of Akbar is featured in Chapter

21. Writer Stephan Zweig probes the sexuality of young men and women in nineteenth-century Vienna in Chapter 26, and a reporter witnesses the bloody climax to Gandhi's civil disobedience in Chapter 30. A Jewish doctor who survived Auschwitz describes the horror of the Nazi death camps in Chapter 32, and poor rural women in today's Third World tell their stories in Chapter 35.

Each "Listening to the Past" section opens with a problem-setting introduction and closes with "Questions for Analysis" that invite students to evaluate the evidence as historians would. Drawn from writings addressing a variety of social, cultural, political, and intellectual issues, these sources promote active involvement and critical interpretation. Selected for their interest and importance and carefully fitted into their historical context, these sources do indeed allow students to listen to the past and to observe how history has been shaped by individual men and women, some of them great aristocrats, others ordinary folk.

Improved Chapter Features

Distinctive features from earlier editions have been retained but improved. To help guide students toward historical understanding, we again pose specific questions at the beginning of each chapter. These questions are answered in the course of each chapter, and each chapter ends with a concise summary. We re-examined and revised the questions and summaries to maximize their usefulness.

Once again in the narrative itself we quote extensively from a wide variety of primary sources, demonstrating in our use of these quotations how historians evaluate evidence. Thus the examination of primary sources is not only highlighted in the "Listening to the Past" material but is an integral part of the narrative as well. We believe that such extensive quotation from primary sources will help students learn to interpret and think critically.

Each chapter again contains an annotated listing of suggestions for further reading. Brief descriptions of each work will help readers know where to turn to continue thinking and learning about specific topics. These bibliographies have been revised and updated.

Revised Timelines

The chapter timelines that appeared in earlier editions are substantially improved, and the comparative timelines that were dispersed throughout the

third edition have been brought together in an appendix at the end of the book. Comprehensive and easy to locate, this useful timeline will allow students to compare simultaneous political, economic, social, cultural, intellectual, and scientific developments over the centuries.

Flexible Format

World history courses differ widely in chronological structure from one campus to another. To accommodate the various divisions of historical time into intervals that fit a two-quarter, three-quarter, or two-semester period, *A History of World Societies* is published in three versions that embrace the complete work:

- One-volume hardcover edition: *A History of World Societies*
- Two-volume paperback edition: *A History of World Societies*, Volume 1, *To 1715* (Chapters 1–17), and Volume 2, *Since 1500* (Chapters 16–36)
- Three-volume paperback edition: *A History of World Societies*, Volume A, *From Antiquity Through the Middle Ages* (Chapters 1–14), Volume B, *From 1100 Through the French Revolution* (Chapters 13–23), and Volume C, *From the French Revolution to the Present* (Chapters 23–36)

Overlapping chapters in the two-volume and three-volume editions facilitate matching the appropriate volume with the opening and closing dates of a specific course.

Ancillaries

Our learning and teaching ancillaries enhance the usefulness of the textbook:

- *Study Guide*
- *Computerized Study Guide*
- *Instructor's Resource Manual*
- *Test Items*
- *Computerized Test Items*
- *Map Transparencies*

The excellent *Study Guide* has been thoroughly revised by Professor James Schmiechen of Central Michigan University. Professor Schmiechen has been a tower of strength ever since he critiqued our initial prospectus, and he has continued to give us many valuable suggestions as well as his warmly appreciated support. His *Study Guide* contains learning objectives, chapter summaries, chapter outlines, review questions, extensive multiple-choice exercises, self-check lists of important concepts and events, and a variety of study aids and suggestions. The fourth edition also retains the study-review exercises on the interpretation of visual sources and major political ideas as well as suggested issues for discussion and essay, chronology reviews, and sections on studying effectively. The sections on studying take the student through reading and studying activities like underlining, summarizing, identifying main points, classifying information according to sequence, and making historical comparisons. To enable both students and instructors to use the *Study Guide* with the greatest possible flexibility, the guide is available in two volumes, with considerable overlapping of chapters. Instructors and students who use only Volumes A and B of the textbook have all the pertinent study materials in a single volume: *Study Guide,* Volume 1 (Chapters 1–23). Those who use only Volumes B and C of the textbook also have all the necessary materials in one volume: *Study Guide*, Volume 2 (Chapters 13–36). The multiple-choice sections of the *Study Guide* are available in a *Computerized Study Guide*, a tutorial version that tells students not only which response is correct but also why each of the other choices is wrong; it also provides the number of the textbook page where each question is discussed. These "rejoinders" to the multiple-choice questions also appear in printed form at the end of the *Study Guide.* The *Computerized Study Guide* is available for IBM® computers.

The *Instructor's Resource Manual*, prepared by John Marshall Carter, contains instructional objectives, annotated chapter outlines, suggestions for lectures and discussion, paper and class activity topics, primary-source exercises, map activities, and lists of audio-visual resources. The accompanying *Test Items*, by Professor Charles Crouch of Georgia Southern University, offer identification, multiple-choice, map, and essay questions for a total of approximately 2,000 test items. These test items are available to adopters in both IBM® and Macintosh versions, both of which include editing capabilities.

In addition, a set of full-color *Map Transparencies* of all the maps in the textbook is available on adoption.

Acknowledgments

It is a pleasure to thank the many instructors who have read and critiqued the manuscript through its development.

Eva Baham
Southern University

Lester Bilsky
University of Arkansas, Little Rock

Kenneth Capalbo
Quincy University

Donald Clark
Trinity University

Frank Coppa
St. John's University

Francis Danquah
Southern University

Gloria-Thomas Emeagwali
Central Connecticut State University

Fuabeh Fonge
North Carolina Agricultural and Technical State University

Bruce Garver
University of Nebraska, Omaha

Ruth Hertzberg
Shippensburg University

Ahmed Ibriham
University of South Carolina

Michelle Scott James
MiraCosta College

Delmarie Klobe
Kapiolani Community College

David Kopf
University of Minnesota

Jim Norris
University of Arkansas, Monticello

Evelyn Rawski
University of Pittsburgh

Edward Reynolds
University of California, San Diego

Cynthia Talbott
University of Northern Arizona

Leila el-Tawil Sarieddine
Southern University

Colonel Steven Wager
United States Military Academy, West Point

Mary Watrous
Washington State University

Colonel James Scott Wheeler
United States Military Academy, West Point

Barbara Woods
South Carolina State University

It is also a pleasure to thank our editors at Houghton Mifflin for their effort and support over many years. To Elizabeth Welch, Senior Basic Book Editor, we owe a special debt of gratitude and admiration. To Jean Woy, Editor-in-Chief for History and Political Science, to Sean Wakely, Senior Sponsoring Editor, and to Jeff Greene, Senior Associate Editor, we express our sincere appreciation. And we thank most warmly Jan Fitter, Leslie Anderson Olney, and Carole Frohlich for their contributions in development, production, and art and photo research.

Many of our colleagues at the University of Illinois continued to provide information and stimulation for our book, often without even knowing it. N. Frederick Nash, Rare Book Librarian, made many helpful suggestions for illustrations, and the World Heritage Museum at the university allowed us complete access to its sizable holdings. James Dengate supplied information on objects from the museum's collection, and Caroline Buckler took many excellent photographs of the museum's objects. Such wide-ranging expertise was a great asset for which we are very appreciative. Bennett Hill wishes to express his sincere appreciation to Ramón de la Fuente for his patience, encouragement, and research assistance in the preparation of the fourth edition.

Each of us has benefited from the generous criticism of his co-authors, although each of us assumes responsibility for what he has written. John Buckler is the author of Chapters 1–7 and 11; Bennett Hill continues the narrative in Chapters 8–10, 12–16, 20–22, and 28; and John McKay is the author of Chapters 17–19, 23–27, and 29–36. Finally, we continue to welcome the many comments and suggestions that have come from our readers, for they have helped us greatly in this ongoing endeavor.

J.P.M.   B.D.H.   J.B.

A HISTORY OF WORLD SOCIETIES

1

Origins

A group of votive stat-
uettes from the Abu
Temple, Square Temple
of the god Abu, Tell
Asmar, 2700–2600 B.C.
*(Source: Courtesy of The
Oriental Institute of the
University of Chicago,
Victor J. Boswell,
photographer)*

Before the dawn of history, bands of people across the earth gradually developed numerous cultures, each unique in some ways while at the same time having features in common. Especially important to the history of the world are events that took place in the ancient Near East (Mesopotamia, Anatolia, and Egypt), India, and China, where human beings abandoned the life of roaming and hunting to settle in stable agricultural communities. From these communities grew cities and civilizations—societies that invented concepts and techniques now integral to contemporary life. Fundamental is the independent development of writing by the Sumerians in Mesopotamia and by the Chinese, an invention that enabled knowledge to be preserved and facilitated the spread and accumulation of learning, lore, literature, and science. Mathematics, astronomy, and architecture were all innovations of ancient civilizations. So, too, were the first law codes and religious concepts, which still permeate daily life across the globe.

- How did nomadic hunters become urban dwellers?
- What geographical factors influenced this change?
- How do geographical factors explain both the elements common to different cultures and the features that differentiate them?

These questions sound the themes of the first four chapters. Chapters 1 and 2 look at how ancient Near Eastern civilizations helped to shape modern Western society. Chapters 3 and 4 explore the responses of the peoples of ancient India and China to these same questions.

❋ WHAT IS HISTORY AND WHY?

History is an effort to reconstruct the past to discover what people thought and did and how their beliefs and actions continue to influence human life. In order to appreciate the past fully, we must put it into perspective so that we can understand the factors that have helped to shape us as individuals, the society in which we live, and the nature of other peoples' societies. Why else should we study societies so separated from ours through time, dis-

tance, and culture as classical Greece, medieval India, early Japan, and modern Russia and Africa?

The matter of perspective is important. In a perfect world all human experience would be equally valuable for its own sake, even if it had little or no impact on the mainstream of history. Yet the evidence on which historians depend for their understanding of the past is far from perfect. Some peoples have left so few traces of themselves that they cannot be understood even in their own right, much less in connection with others. Such peoples are historical enigmas, best left to specialists while other historians examine the principal currents of human development. Historical perspective demands that most attention be devoted to peoples who are best known in their own context.

Historians begin to reconstruct the past by posing questions about it. How and why did cities emerge? How did the political system of a particular society evolve? How did people create an economic system to sustain a complex society? What were a society's religious beliefs, and how did they influence daily life? Historians ask such questions to guide their research and focus their approach to the past.

To answer such questions, historians examine *primary sources,* firsthand accounts of people who lived through the events—men and women who were in the best position to know what happened. Thus historians most commonly rely on the written record of human experience because, no matter how extensive the physical remains of a civilization may be, much of its history will remain a mystery if it has not left records that we can read. Until we are able to decipher the written texts left by the ancient civilization of Minoan Crete, for example, we can draw only vague conclusions about its history.

Of course, the historian's responsibility is to examine all of the evidence, not only written texts but nonverbal evidence. Examined properly, nonverbal sources provide a glimpse of the world as contemporaries saw it. Especially in conjunction with written documents, art can be a valuable and striking means of understanding the past. Similarly, archaeology has proved a valuable avenue to the past, whether an excavation uncovers an ancient Indian city, a medieval temple, or a modern factory building. Things as dissimilar as beautiful paintings and ordinary machines tell historians much about the ways in which people have lived and worked.

When studying written sources—the basic activity in historical research—historians assess the validity and perspective of each account. They try to determine whether sources are honest and accurate, generally by comparing and contrasting the testimony of several different observers. They criticize sources both externally, to attempt to uncover forgeries and errors, and internally, to find an author's motives for writing, inconsistencies within a document, biases, and even cases of outright lying. Some contemporary written accounts, especially from ancient and medieval periods, have been lost; they are known to posterity only because individuals who read the originals incorporated the information into their own writings. These *secondary sources* preserve much history that otherwise would have been lost. Thus historians analyze the viewpoints and accuracy of such derivative writings very carefully. For the modern period historians have a vast supply of primary sources—contemporary accounts of events, memoirs, personal letters, economic statistics, and government reports—all of them useful for understanding the past.

Once historians have pieced together what happened and have determined the facts, they interpret what they have found. Understanding of the past does not necessarily come easily. Unlike the exact physical sciences, history cannot reproduce experiments under controlled conditions, because no two historical events are precisely alike. A historian cannot put people into test tubes. Men, women, and children—the most complex organisms on this planet—are not as predictable as atoms or hydrocarbons.

To complicate matters further, for many epochs only the broad outlines are known, so interpretation is especially difficult. Historians know, for example, that the Hittite Empire collapsed at the height of its power, but interpretations of the causes of the collapse are still speculative. At the other end of the spectrum, some developments are so vast and complex that historians must master mountains of data before they can even begin to venture an interpretation. Events as diverse as the end of the western Roman Empire, the causes of the French Revolution, and the rise of communism in China are very complicated because so many people brought so many different forces to bear for so many different reasons. One simple explanation for such developments will never satisfy everyone, and this fact itself testifies to the complexity of human life.

Still another matter stands in the way of an accurate understanding of the past. Interpretations of the past sometimes change because people's points of view change. The values and attitudes of one generation may not be shared by another. Despite such differences in interpretation, the effort to examine and understand the past can give historians a perspective that is valuable in the present. By analyzing and interpreting evidence, historians come to understand not only the past but the relationship of the past to life today.

Social history, an important subject of this book, is itself an example of historians' reappraisal of the meaning of the past. For centuries historians took the basic facts, details, and activities of life for granted. Obviously, people lived in certain types of houses, ate certain foods that they either raised or bought, and reared families. These matters seemed so ordinary that few serious historians gave them much thought. Yet within our generation a growing number of scholars have demonstrated that the ways in which men, women, and children have lived are as worthy of study as the reigns of monarchs, the careers of great political figures, and the outcomes of big battles.

The topics of history and human societies lead to the question "What is civilization?" *Civilization* is easier to describe than to define. The word comes from the Latin adjective *civilis,* which means "pertaining to, or formed by, a citizen." Citizens willingly and mutually bind themselves in political, economic, and social organizations in which individuals merge themselves, their energies, and their interests in a larger community. In the course of time, *civilization* has come to embrace not only a people's social and political organization but also its particular shared way of thinking and believing, its art, and other facets of its culture—the complex whole that sets one people apart from other peoples who have different shared values and practices.

One way to understand this idea is to observe the origins and development of major civilizations, analyzing similarities and differences among them. At a fundamental level, the similarities are greater than the differences. Almost all peoples share some values, even though they may live far apart, speak different languages, and have different religions and political and social systems. By studying these shared cultural values, which stretch through time and across distance, we can see how the various events of the past have left their impression on the present and how the present may influence the future.

A word about culture is in order. *Culture* is normally defined as a particular type or stage of the intellectual, moral, artistic, and communal practices of a civilization. All people on this planet confront elemental challenges such as how to feed and shelter themselves (the economic aspect of culture) and how to govern their lives in harmony with others (the political and social aspects of culture). Cultures everywhere have felt the need to transmit to future generations what they have learned. Sometimes the content of the transmission is intellectual—for example, the preservation of astronomical information. Sometimes it is religious—for example, beliefs about the relation of the gods to humanity. Appreciation of life and the surrounding world has moved all peoples to create their own forms of art and music. Historians not only note the common themes to be found among various cultures but also study cultural differences. The study of history is the examination of how various peoples confronted and responded to the circumstances of their lives, what their responses had

in common with the responses of others, and how their responses remained individual over time and across the planet earth.

THE FIRST HUMAN BEINGS

On December 27, 1831, young Charles Darwin stepped aboard the H.M.S. *Beagle* to begin a voyage to South America and the Pacific Ocean. In the course of that five-year voyage, he became convinced that species of animals and human beings had evolved from lower forms. At first Darwin was reluctant to publicize his theories because they ran counter to the biblical account of creation, which claimed that God had made Adam in one day. Finally, however, in 1859 he published *On the Origin of Species.* In 1871 he followed it with *The Descent of Man,* in which he argued that human beings and apes are descended from a common ancestor. Even before Darwin had proclaimed his theories, evidence to support them had come to light. In 1856 the fossilized bones of an early form of human

Paleolithic Cave Painting   All Paleolithic peoples relied on hunting for their survival. This scene, painted on the wall of a cave in southern France, depicts the animals normally hunted by the group of which the artist was a member. Paleolithic peoples may have hoped that by drawing these animals they would gain power over them. *(Source: Douglas Mazonowicz/Gallery of Prehistoric Art)*

were discovered in the Neander Valley of Germany. This "Neanderthal man," named after the place of his discovery, was physically more primitive than modern man (*Homo sapiens,* or thinking man). But he was clearly a human being and not an ape. Neanderthal man offered proof of Darwin's theory that *Homo sapiens* had evolved from less-developed forms.

Ideas of human evolution have changed dramatically, particularly in the past few years. Generations of paleoanthropologists—fossil hunters—have sought the "missing link." Ever since Darwin published his theories of evolution, scholars have tried to find the one fossil that would establish the point from which human beings and apes went their own different evolutionary ways. As recently as October 1994 scholars in Ethiopia found remains of a new species of hominid—a humanlike primate, showing both apelike and human skeletal features. The finders proudly suggested the discovery of the missing link, without being able to associate their hominid directly with other anthropological remains. But other recent discoveries have caused other scholars to question the very concept of the missing link and its implications. Fossil remains in China and Southeast Asia suggest that evolution was more complicated than paleoanthropologists previously thought and even that human beings may not have originated in Africa. In the light of the latest findings, paleoanthropologists must reinterpret their data; they must rethink everything that they have discovered.

The fossil record, extensive but incomplete, suggests that thousands of missing links may have existed, no one of them more important than any other. Given the small numbers of these primates and the extent of the globe, there is an almost infinitesimal chance of finding a skeleton that can be considered the missing link between other primates and human beings. A number of years ago Loren Eiseley, a noted American anthropologist, offered the wisest and humblest observation: "The human interminglings of hundreds of thousands of years of prehistory are not to be clarified by a single generation of archaeologists."[1]

Despite the enormous uncertainty surrounding human development, a reasonably clear picture can be drawn of two important early periods: the Paleolithic (Old Stone) Age and the Neolithic (New Stone) Age. The immensely long Paleolithic Age, which lasted from about 400,000 to 7000 B.C., takes its scholarly name from the crude stone tools

the earliest hunters chipped from flint and obsidian, a black volcanic rock. During the much shorter Neolithic Age, which lasted from about 7000 to 3000 B.C., human beings began using new types of stone tools and, more important, pursuing agriculture.*

✳ THE PALEOLITHIC AGE

Paleolithic peoples hunted a huge variety of animals, ranging from elephants in Spain to deer in China. The hunters were thoroughly familiar with the habits and migratory patterns of the animals on which they relied. But success in the hunt also depended on the quality and effectiveness of the hunters' social organization. Paleolithic hunters were organized—they hunted in groups. They used their knowledge of the animal world and their power of thinking to plan how to down their prey. Paleolithic peoples also nourished themselves by gathering nuts, berries, and seeds. Just as they knew the habits of animals, so they had vast knowledge of the plant kingdom. Some Paleolithic peoples even knew how to plant wild seeds to supplement their food supply. Thus they relied on every part of the environment for survival.

The basic social unit of Paleolithic societies was probably the family, and family bonds were no doubt stronger and more extensive than those of families in modern, urban, and industrialized societies. It is likely that the bonds of kinship were strong not just within the nuclear family of father, mother, and children but throughout the extended family of uncles, aunts, cousins, nephews, and nieces. People in nomadic societies typically depend on the extended family for cooperative work and mutual protection. The ties of kinship probably also extended beyond the family to the tribe. A tribe was a group of families led by a patriarch, a dominant male who governed the group. Tribe members considered themselves descendants of a common ancestor. Most tribes probably consisted of from thirty to fifty people.

---

*We follow the traditional practice in the West of expressing historical dates in relation to the birth of Jesus Christ. Dates before his birth are labeled B.C. (for *Before Christ*), and dates after his birth are labeled A.D. (*Anno Domini,* Latin for "in the year of the Lord"). A widely used alternative system refers to these dates as B.C.E. (Before the Common Era) and C.E. (Common Era).

Return of the Iceman   This scene captures the discovery of a Neolithic herdsman who was trapped in the ice about fifty-three hundred years ago. The discovery was made by chance in September 1991. In an ancient accident, the man was sealed in ice with all of his tools, thus providing modern scholars with a unique view of the past. The discovery is so important that scientists have not yet done an autopsy on the corpse. *(Source: Paul Hanny/Liaison)*

As in the hunt, so too in other aspects of life—group members had to cooperate to survive. The adult males normally hunted abroad and between hunts made stone weapons. The women's realm was primarily the camp, but women too ranged through the neighborhood gathering nuts, grains, and fruits to supplement the group's diet. The women's primary responsibility was the bearing of children, who were essential to the continuation of the group. Women also had to care for the children, especially the infants. Part of women's work, too, was tending the fire, which served for warmth, cooking, and protection against wild animals.

Some of the most striking accomplishments of Paleolithic peoples were intellectual. They used reason to govern their actions. Thought and language permitted the lore and experience of the old to be passed on to the young. An invisible world also opened up to *Homo sapiens*. They developed the custom of burying their dead and leaving offerings with the body, perhaps in the belief that somehow life continued after death.

Paleolithic peoples produced the first art. They decorated cave walls with lifelike paintings of animals and scenes of the hunt. Located deep in the caves, some of these paintings still survive. Paleolithic peoples also began to fashion clay models of pregnant women and of animals. The statuettes of pregnant women seem to express a wish for fertile women to have babies and thus ensure the group's survival. The wall paintings and clay statuettes of Paleolithic peoples represent the earliest yearnings of human beings to control their environment.

THE NEOLITHIC AGE

Hunting is at best a precarious way of life, even when the diet is supplemented with seeds and fruits. Paleolithic tribes either moved with the herds and adapted themselves to new circumstances or perished. Several long ice ages—periods when glaciers covered vast parts of Europe—

subjected the small bands of Paleolithic hunters to extreme hardship.

Not long after the last ice age, around 7000 B.C., some hunters and gatherers began to rely chiefly on agriculture for their sustenance. Others continued the old pastoral and nomadic ways. Indeed, agriculture evolved over the course of time. Neolithic peoples had long known how to grow crops. The real transformation of human life occurred only when large numbers of people began to rely primarily and permanently on the grain they grew and the animals they domesticated. Agriculture made possible a more stable and secure life.

Neolithic peoples were responsible for many fundamental inventions and innovations that the modern world takes for granted. First, obviously, is systematic agriculture as the primary source of food. Neolithic peoples developed the primary economic activity of the entire ancient world and the basis of all modern life. With the settled routine of Neolithic farmers came the evolution of towns and eventually cities. Neolithic farmers usually raised more food than they could consume, and their surpluses gave rise to larger, healthier populations. Population growth in turn increased reliance on settled farming, for only systematic agriculture could sustain the growing numbers of people. Since surpluses of food could be bartered for other commodities, the Neolithic era also witnessed the beginnings of the large-scale exchange of goods. In time the increasing complexity of Neolithic societies led to the development of writing, prompted by the need to keep records and later by the urge to chronicle experiences, learning, and beliefs.

The transition to settled life had a profound impact on the family. The shared needs and pressures that encourage extended-family ties are less prominent in settled than in nomadic societies. Bonds to the extended family weakened. In towns and cities, the nuclear family was more dependent on its immediate neighbors than on kinfolk.

Nevertheless, the nomadic way of life and the family relationships it nurtured continued to flourish alongside settled agriculture. Dramatic evidence of this fact came to light on September 19, 1991, when a hiker in the Tyrolean Alps in Italy discovered the frozen body of a Neolithic herdsman. The corpse is the oldest found intact, and its preservation results from the man having been covered for some fifty-three hundred years by glacial ice. Although the discoverers did irreparable

damage to the site, enough remains to give a unique impression of European nomadic life and a surprising glimpse of its sophistication. The "Iceman," as he is now called, was found equipped with the implements of everyday life. Among them are advanced bows and arrows that prove a remarkable knowledge of ballistics. A number of tools, some of bone, wood, and even copper, show that European people were making the transition from the Neolithic Age to the time when they relied primarily on metals for their tools. Dental evidence suggests that the Iceman's diet consisted of milled grain. These findings strongly suggest that the Iceman was a hunter and gatherer but also that he and his society depended on tilled grain as a vital part of their diet. The Iceman proves that nomadic and pastoral life could and did coincide peacefully with the emerging agricultural settlements. Often farmers and nomads bartered with one another, each group trading its surpluses for those of the other. Although nomadic peoples continued to exist throughout the Neolithic period and into modern times, the future belonged to the Neolithic farmers and their descendants. The development of systematic agriculture may not have been revolutionary, but the changes that it ushered in certainly were.

Until recently, scholars thought that agriculture originated in the ancient Near East and gradually spread elsewhere. Contemporary work, however, points to a more complex pattern of development. For unknown reasons people in various parts of the world all seem to have begun domesticating plants and animals at roughly the same time, around 7000 B.C. Four main points of origin have been identified: (1) In the Near East, people in places as far apart as Tepe Yahya in modern Iran, Jarmo in modern Iraq, Jericho in Palestine, and Hacilar in modern Turkey (Map 1.1) raised wheat, barley, peas, and lentils. They also kept herds of sheep, pigs, and possibly goats. (2) In western Africa, Neolithic farmers domesticated many plants, including millet, sorghum, and yams. (3) In northeastern China, peoples of the Yangshao culture developed techniques of field agriculture, animal husbandry, potterymaking, and bronze metallurgy. (4) In Central and South America, Neolithic peoples domesticated a host of plants, among them corn, beans, and squash. CBS

Once people began to rely on farming for their livelihood, they settled in permanent villages and built houses. The location of the village was cru-

stable FOOD : source
- growth of population
- division of labour
- trade

❋ **MAP 1.1 Spread of Cultures in the Ancient Near East** This map illustrates the spread of Mesopotamian and Egyptian culture through a semicircular stretch of land often called the Fertile Crescent. From this area, knowledge and use of agriculture spread throughout the western part of Asia.

cial. Early farmers chose places where the water supply was constant and adequate for their crops and flocks. At first, villages were small, consisting of a few households. But by about 7000 B.C., as the population expanded and prospered, villages usually were transformed into walled towns. The fortifications were so large that they could have been raised only by a large labor force. They indicate that towns were developing social and political organization as well as growing in size and wealth. The fortifications, constructed by the whole community, would have been impossible without central planning.

One of the major effects of the advent of agriculture and settled life was a dramatic increase in population. The number and size of the towns prove that Neolithic society was expanding. Early farmers found that agriculture provided a larger and much more dependable food supply than hunting and gathering. No longer did the long winter months bring the threat of starvation.

Farmers learned to store the surplus for the winter. Because the farming community was better fed than ever before, it was also more resistant to diseases that kill people suffering from malnutrition. Thus Neolithic farmers were healthier and longer-lived than their predecessors.

The surplus of food had two other momentous consequences. First, grain became an article of commerce. The farming community traded surplus grain for items it could not produce itself. The community thus obtained raw materials such as precious gems and metals. Early towns in the region now known as Mesopotamia (see Map 1.1) imported copper from the north, and eventually copper replaced stone for tools and weapons. Trade also brought Neolithic communities into touch with one another, making possible the spread of ideas and techniques.

Second, agricultural surplus made possible the division of labor. It freed some members of the community from the necessity of raising food.

PACIFIC
OCEAN

East
China
Sea

Yellow
Sea

Tropic of Cancer

South China Sea

Anyang
Zhengzhou

CHINA

Millet
Soybeans
Wheat

GOBI DESERT

Southeast Asian
Peasant Farmers and
Hunting Groups

Pastoral Nomads

Largely uninhabited

Mekong

Chang Jiang (Yangtze)

Huang He (Yellow)

HIMALAYA MTS.

Peasant Farmers
and Pastoralists

Ganges

Bay of
Bengal

Cattle
Buffalo
Fowl

Ropar
Harappa
Delhi

INDIA

Wheat
Barley
Vegetables
Cotton

INDUS VALLEY

Mohenjo-daro
Sutkagendor
Lothal

Aral
Sea

Pastoral Nomads of the Steppes

IRANIAN
PLATEAU

Caspian
Sea

Wheat
Barley
Peas
Lentils
Sheep
Pigs
Goats

INDIAN OCEAN

Arabian
Sea

Volga

ARMENIA

MESOPOTAMIA

Tigris

Euphrates

AKKAD
Akkad
Babylon
SUMER

SYRIA

Persian Gulf

Desert Nomads

ARABIA

ARABIAN
DESERT

ANATOLIA

Black Sea

PALESTINE
SINAI

Mediterranean Sea

Danube

European Peasant Farmers

Giza
Memphis
EGYPT

Thebes
(Karnak)

Red Sea

NUBIA

Wheat
Barley
Cattle

SAHARA

Desert Nomads

Equator

0°

Centers of river-valley civilizations

Extent of trading contacts

Wheat Main domesticated crops
Cattle and livestock

Some artisans and craftsmen devoted their attention to making the new stone tools that farming demanded—hoes and sickles for working in the fields and mortars and pestles for grinding grain. Other artisans began to shape clay into pottery vessels, which were used to store grain, wine, and oil and served as kitchen utensils. Still others wove baskets and cloth. People who could specialize in particular crafts produced more and better goods than any single farmer could.

Until recently it was impossible to say much about these goods. But in April 1985 archaeologists announced the discovery near the Dead Sea in modern Israel of a unique deposit of Neolithic artifacts. Buried in a cave were fragments of the earliest cloth yet found, the oldest painted mask, remains of woven baskets and boxes, and jewelry. The textiles are surprisingly elaborate, some woven in eleven intricate designs. These artifacts give eloquent testimony to the sophistication and artistry of Neolithic craftsmanship.

Prosperity and stable conditions nurtured other innovations and discoveries. Neolithic farmers improved their tools and agricultural techniques. They domesticated bigger, stronger animals, such as the bull and the horse, to work for them, and they invented tools such as the plow, which came into use by 3000 B.C. By then the wheel had been invented, and farmers devised ways of hitching bulls and horses to wagons. Neolithic farmers could raise more food more easily, because animals and machines were doing more of the work.

In arid regions such as Mesopotamia and Egypt, farmers learned to irrigate their land and later to drain it to prevent the buildup of salt in the soil. Water diverted from rivers opened new land to cultivation and deposited layers of rich mud, which increased the fertility of the soil. Thus the rivers, together with the manure of domesticated animals, kept replenishing the land. One result was a further increase in population and wealth. Irrigation, especially on a large scale, demanded group effort. The entire community had to plan which land to irrigate and how to lay out the canals. Then everyone had to help dig the canals. The demands of irrigation thus underscored the need for strong central authority within the community. Successful irrigation projects in turn strengthened such central authority by proving it effective and beneficial. Thus corporate spirit and governments to which individuals were subordinate—the makings of urban life—began to evolve.

The development of systematic agriculture was a fundamental turning point in the history of civilization. Farming gave rise to stable, settled societies, which enjoyed considerable prosperity. Settled circumstances and a certain amount of leisure made the accumulation and spread of knowledge easier. Sustained farming prepared the way for urban life.

❋ RIVERS, RESOURCES, AND CIVILIZATIONS

The development of systematic agriculture made possible a huge leap in human development, a leap that took place in several different parts of the world at roughly the same time (Map 1.2). In the ancient Near East, India, and China, Neolithic farmers created the conditions that permitted the evolution of urban civilization.

Certain geographical features were common to these early civilizations. The most important were the mighty river valleys in which they developed. The Egyptians relied on the Nile, the Mesopotamians on the Euphrates and the Tigris. The Indus nourished ancient Indian civilizations, and the great Yellow River in China made the birth of Chinese civilizations possible. Thus those four ancient civilizations could depend on a steady source of water, which also brought nutrients to the soil and fish as a source of food. Except for the violent Tigris and Yellow, the rivers also served as an easy means of communication. It was safer and simpler to use the Nile as a highway than to travel across the deserts surrounding Egypt. Likewise the Indus offered the fastest, most convenient path through the jungle. Communication facilitated the exchange of ideas while breaking down the barriers of isolation. The size and fertility of the broad valleys provided the food, wealth, and population, necessary ingredients to the development of large, sophisticated social structures.

❋ **MAP 1.2 River-Valley Civilizations**   Although systematic agriculture developed in four great river valleys, variations in geography and climate meant that different crops were grown and societies emerged in distinct but similar ways.

Although great rivers were a common feature of these civilizations, soil and climate differed, and these differences left a significant imprint on human development. The rich mud carried by the Nile allowed abundant crops of wheat, and the dry desert air facilitated the preservation of surpluses of grain. The Indus flows through rich subtropical land well suited to growing a large variety of crops, but the humid climate quickly brought rot. Different climates meant that the rivers nurtured different crops and required different methods of agriculture. Geography and the means by which people turned it to their uses, then, influenced the way in which societies evolved.

In addition, the rivers themselves are different, demanding differences in the ways they were used. In Egypt and China, the peoples employed irrigation to bring water to arid land, enabling them to cultivate more fields. That was true in Mesopotamia too, but the farmers there also relied on irrigation to drain land to reclaim it for cultivation. In India farmers protected themselves against the floodwaters of the Indus while taking advantage of the rich mud that the river deposited. Whatever the differences, the rivers challenged early peoples to work together to make the best use of their geographical gifts, whether to divert water to new soil, to draw water from uncultivated fields, or to prevent water from destroying land already being farmed.

As the river-valley societies in the ancient Near East, India, and China outgrew their Neolithic past, they were forced to diversify their activities and abilities. New, centrally organized forms of government were required on a regular, permanent basis to coordinate massive irrigation projects, to administer the land, to govern the people, and to defend the people in time of war. Specialization in government and defense was part of a larger division of labor. Some members of society abandoned the plow to master the technology of metalworking. Others devoted themselves to the study of mathematics and architecture to meet the building needs of society. In the firm belief that they belonged to a world inhabited by gods, some people tried to explain the origin and workings of these higher beings, both to honor them and to teach their mysteries to others so that the divine and human could live in harmony. In the process they preserved traditions not only about their beliefs but also about their own lives—traditions that linked them to the past and helped them shape the future.

Knowledge became too valuable to lose and too complicated to be mastered easily. Whatever their specialization, people increasingly found it necessary to preserve knowledge and experience in a permanent form. To meet this need, they invented writing. They extended the experience of humanity beyond the individual's lifetime to future generations and created the foundations of an intellectual continuity that defied both time and death.

North and South America, Europe, sub-Saharan Africa, and Southeast Asia can all boast of many rivers. Yet only the peoples of Central America and the Incas of Peru in South America established civilizations comparable to those in the Near East, India, and China, though many centuries after the rise of the river-valley civilizations. Thus it seems clear that factors other than rivers were essential to the development of civilization. Climate may have been a limiting factor in places such as equatorial Africa and Southeast Asia. But why did nothing similar to Egyptian, Mesopotamian, Indian, and Chinese advances occur in areas of North America and Europe where the climate is relatively mild?

The answer is that tools in those areas were primitive and totally inadequate. Instead of plowing the soil, early farmers not living in the river valleys of the Near East, India, or China mainly used hoes and digging-sticks. Lacking work animals, they relied on their own labor, not on animal power, to sow, harvest, and process grain. The crop yields that they worked so hard to get were so small that they could not expect sizable surpluses. The lack of food surpluses in turn made it hard for them to develop specialization of labor, to expand population, to build cities, and to accumulate knowledge in a durable form. Furthermore, areas such as parts of sub-Saharan Africa and the Caribbean are so naturally rich in readily available natural food resources that people did not have to toil for a living. Seldom did peoples in such areas develop sophisticated urban cultures.

Thus something more than geography, natural resources, climate, sustained agriculture, and population is needed to constitute a civilization. The significance of urban life to the growth of civilization cannot be overestimated. By banding together and observing common laws and values of life, people could pool their resources. Some people were farmers or craftsmen, and others were magis-

SIGNIFICANT EVENTS IN MESOPOTAMIAN HISTORY

PERIOD	EVENT
ca 3000 B.C.	Sumerians become prevalent in southern Mesopotamia
ca 2600 B.C.	Spread of Mesopotamian culture to northern Mesopotamia
ca 2331 B.C.	Sargon captures Sumer and creates a new capital, the city of Akkad
ca 1792 B.C.	Hammurabi wins control of Mesopotamia; Babylon the new capital of Mesopotamia
ca 1595 B.C.	Hittites and Kassites destroy Hammurabi's dynasty

trates or priests, but all cooperated to sustain and protect the community. Urban life provided the wealth, security, and stability to create civilization in its many forms.

Among the river-valley societies, nowhere can these abstractions be better seen than in the urban culture that flowered in the demanding environment of Mesopotamia, the first of the four societies to attain a level of development that can reasonably be called a civilization.

✤ MESOPOTAMIAN CIVILIZATION

An area roughly equivalent to modern Iraq, Mesopotamia drew its life from the Euphrates and Tigris rivers. Both have their headwaters in the mountains of Armenia in modern Turkey. Both are fed by numerous tributaries, and the entire river system drains a vast mountainous region. Overland routes in Mesopotamia usually followed the Euphrates because the banks of the Tigris are frequently steep and difficult. North of the ancient city of Babylon the land levels out into a barren expanse. The desert continues south of Babylon and still farther south gives way to a 6,000-square-mile region of marshes, lagoons, mud flats, and reed banks. At last, in the extreme south, the Euphrates and the Tigris unite and empty into the Persian Gulf (see Map 1.2).

This area became the home of many folk and the land of the first cities. The region around Akkad, near modern Baghdad, was occupied by bands of nomads related to one another by Semitic languages—languages that include Hebrew and Arabic. Into the south came the Sumerians, farmers and city builders who probably migrated from the east. By 3000 B.C. they had established a number of cities in the southernmost part of Mesopotamia, which became known as Sumer. As the Sumerians pushed north, they came into contact with the Semites, who readily adopted Sumerian culture and turned to urban life. The Sumerians soon changed the face of the land and made Mesopotamia the source of values and techniques that fundamentally influenced the societies of their immediate neighbors in both the West and the East (see Map 1.2).

In the context of world history, the capitalized terms "Western" and "Eastern" and "West" and "East" are *Eurocentric*—they describe events and culture from the viewpoint of European experience and values. This usage dates back to the ancient Greeks, who contrasted their life in "the West" with the lives of their non-Greek neighbors in the "East"—that is, in Africa and western Asia. Peoples in Asia and Africa would probably have dismissed the notion, and no one today uses the categories "West" and "East" to indicate the superiority of one set of historical developments to the other. Despite their flaws, the terms have come into

�֍ **Aerial View of Ur** This photograph gives a good idea of the size and complexity of Ur, one of the most powerful cities in Mesopotamia. In the lower right-hand corner stands the massive ziggurat of Umammu. *(Source: Georg Gerster/Comstock)*

general use as a useful though artificial way to distinguish historical developments in Europe and the Americas from those in Asia.

Another expression already used in these pages, "the ancient Near East," also requires some explanation. It refers to a specific area of western Asia and northeastern Africa. In the north the ancient Near East included the western part of modern Turkey, extending south through the area now called the "Middle East" to Egypt in Africa. The major justification for this term is historical, not geographical. Although various peoples in this area developed their own civilizations to some extent independently, they did not develop in complete isolation but formed a well-defined unit.

Environment and Mesopotamian Culture

From the outset, geography had a profound effect on the evolution of Mesopotamian civilization. In this region agriculture is possible only with irrigation and good drainage. Consequently, the Sumerians and later the Akkadians built cities along the Tigris and Euphrates and their branches. Some major cities, such as Ur and Uruk, took root on tributaries of the Euphrates; others, notably Lagash, were built on tributaries of the Tigris (see Map 1.1). The rivers supplied fish, a major element of the city dwellers' diet. The rivers also provided reeds and clay for building materials. Since this entire area lacks stone, mud brick became the primary building block of Mesopotamian architecture.

Although the rivers sustained life, they also destroyed it by frequent floods that ravaged entire cities. Moreover, they restrained political development by making Sumer a geographical maze. Among the rivers, streams, and irrigation canals stretched open desert or swamp where nomadic tribes roamed. Communication among the isolated cities was difficult and at times dangerous. Thus each Sumerian city became a state, independent of the others and protective of its independence. Any city that tried to unify the country was resisted by the other cities. As a result, the political history of Sumer is one of almost constant warfare. Although Sumer was eventually unified, unification came late and was always tenuous.

The Invention of Writing and the First Schools

The origins of writing probably go back to the ninth millennium B.C., when Near Eastern peoples used clay tokens as counters for record keeping. By the fourth millennium people had realized that drawing pictures of the tokens on clay was simpler than making tokens. This breakthrough in turn suggested that more information could be conveyed by adding pictures of still other objects. The result was a complex system of pictographs in which each sign pictured an object. These pictographs were the forerunners of a Sumerian form of writing known as *cuneiform,* from the Latin term for "wedge-shaped," used to describe the strokes of the stylus.

How did this pictographic system work, and how did it evolve into cuneiform writing? At first, a scribe who wanted to indicate a star just drew a picture of it (line A of Figure 1.1) on a wet clay tablet, which became rock-hard when baked. Anyone looking at the picture knew what it meant and thought of the word for star. This system had serious limitations, for it could not represent abstract ideas or combinations of ideas. For instance, how could it depict a slave woman?

The solution to that problem appeared when the scribe discovered that signs could be combined to express meaning. To refer to a slave woman, the scribe used the sign for woman (line B) and the sign for mountain (line C)—literally, "mountain

Meaning	Pictograph	Ideogram	Phonetic sign
A Star			
B Woman			
C Mountain			
D Slave woman			
E Water In			

FIGURE 1.1 Sumerian Writing *(Source: Excerpted from S. N. Kramer,* The Sumerians: Their History, Culture and Character, *University of Chicago Press, Chicago, 1963, pp. 302–306)*

woman" (line D). Because the Sumerians regularly obtained their slave women from the mountains, this combination of signs was easily understandable.

The next step was to simplify the system. Instead of drawing pictures, the scribe made conventionalized signs that were generally understood to represent ideas. Thus the signs became *ideograms:* they symbolized ideas. The sign for star could also be used to indicate heaven, sky, or even god.

The real breakthrough came when the scribe learned to use signs to represent sounds. For instance, the scribe drew two parallel wavy lines to indicate the word *a* or "water" (line E). Besides water, the word *a* in Sumerian also meant "in." The word *in* expresses a relationship that is very difficult to represent pictorially. Instead of trying to invent a sign to mean "in," some clever scribe used the sign for water because the two words sounded alike. This phonetic use of signs made possible the combining of signs to convey abstract ideas.

The Sumerian system of writing was so complicated that only professional scribes mastered it, and even they had to study it for many years. One graduate of a scribal school had few fond memories of the joy of learning:

My headmaster read my tablet, said:
"There is something missing," caned me.

. . . .

The fellow in charge of silence said:
"Why did you talk without permission," caned me.
The fellow in charge of the assembly said:
"Why did you stand at ease without permission,"
caned me.[2]

The Sumerian system of schooling set the educational standards for Mesopotamian culture, and the Akkadians and later the Babylonians adopted its practices and techniques. Mesopotamian education always had a practical side because of the economic and administrative importance of scribes. Most scribes took administrative positions in the temple or palace, where they kept records of business transactions, accounts, and inventories. But scribal schools did not limit their curriculum to business affairs. They were also centers of culture and scholarship. Topics of study included mathematics, botany, and linguistics. Advanced students copied and studied the classics of Sumerian literature. Talented students and learned scribes wrote compositions of their own. As a result, many literary, mathematical, and religious texts survive today, giving a full picture of Mesopotamian intellectual and spiritual life.

Mesopotamian Thought and Religion

The Mesopotamians made significant and sophisticated advances in mathematics using a numerical system based on units of sixty, ten, and six. They developed the concept of place value—that the value of a number depends on where it stands in relation to other numbers. Mesopotamian mathematical texts are of two kinds: tables and problems. Scribes compiled tables of squares and square roots, cubes and cube roots, and reciprocals. They wrote texts of problems dealing not only with equations and pure mathematics but also with concrete matters such as how to plan irrigation ditches. The building of cities, palaces, temples, and canals demanded practical knowledge of geometry and trigonometry.

Mesopotamian medicine was a combination of magic, prescriptions, and surgery. Mesopotamians believed that demons and evil spirits caused sickness and that magic spells could drive them out.

Or, alternatively, they believed that a physician could force a demon out by giving the patient a foul-tasting prescription. As medical knowledge grew, some prescriptions were found to work and thus were true medicines. Physicians relied heavily on plants, animals, and minerals for recipes, often mixing them with beer to cover their unpleasant taste. Surgeons practiced a dangerous occupation, and the penalties for failure were severe. One section of Hammurabi's law code (see page 21) decreed: "If a physician performed a major operation on a seignior with a bronze lancet and has caused the seignior's death, or he opened up the eye-socket . . . and has destroyed the . . . eye, they shall cut off his hand."[3] No wonder that one medical text warned physicians to avoid a dying person.

Mesopotamian thought had its profoundest impact on theology and religion. The Sumerians originated many beliefs, and the Akkadians and Babylonians added to them. Although the Mesopotamians thought that many gods ran the world, they did not consider all gods and goddesses equal. Some deities had very important jobs, taking care of music, law, sex, and victory. Others had lesser tasks, overseeing leatherworking and basket weaving.

Divine society was a hierarchy. According to the Sumerians the air-god Enlil was king of the gods and laid down the rules by which the universe was run. Enki, the god of wisdom, put Enlil's plans into effect. The Babylonians believed that the gods elected Marduk as their king and that he assigned the lesser gods various duties. Once the gods received their tasks, they carried them out forever.

The Mesopotamians considered natural catastrophes to be the work of the gods. At times the Sumerians described their chief god, Enlil, as "the raging flood which has no rival." The gods, they believed, even used nature to punish the Mesopotamians. According to the myth of the Deluge, which gave rise to the biblical story of Noah, the god Enki warned Ziusudra, the Sumerian Noah:

A flood will sweep over the cult-centers;
To destroy the seed of mankind . . .
Is the decision, the word of the assembly of the gods.[4]

The Mesopotamians did not worship their deities because they believed their gods were benevolent. Human beings were too insignificant to pass judgment on the conduct of the gods, and the gods were too superior to honor human morals. Rather, the Mesopotamians worshiped the gods because they believed their gods were mighty. Likewise, it was not the place of men and women to understand the gods. The Sumerian equivalent to the biblical Job once complained to his god:

The man of deceit has conspired against me,
And you, my god, do not thwart him,
You carry off my understanding.[5]

The motives of the gods were not always clear. In times of affliction one could only pray and offer sacrifices to appease them.

The Mesopotamians had many myths to account for the creation of the universe. According to one Sumerian myth (echoed in Genesis, the first book of the Bible), only the primeval sea existed at first. The sea produced heaven and earth, which were united. Heaven and earth gave birth to Enlil, who separated them and made possible the creation of the other gods. Babylonian beliefs were similar. In the beginning was the primeval sea, the goddess Tiamat, who gave birth to the gods. When Tiamat tried to destroy the gods, Marduk, the chief god of the Babylonians, proceeded to kill her and divide her body and thus created the sky and earth. These myths are the earliest known attempts to answer the question "How did it all begin?" The Mesopotamians obviously thought about these matters, as they thought about the gods, in human terms. They never organized their beliefs into a philosophy, but their myths offered understandable explanations of natural phenomena. The myths were emotionally satisfying, and that was their greatest appeal.

Mesopotamian myths also explained the origin of human beings. In one myth the gods decided to make their lives easier by creating servants in their own image. Nammu, the goddess of the watery deep, brought the matter to Enki. After some thought, Enki instructed Nammu and the others:

Mix the heart of the clay that is over the abyss.
The good and princely fashioners will thicken the
*   clay.*
You, do you bring the limbs into existence.[6]

In Mesopotamian myth, as in Genesis, men and women were made in the divine image but without godlike powers.

Stele of Naramsin Naramsin, the grandson of Sargon, was one of the greatest of the Akkadian kings. The topmost figure on this stele, or commemorative tablet, he displays his power by defeating his enemies in battle. Naramsin's horned crown suggests that he considered himself divine. *(Source: Louvre © Photo R.M.N.)*

One of the Mesopotamians' oldest deities was Inanna, a complicated goddess who represented the passions of love and war. Although she could be kind, she could also be harsh. She took many forms, one of the most important being mother-earth, who gave birth to everything in the world.

Inanna was worshiped by the Semites as Ishtar, and her cult lasted into Roman times.

In addition to myths, the Sumerians produced the first epic poem, the *Epic of Gilgamesh,* which evolved as a reworking of at least five earlier myths (see Listening to the Past). An epic poem is a narration of the achievements, labors, and sometimes the failures of heroes and embodies a people's or a nation's conception of its own past. Historians use epic poems to learn about various aspects of a society. The Sumerian epic recounts the wanderings of Gilgamesh—the semihistorical king of Uruk—and his companion Enkidu, their fatal meeting with the goddess Ishtar, after which Enkidu dies, and Gilgamesh's subsequent search for eternal life. Although Gilgamesh finds a miraculous plant that gives immortality to anyone who eats it, a great snake steals it from him. Despite this loss, Gilgamesh visits the lower world to bring Enkidu back to life, thereby learning of life after death. The *Epic of Gilgamesh* is not only an excellent piece of literature but also an intellectual triumph. It shows the Sumerians grappling with such enduring questions as life and death, humankind and deity, and immortality.

Sumerian Society

Their harsh environment fostered a grim, even pessimistic, spirit among the Mesopotamians. The Sumerians sought to please and calm the gods, especially the patron deity of the city. Encouraged and directed by the traditional priesthood, which was dedicated to understanding the ways of the gods, the people erected shrines in the center of each city and built their houses around them. The best way to honor the gods was to make the shrine as grand and as impressive as possible, for gods who had a splendid temple might think twice about sending floods to destroy the city.

Sumerian society was a complex arrangement of freedom and dependence, and its members were divided into four categories: nobles, free clients of the nobility, commoners, and slaves. The nobility consisted of the king and his family, the chief priests, and high palace officials. Generally, the king, at first elected by the citizenry, rose to power as a war leader. He established a regular army, trained it, and led it into battle. The might of the king and the frequency of warfare quickly made him the supreme figure in the city, and kingship soon became hereditary. The symbol of royal status was the palace, which rivaled the temple in grandeur.

The king and the lesser nobility held extensive tracts of land that, like the estates of the temple, were worked by slaves and clients. Clients were free men and women who were dependent on the nobility. In return for their labor, the clients received small plots of land to work for themselves. Although this arrangement assured the clients of a livelihood, the land they worked remained the possession of the nobility or the temple. Thus the nobility not only controlled most—and probably the best—land but also commanded the obedience of a huge segment of society. They were the dominant force in Mesopotamian society.

Commoners were free citizens. They were independent of the nobility, but they could not rival the nobility in social status and political power. Commoners belonged to large patriarchal families that owned land in their own right. Commoners could sell their land if the family approved, but even the king could not legally take their land without their approval. Commoners had a voice in the political affairs of the city and full protection under the law.

Slavery has been a fact of life throughout history. Some Sumerian slaves were foreigners and prisoners of war. Some were criminals who had lost their freedom as punishment for their crimes. Still others served as slaves to repay debts. These were relatively fortunate because the law required that they be freed after three years. All slaves were subject to whatever treatment their owners might mete out. They could be beaten and even branded. Yet they were not considered dumb beasts. They could borrow money and received at least some legal protection. They engaged in trade and made profits. Indeed, many slaves bought their freedom.

❈ THE SPREAD OF MESOPOTAMIAN CULTURE

The Sumerians established the basic social, economic, and intellectual patterns of Mesopotamia, but the Semites played a large part in spreading Sumerian culture far beyond the boundaries of Mesopotamia. The interaction of the Sumerians and Semites, in fact, gives one of the very first glimpses of a phenomenon that can still be seen today. History provides abundant evidence of peoples of different origins coming together, usually on the borders of an established culture. The result is usually cultural change outweighing any hostility, for each side learns from the other. The outcome in these instances is the evolution of a new culture that consists of two or more old parts. Although the older culture almost invariably looks on the newcomers as inferior, the new just as invariably contributes something valuable to the old. So it was in 2331 B.C. The Semitic chieftain Sargon conquered Sumer and created a new empire. The symbol of his triumph was a new capital, the city of Akkad. Sargon, the first "world conqueror," led his armies to the Mediterranean Sea. Although his empire lasted only a few generations, it spread Mesopotamian culture throughout the Fertile Crescent, the belt of rich farmland that extends from Mesopotamia in the east up through Syria in the north and down to Egypt in the west (see Map 1.1).

Sargon's impact and the extent of Mesopotamian influence even at this early period have been dramatically revealed at Ebla in modern Syria. In 1964 archaeologists there unearthed a once-flourishing Semitic civilization that had assimilated political, intellectual, and artistic aspects of Mesopotamian culture. In 1975 the excavators uncovered thousands of clay tablets that proved that the people of Ebla had learned the art of writing from the Mesopotamians. Eblaite artists borrowed heavily from Mesopotamian art but developed their own style, which in turn influenced Mesopotamian artists. The Eblaites transmitted the heritage of Mesopotamia to other Semitic centers in Syria.

Further evidence of these developments came to light in November 1993, when American and Turkish archaeologists reported evidence of Sumerian influences far removed from Mesopotamia. At Tell Leilan in northern Syria and at Kazam Hoyuk in southern Turkey, researchers found proof of large urban centers that shared Sumerian culture as early as ca 2600 B.C. Finds included evidence of widespread literacy, a functioning bureaucracy, and links with Ebla and Mesopotamia. These discoveries also point to another conclusion. These frontier cities came under Sumerian influence not by conquest but because they found Mesopotamian culture attractive and useful. In this process, a universal culture developed in the ancient Near East, a culture basically Mesopotamian but fertilized by the traditions, genius, and ways of many other peoples.

The question to answer is why Mesopotamian culture had such an immediate and wide appeal. In the first place it was successful and enjoyed the prestige of its success. Newcomers wanted to find a respectable place in this old and venerated culture. It also provided an easy means of communication among people on a broad scale. The Eblaites could efficiently deal with the Mesopotamians and others who embraced this culture in ways that all could understand. Culture ignores borders. Despite local variations, so much common ground existed that similar political and economic institutions, exchange of ideas and religious beliefs, methods of writing, and a shared etiquette served as links among all who embraced Mesopotamian culture.

The Triumph of Babylon

Although the empire of Sargon was extensive, it was short-lived. The Akkadians, too, failed to solve the problems posed by Mesopotamia's geography and population pattern. Most scholars have attributed the fall of the Akkadian empire to internal problems and external invasions. Yet dramatic discoveries announced in August 1993 suggest strongly that climate also played a role in the demise of Akkadian power. Archaeologists have found evidence of a long, harsh drought, perhaps lasting as long as three hundred years, that struck the northern regions of the empire. The areas most severely affected were in modern Iraq, Syria, and parts of southern Turkey. Abandonment of the northern cities led to a stream of refugees to the south, overtaxing the economic resources of the cities there and straining their social and political structures. Cuneiform tablets mention this migration. The turmoil that resulted from this large influx of peoples may have contributed to the fighting that consumed the Akkadian empire.

It was left to the Babylonians to unite Mesopotamia politically and culturally. The Babylonians were Amorites, a Semitic people who had migrated from Arabia and settled on the site of Babylon along the middle Euphrates, where that river runs close to the Tigris. Babylon enjoyed an excellent geographical position and was ideally suited to be the capital of Mesopotamia. It dominated trade on the Tigris and Euphrates rivers: all commerce to and from Sumer and Akkad had to pass by its walls. It also looked beyond Mesopotamia. Babylonian merchants followed the Tigris north to Assyria and Anatolia. The Euphrates led merchants to Syria, Palestine, and the Mediterranean. The city grew great because of its commercial importance and soundly based power.

Sumerian Ram In the art of many Near Eastern cultures, animals were symbols of fertility, linked to the gods. This ram standing behind a thorn bush represents a deity who has taken the form of an animal. (*Source: Courtesy of the Trustees of the British Museum*)

Babylon was also fortunate to have a farseeing and able king, Hammurabi (r. 1792–1750 B.C.). Hammurabi set out to do three things: make Babylon secure, unify Mesopotamia, and win for the Babylonians a place in Mesopotamian civilization. The first two he accomplished by conquering Assyria in the north and Sumer and Akkad in the south. Then he turned to his third goal.

Politically, Hammurabi joined in his kingship the Semitic concept of the tribal chieftain and the Sumerian idea of urban kingship. Culturally, he encouraged the spread of myths that explained how Marduk, the god of Babylon, had been elected king of the gods by the other Mesopotamian deities. Hammurabi's success in making Marduk the god of all Mesopotamians made Babylon the religious center of Mesopotamia. Through Hammurabi's genius the Babylonians made their own contribution to Mesopotamian culture—a culture vibrant enough to maintain its identity while assimilating new influences. Hammurabi's conquests and the activity of Babylonian merchants spread this enriched culture north to Anatolia and west to Syria and Palestine.

Life Under Hammurabi

One of Hammurabi's most memorable accomplishments was the proclamation of a law code that offers a wealth of information about daily life in Mesopotamia. Hammurabi's was not the first law code in Mesopotamia; indeed, the earliest goes back to about 2100 B.C. Like earlier lawgivers, Hammurabi proclaimed that he issued his laws on divine authority "to establish law and justice in the language of the land, thereby promoting the welfare of the people." Hammurabi's code inflicted such penalties as mutilation, whipping, and burning. Despite its severity, a spirit of justice and a sense of responsibility pervade the code. Hammurabi genuinely felt that his duty was to govern the Mesopotamians as righteously as possible. He tried to regulate the relations of his people so that they could live together in harmony.

The Code of Hammurabi has two striking characteristics. First, the law differed according to the social status of the offender. Aristocrats were not punished as harshly as commoners, nor commoners as harshly as slaves. Second, the code demanded that the punishment fit the crime. It called for "an eye for an eye, and a tooth for a tooth," at least among equals. However, an aristocrat who destroyed the eye of a commoner or slave could pay a fine instead of losing his own eye. Otherwise, as long as criminal and victim shared the same social status, the victim could demand exact vengeance.

Hammurabi's code began with legal procedure. There were no public prosecutors or district attorneys, so individuals brought their own complaints before the court. Each side had to produce written documents or witnesses to support its case. In cases of murder, the accuser had to prove the defendant guilty; any accuser who failed to do so was put to death. This strict law was designed to prevent people from lodging groundless charges. The Mesopotamians were very worried about witchcraft and sorcery. Anyone accused of witchcraft, even if the charges were not proved, underwent an ordeal by water. The gods themselves would decide the case. The defendant was thrown into the Euphrates, which was considered the instrument of the gods. A defendant who sank was guilty; a defendant who floated was innocent. (In medieval Europe and colonial America, accused witches also underwent ordeals by water, but they were considered innocent only if they sank.) Another procedural regulation covered the conduct of judges. Once a judge had rendered a verdict, he could not change it. Any judge who did so was fined heavily and deposed. In short, the code tried to guarantee a fair trial and a just verdict.

Consumer protection is not a modern idea; it goes back to Hammurabi's day. Merchants and businessmen had to guarantee the quality of their goods and services. A boatbuilder who did sloppy work had to repair the boat at his own expense. A boatman who lost the owner's boat or sank someone else's boat had to replace it and its cargo. Housebuilders guaranteed their work with their lives. If careless work resulted in the collapse of a house and the death of its inhabitants, the builder was put to death. A merchant who tried to increase the interest rate on a loan forfeited the entire amount. Hammurabi's laws tried to ensure that consumers got what they paid for and paid a just price.

Crime was a feature of Mesopotamian urban life just as it is in modern cities. Burglary was a serious problem, hard to control. Because houses were built of mud brick, it was easy for an intruder to dig through the walls. Hammurabi's punishment

Law Code of Hammurabi Hammurabi ordered his code to be inscribed on a stone pillar and set up in public. At the top of the pillar Hammurabi is depicted receiving the scepter of authority from the god Shamash. (*Source: Hirmer Verlag München*)

for burglary matched the crime. A burglar caught in the act was put to death on the spot, and his body was walled into the breach that he had made. The penalty for looting was also grim: anyone caught looting a burning house was thrown into the fire.

Mesopotamian taverns were notorious haunts of criminals. Tavernkeepers were expected to keep order and arrest anyone overheard planning a crime. Taverns were normally run by women, and they also served as houses of prostitution. Prostitution was disreputable but neither illegal nor regulated by law. Despite their social stigma, taverns were popular places, for Mesopotamians were fond of beer and wine. Tavernkeepers made a nice profit, but if they were caught increasing their profits by watering drinks, they were drowned.

Because farming was essential to Mesopotamian life, Hammurabi's code dealt extensively with agriculture. Tenant farming was widespread. Tenants rented land on a yearly basis, paying a proportion of their crops as rent. Unless the land was carefully cultivated, it quickly reverted to wasteland. Thus tenants faced severe penalties for neglecting the land or not working it at all. Since irrigation was essential to grow crops, tenants had to keep the canals and ditches in good repair. Otherwise the land would be subject to floods and farmers to crippling losses. Anyone whose neglect of the canals resulted in damaged crops had to bear all the expense of the lost crops. If a tenant could not pay the costs of the damaged crops, he would then be sold into slavery.

The oxen that farmers used for plowing and threshing grain were ordinarily allowed to roam the streets. If an ox gored a passerby, its owner had to pad its horns, tie it up, or bear the responsibility for future damages. Sheep raising was very lucrative because textile production was a major Mesopotamian industry (Mesopotamian cloth was famous throughout the Near East). The shepherd was a hired man with considerable responsibility. He was expected to protect the flock from wild animals, which were a standing problem, and to keep the sheep out of the crops. This strict regulation of agriculture paid rich dividends. The Mesopotamians often enjoyed bumper crops of grain, which fostered a large and thriving population.

Hammurabi gave careful attention to marriage and the family. As elsewhere in the Near East, marriage had aspects of a business agreement. The prospective groom and the father of the future bride arranged everything. The man offered the father a bridal gift, usually money. If the man and his bridal gift were acceptable, the father provided his daughter with a dowry. After marriage the dowry belonged to the woman (although the husband normally administered it) and was a means of protecting her rights and status. Once the two men agreed on financial matters, they drew up a contract; no marriage was considered legal without

one. Either party could break off the marriage, but not without paying a stiff penalty. Fathers often contracted marriages while their children were still young. The girl either continued to live in her father's house until she reached maturity or went to live in the house of her father-in-law. During this time she was legally considered a wife. Once she and her husband came of age, they set up their own house.

The wife was expected to be rigorously faithful. The penalty for adultery was death. According to Hammurabi's code: "If the wife of a man has been caught while lying with another man, they shall bind them and throw them into the water."[7] The husband had the power to spare his wife by obtaining a pardon for her from the king. He could, however, accuse his wife of adultery even if he had not caught her in the act. In such a case she could try to clear herself before the city council, which investigated the charge. If she was found innocent, she could take her dowry and leave her husband. If a woman decided to take the direct approach and kill her husband, she was impaled.

The husband had virtually absolute power over his household. He could even sell his wife and children into slavery to pay debts. Sons did not lightly oppose their fathers, and any son who struck his father could have his hand cut off. A father was free to adopt children and include them in his will. Artisans sometimes adopted children to teach them the family trade. Although the father's power was great, he could not disinherit a son without just cause. Cases of disinheritance became matters for the city to decide, and the code ordered the courts to forgive a son for his first offense. Only if a son wronged his father a second time could he be disinherited.

Hammurabi's code restricted married women from commercial pursuits. Financial documents, however, prove that many women engaged in business without hindrance. Some carried on the family business. Others became wealthy landowners in their own right.

Law codes, preoccupied as they are with the problems of society, provide a bleak view of things. Other Mesopotamian documents give a happier glimpse of life. Although the code dealt with marriage in hard-fisted fashion, a Mesopotamian poem tells of two people meeting secretly in the city. Their parting is delightfully modern:

Come now, set me free, I must go home,
Kuli-Enlil . . . set me free, I must go home.
What can I say to deceive my mother?[8]

Countless wills and testaments show that husbands habitually left their estates to their wives, who in turn willed the property to their children. All this suggests happy family life.

Mesopotamians found their lives lightened by holidays and religious festivals. Traveling merchants brought news of the outside world and swapped marvelous tales. Despite their pessimism the Mesopotamians enjoyed a vibrant and creative culture, a culture that left its mark on the entire Near East.

EGYPT, THE LAND OF THE PHARAOHS (3100–1200 B.C.)

The Greek historian and traveler Herodotus in the fifth century B.C. called Egypt the "gift of the Nile." No other single geographical factor had such a fundamental, profound impact on the shaping of Egyptian life, society, and history as the Nile (Map 1.3). Unlike the rivers in Mesopotamia, it rarely brought death and destruction. The Nile was primarily a creative force. The Egyptians never feared the relatively tame Nile in the way the Mesopotamians feared the Tigris. Instead they sang its praises:

Hail to thee, O Nile, that issues from the earth and
  comes to keep Egypt alive! . . .
He that waters the meadows which Re created,
He that makes to drink the desert . . .
He who makes barley and brings emmer [wheat] into
  being . . .
He who brings grass into being for the cattle . . .
He who makes every beloved tree to grow . . .
O Nile, verdant art thou, who makest man and cattle
  to live.[9]

To the Egyptians, the Nile was the supreme fertilizer and renewer of the land. Each September the Nile floods its valley, transforming it into a huge area of marsh or lagoon. By the end of November the water retreats, leaving behind a thin covering of fertile mud ready to be planted with crops.

Dedication to the Sumerian Goddess Inanna
This alabaster and gold votive figurine dates to ca 2850 B.C. and is typical of many other figures dedicated to the gods. This one was found in the excavation of a temple of the goddess Inanna at Nippur. *(Source: Iraqi National Museum, Baghdad)*

The annual flood made the growing of abundant crops almost effortless, especially in southern Egypt. Herodotus, used to the rigors of Greek agriculture, was amazed by the ease with which the Egyptians raised crops:

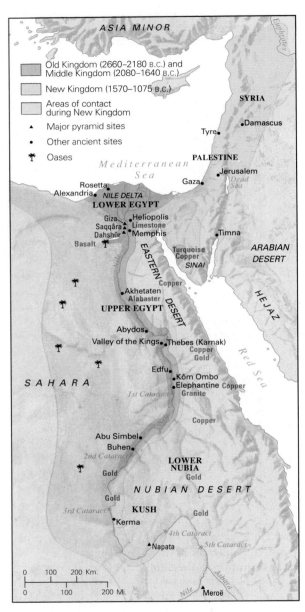

Old Kingdom (2660–2180 B.C.) and
Middle Kingdom (2080–1640 B.C.)

New Kingdom (1570–1075 B.C.)

Areas of contact
during New Kingdom

▲ Major pyramid sites

• Other ancient sites

🌴 Oases

ASIA MINOR

Euphrates

SYRIA

*Mediterranean
Sea*

•Damascus

Tyre•

PALESTINE

Rosetta• •Jerusalem

Alexandria• NILE DELTA   Gaza• *Dead
Sea*

LOWER EGYPT

Giza▲ •Heliopolis
Saqqâra▲ Limestone
Dahshûr▲ •Memphis   •Timna

Basalt 🌴

EASTERN

Turquoise
Copper

SINAI

*ARABIAN
DESERT*

HEJAZ

🌴   Copper

•Akhetaten
Alabaster

UPPER EGYPT

DESERT

🌴

Abydos•

Valley of the Kings•   •Thebes (Karnak)
Copper
Gold

Red Sea

Edfu•

•Kôm Ombo
•Elephantine Copper
1st Cataract Granite

S A H A R A

Copper

Abu Simbel•
Buhen•

2nd Cataract

🌴   **LOWER
NUBIA**

Gold   Gold

N U B I A N   D E S E R T

Gold

3rd Cataract **KUSH**   Gold

•Kerma

4th Cataract

▲Napata   *5th Cataract*

0   100   200 Km.

0   100   200 Mi.

Nile •Meroë

Atbara

✳ **MAP 1.3 Ancient Egypt** Geography and natural resources provided Egypt with centuries of
peace and abundance.

*For indeed without trouble they obtain crops from the
land more easily than all other men. . . . They do not
labor to dig furrows with the plough or hoe or do the
work which other men do to raise grain. But when the
river by itself inundates the fields and the water re-
cedes, then each man, having sown his field, sends*

*pigs into it. When the pigs trample down the seed, he
waits for the harvest. Then when the pigs thresh the
grain, he gets his crop.*[10]

The extraordinary fertility of the Nile Valley made
it easy to produce an annual agricultural surplus,
which in turn sustained a growing and prosperous
population.

Whereas the Tigris and Euphrates and their tributaries carved up Mesopotamia into isolated areas,
the Nile unified Egypt. The river was the region's
principal highway, promoting easy communication
throughout the valley. As individual bands of settlers moved into the Nile Valley, they created stable agricultural communities. By about 3100 B.C.
there were some forty of these communities in
constant contact with one another. This contact,
encouraged and facilitated by the Nile, virtually
ensured the early political unification of Egypt.

Egypt was fortunate because it was nearly self-
sufficient. Besides the fertility of its soil, Egypt
possessed enormous quantities of stone, which
served as the raw material of architecture and
sculpture. Abundant clay was available for pottery,
as was gold for jewelry and ornaments. The raw
materials that Egypt lacked were close at hand.
The Egyptians could obtain copper from Sinai and
timber from Lebanon. They had little cause to
look to the outside world for their essential needs,
which helps to explain the insular quality of Egyptian life.

Geography further encouraged isolation by closing Egypt off from the outside world (see Map
1.3). Yet Egypt was not completely sealed off. As
early as 3250 B.C., Mesopotamian influences, notably architectural techniques and materials and
perhaps even writing, made themselves felt in
Egyptian life. Still later, from 1680 to 1580 B.C.,
northern Egypt was ruled by foreign invaders, the
Hyksos. Infrequent though they were, such periods
of foreign influence fertilized Egyptian culture
without changing it in any fundamental way.

The God-King of Egypt

The geographical unity of Egypt quickly gave rise
to political unification of the country under the
authority of a king whom the Egyptians called
pharaoh. The details of this process have been lost.
Although some scholars have recently suggested

that the origins of Egyptian kingship can be found in Nubia, to the south of Egypt, the evidence is against the idea. First, the concept of kingship is an early and virtually worldwide political notion. Second, the Nubian artifacts so far found can be dated only by Egyptian archaeological finds. That suggests that the Nubians borrowed and adapted some of the symbols of the pharaoh and other aspects of Egyptian culture. What little is known of Nubian kingship indicates typical rule of a single region, in this case much of it mountainous. In contrast, Egyptian kingship is intimately connected with the Nile Valley. The pharaoh was the king of both Upper and Lower Egypt, a geographical situation that did not exist in Nubia.

Most probably, as was the case with the Mesopotamians and the Eblaites, the Egyptians and Nubians enjoyed a long period of mostly peaceful relations during which each learned from the other. Such exchanges of ideas involve the adaptation of certain aspects of culture to fit new, particular, and local circumstances. This situation is precisely what one routinely finds on frontiers. In these cases, all parties bring new ideas and customs together. As a result, they all assimilate what they desire and reject what they find unnecessary. Although the Nubian concept of kingship did not apply to Egyptian geographical conditions, the cultural bonds between the two peoples became so strong that they remained even after the Roman conquest of Egypt centuries later.

The Egyptians themselves told of a great king, Menes, who united Egypt into a single kingdom around 3100 B.C. Thereafter the Egyptians divided their history into *dynasties,* or families of kings. For modern historical purposes, however, it is more useful to divide Egyptian history into periods (see page 29). The political unification of Egypt ushered in the period now known as the Old Kingdom, an era remarkable for prosperity, artistic flowering, and the evolution of religious beliefs.

In religion, the Egyptians developed complex, often contradictory, ideas about an afterlife. These beliefs were all rooted in the environment. The climate of Egypt is so stable that change is cyclical and dependable: the heat of summer bakes the land, and in the fall the Nile always floods and replenishes it. The dry air preserves much that would decay in other climates. Thus there is an air of permanence about Egypt; the past is never far from the present.

This cyclical rhythm permeated Egyptian religious beliefs. According to the Egyptians, Osiris, a fertility god associated with the Nile, died each year, and each year his wife Isis brought him back to life. Osiris eventually became king of the dead, weighing human beings' hearts to determine whether they had lived justly enough to deserve everlasting life. Osiris's care of the dead was shared by Anubis, the jackal-headed god who annually helped Isis resuscitate Osiris. Anubis was the god of mummification, so essential to Egyptian funerary rites.

The focal point of religious and political life in the Old Kingdom was the pharaoh, who commanded the wealth, resources, and people of all Egypt. The pharaoh's power was such that the Egyptians considered him to be the falcon-god Horus in human form. The link between the pharaoh and the god Horus was doubly important. In Egyptian religion Horus was the son of Osiris (king of the dead), which meant that the pharaoh, a living god on earth, became one with Osiris after death. The pharaoh was not simply the mediator between the gods and the Egyptian people. He was the power that achieved the integration between gods and humans, between nature and society, that ensured peace and prosperity for the land of the Nile. The pharaoh was thus a guarantee to his people, a pledge that the gods of Egypt (unlike those of Mesopotamia) cared for their people.

The king's surroundings had to be worthy of a god. Only a magnificent palace was suitable for his home; in fact, the word *pharaoh* means "great house." The king's tomb also had to reflect his might and exalted status. To this day the great pyramids at Giza near Cairo bear silent but magnificent testimony to the god-kings of Egypt. The pharaoh's ability to command the resources and labor necessary to build a huge pyramid amply demonstrates that the god-king was an absolute ruler.

The Pharaoh's People

Because the common folk stood at the bottom of the social and economic scale, they were always at the mercy of grasping officials. The arrival of the tax collector was never a happy occasion. One Egyptian scribe described the worst consequences of such a visit:

Narmer Palette   This ceremonial object celebrates the deeds of Narmer, but it also illustrates several of the attributes of the pharaoh in general. At the top left, the conquering pharaoh views the decapitated corpse of an unknown enemy, showing his duty to defend Egypt by defeating its enemies. This same theme recurs on the right where the pharaoh—also represented by the falcon, symbol of Horus—is about to kill a captive. *(Source: Jean Vertut)*

And now the scribe lands on the river-bank and is about to register the harvest-tax. The janitors carry staves and the Nubians rods of palm, and they say, Hand over the corn, though there is none. The cultivator is beaten all over, he is bound and thrown into a well, soused and dipped head downwards. His wife has been bound in his presence and his children are in fetters.[11]

That was an extreme situation. Nonetheless, taxes might amount to 20 percent of the harvest, and tax collection could be brutal.

Egyptian society seems to have been a curious mixture of freedom and constraint. Slavery did not become widespread until the New Kingdom. There was neither a caste system nor a color bar, and humble people could rise to the highest positions if they possessed talent. Most ordinary folk, however, were probably little more than serfs who could not easily leave the land of their own free will. Peasants were also subject to forced labor, including work on the pyramids and canals. Young men were drafted into the pharaoh's army, which served both as a fighting force and as a labor corps.

The vision of thousands of people straining to build the pyramids and countless artists adorning the pharaoh's tomb brings to the modern mind a distasteful picture of oriental despotism. Indeed, the Egyptian view of life and society is alien to people raised on Western concepts of individual freedom and human rights. To ancient Egyptians the pharaoh embodied justice and order—harmony among human beings, nature, and the divine. If the pharaoh was weak or allowed anyone to challenge his unique position, he opened the way to chaos. Twice in Egyptian history the pharaoh failed to maintain rigid centralization. During those two eras, known as the First and Second Intermediate periods, Egypt was exposed to civil war and invasion. But the monarchy survived, and in each period a strong pharaoh arose to crush the rebels or expel the invaders and restore order.

The Hyksos in Egypt (1640–1570 B.C.)

While Egyptian civilization flourished behind its bulwark of sand and sea, momentous changes were taking place in the ancient Near East, changes that would leave their mark even on rich, insular Egypt. These changes involved enormous and remarkable movements, especially of peoples who spoke Semitic languages.

The original home of the Semites was perhaps the Arabian peninsula. Some tribes moved into northern Mesopotamia, others into Syria and Palestine, and still others into Egypt. Shortly after 1800 B.C. people whom the Egyptians called *Hyksos,* which means "Rulers of the Uplands," began to settle in the Nile Delta. Many scholars have sought the origins of the Hyksos. Available evidence indicates that they entered Egypt from the areas of modern Israel and Lebanon. Yet that is only a partial explanation, for the movements of the Hyksos were part of a larger pattern of migration during this period. The history of Mesopotamia records many such wanderings of people in search of better homes for themselves. Such nomads normally settled in and accommodated themselves with the native cultures. The process was mutually beneficial: each group had something to give and to learn from the other. So it was in Egypt, although Egyptian tradition, as later

The Pyramids at Giza   Giza was the burial place of the pharaohs of the Old Kingdom and of their aristocracy, whose rectangular tombs are visible behind the middle pyramid. The small pyramids at the foot of the foremost pyramid probably belong to the pharaohs' wives. *(Source: Hirmer Verlag München)*

regions of the east men of obscure race, looking forward confidently to victory, invaded our land, and without a battle easily seized it all by sheer force. Having subdued those in authority in the land, they then barbarously burned our cities and razed to the ground the temples of the gods. They fell upon all the natives in an entirely hateful fashion, slaughtering them and leading both their children and wives into slavery. At last they made one of their people king, whose name was Salitis. This man resided at Memphis, leaving in Upper and Lower Egypt tax collectors and garrisons in strategic places.[12]

Although the Egyptians portrayed the Hyksos as a conquering horde, they were probably no more than nomads looking for good land. Their entry into the Nile Delta was probably gradual and generally peaceful. The Hyksos introduced new ideas and techniques into Egyptian life. They brought with them the method of making bronze and casting it into tools and weapons that became standard in Egypt. They thereby brought Egypt fully into the Bronze Age culture of the Mediterranean world, a culture in which the production and use of bronze implements became basic to society. Bronze tools made farming more efficient than ever before because they were sharper and more durable than the copper tools they replaced. The Hyksos's use of bronze armor and weapons, as well as horse-drawn chariots and the composite bow (made of laminated wood and horn and far more powerful than the simple wooden bow), revolutionized Egyptian warfare. But however much the Egyptians learned from the Hyksos, Egyptian culture eventually absorbed the newcomers. The Hyksos came to worship Egyptian gods and modeled their monarchy on the pharaonic system.

The New Kingdom: Revival and Empire (1570–1200 B.C.)

Politically, Egypt was only in eclipse during the Hyksos period. The Egyptian sun shone again when a remarkable line of kings, the pharaohs of the Eighteenth Dynasty, arose to challenge the Hyksos. The pharaoh Ahmose (1558–1533 B.C.) pushed the Hyksos out of the Nile Delta. Thutmose I (1512–1500 B.C.) subdued Nubia in the south, and Thutmose III (1490–1436 B.C.) conquered Palestine and Syria. These warrior-pharaohs

✤ **Hippopotamus Hunt**   This wall painting depicts the success of two men in a small boat who have killed a hippopotamus, seen in the lower right-hand corner. Behind the hippopotamus swims a crocodile hoping for a snack. *(Source: Egyptian Museum SMPK, Berlin/Bildarchiv Preussischer Kulturbesitz)*

recorded by the priest Manetho in the third century B.C., depicted the coming of the Hyksos as a brutal invasion:

In the reign of Toutimaios—I do not know why—the wind of god blew against us. Unexpectedly from the

PERIODS OF EGYPTIAN HISTORY

PERIOD	DATES	SIGNIFICANT EVENTS
Archaic	3100–2660 B.C.	Unification of Egypt
Old Kingdom	2660–2180 B.C.	Construction of the pyramids
First Intermediate	2180–2080 B.C.	Political chaos
Middle Kingdom	2080–1640 B.C.	Recovery and political stability
Second Intermediate	1640–1570 B.C.	Hyksos "invasion"
New Kingdom	1570–1075 B.C.	Creation of an Egyptian empire Akhenaten's religious policy

3rd Intermediate   1100 – 700 Bc   political fragmentation "DARK AGE" [handwritten]

inaugurated the New Kingdom—a period in Egyptian history characterized by enormous wealth and conscious imperialism. During this period and probably for the first time, widespread slavery became a feature of Egyptian life. The pharaoh's armies returned home leading hordes of slaves, who constituted a new labor force for imperial building projects.

The kings of the Eighteenth Dynasty created the first Egyptian empire. Egyptian religion and customs flourished in Nubia, making a huge impact on African culture there and in neighboring areas. The warrior-kings celebrated their success with monuments on a scale unparalleled since the pharaohs of the Old Kingdom had built the pyramids. Even today the colossal granite statues of these pharaohs and the rich tomb objects of Tutankhamen ("King Tut") testify to the might and splendor of the New Kingdom.

One of the most extraordinary of this unusual line of kings was Akhenaten (r. 1367–1350 B.C.), a pharaoh more concerned with religion than with conquest. Nefertiti, his wife and queen, encouraged his religious bent. Akhenaten's religion was often unpopular among the people and the traditional priesthood, and its practice declined in the later years of his reign. After his death, it was condemned and denounced; consequently, not much is known about it. Most historians, however, agree that Akhenaten and Nefertiti were *monotheists*— that is, believers in one universal god, the sun-god

Aton, whom they worshiped. They considered all other Egyptian gods and goddesses frauds and declined to worship them. Yet their belief suffered from an obvious inconsistency. Because the pharaoh himself was considered to be a god, Akhenaten's monotheism somewhat illogically embraced two divine beings. What Akhenaten meant by monotheism was that Aton was the only real god among the traditional Egyptian deities.

Akhenaten's monotheism, imposed from above, failed to find a place among the people. His god had no connection with the past of the Egyptian people, who trusted the old gods and felt comfortable praying to them. The Egyptians had long worshiped a host of gods, chief among whom was Amon-Re, whom they worshiped as king of the gods. Many Egyptians were sincerely devoted to their traditional gods, who they thought had preserved Egypt and would grant them life after death.

To such genuine religious sentiments were added the motives of the traditional priesthood. Many priests were scandalized by Akhenaten's brand of monotheism, and many were concerned about their own welfare. By deposing the old gods, Akhenaten destroyed the priests' livelihood and their reason for existence. Out of pure self-interest, the established priesthood opposed Akhenaten, and their opposition drove the pharaoh to intolerance and persecution. With a vengeance he tried to root out the old gods and their rituals.

To celebrate his break with the past, Akhenaten built a new capital, Akhetaten, present-day El-Amarna (see Map 1.3). There Aton was honored with an immense temple and proper worship. Worship of Aton focused on truth (as Akhenaten defined it) and a desire for the natural. The pharaoh and his queen demanded that the truth be carried over into art. Unlike Old Kingdom painting and sculpture, which blended the actual and the abstract, the art of this period became relentlessly realistic. Sculptors molded exact likenesses of Akhenaten, despite his ugly features and misshapen body. Artists portrayed the pharaoh in intimate family scenes, playing with his infant daughter or expressing affection to members of his family. On one relief Akhenaten appears gnawing a cutlet of meat; on another he lolls in a chair. Akhenaten was being portrayed as a mortal man, not as the divine pharaoh of Egypt.

Average Egyptians were no doubt distressed and disheartened when their familiar gods were outlawed, for those were the gods who they believed had made Egypt powerful and unique. The fanaticism and persecution that accompanied the new monotheism were in complete defiance of the Egyptian tradition of tolerant *polytheism*—the worship of several gods. Thus when Akhenaten died, his religion died with him.

✳ **Akhenaten and Aton** This relief shows the pharaoh and his family giving offerings to Aton, who is represented as the sun. It also demonstrates a new realism in Egyptian art. *(Source: Egyptian Museum, Cairo)*

❖ THE HITTITE EMPIRE

At about the time the Hyksos entered the Nile Delta, the Hittites, who had long been settled in Anatolia (modern Turkey), became a major power in that region and began to expand eastward (Map 1.4). The Hittites were an Indo-European people. The term *Indo-European* refers to a large family of languages that includes English, most of the languages of modern Europe, Greek, Latin, Persian, and Sanskrit, the sacred tongue of ancient India. During the eighteenth and nineteenth centuries, European scholars learned that peoples who spoke related languages had spread as far west as Ireland and as far east as central Asia. In the twentieth century, linguists deciphered the language of the Hittites and the Linear B script of Mycenaean Greece. When both languages proved to be Indo-European, scholars were able to form a clearer picture of these vast movements. Archaeologists were able to date the migrations roughly and put them into their historical context.

Despite the efforts of many scholars, the original home of the Indo-Europeans remains to be identified. Judging primarily from the spread of the lan-

❋ **MAP 1.4 Balance of Power in the Near East**   This map shows the regions controlled by the Hittites and Egyptians at the height of their power. The striped area represents the part of Mesopotamia conquered by the Hittites during their expansion eastward.

guages, linguists have suggested that the migrations started from the steppes region north of the Black and Caspian seas. Although two great waves began around 2000 B.C. and 1200 B.C., these migrations on the whole followed a sporadic and gradual progression. The Celtic-speaking Gauls, for example, did not move into the area of present-day France, Belgium, and Germany until the seventh century B.C., long after most Indo-Europeans had found new homes.

Around 2000 B.C. Indo-Europeans were on the move on a massive scale. Peoples speaking the ancestor of Latin pushed into Italy, and Greek-speaking Mycenaeans settled in Greece. The Hittites came into prominence in Anatolia, and other folk thrust into Iran, India, and central Asia. At first the waves of Indo-Europeans and other peoples disrupted already existing states, but in time the newcomers settled down.

The Rise of the Hittites

Until recently, scholars thought that as part of these vast movements the Hittites entered Anatolia only around 1800 B.C. Current archaeological work and new documents, however, prove that the Hittites had settled there at least as early as 2700 B.C. Nor did they overrun the country in a sweeping invasion, burning, looting, and destroying. Their arrival and diffusion seem to have been rather peaceful, accompanied by intermarriage and alliance with the natives. So well did the Hittites integrate themselves into the local culture of central Anatolia that they even adopted the worship of several native deities.

Their mastery of iron technology set the Hittites apart. Although it is not yet known whether the Hittites were first to discover the possibilities of iron and the ways to use it, they mastered iron technology before anyone else in the Near East. Their knowledge permitted them to craft weapons and tools far superior to those of their neighbors and gave them a decided advantage in both war and commerce.

The rise of the Hittites to prominence in Anatolia is reasonably clear. During the nineteenth century B.C. the native kingdoms in the area engaged in suicidal warfare that left most of Anatolia's once-flourishing towns in ashes and rubble. In this climate of exhaustion the Hittite king Hattusilis I built a hill citadel at Hattusas (modern Boghazköy), from which he led his Hittites against neighboring kingdoms (see Map 1.4). Hattusilis's grandson and successor, Mursilis I (ca 1595 B.C.), extended the Hittite conquests as far as Babylon. With help from the Kassites, a people who had newly settled along the upper reaches of the Euphrates River, Mursilis captured the city and snuffed out the dynasty of Hammurabi. While the Hittites carried off Babylonian loot, the Kassites took control of the territory. Upon his return home, the victorious Mursilis was assassinated by members of his own family, an act that plunged the kingdom into confusion and opened the door to foreign invasion. Mursilis's career is representative of the success and weakness of the Hittites. They were extremely vulnerable to attack by vigilant and tenacious enemies. But once they were united behind a strong king, the Hittites were a power to be reckoned with.

Hittite Society

The geography of central Anatolia encouraged the rise of self-contained agricultural communities. Each was probably originally ruled by a petty king, but under the Hittites a group of local officials known as the Elders handled community affairs. Besides the farming population, Hittite society included a well-defined group of artisans who fashioned pottery, cloth, leather goods, and metal tools. Documents also report that traveling merchants peddled goods and gossip, reminding individual communities that they were part of a larger world. Like many other societies, ancient and modern, the Hittites held slaves, who nonetheless enjoyed certain rights under the law.

At the top of Hittite society was the aristocracy, among whom the relatives of the king constituted a privileged group. The king's relations were a mighty and often unruly group who served as the chief royal administrators. Hittite nobles often revolted against the king, a tendency that weakened central authority and left Hittite society open to outside attack. Below the nobles stood the warriors, who enjoyed the right to meet in their own assembly, the *pankus.* The pankus met to hear the will of the king but could not vote on policy. It was, however, a court of law with the authority to punish criminals.

Above the aristocracy stood the king and queen. The king was the supreme commander of the army, chief judge, and supreme priest. He carried on all diplomatic dealings with foreign powers and in times of war he personally led the Hittite army into the field. The queen held a strong, independent position. She had important religious duties to perform, and some Hittite queens engaged in diplomatic correspondence with foreign queens.

Like many other newcomers to the ancient Near East, the Hittites readily assimilated the cultures that they found. They soon fell under the powerful spell of the more advanced Mesopotamian culture. They adopted the cuneiform script for their own language. Hittite kings published law codes, just as Hammurabi had done, and their royal correspondence followed Mesopotamian forms. The Hittites delighted in Mesopotamian myths, legends, epics, and art. To the credit of the Hittites, they used these Mesopotamian borrowings to create something of their own.

The Era of Hittite Greatness (ca 1475–ca 1200 B.C.)

Like the Egyptians of the New Kingdom, the Hittites eventually produced an energetic and capable line of kings. Those kings restored order and rebuilt Hittite power by controlling the aristocracy, securing central Anatolia, and regaining Syria. Around 1300 B.C. the Hittites stopped the Egyptian army of Rameses II at the battle of Kadesh in Syria. Having fought each other to a standstill, the Hittites and Egyptians first made peace, then an alliance. Alliance was followed by friendship, and friendship by active cooperation. The two greatest powers of the early Near East tried to make war between themselves impossible.

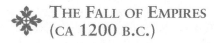 **Hittite Sphinx Gate**   Little praise can be heaped on Hittite art. This sphinx was a symbol of divine protection of the city of Alaca Hüyük. In much of the Near East the placement of ferocious-looking animals at the city gates to ward off evil was common. *(Source: Antonello Perissinotto, Padua)*

They next included the Babylonians in their diplomacy. All three empires developed an official etiquette in which they treated one another as "brothers." They made alliances for offensive and defensive protection and swore to uphold one another's authority. These contacts facilitated the exchange of ideas throughout the Near East. Furthermore, the Hittites passed much knowledge and lore from the Near East to the newly arrived Greeks in Europe (see Chapter 5). The details of Hittite contact with the Greeks are unknown, but enough literary themes and physical objects exist to prove the connection.

THE FALL OF EMPIRES (CA 1200 B.C.)

Like the Hittite kings, Rameses II (ca 1290–1224 B.C.) used the peace after the battle of Kadesh to promote the prosperity of his own kingdom. Free from the expense and waste of warfare, he concentrated the income from the natural wealth and the foreign trade of Egypt on internal affairs. In the age-old tradition of the pharaohs, he began new building projects that brought both employment to his subjects and grandeur to Egypt. From Nubia to the delta of the Nile he bedecked his kingdom with grand, new monuments. Once again, Egypt was wealthy and secure within its natural boundaries. In many ways, he was the last great pharaoh of Egypt.

This stable and generally peaceful situation endured until the late thirteenth century B.C., when invaders destroyed both the Hittite and the Egyptian empires. The most famous of these marauders, called "Sea Peoples" by the Egyptians, remain one of the puzzles of ancient history. Despite much new work, modern archaeology is still unable to identify the Sea Peoples satisfactorily. The reason for this uncertainty is that the Sea Peoples were a collection of peoples who went their own, individual ways after their attacks on the Hittites and Egyptians. It is known, however, that their incursions were part of a larger movement of peoples. Although there is serious doubt about whether the Sea Peoples alone overthrew the Hittites, they did deal both the Hittites and the Egyptians a hard blow, making the Hittites vulnerable to overland invasion from the north and driving the Egyptians back to the Nile Delta. The Hittites fell under the external blows, but the Egyptians, shaken and battered, retreated to the delta and held on.

SUMMARY

During the long span of years covered by this chapter, human beings made astonishing strides, advancing from primitive hunters to become builders of sophisticated civilizations. Four great rivers provided the natural conditions necessary to sustain settled life. Yet because the rivers presented different problems to different peoples, developments across the globe were not identical. By mastering the plant and animal worlds, human beings prospered dramatically. With their basic bodily needs more than satisfied, they realized even greater achievements, including more complex social groupings, metal technology, and long-distance trade. The intellectual achievements of these centuries were equally impressive. Ancient Near Eastern peoples created advanced mathematics, monumental architecture, and engaging literature. Although the societies of the Near East suffered stunning blows in the thirteenth century B.C., more persisted than perished. The great

achievements of Mesopotamia and Egypt survived to enhance the lives of those who came after.

NOTES

1. L. Eiseley, *The Unexpected Universe* (New York: Harcourt Brace Jovanovich, 1969), p. 102.
2. Quoted in S. N. Kramer, *The Sumerians,* (Chicago: University of Chicago Press, 1964), p. 238.
3. J. B. Pritchard, ed., *Ancient Near Eastern Texts,* 3d ed. (Princeton, N.J.: Princeton University Press, 1969), p. 175. Hereafter called *ANET.*
4. *ANET,* p. 44.
5. *ANET,* p. 590.
6. Kramer, *The Sumerians,* p. 150.
7. *ANET,* p. 171.
8. Kramer, *The Sumerians,* p. 251.
9. *ANET,* p. 372.
10. Herodotus, *The Histories* 2.14. Translated by John Buckler.
11. Quoted in A. H. Gardiner, "Ramesside Texts Relating to the Taxation and Transport of Corn," *Journal of Egyptian Archaeology* 27 (1941): 19–20.
12. Manetho, *History of Egypt,* frag. 42.75–77. Translated by John Buckler.

SUGGESTED READING

Those interested in the tangled and incomplete story of human evolution will be rewarded by a good deal of new work, much of it difficult. C. E. Oxnard, *Fossils, Teeth and Sex* (1987), concludes that the search for the "missing link" is the wrong approach because the question is ultimately impossible to answer. I. Rouse, *Migrations in Prehistory* (1989), studies population movements using information from cultural remains. A broad study about women's role in these events comes from M. Ehrenberg, *Women in Prehistory* (1989).

Some very illuminating general studies of Near Eastern developments have recently reached print. H. W. F. Saggs, *Civilization Before Greece and Rome* (1989), provides a fresh analysis of the period that incorporates archaeological and literary evidence to discuss the many achievements of ancient Eastern societies. Similar in nature is A. B. Knapp, *The History and Culture of Ancient Western Asia and Egypt* (1988), a good synthesis by an able scholar. H. J. Nissen examines a broad range of subjects in *The Early History of the Ancient Near East* (1988), which covers the period from 9000 to 2000 B.C., and in *Archaic Bookkeeping* (1993), which discusses the development of early writing and its use in the administration of the ancient economy. Most welcome is the publication of D. Schmandt-Besserat's two-volume work on the origins of writing: *Before Writing;* volume 1 (1992) explores the development of cuneiform writing, and volume 2 (1992) provides the actual evidence. There is nothing to match it on the topic.

H. Crawford, *Sumer and the Sumerians* (1991), gives a fresh appraisal of the Sumerians and poses some intriguing questions. In a very ambitious and thoughtful book, G. Algaze, *The Uruk World System* (1993), examines how the early Mesopotamians expanded their civilization. Older but still valuable is H. W. F. Saggs, *Everyday Life in Babylonia and Assyria* (1965), which offers a delightful glimpse of Mesopotamian life. G. Pettinato, the excavator of Ebla, gives the most thorough description of the site and its importance in *Ebla* (1991).

N. Grimal, *A History of Ancient Egypt* (1992), provides the most recent reassessment of Egyptian history. A bit older but still useful is C. G. Kemp, *Ancient Egypt: Anatomy of a Civilization* (1988), a comprehensive study of Egyptian society. A. Blackman, *Gods, Priests and Men* (1993), is a series of studies in the religion of pharaonic Egypt. B. S. Lesko, *The Remarkable Women of Ancient Egypt,* 2d ed. (1987), is a brief survey of aristocratic and ordinary women that concludes that Egyptian women led freer lives than women of the Greco-Roman period. G.

Robins, *Women in Ancient Egypt* (1993), which is richly illustrated, adds visual information to the literary sources. W. L. Moran, *The Amarna Letters* (1992), has translated the Egyptian documents that are so important to the understanding of events in the New Kingdom. Moran also includes a commentary that explains the significance of the documents. D. B. Redford, *Akenaten: The Heretic King* (1984), puts Akhenaten into his historical context, both political and religious. The title of L. Manniche, *Sexual Life in Ancient Egypt* (1987), aptly describes the book's subject. M. Lichtheim, *Ancient Egyptian Literature,* 3 vols. (1975–1980), is a selection of readings covering the most important periods of Egyptian history.

O. R. Gurney, *The Hittites,* 2d ed. (1954), is still a fine introduction by an eminent scholar. Good also is J. G. MacQueen, *The Hittites and Their Contemporaries in Asia Minor,* 2d ed. (1986). J. P. Mallory, *In Search of the Indo-Europeans* (1989), uses language, archaeology, and myth to study the Indo-Europeans. The 1960s were prolific years for archaeology in Turkey. A brief survey by one of the masters of the field is J. Mellaart, *The Archaeology of Modern Turkey* (1978), which also tests a great number of widely held historical interpretations. The Sea Peoples have been recently studied by T. and M. Dothan, *People of the Sea* (1992), who concentrate their work on the Philistines.

A truly excellent study of ancient religions, from Sumer to the late Roman Empire, is M. Eliade, ed., *Religions of Antiquity* (1989).

LISTENING TO THE
PAST

A Quest for Immortality

The human desire to escape the grip of death, to achieve immortality, is one of the oldest wishes of all peoples. The Sumerian Epic of Gilgamesh *is the earliest recorded treatment of this topic. The oldest elements of the epic go back at least to the third millennium B.C. According to tradition, Gilgamesh was a king of Uruk whom the Sumerians, Babylonians, and Assyrians considered a hero-king and a god. In the story Gilgamesh and his friend Enkidu set out to attain immortality and join the ranks of the gods. They attempt to do so by performing wondrous feats against fearsome agents of the gods, who are determined to thwart them.*

During their quest Enkidu dies. Gilgamesh, more determined than ever to become immortal, begins seeking anyone who might tell him how to do so. His journey involves the effort not only to escape from death but also to reach an understanding of the meaning of life.

The passage begins with Enkidu speaking of a dream that foretells his own death.

Listen, my friend [Gilgamesh], this is the dream I dreamed last night. The heavens roared, and earth rumbled back an answer; between them I stood before an awful being, the sombre-faced man-bird; he had directed on me his purpose. His was a vampire face, his foot was a lion's foot, his hand was an eagle's talon. He fell on me and his claws were in my hair, he held me fast and I smothered; then he transformed me so that my arms became wings covered with feathers. He turned his stare towards me, and he led me away to the palace of Irkalla, the Queen of Darkness [the goddess of the underworld; in other words, an agent of death], to the house from which none who enters ever returns, down the road from which there is no coming back.

At this point Enkidu dies, whereupon Gilgamesh sets off on his quest for the secret of immortality. During his travels he meets with Siduri, the wise and good-natured goddess of wine, who gives him the following advice.

Gilgamesh, where are you hurrying to? You will never find that life for which you are looking. When the gods created man they allotted to him death, but life they retained in their own keeping. As for you, Gilgamesh, fill your belly with good things; day and night, night and day, dance and be merry, feast and rejoice. Let your clothes be fresh, bathe yourself in water, cherish the little child that holds your hand, and make your wife happy in your embrace; for this too is the lot of man.

Ignoring Siduri's advice, Gilgamesh continues his journey, until he finds Utnapishtim. Meeting Utnapishtim is especially important because, like Gilgamesh, he was once a mortal but the gods so favored him that they put him in an eternal paradise. Gilgamesh puts to Utnapishtim the question that is the reason for his quest.

Oh, father Utnapishtim, you who have entered the assembly of the gods, I wish to question you concerning the living and the dead, how shall I find the life for which I am searching?

Utnapishtim said "There is no permanence. Do we build a house to stand forever, do we seal a contract to hold for all time? Do brothers divide an inheritance to keep forever, does the flood-time of rivers endure? . . . What is there between the master and the servant when both have fulfilled their doom? When the Anunnaki [the gods of the underworld], the judges, come together, and Mammetun [the goddess of fate] the mother of destinies, together they decree the fates of men. Life and death they allot but the day of death they do not disclose.

Then Gilgamesh said to Utnapishtim the Faraway, "I look at you now, Utnapishtim, and your appearance is no different from mine; there is nothing strange in your features. I thought I should find you like a hero prepared for battle, but you lie here taking your ease on your back. Tell me truly, how was it that you came to enter the company of the gods and to possess everlasting life?" Utnapishtim said to Gilgamesh, "I shall reveal to you a mystery, I shall tell you a secret of the gods."

Utnapishtim then tells Gilgamesh of a time when the great god Enlil had become angered with the Sumerians and encouraged the other gods to wipe out humanity. The god Ea, however, warned Utnapishtim about the gods' decision to send a great flood to destroy the Sumerians. He commanded Utnapishtim to build a boat big enough to hold his family, various artisans, and all animals in order to survive the flood that was to come. Although Enlil was infuriated by the Sumerians' survival, Ea rebuked him. Then Enlil relented and blessed Utnapishtim with eternal paradise. After telling the story, Utnapishtim foretells Gilgamesh's fate.

Utnapishtim said, ". . . The destiny was fulfilled which the father of the gods, Enlil of the mountain, had decreed for Gilgamesh: In nether-earth the darkness will show him a light: of mankind, all that are known, none will leave a monument for generations to compare with his. The heroes, the wise men, like the new moon have their waxing and waning. Men will say, Who has ever ruled with might and power like his? As in the dark month, the month of shadows, so without him there is no light. O Gilgamesh, this was the meaning of your dream [of immortality]. You were given the kingship, such was your destiny, everlasting life was not your destiny. Because of this do not be sad at heart, do not be grieved or oppressed; he [Enlil] has given you power to bind and to loose, to be the darkness and the light of mankind. He has given unexampled supremacy over the people, victory in battle from which no fugitive re-

Gilgamesh, from the decorative panel of a lyre unearthed at Ur. *(Source: The University Museum, University of Pennsylvania)*

turns, in forays and assaults from which there is no going back. But do not abuse this power, deal justly with your servants in the palace, deal justly before the face of the Sun."

Questions for Analysis

1. What does *The Epic of Gilgamesh* reveal about Sumerian attitudes toward the gods and human beings?

2. At the end of his quest, did Gilgamesh achieve immortality? If so, what was the nature of that immortality?

3. What does the epic tell us about Sumerian views of the nature of human life? Where do human beings fit into the cosmic world?

Source: *The Epic of Gilgamesh,* translated by N. K. Sanders. Copyright © 1972 by Penguin Books, Ltd.

2

Small Kingdoms and Mighty Empires in the East

Reconstruction of the "Ishtar Gate," Babylon, early sixth century B.C. In the Berlin Museum. *(Source: Staatlich e Museen zu Berlin)*

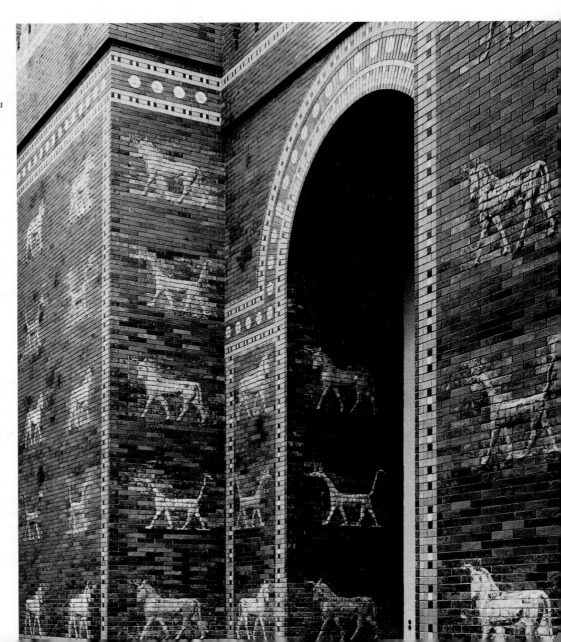

The migratory invasions that brought down the Hittites and stunned the Egyptians in the late thirteenth century B.C. ushered in an era of confusion and weakness. Although much was lost in the chaos, the old cultures of the ancient Near East survived to nurture new societies. In the absence of powerful empires, the Phoenicians, Syrians, Hebrews, and many other peoples carved out small independent kingdoms. During this period Hebrew culture and religion evolved under the influence of urbanism, kings, and prophets.

In the ninth century B.C. this jumble of small states gave way to an empire that for the first time embraced the entire Near East. Yet the very ferocity of the Assyrian Empire led to its downfall only two hundred years later. In 550 B.C. the Persians and Medes, who had migrated into Iran, created a vast empire stretching from Anatolia in the west to the Indus Valley in the east. For over two hundred years the Persians gave the ancient Near East peace and stability.

- How did Egypt, its political greatness behind it, pass on its cultural heritage to its African neighbors?

- How did the Hebrew state and Hebrew religious thought evolve, and what was daily life like in Hebrew society?

- What enabled the Assyrians to overrun their neighbors, and how did their cruelty finally cause their undoing?

- How did Iranian nomads create the Persian Empire?

In this chapter we seek answers to these questions.

❀ MIGRATIONS

The massive migrations of peoples during this period were merely one aspect of the movement of human populations that has been ongoing since the Paleolithic Age. Just as Indo-European and Semitic-speaking peoples sought new land around 1200 B.C., so in the nineteenth and twentieth centuries peoples from Europe and Asia came to North America seeking new opportunities for a more prosperous life. In antiquity, however, the picture is especially complex, and the reasons for movement are varied and unclear. The Hyksos moved into Egypt looking for new land (see pages 27–28). The later onslaught of the Sea Peoples on Egypt seems more like random raids than migrations even though many of the Sea Peoples established permanent homes elsewhere in the Mediterranean (pages 33–34). The Hebrews left Egypt to escape a harsh government (pages 40–41). In short, one major reason for migrations is the poverty of the environment, sometimes combined with overpopulation, which forces people to seek better land. Another is the reaction to vast movements of people. Weaker folk push ahead of the newcomers seeking new homes elsewhere and, as they move, create for others the same problems and challenges that they themselves had confronted. Still other migrants simply try to escape cruel or oppressive governments. In many instances more than one of these factors lie behind the migrations. Each case must be studied individually.

The effects of migrations are as varied as the reasons for them. Some newcomers, like the Hyksos and the Hittites, who came peaceably, draw important lessons from the established peoples whom they encounter, and they contribute something of their own to the cultural environment, which is thereby enriched for both the new arrivals and the native inhabitants. Other migrations result in the obliteration of the native population. As a result, some peoples are known today only by name. No one has yet studied this vast historical phenomenon on its own massive scale, but it can be safely said that the outcome of many of the migrations that occurred around the thirteenth century B.C. was a combination of destruction and fertilization.

❀ EGYPT, A SHATTERED KINGDOM

The invasions of the Sea Peoples brought the great days of Egyptian power to an end. One scribe left behind a somber portrait of Egypt stunned and leaderless:

The land of Egypt was abandoned and every man was a law to himself. During many years there was no leader who could speak for others. Central government lapsed, small officials and headmen took over the whole land. Any man, great or small, might kill his neighbor. In the distress and vacuum that followed . . .

men banded together to plunder one another. They treated the gods no better than men, and cut off the temple revenues.[1]

Egyptians suffered a four-hundred-year period of political fragmentation, a new dark age known to Egyptian specialists as the Third Intermediate Period (eleventh to seventh centuries B.C.). The decline of Egypt was especially sharp in foreign affairs. Whereas the pharaohs of the Eighteenth Dynasty had held sway as far abroad as Syria, their weak successors found it unsafe to venture far from home. In the wake of the Sea Peoples, numerous small kingdoms sprang up in the Near East. Each was fiercely protective of its own independence. To those kingdoms Egypt was a memory, and foreign princes often greeted Egyptian officials with suspicion or even contempt. In the days of Egypt's greatness, petty kings would never have dared to treat Egyptian officials in such a humiliating fashion.

Disrupted at home and powerless abroad, Egypt fell prey to invasion by its African neighbors. Libyans from North Africa filtered into the Nile Delta, where they established independent dynasties. Indeed, from 950 to 730 B.C. northern Egypt was ruled by Libyan pharaohs. The Libyans built cities, and for the first time a sturdy urban life grew up in the delta. Although the coming of the Libyans changed the face of the delta, the Libyans genuinely admired Egyptian culture and eagerly adopted Egypt's religion and way of life.

In southern Egypt, meanwhile, the energetic Africans of Nubia extended their authority northward throughout the Nile Valley. Nubian influence in these years, though pervasive, was not destructive. Since the imperial days of the Eighteenth Dynasty (see pages 29–30), the Nubians, too, had adopted many features of Egyptian culture. Now Nubian kings and aristocrats embraced Egyptian culture wholesale. The thought of destroying the heritage of the pharaohs would have struck them as stupid and barbaric. Thus the Nubians and the Libyans repeated an old phenomenon: new peoples conquered old centers of political and military power and were assimilated into the older culture.

The reunification of Egypt occurred late and unexpectedly. With Egypt distracted and disorganized by foreign invasions, an independent African state, the kingdom of Kush, grew up in modern Sudan with its capital at Nepata. Like the Libyans, the Kushites worshiped Egyptian gods and used

Egyptian hieroglyphs. In the eighth century B.C. their king Piankhy swept through the entire Nile Valley from Nepata in the south to the delta in the north. United once again, Egypt enjoyed a brief period of peace during which Egyptians continued to assimilate their conquerors. In the kingdom of Kush, Egyptian methods of administration and bookkeeping, arts and crafts, and economic practices became common, especially among the aristocracy. Nonetheless, reunification of the realm did not lead to a new Egyptian empire. In the centuries between the fall of the New Kingdom and the recovery of Egypt, several small but vigorous kingdoms had taken root and grown to maturity in the ancient Near East. By 700 B.C. Egypt was once again a strong kingdom but no longer a mighty empire.

Yet Egypt's legacy to its African neighbors remained vibrant and rich. By trading and exploring southward along the coast of the Red Sea, the Egyptians introduced their goods and ideas as far south as the land of Punt, probably a region on the Somali coast. Egypt was the primary civilizing force in Nubia, which became another version of the pharaoh's realm, complete with royal pyramids and Egyptian deities. Egyptian religion penetrated as far south as Ethiopia. Just as Mesopotamian culture enjoyed wide appeal throughout the Near East, so Egyptian culture had a massive impact on northeastern Africa. Nor was Egyptian influence limited to Africa. Through earlier military, economic, and diplomatic contacts with Palestine and Syria, Egyptian ideas and beliefs later found their way to Europe.

❋ THE CHILDREN OF ISRAEL

The fall of the Hittite Empire and Egypt's collapse created in the western Near East a vacuum of power that allowed for the rise of numerous small states. No longer crushed between the Hittites in the north and the Egyptians in the south, various peoples—some of them newcomers—created homes and petty kingdoms in Syria, Phoenicia, and Palestine. After the Sea Peoples had raided Egypt, a branch of them, known in the Bible as Philistines, settled along the coast of Palestine (Map 2.1). Establishing themselves in five cities somewhat inland from the sea, the Philistines set about farming and raising flocks.

Another sturdy new culture was that of the Phoenicians, a Semitic-speaking people who had long inhabited several cities along the coast of modern Lebanon. They had lived under the shadow of the Hittites and Egyptians, but in this period the Phoenicians enjoyed full independence. Unlike the Philistine newcomers, who turned from seafaring to farming, the Phoenicians took to the sea and became outstanding merchants and explorers. In trading ventures they sailed as far west as modern Tunisia, where in 813 B.C. they founded the city of Carthage, which would one day struggle with Rome for domination of the western Mediterranean. Phoenician culture was urban, based on the prosperous commercial centers of Tyre, Sidon, and Byblos.

The Phoenicians' overwhelming cultural achievement was the development of an alphabet: they, unlike other literate peoples, used one letter to designate one sound, a system that vastly simplified writing and reading. The Greeks modified this alphabet and then used it to write their own language. The Phoenicians made another significant contribution by spreading the technical knowledge of ironworking. The Hittites were the first people in the Near East to smelt iron, but the Phoenicians passed the complex technique west to the Greeks and south to the Africans. Once in Africa, the technology spread farther south, though gradually. Most of West Africa had acquired the process by 250 B.C., and sub-Saharan Africa produced steel by A.D. 500.

South of Phoenicia arose another small kingdom, the land of the ancient Jews or Hebrews. It is difficult to say precisely who the Hebrews were and what brought them to this area because virtually the only source for much of their history is the Bible, which is essentially a religious document. Even though it contains much historical material, it also contains many Hebrew myths and legends. Moreover, it was compiled at different times; the earliest parts date to between about 950 and 800 B.C.

Earlier Mesopotamian and Egyptian sources refer to people called "Hapiru," which seems to mean homeless, independent nomads. According to Hebrew tradition, the followers of Abraham migrated from Mesopotamia, but Egyptian documents record Hapiru already in Syria and Palestine in the second millennium B.C. The Hebrews were probably a part of them. Together with other seminomadic peoples they probably migrated into the

✳ **MAP 2.1 Small Kingdoms in the Near East**
This map illustrates the political fragmentation of the Near East after the great wave of invasions that occurred during the thirteenth century B.C.

Nile Delta seeking good land. According to the Bible the Egyptians enslaved them. One group, however, under the leadership of Moses, perhaps a semimythical figure, left Egypt in what the Hebrews remembered as the Exodus. From Egypt they wandered in the Sinai Peninsula until they settled in Palestine in the thirteenth century B.C. Their arrival was by no means peaceful. In a series of vicious wars and savage slaughters they suffered defeats and setbacks but slowly won a place and gradually spread their power northward. Archaeology testifies that the thirteenth century B.C. in Palestine was a time of warfare and disruption. It also shows that the situation in Palestine was far more complicated than the Bible suggests.

In Palestine the Hebrews encountered the Philistines; the Amorites, relatives of Hammurabi's

❈ **Standing Sphinx**   The sphinx was both a decorative and protective figure in ancient art and society. This ivory is a splendid illustration of the sphinx itself—part human, part bird, and part lion. This sphinx also displays the richness of Phoenician art at this period. (*Source: Iraqi National Museum, Baghdad*)

Babylonians; and the Semitic-speaking Canaanites. Despite the numerous wars, contact between the Hebrews and their new neighbors was not always hostile. The Hebrews freely mingled with the Canaanites, and some went so far as to worship Baal, an ancient Semitic fertility god represented as a golden calf. Archaeological research supports the biblical account of these developments. In 1990 an expedition sponsored by Harvard University discovered a statue of a golden calf in its excavations of Ashkelon in modern Israel. Despite the anger expressed in the Bible over Hebrew worship of Baal, there is nothing surprising about the phenomenon. Once again, newcomers adapted themselves to the culture of an older, well-established people.

The greatest danger to the Hebrews came from the Philistines, whose superior technology and military organization at first made them invincible. In Saul (ca 1000 B.C.), a farmer of the tribe of Benjamin, the Hebrews found a champion and a spirited leader. Saul was the Hebrews' first secular king (see Listening to the Past). According to the biblical account, Saul carried the war to the Philistines, often without success. Yet in the meantime he established a monarchy over the twelve Hebrew tribes. Thus, under the peril of the Philistines, the Hebrews evolved from scattered, independent units into a centralized political organization in which the king directed the energies of the people. From this period derives the name *Israelites* for these erstwhile nomads.

Saul's work was carried on by David of Bethlehem, who in his youth had followed Saul into battle against the Philistines. Through courage and cunning, David pushed back the Philistines and waged war against his other neighbors. To give his kingdom a capital, he captured the city of Jerusalem, which he enlarged, fortified, and made the religious and political center of his realm. David's military successes won the Hebrews unprecedented security, and his forty-year reign was a period of vitality and political consolidation.

David's son Solomon (ca 965–925 B.C.) applied his energies to creating a nation out of a collection of tribes ruled by a king. He divided the kingdom, for purposes of effective administration, into twelve territorial districts cutting across the old tribal borders. To bring his kingdom up to the level of its more sophisticated neighbors, he set about a building program to make Israel a respectable Near Eastern state. Work was begun on a magnificent temple in Jerusalem, on cities, palaces, fortresses, and roads. Solomon worked to bring Israel into the commercial mainstream of the world around it and kept up good relations with Phoenician cities to the north. To finance all of the construction and other activities that he initiated, Solomon imposed taxes far greater than any levied before, much to the displeasure of his subjects.

Solomon dedicated the temple in grand style and made it the home of the Ark of the Covenant, the cherished chest that contained the holiest of Hebrew religious articles. The temple in Jerusalem was intended to be the religious heart of the kingdom and the symbol of Hebrew unity. It also became the stronghold of the priesthood, for a legion of priests was needed to conduct religious sacrifices, ceremonies, and prayers. Yet Solomon's efforts were hampered by strife. In the eyes of some people, he was too ready to unite other religions with the worship of the Hebrew god Yahweh, and the financial demands of his building program and his use of forced labor for building projects further fanned popular resentment. However, Solomon turned a rude kingdom into a state with broad commercial horizons and greater knowledge of the outside world. At his death, the Hebrew kingdom broke into two political sections (see Map 2.1). The northern half became Israel, with its capital at Samaria. The southern half was Judah, and Solomon's city of Jerusalem remained its center. With political division went a religious rift: Israel, the northern kingdom, established rival sanctuaries for gods other than Yahweh.

War soon broke out between Israel and Judah, as recorded in the Bible. Unexpected and independent evidence of this warfare came to light in August 1993 when an Israeli archaeologist found an inscription that refers to the "House of David," the royal line of Israel. The stone celebrates an Israelite victory from the early ninth century B.C. This discovery is the first mention of King David's royal family outside the Bible and helps to confirm the biblical account of the fighting between the two kingdoms.

Eventually, the northern kingdom of Israel was wiped out by the Assyrians, but the southern kingdom of Judah survived numerous calamities until the Babylonians crushed it in 587 B.C. The survivors were sent into exile in Babylonia, a period commonly known as the Babylonian Captivity. From 587 B.C. until 538 B.C., men known as prophets kept Yahweh's religion alive in the midst of far older Babylonian religious practices. They predicted that Yahweh would permit their return to their homeland if they remained true only to him. In 538 B.C. the Persians under their king Cyrus the Great permitted some forty thousand exiles to return to Jerusalem. During and especially after the Babylonian Captivity the exiles redefined their beliefs and practices and thus established what they believed was the law of Yahweh. Those who lived by these precepts can be called *Jews*.

The Evolution of Jewish Religion

While evolving politically from fierce nomads to urban dwellers, the Hebrews were also evolving spiritual ideas that still permeate contemporary

Nomadic Semitic Tribe   This Egyptian fresco captures the essentials of nomadic life. These Semites have captured a gazelle and an ibex. The four men behind the leaders hold their weapons, a bow and spears, which they used for both hunting and defense. Bringing up the rear is a domesticated burro. *(Source: Erich Lessing/Art Resource, NY)*

The Golden Calf According to the Hebrew Bible, Moses descended from Mount Sinai, where he had received the Ten Commandments, and found the Hebrews worshiping a golden calf, which was against Yahweh's laws. In July 1990 an American archaeological team found this model of a gilded calf inside a pot. The figurine dates to about 1550 B.C. and proves the existence of the cult represented by the calf in Palestine. *(Source: Courtesy of the Leon Levy expedition to Ashkelon/Carl Andrews)*

societies. Their chief literary product, the Old Testament or Hebrew Bible, has fundamentally influenced both Christianity and Islam and still exerts a compelling force on the modern world.

Fundamental to an understanding of Jewish religion is the concept of the *Covenant,* a formal agreement between Yahweh and the Hebrew people. According to the Bible, the god Yahweh (later called Jehovah by Christians) appeared to Moses on Mount Sinai. There Yahweh made a covenant with the Hebrews that was in fact a contract: if the Hebrews worshiped Yahweh as their only god, he would consider them his chosen people and pro-

tect them from their enemies. The Hebrews believed that Yahweh had led them out of bondage in Egypt and had helped them conquer their new land, the promised land. In return, the Hebrews worshiped Yahweh and Yahweh alone. They also obeyed Yahweh's Ten Commandments, an ethical code of conduct revealed to them by Moses. The Covenant was a powerful force in Hebrew life. The Old Testament records one occasion when the entire nation formally reaffirmed it:

And the king [of the Jews] stood by a pillar, and made a covenant before the lord, to walk after the lord, and to keep his commandments and his testimonies and his statutes with all their heart and all their soul, to perform the words of this covenant that were written in this book [Deuteronomy]. And all the people stood to the covenant.[2]

Yahweh was unique because he was a lone god. Unlike the gods of Mesopotamia and Egypt, Yahweh was not the son of another god, nor did he have a divine wife or family. Initially anthropomorphic, Yahweh gradually lost human form and became totally spiritual. Although Yahweh could assume human form, he was not to be depicted in any form. The Hebrews considered graven images—statues and other physical representations—idolatrous.

At first Yahweh was probably viewed as no more than the god of the Hebrews and sometimes faced competition from Baal and other gods in Palestine. Enlil, Marduk, Amon-Re, and the others sufficed for foreigners, but not for the Hebrews. In time, however, the Hebrews came to regard Yahweh as the only god. This was the beginning of true monotheism. Unlike Akhenaten's brand of monotheism (see pages 29–30), Hebrew monotheism was not an unpopular religion imposed by the ruler. It was the religion of a whole people, deeply felt and cherished. Some might fall away from Yahweh's worship, and various holy men had to exhort the Hebrews to honor the Covenant, but on the whole the people clung to Yahweh.

The Hebrews did not consider it their duty to spread a belief in the one god. They rarely proselytized, as Christians later did. As the chosen people, their chief duty was to maintain the worship of Yahweh as he demanded. That worship was embodied in the Ten Commandments, which forbade the Hebrews to steal, murder, lie, or commit adultery.

Aerial View of Hazor   This sweeping scene illustrates the strength and the economic basis of a Jewish citadel. At the left is the fortified upper city, and in the background is the agricultural land that sustained it. *(Source: Zev Radovan, Jerusalem)*

From the Ten Commandments evolved Hebrew law, a code of law and custom originating with Moses and built on by priests and prophets. The earliest part of this code, the Torah or Mosaic law, was often as harsh as Hammurabi's code, which had a powerful impact on it. Later tradition, largely the work of prophets who lived from the eleventh to the fifth centuries B.C., was more humanitarian. The work of the prophet Jeremiah (ca 626 B.C.) exemplifies this gentler spirit.

Jeremiah's emphasis is on mercy and justice, on avoiding wrongdoing to others because it is displeasing to Yahweh. These precepts replaced the old law's demand for "an eye for an eye." Jeremiah's message is thus representative of a subtle and positive shift in Hebrew thinking. Jeremiah proclaimed that the god of anger was also the god of forgiveness: "Return, thou backsliding Israel, saith the lord; and I will not cause mine anger to

fall upon you; for I am merciful, saith the lord, and I will not keep anger forever."[3] Although Yahweh would punish wrongdoing, he would not destroy those who repented. One generation might be punished for its misdeeds, but Yahweh's mercy was a promise of hope for future generations.

The uniqueness of this phenomenon can be seen by comparing the essence of Hebrew monotheism with the religious outlook of the Mesopotamians. Whereas the Mesopotamians considered their gods capricious, the Hebrews knew what Yahweh expected. The Hebrews believed that their god would protect them and make them prosper if they obeyed his commandments. The Mesopotamians thought human beings insignificant compared to the gods, so insignificant that the gods might even be indifferent to them. The Hebrews, too, considered themselves puny in comparison to Yahweh. Yet they were Yahweh's chosen people, whom he had promised never to abandon. Finally, though the Mesopotamians believed that the gods generally preferred good to evil, their religion did not demand ethical conduct. The Hebrews could please their god only by living up to high moral standards as well as worshiping him.

Many parts of the Old Testament show obvious debts to Mesopotamian culture. Nonetheless, to the Hebrews goes the credit for developing a religion so emotionally satisfying and ethically grand that it not only flourished but also profoundly influenced Christianity and Islam.

Daily Life in Israel

Historians generally know far more about the daily life of the aristocracy and the wealthy in ancient societies than about the conditions of the common people. Jewish society is an exception simply because the Bible, which lays down laws for all Jews, has much to say about peasants and princes alike. Comparisons with the social conditions of Israel's ancient neighbors and modern anthropological work among Palestinian Arabs shed additional light on biblical practices. Thus the life of the common people in ancient Israel is better known than, for instance, the lives of ordinary Romans or ancient Chinese.

The nomadic Hebrews first entered Palestine as tribes, numerous families who thought of themselves as all related to one another. At first, good farmland, pastureland, and water spots were held in common by the tribe. Common use of land was—and still is—characteristic of nomadic peoples. But as formerly nomadic peoples turned increasingly to settled agriculture, communal use of land gave way to family ownership. So it was with the ancient Hebrews. Slowly the shift from nomad to farmer affected far more than just how people fed themselves. Family relationships reflected evolving circumstances. With the transition to settled agriculture, the tribe gradually became less important than the extended family. With the advent of village life and finally full-blown urban life, the extended family in turn gave way to the nuclear family.

For women, the evolution of Jewish society led to less freedom of action, especially in religious life. At first women served as priestesses in festivals and religious cults. Some were considered prophetesses of Yahweh, although they never conducted his official rituals. In the course of time, however, the worship of Yahweh became more male oriented and male dominated. Increasingly, Yahweh became the god of holiness, and to worship him people had to be pure in mind and body. Women were seen as ritually impure because of menstruation and childbirth. Because of these "impurities," women began to play a much reduced role in religion. Even when they did participate in religious rites, they were segregated from men. For the most part, women were confined to the home and the care of the family.

Marriage was one of the most important and joyous events in Hebrew family life. The typical marriage in ancient Israel was monogamous, and a virtuous wife was revered and honored. Perhaps the finest and most fervent song of praise to the good wife comes from the book of Proverbs in the Bible:

Who can find a virtuous woman? for her price is far above rubies. . . . Strength and honour are her clothing; and she shall rejoice in time to come. She openeth her mouth with wisdom; and in her tongue is the law of kindness. She looketh well to the ways of her household, and eateth not the bread of idleness. Her children arise up, and call her blessed; her husband also, and he praiseth her. . . . Favour is deceitful, and beauty is vain: but a woman that feareth the lord, she shall be praised.[4]

The commandment "Honor thy father and thy mother" was fundamental to the Mosaic law. The wife was a pillar of the family, and her work and wisdom were respected and treasured.

Betrothal and marriage were serious matters in ancient Israel. As in Mesopotamia, they were left largely in parents' hands. Boys and girls were often married quite early, and the parents naturally made the arrangements. Rarely were the prospective bride and groom consulted. Marriages were often contracted within the extended family commonly among first cousins—a custom still found among Palestinian Arabs today. Although early Jewish custom permitted marriage with foreigners, the fear of alien religions eventually led to restrictions against mixed marriages.

The father of the groom offered a bridal gift to the bride's father. This custom, the marriage price, also existed among the Mesopotamians and still survives among modern Palestinian Arabs. The gift was ordinarily money, the amount depending on the social status and wealth of the two families. In other instances, the groom could work off the marriage price by performing manual labor. At the time of the wedding the man gave his bride and her family wedding presents; unlike Mesopotamian custom, the bride's father did not provide her with a dowry. A dowry is meant to protect the position of the wife, and the lack of it in Israel made it easier for the husband to divorce his wife without financial loss.

As in Mesopotamia, marriage was a legal contract, not a religious ceremony. At marriage a woman left her own family and joined the family and clan of her husband. The occasion when the bride joined her husband's household was festive. The groom wore a crown and his best clothes. Accompanied by his friends, also dressed in their finest and carrying musical instruments, the bridegroom walked to the bride's house, where she awaited him in her richest clothes, jewels, and a veil, which she removed only later when the couple was alone. The bride's friends joined the group, and together they all marched in procession to the groom's house, their way marked by music and songs honoring the newlyweds. Though the wedding feast might last for days, the couple consummated their marriage on the first night. The next day the blood-stained linen was displayed to prove the bride's virginity.

The right to initiate a divorce was available only to the husband. Even adultery by the husband was not necessarily grounds for divorce, although Jewish law, like the Code of Hammurabi, punished a wife's adultery with death. Jewish custom generally frowned on divorce, and the typical man and woman entered into marriage fully expecting to spend the rest of their lives together.

The newly married couple was expected to begin a family at once. Children, according to the book of Psalms, "are an heritage of the lord: and the fruit of the womb is his reward."[5] The desire for children to perpetuate the family was so strong that if a man died before he could sire a son, his brother was legally obliged to marry the widow. The son born of the brother was thereafter considered the offspring and heir of the dead man. If the brother refused, the widow had her revenge by denouncing him to the elders and publicly spitting in his face.

Sons were especially desired because they maintained the family bloodline and kept the ancestral property within the family. The first-born son had special rights, honor, and responsibilities. At his fa-

ther's death he became the head of the household and received a larger inheritance than did his younger brothers. Daughters were less valued because they would eventually marry and leave the family. Yet in Jewish society, unlike other cultures, infanticide was illegal; Yahweh had forbidden it.

As in most other societies, in ancient Israel the early education of children was in the mother's hands. She taught her children right from wrong and gave them their first instruction in the moral values of society. As boys grew older, they received more education from their fathers in religion and the history of their people. Many children were taught to read and write, and the head of each family was probably able to write. Fathers also taught sons the family craft or trade. Boys soon learned that inattention could be painful, for Jewish custom advised fathers to be strict: "He that spareth his rod hateth his son: but he that loveth him chasteneth him betimes."[6]

Most children grew to adulthood in the context of farm life, whose demands and rhythm changed little over time. Young people began with light tasks. Girls traditionally tended flocks of sheep and drew water from the well for household use. At the well, which was a popular meeting spot, girls could meet other young people and travelers passing through the country with camel caravans. After the harvest, young girls followed behind the reapers to glean the fields. Even this work was governed by law and custom. Once the girls had gone through the fields, they were not to return, for Yahweh had declared that anything left behind belonged to the needy.

Boys also tended flocks, especially in wild areas. Like the young David, they practiced marksmanship with slings and entertained themselves with music. They shared light work such as harvesting grapes and beating the limbs of olive trees to shake the fruit loose. Only when they grew to full strength did they perform the hard work of harrowing, plowing, and harvesting.

The land was precious to the family, not simply because it provided a living but also because it was a link to the past. Ironically, the success of the first Hebrew kings endangered the future of many family farms. With peace, more settled conditions, and increasing prosperity, some Jews began to amass large holdings by buying out the poor and struggling farmers. Far from discouraging this development, the kings created their own huge estates. In many cases slaves, both Jewish and foreign, worked these large farms and estates shoulder to shoulder with paid free men. In still later times, rich land-owners rented plots of land to poor free families; the landowners provided the renters with seed and livestock and normally took half of the yield as rent.

The development of urban life among the Jews created new economic opportunities, especially in crafts and trades. People specialized in certain occupations, such as milling flour, baking bread, making pottery, weaving, and carpentry. All these crafts were family trades. Sons worked with their father, daughters with their mother. If the business prospered, the family might be assisted by a few paid workers or slaves. The practitioners of a craft usually lived in a particular street or section of the town, a custom still prevalent in the Middle East.

Commerce and trade developed later than crafts. In the time of Solomon, foreign trade was the king's domain. Aided by the Phoenicians, Solomon built a fleet to trade with Red Sea ports. He also participated in the overland caravan trade. Otherwise, trade with neighboring countries was handled by foreigners, usually Phoenicians. Jews dealt mainly in local trade, and in most instances craftsmen and farmers sold directly to their customers. Many of Israel's wise men disapproved of commerce and considered it unseemly and immoral to profit from the work of others.

These social and economic developments also left their mark on daily life by prompting the compilation of two significant works, the Torah and the Talmud. The Torah is basically the Mosaic law, or the first five books of the Bible. The Talmud is a later work, begun during the Babylonian Captivity and completed by the end of the sixth century B.C. The Talmud records civil and ceremonial law and Jewish legend.

The dietary rules of the Jews provide an excellent example of both the relationship between the Torah and the Talmud and their effect on ordinary life and culture. According to the Torah, people were not to eat meat that they found in the field. This very sensible prohibition protected them from eating dangerous food. Yet some rules also were needed for meat in the city. The solution, set forth in the Talmud, was a set of regulations for the proper way to conduct ritual slaughter. Some of the rules were very burdensome. The ritual defined the knife to be used in the slaughter and the way in which it was to be used. Accompanying these precise acts were prayers to be given when the animal's throat was cut. So too with the Torah's prohibition against cooking a young goat in its mother's milk. The Talmud's interpretation of this Mosaic law went to such lengths that milk and meat could not be eaten at the same table and different bowls had to be used to serve them. Even different towels had to be used to cleanse them. What began as simple and sensible dietary rules became a complicated ritual, one that many Orthodox Jews follow today.

Between the eclipse of the Hittites and Egyptians and the rise of the Assyrians, the Hebrews moved from nomadism to urban life and full participation in the mainstream of ancient Near Eastern culture. Developing their unique religion and customs, they drew from the practices of other peoples and contributed to the lives of their neighbors.

❈ ASSYRIA, THE MILITARY MONARCHY

Small kingdoms like those of the Phoenicians and the Hebrews could exist only in the absence of a major power. The beginning of the ninth century B.C. saw the rise of such a power: the Assyrians of northern Mesopotamia, whose chief capital was at Nineveh on the Tigris River. The Assyrians were a Semitic-speaking people heavily influenced, like so many other peoples of the Near East, by the Mesopotamian culture of Babylon to the south. They were also one of the most warlike peoples in history, largely because throughout their history they were threatened by neighboring folk. Living in an open, exposed land, the Assyrians experienced frequent and devastating attacks by the wild, war-loving tribes to their north and east and by the Babylonians to the south. The constant threat to survival experienced by the Assyrians promoted political cohesion and military might. Yet they were also a mercantile people who had long pursued commerce both with the Babylonians in the south and other peoples in the north.

The Power of Assyria

For over two hundred years the Assyrians labored to dominate the Near East. Year after relentless year, Assyrian armies hammered at the peoples of the west. These ominous events inaugurated two turbulent centuries marked by Assyrian military campaigns, constant efforts by Syria and the two Jewish kingdoms to maintain or recover their independence, and eventual Assyrian conquest of Babylonia and northern Egypt. In addition, periodic political instability occurred in Assyria itself, which prompted stirrings of freedom throughout the Near East.

By means of almost constant warfare the kings Tiglath-pileser III (r. 774–727 B.C.) and Sargon II (r. 721–705 B.C.) carved out an empire that stretched from east and north of the Tigris River to central Egypt (Map 2.2). Revolt against the Assyrians inevitably promised the rebels bloody battles, prolonged sieges accompanied by starvation, plague, and sometimes even cannibalism, and finally surrender followed by systematic torture and slaughter.

Though atrocity and terrorism struck unspeakable fear into Assyria's subjects, Assyria's success was actually due to sophisticated, farsighted, and effective military organization. By Sargon's time the Assyrians had invented the mightiest military machine the ancient Near East had ever seen. The mainstay of the Assyrian army, the soldier who ordinarily decided the outcome of battles, was the infantryman armed with spear and sword and protected by helmet and armor. The Assyrian army also featured archers, some on foot, others on horseback, still others in chariots. Some infantry archers wore heavy armor. These soldiers served as a primitive field artillery, whose job was to sweep the enemy's walls of defenders so that others could storm the defenses. Slingers also served as artillery in pitched battles. For mobility on the battlefield, the Assyrians organized a corps of chariots.

Assyrian military genius was remarkable for the development of a wide variety of siege machinery and techniques, including excavation to undermine city walls and battering rams to knock down walls and gates. Never before in the Near East had anyone applied such technical knowledge to warfare. The Assyrians even invented the concept of a corps of engineers, who bridged rivers with pontoons or provided soldiers with inflatable skins for swimming. Furthermore, the Assyrians knew how to coordinate their efforts, both in open battle and

Siege of a City   Art here serves to glorify horror. The Assyrian king Tiglath-pileser III launches an assault on a fortified city. The impaled bodies shown at the center demonstrate the cruelty of Assyrian warfare. Also noticeable are the various weapons and means of attack used against the city. *(Source: Courtesy of the Trustees of the British Museum)*

❋   **MAP 2.2 The Assyrian Empire**   The Assyrian Empire at its height (ca 650 B.C.)
included almost all of the old centers of power in the ancient Near East. As comparison with Map 2.3 shows, however, its size was far smaller than that of the later Persian Empire.

in siege warfare. King Sennacherib's account of his
siege of Jerusalem in 701 B.C. is a vivid portrait of
the Assyrian war machine in action:

*As to Hezekiah, the Jew, he did not submit to my yoke,
I laid siege to 46 of his strong cities, walled forts and
to the countless small villages in their vicinity, and
conquered them by means of well-stamped earth-
ramps, and battering rams brought thus near to the
walls combined with the attack by foot soldiers, using
mines, breaches as well as sapper work. . . . Hezekiah
himself, whom the terror-inspiring splendor of my
lordship had overwhelmed and whose irregular and
elite troops which he had brought into Jerusalem, his
royal residence, in order to strengthen it, had deserted
him, did send me, later, to Nineveh, my lordly city, together with 30 talents of gold . . . and all kinds of
valuable treasures.[7]*

Hezekiah and Jerusalem shared the fate of many a
rebellious king and capital and were indeed lucky

to escape severe reprisals. The Assyrians were too
powerful and well organized and far too tenacious
to be turned back by isolated strongholds, no matter how well situated or defended.

Assyrian Rule and Culture

The Assyrians knew not only how to win battles
but also how to use their victories. As early as the
reign of Tiglath-pileser III, the Assyrian kings began to organize their conquered territories into an
empire. The lands closest to Assyria became provinces governed by Assyrian officials. Kingdoms beyond the provinces were not annexed but became
dependent states that followed Assyria's lead. The
Assyrian king chose their rulers either by regulating the succession of native kings or by supporting
native kings who appealed to him. Against more
distant states the Assyrian kings waged frequent
war in order to conquer them outright or make the
dependent states secure.

In the seventh century B.C. Assyrian power seemed secure. Yet the downfall of Assyria was swift and complete. Babylon finally won its independence in 626 B.C. and joined forces with the newly aggressive Medes, an Indo-European-speaking folk from Iran. Together the Babylonians and the Medes destroyed the Assyrian Empire in 612 B.C., paving the way for the rise of the Persians. The Hebrew prophet Nahum spoke for many when he asked: "Nineveh is laid waste: who will bemoan her?"[8] Their cities destroyed and their power shattered, the Assyrians disappeared from history, remembered only as a cruel people of the Old Testament who oppressed the Hebrews. The glory of their empire was forgotten.

Yet modern archaeology has brought the Assyrians out of obscurity. In 1839 the intrepid English archaeologist and traveler A. H. Layard began to excavate Nineveh, then a mound of debris beside the Tigris. His findings electrified the world. Layard's workers unearthed masterpieces, including monumental sculpted figures—huge, winged bulls, human-headed lions, and sphinxes—as well as brilliantly sculpted friezes. Equally valuable were numerous Assyrian cuneiform documents, which ranged from royal accounts of mighty military campaigns to simple letters by common people.

Among the most renowned of Layard's finds were the Assyrian palace reliefs, whose number has been increased by the discoveries of twentieth-century archaeologists. Assyrian kings delighted in scenes of war, which their artists depicted in graphic detail. By the time of Ashurbanipal (r. 668–633 B.C.), Assyrian artists had hit on the idea of portraying a series of episodes—in fact, a visual narrative of events that had actually taken place. Scene followed scene in a continuous frieze, so that the viewer could follow the progress of a military campaign from the time the army marched out until the enemy was conquered. So, too, with another theme of the palace reliefs, the lion hunt. Hunting lions was probably a royal sport, although some scholars have suggested a magical significance, arguing that the hunting scenes depict the

 Royal Lion Hunt   This relief from the palace of Ashurbanipal at Nineveh shows the king fighting a lion and is a typical representation of the energy and artistic brilliance of Assyrian sculptors. The lion hunt was a favorite theme of Assyrian palace reliefs. (*Source: Courtesy of the Trustees of the British Museum*)

king as the protector of his people, the one who wards off evil.

Assyrian art, like much of Egyptian art, was realistic, but the warmth and humor of Egyptian scenes are absent from Assyrian reliefs. Stark and often brutal in subject matter, Assyrian realism is well represented by the illustration reproduced on page 51, which portrays the climax of the royal lion hunt. The king, mounted on horseback, has already fired arrows into two lions, who nonetheless are still full of fight. The king thrusts his spear into another lion, which has begun its spring. The

Persian Warrior This statuette, about fifteen inches in height, of a Persian soldier is elaborate in its portrayal of the warrior's arms and armor. The writing on the base identifies this warrior as the guardian god of a town. (*Source: Teheran Museum, Iran*)

artistic rendering of the figures is exciting, anatomically correct, and in proper proportion and perspective. The whole composition conveys both action and tension. Assyrian art fared better than Assyrian military power. The techniques of Assyrian artists influenced the Persians, who adapted them to gentler scenes.

In fact, many Assyrian innovations, military and political as well as artistic, were taken over wholesale by the Persians. Although the memory of Assyria was hateful throughout the Near East, the fruits of Assyrian organizational genius helped enable the Persians to bring peace and stability to the same regions where Assyrian armies had spread terror.

THE EMPIRE OF THE PERSIAN KINGS

Like the Hittites before them, the Iranians were Indo-Europeans from central Europe and southern Russia. They migrated into the land that now bears their name, the area between the Caspian Sea and the Persian Gulf. Like the Hittites, they then fell under the spell of the more sophisticated cultures of their Mesopotamian neighbors. But the Iranians went on to create one of the greatest empires of antiquity, one that encompassed scores of peoples and cultures. The Persians, the most important of the Iranian peoples, had a farsighted conception of empire. Though as conquerors they willingly used force to accomplish their ends, they normally preferred to depend on diplomacy and toleration to rule.

The Land of Mountains and Plateau

Persia—the modern country of Iran—stretches from the Caspian Sea in the north to the Persian Gulf in the south (Map 2.3). Between the Tigris-Euphrates Valley in the west and the Indus Valley in the east rises an immense plateau surrounded on all sides by lofty mountains that cut off the interior from the sea.

The central plateau is very high, a landscape of broad plains, scattered oases, and two vast deserts. The high mountains, which catch the moisture coming from the sea, generate ample rainfall for the plateau. This semitropical area is fertile, in marked contrast to the aridity of most of Iran. The mountains surrounding the central plateau are dot-

※ **MAP 2.3 The Persian Empire**   By 513 B.C. the Persian Empire included more of the ancient Near East than had the Assyrian Empire, and it extended as far east as western India. With the rise of the Medes and Persians, the balance of power in the Near East shifted east of Mesopotamia for the first time.

ted with numerous oases, often very fertile. From time immemorial they have served as havens for small groups of people. At the center of the plateau lies an enormous depression—a region devoid of water and vegetation, so glowing hot in summer that it is virtually impossible to cross. This depression forms two distinct grim and burning salt deserts, perhaps the most desolate spots on earth. These two deserts form a barrier between East and West.

Iran's geographical position and topography explain its traditional role as the highway between East and West. Throughout history nomadic peoples migrating from the broad steppes of Russia and central Asia have streamed into Iran. Confronting the uncrossable salt deserts, most have turned either eastward or westward, moving on until they reached the advanced and wealthy urban centers of Mesopotamia and India. When cities emerged along the natural lines of East-West communication, Iran became the area where nomads

met urban dwellers, a meeting ground of unique significance for the civilizations of both East and West.

The Coming of the Medes and Persians

The Iranians entered this land around 1000 B.C. They were part of the vast movement of Indo-European-speaking peoples whose wanderings led them in many successive waves into Europe, the Near East, and India (see page 30). These Iranians were nomads who migrated with their flocks and herds. Like their kinsmen the Aryans, who moved into India (see page 53), they were horse breeders, and the horse gave them a decisive military advantage over the native prehistoric peoples of Iran. The Iranians rode into battle in horse-drawn chariots or on horseback and easily swept the natives. Because the influx of Iranians went on for centuries, cultural interchange between victorious newcomers and conquered natives was ongoing.

The Iranians initially created a patchwork of tiny kingdoms. The chieftain or petty king was basically a warlord who depended on fellow warriors for aid and support. This band of noble warriors, like the Greek heroes of the *Iliad,* formed the fighting strength of the army. The king owned estates that supported him and his nobles. For additional income the king levied taxes, which were paid in kind and not in cash. He also demanded labor services from the peasants. Below the king and his warrior nobles were free people who held land and others who owned nothing. Artisans produced the various goods needed to keep society running. At the bottom of the social scale were slaves—probably both natives and newcomers. To them fell the drudgery of hard labor and household service to king and nobles.

This early period saw some significant economic developments. The use of iron increased. By the seventh century B.C., the use of iron farm implements had become widespread. The results were increases in productivity and in overall prosperity and improved standards of living. At the same time Iranian agriculture saw the development of small estates. Farmers worked small plots of land, and the general prosperity of the period gave rise to a sturdy peasantry, who enjoyed greater freedom than the freedom experienced by their peers in Egypt and Mesopotamia.

Iran had considerable mineral wealth, and its iron, copper, and lapis lazuli attracted Assyrian raiding parties. Even more important, mineral wealth and Iranian horse breeding stimulated brisk trade with the outside world. Kings found that merchants, who were not usually Iranians, produced large profits to help fill the royal coffers. Overland trade also put the Iranians in direct contact with their western and eastern neighbors.

Gradually two groups of Iranians began coalescing into larger units. The Persians had settled in

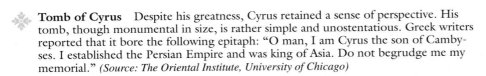

Tomb of Cyrus   Despite his greatness, Cyrus retained a sense of perspective. His tomb, though monumental in size, is rather simple and unostentatious. Greek writers reported that it bore the following epitaph: "O man, I am Cyrus the son of Cambyses. I established the Persian Empire and was king of Asia. Do not begrudge me my memorial." *(Source: The Oriental Institute, University of Chicago)*

Persis, the modern region of Fars, in southern Iran. Their kinsmen the Medes occupied Media, the modern area of Hamadan in the north; the Medes' capital was at Ecbatana. The Medes were vulnerable to attack by nomads from the north, but their greatest threat was the frequent raids by the Assyrian army. Even though distracted by grave pressures from their neighbors, the Medes united under one king around 710 B.C. and extended their control over the Persians in the south. In 612 B.C. the Medes were strong enough to join the Babylonians in overthrowing the Assyrian Empire. With the rise of the Medes, the balance of power in the area for the first time shifted east of Mesopotamia.

The Creation of the Persian Empire

In 550 B.C. Cyrus the Great (r. 559–530 B.C.), king of the Persians and one of the most remarkable statesmen of antiquity, threw off the yoke of the Medes by conquering them and turning their country into his first satrapy, or province. In the space of a single lifetime, Cyrus created one of the greatest empires of antiquity. Two characteristics lifted Cyrus above the common level of warrior kings. First, he thought of Iran, not just Persia and Media, as a state. His concept has survived a long, complex, often turbulent history to play its part in the contemporary world. Second, Cyrus held an enlightened view of empire. Many of the civilizations and cultures that fell to his armies were, he realized, far older, more advanced, and more sophisticated than his. Free of the narrow-minded snobbery of the Egyptians, the religious exclusiveness of the Hebrews, and the calculated cruelty of the Assyrians, Cyrus gave his subject peoples and their cultures respect, toleration, and protection. Conquered peoples continued to enjoy their institutions, religion, language, and way of life under the Persians.

The Persian Empire, which Cyrus created, became a political organization sheltering many different civilizations. To rule such a vast area and so many diverse peoples demanded talent, intelligence, sensitivity, and a cosmopolitan view of the world. These qualities Cyrus and many of his successors possessed in abundance. Though the Persians were sometimes harsh, especially toward those who rebelled against them, they were for the most part enlightened rulers. Consequently, they gave the ancient Near East over two hundred years of peace, prosperity, and security.

With Iran united, Cyrus looked at the broader world. He set out to achieve two goals. First, he wanted to win control of the west and thus of the terminal ports of the great trade routes that crossed Iran and Anatolia. Second, he strove to secure eastern Iran from the pressure of nomadic invaders. In 550 B.C. neither goal was easy to accomplish. To the northwest was the young kingdom of Lydia in Anatolia, whose king Croesus was proverbial for his wealth. To the west was Babylonia, enjoying a new period of power now that the Assyrian Empire had been crushed. To the southwest was Egypt, still weak but sheltered behind its bulwark of sand and sea. To the east ranged tough, mobile nomads, capable of massive and destructive incursions deep into Iranian territory.

Cyrus turned first to Croesus's Lydian kingdom, which fell to him around 546 B.C., along with the Greek cities along the coast of Anatolia. Cyrus thus gained important ports that looked out to the Mediterranean world. In addition, for the first time the Persians came into direct contact with the Greeks, a people with whom their later history was to be intimately connected (see page 129).

From Lydia, Cyrus next marched to the far eastern corners of Iran. In a brilliant campaign he conquered the regions of Parthia and Bactria. All of Iran was now Persian, from Mesopotamia in the west to the western slopes of the Hindu Kush in the east. In 540 B.C. Cyrus moved against Babylonia, now isolated from outside help. When Persian soldiers marched quietly into Babylon the next year, the Babylonians welcomed Cyrus as a liberator. He won the hearts of the Babylonians with humane treatment, toleration of their religion, and support of their efforts to refurbish their capital.

Cyrus was equally generous toward the Jews. He allowed them to return to Palestine, from which they had been deported by the Babylonians. He protected them, gave them back the sacred items they used in worship, and rebuilt the temple of Yahweh in Jerusalem. The Old Testament sings the praises of Cyrus, whom the Jews considered the shepherd of Yahweh, the lord's anointed. Rarely have conquered peoples shown such gratitude to their conquerors. Cyrus's benevolent policy created a Persian Empire in which the cultures and religions of its members were respected and honored. Seldom have conquerors been as wise, sensitive, and farsighted as Cyrus and his Persians.

✳ **Darius the Great and Ahura Mazda** In this rock carving, Darius, king of the Persians, in the presence of the god Ahuramazda and with his blessing, triumphs over lesser and sometimes rebellious kings. The scene asserts the divine approval of Darius's right to rule. *(Source: Robert Harding Picture Library)*

Thus Spake Zarathustra

Iranian religion was originally simple and primitive. Ahuramazda, the chief god, was the creator and benefactor of all living creatures. Yet, unlike Yahweh, he was not a lone god. The Iranians were polytheistic. Mithra the sun-god, whose cult later spread throughout the Roman Empire, saw to justice and redemption. Other Iranian deities personified the natural elements: moon, earth, water, and wind. As in ancient India, fire was a particularly important god. The sacred fire consumed the blood sacrifices that the early Iranians offered to all of their deities.

Early Iranian religion was close to nature and unencumbered by ponderous theological beliefs. A priestly class, the Magi, developed among the Medes to officiate at sacrifices, chant prayers to the gods, and tend the sacred flame. A description of this early worship comes from the German historian Eduard Meyer:

Iranian religion knew neither divine images nor temples. On a hilltop one called upon god and his manifestations—sun and moon, earth and fire, water and wind—and erected altars with their eternal fire. But in other appropriate places one could, without further preparation, pray to the deity and bring him his offerings, with the assistance of the Magi.[9]

In time the Iranians built fire temples for these sacrifices. As late as the nineteenth century, fire was still worshiped in Baku, a major city on the Russian-Iranian border.

Around 600 B.C. the religious thinking of Zarathustra—Zoroaster, as he is better known—breathed new meaning into Iranian religion. So little is known of Zoroaster that even the date of his birth is unknown, but it cannot be earlier than around 1100 B.C. The most reliable information about Zoroaster comes from the *Zend Avesta,* a collection of hymns and poems, the earliest part of which treats Zoroaster and primitive Persian religion.

Zoroaster preached a novel concept of divinity and human life. Life, he taught, is a constant battleground for two opposing forces, good and evil: Ahuramazda, who embodies good and truth, is opposed by Ahriman, a hateful spirit who stands for evil and falsehood. Ahuramazda and Ahriman are locked together in a cosmic battle for the human race. But, according to Zoroaster, people are not mere pawns in this struggle. Each person has to choose which side to join—whether to lead a life of good behavior and truthful dealings with others or one of wickedness and lies.

Zoroaster emphasized the individual's responsibility in this decision. He taught that people possess the free will to decide between Ahuramazda

ANCIENT NEAR EAST

ca 1700 B.C.	Covenant formed between Yahweh and the Hebrews. Emergence of Hebrew monotheism
ca 1570–ca 1075 B.C.	New Kingdom in Egypt
ca 1475–ca 1200 B.C.	Rise and fall of the Hittite Empire
13th century B.C.	Moses leads Exodus of the Hebrews from Egypt into Palestine
ca 1100–700 B.C.	Founding of numerous small kingdoms, including those of the Phoenicians, Syrians, Philistines, and Hebrews
ca 1000 B.C.	Saul establishes monarchy over Hebrews, under threat of Philistines Persians and Medes enter central plateau of Persia
10th century B.C.	David captures Jerusalem, which becomes religious and political center of Judah. Solomon inherits the throne and further unites Hebrew kingdom
925 B.C.	Solomon dies. Hebrew kingdom us divided politically into Israel and Judah
ca 900–612 B.C.	Rise and fall of the Assyrian Empire
813 B.C.	Phoenicians found Carthage
774–705 B.C.	Assyrian kings, Tiglath-pileser III and Sargon II conquer Palestine, Syria, Anatolia, Israel, Judha, and Egypt
ca 710 B.C.	Medes unite under one king and conquer Persians
626 B.C.	Babylonia wins independence from Assyria
612 B.C.	Babylonians and Medes destroy Assyrian capital of Nineveh
ca 600 B.C.	Zoroaster revitalizes Persian religion
550 B.C.	Cyrus the Great conquers Medes, founds Persian Empire
546 B.C.	Cyrus defeats Croesus, wins Lydia
540 B.C.	Persian soldiers under Cyrus enter Babylon
525 B.C.	Cambyses, Cyrus's heir to the throne, conquers Egypt
521–464 B.C.	Darius I and Xerxes complete Persian conquest of ancient East, an area stretching from Anatolia in the west to the Indus Valley in the east Persian attempts to invade Greece unsuccessful

and Ahriman and must rely on their own conscience to guide them. Their decisions are crucial, Zoroaster warned, for there will be a time of reckoning. He promised that Ahuramazda will eventually triumph over evil and lies and that at death each person will stand before the tribunal of good, where Ahuramazda, like the Egyptian god Osiris, will judge whether the dead lived righteously. In short, Zoroaster taught the concept of a Last Judgment at which Ahuramazda will decide each person's eternal fate.

In Zoroaster's thought the Last Judgment was linked to the notion of a divine kingdom after death for those who had been good and truthful.

They would accompany Ahuramazda to what Zoroaster called the "House of Song" and the "Abode of Good Thought," where they would dwell with Ahuramazda forever. Liars and the wicked, denied this blessed immortality, would be condemned to eternal pain, darkness, and punishment. Thus Zoroaster preached a Last Judgment that led to a heaven or a hell.

Though tradition has it that Zoroaster's teachings originally met with opposition and coldness, his thought converted Darius (r. 521–486 B.C.), one of the most energetic men ever to sit on the Persian throne. The Persian royal family adopted Zoroastrianism but did not try to impose it on others. Under the protection of the Persian kings, Zoroastrianism swept through Iran, winning converts and sinking roots that sustained healthy growth for centuries. Zoroastrianism survived the fall of the Persian Empire to influence religious thought in the age of Jesus and to make a vital contribution to Manicheanism, a theology that was to spread through the Byzantine Empire and pose a significant challenge to Christianity. A handful of the faithful still follow the teachings of Zoroaster, whose vision of divinity and human life has transcended the centuries.

Persia's World Empire

Cyrus's successors rounded out the Persian conquest of the ancient Near East. In 525 B.C. Cyrus's son Cambyses (r. 530–522 B.C.) subdued Egypt. Darius (r. 521–486 B.C.) and his son Xerxes (r. 486–464 B.C.) invaded Greece but were fought to a standstill and forced to retreat (see pages 129–130). The Persians never won a permanent foothold in Europe, but Darius carried Persian arms into India. Around 513 B.C. western India became the Persian satrapy of Hindu Kush, which included the valley of the Indus River. Thus within thirty-seven years the Persians transformed themselves from a subject people to the rulers of an empire that included Anatolia, Egypt, Mesopotamia, Iran, and western India. They created an empire encom-

 Lion Weight This formidable lion was a standard weight used to weigh taxes paid in silver and gold. The lion was a royal symbol, and the taxes were sent to the royal treasury at Susa to cover the costs of administering the Persian Empire. *(Source: Louvre © Photo R.M.N.)*

The Royal Palace at Persepolis   Darius began and Xerxes finished building a grand palace worthy of the glory of the Persian Empire. Pictured here is the monumental audience hall, where the king dealt with ministers of state and foreign envoys. *(Source: George Holton/Photo Researchers)*

passing all of the oldest, most honored kingdoms and peoples of the ancient Near East, which never before had been united in one such vast political organization (see Map 2.3).

The Persians knew how to use the peace they had won on the battlefield. The sheer size of the empire made it impossible for one man to rule it effectively. So they divided the empire into some twenty huge satrapies measuring hundreds of square miles, many of them kingdoms in themselves. Each satrapy had a *satrap,* or governor, drawn from the Median and Persian nobility and often a relative of the king. The governor was directly responsible to the king. An army officer, also responsible to the king, commanded the military forces stationed in the satrapy. Still another official collected the taxes. Moreover, the king sent out

royal inspectors to watch the satraps and other officials.

Effective rule of the empire demanded good communication. To meet this need, the Persians established a network of roads. The main highway, known as the Royal Road, spanned some 1,677 miles from the coast of western Asia to western Iran (see Map 2.3). The distance was broken into 111 post stations, each equipped with fresh horses for the king's messengers. Other roads branched out to link all parts of the empire from the coast of western Asia to the valley of the Indus River. This system of communication enabled the Persian king to keep in touch with his subjects and officials. He was able to rule efficiently, keep his ministers in line, and protect the rights of the peoples under his control.

How effective Persian rule could be, even in small matters, is apparent in a letter from King Darius to the satrap of Ionia, the Greek region of Anatolia. The satrap had transplanted Syrian fruit trees in his province, an experiment Darius praised. Yet the governor had also infringed on the rights granted to the sanctuary of the Greek god Apollo, an act that provoked the king to anger:

The King of Kings, Darius the son of Hystaspes says this to Gadatas, his slave [satrap]. I learn that you are not obeying my command in every particular. Because you are tilling my land, transplanting fruit trees from across the Euphrates [Syria] to Asia Minor, I praise your project, and there will be laid up for you great favor in the king's house. But because you mar my dispositions towards the gods, I shall give you, unless you change your ways, proof of my anger when wronged. For you exacted payment from the sacred gardeners of the temple of Apollo, and you ordered them to dig up secular land, failing to understand the attitude of my forefathers towards the god, who told the Persians the truth.[10]

This document alone suggests the efficiency of Persian rule and the compassion of Persian kings. Conquered peoples, left free to enjoy their traditional ways of life, found in the Persian king a capable protector. No wonder many Near Eastern peoples were, like the Jews, grateful for the long period of peace they enjoyed as the subjects of the Persian Empire.

SUMMARY

During the centuries following the Sea Peoples' invasions, Egypt was overrun by its African neighbors, and its long and rich traditions and culture, its firmly established religion, and its administrative techniques became the heritage of these conquerors. The defeat of Egypt also led to conditions that allowed the Hebrews to create their own state. A series of strong leaders fighting hard wars won the Hebrews independence and security. In this atmosphere Hebrew religion evolved and flourished, thanks to priests, prophets, and common piety among the people.

The Assyrians made the Near East tremble in terror of their armies. Their cruelty raised powerful enemies against them. Most important were the

Iranians, who created the Persian Empire. Military and, particularly, political abilities gave the Persians the tools they needed to govern a host of different peoples. For over two hundred years Persian kings offered their subjects enlightened rule. The Persians gave the ancient Near East a period of peace and stability in which peoples enjoyed their native traditions and lived in concord with their neighbors.

Meanwhile, to the east the Indians and Chinese were confronting many of the problems that the peoples farther west were solving. The direction of developments in India and China differed from that in the Near East, largely but not entirely because of geography. The results, however, were essentially the same: sophisticated civilizations based on systematic agriculture and complex social structures, cultures, and religions.

NOTES

1. James H. Breasted, *Ancient Records of Egypt,* vol. 4 (Chicago: University of Chicago Press, 1907), para. 398.
2. 2 Kings 23:3.
3. Jeremiah 3:12.
4. Proverbs 31:10, 25–30.
5. Psalms 128:3.
6. Proverbs 13:24.
7. J. B. Pritchard, ed., *Ancient Near Eastern Texts,* 3d ed. (Princeton, N.J.: Princeton University Press, 1969), p. 288.
8. Nahum 3:7.
9. E. Meyer, *Geschichte des Altertums,* 7th ed., vol. 4, pt. 1 (Darmstadt: Wissenschaftliche Buchgesellschaft, 1975), pp. 114–115. Translated by John Buckler.
10. R. Meiggs and D. M. Lewis, *A Selection of Greek Historical Inscriptions* (Oxford: Clarendon Press, 1969), no. 12.

SUGGESTED READING

Although late Egyptian history is still largely a specialist's field, K. A. Kitchen, *The Third Intermediate Period in Egypt* (1973), is a sturdy synthesis of the period from 1100 to 650 B.C. Valuable, too, is M. L. Bierbrier's monograph, *Late New Kingdom in Egypt, c. 1300–664 B.C.* (1975). D. B. Redford, *Egypt, Canaan, and Israel in Ancient Times* (1992), is an excellent study of relations among the three states. G. Herm,

The Phoenicians (1975), treats Phoenician seafaring and commercial enterprises.

The Jews have been one of the best-studied people in the ancient world, so many good treatments of Jewish history and society are available. E. Anati, *Palestine Before the Hebrews* (1962), though dated, still provides a sound historical treatment of life in Palestine from human origins to the conquest of Canaan. More recent is G. Alon, *The Jews in Their Land* (1989), which covers the Talmudic age. H. Shanks, ed., *The Rise of Ancient Israel* (1991), is a collection of papers that treat numerous aspects of the period. R. Tappy, *The Archaeology of Israelite Samaria* (1993), studies the archaeological remains of the period. S. Niditch, *War in the Hebrew Bible* (1992), addresses the ethics of violence in the Bible. A general introduction to the Bible is B. M. Mezter and M. D. Coogan, eds., *The Oxford Companion to the Bible* (1993). H. W. Attridge, ed., *Of Scribes and Scrolls* (1990), gives a fascinating study of the Hebrew Bible and of Christian origins. Turning to politics, M. Smith, *Palestinian Parties and Politics That Shaped the Old Testament,* 2d ed. (1987), takes a practical look at events. G. W. Ahlstrom, *Royal Administration and National Religion in Ancient Palestine* (1982), treats secular and religious aspects of Hebrew history. W. D. Davis et al., *The Cambridge History of Judaism,* vol. 1 (1984), begins an important new synthesis with work on Judaism in the Persian period. R. Hachlili, *Ancient Jewish Art and Archaeology in the Land of Israel* (1988), attempts to trace the development and meaning of Jewish art in its archaeological context.

The Assyrians, despite their achievements, have not attracted the scholarly attention that other Near Eastern peoples have. Even though woefully outdated, A. T. Olmstead, *History of Assyria* (1928), has the merit of being soundly based in the original sources. H. W. F. Saggs, *Everyday Life in Babylonia and Assyria,* rev. ed. (1987), offers a general and well-illustrated survey of Mesopotamian history from 3000 to 300 B.C. Those who appreciate the vitality of Assyrian art should start with the masterful work of R. D. Barnett and W. Forman, *Assyrian Palace Reliefs,* 2d ed. (1970), an exemplary combination of fine photographs and learned but not difficult discussion.

Several new works on ancient Iran have lately appeared. A comprehensive survey of Persian history is given by one of the leading scholars in the field, R. N. Frye, *History of Ancient Iran* (1984). I. Gershevitch, ed., *The Cambridge History of Iran,* vol. 2 (1985), provides a full account of ancient Persian history, but many of the chapters are already out-of-date. E. Herzfeld, *Iran in the Ancient East* (1987), puts Persian history in a broad context. Most welcome is M. A. Dandamaev, *A Political History of the Achaemenid Empire* (1989), which discusses in depth the history of the Persians and the organization of their empire. M. Boyce, a leading scholar in the field, provides a sound and readable treatment of the essence of Zoroastrianism in her *Zoroastrianism* (1979).

The Covenant Between Yahweh and the Hebrews

This passage from the Hebrew Bible addresses two themes important to the Hebrews: the meaning of kingship and the nature of the Covenant between the Hebrews and Yahweh (here referred to as "the Lord"). The Hebrew Bible tells a great deal about the people who created it. From the following passage we may discern what the Hebrews thought about their own past and religion.

The background of the selection is a political crisis that has some archaeological support. The war with the Philistines put a huge strain on Hebrew society, and new and effective political and military leadership was needed to meet the situation. The elders of the tribes of Israel had previously chosen judges to lead the community only in times of crisis. The Hebrew people now demanded that a secular kingship be established, even though their Covenant declared their god Yahweh to be their king. Samuel, the last of the judges, with Yahweh's approval, anointed Saul as the first Hebrew king. In this excerpt Samuel confronts the Hebrews, reminding them of their obligation to honor the Covenant.

Then said Samuel to the people, Come, and let us go to Gilgal, and renew the kingdom there. And all the people went to Gilgal; and there they made Saul king before the Lord in Gilgal; and there they sacrificed sacrifices of peace offerings before the Lord; and there Saul and all the men of Israel rejoiced greatly.

And Samuel said unto all Israel, Behold, I have hearkened unto your voice in all that you said to me, and have made a king over you. And now, behold, the king walks before you; and I am old and gray-headed; and, behold, my sons are with you: and I have walked before you from my childhood until this day. Behold, here I am: witness against me before the Lord, and before his anointed: whose ox have I taken? or whose ass have I taken? or

whom have I defrauded? whom have I oppressed? or of whose hand have I received any bribe to blind my eyes with it? and I will restore it to you.

And they said, You have not defrauded us, nor oppressed us, neither have you taken anything from any man's hand.

And he said to them, the Lord is witness against you, and his anointed is witness this day, that you have not found anything in my hand. And they answered, he is witness.

At this point Samuel reminds the Hebrews that Yahweh has always been faithful to them, and he lists a number of times in history in which the Hebrews violated their Covenant. Then Samuel gives them stern advice, capped by a threat about any future disobedience.

Now therefore behold the king whom you have chosen, and whom you have desired! and, behold, the Lord has set a king over you. If you will fear the Lord, and serve him, and obey his voice, and not rebel against the commandment of the Lord, then shall both you and also the king who reigns over you continue following the Lord your God: But if you will not obey the voice of the Lord, but rebel against the commandment of the Lord, then shall the hand of the Lord be against you, as it was against your fathers.

Now therefore stand and see this great thing, which the Lord will do before your eyes. Is it not wheat harvest today? I will call to the Lord, and he shall send thunder and rain; that you may perceive and see that your wickedness is great, which you have done in the sight of the Lord, in asking you a king.

So Samuel called to the Lord; and the Lord sent thunder and rain that day: and all the people greatly feared the Lord and Samuel. And all the people said to Samuel, pray for your servants to the Lord your God, so that we will not die: for we have added to all of our sins this evil, to ask us for a king.

And Samuel said to the people, Fear not: you have done all this wickedness; yet turn not aside from following the Lord, but serve the Lord with all your heart; And do not turn aside; for then should you go after vain things, which cannot profit nor deliver; for they are vain. For the Lord will not forsake his people for his great name's sake: because it pleases the Lord to make you his people. Moreover, as for me, God forbid that I should sin against the Lord in ceasing to pray for you: but I will teach you the good and the right way: Only fear the Lord, and serve him in truth with all your heart: for consider how great things he has done for you. But if you shall still act wickedly, you will be consumed, both you and your king.

Questions for Analysis

1. How did Samuel explain his anointment of a king?

2. What was Samuel's attitude toward kingship?

3. What were the duties of the Hebrews toward Yahweh?

4. Might those duties conflict with those toward the secular king? If so, in what ways, and how might the Hebrews avoid the conflict?

Source: Abridged and adapted from 1 Samuel 11:15, 12:1–5, 16–25, *The Holy Bible.* Copyright © 1974 The Gideons International.

Ark of the Covenant, depicted in a relief from Capernaum Synagogue, second century A.D. (*Source: Ancient Art & Architecture Collection*)

CHAPTER

3

Ancient India to ca A.D. 200

The North Gate is one of four ornately carved gates guarding the Buddhist memorial shrine at Sanchi, Madhya Pradesh. Satavahana, 2nd century B.C. *(Source: Jean-Louis Nou)*

While the peoples of the ancient Near East were spreading their cultures and grappling with the political administration of large tracts of land, people in India were wrestling with similar problems—taming the land, settling it, improving agricultural techniques, building cities and urban cultures, and asking basic questions about social organization and the nature of human life.

Like the civilizations of Mesopotamia and Egypt, the earliest Indian civilization centered on a great river, the Indus. Like the people of the ancient Near East, the people of ancient India confronted challenging climate and topography. They suffered monsoons; they faced jungle in some areas and desert in others. The fertile but undeveloped and underpopulated territory offered Neolithic pioneers and their descendants either prosperity or extinction, depending on how well they met the varied demands of the land. As in the ancient Near East, so too in India agriculture promoted an increase in population, and the needs of metal technology encouraged wider contacts.

- How did the ancient Indians respond to the problems that ancient Near Eastern peoples were confronting?
- How did they meet the challenge of the land itself?
- What role did religion play in Indian life?
- What kind of social and political organization developed in India?
- What intellectual and religious values did this society generate?

These questions are the central concerns of this chapter.

THE LAND AND ITS FIRST TAMERS (CA 2500–1500 B.C.)

The subcontinent of India, a landmass as large as western Europe, juts southward into the warm waters of the Indian Ocean. India is a land of contrasts. Some regions are among the wettest on earth; others are dry and even arid desert and scrub land. High mountain ranges in the north drop off to the low river valleys of the Indus and Ganges.

Three regions of India are of overriding geographical significance: (1) the ring of mountains in the north that separates India from its neighbors, (2) the great river valleys of the Indus and Ganges and their tributaries, and (3) the southern peninsula, especially the narrow coastal plains and the large Deccan Plateau (Map 3.1). The lower reaches of the Himalaya Mountains—the northern geographical boundary of the subcontinent—are covered by some of India's densest forests, sustained by heavy rainfall. Immediately to the south the land drops away to the fertile river valleys of the Indus and Ganges. On these lowland plains, which stretch all the way across the subcontinent, agriculture has traditionally flourished. Furthermore, the flat terrain enabled invaders to sweep across and beyond the northern Indian plain, once they passed the area of Delhi. South of these valleys rise the Vindhya Mountains and the dry, hilly Deccan Plateau. Only along the coasts do the hills give way to narrow plains. In short, geography divides India into many subregions, some of them huge, fertile, and capable of sustaining large and vigorous populations.

The Himalayas, which in many places exceed 25,000 feet in height, protected ancient India from wandering peoples in search of new lands to settle. Throughout much of antiquity the Indian Ocean served to keep out invaders while fostering maritime trade with both the Near East and China and Southeast Asia. Only in the northwest—the area between modern Afghanistan and Pakistan—was India accessible to outsiders. This region, penetrated by the Khyber Pass, has traditionally been the highway of invaders—a highway whose other terminus was the flourishing cultures of the ancient Near East. Thus geography segregated India, but it also made possible contact with the ideas, practices, and technology of the earliest civilizations.

The Himalayas shield the subcontinent from the northern cold. They also hold in the monsoon rains that sweep northward from the Indian Ocean each summer. The monsoons and the melting snows of the Himalayas in the north provide India with most of its water. In some areas the resulting moistness and humidity created vast tracts of jungle and swamp. The Ganges, for example, was a particularly forbidding region, and only gradually did settlers move there from the tamer west. Much of India, however, is subtropical and dry. In

Farthest extent of the Persian Empire
The Mauryan Empire
Farthest extent of Alexander's conquest

MAP 3.1 The Development of India from ca 2500 to ca 250 B.C.   This map shows the development of India from the days of the Indus Valley civilization to the reign of Ashoka. Although northwestern India fell to foreign conquerors such as the Persians and Alexander the Great, most of India was unscathed by these incursions. Ashoka created the first real Indian empire.

general, the monsoon area of southwestern India experiences the heaviest rainfall; the driest region is the northeast. Geography and climate, and especially good water resources, combined to make the Punjab and the valley of the Indus River—now in Pakistan—the most attractive regions for India's first settlers.

The story of the first civilization in India, known as the Indus civilization, is one of the most dramatic in the entire ancient world. In 1921 archaeologists discovered astonishing evidence of a thriving and sophisticated urban culture dating to about 2500 B.C. About the tantalizing problem of the origin of the Indus civilization, the eminent English archaeologist Sir Mortimer Wheeler has commented:

By the middle of the 3rd millennium, something very important was happening in the Indus valley, and happening probably at great speed. Who the first leaders were who led their people, however hesitantly, down to the wide and jungle-ridden plain we shall never know, nor why they ventured; but they were bold men, pioneers in the fullest sense, no mere ejects from the highland zone. Some, perhaps many of them, led forlorn hopes and perished. . . . Seemingly the attempted colonization of the valley continued intermittently, failure succeeding failure, until at last a leader, more determined and far-sighted and fortunate than the rest, won through.[1]

This dramatic description of the earliest development of social life in India still possesses merit, but recent discoveries have clarified matters greatly. Wheeler was wrong, when he said that "we shall never know" about the earliest years of Indian life. Contemporary archaeologists and scholars have constructed a more complex interpretation of these events. They have found evidence of a gradual evolution of society from the Neolithic period to the Indus civilization. Scattered settlements consisted of people who made buildings of mud-brick. By at least 5000 B.C., these people had begun to raise crops of barley and wheat and to domesticate cattle, sheep, and goats. They basically laid the foundations of village and later urban life.

They created a thriving and sophisticated urban culture. Like the Mesopotamian city, the Indian city was surrounded by extensive farmland, which fed its inhabitants. These pioneers also developed a script, which is still undeciphered. As early as the reign of Sargon of Akkad in the third millennium B.C., trade between India and Mesopotamia carried goods and ideas between the two cultures, probably by way of the Persian Gulf.

The Indus civilization extended over fully 1.25 million square kilometers in the Indus Valley. Its two best-known cities were Mohenjo-daro in southern Pakistan and Harappa some four hundred miles to the north in the Punjab. Other sites have since been found in southern Pakistan, at Sutkagendor in the west, as far east as Alamgirpur near modern Delhi, and as far north as Ropar (see Map 3.1). Numerous sites are still being excavated, and a full portrait of this vast civilization will have to await archaeologists' findings. It is already clear, however, that the Indus civilization was marked by a striking uniformity of culture and, simultaneously, by regional variation.

Some important new linguistic work suggests that other peoples were also filtering into India from western Asia while the Indus civilization was flourishing. The Dravidians, who are usually considered natives of central and southern India, probably moved through the Indus Valley at about this time. The situation is far from clear because of the many movements of peoples in the subcontinent during these early years. There is, however, nothing to suggest that the Dravidians came as waves of invaders. For all that anyone knows today, they could have been newcomers who adopted various aspects of the Indus civilization, or they could have been an indigenous people who devised their own particular culture, sometimes borrowing heavily from the Harappan culture. Archaeology

Figurine from Mohenjo-daro   Part of the legacy of the Indus civilization is its artistic creations, such as this figurine of a bearded man. The composition is at once bold and sophisticated. Yet even glimpses such as this give little clue to the origins of the creators of the Indus civilization. *(Source: National Museum, Karachi)*

can tell us a great deal about how people lived, but it cannot always tell us how even major developments came about. In short, the movement of ancient peoples into India was a far more complex process than anyone imagined even a few years ago. Only future work in a variety of fields can clarify this immense phenomenon.

Mohenjo-daro and Harappa are currently the best-understood keys to the Indus civilization. Both cities were huge, over three miles in circumference, and housed large populations. Built of fired mud brick, Mohenjo-daro and Harappa were largely unfortified, although both were defended by great citadels that towered 40 or 50 feet above the surrounding plain. Both cities were logically planned from the outset, not merely villages that grew and sprawled haphazardly. In both, blocks of houses were laid out on a grid plan, centuries before the Greeks used this method of urban design. Streets were straight and varied from 9 to 34 feet in width. The houses of both cities were substantial, many two stories tall, some perhaps three, their brick exteriors unadorned. The focal point of the Indus houses was a central open courtyard onto which the rooms opened.

Perhaps the most surprising aspect of the elaborate planning of these cities is their complex system of drainage, well preserved at Mohenjo-daro. Each

house had a bathroom with a drain connected to municipal drains located under the major streets. These brick-built channels, which carried off refuse, had openings to allow clearing of blockages.

Both cities also contained numerous large structures, which excavators think were public buildings. One of the most important is the state granary, a large storehouse for the community's grain. Moreover, a set of tenement buildings next to a series of round working-floors near the granary at Harappa suggests that the central government dominated the storage and processing of the city's cereal crops. The citadel at Mohenjo-daro further testifies to the power of the city's rulers: here stood monumental buildings, including a marketplace or place of assembly, a palace, and a huge bath featur-

�֎ **Mohenjo-daro** The architectural vision and engineering expertise of the Indus civilization are obvious in this view of Mohenjo-daro. The central planning and huge scale of the city reflect a flourishing community. *(Source: Josephine Powell, Rome)*

Bronze Chariot   This bronze figure from Mohenjo-daro is an excellent example of early Indian bronze work. But it poses a problem. The vehicle itself is too slender to be a cart, as usually stated, but is well suited to be a chariot for war. *(Source: National Museum, New Delhi)*

ing a pool some 39 feet by 23 feet and 8 feet deep. The Great Bath, like later Roman baths, was an intricate structure with spacious dressing rooms for the bathers. Because the Great Bath at Mohenjo-daro resembles the ritual purification pools of later Indian society, some scholars have speculated that power was in the hands of a priest-king and that the Great Bath played a role in the religious rituals of the city. But little is yet known about the religious life of Mohenjo-daro and Harappa or about their government. Nonetheless, the power and authority of the government, whether secular or religious, are apparent in the intelligent central planning of these cities.

The prosperity of the Indus civilization depended on constant and intensive cultivation of the rich river valley. The Indus, like the Nile, provided farmers with fertile alluvial soil enriched by annual floods. Farmers built earth embankments to hold the floodwaters. The results of this labor were abundant crops of wheat, barley, vegetables, and cotton. The Indus people also domesticated cattle, buffalo, fowl, and possibly pigs and asses. Their efforts led to a high standard of living and to the surpluses that they traded with Mesopotamia. They were also in contact with neighbors closer to home, trading with the peoples of southern India for gold and with the ancient Afghans for silver.

Despite tantalizing glimpses of a serene and stable society, the intellectual and religious life of the Indus people is largely unknown. Fertility was a major concern to them, as it is to most agricultural people: they apparently worshiped a mother-goddess who looked after the welfare of the community. Some later Indian religious beliefs may have originated in this period. One of the most engaging of the early Indian deities—who is depicted at Mohenjo-daro with his customary three faces, surrounded by wild animals—closely resembles Siva, a major Hindu god. The Indus people's great fondness for animals is apparent in the popularity of terra-cotta animal figurines. Their attitude prefigures the deep respect for the animal world that Indians have traditionally felt. Indeed, they give the impression of having been a people in tune with the world around them, a world they understood and enjoyed. The Indus people maintained their equilibrium with nature for hundreds of years, spreading their culture throughout the valley and enjoying a tranquil development.

Yet this civilization, which appeared in history so suddenly, perished just as mysteriously. After years of prosperity, Mohenjo-daro and Harappa suffered a long decline, perhaps as a result of deforestation, a change in climate, and their huge demands on the land. The first excavators of Mohenjo-daro found some skeletons of men, women, and children, many with ax or sword wounds, scattered across the ground. Contemporary archaeologists, however, point out that too few skeletons at Mohenjo-daro showed signs of violence to indicate wholesale slaughter. Others suggest that the population may have fallen prey to diseases such as malaria. What is not disputed is that many of the Indus people lived on, though disrupted and scattered. With them they carried the accomplishments and values of their culture, which became an important element in the development of later Indian civilization. In fact, the rich religious life of the people proved more important than politics because it was the shared and enduring cultural heritage of the land. Kings came and went; the gods remained, thus religion was the glue that held Indian society together.

THE ASCENDANCY OF THE ARYANS (CA 1500–500 B.C.)

The Aryans, an Indo-European people who entered India from the northwest, may not have reached India until many years after the fall of the Indus civilization. Nevertheless, the Aryans, like the Hittites and later the Greeks, formed part of the widespread migrations that transformed the face of much of the ancient world, an event that forever changed the face of India. The Aryans were part of the enormous movement of Indo-Europeans described in Chapter 1 (see page 3). Their arrival was a turning point in Indian history. Nomadic wanderers, the Aryans came in search of land; the Indus Valley, with its rich plains and predictable climate, lured them on. There they met the native Dravidians, with whom they at first fought. Later the two peoples forged the basis of subsequent Indian society.

Most knowledge of the early Aryans comes from the Rigveda, the oldest and most sacred of the Hindu scriptures. The Rigveda is not a history but a collection of hymns in praise of the Aryan gods. Even so, the hymns contain some historical information that sheds light on the Aryans and on native Indians. The Rigveda and other Vedas, which were also sacred writings, are crucial to understanding the social evolution of India during this period, sometimes called the Dark Ages of India.

The Rigveda portrays the Aryans as a group of battle-loving pastoral tribes, a heroic folk at war with one another and with the native population of India. Their use of horses and bronze weapons in warfare gave them superiority over the natives. At the head of the Aryan tribe was its chief, or *raja,* who led his followers in battle and ruled them in peacetime. Next to the chief was the priest, entrusted with sacrifices to the gods and the knowledge of sacred rituals. In time, as Aryan society (also known as Vedic society) laid increasing emphasis on proper performance of the religious rituals, priests evolved into a distinct class possessing precise knowledge of the complex rituals and of the invocations and formulas that accompanied them. The warrior nobility rode to battle in chariots and perhaps on horseback and expressed its will in assemblies. The commoners supported society by tending herds and, increasingly as conditions settled, working the land. To the non-Aryans fell the drudgery of menial tasks. It is difficult to define precisely their social status. Though probably not slaves at this point, they were certainly dependents of the Aryans, and worked for them in return for support and protection. Women held a more favorable position in this period than in later times: they were not yet given in child-marriage, and widows had the right to remarry.

Gradually the Aryans pushed farther eastward into the valley of the Ganges River, a land of thick jungle populated by tribes. The jungle was as stubborn an enemy as its inhabitants, and clearing it presented a tremendous challenge. For the next six hundred years, the Aryans migrated eastward, finally founding the important city of Delhi. During this time the Aryans and their Indian predecessors blended their cultures, each influencing the other. The resulting synthesis constituted an entirely new Indian society.

The Shaping of Indian Society

Because the push into the jungle demanded an especially large and tightly organized political entity, tribes merged under strong rulers whose power grew increasingly absolute. As rulers claimed sovereignty over specific territory, political rule shifted from tribal chieftainship to kingship. The priests, or *Brahmans,* supported the growth of royal power in return for royal confirmation of their own religious rights, power, and status. The Brahmans also served a political function as advisers to the kings. In the face of this royal-priestly alliance, the old tribal assemblies of warriors withered away.

Development of the newly won territory led to further changes. Cleared land under cultivation needed constant work to keep it from reverting to jungle. The typical response to this challenge was the village. In this period India evolved into the land of villages it still is today. Even the later growth of cities did not eclipse the village as the hallmark of Indian society. Yet villages did not conform to a single social pattern. In the south the typical village consisted of groups of families who considered themselves related to one another, but as always there were exceptions, as when some villagers married outside their own village and outside the family. Each family was a large patriarchal joint or extended family composed of several nuclear families who lived and worked together. In the north, by contrast, marriage outside the village was more common, and families' kinship ties extended over wider areas than in the south. What all Indian villages had in common was a tradition of mutual cooperation born of common interests and obligations. The close-knit society of the village has consistently been a stabilizing element in Indian history. Yet as self-sufficient as it was, the village was far from isolated. It was connected with other villages both socially and economically, and formed the basic component in the various kingdoms of which it was a part. Unfortunately for the villagers, their primary contact with the ruling raja was paying him taxes. Yet in turn they could hope for a stable government and protection from invaders.

Social contact between Aryans and natives led to the development of the complicated system of social organization known as the caste system. A *caste* is a hereditary class of social equals who share the same religion, pursue a specific trade or occupation, and avoid extensive social intercourse with members of other castes. Initially this system had two goals: to distinguish Aryans from non-Aryans and to mark birth or descent. The caste system was fluid at first and allowed for a surprising amount of social mobility. Even in the early days of conquest the Aryans mixed with the conquered population, and that slow mingling eventually resulted in the Indian society that emerged into the full light of history. The blending was intellectual and religious as well as social. Only as conditions stabilized over the years did the system become strict and the number of castes grow.

To further complicate matters there was a system of *jati,* large joint family groups that became

Bronze Sword A striking example of the quality of Aryan arms is this bronze sword, with its rib in the middle of the blade for strength. Native Indians lacked comparable weapons. (*Source: Courtesy of the Trustees of the British Museum*)

incorporated into society. Although the origin of the *jati* is uncertain, they became members of a specific caste, whose function was essentially economic. In effect, they specialized in specific trades, and even enjoyed governance by a ruling council of elders. In time some families branched out into trades not entirely related to the traditional trades of their families. The result was the broadening of the economic and the social importance of the *jati.* Eventually, the castes were subdivided into hundreds and even thousands of *jati.* Although this system may seem hopelessly confusing to others, it actually led to social stability. People know where they stood in society, and the *jati* also provided the opportunity for some social mobility within the caste.

By about 500 B.C. four main groups of Indian society—the priests *(Brahman),* the warriors *(Kshatriya),* the peasants *(Vaishya),* and the serfs *(Shudra)* —were evolving. Indians themselves ascribed this stratification to the gods, as the Rigveda testifies:

> When they divided the [primeval] Man
>   into how many parts did they divide him?
> What was his mouth, what were his arms,
>   what were his thighs and his feet called?
> The Brahman was his mouth, of his
>   arms was made the warrior.
> His thighs became the Vaishya, of
>   his feet the Shudra was born.[2]

According to this division of duties, the priests conducted religious sacrifices and treasured the religious lore. The warriors protected society from external attack and maintained law and order within it, and the peasants grew the food and paid the taxes. The serfs, who were originally the property of the tribe, served the others by performing hard labor. Those without places in this tidy social division—that is, those who entered it later than the others or who had lost their caste status through violations of ritual—were *outcastes.* That simply meant that they belonged to no caste. In time, some of these people became "untouchables," because they were "impure." They were so scorned because they earned their livings by performing such undesirable jobs as slaughtering animals and dressing skins. Although their work was economically valuable, it was considered unworthy and socially polluting.

Slavery was also a feature of social life, as it was elsewhere in antiquity. The scanty evidence available suggests that slavery in Aryan society resembled Mesopotamian slavery. In India there was no caste of slaves, although in practice most slaves would have come from the lower castes, which were economically disadvantaged. In the Aryan period, slaves were often people captured in battle, but these captives could be ransomed by their families. Still later, slavery was less connected with warfare; it was more of an economic and social institution. At birth, slave children automatically became the slaves of their parents' masters. Indian slaves

could be bought, used as collateral, or even given away. As in ancient Mesopotamia, a free man might sell himself and his family into slavery because he could not pay his debts. And, as in Hammurabi's Mesopotamia, he could, if clever, hard working, or fortunate, buy his and his family's way out of slavery.

Slaves in India performed tasks similar to those of slaves in other societies. Like Joseph in ancient Egypt, a man might serve as a royal counselor, having more actual authority than many a free man. Otherwise slaves served in their masters' fields, mines, or houses. Whatever their economic function, socially they were members of their master's household. Indian masters were required to perform the customary duties necessary for the welfare of the soul of a deceased slave. Indian law forbade a master from abandoning slaves in their old age; it also recommended manumission of slaves as an act of piety. Nonetheless, in Indian literature there is ample evidence of the abuse of slaves; and as in other societies—both ancient and modern—it is sometimes impossible to determine to what extent laws and social injunctions were actually put into practice.

Early Indian Religion

In religion and intellectual life, a momentous revolution was occurring in Indian society. The Aryan gods represented natural phenomena. Some of them were great brawling figures, like Agni, the god of fire; Indra, wielder of the thunderbolt and god of war; and Rudra, the divine archer who spread disaster and disease by firing his arrows at people. Others were shadowy figures, like Dyaus, the father of the gods, who appears in Greek as Zeus and in Latin as Jupiter. Varuna, the god of order in the universe, was a hard god, quick to punish those who sinned and thus upset the balance of nature. Ushas, the goddess of dawn, was a refreshingly gentle deity who welcomed the birds, gave delight to human beings, and kept off evil spirits. Although the Aryan gods had their duties, they differed from the Greek deities and Mesopotamian gods in that they rarely had distinctive personalities or extensive mythologies. All the Aryan gods enjoyed sacrifices, however, and ritual was an essential ingredient in early Aryan religion. Gradually, under the priestly monopoly of the Brahmans, correct sacrifice and proper ritual became so important that most Brahmans believed a

Ascetic Instructing Pupils All major branches of Indian intellectual thought, whether philosophical or religious, insisted on the proper education of students. Here an ascetic explains the tenets of his beliefs to a younger generation. *(Source: Indian Museum, Calcutta/Dinodia Picture Agency)*

properly performed ritual would force a god to grant a worshiper's wish. These beliefs became known as Brahmanism.

Religion became sterile and unsatisfying to many, even among the priestly class. In search of a faith richer and more mystical, some Brahmans retreated to the forests to seek a personal road to the gods. Through *asceticism*—severe self-discipline and self-denial—and meditation on the traditional teachings of the Vedas, these pioneers breathed new life into the old rituals. They concluded that disciplined meditation on the ritual sacrifice could produce the same results as the physical ritual it-

self. Thus they reinterpreted the ritual sacrifices as symbolic gestures with mystical meanings. Slowly Indian religion was changing from primitive worship to a way of thought that nourished human needs and eased human fears.

Two cardinal doctrines prevailed: *samsara,* the transmigration of souls by a continual process of rebirth, and *karma,* the tally of good and bad deeds that determined the status of an individual's next life. Good deeds led to better future lives; evil deeds, to worse future lives, even to reincarnation as an animal. Two methods of escape from continual reincarnation were possible: extreme asceticism and *yoga,* or intense meditation. Either method, if pursued successfully, allowed the individual to be absorbed into a timeless and changeless state. Thus gradually arose the concept of a wheel of life that included human beings, animals, and even gods.

To most people, especially those on the low end of the economic and social scale, these concepts were attractive. All existence, no matter how harsh and bitter, could be progress to better things. By living righteously and doing good deeds, people could improve their lot in the next life. Yet there was another side to these ideas: the wheel of life could be seen as a treadmill, giving rise to a yearning for release from the relentless cycle of birth and death. Hence the new concepts created tension in religious thought.

The solution to this baffling problem appears in the Upanishads, a collection of sacred texts created by ascetics who opened up new vistas in religious speculation. The authors of the Upanishads fostered the concept of *moksha,* or release from the wheel of life. All people, they taught, have in themselves an eternal truth and reality called *atman,* which corresponds to an identical but greater all-encompassing reality called *Brahman.* These mystics and ascetics claimed that life in the world is actually an illusion, and the only way to escape it and the wheel of life is to realize that reality is unchanging. By studying the Vedas, by penance, and by meditation, one could join one's individual self with the universal reality. This profound and subtle teaching they summed up in one sentence: "Thou art That." What does this sentence mean? The Chandogya Upanishad tells the story of a father explaining it to his son:

"Believe me, my son, an invisible and subtle essence is the Spirit of the whole universe. That is Reality. That is Atman. THOU ART THAT."

"Explain more to me, father," said Svetaketu.

"So be it, my son.

"Place this salt in water and come to me tomorrow morning."

Svetaketu did as he was commanded, and in the morning his father said to him: "Bring me the salt you put into the water last night."

Svetaketu looked into the water, but could not find it, for it had dissolved.

His father then said: "Taste the water from this side. How is it?"

"It is salt."

"Taste it from the middle. How is it?"

"It is salt."

"Taste it from that side. How is it?"

"It is salt."

"Look for the salt again and come again to me."

The son did so, saying: "I cannot see the salt. I only see water."

His father then said: "In the same way, O my son, you cannot see the Spirit. But in truth he is here.

"An invisible and subtle essence is the Spirit of the whole universe. That is Reality. That is Truth. THOU ART THAT."[3]

Providing a transcendent means to escape the problems presented by the wheel of life, these revolutionary ideas appealed to those who were dissatisfied with the old Brahman religion of sacrifice, and they even won the support of the Brahman and kings. The thought of the Upanishads gave Brahman a high status to which the poor and lowly could aspire in future life; consequently the Brahman greeted these concepts, and those who taught them, with tolerance and understanding. They made a place for them in traditional religious practice. The rulers of Indian society had excellent practical reasons to encourage the new trends. The doctrines of samsara and karma encouraged the poor and oppressed to labor peacefully and dutifully. The revolutionary new doctrines actually promoted stability in social and political life.

By about **500** B.C., all these trends—political, social, and religious—had led to a society, shaped by conqueror and conquered, in which all had a place. Urban life flourished alongside a vigorous village life, both sustained by agriculture. Gone were the warrior chieftains, their place taken by hereditary kings who ruled large territorial states with the support of a hereditary priestly class. Many of India's basic values already had taken shape at this early date.

 ## INDIA'S SPIRITUAL FLOWERING

India's spiritual growth came into full bloom in the sixth and fifth centuries B.C. This period of stunning moral and philosophical thought gave rise to three of the world's greatest religions: Hinduism, Jainism, and Buddhism. The evolution of these sects is complex and somewhat obscure. Hinduism is the most direct descendant of the old Vedic religion. Jainism and Buddhism shared that heritage but reacted against it and against Hinduism. Jainism and Buddhism originated as schools of moral philosophy, preoccupied with the nature of ultimate reality and with ethical conduct.

Hinduism

Hinduism may be the world's oldest flourishing religion. It is certainly one of the world's largest faiths, with millions of adherents in India and other Asian countries, the West Indies, and South Africa. It is also a complex of social customs, doctrines, and beliefs.

Although influenced by Jainism and Buddhism, Hinduism was most firmly rooted in traditional Indian religion. The bedrock of Hinduism is the belief that the Vedas are sacred revelations and that a specific caste system is implicitly prescribed in them. Thus Hinduism is both a collection of religious beliefs and a sacred division of society.

Religiously and philosophically, Hinduism is diverse. It assumes that there are innumerable legitimate ways of worshiping the supreme principle of life. Consequently it readily incorporates new sects, doctrines, beliefs, rites, and deities. The numerous Hindu gods are all considered aspects of Brahma, the supreme and undefinable principle of life. According to Hinduism, Brahma suffuses all things and at the same time transcends all things. The various deities are considered specific manifestations of Brahma. Each of them helps people to reach Brahma by means of rituals.

Hinduism is a guide to life, whose goal is to reach Brahma. There are four steps in this search, progressing from study of the Vedas in youth to complete asceticism in old age. In their quest for Brahma, people are to observe *dharma,* a moral law nearly as complex as Hinduism itself. Dharma stipulates the legitimate pursuits of Hindus: material gain, so long as it is honestly and honorably achieved; pleasure and love, for the perpetuation of the family; and moksha, release from the wheel of life and unity with Brahma. The society that a scrupulous observance of dharma could create is depicted in the *Mahabharata,* a long epic poem in which the law is personified as King Dharma (see Listening to the Past):

All the people, relying on King Dharma, lived happily like souls that rely on their own bodies that are favored with auspicious marks and deeds. The bull of the Bharatas cultivated Law, Profit, and Pleasure

alike, like a family man honoring three kinsmen alike to himself. To Law, Profit, and Pleasure, now incarnated on earth in equal proportions, the king himself appeared as the fourth. In this overlord of men the Vedas found a superb student, the great sacrifices a performer, the four classes a pure guardian. Luck had found her place, wisdom its apex, all Law its kinsman with this lord of the earth.[4]

In short, Hinduism spells out the goals of life and how to attain them.

After the third century B.C., Hinduism began to emphasize the roles and personalities of powerful gods—especially Brahma, the creator; Siva, the cosmic dancer who both creates and destroys; and Vishnu, the preserver and sustainer of creation. Since these gods are personal manifestations of Brahma, Brahma can be known through them. Thus people could reach Brahma by devotion to personal gods. From this emphasis on a god-force in all life came a tradition of nonviolence to all living creatures.

India's best-loved sacred hymn, the Bhagavad Gita, is a spiritual guide to the most serious problem facing a Hindu—how to live in the world and yet honor dharma and thus achieve release. The heart of the Bhagavad Gita is the spiritual conflict confronting Arjuna, a human hero about to ride into battle against his own kinsmen. As he surveys the battlefield, struggling with the grim notion of killing his relatives, Arjuna voices his doubts to his charioteer, none other than the god Krishna himself. When at last Arjuna refuses to spill his family's blood, Krishna instructs him, as he has instructed generations of Hindus, on the true meaning of Hinduism:

Interwoven in his creation, the Spirit Brahma is beyond destruction. No one can bring to an end the Spirit which is everlasting. For beyond time he dwells in these bodies, though these bodies have an end in their time; but he remains immeasurable, immortal. Therefore, great warrior, carry on thy fight. If any man thinks he slays, and if another thinks he is slain, neither knows the ways of truth. The Eternal in man cannot kill; the Eternal in man cannot die. He is never born, and he never dies. He is in Eternity: he is for evermore. Never born and eternal, beyond times gone or to come, he does not die when the body dies. When a man knows him as never-born, everlasting, never-changing, beyond all destruction, how can that man kill a man, or cause another to kill?[5]

Krishna then clarifies the relation between human reality and the eternal spirit. He explains compassionately to Arjuna the duty to act—to live in the world and carry out his duties as a warrior. Indeed, the Bhagavad Gita urges the necessity of action, which is essential for the welfare of the world. Arjuna has the warrior's duty to wage war in compliance with his dharma. Only those who live

Siva   One of the three most important Vedic gods, Siva represented both destruction and procreation. Here Siva, mounted on a bull and carrying a spear, attacks the demon Andhaka. Siva is seen as a fierce and bloodthirsty warrior. *(Source: C. M. Dixon/Photo Resources)*

within the divine law without complaint will be released from karma. One person's dharma may be different from another's, but both must follow their own dharma.

The intimate relation between Hindu religion and the social structure of Indian life merits special attention. They are inseparable parts of a unity that forms the core of Indian civilization. The caste system on the social and economic side forms one part of the equation, and Hinduism on the religious side forms the other. Religion justifies the caste system, and that social system in turn stands as visible proof of the validity of religious teaching. The stability of the village, absolutely basic to Indian civilization, is proof of the strength of this social and religious bond, which allows each village to be almost a complete universe in itself.

Early in India's history Hinduism provided a complex and sophisticated philosophy of life and a religion of enormous emotional appeal. Hinduism also inspired and preserved, in Sanskrit and the major regional languages of India, the vast literature that is India's priceless literary heritage.

Jainism

The founder and most influential thinker of Jainism, Vardhamana Mahavira (ca 540–468 B.C.), the son of an aristocrat, accepted the doctrines of karma and rebirth but developed the animistic philosophy that human beings, animals, plants, and even inanimate objects and natural phenomena all have living souls. Mahavira taught that the universe and everything in it are composed of souls, usually mixed with matter. These souls, though infinite in number, are finite in nature, having definite limits. Souls float or sink, according to Mahavira, depending on the amount of matter with which they are mixed. The only way for any soul to reach eternal happiness is to rid itself of all matter so that it can float to the top of the universe.

Mahavira's followers, known as Jains, believed that people could achieve eternal bliss only by living lives of asceticism and avoiding evil thoughts and actions. The Jains considered all life too sacred to be destroyed. Yet if everything in the world possesses a soul, how can one live without destroying other life? The rigorously logical answer is that one cannot. Strictly speaking, the Jains could adhere to their beliefs only by starving to death. But instead of going to this extreme, the Jains created a hierarchy of life, with human beings at the apex, fol-

Kali Ma The consort of Siva, Kali Ma represented both destructive and procreative powers, as he did. Here she assumes her role as the mother-goddess, but her necklace of skulls reminds viewers of her ferocity. *(Source: C. M. Dixon/Photo Resources)*

lowed by animals, plants, and inanimate objects. A Jain who wished to do the least possible violence to life became a vegetarian.

Nonviolence became a cardinal principle of Jainism and soon took root throughout Indian society. Although Jainism never took hold as widely as Hinduism and Buddhism, it has been an influential strand in Indian thought, and numbers several million adherents in India today. The Jains can claim, perhaps untruly, credit for one of the most practical innovations in Indian history, the creation

Praying Men Around a Stupa The stupa was a domed building erected as a Buddhist shrine. In this picture a group of holy men surround the stupa in prayer and reverence. *(Source: Eliot Elisofon Collection, Harry Ransom Humanities Center, University of Texas, Austin)*

of the Brahman alphabet. Because of the various dialects of the people, a simplified method of writing was needed to unite the kingdom. According to tradition, an aristocratic Jain woman invented an alphabet that made communication easier throughout the subcontinent.

Siddhartha Gautama and Buddhism

Siddhartha Gautama (ca 563–483 B.C.), better known as the Buddha, meaning the "Enlightened One," lived at the time when Jainism and Hinduism were evolving. The Buddha, like Mahavira, also became dissatisfied with settled life and abandoned it for a wandering, ascetic existence. The Buddha was so distressed by human suffering that he abandoned his family's Hindu beliefs in a quest

for a more universal, ultimate enlightenment. He tried techniques of extreme asceticism, including fasting, but found that they led nowhere. Only through meditation did he achieve the universal enlightenment in which he comprehended everything, including how the world of samsara actually worked.

Followers later believed that the Buddha taught them only what was necessary but that he had seen much more. According to this view, what he considered necessary were the "Four Noble Truths" contained in his first sermon: (1) pain and suffering, frustration, and anxiety are ugly but inescapable parts of human life; (2) suffering and anxiety are caused by the human weaknesses of greed, selfishness, and egoism; (3) people can understand these weaknesses and triumph over them;

and (4) this triumph is made possible by following a simple code of conduct, which the Buddha called the "Eightfold Path."

First, the Buddha explained, people have to understand the evils they are suffering. Ultimate release can be achieved only if one has a clear view of the pain and misery of one's life. Second, one has to decide firmly to free oneself from suffering. Third, one can do so by means of what the Buddha called "right conduct" and fourth by "right speech," a way of living in which one practices the virtues of love and compassion, joy, and serenity in daily life. The fifth step on the Eightfold Path is to choose "right livelihood," a means of earning a living that does not interfere with the attainment of ultimate enlightenment. The sixth step is "right endeavor," the conscious effort to eliminate distracting and harmful desires. People can most readily see the worthlessness of desires, according to the Buddha, by recognizing that everything and everyone in the world will pass away. Nothing is permanent. The seventh step is "right awareness," constant contemplation of one's deeds and words, giving full thought to their importance and whether they lead to enlightenment. "Right contemplation" is the last step expected of travelers on the Eightfold Path. This step entails deep meditation on the impermanence of everything in the world.

With the attainment of the eighth step, the traveler achieves *nirvana,* a state of happiness gained by the extinction of self and desires and the release from the effects of karma. Thus the Buddha propounded his own version of karma and how it worked. Though rooted in Hinduism, Buddhism set off on a road of its own, a road that eventually led out of India.

The Buddha also taught that if people understand that everything changes with time, they will neither cling to their egos nor worry about what they believe to be their eternal souls. To Buddhists a human being is a collection of parts, physical and mental. As long as the parts remain combined, that combination can be called "I." When that combination changes, as at death, the various parts remain in existence, ready to become the building blocks of different combinations. According to Buddhist teaching, life is passed from person to person as a flame is passed from candle to candle. Buddhism placed little emphasis on gods. The gods might help people out of difficulties like illness, but they are not judges who reign beyond the

grave or help achieve enlightenment. Nevertheless, the Buddha did conceive of a spiritual state of reality beyond the physical that can be called *nirvana,* which is basically a Hindu concept. In Indian thought *nirvana* is complicated and seen in several ways. For instance, among the Hindus it meant the reunion of the individual with Bramha. Among the Buddhists it meant that people who faithfully followed the Buddha's precepts could escape their mortal life with its tribulations and become united with the cosmic world. In short, the Buddha pointed the way for individuals to merge with the universe. As he told his followers: "There is an unborn, an unoriginated, an unmade, an uncompounded; were there not . . . there would be no escape from the world of the born, the originated, the made and the compounded."[6] This unborn and unmade power had nothing to do with the journey to nirvana. That was entirely up to the individual.

The success of Buddhism largely resulted from the Buddha's teaching that everyone, noble and peasant, educated and ignorant, male and female, could follow the Eightfold Path. Moreover, the Buddha was extraordinarily undogmatic. Convinced that each person must achieve enlightenment alone, he emphasized that the Path was important only because it led the traveler to enlightenment, not for its own sake. He compared it to a raft, essential to cross a river but useless once on the far shore. He warned his followers not to let dogma stand in the way of the journey. Buddhism differed from Hinduism by its willingness to accept anyone who wished to join, and in effect it tacitly rejected the caste system.

Like Mahavira, the Buddha formed a circle of disciples. He continually reminded the *Sangha*—an order of Buddhist monks—that each person must reach ultimate fulfillment by individual effort, but he also recognized the value of a group of people striving for the same goal. Buddhism also established an order of nuns that gave women the opportunity to seek for "truth" as men had traditionally done.

After the Buddha's death, the Sangha met to decide exactly what Buddhist doctrine was and to smooth out differences of interpretation. The result was the split of Buddhism into two great branches: the *Theravada* (or *Hinayana,* Way of the Elders, or Lesser Vehicle) and the *Mahayana* (or Larger Vehicle). The Theravada branch, which found its greatest popularity in Southeast Asia,

INDIA TO CA A.D. 200

ca 2500–1500 B.C.	Indus civilization
ca 1500–500 B.C.	Arrival of the Aryans and development of Vedic society
6th–5th centuries B.C.	Development of Hinduism, Jainism, and Buddhism
ca 513 B.C.	Persian conquest of northwestern India and the Indus Valley
326 B.C.	Alexander the Great conquers northwestern India and the Indus Valley
322–298 B.C.	Reign of Chandragupta
ca 269–232 B.C.	Reign of Ashoka
ca 261 B.C.	Ashoka conquers Kalinga, leading to spread of Buddhism in India
ca 183–145 B.C.	Greek Invasion of India
ca 140 B.C.	First Chinese ambassadors to India
1st century A.D.	Shaka and Kushan invasions of India
A.D. 25–3rd century	Kushan rule in northwestern India
ca A.D. 78	Kushan emperor Kanishka promotes Buddhism

from Sri Lanka to Kampuchea (modern Cambodia), asserted that its tenets rested on the authentic teachings of Buddha—in short, that it represented the oldest and purest form of Buddhism. By ca 20 B.C. the monks of the Theravada branch had met to write down what they considered the authentic teachings of the Buddha and Buddhist tradition. Theravada Buddhism is called the Lesser Vehicle because of its conservative and strict doctrines. Followers believed that the individual is saved only through a rigorous monastic life. These distinctions are solely doctrinal in that the followers of the Buddha defined what they thought Buddhism ought to mean. In that respect, they created divisions of varying interpretations of Buddhism similar to those of later Christians and Muslims, who made similar distinctions in their interpretation of the teachings of Jesus and Mohammed.

Mahayana Buddhism, far more liberal than the Theravada branch, believed that Buddhism was a vast system capable of saving many living things. It also held that the teachings of Buddha were fluid and would evolve over time in different cultures and climates. Mahayana Buddhism emphasized the compassionate side of the Buddha's message. It was known as the Larger Vehicle because it maintained that there were many ways to salvation. Mahayana Buddhism stressed the possibility of other buddhas yet to come and taught that all buddhas follow a path open to everyone in the world. Mahayana held that the Buddha in his previous lives had been a *bodhisattva*—a wise being, a buddha-in-becoming. Bodhisattvas have achieved enlightenment but decline the reward of nirvana to help others. Later Mahayana Buddhism created a huge pantheon of heavenly buddhas and bodhisattvas to whom people could pray for help toward enlightenment.

Mahayana Buddhism eventually won the hearts and minds of the Chinese, Japanese, Koreans, and Vietnamese. Yet not until the dramatic conversion of the Indian king Ashoka, some two centuries after the death of the Buddha, did Buddhist teachings spread much beyond India. Indian merchants, not missionaries, were crucial to the spread of Buddhism. They carried Buddhist beliefs along

The Great Buddha   This figure of Buddha sits grandly and serenely in a cave in Jung-Kang. Here the portrayal of Buddha is typical of Theravada Buddhism, in which individuals sought their salvation alone through asceticism, meditation, and monasticism. *(Source: Werner Forman/Art Resource, NY)*

with their wares far beyond India into Sri Lanka, parts of southeast Asia, and China, Korea, and Japan.

✳ INDIA AND THE WEST (CA 513–298 B.C.)

Between the arrival of the Aryans and the rise of Hinduism, India enjoyed freedom from outside interference. In the late sixth century B.C., however, western India was swept up in events that were changing the face of the ancient Near East. During this period the Persians were creating an empire that stretched from the western coast of Anatolia to the Indus River (see page 58–59). India became

involved in these events when the Persian emperor Darius conquered the Indus Valley about 513 B.C.

Persian control did not reach eastward beyond the banks of the Indus. Even so, as part of the Persian Empire, western India enjoyed immediate contact not only with the old cultures of Egypt and Mesopotamia but also with the young and vital culture of the Greeks. What effects did contact with Persia and the lands farther west have on India?

Culturally the Persian conquest resembled the Hyksos period in Egypt (see page 27) in that it was a fertilizing event, introducing new ideas, techniques, and materials into India. As members of the vast Persian Empire, Indians learned administrative techniques—how to rule large tracts of land

and huge numbers of people. From the Persians the Indians learned the technique of minting silver coins, and they adopted the Persian monetary standard to facilitate trade with other parts of the empire. Even states in the Ganges Valley, which were never part of the empire, adopted the use of coinage. Another innovation was the introduction of the Aramaic language and script, the official language of the Persian Empire. Indians adapted the Aramaic script to their needs and their languages and were able to keep records and publish proclamations just as the Persians did.

Likewise, India participated in the larger economic world created by the Persians. Trade increased dramatically with other regions under Persian rule. Once again hardy merchants took the sea route to the West, as had their predecessors in the Indus civilization. Caravan cities grew in number and wealth as overland trade thrived in the peace brought about by Persian rule. In short, the arrival of the Persians drew India into the mainstream of sophisticated urban, commercial, and political life in the ancient world.

Into this world stormed Alexander the Great, who led his Macedonian and Greek troops through the Khyber Pass into the Indus Valley in 326 B.C. (see pages 149–150). What he found in India is most readily apparent in Taxila, a major center of trade in the Punjab (see Map 3.1). The Greeks described Taxila as "a city great and prosperous, the biggest of those between the Indus River and the Hydaspes [the modern Jhelum River]—a region not inferior to Egypt in size, with especially good pastures and rich in fine fruits."[7] Modern archaeology has proved the Greeks' praise excessive: despite its prosperity and importance as a seat of Hindu learning, Taxila was an unassuming town, a poor town when compared with the cities of the Near East.

From Taxila, Alexander marched to the mouth of the Indus River before turning west and leaving India forever. A riot of bloodshed and destruction, Alexander's invasion facilitated the rise of the first kingdom to embrace all of India.

The Mauryan Empire (ca 322–232 B.C.)

Alexander disrupted the political map of western India and died without organizing his conquests, leaving the area in confusion. Chandragupta, the ruler of a small state in the Ganges Valley, took ad-

vantage of this situation by defeating his enemies piecemeal until, by 322 B.C., he had made himself sole master of India. In 304 B.C. he defeated the forces of Seleucus, a general of Alexander the Great who founded the Seleucid monarchy. In the wake of this battle, Seleucus surrendered the easternmost provinces of his monarchy and concluded a treaty of alliance with Chandragupta. Hence Chandragupta not only defeated one of the mightiest of Alexander's lieutenants but also entered the world of Hellenistic politics (see Chapter 6).

The real heir to Alexander's conquest, Chadragupta created the great Mauryan Empire, which stretched from the Punjab and Himalayas in the north almost to the tip of the subcontinent, from modern Afghanistan in the west to Bengal in the east. In the administration of his empire, Chandragupta adopted the Persian practice of dividing the area into provinces. Each province was assigned a governor, most of whom were drawn from Chandragupta's own family. The smallest unit in this system was typically the village, the mainstay of Indian life. From his capital at Pataliputra, in the valley of the Ganges, the king sent agents to the provinces to oversee the workings of government and to keep him informed of conditions in his realm. Chandragupta also enjoyed the able assistance of his great minister Kautilya, who wrote a practical treatise on statecraft. For the first time in Indian history, one man governed most of the subcontinent, exercising control through delegated power.

With stunning effectiveness Chandragupta applied the lessons learned from Persian rule. He established a complex bureaucracy to see to the operation of the state and a bureaucratic taxation system that financed public services. He also built a regular army, complete with departments for everything from naval matters to the collection of supplies. He exercised tight control, to some degree repressing the people in order to retain power.

Megasthenes, a Greek ambassador of King Seleucus, left a lively description of life at Chandragupta's court. Like many other monarchs, Chandragupta feared treachery, especially assassination, and took elaborate precautions against intrigue. According to Megasthenes:

Attendance on the king's person is the duty of women, who indeed are bought from their fathers. Outside the gates of the palace stand the bodyguards and the rest of the soldiers. . . . Nor does the king sleep during the day, and at night he is forced at various hours to change his bed because of those plotting against him. Of his non-military departures from the palace one is to the courts, in which he passes the day hearing cases to the end, even if the hour arrives for attendance on his person. . . . When he leaves to hunt, he is thickly surrounded by a circle of women, and on the outside by spear-carrying bodyguards. The road is fenced off with ropes, and to anyone who passes within the ropes as far as the women death is the penalty.[8]

Those measures worked: after resigning the kingship, according to the tradition of the Jains, Chandragupta died the peaceful death of a Jain ascetic in 298 B.C. He left behind a kingdom organized to maintain order and defend India from invasion. India enjoyed economic prosperity and communication with its neighbors. At a time when many of the major cultures of the world were in direct touch with one another, the Indians, who had created much from their own experience and had learned much from others, could proudly make their own contributions in both cultural and material spheres.

The Reign of Ashoka (ca 269–232 B.C.)

The years after Chandragupta's death in 298 B.C. were an epoch of political greatness, thanks largely to Ashoka, one of India's most remarkable figures. The grandson of Chandragupta, Ashoka extended the Mauryan Empire to its farthest limits. The era of Ashoka was enormously important in the religious and intellectual history of the world. A man in search of spiritual solace, Ashoka embraced Buddhism and helped to establish it as an important religion. Buddhism would take deep and lasting root throughout much of the East, but not in India itself.

As a young prince, Ashoka served as governor of two important provinces, both seats of Buddhism—at this time still solely an Indian religion—and both commercially wealthy. While governor, Ashoka met and married Devi, a woman of the merchant class who would later end her life spreading Buddhism to Sri Lanka. In religion Ashoka was deeply influenced by Brahmanism and Jainism, which pointed him toward a broad religious outlook.

At the death of his father about 274 B.C., Ashoka rebelled against his older brother, the rightful king, and after four years of fighting succeeded in his bloody bid for the throne. Crowned king of India, Ashoka ruled intelligently and energetically. He was equally serious about his pleasures, especially those of the banquet hall and harem. In short, Ashoka in the early years of his reign was an efficient and contented king whose days were divided between business and pleasure.

The change that occurred in the ninth year of his reign affected not just Ashoka and his subjects but the subsequent history of India and the rest of

Lion Capital of Ashoka This lion capital from a column of Ashoka handsomely represents the emperor's political power. It also illustrates significant Near Eastern and Greek influences on the Indian art of this period. *(Source: Raghubir Singh)*

the world. In that year Ashoka conquered Kalinga, the modern state of Orissa on the east coast of India; in a grim and savage campaign, Ashoka reduced Kalinga by wholesale slaughter. As Ashoka himself admitted, "In that (conquest) one hundred and fifty thousand were killed (or maimed) and many times that number died."[9] Yet instead of exulting like a conqueror, Ashoka was consumed with remorse and revulsion at the horror of war. On the battlefield of Kalinga, the conquering hero looked for a new meaning in life; the carnage of Kalinga gave birth to a new Ashoka. The king embraced Buddhism and used the machinery of his empire to spread Buddhist teachings throughout India.

Ashoka's remarkable crisis of conscience has been the subject of considerable debate, much like the later conversion to Christianity of the Roman emperor Constantine. No one will ever know the content of Ashoka's mind, but the practical results of his conversion led to a more humane governance of India. Ashoka emphasized compassion, nonviolence, and adherence to dharma. He may have perceived dharma as a kind of civic virtue, a universal ethical model capable of uniting the diverse peoples of his extensive empire. Ashoka erected inscriptions to inform the people of his policy. In one edict, he spoke to his people like a father:

Whatever good I have done has indeed been accomplished for the progress and welfare of the world. By these shall grow virtues namely: proper support of mother and father, regard for preceptors and elders, proper treatment of Brahmans and ascetics, of the poor and the destitute, slaves and servants.[10]

Ashoka's new outlook can be seen as a form of *paternalism,* well-meaning government that provides for the people's welfare without granting them much responsibility or freedom. He appointed new officials to oversee the moral welfare of the realm and made sure that local officials administered humanely.

Ashoka felt the need to protect his new religion and keep it pure. Warning Buddhist monks that he would not tolerate *schism*—divisions based on differences of opinion about doctrine or ritual—he threw his support to religious orthodoxy. At the same time, Ashoka honored India's other religions. Hinduism and Jainism were revered and respected,

and the emperor even built shrines for their worshipers.

Despite his devotion to Buddhism, Ashoka never neglected his duties as emperor. He tightened the central government of the empire and kept a close check on local officials. He also built roads and rest spots to improve communication within the realm. Ashoka himself described this work:

On the highways Banyan trees have been planted so that they may afford shade to men and animals; mango-groves have been planted; watering-places have been established for the benefit of animals and men.[11]

These measures also facilitated the march of armies and the armed enforcement of Ashoka's authority. Ashoka's efforts were eminently successful: never before his reign and not again until the modern period did so much of India enjoy peace, prosperity, and humane rule.

India and Its Invaders (ca 250 B.C.–A.D. 200)

Ashoka's reign was the high point of ancient India's political history. His successors remained on the throne until about 185 B.C.; thereafter India was subject to repeated foreign invasions, confined principally to the northwest, that constantly changed the political map of the country. Invaders held northwestern India, and petty Indian kings ruled small realms in the rest of India. For many years the history of India was a tale of relentless war between invaders and Indians and among native Indian kings as well. The energy consumed by these internal wars prevented the Indians from driving out the invaders, from bringing peace and prosperity to the land. Still, even though each wave of newcomers left its mark on the cultural heritage of India, Indian civilization triumphed, changing the invaders as well as being fertilized by them.

The Kushans, whose authority in India lasted until the third century A.D., were particularly significant because their empire encompassed much of central Asia as well as northwestern India. The Kushans put India in closer contact with its eastern neighbors. The Kushan invaders were assimilated into Indian society as Kshatriyas, of higher status than native Vaisya, Shudra, outcastes, and untouchables, and once again a backward nomadic people fell under the spell of a more sophisticated civilization.

The Kushans played a valuable role by giving northwest India a long period in which to absorb the newcomers and adapt the cultural innovations introduced by the various invaders. Kushans and Indians alike absorbed Greek ideas. Greek culture made its greatest impression on Indian art. Greek artists and sculptors working in India adorned Buddhist shrines, modeling the earliest representation of Buddha on Hellenistic statues of Apollo, and they were the leading force behind the Gandhara school of art in India. Only the form, however, was Greek; the content was purely Buddhist. In short, India owes a modest cultural debt to Hellenism. Just as Ashoka's Buddhist missionaries made no impression on the Greek world, so Hellenism gave India some fresh ideas but had no lasting impact on the essence of Indian life. Only Buddhism, which addressed itself to all human beings rather than to any particular culture, was at all significant as a meeting ground for the Greeks, Indians, and Kushans. Otherwise, the outlooks and values of Greek and Indian cultures were too different and too tenacious for one to assimilate the essence of the other.

From the perspective of history, the most significant and lasting gift of these years was the spread of Buddhism to China. India's invaders embraced Buddhism enthusiastically and protected the Buddhist order. They preferred the teachings of the Mahayana sect, more compassionate and flexible than its rival Theravada branch. In the course of their commercial dealings, they carried Mahayana Buddhism across inner Asia to China, transforming it from a purely Indian sect into an international religion.

Kushan Girl   This young woman, splendidly bedecked with jewelry, is carrying a platter of food, presumably for a feast. Indian art of this period is justly noted for its realism and its portrayal of ordinary events. *(Source: Courtesy, Archaeological Museum, Mathura)*

SUMMARY

By roughly 250 B.C. India had developed a highly accomplished urban civilization sustained by systematic agriculture. Many of the fundamental ideals, beliefs, customs, and religious practices that would leave their mark on succeeding generations had already taken shape. These early years of Indian history were especially rich in religion. Not only did the Indians form several different views of the nature of life and visions of an afterlife, but they also made a fundamental impact on life in China by the spread of Buddhism. Hinduism, both religious and social in nature, was for the Indians themselves perhaps the most important development of this period, an ancient heritage that is still a vital factor in Indian life.

NOTES

1. M. Wheeler, *Early India and Pakistan to Ashoka* (London: Thames and Hudson, 1959), pp. 106–107.
2. Rigveda 10.90, translated by A. L. Basham, in *The Wonder That Was India* (New York: Grove Press, 1954), p. 241.
3. J. Mascaro, trans., *The Upanishads* (London: Penguin Books, 1965), pp. 117–118.
4. J. A. B. van Buitenen, trans., *The Mahabharata*, vol. 1, *The Book of the Beginning* (Chicago: University of Chicago Press, 1973), 214.1–7.
5. J. Mascaro, trans., *The Bhagavad Gita* (London: Penguin Books, 1962), 2.17–21.
6. Quoted in N. W. Ross, *Three Ways of Asian Wisdom* (New York: Simon and Schuster, 1966), p. 94.
7. Arrian, *Anabasis* 5.8.2; Plutarch, *Alexander* 59.1. Translated by John Buckler.
8. Strabo, 15.1.55. Translated by John Buckler.
9. Quoted in B. G. Gokhale, *Asoka Maurya* (New York: Twayne Publishers, 1966), p. 157.
10. Pillar Edict 7, quoted ibid., p. 169.
11. Quoted ibid., pp. 168–169.

SUGGESTED READING

Much splendid work has been done on the geographical background of ancient Indian society. Two fine works are B. L. C. Johnson, *South Asia: Selective Studies of the Essential Geography of India, Pakistan, and Ceylon* (1969), and, for the ecological history of India, M. Gadgil and R. Guha, *This Fissured Land* (1993). A masterpiece in its own right is J. Schwartzberg, ed., *An Historical Atlas of South Asia* (1978), the epitome of what a historical atlas should be. Its contents range well into contemporary times.

General histories of India are too numerous to list, with the exception of A. L. Basham, *The Wonder That Was India* (1959), one of the monuments of the field and a good introduction to nearly every aspect of ancient Indian history. Solid too are R. Thapar, *Ancient Indian Social History* (1978), and R. B. Inden, *Imagining India* (1990), a difficult work that controversially covers all essential aspects of Indian life. Both are highly recommended. Especially rewarding are Z. Liu, *Ancient India and Ancient China* (1988); S. F. Mahmud, *A Concise History of Indo-Pakistan,* 2d ed. (1988); and H. Scharff, *The State in Indian Tradition* (1989), which covers the period from the Aryans to the Muslims.

Work on the Indus civilization continues at a rapid pace. A very good survey of the topic is H. Kulke and D. Rothermund, *A History of India* (1990), as is N. N. Bhattacharya, *Ancient Indian History and Civilization* (1988), which focuses on India before A.D. 1000. See also G. L. Possehl, ed., *Harappan Civilization: A Contemporary Perspective* (1982), which combines excavation reports and analysis of material. Possehl's *Ancient Cities of the Indus* (1979) reprints articles by a number of scholars, thus providing a variety of perspectives on early Indus developments. Trade between the Indus and Mesopotamian civilizations is treated in E. C. L. During Caspers, "Sumer, Coastal Arabia and the Indus Valley in Protoliterate and Early Dynastic Eras," *Journal of Economic and Social History of the Orient* 22 (1979): 121–135. See also G. L. Possehl and M. H. Ravel, *Harappan Civilization and Rojdi* (1989), which uses the newest archaeological findings to explore the Harappan civilization. D. K. Chakrabarti, *The Early Use of Iron in India* (1992), uses archaeological evidence to prove that the ancient Indians used iron far earlier than previously thought.

For the arrival of the Aryans and subsequent developments, see R. Thapar, *From Lineage to State* (1990), which examines the historical kingdoms of the mid-first millenium B.C., N. R. Banerjee, *The Iron Age in India* (1965), and C. Chakraborty, *Common Life in the Rig-veda and Atharvaveda* (1977), which treat the period from different points of view. More difficult but rewarding is F. Southworth, "Lexical Evidence for Early Contacts Between Indo-Aryan and Dravidian," in M. M. Deshpande and P. E. Hook, eds., *Aryan and Non-Aryan in India* (1979), pp. 191–234; the book contains a number of other stimulating articles on the period.

Early Indian religion is a complex subject, but a series of books provides a good introduction to the topic. P. S. Jaini, *The Jaina Path of Purification* (1979), and T. Hopkins, *Hindu Religious Tradition* (1971), cover two of the major religions, to which should be added K. K. Klostermaier, *A Survey of Hinduism* (1989), and K. H. Potter, *Guide to Indian Philosophy* (1988).

Buddhism is such a popular topic that the bibliography is virtually endless. H. Akira, *A History of Indian Buddhism* (1990), treats the early history of the Buddha and his followers. Also enlightening is W. Rahula, *What the Buddha Taught* (1971), which sheds light on the Theravada tradition, and R. Robinson and W. Johnson, *The Buddhist Religion,* 3d ed. (1982), which is more comprehensive. Still unsurpassed for its discussion of the relations between Buddhism and Hinduism is the grand work of C. N. Eliot, *Hinduism and Buddhism,* 3 vols. (reprinted 1954), which traces the evolution of theistic ideas in both religions. C. Humphreys has written extensively about Buddhism. The student may wish to consult his *Buddhism* (1962), *Exploring Buddhism* (1975), or *The Wisdom of*

Buddhism (new ed., 1979). More recent is D. Fox, *The Heart of Buddhist Wisdom* (1985).

A stimulating and far-reaching discussion of intellectual developments in India is R. Thapar, "Ethics, Religion, and Social Protest in the First Millennium B.C. in North India," *Daedalus* 104 (Spring 1975): 119–132. Good translations of Indian literature discussed in the chapter are listed in the Notes.

Among the numerous works describing India's relations with the Persian Empire and Alexander the Great are several titles cited in Suggested Reading for Chapters 2 and 6. P. H. L. Eggermont, *Alexander's Campaigns in Sind and Baluchistan* (1975), focuses solely on Alexander's activities in India, as does E. Badian in I. Gershevitch, ed., *The Cambridge History of Iran* (1985). A. J. Dani, *The Historic City of Taxila* (1988), uses anthropological and historic evidence to study this important city and its influence. S. Jones, *Afghanistan* (1992), gives the most recent general history of the area.

Chandragupta's reign is treated in R. K. Mookerji, *Chandragupta Maurya and His Times,* rev. ed. (1966). J. C. Heesterman, "Kautilya and the Ancient Indian State," *Wiener Zeitschrift* 15 (1971): 5–22, analyzes the work and thought of Chandragupta's great minister of state.

The kingdom of Ashoka has attracted much attention. In addition to Gokhale's book cited in the Notes, R. Thapar's excellent *Asoka and the Decline of the Mauryas* (1961) is still an indispensable work on the subject. B. S. Miller, *The Power of Art* (1992), discusses the impact of patronage on art—on those who subsidized works and on those who created them —and the pervasiveness of patronage throughout southern India.

For the Greek invasions, see W. W. Tarn, *The Greeks in Bactria and India* (1951), a difficult book but still valuable. A. K. Narain's more recent treatment, *The Indo-Greeks* (1967), is equally valuable and a bit more readable. For contact between the Hellenistic world and India, see J. W. Sedlar, *India and the Greek World* (1980), which approaches the problem of cultural transmission between the two civilizations. C. Drekmeier, *Kingship and Community in Early India* (1968), takes a broader approach to early developments.

An Account of the Gods and the Creation of the World

Indian religious concepts were very complicated. Poets and priests explained early ideas in a vast poem, the Mahabharata, *written in Sanskrit. The work included epics, theology, ethical and metaphysical doctrine; it also included legends and literary romances. The core of the* Mahabharata *is similar to Homer's* Iliad *in that it treats a political and military clash of epic proportions. In short, it describes the struggle between five heroic brothers, the Pandavas, and their one hundred cousins for the rule of the land. The section presented below has nothing to do with this mighty conflict. Instead it explains the origin of the universe and of human life within it. It also deals with the nature and significance of Brahman.*

The seers said:

Tell us that ancient Lore that was related by the eminent sage Dvaipāyana, which the Gods and brahmin seers honored when they heard it! That divine language of the sublime Histories, in all the varieties of words and books, the sacred Account of the Bhāratas, that language of complex word and meaning, ruled by refinement and reinforced by all sciences, which Vaiśaṃpāyana, at Dvaipāyana's bidding, repeated truthfully to the satisfaction of King Janamejaya at the king's sacrifice. We wish to hear that Grand Collection, now joined to the Collections of the Four Vedas, which Vyāsa the miracle-monger compiled, replete with the Law and dispelling all danger of evil!

The Bard said:

I bow to the Primeval Person the Lord, widely invoked and lauded, who is the True, the One-Syllabled Brahman, manifest and unmanifest, everlasting, at once the existent and the nonexistent, Creator of things high and low. I bow to him who is the Ancient One, supreme, imperishable, blissful and blessing, the most desirable Viṣṇu, faultless and resplendent, who is Kṛṣṇa Hṛṣĩkeśa, the preceptor of all creatures, those that move and those that move not; the God Hari.

I shall speak the entire thought of that great seer and saint who is venerated in all the world, Vyāsa of limitless brilliance. Poets have told it before, poets are telling it now, other poets shall tell this history on earth in the future. It is indeed a great storehouse of knowledge, rooted in the three worlds, which the twiceborn retain in all its parts and summaries. Fine words adorn it, and usages human and divine; many meters scan it; it is the delight of the learned.

When all this was without light and unillumined, and on all its sides covered by darkness, there arose one large Egg, the inexhaustible seed of all creatures. They say that this was the great divine cause, in the beginning of the Eon; and that on which it rests is revealed as the true Light, the everlasting Brahman. Wondrous it was and beyond imagining, in perfect balance in all its parts, this unmanifest subtle cause that is that which is and that which is not.

From it was born the Grandfather, the Sole Lord Prajāpati, who is known as Brahmā, as the Preceptor of the Gods, as Sthāṇu, Manu, Ka, and Parameṣṭhin. From him sprang Dakṣa, son of Pracetas, and thence the seven sons of Dakṣa, and from them came forth the twenty-one Lords of Creation. And the Person of immeasurable soul, the One whom the seers know as the universe; and the Viśve Devas, and the Ādityas as well as the Vasus and the two Aśvins. Yakṣas, Sādhyas, Piśācas, Guhyakas, and the Ancestors were born from it, and the wise and impeccable Seers. So also the many royal seers, endowed with every virtue. Water, Heaven and Earth, Wind, Atmosphere, and Space, the year, the seasons, the months, the fortnights, and days and nights in turn, and whatever else, has all come forth as witnessed by the world. Whatever is found to exist, moving and unmoving, it is all again thrown together, all this world, when the destruction of the Eon has struck. Just as with the change of the season all the various signs of the season appear, so also these beings at the beginning of each Eon. Thus, without beginning and without end, rolls the wheel of existence around in this world, causing origin and destruction, beginningless and endless.

There are thirty-three thousand, thirty-three hundred, and thirty-three Gods—this is the summing-up of creation.

The great Sun is the son of the sky and the soul of the eye, the Resplendent One who is also Savitar, Ṛcīka, Arka, Āśāvaha, the Bringer-of-Hope, and Ravi. Of all the sons of the Sun Vivasvant, the last one was Mahya, who had a son that shone like a God, who is hence known as Subhrāj—the Well-Shining One. Subhrāj had three sons of much fame who had abundant offspring, Daśajyoti, Śatajyoti, and the self-possessed Sahasrajyoti. The great-spirited Daśajyoti had ten thousands sons, Śatajyoti ten times that number, and Sahasrajyoti again ten times that. From them arose the lineage of the Kurus, those of the Yadus and of Bhararta, the lines of Yayāti and Ikṣvāku and of the royal seers in general— many dynasties arose and creations of creatures in their abundant varieties.

All are abodes of being. And there is a triple mystery—Veda, Yoga, and science—Law, Profit, and Pleasure. The seer saw the manifold sciences of Law, Profit, and Pleasure, and the rule that emerged for the conduct of worldly affairs. And the ancient histories with their commentaries, and the various revelations—*everything has been entered here,* and this describes this Book.

Brahmā, the Creator, is seated on a lotus connected to the navel of the reclining Vishnu, the cohesive force of the universe. (*Source: C.L. Bharany, New Delhi. Courtesy, Thames and Hudson*)

Questions for Analysis

1. How does the vision of the creation of the world in this text compare with that found in the first book of the Hebrew Bible?

2. What does the *Mahabharata* tell of the connection between human life and the nature of the universe?

3. Does the poem offer the prospect for ordinary people to understand cosmic and human realities?

Source: *The Mahabharata,* trans. J. A. B. van Buitenen. Copyright © 1973 by University of Chicago Press. Reprinted by permission.

CHAPTER

4

The Rise and Growth of China to ca A.D. 200

Gilt bronze figure of a young woman attendant holding an oil lamp, which consists of twelve component parts. From the tomb of Princess Dou Wan at Mancheng, Hebei province, 2nd century B.C. *(Source: The Cultural Relics Bureau and The Metropolitan Museum of Art)*

Ancient China provides another example of an early people confronting a formidable geographical challenge in order first to survive and then to build a complex and sophisticated civilization. The Chinese had inhabited eastern Asia from at least the Neolithic period. Like the Egyptians, they prospered along a great river. But the Yellow River was hardly the gentle Nile. It needed to be tamed before it would sustain life, and taming it called for group effort on a massive scale. The success of the Chinese in meeting this challenge is reflected in the flowering of Chinese culture, in the overall political stability of the area, and in the prosperity of China's people. As in Mesopotamia, Egypt, and India, so in China there were wars, and dynasty followed dynasty, but political disruption never crippled Chinese cultural evolution. Moreover, the Chinese were remarkably successful in governing a huge population settled over a vast area. Their success resulted in political and social stability seldom, if ever, found elsewhere in the ancient world.

- How did the early Chinese confront the geographical factors of climate, soil, and land?
- What did their response share with the solutions of ancient Near Eastern and Indian peoples to these same problems, and how did it differ?
- What form did Chinese success take in the shaping of society?

These are the questions addressed in this chapter.

❋ THE LAND AND ITS CHALLENGE

Geography had left India an opening to the northwest and thus to the civilizations of the ancient Near East. In contrast, both terrain and distance made China's links to the broader world tenuous (Map 4.1). Between India and China towered the ice-clad and forbidding peaks of the Himalayas and the Pamirs, and beyond lay the vast expanses of Tibet and Chinese Turkestan. Geography isolated China in other directions as well. To the north stretched the Gobi Desert, some 500,000 square miles of desolate waste, and the Mongolian Plateau. To the south rose mountains covered with forests and tracts of jungle. China's main avenue to the major civilizations of the outside world was a threadlike corridor to the northwest, through the vastness of central Asia, past India, and ultimately to Mesopotamia. Though isolated, China was not sealed off completely from other seats of civilization.

China encompasses two immense river basins: those of the Yellow River in the north and the Yangtze in the south. Both rivers rise in the mountains of Tibet and flow eastward across China (see Map 4.1). The Yellow River carries tons of loess, a fine, light-colored dust whose color gives the river its name. Loess is exceptionally fertile and easy to cultivate, and this basin was the site of China's earliest agricultural civilization in the Neolithic Age (see page 7). Yet like the Tigris in Mesopotamia, the Yellow River can be a rampaging torrent, bringing disastrous floods and changing course unpredictably. The Yellow River was frequently called China's Sorrow, because of its flooding. Only in the sixth century B.C. was it somewhat tamed with dikes, which eventually allowed China's great northern plain to nurture a huge population.

The Yangtze river valley was also farmed from Neolithic times, but there is no convincing reason to think that the peoples could be called "Chinese" in the way that modern peoples define "Chinese." As in the West, so also in China various newcomers entered the area, first establishing their own individual cultures before coming together later to make a generally recognized Chinese culture.

The basins of the Yellow and Yangtze rivers are separated in the west by mountains, which give way to hills and finally disappear altogether in the flat country near the coast. The two basins are quite distinct, however, when it comes to farming. Dry farming of wheat and millet characterizes the Yellow River basin in the north; irrigated rice agriculture predominates in the warmer and wetter basin of the Yangtze. In the extreme south is the valley of the Xi, or West, River, an area of mild climate and fertile soil that would later form the southern boundary of China. Except for the river valleys, China is largely mountainous or semidesert land; people could thrive only in certain areas within this enormous expanse of land. Geography thus helped to ensure that human development in China would cling to the mighty river systems.

❋   **MAP 4.1 China Under the Shang and Zhou Dynasties, 1523–221 B.C.**   The heartland of Chinese development is illustrated by this map, which shows the importance of the Yellow River in early Chinese life. Under the Zhou, Chinese authority reached the Yangtze River.

❋ THE SHANG DYNASTY (CA 1523–1027 B.C.)

At about the time the Aryans were transforming Indian life, the kings of the Shang Dynasty rose to power in northern China. Unlike the Aryans, the Shang were natives, very closely linked to indigenous Neolithic peoples. Chinese Neolithic farmers had long ago settled into a life of sustained agriculture and animal domestication. Asia scholars dispute the nature and degree of outside influence on early Chinese development, but most agree that ancient Chinese culture was largely a native growth. China did not suffer massive foreign invasion. Archaeology has recently proved that Neolithic cultures also flourished in Manchuria, along

the southeastern coast, and through the Yangtze Valley. To this relatively self-contained society, the Shang gave a long period of rule. Once considered legendary rather than historical, the Shang Dynasty has been verified from its own written records and the work of modern archaeologists.

Social Organization

The excavations at the modern cities of Anyang, the Shang capital, and Zhengzhou (Chengchou), perhaps the oldest city in China, have shed surprisingly bright light on the Shang kings and the society they ruled. Social divisions among the Shang were apparently simple but sharp: a ruling class of aristocrats, headed by a king and an incipient bureaucracy, directed the work and lives of everyone else. Warfare was a constant feature of Shang life, and the nobles were the warriors of Shang, those who enforced Shang rule. The Shang kings ruled northern China as a kind of family patrimony. The kings and the aristocracy owned slaves, many of whom had been captured in war. They also controlled the peasants, who served as semifree serfs.

The common people—serfs and slaves—performed all the economic functions of society. Most were farmers, whose way of life was basically Neolithic. Even in this remote period, however, Shang farmers knew how to cultivate the silkworm. Silken threads were woven into fine cloth, and under later emperors silk became China's prime export. Nonetheless, Shang farmers worked their fields with Neolithic tools and methods. Their homes too were Neolithic in construction. Each family dug in the ground a pit that served as the living area. Often they dug an entrance passage. The central feature of the house was the hearth, which was dug out of the floor of the pit. The family thatched the roof with reeds and clay, making a conical hutlike house. Although they helped create the wealth of Shang, peasant farmers enjoyed little of it themselves.

Other commoners were artisans. Dependent on the nobles, they manufactured the weapons, ritual vessels, jewelry, and other items demanded by the aristocracy. Shang craftsmen worked in stone, bone, and bronze but are best known for their bronze work. These early Chinese artists created some of the world's most splendid bronze pieces. Among the Shang, bronze was considered a noble metal, fit for weapons and ceremonial vessels but much too precious to be made into tools.

At the top of Shang society lived the king and his nobles, mighty figures elevated far above the common people. They lived in large houses built on huge platforms of pounded earth. The architecture of these houses set a pattern for house building that has flourished into modern times. The king and nobles enjoyed the magnificent bronze work of the artisans and carried bronze weapons into battle. Even after death, the king and his relatives had crucial social roles to play. The living worshiped and entreated them to intercede with the great gods, especially Shangoi, the supreme god, to protect the lives and future hopes of their descendants. At first only the king and his family were worthy of such honors, but this custom was an early form of ancestor worship, which seems to

Ritual Vessel This Shang bronze vessel excellently demonstrates the sophistication and technical mastery of early Chinese artists. The usual interpretation of the piece is that the tiger is protecting the man who is the head of his clan. Or the tiger may be having breakfast. (*Source: Michael Holford*)

have originated in Neolithic times. Whatever its origins, ancestor worship was an abiding element of Chinese religious belief.

Origins of Chinese Writing

Writing developed considerably later in China than in Sumer or India. The origins of Chinese writing appear to be deeply rooted in Shang religion. The kings of Shang were high priests and frequently wanted to ask questions of the gods. Their medium was oracle bones—generally the shoulder

Zhou Ritual Vessel   This bronze vessel is ample proof that Zhou bronzesmiths could rival their Shang predecessors. The bronze work is complicated and the fanciful animal shape delightful. *(Source: Robert Harding Picture Library)*

bones of oxen or the bottom shells of tortoises—on which they wrote their questions. Originally pictographic, the signs used by the Shang contained phonetic values. Even so, the Shang and their successors created thousands of signs. The result was a very complex system. But despite this complexity, mastery of even a few signs (like mastery of a few signs of Sumerian cuneiform) enabled people to keep records. Fluent literacy demanded dedication, time, leisure, and thus wealth.

This system of writing proved popular and enduring. Later, when the script was simplified and standardized, it could be written and understood readily by literate Chinese who spoke different dialects. Since many Chinese dialects were mutually unintelligible, the standardization of the written language, once achieved, proved to be indispensable for political, social, and cultural stability for centuries to come. The script spread throughout China and eventually to Korea and Japan, where it was adapted to local needs. Both the Koreans and

the Japanese adopted their own variations of the Chinese pronunciation of the signs. In effect, both read the signs and adapted them to their own spoken languages.

Literary mastery required such an effort and was so politically important and socially valuable that education and scholarship were revered. The literate elite was essential to the king and deeply respected by the peasants. Literacy made possible a bureaucracy capable of keeping records and conducting correspondence with commanders and governors far from the palace. Hence literacy became the ally of royal rule, facilitating communication with and effective control over the realm. Literacy also preserved the learning, lore, and experience of early Chinese society, a precious historical heritage for future ages.

THE TRIUMPH OF THE ZHOU (CA 1027–221 B.C.)

Some Shang oracle bones mention the king of Zhou (Chou), a small realm in the basin of the Wei River, a tributary of the Yellow River on the western frontier of the Shang domains. The Zhou were an agricultural people who had emigrated into the region, perhaps from the northwest. They were also culturally sophisticated masters of bronze and of horse-drawn chariots. In the eleventh century B.C. the Zhou king, a dependent of the Shang, became increasingly rebellious and ultimately overturned the Shang Dynasty.

The Rule of the Zhou

When the Zhou overthrew the Shang, they led China into the historical period. They extended Chinese rule beyond the boundaries of the Shang, and they grappled with the problems of governing the newly won territory. Because their contact with the Shang resulted in their adoption of much of Shang culture, the political victory of the Zhou caused no cultural break. Nevertheless, the Zhou made significant social and cultural strides. They succeeded in giving China a long period in which to consolidate these advances.

To justify their conquest ideologically, the Zhou founders declared that the last Shang king had forfeited his right to rule because of his excesses and incompetence. They asserted that Heaven itself had transferred its mandate to rule China from the Shang house to its worthier rivals, the Zhou. This justification later served as the basis of the broader concept of the Mandate of Heaven (see page 105).

The victorious Zhou confronted the formidable challenge of governing enormous areas of land. Communication within the realm was poor, and one king could not administer it all effectively. Moreover, the original Zhou capital was near Sian in western China, too remote for efficient rule of the new domain. The Zhou solved these problems by building a second capital at Loyang in the North China Plain (see Map 4.1) and by creating a loosely governed state.

The king of the Zhou gave huge tracts of land to members of the royal family and to others who had demonstrated their talent and loyalty. At the outset, the newly appointed lords received their authority from the king. In a formal ceremony the king handed the new lord a lump of earth, symbolizing the king's gift of land. The lord pledged loyalty to the king and usually promised to send him military forces if he requested them. A written record was made of the grant and of the new lord's obligations and rights—an unprecedented secular use of writing. The Zhou king was also the supreme religious leader of the land; he interceded with the gods for the welfare of Chinese society.

 Shang Oracle Bone   On one side of the bone the Shang diviner wrote his questions to the gods. In this case, the message related to a hunt. On the other side of the bone the diviner applied a hot point. When the cracks in the bone led to the writing, the interpreter read the gods' message. Most questions dealt with the harvest, weather, travel, and hunting. *(Source: Lowell Georgia/Photo Researchers)*

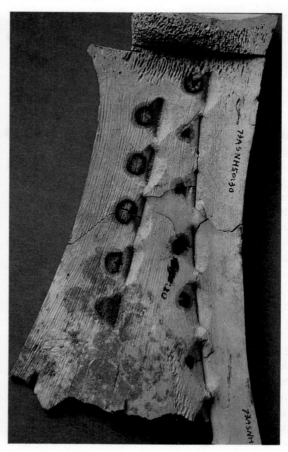

At first the Zhou kings exercised strong control over their political dependencies. Gradually, the power of the lords grew as the prosperity of their holdings increased. The dependencies of the Zhou were actually small islands of settlement scattered all over northern China, separated by wide tracts of undeveloped land. Over several centuries the growing populations of these settlements cleared new land, and eventually permanent cities arose. Once small and vulnerable, these settlements began to coalesce into compact regional states and then to fight among themselves over borders and territories. In this conflict the states in the interior of China were eclipsed by those on the borders, which took advantage of their geographical position to expand. The expansion spread Chinese culture ever wider. While conquering new territory, the lords of the border states were also absolute rulers in their own right. Around them developed a hereditary class of aristocratic ministers of state, warriors, administrators, and tax collectors. China was gradually becoming a land of numerous independent kingdoms.

Along with the growing independence of the lords went a decline in the power and stature of the Zhou kings. The lords used their troops to realize their own ambitions and stopped sending forces to the kings, disregarding their political obligations. In 771 B.C. a Zhou king was defeated and killed by rebel lords. After that the Zhou abandoned their western capital and made Loyang, the eastern capital, their permanent seat.

During the period known as the Era of the Warring States (402–221 B.C.), the entire political organization of the Zhou Dynasty disintegrated. The Zhou kings became little more than figureheads. The dreary cycle of warfare finally ended in 221 B.C., when the ruler of Qin (Ch'in), who had forced the abdication of the last Zhou king in 256 B.C., conquered all the other states.

Social Change and Cultural Advancement in the Zhou Period

The political events of the Zhou period were to have a lasting impact on Chinese society. As the older interior states declined, the aristocracies of these states lost their wealth. Educated, literate, and talented people were forced to seek their fortunes far from home. And the border states, dependent as they were on military and adminis-

trative efficiency, needed capable people to keep the wheels of government turning. The upshot was that impoverished aristocrats gravitated to the border states, where their much-needed talents opened the door to careers as ministers and officials. Merit, not birth, made the difference. This period saw the origins of a trained and able civil service, a group that saw to the daily workings of government and, later, gave a warm reception to the great philosophies of the Zhou period. The rise of Chinese philosophy was largely a response to the political turmoil and warfare that wracked the country, which helps to explain its secular orientation.

Despite the long years of warfare and slaughter, the Zhou period could boast of some remarkable cultural achievements. Around the walled garrisons that the Zhou established to hold down the Shang people, cities grew up, some with huge populations. The roads and canals built to import food and goods to the city dwellers stimulated trade and agriculture. Trade was also stimulated and made easier by the invention of coined money. The significance of these cities is almost incalculable. They were places where people could find the seat of government, meaning that they could visit the palaces of those who governed them. People could also visit major religious shrines and large markets. The centralization of society also led to a more efficient economic exchange between the country and the city, and as usual an easier way for the government to levy and collect taxes.

A surge in technology during the Zhou period permanently altered warfare, agriculture, and ultimately urban life. Under the Zhou, craftsmen and artisans discovered the use of iron and rapidly developed its uses. Zhou metalsmiths produced both wrought and cast iron—a remarkable achievement not matched in Europe until the fourteenth century. Zhou craftsmen turned out an imposing number of weapons, especially dagger-axes and swords.

In agriculture the Chinese under the Zhou Dynasty replaced the Neolithic stone and bone tools of the Shang with iron. Plows with iron shares broke the ground easily. Iron sickles, knives, and spades made the raising and harvesting of crops easier and far more efficient than ever before. By increasing productivity, metal technology gave Zhou farmers the tools to support a thriving urban culture.

THE BIRTH OF CHINESE PHILOSOPHY

The Zhou period was an era of intellectual creativity. Many thoughtful and literate people turned their minds to the basic question of how people could live the happiest and most productive lives in the most efficiently run society. Chinese thinkers were more secular than religious in their outlook. While Indian mystics were creating a complex socioreligious system, the Chinese were exploring philosophies of political development. Fascinated by political, social, and economic problems, they sought universal rules for human conduct. This period gave rise to three branches of thought—Confucianism, Daoism, and Legalism—that along with the popular belief represented by *I Ching* left an indelible stamp on the history of China.

Confucianism

Of the three schools of thought, Confucianism has had the most profound impact on China. The historical Kung Fuci (551–479 B.C.)—better known in the West as Confucius—was primarily a teacher and did not put his thoughts into writing. His fame comes largely from his students, who collected his sayings in a book called the *Analects.*

Confucius's family was aristocratic but poor, and the young man had few immediate prospects of success. His family had him educated so that he could take his place in the civil service, yet he achieved fame not as a minister of state but as a teacher. Confucius taught the sons of nobles but yearned to advise lords. Setting out with a small band of students, he sought employment from the lords of the emerging regional states in northeastern China. He served intermittently as a minor official and continued to spread his ideas. At last Confucius returned home to die among his students, considering himself a failure because he had never held high office.

Confucius's thought centered on the duties and proper behavior of the individual within society. He was far more interested in orderly and stable human relationships than in theology or religious matters. For all his fame, Confucius was not so much an original thinker as a brilliant synthesizer of old ideas. He taught that there is a universal law that even the sun, moon, and stars follow and that human beings too should live according to this law. Confucius considered the family the basic unit of society. Within the family, male was superior to female, age to youth. Thus husband was obeyed by wife, father by son, elder brother by younger. The eldest male was the head of the family. This order was to be respected even when those in authority were wrong:

The Master said, In serving his father and mother a man may gently remonstrate with them. But if he sees that he has failed to change their opinion, he should resume an attitude of deference and not thwart them; he may feel discouraged, but not resentful.[1]

Order in the family was the essential building block of order in society at large.

A man of moderation, Confucius was an earnest advocate of gentlemanly conduct. Only such conduct, which involved a virtuous and ethical life, could bring about peaceful social relations and well-run government. The Confucian gentleman was a man of integrity, education, and culture, a man schooled in proper etiquette. Asked to evaluate Zi-chan, a minister of the Zheng state, Confucius discussed the virtues of a "gentleman":

In him were to be found four of the virtues that belong to the Way of the true gentleman. In his private conduct he was courteous, in serving his master he was punctilious, in providing for the needs of the people he gave them even more than their due; in exacting service from the people, he was just.[2]

The way in which a gentleman disciplined himself is apparent in the conduct of Master Tseng, the most important of Confucius's followers:

Master Tseng said, Every day I examine myself on these three points: in acting on behalf of others, have I always been loyal to their interests? In intercourse with my friends, have I always been true to my word? Have I failed to repeat the precepts that have been handed down to me?[3]

Confucius pointed out that aristocratic birth did not automatically make a man a gentleman. Men of humble birth could reach this exalted level through education and self-discipline. Confucius did not advocate social equality, but his teachings minimized the importance of class distinctions and opened the way for intelligent and talented people

Daoist Painting   One of the finest aspects of Daoism was its appreciation of nature and the feeling that people should find their place in it. This painting vividly illustrates the peacefulness, grace, and charm that Daoists believed people can experience by being in harmony with nature. *(Source: National Palace Museum, Taipei, Taiwan, Republic of China)*

to rise in the social scale. The Confucian gentleman was made, not born.

This gentleman found his calling as a civil servant: he advised the ruler wisely, administered the kingdom intelligently, and dealt with the people humanely. Confucianism urged good government, emphasizing the duty of a good ruler to rule his people wisely and with compassion. Confucius commented on the qualities of a good ruler:

A country of a thousand war-chariots cannot be administered unless the ruler attends strictly to business, punctually observes his promises, is economical in expenditure, shows affection towards his subjects in general, and uses the labour of the peasantry only at the proper times of year.[4]

Confucianism was a vital ingredient in the evolution of an effective civil service. As a social movement, Confucianism was a distinct and specially recruited community whose membership was ideally restricted to learned and talented people who embraced high standards of ethical awareness and conduct. Confucianism offered those in authority a body of expertise on the creation and consolidation of a well-ordered, sound, and powerful state. That expertise, like medical knowledge, demanded to be taken on its own innate merits and was thus offered in the form of advice and persuasion; it could not legitimately be imposed by violence. Neither revolutionaries nor toadies, Confucian scholar-bureaucrats opposed bad government by upholding in nonviolent ways the best ideals of statecraft. The Confucian ideal proved so powerful that it continued to shape Chinese society.

Daoism

The later Zhou period was a time of philosophical ferment. Many others besides Confucius were grappling with the problems of humanity, society, and the universal. Especially significant were the Daoists (often written as Daoists), followers of a school of thought traditionally ascribed to Lao Zi (Lao-tzu). Little is known about Lao Zi's life; he is supposed to have lived in the sixth century B.C., but his very existence has been questioned. The book attributed to him, *Dao De Ching (Book of the Way and Its Power)*, is probably the work of several people and dates only from the fourth century B.C. (see Listening to the Past).

Where Confucian political thought was practical and humanistic, Daoism argued that political authority cannot bestow peace and order if it restricts itself to the rules and customs of society. The only effective social control stems, according to Lao Zi, from adherence to the ultimate nature of reality. The only way to achieve this end, Lao Zi taught, is to follow Dao, or the Way of Nature. *Dao De Ching* portrays the Way as the creative force of nature:

There is a thing confusedly formed,
Born before heaven and earth.
Silent and void
It stands alone and does not change,
Goes round and does not weary.
It is capable of being the mother of the world.
I know not its name
So I style it "the way."[5]

According to Daoists, people could be happy only if they abandoned the world and reverted to nature, living simply and alone. Those who followed the Way had no further need of human society. If the philosophy of Daoism had ever been carried to its logical extreme, Daoism would have created a world of hermits.

Daoism treated the problems of government in a dramatically different way from Confucianism. In essence, the Daoists were convinced that government could do most for people by doing as little as possible. *Dao De Ching* boldly declares that people are better-off left to themselves:

Exterminate the sage, discard the wise,
And the people will benefit a hundredfold;
Exterminate benevolence, discard rectitude,
And the people will again be filial;
Exterminate ingenuity, discard profit,
And there will be no more thieves and bandits.[6]

Lao Zi argued that public works and services, from road building to law courts, led to higher taxes, which in turn led to unhappiness and even popular resistance. The fewer laws and rules, the better, Daoists urged. The Daoists also spelled out how, if there had to be a government at all, the people should be ruled:

Therefore in governing the people, the sage
empties their minds but fills their bellies,

weakens their wills but strengthens their
bones. He always keeps them innocent of
knowledge and free from desire, and ensures
that the clever never dare to act.[7]

The people are to be well treated, according to the Daoists, but they will be happiest if they remain uneducated and materially satisfied.

Daoism was most popular among the rulers and ministers who actually governed Chinese society. It gave them a safety valve in a rough-and-tumble world, a way of coping with the extreme pressures they faced. If a ruler suffered defeat or a minister fell out of favor, he could always resign himself to his misfortune by attributing it to the chaos of the world. In this respect Daoism became a philosophy of consolation—but only for a chosen few. The elite often adopted Daoism for consolation and Confucianism for serious everyday affairs.

Legalism

More pragmatic than Confucianism was Legalism, the collective name later given to a number of distinct but related schools of practical political theory that flourished during the late Zhou period. Among the founders of Legalism were Han Fei Zi (d. 233 B.C.) and Li Su (Li Ssu) (d. 208 B.C.). Both were former Confucians who had been heavily influenced by Daoism. Both were pragmatic realists who thought that the state should possess as much power as possible and extend it relentlessly. Their ideal state was authoritarian: the sensible ruler, in their view, should root out all intellectual dissent or resistance and all competing political ideas. Since human nature is evil, according to the Legalists, the ruler must keep the people disciplined and even suppressed if they are rebellious. The people should be well treated but need not be educated. The ruler should appropriate their labor to feed his armies and their wealth to fill his coffers. No frivolity is to be tolerated: people are to work and produce; they should not waste their time on the study of history, philosophy, and other unproductive pursuits. Rather than refute Confucian political ideas, Legalism repressed or dismissed them, as many twentieth-century ideologies have done to conflicting ideas. Nonetheless, Legalism was realistic and offered Chinese rulers practical solutions to the problems of governing large populations over great distances.

Legalism was at first influential in practical affairs. Both Han Fei Zi and Li Zi were high officials, in a position to put Legalist theories into practice. Though Legalism offered an effective, if harsh, solution to the problems confronting Zhou society, it was ultimately too narrow to compete successfully as an independent school with Confucianism and Daoism.

I Ching and Yin and Yang

Chinese thought was not entirely tied to philosophical schools or outlooks. It remained greatly influenced, especially at the popular level, by a belief that individuals were integral parts of a cosmic whole that they could understand. One aspect of this attitude was the belief that people could learn profound truths and receive dependable guidance to successful lives through interpretations of oracles. *I Ching (The Book of Changes)* also served this purpose. *I Ching* directs readers in how to lead an ethical life and how to live in harmony with the universe. It is thus more ethical than philosophical, yet its philosophical content and importance should not be denied.

The *I Ching* is essentially a book of oracles, and readers used its contents by reading the result of randomly tossed coins. When people wanted answers to questions troubling them, they read the results of the throw of the coins and consulted the appropriate oracle. For instance, for those seeking to understand the continuous flow of life, the appropriate oracle was the following:

Creativity is a constant—flowing through our lives and our world; the very essence of all things. It is one moment built upon its predecessor, the continuous flow of existence. From this, the cosmic example, one must model his inner self, aspiring to consistency in his moments of cosmic unity. It is in this construct of persistent contact and identification with the ceaseless power of heaven that the goal is realized.[8]

For those who wanted to be in harmony with this flow, the best oracle was this:

If one is to be in touch with the cosmic flow, he must develop a consciousness that will permit communication. Through the wide gate of his spirit's awareness, the sage receives the earth-intended force and humbly puts it to use for all men. Through this attitude of serving, he builds cooperation so that men may learn to work together in the shaping of their destinies.[9]

These two examples are enough to demonstrate that the *I Ching* uses ethics, philosophy, and plain common sense to enable people to live a happy, moral life. The *I Ching* did not demand acceptance of any particular philosophical or political doctrine; it simply provided sound advice.

Another attempt to understand the relationship between cosmic forces and human life led to the concept of Yin and Yang. Han thinkers developed the idea that these two elementary powers governed a constant cosmic process. Yang represents the strong, radiant, dry, and manly; Yin represents the weak, dark, moist, and womanly. They constantly work together to bring about a changing but predictable relation of power in the world, a power that is related to the four seasons. Yang becomes strong in spring and comes to fullest strength in summer, only to decline in autumn and still further in winter. Yin reigns supreme in autumn and winter. Together they represent the natural rhythms of the year, those of birth, growth, and death. Both are essential to the process of life, for they are in essence dual. Yin and Yang are not opponents like good and evil. Rather they are complementary. Neither can exist alone.

The concept of Yin and Yang attempted to put the observable facts of human life into an intelligible form. It accounts for the changes in the seasons, their natures, their fruits, the climates of each, and the place of human beings in this natural and eternal cycle. Unlike Hindu religion, which held out the opportunity to escape from the burdens of life, Yin and Yang helped people to think of themselves as a legitimate part of a natural order and not necessarily as an alien or unfortunate part. Both *I Ching* and Yin and Yang gave people an understandable way of orienting themselves in the world.

THE AGE OF EMPIRE

The leader of the state of Qin (Ch'in) who deposed the last Zhou king in 256 B.C. had within thirty-five years made himself sole ruler of China, taking the title Qin Shi Huangdi (Ch'in Shih Huang Ti), or First Emperor (r. 256–210 B.C.).

❉ **Army of the First Emperor**   When the grave of the First Emperor was recently discovered, an army of ceramic soldiers came to light. Six thousand statues, armed with spears, swords, bows, and crossbows, were found intact in a huge pit, here seen still in excavation. The statues give a vivid idea of the army that unified China. *(Source: George Holton/Photo Researchers, Inc.)*

Thus began the Qin Dynasty. Although the Qin Dynasty lasted only some fifteen years, the work of its emperors endured for centuries. Indeed, the Western name for China is derived from the Qin. The First Emperor unified China under a central government, and the Han Dynasty, which replaced the Qin, maintained this unity for centuries. Under the emperors of the Qin and Han, China flourished economically, culturally, and socially.

The Qin and Unification of China

The ancient Chinese historian Sima Qian (Szu-ma Ch'ien) left this vivid description of the victory of the First Emperor:

With its superior strength Ch'in [Qin] pressed the crumbling forces of its rivals, pursued those who had fled in defeat, and overwhelmed and slaughtered the army of a million until their shields floated upon a river of blood. Following up the advantages of its victory, Ch'in gained mastery over the empire and divided up its mountains and rivers. The powerful states begged to submit to its sovereignty and the weaker ones paid homage at its court.[10]

The Qin extended their sway as far south as modern Hong Kong and the South China Sea, introducing Chinese influence into vast new areas. With this hard-won victory came political unity, which the First Emperor was determined to maintain.

The First Emperor considered a highly centralized state necessary to ensure a united China. He and his prime minister, Li Su, a founder of Legalism, embarked on an imaginative, sweeping, and rigorous program of centralization that touched the lives of nearly everyone in China. At the head of the state stood the emperor, an autocrat possessing absolute power. His first act was to cripple the nobility. The First Emperor ordered the nobles to leave their lands and appear at his court. Aristocratic families all across China were torn from their estates and transported to Xianyang (Hsien-yang), the capital of Qin, where they built new homes around the court. The emperor took over their estates and organized China into a system of large provinces subdivided into smaller districts, each governed by three principal officials.

The emperor controlled the provinces by appointing governors and lesser administrators, as well as other officials to keep watch on them. These officers were not drawn from the old aristocracy; they owed their power and position entirely to the favor of the emperor. Unlike the old aristocracy, they could not claim hereditary rights to their positions. The governors kept order in the provinces, enforcing laws and collecting taxes. One of their most important and least popular duties was to draft men for the army and for work on huge building projects.

In the interest of harnessing the enormous human resources of his people, the First Emperor ordered a census of the entire population. Census information helped the imperial bureaucracy to plan its activities—to estimate the costs of public works, the tax revenues needed to pay for them, and the labor force available for military service and building projects.

A highly centralized empire needs good communications. But communication over an area as vast as China presented huge challenges. The emperor met them in several ways. First there was the problem of language itself. During the Zhou period, each state often spoke its own distinct dialect, which contained words borrowed from other dialects. Written language also varied from dialect to dialect; some people used signs that were unintelligible to others. These variations in language made central administration difficult. To solve this problem, the First Emperor and his ministers standardized the written script.

The First Emperor also standardized the weights, measures, and coinage of the realm. The old coinages of conquered states were abolished, and the Qin established its own traditional coinage as the imperial currency. This coinage and system of weights and measures made it much easier for the central government to collect taxes. The emperor also standardized the axle lengths of carts. Most Chinese roads at the time were nothing more than deep tracks cut by the wheels of carts. Uniform axle lengths meant that all carts could use the same ruts, making travel and communication quicker and more convenient.

The First Emperor initiated land reforms that gave peasant farmers greater rights. He furthered irrigation projects and encouraged land reclamation to bring more soil under cultivation. These efforts, together with the widespread use of iron tools, increased agricultural production and fostered prosperity. The emperor also promoted the weaving of textiles, especially silk, which remained the aristocrat of Chinese fabrics. Thanks to the new road system, trade increased. Merchants became important figures, although their social status remained low. The growth of trade stimulated the growth of towns, and the broadened economy enlarged the tax base for the government.

Foreign Danger and Internal Unrest

While the First Emperor was working to bring China unity and prosperity, he faced constant peril on the northern border. For years the Chinese had pushed northward, driving out the nomadic Huns, who in later centuries would carry death, destruction, and terror to the decaying Roman Empire. Chinese encroachment endangered the very survival of the Huns. Each of their scattered tribes was led by its own chieftain. The Huns, on horseback and armed with swords and bows, struck back in quick and repeated raids, plundering prosperous towns and farms, then disappearing into the vastness of the north. The success of the Huns was not always temporary. One chieftain conquered numerous Chinese tribes in the north, thereby creating a Hunnish empire on the Chinese frontier.

Since Chinese expansion in the north had all along met stiff opposition, the northern states had built long walls for self-protection as early as the fourth century B.C. The First Emperor ordered these various stretches of wall to be linked together in one great wall, extending from the sea some fourteen hundred miles to the west (Map 4.2). The number of laborers who worked on the wall

Han Dynasty
Great Wall
Silk Road

MONGOLIAN PLATEAU

HUNS

GOBI DESERT   TOBA

MANCHURIAN PLAIN

Sea of Japan

PAMIRS

WEI

NORTH CHINA PLAIN

KOREA

JAPAN

Yellow Sea

HIMALAYA MTS.

TIBETAN PLATEAU

Huang He (Yellow)

Wei   •Xi'an

Huai

SHU

WU

East China Sea

INDIA

BURMA

Salween

VIETNAM (ANNAM)

Mekong

Xi

•Hong Kong

TAIWAN

South China Sea

Bay of Bengal

0   300   600 Km.

0   300   600 Mi.

MAP 4.2 China Under the Han Dynasty, 206 B.C.–A.D. 220   The glory of the Han Dynasty is evident from this map. The Han pushed the frontiers into central and southeastern Asia and ruled over far more territory than any previous dynasty.

and the sheer amount of construction material needed are stunning tribute to the First Emperor's power. The Great Wall of China is probably humanity's most immense ancient creation. The Great Wall and the huge numbers of troops guarding the frontier gave the north a period of peace.

Despite their achievements the Qin were unpopular rulers. The First Emperor was primarily interested in his own wealth and power and did not tolerate opposition. A Legalist, he distrusted Confucian scholars and reportedly had some 460 of them buried alive. He tried without success to destroy Confucian literature and China's ancient literary heritage by a massive campaign of book burning. He enforced the tenets of Legalism vigorously and ruthlessly in an effort to wipe out any

system of thought that might challenge his autocratic position. The Qin demanded obedience, not intelligence.

The Qin took advantage of the new prosperity to levy heavy taxes, especially on the peasants. Taxation, forced labor on the Great Wall and on other projects, and military service mercilessly disrupted many peasant households. While the men were away, their families worked long, dreary hours to feed themselves and meet the staggering burden of taxes.

The oppressiveness of the Qin bred fierce hatred among the people. One person described the First Emperor as a monster who "had the heart of a tiger and a wolf. He killed men as though he thought he could never finish, he punished men as

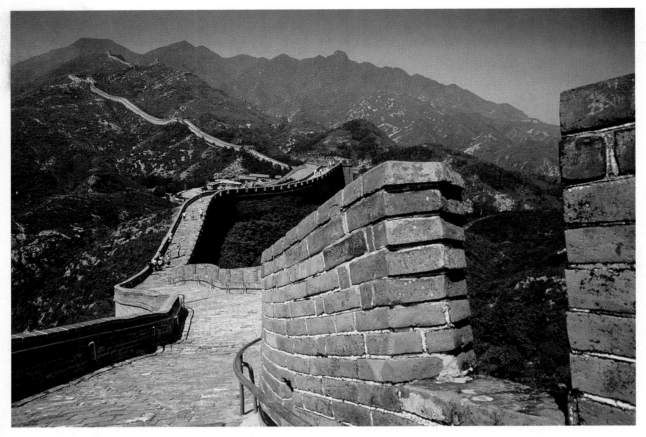

✳ **Great Wall of China** The size and sheer awesomeness of the Great Wall comes through strikingly in this print. Over hill and through valley the Great Wall spanned some 3,000 miles of northern China. *(Tony Stone Images/Chicago Inc.)*

though he were afraid he would never get around to them all."[11] The death of the First Emperor in 210 B.C. sparked massive revolts. Huge bands of peasants took up arms against the new emperor. In the ensuing struggle for power, Liu Bang (Liu Pang), a peasant and petty official of the Qin, defeated his opponents and in 206 B.C. established the Han Dynasty.

The Glory of the Han Dynasty
(206 B.C.–A.D. 220)

The Han Dynasty marked the beginning of China's early imperial age. The dynasty also gave the Chinese their own name: they have traditionally called themselves "men of Han." Liu Bang, the victorious rebel, was no revolutionary. He re-

tained the main features of Qin administration and made no social reforms, but the extreme political centralization of the Qin was relaxed. At least in theory, the Han Empire had an autocratic emperor aided by an educated but nonaristocratic bureaucracy. The basis of the empire, as always, was China's vigorous and hard-working peasants.

Under capable emperors like Liu Bang (r. 206–195 B.C.) and his immediate successors, China recovered from the oppression and turmoil of the Qin period. Unable to conquer the Huns, who were renewing their threats on the northern border, the Chinese first tried to buy them off with lavish presents and stirred up internal trouble among Hun chieftains. In 133 B.C., however, Emperor Han Wudi (Han Wu Ti) went on the attack. In fourteen years of fighting, the Han drove the

Huns still farther north. Chinese armies advanced into western Turkestan, where they opened up direct relations with the subcontinent of India. Equally impressive were the Han emperors' gains in the east. Chinese armies conquered western Korea, where they took over trade with Japan. The Han also extended their rule to the southeastern coast of China, and by 111 B.C. the emperor Han Wudi had conquered northern Vietnam (see Map 4.2).

Han military successes resulted in a dramatic increase in trade with the outside world. After Wudi conquered northern Vietnam, Chinese and foreign merchants moved in and set up trading stations under the supervision of Chinese officials. Southern China and northern Vietnam became meeting grounds for different cultures. The people of northern Vietnam accepted Chinese culture, and regions not far to the south were falling under the influence of Indian culture carried there by Indian merchants. Indeed, an independent state, called Funan by the Chinese, arose in modern southern Vietnam and Cambodia among Malayan people who adopted many aspects of Indian culture.

Under the Han emperors Chinese merchants opened a new route from southwestern China by way of the rivers of Vietnam and Burma to ports on the Bay of Bengal. A Later Han emperor sent an ambassador direct to the West (see page 204). Trade between China and its neighbors, together with the political and social stability of Han rule, gave China an unparalleled time of peace and prosperity.

Han Confucianism and Intellectual Revolt

Confucianism made a comeback during the Han Dynasty, but it was a changed Confucianism. Although many Confucian texts had fed the First Emperor's bonfires, some dedicated scholars had hidden their books, and others had memorized whole books: one ninety-year-old man was able to recite two books virtually in their entirety. These heroic efforts saved much of China's ancient literature and Confucian thought, yet extensive textual corruption introduced non-Confucian elements into traditional Confucian texts.

While trying to reconstruct the past, the new Confucianism was influenced by other schools of thought, even by the hated Legalism. Strengthened by these influences, Confucianism again took

hold. Its hold was so strong that Confucianism endured as the intellectual and cultural basis in China until the present.

During the Han era, Confucian scholars pondering China's past put into systematic form a concept that went back to the Zhou. They elaborated the related theories of the *dynastic cycle* and the *Mandate of Heaven*. The link between the cycle and the mandate was divine approval of the performance of a dynasty. Rule of China was the gift of Heaven, which was considered a deity. With Heaven's blessing the duty of the emperor and his successors was to expand the borders, if possible, or at least to foster prosperity and maintain order for noble and peasant alike, with as little interference as possible in the lives of the people. Once emperors failed in their duty, whether through weakness or corruption, conditions deteriorated, and the empire was left prey to foreign invasion and internal unrest. At that point, Confucian scholars argued, the dynastic cycle came full circle. By failing to maintain the Mandate of Heaven, the last emperor of the dynasty lost his authority to the first man who could restore order and prosperity. That man succeeded because Heaven transferred the mandate to him. Dynasties waxed and waned according to how well they served the requirements of Heaven.

According to Han Confucianism, the emperor was the intermediary between his subjects and Heaven. He served this function by performing all the sacred rites to the deities correctly and scrupulously and by watching for signs that Heaven was displeased. Confucianism explained history by looking to the virtues and vices of individuals, especially emperors and dynasties. Confucian historians saw history not as progressive but as cyclical, as repetitions of the same kinds of events.

Yet the Confucians did not have the field of political thought solely to themselves. Huang Lao Daoism made a considerable impact on Chinese thinking. Owing to the recent discovery of manuscripts from a tomb, we now have a better understanding of this influential political philosophy. Huang Lao held rulers to strict codes of duty and conduct. It expected rulers to serve the people and to keep to a minimum their own material possessions and governmental expenditures. Rulers were obliged to obey the law, not only in public affairs but also in their personal conduct with other individuals. They were to use the army only in just causes or on other appropriate occasions, such as the defense of the people from foreign invasion. They must follow the way (or *dao*), which encompassed law, ethical principles, and forms and names. They must respect the natural order of the world, which included the forces of yin and yang and the cycle of the seasons. Huang Lao drafted a blueprint for efficient and humane conduct and administration of public affairs.

In this climate of thought, the study of history flourished. Generations of Chinese scholars devoted their efforts to studying particular dynasties and events and individual rulers, ministers, and generals. The Chinese, like the Greeks, conceived of history as broader and more complex than the mere chronicling of events. Indeed, during the Han Dynasty China produced one of its finest historians, Sima Qian (Szu-ma Ch'ien) (ca 145–86 B.C.). Like the Greek Thucydides, he believed fervently in visiting the sites where history was made, examining artifacts, and questioning people about events. Sima was also interested in China's geographical variations, local customs, and local history. As an official of the emperor, he had access to important people and documents and to the imperial library. Having decided to write a history of China down to his own time, Sima set about interviewing eyewitnesses and those who had shaped events. He also reviewed official documents and written records. The result, ten years in the making, was his classic *Records of the Grand Historian,* a massive work of literary and historical genius.

Nor did Sima's work die with him. The Ban (Pan), a remarkably creative family, took up his study of the Han. Among the most eminent of them was Ban Zhao (Pan Chao), China's first woman historian and scholar. Ban Zhao also wrote poems and essays, notably *Lessons for Women* on the education of women. Taking up Sima Jian history, the Ban family wrote the first history of a Chinese dynasty. Thereafter, official court historians wrote the history of every dynasty. Like their Greek and Roman counterparts, Chinese historians considered recent and current history important in their investigations.

Han intellectual pursuits were not limited to history. In medicine, the Han period produced its own Hippocrates, Jing Jhi, a practicing physician whose *Treatise on Fevers* became a standard work in Chinese medicine. Chinese surgeons grappled with the problem of reducing the pain of surgery, and the Han physician Hua Duo developed a drug

that, mixed with wine, would render a patient unconscious.

The career of Zhang Heng (A.D. 78–139), the great mathematician, was strikingly similar to that of the Hellenistic philosopher Eratosthenes. Both delved deeply into astronomy and concluded that the world is round, not flat as many of their contemporaries assumed. Not content to speculate, Zhang Heng built models to test his theories. He even designed a seismograph capable of discerning the direction in which an earthquake was taking place, though not its severity. The brilliance of Han intellectual activity shone in its breadth and achievements.

Daily Life During the Han Dynasty

Because the people who chronicled events in Han China were an elite writing for other elites, more is known about the upper levels of society than about the lower levels. The lives of the common people were taken for granted or considered too vulgar to write about. But even though a complete portrayal is beyond reach, it is possible to sketch the outlines of daily life in Han China.

The peasant farmer was the backbone of Han society. Agriculture was considered an important and honorable activity that distinguished the civilized Chinese from their barbaric and nomadic neighbors. Small households of farmers worked the land and generated most of the revenue of the empire. The Chinese peasant family was probably small, four or five people, frequently including a grandparent. Both women and men performed hard manual labor in the fields. Men were typically required to spend time each year in the service of the emperor; and while they were away, their wives ran the farm. Farmers' existence was tenuous, for floods, drought, and unduly harsh taxes could wipe them out. When severely oppressed by harsh, inefficient, and sometimes corrupt government, the peasants revolted, turned to a life of begging or banditry, or put themselves under the protection of powerful landlords. Thus the Han emperors were rightly proud of the peace and security of their reigns, which spared Chinese farmers the worst evils.

The staple grain under cultivation varied with the soil and climate. In the warm and wet south, rice was the traditional crop. In the north, farmers raised millet and wheat wherever possible or barley on land too poor for wheat. Farmers also grew hemp, which was woven into coarse clothing for the common people. Some fortunate farmers had groves of timber or bamboo to supplement their crops; or they grew mulberry trees, the leaves of which nourish silkworms, or groves of lac trees, from which came a resin used on decorative lacquer ware. Wherever possible, farmers grew fruit and nut trees. Farmers near cities found ready profit growing vegetables and ginger and other spices for city folk. Tea and sugar cane were raised in southern China but were still luxury items during the Han period.

Land use became systematic and effective under the Han, probably as a result of experience and of innovations recommended by Chao Kuo, a Han minister. Chao Kuo introduced a systematic ridge-and-furrow system of planting that yielded fairly regular harvests and facilitated crop rotation. To maintain the fertility of the soil, farmers treated their land with manure and crushed bones. The in-

tensive character of Chinese agriculture meant that very little land was available for pasturage. Unlike his Indian counterpart, the Chinese farmer seldom raised cattle, horses, or donkeys. Dogs, pigs, and chickens were the typical domestic farm animals. The lack of draft animals meant that most farm work was done by hand and foot.

Farmers used a variety of tools, but the most important was the plow. The earliest wooden plow was a simple tool, more often pulled by humans than by animals. The new and more effective plow introduced during the Han period was fitted with two plowshares and guided by a pair of handles and was typically pulled by a pair of oxen. Farmers used fans to blow the chaff from kernels of grain, and they used either mortar and pestle or hand mills to grind grain into flour. The Chinese also developed an elaborate system using long hammers to mill grain and pound earth. Eventually, the hammers were driven by waterpower. Irrigation water was pumped into the fields with devices

Han Workers This series of sculptures depict ordinary people and their animals routinely carrying out the basic economic functions of Chinese society. One figure carries a basket, while another leads an ox. These sculptures illustrate the simplicity and hardship of daily life. *(Source: J. L. Klinger, Heidelberg)*

ranging from a simple pole with an attached bucket and counterweight to a sophisticated machine worked by foot.

The agricultural year began in mid-February with the breaking up of heavy soil and manuring of the fields. February was also the beginning of the new year, a time of celebration and an important religious festival. This was the time to sow and transplant seedlings. During the second and third months of the year, farmers practiced their archery to defend themselves against the bandits who infested the countryside; as a further precaution, they repaired the gates and locks of their houses. The fifth month was the time to cut the hay; the sixth, to hoe the fields. Meanwhile, the women of the family nurtured silkworms and made silk cloth, which they would later dye, and they wove the hemp into coarse cloth. With the harvest, processing, and storage of the crop, farmers were ready for winter and the coming year.

City life was varied and hectic compared with the regularity of farming. The wealthiest urbanites lived in splendid houses of two or more stories, surrounded by walls and containing at least one courtyard. These large homes had such features as storage rooms and rooms for animals in the courtyard. The rooms or outhouses used for grain storage were built on stilts to protect against rats and moisture, which could cause rot or mildew.

The house itself was usually four-sided, with the door in one wall. The floors of the poor were covered with animal skins and mats of woven grass;

A Han Manor An excellent representation of a rural manor house, this clay model displays a courtyard, gatehouse, and watchtower—in effect, a small fort. (*Source: Cultural Relics Publishing House, Beijing*)

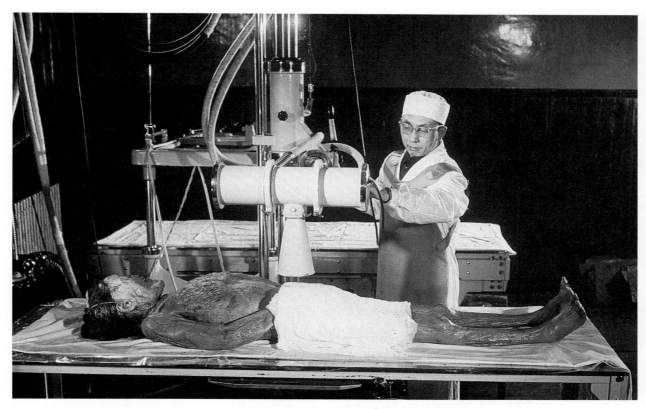

✤ **Corpse of Lady Xin**   Although this may seem no way in which to treat a lady, the scientist and many other experts from across China convened to examine the corpse of Lady Xin, who died some twenty-one hundred years ago. The autopsy revealed that just before her death she had consumed 130 musk-melon seeds. *(Source: China Pictorial, Beijing)*

those of the rich, with finely embroidered cushions and wool rugs. The bedrooms of wealthy homes were furnished with wooden beds, embroidered draperies, and beautiful screens for privacy. Fine furniture of expensive wood and beautifully lacquered bowls graced the houses of the wealthy.

Wealthy urban dwellers loved costly clothes, and everyone who could afford to do so bought fine and brightly colored silks. The wealthy also spent money on furs, usually fox and squirrel and sometimes badger. Expensive shoes lined with silk and decorated with leather became extremely popular. Wealthy women wore jewelry of jade and other precious and semiprecious stones, as well as gold earrings and finger rings. The urban poor probably had easier and somewhat cheaper access to silk garments than did their rural neighbors, but their clothing was primarily made of coarse hemp cloth.

The diet of city folk, like their clothing, could be rich and varied. Owing to general prosperity, people during the Han period began to eat meat more frequently. Demand increased dramatically for wild game and young animals and fish, which were seasoned with leeks, ginger, and herbs. No longer was rice wine, like meat, a luxury for festival days. It began to be consumed avidly, and wealthy Chinese began to age vintages for twenty or thirty years. The Chinese were especially fond of pork, and roast pig was one of the most popular gourmet dishes. The Chinese also enjoyed liver and dog meat. Wood and pottery utensils were standard features of common households, but rich people relegated wood and pottery to the kitchen and dined on dishes decorated with gold and silver.

People with money and taste patronized music. The rich often maintained private musical troupes generally playing bells, drums, and pipes. Flutes and stringed instruments were also popular. People of more common taste flocked to puppet shows and performances of jugglers and acrobats. Magic shows dazzled the impressionable, and cockfighting appealed to bloody tastes. Gambling was popular but considered decidedly vulgar. Archaeologists have found several board games.

As gangs of bandits infested the countryside, so crime plagued the cities. Officials were open to corruption and sometimes connived with criminals and gangs of thugs who had the support of wealthy and powerful families. At times the situation got so far out of hand that private armies roamed the streets, wearing armor and carrying knives and preying on the weak and helpless. Poor people who lacked influence suffered outrages and violence with no hope of justice or retribution.

Silk was in great demand all over the known world during the Han period, and caravans transported bales of it westward. Another distinctive Chinese product was the lacquer ware. Han craftsmen developed lacquer work to a fine art. Because lacquer creates a hard surface that withstands wear, it was ideal for cups, dishes, toilet articles, and even parts of carriages. Such works of art were only for the rich; poor people contented themselves with plain lacquer ware at best. Some of the most splendid examples of lacquer work are elaborately carved and inlaid with precious metals. Chinese craftsmen loved geometric designs. The accuracy of some of their work suggests that they used mechanical tools.

Perhaps the most momentous product of Han imagination was the invention of paper, which the Chinese traditionally date to A.D. 105. Scribes had previously written on strips of bamboo and wood. Fine books for the wealthy were written on silk rolls. Cai Lun, to whom the Chinese attribute the invention of paper, worked the fibers of rags, hemp, bark, and other scraps into sheets of paper. Though far less durable than wood, paper was far cheaper than silk and became a convenient means of conveying the written word. By the fifth century, paper was in common use, preparing the way for the invention of printing.

Han craftsmen continued the Chinese tradition of excellent metallurgy. By the beginning of the first century A.D., China had about fifty state-run ironworking factories. These factories smelted iron ore into ingots before turning it over to the craftsmen who worked it into tools and other articles. Their products demonstrate a sophisticated knowledge of metals. Han workmen turned out iron plowshares, agricultural tools with wooden handles, and weapons and armor. Han metalsmiths were mass-producing superb crossbows long before the crossbow was dreamed of in Europe.

Iron was replacing bronze in tools, but bronze-workers still turned out a host of goods. Bronze was prized for jewelry, mirrors, dishes, and spoons. Bronze was also used for minting coins and for precision tools such as carpenters' rules and adjustable wrenches. Surviving bronze gear-and-cog wheels bear eloquent testimony to the sophistication of Han machinery.

Distribution of the products of Han craftsmen was in the hands of merchants, whom Chinese aristocrats, like ancient Hebrew wise men, considered necessary but lowly. In the Chinese scale of values, agriculture was honorable because farmers worked to win the gifts that nature bestowed. Merchants, however, thrived on the toil of others, and the art of winning profits was considered ungentlemanly and not quite legitimate. The first Han emperor took action to put merchants in their place, as the great historian Sima relates:

After peace had been restored to the empire, Liu Pang issued an order forbidding merchants to wear silk or ride in carriages, and increased the taxes that they were obliged to pay in order to hamper and humiliate them.[12]

Yet the emperors and ministers of Han China realized that merchants had become indispensable. One outcome of this ambiguity was the conclusion that merchants ought to be regulated. Another was an early form of limited socialism—state monopolies on essential commodities like iron and salt, which made for price stability.

Retail merchants set up shop in stalls in the markets, grouped together according to their wares. All the butchers, for example, congregated in one part of the market, each trying to outsell the others. Nearly everything could be found in the markets, from food to horses and cattle, from ox carts and metal hardware to fine silks. The markets were also the haunts of entertainers and fortunetellers. The imperial government stationed officials in the markets to police the selling of goods and to levy taxes on the merchants. In markets public execution of criminals served as an example and a warning to would-be criminals and political agitators in the crowd.

The transportation of goods in bulk was still difficult and expensive. Roads were primitive, but the Han developed several sturdy and effective types of

CHINA TO ca a.d. 400

ca 1523–ca 1027 b.c.	Shang Dynasty and invention of writing
ca 1027–221 b.c.	Zhou Dynasty
551–479 b.c.	Confucius and rise of Confucianism
4th century b.c.	Lao Zi and development of Daoism
ca 250–208 b.c.	Han Fei Zi and Li Su and development of Legalism
221–210 b.c.	Establishment of the Qin Dynasty and unification of China Construction of the Great Wall Destruction of Confucian literature
206 b.c.–a.d. 220	Establishment of the Han Dynasty
111 b.c.	Chinese expansion to the South China Sea and Vietnam
a.d. 221–280	Three Kingdoms era
4th–5th centuries	Barbarian invasions

carts and wagons, and a new harness for horses came into widespread use. Earlier harnesses had fitted around the horse's neck, choking the animal when it pulled a load. The new harness fitted around the horse's chest and over its back, enabling it to pull heavier loads with less effort. This efficient horse collar finally reached medieval Europe in the eighth century a.d., a product of Asian technology that influenced the history of the West.

Because of the difficulty of overland travel, the Chinese relied heavily on water transport. Since the major rivers of China run from east to west, canals were cut between the rivers to make north-south traffic possible. Bulk foodstuffs and goods could be transported fairly cheaply and swiftly on river boats, which also provided reasonably comfortable living quarters for crew and passengers. Maintenance of canals and dikes was expensive and made huge demands on the labor force, but these waterways allowed China to establish a flexible and effective network of communication.

The Fall of Han China

The Han Empire was an imposing political edifice. Eventually, however, wars on the frontiers and the emperors' enormous building projects put an intolerable strain on society. The emperors drew so heavily on the peasants as soldiers and as workers that agricultural production declined severely. Great landlords saw their chance to expand their holdings and to shift the burden of taxation onto the already hard-pressed peasantry. Ground down by ambitious emperors and unscrupulous landowners, many peasants lost their land and sold their children, farm animals, and tools to the landowners, ending as tenants, hired laborers, or outlaws.

The emperor Wang Mang (r. a.d. 9–23), who was a usurper, attempted to reverse these trends. He tried to re-establish a state monopoly on grain so that private speculators could not exploit famines and shortages to make huge profits. He set about redistributing land to the peasants and wanted to abolish slavery. Unfortunately, Wang Mang's commendable efforts did little to improve conditions, and he was killed in a peasant uprising. Han Kuang Wu in turn defeated the rebels and established the later Han Empire in a.d. 25.

After a century of peace, the later Han emperors found themselves facing the same problems that Wang Mang had tried to solve. Once again great landlords took over peasants' land and burdened them with heavy taxes. Disorder, intrigue, and assassination at court distracted the government. A murderous rivalry developed between the old scholar-officials, who had traditionally administered political affairs, and the palace eunuchs, men usually of lowly origin who wielded huge influence from their lair among the women of the imperial harem. Turmoil and palace revolt meant that the great landlords were left unhindered. Once again the peasants staged massive uprisings. When the imperial armies were dispatched to put down the unrest, the victorious generals used their forces to carve out petty kingdoms for themselves. The palace eunuchs revolted against the emperor and his scholar-officials, and the Han Empire collapsed in general turmoil.

In the years that followed, known as the Three Kingdoms Era (A.D. 221–280), the empire was broken into three separate kingdoms. These kingdoms conformed to the natural geographical divisions of the land: the kingdom of Wei held the north; Shu, the upper Yangtze River Valley; and Wu, the lower Yangtze River Valley (see Map 4.2). Throughout this period, China experienced further disorder and barbarian trouble.

The difficulties with barbarians increased in later years, with catastrophic invasions from the north. Most significant were the conquests by the nomadic Toba from Mongolia, who created their own northern dynasty. Early in the fifth century the Toba assumed control of northern China, making the Great Wall their northern boundary. They extended their sway into central Asia and stopped further barbarian invasions of China. Southern China, which remained under Chinese rule, actually benefited from these invasions: thousands of Chinese, among them many scholar-officials, fled to the south, where they devoted their energies and talents to developing southern China economically and culturally.

Barbarian invasions caused China distress and disruption, but the Toba and other nomads quickly came under the spell of Chinese culture linguistically, politically, and economically. The Toba emperor ordered the Toba nobility to speak Chinese at his court and to dress and act like the Chinese elite. The Toba adopted Chinese agricultural techniques and the bureaucratic method of administering the empire. China's political system was so excellently suited to the land and its people

that no barbarian invader could have done without it. That system encompassed not just a bureaucracy fully dependent on the Chinese language, but the culture, religion, and outlook of Chinese society. In that respect, China absorbed its invaders more successfully than India had done.

SUMMARY

Chinese mastery of the land led to the harnessing of China's resources. A vital aspect of this triumph was the development of a systematic method of agriculture capable of sustaining a huge population. Prosperity and growth in population allowed the Chinese to shape their lives as never before. One result was a vibrant and sophisticated intellectual life. Whereas Indian society was largely permeated by religion, Chinese thought was for the most part secular in orientation. Although China sometimes experienced internal disorder and the threat of invasion, political upheaval never destroyed China's cultural heritage. By the end of the Han Dynasty, writing, Confucianism, and the complex political organization of a huge region had left an enduring mark on the Chinese people.

NOTES

1. A. Waley, trans., *The Analects of Confucius* (London: George Allen and Unwin, 1938), 4.18.
2. Ibid., 5.15.
3. Ibid., 1.4.
4. Ibid., 1.5.
5. D. C. Lau, trans., *Lao Tzu, Tao Te Ching* (London: Penguin Books, 1963), 1.25.56.
6. Ibid., 1.19.43.
7. Ibid., 1.3.9.
8. Anonymous, *Change* (Virginia Beach: A.R.E. Press, 1971), p. 1.
9. Ibid., p. 2.
10. B. Watson, trans., *Records of the Grand Historian of China Translated from the Shih chi of Ssu-ma Ch'ien* (New York: Columbia University Press, 1961), 1.31.
11. Ibid., 1.53.
12. Ibid., 2.79.

SUGGESTED READING

In general, see H. T. Zurndorfer, *China Bibliography* (1995), a splendid research guide to reference works about past and present China, which is as remarkably broad as it is deep. E. L. Shaughnessy, *Sources of Eastern Zhou History* (1991), treats the development of bronze technology. M. Loewe, *The Pride That Was China* (1990), is a good general survey by a major scholar who draws heavily on archaeological material. R. S. Dawson, ed., *The Legacy of China* (1990), is a synthesis of all important aspects of early Chinese life, similar to that of P. S. Ropp, ed., *Heritage of China* (1990), which is strong on comparisons between Chinese and Western developments. W. C. Liu, *An Introduction to Chinese Literature* (1991), is an ample survey of all genres of literature, extending to modern times. A lively and charming introduction to daily life in China is *Shih Ching,* more easily accessible in A. Waley, trans., *The Book of Songs* (1960). See also Z. R. Liu, *Ancient India and Ancient China* (1988). Other solid general treatments of East Asia include C. Schirokauer, *A Brief History of Chinese and Japanese Civilizations,* 2d ed. (1989), and J. K. Fairbank, E. O. Reischauer, and A. Craig, *East Asia: Tradition and Transformation,* rev. ed. (1989).

For the development of the Chinese language, see Ho Ping-ti, *The Cradle of the East* (1975). A lively and readable account of early life and the origins of writing, told primarily from an archaeological standpoint, is J. Hay, *Ancient China* (1973). More technical are K. Chang, *The Archaeology of Ancient China,* 4th ed. (1986), and *Food in Chinese Culture* (1977), an edited volume containing historical and anthropological material. H. G. Creel, one of the foremost scholars of early Chinese thought, in *The Origins of Statecraft in China* (1970), argues forcefully that early Zhou emperors maintained firm control over their political dependencies in the first centuries of their dynasty.

A fascinating starting point for the study of early Chinese thought is D. Bodde, *Chinese Thought, Society, and Science* (1991), which ranges widely across those aspects of culture and thought that bore on the development of science. A. C. Graham, *Studies in Chinese Philosophy and Philosophical Literature* (1990), is a sensible, broad treatment of all branches of philosophical thought. Much has been written on Confucius and the Confucian tradition. A. Waley's translation of the *Analects of Confucius* (1938) is an eminently readable version of the work attributed to Confucius.

For a good general approach, see F. W. Mote, *Intellectual Foundations of China,* 2nd ed., (1989). The complexities of Daoism are lucidly set out by H. G. Creel, *What Is Taoism?* (1970), which discusses the differences between purposive and contemplative Daoism. One of the most significant of the contemplative Daoists was Zhuang Zi (Chuang-tzu), whose career is studied by A. C. Graham, *Chuang-tzu: The Seven Inner Chapters* (1981). H. G. Creel provides a sound introduction to Legalism in *Shen Pu-hai* (1974), which demonstrates that, far from being monolithic, Legalism consisted of a number of schools of practical political theory. On the careers of Han Fei Zi and Li Su, see D. Bodde, *China's First Unifier* (1938).

The political and military success of the Qin is the subject of D. Bodde, *China's First Unifier: A Study of the Ch'in Dynasty as Seen in the Life of Li Ssu (280?–208 B.C.)* (1958). P. Nancarrow, *Early China and the Wall* (1978), discusses the importance of the Great Wall of China to early Chinese society. A good account of Qin road building is J. Needham, *Science and Civilization in China,* vol. 4, part 3 (1970).

The Han Dynasty has been amply treated by a master scholar, H. H. Dubs, whose *History of the Former Han Dynasty,* 3 vols. (1938–1955), is comprehensive. The turmoil of Confucianism in this period is ably treated in a series of studies, among them E. Balazs, *Chinese Civilization and Bureaucracy* (1964); H. Welch and A. Seidel, eds., *Facets of Taoism* (1979), which ranges more broadly than its title might suggest; and especially C. Chang, *The Development of Neo-Confucian Thought* (1957), a solid discussion of Han Confucianism. B. Watson has provided two good studies of Ssu-ma Ch'ien (Sima Qian) and his historical work: *Records of the Grand Historian of China* (1961) and *Ssu-ma Ch'ien: Grand Historian of China* (1958). China's most important woman scholar is the subject of N. L. Swann, *Pan Chao: Foremost Woman Scholar of China* (1950). K. Frifelt and P. Sorensen, eds., *South Asian Archaeology* (1988), contains a number of papers devoted to South Asia and its broader connections.

M. Loewe, *Everyday Life in Early Imperial China* (1968), paints a vibrant picture of ordinary life during the Han period, a portrayal that attempts to include all segments of Han society. W. Zhongshu, *Han Civilization* (1982), excellently treats many aspects of material life under the Han, including architecture, agriculture, manufacture, and burial. Last, B. Hinsch, *Passions of the Cut Sleeve* (1990), is the only book in English that treats homosexuality in China.

LISTENING TO THE
PAST

The Daoist Approach to Administering the Empire

The principal writing of the Daoists, the Dao De Jing *is one of the most widespread of Chinese political and philosophical documents. It is a handbook on how to govern the empire. The author or authors take the existence of the empire for granted; they do not account for how it came into being or speculate about its ultimate purpose. The* Dao De Jing *focuses on how to maintain the smooth and peaceful functioning of the machinery of empire. Its advice is both practical and ethical. It also insists on the merits of political and social security. Above all, the work is a cry for stability and how to maintain it. It served as a practical guide for public administrators, giving them precepts about how best to carry out their duties.*

LXII

The way is the refuge for the myriad creatures.
It is that by which the good man protects,
And that by which the bad is protected.
Beautiful words when offered will win high
 rank in return;
Beautiful deeds can raise a man above others.
Even if a man is not good, why should he be
abandoned?
Hence when the emperor is set up and the
three ducal ministers are appointed, he who
makes a present of the way without stirring
from his seat is preferable to one who offers
presents of jade disks followed by a team of
four horses. Why was this way valued of old?
Was it not said that by means of it one got
what one wanted and escaped the consequences when one transgressed?
Therefore it is valued by the empire.

LXIII

Do that which consists in taking no action;
pursue that which is not meddlesome; savour
that which has no flavour.

Make the small big and few many; do good
to him who has done you an injury.
Lay plans for the accomplishment of the difficult before it becomes difficult; make something big by starting with it when small.
Difficult things in the world must needs have
their beginnings in the easy; big things must
needs have their beginnings in the small.
Therefore it is because the sage never attempts to be great that he succeeds in becoming great.
One who makes promises rashly rarely keeps
good faith; one who is in the habit of considering things easy meets with frequent difficulties.
Therefore even the sage treats some things as
difficult. That is why in the end no difficulties
can get the better of him.

LXIV

It is easy to maintain a situation while it is still
 secure;
It is easy to deal with a situation before symp-
 toms develop;
It is easy to break a thing when it is yet brittle;
It is easy to dissolve a thing when it is yet
 minute.
Deal with a thing while it is still nothing;
Keep a thing in order before disorder sets in.
A tree that can fill the span of a man's arms
Grows from a downy tip;
A terrace nine storeys high
Rises from hodfuls of earth;
A journey of a thousand miles
Starts from beneath one's feet.
Whoever does anything to it will ruin it; who-
ever lays hold of it will lose it.
Therefore the sage, because he does nothing,
never ruins anything; and, because he does
not lay hold of anything, loses nothing.
In their enterprises the people

Always ruin them when on the verge of
    success.
Be as careful at the end as at the beginning
And there will be no ruined enterprises.
Therefore the sage desires not to desire
And does not value goods which are hard to
    come by;
Learns to be without learning
And makes good the mistakes of the
    multitude
In order to help the myriad creatures to be
    natural and to refrain from daring to act.

LXV

Of old those excelled in the pursuit of the
way did not use it to enlighten the people but
to hoodwink them. The reason why the peo-
ple are difficult to govern is that they are too
clever.
Hence to rule a state by cleverness
Will be to the detriment of the state;
Not to rule a state by cleverness
Will be a boon to the state.
These two are models.
Always to know the models
Is known as mysterious virtue.
Mysterious virtue is profound and
    far-reaching,
But when things turn back it turns back with
    them.
Only then is complete conformity realized.

The philoshoper Lao-tzû holds his scroll
of the 'Tao-te-ching.' (*Source: National
Palace Museum, Taipei, Taiwan, Republic of
China*)

Questions for Analysis

1. According to the Daoists, what is the primary function of the mandarin scholar-
   official?

2. How is he instructed to perform his official
   duties?

3. Is he in any way expected to reform the imperial system, or should he aim to carry out
   customary duties?

Source: Lao Tzu, *Tao Te Ching*, trans. D. C. Lau.
Copyright 1963 by Penguin Books. Reprinted by permission.

The Legacy of Greece

Bronze statue of Poseidon (Zeus?), fifth century B.C. *(Source: Ancient Art & Architecture Collection)*

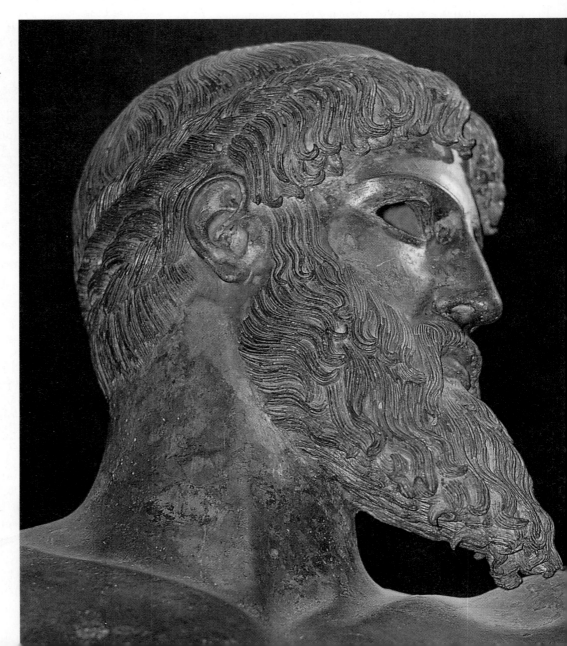

The rocky peninsula of Greece was the home of the civilization that fundamentally shaped European civilization and ultimately influenced the rest of the world. The Greeks were the first to explore questions that continue to concern thinkers to this day. Going beyond mythmaking and religion, the Greeks strove to understand, in logical, rational terms, both the universe and the position of men and women in it. The result was the birth of philosophy and science—subjects that were far more important to most Greek thinkers than religion. The Greeks speculated on human beings and society and created the very concept of politics.

The history of the Greeks is divided into two broad periods: the Hellenic period (the subject of this chapter), roughly the time between the arrival of the Greeks (approximately 2000 B.C.) and the victory over Greece in 338 B.C. by Philip of Macedon; and the Hellenistic period (the subject of Chapter 6), the age beginning with the remarkable reign of Philip's son, Alexander the Great (336–323 B.C.) and ending with the Roman conquest of the Hellenistic East (200–148 B.C.).

- What geographical factors helped to mold the evolution of the city-state?
- How did the impact of the Minoans and Mycenaeans lead to the concept of a heroic past?
- How did the Greeks develop basic and enduring political forms, forms as different as democracy and tyranny?
- What did the Greek intellectual triumph entail, and what were its effects?
- How and why did the Greeks eventually fail?

These questions signal the themes of this chapter.

✻ HELLAS: THE LAND

Hellas, as the ancient Greeks called their land, encompassed the Aegean Sea and its islands as well as the Greek peninsula (Map 5.1). The Greek peninsula itself, stretching in the direction of Egypt and the Near East, is an extension of the Balkan system of mountains. Perhaps the best and most eloquent description of Greece comes from the eminent German historian K. J. Beloch:

Greece is an alpine land, which rises from the waters of the Mediterranean Sea, scenically probably the most beautiful region in southern Europe. The noble contours of the mountains, the bare, rocky slopes, the dusty green of the conifer forests, the white cover of snow that envelops the higher summits for the greatest part of the year, added to which is the profound blue surface of the sea below, and above everything the diffused brightness of the southern sun; this gives a total picture, the charm of which impresses itself unforgettably on the soul of the observer.[1]

The rivers of Greece are never more than creeks, and most of them go dry in the summer. Greece is, however, a land blessed with good harbors. The islands of the Aegean serve as steppingstones between the peninsula and Asia Minor.

Despite the beauty of the region, geography acted as an enormously divisive force in Greek life. The mountains of Greece dominate the landscape, cutting the land into many small pockets and isolating areas of habitation. Innumerable small peninsulas open to the sea. The geographical fragmentation of Greece encouraged political fragmentation. Furthermore, communications were extraordinarily poor. Rocky tracks—usually nothing more than a pair of ruts cut into the rock to accommodate wheels—were far more common than roads. These conditions discouraged the growth of great empires.

✻ THE MINOANS AND MYCENAEANS (CA 1650–CA 1100 B.C.)

Neither historians, archaeologists, nor linguists can confidently establish when Greek-speaking peoples made the Balkan peninsula of Greece their homeland. All that can now safely be said is that they, like the Hittites, Persians, and Aryans, were still another wave of Indo-Europeans who were expanding throughout Europe and Asia during much of antiquity. By about 1650 B.C. Greeks had established themselves at the great city of Mycenae in the Peloponnesus and elsewhere in Greece. Quite probably the Greeks merged with the natives of small farming communities, and from that union emerged the society that modern scholars call Mycenaean, after Mycenae, the most important site of this new Greek-speaking culture.

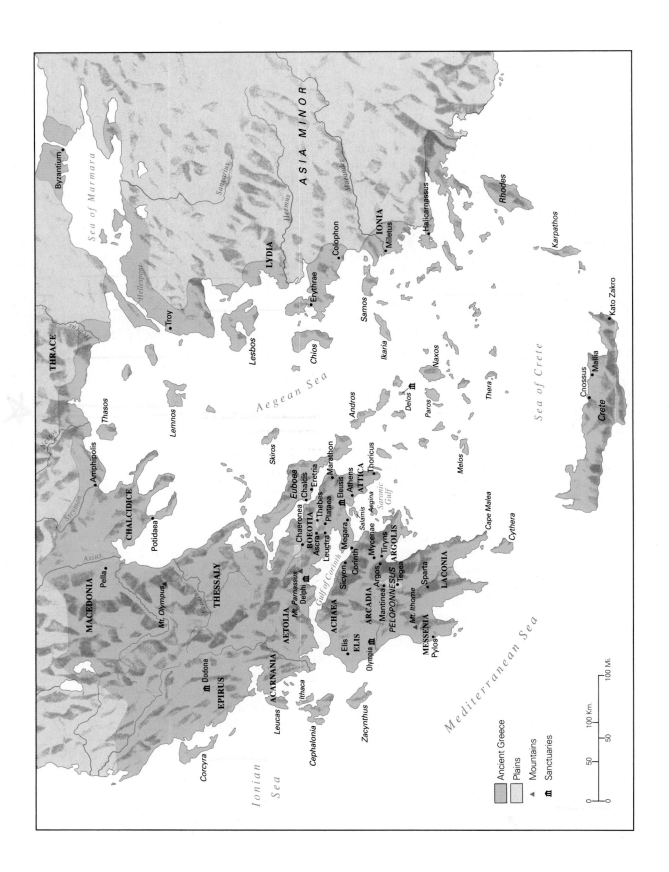

THRACE

Byzantium

Sea of Marmara

Hellespont

Sagarius

ASIA MINOR

Hermus

LYDIA

Maeander

Rhodes

Colophon

IONIA

Erythrae

Karpathos

Miletus

Halicarnassus

Troy

Lesbos

Samos

Chios

Ikaria

Kato Zakro

Skiros

Aegean Sea

Andros

Naxos

Sea of Crete

Delos

Paros

Crossus

Mallia

Thera

Crete

Thasos

Lemnos

Amphipolis

CHALCIDICE

Potidaea

Axius

MACEDONIA

Pella

Mt. Olympus

THESSALY

Melos

Euboea

Marathon

Chaeronea Chalcis

BOEOTIA Eretria

Thoricus

Ascra Thebes

Athens

Leuctra Plataea

ATTICA

Eleusis

Megara

Salamis

Sicyon

Saronic

Mycenae Aegina

Gulf

Corinth

Tiryns

Gulf of Corinth

Argos

ARGOLIS

Cape Malea

Cythera

AETOLIA

Mt. Parnassus

Delphi

ACHAEA

ARCADIA

Mantinea

Tegea

PELOPONNESUS

LACONIA

ACARNANIA

ELIS

Sparta

Elis

Mt. Ithome

Dodona

EPIRUS

Olympia

MESSENIA

Pylos

Ithaca

Leucas

Cephalonia

Corcyra

Zacynthus

Ionian

Sea

Mediterranean Sea

Ancient Greece
Plains
Mountains
Sanctuaries

0   50   100 Km.

0   50   100 Mi.

❋ **Minoan Naval Scene**   This fresco discovered at Thera probably depicts the homecoming of a Minoan fleet of warships. Though later Greeks thought that the Minoans had ruled the sea, fleets such as the one pictured here probably protected Minoan maritime interests and suppressed piracy. Despite its military nature, the scene displays the general air of festivity characteristic of Minoan art. *(Source: National Archaeological Museum, Archaeological Receipts Fund)*

Of this epoch the ancient Greeks themselves remembered almost nothing. The *Iliad* and the *Odyssey,* Homer's magnificent epic poems (eighth century B.C.), retain some dim memory of this period but very little that is authentic. One of the sterling achievements of modern archaeology is the discovery of this lost past. In the nineteenth century Heinrich Schliemann, a German businessman, fell in love with the *Iliad* and decided to find the sites it mentioned. He excavated Troy in modern Turkey, Mycenae, and several other sites in Greece to discover the lost past of the Greek people. At the turn of this century, the English archaeologist

❋ **MAP 5.1 Ancient Greece**   In antiquity the home of the Greeks included the islands of the Aegean Sea and the western shore of Asia Minor as well as the Greek peninsula itself.

Sir Arthur Evans uncovered the remains of an entirely unknown civilization at Cnossus in Crete, and he gave it the name Minoan after the mythical Cretan king Minos. Scholars since then have further illuminated this long-lost era, and despite many uncertainties a reasonably clear picture of the Minoans and Mycenaeans has begun to emerge.

By about 1650 B.C. the island of Crete was the home of the flourishing and vibrant Minoan culture. The Minoans had occupied Crete from at least the Neolithic period. They had also developed a script, now called Linear A, to express their language in writing. Because Linear A is yet undeciphered, however, only archaeology and art offer clues to Minoan life. The symbol of Minoan culture was the palace. Around 1650 B.C. Crete was dotted with palaces, such as those at Mallia on the northern coast and Kato Zakro on the eastern tip of the island. Towering above all others in importance was the palace at Cnossus.

Few specifics are known about Minoan society except that at its head stood a king and his nobles, who governed the lives and toil of Crete's farmers, sailors, shepherds, and artisans. The implements of the Minoans, like those of the Mycenaeans, were bronze, so archaeologists have named this period the Bronze Age. Minoan society was wealthy and, to judge from the absence of fortifications on the island, peaceful. Enthusiastic sailors and merchants, the Minoans traded with Egypt and the cities of the area known today as the Middle East, or Levant. They also established trading posts throughout the Aegean Sea, which brought them into contact with the Mycenaeans on the Greek peninsula.

By about 1650 B.C. Greek-speakers were firmly settled at Mycenae, which became a major city and trading center. Later, other Mycenaean palaces and cities developed at Thebes, Athens, Tiryns, and Pylos. As in Crete, the political unit was the kingdom. The king and his warrior aristocracy stood at the top of society. The seat and symbol of the king's power and wealth was his palace, which was also the economic center of the kingdom. Palace scribes kept records in Greek with a script (now known as Linear B) that was derived from Minoan Linear A. The scribes kept account of taxes and drew up inventories of the king's possessions. Little is known of the king's subjects except that they were the artisans, traders, and farmers of Mycenaean society. The Mycenaean economy was marked by an extensive division of labor, tightly controlled from the palace. At the bottom of the social scale were the slaves, who were normally owned by the king and aristocrats but who also worked for ordinary craftsmen.

Contacts between the Minoans and Mycenaeans were originally peaceful, and Minoan culture flooded the Greek mainland. But around 1450 B.C. the Mycenaeans attacked Crete, destroying many Minoan palaces and taking possession of the grand palace at Cnossus. For about the next fifty years the Mycenaeans ruled much of the island until a further wave of violence left Cnossus in ashes. These events are more disputed than understood. Archaeologists cannot determine whether the Mycenaeans at Cnossus were attacked by other Mycenaeans or whether the conquered Minoans rose in revolt.

Whatever the answer, the Mycenaean kingdoms and their culture in Greece benefited from the fall of Cnossus and the collapse of its trade. Mycenaean commerce quickly expanded throughout the Aegean, reaching as far abroad as Anatolia, Cyprus, and Egypt. Prosperity, however, did not bring peace, and between 1300 and 1000 B.C. kingdom after kingdom suffered attack and destruction.

Later Greeks accused the Dorians, who spoke a particular dialect of Greek, of overthrowing the Mycenaean kingdoms. Yet some modern linguists argue that the Dorians dwelt in Greece during the Mycenaean period. Archaeologists generally conclude that the Dorians, if not already present, could have entered Greece only long after the era of destruction. In fact, the legends preserved by later Greeks told of grim wars between Mycenaean kingdoms and of the fall of great royal families. Apparently Mycenaean Greece destroyed itself in a long series of internecine wars, a pattern that later Greeks would repeat.

The fall of the Mycenaean kingdoms ushered in a period of such poverty, disruption, and backwardness that historians usually call it the Dark Age of Greece (ca 1100–800 B.C.). Even literacy, which was not widespread in any case, was a casualty of the chaos. Yet this period was a time of widespread movements of Greek-speaking peoples. Some Greeks sailed to Crete, where they established new communities. A great wave of Greeks spread eastward through the Aegean to the coast of Asia Minor. These immigrations turned the Aegean into a Greek lake. The people who stayed behind gradually rebuilt Greek society. They thus provided an element of continuity, a link between the Mycenaean period and the Greek culture that emerged from the Dark Age.

❖ HOMER, HESIOD, AND THE HEROIC PAST (1100–800 B.C.)

The Greeks, unlike the Hebrews, had no sacred book that chronicled their past. Instead they had the *Iliad* and the *Odyssey* to describe a time when gods still walked the earth. And they learned the origin and descent of the gods from the *Theogony*, an epic poem by Hesiod (ca 700 B.C.). Instead of authentic history the poems of Homer and Hesiod offered the Greeks an ideal past, a largely legendary Heroic Age. These poems contains scraps of information about the Bronze Age, much about the early Dark Age, and some about the poets' own era. Chronologically, the Heroic Age falls mainly in the period between the collapse of the Mycenaean world and the rebirth of literacy.

The *Iliad* recounts an expedition of Mycenaeans, whom Homer called "Achaeans," to besiege the city of Troy in Asia Minor. The heart of the *Iliad,* however, concerns the quarrel between Agamemnon, the king of Mycenae, and Achilles, the tragic hero of the poem, and how their anger and pride brought suffering to the Achaeans. The *Odyssey,* probably composed later than the *Iliad,* narrates the adventures of Odysseus, one of the Achaean heroes who fought at Troy, during his voyage home from the fighting.

The splendor of these poems does not lie in their plots, although the *Odyssey* is a marvelous adventure story. Rather, both poems portray engaging but often flawed characters who are larger than life and yet typically human. Homer was also strikingly successful in depicting the great gods, who generally sit on Mount Olympus and watch the fighting at Troy like spectators at a baseball game, although they sometimes participate in the action. Homer's deities are reminiscent of Mesopotamian gods and goddesses. Hardly a decorous lot, the Olympians are raucous, petty, deceitful, and splendid. In short, they are human.

Homer at times portrayed the gods in a serious vein, but he never treated them in a systematic fashion, as did Hesiod, who lived somewhat later than Homer. Hesiod's epic poem, the *Theogony,* traces the descent of Zeus. Hesiod was influenced by Mesopotamian myths, which the Hittites had adopted and spread to the Aegean. Like the Hebrews, however, Hesiod envisaged his cosmogony—his account of the way the universe developed—in moral terms. Cronus, the son of Earth and Heaven, like the Mesopotamian Enlil, separated the two and became king of the gods. Zeus, the son of Cronus, defeated his evil father and took his place as king of the gods. He then sired Lawfulness, Right, Peace, and other powers of light and beauty. Thus, in Hesiod's conception, Zeus was the god of righteousness, who loved justice and hated wrongdoing.

In another epic poem, *Works and Days,* Hesiod wrote of his own time and his own village of Ascra in Boeotia, a scenic place set between beautiful mountains and fertile plains. In his will, Hesiod's father had divided his lands between Hesiod and his brother, Perses. Perses bribed the aristocratic authorities to give him the larger part of the inheritance and then squandered his wealth. Undaunted by the injustice of the powerful, Hesiod thundered back:

Bribe-devouring lords, make straight your decisions,
Forget entirely crooked judgments.
He who causes evil to another harms himself.
Evil designs are most evil to the plotter.[2]

Hesiod did not receive justice from the political authorities of the day, but he fully expected divine vindication. Hesiod spoke of Zeus as Jeremiah had spoken of Yahweh, warning that Zeus would see that justice was done and injustice punished. He cautioned his readers that Zeus was angered by those who committed adultery, harmed orphans, and offended the aged.

THE POLIS

After the upheavals that ended the Mycenaean period and the slow recovery of prosperity during the Dark Age, the Greeks developed their basic political and institutional unit, the *polis,* or city-state. Only three city-states were able to muster the resources of an entire region behind them (see Map 5.1): Sparta, which dominated the regions of Laconia and Messenia; Athens, which united the large peninsula of Attica under its rule; and Thebes, which in several periods marshaled the resources of the fertile region of Boeotia. Otherwise, the political pattern of ancient Greece was one of many small city-states, few of which were much stronger or richer than their neighbors.

Physically the term *polis* designated a city or town and its surrounding countryside. The people of a typical polis lived in a compact group of houses within a city. The city's water supply came from public fountains and cisterns. By the fifth century B.C. the city was generally surrounded by a wall. The city contained a point, usually elevated, called the *acropolis,* and a public square or marketplace, the *agora.* On the acropolis, which in the early period was a place of refuge, stood the temples, altars, public monuments, and various dedications to the gods of the polis. The agora was originally the place where the warrior assembly met,

✤ **The Polis of Argos** This view, taken from the east of modern Argos, remarkably illustrates the structure of an ancient polis. Atop the hill in the background are the remains of the ancient acropolis. At its foot to the right are foundations of ancient public and private buildings. In the foreground are modern houses, situated where ancient homes were located. *(Source: John Buckler)*

but it became the political center of the polis. In the agora were porticoes, shops, and public buildings and courts.

The unsettled territory of the polis—arable land, pastureland, and wasteland—was typically its source of wealth. Farmers left the city each morning to work their fields or tend their flocks of sheep and goats, and they returned at night. On the wasteland men often quarried stone or mined for precious metals. Thus the polis was the scene of both urban and agrarian life.

The size of the polis varied according to geographical circumstances. Population figures for Greece are mostly guesswork, because most city-states were too small to need a census. But regardless of its size or wealth, the polis was fundamental to Greek life. The intimacy of the polis was an important factor. The smallness of the polis enabled Greeks to see how the individual fitted into the

overall system—how the human parts made up the social whole. These simple facts go far to explain why the Greek polis was fundamentally different from the great empires of Persia and China. The Greeks knew their leaders and elected them to limited terms of office. They were unlike the subjects of the Mauryan Empire or the Han Dynasty, who might spend their entire lives without ever seeing their emperors. One result of these factors is the absence in Greek politics of a divine emperor. Another is the lack of an extensive imperial bureaucracy and a standing army. The ancient Greeks were their own magistrates, administrators, and soldiers.

Instead of a standing army, the average polis relied on its own citizens for protection. Very rich citizens often served as cavalry. However, the heavily armed infantry was the backbone of the army. The foot soldiers, or *hoplites,* provided their own

The handwritten graffiti at the top reads "THIS BOOK IS A PAIN IN MY ASS!"

equipment and were basically amateurs. When in battle, they stood in several dense lines, in which cohesion and order became as valuable as courage.

The polis could be governed in any of several ways. In a *monarchy,* a term derived from the Greek for "the rule of one man," a king represented the community, reigning according to law and respecting the rights of the citizens. Or the *aristocracy* could govern the state. Or the running of the polis could be the duty and prerogative of an *oligarchy,* which literally means "the rule of a few"—in this case a small group of wealthy citizens, not necessarily of aristocratic birth. Or the polis could be governed as a *democracy,* through the rule of the people, a concept that in Greece meant that all citizens, regardless of birth or wealth, administered the workings of government. How a polis was governed depended on who had the upper hand. When the wealthy held power, they usually instituted oligarchies; when the people could break the hold of the rich, they established democracies. Still another form of Greek government was *tyranny,* rule by a tyrant, a man who had seized power by extralegal means, generally by using his wealth to gain a political following that could topple the existing government.

Because the bonds that held the polis together were so intimate, Greeks were extremely reluctant to allow foreigners to share fully in its life. An alien, even someone Greek by birth, could almost never expect to be made a citizen. Nor could women play a political role. Women participated in the civic cults and served as priestesses, but the polis had no room for them in state affairs. This exclusiveness doomed the polis to a limited horizon.

Although each polis was jealous of its independence, some Greeks banded together to create leagues of city-states. Here was the birth of Greek federalism, a political system in which several states formed a central government while remaining independent in their internal affairs. United in a league, a confederation of city-states was far stronger than any of the individual members and better able to withstand external attack.

The passionate individualism of the polis proved to be another serious weakness. The citizens of each polis were determined to remain free and autonomous. Rarely were the Greeks willing to unite in larger political bodies. The political result in Greece, as in Sumer, was almost constant warfare.

The polis could dominate, but unlike Rome it could not incorporate.

THE LYRIC AGE (800–500 B.C.)

The maturation of the polis coincided with one of the most vibrant periods of Greek history, an era of extraordinary expansion geographically, artistically, and politically. Greeks ventured as far east as the Black Sea and as far west as Spain (Map 5.2). With the rebirth of literacy, this period also witnessed a tremendous literary flowering as poets broke away from the heroic tradition and wrote about their own lives. Politically these were the years when Sparta and Athens—the two poles of the Greek experience—rose to prominence.

Overseas Expansion

Between 1100 and 800 B.C. the Greeks not only recovered from the breakdown of the Mycenaean world but also grew in wealth and numbers. This new prosperity brought with it new problems. Greece is a small and not especially fertile country. The increase in population meant that many men and their families had very little land or none at all. Land hunger and the resulting social and political tensions drove many Greeks to seek new homes outside Greece.

The Mediterranean offered an escape valve, for the Greeks were always a seafaring people. To them the sea was a highway, not a barrier. Through their commercial ventures they had long been familiar with the rich areas of the western Mediterranean. Moreover, the geography of the Mediterranean basin favored colonization. The land and climate of the Mediterranean region are remarkably uniform. Greeks could travel to new areas, whether to Cyprus in the east or to Malta in the west, and establish the kind of settlement they had known in Greece.

From about 750 to 550 B.C. Greeks from the mainland and from Asia Minor poured onto the coasts of the northern Aegean, the Ionian Sea, and the Black Sea and into North Africa, Sicily, southern Italy, southern France, and Spain (see Map 5.2). Just as the migrations of the Dark Age had

MAP 5.2 Colonization of the Mediterranean Though both the Greeks and the Phoenicians colonized the Mediterranean basin at roughly the same time, the Greeks spread over a far greater area.

turned the Aegean into a Greek lake, this later wave of colonization spread the Greeks and their culture throughout the Mediterranean. Colonization on this scale meant that the prevailing culture of the Mediterranean basin would be Greek, the heritage to which Rome would later fall heir.

Lyric Poets

One man can in many ways stand as the symbol of the vital and robust era of colonization. Archilochus, born on the island of Paros, was himself a colonist. He was also a poet of genius, the first of the lyric poets who left an indelible mark on this age. Unlike the epic poets, who portrayed the deeds of heroes, Archilochus sang of himself. He knew the sea, the dangers of sailing, and the price that the sea often exacted. He spoke of one shipwreck in grim terms and even treated the god of the sea with irony: "Of fifty men gentle Poseidon left one, Koiranos, to be saved from shipwreck."

Together with others from Paros he took part in the colonization of Thasos in the northern Aegean. He described the island in less-than-glowing terms: "Like the spine of an ass it stands, crowned to the brim with a wild forest." His opinion of his fellow colonists was hardly kinder: "So the misery of all Greece came together in Thasos." Yet at Thasos he fell in love with a woman named Neoboule. They did not marry because her father opposed the match. In revenge, Archilochus seduced Neoboule's younger sister, railed at the entire family, and left Thasos to live the life of a mercenary.

His hired lance took him to Euboea, and he left a striking picture of the fighting there:

Not many bows will be strung, nor slings be slung
When Ares begins battle in the plain.
There will be the mournful work of the sword:
For in this kind of battle are the spear-famed
Lords of Euboea experienced.[3]

Archilochus exemplifies the energy, restlessness, self-reliance, and sense of adventure that characterize this epoch. People like Archilochus broke old familiar ties, faced homelessness and danger and built new homes for themselves. They made the Mediterranean Greek.

Individualism set a new tone in Greek literature. For the first time in Western civilization, men and women began to write of their own experiences. Their poetry reflected their belief that they had something precious to say about themselves. To them poetry did not belong only to the gods or to the great heroes on the plain of Troy. One of the most unforgettable of these writers is the poet Sappho.

Unlike Archilochus, Sappho neither braved the wilds nor pushed into the unknown, yet she was no less individual than he. Sappho was born in the seventh century B.C. on the island of Lesbos. Her marriage produced a daughter, to whom she wrote some of her poems. Sappho's poetry is personal and intense. She delighted in her surroundings, which were those of aristocratic women, and she celebrated the little things around her. Hers was a world of natural beauty, sacred groves, religious festivals, wedding celebrations, and noble companions. Sappho fondly remembered walks with a woman friend:

There was neither a hill nor a sanctuary
Nor a stream of running water
Which we failed to visit;
Nor when spring began any grove
Filled with the noise of nightingales.[4]

Sappho is best known for erotic poetry, for she expressed her love frankly and without same. She was bisexual, and much of her poetry dealt with her homosexual love affairs. In one of her poems she remembered the words of her lover:

Greek Influence Abroad   This gold comb is a remarkable combination of Greek and Eastern details. The art is almost purely Greek. The mounted horseman is clothed with largely Greek armor, but he attacks an Eastern enemy. The horseman's companion is also Eastern. This splendid piece testifies to the exchange of artistic motifs and styles in the eastern Mediterranean basin. *(Source: Hermitage, Leningrad)*

❈ **Mosaic Portrait of Sappho**   The Greek letters in the upper left corner identify this idealized portrait as that of Sappho. The mosaic, which was found at Sparta, dates to the late Roman Empire and testifies to Sappho's popularity in antiquity. (*Source: Caroline Buckler*)

Sappho, if you don't come out,
Surely I will no longer love you.
O come to us and free your lovely
Strength from your bed.
Lifting off your Chian robe,
Bathe in the waters like a
Pure lily beside a spring.[5]

In antiquity Sappho's name became linked with female homosexual love. Today the English word *lesbian* is derived from Sappho's island home. The Greeks accepted bisexuality—that men and women could enjoy both homosexual and heterosexual lovemaking. Homosexual relationships normally carried no social stigma.

In their poetry Archilochus and Sappho reveal two sides of Greek life in this period. Archilochus exemplifies the energy and adventure of the age; Sappho expresses the intensely personal side of life. The link connecting the two poets is their individualism, their faith in themselves, and their desire to reach out to other men and women in order to share their experiences, thoughts, and wisdom.

The Growth of Sparta

During the Lyric Age the Spartans expanded the boundaries of their polis and made it the leading power in Greece. Like other Greeks, the Spartans faced the problems of overpopulation and land hunger. Unlike other Greeks, the Spartans solved these problems by conquest, not by colonization. To gain more land, the Spartans set out in about 735 B.C. to conquer Messenia, a rich, fertile region in the southwestern Peloponnesus. This conflict, the First Messenian War, lasted for twenty years and ended in a Spartan triumph. The Spartans appropriated Messenian land and turned the Messenians into *helots,* or state serfs.

In about 650 B.C., Spartan exploitation and oppression of the Messenian helots led to a helot revolt so massive and stubborn that it became known as the Second Messenian War. The Spartan poet Tyrtaeus, a contemporary of these events, vividly portrayed the ferocity of the fighting:

For it is a shameful thing indeed
When with the foremost fighters
An elder falling in front of the young men
Lies outstretched,
Having white hair and grey beard,
Breathing forth his stout soul in the dust,
Holding in his hands his genitals
stained with blood.[6]

Confronted with such horrors, Spartan enthusiasm for the war waned. Finally, after some thirty years of fighting, the Spartans put down the revolt. Nevertheless, the political and social strain it caused led to a transformation of the Spartan polis. After the victory the non-nobles, who had done much of the fighting, demanded rights equal to those of the nobility. Their agitation disrupted society until the aristocrats agreed to remodel the state.

Although the Spartans later claimed that the changes brought about by this compromise were the work of Lycurgus, a legendary, semidivine lawgiver, they were really the work of the entire Spartan people. The Lycurgan regimen, as these reforms were called, established an oligarchy of citizens who were all considered legally equal. Sparta was ruled by two kings, assisted by a council of twenty-eight nobles. The civil executive power was in the hands of five *ephors,* overseers elected from and by all the people.

The Hoplite Phalanx When the Greeks adopted heavy armor, weapons, and shields, their lack of mobility forced them to fight in several dense lines, each behind the other. To help the hoplites maintain their pace during the attack, a flute player here plays a marching tune. *(Source: Villa Giulia Museum/Scala/Art Resource, NY)*

To provide for their economic needs, the Spartans divided the land of Messenia among all citizens. Helots worked the land, raised the crops, provided the Spartans with their living, and occasionally served in the army. The Spartans kept the helots in line with systematic terrorism, hoping to beat them down and keep them quiet. Spartan citizens were supposed to devote their time exclusively to military training.

In the Lycurgan system every citizen owed primary allegiance to Sparta. Suppression of the individual together with emphasis on military prowess led to a barracks state. Family life itself was sacrificed to the polis. Once Spartan boys reached the age of twelve, they were enrolled in separate companies with other boys of their age. They slept outdoors on reed mats and underwent rugged physical and military training until age twenty-four, when they became front-line soldiers. For the rest of their lives, Spartan men kept themselves prepared for combat, and the older men were expected to be models of endurance, frugality, and sturdiness to the younger men. In battle Spartans were supposed to stand and die rather than retreat. An anecdote about one Spartan mother sums up Spartan military values. As her son was setting off to battle, the mother handed him his shield and advised him to come back either victorious, carrying the shield, or dead, being carried on it.

Similar rigorous requirements applied to Spartan women, who may have been unique in all of Greek society. They were prohibited from wearing jewelry or ornate clothes. They exercised strenuously in the belief that hard physical training promoted the birth of healthy children. Yet they were hardly oppressed. They enjoyed a more active and open public life than most other Greek women, even though they could neither vote nor hold office.

They were far more emancipated than many other Greek women, in part because Spartan society felt that mothers and wives had to be as hardy as their sons and husbands. Sparta was not a place for weaklings, male or female. Spartan women saw it as their privilege to be the wives and mothers of victorious warriors, and on several occasions their own courage became legendary. They had a reputation for independent spirit and self-assertion. Their position stemmed from their genuine patriotism, but also from their title to much Spartan land. For all of these reasons, they shared with Spartan men a footing that most other Greek women lacked in their own societies.

In addition to emphasizing military values for both sexes, the Lycurgan regimen had another purpose as well: it served to instill in society the civic virtues of dedication to the state and a code of moral conduct. These aspects of the Spartan system were generally admired throughout the Greek world.

The Evolution of Athens

Like Sparta, Athens faced pressing social and economic problems during the Lyric Age, but the Athenian response was far different from that of the Spartans. Instead of creating an oligarchy, the Athenians extended to all citizens the right and duty of governing the polis. Indeed, the Athenian democracy was one of the most thoroughgoing in Greece.

In 621 B.C. Draco, an Athenian aristocrat, published the first law code of the Athenian polis. Although his code was thought harsh, it embodied the idea that the law belonged to the citizens. Nevertheless, by the early sixth century B.C. social and economic conditions had led to an explosive situation. The aristocracy governed Athens oppressively. The aristocrats owned the best land, met in an assembly to govern the polis, and interpreted the law. Noble landowners were forcing small farmers into economic dependence. Many families, unable to repay loans from their wealthy neighbors, were sold into slavery; others were exiled and their land was pledged to the rich.

In many other city-states conditions like those in Athens led to the rise of tyrants. One person who recognized these problems clearly was Solon, an aristocrat and poet and a man opposed to tyrants.

He was also the one man in Athens who enjoyed the respect of both aristocrats and peasants. Like Hesiod, Solon used his poetry to condemn the aristocrats for their greed and dishonesty. He recited his poems in the Athenian agora, where everyone could hear his relentless call for justice and fairness. Around 594 B.C. the nobles elected him *archon,* chief magistrate of the Athenian polis, and gave him extraordinary power to reform the state.

Solon immediately freed all people enslaved for debt, recalled all exiles, canceled all debts on land, and made enslavement for debt illegal. He also divided society into four legal groups on the basis of wealth. In the most influential group were the wealthiest citizens, but even the poorest and least powerful group enjoyed certain rights. Solon allowed them into the old aristocratic assembly, where they could take part in the election of magistrates. His work done, Solon insisted that all swear to uphold his reforms. Then, because many were clamoring for him to become tyrant, he left Athens.

Solon's reforms solved some immediate problems but did not bring peace to Athens. Some aristocrats attempted to make themselves tyrants, while others banded together to oppose them. In 546 B.C. Pisistratus, an exiled aristocrat, returned to Athens, defeated his opponents, and became tyrant. Pisistratus reduced the power of the aristocracy while supporting the common people. Under his rule Athens prospered, and his building program began to transform the city into one of the splendors of Greece.

Athenian acceptance of tyranny did not long outlive Pisistratus, for his son Hippias ruled harshly, committing excesses that led to his overthrow. After a brief period of turmoil between factions of the nobility, Cleisthenes, a wealthy and prominent aristocrat, emerged triumphant in 508 B.C., largely because he won the support of the people. Cleisthenes created the Athenian democracy with the full knowledge and approval of the Athenian people. He reorganized the state completely but presented every innovation to the assembly for discussion and ratification. All Athenian citizens had a voice in Cleisthenes' work.

Cleisthenes created the *deme,* a local unit, to serve as the basis of his political system. Citizenship was tightly linked to the deme, for each deme kept the roll of those within its jurisdiction who were admitted to citizenship. Cleisthenes grouped all the demes into ten tribes, which thus formed the link between the demes and the central government. The central government included an assembly of all citizens and a new council of five hundred members.

The democracy functioned on the idea that all full citizens, the *demos,* were sovereign. Yet not all citizens could take time from work to participate in government. Therefore, they delegated their power to other citizens by creating various offices to run the democracy. The most prestigious of them was the board of ten archons, who were charged with handling legal and military matters. Legislation was in the hands of two bodies, the *boule,* or council, composed of five hundred members, and the *ecclesia,* the assembly of all citizens. The boule was perhaps the major institution of the democracy. By supervising the various committees of government and proposing bills to the assembly, it guided Athenian political life and held the democracy together. The ecclesia, however, had the final word. Open to all male citizens over eighteen years of age, this assembly could accept, amend, or reject bills put before it. Every member could express his opinion on any subject on the agenda. A simple majority vote was needed to pass or reject a bill.

Athenian democracy was to prove an inspiring model. It demonstrated that a large group of people, not just a few, could efficiently run the affairs of state. By heeding the opinions, suggestions, and wisdom of all its citizens, the polis enjoyed the maximum amount of good counsel. Athenian democracy, however, must not be thought of in modern terms. In Athens democracy was a form of government in which in theory poor men as well as rich enjoyed political power and responsibility. In practice, though, most important offices were held by aristocrats. Furthermore, Athenian democracy denied political rights to many people, including women and slaves. Unlike modern democracies, Athenian democracy did not mean that citizens would vote for others who would then run the state. Instead, every citizen was expected to be able to perform the duties of most magistrates. In Athens citizens voted and served. The people were the government. It is this union of the individual and the state—the view that the state exists for the

good of the citizen, whose duty it is to serve it well—that has made Athenian democracy so compelling a model.

✦ THE CLASSICAL PERIOD (500–338 B.C.)

In the years from 500 to 338 B.C. Greek civilization reached its highest peak in politics, thought, and art. In this period the Greeks beat back the armies of the Persian Empire. Then, turning their spears against one another, they destroyed their own political system in a century of warfare. Some thoughtful Greeks felt prompted to record and analyze these momentous events; the result was the creation of history. This era also saw the flowering of philosophy, as Greek thinkers began to ponder the nature and meaning of the universe and human experience. The Greeks also invented drama, and Greek architects reached the zenith of their art. Because Greek intellectual and artistic efforts attained their fullest and finest expression in these years, this age is called the Classical period.

The Deadly Conflicts (499–404 B.C.)

One of the hallmarks of the Classical period was warfare. In 499 B.C. the Greeks of Asia Minor, with the feeble help of Athens, rebelled against the Persian Empire. In 490 B.C. the Persians struck back at Athens but were beaten off at the Battle of Marathon, a small plain in Attica (Map 5.3). In 480 B.C. the Persian king Xerxes retaliated with a mighty invasion force. Facing this emergency, many of the Greeks united to resist the invaders. The Spartans provided the overall leadership and commanded the Greek armies. The Athenians, led by the wily Themistocles, provided the heart of the naval forces.

The first confrontations between the Persians and the Greeks occurred at the pass of Thermopylae and in the waters off Artemisium, the northern tip of Euboea. At Thermopylae the Greek hoplites showed their mettle. Before the fighting began, a report came in that when the Persian archers shot their bows the arrows darkened the sky. One gruff Spartan replied merely, "Fine, then we'll fight in the shade." The Greeks at Thermopylae fought heroically, but the Persians took the position. In

MAP 5.3 The Peloponnesian War   This map shows the alignment of states during the Peloponnesian War and vividly illustrates the large scale of the war and its divisive impact.

480 B.C. the Greek fleet met the Persian armada at Salamis, an island just west of Athens. Though outnumbered by the Persians, the Greek navy won an overwhelming victory (see Listening to the Past). The remnants of the Persian fleet retired, and with them went all hope of Persian victory. In the following year, a coalition of Greek forces smashed the last Persian army at Plataea, a small polis in Boeotia. The Greeks remained free to develop their particular genius. These decisive victories meant that Greek political forms and intellectual concepts would be the heritage of the West.

In 478 B.C. the Athenians and their allies formed the Delian League, a grand naval alliance aimed at liberating Ionia from Persian rule. The Delian League was intended as a free alliance under the leadership of Athens. Athenians provided most of the warships and crews and determined how many ships or how much money each member of the league should contribute to the allied effort.

The Athenians, supported by the Delian League, carried the war against Persia. But Athenian success had a sinister side. While the Athenians drove the Persians out of the Aegean, they also became increasingly imperialistic, even to the point of turning the Delian League into an Athenian empire. Athens began reducing its allies to the status of subjects. Tribute was often collected by force, and the Athenians placed the economic resources of the Delian League under tighter and tighter control.

The expansion of Athenian power and the aggressiveness of Athenian rule alarmed Sparta and its allies. While relations between Athens and Sparta cooled, Pericles (ca 494–429 B.C.) became the leading statesman in Athens. Like the democracy he led, Pericles, an aristocrat of solid intellectual ability, was aggressive and imperialistic. At last, in 459 B.C., Sparta and Athens went to war over conflicts between Athens and some of Sparta's allies. The war ended in 445 B.C. with no serious damage to either side and nothing settled. But this war divided the Greek world between the two great powers.

During the 440s and 430s, Athens continued its severe policies toward its subject allies and came into conflict with Corinth, one of Sparta's leading supporters (see Map 5.3). In response the Spartans convened a meeting of their allies, whose complaints of Athenian aggression ended with a demand that Athens be stopped. Reluctantly the Spartans agreed to declare war. The real reason for war, according to the Athenian historian Thucydides, was very simple: "The truest explanation, though the one least mentioned, was the great growth of Athenian power and the fear it caused the Lacedaemonians [Spartans], which drove them to war."[7]

At the outbreak of this, the Peloponnesian War, a Spartan ambassador warned the Athenians: "This day will be the beginning of great evils for the Greeks." Few have ever spoken more prophetically. The Peloponnesian War lasted a generation (431–404 B.C.) and brought in its wake fearful plagues, famine, civil wars, widespread destruction, and huge loss of life. Thucydides described its cataclysmic effects:

For never had so many cities been captured and destroyed, whether by the barbarians or by the Greeks who were fighting each other. . . . Never had so many men been exiled or slaughtered, whether in the war or because of civil conflicts.[8]

As the war dragged on, older leaders like Pericles died and were replaced by men of the war generation. In Athens the most prominent of this new breed of politicians was Alcibiades (ca 450–404 B.C.), an aristocrat, a kinsman of Pericles, and a student of the philosopher Socrates (see page 140). Brilliant, handsome, charming, and popular with the people, Alcibiades was also self-seeking

The Persian Wars This vase dates to the early fifth century B.C. It depicts fighting between a heavily armed Greek hoplite on the left, carrying a shield and spear, and an Asian soldier who is less heavily armed. *(Source: The Metropolitan Museum of Art, Rogers Fund, 1906 [06.1021.117])*

FRIEZE
COFFERS
TYMPANUM

PEDIMENT
CYMATION
CORNICE
MUTULES
TRIGLYPHS
METOPES
GUTTAE
ARCHITRAVE
ABACUS
ECHINUS

STYLOBATE

Sectional View of the Parthenon This figure both indicates what the Parthenon looked like in antiquity and explains the complex nature of Greek temple building. The Parthenon's apparently simple façade is a work of great architectural sophistication. *(Source:* Guide to Sculptures of the Parthenon, *a British Museum publication)*

and egotistical and a shameless opportunist. His first thoughts were always for himself.

Alcibiades' schemes helped bring Athens down to defeat. Having planned an invasion of Sicily that ended in disaster, he deserted to the Spartans and plotted with the Persians, who had sided with Sparta, against his homeland. In the end, all of Alcibiades' intrigues failed. The Spartans defeated the Athenian fleet in the Aegean and blockaded Athens by land and sea. Finally, in 404 B.C. the Athenians surrendered and watched helplessly while the Spartans and their allies destroyed the walls of Athens to the music of flute girls. The

Peloponnesian War, which lasted twenty-seven years, dealt Greek civilization a serious blow.

The Birth of Historical Awareness

One positive development grew out of the Persian and Peloponnesian wars: the beginnings of historical writing. In his book *The Histories,* Herodotus (ca 485–425 B.C.), known as the father of history, chronicled the rise of the Persian Empire, sketched the background of Athens and Sparta, and described the land and customs of the Egyptians and the Scythians, who lived in the region of the mod-

❄ **The Athenian Acropolis**   This painting, though made in the nineteenth century, gives a vivid impression of what the buildings and their entire setting looked like in antiquity. It demonstrates the artistic appeal of these buildings and proves what Plutarch wrote of them: "Each of them is always in bloom, maintaining its appearance as though untouched by time, as though an ever-green breath and undecaying spirit had been mixed in its construction." *(Source: Neue Pinakothek, Munich)*

ern Crimea. The sheer scope of this work is awesome. Perhaps Herodotus's most striking characteristic was his curiosity. He diligently questioned everyone who could tell him anything about the Persian wars. The confrontation between East and West unfolds relentlessly in *The Histories*.

The outbreak of the Peloponnesian War prompted Thucydides (ca 460–ca 400 B.C.) to write an account of its course in the belief that it would be the greatest war in Greek history. An Athenian politician and general, Thucydides saw action in the war until he was exiled for a defeat. Exile gave him the time and opportunity to question eyewitnesses about the details of events and to visit battlefields.

Thucydides was intensely interested in human nature and how it manifested itself during the war. When a terrible plague struck Athens in 430 B.C., Thucydides described in the same clinical terms both the symptoms of the plague and the reactions of the Athenians. He portrayed the virtual breakdown of a society beset by war, disease, desperation, and despair.

Athenian Arts in the Age of Pericles

In the last half of the fifth century B.C., Pericles turned Athens into the showplace of Greece. He appropriated Delian League funds to pay for a huge building program, planning temples and other buildings to honor Athena, the patron goddess of the city, and to display to all Greeks the glory of the Athenian polis. Thus began the undertaking that turned the Acropolis into a monument for all time. Construction of the Parthenon began in 447 B.C., followed by the Propylaea, the temple of Athena Nike (Athena the Victorious), and the Erechtheum. Even today in their ruined state they still evoke awe.

The planning of the architects and the skill of the workmen who erected these buildings were very sophisticated. Visitors approaching the Acropolis first saw the Propylaea, the ceremonial gateway, a building of complicated layout and grand design whose Doric columns seemed to hold up the sky. On the right was the small temple of Athena Nike, built to commemorate the victory over the Persians. The Ionic frieze above its columns depicted the struggle between the Greeks and the Persians, a tribute to Athenian and Greek valor—and a reminder of Athens's part in the victory. To the left of the visitors, as they passed through the Propylaea, stood the Erechtheum, an Ionic temple that housed several ancient shrines. On its southern side was the famous Portico of the Caryatids, a porch whose roof was supported by statues of Athenian maidens.

As visitors walked on, they obtained a full view of the Parthenon, the chief monument to Athena and her city. The sculptures that adorned the temple portrayed the greatness of Athens and its goddess. The figures on the eastern pediment depicted Athena's birth, those on the west the victory of Athena over the god Poseidon in their struggle for the possession of Attica. Inside the Parthenon stood a huge statue of Athena, the masterpiece of the great sculptor, Phidias.

In many ways the Athenian Acropolis is the epitome of Greek art and its spirit. Although the buildings were dedicated to the gods and most of the sculptures portrayed gods, these works nonetheless express the Greek fascination with the human and the rational. Greek deities were anthropomorphic, and Greek artists portrayed them as human beings. The Acropolis also exhibits the rational side of Greek art. Greek artists portrayed action in a balanced, restrained, and sometimes even serene fashion, capturing the noblest aspects of human beings: their reason, dignity, and promise.

Other aspects of Athenian cultural life were as rooted in the life of the polis as were the architecture and sculpture of the Acropolis. The development of drama was tied to the religious festivals of the city. The polis sponsored the production of plays and required that wealthy citizens pay the expenses of their production. At the beginning of the year, dramatists submitted their plays to the archon. He chose those he considered best and assigned a theatrical troupe to each playwright. Many plays were highly controversial, but the archons neither suppressed nor censored them.

The Athenian dramatists were the first artists in European society to examine such basic questions as the rights of the individual, the demands of society on the individual, and the nature of good and evil. The dramatists used their art to portray, understand, and resolve life's basic conflicts.

Aeschylus (525–456 B.C.), the first of the great Athenian dramatists, was also the first to express the agony of the individual caught in conflict. In his trilogy of plays, *The Oresteia,* Aeschylus deals with the themes of betrayal, murder, and reconciliation, urging that reason and justice be applied to reconcile fundamental conflicts. The final play concludes with a prayer that civil dissension never be allowed to destroy the city and that the life of the city be one of harmony and grace.

Sophocles (496–406 B.C.) also dealt with matters personal and political. In *Antigone* he expressed the precedence of divine law over human defects and touched on the need for recognition of the law and adherence to it as a prerequisite for a tranquil state.

Sophocles' masterpieces have inspired generations of playwrights. Perhaps his most famous plays are *Oedipus the King* and its sequel, *Oedipus at Colonus. Oedipus the King* is the ironic story of a man doomed by the gods to kill his father and marry his mother. Try as he might to avoid his fate, Oedipus's every action brings him closer to its fulfillment. When at last he realizes that he has carried out the decree of the gods, Oedipus blinds himself and flees into exile. In *Oedipus at Colonus* Sophocles dramatizes the last days of the broken king, whose patient suffering and uncomplaining piety win him an exalted position. In the end the gods honor him for his virtue. The interpretation of these two plays has been hotly debated, but Sophocles seems to be saying that human beings should obey the will of the gods, even without fully understanding it, for the gods stand for justice and order.

Euripides (ca 480–406 B.C.), the last of the three great Greek tragic dramatists, also explored the theme of personal conflict within the polis and sounded the depths of the individual. With Euripides drama entered a new, in many ways more personal, phase. To him the gods were far less important than human beings. The essence of Euripides' tragedy is the flawed character—men and women who bring disaster on themselves and their loved ones because their passions overwhelm reason. Although Euripides' plays were less popular in his lifetime than were those of Aeschylus and Sophocles, Euripides was a dramatist of genius whose work later had a significant impact on Roman drama.

Writers of comedy treated the affairs of the polis bawdily and often coarsely. Even so, their plays, too, were performed at religious festivals. The comic playwrights dealt primarily with the political affairs of the polis and the conduct of its leading politicians. Best known are the comedies of Aristophanes (ca 445–386 B.C.), an ardent lover of his city and a merciless critic of cranks and quacks. He lampooned eminent generals, at times depicting them as morons. He commented snidely on Pericles, poked fun at Socrates, and hooted at Euripides. Like Aeschylus, Sophocles, and Euripides, Aristophanes used his art to dramatize his ideas on the right conduct of the citizen and the value of the polis.

Perhaps never were art and political life so intimately and congenially bound together as at Athens. Athenian art was the product of deep and

"Procession of the Horsemen" from the Parthenon Frieze The great temple of Athena on the Acropolis, the Parthenon, was decorated by a band of sculpture depicting the religious procession to celebrate the festival of the payathena. Artists took their subjects from the actual procession. Here an Athenian artist has caught the young riders trying to restrain their unruly horses. The entire frieze blends idealism and realism in its depiction of human activity. *(Source: Courtesy of the Trustees of the British Museum)*

genuine love of the polis. It aimed at bettering the lives of the citizens and the quality of life in the state.

Daily Life in Periclean Athens

In sharp contrast with the rich intellectual and cultural life of Periclean Athens stands the simplicity of its material life. The Athenians—and in this respect they were typical of Greeks in general—lived very happily with comparatively few material possessions. In the first place, there were very few material goods to own. The thousands of machines, tools, and gadgets considered essential for modern life had no counterparts in Athenian life. The inventory of Alcibiades' goods, which the Athenians confiscated after his desertion, is enlightening. His household possessions consisted of chests, beds, couches, tables, screens, stools, baskets, and mats. Other common items of the Greek home included pottery, metal utensils for cooking, tools, luxury goods such as jewelry, and a few other things.

Like its furnishings, the Athenian house was rather simple. Whether large or small, the typical house consisted of a series of rooms built around a central courtyard, with doors opening onto the courtyard. Many houses had bedrooms on an upper floor. Artisans and craftsmen often set aside a room to use as a shop or work area. The two principal rooms were the men's dining room and the room where the women worked wool. Other rooms included the kitchen and bathroom.

In the courtyard were the well, a small altar, and a washbasin. If the family lived in the country, the stalls of the animals faced the courtyard. Even in the city, chickens and perhaps a goat or two roamed the courtyard together with dogs and cats.

Cooking, done over a hearth in the house, provided welcome warmth in the winter. Baking and roasting were done in ovens. Food consisted primarily of various grains, especially wheat and barley, as well as lentils, olives, figs, and grapes. Garlic and onion were popular garnishes, and wine was always on hand. These foods were stored at home in large jars; with them the Greek family sometimes ate fish, chicken, and vegetables. Women ground wheat into flour, baked it into bread, and on special occasions made honey or sesame cakes. The Greeks used olive oil for cooking, as families

still do in modern Greece; they also used it as an unguent and as lamp fuel.

On special occasions, such as important religious festivals, a Greek family ate the animal sacrificed to the god and gave the god the exquisite delicacy of the thighbone wrapped in fat. A successful hunt for rabbits, deer, or wild boar could supplement the family's regular diet. The only Greeks who consistently ate meat were the Spartan warriors. They received a small portion of meat each day, together with the infamous Spartan black broth, a ghastly concoction of pork cooked in blood, vinegar, and salt. One Greek, after tasting the broth, commented that he could easily understand why the Spartans were so willing to die.

In the city a man might support himself as a craftsman—a potter, bronzesmith, sailmaker, or tanner—or he could contract with the polis to work on public buildings, such as the Parthenon and Erechtheum. Men without skills worked as paid laborers but competed with slaves for work. Slaves—usually foreigners, barbarian as well as Greek—were paid the same amount for their employment as were free men.

Slavery was commonplace in Greece, as it was throughout the rest of the ancient world. In its essentials Greek slavery resembled Mesopotamian slavery. Slaves received some protection under the law. Masters could mistreat or neglect their slaves, though killing them was illegal. In addition to doing skilled and unskilled labor, slaves served as domestics and performed light work around the house. Nurses for children, teachers of reading and writing, and guardians for young men were often slaves. The lives of these slaves were much like those of their owners.

The importance of slavery in Athens must not be exaggerated. Athenians did not own huge gangs of slaves as did Roman owners of large estates. Slave labor competed with free labor and kept wages down, but it never replaced the free labor that was the mainstay of the Athenian economy.

Most Athenians supported themselves by agriculture, but on most of the land it was difficult to reap a good crop from the soil. Many people must have consumed nearly everything they raised. Attic farmers were free and, though hardly prosperous, were by no means destitute. They could usually expect yields of five bushels of wheat and ten of barley per acre for every bushel of grain sown. A bad harvest meant a lean year. In many places farmers grew more barley than wheat because of the nature of the soil. Wherever possible, farmers also cultivated grape vines and olive trees.

The social condition of Athenian women has been the subject of much debate and little agreement. One of the difficulties is the fragmentary nature of the evidence. Most Greek historians of the time recounted primarily the political, diplomatic, and military events of the day, events in which women seldom played a notable part. Yet that does not mean that women were totally invisible in the life of the polis. Although women lacked official power, they played a vital role in shaping the society in which they lived. The same situation had existed in Hammurabi's Babylonia, and it would recur in the Hellenistic period.

The status of a free woman of the citizen class was strictly protected by law. Only her children, not those of foreigners or slaves, could be citizens. Only she was in charge of the household and the family's possessions. Yet the law protected her primarily to protect her husband's interests. Raping a free woman was a lesser crime than seducing her, because seduction involved the winning of her affections. This law was not concerned with the husband's feelings but with ensuring that he need not doubt the legitimacy of his children.

Women in Athens and elsewhere in Greece received a certain amount of social and legal protection from their dowries. Upon marriage, the bride's father gave the couple a gift of land or money, which the husband administered. However, the gift was never really his; and in the rare cases of divorce, it returned to the wife's domain. The same is often true in Greece today among the upper class.

Athenian women seem to have enjoyed a social circle of other women of their own class. They also attended public festivals, sacrifices, and funerals. Nonetheless, prosperous and respectable women probably spent much of their time in the house. A white complexion—a sign that a woman did not have to work in the fields—was valued highly.

Courtesans lived the freest lives of all Athenian women. Although some courtesans were simply prostitutes, others added intellectual accomplishments to physical beauty. In constant demand, cultured courtesans moved freely in male society. The most famous was Aspasia, mistress of Pericles and

Women Working   The scene on this vase represents the women of the household at work. It shows how they produced woolen cloth, from the spinning of yarn to the completion of the cloth itself, here held by two women. *(Source: The Metropolitan Museum of Art, Fletcher Fund, 1931)*

supposedly a friend of Socrates. Under Pericles' roof, she participated in intellectual discussions equally with some of the most stimulating thinkers of the day. Yet her position, like that of most other courtesans, was precarious. After Pericles' death, Aspasia fended for herself, ending her days as the madam of a house of prostitution.

A woman's main functions were to raise the children, oversee the domestic slaves and hired labor, and together with her maids work wool into cloth. The woman of the household either did the cooking herself or directed her maids. In a sense, poor women lived freer lives than did wealthier women. They performed manual labor in the fields or sold goods in the agora, going about their affairs much as men did.

A distinctive feature of Athenian life and of Greek life in general was the belief that both homosexual and heterosexual practices were normal parts of life. No one has satisfactorily explained how the Greek attitude toward homosexual love developed or determined how common homosexual behavior was. Homosexuality was probably far more common among the aristocracy than among the lower classes. Even among the aristocracy, attitudes toward homosexuality were complex and sometimes conflicting. Most people saw homosexual love affairs among the young as a stage in the development of a mature heterosexual life. Warrior aristocracies generally emphasized the physical side of the relationship in the belief that warriors who were also lovers would fight all the harder to impress and to protect each other. Whatever their intellectual content, homosexual love affairs were overtly sexual.

One particularly important aspect of social life in Athens and elsewhere in Greece was religion. Yet the Greeks had no uniform faith or creed. Although the Greeks usually worshiped the same deities—Zeus, Hera, Apollo, Athena, and others—the cults of these gods and goddesses varied from polis to polis. Greek religion was often a matter more of ritual than of belief. Nor did cults impose an ethical code of conduct. Unlike the Egyptians and Hebrews, the Greeks lacked a priesthood as the modern world understands the term. In Greece priests and priestesses existed to care for temples and sacred property and to conduct the proper rituals, but not to make religious rules or doctrines, much less to enforce them. In short, there existed in Greece no central ecclesiastical authority and no organized creed.

Although temples to the gods were common, they were unlike modern churches or synagogues in that they were not normally places where a congregation met to worship as a spiritual community. Instead, the individual Greek either visited the temple occasionally on matters of private concern or walked in a procession to a particular temple to celebrate a particular festival. In Greek religion the altar, which stood outside the temple, was important. When the Greeks sought the favor of the gods, they offered them sacrifices. Greek religious observances were generally cheerful. Festivals and sacrifices were frequently times for people to meet together socially, times of high spirits and conviviality rather than of pious gloom.

Besides the Olympian gods, each polis had its own minor deities, each with his or her own local cult. The polis administered the cults and festivals, and all were expected to participate in this civic religion, regardless of whether they believed in the deities being worshiped. Participating unbelievers, who seem to have been a small minority, were not considered hypocrites. Rather, they were seen as patriotic, loyal citizens who in honoring the gods also honored the polis. If this attitude seems contradictory, an analogy may help. Before baseball games Americans stand at the playing of the national anthem, whether they are Democrats, Republicans, or neither, and whether they agree or disagree with the policies of the current administration. They honor their nation as represented by its flag. In somewhat the same way an ancient Greek honored the polis and demonstrated solidarity with it by participating in the state cults.

Some Greeks turned to mystery religions like those of the Eleusinian mysteries in Attica. These cults united individuals in an exclusive religious society with particular deities. Those who joined them went through a period of preparation in which they learned the essential beliefs of the cult and its necessary rituals. Once they had successfully undergone initiation, they were forbidden to reveal the secrets of the cult. In Classical Greece, relatively few except the wealthy could afford the luxuries of time and money to join the mystery religions.

For most Greeks religion was quite simple and close to nature. They believed in the supernatural and the primitive. The religion of the common people was a rich combination of myth, ritual, folklore, and cult. They believed in a world of deities who all around them. The goddess Hestia oversaw the sanctity of the hearth; various nymphs resided at clear springs; and Pan, the lover of wild things and places, protected the herds and flocks. Deities and human beings shared their world so intimately that they could change places within it.

A single, very simple example can give an idea of the nature of this religion, its bond with nature, and its sense of ethics and propriety. Probably no one today thinks much about wading across a stream, unless it is too deep. That attitude would have horrified the Boeotian farmer and poet Hesiod, who would have considered it sacrilegious. Instead, he advises the traveler who encounters a stream:

Never cross the beautifully flowing water of an
*   overflowing river on foot,*
until having looked into the lovely stream and having
*   washed your hands in the very lovely, clear waters,*
you offer a prayer. Whoever crosses a river and
*   with hands unwashed of evil,*
to him the gods will wreak vengeance and will give
*   him pain.*[9]

This is an unaffected example of ritual purification, but no temple or sanctuary is needed for it.

Though Greek religion in general was individual or related to the polis, the Greeks also shared some Pan-Hellenic festivals, the chief of which were held at Olympia in honor of Zeus and at Delphi in honor of Apollo. The festivities at Olympia included athletic contests that have inspired the modern Olympic games. The Pythian games at Delphi also included musical and literary contests. Both the Olympic and the Pythian games were unifying factors in Greek life, bringing Greeks together culturally as well as religiously.

The Flowering of Philosophy

The myths and epics of the Mesopotamians are ample testimony that speculation about the origin of the universe and of mankind did not begin with the Greeks. The signal achievement of the Greeks was the willingness of some to treat these questions in rational rather than mythological terms. Although Greek philosophy did not fully flower until the Classical period, Ionian thinkers had already begun in the Lyric Age to ask what the universe was made of. These men are called the Pre-Socratics, for their work preceded the philosophical revolution begun by the Athenian Socrates.

The first of these Pre-Socratic thinkers, Thales (ca 600 B.C.), learned mathematics and astronomy from the Babylonians and geometry from the Egyptians. Yet there was an immense and fundamental difference between Near Eastern thought

and the philosophy of Thales. The Near Eastern peoples considered events such as eclipses to be evil omens. Thales viewed them as natural phenomena that could be explained in natural terms. In short, he asked why things happened. He believed the basic element of the universe to be water. Although he was wrong, the way in which he had asked the question was momentous: it was the beginning of the scientific method.

Thales' follower Anaximander continued his work. He theorized that the basic element of the universe is the "boundless" or "endless"—something infinite and indestructible. Another Ionian, Heraclitus (ca 500 B.C.), declared the primal element to be fire. He also declared that the world

Golden Chariot By the Classical period the Greeks had stopped using horse-drawn chariots in warfare. Yet they remained a symbol of aristocracy and a memory of the heroic past. Very few ancient artifacts capture that spirit as well as this chariot and its team, which is still trying to win the race. *(Source: Museum of Fine Arts, Boston)*

had neither beginning nor end: "This world, the world of all things, neither any god nor man made, but it always was and it is and it will be: an everlasting fire, measures kindling and measures going out."[10] The culmination of Pre-Socratic thought was the theory that four simple substances make up the universe: fire, air, earth, and water.

Not all of these early philosophers devoted their attention to pure philosophy or natural science. Aesop (d. 564 B.C.) devoted his attention to ethics, the rules of moral behavior. A slave endowed with a keen mind, Aesop made his points metaphorically, by using fables, which were as popular in antiquity as they are today. His tales, in which animals were often the main characters, spread throughout Greece, survived in medieval and modern Europe, and not only can still be enjoyed in books today but also form the plot line of some Bugs Bunny cartoons. They are a reservoir of good sense and simple patterns of behavior. In one fable Aesop tells of a hungry fox who encounters sun-ripened grapes in a vineyard. Try as he might, he cannot reach them. In disgust he leaves, muttering that they were probably sour and wormy anyway, whence comes the expression "sour grapes." The moral is that all fools can criticize what they cannot get. In another fable Aesop tells of a good-natured farmer whose dog falls into a well. The farmer climbs into the well to retrieve the dog, only to be bitten on the hand. Greatly angered, the farmer throws the dog back into the well. The moral again is simple: "Don't bite the hand that feeds you." Many people who never read the writings of philosophers learned from fables such as Aesop's something about life and ethics.

With this impressive heritage behind them, the philosophers of the Classical period ventured into new areas of speculation. This development was partly due to the work of Hippocrates (second half of the fifth century B.C.), the father of medicine. Like Thales, Hippocrates sought natural explanations for natural phenomena. Basing his opinions on empirical knowledge, not on religion or magic, he taught that natural means could be employed to fight disease. But Hippocrates broke away from the mainstream of Ionian speculation by declaring that medicine was a separate craft—just as iron-working was—that had its own principles.

The distinction between natural science and philosophy on which Hippocrates insisted was also promoted by the Sophists, who traveled the Greek world teaching young men. Despite differences of opinion on philosophical matters, the Sophists all agreed that human beings were the proper subject of study. They also believed that excellence could be taught, and they used philosophy and rhetoric to prepare young men for life in the polis. The Sophists laid great emphasis on logic and the meanings of words. They criticized traditional beliefs, religion, rituals, and myth and even questioned the laws of the polis. In essence, they argued that nothing is absolute, that everything is relative.

One of those whose contemporaries thought him a Sophist was Socrates (ca 470–399 B.C.), who sprang from the class of small artisans. Socrates spent his life in investigation and definition. Not, strictly speaking, a Sophist, because he never formally taught or collected fees from anyone, Socrates shared the Sophists' belief that human beings and their environment are the essential subjects of philosophical inquiry. His approach when posing ethical questions and defining concepts was to start with a general topic or problem and to narrow the matter to its essentials. He did so by continuous questioning, conducting a running dialogue with his listeners. Never did he lecture. Socrates thought that by constantly pursuing excellence, an essential part of which was knowledge, human beings could approach the supreme good and thus find true happiness. Yet in 399 B.C. Socrates was brought to trial, convicted, and executed on charges of corrupting the youth of the city and introducing new gods.

Socrates' student Plato (427–347 B.C.) carried on his master's search for the truth. Unlike Socrates, Plato wrote down his thoughts and theories and founded a philosophical school, the Academy. Most people rightly think of Plato as a philosopher. Yet his writings were also literary essays of great charm. They drew out characters, locales, and scenes from ordinary life that otherwise would have been lost to posterity. In addition, Plato used satire, irony, and comedy to relay his thoughts. Behind the elegance of his literary style, however, stand the profound thoughts of a brilliant mind grappling with the problems of his own day and the eternal realities of life. The destruction and chaos of the Peloponnesian War prompted him to ask new and different questions about the nature

PERIODS OF GREEK HISTORY

PERIOD	SIGNIFICANT EVENTS	MAJOR WRITERS
Bronze Age **2000–1100** B.C.	Arrival of the Greeks in Greece Rise and fall of the Mycenaean kingdoms	
Dark Age **1100–800** B.C.	Greek migrations within the Aegean basin Social and political recovery Evolution of the polis Rebirth of literacy	Homer Hesiod
Lyric Age **800–500** B.C.	Rise of Sparta and Athens Colonization of the Mediterranean basin Flowering of lyric poetry Development of philosophy and science in Ionia	Archilochus Sappho Tyrtaeus Solon Anaximander Heraclitus
Classical Period **500–338** B.C.	Persian wars Growth of Athenian empire Peloponnesian War Rise of drama and historical writing Flowering of Greek philosophy Spartan and Theban hegemonies Conquest of Greece by Philip of Macedon	Herodotus Thucydides Aeschylus Sophocles Euripides Aristophanes Plato Aristotle

of human society. He pondered where, why, and how the polis had gone wrong. He gave serious thought to the form that it should take. In these considerations Plato was not only a philosopher but a political scientist and a utopian.

Plato tried to show that a life of ignorance was wretched. From education, he believed, came the possibility of determining an all-comprising unity of virtues that would lead to an intelligent, moral, and ethical life. Plato concluded that only divine providence could guide people to virtue. In his opinion, divine providence was one intelligible and individualistic being. In short, he equated god with the concept of good.

Plato developed the theory that all visible, tangible things are unreal and temporary, copies of "forms" or "ideas" that are constant and indestructible. Only the mind, not the senses, can perceive eternal forms. In Plato's view the highest form is the idea of good. He discussed these ideas in two works. In *The Republic* Plato applied his theory of forms to politics in an effort to describe the ideal polis. His perfect polis was utopian; it aimed at providing the greatest good and happiness to all its members. Plato thought that the ideal polis could exist only if its rulers were philosophers and were devoted to educating their people. He divided society into rulers, guardians of the polis, and workers. The role of individuals in each category would be decided by their education, wisdom, and ability. In Plato's republic men and women would be equal to one another, and women could become rulers. The utopian polis would be a balance, with each individual doing what he or she could to support the state and with each receiving from the state his or her just due. In

The Lion of Chaeronea This stylized lion marks the mass grave of nearly three hundred elite Theban soldiers who died valiantly fighting the Macedonians at the Battle of Chaeronea. After the battle, when Philip viewed the bodies of these brave troops, he said: "May those who suppose that these men did or suffered anything dishonorable perish wretchedly." *(Source: Caroline Buckler)*

The Laws, however, Plato drew a more authoritarian picture of government and society, one not so very different from that of twentieth-century dictatorship.

A student of Plato, Aristotle (384–322 B.C.) went far beyond him in striving to understand the universe. The range of Aristotle's thought is staggering. Everything in human experience was fit subject for his inquiry. In *Politics* Aristotle followed Plato's lead by writing about the ideal polis, approaching the question more realistically than Plato had done. In *Politics* and elsewhere, Aristotle stressed moderation, concluding that the balance of the ideal state depended on people of talent and education who could avoid extremes.

Aristotle was both a philosopher and a scientist. He became increasingly interested in the observation and explanation of natural phenomena. He used logic as his method of scientific discussion, and he attempted to bridge the gap that Plato had created between abstract truth and concrete perception. He argued that the universe was finite, spherical, and eternal. He discussed an immaterial being that was his conception of god. Yet his god neither created the universe nor guided it. The inconsistencies of Aristotle on these matters are obvious. His god was without purpose. Yet for him scientific endeavor, the highest attainable form of living, reached the divine.

Aristotle expressed the heart of his philosophy in *Physics* and *Metaphysics.* In those masterful works he combined empiricism, or observation, and speculative method. In *Physics* he tried to explain how natural physical phenomena interact and how their interactions lead to the results that people see around them daily. He postulated four principles: matter, form, movement, and goal. A seed, for example, possesses both matter and an encoded form. Form determines whether a plant will be a rose or poison ivy. Growth represents movement, and the mature plant the goal of the seed. Although Aristotle considered nature impersonal, he felt that it had its own purposes. In a sense, this notion is a rudimentary ancestor of the concept of evolution.

In *On the Heaven* Aristotle took up the thread of Ionian speculation. His theory of cosmology added ether to air, fire, water, and earth as building blocks of the universe. He concluded that the universe revolves and that it is spherical and eternal. He wrongly thought that the earth is the center of the universe and that the stars and planets revolve around it.

Aristotle possessed one of history's keenest and most curious philosophical minds. While rethinking the old topics explored by the Pre-Socratics, he created whole new areas of study. In short, he tried to learn everything possible about the universe and everything in it.

The Final Act (404–338 B.C.)

Immediately after the Peloponnesian War, with Athens humbled, Sparta began striving for empire over the Greeks. The arrogance and imperialism of the Spartans turned their former allies against them. Even with Persian help Sparta could not maintain its hold on Greece. In 371 B.C. on the plain of Leuctra in Boeotia, a Theban army under the command of Epaminondas destroyed the flower of the Spartan army on a single summer day. But the Thebans were unable to bring peace to Greece. In 362 B.C. Epaminondas was killed in battle, and a period of stalemate set in. The Greek states were virtually exhausted.

The man who turned the situation to his advantage was Philip II, king of Macedonia (359–336 B.C.). Throughout most of Greek history Macedonia, which bordered Greece in the north (see Map 5.3), had been a backward, disunited kingdom, but Philip's genius and courage turned it into a major power. One of the ablest statesmen of antiquity, Philip united his powerful kingdom, built a redoubtable army, and pursued his ambition with drive and determination. His horizon was not limited to Macedonia, for he realized that he could turn the rivalry and exhaustion of the Greek states to his own purposes. By clever use of his wealth and superb army Philip won control of the northern Aegean and awakened fear in Athens, which had vital interests there. A comic playwright depicted one of Philip's ambassadors warning the Athenians:

Do you know that your battle will be with men
Who dine on sharpened swords,
And gulp burning firebrands for wine?
Then immediately after dinner the slave
Brings us desert—Cretan arrows
Or pieces or broken spears.
We have shields and breastplates for

Cushions and at our feet slings and arrows,
And we are crowned with catapults.[11]

In 338 B.C. a combined Theban-Athenian army met Philip's veterans at the Boeotian city of Chaeronea. Philip's army won a hard-fought victory: he had conquered Greece and put an end to Greek freedom. Because the Greeks could not put aside their quarrels, they fell to an invader.

SUMMARY

In a comparatively brief span of time the Greeks progressed from a primitive folk—backward and rude compared with their Near Eastern neighbors—to one of the most influential peoples of history. These originators of science and philosophy asked penetrating questions about the nature of life and society and came up with deathless responses to many of their own questions. Greek achievements range from the development of sophisticated political institutions to the creation of a stunningly rich literature. Brilliant but quarrelsome, they were their own worst enemies. As the Roman historian Pompeius Trogus later said of their fall:

The states of Greece, while each one wished to rule alone, all squandered sovereignty. Indeed, hastening without moderation to destroy one another in mutual ruin, they did not realize, until they were all crushed, that every one of them lost in the end.[12]

Nonetheless, their achievements outlived their political squabbles to become the cornerstone of all later Western development.

NOTES

1. K. J. Beloch, *Griechische Geschichte,* vol. 1, pt. 1 (Strassburg: K. J. Trübner, 1912), p. 49. Unless otherwise credited, all quotations from a foreign language in this chapter have been translated into English by John Buckler.
2. Hesiod, *Works and Days* 263–266.
3. F. Lasserre, *Archiloque* (Paris: Société d'Edition "Les Belles Lettres," 1958), frag. 9, p. 4.
4. W. Barnstable, *Sappho* (Garden City, N.Y.: Doubleday, 1965), frag. 24, p. 22.

5. Ibid., frag. 132, p. 106.

6. J. M. Edmonds, *Greek Elegy and Iambus* (Cambridge, Mass.: Harvard University Press, 1931), I.70, frag. 10.

7. Thucydides, *History of the Peloponnesian War* 1.23.

8. Ibid.

9. Hesiod, *Works and Days* 737–741.

10. E. Diels and W. Krantz, *Fragmente der Vorsokratiker*, 8th ed. (Berlin: Weidmannsche Verlagsbuchhandlung, 1960), Heraclitus frag. B30.

11. J. M. Edmonds, *The Fragments of Attic Comedy* (Leiden: E. J. Brill, 1971), 2.366–369, Mnesimachos frag. 7.

12. Justin 8.1.1–2.

SUGGESTED READING

Translations of the most important writings of the Greeks and Romans can be found in the volumes of the Loeb Classical Library published by Harvard University Press. Paperback editions of the major Greek and Latin authors are available as Penguin Classics. Recent translations of documents include C. Fornara, *Translated Documents of Greece and Rome,* vol. 1 (1977), and P. Harding, vol. 2 (1985).

Among the many general treatments of Greek history is that of H. Bengtson, *History of Greece* (English trans., 1988). Also good is J. Fine, *The Ancient Greeks* (1984).

A number of books on early Greece are available. A careful and learned synthesis can be found in Lord W. Taylour, *The Mycenaeans,* rev. ed. (1983). R. Castledon, *Minoans* (1993), uses archaeology, not always successfully, in an attempt to re-create the life of Bronze Age Crete. C. G. Thomas, *Myth Becomes History* (1993), is an excellent treatment of early Greece and modern historical attitudes toward it. R. Drews, *The Coming of the Greeks* (1988), puts the movement of the Greeks in the broader context of Indo-European migrations. No finer introduction to the Lyric Age can be found that A. R. Burn's *The Lyric Age* (1960). Its sequel, *Persia and the Greeks,* 2d ed. (1984), which is also unsurpassed, carries the history of Greece to the defeat of the Persians in 479 B.C. More recent is J. Boardman et al., *The Cambridge Ancient History,* 2d ed., vol. 4 (1988), but the coverage is very uneven. A. J. Graham, *Colony and Mother City in Ancient Greece,* rev. ed. (1984), gives a good but somewhat dated account of Greek colonization. R. Osborne, *Classical Landscape with Figures* (1985), looks at the relation of the polis to its surrounding landscape. R. A. Tomlinson, *From Mycenae to Constantinople* (1992), is a broad study of the evolution of the city in the Greek and Roman world.

W. Burkert, *The Orientalizing Revolution* (1992), is a masterful discussion of Near Eastern influence on early Greek culture. A good survey of work on Sparta is P. Cartledge, *Sparta and Lakonia* (1979). J. F. Lazenby, *The Spartan Army* (1985), studies the evolution of the Spartan army and hoplite warfare. The Athenian democracy and the society that produced it continue to attract scholarly attention. Interesting and important are M. Ostwald, *From Popular Sovereignty to the Sovereignty of Law* (1986); M. H. Hansen, *The Athenian Assembly* (1987); and J. Ober, *Mass and Elite in Democratic Athens* (1989).

The history of the fifth century B.C. and the outbreak of the Peloponnesian War are treated in M. McGregor, *The Athenians and Their Empire* (1987); A. Ferrill, *The Origins of War* (1985), chap. 4; and E. Badian, *From Plataea to Potidaea* (1993), a collection of essays on major aspects of the period.

The fourth century B.C. has been one of the most fertile fields of recent research. G. Proietti, *Xenophon's Sparta* (1987), and P. Cartledge, *Agesilaos and the Crisis of Sparta* (1987), both treat Spartan government and society in its period of greatness and collapse. J. Buckler, *The Theban Hegemony, 371–362 B.C.* (1980), examines the period of Theban ascendancy, and his *Philip II and the Sacred War* (1989) studies the ways in which Philip of Macedonia used Greek politics to his own ends. J. Cargill, *The Second Athenian League* (1981), a significant study, traces Athenian policy during the fourth century B.C. G. Cawkwell, *Philip of Macedon* (1978), analyzes the career of the great conqueror, and R. M. Errington, *A History of Macedonia* (English trans., 1990), is the best general treatment of the topic published in recent years.

Greek social life has recently received a great deal of attention, constituting a theme of continuing interest among classical scholars. For a general study, see E. Fantham *et al*, eds. *Women in The Classical World* (1994) R. Just, *Women in Athenian Law and Life* (1988), explores such topics as daily life, the family, and women's role in society. N. Loraux, *The Children of Athena* (1993), examines Athenian myths to explore the ideas about citizenship and the status of women in Athenian life. M. Golden, *Children and Childhood in Ancient Athens* (1993), studies a neglected topic. D. Cohen, *Law, Sexuality, and Society* (1992), discusses what the Athenians thought was proper moral behavior and how they tried to enforce it. J. J. Winkler, *The Constraints of Desire* (1989), examines the anthropology of sex and gender in ancient Greece. S. Isager and J. E. Skydsgaard, *Ancient Greek Agriculture* (1992), endorses the theory that agriculture was the main source of wealth in ancient Greece. D. Sansone, *Greek Athletics and the Genesis of Sport* (1988), well illustrated, provides a good and far-ranging treatment of what athletics meant to the classical Greek world. The topic of slavery is addressed in Y. Garlan, *Slavery in Ancient Greece* (1988).

For Greek literature, culture, and science, see A. Lesky's classic *History of Greek Literature* (English trans., 1963), and for drama, H. C. Baldry, *The Greek Tragic Theater* (1971). Still unsurpassed on Greek philosophy is J. Burnet, *Greek Philosophy* (1914), and on science B. Farrington, *Greek Science,* 2 vols. (reprint, 1949). More recent is M. Clagett, *Greek Science in Antiquity* (1971). M. Ferejohn, *The Origins of Aristotelian Science* (1991), discusses earlier Greek scientific thought and Aristotle's response to it. Two new works explore medicine: M. D. Grmek, *Diseases in the Ancient Greek World* (1991), and J. Longrigg,

Greek Rational Medicine (1993), which emphasizes the importance of Greek physicians who concentrated on natural causes of illness and their cure rather than on magic and religion.

Studies of Greek religions and myth include J. D. Mikalson, *Athenian Popular Religion* (reprint, 1987), which opens a valuable avenue to the understanding of Greek popular religion in general. P. N. Hunt, ed., *Encyclopedia of Classical Mystery Religions* (1993), provides more than a thousand entries on mystery religions. It also discusses the later competition between them and Christianity. In general, W. Burkert, *Greek Religion* (1987), gives a masterful survey of ancient religious beliefs. K. Dowden, *The Uses of Greek Mythology* (1992), is a systematic study of the importance of mythology to Greek history, which explores its originality and its relation to Greek culture in general.

PAST

A Veteran's Account of the Battle of Salamis

The battle of Salamis in 480 B.C. was the turning point in the Greek victory over the Persians. One man serving in the Greek fleet that day was the great Athenian dramatist Aeschylus. In his play The Persians *he gave a poetic account of the action. His was the first complete account of a major battle in Greek history, and his historical play was one of the earliest in Attic drama. Though giving few details of the naval maneuvers, which Herodotus recorded later, Aeschylus left a vivid sketch of the battle as seen through the eyes of a veteran.*

The Persian fleet was at sea to prevent the Greeks from escaping from the bay of Salamis (west of Athens), where they had anchored. At dawn the Greek ships lured the Persians into the bay, which became the scene of a furious naval battle.

Aeschylus produced The Persians *probably in 472 B.C., when most of those in the Greek audience could remember these events. The scene begins with a Persian herald reporting news of the battle to the queen, whose husband has not yet returned from the war. One of the remarkable aspects of this play is that Aeschylus uses a Persian in the royal court to praise Greek valor. The herald begins by describing the first movements of the Persian fleet, which expected the Greeks to flee.*

Herald: When the glare of sunlight died,
   and night
  Came on every [Persian] man was at his
   oar,
  Every man at arms who knew them.
  Rank encouraged rank, and long-boats
   sailed
  To stations each had been assigned.
  All night the captains kept the fleet awake;
  And night ran on. No Greek army set
  Secret sail; but when the steeds of day,
  White and luminous, began to cross
  The sky, a song-like, happy tumult sounded

From the Greeks, and island rocks returned
The high-pitched echo. Fear fell among us,
Deceived in hope; for they (and not as if to
  flee)
A solemn paean chanted, and to battle
  Rushed with fervent boldness: trumpets
  flared,
Putting every Greek aflame. At once
  Concordant strokes of oars in dissonance
Slapped the waters' depths: soon we saw
  Them all: first the right wing led in order,
Next advanced the whole fleet:
  A great concerted cry we heard: "O
  Greek
Sons, advance! Free your fathers' land,
Free your sons, your wives, the sanctuaries
Of paternal gods, the sepulchers
Of ancestors. Now the contest is drawn:
All is at stake!" And babel Persian tongues
Rose to meet it: no longer would the ac-
  tion
Loiter. Warships struck their brazen beaks
Together: a Greek man-of-war began
The charge, a Phoenician-ornamented
  stern
Was smashed; and another drove against
  another.
First the floods of Persians held the line,
But when the narrows choked them, and
  rescue hopeless,
Smitten by prows, their bronze jaws gap-
  ing,
Shattered entire was our fleet of oars.
The Greek warships, calculating, dashed
Round, and encircled us: ships showed
  their belly;
No longer could we see the water, charged
With ships' wrecks and men's blood.
Corpses glutted beaches and the rocks.
Every warship urged its own anarchic
Rout; and all who survived that expedition,
Like mackerel or some catch of fish,

Were stunned and slaughtered, boned with
  broken oars
And splintered wrecks: lamentations, cries,
Possessed the open sea, until the black
Eye of evening, closing, hushed them.
  The sum
Of troubles, even if I should rehearse them
For ten days, I could not exhaust. Rest
Content: never in a single day
So great a number died.

. . . .

Queen: Oh wretched am I alas! What doom
Destroyed them?
Herald: There is an island fronting Salamis,
  Small, scarce an anchorage for ships,
  Where the dancer Pan rejoices on the
    shore;
  Whither Xerxes [the Persian king] sent
    those men to kill
  The shipwrecked enemies who sought the
    island
  As a refuge (easily, he thought, the Greek
    arms would be subdued);
  He also bid them rescue friends. He
    conned [studied]
  The future ill. For when a god gave Greeks
  The glory, that very day, fenced in bronze,
  They leaped ashore, and drew the circle
    tight
  At every point: mewed up, we could not
    turn.
  Many rattled to the ground, whom stones
  Had felled, and arrows, shot by bowstring,
  Others killed; and in a final rush,
  The end: they hacked, mangled their
    wretched limbs,
  Until the life of all was gone.
  Xerxes mourned, beholding the lowest
    depths
  Of woe, who, seated on a height that near
  The sea commanded all his host, his robes
  Destroying (and his lamentations shrill),
  Dispatched his regiments on land: they fled
  Orderless. Now you may lament their fate,
  Added to the others' summed before.

Bust of Aeschylus, from the Musei Capi-
tolini, Rome. *(Source: Art Resource, NY)*

Questions for Analysis

1. Why did Aeschylus use a Persian herald to
   narrate the events of the battle at the Persian court?

2. What inspired the Greeks to mount a defense against the Persian invasion?

3. What was the Greek attitude toward the
   victory? Are there any religious overtones
   to the passage? If so, describe and explain
   them.

Source: *The Complete Greek Tragedies,* vol. 1, edited
by D. Grene and R. Lattimore, Copyright (c) 1959 by
University of Chicago Press. Reprinted by permission.

6

Hellenistic Diffusion

Wall-painting from
Pompeii of Pelias and his
daughters. *(Source:
Museo Nazionale Naples)*

Two years after his conquest of Greece, Philip of Macedon fell victim to an assassin's dagger. Philip's twenty-year-old son, historically known as Alexander the Great (r. 336–323 B.C.), assumed the Macedonian throne. This young man, one of the most remarkable personalities of all time, was to have a profound impact on history. By overthrowing the Persian Empire and by spreading *Hellenism*—Greek culture, language, thought, and the Greek way of life—as far as India, Alexander was instrumental in creating a new era, traditionally called Hellenistic to distinguish it from the Hellenic. As a result of Alexander's exploits, the individualistic and energetic culture of the Greeks came into intimate contact with the venerable older cultures of the Near East.

- What did the spread of Hellenism mean to the Greeks and the peoples of the East?
- What did the meeting of West and East hold for the development of economics, religion, philosophy, women's concerns, science, and medicine?

These are the questions we will explore in this chapter.

Bust of Alexander This Roman portrait of Alexander the Great is a copy of a Greek original. Alexander's youth and self-confidence are immediately apparent, yet the style is surprisingly simple for a bust of someone who had conquered the Persian Empire. The Greek inscription is equally simple: "Alexander, the son of Philip, Macedonian." (*Source: Louvre/Giraudon/Art Resource, NY*)

✦ ALEXANDER AND THE GREAT CRUSADE

In 336 B.C. Alexander inherited not only Philip's crown but also his policies. After his victory at Chaeronea, Philip had organized the states of Greece into a huge league under his leadership and announced to the Greeks his plan to lead them and his Macedonians against the Persian Empire. Fully intending to carry out Philip's designs, Alexander proclaimed to the Greek world that the invasion of Persia was to be a great crusade, a mighty act of revenge for the Persian invasion of Greece in 480 B.C. Despite his youth, Alexander was well prepared to lead the attack. In 334 B.C. he led an army of Macedonians and Greeks into western Asia. In the next three years he won three major battles—at the Granicus River, at Issus, and at Gaugamela—victories that stand almost as road signs marking his march to the east (Map 6.1). Having overthrown the Persian Empire, he crossed the Indus

River in 326 B.C. and entered India, where he saw hard fighting. Finally, at the Hyphasis River his troops refused to go farther. Still eager to explore the limits of the world, Alexander turned south to the Indian Ocean and then turned west. In 324 B.C. a long, hard march brought him back to his camp at Susa. The great crusade was over, and Alexander himself died the next year in Babylon.

The political result of Alexander's premature death was chaos. Since several of the chief Macedonian officers aspired to Alexander's position as emperor and others opposed these ambitions, civil war lasting forty-three years tore Alexander's empire apart. By the end of this conflict, the most successful generals had carved out their own small and more or less stable monarchies.

Ptolemy immediately seized Egypt and transformed the native system of administration by appointing Greeks and Macedonians to the chief bureaucratic positions. Meanwhile, Seleucus won the bulk of Alexander's empire; his monarchy extended from western Asia to India. In the third century B.C., however, the eastern parts of Seleucus's monarchy gained their independence: The Parthians came to power in Iran, and the Greeks created a monarchy of their own in Bactria. Antigonus maintained control of the Macedonian monarchy in Europe. Until the arrival of the Romans in the eastern Mediterranean in the second century B.C., these great monarchies were often at war with one another, but without winning any significant political or military advantage. In that respect, the Hellenistic monarchy was no improvement on the Greek polis.

Despite the disintegration of his empire, Alexander was instrumental in changing the face of poli-

tics in the eastern Mediterranean. His campaign swept away the Persian Empire, which had ruled the East for over two hundred years. In its place he established a Macedonian monarchy. More important in the long run was his founding of new cities and military colonies, which scattered Greeks and Macedonians throughout the East. Thus the practical result of Alexander's campaign was to open the East to the tide of Hellenism.

 ## THE SPREAD OF HELLENISM

When the Greeks and Macedonians entered Asia Minor, Egypt, and the more remote East, they encountered civilizations older than their own. In some ways the Eastern cultures were more advanced than the Greek, in others less so. Thus this third great tide of Greek migration differed from

 Alexander at the Battle of Issus At left, Alexander the Great, bareheaded and wearing a breastplate, charges King Darius, who is standing in a chariot. The moment marks the turning point of the battle, as Darius turns to flee from the attack. *(Source: National Museum, Naples/Alinari/Scala/Art Resource, NY)*

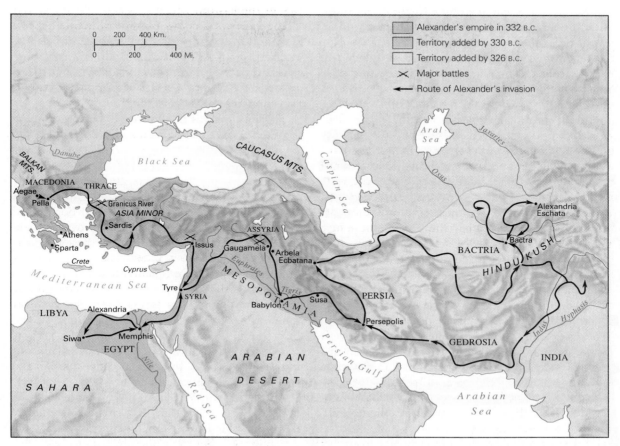

MAP 6.1 Alexander's Conquests   This map shows the course of Alexander's invasion of the Persian Empire and the speed of his progress. More important than the success of his military campaigns was his founding of Hellenistic cities in the East.

preceding waves, which had spread over land that was uninhabited or inhabited by less-developed peoples.

How did Hellenism and the cultures of the East affect one another? What did the meeting of East and West entail for the history of the world?

Cities and Kingdoms

A major development of the Hellenistic kingdoms, the resurgence of monarchy had many repercussions. For most Greeks, monarchs were something out of the heroic past, something found in Homer's *Iliad* but not in daily life. Most Hellenistic

kingdoms encompassed numerous different peoples who had little in common. Hellenistic kings thus attempted to create a ruler cult that linked the king's authority with that of the gods and to establish an easily understandable symbol of political and religious unity within the kingdom.

Monarchy included royal women, who began to play an active part in political and diplomatic life (see Listening to the Past). Some of them did so in their own right, others by manipulating their husbands. Many Hellenistic queens have been depicted as willful or ruthless, especially in power struggles over the throne. In some cases those charges are accurate. Yet for the most part, queens served as examples that women were as capable of shouldering vast responsibilities and performing them successfully as men were.

Hellenistic kings needed large numbers of Greeks to run their kingdoms. Without them, royal business would have ground to a halt, and the conquerors would soon have been swallowed up by the far more numerous conquered population. Obviously, then, the kings had to encourage Greeks to immigrate and build new homes. Since Greek civilization was urban, the kings continued Alexander's policy of establishing cities throughout their kingdoms in order to entice Greeks to immigrate. Yet the creation of these cities posed a serious political problem that the Hellenistic kings failed to solve.

To the Greeks civilized life was unthinkable without the polis, which was far more than a mere city. The Greek polis was by definition sovereign. It was an independent, autonomous state run by its citizens, free of any outside power or restraint. Hellenistic kings, however, refused to grant sovereignty to their cities. They gave their cities all the external trappings of a polis. Each had an assembly of citizens, a council to prepare legislation, and a board of magistrates to conduct the city's political business. But these cities could not pursue their own foreign policy, wage their own wars, or govern their own affairs without interference from the king, who often placed his own officials in the cities to see that his decrees were followed. There were no constitutional links between city and king. The city was simply his possession. Its citizens had no voice in how the kingdom was run and no rights except for those the king granted.

In addition, the Hellenistic city was not homogeneous and could not spark the intensity of feeling that marked the polis. The Greek polis had enjoyed political and social unity even though it was normally composed of citizens, slaves, and resident aliens. The polis had one body of law and one set of customs. In contrast, in the Hellenistic city Greeks were an elite citizen class. Natives and non-Greek foreigners usually possessed lesser rights than Greeks and often had their own laws. In some instances this disparity spurred natives to assimilate Greek culture in order to rise politically and socially. Other peoples, such as many Jews, firmly resisted the essence of Hellenism.

In many respects the Hellenistic city resembled a modern city. It was a cultural center with theaters, temples, and libraries—a seat of learning and a place where people could find amusement. The Hellenistic city was also an economic center—a marketplace, a scene of trade and manufacturing. In short, the Hellenistic city offered cultural and economic opportunities but did not foster a sense of united, integrated enterprise.

Hellenistic kings tried to make the kingdom the political focus of citizens' allegiance. If the king could secure the frontiers of his kingdom, he could give it a geographical identity. He could then hope that his subjects would direct their primary loyalty to the kingdom rather than to a particular city. However, the kings' efforts to fix their borders led only to sustained warfare, and rule by force became the chief political principle of the Hellenistic world (Map 6.2).

Border wars were frequent and exhausting. The Seleucids and Ptolemies, for instance, waged five wars for the possession of southern Syria. Other kings followed Alexander's example and waged wars to reunify his empire under their own authority. By the third century B.C., a weary balance of power was reached, but only as the result of stalemate, not any political principle.

Though Hellenistic kings never built a true polis, that does not mean that their urban policy failed. The Hellenistic city remained the basic social and political unit in the Hellenistic East until the sixth century A.D. Cities were the chief agents of Hellenization, and their influence spread far beyond their walls. Roman rule in the Hellenistic East would later be based on this urban culture. In broad terms, Hellenistic cities were remarkably successful.

The Greeks and the Opening of the East

If the Hellenistic kings failed to satisfy the Greeks' political yearnings, they nonetheless succeeded in giving them unequaled economic and social opportunities. The ruling dynasties of the Hellenistic world were Macedonian, and Greeks filled all important political, military, and diplomatic positions. They constituted an upper class that sustained Hellenism. Besides building Greek cities, Hellenistic kings offered Greeks land and money as lures to further immigration.

The Hellenistic monarchy, unlike the Greek polis, did not depend solely on its citizens to fulfill its

Seleucid Monarchy
Aetolian League
Pergamene Monarchy
Ptolemaic Monarchy
Achaean League
Antigonid Monarchy

❄ **MAP 6.2 The Hellenistic World**   After Alexander's death, no single commander could hold his vast conquests together, and his empire broke up into several kingdoms and leagues.

political needs. Talented Greeks could expect to rise quickly in the government bureaucracy. Appointed by the king, these administrators held their jobs year after year and had ample time to evolve new administrative techniques. The needs of the Hellenistic monarchy and the opportunities it offered thus gave rise to a professional corps of Greek administrators.

Greeks and Macedonians also found ready employment in the armies and navies of the Hellenistic monarchies. Alexander had proved the Greco-Macedonian style of warfare to be far superior to that of the Easterners, and Alexander's successors, themselves experienced officers, realized the importance of trained Greek and Macedonian soldiers. Moreover, Hellenistic kings were extremely

reluctant to allow the native populations to serve in the army, fearing military rebellions among their conquered subjects. The result was the emergence of professional armies and navies consisting entirely of Greeks and Macedonians.

Greeks were able to dominate other professions as well. The kingdoms and cities recruited Greek writers and artists to bring Greek culture to Asian soil. Architects, engineers, and skilled craftsmen found their services in great demand. If Hellenistic kingdoms were to have Greek cities, those cities needed Greek buildings—temples, porticoes, gymnasia, theaters, fountains, and houses. Architects and engineers were sometimes commissioned to design and build whole cities, which they laid out in checkerboard fashion. An enormous wave of

This picture is traumatizing ↓

Old Shepherdess Daily life for the poor and elderly was as hard in the Hellenistic period as in other times. Here a tough, old, scantily clothed shepherdess brings a sheep to market. Such scenes were common during the period; but art, not written sources, has preserved them for posterity. *(Source: Alinari/Art Resource, NY)*

construction took place under the Hellenistic monarchs.

New opportunities opened for women as well, owing in part to the examples of the queens. More women than ever before received educations that enabled them to enter medicine and other professions. Literacy among women increased dramatically, and their options expanded accordingly. Some won fame as poets, while others studied with philosophers and contributed to the intellectual life of the age. Women also began to participate in politics on a limited basis. They served in civil capacities, for which they often received public ac-

knowledgment. A few women received honorary citizenship from foreign cities because of aid given in times of crisis. As a rule, however, these developments touched only wealthy women, and not all of them. Although some poor women were literate, most were not.

The major reason for the new prominence of women was their increased participation in economic affairs. During the Hellenistic period some women took part in commercial transactions. They still lived under legal handicaps. In Egypt, for example, a Greek woman needed a male guardian to buy, sell, or lease land, to borrow money, and to represent her in other transactions. Yet often the guardian was present only to fulfill the letter of the law. The woman was the real agent and handled the business being transacted. In Hellenistic Sparta, women accumulated large fortunes and vast amounts of land. Spartan women, however, were exceptional. In most other areas, even women who were wealthy in their own right were formally under the protection of their male relatives.

Despite the opportunities they offered, the Hellenistic monarchies were hampered by their artificial origins. Their failure to win the political loyalty of their Greek subjects and their policy of wooing Greeks with lucrative positions encouraged a feeling of uprootedness and self-serving individualism among Greek immigrants. Once a Greek had left home to take service with, for instance, the army or the bureaucracy of the Ptolemies, he had no incentive beyond his pay and the comforts of life in Egypt to keep him there. If the Seleucid king offered him more money or a promotion, he might well accept it and take his talents to Asia Minor, where he could find the same sort of life and environment.

As long as Greeks continued to replenish their professional ranks, the Hellenistic kingdoms remained strong. In the process they drew an immense amount of talent from the Greek peninsula, draining the vitality of the Greek homeland. However, the Hellenistic monarchies could not keep recruiting Greeks forever, in spite of their wealth and willingness to spend lavishly. In time, the huge surge of immigration slowed greatly. Even then, the Hellenistic monarchs were reluctant to recruit Easterners to fill posts normally held by Greeks. The result was at first the stagnation of the Hellenistic world and finally, after 202 B.C., its collapse in the face of the young and vigorous Roman republic.

Greeks and Easterners

The Greeks in the East were a minority, but Hellenistic monarchies were remarkably successful in at least partially Hellenizing Easterners and spreading a uniform culture throughout the East. Indeed, the Near East had seen nothing comparable since the days when Mesopotamian culture had spread throughout the area. The spread of Greek culture, however, was wider than it was deep. At best it was a veneer, thicker in some places than in others. Hellenistic kingdoms were never entirely unified in language, customs, and thought. Greek culture took firmest hold along the shores of the Mediterranean, but in the Far East, in Persia and Bactria, it eventually gave way to Eastern cultures.

The Ptolemies in Egypt made no effort to spread Greek culture, and unlike other Hellenistic kings they were not city builders. Indeed, they founded only the city of Ptolemais near Thebes. At first the native Egyptian population, the descendants of the pharaoh's people, retained their traditional language, outlook, religion, and way of life. Initially untouched by Hellenism, the natives continued to be the foundation of the state: they fed it by their labor in the fields and financed its operations with their taxes.

Ay Khanoum This view of a Greek palaestra was found at Ay Khanoum, a city located in modern Afghanistan. The palaestra and other buildings are mute evidence of how the Greeks took their culture with them no matter how far from home. (*Source: French Archaeological Delegation, Afghanistan*)

The bureaucracy of the Ptolemies was ruthlessly efficient, and the native population was viciously and cruelly exploited. Even in times of hardship the king's taxes came first, although payment might mean starvation for the natives. Their desperation was summed up by one Egyptian, who scrawled the warning: "We are worn out; we will run away."[1]

Throughout the third century B.C., the Greek upper class in Egypt had little to do with the native population. But in the second century B.C., Greeks and native Egyptians began to intermarry and mingle their cultures and language. Some natives adopted Greek customs and language and began to play a role in the administration of the kingdom and even to serve in the army. While many Greeks and Egyptians remained aloof from each other, the overall result was the evolution of a widespread Greco-Egyptian culture.

Meanwhile, the Seleucid kings established many cities and military colonies in western Asia Minor and along the banks of the Tigris and Euphrates rivers in order to nurture a vigorous and large Greek population. The Seleucids had no elaborate plan for Hellenizing the native population, but the arrival of so many Greeks was bound to have an impact. Seleucid military colonies were generally founded near native villages, thus exposing Easterners to all aspects of Greek life. In Asia Minor and Syria, numerous native villages and towns developed along Greek lines, and some of them became Hellenized cities. Farther east, the Greek kings who replaced the Seleucids in the third century B.C. spread Greek culture to their neighbors, even into the Indian subcontinent.

For Easterners the prime advantage of Greek culture was its very pervasiveness. The Greek language became the common speech of the East. A common dialect called *koine* even influenced the speech of peninsular Greece itself. Greek became the speech of the royal court, bureaucracy, and army, and any Easterner who wanted to compete in business had to learn it. As early as the third century B.C., some Greek cities were giving citizenship to Hellenized natives.

The vast majority of Hellenized Easterners, however, took only the externals of Greek culture while retaining the essentials of their own way of life. A prime illustration is the impact of Greek culture on the Jews. Jews in Hellenistic cities were allowed to attend to their religious and internal affairs without interference from the Greek municipal government. They obeyed the king's commands, but there was virtually no royal interference with the Jewish religion. Indeed, the Greeks were always reluctant to tamper with anyone's religion.

Some Jews were given the right to become full citizens of Hellenistic cities, but few exercised that right. Citizenship would have obliged them to worship the gods of the city—a practice few Jews chose to follow. But Jews living in Hellenistic cities often embraced a good deal of Hellenism. So many Jews learned Greek, especially in Alexandria, that the Old Testament was translated into Greek. Yet no matter how much of Greek culture or its externals Jews borrowed, most remained attached to their religion. Thus, in spite of Hellenistic trappings, Hellenized Jews remained Jews at heart.

Though Greeks and Easterners adapted to each other's ways, there was never a true fusion of cultures. Nonetheless, each found useful things in the civilization of the other, and the two fertilized each other. This mingling of Greek and Eastern elements is what makes Hellenistic culture unique.

✺ THE ECONOMIC SCOPE OF THE HELLENISTIC WORLD

The Hellenistic period did not see a revolution in the way people lived and worked. The material demands of Hellenistic society remained as simple as those of Athenian society in the fifth century B.C. Clothes and furniture were essentially unchanged, as were household goods, tools, and jewelry. Yet Alexander and his successors brought the East fully into the sphere of Greek economics, linking East and West in a broad commercial network. The spread of Greeks throughout the East created new markets and stimulated trade. The economic unity of the Hellenistic world, like its cultural bonds, would later prove valuable to the Romans.

Commerce

Alexander's conquest of the Persian Empire had immediate effects on trade. In the Persian capitals Alexander had found vast sums of gold, silver, and other treasure. This wealth financed the creation of new cities, the building of roads, and the develop-

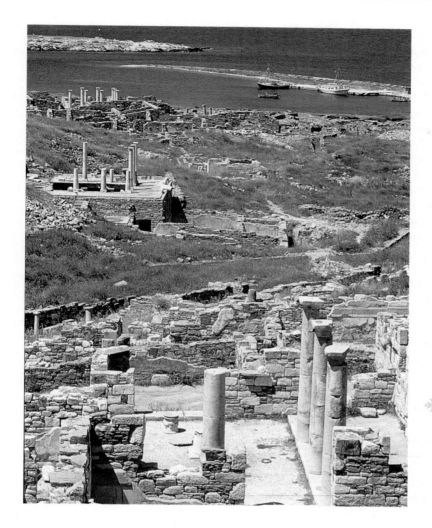

Harbor and Warehouses of Delos   During the Hellenistic period Delos became a thriving trading center. Shown here is the row of warehouses at water's edge. From Delos cargoes were shipped to virtually every part of the Mediterranean. *(Source: Adam Woolfitt/Woodfin Camp & Associates)*

ment of harbors. Most of the great monarchies coined their money on the Attic standard. Traders were less in need of moneychangers than in the days when each major power coined money on a different standard of value. As a result of Alexander's conquests, geographical knowledge of the East increased dramatically. The Greeks spread their law and methods of transacting business throughout the East. In bazaars, ports, and trading centers Greeks learned of Eastern customs and traditions while spreading knowledge of their own culture.

The Seleucid and Ptolemaic dynasties traded as far afield as India, Arabia, and sub-Saharan Africa. Overland trade with India and Arabia was conducted by caravan and was largely in the hands of Easterners. The caravan trade never dealt in bulk items or essential commodities; only luxury goods could be transported in this very expensive fashion. Once the goods reached the Hellenistic monarchies, Greek merchants took a hand in the trade.

In the early Hellenistic period, the Seleucids and Ptolemies ensured that the caravan trade proceeded efficiently. Later in the period—a time of increased war and confusion—they left the caravans unprotected. Taking advantage of this situation, Palmyra in the Syrian desert and Nabataean Petra in Arabia arose as caravan states. Such states protected the caravans from bandits and marauders and served as dispersal areas for caravan goods.

The Ptolemies discovered how to use monsoon winds to establish direct contact with India. One hardy merchant left a firsthand account of sailing this important maritime route:

Hippalos, the pilot, observing the position of the ports and the conditions of the sea, first discovered how to sail across the ocean. Concerning the winds of the ocean in this region, when with us the Etesian winds begin, in India a wind between southwest and south, named for Hippalos, sets in from the open sea. From then until now some mariners set forth from Kanes and some from the Cape of Spices. Those sailing to Dimurikes [in southern India] throw the bow of the ship farther out to sea. Those bound for Barygaza and the realm of the Sakas [in northern India] hold to the land no more than three days; and if the wind remains favorable, they hold the same course through the outer sea, and they sail along past the previously mentioned gulfs.[2]

Although this sea route never replaced overland caravan traffic, it kept direct relations between East and West alive, stimulating the exchange of ideas as well as goods.

More economically important than the exotic caravan trade were commercial dealings in essential commodities like raw materials, grain, and industrial products. The Hellenistic monarchies usually raised enough grain for their own needs as well as a surplus for export. For the cities of Greece and the Aegean this trade in grain was essential, because many of them could not grow enough.

The large-scale wars of the Hellenistic period often interrupted both the production and the distribution of grain. In addition, natural calamities, such as excessive rain or drought, frequently damaged harvests. Throughout the Hellenistic period, famine or severe food shortage remained a grim possibility.

The Greek cities paid for their grain by exporting olive oil and wine. Another significant commodity was fish, which for export was salted, pickled, or dried. This trade was doubly important because fish provided poor people with an essential element of their diet. Also important was the trade in honey, dried fruit, nuts, and vegetables. Of raw materials, wood was high in demand, but little trade occurred in manufactured goods.

Slaves were a staple of Hellenistic trade. The wars provided prisoners for the slave market; to a lesser extent, so did kidnapping and capture by pirates. The number of slaves involved cannot be estimated, but there is no doubt that slavery flourished. Both old Greek states and new Hellenistic kingdoms were ready slave markets, as was Rome

when it emerged triumphant from the Second Punic War (see page 181). Only the Ptolemies discouraged both the trade and slavery itself, and they did so only for economic reasons. Their system had no room for slaves, who would only have competed with free labor. Otherwise, slave labor was to be found in the cities and temples of the Hellenistic world, in the factories and fields, and in the homes of wealthy people. Slaves were vitally important to the Hellenistic economy.

Industry and Agriculture

Although demand for goods increased during the Hellenistic period, no new techniques of production appear to have developed. Manual labor, not machinery, continued to turn out the agricultural produce, raw materials, and few manufactured goods the Hellenistic world used. Nowhere was this truer than in mining.

Invariably miners were slaves, criminals, or forced laborers. The conditions under which they worked were frightful. The Ptolemies ran their gold mines along typically harsh lines. One historian gave a grim picture of the miners' lives:

The kings of Egypt condemn [to the mines] those found guilty of wrong-doing and those taken prisoner in war, those who are victims of false accusations and were put into jail because of royal anger. . . . The condemned—and they are very many—all of them are put in chains, and they work persistently and continually, both by day and throughout the night, getting no rest, and carefully cut off from escape.[3]

The Ptolemies even condemned women and children to work in the mines. The strongest men lived and died swinging iron sledgehammers to break up the gold-bearing quartz rock. Others worked underground, following the seams of quartz; laboring with lamps bound to their foreheads, they were whipped by overseers if they slacked off. Once the diggers had cut out blocks of quartz, young boys gathered up the blocks and carried them outside. All of them—men, women, and boys—worked until they died.

Apart from gold and silver, which were used primarily for coins and jewelry, iron was the most important metal and saw the most varied use. Even so, the method of its production never became very sophisticated.

Pottery remained an important commodity, and most of it was made locally. The pottery used in the kitchen, the coarse ware, did not change at all. Fancier pots and bowls, decorated with a shiny black glaze, came into use during the Hellenistic period. In the second century B.C. a red-glazed ware, often called Samian, burst on the market and soon dominated it. Despite the change in pottery styles, the method of production of all pottery, whether plain or fine, remained essentially unchanged.

Although new techniques of production and wider use of machinery did not develop, the volume of goods produced increased in the Hellenistic period. Small manufacturing establishments existed in nearly all parts of the Hellenistic world.

Just as all kings concerned themselves with trade and industry, they also paid special attention to agriculture. Much of their revenue was derived from the produce of royal lands, rents paid by the tenants of royal land, and taxation of agricultural land. Some Hellenistic kings even sought out and supported agricultural experts. The Ptolemies, who made the greatest strides in agriculture, sponsored experiments to improve seed grain. Hellenistic authors wrote handbooks discussing how farms and large estates could most profitably be run. Whether these efforts had any impact on the average farmer is difficult to determine.

The Ptolemies could decree what crops Egyptian farmers would plant and what animals would be raised. They recognized the need for well-planned and constant irrigation, and much native labor went into the digging and maintenance of canals and ditches. The Ptolemies also reclaimed a great deal of land from the desert. Nevertheless, it can be said that despite royal interest in agriculture and a more studied approach to it in the Hellenistic period, there is no evidence that agricultural productivity increased.

RELIGION IN THE HELLENISTIC WORLD

In religion Hellenism gave Easterners far less than the East gave the Greeks. At first the Hellenistic period saw the spread of Greek religious cults throughout the East. When Hellenistic kings founded cities, they also built temples and established new cults and priesthoods for the old Olympian gods. The new cults enjoyed the prestige of being the religion of the conquerors, and they were supported by public money. The most attractive aspects of the Greek cults were their rituals and festivities, including literary, musical, and athletic contests.

Despite various advantages, Greek cults suffered from some severe shortcomings. They were primarily concerned with ritual. Participation in the civic cults did not even require belief (see page 138). On the whole, the civic cults neither appealed to religious emotions nor embraced matters such as sin and redemption. Greek mystery religions helped fill this gap, but the centers of these religions were in old Greece. Although the new civic cults were lavish in pomp and display, they could not satisfy deep religious feelings or spiritual yearnings.

Even though the Greeks participated in the new cults for cultural reasons, they felt little genuine religious attachment to them and increasingly sought solace from other sources. Educated and thoughtful people turned to philosophy as a guide

Tazza Farnese Bowl This exquisite cameo bowl from Hellenistic Egypt dates to ca 125 B.C. The figure on the left represents the Nile pouring out the horn of plenty. The other figures also personify deities who gave Egypt its great richness. (*Source: National Museum, Naples Wim Swaan*)

Religious Syncretism This relief was found at the Greek outpost of Dura-Europus, located on the Euphrates. In the center sits Zeus Olympius-Baalshamin, a combination of a Greek god and a Semitic god. The Eastern priest at the right is burning incense on an altar, while the figure on the left in Macedonian dress crowns the god. Both the religious sentiments and the style of art show the meeting of East and West. *(Source: Yale University Art Gallery, Dura-Europos Collection)*

to life. Others turned to superstition, magic, or astrology. Still others might shrug and speak of *Tyche*, which meant "Fate" or "Chance" or "Doom"—a capricious and sometimes malevolent force. In view of the decline of Greek religion, it is surprising the Eastern religions did not make more immediate headway among the Greeks. Only in the second century B.C., after a century of exposure to Eastern religions, did Greeks begin to adopt them.

Greek cults were attractive only to those socially aspiring Easterners who adopted Greek culture for personal advancement. Otherwise, Easterners were little affected by Greek religion. Nor did native religions suffer from the arrival of the Greeks. Some Hellenistic kings limited the power of native priest-hoods, but they also subsidized some Eastern cults with public money. Alexander the Great actually reinstated several Eastern cults that the Persians had suppressed.

The only significant junction of Greek and Eastern religious traditions was the growth and spread of new "mystery religions," so called because they featured a body of ritual not to be divulged to anyone not initiated into the cult. The new mystery cults incorporated aspects of both Greek and Eastern religions and had broad appeal for both Greeks and Easterners who yearned for personal immortality. Since the Greeks were already familiar with old mystery cults, such as the Eleusinian mysteries in Attica, the new cults did not strike them as alien or barbarian. The new religions enjoyed one tremendous advantage over the old Greek mystery cults. Whereas old Greek mysteries were tied to particular places, such as Eleusis, the new religions spread throughout the Hellenistic world. People did not have to undertake long and expensive pilgrimages just to become members of the religion.

The mystery religions all claimed to save their adherents from the worst that fate could do and promised life for the soul after death. They all had a single concept in common: the belief that by means of the rites of initiation devotees became united with the god, who had himself died and risen from the dead. The sacrifice of the god and his victory over death saved the devotee from eternal death. Similarly, much like the old Greek mystery cults the Hellenistic mystery religions demanded a period of preparation in which the convert strove to become holy—that is, to live by the religion's precepts. Once aspirants had prepared themselves, they went through an initiation in which they learned the secrets of the religion. The initiation was usually a ritual of great emotional intensity, symbolizing the entry into a new life.

The Eastern mystery religions that took the Hellenistic world by storm were the Egyptian cults of Serapis and Isis. Serapis, who was invented by King Ptolemy, combined elements of the Egyptian god Osiris with aspects of the Greek gods Zeus, Pluto (prince of the underworld), and Asclepius (god of medicine). Serapis was believed to be the judge of souls, who rewarded virtuous and righteous people with eternal life. Like Asclepius, he was a god of healing. Serapis became an international god, and many Hellenistic Greeks thought of him as Zeus.

The cult of Isis enjoyed even wider appeal than that of Serapis. Isis, wife of Osiris, claimed to have conquered Tyche and promised to save any mortal who came to her. She became the most important goddess of the Hellenistic world, and her worship was very popular among women. She was the goddess of marriage, conception, and childbirth. Her priests claimed that she had bestowed on humanity the gift of civilization and had founded law and literature.

There was neither conflict between Greek and Eastern religions nor wholesale acceptance of one or the other. Greeks and Easterners noticed similarities among their respective deities and assumed that they were worshiping the same gods in different garb. These tendencies toward religious universalism and the desire for personal immortality would prove significant when the Hellenistic world came under the sway of Rome, for Hellenistic developments paved the way for the spread of Christianity.

Tyche This statue depicts Tyche as the city-goddess of Antioch, a new Hellenistic foundation of the Seleucid king Antiochus. Some Hellenistic Greeks worshiped Tyche in the hope that she would be kind to them. Philosophers tried to free people from her whimsies. Antiochus tried to win her favor by honoring her. *(Source: Photo Vatican Museums)*

❖ PHILOSOPHY AND THE PEOPLE

Philosophy during the Hellenic period was the exclusive province of the wealthy, for only they had leisure enough to pursue philosophical studies. During the Hellenistic period, however, philosophy reached out to touch the lives of more men and women than ever before. The reasons for this development were several. Since the ideal of the polis had declined, politics no longer offered people an intellectual outlet. Moreover, much of Hellenistic life, especially in the new cities of the East, seemed unstable and without venerable traditions. Many people in search of something permanent, something unchanging in a changing world, turned to philosophy. The decline of traditional religion and a growing belief in Tyche also led many Greeks to look to philosophy to protect against the worst that Tyche could do.

Philosophers themselves became much more numerous, and several new schools of philosophical thought emerged. There was a good deal of rivalry as philosophers tried to demonstrate the superiority of their views, but in spite of their differences the major branches of philosophy agreed on the necessity of making people self-sufficient. They all recognized the need to equip men and women to deal successfully with Tyche. The major schools of Hellenistic philosophy all taught that people could be truly happy only when they had turned their backs on the world and focused full attention on one enduring thing. They differed chiefly on what that enduring thing was.

Cynics

Undoubtedly the most unusual of the new philosophers were the Cynics, who urged a return to nature. They advised men and women to discard traditional customs and conventions (which were in decline anyway) and live simply. The Cynics believed that by rejecting material things people would become free and that nature would provide all necessities.

It was Diogenes of Sinope (ca 412–323 B.C.), one of the most colorful men of the period, who spread the philosophy of the Cynics. Diogenes came to Athens to study philosophy and soon evolved his own ideas on the ideal life. He came to the conclusion that happiness was possible only by living in accordance with nature and forgoing luxuries. He attacked social conventions because he considered them contrary to nature. Throughout Greece he gained fame for the rigorous way in which he put his beliefs into practice.

Diogenes' disdain for luxury and social pretense became legendary. Once, when he was living at Corinth, he was supposedly visited by Alexander the Great: "While Diogenes was sunning himself . . . Alexander stood over him and said: 'Ask me whatever gift you like.' In answer Diogenes said to him: 'Get out of my sunlight.'"[4] The story underlines the essence of Diogenes' teachings: even a great conqueror such as Alexander could give people nothing of any real value, for nature had already provided them with everything essential.

Diogenes did not establish a philosophical school in the manner of Plato and Aristotle. Instead, he and his followers took their teaching to the streets and marketplaces. More than any other philosophical group, the Cynics tried to reach the common people. As part of their return to nature, they often did without warm clothing, sufficient food, or adequate housing, which they considered unnecessary. The Cynics also tried to break down political barriers by declaring that people owed no allegiance to any city or monarchy. They said that all people are cosmopolitan—that is, citizens of the world. The Cynics reached across political boundaries to create a community of people sharing their humanity and living as close to nature as humanly possible. Although comparatively few men and women could follow such rigorous precepts, the Cynics influenced all the other major schools of philosophy.

Epicureans

Epicurus (340–270 B.C.), who founded his own school of philosophy at Athens, based his view of life on scientific theories and put forward a naturalistic theory of the universe. Although he did not deny the existence of the gods, he taught that they had no effect on human life. The essence of Epicurus's belief was that the principal good of human life is pleasure, which he defined as the absence of pain. He was not advocating drunken revels or sexual dissipation, which he thought actually caused pain. Instead, Epicurus concluded that any violent emotion is undesirable. Drawing on the teachings of the Cynics, he advocated mild self-discipline.

Even poverty he considered good, as long as people had enough food, clothing, and shelter. Epicurus also taught that individuals can most easily attain peace and serenity by ignoring the outside world and examining their personal feelings and reactions. Thus Epicureanism led to quietism.

Epicureans taught their followers to ignore politics and issues, for politics led to tumult, which would disturb the soul. Although Epicureans thought that the state originated through a social contract among individuals, they did not care about the political structure of the state, and they never speculated about the ideal state. Their ideals stood outside all political forms.

Stoics

Opposed to the passivity of the Epicureans, Zeno (335–262 B.C.), a philosopher from Citium in Cyprus, advanced a different concept of human beings and the universe. In Athens he formed his own school, the Stoa, named after the building where he preferred to teach.

Stoicism became the most popular Hellenistic philosophy and the one that later captured the mind of Rome. Zeno and his followers considered nature an expression of divine will; in their view, people could be happy only when living in accordance with nature. They stressed the unity of man and the universe, stating that all men were brothers and obliged to help one another.

Unlike the Epicureans, the Stoics taught that people should participate in politics and worldly affairs. Yet this idea never led to the belief that individuals should try to change the order of things. Time and again, the Stoics used the image of an actor in a play: the Stoic plays an assigned part and never tries to change the play. To the Stoics the important question was not whether they achieved anything but whether they lived virtuous lives. In that way they could triumph over Tyche, for Tyche could destroy achievements but not the nobility of their lives.

Like the Epicureans, the Stoics were indifferent to specific political forms. They believed that people should do their duty to the state in which they found themselves. The universal state they preached about was ethical, not political. The Stoics' most significant practical achievement was the creation of the concept of natural law. The Stoics concluded that as all men were brothers, partook

of divine reason, and were in harmony with the universe, one law—a part of the natural order of life—governed them all. The Stoic concept of a universal state governed by natural law is one of the finest heirlooms the Hellenistic world passed on to Rome.

❋ HELLENISTIC SCIENCE

The area in which Hellenistic culture achieved its greatest triumphs was science. Here, too, the ancient Near East made contributions to Greek thought. The patient observations of the Babylonians, who for generations had scanned the skies,

Tower of the Four Winds This remarkable building, which still stands in Athens, was built by an astronomer to serve as a sundial, water-clock, and weather vane. It is one of the few examples of the application of Hellenistic science to daily life. (*Source: Ekdotike Athenon*)

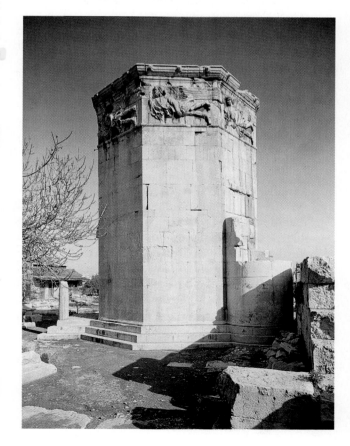

provided the foundation of Hellenistic astronomy. The most notable of the Hellenistic astronomers was Aristarchus of Samos (ca 310–230 B.C.), who was educated in Aristotle's school. Aristarchus concluded that the sun is far larger than the earth and that the stars are exceedingly distant from the earth. He argued against Aristotle's view that the earth is the center of the universe. Instead, Aristarchus propounded the *heliocentric theory*—that the earth and planets revolve around the sun. His work is all the more impressive because he lacked even a rudimentary telescope.

Unfortunately Aristarchus's theories did not persuade the ancient world. In the second century A.D. Claudius Ptolemy, a mathematician and astronomer in Alexandria, accepted Aristotle's theory of the earth as the center of the universe, and their view prevailed for fourteen hundred years. Aristarchus's heliocentric theory lay dormant until resurrected in the sixteenth century by the brilliant Polish astronomer Nicolaus Copernicus.

In geometry Hellenistic thinkers discovered little that was new, but Euclid (ca 300 B.C.), a mathematician who lived in Alexandria, compiled a valuable textbook of existing knowledge. His book *The Elements of Geometry* has exerted immense influence on Western civilization, for it rapidly became the standard introduction to geometry. Generations of students, from the Hellenistic period to the present, have learned the essentials of geometry from it.

The greatest thinker of the Hellenistic period was Archimedes (ca 287–212 B.C.), who was a clever inventor as well. He lived in Syracuse in Sicily and watched Rome emerge as a power in the Mediterranean. When the Romans laid siege to Syracuse in the Second Punic War, Archimedes invented a number of machines to thwart the armed forces. His catapults threw rocks large enough to sink ships and disrupt battle lines. His grappling devices lifted ships out of the water. In a more peaceful vein, Archimedes invented the Archimedean screw and the compound pulley. Plutarch described Archimedes' dramatic demonstration of how easily his pulley could move huge weights with little effort:

A three-masted merchant ship of the royal fleet had been hauled on land by hard work and many hands. Archimedes put aboard her many men and the usual freight. He sat far away from her; without haste, but gently working a compound pulley with his hand, he drew her towards him smoothly and without faltering, just as though she were running on the surface of the sea.[5]

Archimedes was far more interested in pure mathematics than in practical inventions. His mathematical research, covering many fields, was his greatest contribution. In his book *On Plane Equilibriums* Archimedes dealt for the first time with the basic principles of mechanics, including the principle of the lever. He once said that if he were given a lever and a suitable place to stand, he could move the world. With his treatise *On Floating Bodies* Archimedes founded the science of hydrostatics. He concluded that whenever a solid floats in a liquid, the weight of the solid is equal to the weight of liquid displaced. The way he made his discovery has become famous:

When he was devoting his attention to this problem, he happened to go to a public bath. When he climbed down into the bathtub there, he noticed that water in the tub equal to the bulk of his body flowed out. Thus, when he observed this method of solving the problem, he did not wait. Instead, moved with joy, he sprang out of the tub, and rushing home naked he kept indicating in a loud voice that he had indeed discovered what he was seeking. For while running he was shouting repeatedly in Greek, "eureka, eureka" ("I have found it, I have found it.").[6]

Archimedes was willing to share his work with others, among them Eratosthenes (285–ca 204 B.C.), a native of Cyrene and a man of almost universal interests. Around 245 B.C. King Ptolemy invited Eratosthenes to Alexandria. The Ptolemies had done much to make Alexandria an intellectual, cultural, and scientific center. Eratosthenes came to Alexandria to become librarian of the royal library, a position of great prestige. While there, by letter, he struck up his friendship with Archimedes.

Eratosthenes used mathematics to further the geographical studies for which he is most famous. He calculated the circumference of the earth geometrically, estimating it as about 24,675 miles. (He was off by only 185 miles.) Eratosthenes also discussed the shapes and sizes of land and ocean and the irregularities of the earth's surface. He drew a map of the earth and used his own system to explain the divisions of the earth's landmass.

Using geographical information gained by Alexander the Great's scientists, Eratosthenes tried to fit the East into Greek geographical knowledge. He declared that a ship could sail from Spain either around Africa to India or directly westward to India. Not until the great days of Western exploration did sailors such as Vasco da Gama and Magellan actually prove Eratosthenes' theories. Like Eratosthenes, other Greek geographers also turned their attention southward to Africa. During this period the people of the Mediterranean learned of the climate and customs of Ethiopia and gleaned some scant information about equatorial Africa.

In the Hellenistic period the scientific study of botany had its origin. Aristotle's pupil Theophrastus (ca 372–288 B.C.) studied the botanical information made available by Alexander's penetration of the East. Theophrastus wrote two books on the subject, *History of Plants* and *Causes of Plants.* He carefully observed phenomena and based his conclusions on what he had actually seen. Theophrastus classified plants and accurately described their parts. He detected the process of germination and realized the importance of climate and soil to plants. Some of his work found its way into agricultural handbooks, but for the most part Hellenistic science did not carry the study of botany further.

Despite its undeniable brilliance, Hellenistic science suffered from a remarkable weakness almost impossible for practical-minded Americans to understand. Although scientists of this period invented such machines as the air gun, the water organ, and even the steam engine, they never used their discoveries as labor-saving devices. No one has satisfactorily explained why these scientists were so impractical, but one answer is quite possible: they and the rest of society saw no real need for machines. Slave labor was especially abundant and made labor-saving machinery superfluous. Science was applied only to war. Even so, later Hellenistic thinkers preserved the discoveries of Hellenistic science for the modern age.

The Celestial Globe   In Greek mythology the god Atlas held the world on his strong shoulders, thereby preventing it from falling. Hellenistic scientists formed a very accurate idea of the shape and dimension of the earth. Here Atlas holds the globe, which rests on its axis and displays the skies, with figures representing constellations as well as the equator, tropics, and polar circles. *(Source: National Museum, Naples/Alinari/Art Resource, NY)*

❖ HELLENISTIC MEDICINE

The study of medicine flourished during the Hellenistic period, and Hellenistic physicians carried the work of Hippocrates into new areas. Herophi-lus, who lived in the first half of the third century B.C., worked at Alexandria and studied the writings of Hippocrates. He accepted Hippocrates' theory of the four humors and approached the study of medicine in a systematic, scientific fashion. He dissected dead bodies and measured what he observed. He discovered the nervous system and

SPREAD OF HELLENISM

338 B.C.	Battle of Chaeronea: Philip II of Macedonia conquers Greece
336 B.C.	Assassination of Philip II Alexander the Great inherits Macedonian crown
334–330 B.C.	Alexander overthrows the Persian Empire
334 B.C.	Battle of Granicus River
333 B.C.	Battle of Issus: Alexander conquers Asia Minor
331 B.C.	Battle of Gaugamela: Alexander conquers Mesopotamia
330 B.C.	Fall of Persepolis, principal Persian capital Fall of Ecbatana, last Persian capital
330–326 B.C.	Alexander conquers Bactria
326 B.C.	Alexander enters India; mutiny of his troops at the Hyphasis River
323 B.C.	Alexander dies in Babylon at the age of 32
323–275 B.C.	Alexander's empire divided into three monarchies; new dynasties founded by Ptolemy I (Egypt), Antigonus Gonatar (Macedonia, Asia Minor), and Seleucus I (Mesopotamia)
3d century B.C.	Development of the Hellenistic city
ca 300 B.C.	Euclid, *The Elements of Geometry*
ca 300–250 B.C.	Diffusion of philosophy; new schools founded by Epicurus (Epicureans) and Zeno (Stoics) Medical advantages by Herophilus, Erasistratus, Philinus, and Serapion
263 B.C.	Eumenes of Pergamum wins independence from the Seleucids, establishes the Pergamene monarchy
ca 250–200 B.C.	Scientific advances by Archimedes, Eratosthenes, and Aristarchus of Samos

concluded that two types of nerves, motor and sensory, exist. Herophilus also studied the brain, which he considered the center of intelligence. His younger contemporary, Erasistratus, also conducted research on the brain and nervous system and improved on Herophilus's work. He, too, followed in the tradition of Hippocrates and preferred to let the body heal itself by means of diet and air.

Both Herophilus and Erasistratus were members of the Dogmatic school of medicine at Alexandria. In this school speculation played an important part in research. So, too, did the study of anatomy, including dissection. Better knowledge of anatomy led to improvements in surgery. These advances enabled the Dogmatists to invent new surgical instruments and techniques.

In about 280 B.C. Philinus and Serapion, pupils of Herophilus, led a reaction against the Dogmatists. Believing that the Dogmatists had become too speculative, they founded the Empiric school of medicine at Alexandria. Claiming that the Dogmatists' emphasis on anatomy and physiology was misplaced, they concentrated instead on the observation and cure of illnesses. They also laid heavier stress on the use of drugs and medicine to treat illnesses. Heraclides of Tarentum (perhaps first century B.C.) discovered the benefits of opium and worked with other drugs that relieved pain. He also steadfastly rejected the relevance of magic to drugs and medicines.

Hellenistic medicine had its dark side, for many physicians were moneygrubbers, fools, and quacks. One of the angriest complaints comes from the days of the Roman Empire:

Of all men only a physician can kill a man with total impunity. Oh no, on the contrary, censure goes to him who dies and he is guilty of excess, and furthermore he is blamed. . . . Let me not accuse their [physicians'] avarice, their greedy deals with those whose fate hangs in the balance, their setting a price on pain, and their demands for down payment in case of death, and their secret doctrines.[7]

Abuses such as these existed already in the Hellenistic period. As is true today, many Hellenistic physicians did not take the Hippocratic oath very seriously.

Besides incompetent and greedy physicians, the Hellenistic world was plagued by people who claimed to cure illnesses through incantations and magic. Their potions included such concoctions as blood from the ear of an ass mixed with water to cure fever, or the liver of a cat killed when the moon was waning and preserved in salt. Broken bones could be cured by applying the ashes of a pig's jawbone to the break. The dung of a goat mixed with old wine was good for healing broken ribs. One charlatan claimed that he could cure epilepsy by making the patient drink spring water, drawn at night, from the skull of a man who had been killed but not cremated. These quacks even claimed that they could cure mental illness. The

✦ **An Unsuccessful Delivery**   This funeral stele depicts a mother who has perhaps lost her own life as well as her baby's. Maternal and infant mortality was quite common in antiquity. A similar stele elsewhere bears the heartbreaking words attributed to the mother by her grieving family: "All my labor could not bring the child forth; he lies in my womb, among the dead." (*Source: National Museum, Athens*)

treatment for a person suffering from melancholy was calf dung boiled in wine. No doubt the patient became too sick to be depressed.

Quacks who prescribed such treatments were very popular but did untold harm to the sick and injured. They and greedy physicians also damaged the reputation of dedicated doctors who honestly and intelligently tried to heal and alleviate pain. Nonetheless, the work of men like Herophilus and Serapion made valuable contributions to the knowledge of medicine, and the fruits of their work were preserved and handed on to the world.

SUMMARY

Alexander established Macedonian and Greek colonies across western and central Asia for military reasons. They resulted in the spread of Hellenism as a side effect. In the Aegean and Near East the fusion of Greek and Eastern cultures laid the social, intellectual, and cultural foundations on which the Romans would later build. In the heart of the old Persian Empire, Hellenism was only another new influence that was absorbed by older ways of thought and life. Yet overall, in the exchange of ideas and the opportunity for different cultures to learn about one another, a new cosmopolitan society evolved. That society in turn made possible such diverse advances as a wider extent of trade and agriculture, the creation of religious and philosophical ideas that paved the way for Christianity, and greater freedom for women. People of the Hellenistic period also made remarkable advances in science and medicine. They not only built on the achievements of their predecessors, but they also produced one of the most creative intellectual eras of classical antiquity.

NOTES

1. Quoted in W. W. Tarn and G. T. Griffith, *Hellenistic Civilizations,* 3d ed. (Cleveland: Meridian Books, 1961), p. 199.
2. *Periplous of the Erythraian Sea* 57. Unless otherwise credited, all quotations from a foreign language in this chapter have been translated into English by John Buckler.
3. Diodorus 3.12.2–3.
4. Diogenes, *Laertius* 6.38.
5. Ibid., 14.13.
6. Vitruvius, *On Architecture* 9 Preface, 10.
7. Pliny the Elder, *Natural History* 29.8.18, 21.

SUGGESTED READING

General treatments of Hellenistic political, social, and economic history can be found in F. W. Walbank et al., *The Cambridge Ancient History,* 2d ed., vol. 7, pt. 1 (1984). Shorter is F. W. Walbank, *The Hellenistic World* (1981), a fresh appraisal by one of the foremost scholars in the field. The undisputed classic in this area is M. Rostovtzeff, *The Social and Economic History of the Hellenistic World,* 3 vols. (1941). R. M. Errington, *A History of Macedonia,* (English trans., 1990), places Macedonia clearly within a much broader Hellenistic context. Good selections of primary sources in accurate and readable translation can be found in M. M. Austin, *The Hellenistic World from Alexander to the Roman Conquest* (1981), and S. M. Burstein, *The Hellenistic Age from the Battle of Ipsos to the Death of Kleopatra III* (1985).

Each year brings a new crop of biographies of Alexander the Great. Still the best, however, is J. R. Hamilton, *Alexander the Great* (1973). Old but still useful is U. Wilcken, *Alexander the Great* (English trans., 1967), which has had a considerable impact on scholars and students alike. Although many historians have idealized Alexander the Great, recent scholarship has provided a more realistic and unflattering view of him. The foremost expert on Alexander is E. Badian, who gives a succinct account in *The Cambridge History of Iran,* vol. 2 (1985), chap. 8. Recent political studies of the Hellenistic period include A. B. Bosworth, *Conquest and Empire* (1988), which sets Alexander's career in a broad context, and F. L. Holt, *Alexander the Great and Bactria* (1988), which discusses the formation of a Greco-Macedonian frontier in central Asia.

A. K. Bowman, *Egypt After the Pharaohs* (1986), is a readable account of the impact of the Greeks and Macedonians on Egyptian society. The same topic is treated by N. Lewis, a major scholar in the field, in his *Greeks in Ptolemaic Egypt* (1986); and a brief, new study comes from the pen of another major scholar, A. E. Samuel, *The Shifting Sands of History: Interpretations of Ptolemaic Egypt* (1989), which deals with history and historiography. W. Heckel, *The Marshals of Alexander's Empire* (1992), treats the careers of the more than 130 men who were not actually Alexander's chief officers but nonetheless substantially shaped Hellenistic political history. S. Sherwin-White and A. Kuhrt, *From Samarkand to Sardis* (1992), offer a new study of the Seleucid Empire that puts it in an Asian rather than Greek perspective. J. D. Grainger, *Seleukos Nikator* (1990), examines how the Hellenistic king created his empire. R. A. Billows, *Antigone the One-Eyed and the Creation of the Hellenis-*

tic State (1990), examines the career of the one man who most nearly reunited Alexander's empire. E. V. Hansen, *The Attalids of Pergamon,* 2d ed. (1971), though dated, is still the best treatment of that kingdom. B. Bar-Kochva, *Judas Maccabaeus* (1988), treats the Jewish struggle against the Seleucids and Hellenistic influences. A good portrait of one of the busiest ports in the Hellenistic world can be found in R. Garland, *Piraeus* (1987).

Much new work has focused on the spread of Hellenism throughout the Near East. Very extensive is A. Kuhrt and S. Sherwin-White, eds., *Hellenism in the East* (1988), which touches on a broad range of topics, including biblical studies, Christianity, and Islam. A. E. Samuel, *The Promise of the West* (1988), studies the connections among Greek, Roman, and Jewish culture and thought and their significance for Western history. P. McKechnie, *Outsiders in the Greek Cities of the Fourth Century* (1989), provides an interesting study of the social dislocation of the Greeks in the time of Philip II and Alexander the Great.

No specific treatment of women in the Hellenistic world yet exists, but two recent studies shed light on certain aspects of the topic. N. L. Goodrich, *Priestesses* (1989), examines the importance of priestesses in cults from the Near East to Ireland.

Two general studies of religion in the Hellenistic world are F. Grant, *Hellenistic Religion: The Age of Syncretism* (1953), and H. J. Rose, *Religion in Greece and Rome* (1959). L. H. Feldman, *Jew and Gentile in the Ancient World* (1993), argues that the pagan response to Judaism within the Greco-Roman period was not as negative as often thought. R. van den Broek et al., eds., *Knowledge of God in the Graeco-Roman World* (1988), is a difficult but rewarding collection of essays that points out how similarly pagans, Hellenistic Jews, and Christians thought about human attempts to know God. R. E. Witt, *Isis in the Graeco-Roman World* (1971), an illustrated volume, studies the origins and growth of the Isis cult; and more specifically, S. K. Heyob, *The Cult of Isis Among Women in the Graeco-Roman World* (1975), explores its popularity among women. The cult of Isis's consort Osiris is the subject of J. G. Griffiths, *The Origins of Osiris and His Cult* (1980); and for the mystery cults in general, see W. Burkert, *Ancient Mystery Cults* (1987), written by one of the finest scholars in the field.

Hellenistic philosophy and science have attracted the attention of a number of scholars, and the various philosophical schools are especially well covered. A general treatment can be recommended because it deals with the broader question of the role of the intellectual in the Classical period and Hellenistic world: F. L. Vatai, *Intellectuals in Politics in the Greek World from Early Times to the Hellenistic Age* (1984). Broader is S. Blundell's *The Origin of Civilization in Greek and Roman Thought* (1986), a survey of classical political and social theories through a period of ten centuries, from Aristotle to the Stoics and their Roman successors. A convenient survey of Hellenistic philosophy is A. A. Long, *Hellenistic Philosophy* (1974). F. Sayre, *The Greek Cynics* (1948), focuses on Diogenes' thought and manners. H. Jones, *The Epicurean Tradition* (1989), covers Epicurean philosophy from its inception to late Roman times. Three treatments of Stoicism are J. Rist, *Stoic Philosophy* (1969); F. H. Sandbach, *The Stoics* (1975); and M. L. Colish, *The Stoic Tradition from Antiquity to the Early Middle Ages,* 2 vols. (1985), which devotes a great deal of attention to the impact of Stoicism on Christianity. A good survey of Hellenistic science is G. E. R. Lloyd, *Greek Science After Aristotle* (1963), and specific studies of major figures can be found in T. L. Heath's solid work, *Aristarchos of Samos* (1920), still unsurpassed, and E. J. Dijksterhuis, *Archimedes,* rev. ed. (1987).

A Queen's Sacrifice for Her Society

During the Hellenistic period, women in the eastern Mediterranean became prominent in society and more obvious in their public roles. Hellenistic queens became role models for ordinary women. Nevertheless, even Hellenistic queens received criticism from men who felt that they had no business in public life, and they were often portrayed as vicious and vindictive. No one could ever say that of Queen Mother Cratesicleia of Sparta, however.

As described by the Greek biographer Plutarch, the political situation of Sparta at the time of this episode (ca 226 B.C.) was one of extreme danger. Shorn of its might first by the Thebans and later by the Macedonians, Sparta was too weak to compete successfully in the power struggles of the period. As a result, Sparta had to choose sides. When Cleomenes, king of Sparta, asked the help of the Egyptian king Ptolemy against the Macedonians, the cost was high.

Now, Ptolemy the king of Egypt promised him [Cleomenes] aid and assistance, but demanded his mother and his children as hostages. For a long time, therefore, he was ashamed to tell his mother, and though he often went to her and was at the very point of letting her know, he held his peace, so that she on her part became suspicious and enquired of his friends whether there was not something that he wished to tell her but hesitated to do so. Finally, when Cleomenes plucked up courage to speak of the matter, his mother burst into a hearty laugh and said: "Was this the thing that you were often of a mind to tell me but lost your courage? Make haste, put me on board a ship, and send this frail body wheresoever you think it will be of most use to Sparta, before old age destroys it sitting idly here."

Accordingly, when all things were ready, they came to Taenarus [a Spartan port] by land, while the army escorted them with the might of heavy-armed troops. And as Cratesicleia was about to embark, she drew Cleomenes aside by himself into the temple of Poseidon, and after embracing and kissing him in his anguish and deep trouble, said: "Come, O king of the Spartans, when we go forth let no one see us weeping or doing anything unworthy of Sparta. For this lies in our power, and this alone; but as for the issues of fortune, we shall have what the god may grant." After saying this, she composed her countenance and proceeded to the ship with her little grandson, and bade the captain put to sea with all speed.

When she arrived in Egypt, she learned that Sparta's enemies intended to use her and her grandson to pressure Cleomenes into surrender. Hostage though she was, she sent her son a message.

She sent word to him that he must do what was fitting and advantageous for Sparta, and not, because of one old woman and a little boy, be ever in fear of Ptolemy.

When Cleomenes was killed in a major battle, the alliance between Sparta and Ptolemy dissolved. Cleomenes' death sealed Cratesicleia's fate. Ptolemy ordered her execution. She was not at all dismayed and refused to grieve for herself. The words of Plutarch are a fitting tribute to her and other Spartan women.

So, then, Sparta, bringing her women's tragedy into emulous competition with that of her men, showed the world that in the last extremity Virtue cannot be outraged by Fortune.

Questions for Analysis

1. What does this episode tell us about the Spartan concept of duty and how it applies to men and women?

2. What does this episode convey about the importance of Cratesicleia, who held no actual political power?

3. What can be said of Plutarch's literary and historical portrayal of this incident? According to the words he gave Cratesicleia, Sparta would not suffer from the death of one old woman. What sort of model was she setting for others?

Source: Slightly adapted and abbreviated from B. Perrin, trans., *Plutarch's Lives,* vol. 10 (Cambridge, Mass.: Harvard University Press, 1921), pp. 99–141.

Coin depicting Queen Arsinoe II, wife of Ptolemy II, 265–246 B.C. *(Source: Ancient Art & Architecture Collection)*

Rome

QUIRINAL HILL
FIELD OF MARS
Tiber
VIMINAL HILL
CAPITOLINE MT.
Senate House
Forum
Regia
Temple of Jupiter
ESQUILINE MT.
JANICULUM
PALATINE MT.
CAELIAN MT.
Circus Maximus
AVENTINE MT.

ALPS

APENNINES

Adriatic Sea

UMBRIA
ETRURIA
PICENUM
SABINI
AEQUI VESTINI
Veii
Rome
SAMNIUM
LATIUM
APULIA
CAMPANIA
CALABRIA
Tarentum
LUCANIA

CORSICA

SARDINIA

Tyrrhenian Sea

BRUTTIUM

Mediterranean Sea

Messana

SICILY

Syracuse

Carthage
Cape Bon

NORTH AFRICA

— Roman boundary before the Punic wars
-·- Roman boundary before Augustus
— Roman internal regional divisions
— Major road

0   50   100 Km.
0   50   100 Mi.

invaders from the time when peoples began to move into Italy. Among these peoples were the Romans, who established their city on the Tiber River in Latium. The Tiber provided Rome with a constant source of water. Located at an easy crossing point on the Tiber, Rome stood astride the main avenue of communications between northern and southern Italy. The seven hills of Rome were defensible and safe from the floods of the Tiber. Rome was in an excellent position to develop the resources of Latium and maintain contact with the rest of Italy.

THE ETRUSCANS AND THE ROMAN CONQUEST OF ITALY (750–290 B.C.)

In recent years archaeologists have found traces of numerous early peoples in Italy. The origins of these cultures and their precise relations with one another are not yet well understood. In fact, no clear account of the prehistory of Italy is yet possible. Of the period before the appearance of the Etruscans (1200–750 B.C.), one fundamental fact is indisputable: peoples speaking Indo-European languages were moving into Italy from the north, probably in small groups. They were part of the awesome but imperfectly understood movement of peoples that spread the Indo-European family of languages from Spain to India.

Only with the coming of the Greeks does Italy enter the light of history. A great wave of Greek immigration swept into southern Italy and Sicily during the eighth century B.C. (see pages 123–124). The Greeks brought urban life to these regions, spreading cultural influence far beyond their city-states.

In the north the Greeks encountered the Etruscans, one of the truly mysterious peoples of antiquity. Who the Etruscans were and where they came from are unknown. Nonetheless, this fascinating people was to leave an indelible mark on the Romans. Skillful metalworkers, the Etruscans amassed extensive wealth by trading their manufactured

goods in Italy and beyond. The strength of their political and military institutions enabled them to form a loosely organized league of cities whose dominion extended as far north as the Po Valley and as far south as Latium and Campania (see Map 7.1). In Latium they founded cities and took over control of Rome. Like the Greeks, the Etruscans promoted urban life, and one of the places that benefited from Etruscan influence was Rome.

Early Roman history is an uneven mixture of fact and legend. Roman traditions often contain an important kernel of truth, but that does not make them history. In many cases they are significant because they illustrate the ethics, morals, and ideals that Roman society considered valuable. According to Roman legend, Romulus and Remus founded Rome in 753 B.C. During the years 753 to 509 B.C., the Romans embraced many Etruscan customs. They adopted the Etruscan alphabet, which the Etruscans themselves had adopted from the Greeks. The Romans later handed on this alphabet to medieval Europe and thence to the modern Western world. It was also thanks to the Etruscans that the Romans truly became urban dwellers.

Etruscan power and influence at Rome were so strong that Roman traditions preserved the memory of Etruscan kings who ruled the city. Under the Etruscans, Rome enjoyed contacts with the larger Mediterranean world, and the city began to grow. In the years 575 to 550 B.C., temples and public buildings began to grace the city. The Capitoline Hill became the religious center of the city when the temple of Jupiter Optimus Maximus (Jupiter the Best and Greatest) was built there. The Forum, located on the site of a former cemetery, began its history as a public meeting place, a development parallel to that of the Greek agora. Trade in metalwork became common, and the wealthier Roman classes began to import large numbers of fine Greek vases. The Etruscans had found Rome a collection of villages and made it a city.

According to Roman tradition, the Romans expelled the Etruscan king Tarquin the Proud from Rome in 509 B.C. and founded the republic. In the years that followed, the Romans fought numerous wars with their neighbors on the Italian peninsula. They became soldiers, and the grim fighting bred tenacity, a prominent Roman trait. At an early date the Romans also learned the value of alliances and

MAP 7.1 Italy and the City of Rome The geographical configuration of the Italian peninsula shows how Rome stood astride north-south communications and how the state that united Italy stood poised to move into Sicily and northern Africa.

❀ **Sarcophagus of Lartie Seianti**   The woman portrayed on this lavish sarcophagus is the noble Etruscan Lartie Seianti. Although the sarcophagus is her place of burial, she is portrayed as in life, comfortable and at rest. The influence of Greek art on Etruscan is apparent on almost every feature of the sarcophagus. *(Source: Archaeological Museum, Florence/Nimatallah/Art Resource, NY)*

how to provide leadership for their allies. Alliances with the Latin towns around them provided them with a large reservoir of manpower. Their alliances involved the Romans in still other wars and took them farther afield in the Italian peninsula.

The growth of Roman power was slow but steady. Not until roughly a century after the founding of the republic did the Romans drive the Etruscans entirely out of Latium. Around 390 B.C. the Romans suffered a major setback when a new people, the Celts—or "Gauls," as the Romans called them—swept aside a Roman army and sacked Rome. More intent on loot than on land, they agreed to abandon Rome in return for a thousand pounds of gold.

During the century from 390 B.C. to 290 B.C., Romans rebuilt their city and recouped their losses. They also reorganized their army to create the mobile legion, a flexible unit capable of fighting on either broken or open terrain. The Romans finally brought Latium and their Latin allies fully under their control and conquered Etruria (see Map 7.1). In 343 B.C. they grappled with the Sam-

nites in a series of bitter wars for the possession of Campania and southern Italy. The Samnites were a formidable enemy and inflicted serious losses on the Romans. But the superior organization, institutions, and manpower of the Romans won out in the end. Although Rome had yet to subdue the whole peninsula, for the first time in history the city stood unchallenged in Italy.

Rome's success in diplomacy and politics was as important as its military victories. Unlike the Greeks, the Romans did not simply conquer and dominate. Instead, they shared with other Italians both political power and degrees of Roman citizenship. With many of their oldest allies, such as the Latin cities, they shared full Roman citizenship. In other instances they granted citizenship without the franchise (*civitas sine suffragio*). Allies who held this status enjoyed all the rights of Roman citizenship except that they could not vote or hold Roman offices. They were subject to Roman taxes and calls for military service but ran their own local affairs. The Latin allies were able to acquire full Roman citizenship by moving to Rome.

❈ THE ROMAN REPUBLIC

By their willingness to extend their citizenship, the Romans took Italy into partnership. Rome proved itself superior to the Greek polis because it not only conquered but shared the fruits of conquest with the conquered. Rome could consolidate where Greece could only dominate. The unwillingness of the Greek polis to share its citizenship condemned it to a limited horizon. Not so with Rome. The extension of Roman citizenship strengthened the state, gave it additional manpower and wealth, and laid the foundation of the Roman Empire.

The Roman State and Social Conflict

The Romans summed up their political existence in a single phrase: *senatus populusque Romanus,* "the Roman senate and the people." The real genius of the Romans lay in the fields of politics and law. Unlike the Greeks, they did not often speculate on the ideal state or on political forms. Instead, they realistically met actual challenges and created institutions, magistracies, and legal concepts to deal with practical problems. Change was consequently commonplace in Roman political life; thus the constitution of 509 B.C. was far simpler than that of 27 B.C. Moreover, the Roman constitution was not a single written

❈ **The Roman Forum**   The Forum was the center of Roman political life. From simple beginnings it developed into the very symbol of Rome's imperial majesty. *(Source: Josephine Powell, Rome)*

document but a set of traditional beliefs, customs, and laws.

In the early republic, social divisions determined the shape of politics. Political power was in the hands of the aristocracy—the *patricians,* who were wealthy landowners. Patrician families formed clans, as did aristocrats in early Greece. They dominated the affairs of state, provided military leadership in time of war, and monopolized knowledge of law and legal procedure. The common people of Rome, the *plebeians,* had few of the patricians' advantages. Some plebeians formed their own clans and rivaled the patricians in wealth, but most plebeians were poor. They were the artisans, small farmers, and landless urban dwellers. The plebeians, rich and poor alike, were free citizens with a voice in politics. Nonetheless, they were overshadowed by the patricians.

Perhaps the greatest institution of the republic was the senate, which had originated under the Etruscans as a council of noble elders who advised the king. During the republic the senate advised the consuls and other magistrates. Because the senate sat year after year, while magistrates changed annually, it provided stability and continuity. It also served as a reservoir of experience and knowledge. Technically, the senate could not pass legislation; it could only offer its advice. But increasingly, because of the senate's prestige, its advice came to have the force of law.

The Romans created several assemblies through which the people elected magistrates and passed legislation. Patricians generally dominated, but in 471 B.C. the plebeians won the right to meet in an assembly of their own, the *concilium plebis,* and to pass ordinances.

The chief magistrates of the republic were two consuls, elected for one-year terms. At first the consulship was open only to patricians. The consuls commanded the army in battle, administered state business, and supervised financial affairs. In effect, they and the senate ran the state.

In 366 B.C. the Romans created the office of *praetor,* and in 227 B.C. the number of praetors was increased to four. When the consuls were away from Rome, the praetors could act in their place. The praetors dealt primarily with the administration of justice. When a praetor took office, he issued a proclamation declaring the principles by which he would interpret the law. These proclamations became very important because they usually covered areas where the law was vague and thus helped clarify the law.

After the age of overseas conquest (see pages 179–181), the Romans divided the Mediterranean area into provinces governed by former consuls and former praetors. Because of their experience in Roman politics, they were well suited to administer the affairs of the provincials and to fit Roman law and custom into new contexts.

The development of law was one of the Romans' most splendid achievements. Roman law began as a set of rules that regulated the lives and relations of citizens. This civil law, or *ius civile,* consisted of statutes, customs, and forms of procedure. Roman assemblies added to the body of law, and praetors interpreted it. The spirit of the law aimed at protecting the property, lives, and reputations of citizens, redressing wrongs, and giving satisfaction to victims of injustice.

As the Romans came into more frequent contact with foreigners, they had to devise laws to deal with disputes between Romans and foreigners and between foreigners living under Roman jurisdiction. In these instances, where there was no precedent to guide the Romans, the legal decisions of the praetors proved of immense importance. The praetors adopted aspects of other legal systems and resorted to the law of equity—what they thought was right and just to all parties. Free, in effect, to determine law, the praetors enjoyed a great deal of flexibility. This situation illustrates the practicality and the genius of the Romans. By addressing specific, actual circumstances the praetors developed a body of law, the *ius gentium,* "the law of peoples," that applied to Romans and foreigners and that laid the foundation for a universal conception of law. By the time of the late republic, Roman jurists were reaching decisions on the basis of the Stoic concept of *ius naturale,* "natural law," a universal law that could be applied to all societies.

Another important aspect of early Roman history was a great social conflict, usually known as the Struggle of the Orders, which developed between patricians and plebeians. What the plebeians wanted was real political representation and safeguards against patrician domination. The plebeians' efforts to obtain recognition of their rights is the crux of the Struggle of the Orders.

Rome's early wars gave the plebeians the leverage they needed: Rome's survival depended on the army, and the army needed the plebeians. The first

Evolution of Law:
Pat
{ Plebs — 12 Tables = Romans
Struggle of Orders
Lex Hortensia (civil Law) ⟹ Romans natives ⟹ natural law, everyone equal
THE ROMAN REPUBLIC 179

showdown between plebeians and patricians came, according to tradition, in 494 B.C. To force the patricians to grant concessions, the plebeians seceded from the state; they literally walked out of Rome and refused to serve in the army. The plebeians' general strike worked. Because of it the patricians made important concessions. One of these was social. In 445 B.C. the patricians passed a law, the *lex Canuleia,* which for the first time allowed patricians and plebeians to marry one another. Furthermore, the patricians recognized the right of plebeians to elect their own officials, the *tribunes.* The tribunes in turn had the right to protect the plebeians from the arbitrary conduct of patrician magistrates. The tribunes brought plebeian grievances to the senate for resolution. The plebeians were not bent on undermining the state. Rather, they used their gains only to win full equality under the law.

The law itself was the plebeians' next target. Only the patricians knew what the law was, and only they could argue cases in court. All too often they had used the law for their own benefit. The plebeians wanted the law codified and published. The result of their agitation was the Law of the Twelve Tables. Later still, the plebeians forced the patricians to publish legal procedures as well. The plebeians had broken the patricians' legal monopoly and henceforth enjoyed full protection under the law.

The decisive plebeian victory came in 367 B.C. after rich plebeians joined the poor to mount a sweeping assault on patrician privilege. Wealthy plebeians demanded that the patricians allow them access to all the magistracies of the state. The senate did approve a law that stipulated that one of the two consuls had to be a plebeian. Though decisive, this victory did not automatically end the Struggle of the Orders. That happened only in 287 B.C. with the passage of a law, the *lex Hortensia,* that gave the resolutions of the concilium plebis the force of law for patricians and plebeians alike.

The Struggle of the Orders resulted in a Rome stronger and better united than before. It could have led to class warfare and anarchy, but again certain Roman traits triumphed. The values fostered by their social structure predisposed the Romans to compromise, especially in the face of common danger. Important, too, were Roman patience, tenacity, and a healthy sense of the practical. These qualities enabled both sides to keep working until they had resolved the crisis. The

Struggle of the Orders ended in 287 B.C. with a new concept of Roman citizenship. All citizens shared equally under the law. Theoretically, all could aspire to the highest political offices. Patrician or plebeian, rich or poor, Roman citizenship was equal for all.

The Age of Overseas Conquest (282–146 B.C.)

In 282 B.C. Rome embarked on a series of wars that left it the ruler of the Mediterranean world. There was nothing ideological about these wars. Unlike Napoleon or Hitler, the Romans did not map out grandiose strategies for world conquest. They had no idea of what lay before them. If they could have looked into the future, they would have stood amazed. In many instances the Romans did not even initiate action; they simply responded to situations as they arose. Though they sometimes declared war reluctantly, they nonetheless felt the need to dominate, to eliminate any state that could threaten them.

The Samnite wars had drawn the Romans into the political world of southern Italy. In 282 B.C., alarmed by the powerful newcomer, the Greek city of Tarentum in southern Italy called for help from Pyrrhus, king of Epirus in western Greece. A relative of Alexander the Great and an excellent general, Pyrrhus won two furious battles but suffered heavy casualties—thus the phrase "Pyrrhic victory" for a victory involving severe losses. Roman bravery and tenacity led him to comment: "If we win one more battle with the Romans, we'll be completely washed up." In 275 B.C. the Romans drove Pyrrhus from Italy and extended their sway over southern Italy. Once they did, the island of Sicily became a key for them to block Carthaginian expansion northward.

Pyrrhus once described Sicily as a future "wrestling ground for the Carthaginians and Romans." The Phoenician city of Carthage in North Africa (Map 7.2) had for centuries dominated the western Mediterranean. Sicily had long been a Carthaginian target. Since Sicily is the steppingstone to Italy, the Romans could not let it fall to an enemy. In 264 B.C. Carthage and Rome came to blows over the city of Messana, which commanded the strait between Sicily and Italy.

This conflict, the First Punic War, lasted for twenty-three years (264–241 B.C.). The Romans

❋ **Scene of the Life of a Child**   This scene depicts the life of Marcus Cornelius—his infancy, his playing with his ponies, and his death. The entire scene suggests a pleasant and loving, though brief, childhood. *(Source: Louvre/Bildarchiv Foto Marburg/Art Resource, NY)*

from hindsight, complained that the acquisition of an empire was the beginning of Rome's troubles:

But when through labor and justice our Republic grew powerful, great kings defeated in war, fierce nations and mighty peoples subdued by force, when Carthage the rival of the Roman people was wiped out root and branch, all the seas and lands lay open, then fortune began to be harsh and to throw everything into confusion. The Romans had easily borne labor, danger, uncertainty, and hardship. To them leisure, riches—otherwise desirable—proved to be burdens and torments. So at first money, then desire for power grew great. These things were a sort of cause of all evils.[2]

Sallust was not alone in his feelings. At the time, some senators had opposed the destruction of Carthage on the grounds that fear of their old rival would keep the Romans in check. In the second century B.C., Romans learned that they could not return to what they fondly considered a simple life. They were world rulers. The responsibilities they faced were complex and awesome. They had to change their institutions, social patterns, and way of thinking to meet the new era. They were in fact building the foundations of a great imperial system.

How did the Romans of the day meet these challenges? How did they lead their lives and cope with these momentous changes? Obviously there are as many answers to these questions as there were Romans. Yet two attitudes represent the major trends of the second century B.C. One was a

longing for the good old days and an idealized view of the traditional agrarian way of life. The other was an embracing of the new urban life, with its eager acceptance of Greek culture.

In Roman society ties within the family were very strong. The head of the family was the *paterfamilias,* a term that meant far more than merely "father." The paterfamilias was the oldest dominant male of the family. He held nearly absolute power over the lives of his wife and children as long as he lived. He could legally kill his wife for adultery or divorce her at will. He could kill his children or sell them into slavery. He could force them to marry against their will. Until the paterfamilias died, his sons could not legally own property. At his death, the wife and children of the paterfamilias inherited his property.

Despite his immense power, the paterfamilias did not necessarily act alone or arbitrarily. To deal with important family matters, he usually called a council of the adult males. In this way the leading members of the family aired their views. In these councils the women of the family had no formal part, but it can safely be assumed that they played an important role behind the scenes. Although the possibility of serious conflicts between a paterfamilias and his grown sons is obvious, no one in ancient Rome ever complained about the institution. Perhaps in practice the paterfamilias preferred to be lenient rather than absolute.

In the traditional Roman family, the wife was the matron of the family, a position of authority and respect. The virtues expected of a Roman matron were fidelity, chastity, modesty, and dedication to the family. She ran the household. She supervised the domestic slaves, planned the meals, and devoted a good deal of attention to her children. In wealthy homes during this period, the matron had begun to employ a slave as a wet nurse, but most ordinary Roman women nursed their babies and bathed and swaddled them daily. After the age of seven, sons—and in many wealthy households daughters too—began to undertake formal education.

The agricultural year followed the sun and the stars—the farmer's calendar. Farmers used oxen and donkeys to pull the plow, collecting the dung of the animals for fertilizer. The main money crops, at least for rich soils, were wheat and flax. Forage crops included clover, vetch, and alfalfa. Prosperous farmers raised olive trees chiefly for the oil. They also raised grapevines for the production of wine. Harvests varied depending on the soil, but farmers could usually expect yields of $5\frac{1}{2}$ bushels of wheat or $10\frac{1}{2}$ bushels of barley per acre.

An influx of slaves resulted from Rome's wars and conquests. Prisoners from Spain, Africa, and the Hellenistic East and even some blacks and other prisoners from Hannibal's army came to Rome as the spoils of war. The Roman attitude toward slaves and slavery had little in common with modern views. To the Romans slavery was a misfortune that befell some people, but it did not entail any racial theories. Races were not enslaved because the Romans thought them inferior. The black African slave was treated no worse—and no better—than the Spaniard. Indeed, some slaves were valued because of their physical distinctiveness: black Africans and blond Germans were particular favorites. For the talented slave, the Romans always held out the hope of eventual freedom. *Manumission*—the freeing of individual slaves by their masters—became so common that it had to be limited by law. Not even Christians questioned the institution of slavery. It was just a fact of life.

For most Romans, religion played an important part in life. Originally the Romans thought of the gods as invisible, shapeless natural forces. Only through Etruscan and Greek influence did Roman deities take on human form. Jupiter, the sky-god, and his wife, Juno, became equivalent to the Greek Zeus and Hera. Mars was the god of war but also guaranteed the fertility of the farm and protected it from danger. The gods of the Romans were not loving and personal. They were stern, powerful, and aloof. But as long as the Romans honored the cults of their gods, they could expect divine favor.

In addition to the great gods, the Romans believed in spirits who haunted fields, forests, crossroads, and even the home itself. Some of the deities were hostile; only magic could ward them off (see Listening to the Past). The spirits of the dead, like ghosts in modern horror films, frequented places where they had lived. They, too,

 Vase Portrait of an Ethiopian Woman This vase, dating to ca 100 B.C., reflects Roman curiosity about different peoples. The portrait is realistic and not exaggerated. The silver inlay used for the whites of the eyes indicates that this was an expensive vase. (*Source: Courtesy of the Trustees of the British Museum*)

had to be placated but were ordinarily benign. As the poet Ovid (43 B.C.–A.D. 17) put it:

The spirits of the dead ask for little.
They are more grateful for piety than for an expensive
* gift—*
Not greedy are the gods who haunt the Styx below.
A rooftile covered with a sacrificial crown,
Scattered kernels, a few grains of salt,
Bread dipped in wine, and loose violets—
These are enough.
Put them in a potsherd and leave them in the middle
* of the road.*[3]

A good deal of Roman religion consisted of rituals such as those Ovid describes. These practices lived on long after the Romans had lost interest in the great gods. Even Christianity could not entirely wipe them out. Instead, Christianity was to incorporate many of these rituals into its own style of worship.

By the second century B.C. the ideals of traditional Roman society came into conflict with a new spirit of wealth and leisure. The conquest of the Mediterranean world and the spoils of war made Rome a great city. Roman life, especially in the cities, was changing and becoming less austere. The spoils of war went to build baths, theaters, and other places of amusement. Simultaneously, the new responsibilities of governing the world produced in Rome a sophisticated society. Romans developed new tastes and a liking for Greek culture and literature. They began to learn the Greek language. Hellenism dominated the cultural life of Rome. The poet Horace (64–8 B.C.) summed it up well: "Captive Greece captured her rough conqueror and introduced the arts into rustic Latium."

The new Rome produced a new Roman—imperial, cultured, and independent. In education and interests Romans began to break with the past. The new Hellenism profoundly stimulated the growth and development of Roman art and literature. The Roman conquest of the Hellenistic East resulted in wholesale confiscation of Greek paintings and sculpture to grace Roman temples, public buildings, and private homes. Roman artists copied many aspects of Greek art, but their emphasis on realistic portraiture carried on a native tradition.

Fabius Pictor (second half of the third century B.C.), a senator, wrote the first *History of Rome* in Greek. Other Romans translated Greek classics into Latin. Still others, such as the poet Ennius (239–169 B.C.), the father of Latin poetry, studied Greek philosophy, wrote comedies in Latin, and adapted many of Euripides' tragedies for the Roman stage. Ennius also wrote a history of Rome in Latin verse. Plautus (ca 254–184 B.C.) specialized in rough humor. He, too, decked out Greek plays in Roman dress but was no mere imitator. The Roman dramatist Terence (ca 195–159 B.C.) wrote comedies of refinement and grace that owed their essentials to Greek models. His plays lacked the energy and the slapstick of Plautus's rowdy plays. All of early Roman literature was derived from the Greeks, but it managed in time to speak in its own voice and to flourish because it had something of its own to say.

The conquest of the Mediterranean world brought the Romans leisure, and Hellenism influenced how they spent their free time. During the second century B.C. the Greek custom of bathing became a Roman passion and an important part of the day. In the early republic Romans had bathed infrequently, especially in the winter. Now large buildings containing pools and exercise rooms went up in great numbers, and the baths became an essential part of the Roman city. Architects built intricate systems of aqueducts to supply the bathing establishments with water. Conservatives railed at this Greek custom, calling it a waste of time and an encouragement to idleness. But the baths were socially important places where men and women went to see and be seen. Social climbers tried to talk to the "right people" and wangle invitations to dinner; politicians took advantage of the occasion to discuss the affairs of the day.

Did Hellenism and new social customs corrupt the Romans? Perhaps the best answer is this: the Roman state and the empire it ruled continued to exist for six more centuries. Rome did not collapse; the state continued to prosper. The golden age of Roman literature was still before it. The high tide of Roman prosperity still lay in the future. The Romans did not like change but took it in stride. That was part of their practical turn of mind and their strength.

The Late Republic (133–31 B.C.)

The wars of conquest created serious problems for the Romans. Some of the most pressing were political. The republican constitution had suited the needs of a simple city-state but was inadequate to meet the requirements of Rome's new position in international affairs (see Map 7.2). Sweeping changes and reforms were necessary to make it serve the demands of empire. A system of provincial administration had to be established. Armies had to be provided for defense, and a system of tax collection had to be created.

Other political problems were equally serious. During the wars Roman generals commanded huge numbers of troops for long periods of time. Men such as Scipio Aemilianus were on the point of becoming too mighty for the state to control. Although Rome's Italian allies had borne much of the burden of the fighting, they received fewer rewards than did Roman officers and soldiers. Italians began to agitate for full Roman citizenship and a voice in politics.

There were serious economic problems, too. Hannibal's operations and the warfare in Italy had left the countryside a shambles. The movements of numerous armies had disrupted agriculture. The prolonged fighting had also drawn untold numbers of Roman and Italian men away from their farms for long periods. The families of these soldiers could not keep the land under full cultivation. The people who defended Rome and conquered the world for Rome became impoverished for having done their duty. These problems, complex and explosive, largely account for the turmoil of the closing years of the republic.

When the legionaries returned to their farms in Italy, they encountered an appalling situation. All too often their farms looked like the farms of the people they had conquered. Many thus chose to sell their holdings. The wars of conquest had made some men astoundingly rich. These men bought up small farms to create huge estates, which the Romans called *latifundia*. Most landless veterans migrated to the cities, especially to Rome. Although some found work, most did not. Industry and small manufacturing were generally in the hands of slaves. Even when there was work, slave labor kept the wages of free men low. This trend held ominous consequences for the strength of Rome's armies. Landless men, even if they were Roman veterans and lived in Rome, could not be conscripted into the army. A large pool of experienced manpower was going to waste.

The landless former legionaries wanted a new start, and they were willing to support any leader who would provide it. One man who recognized the plight of Rome's peasant farmers and urban

Roman Table Manners   This mosaic is a floor that can never be swept clean. It whimsically suggests what a dining-room floor looked like after a lavish dinner, and it also tells something about the menu: a chicken head, a wishbone, remains of various seafoods, vegetables, and fruit are easily recognizable. (*Source: Museo Gregoria-Profano/Scala/Art Resource, NY*)

poor was an aristocrat, Tiberius Gracchus (163–133 B.C.). Appalled by what he saw, Tiberius warned his countrymen that the legionaries were losing their land while fighting Rome's wars:

The wild beasts that roam over Italy have every one of them a cave or lair to lurk in. But the men who fight and die for Italy enjoy the common air and light, indeed, but nothing else. Houseless and homeless they wander about with their wives and children. And it is with lying lips that their generals exhort the soldiers in their battles to defend sepulchres and shrines from

THE ROMAN REPUBLIC

509 B.C.	Expulsion of the Etruscan king and founding of the Roman republic
471 B.C.	Plebeians win official recognition of their assembly, the *concilium plebis*
ca 450 B.C.	Law of the Twelve Tables
390 B.C.	The Gauls sack Rome
390–290 B.C.	Rebuilding of Rome Reorganization of the army Roman expansion in Italy
367 B.C.	Licinian-Sextian rogations
287 B.C.	Legislation of the *concilium plebis* made binding on entire population
282–146 B.C.	The era of overseas conquest
264–241 B.C.	First Punic War: Rome builds a navy, defeats Carthage, acquires Sicily
218–202 B.C.	Second Punic War: Scipio defeats Hannibal Rome dominates the western Mediterranean
200–148 B.C.	Rome conquers the Hellenistic east
149–146 B.C.	Third Punic War: savage destruction of Carthage
133–121 B.C.	The Gracchi introduce land reform Murder of the Gracchi by some senators
107 B.C.	Marius becomes consul and begins the professionalization of the army
91–88 B.C.	War with Rome's Italian allies
88 B.C.	Sulla marches on Rome and seizes dictatorship
79 B.C.	Sulla abdicates
78–27 B.C.	Era of civil war
60–49 B.C.	First Triumvirate: Pompey, Crassus, Julius Caesar
45 B.C.	Julius Caesar defeats Pompey's forces and becomes dictator
44 B.C.	Assassination of Julius Caesar
43–36 B.C.	Second Triumvirate: Marc Antony, Lepidus, Augustus
31 B.C.	Augustus defeats Antony and Cleopatra at Actium

the enemy, for not a man of them has an hereditary altar, not one of all these many Romans an ancestral tomb, but they fight and die to support others in luxury, and though they are styled masters of the world, they have not a single clod of earth that is their own.[4]

After his election as tribune of the people in 133 B.C., Tiberius proposed that public land be given to the poor in small lots. His was an easy and sensible plan, but it drew bitter resistance from many of the wealthy aristocrats who had usurped large tracts of public land for their own use. Violence broke out when a large body of senators killed Tiberius in cold blood. The death of Tiberius was the beginning of an era of political violence. In the end that violence would bring down the republic.

Although Tiberius was dead, his land bill became law. Furthermore, Tiberius's brother Gaius Gracchus (153–121 B.C.) took up the cause of reform. A veteran soldier with an enviable record and a fiery orator, Gaius also became tribune and demanded even more extensive reform than his brother. Gaius pushed legislation to provide the urban poor with cheap grain for bread. He proposed that Rome send many of its poor and propertyless people out to form colonies in southern Italy. The poor would have a new start and lead productive lives. As nonproductive families left for new opportunities abroad, Rome would be less crowded, sordid, and dangerous.

Gaius went a step further and urged that all Italians be granted full rights of Roman citizenship. This measure provoked a storm of opposition, and reactionary senators rose against Gaius Gracchus and murdered him and three thousand of his supporters. Once again the cause of reform had met with violence. Once again it was Rome's leading citizens who flouted the law.

In 107 B.C., Gaius Marius, an Italian "new man" (a politician not from the traditional Roman aristocracy), became consul. A man of fierce vigor and courage, Marius saw the army as the tool of his ambition. To prepare for war in North Africa against Jugurtha, a rebellious Numidian king, Marius reformed the Roman army. He took the unusual but not wholly unprecedented step of recruiting an army by permitting the landless to serve in the legions. Marius thus tapped Rome's vast reservoir of idle manpower. His volunteer army was a professional force, not a body of draftees, and in 106 B.C. it handily defeated Jugurtha.

There was, however, a disturbing side to Marius's reforms, one that later would haunt the republic. To encourage enlistments, Marius promised land to his volunteers after the war. Poor and landless veterans flocked to him, but when Marius proposed a bill to grant land to his veterans, the senate refused to act, in effect turning its back on the soldiers of Rome. This was a disastrous mistake. Henceforth, the legionaries expected their commanders—not the senate or the state—to protect their interests. By failing to reward the loyalty of Rome's troops, the senate set the stage for military rebellion and political anarchy.

Trouble was not long in coming. The senate's refusal to honor Marius's promises to his soldiers and a brief but bitter war between the Romans and their Italian allies over the issue of full citizenship (91–88 B.C.) set off serious political disturbances in Rome. In 88 B.C. the Roman general and conqueror Sulla (138–78 B.C.) marched on Rome with his army to put an end to the turmoil. Sulla made himself dictator, put his enemies to death, and confiscated their land. The constitution thus disrupted never was put back together effectively.

In 79 B.C. Sulla voluntarily abdicated his dictatorship and permitted the republican constitution to function once again. Yet dictatorship and civil war were to be the constant lot of Rome for the next fifty years. In the late republic the Romans were grappling with the simple and inescapable fact that their old city-state constitution was unequal to the demands of overseas possessions and the governing of provinces. Thus even Sulla's efforts to put the constitution back together proved hollow. Once the senate and other institutions of the Roman state had failed to come to grips with the needs of empire, once the authorities had lost control of their own generals and soldiers, and once the armies put their faith in commanders instead of in Rome, the republic was doomed.

The history of the late republic is the story of the power struggles of some of Rome's most famous figures: Julius Caesar and Pompey, Augustus and Marc Antony. One figure who stands apart is Cicero (106–43 B.C.), a practical politician whose greatest legacy to the Roman world and to Western civilization is his mass of political and oratorical writings.

Pompous, vain, and sometimes silly, Cicero was nonetheless one of the few men of the period to urge peace and public order. As consul in 63 B.C. he put down a conspiracy against the republic but

Julius Caesar This realistic bust of Caesar captures the power, intensity, and brilliance of the man. It is a study of determination and an excellent example of Roman portraiture. *(Source: Museo Nationale, Naples/Alinari/Art Resource, NY)*

refused to use force to win political power. Instead, he developed the idea of "concord of the orders," an idealistic, probably unattainable balance among the elements that constituted the Roman state. Yet Cicero commanded no legions, and only legions commanded respect.

Sulla's real political heirs were Pompey and Julius Caesar. A man of boundless ambition, Pompey began his career as one of Sulla's lieutenants. After his army put down a rebellion in Spain, he himself threatened to rebel unless the senate allowed him to run for consul. He and another ambitious politician, Crassus, pooled political re-

sources, and both won the consulship. They dominated Roman politics until the rise of Julius Caesar, who became consul in 59 B.C. Together the three concluded a political alliance, the First Triumvirate, in which they agreed to advance one another's interests.

The man who cast the longest shadow over these troubled years was Julius Caesar (100–44 B.C.). More than a mere soldier, Caesar was a cultivated man. Born of a noble family, he received an excellent education, which he furthered by studying in Greece with some of the most eminent teachers of the day. He was also a shrewd politician of unbridled ambition. Since military service was an effective steppingstone to politics, Caesar launched his military career in Spain, where his courage won the respect and affection of his troops. Personally brave and tireless, Caesar was a military genius who knew how to win battles and turn victories into permanent gains. By 50 B.C. he had conquered all of Gaul (modern France). By 49 B.C. the First Triumvirate had fallen apart. Crassus had died in battle, and Caesar and Pompey, each suspecting the other of treachery, came to blows in a long and bloody civil war. Although Pompey enjoyed the official support of the government, Caesar finally defeated Pompey's forces in 45 B.C. He had overthrown the republic and made himself dictator.

Julius Caesar was not merely another victorious general. Politically brilliant, he was determined to make basic reforms, even at the expense of the old constitution. He took the first long step to break down the barriers between Italy and the provinces, extending citizenship to many of the provincials who had supported him. To cope with Rome's burgeoning population, Caesar sent his veterans and some eighty thousand of the poor and unemployed to colonies throughout the Mediterranean. Mostly located in Gaul, Spain, and North Africa, these colonies were important agents in spreading Roman culture in the western Mediterranean. A Roman empire composed of citizens, not subjects, was the result.

In 44 B.C. a group of conspirators assassinated Caesar and set off another round of civil war. Caesar had named his eighteen-year-old grandnephew, Octavian, as his heir. Octavian joined forces with two of Caesar's lieutenants, Marc Antony and Lepidus, in a pact known as the Second Triumvirate, and together they hunted down and defeated Caesar's murderers. In the process, however, Octavian came into conflict with Antony, "boastful, arrogant, and full of empty exultation and capricious ambition."[5] Octavian painted lurid pictures of Antony lingering in the eastern Mediterranean, a romantic and foolish captive of the seductive Cleopatra, queen of Egypt and bitter enemy of Rome. In 31 B.C., with the might of Rome at his back, Octavian met and defeated the army and navy of Antony and Cleopatra at the Battle of Actium in Greece. Octavian's victory put an end to an age of civil war that had lasted since the days of Sulla. For this success, in 27 B.C. the senate voted Octavian the name *Augustus*.

�֎ THE PAX ROMANA

When Augustus put an end to the civil wars that had raged since 83 B.C., he faced monumental problems of reconstruction. He could easily have declared himself dictator, as Caesar had done, but the thought was repugnant to him. Augustus was neither an autocrat nor a revolutionary. His solution, as he put it, was to restore the republic. But was that possible? Some eighteen years of anarchy and civil war had shattered the republican constitution. From 29 to 23 B.C., Augustus toiled to heal Rome's wounds. The first problem facing him was to rebuild the constitution and the organs of government. Next he had to demobilize much of the army and care for the welfare of the provinces. Then he had to meet the danger of barbarians at Rome's European frontiers. Augustus was highly successful in meeting these challenges. His gift of peace to a war-torn world sowed the seeds of the empire's golden age.

Augustus's Settlement (31 B.C.–A.D. 14)

Augustus claimed that in restoring constitutional government he was also restoring the republic. Typically Roman, he preferred not to create anything new; he intended instead to modify republican forms and offices to meet new circumstances. Augustus expected the senate to administer some of the provinces, continue to be the chief deliberative body of the state, and act as a court of law. But he did not give the senate enough power to become his partner in government. As a result, the senate could not live up to the responsibilities that

Augustus assigned. Many of its prerogatives shifted by default to Augustus and his successors.

Augustus's own position in the restored republic was something of an anomaly. He could not simply surrender the reins of power, for someone else would have seized them. But how was he to fit into a republican constitution? Again Augustus had his own answer. He became *princeps civitatis*, the "first citizen of the state." This prestigious title carried no power; it indicated only that Augustus was the most distinguished of all Roman citizens. In effect, it designated Augustus as the first among

Augustus as Imperator Here Augustus, dressed in breastplate and uniform, emphasizes the imperial majesty of Rome and his role as *imperator*. The figures on his breastplate represent the restoration of peace, one of Augustus's greatest accomplishments and certainly one that he frequently stressed. (*Source: Alinari/Art Resource, NY*)

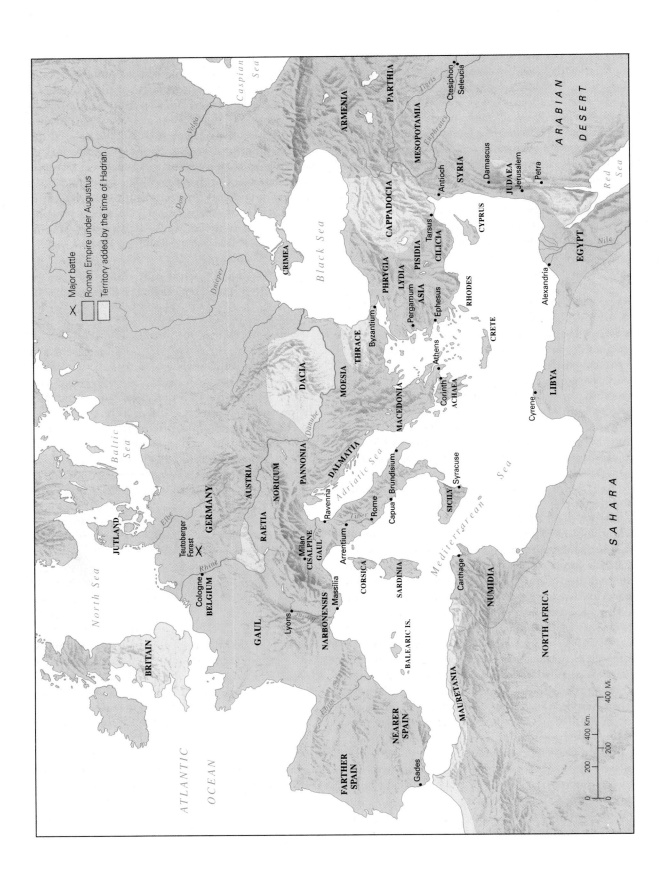

Major battle

Roman Empire under Augustus

Territory added by the time of Hadrian

ARABIAN DESERT

ARMENIA

PARTHIA

Ctesiphon

Seleucia

MESOPOTAMIA

Tigris

Euphrates

SYRIA

Antioch

Damascus

JUDAEA

Jerusalem

Petra

CAPPADOCIA

Red Sea

CYPRUS

EGYPT

Nile

PHRYGIA

LYDIA

PISIDIA

CILICIA

Tarsus

ASIA

Pergamum

Ephesus

RHODES

Alexandria

Caspian Sea

Volga

Don

CRIMEA

Black Sea

Dnieper

THRACE

Byzantium

Athens

CRETE

MACEDONIA

Corinth

ACHAEA

Cyrene

LIBYA

Mediterranean Sea

DACIA

MOESIA

Danube

PANNONIA

DALMATIA

Adriatic Sea

Ravenna

Po

Rome

Tiber

Capua

Brundisium

SICILY

Syracuse

Carthage

NUMIDIA

Baltic Sea

Elbe

JUTLAND

GERMANY

AUSTRIA

NORICUM

RAETIA

Teutoberger Forest X

Rhine

Cologne

BELGIUM

Milan

CISALPINE GAUL

Po

Arrentium

CORSICA

SARDINIA

NORTH AFRICA

North Sea

BRITAIN

GAUL

Lyons

Rhone

NARBONENSIS

Massilia

BALEARIC IS.

MAURETANIA

SAHARA

ATLANTIC OCEAN

FARTHER SPAIN

NEARER SPAIN

Ebro

Gades

0   200   400 Mi.

0   200   400 Km.

equals, a little "more equal" than anyone else in the state. His real power resided in the magistracies he held, in the powers granted him by the senate, and above all in his control of the army, which he turned into a permanent, standing organization.

What is to be made of Augustus's constitutional settlement? Despite his claims to the contrary, Augustus did not restore the republic. He created a constitutional monarchy, something completely new in Roman history. He was not exactly being a hypocrite, but he carefully kept his real military power in the background. As consul he had no more constitutional and legal power than his fellow consul. But in addition to the consulship, Augustus held many magistracies that his fellow consul did not hold. At first he held the consulship annually; then the senate voted him proconsular power on a regular basis. The senate also voted him *tribunicia potestas*—the "full power of the tribunes." Tribunician power gave Augustus the right to call the senate into session, present legislation to the people, and defend their rights. He held either high office or the powers of chief magistrate year in and year out. No other magistrate could do the same. Without specifically saying so, he had created the office of emperor, which included many traditional powers separated from their traditional offices.

Augustus's title as commander of the Roman army was *imperator,* with which Rome customarily honored a general after a major victory, and it came to mean "emperor" in the modern sense of the term. Augustus governed the provinces where troops were needed for defense. The frontiers were his special concern. There, Roman legionaries held the German barbarians at arm's length. Augustus made sure that Rome went to war only at his command. He controlled deployment of the Roman army and paid its wages. He granted it bonuses and gave veterans retirement benefits. To employ Rome's surplus of soldiers he also founded at least forty new colonies, which, like Julius Caesar's, were a significant tool in the spread of Roman culture. Thus he avoided the problems with the army that the old senate had created for itself. Augustus never shared control of the army, and no Roman found it easy to defy him militarily.

Augustus, however, failed to solve a momentous problem. He never found a way to institutionalize his position with the army. The ties between the princeps and the army were always personal. The army was loyal to the princeps but not necessarily to the state. The Augustan principate worked well at first, but by the third century A.D. the army would make and break emperors at will. Nonetheless, it is a measure of Augustus's success that his settlement survived as long and as well as it did.

Administration and Expansion Under Augustus

To gain an accurate idea of the total population of the empire Augustus ordered a census to be taken in 28 B.C. In Augustus's day the population of the Roman Empire was between 70 million and 100 million people, fully 75 percent of whom lived in the provinces. In the areas under his immediate jurisdiction, Augustus put provincial administration on an orderly basis and improved its functioning. Believing that the cities of the empire should look after their own affairs, he encouraged local self-government and urbanism. Augustus respected local customs and ordered his governors to do the same.

As a spiritual bond between the provinces and Rome, Augustus encouraged the cult of Roma, goddess and guardian of the state. In the Hellenistic East, where king-worship was an established custom, the cult of *Roma et Augustus* (Rome and Augustus) grew and spread rapidly. Augustus then introduced it in the West. By the time of his death in A.D. 14, nearly every province in the empire could boast an altar or shrine to Roma et Augustus. In the West it was not the person of the emperor who was worshiped but his *genius*—his guardian spirit. In praying for the good health and welfare of the emperor, Romans and provincials were praying for the empire itself. The cult became a symbol of Roman unity.

For the history of Western civilization one of the most momentous aspects of Augustus's reign was Roman expansion into the wilderness of northern and western Europe (Map 7.3). Carrying on Caesar's work, Augustus pushed Rome's frontier into the region of modern Germany.

MAP 7.3 Roman Expansion Under the Empire Augustus added vast tracts of Europe to the Roman Empire, which the emperor Hadrian later enlarged by assuming control over parts of central Europe, the Near East, and North Africa.

Augustus began his work in the west and north by completing the conquest of Spain. In Gaul, apart from minor campaigns, most of his work was peaceful. He founded twelve new towns, and the Roman road system linked new settlements with one another and with Italy. But the German frontier, along the Rhine River, was the scene of hard fighting. In 12 B.C. Augustus ordered a major invasion of Germany beyond the Rhine. In 9 A.D. Augustus's general Varus lost some twenty thousand troops at the Battle of the Teutoburger Forest. Thereafter the Rhine remained the Roman frontier.

Meanwhile, more successful generals extended the Roman standards as far as the Danube. Roman legions penetrated the area of modern Austria, southern Bavaria, and western Hungary. The regions of modern Serbia, Bulgaria, and Romania fell. Within this area the legionaries built fortified camps. Roads linked these camps with one another, and settlements grew up around the camps. Amid the vast expanse of forests, Roman towns, trade, language, and law began to exert a civilizing influence on the barbarians. Many military camps became towns, and many modern European cities owe their origins to the forts of the Roman army. For the first time, the barbarian north came into direct, immediate, and continuous contact with Mediterranean culture. The arrival of the Romans often provoked resistance from barbarian tribes that simply wanted to be left alone. In other cases, the prosperity and wealth of the new Roman towns lured barbarians eager for plunder. The Romans maintained peaceful relations with the barbarians whenever possible, but Roman legions remained on the frontier to repel hostile barbarians. The result was the evolution of a consistent, systematic frontier policy.

Literary Flowering

The Augustan settlement's gift of peace inspired a literary flowering unparalleled in Roman history. Augustus and many of his friends actively encouraged poets and writers. Horace, one of Rome's finest poets, offered his own opinion of Augustus and his era:

With Caesar Augustus the guardian of the state
Not civil rage nor violence shall drive out peace,
Nor wrath which forges swords
And turns unhappy cities against each other.[6]

To a generation that had known only vicious civil war, Augustus's settlement was an unbelievable blessing.

The tone and ideal of Roman literature, like that of the Greeks, was humanistic and worldly. Roman poets and prose writers celebrated the dignity of humanity and the range of its accomplishments. They stressed the physical and emotional joys of a comfortable, peaceful life. Their works were highly polished, elegant in style, and intellectual in conception. Roman poets referred to the gods often and treated mythological themes, but always the core of their work was human, not divine.

Virgil (70–19 B.C.), Rome's greatest poet, celebrated the new age in the *Georgics,* a poetic work on agriculture in four books. Virgil delighted in his own farm, and his poems sing of the pleasures of peaceful farm life. The poet also tells how to keep bees, grow grapes and olives, plow, and manage a farm. A sensitive man who delighted in simple things, Virgil left in his *Georgics* a charming picture of life in the Italian countryside during a period of peace.

Virgil's masterpiece is the *Aeneid,* an epic poem that is the Latin equivalent of the Greek *Iliad* and *Odyssey.* Virgil's account of the founding of Rome and the early years of the city gave final form to the legend of Aeneas, the Trojan hero who escaped to Italy at the fall of Troy. The principal Roman tradition held that Romulus was the founder of Rome, but the legend of Aeneas was known as early as the fifth century B.C. Virgil linked the legends of Aeneas and Romulus and preserved them both; in so doing, he connected Rome with Greece's heroic past. He also mythologized later aspects of Roman history. Recounting the story of Aeneas and Dido, the queen of Carthage, Virgil made their ill-fated love affair the cause of the Punic wars. But, above all, the *Aeneid* is the expression of Virgil's passionate belief in Rome's greatness. It is a vision of Rome as the protector of the good and noble against the forces of darkness and disruption.

The poet Ovid shared Virgil's views of the simple pleasures of life and also celebrated the popular culture of the day. In his *Fasti* (ca A.D. 8) he takes a personal approach to discuss and explain the ordinary festivals of the Roman year, festivals that most Romans took for granted. Without his work the modern world would be much the poorer in its knowledge of the popular religion of imperial Rome. For instance, he tells his readers that on a journey to Rome he encountered a white-robed

✤ **Ara Pacis**   This scene from the Ara Pacis, the Altar of Peace, celebrates Augustus's restoration of peace and the fruits of peace. Here Mother Earth is depicted with her children. The cow and the sheep under the goddess represent the prosperity brought by peace, especially the agricultural prosperity so highly cherished by Virgil. *(Source: Art Resource, NY)*

crowd in the middle of the road. A priest and farmers were performing an annual festival. Ovid stopped to ask the priest what was happening. The priest explained that they were sacrificing to Mildew, not a farmer's favorite goddess. By burning the offerings the priest and his friends asked the goddess to be so content with them that she would not attack the crops. He further asked her not to attack the farmer's tools but to be satisfied with swords and other weapons of iron. He reminded her that "there is no need for them; the world lives in peace."[6] In his poetry Ovid, like Virgil, celebrated the pax Romana, while giving a rare glimpse of ordinary Roman life.

In its own way Livy's history of Rome, entitled simply *Ab Urbe Condita (From the Founding of the City),* is the prose counterpart of the *Aeneid.* Livy (59 B.C.–A.D. 17) received training in Greek and Latin literature, rhetoric, and philosophy. He even

urged the future emperor Claudius to write history. Livy loved and admired the heroes and great deeds of the republic, but he was also a friend of Augustus and a supporter of the principate. He especially approved of Augustus's efforts to restore republican virtues.

The poet Horace (65–8 B.C.) rose from humble beginnings to friendship with Augustus. The son of a former slave and a tax collector, Horace nonetheless received an excellent education. He loved Greek literature and finished his education in Athens. After Augustus's victory he returned to Rome and became Virgil's friend. Horace happily turned his pen to celebrating Rome's newly won peace and prosperity. One of his finest odes commemorates Augustus's victory over Cleopatra at Actium in 31 B.C. Cleopatra is depicted as a frenzied queen, drunk with desire to destroy Rome. Horace saw in Augustus's victory the triumph of

West over East, of simplicity over excess. One of the truly moving aspects of Horace's poetry, like Virgil's and Ovid's, is his deep and abiding gratitude for the pax Romana.

For Rome, Augustus's age was one of hope and new beginnings. Augustus had put the empire on a new foundation. Constitutional monarchy was firmly established, and government was to all appearances a partnership between princeps and senate. The Augustan settlement was a delicate structure, and parts of it would in time be discarded. Nevertheless, it worked, and by building on it later emperors would carry on Augustus's work.

The solidity of Augustus's work became obvious at his death in A.D. 14. Since the principate was not technically an office, Augustus could not legally hand it to a successor. Augustus had recognized this problem and long before his death had found a way to solve it. He shared his consular and tribunician powers with his adopted son, Tiberius, thus grooming him for the principate. In his will Augustus left most of his vast fortune to Tiberius, and the senate formally requested Tiberius to assume the burdens of the principate. Formalities apart, Augustus had succeeded in creating a dynasty.

 ## THE COMING OF CHRISTIANITY

During the reign of the emperor Tiberius (r. A.D. 14–37), perhaps in A.D. 29, Pontius Pilate, prefect of Judaea, the Roman province created out of the Jewish kingdom of Judah, condemned Jesus of Nazareth to death. Jesus lived in a troubled time,

Pontius Pilate and Jesus This Byzantine mosaic from Ravenna illustrates a dramatic moment in Jesus' trial and crucifixion. Jesus stands accused before Pilate, and Pilate symbolically washes his hands of the whole affair. *(Source: Scala/Art Resource, NY)*

Nitasha Gupta is a poop face!
-Nikhil Gupta

when Roman rule aroused hatred and unrest among the Jews. This climate of hostility formed the backdrop of Jesus' life and his ministry.

The entry of Rome into Jewish affairs was anything but peaceful. The civil wars that destroyed the republic wasted the prosperity of Judaea and the entire eastern Mediterranean world. Jewish leaders took sides in the fighting, and Judaea suffered its share of ravages and military confiscations. Peace brought little satisfaction to the Jews. Although Augustus treated Judaea generously, the Romans won no popularity by making Herod king of Judaea (ca 73–4 B.C.). King Herod gave Judaea prosperity and security, but the Jews hated his acceptance of Greek culture. He was also a bloodthirsty prince who murdered his own wife and sons. At his death the Jews broke out in revolt. For the next ten years Herod's successor waged almost constant war against the rebels. Added to the horrors of civil war were years of crop failure, which caused famine and plague.

At length the Romans intervened to restore order. Augustus put Judaea under the charge of a prefect answerable directly to the emperor. Religious matters and local affairs became the responsibility of the *Sanhedrin,* the highest Jewish judicial body. Although many prefects in Judaea tried to perform their duties scrupulously and conscientiously, many others were rapacious and indifferent to Jewish culture. Especially hated were the Roman tax collectors, called "publicans," many of whom pitilessly gouged the Jews. *Publicans* and *sinners*—the words became synonymous. Clashes between Roman troops and Jewish guerrillas inflamed the anger of both sides.

Among the Jews two movements spread. First was the rise of the Zealots, extremists who worked and fought to rid Judaea of the Romans. Resolute in their worship of Yahweh, they refused to pay any but the tax levied by the Jewish temple. Their battles with the Roman legionaries were marked by savagery on both sides. The second movement was the growth of militant apocalyptic sentiment—the belief that the coming of the Messiah was near. This belief was an old one among the Jews. But by the first century A.D. it had become more widespread and fervent than ever before. Typical was the Apocalypse of Baruch, which foretold the Messiah's appearance and the destruction of the Roman Empire, after which the Messiah would inaugurate a period of happiness and plenty for the Jews.

As the ravages of war became more widespread and conditions worsened, more and more people prophesied the imminent coming of the Messiah. One such was John the Baptist, "the voice of one crying in the wilderness, Prepare ye the way of the lord."[7] The sect described in the Dead Sea Scrolls readied itself for the end of the world. Its members were probably Essenes, who shared possessions, precisely as John the Baptist urged people to do. This sect also made military preparations for the day of the Messiah.

Jewish religious aspirations were only one part of the story, for Christianity was born into the pagan world of Rome and its empire. The term *pagans* refers to all those who believed in the Greco-Roman gods. Paganism at the time of Jesus' birth can be broadly divided into three types: the official state religion of Rome, the traditional Roman cults of hearth and countryside, and the new mystery religions that flowed from the Hellenistic East. The official state religion and its cults honored the traditional deities: Jupiter, Juno, Mars, and such newcomers as Isis (see page 161). This very formal religion of ritual and grand spectacle provided little emotional or spiritual comfort for the people. The state cults were a bond between the gods and the people, a religious contract to ensure the well-being of Rome.

For emotional and spiritual satisfaction, many Romans observed the old cults of home and countryside. These traditional cults brought the Romans back in touch with nature and with something elemental to Roman life. Particularly popular were rustic shrines—often a small building or a sacred tree in an enclosure—to honor the native spirit of the locality. Though familiar and simple, even this traditional religion was not enough for many. They wanted something more personal and immediate.

Many people in the Roman Empire found the answer to their need for emotionally satisfying religion and spiritual security in the various Hellenistic mystery cults (see pages 160–161). The appeal of the mystery religions was not simply that they provided emotional release. They gave their adherents what neither the traditional cults nor philosophy could—above all, security. But the mystery religions were by nature exclusive, and none was truly international, open to everyone.

Into this climate of Roman religious yearning, political severity, fanatical Zealotry, and messianic hope came Jesus of Nazareth (ca 5 B.C.–A.D. 29).

He was raised in Galilee, stronghold of the Zealots. Yet Jesus himself was a man of peace. Jesus urged his listeners to love God as their father and one another as God's children.

Jesus' teachings were Jewish. He declared that he would change not one jot of the Jewish law. His major deviation from orthodoxy was his insistence that he taught in his own name, not in the name of Yahweh. Was he then the Messiah? A small band of followers thought so, and Jesus claimed that he was. But Jesus had his own conception of the Messiah. Jesus would not destroy the Roman Empire. He told his disciples flatly that they were to "render unto Caesar the things that are Caesar's." Jesus would establish a spiritual kingdom, not an earthly one. Repeatedly he told his disciples that his kingdom was "not of this world," but one of eternal happiness in a life after death.

Of Jesus' life and teachings the prefect Pontius Pilate knew little and cared even less. All that concerned him was the maintenance of peace and order. The crowds following Jesus at the time of the Passover, a highly emotional time in the Jewish year, alarmed Pilate, who faced a volatile situation. Some Jews believed that Jesus was the long-awaited Messiah. Others were disappointed because he refused to preach rebellion against Rome. Still others hated and feared Jesus and wanted to be rid of him. The last thing Pilate wanted was a riot. These were the problems on Pilate's mind when Jesus stood before him. Jesus as king of the Jews did not worry him. The popular agitation surrounding Jesus did. To avert riot and bloodshed, Pilate condemned Jesus to death. It is a bitter historical irony that such a gentle man died such a cruel death. After being scourged, he was hung from a cross until he died in the sight of family, friends, enemies, and the merely curious.

Once Pilate's soldiers had carried out the sentence, the entire matter seemed to be closed. Then on the third day after Jesus' crucifixion, an odd rumor began to circulate in Jerusalem. Some of Jesus' followers were saying he had risen from the dead, while others accused them of having stolen his body. For the earliest Christians and for generations to come, the resurrection of Jesus became a central element of faith—and more than that, a promise: Jesus had triumphed over death, and his resurrection promised all Christians immortality.

In Jerusalem, meanwhile, the tumult subsided. Jesus' followers lived quietly and peacefully, unmolested by Roman or Jew. Pilate had no quarrel with

them. Judaism already had many minor sects. Peter (d. A.D. 67?), the first of Jesus' followers, became the head of a sect that continued to observe Jewish law and religious customs. A man of traditional Jewish beliefs, Peter felt Jesus' teachings were meant exclusively for the Jews. Only in their practices of baptism and the Lord's Supper (the Eucharist) did the sect differ from normal Jewish custom.

Christianity might have remained a purely Jewish sect had it not been for Paul of Tarsus (A.D. 5?–67?). Questions about the conversion of Hellenized Jews and of Gentiles (non-Jews) to Christianity caused the sect grave problems. Were the Gentiles subject to the law of Moses? If not, was Christianity to have two sets of laws? The answer to these questions was Paul's momentous contribution to Christianity. Paul was unlike Jesus or Peter. Born in a thriving, busy city filled with Romans, Greeks, Jews, Syrians, and others, he was at home in the world of Greco-Roman culture. After his conversion to Christianity, he taught that his native Judaism was the preparation for the Messiah and that Jesus by his death and resurrection had fulfilled the prophecy of Judaism and initiated a new age. Paul taught that Jesus was the son of God, the giver of a new law, and he preached that Jesus' teachings were to be proclaimed to all, whether Jew or Gentile. Paul thus made a significant break with Judaism, Christianity's parent religion, for Judaism was exclusive and did not usually seek converts.

Paul's influence was far greater than that of any other early Christian. He traveled the length and breadth of the eastern Roman world, spreading his doctrine and preaching of Jesus. To little assemblies of believers in cities as distant as Rome and Corinth, he taught that Jesus had died to save all people. Paul's vision of Christianity won out over Peter's traditionalism. Christianity broke with Judaism and embarked on its own course.

What was Christianity's appeal to the Roman world? What did this obscure sect give people that other religions did not? Christianity possessed many different attractions. One of its appeals was its willingness to embrace both men and women, slaves and nobles. Many of the Eastern mystery religions with which Christianity competed were exclusive in one way or another, permitting only men or only Greeks and Romans to become devotees, for example.

Nevertheless, Christianity had many features in common with mystery religions (see pages 160–

161). Once people had prepared themselves for conversion by learning of Jesus' message and committing themselves to live by it, they were baptized. Like initiates in mystery religions, they entered a community of believers. The Christian community of believers was strengthened by the sacrament of the Eucharist, the communal celebration of the Lord's Supper. Like the mystery religions, Christianity had a priesthood to officiate at rituals, and offered adherents the promise of salvation. Christians believed that Jesus on the cross had defeated evil and that he would reward his followers with eternal life after death. Christianity also offered the possibility of forgiveness. Human nature was weak, and even the best Christians would fall into sin. But Jesus loved sinners and forgave those who repented. In its doctrine of salvation and forgiveness alone, Christianity had a powerful ability to give solace and strength to believers.

Christianity was attractive to many because it gave the Roman world a cause. Hellenistic philosophy had attempted to make men and women self-sufficient: people who became indifferent to the outside world could no longer be hurt by it. That goal alone ruled out any cause except the attainment of serenity. The Romans, never innovators in philosophy, merely elaborated this lonely and austere message. Instead of passivity, Christianity stressed the ideal of striving for a goal. Each and every Christian, no matter how poor or humble, supposedly worked to realize the triumph of Christianity on earth. This was God's will, a sacred duty for every Christian. By spreading the word of Christ, Christians played their part in God's plan. No matter how small, the part each Christian played was important. Since this duty was God's will, Christians believed that the goal would be achieved. The Christian was not discouraged by temporary setbacks, believing Christianity to be invincible.

Christianity gave its devotees a sense of community. No Christian was alone. All members of the Christian community strove toward the same goal of fulfilling God's plan. Each individual community was in turn a member of a greater community. And that community, the Church General, was indestructible.

So Christianity's attractions were many, from forgiveness of sin to an exalted purpose for each individual. Its insistence on the individual's importance gave solace and encouragement, especially to the poor and meek. Its claim to divine protection fed hope in the eventual success of the Christian community. Christianity made participation in the universal possible for everyone. The ultimate reward promised by Christianity was eternal bliss after death.

�֎ THE GOLDEN AGE

For fifty years after Augustus's death the dynasty that he established—known as the Julio-Claudians because they were all members of the Julian and Claudian clans—provided the emperors of Rome. Some of the Julio-Claudians, including Caligula and Nero, were weak and frivolous men who exercised their power stupidly and brought misery to the empire. But others, such as Tiberius and Claudius, were sound rulers and able administrators who were responsible for some notable achievements. During their reigns the empire largely prospered.

One of the most momentous achievements of the Julio-Claudians was Claudius's creation of an imperial bureaucracy composed of professional administrators. The numerous duties and immense responsibilities of the emperor prompted Claudius to delegate power. He began by giving the freedmen of his household official duties, especially in finances. It was a simple, workable system, and Claudius's innovations enabled the emperor to rule the empire more easily and efficiently.

In A.D. 68 Nero's inept rule led to military rebellion and his death, thus opening the way for widespread disruption. In A.D. 69, four men claimed the position of emperor. Roman armies in Gaul, on the Rhine, and in the East marched on Rome to make their commanders emperor. The man who emerged triumphant was Vespasian, commander of the eastern armies, who entered Rome in 70 and restored order.

By establishing the Flavian Dynasty (named after his clan), Vespasian turned the principate into an open and admitted monarchy. The Flavians (A.D. 69–96) carried on Augustus's work on the frontiers, gave the Roman world peace, and kept the legions in line. Their work paved the way for the era of the "five good emperors," the golden age of the empire (A.D. 96–180).

Beginning in the second century A.D., the era of the five good emperors was a period of almost unparalleled prosperity for the empire. Wars generally

Scene from Trajan's Column From 101 to 107 Trajan fought the barbarian tribes along the Danube. With remarkable realism, a feature of Roman art, this scene portrays Roman soldiers building fieldworks outside a city. *(Source: Ancient Art & Architecture Collection)*

ended in victories and were confined to the frontiers. The five good emperors—Nerva, Trajan, Hadrian, Antoninus Pius, and Marcus Aurelius—were among the noblest, most dedicated, ablest men in Roman history.

Under the Flavians the principate became a full-blown monarchy, and by the time of the five good emperors the principate was an office with definite rights, powers, and prerogatives. In the years between Augustus and the era of the five good emperors, the emperor had become an indispensable part of the imperial machinery. In short, without the emperor the empire would quickly have fallen to pieces. Augustus had been monarch in fact but not in theory; during their reigns, the five good emperors were monarchs in both.

The five good emperors were not power-hungry autocrats. The concentration of power was the result of empire. The easiest and most efficient way to run the Roman Empire was to invest the emperor with vast powers. Furthermore, Roman emperors on the whole proved to be effective rulers and administrators. As capable and efficient emperors took on new tasks and functions, the emperor's hand was felt in more areas of life and government. The five good emperors were benevolent and exercised their power intelligently, but they were absolute kings all the same. Lesser men would later throw off the façade of constitutionality and use this same power in a despotic fashion.

One of the most significant changes in Roman government since Augustus's day was the enormous growth of the imperial bureaucracy created by Claudius. Hadrian, who became emperor in A.D. 117, reformed this system by putting the bureaucracy on an organized, official basis. He established imperial administrative departments to handle the work formerly done by imperial freedmen.

Hadrian also separated civil service from military service. Men with little talent or taste for the army could instead serve the state as administrators. Hadrian's bureaucracy demanded professionalism from its members. Administrators made a career of the civil service. These innovations made for more efficient running of the empire and increased the authority of the emperor—the ruling power of the bureaucracy.

The Roman army had also changed since Augustus's time. The Roman legion had once been a mobile unit, but its duties under the empire no longer called for mobility. The successors of Augustus generally called a halt to further conquests. The army was expected to defend what had already been won. Under the Flavian emperors (A.D. 69–96), the frontiers became firmly fixed. Forts and watch stations guarded the borders. Behind the forts the Romans built a system of roads that allowed the forts to be quickly supplied and reinforced in times of trouble. The army had evolved into a garrison force, with legions guarding specific areas for long periods.

The personnel of the legions was also changing. Italy could no longer supply all the recruits needed for the army. Increasingly, only the officers came from Italy and from the more Romanized provinces. The legionaries were mostly drawn from the less civilized provinces, especially the ones closest to the frontiers. In the third century A.D. the barbarization of the army would result in an army indifferent to Rome and its traditions. In the era of the five good emperors, however, the army was still a source of economic stability and a Romanizing agent. Men from the provinces and even barbarians joined the army to learn a trade and to gain Roman citizenship. Even so, the signs were ominous. Veterans from Julius Caesar's campaigns would hardly have recognized Hadrian's troops as Roman legionaries.

LIFE IN THE GOLDEN AGE: IMPERIAL ROME AND THE PROVINCES

Many people, both ancient and modern, have considered these years one of the happiest epochs in Western history. But popular accounts have also portrayed Rome as already decadent by the time of the five good emperors. If Rome was decadent, who kept the empire running? For that matter, can life in Rome itself be taken as representative of life in other parts of the empire? Rome was unique and must be seen as such. Rome no more resembled a provincial city like Cologne than New York resembles Keokuk, Iowa. Only when the uniqueness of Rome is understood in its own right can one turn to the provinces to obtain a full and reasonable picture of the empire under the five good emperors.

Rome was truly an extraordinary city, especially by ancient standards. It was enormous, with a population somewhere between 500,000 and 750,000. Although it could boast of stately palaces, noble buildings, and beautiful residential areas, most people lived in jerrybuilt apartment houses. Fire and crime were perennial problems even after Augustus created fire and urban police forces. Streets were narrow, and drainage was inadequate. During the republic, sanitation had been a common problem. Numerous inscriptions record prohibitions against dumping human refuse and even cadavers on the grounds of sanctuaries and cemeteries. Under the empire this situation improved. By comparison with medieval and early modern European cities, Rome was a healthy enough place to live.

Rome was such a huge city that the surrounding countryside could not feed it. Because of the danger of starvation, the emperor, following republican practice, provided the citizen population with free grain for bread and, later, oil and wine. By feeding the citizenry, the emperor prevented bread riots caused by shortages and high prices. For the rest of the urban population who did not enjoy the rights of citizenship, the emperor provided grain at low prices. This measure was designed to prevent speculators from forcing up grain prices in times of crisis. By maintaining the grain supply, the emperor kept the favor of the people and ensured that Rome's poor and idle did not starve.

The emperor also entertained the Roman populace, often at vast expense. The most popular forms of public entertainment were gladiatorial contests and chariot racing. Gladiatorial fighting was originally an Etruscan funerary custom, a blood sacrifice for the dead. Many gladiators were criminals; some were the slaves of gladiatorial trainers; others were prisoners of war. Still others were free men who volunteered for the arena. Even women at times engaged in gladiatorial combat. Although some Romans protested gladiatorial fighting, most delighted in it. Not until the fifth century did Christianity put a stop to it.

The Romans were even more addicted to chariot racing than to gladiatorial shows. Under the empire, four permanent teams competed against one another. Each had its own color—red, white, green, or blue. Some Romans claimed that people cared more about their favorite team than about the race itself. Two-horse and four-horse chariots ran a course of seven laps, about five miles. A successful driver could be the hero of the hour. One charioteer, Gaius Appuleius Diocles, raced for twenty-four years. During that time he drove 4,257 starts and won 1,462 of them. His admirers honored him with an inscription that proclaimed him champion of all charioteers.

But people like the charioteer Diocles were no more typical of the common Roman than Babe Ruth is of the average American. Ordinary Romans left their mark in the inscriptions that grace their graves. They were proud of their work and accomplishments, affectionate toward their families and friends, and eager to be remembered after death. The funerary inscription of Paprius Vitalis to his wife is particularly engaging: "If there is anything good in the lower regions—I, however, finish a poor life without you—be happy there too, sweetest Thalassia . . . married to me for 40 years."[8]

The personal philosophies of typical Romans have come down from antiquity: "All we who are dead below have become bones and ashes, but nothing else."[9] "I was, I am not, I don't care." "To each his own tombstone." These Romans went about their lives as people have always done. Though fond of brutal spectacles, they also had their loves and dreams.

In the provinces and even on the frontiers, the era of the five good emperors was one of extensive prosperity, especially in western Europe. The Roman army had beaten back the barbarians and exposed them to the civilizing effects of Roman traders. The resulting peace and security opened Britain, Gaul, Germany, and the lands of the Danube to immigration. Agriculture flourished as large tracts of land came under cultivation. Most of this land was in the hands of free tenant farmers. From the time of Augustus slavery had declined in the empire, as had the growth of latifundia (see page 185). Augustus and his successors encouraged the rise of free farmers. Under the five good emperors this trend continued, and the holders of small parcels of land throve as never before. The emperors provided loans on easy terms to farmers, enabling them to rent land previously worked by slaves. They also permitted them to cultivate the new lands that were being opened up. Consequently, the small tenant farmer was becoming the backbone of Roman agriculture.

Chariot Racing   This brilliant mosaic found near Lyons, France, captures a typical chariot race. In the center around which the chariots are racing is a decorative pond with gushing water, dolphins, and egg-shaped spheres. *(Source: Cliché Musée de la Civilisation Gallo-Romaine de Lyons)*

In continental Europe the army was largely responsible for the new burst of expansion. The areas where legions were stationed readily became Romanized. When legionaries retired from the army, they often settled where they had served. Since they had usually learned a trade in the army, they brought essential skills to areas that badly needed trained men. These veterans took their retirement pay and used it to set themselves up in business.

The eastern part of the empire also participated in the boom. The Roman navy had swept the sea of pirates, and Eastern merchants traded throughout the Mediterranean. The flow of goods and produce in the East matched that of the West. Venerable cities like Corinth, Antioch, and Ephesus flourished as rarely before. The cities of the East built extensively, bedecking themselves with new amphitheaters, temples, fountains, and public buildings. For the East this age was the heyday of the city. Life there grew ever richer and more comfortable.

Trade among the provinces increased dramatically. Britain and Belgium became prime grain producers, much of their harvests going to the armies of the Rhine. Britain's wool industry probably got its start under the Romans. Italy and southern Gaul produced wine in huge quantities. Roman colonists had introduced the olive to southern Spain and northern Africa, an experiment so successful that these regions produced most of the oil consumed in the Western empire. In the East, Syrian farmers continued to cultivate the olive, and oil production reached an all-time high. Egypt was the prime grain producer of the East, and tons of Egyptian wheat went to feed the Roman populace. The Roman army in Mesopotamia consumed a high percentage of the raw materials and manufactured products of Syria and Asia Minor. The spread of trade meant the end of isolated and self-contained economies. By the time of the five good emperors, the empire had become an economic as well as a political reality (Map 7.4).

One of the most striking features of this period was the growth of industry in the provinces. Cities in Gaul and Germany eclipsed the old Mediterranean manufacturing centers. Italian cities were particularly hard hit by this development. Cities like Arretium and Capua had dominated the production of glass, pottery, and bronze ware. Yet in the second century A.D., Gaul and Germany took over the pottery market. Lyons in Gaul and later Cologne became the new center of the glassmaking industry. The cities of Gaul were nearly unrivaled in the manufacture of bronze and brass. For the first time in history, northern Europe was able to rival the Mediterranean as a producer of manufactured goods. Europe had entered fully into the economic and cultural life of the Mediterranean world.

The age of the five good emperors was generally one of peace, progress, and prosperity. The work of the Romans in northern and western Europe was a permanent contribution to the history of Western society. This period was also one of consolidation. Roads and secure sea lanes linked the empire in one vast web. The empire had become a commonwealth of cities, and urban life was its hallmark.

 ## ROME AND THE EAST

Their march to empire and their growing interest in foreign peoples brought the Romans into contact with a world much larger than Europe and the Mediterranean. As early as the late republic, Roman commanders in the East encountered peoples who created order out of the chaos left by Alexander the Great and his Hellenistic successors. This meeting of West and East had two immediate effects. The first was a long military confrontation between the Romans and their Iranian neighbors. Second, Roman military expansion to the east coincided with Chinese expansion to the west, and the surprising result was a period when the major ancient civilizations of the world were in touch with one another. For the first time in history, peoples from the Greco-Roman civilization of the Mediterranean and peoples from central Asia, India, and China met one another and observed one another's cultures at first hand.

Romans Versus Iranians

When Roman armies moved into Mesopotamia in 92 B.C., they encountered the Parthians, a people who had entered the Iranian Plateau from central Asia in the time of the Persian kings. The disintegration of Alexander's eastern holdings enabled them to reap the harvest of his victory. They created an empire that once stretched from Armenia and Babylonia in the west to the Hellenistic kingdom of Bactria in the east (Map 7.5). They divided

Roman Empire at its height, ca. A.D. 200

Principal trade routes by sea

Principal trade routes by land

Grain Principal products

their realm into large provinces, or *satrapies,* and created a flexible political organization to administer their holdings. Unlike China, however, Parthia never had a sophisticated bureaucracy. Nonetheless, the loose provincial organization enabled the Parthians to govern the many different peoples who inhabited their realm. The Romans marveled at Parthia's success, as the Greek geographer Strabo (ca 65 B.C.–A.D. 19) attests:

and now they rule so much territory and so many people that they have become in a way rivals of the Romans in the greatness of their empire.[10]

In the process the Parthians won their place in history as the heirs of the Persian Empire.

Although Augustus sought peace with the Parthians, later Roman emperors, beginning with Nero in A.D. 58, struggled to wrest Armenia and Mesopotamia from them. Until their downfall in 226, the Parthians met the Roman advance to the east with iron and courage.

The Romans found nothing to celebrate in the eclipse of the Parthians, for their place was immediately taken by the Sassanids, a people indigenous to southern Iran. As early as 230 the Sassanids launched a campaign to the west, which the Romans blunted. The setback was only temporary, for in 256 the great Persian king Shapur overran Mesopotamia and the Roman province of Syria. Four years later Shapur defeated the legions of the emperor Valerian, whom he took prisoner. Thereafter, the Romans and Sassanids fought long, bitter, and destructive wars in western Asia as the Romans battled to save their eastern provinces. Not until the reigns of Diocletian and Constantine was Roman rule again firmly established in western Asia.

Trade and Contact

Although warfare between Roman emperors and Iranian kings disrupted western Asia, it did not prevent Iran from becoming a link between East and West. Iran's geographical position facilitated communications and trade between the Roman and Chinese empires, the two wealthiest and most commercially active realms in the ancient world. As the middlemen in this trade, the Parthians tried to keep the Chinese and Romans from making direct contact—and thus from learning how large a cut the Parthians took in commercial transactions.

An elaborate network of roads linked Parthia to China in the east, India in the south, and the Roman Empire in the west. The many branch roads even included routes to southern Russia. The most important of the overland routes was the Silk Road, named for the shipments of silk that passed from China through Parthia to the Roman Empire (see Map 7.5). Many other luxury items also passed along this route: the Parthians exported exotic fruits, rare birds, ostrich eggs, and other dainties to China in return for iron and delicacies like apricots. Other easily portable luxury goods included gems, gold, silver, spices, and perfumes. From the Roman Empire came glassware, statuettes, and slaves trained as jugglers and acrobats.

Rarely did a merchant travel the entire distance from China to Mesopotamia. Chinese merchants typically sold their wares to Parthians at the Stone Tower, located at modern Tashkurghan in Afghanistan. From there Parthian traders carried goods across the Iranian Plateau to Mesopotamia or Egypt. This overland trade fostered urban life in Parthia as cities arose and prospered along the caravan routes. In the process, the Parthians themselves became important consumers of goods, contributing to the volume of trade and reinforcing the commercial ties between East and West.

More than goods passed along these windswept roads. Ideas, religious lore, and artistic inspiration also traveled the entire route. A fine example of how ideas and artistic influences spread across long distances is a Parthian coin that caught the fancy of an artist in China. The coin bore an inscription—a practice the Parthians had adopted from the Greeks—and although the artist could not read it, he used the lettering as a motif on a bronze vessel. Similarly, thoughts, ideas, and literary works found ready audiences; Greek plays were performed at the court of the Parthian king. At a time when communication was difficult and often dangerous, trade routes were important avenues for the spread of knowledge about other societies.

MAP 7.4 The Economic Aspect of the Pax Romana   The Roman Empire was not only a political and military organization but also an intricate economic network through which goods from Armenia and Syria were traded for Western products from as far away as Spain and Britain.

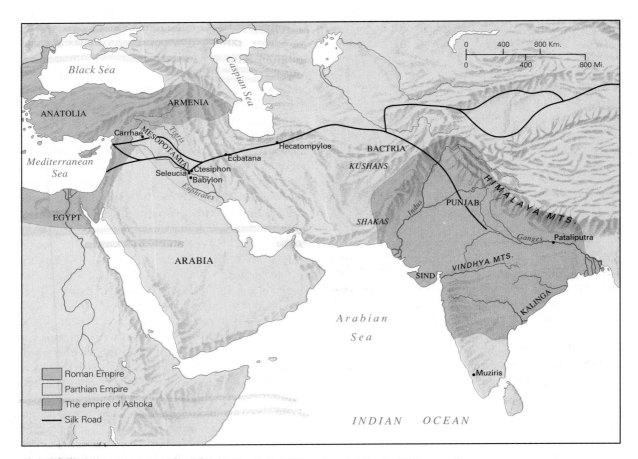

�֍ **MAP 7.5** **The Major Empires of Central and Southern Asia, ca 250 B.C.** From Anatolia in the West to the Himalayas in the East, three great empires ruled western, central, and southern Asia. During these years, frontiers fluctuated, but the Silk Road served as a thread connecting them all.

This was also an era of exciting maritime exploration. Roman ships sailed from Egyptian ports to the mouth of the Indus River, where they traded local merchandise and wares imported by the Parthians. Merchants who made the voyage had to contend with wind, shoal waters, and pirates. Despite such dangers and discomforts, hardy mariners pushed into the Indian Ocean and beyond, reaching Malaya, Sumatra, and Java.

Direct maritime trade between China and the West began in the second century A.D. The period of this contact coincided with the era of Han greatness in China. It was the Han emperor Wu Ti who took the momentous step of opening the Silk Road to the Parthian Empire. Indeed, a later Han emperor sent an ambassador directly to the Roman Empire by sea. The ambassador, Kan Ying, sailed to the Roman province of Syria, where during the reign of the Roman emperor Nerva (96–98) he became the first Chinese official to have a firsthand look at the Greco-Roman world. Kan Ying enjoyed himself thoroughly, and in A.D. 97 delivered a fascinating report of his travels to his emperor:

The inhabitants of that country are tall and well-proportioned, somewhat like the Chinese, whence they are called Ta-ts'in. The country contains much gold, silver, and rare precious stones . . . corals, amber, glass . . . gold embroidered rugs and thin silk-cloth and asbestos cloth. All the rare gems of other foreign countries come from there. They make coins of gold and silver. Ten units of silver are worth one of gold. They traffic by sea with An-hsi (Parthia) and Tien-chu (India), the profit of which trade is ten-fold. They are honest in their transactions and there are no double prices. Cereals are always cheap. . . . Their kings always desired to send embassies to China, but the An-hsi (Parthians) wished to carry on trade with them in Chinese silks, and it is for this reason that they were cut off from communication.[11]

The sea route and to a lesser extent the Silk Road included India in this long web of communications that, once established, was never entirely broken.

THE EMPIRE IN CRISIS

The era of the five good emperors gave way to a period of chaos and stress. During the third century A.D. the Roman Empire was stunned by civil wars and barbarian invasions. By the time peace was restored, the economy was shattered, cities had shrunk in size, and agriculture was becoming manorial. In the disruption of the third century and the reconstruction of the fourth, the medieval world had its origins.

Civil Wars and Invasions in the Third Century

After the death of Marcus Aurelius, the last of the five good emperors, his son Commodus, a man totally unsuited to govern the empire, came to the throne. His misrule led to his murder and a renewal of civil war. After a brief but intense spasm of fighting, the African general Septimius Severus defeated other rival commanders and established the Severan Dynasty (A.D. 193–235). Although Septimius Severus was able to stabilize the empire, his successors proved incapable of disciplining the legions. When the last of the Severi was killed by one of his own soldiers, the empire plunged into still another grim, destructive, and this time prolonged round of civil war.

Over twenty different emperors ascended the throne in the forty-nine years between 235 and 284, and many rebels died in the attempt to seize power. So many military commanders seized rule that the middle of the third century has become known as the age of the barracks emperors. The Augustan principate had become a military monarchy, and that monarchy was nakedly autocratic.

The first and most disastrous result of the civil wars was trouble on the frontiers. It was Rome's misfortune that this era of anarchy coincided with immense movements of barbarian peoples, still another example of the effects of mass migrations in ancient history, this time against one of the best organized empires of antiquity. Historians still dispute the precise reason for these migrations, though their immediate cause was pressure from tribes moving westward across Asia. In the sixth century A.D., Jordanes, a Christianized Goth, preserved the memory of innumerable wars among the barbarians in his *History of the Goths*. Goths fought Vandals; Huns fought Goths. Steadily the defeated and displaced tribes moved toward the Roman frontiers. Finally, like "a swarm of bees"— to use Jordanes's image—the Goths, one such people, burst into Europe in A.D. 258.

When the barbarians reached the Rhine and Danube frontiers, they often found huge gaps in the Roman defenses. During much of the third century A.D., bands of Goths devastated the Balkans as far south as Greece. The Alamanni, a German people, at one point entered Italy and reached Milan before they were beaten back. Meanwhile, the Franks, still another German folk, invaded eastern and central Gaul and northeastern Spain. Saxons from Scandinavia sailed into the English Channel in search of loot. In the East the Sassanids overran Mesopotamia. If the Roman army had been guarding the borders instead of creating and destroying emperors, none of these invasions would have been possible. The barracks emperors should be credited with one accomplishment, however: they fought barbarians when they were not fighting one other. Only that kept the empire from total ruin.

Reconstruction Under Diocletian and Constantine (A.D. 284–337)

At the close of the third century A.D., the emperor Diocletian (r. 284–305) put an end to the period of turmoil. Repairing the damage done in the third century was the major work of the emperor Constantine (r. 306–337) in the fourth. But the price was high.

Under Diocletian, the princeps became *dominus*—"lord." The emperor claimed that he was "the elect of God"—that he ruled because of God's favor. Constantine even claimed to be the equal of Jesus' first twelve followers.

No mere soldier but rather an adroit administrator, Diocletian gave serious thought to the

Prefecture of Gaul
Prefecture of Italy
Prefecture of Illyricum
Prefecture of the East

ATLANTIC OCEAN

North Sea

Baltic Sea

Caspian Sea

Black Sea

Mediterranean Sea

Adriatic Sea

Red Sea

BRITAIN

GERMANY

GAUL

FARTHER SPAIN

NEARER SPAIN

NARBONENSIS

Massilia

Lyons

Rhône

Ebro

Rhine

Elbe

Danube

RAETIA

NORICUM

CISALPINE GAUL

Ravenna

Rome

Tiber

Po

PANNONIA

DALMATIA

DACIA

MOESIA

THRACE

MACEDONIA

Athens

Corinth

Byzantium

PHRYGIA

LYDIA

ASIA

Pergamum

Smyrna

CAPPADOCIA

ARMENIA

CILICIA

Tarsus

CYPRUS

RHODES

CRETE

SYRIA

Antioch

Damascus

JUDAEA

Jerusalem

Petra

EGYPT

Alexandria

Nile

LIBYA

Cyrene

ARABIAN DESERT

Tigris

Euphrates

CRIMEA

Dnieper

Don

Volga

Line of division between East and West

Brundisium

SICILY

Syracuse

CORSICA

SARDINIA

BALEARIC IS.

Carthage

NUMIDIA

NORTH AFRICA

MAURETANIA

SAHARA

400 Mi.

400 Km.

200

200

0

To solve the first of these problems

empire's ailments. He recognized that the empire and its difficulties had become too great for one man to handle. He also realized that during the third century provincial governors had frequently used their positions to foment or participate in rebellions. To solve the first of these problems, Diocletian divided the empire into a western and an eastern half (Map 7.6). Diocletian assumed direct control of the eastern part; he gave the rule of the western part to a colleague, along with the title *augustus*, which had become synonymous with *emperor*. Diocletian and his fellow augustus further delegated power by appointing two men to assist them. Each man was given the title *caesar* to indicate his exalted rank. Although this system is known as the *Tetrarchy* because four men ruled the empire, Diocletian was clearly the senior partner and final source of authority.

Each half of the empire was further split into two prefectures, each governed by a prefect responsible to an augustus. Diocletian reduced the power of the old provincial governors by dividing provinces into smaller units. He organized the prefectures into small administrative units called *dioceses,* which were in turn subdivided into small provinces. Provincial governors were also deprived of their military power, retaining only their civil and administrative duties.

Diocletian's political reforms were a momentous step. The Tetrarchy soon failed, but Diocletian's division of the empire into two parts became permanent. Constantine and later emperors tried hard but unsuccessfully to keep the empire together. Throughout the fourth century A.D., the eastern and the western sections drifted apart. In later centuries the western part witnessed the fall of Roman government and the rise of barbarian kingdoms, while the eastern empire evolved into the majestic Byzantine Empire.

The most serious immediate matters confronting Diocletian and Constantine were economic, social, and religious. They needed additional revenues to support the army and the imperial court. Yet the wars and the barbarian invasions had caused widespread destruction and poverty. The fighting had struck a serious blow to Roman agriculture, which the emperors tried to revive. Christianity had become too strong either to ignore or to crush. The responses to these problems by Diocletian, Constantine, and their successors helped create the economic and social patterns that medieval Europe inherited.

The barracks emperors had dealt with economic hardship by depreciating the currency, cutting the silver content of coins until money was virtually worthless. As a result, the entire monetary system fell into ruin. In Egypt, governors had to order bankers to accept imperial money. The immediate result was crippling inflation throughout the empire.

The empire was less capable of recovery than in earlier times. Wars and invasions had disrupted normal commerce and the means of production and had hit the cities especially hard. Markets were disrupted, and travel became dangerous. Craftsmen, artisans, and traders rapidly left devastated regions. Cities were no longer places where trade and industry thrived. The devastation of the countryside increased the difficulty of feeding and supplying the cities. So extensive was the destruction that many wondered whether the ravages could be repaired at all.

The response of Diocletian and Constantine to these problems was marked by compulsion, rigidity, and loss of individual freedom. Diocletian's attempt to curb inflation illustrates the methods of absolute monarchy. In a move unprecedented in Roman history, he issued an edict that fixed maximum prices and wages throughout the empire. The measure proved a failure because it was unrealistic as well as unenforceable.

With the monetary system in ruins, most imperial taxes became payable in kind—that is, in goods or produce instead of money. The major drawback of payment in kind is its demands on transportation. Goods have to be moved from where they are grown or manufactured to where they are needed. Accordingly, the emperors locked into their occupations all people involved in the growing, preparation, and transportation of food and essential commodities. A baker or shipper could not go into any other business, and his son took up the trade at his death. The late Roman Empire had a place for everyone, and everyone had a place.

MAP 7.6 The Roman World Divided Diocletian divided the Roman Empire into a western and an eastern half. This development foreshadowed the medieval division between the Latin West and the Byzantine East.

Diocletian's Tetrarchy The emperor Diocletian's attempt to reform the Roman Empire by dividing rule among four men is represented in this sculpture, which in many features illustrates the transition from ancient to medieval art. The four tetrarchs demonstrate their solidarity by clasping one another on the shoulder. Nonetheless, each man has his other hand on his sword—a gesture that proved prophetic when Diocletian's reign ended and another struggle for power began. *(Source: Alinari/Art Resource, NY)*

The late Roman heritage to medieval Europe is most evident in agriculture. During the third century A.D., many free tenant farmers were killed or abandoned farms that had been ravaged in the fighting. Consequently, large tracts of land lay deserted. Great landlords with ample resources began to reclaim land and amass the huge estates that were the forerunners of medieval manors. In return for the protection and security that landlords could offer, free men and their families became the landlords' clients. To ensure a steady supply of labor for themselves, the landlords bound the free men to the soil. Henceforth they worked their patrons' land, not their own, and could not move elsewhere. Free men and women were in effect becoming serfs.

The Acceptance of Christianity

In religious affairs Constantine took the decisive step of recognizing Christianity as a legitimate religion. No longer would Christians suffer persecution for their beliefs as they had occasionally experienced earlier. Constantine himself died a Christian in 337. Why had the pagans persecuted Christians in the first place? Polytheism is by nature tolerant of new gods and accommodating in religious matters. Why was Christianity singled out for violence? These questions are still matters of scholarly debate, but some broad answers can be given.

A splendid approach to these problems has come from the eminent Italian scholar Marta Sordi.[12] Confronting a very complicated topic, she offers evidence that the Christians exaggerated the degree of pagan hostility to them and that most of the gory stories about the martyrs are fictitious. There were indeed some cases of pagan persecution of the Christians, but with few exceptions they were local and sporadic. Even Nero's notorious persecution was temporary and limited to Rome. No constant persecution of Christians occurred. Instead, pagans and Christians alike enjoyed long periods of tolerance and even friendship. Nonetheless, some pagans thought that Christians were atheists because they scorned the traditional pagan gods. Christians in fact either denied the existence of pagan gods or called them evil spirits. They went so far as to urge people not to worship pagan gods. In turn, pagans, who believed in their gods as fervently as the Christians believed in their one god, feared that the gods would withdraw their favor from the Roman Empire because of Christian blasphemy.

At first many pagans genuinely misunderstood Christian practices and rites. Even educated and cultured people like the historian Tacitus opposed Christianity because they saw it as a bizarre new sect. Tacitus believed that Christians hated the whole human race. As a rule, early Christians kept to themselves. Romans distrusted and feared their exclusiveness, which seemed unsociable and even subversive. They thought the Lord's Supper, at

ROMAN HISTORY AFTER AUGUSTUS

Period	Important Emperors	Significant Events
Julio-Claudians 27 B.C.–A.D. 68	Augustus, 27 B.C.–A.D. 14 Tiberius, 14–37 Caligula, 37–41 Claudius, 41–54 Nero, 54–68	Augustan settlement Beginning of the principate Birth and death of Jesus Expansion into northern and Western Europe Creation of the imperial bureaucracy
Year of the Four Emperors 68–69	Nero Galba Otho Vitellius	Civil war Major breakdown of the concept of the principate
Flavians 69–96	Vespasian, 69–79 Titus, 79–81 Domitian, 81–96	Growing trend toward the concept of monarchy Defense and further consolidation of the European frontiers
Antonines 96–192	Nerva, 96–98 Trajan, 98–117 Hadrian, 117–138 Antoninus Pius, 138–161 Marcus Aurelius, 161–180 Commodus, 180–192	The "golden age"—the era of the "five good emperors" Economic prosperity Trade and growth of cities in northern Europe Beginning of barbarian menace on the frontiers
Severi 193–235	Septimius Severus, 193–211 Caracalla, 211–217 Elagabalus, 218–222 Severus Alexander, 222–235	Military monarchy All free men within the empire given Roman citizenship
"Barracks Emperors" 235–284	Twenty-two emperors in forty-nine years	Civil war Breakdown of the empire Barbarian invasions Severe economic decline
Tetrarchy 284–337	Diocletian, 284–305 Constantine, 306–337	Political recovery Autocracy Legalization of Christianity Transition to the Middle Ages in the West Birth of the Byzantine Empire in the East

which Christians said that they ate and drank the body and blood of Jesus, was an act of cannibalism. Pagans also thought that Christians indulged in immoral and indecent rituals. They considered Christianity one of the worst of the Eastern mystery cults, for one of the hallmarks of many of those cults was disgusting rituals.

Another source of misunderstanding was that the pagans did not demand that Christians *believe* in pagan gods. Greek and Roman religion was never a matter of belief or ethics. It was purely a religion of ritual. One of the clearest statements of pagan theological attitudes comes from the Roman senator Symmachus in the later fourth century A.D.:

We watch the same stars; heaven is the same for us all; the same universe envelops us: what importance is it in what way anyone looks for truth? It is impossible to arrive by one route at such a great secret.[13]

Yet Roman religion was inseparable from the state. An attack on one was an attack on the other. The Romans were being no more fanatical or intolerant than the eighteenth-century English judge who declared the Christian religion part of the law of the land. All the pagans expected was performance of the ritual act, a small token of sacrifice. Those Christians who sacrificed went free, no matter what they personally believed.

As time went on, pagan hostility decreased. Pagans realized that Christians were not working to overthrow the state and that Jesus was no rival of Caesar. The emperor Trajan forbade his governors to hunt down Christians. Trajan admitted that he thought Christianity an abomination, but he preferred to leave Christians in peace.

The stress of the third century, however, seemed to some emperors the punishment of the gods. What else could account for such anarchy? With the empire threatened on every side, a few emperors thought that one way to appease the gods was by offering them the proper sacrifices. Such sacrifices would be a sign of loyalty to the empire, a show of Roman solidarity and religious piety. Consequently, a new wave of persecutions began out of desperation. Although the Christians depicted the emperor Diocletian as a fiend, he persecuted them in the hope that the gods would restore their blessings on Rome. Yet even these persecutions were never very widespread or long-lived; most pagans were not greatly sympathetic to the new round of persecutions. Pagan and Christian alike must have been relieved when Constantine legalized the Christian religion.

In time the Christian triumph would be complete. In 380 the emperor Theodosius made Christianity the official religion of the Roman Empire. At that point Christians began to persecute the pagans for their beliefs. History had come full circle.

The Construction of Constantinople

The triumph of Christianity was not the only event that made Constantine's reign a turning point in Roman history. Constantine took the bold step of building a new capital for the empire. Constantinople, the New Rome, was constructed on the site of Byzantium, an old Greek city on then Bosporus. Throughout the third century, emperors had found Rome and the West hard to defend. The eastern part of the empire was more easily defensible and escaped the worst of the barbarian devastation. It was wealthy and its urban life still vibrant. Moreover, Christianity was more widespread in the East than in the West, and the city of Constantinople was intended to be a Christian center.

SUMMARY

The Romans conquered the Mediterranean world only to find that conquest required them to change their way of life. Politically, their city-state constitution broke down and expired in the wars of the republic. Even so, men like Caesar and later Augustus sought new solutions to the problems confronting Rome. The result was a system of government capable of administering an empire with justice and fairness. Out of the failure of the republic arose the pax Romana of the empire.

The Roman Empire created by Augustus nearly collapsed before being restored by Diocletian and Constantine. Constantine's legalization and patronage of Christianity and his shift of the capital from Rome to Constantinople marked a new epoch in Western history as the ancient world gave way to the medieval. In the process the Roman Empire came into direct contact with its Asian neighbors, sometimes in anger but more often in peace. Never before in Western history and not again until modern times did one state govern so much territory for so long a time.

The true heritage of Rome is its long tradition of law and freedom. Under Roman law and government, the empire enjoyed relative peace and security for extensive periods of time. Through Rome the best of ancient thought and culture was preserved to make its contribution to modern life. Perhaps no better epitaph for Rome can be found than the words of Virgil:

While rivers shall run to the sea,
While shadows shall move across the valleys of
* mountains,*
While the heavens shall nourish the stars,
Always shall your honor and your name and your
* fame endure.*[14]

NOTES

1. Polybius, *The Histories* 1.1.5. Unless otherwise credited, all quotations from a foreign language in this chapter have been translated into English by John Buckler.
2. Sallust, *War with Catiline* 10.1–3.
3. Ovid, *Fasti* 2.535–539.
4. Plutarch, *Life of Tiberius Gracchus* 9.5–6.
5. Plutarch, *Life of Antony* 2.8.
6. Horace, *Odes* 4.15.
7. Matthew 3:3.
8. *Corpus Inscriptionum Latinarum,* vol. 6 (Berlin: G. Reimer, 1882), no. 9792.
9. Ibid., vol. 6, no. 14672.
10. Strabo, 11.9.2.
11. Quoted in W. H. Schoff, *The Periplus of the Erythraean Sea* (London: Longmans, Green, 1912), p. 276.
12. See M. Sordi, *The Christians and the Roman Empire,* trans. A. Bedini (Norman: University of Oklahoma Press, 1986).
13. Symmachus, *Relations* 3.10.
14. Virgil, *Aeneid* 1.607–609.

SUGGESTED READING

R. T. Ridley, *The History of Rome* (1989), is an undogmatic history of Rome, firmly based in the sources. The Etruscans have inspired a great deal of work, most notably M. Pallottino, *A History of Earliest Italy* (1991), which treats the entire period of early relations among peoples; E. Gabba, *Dionysius and the History of Archaic Rome* (1991), is the study of the origins of Rome. J. F. Gardner, *Being a Roman Citizen* (1993), is a broad work that includes material on former slaves, the lower classes, and much else. S. L. Dyson, *The Creation of the Roman Frontier* (1985), deals with the process by which the Romans established their frontiers. See also E. S. Gruen, *Culture and National Identity in Republican Rome* (1992).

A. M. Eckstein's *Senate and Generals* (1987) discusses how the decisions of individual generals affected both the senate and Roman foreign relations.

K. D. White, *Roman Farming* (1970), deals with agriculture. Work on Roman social history has advanced in several areas. A wealth of research on the Roman family and related topics has recently appeared, including K. R. Bradley, *Discovering the Roman Family* (1990), a series of essays on Roman social history; S. Dixon, *The Roman Family* (1992); S. Treggiari, *Roman Marriage* (1991); and R. A. Baumann, *Women and Politics in Ancient Rome* (1992). E. Eyben, *Restless Youth in Ancient Rome* (1993), explores the mores of youth of the upper class.

Some good general treatments of the empire include J. Wacher, ed., *The Roman World,* 2 vols. (1987), which attempts a comprehensive survey of the world of the Roman Empire.

R. MacMullen, *Enemies of the Roman Order* (1993), treats the ways in which the Romans dealt with alien and sometimes hostile behavior within the empire. V. Rudich, *Political Dissidence Under Nero* (1993), provides an unorthodox treatment of the subject that examines the reasons behind some popular rejections of official policy. D. J. Breeze and B. Dobson, *Roman Officers and Frontiers* (1993), analyze the careers of officers and how they defended the frontiers.

The commercial life of the empire is the subject of M. Rostovtzeff, *The Economic and Social History of the Roman Empire* (1957). J. Rich, *The City in Late Antiquity* (1992), traces the influence of late Roman cities on their medieval successors.

Social aspects of the empire are the subject of L. A. Thompson, *Romans and Blacks* (1989). J. Humphrey, *Roman Circuses and Chariot Racing* (1985), treats a topic very dear to the hearts of ancient Romans. C. A. Barton, *The Sorrows of the Ancient Romans* (1993), is an intriguing attempt to understand the Roman fascination with gladiatorial games. K. R. Bradley, *Slaves and Masters in the Roman Empire* (1988), discusses social controls in a slaveholding society.

Christianity, paganism, Judaism, and the ways in which they all met have received much attention of A. Chester, *The Social Context of Early Christianity* (1989). Jesus and the history of early Christianity are the subjects of much recent scholarship. In general, see J. T. Burtchaell, *From Synagogue to Church* (1992); related is J. Lieu, ed., *The Jews Among Pagans and Christians* (1992), which explores relations among all three sets of beliefs. More dramatic perhaps are J. D. Crossan, *The Historical Jesus* (1991); J. Meier, *A Marginal Jew* (1992); and *The Lost Gospel* (1993), which studies "The Book of Q" and its relation to Christian origins. F. R. Trombley, *Hellenic Religion and Christianization, c. 370–529,* 2 vols. (1993), is an excellent examination of how Greek religion influenced the development of Christianity in the eastern parts of the later Roman Empire.

New treatments of two of the most important Augustan poets are C. Kallendorf, ed., *Virgil* (1993), and W. S. Anderson, ed., *Ovid* (1993).

S. N. C. Lieu and M. Dodgeon, *Rome's Eastern Frontier, A.D. 226–363* (1988), rely primarily on documents to trace Rome's policy in the East during this difficult period. R. MacMullen, *Constantine* (1988), written by a leading scholar in the field, provides a broad and lucid interpretation of Constantine and the significance of his reign.

8

The Making of Europe

Interior (view from the apse) of the Byzantine church San Vitale, Ravenna, 526–7 A.D. *(Source: Scala/Art Resource, NY)*

The five centuries between approximately 400 and 900 present a paradox. They witnessed the disintegration of the Western Roman Empire, which had been one of humanity's great political and cultural achievements. But they were also a creative and seminal period during which Europeans laid the foundations for medieval and modern Europe. It is not overstatement to say that this period saw the making of Europe.

The basic ingredients that went into the making of a distinctly European civilization were the cultural legacy of Greece and Rome, the customs and traditions of the Germanic peoples, and the Christian faith. The most important of these was Christianity. It absorbed and assimilated the other two. It reinterpreted the classics in a Christian sense. It instructed the Germanic peoples and gave them new ideals of living and social behavior. Christianity became the cement that held European society together.

During this period the Byzantine Empire, centered at Constantinople, served as a protective buffer between Europe and peoples to the east. The Byzantine Greeks and the Muslims (see Chapter 9) preserved the philosophical and scientific texts of the ancient world, which later formed the basis for study in science and medicine. The Byzantines also produced a great synthesis of Roman law, Justinian's *Code*. Living an urbane and sophisticated life at Constantinople, the Greeks set a standard far above the primitive existence of the West.

- How did the Greco-Roman heritage, Germanic traditions, and the Christian faith act on one another?
- How did they lead to the making of Europe?
- What influence did Byzantine culture have on the making of Europe?

This chapter will focus on these questions.

❈ THE GROWTH OF THE CHRISTIAN CHURCH

As we have seen, Christianity was a syncretic faith, absorbing and adapting many of the religious ideas of the eastern Mediterranean world. From Judaism came the concept, unique in the ancient world, of monotheism—belief in one God—together with the rich ethical and moral precepts of the Old Testament Scriptures. From Orphism, a set of sixth-century B.C. religious ideas, came the belief that the body is the prison of the soul. From Hellenistic thought came the notion of the superiority of spirit over matter. Likewise, scholars have noticed the similarity between the career of Jesus and that of the gods of Eastern mystery cults (see page 160).

While many elements of the Roman Empire disintegrated, the Christian church survived and grew. What is the church? Scriptural scholars tell us that the earliest use of the word *church* (in Greek, *ekklesia*) in the New Testament appears in Saint Paul's Letter to the Christians of Thessalonica in northern Greece, written about A.D. 51. By *ekklesia* Paul meant the local community of Christian believers. In Paul's later letters, the term *church* refers to the entire Mediterranean-wide assembly of Jesus' followers. After the legalization of Christianity by the emperor Constantine (see page 208) and the growth of institutional offices and officials, the word *church* was sometimes applied to those officials—much as the terms *the college* or *the university* are used today to refer to academic administrators. Then the bishops of Rome—known as popes from the Latin word *papa,* meaning "father"—claimed to speak and act as the source of unity for all Christians. The popes claimed to be the successors of Saint Peter and heirs to his authority as chief of the apostles, on the basis of Jesus' words:

You are Peter, and on this rock I will build my church, and the jaws of death shall not prevail against it. I will entrust to you the keys of the kingdom of heaven. Whatever you declare bound on earth shall be bound in heaven; whatever you declare loosed on earth shall be loosed in heaven.[1]

Roman bishops used this text, known as the Petrine Doctrine, to support their assertions of authority over other bishops in the church. Thus the popes maintained that they represented "the church." The word *church,* therefore, has several connotations. Modern Catholic theology frequently defines the church as "the people of God" and identifies it with local and international Christian communities, but in the Middle Ages the institutional and monarchial interpretations tended to be stressed.

Having gained the support of the fourth-century emperors, the church gradually adopted the Roman system of organization. Christianity had a dynamic missionary policy, and the church slowly succeeded in *assimilating*—that is, adapting—pagan peoples, both Germans and Romans, to Christian teaching. Moreover, the church possessed able administrators and leaders and highly literate and creative thinkers. These factors help to explain the survival and growth of the Christian church in the face of repeated Germanic invasions.

The Church and the Roman Emperors

The church benefited considerably from the emperors' support. In return, the emperors expected the support of the Christian church in maintaining order and unity. After legalizing its practice, Constantine encouraged Christianity throughout his reign. In 380 the emperor Theodosius went further than Constantine and made Christianity the official religion of the empire. Theodosius stripped Roman pagan temples of statues, made the practice of the old Roman state religion a treasonable offense, and persecuted Christians who dissented from orthodox doctrine. Most significant, he allowed the church to establish its own courts. Church courts began to develop their own body of law, called *canon law*. These courts, not the Roman government, had jurisdiction over the clergy and ecclesiastical disputes. At the death of Theodosius, the Christian church was considerably independent of the Roman state. The foundation for the medieval church's power had been laid.

In the fourth century, theological disputes frequently and sharply divided the Christian community. Some disagreements had to do with the nature of Christ. For example, Arianism, which originated with Arius (ca 250–336), a priest of Alexandria, denied that Christ was divine and co-eternal with God the Father—two propositions of orthodox Christian belief. Arius held that God the Father was by definition uncreated and unchangeable. Jesus, however, was born of Mary, grew in wisdom, and suffered punishment and death. Jesus was created by the will of the Father and thus was not co-eternal with the Father. Therefore, Arius reasoned, Jesus the Son must be less than or inferior to the Unbegotten Father, who is incapable of

suffering and did not die. This argument implies that Jesus stands somewhere between God the Creator and humanity in need of redemption. Orthodox theologians branded Arius's position a *heresy*—denial of a basic doctrine of faith.

Arianism enjoyed such popularity and provoked such controversy that Constantine, to whom religious disagreement meant civil disorder, interceded. In 325 he summoned a council of church leaders to Nicaea in Asia Minor and presided over it personally. The council produced the Nicene Creed, which defined the orthodox position that Christ is "eternally begotten of the Father" and of the same substance as the Father. Arius and those who refused to accept the creed were banished, the first case of civil punishment for heresy. This participation of the emperor in a theological dispute within the church paved the way for later emperors to claim that they could do the same.

So active was the emperor Theodosius's participation in church matters that he eventually came to loggerheads with Bishop Ambrose of Milan (339–397). Theodosius ordered Ambrose to hand over his cathedral church to the emperor. Ambrose's response had important consequences for the future:

At length came the command, "Deliver up the Basilica"; I reply, "It is not lawful for us to deliver it up, nor for your Majesty to receive it. . . . It is asserted that all things are lawful to the Emperor, that all things are his. But do not burden your conscience with the thought that you have any right as Emperor over sacred things. Exalt not yourself, but if you would reign the longer, be subject to God. It is written, God's to God and Caesar's to Caesar. The palace is the Emperor's, the Churches are the Bishop's. To you is committed jurisdiction over public, not over sacred buildings."[2]

Ambrose insisted that the church was independent of the state's jurisdiction. He insisted that, in matters relating to the faith or the church, the bishops were to be the judges of emperors, not the other way around. In a Christian society, harmony and peace depended on agreement between the bishop and the secular ruler. But if disagreement developed, Ambrose maintained, the church was ultimately the superior power because the church was responsible for the salvation of all (including the emperor). Throughout the Middle Ages, theologians, canonists, and propagandists repeatedly cited Ambrose's position as the basis of relations between the two powers.

Inspired Leadership

The early Christian church benefited from the brilliant administrative abilities of some church leaders and from identification of the authority and dignity of the bishop of Rome with the imperial traditions of the city. With the empire in decay, educated people joined and worked for the church in the belief that it was the one institution able to provide leadership. Bishop Ambrose, for example, the son of the Roman prefect of Gaul, was a trained lawyer and governor of a province. He is typical of those Roman aristocrats who held high public office, were converted to Christianity, and subsequently became bishops. Such men later provided social continuity from Roman to Germanic rule.

During the reign of Diocletian (284–305), the Roman Empire had been divided for administrative purposes into geographical units called *dioceses.* Gradually the church made use of this organizational structure. Christian bishops established their headquarters, or *sees,* in the urban centers of the old Roman dioceses. A bishop's jurisdiction extended throughout all parts of his diocese. The center of the bishop's authority was his cathedral (the word derives from the Latin *cathedra,* meaning "chair"). Thus church leaders capitalized on the Roman imperial method of organization and adapted it to ecclesiastical purposes.

After the removal of the imperial capital and the emperor to Constantinople (see page 210), the bishop of Rome exercised considerable influence in the West because he had no real competitor there. Successive bishops of Rome stressed the special importance of Rome in the framework of the old empire. They reminded Christians in other parts of the world that Rome was the burial place of Saint Peter and Saint Paul. Moreover, according to tradition, Saint Peter, the chief of Christ's first twelve followers, had lived and been executed in Rome. No other city in the world could make such claims.

In the fifth century the bishops of Rome began to stress their supremacy over other Christian communities and to urge other churches to appeal to Rome for the resolution of disputed doctrinal issues. Thus Pope Innocent I (r. 401–417) wrote to the bishops of north Africa:

Pope Gregory I (r. 590–604) and Scribes   One of the four "Doctors" (or Learned Fathers) of the Latin church, Gregory is shown in this tenth-century ivory book cover writing at his desk while the Holy Spirit in the form of a dove whispers in his ear. Below, scribes copy Gregory's works. *(Source: Kunsthistorisches Museum, Vienna)*

We approve your action in following the principle that nothing which was done even in the most remote and distant provinces should be taken as finally settled unless it came to the notice of this See, that any just pronouncement might be confirmed by all the authority of this See, and that the other churches might from thence gather what they should teach.[3]

The prestige of Rome and the church as a whole was also enhanced by the courage and leadership of the Roman bishops. According to tradition, Pope Leo I (r. 440–461) met the advancing army of Attila the Hun in 452 and, through his power of persuasion, saved Rome from destruction. According to legend, three years later, Leo persuaded the Vandal leader Gaiseric not to burn the city, though the pope could not prevent a terrible sacking.

By the time Gregory I (r. 590–604) became pope, there was no civic authority left to handle the problems pressing the city. Flood, famine, plague, and invasion by the Lombards made for an almost disastrous situation. Pope Gregory concluded a peace with the Lombards, organized relief services that provided water and food for the citizens, and established hospitals for the sick and dying. The fact that it was Christian leaders, rather than imperial administrators, who responded to the city's dire needs could not help but increase the prestige and influence of the church.

Although Innocent I and Leo I strongly asserted the primacy of the Roman papacy, those assertions were not universally accepted. Local Christian communities and their leaders often exercised decisive authority over their local churches. Particular social and political conditions determined the actual power of the bishop of Rome in a given circumstance. The importance of arguments for the Roman primacy, holding the first place among Christian bishops, rests in the fact that they served as precedents for later appeals.

Missionary Activity

The word *catholic* derives from a Greek word meaning "general," "universal," or "worldwide." Christ had said that his teaching was for all peoples, and Christians sought to make their faith catholic—that is, believed everywhere. This could be accomplished only through missionary activity. As Saint Paul had written to the Christian community at Colossae in Asia Minor:

You have stripped off your old behavior with your old self, and you have put on a new self which will progress towards true knowledge the more it is renewed in the image of its creator; and in that image there is no room for distinction between Greek and Jew, between the circumcised or the uncircumcised, or between barbarian or Scythian, slave and free man. There is only Christ; he is everything and he is in everything.[4]

Paul urged Christians to bring the "good news" of Christ to all peoples. The Mediterranean served as the highway over which Christianity spread to the cities of the empire (Map 8.1).

Christian communities were scattered throughout Gaul and Britain during the Roman occupation. The effective beginnings of Christianity in Gaul can be traced to Saint Martin of Tours (ca 316–397), a Roman soldier who, after giving half of his cloak to a naked beggar, had a vision of Christ and was baptized. Martin founded the monastery of Ligugé, the first in Gaul; it became a center for the evangelization of the country districts. In 372 he became bishop of Tours and introduced a rudimentary parish system.

Tradition identifies the conversion of Ireland with Saint Patrick (ca 385–461), one of the most effective missionaries in history. Born in western England to a Christian family of Roman citizenship, Patrick was captured and enslaved by Irish raiders and taken to Ireland, where he worked for six years as a herdsman. He escaped and returned to England, where a vision urged him to Christianize Ireland. In preparation, Patrick studied in Gaul and in 432 was consecrated a bishop. He converted the Irish tribe by tribe, having first baptized each tribal chief.

In 445, with the approval of Pope Leo I, Patrick established his see in Armagh. Armagh was a monastery, and the monastery, rather than the diocese, served as the center of ecclesiastical organization in Ireland. Local tribes and the monastery were interdependent. The tribes supported the monastery economically, and the monastery provided religious and educational services for the tribes. Patrick also introduced the Roman alphabet and supported the codification of traditional laws. By the time of his death, the majority of the Irish people had received Christian baptism.

The Christianization of the English really began in 597, when Pope Gregory I sent a delegation of monks under the Roman Augustine to Britain to convert the English. Augustine's approach, like Patrick's, was to concentrate on converting the chief or king. When he succeeded in converting Ethelbert, king of Kent, the baptism of Ethelbert's people took place as a matter of course. Augustine established his see at Canterbury, the capital of Kent.

The conversion of the English had far-reaching consequences because Britain later served as a base

MAP 8.1 The Spread of Christianity   Originating in Judaea, the southern part of modern Israel and Jordan, Christianity spread throughout the Roman world. Roman sea lanes and Roman roads facilitated its expansion.

for the Christianization of the European continent (see Map 8.1). Between the fifth and tenth centuries, the great majority of peoples living on the European continent and the nearby islands accepted the Christian religion—that is, they received baptism, though baptism in itself did not automatically transform people into Christians.

Religion influenced all aspects of tribal life. All members of a tribe participated in religious observances because doing so was a social duty. Religion was not a private or individual matter; the religion of the chief or king determined the religion of the people. Thus Patrick, Augustine, and other missionaries concentrated their initial efforts on kings or tribal chieftains. According to custom, tribal chiefs negotiated with all foreign powers, including

the gods. Because the Christian missionaries represented a "foreign" power (the Christian God), the king dealt with them. Germanic kings accepted Christianity for various reasons: because they believed that the Christian God was more powerful than pagan gods and would deliver victory in battle; because Christianity taught obedience to (kingly) authority; or because Christian priests possessed knowledge and charisma that they associated with kingly power. Whatever the reason, if the ruler accepted Christian baptism, his people did so too. With the resulting mass baptism, however, the work of Christianization had only begun. Baptism meant either sprinkling the head or immersing the body in water. Conversion meant mental and heartfelt acceptance of the beliefs of Christianity.

The Germanic peoples were warriors who idealized the military virtues of physical strength, ferocity in battle, and loyalty to the leader. Victors in battle enjoyed the spoils of success and plundered the vanquished. The greater the fighter, the more trophies and material goods he collected. Thus the Germans had trouble accepting the Christian precepts of "love your enemies" and "turn the other cheek," and they found the Christian notions of sin and repentance virtually incomprehensible. Sin in Christian thought meant disobedience to the will of God as revealed in the Ten Commandments and the teaching of Christ. Good or "moral" behavior to the barbarians meant the observance of tribal customs and practices. In Germanic society, dishonorable behavior brought social ostracism. The inculcation of Christian ideals took a very long time.

How effective was Christian missionary activity? Between the fifth and tenth centuries most people in Europe received Christian baptism, learned something about the commandments and teachings of Jesus, and eventually identified themselves as Christian. So from a social and formal point of view the missionaries were "successful." But the chronic violence and warfare, theft, arson, rape, and pillage that characterized so much of society attest to the incomplete conversion of the European peoples and their unwillingness to follow Jesus' fundamental message to love God and one's neighbor.

Conversion and Assimilation

In Christian theology, conversion involves a turning toward God—that is, a conscious effort to live according to the Gospel message. How did missionaries and priests get masses of pagan and illiterate peoples to understand and live by Christian ideals and teachings? Through preaching, through assimilation, and through the penitential system.

Preaching aimed at instruction and edification. Instruction presented the basic teachings of Christianity. Edification was intended to strengthen the newly baptized in their faith through stories about the lives of Christ and the saints. Deeply ingrained pagan customs and practices, however, could not be stamped out by words alone or even by imperial edicts. Christian missionaries often pursued a policy of assimilation, easing the conversion of pagan men and women by stressing similarities between their customs and beliefs and those of Christianity.

A letter from Pope Gregory I to Augustine of Canterbury in 601 beautifully illustrates this policy:

we have been giving careful thought to the affairs of the English, and have come to the conclusion that the temples of the idols among that people should on no account be destroyed. The idols are to be destroyed, but the temples themselves are to be aspersed with holy water, altars set up in them, and relics deposited there. For if these temples are well-built, they must be purified from the worship of demons and dedicated to the service of the true God. In this way, we hope that the people, seeing that their temples are not destroyed, may abandon their error and, flocking more readily to their accustomed resorts, may come to know and adore the true God.[5]

How assimilation works is perhaps best appreciated through the example of a festival familiar to all Americans, Saint Valentine's Day. There were two Romans named Valentine. Both were Christian priests, and both were martyred for their beliefs around the middle of February in the third century A.D. Since about 150 B.C. the Romans had celebrated the festival of Lupercalia, at which they asked the gods for fertility for themselves, their fields, and their flocks, in mid-February, before the arrival of spring. Thus the early church "converted" the old festival of Lupercalia into Saint Valentine's Day. (Nothing in the lives of the two Christian martyrs connects them with lovers or the exchange of messages and gifts. That practice began in the later Middle Ages.)

In the early church confession meant that the sinner *publicly* acknowledged charges laid against him or her and *publicly* carried out the penitential works that the priest or bishop prescribed. For example, an adulterer might have to stand outside the church before services, wearing a sign naming his or her sin and asking for the prayers of everyone who entered. Beginning in the late sixth century, Irish and English missionaries brought the penitential system to continental Europe. The illiterate penitent knelt before the priest, who questioned the penitent about the sins he or she might have committed. The priest then imposed a penance. Penance usually meant fasting for a period of time on bread and water, which was intended as a medicine for the soul. Here is a section of the penitential prepared by Archbishop Theodore of Canterbury (668–690), which circulated widely at the time:

If anyone commits fornication with a virgin he shall do penance for one year. If with a married woman, he shall do penance for four years, two of these entire. . . .

A male who commits fornication with a male shall do penance for three years.

If a woman practices vice with a woman, she shall do penance for three years.

Whoever has often committed theft, seven years is his penance, or such a sentence as his priest shall determine, that is, according to what can be arranged with those whom he has wronged. . . .

If a layman slays another with malice aforethought, if he will not lay aside his arms, he shall do penance for seven years; without flesh and wine, three years.

He who defiles his neighbor's wife, deprived of his own wife, shall fast for three years two days a week and in the three forty-day periods.

Women who commit abortion before [the fetus] has life, shall do penance for one year or for the three forty-day periods or for forty days, according to the nature of the offense; and if later, that is, more than forty days after conception, they shall do penance as murderesses.[6]

As this sample suggests, writers of penitentials were preoccupied with sexual transgressions.

Penitentials provide an enormous amount of information about the ascetic ideals of early Christianity and about the crime-ridden realities of Celtic and Germanic societies. Penitentials also reveal the ecclesiastical foundations of some modern attitudes toward sex, birth control, and abortion. Unlike the earlier public penances, Celtic forms permitted the repeated reconciliation of the same

The Pantheon (Interior)   Originally a temple for the gods, the Pantheon later served as a Christian church. As such, it represents the adaptation of pagan elements to Christian purposes. *(Source: Alinari/Art Resource, NY)*

✤ **The Two Marys at the Sepulcher** This late-fourth-century ivory panel tells the story (Matthew 28:1–6) of Mary Magdalene and another woman named Mary, who went to Jesus' tomb. They discovered the stone at the entrance rolled away and an angel (lower panel, at left) sitting on it. The guards assigned to watch the tomb "trembled and became like dead men" (upper panel). The angel told the women that Jesus had risen. The blend of Roman artistic style—in spacing, drapery, men's hair fashion—and Christian subject matter shows the assimilation of classical form and Christian teaching. (*Source: Castello Sforzesco/Scala/Art Resource, NY*)

sinner in a *private* situation involving only the priest and penitent. We do not know whether these severe penances were actually enforced; some scholars believe they were not. In any case, the penitential system contributed to the growth of a different attitude toward religion: formerly public, corporate, and social, religious observances became private, personal, and individual.[7]

✤ CHRISTIAN ATTITUDES TOWARD CLASSICAL CULTURE

Probably the major dilemma the early Christian church faced concerned Greco-Roman culture. In Greek philosophy, art, and architecture, in Roman law, literature, education, and engineering, the legacy of a great civilization continued. The Christian religion had begun and spread within this intellectual and psychological milieu. What was to be the attitude of Christians to the Greco-Roman world of ideas?

Adjustment

Christians in the first and second centuries believed that Christ would soon fulfill his promise to return and that the end of the world was near. Thus they considered knowledge useless and learning a waste of time, and they preached the duty of Christians to prepare for the Second Coming of the Lord. Good Christians who sought the Kingdom of Heaven by imitating Christ believed they had to disassociate themselves from the "filth" that Roman culture embodied.

Saint Paul (A.D. 5?–67?) had written, "The wisdom of the world is foolishness, we preach Christ crucified." And about a century and a half later, Tertullian (ca 160–220), an influential African Christian writer, condemned all secular literature as foolishness in the eyes of God. He called the Greek philosophers, such as Aristotle, "hucksters of eloquence" and compared them to "animals of self-glorification." "What has Athens to do with Jerusalem," he demanded, "the Academy with the Church? We have no need for curiosity since Jesus Christ, nor for inquiry since the gospel." Tertullian insisted that Christians would find in the Bible all the wisdom they needed.

Nevertheless, Christianity encouraged adjustment to the ideas and institutions of the Roman world. Specifically addressing Christians living among non-Christians in the hostile environment of Rome, for example, the author of the First Letter of Peter had written about the obligations of Christians toward civil authority:

For the sake of the Lord, accept the authority of every social institution: the emperor, as the supreme authority, and the governors as commissioned by him to punish criminals and praise good citizenship. God wants you to be good citizens. . . . Have respect for everyone and love for your community; fear God and honour the emperor.[8]

Christians really had little choice. Christianity did not emerge in a social or intellectual vacuum; Jewish and Roman cultures were the only cultures early Christians knew. Thus they had to adapt their Roman education to their Christian beliefs. Saint Paul himself believed there was a good deal of truth in pagan thought, as long as it was correctly interpreted and understood. The result was compromise.

Christians gradually came to terms with Greco-Roman culture. Saint Jerome (340–419), a distinguished theologian and linguist, remains famous for his translation of the Old and New Testament from Hebrew and Greek into the vernacular Latin. Called the Vulgate, his edition of the Bible served as the official translation until the sixteenth century; even today, scholars rely on it. Familiar with the writings of classical authors, Saint Jerome also believed that Christians should study the best of ancient thought because it would direct their minds to God. Christian attitudes toward women and toward homosexuality illustrate the ways early Christians adopted the views of their contemporary world.

Jesus, whom Christians accept as the Messiah, considered women the equal of men in his plan of salvation. He attributed no disreputable qualities to women, made no comment on the wiles of women, made no reference to them as inferior creatures. On the contrary, women were among his earliest and most faithful converts. He discussed his mission with them (John 4:21–25); he accepted the ministrations of a reformed prostitute; and women were the first persons to whom he revealed himself after his resurrection (Matthew 28:9–10). The influence of Jewish and Christian writers on the formation of medieval (and modern) attitudes toward women, however, was greater than Jesus' influence.

Jesus' message emphasized love for God and for one's fellow human beings. Later writers tended to stress Christianity as a religion of renunciation and asceticism, and they equated sexual activity with women. Their views derive from Platonic-Hellenistic ideas of the contemporary Mediterranean world. The Hellenistic Jewish philosopher Philo of Alexandria (ca 20 B.C.–ca 50 A.D.), for example, held that since the female represented sense perception and the male the higher, rational soul, the female was inferior to the male. Female beauty may come from God who created everything, the African church father Tertullian wrote, but it should be feared. Women should wear veils, he warned; otherwise, men will be endangered by the sight of them. Perhaps the most revolting image of women comes from Saint John Chrysostom (347–407), patriarch of Constantinople. This ruthless critic of contemporary morals characterized female beauty as "a white sepulchre; the parts within are full of so much uncleanliness."[9]

The church fathers acknowledged that God had established marriage for the generation of children, but they believed marriage was a concession to weak people who could not bear celibacy. Saint Augustine (see page 224) considered sexual intercourse a great threat to spiritual freedom. In daily life every act of intercourse was evil, he taught; every child was conceived by a sinful act and came into the world tainted with original sin. Celibacy was the highest good; intercourse little more than animal lust.

Women were considered incapable of writing on the subject, so we have none of their views. The church fathers, by definition, were men. Because many of them experienced physical desire when in the presence of women, misogyny (hatred of women) entered Christian thought. Although early Christian writers believed women the spiritual equals of men, and although Saint Melania, Saint Scholastica (see page 236), and some other women exercised influence as teachers and charismatic leaders, Christianity became a male-centered and sex-negative religion. "The Church Fathers regarded sex as at best something to be tolerated, an evil whose only good was procreation."[10] Until perhaps very recently, this attitude dominated Western thinking on human sexuality.

Toward homosexuality, according to a controversial study, Christians of the first three or four centuries simply imbibed the attitude of the world in which they lived. Many Romans indulged in homosexual activity, and contemporaries did not consider such behavior (or inclinations to it) immoral, bizarre, or harmful. Early Christians, too, considered homosexuality a conventional expression of physical desire and were no more susceptible to antihomosexual prejudices than pagans were. Some prominent Christians experienced loving same-gender relationships that probably had a sexual element. What eventually led to a change in public and Christian attitudes toward sexual behavior was the shift from the sophisticated urban culture of the Greco-Roman world to the rural culture of medieval Europe.[11]

Synthesis: Saint Augustine

The finest representative of the blending of classical and Christian ideas, and indeed one of the most brilliant thinkers in the history of the Western world, was Saint Augustine of Hippo (354–430). Aside from the scriptural writers, no one else has had a greater impact on Christian thought in succeeding centuries. Saint Augustine was born into an urban family in what is now Algeria in North Africa. His father was a pagan; his mother, Monica, a devout Christian. Because his family was poor—his father was a minor civil servant—the only avenue to success in a highly competitive world was a classical education.

Augustine received his basic education in the local school. By modern and even medieval standards, that education was extremely narrow: textual study of the writings of the poet Virgil, the orator-politician Cicero, the historian Sallust, and the playwright Terence. As in the Islamic and Chinese worlds (see pages 273 and 720), learning in the Christian West meant memorization. Education in the late Roman world aimed at appreciation of words, particularly those of renowned and eloquent orators.

At the age of seventeen, Augustine went to nearby Carthage to continue his education. There he took a mistress with whom he lived for fifteen years. At Carthage, Augustine began an intellectual and spiritual pilgrimage that led him through experiments with several philosophies and heretical Christian sects. In 383 he traveled to Rome, where he endured not only illness but also disappointment in his teaching: his students fled when their bills were due.

Finally, in Milan in 387, Augustine received Christian baptism. He later became bishop of the seacoast city of Hippo Regius in his native North Africa. He was a renowned preacher to Christians there, a vigorous defender of orthodox Christianity, and the author of over ninety-three books and treatises.

Augustine's autobiography, *The Confessions,* is a literary masterpiece and one of the most influential books in the history of Europe. Written in the form of a prayer, *The Confessions* describes Augustine's moral struggle: the conflict between his spiritual and intellectual aspirations and his sensual and material self.

The Confessions, written in the rhetorical style and language of late Roman antiquity, marks the synthesis of Greco-Roman forms and Christian thought. Many Greek and Roman philosophers had taught that knowledge and virtue are the same—that a person who really knows what is right will do what is right. Augustine rejected this idea. He believed that a person may know what is right but fail to act righteously because of the innate weakness of the human will. He pointed out that people do not always act on the basis of rational knowledge. A learned person can be corrupt and evil.

Augustine's ideas on sin, grace, and redemption became the foundation of all subsequent Christian theology, Protestant as well as Catholic. He wrote that the basic or dynamic force in any individual is the *will,* which he defined as "the power of the soul to hold on to or to obtain an object without constraint." The end or goal of the will determines the moral character of the individual. When Adam ate the fruit forbidden by God in the garden of Eden (Genesis 3:6), he committed "the original sin" and corrupted the will. By concupiscence or sexual desire, which all humans have, Adam's sin has been passed on by hereditary transmission through the flesh to all humanity. Original sin thus became a common social stain. Because Adam disobeyed God and fell, so all human beings have an innate tendency to sin: their will is weak. But, according to Augustine, God restores the strength of the will through grace (his love, assistance, support), which is transmitted through the sacraments, such as penance, or reconciliation, by the action of the Spirit.

Augustine also argued against the idea that the church consisted of a spiritual elite that was an alternative to society. Rather than seeing themselves as apart from society, Augustine said, Christians must live in and transform society. The notion of the church as a special spiritual elite, distinct from and superior to the rest of society, recurred many times in the Middle Ages. Each time it was branded a heresy, and Augustine's arguments were marshaled against it.

When the Visigothic chieftain Alaric conquered Rome in 410, horrified pagans blamed the disaster on the Christians. In response, Augustine wrote *City of God.* This profoundly original work contrasts Christianity with the secular society in which it existed. *City of God* presents a moral interpretation of the Roman government—in fact, of all history. Filled with references to ancient history and mythology, it remained for centuries the standard statement of the Christian philosophy of history.

According to Augustine, history is the account of God acting in time. Human history reveals that there are two kinds of people: those who live according to the flesh in the City of Babylon and those who live according to the spirit in the City of God. The former will endure eternal hellfire, the latter eternal bliss.

Augustine maintained that states came into existence as the result of Adam's fall and people's inclination to sin. The state is a necessary evil, but it can work for the good by providing the peace, justice, and order that Christians need in order to pursue their pilgrimage to the City of God. The particular form of government—whether monarchy, aristocracy, or democracy—is basically irrelevant. Any civil government that fails to provide justice is no more than a band of gangsters.

Although the state results from moral lapse—from sin—the church (the Christian community) is not entirely free from sin. The church is certainly not equivalent to the City of God. But the church, which is concerned with salvation, is responsible for everyone, including Christian rulers. Churches in the Middle Ages used Augustine's theory to defend their belief in the ultimate superiority of the spiritual power over the temporal. This remained the dominant political theory until the late thirteenth century.

❈ CHRISTIAN MONASTICISM

Christianity began and spread as a city religion. Since the first century, however, some especially pious Christians had felt that the only alternative to the decadence of urban life was complete separation from the world. The fourth century witnessed a significant change in the relationship between Christianity and the broader society. Until Constantine's legalization of Christianity, Christians were a persecuted minority. Some were tortured and killed. Christians greatly revered these *martyrs* who, like Jesus, suffered and died for their faith. When Christianity was legalized and the persecutions ended, a new problem arose.

Where Christians had been a suffering minority, now they came to be identified with the state: non-Christians could not advance in the imperial service. But if Christianity had triumphed, so had "the world," for secular attitudes and values pervaded the church. The church of martyrs no longer existed. Some scholars believe the monasteries provided a way of life for those Christians who wanted to make a total response to Christ's teachings—people who wanted more than a lukewarm Christianity. The monks became the new martyrs. Saint Anthony of Egypt (d. 356), the first monk for whom there is concrete evidence and the person later considered the father of monasticism, went to Alexandria during the last persecution in the hope of gaining martyrdom. Christians believed that monks, like the martyrs before them, could speak to God and that their prayers had special influence with him.

Western Monasticism

Monasticism began in Egypt in the third century. At first individuals and small groups withdrew from cities and organized society to seek God through prayer in caves and shelters in the desert or mountains. Gradually large colonies of monks emerged in the deserts of upper Egypt. They were called hermits from the Greek word *eremos,* meaning "desert." Many devout women also were attracted to the monastic life. Although monks (and nuns) led isolated lives and the monastic movement represented the antithesis of the ancient ideal of an urban social existence, ordinary people soon recognized the monks and nuns as holy people and sought them as spiritual guides.

When monasticism spread to western Europe, several factors worked against the continuation of the eremitical form. The cold, snow, ice, and fog that covered much of northern Europe for many months of the year discouraged isolated living. Dense forests filled with wild animals and wandering Germanic tribes presented obvious dangers.

✥ **Saint Benedict**   Holding his *Rule* in his left hand, the seated and cowled patriarch of Western monasticism blesses a monk with his right hand. His monastery, Monte Cassino, is in the background. *(Source: Biblioteca Apostolica Vaticana)*

Moreover, church leaders did not really approve of eremitical life. Hermits sometimes claimed to have mystical experiences—direct communications with God. If hermits could communicate directly with the Lord, what need had they for the priest and the institutional church? The scholarly bishop Basil of Caesarea in Cappadocia in Asia Minor argued that the eremitical life posed the danger of excessive concern with the self and did not provide the opportunity for the exercise of charity, the first virtue of any Christian. Saint Basil and the church hierarchy encouraged *coenobitic monasticism,* communal living in monasteries, which provided an environment for training the aspirant in the virtues of charity, poverty, and freedom from self-deception.

In the fourth, fifth, and sixth centuries, many experiments in communal monasticism were made in Gaul, Italy, Spain, Anglo-Saxon England, and Ireland. While at Rome, Saint Jerome attracted a group of aristocratic women whom he instructed in Scripture and the ideals of ascetic life. After studying both eremitical and coenobitic monasticism in Egypt and Syria, John Cassian established two monasteries near Marseilles in Gaul around 415. The abbey or monastery of Lérins on the Mediterranean Sea near Cannes (ca 410) encouraged the severely penitential and extremely ascetic behavior common in the East, such as long hours of prayer, fasting, and self-flagellation. It was this tradition of harsh self-mortification that the

Roman-British monk Saint Patrick carried from Lérins to Ireland in the fifth century. Church organization in Ireland became closely associated with the monasteries, and Irish monastic life followed the ascetic Eastern form.

Around 540 the former Roman senator Cassiodorus established a monastery, the Vivarium, on his estate in Italy. Cassiodorus enlisted highly educated and sophisticated men to copy both sacred and secular manuscripts, intending this to be their sole occupation. Cassiodorus started the association of monasticism with scholarship and learning. This developed into a great tradition in the medieval and modern worlds. The fifth and sixth centuries witnessed the appearance of many other monastic lifestyles.

The Rule of Benedict

In 529 Benedict of Nursia (480–543), who had experimented with both the eremitical and the communal forms of monastic life, wrote a brief set of regulations for the monks who had gathered around him at Monte Cassino between Rome and Naples. Benedict's *Rule* derives from a longer, repetitious, and sometimes turgid document called *The Rule of the Master.* Benedict's guide for monastic life proved more adaptable and slowly replaced all others. *The Rule of Saint Benedict* has influenced all forms of organized religious life in the Roman church.

Saint Benedict conceived of his *Rule* as a simple code for ordinary men. It outlined a monastic life of regularity, discipline, and moderation. Each monk had ample food and adequate sleep. Self-destructive acts of mortification were forbidden. In an atmosphere of silence, the monk spent part of the day in formal prayer, which Benedict called the "Work of God." This consisted of chanting psalms and other prayers from the Bible. The rest of the day was passed in study and manual labor. After a year of probation, the monk made three vows.

First, the monk vowed stability: he promised to live his entire life in the monastery of his profession. The object of this vow was to prevent the wandering so common in Saint Benedict's day. Second, the monk vowed conversion of manners—that is, to strive to improve himself and to come closer to God. Third, he promised obedience to the *abbot,* or head of the monastery.

The Rule of Saint Benedict expresses the assimilation of the Roman spirit into Western monasticism. It reveals the logical mind of its creator and the Roman concern for order, organization, and respect for law. Its spirit of moderation and flexibility is reflected in the patience, wisdom, and understanding with which the abbot is to govern and, indeed, with which life is to be led.

Saint Benedict's *Rule* implies that a person who wants to become a monk or nun need have no previous ascetic experience or even a particularly strong bent toward the religious life. Thus it allowed for the admission of newcomers with different backgrounds and personalities. From Chapter 59, "The Offering of Sons by Nobles or by the Poor," and from Benedict's advice to the abbot— "The abbot should avoid all favoritism in the monastery. . . . A man born free is not to be given higher rank than a slave who becomes a monk" (Chapter 2)—we know that men of different social classes belonged to his monastery. This flexibility helps to explain the attractiveness of Benedictine monasticism throughout the centuries.

The Rule of Saint Benedict had one fundamental purpose. The exercises of the monastic life were designed to draw the individual slowly but steadily away from attachment to the world and love of self and toward the love of God. But the monastic life as conceived by Saint Benedict did not lean too heavily in any one direction. With its division of the day into prayer, study, and manual labor, it struck a balance between asceticism and idleness. It thus provided opportunities for persons of entirely different abilities and talents—from mechanics to gardeners to literary scholars. Benedict's *Rule* contrasts sharply with Cassiodorus's narrow concept of the monastery as a place for aristocratic scholars and bibliophiles.

Benedictine monasticism also suited the social circumstances of early medieval society. The Germanic invasions had fragmented European life: the self-sufficient rural estate replaced the city as the basic unit of civilization. A monastery, too, had to be economically self-sufficient. It was supposed to produce from its lands and properties all that was needed for food, clothing, shelter, and liturgical service of the altar. The monastery fitted in—indeed, represented—the trend toward localism. The Benedictine form of religious life also proved congenial to women. Five miles from Monte Cassino at Plombariola, Benedict's twin sister Scholastica

(480–543) adapted the *Rule* for the use of her community of nuns. Many other convents for nuns were established in the early Middle Ages.

Benedictine monasticism also succeeded partly because it was so materially successful. In the seventh and eighth centuries, monasteries pushed back forest and wasteland, drained swamps, and experimented with crop rotation. The abbey of Jumièges, in the diocese of Rouen, followed this pattern. Such Benedictine houses made a significant contribution to the agricultural development of Europe, earning immense wealth in the process. The communal nature of their organization, whereby property was held in common and profits were pooled and reinvested, made this contribution possible.

Finally, monasteries conducted schools for local young people. Some learned about prescriptions and herbal remedies and went on to provide medical treatment for their localities. A few copied manuscripts and wrote books. This training did not go unappreciated in a society desperately in need of it. Local and royal governments drew on the services of the literate men and able administrators the monasteries produced.

❖ THE MIGRATION OF THE GERMANIC PEOPLES

The migration of peoples from one area to another has been a dominant and continuing feature of world history. The causes of early migrations varied and are not thoroughly understood by scholars. But there is no question that they profoundly affected both the regions to which peoples moved and the regions they left behind.

The *Völkerwanderungen,* or migrations of the Germanic peoples, were important in the decline of the Western Roman Empire and in the making of European civilization. Since about 150, Germanic tribes from the regions of the northern Rhine, Elbe, and Oder rivers had pressed along the Rhine-Danube frontier of the Roman Empire. Some tribes, such as the Visigoths and Ostrogoths, led a settled existence, engaged in agriculture and trade, and accepted Arian Christianity. Other tribes, such as the Angles, Saxons, and Huns, led a nomadic life unaffected by Roman influences. Scholars do not know exactly when the Mongolian tribe called the Huns began to move westward from China, but about 370 they pressured the Goths along the Rhine-Danube frontier.

Why did the Germans migrate? Although many twentieth-century scholars have tried to answer this question, the answer is not known. Perhaps overpopulation and the resulting food shortages caused migration. Perhaps victorious tribes forced the vanquished to move southward. Probably "the primary stimulus for this gradual migration was the Roman frontier, which increasingly offered service in the army and work for pay around the camps."[12]

By the late third century, a large percentage of military recruits came from the Germanic peoples. Besides army recruits, several types of barbarian peoples entered the empire and became affiliated with Roman government. The *laeti,* refugees or prisoners of war, were settled with their families in areas of Gaul and Italy under the supervision of Roman prefects and landowners. Generally isolated from the local Roman population, the laeti farmed regions depopulated by plague. The men had to serve in the Roman army.

Free barbarian units called *foederati,* stationed near major provincial cities, were a second type of affiliated barbarian group. Research has suggested that rather than giving them land, the Romans assigned the foederati shares of the tax revenues from the region.[13] Living close to Roman communities, the foederati quickly assimilated into Roman culture. In fact, in the fourth century, some foederati rose to the highest ranks of the army and moved in the most cultured and aristocratic circles.

The arrival of the Huns in the West in 376 precipitated the entry of entire peoples, the *gentes,* into the Roman Empire. Pressured by defeat in battle, starvation, or the movement of other peoples, tribes such as the Ostrogoths and Visigoths entered in large numbers, perhaps as many as twenty thousand men, women, and children.[14] Once the Visigoths were inside the empire, Roman authorities exploited their hunger by forcing them to sell their own people in exchange for dogflesh: "the going rate was one dog for one Goth." The bitterness of those enslaved was aggravated by the arrival of the Ostrogoths. A huge rebellion erupted, and the Goths crushed the Roman army at Adrianople on August 9, 378.[15] This date marks the beginning of massive Germanic invasions into the empire (Map 8.2).

Except for the Lombards, whose conquests of Italy persisted into the mid-eighth century, the movements of Germanic peoples on the European

MAP 8.2 The Germanic Migrations The Germanic tribes infiltrated and settled in all parts of western Europe. The Huns, who were Mongolian, not Germanic, originated in central Asia. Their victory over the Ostrogoths led the emperor to allow the Visigoths to settle within the empire, a decision that proved disastrous for Rome.

continent ended about 600. Between 450 and 565 the Germans established a number of kingdoms, but none except the Frankish kingdom lasted very long. Unlike modern nation-states, the Germanic kingdoms did not have definite geographical boundaries. The Visigoths overran much of southwestern Gaul. Establishing their headquarters at Toulouse, they exercised a weak domination over Spain until a great Muslim victory at Guadalete in 711 ended Visigothic rule. The Vandals, whose destructive ways are commemorated in the word *vandal,* settled in North Africa. In northern and western Europe in the sixth century, the Burgundians established rule over lands roughly circumscribed by old Roman army camps at Lyons, Besançon, Geneva, and Autun.

In northern Italy the Ostrogothic king Theodoric (r. 471–526) established his capital at Ravenna and gradually won control of all Italy, Sicily, and the territory north and east of the upper Adriatic. Though attached to the customs of his people, Theodoric pursued a policy of assimilation between Germans and Romans. He maintained close relations with the emperor at Constantinople and attracted to his administration able scholars such as Cassiodorus (see page 227). Theodoric's accomplishments were not insignificant, but after his death his administration fell apart.

The most enduring Germanic kingdom was established by the Frankish chieftain Clovis (r. 481–511). Originally only a petty chieftain in northwestern Gaul (modern Belgium), Clovis began to

Helmet of King Agiluf   Germanic chieftains wanted to be portrayed as Roman-style rulers in order to convey Roman ideals of power. On this plaque for the helmet of the Lombard king Agiluf, the king sits enthroned in majesty flanked by bodyguards while subject cities bring tribute. *(Source: Scala/Art Resource, NY)*

expand his territories in 486. His Catholic wife Clothilde worked to convert her husband and supported the founding of churches and monasteries. Clothilde is representative of the role women played in the Christianization and Romanization of the Germanic kingdoms (see Listening to the Past). Clovis's conversion to orthodox Christianity in 496 won him the crucial support of the papacy and the bishops of Gaul. As the defender of Roman Catholicism against heretical Germanic tribes, Clovis went on to conquer the Visigoths, extending his domain as far as the Pyrenees and making Paris his headquarters. Because he was descended from the half-legendary chieftain Merovech, the dynasty that Clovis founded has been called Merovingian (see pages 345–346).

The island of Britain, conquered by Rome during the reign of Claudius, shared fully in the life of the Roman Empire during the first four centuries of the Christian era. A military aristocracy governed, and the official religion was the cult of the emperor. Towns were planned in the Roman fashion, with temples, public baths, theaters, and amphitheaters. In the countryside, large manors controlled the surrounding lands. Roman merchants brought Eastern luxury goods and Eastern religions—including Christianity—into Britain. The native Britons, a peaceful Celtic people, became thoroughly Romanized. Their language was Latin. Their lifestyle was Roman.

After the Visigothic defeat of the Roman emperor at Adrianople, however, Roman troops were withdrawn from Britain, leaving it unprotected. The savage Picts from Scotland harassed the north. Teutonic tribes from modern-day Norway, Sweden, and Denmark—the Angles, Saxons, and Jutes—stepped up their assaults. Germans took over the best lands and humbled the Britons. The sporadic raids continued for over a century and led to Germanic control of most of Britain. Historians have labeled the period from 500 to 1066 "Anglo-Saxon." Germanic tribes never subdued Scotland, where the Picts remained strong, or Wales, where the Celts and native Britons continued to put up stubborn resistance.

�֍ GERMANIC SOCIETY

After the Germans replaced the Romans, Germanic customs and traditions shaped European society for centuries. What sorts of social, political, and economic life did the Germans have? Scholars are hampered in answering such questions because the Germans did not write and thus kept no written records before their conversion to Christianity. The earliest information about them comes from moralistic accounts by Romans such as the historian Tacitus, who was acquainted only with the tribes living closest to the borders of the Roman Empire and imposed Greco-Roman categories of tribes and nations on the Germanic peoples he described. Tacitus's ethnographic classifications dominated scholarly writing until fairly recently. Only in the past few decades have anthropologists begun to study early Germanic society on its own terms.

Kinship, Class, and Law

The Germans had no notion of the state as we in the twentieth century use the term; they thought in social, not political, terms. The basic Germanic social unit was the tribe, or *folk.* Members of the folk believed that they were all descended from a common ancestor. Blood united them. Kinship protected them. Law was custom—unwritten and handed down by word of mouth from generation to generation. Custom regulated everything. Members were subject to their tribe's customary law wherever they went, and friendly tribes respected one another's laws.

Germanic tribes were led by kings or tribal chieftains. The chief, recognized as the strongest and bravest in battle, was elected from among the male members of the strongest family. He led the tribe in war, settled disputes among its members, conducted negotiations with outside powers, and offered sacrifices to the gods.

Closely associated with the chief in some southern tribes was the *comitatus,* or "war band." Writing at the end of the first century, Tacitus described the war band as the bravest young men in the tribe. They swore loyalty to the chief, fought with him in battle, and were not supposed to leave the battlefield without him; to do so implied cowardice and disloyalty and resulted in social disgrace. Social egalitarianism existed among members of the war band.

During the migrations of the third and fourth centuries, and as a result of constant warfare, the war band was transformed into a system of stratified ranks. Armbands, first obtained through contact with the Romans, came to be coveted as marks of rank, especially the gold ones reserved for the "royal families." During the Ostrogothic conquest of Italy under Theodoric, warrior nobles also

sought to acquire land, both as a mark of prestige and as a means to power. As land and wealth came into the hands of a small elite class, social inequalities emerged and gradually grew stronger.[16] These inequalities help to explain the origins of the European noble class (see pages 349–350).

King Lhodari of the Alemanni The Alemanni occupied territory in southwestern Germany and Switzerland in the fifth century but did not accept Christianity until the late seventh or early eighth century. King Lhodari had Alemanni law (hitherto transmitted orally) written down in Latin. (In French speech the name *Allemands* came to signify all Germans.) Here the ninth-century artist portrays Lhodari in Roman military garb. *(Source: Bibliothèque Nationale, Paris)*

As long as custom determined all behavior, the early Germans had no need for written law. Beginning in the late sixth century, however, German tribal chieftains began to collect, write, and publish lists of their customs. Why then? The Christian missionaries who were slowly converting the Germans to Christianity wanted to read about German ways in order to assimilate the tribes to Christianity, and they encouraged German rulers to write their customs down. Moreover, by the sixth century the Germanic rulers needed regulations that applied to the Romans under their jurisdiction as well as to their own people.

Today, if a person holds up a bank, American law maintains that the robber attacks both the bank and the state in which it exists—a sophisticated notion involving the abstract idea of the state. In early Germanic law, all crimes were regarded as crimes against a person.

According to the code of the Salian Franks, every person had a particular monetary value to the tribe. This value was called the *wergeld,* which literally means "man-money" or "money to buy off the spear." Men of fighting age had the highest wergeld, then women of childbearing age, then children, and finally the aged. If a person accused of a crime agreed to pay the wergeld and if the victim and his or her family accepted the payment, there was peace. If the accused refused to pay the wergeld or if the victim's family refused to accept it, a blood feud ensued. Individuals depended on their kin for protection, and kinship served as a force of social control.

The early law codes are patchwork affairs studded with additions made in later centuries. Yet much historical information can be gleaned from them. The law code of the Salian Franks issued by Clovis offers a general picture of Germanic life and problems in the early Middle Ages and is typical of the law codes of other tribes. The Salic Law lists the money fines to be paid to the victim or the family for injuries such as theft, rape, assault, arson, and murder. It is not really a code of law at all but a list of tariffs or fines for particular offenses.

If any person strike another on the head so that the brain appears, and the three bones which lie above the brain shall project, he shall be sentenced to 1200 denars, which make 300 shillings. . . .

If any one have killed a free woman after she has begun bearing children, he shall be sentenced to 2400 denars, which make 600 shillings. . . .

If any one shall have drawn a harrow through another's harvest after it has sprouted, or shall have gone through it with a wagon where there was no road, he shall be sentenced to 120 denars, which make 30 shillings. . . . [17]

Germanic law aimed at the prevention or reduction of violence. It was not concerned with abstract justice.

As Germanic kings accepted Christianity and as Romans and Germans increasingly intermarried, the distinction between Germanic and Roman law blurred and, in the course of the seventh and eighth centuries, disappeared. The result would be the new feudal law.

Germanic Life

The Germans usually resided in small villages. Climate and geography determined the basic patterns of agricultural and pastoral life. In the flat or open coastal regions, men engaged in animal husbandry, especially cattle raising. Many tribes lived in small settlements on the edges of clearings where they raised barley, wheat, oats, peas, and beans. They tilled their fields with a simple wooden scratch plow and harvested their grains with a small iron sickle. Women ground the kernels of grain with a grindstone and made the resulting flour into a dough that they shaped into flat cakes and baked on clay trays. Much of the grain was fermented into a strong, thick beer. Women performed the heavy work of raising, grinding, and preserving cereals, a mark, some scholars believe, of their low status in a male-dominated society. Women were also responsible for weaving and spinning.

Within the small villages there were great differences in wealth and status. Free men constituted the largest class. The number of cattle a man possessed indicated his wealth and determined his social status. "Cattle were so much the quintessential indicator of wealth in traditional society that the modern English term 'fee' (meaning cost of goods or services), which developed from the medieval term 'fief,' had its origin in the Germanic term *fihu* . . . , meaning cattle, chattels, and hence, in general, wealth."[18] Free men also shared in tribal warfare. Slaves (prisoners of war) worked as farm laborers, herdsmen, or household servants.

Germanic society was patriarchal: within each household the father had authority over his wives, children, and slaves. The Germans practiced

Vandal Landowner   The adoption of Roman dress—short tunic, cloak, and sandals—reflects the way the Germanic tribes accepted Roman lifestyles. Likewise both the mosaic art form and the man's stylized appearance show the Germans' assimilation of Roman influences. Notice that the rider has a saddle but no stirrups. *(Source: Courtesy of the Trustees of the British Museum)*

polygamy, and men who could afford them had more than one wife.

Did the Germans produce goods for trade and exchange? Ironworking was the most advanced craft of the Germanic peoples. Much of northern Europe had iron deposits at or near the earth's surface, and the dense forests provided wood for charcoal. Most villages had an oven and smiths who produced agricultural tools and instruments of war—one-edged swords, arrowheads, and shields. In the first two centuries A.D., the quantity and quality of German goods increased dramatically, and the first steel swords were superior to the weapons of Roman troops. Germanic goods, however, were produced for war and the subsistence economy, not for trade. Goods were also used for gift giving, a social custom that conferred status on the giver. Gift giving showed the higher (economic) status of the giver, cemented friendship, and placed the receiver in the giver's debt.[19] Goods that could not be produced in the village were acquired by raiding and warfare rather than by commercial exchanges. Raids between tribes brought the victors booty; captured cattle and slaves were traded or given as gifts. Warfare determined the economy and the individual's status within Germanic society.

What was the position of women in Germanic society? Did they have, as some scholars contend, a higher status than they were to have later in the Middle Ages? The law codes provide the best evidence. The codes show societies that regarded women as family property. A marriageable daughter went to the highest bidder. A woman of childbearing years had a very high wergeld. The codes also protected the virtue of women. For example, the Salic Law of the Franks fined a man a large amount if he pressed the hand of a woman and even more if he touched her above the elbow. But heavy fines did not stop injury, rape, or abduction. Widows were sometimes seized on the battlefields where their dead husbands lay and were forced to marry the victors.

A few slaves and peasant women used their beauty and their intelligence to advance their positions. The slave Fredegunda, for whom King Chilperic murdered his Visigothic wife, became a queen and held her position after her husband's death. Another slave, Balthilda, became the wife of Clovis II. During her sons' minority she worked to alleviate the evils of the slave trade.[20]

❋ THE BYZANTINE EAST (CA 400–788)

Constantine (r. 306–337) and later emperors tried to maintain the unity of the Roman Empire, but during the fifth and sixth centuries the western and eastern halves drifted apart. Justinian (r. 527–565) waged long and hard-fought wars against the Ostrogoths and temporarily regained Italy and North Africa. But his conquests had disastrous consequences. Justinian's wars exhausted the resources of the Byzantine state, destroyed Italy's economy, and killed a large part of Italy's population. The wars paved the way for the easy conquest of Italy by the Lombards shortly after Justinian's death. In the late sixth century, the territory of the Western Roman Empire came under Germanic sway, while in the East the Byzantine Empire continued the traditions and institutions of the caesars.

Latin Christian culture was only one legacy the Roman Empire bequeathed to the Western world. The Byzantine culture centered at Constantinople—Constantine's "new Rome"—was another. The Byzantine Empire maintained a high standard of living, and for centuries the Greeks were the most civilized people in the Western world. The Byzantine Empire held at bay, or at least hindered, barbarian peoples who otherwise could have wreaked additional devastation on western Europe, retarding its development. Most important, however, is the role of Byzantines, together with the Muslims (see pages 272–276), as preservers of

the wisdom of the ancient world. Throughout the long years when barbarians in western Europe trampled down the old and then painfully built something new, Byzantium protected and then handed on to the West the intellectual heritage of Greco-Roman civilization.

Byzantine East and Germanic West

As imperial authority disintegrated in the West during the fifth century, civic functions were performed first by church leaders and then by Germanic chieftains. Meanwhile, in the East, the Byzantines preserved the forms and traditions of the old Roman Empire and even called themselves Romans. Byzantine emperors traced their lines back past Constantine to the emperor Augustus. The senate that sat in Constantinople carried on the traditions and preserved the glory of the old Roman senate. The army that defended the empire was the direct descendant of the old Roman legions. Even the chariot factions of the Roman Empire lived on under the Greeks, who cheered their favorites as enthusiastically as had the Romans of Hadrian's day.

The position of the church differed considerably in the Byzantine East and the Germanic West. The fourth-century emperors Constantine and Theodosius had wanted the church to act as a unifying force within the empire, but the Germanic invasions made that impossible. The bishops of Rome repeatedly called on the emperors at Constantinople for military support against the invaders, but rarely could the emperors send it. The church in the West steadily grew away from the empire and became involved in social and political affairs. Nevertheless, until the eighth century, the popes, who were often selected by the clergy of Rome, continued to send announcements of their election to the emperors at Constantinople—a sign that the Roman popes long thought of themselves as bishops of the Roman Empire.

The popes were preoccupied with conversion of the Germans, the Christian attitude toward classical culture, and relations with Germanic rulers. Because the Western church concentrated on its missionary function, it took centuries for the clergy to be organized. Most church theology in the West came from the East, and the overwhelming majority of popes were of Eastern origin.

Tensions occasionally developed between church officials and secular authorities in the West. Pope Gelasius I (r. 492–496) insisted that bishops, not civil authorities, were responsible for the administration of the church. Gelasius maintained that two powers governed the world: the sacred authority of popes and the royal power of kings. And, he insisted, the sacred power was the greater, because priests had to answer to God even for the actions of kings.

Such an assertion was virtually unheard-of in the East, where the emperor's jurisdiction over the church was fully acknowledged. The emperor in Constantinople nominated the *patriarch,* as the highest prelate of the Eastern church was called. The Eastern emperor looked on religion as a branch of the state. Religion was such a vital aspect of the social life of the people that the emperor devoted considerable attention to it. He considered it his duty to protect the faith, not only against heathen enemies but also against heretics within the empire. In case of doctrinal disputes, the emperor, following Constantine's example at Nicaea, summoned councils of bishops and theologians to settle problems.

The steady separation of the Byzantine East and the Germanic West reflects differences in the ways Christianity and classical culture were received in the two parts of the Roman Empire. In the West, Christians at first were a small, alien minority within the broad Roman culture. They kept apart from the rest of society, condemning, avoiding, and demystifying Roman society and classical culture. In Byzantium, by contrast, most Greeks were Christian. Greek *apologists,* or defenders, of Christianity insisted on harmony between Christianity and classical culture: they used Greek philosophy to buttress Christian tenets.

The Empress Theodora and Her Attendants   This mosaic detail is composed of thousands of tiny cubes of colored glass or stone set in plaster against a blazing golden background. A halo, symbol of power in Eastern art, surrounds the empress's head. An attempt has been made at naturalistic portraiture. *(Source: Scala/Art Resource, NY)*

Eastern Monasticism

From Egypt, Christian monasticism had spread to the Greek provinces of Syria and Palestine and to Byzantium itself. Saint Basil composed a rule that influenced all Eastern monasticism—the *Long Rules*. Basil recommended the establishment of communities of economically self-sufficient monks (or nuns) living lives of moderation. He discouraged the severe asceticism (flagellation of the body, excessive fasting, lengthy vigils with little sleep) that was so common in Egypt. Basil also supported the establishment of urban monasteries.

With the financial assistance of the emperor Justinian I (r. 527–565) and that of wealthy noble men and women, monasteries soon spread throughout the Eastern empire. Seventy abbeys were erected in Constantinople alone. Beginning in the tenth century, the monasteries acquired fields, pastures, livestock, mills, saltworks, and urban rental properties, as well as cash and precious liturgical vessels. The exemption of Byzantine monasteries from state taxes also served to increase monastic wealth.

What did the monasteries do with their revenues? Did the Greek monasteries have an impact on the broader society? Implementing Saint Basil's belief that *philanthropia,* active love for humankind, was a central part of the monastic vocation, monasteries performed important social services: they distributed food, clothing, and money to the poor and needy. Many monasteries contained within their compounds hospitals for the sick (see page 240); homes for the destitute elderly staffed by monks or nuns; and inns for travelers where the food and lodging were free. Orphans, cripples, the mentally ill, and battered women also found temporary or permanent refuge in the monasteries of monks or nuns. The Byzantine scholar Norman Baynes has written, "The Byzantine in his hour of need turned instinctively to the ascete (monk) in the full assurance of his sympathy and succor." A few monks undertook evangelical work. For example, Saint Nikon (c. 930–1000) reconverted the peoples of Crete after the Muslim occupation and preached among the pagan Slavs of the Peloponnesus. The Christian East, however, never regarded missionary or charitable work as the primary work of monasticism.

The main duty of the monk or nun was to pray. Monks and nuns served the world not so much by what they *did* as by what they *were*: people of prayer, of holiness. The monastery was the scene of the daily and continuous ritual of the divine office. The monks spent heavily on the sacred vestments and vessels used in their liturgies, which in the course of the centuries became famous for their elaborateness and splendor. The holy and charismatic *elder* (or *starets* in Slavonic) became a characteristic figure in Eastern monasticism: he or she was the spiritually mature physician capable of guiding others and healing their souls. Thus Saint Melania (383–439), abbess of a community of nuns at the Mount of Olives in Jerusalem, guided Evagrius of Pontus (ca 345–ca 399), a Syrian who later served as the spiritual father of many of the Egyptian monks at Nitria and Kellia in upper Egypt.

Monasticism in the Greek world differed in fundamental ways from the monasticism that evolved in western Europe. First, while *The Rule of Saint Benedict* gradually became the universal guide or constitution for all European monasteries, each individual house in the Byzantine world developed its own *typikon,* or set of rules for organization and behavior. The *typika* contain regulations about novitiate, diet, clothing, liturgical functions, commemorative services for benefactors, and the election of officials, such as the *hegoumenos,* or superior of the house. Second, while stability in the monastery eventually characterized Western monasticism (see page 227), many Eastern monks, especially those with a reputation for holiness, "moved frequently from one monastery to another or alternated between a coenobitic monastery and a hermit's kellion"[21] (cell). Finally, unlike the case in the West, where monasteries often established schools for the youth of the neighborhood, education never became a central feature of the Greek monasteries. Children destined for the monastic life were taught to read and write in some monasteries where monks or nuns devoted themselves to study and writing. But those houses were very few, and no monastery assumed responsibility for the general training of the local young. Since bishops and patriarchs of the Greek church were recruited only from the monasteries, Greek monasteries did exercise a cultural influence.

External Threats and Internal Conflicts

The wars of Justinian's reign left the Byzantine Empire economically and demographically weakened. Over the next two centuries, two additional troubles threatened its very survival: foreign invasion and internal theological disputes.

Beginning around 560, the Avars, a mounted Asiatic nomad group, and the Slavs, an Indo-European people probably originating in Galicia (southeastern Poland and western Ukraine), burst into the Balkan Peninsula. In the meantime, the Sassanid Persians threatened the eastern provinces. By 602 both the northern and the eastern frontiers of the Byzantine Empire had collapsed. In 626 a combined force of Persians and Avars attacked Constantinople itself. Only Byzantine control of the sea and the superhuman exertions of the emperor Heraclius (r. 610–641) saved the empire. But this effort so thoroughly exhausted both the Persians and the Greeks that they proved no match for the Arabs, who overran the eastern provinces of the empire between 632 and 640 (see pages 251–252).

Constantinople again faced sieges between 674 and 678 and from 717 to 718. Again Byzantine naval supremacy and the use of "Greek fire" (see page 239) saved the day. The Balkans, however, were lost to the Slavs; the eastern provinces, to the Arabs.

From all of these military disruptions certain benefits did result. First, the territories lost to the empire contained peoples of very diverse ethnic origins, languages, and religions. The territories that continued under imperial authority gradually achieved a strong cultural unity. They were Greek in culture and administration, orthodox in religion.

Second, foreign invasions created the need for internal reorganization. Heraclius and his successors militarized the administration. The empire was divided into *themes,* or military districts, governed by *strategoi,* or generals, who held both civil and military authority. The strategoi were directly responsible to the emperor. This reorganization brought into being a new peasant army. Foreign invasion had broken up the great landed estates of the empire, and the estate land was distributed to peasant soldiers, who equipped and supported themselves from the profits of the land. Formerly the Byzantine state had relied on foreign mercenaries. Now each theme had an army of native soldiers with a permanent (landed) interest in the preservation of the empire. The government saved the costs of hiring troops and was assured the loyalty of native soldiers. The elevation of peasants to military status revitalized the social structure.

In addition, some scholars maintain that the military disasters of the period led to an increase in popular piety and devotion to *icons*—images or representations in painting, bas-relief, or mosaic of God the Father, Jesus, the Virgin, or the saints. Since the third century, the church had allowed people to venerate icons. Although all prayer had to be directed to God the Father, Christian teaching held that icons representing the saints fostered reverence and that Jesus and the saints could most effectively plead a cause to God the Father. *Iconoclasts,* those who favored the destruction of icons, argued that people were worshiping the image itself rather than what it signified. This, they claimed, constituted *idolatry,* a violation of the Mosaic prohibition of graven images in the Ten Commandments.

The result of the controversy over icons was a terrible theological conflict that split the Byzantine world for a century. In 730 the emperor Leo III (r. 717–741) ordered the destruction of the images. The removal of icons from Byzantine churches provoked a violent reaction: entire provinces revolted, and the empire and Roman papacy severed relations. Since Eastern monasteries were the fiercest defenders of icons, Leo's son Constantine V (r. 741–775), nicknamed "Copronymous" ("Dung-name") by his enemies, took the war to the monasteries. He seized their properties, executed some of the monks, and forced others into the army. Theological disputes and civil disorder over the icons continued intermittently until 843, when the icons were restored.

The implications of the iconoclastic controversy extended far beyond strictly theological issues. Iconoclasm raised the question of the right of the emperor to intervene in religious disputes—a central problem in the relations of church and state. Iconoclasm antagonized the pope and served to encourage him in his quest for an alliance with the Frankish monarchy (see page 346). Iconoclasm thus contributed to the end of Byzantine political influence in central Italy. Arab control of the Mediterranean in the seventh and eighth centuries furthered the separation of the Roman and Byzantine churches by dividing the two parts of Christendom. Separation bred isolation. Isolation, combined with prejudice on both sides, bred hostility.

In 1054 a theological disagreement led the bishop of Rome and the patriarch of Constantinople to excommunicate each other. The outcome was a continuing *schism,* or split, between the Roman Catholic and the Greek Orthodox churches. The bitterness generated by iconoclasm contributed to that schism. Finally, the acceptance of icons profoundly influenced subsequent religious art. That art rejected the Judaic and Islamic prohibition of figural representation and continued in the Greco-Roman tradition of human representation.

Despite religious differences, the Byzantine Empire served as a bulwark for the West, protecting it against invasions from the East. The Greeks stopped the Persians and blunted Arab attacks, and they fought courageously against Turkish invaders until the fifteenth century, when they were finally overwhelmed. Byzantine Greeks slowed the impetus of Slavic incursions in the Balkans and held the Russians at arm's length.

Turning from war to peace, the Byzantines set about civilizing the Slavs, both in the Balkans and in Russia. Byzantine missionaries spread the word of Christ, and one of their triumphs was the conversion of the Russians in the tenth century. The Byzantine missionary Cyril invented a Slavic alphabet using Greek characters, and this script (called the Cyrillic alphabet) is still in use today. Cyrillic script made possible the birth of Russian literature. Similarly, Byzantine art and architecture became the basis and inspiration of Russian forms. The Byzantines were so successful that the Russians claimed to be the successors of the Byzantine Empire. For a time, Moscow was even known as the "Third Rome" (the second Rome being Constantinople).

The Law Code of Justinian

One of the most splendid achievements of the Byzantine emperors was the preservation of Roman law for the medieval and modern worlds. Roman law had developed from many sources—decisions by judges, edicts of the emperors, legislation passed by the senate, and the opinions of jurists expert in the theory and practice of law. By the fourth century, Roman law had become a huge, bewildering mass. Its sheer bulk made it almost unusable. Some laws had become outdated; some repeated or contradicted others.

The emperor Justinian appointed a committee of eminent jurists to sort through and organize the laws. The result was the *Code,* which distilled the legal genius of the Romans into a coherent whole,

eliminated outmoded laws and contradictions, and clarified the law itself.

Justinian next set about bringing order to the equally huge body of Roman *jurisprudence,* the science or philosophy of law. To harmonize the often differing opinions of Roman jurists, Justinian directed his jurists to clear up disputed points and to issue definitive rulings. Accordingly, in 533 his lawyers published the *Digest,* which codified Roman legal thought. Then Justinian's lawyers compiled a handbook of civil law, the *Institutes.*

These three works—the *Code, Digest,* and *Institutes*—are the backbone of the *corpus juris civilis,* the "body of civil law," which is the foundation of law for nearly every modern European nation. The following excerpts on marriage and adultery provide valuable information on the status of women in Roman and Byzantine law:

Roman citizens unite in legal marriage when they are joined according to the precepts of the law, and males have attained the age of puberty and the females are capable of childbirth, whether they are the heads of families or the children of families, if the latter have also the consent of the relatives under whose authority they may be, for this should be obtained and both civil and natural law require that it should be secured.

The lex Julia ("Julian law," dating from 18 B.C.) declares that wives have no right to bring criminal accusations for adultery against their husbands, even though they may desire to complain of the violation of the marriage vow, for while the law grants this privilege to men it does not concede it to women. . . .

The right is granted to the father to kill a man who commits adultery with his daughter while she is under his control.[22]

Byzantine Intellectual Life

Among the Byzantines, education was highly prized, and because of them many masterpieces of ancient Greek literature survived to influence the intellectual life of the modern world. The literature of the Byzantine Empire was predominately Greek, although Latin was long spoken by top politicians, scholars, and lawyers. Among members of the large reading public, history was a favorite subject. Generations of Byzantines read the historical works of Herodotus, Thucydides, and others. Some Byzantine historians condensed long histories, such as those of Polybius; others wrote detailed narratives of their own days.

The most remarkable Byzantine historian was Procopius (ca 500–ca 562), who left a rousing account praising Justinian's reconquest of North Africa and Italy. Procopius's *Secret History,* however, is a vicious and uproarious attack on Justinian and his wife, the empress Theodora. The Byzantines are often depicted as dull and lifeless, but such opinions are hard to defend in the face of Procopius's description of Justinian's character:

For he was at once villainous and amenable; as people say colloquially, a moron. He was never truthful with anyone, but always guileful in what he said and did, yet easily hoodwinked by any who wanted to deceive him. His nature was an unnatural mixture of folly and wickedness.[23]

How much of this is true, how much the hostility of a sanctimonious hypocrite relishing the gossip he spreads, we will never know. Certainly *The Secret History* is robust reading.

Later Byzantine historians chronicled the victories of their emperors and the progress of their barbarian foes. Like Herodotus before them, they were curious about foreigners and left striking descriptions of the Turks, who eventually overwhelmed Byzantium. They sometimes painted unflattering pictures of the uncouth and grasping princes of France and England, whom they encountered on the Crusades.

In mathematics and geometry the Byzantines discovered little that was new. Yet they were exceptionally important as catalysts, for they passed Greco-Roman learning on to the Arabs, who assimilated it and made remarkable advances with it. The Byzantines were equally uncreative in astronomy and natural science, but at least they faithfully learned what the ancients had to teach.

Only when science could be put to military use did the Byzantines make advances. The best-known Byzantine scientific discovery was chemical—"Greek fire" or "liquid fire," an explosive compound made of crude oil mixed with resin and sulphur, which was heated and propelled by a pump through a bronze tube. As the liquid jet left the tube, it was ignited. The Byzantines zealously guarded details of Greek fire's composition. The equivalent of a modern flamethrower, it saved Constantinople from Arab assault in 678. In me-

Woman Carrying Pitcher This detail from a floor mosaic in the Great Palace at Constantinople shows a woman balancing a huge water ewer on her shoulder, which suggests part of her daily work. Notice the large earrings and the coiffured hair. *(Source: Scala/Art Resource, NY)*

chanics the Byzantines continued the work of Hellenistic and Roman inventors of artillery and siege machinery.

The Byzantines devoted a great deal of attention to medicine, and the general level of medical competence was far higher in the Byzantine Empire than it was in the medieval West. The Byzantines assimilated the discoveries of Hellenic and Hellenistic medicine but added very few of their own. The basis of their medical theory was Hippocrates' concept of the four humors (see page 140). Byzantine physicians emphasized the importance of diet and rest and relied heavily on herbal drugs. Perhaps their chief weakness was excessive use of bleeding and burning, which often succeeded only in further weakening an already feeble patient.

Greek medical science, however, could not cope with the terrible disease, often called "the Justinian plague," that swept through the Byzantine Empire, Italy, southern France, Iberia, and the Rhine Valley between 541 and approximately 700. Probably originating in northwestern India and carried to the Mediterranean region by ships, the disease was similar to modern forms of bubonic plague. Characterized by high fevers, chills, delirium, and enlarged lymph nodes, or by inflammation of the lungs that caused hemorrhages of black blood, the plague carried off tens of thousands of people. It reappeared in eight- or twelve-year cycles (558–561, 580–582, 599–600, and so on) but killed fewer people each time.

The epidemic had profound political as well as social consequences. It weakened Justinian's military resources, thus hampering his efforts to restore unity to the Mediterranean world (see page 181). Demographic disasters resulting from the plague also prevented Byzantine and Persian forces from offering more than token opposition to the Muslim armies when the Arabs swarmed out of Arabia in 634[24] (see page 252).

Still, by the ninth or tenth century, most major Greek cities had hospitals for the care of the sick. The hospital operated by the Pantokrator monastery in Constantinople possessed fifty beds divided into five wards for different illnesses. A female gynecologist practiced in the women's ward. The hospital staff also included an ophthalmologist (specialist in the functions and diseases of the eye), a surgeon who performed hernia repairs, two general practitioners, two surgeons who worked an outpatient clinic, and an attendant responsible for keeping instruments clean. The imperial Byzantine government, more caring than some twentieth-century ones, bore the costs of this hospital and others.

Constantinople: The Second Rome

In the tenth century Constantinople was the greatest city in the Christian world: the seat of the imperial court and administration, a large population center, and the pivot of an extensive volume of international trade. As a natural geographical entrepôt between East and West, the city's markets offered goods from many parts of the world. About 1060 the Spanish Jew Benjamin of Tudela reported that Constantinople had merchant communities from Babylon, Canaan, Egypt, Hungary, Persia, Russia, Sennar (in the Sudan), and Spain, plus two thousand Jews.

But Constantinople did not enjoy constant political stability. Between the accession of Heraclius in 610 and the fall of the city to Western Crusaders in 1204 (see page 371), four separate dynasties ruled at Constantinople. Imperial government involved such intricate court intrigue, assassinations, and military revolts that the word *byzantine* is sometimes used in English to mean extremely entangled and complicated politics. For example, in 963 the emperor Nicephorus I Phocas married Theophano, the widow of the emperor Romanus II. In 969 Nicephorus was murdered and replaced by his nephew John I Tzimisces, Theophano's lover and an exceptionally able general.

In commerce, Jewish, Muslim (see pages 269–271), and Italian merchants controlled most foreign trade. Beginning in the eleventh century, the Venetians acquired important commercial concessions in Byzantium, thereby laying the foundations for future Venetian prosperity (see pages 360, 467). Among the Greeks, commerce faced ancient prejudices, and aristocrats and monasteries usually invested their wealth in real estate, which involved little risk but brought little gain. As in the medieval West and early modern China, rural ideals permeated Byzantine society. The landed aristocracy always held the dominant social position in the empire. Greek merchants and craftsmen, even when they acquired considerable wealth, never won social prominence.

Behind the public life of the imperial court with its assassinations and complicated politics, beyond the noise and bustle of the marketplaces thronged with Venetian and Eastern merchants, and behind the monastery walls enclosing the sophisticated theological debates of the monks, what do we know of the private life of the Constantinopolitan Greeks? Recent research has revealed a fair amount about the Byzantine *oikos,* or household. The Greek household included family members and servants, some of whom were slaves. Artisans lived and worked in their shops. Clerks, civil servants, minor officials, business people—those who today would be called middle class—commonly dwelled in multistory buildings perhaps comparable to the apartment complexes of modern American cities. Wealthy aristocrats resided in free-standing mansions that frequently included interior courts, galleries, large reception halls, small sleeping rooms, reading and writing rooms, baths, and *oratories,* chapels where all members of the household met for religious services. A complicated system of locks protected most houses from intrusion.

In the homes of the upper classes, the segregation of women seems to have been the first principle of interior design. Private houses contained a *gynaikonitis,* or women's apartment, where women were kept strictly separated from the outside world (the Muslim harem, discussed on page 269, probably derives from this Greek institution). The fundamental reason for this segregation was the family's honor: "An unchaste daughter is guilty of harming not only herself but also her parents and relatives. That is why you should keep your daughters under lock and key, as if proven guilty or imprudent, in order to avoid venomous bites," as an eleventh-century Byzantine writer put it.[25] Women did not receive outside guests, at least in theory. Although they were allowed at family banquets, they could not attend if wine was served or questionable entertainment was given. To do so gave a husband grounds for divorce.

Marriage served as part of a family's strategy for social advancement. The family and the entire kinship group participated in the selection of brides and grooms. Wealth and social connections were the chief qualities sought in potential candidates. Weddings could take place at home, in the oratory of the bride's house, or in the local church.

Scholars know a great deal about the sleeping arrangements of the imperial couples. The emperor Romanus III (r. 1028–1034), for example, shared the bed of his wife, the empress Zoe; she shared the bed of her lover, later the emperor Michael IV (r. 1034–1041). The domestic arrangements of Byzantine rulers, however, were hardly typical, and little is known about the sleeping and sexual practices of lesser mortals. The church prescribed periods of abstinence, especially during Lent (the forty days before Easter) and on Saturday and Sunday. How closely practice conformed to precept is not known. The availability of relatively good medical attention suggests that those who could afford a physician secured his services. Women delivered children seated or standing up.

SUMMARY

Saint Augustine died in 430 as the Vandals approached the coastal city of Hippo. Scholars have sometimes described Augustine as standing with one foot in the ancient world and one in the Middle Ages. Indeed, Augustine represents the end of ancient culture and the birth of what has been called the Middle Ages. A new and different kind of society was gestating in the mid-fifth century.

The world of the Middle Ages combined Germanic practices and institutions, classical ideas and patterns of thought, Christianity, and a significant dash of Islam (see Chapter 9). Christianity, because it creatively and energetically fashioned the Germanic and classical legacies, was the most powerful agent in the making of Europe. Saint Augustine of Hippo, dogmatic thinker and Christian bishop, embodied the coming world-view. In the Byzantine Empire a vigorous intellectual life, which preserved Greek scientific and medical knowledge and Roman law, flourished.

NOTES

1. Matthew 16:18–19.
2. R. C. Petry, ed., *A History of Christianity: Readings in the History of Early and Medieval Christianity* (Englewood Cliffs, N.J.: Prentice-Hall, 1962), p. 70.
3. H. Bettenson, ed., *Documents of the Christian Church* (Oxford: Oxford University Press, 1947), p. 113.
4. Colossians 3:9–11.
5. L. Sherley-Price, trans., *Bede: A History of the English Church and People* (Baltimore: Penguin Books, 1962), pp. 86–87.
6. J. T. McNeill and H. Gamer, trans., *Medieval Handbooks of Penance* (New York: Octagon Books, 1965), pp. 184–197.
7. L. White, "The Life of the Silent Majority," in *Life and Thought in the Early Middle Ages,* ed. R. S. Hoyt (Minneapolis: University of Minnesota Press, 1967), p. 100.
8. 1 Peter 2:11–20.
9. Quoted in V. L. Bullough, *The Subordinate Sex: A History of Attitudes Toward Women* (Urbana: University of Illinois Press, 1973), p. 114.
10. Ibid., pp. 118–119.
11. See J. Boswell, *Christianity, Social Tolerance, and Homosexuality: Gay People in Western Europe from the Beginning of the Christian Era to the Fourteenth Century* (Chicago: University of

Chicago Press, 1980), Chs. 3 and 5, esp. pp. 87, 127–131.

12. T. Burns, *A History of the Ostrogoths* (Bloomington: Indiana University Press, 1984), pp. 18, 21.

13. See W. Goffart, *Barbarians and Romans: The Techniques of Accommodation* (Princeton, N.J.: Princeton University Press, 1980), Ch. 3, and esp. Conclusion, pp. 211–230.

14. See P. J. Geary, *Before France and Germany: The Creation and Transformation of the Merovingian World* (New York: Oxford University Press, 1988), pp. 18–25.

15. Ibid., p. 24.

16. Ibid., pp. 108–112.

17. E. F. Henderson, ed., *Select Historical Documents of the Middle Ages* (London: G. Bell & Sons, 1912), pp. 176–189.

18. Geary, *Before France and Germany,* p. 46.

19. Ibid., p. 50.

20. See S. F. Wemple, "Sanctity and Power: The Dual Pursuit of Early Medieval Women," in *Becoming Visible: Women in European History,* 2d ed., ed. R. Bridenthal et al. (Boston: Houghton Mifflin, 1987), pp. 133–136.

21. A.-M. Talbot, "Monasteries," in *The Oxford Dictionary of Byzantium,* vol. 2, ed. A. Kazhdan (New York: Oxford University Press, 1991), p. 1393.

22. Quoted in E. Amt, ed., *Women's Lives in Medieval Europe: A Sourcebook* (New York: Routledge, 1993), pp. 34–35.

23. R. Atwater, trans., *Procopius: The Secret History* (Ann Arbor: University of Michigan Press, 1963), bk. 8.

24. W. H. McNeill, *Plagues and Peoples* (New York: Doubleday, 1976), pp. 127–128.

25. Quoted in E. Patlagean, "Byzantium in the Tenth and Eleventh Centuries," in *A History of Private Life: From Pagan Rome to Byzantium,* ed. P. Ariès and G. Duby (Cambridge, Mass.: Harvard University Press, 1987), p. 573.

SUGGESTED READING

Students seeking information on the early Christian church will find sound material in these reference works: *Encyclopedia of the Early Church,* ed. Angelo Di Berardino, trans. A. Walford, 2 vols. (1992); J. F. Kelly, *The Concise Dictionary of Early Christianity* (1992); *The Oxford Illustrated History of Christianity,* ed. J. McManners (1990); and *The Oxford Dictionary of Byzantium,* ed. A. Kazhdan (1991), which is cited in the Notes.

J. Herrin's *The Formation of Christendom* (1987) is unquestionably the best recent synthesis of the history of the early Middle Ages; it also contains an excellent discussion of Byzantine, Muslim, and Western art. In addition to the other studies listed in the Notes, students may consult the following works for a more detailed treatment of the early Middle Ages. Both M. Grant, *The Dawn of the Middle Ages* (1981), which emphasizes innovation and development, and P. Brown, *The World of Late Antiquity, A.D. 150–750,* rev. ed. (1989), which stresses social and cultural change, are lavishly illustrated and lucidly written introductions to the entire period. Grant has especially valuable material on the Germanic kingdoms, Byzantium, and eastern Europe. J. Pelikan, *The Excellent Empire: The Fall of Rome and the Triumph of the Church* (1987), describes how interpretations of the fall of Rome have influenced our understanding of Western culture. *The Cambridge Illustrated History of the Middle Ages, 350–950,* ed. R. Fossier, trans. J. Sondheimer (1989), contains some of the best recent French research on the period, though the style is often abstruse.

There is a rich literature on the Christian church and its role in the transition from ancient to medieval civilization. J. Pelikan, *Jesus Through the Centuries: His Place in the History of Culture* (1985), discusses the image of Jesus held by various cultures over the centuries and its function in the development of these cultures. F. Oakley, *The Medieval Experience: Foundations of Western Cultural Singularity* (1974), emphasizes the Christian roots of Western cultural uniqueness. W. Meeks, *The First Urban Christians: The Social World of the Apostle Paul* (1983), provides fascinating material on the early Christians and shows that they came from all social classes. For a solid appreciation of Christian life in a non-Christian society, see M. Mullin, *Called to Be Saints: Christian Living in First Century Rome* (1992). J. Richards, *Consul of God: The Life and Times of Gregory the Great* (1980), is the first significant study in seventy years of this watershed pontificate. P. Brown, *The Cult of the Saints: Its Rise and Function in Latin Christianity* (1982), describes the significance of the saints in popular religion. Students seeking to understand early Christian attitudes on sexuality and how they replaced Roman ones should consult the magisterial work of P. Brown, *The Body and Society: Men, Women, and Sexual Renunciation in Early Christianity* (1988); the profound study of J. Cohen, *"Be Fertile and Increase, Fill the Earth and Master It": The Ancient and Medieval Career of a Biblical Text* (1992), gives a lucid analysis of the church fathers' commentaries on the biblical text implied in the title and thus their views on marriage.

For the synthesis of classical and Christian cultures, see C. N. Cochrane, *Christianity and Classical Culture*

(1957), a deeply learned monograph. The best biography of Saint Augustine is P. Brown, *Augustine of Hippo* (1967), which treats him as a symbol of change. J. B. Russell, *Dissent and Order in the Middle Ages: The Search for Legitimate Authority* (1992), offers a provocative discussion of religious orthodoxy and heresy in the church.

For the Germans see, in addition to Burns's work cited in the Notes, J. M. Wallace-Hadrill, *The Barbarian West: The Early Middle Ages, A.D. 400–1000* (1962), and A. Lewis, *Emerging Europe, A.D. 400–1000* (1967), both of which describe Germanic customs and society and the Germanic impact on the Roman Empire. A rich but difficult study is H. Wolfram, *History of the Goths,* trans. T. J. Dunlop (1988), which explores Germanic tribal formation and places Gothic history within the context of late Roman society and institutions. F. Lot, *The End of the Ancient World* (1965), emphasizes the economic and social causes of Rome's decline. G. Le Bras, "The Sociology of the Church in the Early Middle Ages," in S. L. Thrupp, ed., *Early Medieval Society* (1967), discusses the Christianization of the barbarians. E. Amt, ed., *Women's Lives in Medieval Europe: A Sourcebook* (1993), is perhaps the best available collection of primary materials on women from biblical times through the thirteenth century.

The phenomenon of monasticism has attracted interest throughout the centuries. The best modern edition of the document is T. Fry et al., eds., *RB 1980: The Rule of St. Benedict in Latin and English with Notes* (1981), which contains a history of Western monasticism and a scholarly commentary on the *Rule*.

L. Eberle, trans., *The Rule of the Master* (1977), offers the text of and a commentary on Benedict's major source. Especially useful for students is O. Chadwick, *The Making of the Benedictine Ideal* (1981), a short but profound essay that emphasizes the personality of Saint Benedict in the development of the Benedictine ideal. G. Constable, *Medieval Monasticism: A Select Bibliography* (1976), is a useful research tool. Two beautifully illustrated syntheses by leading authorities are D. Knowles, *Christian Monasticism* (1969), which sketches monastic history through the middle of the twentieth century, and G. Zarnecki, *The Monastic Achievement* (1972), which focuses on the medieval centuries. L. J. Daly, *Benedictine Monasticism* (1965), stresses day-to-day living; H. W. Workman, *The Evolution of the Monastic Ideal* (1962), shows the impact of the monastic ideal on later religious orders. For women in monastic life, see S. F. Wemple, *Women in Frankish Society: Marriage and the Cloister, 500–900* (1981), an important book with a good bibliography.

For Byzantium, see J. J. Norwich, *Byzantium: The Early Centuries* (1989), an elegantly written sketch; E. Patlagean, "Byzantium in the Tenth and Eleventh Centuries," in *A History of Private Life,* vol. 1, *From Pagan Rome to Byzantium* (1987); J. Hussey, *The Byzantine World* (1961); S. Runciman, *Byzantine Civilization* (1956); and A. Bridge, *Theodora: Portrait in a Byzantine Landscape* (1984), a romantic and amusing biography of the courtesan who became empress. A. Harvey, *Economic Expansion in the Byzantine Empire, 900–1200* (1989), should prove useful for research on social and economic change.

The Conversion of Clovis

Modern Christian doctrine holds that conversion is a process, the gradual turning toward Jesus and the teachings of the Christian Gospels. But in the early medieval world, conversion was perceived more as a onetime event determined by the tribal chieftain. If he accepted baptism, the mass conversion of his people followed. The selection here about the Frankish king Clovis is from the History of the Franks *by Gregory, bishop of Tours (ca 540–594), written about a century after the events it describes.*

The first child which Clotild bore for Clovis was a son. She wanted to have her baby baptized, and she kept urging her husband to agree to this. "The gods who you worship are no good," she would say. "They haven't even been able to help themselves, let alone others. . . . Take your Saturn, for example, who ran away from his own son to avoid being exiled from his kingdom, or so they say; and Jupiter, that obscene perpetrator of all sorts of mucky deeds, who couldn't keep his hands off other men, who had his fun with all his female relatives and couldn't even refrain from intercourse with his own sister. . . .

"You ought instead to worship Him who created at a word and out of nothing heaven, and earth, the sea and all that therein is, who made the sun to shine, who lit the sky with stars, who peopled the water with fish, the earth with beasts, the sky with flying creatures, by whose hand the race of man was made, by whose gift all creation is constrained to serve in deference and devotion the man He made." However often the Queen said this, the King came no nearer to belief. . . .

The Queen, who was true to her faith, brought her son to be baptized. . . . The child was baptized; he was given the name Ingomer; but no sooner had he received baptism than he died in his white robes. Clovis was extremely angry. He began immediately

to reproach his Queen. "If he had been dedicated in the name of my gods," he said, "he would have lived without question; but now that he has been baptized in the name of your God he has not been able to live a single day!" "I give thanks to Almighty God," replied Clotild, "the Creator of all things who has not found me completely unworthy, for He has deigned to welcome into his Kingdom a child conceived in my womb. . . ."

Some time later Clotild bore a second son. He was baptized Chlodomer. He began to ail and Clovis said, "What else do you expect? It will happen to him as it happened to his brother: no sooner is he baptized in the name of your Christ than he will die!" Clotild prayed to the Lord and at His commands the baby recovered.

Queen Clotild continued to pray that her husband might recognize the true God and give up his idol-worship. Nothing could persuade him to accept Christianity. Finally war broke out against the Alamanni and in this conflict he was forced by necessity to accept what he had refused of his own free will. It so turned out that when the two armies met on the battlefield there was a great slaughter and the troops of Clovis were rapidly being annihilated. He raised his eyes to heaven when he saw this, felt compunction in his heart and was moved to tears. "Jesus Christ," he said, "you who Clotild maintains to be the Son of the living God, you who deign to give help to those in travail and victory to those who trust in you, in faith I beg the glory of your help. If you will give me victory over my enemies, and if I may have evidence to that miraculous power which the people dedicated to your name say that they have experienced, then I will believe in you and I will be baptized in your name. I have called upon my own gods, but, as I see only too clearly, they have no intention of helping me. I therefore cannot believe that they possess any power for they do not come to the assistance of those who trust them. I now call upon you. I want to believe in you, but I must first be saved from my enemies." Even as he said this the Alamanni turned their backs and began to run away. As soon as they saw that their King was killed, they submitted to Clovis. "We beg you," they said, "to put an end to this slaughter. We are prepared to obey you." Clovis stopped the war. He made a speech in which he called for peace. Then he went home. He told the Queen how he had won a victory by calling on the name of Christ. This happened in the fifteenth year of his reign (496).

The Queen then ordered Saint Remigius, Bishop of the town of Rheims, to be summoned in secret. She begged him to impart the word of salvation to the King. The Bishop asked Clovis to meet him in private and began to urge him to believe in the true God, Maker of heaven and earth, and to forsake his idols, which were powerless to help him or anyone else. The King replied: "I have listened to you willingly, holy father. There remains one obstacle. The people under my command will not agree to forsake their gods. I will go and put to them what you have said to me." He arranged a meeting with this people, but God in his power had preceded him, and before he could say a word all those present shouted in unison: "We will give up worshipping our mortal gods, pious King, and we are prepared to follow the immortal God about whom Remigius preaches." This news was reported to the Bishop. He was greatly pleased and he ordered the baptismal pool to be made ready. . . . The baptistry was prepared, sticks of incense gave off clouds of perfume, sweet-smelling candles gleamed bright and the holy place of baptism was filled with divine fragrance. God filled the hearts of all present with such grace that they imagined themselves to have been transported to some perfumed paradise. King Clovis asked that he might be baptized first by the Bishop. Like some new Constantine he stepped forward to the baptismal pool, ready to wash away the sores of his old leprosy and to be cleansed in flowing water from the sordid stains which he had borne so long.

King Clovis confessed his belief in God Almighty, three in one. He was baptized in the name of the Father, the Son and the Holy

Ninth-century ivory carving showing Clovis being baptized by Saint Remi. *(Source: Musée Condé, Chantilly/Laurie Platt Winfrey, Inc.)*

Ghost, and marked in holy chrism [an anointing oil] with the sign of the Cross of Christ. More than three thousand of his army were baptized at the same time.

Questions for Analysis

1. Who took the initiative in urging Clovis's conversion? What can we deduce from that?

2. According to this account, why did Clovis ultimately accept Christianity?

3. For the Salian Franks, what was the best proof of divine power?

4. On the basis of this selection, do you consider the *History of the Franks* reliable history? Why or why not?

Source: L. Thorpe, trans., *The History of the Franks by Gregory of Tours* (Harmondsworth, Eng.: Penguin, 1974), p. 159; and P. J. Geary, ed., *Readings in Medieval History* (Peterborough, Ont.: Broadview Press, 1991), pp. 165–166.

The Islamic World, ca 600–1400

Arch before the *mihrab* (small niche) in the beautiful mosque of Cordova, which was begun by Abd er Rahman I in 795. *(Source: MAS Barcelona)*

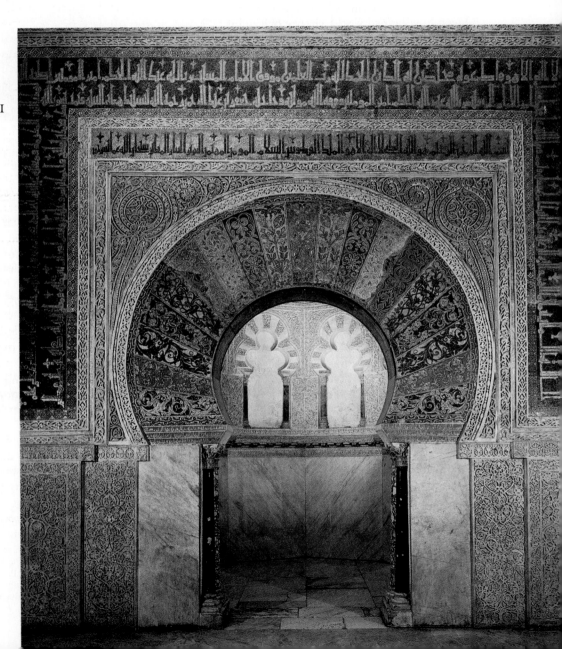

Around 610, in the important commercial city of Mecca in what is now Saudi Arabia, a merchant called Muhammad began to have religious visions. By the time he died in 632, most of Arabia had accepted his creed. A century later, his followers controlled Syria, Palestine, Egypt, Iraq, Persia (present-day Iran), northern India, North Africa, Spain, and part of France. Within another century Muhammad's beliefs had been carried across central Asia to the borders of China. In the ninth, tenth, and eleventh centuries the Muslims created a brilliant civilization centered at Baghdad in Iraq, a culture that profoundly influenced the development of both Eastern and Western civilizations.

- Who were the Arabs?
- What are the main tenets of the Muslim faith?
- What factors account for the remarkable spread of Islam?
- How did the Muslims govern the vast territories they conquered?
- Why did the Shi'ite Muslim tradition arise, and how did the split between Shi'ites and Sunnis affect the course of Islam?
- What position did women hold in Muslim society?
- What features characterized the societies of the great Muslim cities of Baghdad and Cordoba?
- How did the Muslims view Western society and culture?

This chapter explores those questions.

�֎ THE ARABS BEFORE ISLAM

The Arabian peninsula, perhaps a third of the size of Europe or the United States, covers about a million square miles. Ancient Greek geographers named the peninsula *Arabian* after the Bedouin Arabs, nomads who grazed their animals in the sparse patches of grass that dotted the vast, semi-arid land. Thus *Arab* originally meant a native of Arabia. After Islam spread and peoples of various ethnic backgrounds attached themselves to or intermarried with the Arabs, they assumed an Arab identity. Today, the term *Arab* refers to an ethnic identity; *Arabic* means a linguistic and cultural heritage.

In the sixth century A.D. most Arabs were not nomads; most led a settled existence. In the southwestern mountain valleys of the Arabian peninsula, plentiful rainfall and sophisticated irrigation techniques resulted in highly productive agriculture that supported fairly dense population settlements. In other areas scattered throughout the peninsula, oasis towns based on the cultivation of date palms grew up around wells. Some oasis towns sustained sizable populations including artisans, merchants, and religious leaders. Some, such as Mecca, served as important trading outposts. The presence of the Ka'ba, a temple containing a black stone thought to be a god's dwelling place, also attracted pilgrims and enabled Mecca to become the metropolis of western Arabia. Mecca served economic and religious/cultic functions.

Thinly spread over the entire peninsula, the nomadic Bedouins migrated from place to place, grazing their sheep, goats, and camels. Though always small in number, Bedouins were the most important political and military force in the region because of their toughness, solidarity, fighting traditions, and ability to control trade and lines of communication. Between the peoples settled in oasis towns and the Bedouin nomads were seminomads. As the agricultural conditions around them fluctuated, they practiced either settled agriculture or nomadic pastoralism.

For all Arabs the basic social unit was the *tribe*—a group of blood relations that descended in the male line. The tribe provided protection and support and in turn received members' total loyalty. Like the Germanic peoples in the age of their migrations (see pages 228–229), Arab tribes were not static entities but continually evolving groups. A particular tribe might include both nomadic and sedentary members.

Strong economic links joined all Arab peoples. Nomads and seminomads depended on the agriculturally productive communities for food they could not produce, cloth, metal products, and weapons. Nomads paid for these goods with the livestock, milk and milk products, hides, and hair wanted by oasis towns. Nomads acquired income by serving as desert guides and as guards for caravans. Plundering caravans and extorting protection money also yielded funds.

In northern and central Arabia, tribal confederations dominated by a warrior aristocracy characterized Arab political organization. The warrior aristocrats possessed several assets that help to explain their power. They had tremendous physical toughness, and they had a few horses, which though difficult to maintain in desert conditions gave them speed and mobility. They paid tribute to no one and claimed blood descent from some great chief. Within a confederation, tribes competed for preeminence.

In the southern parts of the peninsula in the early seventh century, religious aristocracies tended to hold political power. Many oasis or market towns contained members of one holy family who claimed to be servants or priests of the deity who resided in the town, and they served as guardians of the deity's shrine, or *haram*. The family imposed rules for behavior at the shrine. Murder was forbidden at the shrine, and a tribesman knew that even his bitterest enemy would not attack him there. At the haram, a *mansib*, or cultic leader, adjudicated disputes and tried to get agreements among warrior tribes. All Arabs respected the harams because they feared retribution if the gods' shrines were desecrated and because the harams served as neutral places for arbitration among warring tribes.

The power of the northern warrior aristocracy rested on its fighting skills. The southern religious aristocracy, by contrast, depended on its cultic and economic power. Located in agricultural areas that were also commercial centers, the religious aristocracy had a stronger economic base than the warrior aristocrats. Scholarship has shown that the arbitrator role of the mansib marks a step toward a society governed by law.[1] The political genius of Muhammad was to bind together these different tribal groups into a strong unified state.

�֎ MUHAMMAD AND THE FAITH OF ISLAM

A fair amount is known about Jesus after he began his public ministry at about age thirty, but little is known about his early life. Similarly, a good deal is known about Muhammad after his "call" as God's messenger at age forty, but little is known about him before then. Except for a few vague remarks in the Qur'an, the sacred book of Islam, no contemporary account of Muhammad's life (ca 570–632) survives. Arabic tradition accepts as historically true some of the sacred legends that developed about him, but those legends were not written down until about a century after his death. (Similarly, the earliest accounts of the life of Jesus, the Christian Gospels, were not written down until forty or fifty years after his death.)

Orphaned at the age of six, Muhammad was brought up by his paternal uncle. As a young man he became a merchant in the caravan trade. Later he entered the service of a wealthy widow, Khadija, and their subsequent marriage brought him financial security while she lived. Muhammad apparently was extremely pious, self-disciplined, and devoted to contemplation. At about forty, in a cave in the hills near Mecca where he was accustomed to pray, Muhammad had a profound religious experience. In a vision an angelic being (whom Muhammad later interpreted to be Gabriel, God's messenger) commanded him to preach the revelations that God would be sending him. Muhammad began to preach to the people of Mecca, urging them to give up their idols and submit to the one indivisible God. During his lifetime Muhammad's followers jotted down his revelations haphazardly. After his death scribes organized the revelations into chapters. In 651 they published the version of them that Muslims consider authoritative, the *Qur'an* (from an Arabic word meaning "reading" or "recitation"). Muslims revere the Qur'an for its sacred message and for the beauty of its Arabic language.

Islam, the strict monotheistic faith that is based on the teachings of Muhammad, rests on the principle of the absolute unity and omnipotence of Allah, God. The word *Islam* means "submission to God," and *Muslim* means "a person who submits." Thus the community of Muslims consists of people who have submitted to God by accepting his teachings as revealed by Muhammad, the Prophet. Muslims believe that Muhammad was the last of the prophets, completing the work begun by Abraham, Moses, and Jesus. According to the Qur'an, both Jewish and Christian authorities acknowledged the coming of a final prophet. The Jewish rabbi Kab al-Ahbar, an early convert to Islam and the source of much of the Jewish material in the early Islamic tradition, asserted "the disciples of Jesus asked, O Spirit of God, will there be another religious community after us?" And, the rabbi re-

✳ Qur'an with Kufic Script   Kufic takes its name from the town of Kufa, south of Baghdad in Iraq, at one time a major center of Muslim learning. The script relates to the angular form of the Arabic alphabet used in producing fine copies of the Qur'an. *(Source: Mashed Shrine Library, Iran/Robert Harding Picture Library)*

ported, Jesus said: "Yes, the community of Ahmad [that is Muhammad]. It will comprise people who are wise, knowing, devout, and pious."[2]

Muslims believe that they worship the same God as Jews and Christians. Islam's uncompromising monotheism—belief in the oneness of God—

spelled the end of paganism everywhere that Islam was accepted.

Monotheism, however, had flourished in Middle Eastern Semitic and Persian cultures for centuries before Muhammad. According to one scholar, "Muhammad was not the founder of Islam; he did not start a new religion." Instead, like the Old Testament prophets, Muhammad came as a reformer. In Jewish, Christian, and Muslim theology, a prophet is not someone who predicts the future; a prophet speaks the word of God. Muhammad insisted that he was not preaching a new message; rather, he was calling people back to the one true God, urging his contemporaries to reform their lives, to return to the faith of Abraham, the first monotheist.[3]

Muhammad's social and political views are inseparable from his religious ideas. Muhammad displayed genius as both political strategist and religious teacher. He gave Arabs the idea of a unique and unified *umma*, or community, which consisted of all those whose primary identity and bond was a common religious faith and commitment, not a tribal tie. The umma was to be a religious and political community led by Muhammad for the achievement of God's will on earth.

In the early seventh century the southern Arab tribal confederations, which centered around sacred enclaves, lacked cohesiveness and unity and were constantly warring; they recognized no single higher authority. The Islamic notion of an absolute higher authority transcended the boundaries of individual tribal units and fostered the political consolidation of the tribal confederations. Islam teaches that God is not only all-powerful and all-knowing but has set forth a law against which *all* human actions are measured. The fundamental tenet of Islam, to which any believer must subscribe, is "There is no God but God, and Muhammad is his Prophet." If one accepts the idea of

Jonah and the Whale The story of Jonah in the Old Testament describes a prophet who tried to avoid his responsibilities and is swallowed by a whale; it is a parable of divine mercy, urging people to repent and seek forgiveness. The Chinese artist who executed this superb painting had never seen a whale, but he possessed imagination, delicacy, and mastery of movement. *(Source: Edinburgh University Library)*

God's oneness and Muhammad's claim to be his Prophet, then it follows that all authority comes from God *through Muhammad*. Within the umma, the law of God was discerned and applied through Muhammad. Thus, in the seventh century, Islam centralized authority, both political and religious, in Muhammad's hands.[4]

The Qur'an is much holier to Muslims than the Torah and the Gospels are to Jews and Christians. The Qur'an prescribes a strict code of moral behavior. A Muslim must recite the profession of faith in God and in Muhammad as his prophet: "There is no God but God, and Muhammad is his Prophet." A believer must also pray five times a day, fast and pray during the sacred month of Ramadan, make a pilgrimage to the holy city of Mecca once during his or her lifetime, and give alms to the Muslim poor. The Qur'an forbids alcoholic beverages and gambling. It condemns usury in business—that is, lending money and charging the borrower interest—and taking advantage of market demand for products by charging high prices. Some foods, such as pork, are forbidden, a dietary regulation perhaps adopted from the Mosaic law of the Hebrews.

Compared with earlier Arab standards, the Qur'an sets forth an austere sexual code. Muslim jurisprudence condemned licentious behavior by both men and women, and the status of women improved. About marriage, illicit intercourse, and inheritance, the Qur'an states:

Of . . . women who seem good in your eyes, marry but two, three, or four; and if ye still fear that ye shall not act equitably, then only one. . . .

The whore and the fornicator: whip each of them a hundred times. . . .

The fornicator shall not marry other than a whore; and the whore shall not marry other than a fornicator. . . .

Men who die and leave wives behind shall bequeath to them a year's maintenance. . . . And your wives shall have a fourth part of what you leave, if you have no issue; but if you have issue, then they shall have an eighth part.

With regard to your children, God commands you to give the male the portion of two females; and if there be more than two females, then they shall have two-thirds of what their father leaves; but if there be one daughter only, she shall have the half.[5]

By contrast, Western law has tended to punish prostitutes, not their clients.

With respect to matters of property in the seventh and eighth centuries, Muslim women were more emancipated than Western women. Islamic law gave a woman control of all the property she brought to her marriage, except for the dowry. Half of the dowry went to the husband; the other half remained hers in case the marriage failed. A Muslim woman could dispose of her property in any way she wished. A Western woman had no such power.

Islam warns about the Last Judgment and the importance of the life to come. The Islamic Last Judgment bears striking resemblance to the Christian one: on that day God will separate the saved and the damned. The Qur'an describes in detail the frightful tortures with which God will punish the damned: scourgings, beatings with iron clubs, burnings, and forced drinking of boiling water. Muhammad's account of the heavenly rewards of the saved and the blessed are equally graphic but are different in kind from those of Christian theology. The Muslim vision of heaven features lush green gardens surrounded by refreshing streams. There, the saved, clothed in rich silks, lounge on brocaded couches, nibbling ripe fruits, sipping delicious beverages, and enjoying the companionship of physically attractive people.

How do the Muslim faithful merit the rewards of heaven? Salvation is by God's grace and choice alone. Because God is all-powerful, he knows from the moment of conception whether a person will be saved. But predestination does not mean that believers have no reason to try to achieve heaven. Muslims who suffer and die for the faith in battle are ensured the rewards of heaven. For others, the Qur'anic precepts mark the path to salvation.

THE EXPANSION OF ISLAM

Muhammad's preaching at first did not appeal to many people. Legend has it that for the first three years he attracted only fourteen believers. Muhammad's teaching constituted social revolution. He preached a revelation that opposed the undue accumulation of wealth and social stratification and that held all men as brothers within a social order ordained by God. Moreover, he urged the destruction of the idols in the Ka'ba at Mecca, a site that drew thousands of devout Arabs annually and thus brought important revenue to the city. The bankers and merchants of Mecca fought him. The townspeople turned against him, and he and his followers were forced to flee to Medina. This *hijra,* or emigration, occurred in 622, and Muslims later dated the beginning of their era from that event. At Medina, Muhammad attracted increasing numbers of believers, and his teachings began to have an impact.

Expansion to the West

By the time Muhammad died in 632, he had welded together all the Bedouin tribes. The crescent of Islam, the Muslim symbol, controlled most of the Arabian peninsula. In the next hundred years, one rich province of the old Roman Empire after another came under Muslim domination—first Syria, then Egypt, then all of North Africa (Map 9.1).

In 711 a Muslim force crossed the Strait of Gibraltar and at the Guadalete River easily defeated the weak Visigothic kingdom in Spain. A few Christian princes supported by the Frankish rulers held out in the Pyrenees Mountains, but the Muslims controlled most of Spain until the twelfth century. The political history of Christian Spain in the Middle Ages is the history of the *reconquista,* the Christian reconquest of that country.

In 719 the Muslims pushed beyond the Pyrenees into the kingdom of the Franks. At the Battle of Tours in 733, the Frankish chieftain Charles Martel defeated the Arabs and halted their northern expansion. The Muslims had greatly overextended their forces. Ultimately, Charlemagne expelled them from France.

Expansion to the East

Between 632 and 640, the Arabs surged to the east into the Sassanid kingdom of Persia (see page 55). When they defeated the Persians at Nihawand in 651, Muslim control of the Persian Empire was completed. The wealth seized at the Persian capital, Ctesiphon, astounded the victorious, uneducated Bedouin tribesmen, who according to one modern scholar did not understand what they had won:

Some of the warriors, unfamiliar with gold pieces, were willing to exchange them for silver ones. Others, who had never seen camphor before, took it for salt and used it in cooking. When blamed at Hira for selling an aristocratic woman who had fallen as his share of booty for only a thousand silver pieces, an Arabian replied that he never thought there was a number higher than ten hundred.[6]

The government headquarters of the vast new empire was transferred from Medina to Damascus in Syria. A contemporary proverb speaks of the Mediterranean as a Muslim lake.

The Muslims continued their drive eastward. In the mid-seventh century, they occupied the province of Khorasan, where the city of Merv became the center of Muslim control over eastern Persia (Map 9.2) and the base for campaigns farther east. By 700 the Muslims had crossed the Oxus River and swept toward Kabul, today the capital of Afghanistan. They penetrated Kazakhstan and then seized Tashkent, one of the oldest cities in central Asia. The clash of Muslim horsemen with a Chinese army at the Talas River in 751 seems to mark the farthest Islamic penetration into central Asia.

From Makran in southern Persia a Muslim force marched into the Indus Valley in northern India and in 713 founded an Islamic community at Multan. Beginning in the eleventh century, Muslim dynasties from Ghazni in Afghanistan carried Islam deeper into the Indian subcontinent.

Reasons for the Spread of Islam

By the beginning of the eleventh century the crescent of Islam flew from the Iberian heartlands to northern India. How can this rapid and remarkable expansion be explained? Muslim historians attribute Islamic victories to God's support for the Muslim faith. True, the Arabs won their military successes because they possessed a religious fervor and loyalty that their enemies could not equal. They were convinced of the necessity of the *jihad,* or holy war. The Qur'an does not explicitly mention this subject, but because the Qur'an does suggest that God sent the Prophet to establish justice on earth, it follows that justice will take effect only where Islam triumphs. Just as Christians have the

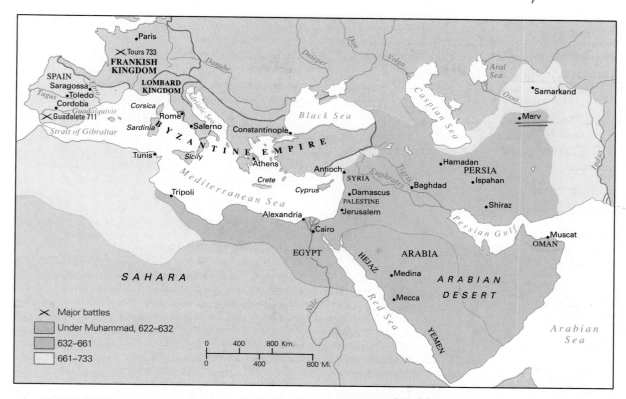

MAP 9.1 **Expansion of Islam to 733**   Political weaknesses in the territories they conquered, as well as superior fighting skills, help explain the speed with which the Muslims expanded.

missionary obligation to spread their faith, so Muslims have the obligation, as individuals and as a community, and to extend Islam. *Jihad* also came to mean the struggle to defend Islam. Those who waged it were assured happiness in the world to come.

The Muslim outburst from Arabia and subsequent successes had strong economic, political, and military, as well as religious, causes. The Arab surge reflects the economic needs of a tough people squeezed into a semibarren, overpopulated area and the desire to share in the rich life of the Fertile Crescent. Arab expansion in the seventh and eighth centuries was another phase of the infiltration that had taken the ancient Hebrews to the other end of the Fertile Crescent (see Map 1.1, page 9). Also, recent conflicts between the Byzantine and Sassanid empires had left both weak and divided.

In the Byzantine provinces of Egypt and Syria, moreover, theological squabbles and factional divisions helped the Muslim advance. Groups alienated from Byzantine rule expressed their dissatisfaction by quickly capitulating to the Arabs in return for promises of religious freedom and the protection of their property. In the period between 642 and 643, an Arab army officer recorded his pledges to the people of Qum, in Persia:

In the name of God, the Merciful and the Compassionate. This is what Suwayd ibn Muqarrin gave to the inhabitants of Qumis and those who are dependent on them, concerning safe-conduct for themselves, their religions and their property, on condition that they pay the jizya [a poll tax] from the hand of every adult male, according to his capacity, that they show goodwill and do not deceive, that they guide the Muslim traveler, and that they accommodate Muslims who

MAP 9.2 Expansion of Islam to 1500   Islam spread along the commercial arteries that extended from the eastern Mediterranean all the way to China, Southeast Asia, and Malaysia.

make a halt with them for a day and a night with their average food. If they change this or make light of their obligations, the pact [dhimma] with them is void.[7]

The Muslim conquest of Syria provides an example of the combination of motives—economic, religious, and political—that propelled early Muslim expansion. Situated to the north of the Arabian peninsula, Syria had been under Byzantine-Christian (or Roman) rule for centuries. Arab caravans knew the market towns of southern Syria and the rich commercial centers of the north, such as Edessa, Aleppo, and Damascus. Syria's economic prosperity attracted the Muslims, and perhaps Muhammad saw the lands as a potential means of support for the poor who flooded Medina. Syria also contained sites important to the Muslim faith: Jerusalem, where Jesus and other prophets mentioned in the Qur'an had lived and preached; and Hebron, the traditional burial place of Abraham, the father of monotheism. Finally, a practical polit-

ical reason encouraged expansion. The centralization of the Islamic state depended on the control of the nomadic tribes of the Arabian and Syrian deserts. In the 630s the Byzantine state, barely recovering from a long war with the Sassanid empire of Persia over Syria, was trying to forge alliances with the nomadic tribes. From the Muslim perspective, the Islamic state had to win over these peoples before the Byzantines did so. Expansion in Syria, therefore, was absolutely essential.[8]

Military organization also helps account for the Muslims' rapid success. The leadership maintained a cohesive hold on the troops, and internal conflicts did not arise to slow their initial advances. The military elite solved the problem of recruitment for the army. Fixed salaries, regular pay, and the lure of battlefield booty attracted the rugged tribesmen. In the later campaigns to the east, many recruits were recent converts to Islam from Christian, Persian, and Berber backgrounds. The assurance of army wages secured the loyalty of these very diverse men. Here is an eleventh-century description of the Egyptian army (medieval numbers were always greatly exaggerated):

Each corps has its own name and designation. One group are called Kitamis [a Berber tribe]. These came from Qayrawan in the service of al-Mu'izz li-Din Allah. They are said to number 20,000 horsemen. . . . Another group is called Masmudis. They are blacks from the land of the Masmudis and said to number 20,000 men. Another group are called the Easterners, consisting of Turks and Persians. They are so-called because they are not of Arab origin. Though most of them were born in Egypt, their name derives from their origin. They are said to number 10,000 powerfully built men. Another group are called the slaves by purchase. . . . They are slaves bought for money and are said to number 30,000 men. Another group are called Bedouin. They are from the Hijaz [Hejaz] and are all armed with spears. They are said

to number 50,000 horsemen. Another group are called Ustads. These are servants [eunuchs], black and white, bought for service. They number 30,000 horsemen.[9]

In classical Islam, ethnicity and concepts of nation, country, and political sovereignty played a very small role in defining political power and authority in territorial terms. For Muslims, religion was the core of identity. They divided the world into two fundamental sections: the House of Islam, which consisted of all those regions where the law of Islam prevailed, and the House of War, which was the rest of the world. "As there is one God in heaven, so there can be only one ruler on earth." By the logic of Islamic law, no political entity outside of Islam can exist permanently. Every Muslim, accordingly, has the religious duty of the jihad—carrying out the war of conversion. Consequently, a state of war exists permanently between

Muezzin Calling People to Prayer   A mosque is usually surrounded by an open courtyard containing a fountain for ritual ablutions and a *minaret*, or lofty tower surrounded by projecting balconies from which an official, the muezzin, summons the faithful to prayer. *(Source: Ian Graham)*

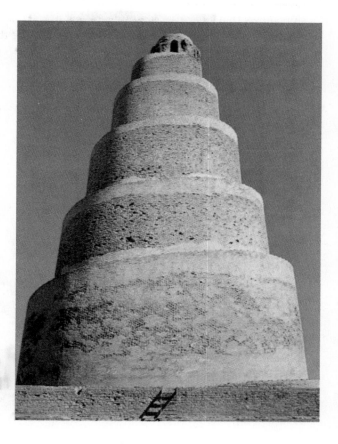

the House of Islam and the House of War. With the conversion or conquest of all humankind, the war will end.

In practice, of course, Muslims did recognize divisions among unbelievers. The most basic distinction was between those who possessed revealed religions—Jews and Christians, whose faiths are based on the revelations in the Scriptures—and those who did not. Jews and Christians who submitted to Islam enjoyed the protection of the state. They were known as *dhimmis*, or "protected people." Islam also accommodated Zoroastrians, Hindus, Buddhists, and other polytheists. Europeans regarded Muslims as "heretics" or "infidels" who when conquered had to choose between conversion and death.[10] There were, of course, many exceptions, but in general the Christian attitude toward Islam was far more bigoted and intolerant than was the attitude of Islam toward Christianity (see page 380).

What was the fate of Jews living under Islam? How does their experience compare with that of Jews living in Christian Europe? Recent scholarship shows that in Europe, Jews were first marginalized in the Christian social order, then completely expelled from it (see pages 379–380). In Islam, though marginalized, Jews participated fully in commercial and professional activities, some attaining an economic equality with their Muslim counterparts. Why? The 17th Sur (chapter) of the Qur'an, entitled Bani Isra'il, "The Children of Israel," accords to the Jews a special respect because they were "the people of the Book." Scriptural admonitions of the Qur'an carried over into social and political legislation, and "the relative stability over time of the basic law regarding their (Jews') legal status assured them a considerable degree of continuity."[11] In contrast, Western Christian legislation about the Jews fluctuated, making their legal position more ambiguous, tenuous, and insecure. Also, Islamic culture was an urban and commercial culture that gave the merchant considerable respect; medieval Christian culture was basically rural and agricultural; it did not revere the business person.

Finally, the Muslim practice of establishing camp cities in newly conquered territories facilitated expansion. New military towns, such as Al-Fustat in Egypt and Basra in Iraq, became sites from which future conquests were planned and directed. They safeguarded Muslim identity and prevented the Muslim conquerors, at first a small minority, from being assimilated into the larger indigenous population. As the subject peoples became Muslim, the army towns became major centers for the spread of Islamic culture.

CONSOLIDATION OF THE ISLAMIC STATE

Although centered in towns, Islam arose within a tribal society that lacked stable governing institutions. When Muhammad died in 632, he left a large Muslim *umma*, but this community stood in danger of disintegrating into separate tribal groups. Some tribespeople even attempted to elect new chiefs. What provisions did Muhammad make for the religious and political organization of his followers? How was the vast and hastily acquired empire that came into existence within one hundred years of his death to be governed?

The Caliphate

Muhammad fulfilled his prophetic mission, but his religious work remained. The Muslim umma had to be maintained and Islam carried to the rest of the world. To achieve these goals, political and military power had to be exercised. But neither the Qur'an nor the Sunna, the account of the Prophet's sayings and conduct in particular situations, offered guidance for the succession (see page 248).

In this crisis, a group of Muhammad's ablest followers elected Abu Bakr (573–634), a close supporter of the Prophet, and hailed him as *khalifa*, or caliph, an Arabic term combining the ideas of leader, successor, and deputy (of the Prophet). This election marked the decisive victory of the concept of a universal community of Muslim believers. The goals of the Muslim umma were set down in the Qur'an to make the faith revealed to Muhammad the cornerstone of Muslim law, government, and personal behavior.

Because the law of the Qur'an was to guide the community, there had to be an authority to enforce the law. Muslim teaching held that the law was paramount. God is the sole source of the law, and the ruler is bound to obey the law. Government exists not to make law but to enforce it. Muslim teaching also maintained that there is no distinction between the temporal and spiritual domains: social law is a basic strand in the fabric of comprehensive religious law. Thus religious belief and political power are inextricably intertwined: the first sanctifies the second, and the second sustains the first.[12] The creation of Islamic law in an institutional sense took three or four centuries and is one of the great achievements of medieval Islam.

In the two years of his rule (632–634), Abu Bakr governed on the basis of his personal prestige within the Muslim umma. He sent out military expeditions, collected taxes, dealt with tribes on behalf of the entire community, and led the community in prayer. Gradually, under Abu Bakr's first three successors, Umar (r. 634–644), Uthman (r. 644–656), and Ali (r. 656–661), the caliphate emerged as an institution. Umar succeeded in ex-

erting his authority over the Bedouin tribes involved in ongoing conquests. Uthman asserted the right of the caliph to protect the economic interests of the entire umma. Uthman's publication of the definitive text of the Qur'an showed his concern for the unity of the umma. But Uthman's enemies accused him of nepotism—of using his position to put his family in powerful and lucrative jobs—and of unnecessary cruelty. Opposition coalesced around Ali, and when Uthman was assassinated in 656, Ali was chosen to succeed him.

The issue of responsibility for Uthman's murder raised the question of whether Ali's accession was legitimate. Uthman's cousin Mu'awiya, a member of the Umayyad family, who had built a power base as governor of Syria, refused to recognize Ali as caliph. In the ensuing civil war, Ali was assassinated, and Mu'awiya (r. 661–680) assumed the caliphate. Mu'awiya founded the Umayyad Dynasty

Woven Silk Fragment This tenth-century piece from Khurasan, in northern Iran, shows elephants used as pack animals and an elegant Kufic border inscription reading "Glory and prosperity to Qa'id Abu-l-Mansur Bakht-tegin, may Allah perpetuate his happiness," which identifies the original owner. (Source: Louvre © Photo R.M.N.)

and shifted the capital of the Islamic state from Medina to Damascus in Syria. From 661 to 750 Damascus served as the center of the Muslim government bureaucracy.

The first four caliphs were elected by their peers, and the theory of an elected caliphate remained the Islamic legal ideal. Three of the four "patriarchs," as they were called, were murdered, however, and civil war ended the elective caliphate. Beginning with Mu'awiya, the office of caliph was in fact, but never in theory, dynastic. Two successive dynasties, the Umayyad (661–750) and the Abbasid (750–1258), held the caliphate.

From its inception with Abu Bakr, the caliphate rested on the principle that Muslim political and religious unity transcended tribalism. Mu'awiya sought to enhance the power of the caliphate by making the tribal leaders dependent on him for concessions and special benefits. At the same time, his control of a loyal and well-disciplined army enabled him to develop the caliphate in an authoritarian direction. Through intimidation he forced the tribal leaders to accept his son Yazid as his heir—thereby establishing the dynastic principle of succession. By distancing himself from a simple life within the umma and withdrawing into the palace that he built at Damascus, and by surrounding himself with symbols and ceremony, Mu'awiya laid the foundations for an elaborate caliphal court. Many of Mu'awiya's innovations were designed to protect him from assassination. A new official, the *hajib*, or chamberlain, restricted access to the caliph, who received visitors seated on a throne surrounded by bodyguards. Beginning with Mu'awiya, the Umayyad caliphs developed court ritual into a grand spectacle.

The assassination of Ali and the assumption of the caliphate by Mu'awiya had another profound consequence. It gave rise to a fundamental division in the umma and in Muslim theology. Ali had claimed the caliphate on the basis of family ties—he was Muhammad's cousin and son-in-law. When Ali was murdered, his followers argued—partly because of the blood tie, partly because Muhammad had designated Ali *imam*, or leader in community prayer—that Ali had been the Prophet's designated successor. These supporters of Ali were called *Shi'ites*, or *Shi'at Ali*, or simply *Shi'a*—Arabic terms all meaning "supporters" or "partisans" of Ali. In succeeding generations, opponents of the

Umayyad Dynasty emphasized their blood descent from Ali and claimed to possess divine knowledge that Muhammad had given them as his heirs.

Other Muslims adhered to the practice and beliefs of the umma, based on the precedents of the Prophet. They were called *Sunnis*, which derived from *Sunna*. When a situation arose for which the Qur'an offered no solution, Sunnite scholars searched for a precedent in the Sunna, which gained an authority comparable to the Qur'an itself.

What basically distinguished Sunni and Shi'ite Muslims was the Shi'ite doctrine of the *imamate*. According to the Sunnites, the caliph, the elected successor of the Prophet, possessed political and military leadership but not Muhammad's religious authority. In contrast, according to the Shi'ites, the imam (leader) is directly descended from the Prophet and is the sinless, divinely inspired political leader and religious guide of the community. Put another way, both Sunnites and Shi'ites maintain that authority within Islam lies first in the Qur'an and then in the Sunna. Who interprets these sources? Shi'ites claim that the imam does, for he is invested with divine grace and insight. Sunnites insist that interpretation comes from the consensus of the *ulema*, a group of religious scholars.

The Umayyad caliphs were Sunnis, and throughout the Umayyad period the Shi'ites constituted a major source of discontent. Shi'ite rebellions expressed religious opposition in political terms. The Shi'ites condemned the Umayyads as worldly and sensual rulers, in contrast to the pious and true "successors" of Muhammad.

The Abbasid clan, which based its claim to the caliphate on the descent of Abbas, Muhammad's uncle, exploited the situation. The Abbasids agitated the Shi'ites, encouraged dissension among tribal factions, and contrasted Abbasid piety with the pleasure-loving style of the Umayyads. Through open rebellion in 747, the Abbasids overthrew the Umayyads. In 750 the Abbasids won recognition as caliphs and later set up their capital at Baghdad in Iraq. The Abbasid Dynasty lasted until 1258, but its real power began to disintegrate in the mid-ninth century.

Scholars agree that the Abbasid revolution established a basis for rule and citizenship more cosmopolitan and Islamic than the narrow, elitist,

THE ISLAMIC WORLD, CA 600–1258

610	Muhammad preaches reform, monotheism
610–733	Spread of Islam across Arabia, southern Europe, North Africa, and Asia as far as India
622	The hijra—Muhammad and his followers emigrate to Medina
632	Muhammad dies
632–661	Caliphate emerges as an institution
642	Muslims' victory at Nihawand signals their control of the Persian Empire
651	Publication of the Qur'an, the sacred book of Islam
661–750	The Umayyad Dynasty
661	Umayyads move Muslim capital from Medina to Damascus
713	Spread of Islam to India, with the founding of a Muslim community at Multan
733	Charles Martel defeats Arabs at Battle of Tours, halting spread of Islam in northwestern Europe
750–1258	The Abbasid Dynasty
751	Battle at Talas River slows Islamic penetration of central Asia
762	Abbasids move Muslim capital from Damascus to Baghdad
945	Buyids occupy Baghdad
946	Blinding of Caliph al-Mustakfi signals the practical end of the Abbasid Dynasty
1055	Baghdad falls to the Seljuk Turks
1258	Mongols destroy Baghdad and kill the last of the Abbasid caliphs

and Arab basis that had characterized Umayyad government. Moreover, under the Umayyads the Muslim state had been governed by one ruler; during the Abbasid caliphate, steady disintegration occurred as provincial governors gradually won independent power. Although at first Muslims represented only a small minority of the conquered peoples, Abbasid rule provided the political and re-ligious milieu in which Islam gained, over the centuries, the allegiance of the vast majority of the population from Spain to Afghanistan.

Administration of the Islamic State

The Islamic conquests brought into being a new imperial system that dominated southwestern Asia and North Africa. The Muslims adopted the patterns of administration used by the Byzantines in Egypt and Syria and by the Sassanids in Persia. Arab emirs, or governors, were appointed and given overall responsibility for good order, the maintenance of the armed forces, and tax collecting. Below them, experienced native officials—Greeks, Syrians, Copts (Egyptian Christians)—remained in office. Thus there was continuity with previous administrations.

The Arab conquerors developed devices to meet the changing needs of their empire. Tradition holds that the second caliph, Umar, established the diwan, or financial bureau. This agency recorded the names of soldiers, together with their salaries from state revenues. The diwan converted payments in kind to monetary equivalents and dispersed sums to tribal chieftains for distribution to their followers. All later departments of Muslim administration derive from this core.

The Umayyad caliphate witnessed the further development of the imperial administration. At the head stood the caliph, who led the holy war against unbelievers. Theoretically, he had the ultimate responsibility for the interpretation of the sacred law. In practice, the ulema interpreted the law as revealed in the Qur'an and in the Sunna. In the course of time the ulema's interpretations constituted a rich body of law, the shari'a, which covered social, criminal, political, commercial, and ritualistic matters. The ulema enjoyed great prestige in the Muslim community and was consulted by the caliph on difficult legal and spiritual matters. The qadis, or judges, who were well versed in the sacred law, carried out the judicial functions of the state. Nevertheless, Muslim law prescribed that all people have access to the caliph, and he set aside special times for hearing petitions and for the direct redress of grievances.

The central administrative organ was the diwan al-kharaj, which collected the taxes that paid soldiers' salaries and financed charitable and public works that the caliph undertook, such as aid to the poor (as the Qur'an prescribed), and construction of mosques, irrigation works, and public baths.

As Arab conquests extended into Spain, central Asia, and Afghanistan, lines of communication had to be kept open. Emirs and other officials, remote from the capital at Damascus and later Baghdad, might revolt. Thus a relay network known as the barid was established to convey letters and intelligence reports between the capital and the various outposts. The barid employed a special technical vocabulary, as similar networks used by the Byzantine and Sassanid empires had done.

The early Abbasid period witnessed considerable economic expansion and population growth, so the work of government became more complicated. New and specialized departments emerged, each with a hierarchy of officials. The most important new official was the vizier, a position that the Abbasids adopted from the Persians. Initially, the vizier was the caliph's chief assistant. The vizier advised the caliph on matters of general policy, supervised the bureaucratic administration, and, under the caliph, superintended the army, the provincial governors, and relations with foreign governments. As the caliphs withdrew from leading Friday prayers and other routine functions, the viziers gradually assumed power. But the authority and power of the vizier usually depended on the caliph's personality and direct involvement in state affairs. Many viziers used their offices for personal gain and wealth. Although some careers ended with the vizier's execution, there were always candidates seeking the job.

The vizier al-Fustat (d. 924) set down some of his reflections on government. They sound more like cynical aphorisms than serious policy principles:

A terse saying embodying a general truth or astute observation.

The basis of government is trickery; if it succeeds and endures, it becomes policy.

It is better to keep the affairs of government moving on the wrong path than to stand still on the right one.[13]

In theory, the caliph and his central administration governed the whole empire. In practice, the many parts of the empire enjoyed considerable local independence; and as long as public order was maintained and taxes were forwarded to the diwan al-kharaj, the central government rarely interfered. In theory, Muslim towns did not possess the chartered self-governing status of the towns and cities of medieval Europe (see pages 381–382). In practice, although a capable governor kept a careful eye on municipal activities, wealthy merchants and property owners had broad local autonomy.

DECENTRALIZATION OF THE ISLAMIC STATE

The Umayyad state virtually coincided with all Islamic states. Under the Abbasids, decentralization began nearly from the start of the dynasty. In 755 a Umayyad prince who had escaped death at the hands of the triumphant Abbasids and fled to Spain set up an independent regime at Cordoba (see Map 9.2). In 800, the emir in Tunisia in North Africa set himself up as an independent ruler and refused to place the caliph's name on the local coinage. In 820, Tahir, the son of a slave, was rewarded with the governorship of Khorasan because he had supported the caliphate. Once there, Tahir ruled independently of Baghdad, not even mentioning the caliph's name in the traditional Friday prayers in recognition of caliphal authority.

This sort of decentralization occurred all over the Muslim world. The enormous distance separating many provinces from the imperial capital enabled the provinces to throw off the caliph's jurisdiction. Particularism and ethnic or tribal tendencies, combined with strength and fierce ambition, led to the creation of local dynasties. Incompetent or immature caliphs at Baghdad were unable to enforce their authority over distant and strong local rulers. This pattern led to the decline of the Abbasids and invasion by foreign powers.

Decline of the Abbasids

In the later ninth century, rebellions shook Arabia, Syria, and Persia, and a slave revolt devastated Iraq. These disorders hurt agricultural productivity and in turn cut tax receipts. Having severely taxed the urban mercantile groups, the caliphate had already alienated the commercial classes. Disorder and disintegration threatened the Muslim state.

In the meantime, the luxury and extravagance of the caliphal court imposed a terrible financial burden. In the caliph's palace complexes, maintained by staffs numbering in the tens of thousands, an important visitor would be conducted through elaborate rituals and confronted with indications of the caliph's majesty and power: rank upon rank of

Embassy to the Court of Ethiopia   Describing an event that happened centuries before, a fourteenth-century artist depicts a Muslim embassy to the king of Ethiopia to arrange for the extradition of early converts to Islam who had fled to Ethiopia. The easy movement of the figures suggests the influence of Chinese artists who immigrated to Baghdad and Persia during the Mongol period. Both Chinese and Muslim artists believed the blacks dressed very simply. *(Source: Edinburgh University Library)*

lavishly appointed guards, pages, servants, slaves, and other retainers; lush parks full of exotic wild beasts; fantastic arrays of gold and silver objects, ornamented furniture, precious carpets and tapestries, pools of mercury, and ingenious mechanical devices. The most famous of the mechanical devices was a gold and silver tree with leaves that rustled, branches that swayed, and mechanical birds that sang as the breezes blew.[14]

Some caliphs in the early tenth century worked to halt the process of decay. But in 945, the Buyids, a Shi'ite clan originating in Daylam, the mountainous region on the southern shores of the Caspian Sea, overran Iraq and occupied Baghdad. The caliph, al-Mustakfi, was forced to recognize the Buyid leader Mu'izz al-Dawla as *amir al-umara,* emir of emirs, and to allow the celebration of Shi'ite festivals—though the caliph and most of the people were Sunnites. A year later the caliph was accused of plotting against his new masters. He was snatched from his throne, dragged through the streets to Mu'izz al-Dawla's palace, and blinded. Blinding was a practice that the Buyids adopted from the Byzantines as a way of rendering a ruler incapable of carrying out his duties. This incident marks the practical collapse of the Abbasid caliphate, although the caliphs remained as puppets of the Buyids and symbols of Muslim unity until the Mongols killed the last of them in 1258.

The Assault of the Turks and Mongols

In the mid-tenth century, the Seljuk Turks began to besiege the Islamic world. Originating in Turkestan in central Asia and displaying great physical endurance and mobility, the Turks surged westward. They accepted Sunnite Islam near Bukhara (then a great Persian commercial and intellectual center), swarmed over the rest of Persia, and pushed through Iraq and Syria. Baghdad fell to them on December 18, 1055, and the caliph became a puppet of the Turkish sultan—literally, "he with authority." The sultans replaced the Buyids as masters of the Abbasid caliphate. The Turks did not acquire all of the former Abbasid state. To the west, the Shi'ite Fatimids, so-called because they claimed descent from Muhammad's daughter Fatima, had conquered present-day central Algeria, Sicily, and, in 969, Egypt.

Thus by the middle of the eleventh century, there were three centers of Muslim power: Cordoba in Spain, Cairo in Egypt, and Baghdad in Iraq. Within the Baghdad caliphate the construction of mosques, schools, canals, and roads for commerce and pilgrimages by Nizam al-Mulk (1018–1092), the vizier of three sultans, signaled new intellectual and spiritual vitality. A Turkish sultan ruled in a Muslim state.

Into this world in the early thirteenth century exploded the Mongols, a people descended from an ethnic group that originated in the area that is present-day Siberia. The Mongols adhered to shamanism, a religion in which unseen gods, demons, and ancestral spirits are thought to be responsive only to *shamans,* or priests. In 1206 their leader Jenghiz Khan (1162–1227), having welded the Mongols and related Turkish tribes into a strong confederation, swept westward.

Whether the Mongols were driven by economic or military pressures, or were attracted by the sophisticated life to the west, scholars do not know. With perhaps sixty thousand highly disciplined soldiers, the Mongols left a trail of blood and destruction. They used terror as a weapon, and out of fear the rich commercial centers of central Asia—Khwarizm, Bukhara (whose mosques were turned into stables), Herat, Samarkand, Baikal (whose peoples were all slaughtered or enslaved)—fell before them. When Jenghiz Khan died, his empire stretched from northern China and Korea to the Caspian Sea and from the Danube River to the Arctic. In 1242 the Mongols sacked Kiev. By 1250 they controlled all of southern Russia under the title "Khanate of the Golden Horde," and they ruled it for two hundred years.

Under Jenghiz Khan's grandsons, Hulagu (1217–1265) and Kublai Khan (1216–1294), the Mongol Empire expanded farther. In the west, Hulagu sacked and burned Baghdad and killed the last Abbasid caliph (1258). His hordes captured Damascus in 1260, and only a major defeat at Ayn Jalut in Syria saved Egypt and the Muslim lands in North Africa and perhaps Spain. In the east, meanwhile, Kublai Khan campaigned in China. His defeat of the Song (Sung) Dynasty and establishment of the Yuan Dynasty marked the greatest territorial extent of the Mongol Empire.

Hulagu tried to eradicate Muslim culture, but his descendant Ghazan embraced Islam in 1295 and worked for the revival of Muslim culture. As the Turks had done earlier, so did the Mongols, once converted, inject new vigor into the faith and spirit of Islam. In the Middle East the Mongols governed through Persian viziers and native financial officials.

THE LIFE OF THE PEOPLE

When the Prophet appeared, Arab society consisted of independent Bedouin tribal groups, loosely held together by loyalty to a strong leader and by the belief that all members of a tribe were descended from a common ancestor. Heads of families elected the *sheik*, or tribal chief. He was usually chosen from among aristocratic warrior families whose members had a strong sense of their superiority. Birth determined aristocracy.

According to the Qur'an, however, birth counted for nothing; zeal for Islam was the only criterion for honor: "O ye folk, verily we have created you male and female. . . . Verily the most honourable of you in the sight of God is the most pious of you."[15] The idea of social equality founded on piety was a basic Muslim doctrine. As a thirteenth-century commentator explained:

We have created everyone of you by means of a father and mother. All are equal in this and there is no reason therefore for boasting of one's lineage (the old Arab view being that in lineage lay honour). Through piety are souls brought to perfection and persons may compete for excellence in it; and let him who desires honour seek it in piety.[16]

When Muhammad defined social equality, he was thinking about equality among Muslims alone. But even among Muslims a sense of pride in ancestry could not be destroyed by a stroke of the pen. Claims of birth remained strong among the first Muslims; and after Islam spread outside of Arabia, full-blooded Bedouin tribesmen regarded themselves as superior to foreign converts.

The Classes of Society

In the Umayyad period, Muslim society consisted of four classes. At the top were the caliph's household and the ruling Arab Muslims. Descended from Bedouin tribespeople and composed of warriors, veterans, governing officials, and town settlers, this class constituted the aristocracy. Because birth continued to determine membership, it was more a caste than a class. It was also a relatively small group, greatly outnumbered by villagers and country people.

Converts constituted the second class in Islamic society. Converts to Islam had to attach themselves to one of the Arab tribes as clients. For economic, social, and cultural reasons they greatly resented having to do this. They believed they represented a culture superior to the culture of the Arab tribespeople. From the Muslim converts eventually came the members of the commercial and learned professions—merchants, traders, teachers, doctors, artists, and interpreters of the shari'a. Second-class citizenship led some Muslim converts to adopt Shi'ism (see page 258) and other unorthodox doctrines inimical to the state. Over the centuries, Berber, Copt, Persian, Aramaean, and other converts to Islam intermarried with their Muslim conquerors. Gradually assimilation united peoples of various ethnic and "national" backgrounds. However, in the words of one scholar, "an Arabian remained a native of the peninsula, but an Arab became one who professed Islam and spoke Arabic, regardless of national origin."[17]

Dhimmis, or "protected peoples"—Jews, Christians, and Zoroastrians—formed the third class. They were allowed to practice their religions, maintain their houses of worship, and conduct their business affairs, as long as they gave unequivocal recognition to Muslim political supremacy. Here is a formula drawn up in the ninth century as a pact between Muslims and their nonbelieving subjects:

I accord to you and to the Christians of the city of so-and-so that which is accorded to the dhimmis . . . safe-conduct . . . namely:

You will be subject to the authority of Islam and to no contrary authority. You will not refuse to carry out any obligation which we think fit to impose upon you by virtue of this authority.

If any one of you speaks improperly of Muhammed, may God bless and save him, the Book of God, or of His religion, he forfeits the protection [dhimma] of God, of the Commander of the Faithful, and of all the

✳ **Lustre Dish: Prince Khusraw Discovers Shirin Bathing** Major Persian pottery centers at Ravy and Kashan produced ceramic masterpieces often in styles influenced by Chinese artists or by imported Chinese porcelains. The subjects derived from Persian literature. *(Source: Courtesy of the Freer Gallery of Art, Smithsonian Institution, Washington, D.C.)*

Muslims; his property and his life are at the disposal of the Commander of the Faithful. . . .

If any one of them commits fornication with a Muslim woman or goes through a form of marriage with her or robs a Muslim on the highway or subverts a Muslim from his religion or aids those who made war against the Muslims by fighting with them or by showing them the weak points of the Muslims, or by harboring their spies, he has contravened his pact . . . and his life and his property are at the disposal of the Muslims. . . .

You may not display crosses in Muslim cities, nor proclaim polytheism, nor build churches or meeting places for your prayers . . . nor proclaim your polytheistic beliefs on the subject of Jesus [beliefs relating to the Trinity]. . . .

Every adult male of sound mind among you shall have to pay a poll tax [jizya] of one dinar, in good coin, at the beginning of each year.[18]

Restrictions placed on Christians and Jews were not severe, and both groups seem to have thrived under Muslim rule. Rare outbursts of violence against Christians and Jews occurred only when Muslims felt that the dhimmis had stepped out of line and broken the agreement. The social position of the "protected peoples" deteriorated during the Crusades (see pages 369–370) and the Mongol invasions, when there was a general rise of religious loyalties. At those times Muslims suspected the dhimmis, often rightly, of collaborating with the enemies of Islam.

At the bottom of the social scale were slaves. The Qur'an's acceptance of slavery parallels that of the Old and New Testaments. The Qur'an forbids the enslavement of Muslims or "protected peoples," and Muhammad had recommended the humane treatment of slaves. Emancipation was a meritorious act, but the Qur'an did not grant freedom to slaves who accepted Islam.

The Muslim duty of the holy war ensured a steady flow of slaves. Prisoners of war or people captured in raids or purchased in the slave markets, slaves constituted very large numbers in the Muslim world. The great Muslim commander Musa ibn Nusayr, the son of a Christian enslaved in Iraq, is reputed to have taken 300,000 prisoners of war in his North African campaigns (708–718) and 30,000 virgins from the Visigothic nobility of Spain (these numbers are surely greatly inflated). Every soldier, from general to private, had a share of slaves from the captured prisoners. In the slave

Muslim Slave Market   Slaves of several races were available at this thirteenth-century market at Zabid in Yemen. Women and children were wanted more than men: boys for military or administrative service, attractive women for the harem. Emancipation or the attainment of high political or military positions worked against the growth of class consciousness among slaves. *(Source: Bibliothèque Nationale, Paris)*

markets of Damascus and Baghdad in the tenth and eleventh centuries, a buyer could select from white slaves brought from Spain, Sicily, and southeastern Europe, yellow slaves from central Asia, brown slaves from India, and black slaves from sub-Saharan Africa.

Most slaves in the Islamic world went into the army or worked as household servants. Some were entrusted with business or administrative responsibilities. Few performed the kinds of agricultural labor commonly associated with slavery in the Western Hemisphere. Islamic law declared the children of a female slave to be slaves, but the offspring of a free male and a slave woman were free because lineage was in the paternal line. Many Muslims took slave women as concubines; the children belonged to the father and were free. In classical Islamic civilization, slaves played a large and sometimes distinguished role in the military, politics, religion, and the arts and sciences. Many caliphs were the emancipated sons of Turkish, Greek, and black slave women.

By the beginning of the tenth century, Islamic society had undergone significant change. The courtier al-Fadl b. Yahya, writing in 903, divided humankind into four classes:

Firstly, rulers elevated to office by their deserts; secondly, viziers, distinguished by their wisdom and understanding; thirdly, the upper classes, elevated by their wealth; and fourthly, the middle classes to which belong men marked by their culture. The remainder are filthy refuse, a torrent of scum, base cattle, none of whom thinks of anything but his food and sleep.[19]

The last category hardly reflects compassion for the poor and unfortunate. However, it is clear that birth as a sign of social distinction had yielded to wealth and talent.

Women in Classical Islamic Society

Arab tribal law gave women virtually no legal status. According to tribal law, at birth girls could be buried alive by their fathers. They were sold into marriage by their guardians for a price. Their husband could terminate the union at will. And women had virtually no property or succession rights. The Qur'an sought to improve the social position of women.

The Qur'an, like the religious writings of all traditions, represents moral precept rather than social

practice, and the texts are open to different interpretations. Yet modern scholars tend to agree that the Islamic sacred book intended women as the spiritual and sexual equals of men and gave women considerable economic rights. In the early Umayyad period, moreover, women played an active role in the religious, economic, and political life of the community. They owned property. They had freedom of movement and traveled widely. They participated in the politics of the caliphal succession. Women participated with men in the public religious rituals and observances. But this Islamic ideal of women and men of equal value to the community did not last.[20] As Islamic society changed, the precepts of the Qur'an were interpreted to meet different circumstances.

In the later Umayyad period, the status of women declined. The rapid conquest of vast territories led to the influx of large numbers of slave women. As wealth replaced birth as the criterion of social status, men more and more viewed women as possessions, as a form of wealth. The increasingly inferior status of women is revealed in three ways: in the relationship of women to their husbands, in the practice of veiling women, and in the seclusion of women in harems.

On the rights and duties of a husband to his wife, the Qur'an states that "men are in charge of women because Allah hath made the one to excel the other, and because they (men) spend of their property (for the support of women). So good women are obedient, guarding in secret that which Allah hath guarded."[21] A tenth-century interpreter, Abu Ja'far Muhammad ibn-Jarir al-Tabari, commented on that passage in this way:

Men are in charge of their women with respect to disciplining (or chastising) them, and to providing them with restrictive guidance concerning their duties toward God and themselves (i.e., the men), by virtue of that by which God has given excellence (or preference) to the men over their wives: i.e., the payment of their dowers to them, spending of their wealth on them, and providing for them in full.[22]

A thirteenth-century commentator on the same Qur'anic passage goes into more detail and argues that women are incapable of and unfit for any public duties, such as participating in religious rites, giving evidence in the law courts, or being involved in any public political decisions.[23] Muslim

Birth of Prince Rustaw Childbirth in the Islamic world, as in medieval Europe, was a process entirely in the hands of midwives. The presence of a male physician as here suggests a very difficult birth: the doctor has performed a caesarean section. This manuscript painting was executed in Egypt ca 1510 as an illustration of the Persian hero Rustaw. *(Source: Topkapi Saray Museum, Istanbul)*

society fully accepted this view, and later interpreters further categorized the ways in which men were superior to women.

The Sunni aphorism "There shall be no monkery Islam" captures the importance of marriage in Muslim culture and the Muslim belief that a sexually frustrated person was dangerous to the community. Islam vehemently discouraged sexual abstinence. Islam expected that every man and woman, unless physically incapable or financially unable, would marry: marriage was a safeguard of chastity, essential to the stability both of the family and of society. Marriage in Muslim society was a sacred contract between two families.

As in medieval Europe (see pages 428–429) and in Ming China (pages 719–720), marriage was considered too important an undertaking to be left to the romantic emotions of the young. Families or guardians, not the prospective bride and groom, identified suitable partners and finalized the contract. The official wedding ceremony consisted of an offer and its acceptance by representatives of the bride and groom's parents at a meeting before witnesses. A wedding banquet followed at which men and women feasted separately; the quality of the celebration, of the gifts, and of the food depended on the relative wealth of the two families. Because it was absolutely essential that the bride be a virgin, marriages were arranged shortly after the onset of the girl's menarche at age twelve or thirteen. Youthful marriages ensured a long period of fertility.

A wife's responsibilities depended on the financial status of her husband. A farmer's wife helped in the fields, ground the corn, carried water, prepared food, and did the myriad of tasks necessary in rural life. Shopkeepers' wives in the cities often helped in business. In an upper-class household, the lady supervised servants, looked after all domestic arrangements, and did whatever was needed for her husband's comfort.

In every case, children were the wife's special domain. A mother exercised authority over her children and enjoyed their respect. A Muslim tradition asserts that "Paradise is at the mother's feet." Thus, as in Chinese culture, the prestige of the young wife depended on the production of children—especially sons—as rapidly as possible. A wife's failure to have children was one of the main reasons for a man to take a second wife or to divorce his wife entirely.

Like the Jewish tradition, Muslim law permitted divorce, but the Qur'an seeks to preserve the union and to protect a possible child's paternity. The law prescribed that if a man intended to divorce his wife, he should avoid hasty action and not have intercourse with her for four months; hopefully, they would reconcile. If the woman became pregnant during that period, the father could be identified:

Women who are divorced have to wait for three monthly periods (before remarriage), and if they believe in God and the Last Day, they must not hide unlawfully what God has formed within their wombs. Their (ex)husbands would do well to take them back in that period, if they wish to be reconciled. Women also have recognized rights as men have, though men are over them in rank.[24]

Some interpreters of the Islamic traditions on divorce show a marked similarity to the Christian attitude. For example, some Pharisees asked Jesus whether it was permissible for a man to divorce his wife. When the Pharisees quoted the Mosaic law as allowing divorce, Jesus discussed the Mosaic law as a concession to human weakness, arguing that what God has joined together no one should separate. In other words, Jesus held that divorce is wrong, whatever the law does to regulate it (Mark 10:2–9). Likewise, the commentator Ibn Urnan reported the Prophet as saying, "The lawful thing which God hates most is divorce."[25]

Interpretations of the Qur'an's statements on polygamy give an example of the declining status of women. The Qur'an permitted a man to have four wives, provided "that all are treated justly. . . . Marry of the women who seem good to you, two or three or four; and if ye fear that you cannot do justice (to so many) then one (only) or the captives that your right hand possess."[26] Where the Qur'an permitted polygamy, Muslim jurists interpreted the statement as having legal force. The Prophet's emphasis on justice to the several wives, however, was understood as a mere recommendation.[27] Although the Qur'an allowed polygamy, only very wealthy men could afford several wives. The vast majority of Muslim males were monogamous because women could not earn money and men had difficulty enough supporting one wife.

In contrast to the Christian view of sexual activity as something inherently shameful and even within marriage only a cure for sexual desire, Islam maintained a healthy acceptance of sexual pleasure for both males and females. Islam held that sexual satisfaction for both partners in marriage was necessary to prevent extramarital activity. Men, however, were entitled to as many as four legal partners. Women had to be content with one. Because satisfaction of the sexual impulse for males allowed polygamy,

one can speculate that fear of its inverse—one woman with four husbands—might explain the assumption of women's insatiability, which is at the core of the Muslim concept of female sexuality. Since Islam assumed that a sexually frustrated individual is a very problematic believer and a troublesome citizen, . . . the distrust of women is even greater.[28]

Modern sociologists contend that polygamy affects individuals' sense of identity. It supports men's self-images as primarily sexual beings. And, by emphasizing wives' inability to satisfy their husbands, it undermines women's confidence in their sexuality. The function of polygamy as a device to humiliate women is evident in an aphorism from Moroccan folklore: "Debase a woman by bringing in (the house) another one."[29]

In many present-day Muslim cultures, few issues are more sensitive than those of the veiling and the seclusion of women. These practices have their roots in pre-Islamic times, and they took firm hold in classical Islamic society. The head veil seems to have been the mark of free-born urban women; wearing the veil distinguished free women from slave women. Country and desert women did not wear veils because they interfered with work. Probably of Byzantine or Persian origin, the veil indicated respectability and modesty. As the Arab conquerors subjugated various peoples, they adopted some of the vanquished peoples' customs, one of which was veiling. The Qur'an contains no specific rule about the veil, but its few vague references have been interpreted as sanctioning the practice. Gradually, all parts of a woman's body were considered *pudendal* (shameful because they were capable of arousing sexual desire) and were not allowed to be seen in public.

Even more restrictive of the freedom of women than veiling was the practice of *purdah*, literally seclusion behind a screen or curtain—the harem system. The English word *harem* comes from the Arabic *haram*, meaning "forbidden" or "sacrosanct," which the women's quarters of a house or palace were considered to be. The practice of secluding women in a harem also derives from Arabic contacts with other Eastern cultures. Scholars do not know precisely when the harem system began, but within "one-and-a-half centuries after the death of the Prophet, the (harem) system was fully established. . . . Amongst the richer classes, the women were shut off from the rest of the household."[30] The harem became another symbol of male prestige and prosperity, as well as a way to distinguish and set apart upper-class women from peasants.

Trade and Commerce

Islam had a highly positive disposition toward profit-making enterprises. In the period from 1000 to 1500, there was less ideological resistance to the striving for profit in trade and commerce than there was in the Christian West. Christianity tended to condemn the acquisition of wealth beyond one's basic needs. "For Islam, the stress is laid rather upon the good use to be made of one's possessions, the merit that lies in expending them intelligently and distributing them with generosity—an attitude more favourable to economic expansion than that of the Christian theologians."[31]

Since Muslim theology and law were fully compatible with profitable economic activity, trade and commerce played a prominent role in the Islamic world. Muhammad had earned his living in business as a representative of the city of Mecca, which carried on a brisk trade from southern Palestine to southwestern Arabia. Although Bedouin nomads were among the first converts to Islam, Islam arose in a mercantile, not an agricultural, setting. The merchant had a respectable place in Muslim society. According to the sayings of the Prophet:

The honest, truthful Muslim merchant will stand with the martyrs on the Day of Judgment.

I commend the merchants to you, for they are the couriers of the horizons and God's trusted servants on earth.[32]

In contrast to the social values of the medieval West and of Confucian China, Muslims tended to look with disdain on agricultural labor and to hold trade in esteem. The Qur'an, moreover, had no prohibition against trade with Christians or other unbelievers.

Western scholars have tended to focus attention on the Mediterranean Sea as the source of Islamic mercantile influence on Europe in the Middle Ages. From the broad perspective of Muslim commerce, however, the Mediterranean held a position much subordinate to other waterways: the Black Sea; the Caspian Sea and the Volga River, which gave access deep into Russia; the Aral Sea, from which region caravans departed for China; the Gulf of Aden; and the Arabian Sea and the Indian Ocean, which linked the Arabian gulf region with eastern Africa, the Indian subcontinent, and eventually Indonesia and the Philippines. These served as the main commercial seaways of the Islamic world.

By land Muslim traders pushed south from North Africa across the Sahara into west-central Africa (see Map 9.2). By the tenth century they

Muslim Dhow Hundreds of these lateen-rigged Arab vessels gave Islam mastery of the Indian Ocean. The Muslim fleet in the Mediterranean never equaled the one in the Indian Ocean, a circumstance that helps to explain Venetian and Genoese power in the Mediterranean in the thirteenth century. *(Source: Bibliothèque Nationale, Paris)*

had penetrated as far east as China and possibly Korea. They were pursuing silk, which was the earliest Chinese gift to the world. Travelers called the land route going through Samarkand, Bukhara, and other Turkestan towns the "great silk way," and along that way caravans collected the merchandise of Transoxiana and Turkestan. A private ninth-century list mentions a great variety of commodities transported into and through the Islamic world by land and by sea:

Imported from India: tigers, leopards, elephants, leopard skins, red rubies, white sandalwood, ebony, and coconuts

From China: aromatics, silk, porcelain, paper, ink, peacocks, fiery horses, saddles, felts, cinnamon

From the Byzantines: silver and gold vessels, embroidered cloths, fiery horses, slave girls, rare articles in red copper, strong locks, lyres, water engineers, specialists in plowing and cultivation, marble workers, and eunuchs

From Arabia: Arab horses, ostriches, thoroughbred she-camels, and tanned hides

From Barbary and Maghrib (the Arabic name for northwest Africa, an area that included Morocco, Algeria, and Tunisia): leopards, acacia, felts, and black falcons

From Egypt: ambling donkeys, fine cloths, papyrus, balsam oil, and, from its mines, high-quality topaz

From the Khazars (a people living on the northern shore of the Black Sea): slaves, slave women, armor, helmets, and hoods of mail

From Samarkand: paper

From Ahwaz (a city in southwestern Persia): sugar, silk brocades, castanet players and dancing girls, kinds of dates, grape molasses, and candy.[33]

Camels made long-distance land transportation possible. Stupid and vicious, camels nevertheless proved more efficient for desert transportation than horses or oxen. The use of the camel to carry heavy and bulky freight facilitated the development of world commerce.

Between the eighth and twelfth centuries, the Islamic world functioned virtually as a free-trade area in which goods circulated freely. The Muslims developed a number of business techniques that facilitated the expansion of trade. For example, they originated the concept of the bill of exchange, which made the financing of trade more flexible. The Muslims also seem to have come up with the idea of the joint stock company—an arrangement that lets a group of people invest in a venture and share in its profits and losses in proportion to the amount each has invested. Also, many financial and business terms—check, coffer, cipher, nadir, zenith, zero, and risk—entered the English language from Arabic.

Vigorous long-distance trade had significant consequences. Commodities produced in one part of the world became available in many other places, providing a uniformity of consumer goods among diverse peoples living over a vast area. Trade promoted scientific advances in navigation, shipbuilding, and cartography. For example, from the Chinese, Arabic sailors seem to have learned about the compass, an instrument that mariners used to determine directions on the earth's surface by means of a magnetic needle. Muslims carried the compass to Europe, and in the twelfth century it came into wide navigational use. Muslim mariners also developed the astrolabe, an instrument used to determine latitude and the time of day.

Long-distance trade brought some merchants fabulous wealth. A jeweler in Baghdad remained rich even after the caliph al-Muqtadir (r. 908–937) had seized 16 million dinars of his property. Many merchants in Siraf owned homes worth 30,000 dinars and had fortunes of 4 million dinars.[34] To appreciate the value of these sums in terms of present-day buying power, more information about the cost of living in tenth- and eleventh-century Muslim cities is needed. Nevertheless, it can be said that the sums represent very great riches.

Did Muslim economic activity amount to a kind of capitalism? If by capitalism is meant private (not state) ownership of the means of production, the production of goods for market sale, profit as the main motive for economic activity, competition, a money economy, and the lending of money at interest, then, unquestionably, the medieval Muslim economy had capitalistic features. Students of Muslim economic life have not made a systematic and thorough investigation of Muslims' industries, businesses, and seaports, but the impressionistic evidence is overwhelming: "Not only did the Muslim world know a capitalist sector, but this sector was apparently the most extensive in history before the establishment of the world market created by the Western European bourgeoisie, and this did not outstrip it in importance until the sixteenth century."[35]

Urban Centers

Long-distance trade provided the wealth that made possible a gracious and sophisticated culture in the cities of the Muslim world. Although cities and mercantile centers dotted the entire Islamic empire, the cities of Baghdad and Cordoba at their peak in the tenth century stand out as the finest examples of cosmopolitan Muslim civilization. Baghdad was founded in 762 by the second Abbasid caliph, al-Mansur, on the Tigris River, astride the major overland highways. It became the administrative, strategic, and commercial capital of the Muslim world. The presence of the caliph and his court and administration, caliphal patronage of learning and the arts, and Baghdad's enormous commercial advantages gave the city international prestige. On its streets thronged a kaleidoscope of races, creeds, costumes, and cultures, an almost infinite variety of peoples: returning travelers, administrative officials, slaves, visitors, merchants from Asia, Africa, and Europe. Shops and marketplaces offered the rich and extravagant a dazzling and exotic array of goods from all over the world.

The caliph Harun al-Rashid (r. 786–809) presided over a glamorous court. His vast palace with hundreds of officials, his harems with thousands of slave girls, his magnificent banquets, receptions, and ceremonies—all astounded foreign visitors. Harun al-Rashid invited writers, dancers, musicians, poets, and artists to live in Baghdad, and he is reputed to have rewarded one singer with a hundred thousand silver pieces for a single song. This brilliant era provided the background for the tales that appear in *A Thousand and One Nights,* the great folk classic of Arabic literature.

The central plot of the fictional tales involves the efforts of Scheherazade to keep her husband, Schariar, legendary king of Samarkand, from killing her. She entertains him with one tale a night for 1,001 nights. The best-known tales are "Aladdin and His Lamp," "Sinbad the Sailor," and "Ali Baba and the Forty Thieves." Also known as *The Arabian Nights,* this book offers a sumptuous collection of caliphs, viziers, and genies, varieties of sexual experiences, and fabulous happenings. *The Arabian Nights,* though folklore, has provided many of the images that Europeans have used since the eighteenth century to describe the Islamic world.

Cordoba in southern Spain competed with Baghdad for the cultural leadership of the Islamic world. In the tenth century, no city in Asia or Europe could equal dazzling Cordoba. Its streets were well paved and lighted, and the city had an abundant supply of fresh water. With a population of about 1 million, Cordoba contained 1,600 mosques, 900 public baths, 213,177 houses for ordinary people, and 60,000 mansions for generals, officials, and the wealthy. In its 80,455 shops, 13,000 weavers produced silks, woolens, and brocades that were internationally famous. The English language has memorialized the city's leather with the word *cordovan.* Cordoba invented the process of manufacturing crystal. Cordoba was a great educational center with 27 free schools and a library containing 400,000 volumes. (By contrast, the great Benedictine abbey of Saint-Gall in Switzerland had about 600 books. The use of paper—whose manufacture the Muslims had learned from the Chinese—instead of vellum, gave rise to this great disparity.) Through Iran and Cordoba the Indian game of chess entered western Europe.

Cordoba's scholars made contributions in chemistry, medicine and surgery, music, philosophy, and mathematics. Cordoba's fame was so great it is no wonder that the contemporary Saxon nun Hroswhita of Gandersheim (d. 1000) could describe the city as the "ornament of the world."[36]

Education and Intellectual Life

Urban and sophisticated Muslim culture possessed a strong educational foundation. Recent scholarly research provides exciting information about medieval Muslim education. Muslim culture placed extraordinary emphasis on knowledge, especially religious knowledge; indeed, knowledge and learning were esteemed above every other human activity. Knowledge provided the guidelines by which men and women should live. What kinds of educational institutions existed in the Muslim world? What was the method of instruction? What social or practical purposes did Muslim education serve?

Islam is a religion of the law, and the institution for instruction in Muslim jurisprudence was the *madrasa,* the school for the study of Muslim law and religious science. The Arabic noun *madrasa* derives from a verb meaning "to study." The first madrasas were probably established in Khurasan in northeastern Persia. By 1193, thirty madrasas existed in Damascus; between 1200 and 1250, sixty more were established there. Aleppo, Jerusalem, Alexandria, and above all Cairo also witnessed the foundation of madrasas. Schools were urban phenomena.

Wealthy merchants endowed these schools, providing salaries for the teachers, stipends for students, and living accommodations for both (see Listening to the Past). The *shaykh,* or teacher, served as a guide to the correct path of living. All Islamic higher education rested on a close relationship between teacher and students, so in selecting a teacher, the student (or his father) considered the character and intellectual reputation of the shaykh, not that of any institution. Students built their subsequent careers on the reputation of their teachers.

Learning depended heavily on memorization. In primary school, which was often attached to the institution of higher learning, a boy began his education by memorizing the entire Qur'an. Normally, he achieved this feat by the time he was seven or eight! In adolescence students learned by

Public Library at Hulwan near Baghdad   In this scene from everyday life, the teacher, second from left with open book, instructs students by commenting on the text. Library books rest on the shelves in the background. *(Source: Bibliothèque Nationale, Paris)*

heart an introductory work in one of the branches of knowledge, such as jurisprudence or grammar. Later he analyzed the texts in detail. Because the hadith—traditions containing the sayings, commands of, or stories about the Prophet and his companions—laid great stress on memory, students learned the entire texts through memory and will-power. Memorizing from 400 to 500 lines a day was considered outstanding. Every class day, the shaykh examined the student on the previous day's learning and determined whether the student fully understood what he had memorized. Students of course learned to write, for they had to write down the teacher's commentary on a particular text. But the overwhelming emphasis was on the oral transmission of knowledge.

Because Islamic education focused on particular books or texts, when the student had mastered that text to his teacher's satisfaction, the teacher issued the student a *ijaza,* or license, certifying that he had studied a book or collection of traditions with his teacher. The ijaza allowed the student to transmit on the authority of his teacher a text to the next generation. The ijaza legalized the transmission of sacred knowledge.[37]

Apart from the fundamental goal of preparing men to live wisely and in accordance with God's law, Muslim higher education aimed at preparing men to perform religious and legal functions in the umma, or community: as Qur'an- or hadith-readers, as preachers in the mosques, as professors, educators, copyists, and especially as judges. Judges issued *ifta,* or legal opinions, in the public courts; their training was in the Qur'an, hadith, or some text forming part of the shar'ia. Islam did not know the division between religious and secular knowledge characteristic of the modern Western world.

What about women—what educational opportunities were available to them? "The seeking of knowledge is a duty of every Muslim," Muhammad had said, but Islamic culture was ambivalent on the issue of female education. Because of the basic Islamic principle that "Men are the guardians of women, because God has set the one over the other," the law excluded women from participation in the legal, religious, or civic occupations for which the madrasa prepared young men. Moreover, educational theorists insisted that men should study in a sexually isolated environment because feminine allure would distract male students. Rich evidence shows that no woman studied or held a professorship in the schools of Cairo, for example. Nevertheless, many young women received substantial educations from their parents or family members; the initiative invariably rested with their fathers or older brothers. The daughter of Ali ibn Muhammad al-Diruti al Mahalli, for example, memorized the Qur'an, learned to write, and received instruction in several sacred works. One biographical dictionary containing the lives of 1,075 women reveals that 411 had memorized the Qur'an, studied with a particular teacher, and received the ijaza. After marriage, responsibility for a woman's education belonged to her husband.[38]

How does Islamic higher education compare with that available in medieval Europe (see page 395) or Ming China (see pages 720–721)? There are some striking similarities and some major differences. In the Christian West and in China, primary and higher education was institutional. The church operated schools and universities in Europe. Local villages or towns ran schools in China. In contrast, in the Islamic world the transmission of knowledge depended overwhelmingly on the personal relationship of teacher and student: though dispensed through the madrasa, education was not institutional. In Europe the reward for satisfactory completion of a course of study was a degree granted by the university. In Muslim culture, it was not the school but the individual teacher who granted the ijaza. In China, the imperial civil service examination tested candidates' knowledge and rewarded achievement with appointments in the state bureaucracy.

In all three cultures education rested heavily on the study of basic religious, legal, or philosophical texts: the Old and New Testaments or the Justinian Code in Europe; the ethical writings of Confucian philosophy in China; the Qur'an, hadith, and legal texts deriving from these in the Muslim world. In all three cultures memorization played a large role in the acquisition and transmission of information. In the European university, however, the professor lectured on biblical text or passages of the Code, and in the Muslim madrasa the shaykh commented on a section of the Qur'an or hadith. Both professors and shaykhs sometimes disagreed fiercely about the correct interpretations of a particular text, forcing students to question, to think critically, to choose between divergent opinions. Such does not appear to be the case in China; there, critical thinking and individual imagination were discouraged.

Finally, educated people in each culture shared the same broad literary and religious or ethical culture, giving that culture cohesion and stability. Just as a man who took a degree at Cambridge University in England shared the Latin language and general philosophical outlook of someone with a degree from Montpellier in France or Naples in Italy, so a Muslim gentleman from Cairo spoke and read the same Arabic and knew the same hadith as a man from Baghdad or Samarkand. Such education as women received in Christian Europe, the Islamic world, or Ming China began and usually ended in the home and with the family.

The cosmopolitan nature of the Muslim world gave rise to a period of intellectual vitality. In spite of schism, warfare, and dynastic conflicts, the sacred Arabic language and dedication to scholarship and learning combined Semitic, Hellenic, and Persian knowledge. "A scholar might publish in Samarkand the definitive work on arithmetic used in the religious schools of Cairo. Or, in a dialogue with colleagues in Baghdad and Hamadan, he could claim to have recovered the unalloyed teachings of Aristotle in the libraries of Fez and Cordoba."[39] Modern scholars consider Muslim creativity and vitality from about 900 to 1200 one of the most brilliant periods in the world's history.

The Persian scholar al-Khwarizmi (d. ca 850) harmonized Greek and Indian findings to produce astronomical tables that formed the basis for later Eastern and Western research. Al-Khwarizmi also studied mathematics, and his textbook on algebra (from the Arabic *al-Jabr*) was the first work in which the word *algebra* is used to mean the "transposing of negative terms in an equation to the opposite side."

Muslim medical knowledge far surpassed that of the West. The Baghdad physician al-Razi (865–925) produced an encyclopedic treatise on medicine that was translated into Latin and circulated widely in the West. Al-Razi was the first physician to make the clinical distinction between measles and smallpox. The great surgeon of Cordoba, al-Zahrawi (d. 1013), produced an important work in which he discussed the cauterization of wounds (searing with a branding iron) and the crushing of stones in the bladder. In Ibn Sina of Bukhara (980–1037), known in the West as Avicenna, Muslim science reached its peak. His *al-Qanun* codified all Greco-Arabic medical thought, described the contagious nature of tuberculosis and the spreading of diseases, and listed 760 pharmaceutical drugs. Muslim scholars also wrote works on geography and jurisprudence.

Man Bitten by a Dog Alert to the dangers of rabies and other diseases transmitted by animals, the author of this text discusses pharmaceutical remedies. Medical manuscripts were greatly valued. *(Source: Courtesy of the Freer Gallery of Art, Smithsonian Institution, Washington, DC)*

Likewise, in philosophy the Muslims made significant contributions. The Arabs understood philosophy not as a separate and distinct discipline but as a branch of theology related, like theology, to the study of the Qur'an. The Abbasid caliph al-Ma'mun (r. 813–833) established at Baghdad in 830 the House of Wisdom, a center for research and translation. Under the direction of Humayn ibn-Ishaq (d. 873), the House of Wisdom made a systematic effort to acquire and translate the chief works of ancient Greek philosophy and science. Humayn supervised the translation of almost all of Aristotle's works and the complete medical writings of Hippocrates. At the same research center al-Kindi (d. ca 870) was the first Muslim thinker to try to harmonize Greek philosophy and the religious precepts of the Qur'an. Al-Kindi sought to integrate Islamic concepts of human beings and their relations to God and the universe with the principles of ethical and social conduct discussed by Plato and Aristotle.

Inspired by Plato's *Republic* and Aristotle's *Politics,* the distinguished philosopher al-Farabi (d. 950) wrote a political treatise describing an ideal city whose ruler is morally and intellectually perfect and who has as his goal the citizens' complete happiness. Avicenna maintained that the truths found by human reason cannot conflict with the truths of revelation as given in the Qur'an. Ibn Rushid, or Averroës (1126–1198), of Cordoba, a judge in Seville and later royal court physician, paraphrased and commented on the works of Aristotle. He insisted on the right to subject all knowledge, except the dogmas of faith, to the test of reason.

Through Latin translations of these Muslim philosophers, Arabic and Hebrew writings and Greek philosophy were transmitted to the European West (see page 396). Scholasticism, the leading philosophical system of medieval Europe (see page 396), leaned heavily on Aristotelian thought. Europeans gained their knowledge of Aristotle primarily from Muslim translators and commentators.

Sufism

In the ninth and tenth centuries, in Arabia, Syria, Egypt, and Iraq, a popular religious movement arose within Islam. Some especially devout individuals within the community rejected what they considered the increasing materialism of Muslim life and sought a return to the simplicity of the Prophet's time. Called *Sufis* from the simple coarse woolen (*suf*) garments they wore, these men and women followed an ascetic lifestyle, dedicating themselves to fasting, prayer, and meditation on the Qur'an. Through asceticism and a deep love of God, Sufis sought a direct or mystical union with God. Sufi ideals—careful following of the Qur'an, the avoidance of sin, and a humble yearning toward God—were embodied in the word *zuhd,* renunciation.

The woman mystic Rabia (d. 801) epitomizes this combination of renunciation and devotionalism. An attractive woman who refused marriage so that nothing would distract her from a total commitment to God, Rabia attracted followers, whom she served as a spiritual guide. Her poem in the form of prayer captures her deep devotion:

O my lord, if I worship thee from fear of hell, and if I worship thee in hope of paradise, exclude me thence, but if I worship thee for thine own sake, then withhold not from me thine eternal beauty.

Sufism grew into a mass movement that drew people from all social classes. Though its sources were the Qur'an and the Sunna, Sufism accepted ideas from Christian and Buddhist monasticism and from Hindu devotionalism. Consequently, the ulema, the religious scholars who interpreted the Qur'an and Muslim law, looked on Sufism as a heretical movement and an unnecessary deviation from orthodoxy. The ulema also felt that the Sufis challenged their religious authority. Just as ecclesiastical authorities in Europe looked on Christian mystics with suspicion because the direct mystical union with God denied the need for the institutional church, so the Muslim ulema condemned and persecuted extreme Sufis for their rejection of religious formalism.

The Muslim View of the West

Europeans and Muslims of the Middle East were geographical neighbors. The two peoples shared a common cultural heritage from the Judeo-Christian past. But a thick psychological iron curtain restricted contact between them. The Muslim assault on Christian Europe in the eighth and ninth centuries—villages were burned, monasteries sacked,

کوشیاز عشرت ونوشته رحمت   زجرہ سر رخ حوار و پری کلاب د

Sufi Collective Ritual   Collective or group rituals, in which Sufis tried through ec-static experiences to come closer to God, have always fascinated outsiders, including non-Sufi Muslims. Here the sixteenth-century Persian painter Sultan Muhammad il-lustrates the writing of the fourteenth-century lyric poet Hafiz. Just as Hafiz's poetry moved back and forth between profane and mystical themes, so it is difficult to de-termine whether the ecstasy achieved here is alcoholic or spiritual. Many figures seem to enjoy wine. Notice the various musical instruments and the delicate floral patterns so characteristic of Persian art. *(Source: Courtesy of The Arthur M. Sackler Museum, Har-vard University)* and Christians sold into slavery (see page 357)—left a legacy of bitter hostility. Europeans' fierce intolerance also helped buttress the barrier between the two peoples. Christians felt threatened by a faith that acknowledged God as creator of the universe but denied the doctrine of the Trinity; that accepted Christ as a prophet but denied his divinity; that believed in the Last Judgment but seemed to make sex heaven's greatest reward. Popes preached against the Muslims; theologians penned tracts against them; and church councils condemned them. Europeans' perception of Islam as a menace helped inspire the Crusades of the eleventh through thirteenth centuries (see pages 368–372). The knightly class believed that it had a sacred obligation to fight the Muslims. As a popular song during the Second Crusade put it:

God has brought before you his suit against the Turks and Saracens [Crusaders' hostile term for Muslims], who have done him great despite [injury]. They have seized his fiefs, where God was first served [that is, the holy places in Palestine] and recognized as Lord.[40]

During the Crusades, Europeans imposed Christianity on any lands they conquered from Islam, and they compelled Muslims to choose among conversion, exile, and death. By the thirteenth century, Western literature, such as the Florentine poet Dante's *Divine Comedy,* portrayed the Muslims as the most dreadful of Europe's enemies, guilty of every kind of crime.

Muslims had a strong aversion to travel in Europe. They were quite willing to trade with Europeans, but they rejected European culture. Medieval Europe had no resident Muslim communities where a traveler could find the mosques, food, or other things needed for the Muslim way of life. Muslims generally had a horror of going among those they perceived as infidels, and often when compelled to make diplomatic or business contacts, they preferred to send Jewish or Christian intermediaries, the dhimmis. Commercially, from the Muslim perspective, Europe had very little to offer, apart from fine English woolens, which the Muslims admired. There was only a trickle of slaves from central and southeastern Europe.

Did Western culture have any impact on Islam? Muslims considered Christianity to be a flawed religion superseded by Islam. "For the Muslim, Christ was a precursor, for the Christian Muhammad was an impostor. For the Muslim, Christianity was an early, incomplete, and obsolete form of the true religion."[41] Religion dominated the Islamic perception of Europe. Muslims understood Europe not as Western, European, or white but as Christian. And the fact that European culture was Christian immediately discredited it in Muslim eyes. Christians were presumed to be hostile to Islam and were thought to be culturally inferior. Thus Muslims had no interest in them.

An enormous quantity of Muslim historical writing survives from the period between about 800 and 1600. Although the material reflects some knowledge of European geography, it shows an almost total lack of interest among Muslim scholars in European languages, life, and culture. Before the nineteenth century, not a single grammar book or dictionary of any Western language existed in the Muslim world. By contrast, Western scholarship on the Middle East steadily advanced. By the early seventeenth century, a curious European student could find an extensive literature on the history, religion, and culture of the Muslim peoples. In 1633, a professorship in Arabic studies was founded at Cambridge University in England.[42]

As in language and literature, so in science, engineering, and medicine: the medieval West had no influence on the Muslim world. Muslims had only contempt for Western science. Here is a twelfth-century account of a Muslim's impression of European medical practice:

The Lord of Munaytira (a Crusading Baron) wrote to my uncle asking him to send a physician to treat one of his companions who was sick. He sent him a . . . physician called Thabit. He had hardly been away for ten days, when he returned, and we said to him: "How quickly you have healed the sick!" and he replied, "They brought me two patients, a knight with an abscess on his leg, and a woman afflicted with a mental disorder. I made the knight a poultice, and the abscess burst and he felt better. I put the woman on a diet and kept her humour moist. Then a Frankish physician came to them and said to them: 'This man knows nothing about how to treat them!' Then he said to the knight: 'Which do you prefer, to live with one leg or to die with two?' and the knight said: 'To live with one.' Then the physician said: 'Bring me a strong knight and an ax,' and they brought them. Meanwhile I stood by. Then he put the sick man's leg on a wooden block and said to the knight: 'Strike his leg with the ax and cut it off with one blow!' Then, while I watched, he struck one blow, but the leg was not severed; then he struck a second blow, and the marrow of the leg spurted out, and the man died at once.

"The physician then turned to the woman, and said: 'This woman has a devil in her head who has fallen in love with her. Shave her hair off.' So they shaved her head, and she began once again to eat their usual diet, with garlic and mustard and such like. Her disorder got worse, and he said:

"'The devil has entered her head.' Then he took a razor, incised a cross on her head and pulled off the skin in the middle until the bone of the skull appeared; this he rubbed with salt, and the woman died forthwith.

"Then I said to them: 'Have you any further need of me?' and they said no and so I came home, having learned things about their medical practice which I did not know before."[43]

Only in the art of warfare did Muslims show an interest in European knowledge. During the Crusades, the Muslims adopted Frankish weapons and methods of fortification. Overall, though, medieval Muslims considered Christian Europe a backward land and almost always described Europeans as "ignorant infidels."[44]

SUMMARY

Islam is an extraordinary phenomenon in world history. Its universal monotheistic creed helps to explain its initial attractiveness to Bedouin tribes. Driven by the religious zeal of the jihad, Muslims carried their faith from the Arabian peninsula through the Middle East to North Africa, Spain, and southern France in the west and to the borders of China and northern India in the east—within the short span of one hundred years. Economic need, the political weaknesses of their enemies, strong military organization, and the practice of establishing army cities in newly conquered territories account for their expansion.

Two successive dynasties—the Umayyad, centered at Damascus in Syria, and the Abbasid, located at Baghdad in Iraq—governed the Islamic state. A large imperial bureaucracy headed by a vizier supervised the administration of the state.

All government agencies evolved from the diwan. As provincial governors acquired independent power, which the caliphs could not check, centralized authority within the Islamic state disintegrated.

Commerce and trade also spread the faith of Muhammad. Although its first adherents were nomads, Islam developed and flourished in a mercantile milieu. By land and sea, Muslim merchants transported a rich variety of goods across Asia, the Middle East, Africa, and western Europe. Muslim business procedures and terminology have greatly influenced the West.

On the basis of the wealth that trade generated, a gracious, sophisticated, and cosmopolitan culture developed with centers at Baghdad and Cordoba. In the tenth and eleventh centuries, the Islamic world witnessed enormous intellectual vitality and creativity. Muslim scholars produced important work in many disciplines, especially mathematics, medicine, and philosophy. Muslim civilization in the Middle Ages was far in advance of that of Christian Europe, and Muslims, with some justification, looked on Europeans as ignorant barbarians.

NOTES

1. See F. McG. Donner, *The Early Islamic Conquests* (Princeton, N.J.: Princeton University Press, 1981), pp. 14–37.
2. Quoted in F. E. Peters, *A Reader on Classical Islam* (Princeton, N.J.: Princeton University Press, 1994), p. 47.
3. J. L. Esposito, *Islam: The Straight Path* (New York: Oxford University Press, 1988), pp. 6–17; the quotation is on p. 15.
4. Donner, *The Early Islamic Conquests,* pp. 57–60.
5. Quoted in J. O'Faolain and L. Martines, eds., *Not in God's Image: Women in History from the Greeks to the Victorians* (New York: Harper & Row, 1973), pp. 108–115.
6. Quoted in P. K. Hitti, *The Near East in History* (Princeton, N.J.: Van Nostrand, 1961), p. 211.
7. B. Lewis, ed. and trans., *Islam: From the Prophet Muhammad to the Capture of Constantinople, vol. 1, Politics and War* (New York: Harper & Row, 1974), p. 239.
8. Donner, *The Early Islamic Conquests,* pp. 92–101.
9. Quoted ibid., p. 217.

10. See B. Lewis, *The Muslim Discovery of Europe* (New York: Norton, 1982), pp. 59–63. Discussion herein is based heavily on this important work by Lewis.

11. See M. R. Cohen, *Under Crescent and Cross: The Jews in the Middle Ages* (Princeton, N.J.: Princeton University Press, 1994), Ch. 4; the quotation is on p. 74.

12. See G. E. von Grunebaum, *Medieval Islam: A Study in Cultural Orientation* (Chicago: University of Chicago Press, 1954), pp. 142–150.

13. Quoted in Lewis, *Politics and War,* p. 201.

14. L. I. Conrad, "Caliphate," in *Dictionary of the Middle Ages,* vol. 3, ed. J. R. Strayer (New York: Scribner's, 1983), p. 45.

15. Quoted in R. Levy, *The Social Structure of Islam,* 2d ed. (Cambridge: Cambridge University Press, 1957), p. 55.

16. Ibid.

17. Hitti, *The Near East in History,* p. 229.

18. B. Lewis, ed. and trans., *Islam: From the Prophet Muhammad to the Capture of Constantinople, vol. 2, Religion and Society* (New York: Harper & Row, 1975), pp. 219–221.

19. Quoted in Levy, *The Social Structure of Islam,* p. 67.

20. N. Coulson and D. Hinchcliffe, "Women and Law Reform in Contemporary Islam," in *Women in the Muslim World,* ed. L. Beck and N. Keddie (Cambridge, Mass.: Harvard University Press, 1982), p. 37.

21. Quoted in B. F. Stowasser, "The Status of Women in Early Islam," in *Muslim Women,* ed. F. Hussain (New York: St. Martin's Press, 1984), p. 25.

22. Quoted ibid., pp. 25–26.

23. Quoted ibid., p. 26.

24. Peters, *A Reader on Classical Islam,* pp. 249–250; the quotation is on p. 250.

25. Ibid.

26. Quoted ibid., p. 16.

27. G. Nashat, "Women in Pre-Revolutionary Iran: A Historical Overview," in *Women and Revolution in Iran,* ed. G. Nashat (Boulder, Colo.: Westview Press, 1983), pp. 47–48.

28. F. Mernissi, *Beyond the Veil: Male-Female Dynamics in Modern Muslim Society* (New York: Schenkman, 1975), p. 16.

29. Ibid.

30. Quoted in D. J. Gerner, "Roles in Transition: The Evolving Position of Women in Arab Islamic Countries," in Hussain, *Muslim Women,* p. 73.

31. Quoted in Cohen, *Under Crescent and Cross,* p. 90.

32. Lewis, *Religion and Society,* pp. 126–127.

33. Adapted from Lewis, ibid., pp. 154–157.

34. Hitti, *The Near East in History,* p. 278.

35. M. Rodinson, *Islam and Capitalism,* trans. Brian Pearce (Austin: University of Texas Press, 1981), p. 56.

36. R. Hillenbrand, "Cordoba," in Strayer, *Dictionary of the Middle Ages,* vol. 3, pp. 597–601.

37. I have leaned heavily here on the important study of J. Berkey, *The Transmission of Knowledge in Medieval Cairo. A Social History of Islamic Education* (Princeton, N.J.: Princeton University Press, 1992), pp. 22–43.

38. Ibid., pp. 161–181; the quotation is on p. 161.

39. P. Brown, "Understanding Islam," *New York Review of Books,* February 22, 1979, pp. 30–33.

40. Quoted in R. W. Southern, *The Making of the Middle Ages* (New Haven, Conn.: Yale University Press, 1961), p. 55.

41. Lewis, *The Muslim Discovery of Europe,* p. 297.

42. Ibid., pp. 296–297.

43. Quoted ibid., p. 222.

44. Ibid.

SUGGESTED READING

The titles by F. E. Peters and M. R. Cohen cited in the Notes are especially useful: Peters for its rich collection of documents on many facets of the culture of classical Islam, Cohen for the study of Jews and Christians living in Muslim societies. C. Lindholm, *The Anthropology of Islam* (1995), argues that Islam is the most egalitarian of the Middle Eastern religions. Perhaps the best introduction to Shi'ism is Y. Richard, *Shi'ite Islam* (1994). For the social, commercial, and political significance of the obligatory Muslim pilgrimage to Mecca, see F. E. Peters, *The Hajj: The Muslim Pilgrimage to Mecca and the Holy Places* (1994). For general surveys, the curious student may consult A. Hourani, *A History of the Arab Peoples* (1991), a readable and important synthesis, and S. Fisher and W. Ochsenwald, *The Middle East: A History* (1990), which has helpful bibliographical material. The older studies of H. A. R. Gibb, *Mohammedanism: An Historical Survey,* 2d. ed. (1970), and J. J. Saunders, *A History of Medieval Islam* (1965), are still useful. For the Prophet, see W. M. Watt, *Muhammad at Mecca* (1953) and *Muhammad at Medina* (1956), and M. Rodinson, *Mohammed,* trans. A. Carter (1971). M. G. S. Hodgson, *The Classical Age of Islam,* vol. 1 of *The Venture of Islam* (1964), is comprehensive but for the specialist. K. Cragg and R. M. G. Speight, eds., *Islam from Within: Anthology of a*

Religion (1980), offers a fine collection of primary materials on the beginnings of Islam. For the cultural impact of Islam, G. E. von Grunebaum, *Classical Islam: A History 600–1258,* trans. K. Watson, (1970), remains valuable.

The best recent study of Muslim expansion is F. M. Donner, *The Early Islamic Conquests* (1986). For law and religious authority, see, in addition to the title by J. Berkey cited in the Notes, N. J. Coulson, *A History of Islamic Law* (1964); J. N. D. Anderson, *Islamic Law in the Modern World* (1959); R. P. Mottahedeh, *Loyalty and Leadership in Early Islamic Society* (1986); and S. D. Gottein, *Studies in Islamic History and Institutions* (1966).

For Muslim commercial practices, see A. L. Udovitch, *Partnership and Profit in Medieval Islam* (1970), but its thesis should be compared with the work by Rodinson cited in the Notes. For agricultural practices, see A. M. Watson, *Agricultural Innovation in the Early Islamic World* (1983), and the fascinating material in T. F. Glick, *Islamic and Christian Spain in the Early Middle Ages* (1979). For slavery in the Arab world, see B. Lewis, *Race and Slavery in the Middle East* (1990), which demythologizes the Western view of the Middle East as free of racial prejudice, and G. Murray, *Slavery in the Arab World* (1989), which explains the persistence of slavery in Muslim societies in sexual, not economic, terms. W. M. Watson, *Islam and the Integration of Society* (1961), provides an important sociological interpretation of factors that led to the unity of very diverse peoples.

In the avalanche of material that has recently appeared on women and gender in Islamic societies, J. Tucker, *Gender and Islamic History* (1993), which offers a broad sketch and an excellent introduction to the many problems in the study of gender, is especially recommended. B. F. Stowasser, *Women in the Qur'an, Traditions, and Interpretation* (1994), gives a fine analysis of the Qur'an's statement on women. The following studies contain fascinating and important discussions: L. Ahmed, *Women and Gender in Islam: Historical Roots of a Modern Debate* (1992); D. Kandiyoti, "Islam and Patriarchy: A Comparative Perspective," in *Women in Middle Eastern History,* ed. B. Baron and N. Keddie (1991), pp. 23–42; J. F. Tucker, "The Arab Family in History: 'Otherness' and the Study of the Family," in *Arab Women: Old Boundaries, New Frontiers,* ed. J. F. Tucker (1993), which although focusing on the period since 1800 will interest students of any period; N. Hijab, *Womanpower* (1988); and G. Nashat, "Women in the Middle East, 8000 B.C.–A.D. 1800," in *Restoring Women to History* (1988).

For Islamic art, see the stunning achievement of S. S. Blair and J. M. Bloom, *The Art and Architecture of Islam, 1250–1800* (1994), which authoritatively treats the trends in Islamic art and discusses virtually all masterpieces in Islamic lands. The older studies of O. Grabar, *The Formation of Islamic Art* (1987), and D. Talbot Rice, *Islamic Art,* rev. ed. (1985), provide valuable material.

On the Mongols, see P. Ratchnevsky, *Genghis Khan* (1993), which is based on Chinese, Mongol, and Persian sources, as well as European ones, to give a balanced account of the great world conqueror; M. Rossabi, *Khubilai Khan: His Life and Times* (1988); and D. Morgan, *The Mongols* (1986), an especially readable study. R. E. Dunn, *The Adventures of Ibn Battuta: A Muslim Traveler of the Fourteenth Century* (1987), gives a fascinating account of Asian and African societies by a Muslim world-traveler.

LISTENING TO THE
PAST

The Endowment of a Madrasa

In classical Islam, learning was considered an act of piety, a way of worshiping God. The emphasis Muslims place on learning inspired wealthy people to establish and endow madrasas, schools for the study of Muslim jurisprudence. The patron or benefactor shared in the good that the school did. This inscription (1339) from a marble tablet on a mosque in Tlemcen (modern northwest Algeria) served as a memorial to the donors and as a legal record.

In the name of God, the Merciful and the Compassionate: May God bless our Lord and our Master Muḥammad and his family and save them. Praise be to God the Lord of the Worlds, and a good end for the pious [Qur'ān, vii, 128].

The building of this blessed mosque, with the college [*madrasa*] attached to it on the western side, was ordered by our master the very just Sultan, the amir of the Muslims, the fighter in the Holy War [*mujāhid*] for the sake of the Lord of the Worlds, Abu'l-Ḥasan, the son of our master, the amir of the Muslims, the fighter in the Holy War for the sake of the Lord of the Worlds Abū Sa'īd, the son of our master the amir of the Muslims, the fighter in the Holy War for the sake of the Lord of the Worlds Abū Yūsuf ibn 'Abd al-Ḥaqq, may God support his rule and perpetuate his memory by good works. He showed his sincerity toward God by his pious works, both private and public, and he consecrated the said college for the benefit of students of the noble science and for its teaching. He consecrated the following, from his royal bounty, to the said mosque and the said college, may God enable them to profit from it:

The whole of the garden of al-Quṣayr, situated in upper al-'Ubbād, bought from the two children of 'Abd al-Wāḥid al-Quṣayr. . . .

The whole of the large garden and the house adjoining it on the western side known by the name of Dāwūd ibn 'Alī, bought from his heirs, situated in the lowest part of a lower al-'Ubbād. . . .

The whole of the garden known as the garden of al-Bādisī, also inherited from him, bought from Yaḥyā the son of the said Dāwūd, situated in the lowest part of lower al-'Ubbād.

The whole of the garden called Ibn Qar'ūsh, near the said garden of al-Bādisī, also inherited from him and bought from the son of 'Abd al-Wāḥid and 'Isā.

The whole of four orchards of which the highest is known by the name of Ibn Makkiyya, the second, of Muḥammad ibn al-Sarrāj, the third, of Faraj al-Madlisī, and the fourth, of Ibn al-Qudā Qā'isa, also inherited from him and bought from all the heirs.

The whole of his two houses which are to the north of the mosque of lower al-'Ubbād, bought from them likewise.

A half-share of the garden of al-Zuhrī, with the whole of two mills built nearby, in the direction of al-Warīṭ.

The whole of two mills also built at Qal'at Banī Mu'allā, outside the Kashūṭ gate of Tlemcen, may God guard it.

The whole of the bathhouse known as the bathhouse of al-'Āliya,[1] which is inside the

---

1. Few private houses had bathing facilities. Thus, following the practice of ancient Roman cities, most Muslim cities had public bathhouses (segregated for the two sexes) where people could cleanse themselves for a cheap price. Bathhouses were a source of revenue for their owners.

said city in the neighborhood of the iron gate, with its two adjoining shops to the right as one goes out by the southern gate, the small house adjoining it on the inner side and the upper chamber above the vestibule.

A half-share of the old bathhouse inside the city of al-Manṣūra, may God protect it.

A piece of plough-land, of the size of 20 yokes, at Tīman Yubīn in Zīdūr in the territory of Tlemcen, to provide foodstuffs for the convent of al-Ubbād, may God cause it to flourish, for the poor and for pilgrims, resident and transient.

Another piece of land of 10 yokes in the said place for those who lodge in the said college at the rate of 15 ṣāʿ per student per month. . . .

The rest of the square adjoining the said mosque, being the remainder of the garden on which the mosque was built, bought from the heirs of Muḥammad ibn ʿAbd al-Wāḥid, from the heirs of his father, his mother, and of their maternal aunt Maymūna, so that the heirs retain no claim or right of any kind.

Manuscript Illustration of teacher and pupil. (*Source: Bibliothèque Nationale, Paris*)

Questions for Analysis

1. What were the donors' motives in the foundation and endowment of the madrasa? Why were all the donors listed in the inscription?

2. What kinds of gifts were given, and why were the gifts and their locations described in such detail?

3. How would you compare the endowment of this Muslim school and the endowment of your college of university?

Source: *Repertoire chronologique d'epigraphie arabe*, vol. 15, pp. 103–107, no. 5764. Reprinted from *Islam: From the Prophet Muhammad to the Capture of Constantinople*, vol. 2, *Religion and Society*, ed. and trans. Bernard Lewis (New York: Oxford University Press, 1987), pp. 16–18.

EUROPE

Azores

Lisbon

Cadiz

Madeira Islands

Fez

BERBERS ATLAS MTS.

Sijilmassa

Canary Islands

Taghaza

Awdaghost

Walata

Timbuktu

GHANA

Kumbi
(Kumbi-Saheh)

Niani

Jenne

Gao

Takedda

S A H E L

NIGERIA

JOS PLATEAU

S A H A R A

Ghat

Agades

Tripoli

Tajura

Black Sea

Mediterranean Sea

Alexandria

Cairo

EGYPT

Nile

Lake Chad

Dongola

Meroë

Axum

ETHIOPIA

Aral Sea

Caspian Sea

PERSIA

IRAQ

Basra

Shiraz

Persian Gulf

ARABIA

Mecca

Red Sea

Adulis

Aden *Gulf of Aden*

Berbera

Cape Guardafui

SOMALIA

MALI

Senegal

Niger

Gulf of Guinea

PORTUGUESE ROUTE

ATLANTIC OCEAN

Congo (Zaire)

Olduvai Gorge

Malindi

Mombasa

TANGANYIKA

KATANGA

Mogadishu

Brava

MUSLIM ROUTE

Pemba

Zanzibar

Mafia

Kilwa

Cape Delgado

Zambezi

MUTAPA REGION

Great Zimbabwe

Sofala

MADAGASCAR

NAMIB DESERT

KALAHARI DESERT

Cape of Good Hope

INDIAN OCEAN

——— Trans-Saharan trade routes

——— Coastal trade routes

Major Climatic Zones of Africa

Wet equatorial

Humid tropical and subtropical

Tropical with long dry season (6–9 months)

Sahelian or subdesert

Desert

Mediterranean

Highland (climate moderated by altitude)

Savannah

0   500   1000 Km.

0   500   1000 Mi.

Tassili Rock Painting   This scene of cattle grazing near the group of huts (represented on the left by stylized white ovals) reflects the domestication of animals and the development of settled pastoral agriculture. Women and children seem to perform most of the domestic chores. Tassili is a mountainous region in the Sahara. *(Source: Henri Lhote, Montrichard, France)*

Black Africans inhabited the region south of the Sahara, an area of savanna and rain forest. In describing them, the ancient Greeks used the term *Ethiopians,* which meant "people with burnt faces." The Berbers coined the term *Akal-n-Iquinawen,* which survives today as *Guinea.* The Arabs introduced another term, *Bilad al-Sudan,* which survives as *Sudan.* The Berber and Arab words both mean the "land of the blacks." Short-

statured peoples sometimes called Pygmies inhabited the equatorial rain forests. South of those forests, in the southern third of the continent, lived the Khoisan, a small people of yellow-brown skin color who primarily were hunters.

EARLY AFRICAN SOCIETIES

Africa was one of the sites where agriculture began. Archaeological investigations suggest that knowledge of cultivation moved west from ancient Judaea (southern Palestine) and arrived in the Nile Delta in Egypt about the fifth millennium before Christ. Settled agriculture then traveled down the Nile Valley and moved west across the southern

MAP 10.1 Africa Before 1500   For centuries trade linked West Africa with Mediterranean and Asian societies. Note the various climatic zones, the trans-Saharan trade routes, and the trade routes along the coast of East Africa.

edge of the Sahara to the central and western Sudan. By the first century B.C. settled agriculture existed in West Africa. From there it spread to the equatorial forests. African farmers learned to domesticate plants, including millet, sorghum, and yams. Cereal-growing people probably taught forest people to plant regular fields. Gradually African farmers also learned to clear land by burning. They evolved a sedentary way of life: living in villages, clearing fields, relying on root crops, and fishing.

Nok Woman   Hundreds of terra-cotta sculptures such as the head of this woman survive from the Nok culture, which originated in the central plateau of northern Nigeria in the first millennium B.C. *(Source: National Museum, Lagos, Nigeria/Werner Forman Archive/Art Resource, NY)*

Between 1500 and 1000 B.C. settled agriculture also spread southward from Ethiopia along the Rift Valley of present-day Kenya and Tanzania. Archaeological evidence reveals that the peoples of this region grew cereals, raised cattle, and used tools made of wood and stone. Cattle raising spread more quickly than did planting. Early African peoples prized cattle highly. Many trading agreements, marriage alliances, political compacts, and treaties were negotiated in terms of cattle.

Cereals such as millet and sorghum are indigenous to Africa. Scholars speculate that traders brought bananas, taros (a type of yam), sugar cane, and coconut palms to Africa from Southeast Asia. Because tropical forest conditions were ideal for banana trees, their cultivation spread rapidly; they were easier to raise than cereal grains. Donkeys, pigs, chickens, geese, and ducks were also domesticated.

The evolution to a settled life had profound effects. In contrast to nomadic conditions, settled societies made shared or common needs more apparent, and those needs strengthened ties among extended families. Population also increased:

The change from a hunter-gatherer economy to a settled farming economy affected population numbers. . . . What remains uncertain is whether in the agricultural economy there were more people, better fed, or more people, less well fed. . . . In precolonial Africa agricultural and pastoral populations may not have increased steadily over time, but fluctuated cyclically, growing and declining, though overall slowly growing.[2]

Scholars dispute the route by which ironworking spread to sub-Saharan Africa. Some believe that the Phoenicians brought the technique for smelting iron to northwestern Africa and that from the north it spread southward. Others insist that it spread from the Meroe region on the Nile westward. Most of West Africa had acquired knowledge of ironworking by 250 B.C. and archaeologists believe that Meroe achieved pre-eminence as an iron-smelting center only in the first century B.C. Thus a stronger case can probably be made for the Phoenicians. The great African overland trade routes may have carried knowledge of ironworking southward; in any case, by about A.D. 600 it was widely understood in sub-Saharan Africa. Ancient iron tools found at the village of Nok on the Jos

Plateau in present-day Nigeria seem to prove a knowledge of ironworking in West Africa. Nok culture (ca 800 B.C.–A.D. 200) enjoys enduring fame for its fine terra-cotta (baked clay) sculptures.

Around the time of Christ, Bantu-speakers—a small group of people who had long occupied modern-day Nigeria on Africa's west coast—began to move southeastward, settling for a time in central Africa, south of the equatorial rain forests. Because much of central Africa is a plateau, its topsoil is thin and ground water is scarce. These conditions promote migratory rather than settled agriculture. The Bantu continued to move gradually south and east, reaching present-day Zimbabwe by the eighth century and the southeastern coast by the sixteenth century. Knowledge of ironworking gave the Bantu a distinct advantage over hunters and gatherers such as the Khoisan people they encountered, whom they absorbed and displaced.

Describing the village life of Bantu people in the nineteenth century, the Scottish missionary explorer David Livingstone (1813–1873) wrote,

Food abounds, and very little labor is required for its cultivation. . . . When a garden becomes too poor for good crops . . . the owner removes a little farther into the forest, applies fire round the roots of the larger trees to kill them, cuts down the smaller, and a new, rich garden is ready for the seed.[3]

Livingstone's evaluation aside, farming always requires considerable skill and labor—and even more effort if performed by women, as much of it was in Africa.

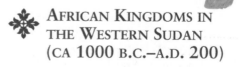

❖ AFRICAN KINGDOMS IN THE WESTERN SUDAN (CA 1000 B.C.–A.D. 200)

The region bounded on the north by the Sahara, on the south by the Gulf of Guinea, on the west by the Atlantic Ocean, and on the east by the mountains of Ethiopia is known as the Sudan. In the savanna lands of the western Sudan—where the Bantu migrations originated—a series of dynamic kingdoms emerged in the millennium before European intrusion.

Between 1000 B.C. and A.D. 200, the peoples of the western Sudan made the momentous shift from nomadic hunting to settled agriculture. The rich savanna proved ideally suited to the production of cereals, especially rice, millet, and sorghum, and people situated near the Senegal River and Lake Chad supplemented their diet with fish. Food supply tends to affect population, and the peoples of the region—known as the Mande-speakers and the Chadic-speakers, or Sao—increased dramatically in number. By A.D. 400 the entire savanna, particularly the areas around Lake Chad, the Niger River bend, and present-day central Nigeria (see Map 10.1), had a large population.

Families and clans affiliated by blood kinship lived together in villages or small city-states. The basic social unit was the extended family. A chief, in consultation with a council of elders, governed a village. Some villages seem to have formed kingdoms. Village chiefs were responsible to regional heads, who answered to provincial governors, who in turn were responsible to a king. The chiefs and their families formed an aristocracy.

Kingship in the Sudan may have emerged from the priesthood, whose members were believed to make rain and to have contact with spirit powers. African kings always had religious sanction or support for their authority and were often considered divine. In this respect, early African kingship bears a strong resemblance to Germanic kingship of the same period: the authority of the king rested in part on the ruler's ability to negotiate with outside powers, such as the gods.

African religions were animistic and polytheistic. Most people believed that a supreme being had created the universe and was the source of all life. The supreme being breathed spirit into all living things, and the *anima*, or spirit, residing in such things as trees, water, and earth had to be appeased. In the cycle of the agricultural year, for example, all the spirits had to be propitiated from the time of clearing the land through sowing the seed to the final harvest. Because special ceremonies were necessary to satisfy the spirits, special priests with the knowledge and power to communicate with them through sacred rituals were needed. Thus the heads of families and villages were likely to be priests. The head of each family was responsible for maintaining the family ritual cults—ceremonies honoring the dead and living members of the family.[4]

In sum, the most prominent feature of early African society was a strong sense of community, based on the blood relationship and on religion.

Extended families made up the villages that collectively formed small kingdoms. What spurred the expansion of these small kingdoms into formidable powers controlling sizable territory was the development of long-distance trade. And what made long-distance or trans-Saharan trade possible was the camel.

❖ THE TRANS-SAHARAN TRADE

The expression "trans-Saharan trade" refers to the north-south trade across the Sahara (see Map 10.1). The camel had an impact on this trade comparable to the impact of the horse on European agriculture (see page 403). Although scholars dispute exactly when the camel was introduced from central Asia—first into North Africa, then into the Sahara and the Sudan—they agree that it was before A.D. 200. Camels can carry about 500 pounds as far as 25 miles a day and can go for days without drinking, living on the water stored in their stomachs. Sometimes stupid and vicious, camels had to be loaded on a daily, sometimes twice-daily, basis. And much of the cargo for a long trip was provisions for the journey itself. Nevertheless, camels proved more efficient for desert transportation than horses or oxen, and the use of this beast to carry heavy and bulky freight not only brought economic and social change to Africa but affected the development of world commerce.

Sometime in the fifth century the North African Berbers fashioned a saddle for use on the camel. This saddle had no direct effect on commercial operations, for a merchant usually walked and guided the camel on foot. But the saddle gave the Berbers and later the Arabian inhabitants of the region maneuverability on the animal and thus a powerful political and military advantage: they came to dominate the desert and to create lucrative routes across it. The Berbers determined who could enter the desert, and they extracted large sums of protection money from merchant caravans in exchange for a safe trip.

Between A.D. 700 and 900 the Berbers developed a network of caravan routes between the Mediterranean coast and the Sudan (see Map 10.1). The Morocco-Niger route ran from Fez to Sijilmassa on the edge of the desert and then south by way of Taghaza and Walata and back to Fez. Another route originated at Sijilmassa and extended due south to Timbuktu with a stop at Taghaza. A third route ran south from Tripoli to Lake Chad. A fourth ran from Egypt to Gao by way of the Saharan oases of Ghat and Agades and then on to Takedda.

The long expedition across the Sahara testifies to the spirit of the traders and to their passion for wealth. Because of the blistering sun and daytime temperatures of 110 degrees, the caravan drivers preferred to travel at night, when the temperature might drop to the low 20s. Ibn Battuta, an Arab traveler who made the journey in the fourteenth century when trans-Saharan traffic was at its height, wrote an account of the experience.

Nomadic raiders, the Tuareg Berbers, posed a serious threat. The Tuaregs lived in the desert uplands and preyed on the caravans as a way of life. Thus merchants made safe-conduct agreements with them and selected guides from among them. Caravans of twelve thousand camels were reported in the fourteenth century. Large numbers of merchants crossed the desert together to discourage attack. Blinding sandstorms often isolated part of a line of camels and on at least one occasion buried alive some camels and drivers. Water was the biggest problem. The Tuaregs sometimes poisoned wells to wipe out caravans and steal their goods. To satisfy normal thirst and to compensate for constant sweating, a gallon of water a day per person was required. Desperate thirst sometimes forced the traders to kill camels and drink the foul, brackish water in their stomachs. It took Ibn Battuta twenty-five days to travel from Sijilmassa to the oasis of Taghaza and another sixty-five days to travel from Taghaza to the important market town of Walata.

The Arab-Berber merchants from North Africa who controlled the caravan trade carried manufactured goods—silk and cotton cloth, beads, mirrors—as well as dates and salt (essential in tropical climates to replace the loss from perspiration) from the Saharan oases and mines to the Sudan. These products were exchanged for the much-coveted commodities of the West African savanna—gold, ivory, gum, kola nuts (eaten as a stimulant), and captive slaves.

The steady growth of trans-Saharan trade had three important effects on West African society.

The trade stimulated gold mining and the search for slaves. Parts of modern-day Senegal, Nigeria, and Ghana contained rich veins of gold. Both sexes shared in mining it. Men sank the shafts and hacked out gold-bearing rocks and crushed them, separating the gold from the soil. Women washed the gold in gourds. Alluvial gold (mixed with soil, sand, or gravel) was separated from the soil by panning. Scholars estimate that by the eleventh century nine tons were exported to Europe annually—a prodigious amount for the time, since even with modern machinery and sophisticated techniques the total gold exports from the same region in 1937 amounted to only twenty-one tons. A large percentage of this metal went to Egypt. From there it was transported down the Red Sea and eventually to India (see Map 10.3) to pay for the spices and silks demanded by Mediterranean commerce. West African gold proved "absolutely vital for the monetization of the medieval Mediterranean economy and for the maintenance of its balance of payments with South Asia."[5] African gold linked the entire world, exclusive of the Western Hemisphere.

Slaves were West Africa's second most valuable export (after gold). African slaves, like their early European and Asian counterparts, seem to have been peoples captured in war. In the Muslim cities of North Africa, southern Europe, and southwestern Asia, the demand for household slaves was high among the elite. Slaves were also needed to work the gold and salt mines. Recent research suggests, moreover, that large numbers of black slaves were recruited through the trans-Saharan trade for Muslim military service. High death rates from disease, manumission, and the assimilation of some blacks into Muslim society meant that the demand for slaves remained high for centuries. Table 10.1 shows one scholar's tentative conclusions, based on many kinds of evidence, about the scope of the trans-Saharan slave trade. The total number of blacks enslaved over an 850-year period may be tentatively estimated at over 4 million.[6]

Slavery in Muslim societies, as in European and Asian countries before the fifteenth century, was not based strictly on skin color. Muslims also enslaved Caucasians who had been purchased, seized in war, or kidnapped from Europe. The households of wealthy Muslims in Cordoba, Alexandria, or Tunis often included slaves of a number of

Bust of Man from Jenne Founded in the eighth century on the Bani River in Mali, and by the thirteenth a thriving entrepôt for gold, slaves, and salt, Jenne must have been an important artistic center, since many terra-cotta figures have been discovered there. The beautiful stole suggests the figure was a ruler or member of the elite. *(Source: Detroit Institute of Arts, Eleanor Clay Ford Fund. Acc. #78.32)*

TABLE 10.1 ESTIMATED MAGNITUDE OF TRANS-SAHARAN SLAVE TRADE, 650–1500

Years	Annual Average of Slaves Traded	Total
650–800	1,000	150,000
800–900	3,000	300,000
900–1100	8,700	1,740,000
1100–1400	5,500	1,650,000
1400–1500	4,300	430,000

Source: From R. A. Austen, "The Trans-Saharan Slave Trade: A Tentative Census," in The Uncommon Market: Essays in the Economic History of the Atlantic Slave Trade, *ed. H. A. Gemery and J. S. Hogendorn (New York: Academic Press, 1979). Used with permission.*

races, all of whom had been completely cut off from their cultural roots. Likewise, West African kings who sold blacks to traders from the north also bought a few white slaves—Slavic, British, and Turkish—for their domestic needs. Race had little to do with the phenomenon of slavery.[7]

The trans-Saharan trade also stimulated the development of vigorous urban centers in West Africa. Scholars date the growth of African cities from around the beginning of the ninth century. Families that had profited from trade tended to congregate in the border zones between the savanna and the Sahara. They acted as middlemen between the miners to the south and Muslim merchants from the north. By the early thirteenth century, these families had become powerful black merchant dynasties. Muslim traders from the Mediterranean settled permanently in the trading depots, from which they organized the trans-Saharan caravans. The concentration of people stimulated agriculture and the craft industries. Gradually cities of sizable population emerged. Jenne, Gao, and Timbuktu, which enjoyed commanding positions on the Niger River bend, became centers of the export-import trade. Sijilmassa grew into a thriving market center. Kumbi, with between 15,000 and 20,000 inhabitants, was probably the largest city in the western Sudan in the twelfth century. (By European standards Kumbi was a metropolis; London and Paris achieved its size only in the late thirteenth century.) Between 1100 and 1400 these cities played a dynamic role in the commercial life of West Africa and Europe and became centers of intellectual creativity.

Perhaps the most influential consequence of the trans-Saharan trade was the introduction of Islam to West African society. Muslim expansion began soon after Muhammad's death in 632 (see pages 251–252). By the tenth century, Muslim Berbers controlled the north-south trade routes to the savanna. By the eleventh century, African rulers of Gao and Timbuktu had accepted Islam. The king of Ghana was also influenced by Islam. Muslims quickly became integral to West African government and society.

Conversion to Islam introduced West Africans to a rich and sophisticated culture. By the late eleventh century, Muslims were guiding the ruler of Ghana in the operation of his administrative machinery. The king of Ghana adopted the Muslim diwan, the agency for keeping financial records (see page 260). Because efficient government depends on the preservation of records, the arrival of Islam in West Africa marked the advent of written documents there. Arab Muslims also taught the rulers of Ghana how to manufacture bricks, and royal palaces and mosques began to be built of brick. African rulers corresponded with Muslim architects, theologians, and other intellectuals, who advised them on statecraft and religion. Islam accelerated the development of the African empires of the ninth through fifteenth centuries.

❋ AFRICAN KINGDOMS AND EMPIRES (CA 800–1450)

All African societies shared one basic feature: a close relationship between political and social organization. Ethnic or blood ties bound clan members together. What scholars call "stateless societies" were culturally homogeneous ethnic societies. The smallest ones numbered fewer than a hundred people and were nomadic hunting groups. Larger stateless societies of perhaps several thousand people lived a settled and often agricultural or herding life.

The period from about 800 to 1450 witnessed the flowering of several powerful African states. In the western Sudan, the large empires of Ghana and Mali developed, complete with massive royal bureaucracies. On the east coast emerged powerful city-states based on sophisticated mercantile activities and, like Sudan, very much influenced by Islam. In Ethiopia, in central East Africa, kings relied on the Christian faith of their people to strengthen political authority. In South Africa the empire of Great Zimbabwe, built on the gold trade with the east coast, flourished.

The Kingdom of Ghana (ca 900–1100)

So remarkable was the kingdom of Ghana during the age of Africa's great empires that writers throughout the medieval world, such as the four-teenth-century Muslim historian Ibn Khaldun, praised it as a model for other rulers. Medieval Ghana also holds a central place in the historical consciousness of the modern state of Ghana. Since this former British colony attained independence in 1957, its political leaders have hailed the medieval period as a glorious heritage. The name of the modern republic of Ghana—which in fact lies far from the site of the old kingdom—was selected to signify the rebirth of an age of gold in black Africa.

The nucleus of the territory that became the kingdom of Ghana was inhabited by Soninke people who called their ruler *ghana,* or war chief. By the late eighth century Muslim traders and other foreigners applied the word to the region where the Soninke lived, the black kingdom south of the Sahara. The Soninke themselves called their land "Aoukar" or "Awkar," by which they meant the region north of the Senegal and Niger Rivers. Only the southern part of Aoukar received enough rainfall to be agriculturally productive, and it was in this area that the civilization of Ghana developed. Skillful farming and an efficient system of irrigation led to the production of abundant crops, which eventually supported a population of as many as 200,000.

The Soninke name for their king—war chief—aptly describes the king's major preoccupation in the tenth century. In 992 Ghana captured the Berber town of Awdaghost, strategically situated on the trans-Saharan trade route (see Map 10.1). Thereafter Ghana controlled the southern portion of a major caravan route. Before the year 1000 the rulers of Ghana had extended their influence almost to the Atlantic coast and had captured a number of small kingdoms in the south and east. By the beginning of the eleventh century, the king exercised sway over a territory approximately the size of Texas. No other power in the West African region could successfully challenge him.

Throughout this vast West African area, all authority sprang from the king. Religious ceremonies and court rituals emphasized the king's sacredness and were intended to strengthen his authority. The king's position was hereditary in the matrilineal line—that is, the heir of the ruling king was one of the king's sister's sons (presumably the eldest or fittest for battle). According to the eleventh-century Spanish Muslim geographer al-Bakri (1040?–1094): "This is their custom . . . the kingdom is inherited only by the son of the king's sister. He the king has no doubt that his successor is a son of his sister, while he is not certain that his son is in fact his own."[8]

A council of ministers assisted the king in the work of government, and from the ninth century on, most of these ministers were Muslims. Detailed evidence about the early Ghanaian bureaucracy has not survived, but scholars suspect that separate agencies were responsible for taxation, royal property, foreigners, forests, and the army. The royal administration was well served by Muslim ideas, skills, and especially literacy. The king and his people, however, clung to their ancestral religion, and the basic political institutions of Ghana remained African.

The king of Ghana held his court in Kumbi. Al-Bakri provides a valuable picture of the city in the eleventh century:

The city of Ghana consists of two towns lying on a plain, one of which is inhabited by Muslims and is large, possessing twelve mosques—one of which is a congregational mosque for Friday prayer; each has its imam, its muezzin and paid reciters of the Quran. The town possesses a large number of jurisconsults and learned men.[9]

Benin Queen Mother Queens wore a specially woven crown with a high forward-pointing peak, called a "chicken's beak" that symbolized rank. This projection, known as an *ede,* was believed to possess spiritual powers. Notice the roped necklace, probably made of strands of woven gold. *(Source: British Museum/Michael Holford)*

Either for their own protection or to preserve their special identity, the Muslims lived separate from the African artisans and tradespeople. The Muslim community in Ghana must have been large and prosperous to have supported twelve mosques. The *imam* was the religious leader who conducted the ritual worship, especially the main prayer ser-

vice on Fridays. The *muezzin* led the prayer responses after the imam; he needed a strong voice so that those at a distance and the women in the harem, or enclosure, could hear. Muslim religious leaders exercised civil authority over their coreligionists. Their presence and that of other learned Muslims also suggests vigorous intellectual activity.

Al-Bakri describes the town where the king lived and the royal court:

The town inhabited by the king is six miles from the Muslim one and is called Al Ghana. . . . The residence of the king consists of a palace and a number of dome-shaped dwellings, all of them surrounded by a strong enclosure, like a city wall. In the town . . . is a mosque, where Muslims who come on diplomatic missions to the king pray. The town where the king lives is surrounded by domed huts, woods, and copses where priest-magicians live; in these woods also are the religious idols and tombs of the kings. Special guards protect this area and prevent anyone from entering it so that no foreigners know what is inside. Here also are the king's prisons, and if anyone is imprisoned there, nothing more is heard of him.[10]

The king adorns himself, as do the women here, with necklaces and bracelets; on their heads they wear caps decorated with gold, sewn on material of fine cotton stuffing. When he holds court in order to hear the people's complaints and to do justice, he sits in a pavilion around which stand ten horses wearing golden trappings; behind him ten pages stand, holding shields and swords decorated with gold; at his right are the sons of the chiefs of the country, splendidly dressed and with their hair sprinkled with gold. The governor of the city sits on the ground in front of the king with other officials likewise sitting around him. Excellently pedigreed dogs guard the door of the pavilion. . . . The noise of a sort-of drum, called a daba, and made from a long hollow log, announces the start of the royal audience. When the king's coreligionists appear before him, they fall on their knees and toss dust on their heads—this is their way of greeting their sovereign. Muslims show respect by clapping their hands.[11]

What sort of juridical system did Ghana have? How was the guilt or innocence of an accused person determined? Justice derived from the king, who heard cases at court or on his travels throughout his kingdom. As al-Bakri recounts:

When a man is accused of denying a debt or of having shed blood or some other crime, a headman (village chief) takes a thin piece of wood, which is sour and bitter to taste, and pours upon it some water which he then gives to the defendant to drink. If the man vomits, his innocence is recognized and he is congratulated. If he does not vomit and the drink remains in his stomach, the accusation is accepted as justified.[12]

This appeal to the supernatural for judgment was very similar to the justice by ordeal that prevailed among the Germanic peoples of western Europe at the same time. Complicated cases in Ghana seem to have been appealed to the king, who often relied on the advice of Muslim legal experts.

The king's elaborate court, the administrative machinery he built, and the extensive territories he governed were all expensive. The king of Ghana needed a lot of money, and he apparently had four main sources of support. The royal estates—some hereditary, others conquered in war—produced annual revenue, mostly in the form of foodstuffs for the royal household. The king also received tribute annually from subordinate chieftains (lack of evidence prevents an estimate of the value of this tax). Customs duties on goods entering and leaving the country generated revenues. Salt was the largest import. Berber merchants paid a tax to the king on the cloth, metalwork, weapons, and other goods that they brought into the country from North Africa; in return these traders received royal protection from bandits. African traders bringing gold into Ghana from the south also paid the customs duty.

Finally, the royal treasury held a monopoly on the export of gold. The gold industry was undoubtedly the king's largest source of income. It was on gold that the fame of medieval Ghana rested. The ninth century geographer al-Ya-qubi wrote, "its king is mighty, and in his lands are gold mines. Under his authority are various other kingdoms—and in all this region there is gold."[13]

The governing aristocracy—the king, his court, and Muslim administrators—occupied the highest rung on the Ghanaian social ladder. On the next rung stood the merchant class. Considerably below the merchants stood the farmers, cattle breeders, supervisors of the gold mines, and skilled craftsmen and weavers—what today might be called the middle class. Some merchants and miners must have enjoyed great wealth, but, as in all aristocratic

societies, money alone did not suffice. High status was based on blood and royal service. At the bottom of the social ladder were slaves, who worked in households, on farms, and in the mines. As in Asian and European societies of the time, slaves accounted for only a small percentage of the population.

Apart from these social classes stood the army. According to al-Bakri, "the king of Ghana can put 200,000 warriors in the field, more than 40,000 being armed with bow and arrow."[14] Like most medieval estimates, this is probably a gross exaggeration. Even a modern industrialized state with

Oni Obalufon African masks always had religious significance. Some were intended as a disguise, some filled a ritual function in religious festivals, and some served as funerary representations of the deceased. This fourteenth-century copper mask was made for Oni (king) Obalufon. (*Source: Ife Museum/National Commission for Museums and Monuments, Lagos, Nigeria*)

❋ **MAP 10.2 The Kingdom of Mali**   The economic strength of the kingdom of Mali rested heavily on the trans-Saharan trade.

The Kingdom of Mali (ca 1200–1450)

During the century after the collapse of Kumbi, a cloud of obscurity hung over the western Sudan. The kingdom of Ghana split into several small kingdoms that feuded among themselves. One people, the Mandinke, lived in the kingdom of Kangaba on the upper Niger River. The Mandinke had long been part of the Ghanaian empire, and the Mandinke and Soninke belonged to the same language group. Kangaba formed the core of the new empire of Mali. Building on Ghanaian foundations, Mali developed into a better-organized and more powerful state than Ghana.

The kingdom of Mali (Map 10.2) owed its greatness to two fundamental assets. First, its strong agricultural and commercial base provided for a large population and enormous wealth. Second, Mali had two rulers, Sundiata and Mansa Musa, who combined military success with exceptionally creative personalities.

The earliest surviving evidence about the Mandinke, dating from the early eleventh century, indicates that they were extremely successful at agriculture. Consistently large harvests throughout the twelfth and thirteenth centuries meant a plentiful supply of food, which encouraged steady population growth. The geographical location of Kangaba also placed the Mandinke in an ideal position in West African trade. Earlier, during the period of Ghanaian hegemony, the Mandinke had acted as middlemen in the gold and salt traffic flowing north and south. In the thirteenth century Mandinke traders formed companies, traveled widely, and gradually became a major force in the entire West African trade.

Sundiata (r. ca 1230–1255) set up his capital at Niani, transforming the city into an important financial and trading center. He then embarked on a policy of imperial expansion. Through a series of military victories, Sundiata and his successors absorbed into Mali other territories of the former kingdom of Ghana and established hegemony over the trading cities of Gao, Jenne, and Walata.

These expansionist policies were continued in the fourteenth century by Sundiata's descendant Mansa Musa (r. ca 1312–1337), early Africa's most famous ruler. In the language of the Mandinke, *mansa* means "emperor." Mansa Musa fought many campaigns and checked every attempt at re-

sophisticated means of transportation, communication, and supply lines would have enormous difficulty mobilizing so many men for battle. The king of Ghana, however, was not called "war chief" for nothing. He maintained at his palace a crack standing force of a thousand men, comparable to the Roman Praetorian Guard. These thoroughly disciplined, well-armed, totally loyal troops protected the king and the royal court. They lived in special compounds, enjoyed the favor of the king, and sometimes acted as his personal ambassadors to subordinate rulers. In wartime, this regular army was augmented by levies of soldiers from conquered peoples and by the use of slaves and free reserves. The force that the king could field was sizable, if not as huge as al-Bakri estimated.

Timbuktu   Begun as a Tuareg seasonal camp in the eleventh century, Timbuktu emerged as a great commercial entrepôt in the fourteenth century and as an important Muslim educational center in the sixteenth. A strong agricultural base, watered by the nearby Niger River, supported a sizable population. *(Source: Library of Congress)*

bellion. Ultimately his influence extended northward to several Berber cities in the Sahara, eastward to Timbuktu and Gao, and westward as far as the Atlantic Ocean. Throughout his territories he maintained strict royal control over the rich trans-Saharan trade. Thus this empire, roughly twice the size of the Ghanaian kingdom and containing perhaps 8 million people, brought Mansa Musa fabulous wealth.

Mansa Musa built on the foundations of his predecessors. The stratified aristocratic structure of Malian society perpetuated the pattern set in Ghana, as did the system of provincial administration and annual tribute. The emperor took responsibility for the territories that formed the heart of the empire and appointed governors to rule the outlying provinces or dependent kingdoms. But Mansa Musa made a significant innovation: in a practice strikingly similar to a system used in both China and France at that time, he appointed members of the royal family as provincial governors. He could count on their loyalty, and they received valuable experience in the work of government.

In another aspect of administration, Mansa Musa also differed from his predecessors. He became a devout Muslim. Although most of the Mandinke clung to their ancestral animism, Islamic practices and influences in Mali multiplied.

The most celebrated event of Mansa Musa's reign was his pilgrimage to Mecca in 1324–1325, during which he paid a state visit to the sultan of Egypt. Mansa Musa's entrance into Cairo was magnificent. Preceded by five hundred slaves, each carrying a six-pound staff of gold, he followed with a huge host of retainers including one hundred elephants each bearing one hundred pounds of gold. The emperor lavished his wealth on the citizens of the Egyptian capital. Writing twelve years later, al-Omari, one of the sultan's officials, recounts:

This man Mansa Musa spread upon Cairo the flood of his generosity: there was no person, officer of the court, or holder of any office of the Sultanate who did not receive a sum of gold from him. The people of Cairo earned incalculable sums from him, whether by buying and selling or by gifts. So much gold was current in Cairo that it ruined the value of money.[15]

Mansa Musa's gold brought about terrible inflation throughout Egypt. For the first time, the Mediterranean world gained concrete knowledge of the wealth and power of the black kingdom of Mali, and it began to be known as one of the great empires of the world. Mali retained this international reputation into the fifteenth century.

Musa's pilgrimage also had significant consequences within Mali. He gained some understanding of the Mediterranean countries and opened diplomatic relations with the Muslim rulers of Morocco and Egypt. His zeal for the Muslim faith and Islamic culture increased. Musa brought back from Arabia the distinguished architect al-Saheli, whom he commissioned to build new mosques at Timbuktu and other cities. These mosques served as centers for the conversion of Africans. Musa employed Muslim engineers to build in brick. He also encouraged Malian merchants and traders to wear the distinctive flowing robes and turbans of Muslim males.

Timbuktu began as a campsite for desert nomads. Under Mansa Musa it grew into a thriving entrepôt, attracting merchants and traders from North Africa and all parts of the Mediterranean world. These people brought with them cosmopolitan attitudes and ideas. In the fifteenth century Timbuktu developed into a great center for scholarship and learning. Architects, astronomers, poets, lawyers, mathematicians, and theologians flocked there. One hundred fifty schools were devoted to the study of the Qur'an. The school of

Islamic law enjoyed a distinction in Africa comparable to the prestige of the school at Cairo (see page 272). A vigorous trade in books flourished in Timbuktu. Leo Africanus, a sixteenth-century Muslim traveler and writer who later converted to Christianity, recounts that around 1500 Timbuktu had a

great store of doctors, judges, priests, and other learned men that are bountifully maintained at the king's cost and charges. And hitherto are brought diverse manuscripts or written books out of Barbarie the north African states, from Egypt to the Atlantic Ocean which are sold for more money than any other merchandise.

It is easy to understand why the university at Timbuktu was called by a contemporary writer "the Queen of the Sudan." Timbuktu's tradition and reputation for African scholarship lasted until the eighteenth century.

Moreover, in the fourteenth and fifteenth centuries many Muslim intellectuals and Arabic traders married native African women. These unions brought into being a group of racially mixed people. The necessity of living together harmoniously, the traditional awareness of diverse cultures, and the cosmopolitan atmosphere of Timbuktu all contributed to a rare degree of racial toleration and understanding. After visiting the court of Mansa Musa's successor in 1352–1353, Ibn Battuta observed that

the Negroes possess some admirable qualities. They are seldom unjust, and have a greater abhorrence of injustice than any other people. Their sultan shows no mercy to anyone who is guilty of the least act of it. There is complete security in their country. Neither traveler nor inhabitant in it has anything to fear from robbers. . . . They do not confiscate the property of any white man who dies in their country, even if it be uncounted wealth. On the contrary, they give it into the charge of some trustworthy person among the whites, until the rightful heir takes possession of it.[16]

Ethiopia: The Christian Kingdom of Axum

Egyptian culture exerted a profound influence on the sub-Saharan kingdom of Nubia in northeastern Africa (Map 10.3). Nubia's capital was at Meroe; thus the country is often referred to as the Nubian

Church of Saint George, Lalibela   Shortly before A.D. 1100 the political capital of Ethiopia was moved south from Axum to Lalibela. Legend holds that Saint George, the third-century Christian martyr, ordered villagers here to construct a church in his honor. They carved it from a hillside of volcanic rock. Worshipers entered through the subterranean trench to the left of the building. Concentric Greek crosses, formed of four equal arms and symbolizing the universal Christian Church, made up the roof. *(Source: Kal Muller/Woodfin Camp & Associates)*

kingdom of Meroe. As part of the Roman Empire, Egypt was naturally subject to Hellenistic and Roman cultural forces, and it became an early center of Christianity. Nubia, however, was never part of the Roman Empire; its people clung to ancient Egyptian religious ideas. Christian missionaries went to the upper Nile region and succeeded in converting the Nubian rulers around A.D. 600. By that time there were three separate Nubian states, of which the kingdom of Nobatia, centered at

❋ **MAP 10.3 Trade Routes Between East Africa and India**   The Indian Ocean, controlled by the Muslim merchant fleet until the arrival of the Portuguese in the late fifteenth century, was of far greater importance for world trade than the Mediterranean. Gold from Great Zimbabwe passed through the cities on the East African coast before shipment north to the Middle East and east to India and China.

Dongola, was the strongest. The Christian rulers of Nobatia had close ties with Ethiopia.

The kingdom of Ethiopia, centered at Axum (see Map 10.3), had had important commercial contacts with the Roman world. Perhaps partly for that reason, Axum officially adopted Christianity in A.D. 350, just a short time after Christianity be-

came legal within the Roman Empire itself. Ethiopia adopted the Egyptian or Coptic form of Christianity. According to its Monophysitic doctrine, Christ has only one, divine, nature. Orthodox teaching holds that Christ's nature is both human and divine. The Egyptian partriarch of Alexandria appointed the first bishop of Axum, an appointment that led to close religious ties between Egypt and Ethiopia. At the time Axum was a powerful cosmopolitan center whose mercantile activities played a major part in international commerce and whose military and political power was the dominant influence in East Africa.

The expansion of Islam in the eighth century severed Axum's commercial contacts with the Byzantine Empire and ended its control of the Red Sea routes. The kingdom declined as a major power. Ethiopia's high mountains encouraged an inward concentration of attention and hindered access from the outside. Twelfth-century Crusaders returning from the Middle East told of a powerful Christian ruler, Prester John, whose lands lay behind Muslim lines and who was eager to help restore the Holy Land to Christian control. Europeans identified that kingdom with Ethiopia. In the later thirteenth century, the dynasty of the Solomonid kings witnessed a literary and artistic renaissance particularly notable for works of hagiography (biographies of saints), biblical exegesis, and manuscript illumination. The most striking feature of Ethiopian society in the period from 500 to 1500 was the close relationship between the church and the state. Coptic Christianity inspired a fierce devotion and tended to equate doctrinal heresy with political rebellion, thus reinforcing central monarchial power.

The East African City-States

In the first century A.D., a merchant-seaman from Alexandria in Egypt sailed down the Red Sea and out into the Indian Ocean. Along the coasts of East Africa and India he found seaports. He took careful notes on all he observed, and the result, *Periplus of the Erythraean Sea* (as the Greeks called the Indian Ocean), is the earliest surviving literary evidence of the city-states of the East African coast. Although primarily preoccupied with geography and navigation, the *Periplus* includes accounts of the local peoples and their commercial activities. Even in the days of the Roman emperors, the *Periplus* testifies, the East African coast had strong commercial links with India and the Mediterranean.

Greco-Roman ships traveled from Adulis on the Red Sea around the tip of the Gulf of Aden and down the African coast that the Greeks called "Azania," in modern-day Kenya and Tanzania (see Map 10.3). These ships carried manufactured goods—cotton cloth, copper and brass, iron tools, and gold and silver plate. At the African coastal emporiums, Mediterranean merchants exchanged these goods for cinnamon, myrrh and frankincense, captive slaves, and animal byproducts such as ivory, rhinoceros horns, and tortoise shells. Somewhere around Cape Guardafui on the Horn of Africa, the ships caught the monsoon winds eastward to India, where ivory was in great demand.

An omission in the *Periplus* has created a debate over the racial characteristics of the native peoples in East Africa and the dates of Bantu migrations into the area. The author, writing in the first century, did not describe the natives; apparently he did not find their skin color striking enough to comment on. Yet in the fifth century, there are references to these peoples as "Ethiopians." Could this mean that migrating black Bantu-speakers reached the east coast between the first and the fifth centuries? Possibly. The distinguished archaeologist Neville Chittick, however, thinks not: "The writer of the *Periplus* made few comments on the physical nature of the inhabitants of the countries which he described . . . therefore nothing can be based on the mere omission of any mention of skin color."[17]

In the first few centuries of the Christian era, many merchants and seamen from the Mediterranean settled in East African coastal towns. Succeeding centuries saw the arrival of more traders. The great emigration from Arabia after the death of Muhammad accelerated Muslim penetration of the area, which the Arabs called the *Zanj*, "land of the blacks." Arabic Muslims established along the coast small trading colonies whose local peoples were ruled by kings and practiced various animistic religions. Eventually—whether through Muslim political hegemony or gradual assimilation—the coastal peoples slowly converted to Islam. Indigenous African religions, however, remained strong in the interior of the continent.

Beginning in the late twelfth century, fresh waves of Arabs and of Persians from Shiraz poured down the coast, first settling at Mogadishu, then pressing southward to Kilwa (see Map 10.3). Everywhere they landed, they introduced Islamic culture to the indigenous population. Similarly, from the earliest Christian centuries through the Middle Ages, Indonesians crossed the Indian

Ocean and settled on the African coast and on the large island of Madagascar, or Malagasy, an Indonesian word. All these immigrants intermarried with Africans, and the resulting society combined Asian, African, and especially Islamic traits. The East African coastal culture was called Swahili, after a Bantu language whose vocabulary and poetic forms exhibit a strong Arabic influence. The thirteenth-century Muslim mosque at Mogadishu and the fiercely Muslim populations of Mombasa and Kilwa in the fourteenth century attest to strong Muslim influence.

By the late thirteenth century Kilwa had become the most powerful city on the coast, exercising political hegemony as far north as Pemba and as far south as Sofala (see Map 10.3). In the fourteenth and fifteenth centuries the coastal cities were great commercial empires comparable to Venice and

Great Mosque at Kilwa　Built between the thirteenth and fifteenth centuries to serve the Muslim commercial aristocracy of Kilwa on the Indian Ocean, the mosque attests to the wealth and power of the East African city-states. *(Source: Werner Forman Archive/Art Resource, NY)*

Genoa (see page 385). Like those Italian city-states, Kilwa, Mombasa, and Mafia were situated on offshore islands. The tidal currents that isolated them from the mainland also protected them from landside attack.

Much current knowledge about life in the East African trading societies rests on the account of Ibn Battuta. When he arrived at Kilwa, he found, in the words of a modern historian,

the city large and elegant, its buildings, as was typical along the coast, constructed of stone and coral rag [roofing slate]. Houses were generally single storied, consisting of a number of small rooms separated by thick walls supporting heavy stone roofing slabs laid across mangrove poles. Some of the more formidable structures contained second and third stories, and many were embellished with cut stone decorative borders framing the entranceways. Tapestries and ornamental niches covered the walls and the floors were carpeted. Of course, such appointments were only for the wealthy; the poorer classes occupied the timeless mud and straw huts of Africa, their robes a simple loincloth, their dinner a millet porridge.[18]

On the mainland were fields and orchards of rice, millet, oranges, mangoes, and bananas, and pastures and yards for cattle, sheep, and poultry. Yields were apparently high; Ibn Battuta noted that the rich enjoyed three enormous meals a day and were very fat.

From among the rich mercantile families that controlled the coastal cities arose a ruler who by the fourteenth century had taken the Arabic title *sheik*. The sheik governed both the island city and the nearby mainland. Farther inland, tribal chiefs ruled with the advice of councils of elders.

The Portuguese, approaching the East African coastal cities in the late fifteenth century, were astounded at their enormous wealth and prosperity. This wealth rested on monopolistic control of all trade in the area. Some coastal cities manufactured goods for export: Mogadishu produced a cloth for the Egyptian market; Mombasa and Malindi processed iron tools; and Sofala made Cambay cottons for the interior trade. The bulk of the cities' exports, however, consisted of animal products—leopard skins, tortoise shell, ambergris, ivory—and gold. The gold originated in the Mutapa region south of the Zambezi River, where the Bantu

mined it. As in tenth-century Ghana, gold was a royal monopoly in the fourteenth-century coastal city-states. The Mutapa kings received it as annual tribute, prohibited outsiders from entering the mines or participating in the trade, and controlled shipments down the Zambezi to the coastal markets. The prosperity of Kilwa rested on its traffic in gold.

African goods satisfied the widespread aristocratic demand for luxury goods. In Arabia, leopard skins were made into saddles, shells were made into combs, and ambergris was used in the manufacture of perfumes. Because the tusks of African elephants were larger and more durable than the tusks of Indian elephants, African ivory was in great demand in India for sword and dagger handles, carved decorative objects, and the ceremonial bangles used in Hindu marriage rituals. In China, the wealthy valued African ivory for use in the construction of sedan chairs.

In exchange for these natural products, the Swahili cities bought pottery, glassware and beads, and many varieties of cloth. Swahili kings imposed enormous duties on imports, perhaps more than 80 percent of the value of the goods themselves. Even so, traders who came to Africa made fabulous profits.

Slaves were another export from the East African coast. Reports of slave trading began with the *Periplus*. The trade accelerated with the establishment of Muslim settlements in the eighth century and continued down to the arrival of the Portuguese in the late fifteenth century. In fact, the East African coastal trade in slaves persisted at least to the beginning of the twentieth century.

As in West Africa, traders obtained slaves primarily through raids and kidnapping. As early as the tenth century, Arabs from Oman enticed hungry children with dates. When the children accepted the sweet fruits, they were abducted and enslaved. Profit was the traders' motive.

The Arabs called the northern Somalia coast *Ras Assir* ("Cape of Slaves"). From there, Arab traders transported slaves northward up the Red Sea to the markets of Arabia, Persia, and Iraq. Muslim dealers also shipped blacks from the region of Zanzibar across the Indian Ocean to markets in India. Rulers of the Deccan Plateau in central India used large numbers of black soldier-slaves in their military campaigns. Slaves also worked on the

AFRICA, CA 400–1500

ca 1st century A.D.	Beginning of Bantu migrations
ca A.D. 200	First use of the camel for trans-Saharan transportation
4th century	Ethiopia accepts Christianity
600–1500	Extensive slave trade from sub-Saharan Africa to the Mediterranean
6th and 7th centuries	Political and commercial ascendancy of Ethiopia
9th century	Decline of Ethiopia
11th century	Islam penetrates sub-Saharan Africa Height of the kingdom of Ghana
13th and 14th centuries	Kingdom of Mali
ca 1312–1337	The reign of Mansa Musa, medieval Africa's most famous ruler
14th and 15th centuries	Height of the Swahili (East African) city-states

docks and *dhows* (typical Arab lateen-rigged ships) in the Muslim-controlled Indian Ocean and as domestic servants and concubines throughout South and East Asia.

As early as the tenth century, sources mention persons with "lacquer-black bodies" in the possession of wealthy families in Song (Sung) China.[19] In 1178 a Chinese official noted in a memorial to the emperor that Arab traders were shipping thousands of blacks from East Africa to the Chinese port of Guangzhou (Canton) by way of the Malay Archipelago. The Chinese employed these slaves as household servants, as musicians, and, because East Africans were often expert swimmers, as divers to caulk the leaky seams of ships below the water line.

By the thirteenth century, Africans living in many parts of South and East Asia had made significant economic and cultural contributions to their societies. Neither Asian nor Western scholars have adequately explored this subject. It appears, however, that in Indian, Chinese, and East African markets, slaves were never as valuable a commodity as ivory. Thus the volume of the eastern slave trade did not approach that of the trans-Saharan trade.[20]

South Africa

South Africa, the region bordered on the northwest by tropical grasslands and on the northeast by the Zambezi River (see Map 10.3), enjoys a mild and temperate climate. Desert conditions prevail along the Atlantic coast, which gets less than five inches of annual rainfall. Eastward, rainfall increases, though some areas receive less than twenty inches a year. Although the Limpopo Valley in the east is very dry, temperate grasslands characterize the highlands to the north and northwest (the region of the modern Orange Free State, the Transvaal, and Zimbabwe). Considerable variations in climate occur throughout much of South Africa from year to year.

Located at the southern extremity of the Afro-Eurasian landmass, South Africa has a history that is very different from the histories of West Africa, the Nile Valley, and the east coast. Over the centuries, North and West Africa felt the influences of Phoenician, Greek, Roman, and Muslim cultures; the Nile Valley experienced the impact of major Egyptian, Assyrian, Persian, and Muslim civilizations; and the coast of East Africa had important contacts across the Indian Ocean with southern and eastern Asia and across the Red Sea with Arabia and Persia. South Africa, however, remained far removed from the outside world until the arrival of the Portuguese in the late fifteenth century—with one important exception. Bantu-speaking people reached South Africa in the eighth century. They brought with them skills in ironworking and mixed farming (settled crop production plus cattle and sheep raising) and an immunity to the kinds of diseases that later decimated the Amerindians of South America (see pages 524–525).

The earliest residents of South Africa were hunters and gatherers. In the first millennium after the birth of Christ, new farming techniques from the north arrived. A lack of water and timber (which were needed to produce the charcoal used in iron smelting) slowed the spread of iron technology and tools and thus of crop production in western South Africa. These advances, however, reached the western coastal region by 1500. By that date Khoisan-speakers were farming in the arid western regions. To the east, descendants of Bantu immigrants grew sorghum, raised sheep and cattle, and fought with iron-headed spears. They practiced polygamy and traced their descent in the male line.

In 1871 a German explorer discovered the ruined city of Great Zimbabwe southeast of the modern Rhodesian town of Fort Victoria. Archaeologists consider Great Zimbabwe the most

Ruins of Great Zimbabwe   Considered the most impressive monument in the African interior south of the Ethiopian highlands, these ruins of Great Zimbabwe consist of two complexes of dry-stone buildings, some surrounded by a massive serpentine wall 32 feet high and 17 feet thick at its maximum. Great Zimbabwe was the center of a state whose wealth rested on gold. *(Source: Robert Aberman/Barbara Heller Archive/Art Resource, NY)*

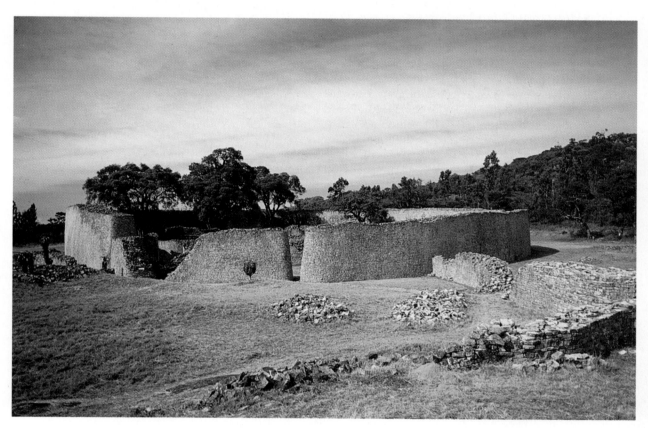

powerful monument in Africa south of the Nile Valley and the Ethiopian highlands. The ruins consist of two vast complexes of dry-stone buildings, a fortress, and an elliptically shaped enclosure commonly called the Temple. Stone carvings, gold and copper ornaments, and Asian ceramics once decorated the buildings. The ruins extend over sixty acres and are encircled by a massive wall. The entire city was built from local granite between the eleventh and fifteenth centuries without any outside influence.

These ruins tell a remarkable story. Great Zimbabwe was the political and religious capital of a vast empire. During the first millennium A.D., settled crop cultivation, cattle raising, and work in metal led to a steady buildup in population in the Zambezi-Limpopo region. The area also contained a rich gold-bearing belt. Gold ore lay near the surface; alluvial gold lay in the Zambezi River tributaries. In the tenth century the inhabitants collected the alluvial gold by panning and washing; after the year 1000 the gold was worked in open mines with iron picks. Traders shipped the gold eastward to Sofala (see Map 10.3). The wealth and power of Great Zimbabwe rested on this gold trade.[21]

Great Zimbabwe declined in the fifteenth century, perhaps because the area had become agriculturally exhausted and could no longer support the large population. Some people migrated northward and settled in the valley of the Mazoe River, a tributary of the Zambezi. This region also contained gold, and there the settlers built a new empire in the tradition of Great Zimbabwe. Rulers of this empire were called "Mwene Mutapa," and their power too was based on the gold trade carried on by means of the Zambezi River and Indian Ocean ports. It was this gold that the Portuguese sought when they arrived on the East African coast in the late fifteenth century.

Summary

In the fifteenth century, the African continent contained a number of very different societies and civilizations. In West Africa, Mali continued the brisk trade in gold, salt, and slaves that had originated many centuries earlier. Islam, which had spread to sub-Saharan Africa through the caravan trade, had tremendous influence on the peoples of the western Sudan, their administrative forms, and their cities. The impact of the Islamic faith was also felt in East Africa, whose bustling port cities were in touch with the cultures of the Mediterranean and the Indian Ocean. While the city-states of the eastern coast conducted complicated mercantile activities with foreign powers, the Christian kingdom of Ethiopia led an isolated, inward-looking existence. In South Africa, the vast empire of Great Zimbabwe was giving way to yet another kingdom whose power was based on precious gold.

Notes

1. See J. Hiernaux, *The People of Africa* (New York: Scribner's, 1975), pp. 46–48.
2. "African Historical Demography" (proceedings of a seminar held in the Centre of African Studies, University of Edinburgh, April 29–30, 1977), p. 3.
3. Quoted in R. W. July, *Precolonial Africa: An Economic and Social History* (New York: Scribner's, 1975), p. 135.
4. J. S. Trimingham, *Islam in West Africa* (Oxford: Oxford University Press, 1959), pp. 6–9.
5. R. A. Austen, *Africa in Economic History* (London: James Currey/Heinemann, 1987), p. 36.
6. R. A. Austen, "The Trans-Saharan Slave Trade: A Tentative Census," in *The Uncommon Market: Essays in the Economic History of the Atlantic Slave Trade,* ed. H. A. Gemery and J. S. Hogendorn (New York: Academic Press, 1979), pp. 1–71, esp. p. 66.
7. July, *Precolonial Africa,* pp. 124–129.
8. Quoted in J. O. Hunwick, "Islam in West Africa, A.D. 1000–1800," in *A Thousand Years of West African History,* ed. J. F. Ade Ajayi and I. Espie (New York: Humanities Press, 1972), pp. 244–245.
9. Quoted in A. A. Boahen, "Kingdoms of West Africa, c. A.D. 500–1600," in *The Horizon History of Africa* (New York: American Heritage, 1971), p. 183.
10. Al-Bakri, *Kitab al-mughrib fdhikr bilad Ifriqiya wa'l-Maghrib (Description de l'Afrique Septentrionale),* trans. De Shane (Paris: Adrien-Maisonneuve, 1965), pp. 328–329.
11. Quoted in R. Oliver and C. Oliver, eds., *Africa in the Days of Exploration* (Englewood Cliffs, N.J.: Prentice-Hall, 1965), p. 10.
12. Quoted in Boahen, "Kingdoms of West Africa, c. A.D. 500–1600," p. 184.

13. Quoted in E. J. Murphy, *History of African Civilization* (New York: Delta, 1972), p. 109.
14. Quoted ibid., p. 111.
15. Quoted ibid., p. 120.
16. Quoted in Oliver and Oliver, *Africa in the Days of Exploration,* p. 18.
17. H. N. Chittick, "The Peopling of the East African Coast," in *East Africa and the Orient: Cultural Syntheses in Pre-Colonial Times,* ed. H. N. Chittick and R. I. Rotberg (New York: Africana Publishing, 1975), p. 19.
18. July, *Precolonial Africa,* p. 209.
19. See Austen, "The Trans-Saharan Slave Trade," p. 65; J. H. Harris, *The African Presence in Asia* (Evanston, Ill.: Northwestern University Press, 1971), pp. 3–6, 27–30; and P. Wheatley, "Analecta Sino-Africana Recensa," in Chittick and Rotberg, *East Africa and the Orient,* p. 109.
20. See I. Hrbek, ed., *Africa from the Seventh to the Eleventh Century, General History of Africa,* vol. 3 (Berkeley: University of California Press; New York: UNESCO, 1991), pp. 294–295, 346–347.
21. P. Curtin et al., *African History,* rev. ed. (New York: Longman, 1984), pp. 284–287.

SUGGESTED READING

The titles by Austen, Chittick, Curtin et al., Hiernaux, Hrbek, and Wheatley listed in the Notes represent some of the most reliable scholarship on early African history, and they are especially recommended. Most contain useful bibliographies. The enterprising student should also see B. Davidson, *African Civilization Revisited* (1991), a useful collection of primary documents with material on all parts of Africa; R. O. Collins, ed., *Problems in African History: The Precolonial Centuries* (1993), another collection of sources; and V. B. Khapoya, *The African Experience* (1994), and R. Oliver, *The African Experience* (1991), both of which offer broad interpretations.

For specific topics in early African history, see, in addition to the topics in the Notes, J. Suret-Canale, "The Traditional Societies in Tropical Africa and the Concept of the 'Asiatic Production,'" in J. Suret-Canale, *Essays on African History* (1988), which explores a Marxist understanding of pre-colonial African societies. For the east coast, see J. de Vere Allen, *Swahili Origins* (1993), a study of the problem of Swahili identity; R. Oliver and G. Mathews, eds., *History of East Africa* (1963), perhaps still the standard general work on this part of the continent; and G. S. P. Freeman-Grenville, *The East African Coast: Select Documents from the First to the Earlier Nineteenth Century* (1962), which has valuable material from Arabic, Chinese, and Portuguese perspectives. The works of J. S. Trimingham, *A History of Islam in West Africa* (1970) and *Islam in East Africa* (1974), remain standard studies on the important issue of Islam. J. Kritzeck and W. H. Lewis, eds., *Islam in Africa* (1969), and M. Lombard, *The Golden Age of Islam* (1975), are also helpful. For the importance of the camel to African trade, R. W. Bulliet, *The Camel and the Wheel* (1975), is basic.

Students interested in the art of early Africa will find the following titles provocative and attractively produced: K. Ezra, *Royal Art of Benin* (1992); E. Eyo and F. Willett, *Treasures of Ancient Nigeria* (1980); and P. Ben-Amos, *The Art of Benin* (1980), which describes the political, social, and religious significance of Benin art through beautiful illustrations.

The Epic of Old Mali

Just as the Greek epic poems the Iliad *and the* Odyssey *serve as essential sources for the early history of ancient Greece, so the testimony of African griots provide information about early West African societies. There were three classes of griots. Musician-entertainers in the service of nobles formed the lowest group. In the middle group were griots who acted as praise-singers of kings and as their advisers. "Traditionalists" who were attached to a royal household and whose function was to recite from memory in sung poems the royal family's historic traditions and to stress the family's rights and precedence constituted the highest-ranking griots. The Mandinke griot Djeli Mamadou Kouyate was a member of this third group. This selection is from the beginning of his account of old Mali, which is an important source for the early history of the kingdom of Mali.*

I am a griot. It is I, Djeli Mamadou Kouyate, son of Bintou Kouyate and Djeli Kediane Kouyate, master in the art of eloquence. Since time immemorial the Kouyates have been in the service of the Keita princes of Mali; we are vessels of speech, we are the repositories which harbor secrets many centuries old. The art of eloquence has no secrets for us; without us the names of kings would vanish into oblivion, we are the memory of mankind; by the spoken word we bring to life the deeds and exploits of kings for younger generations. . . . I know the list of all the sovereigns who succeeded to the throne of Mali. . . . I teach kings the history of their ancestors so that the lives of the ancients might serve them as an example, for the world is old, but the future springs from the past. . . . Listen to my word, you who want to know; by my mouth you will learn the history of Mali. . . . Listen to the story of the Buffalo. I am going to tell you of Maghan Sundiata, of Mari-Djata, of Sogolon Djata, of Nare Maghan Djata: the man of many names against whom sorcery could avail nothing. . . . Listen then, sons of Mali, children of the black people, listen to my word, for I am going to tell you of Sundiata, the father of the Bright Country, of the savanna land, the ancestor of those who draw the bow, the master of a hundred vanished kings.

Questions for Analysis

1. How did Djeli Mamadou Kouyate secure his position as a griot?

2. What did Kouyate understand his social function to be?

3. According to Kouyate, what purpose did history serve among the Mali? Does this purpose resemble that among any other people you have studied, such as the Christians, Muslims, or Chinese?

4. Consider the value of oral history for the modern historian.

Source: B. Davidson, *African Civilization Revisited* (Trenton, N.J.: Africa World Press, 1991), p. 90.

A griot retells the history of his people. *(Source: Bibliothèque Nationale, Paris)*

Tai-tsung receiving Tibetan Envoy, by Yen Li-pên (d. 673); ink and color on silk. *(Source: The Palace Museum Beijing. Photo: Wan-go Weng)*

Between approximately 320 and 1400 the various societies of Asia continued to evolve their own distinct social, political, and religious institutions. These years saw momentous changes sweep across Asia. The tide of change surged back and forth between East and West. In the first half of the period Arab conquerors and their new Muslim faith reached the Indian subcontinent and Afghanistan. In central Asia they met the Turks moving westward from the borders of China. The result of this contact was widespread conversion of the Turks to Islam. Muslim Turks then spread their new religion to northern India, which they conquered. Others continued westward, settling in Anatolia and sinking the ethnic and cultural roots of modern Turkey. Meanwhile, Japan emerged into the light of history. Although affected by Chinese culture, philosophy, and religion, the Japanese adapted these influences to their way of life.

In the second half of the period the Mongols swept from their homeland north of China. They conquered China and unsuccessfully hurled two vast fleets at Japan. Toward the end of the period, the travels of the Venetian merchant Marco Polo to Beijing (Peking) gave promise of a new era of East-West contact.

- What effect did these great movements of peoples have on the traditional societies of Asia?
- How were new religious and cultural ideas received by the long-established cultures of the East?
- What political and economic effects did these events have on newcomer and native alike?

This chapter explores these three questions.

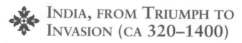

INDIA, FROM TRIUMPH TO INVASION (CA 320–1400)

Under the Gupta kings, India enjoyed one of the most magnificent cultural flowerings in its long history. By about 800 the caste system (see pages 71–72) had fully evolved, dividing Indian society into thousands of self-contained subcastes. The incursion of the Muslim Turks—the second permanent foreign influence on India—introduced a new religion that also accelerated the decline of Buddhism in India.

The Gupta Empire (ca 320–480)

For years after the end of Mauryan power, India suffered fragmentation and foreign domination, though even political turmoil did not interrupt the evolution of Indian culture. Not until about 320 did another line of Indian kings, the Guptas, extend their authority over much of the subcontinent. Founded by Chandragupta—unrelated to the founder of the Mauryan Empire by the same name—the Guptas' original home was in the area of modern Bihar in the Ganges Valley (Map 11.1). The Guptas consciously modeled their rule after that of the Mauryan Empire. Although the Guptas failed to restore Ashoka's empire, they united northern India and received tribute from states in Nepal and the Indus Valley. They also gave large parts of India a period of peace and political unity.

The real creator of the Gupta Empire was Chandragupta's son Samudragupta (ca 335–375), who defeated many of the rulers of southern India and then restored them to their thrones as his subjects. With frontier states he made alliances, and over them he extended his protection. By means of military conquest and political shrewdness, Samudragupta brought much of India from the Himalayas in the north to the Vindhya Mountains in the south under his government.

Samudragupta boasted of his accomplishments:

His far-reaching fame, deep-rooted in peace, emanated from the restoration of the sovereignty of many fallen royal families. . . . He, who had no equal in power in the world, eclipsed the fame of the other kings by the radiance of his versatile virtues, adorned by innumerable good actions. He, who was enigmatic, was the real force that generated good and destroyed the evil. Having a compassionate heart, he could easily be won over by faithfulness, loyalty, and homage.[1]

In fact, Samudragupta had reason to boast of his accomplishments. By putting an end to weakness and fragmentation, he laid the foundations of India's golden age.

Under Samudragupta's son Chandragupta II (ca 375–415), the glory of the Guptas reached its height. Perhaps Chandragupta's most significant exploit was the overthrow of the Shakas (invaders from the borders of China) in western India. As a result, the busy maritime trade between western India and the Middle East and China came under

MAP 11.1 Political Map of India from ca 400 to ca 1294   This map and inset show the political face of India from the time of the imperial Guptas to the arrival of Muslim invaders. They also demonstrate the importance of the Indus and Ganges river valleys, perhaps the most coveted area in India.

the protection of the Guptas, and the Indian people were once again in direct touch with the wider world.

The great crisis of the Gupta Empire was the invasion of the Huns. The migration of these nomads from central Asia shook the known world. By at least 450 a group of them known as the White Huns thundered into India. Mustering his full might, the ruler Skandagupta (ca 455–467) threw back the invaders. Although the Huns failed to uproot the Gupta Empire, they dealt the dynasty a fatal blow. By 500 the glory of the Gupta kings was past. Soon the country once again reverted to a pattern of local kingdoms in constant conflict.

Even though the Guptas failed to unite India permanently, they saved India for a period from political fragmentation, foreign domination, and

confusion. The peace they established released cultural and intellectual energies that shaped one of the sunniest epochs in India's long history. A prominent feature was interest in the literature of the Aryans, written in Sanskrit, which was the spoken language of India. Sanskrit masterpieces were preserved, and traditional epic poems and verses on mythological themes were reworked and polished. The Gupta period also saw the rise of Indian drama. India's greatest poet, Kalidasa (ca 380–450), like Shakespeare, melded poetry and drama. Poets composed epics for the courts of the Gupta kings, and other writers experimented with prose romances and popular tales.

The Guptas also made a lasting impact on Indian religion. For political purposes they promoted Hinduism to the detriment of Buddhism. In effect,

The Mriga Jataka   The Buddhist caves at Ajanta contain the most important surviving collection of wall paintings from the Gupta period. Religious in inspiration, they are also spontaneous and unrestrained, as this detail of a royal servant holding an energetic dog on a leash reflects. (*Source: Satish Pavashav/Dinodia Picture Agency*)

they pushed Buddhism into decline. By the time that Islam reached India, Buddhism had virtually disappeared. In the future, India would be divided between Muslim and Hindu.

In science, too, the Gupta period could boast of impressive intellectual achievements. Science never appealed to the Indians as much as religion, but Indian mathematicians arrived at the concept of zero, which is necessary for higher mathematics. Other scientific thinkers wrestled with the concept of gravitation centuries before Sir Isaac Newton (1642–1727).

Daily Life in India

The first reliable and abundant information about the daily life of the Indian people dates from the period of the Gupta Empire. One of the most instructive and, to modern minds, amazing characteristics of Indian society is its remarkable stability and veneration for its age-old customs and traditions. Indian society changed slowly, so it is possible to take a look at daily life and social customs in the millennium between the fourth and fourteenth centuries.

Although Indian agriculture ranged from subsistence farming to the working of huge estates, agricultural life ordinarily meant village life. The average farmer worked a small plot of land outside the village, aided by the efforts of the extended family. All the family members pooled their resources—human, animal, and material—under the direction of the head of the family. Shared work, shared sacrifice, and joint confrontation of hazards strengthened family ties. The Indian farming family usually lived close to the bone: bad weather and heavy taxes frequently condemned its members to a lean year of poverty and hardship.

To all Indian farmers, rich and poor, water supply was crucial. India's great scourge is merciless droughts, which cause plants to wither, the earth to crack, and famine to stalk the countryside. Indian farmers quickly learned to drill deep into the ground to tap permanent sources of water. They also irrigated their fields by diverting rivers and digging reservoirs and canals. As in Hammurabi's Mesopotamia, maintenance of waterworks demanded constant effort, and disputes over water rights often led to local quarrels.

The agricultural year began with spring plowing. The ancient plow, drawn by two oxen wearing yokes and collars, had an iron-tipped share and a handle with which the farmer guided it. Similar plows are still used in parts of India. Once plowed and sown, the land yielded a rich variety of crops. Rice, the most important and popular grain, was sown at the beginning of the long rainy season. Beans, lentils, and peas were the farmer's friends, for they grew during the cold season and were harvested in the spring when fresh food was scarce. Cereal crops like wheat, barley, and millet provided carbohydrates and other nutrients. Large estates grew sugar cane. Some families cultivated vegetables, spices, and flowers in their gardens. Village orchards kept people supplied with fruit, and the inhabitants of well-situated villages could eat their fill of fresh and dried fruit and sell the surplus at a nearby town.

Indian farmers raised and bred livestock. Most highly valued were cattle. They were used for plowing and esteemed for their milk. Their hides and horns were precious raw materials, as were the fleeces of sheep. All the animals of the community were in the hands of the village cowherd or shepherd, who led them to and from pasture and protected them from wild animals and thieves.

Farmers fortunate enough to raise surpluses found ready markets in towns and cities. There they came into contact with merchants and traders, some of whom dealt in local commodities and others in East-West trade. Like their Muslim counterparts, Indian merchants enjoyed a respectable place in society. There were huge profits to be made in foreign commerce. Daring Indian sailors founded new trading centers along the coasts of Southeast Asia and in the process spread Indian culture. Other Indian merchants specialized in the caravan trade that continued to link China, Iran, India, and the West.

Local craftsmen and tradesmen lived and worked in specific parts of a town or village. Their shops were open to the street; the family lived on the floor above. The busiest tradesmen dealt in milk and cheese, oil, spices, and perfumes. Equally prominent but disreputable were tavernkeepers. Indian taverns were haunts of criminals and con artists, and in the worst of them fighting was as common as drinking. In addition to these tradesmen and merchants a host of peddlers shuffled through towns and villages selling everything from bath salts to fresh-cut flowers.

Leatherworkers were economically important but were considered *outcastes* (those without places in the traditional social structure). Indian religious and social customs condemned those who made a living handling the skins of dead animals. Masons, carpenters, and brickmakers were more highly respected. As in all agricultural societies, blacksmiths were essential. Pottery was used in all households, but Indian potters, unlike their counterparts in the ancient Near East and the Greco-Roman world, neither baked their wares in kilns nor decorated them. The economic life of the village, then, consisted of a harmonious balance of agriculture and small business.

What of the village itself—its people and its daily sights? Encircled by walls, the typical village was divided into quarters by two main streets that intersected at the center of the village. The streets were unpaved, and the rainy season turned them into a muddy soup. Cattle and sheep roamed as freely as people. The villagers shared their simple houses with such household pets as cats, parrots, and geese. Half-wild mongooses served as effective protection against snakes. The pond outside the village served as its main source of water and also as a spawning ground for fish, birds, and mosquitoes. Women drawing water frequently encountered water buffaloes wallowing in the shallows. After the farmers returned from the fields in the evening, the village gates were closed until morning.

The period following the fall of the Guptas saw the slow proliferation and hardening of the caste system. Early Indian society was divided into four major groups: priests (*Brahman*), warriors (*Kshatriya*), peasants (*Vaishya*) and serfs (*Shudra*) (see page 72). Further subdivisions arose, reflecting differences in trade or profession, tribal or racial affiliation, religious belief, and place of residence. By about 800 these distinctions had solidified into an approximation of the caste system as it is known today. Eventually Indian society comprised perhaps as many as three thousand castes. Each caste had its own governing body, which enforced the rules of the caste. Those incapable of living up to the rules were expelled, becoming outcastes. These unfortunates lived hard lives, performing tasks that others considered unclean or lowly.

For all members of Indian society, regardless of caste, marriage and the family were the focus of life. Once again, far more is known about the upper levels of society than about the lower levels. As in earlier eras, the Indian family of this period was an extended family: grandparents, uncles and aunts, cousins, and nieces and nephews all lived together in the same house or compound. The joint family was under the authority of the eldest male, who might even take several wives. The family affirmed its solidarity by the religious ritual of honoring its dead ancestors—a ritual that linked the living and the dead.

Special attention was devoted to the raising of sons, but all children were pampered. The great poet Kalidasa depicts children as the greatest joy of their father's life:

With their teeth half-shown in causeless laughter,
and their efforts at talking so sweetly uncertain,
when children ask to sit on his lap
a man is blessed, even by the dirt on their bodies.[2]

Children in poor households worked as soon as they were able. Children in wealthier households faced the age-old irritations of reading, writing, and arithmetic. Less attention was paid to daughters, though in the most prosperous families they were usually literate.

Boys of the three upper castes underwent a religious initiation symbolizing a second birth. Ideally, they then entered into a period of asceticism and religious training at the hands of *gurus,* Brahman teachers with whom the boys boarded. In reality,

Young Girl Writing This illustration catches, like a photograph, a young girl writing on a tablet. The artist portrays her attentiveness to her work and her natural grace. She was more fortunate than most women in the ancient world: literacy among women was uncommon and in some cases was considered undesirable. *(Source: Indian Museum, Calcutta/Dinodia Picture Agency)*

relatively few went through this expensive education. Having completed their education, young men were ready to lead adult lives, the first and foremost step in which was marriage.

Child-marriage, unknown in earlier periods, later became customary. Indians considered child-marriage desirable, in part because of their attitudes toward women. Girls were thought to be unusually fascinated by sex. Lawgivers feared that young girls left to their own whims would take lovers as soon as they reached puberty and become pregnant before they were married. Girls who had lost their virginity could seldom hope to find good husbands; most became financial burdens and social disgraces to their families. Daughters were customarily betrothed before their first menstrual period, often to men whom they had never seen. The wedding and consummation of the marriage did not take place until after a girl had reached puberty and could start a family.

After an elaborate wedding ceremony, a newly married couple set up quarters in the house or compound of the bridegroom's father. In contrast to ancient Jewish practice, newlyweds were not expected to consummate their marriage on the first night. Indian custom delicately acknowledged that two strangers, though married, might need some time to adjust to their new mode of life.

An Indian wife had two main duties: to manage the house and to produce children, preferably sons. Her husband was her master, to whom she owed obedience. Indian women spent their entire lives, from childhood to old age, under the authority of men. Indian law was blunt:

A woman is not independent, the males are her masters. . . . Their fathers protect them in childhood, their husbands protect them in youth, and their sons protect them in age; a woman is never fit for independence.[3]

Denied a significant role in life outside the home, wives made the household their domain. All domestic affairs were under their control. As a rule, women rarely left the house, and then only with a chaperone. Among one stratum of high-caste Hindus, the Kshatriyas, wives' bonds with their husbands were so strong that it was felt a wife should have no life apart from her husband. A widow was expected to perform the act of *sati,* throwing herself on his funeral pyre. Yet there is reason to think that this custom did not become common practice.

Within the home, the position of a wife often depended chiefly on her own intelligence and strength of character. In the best of cases a wife was considered a part of her husband, his friend and comforter as well as his wife. Wives were traditionally supposed to be humble, cheerful, and diligent even toward worthless husbands. In reality, some women, far from being docile, ruled the roost. An Indian verse paints a vivid picture of what a henpecked husband could expect:

But when she has him in her clutches
*   it's all housework and errands!*
"Fetch a knife to cut this gourd!"
*   "Get me some fresh fruit!"*

"We want wood to boil the greens,
*   and for a fire in the evening!"*
"Now paint my feet!"
*   "Come and massage my back!"*

So . . . resist the wiles of women,
*   avoid their friendship and company.*
The little pleasure you get from them
*   will only lead you into trouble!*[4]

Most women, however, were frankly and unashamedly subservient to their husbands. Nevertheless, despite the severe limitations of her society, the typical wife lived her days honored, cherished, and loved by her husband and family.

The most eagerly desired event was the birth of children. Marriage had no other purpose. Before consummating their marriage, the newlyweds repeated traditional prayers for the wife to become pregnant immediately. While pregnant, the wife was treated like a queen, nearly suffocated with affection and attention, and rigorously circumscribed by religious ritual. At labor and birth, while the women of the household prepared for the birth, the husband performed rituals intended to guarantee an easy delivery and a healthy child. After the birth, the parents performed rituals intended to bring the baby happiness, prosperity, and desirable intellectual, physical, and moral qualities. Infants were pampered until they reached the age of schooling and preparation for the adult world.

India and Southeast Asia

Between about 650 and 1250, Indian merchants and missionaries disseminated Indian culture throughout Southeast Asia. The earlier history of the area is the product of archaeological studies. So far the evidence has allowed scholars to trace the movements of numerous peoples without being able to tell very much about them. It is known that Indian penetration of Southeast Asia changed things considerably, and Sanskrit gave peoples a common mode of written expression. The demands of trade frequently led to small Indian settlements, generally located on the coast, stretching from modern Thailand in the west to the Mekong Delta of modern Vietnam (Map 11.2). In these trading posts Indians met natives, and the result was often intermarriage and the creation of a cul-ture fertilized by both. The greatest influence of India on Southeast Asian societies came in the courts of local rulers, who often adopted Indian customs and values, embraced Hinduism and Buddhism, and learned Sanskrit.

Although there is no denying Indian influence on Southeast Asia, its strength should not be exaggerated. Outside the courts of the rulers, native societies maintained their own cultural identity even when they assimilated various Indian customs. Perhaps two examples can illustrate the process. Taking up the *Ramayana,* an Indian epic poem describing the deeds of the Vedic heroes, the Javanese retained the essentials of the Indian narrative but added to it native Javanese legends, thus creating a work that did not belong solely to either culture. So, too, with religion. Early peoples in the region of Cambodia and in Tibet adapted Buddhism to

MAP 11.2 States of Southeast Asia from ca 650 to ca 1250   This map illustrates the greatest extent of several major Southeast Asian states. The boundaries are somewhat approximate, for states gained and lost territory several times during this long period.

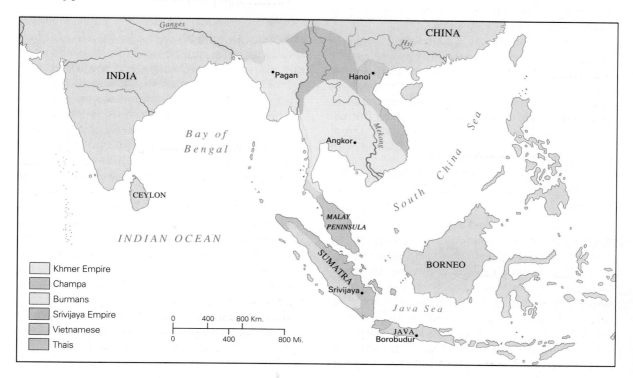

their own values, attitudes, and customs. In both cases local tradition shaped Buddhism in its own likeness.

When the Indians entered Southeast Asia, they encountered both indigenous peoples and newcomers moving southward from the frontiers of China. Their relations with these peoples varied greatly. Contact with the vigorous tribes moving into the southern areas of the mainland was generally peaceful. But commercial rivalry sometimes led to active warfare with the native states in the Malay Peninsula and the islands of the Indian Ocean. Although many of the events of these years are imperfectly known, a fairly clear picture has emerged of the situation in the region (see Map 11.2).

On the mainland three major groups of newcomers pushed southward toward the Indian Ocean from the southern borders of China. Their movements entailed prolonged fighting. As in other such extensive migrations, the newcomers fought one another as often as they fought the native populations. The Vietnamese, the group least influenced by Indian culture, established themselves on the eastern coast of the mainland. In 939 they became independent of China and extended their power southward along the coast of present-day Vietnam. The Thais lived to the west in what is today southwestern China and northern Burma. In the eighth century the Thai tribes united in a confederacy and even expanded northward against Tang China; like China, however, the Thai confederacy fell to the Mongols in 1253. Still farther west another tribal people, the Burmans, migrated in the eighth century to the area of modern Burma. They too established a state, which they ruled from their capital, Pagan, and came into contact with India and Ceylon.

The most important mainland state was the Khmer Empire of Cambodia, which controlled the heart of the region. The Khmers were indigenous to the area, and by around 400 they had created an independent state. Founded in 802, their empire eventually extended its southern borders to the sea and the northeastern Malay Peninsula. Generally successful in a long series of wars with the Vietnamese, the Khmers reached the peak of their power in 1219 and then declined.

Far different from these land-based states was the maritime empire of Srivijaya, which originated as a city-state on the island of Sumatra. Like the Khmers, the people of Srivijaya were indigenous.

Their wealth was based on seaborne trade and on tolls that they exacted from ships passing through their waters. Their navy ruled the waters around Sumatra, Borneo, and Java. Though long predominant in the area, Srivijaya suffered a stunning blow in 1025: a commercial rival in southern India launched a large naval raid that succeeded in capturing the king and capital of the empire. Unable to hold their gains, the Indians retreated, but the Srivijaya Empire never recovered its former vigor. By the mid-thirteenth century the arrival of Chinese traders further weakened the empire, and eventually it fell to local rivals.

Although the political histories of all these peoples varied, their responses to Indian culture were similar. The coastal states, influenced by the presence of trading stations, were the first to adopt and adapt Indian ways. The very concept of kingship came from India. Local rulers and their elites, like good Indian kings, began to observe *dharma* (the moral law) and to govern their peoples by its precepts. Sanskrit, both the Indian language and the script in which it was written, surmounted the barriers raised by the many different native languages of the region. Indian mythology took hold, as did Indian architecture and sculpture. Some of the world's greatest edifices were erected in central Java and Cambodia, inspired by Indian building principles, techniques, and cultural ideals. Kings and their courts, the first to embrace Indian culture, consciously spread it to their subjects.

Indian religion was also instrumental in this process. Certain aspects of Hinduism proved popular, but Buddhism took Southeast Asia by storm. Buddhism emphasized the value of popular education, and its temples, monasteries, and missionaries helped bring education to the common people. Especially influential was the Buddhist concept of the *bodhisattva*, a buddha-in-becoming (see page 80). Inspired by this ideal, many kings and local rulers strove to give their subjects good and humane government. Buddhist missionaries from India played a prominent role in these developments. Local converts continued the process by making pilgrimages to India and Sri Lanka to worship and to observe Indian life for themselves.

By the twelfth century, Indian culture, secular and religious, had found a permanent new home in Southeast Asia. The process was for the most part peaceful; unlike the case with Western newcomers in modern times, no truly forced colonization

✻ **Angkor Wat** This aerial view of Angkor Wat illustrates the great artistic achievements of the Khmers, who planned and built this architectural monument. The temple also reflects Indian influence, for the god chiefly honored here is Vishnu. *(Source: Photography Collection, Harry Ransom Humanities Research Center, the University of Texas at Austin)*

seems to have occurred. Chinese influence flourished more strongly among the Vietnamese, and Islam would later rival Buddhism; but Indian culture persisted, especially in the southern part of the region. Seldom has the world seen such a protracted and pervasive cultural diffusion. It stands as a monument to the vitality and magnetism of Indian civilization.

India Under Siege

Between roughly 650 and 1400 India experienced turmoil and invasion as wave after wave of foreign armies moved into the subcontinent. Arabs, Turks, and Mongols all swept into India. Particularly during the six centuries from 636 to 1296, invaders

beat against India and its neighbors. This complex and imperfectly understood phenomenon had four distinct phases. The Muslim Arabs' attack on the Sind area (636–713) was followed by the battle for Afghanistan (643–870). Muslims next pushed into the Punjab (870–1030) and finally conquered the valley of the Ganges (1175–1206). Between onslaughts, conflict persisted between newcomer and native.

Arabs under the leadership of Muhammad ibn-Qasim reached the western coast of modern Pakistan in 636 and pushed on into the Sind and the Indus Valley (see Map 11.1). But the Islamic conquest of northern India came at the hands of Turkish converts to Islam. While huge numbers of Turks advanced on the Byzantine Empire and won

INDIA, CA 320–CA 1400

ca 320–480	Gupta Empire
ca 380–450	Kalidasa, India's greatest poet
636–1206	Muslim invasions of India
ca 1193	Destruction of Buddhism in India
1290–1320	Sultanate of Delhi
1398	Timur conquers the Punjab and Delhi

control of Asia Minor, others remained in the East. In 986 Sabuktigin, a Turkish chieftain in Afghanistan and a devout Muslim, launched his initial raid into the Punjab. Once again, India suffered its age-old fate: invasion by a strong and confident power through the northwestern corridor. Sabuktigin's son Mahmud stepped up the frequency and intensity of the raids until he had won the Punjab. Then, like other invaders before him, he began pushing toward the Ganges. Mahmud systematically looted secular palaces and Hindu shrines, and he destroyed Indian statues as infidel idols. Even the Arab conquerors of the Sind fell to him. The Indus Valley, the Punjab, and the rest of northwestern India were in the grip of the invader.

Mahmud's death gave India roughly a century and a half of fitful peace marred by local conflicts. Then a new line of Turkish rulers that had arisen in Afghanistan, with its capital at Ghur (see Map 11.1), renewed Muslim attacks on India. After conquering Mahmud's Indian holdings, Muhammad of Ghur struck eastward toward the Ganges in 1192. Muhammad's generals captured Delhi and extended their control nearly throughout northern India. Like Mahmud, Muhammad and his generals considered Hindu and Buddhist religious statues nothing more than idols; Muslim troops destroyed them in vast numbers. Buddhist centers of worship and learning suffered grievously. In 1193 a Turkish raiding party destroyed the great Buddhist university at Nalanda in Bihar. Most Buddhists took refuge from this dual military and religious assault in Tibet and places farther east. Buddhism, which

had thrived so long in peaceful and friendly competition with Hinduism, was pushed out of its native soil by the invaders.

When Muhammad of Ghur fell to an assassin in 1206, one of his generals, the former slave Qutb-ud-din, seized the reins of power and made his capital at Delhi. To prevent assimilation by the far more numerous Indians, the Muslims recruited Turks and Iranians from outside India, many of whom were fleeing the widespread Mongol devastation of Iran and the Middle East. Under the sultanate of Delhi, Iranian influences deeply affected Hindu art and architecture. Iranians introduced the minaret—an essential architectural feature of the mosque—as well as the arch and the dome. So great was the impact of Iranian Muslims that Urdu, the official language of modern Pakistan, evolved as a mixture of Persian with Arabic and Hindi.

The most lasting impact of the invader was religious. Islam replaced Hinduism and Buddhism in the Indus Valley (modern Pakistan) and in Bengal at the mouth of the Ganges (modern Bangladesh). Elsewhere in India, where Muslim influence was far less powerful, Hinduism resisted the newcomers and their religion. Most Indians looked on the successful invaders simply as a new ruling caste, capable of governing and taxing them but otherwise peripheral to their lives. The myriad castes largely governed themselves, isolating the newcomers.

Hinduism enjoyed profound devotion from the Indian people. The years of war and invasion had not hindered the development of a pious, devotional Hinduism called Bhakti. Bhakti emphasized personal reverence for and worship of a Hindu deity such as Krishna, Shiva, or Rama. Bhakti nourished impassioned love of the Hindu gods among ordinary folk. There was a certain amount of mutual borrowing between Islam and Hindu tradition. But in general, Hinduism's beliefs and social organization had a strong hold over the people of India; roughly 75 percent remained Hindu.

By about 1400 India was as politically divided as it had been before the Gupta Empire. Yet the events of the preceding millennium had had more than political and military significance. The march of armies had brought Islam into India and driven out Buddhism. Meanwhile, Hinduism had flourished. These developments were to be critically important for the future of the entire region, for in them lie the origins of the modern nations of India, Pakistan, and Bangladesh.

CHINA'S GOLDEN AGE (580–CA 1400)

The years between the fall of the Han Dynasty in the third century and the rise of the Ming in the fourteenth brought some of China's brightest days and some of its darkest. During this period the Chinese absorbed foreign influences, notably Buddhism, that fundamentally shaped their society. Chinese cultural traditions, especially Confucianism, drew new strength and vitality from abroad. This was a golden era of enormous intellectual and artistic creativity in Chinese history.

Sui, Tang, and Song (Sung) emperors and statesmen reunited the empire, repaired the foundations of national strength, and once again made China one of the world's unrivaled states. Even later political disruption, particularly the invasion of the Mongols, could not undo the achievements of those who shaped the history of these years. The Mongols were the first foreigners ever to rule all of China, but their domination lasted only ninety-seven years, until the Ming emperors once again united the land under a native dynasty.

Buddhism Flourishes in China

Buddhism reached China from the west before the Han Dynasty, but it flourished between the fall of the Han in 220 and the rise of the Sui in 581. Buddhism reached China by means of merchants and travelers from India. It initially won a place for itself in China because it offered a refreshing and novel solution to social disruption and political chaos (see pages 80–81). It was ultimately successful in China because it had powerful appeal for many different segments of society.

To Chinese scholars, the Buddhist concepts of transmigration of souls, karma, and nirvana posed a stimulating intellectual challenge. For rulers the Buddhist church was a source of magical power and a political tool. Because it was neither barbarian nor Chinese, this foreign faith could embrace both groups equally. To the middle and lower classes, Buddhism's egalitarianism came as a breath of fresh air. The lower orders of society had as much chance as the elites to live according to Buddha's precepts. Simple faith and devotion alone could win enlightenment and salvation. For many, regardless of social status, Buddhism's promise of eternal bliss as the reward for a just and upright life was deeply comforting. In a rough and tumultuous age, moreover, Buddhism's emphasis on kindness, charity, and the value of human life offered hope of a better life on earth.

If Buddhism changed Chinese life, China likewise changed Buddhism. Mahayana Buddhism, the more flexible and widespread of Buddhism's two schools (see pages 79–80), gave rise to several new sects responsive to specific Chinese needs. The Tian-tai sect, which later gave rise to the Tendai sect in Japan (see page 336), was favored by Chinese scholars, who attempted to resolve the numerous intellectual problems in Buddhism and to organize its doctrines in keeping with traditional Chinese thought. Most popular was the Pure Land sect. It too would later have a vast impact on Japanese society. Like its Indian counterpart, this sect was very lenient. Instead of following Buddha's Eightfold Path, people had only to declare their sincere faith in Buddha to reach paradise, the "pure land." Many simple and uneducated people found in the Pure Land sect a comforting route to joy scarcely attainable on earth.

The True Word sect, which won more popularity in Japan than in China, promised adherents immortality through magic, rituals, and chants. The Chan sect, the forerunner of Zen Buddhism in Japan, combined elements of Daoism and Buddhism. Like Daoism itself, Chan dreamed of a return to nature and simplicity. Chan emphasized

❀ **Buddhism Reaches China** This scene illustrates the spread of Buddhism from India to China. The writing at the left, printed in Chinese characters, is a translation of a Buddhist text originally written in Sanskrit. This scene of Buddha addressing a follower is the earliest dated example of block-printing. *(Source: The British Library)*

meditation and preached that individuals were responsible for their own ultimate enlightenment. In this respect Chan was quite similar to Buddha's teaching that each person must tread the path of enlightenment alone. One of the prime reasons for Buddhism's success in China was its extraordinary ability to accommodate itself to local thought, beliefs, and conditions.

Buddhist monks from abroad introduced monasticism to China, and the resulting monasteries became more than merely centers for religious practice and study. Like their Christian counterparts in medieval Europe, Buddhist monasteries played an active role in social, economic, and political life. Buddhist missionary monks traveled the trade routes with Buddhist merchants, who gave

the newly formed monasteries a secular function: increasingly, they entrusted their money and wares to the monasteries for safekeeping, in effect transforming the monasteries into banks and warehouses. Buddhist merchants often endowed monks with money or land to support temples and monasteries. The monks, who thus became powerful landlords, hired peasants to work the monastic and temple lands, and the tenants in turn became ready converts to Buddhism. Formidable in wealth and numbers, monasteries became influential participants in politics, rivaling the power of the traditional Chinese landlords. The monasteries' prosperity and political power further protected converts from local Chinese lords and reinforced the spread of Buddhism.

Buddhism also had a profound impact on the artistic life of China. Buddhist art, like the faith's religious message, first reached China along the Silk Road. At Tun-huang in northwestern China, thousands of artists worked for centuries to transform a mile-long stretch of hillside into a monumental shrine. The life of Buddha offered Chinese painters and sculptors a wealth of new themes. From the fourth century on, Buddha and his life became inseparable from Chinese art.

Thus Buddhism's appeal to the Chinese was religious, social, and artistic. Its message struck a sympathetic chord among nobles and peasants alike. It endowed China with a new view of human dignity, the promise of personal salvation, and a compelling vision of peace.

The Tang Dynasty (618–907)

The Tang emperors rose to greatness on the shoulders of their predecessors, the Sui Dynasty (581–618). Sui land reforms helped to restore prosperity to a storm-tossed land, and Sui waterworks strengthened ties between northern and southern China. The crowning achievement of the Sui was the Grand Canal, connecting the eastern reaches of the Yellow River to the eastern waters of the Huai and Yangtze Rivers (Map 11.3). The canal facilitated the shipping of tax grain from the recently developed Yangtze Delta to the centers of political and military power in northern China. Henceforth the rice-growing Yangtze Valley and southern China generally played an ever more influential role in the country's economic and political life, strengthening China's internal cohesion.

Though successful as reformers, the Sui emperors fell prey to a grim combination of military defeat and massive peasant uprisings. From these unlikely conditions rose the Tang Dynasty (618–907), probably the greatest dynasty in Chinese history. Its founder, who took the imperial name Tai Zong, was an able general and astute politician. He was also an educated and far-sighted administrator who followed conscientiously the lessons of Chinese history. Having seen the results of oppression, Tai Zong avoided extravagance and continued Sui reforms.

Tai Zong tried first to alleviate the poverty of the peasants. Building on the Sui system, he ordered that land be divided among the peasants as equally as possible and that imperial officials safe-

Justice in Court This picture gives an idealized look at the system of law, but that does not mean that it is misleading. A council of judges review the law, examine the testimony, and deliver a verdict. This is a fine example of the mandarin scholar-official serving the state. (*Source: Courtesy, Museum of Fine Arts, Boston. Denman Waldo Ross Collection, Acc. no. 06.317*)

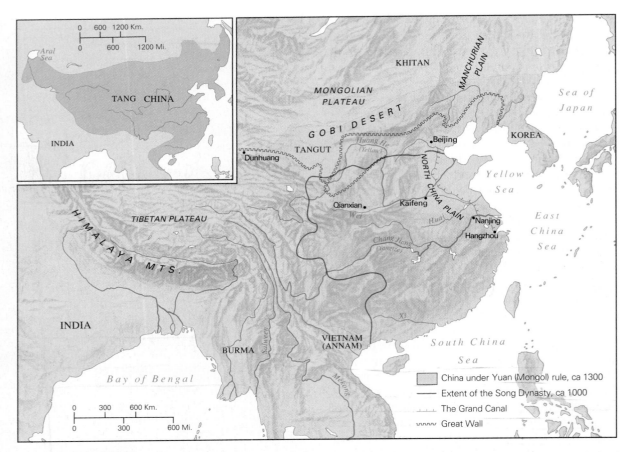

MAP 11.3 **Political Divisions of China from the Tang to the Yuan Dynasty, 618–1368** This map and inset illustrate how the Tang Dynasty and its successors were able to sustain the expanded frontiers of the Han Dynasty, although their hold in the west was always somewhat tenuous.

guard the peasants' holdings. A prosperous peasantry, in Tai Zong's view, would provide a secure and steady base of income for the empire. In practice, the attempt to equalize landholdings quickly broke down, and by 780 the law was revoked. Even so, Tai Zong's efforts were not entirely in vain: he had done enough to give agriculture a much-needed boost, and productivity increased in both grain and livestock. Not since the Han Dynasty had the peasants been so well off.

In the civil sphere, Tang accomplishments far outstripped anything known in Europe until the growth of national states in the seventeenth century. Tang emperors subdivided the administration of the empire into departments, much like the nu-

merous agencies of modern governments. Tang departments oversaw military organization, maintenance and supply of the armies, foreign affairs, administration of justice, finance, building and transportation, education, and much else. During this period no other state on earth was as politically sophisticated as the Tang Empire.

A bureaucracy of this scope demanded huge numbers of educated and trained personnel. Tang emperors revived and expanded the Han method of hiring and promoting government officials on the basis of education, ability, and merit. This process reinforced Confucian values, ethics, and emphasis on scholarship. Candidates for official positions were expected to learn the Confucian classics, to master the rules of poetry, and to discuss practical administrative and political matters. Universities were founded to train able and dedicated young men. Graduates passed a demanding battery of oral and written examinations to prove their ability. Training was hard and long; although students did not endure the physical discipline of Mesopotamian scribes, they sacrificed much to achieve success.

Mandarin scholar-officials also played an important cultural role. Since much of an official's training involved the study of literature, history, and politics, China's literary heritage became integral to contemporary life. Because nearly any literate man in the empire could take the examinations, centers for study sprouted throughout China. Knowledge of the classics spread throughout the empire, fostering cultural unity. The mandarin system became an institution in which people from every part of China could meet on a common ground.

In foreign affairs the Tang turned their attention first to the Turks, who had spread their power from the northern borders of China to the Byzantine Empire in Asia Minor. By Tai Zong's death in 649, Chinese armies had conquered all of Turkestan in the west.

Chinese influence in Tibet came somewhat more peacefully, despite some Sino-Tibetan rivalries and wars. For years the Tibetans had lived a partly nomadic and partly agricultural life on China's western border. Then in the early seventh century one of their chieftains unified the Tibetan tribes and sought a marriage alliance with Tai Zong. The emperor sent his daughter to Tibet with musicians, craftsmen, and technicians to introduce new tools and techniques, along with books on Chinese agricultural methods. The Tibetans modeled their culture partially on the Tang. The Koreans and Japanese adopted Chinese culture more enthusiastically. China's script and literature, Buddhism, crafts, and political ideas and techniques spread widely, making Chinese culture dominant throughout eastern Asia.

The Song Dynasty (960–1279)

In the middle of the eighth century, Tang foreign policy collapsed in rout and rebellion. The defeat of Chinese armies in central Asia and on the south-

Head of the Dragon Just as the Greeks built their Tower of the Four Winds for astronomical functions, so did the astronomer Guo Shoujing. His calculation of the length of the solar year was accurate to within twenty seconds. Like the Greeks, he produced an architectural masterpiece. (*Source: Patrick Lui & Associates*)

western border undercut the emperor's authority. Beginning in 755 powerful generals revolted in response to imperial malfeasance. The Tang Dynasty ended in a conflagration of military rebellions, peasant uprisings, and barbarian invasions. The period from 907 to 960, known as the Era of the Five Dynasties, resembled the age of the barracks emperors of the Roman Empire (see page 205). Weak and distracted, China presented an easy target to the barbarians, and one group of nomads, known as the Khitan, captured Beijing and most of northeastern China and Manchuria.

The founder of the Song Dynasty, the northern general Zhao Kuangyin, made his bid for empire in 960. Against great odds and with great effort Zhou Kuangyin—known as Emperor Song Tai Zu—stabilized northern China and extended control over the south, not only in China but as far as Indonesia.

Despite sporadic warfare, the early Song period enjoyed broad-based prosperity for a variety of demographic and economic reasons. The population had increased to an unprecedented 100 million. Rapidly increasing urbanization went hand in hand with greatly expanded agricultural productivity. Advances in the technology and production of coal and iron also played a significant part, as did improvements in communications. Efficient water transport fostered the development of a national market for domestic products. The tea trade boomed. In the Han period tea had been a luxury item, but during the Tang period tea became immensely popular throughout China. Trade was brisk in other commodities as well. Porcelain continued to be a prime export and domestic product. Salt continued to be a state monopoly.

The political and economic success of the Song permitted the technological innovations of the Tang period to reach full growth. Foremost among them was the invention of printing, which changed the history of China and the entire world. Tang craftsmen developed the art of carving words and pictures onto wooden blocks, inking them, and then pressing the blocks onto paper. Each block consisted of an entire page of text and illustrations. Such whole-page blocks were being printed as early as the middle of the ninth century, and in the eleventh century movable type was invented. Movable type was never widely used in China, but when this Chinese invention reached Europe in the fifteenth century, it revolutionized the communication of ideas. In China as well as in Europe, the invention and spread of printing dramatically increased the availability of books and lowered their price. Scholarship flourished, and literacy spread rapidly among the general population.

The Tang also invented gunpowder, originally for use in fireworks. By the early Song period people were using gunpowder to propel arrows—in effect, the first rockets. Later, projectiles were given a gunpowder charge so that they exploded on impact.

In this period the abacus, perhaps already introduced by the Han period, saw broader use. Inventions included the combination of the water wheel and the bellows that enabled smelters to increase the output of pig iron. Under the Song, government-operated spinning and weaving mills produced cheap, durable, and comfortable cotton clothing.

Economic vitality and the consolidation of Song rule gave a great impetus to urbanization. City dwellers were becoming economically more important than the landed gentry. Rich urbanites indulged in increasingly costly dress and food. Well-to-do urban women, however, suffered a severe decline in social standing. The most obvious sign of their changed status was the custom of foot-binding, which made a woman's feet nearly useless. As long as women's labor was needed to help keep starvation from the door, women possessed a certain status, albeit lowly. But in prosperous urban households, women no longer fulfilled an economic function and, in effect, became ornaments. To show the world that their men were prosperous enough to support them, women bound the feet of their infant daughters until the arches broke and the foot healed to half its normal growth. Not until the twentieth century was this custom abandoned.

In international affairs, the Song used diplomacy to avoid war and play off one state against the other. In 1114, however, the Jurchen, a people from the northeastern frontier, marched against the Song. In 1126 they sacked the Song capital and drove the remnants of the imperial court to the southern city of Hangzhou (Hangchow).

The Song emperors who governed from Hangzhou, commonly known as the Southern Song Dynasty, held on to the area below the Yangtze River from 1127 to 1279. The Southern Song resisted the northerners but established a stable border with them. Although there never was genuine peace between the two, fighting was usually limited to border areas. For 152 years the Southern Song flourished, despite the annual tribute they paid to the northerners.

The Southern Song period is especially notable for a great increase in the volume of maritime trade, both oceanic and coastal. Chinese shipwrights built large, stable junks with huge cargo capacity. These ships enabled Chinese merchants to sail directly to Korea and Japan, which became

CHINA, CA 320–CA 1400

220–589	Buddhism flourishes in China
581–618	Sui Dynasty and restoration of public order
618–907	Tang Dynasty: economic, political, and artistic flowering
907–960	Era of the Five Dynasties: warfare and revolt
960–1279	Song Dynasty and Neo-Confucian thought
1021–1086	Wang Anshi, author and political reformer
1215–1279	Mongol conquest of China
ca 1300	Marco Polo travels in China

eager importers of Chinese goods. Ocean voyages were rendered considerably easier and safer by the Chinese invention of the magnetic compass, which was widely used in China at least two centuries earlier than in the rest of the world. The shipping of Chinese goods to the West was mostly in the hands of Arabs. Thus southern China under the Song entered fully and prosperously into a commercial network that stretched from Japan all the way to the Mediterranean.

The invention of printing and the increased volume of trade led to two momentous innovations: the use of paper money and the development of banking. Paper money originated under the Song as notes of deposit—documents certifying that a person had deposited a specific amount of copper coinage with the government. Notes of deposit rapidly gave way to true paper money, which anyone could cash in for copper coins. The legendary Venetian merchant and adventurer Marco Polo (ca 1254–1342) wrote one of the earliest descriptions of how Chinese paper money was issued:

The coinage of this paper money is authenticated with as much form and ceremony as if it were actually of pure gold or silver; for to each note a number of officers, specially appointed, not only subscribe their names, but affix their signets also; and when this has been regularly done by the whole of them, the principal officer . . . having dipped into vermillion the royal seal committed to his custody, stamps with it the piece of paper, so that the form of the seal tinged with the vermillion remains impressed upon it.[5]

To this day American paper money carries the signatures of federal officials, the seals of the Federal Reserve Bank, and the Great Seal of the United States; only the vermillion is absent.

The popularity of the convenient and portable paper money also gave rise to the new profession of counterfeiting; Chinese counterfeiters risked their heads, for those inept or unlucky enough to be caught were decapitated. Paper money in turn gave rise to a system of credit and banking that enabled merchants to deposit money, take out loans, and invest in commercial ventures. Facilitated by the new monetary and banking systems, trade burgeoned so much that the Song government derived more revenue from trade and taxes on trade than from the traditional land tax.

Cultural Blossoming of the Tang and Song

The economic reforms, political stability, and military successes of the Tang and Song nourished a splendid era in the history of Chinese culture. Although the Tang period is best known for its poetry, many forms of art flourished during these years. Potters produced porcelain of extraordinarily high quality and delicate balance. Porcelain of

Song Baby Pillow This imaginative piece of art was surely more decorative than practical. It represents an uncomfortable-looking pillow for the head, supported by the form of a sleeping, plump infant. During the Song period children became a popular motif in art. *(Source: The Avery Brundage Collection/Laurie Platt Winfrey, Inc.)*

uniformly high quality became a major item of export to western Asia and Europe.

Within the past seventeen years the excavations of Tang imperial tombs at Qianxian in Shaanxi province have shed welcome light on the sculpture and painting of this vibrant period. At Qianxian scores of life-size statues of horses and warriors guard the tombs of emperors while rows of statues of dignitaries, lions, and sheep stand in silent audience. Inside the tombs, ceramic statuettes of ceremonial troops serve as guardians.

The royal tombs display Tang painting at its best. The walls are graced with the painted figures of respectful mandarins, court ladies, and warrior guards. Scenes of hunting and polo lend an air of energy and vivacity. Mythological creatures ward off evil spirits. Realistic and graceful in form, the paintings exhibit a sophisticated sense of perspective. The total effect is joyous, even gay. Tang painters captured life accurately and with a deft touch.

The glory of Tang literature was poetry, which achieved unmatched elegance and brilliance. Tang poetry was sophisticated, urbane, and learned. Thoroughly familiar with earlier poetry and with history, Tang poets were also influenced by Chinese and foreign folk songs. They were consummate masters of meter and rhythm, their poems often gemlike. Though formal and rigorous in composition, Tang poetry expresses genuine emotion, frequently with humor and sensitivity. Some poets strung songs together to accompany drama, in effect creating Chinese opera. Tang poets created new vehicles for verse, and they themselves became the models for their Song successors and all later Chinese poets (see Listening to the Past).

One of the most delightful of the Tang poets was Li Bo (701–762), whose poetry is polished, learned, and good-natured. Unlike most Tang poets, Li Bo was never a mandarin official, although he was familiar with the cultivated life of the imperial court. He was a member in good standing of the literary circle known as the Eight Immortals of the Wine Cup, and his poems allude often to his love of wine. Even banishment from the court did not dampen his spirits, for Li Bo loved his wine, his art, and all of nature too much ever to become morose. One of his most famous poems describes an evening of drinking with only the moon and his shadow for company:

A cup of wine, under the flowering trees;
I drink alone, for no friend is near.
Raising my cup I beckon the bright moon,
For he, with my shadow, will make three men.
The moon, alas, is no drinker of wine;
Listless, my shadow creeps about at my side.

. . . .

Now we are drunk, each goes his way.
May we long share our odd, inanimate feast,
And we meet at last on the cloudy River of the sky.[6]

Another poem captures a moment of joy that the poet experienced while walking in the mountains on a summer day:

Gently I stir a white feather fan,
With open shirt sitting in a green wood.
I take off my cap and hang it on a jutting stone;
A wind from the pine-trees trickles on my bare head.[7]

Li Bo is said to have died one night in the company of his old friend the moon.

Chinese River Festival   The beauty and delicacy of Chinese painting are obvious in this lively scene of people enjoying a river festival. Like the great poets, Chinese painters delighted in scenes from daily life. *(Source: The Metropolitan Museum of Art, Fletcher Fund, 1947, A. W. Bahr Collection)*

Less cheerful but no less talented was Bo Juyi (772–846), whose poems often reflect the concerns of a scholar-official. He felt the weight of his responsibilities as governor of several small provinces and sympathized with the people whom he governed. At times Bo Juyi worried about whether he was doing his job justly and well:

From my high castle I look at the town below
Where the natives of Pa cluster like a swarm of flies.
How can I govern these people and lead them aright?
I cannot even understand what they say.

But at least I am glad, now that the taxes are in,
To learn that in my province there is no discontent.[8]

Watching the reapers in the fields, he described their work and wondered about their fate and his:

Tillers of the soil have few idle months;

. . . .

Suddenly the hill is covered with yellow corn.
Wives and daughters shoulder baskets of rice;
Youths and boys carry the flasks of wine.
Following after they bring a wage of meat
To the strong reapers toiling on the southern hill,
Whose feet are burned by the hot earth they tread,
Whose backs are scorched by flames of the shining sky.

. . . .

And I to-day . . . by virtue of what right
Have I never once tended field or tree?

. . . .

Thinking of this, secretly I grew ashamed;
And all day the thought lingered in my head.[9]

Though a high official, he enjoyed such simple things as the pine trees growing around his house and a river babbling over its stony bed. At age seventy-four he died of a stroke, comforted by his wine and poetry.

The artists and thinkers of the Song period brought to fulfillment what the Tang had so brilliantly begun. Buoyed by political stability and economic prosperity, the Song explosion of learning and thought was a direct result of the invention of printing. The availability of books enabled scholars to amass their own libraries and thus to pursue their studies more easily and deeply. Song scholars formed circles to discuss their interests and ideas and to share their work with others. Song publishers printed the classics of Chinese literature in huge editions to satisfy scholarly appetites. Works on philosophy, science, and medicine were also consumed avidly. Han and Tang poetry and historical works became the models for Song writers' own work. One popular literary innovation was the encyclopedia, which first appeared in the Song period, at least five centuries before publication of a European encyclopedia.

One of the most influential Song schools of thought (which gave rise to an intellectual trend known as Neo-Confucianism) was that of Wang Anshi (1021–1086), whose interests embraced economics, politics, literary style, and the classics of Chinese literature. As a Song minister of state, Wang Anshi launched a series of political and economic innovations with his "New Laws." The "Young Shoots" law extended low-interest loans to poor farmers, as some governments do today. Another law substituted a graduated tax for forced labor on state work projects. Like the Roman emperor Diocletian (see page 207), Wang Anshi introduced official price controls and limitations on profits; he went further than Diocletian by coupling this measure with a plan to equalize the land tax. Though marked by realism and good sense, Wang Anshi's innovations ultimately failed against bureaucratic infighting among officials and serious opposition from wealthy merchants and great landowners.

Other schools of Neo-Confucian thought confronted purely intellectual problems and left a more enduring imprint. The Cheng-Zu school achieved one of the greatest intellectual feats of a great age by adding a metaphysical dimension to traditional Confucianism's secular approach to human life and the universe. Metaphysics—the theoretical philosophy of being—gave Confucianism an intellectual depth and sophistication that equipped it to challenge what had long been a Buddhist monopoly of ultimate truth.

Neo-Confucians mined Confucian, Buddhist, and Daoist thought to create this new metaphysics. Meanwhile, one of the finest minds of the age, Zu Xi (1120–1200), addressed himself to the metaphysical problem of evil. He was primarily responsible for formulating Rational Neo-Confucianism. He read the commentaries of other scholars and then sought to explain them in his own terms. He concluded that people are born with principle (*li*) and matter (*Ch'i*). Purity of matter allows people clearly to appreciate principle. Impurity of matter means that people improperly realize principle and leads to various degrees of evil behavior. People can correct this imbalance, Zu Xi taught, through Confucian study and Buddhist meditation. In effect, Zu Xi explained not only how evil develops in the world but how it can be corrected.

Zu Xi wrote learned commentaries on the classics of Chinese literature. He was also the premier historian of his day. In striving for a unified view of life and the universe, he interpreted history and literature in support of his philosophical ideas. Unparalleled among the works of Neo-Confucians, Zu Xi's writings became classics; they have been read, revered, and imitated for centuries. He and other intellectuals breathed new life into Confucianism to meet the challenge of Buddhism.

Song poets and painters matched the greatness of their Tang predecessors. The Song particularly excelled at painting. Two dramatically dissimilar approaches to art arose. Some painters, like Li Longmian (ca 1040–1106), stressed exact realism. Others, like Mi Fei (ca 1051–1107), pursued a mystical romanticism in which space and natural elements were suggested with a few brush strokes.

The culture of the Tang and Song periods is remarkable for its breadth and variety, as well as its brilliance. From painting to poetry, from philosophy to history, these years gave rise to exquisite masterpieces. Yet despite cultural brilliance and political and economic success, the Southern Song emperors lived in the twilight of a great era. In the north a new and unforeseen danger, the Mongols, was on the verge of shaking the world from China to Hungary.

The Mongol Conquest (1215–1368)

In 1215 the Southern Song and their northern neighbors felt the first tremor of what was to be among the most remarkable movements of people in all history. Jenghiz Khan (1162–1227) and his huge band of Mongols, Tatars, and Turks burst into northern China. Marco Polo left a vivid description of their endurance and military skill:

They are brave in battle, almost to desperation, setting little value upon their lives, and exposing themselves without hesitation to all manner of danger.

Their disposition is cruel. They are capable of supporting every kind of privation, and when there is a necessity for it, can live for a month on the milk of their mares, and upon such wild animals as they may chance to catch. The men are habituated to remain on horseback during two days and two nights, without dismounting, sleeping in that situation whilst their horses graze. No people on earth can surpass them in fortitude under difficulties, nor show greater patience under wants of every kind.[10]

In 1215 the Mongols overwhelmed the Jurchens in the north and captured Beijing. All of northern China fell in 1234. The Southern Song held on tenaciously against the invaders, but Jenghiz Khan's grandson Kublai Khan (1216–1294) extinguished the dynasty and annexed all of southern China by 1279 (see Map 11.3). For the first time in history, all of China was ruled by foreigners. By 1271 Kublai Khan (also known as the Great Khan) had proclaimed himself emperor of China and founder of the Yuan Dynasty (1271–1368).

The Mongols distrusted the traditional mandarin class yet needed the mandarin's bureaucratic system. They compromised by assigning foreigners—Turks, Muslims from central Asia, and even a handful of European adventurers—to the highest administrative posts and allowing Chinese to hold lower offices. The Mongol conquest did not hinder China's trade: the expansion begun under the Song continued. By establishing his capital at Beijing, Kublai Khan helped reunite northern and southern China commercially: the wealth of the south flowed north to sustain the capital.

A conquering minority, the Mongols proclaimed repressive laws against the far more numerous Chinese. The northern Chinese, who were conquered first, had broader political and legal rights than the southerners but bore a far heavier burden of taxes and services. The Mongols disarmed the Chinese people and forbade them to assemble in large numbers and even to travel by night. The Chinese were captives in their own country.

The Mongols linked their internal policy with their dealings with the outside world. Some scholars argue that the Mongols provided a climate of peace and tolerance that facilitated friendly relations with those involved in long-distance trade. A realistic or even cynical view is that it served the Mongols, who were outsiders, very handsomely to

The Silk Road   The Mongol conquest at least secured the safety of merchants traveling the Silk Road. There were few inns or hostels along the route, except in the cities. Most merchants, like those shown here, pitched camp each night by their camels. *(Source: National Palace Museum, Taiwan)*

seek outside economic support for their rule, all the while keeping the Chinese in their place.

Into this world wandered Marco Polo with his father and uncle. The three Polos had journeyed by land across Asia to the court of Kublai Khan, who received them with warmth and curiosity. Adept in four Asian languages, Marco Polo was uniquely equipped to collect accurate information about China. Although he visited South China, he probably seldom traveled far from Beijing. Instead, he seems to have drawn heavily on Chinese accounts for his information. He trained his insatiable curiosity on the land of China, its people and their customs, and everything likely to stimulate commerce. After seventeen years in China, the Polos returned to Italy, where Marco wrote a vivid ac-

count of their travels. At first considered sheer fantasy, his book was widely read and contributed enormously to familiarizing Europeans with Asia.

Mongol repression bred bitter resentment throughout China. By the middle of the fourteenth century, moreover, the Mongol hold on East Asia was weakening. Struggles among claimants to the Yuan throne seriously compromised the Great Khan's power and prestige, and Kublai Khan's successors proved weak and incompetent. In this atmosphere of crisis, some Chinese formed secret societies dedicated to overthrowing the oppressor. The most effective secret society, known as the Red Turbans, consisted of peasants and artisans, who had suffered the most from Mongol rule. Their rebellion in 1351 caught the Mongols totally off-guard. One of the rebels was a poor peasant and former monk best known to history as Hong Wu.

In 1356 Hong Wu and his followers stormed the important city of Nanjing (Nanking). Securing control over southern and central China, they pushed the Mongols northward, and by 1368 the Chinese had driven the Mongols completely out of China. Hung Wu established the Ming Dynasty (1368–1644). Once again China was united under one of its sons. In the following years Ming emperors would continue to push the Mongols north. They also rebuilt the Chinese economy by reclaiming abandoned farmland, by repairing neglected dikes and canals that were essential to fruitful agriculture, and by reforesting the countryside. As a result, under Ming rule China again prospered.

JAPAN, DAWN OF THE RISING SUN

Japan entered the light of history late, and Japanese historical writing originated even later. The earliest reliable information on Japan comes from sporadic notices in Chinese histories; the first of them dates from A.D. 57. The Japanese people, by the time of their first appearance in history, had already had extensive exposure to Chinese culture. The Japanese derived much from the Chinese, but they molded their borrowings to suit their special needs. Early Japan saw the growth of an indigenous culture that the Chinese influenced but never overwhelmed.

The Japanese Islands

The heart of Japan is four major islands (Map 11.4). The largest and most important is Honshu. Honshu and the two southern islands surround the Inland Sea, a narrow stretch of water dotted with smaller islands. All four major islands are mountainous, with craggy interiors and some active volcanoes. Rugged terrain divides the land into numerous small valleys watered by streams. There is little flat land, and only 16 percent of the total area is arable. Japan's climate ranges from subtropical in the south, which the Pacific bathes in warm currents, to a region of cold winters in the north. Rainfall is abundant, favoring rice production. Yet nature can be harsh: Japan is a land buffeted by earthquakes, typhoons, and tidal waves.

Suitable for farming

Creation of Japan This Japanese painting portrays two deities standing in the clouds above the Pacific Ocean. The god, sword at his side, stirs the waters with a lance and thereby creates the home islands of Japan. *(Source: Courtesy, Museum of Fine Arts, Boston, William Sturgis Bigelow Collection, Acc. no. 11.7972)*

✳ **MAP 11.4 The Islands of Japan, ca 1185**
This map illustrates the importance of the island of Honshu and the Inland Sea in the development of early Japanese society.

Despite occasional rages, the sea provides a rich harvest, and the Japanese have traditionally been fishermen and mariners. Since the land is rugged and lacking in navigable waterways, the Inland Sea, like the Aegean in Greece, was the readiest avenue of communication. Hence the land bordering the Inland Sea developed as the political and cultural center of early Japan. Geography also blessed Japan with a moat—the Korea Strait and the Sea of Japan. Consequently, the Japanese for long periods were free to develop their way of life without external interference. Continuity has been a hallmark of Japanese history.

Early Japan and the Yamato State

The beginnings of Japanese history are lost in the mists of legend. The Chinese historian Wei Zhi wrote one of the earliest reliable descriptions of Japanese life in A.D. 297:

The land of Wa [Japan] is warm and mild. In winter as in summer the people live on raw vegetables and go barefooted. They live in houses; father and mother, elder and younger, sleep separately. They smear their bodies with pink and scarlet, just as the Chinese use powder. They serve food on bamboo and wooden trays, helping themselves with their fingers.[11]

The society that Wei Zhi and other Chinese sources portray was based on agriculture and dominated by a warrior aristocracy. Clad in helmet and armor, these warriors wielded swords and battle-axes and often the bow. Some of them rode into battle on horseback. Social stratification was rigid. Peasants served at the command of nobles. At the bottom of the social scale were slaves—usually house servants. Slaves may have accounted for about 5 percent of the total population.

Early Japan was divided into numerous political units, although by about 513 their number had been greatly reduced. Each pocket of local authority was under the rule of a particular clan—a large group of families that claimed descent from a common ancestor and worshiped a common deity. Each clan had its own chieftain, who marshaled clan forces for battle and served as clan chief priest. In Japan as in many other ancient societies, political power was a function of family strength, organization, and cohesion.

By the third century A.D. the Yamato clan had seized the fertile area south of Kyoto, near Osaka Bay (see Map 11.4). At the center of the Yamato holdings was a rich plain, which constituted the chief economic resource of the clan. Gradually the Yamato clan, which traced its descent from the sun-goddess, subordinated a huge number of other clans to create the Yamato state. The chieftain of the Yamato clan proclaimed himself emperor and ruler over the other chieftains. Clans that recognized Yamato dominion continued to exercise local authority, and some clans were given specific military or religious functions to fulfill. In an effort to centralize further the administration of the state, the emperor created a council of chieftains, whose members were treated as though they were appointed officials.

The Yamato also used their religion to subordinate the gods of their supporters, much as Hammurabi had used Marduk (see page 20). Creating a hierarchy of gods under the authority of their sun-goddess, the Yamato established her chief shrine in eastern Honshu, where she could catch the first rays of the rising sun. Around the shrine there grew up local clan cults, giving rise to a native religion known as Shinto, the Way of the Gods. Shinto was a unifying force: the chief deity of Shinto, the sun-goddess, became the nation's protector. Shinto also stressed the worship of ancestors, thus strengthening the link between the present and the past. Much of its appeal rose from the fact that it was a happy religion. Its rituals celebrated the beauty of nature instead of invoking the hazards of fate or divine wrath. Shinto emphasized ritual cleanliness, and its festivals were marked by wine, song, and good cheer.

By the sixth century the powerful Yamato state was struggling to dominate Korea. From the dawn of their history the Japanese had held parts of Korea, but by 562 the Koreans had driven them out. Much more important was Korea's role as the avenue through which Chinese influence reached Japan. The Japanese adapted the Chinese systems of writing and record keeping, which allowed for bureaucratic administration along Chinese lines and set the stage for literature, philosophy, and written history.

Another influence of lasting importance to the Japanese was Buddhism. In 538 a Korean king sent the Yamato court Buddhist images and scriptures. The new religion immediately became a political football. One faction of the ruling clan favored its official adoption, and other factions opposed it. The resulting turmoil, both religious and political, ended only in 587, when members of the pro-Buddhist group defeated their opponents on the battlefield. Buddhism proved important to Japanese life for three broad reasons. First, it was a new and sophisticated but appealing religion that met needs not envisaged by Shinto. Second, it served as an influential carrier of Chinese culture. Finally, its acceptance by Japan's rulers enabled it to play an influential role in politics.

The victorious pro-Buddhist faction undertook a sweeping reform of the state, partly to strengthen Yamato rule and partly to introduce Chinese political and bureaucratic concepts. The architect of this effort was Prince Shotoku (574–622), the author of the "Seventeen Article Constitution," a triumph of Buddhist ethical and Confucian political thought. Issued in 604, the constitution was not a blueprint for government but a list of moral and ethical Buddhist precepts stressing righteous political conduct. It upheld the rights of the ruler and commanded his subjects to obey him. The constitution recommended an intricate bureaucracy like China's and admonished the nobility to avoid strife and opposition. Although the "Seventeen Article Constitution" never became the law of the entire land, it spelled out what Shotoku considered the proper goals of government and pointed the way to future reform.

Prince Shotoku   The author of the "Seventeen Article Constitution" is shown here with many of the attributes of a Chinese mandarin official. His sword shows that he was more than a mere administrator and was ready to resist those who opposed his reforms. *(Source: Imperial Household Collection, Kyoto)*

The death of Prince Shotoku in 622 set off some twenty years of political chaos. Finally in 645 supporters of his policies overthrew the government. The following year they proclaimed the Taika Reforms, a bold effort to create a complete imperial and bureaucratic system like that of the Tang Empire. For all their hopes, the Taika Reforms failed to make Japan a small-scale copy of Tang China. Nonetheless, the reformers created a nation with all the political trappings of its neighbors. The symbol of this new political awareness was the establishment in 710 of Japan's first true capital and first city, at Nara, just north of modern Osaka.

Nara, which was modeled on the Tang capital, gave its name to an era that lasted until 794, an era characterized by the continued importation of Chinese ideas and methods. Buddhism triumphed both religiously and politically. The Buddhist monasteries that ringed the capital were both religious centers and wealthy landlords, and the monks were active in the political life of the capital. In the Nara era, Buddhism and the imperial court were hand in glove.

The Heian Era (794–1185)

Buddhist influence at Nara showed its dark side in 765 when a Buddhist monk usurped the throne. He deposed the emperor but five years later lost power and was banished. The results were twofold. The imperial family moved the capital to Heian—modern Kyoto—where it remained until 1867. And a strong reaction against Buddhism and Chinese culture soon set in, strikingly symbolized by the severance of relations with China after 838. Thereafter the Japanese assimilated and adapted what they had imported. In a sense their intellectual and cultural childhood had come to an end, and they were ready to go their own way.

Though under a cloud, Buddhism not only survived the reaction but actually made gains. Before closing the door on China, the Japanese admitted two new Buddhist cults that gradually became integral parts of Japanese life. In 805 a Japanese monk introduced the Tendai (Chinese Tiantai) sect (see page 321). Though a complex product of China's high culture, Tendai proved popular because it held out the possibility of salvation to all. In addition to its religious message, Tendai preached the Confucian ideal of service to the state. The Shingon (True Word) sect arrived in 806 on the heels of Tendai. Like its Chinese precursor, this Japanese sect promised salvation through ritual, magical incantations, and masses for the dead.

Patronized initially by the nobility, both sects held the seeds of popular appeal. The common people cared nothing for Tendai and Shingon as metaphysical and intellectual systems but were strongly attracted by their magic and by the prospect of personal salvation. As Tendai and Shingon spread Buddhism throughout Japan, they were gradually transformed into distinctively Japanese religions. Furthermore, Buddhist art had an aesthetic appeal to the Japanese people.

Only later, during the Kamakura Shogunate (1185–1333), did Buddhism begin a vigorous proselytizing campaign. The emphasis on equality and salvation that was the hallmark of both Tendai and Shingon prepared the way for two sects that promised their followers sure and immediate salvation. The Pure Land sect (see page 321) preached that paradise could be reached through simple faith in Buddha. Neither philosophical understanding of Buddhist scriptures nor devotion to rituals was necessary. The second sect, an offshoot of the first, was the Lotus Sutra sect of Nichiren (1222–1281), a fiery and intolerant preacher. To be saved, according to Nichiren, people only had to invoke sincerely the Lotus Sutra, not the Buddha himself. Nichiren wanted to create a national faith, one that opposed Pure Land Buddhism (which called on Amida Buddha) and all other Buddhist sects but his own. Stripped of its intellectual top-weight, Buddhism made greater headway in the countryside than ever before.

The eclipse of Chinese influence liberated Japanese artistic and cultural impulses. The Japanese continued to draw on Chinese models but forged new paths of their own. They made great strides in writing. To express themselves more easily and clearly, Japanese scholars modified the Chinese script that they had adopted during the Yamato period. For the first time it became possible to write the Japanese language using the native syntax.

The reform of their written language unshackled Japanese writers. No longer bound in the straitjacket of Chinese, they created their own literary style and modes of expression. The writing of history, which had begun in the Nara era, received a huge boost, as did poetry. Completely original was the birth of the novel. One of the finest novels is

The Tale of Genji, by the court lady Murasaki Shikibu (978–ca 1016). This ageless work treats court life, paying minute attention to dialogue and exploring personalities. Not merely a novelist, Murasaki wrote about the mission of the novelist and the purpose of the novel. Other writers also produced novels. Sei Shonagon's *Pillow Book* is another masterpiece. These works bore no resemblance to any works in Chinese literature. The Japanese had launched their own independent and fertile literary tradition.

Politically, the Heian era saw aristocrats striving to free themselves from imperial control. The aristocrats quickly won out over the emperors. The biggest winners were the Fujiwara family. In the ninth century members of this family had regularly served as regents for the emperors and had married and connived their way into almost complete domination of the imperial line of rulers. As other families rose to prominence, setting the stage for intrigue and infighting at court, the effectiveness of the imperial government was further diminished.

In 1156, fed by declining central power, feuds among the great families, and the ambitions of local lords, open rebellion and civil war erupted. The two most powerful contenders in the struggle were the Taira and Minamoto clans, who quickly outstripped both the emperor and the Fujiwara. Both clans relied on *samurai,* skilled warriors who were rapidly consolidating as a new social class. By 1192 the Minamoto had vanquished all opposition, and their leader Yoritomo (1147–1199) became *shogun,* or general-in-chief. With him began the Kamakura Shogunate, which lasted until 1333.

The Land and the Samurai

The twelfth-century events that culminated in the Kamakura Shogunate involved a new relation between the samurai and the land. That relation eventually led to a fusion of the military, civil, and judicial aspects of government into a single authority. The Japanese samurai were a very important part of a larger system. Without an independent income of their own, the samurai needed the economic support of others. They depended economically on the *shoen,* a private domain outside imperial control. The shoen typically consisted of a village and its farmland, normally land capable of growing rice. Land was essential to the maintenance of the samurai.

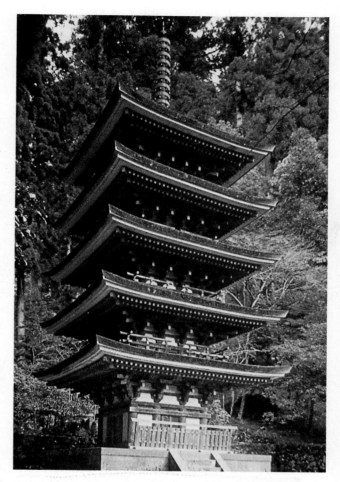

Five-Story Pagoda   This pagoda is a splendid example of Japanese architecture of the Heian period. Such buildings were intended to complement their natural surroundings. *(Source: Courtesy, Horyuji Temple)*

Both samurai and shoen owed their origins directly to the gradual breakdown of central authority in the Heian era. The shoen had its roots in the ninth century, when local lords began escaping imperial taxes and control by formally giving their land to a Buddhist monastery, which was exempt from taxes, or to a court official who could get special privileges from the emperor. The local lord then received his land back as a tenant and paid his protector a nominal rent. The monastery or official received a steady income from the land, and the tenant was thereafter free of imperial taxes and jurisdiction. In spite of his legal status as a tenant,

Shogun → Daimyo → Samurai

the local lord continued to exercise actual authority over the land—all the more so, in fact, since imperial officials could no longer touch him.

The many other people who were economically, politically, and legally dependent on the shoen, and who had various functions within it, enjoyed the rights of the *shiki*, a share of the produce of the land. The shoen was cultivated by independent farmers *(myoshu)* who owned specific fields, by dependent farmers, or, typically, by a combination of both. Unlike peasants in medieval Europe, dependent farmers never became serfs.

To keep order on the shoen and to protect it from harm, lords organized private armies. As the central government weakened, local lords and their armies of professional soldiers—the samurai—grew stronger. They were the only source of law and order in the countryside. The samurai and his lord had a double bond. The lord extended his authority over the samurai in return for the latter's loyalty and service. The samurai originally received from his lord only shiki rights to produce. Later the samurai received grants of land for their service. Each samurai entered into his lord's service in a formal ceremony that included a religious element.

The samurai had their own military and social code of conduct, later called *Bushido,* or "Way of the Warrior." The bedrock of the samurai code was loyalty to the lord, to which everything else was secondary. Preferring death to dishonor, the samurai showed complete dedication in the act of *seppuku* (sometimes incorrectly called *harakiri*), ritual suicide by disemboweling oneself. Yoritomo founded the Kamakura Shogunate on the samurai and their code. Attitudes that blossomed in Yoritomo's lifetime long outlasted the political system he built.

By the end of the twelfth century the samurai constituted the ruling class at the local level; they were warrior aristocrats who were close to the land and to those who worked it. Their code of conduct embraced religion, personal conduct, and practical affairs. According to the *Bushido,* samurai were expected to respect the gods, keep honorable company, be fair and even generous to others, and be sympathetic to the weak and helpless.

The symbols of the samurai were their swords, with which they were expected to be expert, and the cherry blossom, which falls with the spring wind, signifying the way in which samurai gave their lives for their lords. Like knights, samurai went into battle in armor and often on horseback. Like the ancient Spartans, samurai were expected to make do with little and like it. Physical hardship became routine, and soft living was despised as weak and unworthy. Although the full-blown samurai code did not take final shape until the later Ashikaga Shogunate, by the end of the twelfth century the samurai had left their mark on Japanese cultural life as well as on military affairs.

The Kamakura Shogunate (1185–1333)

The Kamakura Shogunate derives its name from Kamakura, the seat both of the Minamoto clan and of Yoritomo's shogunate. Yoritomo's victory meant that the emperor was still an ornament, honored and esteemed but mostly powerless.

Based on the loyalty of his followers, Yoritomo's rule was an extension of the way in which he ran his own estate. Having established his *bakufu* (tent government) at Kamakura, Yoritomo created three bodies, staffed by his retainers, to handle political and legal matters. His administrative board drafted government policy. Another board regulated lords and samurai, and a board of inquiry served as the court of the land.

For administration at the local level, Yoritomo created two groups of officials: military land stewards and military governors. The military land stewards were responsible for the collection of taxes. Charged with governing most estates, they saw to the estates' proper operation and maintained law and order in return for a share of the produce. The military governors oversaw the military and police protection of the provinces. They supervised the conduct of the military land stewards in peacetime and commanded the provincial samurai in war.

Yoritomo's successors did not inherit his ability, and in 1219 the Hojo family, a powerful vassal, reduced the shogun to a figurehead. Until 1333, the Hojo family held the reins of power by serving as regents of the shogun. The shogun had joined the emperor as a political ornament.

Internal affairs continued unchanged during the Hojo Regency, but a formidable challenge appeared from abroad. A massive seaborne invasion rudely interrupted Japan's self-imposed isolation in the thirteenth century. Its lingering effects weakened the Hojo Regency and eventually led to the

JAPAN, CA 320–CA 1400

3d century A.D.	Creation of the Yamato state
538	Introduction of Buddhism
604	Shotoku's "Seventeen Article Constitution"
646	Taika Reforms
710	Establishment of Nara as Japan's first capital and first city
710–794	Nara era
794–1185	Heian era and literary flowering
1185–1333	Kamakura Shogunate and Japanese feudalism
1274 and 1281	Unsuccessful Mongol invasions of Japan

downfall of the Kamakura Shogunate. The Mongol leader Kublai Khan, having overrun China and Korea, turned his eyes toward Japan. In 1274 and again in 1281 he sent huge numbers of ships and men to storm the islands. On both occasions the Mongols managed to land but were beaten back by samurai. What proved decisive, however, were two fierce storms that destroyed the Mongol fleets. Marco Polo recounted what he heard about one invasion force:

It happened, after some time, that a north wind began to blow with great force, and the ships of the Tartars, which lay near the shore of the island, were driven foul of each other. . . . The gale, however, increased to so violent a degree that a number of vessels foundered. The people belonging to them, by floating upon the pieces of the wreck, saved themselves upon an island lying about four miles from the coast of Zipangu [Japan].[12]

The Japanese claimed that they were saved by the *kamikaze*, the Divine Wind—which lent its name to the thousands of Japanese aviators who tried to become a sort of divine wind in World War II by crashing their airplanes onto American warships. The Hojo regents successfully defended Japan but were unable to reward their vassals satisfacto-

rily because little booty was found among the wreckage of the Mongol fleets. Discontent grew among the samurai, and by the fourteenth century the entire political system was breaking down. Both the imperial and the shogunate families were divided among themselves. Because the land could not support more samurai, who were rapidly growing in number, many samurai families became impoverished. Poverty created a pool of warriors ready for plunder, and the samurai shifted their loyalty to local officials who could offer them adequate maintenance.

The combination of factional disputes among Japan's leading families and among the samurai remained explosive until 1331, when the emperor Go-Daigo tried to recapture real power. His attempt sparked an uprising by the great families, local lords, samurai, and even Buddhist monasteries, which commanded the allegiance of thousands of samurai. Go-Daigo destroyed the Kamakura Shogunate in 1333 but lost the loyalty of his followers. By 1338 one of his most important military leaders, Ashikaga Takauji, had defeated the emperor and established the Ashikaga Shogunate, which lasted until 1573. Takauji's victory was also a victory for the samurai, who took over civil authority throughout Japan. The day of the samurai had fully dawned.

SUMMARY

By about 1400, traditional religious, social, and intellectual values had been challenged and fertilized by new peoples and new ideas throughout Asia. Most of India clung to Hinduism while Islam took root in modern Pakistan and Bangladesh. China incorporated and distilled Buddhism, which won a place next to Confucianism in Chinese life. Japan imported much of Chinese culture only to mold it into something distinctly Japanese. Finally, firm economic and cultural links made it virtually impossible for any Asian people to continue to develop in isolation.

NOTES

1. O. P. Singh Bhatia, trans., *The Imperial Guptas* (New Delhi: New India Press, 1962), p. 79.
2. A. L. Basham, trans., *The Wonder That Was India* (New York: Grove Press, 2nd ed., 1959), p. 161.
3. *Vasishtha* 4.5.1–2, trans. G. Bühler, in *The Sacred Laws of the Aryas,* part 2, *Vasishtha and Baudhayana* (Oxford: Clarendon Press, 1882), p. 31.
4. *Sutrakritanga* 1.4.2, quoted in Basham, *The Wonder That Was India,* pp. 459–460.
5. *The Travels of Marco Polo, the Venetian* (London: J. M. Dent and Sons, 1908), p. 203.
6. A. Waley, trans., *More Translations from the Chinese* (New York: Knopf, 1919), p. 27.
7. Ibid., p. 29.
8. Ibid., p. 71.
9. Ibid., p. 41.
10. *The Travels of Marco Polo,* p. 128.
11. R. Tsunoda et al., *Sources of the Japanese Tradition* (New York: Columbia University Press, 1958), p. 6.
12. *The Travels of Marco Polo,* pp. 325–326.

SUGGESTED READING

K. N. Chaudhuri, *Asia Before Europe* (1990), discusses the economy and civilization of cultures within the basin of the Indian Ocean. P. B. Golden, *An Introduction to the History of the Turkic Peoples* (1992), is a broad survey that covers the spread of Turks through central Asia and the Middle East. D. Simon, ed., *The Cambridge History of Early Inner Asia* (1990), is an ambitious and successful collection that ranges in time from prehistory to the early thirteenth century A.D. and in space from the Near East to India. A. Wink, Al-Hind, *The Making of the Indo-Islamic World,* vol. 1 (1990), is a massive and often difficult volume that examines economic expansion in India and its links to the Middle East. The reign of the Guptas is especially well documented. O. P. Singh Bhatia, trans., *The Imperial Guptas* (1962), treats the entire dynasty. In a series of works S. K. Maity covers many facets of the period: *Gupta Civilization: A Study* (1974), *The Imperial Guptas and Their Times* (1975), and *Economic Life in North India in the Gupta Period* (1975). Good treatments of Indian society and daily life can be found in A. L. Basham, *The Wonder That Was India,* 2nd ed. (1959), Ch. 6, and J. Auboyer, *Daily Life in Ancient India from 200 B.C. to A.D. 700* (1965).

Broad in scope are two books by H. G. Q. Wales: *The Indianization of China and of South-East Asia* (1967) and *The Making of Greater India,* 3d ed. (1974). H. Akira, *A History of Indian Buddhism* (1990), studies Buddhist influence on commerce, which so facilitated the spread of Buddhism beyond India.

An extensive survey of the Islamic invasions of India is J. F. Richards, "The Islamic Frontier in the East: Expansion into South Asia," *South Asia* 4 (1974): 90–109, in which Richards makes the point that many Indian princes put up stiff resistance to the invaders. A good treatment of early Islam in India is K. A. Nizami, *Some Aspects of Religion and Politics in India During the Thirteenth Century* (repr. 1970). In two books, *Islam in the Indian Subcontinent* (1980) and *Islam in India and Pakistan* (1982), A. Schimmel surveys many aspects of Islam, including architecture, life, art, and traditions in the subcontinent. G. S. Pomerantz, "The Decline of Buddhism in India," *Diogenes* 96 (1976): 38–66, treats the demise of Buddhism on its native soil.

Two works concentrate on the sultanate of Delhi: M. Habib and K. A. Nizami, eds., *Comprehensive History of India,* vol. 5, *Delhi Sultanate* (1970), and P. Hardy, "The Growth of Authority over a Conquered Political Elite: The Early Delhi Sultanate as a Possible Case Study," in J. F. Richards, ed., *Kingship and Authority in South Asia* (1978).

The standard work on the arrival of Buddhism in China is E. Zürcher, *The Buddhist Conquest of China,* 2 vols. (1959) C. W. Ernst, *Eternal Garden* (1992), is a far-ranging study of the mysticism, history, and politics at a major religious center, enlightening because of its emphasis on the relations between Muslim religion and politics. V. Hansen, *Changing Gods in Medieval China, 1127–1276* (1990), studies the social history of popular religion. Also good on the intellectual climate of the time are E. Balazs, *Chinese Civilization and Bureaucracy* (1964), and H. Welch and A. Seidel, eds., *Facets of Taoism* (1979). L. Kohn, *Taoist Mystical Philosophy* (1991), discusses Daoist mysticism in connection with controversies in Buddhist thought. Shorter and more popular is A. Wright, *Buddhism in Chinese History* (1959). Two books by K. Ch'en, *Buddhism in China* (1964) and *The Chinese Transformation of Buddhism* (1973), cover the early evolution of Buddhism in China. B. Gray, *Buddhist Cave Paintings at Tunhuang* (1959), is the place to begin study of the artistic impact of Buddhism on China.

Political events from the time of the Sui to the Song Dynasty are particularly well covered. A. F. Wright, *The Sui Dynasty* (1978), has become the standard work on this important dynasty. Though old, W. Bingham, *The Founding of the T'ang Dynasty: The Fall of Sui and Rise of T'ang* (1941), is still useful. C. P. Fitzgerald, *Son of Heaven: A Biography of Li Shih-min, Founder of the T'ang Dynasty* (1933), is likewise an old treatment of the first Tang emperor. Newer and broader is J. Perry and B. Smith, eds., *Essays on T'ang Society* (1976). The career of An Lu-shan is admirably discussed by E. G. Pullyblank, *The Background of the Rebellion of An Lu-shan* (1955). The difficult Era of the Five Dynasties is well covered by G. Wang, *The Structure of Power in North China During the Five Dynasties* (1963). Various aspects of Song developments receive attention in J. T. C. Liu and P. Golas, eds., *Changes in Sung China* (1969), and E. A. Kracke, Jr., *Civil Service in Early Sung China (960–1067)* (1953).

A brief treatment of the Tang tombs at Jianxian, well illustrated with color plates, is N. H. Dupree, "T'ang Tombs in Chien County, China," *Archaeology* 32, no. 4 (1979): 34–44. Students interested in further discussion of the great poets of the period can find no better place to start than the work of A. Waley, a gifted translator: *The Life and Times of Po Chü-i* (1949) and *The Poetry and Career of Li Po, 701–762* (1950). Wang Anshi still generates controversy, and a variety of views can be found in J. T. C. Liu, *Reform in Sung China: Wang An-shih (1021–1086) and His New Policies* (1959), and in J. Meskill, ed., *Wang An-shih— Practical Reformer?* (1963).

For the Mongols in their native setting, see L. Kwanten, *Imperial Nomads: A History of Central Asia, 500–1500 A.D.* (1979), a comprehensive picture of central Asian developments. H. D. Martin, *The Rise of Chinghis Khan and His Conquest of North China* (1950), studies the rise of the Mongols to greatness. J. Dardess's "From Mongol Empire to Yuan Dynasty: Changing Forms of Imperial Rule in Mongolia and Central Asia," *Monumenta Serica* 30 (1972–1973): 117–165, traces the evolution of Mongol government. His *Conquerors and Confucians: Aspects of Political Change in Late Yuan China* (1973) continues the

study for a somewhat later period. Dardess's "The Transformations of Messianic Revolt and the Founding of the Ming Dynasty," *Journal of Asian Studies* 29 (1970): 539–558, treats some of the factors behind the overthrow of the Yuan Dynasty.

Among the many fine general works on Japan, the following are especially recommended in addition to those cited in the Notes: G. Trewartha, *Japan: A Geography* (1965); and E. O. Reischauer and J. K. Fairbank, *East Asia: The Great Tradition* (1960). More recent works include C. Schirokauer, *A Brief History of Chinese and Japanese Civilizations,* 2d ed. (1989); J. K. Fairbank, E. O. Reischauer, and A. Craig, *East Asia: Tradition and Transformation,* rev. ed. (1989); C. Totman, *Japan Before Perry* (1981); and A. Tiedmann, ed., *An Introduction to Japanese Civilization* (1974).

For early Japanese history, W. G. Aston, trans., *Nihongi: Chronicles of Japan from Earliest Times to A.D. 697* (1896, repr. 1990), despite its age, is still the only English translation of the earliest historical chronicle. J. P. Maas, *Antiquity and Anachronism in Japanese History* (1992), makes the bold suggestion that an exaggerated history of antiquity led to a distorted perception of the past. G. J. Groot, *The Prehistory of Japan* (1951), is still useful though rapidly becoming dated. The same is true of J. E. Kidder, *Japan Before Buddhism* (1959). Newer and quite readable is Kidder, *Early Buddhist Japan* (1972), which is well illustrated. J. M. Kitagawa, *Religion in Japanese History* (1966), discusses both Shinto and Buddhism.

Early Japanese literary flowering has attracted much attention. I. Morris, *The World of the Shining Prince: Court Life in Ancient Japan* (1964), provides a general treatment of the climate in which early Japanese artists lived. Murasaki Shikibu, *The Tale of Genji,* has been recently translated by R. Bowring (1988); I. Morris translated *The Pillow Book of Sei Shonagon,* 2 vols. (1967).

Japanese feudalism, like its medieval European counterpart, continues to excite discussion and disagreement. Some provocative works include P. Duus, *Feudalism in Japan,* 2d ed. (1976); E. O. Reischauer, "Japanese Feudalism," in R. Coulborn, ed., *Feudalism in History* (1956), pp. 26–48, and T. Keirstead, *The Geography of Power in Medieval Japan* (1992), which attempts to determine the cultural framework of the existence and development of the shoen system. For military affairs, see W. W. Farris, *Heavenly Warriors* (1992), which studies the early development of military organization and methods of warfare, and K. F. Friday, *Hired Swords* (1992), which treats the evolution of state military development in connection with the emergence of the samurai.

LISTENING TO THE
PAST

Women in Chinese Society

Women seldom made their voices heard in antiquity. Literature, like politics, was mostly a male preserve. Two moving exceptions to the norm are the poems reprinted here.

In the first, a woman has been divorced by her husband. She has lived her adult life in a region far from her home. She will return to the land of her brothers, who hold no sympathy for her plight. Her lament is poignant but without bitterness. This work is a striking example of popular culture. The situation that it described was surely not unique but one that happened all too often.

The mulberry leaves have fallen
All yellow and seared.
Since I came to you,
Three years I have eaten poverty.
The waters of the Ch'i were in flood;
They wetted the curtains of the carriage.
It was not I who was at fault;
It is you who have altered your ways,
It is you who are unfaithful,
Whose favours are cast this way and that.

Three years I was your wife.
I never neglected my work.
I rose early and went to bed late;
Never did I idle.
First you took to finding fault with me,
Then you became rough with me.
My brothers disowned me;
'Ho, ho,' they laughed.
And when I think calmly over it,
I see that it was I who brought all this upon
    myself.

I swore to grow old along with you;
I am old, and have got nothing from you but
    trouble.
The Ch'i has its banks,

The swamp has its sides;
With hair looped and ribboned
How gaily you talked and laughed,
And how solemnly you swore to be true,
So that I never thought there could be a
    change.
No, of a change I never thought;
and that *this* should be the end!

The next poem is the lament of a widow who has lost her husband in war. To describe the nature of her marriage, she uses the analogy of plants that bind themselves together. At the end of the poem, she looks forward to the day when she will join her husband at the end of her life.

The cloth-plant grew till it covered the thorn
    bush;
The bindweed spread over the wilds.
My lovely one is here no more.
With whom? No, I sit alone.

The cloth-plant grew till it covered the
    brambles;
The bindweed spread across the borders of
    the field.
My lovely one is here no more.
With whom? No, I lie down alone.

The horn pillow so beautiful,
The worked coverlet so bright!
My lovely one is here no more.
With whom? No, alone I watch till dawn.

Summer days, winter nights—
Year after year of them must pass
Till I go to him where he dwells.
Winter nights, summer days—
Year after year of them must pass
Till I go to his home.

Questions for Analysis

1. What does the first poem tell about the social status of women? What rights did they have, what powers, what means of protection?

2. Why do the brothers laugh at the woman in the first poem rather than showing sympathy for her misfortunes?

3. Does the widow in the second poem face the same situation as the one in the first? What are the differences between the two women, and how can we account for them?

Source: A. Waley, trans., *The Book of Songs.* Copyright 1937 Houghton Mifflin Company. Reprinted by permission.

Ch'ing dynasty painting of woman peeking from behind baton door. *(Source: By courtesy of the Trustees of the Victoria & Albert Museum)*

343

Cover of *Codex Aureus* of
Saint Emmeram, ca 870
A.D. *(Source: Bayerische
Staatsbibliothek)*

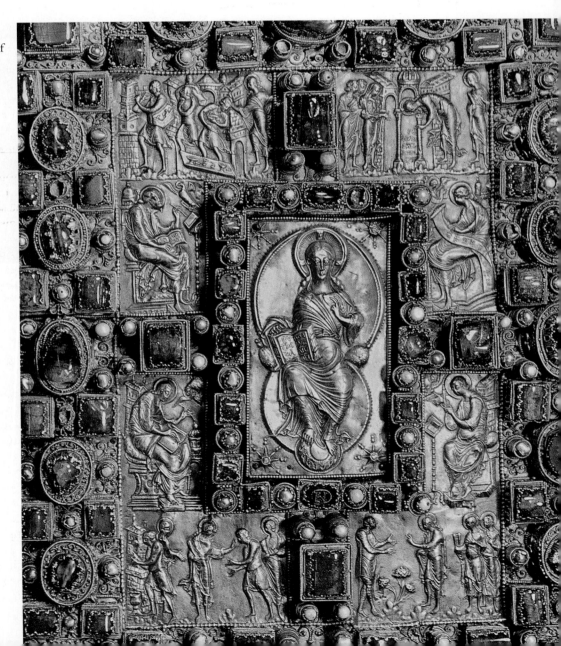

The Frankish chieftain Charles Martel defeated Muslim invaders in 733 at the Battle of Tours in central France.[1] Muslims and Christians have interpreted the battle differently. Muslims considered it a minor skirmish and attributed the Frankish victory to Muslim difficulties in maintaining supply lines over long distances and to ethnic conflicts and unrest in Islamic Spain. Christians considered the Frankish victory one of the great battles of history because it halted Muslim expansion in Europe. A century later, in 843, Charles Martel's three great-great-grandsons, after a bitter war, concluded the Treaty of Verdun, which divided the European continent among themselves. Civil disorder and foreign invasion then wracked Europe for about the next 150 years. Between 733 and 843, a distinctly European society emerged. A new kind of social and political organization, later called feudalism, appeared. And for the first time since the collapse of the Roman Empire, most of western Europe was united under one government, which reached its peak under Charles Martel's grandson, Charlemagne. Christian missionary activity among the Germanic peoples continued, and strong ties were forged with the Roman papacy. A revival of study and learning—the Carolingian Renaissance—occurred during the reign of Charlemagne.

By the last quarter of the tenth century, after a long and bitter winter of discontent, signs of a European spring appeared. That spring lasted from the early eleventh to the end of the thirteenth century. The period from about 1050 to 1300, the central Middle Ages, was a time of creativity and vitality between two eras of crisis. During the central Middle Ages, European society experienced demographic growth, religious reform, increasing political stability, and enormous economic development.

- How did Charlemagne acquire and govern his vast empire, and what was the Carolingian Renaissance?

- What was feudalism, and how did it come about?

- What factors contributed to the disintegration of the Carolingian Empire, and what were the ingredients of the revival of Europe?

- How did the Christian church and civil government develop and influence one another during the early and central Middle Ages?

- How did medieval rulers work to solve their problems of government, thereby laying the foundations of the modern state?

- How did medieval towns originate, and how do they reveal the beginnings of radical change in medieval society?

These are the questions this chapter will explore.

❖ THE CAROLINGIAN ERA

The Frankish kingdom that had emerged under Clovis by the early sixth century included most of what is now France and a large section of southwestern Germany. Clovis's baptism into orthodox Christianity won him church support against other Germanic tribes. Clovis died in 511, and the Merovingian Dynasty went on to rule for two centuries.

Rule is, of course, too strong a verb. Conquering the vast territories proved easier for the Merovingians than governing them, given their inadequate political institutions. When he died, Clovis divided his kingdom among his four sons, according to Frankish custom. Because of the vast size of the kingdom, the division made sense. Practically, however, Clovis's decision was disastrous, because it led to civil war. The four Merovingian heirs hated each other, and each one fought to deprive his relatives of their portions of the kingdom. Thus in 558 Clovis's youngest son, Lothair, acquired the whole kingdom after he had murdered two of his nephews and eliminated one rebellious brother by burning him and his family alive. After Lothair died, the two remaining sons of Clovis continued the civil war until just one of them survived.

In this domestic violence the remarkable Queen Brunhilda (d. 631), wife of King Sigebert of the East Frankish kingdom, played an important role. Chilperic, ruler of the West Frankish kingdom, murdered his wife Galswintha so that he could marry his mistress Fredegunda. Galswintha and Brunhilda were sisters, and Brunhilda promptly instigated war between the East and West Frankish kingdoms. Hatred of Fredegunda led her to continue the war even after the deaths of both Sigebert and Chilperic. During the reigns of her son and grandson, Brunhilda actually ruled the East Frankish kingdom, displaying considerable political skill and a merciless use of violence in pursuit of royal goals.

The long period of civil war in the Frankish kingdom may have provided the opportunity for the emergence of a distinct aristocratic class. Research in Frankish family history has revealed that a noble ruling class existed before the mid-sixth century. Members of this class belonged to families of high reputation, who gradually intermarried with members of the old Gallo-Roman senatorial class. They possessed wealth and great villas and led an aristocratic lifestyle. They exercised rights of lordship over their lands and tenants, dispensing local customary, not royal, law. From these families came almost all the bishops of the church. Because they had a political distinction from the rest of society, they constituted a noble class.[2]

The Rise of the Carolingian Dynasty

The rise of the Carolingians—their name derives from the Latin *Carolus*, for "Charles"—was partly due to papal support. In the early eighth century, missionaries supported Charles Martel and his son Pippin III as they attempted to bring the various Germanic tribes under their jurisdiction. The Anglo-Saxon missionary Wynfrith, or Boniface (680–754), as he was later called, was the most important. Boniface's achievements were remarkable. He helped shape the structure of the German church. He established *The Rule of Saint Benedict* in all the monasteries he founded or reformed, thus promoting monastic unity. And, with the support of the king, he held councils to reform the church in the Frankish kingdom.

Saint Boniface preached throughout Germany against divorce, polygamous unions, and incest. On these matters German custom and ecclesiastical law completely disagreed. The Germans allowed divorce: a man simply repudiated his wife (divorce did not require her consent). The Germanic peoples also practiced polygamy and incest—sexual relations between brothers and sisters or parents and children—on a wide scale. Church councils and theologians stressed that marriage, validly entered into—that is, freely consented to—could not be ended.

Boniface's preaching was not without impact. Some fifty years later, in 802, Charles Martel's grandson Charlemagne would prohibit incest. Charlemagne also would decree that a husband might separate from an adulterous wife, that the woman could be punished, and that the man could not remarry in her lifetime. Charlemagne would

also encourage severe punishment for adulterous men. The publication of laws does not usually or instantly end deeply rooted social practices, but Charlemagne's efforts brought new dignity to marriage and to women.

Charles Martel had been king of the Franks in fact but not in title. His son Pippin III (r. 751–768) made himself king in title as well as in fact. According to Germanic custom, which had the force of law, the kingship had to pass to someone of royal blood. Pippin did not want to murder the ineffectual Merovingian king, but he did want the kingship. So he consulted the pope, who tacitly supported the deposition of the last Merovingian king and recognized the Carolingians. The Merovingian ruler was removed and forced to become a monk.

Pippin was the first ruler to be anointed by the pope with the sacred oils and acknowledged as *rex et sacerdos* ("king and priest"). Anointment, rather than royal blood, set the Christian king apart. Pippin also cleverly eliminated possible threats to the Frankish throne, and the pope promised him support in the future. When Pippin died, his son Charlemagne succeeded him.

The Empire of Charlemagne

Charles the Great (r. 768–814), generally known as Charlemagne, built on the military and diplomatic foundations of his ancestors. Einhard, his secretary and biographer, wrote a lengthy idealization of the warrior-ruler. It has serious flaws but is the earliest medieval biography of a layman, and historians consider it generally accurate:

Charles was large and strong, and of lofty stature, though not disproportionately tall . . . the upper part of his head was round, his eyes very large and animated, nose a little long, hair fair, and face laughing and merry. Thus his appearance was always stately and dignified . . . although his neck was thick and somewhat short, and his belly rather prominent; but the symmetry of the rest of his body concealed these defects. His health was excellent, except during the four years preceding his death.[3]

Though crude and brutal, Charlemagne was a man of enormous intelligence. He appreciated good literature, such as Saint Augustine's *City of God,* and Einhard considered him an unusually effective speaker. Recent scholarship disputes Ein-

❖ **Merovingian Army**   This sixth- or seventh-century ivory depicts a nobleman in civilian dress followed by seven warriors. Notice that the mounted men do not have stirrups and seem to have fought with spears and bows and arrows. The power of the Frankish aristocracy rested on these private armies. *(Source: Landesmuseum, Trier)*

hard's claim that Charlemagne could not write. Charlemagne had four legal wives and six concubines and even after the age of sixty-five continued to sire children. Three of his sons reached adulthood, but only one outlived him. Four surviving grandsons, however, ensured perpetuation of the family.

Charlemagne's most striking characteristic was his phenomenal energy, which helps to explain his great military achievements.[4] Continuing the expansionist policies of his ancestors, Charlemagne fought more than fifty campaigns and became the greatest warrior of the early Middle Ages. He subdued all of the north of modern France and, in the course of a thirty-year war against the semibarbaric Saxons, added most of the northwestern German tribes to the Frankish kingdom. Because of repeated rebellions by the Saxons, Charlemagne, according to Einhard, ordered more than four thousand Saxons slaughtered in one day.

To the south, he also achieved spectacular results. In 773–774 the Lombards in northern Italy were threatening the papacy. Charlemagne marched south, overran fortresses at Pavia and Spoleto, and incorporated Lombardy into the Frankish kingdom and to his title as king of the Franks he added king of the Lombards. He successfully fought the Byzantine Empire for Venetia (excluding the city of Venice), Istria, and Dalmatia and temporarily annexed those areas to his kingdom.

In the west, Charlemagne tried to occupy Basque territory in northwestern Spain. When his long siege of Saragossa proved unsuccessful and the Saxons on his northeastern borders rebelled, Charlemagne decided to withdraw. At Roncesvalles in 778, the Basques annihilated his rear guard, which was under the command of Count Roland. This attack was Charlemagne's only defeat, and he forbade people to talk about it. The expedition, however, inspired the great medieval epic *The Song of Roland,* written down around 1100, which portrays Roland as the ideal chivalric knight and Charlemagne as exercising a sacred kind of kingship. Although many of the epic's details differ from the historical evidence, *The Song of Roland* is important because it reveals the popular image of Charlemagne in later centuries.

By around 805, the Frankish kingdom included all of continental Europe except Spain, Scandinavia, southern Italy, and the Slavic fringes of the

❋ **MAP 12.1 The Carolingian World** The extent of Charlemagne's nominal jurisdiction was extraordinary: it was not equaled until the nineteenth century.

East (Map 12.1). The Muslims in northeastern
Spain were checked by the establishment of
strongly fortified areas known both as *marches* and
as *marks*. Not since the third century A.D. had any
ruler controlled so much of the Western world.

Charlemagne ruled a vast rural world dotted
with isolated estates and characterized by constant
petty violence. His empire was not a state as people today understand that term; it was a collection
of primitive peoples and semibarbaric tribes. Apart

from a small class of warrior aristocrats and clergy, almost everyone engaged in agriculture. Trade and commerce played only a small part in the economy. Cities served as the headquarters of bishops and as ecclesiastical centers.

By constant travel, personal appearances, and the sheer force of his personality, Charlemagne sought to awe conquered peoples with his fierce presence and terrible justice. By confiscating the estates of great territorial magnates, he acquired lands and goods with which to gain the support of lesser lords, further expanding the territory under his control.

The political power of the Carolingians rested on the cooperation of the dominant social class, the Frankish aristocracy. By the seventh century, through mutual cooperation and frequent marriage alliances, these families exercised great power that did not derive from the Merovingian kings. The Carolingians themselves had emerged from this aristocracy, and their military and political success depended on the support of the nobility. The lands and booty with which Charles Martel and Charlemagne rewarded their followers in these noble families enabled the nobles to improve their economic position. In short, Carolingian success was a matter of reciprocal help and reward.[5]

Two or three hundred counts from this imperial aristocracy governed at the local level. They had full military and judicial power and held their offices for life but could be removed by the emperor for misconduct. As a link between local authorities and the central government, Charlemagne appointed officials called *missi dominici,* "agents of the lord king." The empire was divided into visitorial districts. Each year, beginning in 802, two missi, usually a count and a bishop or abbot, visited assigned districts. They held courts and investigated their districts' judicial, financial, and clerical activities. They held commissions to regulate crime, moral conduct, the clergy, education, the poor, and many other matters. The missi checked up on the counts and worked to prevent the counts' positions from becoming hereditary: strong counts with hereditary estates would have weakened Charlemagne's power. In the marks—especially in unstable areas—officials called margraves had extensive powers to govern.

A modern state has institutions of government such as a civil service, courts of law, financial agencies for collecting and apportioning taxes, and police and military powers. These did not exist in Charlemagne's empire. Instead, dependent relationships cemented by oaths promising faith and loyalty held society together. Nevertheless, although the empire lacked viable institutions, some Carolingians involved in governing did have vigorous political ideas. The abbots and bishops who served as Charlemagne's advisers worked out what was for their time a sophisticated political ideology.

In letters and treatises, churchmen set before their ruler high standards of behavior and of government. They wrote that although a ruler holds power from God the ruler is obliged to respect the law just as all subjects of the empire were required to obey the ruler. The abbots and bishops envisioned a unified Christian society presided over by a king who was responsible for maintaining peace, law, and order and dispensing justice, without which, they pointed out, neither the ruler nor the kingdom had any justification. These views derived largely from Saint Augustine's theories of kingship. Inevitably, they could not be realized in an illiterate, preindustrial society. But they were the seeds from which medieval and even modern ideas of government were to develop.

In the autumn of the year 800, Charlemagne paid a momentous visit to Rome. Einhard gave his account of what happened:

His last journey there [to Rome] was due to another factor, namely that the Romans, having inflicted many injuries on Pope Leo—plucking out his eyes and tearing out his tongue, he had been compelled to beg the assistance of the king. Accordingly, coming to Rome in order that he might set in order those things which had exceedingly disturbed the condition of the Church, he remained there the whole winter. It was at the time that he accepted the name of Emperor and Augustus. At first he was so much opposed to this that he insisted that although that day was a great [Christian] feast, he would not have entered the Church if he had known beforehand the pope's intention. But he bore very patiently the jealousy of the Roman Emperors [that is, the Byzantine rulers] who were indignant when he received these titles. He overcame their arrogant haughtiness with magnanimity, a virtue in which he was considerably superior to them, by sending frequent ambassadors to them and in his letters addressing them as brothers.[6]

For centuries scholars have debated the significance of the imperial coronation of Charlemagne by the pope. Did Charles plan the ceremony in

Saint Peter's on Christmas Day, or did he merely accept the title of emperor? What did he have to gain from it?

Three points seem certain. First, Charlemagne gained the imperial *title* "Holy Roman emperor" and considered himself a Christian king ruling a Christian people. His motto, *Renovatio romani imperi* ("Revival of the Roman Empire"), reinforces the notion that Charles was consciously perpetuating old Roman imperial notions while at the same time identifying with the new Rome of the Christian church. Charlemagne and his government represented a combination of Frankish practices and Christian ideals—the two basic elements of medieval European society. Second, later German rulers were anxious to gain the imperial title and to associate themselves with the legends of Charlemagne and ancient Rome. Third, ecclesiastical authorities continually cited the event as proof that the dignity of the imperial crown could be granted only by the pope. The imperial coronation of Charlemagne, whether planned by the Carolingian court or by the papacy, was to have a profound effect on the course of German history and on the later history of Europe.

The Carolingian Intellectual Revival

It is ironic that Charlemagne's most enduring legacy was the stimulus he gave to scholarship and learning. Barely literate, preoccupied with the control of vast territories, much more a warrior than a thinker, Charlemagne nevertheless set in motion a cultural revival that had widespread and long-lasting consequences.

The revival of learning associated with Charlemagne and his court at Aachen drew its greatest inspiration from seventh- and eighth-century intellectual developments in the Anglo-Saxon kingdom of Northumbria, situated at the northernmost tip of the old Roman world (see Map 12.1). Northumbrian monasteries produced scores of religious books, commentaries on the Scriptures, illuminated manuscripts, law codes, and collections of letters and sermons. The finest product of Northumbrian art is probably the Gospel book produced at Lindisfarne around 700. The incredible expense involved in the publication of such a book—for vellum (calfskin or lambskin specially prepared for writing), coloring, and gold leaf—represents in part an aristocratic display of wealth.

In Gaul and Anglo-Saxon England, women shared with men in the work of evangelization and in the new Christian learning. Kings and nobles, seeking suitable occupations for daughters who did not or would not marry, founded monasteries for nuns. Some were *double monasteries,* housing both men and women in two adjoining establishments and governed by a woman—the *abbess*. Double monasteries provided women of the ruling class with something to rule. Nuns and monks worked together. Nuns looked after the children given to the monastery as *oblates* ("offerings"), the elderly who retired at the monastery, and travelers who needed hospitality. Monks provided protection, for

Lindisfarne Gospels "In the beginning was the Word" (John 1:1), and the crucial texts for the preservation and spread of the Christian faith were the Gospels. Bishop Eadfrith of Lindisfarne (ca 690) produced this carpet, or cover page, for a Gospel book. Reflecting the Celtic tradition of interlaced ornaments and figurative imagery, this work is a superb example of Northumbrian culture. The style became celebrated throughout Christian Europe. *(Source: The British Library)*

in a violent age an isolated house of women invited attack. The monks also did the heavy work on the land. Perhaps the most famous abbess of the Anglo-Saxon period was Saint Hilda (d. 680). A noblewoman of considerable learning and administrative ability, she ruled the double monastery of Whitby on the Northumbrian coast, advised kings and princes, hosted a synod in 664, and encouraged scholars and poets. Several generations after Hilda, Saint Boniface wrote many letters to Whitby and to other houses of nuns, pleading for copies of books.[7]

The finest representative of Northumbrian and indeed all Anglo-Saxon scholarship is the Venerable Bede (ca 673–735). At the age of seven he was given by his parents as an oblate to Abbot Benet Biscop's monastery at Wearmouth. Later he was sent to the new monastery at Jarrow, five miles away. There, surrounded by the books that Benet Biscop had brought from Italy, Bede spent the rest of his life.

The author of learned commentaries on the Scriptures, Bede also devoted himself to other scholarly fields. Modern scholars praise him for his *Ecclesiastical History of the English Nation*, which is the chief source of information about early Britain. Bede searched far and wide for his information, discussed the validity of his evidence, compared various sources, and exercised a rare critical judgment. For these reasons, he has been called "the first scientific intellect among the Germanic peoples of Europe."[8]

At about the time that monks at Lindisfarne were producing their Gospel book and Bede at Jarrow was writing his *History,* another Northumbrian monk was at work on a nonreligious epic poem that provides considerable information about the society that produced it. In contrast to the works of Bede, which were written in Latin, the poem *Beowulf* was written in the vernacular Anglo-Saxon. Although *Beowulf* is the only native English heroic epic, all the events of the tale take place in Denmark and Sweden, suggesting the close relationship between England and Scandinavia in the eighth century. Scholars have hailed it as a masterpiece of Western literature.[9]

The physical circumstances of life in the seventh and eighth centuries make Northumbrian cultural achievements all the more remarkable. Learning was pursued under terribly difficult circumstances. Monasteries such as Jarrow and Lindisfarne stood on the very fringes of the European world (see

❈ **Plan for an Ideal Monastery**   This is a ninth-century architectural design for a self-supporting monastic community of 270 members. The primary focus of the monks' lives was the church and the cloister, which appropriately appear in the center of the plan. Notice the herb garden close to the physician's quarters. The western entrance for visitors was surrounded by the hostel for poor guests and pens for farm animals—with all the inevitable smells. (*Source: Kenneth John Conant,* Carolingian and Romanesque Architecture, 800–1200. *Pelican History of Art, 2d rev. ed. New York: Pelican, 1978, p. 57*)

Map 12.1). The barbarian Picts, just an afternoon's walk from Jarrow, were likely to attack at any time. Winter could be extremely harsh. In 664, for example, deep snow was hardened by frost from early winter until mid-spring. When it melted away, many animals, trees, and plants were found dead. To make matters worse, disease could take terrible tolls. Bede described events in the year 664:

In the same year of our Lord 664 . . . a sudden pestilence first depopulated the southern parts of Britain and then attacked the kingdom of the Northumbrians as well. Raging far and wide for a long time with cruel devastation it struck down a great multitude of men. . . . This same plague oppressed the island of Ireland with equal destruction.[10]

Damp cold with bitter winds blowing across the North Sea must have pierced everything, even stone monasteries. Inside, only one room, the *calefactory,* or "warming room," had a fire. Scribes in the *scriptorium,* or "writing room," had to stop frequently to rub circulation back into their numb hands. These monk-artists and monk-writers paid a high physical price for what they gave to posterity.

If Northumbrian cultural achievements had remained entirely insular, they would have been of slight significance. As it happened, an Englishman from Northumbria played a decisive role in the transmission of English learning to the Carolingian Empire and continental Europe, where Charlemagne promoted a revival that later scholars named the Carolingian Renaissance. The support Charlemagne gave to education and learning preserved the writings of the ancients and laid the foundations for all subsequent medieval culture.

At his court at Aachen, Charlemagne assembled learned men from all over Europe. The most important scholar and the leader of the palace school was the Northumbrian Alcuin (ca 735–804). From 781 until his death, Alcuin was the emperor's chief adviser on religious and educational matters. An unusually prolific scholar, Alcuin prepared some of the emperor's official documents and wrote many moral *exempla,* or "models," which set high standards for royal behavior and constitute a treatise on kingship. Alcuin's letters to Charlemagne set forth political theories on the authority, power, and responsibilities of a Christian ruler.

Aside from Alcuin's literary efforts, scholars at Charlemagne's court copied books and manuscripts and built up libraries. They used the beautifully clear handwriting now known as Carolingian minuscule, from which modern Roman type is derived. This script is called "minuscule" because it has lower-case as well as capital letters; the script that the Romans used had only capitals. Because lower-case letters are smaller than capitals, scribes using Carolingian minuscule could put more words on each sheet of vellum and could increase the number of texts they copied.

The development of Carolingian minuscule illustrates the way a seemingly small technological change can have broad cultural consequences.

✳ **Saint Luke from the Ada Gospels** After the cross, the most famous early Christian symbols were representations of the four evangelists: Matthew (man), Mark (lion), Luke (a winged ox), and John (eagle), based on the text in Revelation 4:7. The Ada School of painting, attached to the court of Charlemagne, gets its name from Ada, Charlemagne's sister, who commissioned some of the school's work. In this lavishly illuminated painting dating from the late eighth or early ninth century, a statuesque Saint Luke sits enthroned, his draperies falling in nervous folds reminiscent of Byzantine art, and surrounded by an elaborate architectural framework. This is a splendid example of Carolingian Renaissance art. (*Source: Municipal Library, Trier*)

Scholars established schools all across Europe, attaching them to monasteries and cathedrals. They placed great emphasis on the education of priests, trying to make all priests at least able to read, write, and do simple arithmetic. The greatest contribution of the scholars at Aachen was not so much the originality of their ideas as their hard work of salvaging and preserving the thought and writings of the ancients. The Carolingian Renaissance was a rebirth of interest in, study of, and preservation of the language, ideas, and achievements of classical Greece and Rome.

Although the scholars worked with Latin, the common people spoke their vernacular languages. The Bretons, for example, retained the local dialect of Britanny; and the Saxons and Bavarians, despite their geographical closeness, could not understand each other (see Map 12.1). Communication among the diverse peoples of the Carolingian Empire was possible only through the medium of Latin.

Once basic literacy was established, monastic and other scholars went on to more difficult work. By the middle years of the ninth century, there was a great outpouring of more sophisticated books. Ecclesiastical writers, imbued with the legal ideas of ancient Rome and the theocratic ideals of Saint Augustine, instructed the semibarbaric rulers of the West. And it is no accident that medical study in the West began, at Salerno in southern Italy, in the late ninth century, *after* the Carolingian Renaissance.

Alcuin completed the work of his countryman Boniface—the Christianization of northern Europe. Latin Christian attitudes penetrated deeply into the consciousness of European peoples. By the tenth century, the patterns of thought and lifestyles of educated western Europeans were those of Rome and Latin Christianity. Even the violence and destruction of the great invasions of the late ninth and tenth centuries could not destroy the strong foundations laid by Alcuin and his colleagues.

❋ DIVISION AND DISINTEGRATION OF THE CAROLINGIAN EMPIRE (814–987)

Charlemagne left his vast empire to his only surviving son, Louis the Pious (814–840), who was crowned emperor in his father's lifetime. Deeply religious and well educated, Louis was no soldier,

and he could not retain the respect and loyalty of the warrior aristocracy on whom he depended for troops and for administration of his territories. The disintegration that had begun in Charlemagne's last years accelerated as soon as he died.

The basic reason for the collapse of the Carolingian Empire is that it was too big. Bad roads swarming with thugs and rivers infested with pirates made communication within the empire very difficult. In Charlemagne's lifetime the empire was held together by the sheer force of his personality and driving energy. After his death, it began to fall apart. The empire lacked a bureaucracy like that of the Roman Empire—the administrative machinery necessary for strong and enduring government. It was a collection of tribes held together at the pleasure of warrior aristocrats, men most interested in strengthening their own local positions and ensuring that they could pass on to their sons the offices and estates they had amassed. Why should counts, abbots, and bishops obey the unimpressive, distant Louis the Pious, who represented a centralizing power that threatened their local interests? What counted was strength in one's own region and the preservation of family holdings.

The Frankish custom of dividing estates among all male heirs hastened the empire's disintegration. Between 817 and his death in 840, Louis the Pious made several divisions of the empire. Dissatisfied with their portions and anxious to gain the imperial title, Louis's three sons—Lothair, Louis the German, and Charles the Bald—fought bitterly among themselves. Finally, in the Treaty of Verdun of 843, the brothers agreed to partition the empire (Map 12.2).

Lothair, the eldest, received the title "emperor," still a source of prestige, and the so-called middle kingdom, an area extending diagonally across Europe from Flanders to Lombardy. Almost immediately, this kingdom broke up into many petty principalities. From the tenth century to the twelfth and thirteenth centuries, when French and German monarchs were trying to build strong central governments, the "middle kingdom" was constantly contested among them.

The eastern and most Germanic part of the Carolingian Empire passed to Louis the German. The western kingdom went to Charles the Bald; it included the provinces of Aquitaine and Gascony and formed the basis of medieval and modern France. The descendants of Charles the Bald held on in the west until 987, when the leading

MAP 12.2 Division of the Carolingian Empire, 843   The Treaty of Verdun (843), which divided the empire among Charlemagne's grandsons, is frequently taken as the start of the separate development of Germany, France, and Italy. The "middle kingdom" of Lothair, however, lacked defensive borders and any political or linguistic unity and quickly broke up into numerous small territories.

magnates elected Hugh Capet as king. The heirs of Louis the German ruled the eastern kingdom until 911, but real power was in the hands of local chieftains. Everywhere in the tenth century, fratricidal warfare among the descendants of Charlemagne accelerated the spread of feudalism.

FEUDALISM AND MANORIALISM

Feudalism, which emerged in western Europe in the ninth century, was a type of government "in which political power was treated as a private possession and was divided among a large number of lords."[11] This kind of government characterized most parts of western Europe from about 900 to 1300. Feudalism actually existed at two social levels: (1) at the level of armed retainers who became knights and (2) at the level of counts and other

royal officials who ruled great feudal principalities. A wide and deep gap in social standing and political function separated these social levels.

In the early eighth century, the Carolingian kings and other powerful men needed bodyguards and retainers—armed men who could fight. Charles Martel, using techniques common among his Merovingian predecessors, purchased the support and loyalty of his followers with grants of land or estates taken from churchmen or laymen or with movable wealth such as weapons or jewelry captured in battle.[12] Charles and other powerful men bound their retainers by oaths of loyalty and ceremonies of homage. Personal ties of loyalty cemented the relationship between lord and retainer. These retainers became known as *vassals*, from a Celtic term meaning "servant." Since knights were not involved in any government activity, and since only men who exercised political power were considered noble, knights were not part of the noble class. Down to the eleventh century, political power was concentrated in a small group of counts.

Counts, descended from the old Frankish aristocracy (see page 349), constituted the second level of feudalism. Under Charles Martel and his heirs, counts monopolized the high offices in the Carolingian Empire. At the local level, they had full judicial, military, and financial power. They held courts that dispensed justice, collected taxes, and waged wars. For most ordinary people, the counts were the government. Charlemagne regularly sent missi to inspect the activities of the counts, but there was slight chance of a corrupt or wicked count being removed from office.

Countships were not hereditary in the eighth century, but they tended to remain within the same family. In the eighth and early ninth centuries, regional concentrations of power depended on family connections and political influence at the king's court. The disintegration of the Carolingian Empire, however, served to increase the power of regional authorities. Civil wars and the great invasions of the ninth century (see pages 355–358) weakened the power and prestige of kings because they could do little about domestic violence. Common people turned for protection to the strongest local power, the counts, whom they considered their rightful rulers. Thus, in the ninth and tenth centuries, great aristocratic families governed virtually independent territories in which distant and weak kings could not interfere. "Political power had become a private, heritable property for great counts and lords."[13] This is what is meant by feudalism as a form of government.

Because feudal society was a military society, men held the dominant positions in it. A high premium was put on physical strength, fighting skill, and bravery. The legal and social position of women was not as insignificant as might be expected, however. Charters recording gifts to the church indicate that women held land in many areas. Women frequently endowed monasteries, churches, and other religious establishments. The possession of land obviously meant economic power. Moreover, women inherited *fiefs*, or landed estates. In southern France and Catalonia in Spain, women inherited feudal property as early as the tenth century. Other evidence also attests to women's status. In parts of northern France, children sometimes identified themselves in legal documents by their mother's name rather than their father's, indicating that the mother's social position in the community was higher than the father's.

In a treatise he wrote in 822 on the organization of the royal household, Archbishop Hincmar of Reims placed the queen directly above the treasurer. She was responsible for giving the knights their annual salaries. She supervised the manorial accounts. Thus, in the management of large households with many knights to oversee and complicated manorial records to supervise, the lady of the manor was likely to have highly important responsibilities. With such responsibility went power and influence.[14]

Feudalism concerned the rights, powers, and lifestyle of the military elite. *Manorialism* involved the services and obligations of the peasant classes who worked on the landed estates of the warring class. Feudalism and manorialism were inextricably linked. Peasants needed protection, and lords demanded something in return for providing that protection. Free farmers surrendered themselves and their lands to the lord's jurisdiction. The land was given back to them to farm, but they became tied to the land by various kinds of payments and services. In France, England, Germany, and Italy, local custom determined precisely what those services were, but certain practices became common everywhere. The peasant was obliged to turn over to the lord a percentage of the annual harvest, usually in produce, sometimes in cash. The peasant paid a fee to marry someone from outside the

lord's estate. To inherit property, the peasant paid a fine—often the best sheep or cow the person owned. Most significant, the peasant became a *serf*—part of the lord's permanent labor force, bound to the land and not allowed to leave it without the lord's permission. With vast stretches of uncultivated virgin land and a tiny labor population, the most profitable form of capital was not land but laborers.

The transition from freedom to serfdom was slow; its speed was closely related to the degree of political order in a given region. Even in the late eighth century, there were still many free peasants. And within the legal category of serfdom there were many economic levels, ranging from the highly prosperous to the desperately poor. Nevertheless, a social and legal revolution was taking place. By the year 800, perhaps 60 percent of the population of western Europe—completely free a century before—had been reduced to serfdom. The ninth-century Viking assaults on Europe created extremely unstable conditions and individual insecurity, leading to additional loss of personal freedom.

GREAT INVASIONS OF THE NINTH CENTURY

After the Treaty of Verdun and the division of Charlemagne's empire among his grandsons, continental Europe presented an easy target for foreign invaders. All three kingdoms were torn by domestic dissension and disorder. No European political power was strong enough to put up effective resistance to external attacks.

Assaults on Western Europe

From the moors of Scotland to the mountains of Sicily, there arose in the ninth century the Christian prayer, "Save us, O God, from the violence of the Northmen." The Northmen, also known as Normans or Vikings, were pagan Germanic peoples from Norway, Sweden, and Denmark who had remained beyond the sway of the Christianizing and civilizing influences of the Carolingian Empire. Some scholars believe that the name Viking derives from the Old Norse word *vik*, meaning "creek." A *Viking*, then, was a pirate who waited in a creek or bay to attack passing vessels.

✳ **Vikings Invade Britain**   In this twelfth-century representation of the Viking invasions, warriors appear to be armed with helmets, spears, and shields. Rowing their open boats across the rough North Sea and English Channel, they had great courage. *(Source: The Pierpont Morgan Library/Art Resource, NY)*

Viking ship could carry between forty and sixty men—quite enough to harass an isolated monastery or village. Against these ships navigated by thoroughly experienced and utterly fearless sailors, the Carolingian Empire, with no navy, was helpless. The Vikings moved swiftly, attacked, and escaped to return again.

Scholars disagree about the reasons for Viking attacks and migrations. Some maintain that overpopulation forced the Vikings to emigrate. Others argue that climatic conditions and crop failures forced migration. Still others insist that the Vikings were looking for trade and new commercial contacts, along with targets for plunder. Plunder they did. Viking attacks were savage. At first they attacked and sailed off laden with booty. Later, on returning, they settled down and colonized the areas they had conquered (Map 12.4). Between 876 and 954, Viking control extended from Dublin across the Irish Sea to Britain, then across northern Britain and the North Sea to the Vikings' Scandinavian homelands. These invaders also overran a large part of northwestern France and called the territory Norsemanland, from which the word *Normandy* derives.

Scarcely had the savagery of the Viking assaults begun to subside when Europe was hit from the east and south. Beginning about 890, Magyar tribes crossed the Danube and pushed steadily westward. (People thought of them as returning Huns, so the Magyars came to be known as Hungarians.) They subdued northern Italy, compelled Bavaria and Saxony to pay tribute, and penetrated even into the Rhineland and Burgundy. These roving bandits attacked isolated villages and monasteries, taking prisoners and selling them in the Eastern slave markets. The Magyars were not colonizers; their sole object was booty and plunder.

The Vikings and Magyars depended on fear. In their initial attacks on isolated settlements, they put many people to the sword. The Vikings also seized thousands of captives as slaves. From the British Isles and from territories along the Baltic, the Vikings took *thralls* (slaves) to be sold in the markets of Magdeburg on the Elbe River and Regensburg in Bavaria on the Danube and to supply the huge demand for slaves in the Muslim world. The slave trade represented an important part of Viking commerce. The Icelander Hoskuld Dala-Kolsson of Laxardal paid three marks of silver— three times the price of a common concubine—for

Viking assaults began around 787, and by the mid-tenth century the Vikings had brought large sections of continental Europe and Britain under their sway (Map 12.3). In the east they pierced the rivers of Russia as far as the Black Sea. In the west they sailed as far as Iceland, Greenland, and even the coast of North America, perhaps as far south as Long Island Sound, New York.

The Vikings were superb seamen with advanced methods of boatbuilding. Propelled either by oars or by sails, deckless, and about 65 feet long, a

MAP 12.3 The Great Invasions of the Ninth Century   Note the Vikings' penetration of eastern Europe and their probable expeditions to North America. What
impact did their various invasions have on European society?

a pretty Irish girl; she was one of twelve offered by
a Viking trader.

From the south the Muslims also began new encroachments, concentrating on the two southern
peninsulas, Italy and Spain. Seventh- and early-
eighth-century Islamic movements had been for

conquest and colonization, but the goal of ninth-
and tenth-century incursions was plunder. In Italy
the Muslims drove northward and sacked Rome in
846. Most of Spain had remained under their
domination since the eighth century. Expert seamen, they sailed around the Iberian Peninsula and

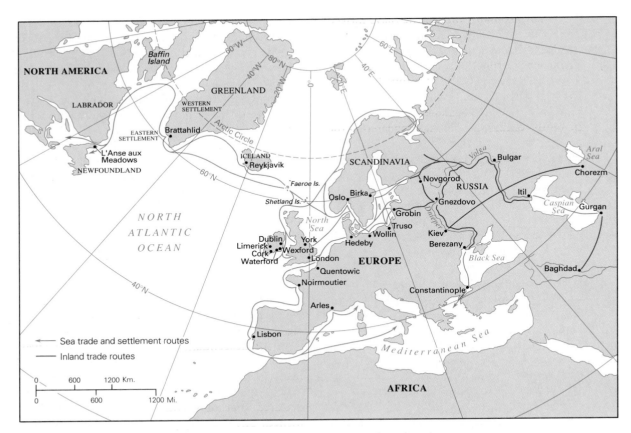

❋ **MAP 12.4 Viking Settlement and Trade Routes** Viking trade and settlements extended from Newfoundland and Greenland to deep into Russia.

braved the dangerous shoals and winds of the Atlantic coast. They also attacked Mediterranean settlements along the coast of Provence. But Muslim attacks on the European continent in the ninth and tenth centuries were less destructive than the assaults of the more primitive Vikings and Magyars.

What was the effect of these invasions on the structure of European society? Viking, Magyar, and Muslim attacks accelerated the development of feudalism. Lords capable of rallying fighting men, supporting them, and putting up resistance to the invaders did so. They also assumed political power in their territories. Weak and defenseless people sought the protection of local strongmen. Free peasants sank to the level of serfs. Consequently, European society became further fragmented. Public power became increasingly decentralized.

The ninth-century invaders left significant traces of their own cultures. The Muslims made an important contribution to European agriculture, primarily through their influence in Spain. The

Vikings, too, made positive contributions to the areas they settled. They carried everywhere their unrivaled knowledge of shipbuilding and seamanship. The northeastern and central parts of England where the Vikings settled became known as the Danelaw because Danish law and customs, not English, prevailed there. York in northern England, once a Roman army camp and then an Anglo-Saxon town, became a thriving center of Viking trade with Scandinavia (see Map 12.4). At Dublin on the east coast of Ireland, Viking iron and steel workers and comb makers established a center for trade with the Hebrides, Iceland, and Norway. The Irish cities of Limerick, Cork, Wexford, and Waterford trace their origins to Viking trading centers.

The Vikings and the Kievan Principality

In antiquity the Slavs lived as a single people in central Europe. With the start of the mass migrations of the late Roman Empire, the Slavs moved in different directions and split into three groups. Between the fifth and ninth centuries, the eastern Slavs, from whom the Ukrainians, the Russians, and the White Russians descend, moved into the vast and practically uninhabited area of present-day European Russia and the Ukraine.

In the ninth century, the Vikings appeared in the lands of the eastern Slavs. Called Varangians in the old Russian chronicles, the Vikings were interested primarily in international trade. Moving up and down the rivers, the Vikings soon linked Scandinavia and northern Europe to the Black Sea and to the Byzantine Empire with its capital at Constantinople (see Map 12.4). They built a few strategic forts along the rivers, from which they raided the neighboring Slavic tribes and collected tribute. Slaves were the most important article of tribute, and *Slav* even became the word for "slave" in several European languages.

To increase and protect their international commerce, the Vikings declared themselves the rulers of the eastern Slavs. According to tradition, the semilegendary chieftain Ruirik founded the princely dynasty about 860. In any event, the Varangian ruler Oleg (r. 878–912) established his residence at Kiev. He and his successors ruled over a loosely united confederation of Slavic territories—the Kievan principality—until 1054. The Viking prince and his clansmen quickly became assimilated into the Slavic population, taking local wives and emerging as the noble class.

Assimilation and loss of Scandinavian ethnic identity was speeded up by the conversion of the Vikings and local Slavs to Eastern Orthodox Christianity by missionaries of the Byzantine Empire. The written language of these missionaries, an early form of Slavic now known as Old Church Slavonic, was subsequently used in all religious and nonreligious documents in the Kievan state. Thus the rapidly Slavified Vikings left two important legacies: they created a loose unification of Slavic territories under a single ruling prince and a single ruling dynasty, and they imposed a basic religious unity by accepting Orthodox Christianity (as opposed to Roman Catholicism) for themselves and the eastern Slavs.

Even at its height under Great Prince Iaroslav the Wise (r. 1019–1054), the unity of the Kievan principality was extremely tenuous. Trade, rather than government, was the main concern of the rulers. Moreover, the Slavified Vikings failed to find a way of peacefully transferring power from one generation to the next. In medieval western Europe this fundamental problem of government was increasingly resolved by resort to the principle of *primogeniture:* the king's eldest son received the crown as his rightful inheritance when his father died. In early Kiev, however, there were apparently no fixed rules, and much strife accompanied each succession. Between 1054 and 1237, Kiev disintegrated into more and more competing units, each ruled by a prince claiming to be a descendant of Ruirik. Even when only one prince was claiming to be the great prince, the whole situation was very unsettled.

A given prince owned a certain number of farms or landed estates and had them worked directly by his people, mainly slaves, called *kholops* in Russian. Outside of these estates, the prince exercised only very limited authority in his principality. Excluding the clergy, two kinds of people lived there: the noble *boyars* and the commoner peasants. The boyars were the descendants of the original Viking warriors, and they also held their lands as free and clear private property. Although the boyars normally fought in princely armies, the customary law declared that they could serve any prince they wished. The ordinary peasants were also truly free. They could move at will wherever opportunities were greatest. In the touching phrase of the times, theirs was "a clean road, without boundaries."[15] In short, fragmented princely power, private property, and personal freedom all went together.

❈ REVIVAL AND RECOVERY

The eleventh century witnessed the beginnings of political stability in western Europe. Foreign invasions gradually declined, and domestic disorder subsided. This development gave people security in their persons and property. Political order and security provided the foundation for economic recovery and contributed to a slow increase in population.

The Decline of Invasion and Civil Disorder

In the tenth century Charlemagne's descendants continued to hold the royal title in the West Frankish kingdom, but they exercised no effective control over the great feudal lords. Research on medieval France has focused on regions and principalities, emphasizing the diversity of languages and cultures, the differences in social structure, and the division of public authority. Northern French society, for example, had strong feudal elements, but in the south the fief and vassalage were almost unknown. The southern territories used Roman law, but the northern counties and duchies relied on unwritten customary law that was not codified until the thirteenth century. The kings of France in the eleventh century were kings in name but petty barons in fact; no ruler exercised wide jurisdiction. Broad generalizations about France are difficult to make.[16]

Normandy gradually emerged as the strongest territory with the greatest relative level of peace. At Saint-Clair-sûr-Epte in Normandy in 911 the West Frankish ruler Charles the Simple, unable to oust the Vikings, officially recognized their leader Rollo and later invested him with more lands. In return, Rollo gave allegiance to Charles and agreed to hold the region as a barrier against future Viking attacks. Rollo and his men were baptized as Christians and supported the West Frankish ruler when he needed their help. Additional Northmen arrived but were easily pacified. The late tenth and early eleventh centuries saw the assimilation of Norman and French. Major assaults on France had ended.

After the death of the last Carolingian ruler in 987, an assembly of nobles met to choose a successor. The nobles selected Hugh Capet, who was *dux Francorum*—duke, or leader, of the Franks—and head of a powerful clan in the West Frankish kingdom. The history of France as a separate kingdom starts with the selection of Hugh Capet as king. The first Capetian kings (so called from the *côpe,* or cloak, that Hugh Capet wore as abbot of Saint-Denis) were weak in comparison with the duke of Normandy; but by hanging on to what they had, they laid the foundations for later political stability.

In Anglo-Saxon England recovery followed a different pattern. The Vikings had made a concerted effort to conquer and rule the whole island, and probably no part of Europe suffered more. The victory of the remarkable Alfred, king of the West Saxons, over Guthrun the Dane at Edington in 878 inaugurated a great political revival. Alfred and his immediate successors built a system of local defenses and slowly extended royal rule beyond Wessex (the area controlled by the West Saxons) to other Anglo-Saxon peoples until one law—royal law—replaced local custom. Alfred and his successors also laid the foundations for an efficient system of local government responsible directly to the king. Under the pressure of the Vikings, the seven kingdoms of England were gradually united under one ruler.

In the east, the German king Otto I (r. 936–973) inflicted a crushing defeat on the Hungarians at the banks of the Lech River in 955. This battle halted the Magyars' westward expansion and threat to Germany and made Otto a great hero to the Germans. It also signified the revival of the German monarchy and demonstrated that Otto was a worthy successor to Charlemagne.

When chosen king, Otto had selected Aachen as the site of his coronation to symbolize his intention to continue the tradition of Charlemagne. The basis of his power was to be alliance with and control of the church. Otto asserted the right to control ecclesiastical appointments. Before receiving religious consecration, bishops and abbots had to perform feudal homage for the lands that accompanied the church office. This practice, later known as investiture, was to create a grave crisis in the eleventh century (see pages 364–368).

Some of our knowledge of Otto derives from *The Deeds of Otto,* a history of his reign in heroic verse written by a nun, Hrotswitha of Gandersheim (ca 935–ca 1003). A learned poet, she also produced six verse plays and is considered the first dramatist after the fall of the ancient classical theater.

Otto's coronation by the pope in 962 revived the imperial dignity and laid the foundation for what was later called the Holy Roman Empire. Having the support of the church in Germany and Italy, Otto filled a power vacuum in northern Italy and brought peace among the great aristocratic families. Peace and political stability in turn promoted the revival of Venice and other northern Italian cities.

Although plague, climatic deterioration (which reduced agricultural productivity), and invasions had drastically reduced population throughout Italy, most of the northern Italian city-states survived the disorders of the early Middle Ages. By the ninth century, some Italian cities showed considerable economic dynamism, in particular Venice. Venice won privileged access to Byzantine markets; imported silk, textiles, cosmetics, and Crimean slaves; and sold these to Padua and other cities. By the eleventh century Venetian commerce had stimulated economic growth in the Lombard cities such as Milan and Cremona. Those cities and Sicily supplied Venice with food in exchange for luxury goods from the East. The rising economic importance of Venice and later of Genoa, Pisa, and other Italian cities became a central factor in the struggle between the papacy and the German empire.

Population, Climate, and Mechanization

A steady growth of population also contributed to Europe's general recovery. The decline of foreign invasions and internal civil disorder reduced the number of people killed and maimed. Feudal armies in the eleventh through thirteenth centuries continued their destruction, but they were small by modern standards and fought few pitched battles. Most medieval conflicts consisted of sieges directed at castles or fortifications. As few as twelve men with sufficient food and water could defend a castle for a long time. The survival of more young people—those most often involved in war and usually the most sexually active—meant a population rise.

The weather cooperated with the revival. Meteorologists believe that a significant warming trend occurred from the ninth century until about 1200. In the century between 1080 and 1180, England, France, and Germany experienced exceptionally mild winters and dry summers. Good weather helps to explain advances in population growth, land reclamation, and agricultural yield. Increased agricultural output profoundly affected Europeans' health, commerce, industry, and general lifestyle. A better diet had an enormous impact on women's lives: a better diet meant increased body fat and increased fertility; more iron in the diet meant that women were less anemic and less subject to opportunistic diseases. Some students believe that it was in the central Middle Ages that Western women began to outlive men.

The tenth and eleventh centuries also witnessed a remarkable spurt in mechanization, especially in

Arabic Water Mill Irrigation, essential to the growth of an agricultural economy, was greatly advanced by Arab inventions such as this *noria,* or water wheel, which harnessed the power of moving water. *(Source: Biblioteca Apostolica Vaticana)*

the use of energy. The increase in the number of water mills was spectacular. The abundance of slave labor in the ancient world had retarded the development of mills, but by the mid-ninth century, on the lands of the abbey of Saint-Germain-des-Prés near Paris, there were 59 mills powered by water. Succeeding generations saw a continued increase. *Domesday Book,* William the Conqueror's great survey of English economic resources in the late eleventh century (see page 373), recorded 5,624 water mills. One scholar has calculated that on average each mill supplied fifty households. Besides grinding wheat or other grains to produce flour, water mills became essential in fulling—the process of scouring, cleansing, and thickening cloth. In the past, to clean and increase the bulk and weight of cloth, men or women had trampled the cloth in a trough. Now, wooden hammers were raised and dropped on the cloth by means of a revolving drum connected to the spindle of a water wheel. Water mills revolutionized grinding and fulling by using natural, rather than human, energy.

Successful at adapting waterpower to human needs, medieval engineers soon harnessed windpower. They replaced the wheels driven by water with sails. Unlike water, which always flows in the same direction, wind can blow from many directions. Windmill engineers solved this problem very ingeniously by mounting the framed wooden body, which contained the machinery and carried the sails, on a massive upright post free to turn with the wind.[17]

❊ REVIVAL AND REFORM IN THE CHRISTIAN CHURCH

The eleventh century witnessed the beginnings of a remarkable religious revival. Monasteries, always the leaders in ecclesiastical reform, remodeled themselves under the leadership of the Burgundian abbey of Cluny. Subsequently, new religious orders, such as the Cistercians, were founded and became a broad spiritual movement.

The papacy itself, after a century of corruption and decadence, was cleaned up. The popes worked to clarify church doctrine and codify church law. They and their officials sought to communicate with all the clergy and peoples of Europe through a clearly defined, obedient hierarchy of bishops. Pope Gregory VII's strong assertion of papal power led to profound changes and serious conflict with secular authorities. The revival of the church manifested itself in the crusading movement.

Monastic Revival

The Viking, Magyar, and Muslim invaders attacked and ransacked many monasteries across Europe. Some religious communities fled and dispersed. In the period of political disorder that followed the disintegration of the Carolingian Empire, many religious houses fell under the control and domination of local feudal lords. Powerful laymen appointed themselves as abbots but kept their wives or mistresses. They took for themselves the lands and goods of monasteries, spending monastic revenues and selling monastic offices. All over Europe, temporal powers dominated the monasteries. The level of spiritual observance and intellectual activity declined.

In 909 William the Pious, duke of Aquitaine, established the abbey of Cluny near Macon in Burgundy. In his charter of endowment, Duke William declared that Cluny was to enjoy complete independence from all feudal (or secular) and episcopal lordship. The new monastery was to be subordinate only to the authority of Saints Peter and Paul as represented by the pope.

This monastery and its foundation charter came to exert vast religious influence. The first two abbots of Cluny, Berno (910–927) and Odo (927–942), set very high standards of religious behavior and stressed strict observance of *The Rule of Saint Benedict.* Cluny gradually came to stand for clerical celibacy and the suppression of *simony* (the sale of church offices). In the eleventh century, a series of highly able abbots ruled Cluny for a long time. These abbots paid careful attention to sound economic management. In a disorderly world, Cluny represented religious and political stability. Lay persons placed lands under Cluny's custody and monastic houses under its jurisdiction for reform. Benefactors wanted to be associated with Cluniac piety. Moreover, properties and monasteries under Cluny's jurisdiction enjoyed special protection, at least theoretically, from violence.[18] In this way hundreds of monasteries, primarily in France and Spain, came under Cluny's authority. Cluny was not the only center of monastic reform. The abbey of Gorze in Lotharingia (modern Lorraine) exercised a correcting influence on German

Consecration of the Church of Cluny Pope Urban II surrounded by mitred bishops appears on the left, Abbot Hugh of Cluny with cowled monks on the right. A French nobleman who had been a monk of Cluny, Urban coined the term *curia* as the official designation of the central government of the church. *(Source: Bibliothèque Nationale, Paris)*

religious houses and directed a massive reform of monasteries in central Europe.

Deeply impressed lay people showered gifts on monasteries with good reputations. Jewelry, rich vestments, elaborately carved sacred vessels, and even lands and properties poured into some houses. But with this wealth came lay influence. And as the monasteries became richer, the lifestyle of the monks grew increasingly luxurious, monastic observance and spiritual fervor declined. Soon fresh demands for reform were heard. The result was the founding of new religious orders in the late eleventh and early twelfth centuries. The best representatives of the new reforming spirit were the Cistercians.

In 1098 a group of monks left the rich abbey of Molesmes in Burgundy and founded a new house in the swampy forest of Cîteaux, planning to avoid all involvement with secular feudal society. They decided to accept only uncultivated lands far from regular habitation. They intended to refuse all gifts of mills, serfs, tithes, ovens—the traditional manorial sources of income. The early Cistercians determined to avoid elaborate liturgy and ceremony and to keep their chant simple. And they refused to allow the presence of powerful lay people in their monasteries, because they knew that such influence was usually harmful to careful observance.

The first monks at Cîteaux experienced sickness, a dearth of recruits, and terrible privation, but their sincerity and idealism attracted attention. In 1112 a twenty-three-year-old nobleman called Bernard joined the community at Cîteaux, together with thirty of his aristocratic companions. Thereafter, this reforming movement gained impetus. Cîteaux founded 525 new monasteries in the course of the twelfth century, and its influence on European society was profound. Unavoidably, however, Cistercian success brought wealth, and wealth brought power, both of which by the later twelfth century had begun to compromise Cistercian ideals.

Reform of the Papacy

Some scholars believe that the monastic revival spreading from Cluny influenced reform of the Roman papacy and eventually the reform of the entire Christian church. Important figures in this reform movement, such as Pope Gregory VII (r. 1073–1085) had spent some time at Cluny. And the man who consolidated the reform movement and strengthened the medieval papal monarchy, Pope Urban II (r. 1088–1099), had been a monk and prior at Cluny. But the precise degree of Cluny's impact on the reform movement cannot be measured. The broad goals of the Cluniac movement and those of the Roman papacy, however, were the same.

In the tenth century the papacy provided little leadership to the Christian peoples of western Europe. Factions in Rome sought to control the papacy for their own material gain. Popes were appointed to advance the political ambitions of their families—the great aristocratic families of Rome—and not because of special spiritual qualifications.

At the local parish level there were many married priests. Taking Christ as the model for the priestly life, the Roman church had always encouraged clerical celibacy, and it had been an obligation for ordination since the fourth century. But in the tenth and eleventh centuries, probably a majority of European priests were married or living with a woman.

Serious efforts at reform began under Pope Leo IX (r. 1049–1054). Leo traveled widely and held councils at Pavia, Reims, and Mainz that issued decrees against simony, clerical marriage, and violence. His representatives held church councils across Europe, pressing for moral reform. They urged those who could not secure justice at home to appeal to the pope, the ultimate source of justice. By his character and actions, Leo set high moral standards for the West.

During the short reign of Nicholas II (r. 1058–1061), a council held in the ancient church of Saint John Lateran at Rome in 1059 devised a new method of electing the pope to remove the influence of Roman aristocratic factions from papal elections. Since the eighth century, the priests of the major churches in and around Rome had constituted a special group, called a "college," that advised the pope when he summoned them to meetings. These chief priests were called "cardinals" from the Latin *cardo,* meaning "hinge." The cardinals were the hinges on which the church turned. The Lateran Synod of 1059 decreed that the authority and power to elect the pope rested solely in this college of cardinals. The college retains that power today.

When the office of pope was vacant, the cardinals were responsible for governing the church. (In the Middle Ages the college of cardinals numbered around twenty-five or thirty, most of them from Italy. In 1586 the figure was set at seventy. In the 1960s Pope Paul VI virtually doubled that number, appointing men from all parts of the globe to reflect the international character of the church.) By 1073 the progress of reform in the Christian church was well advanced. The election of Cardinal Hildebrand as Pope Gregory VII in 1073 changed the direction of reform from a moral to a political one.

Cardinal Hildebrand had received a good education at Rome and spent some time at Cluny, where his strict views of clerical life were strengthened. He believed that the pope, as the successor of Saint Peter, was the Vicar of God on earth and that papal orders were the orders of God. Once Hildebrand became pope, he and his assistants began to insist on the "freedom of the church." By this they meant the freedom of churchmen to obey canon law and their freedom from control and interference by lay people.

"Freedom of the church" pointed to the end of *lay investiture*—the selection and appointment of church officials by secular authorities. Bishops and abbots were invested with a staff representing pastoral jurisdiction and a ring signifying union with the diocese or monastic community. When laymen gave these symbols, they appeared to be distributing spiritual authority. Ecclesiastical opposition to lay investiture was not new in the eleventh century. It, too, had been part of church theory for centuries. But Gregory's attempt to put theory into practice was a radical departure from long usage. Since feudal monarchs depended on the literacy and administrative knowledge of churchmen for the operation of their governments, Gregory's program seemed to spell disaster for stable royal administration. It provoked a terrible crisis.

The Controversy over Lay Investiture

In February 1075 Pope Gregory held a council at Rome that published a decree against lay investiture:

If anyone henceforth shall receive a bishopric or abbey from the hands of a lay person, he shall not be considered as among the number of bishops and abbots. . . . Likewise if any emperor, king . . . or any one at all of the secular powers, shall presume to perform investiture with bishoprics or with any other ecclesiastical dignity . . . he shall feel the divine displeasure as well with regard to his body as to his other belongings.[19]

In short, clerics who accepted investiture from laymen were to be deposed, and laymen who invested clerics were to be *excommunicated*—cut off from the sacraments and the Christian community.

The church's penalty of excommunication relied for its effectiveness on public opinion. Gregory believed the strong support he enjoyed for his moral reform would carry over to his political reforms; he thought that excommunication would compel rulers to abide by his changes. Immediately, however, Henry IV in the Holy Roman Empire, William the Conqueror in England, and Philip I in France protested.

The strongest reaction came from Germany and Henry IV. In two basic ways, the relationship of the German kings to the papacy differed from that of other monarchs: the pope crowned the German emperor, and both the empire and the papal states claimed northern Italy. Since the time of Charlemagne the emperor had controlled some territory and bishops in Italy.

In addition to the subject of lay investiture, a more fundamental issue was at stake. Gregory's decree raised the question of the proper role of the monarch in a Christian society. Did a king have ultimate jurisdiction over all his subjects, including the clergy? For centuries, tradition had answered this question in favor of the ruler, so it is no wonder that Henry protested the papal assertions about investiture. Indirectly, they undermined imperial power and sought to make papal authority supreme.

An increasingly bitter exchange of letters ensued. Gregory accused Henry of lack of respect for the papacy and insisted that disobedience to the pope was disobedience to God. Henry protested in a letter beginning, "Henry King not by usurpation, but by the pious ordination of God, to Hildebrand, now not Pope, but false monk."

Within the empire, in January 1076, the German bishops who had been invested by Henry withdrew their allegiance from the pope. Gregory replied by excommunicating them and suspending Henry from the kingship. The lay nobility delighted in the bind the emperor had been put in: with Henry IV excommunicated and cast outside the Christian fold, they did not have to obey him and could advance their own interests. Gregory hastened to support them. The Christmas season of 1076 witnessed an ironic situation in Germany: the clergy supported the emperor, and the great nobility favored the pope.

Henry outwitted Gregory. Crossing the Alps in January 1077, he approached the pope's residence at Canossa in northern Italy. According to legend, Henry stood for three days in the snow seeking forgiveness. As a priest, Pope Gregory was obliged to grant absolution and to readmit the emperor to the Christian community. Although the emperor, the most powerful ruler in Europe, bowed before the pope, Henry actually scored only a temporary victory. When the sentence of excommunication was lifted, he regained the kingship and authority over his rebellious subjects. But for the next two hundred years, in Germany and elsewhere, secular rulers were reluctant to pose a serious challenge to the papacy.

For Germany the incident at Canossa settled nothing. The controversy over lay investiture and the position of the king in Christian society continued. Finally, in 1122, at a conference held at Worms, a compromise settled the issue. Bishops were to be chosen according to canon law—that is, by the clergy—in the presence of the emperor or his delegate. The emperor surrendered the right to invest bishops with the ring and staff. The papacy achieved technical success, because rulers could not longer invest. But lay rulers still possessed an effective veto over ecclesiastical appointments, because they were permitted to be present at ecclesiastical elections and to accept or refuse feudal homage from the new prelates. Papal power was enhanced, but neither side won a clear victory.

William the Conqueror of England and Philip I of France were just as guilty of lay investiture as the German emperor, and both quarreled openly with Gregory. However, Rome's conflict with the western rulers never reached the proportions of the dispute with the German emperor. Gregory VII and his successors had the diplomatic sense to avoid creating three enemies at once.

The long controversy had tremendous social and political consequences in Germany. For half a century, between 1075 and 1125, civil war was chronic in the empire. Preoccupied with Italy and the quarrel with the papacy, the German emperors could do little about it. The lengthy struggle between papacy and emperor allowed emerging noble dynasties, such as the Zähringer of Swabia, to enhance their position. By the eleventh century these great German families had achieved a definite sense of themselves as noble.[20] To control their lands, the great lords built castles, which were both military strongholds and centers of administration for the surrounding territories. The German aristocracy subordinated the knights and reinforced their dependency with strong feudal ties. They reduced free men and serfs to an extremely servile position. Henry IV and Henry V were compelled to surrender rights and privileges to the nobility. When the papal-imperial conflict ended in 1122, the nobility held the balance of power in Germany, and later German kings, such as Frederick Barbarossa (see page 375), would fail in their efforts to strengthen the monarchy against the princely families. For these reasons, particularism, localism, and feudal independence characterized the Holy Roman Empire in the central Middle Ages. The investiture controversy had a catastrophic effect there, severely retarding development of a strong centralized monarchy.

In the late eleventh century and throughout the twelfth, the papacy pressed Gregory's campaign for reform of the church. Pope Urban II laid the foundations for the papal monarchy by reorganizing the central government of the Roman church. He recognized the college of cardinals as a definite consultative body. This agency, together with the papal chapel, constituted the papal court, or *curia Romana*—the papacy's administrative and financial bureaucracy and its court of law. The papal court, though not fully developed until the mid-twelfth century, was the first well-organized institution of monarchial authority in medieval Europe.

The Roman curia had its greatest impact as a court of law. As the highest ecclesiastical tribunal, it formulated canon law for all of Christendom. It was the instrument with which the popes pressed the goals of reform and centralized the church. The curia sent legates to hold councils in various parts of Europe. Councils published decrees and sought to enforce the law. When individuals in any part of Christian Europe felt they were being denied justice in their local church courts, they could appeal to Rome. Slowly but surely, in the central Middle Ages the papal curia developed into the court of final appeal for all of Christian Europe. The majority of cases that came to the Roman curia related to disputes over church property or ecclesiastical elections and, especially, to questions of marriage and annulment. Since the fourth century, Christian values had influenced the administration of the law, and bishops frequently sat in civil courts that heard marriage cases. In the tenth and eleventh centuries, church officials began to claim that they had exclusive jurisdiction over marriage. Appeals to an ecclesiastical tribunal, rather than to a civil court, or appeals from a civil court to a church court, implied the acceptance of a church court's jurisdiction.

Most of the popes in the twelfth and thirteenth centuries were canon lawyers who recognized the authority of church courts. The most famous of them, the man whose pontificate represented the height of medieval papal power, was Innocent III (r. 1198–1216). Innocent judged a vast number of cases. He compelled King Philip Augustus of France to take back his wife, Ingeborg of Denmark. He arbitrated the rival claims of two disputants to the imperial crown of Germany. He forced King John of England to accept as archbishop of Canterbury a man John did not really want.

By the early thirteenth century, papal efforts at reform begun more than a century before had attained phenomenal success. The popes themselves were men of high principles and strict moral behavior. The frequency of clerical marriage and the level of violence had declined considerably. The practice of simony was much more the exception than the rule. Yet the seeds of future difficulties were being planted. As the volume of appeals to Rome multiplied, so did the size of the papal bureaucracy. As the number of lawyers increased, so did concern for legal niceties and technicalities,

EUROPE IN THE MIDDLE AGES

ca 700	Publication of the Lindisfarne Gospel book, Bede's *Ecclesiastical History of the English Nation,* and *Beowulf*
ca 710–750	Missionary work of Wynfrith (Boniface) supports the efforts of Charles Martel and Pippin III to assimilate Germanic tribes
733	Charles Martel defeats Muslims at Battle of Tours
751	Pippin III elected king by Frankish magnates
754	The pope anoints Pippin III king at Paris, establishing an important alliance between the Christian church and the Frankish ruler
756	Pippin III donates the Papal States to the papacy
768	Charlemagne succeeds to the Frankish throne
768–805	Charlemagne conquers all of continental Europe except Spain, Scandinavia, southern Italy, and Slavic fringes of the East
781	Alcuin enters Charlemagne's court at Aachen as chief adviser on religious and educational matters
ca 787	Viking raids of Carolingian territories begin
800	Imperial coronation of Charlemagne
814	Louis the Pious succeeds to Charlemagne's empire
843	Treaty of Verdun: Charlemagne's empire divided among his grandsons Lothair, Louis the German, and Charles the Bald
ca 845–900	Viking, Magyar, and Muslim invasions complete the disintegration of the Carolingian Empire
878	King Alfred's victory over Guthrun inaugurates political recovery in Anglo-Saxon England
909	Founding of the abbey of Cluny—first step in the revival of monasticism and reform of the church
955	Otto I's victory at Lech River ends Magyar incursions in Germany
962	Otto's coronation lays the foundation for the Holy Roman Empire
987	Election of Hugh Capet as king of the West Frankish kingdom
1049	Pope Leo IX begins serious reform of the church
1059	Lateran Synod gives power of papal election to the college of cardinals
1073	Cardinal Hildebrand becomes Pope Gregory VII
1075	Church issues decree against lay investiture that leads to conflict between the pope and the rulers of Germany, England, and France
1096–1099	The First Crusade
1098	Founding of the Cistercian order
1122	Compromise at Worms removes power of investiture from lay rulers but grants them effective veto over ecclesiastical appointments
1202–1204	The Fourth Crusade; sacking of Constantinople cements the split between Eastern and Western churches

fees, and church offices. As early as the mid-twelfth century, John of Salisbury, an Englishman working in the papal curia, had written that the people condemned the curia for its greed and indifference to human suffering. Nevertheless, the power of the curia continued to grow, as did its bureaucracy.

Thirteenth-century popes devoted their attention to the bureaucracy and their conflicts with the German emperor Frederick II. Some, like Gregory IX (r. 1227–1241), abused their prerogatives to such an extent that their moral impact was seriously weakened. Even worse, Innocent IV (r. 1243–1254) used secular weapons, including military force, to maintain his leadership. These popes badly damaged papal prestige and influence. By the early fourteenth century, the seeds of disorder would grow into a vast and sprawling tree, and once again cries for reform would be heard.

The Crusades

The Crusades of the eleventh and twelfth centuries were the most obvious manifestation of the papal claim to the leadership of Christian society. The enormous popular response to papal calls for crusading reveals the influence of the reformed papacy. The Crusades also reflect the church's new understanding of the noble warrior class. As a distinguished scholar of the Crusades wrote, "just as rulership earlier had been Christianized . . . , so now was the military profession; it acquired a direct ecclesiastical purpose, for war in the service of the church or for the weak came to be regarded as holy and was declared to be a religious duty not only for the king but also for every individual knight."[21]

Crusades in the late eleventh and early twelfth centuries were holy wars sponsored by the papacy for the recovery of the Holy Land from the Muslim Arabs or the Turks. They grew out of the long conflict between Christians and Muslims in Spain, where by about 1250 Christian kings had regained roughly 90 percent of the peninsula. Although people of all ages and classes participated in the Crusades, so many knights did so that crusading became a distinctive feature of the upper-class lifestyle. In an aristocratic, military society, men coveted reputations as Crusaders; the Crusades manifested the religious and chivalric ideals—as well as the tremendous vitality—of medieval society.

The Roman papacy supported the holy war in Spain and by the late eleventh century, amid the bitter struggle over investiture with the German emperors, had strong reasons for wanting to launch an expedition against Muslim infidels in the Middle East as well. If the pope could muster a large army against the enemies of Christianity, his claim to be leader of Christian society in the West would be strengthened. Moreover, in 1054 a serious theological disagreement had split the Greek church of Byzantium and the Roman church of the West. The pope believed that a crusade would lead to strong Roman influence in Greek territories and eventually the reunion of the two churches.

In 1071 at Manzikert in eastern Anatolia, Turkish soldiers in the pay of the Arabs defeated a Greek army and occupied much of Asia Minor (Map 12.5). The emperor at Constantinople appealed to the West for support. Shortly afterward, the holy city of Jerusalem fell to the Turks, and the papacy claimed to be outraged that the holy city was in the hands of unbelievers. Since the Muslims had held Palestine since the eighth century, what the papacy actually feared was that the Seljuk Turks would be less accommodating to Christian pilgrims than the Muslims had been.

In 1095 Pope Urban II journeyed to Clermont in France and called for a great Christian holy war against the infidels. He urged Christian knights who had been fighting one another to direct their energies against the true enemies of God, the Muslims. Urban proclaimed an *indulgence,* or remission of the temporal penalties imposed by the church for sin, to those who would fight for and regain the holy city of Jerusalem.

Few speeches in history have had such a dramatic effect as Urban's call at Clermont for the First Crusade. Godfrey of Bouillon, Geoffrey of Lorraine, and many other great lords from northern France immediately had the cross of the Crusader sewn on their tunics. Encouraged by popular preachers, thousands of people of all classes joined the crusade. Although most of the Crusaders were French, pilgrims from many regions streamed southward from the Rhineland, through Germany and the Balkans. Of all of the developments of the central Middle Ages, none better reveals Europeans' religious and emotional fervor and the influence of the reformed papacy than the extraordinary outpouring of support for the First Crusade.

Religious convictions inspired many, but mundane motives were also involved. For the curious

MAP 12.5 Routes of the Crusades   The Crusades led to a major cultural encounter between Muslim and Christian values. What significant intellectual and economic effects resulted?

and the adventurous, the crusade offered foreign travel and excitement. It provided kings, who were trying to establish order and build states, the perfect opportunity to get rid of troublemaking knights. It gave land-hungry younger sons a chance to acquire fiefs in the Middle East.

The Crusades brought to the surface latent Christian prejudice against the Jews. Between the sixth and tenth centuries, descendants of Sephardic (from the modern Hebrew word *Separaddi,* meaning "Spaniard") Jews had settled along the trade routes of western Europe. In the eleventh century, they played a major role in the international trade between the Muslim Middle East and the West. Jews also lent money to peasants, townspeople, and nobles. Because the Jews performed these useful economic services, kings and lords protected them. When the First Crusade was launched, many poor knights had to borrow from Jews to equip themselves for the expedition. Debt bred resentment against Jews. Christian preachers often focused their remarks on Jerusalem, blaming the

Jews there for Jesus' crucifixion. They conveniently ignored the fact that Jesus had forgiven all his executioners—Luke 22:34. With the atmosphere thus poisoned, as crusading armies passed through the Rhineland in May and June 1096, they directed assaults on Jewish communities in Speyer, Worms, Mainz, Cologne, Trier, and Metz. The resulting massacres testify to the general ignorance, bigotry, and lack of concentrated strategy that characterized the entire crusading movement.

The First Crusade was successful mostly because of the enthusiasm of the participants. The Crusaders had little more than religious zeal. They knew nothing about the geography, climate, or culture of the Middle East. Although there were several counts with military experience among the throng, the Crusaders could never agree on a leader, and the entire expedition was marked by disputes among the great lords. Lines of supply were never set up. Starvation and disease wracked the army, and the Turks slaughtered hundreds of noncombatants. Nevertheless, convinced that

❋ **The Capture of Jerusalem in 1099**   As engines hurl stones to breach the walls, Crusaders enter on scaling ladders. Scenes from Christ's Passion (above) identify the city as Jerusalem. *(Source: Bibliothèque Nationale, Paris)*

"God wills it"—the war cry of the Crusaders—the army pressed on and in 1099 captured Jerusalem. Although the Crusaders fought bravely, Arab disunity was a chief reason for their victory. At Jerusalem, Edessa, Tripoli, and Antioch, Crusader kingdoms were founded on the Western feudal model.

Between 1096 and 1270, the crusading ideal was expressed in eight papally approved expedi-

tions to the East. Despite the success of the First Crusade, none of the later ones accomplished very much. The Third Crusade (1189–1192) was precipitated by the recapture of Jerusalem by the sultan Saladin in 1187. Frederick Barbarossa of the Holy Roman Empire, Richard (Lion-Heart) of England, and Philip Augustus of France participated, and the Third Crusade was better financed than previous ones. But disputes among the leaders and strategic problems prevented any lasting results.

During the Fourth Crusade (1202–1204), careless preparation and inadequate financing had disastrous consequences for Latin-Byzantine relations. When the Crusaders could not pay the Venetians the money promised for transport to the Holy Land, the Venetians agreed to postpone the debt if the Crusaders attacked Zara, a *Christian* city on the Dalmatian coast (the Dalmatian forests were the source of the oak that the Venetians used for shipbuilding). The Crusaders took Zara on November 24, 1202. At Zara, envoys from the dethroned Byzantine emperor Isaac II and his son Alexius promised reunification of the Greek and Latin churches, large payments to the Venetians, and Byzantine support for the expedition to the Holy Land. Thus in April 1204, the Crusaders and Venetians stormed Constantinople, sacked the city destroying its magnificent library, and grabbed thousands of relics that were later sold in Europe. From this destruction the Byzantine Empire as a political unit never recovered. Moreover, the assault of one Christian people on another—when one of the goals of the Fourth Crusade was reunion of Greek and Latin churches—made the split between the Greek and Latin churches permanent. It also helped to discredit the entire crusading movement.

In 1208, two expeditions of children set out on a crusade to the Holy Land. One contingent turned back; the other was captured and sold into slavery. Two later crusades against the Muslims were undertaken by King Louis IX of France and added to his prestige as a pious ruler. Apart from that, the last of the official crusades accomplished nothing at all.

Crusades were also mounted against groups perceived as Christendom's social enemies. In 1208 Pope Innocent III proclaimed a crusade against the Albigensians, a heretical sect concentrated in southern France that rejected orthodox doctrine on the relationship of God and man, on the sacraments, and on the clerical hierarchy. Fearing that religious division would lead to civil disorder, the French monarchy joined the crusade and inflicted a savage defeat on the Albigensians at Muret in 1213. Fearful of encirclement by imperial territories, the popes also promoted crusades against Emperor Frederick II in 1227 and 1239. This use of force against a Christian ruler backfired, damaging the credibility of the papacy as the sponsor of peace.

What impact did the Crusades have on women? That is a difficult question. Fewer women than men directly participated (societies usually perceive war as a masculine enterprise). Given the aristocratic bias of the chroniclers, we have more information about royal and noble ladies who went to the Holy Land than about middle-class and peasant women, though the latter groups contributed the greater numbers. Eleanor of Aquitaine (1122?–1204) accompanied her husband King Louis VII on the Second Crusade (1147–1149), and the thirteenth-century English chronicler Matthew Paris says that large numbers of women went on the Seventh Crusade (1248–1254) so that they could obtain the crusading indulgence. The Crusades illustrate that women in feudal society exercised considerable power. Women who stayed home assumed their husbands' responsibilities in the management of estates, the dispensation of justice to vassals and serfs, and the protection of property from attack. Since Crusaders frequently could finance the expedition only by borrowing, it fell to their wives to repay the loans. These heavy responsibilities brought women a degree of power. The many women who operated inns and shops in the towns through which crusading armies passed profited from the rental of lodgings and the sale of foodstuffs, clothing, arms, and fodder for animals. For prostitutes, also, crusading armies offered business opportunities.

The Crusades introduced some Europeans to Eastern luxury goods, but the Crusades' overall cultural impact on the West remains debatable. By the late eleventh century, strong economic and intellectual ties with the East had already been made. The Crusades testify to the religious enthusiasm of the central Middle Ages. But, as Steven Runciman, a distinguished scholar of the Crusades, concluded in his three-volume history: "The triumphs of the Crusade were the triumphs of faith. But faith without wisdom is a dangerous thing. . . . In the long sequence of interaction and fusion between Orient and Occident out of which our civilization has grown, the Crusades were a tragic and destructive episode."[22]

In addition to the feudal states that the Crusaders set up along the Syrian and Palestinian coasts, which managed to survive for about two centuries before the Muslims reconquered them, the Crusaders left in the Middle East two legacies that continue to resonate. First, the long struggle between Islam and Christendom and the example of persecution set by Christian kings and prelates left an inheritance of deep bitterness; relations between Muslims and their Christian and Jewish subjects worsened. Second, European merchants, primarily Italians, had established communities in the Crusader states. After those kingdoms collapsed, Muslim rulers still encouraged trade with European businessmen. Commerce with the West benefited both Muslims and Europeans, and it continued to flourish.[23]

✦ MEDIEVAL ORIGINS OF THE MODERN STATE

Rome's great legacy to Western civilization had been the concepts of the state and the law. But for almost five hundred years after the disintegration of the Roman Empire in the West, the state as a reality did not exist. Political authority was completely decentralized. Power was spread among many feudal lords, who gave their localities such protection and security as their strength allowed and whose laws affected a relative few. In the mid-eleventh century, many overlapping layers of authority—earls, counts, barons, knights—existed between a king and the ordinary people.

In these circumstances, medieval rulers had common goals. To increase public order, they wanted to establish an effective means of communication with all peoples. They also wanted more revenue and efficient bureaucracies. The solutions they found to these problems laid the foundations for modern national states.

The modern state is an organized territory with definite geographical boundaries that are recognized by other states. It has a body of law and institutions of government. If the state claims to govern according to law, it is guided in its actions by the law. The modern national state counts on the loyalty of its citizens, or at least of a majority of them. In return, it provides order so that citizens can go about their daily work and other activities. It protects its citizens in their persons and property. The state tries to prevent violence and to ap-

✦ **The Bayeux Tapestry** Measuring 231 feet by 19½ inches, the Bayeux Tapestry gives a narrative description of the events surrounding the Norman conquest of England. The tapestry provides an important historical source for the clothing, armor, and lifestyles of the Norman and Anglo-Saxon warrior class. *(Source: Tapisserie de Bayeux et avec autorisation spéciale de la Ville de Bayeux)*

prehend and punish those who commit it. It supplies a currency or medium of exchange that permits financial and commercial transactions. The state conducts relations with foreign governments. In order to accomplish even these minimal functions, the state must have officials, bureaucracies, laws, courts of law, soldiers, information, and money. States with these attributes are relatively recent developments.

Unification and Communication

Political developments in England, France, and Germany provide good examples of the beginnings of the national state in the central Middle Ages. Under the pressure of the Viking invasions of the ninth and tenth centuries, the seven kingdoms of Anglo-Saxon England united under one king. At the same time, for reasons historians still cannot fully explain, England was divided into local *shires,* or counties, each under the jurisdiction of a sheriff appointed by the king. The kingdom of England, therefore, had a political head start on the rest of Europe.

When Edward the Confessor (r. 1042–1066) died, his cousin Duke William of Normandy—known in English history as William the Conqueror—claimed the English throne and in 1066 defeated the Anglo-Saxon claimant on the battlefield of Hastings. As William subdued the rest of the country, he distributed lands to his Norman followers and required all feudal lords to swear an oath of allegiance to him as king.

William the Conqueror (r. 1066–1087) preserved the Anglo-Saxon institution of sheriffs representing the king at the local level but replaced Anglo-Saxon sheriffs with Normans. A sheriff had heavy duties. He maintained order in the shire. He caught criminals and had them tried in the shire court over which his deputy, the undersheriff, presided. He collected taxes and, when the king ordered him to do so, raised an army of foot soldiers. For all his efforts, the sheriff received no pay. This system, whereby unpaid officials governed the county, served as the basic pattern of English local government for many centuries. It cost the Crown nothing, but it restricted opportunities for public service to the well-to-do.

William also retained another Anglo-Saxon device, the *writ*. This brief administrative order, written in the vernacular (Anglo-Saxon) by a government clerk, was the means by which the central government communicated with people at the local level. Sheriffs were empowered to issue writs relating to matters in their counties.

At his Christmas court in 1085, William decided to conduct a systematic investigation of the entire country to determine how much wealth there was in his new kingdom and who held what land. Groups of royal officials or judges were sent to every part of England. In every village and farm, the priest and six local people were put under oath to answer the questions of the king's commissioners truthfully. In the words of a contemporary chronicler:

He sent his men over all England into every shire and had them find out how many hundred hides there were in the shire [a hide was a measure of land large enough to support one family], or what land and cattle the king himself had, or what dues he ought to have in twelve months from the shire. Also . . . what or how much everybody had who was occupying land in England, in land or cattle, and how much money it was worth. So very narrowly did he have it investigated, that there was no single hide nor yard of land, nor indeed . . . one ox nor one cow nor one pig was there left out, and not put down in his record: and all these records were brought to him afterwards.[24]

The resulting record, called *Domesday Book* from the Anglo-Saxon word *doom* meaning "judgment," provided William and his descendants with information vital for the exploitation and government of the country. Knowing the amount of wealth every area possessed, the king could tax accordingly. Knowing the amount of land his vassals had, he could allot knight service fairly.

In 1128 the Conqueror's granddaughter Matilda was married to Geoffrey of Anjou. Their son, who became Henry II of England and inaugurated the Angevin (from Anjou) Dynasty, inherited the French provinces of Normandy, Anjou, Maine, and Touraine in northwestern France (Map 12.6). When Henry married the great heiress Eleanor of Aquitaine in 1152, he claimed lordships over Aquitaine, Poitou, and Gascony in southwestern France. The so-called Angevin empire included most of the British Isles and half of France. The histories of England and France in the central Middle Ages were thus closely intertwined.

In the early twelfth century, France consisted of a number of virtually independent provinces, each

ENGLAND

• Bruges
Ghent •
Calais • • Ypres
FLANDERS
× Bouvines
1214
ARTOIS
Arras •

English Channel

• Amiens
VERMANDOIS

• Rouen   PICARDY
• Soissons
• Reims

NORMANDY   CHAMPAGNE

Paris •
• Chartres   *Seine*   • Troyes
ÎLE-DE-FRANCE
(ROYAL DOMAIN)
MAINE   BLOIS   • Orléans

BRITTANY

ANJOU   *Loire*

• Nantes   Tours •
TOURAINE   BURGUNDY
• Bourges

POITOU
Poitiers •   BOURBON
• Cluny

Bay

of

Biscay

AQUITAINE   Clermont •
• Lyons

• Bordeaux

Garonne   *Rhône*

• Avignon
TOULOUSE   PROVENCE
GASCONY
• Toulouse   Montpellier •
• Marseilles

Mediterranean Sea

LANGUEDOC
SPAIN

HOLY

ROMAN

EMPIRE

Meuse

☐ Crown lands in 1180
☐ Added by Philip Augustus, 1180–1223
☐ Added 1223–1270
☐ Added 1270–1314
☐ Royal fiefs
× Major battle

0   50   100 Km.
0   50   100 Mi.

✿ **MAP 12.6 Growth of the Kingdom of France**   Some scholars believe that Philip II received the title "Augustus" (from a Latin word meaning "to increase") because he vastly expanded the territories of the kingdom of France.

governed by its local ruler. Unlike the king of England, the king of France had jurisdiction over a very small area. Chroniclers called King Louis VI (r. 1108–1137) *roi de Saint-Denis,* king of Saint-Denis, because the territory he controlled was limited to Paris and the Saint-Denis area surrounding the city. This region, the Île-de-France or royal do-

main, became the nucleus of the French state. The clear goal of the medieval French king was to increase the royal domain and extend his authority.

The work of unifying France began under Louis VI's grandson Philip II (r. 1180–1223). Rigord, Philip's biographer, gave him the title "Augustus" (from a Latin word meaning "to increase") because he vastly enlarged the territory of the kingdom of France (see Map 12.6). By defeating a baronial plot against the Crown, Philip Augustus acquired the northern counties of Artois and Vermandois. The rich province of Normandy, held by King John of England, who was Philip's vassal, fell to the French in 1204. Within two years Philip also gained the farmlands of Maine, Touraine, and Anjou. By the end of his reign Philip was effectively master of northern France.

In the thirteenth century, Philip Augustus's descendants acquired important holdings in the south, and by the end of the thirteenth century, most of the provinces of modern France had been added to the royal domain through diplomacy, marriage, war, and inheritance. The king of France was stronger than any group of nobles who might try to challenge his authority.

Philip Augustus devised a method of governing the provinces and providing for communication between the central government in Paris and local communities. He decided that each province would retain its own institutions and laws. But royal agents, called *baillis* in the north and *seneschals* in the south, were sent from Paris into the provinces as the king's official representatives with authority to act for him. The baillis and seneschals were appointed by, paid by, and responsible to the king. Unlike the English sheriffs, they were never natives of the provinces to which they were assigned, and they could not own land there. This policy reflected the fundamental principle of French administration that royal interests superseded local interests. But although France was administered by a centralized professional royal bureaucracy, the French system was characterized by a great variety of customs, laws, and provincial institutions at the local level. Although it sometimes fell into disrepair, although one scholar has called it decrepit from the start, the basic system that Philip Augustus created lasted until the Revolution of 1789.

The political problems of Germany differed from those of France and England. The eleventh-century investiture controversy between the German emperor and the Roman papacy had left Germany shattered and divided (see pages 364–365). In the twelfth and thirteenth centuries, Germany was split into hundreds of independent provinces, principalities, bishoprics, duchies, and free cities.

There were several barriers to the development of a strong central government. Unlike the French kings, the German rulers lacked a strong royal domain to use as a source of revenue and a base from which to expand royal power. No accepted principle of succession to the throne existed; as a result, the death of the Holy Roman emperor was often followed by disputes, civil war, and anarchy. Moreover, German rulers were continually attracted south by the wealth of the northern Italian cities or by dreams of restoring the imperial glory of Charlemagne. Time after time the German kings got involved in Italian affairs, and in turn the papacy, fearful of a strong German power in northern Italy, interfered in German affairs. German princes took bribes from whichever authority—the emperor or the pope—best supported their own particular ambitions. Consequently, in contrast to France and England, the German empire witnessed little royal centralization.

Frederick Barbarossa (r. 1152–1190) of the House of Hohenstaufen tried valiantly to unify the empire. Just as the French rulers branched out from the Île-de-France, Frederick tried to use his family duchy of Swabia in southwestern Germany as a power base (Map 12.7). Like William the Conqueror, Frederick required all his vassals to take an oath of allegiance to him as emperor.

Outside Swabia, Frederick tried to make feudalism work as a system of government. He made alliances with the great lay princes: they acknowledged that their lands were fiefs of the emperor, and he in turn recognized their military and political jurisdiction over their territories. Frederick also compelled the great churchmen to become his vassals, so that when they died he could control their estates. In 1158 Frederick forbade private warfare and ordered severe penalties for violations of the peace.

Unfortunately, Frederick Barbarossa did not concentrate his efforts and resources in one area. He, too, became embroiled in the affairs of Italy. In the eleventh and twelfth centuries, the northern Italian cities had grown rich on trade, and Frederick believed that if he could gain the imperial crown, he could cash in on Italian wealth.

Between 1154 and 1188, Frederick made six expeditions into Italy. His scorched-earth policy was successful at first, resulting in significant conquests in the north. The brutality of his methods, however, provoked revolts, and the Italian cities formed an alliance with the papacy. In 1176 Frederick suffered a defeat at Legnano (see Map 12.7). This battle marked the first time a feudal cavalry of

armed knights was decisively defeated by bourgeois infantrymen. Frederick was forced to recognize the municipal autonomy of the northern Italian cities. Germany and Italy remained separate and followed separate courses of development.

Frederick Barbarossa's Italian ventures contributed nothing to the unification of the German states. Because the empire lacked a stable bureaucratic system of government, his presence was essential for the maintenance of peace. During Frederick's absences, the fires of independence and disorder spread, and the princes and magnates consolidated their power. By 1187 Frederick had to accept again the reality of private warfare. The power of the princes cost the growth of a centralized monarchy.

Law and Justice

Throughout Europe in the twelfth and thirteenth centuries, the law was a hodgepodge of Germanic customs, feudal rights, and provincial practices. Kings wanted to blend these elements into a uniform system of rules acceptable and applicable to all their peoples. In France and England, kings successfully contributed to the development of national states through the administration of their laws.

The French king Louis IX (r. 1226–1270) was famous in his time for his concern for justice. Each French province, even after being made part of the kingdom of France, retained its unique laws and procedures, but Louis IX created a royal judicial system. He established the Parlement of Paris, a kind of supreme court that welcomed appeals from local administrators and from the courts of feudal lords throughout France. By the very act of appealing the decisions of feudal courts to the Parlement of Paris, French people in far-flung provinces were recognizing the superiority of royal justice.

Louis was the first French monarch to publish laws for the entire kingdom. The Parlement of Paris registered (or announced) these laws, which forbade private warfare, judicial duels, gambling, blaspheming, and prostitution. Louis sought to

✤ MAP 12.7 The Holy Roman Empire, ca 1200 Frederick Barbarossa tried to use the feudal bond to tie the various provinces, principalities, bishop-rics, duchies, and free cities to the imperial monarchy.

identify justice with the kingship, and gradually royal justice touched all parts of the kingdom.

Under Henry II (r. 1154–1189), England developed and extended *common law*—a law common to and accepted by the entire country. No other country in medieval Europe did so. Each year Henry sent out *circuit judges* (royal officials who traveled in a given circuit or district) to hear civil and criminal cases. Wherever the king's judges sat, there sat the king's court. Slowly, the king's court gained jurisdiction over all property disputes and criminal actions.

An accused person formally charged with a crime did *not* undergo trial by jury, however. He or she was tried by ordeal. The accused was tied hand and foot and dropped in a lake or river. People believed that water was a pure substance and would reject anything foul or unclean. Thus a person who sank was considered innocent, and a person who floated was considered guilty. Although the community decided whether the accused had sunk or floated, people believed that God determined innocence or guilt. Thus a priest had to be present to bless the water.

Henry II and others considered this ancient Germanic method irrational and disliked community control of the process. But Henry had no alternative. Then in 1215, the Fourth Lateran Council of the church forbade the presence of priests at trials by ordeal and thus effectively abolished them. Gradually, in the course of the thirteenth century, the king's judges adopted the practice of calling upon twelve people (other than the accusing jury) to consider the question of innocence or guilt. This became the jury of trial, but it was very slowly accepted because medieval people had more confidence in the judgment of God than in the judgment of twelve ordinary people.

One aspect of Henry's judicial reforms encountered stiff resistance from an unexpected source: Thomas Becket, a friend and former chief adviser whom Henry had made archbishop of Canterbury. When Henry wanted to bring all persons in the kingdom under the jurisdiction of the royal courts, Thomas Becket's opposition led to another dramatic conflict between temporal and spiritual powers.

In the 1160s many literate people accused of crimes claimed "benefit of clergy" even though they were not clerics and often had no intention of being ordained. Benefit of clergy gave the accused

Limoges Casket   The principal city of Limousin in west-central France, Limoges was famous for the superb work of its enamelers and goldsmiths. This casket, or chest, showing Thomas Becket's execution (lower panel) and burial (upper panel) was used to preserve relics of Becket. The two scenes are done on gilded copper plaques nailed over wood. *(Source: British Rail Pension Fund)*

the right to be tried in church courts, which meted out mild punishments. A person found guilty in the king's court might suffer mutilation—loss of a hand, loss of a foot, castration—or even death. Ecclesiastical punishments, in contrast, tended to be an obligation to say certain prayers or to make a pilgrimage. In 1164 Henry II insisted that everyone, including clerics, be subject to the royal courts. Becket vigorously protested that church law required clerics to be subject to church courts. The disagreement between the king and the archbishop dragged on for years. The king grew increasingly bitter that his appointment of Becket had proved to be such a mistake. Late in December 1170, in a fit of rage, Henry expressed the wish that Becket be destroyed. Four knights took the king at his word, went to Canterbury, and killed the archbishop in his cathedral as he was leaving evening services.

What Thomas Becket could not achieve in life, he gained in death. The assassination of an archbishop in his own church during the Christmas season turned public opinion in England and throughout western Europe against the king. Within months, miracles were recorded at Becket's tomb, and in a short time Canterbury Cathedral became a major pilgrimage and tourist site. Henry had to back down. He did public penance for the murder and gave up his attempts to bring clerics under the authority of the royal court.

Henry II's son John (r. 1199–1216) inherited a heavy debt from his father and from his brother, Richard I (r. 1189–1199), whose crusading zeal had cost the country dearly. While returning from the Holy Land, Richard had been captured by the duke of Austria, with whom he had quarreled, and England had paid an enormous ransom to secure his release. Between 1180 and 1220, England experienced severe inflation, which drove prices up. In 1204 John lost the rich province of Normandy to Philip Augustus of France and then spent the rest of his reign trying to get it back. To finance that war, he got in deeper and deeper trouble with his barons. John squeezed as much money as possible from his position as feudal lord. He forced widows to pay exorbitant fines to avoid unwanted marriages. He sold young girls who were his feudal wards to the highest bidder. These actions antagonized the nobility.

John also alienated the church and the English townspeople. He rejected Pope Innocent III's nominee to the see of Canterbury. And he infuriated the burghers of the towns by extorting money from them and threatening to revoke the towns' charters of self-government.

All the money John raised did not bring him success. In July 1214, John's coalition of Flemish, German, and English cavalry suffered a severe defeat at the hands of Philip Augustus of France at Bouvines in Flanders. This battle ended English hopes for the recovery of territories from France and also strengthened the barons' opposition to John. On top of his heavy taxation, his ineptitude as a soldier in a society that idealized military glory was the final straw. Rebellion begun by northern barons eventually grew to involve many of the English nobility, including the archbishop of Canterbury and the earl of Pembroke, respectively the leading ecclesiastical and lay peers. After lengthy negotiations, John met the barons at Runnymede, a meadow along the Thames River. There he was forced to approve and to attach his seal to Magna Carta, the treaty that became the cornerstone of English justice and law.

Magna Carta—the Great Charter—signifies the principle that the king and the government shall be under the law, that everyone—including the king—must obey the law. It defends the interests of widows, orphans, townspeople, free men, and the church. Some clauses contain the germ of the ideas of due process of law and the right to a fair and speedy trial. Every English king in the Middle Ages reissued Magna Carta as evidence of his promise to observe the law. Because it was reissued frequently and because later generations appealed to Magna Carta as a written statement of English liberties, it acquired an almost sacred importance as a guarantee of law and justice.

In the later Middle Ages, English common law developed features that differed strikingly from the system of Roman law operative in continental Europe. Common law relied on precedents: a decision in an important case served as an authority for deciding similar cases. By contrast, continental judges, trained in Roman law, used the fixed legal maxims of the sixth century text known as the Justinian *Code* to decide their cases. Thus the com-

mon-law system evolved and reflected the changing experience of the people, while the Roman-law tradition tended toward an absolutist approach. In countries influenced by common law, such as Canada and the United States, the court is open to the public; in countries with Roman-law traditions, such as France and the Latin American nations, courts need not be public. Under common law, people accused in criminal cases have a right to see the evidence against them; under the other system, they do not. Common law urges judges to be impartial; in the Roman-law system, judges interfere freely in activities in their courtrooms. Finally, whereas torture is foreign to the common-law tradition, it was once widely used in the Roman legal system.

The extension of law and justice led to a phenomenal amount of legal codification all over Europe. Legal texts and encyclopedias exalted royal authority, consolidated royal power, and emphasized political and social uniformity. The pressure for social conformity in turn contributed to a rising hostility toward minorities, Jews, and homosexuals.

By the late eleventh century, many towns in western Europe had small Jewish populations. The laws of most countries forbade Jews to own land, though they could hold land pledged to them for debts. By the twelfth century, many Jews were usurers: they lent to consumers but primarily to new or growing business enterprises. New towns and underdeveloped areas where cash was scarce welcomed Jewish settlers. Like other business people, the Jews preferred to live near their work; they also settled close to their synagogue or school. Thus originated the Jews' street or quarter or ghetto. Such neighborhoods gradually became legally defined sections where Jews were required to live.

Jews had been generally tolerated and had become important parts of the urban economies through trade and finance. Some Jews had risen to positions of power and prominence. Through the twelfth century, for example, Jews managed the papal household. The later twelfth and entire thirteenth centuries, however, witnessed increasingly ugly anti-Semitism. Why? Present scholarship does not provide completely satisfactory answers, but we have some clues. Shifting agricultural and economic patterns aggravated social tensions. The indebtedness of peasants and nobles to Jews in an increasingly cash-based economy; the xenophobia that accompanied and followed the Crusades; Christian merchants' and financiers' resentment of Jewish business competition; the spread of vicious accusations of ritual murders or sacrileges against Christian property and persons; royal and papal legislation aimed at social conformity—these factors all contributed to rising anti-Semitism. Philip Augustus of France used hostility to Jews as an excuse to imprison them and then to demand heavy ransom for their release. The Fourth Lateran Council of 1215 forbade Jews to hold public office, restricted their financial activities, and required them to wear distinctive clothing. In 1290 Edward I of England capitalized on mercantile and other resentment of Jews to expel them from the country in return for a large financial grant. In 1302 Philip IV of France followed suit and confiscated their property. Fear, ignorance, greed, stupidity, and the pressure for social conformity all played a part in anti-Semitism of the central Middle Ages.

Early Christians displayed no special prejudice against homosexuals. Some of the church fathers, such as Saint John Chrysostom (347–407), preached against them, but a general indifference to homosexual activity prevailed throughout the early Middle Ages. In the early twelfth century, a large homosexual literature circulated. Publicly known homosexuals—for example, Ralph, archbishop of Tours (1087–1118), and King Richard I of England—held high ecclesiastical and political positions.

Beginning in the late twelfth century, however, a profound change occurred in public attitudes toward homosexual behavior. Scholars have only begun to investigate why this occurred, and the root cause of intolerance rarely yields to easy analysis. In the thirteenth century, a fear of foreigners, especially Muslims, became associated with the crusading movement. Heretics were the most despised minority in an age that stressed religious and social uniformity. The notion spread that both Muslims and heretics, the great foreign and domestic menaces to the security of Christian Europe, were inclined to homosexual relations. In addition, the systematization of law and the rising strength of the state made any religious or sexual distinctiveness increasingly unacceptable. Whatever the precise cause, "between 1250 and 1300 homosexual activity passed from being completely legal in most of Europe to incurring the death penalty in all but a few legal compilations."[25] Spain, France, England, Norway, and several Italian city-states adopted laws condemning homosexual acts. Most of these laws remained on statute books until the twentieth century. Anti-Semitism and hostility to homosexuals were at odds with the general creativity and vitality of the period.

✳ **A Jewish Expulsion**   Subject to ancient and irrational prejudices and lacking legal rights, Jewish people lived and worked in an area according to the pleasure of kings and lords. The increasing anti-Semitism of the thirteenth century led to their expulsion from many places. *(Source: Bibliothèque royale Albert 1er, Brussels/ms 5 fol. 265 recto)*

�֍ ECONOMIC REVIVAL

A salient manifestation of Europe's recovery after the tenth-century disorders and of the vitality of the central Middle Ages was the rise of towns and the growth of a new business and commercial class.

These developments were to lay the foundations for Europe's transformation, centuries later, from a rural agricultural society into an industrial urban society—a change with global implications.

Why and how did these developments occur when they did? Part of the answer has already been given. Without increased agricultural output, there would not have been an adequate food supply for new town dwellers. Without a rise in population, there would have been no one to people the towns. Without a minimum of peace and political stability, merchants could not have transported and sold goods.

The Rise of Towns

Early medieval society was traditional, agricultural, and rural. The emergence of a new class that was none of these constituted a social revolution. The new class—artisans and merchants—came from the peasantry. They were landless younger sons of large families, driven away by land shortage. Or they were forced by war and famine to seek new possibilities. Or they were unusually enterprising and adventurous, curious and willing to take a chance.

Few towns of the tenth and eleventh centuries were "new" in the sense that they had been carved out of forest and wilderness. Some medieval towns that had become flourishing centers of trade by the mid-twelfth century had originally been Roman army camps, or perhaps forts erected during the ninth-century Viking invasions. York in northern England, Bordeaux in west-central France, and Cologne in west-central Germany are good examples of ancient towns that underwent revitalization in the eleventh century. Great cathedrals and monasteries, which represented a demand for goods and services, also attracted concentrations of people. Italian seaport cities such as Venice, Pisa, and Genoa had been centers of shipping and commerce in earlier times. Muslim attacks and domestic squabbles had cut their populations and drastically reduced the volume of their trade in the early Middle Ages, but trade with Constantinople and the East had never stopped entirely. The restoration of order and political stability promoted rebirth and new development. Medieval towns had a few characteristics in common. Walls enclosed the town. (The terms *burgher* and *bourgeois* derive from the Old English and Old German words

burg, burgh, borg, and *borough* for "a walled or fortified place.") The town had a marketplace. It often had a mint for the coining of money and a court to settle disputes.

In each town, many people inhabited a small, cramped area. As population increased, towns rebuilt their walls, expanding the living space to accommodate growing numbers. Through an archaeological investigation of the amount of land gradually enclosed by walls, historians have gained a rough estimate of medieval town populations. For example, the walled area of the German city of Cologne equaled 100 hectares in the tenth century (1 hectare = 2.471 acres), about 185 hectares in 1106, about 320 in 1180, and 397 in the fourteenth century. In 1180 Cologne's population was at least 32,000; in the mid-fourteenth century, perhaps 40,000.[26] The concentration of the textile industry in the Low Countries brought into being the most populous cluster of cities in western Europe: Ghent with about 56,000 people, Bruges with 27,000, Tournai and Brussels each with perhaps 20,000.[27] Paris, together with Milan, Venice, and Florence, each with about 80,000, led all Europe in population.

The aristocratic nobility glanced down with contempt and derision at the moneygrubbing townspeople but were not above borrowing from them. The rural peasantry peered up with suspicion and fear at the town dwellers. Some farmers fled to the towns seeking wealth and freedom. But most farmers wondered what was the point of making money. They believed that only land had real permanence. Nor did the new commercial class make much sense initially to churchmen. The immediate goal of the middle class was obviously not salvation. It would be a long while before churchmen developed a theological justification for the new class.

Town Liberties and Town Life

The history of towns in the eleventh through thirteenth centuries consists largely of merchants' efforts to acquire liberties. In the Middle Ages, *liberties* meant special privileges. For the town dweller, liberties included the privilege of living and trading on the lord's land. The most important privilege a medieval townsperson could gain was personal freedom. It gradually developed that an individual who lived in a town for a year and a day, and was accepted by the townspeople, was free of servile obligations and servile status. More than anything else, perhaps, the personal freedom that came with residence in a town contributed to the emancipation of the serfs in the central Middle Ages. Liberty meant citizenship, and, unlike foreigners and outsiders of any kind, a full citizen of a town did not have to pay taxes and tolls in the market. Obviously, this exemption increased profits.

In the twelfth and thirteenth centuries, towns fought for, and slowly gained, legal and political rights. Gradually, towns across Europe acquired the right to hold municipal courts that alone could judge members of the town. In effect, this right gave them judicial independence.[28]

In the acquisition of full rights of self-government, the *merchant guilds* played a large role. Medieval people were long accustomed to communal enterprises. In the late tenth and early eleventh centuries, those who were engaged in foreign trade joined together in merchant guilds; united enterprise provided them greater security and less risk of losses than did individual action. At about the same time, the artisans and craftsmen of particular trades formed their own guilds. These were the butchers, bakers, and candlestick makers. Members of the *craft guilds* determined the quality, quantity, and price of the goods produced and the number of apprentices and journeymen affiliated with the guild.

Research indicates that, by the fifteenth century, women composed the majority of the adult urban population. Many women were heads of households.[29] They engaged in every kind of urban commercial activity, both as helpmates to their husbands and independently. In many manufacturing trades women predominated, and in some places women were a large percentage of the labor force. In fourteenth-century Frankfurt, for example, about 33 percent of the crafts and trades were entirely female, about 40 percent wholly male, and the remaining crafts roughly divided between the sexes. Craft guilds provided greater opportunity for women than did merchant guilds. Most members of the Paris silk and woolen trades were women, and some achieved the mastership. Widows frequently followed their late husbands' professions, but if they remarried outside the craft, they lost the mastership. Between 1254 and 1271, the chief magistrate of Paris drew up the following regulations for the silk industry:

Any woman who wishes to be a silk spinster [woman who spins] on large spindles in the city of Paris . . . may freely do so, provided she observe the following customs and usages of the crafts:

No spinster on large spindles may have more than three apprentices, unless they be her own or her husband's children born in true wedlock; nor may she contract with them for an apprenticeship of less than seven years. . . . If a working woman comes from outside Paris and wishes to practice the said craft in the city, she must swear before the guardians of the craft that she will practice it well and loyally and conform to its customs and usages.[30]

Guild records show that women received lower wages than men for the same work, on the grounds that they needed less income.

Recent research demonstrates that women with ready access to cash—such as female innkeepers, alewives, and women in trade—"extended credit on purchases, gave cash advances to good customers or accepted articles on pawn . . . and many widows supplemented their earnings from their late husbands' businesses or homesteads by putting out cash at interest." Likewise, Christian noblewomen, nuns, and Jewish businesswomen participated in money lending. Wherever Jews lived, Jewish women were active moneylenders—for example, in northern France (where in the thirteenth century Jewish women constituted a third of all Jewish lenders), the German-speaking parts of Europe, Navarre, Catalonia, and throughout Italy. Loans made by all women tended to be very small (in comparison to those extended by men), for domestic consumption (to tide over a household in some emergency, in contrast to productive loans such as those to repair or replace a piece of farm equipment), and for short terms (a few weeks or a month).[31]

By the late eleventh century, especially in the towns of the Low Countries and northern Italy, the leaders of the merchant guilds were quite rich and powerful. They constituted an oligarchy in their towns, controlling economic life and bargaining with kings and lords for political independence. Full rights of self-government included the right to hold a town court, the right to select the mayor and other municipal officials, and the right to tax and collect taxes.

A charter that King Henry II of England granted to the merchants of Lincoln around 1157 nicely illustrates the town's rights. The passages quoted clearly suggest that the merchant guild had been the governing body in the city for almost a century and that anyone who lived in Lincoln for a year and a day was considered free:

Henry, by the grace of God, etc. . . . Know that I have granted to my citizens of Lincoln all their liberties and customs and laws which they had in the time of Edward [King Edward the Confessor] and William and Henry, kings of England. And I have granted them their gild-merchant, comprising men of the city and other merchants of the shire, as well and freely as they had it in the time of our aforesaid predecessors. . . . I also confirm to them that if anyone has lived in Lincoln for a year and a day without dispute from any claimant, and has paid the customs [tax levied by the king] . . . then let the defendant remain in peace in my city of Lincoln as my citizen, without [having to defend his] right.[32]

Kings and lords discovered that towns attracted increasing numbers of people—people whom the lords could tax. Moreover, when burghers bargained for a town's political independence, they offered sizable amounts of ready cash. Consequently, feudal lords ultimately agreed to self-government.

Gates pierced the town walls, and visitors waited at the gates to gain entrance to the town. When the gates were opened early in the morning, guards inspected the quantity and quality of the goods brought in, and they collected the customary taxes. Part of the taxes went to the lord on whose land the town stood, part to the town council for civic purposes. Constant repair of the walls was usually the town's greatest expense.

Medieval cities served, above all else, as markets. In some respects the entire city was a marketplace. The place where a product was made and sold was

Hammering Cobblestones Laborers pave the highway leading from the walled city of Bavay in France. The original roadbed was loose earth. Upkeep of the roads and walls was often a town's greatest expense. *(Source: Bibliothèque royale Albert 1er, Brussels/ms 9242, fol. 48 verso)*

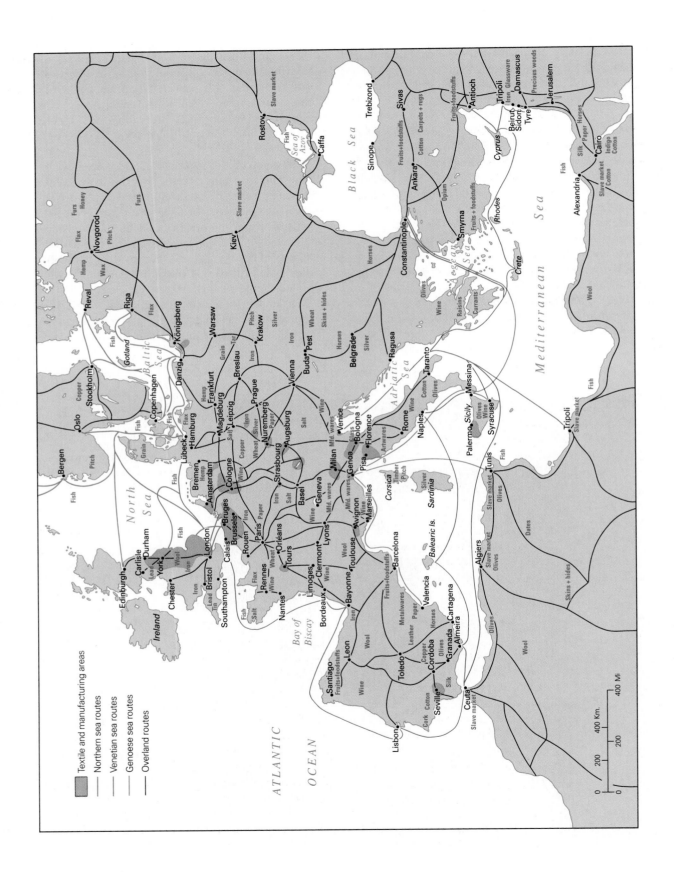

ATLANTIC
OCEAN

Bay of
Biscay

North
Sea

Baltic
Sea

Black
Sea

Sea of
Azov

Aegean
Sea

Adriatic
Sea

Mediterranean
Sea

Ireland
Gotland
Corsica
Sardinia
Balearic Is.
Sicily
Crete
Cyprus
Rhodes

Textile and manufacturing areas

Northern sea routes

Venetian sea routes

Genoese sea routes

Overland routes

Bergen
Fish
Pitch
Edinburgh
Carlisle
Durham
York
Chester
Southampton
Bristol
Nantes
Rennes
London
Calais
Bruges
Brussels
Rouen
Paris
Orléans
Tours
Limoges
Clermont
Bordeaux
Bayonne
Toulouse
Santiago
Leon
Lisbon
Toledo
Cordoba
Seville
Granada
Almeira
Cartagena
Valencia
Barcelona
Ceuta
Algiers
Tunis
Tripoli

Oslo
Stockholm
Copenhagen
Hamburg
Bremen
Amsterdam
Cologne
Lübeck
Danzig
Königsberg
Reval
Riga
Novgorod
Kiev
Rostov
Caffa
Sinope
Trebizond
Sivas
Ankara
Smyrna
Constantinople
Belgrade
Ragusa
Taranto
Rome
Naples
Palermo
Messina
Syracuse

Frankfurt
Magdeburg
Leipzig
Prague
Nuremberg
Augsburg
Breslau
Krakow
Warsaw
Vienna
Buda
Pest
Basel
Geneva
Lyons
Strasbourg
Avignon
Marseilles
Milan
Genoa
Pisa
Florence
Bologna
Venice

Alexandria
Cairo
Jerusalem
Tripoli
Damascus
Antioch
Beirut
Sidon
Tyre

Furs
Honey
Flax
Wax
Pitch
Hemp
Copper
Grain
Fish
Salt
Wool
Iron
Lead
Tin
Wine
Wheat
Flax
Salt
Paper
Hemp
Copper
Iron
Salt
Silver
Wine
Glass
Mfd. wares
Mfd. wares
Artwares
Olives
Wine
Raisins
Currants
Olives
Wool
Fish
Dates
Skins + hides
Olives
Wool
Olives
Slave market
Cotton
Olives
Silver
Timber
Pitch
Olives
Wine
Cotton
Fruits + foodstuffs
Opium
Horses
Skins + hides
Wheat
Silver
Iron
Pitch
Tar
Flax
Silver
Iron
Salt
Horses
Slave market
Silk
Paper
Indigo
Cotton
Slave market
Cotton
Horses
Silk
Glassware
Iron
Precious woods
Fruits+foodstuffs
Carpets + rugs
Fruits+foodstuffs

400 Mi
400 Km.
200
0

also typically the merchant's residence. Usually the ground floor was the scene of production. A window or door opened from the main workroom directly onto the street, and passersby could look in and see the goods being produced. The merchant's family lived above the business on the second or third floor. As the business and the family expanded, the merchant built additional stories on top of the house.

Because space within the town walls was limited, expansion occurred upward. Second and third stories were built jutting out over the ground floor and thus over the street. Since the streets were narrow to begin with, houses lacked fresh air and light. Initially, houses were made of wood and thatched with straw. Fire was a constant danger and spread rapidly. Municipal governments consequently urged construction in stone or brick.

Most medieval cities developed haphazardly. There was little town planning. As the population increased, space became more and more limited. Air and water pollution presented serious problems. Many families raised pigs for household consumption in sties next to the house. Horses and oxen, the chief means of transportation and power, dropped tons of dung on the streets every year. It was universal practice in the early towns to dump household waste, both animal and human, into the road in front of one's house. The stench must have been abominable. Lack of space, air pollution, and sanitation problems bedeviled urban people in medieval times, as they do today. Still, people wanted to get into medieval cities because they represented opportunities for economic advancement, social mobility, and improvement in legal status.

The Revival of Long-Distance Trade

The eleventh century witnessed a remarkable revival of trade, as artisans and craftsmen manufactured goods for local and foreign consumption (Map 12.8). Most trade centered in towns and was controlled by professional traders. The transportation of goods involved serious risks. Shipwrecks were common. Pirates infested the sea lanes, and

robbers and thieves roamed virtually all of the land routes. Since the risks were so great, merchants preferred to share them. A group of people would thus pool some of their capital to finance an expedition to a distant place. When the ship or caravan returned and the goods brought back were sold, the investors would share the profits. If disaster struck the caravan, an investor's loss was limited to the amount of that individual's investment.

What goods were exchanged? What towns took the lead in medieval international trade? The Italian cities, especially Venice, led the West in trade in general and completely dominated the Asian market. Ships carried salt from the Venetian lagoon, pepper and other spices from North Africa, slaves and silks and purple textiles from the East to northern and western Europe. Lombard and Tuscan merchants exchanged those goods at the town markets and regional fairs of France, Flanders, and England. (Fairs were periodic gatherings that attracted buyers, sellers, and goods from all over Europe.) Flanders controlled the cloth industry: the towns of Bruges, Ghent, and Ypres built up a vast industry in the manufacture of cloth. Italian merchants exchanged their products for Flemish tapestries, fine broadcloth, and other textiles.

Two circumstances help to explain the lead Venice and the Flemish towns gained in long-distance trade. Both enjoyed a high degree of peace and political stability, but geographical factors were equally, if not more, important (see Map 12.8). Venice was ideally located at the northwestern end of the Adriatic Sea, with easy access to the transalpine land routes as well as the Adriatic and Mediterranean sea lanes. The markets of North Africa, Byzantium, and Russia and the great fairs of Ghent in Flanders and Champagne in France provided commercial opportunities that Venice quickly seized. The geographical situation of Flanders also offered unusual possibilities. Just across the Channel from England, Flanders had easy access to English wool. Indeed, Flanders and England developed a very close economic relationship.

Wool was the cornerstone of the English medieval economy. Scholars have estimated that, by the end of the twelfth century, roughly 6 million sheep grazed on the English moors and downs.[33] Population growth in the twelfth century and the success of the Flemish and Italian textile industries created foreign demand for English wool. The production of English wool stimulated Flemish

✤ **MAP 12.8 Trade and Manufacturing in Medieval Europe** Notice the number of cities and the sources of silver, iron, copper, lead, paper, wool, carpets and rugs, and slaves.

manufacturing, and the expansion of the Flemish cloth industry in turn spurred the production of English wool. The availability of raw wool also encouraged the development of domestic cloth manufacture within England. The port cities of London, Hull, Boston, and Bristol thrived on the wool trade. In the thirteenth century, commercial families in these towns grew fabulously rich.

The Commercial Revolution

A steadily expanding volume of international trade from the late eleventh through the thirteenth centuries was a sign of the great economic surge, but it was not the only one. In cities all across Europe, trading and transportation firms opened branch offices. Credit was widely extended, considerably facilitating exchange. Merchants devised the letter of credit, which made unnecessary the slow and dangerous shipment of coin for payment.

A new capitalistic spirit developed. Professional merchants were always on the lookout for new markets and opportunities. They invested surplus capital in new enterprises. They became involved in a wide variety of operations. The typical prosperous merchant in the later thirteenth century might well be involved in buying and selling, shipping, lending some capital at interest, and other types of banking. Medieval merchants were fiercely competitive. Some scholars consider capitalism a modern phenomenon, beginning in the fifteenth or sixteenth century. But in their use of capital to make more money, in their speculative pursuits and willingness to gamble, in their competitive spirit, and in the variety of their interests and operations, medieval businessmen displayed the traits of capitalists.

The ventures of the German Hanseatic League illustrate these impulses. The Hanseatic League was a mercantile association of towns formed to achieve mutual security and exclusive trading rights. During the thirteenth century, perhaps two hundred cities from Holland to Poland joined the league, but Lübeck always remained the dominant member. From the thirteenth to the sixteenth century, the Hanseatic League controlled trade over a Novgorod-Reval-Lübeck-Hamburg-Bruges-London axis—that is, the trade of northern Europe (see Map 12.8). In the fourteenth century, Hanseatic merchants branched out into southern Germany and Italy by land and into French, Spanish, and Portuguese ports by sea.

The ships of league cities carried furs, wax, copper, fish, grain, timber, and wine. These goods were exchanged for finished products, mainly cloth and salt, from western cities. At cities such as Bruges and London, Hanseatic merchants secured special trading concessions exempting them from all tolls and allowing them to trade at local fairs. Hanseatic merchants established foreign trading centers called "factories." The most famous was the London Steelyard, a walled community with warehouses, offices, a church, and residential quarters for company representatives.[34]

By the late thirteenth century, Hanseatic merchants had developed an important business tool, the business register. Merchants publicly recorded their debts and contracts and received a league guarantee for them. This device proved a decisive factor in the later development of credit and commerce in northern Europe.[35] These activities required capital, risk taking, and aggressive pursuit of opportunities—the essential ingredients of capitalism. They also yielded fat profits.

These developments added up to what one modern scholar has called "a commercial revolution, . . . probably the greatest turning point in the history of our civilization."[36] This is not a wildly extravagant statement. In the long run, the commercial revolution of the central Middle Ages brought about radical change in European society. One remarkable aspect of this change is that the commercial classes did not constitute a large part of the total population—never more than 10 percent. They exercised an influence far in excess of their numbers.

The commercial revolution created a great deal of new wealth. Wealth meant a higher standard of living. The new availability of something as simple as spices, for example, allowed for variety in food. Dietary habits gradually changed. Tastes became more sophisticated. Contact with Eastern civilizations introduced Europeans to eating utensils, and table manners improved. Nobles learned to eat with forks and knives instead of tearing the meat from a roast with their fingers. They began to use napkins instead of wiping their greasy fingers on the dogs lying under the table.

The existence of wealth did not escape the attention of kings and other rulers. Wealth could be taxed, and through taxation kings could create strong and centralized states. In the years to come, alliances with the middle classes were to enable kings to defeat feudal powers and aristocratic interests and to build the states that came to be called "modern."

The commercial revolution also provided the opportunity for thousands of serfs to improve their social position. The slow but steady transformation of European society from almost completely rural and isolated to a relatively more sophisticated one constituted the greatest effect of the commercial revolution that began in the eleventh century.

Still, most towns remained small. The castle, the manorial village, and the monastery dominated the landscape. The feudal nobility and churchmen determined the prevailing social attitudes, values, and patterns of thought and behavior. The commercial changes of the eleventh through thirteenth centuries did, however, lay the economic foundations for the later development of urban life and culture.

SUMMARY

The culture that emerged in Europe between 733 and 843 has justifiably been called the "first" European civilization. That civilization had definite characteristics: it was Christian, feudal, and infused with Latin ideas and models. Almost all people were baptized Christians. Latin was the common language—written as well as spoken—of educated people everywhere. This culture resulted from the mutual cooperation of civil and ecclesiastical authorities. Kings and church leaders supported each other's goals and utilized each other's prestige and power. Kings encouraged preaching and publicized church doctrines, such as the stress on monogamous marriage. In return, church officials urged obedience to royal authority. The support that Charlemagne gave to education and learning, the intellectual movement known as the Carolingian Renaissance, proved his most enduring legacy.

The enormous size of Charlemagne's empire, its lack of viable administrative institutions, the domestic squabbles among his descendants, and the invasions of the Vikings, Magyars, and Muslims—these factors all contributed to the empire's disintegration. As the empire broke down, a new form of decentralized government, later known as feudalism, emerged. In a feudal society public and political power was held by a small group of military leaders. No civil or religious authority could maintain stable government over a very wide area. Local strongmen provided what little security existed.

Commerce and long-distance trade were drastically reduced. Because of their agricultural and commercial impact, the Viking and Muslim invaders were the most dynamic and creative forces of the period.

In the year 1000, having enough to eat was the rare privilege of a few nobles, priests, and monks. By the eleventh century, however, manorial communities were slowly improving their agricultural output through increased mechanization, especially the use of waterpower and windpower; these advances, aided by warmer weather, meant more food and increasing population.

In the eleventh century, rulers and local authorities gradually imposed some degree of order within their territories. Peace and domestic security contributed to the rise in population, bringing larger crops for the peasants and improving trading conditions for the townspeople. The church overthrew the domination of lay influences, and the spread of the Cluniac and Cistercian orders marked the ascendancy of monasticism. The Gregorian reform movement with its stress on the "freedom of the church" led to a grave conflict with kings over lay investiture. The papacy achieved a technical success on the religious issue, but in Germany the greatly increased power of the nobility, at the expense of the emperor, represents the significant social consequence. Having put its own house in order, the Roman papacy in the twelfth and thirteenth centuries built the first strong government bureaucracy. In the central Middle Ages, the church exercised general leadership of European society. The Crusades exhibit that leadership, though their consequences for Byzantine-Western and for Christian-Muslim relations proved disastrous.

Through the instruments of justice and finance, the kings of England and France attacked feudal rights and provincial practices, built centralized bureaucracies, and gradually came in contact with all their subjects. In so doing, these rulers laid the foundations for modern national states. The German emperors, preoccupied with Italian affairs and with a quest for the imperial crown, allowed feudal and local interests to triumph. Medieval cities recruited people from the countryside and brought into being a new social class: the middle class. Cities provided economic opportunity, which, together with the revival of long-distance trade and a new capitalistic spirit, led to greater wealth, a higher standard of living, and upward social mobility.

NOTES

1. For the date of this battle, October 17, 733, see L. White, *Medieval Technology and Social Change* (Oxford: Clarendon Press, 1962), p. 3 n. 3 and p. 12.

2. See F. Irsigler, "On the Aristocratic Character of Early Frankish Society," in *The Medieval Nobility: Studies on the Ruling Class of France and Germany from the Sixth to the Twelfth Century,* ed. and trans. T. Reuter (New York: North-Holland, 1978), pp. 105–136, esp. p. 123.

3. Einhard, *The Life of Charlemagne,* with a Foreword by S. Painter (Ann Arbor: University of Michigan Press, 1960), pp. 50–51.

4. P. Stafford, *Queens, Concubines, and Dowagers: The King's Wife in the Early Middle Ages* (Athens: University of Georgia Press, 1983), pp. 60–62.

5. See K. F. Werner, "Important Noble Families in the Kingdom of Charlemagne," in Reuter, *The Medieval Nobility,* pp. 174–184.

6. Quoted in B. D. Hill, ed., *Church and State in the Middle Ages* (New York: Wiley, 1970), pp. 46–47.

7. J. Nicholson, "Feminae Gloriosae: Women in the Age of Bede," in *Medieval Women,* ed. D. Baker (Oxford: Basil Blackwell, 1978), pp. 15–31, esp. p. 19, and C. Fell, *Women in Anglo-Saxon England and the Impact of 1066* (Bloomington: Indiana University Press, 1984), p. 109.

8. R. W. Southern, *Medieval Humanism and Other Studies* (Oxford: Basil Blackwell, 1970), p. 3.

9. D. Wright, trans., *Beowulf* (Baltimore: Penguin Books, 1957), pp. 9–19.

10. L. Sherley-Price, trans., *Bede: A History of the English Church and People* (Baltimore: Penguin Books, 1962), bk. 3, chap. 27, p. 191.

11. J. R. Strayer, "The Two Levels of Feudalism," in *Medieval Statecraft and the Perspectives of History* (Princeton, N.J.: Princeton University Press, 1971), p. 63. This section leans heavily on this seminal study.

12. See B. S. Bachrach, "Charles Martel, Mounted Shock Combat, the Stirrup, and Feudalism," in *Studies in Medieval and Renaissance History,* vol. 7 (1970), pp. 49–75, esp. pp. 66–75.

13. Strayer, "The Two Levels of Feudalism," pp. 65–76, esp. p. 71.

14. See D. Herlihy, "Land, Family, and Women in Continental Europe, 701–1200," in *Women in Medieval Society,* ed. S. M. Stuard (Philadelphia: University of Pennsylvania Press, 1976), pp. 13–45.

15. Quoted in R. Pipes, *Russia Under the Old Regime* (New York: Charles Scribner's Sons, 1974), p. 48.

16. See E. M. Hallam, *Capetian France, 987–1328* (New York: Longman, 1980), pp. 12–43.

17. J. Gimpel, *The Medieval Machine: The Industrial Revolution of the Middle Ages* (New York: Penguin Books, 1976), pp. 7, 10–15.

18. See B. Rosenwein, *Rhinoceros Bound: Cluny in the Tenth Century* (Philadelphia: University of Pennsylvania Press, 1982), Ch. 2.

19. Quoted in Hill, ed., *Church and State in the Middle Ages,* p. 68.

20. See J. B. Freed, *The Counts of Falkenstein: Noble Self-consciousness in Twelfth-Century Germany,* Transactions of the American Philosophical Society, vol. 74, pt. 6 (Philadelphia, 1984), pp. 9–11.

21. C. Erdmann, *The Origin of the Idea of the Crusade,* trans. M. Baldwin and W. Goffart (Princeton, N.J.: Princeton University Press, 1977), p. 57.

22. S. Runciman, *A History of the Crusades,* vol. 3, *The Kingdom of Acre* (Cambridge: Cambridge University Press, 1955), p. 480.

23. Cited ibid., pp. 23–25.

24. Quoted in D. C. Douglas and G. E. Greenaway, eds., *English Historical Documents,* vol. 2 (London: Eyre & Spottiswoode, 1961), p. 853.

25. J. Boswell, *Christianity, Social Tolerance, and Homosexuality: Gay People in Western Europe from the Beginning of the Christian Era to the Fourteenth Century* (Chicago: University of Chicago Press, 1980), pp. 270–293; the quotation is from p. 293. For alternative interpretations, see K. Thomas, "Rescuing Homosexual History," *New York Review of Books,* December 4, 1980, pp. 26ff.; and J. DuQ. Adams, *Speculum* 56 (April 1981): 350ff. For the French monarchy's persecution of the Jews, see J. W. Baldwin, *The Government of Philip Augustus: Foundations of French Royal Power in the Middle Ages* (Berkeley: University of California Press, 1986), pp. 51–52, and W. C. Jordan, *The French Monarchy and the Jews* (Philadelphia: University of Pennsylvania Press, 1989).

26. J. C. Russell, *Medieval Regions and Their Cities* (Bloomington: University of Indiana Press, 1972), p. 91.

27. Ibid., pp. 113–117.

28. H. Pirenne, *Economic and Social History of Medieval Europe* (New York: Harcourt, Brace, 1956), p. 53.

29. See D. Herlihy, *Medieval and Renaissance Pistoia: The Social History of an Italian Town, 1200–1430* (New Haven, Conn.: Yale University Press, 1967), p. 257.

30. Quoted in J. O'Faolain and L. Martines, eds., *Not in God's Image: Women in History from the*

Greeks to the Victorians (New York: Harper & Row, 1973), pp. 155–156.

31. W. C. Jordan, *Women and Credit in Pre-Industrial and Developing Societies* (Philadelphia: University of Pennsylvania Press, 1993), pp. 20ff.

32. Quoted in Douglas and Greenaway, *English Historical Documents,* pp. 969–970.

33. M. M. Postan, *The Medieval Economy and Society: An Economic History of Britain in the Middle Ages* (Baltimore: Penguin Books, 1975), pp. 213–214.

34. See P. Dollinger, *The German Hansa,* trans. and ed. D. S. Ault and S. H. Steinberg (Stanford, Calif.: Stanford University Press, 1970).

35. C. M. Cipolla, *Before the Industrial Revolution: European Society and Economy, 1000–1700,* 2d ed. (New York: Norton, 1980), p. 197.

36. R. S. Lopez, "The Trade of Medieval Europe: The South," in *The Cambridge Economic History of Europe,* vol. 2, ed. M. M. Postan and E. E. Rich (Cambridge: Cambridge University Press, 1952), p. 289.

SUGGESTED READING

The best general treatment of the Carolingian world is R. McKitterick, *The Frankish Kingdom Under the Carolingians, 751–987* (1983). The same author's *The Carolingians and the Written Word* (1989) will prove essential for many aspects of the Carolingian Renaissance, as will her edited *The Uses of Literacy in Early Medieval Europe* (1990), which includes articles on Ireland, Anglo-Saxon England, Merovingian Gaul, Muslim Spain, and Byzantium.

Einhard's *Life of Charlemagne,* cited in the Notes, is a good starting point for study of the great chieftain. The best general biography of Charlemagne is D. Bullough, *The Age of Charlemagne* (1965). P. Riche, *Daily Life in the World of Charlemagne,* trans. J. McNamara (1978), is a richly detailed study of many facets of Carolingian society by a distinguished authority. The same scholar's *Education and Culture in the Barbarian West: From the Sixth Through the Eighth Century,* trans. J. J. Contreni (1976), provides an excellent though technical treatment of Carolingian intellectual activity. For agricultural and economic life, G. Duby, *The Early Growth of the European Economy: Warriors and Peasants from the Seventh to the Twelfth Century* (1978), relates economic behavior to other aspects of human experience in a thoroughly readable style. The importance of technological developments in the Carolingian period is described by L. White, *Medieval Technology and Social Change* (1962), now a classic work.

In addition to the references to Bede and *Beowulf* in the Notes, D. L. Sayers, trans., *The Song of Roland* (1957), provides an excellent key, in epic form, to the values and lifestyles of the feudal classes, and the beautifully written evocation by P. H. Blair, *Northumbria in the Days of Bede* (1976), is highly recommended.

For the Christian church, its development as an institution, and its impact on pagan Germanic peoples, see the monumental work of F. Kempf et al., *The Church in the Age of Feudalism,* trans. A. Biggs (1980), vol. 3 of the *History of the Church* series edited by H. Jedin and J. Dolan. The scope of G. Tellenbach, *The Church in Western Europe from the Tenth to the Early Twelfth Century,* trans. T. Reuter (1993), is indicated by its title, but see also C. Morris, *The Papal Monarchy: The Western Church, 1050–1250* (1989). F. Paxton, *Christianizing Death: The Creation of Ritual Process in Early Medieval Europe* (1990), and T. Head, *Hagiography and the Cult of the Saints* (1990), are valuable books dealing with specialized topics.

For feudalism and manorialism, see, in addition to the references given in the Notes, S. Reynolds, *Fiefs and Vassals* (1994); F. L. Ganshof, *Feudalism* (1961); and J. R. Strayer, "Feudalism in Western Europe," in *Feudalism in History,* ed. R. Coulborn (1956). M. Bloch, *Feudal Society,* trans. L. A. Manyon (1961), remains important. The best broad treatment of peasant life and conditions is G. Duby, *Rural Economy and Country Life in the Medieval West,* trans. C. Postan (1968).

J. Brondsted, *The Vikings* (1960), is an excellently illustrated study of many facets of Viking culture. G. Jones, *A History of the Vikings,* rev. ed. (1984), provides a comprehensive survey of the Viking world based on the latest archaeological findings and numismatic evidence; P. H. Sawyer, *Kings and Vikings: Scandinavia and Europe, A.D. 700–1100* (1983), relies heavily on the literary evidence.

R. Bartlett, *The Making of Europe: Conquest, Colonization and Cultural Change, 950–1350* (1993), is a superb synthesis emphasizing expansion. Two broad surveys, D. Nicholas, *The Evolution of the Medieval World: Society, Government and Thought in Europe, 312–1500* (1992), and G. Holmes, ed., *The Oxford History of Medieval Europe* (1992), contain useful, up-to-date material. D. Bates, *Normandy Before 1066* (1982), traces the history of the region from the earliest Viking settlement to the time of ducal government and presents important material on social history. For Spain, R. Fletcher, *The Quest for El Cid* (1990), provides an excellent introduction to Spanish social and political conditions through a study of Rodrigo Dias, the eleventh-century soldier of fortune who became the Spanish national hero. Fletcher's *Moorish Spain* (1992) provides a highly readable

An Arab View of the Crusades

The Crusaders helped shape the understanding that Arabs and Europeans had of each other and all subsequent relations between the Christian West and the Arab world. To medieval Christians, the crusades were papally approved military expeditions for the recovery of holy places in Palestine; to the Arabs, these campaigns were "Frankish wars" or "Frankish invasions" for the acquisition of territory.

Early in the thirteenth century, Ibn Al-Athir (1160–1223), a native of Mosul, an important economic and cultural center in northern Mesopotamia (modern Iraq), wrote a history of the First Crusade. He relied on Arab sources for the events he described. Here is his account of the Crusaders' capture of Antioch:

The power of the Franks first became apparent when in the year 478/1085–86[1] they invaded the territories of Islam and took Toledo and other parts of Andalusia. Then in 484/1091 they attacked and conquered the island of Sicily and turned their attention to the African coast. Certain of their conquests there were won back again but they had other successes, as you will see.

In 490/1097 the Franks attacked Syria. This how it all began: Baldwin, their King, a kinsman of Roger the Frank who had conquered Sicily, assembled a great army and sent word to Roger saying: "I have assembled a great army and now I am on my way to you, to use your bases for my conquest of the African coast. Thus you and I shall become neighbors."

Roger called together his companions and consulted them about these proposals. "This will be a fine thing for them and for us!" they declared, "for by this means these lands will be converted to the Faith!" At this Roger raised one leg and farted loudly, and swore that it was of more use than their advice. "Why?" "Because if this army comes here it will need quantities of provisions and fleets of ships to transport it to Africa, as well as reinforcements from my own troops. Then, if the Franks succeed in conquering this territory they will take it over and will need provisioning from Sicily. This will cost me my annual profit from the harvest. If they fail they will return here and be an embarrassment to me here in my own domain." . . .

He summoned Baldwin's messenger and said to him: "If you have decided to make war on the Muslims your best course will be to free Jerusalem from their rule and thereby win great honor. I am bound by certain promises and treaties of allegiance with the ruler of Africa." So the Franks made ready to set out to attack Syria.

Another story is that the Fatimids of Egypt were afraid when they saw the Seljuqids extending their empire through Syria as far as Gaza, until they reached the Egyptian border and Atsiz invaded Egypt itself. They therefore sent to invite the Franks to invade Syria and so protect Egypt from the Muslims.[2] But God knows best.

When the Franks decided to attack Syria they marched east to Constantinople, so that they could cross the straits and advance into Muslim territory by the easier, land route. When they reached Constantinople, the Emperor of the East refused them permission to pass through his domains. He said: "Unless you first promise me Antioch, I shall not allow you to cross into the Muslim empire." His real intention was to incite them to attack the Muslims, for he was convinced that the Turks, whose invincible control over Asia Minor he had observed, would exterminate every one of them. They accepted his conditions and in 490/1097 they crossed the Bosphorus at

Constantinople. . . . They . . . reached Antioch, which they besieged.

When Yaghi Siyan, the ruler of Antioch, heard of their approach, he was not sure how the Christian people of the city would react, so he made the Muslims go outside the city on their own to dig trenches, and the next day sent the Christians out alone to continue the task. When they were ready to return home at the end of the day he refused to allow them. "Antioch is yours," he said, "but you will have to leave it to me until I see what happens between us and the Franks." Who will protect our children and our wives?" they said. "I shall look after them for you." So they resigned themselves, to their fate, and lived in the Frankish camp for nine months, while the city was under siege.

Yaghi Siyan showed unparalleled courage and wisdom, strength and judgment. If all the Franks who died had survived they would have overrun all the lands of Islam. He protected the families of the Christians in Antioch and would not allow a hair of their heads to be touched.

After the siege had been going on for a long time the Franks made a deal with . . . a cuirass-maker called Ruzbih whom they bribed with a fortune in money and lands. He worked in the tower that stood over the riverbed, where the river flowed out of the city into the valley. The Franks sealed their pact with the cuirass-maker, God damn him! and made their way to the water-gate. They opened it and entered the city. Another gang of them climbed the tower with their ropes. At dawn, when more than 500 of them were in the city and the defenders were worn out after the night watch, they sounded their trumpets. . . . Panic seized Yaghi Siyan and he opened the city gates and fled in terror, with an escort of thirty pages. His army commander arrived, but when he discovered on enquiry that Yaghi Siyan had fled, he made his escape by another gate. This was of great help to the Franks, for if he had stood firm for an hour, they would have been wiped out. They entered the city by the gates and sacked it, slaughtering all the Muslims they found there. This happened in jumada I (491/April/May 1098). . . .

It was the discord between the Muslim princes . . . that enabled the Franks to overrun the country.

Miniature showing lightly clad Muslims. *(Source: Bibliothèque Nationale, Paris)*

Questions for Analysis

1. From the Arab perspective, when did the Crusade begin?

2. How did Ibn Al-Athir explain the Crusaders' expedition to Syria?

3. Why did Antioch fall to the Crusaders?

4. The use of dialogue in historical narrative is a very old device dating from the Greek historian Thucydides (fifth century B.C.). Assess the value of Ibn Al-Athir's dialogues for the modern historian.

Notes: 1. Muslims traditionally date events from Muhammad's hegira, or emigration, to Medina which occurred in 622 according to the Christian calendar. 2. Although Muslims, Fatimids were related doctrinally to the Shi'ites, and the dominant Sunni Muslims therefore considered the Fatimids heretics.

(Sources: P. J. Geary, ed., *Readings in Medieval History* (Peterborough, Ontario: Broadview Press, 1991), pp. 443–444; E. J. Costello, trans., *Arab Historians of the Crusades* (Berkeley and Los Angeles: University of California Press, 1969).

sketch of the history of Islamic Spain from the eighth to the seventeenth century. For the developing social and economic importance of the Flemish towns, see D. Nicholas, *Medieval Flanders* (1992).

The relationship of the monks to the ecclesiastical crisis of the late eleventh century is discussed by N. F. Cantor, "The Crisis of Western Monasticism," *American Historical Review* 66 (1960), but see also the essential analysis of J. Van Engen, "The 'Crisis of Cenobitism' Reconsidered: Benedictine Monasticism in the Years 1050–1150," *Speculum* 61 (1986): 269–304, as well as H. E. J. Cowdrey, *The Cluniacs and the Gregorian Reform* (1970), an impressive but difficult study. Cowdrey's *The Age of Abbot Desiderius: Monte Cassino, the Papacy, and the Normans in the Eleventh and Early Twelfth Centuries* (1983) focuses on Monte Cassino, the oldest black monk monastery. The advanced student will benefit considerably from the works by C. Erdmann, J. B. Freed, and B. Rosenwein that are cited in the Notes. I. S. Robinson, *The Papacy, 1073–1198: Continuity and Innovation* (1990), explores the changing role of the papacy in the eleventh and twelfth centuries and the development of the new model of papal government.

The following studies provide exciting and highly readable general accounts of the Crusades: J. Riley-Smith, *What Were the Crusades?* (1977), and R. C. Finucane, *Soldiers of the Faith: Crusaders and Muslims at War* (1983). There are excellent articles on many facets of the Crusades, including "The Children's Crusade," "Crusade Propaganda," "Crusader Art and Architecture," and "The Political Crusades"—all written by authorities—in J. R. Strayer, ed., *The Dictionary of the Middle Ages,* vol. 4 (1984). For the Fourth Crusade, see the excellent study of D. E. Queller, *The Fourth Crusade: The Capture of Constantinople* (1977), which gives an important revisionist interpretation. B. Lewis, *The Muslim Discovery of Europe* (1982), gives the Muslim view of the Crusades. Serious students will eventually want to consult the multivolume work of K. M. Setton, gen. ed., *A History of the Crusades* (1955–1977). C. Tyerman, *England and the Crusades, 1095–1588* (1988), treats the central topics of financing and the impact of the Crusades on economic, political, and social life.

G. O. Sayles, *The Medieval Foundations of England* (1961), traces political and social conditions to the end of the twelfth century. H. G. Richardson and G. O. Sayles, *The Governance of Medieval England from the Conquest to Magna Carta* (1963), focuses on administrative developments. For the Becket controversy, see F. Barlow, *Thomas Becket* (1986), the best recent study, and D. Knowles, *Thomas Becket* (1970). J. C. Holt, *Magna Carta* (1969), remains the best modern treatment of the document.

For France, both E. Hallam, *The Capetian Kings of France, 987–1328* (1980), and R. Fawtier, *The Capetian Kings of France* (1962), are readable introductions. Advanced students of medieval French administrative history should see J. Baldwin, *The Government of Philip Augustus: Foundations of French Royal Power in the Middle Ages* (1986), and J. R. Strayer, *The Reign of Philip the Fair* (1980). On Germany, H. Furhman, *Germany in the High Middle Ages,* trans. T. Reuther (1986), and G. Barraclough, *The Origins of Modern Germany* (1963), provide an excellent explanation of the problems and peculiarities of the Holy Roman Empire; the latter is a fine example of the Marxist interpretation of medieval history. M. Pacaut, *Frederick Barbarossa,* trans. A. J. Pomerans (1980), is perhaps the best one-volume treatment of that important ruler.

For the economic revival of Europe, see in addition to the titles by Dollinger, Herlihy, Postan, and Russell given in the Notes, T. H. Lloyd, *England and the German Hanse, 1157–1611: A Study in Their Trade and Commercial Diplomacy* (1992), which is essential for northern European commercial development. See also C. M. Cipolla, *Before the Industrial Revolution of the Middle Ages* (1976). The effect of climate on population and economic growth is discussed in the remarkable work of E. L. Ladurie, *Times of Feast, Times of Famine: A History of Climate Since the Year 1000,* trans. B. Bray (1971).

For women, see S. F. Wemple, *Women in Frankish Society: Marriage and the Cloister, 500 to 900* (1981), a basic work; C. Klapisch-Zuber, ed., *A History of Women,* vol. 2, *Silences of the Middle Ages* (1992), which contains useful essays on many aspects of women's lives and status; and S. Shahar, *The Fourth Estate: Women in the Middle Ages* (1983), a provocative work. J. M. Bennett, *Women in the Medieval English Countryside: Gender and Household in Brigstock Before the Plague* (1987), is a fascinating case study. E. Amt, ed., *Women's Lives in Medieval Europe: A Sourcebook* (1993), has fresh primary material on many aspects of the lives of noble, business, and peasant women.

Those interested in the origins of medieval towns and cities will learn how historians use the evidence of coins, archaeology, tax records, geography, and laws in J. F. Benton, ed., *Town Origins: The Evidence of Medieval England* (1968). S. Reynolds, *An Introduction to the History of English Medieval Towns* (1982), explores the social structure, political organization, and economic livelihood of English towns. R. H. Hilton, *English and French Towns in Feudal Society* (1992), is an exciting comparative study. C. Platt's well-illustrated *The English Medieval Town* (1979) makes excellent use of archaeological data and contains detailed information on the wool and cloth trades.

13

Creativity and Crisis in the Central and Later Middle Ages

Miniature of King Charles VII presiding at the trial of the Duc d'Alençon. *(Source: Bayerische Staatsbibliothek, Munich)*

The central Middle Ages witnessed some of the most remarkable achievements in the history of the Western world. Europeans displayed tremendous creativity in many facets of culture. The university, a unique Western contribution to civilization, came into being. The Gothic cathedral manifested medieval people's deep Christian faith, their sense of community, and their appreciation of the worlds of nature, humanity, and God.

In the medieval world, the nobility fought, the clergy prayed, and the peasantry worked to produce the food on which all depended. The lives of the vast majority of ordinary people continued to be conditioned by their local geography, climate, religion, and parish. For the peasantry, considerable social mobility existed in the central Middle Ages. Then, between 1300 and 1450, Europeans experienced a series of frightful shocks: economic dislocation, plague, war, and social upheaval. The last book of the New Testament—the Book of Revelation, dealing with visions of the end of the world, disease, war, famine, and death—inspired thousands of sermons and religious tracts. Death and preoccupation with death make the fourteenth century one of the most wrenching periods of Western civilization.

The progression from the vitality and creativity of the central Middle Ages to the crises of the later Middle Ages brings to mind a number of questions:

- How did the universities, the Gothic cathedrals, and troubadour poetry evolve, and what do they reveal about medieval ideals and society?
- How did people actually live, and what were their major preoccupations and lifestyles?
- What were the social and psychological effects of economic difficulties, disease, and war in the later Middle Ages?
- What impact did schism in the Christian church have on the lives of ordinary people?
- What political and social factors were reflected in the development of national literatures and in the expansion of literacy?

These are among the questions this chapter will explore.

MEDIEVAL UNIVERSITIES

Just as the first strong secular states emerged in the thirteenth century, so did the first universities. This was no coincidence. The new bureaucratic states and the church needed educated administrators, and universities were a response to this need.

Since the time of the Carolingian Empire, monasteries and cathedral schools had offered the only formal instruction available. Monasteries were geared to religious concerns. They wished to maintain an atmosphere of seclusion and silence and were unwilling to accept large numbers of noisy lay students. In contrast, schools attached to cathedrals and run by the bishop and his clergy were frequently situated in bustling cities, and in the eleventh century in Bologna and other Italian cities wealthy businessmen established municipal schools. Inhabited by peoples of many backgrounds and "nationalities," cities stimulated the growth and exchange of ideas. In the course of the twelfth century, cathedral schools in France and municipal schools in Italy developed into universities.

The growth of the University of Bologna coincided with a revival of interest in Roman law. The study of Roman law as embodied in Justinian's *Code* had never completely died out in the West, but this sudden burst of interest seems to have been inspired by Irnerius (d. 1125), a great teacher at Bologna. His fame attracted students from all over Europe. Irnerius not only explained the Roman law of Justinian's *Code* but applied it to difficult practical situations. An important school of civil law was founded at Montpellier in France, but Bologna remained the greatest law school throughout the Middle Ages.

At Salerno, interest in medicine had persisted for centuries. Greek and Muslim physicians there had studied the use of herbs as cures and experimented with surgery. The twelfth century ushered in a new interest in Greek medical texts and in the work of Arab and Greek doctors. Students of medicine poured into Salerno and soon attracted royal attention. In 1140, when King Roger II (r. 1130–1154) of Sicily took the practice of medicine under royal control, his ordinance stated:

Who, from now on, wishes to practice medicine, has to present himself before our officials and examiners, in order to pass their judgment. Should he be bold enough to disregard this, he will be punished by imprisonment and confiscation of his entire property. In this way we are taking care that our subjects are not endangered by the inexperience of the physicians.[1]

In the first decades of the twelfth century, students converged on Paris. They crowded into the cathedral school of Notre Dame and spilled over into the area later called the Latin Quarter—whose name probably reflects the Italian origin of many of the students. The cathedral school's international reputation had already drawn to Paris scholars from all over Europe. One of the most famous of them was Peter Abélard.

The son of a minor Breton knight, Peter Abélard (1079–1142) studied in Paris, quickly absorbed a large amount of material, and set himself up as a teacher. Fascinated by logic, which he believed could be used to solve most problems, Abélard used a method of systematic doubting in his writing and teaching. As he put it, "By doubting we come to questioning, and by questioning we perceive the truth." Other scholars merely asserted theological principles; Abélard discussed and analyzed them.

The influx of students eager for learning and the presence of dedicated and imaginative teachers created the atmosphere in which universities grew. In northern Europe—at Paris and later at Oxford and Cambridge in England—associations or guilds of professors organized universities. They established the curriculum, set the length of time for study, and determined the form and content of examinations. University faculties grouped themselves according to academic disciplines, or schools—law, medicine, arts, and theology. The professors, known as "Schoolmen" or "Scholastics," developed a method of thinking, reasoning, and writing in which questions were raised and authorities cited on both sides of a question. The goal of the Scholastic method was to arrive at definitive answers and to provide a rational explanation for what was believed on faith.

The Scholastic approach rested on the recovery of classical philosophical texts and on ancient Greek and Arabic texts that had entered Europe in the early twelfth century. Thirteenth-century philosophers relied on Latin translations of these texts, especially translations of Aristotle. The Scholastics reinterpreted Aristotelian texts in a Christian sense.

In exploration of the natural world, Aristotle's axioms were not precisely followed. Medieval scientists argued from authority, such as the Bible, Justinian's *Code,* or ancient scientific treatises, rather than from direct observation and experimentation, as modern scientists do. Thus the conclusions of medieval scientists were often wrong. Nevertheless, natural science gradually emerged as a discipline distinct from philosophy.

Many of the problems that Scholastic philosophers raised dealt with theological issues. For example, they addressed the question that interested all Christians, educated and uneducated: How is a person saved? Saint Augustine's thesis—that, as a result of Adam's fall, human beings have a propensity to sin—had become a central feature of medieval church doctrine. The church taught that it possessed the means to forgive the sinful: grace conveyed through the sacraments. The Scholastics held that one must also *decide* to use the grace received. In other words, a person must use his or her reason to advance to God.

Thirteenth-century Scholastics devoted an enormous amount of time to collecting and organizing knowledge on all topics. These collections were published as *summa,* or reference books. There were summa on law, philosophy, vegetation, animal life, and theology. Saint Thomas Aquinas (1225–1274), a professor at Paris, produced the most famous collection, the *Summa Theologica,* which deals with a vast number of theological questions.

Aquinas drew an important distinction between faith and reason. He maintained that, although reason can demonstrate many basic Christian principles such as the existence of God, other fundamental teachings such as the Trinity and original sin cannot be proved by logic. That reason cannot establish them does not, however, mean they are contrary to reason. Rather, people understand such doctrines through revelation embodied in Scripture. Scripture cannot contradict reason, nor reason Scripture:

The light of faith that is freely infused into us does not destroy the light of natural knowledge [reason] implanted in us naturally. For although the natural light of the human mind is insufficient to show us these things made manifest by faith, it is nevertheless impossible that these things which the divine principle gives us by faith are contrary to these implanted in us by nature [reason]. Indeed, were that the case, one or the other would have to be false, and, since both are given to us by God, God would have to be the author of untruth, which is impossible.[2]

Thomas Aquinas and all medieval intellectuals held that the end of both faith and reason was the knowledge of, and union with, God. His work later became the fundamental text of Roman Catholic doctrine.

At all universities, the standard method of teaching was the *lecture*—that is, a reading. The professor read a passage from the Bible, Justinian's *Code,* or one of Aristotle's treatises. He then explained and interpreted the passage; his interpretation was called a *gloss.* Students wrote down everything. Because books had to be copied by hand, they were extremely expensive, and few students could afford them. Students therefore depended for study on their own or on friends' notes accumulated over a period of years. Examinations were given after three, four, or five years of study, when the student applied for a degree. The professors determined the amount of material students had to know for each degree, and students frequently insisted that the professors specify precisely what that material was. Examinations were oral and very difficult. If the candidate passed, he was awarded the first, or bachelor's, degree. Further study, about as long, arduous, and expensive as it is today, enabled the graduate to try for the master's and doctor's degrees. Degrees were technically licenses to teach. Most students, however, did not become teachers. They staffed the expanding royal and papal administrations.

FROM ROMANESQUE GLOOM TO "UNINTERRUPTED LIGHT"

It is difficult for twentieth-century people to appreciate the extraordinary amounts of energy, imagination, and money involved in building medieval churches. Between 1180 and 1270 in France alone, eighty cathedrals, about five hundred abbey churches, and tens of thousands of parish churches were constructed. This construction represents a remarkable investment for a country of scarcely 18 million people. More stone was quarried for churches in medieval France than had been mined in ancient Egypt, where the Great Pyramid alone consumed 40.5 million cubic feet of stone. All these churches displayed a new architectual style. Fifteenth-century critics called the new style

Gothic because they mistakenly believed the fifth-century Goths had invented it. It actually developed partly in reaction to the earlier Romanesque style, which resembled ancient Roman architecture.

The manner in which a society spends its wealth expresses its values. Cathedrals, abbeys, and village churches testify to the deep religious faith and piety of medieval people. If the dominant aspect of medieval culture had not been the Christian faith, the builder's imagination and the merchant's money would have been used in other ways.

Interior of La Sainte Chapelle, Paris   The central features of the Gothic style—pointed arch, ribbed vaulting, and flying buttress—made possible the construction of churches higher than ever before and the use of stained glass to replace stone walls. King Louis IX built this church to house the crown of thorns and other relics that he brought back from the Crusades. The result is a building of breathtaking beauty, a jeweled reliquary. *(Source: Art Resource, NY)*

In the ninth and tenth centuries, the Vikings and Magyars had burned hundreds of wooden churches. In the eleventh century, the abbots wanted to rebuild in a more permanent fashion, and after the year 1000, church building increased on a wide scale. Because fireproofing was essential, ceilings had to be made of stone. Therefore, builders replaced wooden roofs with arched stone ceilings called vaults. The stone ceilings were heavy; only thick walls would support them. Because the walls were so thick, the windows were small, allowing little light into the interior of the church. In northern Europe, twin bell towers often crowned these Romanesque churches, giving them a powerful, fortresslike appearance. Built primarily by monasteries, Romanesque churches reflect the quasi-military, aristocratic, and pre-urban society that built them.

The inspiration for the Gothic style originated in the brain of one monk, Suger, abbot of Saint-Denis (1122–1151). When Suger became abbot, he decided to reconstruct the old Carolingian abbey church at Saint-Denis. Work began in 1137. On June 11, 1144, King Louis VII and a large crowd of bishops, dignitaries, and common people witnessed the solemn consecration of the first Gothic church in France.

Not unknown before 1137, the basic features of Gothic architecture—the pointed arch, the ribbed vault, and the flying buttress—allowed unprecedented interior lightness. Since the ceiling of a Gothic church weighed less than that of a Romanesque church, the walls could be thinner. Stained-glass windows were cut into the stone, flooding the church with light. The interior, Suger exulted, "would shine with the wonderful and uninterrupted light of most sacred windows, pervading the interior beauty."[3]

Begun in the Île-de-France, Gothic architecture spread throughout France with the expansion of royal power. French architects were soon invited to design and supervise the construction of churches in other parts of Europe, and the new style traveled rapidly.

The construction of a Gothic cathedral represented a gigantic investment of time, money, and corporate effort. The bishop and the clergy of the cathedral made the decision to build, but they depended on the support of all social classes. Bishops raised revenue from contributions by people in their dioceses, and the clergy appealed to the king and the nobility. Above all, the church relied on the financial help of those with the greatest amount of ready cash, the commercial classes.

Money was not the only need. A great number of craftsmen had to be assembled: quarrymen, sculptors, stonecutters, masons, mortar makers, carpenters, blacksmiths, glassmakers, roofers. Unskilled laborers had to be recruited for the heavy work. The construction of a large cathedral was rarely completed in one lifetime; many cathedrals were never finished at all. Because generation after generation added to the building, many Gothic churches show the architectural influences of two or even three centuries.

Towns competed to build the largest and most splendid church. In northern France in the late twelfth and early thirteenth centuries, cathedrals grew progressively taller. The people of Beauvais exceeded everyone: their church, started in 1247, reached 157 feet. Unfortunately, the weight imposed on the vaults was too great, and the building collapsed in 1284. Medieval people built cathedrals to glorify God—and if mortals were impressed, so much the better.[4]

Cathedrals served secular as well as religious purposes. The sanctuary containing the altar and the bishop's chair belonged to the clergy, but the rest of the church belonged to the people. In addition to marriages, baptisms, and funerals, there were scores of feast days on which the entire town gathered in the cathedral for festivities. Local guilds met in the cathedrals to arrange business deals, plan recreational events and the support of disabled members. Magistrates and municipal officials held political meetings there. Pilgrims slept there, lovers courted there, and traveling actors staged plays there. The cathedral belonged to all.

First and foremost, however, the cathedral was intended to teach the people the doctrines of Christian faith through visual images. Architecture became the servant of theology. The west front of the cathedral faced the setting sun, and its wall was usually devoted to the scenes of the Last Judgment. The north side, which received the least sunlight, displayed events from the Old Testament. The south side, washed in warm sunshine for much of the day, depicted scenes from the New Testament. This symbolism implied that the Jewish people of the Old Testament lived in darkness and that the Gospel brought by Christ illuminated the world. Every piece of sculpture, furniture, and stained glass had some religious or social significance.

Stained glass beautifully reflects the creative energy of the central Middle Ages. It is both an integral part of Gothic architecture and a distinct form of painting. The glassmaker "painted" the picture with small fragments of glass held together with strips of lead. As Gothic churches became more skeletal and had more windows, stained glass replaced manuscript illumination as the leading kind of painting. Thousands of scenes in the cathedral celebrate nature, country life, and the activities of ordinary people. All members of medieval society had a place in the City of God, which the Gothic cathedral represented.

The drama, derived from the church's liturgy, emerged as a distinct art form during the same period. For centuries, skits based on Christ's Nativity and Resurrection had been performed in monasteries and cathedrals. Beginning in the thirteenth century, plays based on these and other biblical themes and on the lives of the saints were performed in the towns. Guilds financed these "mystery plays"—so called because they were based on the mysteries of the Christian faith. Performed first at the cathedral altar, then in the church square, and later in the town marketplace, mystery plays enjoyed great popularity. By combining comical farce based on ordinary life with serious religious scenes, they allowed the common people to understand and identify with religious figures and the mysteries of their faith.

❖ TROUBADOUR POETRY

In the twelfth and thirteenth centuries a remarkable literary culture blossomed in southern France. The word *troubadour* comes from the Provençal word *trobar,* which in turn derives from the Arabic *taraba,* meaning "to sing" or "to sing poetry." A troubadour was a poet of Provence who wrote lyric verse in his or her native language and sang it at one of the noble courts. Troubadour songs had a variety of themes. Men sang about "courtly love," the pure love a knight felt for his lady, whom he sought to win by military prowess and patience; about the love a knight felt for the wife of his feudal lord; or about carnal desires seeking satisfac-

tion. Women troubadours *(trobairitz)* focused on their emotions, their intimate feelings, or their experiences with men. Some poems exalted the married state, and others idealized adulterous relationships; some were earthy and bawdy, and others advised young girls to remain chaste in preparation for marriage. Many poems celebrate the beauties of nature; a few speak of the sexual frustrations of nuns. The married Countess Beatrice of Dia (1150–1200?) expresses the hurt she feels after being jilted by a young knight:

I've suffered great distress
From a knight whom I once owned.
Now, for all time, be it known:
I loved him-yes, to excess.
　　His jilting I've regretted,
Yet his love I never really returned.
Now for my sin I can only burn:
　　Dressed, or in my bed.

O if I had that knight to caress
Naked all night in my arms,
He'd be ravished by the charm
Of using, for cushion, my breast.
　　His love I more deeply prize
Than Floris did Blancheflor's
Take that love, my core,
　　My sense, my life, my eyes!

Lovely lover, gracious, kind,
When will I overcome your fight?
O if I could lie with you one night!
Feel those loving lips on mine!
　　Listen, one thing sets me afire:
Here in my husband's place I want you,
If you'll just keep your promise true:
　　Give me everything I desire.[5]

Because of its varied and contradictory themes, courtly love has been one of the most hotly debated topics in all medieval studies. One scholar concludes that it was at once "a literary movement, an ideology, an ethical system, an expression of the play element in culture, which arose in an aristocratic Christian environment exposed to Hispano-Arabic influences."[6] Another scholar insists there is no evidence for the practice of courtly love. If, however, the knight's love represented the respect of a vassal for his lady, a respect that inspired him to noble deeds, then perhaps courtly love contributed to an improvement in the status of women.

Troubadours certainly felt Hispano-Arabic influences. In the eleventh century, Christians of southern France were in intimate contact with the Arabized world of Andalusia, where reverence for the lady in a "courtly" tradition had long existed. In 1064 the Provençal lord Guillaume de Montreuil captured Barbastro and, according to legend, took a thousand slave girls from Andalusia back to Provence. Even if this figure is an exaggeration, those women who came to southern France would have been familiar with the Arabic tradition of sung poetry and continued it in their new land. Troubadour poetry thus represents another facet of the strong Muslim influence on European culture and life.[7]

The romantic motifs of the troubadours also influenced the northern French *trouvères,* who wrote adventure-romances in the form of epic poems. At the court of his patron Marie of Champagne, Chrétien de Troyes (ca 1135–1183) used the legends of the fifth-century British king Arthur to discuss contemporary chivalric ideals and their moral implications. Such poems as *Lancelot, Percival and the Holy Grail,* and *Tristan and Isolde* reveal Chrétien as the founding father of the Western romantic genre. The theme of these romances centers on the knight-errant who seeks adventures and who, when faced with crises usually precipitated by love, acquires new values and grows in wisdom.

The songs of the troubadours and trouvères were widely imitated in Italy, England, and Germany, and they spurred the development of vernacular languages (see pages 432–433). Most of the troubadours and trouvères came from and wrote for the aristocratic classes, and their poetry suggests the interests and values of noble culture in the central Middle Ages.

❋ LIFE IN CHRISTIAN EUROPE IN THE CENTRAL MIDDLE AGES

In the late ninth century, medieval intellectuals described Christian society as composed of those who pray (the monks), those who fight (the nobles), and those who work (the peasants). According to this image of social structure, function determined social classification.[8] Reality, however, was somewhat different. In the eleventh and twelfth centuries, most clerics and monks descended from the noble class and retained aristo-cratic attitudes and values, and the lay brothers who did most of the agricultural labor on monastic estates came from the peasant classes. The division of society into fighters, monks, and peasants also presents too static a view of a world in which there was considerable social mobility. Moreover, such a social scheme does not take into consideration townspeople and the emerging commercial classes. That omission, however, is easy to understand. Traders and other city dwellers were not typical members of medieval society. Medieval people were usually contemptuous (at least officially) of profit-making activities, and even after the appearance of urban commercial groups, the ideological view of medieval Christian society remained the one formulated in the ninth century: the three-part division among peasants, nobles, and monks.

Those Who Work

According to one modern scholar, "Peasants were rural dwellers who possess (if they do not own) the means of agricultural production."[9] Some peasants worked continuously on the land. Others supplemented their ordinary work as brewers, carpenters, tailors, or housemaids with wage labor in the field. In either case, all peasants supported lords, clergy, townspeople, as well as themselves. The men and women who worked the land in the twelfth and thirteenth centuries made up the overwhelming majority of the population, probably more than 90 percent. Yet it is difficult to form a coherent picture of them. The records that serve as historical sources were written by and for the aristocratic classes.

It is important to remember that peasants' conditions varied widely across Europe and that geography and climate as much as human initiative and local custom determined the peculiar quality of rural life.[10] The problems that faced the farmer in Yorkshire, England, where the soil was rocky and the weather rainy, were very different from those of the Italian peasant in the sun-drenched Po Valley.

Another obstacle to the creation of a coherent picture of the peasants has been historians' tendency to group all peasants into one social class. Although medieval theologians lumped everyone who worked the land into the "those who work" category, there were many kinds of peasants—ranging from complete slaves to free and very rich

The Three Classes   Medieval people believed that their society was divided among clerics, warriors, and workers, here represented by a monk, a knight, and a peasant. The new commercial class had no recognized place in the agrarian military world. *(Source: The British Library)*

farmers. The status of the peasantry fluctuated widely all across Europe. The period from 1050 to 1250 was one of considerable social mobility.

Slaves were found in western Europe in the central Middle Ages, but in steadily declining numbers. That the word *slave* derives from *Slav* attests to the widespread trade in men and women from the Slavic areas in the Middle Ages. Around the year 1200, there were in aristocratic and upper-middle-class households in Provence, Catalonia, Italy, and Germany a few slaves—blond Slavs from the Baltic, olive-skinned Syrians, and blacks from Africa. Legal language differed considerably from place to place,

and the distinction between slave and serf was not always clear. Both lacked freedom—the power to do as one wished—and both were subject to the arbitrary will of one person, the lord. A serf, however, could not be bought and sold like an animal or an inanimate object, as the slave could.

The serf was required to perform labor services on the lord's land. The number of workdays varied, but it was usually three days a week except in the planting or harvest seasons, when it increased. Serfs frequently had to pay arbitrary levies, as for marriage or inheritance (see page 355). The precise amounts of tax paid to the lord depended on local custom and tradition. A free person had to do none of these things. For his or her landholding, rent had to be paid to the lord, and that was often the sole obligation. A free person could move and live as he or she wished.

Serfs were tied to the land, and serfdom was a hereditary condition. A person born a serf was likely to die a serf, though many did secure their freedom. About 1187 Glanvill, an official of King Henry II and an expert on English law, described how *villeins* (literally, "inhabitants of small villages")—as English serfs were called—could be made free:

A person of villein status can be made free in several ways. For example, his lord, wishing him to achieve freedom from the villeinage by which he is subject to him, may quit-claim [release] him from himself and his heirs; or he may give or sell him to another with intent to free him. . . . No person of villein status can seek his freedom with his own money, . . . because all the chattels of a villein are deemed to be the property of his lord that he cannot redeem himself from villeinage with his own money, as against his lord. If, however, a third party provides the money and buys the villein in order to free him, then he can maintain himself for ever in a state of freedom as against his lord who sold him. . . . If any villein stays peaceably for a year and a day in a privileged town and is admitted as a citizen into their commune, that is to say, their gild, he is thereby freed from villeinage.[11]

Thus, with the advent of a money economy, serfs could save money and, through a third-person intermediary, buy their freedom.

The economic revival that began in the eleventh century (see pages 380–386) advanced the cause of individual liberty. Hundreds of new towns arose in Ireland, in Mecklenburg and Pomerania in northeastern Germany, and in reconquest Spain; their settlers often came from long distances. Some colonial towns were the offspring of colonial traders. For example, Venetian and Genoese merchants founded in the Crimean region trading posts that served as entrepôts on the routes to China. The thirteenth century witnessed enormous immigration to many parts of Europe that previously had been sparsely settled. Immigration and colonization provided the opportunity for freedom and social mobility.[12]

Another opportunity for increased personal freedom, or at least for a reduction in traditional manorial obligations and dues, was provided by the reclamation of waste and forest land in the eleventh and twelfth centuries. Marshes and fens were drained and slowly made arable. This type of agricultural advancement frequently improved the peasants' social and legal condition. A serf could clear a patch of fen or forest land, make it productive, and, through prudent saving, buy more land and eventually purchase freedom. Settlers on the lowlands of the abbey of Bourbourg in Flanders, who had erected dikes and extended the arable land, possessed hereditary tenures by 1159. They secured personal liberty and owed their overlord only small payments.

In the thirteenth century, the noble class frequently needed money to finance crusading, building, or other projects. For example, in 1240 when Geoffrey de Montigny became abbot of Saint-Pierre-le-Vif in the Senonais region of France, he found the abbey church in bad disrepair and needed revenues to rebuild it. Geoffrey also discovered that the descendants of families who had once owed the abbey servile obligations now refused to recognize their bondage. Some of these peasants had grown wealthy. When the abbot determined to reclaim these peasants in order to get the revenues to rebuild his church, a legal struggle ensued. In 1257 a compromise was worked out whereby Geoffrey manumitted 366 persons who in turn agreed to pay him £500 a year over a twelve-year period.[13]

In the central Middle Ages, most European peasants, free and unfree, lived on a *manor*, the estate of a lord. The manor was the basic unit of medieval rural organization and the center of rural life. All other generalizations about manors and manorial life have to be limited by variations in the quality of the soil, local climatic conditions, and methods of cultivation. Manors varied from several thousand acres to as little as 120 acres. Recent archaeological evidence suggests that a manor might include several villages, one village whose produce was divided among several lords, or an isolated homestead.

The arable land of the manor was divided into two sections. The *demesne,* or home farm, was cultivated by the peasants for the lord. The other, usually larger section was held by the peasantry. All the arable land, both the lord's and the peasants', was divided into strips, and the strips belonging to any given individual were scattered throughout the manor. All peasants cooperated in the cultivation of the land, working it as a group. All shared in any disaster as well as in any large harvest.

A manor usually held pasture or meadowland for the grazing of cattle, sheep, and sometimes goats. Often the manor had some forest land as well. Forests had enormous economic importance. They were the source of wood for building and fuel, resin for lighting, ash for candles, and ash and lime for fertilizers and all sorts of sterilizing products. The forests were used for feeding pigs, cattle, and domestic animals on nuts, roots, and wild berries.

The fundamental objective of all medieval agriculture was the production of an adequate food supply. Using the method that historians have called the open-field system, peasants divided the arable land of a manor into two or three fields without hedges or fences to mark the individual holdings of the lord, serfs, and freemen. Beginning in the eleventh century in parts of France, England, and Germany, peasants divided all the arable land into three large fields. In any one year, two of the fields were cultivated and one lay fallow. One part of the land was sown with winter cereals such as rye and wheat, the other with spring crops such as peas, beans, and barley. Each year the crop was rotated. Local needs, the fertility of the soil, and dietary customs determined what was planted and the method of crop rotation.

In the early twelfth century, the production of iron increased greatly. In the thirteenth century, the wooden plow continued to be the basic instrument of agricultural production, but its edge was strengthened with iron. Only after the start of the fourteenth century, when lists of manorial equipment began to be kept, is there evidence for pitchforks, spades, axes, and harrows.

The plow and the harrow (a cultivating instrument with heavy teeth that breaks up and smoothes the soil) were increasingly drawn by horses. The development of the padded horse collar, resting on the horse's shoulders and attached to the load by shafts, led to an agricultural revolution. The horse collar let the animal put its entire weight into the task of pulling. In the twelfth century, the use of horses, rather than oxen, spread because horses' greater strength brought greater efficiency to farming. Horses, however, were an enormous investment, perhaps comparable to a modern tractor. They had to be shod (another indication of increased iron production), and the oats they ate were costly. Although horses represent a crucial element in the improvement of husbandry, students of medieval agriculture are not sure whether the greater use of horses increased crop yields.

The thirteenth century witnessed a tremendous spurt in the use of horses to haul carts to market. Large and small farmers increasingly relied on horses to pull wagons because they could travel much faster than oxen. Consequently, goods

Boarstall Manor, Buckinghamshire In 1440, Edmund Rede, lord of this estate, had a map made showing his ancestor receiving the title from King Edward I (lower field). Notice the manor house, church, and peasants' cottages along the central road. In the common fields, divided by hedges, peasants cultivated on a three-year rotation cycle— winter wheat, spring oats, and fallow. Peasants' pigs grazed freely in the woods, indicated by trees. We don't know whether the peasants could hunt the deer. *(Source: Buckinghamshire Record Office, Aylesbury)*

reached a market faster, and the number of markets within an area to which the peasant had access increased. The opportunities and temptations for consumer spending on nonagricultural goods multiplied.[14]

Agricultural yields varied widely from place to place and from year to year. By twentieth-century standards, they were very low. Inadequate soil preparation, poor seed selection, lack of manure—all made low yields virtually inevitable. And, like farmers of all times and places, medieval peasants were at the mercy of the weather. Yet there was striking improvement over time. Researchers have tentatively concluded that between the ninth and early thirteenth centuries, yields of cereals approximately doubled, and on the best-managed estates farmers harvested five bushels of grain for every bushel of seed planted. Grain yields were probably greatest on large manorial estates, where there was more professional management.

A modern Illinois farmer expects to get 40 bushels of soybeans, 150 bushels of corn, and 50 bushels of wheat for every bushel of seeds planted. Of course, modern costs of production in labor, seed, and fertilizer are quite high, but this yield is at least ten times that of the farmer's medieval ancestor. Some manors may have achieved a yield of 12 or even 15 to 1, but the *average* manor probably got a yield of only 5 to 1 in the thirteenth century.[15]

Life on the Manor For most people in medieval Europe, life meant country life. A person's horizons were not likely to extend beyond the manor on which he or she was born. True, peasants who colonized sparsely settled regions such as eastern Germany must have traveled long distances. But most people rarely traveled more than twenty-five miles beyond their villages. Their world was small, narrow, and provincial in the original sense of the

Late Medieval Wheelless Plow The sharp-pointed colter of this plow cut the earth while the attached moldboard lifted, turned, and pulverized the soil. As the man steers the plow, his wife prods the oxen. The caption reads, "God speed the plow, and send us corn [wheat] enough." *(Source: Trinity College Library, Cambridge)*

word: limited by the boundaries of the province. This way of life did not have entirely unfortunate results. A farmer had a strong sense of family and the certainty of its support and help in time of trouble. People knew what their life's work would be—the same as their mother's or father's. They had a sense of place, and pride in that place was reflected in adornment of the village church. Religion and the village gave people a sure sense of identity and with it psychological peace. Modern people—urban, isolated, industrialized, rootless, and thoroughly secularized—have lost many of these reinforcements.

But, even aside from the unending physical labor, life on the manor was dull. Medieval men and women must have had a crushing sense of frustration. Often they sought escape in heavy drinking. English judicial records of the thirteenth century reveal a surprisingly large number of "accidental" deaths. Strong, robust, commonsensical farmers do not ordinarily fall on their knives and stab themselves, or slip out of boats and drown, or get lost in the woods on a winter's night. They were probably drunk. Many of these accidents occurred, as the court records say, "coming from an ale." Brawls and violent fights were frequent at taverns.

Scholars have recently spent much energy investigating the structure of medieval peasant households. Because little concrete evidence survives, conclusions are very tentative. It appears, however, that a peasant household consisted of a simple nuclear family: a married couple alone, a couple of children, or a widow or widower with children. Peasant households were *not* extended families containing grandparents or married sons and daughters and their children. The simple family predominated in thirteenth-century England, in northern France in the fourteenth century, and in fifteenth-century Tuscany. Before the first appearance of the Black Death (see pages 419–421), perhaps 94 percent of peasant farmers married, and both bride and groom were in their early twenties. The typical household numbered about five people—the parents and three children.[16]

Women played a significant role in the agricultural life of medieval Europe. Historians often overlook this obvious fact. Women worked with men in wheat and grain cultivation, in the vineyards, and in the harvest and preparation of crops needed by the textile industry—flax and plants used for dyeing cloth, such as madder (which pro-duces shades of red) and woad (which yields blue dye). Especially at harvest time women shared with their fathers and husbands the backbreaking labor in the fields, work that was especially difficult for them because of weaker muscular development and frequent pregnancies. Lords of great estates commonly hired female day laborers to shear sheep, pick hops (used in the manufacture of beer and ale), tend gardens, as well as do household chores such as cleaning, laundry, and baking. Servant girls in the country considered their hired status as temporary, until they married. Thrifty farm wives contributed to the family income by selling for cash the produce of their gardens or kitchen: butter, cheese, eggs, fruit, soap, mustard, cucumbers. In a year of crisis, careful management was often all that separated a household from starvation. And starvation was a very real danger to the peasantry down to the eighteenth century.

Women managed the house. The size and quality of peasants' houses varied according to their relative prosperity, and usually depended on the amount of land held. The poorest peasants lived in windowless cottages built of wood and clay or wattle and thatched with straw. These cottages consisted of one large room that served as the kitchen and living quarters for all. Everyone slept there. The house had an earthen floor and a fireplace. The lack of windows meant that the room was very sooty. A trestle table, several stools, one or two beds, and a chest for storing clothes constituted the furniture. A shed attached to the house provided storage for tools and shelter for animals. Prosperous peasants added rooms and furniture as they could be afforded, and some wealthy peasants in the early fourteenth century had two-story houses with separate bedrooms for parents and children.

Every house had a small garden and an outbuilding. Onions, garlic, turnips, and carrots were grown and stored through the winter. Cabbage was raised and pickled almost everywhere. Preserving and storing other foods were the basic responsibility of the women and children.

Women dominated in the production of ale for the community market. They had to know how to mix the correct proportions of barley, water, yeast, and hops in 12-gallon vats of hot liquid. Brewing was hard and dangerous work. Records of the English coroners' courts reveal that 5 percent of women who died lost their lives in brewing accidents, falling into the vats of boiling liquid.[17] Ale was the universal drink of the common people in northern Europe. By modern American standards the rate of consumption was heroic. Each monk of Abingdon Abbey in twelfth-century England was allotted 3 gallons a day, and a man working in the fields for ten hours probably drank much more.[18]

The mainstay of the diet for peasants everywhere—and for all other classes—was bread. It was a hard, black substance made of barley, millet, and oats, rarely of expensive wheat flour. The housewife usually baked the household supply once a week. If sheep, cows, or goats were raised, she also made cheese.

The diet of those living in an area with access to a river, lake, or stream was supplemented with fish, which could be preserved by salting. In many places there were severe laws against hunting and trapping in the forests. Deer, wild boars, and other game were strictly reserved for the king and nobility. These laws were flagrantly violated, however, and stolen rabbits and wild game often found their way to the peasants' tables.

Lists of peasant obligations and services to the lord, such as the following from Battle Abbey, commonly included the payment of chickens and eggs:

John of Coyworth holds a house and thirty acres of land, and owes yearly 2 p at Easter and Michaelmas; and he owes a cock and two hens at Christmas, of the value of 4 d.[19]

Except for the rare chicken or illegally caught wild game, meat appeared on the table only on the great feast days of the Christian year: Christmas, Easter, and Pentecost. Then the meat was likely to be pork from the pig slaughtered in the fall and salted for the rest of the year. Some scholars believe that, by the mid-thirteenth century, there was a great increase in the consumption of meat generally. If so, this improvement in diet is further evidence of an improved standard of living.

Breakfast, eaten at dawn before people departed for their farmwork, might well consist of bread, an onion (easily stored through the winter months), and a piece of cheese, washed down with milk or ale. Farmers, then as now, ate their main meal around noon. This was often soup—a thick *potage* of boiled cabbage, onions, turnips, and peas, seasoned with a bone or perhaps a sliver of meat. The

evening meal, taken at sunset, consisted of leftovers from the noon meal, perhaps with bread, cheese, milk, or ale.

Once children were able to walk, they helped their parents in the hundreds of chores that had to be done. Small children were set to collecting eggs, if the family had chickens, or gathering twigs and sticks for firewood. As they grew older, children had more responsible tasks, such as weeding the family vegetable garden, shearing the sheep, helping with the planting or harvesting, and assisting their mothers in the endless tasks of baking, cooking, and preserving. Because of poor diet, terrible sanitation, and lack of medical care, the death rate among children was phenomenally high.

Health Care What medical attention was available to the sick person in Western Europe between 1050 and 1300? Scholars are only beginning to explore this question, and there are many aspects of public health that we know little about. The steady rise in population in these centuries is usually attributed to the beginnings of political stability, the reduction of violence, and the increases in cultivated land and food supply. It may also be ascribed partly to better health care. Survival to adulthood probably meant a tough people. A recent study of skeletal remains in the village of Brandes in Orisans in Burgundy showed that peasants enjoyed very good health: they were well built, they had excellent teeth, and their bones revealed no signs of chronic disease. This evidence comes from only one village, but preliminary research confirms the impression that is given by romantic literature: in the prime of life the average person had an innocent raw vitality that enabled him or her to eat, drink, and make love with great gusto.[20]

In recent years scholars have produced some exciting information relating to the natural processes of pregnancy and childbirth. But the acquisition of information has not been easy. Because modesty forbade the presence of men at the birth of a child, very few men could write about it, and there was general illiteracy among women. One woman who wrote extensively, the twelfth-century physician Trotula of Salerno, tended to explain problems of gynecology (women's health) and obstetrics (pregnancy and childbirth) in terms of the relative degree of heat and cold and moisture and dryness within the female body. On the potential difficulty of childbirth she wrote

There are, however, certain women so narrow in the function of childbearing that scarcely ever or never do they succeed. . . . Sometimes external heat comes up around the internal organs and they are straightened in the act of giving birth. Sometimes the exit from the womb is too small, the woman is too fat, or the foetus is dead, not helping nature by its own movements. This often happens to a woman giving birth in winter. If she has by nature a tight opening of the womb, the coldness of the season constricts the womb still more. Sometimes the heat all goes out of the woman herself and she is left without strength to help herself in childbearing. . . . Let her sides, abdomen, hips, and flanks be rubbed with oil of roses or oil of violets.[21]

Trotula believed that sneezing, which forced the woman to push her inner organs downward, should be induced. Her general knowledge cannot be called scientific.

Midwives learned their work through a practical apprenticeship, not through any sort of professional study. Most could not read, and even if they could, few medical texts existed. Because the first pregnancy of many women ended fatally, women of all social classes had a great fear of childbirth. Trotula, Hildegard of Bingen, and other writers on obstetrics urged pregnant women to pray that Christ would grant them a safe childbed.[22]

In the thirteenth century midwives began the practice of delivery by caesarean section—birth by an incision through the abdominal wall and uterus—so called from the traditional belief that the Roman statesman Julius Caesar had been born by means of this operation. Caesarean sections were performed only if the mother had died in labor; the purpose of the operation was the baptism of the child to assure its salvation.

Caesarean sections posed serious ethical problems. Who was to decide whether the mother was

A Caesarean Birth The midwife lifts a male child from the abdominal opening in the mother's dead body. Her helper prepares a tub of water to bathe the child. Since few infants survived the procedure, midwives needed witnesses to assert that they had not bungled the birth or deliberately killed the infant. *(Source: The British Library)*

dead? (The stethoscope was not invented until 1819.) Who could decide whether the fetus was alive after the mother's death? In a very difficult birth should the life of the mother be sacrificed for the sake of the child? An Old English translation of Trotula's advice to midwives states that "whan the woman is feble and the chylde may noght comyn out, then it is better that the chylde is slayne than that the moder of the child also dye." The greatest theologian of the age, Saint Thomas Aquinas in his treatise on baptism is also explicit: "Evil should not be done that good may come. Therefore one should not kill the mother in order to baptize the child; if, however, the child be still alive in the womb after the mother has died, the mother should be opened in order to baptize the child."[23] Since caesarean sections were performed only after the mother was dead, the choice of the mother's life or the child's never arose.[24] About 1400, male surgeons, motivated by professional, scientific, and probably financial interests, began to perform caesarean sections. Thus through caesarean births men entered the field of obstetrics.[25]

Childhood diseases, poor hygiene, tooth decay, wounds received in fighting, and the myriad ail-ments and afflictions for which even modern medical science has no cure—from cancer to the common cold—must have caused considerable suffering. For the sick what care existed?

As in all ages, the sick everywhere depended above all on the private nursing care of relatives and friends. For public health, English sources provide the largest evidence to date. In the British Isles the twelfth century witnessed a momentous breakthrough in the establishment of institutional care in hospitals. In addition to the infirmaries run by monks and nuns, there were at least 113 hospitals in England with possibly as many as 3,494 beds. Medieval hospitals were built by the royal family, the clergy, barons, and ordinary people to alleviate the suffering of the sick, not just to house them. Hospitals attracted considerable popular support, and in their charitable contributions women played an especially strong role in the endowment of hospitals.[26]

As in the developed modern world, persons living in or near a town or city had a better chance of receiving some form of professional attention than did those in remote rural areas. English documents label at least ninety practitioners as *medicus*, mean-

Saint Maurus, Healing   A rich body of legend developed around Maurus, a nobleman's son given as an oblate to Saint Benedict. In the eleventh century, Maurus had a reputation, unsupported by evidence, for medical knowledge and curative powers. Here he is depicted giving a patient some kind of pharmaceutical preparation. *(Source: Bibliothèque municipale de Troyes)*

ing physician, surgeon, or medical man, but that is a pitifully small number in a population of perhaps 2 million. With so few doctors, only the largest cities—such as London, York, Winchester, and Canterbury, which all catered to pilgrims and travelers—had resident physicians. At other hospitals, physician consultants were brought in as the occasion required. Most people, of course, did not live in or near large towns. They relied for assistance on the chance presence of a local monk or nun with herb and pharmaceutical knowledge, a local person skilled in setting broken bones, or the wise village person experienced in treating diseases.

Since public morality and ancient tradition forbade the examination of female patients by men, women could practice obstetrics and gynecology. But although women played active roles as healers and in the general care of the sick, male doctors jealously guarded their status and admitted very few women to university medical schools when they were founded; "Francesca Romano, who was licensed as a surgeon in 1321 by Duke Carl of Calabria is the exception that proves the rule."[27] The medical faculty at the University of Paris in the fourteenth century penalized women who practiced medicine because they lacked a degree—which they were not allowed to get.

Popular Religion   Apart from the land, the weather, and the peculiar conditions that existed on each manor, the Christian religion had the greatest impact on the daily lives of ordinary people in the central Middle Ages. Religious practices varied widely from country to country and even from province to province. But nowhere was religion a one-hour-on-Sunday or High Holy Days affair. Christian practices and attitudes permeated virtually all aspects of everyday life.

As the Germanic and Celtic peoples were Christianized, their new religion became a fusion of Jewish, pagan, Roman, and Christian practices. In the central Middle Ages, all people shared as a natural and public duty in the religious life of the community.

The village church was the center of community life—social, political, and economic as well as religious. Most of the important events in a person's life took place in or around the church. A person was baptized there, within hours of birth. Men and women confessed their sins to the village priest there and received, usually at Easter and Christmas, the sacrament of the Eucharist. In front of the church, the bishop reached down from his horse and confirmed a person as a Christian by placing his hands over the candidate's head and making the sign of the cross on the forehead. (Bishops Thomas Becket of Canterbury and Hugh of Lincoln were considered especially holy men because they got down from their horses to confirm.) Young people courted in the churchyard and, so the sermons of the priests complained, made love in the church cemetery. Priests urged couples to marry publicly in the church, but many married privately, without witnesses (see page 429).

In the church, women and men could pray to the Virgin and the local saints. The stone in the church altar contained relics of the saints, often a local saint to whom the church itself had been dedicated. The saints had once lived on earth and thus, people believed, understood human problems. They could be helpful intercessors with Christ or with God the Father. They could perform miracles. The saint became the special property of the locality where his or her relics rested. Thus to secure the saint's support and to guarantee the region's prosperity, a busy traffic in relics developed—bones, articles of clothing, the saint's tears or saliva, even dust from the saint's tomb. The understanding that existed between the saint and the peasants rested on the customary medieval relationship of mutual fidelity and aid: peasants would offer the saint prayers, loyalty, and gifts to the shrine or church in return for the saint's healing and support. When saints failed to receive the attention they felt they deserved, they sometimes took offense and were vindictive. An English knight whose broken arm was healed by Saint James forgot to thank the saint at his shrine at Reading, whereupon the saint punished the knight by breaking his other arm.

What had been the saints' social background when alive? "The initiative in creating a cult (of a saint) always belonged to believers"[28] (ordinary people). Although papal authorities insisted that they had the exclusive right to examine the lives and activities of candidates for sainthood in a formal "trial," popular opinion declared people saints. Between 1185 and 1431, only seventy official investigations were held at Rome, but hundreds of new persons across Europe were venerated as saints. Church officials and educated clergy evaluated candidates according to the "heroic virtue" of their lives, but lay people judged solely by the candidates' miracles.

Modern research suggests a connection between the models of holiness and the social structures in different parts of Europe. Northern Europeans and southern Europeans chose saints of different social backgrounds or classes. In France and Germany, saints were primarily men and women of the nobility. In Italy and Mediterranean lands, saints tended to be *popolani*—non-nobles, nonaristocrats. The cult of the saints, which developed in a rural environment among uneducated people, is a central feature of popular culture in the Middle Ages.[29]

Popular religion consisted largely of rituals heavy with symbolism. Before slicing a loaf of bread, the good wife tapped the sign of the cross on the loaf with her knife. Before the planting, the village priest customarily went out and sprinkled the fields with water, symbolizing refreshment and life. Shortly after a woman had successfully delivered a child, she was "churched." Churching was a ceremony of thanksgiving based on the Jewish rite of purification. When a child was baptized, a few grains of salt were dropped on its tongue. Salt had been the symbol of purity, strength, and incorruptibility for the ancient Hebrews, and the Romans had used it in their sacrifices. It was used in Christian baptism to drive away demons and to strengthen the infant in its new faith.

The entire calendar was designed with reference to Christmas, Easter, and Pentecost. Saints' days were legion. Everyone participated in village processions. The colored vestments the priests wore at Mass gave the villagers a sense of the changing seasons of the church's liturgical year. The signs and symbols of Christianity were visible everywhere.

What did people actually *believe*? It is difficult to say, partly because medieval peasants left few written records of their thoughts, partly because in any age there is often a great disparity between what people profess to believe and their conduct or the ways they act on their beliefs. Peasants accepted what family custom and the clergy taught them. Recent research has shown that in the central Middle Ages a new religious understanding emerged. "Whereas early Christianity looked to holy men and women and early medieval society turned to saints to effect the connection between God and humankind through prayers of intercession," in the twelfth century a sacramental system developed. The seven sacraments—Baptism, Penance, Eucharist, Confirmation, Marriage, Holy Orders,

Extreme Unction—brought grace, the divine assistance or help needed to lead a good Christian life and to merit salvation. At the center of the sacramental system stood the Eucharist, the small piece of bread that through the words of priestly consecration at the Mass, became the living body of Christ and, when worthily consumed, became a channel of Christ's grace. The ritual of consecration, repeated at every altar of Christendom, became a unifying symbol in a complex world.[30]

The Mass was in Latin, but the priest delivered sermons on the Gospel in the vernacular—or he was supposed to. An almost universal criticism of the parish clergy in the twelfth and thirteenth centuries was that they were incapable of explaining basic Christian teaching to their parishioners. The growth of the universities did not improve the situation, because few diocesan clerics attended them and those who did obtain degrees secured administrative positions. The only parish priest to be canonized in the entire Middle Ages, the Breton lawyer and priest Saint Yves (d. 1303), had resigned a position as a diocesan judge to serve rural parishioners. At the trial for his canonization, laypeople stressed not only that he led a simple and frugal life but that he put his forensic skills to the service of preaching the Christian gospels. Saint Yves is the great exception that proves the rule that the medieval parish clergy were generally incapable of preaching in a rural milieu. Parish priests celebrated the liturgy and administered the sacraments, but they had other shortcomings. A thirteenth-century Alsatian chronicler said that the peasants of the region did not complain that their pastors lived in concubinage, because that made them less fearful for the virtue of their daughters.[31]

Christians had long had special reverence and affection for the Virgin Mary as the Mother of Christ. In the eleventh century, theologians began to emphasize the depiction of Mary at the crucifixion in the Gospel of John (19:25–27):

But standing by the cross of Jesus were his mother, and his mother's sister, Mary the wife of Clopas, and Mary Magdalene. When Jesus saw his mother and the disciple whom he loved standing near, he said to his mother, "Woman, behold, your son!" Then he said to the disciple, "Behold, your mother!"

Medieval scholars interpreted this passage as expressing Christ's compassionate concern for all humanity and Mary's spiritual motherhood of all Christians. The huge outpouring of popular devotions to Mary concentrated on her role as Queen of Heaven and, because of her special relationship to Christ, as all-powerful intercessor with him. Masses on Saturdays specially commemorated her, sermons focused on her unique influence with Christ, and hymns and prayers to her multiplied.

Those Who Fight

The nobility, though a small fraction of the total population, strongly influenced all aspects of medieval culture—political, economic, religious, educational, and artistic. For that reason, European society in the twelfth and thirteenth centuries may be termed aristocratic.

Members of the nobility enjoyed a special legal status. A nobleman was free personally and in his possessions. He was limited only by his military obligation to king, duke, or prince. As the result of his liberty, he had certain rights and responsibilities. He raised troops and commanded them in the field. He held courts that dispensed a sort of justice. Sometimes he coined money for use within his territories. As lord of the people who settled on his lands, he made political decisions affecting them, resolved disputes among them, and protected them in time of attack. The liberty and privileges of the noble were inheritable, perpetuated by blood and not by wealth alone.

The nobleman was a professional fighter. His social function, as churchmen described it, was to protect the weak, the poor, and the churches by arms. He possessed a horse and a sword. These, and the leisure time in which to learn how to use them in combat, were the visible signs of his nobility. He was encouraged to display chivalric virtues—courtesy, loyalty to his commander, and generosity. All nobles were knights, but not all knights were noble.[32]

Those who aspired to the aristocracy desired a castle, the symbol of feudal independence and military lifestyle. Through military valor, a fortunate marriage, or outstanding service to king or lord, poor knights could and did achieve positions in the upper nobility of France and England. Not so in Germany, where a large class of unfree knights, or *ministerials,* fought as warriors or served as stewards who managed nobles' estates or households. In the twelfth century, ministerials sometimes ac-

quired fiefs and wealth. The most important ministerials served the German kings and had significant responsibilities. Legally, however, they remained of servile status: they were not noble.[33]

Infancy, Childhood, and Youth The rate of infant mortality (the number of babies who died before their first birthday) in the central Middle Ages must have been staggering. The limited information indicates that midwives had surely contributed to the death rate of both the newborn and the mother. Natural causes—disease and poor or insufficient food—also resulted in many deaths. Infanticide, however, which was common in the ancient world, seems to have declined in the central Middle Ages. Ecclesiastical pressure worked steadily against it. Infanticide in medieval Europe is another indication of the slow and very imperfect Christianization of European peoples.

On the other hand, the abandonment of infant children seems to have been the most favored form of family limitation, widely practiced throughout the entire Middle Ages. Abandonment was "the voluntary relinquishing of control over children by their natal parents or guardians, whether by leaving them somewhere, selling them, or legally consigning authority to some other person or institution."[34] Why did parents do this? What became of the children? What was the rate of abandonment? What attitudes did medieval society have toward this practice?

Poverty or local natural disaster led some parents to abandon their children because they could not support them. Thus Saint Patrick wrote that, in times of famine, fathers would sell their sons and daughters so that the children could be fed. Parents sometimes gave children away because they were illegitimate or the result of incestuous unions.

Sometimes parents believed that someone of greater means or status might find the child and bring it up in better circumstances than the natal parents could provide. Disappointment in the sex of the child or its physical weakness or deformity might also lead parents to abandon it. Finally, some parents were indifferent—they "simply could not be bothered" with the responsibilities of parenthood.[35]

The Christian Middle Ages witnessed a significant development in the disposal of superfluous children: they were given to monasteries as *oblates* or "offerings." Boys and girls were given to

✤ **Children Given to Creditors** Ecclesiastical laws against lending money at interest were widely flouted, and many nobles, having borrowed beyond their ability to repay, fell heavily into debt. The selling or giving of children to creditors, illustrated here, was one solution to indebtedness. *(Source: The Bodleian Library, Oxford)*

monasteries or convents as permanent gifts. By the seventh century, church councils and civil codes had defined the practice: "Parents of any social status could donate a child, of either sex, at least up to the age of ten." Contemporaries considered oblation a religious act, for the child was offered to God often in recompense for parental sin. But oblation also served social and economic functions. The monastery nurtured and educated the child in a familial atmosphere, and it provided career opportunities for the mature monk or nun despite his or her humble origins.[36] In the twelfth and thirteenth centuries, the incidence of noble parents giving their younger sons and daughters to religious houses increased dramatically; nobles wanted to preserve the estate intact for the eldest son. In

the early thirteenth century, the bishop of Paris observed that children were "cast into the cloister by parents and relatives just as if they were kittens or piglets whom their mothers could not nourish; so that they may die to the world not spiritually but . . . civilly, that is—so that they may be deprived of their hereditary position and that it may devolve on those who remain in the world." The abandonment of children remained a socially acceptable institution. Ecclesiastical and civil authorities never legislated against it.[37]

For children of aristocratic birth, the years from infancy to around the age of seven or eight were primarily years of play. Infants had their rattles, as the twelfth-century monk Guibert of Nogent reports, and young children their special toys. Guibert of Nogent speaks in several places in his autobiography of "the tender years of childhood"—the years from six to twelve. Describing the severity of the tutor whom his mother assigned to him, Guibert wrote:

Placed under him, . . . I was kept from ordinary games and never allowed to leave my master's company, or to eat anywhere else than at home, in everything I had to show self-control in word, look, and deed, so that he seemed to require of me the conduct of a monk rather than a clerk. While others of my age wandered everywhere at will and were unchecked in the indulgence of such inclinations as were natural at their age, I, hedged in with constant restraints and dressed in my clerical garb, would sit and look at the troops of players like a beast awaiting sacrifice. Even on Sundays and saints' days I had to submit to the severity of school exercises.[38]

Guibert's mother had intended him for the church. At about the age of seven, a boy of the noble class who was not intended for the church was placed in the household of one of his father's friends or relatives. There he became a servant to the lord and received his formal training in arms. He was expected to serve the lord at the table, to assist him as a private valet when called on to do so, and, as he gained experience, to care for the lord's horses and equipment. The boy might have a great deal of work to do, depending on the size of the household and the personality of the lord. The work that children did, medieval people believed, gave them experience and preparation for later life.

Training was in the arts of war. The boy learned to ride and to manage a horse. He had to acquire skill in wielding a sword, which sometimes weighed as much as twenty-five pounds. He had to be able to hurl a lance, shoot with a bow and arrow, and care for armor and other equipment. Increasingly, in the eleventh and twelfth centuries, noble youths learned to read and write some Latin. Still, on thousands of charters from that period, nobles signed with a cross (+) or some other mark. Literacy for the nobility became more common in the thirteenth century. Formal training was concluded around the age of twenty-one with the ceremony of knighthood. The custom of knighting, though never universal, seems to have been widespread in France and England but not in Germany. Once knighted, a young man was supposed to be

courteous, generous, and, if possible, handsome and rich. Above all, he was to be loyal to his lord and brave in battle. In a society lacking strong institutions of government, loyalty was the cement that held aristocratic society together. The greatest crime was called a *felony,* which meant treachery to one's lord.

Parents often wanted to settle daughters' futures as soon as possible. Men tended to prefer young brides. A woman in her late twenties or thirties had relatively few years in which to produce children; thus aristocratic girls in the central Middle Ages were married at around the age of sixteen.

The future of many young women was not enviable. For a girl of sixteen, marriage to a man in his thirties was not the most attractive prospect, and marriage to a widower in his forties and fifties was even less so. If there were a large number of marriageable young girls in a particular locality, their "market value" was reduced. In the early Middle Ages, it had been the custom for the groom to present a dowry to the bride and her family, but by the late twelfth century the process was reversed. Thereafter, the size of the marriage portions that brides and their families offered to prospective husbands rose higher and higher.

What was a young woman unhappily married to a much older man to do? The literature of courtly love is filled with stories of young bachelors in love with young married women. How hopeless their love was is not known. The cuckolded husband is a stock figure in masterpieces such as *The Romance of Tristan and Isolde,* Chaucer's *The Merchant's Tale,* and Boccaccio's *Fiammetta's Tale.*

Power and Responsibility   The responsibilities of a noble in the central Middle Ages depended on the size and extent of his estates, the number of his dependents, and his position in his territory relative to others of his class and to the king. As a vassal a noble was required to fight for his lord or for the king when called on to do so. By the mid-twelfth century, this service was limited in most parts of western Europe to forty days a year. The noble was obliged to attend his lord's court on important occasions when the lord wanted to put on great displays, such as at Easter, Pentecost, and Christmas. When the lord knighted his eldest son or married off his eldest daughter, he called his vassals to his court. They were expected to attend and to present a contribution known as a "gracious aid."

Until the late thirteenth century, when royal authority intervened, a noble in France or England had great power over the knights and peasants on his estates. He maintained order among them and dispensed justice to them. The quality of justice varied widely: some lords were vicious tyrants who exploited and persecuted their peasants; others were reasonable and evenhanded. In any case, the quality of life on the manor and its productivity were related in no small way to the temperament and decency of the lord—and his lady.

Women played a large and important role in the functioning of the estate (see Listening to the Past). They were responsible for the practical management of the household's "inner economy"—cooking, brewing, spinning, weaving, caring for yard animals. The lifestyle of the medieval warrior nobles required constant travel, both for purposes of war and for the supervision of distant properties. Frequent pregnancies and the reluctance to expose women to hostile conditions kept the lady at home and therefore able to assume supervision of the family's fixed properties. When the lord was away for long periods—on crusade, for instance, the lord could be gone from two to five years, if he returned at all—his wife often became the sole manager of the family properties. Between 1060 and 1080, the lady Hersendis was the sole manager of her family's properties in northern France while her husband was on crusade in the Holy Land.

Women Defending Castle
Women shared with men the difficulties and dangers of defending castles. Armed with rocks and bows and arrows, and not hesitating to poke a finger through a chain-mail helmet and into the eye of a knight scaling the walls on a ladder, these noble ladies try to fight off attackers. *(Source: Bibliothèque royale Albert 1er, Brussels)*

Nor were women's activities confined to managing households and estates in their husbands' absence. Medieval warfare was largely a matter of brief skirmishes, and few men were killed in any single encounter. But altogether the number slain ran high, and there were many widows. Aristocratic widows frequently controlled family properties and fortunes and exercised great authority. Although the evidence is scattered and sketchy, there are indications that women performed many of the functions of men. In Spain, France, and Germany they bought, sold, and otherwise transferred property. Gertrude, labeled "Saxony's almighty widow" by the chronicler Ekkehard of Aura, took a leading role in conspiracies against the emperor Henry V.

Those Who Pray

Monasticism represented some of the finest aspirations of medieval civilization. The monasteries were devoted to prayer, and their standards of Christian behavior influenced the entire church. The monasteries produced the educated elite that was continually drawn into the administrative service of kings and great lords. Monks kept alive the remains of classical culture and experimented with new styles of architecture and art. They introduced new techniques of estate management and land reclamation. Although relatively few in number in the central Middle Ages, the monks played a significant role in medieval society.

Toward the end of his *Ecclesiastical History of England and Normandy,* when he was well into his sixties, Orderic Vitalis, a monk of the Norman abbey of Saint Evroul, interrupted his narrative to explain movingly how he happened to become a monk:

And so, O glorious God, you didst inspire my father Odeleric to renounce me utterly and submit me in all things to thy governance. So, weeping, he gave me, a weeping child, into the care of the monk Reginald, and sent me away into exile for love of thee, and never saw me again. And I, a mere boy, did not presume to oppose my father's wishes, but obeyed him in all things, for he promised me for his part that if I became a monk I should taste of the joys of Heaven with the Innocents after my death. . . . And so, a boy of ten, I crossed the English channel and came into Normandy as an exile, unknown to all, knowing no one.[39]

Orderic Vitalis (ca 1075–ca 1140) was one of the leading scholars of his time. As such, he is not a representative figure or even a typical monk. Intellectuals, those who earn their living or spend most of their time working with ideas, are never typical figures of their times. In one respect, however, Orderic was quite representative of the monks of the central Middle Ages: although he had no doubt that God wanted him to be a monk, the decision was actually made by his parents. Orderic was the third son of a knight who held lands in western England. Concern for the provision of his two older sons probably led the knight to give his youngest boy to the monastery. Medieval monasteries were religious institutions whose organization and structure fulfilled the social needs of the feudal nobility. The monasteries provided noble children with both an honorable and aristocratic life and opportunities for ecclesiastical careers.[40] As medieval society changed economically, and as European society ever so slowly developed middle-class traits, the monasteries almost inevitably drew their manpower, when they were able, from the middle classes. Until that time, they were preserves of the aristocratic nobility.

Through the Middle Ages, social class also defined the kinds of religious life open to women. Kings and nobles usually established convents for their daughters, sisters, aunts, or aging mothers. Entrance was restricted to women of the founder's class. Since a well-born lady could not honorably be apprenticed to a tradesperson or do any kind of manual labor, the sole alternative to life at home was the religious life.

The founder's endowment and support greatly influenced the later social, economic, and political status of the convent. A few convents received large endowments and could accept many women. Amesbury Priory in Wiltshire, England, for example, received handsome endowments from King Henry II and his successors. In 1256 Amesbury supported a prioress and 76 nuns, 7 priests, and 16 lay brothers. The convent raised £100 in annual rents and £40 from the wool clip—very large sums at the time. By 1317 Amesbury had 177 nuns.[41] Most houses of women, however, possessed limited resources and remained small in numbers.

The office of abbess or prioress, the house's superior, customarily went to a nun of considerable social standing. Since an abbess or prioress had responsibility for governing her community and

✳ **Synagogue** Hildegard of Bingen, the first major German mystic, developed a rich theology on the basis of her visions. Here Synagogue is portrayed as a tall woman commanded by God to prepare humanity for the coming of Christ. In her arms Moses holds up the stone tablets of the Ten Commandments; in her lap are the patriarchs and prophets who foretold the birth of Christ. The headband symbolizes the Virgin Mary: because Mary gave the world the savior, Hildegard makes Synagogue the Mother of the Incarnation. *(Source: Rheinische Bildarchiv)*

for representing it in any business with the outside world, she was a woman of local, sometimes national, power and importance. Although the level of intellectual life in the women's houses varied widely, the career of Hildegard of Bingen suggests the activities of some nuns in the central Middle Ages. The tenth child of a lesser noble family, Hildegard (1098–1179) was given when eight years old as an oblate to an abbey in the Rhineland, where she learned Latin and received a good education. In 1147 Hildegard founded the convent of Rupertsberg near Bingen. There she produced a body of writings including the *Scivias (Know the Ways)*, a record of her mystical visions that incorporates vast theological learning; the *Physica (On the Physical Elements)*, a classification of the natural elements, such as plants, animals, metals, and the movements of the heavenly bodies; a mystery play; and a medical work that led a distinguished twentieth-century historian of science to describe Hildegard as "one of the most original writers of the Latin West in the twelfth century." At the same time, she carried on a vast correspondence with scholars, prelates, and ordinary people and had such a reputation for wisdom that a recent writer has called her "the Dear Abby of the twelfth century to whom everyone came or wrote for advice or comfort."[42] An exceptionally gifted person, Hildegard represents the Benedictine ideal of great learning combined with a devoted monastic life. Like intellectual monks, however, intellectual nuns were not typical of the era.

In medieval Europe the monasteries of men greatly outnumbered those of women. The pattern of life within individual monasteries varied widely from house to house and from region to region. One central activity, however—the work of God—was performed everywhere. Daily life centered around the liturgy.

Seven times a day and once during the night, the monks went to choir to chant the psalms and other prayers prescribed by Saint Benedict. Prayers were offered for peace, rain, good harvests, the civil authorities, the monks' families, and their benefactors. Monastic patrons in turn lavished gifts on the monasteries, which often became very wealthy. Through their prayers the monks performed a valuable service for the rest of society.

Prayer justified the monks' spending a large percentage of their income on splendid objects to enhance the liturgy; monks praised God, they believed, not only in prayer but in everything connected with prayer. They sought to accumulate priestly vestments of the finest silks, velvets, and embroideries, as well as sacred vessels of embossed silver and gold and ornamented and bejeweled Gospel books. Every monastery tried to acquire the relics of its patron saint, which necessitated the production of a beautiful reliquary to house the relics. The liturgy, then, inspired a great deal of art, and the monasteries became the crucibles of art in Western Christendom.

The monks fulfilled their social responsibility by praying. It was generally agreed that they could best carry out this duty if they were not distracted by worldly needs. Thus great and lesser lords gave the monasteries lands that would supply the community with necessities.

The usual method of economic organization was the manor. Many monastic manors were small enough and close enough to the abbey to be supervised directly by the abbot. But if a monastery held and farmed vast estates, the properties were divided into administrative units under the supervision of one of the monks of the house.

The Cistercians, whose constitution insisted that they accept lands far from human habitation, were ideally suited to the agricultural needs and trends

Beekeeping at Monte Cassino   Because of the scarcity and expense of sugar, honey was the usual sweetener for pastries and liquids throughout the Middle Ages. This illustrator had never actually seen the process of gathering honey: without veils, nets, and gloves, the beekeepers would be badly stung. (*Source: Biblioteca Apostolica Vaticana*)

of their times. In the Low Countries they built dikes to hold back the sea, and the reclaimed land was put to the production of cereals. In the eastern parts of Germany they took the lead in draining swamps and cultivating wasteland. As a result of their efforts, the rich, rolling land of French Burgundy was turned into lush vineyards, and the rocky soil and damp downs of northern and central England were turned into sheep runs.

Some monasteries lent their surplus revenues to the local nobility and peasantry. In the twelfth century the abbey of Savigny in Normandy, for example, acted as a banking house, providing loans at interest to many noble families of Normandy and Brittany. Although church law opposed usury—lending at interest—one reliable scholar has recently written that "it was clerics and ecclesiastical institutions (monasteries and nunneries) that constituted the main providers of credit."[43]

Whatever work particular monks did and whatever economic activities individual monasteries were involved in, monks also performed social services and exerted an influence for the good. In addition to running schools and "hospitals," monasteries like Saint Albans, situated north of London on a busy thoroughfare, served as hotels and resting places for travelers. In short, monasteries performed a variety of social services in an age when there was no "state" and no conception of social welfare as a public responsibility.

✤ CRISES OF THE LATER MIDDLE AGES

In the later years of the thirteenth century, Europeans seemed to run out of steam. The crusading movement gradually fizzled out. Few new cathedrals were constructed, and if a cathedral had not been completed by 1300, the chances were high that it never would be. The strong rulers of England and France, building on the foundations of their predecessors, increased their authority and gained the loyalty of all their subjects. The vigor of those kings, however, did not pass to their immediate descendants. Meanwhile, the church, which for two centuries had guided Christian society, began to face grave difficulties. A violent dispute between the papacy and the kings of England and France badly damaged the prestige of the pope.

But religious struggle was only one of the crises that would face European society in the fourteenth century.

A Challenge to Religious Authority

In 1294, King Edward I of England and Philip the Fair of France declared war on each other. To finance this war, both kings laid taxes on the clergy. Kings had been taxing the church for decades. Pope Boniface VIII (r. 1294–1303), arguing from precedent, insisted that kings gain papal consent for taxation of the clergy and forbade churchmen to pay the taxes. But Edward and Philip refused to accept this decree, partly because it hurt royal finances and partly because the papal order threatened royal authority within their countries. Edward immediately denied the clergy the protection of the law, an action that meant its members could be attacked with impunity. Philip halted the shipment of all ecclesiastical revenue to Rome. Boniface had to back down.

Philip the Fair and his ministers continued their attack on all powers in France outside royal authority. Philip arrested a French bishop who was also the papal legate. When Boniface defended the ecclesiastical status and diplomatic immunity of the bishop, Philip replied with the trumped-up charge that the pope was a heretic. The papacy and the French monarchy waged a bitter war of propaganda. Finally, in 1302, in a letter entitled *Unam Sanctam* (because its opening sentence spoke of one holy Catholic church), Boniface insisted that all Christians, including kings, are subject to the pope. Philip's university-trained advisers, with an argument drawn from Roman law, maintained that the king of France was completely sovereign in his kingdom and responsible to God alone. French mercenary troops went to Italy and arrested the aged pope at Anagni. Although Boniface was soon freed, he died shortly afterward.

The Black Death

Economic difficulties originating in the later thirteenth century were fully manifest by the start of the fourteenth. In the first decade, the countries of northern Europe experienced considerable price inflation. The costs of grain, livestock, and dairy products rose sharply. Severe weather, which historical geographers label "the Little Ice Age," made a serious situation frightful. An unusual number of storms brought torrential rains, ruining the wheat, oat, and hay crops on which people and animals depended almost everywhere. Population had steadily increased in the twelfth and thirteenth centuries, and large amounts of land had been put under cultivation. The amount of food yielded, however, did not match the level of population growth. Bad weather had disastrous results. Poor harvests—one in four was likely to be poor—led to scarcity and starvation. Almost all of northern Europe suffered a terrible famine in the years 1315 to 1317. Then in 1318 disease hit cattle and sheep, drastically reducing the herds and flocks. Another bad harvest in 1321 brought famine, starvation, and death. The undernourished population was ripe for the Grim Reaper, who appeared in 1348 in the form of the Black Death.

In October 1347, Genoese ships traveling from the Crimea in southern Russia brought the bubonic plague to Messina, from where it spread across Sicily and up into Italy. By late spring of 1348, southern Germany was attacked. Frightened French authorities chased a galley bearing the disease from the port of Marseilles, but not before plague had infected the city. In June 1348 two ships entered the Bristol Channel and introduced it into England. All Europe felt the scourge of this horrible disease (Map 13.1).

The bacillus that causes the plague, *Pasteurella pestis,* likes to live in the bloodstream of an animal or, ideally, in the stomach of a flea. The flea in turn resides in the hair of a rodent, sometimes a squirrel but preferably the hardy, nimble, and vagabond black rat. In the fourteenth century, the host black rat traveled by ship, where it could feast for months on a cargo of grain or live snugly among bales of cloth. Fleas bearing the bacillus also had no trouble nesting in saddlebags.[44] Comfortable, well fed, and often having greatly multiplied, the black rats ended their ocean voyage and descended on the great cities of Europe.

The plague took two forms—bubonic and pneumonic. The rat was the transmitter of the bubonic form of the disease. The pneumonic form was communicated directly from one person to another.

Although by the fourteenth century urban authorities from London to Paris to Rome had begun to try to achieve a primitive level of sanitation, urban conditions remained ideal for the spread of

disease. Narrow streets filled with mud, refuse, and human excrement were as much cesspools as thoroughfares. Dead animals and sore-covered beggars greeted the traveler. Houses whose upper stories

Saint Dominic and the Inquisition   The fifteenth-century court painter to the Spanish rulers Ferdinand and Isabella, Pedro Berruguete (d. 1504) here portrays an event from the life of Saint Dominic. Dominic presides at the trial of Count Raymond of Toulouse, who had supported the Albigensian heretics. Raymond, helmeted and on horseback, repented and was pardoned; his companions, who would not repent, were burned. Smoke from the fire has put one of the judges to sleep, and other officials, impervious to the human tragedy, chat among themselves. (*Source: Museo del Prado, Madrid*)

MAP 13.1 The Course of the Black Death in Fourteenth-Century Europe
Notice the routes that the bubonic plague took across Europe. How do you account for the fact that several regions were spared the "dreadful death"?

projected over the lower ones eliminated light and air. And extreme overcrowding was commonplace. When all members of an aristocratic family lived and slept in one room, it should not be surprising that six or eight persons in a middle-class or poor household slept in one bed—if they had one.

Standards of personal hygiene remained frightfully low. Fleas and body lice were universal afflictions: everyone from peasants to archbishops had them. One more bite did not cause much alarm. But if that nibble came from a bacillus-bearing flea, an entire household or area was doomed.

The symptoms of the bubonic plague started with a growth the size of a nut or an apple in the armpit, in the groin, or on the neck. This was the boil, or *buba,* that gave the disease its name and caused agonizing pain. If the buba was lanced and the pus thoroughly drained, the victim had a chance of recovery. The secondary stage was the appearance of black spots or blotches caused by bleeding under the skin. Finally, the victim began to cough violently and spit blood. This stage, indicating the presence of thousands of bacilli in the bloodstream, signaled the end, and death followed in two or three days. Rather than evoking compassion for the victim, a French scientist has written, everything about the bubonic plague provoked horror and disgust: "All the matter which exuded from their bodies let off an unbearable stench;

sweat, excrement, spittle, breath, so fetid as to be overpowering; urine turbid, thick, black or red."[45]

Fourteenth-century medical literature indicates that physicians had no rational explanation for the disease, could sometimes ease the pain, but had no cure. Most people—lay, scholarly, and medical—believed that the Black Death was caused by some "vicious property in the air" that carried the disease from place to place. When ignorance was joined to fear and ancient bigotry, savage cruelty sometimes resulted. Many people believed that the Jews had poisoned the wells of Christian communities and thereby infected the drinking water. This charge led to the murder of thousands of Jews across Europe. According to one chronicler, sixteen thousand were killed at the imperial city of Strasbourg alone in 1349. That sixteen thousand is probably a typically medieval numerical exaggeration does not lessen the horror of the massacre.

The Italian writer Giovanni Boccaccio (1313–1375), describing the course of the disease in Florence in the preface to his book of tales, *The Decameron,* pinpointed the cause of the spread:

Moreover, the virulence of the pest was the greater by reason that intercourse was apt to convey it from the sick to the whole, just as fire devours things dry or greasy when they are brought close to it. Nay, the evil went yet further, for not merely by speech or association with the sick was the malady communicated to the healthy with consequent peril of common death, but any that touched the clothes of the sick or aught else that had been touched or used by them, seemed thereby to contract the disease.[46]

The highly infectious nature of the plague, especially in areas of high population density, was recognized by a few sophisticated Arabs. When the disease struck the town of Salé in Morocco, Ibu Abu Madyan shut in his household with sufficient food and water and allowed no one to enter or leave until the plague had passed. Madyan was entirely successful. The rat that carried the disease-bearing flea avoided travel outside the cities. Thus the countryside was relatively safe. City dwellers who could afford to move fled to the country districts.

Because population figures for the period before the arrival of the plague do not exist for most countries and cities, only educated guesses can be made about mortality rates. Of a total English population of perhaps 4.2 million, probably 1.4 million died of the Black Death in its several visits.[47] Densely populated Italian cities endured incredible losses. Florence lost between half and two-thirds of its 1347 population of 85,000 when the plague visited in 1348. The disease recurred intermittently in the 1360s and 1370s and reappeared many times down to 1700. Population losses in Bohemia and Poland seem to have been much less. Historians of medicine have recently postulated that people with blood type O are immune to the bubonic disease; since this blood type predominated in Hungary, that region would have been slightly affected. No estimates of population losses have ever been attempted for Russia and the Balkans.

Economic historians and demographers sharply dispute the impact of the plague on the economy in the late fourteenth century. The traditional view that the plague had a disastrous effect has been greatly modified. The clearest evidence comes from England, where the agrarian economy showed remarkable resilience. Although the severity of the disease varied from region to region, it appears that by about 1375 most landlords enjoyed revenues near those of the pre-plague years. By the early fifteenth century seigneurial prosperity reached a medieval peak. Why? The answer appears to lie in the fact that England and many parts of Europe suffered from overpopulation in the early fourteenth century. Population losses caused by the Black Death "led to increased productivity by restoring a more efficient balance between labour, land, and capital."[48] Population decline meant a sharp increase in per capita wealth. Increased demand for labor meant greater mobility among peasant and working classes. Wages rose, providing better distribution of income. The shortage of labor and steady requests for higher wages put landlords on the defensive. Some places, such as Florence, experienced economic prosperity as a long-term consequence of the plague.

Even more significant than the social effects were the psychological consequences. The knowledge that the disease meant almost certain death provoked the most profound pessimism. Imagine an entire society in the grip of the belief that it was at the mercy of a frightful affliction about which nothing could be done, a disgusting disease from which family and friends would flee, leaving one to die alone and in agony. It is not surprising that

Procession of Saint Gregory According to the *Golden Legend,* a thirteenth-century collection of saints' lives, in 590 when plague ravaged Rome, Pope Gregory I ordered a procession around the city to beg heaven to end the epidemic. As the people circle the walls, a deacon falls victim, and Pope Gregory sees an angel on top of Hadrian's tomb (thereafter called Castel Sant'Angelo), which Gregory interprets to mean the plague is ending. *(Source: Musée Condé, Chantilly/The Bridgeman Art Library, London)*

some sought release in orgies and gross sensuality while others turned to the severest forms of asceticism and frenzied religious fervor. Some extremists joined groups of *flagellants,* men and women who whipped and scourged themselves as penance for their and society's sins, in the belief that the Black Death was God's punishment for humanity's wickedness.

The literature and art of the fourteenth century reveal a terribly morbid concern with death. One highly popular artistic motif, the Dance of Death, depicted a dancing skeleton leading away a living person. No wonder survivors experienced a sort of shell shock and a terrible crisis of faith. Lack of confidence in the leaders of society, lack of hope for the future, defeatism, and malaise wreaked enormous anguish and contributed to the decline of the Middle Ages. A long international war added further misery to the frightful disasters of the plague.

The Hundred Years' War (ca 1337–1453)

Another phase of the centuries-old struggle between the English and French monarchies, the Hundred Years' War was fought intermittently

116 years

from 1337 to 1453. Its causes were both distant and immediate. The English claimed Aquitaine as an ancient feudal inheritance. In 1329 England's King Edward III (r. 1327–1377) paid homage to Philip VI (r. 1328–1350) for Aquitaine. French policy, however, was strongly expansionist, and in 1337 Philip, determined to exercise full jurisdiction there, confiscated the duchy. This action was the immediate cause of the war. Edward III maintained that the only way he could exercise his rightful sovereignty over Aquitaine was by assuming the title of king of France.[49] As the grandson and eldest surviving male descendant of Philip the Fair, he believed he could rightfully make this claim.

For centuries, economic factors involving the wool trade and the control of Flemish towns had served as justifications for war between France and England. The wool trade between England and Flanders was the cornerstone of both countries' economies; they were closely interdependent. Flanders was a fief of the French crown, and the Flemish aristocracy was highly sympathetic to the monarchy in Paris. But the wealth of Flemish merchants and cloth manufacturers depended on English wool, and Flemish burghers strongly supported the claims of Edward III.

The governments of both England and France manipulated public opinion to support the war. Edward III issued letters to the sheriffs describing in graphic terms the evil deeds of the French and listing royal needs. Kings in both countries instructed the clergy to deliver sermons filled with patriotic sentiment. The royal courts sensationalized the wickedness of the other side and stressed the great fortunes to be made from the war. Philip VI sent agents to warn communities about the dangers of invasion and to stress the French crown's revenue needs to meet the attack.[50]

The Hundred Years' War was popular because it presented unusual opportunities for wealth and advancement. Poor knights and knights who were unemployed were promised regular wages. Criminals who enlisted were granted pardons. The great nobles expected to be rewarded with estates. Royal exhortations to the troops before battles repeatedly stressed that, if victorious, the men might keep whatever they seized. The French chronicler Jean Froissart wrote that, at the time of Edward III's expedition of 1359, men of all ranks flocked to the English king's banner. Some came to ac-

quire honor, but many came in order "to loot and pillage the fair and plenteous land of France."[51]

The period of the Hundred Years' War witnessed the final flowering of the aristocratic code of medieval chivalry. Indeed, the enthusiastic participation of the nobility in both France and England was in response primarily to the opportunity the war provided to display chivalric behavior. War was considered an ennobling experience: there was something elevating, manly, fine, and beautiful about it. Describing the French army before the Battle of Poitiers (1356), a contemporary said:

Then you might see banners and pennons unfurled to the wind, whereon fine gold and azure shone, purple, gules and ermine. Trumpets, horns and clarions—you might hear sounding through the camp; the Dauphin's [title borne by the eldest son of the king of France] great battle made the earth ring.[52]

Doogie Howser!

This romantic and "marvelous" view of war holds little appeal for modern men and women, who are more conscious of the slaughter, brutality, dirt, and blood that war inevitably involves. Also, modern thinkers are usually conscious of the broad mass of people, while the chivalric code applied only to the aristocratic military elite. When English knights fought French ones, they were social equals fighting according to a mutually accepted code of behavior. The infantry troops were looked on as inferior beings. When a peasant force at Longueil destroyed a contingent of English knights, their comrades mourned them because "it was too much that so many good fighters had been killed by mere peasants."[53]

The war was fought almost entirely in France and the Low Countries (Map 13.2). It consisted mainly of a series of random sieges and cavalry raids. During the war's early stages, England was highly successful. At Crécy in northern France in 1346, English longbowmen scored a great victory over French knights and crossbowmen. Although the fire of the longbow was not very accurate, it allowed for rapid reloading, and English archers could send off three arrows to the French crossbowmen's one. The result was a blinding shower of arrows that unhorsed the French knights and caused mass confusion. The firing of cannon— probably the first use of artillery in the West—created further panic. Thereupon the English horsemen charged and butchered the French.

1337
(before the Battle of Crécy)
Held by the kings
of England

1360
(after the Battle of Poitiers)
Held by the kings
of England
✕ Major battles

ca 1429
(after the siege of Orléans)
Held by the kings
of England
✕ Major battle

1453
(end of war)
Held by the kings
of England

The Battle of Crécy, 1346
Pitched battles were unusual
in the Hundred Years' War.
At Crécy, the English scored a
spectacular victory. The longbow proved a more effective
weapon than the French
crossbow, but characteristically the artist concentrated
on the aristocratic knights.
*(Source: Bibliothèque Nationale,
Paris)*

Ten years later, Edward the Black Prince, using
the same tactics as at Crécy, smashed the French at
Poitiers, captured the French king, and held him
for ransom. Again, at Agincourt near Arras in
1415, the chivalric English soldier-king Henry V
(r. 1413–1422) gained the field over vastly superior numbers. By 1419 the English had advanced
to the walls of Paris. But the French cause was not
lost. Though England scored the initial victories,
France won the war.

The ultimate French success rests heavily on the
actions of an obscure French peasant girl, Joan of
Arc, whose vision and work revived French fortunes and led to victory. Born in 1412 to well-
to-do peasants in the village of Domrémy in

Champagne, Joan of Arc grew up in a religious
household. During adolescence she began to hear
voices, which she later said belonged to Saint
Michael, Saint Catherine, and Saint Margaret. In
1428 these voices spoke to her with great urgency,
telling her that the dauphin (the uncrowned King
Charles VII) had to be crowned and the English
expelled from France. Joan went to the French
court, persuaded the king to reject the rumor
that he was illegitimate, and secured his support
for her relief of the besieged city of Orléans (see
Map 13.2).

Joan arrived before Orléans on April 28, 1429.
Seventeen years old, she knew little of warfare and
believed that if she could keep the French troops
from swearing and frequenting brothels, victory
would be theirs. On May 8 the English, weakened
by disease and lack of supplies, withdrew from Orléans. Ten days later, Charles VII was crowned
king at Reims. These two events marked the turning point in the war.

**MAP 13.2 English Holdings in France During
the Hundred Years' War** The year 1429
marked the greatest extent of English holdings in
France. Why was it unlikely that England could
have held these territories permanently?

In 1430 England's allies, the Burgundians, captured Joan and sold her to the English. When the English handed her over to the ecclesiastical authorities for trial, the French court did not intervene. The English wanted Joan eliminated for obvious political reasons, but sorcery (witchcraft) was the charge at her trial. Witch persecution was increasing in the fifteenth century, and Joan's wearing of men's clothes appeared not only aberrant but indicative of contact with the Devil. In 1431 the court condemned her as a heretic. Her claim of direct inspiration from God, thereby denying the authority of church officials, constituted heresy. She was burned at the stake in the marketplace at Rouen. A new trial in 1456 rehabilitated her name. In 1920 she was canonized and declared a holy maiden, and today she is revered as the second patron saint of France.

The relief of Orléans stimulated French pride and rallied French resources. As the war dragged on, loss of life mounted, and money appeared to be flowing into a bottomless pit, demands for an end increased in England. The clergy and intellectuals pressed for peace. Parliamentary opposition to additional war grants stiffened. Slowly the French reconquered Normandy and finally ejected the English from Aquitaine. At the war's end in 1453, only the town of Calais remained in English hands (see Map 13.2).

For both France and England, the war proved a disaster. In France the English had slaughtered thousands of soldiers and civilians. In the years after the sweep of the Black Death, this additional killing meant a grave loss of population. The English had laid waste to hundreds of thousands of acres of rich farmland, leaving the rural economy of many parts of France a shambles. The war had disrupted trade and the great fairs, resulting in the drastic reduction of French participation in international commerce. Defeat in battle and heavy taxation contributed to widespread dissatisfaction and aggravated peasant grievances.

The costs of the war were tremendous. England spent over £5 million on the war effort, a huge sum in the fourteenth and fifteenth centuries. Manpower losses had greater social consequences. The knights who ordinarily handled the work of local government as sheriffs, coroners, jurymen, and justices of the peace were abroad, and their absence contributed to the breakdown of order at the local level. The English government attempted to finance the war effort by raising taxes on the wool crop. Because of steadily increasing costs, the Flemish and Italian buyers could not afford English wool. Consequently, raw wool exports slumped drastically between 1350 and 1450.[54]

The long war also had a profound impact on the political and cultural lives of the two countries. Most notably, it stimulated the development of the English Parliament. Between 1250 and 1450, representative assemblies from several classes of society flourished in many European countries. In the English Parliaments, French Estates, German Diets, and Spanish Cortes, deliberative practices developed that laid the foundations for the representative institutions of modern liberal-democratic nations. Representative assemblies declined in most countries after the fifteenth century, but the English Parliament endured. Edward III's constant need for money to pay for the war compelled him to summon not only the great barons and bishops but knights of the shires and burgesses from the towns as well. Between the outbreak of the war in 1337 and the king's death in 1377, parliamentary assemblies met twenty-seven times. Parliament met in thirty-seven of the fifty years of Edward's reign.[55]

In England theoretical consent to taxation and legislation was given in one assembly for the entire country. France had no such single assembly; instead, there were many regional or provincial assemblies. Why did a national representative assembly fail to develop in France? The initiative for convening assemblies rested with the king, who needed revenue almost as much as the English ruler.

No one in France wanted a national assembly. Linguistic, geographic, economic, legal, and political differences were very strong. People tended to think of themselves as Breton, Norman, Burgundian, or whatever, rather than French. Through much of the fourteenth and early fifteenth centuries, weak monarchs lacked the power to call a national assembly. Provincial assemblies, highly jealous of their independence, did not want a national assembly. The costs of sending delegates to it would be high, and the result was likely to be increased taxation. Finally, the Hundred Years' War itself hindered the growth of a representative body of government. Possible violence on dangerous roads discouraged people from travel.

In both countries, however, the war did promote nationalism—the feeling of unity and identity that binds together a people who speak the same language, have a common ancestry and customs, and live in the same area. In the fourteenth century, nationalism largely took the form of hostility toward foreigners. Both Philip VI and Edward III drummed up support for the war by portraying the enemy as an alien, evil people. Edward III sought to justify his personal dynastic quarrel by linking it with England's national interests. As the Parliament Roll of 1348 states:

The Knights of the shires and the others of the Commons were told that they should withdraw together and take good counsel as to how, for withstanding the malice of the said enemy and for the salvation of our said lord the King and his Kingdom of England . . . the King could be aided.[56]

After victories, each country experienced a surge of pride in its military strength. Just as English patriotism ran strong after Crécy and Poitiers, so French national confidence rose after Orléans. French national feeling demanded the expulsion of the enemy not merely from Normandy and Aquitaine but from French soil. Perhaps no one expressed this national consciousness better than Joan of Arc, when she exulted that the enemy had been "driven out of *France.*"

Religious Crisis

In times of crisis or disaster, people of all faiths have sought the consolation of religion. In the fourteenth century, however, the official Christian church offered very little solace. In fact, the leaders of the church added to the sorrow and misery of the times.

From 1309 to 1376, the popes lived in the city of Avignon in southeastern France. In order to control the church and its policies, Philip the Fair of France pressured Pope Clement V to settle in Avignon. Critically ill with cancer, Clement lacked the will to resist Philip. This period in church history is often called the Babylonian Captivity (referring to the seventy years the ancient Hebrews were held captive in Mesopotamian Babylon).

The Babylonian Captivity badly damaged papal prestige. The Avignon papacy reformed its financial administration and centralized its government. But the seven popes at Avignon concentrated on bureaucratic matters to the exclusion of spiritual objectives. In 1377 Pope Gregory XI (r. 1370–

1378) brought the papal court back to Rome. Unfortunately, he died shortly after the return. At Gregory's death, Roman citizens demanded an Italian pope who would remain in Rome.

Urban VI (r. 1378–1389), Gregory's successor, had excellent intentions for church reform. He wanted to abolish simony, pluralism (holding several church offices at the same time), absenteeism, clerical extravagance, and ostentation, but he went about the work of reform in a tactless, arrogant, and bullheaded manner. He delivered blistering attacks on cardinals and threatened to excommunicate some of them. When he was advised that such excommunications would not be lawful unless the guilty had been warned three times, he shouted, "I can do anything, if it be my will and judgment."[57] Urban's quick temper and irrational behavior have led scholars to question his sanity. His actions brought disaster.

The cardinals slipped away from Rome, met at Anagni, and declared Urban's election invalid because it had come about under threats from the Roman mob. The cardinals then proceeded to elect Cardinal Robert of Geneva, the cousin of King Charles V of France, as pope. Cardinal Robert took the name Clement VII (r. 1378–1394) and set himself up at Avignon in opposition to the legally elected Urban. So began the Great Schism, which divided Western Christendom until 1417.

The powers of Europe aligned themselves with Urban or Clement along strictly political lines. France recognized the Frenchman, Clement; England, France's historic enemy, recognized Urban. The scandal provoked horror and vigorous cries for reform. The common people—hard-pressed by inflation, wars, and plague—were thoroughly confused about which pope was legitimate. The schism weakened the religious faith of many Christians and gave rise to instability and religious excesses. At a time when ordinary Christians needed the consolation of religion and confidence in religious leaders, church officials were fighting among themselves for power.

The English scholar and theologian John Wyclif (1329–1384) wrote that papal claims of temporal power had no foundation in the Scriptures and that the Scriptures alone should be the standard of Christian belief and practice. He urged the abolition of such practices as the veneration of saints, pilgrimages, pluralism, and absenteeism. Sincere Christians, Wyclif said, should read the Bible for themselves. Wyclif's views had broad social and economic significance. He urged that the church be stripped of its property. His idea that every Christian free of mortal sin possessed lordship was seized on by peasants in England during a revolt in 1381 and used to justify their goals.

Although Wyclif's ideas were vigorously condemned by ecclesiastical authorities, they were widely disseminated by humble clerics and enjoyed great popularity in the early fifteenth century. The teachings of Wyclif's followers, called Lollards, allowed women to preach and to consecrate the Eucharist. Women, some well educated, played a significant role in the movement. After Anne, sister of Wenceslaus, king of Germany and Bohemia, married Richard II of England, members of Queen Anne's household carried Lollard principles back to Bohemia, where they were spread by John Hus, rector of the University of Prague.

In response to continued calls throughout Europe for a council, the two colleges of cardinals—one at Rome, the other at Avignon—summoned a council at Pisa in 1409. A distinguished gathering of prelates and theologians deposed both popes and selected another. Neither the Avignon pope nor the Roman pope would resign, however, and the appalling result was the creation of a threefold schism.

Finally, because of the pressure of the German emperor Sigismund, a great council met at the imperial city of Constance (1414–1418). It had three objectives: to end the schism, to reform the church "in head and members" (from top to bottom), and to wipe out heresy. The council condemned the Lollard ideas of John Hus, and he was burned at the stake. The council eventually deposed the three schismatic popes and elected a new leader, the Roman cardinal Colonna, who took the name Martin V (1417–1431).

Martin proceeded to dissolve the council. Nothing was done about reform. The schism was over, and though councils subsequently met at Basel and at Ferrara-Florence, in 1450 the papacy held a jubilee, celebrating its triumph over the conciliar movement. In the later fifteenth century, the papacy concentrated on Italian problems to the exclusion of universal Christian interests. The schism and the conciliar movement, however, had exposed the crying need for ecclesiastical reform, thus laying the foundations for the great reform efforts of the sixteenth century.

 ## MARRIAGE AND THE PARISH IN THE LATER MIDDLE AGES

Marriage and the local parish church continued to be the center of the lives of most people. Scholars long believed that because peasants were illiterate and left very few statements about their marriages, generalizations could not be made about them. Recent research in English manorial, ecclesiastical, and coroners' records, however, has uncovered fascinating material. Evidence abounds of teenage flirtations, and many young people had sexual contacts—some leading to conception. Premarital pregnancy may have been deliberate: because children were economically important, the couple wanted to be sure of fertility before entering marriage.

"Whether rich or poor, male or female, the most important rite de passage for peasant youth was marriage."[58] Did they select their own spouses or accept their parents' choices? Church law stressed that for a marriage to be valid both partners had to freely consent to it. Nevertheless, the evidence overwhelmingly shows, above all where land or other property accompanied the union, that parents took the lead in arranging their children's marriages. Parents might have to depend on a son- or daughter-in-law for care in old age. Marriage determined the life partner, the economic circumstances in which the couple would live, and the son-in-law who might take on the family land. Most marriages were between men and women of the same village; where the name and residence of a husband are known, perhaps 41 percent were outsiders. Once the prospective bride or groom had been decided on, parents paid the lord's fee. To allow for objections to the union, parents saw that the parish priest published on three successive Sundays the banns—public announcements that the couple planned to marry. And parents made the financial settlement. The couple then proceeded to the church door. There they made the vows, rings were blessed and exchanged, and the ceremony concluded with some kind of festivity.[59]

The general pattern in late medieval Europe was marriage between men in their middle or late twenties and women under twenty.[60] Poor peasants and wage laborers, both men and women, did not marry until their mid or late twenties. In the later Middle Ages, as earlier—indeed, until the late nineteenth century—economic factors rather than romantic love or physical attraction determined whom and when a person married. The young agricultural laborer on the manor had to wait until he had sufficient land. Thus most men had to wait until their fathers died or yielded the holding. The late age of marriage affected the number of children a couple had. The journeyman craftsman in the urban guild faced the same material difficulties. Prudent young men selected (or their parents selected for them) girls who would bring the most land or money to the union.

With marriage for men postponed, was there any socially accepted sexual outlet? Municipal authorities in many European towns set up legal houses of prostitution or red-light districts either outside the city walls or away from respectable neighborhoods. For example, authorities in Montpellier set aside Hot Street for prostitution, required public women to live there, and forbade anyone to molest them. Prostitution thus passed from being a private concern to a social matter requiring public supervision.[61] Publicly owned brothels were more easily policed and supervised than privately run ones.

Prostitution was an urban phenomenon because only populous towns had large numbers of unmarried young men, communities of transient merchants, and a culture accustomed to a cash exchange. Although the risk of disease limited the number of years a woman could practice this profession, many women prospered. Some acquired sizable incomes. In 1361 Françoise of Florence, a prostitute working in a brothel in Marseilles, made a will in which she made legacies to various charities and left a large sum as a dowry for a poor girl to marry. Legalized prostitution suggests that public officials believed the prostitute could make a positive contribution to the society; it does not mean the prostitute was respected. Rather, she was scorned and distrusted. Legalized brothels also reflect a greater tolerance for male than for female sexuality.[62]

Once a couple married, the union ended only with the death of one partner. Deep emotional bonds knit members of medieval families. Most parents delighted in their children, and the church encouraged a cult of paternal care. Divorce did not exist. The church held that a marriage validly entered into, with mutual oral consent or promise of two parties, could not be dissolved. Annulments were granted in extraordinary circumstances, such

❖ **Shepherds Dancing**   As in all ages, young people (and some not so young) enjoyed dancing, and the marriage or baptismal feast or harvest celebration provided an opportunity, perhaps accompanied by singing or the music of someone talented on the harmonica or as seen here (lower right) on a bagpipe. (*Source: Bibliothèque Nationale, Paris*)

as male impotence, on the grounds that a lawful marriage had never existed.[63]

Theologians of the day urged that the couple's union be celebrated and witnessed in a church ceremony and blessed by a priest. A great number of couples, however, treated marriage as a private act. They made the promise and spoke the words of marriage to each other without witnesses and then proceeded to enjoy the sexual pleasures of marriage. This practice led to a great number of disputes, because one or the other of the two parties could later deny having made a marriage agreement. The records of the ecclesiastical courts reveal evidence of marriages contracted in a garden, in a blacksmith's shop, at a tavern, and, predictably, in a bed.

Marriage and collective work on the land remained the focus of life for the European peasantry in the thirteenth century. Craft guilds, however, provided the small minority of men and women living in towns and cities with the psychological satisfaction of involvement in the manufacture of a superior product. The guild member also had economic security. The guilds looked after the sick, the poor, the widowed, and the orphaned. Masters and employees worked side by side.

In the fourteenth century, those ideal conditions began to change. The fundamental objective of the craft guild was to maintain a monopoly on its product, and to do so recruitment and promotion were carefully restricted. Some guilds required a high entrance fee for apprentices; others admitted only relatives of members. Restrictions limited the number of apprentices and journeymen to match the anticipated openings for masters. Women experienced the same exclusion. A careful study of the records of forty-two craft guilds in Cologne, for example, shows that in the fifteenth century all but six became virtual male preserves.[64] The decreasing number of openings created serious frustrations. Strikes and riots occurred in the Flemish towns, in France, and in England.

The recreation of all classes reflected the fact that late medieval society was organized for war and that violence was common. The aristocracy engaged in tournaments or jousts; archery and wrestling had great popularity among ordinary people. Everyone enjoyed the cruel sports of bullbaiting and bearbaiting. The hangings and mutilations of criminals were exciting and well-attended events, with all the festivity of a university town before a Saturday football game. Chroniclers exulted in describing executions, murders, and massacres. Here a monk gleefully describes the gory execution of William Wallace in 1305:

Wilielmus Waleis, a robber given to sacrilege, arson and homicide . . . was condemned to most cruel but justly deserved death. He was drawn through the streets of London at the tails of horses, until he reached a gallows of unusual height, there he was suspended by a halter; but taken down while yet alive, he was mutilated, his bowels torn out and burned in a fire, his head then cut off, his body divided into four, and his quarters transmitted to four principal parts of Scotland.[65]

Violence was as English as roast beef and plum pudding, as French as bread, cheese, and *potage*.

 PEASANT REVOLTS

In the fourteenth century, economic and political difficulties, disease, and war profoundly affected the lives of European peoples. Decades of slaughter and destruction, punctuated by the decimating visits of the Black Death, made a grave economic situation virtually disastrous. In many parts of France and the Low Countries, fields lay in ruin or untilled for lack of labor power. In England, as taxes increased, criticisms of government policy and mismanagement multiplied.

Peasant revolts occurred often in the Middle Ages. Early in the thirteenth century, the French preacher Jacques de Vitry asked rhetorically, "How many serfs have killed their lords or burnt their castles?"[66] And in the fourteenth and fifteenth centuries, social and economic conditions caused a great increase in peasant uprisings.

In 1358, when French taxation for the Hundred Years' War fell heavily on the poor, the frustrations of the French peasantry exploded in a massive uprising called the *Jacquerie*, after a supposedly happy agricultural laborer, Jacques Bonhomme (Good Fellow). Two years earlier, the English had captured the French king John and many nobles and held them for ransom. The peasants resented paying for their lords' release. Recently hit by plague, experiencing famine in some areas, and harassed by fur-collar criminals, peasants erupted in anger and frustration in Picardy, Champagne, and the area around Paris. Crowds swept through the countryside slashing the throats of nobles, burning their castles, raping their wives and daughters, killing or maiming their horses and cattle. Artisans, small merchants, and parish priests joined the peasants. Urban and rural groups committed terrible destruction, and for several weeks the nobles were on the defensive. Then the upper class united to repress the revolt with merciless ferocity. Thousands of the "Jacques," innocent as well as guilty, were cut down.

The Peasants' Revolt in England in 1381, involving perhaps a hundred thousand people, was probably the largest single uprising of the entire Middle Ages. The causes of the rebellion were complex and varied from place to place. In general, though, the thirteenth century had witnessed the steady commutation of labor services for cash rents, and the Black Death had drastically cut the labor supply. As a result, peasants demanded higher wages and fewer manorial obligations. Thirty years earlier the parliamentary Statute of Laborers of 1351 had declared:

Whereas to curb the malice of servants who after the pestilence were idle and unwilling to serve without securing excessive wages, it was recently ordained . . . that such servants, both men and women, shall be bound to serve in return for salaries and wages that were customary . . . five or six years earlier.[67]

This attempt by landlords to freeze wages and social mobility could not be enforced. As a matter of fact, the condition of the English peasantry steadily improved in the course of the fourteenth century. Why then was the outburst in 1381 so serious? It was provoked by a crisis of rising expectations.

The relative prosperity of the laboring classes led to demands that the upper classes were unwilling to grant. Unable to climb higher, the peasants found release for their economic frustrations in revolt. But economic grievances combined with other factors. The south of England, where the revolt broke out, had been subjected to frequent and destructive French raids. The English government did little to protect the south, and villages grew increasingly scared and insecure. Moreover, decades of aristocratic violence, much of it perpetrated against the weak peasantry, had bred hostility and bitterness. In France frustration over the lack of permanent victory increased. In England the social and religious agitation of the popular preacher John Ball fanned the embers of discontent. Sayings such as Ball's famous couplet "When Adam delved and Eve span; Who was then the gentleman?" reflect real revolutionary sentiment.

The straw that broke the camel's back in England was the reimposition of a head tax on all adult males. Beginning with assaults on the tax collectors, the uprising in England followed much the same course as had the Jacquerie in France. Castles and manors were sacked; manorial records were destroyed. Many nobles, including the archbishop of Canterbury, who had ordered the collection of the tax, were murdered. Urban discontent merged with rural violence. Apprentices and journeymen, frustrated because the highest positions in the guilds were closed to them, rioted.

The boy-king Richard II (r. 1377–1399) met the leaders of the revolt, agreed to charters ensuring peasants' freedom, tricked them with false promises, and then proceeded to crush the uprising with terrible ferocity. Although the nobility tried to restore ancient duties of serfdom, virtually a century of freedom had elapsed, and the

John Ball Outdoors after Mass the priest from Kent preached his radical egalitarianism: "matters goeth not well . . . in England nor shall (they) till everything be common and . . . there be no villains (serfs) nor gentlemen . . . What have we deserved, or why should we be kept thus in servage (servitude)?" All contemporary writers blamed Ball for fomenting the rebellion of 1381. But the evidence shows that peasant demands were limited and local: hunting rights in the woods, freedom from miscellaneous payments, exemption from special work on the lord's bridges or parks. (*Source: Private Collection*)

commutation of manorial services continued. Rural serfdom had disappeared in England by 1550.

Conditions in England and France were not unique. In Florence in 1378, the *ciompi,* the poor propertyless workers, revolted. Serious social trouble occurred in Lübeck, Brunswick, and other German cities. In Spain in 1391, massive uprisings in Seville and Barcelona took the form of vicious attacks on Jewish communities. Rebellions and uprisings everywhere reveal deep peasant and working-class frustration and the general socioeconomic crisis of the time.

 ## VERNACULAR LITERATURE IN THE LATER MIDDLE AGES

Few developments express the emergence of national consciousness more vividly than the emergence of national literatures. Across Europe people spoke the language and dialect of their particular locality and class. In England, for example, the common people spoke regional English dialects, and the upper classes conversed in French. Official documents and works of literature were written in Latin or French. Beginning in the fourteenth century, however, national languages—the vernacular—came into widespread use not only in verbal communication but in literature as well. Two masterpieces of European culture, Dante's *Divine Comedy* (1310–1320), and Chaucer's *Canterbury Tales* (1387–1400), brilliantly manifest this new national pride.

Dante Alighieri (1265–1321) descended from an aristocratic family in Florence, where he held several positions in the city government. Dante called his work a "comedy" because he wrote it in Italian and in a different style from the "tragic" Latin; a later generation added the adjective "divine," referring both to its sacred subject and to Dante's artistry. Each of the *Divine Comedy*'s three parts describes one of the three realms of the next world—Hell, Purgatory, and Paradise. Dante recounts his imaginary journey through these regions toward God. The Roman poet Virgil, representing reason, leads Dante through Hell, where he observes the torments of the damned and denounces the disorders of his own time, especially ecclesiastical ambition and corruption. Passing up into Purgatory, Virgil shows the poet how souls are purified of their disordered inclinations. From Purgatory, Beatrice, a woman Dante once loved

and the symbol of divine revelation in the poem, leads Dante to Paradise. In Paradise, home of the angels and saints, Saint Bernard—representing mystic contemplation—leads Dante to the Virgin Mary. Through her intercession he at last attains a vision of God.

The *Divine Comedy* portrays contemporary and historical figures, comments on secular and ecclesiastical affairs, and draws on Scholastic philosophy. Within the framework of a symbolic pilgrimage to the City of God, the *Divine Comedy* embodies the psychological tensions of the age. A profoundly Christian poem, it also contains bitter criticism of some church authorities. In its symmetrical structure and use of figures from the ancient world, such as Virgil, the poem perpetuates the classical tradition. But as the first major work of literature in the Italian vernacular, it is distinctly modern.

Geoffrey Chaucer (1340–1400), the son of a London wine merchant, was an official in the administrations of the English kings Edward III and Richard II and wrote poetry as an avocation. Chaucer's *Canterbury Tales* is a collection of stories in lengthy, rhymed narrative. On a pilgrimage to the shrine of Saint Thomas Becket at Canterbury (see page 378), thirty people of various social backgrounds each tell a tale. The Prologue sets the scene and describes the pilgrims, whose characters are further revealed in the story each one tells. For example, the gentle Christian Knight relates a chivalric romance; the gross Miller tells a vulgar story about a deceived husband; the earthy Wife of Bath, who has buried five husbands, sketches a fable about the selection of a spouse. In depicting the interests and behavior of all types of people, Chaucer presents a rich panorama of English social life in the fourteenth century. Like the *Divine Comedy, Canterbury Tales* reflects the cultural tensions of the times. Ostensibly Christian, many of the pilgrims are also materialistic, sensual, and worldly, suggesting the ambivalence of the broader society's concern for the next world and frank enjoyment of this one.

Perhaps the most versatile and prolific French writer of the later Middle Ages was Christine de Pisan (1363?–1434?). The daughter of a professor of astrology, Christine had acquired a broad knowledge of Greek, Latin, French, and Italian literature. The deaths of her father and husband left her with three small children and her mother to support, and she resolved to earn her living with her pen. In addition to poems and books on love, religion, and morality, Christine produced major historical works and many letters. *The City of Ladies* (1404) lists the great women of history and their contributions to society, and *The Book of Three Virtues* provides prudent and practical advice on household management for women of all social classes and at all stages of life. Christine de Pisan's wisdom and wit are illustrated in her autobiographical *Avison-Christine.* She records that a man told her that an educated woman is unattractive because there are so few, to which she responded that an ignorant man was even less attractive because there are so many.

From the fifth through the thirteenth century, the overwhelming majority of people who could read and write were priests, monks, and nuns. Beginning in the fourteenth century, a variety of evidence attests to the increasing literacy of laypeople. In England, as one scholar has recently shown, the number of schools in the diocese of York quadrupled between 1350 and 1500; information from the Flemish and German towns is similar: children were sent to schools and received the fundamentals of reading, writing, and arithmetic. The penetration of laymen into the higher positions of government administration, long the preserve of clerics, indicates the rising lay literacy.

The spread of literacy represents a response to the needs of an increasingly complex society. Trade, commerce, and expanding government bureaucracies required more and more literate people. Late medieval culture remained an oral culture in which most people received information by word of mouth. But by the mid-fifteenth century, even before the printing press was turning out large quantities of reading materials, the evolution toward a literary culture is already perceptible.[68]

The Wife of Bath   The fame of medieval England's greatest poet, Geoffrey Chaucer, rests on *The Canterbury Tales,* consisting of a Prologue and the stories of twenty-four pilgrims on their way to Canterbury. The earthy, vivacious Wife of Bath, having had five husbands "not counting other company in youth," is very blunt about her charms and her power:

> *In wyfhode I wol use myn instrument*
> *As freely as my Maker hath it sent.*

Faithful to Chaucer's description, the artist shows her with wide-brimmed hat, hair in a net, and riding astride, not sidesaddle as ladies were expected to do. *(Source: Reproduced by permission of The Huntington Library, San Marino, California)*

SUMMARY

Universities—institutions of higher learning unique to the West—emerged from cathedral and municipal schools and provided trained officials for the new government bureaucracies. The soaring Gothic cathedrals that medieval towns erected demonstrate civic pride, deep religious faith, and economic vitality.

The performance of agricultural services and the payment of rents preoccupied peasants throughout the Middle Ages. Though peasants led hard lives, the reclamation of waste and forest lands, migra-tion to frontier territory, or flight to a town offered means of social mobility. The Christian faith, though perhaps not understood at an intellectual level, provided a strong emotional and spiritual solace.

By 1100 the nobility possessed a strong class consciousness. Aristocratic values and attitudes shaded all aspects of medieval culture. Trained for war, nobles often devoted considerable time to fighting, and intergenerational squabbles were common. Yet a noble might shoulder heavy judicial, political, and economic responsibilities, depending on the size of his estates.

The monks and nuns exercised a profound influence on matters of the spirit. In their prayers, monks and nuns battled for the Lord, just as the chivalrous knights clashed on the battlefield. In their chant and rich ceremonial, in their architecture and literary productions, and in the example of many monks' lives, the monasteries inspired Christian peoples to an incalculable degree. As the crucibles of sacred art, the monasteries became the cultural centers of Christian Europe.

Late medieval preachers likened the crises of their times to the Four Horsemen of the Apocalypse in the Book of Revelation, who brought famine, war, disease, and death. The crises of the fourteenth and fifteenth centuries were acids that burned deeply into the fabric of traditional medieval European society. Bad weather—beyond human control—brought poor harvests, which contributed to the international economic depression. Disease, fostered widespread depression and dissatisfaction. Population losses caused by the Black Death and the Hundred Years' War encouraged the working classes to try to profit from the labor shortage by selling their services higher. When peasant frustrations exploded in uprisings, the frightened nobility and upper middle class joined to crush the revolts. But events had heightened social consciousness among the poor.

The increasing number of schools leading to the growth of lay literacy represents a positive achievement of the later Middle Ages. So also does the development of national literatures. The first sign of a literary culture appeared.

Religion held society together. European culture was a Christian culture. But the Great Schism weakened the prestige of the church and people's faith in papal authority. The conciliar movement, by denying the church's universal sovereignty, strengthened the claims of secular governments to jurisdiction over all their peoples. The later Middle Ages witnessed a steady shift of loyalty away from the church and toward the emerging national states.

NOTES

1. Quoted in H. E. Sigerist, *Civilization and Disease* (Chicago: University of Chicago Press, 1943), p. 102.

2. Quoted in J. H. Mundy, *Europe in the High Middle Ages, 1150–1309* (New York: Basic Books, 1973), pp. 474–475.

3. E. Panofsky, trans. and ed., *Abbot Suger on the Abbey Church of St.-Denis and Its Art Treasures* (Princeton, N.J.: Princeton University Press, 1946), p. 101.

4. See J. Gimpel, *The Cathedral Builders* (New York: Grove Press, 1961), pp. 42–49.

5. Quoted in J. J. Wilhelm, ed., *Lyrics of the Middle Ages: An Anthology* (New York: Garland Publishers, 1993), pp. 94–95.

6. R. Boase, *The Origin and Meaning of Courtly Love* (Manchester, Eng.: 1977), pp. 129–130.

7. I have leaned on the very persuasive interpretation of M. R. Menocal, *The Arabic Role in Medieval Literary History* (Philadelphia: University of Pennsylvania Press, 1990), pp. ix–xv and 27–33.

8. G. Duby, *The Chivalrous Society,* trans. C. Postan (Berkeley: University of California Press, 1977), pp. 90–93.

9. B. A. Hanawalt, *The Ties That Bound: Peasant Families in Medieval England* (New York: Oxford University Press, 1986), p. 5.

10. E. Power, "Peasant Life and Rural Conditions," in J. R. Tanner et al., *The Cambridge Medieval History,* vol. 7 (Cambridge: Cambridge University Press, 1958), p. 716.

11. Glanvill, "De Legibus Angliae," bk. 5, chap. 5, in *Social Life in Britain from the Conquest to the Reformation,* ed. G. G. Coulton (London: Cambridge University Press, 1956), pp. 338–339.

12. See R. Bartlett, "Colonial Towns and Colonial Traders," in *The Making of Europe: Conquest, Colonization, and Cultural Change, 950–1350* (Princeton, N.J.: Princeton University Press, 1993), pp. 167–196.

13. See W. C. Jordan, *From Servitude to Freedom: Manumission in the Senonais in the Thirteenth Century* (Philadelphia: University of Pennsylvania Press, 1986), esp. Ch. 3, pp. 37–58.

14. See John L. Langdon, *Horses, Oxen, and Technological Innovation: The Use of Draught Animals in English Farming, 1066–1500* (New York: Cambridge University Press, 1986), esp. pp. 254–270.

15. G. Duby, *The Early Growth of the European Economy: Warriors and Peasants from the Seventh to the Twelfth Century* (Ithaca, N.Y.: Cornell University Press, 1978), pp. 213–219.

16. See Hanawalt, *The Ties That Bound,* pp. 90–100.

17. Ibid., p. 149.

18. On this quantity and medieval measurements, see D. Knowles, "The Measures of Monastic

Beverages," in *The Monastic Order in England* (Cambridge: Cambridge University Press, 1962), p. 717.

19. S. R. Scargill-Bird, ed., *Custumals of Battle Abbey in the Reigns of Edward I and Edward II* (London: Camden Society, 1887), pp. 213–219.

20. G. Duby, ed., *A History of Private Life,* vol. 2, *Revelations of the Middle Ages* (Cambridge, Mass.: Harvard University Press, 1988), p. 585.

21. Quoted in E. Amt, ed., *Women's Lives in the Middle Ages: A Sourcebook* (New York: Routledge, 1992), pp. 103–104.

22. See C. Klapisch-Zuber, ed., *A History of Women,* vol. 2, *Silences of the Middle Ages* (Cambridge, Mass.: Harvard University Press, 1992), p. 289 et seq.

23. See R. Blumenfeld-Kosinski, *Not of Woman Born: Representations of Caesarian Birth in Medieval and Renaissance Culture* (Ithaca, N.Y.: Cornell University Press, 1990), p. 27.

24. Ibid.

25. Ibid., p. 47.

26. E. J. Kealey, *Medieval Medicus: A Social History of Anglo-Norman Medicine* (Baltimore: Johns Hopkins University Press, 1981), p. 102.

27. Klapisch-Zuber, *Silences of the Middle Ages,* p. 299.

28. See A. Gurevich, *Medieval Popular Culture: Problems of Belief and Perception,* trans. J. M. Bak and P. A. Hollingsworth (New York: Cambridge University Press, 1990), Ch. 2, pp. 39–77, esp. p. 76.

29. Ibid.

30. See M. Rubin, *Corpus Christi: The Eucharist in Late Medieval Culture* (New York: Cambridge University Press, 1992), p. 13 et seq.

31. A. Vauchez, *The Laity in the Middle Ages: Religious Beliefs and Devotional Practices,* ed. D. E. Bornstein, trans. M. J. Schneider (Notre Dame, Ind.: University of Notre Dame Press, 1993), pp. 99–102.

32. Duby, *The Chivalrous Society,* p. 98.

33. J. B. Freed, "The Origins of the European Nobility: The Problem of the Ministerials," *Viator* 7 (1976): 214.

34. J. Boswell, *The Kindness of Strangers: The Abandonment of Children in Western Europe from Late Antiquity to the Renaissance* (New York: Pantheon Books, 1989), p. 24. This section relies heavily on this important work.

35. Ibid., pp. 428–429.

36. Ibid., pp. 238–239.

37. Ibid., pp. 297, 299, and the Conclusion.

38. J. F. Benton, ed. and trans., *Self and Society in Medieval France: The Memoirs of Abbot Guibert of Nogent* (New York: Harper & Row, 1970), p. 46.

39. M. Chibnall, ed. and trans., *The Ecclesiastical History of Orderic Vitalis* (Oxford: Oxford University Press, 1972), 2.xiii.

40. R. W. Southern, *Western Society and the Church in the Middle Ages* (Baltimore: Penguin Books, 1970), pp. 224–230, esp. p. 228.

41. See M. W. Labarge, *A Small Sound of the Trumpet: Women in Medieval Life* (Boston: Beacon Press, 1986), pp. 104–105.

42. J. M. Ferrante, "The Education of Women in the Middle Ages in Theory, Fact, and Fantasy," in *Beyond Their Sex: Learned Women of the European Past,* ed. P. H. Labalme (New York: New York University Press, 1980), pp. 22–24.

43. W. C. Jordan, *Women and Credit in Pre-Industrial and Developing Societies* (Philadelphia: University of Pennsylvania Press, 1993), p. 61.

44. W. H. McNeill, *Plagues and Peoples* (New York: Doubleday, 1976), pp. 151–168.

45. Quoted in P. Ziegler, *The Black Death* (Harmondsworth, Eng.: Pelican Books, 1969), p. 20.

46. J. M. Rigg, trans., *The Decameron of Giovanni Boccaccio* (London: J. M. Dent & Sons, 1903), p. 6.

47. Ziegler, *The Black Death,* pp. 232–239.

48. J. Hatcher, *Plague, Population and the English Economy, 1348–1530* (London: Macmillan Education, 1986), p. 33.

49. See G. P. Cuttino, "Historical Revision: The Causes of the Hundred Years' War," *Speculum* 31 (July 1956): 463–472.

50. J. Barnie, *War in Medieval English Society: Social Values and the Hundred Years' War* (Ithaca, N.Y.: Cornell University Press, 1974), p. 6.

51. Quoted ibid., p. 34.

52. Quoted ibid., p. 73.

53. Ibid., pp. 72–73.

54. M. M. Postan, "The Costs of the Hundred Years' War," *Past and Present* 27 (April 1964): 34–53.

55. See G. O. Sayles, *The King's Parliament of England* (New York: Norton, 1974), app., pp. 137–141.

56. C. Stephenson and G. F. Marcham, eds., *Sources of English Constitutional History,* rev. ed. (New York: Harper & Row, 1972), p. 217.

57. Quoted in J. H. Smith, *The Great Schism 1378: The Disintegration of the Medieval Papacy* (New York: Weybright & Talley, 1970), p. 141.

58. Hanawalt, *The Ties That Bound,* p. 197. This section leans heavily on Hanawalt's important work.

59. Ibid., pp. 194–204.

60. See D. Herlihy, *Medieval Households* (Cam-

bridge, Mass.: Harvard University Press, 1985), pp. 103–111.

61. L. L. Otis, *Prostitution in Medieval Society: The History of an Urban Institution in Languedoc* (Chicago: University of Chicago Press, 1987), p. 2.

62. Ibid., pp. 118–130.

63. See R. H. Helmholz, *Marriage Litigation in Medieval England* (Cambridge: Cambridge University Press, 1974), pp. 28–29 and passim.

64. See M. C. Howell, *Women, Production, and Patriarchy in Late Medieval Cities* (Chicago: University of Chicago Press, 1986), pp. 134–135.

65. A. F. Scott, ed., *Everyone a Witness: The Plantagenet Age* (New York: Thomas Y. Crowell, 1976), p. 263.

66. Quoted in M. Bloch, *French Rural History,* trans. J. Sondeimer (Berkeley: University of California Press, 1966), p. 169.

67. Stephenson and Marcham, *Sources of English Constitutional History,* p. 225.

68. See M. Keen, *English Society in the Later Middle Ages, 1348–1500* (New York: Penguin Books, 1990), pp. 219–239.

SUGGESTED READING

The achievements of the central and later Middle Ages have attracted considerable scholarly attention, and the curious student will have no difficulty finding exciting material. Three general surveys of the period 1050 to 1300 are especially recommended: D. Nicholas, *The Evolution of the Medieval World* (1992), explores the major themes of the age in depth; G. Holmes, ed., *The Oxford History of Medieval Europe* (1992), discusses the creativity of the period in a series of essays; and J. R. Strayer, *Western Europe in the Middle Ages* (1955), is a masterful synthesis.

N. Orme, *Education and Society in Medieval and Renaissance England* (1989), focuses on early education, schools, and literacy in English medieval society. J. Leclercq, *The Love of Learning and the Desire of God* (1974), discusses monastic literary culture. For the development of literacy among laypeople and the formation of a literate mentality, the advanced student should see M. T. Clanchy, *From Memory to Written Record: England, 1066–1307* (1979).

For the new currents of thought in the central Middle Ages, see C. Brooke, *The Twelfth Century Renaissance* (1970), a splendidly illustrated book with copious quotations from the sources; E. Gilson, *Héloise and Abélard* (1960), which treats the medieval origins of modern humanism against the background of Abélard the teacher; D. W. Robertson, Jr., *Abélard and Héloise* (1972), which is highly readable, com-

monsensical, and probably the best recent study of Abélard and the love affair he supposedly had; C. H. Haskins, *The Renaissance of the Twelfth Century* (1971), a classic; and C. W. Hollister, ed., *The Twelfth Century Renaissance* (1969), a well-constructed anthology with source materials on many aspects of twelfth-century culture.

On the medieval universities, C. H. Haskins, *The Rise of the Universities* (1959), is a good introduction. H. De Ridder-Symoens, ed., *A History of the University in Europe,* vol. 1, *Universities in the Middle Ages* (1991) offers up-to-date interpretations by leading scholars. H. Rashdall, *The Universities of Europe in the Middle Ages* (1936), is the standard scholarly work. G. Leff, *Paris and Oxford Universities in the Thirteenth and Fourteenth Centuries* (1968), gives a fascinating sketch and includes a useful bibliography.

F. and J. Gies, *Cathedral, Forge, and Waterwheel* (1993), provides an exciting and illustrated survey of medieval technological achievements. The following studies are all valuable for the evolution and development of the Gothic style: P. Frankl, *The Gothic* (1960); O. von Simson, *The Gothic Cathedral* (1973); and J. Bony, *French Gothic Architecture of the 12th and 13th Centuries* (1983). H. Kraus, *Gold Was the Mortar: The Economics of Cathedral Building* (1979), describes how the cathedrals were financed. D. Grivot and G. Zarnecki, *Gislebertus, Sculptor of Autun* (1961), is the finest appreciation of Romanesque architecture written in English. For the actual work of building, see D. Macaulay, *Cathedral: The Story of Its Construction* (1961), which explores the engineering problems involved in cathedral building and places the subject within its social context. For the most important cathedrals in France, architecturally and politically, see A. Temko, *Notre Dame of Paris: The Biography of a Cathedral* (1968); G. Henderson, *Chartres* (1968); and A. Katzenellengoben, *The Sculptural Programs of Chartres Cathedral* (1959), by a distinguished art historian. E. Panofsky, *Abbot Suger on the Abbey Church of St.-Denis and Its Art Treasures* (1946), provides a contemporary background account of the first Gothic building. C. A. Bruzelius, *The Thirteenth-Century Church at St.-Denis* (1985), traces later reconstruction. J. Gimpel, *The Medieval Machine: The Industrial Revolution of the Middle Ages* (1977), an extremely useful book, discusses the mechanical and scientific problems involved in early industrialization and shows how construction affected the medieval environment.

On troubadour poetry, see, in addition to the titles by R. Boase and J. J. Wilhelm cited in Notes, M. Bogin, *The Women Troubadours* (1980).

For the Black Death, see P. Ziegler, *The Black Death* (1969), a fascinating and highly readable study. For the social implications of disease, see W. H. Mc-

Neill, *Plagues and Peoples* (1976); F. F. Cartwright, *Disease and History* (1972); and H. E. Sigerist, *Civilization and Disease* (1970). For the economic effects of the plague, see J. Hatcher, *Plague, Population, and the English Economy, 1348–1550* (1977).

The standard study of the long military conflicts of the fourteenth and fifteenth centuries remains E. Perroy, *The Hundred Years' War* (1959). J. Barnie's *War in Medieval English Society* treats the attitudes of patriots, intellectuals, and the general public. D. Seward, *The Hundred Years' War: The English in France, 1337–1453* (1981), tells an exciting story, and J. Keegan, *The Face of Battle* (1977), Ch. 2, "Agincourt," describes what war meant to the ordinary soldier. B. Tuchman, *A Distant Mirror: The Calamitous Fourteenth Century* (1980), gives a vivid picture of many facets of fourteenth-century life while concentrating on the war. The best treatment of the financial costs of the war is probably M. M. Postan, "The Costs of the Hundred Years' War," cited in the Notes. E. Searle and R. Burghart, "The Defense of England and the Peasants' Revolt," *Viator* 3 (1972), is a fascinating study of the peasants' changing social attitudes. R. Barber, *The Knight and Chivalry* (1982), and M. Keen, *Chivalry* (1984), give fresh interpretations of the cultural importance of chivalry.

For political and social conditions in the fourteenth and fifteenth centuries, see the works by Sayles, Bloch, Hanawalt, and Helmholz cited in the Notes. The following studies are also useful: P. S. Lewis, *Later Medieval France: The Polity* (1968); L. Romier, *A History of France* (1962); A. R. Meyers, *Parliaments and Estates in Europe to 1789* (1975); R. G. Davies and J. H. Denton, eds., *The English Parliament in the Middle Ages* (1981); I. Kershaw, "The Great Famine and Agrarian Crisis in England, 1315–1322," *Past and Present* (May 1973); K. Thomas, "Work and Leisure in Pre-industrial Society," *Past and Present* 29 (December 1964); R. Hilton, *Bond Men Made Free: Medieval Peasant Movements and the English Rising of 1381* (1973), a comparative study; M. Keen, *The Outlaws of Medieval Legend* (1961) and "Robin Hood—Peasant or Gentleman?" *Past and Present* 19 (April 1961): 7–18; and P. Wolff, "The 1391 Pogrom in Spain: Social Crisis or Not?" *Past and Present* 50 (February 1971): 4–18. Students are especially encouraged to consult the brilliant achievement of E. L.

Ladurie, *The Peasants of Languedoc,* trans. J. Day (1976). R. H. Hilton, ed., *Peasants, Knights, and Heretics: Studies in Medieval English Social History* (1976), contains a number of valuable articles primarily on the social implications of agricultural change. J. C. Holt, *Robin Hood* (1982), is a soundly researched and highly readable study of the famous outlaw.

For women's economic status in the late medieval period, see the important study of M. C. Howell, *Women, Production, and Patriarchy in Late Medieval Cities* (1986). B. Hanawalt, *The Ties That Bind,* cited in the Notes, gives a living picture of the family lives of ordinary people in rural communities. D. Nicholas, *The Domestic Life of a Medieval City: Women, Children, and the Family in Fourteenth-Century Ghent* (1985), focuses on an urban society. C. Klapisch-Zuber, ed., *A History of Women,* vol. 2, *Silences of the Middle Ages* (1992), contains useful essays on many aspects of women's lives and status. S. Shahar, *The Fourth Estate: Women in the Middle Ages* (1983), is a provocative work. J. M. Bennett, *Women in the Medieval English Countryside: Gender and Household in Brigstock Before the Plague* (1987), is a fascinating case study. E. Amt, ed., *Women's Lives in Medieval Europe: A Sourcebook* (1993), has fresh primary material on many aspects of the lives of noble, business, and peasant women.

The poetry of Dante and Chaucer may be read in the following editions: D. Sayers, trans., *Dante: The Divine Comedy,* 3 vols. (1963); and N. Coghill, trans., *Chaucer's Canterbury Tales* (1977). The social setting of *Canterbury Tales* is brilliantly evoked in D. W. Robertson, Jr., *Chaucer's London* (1968).

For the religious history of the period, F. Oakley, *The Western Church in the Later Middle Ages* (1979), is an excellent introduction. R. N. Swanson, *Church and Society in Late Medieval England* (1989), provides a good synthesis of English conditions. S. Ozment, *The Age of Reform, 1250–1550* (1980), discusses the Great Schism and the conciliar movement in the intellectual context of the ecclesio-political tradition of the Middle Ages. Students seeking a highly detailed and comprehensive work should consult H. Beck et al., *From the High Middle Ages to the Eve of the Reformation,* trans. A. Biggs, vol. 14 in the History of the Church series, ed. H. Jedin and J. Dolan (1980).

A Medieval Noblewoman

In 1115 Guibert (ca 1064?–1124), descendant of a noble family and abbot of Noyon in Picardy, wrote an autobiography, one of the rare examples in the Middle Ages of this literary genre. Cast in the form of a prayer to God, like Saint Augustine's Confessions, *on which it was modeled, Guibert's autobiography includes a sketch of his mother's life. Guibert deeply loved his mother, was dependent on her, and seems to have concentrated on her virtues. He thus gives us an informed, if perhaps idealized, picture of a twelfth-century French noblewoman.*

First and above all, therefore, I render thanks to Thee for that Thou didst bestow on me a mother fair, yet chaste, modest and most devout. . . .

Almost the whole of Good Friday had my mother passed in excessive pain of travail. . . . Racked, therefore, by pains long-endured, and her tortures increasing as her hour drew near, when she thought I had at last in a natural course come to the birth, instead I was returned within the womb. By this time my father, friends, and kinsfolk were crushed with dismal sorrowing for both of us, for whilst the child was hastening the death of the mother, and she her child's in denying him deliverance, all had reason for compassion. . . . So they ask[ed] counsel in their need and [fled] for help to the altar of the Lady Mary, and to her . . . this vow was made and in the place of an offering this gift laid upon the Gracious Lady's altar: that should a male child come to the birth, he should be given up to the service of God and of herself in the ministry, but if one of the weaker sex, she should be handed over to the corresponding calling. At once was born a weak little being, almost an abortion, and at that timely birth there was rejoicing only for my mother's deliverance, the child being such a miserable object. . . . On that same day . . . I was put into the cleansing water [baptized, for fear of death]. . . .

Once I had been beaten in school—the school being no other than the dining-hall in our house, for he had given up the charge of others to take me alone, my mother having wisely required him to do this for a higher emolument and a better position. When, therefore, at a certain hour in the evening, my studies, such as they were, had come to an end, I went to my mother's knees after a more severe beating than I had deserved. And when she, as she was wont, began to ask me repeatedly whether I had been whipped that day, I, not to appear a tell-tale, entirely denied it. Then she, whether I liked it or not, threw off the inner garments which they call a vest or shirt, and saw my little arms blackened and the skin of my back everywhere puffed up with the cuts from the twigs. And being grieved to the heart by the very savage punishment inflicted on my tender body, troubled, agitated and weeping with sorrow, she said: "You shall never become a clerk, nor any more suffer so much to get learning." At that I, looking at her with what reproach I could, replied: "If I had to die on the spot, I would not give up learning my book and becoming a clerk." Now she had promised that if I wished to become a knight, when [I] reached the age for it, she would give me the arms and equipment.

She, when hardly of marriageable age, was given to my father, a mere youth, by provision of my grandfather. . . . Now it so happened that at the very beginning of that lawful union conjugal intercourse was made ineffective through the bewitchments of certain persons. For it was said that their marriage drew upon them the envy of a step-mother, who, having nieces of great beauty and nobility, was plotting to entangle one of them with my father.

Meeting with no success in her designs, she is said to have used magical arts to prevent entirely the consummation of the marriage. His wife's virginity thus remaining intact for three years, during which he endured his great misfortune in silence, at last, driven to it by his kinsfolk, my father was the first to reveal the facts. Imagine how my kinsmen tried hard in every way to bring about a divorce, and their constant pressure upon my father, young and raw, to become a monk. . . . This, however, was not done for his soul's good, but with the purpose of getting possession of his property. But when their suggestion produced no effect, they began to hound the girl herself, far away as she was from her kinsfolk and harassed by the violence of strangers, into voluntary flight out of sheer exhaustion under their insults, and without waiting for divorce. Meanwhile she endured all this, bearing with calmness the abuse that was aimed at her, and, if out of this rose any strife, pretending ignorance of it. Besides certain rich men perceiving that she was not in fact a wife, began to assail the heart of the young girl; but Thou, O lord, the builder of inward chastity, didst inspire her with purity stronger than her nature or her youth. . . .

In plainness of living there was nothing that she could do, for her delicacy and her sumptuous rearing did not admit of a meagre diet. In other matters no one knew what self-denial she practised. With these eyes I have seen and made certain by touch that whereas over all she wore garments of rich material, next to her skin she was covered with the roughest haircloth, which she wore not only in the daytime, but, what was a great hardship for a delicate body, she even slept in it at night.

The night offices she hardly ever missed, being as regular at the services attended by all God's people in holy seasons; in such fashion that scarcely ever in her house was there rest from the singing of God's praises by her chaplains. . . . A few years before her death she conceived a strong desire to take the sacred veil. When I tried to dissuade her, putting forward as authority the passage where it is written, "Let no prelate attempt to veil widows," saying that her most chaste life would be sufficient without the external veil . . . yet so

Medieval noblewoman at work, from a fifteenth-century manuscript. *(Source: The British Library)*

much more was she inflamed and by no reasoning could be driven from her resolve. So she prevailed, and when taking the veil in the presence of John, the Abbot of that place, gave satisfactory reasons for this act, and in the end she proved that . . . her consecration was invited by signs from heaven.

Questions for Analysis

1. What values shaped Guibert's representation of his mother?

2. How did her marriage come about, and how would you describe her married life?

3. What is the value of this picture of a noblewoman for a present-day historian?

Source: C. C. Swinton Bland, trans., *The Autobiography of Guibert of Nogentsous-Coucy* (New York, 1925); and E. Amt, ed., *Women's Lives in Medieval Europe* (New York: Routledge, 1993), pp. 142–149.

14

The Americas Before European Intrusion, ca 400–1500

This plate from the *Codex Mendoza* dipicts the Aztec legend of the founding of Mexico-Tenochtitlan on the spot where an eagle—an incarnation of Huitzilopochtli—perched on a cactus. *(Source: The Bodleian Library, Oxford)*

Between approximately A.D. 300 and 1500, sophisticated civilizations developed in the Western Hemisphere. But unlike most other societies in the world, which felt the influences of other cultures—sub-Saharan Africa, for example, experienced the impact of Muslims, Asians, and Europeans—Amerian societies grew in almost total isolation from other peoples. Then, in 1501–1502, the Florentine explorer Amerigo Vespucci (1451–1512) sailed down the eastern coast of South America to Brazil. Convinced that he had found a new world, Vespucci published an account of his voyage. Shortly thereafter the German geographer Martin Waldseemüller proposed that this new world be called "America" to preserve Vespucci's memory. Initially applied only to South America, by the end of the sixteenth century the term *America* was used for both continents in the Western Hemisphere.

To the peoples of the Americas, the notion of discovery meant nothing. They did not write about it, and most of the information we have about the Americas derives from European sources. Thus the "new world" was in a very real sense a European invention. Even for Europeans the concept of discovery presented problems. In matters of geography, as in other branches of knowledge, medieval Europeans believed that all human knowledge was contained in the Scriptures, the writings of the church fathers, and the Greek and Roman authors, none of whom mentioned a new world. The adventurous explorers of the fifteenth and sixteenth centuries sailed west searching for Asia and Africa because Europeans believed that those continents and Europe composed the only world that existed. They did not expect to find new continents. Long before the arrival of Europeans, however, sophisticated civilizations were flourishing in Central and South America.

- What is the geography of the Americas, and how did it shape the lives of the peoples?

- What patterns of social and political organization did Amerindian peoples display before the European intrusion?

- What are the significant cultural achievements of the Maya, the Aztecs, and the Incas?

This chapter considers these questions.

THE GEOGRAPHY AND PEOPLES OF THE AMERICAS

The distance from the Bering Strait, which separates Asia from North America, to the southern tip of South America is about eleven thousand miles. A mountain range extends all the way from Alaska to the tip of South America, crossing Central America from northwest to southeast and making for rugged country along virtually the entire western coast of both continents.

Scholars use the term *Mesoamerica* to designate the area of present-day Mexico and Central America. Mexico is dominated by high plateaus bounded by coastal plains. Geographers have labeled the plateau regions "cold lands," the valleys between the plateaus "temperate lands," and the Gulf and Pacific coastal regions "hot lands." The Caribbean coast of Central America—modern Belize, Guatemala, Honduras, Nicaragua, El Salvador, Costa Rica, and Panama—is characterized by thick jungle lowlands, heavy rainfall, and torrid heat; it is an area generally unhealthy for humans. Central America's western uplands, with their more temperate climate and good agricultural land, support the densest population in the region.

Like Africa, South America is a continent of extremely varied terrain (see Map 14.3). The entire western coast is edged by the Andes, the highest mountain range in the Western Hemisphere. On the east coast another mountain range—the Brazilian Highlands—accounts for one-fourth of the area of modern-day Brazil. Three-fourths of South America—almost the entire interior of the continent—is lowland plains. The Amazon River, at 4,000 miles the second longest river in the world, bisects the north-central part of the continent, draining 2.7 million square miles of land. Tropical lowland rain forests with dense growth and annual rainfall in excess of 80 inches extend from the Amazon and Orinoco river basins northward all the way to southern Mexico.

Most scholars believe that people began crossing the Bering Strait from Russian Siberia between fifty thousand and twenty thousand years ago, when the strait was narrower than it is today. Skeletal finds indicate that these immigrants belonged to several ethnic groups now known collectively as American Indians, or Amerindians. Amerindians were nomadic and technologically

❖ **Colossal Head Monument from San Lorenzo** Measuring 9 feet, 4 inches in height, and over 10 tons in weight, this basalt head is a superb example of Olmec sculpture intended as architecture. The facial features have led some scholars to suggest African influences, but that hypothesis has not been proven. *(Source: National Tarn/Photo Researchers, Inc.)*

primitive people who lived by hunting small animals, fishing, and gathering wild fruits. As soon as an area had been exploited and a group had grown too large for the land to support, some families broke off from the group and moved on, usually southward. Gradually the newcomers spread throughout the Americas, losing contact with one another.

At the time the Europeans arrived, most of the peoples of North America and the huge Amazon basin were Neolithic hunters and farmers, some migratory and some living in villages. Hunters of big game (bison, elk, boar) armed with heavy stone missiles, traveled in small groups. Sizable groups of people who had learned to cultivate the soil lived a more settled life. Archaeological excavations indicate that corn was grown in Mexico City around 2500 B.C. Before 2300 B.C. the

Amerindians also were raising beans, squash, pumpkins, and, in the area of modern Peru, white potatoes.

Amerindians in central Mexico built chinampas, floating gardens. They dredged soil from the bottom of a lake or pond, placed the soil on mats of woven twigs, and then planted crops in the soil. Chinampas were enormously productive, yielding up to three harvests a year. So extensive was this method of agriculture that central Mexico became known as the chinampas region. In Peru, meanwhile, people terraced the slopes of the Andes with stone retaining walls to keep the hillsides from sliding. Both chinampas and terraced slopes required the large labor force that became available with stable settlement.

Agricultural advancement had definitive social and political consequences. Careful cultivation of the land brought a reliable and steady food supply, which contributed to a relatively high fertility rate and in turn to a population boom. Because corn and potatoes require much less labor than does grain, Amerindian civilizations had a large pool of people who were not involved in agriculture and thus were available to construct religious and political buildings and serve in standing armies.[1]

MESOAMERICAN CIVILIZATIONS FROM THE OLMECS TO THE TOLTECS

Several American civilizations arose between roughly 1500 B.C. and A.D. 900: the civilizations of the Olmecs, the Maya, Teotihuacán, and the Toltecs. Archaeological investigations of these civilizations are under way, and more questions than answers about them remain, but scholars generally accept a few basic conclusions about them.

Scholars believe that Olmec civilization is the oldest of the early advanced Amerindian civilizations. Olmec culture, based on agriculture, spread over regions in central Mexico that lie thousands of miles apart. The Olmec practice of building scattered ceremonial centers found its highest cultural expression in the civilization of the Maya. The Maya occupied the area of present-day Yucatán, the highland crescent of eastern Chiapas in Mexico, and much of Guatemala and western Honduras. In the central plateau of Mexico an "empire" centered at Teotihuacán arose. Scholars hotly debate whether the Teotihuacán territory constituted an empire, but they agree that Teotihuacán society was heavily stratified and that it exercised military, religious, and political power over a wide area. The Toltecs, whose culture adopted many features of Teotihuacán and Olmec civilizations, was the last advanced Amerindian civilization before the rise of the Aztecs.

The Olmecs

Population growth in the region of southern Veracruz and Tabasco (see Map 14.2) led to the development of the first distinct Mesoamerican civilization: the Olmec. Scholars estimate that the Olmecs thrived from approximately 1500 B.C. to A.D. 300. All subsequent Mesoamerican cultures derive from their culture. At present-day San Lorenzo, the center of Olmec society, were groups of

large stone buildings where the political elite and the priestly hierarchy resided with their retainers. Peasant farmers inhabited the surrounding countryside. From careful study of the surviving architectural structures and their richly carved jade sculptures, scholars have learned that a small hereditary elite governed the mass of workers and that the clustered buildings served as sites for religious ceremonies and as marketplaces for the exchange of agricultural produce and manufactured goods. The Olmecs also possessed a form of writing.

Around 900 B.C. San Lorenzo was destroyed, probably by migrating peoples from the north, and power passed to La Venta in Tabasco. Archaeological excavation at La Venta has uncovered a huge volcano-shaped pyramid. Standing 110 feet high at an inaccessible site on an island in the Tonala River, the so-called Great Pyramid was the center of the Olmec religion. The upward thrust of this monument, like that of the cathedrals of medieval Europe, may have represented the human effort to get closer to the gods. Built of huge stone slabs, the Great Pyramid required, scholars estimated, some 800,000 man-hours of labor. It testifies to the region's bumper harvests, which were able to support a labor force large enough to build such a monument. Around 300 B.C., La Venta fell, and Tres Zapotes, 100 miles to the northwest, became the leading Olmec site.

Olmec ceremonialism, magnificent sculpture, skillful stone work, social organization, and writing were important cultural advances that paved the way for the developments of the Classic period (A.D. 300–900), the golden age of Mesoamerican civilization.

The Maya of Central America

In the Classic period the Maya attained a level of intellectual and artistic achievement equaled by no other Amerindian people and by few peoples anywhere. The Maya developed a sophisticated system of writing, perhaps derived partly from the Olmec. They invented a calendar more accurate than the European Gregorian calendar. And they made advances in mathematics that Europeans did not match for several centuries.

Who were the Maya, and where did they come from? What was the basis of their culture? What is the significance of their intellectual and artistic achievement? The word *Maya* seems to derive from

Zamna, the name of a Maya god. Linguistic evidence leads scholars to believe that the first Maya were a small North American Indian group that emigrated from southern Oregon and northern California to the western highlands of Guatemala. Between the third and second millennia B.C. various groups, including the Cholans and Tzeltalans, broke away from the parent group and moved north and east into the Yucatán peninsula. The Cholan-speaking Maya, who occupied the area during the time of great cultural achievement, apparently created the culture.

Maya culture rested on agriculture. The staple crop in Mesoamerica was maize (corn). In 1972, a geographer and an aerial photographer studying the Campeche region of the Yucatán peninsula (Map 14.1) proved that the Maya practiced intensive agriculture in raised narrow rectangular plots that they built above the low-lying, seasonally flooded land bordering rivers. Because of poor soil caused by heavy tropical rainfall and the fierce sun, farmers may also have relied on *milpa* for growing maize. Using this method, farmers cut down the trees in a patch of forest and set the wood and brush afire. They then used a stick to poke holes through the ash and planted maize seed in the holes. A milpa (the word refers to both the area and the method) produced for only two years, after which it had to lie fallow for between four and seven years. Throughout the Yucatán Peninsula, the method of burning and planting in the fertile ashes, known as *swidden agriculture,* remains the typical farming practice today.

In addition to maize, the Maya grew beans, squash, chili peppers, some root crops, and fruit trees. Turkeys were domesticated, but barkless

Cylindrical Vessel Because the Maya suffered a high death rate from warfare, sacrificial ritual, and natural causes, the subject of death preoccupied them. Many art objects depict death as a journey into Xibalba, the Maya hell, and to rebirth for the Maya in children and grandchildren who replace them. Here three Xibalbans receive a sacrificial head on a drum. The scrawny torso of one has the look of starvation, and the excrement implies a revolting smell. The next figure, with a skeletal head, insect wings, and a distended stomach, suggests a parasitic disease. A common if nauseating scene. *(Source: © Justin Kerr 1985. Courtesy Houston Art Museum)*

dogs that were fattened on corn seem to have been the main source of protein. In the Yucatán, men trapped fish along the shores. The discovery of rich Maya textiles all over Mesoamerica indicates that cotton was widely exported.

The raised-field and milpa systems of intensive agriculture yielded food sufficient to support large population centers. The entire Maya region could have had as many as 14 million inhabitants. At Uxmal, Uaxactún, Copán, Piedras Negras, Tikal, Palenque, and Chichén Itzá (see Map 14.1), archaeologists have uncovered the palaces of nobles, elaborate pyramids where nobles were buried, engraved steles (stone-slab monuments), masonry temples, altars, sophisticated polychrome pottery, and courts for games played with a rubber ball. The largest site, Tikal, may have had 40,000 people. Since these centers lacked industrial activities, scholars avoid calling them cities. Rather they were religious and ceremonial centers.

Public fairs accompanying important religious festivals in population centers seem to have been the major Maya economic institutions. Jade, obsidian, beads of red spiny oyster shell, lengths of cloth, and cacao (chocolate) beans—all in high demand in the Mesoamerican world—served as the medium of exchange. The extensive trade among Maya communities, plus a common language, promoted the union of the peoples of the region and gave them a common sense of identity. Merchants trading beyond Maya regions, such as with the Mije-speaking peoples of the Pacific coast, the post-Olmec people of the Gulf coast, the Zapotecs of the Valley of Oaxaca, and the Teotihuacanos of the central valley of Mexico were considered state ambassadors bearing "gifts" to royal neighbors who reciprocated with their own "gifts." Since this long-distance trade played an important part in international relations, merchants conducting it were high nobles or even members of the royal family.

The Maya were a Stone Age people. Lacking iron tools until a few centuries before the Spanish conquest and beasts of burden until after the conquest, how were goods transported to distant regions? The extensive networks of rivers and swamps were the main arteries of transportation; over them large canoes carved out of hardwood trees carried cargoes of cloth and maize. Wide roads also linked Maya centers; on the roads merchants and lords were borne in litters, goods and produce on human backs. Trade produced considerable wealth that seems to have been concen-

MAP 14.1 The Maya World, a.d. 300–900
Archaeologists have discovered the ruins of dozens of Mayan city-states. Only the largest of them are shown here. Called the "Greeks of the New World," the Maya perfected the only written language in the Western Hemisphere, developed a sophisticated political system and a flourishing trade network, and created elegant art.

trated in a noble class, for the Maya had no distinctly mercantile class. They did have a sharply defined hierarchical society. A hereditary elite owned private land, defended society, carried on commercial activities, exercised political power, and directed religious rituals. The intellectual class also belonged to the ruling nobility. The rest of the people were free workers, serfs, and slaves.

The Maya developed a system of hieroglyphic writing with 850 characters and used it to record chronology, religion, and astronomy in books made of bark paper and deerskin. The recent deciphering of this writing has demonstrated that inscriptions on steles are actually historical documents recording the births, accessions, marriages, wars, and deaths of Maya kings. An understanding of the civilization's dynastic history allows scholars to interpret more accurately Maya pictorial imagery and to detect patterns in Maya art. They are

Palace Doorway Lintel at Yaxchilan, Mexico Lady Xoc, principal wife of King Shield-Jaguar, who holds a torch over her, pulls a thorn-lined rope through her tongue to sanctify with her blood the birth of a younger wife's child—reflecting the importance of blood sacrifice in Maya culture. The elaborate headdresses and clothes of the royal couple show their royal status. (*Source: © Justin Kerr 1985*)

finding that the imagery explicitly portrays the text in pictorial scenes and on stelar carvings.[2]

In the sixteenth century, Spanish friars taught Maya students to write their language in the Roman script so that the friars could understand Maya culture. Maya deities and sacrificial customs, however, provoked Spanish outrage. To hasten Maya conversion to Christianity, the priests tried to extirpate all native religion by destroying Maya sculpture and books. Only one Maya hieroglyphic book survived: the *Popul Vuh*, or Book of Council, which was written in European script by a young Quiche noble. Scholars call this document the Maya "Bible," meaning that like the Judeo-Christian scriptures the *Popul Vuh* gives the Maya view of the creation of the world, concepts of good and evil, and the entire nature and purpose of the living experience.

A method of measuring and recording time to arrange and commemorate events in the life of a society and to plan the agricultural and ceremonial year is a basic feature of all advanced societies. From careful observation of the earth's movements around the sun, the Maya invented a calendar of eighteen 20-day months and one 5-day month, for a total of 365 days. Using a system of bars (— = 5) and dots (∘ = 1), the Maya devised a form of mathematics based on the vigesimal (20) rather than the decimal (10) system. They proved themselves masters of abstract knowledge—notably in astronomy, mathematics, calendric development, and the recording of history.

Maya civilization lasted about a thousand years, reaching its peak between approximately A.D. 600 and 900, the period when the Tang Dynasty was flourishing in China, Islam was spreading in the Middle East, and Carolingian rulers were extending their sway in Europe. Between the eighth and tenth centuries, the Maya abandoned their cultural and ceremonial centers, and Maya civilization collapsed. Archaeologists and historians attribute the collapse to some combination of foreign invasions led by peoples attracted to the wealth of the great Maya centers, domestic revolts of subject peoples, disease, overpopulation resulting from crop failures, and the acquisition of so much territory by expansionist kings that rulers could not govern effectively. Just as scholars give no single reason for the decline and fall of the Roman Empire in Europe, so current scholarship holds that many factors were responsible for the fall of Maya civilization. The Maya, however, were not totally vanquished. Having resisted Indian invaders and the encroachments of Spanish American civilization, about 2 million Maya survive today on the Yucatán peninsula.

Teotihuacán and Toltec Civilizations

During the Classic period the Teotihuacán Valley in central Mexico witnessed the flowering of a remarkable civilization built by a new people from regions east and south of the Valley of Mexico. The city of Teotihuacán had a population of over 200,000—larger than any European city at the time. The inhabitants were stratified into distinct social classes. The rich and powerful resided in a special precinct, in houses of palatial splendor. Ordinary working people, tradespeople, artisans, and obsidian craftsmen lived in apartment compounds, or barrios, on the edge of the city. The inhabitants of the barrios seem to have been very poor and related by kinship ties and perhaps by shared common ritual interests. Agricultural laborers lived outside the city. Teotihuacán was a great commercial center, the entrepôt for trade and culture for all of Mesoamerica. It was also the ceremonial center of an entire society, a capital filled with artworks, a mecca that attracted thousands of pilgrims a year.

In the center of the city stood the Pyramids of the Sun and the Moon. The Pyramid of the Sun was built of sun-dried bricks and faced with stone. Each of its sides is 700 feet long and 200 feet high.

The smaller Pyramid of the Moon is similar in construction. In lesser temples, natives and outlanders worshiped the rain-god and the feathered serpent later called Quetzalcoatl. These gods were associated with the production of corn, the staple of the people's diet.

Although Teotihuacán dominated Mesoamerican civilization during the Classic period, other centers also flourished. In the isolated valley of Oaxaca at modern-day Monte Albán (see Map 14.2), for example, Zapotecan-speaking peoples established a great religious center whose temples and elaborately decorated tombs testify to the wealth of the nobility. The art—and probably the entire culture—of Monte Albán and other centers derived from Teotihuacán.

As had happened to San Lorenzo and La Venta, Teotihuacán collapsed before invaders. Around A.D. 700 semibarbarian hordes from the southwest burned Teotihuacán; Monte Albán fell shortly afterward. By 900 the golden age of Mesoamerica had ended. There followed an interregnum known as the "Time of Troubles" (ca A.D. 800–1000), characterized by disorder and extreme militarism. Whereas nature gods and their priests seem to have governed the great cities of the earlier period, militant gods and warriors dominated the petty states that now arose. Among these states, the most powerful heir to Teotihuacán was the Toltec confederation, a weak union of strong states. The Toltecs admired the culture of their predecessors and sought to absorb and preserve it. Through intermarriage, they assimilated with the Teotihuacán people. In fact, every new Mesoamerican confederation became the cultural successor of earlier confederations.

Under Toliptzin (ca 980–1000), the Toltecs extended their hegemony over most of central Mexico. Toliptzin established his capital at Tula. Its splendor and power became legendary during his reign. Apparently he took the name "Quetzalcoatl," signifying his position as high priest of the Teotihuacán god worshiped by the Toltecs. According to the "Song of Quetzalcoatl," a long Aztec glorification of Toliptzin,

he was very rich and had everything necessary to eat and drink, and the corn under his reign was in abundance, and the squash very fat, an arm's length around, and the ears of corn were so tall that they were carried with both arms. . . . And more than that the said Quetzalcoatl had all the wealth of the world, gold and silver and green stones jade and other precious things and a great abundance of coca trees in different colors, and the said vassals of the said Quetzalcoatl were very rich and lacked nothing. . . . Nor did they lack corn, nor did they eat the small ears but rather they used them like firewood to heat up their baths.[3]

Later, Aztec legends described a powerful struggle between the Toltecs' original tribal god, Tezcatlipoca, who required human sacrifices, and the newer Toltec-Teotihuacán god Quetzalcoatl, who gave his people bumper corn crops, fostered learning and the arts, and asked only the sacrifice of animals like butterflies and snakes. Tezcatlipoca won

Tezcatlipoca and Quetzalcoatl The Aztecs were deeply concerned with the passage of time, and like the Maya they had a solar year of 365 days divided into 18 months of 20 days each. The Aztec *tonalamatl*, or sacred "book of days," included a ritual calendar that portrayed thirteen Lords of the Day and nine Lords of the Night, each of them associated with a particular bird. This early-sixteenth-century illustration of a book of days shows Tezcatlipoca and Quetzalcoatl, who were major Lords of the Day. (*Source: Bibliothèque de l'Assemblée, Paris*)

this battle, and the priest-king Toliptzin-Quetzal-coatl was driven into exile. As he departed, he promised to return and regain his kingdom.

Whatever reality lies behind this legend, it became a cornerstone of Aztec tradition. It also played a profound role in Mexican history: by a remarkable coincidence, Quetzalcoatl promised to return in the year that happened to be 1519, the year in which the Spanish explorer Hernando Cortés landed in Mexico. Belief in the Quetzalcoatl legend helps explain the Aztec emperor Montezuma's indecisiveness about the Spanish adventurers and his ultimate fate (see pages 522–523).

After the departure of Toliptzin-Quetzalcoatl, troubles beset the Toltec state. Drought led to crop failure. Northern barbarian peoples, the Chichimec, attacked the borders in waves. Weak, incompetent rulers could not quell domestic uprisings. When the last Toltec king committed suicide in 1174, the Toltec state collapsed. In 1224 the Chichimec captured Tula.

The last of the Chichimec to arrive in central Mexico were the Aztecs. As before, the vanquished strongly influenced the victors: the Aztecs absorbed the cultural achievements of the Toltecs. The Aztecs—building on Olmec, Maya, Teotihuacán, and Toltec antecedents—created the last unifying civilization in Mexico before the arrival of the Europeans.

✳ AZTEC SOCIETY: RELIGION AND WAR

Although the terms *Aztec* and *Mexica* are used interchangeably here, *Mexica* is actually the more accurate word because it is a pre-Columbian term designating the dominant ethnic people of the island capital of Tenochtitlán-Tlalelolco. Aztec derives from *Aztlan,* the legendary homeland of the Mexica people before their migration into the Valley of Mexico, is *not* a pre-Columbian word, and was popularized by nineteenth-century historians.[4]

The Aztecs who appeared in the Valley of Mexico spoke the same Nahuatl language as the Toltecs but otherwise had nothing in common with them. Poor, unwelcome, looked on as foreign barbarians, the Aztecs had to settle on a few swampy islands in Lake Texcoco. From these unpromising beginnings they rapidly assimilated the culture of the

Toltecs and in 1428 embarked on a policy of territorial expansion. By the time Cortés arrived in 1519, the Aztec confederation encompassed all of central Mexico from the Gulf of Mexico to the Pacific Ocean as far south as Guatemala (Map 14.2). Thirty-eight subordinate provinces paid tribute to the Aztec king.

The growth of a strong mercantile class led to an influx of tropical wares and luxury goods: cotton, feathers, cocoa, skins, turquoise jewelry, and gold. The upper classes enjoyed an elegant and extravagant lifestyle; the court of Emperor Montezuma II (r. 1502–1520) was more magnificent than anything in western Europe. How, in less than two hundred years, had the Mexicans (from the Aztec word *mizquitl,* meaning "desolate land," or from *Mixitli,* the Aztec god of war) grown from an insignificant tribe of wandering nomads to a people of vast power and fabulous wealth?

The Aztecs' pictorial records attribute their success to the power of their war-god Huitzilopochtli and to their own drive and willpower. Will and determination they unquestionably had, but there is another explanation for their success: the Aztec state was geared for war. In the course of the fifteenth century, the primitive tribesmen who had arrived in the Valley of Mexico in 1325 transformed themselves into professional soldiers. Military campaigns continued; warriors were constantly subduing new states and crushing rebellions. A strong standing army was the backbone of the Aztec state, and war became the central feature of Mexica culture.

Warfare was a formal stylized ritual conducted according to rules whose goal was the capture, not the execution, of the enemy. Warriors hurled projectiles into their massed foes, intending to demoralize, not to kill. Then, a crippling blow with his obsidian "sword" to a foe's knees or to one of the muscles in the back of the thigh enabled the Aztec warrior to bring him to the ground. Once subdued, men with ropes tied the captive and took him to the rear of the battlefield.[5]

Religion and Culture

In Mexica society, religion was the dynamic factor that transformed other aspects of the culture: economic security, social mobility, education, and especially war. War was an article of religious faith. The state religion of the Aztecs initially gave them powerful advantages over other groups in central

MAP 14.2 The Aztec Empire, 1519 Aztecs controlled much of central Mexico. The Maya survived in the Yucatán Peninsula and some of present-day Guatemala. Notice the number of cities.

Mexico; it inspired them to conquer vast territories in a remarkably short time.[6] But that religion also created economic and political stresses that could not easily be resolved and that ultimately contributed heavily to the society's collapse.

Chief among the Aztecs' many gods was Huitzilopochtli, who symbolized the sun blazing at high noon. The sun, the source of all life, had to be kept moving in its orbit if darkness was not to overtake the world. To keep it moving, Aztecs believed, the sun had to be fed frequently precious fluids—that is, human blood. Human sacrifice was a sacred duty, essential for the preservation and prosperity of humankind. Black-robed priests carried out the ritual:

The victim was stretched out on his back on a slightly convex stone with his arms and legs held by four priests, while a fifth ripped him open with a flint knife and tore out his heart. The sacrifice also often took place in a manner which the Spanish described as gladiatorio: the captive was tied to a huge disk of stone . . . by a rope that left him free to move; he was armed with wooden weapons, and he had to fight several normally-armed Aztec warriors in turn. If, by an extraordinary chance, he did not succumb to their attacks, he was spared; but nearly always the "gladia-tor" fell, gravely wounded, and a few moments later he died on the stone, with his body opened by the black-robed, long-haired priests.[7]

Mass sacrifice was also practiced:

Mass sacrifices involving hundreds and thousands of victims could be carried out to commemorate special events. The Spanish chroniclers were told, for example, that at the dedication in 1487, of the great pyramid of Tenochtitlán four lines of prisoners of war stretching for two miles each were sacrificed by a team of executioners who worked night and day for four days. Allotting two minutes for sacrifice, the demographer and historian Sherbourne Cook estimated that the number of victims associated with that single event was 14,100. The scale of these rituals could be dismissed as exaggerations were it not for the encounters of Spanish explorers with . . . rows of human skulls in the plazas of the Aztec cities. . . . In the plaza of Xocotlan "there were . . . more than one hundred thousand of them."[8]

The Mexica did not invent human sacrifice; it seems to have been practiced by many Mesoamerican peoples. The Maya, for example, dedicated their temples with the blood of freshly executed victims. Anthropologists have proposed several explanations—none of them completely satisfactory—for the Aztecs' practice of human sacrifice and the cannibalism that often accompanied it. Some suggest that human sacrifice served to regulate population growth. Yet ritual slaughter had been practiced by earlier peoples—the Olmecs, the Maya, the dwellers of Teotihuacán, and the Toltecs—in all likelihood before population density had reached the point of threatening the food supply. Moreover, since almost all the victims were men—warriors captured in battle—population growth could still have exceeded the death rate. Executing women of child-bearing age would have had more effect on population growth.

According to a second hypothesis, the ordinary people were given victims' bodies as a source of protein.[9] These people lived on a diet of corn, beans, squash, tomatoes, and peppers. Wildlife was scarce, and dog meat, chicken, turkey, and fish were virtually restricted to the upper classes. The testimony of modern nutritionists that beans supply ample protein, and the evidence that, in an area teeming with wild game, the Huron Indians of North America ritually executed captives and feasted on their stewed bodies, weaken the validity of this theory.

A third, more plausible, theory holds that ritual human sacrifice was an instrument of state terrorism—that the Aztec rulers crushed dissent with terror. The Aztecs controlled a large confederation of city-states by sacrificing prisoners seized in battle; by taking hostages from among defeated peoples as ransom against future revolt; and by demanding from subject states an annual tribute of people to be sacrificed to Huitzilopochtli. Unsuccessful generals, corrupt judges, and careless public officials, even people who accidentally entered forbidden precincts of the royal palaces, were routinely sacrificed. When the supply of such victims ran out, slaves, plebeians, and even infants torn from their mothers suffered ritual execution. The emperor Montezuma II, who celebrated his coronation with the sacrifice of fifty-one hundred people, could be said to have ruled by holocaust. Trumpets blasted and drums beat all day long announcing the sacrifice of yet another victim. Blood poured down the steps of the pyramids. Death and fear stalked everywhere. Ordinary people appear to have endured this living nightmare by escaping into intoxicating drink and drugs.[10] Even this in-

terpretation, however, does not put the practice of human sacrifice in its full cultural context.

The Mexica state religion required constant warfare for two basic reasons. One was to meet the gods' needs for human sacrifice; and, secondly, warriors for the next phase of imperial expansion. ". . . the sacred campaigns of Huitzilopochtli were synchronized with the political and economic needs of the Mexica nation as a whole."[11] Nobles, warriors, and commoners who secured captives on the battlefield shared in the booty, lands, and the

❋ **The Goddess Tlazolteotl**   The Aztecs believed that Tlazolteotl (sometimes called "Mother of the Gods"), by eating refuse, consumed the sins of humankind. As the goddess of childbirth, Tlazolteotl was extensively worshiped. Notice the squatting position for childbirth, then common all over the world. (*Source: Dumbarton Oaks Research Library and Collections, Washington, D.C.*)

emperor's rich rewards of gold and silver jewelry, feathered costumes, and other articles of distinctive dress—depending on the number of captives they won. Nobles could grow wealthier, and the ordinary soldier could be promoted to the nobility. Social status, especially in the early period of Aztec expansion, depended on military performance. Warfare, therefore, offered the powerful incentive of upward social mobility. Moreover, defeated peoples had to pay tribute in foodstuffs to support rulers, nobles, warriors, and the imperial bureaucracy. The vanquished supplied laborers for agriculture, the economic basis of Mexica society. Likewise, conquered peoples had to produce workers for the construction and maintenance of the entire Aztec infrastructure—roads, dike systems, aqueducts, causeways, and the royal palaces. Finally, merchants also benefited, for war opened new markets for traders' goods in subject territories.

When the Spaniards under Hernando Cortés (1485–1547) arrived in central Mexico in 1519, the sacred cult of Huitzilopochtli had created a combination of interrelated problems for the emperor Montezuma II. The thirty-eight provinces of the empire, never really assimilated into the Mexica state and usually governed by members of the defeated dynasty, seethed with rebellion. Population increases at the capital Tenochtitlán had forced the emperor to lay increasingly heavier tribute on conquered provinces, which in turn, murdered the tribute collectors. Invasion and reconquest followed. "The provinces were being crushed beneath a cycle of imperial oppression: increases in tribute, revolt, reconquest, retribution, higher tribute, resentment, and repeated revolt."[12] By causing the death in battle and by sacrifice of thousands of food producers, Mexica religion destroyed the very economic basis of the empire.

Faced with grave crisis, Montezuma attempted to solve the problem by freezing social positions. He purged the court of many officials, drastically modified the dress and behavior of the merchant class, and severely limited the honors given to low-born warriors and all but the highest nobility. These reforms provoked great resentment, reduced incentive, and virtually ended social mobility. Scholars have traditionally portrayed Montezuma as weak-willed and indecisive when faced by the Spaniards. But recent research has shown that he was a very determined, even autocratic ruler. Terrible domestic problems whose roots lay

in a religious cult requiring appalling human slaughter offer the fundamental explanation for the Mexica collapse.[13]

The Life of the People

A wealth of information has survived about fifteenth- and sixteenth-century Mexico. The Aztecs were deeply interested in their own past, and in their pictographic script they wrote many books recounting their history, geography, and religious practices. They loved making speeches, and every public or social occasion gave rise to lengthy orations, which scribes copied down. The Aztecs also preserved records of their legal disputes, which alone amounted to vast files. The Spanish conquerors subsequently destroyed much of this material. But enough documents remain to construct a picture of the Mexica people at the time of the Spanish intrusion.

No sharp social distinctions existed among the Aztecs during their early migrations. All were equally poor. The head of a family was both provider and warrior, and a sort of tribal democracy prevailed in which all adult males participated in important decision making. By the early sixteenth century, however, Aztec society had changed. A stratified social structure had come into being, and the warrior aristocracy exercised great authority.

Scholars do not yet understand precisely how this change evolved. According to Aztec legend, the Mexicans admired the Toltecs and chose their first king, Acamapichtli, from among them. The many children he fathered with Mexica women formed the nucleus of the noble class. At the time of the Spanish intrusion into Mexico, men who had distinguished themselves in war occupied the highest military and social positions in the state. Generals, judges, and governors of provinces were appointed by the emperor from among his servants who had earned reputations as war heroes. These great lords, or tecuhtli, dressed luxuriously and lived in palaces. Like feudal lords, the provincial governors exercised full political, judicial, and military authority on the emperor's behalf. In their territories they maintained order, settled disputes, and judged legal cases; oversaw the cultivation of land; and made sure that tribute—in food or gold—was paid. The governors also led troops in wartime. These functions resembled those of feudal lords in western Europe during the Middle

Ages (see pages 413–414). Just as only nobles of France and England could wear fur and carry a sword, just as gold jewelry and elaborate hairstyles for women distinguished royal and noble classes in African kingdoms, so in Mexica societies only the techutli could wear jewelry and embroidered cloaks.

Beneath the great nobility of soldiers and imperial officials was the class of warriors. Theoretically every freeman could be a warrior, and parents dedicated their male children to war, burying a male child's umbilical cord with some arrows and a shield on the day of his birth. In actuality the sons of nobles enjoyed advantages deriving from their fathers' position and influence in the state. At the age of six, boys entered a school that trained them for war. Future warriors were taught to fight with a *macana,* a paddle-shaped wooden club edged with bits of obsidian (a volcanic rock similar to granite but as sharp as glass). This weapon could be brutally effective: during the Spanish invasion, Aztec warriors armed with macanas slashed off horses' heads with one blow. Youths were also trained in the use of spears, bows and arrows, and lances fitted with obsidian points. They learned to live on little food and sleep and to accept pain without complaint. At about age eighteen a warrior fought his first campaign. If he captured a prisoner for ritual sacrifice, he acquired the title *iyac,* or warrior. If in later campaigns he succeeded in killing or capturing four of the enemy, he became a *tequiua*—one who shared in the booty and thus was a member of the nobility. Warriors enjoyed a privileged position in Mexica society because they provided the state with the victims necessary for its survival. If a young man failed in several campaigns to capture the required four prisoners, he joined the *maceualtin,* the plebeian or working class.

The maceualtin were the ordinary citizens—the backbone of Aztec society and the vast majority of the population. The word *maceualti* means "worker" and implied boorish speech and vulgar behavior. Members of this class performed all sorts of agricultural, military, and domestic services and carried heavy public burdens not required of noble warriors. Government officials assigned the maceualtin work on the temples, roads, and bridges. Army officers called them up for military duty, but Mexicans considered this an honor and a religious rite, not a burden. Unlike nobles, priests, orphans, and slaves, maceualtin paid taxes. Maceualtin in the capital, however, possessed certain rights: they

Coronation Stone of Montezuma Originally located within the ritual center at Tenochtitlán, this quadrangular stone, carved with hieroglyphics in the Nahual language of the Aztecs, commemorates the start of Montezuma's reign, July 15, 1503, the date of his coronation. The sculpture associates his rule with the cycle of birth, death, and renewal. (*Source: Art Institute of Chicago, Major Acquisitions Centennial Endowment*)

held their plots of land for life, and they received a small share of the tribute paid by the provinces to the emperor.

Beneath the maceualtin were the *thalmaitl,* the landless workers or serfs. Some social historians speculate that this class originated during the "Time of Troubles," a period of migrations and upheavals in which weak and defenseless people placed themselves under the protection of strong warriors. The thalmaitl provided agricultural labor at times of planting and harvesting, paid rents in kind, and were bound to the soil—they could not move off the land. The thalmaitl resembled in many ways the serfs of western Europe, but unlike serfs they performed military service when called on to do so. They enjoyed some rights as citizens and generally were accorded more respect than slaves.

Slaves were the lowest social class. Like Asian, European, and African slaves, most were prisoners captured in war or kidnapped from enemy tribes.

¿como estás? ¡Yo he llegado!

But Aztecs who stole from a temple or private house or plotted against the emperor could also be enslaved, and people in serious debt sometimes voluntarily sold themselves into slavery. Female slaves often became their masters' concubines. Mexican slaves, however, differed fundamentally from European ones: "Tlatlocotin slaves could possess goods, save money, buy land and houses and even slaves for their own service."[14] Slaves could purchase their freedom. If a male slave married a free woman, their offspring were free, and a slave who escaped and managed to enter the emperor's palace was automatically free. Most slaves eventually gained their freedom. Mexican slavery, therefore, had humane qualities, in marked contrast with the slavery that the Spanish later introduced into South America and that the English imposed in North America.

Women of all social classes played important roles in Mexica society, but those roles were restricted entirely to the domestic sphere. As the little hands of the new-born male child were closed around a tiny bow and arrow indicating his warrior destiny, so the infant female's hands were wrapped around miniature weaving instruments and a small broom: weaving was a sacred and exclusively female art; the broom signalled a female's responsibility for the household shrines and for keeping the household swept and free of contamination. Almost all of the Mexica people married, a man at about twenty when he had secured one or two captives, a woman a couple years earlier. As in premodern Asian and European societies, parents selected their children's spouse, using neighborhood women as go-betweens. Save for the few women vowed to the service of the temple, marriage and the household was woman's fate; marriage represented social maturity for both sexes. Pregnancy became the occasion for family and neighborhood feasts, and a successful birth launched celebrations lasting from ten to twenty days. The rich foods available, such as frogs stewed with green chilis or gophers with sauce, as well as the many varieites of tamales, suggest that women had a sophisticated knowledge of food preparation. Women also had the care of small children.

Women took no part in public affairs—with a few notable exceptions. As the bearing of children was both a social duty and a sacred act, midwives enjoyed great respect. The number of midwives at a confinement indicated rank: a noblewoman often had two or three midwives. As in the medieval European West, in a very difficult birth midwives sacrificed the life of the child for that of the mother. Mexica society also awarded high status and authority to female physicians and herbalists. They treated men as well as women, setting broken bones and prescribing herbal remedies for a variety of ailments. The sources, though limited, imply that a few women skilled at market trading achieved economic independence. The woman weaver capable of executing complicated designs also had the community's esteem. Prostitutes in the state brothels, not local Mexica but tribute girls from the provinces given to successful warriors as part of their rewards, probably did not enjoy esteem.[15]

Alongside the secular social classes stood the temple priests. Huitzilopochtli and each of the numerous lesser gods had many priests to oversee the upkeep of the temple, assist at religious ceremonies, and perform ritual sacrifices. The priests also did a brisk business in foretelling the future from signs and omens. Aztecs consulted priests on the selection of wives and husbands, on the future careers of newborn babies, and before leaving on journeys or for war. Temples possessed enormous wealth in gold and silver ceremonial vessels, statues, buildings, and land. Fifteen provincial villages had to provide food for the temple at Texcoco and wood for its eternal fires. The priests who had custody of all this property did not marry and were expected to live moral and upright lives. From the temple revenues and resources, the priests supported schools, aided the poor, and maintained hospitals. The chief priests had the ear of the emperor and often exercised great power and influence.

At the peak of the social pyramid stood the emperor. The various Aztec historians contradict one another about the origin of the imperial dynasty, but modern scholars tend to accept the verdict of one sixteenth-century authority that the "custom has always been preserved among the Mexicans (that) the sons of kings have not ruled by right of inheritance, but by election."[16] A small oligarchy of the chief priests, warriors, and state officials made the selection. If none of the sons proved satisfactory, a brother or nephew of the emperor was chosen, but election was always restricted to the royal family.

The Aztec emperor was expected to be a great warrior. He led Mexican and allied armies into battle. All his other duties pertained to the welfare of

bad peeps

marr. rights

his people. It was up to the emperor to see that justice was done—he was the final court of appeal. He also held ultimate responsibility for ensuring an adequate food supply. The emperor Montezuma I (r. 1440–1467) distributed twenty thousand loads of stockpiled grain when a flood hit Tenochtitlán. The records show that the Aztec emperors took their public duties seriously.

The Cities of the Aztecs

When the Spanish entered Tenochtitlán (which they called "Mexico City") in November 1519, they could not believe their eyes. According to Bernal Díaz, one of Cortés's companions,

when we saw all those cities and villages built in the water, and other great towns on dry land, and that straight and level causeway leading to Mexico, we were astounded. These great towns and cues (temples)

and buildings rising from the water, all made of stone, seemed like an enchanted vision. . . . Indeed, some of our soldiers asked whether it was not all a dream.[17]

Tenochtitlán had about 60,000 households. The upper class practiced polygamy and had many children, and many households included servants and slaves. The total population probably numbered around 250,000. At the time, no European city and few Asian ones could boast a population even half that size. The total Aztec Empire has been estimated at around 5 million inhabitants.

Originally built on salt marshes, Tenochtitlán was approached by four great highways that connected it with the mainland. Wide straight streets and canals crisscrossed the city. Boats and canoes plied the canals. Lining the roads and canals stood thousands of rectangular one-story houses of mortar faced with stucco. Although space was limited, many small gardens and parks were alive with the

Tenochtitlán The great Mexican archaeologist Ignacio Marquina reconstructed the central plaza of the Aztec capital as it looked in 1519. The huge temple of the god of war dominates the area; royal palaces are on each side. On the right stands the rack with tens of thousands of human skulls; in the center is the platform where captives met sacrificial death. *(Source: Library of Congress)*

colors·and scents of flowers. The Mexicans loved flowers and used them in ritual ceremonies.

A large aqueduct whose sophisticated engineering astounded Cortés carried pure water from distant springs and supplied fountains in the parks. Streets and canals opened onto public squares and marketplaces. Tradespeople offered every kind of merchandise. Butchers hawked turkeys, ducks, chickens, rabbits, and deer; grocers sold kidney beans, squash, avocados, corn, and all kinds of peppers. Artisans sold intricately designed gold, silver, and feathered jewelry. Seamstresses offered sandals, loincloths and cloaks for men, and blouses and long skirts for women—the clothing customarily worn by ordinary people—and embroidered robes and cloaks for the rich. Slaves for domestic

service, wood for building, herbs for seasoning and medicine, honey and sweets, knives, jars, smoking tobacco, even human excrement used to cure animal skins—all these wares made a dazzling spectacle.

At one side of the central square of Tenochtitlán stood the great temple of Huitzilopochtli. Built as a pyramid and approached by three flights of 120 steps each, the temple was about 100 feet high and dominated the city's skyline. According to Cortés it was

so large that within the precincts, which are surrounded by a very high wall, a town of some five hundred inhabitants could easily be built. All round inside this wall there are very elegant quarters with very large rooms and corridors where their priests live.[18]

Describing the Aztec way of life for the emperor Charles V, Cortés concluded: "considering that they are barbarous and so far from the knowledge of God and cut off from all civilized nations, it is truly remarkable to see what they have achieved in all things."[19] Certainly Cortés's views reflect his own culture and outlook, but it is undeniable that Mexica culture was remarkable.

✺ MAP 14.3 The Inca Empire, 1463–1532
South America, which extends 4,750 miles in length and 3,300 miles from east to west at its widest point, contains every climatic zone and probably the richest variety of vegetation on earth. Roads built by the Incas linked most of the Andean region.

✸ THE INCAS OF PERU

In the late 1980s archaeologists working in the river valleys on the west coast of present-day Peru uncovered stunning evidence of complex societies that flourished between 5,000 and 3,000 years ago—roughly the same period as the great pyramids of Egypt. In spite of the altitude and dryness of the semidesert region, scores of settlements existed (Map 14.3). Perhaps the most spectacular was the one at Pampa de las Llamas-Moxeke in the Casma Valley. Stepped pyramids and U-shaped buildings, some more than ten stories high, dominated these settlements. Were these structures warehouses for storing food or cultic temples? Were these settlements connected in some sort of political association? Was there sufficient commercial activity to justify calling them cities? Why did these peoples, who lived on a diet of fish, sweet potatoes, beans, and peanuts, suddenly abandon their settlements and move into the Andean highlands? Scholars have only begun to process these

Boom Boom Boom
I want you in my room

vast remains, but radio carbon dating has already demonstrated that the settlements are older than the Maya and Aztec structures.[20]

Another archaeological discovery is providing scholars with rich information about pre-Columbian society. For some time, the villagers of Sipán in northern Peru supplemented their meager incomes by plundering ancient cemeteries and pyramids. One night in 1987 while digging deep in a pyramid, they broke into one of the richest funerary chambers ever located, and they filled their sacks with ceramic, gold, and silver objects. A dispute about the distribution of the loot led one dissatisfied thief to go to the police. When archaeologists from Lima and the United States arrived, they ranked the discoveries at Sipán with those at Tutankhamen's tomb in Egypt and the terra-cotta statues of the Qin Dynasty warriors near Xian, China.

The treasures from the royal tombs at Sipán derive from the Moche civilization, which flourished along a 250-mile stretch of Peru's northern coast between A.D. 100 and 800. Rivers that flowed out of the Andes Mountains into the valleys allowed the Moche people to develop complex irrigation systems for agricultural development. Each Moche valley contained a large ceremonial center with palaces and pyramids surrounded by settlements of up to 10,000 people. The dazzling gold and silver artifacts, elaborate hairdresses, and ceramic vessels display a remarkable skill in metalwork. Much of later Inca technology seems clearly based on the work of the Moche.[21]

The Aztec civilization of Mexico had already passed its peak when the Spanish landed in America. So too had a greater culture to the south, that of the Incas of Peru. Like the Aztecs, the Incas were "a small militaristic group that came to power late, conquered surrounding groups, and established one of the most extraordinary empires in the world."[22] Gradually, Inca culture spread throughout Peru. Modern knowledge of the Incas is concentrated on the last century before Spanish intrusion (1438–1532); today's scholars know far less about earlier developments.

In the center of Peru rise the cold highlands of the Andes Mountains. Six valleys of fertile and wooded land at altitudes ranging from 8,000 to 11,000 feet punctuate highland Peru. The largest of these valleys are Huaylas, Cuzco, and Titicaca. It was there that Inca civilization developed and flourished.

Portrait Vessel of a Ruler   Artisans of the Moche culture on the northern coast of Peru produced objects representing many aspects of their world, including this flat-bottomed stirrup-spout jar with a ruler's face. The commanding expression conveys a strong sense of power, as does the elaborate headdress with the geometric designs of Moche textiles worn only by elite persons. *(Source: Art Institute of Chicago. Kate S. Buckingham Endowment, 1955.2338)*

Archaeologists still do not understand how people of the Andean region acquired a knowledge of agriculture. Around 2500 B.C. they were relying on fish and mussels for food. Early agriculture seems to have involved cultivating cotton for ordinary clothing, ceremonial dress, and fish nets. Beautifully dyed cotton textiles, swatches of which

✳ **Machu Picchu** The citadel of Machu Picchu, surrounded by mountains in the clouds, clings to a spectacular crag in upland Peru. It was discovered in 1911 by the young American explorer Hiram Bingham. Its origin and the reason for its abandonment remain unknown. (*Source: Photo Researchers*)

have been found in ancient gravesites, may also have served as articles for trade. The central highland region of the Andes is much less well suited to agriculture than is Mesoamerica; in the Andes arable land is scarce. Yet between A.D. 600 and 1000, remarkable agricultural progress was made.

The Incas constructed great terraces along the mountain slopes and shored them up with walls to retain moisture. With only a foot plow, bronze hoe, and *guano* (the dried excrement of sea birds) as fertilizer, the Amerindians of Peru produced bumper crops of white potatoes. Potatoes ordinarily cannot be stored for long periods, but the Inca

of the Andean highlands developed a product called *chuñu*, freeze-dried potatoes made by subjecting potatoes alternately to nightly frosts and daily sun. Chuñu will keep unspoiled for several years. The construction of irrigation channels also facilitated the cultivation of corn. Potatoes and corn required far less labor and time than did the cultivation of wheat in Europe or rice in China.

By the fifteenth century, enough corn, beans, chili peppers, squash, tomatoes, sweet potatoes, peanuts, avocados, and white potatoes were harvested to feed not only the farmers themselves but also massive armies and administrative bureaucracies and thousands of industrial workers. Wild animals had become almost extinct in the region and were the exclusive preserve of the nobility. Common people rarely ate any meat other than guinea pigs, which most families raised. Chicha, a beer fermented from corn, was the staple drink.

Inca Imperialism

Who were the Incas? *Inca* was originally the name of the governing family of an Amerindian group that settled in the basin of Cuzco (see Map 14.3). From that family, the name was gradually extended to all people living in the Andes valleys. The Incas themselves used the word to identify their chief or emperor. Here the term is used for both the ruler and the people.

As with the Aztecs, so with the Incas: religious ideology was the force that transformed the culture. Religious concepts created pressure for imperialist expansion—with fatal consequences.

The Incas believed their ruler descended from the sun-god and that the health and prosperity of the state depended on him. Dead rulers were thought to link the people to the sun-god. When the ruler died, his corpse was preserved as a mummy in elaborate clothing and housed in a sacred and magnificent chamber. The mummy was brought in procession to all important state ceremonies, his advice was sought in time of crisis, and hundreds of human beings were sacrificed to him. In ordinary times, the dead ruler was carried to visit his friends, and his heirs and relatives came to dine with him. Some scholars call this behavior the "cult of the royal mummies" because it was a kind of ancestor worship.

The mummies were not only the holiest objects in the Inca world, but also a powerful dynamic force in Inca society. According to the principle of the "split inheritance," when an Inca ruler died, the imperial office, insignia, and rights and duties of the monarchy passed to the new king. The dead ruler, however, retained full and complete ownership of all his estates and properties. His royal descendants as a group managed his lands and sources of income for him and used the revenues to care for his mummy and to maintain his cult. Thus a new ruler came to the throne land- or property-poor. In order to live in the royal style, strengthen his administration, and reward his supporters, he had to win his own possessions by means of war and imperial expansion.[23]

Around A.D. 1000 the Incas were one of many small groups fighting among themselves for land and water. As they began to conquer their neighbors, a body of religious lore came into being that ascribed divine origin to their earliest king, Manco Capac (ca 1200) and promised warriors the gods' favor and protection. Strong historical evidence, however, dates only from the reign of Pachacuti Inca (1438–1471), who launched the imperialist phase of Inca civilization.

If the cult of ancestor or mummy worship satisfied some Inca social needs, in time it also created serious problems. The desire for conquest provided incentives for courageous (or ambitious) nobles: those who were victorious in battle and gained new territories for the state could expect lands, additional wives, servants, herds of llamas, gold, silver, fine clothes, and other symbols of high status. And even common soldiers who distinguished themselves in battle could be rewarded with booty and raised to noble status. The imperial interests of the emperor paralleled those of other social groups. Thus, under Pachacuti Inca and his successors Topa Inca (1471–1493) and Huayna Capac (1493–1525), Inca domination was gradually extended by warfare to the frontier of present-day Ecuador and Colombia in the north and to the Maule River in present-day Chile in the south (see Map 14.3), an area of about 350,000 square miles. Eighty provinces, scores of ethnic groups, and 16 million people came under Inca control. A remarkable system of roads held the empire together.

Before Inca civilization, each group that entered the Andes valleys had its own distinct language. These languages were not written and have become extinct. Scholars will probably never understand the linguistic condition of Peru before the fifteenth century when Pachacuti made Quechua (pronounced "keshwa") the official language of his people and administration. Conquered peoples were forced to adopt the language, and Quechua spread the Inca way of life throughout the Andes. Though not written until the Spanish in Peru adopted it as a second official language, Quechua had replaced local languages by the seventeenth and eighteenth centuries and is still spoken by most Peruvians today.

Whereas the Aztecs controlled their subject peoples through terror, the Incas governed by means of imperial unification. They imposed not only their language but their entire panoply of gods: the sun-god, divine ancestor of the royal family; his wife the moon-god; and the thunder-god, who brought life-giving rain. Magnificent temples scattered throughout the expanding empire housed idols of these gods and the state-appointed priests who attended them. Priests led prayers and elaborate rituals, and, on such occasions as a terrible natural disaster or a great military victory, they sacrificed human beings to the gods. Subject peoples were required to worship the state gods. Imperial unification was also achieved through the forced participation of local chieftains in the central bureaucracy and through a policy of colonization called *mitima*. To prevent rebellion in newly conquered territories, Pachacuti transferred all their inhabitants to other parts of the empire, replacing them with workers who had lived longer under Inca rule and whose independent spirit had been broken.[24] An excellent system of roads—averaging three feet in width, some paved and others not—facilitated the transportation of armies and the rapid communication of royal orders by runners. The roads followed straight lines wherever possible but also crossed pontoon bridges and tunneled through hills. This great feat of Inca engineering bears striking comparison with ancient Roman roads, which also linked an empire.

Rapid Inca expansion, however, produced stresses. Although the pressure for growth remained unabated, in the reign of Topa Inca open lands began to be scarce. Topa Inca had some success in attacks on the eastern slopes of the Andes, but his attempts to penetrate the tropical Amazon forest east of the Andes led to repeated military disasters. The Incas waged wars with highly trained armies drawn up in massed formation and fought pitched battles on level ground, often engaging in hand-to-hand combat, or they launched formal assaults on fortresses. But in dense jungles, the troops could not maneuver or maintain order against enemies using guerrilla tactics and sniping at them with deadly blowguns. Another source of stress was discontent among subject peoples in conquered territories. Many revolted. It took Huayna Capac several years to put down a revolt in Ecuador. Even the system of roads and trained runners eventually caused administrative problems. The average runner could cover about 50 leagues or 175 miles per day—a remarkable feat of physical endurance, especially at high altitude—but the larger the empire became, the greater the distances to be covered. The round trip from the capital at Cuzco to Quito in Ecuador, for example,

took from 10 to 12 days, so that an emperor might have to base urgent decisions on incomplete or out-of-date information. The empire was overextended. "In short, the cult of the royal mummies helped to drive the Inca expansion, but it also linked economic stress, administrative problems, and political instabilities in a cyclical relationship."[25]

In 1525 the Inca Huayna Capac died of plague while campaigning in Ecuador. Between that date and the arrival of the Spanish conquistador Francisco Pizarro in 1532, the Inca throne was bitterly contested by two of Huayna's sons, the half-brothers Huascar and Atauhualpa. Inca law called for a dying emperor to assign the throne to his most competent son by his principal wife, who had to be the ruler's full sister. Huascar, unlike Atauhualpa, was the result of such an incestuous union and thus had a legitimate claim to the throne. Atauhualpa, who had fought with Huayna Capac in his last campaign, tried to convince Huascar that their father had divided the kingdom and had given him (Atauhualpa) the northern part. Huascar bitterly rejected his half-brother's claim.

When Huascar came to the throne, the problems facing the Inca Empire had become critical: the dead rulers controlled too much of Peru's land and resources. Huascar proposed a radical solution:

annoyed one day with these dead (his ancestors), [he] said that he ought to order them all buried and take from them all that they had, and that there should not be dead men but living ones, because (the dead) had all that was best in the country.[26]

Although Atauhualpa had the grave liability of being born of a nonincestuous union, to the great nobility responsible for the cult of the royal mummies, Huascar's proposal represented a far graver threat to the established order: Huascar intended to insult the mummies who linked the Inca people to the gods, and if his proposals were enacted, the anger of the mummies would ensure a disastrous future. (The nobility did not say the obvious—that if Huascar buried the dead and took their vast properties, the nobles would be deprived of wealth and power.) Not surprisingly, the nobles threw their support behind Atauhualpa.

In the civil war that began in 1532, Atauhualpa's veteran warriors easily defeated Huascar's green recruits. On his way to his coronation at Cuzco,

THE AMERICAS, CA 400–1500

ca 20,000 b.c.	Migration across the Bering Strait to the Americas
ca 1500 b.c.–a.d. 300	Rise of Olmec culture
ca a.d. 400–600	Height of Teotihuacán civilization
ca 600–900	Peak of Maya civilization
ca 800–1000	"Time of Troubles" in Mesoamerica
ca 980–1000	Toltec hegemony
ca 1000	Beginning of Inca expansion
ca 1325	Arrival of the Aztecs in the Valley of Mexico
mid-15th century	Height of Aztec culture
1438–1493	Great Age of Inca imperialism
1519	Arrival of the Spanish
1521	Collapse of the Aztecs
1532	Spanish execution of the Inca king and decline of Inca Empire

Atauhualpa encountered Pizzaro and 168 Spaniards who had recently entered the kingdom. The Spaniards quickly became the real victors in the Inca kingdom (see pages 523–524). The cult of the royal mummies had brought, or at least contributed heavily to, Inca collapse.

Inca Society

The fundamental unit of early Inca society was the *ayllu*, or clan, whose members were all those who claimed a common male ancestor. A village typically consisted of several ayllus. Each had its own farmland and woodland, which all members tended. The chief, or *curacas*, of an ayllu, to whom all members owed allegiance, conducted relations with outsiders.

In the fifteenth century, Pachacuti Inca and Topa Inca superimposed imperial institutions on those of kinship. They ordered allegiance to be paid to the ruler at Cuzco rather than to the curacas. They drafted local men for distant wars and relocated the entire populations of certain regions through the mitima system. Entirely new ayllus were formed, based on residence rather than kinship.

The emperors sometimes gave newly acquired lands to victorious generals, distinguished civil servants, and favorite nobles. These lords subsequently exercised authority previously held by the native curacas. Whether long-time residents or new colonists, common people had the status of peasant farmers, which entailed heavy agricultural or other obligations. Just as in medieval Europe peasants worked several days each week on their lord's lands, so the Inca people had to work on state lands (that is, the emperor's lands) or on lands assigned to the temple. Peasants also labored on roads and bridges; terraced and irrigated new arable land; served on construction crews for royal palaces, temples, and public buildings such as fortresses; acted as runners on the post roads; and excavated in the imperial gold, silver, and copper mines. The imperial government annually determined the number of laborers needed for these various undertakings, and each district had to supply an assigned quota. The government also made an ayllu responsible for the state-owned granaries and for the production of cloth for army uniforms.

The state required everyone to marry and even decided when and sometimes whom a person should marry. Men married around the age of twenty, women a little younger. A young man who wanted a certain girl hung around her father's house and shared in the work. The Incas did not especially prize virginity; premarital sex was common. The marriage ceremony consisted of the joining of hands and the exchange of a pair of sandals. This ritual was followed by a large wedding feast, at which the state presented the bride and groom with two complete sets of clothing, one for everyday wear and one for festive occasions. If a man or woman did not find a satisfactory mate, the provincial governor selected one for him or her. Travel was forbidden, so couples necessarily came from the same region. Like most warring societies with high male death rates, the Incas practiced polygamy, though the cost of supporting many wives restricted it largely to the upper classes.

In many aspects of daily life, the common people were regimented, denied both choice and initiative. The Incas, however, took care of the poor and aged who could not look after themselves, distributed grain in time of shortage and famine, and supplied assistance in natural disasters. Scholars have debated whether Inca society was socialistic, totalitarian, or a forerunner of the welfare state; it may be merely a matter of definition. Although the Inca economy was strictly regulated, there certainly was not an equal distribution of wealth. Everything above and beyond the masses' basic needs went to the emperor and the nobility.

The backbreaking labor of ordinary people in the fields and mines made possible the luxurious lifestyle of the great Inca nobility. The nobles—called *Orejones*, or "Big Ears," by the Spanish because they pierced their ears and distended the lobes with heavy jewelry—were the ruling Inca's kinsmen. Lesser nobles included the curacas, royal household servants, public officials, and entertainers. As the empire expanded in the fifteenth century, there arose a noble class of warriors, governors, and local officials, whose support the ruling Inca secured with gifts of land, precious metals, and llamas and alpacas (llamas were used as beasts of burden; alpacas were raised for their long fine wool). The nobility was exempt from agricultural work and from other kinds of public service.

SUMMARY

Several strong Amerindian civilizations flourished in the Western Hemisphere in the years between 400 and 1500. The Maya are justly renowned for their art and their accomplishments in abstract thought, especially mathematics. The Aztecs built a unified culture based heavily on the Toltec heritage and distinguished by achievements in engineering, sculpture, and architecture. The Incas revealed a genius for organization, and their state was virtually unique in its time for assuming responsibility for all its people. In both the Mexica and the Inca societies religious ideology shaped other facets of the culture. The Mexica cult of war and human sacrifice and the Inca cult of the royal mummies proved fatal weaknesses and contributed to the decline of those societies.

Inca culture did not die with the Spaniard Pizarro's strangulation of Atauhualpa (p. 524). In May 1536 his successor Inca Mancu Yupanki led a massive revolt against the Spanish and then led his people to Machu Picchu deep in the Valcahamba range of the Andes. Inca military resistance to Spanish domination continued throughout the sixteenth to eighteenth centuries. In 1780 Jose Gabriel Kunturkanki, a highly educated businessman and landowner, proclaimed himself Inca Tupac Amaru II and launched a native independence movement that the Spanish put down with the greatest difficulty (p. 919).

NOTES

1. See F. Braudel, *The Structures of Everyday Life: Civilization and Capitalism, 15th–18th Century,* vol. 1, trans. S. Reynolds (New York: Harper & Row, 1981), pp. 160–161.
2. See L. Schele and M. E. Miller, *The Blood of Kings: Dynasty and Ritual in Maya Art* (New York: Braziller, 1986), pp. 14–15, passim.
3. Quoted in I. Bernal, *Mexico Before Cortez: Art, History, and Legend,* rev. ed., trans. Willis Barnstone (New York: Anchor Books, 1975), p. 68.
4. G. W. Conrad and A. A. Demarest, *Religion and Empire: The Dynamics of Aztec and Inca Expansionism* (New York: Cambridge University Press, 1993), p. 71.
5. See I. Clendinnen, *Aztecs: An Interpretation* (New York: Cambridge University Press, 1992), pp. 115–117.
6. J. Soustelle, *Daily Life of the Aztecs on the Eve of the Spanish Conquest,* trans. P. O'Brian (Stan-

ford, Calif.: Stanford University Press, 1970), p. 97.

7. See M. Harris, *Cannibals and Kings* (New York: Random House, 1977), pp. 99–110; the quotation is from p. 106.

8. Ibid., pp. 109–110.

9. See R. Padden, *The Hummingbird and the Hawk* (Columbus: Ohio State University Press, 1967), pp. 76–99.

10. I am relying heavily here on Conrad and Demarest, *Religion and Empire,* pp. 37–44.

11. Ibid., p. 49.

12. Ibid., p. 57.

13. Ibid., pp. 66–70.

14. Soustelle, *Daily Life of the Aztecs,* p. 74.

15. See Clendinnen, pp. 153–173.

16. Quoted in Soustelle, p. 89.

17. B. Díaz, *The Conquest of New Spain,* trans. J. M. Cohen (New York: Penguin Books, 1978), p. 214.

18. Quoted in J. H. Perry, *The Discovery of South America* (New York: Taplinger, 1979), pp. 161–163.

19. Quoted ibid., p. 163.

20. William K. Stevens, "Andean Culture Found to Be as Old as the Great Pyramids," *New York Times,* October 3, 1989, p. C1.

21. John Noble Wilford, "Lost Civilization Yields Its Riches as Thieves Fall Out," *New York Times,* July 29, 1994, pp. C1, C28.

22. J. A. Mason, *The Ancient Civilizations of Peru* (New York: Penguin Books, 1978), p. 108.

23. Conrad and Demarest, *Religion and Empire,* pp. 91–94.

24. Mason, *The Ancient Civilization of Peru,* p. 123.

25. Ibid., p. 132.

26. Ibid., p. 136.

SUGGESTED READING

The titles by Clendinnen, Conrad and Demarest, and Schele and Miller, cited in the Notes, represent some of the most exciting recent research on pre-Columbian Mesoamerican societies. For the Maya, students should also see L. Schele and D. Freidel, *A Forest of Kings: The Untold Story of the Ancient Maya* (1990), a splendidly illustrated work, providing expert treatment of many facets of the Maya world; R. Wright, *Time Among the Maya* (1989), which gives a highly readable account of the important Maya agricultural and religious calendars; M. D. Coe, *The Maya,* 4th ed. (1987), a sound and well-illustrated survey. For the Aztecs, R. F. Townsend, *The Aztecs* (1992), discusses the various classes of Mexica society, as well as expansion, education, and religious ritual in a clearly illustrated study. M. León-Portilla, *The Aztec Image of Self and Society: An Introduction to Nahua Culture* (1992), is perhaps the best appreciation of Aztec religious ritual and symbolism. For warfare, R. Hassig, *Aztec Warfare: Imperial Expansion and Political Control* (1988), is probably the standard work.

Students desiring books exploring the entire hemisphere before the arrival of Columbus might see B. Fagan, *Kingdoms of Gold, Kingdoms of Jade* (1991), a fine work in comparative anthropology, and *America in 1492,* ed. A. M. Josephy (1992), an interesting collection of essays, many written by leading scholars. For the impact of the Spanish on Mesoamerican peoples, see I. Clendinnen, *Ambivalent Conquests: Maya and Spanish in Yucatan, 1517–1570* (1987), a profoundly sensitive, learned, and important study; R. Wright, *Stolen Continents: The Americas through Indian Eyes since 1492* (1992), which emphasizes the persistence and survival of native American cultures and peoples; and *In the Wake of Contact: Biological Responses to Conquest,* ed. C. S. Larsen and G. Milner (1994), a useful collection of articles dealing with many parts of the world.

The following older studies may also prove helpful for particular topics: S. Masuda, I. Shimada, and C. Morris, eds., *Andean Ecology and Civilization* (1985) and E. R. Wolfe, ed., *The Valley of Mexico: Studies in Pre-Hispanic Ecology and Society* (1976), are important for environmental research; L. Baudin, *A Socialist Empire: The Incas of Peru* (1961), which gives a provocative interpretation of the Incas, while V. W. Van Hagen, *Realm of the Incas* (1961), offers a popular account; and F. Katz, *The Ancient American Civilisations* (1972), a standard anthropological work that surveys all the major Mesoamerican cultures, and T. Todorov, *The Conquest of America,* trans. R. Howard (1984), an important, but difficult, study in cross-cultural perceptions.

LISTENING TO THE
PAST

The Installation of the Inca

All societies have special ceremonies in which the head of state, ruler, or king is officially constituted or consecrated. These rites, often involving religious ritual, set the head of state apart from all others.

In 1653 the Spanish Jesuit Bernabe Cobo (1580–1657) completed his Historia del Nuevo Mundi *(History of the New World), a major Spanish source for Inca history and institutions. Cobo's work is not based on firsthand observation. Modern scholars believe it rests on lost sixteenth-century manuscripts, but, taking into account Cobo's period and prejudices, they consider it highly reliable. Here is Cobo's account of an Inca's installation, his majesty and splendor.*

. . . The prince was not crowned until the funeral rites of his father were concluded, and after this, all of the great lords and gentlemen who resided in the court and whoever could comfortably come from all over the kingdom gathered in the plaza of Cuzco for the installation and coronation. . . . The Inca took possession of the kingdom when he put the fringe on his forehead, which was like the royal crown, and after it, he put on the rest of the insignias that the Peruvian kings used; besides the fringe there was the *sunturpaucar*, the *champi*, the rainbow and two serpents, and the other emblems that each one picked out.

The way his vassals installed him and swore allegiance to him is as follows. Once all the lords were together in the plaza and the king was seated in the middle on his *duho*,[1] one by one the lords stood up, first the *orejones*[2] and after them the caciques and lords in charge of the most towns. In their hands they had some little feathers called *tocto* from certain birds . . . . They stood barefooted before the Inca and turned the palms of their hands toward him, showing their reverence. They also swore allegiance by the Sun, raising their faces toward

it, and by the earth, to be loyal to the Inca and serve him in whatever he ordered them to do.

The king was dressed and adorned in the same clothing as the Inca nobles and *orejones*. The king was distinguished only by having larger holes pierced in his ears and larger and more lavish earplugs, by having his hair cut short to the breadth of one or two fingers, and by his *lluato* [headband] which was many-colored. The braided headbands worn by other members of the Inca lineage were of a single color. The Inca wore a cloak and a shirt, with *ojotas* on his feet; in this respect he followed the custom of the common people, but his clothing was . . . made of the finest wool and the best cloth that was woven in his whole kingdom, with more brilliant colors and finer-quality weaving. The *mamaconas*[3] made his clothing for him, and most of it was made from vicuña wool, which is almost as fine as silk. . . .

The fringe (royal insignia that they always wore in place of a crown or diadem) was called *maxcapaycha*; it was made of very fine red wool. They had it sewn to the *llauto* and hanging in the middle of their forehead, and it reached down to their eyebrows. . . . The *sunturpaucar* and the *champi* were two of the king's other insignias, besides the royal standard. The *sunturpaucar* was a staff, a little shorter than a pike, all covered and adorned from top to bottom with short feathers of various colors. . . . The *champi*[4] was a certain kind of weapon with which they fought in wars. In front of the Inca, at the sides of the royal standard, two *champis* on two long staves were held and the Inca himself, instead of a scepter, carried a short *champi*, like a baton with a golden head. The royal banner or standard was a small, square pennant, about ten or twelve palms around the edge, made of cotton or wool cloth; it was fixed on the end of a long pole so as to stand out stiffly and not wave in the wind. Each king had his arms and emblems painted on it. . . .

The Incas made a majestic display both in their personal style of life and adornment and in the pomp and splendor that accompanied them and with which they were served inside and outside of their homes. The multitude of servants that they had in their palace was incredible. Many of these servants were the children of caciques and noblemen. These youngsters were raised in the royal house so that they would learn civil customs. The Incas felt that it was a sign of grandeur to support many servants and have many wives and concubines. They were served all the exquisite, precious, and rare things that the land produced, and they had these things brought for their pleasure from the most distant corners of their empire. . . . Serving women brought him all of his food on gold, silver, and pottery plates and set them before him on some very thin, small green rushes.

Wherever he went, and many times within a town, the Inca was carried on the shoulders of bearers supporting a splendid litter covered on the inside with gold; carrying this litter was a special favor and honor. When the Inca traveled, he had a large following of *orejones*; these were the nobles and military men, who added security as well as authority to the Inca's group.

The riches of these barbarian kings were so immense that it is not easy to describe. They never found that their wealth was insufficient, nor were they ever worried about finding a way to remedy their needs, because they never had any; rather they had peace of mind and abundance of everything, for they were more concerned about how to divest themselves of what was left over from their large income than in seeking new ways to obtain and keep treasures. This was due to the fact that whatever their vassals produced or acquired was at their service and disposal. . . .
The riches that were collected and gathered together just in the city of Cuzco, as the capital and court of the empire, were incredible; in it there were many important houses of the dead kings with all the treasure that each one had accumulated in his life. Since the one who ascended to the throne did not touch his predecessor's property and riches, which were given over to the *guaca* and service of the deceased, the new king had his own house built and acquired silver and gold and all the rest; thus the treasure in the city was immense. . . .

So Cuzco was the richest city that has been found in this New World, and the reason why

Painting of Inca chief (Pretender) Lloque Yupanqui, ca. 1615. *(Source: Collection Musée de l'Homme, Paris)*

it had such a great amount of wealth in silver and gold and precious stones was because the caciques and governors made presents of all of these things to the Inca when they visited him in his court and when he passed through their lands as he was visiting his kingdom. . . .

Questions for Analysis

1. What symbols were used in the installation of the Inca, and what do they represent?

2. Why did the Inca travel by litter? What does this method of conveyance tell us about Inca society and technology?

3. Compare the lifestyle of the Inca and the Chinese emperor K'ang-hsi or the French king Louis XIV. What do they all have in common? How does religious ideology support the rule of each?

4. Why does Cobo dwell on the wealth and riches of the Inca?

Source: *History of the Inca Empire by Father Bernabe Cobo,* trans. and ed. R. Hamilton (Austin: University of Texas Press, 1979), pp. 244–49.

Notes: 1. A low stool or bench, the symbol of the Inca's high office. 2. Nobles distinguished by their big ears, from which heavy jewelry extended. 3. Cloistered women who were dedicated to the service of the Inca gods and who also trained all royal household servants. 4. Similar to a mace and carried by the Inca, in war; like the scepter carried by European monarchs, the *champi* was an emblem of authority and of the Inca's duty to defend his people and extend his empire.

15

European Society in the Age of the Renaissance and Reformation

Michelangelo painted the entire Sistine Chapel ceiling by himself, 1508–1512. *(Source: Nippon Television Network Corporation, Tokyo, 1994)*

While the Four Horsemen of the Apocalypse were carrying war, plague, famine, and death across the continent of Europe, a new culture was emerging in southern Europe. The fourteenth century witnessed the beginnings of remarkable changes in many aspects of Italian society. In the fifteenth century, these phenomena spread beyond Italy and gradually influenced society in northern Europe. These cultural changes have collectively been labeled the Renaissance.

The idea of reform is as old as Christianity itself: the need for reform of the individual Christian and of the institutional church is central to the Christian faith. The Christian humanists of the late fifteenth and early sixteenth centuries called for reform of the church on the pattern of the early church, primarily through educational and social change. These cries for reformation were not new. Men and women of every period believed the early Christian church represented a golden age. What was new were the criticisms of educated lay people whose religious needs were not being met. In the sixteenth century, demands for religious reform became so strong that they became enmeshed with social, political, and economic factors.

- What does the term *Renaissance* mean?
- How did the Renaissance manifest itself in politics, government, art, and social organization?
- Why did the theological ideas of Martin Luther trigger political, social, and economic reactions?
- What response did the Catholic church make to the movements for reform?

This chapter explores these questions.

❋ ECONOMIC AND POLITICAL ORIGINS OF THE ITALIAN RENAISSANCE

The period extending roughly from 1050 to 1300 witnessed phenomenal commercial and financial development, the growing political power of self-governing cities in northern Italy, and great population expansion. The period from the late thirteenth to the late sixteenth century was characterized by an amazing flowering of artistic energies.[1] Scholars commonly use the term *Renaissance* to describe the cultural achievements of the four-teenth through sixteenth centuries. Those achievements rest on the economic and political developments of earlier centuries.

In the great commercial revival of the eleventh century, northern Italian cities led the way. By the middle of the twelfth century, Venice, supported by a huge merchant marine, had grown enormously rich from overseas trade. It profited tremendously from the diversion of the Fourth Crusade to Constantinople (see page 371). Genoa and Milan enjoyed the benefits of a large volume of trade with the Middle East and northern Europe. These cities fully exploited their geographical positions as natural crossroads for mercantile exchange between the East and West.

Florence too possessed enormous wealth despite geographical constraints. It was an inland city without easy access to water transportation. But toward the end of the thirteenth century, Florentine merchants and bankers acquired control of papal banking. From their position as tax collectors for the papacy, Florentine mercantile families began to dominate European banking on both sides of the Alps. The profits from loans, investments, and money exchanges that poured back to Florence were pumped into urban industries, such as the Florentine wool industry, which was the major factor in the city's financial expansion and population increase. Florence purchased the best-quality wool from England and Spain, developed remarkable techniques for its manufacture into cloth, and employed thousands of workers in the manufacturing process. Florentine woolen cloth brought the highest prices in the fairs, markets, and bazaars of Europe, Asia, and Africa. Scholars tend to agree that the first artistic and literary manifestations of the Italian Renaissance appeared in Florence.

In the course of the twelfth century, Milan, Florence, Genoa, Siena, and Pisa fought for and won political and economic independence from surrounding feudal nobles. The nobles, attracted by the opportunities of long-distance and maritime trade, the rising value of urban real estate, the new public offices available in the expanding cities, and the chances for advantageous marriages into rich commercial families, frequently settled within the cities. Marriage vows often sealed business contracts between the rural nobility and the mercantile aristocracy. This merger of the northern Italian feudal nobility and the commercial aristocracy brought into being a new social class—an urban nobility.

467

This new class made citizenship and political participation in the city-states dependent on a property qualification, years of residence within the city, and social connections. Only a tiny percentage of the male population possessed these qualifications. A new group, called the *pòpolo,* disenfranchised and heavily taxed, bitterly resented its exclusion from power. Throughout most of the thirteenth century, in city after city, the pòpolo used armed force and violence to take over the city governments. Members of the pòpolo could not establish civil order within their cities, however. Consequently, these movements for republican government—government in which political power theoretically resides in the people and is exercised by their chosen representatives—failed. By the year 1300 *signori* (despots, or one-man rulers) or *oligarchies* (the rule of merchant aristocracies) had triumphed everywhere.[2]

For the next two centuries, the Italian city-states were ruled by signori or by constitutional oligarchies. In the signories, despots pretended to observe the law while actually manipulating it to conceal their basic illegality. Oligarchic regimes possessed constitutions, but through a variety of schemes a small, restricted class of wealthy merchants exercised the judicial, executive, and legislative functions of government. Thus in 1422 Venice had a population of 84,000, but 200 men held all power; and Florence had about 40,000 people, but 600 men ruled. Oligarchic regimes maintained only a façade of republican government. Nostalgia for the Roman form of government, combined with calculating shrewdness, prompted the leaders of Venice, Milan, and Florence to use the old forms.

In the fifteenth century, political power and elite culture centered at the princely courts of despots and oligarchs. "A court was the space and personnel around a prince as he made laws, received ambassadors, made appointments, took his meals, and proceeded through the streets."[3] The princely court afforded the despot or oligarchs the opportunity to display and assert their wealth and power. They flaunted their patronage of learning and the arts by munificent gifts to writers, philosophers, and artists, and they promoted occasions for magnificent pageantry and elaborate ritual—all designed to assert their wealth and power. The rulers of the city-states governed as monarchs. They crushed urban revolts, levied taxes, and killed their enemies. And they used massive building programs to employ, and the arts to overawe, the masses.

Renaissance Italians had a passionate attachment to their individual city-states. This intensity of local feeling perpetuated the dozens of small states and hindered the development of a unified Italian state.

In the fifteenth century, five powers dominated the Italian peninsula: Venice, Milan, Florence, the Papal States, and the kingdom of Naples. Venice had a sophisticated constitution and was a republic in name, but an oligarchy of merchant-aristocrats actually ran the city. Milan was also called a republic, but despots of the Sforza family ruled harshly and dominated the smaller cities of the north. Likewise in Florence the form of government was republican, but between 1434 and 1494 power in Florence was held by the great Medici banking family. Though not public officers, Cosimo de' Medici (1434–1464) and Lorenzo de' Medici (1469–1492) ruled from behind the scenes. Central Italy consisted mainly of the Papal States, which during the Babylonian Captivity (see page 427) had come under the sway of important Roman families. Pope Alexander VI (r. 1492–1503), aided militarily and politically by his son Cesare Borgia, reasserted papal authority in the papal lands. Cesare Borgia, the inspiration of Machiavelli's *The Prince* (see page 478), began the work of uniting the peninsula by ruthlessly conquering and exacting total obedience from the principalities making up the Papal States. South of the Papal States, the kingdom of Naples had long been disputed by the Aragonese and by the French. In 1435 it passed to Aragon.

The five major Italian city-states competed furiously among themselves for territory. They used diplomacy, spies, paid informers, and any other means to advance their ambitions. While the states of northern Europe were moving toward centralization and consolidation, the world of Italian politics resembled a jungle where the powerful dominated the weak.

In one significant respect, however, the Italian city-states anticipated future relations among competing European states after 1500. Whenever one Italian state appeared to gain a dominant position on the peninsula, the other states joined forces to establish a *balance of power* against the major threat. In forming these shifting alliances, Renaissance Italians invented the machinery of modern diplomacy: permanent embassies with resident ambassadors in capitals where political relations and commercial ties needed continual monitoring. The

❊ **A Bank Scene, Florence**   Originally a "bank" was just a counter; if covered with a carpet like this Ottoman geometric rug with a kufic border, it became a bank of distinction. Moneychangers who sat behind the counter became "bankers," exchanging different currencies and holding deposits for merchants and business people. *(Source: Prato, San Francesco/Scala/Art Resource, NY)*

resident ambassador is one of the great achievements of the Italian Renaissance.

At the end of the fifteenth century, Venice, Florence, Milan, and the Papal States possessed great wealth and represented high cultural achievement. However, their imperialistic ambitions at one another's expense, and their resulting inability to form a common alliance against potential foreign enemies, made Italy an inviting target for invasion. When Florence and Naples entered into an agreement to acquire Milanese territories, Milan called on France for support.

In Florence a Dominican friar, Girolamo Savonarola (1452–1498), had been predicting an invasion by France. In a number of fiery sermons between 1491 and 1494, Savonarola attacked what he considered the paganism and moral vice of the city, the undemocratic government of Lorenzo de' Medici, and the corruption of Pope Alexander VI. For a time he enjoyed wide support among the ordinary people; he became the religious leader of

Florence and as such contributed to the fall of the Medicis. Savonarola stands as proof that the common people did not share the worldly outlook of the commercial and intellectual elite. Eventually, however, people wearied of his moral denunciations, and he was excommunicated by the pope and executed.

The invasion of Italy in 1494 by the French king Charles VIII (r. 1483–1498) inaugurated a new period in Italian and European power politics. Italy became the focus of international ambitions and the battleground of foreign armies. Charles swept the peninsula with little opposition. Florence, Rome, and Naples soon bowed before him. When Piero de' Medici, Lorenzo's son, went to the French camp seeking peace, the Florentines exiled the Medicis and restored republican government.

In the sixteenth century, the political and social life of Italy was upset by the relentless competition for dominance between France and the Holy Roman Empire. In 1519 Charles V succeeded his grandfather Maximilian as Holy Roman emperor. When the French returned to Italy in 1521, there began a series of conflicts called the Habsburg-Valois Wars (named for the German and French dynasties), whose battlefield was often Italy. The Italian cities suffered severely from the continual warfare, especially in the frightful sack of Rome in 1527 by imperial forces under Charles V. Thus the failure of the Italian city-states to form a common alliance against foreign enemies led to the continuation of the centuries-old subjection of the Italian peninsula by outside invaders.

✿ INTELLECTUAL HALLMARKS OF THE RENAISSANCE

Some Italians in the fourteenth and fifteenth centuries believed that they were living in a new era. The realization that something new and unique was happening first came to men of letters in the fourteenth century, especially to poet and humanist Francesco Petrarch (1304–1374). Petrarch thought that the Germanic invasions had caused a sharp cultural break with the glories of Rome and had ushered in what he called the "Dark Ages." Medieval people had recognized no cultural division between the world of the Roman emperors and their own times, but in the opinion of Petrarch and many of his contemporaries, the thousand-year period between the fourth and the fourteenth centuries constituted a barbarian, or Gothic, or "middle" age (hence historians' use of the expression "Middle Ages"). The sculptors, painters, and writers of the Renaissance spoke contemptuously of their medieval predecessors and identified themselves with the thinkers and artists of Greco-Roman civilization. Petrarch believed he was witnessing a new golden age of intellectual achievement—a rebirth or, to use the French word that came into English, a *renaissance.*

The division of historical time into periods is often arbitrary and done by historians for their own convenience. In terms of the way most people lived and thought, no sharp division existed between the Middle Ages and the Renaissance. The guild and the parish, for example, continued to provide strong support for the individual and to exercise great social influence. Renaissance intellectuals, however, developed a new sense of historical distance and some important poets, writers, and artists believed they were living in a new age.

The Renaissance also manifested itself in new attitudes towards individuals, learning, and the world at large. There was a renewal of belief in the importance of the individual, a rebirth of interest in the Latin classics and in antique lifestyles, and a restoration of interest in the material world.

Individualism

Though the Middle Ages had seen the appearance of remarkable individuals, recognition of such persons was limited. Saint Augustine in the fifth century and Peter Abélard and Guibert of Nogent in the twelfth—men who perceived themselves as unique and produced autobiographical statements—stand out, for Christian humility discouraged self-absorption. In the fourteenth and fifteenth centuries, however, a large literature presenting a distinctly Renaissance individualism emerged.

Many distinctive individuals gloried in their uniqueness. Italians of unusual abilities were self-consciously aware of their singularity and unafraid to be different from their neighbors; they had enormous confidence in their ability to achieve great things. Leon Battista Alberti (1404–1474), a writer, architect, and mathematician, remarked, "Men can do all things if they will."[4] The Florentine goldsmith and sculptor Benvenuto Cellini (1500–1574) prefaced his *Autobiography* with a sonnet that declares:

My cruel fate hath warr'd with me in vain:
Life, glory, worth, and all unmeasur'd skill,
Beauty and grace, themselves in me fulfill
That many I surpass, and to the best attain.[5]

Certain of his genius, Cellini wrote so that the whole world might appreciate it.

Individualism stressed personality, genius, uniqueness, and the fullest development of capabilities and talents. Artist, athlete, painter, scholar, sculptor, whatever—a person's abilities should be stretched until fully realized. Thirst for fame, a driving ambition, a burning desire for success drove such people to achieve their potential. The quest for glory was a central component of Renaissance individualism.

Humanism

In the cities of Italy, especially Rome, civic leaders and the wealthy populace showed great archaeological zeal for the recovery of manuscripts, statues, and monuments. The Vatican Library, planned in the fifteenth century to house the nine thousand manuscripts collected by Pope Nicholas V (r. 1447–1455), remains one of the richest repositories of ancient and medieval documents. Patrician Italians consciously copied the lifestyle of the ancients and tried to trace their genealogies back to ancient Rome.

The revival of interest in antiquity was also apparent in the serious study of the Latin classics. This feature of the Renaissance became known as the "new learning," or simply "humanism," the term used by the Florentine rhetorician and historian Leonardo Bruni (1370–1444). The words *humanism* and *humanist* derived from the Latin *humanitas,* which Cicero used to refer to the literary culture needed by anyone who wanted to be considered educated and civilized. Humanism focused on human beings—their achievements, interests, and capabilities. Although churchmen supported the new learning, by the later fifteenth century Italian humanism was increasingly a lay phenomenon.

Appreciation of the literary culture of the Romans had never died in the West. Bede and John of Salisbury (see page 368), for example, had studied and imitated the writings of the ancients. But medieval writers had accepted pagan and classical authors uncritically. Renaissance humanists, in contrast, were skeptical of their authority, conscious of the historical distance separating themselves from the ancients, and fully aware that classical writers often disagreed among themselves. Medieval writers looked to the classics to reveal God. Renaissance humanists studied the classics to understand human nature, though from a strongly Christian perspective. For example, in a remarkable essay, *On the Dignity of Man,* the Florentine writer Pico della Mirandola (1463–1494) stressed that man possesses great dignity because he was made as Adam in the image of God before the Fall and as Christ after the Resurrection. According to Pico, man's place in the universe is somewhere between the beasts and the angels, but, because of the divine image planted in him, there are no limits to what man can accomplish. Humanists rejected classical ideas that were opposed to Christianity. Or they sought through reinterpretation an underlying harmony between the pagan and secular and the Christian faith. The fundamental difference between medieval humanists and Renaissance ones is that the latter were more self-conscious about what

they were doing and stressed the realization of human potential.[6]

The leading humanists of the early Renaissance were rhetoricians, seeking effective and eloquent communication, both oral and written. They loved the language of the classics and scorned the corrupt, "barbaric" Latin of the medieval schoolmen. Literary humanists of the fourteenth century wrote each other highly stylized letters imitating ancient authors, and they held witty philosophical dialogues in conscious imitation of Plato's Academy of the fourth century B.C. Renaissance writers were very excited by the purity of ancient Latin. Eventually, however, they became concerned more about form than about content, more about the way an idea was expressed than about the significance and validity of the idea.

Secular Spirit

Secularism is a basic concern with the material world instead of with eternal and spiritual matters. A secular way of thinking tends to find the ultimate explanation of everything and the final end of human beings within the limits of what the senses can discover. Medieval business people ruthlessly pursued profits while medieval monks fought fiercely over property. But medieval society was religious, not secular: the dominant ideals focused on the otherworldly, on life after death. Renaissance people often held strong and deep spiritual beliefs. But Renaissance society was secular: attention is concentrated on the here and now, often on the acquisition of material things. The fourteenth and fifteenth centuries witnessed the slow but steady growth of secularism in Italy.

The economic changes and rising prosperity of the Italian cities in the thirteenth century worked a fundamental change in social and intellectual attitudes and values. Worries about shifting rates of interest, shipping routes, personnel costs, and employee relations did not leave much time for thoughts about penance and purgatory. Wealth made possible greater material pleasures, a more comfortable life, the leisure time to appreciate and patronize the arts. Money could buy many sensual gratifications, and the rich, social-climbing bankers and merchants of the Italian cities came to see life more as an opportunity to be enjoyed than as a painful pilgrimage to the City of God.

In *On Pleasure,* the humanist Lorenzo Valla (1406–1457) defended the pleasures of the senses as the highest good. Scholars praise Valla as a father of modern historical criticism. His study *On the False Donation of Constantine* (1444) demonstrated by careful textual examination that an anonymous eighth-century document supposedly giving the papacy jurisdiction over vast territories in western Europe was a forgery. Medieval people had accepted the Donation of Constantine as valid, and the proof that it was a forgery weakened the foundations of papal claims to temporal authority. Lorenzo Valla's work exemplifies the application of critical scholarship to old and almost-sacred writings, as well as the new secular spirit of the Renaissance.

The tales in *The Decameron* (1353), by the Florentine Giovanni Boccaccio (1313–1375), describe ambitious merchants, lecherous friars, and cuckolded husbands and portray a frankly acquisitive, sensual, and worldly society. Historians, however, must be cautious in basing conclusions solely on literature. Boccaccio's figures were stock literary characters not unknown in the Middle Ages, and writers draw on their imagination as well as on social experience. Nevertheless, *The Decameron* contains none of the "contempt of the world" theme so pervasive in medieval literature.

Renaissance writers justified the accumulation and enjoyment of wealth with references to ancient authors, and church leaders did little to combat the new secular spirit. In the fifteenth and early sixteenth centuries, the papal court and the households of the cardinals were just as worldly as those of great urban patricians. Renaissance popes beautified the city of Rome, patronized artists and men of letters, and expended enormous enthusiasm and huge sums of money. A new papal chancellery, begun in 1483 and finished in 1511, stands as one of the architectural masterpieces of the High Renaissance. Pope Julius II (r. 1503–1513) tore down the old Saint Peter's Basilica and began work on the present structure in 1506. Michelangelo's dome for Saint Peter's is still considered his greatest work.

Although papal interests fostered the new worldly attitude, the broad mass of the people and the intellectuals and leaders of society remained faithful to the Christian church. Few questioned the basic tenets of the Christian religion. The thousands of pious paintings, sculptures, processions, and pilgrimages of the Renaissance period prove that strong religious feeling persisted.

Art and the Artist

No feature of the Renaissance evokes greater admiration than its artistic masterpieces. The 1400s (called *quattrocento* in Italian) and 1500s (*cinquecento*) bore witness to a dazzling creativity in painting, architecture, and sculpture. In all the arts, the city of Florence first led the way. In the period art historians describe as the High Renaissance (1500–1527) Rome took the lead. The main characteristics of High Renaissance art—classical balance, harmony, and restraint—are revealed in the masterpieces of Leonardo da Vinci (1452–1519), Raphael (1483–1520), and Michelangelo (1475–1564), all of whom worked in Rome.

In early Renaissance Italy, art manifested corporate power. Powerful urban groups such as guilds and religious confraternities commissioned works of art. The Florentine cloth merchants, for example, delegated Filippo Brunelleschi (1377–1446) to build the magnificent dome on the cathedral of Florence and selected Lorenzo Ghiberti (1378–1455) to design the bronze doors of the baptistry. These works were signs of the merchants' dominant influence in the community. Corporate patronage is also reflected in the Florentine government's decision to hire Michelangelo to create a sculpture of David, the great Hebrew hero and king. The subject matter of art through the early fifteenth century, as in the Middle Ages, remained overwhelmingly religious.

Increasingly in the later quattrocento, individuals and oligarchs, rather than corporate groups, sponsored works of art. Merchants, bankers, popes, and princes supported the arts as a means of glorifying themselves, their families, and their power. Vast sums were spent on family chapels, frescoes, religious panels, and tombs. Writing about 1470, the Florentine oligarch Lorenzo de' Medici declared that over the past thirty-five years his family had spent the astronomical sum of 663,755 gold florins for artistic and architectural commissions. And, he said, "I think it casts a brilliant light on our estate [public reputation] and it seems to me that the monies were well spent and I am very pleased with this."[7]

As the fifteenth century advanced, the subject matter of art became steadily more secular. Religious topics, such as the Annunciation of the Virgin, remained popular among both patrons and artists, but classical themes and motifs, such as the lives and loves of pagan gods and goddesses, figured increasingly in painting and sculpture. The individual portrait emerged as a distinct artistic genre. People were conscious of their physical uniqueness and wanted their individuality immortalized. In the fifteenth century, members of the newly rich middle class often had themselves painted in a scene of romantic chivalry or in courtly society. Rather than reflecting a spiritual ideal, as medieval painting and sculpture tended to do, Renaissance portraits mirrored reality.

The Florentine painter Giotto (1276–1337) led the way in the use of realism; his treatment of the human body and face replaced the formal stiffness and artificiality that had for so long characterized the representation of the human body. The sculptor Donatello (1386–1466) probably exerted the greatest influence of any Florentine artist before Michelangelo. His many statues express an appreciation of the incredible variety of human nature. Medieval artists had depicted the nude body only in a spiritualized and moralizing context. Donatello revived the classical figure with its balance and self-awareness. The short-lived Florentine Masaccio (1401–1428), sometimes called the father of modern painting, inspired a new style characterized by great realism, narrative power, and effective use of light and dark.

Narrative artists depicted the body in a more scientific and natural manner. The female figure is voluptuous and sensual. The male body, as in Michelangelo's *David* (1501–1504) and *The Last Judgment* (1534–1541), is strong and heroic. This glorification of the human body is a sign of the secular spirit of the age. Brunelleschi and Piero della Francesca (1420–1492) seem to have pioneered *perspective* in painting—the linear representation of distance and space on a flat surface. *The Last Supper* (ca 1495–1498) of Leonardo da Vinci, with its stress on the tension between Christ and the disciples, is a subtle psychological interpretation.

As important as realism was the new "international style," so called because of the wandering careers of influential artists, the close communications and rivalry of princely courts, and the increased trade in works of art. Rich color, decorative detail, curvilinear rhythms, and swaying forms characterized the international style. As the term *international* implies, this style was European, not merely Italian.

The growing secular influences on art are reflected in the improved social status of the artist in the Renaissance. The lower-middle-class medieval master mason had been viewed in the same light as a mechanic. The artist in the Renaissance was considered a free intellectual worker. Artists did not produce unsolicited pictures or statues for the general public; that could mean loss of status. They usually worked on commission from a powerful prince. The artist's reputation depended on the support of powerful patrons, and through them some artists and architects achieved not only economic security but great wealth. All aspiring artists received a practical (not theoretical) education in a recognized master's workshop. For example, Michelangelo was apprenticed at age thirteen to the artist Ghirlandaio (1449–1494), although he later denied that fact to make it appear he never had any formal training. The more famous an artist was, the more he attracted assistants or apprentices.

Renaissance society respected and rewarded the distinguished artist. At a time when a person could live in a princely fashion on 300 ducats a year, Leonardo da Vinci was making 2,000 ducats annually. Michelangelo was paid 3,000 ducats for painting the ceiling of the Sistine Chapel. When he agreed to work on Saint Peter's Basilica, he refused a salary; he was already a wealthy man.[8] In 1537 the prolific letter writer, humanist, and satirizer of princes Pietro Aretino (1492–1556) wrote to Michelangelo while he was painting the Sistine Chapel:

To the Divine Michelangelo:
Sir, just as it is disgraceful and sinful to be unmindful of God so it is reprehensible and dishonourable for any man of discerning judgement not to honour you as a brilliant and venerable artist whom the very stars use as a target at which to shoot the rival arrows of their favour. You are so accomplished, therefore, that hidden in your hands lives the idea of a new king of creation. . . . And it is surely my duty to honour you with this salutation, since the world has many kings but only one Michelangelo.[9]

The Renaissance witnessed the birth of the concept of the artist as genius. In the Middle Ages, people believed that only God created, albeit through individuals; the medieval conception recognized no particular value in artistic originality. Boastful Renaissance artists and humanists came to think that a work of art was the deliberate creation of a unique personality, of an individual who transcended traditions, rules, and theories. A genius had a peculiar gift, which ordinary laws should not inhibit. Cosimo de' Medici described a painter, because of his genius, as "divine," implying that the artist shared in the powers of God. Aretino and others applied the word *divine* to Michelangelo.

But the student must remember that Italian Renaissance culture was that of a small mercantile elite, a business patriciate with aristocratic pretensions. Renaissance culture did not directly affect the broad middle classes, let alone the vast urban proletariat. Renaissance humanists were a smaller and narrower group than the medieval clergy had ever been. In the Middle Ages, high churchmen had commissioned the construction of the Gothic cathedrals, but, once finished, the buildings were for all to enjoy. Nothing comparable was built in the Renaissance. A small, highly educated group of literary humanists and artists created the culture of and for an exclusive elite. They cared little for ordinary people.[10]

The Renaissance in the North

In the last quarter of the fifteenth century, Italian Renaissance thought and ideals penetrated north-

Benozzo Gozzoli: Journey of the Magi   Few Renaissance paintings better illustrate art in the service of the princely court, in this case the Medici. Commissioned by Piero de' Medici to adorn his palace chapel, everything in this fresco—the large crowd, the feathers and diamonds adorning many of the personages, the black servant in front—serve to flaunt the power and wealth of the House of Medici. There is nothing especially religious about it; the painting could more appropriately be called "Journey of the Medici." *(Source: Scala/Art Resource, NY)*

ern Europe. Students from the Low Countries, France, Germany, and England flocked to Italy, imbibed the "new learning," and carried it back to their countries. However, cultural traditions of northern Europe tended to remain more distinctly Christian, or at least pietistic, than those of Italy. Italian humanists certainly were strongly Christian, as the example of Pico della Mirandola shows. But in Italy secular and pagan themes and Greco-Roman motifs received more humanistic attention than they received north of the Alps. The Renaissance in northern Europe had a distinctly religious character, and what fundamentally distinguished Italian humanists from northern ones is that the latter had a program for broad social reform based on Christian ideals.

Christian humanists in northern Europe were interested in the development of an ethical way of life. To achieve it, they believed, the best elements of classical and Christian cultures should be combined. For example, the classical ideals of calmness, stoical patience, and broad-mindedness should be joined in human conduct with the Christian virtues of love, faith, and hope. Northern humanists also stressed the use of reason, rather than acceptance of dogma, as the foundation for an ethical way of life. Like the Italians, they were impatient with Scholastic philosophy. Christian humanists had a profound faith in the power of human intellect to bring about moral and institutional reform. They believed that human nature had been corrupted by sin but nevertheless was fundamentally good and capable of improvement through education, which would lead to piety and an ethical way of life.

The Englishman Thomas More (1478–1535) towers above other figures in sixteenth-century English social and intellectual history. More's political stance and his resulting fate later, at the time of the Reformation (see page 501), have tended to obscure his contribution to Christian humanism. More, who practiced law, was deeply interested in the classics; his household served as a model of warm Christian family life and as a mecca for foreign and English humanists. He entered government service during the reign of Henry VIII and was sent as ambassador to Flanders. There More found the time to write *Utopia* (1516), which presented a revolutionary view of society.

Utopia, which literally means "nowhere," describes an ideal socialistic community on an island somewhere off the mainland of the New World. All

its children receive a good education, and since the goal of all education is to develop rational faculties, adults divide their days equally between manual labor or business pursuits and various intellectual activities. The profits from business and property are held strictly in common, so there is absolute social equality. The Utopians use gold and silver both to make chamber pots and to prevent wars by buying off their enemies. By this casual use of precious metals, More meant to suggest that the basic problems in society were caused by greed. Utopian law exalts mercy above justice. Citizens of Utopia lead a nearly perfect existence because they live by reason. More punned on the word *Utopia*, which he termed "a good place. A good place which is no place."

More's ideas were profoundly original in the sixteenth century. The long-prevailing view was that vice and violence exist because women and men are basically corrupt. But More maintained that acquisitiveness and private property promote all sorts of vices and civil disorders and that because society protects private property, *society's* flawed institutions are responsible for corruption and war. Today people take this view so much for granted that it is difficult to appreciate how radical it was in the sixteenth century. According to More, the key to improvement and reform of the individual was reform of the social institutions that mold the individual.

Better known by contemporaries than Thomas More was the Dutch humanist Desiderius Erasmus of Rotterdam (1466?–1536), whose life work became the application of the best humanistic learning to the study and explanation of the Bible. As a mature scholar with an international reputation stretching from Cracow to London, a fame that rested largely on his exceptional knowledge of Greek, Erasmus could boast with truth, "I brought it about that humanism, which among the Italians . . . savored of nothing but pure paganism, began nobly to celebrate Christ."[11]

Erasmus's long list of publications includes *The Adages* (1500), a list of Greek and Latin precepts on ethical behavior; *The Education of a Christian Prince* (1504), which combines idealistic and practical suggestions for the formation of a ruler's character; *The Praise of Folly* (1509), a satire of worldly wisdom and a plea for the simple and spontaneous Christian faith of children; and, most important of all, a critical edition of the Greek New Testament (1516). In the preface to the New

Testament, Erasmus explained the purpose of his great work:

Only bring a pious and open heart, imbued above all things with a pure and simple faith. . . . For I utterly dissent from those who are unwilling that the sacred Scriptures should be read by the unlearned translated into their vulgar tongue, as though Christ had taught such subtleties that they can scarcely be understood even by a few theologians. . . . Christ wished his mysteries to be published as openly as possible. I wish that even the weakest woman should read the Gospel—should read the epistles of Paul. And I wish these were translated into all languages, so that they might be read and understood, not only by Scots and Irishmen, but also by Turks and Saracens. . . . Why do we prefer to study the wisdom of Christ in men's writings rather than in the writing of Christ himself?[12]

Two fundamental themes run through all of Erasmus's scholarly work. First, education—study of the Bible and the classics—is the means to reform, the key to moral and intellectual improvement. Second, the essence of Erasmus's thought is, in his own phrase, "the philosophy of Christ." By this Erasmus meant that Christianity is an inner attitude of the heart or spirit. Christianity is not formalism, special ceremonies, or law; Christianity is Christ—his life and what he said and did, not what theologians have written about him.

Whereas the writings of Erasmus and More have strong Christian themes and have drawn the attention primarily of scholars, the stories of the French humanist François Rabelais (1490?–1553) possess a distinctly secular flavor and have attracted broad readership. The most roguishly entertaining Renaissance writer, Rabelais was convinced that "laughter is the essence of manhood." Rabelais's *Gargantua* and *Pantagruel* (serialized between 1532 and 1552) belong among the great comic masterpieces of world literature. These stories' gross and robust humor introduced the adjective *Rabelaisian* into the language.

In *Gargantua* and *Pantagruel* the reader enters a world of Renaissance vitality, ribald joviality, and intellectual curiosity. On his travels Gargantua meets various absurd characters, and within their hilarious exchanges there occur serious discussions on religion, politics, philosophy, and education. Rabelais had received an excellent humanistic education in a monastery, and Gargantua discusses the disorders of contemporary religious and secular life. Like Erasmus, Rabelais satirized hypocritical monks, pedantic academics, and pompous lawyers. But unlike Erasmus, Rabelais applied wild and gross humor. Like Thomas More, Rabelais believed that institutions molded individuals and that education was the key to a moral and healthy life. The aristocratic residents of Rabelais's Thélèma, the abbey that Gargantua establishes, live for the full gratification of their physical instincts and rational curiosity. Thélèma, whose motto is "Do as Thou Wilt," admits women *and* men; allows all to eat, drink, sleep, and work when they choose; provides excellent facilities for swimming, tennis, and football; and encourages sexual experimentation and marriage. Rabelais believed profoundly in the basic goodness of human beings and the rightness of instinct.

The distinctly religious orientation of the literary works of the Renaissance in the north also characterized northern art and architecture. Some Flemish painters, notably Rogier van der Weyden (1399/1400–1464) and Jan van Eyck (1366–1441), were considered the artistic equals of Italian painters, were much admired in Italy, and worked a generation before Leonardo and Michelangelo. One of the earliest artists successfully to use oil-based paints, van Eyck, in paintings such as *Ghent Altarpiece* and the portrait *Giovanni Arnolfini and His Bride,* shows the Flemish love for detail; the effect is great realism and remarkable attention to human personality.

Another Flemish painter, Hieronymous Bosch (ca 1450–1516), frequently used religious themes, but in combination with grotesque fantasies, colorful imagery, and peasant folk legends. Many of Bosch's paintings reflect the confusion and anguish often associated with the end of the Middle Ages. In *Death and the Miser,* Bosch's dramatic treatment of the Dance of Death theme, the miser's gold, increased by usury, is ultimately controlled by diabolical rats and toads, and his guardian angel urges him to choose the crucifix.

A quasi-spiritual aura likewise infuses architectural monuments in the north. The city halls of wealthy Flemish towns such as Bruges, Brussels, Louvain, and Ghent strike the viewer more as shrines to house the bones of saints than as settings for the mundane decisions of politicians and business people. Northern architecture was little influenced by the classical revival so obvious in Renaissance Rome and Florence.

Jan van Eyck: Madonna of Chancellor Rodin The tough and shrewd chancellor who ordered this rich painting visits the Virgin and Christ-Child (though they seem to be visiting him). An angel holds the crown of heaven over the Virgin's head while Jesus, the proclaimed savior of the world, holds it in his left hand and raises his right hand in blessing. Through the colonnade, sculpted with scenes from Genesis, is the city of Bruges. Van Eyck's achievement in portraiture is extraordinary; his treatment of space and figures and his ability to capture the infinitely small and the very large prompted art historian Erwin Panofsky to write that "his eye was at one and the same time a microscope and a telescope." *(Source: © Louvre/Photo R.M.N.)*

 ## SOCIAL CHANGE DURING THE RENAISSANCE

The Renaissance changed many aspects of Italian and, subsequently, European society. The new developments brought about real breaks with the medieval past in education and political thought, through new printing technology, and in the experience of women and blacks.

Education and Political Thought

Education and moral behavior were central preoccupations of the humanists. Humanists poured out treatises, often in the form of letters, on the structure and goals of education and the training of rulers. In one of the earliest systematic programs for the young, Peter Paul Vergerio (1370–1444) wrote Ubertinus, the ruler of Carrara:

For the education of children is a matter of more than private interest; it concerns the State, which indeed regards the right training of the young as, in certain aspects, within its proper sphere. . . . Above all, respect for Divine ordinances is of the deepest importance; it should be inculcated from the earliest years.

Reverence towards elders and parents is an obligation closely akin.

We call those studies liberal which are worthy of a free man; those studies by which we attain and practice virtue and wisdom; that education which calls forth, trains and develops those highest gifts of body and of mind which ennoble men, and which are rightly judged to rank next in dignity to virtue only.[13]

Part of Vergerio's treatise specifies subjects for the instruction of young men in public life: history teaches virtue by examples from the past; ethics focuses on virtue itself; and rhetoric, or public speaking, trains for eloquence.

No book on education had broader influence than Baldassare Castiglione's *The Courtier* (1528). This treatise sought to train, discipline, and fashion the young man into the courtly ideal, the gentleman. According to Castiglione (1478–1529), the educated man of the upper class should have a broad background in many academic subjects, and his spiritual and physical, as well as intellectual, capabilities should be trained. The courtier should have easy familiarity with dance, music, and the arts. Castiglione envisioned a man who could compose a sonnet, wrestle, sing a song and accompany himself on an instrument, ride expertly, solve difficult mathematical problems, and above all speak and write eloquently (see Listening to the Past). In the sixteenth and seventeenth centuries, the courtier envisioned by Castiglione became the model of the European gentleman.

No Renaissance book on any topic has been more widely read and studied in all the centuries since its publication in 1513 than the short political treatise *The Prince,* by Niccolò Machiavelli (1469–1527). Some political scientists maintain that Machiavelli was describing the actual competitive framework of the Italian states with which he was familiar. Other thinkers praise *The Prince* because it revolutionized political theory and destroyed medieval views of the nature of the state. Still other scholars consider this work a classic because it deals with eternal problems of government and society.

Born to a modestly wealthy Tuscan family, Machiavelli received a good education in the Latin classics. He entered the civil service of the Florentine government and served on thirty diplomatic missions. When the exiled Medicis returned to power in Florence in 1512, they expelled Machiavelli from his position as an officer of the city government. In exile he wrote *The Prince.*

The subject of *The Prince* is political power: how the ruler should gain, maintain, and increase it. A good humanist, Machiavelli explores the problems of human nature and concludes that human beings are selfish and out to advance their own interests. This pessimistic view of humanity leads him to maintain that the prince may have to manipulate the people in any way he finds necessary:

For a man who, in all respects, will carry out only his professions of good, will be apt to be ruined amongst so many who are evil. A prince therefore who desires to maintain himself must learn to be not always good, but to be so or not as necessity may require.[14]

The prince should combine the cunning of a fox with the ferocity of a lion to achieve his goals. Pondering the question of whether it is better for a ruler to be loved or feared, Machiavelli wrote:

It will naturally be answered that it would be desirable to be both the one and the other; but as it is difficult to be both at the same time, it is much more safe to be feared than to be loved, when you have to choose between the two. For it may be said of men in

general that they are ungrateful and fickle, dissemblers, avoiders of danger, and greedy of gain. So long as you shower benefits upon them, they are all yours.[15]

Medieval political theorists and theologians had stressed the way government *ought* to be. They had set high moral and Christian standards for the ruler's conduct. In their opinion, the test of good government was whether it provided justice, law, and order. Machiavelli maintained that the ruler should be concerned not with the way things ought to be but with the way things actually are. The sole test of whether a government was "good" was whether it was effective, whether the ruler increased his power. Machiavelli believed that political action cannot be restricted by moral considerations, but he did not advocate amoral behavior. In the *Discourses of the Ten Books of Titus Livy,* he even showed his strong commitment to republican government. Nevertheless, on the basis of a simplistic interpretation of *The Prince,* the adjective *Machiavellian* entered the language as a synonym for devious, corrupt, and crafty politics in which the end justifies the means. Machiavelli's ultimate significance rests on two ideas: that one permanent social order reflecting God's will cannot be established and that politics has its own laws and ought to be considered a science.[16]

Movable Type and the Spread of Literacy

Sometime in the thirteenth century, paper money and playing cards from China reached the West. They were *block-printed*—that is, each word, phrase, or picture was carved on a separate wooden block to be inked and used for printing. This method of reproduction was extraordinarily expensive and slow. By the middle of the fifteenth century, Europeans had mastered paper manufacture, which also originated in China and was introduced by the Arabs to the West in the twelfth century. Then around 1455, probably through the combined efforts of three men—Johann Gutenberg, Johann Fust, and Peter Schöffer, all experimenting at Mainz—movable type came into being in the West. The mirror image of each letter (rather than entire words or phrases) was carved in relief on a small block. Individual letters, easily movable, were put together to form words in lines of type that made up a page. An infinite variety of texts could be printed by reusing and rearranging pieces of type.

The effects of the invention of movable-type printing were not obvious overnight. But within a half-century of the publication of Gutenberg's Bible of 1456, printing from movable type brought about radical changes. It transformed both the private and the public lives of Europeans. Governments that "had employed the cumbersome methods of manuscripts to communicate with their subjects switched quickly to print to announce declarations of war, publish battle accounts, promulgate treaties or argue disputed points in pamphlet form. Theirs was an effort 'to win the psychological war.'" Printing made propaganda possible, emphasizing differences between opposing groups such as Crown and nobility, church and state. These differences laid the basis for the formation of distinct political parties.

Printing also stimulated the literacy of lay people and eventually came to have a deep effect on their private lives. Although most of the earliest books and pamphlets dealt with religious subjects, students, housewives, businessmen, and upper- and middle-class people sought books on all subjects. Printers responded with moralizing, medical, practical, and travel manuals. Pornography as well as piety assumed new forms. For example, the satirist Pietro Aretino used the shock of sex in pornography as a vehicle to criticize: his *Sonnetti lussuriosi* (1527) and *Ragionamenti* (1534–1536), sonnets accompanying sixteen engravings of as many sexual positions, attacked princely court life, humanist education, and false clerical piety.[17] Broadsides and flysheets allowed great public festivals, religious ceremonies, and political events to be experienced vicariously by the stay-at-home. Since books and other printed materials were read aloud to illiterate listeners, print bridged the gap between written and oral cultures.[18]

Women in Renaissance Society

How did women experience the Renaissance? Did they participate in the intellectual and artistic changes of the period? How did the status of women in the fourteenth to sixteenth centuries compare with that of women in the eleventh to thirteenth centuries?

During the Renaissance the status of upper-class women declined. If women in the High Middle Ages are compared with those of fifteenth- and sixteenth-century Italy with respect to the kind of work they performed, their access to property and

political power, and their role in shaping the outlook of their society, it is clear that ladies in the Renaissance ruling classes generally had less power than comparable ladies in the feudal age.

In the cities of Renaissance Italy, well-to-do girls received an education similar to boys'. Young ladies learned their letters and studied the classics. Many read Greek as well as Latin, knew the poetry of Ovid and Virgil, and could speak one or two "modern" languages, such as French or Spanish. In this respect, Renaissance humanism represented a real educational advance for women. Some women, though a small minority among humanists, acquired great learning and fame. Some Italian women published books, and Sofonisba Anguissola (1530–1625) achieved international renown for her paintings.

Laura Cereta (1469–1499) illustrates the successes and failures of educated Renaissance women. Educated by her father, who was a member of the governing elite of Brescia in Lombardy, she learned languages, philosophy, theology, and mathematics. She also gained self-confidence and a healthy respect for her own potential. By the age of fifteen, when she married, her literary career was already launched, as her letters to several cardinals attest. For Laura Cereta, however, as for all educated women of the period, the question of marriage forced the issue: she could choose a husband, family, and full participation in social life or else study and withdrawal from the world. Cereta chose marriage but was widowed at eighteen and was able to spend the remaining twelve years of her life in study. Responding to the envy of other women and the hostility of men who felt threatened, Laura Cereta criticized "empty women, who strive for no good but exist to adorn themselves . . . these women of majestic pride, fantastic coiffures, outlandish ornament, and necks bound with gold or pearls [which] bear the glittering symbols of their captivity to men." She believed that women's inferior status derived not from the divine order of things but from the choices women were making: "For knowledge is not given as a gift, but through study. . . . The free mind, not afraid of labor, presses on to attain the good."[19] Despite Laura Cereta's faith in women's potential, most men believed that a woman who became learned violated nature and thus ceased to be a woman. Brilliant women such as Laura Cereta were severely attacked by men who feared threats to male dominance in the intellectual realm.

Sofonisba Anguissola: The Artist's Sister Minerva   A nobleman's daughter and one of the first Italian women to become a recognized artist, Sofonisba did portraits of her five sisters and of prominent people. The coiffure, elegant gown, necklaces, and rings depict aristocratic dress in the mid-sixteenth century. *(Source: Milwaukee Art Museum)*

Laura Cereta was a prodigy. Ordinary girls of the urban upper middle class received some training in painting, music, and dance, in addition to a classical education. What were they to do with this training? They were to be gracious, affable, charming—in short, decorative. Renaissance women were better educated than their medieval counterparts. But whereas education trained a young man to participate in the public affairs of the city, it prepared a woman for the social functions of the home. An educated lady was supposed to know how to attract artists and literati to her husband's court and how to grace her husband's household. An educated man was supposed to know how to rule and participate in public affairs.

With respect to love and sex, the Renaissance witnessed a downward shift in women's status. In the medieval literature of courtly love—the etiquette books and romances—manners shaped the man to please the woman. According to *The Courtier,* Castiglione's manual on courtesy and good behavior, the woman was to make herself pleasing to the man. In contrast to the medieval tradition of relative sexual equality, Renaissance humanists laid the foundations for the bourgeois double standard. Men, and men alone, operated in the public sphere; women belonged in the home. Castiglione, the foremost spokesman of Renaissance love and manners, completely separated love from sexuality. For women, sex was restricted entirely to marriage. Ladies were bound to chastity, to the roles of wife and mother in a politically arranged marriage. Men, however, could pursue sensual indulgence outside marriage.[20]

Did the Renaissance have an impact on the lives of ordinary women? Women, of course, continued to perform economic functions in the expanding industries. Rural women assisted husbands and fathers in agricultural tasks. Urban women helped in the shops and were heavily involved in the Florentine textile industry, weaving cloth and reeling and winding silk. In the Venetian Arsenal, the state-controlled dock and ship construction area—the largest single industrial plant in Europe—women made sails. Widows frequently ran their husbands' businesses, and in Italy and France some became full members of guilds.

Educational opportunities being severely limited, few girls received an education. Women may have taken civic pride in the new monuments and art works in their localities, as far as they could understand them. But apart from that, the literary and art works of the Renaissance had no effect on ordinary women—or men. Many scholars believe the period of the Renaissance witnessed the emergence of the irreversible divide between an educated elite that participates in a "high culture" of art, music, literature, and learning, and the broad mass whose "popular culture" involves tools, houses, and the man-made environment.[21]

Official attitudes toward rape provide another index of the status of women in the Renaissance. A careful study of the legal evidence from Venice from 1338 to 1358 shows that rape was not considered a particularly serious crime against either the victim or society. The rape of a young girl of marriageable age or a child under twelve was considered a graver crime than the rape of a married woman. Still, the punishment for rape of a noble, marriageable girl was only a fine or about six months' imprisonment. In an age when theft and robbery were punished by mutilation, and forgery and sodomy by burning, this penalty was very mild indeed. In the eleventh century, William the Conqueror had decreed that rapists be castrated, implicitly according women protection and a modicum of respect. But in the early Renaissance, Venetian laws and their enforcement show that the governing oligarchy believed that rape damaged, but only slightly, men's property—women.[22]

Evidence from Florence in the fifteenth century also sheds light on infanticide, which historians are only now beginning to study in the Middle Ages and Renaissance. Early medieval penitentials and church councils legislated against abortion and infanticide. Nevertheless, Pope Innocent III (r. 1198–1216) was moved to establish an orphanage "because so many women were throwing their children into the Tiber."[23] In the fourteenth and early fifteenth centuries, a considerable number of children died in Florence under suspicious circumstances such as exposure or suffocation. These deaths occurred too frequently to have all been accidental, and far more girls than boys died, thus reflecting societal discrimination against girl children as inferior and less useful than boys. Dire poverty led some parents to do away with unwanted children.

The gravity of the problem of infanticide, which violated both the canon law of the church and the civil law of the state, forced the Florentine government to build the Foundling Hospital. Supporters of the institution maintained that, without public responsibility, "many children would soon be found dead in the rivers, sewers, and ditches, unbaptized."[24] The large size of the hospital suggests that great numbers of children were abandoned.

Blacks in Renaissance Society

Ever since the time of the Roman republic, a few black people had lived in western Europe. They had come, along with white slaves, as the spoils of war. Even after the collapse of the Roman Empire, Muslim and Christian merchants continued to import them. The evidence of medieval art attests to the presence of Africans in the West and Europeans' awareness of them. In the twelfth and thirteenth centuries, a large cult surrounded Saint Maurice, who was portrayed as a black knight martyred in the fourth century for refusing to renounce his Christian faith. Saint Maurice received the special veneration of the nobility.

Until the fifteenth century, the number of blacks living in western Europe was small. Then, in the fifteenth century, sizable numbers of black slaves began to enter Europe. Portuguese explorers imported perhaps a thousand a year and sold them at the markets of Seville, Barcelona, Marseilles, and Genoa. By the mid-sixteenth century, blacks, slave and free, constituted about 10 percent of the populations of the Portuguese cities of Lisbon and Évora; other cities had smaller percentages. In all, blacks made up roughly 3 percent of the Portuguese population. The Venetians specialized in the import of white slaves, but blacks were so greatly in demand at the Renaissance courts of northern Italy that the Venetians defied papal threats of excommunication to secure them.

What roles did blacks play in Renaissance society? What image did Europeans have of Africans? The medieval interest in curiosities, the exotic, and the marvelous continued into the Renaissance. Because of their rarity, black servants were highly prized and a symbol of wealth. In the late fifteenth century, Isabella, the wife of Gian Galazzo Sforza, took pride in the fact that she had ten black servants. In 1491 Isabella of Este, duchess of Mantua, instructed her agent to secure a black girl between four and eight years old, "shapely and as black as possible." The duchess saw the child as a source of entertainment: "we shall make her very happy and shall have great fun with her." She hoped that the little girl would become "the best buffoon in the world."[25] The cruel ancient tradition of retaining a professional "fool" for the amusement of a noble family persisted through the Renaissance—and even down to the twentieth century.

Adult black slaves filled a variety of positions. Many served as maids, valets, and domestic servants. The Venetians employed blacks—slave and free—as gondoliers and stevedores on the docks. In Portugal, they supplemented the labor force in virtually all occupations.[26] In Renaissance Spain and Italy, blacks performed as dancers, as actors and actresses in courtly dramas, and as musicians, sometimes making up full orchestras.[27] Slavery during the Renaissance foreshadowed the American, especially the later Brazilian, pattern.

Before the sixteenth-century "discoveries" of the non-European world, Europeans had little concrete knowledge of Africans and their cultures. Europeans knew little about them beyond biblical accounts and their attitude toward Africans was ambivalent.[28] On the one hand, Europeans perceived Africa as a remote place, the home of strange people isolated by heresy and Islam from supposedly superior European civilization. They believed that contact with Christian Europeans could only "improve" black Africans, even slaves. Theologians taught that God was light, and blackness, the opposite of light, was believed to represent the hostile forces of evil, sin, and the devil. Thus in medieval and early Renaissance art the devil was commonly represented as a black man. On the other hand, blackness was also associated with certain positive qualities. It symbolized the emptiness of worldly goods and the humility of the monastic way of life. Black vestments and funeral trappings indicated grief, and Christ had said that those who mourn are blessed. Thus in Renaissance society blacks—like women—were signs of wealth; both were used for display.

POLITICS AND THE STATE IN THE RENAISSANCE (CA 1450–1521)

The High Middle Ages witnessed the beginnings of many of the basic institutions of the modern state. Sheriffs, inquests, juries, circuit judges, professional bureaucracies, and representative assemblies all trace their origins to the twelfth and thirteenth centuries (see pages 375, 377). The linchpin for the development of states, however, was strong monarchy, and during the period of the Hundred Years' War, no ruler in western Europe was able to provide effective leadership. The resurgent power of feudal nobilities weakened the centralizing work begun earlier.

Beginning in the fifteenth century, rulers utilized the aggressive methods implied by Renaissance political ideas to rebuild their governments. First in Italy (see pages 468–469), then in France, England, and Spain, rulers began the work of reducing violence, curbing unruly nobles and troublesome elements, and establishing domestic order. The Holy Roman Empire of Germany, however, remained divided into scores of independent principalities.

The despots and oligarchs of the Italian city-states, together with Louis XI of France, Henry VII of England, and Ferdinand of Aragon, were tough, cynical, calculating rulers. In their ruthless push for power and strong governments, they subordinated morality to hard results. They preferred to be secure and feared rather than loved. They could not have read Machiavelli's *The Prince,* but their actions were in harmony with its ideas.

Some historians have called Louis XI (r. 1461–1483), Henry VII (r. 1485–1509), and Ferdinand and Isabella in Spain (r. 1474–1516) "new monarchs" because they invested kingship with a strong sense of royal authority and national purpose. They stressed that the monarchy was the one institution that linked all classes and peoples within definite territorial boundaries. They insisted on the respect and loyalty of all subjects and ruthlessly suppressed opposition and rebellion, especially from the nobility. And they loved the business of kingship and worked hard at it.

In other respects, however, the methods of these rulers, which varied from country to country, were not so new. They reasserted long-standing ideas and practices of strong monarchs in the Middle Ages. To advance their authority, they seized on the maxim of the Justinian *Code:* "What pleases the prince has the force of law." Like medieval rulers, Renaissance rulers tended to rely on middle-class civil servants. Using tax revenues, medieval rulers had built armies to crush feudal anarchy. Renaissance townspeople with commercial and business interests wanted a reduction of violence and usually they were willing to pay taxes in order to achieve it.

France

The Hundred Years' War left France badly divided, drastically depopulated, commercially ruined, and agriculturally weak. Nonetheless, the ruler whom Joan of Arc had seen crowned at Reims, Charles VII (r. 1422–1461), revived the monarchy and France. He seemed an unlikely person to do so. Frail, indecisive, and burdened with questions about his paternity (his father was deranged, his mother notoriously promiscuous), Charles VII nevertheless began France's long recovery.

Charles reorganized the royal council, giving increased influence to the middle-class men, and strengthened royal finances through such taxes as the *gabelle* (on salt) and the *taille* (on land). By establishing regular companies of cavalry and archers—recruited, paid, and inspected by the state—Charles created the first permanent royal army. In 1438 he published the Pragmatic Sanction of Bourges, giving the French crown major control over the appointment of bishops, and depriving the pope of French ecclesiastical revenues. The Pragmatic Sanction established the Gallican (or French) liberties because it affirmed the special rights of the French crown over the French church. Greater control over the church and the army helped to consolidate the authority of the French crown.

Charles's son Louis XI (r. 1461–1483), called the "Spider King" by his subjects because of his treacherous and cruel character, was very much a Renaissance prince. Facing the perpetual French problems of unification of the realm and reduction of feudal disorder, he saw money as the answer. Louis promoted new industries, such as silk weaving at Lyons and Tours, and entered into commercial treaties with other countries. The revenues raised through these economic activities and severe taxation were used to improve the army. With the army Louis stopped aristocratic brigandage and slowly cut into urban independence. He was also able to gain territory that furthered his goal of expanding royal authority and unifying the kingdom. Some scholars have credited Louis XI with laying the foundations for later French royal absolutism. Indeed, he worked tirelessly to remodel the government after the disorders of the fourteenth and early fifteenth centuries. In his reliance on finances supplied by the middle classes to fight the feudal nobility, Louis was thought to be typical of the new monarchs.

England

English society suffered severely from the disorders of the fifteenth century. The aristocracy dominated the government and indulged in mischievous violence at the local level. Population, decimated by the Black Death, continued to decline. Then between 1455 and 1471, supporters of the ducal houses of York and Lancaster waged civil war, commonly called the Wars of the Roses because the symbol of the Yorkists was a white rose and that of the Lancastrians a red one. The chronic disorder hurt trade, agriculture, and domestic industry, and the authority of the monarchy sank lower than it had been in centuries.

The Yorkist Edward IV (r. 1461–1483) began re-establishing domestic tranquillity. He defeated the Lancastrian forces and after 1471 began to reconstruct the monarchy and consolidate royal power. Henry VII (r. 1485–1509) of the Welsh

house of Tudor advanced the work of restoring royal prestige by crushing the power of the nobility and establishing order and law at the local level.

The Hundred Years' War had cost the nation dearly, and the money to finance it had been raised by Parliament, the arena where the nobility exerted its power. As long as the monarchy was dependent on the Lords and the Commons for revenue, the king had to call Parliament. Thus Edward IV, and subsequently the Tudors except for Henry VIII, conducted foreign policy by means of diplomacy and avoided expensive wars. Unlike the continental countries of Spain and France, England had no standing army or professional civil service bureacracy. The Tudors relied on the support of unpaid local justices of the peace—influential landowners in the shires—to handle the work of local government. From the royal point of view, they were an inexpensive method of government. Thus for a time the English monarchy did not depend on Parliament for money, and the Crown undercut that source of aristocratic influence.

Henry VII did summon several meetings of Parliament in the early years of his reign, primarily to confirm laws, but the center of royal authority while he was king was the royal council, which governed at the national level. The royal council handled any business the king put before it—executive, legislative, judicial. It also dealt with real or potential aristocratic threats through a judicial offshoot, the Court of Star Chamber, so called because of the stars painted on the ceiling of the room in which it met. The court applied principles of Roman law, a system that exalted the power of the Crown as the embodiment of the state. The court's methods were sometimes terrifying: evidence and proceedings were secret, torture could be applied, and juries were not called. These procedures ran directly counter to English common-law precedents, but they effectively reduced aristocratic troublemaking.

The Tudors won the support of the influential upper middle class because the Crown linked government policy with the interests of that class. A commercial or agricultural upper class fears and dislikes few things more than disorder and violence. Grave, secretive, cautious, and always thrifty, Henry VII promoted peace and social order, and the gentry did not object to arbitrary methods, like those used by the Court of Star Chamber, because the government had ended the long period of anarchy. At the same time both English exports of wool and the royal export tax on that wool steadily increased. When Henry VII died in 1509, he left a country at peace both domestically and internationally, a substantially augmented treasury, and the dignity and role of the royal majesty much enhanced.

Spain

Political development in Spain followed a pattern different from that of France and England. The central theme in the history of medieval Spain's separate kingdoms was disunity and plurality. Different languages, laws, and religious communities made for a rich cultural diversity shaped by Hispanic, Roman, Visigothic, Muslim, and Jewish traditions.

By the middle of the fifteenth century, the centuries-long *reconquista*—the attempts of the northern Christian kingdoms to control the entire peninsula—was nearing completion. The kingdoms of Castile and Aragon dominated weaker kingdoms, and with the exception of Granada, the Iberian Peninsula had been won for Christianity. The wedding in 1469 of the dynamic and aggressive Isabella, heiress of Castile, and the crafty and persistent Ferdinand, heir of Aragon, was the final major step in the unification and Christianization of Spain.

Ferdinand and Isabella pursued a common foreign policy. Under their rule Spain remained a loose confederation of separate states, but they determined to strengthen royal authority. To curb rebellious and warring aristocrats, they revived an old medieval institution. In the towns, popular groups called *hermandades,* or brotherhoods, were given the authority to act both as local police forces and as judicial tribunals. The hermandades repressed violence with such savage punishments that by 1498 they could be disbanded. The decisive step that Ferdinand and Isabella took to curb aristocratic power was the restructuring of the royal council. The king and queen appointed to the council only people of middle-class background; they rigorously excluded aristocrats and great territorial magnates. The council and various government boards recruited men trained in Roman law.

In the extension of royal authority and the consolidation of the territories of Spain, the church was the linchpin. Through a diplomatic alliance with the Spanish pope Alexander VI, the Spanish monarchs secured the right to appoint bishops in Spain and in the Hispanic territories in America. This power enabled the "Most Catholic Kings of Spain," a title that the pope granted to Ferdinand and Isabella, to establish, in effect, a national church.[29] Revenues from ecclesiastical estates provided the means to raise an army to continue the reconquista. The victorious entry of Ferdinand and Isabella into Granada on January 6, 1492, signaled the conclusion of eight centuries of Spanish struggle against the Arabs in southern Spain. In 1512 Ferdinand conquered Navarre in the north.

Although the Muslims had been defeated, there still remained a sizable and, in the view of the Catholic sovereigns, potentially dangerous minority, the Jews. Since ancient times, Christian governments had usually suppressed religious faiths that differed from the official state religion, considering them politically dangerous. France and England had expelled their Jewish populations in the Middle Ages, but in Spain Jews had been tolerated and had played a decisive role in the economic and intellectual life of the several Spanish kingdoms. Then, in the late fourteenth century, anti-Semitic riots and pogroms led many Spanish Jews to convert to Christianity; such people were called *conversos.*

By the middle of the fifteenth century, many conversos held high positions in Spanish society as financiers, physicians, merchants, tax collectors, and even officials of the church hierarchy. Numbering perhaps 200,000 in a total population of about 7.5 million, Jews exercised an influence quite disproportionate to their numbers. Aristocratic grandees who borrowed heavily from Jews resented their financial dependence, and churchmen questioned the sincerity of Jewish conversions. At first, Isabella and Ferdinand continued the policy of royal toleration—Ferdinand himself had inherited Jewish blood from his mother. But many conversos apparently reverted to the faith of their ancestors, prompting Ferdinand and Isabella in 1478 to secure Rome's permission to revive the Inquisition, a medieval judicial procedure for the punishment of heretics.

Although the Inquisition was a religious institution established to safeguard the Catholic faith, in Spain it was controlled by the Crown and served primarily as a political unifying force. Because the Spanish Inquisition commonly applied torture to extract confessions, first from lapsed conversos, then from Muslims, and later from Protestants, it

van Schwanenburgh: The Spinners   In the late sixteenth century, the prosperity of Leyden in Holland rested on the textile industry, which in turn depended on the import of merino wool from Spain. In this lush scene three large spinning wheels are operated simultaneously. Women composed 30 percent of the work force but earned much less than men. *(Source: Stedelijk Museum, "De Lakenhal," Leiden, Holland)*

gained a notorious reputation. Thus the word *inquisition,* meaning "any judicial inquiry conducted with ruthless severity," came into the English language.

In 1492, Isabella and Ferdinand took a further dire and drastic step against backsliding conversos. They issued an edict expelling all practicing Jews from Spain. Of the community of perhaps 200,000 Jews, 150,000 fled. (Efforts were made, through last-minute conversions, to retain good Jewish physicians.) Absolute religious orthodoxy and purity of blood (untainted by Jews or Muslims) became the theoretical foundation of the Spanish national state.

The diplomacy of the Catholic rulers of Spain achieved a success they never anticipated. Partly out of hatred for the French and partly to gain international recognition for their new dynasty, Ferdinand and Isabella in 1496 married their second daughter, Joanna, heiress to Castile, to the archduke Philip, heir through his mother to the Burgundian Netherlands and through his father to the Holy Roman Empire.

Germany and the Habsburg Dynasty

The marriage in 1477 of Maximilian I of the house of Habsburg and Mary of Burgundy was a decisive event in early modern European history. Burgundy consisted of two parts: the French duchy with its capital at Dijon, and the Burgundian Netherlands with its capital at Brussels. Through this union with the rich and powerful duchy of Burgundy, the Austrian House of Habsburg, the strongest ruling family in the empire, started to become an international power.

In the fifteenth and sixteenth centuries, as in the Middle Ages, relations among states continued to be greatly affected by the connections of royal families. Marriage often determined the diplomatic status of states. The Habsburg-Burgundian marriage angered the French, who considered Burgundy part of French territory. Within the empire, German principalities that resented Austria's preeminence began to see that they shared interests with France. The marriage of Maximilian and Mary inaugurated centuries of conflict between the Austrian House of Habsburg and the kings of France. Germany was to be the chief arena of the struggle.

"Other nations wage war; you, Austria, marry." Historians dispute the origins of the adage, but no one questions its accuracy. The heir of Mary and Maximilian, Philip of Burgundy, married Joanna of Castile, daughter of Ferdinand and Isabella of Spain. Philip and Joanna's son Charles V (1500–1558) fell heir to a vast conglomeration of territories. Through a series of accidents and unexpected deaths, Charles inherited Spain from his mother, together with her possessions in the Americas and the Spanish dominions in Italy, Sicily, Sardinia, and Naples. From his father he inherited the Habsburg lands in Austria, southern Germany, the Low Countries, and Franche-Comté in east-central France.

Charles's inheritance was an incredibly diverse collection of states and peoples, each governed in a different manner and held together only by the person of the emperor (Map 15.1). Charles's Italian adviser, the grand chancellor Gattinara, told the young ruler: "God has set you on the path toward world monarchy." Charles not only believed this; he was convinced that it was his duty to maintain the political and religious unity of Western Christendom. In this respect Charles V was the last medieval emperor.

Charles needed and in 1519 secured the imperial title from the electors. Forward-thinking Germans proposed government reforms. They urged placing the administration in the hands of an imperial council whose president, the emperor's appointee, would have ultimate executive power. They also recommended reforms of the imperial finances, the army, and the judiciary. Such ideas did not interest the young emperor at all. When he finally arrived in Germany from Spain and opened his first Diet (assembly of the estates of the empire) at Worms in January 1521, he naively announced that "the empire from of old has had not many masters, but one, and it is our intention to be that one." Charles went on to say that he was to be treated as of greater account than his predecessors because he was more powerful than they had been. In view of the long history of aristocratic power in the Holy Roman Empire, Charles's notions were pure fantasy.

Charles continued the Burgundian policy of his grandfather Maximilian. German revenues and German troops were subordinated to the needs of other parts of the empire, first Burgundy and then Spain. Habsburg international interests came before the need for reform in Germany. Two years before the electors chose as emperor the nineteen-year-old Charles, Martin Luther had launched a movement to reform the church.

THE CONDITION OF THE CHURCH (CA 1400–1517)

The papal conflict with the German emperor Frederick II in the thirteenth century, followed by the Babylonian Captivity and then the Great Schism (see pages 427–428), badly damaged the prestige of church leaders. In the fourteenth and fifteenth centuries, leaders of the conciliar movement reflected educated public opinion when they called for the reform of the church "in head and members" (see page 428). The humanists of Italy and the Christian humanists of northern Europe denounced corruption in the church. As Machiavelli put it, "We Italians are irreligious and corrupt above others, because the Church and her representatives set us the worst example."[30] In *The Praise of Folly,* Erasmus condemned the absurd superstitions of the parish clergy and the excessive rituals of the monks. The records of episcopal visitations of parishes, civil court records, and even such literary masterpieces as Chaucer's *Canterbury Tales* and Boccaccio's *The Decameron* tend to confirm the perceptions of corruption.

Signs of Disorder

In the early sixteenth century, critics of the church concentrated their attacks on three disorders: cleri-

MAP 15.1 The European Empire of Charles V   Charles V exercised theoretical jurisdiction over more territory than anyone since Charlemagne. This map does not show his Latin American and Asian possessions.

cal immorality, clerical ignorance, and clerical pluralism. There was little pressure for doctrinal change; the emphasis was on moral and administrative reform.

Since the fourth century, church law had required candidates for the priesthood to accept absolute celibacy. The requirement had always been difficult to enforce. Many priests, especially those ministering to country people, had concubines, and reports of neglect of the rule of celibacy were common. Immorality, of course, included more than sexual transgressions. Clerical drunkenness, gambling, and indulgence in fancy dress were frequent charges. There is no way of knowing how many priests were guilty of such behavior. But because such conduct was so much at odds with the church's rules and moral standards, it scandalized the educated faithful.

The bishops enforced regulations regarding the education of priests casually. As a result, standards for ordination were shockingly low. The evidence points consistently to the low quality of the Italian clergy. In northern Europe—in England, for ex- ample—recent research shows an improvement in clerical educational standards in the early sixteenth century. Nevertheless, parish priests throughout Europe were not as educated as the educated laity. Predictably, Christian humanists, with their con- cern for learning, condemned the ignorance or low educational level of the clergy. Many priests could barely read and write, and critics laughed at the il- literate priest mumbling Latin words to the Mass that he could not understand.

Pluralism and absenteeism constituted the third major abuse. Many clerics, especially higher eccle- siastics, held several *benefices,* or offices, simultane- ously but seldom visited them, let alone performed the spiritual responsibilities those offices entailed.

The Folly of Indulgences This woodcut viciously satirizes the church's sale of indulgences. With one foot in the holy water symboliz- ing the rite of purification (Psalm 50) and the other foot resting on the coins paid for indulgences, the church, portrayed as a rapacious ea- gle with its right hand stretched out for offerings, writes out an indul- gence with excrement—which rep- resents its worth. Fools with a false sense of security sit in the animal's gaping mouth, representing hell, to which a devil delivers the pope wear- ing a three-tiered crown and hold- ing the keys to heaven originally given to Saint Peter. (*Source: Kunst- sammlungen der Veste Coburg*)

Instead, they collected revenues from each benefice and paid a poor priest a fraction of the income to fulfill the spiritual duties of a particular local church. The French king Louis XII's diplomat Antoine du Prat is perhaps the most notorious example of absenteeism. He was archbishop of Sens, but the first time he entered his cathedral was in his own funeral procession.

Critics condemned pluralism, absenteeism, and the way money seemed to change hands when a bishop entered into his office. Although royal governments strengthened their positions and consolidated their territories in the fifteenth and sixteenth centuries, rulers lacked sufficient revenues to pay and reward able civil servants. The Christian church, with its dioceses and abbeys, possessed a large proportion of the wealth of the countries of Europe. What better way for a ruler to reward government officials, who were usually clerics, than with bishoprics and other high church offices? The practice was sanctioned by centuries of tradition. Thus churchmen who served as royal councilors, diplomats, treasury officials, chancellors, viceroys, and judges were paid by the church for their services to the state. It is astonishing that so many conscientiously tried to carry out their religious duties on top of their public burdens.

In most countries except England, members of the nobility occupied the highest church positions. The spectacle of proud, aristocratic prelates living in magnificent splendor contrasted very unfavorably with the simple fishermen who were Christ's disciples. Nor did the popes of the period 1450 to 1550 set much of an example. They lived like secular Renaissance princes, supporting artists and undertaking building projects, often making the papal court a model of luxury and scandal. Some popes used papal power and wealth to advance the material interests of their own families.

The court of the Spanish pope Rodrigo Borgia, Alexander VI (r. 1492–1503), who publicly acknowledged his mistress and children, reached new heights of impropriety. Because of the prevalence of intrigue, sexual promiscuity, and supposed poisonings, the name Borgia became a synonym for moral corruption. Pope Julius II (r. 1503–1513) donned military armor and personally led papal troops against the French invaders of Italy in 1506. After him, Giovanni de' Medici, the son of Lorenzo de' Medici, carried on as Pope Leo X (r. 1513–1521) the Medicean tradition of being a great patron of the arts.

Signs of Vitality

Calls for reform testify to the spiritual vitality of the church as well as to its problems. In the late fifteenth and early sixteenth centuries, both individuals and groups within the church were working actively for reform. In Spain, for example, Cardinal Francisco Jiménez (1436–1517) visited religious houses, encouraged the monks and friars to obey their rules and constitutions, and set high standards for the training of the diocesan clergy.

In Holland, beginning in the late fourteenth century, a group of pious lay people called Brethren of the Common Life sought to make religion a personal, inner experience. They lived in stark simplicity while daily carrying out the Gospel teaching of feeding the hungry, clothing the naked, and visiting the sick. The Brethren also taught in local schools to prepare devout candidates for the priesthood and the monastic life. The spirituality of the Brethren of the Common Life found its finest expression in the classic *The Imitation of Christ* by Thomas à Kempis, which urges Christians to take Christ as their model and seek perfection in a simple way of life. As Protestants would do later, the Brethren stressed the centrality of Scripture in the spiritual life.[31] In the mid-fifteenth century, the movement had houses in the Netherlands, in central Germany, and in the Rhineland; it was a true religious revival.

If external religious observances are a measure of depth of heartfelt conviction, Europeans in the early sixteenth century remained deeply pious and loyal to the Roman Catholic church. Villagers participated in processions honoring the local saints. Middle-class people made pilgrimages to the great shrines such as Saint Peter's in Rome. The upper classes continued to remember the church in their wills.

The papacy also expressed concern for reform. Pope Julius II summoned an ecumenical, or universal, council, which met in the church of Saint John Lateran in Rome from 1512 to 1517. Most of the bishops were Italian and did not represent a broad cross section of international opinion, so the designation *ecumenical* was not really appropriate. Nevertheless, the bishops and theologians who attended the Lateran Council strove earnestly to reform the church. The council recommended higher standards for education of the clergy and instruction of the common people. The bishops placed the responsibility for eliminating

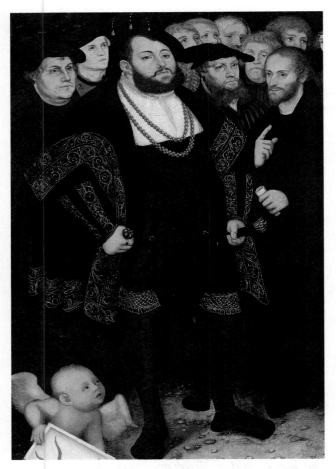

Lucas Cranach the Younger: Luther and the Wittenberg Reformers The massive figure of John Frederick, elector of Saxony, who protected and supported Luther, dominates this group portrait. Luther is on the far left, his associate Philip Melancthon far right in the front. Luther's face shows a quiet determination. *(Source: The Toledo Museum of Art, Toledo, Ohio; Gift of Edward Drummond Libbey)*

bureaucratic corruption squarely on the papacy and suggested significant doctrinal reforms. But many obstacles stood in the way of ecclesiastical change. Nor did the actions of an obscure German friar immediately force the issue.

MARTIN LUTHER AND THE BIRTH OF PROTESTANTISM

As a result of a personal religious struggle, a German Augustinian friar, Martin Luther (1483–1546) launched the Protestant Reformation of the

sixteenth century. Luther articulated the widespread desire for reform of the Christian church and the deep yearning for salvation that were typical of his time.

Martin Luther was born at Eisleben in Saxony, the second son of a copper miner who later became a mine owner. At considerable sacrifice, his father sent him to school and then to the University of Erfurt. Hans Luther intended his son to study law and have a legal career, which for centuries had been the steppingstone to public office and material success. Badly frightened during a thunderstorm, however, young Luther vowed to become a friar. Without consulting his father, he entered a monastery at Erfurt in 1505. Luther was ordained a priest in 1507 and after additional study earned the doctorate of theology. From 1512 until his death, he served as professor of Scripture at the new University of Wittenberg.

Martin Luther was exceedingly scrupulous in his monastic observances and was devoted to prayer, penances, and fasting; but the doubts and conflicts that trouble any sensitive young person who has just taken a grave step were especially intense in young Luther. He had terrible anxieties about sin, and he worried continually about his salvation. Luther intensified his monastic observances but still found no peace of mind.

Luther's wise and kindly confessor, Staupitz, directed him to the study of Saint Paul's letters. Gradually, Luther arrived at a new understanding of the Pauline letters and of all Christian doctrine. He came to believe that salvation comes not through external observances and penances but through a simple faith in Christ. Faith is the means by which God sends humanity his grace, and faith is a free gift that cannot be earned.

The Ninety-five Theses

An incident illustrative of the condition of the church in the early sixteenth century propelled Martin Luther onto the stage of history and brought about the Reformation in Germany. The University of Wittenberg lay within the archdiocese of Magdeburg. The archbishop of Magdeburg, Albert, held two other high ecclesiastical offices. To hold all three offices simultaneously—blatant pluralism—required papal dispensation. Archbishop Albert borrowed money from the Fuggers, a wealthy banking family of Augsburg, to pay Pope Leo X for the dispensation (the pope wanted the money to complete work on Saint Peter's Basilica). Leo X then authorized Archbishop Albert to sell indulgences in Germany to repay the Fuggers.

Medici

Wittenberg was in the political jurisdiction of the elector Frederick of Saxony. When Frederick forbade the sale of indulgences within his duchy, people of Wittenberg, including some of Professor Luther's students, streamed across the border from Saxony into Jütenborg in Thuringia to buy them.

What exactly was an *indulgence*? According to Catholic theology, individuals who sin alienate themselves from God and his love. In order to be reconciled to God, the sinner must confess his or her sins to a priest and do the penance that the priest assigns. The doctrine of indulgence rested on three principles. First, God is merciful, but he is also just. Second, Christ and the saints, through their infinite virtue, established a "treasury of merits" on which the church, because of its special relationship with Christ and the saints, can draw. Third, the church has the authority to grant sinners the spiritual benefits of those merits. Originally an indulgence was a remission of the temporal (priest-imposed) penalties for sin. Beginning in the twelfth century, the papacy and bishops had given Crusaders such indulgences. By the later Middle Ages people widely believed that an indulgence secured total remission of penalties for sin—on earth or in purgatory—and ensured swift entry into heaven.

Archbishop Albert hired the Dominican friar John Tetzel to sell the indulgences. Tetzel mounted an advertising blitz. One of his slogans—"As soon as coin in coffer rings, the soul from purgatory springs"—brought phenomenal success. Men and women bought indulgences not only for themselves but for deceased parents, relatives, or friends.

Luther was severely troubled that ignorant people believed they had no further need for repentance once they had purchased an indulgence. Thus, according to historical tradition, in the academic fashion of the times, on the eve of All Saints' Day (October 31), 1517, he attached to the door of the church at Wittenberg Castle a list of ninety-five theses (or propositions) on indulgences. By this act Luther intended only to start a theological discussion of the subject and to defend the theses publicly.

Luther's theses were soon translated from Latin into German, printed, and read throughout the empire. Immediately, broad theological issues were raised. When questioned, Luther rested his fundamental argument on the principle that there was no biblical basis for indulgences. But, replied Luther's opponents, to deny the legality of indulgences was to deny the authority of the pope who had authorized them. The issue was drawn: where did authority lie in the Christian church?

The papacy responded with a letter condemning some of Luther's propositions, ordering that his books be burned, and giving him two months to recant or be excommunicated. Luther retaliated by publicly burning the letter. By January 3, 1521, when the excommunication was supposed to become final, the controversy involved more than theological issues. The papal legate wrote, "All Germany is in revolution. Nine-tenths shout 'Luther' as their warcry; and the other tenth cares nothing about Luther, and cries 'Death to the court of Rome.'"[32]

In this highly charged atmosphere the twenty-one-year-old emperor Charles V held his first Diet at Worms and summoned Luther to appear before it. When ordered to recant, Luther replied in language that rang all over Europe:

Unless I am convinced by the evidence of Scripture or by plain reason—for I do not accept the authority of the Pope or the councils alone, since it is established that they have often erred and contradicted themselves—I am bound by the Scriptures I have cited and my conscience is captive to the Word of God. I cannot and will not recant anything, for it is neither safe nor right to go against conscience. God help me. Amen.[33]

The emperor declared Luther an outlaw of the empire and denied him legal protection. Duke Frederick of Saxony, however, protected him.

Protestant Thought

Between 1520 and 1530, Luther worked out the basic theological tenets that became the articles of faith for his new church and subsequently for all Protestant groups. At first the word *Protestant* meant "Lutheran," but with the appearance of many protesting sects it became a general term applied to all non-Catholic Christians. Ernst Troeltsch, a German student of the sociology of religion, has defined *Protestantism* as a "modification of Catholicism, in which the Catholic formulation of questions was retained, while a different answer was given to them." Luther provided new answers to four old, basic theological issues.[34]

First, how is a person to be saved? Traditional Catholic teaching held that salvation was achieved by both faith *and* good works. Luther held that salvation comes by faith alone. Women and men are saved, said Luther, by the arbitrary decision of God, irrespective of good works or the sacraments. God, not people, initiates salvation.

Second, where does religious authority reside? Christian doctrine had long maintained that authority rests both in the Bible and in the traditional teaching of the church. Luther maintained that authority rests in the Word of God as revealed in the Bible alone and as interpreted by an individual's conscience. He urged that each person read and reflect on the Scriptures.

Third, what is the church? Medieval churchmen had tended to identify the church with the clergy. Luther re-emphasized the Catholic teaching that the church consists of the entire community of Christian believers.

Finally, what is the highest form of Christian life? The medieval church had stressed the superiority of the monastic and religious life over the secular. Luther argued that all vocations, whether ecclesiastical or secular, have equal merit and that every person should serve God according to his or her individual calling. Protestantism, in sum, represented a reformulation of the Christian heritage.

The Social Impact of Luther's Beliefs

As early as 1521, Luther had a vast following. By the time of his death in 1546, people of all social classes had become Lutheran. What was the immense appeal of Luther's religious ideas?

Historical research on the German towns has shown that two significant late medieval developments prepared the way for Luther's ideas. First, since the fifteenth century, city governments had expressed resentment at clerical privileges and immunities. Religious orders frequently held large amounts of urban property, but priests, monks, and nuns paid no taxes and were exempt from civic responsibilities such as defending the city. City governments were determined to integrate the clergy into civic life by reducing their privileges and giving them public responsibilities.

Second, critics of the late medieval church, especially informed and intelligent townspeople, had condemned the irregularity and poor quality of sermons. As a result, prosperous burghers in many towns had established preacherships. Preachers were men of superior education who were required to deliver about a hundred sermons a year, each lasting about forty-five minutes. Luther's ideas attracted many preachers, and in Stuttgart, Reutlingen, and other towns, preachers became Protestant

Hans Holbein the Younger: Christ as the Man of Sorrows   The scriptural basis of this concept is Isaiah 53:3–5: "He was pierced for our offenses, crushed by our sins. Upon him was the chastisement that makes us whole; by his stripes we were healed." Using a theme characteristic of early-sixteenth-century German piety, and placing the subject within a Renaissance architectural structure, Holbein produced this devotional painting in 1520 for the private use of the donor. *(Source: Öffentliche Kunstsammlung Basel)*

leaders. Preacherships also encouraged the Protestant form of worship, in which the sermon, not the Eucharist, was the central part of the service.[35]

In the countryside the attraction of the German peasants to Lutheran beliefs was almost predictable. Luther himself came from a peasant background and admired the peasants' ceaseless toil. Peasants respected Luther's defiance of church authority. Moreover, they thrilled to the words Luther used in his treatise *On Christian Liberty* (1520): "A Christian man is the most free lord of all and subject to none." Taken out of context, these words easily stirred social unrest.

Fifteenth-century Germany had witnessed several peasant revolts. In the early sixteenth century, the economic condition of the peasantry varied from place to place but was generally worse than it had been in the fifteenth century and was deteriorating. Crop failures in 1523 and 1524 aggravated an explosive situation. In 1525 representatives of the Swabian peasants met at the city of Memmingen and drew up twelve articles that expressed their grievances. The peasants complained that nobles had seized village common lands, which traditionally had been used by all; that nobles had imposed new rents and services on the peasants working properties; and that nobles had forced poor peasants to pay unjust death duties in the form of their best horses or cows. Wealthy, socially mobile peasants especially resented these burdens, which, they maintained, were new.[36] The peasants believed their demands conformed to Scripture and cited Luther as a theologian who could prove that they did.

Luther wanted to prevent rebellion. At first he sided with the peasants and in his tract *An Admonition to Peace* blasted the nobles:

We have no one on earth to thank for this mischievous rebellion, except you lords and princes, especially you blind bishops and mad priests and monks. . . . In your government you do nothing but flay and rob your subjects in order that you may lead a life of splendor and pride, until the poor common folk can bear it no longer.[37]

But nothing justified the use of armed force, he warned: "The fact that rulers are unjust and wicked does not excuse tumult and rebellion; to punish wickedness does not belong to everybody, but to the worldly rulers who bear the sword."[38] As for biblical support for the peasants' demands,

he maintained that Scripture had nothing to do with earthly justice or material gain.

Massive revolts first broke out near the Swiss frontier and then swept through Swabia, Thuringia, the Rhineland, and Saxony. The crowds' slogans came directly from Luther's writings. "God's righteousness" and the "Word of God" were invoked in the effort to secure social and economic justice. The peasants who expected Luther's support were soon disillusioned. He had written of the "freedom" of the Christian, but he had meant the freedom to obey the Word of God, for in sin men and women lose their freedom and break their relationship with God. To Luther, freedom meant independence from the authority of the Roman church; it did *not* mean opposition to legally established secular powers. Firmly convinced that rebellion hastened the end of civilized society, he wrote a tract *Against the Murderous, Thieving Hordes of the Peasants:* "Let everyone who can smite, slay, and stab [the peasants], secretly and openly, remembering that nothing can be more poisonous, hurtful or devilish than a rebel."[39] The nobility ferociously crushed the revolt. Historians estimate that over seventy-five thousand peasants were killed in 1525.

Luther took literally these words in Saint Paul's Letter to the Romans: "Let every soul be subject to the higher powers. For there is no power but of God: the powers that be are established by God. Whosoever resists the power, resists the ordinance of God: and they that resist shall receive to themselves damnation."[40] As it developed, Lutheran theology exalted the state, subordinated the church to the state, and everywhere championed "the powers that be." The revolt of 1525 strengthened the authority of lay rulers. Peasant economic conditions, however, moderately improved. For example, in many parts of Germany, enclosed fields, meadows, and forests were returned to common use.

Like the peasants, educated people and humanists were much attracted by Luther's words. He advocated a simpler, personal religion based on faith and the Scriptures, a return to the spirit of the early church, the abolition of elaborate ceremonial—precisely the reforms the northern humanists had been calling for. Ulrich Zwingli (1484–1531), for example, a humanist of Zurich, was strongly influenced by Luther's bold stand. It stimulated Zwingli's reforms in the Swiss city of Zurich and later in Bern.

Luther's linguistic skill, together with his translation of the New Testament in 1523, led to the acceptance of his dialect of German as the standard version of German. His insistence that everyone should read and reflect on the Scriptures attracted the literate and thoughtful middle classes partly because he appealed to their intelligence. Moreover, the business classes, preoccupied with making money, envied the church's wealth, disapproved of the luxurious lifestyle of some churchmen, and resented tithes and ecclesiastical taxation. Luther's doctrines of salvation by faith and the priesthood of all believers not only raised the religious status of the commercial classes but protected their pocketbooks as well.

Hymns, psalms, and Luther's two catechisms (1529)—compendiums of basic religious knowledge—also show the power of language in spreading the ideals of the Reformation. The reformers knew "that rhyme, meter, and melodies could forcefully impress minds and affect sensibilities." Lutheran hymns such as "A Mighty Fortress Is Our God" expressed deep feelings, were easily remembered, and imprinted on the mind central points of doctrine. Luther's *Larger Catechism* contained brief sermons on the main articles of faith; his *Shorter Catechism* gave concise explanations of doctrine in question-and-answer form. Both catechisms stressed the importance of the Ten Commandments, the Lord's Prayer, the Apostle's Creed, and the sacraments for the believing Christian. Though originally intended for the instruction of pastors, these catechisms became powerful tools for the indoctrination of men and women of all ages, especially the young.[41]

What appeal did Luther's message have for women? Luther's argument that all vocations have equal merit in the sight of God gave dignity to those who performed ordinary, routine, domestic tasks. The abolition of monasticism in Protestant territories led to the exaltation of the home, which Luther and other reformers stressed as the special domain of the wife. The Christian home, in contrast to the place of business, became the place for the exercise of the gentler virtues—love, tenderness, reconciliation, the carrying of one another's burdens. The Protestant abolition of private confession to a priest freed women from embarrassing explorations of their sexual lives. Protestants established schools where girls, as well as boys, became literate in the catechism and the Bible. The reformers stressed marriage as the cure for clerical concupiscence. Protestantism thus proved attractive to the many women who had been priests' concubines and mistresses: they became legal and honorable wives.[42]

For his time, Luther held enlightened views on matters of sexuality and marriage. He wrote to a young man, "Dear lad, be not ashamed that you desire a girl, nor you my maid, the boy. Just let it lead you into matrimony and not into promiscuity, and it is no more cause for shame than eating and drinking."[43] Luther was confident that God took delight in the sexual act and denied that original sin affected the goodness of creation. He believed, however, that marriage was a woman's career. A student recorded Luther as saying, early in his public ministry, "Let them bear children until they are dead of it; that is what they are for." A happy marriage to the former nun Katharine von Bora mellowed him, and another student later quoted him as saying, "Next to God's Word there is no more precious treasure than holy matrimony. God's highest gift on earth is a pious, cheerful, God-fearing, home-keeping wife, with whom you may live peacefully, to whom you may entrust your goods, and body and life."[44] Though Luther deeply loved his "dear Katie," he believed that women's principal concerns were children, the kitchen, and the church.

�֍ GERMANY AND THE PROTESTANT REFORMATION

The history of the Holy Roman Empire in the later Middle Ages is a story of dissension, disintegration, and debility. Unlike Spain, France, and England, the empire lacked a strong central power. In 1356 the Golden Bull legalized what had long existed—government by an aristocratic federation. Each of seven electors gained virtual sovereignty in his own territory. The agreement ended disputed elections in the empire; it also reduced the central authority of the Holy Roman emperor. The empire was characterized by weak borders, localism, and chronic disorder. The nobility strengthened their territories, while imperial power declined.

The Political Impact of Luther's Beliefs

In the sixteenth century, the practice of religion remained a public matter. Everyone participated in the religious life of the community, just as almost everyone shared in the local agricultural work.

Peasants Sack the Abbey of Weissenau   Convinced that the monks lived idle, luxurious lives on money squeezed from the poor, peasants sacked the abbeys during the great revolt of 1525. *(Source: Château de Waldburg, Archives/Schneiders/Artephot)*

Whatever spiritual convictions individuals held in the privacy of their consciences, the emperor, king, prince, magistrate, or other civil authority determined the official form of religious practice within his jurisdiction. Almost everyone believed that the presence of a faith different from that of the majority represented a political threat to the security of the state. Only a tiny minority, and certainly none of the princes, believed in religious liberty.

Against this background, the religious storm launched by Martin Luther swept across Germany. Several elements in his religious reformation stirred patriotic feelings. Anti-Roman sentiment ran high. Humanists lent eloquent intellectual support. And Luther's translation of the New Testament into German evoked national pride.

For decades devout lay people and churchmen had called on the German princes to reform the church. In 1520 Luther took up the cry in his *Appeal to the Christian Nobility of the German Nation.* Unless the princes destroyed papal power in Germany, Luther argued, reform was impossible. He urged the princes to confiscate ecclesiastical wealth and to abolish indulgences, dispensations, pardons, and clerical celibacy. He told them that it was their public duty to bring about the moral reform of the church. Luther based his argument in part on the papacy's financial exploitation of Germany:

How comes it that we Germans must put up with such robbery and such extortion of our property at the hands of the pope? Why do we Germans let them make such fools and apes of us? It would all be more bearable if in this way they only stole our property; but they lay waste the churches and rob Christ's sheep of their pious shepherds, and destroy the worship and the Word of God.[45]

These words fell on welcome ears and itchy fingers. Luther's appeal to German patriotism gained him strong support, and national feeling influenced many princes otherwise confused by or indifferent to the complexities of the religious issues.

The church in Germany possessed great wealth. And, unlike other countries, Germany had no strong central government to check the flow of gold to Rome. Rejection of Roman Catholicism and adoption of Protestantism would mean the legal confiscation of lush farmlands, rich monasteries, and wealthy shrines. Some German princes were sincerely attracted to Lutheranism, but many civil authorities realized that they had a great deal to gain by embracing the new faith. A steady stream of duchies, margraviates, free cities, and bishoprics did so and secularized church property. The decision reached at Worms in 1521 to condemn Luther and his teaching was not enforced because the German princes did not want to enforce it.

Many princes used the religious issue to extend their financial and political independence. The results were unfortunate for the improvement of German government. The Protestant movement ultimately proved a political disaster for Germany.

Charles V must share blame with the German princes for the disintegration of imperial authority in the empire. He neither understood nor took an interest in the constitutional problems of Germany, and he lacked the material resources to oppose Protestantism effectively there. Throughout his reign he was preoccupied with his Flemish, Spanish, Italian, and American territories. Moreover, the Turkish threat prevented him from acting effectively against the Protestants; Charles's brother Ferdinand needed Protestant support against the Turks who besieged Vienna in 1529.

Five times between 1521 and 1555, Charles V went to war with the Valois kings of France. The issue each time was the Habsburg lands acquired by the marriage of Maximilian and Mary of Burgundy. Much of the fighting occurred in Germany. The cornerstone of French foreign policy in the sixteenth and seventeenth centuries was the desire to keep the German states divided. Thus Europe witnessed the paradox of the Catholic king of France supporting the Lutheran princes in their challenge to his fellow Catholic, Charles V. Habsburg-Valois Wars advanced the cause of Protestantism and promoted the political fragmentation of the German empire.

Finally, in 1555, Charles agreed to the Peace of Augsburg, which, in accepting the status quo, officially recognized Lutheranism. Each prince was permitted to determine the religion of his territory. Most of northern and central Germany became Lutheran; the south remained Roman Catholic. There was no freedom of religion, however.

Princes or town councils established state churches to which all subjects of the area had to belong. Dissidents, whether Lutheran or Catholic, had to convert or leave. The political difficulties Germany inherited from the Middle Ages had been compounded by the religious crisis of the sixteenth century.

THE GROWTH OF THE PROTESTANT REFORMATION

By 1555 much of northern Europe had broken with the Roman Catholic church. All of Scandinavia, England (except during the reign of Mary Tudor), Scotland, and large parts of Switzerland, Germany, and France had rejected the religious authority of Rome and adopted new faiths. Because a common religious faith had been the one element uniting all of Europe for almost a thousand years, the fragmentation of belief led to profound changes in European life and society. The most significant new form of Protestantism was Calvinism, of which the Peace of Augsburg had made no mention at all.

Calvinism

In 1509, while Luther was studying for the doctorate at Wittenberg, John Calvin (1509–1564) was born in Noyon in northwestern France. Luther inadvertently launched the Protestant Reformation. Calvin, however, had the greater impact on future generations. In 1533 he experienced a religious crisis, as a result of which he converted to Protestantism. His theological writings profoundly influenced the social thought and attitudes of Europeans and English-speaking peoples all over the world, especially in Canada and the United States.

Convinced that God selects certain people to do his work, Calvin believed that God had specifically called him to reform the church. Accordingly, he accepted an invitation to assist in the reformation of the city of Geneva. There, beginning in 1541, Calvin worked assiduously to establish a Christian society ruled by God through civil magistrates and reformed ministers. Geneva, "a city that was a Church," became the model of a Christian community for sixteenth-century Protestant reformers.

To understand Calvin's Geneva, it is necessary to understand Calvin's ideas. These he embodied in *The Institutes of the Christian Religion,* first published in 1536 and definitively issued in 1559. The cornerstone of Calvin's theology was his belief in the absolute sovereignty and omnipotence of God and the total weakness of humanity. Before the infinite power of God, he asserted, men and women are as insignificant as grains of sand.

Calvin did not ascribe free will to human beings, because that would detract from the sovereignty of God. Men and women cannot actively work to achieve salvation; rather, God in his infinite wisdom decided at the beginning of time who would be saved and who damned. This viewpoint constitutes the theological principle called *predestination:*

Predestination we call the eternal decree of God, by which he has determined in himself, what he would have become of every individual of mankind. . . . God has once for all determined, both whom he would admit to salvation, and whom he would condemn to destruction. We affirm that this counsel, as far as concerns the elect, is founded on his gratuitous mercy, totally irrespective of human merit; but that to those whom he devotes to condemnation, the gate of life is closed by a just and irreprehensible, but incomprehensible, judgment. How exceedingly presumptuous it is only to inquire into the causes of the Divine will; which is in fact, and is justly entitled to be, the cause of everything that exists. . . . For the will of God is the highest justice; so that what he wills must be considered just, for this very reason, because he wills it.[46]

Many people have found the doctrine of predestination, which dates back to Saint Augustine and Saint Paul, a pessimistic view of the nature of God, who, they feel, revealed himself in the Old and New Testaments as merciful as well as just. But "this terrible decree," as even Calvin called it, did not lead to pessimism or fatalism. Rather, the Calvinist believed in the redemptive work of Christ and was confident that God had elected (saved) him or her. Predestination served as an energizing dynamic, forcing a person to undergo hardships in the constant struggle against evil.

Calvin aroused Genevans to a high standard of morality. Using his sermons and a program of religious education, God's laws and man's were enforced in Geneva. Using his *Genevan Catechism,* published in 1541, children and adults memorized set questions and answers and acquired a summary of their faith and a guide for daily living. Calvin's sermons and his *Catechism* gave a whole generation of Genevans thorough instruction in the reformed religion.[47]

In the reformation of the city, the Genevan Consistory also exercised a powerful role. This body consisted of twelve laymen, plus the Company of Pastors, of which Calvin was the permanent moderator (presider). The duties of the Consistory were "to keep watch over every man's life [and] to admonish amiably those whom they see leading a disorderly life." Calvin emphasized that the Consistory's activities should be thorough and "its eyes may be everywhere," but corrections were only "medicine to turn sinners to the Lord."[48]

Although all municipal governments in early modern Europe regulated citizens' conduct, none did so with the severity of Geneva's Consistory under Calvin's leadership. Nor did it make any distinction between what we would consider crimes against society and simple unchristian conduct. The Consistory investigated and punished absence from sermons, criticism of ministers, dancing, playing cards, family quarrels, and heavy drinking. The civil authorities handled serious crimes and heresy and, with the Consistory's approval, sometimes used torture to extract confessions. Between 1542 and 1546 alone seventy-six persons were banished from Geneva and fifty-eight executed for heresy, adultery, blasphemy, and witchcraft.

Calvin reserved his harshest condemnation for religious dissenters, declaring them "dogs and swine":

God makes plain that the false prophet is to be stoned without mercy. We are to crush beneath our heel all affections of nature when His honor is concerned. The father should not spare his child, nor brother his brother, nor husband his own wife or the friend who is dearer to him than life. No human relationship is more than animal unless it be grounded in God.[49]

Calvin translated his words into action. He made an example of the Spanish humanist Michael Servetus, who, persecuted by the Spanish Inquisition, escaped to Geneva. In addition to denying the Trinity—which identifies God as three divine persons, Father, Son, and Holy Spirit—Servetus insisted that a person under twenty cannot commit a mortal sin. The city fathers considered this idea dangerous to public morality, "especially in these days when the young are so corrupted." Servetus was burned at the stake.

To many sixteenth-century Europeans, Calvin's Geneva seemed "the most perfect school of Christ since the days of the Apostles." Religious refugees from France, England, Spain, Scotland, and Italy

THE LATER MIDDLE AGES, RENAISSANCE, AND PROTESTANT AND CATHOLIC REFORMATIONS, 1300–1600

1309–1376	Babylonian Captivity of the papacy
1310–1320	Dante, *The Divine Comedy*
1337–1453	Hundred Years' War
1347–1351	The Black Death (returned intermittently until ca 1700)
1356	Golden Bull transforms the Holy Roman Empire into an aristocratic confederation
ca 1376	John Wyclif attacks the church's temporal power and asserts the supremacy of the Scriptures
1378–1417	The Great Schism
1381	Peasants' revolt in England
1387–1400	Chaucer, *Canterbury Tales*
1404	Christine de Pisan, *The City of Ladies*
1414–1418	Council of Constance ends the schism, postpones reform, executes John Hus
1453	Capture of Constantinople by the Ottoman Turks, ending the Byzantine Empire
1455–1471	Wars of the Roses in England
1456	Gutenberg Bible
1492	Unification of Spain under Ferdinand and Isabela; expulsion of Jews and Muslims from Spain Columbus reaches the Americas
1494	France invades Italy, inaugurating sixty years of war on Italian soil
1513	Machiavelli, *The Prince*
1517	Martin Luther publishes the Ninety-five Theses
1523	Luther's translation of the New Testament into German
1525	Peasants' revolt in Germany
1533	Act in Restraint of Appeals inaugurates the English Reformation
1536	Calvin, *The Institutes of the Christian Religion*
1540	Loyola founds the Society of Jesus (Jesuits)
1541	Calvin establishes a theocracy in Geneva
1543	Copernicus, *On the Revolutions of the Heavenly Spheres*
1545–1563	Council of Trent
1555	Peace of Augsburg officially recognized
1588	Spanish Armada
1603	Shakespeare, *Hamlet*
1611	Authorized or King James Version of the Bible

Calvinist Worship A converted house in Lyons, France, serves as a church for the simple Calvinist service. Although Calvin's followers believed in equality and elected officials administered the church, here men and women are segregated, and some people sit on hard benches while others sit in upholstered pews. Beside the pulpit an hourglass hangs to time the preacher's sermon. (Could the dog sit still for that long?) (*Source: Bibliothèque publique et universitaire, Geneva*)

visited the city. Subsequently, the Reformed church of Calvin served as the model for the Presbyterian church in Scotland, the Huguenot church in France, and the Puritan churches in England and New England. The Calvinist provision for congregational participation and vernacular liturgy helped to satisfy women's desire to belong to and participate in a meaningful church organization. The Calvinist ethic of the "calling" dignified all work with a religious aspect: hard work, well done, was said to be pleasing to God. This doctrine encouraged an aggressive, vigorous activism. In the *Institutes* Calvin provided a systematic theology for Protestantism. The Reformed church of Calvin had a strong and well-organized machinery of government. These factors, together with the social

and economic applications of Calvin's theology, made Calvinism the most dynamic force in sixteenth- and seventeenth-century Protestantism.

The Anabaptists

The name *Anabaptist* derives from a Greek word meaning "to baptize again." The Anabaptists, sometimes described as the left wing of the Reformation, believed that only adults could make a free choice about religious faith, baptism, and entry into the Christian community. Thus they considered the practice of baptizing infants and children preposterous and wanted to rebaptize believers who had been baptized as children. Anabaptists took the Gospel and, at first, Luther's teachings absolutely literally and favored a return to the kind of church that had existed among the earliest Christians—a voluntary association of believers who had experienced an inner light.

Anabaptists maintained that only a few people would receive the inner light. This position meant that the Christian community and the Christian state were not identical. In other words, Anabaptists believed in the separation of church and state and in religious tolerance. They almost never tried to force their values on others. In an age that believed in the necessity of state-established churches, Anabaptist views on religious liberty were thought to undermine that concept.

Each Anabaptist community or church was entirely independent; it selected its own ministers and ran its own affairs. In 1534 the community at Münster in Germany, for example, established a legal code that decreed the death penalty for insubordinate wives. Moreover, the Münster community also practiced polygamy and forced all women under a certain age to marry or face expulsion or execution.

Anabaptists admitted women to the ministry. They shared goods as the early Christians had done, refused all public offices, and would not serve in the armed forces. In fact, they laid great stress on pacifism. A favorite Anabaptist scriptural quotation was "By their fruits you shall know them," suggesting that if Christianity was a religion of peace, the Christian should not fight. With such beliefs Anabaptists were inevitably a minority. Anabaptism later attracted the poor, the unemployed, the uneducated. Geographically, Anabaptists drew their members from depressed urban areas.

Ideas such as absolute pacifism and the distinction between the Christian community and the state brought down on these unfortunate people fanatical hatred and bitter persecution. Zwingli, Luther, Calvin, and Catholics all saw—quite correctly—the separation of church and state as leading ultimately to the complete secularization of society. The powerful rulers of Swiss and German society immediately feared that the combination of religious differences and economic grievances would lead to civil disturbances. In Saxony, in Strasbourg, and in the Swiss cities, Anabaptists were either banished or executed by burning, beating, or drowning. Their community spirit and the edifying example of their lives, however, contributed to the survival of Anabaptist ideas.

The Quakers with their gentle pacifism, the Baptists with their emphasis on an inner spiritual light, the Congregationalists with their democratic church organization, and, in 1787, the authors of the U.S. Constitution with their concern for the separation of church and state—all trace their origins in part to the Anabaptists of the sixteenth century.

The English Reformation

As on the continent of Europe, the Reformation in England had social and economic causes as well as religious ones. As elsewhere, too, Christian humanists had for decades been calling for the purification of the church. When the personal matter of the divorce of King Henry VIII (r. 1509–1547) became enmeshed with political issues, a complete break with Rome resulted.

Demands for ecclesiastical reform dated back at least to the fourteenth century. The Lollards (see page 428) had been driven underground in the fifteenth century but survived in parts of southern England and the Midlands. Working-class people, especially cloth workers, were attracted to their ideas. The Lollards stressed the individual's reading and interpretation of the Bible, which they considered the only standard of Christian faith and holiness. They put no stock in the value of the sacraments and were vigorously anticlerical. Lollards opposed ecclesiastical wealth, the veneration of the saints, prayers for the dead, and all war. Although they had no notion of justification by faith, like Luther they insisted on the individual soul's direct responsibility to God.

Still, traditional Catholicism exerted an enormously strong, diverse, and vigorous hold over the imagination and loyalty of the people. The teachings of Christianity were graphically represented in the liturgy, constantly reiterated in sermons, enacted in plays, and carved and printed on walls, screens, and the windows of parish churches. A zealous clergy, increasingly better educated, engaged in a "massive catechetical enterprise." No substantial gulf existed between the religion of the clergy and educated elite and the broad mass of the English people.[50] The Reformation in England was an act of state, initiated by the king's emotional life.

In 1527, having fallen in love with Anne Boleyn, Henry wanted his marriage to Catherine of Aragon annulled. Catherine had failed to bear a boy child, and Henry claimed that only a male heir to the throne could prevent a disputed succession. He thus petitioned Pope Clement VII (r. 1523–1534) for an annulment. When Henry had married Catherine, he had secured a dispensation from Pope Julius II eliminating all legal technicalities about Catherine's previous union with Henry's late brother, Arthur. Henry now argued that Pope Julius's dispensation had contradicted the law of God—that a man may not marry his brother's widow. The English king's request reached Rome at the very time that Luther was widely publishing tracts condemning the papacy. If Clement had granted Henry's annulment and thereby admitted that Julius II had erred, Clement would have given support to the Lutheran assertion that popes substitute their own evil judgments for the law of God. This Clement could not do, so he delayed acting on Henry's request.[51] The capture and sack of Rome in 1527 by mercenaries working for the emperor Charles V, Queen Catherine's nephew, thoroughly tied the pope's hands.

Since Rome appeared to be thwarting Henry's matrimonial plans, he decided to remove the English church from papal jurisdiction. Henry used Parliament to legalize the Reformation in England. The Act in Restraint of Appeals (1533) declared the king to be the supreme sovereign in England and forbade judicial appeals to the papacy, thus establishing the Crown as the highest legal authority in the land. The Act for the Submission of the Clergy (1534) required churchmen to submit to the king and forbade the publication of ecclesiastical laws without royal permission. The Supremacy Act of 1534 declared the king the supreme head of the Church of England.

An authority on the Reformation Parliament has written that probably only a small number of those who voted for the Restraint of Appeals actually knew they were voting for a permanent break with Rome.[52] Some opposed the king. John Fisher, the bishop of Rochester, a distinguished scholar and humanist, lashed the clergy with scorn for their cowardice. Thomas More, who had written *Utopia* nearly two years before (see page 475), resigned the chancellorship rather than acknowledge the rejection of papal authority. Fisher, More, and other dissenters were beheaded for treason in 1535.

When Anne Boleyn failed twice to produce a male child, Henry VIII charged her with adulterous incest and in 1536 had her beheaded. His third wife, Jane Seymour, gave Henry the desired son, Edward, but died in childbirth. Henry went on to three more wives before he passed to his reward in 1547.

Between 1535 and 1539, under the influence of his chief minister, Thomas Cromwell, Henry decided to dissolve the English monasteries because he wanted their wealth. The king ended nine hundred years of English monastic life, dispersed the monks and nuns, and confiscated their lands. Hundreds of properties were sold to the middle and upper classes and the proceeds spent on war. The closing of the monasteries did not achieve a more equitable distribution of land and wealth. Rather, the "bare ruined choirs where late the sweet birds sang"—as Shakespeare's Sonnet 73 describes the desolate religious houses—testified to the loss of a valuable cultural force in English life. The redistribution of land, however, strengthened the upper classes and tied them to the Tudor Dynasty.

Henry retained such traditional Catholic practices and doctrines as auricular confession, clerical celibacy, and *transubstantiation* (the doctrine that the bread and wine of the Eucharist are transformed into the body and blood of Christ although their appearance does not change). But Protestant literature circulated, and Henry approved the selection of men of Protestant sympathies as tutors for his son.

Did the religious changes have broad popular support? Recent scholarship has emphasized that the English Reformation came from above. The surviving evidence does not allow us to gauge the degree of opposition to (or support for) Henry's break with Rome. Certainly, many lay people wrote to the king, begging him to spare the monasteries. "Most laypeople acquiesced in the Reformation because they hardly knew what was going on, were understandably reluctant to jeopardise life or limb, a career or the family's good name."[53] But not all quietly acquiesced. In 1536 popular opposition in the north to the religious changes led to the Pilgrimage of Grace, a massive multiclass rebellion that proved the largest in English history. In 1546 serious rebellions in East Anglia and in the west, despite possessing economic and Protestant components, reflected considerable public opposition to the state-ordered religious changes.[54]

After Henry's death, the English church shifted left and right. In the short reign of Henry's sickly son Edward VI (r. 1547–1553), strongly Protestant ideas exerted a significant influence on the

Lutheran

Calvinist (Reformed)

Church of England

Roman Catholic

▲ Huguenot centers

→ Spread of Calvinism

0   150   300 Km.

0   150   300 Mi.

ATLANTIC

OCEAN

North Sea

Baltic Sea

Black Sea

Adriatic Sea

Mediterranean Sea

NORWAY 1536/1607

Bergen

SWEDEN

Stockholm

Helsinki

Riga

LITHUANIA

PRUSSIA

Warsaw

POLAND

DENMARK

Copenhagen

BRANDENBURG

Hamburg

SAXONY

Amsterdam

NETHERLANDS

Münster

Antwerp

Brussels

Wittenberg, Martin Luther

Birthplace of Martin Luther, ~1483–1546

Eisleben,

Erfurt,

Leipzig

Marburg

Worms

Edict of Worms, 1521

Noyon,

Birthplace of John Calvin, 1509–1564

Paris

HOLY ROMAN EMPIRE

Speyer

Nuremberg

Stuttgart

Augsburg

Munich

BOHEMIA

Prague

John Hus, 1369–1415

MORAVIA

Vienna

AUSTRIA

Buda

Pest

HUNGARY

TRANSYLVANIA

OTTOMAN EMPIRE

Lepanto

Strasbourg

Basel

Zurich

Ulrich Zwingli, 1484–1531

Geneva

John Calvin

Council of Trent, 1545–1563

Trent

Milan

Pavia

Genoa

Venice

Pisa

Florence

ITALY

Rome

Roman Inquisition established, 1542

Naples

Bari

Corsica

Sardinia

Sicily

Marseilles

Avignon

Toulouse

FRANCE

Rennes

Orléans

Nantes

Edict of Nantes, 1598

La Rochelle

Bordeaux

Loyola,

Birthplace of Ignatius Loyola, 1491

Barcelona

Valencia

SPAIN

Madrid

Toledo

Granada

Seville

PORTUGAL

Lisbon

Balearic Is.

MUSLIM STATES

IRELAND

Dublin

SCOTLAND 1560

Edinburgh

John Knox, 1505–1572

Penetration of Calvinism to England after 1558

ENGLAND 1536

Oxford

John Wyclif, 1320–1384

London

Plymouth

religious life of the country. Archbishop Thomas Cranmer simplified the liturgy, invited Protestant theologians to England, and prepared the first *Book of Common Prayer* (1549). In stately and dignified English, the *Book of Common Prayer* included, together with the Psalter, the order for all services of the Church of England.

The equally brief reign of Mary Tudor (r. 1553–1558) witnessed a sharp move back to Catholicism. The devoutly Catholic daughter of Catherine of Aragon and Henry, Mary rescinded the Reformation legislation of her father's reign and fully restored Roman Catholicism. Mary's marriage to her cousin Philip of Spain, son of the emperor Charles V, proved highly unpopular in England, and her persecution and execution of several hundred Protestants further alienated her subjects. Mary's death raised to the throne her sister Elizabeth (r. 1558–1603) and inaugurated the beginnings of religious stability.

Elizabeth had been raised a Protestant, but at the start of her reign sharp differences existed in England. Catholics wanted a Roman Catholic ruler, but a vocal number of returning exiles wanted all Catholic elements in the Church of England eliminated. Members of the latter group were called Puritans because they wanted to "purify" the church. Probably one of the shrewdest politicians in English history, Elizabeth chose a middle course between Catholic and Puritan extremes. She insisted on dignity in church services and political order in the land. She did not care what people believed as long as they kept quiet about it. Avoiding precise doctrinal definitions, Elizabeth had herself styled "Supreme Governor of the Church of England, Etc.," and left it to her subjects to decide what the "Etc." meant.

The parliamentary legislation of the early years of Elizabeth's reign—laws sometimes labeled the "Elizabethan Settlement"—required outward conformity to the Church of England and uniformity in all ceremonies. Everyone had to attend Church of England services; those who refused were fined. During Elizabeth's reign, the Anglican church

❧ **MAP 15.2 The Protestant and the Catholic Reformations**   The reformations shattered the religious unity of Western Christendom. What common cultural traits predominated in regions where a particular branch of the Christian faith was maintained or took root?

(from the Latin *Ecclesia Anglicana*), as the Church of England was called, moved in a moderately Protestant direction. Services were conducted in English, monasteries were not re-established, and the clergy were allowed to marry. But the bishops remained as church officials, and apart from language, the services were quite traditional.

❧ THE CATHOLIC AND THE COUNTER-REFORMATIONS

Between 1517 and 1547, the reformed versions of Christianity known as Protestantism made remarkable advances. All of England, Scandinavia, much of Scotland and Germany, and sizable parts of France and Switzerland adopted the creeds of Luther, Calvin, and other reformers. Still, the Roman Catholic church made a significant comeback. After about 1540, no new large areas of Europe, except for the Netherlands, accepted Protestant beliefs (Map 15.2).

Historians distinguish between two types of reform within the Catholic church in the sixteenth and seventeenth centuries. The Catholic Reformation began before 1517 and sought renewal basically through the stimulation of a new spiritual fervor. The Counter-Reformation started in the 1540s as a reaction to the rise and spread of Protestantism. The Counter-Reformation was a Catholic effort to convince or coerce dissidents or heretics to return to the church.

The Renaissance princes who sat on the throne of Saint Peter were not blind to the evils that existed. Modest reform efforts had begun with the Lateran Council that Pope Julius II called in 1512. The Dutch pope Adrian VI (r. 1522–1523) instructed his legate in Germany "to say that we frankly confess that God permits this [Lutheran] persecution of his church on account of the sins of men, especially those of the priests and prelates."[55]

Overall, why did the popes, spiritual leaders of the Western church, move so slowly? The answers lie in the personalities of the popes themselves, in their preoccupation with political affairs in Italy, and in the awesome difficulty of reforming so complicated a bureaucracy as the Roman curia. Clement VII, a true Medici, was far more interested in elegant tapestries and Michelangelo's painting of the Last Judgment than in theological disputes in barbaric Germany or far-off England.

In the Habsburg-Valois conflicts in Italy Clement first backed the emperor Charles. He then switched to the French ruler. Shortly afterward, the emperor's Spanish and German mercenaries sacked and looted Rome and took him captive.

The idea of reform was closely linked to the idea of a general council representing the entire church. Popes such as Clement VII, remembering fifteenth-century conciliar attempts to limit papal authority, resisted calls for a council, fearing loss of power, revenue, and prestige.

The Council of Trent

In the papal conclave that followed the death of Clement VII, Cardinal Alexander Farnese promised two German cardinals that if he were elected pope he would summon a council. He won the election and ruled as Pope Paul III (r. 1534–1549). This Roman aristocrat, humanist, and astrologer, who immediately made his teenage grandsons cardinals, seemed an unlikely person to undertake serious reform. Yet Paul III appointed as cardinals several learned and reform-minded men; established the Inquisition in the Papal States; and called a council, which finally met at Trent, an imperial city close to Italy (see Map 15.2).

The Council of Trent met intermittently from 1545 to 1563. It was called not only to reform the church but to secure reconciliation with the Protestants. Lutherans and Calvinists were invited to participate, but their insistence that the Scriptures be the sole basis for discussion made reconciliation impossible. International politics repeatedly cast a shadow over the theological debates. Charles V opposed discussions on any matter that might further alienate his Lutheran subjects. The French kings worked against any reconciliation of Roman Catholicism and Lutheranism, wanting the German states to remain divided. Portugal, Poland, Hungary, and Ireland sent representatives, but very few German bishops attended.

Another problem was the persistence of the conciliar theory of church government. Some bishops wanted a concrete statement asserting the supremacy of a church council over the papacy. The adoption of the conciliar principle could have led to a divided church. The bishops had a provincial and national outlook; only the papacy possessed an international religious perspective. The centralizing tenet was established that all acts of the council required papal approval.

In spite of the obstacles, the achievements of the Council of Trent are impressive. It dealt with both doctrinal and disciplinary matters. The council gave equal validity to the Scriptures and to tradition as sources of religious truth and authority. It reaffirmed the seven sacraments and the traditional Catholic teaching on transubstantiation, rejecting Lutheran and Calvinist positions.

The council tackled the problems arising from ancient abuses by strengthening ecclesiastical discipline. Tridentine (from *Tridentum,* the Latin word for "Trent") decrees required bishops to reside in their own dioceses, suppressed pluralism and simony, and forbade the sale of indulgences. Clerics who kept concubines were to give them up. In a highly original canon, the council required every diocese to establish a seminary for the education and training of the clergy and insisted that preference for admission be given to sons of the poor. Seminary professors were to determine whether candidates for ordination had *vocations*—genuine callings as evidenced by purity of life, detachment from the broader secular culture, and a steady inclination toward the priesthood. This was a novel idea, since from the time of the early church, parents had determined their sons' (and daughters') religious careers. Also, great emphasis was laid on preaching and instructing the laity, especially the uneducated.

One decision had especially important social consequences for lay people. Since the time of the Roman Empire, many couples had treated marriage as a completely personal matter, exchanged vows privately without witnesses, and thus formed clandestine (secret) unions. This widespread practice frequently led later to denials by one party that a marriage had taken place, to conflicts over property, and to disputes in the ecclesiastical courts that had jurisdiction over marriage. The Tridentine decree *Tametsi* (1563) stipulated that for a marriage to be valid, consent (the essence of marriage) as expressed in the vows had to be given publicly before witnesses, one of whom had to be the parish priest. Trent thereby ended secret marriages in Catholic countries.

The Council of Trent did not bring about reform immediately. But the Tridentine decrees laid a solid basis for the spiritual renewal of the church and for the enforcement of correction. For four centuries, the doctrinal and disciplinary legislation of Trent served as the basis for Roman Catholic faith, organization, and practice.

New Religious Orders and the Inquisition

The establishment of new religious orders within the church reveals a central feature of the Catholic Reformation. These new orders developed in response to the need to raise the moral and intellectual level of the clergy and people. Education was a major goal of them all.

The Ursuline order of nuns, founded by Angela Merici (1474–1540), attained enormous prestige for the education of women. The daughter of a country gentleman, Angela Merici worked for many years among the poor, sick, and uneducated around her native Brescia in northern Italy. In 1535 she established the Ursuline order to combat heresy through Christian education of young girls. The Ursulines sought to re-Christianize society by training future wives and mothers. Approved as a religious community by Paul III in 1544, the Ursulines rapidly grew and spread to France and the New World. Their schools in North America, stretching from Quebec to New Orleans, provided superior education for young women and inculcated the spiritual ideals of the Catholic Reformation.

The Society of Jesus, founded by Ignatius Loyola (1491–1556), a former Spanish soldier, played a powerful international role in resisting the spread of Protestantism, converting Asians and Latin American Indians to Catholicism, and spreading Christian education all over Europe. While recuperating from a severe battle wound to his legs, Loyola studied a life of Christ and other religious books and decided to give up his military career and become a soldier of Christ. His great classic, *Spiritual Exercises,* directed the individual imagination and will to the reform of life and a new spiritual piety.

Loyola was apparently a man of considerable personal magnetism. After study at the universities

Juan de Valdes Leal: Pope Paul III Approves the Jesuit Constitutions Although Paul III devoted considerable energy to advancing the interests of his (Farnese) family, he also tried to meet the challenge of Protestantism—by means of the Council of Trent and new religious orders. When the Jesuit constitutions were read to him, Paul III supposedly murmured, "There is the finger of God." The portrait of Ignatius Loyola (holding the paper) is a reasonable likeness; that of the pope is an idealization: in 1540 he was a very old man. (*Source: MAS, Barcelona*)

in Salamanca and Paris, he gathered a group of six companions and in 1540 secured papal approval of the new Society of Jesus, whose members were called Jesuits. The first Jesuits were recruited primarily from the wealthy merchant and professional classes. They saw the Reformation as a pastoral problem, its causes and cures related not to doctrinal issues but to people's spiritual condition. Reform of the church as Luther and Calvin understood the word *reform* played no role in the future the Jesuits planned for themselves. Their goal was "to help souls." Loyola also possessed a gift for leadership that consisted in spotting talent and "in the ability to see how at a given juncture change is more consistent with one's scope than staying the course."[56]

The Society of Jesus developed into a highly centralized, tightly knit organization. Candidates underwent a two-year novitiate, in contrast to the usual one-year probation required by older religious orders. In addition to the traditional vows of poverty, chastity, and obedience, professed members vowed "special obedience to the sovereign pontiff regarding missions."[57] Thus, as stability—the promise to live one's life in the monastery—was what made a monk, so mobility—the commitment to go anywhere for the help of souls—was the defining characteristic of a Jesuit. Flexibility and the willingness to respond to the needs of time and circumstance formed the Jesuit tradition. In this respect they were very modern, and they attracted many recruits.

The Society of Jesus achieved phenomenal success for the papacy and the reformed Catholic church. Jesuit schools adopted the modern humanist curricula and methods. They first concentrated on the children of the poor but soon were educating the sons of the nobility. As confessors and spiritual directors to kings, Jesuits exerted great political influence. Operating on the principle that the end sometimes justifies the means, they were not above spying. Indifferent to physical comfort and personal safety, they carried Christianity to India and Japan before 1550 and to Brazil, North America, and the Congo in the seventeenth century. Within Europe, the Jesuits brought southern Germany and much of eastern Europe back to Catholicism.

In 1542 Pope Paul III established the Sacred Congregation of the Holy Office with jurisdiction over the Roman Inquisition, a powerful instrument of the Counter-Reformation. A committee of six cardinals, the Roman Inquisition had judicial authority over all Catholics and the power to arrest, imprison, and execute. Under the fanatical Cardinal Caraffa, it vigorously attacked heresy. The Roman Inquisition operated under the principles of Roman law. It accepted hearsay evidence, was not obliged to inform the accused of charges against them, and sometimes used torture. Echoing one of Calvin's remarks about heresy, Cardinal Caraffa wrote, "No man is to lower himself by showing toleration towards any sort of heretic, least of all a Calvinist."[58] The Holy Office published the *Index of Prohibited Books*, a catalogue of forbidden reading.

Within the Papal States, the Roman Inquisition effectively destroyed heresy (and some heretics). Outside the papal territories, its influence was slight. Governments had their own judicial systems for the suppression of treasonable activities, as religious heresy was then considered.[59]

SUMMARY

From about 1050 to 1300, a new economy emerged in Italy, based on Venetian and Genoese shipping and long-distance trade and on Florentine banking and cloth manufacture. The combination of these commercial activities and the struggle of urban communities for political independence from surrounding feudal lords led to the appearance of a new wealthy aristocratic class. With this foundation, Italy was the scene of a remarkable intellectual and artistic flowering. Based on renewed interest in the Greco-Roman world, the Renaissance had a classicizing influence on many facets of culture. Despots or oligarchs ruled the city-states of fifteenth- and sixteenth-century Italy and manipulated Renaissance culture to enhance their personal power. Moving beyond Italy, the individualism, humanism, and secular spirit characteristic of the Italian Renaissance affected the culture of all Europe.

In northern Europe, city merchants and rural gentry allied with rising monarchies. Using taxes provided by business people, kings provided a greater degree of domestic peace and order, conditions essential for trade. In Spain, France, and England, rulers also emphasized royal dignity and authority. Except in the Holy Roman Empire, feudal monarchies gradually evolved in the direction of nation-states.

In the sixteenth century and through most of the seventeenth, religion and religious issues continued to play a major role in the lives of individuals and in the policies and actions of governments. The age of the Reformation presents very real paradoxes. The break with Rome and the rise of Lutheran, Anglican, Calvinist, and other faiths destroyed the unity of Europe as an organic Christian society. The strength of religious convictions caused political fragmentation, and religion, whether Protestant or Catholic, decisively influenced the growth of national states. Although most reformers rejected religious toleration, they helped pave the way for it.

Scholars have maintained that the sixteenth century witnessed the beginnings of the modern world. They are both right and wrong. The sixteenth-century revolt from the church laid the groundwork for the eighteenth-century revolt from the Christian God, one of the strongest supports of life in Western culture. In this respect, the Reformation marks the beginning of the modern world, with its secularism and rootlessness. At the same time, it can be argued that the sixteenth century represents the culmination of the Middle Ages. Martin Luther's anxieties about salvation show him to be very much a medieval man. His concerns had deeply troubled serious individuals since the time of Saint Augustine. Modern people tend to be less troubled by them.

NOTES

1. See L. Martines, *Power and Imagination: City-States in Renaissance Italy* (New York: Vintage Books, 1980), esp. pp. 332–333.
2. Ibid., pp. 22–61.
3. Ibid., pp. 221–237, esp. p. 221.
4. Quoted in J. Burckhardt, *The Civilization of the Renaissance in Italy* (London: Phaidon Books, 1951), p. 89.
5. *Memoirs of Benvenuto Cellini; A Florentine Artist; Written by Himself* (London: J. M. Dent & Sons, 1927), p. 2.
6. See C. Trinkaus, *In Our Image and Likeness: Humanity and Divinity in Italian Humanist Thought,* vol. 2 (London: Constable, 1970), pp. 505–529.
7. See Martines, *Power and Imagination,* Ch. 13, esp. pp. 241, 243.
8. See A. Hauser, *The Social History of Art,* vol. 2 (New York: Vintage Books, 1959), Ch. 3, esp. pp. 60, 68.
9. G. Bull, trans., *Aretino: Selected Letters* (Baltimore: Penguin Books, 1976), p. 109.
10. Hauser, *The Social History of Art,* pp. 48–49.
11. Quoted in E. H. Harbison, *The Christian Scholar and His Calling in the Age of the Reformation* (New York: Charles Scribner's Sons, 1956), p. 109.
12. Quoted in F. Seebohm, *The Oxford Reformers* (London: J. M. Dent & Sons, 1867), p. 256.
13. Quoted in W. H. Woodward, *Vittorino da Feltre and Other Humanist Educators* (Cambridge: Cambridge University Press, 1897), pp. 96–97.
14. C. E. Detmold, trans., *The Historical, Political and Diplomatic Writings of Niccolò Machiavelli* (Boston: J. R. Osgood, 1882), pp. 51–52.
15. Ibid., pp. 54–55.
16. See F. Gilbert, *Machiavelli and Guicciardini: Politics and History in Sixteenth Century Florence* (New York: Norton, 1984), pp. 197–200.
17. See L. Hunt, *The Invention of Pornography: Obscenity and the Origins of Modernity, 1500–1800* (New York: Zone Books, 1993), pp. 10, 93–95.
18. Quoted in E. L. Eisenstein, *The Printing Press as an Agent of Change: Communications and Cultural Transformations in Early Modern Europe,* vol. 1 (New York: Cambridge University Press, 1979), p. 135; for an overall discussion, see pp. 126–159.
19. M. L. King, "Book-lined Cells: Women and Humanism in the Early Italian Renaissance," in *Beyond Their Sex: Learned Women of the European Past,* ed. P. H. Labalme (New York: New York University Press, 1980), pp. 66–81, esp. p. 73.
20. This account rests on J. Kelly-Gadol, "Did Women Have a Renaissance?" in *Becoming Visible: Women in European History,* ed. R. Bridenthal and C. Koontz (Boston: Houghton Mifflin, 1977), pp. 137–161, esp. p. 161.
21. See Peter Burke, "What Is the History of Popular Culture," in *What Is History Today?* ed. J. Gardiner (Atlantic Highlands, N.J.: Humanities Press, 1989), pp. 121–123.
22. G. Ruggerio, "Sexual Criminality in Early Renaissance Venice, 1338–1358," *Journal of Social History* 8 (Spring 1975): 18–31.
23. Quoted in R. C. Trexler, "Infanticide in Florence: New Sources and First Results," *History of Childhood Quarterly* 1 (Summer 1973): 99.
24. Ibid., p. 100.
25. J. Devisse and M. Mollat, *The Image of the Black in Western Art,* trans. W. G. Ryan, vol. 2 (New York: Morrow, 1979), pt. 2, pp. 187–188.
26. See C. M. Saunders, *A Social History of Black Slaves and Freedmen in Portugal, 1441–1555* (New York: Cambridge University Press, 1982), pp. 59, 62–88, 176–179.

27. Ibid., pp. 190–194.

28. Ibid., pp. 255–258.

29. See J. H. Elliott, *Imperial Spain, 1469–1716* (New York: Mentor Books, 1963), esp. pp. 75, 97–108.

30. Quoted in Burckhardt, *The Civilization of the Renaissance in Italy,* p. 262.

31. See R. R. Post, *The Modern Devotion: Confrontation with Reformation and Humanism* (Leiden: E. J. Brill, 1968), esp. pp. 237–238, 255, 323–348.

32. Quoted in O. Chadwick, *The Reformation* (Baltimore: Penguin Books, 1976), p. 55.

33. Quoted in E. H. Harbison, *The Age of Reformation* (Ithaca, N.Y.: Cornell University Press, 1963), p. 52.

34. This discussion is based heavily on Harbison, *The Age of Reformation,* pp. 52–55.

35. See S. E. Ozment, *The Reformation in the Cities: The Appeal of Protestantism to Sixteenth-Century Germany and Switzerland* (New Haven, Conn.: Yale University Press, 1975), pp. 32–45.

36. See S. E. Ozment, *The Age of Reform, 1250–1550: An Intellectual and Religious History of Late Medieval and Reformation Europe* (New Haven, Conn.: Yale University Press, 1980), pp. 273–279.

37. Quoted ibid., p. 280.

38. Quoted ibid., p. 281.

39. Quoted ibid., p. 284.

40. Romans 13:1–2.

41. G. Strauss, *Luther's House of Learning: Indoctrination of the Young in the German Reformation* (Baltimore: Johns Hopkins University Press, 1978), esp. pp. 159–162, 231–233.

42. See R. H. Bainton, *Women of the Reformation in Germany and Italy* (Minneapolis: Augsburg, 1971), pp. 9–10; and Ozment, *The Reformation in the Cities,* pp. 53–54, 171–172.

43. Quoted in H. G. Haile, *Luther: An Experiment in Biography* (Garden City, N.Y.: Doubleday, 1980), p. 272.

44. Quoted in J. Atkinson, *Martin Luther and the Birth of Protestantism* (Baltimore: Penguin Books, 1968), pp. 247–248.

45. *Martin Luther: Three Treatises* (Philadelphia: Muhlenberg Press, 1947), pp. 28–31.

46. J. Allen, trans., *John Calvin: The Institutes of the Christian Religion* (Philadelphia: Westminster Press, 1930), bk. 3, chap. 21, paras. 5, 7.

47. E. W. Monter, *Calvin's Geneva* (New York: Wiley, 1967), pp. 98–108.

48. Ibid., p. 137.

49. Quoted in Bainton, *Women of the Reformation in Germany and Italy,* pp. 69–70.

50. E. Duffy, *The Stripping of the Altars: Traditional Religion in England, 1400–1580* (New Haven, Conn.: Yale University Press, 1992), pp. 2–6, and passim.

51. See R. Marius, *Thomas More: A Biography* (New York: Knopf, 1984), pp. 215–216.

52. See S. E. Lehmberg, *The Reformation Parliament 1529–1536* (Cambridge: Cambridge University Press, 1970), pp. 174–176, 204–205.

53. J. J. Scarisbrick, *The Reformation and the English People* (Oxford: Basil Blackwell, 1984), pp. 81–84, esp. p. 81.

54. Ibid.

55. Quoted in P. Smith, *The Age of the Reformation,* rev. ed. (New York: Henry Holt, 1951), p. 346.

56. See J. W. O'Malley, *The First Jesuits* (Cambridge, Mass.: Harvard University Press, 1993), p. 376.

57. Ibid., p. 298.

58. Quoted in Chadwick, *The Reformation,* p. 270.

59. See P. Grendler, *The Roman Inquisition and the Venetian Press, 1540–1605* (Princeton, N.J.: Princeton University Press, 1977).

SUGGESTED READING

Scores of exciting studies are available on virtually all aspects of the Renaissance. In addition to the titles given in the Notes, the curious student should see P. Burke, *The Italian Renaissance: Culture and Society in Italy* (1986), an important sociological interpretation relating culture and society, and J. H. Plumb, *The Italian Renaissance* (1965), a superbly written book. P. Burke, *The Historical Anthropology of Early Modern Italy* (1987), contains many useful essays on Italian cultural history in a comparative European framework. J. R. Hale, *Renaissance Europe: The Individual and Society, 1480–1520* (1978), is an excellent treatment of individualism by a distinguished authority. Hale's magisterial achievement, *The Civilization of Europe in the Renaissance* (1994) reveals how the very idea of "Europe" crystallized. For Renaissance humanism and education, see P. F. Grendler, *Schooling in Renaissance Italy: Literacy and Learning, 1300–1600* (1989); J. H. Moran, *The Growth of English Schooling, 1340–1548: Learning, Literacy, and Laicization in Pre-Reformation York Diocese* (1985); and J. F. D'Amico, *Renaissance Humanism in Papal Rome: Humanists and Churchmen on the Eve of the Reformation* (1983), which are all highly readable works of outstanding scholarship. For the city where much of it originated, G. A. Brucker, *Renaissance Florence* (1969), gives a good description of Florentine economic, political, social, and cultural history. Learned, provocative, and beautifully written, and a work on which this chapter leans heavily, L. Martines, *Power and Imagination: City-States in Renaissance Italy* (1980), is probably the best broad appreciation of the period produced in several decades. For the Renaissance court, see the splendid achievement of G. Lubkin, *A Renaissance Court: Milan Under Galeazzo Maria Sforza* (1994).

J. R. Hale, *Machiavelli and Renaissance Italy* (1966), is a sound short biography, but advanced students may want to consult the sophisticated intellectual biography of S. de Grazia, *Machiavelli in Hell* (1989). F. Gilbert, *Machiavelli and Guicciardini,* mentioned in the Notes, places the two thinkers in their intellectual and social context.

The best introduction to the Renaissance in northern Europe and a book that has greatly influenced twentieth-century scholarship is J. Huizinga, *The Waning of the Middle Ages: A Study of the Forms of Life, Thought, and Art in France and the Netherlands in the Dawn of the Renaissance* (1954). This book challenges the whole idea of a Renaissance. R. J. Knecht, *Renaissance Warrior and Patron: The Reign of Francis I* (1994), is the standard study of that important French ruler. W. Blockman and W. Prevenier, *The Burgundian Netherlands* (1986) is essential for the culture of the Burgundy. The leading northern humanist is sensitively treated in M. M. Phillips, *Erasmus and the Northern Renaissance* (1956), and J. Huizinga, *Erasmus of Rotterdam* (1952). R. Marius, *Thomas More: A Biography* (1984), is an original study of the great English humanist and statesman. J. Leclercq, trans., *The Complete Works of Rabelais* (1963), is easily available.

The following titles should prove useful for various aspects of Renaissance social history: G. Ruggerio, *Violence in Early Renaissance Venice* (1980), a pioneering study of crime and punishment in a stable society; J. C. Brown, *Immodest Acts: The Life of a Lesbian Nun in Renaissance Italy* (1985), which is helpful for an understanding of the role and status of women; and I. Maclean, *The Renaissance Notion of Women* (1980). The student who wishes to study blacks in medieval and early modern European society should see the rich and original achievement of J. Devisse and M. Mollat, *The Image of the Black in Western Art,* cited in the Notes.

Renaissance art has inspired vast research. M. Baxandall, *Painting and Experience in Fifteenth Century Italy* (1988), is essential, and A. Martindale, *The Rise of the Artist in the Middle Ages and Early Renaissance* (1972), is a splendidly illustrated introduction. One of the finest appreciations of Renaissance art, written by one of the greatest art historians of this century, is E. Panofsky, *Meaning in the Visual Arts* (1955). Both Italian and northern painting are treated in the brilliant study of M. Meiss, *The Painter's Choice: Problems in the Interpretation of Renaissance Art* (1976), a collection of essays dealing with Renaissance style, form, and meaning. L. Steinberg, *The Sexuality of Christ in Renaissance Art and in Modern Oblivion*

(1983), is a brilliant work that relates Christ's sexuality to incarnational theology. J. M. Saslow, *Ganymede in the Renaissance* (1986), which uses images of Ganymede as a metaphor for emotional and sexual relations between men and youths, provides information on social attitudes toward homosexuality. R. Jones and N. Penny, *Raphael* (1983), celebrates the achievements of that great master.

Students interested in the city of Rome might consult P. Partner, *Renaissance Rome, 1500–1559: A Portrait of a Society* (1979), and the elegantly illustrated study of C. Hibbert, *Rome: The Biography of a City* (1985). Da Vinci's scientific and naturalist ideas and drawings are available in I. A. Richter, ed., *The Notebooks of Leonardo da Vinci* (1985). The magisterial achievement of J. Pope-Hennessy, *Cellini* (1985), is a superb evocation of that artist's life and work.

The following works not only are useful for the political and economic history of the Renaissance but also contain valuable bibliographical information: A. J. Slavin, ed., *The "New Monarchies" and Representative Assemblies* (1965), a collection of interpretations, and R. Lockyer, *Henry VII* (1972), a biography with documents illustrative of the king's reign. For Spain, see P. Liss, *Isabel the Queen: Life and Times* (1992); N. Rubin, *Isabella of Castile: The First Renaissance Queen* (1991); J. S. Gerber, *The Jews of Spain: A History of the Sephardic Experience* (1992); H. Kamen, *Inquisition and Society in Spain in the Sixteenth and Seventeenth Centuries* (1985); B. Bennasar, *The Spanish Character: Attitudes and Mentalities from the Sixteenth to the Nineteenth Century,* trans. B. Keen (1979). For the Florentine business classes, see I. Origo, *The Merchant of Prato* (1957); G. Brucker, *Two Memoirs of Renaissance Florence: The Diaries of Buonaccorso Pitti and Gregorio Dati,* trans. J. Martines (1967); and Paul Grendler, ed., *An Italian Renaissance Reader* (1987).

There are many easily accessible and lucidly written general studies of the religious reformations of the sixteenth century. P. Chaunu, ed., *The Reformation* (1989), is a lavishly illustrated anthology of articles by an international team of scholars, a fine appreciation of both theological and historical developments with an up-to-date bibliography. E. Cameron, *The European Reformation* (1991), provides a comprehensive survey based on recent research. A. Pettegree, ed., *The Early Reformation in Europe* (1992), explores the Reformation as an international movement and compares developments in different parts of Europe. L. W. Spitz, *The Protestant Reformation, 1517–1559* (1985), provides a comprehensive survey. For the recent trend in scholarship, interpreting the Reformation against the background of fifteenth-century reforming developments, see the excellent study of J. F. D'Amico, cited above, and J. H. Overfield, *Humanism and Scholasticism in Late Medieval Germany* (1984), which portrays the intellectual life of the

A Universal Man

Some people of the Renaissance believed in the ideal of universality, the achievement of distinction in many different skills and branches of knowledge. As one humanist put it, "A man is able to learn many things and make himself universal in many excellent arts." (Not everyone thought this: while Michelangelo was painting the Sistine Chapel, he complained to his father that "painting is not my profession.") Leon Battista Alberti (1404–1474), the illegitimate son of a family exiled from Florence, strongly believed he could be a universal man. A scholar-humanist, mathematician, and musician, he wrote treatises on domestic morality, the physical remains of antiquity, painting, and architecture. Here is a section of Alberti's autobiography.

And finally he embraced with zeal and forethought everything which pertained to fame. To omit the rest, he strove so hard to attain a name in modeling and painting that he wished to neglect nothing by which he might gain the approbation of good men. His genius was so versatile that you might almost judge all the fine arts to be his. . . .

He played ball, hurled the javelin, ran, leaped, wrestled, and above all delighted in the steep ascent of mountains; he applied himself to all these things for the sake of health rather than sport or pleasure. As a youth he excelled in warlike games. With his feet together, he could leap over the shoulders of men standing by; he had almost no equal among those hurling the lance. An arrow shot by his hand from his chest could pierce the strongest iron breastplate. . . . On horseback, holding in his hand one end of a long wand, while the other was firmly fixed to his foot, he could ride his horse violently in all directions for hours at a time as he wished, and the wand would remain completely immobile. Strange and marvelous! that the most spirited horses and those most impatient of riders would, when he first mounted them, tremble vio-

lently and shudder as if in great fear. He learned music without teachers, and his compositions were approved by learned musicians. He sang throughout his whole life, but in private, or alone. . . . He delighted in the organ and was considered an expert among the leading musicians.

When he had begun to mature in years, neglecting everything else, he devoted himself entirely to the study of letters, and spent some years of labour on canon and civil law. Finally after so many nightly vigils and such great constancy, he fell gravely ill from the exertion of his studies. Since his relatives were neither kind nor humane to him in his illness, by way of consoling himself between his convalescence and cure he wrote the play *Philodoxeos*, putting aside his legal studies—this when he was only twenty years old. And as soon as his health permitted, he resumed his studies, intending to complete the law, but again he was seized by a grave illness. . . .

At length, on the orders of his doctors, he desisted from those studies which were most fatiguing to the memory, just when they were about to flourish. But in truth, because he could not live without letters, at the age of twenty-four he turned to physics and the mathematical arts. . . .

Although he was affable, gentle, and harmful to no one, nevertheless he felt the animosity of many evil men, and hidden enmities, both annoying and very burdensome; in particular the harsh injuries and intolerable insults from his own relatives. He lived among the envious and malevolent with such modesty and equanimity that none of his detractors or rivals, although very hostile towards him, dared to utter a word about him in the presence of good and worthy men unless it was full of praise and admiration. . . .

When he heard that a learned man of any kind had arrived, he would at once work his way into a position of familiarity with him and thus from any source whatsoever he began to learn what he was ignorant of. From craftsmen, architects, shipbuilders, and even from cobblers he sought information to see if by chance they preserved anything rare or unusual or special in their arts; and he would then communicate such things to those citizens who wished to know them. He pretended to be ignorant in many things so that he might observe the talents and habits and skill of others. And so he was a zealous observer of whatsoever pertained to inborn talent of the arts.

He wholly despised the pursuit of material gain. He gave his money and goods to his friends to take care of and to enjoy. Among those by whom he believed himself loved, he was not only outgoing about his affairs and his habits but even about his secrets. He never betrayed the secrets of another but remained silent forever. . . .

He was by nature prone to wrath and bitter in spirit, but he could repress his rising indignation immediately by taking thought. Sometimes he deliberately fled from the verbose and the headstrong because with them he could not subdue his wrath. At other times he voluntarily submitted to the bold, in order to grow in patience. . . .

He wrote some books entitled *On Painting*, and in this very art of painting he created works unheard of and unbelievable to those who saw them. . . .

He had within himself a ray by which he could sense the good or evil intentions of men towards himself. Simply by looking at them, he could discover most of the defects of anyone in his presence. He used all kinds of reasoning and great effort, but in vain, to make more gentle towards himself those whom he had learned at one glance would be inimical. . . .

He could endure pain and cold and heat. When, not yet fifteen, he received a serious wound in the foot, and the physician, according to his custom and skill, drew together the broken parts of the foot and sewed them through the skin with a needle, he scarcely uttered a sound of pain. With his own hands, though in such great pain, he even aided the ministering doctor and treated his own wound though he was burning with fever. . . . By some defect in his nature he loathed garlic and also honey, and the mere sight of them, if by chance they were offered to him, brought on vomiting. But he conquered himself by

Bronze medallion of Leon Battista Alberti, by Matteo di Andrea de' Pasti. *(Source: Alinari/Art Resource, NY)*

force of looking at and handling the disagreeable objects, so that they came to offend him less, thus showing by example that men can do anything with themselves if they will.

He took extraordinary and peculiar pleasure in looking at things in which there was any mark of beauty or adornment. He never ceased to wonder at old men who were endowed with dignity of countenance, and unimpaired and vigorous, and he proclaimed that he honoured them as "delights of nature." He declared that quadrupeds, birds, and other living things of outstanding beauty were worthy of benevolence because by the very distinction of their nature they deserved favour. When his favorite dog died he wrote a funeral oration for him.

Questions for Analysis

1. What distinctively Renaissance traits did Alberti show?

2. According to his own assessment, what personal or human qualities did Alberti possess?

3. Did Alberti appear to have any psychological complexes or difficulties? How would you explain them?

Source: "Self-Portrait of a Universal Man" by Leon Battista Alberti from *The Portable Renaissance Reader*, edited by J. B. Ross and M. M. McLaughlin. Copyright 1968 by Penguin USA.

German universities, the milieu from which the Protestant Reformation emerged. For the condition of the church in the late fifteenth and early sixteenth centuries, see D. Hay, *The Church in Italy in the Fifteenth Century* (1977), and P. Heath, *The English Parish Clergy on the Eve of the Reformation* (1969).

For the central figure of the early Reformation, Martin Luther, students should see the works by Atkinson and Haile mentioned in the Notes, as well as E. Erikson, *Young Man Luther: A Study in Psychoanalysis and History* (1962); G. Brendler, *Martin Luther: Theology and Revolution* (1991), a response to the Marxist interpretation of Luther as the tool of the aristocracy who sold out the peasantry; and H. Boehmer, *Martin Luther: Road to Reformation* (1960), a well-balanced work treating Luther's formative years.

The best study of John Calvin is W. J. Bouwsma, *John Calvin: A Sixteenth-Century Portrait* (1988), an authoritative study that places Calvin within Renaissance culture. R. T. Kendall, *Calvinism and English Calvinism to 1649* (1981), presents English conditions. R. M. Mitchell, *Calvin and the Puritan's View of the Protestant Ethic* (1979), interprets the socioeconomic implications of Calvin's thought. Students interested in the left wing of the Reformation should see the profound though difficult work of G. H. Williams, *The Radical Reformers* (1962). For reform in other parts of Switzerland, see T. Brady, *Turning Swiss* (1990), and L. P. Wendel, *Always Among Us: Images of the Poor in Zwingli's Zurich* (1990).

For various aspects of the social history of the period, see in addition to the titles by Bainton and Ozment cited in the Notes, S. E. Ozment, *Magdalena and Balthasar* (1987), which reveals many features of social life through the letters of a Nuremburg couple; and K. von Greyerz, ed., *Religion and Society in Early Modern Europe, 1500–1800* (1984), both of which contain interesting essays on religion, society, and popular culture. For women, see M. E. Wiesner, *Women and Gender in Early Modern Europe* (1993); L. Roper, *The Holy Household: Women and Morals in Reformation Augsburg* (1991), an important study in local religious history as well as the history of gender; M. Wiesner, *Women in the Sixteenth Century: A Bibliography* (1983), a useful reference tool; and S. M. Wyntjes, "Women in the Reformation Era," in *Becoming Visible: Women in European History,* ed. R. Bridenthal and C. Koonz (1977), an interesting general survey. The best recent treatment of marriage and the family is S. E. Ozment, *When Fathers Ruled: Family Life in Reformation Europe* (1983). Ozment's

edition of *Reformation Europe: A Guide to Research* (1982) contains not only helpful references but valuable articles on such topics as "The German Peasants," "The Anabaptists," and "The Confessional Age: The Late Reformation in Germany." For Servetus, see R. H. Bainton, *Hunted Heretic: The Life and Death of Michael Servetus* (1953), which remains valuable.

For England, in addition to the fundamental work by Duffy cited in the Notes, see A. G. Dickens, *The English Reformation* (1964). K. Thomas, *Religion and the Decline of Magic* (1971), provides a useful treatment of pre-Reformation popular religion. S. J. Gunn and P. G. Lindley, eds., *Cardinal Wolsey: Church, State and Art* (1991), is a useful study of that important prelate. The marital trials of Henry VIII are treated in both the sympathetic study of G. Mattingly, *Catherine of Aragon* (1949), and A. Fraser, *The Wives of Henry VIII* (1992). The legal implications of Henry VIII's divorces have been thoroughly analyzed in J. J. Scarisbrick, *Henry VIII* (1968), an almost definitive biography. On the dissolution of the English monasteries, see D. Knowles, *The Religious Orders in England,* vol. 3 (1959), one of the finest examples of historical prose in English written in the twentieth century. Knowles's *Bare Ruined Choirs* (1976) is an attractively illustrated abridgment of *The Religious Orders in England.* G. R. Elton, *The Tudor Revolution in Government* (1959), discusses the modernization of English government under Thomas Cromwell; the same author's *Reform and Reformation: England, 1509–1558* (1977) combines political and social history in a broad study. Many aspects of English social history are discussed in J. Youings, *Sixteenth Century England* (1984), a beautifully written work that is highly recommended.

P. Janelle, *The Catholic Reformation* (1951), is a comprehensive treatment of the Catholic Reformation from a Catholic point of view, and A. G. Dickens, *The Counter Reformation* (1969), gives the Protestant standpoint in a beautifully illustrated book. The definitive study of the Council of Trent was written by H. Jedin, *A History of the Council of Trent,* 3 vols. (1957–1961). For the Jesuits, see W. W. Meissner, *Ignatius of Loyola: The Psychology of a Saint* (1993), and J. W. O'Malley, *The First Jesuits* (1993); these books are basic not only for the beginnings of the Society of Jesus but for the refutation of many myths about the Jesuits. Perhaps the best recent work on the Spanish Inquisition is W. Monter, Frontiers of Heresy: *The Spanish Inquisition from the Basque Lands to Sicily* (1990).

16

The Age of European Expansion and Religious Wars

A detail from an early 17th-century Flemish painting depiction maps, illustrated travel books, a globe, a compass, and an astrolabe. *(Source: Reproduced by courtesy of the Trustees, The National Gallery, London)*

Between 1450 and 1650 two developments dramatically altered the world: Europeans' overseas expansion and the reformations of the Christian church. Europeans carried their cultures to other parts of the globe. Overseas expansion brought them into confrontation with ancient civilizations in Africa, Asia, and the Americas. These confrontations led first to conquest, then to exploitation, and finally to profound social changes in both Europe and the conquered territories. Likewise, the Renaissance and the religious reformations drastically changed intellectual, political, religious, and social life in Europe. War and religious issues dominated the politics of European states. Although religion was commonly used to rationalize international conflict, wars were fought for power and territory.

- Why, in the sixteenth and seventeenth centuries, did a relatively small number of people living on the edge of the Eurasian landmass gain control of the major sea lanes of the world and establish political and economic hegemony on distant continents?

- How were a few Spaniards, fighting far from home, able to overcome the powerful Aztec and Inca Empires in America?

- What effect did overseas expansion have on Europe and on conquered societies?

- What were the causes and consequences of the religious wars in France, the Netherlands, and Germany?

- How did the religious crises of this period affect the status of women?

- How and why did African slave labor become the dominant form of labor organization in the New World?

- What religious and intellectual developments led to the growth of skepticism?

- What literary masterpieces of the English-speaking world did this period produce?

This chapter addresses these questions.

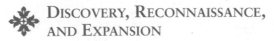 DISCOVERY, RECONNAISSANCE, AND EXPANSION

Historians of Europe have called the period from 1450 to 1650 the "Age of Discovery," "Age of Reconnaissance," and "Age of Expansion." All three labels are appropriate. "Age of Discovery" refers to the era's phenomenal advances in geographical knowledge and technology, often achieved through trial and error. In 1350 it took as long to sail from the eastern end of the Mediterranean to the western end as it had taken a thousand years earlier. Even in the fifteenth century, Europeans knew little more about the earth's surface than the Romans had known. By 1650, however, Europeans had made an extensive reconnaissance—or preliminary exploration—and had sketched fairly accurately the physical outline of the whole earth. Much of the geographical information they had gathered was tentative and not fully understood—hence the appropriateness of "Age of Reconnaissance."

The designation "Age of Expansion" refers to the migration of Europeans to other parts of the world. This colonization resulted in political control of much of South and North America; coastal regions of Africa, India, China, and Japan; and many Pacific islands. Political hegemony was accompanied by economic exploitation, religious domination, and the introduction of European patterns of social and intellectual life. The sixteenth-century expansion of European society launched a new age in world history. None of the three "Age" labels reflects the experiences of non-European peoples. Africans, Asians, and native Americans had known the geographies of their regions for centuries. They made no "discoveries" and undertook no reconnaissance, and they experienced "expansion" only as forced slave laborers.

Overseas Exploration and Conquest

The outward expansion of Europe began with the Viking voyages across the Atlantic in the ninth and tenth centuries. Under Eric the Red and Leif Ericson, the Vikings discovered Greenland and the eastern coast of North America. They made permanent settlements in, and a legal imprint on, Iceland, Ireland, England, Normandy, and Sicily. The Crusades of the eleventh through thirteenth centuries were another phase in Europe's attempt to explore and exploit peoples on the periphery of the continent. But the lack of a strong territorial base, superior Muslim military strength, and sheer misrule combined to make the Crusader kingdoms short-lived. In the mid-fifteenth century, Europe seemed ill prepared for further international

ARCTIC OCEAN

PACIFIC OCEAN

ASIA

JAPAN 1542
Kyushu
CHINA
Macao 1517
Canton 1513
PHILIPPINES
New Guinea
AUSTRALIA

1521

Moluccas 1511
Malacca 1509
Borneo
Sumatra
Java

INDIA
Goa 1510
Ceylon 1505
Calicut 1498

PERSIA
Ormuz 1507
Muscat
ARABIA
Aden 1513
ETHIOPIA

INDIAN OCEAN

MADAGASCAR 1500

1522

Constantinople

EUROPE
Amsterdam
Antwerp

Mombasa 1498
Mozambique

Lisbon
Seville
Ceuta 1415
SAHARA
Timbuktu
Niani
CAPE VERDE 1444
GUINEA
GOLD COAST

AFRICA

Cape of Good Hope

1497

ATLANTIC OCEAN

1522

Azores
Canary Is.
Cape Verde Is. 1456

1519

1498

GREENLAND

Newfoundland 1497

1493

1492

NORTH AMERICA

Quebec 1608

St. Augustine 1565
Cuba
San Salvador 1492
Puerto Rico 1492
Hispaniola 1492
Jamaica
Trinidad 1498
SPANISH MAIN

Rio de Janeiro 1516

BRAZIL

SOUTH AMERICA

Honduras
Cartagena
Panama
Quito 1534
Lima 1535
PERU
Potosi

Santiago
Buenos Aires

NEW SPAIN
Guanajuato
Zacatecas
Mexico City 1519
Vera Cruz

PACIFIC OCEAN

Strait of Magellan

Cape Horn

1520

→ Magellan and crew
→ Columbus
→ Da Gama
→ Other

Spanish holdings
Portuguese holdings

0   1500   3000 Km.
0   1500   3000 Mi.

ventures. By 1450 a grave new threat had appeared in the East: the Ottoman Turks.

Combining excellent military strategy with efficient administration of their conquered territories, the Turks had subdued most of Asia Minor and begun to settle on the western side of the Bosporus. The Muslim Ottoman Turks under Sultan Mohammed II (r. 1451–1481) captured Constantinople in 1453, pressed northwest into the Balkans, and by the early sixteenth century controlled the eastern Mediterranean. The Turkish menace badly frightened Europeans. In France in the fifteenth and sixteenth centuries, twice as many books were printed about the Turkish threat as about the American discoveries. Yet the fifteenth and sixteenth centuries witnessed a fantastic continuation, on a global scale, of European expansion.

Political centralization in Spain, France, and England helps to explain those countries' outward push. In the fifteenth century, Isabella and Ferdinand had consolidated their several kingdoms to achieve a more united Spain. The Catholic rulers revamped the Spanish bureaucracy and humbled dissident elements, notably the Muslims and the Jews. The Spanish monarchy was stronger than ever before and in a position to support foreign ventures; it could bear the costs and dangers of exploration. But Portugal, situated on the extreme southwestern edge of the European continent, got the start on the rest of Europe. Still insignificant as a European land power despite its recently secured frontiers, Portugal sought greatness in the unknown world overseas.

Portugal's taking of Ceuta, an Arab city in northern Morocco, in 1415 marked the beginning of European exploration and control of overseas territory (Map 16.1). The objectives of Portuguese policy included the historic Iberian crusade to Christianize Muslims and the search for gold, for an overseas route to the spice markets of India, and for the mythical Christian ruler of Ethiopia, Prester John.

In the early phases of Portuguese exploration, Prince Henry (1394–1460), called "the Naviga-

tor" because of the annual expeditions he sent down the western coast of Africa, played the leading role. In the fifteenth century, most of the gold that reached Europe came from the Sudan in West Africa and from the Akan peoples living near the area of present-day Ghana. Muslim caravans brought the gold from the African cities of Niani and Timbuktu and carried it north across the Sahara to Mediterranean ports. Then the Portuguese muscled in on this commerce in gold. Prince Henry's carefully planned expeditions succeeded in reaching Guinea, and under King John II (r. 1481–1495) the Portuguese established trading posts and forts on the Guinea coast and penetrated into the continent all the way to Timbuktu (see Map 16.1). Portuguese ships transported gold to Lisbon, and by 1500 Portugal controlled the flow of gold to Europe. The golden century of Portuguese prosperity had begun.

The spices Europeans wanted, however, came from South Asia and the Moluccan islands, not from African kingdoms. Thus the Portuguese pushed farther south down the west coast of Africa. In 1487 Bartholomew Diaz rounded the Cape of Good Hope at the southern tip, but storms and a threatened mutiny forced him to turn back. On a second expedition (1497–1499), the Portuguese mariner Vasco da Gama reached India and returned to Lisbon loaded with samples of Indian wares. King Manuel (r. 1495–1521) promptly dispatched thirteen ships under the command of Pedro Alvares Cabral, assisted by Diaz, to set up trading posts in India. On April 22, 1500, the coast of Brazil in South America was sighted and claimed for the crown of Portugal. Cabral then proceeded south and east around the Cape of Good Hope and reached India. Half of the fleet was lost on the return voyage, but the six spice-laden vessels that dropped anchor in Lisbon harbor in July 1501 more than paid for the entire expedition. Thereafter, convoys were sent out every March. Lisbon became the entrance port for Asian goods into Europe—but not without a fight.

For centuries the Muslims had controlled the rich spice trade of the Indian Ocean, and they did not surrender it willingly. Portuguese commercial activities were accompanied by the destruction or seizure of strategic Muslim coastal forts, which later served Portugal as both trading posts and military bases. Alfonso de Albuquerque, whom the Portuguese crown appointed as governor of India

❉ **MAP 16.1 Overseas Exploration and Conquest in the Fifteenth and Sixteenth Centuries** The voyages of discovery marked another phase in the centuries-old migrations of European peoples. Consider the major contemporary significance of each of the three voyages depicted on this map.

The Cantino Map   This map (1502) is named for the agent secretly commissioned to design it in Lisbon for the duke of Ferrara, an avid Italian map collector. It reveals such good knowledge of the African continent, of the islands of the West Indies, and of the shoreline of present-day Venezuela, Guiana, and Brazil in South America that modern scholars suspect there may have been clandestine voyages to the Americas shortly after Columbus's. (*Source: Biblioteca Estense Universitaria, Modena*)

(1509–1515), decided that these bases and not inland territories should control the Indian Ocean. Accordingly, his cannon blasted open the ports of Calicut, Ormuz, Goa, and Malacca, the vital centers of Arab domination of south Asian spice trade (see Map 16.1). This bombardment laid the foundation for Portuguese imperialism in the sixteenth and seventeenth centuries—a strange way to bring Christianity to "those who were in darkness." As one scholar wrote about the opening of China to the West, "while Buddha came to China on white elephants, Christ was borne on cannon balls."[1]

In March 1493, between the voyages of Diaz and da Gama, Spanish ships entered Lisbon harbor bearing a triumphant Italian explorer in the service of the Spanish monarchy. Christopher Columbus (1451–1506), a Genoese mariner, had secured Spanish support for an expedition to the East (see Listening to the Past). He sailed from Palos, Spain, to the Canary Islands and crossed the Atlantic to the Bahamas, landing in October 1492 on an island that he named San Salvador and believed to be the coast of India.

Technological Stimuli to Exploration

Technological developments were the key to Europe's remarkable outreach. By 1350 cannon made of iron or bronze and able to fire iron or stone balls had been fully developed in western Europe. This artillery emitted frightening noises and great flashes of fire and could batter down fortresses and even city walls. Sultan Mohammed II's siege of Constantinople in 1453 provides a classic illustration of the effectiveness of cannon fire.

Constantinople had very strong walled fortifications. The sultan secured the services of a Western technician, who built fifty-six small cannon and a gigantic gun that could hurl stone balls weighing about eight hundred pounds. The gun had to be moved by several hundred oxen and could be loaded and fired only by about a hundred men working together. Reloading took two hours. This awkward but powerful weapon breached the walls of Constantinople before it cracked on the second day of the bombardment. Lesser cannon finished the job.

Although early cannon posed serious technical difficulties for land warfare, they could be used at sea. The mounting of cannon on ships and improved techniques of shipbuilding gave impetus to European expansion. Since ancient times, most seagoing vessels had been narrow, open boats called *galleys,* propelled largely by oarsmen: slaves or convicts who had been sentenced to the galleys manned the oars of the cargo and war ships that sailed the Mediterranean (both types of ship carried soldiers for defense). Well suited to the calm and thoroughly explored waters of the Mediterranean, galleys could not withstand the rough winds and uncharted shoals of the Atlantic. The need for sturdier craft, as well as population losses caused by the Black Death, forced the development of a new style of ship that did not require soldiers for defense or a large crew of oarsmen.

In the course of the fifteenth century, the Portuguese developed the *caravel,* a small, light, three-masted sailing ship. Though somewhat slower than the galley, the caravel held more cargo and was highly maneuverable. When fitted with cannon, it could dominate larger vessels, such as the round ships commonly used in commerce. The substitution of windpower for manpower, and artillery fire for soldiers, signaled a great technological advance and gave Europeans navigational and fighting ascendancy over the rest of the world.[2]

Other fifteenth-century developments in navigation helped make possible the conquest of the Atlantic. The magnetic compass enabled sailors to determine their direction and position at sea. The astrolabe, an instrument developed by Muslim navigators in the twelfth century and used to determine the altitude of the sun and other celestial bodies, permitted mariners to plot their latitude, or position north or south of the equator. Steadily improved maps and sea charts provided information about distances, sea depths, and geography.

The Explorers' Motives

The expansion of Europe was not motivated by demographic pressures. The Black Death had caused serious population losses from which Europe had not recovered in 1500. Few Europeans emigrated to North or South America in the sixteenth century. Half of those who did sail to begin a new life in America died en route; half of those who reached what they regarded as the New World eventually returned to their homeland. Why, then,

did explorers brave the Atlantic and Pacific Oceans, risking their lives to discover new continents and spread European culture?

The reasons are varied and complex. People of the sixteenth century were still basically medieval: their attitudes and values were shaped by religion and expressed in religious terms. In the late fifteenth century, crusading fervor remained a basic part of the Portuguese and Spanish national ideal. The desire to Christianize Muslims and pagan peoples played a central role in European expansion. Queen Isabella of Spain, for example, showed a fanatical zeal for converting the Muslims to Christianity and concentrated her efforts on the Muslims in Granada. But after the abortive crusading attempts of the thirteenth century, Isabella and other rulers realized full well that they lacked the material resources to mount the full-scale assault on Islam necessary for victory. Crusading impulses thus shifted from the Muslims to the pagan peoples of Africa and the Americas.

Moreover, after the *reconquista*—the Christian reconquest of Muslim areas—enterprising young men of the Spanish upper classes found economic and political opportunities severely limited. As a study of the Castilian city Ciudad Real shows, the traditional aristocracy controlled the best agricultural land and monopolized urban administrative posts. Great merchants and a few nobles (surprisingly, since Spanish law forbade noble participation in commercial ventures) dominated the textile and leather-glove manufacturing industries. Thus many ambitious men emigrated to the Americas to seek their fortunes.[3]

Government sponsorship and encouragement of exploration also help to account for the results of the various voyages. Individual mariners and explorers could not afford the massive sums needed to explore mysterious oceans and to control remote continents. The strong financial support of Prince Henry the Navigator led to Portugal's phenomenal success in the spice trade. Even the grudging and modest assistance of Isabella and Ferdinand eventually brought untold riches—and complicated problems—to Spain. The Dutch in the seventeenth century, through such government-sponsored trading companies as the Dutch East India Company, reaped enormous wealth, and although the Netherlands was a small country in size, it dominated the European economy in 1650.

Scholars have frequently described the European discoveries as a manifestation of Renaissance curiosity about the physical universe—the desire to know more about the geography and peoples of the world. There is truth to this explanation. Cosmography, natural history, and geography aroused enormous interest among educated people in the fifteenth and sixteenth centuries. Just as science fiction and speculation about life on other planets excite readers today, quasi-scientific literature about Africa, Asia, and the Americas captured the imaginations of Europeans. Oviedo's *General History of the Indies* (1547), a detailed eyewitness account of plants, animals, and peoples, was widely read.

Spices were another important incentive to voyages of discovery. Introduced into western Europe by the Crusaders in the twelfth century, nutmeg, mace, ginger, cinnamon, and pepper added flavor and variety to the monotonous diet of Europeans. Spices were also used in the preparation of medicinal drugs and incense for religious ceremonies. In the late thirteenth century, the Venetian Marco Polo (1254?–1324?), the greatest of medieval travelers, had visited the court of the Chinese emperor. The widely publicized account of his travels in the *Book of Various Experiences* stimulated the trade in spices between Asia and Italy. The Venetians came to hold a monopoly of trade in western Europe.

Spices were grown in India and China, shipped across the Indian Ocean to ports on the Persian Gulf, and then transported by Arabs across the Arabian Desert to Mediterranean ports. But the rise of the Ming Dynasty in China in the late fourteenth century resulted in the expulsion of foreigners. And the steady penetration of the Ottoman Turks into the eastern Mediterranean and of Muslims across North Africa forced Europeans to seek a new route to the Asian spice markets.

The basic reason for European exploration and expansion, however, was the quest for material profit. Mariners and explorers frankly admitted this. As Bartholomew Diaz put it, his motives were "to serve God and His Majesty, to give light to those who were in darkness and to grow rich as all men desire to do." When Vasco da Gama reached the port of Calicut, India, in 1498, a native asked what the Portuguese wanted. Da Gama replied, "Christians and spices."[4] The bluntest of the Spanish conquistadors, Hernando Cortés, announced as he prepared to conquer Mexico, "I have come to win gold, not to plow the fields like a peasant."[5]

A sixteenth-century diplomat, Ogier Gheselin de Busbecq, summed up explorers' paradoxical attitude: in expeditions to the Indies and the Antipodes, he said, "religion supplies the pretext and gold the motive."[6]

The Problem of Christopher Columbus

The year 1992, which marked the quincentenary of Columbus's first voyages to the Americas, spawned an enormous amount of discussion about the significance of his voyages. Journalists, scholars, amateurs, and polemicists debated Columbus's accomplishments and failures. Until the 1980s most writers generally would have agreed with the Harvard historian Samuel Eliot Morison in his 1942 biography of Columbus:

The whole history of the Americas stems from the Four Voyages of Columbus; and as the Greek city-states looked back to the deathless gods as their founders, so today a score of independent nations and dominions unite in homage to Columbus, the stout-hearted son of Genoa, who carried Christian civilization across the Ocean Sea.[7]

In 1942, we must remember, the Western Powers believed they were engaged in a life-and-death struggle to defend "Christian civilization" against the evil forces of fascism. As the five hundredth anniversary of his famous voyage approached, however, Columbus underwent severe criticism. Critics charged that he enslaved and sometimes killed the Indians and was a cruel and ineffective governor of Spain's Caribbean colony. Moreover, they said, he did not discover a previously unknown continent: Africans and other Europeans had been to the Western Hemisphere before him. And not only did he not discover a "new" continent, he not not realize what he had found. In short, according to his harshest critics, he was a fool who didn't know what was going on around him. Some claim that he was the originator of European exploitation of the non-European world and destroyed the paradise that had been the New World.[8]

Because those judgments rest on social and ethical standards that did not exist in Columbus's world, responsible scholars consider them ahistorical. Instead, using the evidence of his journal (sea log) and letters, let us ask three basic questions: (1) What kind of man was Columbus, and what forces or influences shaped him? (2) In sailing westward from Europe, what were his goals? (3) Did he achieve his goals, and what did he make of his discoveries?

✤ **Pepper Harvest** To break the monotony of their bland diet, Europeans had a passion for pepper, which—along with cinnamon, cloves, nutmeg, and ginger—was the main object of the Asian trade. Since one kilo of pepper cost 2 grams of silver at the place of production in the East Indies and from 10 to 14 grams of silver in Alexandria, 14 to 18 grams in Venice, and 20 to 30 grams at the markets of northern Europe, we can appreciate the fifteenth-century expression "As dear as pepper." Here natives fill vats, and the dealer tastes a peppercorn for pungency. *(Source: Bibliothèque Nationale, Paris)*

The central feature in the character of Christopher Columbus is that he was a deeply religious man. He began the *Journal* of his voyage to the Americas, written as a letter to Ferdinand and Isabella of Spain, with this recollection:

On 2 January in the year 1492, when your Highnesses had concluded their war with the Moors who reigned in Europe, I saw your Highnesses' banners victoriously raised on the towers of the Alhambra, the citadel of the city, and the Moorish king come out of the city gates and kiss the hands of your Highnesses and the prince, My Lord. And later in that same month, on the grounds of information I had given your Highnesses concerning the lands of India . . . your Highnesses decided to send me, Christopher Columbus, to see these parts of India and the princes and peoples of those lands and consider the best means for their conversion.[9]

He had witnessed the Spanish reconquest of Granada and shared fully in the religious and nationalistic fervor surrounding that event. Just seven months separated Isabella and Ferdinand's entry

into Granada on January 6 and Columbus's departure westward on August 3, 1492. In his mind, the two events were clearly linked. Long after Europeans knew something of Columbus's discoveries in the Caribbean, they considered the restoration of Muslim Granada to Christian hands as Ferdinand and Isabella's greatest achievements; for the conquest, in 1494 the Spanish pope Alexander VI (r. 1492–1503) rewarded them with the title of "Most Catholic Kings." Like the Spanish rulers and most Europeans of his age, Columbus understood Christianity as a missionary religion that should be carried to places and peoples where it did not exist. Although Columbus's character certainly included material and secular qualities, first and foremost, as he wrote in 1498, he believed he was a divine agent:

God made me the messenger of the new heaven and the new earth of which he spoke in the Apocalypse of St. John after having spoken of it through the mouth of the prophet Isaiah; and he showed me the post where to find it.[10]

A second and fundamental facet of Columbus the man is that he was very knowledgeable about the sea. He was familiar with fifteenth-century Portuguese navigational aids such as portolans—written descriptions of routes showing bays, coves, capes, ports, and the distances between these places—and the magnetic compass. He had spent years consulting geographers, mapmakers, and navigators. And, as he implies in his *Journal,* he had acquired not only theoretical but practical experience:

I have spent twenty-three years at sea and have not left it for any length of time worth mentioning, and I have seen everything from east to west [meaning he had been to England] and I have been to Guinea" [North and West Africa].[11]

Some of Columbus's calculations, such as his measurement of the distance from Portugal to Japan as 2,760 miles (it is actually 12,000), proved inaccurate. But his successful thirty-three-day voyage to the Caribbean owed a great deal to his seamanship and his knowledge and skillful use of instruments.

What was the object of his first voyage? What did Columbus set out to do? He gives the answer in the very title of the expedition, "The Enterprise of the Indies." He wanted to find a direct ocean route to Asia, which would provide the opportunity for a greatly expanded trade, a trade in which the European economy, and especially Spain, would participate. Two scholars have recently written, "If Columbus had not sailed westward in search of Asia, someone else would have done so. The time was right for such a bold undertaking."[12] Someone else might have done so, but the fact remains that Columbus, displaying a characteristic Renaissance curiosity and restless drive, actually accepted the challenge.

How did Columbus interpret what he had found, and did he think he had achieved what he set out to do? His mind had been formed by the Bible and the geographical writings of classical authors, as were the minds of most educated people of his time. Thus, as people in every age have often done, Columbus ignored the evidence of his eyes; he described what he saw in the Caribbean as an idyllic paradise, a peaceful garden of Eden. When accounts of his travels were published, Europeans' immediate fascination with this image of the New World meant that Columbus's propaganda created an instant myth. But when he sensed that he had not found the spice markets and bazaars of Asia,

his goal changed from establishing trade with the (East) Indians and Chinese to establishing the kind of trade the Portuguese were then conducting with Africa and with Cape Verde and other islands in the Atlantic (see Map 16.1). That meant setting up some form of government in the Caribbean islands, even though Columbus had little interest in, or capacity for, governing. In 1496, he forcibly subjugated the island of Hispaniola, enslaved the Indians, and laid the basis for a system of land grants tied to the Indians' labor service. Borrowing practices and institutions from reconquest Spain and the Canary Islands, Columbus laid the foundation for Spanish imperial administration. In all of this, Columbus was very much a man of his times. He never understood, however, that the scale of his discoveries created problems of trade, settlers, relations with the Indians, and, above all, government bureaucracy.[13]

The Conquest of Aztec Mexico and Inca Peru

Technological development also helps to explain the Spanish conquest of Aztec Mexico and Inca Peru.

The strange end of the Aztec nation remains one of the most fascinating events in the annals of human societies. The Spanish adventurer Hernando Cortés (1485–1547) landed at Vera Cruz in February 1519. In November he entered Tenochtitlán (Mexico City) and soon had the emperor Montezuma II (r. 1502–1520) in custody. In less than two years Cortés destroyed the monarchy, gained complete control of the Mexican capital, and extended his jurisdiction over much of the Aztec Empire. Why did a strong people defending its own territory succumb so quickly to a handful of Spaniards fighting in dangerous and completely unfamiliar circumstances? How indeed, since Montezuma's scouts sent him detailed reports of the Spaniards' movements? The answers to these questions lie in the fact that at the time of the Spanish arrival the Aztec and Inca Empires faced grave internal difficulties brought on by their religious ideologies; by the Spaniards' boldness, timing, and technology; and by Aztec and Incan psychology and attitudes toward war.

The Spaniards arrived in late summer, when the Aztecs were preoccupied with harvesting their crops and not thinking of war. From the Spaniards' perspective, their timing was ideal. A series of naters and drifters unable to find work in Spain, they did not intend to work in the New World. After assisting in the conquest of the Aztecs and the subjugation of the Incas, these drifters wanted to settle down and become a ruling class. In temperate grazing areas they carved out vast estates and imported Spanish sheep, cattle, and horses for the kinds of ranching with which they were familiar. In the coastal tropics, unsuited for grazing, the Spanish erected huge sugar plantations. Columbus had introduced sugar into the West Indies; Cortés had introduced it into Mexico. Sugar was a great luxury in Europe, and demand for it was high. Around 1550 the discovery of silver at Zacatecas and Guanajuato in Mexico and Potosí in present-day Bolivia stimulated silver rushes. How were the cattle ranches, sugar plantations, and silver mines to be worked? Obviously, by the Indians.

The Spanish quickly established the *encomienda* system, whereby the Crown granted the conquerors the right to employ groups of Indians in a town or area as agricultural or mining laborers or as tribute-payers. Theoretically, the Spanish were forbidden to enslave the Indian natives; in actuality, the encomiendas were a legalized form of slavery. The European demand for sugar, tobacco, and silver prompted the colonists to exploit the Indians mercilessly. Unaccustomed to forced labor, especially in the blistering heat of tropical cane fields or the dark, dank, and dangerous mines, Indians died like flies. Recently scholars have tried to reckon the death rate of the Amerindians in the sixteenth century. Some historians maintain that the Indian population of Peru fell from 1.3 million in 1570 to 600,000 in 1620; central Mexico had 25.3 million Indians in 1519 and 1 million in 1605.[18] Some demographers dispute these figures, but all agree that the decline of the native Indian population in all of Spanish-occupied America amounted to a catastrophe greater in scale than any that has occurred even in the twentieth century.

What were the causes of this devastating slump in population? Students of the history of medicine have suggested the best explanation: disease. The

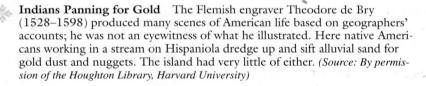

Indians Panning for Gold   The Flemish engraver Theodore de Bry (1528–1598) produced many scenes of American life based on geographers' accounts; he was not an eyewitness of what he illustrated. Here native Americans working in a stream on Hispaniola dredge up and sift alluvial sand for gold dust and nuggets. The island had very little of either. *(Source: By permission of the Houghton Library, Harvard University)*

major cause of widespread epidemics is migration, and those peoples isolated longest from other societies suffer most. Contact with disease builds up bodily resistance. At the beginning of the sixteenth century, Amerindians probably had the unfortunate distinction of longer isolation from the rest of humankind than any other people on earth. Crowded concentrations of laborers in the mining camps bred infection, which the miners carried to their home villages. With little or no resistance to diseases brought from the Old World, the inhabitants of the highlands of Mexico and Peru, especially, fell victim to smallpox. According to one expert, smallpox caused "in all likelihood the most severe single loss of aboriginal population that ever occurred."[19]

Although disease was the prime cause of the Indian holocaust, the Spaniards themselves contributed heavily to the Indians' death rate.[20] According to the Franciscan missionary Bartolomé de Las Casas (1474–1566), the Spanish maliciously murdered thousands:

This infinite multitude of people [the Indians] was . . . without fraud, without subtilty or malice . . . toward the Spaniards whom they serve, patient, meek and peaceful. . . .

To these quiet Lambs . . . came the Spaniards like most c(r)uel Tygres, Wolves and Lions, enrag'd with a sharp and tedious hunger; for these forty years past, minding nothing else but the slaughter of these unfortunate wretches, whom with divers kinds of torments neither seen nor heard of before, they have so cruelly and inhumanely butchered, that of three millions of people which Hispaniola it self did contain, there are left remaining alive scarce three hundred persons.[21]

Las Casas's remarks concentrate on the tropical lowlands, but the death rate in the highlands was also staggering.

The Christian missionaries who accompanied the conquistadors and settlers—Franciscans, Dominicans, and Jesuits—played an important role in converting the Indians to Christianity, teaching them European methods of agriculture, and inculcating loyalty to the Spanish crown. In terms of numbers of people baptized, missionaries enjoyed phenomenal success, though the depth of the Indians' understanding of Christianity remains debatable. Missionaries, especially Las Casas, asserted that the Indians had human rights, and through Las Casas's persistent pressure the emperor Charles V in 1531 abolished the worst abuses of the encomienda system.

Some scholars offer a psychological explanation for the colossal death rate of the Indians, suggesting that they simply lost the will to survive because their gods appeared to have abandoned them to a world over which they had no control. Hopelessness, combined with abusive treatment and overwork, pushed many men to suicide, many women to abortion or infanticide.

Whatever its precise causes, the astronomically high death rate created a severe labor shortage in Spanish America. As early as 1511, King Ferdinand of Spain observed that the Indians seemed to be "very frail" and that "one black could do the work of four Indians."[22] Thus was born an absurd myth and the massive importation of black slaves from Africa (see pages 665–674).

Colonial Administration

Having seized the great Indian ceremonial centers in Mexico and Peru, the Spanish conquistadors proceeded to subdue the main areas of native American civilization in the New World. Columbus, Cortés, and Pizarro claimed the lands they had "discovered" for the crown of Spain. How were these lands to be governed?

According to the Spanish theory of absolutism, the Crown was entitled to exercise full authority over all imperial lands. In the sixteenth century the Crown divided Spain's New World territories into four *viceroyalties*, or administrative divisions. New Spain, with its capital at Mexico City, consisted of Mexico, Central America, and present-day California, Arizona, New Mexico, and Texas. Peru, with its viceregal seat at Lima, originally consisted of all the lands in continental South America but later was reduced to the territory of modern Peru, Chile, Bolivia, and Ecuador. New Granada, with Bogotá as its administrative center, included present-day Venezuela, Colombia, Panama, and, after 1739, Ecuador. La Plata, with Buenos Aires as its capital, consisted of Argentina, Uruguay, and Paraguay. Within each territory a *viceroy*, or imperial governor, had broad military and civil authority as the Spanish sovereign's direct representative. The viceroy presided over the *audiencia*, twelve to fifteen judges who served as advisory council and as the highest judicial body.

From the early sixteenth century to the beginning of the nineteenth, the Spanish monarchy acted on the mercantilist principle that the colonies existed for the financial benefit of the mother country. The mining of gold and silver was always the most important industry in the colonies. The Crown claimed the *quinto,* one-fifth of all precious metals mined in the Americas. Gold and silver yielded the Spanish monarchy 25 percent of its total income. In return, Spain shipped manufactured goods to the New World and discouraged the development of native industries.

The Portuguese governed their colony of Brazil in a similar manner. After the union of the crowns of Portugal and Spain in 1580, Spanish administrative forms were introduced. Local officials called *corregidores* held judicial and military powers. Mercantilist policies placed severe restrictions on Brazilian industries that might compete with those of Portugal. In the seventeenth century the use of black slave labor made possible the cultivation of coffee, cotton, and sugar. In the eighteenth century Brazil led the world in the production of sugar. The unique feature of colonial Brazil's culture and society was its thoroughgoing mixture of Indians, whites, and blacks.

The Economic Effects of Spain's Discoveries on Europe

The sixteenth century has often been called Spain's golden century. The influence of Spanish armies, Spanish Catholicism, and Spanish wealth was felt all over Europe. This greatness rested largely on the influx of precious metals from the Americas.

The mines at Zacatecas, Guanajuato, and Potosí in Peru poured out huge quantities of precious metals. To protect this treasure from French and English pirates, armed convoys transported it each year to Spain. Between 1503 and 1650, 16 million kilograms of silver and 185,000 kilograms of gold entered Seville's port. Spanish predominance, however, proved temporary.

In the sixteenth century, Spain experienced a steady population increase, creating a sharp rise in the demand for food and goods. Spanish colonies in the Americas also represented a demand for products. Since Spain had expelled some of the best farmers and businessmen—the Muslims and Jews—in the fifteenth century, the Spanish economy was suffering and could not meet the new demands. Prices rose. Because the cost of manufacturing cloth and other goods increased, Spanish products could not compete in the international market with cheaper products made elsewhere. The textile industry was badly hurt. Prices spiraled upward faster than the government could levy taxes to dampen the economy. (Higher taxes would have cut the public's buying power; with fewer goods sold, prices would have come down.)

Did the flood of silver bullion from America cause the inflation? Prices rose most steeply before 1565, but bullion imports reached their peak between 1580 and 1620. Thus there is no direct correlation between silver imports and the inflation rate. Did the substantial population growth accelerate the inflation rate? It may have done so. After 1600, when the population pressure declined, prices gradually stabilized. One fact is certain: the price revolution severely strained government budgets. Several times between 1557 and 1647, Spain's king Philip II and his successors repudiated the state debt, thereby undermining confidence in the government and leading the economy into shambles.

As Philip II paid his armies and foreign debts with silver bullion, Spanish inflation was transmitted to the rest of Europe. Between 1560 and 1600, much of Europe experienced large price increases. Prices doubled and in some cases quadrupled. Spain suffered most severely, but all European countries were affected. People who lived on fixed incomes, such as the continental nobles, were badly hurt because their money bought less. Those who owed fixed sums of money, such as the middle class, prospered: in a time of rising prices, debts had less value each year. Food costs rose most sharply, and the poor fared worst of all.

Seaborne Trading Empires

By 1550, European overseas reconnaissance had led to the first global seaborne trade. For centuries the Muslims had controlled the rich spice trade of the Indian Ocean; Muslim expeditions had been across Asian and African land routes. The Europeans' discovery of the Americas and their exploration of the Pacific for the first time linked the entire world by intercontinental seaborne trade. That trade brought into being three successive commercial empires: the Portuguese, the Spanish, and the Dutch.

In the sixteenth century, naval power and shipborne artillery gave Portugal hegemony over the sea route to India. To Lisbon the Portuguese fleet brought spices, which the Portuguese paid for with

textiles produced at Gujarat and Coromandel in India and with gold and ivory from East Africa (Map 16.2). From their fortified bases at Goa on the Arabian Sea and at Malacca on the Malay Peninsula, ships of Malabar teak carried goods to the Portuguese settlement at Macao in the South China Sea. From Macao, loaded with Chinese silks and porcelains, Portuguese ships sailed to the Japanese port of Nagasaki and to the Philippine port of Manila, where Chinese goods were exchanged for Spanish (that is, Latin American) silver. Throughout Asia, the Portuguese traded in slaves—black Africans, Chinese, and Japanese. The Portuguese imported to India horses from Mesopotamia and copper from Arabia; from India they exported hawks and peacocks for the Chinese and Japanese markets.

Across the Atlantic, Portuguese Brazil provided most of the sugar consumed in Europe in the sixteenth and early seventeenth centuries. African slave labor produced the sugar on the plantations of Brazil, and Portuguese merchants, some of them Jewish, controlled both the slave trade between West Africa and Brazil (see pages 545–546) and the commerce in sugar between Brazil and Portugal. The Portuguese were the first worldwide traders, and Portuguese was the language of the Asian maritime trade.

Spanish possessions in the New World constituted basically a land empire and, as already described, in the sixteenth century the Spaniards devised a method of governing that empire. But across the Pacific the Spaniards also built a seaborne empire, centered at Manila in the Philippines, which had been "discovered" by Ferdinand Magellan in 1521. Between 1564 and 1571, the Spanish navigator Miguel Lopez de Legazpi sailed from Mexico and through a swift and almost bloodless conquest took over the Philippine Islands. Legazpi founded Manila, which served as the trans-Pacific bridge between Spanish America and the extreme Eastern trade.

Chinese silk, sold by the Portuguese in Manila for American silver, was transported to Acapulco in Mexico, from which it was carried overland to Vera Cruz for re-export to Spain. Because hostile Pacific winds prohibited direct passage from the Philippines to Peru, large shipments of silk also went south from Acapulco to Peru (see Map 16.2). Spanish merchants could never satisfy the European demand for silk, so huge amounts of bullion went from Acapulco to Manila. For example, in 1597, 12 million pesos of silver, almost the total value of the transatlantic trade, crossed the Pacific. After about 1640, the Spanish silk trade declined because it could not compete with Dutch imports.

In the latter half of the seventeenth century, the worldwide Dutch seaborne trade predominated. The Dutch Empire was built on spices. In 1599 a Dutch fleet returned to Amsterdam carrying 600,000 pounds of pepper and 250,000 pounds of cloves and nutmeg. Those who had invested in the expedition received a 100 percent profit. The voyage led to the establishment in 1602 of the Dutch East India Company, founded with the stated intention of capturing the spice trade from the Portuguese.

The Dutch fleet, sailing from the Cape of Good Hope and avoiding the Portuguese forts in India, steered directly for the Sunda Strait in Indonesia (see Map 16.2). The Dutch wanted direct access to and control of the Indonesian sources of spices. In return for assisting Indonesian princes in local squabbles and disputes with the Portuguese, the Dutch won broad commercial concessions. Through agreements, seizures, and outright war, they gained control of the western access to the Indonesian archipelago. Gradually, they acquired political domination over the archipelago itself. Exchanging European manufactured goods—armor, firearms, linens, and toys—the Dutch soon had a monopoly on the very lucrative spice trade.[23]

The seaborne empires profited from the geographical reconnaissance and technological developments of the sixteenth century. The empires of Portugal, Spain, and Holland had strong commercial ambitions. They also paved the way for the eighteenth-century mercantilist empires of France and Great Britain.

The Chinese and Japanese Discovery of the West

The desire to Christianize pagan peoples was a major motive in Europeans' overseas expansion. The Indians of Central and South America, the

❋ **MAP 16.2 Seaborne Trading Empires in the Sixteenth and Seventeenth Centuries** In the sixteenth century, for the first time, the entire globe was linked by seaborne trade. In the seventeenth century American silver paid for Asian silks and spices, and African slaves in Latin America produced sugar for the tables of Europe.

Muslims and polytheistic peoples of the Pacific, and the Confucian, Buddhist, and Shinto peoples of China and Japan became objects of Christianizing efforts. In this missionary activity the new Jesuit Order was dominant and energetic.

In 1582 the Jesuit Matteo Ricci (1552–1610) settled at Macao on the mouth of the Canton River. Like the Christian monks who had converted the Germanic tribes of early medieval Europe, Ricci sought first to convert the emperor and elite groups and then, through gradual assimilation, to win the throngs of Chinese. He tried to present Christianity to the Chinese in Chinese terms. He understood the Chinese respect for learning and worked to win converts among the scholarly class. When Ricci was admitted to the Imperial City at Beijing (Peking), he addressed the emperor Wan-li:

Li Ma-tou [Ricci's name transliterated into Chinese], your Majesty's servant, comes from the Far West, addresses himself to Your Majesty with respect, in order to offer gifts from his country. Despite the distance, fame told me of the remarkable teaching and fine institutions with which the imperial court has endowed all its peoples. I desired to share these advantages and live out my life as one of Your Majesty's subjects, hoping in return to be of some small use.[24]

Ricci presented the emperor with two clocks, one of them decorated with dragons and eagles in the Chinese style. The emperor's growing fascination with clocks gave Ricci the opportunity to display other examples of Western technology. He instructed court scholars about astronomical equipment and the manufacture of cannon and drew for them a map of the world—with China at its center. These inventions greatly impressed the Chinese intelligentsia. Over a century later a Jesuit wrote, "The Imperial Palace is stuffed with clocks, . . . watches, carillons, repeaters, organs, spheres, and astronomical clocks of all kinds—there are more than four thousand pieces from the best masters of Paris and London."[25] The Chinese first learned about Europe from the Jesuits.

But the Christians and the Chinese did not understand one another. Because the Jesuits served the imperial court as mathematicians, astronomers, and cartographers, the Chinese emperors allowed them to remain in Beijing. The Jesuits, however, were primarily interested in converting the Chinese to Christianity. The missionaries thought that

by showing the pre-eminence of Western science, they were demonstrating the superiority of Western religion. This was a relationship that the Chinese did not acknowledge. They could not accept a religion that required total commitment and taught the existence of an absolute. Only a small number of the highly educated, convinced of a link between ancient Chinese tradition and Christianity, became Christians. Most Chinese were hostile to the Western faith. They accused Christians of corrupting Chinese morals because they forbade people to honor their ancestors—and corruption of morals translated into disturbing the public order. They also accused Christians of destroying Chinese sanctuaries, of revering a man (Christ) who had been executed as a public criminal, and of spying on behalf of the Japanese.

The "Rites Controversy," a dispute over ritual between the Jesuits and other Roman Catholic religious orders, sparked a crisis. The Jesuits supported the celebration of the Mass in Chinese and the performance of other ceremonies in terms understandable to the Chinese. The Franciscans and other missionaries felt that the Jesuits had sold out the essentials of the Christian faith in order to win converts.

One burning issue was whether Chinese reverence for ancestors was homage to the good that the dead had done during their lives or an act of worship. The Franciscans secured the support of Roman authorities who considered themselves authorities on Chinese culture and decided against the Jesuits. In 1704 and again in 1742 Rome decreed that Roman ceremonial practice in Latin (not in Chinese) was to be the law for Chinese missions. (This decision continued to govern Roman Catholic missionary activity until the Second Vatican Council in 1962.) Papal letters also forbade Chinese Christians from participating in the rites of ancestor worship. The emperor in turn banned Christianity in China, and the missionaries were forced to flee.

The Christian West and the Chinese world learned a great deal from each other. The Jesuits probably were "responsible for the rebirth of Chinese mathematics in the seventeenth and eighteenth centuries," and Western contributions stimulated the Chinese development of other sciences.[26] From the Chinese, Europeans got the idea of building bridges suspended by chains. The first Western experiments in electrostatics and magnetism in the seventeenth century derived from

Chinese models. Travel accounts about Chinese society and customs had a profound impact on Europeans, making them more sensitive to the beautiful diversity of peoples and manners, as the essays of Montaigne (see pages 546–547) and other Western thinkers reveal.

Initial Japanese contacts with Europeans paralleled those of the Chinese. In 1542, Portuguese merchants arrived in Japan and quickly won large profits carrying goods between China and Japan. Dutch and English ships followed, also enjoying the rewards of the East Asian trade. The Portuguese merchants vigorously supported Christian missionary activity, and in 1547 the Jesuit missionary Saint Francis Xavier landed at Kagoshima, preached widely, and in two years won many converts. From the beginning, however, the Japanese government feared that native converts might have conflicting political loyalties. Divided allegiance could encourage European invasion of the islands—the Japanese authorities had the example of the Philippines, where Spanish conquest followed missionary activity.

Convinced that European merchants and missionaries had contributed to the general civil disorder, which the regime was trying to eradicate, the Japanese government decided to expel the Spanish and Portuguese and to close Japan to all foreign influence. A decree of 1635 was directed at the commissioners of the port of Nagasaki, a center of Japanese Christianity:

If there is any place where the teachings of the padres (Catholic priests) is practiced, the two of you must order a thorough investigation. . . . If there are any Southern Barbarians (Westerners) who propagate the teachings of the padres, or otherwise commit crimes, they may be incarcerated in the prison.[27]

In 1639, an imperial memorandum decreed: "hereafter entry by the Portuguese galeota [galleon or large oceangoing warship] is forbidden. If they insist on coming [to Japan], the ships must be destroyed and anyone aboard those ships must be beheaded.[28]

When tens of thousands of Japanese Christians made a stand on the peninsula of Shimabara, the Dutch lent the Japanese government cannon. The Protestant Dutch hated Catholicism, and as businessmen they hated the Portuguese, their great commercial rivals. Convinced that the Dutch had come only for trade and did not want to proselytize, the imperial government allowed the Dutch to remain. But Japanese authorities ordered them to remove their factory-station from Hirado on the western tip of Kyushu to the tiny island of Deshima, which covered just 2,100 square feet. The government limited Dutch trade to one ship a year, watched the Dutch very closely, and required Dutch officials to pay an annual visit to the capital to renew their loyalty. The Japanese also compelled the Dutch merchants to perform servile acts that other Europeans considered humiliating.

Long after Christianity ceased to be a potential threat to the Japanese government, the fear of Christianity sustained a policy of banning Western books on science or religion. Until well into the eighteenth century, Japanese intellectuals were effectively cut off from Western developments. The Japanese opinion of Westerners was not high. What little the Japanese knew derived from the few Dutch businessmen at Deshima. Very few Japanese people ever saw Europeans. If they did, they considered them "a special variety of goblin that bore only a superficial resemblance to a normal human being." The widespread rumor was that when Dutchmen urinated they raised one leg like dogs.[29]

POLITICS, RELIGION, AND WAR

In 1559 France and Spain signed the Treaty of Cateau-Cambrésis, which ended the long conflict known as the Habsburg-Valois Wars. This event marks a watershed in early modern European history. Spain (the Habsburg side) was the victor. France, exhausted by the struggle, had to acknowledge Spanish dominance in Italy, where much of the war had been fought. Spanish governors ruled in Sicily, Naples, and Milan, and Spanish influence was strong in the Papal States and Tuscany. The Treaty of Cateau-Cambrésis ended an era of strictly dynastic wars and initiated a period of conflicts in which politics and religion played the dominant roles.

The wars of the late sixteenth century differed considerably from earlier wars. Sixteenth- and seventeenth-century armies were bigger than medieval ones; some forces numbered as many as fifty thousand men. Because large armies were expensive, governments had to reorganize their administrations to finance them. The use of gunpowder altered both the nature of warfare and popular attitudes toward it. Guns and cannon killed and wounded from a distance, indiscriminately. Writers scorned gunpowder as a coward's weapon that allowed a common soldier to kill a gentleman. Gunpowder weakened the notion, common during the Hundred Years' War (1337–1453), that warfare was an ennobling experience. Governments utilized propaganda, pulpits, and the printing press to arouse public opinion to support war.[30]

Late sixteenth-century conflicts fundamentally tested the medieval ideal of a unified Christian society governed by one political ruler—the emperor—to whom all rulers were theoretically subordinate, and one church, to which all people belonged. The Protestant Reformation had killed this ideal, but few people recognized it as dead. Catholics continued to believe that Calvinists and Lutherans could be reconverted; Protestants persisted in thinking that the Roman church should be destroyed. Most people believed that a state could survive only if its members shared the same faith. The settlement finally achieved in 1648, known as the Peace of Westphalia, signaled the end of the medieval ideal.

The Origins of Difficulties in France (1515–1559)

In the first half of the sixteenth century, France continued the recovery begun during the reign of Louis XI (r. 1461–1483). The population losses caused by the plague and the disorders accompanying the Hundred Years' War had created such a labor shortage that serfdom virtually disappeared. Cash rents replaced feudal rents and servile obligations. This development clearly benefited the peasantry. Meanwhile, the declining buying power of money hurt the nobility. Domestic and foreign trade picked up; mercantile centers expanded.

The charming and cultivated Francis I (r. 1515–1547) and his athletic, emotional son Henry II (r. 1547–1559) governed through a small, efficient council. In 1539 Francis issued an ordinance that placed the whole of France under the jurisdiction of the royal law courts and made French the language of those courts. This act had a powerful centralizing impact. The *taille*, a tax on land, provided what strength the monarchy had and supported a strong standing army. Unfortunately, the tax base was too narrow to support France's extravagant promotion of the arts and ambitious foreign policy.

Deliberately imitating the Italian Renaissance princes, the Valois monarchs lavished money on a vast building program and on Italian artists. Francis I commissioned the Paris architect Pierre Lescot to rebuild the palace of the Louvre and Michelangelo's star pupil, Il Rosso, to decorate the wing of the Fontainebleau chateau. After acquiring Leonardo da Vinci's painting *Mona Lisa,* Francis brought Leonardo himself to France. Whatever praise Francis I and Henry II deserve for importing Italian Renaissance art and architecture to France, they spent far more than they could afford.

The Habsburg-Valois Wars, which had begun in 1522, also cost more than the government could afford. In addition to the time-honored practices of increasing taxes and heavy borrowing, Francis I tried two new devices to raise revenue: the sale of public offices and a treaty with the papacy. The former proved to be only a temporary source of money. The offices sold tended to become hereditary within a family, and once a man bought an office he and his heirs were tax-exempt. The sale of public offices thus created a tax-exempt class known as the "nobility of the robe."

The treaty with the papacy was the Concordat of Bologna (1516), in which Francis agreed to recognize the supremacy of the papacy over a universal council, thereby accepting a monarchial, rather than a conciliar view of church government. In return, the French crown gained the right to appoint all French bishops and abbots. This understanding gave the monarchy a rich supplement of money and offices and power over ecclesiastical organization that lasted until the Revolution of 1789. The Concordat of Bologna helps to explain why France did not later become Protestant: in effect, it established Catholicism as the state religion. The Concordat, however, perpetuated disorders within the French church. The government used ecclesiastical offices to pay and reward civil servants, who were likely to be worldly priests who possessed few special spiritual qualifications and were not inclined to work to elevate the intellectual and moral standards of the parish clergy. Thus the teachings of Luther and Calvin, spread far and wide because of the invention of printing from movable type some sixty years before, found a receptive audience.

After the publication of Calvin's *Institutes of the Christian Religion* in 1536, sizable numbers of French people were attracted to the "reformed religion," as Calvinism was called. Because Calvin wrote in French rather than Latin, his ideas gained wide circulation. At first, Calvinism drew converts from among reform-minded members of the

gabelle

Rossi and Primaticcio: The Gallery of Francis I Flat paintings alternating with rich sculpture provide a rhythm that directs the eye down the long gallery at Fontainebleau, constructed between 1530 and 1540. Francis I sought to re-create in France the elegant Renaissance lifestyle found in Italy. *(Source: Art Resource, NY)*

Catholic clergy, the industrious middle classes, and artisan groups. Most Calvinists lived in Paris, Lyons, Meaux, Grenoble, and other major cities.

In spite of condemnation by the universities, government bans, and massive burnings at the stake, the numbers of Protestants in France grew steadily. When Henry II died in 1559, perhaps one-tenth of the population had become Calvinist.

Religious Riots and Civil War in France (1559–1589)

For thirty years, from 1559 to 1589, violence and civil war divided and shattered France. The feebleness of the monarchy was the seed from which the weeds of civil violence germinated. The three weak sons of Henry II could not provide the necessary leadership, and the French nobility took advantage of this monarchial weakness. In the second half of the sixteenth century, between two-fifths and one-half of the nobility at one time or another became Calvinist, frequently adopting the "reformed religion" as a religious cloak for their independence from the monarchy. Armed clashes between Catholic royalist lords and Calvinist antimonarchial lords occurred in many parts of France.

Among the upper classes, the fundamental object of the struggle was power. At lower social levels, however, religious concerns were paramount.

Working-class crowds composed of skilled craftsmen and the poor wreaked terrible violence on people and property. Both Calvinists and Catholics believed that the others' books, services, and ministers polluted the community. Preachers incited violence, and ceremonies like baptisms, marriages, and funerals triggered it. Protestant pastors encouraged their followers to destroy statues and liturgical objects in Catholic churches. Catholic priests urged their flocks to shed the blood of the Calvinist heretics.

In the fourteenth and fifteenth centuries, crowd action—attacks on great nobles and rich prelates—had expressed economic grievances. In contrast, religious rioters of the sixteenth century believed that they could assume the power of public magistrates and rid the community of corruption. Municipal officials criticized the crowds' actions, but the participation of pastors and priests in these riots lent them some legitimacy.[31]

A savage Catholic attack on Calvinists in Paris on August 24, 1572 (Saint Bartholomew's Day), followed the usual pattern. The occasion was a religious ceremony—the marriage of the king's sister Margaret of Valois to the Protestant Henry of Navarre—that was intended to help reconcile Catholics and Huguenots, as French Calvinists were called. The night before the wedding, the leader of the Catholic aristocracy, Henry of Guise, had Gaspard de Coligny, leader of the Huguenot party, attacked. Rioting and slaughter followed. The Huguenot gentry in Paris was massacred, and religious violence spread to the provinces. Between August 25 and October 3, perhaps twelve thousand Huguenots perished at Meaux, Lyons, Orléans, and Paris.

The Saint Bartholomew's Day massacre led to the War of the Three Henrys, a civil conflict among factions led by the Protestant Henry of Navarre, by King Henry III (who succeeded the tubercular Charles IX), and by the Catholic Henry of Guise. The Guises wanted not only to destroy Calvinism but to replace Henry III with a member of the Guise family. France suffered fifteen more years of religious rioting and domestic anarchy. Agriculture in many areas was destroyed; commercial life declined severely; starvation and death haunted the land.

What ultimately saved France was a small group of Catholic moderates called *politiques*. They believed that no religious creed was worth the incessant disorder and destruction and that only the restoration of a strong monarchy could reverse the trend toward collapse. The death of Queen Catherine de' Medici, followed by the assassinations of Henry of Guise and King Henry III, paved the way for the accession of the politique and Protestant Henry of Navarre, who ascended the throne as Henry IV (r. 1589–1610).

This glamorous prince, "who knew how to fight, to make love, and to drink," as a contemporary remarked, knew that the majority of the French were Roman Catholics. Declaring "Paris is worth a Mass," Henry knelt before the archbishop of Bourges and was received into the Roman Catholic church. Henry's willingness to sacrifice religious principles in the interest of a strong monarchy saved France. The Edict of Nantes, which Henry published in 1598, granted to Huguenots liberty of conscience and liberty of public worship in two hundred fortified towns, such as La Rochelle. The reign of Henry IV and the Edict of Nantes prepared the way for French absolutism in the seventeenth century (see page 558) by helping to restore internal peace in France.

The Revolt of the Netherlands and the Spanish Armada

In the last quarter of the sixteenth century, the political stability of England, the international prestige of Spain, and the moral influence of the Roman papacy all became mixed up with a religious crisis in the Low Countries. By this time, the Netherlands was the pivot around which European money, diplomacy, and war revolved. What began as a movement for the reformation of the Catholic church developed into a struggle for Dutch independence from Spanish rule.

The Habsburg emperor Charles V (r. 1519–1556) had inherited the seventeen provinces that compose present-day Belgium and Holland. The French-speaking southern towns produced fine linens and woolens; the wealth of the Dutch-speaking northern cities rested on fishing, shipping, and international banking. In the cities of both regions of the Low Countries, trade and commerce had produced a vibrant cosmopolitan atmosphere.

Each of the seventeen provinces of the Netherlands was self-governing and enjoyed the right to make its own laws and collect its own taxes. Only economic connections and the recognition of a common ruler in the person of the emperor Charles V united the provinces. Delegates from each province met together in the Estates General, but important decisions had to be referred back to each provincial Estate for approval. In the middle of the sixteenth century, the provinces of the Netherlands had a limited sense of federation.

In the Low Countries, as elsewhere, corruption in the Roman church and the critical spirit of the Renaissance provoked pressure for reform. Lutheran tracts and Dutch translations of the Bible flooded the seventeen provinces in the 1520s and 1530s, and Protestant ideas circulated freely in the cosmopolitan atmosphere of the commercial centers. But Charles's Flemish loyalty checked the spread of Lutheranism. Charles had been born in Ghent and raised in the Netherlands; he was Flemish in language and culture. He identified with the Flemish and they with him.

In 1556, however, Charles V abdicated and divided his territories. His younger brother Ferdinand received Austria and the Holy Roman Empire and ruled as Ferdinand I (r. 1558–1564). His son Philip inherited Spain, the Low Countries, Milan and the kingdom of Sicily, and the Spanish possessions in America and ruled as Philip II (r. 1556–1598).

Lutheranism posed no serious threat to Spanish rule in the Low Countries; it was the spread of Calvinism that upset the applecart. By the 1560s,

To Purify the Church   The destruction of pictures and statues representing biblical events, Christian doctrine, or sacred figures was a central feature of the Protestant Reformation. Here Dutch Protestant soldiers destroy what they consider idols in the belief that they are purifying the church. *(Source: Fotomas Index)*

there was a strong, militant minority of Calvinists to whom Calvinism appealed because of its intellectual seriousness, moral gravity, and approval of any form of labor well done. Many working-class people converted because Calvinist employers would hire only fellow Calvinists. Well organized and with the backing of rich merchants, Calvinists quickly gained a wide following, and the Calvinist reformed religion tended in the 1570s to encourage opposition to "illegal" civil authorities.

In August of 1566, a year of very high grain prices, fanatical Calvinists, primarily of the poorest classes, embarked on a rampage of frightful destruction. As in France, Calvinist destruction in the Low Countries was incited by popular preaching, and attacks were aimed at religious images as symbols of false doctrines, not at people. The cathedral of Notre Dame at Antwerp was the first target. Begun in 1124 and finished only in 1518, this church stood as a monument to the commercial prosperity of Flanders, the piety of the business classes, and the artistic genius of centuries. On six succes-

sive summer evenings, crowds swept through the nave, attacking the greatest concentration of artworks in northern Europe: altars, paintings, books, tombs, ecclesiastical vestments, missals, manuscripts, ornaments, stained-glass windows, and sculptures. Before the havoc was over, thirty more churches had been sacked and irreplaceable libraries burned. From Antwerp the destruction spread to Brussels and Ghent and north to the provinces of Holland and Zeeland.

From Madrid, Philip II sent twenty thousand Spanish troops led by the duke of Alva to pacify the Low Countries. Alva interpreted "pacification" to mean the ruthless extermination of religious and political dissidents. His repressive measures and heavy taxation triggered widespread revolt.

For ten years, between 1568 and 1578, civil war raged in the Netherlands between Catholics and Protestants and between the seventeen provinces and Spain. Spanish generals could not halt the fighting. In 1576 the seventeen provinces united under the leadership of Prince William of Orange, called "the Silent" because of his remarkable discretion. In 1578 Philip II sent his nephew Alexander Farnese, duke of Parma, with an army of German mercenaries to crush the revolt once and for all. Avoiding pitched battles, Farnese fought by patient sieges. One by one the cities of the south fell and finally Antwerp, the financial capital of northern Europe.

Antwerp marked the farthest extent of Spanish jurisdiction and ultimately the religious division of the Netherlands. The ten southern provinces, the Spanish Netherlands (the future Belgium), remained Catholic and under the control of the Spanish Habsburgs. The seven northern provinces were Protestant and, led by Holland, formed the Union of Utrecht and in 1581 declared their independence from Spain. Thus was born the United Provinces of the Netherlands (Map 16.3).

Geography and sociopolitical structure differentiated the two countries. The northern provinces were ribboned with sluices and canals and therefore were highly defensible. Several times the Dutch had broken the dikes and flooded the countryside to halt the advancing Farnese. In the southern provinces the Ardennes Mountains interrupt the otherwise flat terrain. In the north the commercial aristocracy possessed the predominant power; in the south the landed nobility had the greater influence. The north was Protestant; the south remained Catholic.

Philip II and Alexander Farnese did not accept the division of the Low Countries, and the strug-

❋ **The Battle of Lepanto**   On October 7, 1571, the fleet of the Holy League (Spain, Venice, the papacy), under Don Juan of Austria, met the Ottoman Turkish navy at a bay in the mouth of the Gulf of Patros off Lepanto in western Greece. Since most of the Ottoman sailors had been sent home for the winter, the Turkish fleet was not ready for battle. Superior European numbers and command prevailed, and the Ottomans were routed. The battle broke the spell of complete Turkish supremacy in the Mediterranean, Europe celebrated a great victory, and the Christian galleys gained a huge crop of prisoners to man the oars. But the Turks quickly rebuilt their navy and regained effective control of the Mediterranean. *(Source: National Maritime Museum, London)*

gle continued after 1581. The Protestant United Provinces repeatedly asked the Protestant Queen Elizabeth of England for assistance. But she was reluctant to antagonize Philip II by supporting the Dutch against the Spanish. The Spanish king had the steady flow of silver from the Americas at his disposal, and Elizabeth, lacking such treasure, wanted to avoid war. She realized, however, that if she did not help the Protestant Netherlands and they were crushed by Farnese, the Spanish were likely to invade England.

Three developments forced Elizabeth's hand. First, the wars in the Low Countries—the chief market for English woolens—badly hurt the English economy. When wool was not exported, the Crown lost valuable customs revenues. Second, the murder of William the Silent in July 1584 eliminated not only a great Protestant leader but the chief military check on the Farnese advance. Third, the collapse of Antwerp appeared to signal a Catholic sweep through the Netherlands. The next step, the English feared, would be a Spanish invasion of their island. For these reasons, Elizabeth pumped £250,000 and two thousand troops into the Protestant cause in the Low Countries between 1585 and 1587. Increasingly fearful of plots orchestrated by the Catholic Mary, Queen of Scots, Elizabeth's cousin and probable heir, Elizabeth finally signed her death warrant. Mary was beheaded on February 18, 1587. Sometime between March 24 and 30, the news of Mary's death reached Philip II.

Philip of Spain considered himself the international defender of Catholicism and heir to the medieval imperial power. When Pope Sixtus V (r. 1585–1590) heard of the death of the Queen of Scots, he promised to pay Philip a million gold ducats the moment Spanish troops landed in England. Alexander Farnese had repeatedly warned that, to subdue the Dutch, he would have to conquer England and cut off the source of Dutch support.

In these circumstances Philip prepared a vast fleet to sail from Lisbon to Flanders, fight off Elizabeth's navy *if* it attacked, rendezvous with Farnese, and escort his barges across the English Channel. The expedition's purpose was to transport the Flemish army for a cross-Channel assault. Philip expected to receive the support of English Catholics and anticipated a great victory for Spain.

On May 9, 1588, *la felicissima armada*—"the most fortunate fleet" of 130 vessels as it was called in official documents—sailed from Lisbon harbor.

MAP 16.3 The Netherlands, 1578–1609 Though small in geographical size, the Netherlands held a strategic position in the religious struggles of the sixteenth century.

An English fleet of about 150 ships—smaller, faster, and more maneuverable than the Spanish ships, and many having greater firepower—met the Spanish fleet in the Channel. A combination of storms and squalls, spoiled food and rank water aboard the Spanish ships, inadequate Spanish ammunition, and, to a lesser extent, English fire ships that caused the Spanish to scatter gave England the victory. Many Spanish ships sank on the journey home around Ireland; perhaps 65 managed to reach home ports.

The battle in the Channel had mixed consequences. Spain soon rebuilt its navy, and after 1588 the quality of the Spanish fleet improved. More silver reached Spain from the New World between 1588 and 1603 than in any other fifteen-year period. The war between England and Spain dragged on for years.

RUSSIA

FINLAND

SWEDEN

NORWAY

Vilna

ESTONIA

LIVONIA

POLAND

Warsaw

Baltic Sea

PRUSSIA

Danzig

Vistula

CRIMEA

Black Sea

MOLDAVIA

TRANSYLVANIA

WALLACHIA

Dnieper

Dniester

OTTOMAN

E M P I R E

Constantinople*

*Athens

CRETE
(To Rep. of Venice)

DENMARK

*Copenhagen

JUTLAND

SCHLESWIG

Lübeck*

Hamburg*

Bremen*

POMERANIA

MECKLENBURG

BRANDENBURG

Berlin*

Breitenfeld

×·1631

SILESIA

White Mountain 1620

*Prague

BOHEMIA

Elbe

SAXONY

×

Lützen 1632

Magdeburg*

Osnabrück*

Münster*

Essen*

Cologne*

Rhine

UNITED
NETHERLANDS

Amsterdam*

Antwerp*

SPANISH
NETHERLANDS

*Paris

London*

ENGLAND

Nantes*

Loire

FRANCE

Metz*

ALSACE

FRANCHE-
COMTÉ

Geneva*

SWITZERLAND

Zurich*

SAVOY

PIEDMONT

MILAN

GENOA

FLORENCE

REPUBLIC OF VENICE

CORSICA
(To Genoa)

SARDINIA

MORAVIA

Nördlingen 1634

×

BAVARIA

Augsburg*

STYRIA

CARNIOLA

Vienna*

Danube

Buda*

Pest*

Belgrade*

PAPAL
STATES

Rome*

NAPLES

Naples*

Palermo*

SICILY

Mediterranean Sea

BALEARIC IS.

SPAIN

Madrid*

Tagus

Ebro

PORTUGAL

Lisbon*

ATLANTIC
OCEAN

North Sea

SCOTLAND

Edinburgh*

IRELAND

Dublin*

Austrian Habsburg lands
Spanish Habsburg lands
Prussian lands
German states
Swedish lands
Boundary of Holy Roman Empire
× Major battles

0   150   300 Km.

0   150   300 Mi.

The defeat of the Spanish Armada was decisive, however, in the sense that it prevented Philip II from reimposing unity on western Europe by force. He did not conquer England, and Elizabeth continued her financial and military support of the Dutch. In the Netherlands neither side gained significant territory. The borders of 1581 tended to become permanent. In 1609 Philip III of Spain (r. 1598–1621) agreed to a truce, in effect recognizing the independence of the United Provinces. In seventeenth-century Spain the memory of the defeat of the Armada contributed to a spirit of defeatism. In England the victory gave rise to a David and Goliath legend that enhanced English national sentiment.

The Thirty Years' War (1618–1648)

Meanwhile, the political-religious situation in central Europe deteriorated. An uneasy truce had prevailed in the Holy Roman Empire since the Peace of Augsburg of 1555. The Augsburg settlement, recognizing the independent power of the German princes, had undermined the authority of the central government. According to the Augsburg settlement, the faith of the prince determined the religion of his subjects. There was no freedom of religion. If a prince was Lutheran, his subjects would be Lutheran. If a prince was Catholic, his subjects would be too. Dissidents had to convert or move to an area where their religion was recognized. Later in the century, Catholics grew alarmed because Lutherans, in violation of the Peace of Augsburg, were steadily acquiring German bishoprics. And Protestants were not pleased by militant Jesuits' success in reconverting several Lutheran princes to Catholicism. The spread of Calvinism further confused the issue. Lutherans feared that Catholic and Calvinist gains would totally undermine the Augsburg principles. In an increasingly tense situation, Lutheran princes formed the Protestant Union (1608). Catholics retaliated with the Catholic League (1609). The Holy Roman Empire was divided into two armed camps.

✳ **MAP 16.4 Europe in 1648** Which country emerged from the Thirty Years' War as the strongest European power? What dynastic house was that country's major rival in the early modern period?

Dynastic interests were also at stake. The Spanish Habsburgs strongly supported the goals of the Austrian Habsburgs: the unity of the empire under Habsburg rule and the preservation of Catholicism within the empire.

Violence erupted first in Bohemia (Map 16.4). The Bohemians were Czech and German in nationality, and Lutheran, Calvinist, Catholic, and Hussite in religion; all these faiths enjoyed a fair degree of religious freedom in Bohemia. In 1617 Ferdinand of Styria, the new Catholic king of Bohemia, closed some Protestant churches. In retaliation, on May 23, 1618, Protestants hurled two of Ferdinand's officials from a castle window in Prague. They fell 70 feet but survived: Catholics claimed that angels had caught them; Protestants said the officials fell on a heap of soft horse manure. Called the "defenestration of Prague," this event marked the beginning of the Thirty Years' War (1618–1648).

Historians traditionally divide the war into four phases. The first, or Bohemian, phase (1618–1625) was characterized by civil war in Bohemia, as Bohemians fought for religious liberty and independence from Austrian Habsburg rule. In 1620 Ferdinand, newly elected Holy Roman Emperor Ferdinand II (r. 1619–1637), totally defeated Protestant forces at the Battle of the White Mountain and followed up his victories by wiping out Protestantism in Bohemia.

The second, or Danish, phase of the war (1625–1629)—so called because of the participation of King Christian IV of Denmark (r. 1588–1648), the ineffective leader of the Protestant cause—witnessed additional Catholic victories. The year 1629 marked the peak of Habsburg power. The Jesuits persuaded Ferdinand to issue the Edict of Restitution. It specified that all Catholic properties lost to Protestantism since 1552 were to be restored and only Catholics and Lutherans (*not* Calvinists, Hussites, or other sects) were to be allowed to practice their faiths. Ferdinand appeared to be embarked on a policy to unify the empire. Protestants throughout Europe feared collapse of the balance of power in north-central Europe.

The third, or Swedish, phase of the war (1630–1635) began when Swedish king Gustavus Adolphus (1594–1632) intervened to support the Protestant cause within the empire. In 1631, with French support, Gustavus Adolphus won a brilliant victory at Breitenfeld (see Map 16.4). Again in

1632 he was victorious at Lützen, though he was fatally wounded in the battle. The participation of the Swedes in the Thirty Years' War proved decisive for the future of Protestantism and later German history. The Swedish victories ended the Habsburg ambition of uniting all the German states under imperial authority.

The death of Gustavus Adolphus, followed by the defeat of the Swedes at the Battle of Nördlingen in 1634, prompted the French to enter the war on the side of the Protestants. Thus began the French, or international, phase of the Thirty Years' War (1635–1648). For almost a century, French foreign policy had been based on opposition to the Habsburgs, because a weak Holy Roman Empire enhanced France's international stature. Now, in 1635, France declared war on Spain and again sent financial and military assistance to the Swedes and the German Protestant princes. The war dragged on; neither side had the resources to win a quick, decisive victory. French, Dutch, and Swedes, supported by Scots, Finns, and German mercenaries, burned, looted, and destroyed German agriculture and commerce.

Finally, in October 1648, peace was achieved. The treaties signed at Münster and Osnabrück— the Peace of Westphalia—mark a turning point in European political, religious, and social history. The treaties recognized the sovereign, independent authority of the German princes. Each ruler could govern his particular territory and make war and peace as well. With power in the hands of more than three hundred princes, with no central government, courts, or means of controlling unruly rulers, the Holy Roman Empire as a real state was effectively destroyed.

The independence of the United Provinces of the Netherlands was acknowledged. The political divisions within the empire, and the acquisition of the province of Alsace increased France's size and prestige, and the treaties allowed France to intervene at will in German affairs. Sweden achieved a powerful presence in northeastern Germany (see Map 16.4). The treaties also denied the papacy the right to participate in German religious affairs— a restriction symbolizing the reduced role of the church in European politics.

The Westphalian treaties stipulated that the Augsburg religious agreement of 1555 should stand permanently. The sole modification made Calvinism, along with Catholicism and Lutheranism, a legally permissible creed. In practice, the north German states remained Protestant, the south German states Catholic.

The Thirty Years' War settled little but was a disaster for the German economy and society—probably the most destructive event in German history before the twentieth century. Population losses were frightful. Perhaps one-third of the urban residents and two-fifths of the inhabitants of rural areas died. Entire areas of Germany were depopulated, partly by military actions, partly by disease— typhus, dysentery, bubonic plague, and syphilis (brought to Europe from the Americas) accompanied the movements of armies—and partly by the thousands of refugees who fled to safer areas.

In Germany the European-wide economic crisis caused primarily by the influx of silver from South America was badly aggravated by the war. Scholars still cannot estimate the value of losses in agricultural land and livestock, in trade and commerce. Those losses, compounded by the flood of Spanish silver, brought on severe price increases. Inflation was worse in Germany than anywhere else in Europe.

The population decline caused a rise in the value of labor. Owners of great estates had to pay more for agricultural workers. Farmers who needed only small amounts of capital to restore their lands started over again. Many small farmers, however, lacked the revenue to rework their holdings and became day laborers. Nobles and landlords were able to buy up many small holdings and amass great estates. In some parts of Germany, especially east of the Elbe River in areas like Mecklenburg and Pomerania, peasants' loss of land led to a new serfdom.[32] The Thirty Years' War contributed to the legal and economic decline of the largest segment of German society.

✤ CHANGING ATTITUDES

What were the cultural consequences of the religious wars and of the worldwide discoveries? What impact did the discoveries and wars have on Europeans' attitudes? The clash of traditional religious and geographical beliefs with the new knowledge provided by explorers—combined with decades of devastation and disorder within Europe—bred confusion, uncertainty, and insecurity. Geographical evidence based on verifiable scientific proofs contradicted the evidence of the Scriptures and of the classical authors.

✥ **The Horrors of War**   Following Richelieu's invasion of Lorraine in 1633, the French engraver Jacques Callot (1592/3–1635) produced a series of etchings collectively titled *The Great Miseries of War*, depicting the theft, rape, and brutality for which soldiers of the Thirty Years' War gained an enduring reputation. *(Source: Courtesy of the Trustees of the British Museum)*

The age of religious wars revealed extreme and violent contrasts. It was a deeply religious period in which men fought passionately for their beliefs; 70 percent of the books printed dealt with religious subjects. Yet the times saw the beginnings of religious skepticism. Europeans explored new continents, partly with the missionary aim of Christianizing the peoples they encountered. Yet the Spanish, Portuguese, Dutch, and English proceeded to dominate and enslave the Indians and blacks they encountered. While Europeans indulged in gross sensuality, the social status of women declined. The exploration of new continents reflects deep curiosity and broad intelligence. Yet Europeans believed in witches and burned thousands at the stake. Sexism, racism, and skepticism had all originated in ancient times. But late in the sixteenth century they began to take on their familiar modern forms.

The Status of Women

Did new ideas about women appear in this period? Theological and popular literature on marriage published in Reformation Europe helps to answer this question. Manuals emphasized the qualities expected of each partner. A husband was obliged to provide for the material welfare of his wife and children, to protect his family while remaining steady and self-controlled. He was to rule his household firmly but justly; he was not to behave like a tyrant—a guideline that counselors repeated frequently. A wife was to be mature, a good household manager, and subservient and faithful to her spouse. The husband also owed fidelity. Both Protestant and Catholic moralists rejected the double standard of sexual morality, considering it a threat to family unity. Counselors believed that marriage should be based on mutual respect and trust. Although they discouraged impersonal unions arranged by parents, they did not think romantic attachments—based on physical attraction and love—a sound basis for an enduring relationship.

A woman might assist in her own or her husband's business and do charitable work. But moralists held that involvement in social or public activities was inappropriate because it distracted the wife from her primary responsibility: her household. If a woman suffered under her husband's yoke, writers explained, her submission, like the pain of childbearing, was a punishment inherited from Eve, penance for man's fall. Moreover, they said, a woman's lot was no worse than a man's: he had to earn the family's bread by the sweat of his brow.[33]

Catholics viewed marriage as a sacramental union; validly entered into, it could not be dissolved. Protestants stressed the contractual nature of marriage: each partner promised the other support, companionship, and the sharing of mutual property. Protestants recognized the right of both parties to divorce and remarry for various reasons, including adultery and irreparable breakdown.[34]

Society in the early modern period was patriarchal. Women neither lost their identity nor lacked meaningful work, but the all-pervasive assumption was that men ruled. Leading students of the Lutherans, Catholics, French Calvinists, and English Puritans tend to agree that there was no improvement in women's long-standing subordinate status.

Artists' drawings of plump, voluptuous women and massive, muscular men reveal the contemporary standards of physical beauty. It was a sensual age that gloried in the delights of the flesh. Some people, such as the humanist poet Pietro Aretino (1492–1556), found sexual satisfaction with people of either sex. Reformers and public officials simultaneously condemned and condoned sexual "sins."

Prostitution was common because desperate poverty forced women and young men into it. Since the later Middle Ages, licensed houses of prostitution had been common in urban centers. When in 1566 Pope Pius IV (r. 1559–1565) expelled all the prostitutes from Rome, so many people left and the city suffered such a loss of revenue that in less than a month the pope was forced to rescind the order. Scholars debated Saint Augustine's notion that prostitutes serve a useful social function by preventing worse sins. Civil authorities in both Catholic and Protestant countries licensed houses of public prostitution. These establishments were intended for the convenience of single men, and some Protestant cities, such as Geneva and Zurich, installed officials in the brothels with the express purpose of preventing married men from patronizing them.

Single women of the middle and working classes in the sixteenth and seventeenth centuries worked in many occupations and professions—as butchers, shopkeepers, nurses, goldsmiths, and midwives and in the weaving and printing industries. Most women who were married assisted in their husbands' businesses. What became of the thousands of women who left convents and nunneries during the Reformation? This question pertains primarily to women of the upper classes, who formed the dominant social group in the religious houses of late medieval Europe. Luther and the Protestant reformers believed that celibacy had no scriptural

basis and that young girls were forced by their parents into convents and, once there, were bullied by men into staying. Therefore, reformers favored the suppression of women's religious houses and encouraged former nuns to marry. Marriage, the reformers maintained, not only gave women emotional and sexual satisfaction but freed them from clerical domination, cultural deprivation, and sexual repression.[35] It appears that these women passed from clerical domination to subservience to husbands.

Some nuns in the Middle Ages probably did lack a genuine religious vocation, and some religious houses did witness financial mismanagement and moral laxness. Nevertheless, convents had provided women of the upper classes with an outlet for their literary, artistic, medical, or administrative talents if they could not or would not marry. When the convents were closed, marriage became virtually the only occupation available to upper-class Protestant women.

The great European witch scare reveals more about contemporary attitudes toward women.

The Great European Witch-Hunt

The period of the religious wars witnessed a startling increase in the phenomenon of witch-hunting, whose prior history was long but sporadic. "A witch," according to Chief Justice Edward Coke of England (1552–1634), "was a person who hath conference with the Devil to consult with him or to do some act." This definition by the highest legal authority in England demonstrates that educated people, as well as the ignorant, believed in witches. Witches were thought to be individuals who could mysteriously injure other people or animals—by causing a person to become blind or impotent, for instance, or by preventing a cow from giving milk.

Belief in witches dates back to the dawn of time. For centuries, tales had circulated about old women who made nocturnal travels on greased broomsticks to *sabbats,* or assemblies of witches, where they participated in sexual orgies and feasted on the flesh of infants. In the popular imagination witches had definite characteristics. The vast majority were married women or widows between fifty and seventy years old, crippled or bent with age, with pockmarked skin. They often practiced midwifery or folk medicine, and most had sharp tongues and were quick to scold.

Religious reformers' extreme notions of the Devil's powers and the insecurity created by the religious wars contributed to the growth of belief in witches. The idea developed that witches made pacts with the Devil in return for the power to work mischief on their enemies. Since pacts with the Devil meant the renunciation of God, witchcraft was considered heresy, and persecution for it had actually begun in the later fourteenth century when it was so declared. Persecution reached its most virulent stage in the late sixteenth and seventeenth centuries.

Fear of witches took a terrible toll of innocent lives in several parts of Europe. In southwestern Germany, 3,229 witches were executed between 1561 and 1670, most by burning. The communities of the Swiss Confederation in central Europe tried 8,888 persons between 1470 and 1700 and executed 5,417 of them as witches. In all the centuries before 1500, witches in England had been suspected of causing perhaps "three deaths, a broken leg, several destructive storms and some bewitched genitals." Yet between 1559 and 1736, almost 1,000 witches were executed in England.[36]

Historians and anthropologists have offered a variety of explanations for the great European witch-hunt. Some scholars maintain that charges of witchcraft were a means of accounting for inexplicable misfortunes. The English in the fifteenth century had blamed their military failures in France on Joan of Arc's witchcraft. In the seventeenth century the English Royal College of Physicians attributed undiagnosable illnesses to witchcraft. Some scholars think that in small communities, which typically insisted on strict social conformity, charges of witchcraft were a means of attacking and eliminating the nonconformist; witches, in other words, served the collective need for scapegoats. The evidence of witches' trials, some writers suggest, shows that women were not accused because they harmed or threatened their neighbors; rather, people believed such women worshiped the Devil, engaged in wild sexual activities with him, and ate infants. Other scholars argue the exact opposite: that people were tried and executed as witches because their neighbors feared their evil powers. According to still another theory, the unbridled sexuality attributed to witches was a figment of their accusers' imagination—a psychological projection by their accusers resulting from Christianity's repression of sexuality.

Witches Worshiping the Devil In medieval Christian art, a goat symbolizes the damned at the Last Judgment, following Christ's statement that the Son of Man would separate believers from nonbelievers as a shepherd separates the sheep from the goats (Matthew 25:31–32). In this manuscript illustration, a witch arrives at a sabbat and prepares to venerate the Devil in the shape of a goat by kissing its anus. *(Source: The Bodleian Library, Oxford)*

Despite an abundance of hypotheses, scholars cannot fully understand the phenomenon. Specific reasons for the persecution of women as witches probably varied from place to place. Nevertheless, given the broad strand of misogyny (hostility to women) in Western religion, the ancient belief in the susceptibility of women (the so-called weaker vessels) to the Devil's allurements, and the pervasive seventeenth-century belief about women's multiple and demanding orgasms and thus their sexual insatiability, it is not difficult to understand why women were accused of all sorts of mischief and witchcraft. Charges of witchcraft provided a legal basis for the execution of tens of thousands of women. The most important capital crime for women in early modern times, witchcraft has considerable significance for the history and status of women.[37]

African Slave and Indian Woman A black slave approaches an Indian prostitute. Unable to explain what he wants, he points with his finger; she eagerly grasps for the coin. The Spanish caption above moralizes on the black man using stolen money—yet the Spaniards ruthlessly expropriated all South American mineral wealth. (*Source: New York Public Library*)

European Slavery and the Origins of American Racism

Except for the Aborigines of Australia, almost all peoples in the world have engaged in the enslavement of other human beings at some time in their histories. Since ancient times, victors in battle have enslaved conquered peoples. In the later Middle Ages slavery was deeply entrenched in southern Italy, Sicily, Crete, and Mediterranean Spain. The bubonic plague, famines, and other epidemics created a severe shortage of agricultural and domestic workers throughout Europe, encouraging Italian merchants to buy slaves from the Balkans, Thrace,

southern Russia, and central Anatolia for sale in the West. In 1364 the Florentine government allowed the unlimited importation of slaves as long as they were not Catholics. Between 1414 and 1423, at least ten thousand slaves were sold in Venice alone. The slave trade was a lucrative business enterprise in Italy during the Renaissance. Where profits were high, papal threats of excommunication completely failed to stop it. Genoese slave traders set up colonial stations in the Crimea and along the Black Sea, and according to an international authority on slavery, these outposts were "virtual laboratories" for the development of slave plantation agriculture in the New World.[38] This form of slavery had nothing to do with race; almost all of these slaves were white. How, then, did black African slavery enter the European picture and take root in the New World?

The capture of Constantinople by the Ottoman Turks in 1453 halted the flow of white slaves from the Black Sea region and the Balkans. Mediterranean Europe, cut off from its traditional source of slaves, had no alternative source for slave labor but sub-Saharan Africa. The centuries-old trans-Saharan trade in slaves was greatly stimulated by the existence of a ready market for slaves in the vineyards and sugar plantations of Sicily and Majorca. By the later fifteenth century, before the discovery of America, the Mediterranean had developed an "American" form of slavery.

Meanwhile, the Genoese and other Italians had colonized the Canary Islands in the western Atlantic. And sailors working for Portugal's Prince Henry the Navigator (see page 517) discovered the Madeira Islands and made settlements there. In this stage of European expansion, "the history of slavery became inextricably tied up with the history of sugar."[39] Population increases and monetary expansion in the fifteenth century led to an increasing demand for sugar even though it was an expensive luxury that only the affluent could afford. Between 1490 and 1530, between 300 and 2,000 black slaves arrived annually at the port of Lisbon (Map 16.5). From Lisbon, where African slaves performed most of the manual labor and constituted 10 percent of the city's population, slaves were transported to the sugar plantations of Madeira, the Azores, the Cape Verde Islands, and then Brazil. Sugar and those small Atlantic islands gave slavery in the Americas its distinctive shape. Columbus himself spent a decade in Madeira and took sugar plants on his voyages to "the Indies."

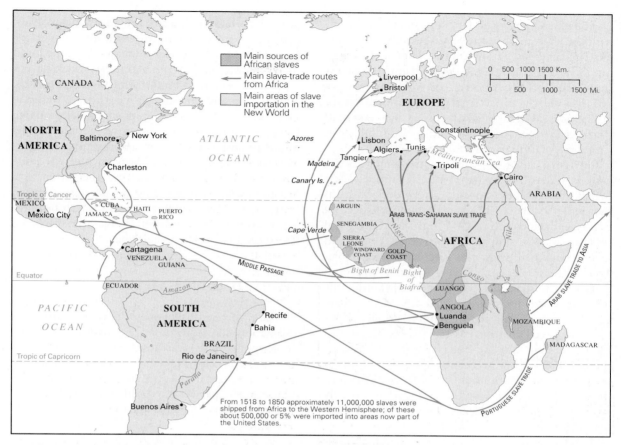

Main sources of
African slaves
Main slave-trade routes
from Africa
Main areas of slave
importation in the
New World

From 1518 to 1850 approximately 11,000,000 slaves were
shipped from Africa to the Western Hemisphere; of these
about 500,000 or 5% were imported into areas now part of
the United States.

MAP 16.5 The African Slave Trade   Decades before the discovery of America,
Greek, Russian, Bulgarian, Armenian, and then black slaves worked the plantation
economies of southern Italy, Sicily, Portugal, and Mediterranean Spain—thereby
serving as models for the American form of slavery.

As European economic exploitation of the
Americas proceeded, the major problem settlers
faced was a shortage of labor. As early as 1495, the
Spanish solved the problem by enslaving the native
Indians. In the next two centuries, the Portuguese,
Dutch, and English followed suit.

Unaccustomed to any form of forced labor, certainly not to panning gold for more than twelve
hours a day in the broiling sun, the Indians died
"like fish in a bucket," as one Spanish settler reported.[40] In 1515 the Spanish missionary Bartolomé de Las Casas (see page 526), who had seen
the evils of Indian slavery, urged the future emperor Charles V to end Indian slavery in his American dominions. Las Casas recommended the importation of blacks from Africa, both because
church law did not strictly forbid black slavery and

because he thought blacks could better survive under South American conditions. Charles agreed,
and in 1518 the African slave trade began. (When
the blacks arrived, Las Casas immediately regretted
his suggestion.) Columbus's introduction of sugar
plants, moreover, stimulated the need for black
slaves, and the experience and model of plantation
slavery in Portugal and on the Atlantic islands encouraged the establishment of a similar agricultural
pattern in the New World.

Several European nations participated in the
African slave trade. Portugal brought the first
slaves to Brazil; by 1600, 4,000 were being imported annually. After its founding in 1621, the
Dutch West India Company, with the full support
of the government of the United Provinces, transported thousands of Africans to Brazil and the

Caribbean. Only in the late seventeenth century, with the chartering of the Royal African Company, did the English get involved. Thereafter, large numbers of African blacks poured into the West Indies and North America. In 1790 there were 757,181 blacks in a total U.S. population of 3,929,625. When the first census was taken in Brazil in 1798, blacks numbered about 2 million in a total population of 3.25 million.

European settlers brought to the Americas the racial attitudes they had absorbed in Europe. Their beliefs and attitudes toward blacks derived from two basic sources: Christian theological speculation about the nature of God (light) and the Devil (black), and Muslim ideas. In the sixteenth and seventeenth centuries, the English, for example, were extremely curious about Africans' lives and customs, and slavers' accounts were extraordinarily popular. Travel literature depicted Africans as savages because of their eating habits, morals, clothing, and social customs; as barbarians because of their language and methods of war; and as heathens because they were not Christian. English people saw similarities between apes and Africans; thus the terms *bestial* and *beastly* were frequently applied to Africans. Africans were believed to possess a potent sexuality. One seventeenth-century observer considered Africans "very lustful and impudent, . . . their members' extraordinary greatness is a token of their lust." African women were considered sexually aggressive with a "temper hot and lascivious."[41]

"At the time when Columbus sailed to the New World, Islam was the largest world religion, and the only world religion that showed itself capable of expanding rapidly in areas as far apart and as different from each other as Senegal [in northwest Africa], Bosnia [in the Balkans], Java, and the Philippines."[42] Medieval Arabic literature emphasized blacks' physical repulsiveness, mental inferiority, and primitivism. In contrast to civilized peoples from the Mediterranean to China, some Muslim writers claimed, sub-Saharan blacks were the only peoples who had produced no sciences or stable states. The fourteenth-century Arab historian Ibn Khaldun (1332–1406) wrote that "the only people who accept slavery are the Negroes, owing to their low degree of humanity and their proximity to the animal stage." Though black kings, Khaldun alleged, sold their subjects without even a pretext of crime or war, the victims bore no resentment because they gave no thought to the future and had "by nature few cares and worries; dancing and rhythm are for them inborn."[43] It is easy to see how such absurd images developed into the classic stereotypes used to justify black slavery in South and North America in the seventeenth, eighteenth, and nineteenth centuries. Medieval Christians and Muslims had similar notions of blacks as inferior and primitive people ideally suited to enslavement. Perhaps centuries of commercial contacts between Muslim and Mediterranean peoples had familiarized the latter with Muslim racial attitudes. The racial beliefs that the Portuguese, Spanish, Dutch, and English brought to the New World, however, derive primarily from Christian theological speculation.

❈ LITERATURE AND ART

The age of religious wars and overseas expansion also witnessed extraordinary intellectual and artistic ferment. This effervescence can be seen in prose, poetry, and drama, in art, and in music. In many ways, the literature, visual arts, music, and drama of the period mirrored the social and cultural conditions that gave rise to them.

The Essay: Michel de Montaigne

Decades of religious fanaticism brought famine, civil anarchy, and death and led both Catholics and Protestants to doubt that any one faith contained absolute truth. The late sixteenth and seventeenth centuries witnessed the beginning of modern *skepticism,* a school of thought founded on doubt that total certainty or definitive knowledge is ever attainable. The skeptic is cautious and critical and suspends judgment. Perhaps the finest representative of early modern skepticism is the Frenchman Michel de Montaigne (1533–1592).

Montaigne came from a bourgeois family that had made a fortune selling salted herring and wine and in 1477 had purchased the title and property of Montaigne in Gascony; his mother descended from a Jewish family that had been forced to flee Spain. Montaigne received a classical education before studying law and securing a judicial appointment in 1554. At the age of thirty-eight, Montaigne resigned his judicial post, retired to his estate, and devoted the rest of his life to study, contemplation, and the effort to understand himself. His wealth provided him the leisure time to do so. Like the Greeks, he believed that the object of life was to "know thyself," for self-knowledge teaches men and women how to live in accordance with nature and God.

Montaigne developed a new literary genre, the essay—from the French word *essayer,* meaning "to test or try"—to express his thoughts and ideas. His *Essays* provide insight into the mind of a remarkably humane, tolerant, and civilized man. Montaigne was a humanist; he loved the Greek and Roman writers and was always eager to learn from them. From the ancient authors, especially the Roman Stoic Seneca, he acquired a sense of calm, inner peace, and patience and broad-mindedness.

Montaigne grew up during the French civil wars—a period when religious ideology had set family against family, even brother against brother. He wrote:

In this controversy . . . France is at present agitated by civil wars. . . . [Even] among the good men . . . we see many whom passion drives outside the bounds of reason, and makes them sometimes adopt unjust, violent, and even reckless courses.[44]

Though he remained a Catholic, Montaigne possessed a detachment and a willingness to look at all sides of a question:

I listen with attention to the judgment of all men; but so far as I can remember, I have followed none but my own. Though I set little value upon my own opinion, I set no more on the opinions of others.

In the book-lined tower where he passed his days, Montaigne became a deeply learned man. Yet he was not ignorant of the world of affairs, and he criticized scholars and bookworms who ignored the life around them. His essay "On Cannibals" reflects the impact of overseas discoveries on Europeans' consciousness. His tolerant mind rejected the notion that one culture is superior to another:

I long had a man in my house that lived ten or twelve years in the New World, discovered in these latter days, and in that part of it where Villegaignon landed [Brazil]. . . .

I find that there is nothing barbarous and savage in [that] nation, by anything that I can gather, excepting, that every one gives the title of barbarism to everything that is not in use in his own country. As, indeed, we have no other level of truth and reason, than the example and idea of the opinions and customs of the place wherein we live.[45]

In his belief in the nobility of human beings in the state of nature, uncorrupted by organized society, and in his cosmopolitan attitude toward different civilizations, Montaigne anticipated many eighteenth-century thinkers.

The thought of Michel de Montaigne marks a sharp break with the past. Faith and religious certainty had characterized the intellectual attitudes of Western society for a millennium. Montaigne's rejection of any kind of dogmatism, his secularism, and his skepticism thus represent a basic change. In his own time and throughout the seventeenth century, few would have agreed with him. Montaigne inaugurated an era of doubt. "Wonder," he said, "is the foundation of all philosophy, research is the means of all learning, and ignorance is the end."[46]

Elizabethan and Jacobean Literature

In addition to the development of the essay as a literary genre, the period fostered remarkable creativity in other branches of literature. England, especially in the latter part of Elizabeth's reign and in the first years of her successor James I (r. 1603–1625), witnessed unparalleled brilliance. The terms *Elizabethan* and *Jacobean* (the latter refers to the reign of James) are used to designate the English music, poetry, prose, and drama of this period. The poetry of Sir Philip Sidney (1554–1586), such as *Astrophel and Stella,* strongly influenced later poetic writing. *The Faerie Queene* of Edmund Spenser (1552–1599) endures as one of the greatest moral epics in any language. Above all, the immortal dramas of Shakespeare and the stately prose of the Authorized or King James Version of the Bible mark the Elizabethan and Jacobean periods as the golden age of English literature.

William Shakespeare (1564–1616), the son of a successful glove manufacturer who rose to the highest municipal office in the Warwickshire town of Stratford-on-Avon, chose a career on the London stage. By 1592 he had gained recognition as an actor and playwright. Between 1599 and 1603, Shakespeare performed in the Lord Chamberlain's Company and became co-owner of the Globe Theatre, which after 1603 presented his plays.

Shakespeare's genius lies in the originality of his characterizations, the diversity of his plots, his understanding of human psychology, and his unexcelled gift for language. Shakespeare was a Renaissance man in his deep appreciation for classical culture, individualism, and humanism. Such plays as *Julius Caesar, Pericles,* and *Antony and Cleopatra* deal with classical subjects and figures. Several of his comedies have Italian Renaissance settings. The nine history plays, including *Richard II, Richard III,* and *Henry IV,* enjoyed the greatest popularity among Shakespeare's contemporaries. Written during the decade after the defeat of the Spanish Armada, the history plays express English national consciousness. Lines such as these from *Richard II* reflect this sense of national greatness with unparalleled eloquence:

This royal Throne of Kings, this sceptre'd Isle,
This earth of Majesty, this seat of Mars,
This other Eden, demi-paradise,
This fortress built by Nature for herself,
Against infection and the hand of war:
This happy breed of men, this little world,
This precious stone, set in the silver sea,
Which serves it in the office of a wall,
Or as a moat defensive to a house,
Against the envy of less happier Lands,
This blessed plot, this earth, this Realm, this
  England.

Shakespeare's later plays, above all the tragedies *Hamlet, Othello,* and *Macbeth,* explore an enormous range of human problems and are open to an almost infinite variety of interpretations. *Othello,* which the nineteenth-century historian Thomas Macaulay called "perhaps the greatest work in the world," portrays an honorable man destroyed by a flaw in his own character and the satanic evil of his supposed friend Iago. The central figure in *Hamlet,* a play suffused with individuality, wrestles with moral problems connected with revenge and with man's relationship to life and death. The soliloquy in which Hamlet debates suicide is perhaps the most widely quoted passage in English literature:

To be, or not to be: that is the question:
Whether 'tis nobler in the mind to suffer
The slings and arrows of outrageous fortune,
Or to take arms against a sea of troubles,
And by opposing end them?

Hamlet's sad cry, "There is nothing either good or bad but thinking makes it so," expresses the anguish and uncertainty of modern man. *Hamlet* has always enjoyed great popularity, because in his many-faceted personality people have seen an aspect of themselves.

In 1929, in lectures at Oxford University, the novelist Virginia Woolf created an imaginary situation. What would have happened, she wondered, if Shakespeare had had a gifted sister who wanted to be an actress and to write poetry or plays? Unlike her brother, she would not have been sent to grammar school. If on her own she learned to read and write and occasionally picked up a book, her parents soon would have interrupted and told her to mend the stockings or mind the stew. Before she was out of her teens, her parents, loving though they were, would have selected a husband for her. If the force of her gift for learning and the stage was strong enough, she would have the choice of obeying her parents or leaving their home. If she succeeded in getting to London, she would discover that the theater did not hire women. Dependent on the kindness of strangers even for food, she probably would have found herself pregnant. And then "who shall measure the heat and violence of the poet's heart when caught and tangled in a woman's body?—she kills herself." Woolf concludes her story:

This may be true or it may be false—who can say?—but what is true in it, so it seemed to me, reviewing the story of Shakespeare's sister as I have made it, is that any woman born with a great gift in the sixteenth century would certainly have gone crazed, shot herself, or ended her days in some lonely cottage outside the village, half witch, half wizard, feared and mocked at.[47]

Unlike her contemporary Montaigne, Shakespeare's sister would not have had "a room of her own"—that is, the financial means to study and to write, even apart from the social and cultural barriers against a woman doing so.

The other great masterpiece of the Jacobean period was the Authorized or King James Version of the Bible (1611). Based on the best scriptural research of the time and divided into chapters and verses, the Authorized Version is actually a revision of earlier versions of the Bible rather than an original work. Yet it provides a superb expression of the mature English vernacular in the early seventeenth century. Thus Psalm 37:

Fret not thy selfe because of evill doers, neither bee
  thou envious against the workers of iniquitie.
For they shall soone be cut downe like the grasse;
  and wither as the greene herbe.

*Trust in the Lord, and do good, so shalt thou dwell in
the land, and verely thou shalt be fed.*

*Delight thy selfe also in the Lord; and he shall give
thee the desires of thine heart.*

*Commit thy way unto the Lord: trust also in him, and
he shall bring it to passe.*

*And he shall bring forth thy righteousness as the
light, and thy judgement as the noone day.*

The Authorized Version, so called because it was
produced under royal sponsorship—it had no official ecclesiastical endorsement—represented the
Anglican and Puritan desire to encourage lay people to read the Scriptures. It quickly achieved great
popularity and displaced all earlier versions. British
settlers carried this Bible to the North American
colonies, where it became known as the "King
James Bible." For centuries this version of the
Bible has had a profound influence on the language and lives of English-speaking peoples.

Baroque Art and Music

Throughout European history, the cultural tastes
of one age have often seemed quite unsatisfactory
to the next. So it was with the baroque. The term
baroque may have come from a Portuguese word

for an "odd-shaped, imperfect pearl." Late-eighteenth-century art critics used it as an expression of
scorn for what they considered an overblown, unbalanced style. The hostility of these critics has
long since passed, and modern specialists agree
that the triumphs of the baroque mark one of the
high points in the history of Western culture.

The early development of the baroque is complex. Most scholars stress the influence of Rome
and the revitalized Catholic church of the later sixteenth century. The papacy and the Jesuits encouraged the growth of an intensely emotional, exuberant art. These patrons wanted artists to go beyond
the Renaissance focus on pleasing a small, wealthy
cultural elite. They wanted artists to appeal to the
senses and thereby touch the souls and kindle the
faith of ordinary churchgoers while proclaiming
the power and confidence of the reformed Catholic church. In addition to this underlying religious emotionalism, the baroque drew its sense of
drama, motion, and ceaseless striving from the
Catholic Reformation. The interior of the famous
Jesuit Church of Jesus in Rome—the Gesù—combined all these characteristics in its lavish, shimmer-
ing, wildly active decorations and frescoes.

Taking definite shape in Italy after 1600, the
baroque style in the visual arts developed with

Veronese: Feast in the House of Levi Using the story in Mark 2:15, which says
that many tax collectors and sinners joined Jesus at dinner, the Venetian painter celebrated patrician wealth and luxury in Venice's golden age. The black servants,
dwarfs, and colonnades all contribute to the sumptuous setting. *(Source: Gallerie
dell'Accademia/Archivio Cameraphoto Venezia/Art Resource, NY)*

Velázquez: Juan de Pareja This portrait (1650) of the Spanish painter Velázquez's one-time assistant, a black man of obvious intellectual and sensual power and himself a renowned religious painter, suggests the integration of some blacks in seventeenth-century society. The elegant lace collar attests to his middle-class status. *(Source: The Metropolitan Museum of Art)*

sensuous, colorful style, characterized by animated figures, melodramatic contrasts, and monumental size. Rubens excelled in glorifying monarchs such as Queen Mother Marie de' Medici of France. He was a devout Catholic—nearly half of his pictures treat Christian subjects—yet among his trademarks are the fleshy, sensual nudes who populate his canvases as Roman goddesses, water nymphs, and remarkably voluptuous saints and angels.

In music, the baroque style reached its culmination almost a century later in the dynamic, soaring lines of the endlessly inventive Johann Sebastian Bach (1685–1750), one of the greatest composers of the Western world. Organist and choirmaster of several Lutheran churches across Germany, Bach was equally at home writing secular concertos and sublime religious cantatas. Bach's organ music, the greatest ever written, combines the baroque spirit of invention, tension, and emotion in an unforgettable striving toward the infinite. Unlike Rubens, Bach was not fully appreciated in his lifetime, but since the early nineteenth century his reputation has grown steadily.

exceptional vigor in Catholic countries—in Spain and Latin America, Austria, southern Germany, and Poland. Yet baroque art was more than just "Catholic art" in the seventeenth century and the first half of the eighteenth. True, neither Protestant England nor the Netherlands ever came fully under the spell of the baroque, but neither did Catholic France. And Protestants accounted for some of the finest examples of baroque style, especially in music. The baroque style spread partly because its tension and bombast spoke to an agitated age, which was experiencing great violence and controversy in politics and religion.

In painting, the baroque reached maturity early in the work of Peter Paul Rubens (1577–1640), the most outstanding and representative of baroque painters. Studying in his native Flanders and in Italy, where he was influenced by such masters as Michelangelo, Rubens developed his own rich,

SUMMARY

In the sixteenth and seventeenth centuries, Europeans for the first time gained access to large parts of the globe. European peoples had the intellectual curiosity, driving ambition, and scientific technology to attempt feats that were as difficult and expensive then as going to the moon is today. Exploration and exploitation contributed to a more sophisticated standard of living in the form of spices and Asian luxury goods and to a terrible international inflation resulting from the influx of South American silver and gold. Governments, the upper classes, and especially the peasantry were badly hurt by the inflation. Meanwhile, the middle class of bankers, shippers, financiers, and manufacturers prospered for much of the seventeenth century.

Europeans' technological development contributed to their conquest of Aztec Mexico and Inca Peru. Along with technology, Europeans brought disease to the New World and thereby caused a holocaust among the Indians. Overseas reconnaissance led to the first global seaborne commercial empires of the Portuguese, the Spanish, and the Dutch.

European expansion and colonization took place against a background of religious conflict and rising national consciousness. The sixteenth and seventeenth centuries were by no means a secular period. Although the medieval religious framework had broken down, people still thought largely in religious terms. Europeans used religious doctrine to explain what they did politically and economically. Religious ideology served as a justification for a variety of conflicts: the French nobles' opposition to the Crown, the Dutch struggle for political and economic independence from Spain. In Germany, religious pluralism and foreign ambitions added to political difficulties. After 1648 the divisions between Protestants and Catholics tended to become permanent. Sexism, racism, and religious skepticism were harbingers of developments to come.

NOTES

1. Quoted in C. M. Cipolla, *Guns, Sails, and Empires: Technological Innovation and the Early Phases of European Expansion, 1400–1700* (New York: Minerva Press, 1965), pp. 115–116.
2. J. H. Parry, *The Age of Reconnaissance* (New York: Mentor Books, 1963), Chs. 3 and 5.
3. See C. R. Phillips, *Ciudad Real, 1500–1750: Growth, Crisis, and Readjustment in the Spanish Economy* (Cambridge, Mass.: Harvard University Press, 1979), pp. 103–104, 115.
4. Quoted in Cipolla, *Guns, Sails, and Empires,* p. 132.
5. Quoted in F. H. Littell, *The Macmillan Atlas History of Christianity* (New York: Macmillan, 1976), p. 75.
6. Quoted in Cipolla, *Guns, Sails, and Empires,* p. 133.
7. Quoted in S. E. Morison, *Admiral of the Ocean Sea: A Life of Christopher Columbus* (Boston: Little, Brown, 1942), p. 339.
8. T. K. Rabb, "Columbus: Villain or Hero," *Princeton Alumni Weekly,* October 14, 1992, pp. 12–17.
9. J. M. Cohen, ed. and trans., *The Four Voyages of Christopher Columbus* (New York: Penguin Books, 1969), p. 37.
10. Quoted in R. L. Kagan, "The Spain of Ferdinand and Isabella," in *Circa 1492: Art in the Age of Exploration,* ed. J. A. Levenson (Washington, D.C.: National Gallery of Art, 1991), p. 60.
11. Quoted in F. Maddison, "Tradition and Innovation: Columbus' First Voyage and Portuguese Navigation in the Fifteenth Century," ibid., p. 69.
12. W. D. Phillips and C. R. Phillips, *The Worlds of Christopher Columbus* (Cambridge: Cambridge University Press, 1992), p. 273.
13. See ibid.
14. See G. W. Conrad and A. A. Demarest, *Religion and Empire: The Dynamics of Aztec and Inca Expansionism* (New York: Cambridge University Press, 1993), pp. 67–69.
15. G. C. Vaillant, *Aztecs of Mexico* (New York: Penguin Books, 1979), p. 241. Chapter 15, on which this section leans, is fascinating.
16. V. W. Von Hagen, *Realm of the Incas* (New York: New American Library, 1961), pp. 204–207.
17. Conrad and Demarest, *Religion and Empire,* pp. 135–139.
18. N. Sanchez-Albornoz, *The Population of Latin America: A History,* trans. W. A. R. Richardson (Berkeley: University of California Press, 1974), p. 41.
19. Quoted in A. W. Crosby, *The Columbian Exchange: Biological and Cultural Consequences of 1492* (Westport, Conn.: Greenwood, 1972), p. 39.
20. Ibid., pp. 35–59.
21. Quoted in C. Gibson, ed., *The Black Legend: Anti-Spanish Attitudes in the Old World and the New* (New York: Knopf, 1971), pp. 74–75.
22. Quoted in L. B. Rout, Jr., *The African Experience in Spanish America* (New York: Cambridge University Press, 1976), p. 23.
23. See Parry, *The Age of Reconnaissance,* Chs. 12, 14, and 15.
24. Quoted in S. Neill, *A History of Christian Missions* (New York: Penguin Books, 1977), p. 163.
25. Quoted in C. M. Cipolla, *Clocks and Culture: 1300–1700* (New York: Norton, 1978), p. 86.
26. J. Gernet, *A History of Chinese Civilization* (New York: Cambridge University Press, 1982), p. 458.
27. Quoted in A. J. Andrea and J. H. Overfield, *The Human Record,* vol. 1 (Boston: Houghton Mifflin, 1990), pp. 406–407.
28. Ibid., p. 408.
29. See D. Keene, *The Japanese Discovery of Europe,* rev. ed. (Stanford, Calif.: Stanford University Press, 1969), pp. 1–17. The quotation is on page 16.
30. See J. Hale, "War and Public Opinion in the Fifteenth and Sixteenth Centuries," *Past and Present* 22 (July 1962): 29.
31. See N. Z. Davis, "The Rites of Violence: Religious Riot in Sixteenth Century France," *Past and Present* 59 (May 1973): 51–91.
32. H. Kamen, "The Economic and Social Consequences of the Thirty Years' War," *Past and Present* 39 (April 1968): 44–61.
33. This passage is based heavily on S. E. Ozment, *When Fathers Ruled: Family Life in Reformation*

Europe (Cambridge, Mass.: Harvard University Press, 1983), pp. 50–99.

34. Ibid., pp. 85–92.
35. Ibid., pp. 9–14.
36. N. Cohn, *Europe's Inner Demons: An Enquiry Inspired by the Great Witch-Hunt* (New York: Basic Books, 1975), pp. 253–254; K. Thomas, *Religion and the Decline of Magic* (New York: Charles Scribner's Sons, 1971), pp. 450–455.
37. See E. W. Monter, "The Pedestal and the Stake: Courtly Love and Witchcraft," in *Becoming Visible: Women in European History,* ed. R. Bridenthal and C. Koonz (Boston: Houghton Mifflin, 1977), pp. 132–135; and A. Fraser, *The Weaker Vessel* (New York: Random House, 1985), pp. 100–103.
38. C. Verlinden, *The Beginnings of Modern Colonization,* trans. Y. Freccero (Ithaca, N.Y.: Cornell University Press, 1970), pp. 5–6, 80–97.
39. This section leans heavily on D. B. Davis, *Slavery and Human Progress* (New York: Oxford University Press, 1984), pp. 54–62.
40. Quoted in D. P. Mannix with M. Cowley, *Black Cargoes: A History of the Atlantic Slave Trade* (New York: Viking Press, 1968), p. 5.
41. Ibid., p. 19.
42. See P. Brown, "Understanding Islam," *New York Review of Books,* February 22, 1979, pp. 30–33.
43. Davis, *Slavery and Human Progress,* pp. 43–44.
44. D. M. Frame, trans., *The Complete Works of Montaigne* (Stanford, Calif.: Stanford University Press, 1958), pp. 175–176.
45. C. Cotton, trans., *The Essays of Michel de Montaigne* (New York: A. L. Burt, 1893), pp. 207, 210.
46. Ibid., p. 523.
47. V. Woolf, *A Room of One's Own* (New York: Harcourt, Brace & World, 1957), p. 51.

SUGGESTED READING

Perhaps the best starting point for the study of European society in the age of exploration is Parry's *Age of Reconnaissance,* cited in the Notes, which treats the causes and consequences of the voyages of discovery. Parry's splendidly illustrated *The Discovery of South America* (1979) examines Europeans' reactions to the maritime discoveries and treats the entire concept of new discoveries. For the earliest British reaction to the Japanese, see *A World Elsewhere: Europe's Encounter with Japan in the Sixteenth and Seventeenth Centuries* (1990). The urbane studies of C. M. Cipolla present fascinating material on technological and sociological developments written in a lucid style. In addition to the titles cited in the Notes, see *Cristofano and the Plague: A Study in the History of Public Health in the Age of Galileo* (1973) and *Public Health and the Medical Profession in the Renaissance* (1976). Morison's *Admiral of the Ocean Sea,* also listed in the Notes, is the standard biography of Columbus. The advanced student should consult F. Braudel, *Civilization and Capitalism, 15th–18th Century,* trans. S. Reynolds, vol. 1, *The Structures of Everyday Life* (1981); vol. 2, *The Wheels of Commerce* (1982); and vol. 3, *The Perspective of the World* (1984). These three fat volumes combine vast erudition, a global perspective, and remarkable illustrations. For the political ideas that formed the background of the first Spanish overseas empire, see A. Pagden, *Spanish Imperialism and the Political Imagination* (1990).

For the religious wars, in addition to the references cited in the Notes to this chapter, see J. H. M. Salmon, *Society in Crisis: France in the Sixteenth Century* (1975), which traces the fate of French institutions during the civil wars. A. N. Galpern, *The Religions of the People in Sixteenth-Century Champagne* (1976), is a useful case study in religious anthropology, and W. A. Christian, Jr., *Local Religion in Sixteenth Century Spain* (1981), traces the attitudes and practices of ordinary people.

A cleverly illustrated introduction to the Low Countries is K. H. D. Kaley, *The Dutch in the Seventeenth Century* (1972). The study by J. L. Motley, *The Rise of the Dutch Republic,* vol. 1 (1898), still provides a good comprehensive treatment and is fascinating reading. For Spanish military operations in the Low Countries, see G. Parker, *The Army of Flanders and the Spanish Road, 1567–1659: The Logistics of Spanish Victory and Defeat in the Low Countries' Wars* (1972). The same author's *Spain and the Netherlands, 1559–1659: Ten Studies* (1979), contains useful essays, of which students may especially want to consult "Why Did the Dutch Revolt Last So Long?" For the later phases of the Dutch-Spanish conflict, see J. I. Israel, *The Dutch Republic and the Hispanic World, 1606–1661* (1982), which treats the struggle in global perspective.

Of the many biographies of Elizabeth of England, W. T. MacCaffrey, *Queen Elizabeth and the Making of Policy, 1572–1588* (1981), examines the problems posed by the Reformation and how Elizabeth solved them. J. E. Neale, *Queen Elizabeth I* (1957), remains valuable, and L. B. Smith, *The Elizabethan Epic* (1966), is a splendid evocation of the age of Shakespeare with Elizabeth at the center. The best recent biography is C. Erickson, *The First Elizabeth* (1983), a fine, psychologically resonant portrait.

Nineteenth- and early-twentieth-century historians described the defeat of the Spanish Armada as a great victory for Protestantism, democracy, and capitalism, which those scholars tended to link together. Recent historians have focused on its contemporary significance. For a sympathetic but judicious portrait of the man who launched the Armada, see G. Parker, *Philip II* (1978). The best recent study of the leader of the Armada is P. Pierson, *Commander of the Armada: The Seventh Duke of Medina Sidonia* (1989). D. Howarth, *The Voyage of the Armada* (1982), discusses the expedition largely in terms of the individuals involved, and G. Mattingly, *The Armada* (1959), gives the diplomatic and political background; both Howarth and Mattingly tell very exciting tales. M. Lewis, *The Spanish Armada* (1972), also tells a good story, but strictly from the English perspective. Significant aspects of Portuguese culture are treated in A. Hower and R. Preto-Rodas, eds., *Empire in Transition: The Portuguese World in the Time of Camões* (1985).

C. V. Wedgwood, *The Thirty Years' War* (1961), must be qualified in light of recent research on the social and economic effects of the war, but it is still a good (though detailed) starting point on a difficult period. Various opinions on the causes and results of the war are given in T. K. Rabb's anthology, *The Thirty Years' War* (1981). In addition to the articles by Hale and Kamen cited in the Notes, the following articles, both of which appear in the scholarly journal *Past and Present,* provide some of the latest important findings: J. V. Polisensky, "The Thirty Years' War and the Crises and Revolutions of Sixteenth Century Europe," 39 (1968), and M. Roberts, "Queen Christina and the General Crisis of the Seventeenth Century," 22 (1962).

As background to the intellectual changes instigated by the Reformation, D. C. Wilcox, *In Search of God and Self: Renaissance and Reformation Thought* (1975), contains a perceptive analysis, and T. Ashton, ed., *Crisis in Europe, 1560–1660* (1967), is fundamental. For women, marriage, and the family, see L. Stone, *The Family, Sex, and Marriage in England, 1500–1800* (1977), an important but controversial work; D. Underdown, "The Taming of the Scold," and S. Amussen, "Gender, Family, and the Social Or-

der," in *Order and Disorder in Early Modern England,* ed. A. Fletcher and J. Stevenson (1985); A. Macfarlane, *Marriage and Love in England: Modes of Reproduction, 1300–1848* (1986); C. R. Boxer, *Women in Iberian Expansion Overseas, 1415–1815* (1975), an invaluable study of women's role in overseas immigration; and S. M. Wyntjes, "Women in the Reformation Era," a quick survey of conditions in different countries, in Bridenthal and Koonz's *Becoming Visible.* Ozment's *When Fathers Ruled,* cited in the Notes, is a seminal study concentrating on Germany and Switzerland.

On witches and witchcraft see, in addition to the titles by Cohn and Thomas in the Notes, J. B. Russell, *Witchcraft in the Middle Ages* (1976) and *Lucifer: The Devil in the Middle Ages* (1984); M. Summers, *The History of Witchcraft and Demonology* (1973); and H. R. Trevor-Roper, *The European Witch-Craze of the Sixteenth and Seventeenth Centuries* (1967), an important collection of essays.

As background to slavery and racism in North and South America, students should see J. L. Watson, ed., *Asian and African Systems of Slavery* (1980), a valuable collection of essays. Davis's *Slavery and Human Progress,* cited in the Notes, shows how slavery was viewed as a progressive force in the expansion of the Western world. For North American conditions, interested students should consult W. D. Jordan, *The White Man's Burden: Historical Origins of Racism in the United States* (1974), and the title by Mannix listed in the Notes, a hideously fascinating account. For Caribbean and South American developments, see F. P. Bowser, *The African Slave in Colonial Peru* (1974); J. S. Handler and F. W. Lange, *Plantation Slavery in Barbados: An Archeological and Historical Investigation* (1978); and R. E. Conrad, *Children of God's Fire: A Documentary History of Black Slavery in Brazil* (1983).

The leading authority on Montaigne is D. M. Frame. In addition to his translation of Montaigne's works cited in the Notes, see his *Montaigne's Discovery of Man* (1955).

Columbus Describes His First Voyage

On his return voyage to Spain in January 1493, Christopher Columbus composed a letter intended for wide circulation and had copies of it sent ahead to Isabella and Ferdinand and others when the ship docked at Lisbon. Because the letter sums up Columbus's understanding of his achievements, it is considered the most important document of his first voyage. Remember that his knowledge of Asia rested heavily on Marco Polo's Travels, *published around 1298.*

Since I know that you will be pleased at the great success with which the Lord has crowned my voyage, I write to inform you how in thirty-three days I crossed from the Canary Islands to the Indies, with the fleet which our most illustrious sovereigns gave me. I found very many islands with large populations and took possession of them all for their Highnesses; this I did by proclamation and unfurled the royal standard. No opposition was offered.

I named the first island that I found 'San Salvador,' in honour of our Lord and Saviour who has granted me this miracle. . . . When I reached Cuba, I followed its north coast westwards, and found it so extensive that I thought this must be the mainland, the province of Cathay.[1] . . . From there I saw another island eighteen leagues eastwards which I then named 'Hispaniola.'[2] . . .

Hispaniola is a wonder. The mountains and hills, the plains and meadow lands are both fertile and beautiful. They are most suitable for planting crops and for raising cattle of all kinds, and there are good sites for building towns and villages. The harbours are incredibly fine and there are many great rivers with broad channels and the majority contain gold.[3] The trees, fruits and plants are very different from those of Cuba. In Hispaniola there are many spices and large mines of gold and other metals. . . .[4]

The inhabitants of this island, and all the rest that I discovered or heard of, go naked, as their mothers bore them, men and women alike. A few of the women, however, cover a single place with a leaf of a plant or piece of cotton which they weave for the purpose. They have no iron or steel or arms and are not capable of using them, not because they are not strong and well built but because they are amazingly timid. All the weapons they have are canes cut at seeding time, at the end of which they fix a sharpened stick, but they have not the courage to make use of these, for very often when I have sent two or three men to a village to have conversation with them a great number of them have come out. But as soon as they saw my men all fled immediately, a father not even waiting for his son. And this is not because we have harmed any of them; on the contrary, wherever I have gone and been able to have conversation with them, I have given them some of the various things I had, a cloth and other articles, and received nothing in exchange. But they have still remained incurably timid. True, when they have been reassured and lost their fear, they are so ingenuous and so liberal with all their possessions that no one who has not seen them would believe it. If one asks for anything they have they never say no. On the contrary, they offer a share to anyone with demonstrations of heartfelt affection, and they are immediately content with any small thing, valuable or valueless, that is given them. I forbade the men to give them bits of broken crockery, fragments of glass or tags of laces, though if they could get them they fancied them the finest jewels in the world.

I hoped to win them to the love and service of their Highnesses and of the whole Spanish nation and to persuade them to collect and give us of the things which they possessed in abundance and which we needed. They have no religion and are not idolaters; but all believe that power and goodness dwell in the sky and they are firmly convinced that I have come from the sky with these ships and people. In this belief they gave me a good reception everywhere, once they had overcome their fear; and this is not because they are stupid—far from it, they are men of great intelligence, for they navigate all those seas, and give a marvellously good account of everything—but because they have never before seen men clothed or ships like these. . . .

In all these islands the men are seemingly content with one woman, but their chief or king is allowed more than twenty. The women appear to work more than the men and I have not been able to find out if they have private property. As far as I could see whatever a man had was shared among all the rest and this particularly applies to food. . . . In another island, which I am told is larger than Hispaniola, the people have no hair. Here there is a vast quantity of gold, and from here and the other islands I bring Indians as evidence.

In conclusion, to speak only of the results of this very hasty voyage, their Highnesses can see that I will give them as much gold as they require, if they will render me some very slight assistance; also I will give them all the spices and cotton they want . . . I will also bring them as much aloes as they ask and as many slaves, who will be taken from the idolaters. I believe also that I have found rhubarb and cinnamon and there will be countless other things in addition . . .

So all Christendom will be delighted that our Redeemer has given victory to our most illustrious King and Queen and their renowned kingdoms, in this great matter. They should hold great celebrations and render solemn thanks to the Holy Trinity with many solemn prayers, for the great triumph which they will have, by the conversion of so many peoples to our holy faith and for the temporal benefits which will follow, for not only Spain, but all Christendom will receive encouragement and profit.

This is a brief account of the facts.
Written in the caravel off the Canary Islands.[5]

15 February 1493

At your orders
THE ADMIRAL

German woodcut depicting Columbus's landing at San Salvador. (*Source: John Carter Brown Library*)

2. What was Columbus's view of the native Americans he met?

3. Evaluate Columbus's statements that the Caribbean islands possessed gold, cotton, and spices.

4. Why did Columbus cling to the idea that he had reached Asia?

Source: J. M. Cohen, ed. and trans., *The Four Voyages of Christopher Columbus.* Copyright © 1969 Penguin Books Ltd.

1. Cathay is the old name for China. In the logbook and later in this letter Columbus accepts the native story that Cuba is an island which they can circumnavigate in something more than twenty-one days, yet he insists here and later, during the second voyage, that it is in fact part of the Asiatic mainland. 2. Hispaniola is the second largest island of the West Indies; Haiti occupies the western third of the island, the Dominican Republic the rest. 3. This did not prove to be true. 4. These statements are also inaccurate. 5. Actually Columbus was off Santa Maria in the Azores.

Questions for Analysis

1. How did Columbus explain the success of his voyage?

17

Absolutism and Constitutionalism in Europe, ca 1589–1725

The Queen's Staircase is among the grandest of the surviving parts of Louis XIV's palace at Versailles. *(Source: © Photo R.M.N.)*

The seventeenth century in Europe was an age of intense conflict and crisis. The crisis had many causes, but the era's almost continuous savage warfare was probably the most important factor. War drove governments to build enormous armies and levy ever higher taxes on an already hard-pressed, predominately peasant population. Deteriorating economic conditions also played a major role. Europe as a whole experienced an unusually cold and wet climate over many years—a "little ice age" that brought small harvests, periodic food shortages, and even starvation. Not least, the combination of war, increased taxation, and economic suffering triggered social unrest and widespread peasant revolts, which were both a cause and an effect of profound dislocation.

The many-sided crisis of the seventeenth century posed a grave challenge to European governments: how were they to maintain order? The most common response of monarchial governments was to seek more power to deal with the problems and the threats that they perceived. Indeed, European rulers in this period generally sought to attain *absolute,* or complete, power and build absolutist states. Thus monarchs regulated religious sects, and they abolished the liberties long held by certain areas, groups, or provinces. Absolutist rulers also created new state bureaucracies to enhance their power and to direct the economic life of the country in the interest of the monarch. Above all, monarchs fought to free themselves from the restrictions of custom, competing institutions, and powerful social groups. In doing so, they sought freedom from the nobility and from traditional representative bodies—most commonly known as Estates or Parliament—that were usually dominated by the nobility.

The monarchial demand for freedom of action upset the status quo and led to bitter political battles. Nobles and townspeople sought to maintain their traditional rights, claiming that monarchs could not rule at will but rather had to respect representative bodies and follow established constitutional practices. Thus opponents of absolutism argued for *constitutionalism*—the limitation of the state by law. In seventeenth-century Europe, however, advocates of constitutionalism generally lost out and would-be absolutists triumphed in most countries.

There were important national variations in the development of absolutism. The most spectacular example occurred in western Europe, where Louis XIV built on the heritage of a well-developed monarchy and a strong royal bureaucracy. Moreover, when Louis XIV came to the throne, the powers of the nobility were already somewhat limited, the French middle class was relatively strong, and the peasants were generally free from serfdom. In eastern Europe and Russia, absolutism emerged out of a very different social reality: a powerful nobility, a weak middle class, and an oppressed peasantry composed of serfs. Eastern monarchs generally had to compromise with their nobilities as they fashioned absolutist states. Finally, in Holland and England, royal absolutism did not triumph. In England especially, the opponents of unrestrained monarchial authority succeeded in firmly establishing a constitutional state, which guaranteed that henceforth Parliament and the monarch would share power.

Thus in the period between roughly 1589 and 1725, two basic patterns of government emerged in Europe: absolute monarchy and the constitutional state. Almost all subsequent governments in the West have been modeled on one of these patterns, which have also influenced greatly the rest of the world in the last three centuries.

- How and why did Louis XIV of France lead the way in forging the absolute state?

- How did Austrian, Prussian, and Russian rulers in eastern Europe build absolute monarchies—monarchies that proved even more durable than that of Louis XIV?

- How did the absolute monarchs' interaction with artists, architects, and writers contribute to the splendid cultural achievements of both western and eastern Europe in this period?

- How and why did the constitutional state triumph in Holland and England?

This chapter explores these questions.

✦ FRANCE: THE MODEL OF ABSOLUTE MONARCHY

France had a long history of unifying and centralizing monarchy, although the actual power and effectiveness of the French kings had varied enormously over time. Passing through a time of troubles and civil war after the death of Henry II in

1559, both France and the monarchy recovered under Henry IV and Cardinal Richelieu in the early seventeenth century. They laid the foundations for fully developed French absolutism under the "Great Monarch," Louis XIV. Providing inspiration for rulers all across Europe, Louis XIV and the mighty machine he fashioned deserve special attention

The Foundations of French Absolutism

Henry IV, the ingenious Huguenot-turned-Catholic, ended the French religious wars with the Edict of Nantes in 1598 (see page 534). The first of the Bourbon dynasty, Henry IV and his great minister Maximilian de Béthune, duke of Sully (1560–1641), then laid the foundations of later French absolutism.

Henry denied influence on the royal council to the nobility, which had harassed the countryside for half a century. Maintaining that "if we are without compassion for the people, they must succumb and we all perish with them," Henry also lowered taxes paid by the overburdened peasantry. Sully reduced the crushing royal debt accumulated during the era of religious conflict, encouraged French trade, and started a countrywide highway system. Within twelve years, Henry IV and his minister had restored public order in France and laid the foundation for economic prosperity. Unfortunately, the murder of Henry IV in 1610 by a crazed fanatic led to a severe crisis.

After the death of Henry IV, the queen-regent Marie de' Medici led the government for the child-king Louis XIII (r. 1610–1643), but feudal nobles and princes of the blood dominated the political scene. In 1624 Marie de' Medici secured the appointment of Armand Jean du Plessis—Cardinal Richelieu (1585–1642)—to the council of ministers. It was a remarkable appointment. The next year Richelieu became president of the council, and after 1628 he was first minister of the French crown. Richelieu used his strong influence over King Louis XIII to exalt the French monarchy as the embodiment of the French state.

Richelieu's policy was the total subordination of all groups and institutions to the French monarchy. The French nobility, with its selfish and independent interests, had long constituted the foremost threat to the centralizing goals of the Crown and to a strong national state. Now Richelieu crushed aristocratic conspiracies with quick execu-

tions, and he never called a session of the Estates General—the ancient representative body of the medieval orders that was primarily a representative of the nobility.

The genius of Cardinal Richelieu was reflected in the administrative system he established. He extended the use of the royal commissioners called *intendants,* each of whom held authority in one of France's thirty-two *généralités* (districts). The intendants were authorized "to decide, order and execute all that they see good to do." Usually members of the upper middle class or minor nobility, the intendants were appointed directly by the monarch, to whom they were solely responsible. They recruited men for the army, supervised the collection of taxes, presided over the administration of local law, checked up on the local nobility, and regulated economic activities—commerce, trade, the guilds, marketplaces—in their districts. As the intendants' power grew during Richelieu's administration, so did the power of the centralized state.

The cardinal perceived that Protestantism often served as a cloak for the political intrigues of ambitious lords. When the Huguenots revolted in 1625, Richelieu personally supervised the siege of their walled city, La Rochelle, and forced it to surrender. Thereafter, fortified cities were abolished. Huguenots were allowed to practice their faith, but they no longer possessed armed strongholds or the means to be an independent party in the state.

French foreign policy under Richelieu was aimed at the destruction of the fence of Habsburg territories that surrounded France. Consequently, in the Thirty Years' War Richelieu supported the Habsburgs' enemies, like the Lutheran king Gustavus Adolphus (see page 539). French influence became an important factor in the political future of the German Empire.

These new policies, especially war, cost money. Richelieu fully realized the need for greater revenues through increased taxation. But seventeenth-century France remained "a collection of local economies and local societies dominated by local elites." The government's power to tax was limited by the rights of assemblies in some provinces (such as Brittany) to vote their own taxes, the hereditary exemption from taxation of many wealthy members of the nobility and the middle class, and the royal pension system. Therefore, Richelieu—and later Louis XIV—temporarily solved their financial problems by securing the cooperation of local elites. Even in France royal absolutism was restrained by its need to compromise with the financial interests of well-entrenched groups.[1]

In building the French state, Richelieu believed that he had to take drastic measures against persons and groups within France and conduct a tough anti-Habsburg foreign policy. He knew that his actions sometimes seemed to contradict traditional Christian teaching. As a priest and bishop, how did he justify his policies? He developed his own *raison d'état* (reason of state): "What is done for the state is done for God, who is the basis and foundation of it." This being so, Richelieu maintained that, "Where the interests of the state are concerned, God absolves actions which, if privately committed, would be a crime."[2]

Richelieu persuaded Louis XIII to appoint his protégé Jules Mazarin (1602–1661) as his successor. Governing for the child-king Louis XIV, Mazarin became the dominant power in the government. He continued the centralizing policies of Richelieu, but in 1648 his unpopular attempts to increase royal revenues and expand the state bureaucracy resulted in a widespread rebellion known as the Fronde. Bitter civil war ensued between the monarchy and the opposition, led by the nobility and middle class. Riots and turmoil wracked Paris and the nation. Violence continued intermittently for the next twelve years.

Conflicts during the Fronde had a traumatic effect on the young Louis XIV. The king and his mother were frequently threatened and sometimes treated as prisoners by aristocratic factions. This period formed the cornerstone of Louis's political education and of his conviction that the sole alternative to anarchy was to concentrate as much power as possible in his own hands. Yet Louis XIV also realized that he would have to compromise with the bureaucrats and social elites who controlled local institutions and constituted the state bureaucracy. And he did so.

The Monarchy of Louis XIV

In the reign of Louis XIV (r. 1643–1715), the longest in European history, the French monarchy reached the peak of its absolutist development. In the magnificence of his court, in his absolute power, in the brilliance of the culture over which he presided and which permeated all of Europe, and in his remarkably long life, the "Sun King"

Philippe de Champaigne: Cardinal Richelieu
This portrait, with its penetrating eyes, expression of haughty and imperturbable cynicism, and dramatic sweep of red robes, suggests the authority, grandeur, and power that Richelieu wished to convey as first minister of France. *(Source: Reproduced by courtesy of the Trustees, The National Gallery, London)*

dominated his age. It was said that when Louis sneezed, all Europe caught cold.

Born in 1638, king at the age of five, Louis entered into personal, or independent, rule in 1661. Always a devout Catholic, Louis believed that God had established kings as his rulers on earth. The royal coronation consecrated Louis to God's service, and he was certain that although kings were a race apart, they had to obey God's laws and rule for the good of the people.

Louis's education was more practical than formal. He learned statecraft by direct experience.

Louis XIV   A skilled horseman and an enthusiastic hunter, Louis XIV rode with his armies on their many campaigns. This painting of Louis as a Roman general by Mignard Pierre (1612–1695) captures the king's enormous physical energy and proud self-confidence. *(Source: Galleria Sabauda, Turin/Scala/Art Resource, NY)*

hundreds of candles illuminated the domed ceiling, where allegorical paintings celebrated the king's victories. Louis skillfully used the art and architecture of Versailles to overawe his subjects and visitors and reinforce his power. Many monarchs subsequently imitated Louis XIV's example, and French became the language of diplomatic exchange and of royal courts all across Europe.

Historians have often said that Louis XIV was able to control completely the nobility, which historically had opposed the centralizing goals of the French monarchy. The duke of Saint-Simon, a high-ranking noble and fierce critic of the king, wrote in his memoirs, that Louis XIV

reduced everyone to subjection, and brought to his court those very persons he cared least about. Whoever was old enough to serve did not dare demur. It was still another device to ruin the nobles by accustoming them to equality and forcing them to mingle with everyone indiscriminately. . . .

Upon rising, at bedtime, during meals, in his apartments, in the gardens of Versailles, everywhere the courtiers had a right to follow, he would glance right and left to see who was there; he saw and noted everyone; he missed no one, even those who were hoping they would not be seen. . . .

Louis XIV took great pains to inform himself on what was happening everywhere, in public places, private homes, and even on the international scene. . . . Spies and informers of all kinds were numberless.[3]

The misery he suffered during the Fronde gave him an eternal distrust of the nobility and a profound sense of his own isolation. Accordingly, silence, caution, and secrecy became political tools for the achievement of his goals. His characteristic answer to requests of all kinds became the enigmatic "Je verrai" ("I shall see").

Louis XIV installed his royal court at Versailles, an old hunting lodge ten miles from Paris. His architects, Le Nôtre and Le Vau, turned what the duke of Saint-Simon called "the most dismal and thankless of sights" into a veritable paradise. Louis XIV required all the great nobility of France—at the peril of social, political, and sometimes economic disaster—to live at Versailles for at least part of the year. Versailles became a model of rational order, the center of France, and the perfect symbol of the king's power. In the gigantic Hall of Mirrors

As Saint-Simon suggests, the king did use court ceremonial to curb the great nobility. By excluding the highest nobles from his councils, he also weakened their ancient right to advise the king and to participate in government. They became mere instruments of policy, their time and attention occupied with operas, balls, gossip, and trivia.

Recent research, however, has demonstrated that Louis XIV actually secured the active collaboration of the nobility. Thus Louis XIV separated power from status and grandeur at Versailles: he secured the nobles' cooperation, and the nobility enjoyed their status and the grandeur in which they lived. The nobility agreed to participate in projects that both exalted the monarchy and reinforced their own ancient aristocratic prestige. Thus French government in the seventeenth century rested on a social and political structure in which the nobility continued to exercise great influence.[4]

In day-to-day government Louis utilized several councils of state, which he personally attended, and the intendants, who acted for the councils throughout France. A stream of questions and instructions flowed between local districts and Versailles, and under Louis XIV a uniform and centralized administration was imposed on the country. The councilors of state came from the upper middle class or from the recently ennobled, who were popularly known as "nobility of the robe" (because of the long judicial robes many of them wore). These ambitious professional bureaucrats served the state in the person of the king.

Throughout Louis's long reign and despite increasing financial problems, he never called a meeting of the Estates General. Thus his critics had no means of united action. French government remained highly structured, bureaucratic, centered at Versailles, and responsible to Louis XIV.

Economic Management and Religious Policy

Louis XIV's bureaucracy, court, and army cost a great amount of money, and the French method of collecting taxes consistently failed to produce the necessary revenue. An old agreement between the Crown and the nobility permitted the king to tax the common people if he did not tax the nobles. Because many among the rich and prosperous classes were exempt, the tax burden fell heavily on those least able to pay: the poor peasants.

The king named Jean-Baptiste Colbert (1619–1683), the son of a wealthy merchant-financier, as controller-general of finances. Colbert came to manage the entire royal administration and proved himself a financial genius. His central principle was that the French economy should serve the state, and he rigorously applied to France the system called mercantilism.

Hall of Mirrors, Versailles The grandeur and elegance of the Sun King's reign are reflected in the Hall of Mirrors at the Versailles palace. The king's victories were celebrated in paintings on the domed ceiling. Hundreds of candles lit up the dome. (*Source: Giraudon/Art Resource, NY*)

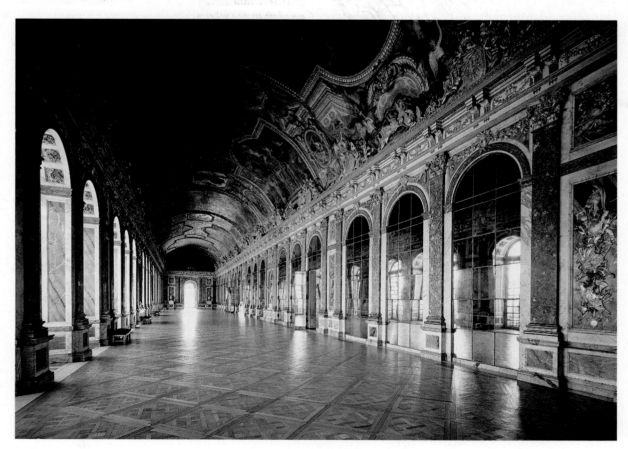

Mercantilism is a collection of government policies for the regulation of economic activities, especially commercial activities, by and for the state. In the seventeenth and eighteenth centuries, a nation's international power was thought to be based on its wealth—specifically on the gold so necessary for fighting wars. To accumulate gold, economic theory suggested, a country should always sell more goods abroad than it bought. Colbert insisted that France should be self-sufficient, able to produce within its borders everything needed by the subjects of the French king. If France were self-sufficient, the outflow of gold would be halted, debtor states would pay in bullion, and, with the wealth of the nation increased, France's power and prestige would be enhanced.

Colbert attempted to accomplish self-sufficiency through state support for both old industries and newly created ones. New factories in Paris manufactured mirrors to replace Venetian imports, for example. To ensure a high-quality finished product, Colbert set up a system of state inspection and regulation. He compelled all craftsmen to organize into guilds, and he encouraged skilled foreign craftsmen and manufacturers to immigrate to France. To improve communications, he built roads and canals. To protect French products, he placed high tariffs on foreign goods. His most important accomplishment was the creation of a powerful merchant marine to transport French goods. Colbert tried to organize and regulate the entire French economy for the glory of the French state as embodied in the king.

Colbert's achievement in the development of manufacturing was prodigious. The commercial classes prospered, and between 1660 and 1700 their position steadily improved. The national economy, however, rested on agriculture. Although French peasants were not serfs, as were the peasants of eastern Europe, they were mercilessly taxed. After 1685 other hardships afflicted them: savage warfare, poor harvests, continuing deflation of the currency, and fluctuation in the price of grain. Many peasants emigrated. A totally inadequate tax base and heavy expenditure for war in the later years of Louis's reign made Colbert's goals unattainable.

Economic policy was complicated in 1685 by Louis XIV's revocation of the Edict of Nantes. The new law ordered the destruction of churches, the closing of schools, the Catholic baptism of Huguenots, and the exile of Huguenot pastors who refused to renounce their faith. Why did Louis, by revoking the edict, persecute some of his most loyal and industrially skilled subjects?

Recent scholarship has convincingly shown that Louis XIV was basically tolerant. He insisted on religious unity not for religious but for political reasons. His goal was "one king, one law, one faith." He hated division within the realm and insisted that religious unity was essential to his royal dignity and to the security of the state. Thus after permitting religious liberty in the early years of his reign, Louis finally decided to crack down on Protestants.

Although France's large Catholic majority applauded Louis XIV, writers in the eighteenth century and later damned him for intolerance and for the adverse impact that revocation had on the economy and foreign affairs. They claimed that tens of thousands of Huguenot craftsmen, soldiers, and business people emigrated, depriving France of their skills and tax revenues and carrying their bitterness to Holland, England, and Prussia. Although the claims of economic damage were exaggerated, the revocation of the Edict of Nantes certainly aggravated Protestant hatred for Louis and for his armies.

French Classicism

Scholars characterize French art and literature during the age of Louis XIV as "French classicism." French artists and writers of the late seventeenth century deliberately imitated the subject matter and style of classical antiquity; their work resembled that of Renaissance Italy. French art possessed the classical qualities of discipline, balance, and restraint. Classicism was the official style of Louis's court.

After Louis's accession to power, the principles of absolutism molded the ideals of French classicism. Individualism was not allowed, and artists glorified the state as personified by the king. Precise rules governed all aspects of culture. Formal and restrained perfection was the goal.

Contemporaries said that Louis XIV never ceased playing the role of grand monarch on the stage of his court, and he used music and theater as a backdrop for court ceremonial. Among composers Louis favored Jean-Baptiste Lully (1632–1687), whose orchestral works and court ballets combine lively animation with the restrained austerity typical of French classicism. His operatic pro-

Lully Gavotte

ductions were a powerful influence throughout Europe. Louis also supported François Couperin (1668–1733), whose harpsichord and organ works possess the grandeur the king loved, and Marc-Antoine Charpentier (1634–1704), whose solemn religious music entertained him at meals.

Louis XIV loved the stage, and in the plays of Molière and Racine his court witnessed the finest achievements of the French theater. Playwright, stage manager, director, and actor, Molière produced comedies that exposed the hypocrisies and follies of society through brilliant caricature. *Tartuffe* satirized the religious hypocrite; *Les Femmes Savantes (The Learned Women)* mocked the fashionable pseudointellectuals of the day. Molière made the bourgeoisie the butt of his ridicule; he stopped short of criticizing the nobility, thus reflecting the policy of his royal patron.

While Molière dissected social mores, his contemporary Jean Racine (1639–1699) analyzed the power of love. Racine based his tragic dramas on Greek and Roman legends, and his persistent theme is the conflict of good and evil. Several of his plays—*Andromaque, Bérénice, Iphigénie,* and *Phèdre*—bear the names of women and deal with the power of passion in women. For simplicity of language, symmetrical structure, and calm restraint, the plays of Racine represent the finest examples of French classicism.

Jean-Baptiste Poquelin, also known as Molière
This is an elegant, sensuous, and romantic portrait of the playwright whose works set the moral tone of Louis's court. Louis basked in Molière's admiration, approved his social criticism, and amply rewarded him. *(Source: Musée de Versailles/Photographie Bulloz)*

The Wars of Louis XIV

Visualizing himself as a great military hero, Louis XIV used almost endless war to exalt himself above the other rulers of Europe. Military glory was his aim. In 1666 Louis appointed François le Tellier (later marquis of Louvois) secretary of war. Louvois created a professional army, which was modern in the sense that the French state, rather than private nobles, employed the soldiers.

A commissariat was established to feed the troops, taking the place of the usual practice of living off the countryside. Uniforms and weapons were standardized. A rational system of recruitment, training, discipline, and promotion was imposed. With this new military machine, one national state, France, was able to dominate the politics of Europe for the first time.

Louis continued on a broader scale the expansionist policy begun by Cardinal Richelieu. In 1667, using a dynastic excuse, he invaded Flanders, part of the Spanish Netherlands, and

Franche-Comté. He thus acquired twelve towns, including the important commercial centers of Lille and Tournai (Map 17.1). Five years later, Louis personally led an army of over a hundred thousand men into Holland. The Dutch ultimately saved themselves only by opening the dikes and flooding the countryside. This war, which lasted six years and eventually involved the Holy Roman Empire and Spain, was concluded by the Treaty of Nijmegen (1678). Louis gained additional Flemish towns and all of Franche-Comté.

Encouraged by his successes, by the weakness of the German Empire, and by divisions among the other European powers, Louis continued his aggression. In 1681 he seized the city of Strasbourg and three years later sent his armies into the province of Lorraine. At that moment the king seemed invincible. In fact, Louis had reached the limit of his expansion at Nijmegen. The wars of the

MAP 17.1 Acquisitions of Louis XIV, 1668–1713 The desire for glory and the weakness of his German neighbors encouraged Louis's expansionist policy. But he paid a high price for his acquisitions.

1680s and 1690s brought him no additional territories. In 1689 the Dutch prince William of Orange, a bitter foe, became king of England. William joined the League of Augsburg—which included the Habsburg emperor, the kings of Spain and Sweden, and the electors of Bavaria, Saxony, and the Palatinate—adding British resources and men to the alliance. Neither the French nor the league won any decisive victories. France lacked the means to win; it was financially exhausted.

At the same time a series of bad harvests between 1688 and 1694 brought catastrophe. Cold, wet summers reduced the harvests by an estimated one-third to two-thirds, and in many provinces the death rate rose to several times the normal figure. Rising grain prices, new taxes, a slump in manufac-

turing, and the constant nuisance of pillaging troops—all these meant great suffering for the French people. France wanted peace at any price. Louis XIV granted a respite for five years while he prepared for the conflict later known as the War of the Spanish Succession.

This struggle (1701–1713) involved the dynastic question of the succession to the Spanish throne. When Charles I (r. 1665–1700) died in 1700, his will left the Spanish crown and the worldwide Spanish Empire to Philip of Anjou, Louis XIV's grandson. By accepting this will, Louis obviously would gain power in Spain; he would also be reneging on an earlier treaty to divide the vast Spanish possessions between himself and the Holy Roman emperor. He accepted the will, thereby provoking a great war.

The Dutch and the English would not accept French acquisition of the Spanish Netherlands and of the rich trade with the Spanish colonies, which would make France too strong in Europe and in North America. Thus in 1701 they joined with the Austrians and Prussians in the Grand Alliance. In the ensuing series of conflicts, Louis suffered major defeats and finally sued for peace.

The war was concluded at Utrecht in 1713, where the principle of partition was applied. Louis's grandson Philip remained the first Bourbon king of Spain on the understanding that the French and Spanish crowns would never be united. France surrendered Newfoundland, Nova Scotia, and the Hudson Bay territory to England, which also acquired Gibraltar, Minorca, and control of the African slave trade from Spain. The Dutch gained little because Austria received the former Spanish Netherlands (Map 17.2).

The Peace of Utrecht represented the balance-of-power principle in operation, setting limits on the extent to which any one power, in this case France, could expand. The treaty completed the decline of Spain as a great power. It vastly expanded the British Empire. The Peace of Utrecht also marked the end of French expansionist policy. In Louis's thirty-five-year quest for military glory, his main territorial acquisition after 1678 was Strasbourg. Even revisionist historians sympathetic to Louis acknowledge "that the widespread misery in France during the period was in part due to royal policies, especially the incessant wars."[5] The news of Louis's death in 1715 brought rejoicing throughout France.

✤ THE DECLINE OF ABSOLUTIST SPAIN IN THE SEVENTEENTH CENTURY

Spanish absolutism and greatness had preceded that of the French. In the sixteenth century, Spain (or, more precisely, the kingdom of Castile) had developed the standard features of absolute monarchy: a permanent professional bureaucracy, a standing army, and national taxes that fell most heavily on the poor. Spain developed its mighty international absolutism on the basis of silver bullion from Peru. But by the 1590s the seeds of disaster were sprouting, and in the seventeenth century Spain experienced a steady decline. The lack of a strong middle class (largely the result of the expul-sion of the Jews and Moors), agricultural crisis and population decline, failure to invest in productive enterprises, intellectual isolation and psychological malaise—by 1715 all combined to reduce Spain to a second-rate power.

The fabulous flow of silver from Mexico and Peru had led Philip II to assume the role of defender of Roman Catholicism in Europe (see pages 534–539). But when the "Invincible Armada" went down in 1588, a century of Spanish pride and power went with it. After 1590 a spirit of defeatism and disillusionment crippled most reform efforts.

Philip II's Catholic crusade had been financed by the revenues of the Spanish-Atlantic economy. In the early seventeenth century, the Dutch and English began to trade with the Spanish colonies, and Mexico and Peru developed local industries. Between 1610 and 1650, Spanish trade with the colonies fell 60 percent, and the American silver lodes started to run dry. Yet in Madrid royal expenditures remained high. The result was chronic deficits and frequent cancellations of Spain's national debt. These brutal cancellations—a form of bankruptcy—shook public confidence in the state.

Spain, in contrast to the other countries of western Europe, developed only a tiny middle class. Public opinion, taking its cue from the aristocracy, condemned moneymaking as vulgar and undignified. Those with influence or connections sought titles of nobility and social prestige, or they became priests, monks, and nuns. The flood of gold and silver had produced severe inflation, and many businessmen found so many obstacles in the way of profitable enterprise that they simply gave up.

Spanish aristocrats, attempting to maintain an extravagant lifestyle that they could no longer afford, increased the rents on their estates. High rents and heavy taxes in turn drove the peasants from the land. Agricultural production suffered, and the peasants departed for the large cities, where they swelled the ranks of beggars.

Their most Catholic majesties, the kings of Spain, had no solutions to these dire problems. Philip IV (r. 1622–1665) left the management of his several kingdoms to Count Olivares. An able administrator, the count devised new sources of revenue, but he clung to the grandiose belief that the solution to Spain's difficulties rested in a return to the imperial tradition. Unfortunately, the imperial tradition demanded the revival of war with the Dutch in 1622 and a long war with France over Mantua (1628–1659). These conflicts, on top of

RUSSIAN EMPIRE

Moscow

Dnieper

Kiev

Dniester

POLAND

Warsaw

MOLDAVIA

WALLACHIA

Danube

OTTOMAN EMPIRE

Black Sea

Constantinople

MOREA
(Rep. of Venice)

Mediterranean Sea

SWEDEN

NORWAY

INGRIA

ESTONIA

LIVONIA

LITHUANIA

EAST
PRUSSIA

Baltic Sea

Oder

SILESIA

HUNGARY

Buda Pest

Vienna

AUSTRIA

BOHEMIA

CORFU
(Rep. of Venice)

KINGDOM
OF
DENMARK

DENMARK

BRANDENBURG-PRUSSIA

Berlin

BRANDENBURG

SAXONY

HOLY ROMAN EMPIRE

BAVARIA

Danube

REPUBLIC OF VENICE

PAPAL
STATES

TUSCANY

KINGDOM
OF
NAPLES

SICILY
(Savoy)

Naples

Rome

HANOVER

North Sea

Rhine

PALATINATE

SWITZERLAND

SAVOY

MILAN

GENOA

CORSICA
(Genoa)

SARDINIA
(Austria)

UNITED
NETHERLANDS

Utrecht

AUSTRIAN
NETHERLANDS

LORRAINE

Strasbourg

Paris

Seine

FRANCE

Loire

Rhône

Marseilles

MINORCA
(Gr. Br.)

Balearic Is.

SCOTLAND

GREAT BRITAIN

ENGLAND

London

Thames

IRELAND

ATLANTIC
OCEAN

SPAIN

Madrid

Tagus

PORTUGAL

Lisbon

GIBRALTAR
(Great Britain)

French Bourbon lands
Spanish Bourbon lands
Austrian Habsburg lands
Prussian lands
Great Britain
Boundary of Holy Roman Empire

300 Mi.
300 Km.
0   150   150   300
0

an empty treasury, brought disaster. The Treaty of the Pyrenees of 1659, which ended the French-Spanish wars, compelled Spain to surrender extensive territories to France. After this treaty, Spain's decline as a great power became irreversible.

Seventeenth-century Spain was the victim of its past. It could not forget the grandeur of the sixteenth century and look to the future. The most cherished Spanish ideals were military glory and strong Roman Catholic faith. In the seventeenth century, Spain lacked the finances and the manpower to fight long, expensive wars. Spain also ignored the new mercantile ideas and scientific methods because they came from heretical nations, Holland and England.

In the brilliant novel *Don Quixote,* the Spanish writer Miguel de Cervantes (1547–1616) produced one of the masterpieces of world literature. *Don Quixote* delineates the whole fabric of sixteenth-century Spanish society. The main character, Don Quixote, lives in a dream world, traveling about the countryside seeking military glory. A leading scholar wrote, "The Spaniard convinced himself that reality was what he felt, believed, imagined. He filled the world with heroic reverberations. Don Quixote was born and grew."[6]

ABSOLUTISM IN EASTERN EUROPE: AUSTRIA, PRUSSIA, AND RUSSIA

The rulers of eastern Europe also labored to build strong absolutist states in the seventeenth century. But they built on social and economic foundations different from those in western Europe. These foundations were laid between 1400 and 1650,

MAP 17.2 Europe in 1715 The Peace of Utrecht ended the War of the Spanish Succession and redrew the map of Europe. A French Bourbon king succeeded to the Spanish throne on the understanding that the French would not attempt to unite the French and Spanish crowns. France surrendered to Austria the Spanish Netherlands (later Belgium), then in French hands; and France recognized the Hohenzollern rulers of Prussia. Spain ceded Gibraltar to Great Britain, for which it has been a strategic naval station ever since. Spain also granted to Britain the *asiento,* the contract for supplying African slaves to America.

when the princes and the landed nobility of eastern Europe rolled back the gains made by the peasantry during the High Middle Ages and reimposed serfdom on the rural masses. The nobility also enhanced its power as the primary social force by reducing the importance of the towns and the middle classes.

Despite the strength of the nobility, strong kings did begin to emerge in many eastern European lands in the course of the seventeenth century. There were endless wars, and in this atmosphere of continuous military emergency monarchs found ways to reduce the political power of the landlord nobility. Cautiously leaving the nobles the unchallenged masters of their peasants, eastern monarchs gradually monopolized political power in three key areas. They imposed and collected permanent taxes without consent. They maintained permanent standing armies, which policed their subjects in addition to fighting abroad. And they conducted relations with other states as they pleased.

There were important variations on the absolutist theme in eastern Europe. The royal absolutism created in Prussia was stronger and more effective than that established in Austria. This advantage gave Prussia a thin edge over Austria in the struggle for power in east-central Europe in the eighteenth century, and it prepared the way for Prussia's unification of the German people in the nineteenth century. As for Russia, it developed its own form of autocratic government at an early date, and its political absolutism was quite different from that of France or even Prussia.

Lords and Peasants

Lords and peasants were the basic social groups in eastern Europe, a vast region including Bohemia, Silesia, Hungary, eastern Germany, Poland, Lithuania, and Russia. Peasants in eastern Europe had done relatively well in the period from roughly 1050 to 1300, a time of gradual economic expansion and population growth. Eager to attract German settlers to their sparsely populated lands, the rulers and nobles of eastern Europe had offered potential newcomers economic and legal incentives. Large numbers of incoming settlers had obtained land on excellent terms and gained much personal freedom. These benefits were gradually extended to the local Slavic populations, even

THE RISE OF WESTERN ABSOLUTISM AND CONSTITUTIONALISM

1581	Formation of the Republic of the United Provinces of the Netherlands
1588	Defeat of the Spanish Armada
1589–1610	Reign of Henry IV of France; economic reforms help to restore public order, lay foundation for absolutist rule
1598	Edict of Nantes: Henry IV ends the French wars of religion
1610–1650	Spanish trade with the New World falls by 60 percent
1618–1648	Thirty Years' War
1624–1642	Richelieu dominates French government
1625	Huguenot revolt in France; siege of La Rochelle
1629–1640	Charles I attempts to rule England without Parliament
1640–1660	Long Parliament in England
1642–1649	English civil war
1643–1715	Reign of Louis XIV
1648–1660	The Fronde: French nobility opposes centralizing efforts of monarchy
1648	Peace of Westphalia confirms Dutch independence from Spain
1649	Execution of Charles I; beginning of the Interregnum in England
1653–1658	Cromwell rules England as military dictator
1659	Treaty of the Pyrenees forces Spain to cede extensive territories to France
1660	Restoration of the English monarchy: Charles II returns from exile
1661	Louis XIV enters into independent rule
ca 1663–1683	Colbert directs Louis XIV's mercantilist economic policy
1667	France invades Holland
1673	Test Act excludes Roman Catholics from public office in England
1685	Louis XIV revokes the Edict of Nantes
1685–1688	James II rules England, attempts to restore Roman Catholicism as state religion
1688	The Glorious Revolution establishes a constitutional monarchy in England under Mary and William III
1689	Enactment of the Bill of Rights in England
1701–1713	War of the Spanish Succession
1713	Peace of Utrecht ends French territorial acquisitions, expands the British Empire, completes decline of Spain as a great power

THE RISE OF ABSOLUTISM IN EASTERN EUROPE

1050–1300	Increasing economic development in eastern Europe encourages decline in serfdom
1054	Death of Prince Iaroslav the Wise, under whom the Kievan state reached its highest development
1054–1237	Kiev is divided into numerous territories ruled by competing princes
1237–1242	Mongol invasion and conquest of Russia
1252	Alexander Nevsky, prince of Moscow, recognizes Mongol overlordship
1327–1328	Suppression of the Tver revolt; Mongol khan recognizes Ivan I as great prince
1400–1650	The nobility reimposes serfdom in eastern Europe
ca 1480	Ivan III rejects Mongol overlordship and begins to use the title of tsar
1533–1584	Rule of Tsar Ivan IV (the Terrible): defeat of the khanates of Kazan and Astrakhan; subjugation of the boyar aristocracy
1598–1613	Time of Troubles in Russia
1613	Election of Michael Romanov as tsar: re-establishment of autocracy
1640–1688	Rule of Frederick William, the Great Elector, in Brandenburg-Prussia
1652	Patriarch Nikon's reforms split the Russian Orthodox church
1670–1671	Cossack revolt of Stenka Razin in Russia
1683	Siege of Vienna by the Ottoman Turks
1682–1725	Rule of Tsar Peter the Great
1683–1699	Habsburg conquest of Hungary and Transylvania
1703	Founding of St. Petersburg
1713–1740	Rule of King Frederick William I in Prussia

those of central Russia. Thus by 1300 serfdom had all but disappeared in eastern Europe. Peasants were able to bargain freely with their landlords and move about as they pleased.

After about 1300, however, as Europe's population and economy declined grievously, mainly because of the Black Death, noble landlords sought to solve their tough economic problems by more heavily exploiting the peasantry. In western Europe this attempt generally failed, but in the vast region east of the Elbe River in Germany the landlords were successful in degrading peasants. By 1500 eastern peasants were on their way to becoming serfs again.

Eastern lords triumphed because they made their kings and princes issue laws that restricted the right of their peasants to move to take advantage of better opportunities elsewhere. In Prussian territories by 1500, the law required that runaway peasants be hunted down and returned to their lords, and a runaway servant was to be nailed to a post by one ear and given a knife to cut himself loose. Moreover, lords steadily took more and more of their peasants' land and arbitrarily imposed heavier and heavier labor obligations. By the early 1500s, lords in many territories could command their peasants to work for them without pay for as many as six days a week.

Punishing Serfs This seventeenth-century illustration from Adam Olearius's *Travels in Moscovy* suggests what eastern serfdom really meant. The scene is eastern Poland. There, according to Olearius, a common command of the lord was, "Beat him till the skin falls from the flesh." Selections from Olearius's book are found in this chapter's Listening to the Past. *(Source: University of Illinois Library, Champaign)*

The gradual erosion of the peasantry's economic position was bound up with manipulation of the legal system. The local lord was also the local prosecutor, judge, and jailer. There were no independent royal officials to provide justice or uphold the common law.

Between 1500 and 1650, the social, legal, and economic conditions of peasants in eastern Europe continued to decline. In Poland, for example, nobles gained complete control over their peasants in 1574. In Russia the right of peasants to move from a given estate was abolished in 1603. In 1649 a new law code completed the legal re-establishment of permanent hereditary serfdom. The common fate of peasants in eastern Europe by the middle of the seventeenth century was serfdom.

The consolidation of serfdom between 1500 and 1650 was accompanied by the growth of estate agriculture, particularly in Poland and eastern Germany. In the sixteenth century, European economic expansion and population growth resumed after the great declines of the late Middle Ages. Eastern lords had powerful economic incentives to increase the production of their estates, and they did so. Generally, the estates were inefficient and technically backward, but they nevertheless succeeded in squeezing sizable surpluses out of the impoverished peasants. These surpluses were sold to foreign merchants, who exported them to the growing cities of wealthier western Europe.

The re-emergence of serfdom in eastern Europe in the early modern period was a momentous human development. Above all, it reflected the fact that eastern lords enjoyed much greater political power than their western counterparts. In the late Middle Ages, when much of eastern Europe was experiencing innumerable wars and general political chaos, the noble landlord class had greatly increased its political power at the expense of the ruling monarchs. Moreover, the western concept and reality of sovereignty, as embodied in a king who protected the interests of all his people, was not well developed in eastern Europe before 1650.

Finally, with the approval of weak kings, the landlords systematically undermined the medieval privileges of the towns and the power of the urban classes. For example, instead of selling their products to local merchants in the towns, as required in the Middle Ages, the landlords often sold directly to foreign capitalists. Eastern towns also lost their medieval right of refuge and were compelled to return runaways to their lords. The population of the towns and the urban middle classes declined greatly. This development both reflected and promoted the supremacy of noble landlords in most of eastern Europe in the sixteenth century.

Austria and the Ottoman Turks

The Habsburgs of Austria emerged from the Thirty Years' War (see pages 539–540) impoverished and exhausted. The effort to root out Protestantism in the German lands had failed utterly, and the authority of the Holy Roman Empire and its Habsburg emperors had declined almost to the vanishing point. Yet defeat in central Europe also opened new vistas. The Habsburg monarchs were forced to turn inward and eastward in an attempt to fuse their diverse holdings into a strong, unified state.

An important step in this direction had actually been taken in Bohemia during the Thirty Years' War. Protestantism had been strong among the Czechs, a Slavic people concentrated in Bohemia. In 1618 the Czech nobles who controlled the Bohemian Estates—the representative body of the different legal orders—had risen up against their Habsburg king. This revolt was crushed, and then the Czech nobility was totally restructured to ensure its loyalty to the monarchy. With the help of this new nobility, the Habsburgs established strong direct rule over reconquered Bohemia. The condition of the enserfed peasantry worsened. Protestantism was also stamped out, and religious unity began to emerge. The reorganization of Bohemia was a giant step toward royal absolutism.

After the Thirty Years' War, Ferdinand III (r. 1637–1657) centralized the government in the hereditary German-speaking provinces, most notably Austria, Styria, and the Tyrol. The king created a permanent standing army ready to put down any internal opposition. The Habsburg monarchy was then ready to turn toward the vast plains of Hungary, in opposition to the Ottoman Turks.

The Ottomans had come out of Anatolia, in present-day Turkey, to create one of history's greatest military empires. Their armies had almost captured Vienna in 1529, and for more than 150 years

thereafter the Ottomans ruled all of the Balkan territories, almost all of Hungary, and part of southern Russia. In the late seventeenth century, under vigorous reforming leadership, the Ottoman Empire succeeded in marshaling its forces for one last mighty blow at Christian Europe. A huge Turkish army surrounded Vienna and laid siege to it in 1683. After holding out against great odds for two months, the city was relieved at the last minute, and the Ottomans were forced to retreat. As their Russian and Venetian allies attacked on other fronts, the Habsburgs conquered all of Hungary and Transylvania (part of present-day Romania) by 1699 (Map 17.3).

The Turkish wars and this great expansion strengthened the Habsburg army and promoted some sense of unity in the Habsburg lands. But Habsburg efforts to create a fully developed, highly centralized, absolutist state were only partly successful. The Habsburg state remained a composite of three separate and distinct territories: the old "hereditary provinces" of Austria, the kingdom of Bohemia, and the kingdom of Hungary. Each part had its own laws and political life, for the three noble-dominated Estates continued to exist, though with reduced powers. Above all, the Hungarian nobility effectively thwarted the full development of Habsburg absolutism. Time and again throughout the seventeenth century, Hungarian nobles rose in revolt against the attempts of Vienna to impose absolute rule. They never triumphed decisively, but neither were they ever crushed.

Hungarians resisted because many of them were Protestants, especially in the area long ruled by the more tolerant Turks, and they hated the heavy-handed attempts of the conquering Habsburgs to re-Catholicize everyone. Moreover, the lords of Hungary and even part of the Hungarian peasantry had become attached to a national ideal long before most of the other European peoples. They were determined to maintain as much independence and local control as possible. Thus when the Habsburgs were bogged down in the War of the Spanish Succession (see page 564), the Hungarians rose in one last patriotic rebellion under Prince Francis Rákóczy in 1703. Rákóczy and his forces were eventually defeated, but this time the Habsburgs had to accept many of the traditional privileges of the Hungarian aristocracy in return for Hungarian acceptance of hereditary Habsburg rule. Thus Hungary, unlike Austria or Bohemia,

MAP 17.3 Growth of Austria and Brandenburg-Prussia to 1748 Austria expanded to the southwest into Hungary and Transylvania at the expense of the Ottoman Empire. It was unable to hold the rich German province of Silesia, however, which was conquered by Brandenburg-Prussia.

Hungary never came close to being fully integrated into a centralized, absolute Habsburg state.

The Emergence of Prussia

As the status of east German peasants declined steadily after 1400, local princes lost political power, and a revitalized landed nobility became the undisputed ruling class. The Hohenzollern family, which ruled through different branches as the electors of Brandenburg and the dukes of Prussia, were little more than the largest landowners in a landlord society. Nothing suggested that the Hohenzollerns and their territories would ever play an important role in European or even German affairs.

Brandenburg was a helpless spectator in the Thirty Years' War, its territory alternately ravaged by Swedish and Habsburg armies. Yet the country's devastation prepared the way for Hohenzollern absolutism, because foreign armies dramatically weakened the political power of the Estates—the representative assemblies of the realm. The weakening of the Estates helped the very talented young elector Frederick William (r. 1640–1688), later known as the "Great Elector," to ride roughshod over traditional constitutional liberties and to take a giant step toward royal absolutism.

When Frederick William came to power in 1640, the twenty-year-old ruler was determined to unify his three quite separate provinces and to add to them by diplomacy and war. These provinces were Brandenburg itself, the area around Berlin; Prussia, inherited in 1618 when the junior branch of the Hohenzollern family died out; and scattered holdings along the Rhine in western Germany (see Map 17.3). Each province was inhabited by Germans; but each had its own Estates, dominated by the nobility and the landowning classes.

The struggle between the Great Elector and the provincial Estates was long, complicated, and intense. After the Thirty Years' War, the representatives of the nobility zealously reasserted the right of the Estates to vote taxes, a right the Swedish armies of occupation had simply ignored. Yet first in Brandenburg and then in Prussia, the Great Elector eventually had his way. To pay for the permanent standing army that he first established in 1660, Frederick William forced the Estates to accept the introduction of permanent taxation without consent. The soldiers doubled as tax collectors and policemen, becoming the core of the expanding state bureaucracy. The power of the Estates declined rapidly thereafter, and the Great Elector turned the screws of taxation. State revenue tripled and the size of the army leaped about tenfold during his reign.

In accounting for the Great Elector's fateful triumph, two factors appear central. First, as in the formation of every absolutist state, war was a decisive factor. The ongoing struggle between Sweden and Poland for control of the Baltic after 1648 and the wars of Louis XIV in western Europe created an atmosphere of permanent crisis. It was no accident that, except in commercially minded Holland, constitutionalism won out only in England, the only major country to escape devastating foreign invasions in the seventeenth century.

Second, the nobility had long dominated the government through the Estates but only for its own narrow self-interest. When, therefore, the Great Elector reconfirmed the nobility's freedom from taxation and its unlimited control over the peasants in 1653 and after, the nobility accepted a self-serving compromise. While Frederick William reduced the nobility's political power, the bulk of the Great Elector's new taxes fell on towns, and royal authority stopped at the landlords' gates.

By the time of his death in 1688, the Great Elector had created a single state out of scattered principalities. But his new creation was still small and fragile. It was Frederick William I, "the Soldiers' King" (r. 1713–1740), who truly established

A Prussian Giant Grenadier   Frederick William I wanted tall, handsome soldiers. He dressed them in tight, bright uniforms to distinguish them from the peasant population from which most soldiers came. He also ordered several portraits of his favorites from his court painter, J. C. Merk. Grenadiers wore the distinctive mitre cap instead of an ordinary hat so that they could hurl their heavy hand grenades unimpeded by a broad brim. *(Source: Copyright reserved to Her Majesty Queen Elizabeth II)*

wonderful

Prussian absolutism and gave it its unique character. A dangerous psychoneurotic as well as a talented reformer, Frederick William I created the best army in Europe, for its size, and he infused military values into a whole society.

Frederick William's attachment to the army and military life was intensely emotional. He had, for example, a bizarre, almost pathological love for tall soldiers, whom he credited with superior strength and endurance. Like some fanatical modern-day basketball coach in search of a championship team, he sent his agents throughout both Prussia and all of Europe, tricking, buying, and kidnapping top recruits. Neighboring princes sent him their giants as gifts to win his gratitude. Prussian mothers told their sons: "Stop growing or the recruiting agents will get you."[7] Frederick William's love of the army was also based on a hardheaded conception of the struggle for power and a dog-eat-dog view of international politics. Throughout his long reign he never wavered in his conviction that the welfare of king and state depended above all else on the army.

As in France, the cult of military power provided the rationale for a great expansion of royal absolutism. As the ruthless king himself put it: "I must be served with life and limb, with house and wealth, with honour and conscience, everything must be committed except eternal salvation—that belongs to God, but all else is mine."[8] To make good these extraordinary demands, Frederick William created a strong and exceptionally honest bureaucracy, which administered the country and tried to develop it economically. The last traces of the parliamentary Estates and local self-government vanished.

The king's grab for power brought him into considerable conflict with the noble landowners, the Junkers. In the end the Prussian nobility responded to a combination of threats and opportunities and became the officer caste. By 1739 all but 5 of 245 officers with the rank of major or above were aristocrats. A new compromise had been worked out: the nobility imperiously commanded the peasantry in the army as well as on its estates.

Coarse and crude, penny-pinching and hard working, Frederick William achieved results. Above all, he built a first-rate army out of third-rate resources. Twelfth in Europe in population, Prussia had the fourth largest army by 1740, behind France, Russia, and Austria. Soldier for soldier, the Prussian army became the best in Europe, astonishing foreign observers with its precision,

can we say "psycho"?

skill, and discipline. Curiously, the king loved his "blue boys" so much that he hated to "spend" them. This most militaristic of kings was, paradoxically, almost always at peace.

Nevertheless, the Prussian people paid a heavy and lasting price for the obsessions of the royal drillmaster. Civil society became rigid and highly disciplined. Prussia became the "Sparta of the North"; unquestioning obedience was the highest virtue. As a Prussian minister later summed up, "To keep quiet is the first civic duty."[9] Thus the absolutism of Frederick William I combined with harsh peasant bondage and Junker tyranny to lay the foundations for probably the most militaristic country of modern times.

The Rise of Moscow

In the ninth century, the Vikings, those fearless warriors from Scandinavia, appeared in the lands of the eastern Slavs. Called "Varangians" in the old Russian chronicles, the Vikings were interested primarily in international trade. In order to increase and protect their international commerce, they declared themselves the rulers of the eastern Slavs. The Varangian ruler Oleg (r. 878–912) established his residence at Kiev. He and his successors ruled over a loosely united confederation of Slavic territories—the Kievan state—which reached its height under Prince Iaroslav the Wise (r. 1019–1054).

After Iaroslav's death in 1054, Kiev disintegrated into more and more competing units, each ruled by a prince. A given prince owned a certain number of farms or landed estates and had them worked directly by his people, mainly slaves, called *kholops* in Russian. Outside of these estates, the prince exercised limited authority in his principality. Excluding the clergy, two kinds of people lived there: the noble boyars and the commoner peasants.

Like the Germans and the Italians, the eastern Slavs might have emerged from the Middle Ages weak and politically divided had it not been for the Mongol conquest of the Kievan state. Wild nomadic tribes from present-day Mongolia, the Mongols were temporarily unified in the thirteenth century by Jenghiz Khan (1162–1227), one of history's greatest conquerors. In five years his armies subdued all of China. His successors then wheeled westward, smashing everything in their path and reaching the plains of Hungary victorious before they pulled back in 1242. The Mongol army—the

Golden Horde—was savage in the extreme, often slaughtering entire populations of cities before burning them to the ground.

Having devastated and conquered, the Mongols ruled the eastern Slavs for more than two hundred years. They forced all the bickering Slavic princes to submit to their rule and to give them tribute and slaves. If the conquered peoples rebelled, the Mongols were quick to punish with death and destruction. Thus the Mongols unified the eastern Slavs, for the Mongol khan was acknowledged by all as the supreme ruler.

Beginning with Alexander Nevsky in 1252, the previously insignificant princes of Moscow became particularly adept at serving the Mongols. They loyally put down popular uprisings and collected the khan's harsh taxes. By way of reward, the princes of Moscow emerged as hereditary great princes. Eventually the Muscovite princes were able to destroy their princely rivals and even to replace the khan as supreme ruler.

One of the more important Muscovite princes was Ivan I (r. 1328–1341), popularly known as "Ivan the Moneybag." Extremely stingy, Ivan I built up a large personal fortune and increased his influence by loaning money to less frugal princes to pay their Mongol taxes. Ivan's most serious rival was the prince of Tver, who joined his people in 1327 in a revolt against Mongol oppression. Appointed commander of a large Russian-Mongol army, Ivan laid waste to Tver and its lands. For this proof of devotion, the Mongols made Ivan the general tax collector for all the Slavic lands they had subjugated and named him great prince. Ivan also convinced the metropolitan of Kiev, the leading churchman of all eastern Slavs, to settle in Moscow. Ivan I thus gained greater prestige.

In the next hundred-odd years, the great princes of Moscow significantly increased their holdings. Then, in the reign of Ivan III (r. 1462–1505), the process of gathering in the territories around Moscow was largely completed. Of the principalities that Ivan III purchased and conquered, Novgorod with its lands extending almost to the Baltic Sea was most crucial (Map 17.4). Thus the princes of Moscow defeated all rivals to win complete princely authority.

Not only was the prince of Moscow the *unique* ruler, he was the *absolute* ruler, the autocrat, the *tsar*—the Slavic contraction for "caesar," with all its connotations. This imperious conception of absolute power was powerfully reinforced by two developments. First, about 1480 Ivan III stopped acknowledging the khan as his supreme ruler. There is good evidence to suggest that Ivan and his successors saw themselves as khans. Certainly they assimilated the Mongol concept of kingship as the exercise of unrestrained and unpredictable power.

Second, after the fall of Constantinople to the Turks in 1453, the tsars saw themselves as the heirs of both the caesars and Orthodox Christianity, the one true faith. All the other kings of Europe were heretics: only the tsars were rightful and holy rulers. This idea was promoted by Orthodox churchmen, who spoke of "holy Russia" as the "Third Rome." Ivan's marriage to the daughter of the last Byzantine emperor further enhanced the aura of an imperial inheritance for Moscow. Worthy successor to the mighty khan and the true Christian emperor, the Muscovite tsar was a king claiming unrestricted power as his God-given right. The Mongol inheritance weighed heavily on Russia.

As peasants had begun losing their freedom of movement in the fifteenth century, so had the noble boyars begun losing power and influence. For example, when Ivan III conquered the principality of Novgorod in the 1480s, he confiscated fully 80 percent of the land, executing the previous owners or resettling them nearer Moscow. He then kept more than half of the confiscated land for himself and distributed the remainder to members of a newly emerging service nobility, who held the tsar's land on the explicit condition that they serve in the tsar's army. Moreover, Ivan III began to require boyars outside Novgorod to serve him if they wished to retain their lands.

The rise of the new service nobility accelerated under Ivan IV (r. 1533–1584), the famous "Ivan the Terrible." Having ascended the throne at age three, Ivan suffered insults and neglect at the hands of the haughty boyars after his mother died. But at age sixteen he suddenly pushed aside his hated boyar advisers and crowned himself. Selecting the beautiful and kind Anastasia of the popular Romanov family for his wife and queen, the young tsar soon declared war on the remnants of Mongol power. He defeated the faltering khanates of Kazan and Astrakhan between 1552 and 1556, adding vast new territories to Russia. In the course of these wars, Ivan virtually abolished the old distinction between hereditary boyar private property and land granted temporarily for service. All nobles, old and new, had to serve the tsar in order to hold any land.

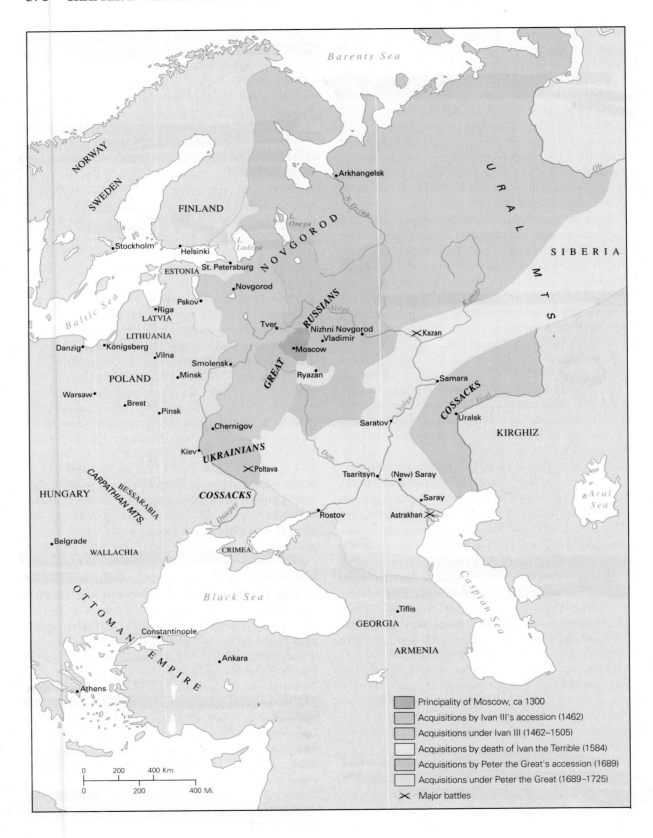

NORWAY

SWEDEN

FINLAND

Barents Sea

•Arkhangelsk

N. Dvina

U R A L

S I B E R I A

L. Onega

NOVGOROD

•Stockholm

•Helsinki

L. Ladoga

ESTONIA

St. Petersburg

•Novgorod

Baltic Sea

Pskov•

•Riga

LATVIA

RUSSIANS

Tver•

•Nizhni Novgorod

•Vladimir

×Kazan

Volga

Kama

M T S.

LITHUANIA

Danzig•

•Königsberg

•Vilna

•Moscow

GREAT

Smolensk•

•Minsk

•Ryazán

Samara•

COSSACKS

•Uralsk

Ural

KIRGHIZ

POLAND

Warsaw•

•Brest

•Pinsk

•Chernigov

Saratov•

Volga

Kiev•

UKRAINIANS

×Poltava

HUNGARY

BESSARABIA

CARPATHIAN MTS.

COSSACKS

Tsaritsyn•

(New) Saray

Don

Dnieper

•Rostov

Astrakhan×

•Saray

Aral Sea

•Belgrade

WALLACHIA

CRIMEA

Black Sea

•Tiflis

Caspian Sea

GEORGIA

O T T O M A N

•Constantinople

•Ankara

E M P I R E

ARMENIA

•Athens

0   200   400 Km.

0   200   400 Mi.

■	Principality of Moscow, ca 1300
□	Acquisitions by Ivan III's accession (1462)
■	Acquisitions under Ivan III (1462–1505)
□	Acquisitions by death of Ivan the Terrible (1584)
■	Acquisitions by Peter the Great's accession (1689)
□	Acquisitions under Peter the Great (1689–1725)
×	Major battles

Ivan the Terrible   Ivan IV, the first to take the title Tsar of Russia, executed many Muscovite boyars and their peasants and servants. His control of all land, trade, and industry restricted Russian social and economic development. *(Source: National Museum, Copenhagen, Denmark)*

The transformation of the entire nobility into a service nobility was completed in the second part of Ivan the Terrible's reign. In 1557 Ivan turned westward, and for the next twenty-five years Muscovy waged an exhausting, unsuccessful war primarily with the large Polish-Lithuanian state, which controlled not only Poland but much of the Ukraine in the sixteenth century. Quarreling with the boyars over the war and blaming them for the sudden death of his beloved Anastasia in 1560, the increasingly cruel and demented Ivan turned to strike down all who stood in his way.

Above all, he reduced the ancient Muscovite boyar families with a reign of terror. Leading boyars, their relatives, and even their peasants were executed en masse by a special corps of unquestioning servants. Dressed in black and riding black horses, they were forerunners of the modern dictator's secret police. Large estates were confiscated, broken up, and reapportioned to the lower service nobility, which was totally dependent on the autocrat.

Ivan also took giant strides toward making all commoners servants of the tsar. As the service nobles demanded more from their peasants, more and more peasants fled toward the wild, recently conquered territories to the east and south. There they formed free groups and outlaw armies known as Cossacks. The Cossacks maintained a precarious independence beyond the reach of the oppressive landholders and the tsar's hated officials. The solution to this problem was to complete the tying of the peasants to the land, making them serfs perpetually bound to serve the noble landholders, who were bound in turn to serve the tsar.

In the time of Ivan the Terrible, urban traders and artisans were also bound to their towns and

MAP 17.4 Expansion of Russia to 1725   After the disintegration of the Kievan state and the Mongol conquest, the princes of Moscow and their descendants gradually extended their rule over an enormous territory.

jobs so that the tsar could tax them more heavily. The urban classes had no security in their work or property and remained weak and divided. Even the wealthiest merchants were basically dependent agents of the tsar.

As has so often occurred in Russia, the death of an iron-fisted tyrant—in this case, Ivan the Terrible in 1584—ushered in an era of confusion and violent struggles for power. Events were particularly chaotic after Ivan's son Theodore died in 1598 without an heir. The years 1598 to 1613 are aptly called the Time of Troubles.

Close relatives of the deceased tsar intrigued against and murdered each other, alternately fighting and welcoming the invading Swedes and Poles, who even occupied Moscow. Most serious for the cause of autocracy, there was a great social upheaval as Cossacks marched northward, rallying peasants and slaughtering nobles and officials. This social explosion from below, which combined with a belated surge of patriotic opposition to the Polish invaders, brought the nobles to their senses. In 1613 they elected Ivan's sixteen-year-old grandnephew, Michael Romanov, the new hereditary tsar and rallied around him in the face of common internal and external threats.

Michael's reign saw the gradual re-establishment of tsarist autocracy (see Listening to the Past). The recently rebellious peasants were ground down further, while Ivan's heavy military obligations on the nobility were relaxed considerably, a trend that continued after his death. The result was a second round of mass upheaval and protest.

In the mid-seventeenth century, the unity of the Russian Orthodox church was torn apart by the religious reforms of the patriarch Nikon, a dogmatic purist who wished to bring "corrupted" Russian practices of worship into line with the Greek Orthodox model. The self-serving church hierarchy quickly went along, but the intensely religious common people resisted. Great numbers left the church and formed illegal communities of "Old Believers," who were hunted down and persecuted. After the great split, the Russian masses were alienated from the established church, which became totally dependent on the state for its authority.

Again the Cossacks revolted against the state, which was doggedly trying to catch up with them on the frontiers and reduce them to serfdom. Under the leadership of Stenka Razin they moved up the Volga River in 1670 and 1671, attracting a great undisciplined army of peasants, murdering landlords, and high church officials, and proclaiming freedom from oppression. In response to this rebellion, finally defeated by the government, the thoroughly scared upper classes tightened the screws of serfdom even further.

The Reforms of Peter the Great

It is now possible to understand the reforms of Peter the Great (r. 1682–1725) and his kind of monarchial absolutism. Contrary to some historians' assertions, Peter was interested primarily in military power and not in some grandiose westernization plan. A giant for his time, at six feet seven inches, and possessing enormous energy and determination, Peter was determined to increase Russia's power and to continue the territorial expansion that had gained a large part of the Ukraine in 1667 and had completed the conquest of Siberia in the seventeenth century. Little wonder that the forty-three years of Peter's rule knew only one year of peace.

When Peter took full control in 1689, the heart of his part-time army still consisted of cavalry made up of boyars and service nobility. The Russian army was lagging behind the professional standing armies being formed in Europe in the seventeenth century. The core of such armies was a highly disciplined infantry—an infantry that fired and refired rifles as it fearlessly advanced, before charging with fixed bayonets. Such a large, permanent army was enormously expensive. Given the desire to conquer more territory, Peter's military problem was serious.

Peter's solution was, in essence, to tighten up Muscovy's old service system and really make it work. He put the nobility back in harness with a vengeance. Every nobleman, great or small, was once again required to serve in the army or in the civil administration—for life. Since a more modern army and government required skilled technicians and experts, Peter created schools and even universities. One of his most hated reforms required five years of compulsory education away from home for every young nobleman. Peter established a merit-based military-civilian bureaucracy in which some people of non-noble origin rose to high positions. He also searched out talented foreigners—twice in his reign he went abroad to study and observe—and placed them in his service. These measures combined to make the army and government more powerful and efficient.

Peter also greatly increased the service requirements of the commoners. He established a regular standing army of more than 200,000 soldiers. In addition, special forces of Cossacks and foreigners numbered more than 100,000. The departure of a drafted peasant boy was regarded by his family and village as almost like a funeral, as indeed it was, since the recruit was drafted for life. The peasantry also served with its taxes, which increased threefold during Peter's reign. Serfs were arbitrarily assigned to work in the growing number of factories and mines.

The constant warfare of Peter's reign consumed from 80 to 85 percent of all revenues but brought only modest territorial expansion. Yet after initial losses in the Great Northern War with Sweden, which lasted from 1700 to 1721, Peter's new war machine crushed Sweden's smaller army in the Ukraine at Poltava in 1709, one of the most significant battles in Russian history. Sweden never really regained the offensive. Annexing Estonia and much of present-day Latvia (see Map 17.4), Russia became the dominant power on the Baltic Sea and very much a European Great Power. If victory or defeat is the ultimate historical criterion, Peter's reforms were a success.

There were other important consequences of Peter's reign. Because of his feverish desire to use modern technology to strengthen the army, many Westerners and Western ideas flowed into Russia for the first time. A new class of educated Russians began to emerge. At the same time, vast numbers of Russians, especially among the poor and weak, hated Peter's massive changes. The split between the enserfed peasantry and the educated nobility thus widened, even though all were caught up in the endless demands of the sovereign.

A new idea of state interest, distinct from the tsar's personal interests, began to take hold. Peter claimed to act for the common good, and he attached explanations to his decrees in an attempt to gain the support of the populace. Yet, as before, the tsar alone decided what the common good was.

In sum, Peter built on the service obligations of old Muscovy. His monarchial absolutism was truly the culmination of the long development of a unique Russian civilization. Yet the creation of a more modern army and state introduced much that was new and Western to that civilization. This development paved the way for Russia to move much closer to the European mainstream in its thought and institutions during the Enlightenment under Catherine the Great.

Absolutism and the Baroque

The rise of royal absolutism in eastern Europe had major cultural consequences. Inspired in part by Louis XIV of France, the great and not-so-great rulers called on the artistic talent of the age to glorify their power and magnificence. This exaltation of despotic rule was particularly striking in architecture and city planning.

As soaring Gothic cathedrals expressed the idealized spirit of the High Middle Ages, so dramatic baroque palaces symbolized the age of absolutist power. By 1700 palace building had become an obsession for the rulers of central and eastern Europe. Their baroque palaces were clearly intended to overawe the people with the monarch's strength. One such palace was Schönbrunn, an enormous Viennese Versailles begun in 1695 by Emperor Leopold I to celebrate Austrian military victories and Habsburg might.

Petty princes also contributed mightily to the mania of palace building. The not-very-important elector-archbishop of Mainz, the ruling prince of that city, confessed apologetically that "building is a craze which costs much, but every fool likes his own hat."[10] The archbishop of Mainz's own "hat" was an architectural gem, like that of another churchly ruler, the prince-bishop of Würzburg. In central and eastern Europe, the favorite noble servants of royalty became extremely rich and powerful, and they, too, built grandiose palaces in the capital cities. These palaces were in part an extension of the monarch, for they surpassed the buildings of less favored nobles.

Palaces like Schönbrunn and Würzburg were magnificent examples of the baroque style. They expressed the baroque delight in bold, sweeping statements intended to provide a dramatic emotional experience. To create this experience, baroque masters dissolved the traditional artistic frontiers: the architect permitted the painter and the artisan to cover the undulating surfaces with wildly colorful paintings, graceful sculptures, and fanciful carvings. Space was used in a highly original way, to blend everything together in a total environment.

Not content with fashioning ostentatious palaces, absolute monarchs and baroque architects remodeled existing capital cities or built new ones to

Würzburg, the Prince-Bishop's Palace The baroque style brought architects, painters, and sculptors together in harmonious, even playful partnership. This magnificent monumental staircase, designed by Johann Balthasar Neumann in 1735, merges into the vibrant ceiling frescoes by Giovanni Battista Tiepolo. A man is stepping out of the picture, and a painted dog resembles a marble statue. *(Source: Erich Lessing/Art Resource, NY)*

reflect royal magnificence and the centralization of political power. Karlsruhe, founded in 1715 as the capital city of a small German principality, is one extreme example. There, broad, straight avenues radiated out from the palace, so that all roads—like all power—were focused on the ruler. More typically, the monarch's architects added new urban areas alongside the old city, and these areas became the real heart of the expanding capital.

The distinctive features of the new additions were their broad avenues, their imposing government buildings, and their rigorous mathematical layout. Along major thoroughfares the nobles built elaborate townhouses; stables and servants' quarters were built on the alleys behind. Under arcades along the avenues appeared smart and expensive shops, the first department stores, with plate-glass windows and fancy displays. The additions brought reckless speed to the European city. Whereas everyone had walked through the narrow, twisting streets of the medieval town, the high and mighty raced down the broad boulevards in elegant carriages. A social gap opened between the wealthy riders and the gaping, dodging pedestrians.

No city illustrates better than St. Petersburg the close ties among politics, architecture, and urban development in this period. In 1702 Peter the Great's armies seized a desolate Swedish fortress on one of the water-logged islands at the mouth of the Neva River on the Baltic Sea. Within a year the tsar had decided to build a new city there and to make it, rather than ancient Moscow, his capital. The land was swampy and inhospitable. But for Peter it was a future metropolis gloriously bearing his name. After the decisive Russian victory at Poltava in 1709, he moved into high gear. In one imperious decree after another, he ordered his people to build a new city, his "window on Europe."

Peter believed that it would be easier to reform the country militarily and administratively from such a city than from Moscow, and his political goals were reflected in his architectural ideas. First Peter wanted a comfortable, "modern" city. Modernity meant broad, straight, stone-paved avenues, houses built in a uniform line, large parks, canals for drainage, stone bridges, and street lighting. Second, all building had to conform strictly to detailed architectural regulations set down by the government. Finally, each social group—the nobility, the merchants, the artisans, and so on—was to live in a certain section of town. In short, the city and its population were to conform to a carefully defined urban plan of the baroque type.

Peter used the methods of Russian autocracy to build his modern capital. The creation of St. Petersburg was just one of the heavy obligations he dictatorially imposed on all social groups in Russia. The peasants bore the heaviest burdens. Just as the government drafted peasants for the army, it also drafted from 25,000 to 40,000 men each summer to labor in St. Petersburg for three months, without pay. Peasants hated forced labor in the capital, and each year from one-fourth to one-third of those sent risked brutal punishment and ran away. Many peasant construction workers died each summer from hunger, sickness, and accidents. Beautiful St. Petersburg was built on the shoveling, carting, and paving of a mass of conscripted serfs.

Peter also drafted more privileged groups to his city, but on a permanent basis. Nobles were sum-

St. Petersburg, ca 1760   Rastrelli's remodeled Winter Palace, which housed the royal family until the Russian Revolution of 1917, stands on the left along the Neva River. The Navy Office with its golden spire and other government office buildings are nearby and across the river. Russia became a naval power and St. Petersburg a great port. *(Source: Michael Holford)*

marily ordered to build costly stone houses and palaces in St. Petersburg and to live in them most of the year. Merchants and artisans were also commanded to settle and build in St. Petersburg. These nobles and merchants were then required to pay for the city's avenues, parks, canals, embankments, pilings, and bridges. The building of St. Petersburg was, in truth, an enormous direct tax levied on the wealthy, who in turn forced the peasantry to do most of the work. No wonder so many Russians hated Peter's new city.

Yet the tsar had his way. By the time of his death in 1725, there were at least six thousand houses and numerous impressive government buildings in St. Petersburg. Under the remarkable women who ruled Russia throughout most of the eighteenth century, St. Petersburg blossomed as a majestic and well-organized city, at least in its wealthy showpiece sections. Chief architect Bartolomeo Rastrelli combined Italian and Russian traditions into a unique, wildly colorful St. Petersburg style in many noble palaces and government buildings. All the while St. Petersburg grew rapidly, and its almost 300,000 inhabitants in 1782 made it one of the world's largest cities. A magnificent and harmonious royal city, St. Petersburg proclaimed the power of Russia's rulers and the creative potential of the absolutist state.

❊ ENGLAND: THE TRIUMPH OF CONSTITUTIONAL MONARCHY

defeat of Spanish Armada

In 1588 Queen Elizabeth I of England exercised great personal power, but by 1689 the power of the English monarchy was severely limited. Change in England was anything but orderly. Seventeenth-century England displayed little political stability. It executed one king, experienced a bloody civil war, experimented with military dictatorship, then restored the son of the murdered king, and finally, after a bloodless revolution, established constitutional monarchy. Political stability came only in the 1690s. Yet out of this tumultuous century England built the foundations for a strong and enduring constitutional monarchy.

In the middle years of the seventeenth century, the problem of sovereignty was vigorously debated. In *Leviathan,* the English philosopher and political theorist Thomas Hobbes (1588–1679) maintained that sovereignty is ultimately derived from the people, who transfer it to the monarchy by implicit contract. The power of the ruler is absolute, Hobbes said, but kings do not hold their power by divine right. This abstract theory pleased no one in the seventeenth century, but it did stimulate fruitful thinking about England's great seventeenth-century problem—the problem of order and political power.

The Decline of Absolutism in England (1603–1660)

Elizabeth I's extraordinary success was the result of her political shrewdness and flexibility, her careful management of finances, her wise selection of ministers, her clever manipulation of Parliament, and her sense of royal dignity and devotion to hard work. After her Scottish cousin James Stuart succeeded her as James I (r. 1603–1625), Elizabeth's strengths seemed even greater.

King James was learned and, with thirty-five years' experience as king of Scotland, politically shrewd. But he was not as interested in displaying the majesty and mystique of monarchy as Elizabeth had been, and he lacked the common touch. Moreover, James was a dogmatic proponent of the theory of divine right of kings. "There are no privileges and immunities," said James, "which can stand against a divinely appointed King." This typically absolutist notion implied total royal jurisdiction over the liberties, persons, and properties of English men and women. Such a view ran directly counter to many long-standing English ideas, including the belief that a person's property could not be taken away without due process of law. And in the House of Commons the English had a strong representative body to question these absolutist pretensions.

The House of Commons guarded the state's pocketbook, and James and later Stuart kings badly needed to open that pocketbook. James I looked on all revenues as a windfall to be squandered on a lavish court and favorite courtiers. The extravagance displayed in James's court, as well as the public flaunting of his male lovers, weakened respect for the monarchy. These actions also stimulated the knights and burgesses who sat in the House of Commons at Westminster to press for a thorough discussion of royal expenditures, religious reform, and foreign affairs. In short, the Commons aspired to sovereignty—the ultimate political power in the realm.

During the reigns of James I and his son Charles I (r. 1625–1649) the English House of Commons was very different from the assembly that Henry VIII had manipulated into passing his Reformation legislation. The class that dominated the Commons during the Stuarts' reign wanted political power corresponding to its economic strength. A social revolution had brought about this change. The dissolution of the monasteries and the sale of monastic land had enriched many people. Agricultural techniques like the draining of wasteland had improved the land and increased its yield. In the seventeenth century old manorial common land was enclosed and profitably turned into sheep runs. Many invested in commercial ventures at home, such as the expanding cloth industry, and in foreign trade. Many also made prudent marriages. These developments increased social mobility. The typical pattern was for the commercially successful to set themselves up as country gentry. This elite group possessed a far greater proportion of the land and of the nation's wealth in 1640 than in 1540. Increased wealth resulted in a better-educated and more articulate House of Commons.

In England, unlike France, no social stigma was attached to paying taxes. Members of the House of Commons were willing to tax themselves provided they had some say in state spending and state policies. The Stuart kings, however, considered such ambitions intolerable presumption and a threat to their divine-right prerogative. Consequently, at every Parliament between 1603 and 1640, bitter squabbles erupted between Crown and Commons. Like the Great Elector in Prussia, Charles I tried to govern without Parliament (1629–1640) and to finance his government by arbitrary levies. And as in Prussia these absolutist measures brought intense political conflict.

Religion was another source of conflict. In the early seventeenth century, increasing numbers of English people felt dissatisfied with the Church of England established by Henry VIII and reformed by Elizabeth. Many Puritans (see page 535) remained committed to "purifying" the Anglican church of Roman Catholic elements—elaborate vestments and ceremonies, the position of the altar in the church, even the giving and wearing of wedding rings.

Many Puritans were also attracted by the socioeconomic implications of John Calvin's theology. Calvinism emphasized hard work, sobriety, thrift, competition, and postponement of pleasure, and it tended to link sin and poverty with weakness and moral corruption. These attitudes, which have frequently been called the "Protestant ethic," "middle-class ethic," or "capitalist ethic," fit in precisely with the economic approaches and practices of many (successful) business people and farmers. These "Protestant virtues" represented the prevailing values of members of the House of Commons.

James I and Charles I both gave the impression of being highly sympathetic to Roman Catholicism. Charles supported the policies of Archbishop of Canterbury William Laud (1573–1645), who tried to impose elaborate ritual and rich ceremonial on all churches. People believed that the country was being led back to Roman Catholicism. In 1637 Laud attempted to impose two new elements on the church organization in Scotland: a new prayer book, modeled on the Anglican Book of Common Prayer, and bishoprics, which the Presbyterian Scots firmly rejected. The Scots revolted. To finance an army to put down the Scots, King Charles was compelled to summon Parliament in November 1640. It was a fatal decision.

For eleven years Charles I had ruled without Parliament, financing his government through extraordinary stopgap levies considered illegal by most English people. Most members of Parliament believed that such taxation without consent amounted to absolutist despotism. Thus they were not willing to trust the king with an army. Accordingly, the Parliament summoned in November 1640 (commonly called the Long Parliament because it sat from 1640 to 1660) enacted legislation that limited the power of the monarch and made arbitrary government impossible.

In 1641 the Commons passed the Triennial Act, which compelled the king to summon Parliament every three years. The Commons impeached Archbishop Laud and abolished the House of Lords and the ecclesiastical Court of High Commission. King Charles reluctantly accepted these measures. But understanding and peace were not achieved, and an uprising in Ireland precipitated civil war.

Ever since Henry II had conquered Ireland in 1171, English governors had mercilessly ruled the land, and English landlords had ruthlessly exploited the Irish people. The English Reformation had made a bad situation worse: because the Irish remained Catholic, religious differences united with economic and political oppression. Without an army, Charles I could neither come to terms with the Scots nor put down the Irish rebellion, and the Long Parliament remained unwilling to place an army under a king it did not trust. Charles thus recruited an army drawn from the nobility and the nobility's cavalry staff, the rural gentry, and mercenaries. The parliamentary army that rose in opposition was composed of the militia of the city of London, country squires with business connections, and men with a firm belief that serving was their spiritual duty.

The English civil war (1642–1649) tested whether ultimate political power in England was to reside in the king or in Parliament. The civil war did not resolve that problem, although it ended in 1649 with the execution of King Charles on the charge of high treason and thus dealt a severe blow to the theory of divine-right, absolute monarchy in England. Kingship was abolished in England, and a *commonwealth,* or republican form of government, was proclaimed.

In fact, the army that had defeated the royal forces controlled the government, and Oliver Cromwell controlled the army. Indeed, the period from 1649 to 1660, known as the Interregnum because it separated two monarchial periods, was a transitional time of military dictatorship, and for most of that time Cromwell was head of state.

Oliver Cromwell (1599–1658) came from the country gentry, the class that dominated the House of Commons in the early seventeenth century. He was a member of the Long Parliament. Cromwell rose in the parliamentary army and achieved nationwide fame by infusing the army with his Puritan convictions and molding it into the highly effective military machine, called the New Model Army, that defeated the royalist forces. The army prepared a constitution, the Instrument of Government (1653), that invested executive power in a lord protector (Cromwell) and a council of state. The instrument provided for triennial parliaments and gave Parliament the sole power to raise taxes. But after repeated disputes, Cromwell tore up the document and proclaimed quasi-martial law.

On the issue of religion, Cromwell favored broad toleration, and the Instrument of Government gave all Christians, except Roman Catholics, the right to practice their faith. Cromwell welcomed the immigration of Jews, because of their skills, and they began to return to England after four centuries of absence. As for Irish Catholicism, Cromwell identified it with sedition. In 1649 he crushed rebellion in Ireland with merciless savagery, leaving a legacy of Irish hatred for England. He also rigorously censored the press, forbade sports, and kept the theaters closed in England.

Cromwell pursued mercantilist economic policies similar to those that Colbert established in France. He enforced a navigation act requiring that English goods be transported on English ships. The navigation act was a great boost to the development of an English merchant marine and brought about a short but successful war with the commercially threatened Dutch.

✳ **Periodical Sheet on the English Civil War** Single sheets or broadsides spread the positions of the opposing sides to the nonliterate public. *Mercurius Rusticus*, intended for country people, conveyed the royalist argument. *(Source: The British Library)*

Military government collapsed when Cromwell died in 1658. Fed up with military rule, the English longed for a return to civilian government, restoration of the common law, and social and religious stability. Moreover, the strain of creating a community of puritanical saints proved too psychologically exhausting. Government by military dictatorship was an experiment in absolutism that the English never forgot or repeated. By 1660 they were ready to try a restoration of monarchy.

The Restoration of the English Monarchy

The Restoration of 1660 re-established the monarchy in the person of Charles II (r. 1660–1685), eldest son of Charles I. At the same time both houses of Parliament were also restored, together with the established Anglican church. The Restoration failed to resolve two serious problems. What was to be the attitude of the state toward Puritans, Catholics, and dissenters from the established church? And what was to be the constitutional relationship between the king and Parliament?

Charles II, a relaxed, easygoing, and sensual man, was basically not much interested in religious issues. But the new members of Parliament were, and they proceeded to enact a body of laws that sought to compel religious uniformity. Those who refused to receive the sacrament of the Church of England could not vote, hold public office, preach, teach, attend the universities, or even assemble for meetings, according to the Test Act of 1673.

In politics, Charles II was at first determined to get along with Parliament and share power with it. His method for doing so had profound importance for later constitutional development. The king appointed a council of five men who served both as his major advisers and as members of Parliament, thus acting as liaison agents between the executive and the legislature. It gradually came to be accepted that the council of five was answerable in Parliament for the decisions of the king.

Harmony between the Crown and Parliament rested on the understanding that Charles would summon Parliament frequently and Parliament would vote him sufficient revenues. However, although Parliament believed that Charles should have large powers, it did not grant him an adequate income. Accordingly, in 1670 Charles entered into a secret agreement with Louis XIV. The French king would give Charles £200,000 annually. In return Charles would relax the laws against Catholics, gradually re-Catholicize England, support French policy against the Dutch, and convert to Catholicism himself.

When the details of this secret treaty leaked out, a wave of anti-Catholic fear swept England. Charles had produced only bastards, and therefore it appeared that his brother and heir, James, duke of York, who had publicly acknowledged his Catholicism, would inaugurate a Catholic dynasty. The combination of hatred for the French absolutism embodied in Louis XIV and hostility to Roman Catholicism led the Commons to pass an exclusion bill denying the succession to a Roman Catholic. But Charles quickly dissolved Parliament, and the bill never became law.

James II (r. 1685–1688) succeeded his brother. Almost at once the worst English anti-Catholic fears, already aroused by Louis XIV's recent revocation of the Edict of Nantes, were realized. In direct violation of the Test Act, James appointed Roman Catholics to positions in the army, the universities, and local government. The king was suspending the law at will and appeared to be reviving the absolutism of his father (Charles I) and grandfather (James I). He went further. Attempting to broaden his base of support with Protestant dissenters and nonconformists, James issued a declaration of indulgence granting religious freedom to all.

Two events gave the signals for revolution. First, seven bishops of the Church of England petitioned the king that they not be forced to read the declaration of indulgence because of their belief that it was an illegal act. They were imprisoned in the Tower of London but subsequently acquitted amid great public enthusiasm. Second, in June 1688 James's second wife produced a male heir. A Catholic dynasty seemed assured. The fear of a Roman Catholic monarchy, supported by France and ruling outside the law, prompted a group of eminent persons to offer the English throne to James's Protestant daughter, Mary, and her Dutch husband, Prince William of Orange. In December 1688 James II, his queen, and their infant son fled to France and became pensioners of Louis XIV. Early in 1689, William and Mary were crowned king and queen of England.

The English call the events of 1688 to 1689 the "Glorious Revolution." The revolution was indeed glorious in the sense that it replaced one king with another with a minimum of bloodshed. It also represented the destruction, once and for all, of the idea of divine-right absolutism in England. William and Mary accepted the English throne from Parliament and in so doing explicitly recognized the supremacy of Parliament.

The men who brought about the revolution quickly framed their intentions in the Bill of Rights, the cornerstone of the modern British constitution. The basic principles of the Bill of Rights were formulated in direct response to Stuart absolutism. Law was to be made in Parliament; once made, it could not be suspended by the Crown. Parliament had to be called at least every three years. Both elections to and debate in Parliament were to be free, in the sense that the Crown was not to interfere in them. Judges would hold their offices "during good behavior," a provision that assured judicial independence.

In striking contrast to the states of continental Europe, there was to be no standing army that could be used against the English population in peacetime. Moreover, the Bill of Rights granted Protestants the right to possess firearms. Additional legislation granted freedom of worship to Protestant dissenters and nonconformists and required that the English monarch always be Protestant.

The Glorious Revolution found its best defense in John Locke's *Second Treatise of Civil Government* (1690). The political philosopher Locke (1632–1704) maintained that people set up civil governments in order to protect life, liberty, and property. A government that oversteps its proper function—protecting the natural rights of life, liberty, and property—becomes a tyranny. (By "natural" rights, Locke meant rights basic to all men because all have the ability to reason.) Under a tyrannical government, the people have the natural right to rebellion. Recognizing the close relationship between economic and political freedom, Locke linked economic liberty and private property with political freedom.

Locke served as the great spokesman for the liberal English revolution of 1688 to 1689 and for representative government. His idea, inherited from ancient Greece and Rome, that there are natural or universal rights equally valid for all peoples and societies, played a powerful role in eighteenth-century Enlightenment thought. His ideas on liberty and tyranny were especially popular in colonial America.

The events of 1688 to 1689 did not constitute a *democratic* revolution. The revolution formalized Parliament's great power, and Parliament represented the upper classes. The great majority of English people had little say in their government. The English revolution established a constitutional monarchy; it also inaugurated an age of aristocratic government.

In the course of the eighteenth century, the cabinet system of government evolved out of Charles II's old council-of-five system. The term *cabinet* derives from the small private room in which English rulers consulted their chief ministers. In a cabinet system, the leading ministers formulate common policy and conduct the business of the country. During the administration of one royal minister, Sir Robert Walpole, who led the cabinet from 1721 to 1742, the idea developed that the cabinet was responsible to the House of Commons. Walpole enjoyed the favor of the monarchy and of the House of Commons and came to be called the king's first, or "prime," minister. In the English cabinet system, both legislative and executive power are held by the leading ministers, who form the government.

❋ THE DUTCH REPUBLIC IN THE SEVENTEENTH CENTURY

In the late sixteenth century, the seven northern provinces of the Netherlands, of which Holland and Zeeland were the most prosperous, had thrown off Spanish domination (see pages 534–539). The seventeenth century then witnessed an unparalleled flowering of Dutch scientific, artistic, and literary achievement. In this period, often called the golden age of the Netherlands, Dutch ideas and attitudes played a profound role in shaping a new and modern world-view.

The Republic of the United Provinces of the Netherlands represents a variation in the development of the modern constitutional state. Within each province an oligarchy of wealthy merchants called regents handled domestic affairs in the local Estates. The provincial Estates held virtually all the power. A federal assembly, or States General, handled matters of foreign affairs, such as war, but all issues had to be referred back to the local Estates for approval. The regents in each province jealously guarded local independence and resisted efforts at centralization. Nevertheless, Holland, which had the largest navy and the most wealth, dominated the republic and the States General.

The government of the United Provinces conforms to none of the standard categories of seventeenth-century political organization. The Dutch were not monarchial but fiercely republican. The government was controlled by wealthy merchants and financiers. Though rich, their values were not aristocratic but strongly middle class. The political success of the Dutch rested on the phenomenal commercial prosperity of the Netherlands. The moral and ethical bases of that commercial wealth were thrift, hard work, and simplicity in living.

John Calvin had written, "From where do the merchant's profits come except from his own diligence and industry." This attitude undoubtedly encouraged a sturdy people who had waged a centuries-old struggle against the sea. Louis XIV's hatred of the Dutch was proverbial. They represented all that he despised—middle-class values, religious toleration, and independent political institutions.

Alone of all European peoples in the seventeenth century, the Dutch practiced religious toleration. Peoples of all faiths were welcome within their borders. Jews enjoyed a level of acceptance and absorption in Dutch business and general culture unique in early modern Europe. It is a testimony to the urbanity of Dutch society that in a century when patriotism was closely identified with religious uniformity, the Calvinist province of Holland allowed its highest official, Jan van Oldenbarneveldt, to continue to practice his Roman Catholic faith. As long as business people conducted their religion in private, the government did not interfere with them.

Toleration paid off. It attracted a great amount of foreign capital and business expertise. The Bank of Amsterdam became Europe's best source of cheap credit and commercial intelligence and the main clearing-house for bills of exchange. People of all races and creeds traded in Amsterdam, at whose docks on the Amstel River five thousand ships were berthed. Joost van den Vondel, the poet of Dutch imperialism, exulted:

Rembrandt: The Jewish Bride   Holland's greatest painter, Rembrandt (1606–1669) combined an expressive mastery of technique, emotional depth, psychological penetration, and enormous range—religious scenes, still lifes, portraits. The so-called Jewish Bride (ca 1665), perhaps a wedding portrait of two wealthy people, reveals the artist's unsurpassed handling of light, so characteristic of his later work. (*Source: Rijksmuseum-Stichting*)

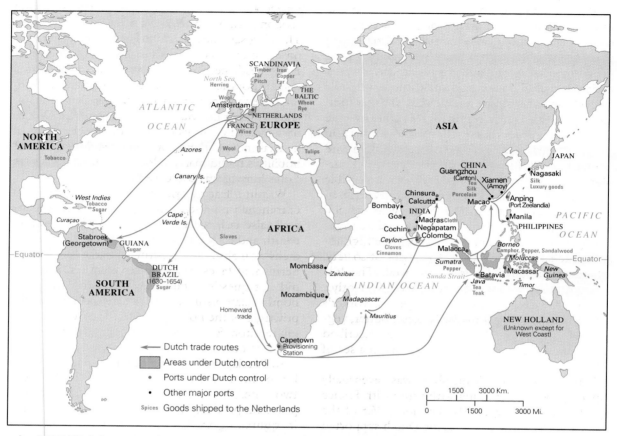

✤ **MAP 17.5 Seventeenth-Century Dutch Commerce**   Dutch wealth rested on commerce, and commerce depended on the huge Dutch merchant marine, manned by perhaps forty-eight thousand sailors. The fleet carried goods from all parts of the globe to the port of Amsterdam.

God, God, the Lord of Amstel cried, hold every
  conscience free;
And Liberty ride, on Holland's tide, with billowing
  sails to sea,
And run our Amstel out and in; let freedom gird the
  bold,
And merchant in his counting house stand elbow deep
  in gold.[11]

The fishing industry was a cornerstone of the Dutch economy. For half of the year, from June to December, fishing fleets combed the dangerous English coast and the North Sea, raking in tiny herring. Profits from herring stimulated shipbuilding, and even before 1600 the Dutch were offering the lowest shipping rates in Europe. In 1650 the Dutch merchant marine was the largest in Europe,

comprising roughly half of the European total. All the wood for these ships had to be imported: the Dutch bought whole forests from Norway. They controlled the Baltic grain trade, buying entire wheat and rye crops in Poland, east Prussia, and Swedish Pomerania. Foreign merchants coming to Amsterdam could buy anything from precision lenses for the newly invented microscope to muskets for an army of five thousand.

In 1602 a group of the regents of Holland formed the Dutch East India Company, a joint stock company. Each investor received a percentage of the profits proportional to the amount of money he had put in. Within a half-century, the Dutch East India Company had cut heavily into Portuguese trading in East Asia. The Dutch seized the Cape of Good Hope, Ceylon, and Malacca and established trading posts in each place. In the 1630s the Dutch East India Company was paying its investors about a 35 percent annual return on their investments. The Dutch West India Company, founded in 1621, traded extensively with Latin America and Africa (Map 17.5).

Trade and commerce brought the Dutch prodigious wealth. In the seventeenth century, the Dutch enjoyed the highest standard of living in Europe, perhaps in the world. Amsterdam and Rotterdam built massive granaries where the surplus of one year could be stored against possible shortages the next. Thus food prices fluctuated very little, except during the 1650s when several bad harvests reduced supplies. By the standards of Cologne, Paris, or London, salaries were high for all workers, except women. All classes of society, including unskilled laborers, ate well. The low price of bread meant that, compared with other places in Europe, a higher percentage of a worker's income could be spent on fish, cheese, butter, vegetables, even meat. A scholar recently described the Netherlands as "an island of plenty in a sea of want."[12]

Dutch economic leadership was eventually sapped by wars, beginning with those with France and England in the 1670s. The long War of the Spanish Succession, in which the Dutch supported England against France, was a costly drain on Dutch manpower and financial resources. The peace signed in 1713 to end that war marked the beginning of Dutch economic decline.

SUMMARY

War, religious strife, economic depression, and peasant revolts were all aspects of a deep crisis in seventeenth-century Europe. Rulers responded by aggressively seeking to expand their power, which they claimed was essential to meet emergencies and quell disorders. Claiming also that they ruled by divine right, monarchs sought the freedom to wage war, levy taxes, and generally make law as they saw fit. Although they were limited by technology and inadequate financial resources, monarchial governments on the European continent succeeded to a large extent, overpowering organized opposition and curbing the power of the nobility and the traditional representative institutions.

The France of Louis XIV led the way to royal absolutism. France developed a centralized bureaucracy, a professional army, a state-directed economy, all of which Louis personally supervised. The king saw himself as the representative of God on earth and accountable to no one here below. His majestic bearing and sumptuous court dazzled contemporaries. Yet behind the grand façade of unchallenged personal rule and obedient bureaucrats working his will there stood major limitations on Louis XIV's power. Most notable were the financial independence of some provinces and the nobility's traditional freedom from taxation, which Louis himself was compelled to reaffirm.

Within a framework of resurgent serfdom and entrenched nobility, Austrian and Prussian monarchs also fashioned absolutist states in the seventeenth and early eighteenth centuries. These monarchs won absolutist control over standing armies, permanent taxes, and legislative bodies. But they did not question the underlying social and economic relationships. Indeed, they enhanced the privileges of the nobility, which furnished the leading servitors for enlarged armies and growing government bureaucracies.

In Russia, social and economic trends were similar to those in Austria and Prussia. Unlike those two states, however, Russia had a long history of powerful princes. Tsar Peter the Great succeeded in tightening up Russia's traditional absolutism and modernizing it by reforming the army, the bureaucracy, and the defense industry. In Russia and throughout eastern Europe, war and the needs of the state in time of war weighed heavily in the triumph of absolutism.

Triumphant absolutism interacted spectacularly with the arts. It molded the ideals of French classicism, which glorified the state as personified by Louis XIV. Baroque art, which had grown out of the Catholic Reformation's desire to move the faithful and exalt the faith, admirably suited the secular aspirations of eastern European rulers. Thus baroque art attained magnificent heights in eastern Europe, symbolizing the ideal and harmonizing with the reality of imperious royal absolutism.

Holland and England defied the general trend toward absolute monarchy. While Holland prospered under a unique republican confederation that placed most power in the hands of the different provinces, England—fortunately shielded from continental armies and military emergencies by its navy and the English Channel—evolved into the first modern constitutional state. The bitter conflicts between Parliament and the first two Stuart rulers, James I and Charles I, tested where supreme power would rest in the state. The resulting civil war deposed the king, but it did not settle the question. A revival of absolutist tendencies under James II brought on the Glorious Revolution of 1688, and the people who made that revolution settled three basic issues. Power was divided between king and Parliament, with Parliament enjoying the greater share. Government was to be based on the rule of law. And the liberties of English people were to be made explicit in written form, in the Bill of Rights. This constitutional settlement marked an important milestone in world history, although the framers left to later generations the task of making constitutional government work.

NOTES

1. J. B. Collins, *Fiscal Limits of Absolutism: Direct Taxation in Early Seventeenth Century France* (Berkeley: University of California Press, 1988), pp. 1, 3–4, 215–222.
2. Quoted in J. H. Elliot, *Richelieu and Olivares* (Cambridge: Cambridge University Press, 1984), p. 135; and in W. F. Church, *Richelieu and Reason of State* (Princeton, N.J.: Princeton University Press, 1972), p. 507.
3. S. de Gramont, ed., *The Age of Magnificence: Memoirs of the Court of Louis XIV by the Duc de Saint Simon* (New York: Capricorn Books, 1964), pp. 141–145.
4. See W. Beik, *Absolutism and Society in Seventeenth Century France: State Power and Provincial Aristocracy in Languedoc* (Cambridge: Cambridge University Press, 1985), pp. 279–302.
5. W. F. Church, *Louis XIV in Historical Thought: From Voltaire to the Annales School* (New York: Norton, 1976), p. 92.
6. B. Bennassar, *The Spanish Character: Attitudes and Mentalities from the Sixteenth to the Nineteenth Century,* trans. B. Keen (Berkeley: University of California Press, 1979), p. 125.
7. Quoted in R. Ergang, *The Potsdam Fuhrer: Frederick William I, Father of Prussian Militarism* (New York: Octagon Books, 1972), pp. 85, 87.
8. Quoted in R. A. Dorwart, *The Administrative Reforms of Frederick William I of Prussia* (Cambridge, Mass.: Harvard University Press, 1953), p. 226.
9. Quoted in H. Rosenberg, *Bureaucracy, Aristocracy, and Autocracy: The Prussian Experience,*

1660–1815 (Boston: Beacon Press, 1966), p. 38.
10. Quoted in J. Summerson, in *The Eighteenth Century: Europe in the Age of Enlightenment,* ed. A. Cobban (New York: McGraw-Hill, 1969), p. 80.
11. Quoted in D. Maland, *Europe in the Seventeenth Century* (New York: Macmillan, 1967), pp. 198–199.
12. S. Schama, *The Embarrassment of Riches: An Interpretation of Dutch Culture in the Golden Age* (New York: Knopf, 1987), pp. 165–170.

SUGGESTED READING

Students who wish to explore the problems presented in this chapter will find a rich and exciting literature. G. Parker, *Europe in Crisis, 1598–1618* (1980), provides a sound introduction to the social, economic, and religious tensions of the period, as does R. S. Dunn, *The Age of Religious Wars, 1559–1715,* 2d ed. (1979). T. Aston, ed., *Crisis in Europe, 1560–1660* (1967), contains essays by leading historians. P. Anderson, *Lineages of the Absolutist State* (1974), is a stimulating Marxist interpretation of absolutism in western and eastern Europe.

Louis XIV and his age have attracted the attention of many scholars. J. Wolf, *Louis XIV* (1968), remains the best available biography. Two works of W. H. Lewis, *The Splendid Century* (1957) and *The Sunset of the Splendid Century* (1963), make delightful light reading. The advanced student will want to consult the excellent historiographical analysis by W. F. Church mentioned in the Notes, *Louis XIV in Historical Thought.* Perhaps the best works of the Annales school on the period are P. Goubert, *Louis XIV and Twenty Million Frenchmen* (1972), and Goubert's heavily detailed *The Ancien Régime: French Society, 1600–1750,* 2 vols. (1969–1973), which contains invaluable material on the lives and work of ordinary people. R. Bonney, *The King's Debts: Finance and Politics in France, 1589–1661* (1981), and A. Trout, *Jean-Baptiste Colbert* (1978), consider economy and financial conditions. R. Hatton, *Europe in the Age of Louis XIV* (1979), is a splendidly illustrated survey of many aspects of seventeenth-century European culture.

For Spain, M. Defourneaux, *Daily Life in Spain in the Golden Age* (1976), is extremely useful. See also C. R. Phillips, *Ciudad Real, 1500–1750: Growth, Crisis, and Readjustment in the Spanish Economy* (1979), a significant case study. V. L. Tapie, *The Age of Grandeur: Baroque Art and Architecture* (1960), emphasizes the relationship between art and politics with excellent illustrations. Art and architecture are also treated admirably in E. Hempel, *Baroque Art and Architecture in Central Europe* (1965), and G. Hamilton, *The Art and Architecture of Russia* (1954).

The best study on early Prussian history is still F. L. Carsten, *The Origin of Prussia* (1954). Rosenberg, *Bureaucracy, Aristocracy, and Autocracy,* cited in the Notes, is a masterful analysis of the social context of Prussian absolutism. Ergang, *The Potsdam Fuhrer,* also cited in the Notes, is an exciting and critical biography of ramrod Frederick William I. G. Craig, *The Politics of the Prussian Army, 1640–1945* (1964), expertly traces the great influence of the military on the Prussian state over three hundred years. R. J. Evans, *The Making of the Habsburg Empire, 1550–1770* (1979), analyzes the development of absolutism in Austria, as does A. Wandruszka, *The House of Habsburg* (1964). D. McKay and H. Scott, *The Rise of the Great Powers, 1648–1815* (1983), is a good general account. R. Vierhaus, *Germany in the Age of Absolutism* (1988), offers a thorough survey of the different German states.

On eastern European peasants and serfdom, D. Chirot, ed., *The Origins of Backwardness in Eastern Europe: Economics and Politics from the Middle Ages Until the Twentieth Century* (1989), is a wide-ranging introduction. E. Levin, *Sex and Society in the World of the Orthodox Slavs, 900–1700* (1989), carries family history to eastern Europe. J. Blum, *Lord and Peasant in Russia from the Ninth to the Nineteenth Century* (1961), provides a good look at conditions in rural Russia, and P. Avrich, *Russian Rebels, 1600–1800* (1972), treats some of the violent peasant upheavals that those conditions produced. R. Hellie, *Enserfment and Military Change in Muscovy* (1971), is outstanding. In addition to the fine survey by N. V. Riasanovsky, *A History of Russia* (1963), J. Billington, *The Icon and the Axe* (1970), is a stimulating history of early Russian intellectual and cultural developments. B. H. Sumner, *Peter the Great and the Emergence of Russia* (1962), is a good brief introduction, which may be compared with N. V. Riasanovsky, *The Image of Peter the Great in Russian History and Thought* (1985).

English political and social issues of the seventeenth century are considered by M. Ashley, *The House of Stuart: Its Rise and Fall* (1980); C. Hill, *A Century of Revolution* (1961); and K. Wrightson, *English Society, 1580–1680* (1982). Comprehensive treatments of Parliament include C. Russell's *Crisis of Parliaments, 1509–1660* (1971), and *Parliaments and English Politics, 1621–1629* (1979). L. Stone, *The Causes of the English Revolution* (1972), and B. Manning, *The English People and the English Revolution* (1976), are recommended. D. Underdown, *Revel, Riot, and Rebellion* (1985), discusses the extent of popular involvement. For English intellectual currents, see J. O. Appleby, *Economic Thought and Ideology in Seventeenth Century England* (1978). Other recommended works include P. Collinson, *The Religion of Protestants* (1982); R. Thompson, *Women in Stuart England and America* (1974); and A. Fraser, *The Weaker Vessel* (1985). For Cromwell and the Interregnum, A. Fraser, *Cromwell, the Lord Protector* (1973), is valuable. C. Hill, *The World Turned Upside Down* (1972), discusses radical thought during the period. For the Restoration and the Glorious Revolution, see R. Hutton, *Charles II: King of England, Scotland and Ireland* (1989); J. Childs, *The Army, James II, and the Glorious Revolution* (1980); and L. G. Schwoerer, *The Declaration of Rights, 1689* (1981), a fine assessment of that fundamental document. The ideas of John Locke are analyzed by J. P. Kenyon, *Revolution Principles: The Politics of Party, 1689–1720* (1977).

On Holland, K. H. D. Haley, *The Dutch Republic in the Seventeenth Century* (1972), is a splendidly illustrated appreciation of Dutch commercial and artistic achievements, and Schama, *The Embarrassment of Riches,* cited in the Notes, is a lively recent synthesis. R. Boxer, *The Dutch Seaborne Empire* (1980), is useful for Dutch overseas expansion. V. Barbour, *Capitalism in Amsterdam in the Seventeenth Century* (1950), and D. Regin, *Traders, Artists, Burghers: A Cultural History of Amsterdam in the Seventeenth Century* (1977), focus on the leading Dutch city. The leading statesmen of the period may be studied in these biographies: H. H. Rowen, *John de Witt, Grand Pensionary of Holland, 1625–1672* (1978); S. B. Baxter, *William the III and the Defense of European Liberty, 1650–1702* (1966); and J. den Tex, *Oldenbarnevelt,* 2 vols. (1973).

LISTENING TO THE
PAST

A Foreign Traveler in Russia

*Russia in the seventeenth century remained a re-
mote and mysterious land for western and even
central Europeans, who had few direct contacts
with the tsar's dominion. Knowledge of Russia
came mainly from occasional travelers who had
visited Muscovy and sometimes wrote accounts
of what they had seen.*

*The most famous of these accounts was by the
German Adam Olearius (ca 1599–1671), who
was send to Moscow by the duke of Holstein on
three diplomatic missions in the 1630s. These
missions ultimately proved unsuccessful, but they
provided Olearius with a rich store of information for his* Travels in Moscovy, *from which the
following excerpts are taken. Published in German in 1647 and soon translated into several
languages (but not Russian), Olearius's unflattering but well-informed study played a major
role in shaping European ideas about Russia.*

The government of the Russians is what political theorists call a "dominating and despotic
monarchy," where the sovereign, that is, the
tsar or the grand prince who has obtained the
crown by right of succession, rules the entire
land alone, and all the people are his subjects,
and where the nobles and princes no less than
the common folk—townspeople and peasants—are his serfs and slaves, whom he rules
and treats as a master treats his servants. . . .

If the Russians be considered in respect to
their character, customs, and way of life, they
are justly to be counted among the barbarians. . . . The vice of drunkenness is so common in this nation, among people of every
station, clergy and laity, high and low, men
and women, old and young, that when they
are seen now and then lying about in the
streets, wallowing in the mud, no attention is
paid to it, as something habitual. If a cart
driver comes upon such a drunken pig whom
he happens to know, he shoves him onto his
cart and drives him home, where he is paid his
fare. No one ever refuses an opportunity to
drink and to get drunk, at any time and in any
place, and usually it is done with vodka. . . .

The Russians being naturally tough and
born, as it were, for slavery, they must be kept
under a harsh and strict yoke and must be
driven to do their work with clubs and whips,
which they suffer without impatience, because
such is their station, and they are accustomed
to it. Young and half-grown fellows sometimes come together on certain days and train
themselves in fisticuffs, to accustom themselves to receiving blows, and, since habit is
second nature, this makes blows given as punishment easier to bear. Each and all, they are
slaves and serfs. . . .

Because of slavery and their rough and hard
life, the Russians accept war readily and are
well suited to it. On certain occasions, if need
be, they reveal themselves as courageous and
daring soldiers. . . .

Although the Russians, especially the common populace, living as slaves under a harsh
yoke, can bear and endure a great deal out of
love for their masters, yet if the pressure is beyond measure, then it can be said of them:
"Patience, often wounded, finally turned into
fury." A dangerous indignation results, turned
not so much against their sovereign as against
the lower authorities, especially if the people
have been much oppressed by them and by
their supporters and have not been protected
by the higher authorities. And once they are
aroused and enraged, it is not easy to appease
them. Then, disregarding all dangers that may
ensue, they resort to every kind of violence
and behave like madmen. . . . They own little;
most of them have no feather beds; they lie on
cushions, straw, mats, or their clothes; they
sleep on benches and, in winter, like the non-
Germans [i.e., natives] in Livonia, upon the

oven, which serves them for cooking and is flat on the top; here husband, wife, children, servants, and maids huddle together. In some houses in the countryside we saw chickens and pigs under the benches and the ovens. . . .

Russians are not used to delicate food and dainties; their daily food consists of porridge, turnips, cabbage, and cucumbers, fresh and pickled, and in Moscow mostly of big salt fish which stink badly, because of the thrifty use of salt, yet are eaten with relish. . . .

The Russians can endure extreme heat. In the bathhouse they stretch out on benches and let themselves be beaten and rubbed with bunches of birch twigs and wisps of bast (which I could not stand); and when they are hot and red all over and so exhausted that they can bear it no longer in the bathhouse, men and women rush outdoors naked and pour cold water over their bodies; in winter they even wallow in the snow and rub their skin with it as if it were soap; then they go back into the hot bathhouse. And since bathhouses are usually near rivers and brooks, they can throw themselves straight from the hot into the cold bath. . . .

Generally noble families, even the small nobility, rear their daughters in secluded chambers, keeping them hidden from outsiders; and a bridegroom is not allowed to have a look at his bride until he receives her in the bridal chamber. Therefore some happen to be deceived, being given a misshapen and sickly one instead of a fair one, and sometimes a kinswoman or even a maidservant instead of a daughter; of which there have been examples even among the highborn. No wonder therefore that often they live together like cats and dogs and that wife-beating is so common among Russians. . . .

In the Kremlin and in the city there are a great many churches, chapels, and monasteries, both within and without the city walls, over two thousand in all. This is so because every nobleman who has some fortune has a chapel built for himself, and most of them are of stone. The stone churches are round and vaulted inside. . . . They allow neither organs nor any other musical instruments in their churches, saying: Instruments that have neither souls nor life cannot praise God. . . .

In their churches there hang many bells, sometimes five or six, the largest not over two hundredweights. They ring these bells to

✳ V. Vasnetsou (1848–1926), Red Square in the late seventeenth century. *(Source: Sovfoto/Eastfoto)*

summon people to church, and also when the priest during mass raises the chalice. In Moscow, because of the multitude of churches and chapels, there are several thousand bells, which during the divine service create such a clang and din that one unaccustomed to it listens in amazement.

Questions for Analysis

1. In what ways were all social groups in Russia similar, according to Olearius?

2. How did Olearius characterize the Russians in general? What supporting evidence did he offer for his judgment?

3. Did Olearius find any positive or admirable traits in the Russian people? What were they?

4. On the basis of these representative passages, why do you think Olearius's book was so popular and influential in central and western Europe?

Source: G. Vernadsky and R. T. Fisher Jr., eds., *A Source Book for Russian History.* Copyright © 1972 by Yale University Press. Reprinted by permission.

18

Toward a New World-View in the West

Painting by Jean-Honoré Fragonard (1732–1806) of Denis Diderot, one of the editors of the *Encyclopedia,* the greatest intellectual achievement of the Enlightenment. *(Source: Louvre © Photo R.M.N.)*

Most people are not philosophers, but they nevertheless have a basic outlook on life, a more or less coherent world-view. At the risk of oversimplification, one may say that the world-view of medieval and early modern Europe was primarily religious and theological. Not only did Christian or Jewish teachings form the core of people's spiritual and philosophical beliefs, but religious teachings also permeated all the rest of human thought and activity. Political theory relied on the divine right of kings, for example, and activities ranging from marriage and divorce to eating habits and hours of business were regulated by churches and religious doctrines.

In the course of the eighteenth century, this religious and theological world-view underwent a fundamental transformation among the European upper and comfortable classes. Economically secure and increasingly well educated, these privileged groups of preindustrial Europe often came to see the world primarily in secular and scientific terms. And while few individuals abandoned religious beliefs altogether, the role of churches and religious thinking in earthly affairs and in the pursuit of knowledge was substantially reduced. Among many in the aristocracy and solid middle classes, a new critical, scientific, and very modern world-view took shape.

- Why did this momentous change occur?
- How did this new world-view affect the way people thought about society and human relations?
- What impact did this new way of thinking have on political developments and monarchial absolutism?

This chapter will focus on these questions.

THE SCIENTIFIC REVOLUTION

The foremost cause of the change in world-view was the scientific revolution. Modern science—precise knowledge of the physical world based on the union of experimental observations with sophisticated mathematics—crystallized in the seventeenth century. Whereas science had been secondary and subordinate in medieval intellectual life, it became independent and even primary for many educated people in the eighteenth century.

The emergence of modern science was a development of tremendous long-term significance. A noted historian has even said that the scientific revolution of the late sixteenth and seventeenth centuries "outshines everything since the rise of Christianity" and was "the real origin both of the modern world and the modern mentality."[1] This statement is an exaggeration, but not much of one. Of all the great civilizations, only that of the West developed modern science. With the scientific revolution Western society began to acquire its most distinctive traits. Let us examine the milestones on the fateful march toward modern science first and then search for the nonscientific influences along the route.

Scientific Thought in 1500

Since developments in astronomy and physics were at the heart of the scientific revolution, one must begin with the traditional European conception of the universe and movement within it. In the early 1500s, traditional European ideas about the universe were still based primarily on the ideas of Aristotle, the great Greek philosopher of the fourth century B.C. These ideas had been recovered gradually during the Middle Ages and then brought into harmony with Christian doctrines by medieval theologians. According to this revised Aristotelian view, a motionless earth was fixed at the center of the universe. Around it moved ten separate transparent crystal spheres. In the first eight spheres were embedded, in turn, the moon, the sun, the five known planets, and the fixed stars. Then followed two spheres that theologians added during the Middle Ages to account for slight changes in the positions of the stars over the centuries. Beyond the tenth sphere was heaven, with the throne of God and the souls of the saved. Angels kept the spheres moving in perfect circles.

Aristotle's views, suitably revised by medieval philosophers, also dominated thinking about physics and motion on earth—the sublunar world. The sublunar world was made up of four imperfect, changeable elements. The "light" elements (air and fire) naturally moved upward; the "heavy" elements (water and earth) naturally moved downward. These natural directions of motion did not always prevail, however, for elements were often mixed together and could be affected by an outside force such as a human being. Aristotle and his

Ptolemy's System   This 1543 drawing shows how the changing configurations of the planets moving around the earth form the twelve different constellations, or "signs," of the zodiac. The learned astronomer on the right is using his knowledge to predict the future for the king on the left. *(Source: Mary Evans Picture Library/Photo Researchers)*

followers also believed that a uniform force moved an object at a constant speed and that the object would stop as soon as that force was removed.

Aristotle's science as interpreted by Christian theologians fit neatly with Christian doctrines. It established a home for God and a place for Christian souls. It put human beings at the center of the universe and made them the critical link in a "great chain of being" that stretched from the throne of God to the most lowly insect on earth. Thus science was primarily a branch of theology, and it reinforced religious thought.

The Copernican Hypothesis

The desire to explain and thereby glorify God's handiwork led to the first great departure from the medieval system. This departure was the work of the Polish clergyman and astronomer Nicolaus Copernicus (1473–1543). As a young man, Copernicus studied church law and astronomy in various European universities. He saw how professional astronomers still depended for their most accurate calculations on the work of Ptolemy, the last great ancient astronomer, who had lived in Alexandria in the second century A.D. Ptolemy's achievement had been to work out complicated rules to help stargazers and astrologers to track the planets with greater precision. Many people then (and now) believed that the changing relationships between planets and stars influenced and even determined the future.

The young Copernicus was uninterested in astrology and felt that Ptolemy's cumbersome and occasionally inaccurate rules detracted from the majesty of a perfect Creator. He preferred an old Greek idea being discussed in Renaissance Italy—the idea that the sun, rather than the earth, was at the center of the universe. Working on his hypothesis from 1506 to 1530, Copernicus indeed theorized that the stars and planets, including the earth, revolve around a fixed sun. Yet Copernicus was a cautious man. Fearing the ridicule of other astronomers, he did not publish his *On the Revolutions of the Heavenly Spheres* until 1543, the year of his death.

Copernicus's theory had enormous scientific and religious implications, many of which the conservative Copernicus did not anticipate. Perhaps most significant from a religious standpoint was that by characterizing the earth as just another planet in an immense universe, Copernicus destroyed the basic idea of Aristotelian physics—the idea that the earthly world was quite different from the heavenly one. Where was the realm of perfection? Where were heaven and the throne of God?

The Copernican theory quickly brought sharp attacks from religious leaders, especially Protestants. Hearing of Copernicus's work even before it was published, Martin Luther spoke of him as the "new astrologer who wants to prove that the earth moves and goes round. . . . The fool wants to turn the whole art of astronomy upside down." Luther noted that "as the Holy Scripture tells us, so did Joshua bid the sun stand still and not the earth."[2]

John Calvin also condemned Copernicus. Catholic reaction was milder at first, but in 1616 the church officially declared the Copernican theory false.

Other events were almost as influential in creating doubts about traditional astronomical ideas. In 1572 a new star appeared and shone very brightly for almost two years. The new star, which was actually a distant exploding star, made an enormous impression on people. It seemed to contradict the idea that the heavenly spheres were unchanging and therefore perfect. In 1577 a new comet suddenly moved through the sky, cutting a straight path across the supposedly impenetrable crystal spheres. It was time, as a typical scientific writer put it, for "the radical renovation of astronomy."[3]

From Brahe to Galileo

One astronomer who agreed was Tycho Brahe (1546–1601) of Denmark. He established himself as Europe's leading astronomer with his detailed observations of the new star of 1572. For twenty years thereafter he meticulously observed the stars and planets with the naked eye. An imposing man who had lost a piece of his nose in a duel and replaced it with a special bridge of gold and silver alloy, Brahe was a noble who exploited his peasants arrogantly and approached the heavens humbly. His great contribution was his mass of data. His limited understanding of mathematics, however, prevented him from making much sense out of his data. That was left to his brilliant young assistant, the German Johannes Kepler (1571–1630).

Working and reworking Brahe's mountain of observations in a staggering sustained effort, Kepler formulated three famous laws of planetary motion. First, building on Copernican theory, he demonstrated in 1609 that the orbits of the planets around the sun are elliptical rather than circular. Second, he demonstrated that the planets do not move at a uniform speed in their orbits. Third, in 1619 he showed that the time a planet takes to make its complete orbit is precisely related to its distance from the sun. Kepler's contribution was monumental. Whereas Copernicus had speculated, Kepler proved mathematically the precise relations of a sun-centered (solar) system. His work demolished the old system of Aristotle and Ptolemy, and in his third law he came close to formulating the idea of universal gravitation.

While Kepler was unraveling planetary motion, a young Florentine named Galileo Galilei (1564–1642) was challenging all the old ideas about motion. Like so many early scientists, Galileo was a poor nobleman first marked for a religious career. However, he soon became fascinated by mathematics. A brilliant student, Galileo became a professor of mathematics in 1589 at age twenty-five. He proceeded to examine motion and mechanics in a new way. Indeed, his great achievement was the elaboration and consolidation of the modern experimental method: rather than speculate about what might or should happen, Galileo conducted controlled experiments to find out what actually *did* happen.

In his famous acceleration experiment, by rolling brass balls down an inclined plane, he showed that a uniform force—in this case, gravity—produces a uniform acceleration. With this and other experiments, Galileo went on to formulate the law of inertia: rather than rest being the natural state of objects, an object continues in motion forever unless stopped by some external force. Aristotelian physics was in a shambles.

On hearing details about the invention of the telescope in Holland, Galileo made one for himself and trained it on the heavens. He quickly discovered the first four moons of Jupiter, providing new evidence for the Copernican theory, in which Galileo already believed. Galileo then pointed his telescope at the moon. He wrote in 1610 in *Siderus Nuncius*:

I feel sure that the moon is not perfectly smooth, free from inequalities, and exactly spherical, as a large school of philosophers considers with regard to the moon and the other heavenly bodies. On the contrary, it is full of inequalities, uneven, full of hollows and protuberances, just like the surface of the earth itself, which is varied. . . . The next object which I have observed is the essence or substance of the Milky Way. By the aid of a telescope anyone may behold this in a manner which so distinctly appeals to the senses that all the disputes which have tormented philosophers through so many ages are exploded by the irrefutable evidence of our eyes, and we are freed from wordy disputes upon the subject. For the galaxy is nothing else but a mass of innumerable stars planted together in clusters.[4]

Reading these famous lines, one feels a crucial corner in Western civilization being turned. The traditional religious and theological world-view, which rested on identifying and accepting the proper established authority, was beginning to give way in certain fields to a critical, scientific method. This new method of learning and investigating was the greatest accomplishment of the entire scientific revolution, for it proved capable of great extension. A historian investigating documents of the past, for example, is not so different from a Galileo studying stars and rolling balls.

Galileo's work eventually aroused the ire of some theologians. After the publication in Italian of his widely read *Dialogue on the Two Chief Systems of the World* in 1632, which openly lampooned the traditional views of Aristotle and Ptolemy and defended those of Copernicus, Galileo was tried for heresy by the papal Inquisition. Imprisoned and threatened with torture, the aging Galileo recanted, "renouncing and cursing" his Copernican errors. Of minor importance in the development of science, Galileo's trial later became for some writers the perfect symbol of the inherent conflict between religious belief and scientific knowledge.

Newton's Synthesis

The accomplishments of Kepler, Galileo, and other scientists had taken effect by about 1640. The old astronomy and physics were in ruins, and several fundamental breakthroughs had been made. The fusion of the new findings in a new synthesis, a single explanatory system that would comprehend motion both on earth and in the skies, was the work of Isaac Newton (1642–1727).

Newton was born into lower English gentry and attended Cambridge University. Fascinated by alchemy, he sought the elixir of life and a way to change base metals into gold and silver. Not without reason did the twentieth-century economist John Maynard Keynes call him the "last of the magicians." Newton was also intensely religious. He

Galileo's Paintings of the Moon When Galileo published the results of his telescopic observations of the moon, he added these paintings to illustrate the marvels he had seen with his telescopes. *(Source: Biblioteca Nazionale Centrale, Florence/Scala/Art Resource, NY)*

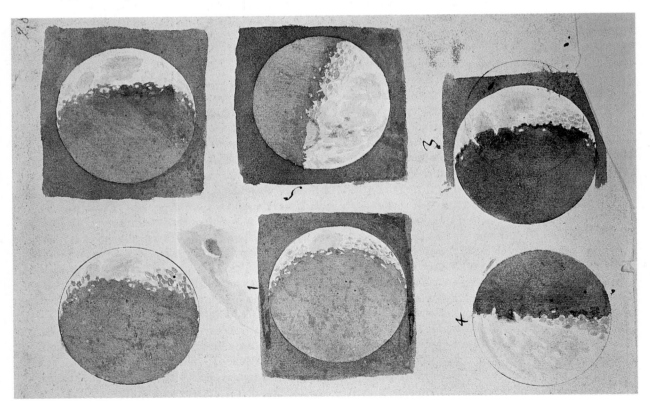

had a highly suspicious nature, lacked interest in women and sex, and in 1693 suffered a nervous breakdown from which he later recovered. He was far from being the perfect rationalist so endlessly eulogized by writers in the eighteenth and nineteenth centuries.

Of his intellectual genius and incredible powers of concentration there can be no doubt, however. Arriving at some of his most basic ideas about physics in 1666 at age twenty-four, but unable to prove these theories mathematically, he attained a professorship and studied optics for many years. In 1684 Newton returned to physics for eighteen extraordinarily intensive months. Seldom leaving his room, he neglected even the meals sent up, his mind fastened like a vise on the laws of the universe. He opened the third book of his immortal *Principia,* published in Latin in 1687, with these lines: "In the preceding books I have laid down the principles . . . [that] are the laws of certain motions, and powers or forces. . . . It remains that from the same principles I now demonstrate the frame of the System of the World."

Newton made good his grandiose claim. He integrated the astronomy of Copernicus, as corrected by Kepler's laws, with the physics of Galileo and his predecessors. Newton did this by means of a set of mathematical laws that explain motion and mechanics. These laws of dynamics are complex, and it took scientists and engineers two hundred years to work out all their implications. Nevertheless, the key feature of the Newtonian synthesis was the law of universal gravitation. According to this law, every body in the universe attracts every other body in the universe in a precise mathematical relationship, based on mass and distance. The whole universe—from Kepler's elliptical orbits to Galileo's rolling balls—was unified in one majestic system.

Causes of the Scientific Revolution

With a charming combination of modesty and self-congratulation, Newton once wrote, "If I have seen further [than others], it is by standing on the shoulders of Giants."[5] Surely the path from Copernicus to Newton confirms the "internal" view of the scientific revolution as the product of towering individual genius. Yet there were certainly broader causes as well.

First, the long-term contribution of medieval intellectual life and medieval universities to the scien-

Isaac Newton   This portrait suggests the depth and complexity of the great genius. Is the powerful mind behind those piercing eyes thinking of science or of religion, or perhaps of both? *(Source: Scala/Art Resource, NY)*

tific revolution was much more considerable than historians unsympathetic to the Middle Ages once believed. By the thirteenth century, permanent universities with professors and large student bodies had been established in western Europe to train the lawyers, doctors, and church leaders that society required. By 1300 philosophy had taken its place alongside law, medicine, and theology. Medieval philosophers developed a limited but real independence from theologians and a sense of free inquiry. They nobly pursued a body of knowledge and tried to arrange it meaningfully by means of abstract theories.

Within this framework, science was able to emerge as a minor but distinct branch of philosophy. In the fourteenth and fifteenth centuries, first in Italy and then elsewhere in Europe, leading universities established new professorships of mathematics, astronomy, and physics (natural philosophy) within their faculties of philosophy. Although the prestige of the new fields was low among both professors and students, rational, critical thinking was applied to scientific problems by a permanent community of scholars. And an outlet existed for the talents of a Galileo or a Newton: all the great pathfinders either studied or taught at universities.

Second, the Renaissance also stimulated scientific progress. The recovery of the finest works of Greek mathematics—a byproduct of Renaissance humanism's ceaseless search for the knowledge of antiquity—greatly improved European mathematics well into the early seventeenth century. Finally, in the Renaissance pattern of patronage, especially in Italy, various rulers and wealthy business people supported scientific investigations, as the Medicis of Florence, for instance, did those of Galileo.

The navigational problems of long sea voyages in the age of overseas expansion were a third factor in the scientific revolution. As early as 1484, the king of Portugal appointed a commission of mathematicians to perfect tables to help seamen find their latitude. This resulted in the first European navigation manual.

The problem of fixing longitude was much more difficult. In England the government and the great capitalistic trading companies turned to science and scientific education in an attempt to solve this pressing practical problem. At Gresham College in London, the main center of scientific activity in England in the first half of the seventeenth century, the professor of astronomy was directed to teach courses on the science of navigation. Scientists at Gresham College enjoyed close ties with top officials of the Royal Navy and with leading merchants and shipbuilders. The close tie between practical men and scientists also led to the establishment in 1662 of the Royal Society of London, which published scientific papers and sponsored scientific meetings.

Navigational problems were also critical in the development of many new scientific instruments, such as the telescope, barometer, thermometer, pendulum clock, microscope, and air pump. Better instruments, which permitted more accurate observations, were part of a fourth factor in the scientific revolution, the development of better ways of obtaining knowledge about the world. Two important thinkers, Francis Bacon (1561–1626) and René Descartes (1596–1650), represented key aspects of this improvement in scientific methodology.

The English politician and writer Francis Bacon was the greatest early propagandist for the new experimental method, as Galileo was its greatest early practitioner. Rejecting the Aristotelian and medieval method of using speculative reasoning to build general theories, Bacon argued that new knowledge had to be pursued through empirical, experimental research. A researcher who wants to learn more about leaves or rocks should not speculate about the subject but rather collect a multitude of specimens and then compare and analyze them. Thus freed from sterile medieval speculation, the facts will speak for themselves, and important general principles will then emerge. Knowledge will increase. Bacon's contribution was to formalize the empirical method, which had already been used by Brahe and Galileo, into the general theory of inductive reasoning known as *empiricism.*

Bacon claimed that the empirical method would result not only in more knowledge but also in highly practical, useful knowledge. According to Bacon, scientific discoveries would bring about much greater control over the physical environment and make people rich and nations powerful. Thus Bacon helped provide a radically new and effective justification for private and public support of scientific inquiry.

The French philosopher René Descartes was a true genius who made his first great discovery in mathematics. As a twenty-three-year-old soldier serving in the Thirty Years' War, he experienced on a single night in 1619 a life-changing intellectual vision. Descartes saw that there was a perfect correspondence between geometry and algebra and that geometrical, spatial figures could be expressed as algebraic equations and vice versa. A major step forward in the history of mathematics, Descartes' discovery of analytic geometry provided scientists with an important new tool. But his greatest achievement was to develop his initial vision into a whole philosophy of knowledge and science.

Like Bacon, Descartes scorned traditional science and had great faith in the powers of the human mind. Yet Descartes was much more systematic and mathematical than Bacon. He decided it was necessary to doubt everything that could reasonably be doubted and then, as in geometry, to use deductive reasoning from self-evident principles to ascertain scientific laws. Descartes' reasoning ultimately reduced all substances to "matter" and "mind"—that is, to the physical and the spiri-

✳ **Descartes in Sweden**   Queen Christina of Sweden (r. 1632–1654) encouraged art
and science and invited many foreign artists and scholars to visit her court. She
speaks here with French mathematician and philosopher René Descartes in 1649.
The strong-minded daughter of Protestant hero Gustavus Adolphus, Christina rejected marriage, abdicated in 1654, converted to Catholicism, and died in Rome.
(Source: Versailles/Photographie Bulloz)

tual. His view of the world as consisting of two
fundamental entities is known as *Cartesian dualism.*
Descartes was a profoundly original and extremely
influential thinker.

Bacon's inductive experimentalism and Descartes' deductive, mathematical rationalism are
combined in the modern scientific method, which
began to crystallize in the late seventeenth century.
Neither man's extreme approach was sufficient by
itself. Thus the modern scientific method has
joined precise observations and experimentalism
with the search for general laws that may be expressed in rigorously logical, mathematical language.

Finally, there is the question of the role of religion in the development of science. Just as some
historians have argued that Protestantism led to
the rise of capitalism, others have concluded that
Protestantism, by supposedly making scientific inquiry a question of individual conscience and not
of religious doctrine, was a fundamental factor in
the rise of modern science. However, all religious
authorities in the West—Catholic, Protestant, and
Jewish—opposed the Copernican system to a
greater or lesser extent until about 1630, by which
time the scientific revolution was definitely in
progress. The Catholic church was initially less
hostile than Protestant and Jewish religious leaders. This early Catholic toleration and the scientific
interests of Renaissance Italy helped account for
the crucial role that Italian scientists played in scientific progress right up to the trial of Galileo
in 1633. Thereafter, the Counter-Reformation
church became more hostile to science, a change
that helped account for the decline of science in
Italy (but not in Catholic France) after 1640. At
the same time, some Protestant countries became
quite proscience, especially if the country lacked a
strong religious authority capable of imposing religious orthodoxy on scientific questions, as did
Protestant England after 1630. English religious
conflicts became so intense that the authorities
could not impose religious unity on anything, including science. Neutral and useful, science became an accepted part of life and developed rapidly
in England after about 1640.

Some Consequences of the Scientific Revolution

The rise of modern science had many consequences, some of which are still unfolding. First, it went hand in hand with the rise of a new and expanding social group—the international scientific community. Members of this community were linked together by common interests and shared values as well as by journals and the learned scientific societies founded in many countries in the later seventeenth and the eighteenth centuries. Expansion of knowledge was the primary goal of this community, and scientists' material and psychological rewards depended on their success in this endeavor. Thus science became quite competitive, and even more scientific advance was inevitable.

Second, the revolutionary modern scientific method, in addition to being both theoretical and experimental, was highly critical, and it differed profoundly from the old way of getting knowledge about nature. It refused to base its conclusions on tradition and established sources, on ancient authorities and sacred texts.

The scientific revolution had few consequences for economic life and the living standards of the masses until the late eighteenth century at the very earliest. True, improvements in the techniques of navigation facilitated overseas trade and helped enrich leading merchants. But science had relatively few practical economic applications, and the hopes of the early Baconians were frustrated. The close link between theoretical, or pure, science and applied technology, which we take for granted today, simply did not exist before the nineteenth century. Thus the scientific revolution of the seventeenth century was first and foremost an intellectual revolution. For more than a hundred years its greatest impact was on how people thought and believed.

❖ THE ENLIGHTENMENT

The scientific revolution was the single most important factor in the creation of the new world-view of the eighteenth-century Enlightenment. This world-view, which has played a large role in shaping the modern mind, grew out of a rich mix of ideas. These ideas were diverse and often conflicting, for the talented (and not-so-talented) writers who espoused them competed vigorously for the attention of a growing public of well-educated but fickle readers, who remained a small minority of the population. Despite this diversity, three central concepts stand at the core of Enlightenment thinking.

The most important and original idea of the Enlightenment was that the methods of natural science could and should be used to examine and understand all aspects of life. This was what intellectuals meant by *reason,* a favorite word of Enlightenment thinkers. Nothing was to be accepted on faith. Everything was to be submitted to the rational, critical, scientific way of thinking. This approach often brought the Enlightenment into a head-on conflict with established churches, which rested their beliefs on the special authority of the Bible and Christian theology. A second important Enlightenment concept was that the scientific method was capable of discovering the laws of human society as well as those of nature. Thus was social science born. Its birth led to the third key idea, that of progress. Armed with the proper method of discovering the laws of human existence, Enlightenment thinkers believed it was at least possible for human beings to create better societies and better people. Their belief was strengthened by some modest improvements in economic and social life during the eighteenth century.

The Enlightenment was therefore profoundly secular. It revived and expanded the Renaissance concentration on worldly explanations. In the course of the eighteenth century, the Enlightenment had a profound impact on the thought and culture of the urban middle classes and the aristocracy. It did not, however, have much appeal for the urban poor and the peasants, who were preoccupied with the struggle for survival and who often resented the Enlightenment attack on traditional popular beliefs (see Chapter 19).

The Emergence of the Enlightenment

Loosely united by certain key ideas, the European Enlightenment was a broad intellectual and cultural movement that gained strength gradually and did not reach its maturity until about 1750. Yet it was the generation that came of age between the publication of Newton's *Principia* in 1687 and the death of Louis XIV in 1715 that tied the crucial knot between the scientific revolution and a new outlook on life. Talented writers of that generation popularized hard-to-understand scientific achievements for the educated elite.

The most famous and influential popularizer was a versatile French man of letters, Bernard de Fontenelle (1657–1757). He set out to make science witty and entertaining for a broad nonscientific audience—as easy to read as a novel. This was a tall order, but Fontenelle largely succeeded. His most famous work, *Conversations on the Plurality of Worlds* (1686), begins with two elegant figures walking in the gathering shadows of a large park. One is a woman, a sophisticated aristocrat, and the other is her friend, perhaps even her lover. They gaze at the stars, and their talk turns to a passionate discussion of . . . astronomy! He confides that "each star may well be a different world," then gently stresses how error is giving way to truth. At one point he explains:

There came on the scene . . . one Copernicus, who made short work of all those various circles, all those solid skies, which the ancients had pictured to themselves. . . . Fired with the noble zeal of a true astronomer, he took the earth and spun it very far away from the center of the universe, where it had been installed, and in that center he put the sun, which had a far better title to the honor.[6]

Rather than despair at this dismissal of traditional understanding, Fontenelle's lady rejoices in the knowledge that the human mind is capable of making great progress.

Fontenelle and other writers of his generation were instrumental in bringing science into conflict with religion. Many seventeenth-century scientists, both Catholic and Protestant, believed that their work exalted God. They did not draw antireligious implications from their scientific findings. Fontenelle, in contrast, was skeptical about absolute truth and cynical about the claims of organized religion. In *Eulogies of Scientists,* Fontenelle exploited with endless variations the basic theme of rational, progressive scientists versus prejudiced, reactionary priests.

The progressive and antireligious implications that writers such as Fontenelle drew from the scientific revolution reflected a crisis in European thought at the end of the seventeenth century. This crisis had its roots in several intellectual uncertainties and dissatisfactions, of which the demolition of Aristotelian-medieval science was only one.

A second uncertainty involved the whole question of religious truth. The destructive wars of religion had been fought, in part, because religious freedom was an intolerable idea in Europe in the early seventeenth century. Both Catholics and Protestants had believed that religious truth was absolute and therefore worth fighting and dying for. Most Catholics and Protestants also believed that a strong state required unity in religious faith. Yet the disastrous results of the many attempts to impose such religious unity led some people to ask if it was really necessary. Others skeptically asked if religious truth could ever be known with absolute certainty and concluded that it could not.

The most famous of these skeptics was Pierre Bayle (1647–1706), a French Huguenot who despised Louis XIV and found refuge in the Netherlands. Critically examining the religious beliefs and

Popularizing Science   The frontispiece illustration of Fontenelle's *Conversations on the Plurality of Worlds* invites the reader to share the pleasures of astronomy with an elegant lady and an entertaining teacher. The drawing shows the planets revolving around the sun. *(Source: University of Illinois Library, Champaign)*

persecutions of the past, Bayle demonstrated that human beliefs had been extremely varied and very often mistaken. He concluded that nothing can ever be known beyond all doubt and that in religion, as in philosophy, humanity's best hope was open-minded toleration. Bayle's skeptical views were very influential. Many eighteenth-century writers mined his inexhaustible vein of critical skepticism for ammunition in their attacks on superstition and theology.

The rapidly growing travel literature on non-European lands and cultures was a third cause of uncertainty. In the wake of the great discoveries, Europeans were learning that the peoples of China, India, Africa, and the Americas all had their own very different beliefs and customs. Europeans shaved their faces and let their hair grow. Turks shaved their heads and let their beards grow. In Europe a man bowed before a woman to show respect. In Siam a man turned his back on a woman when he met her because it was disrespectful to look directly at her. Countless similar examples discussed in the travel accounts helped change the perspective of educated Europeans. They began to look at truth and morality in relative, rather than absolute, terms. If anything was possible, who could say what was right or wrong?

A fourth cause and manifestation of European intellectual turmoil was John Locke's epoch-making *Essay Concerning Human Understanding.* Published in 1690—the same year Locke published his *Second Treatise of Civil Government* (see page 586) —Locke's essay brilliantly set forth a new theory about how human beings learn and form their ideas. In doing so, he rejected the prevailing view of Descartes, who had held that all people are born with certain basic ideas and ways of thinking. Locke insisted that all ideas are derived from experience. The human mind at birth is like a blank tablet (*tabula rasa*) on which the environment writes the individual's understanding and beliefs. Human development is therefore determined by education and social institutions, for good or for evil. Locke's *Essay* was, along with Newton's *Principia,* one of the dominant intellectual inspirations of the Enlightenment.

The Philosophes and the Public

By the time Louis XIV died in 1715, many of the ideas that would soon coalesce into the new world-view had been assembled. Yet Christian Europe was still strongly attached to its traditional beliefs, as witnessed by the powerful revival of religious orthodoxy in the first half of the eighteenth century (see Chapter 19). By the outbreak of the American Revolution in 1775, however, a large portion of western Europe's educated elite had embraced many of the new ideas. This acceptance was the work of one of history's most influential groups of intellectuals, the philosophes. It was the philosophes who proudly and effectively proclaimed that they, at long last, were bringing the light of knowledge to their ignorant fellow creatures in a great age of enlightenment.

Philosophe is the French word for "philosopher," and it was in France that the Enlightenment reached its highest development. The French philosophes were indeed philosophers, asking fundamental philosophical questions about the meaning of life, God, human nature, good and evil, and cause and effect. But in the tradition of Bayle and Fontenelle, they were not content with abstract arguments or ivory-tower speculations. They were determined to reach and influence all the economic and social elites, whom they perceived as the educated or enlightened public, or simply the "public."

As a wealth of recent scholarship has shown, this public was quite different from the great majority of the population, which was known as the common people, or simply the "people." French philosophe Jean le Rond d'Alembert (1717–1783) characteristically made a sharp distinction between "the truly enlightened public" and "the blind and noisy multitude."[7] The philosophes believed that the great majority of the common people was doomed to superstition and confusion because it lacked the money and leisure to look beyond its bitter struggle with grinding poverty (see Chapter 19).

The great philosophes and their imitators were not free to write as they wished, for it was illegal in France to criticize openly either church or state. Their most radical works had to circulate in manuscript form. Knowing that direct attacks would probably be banned or burned, the philosophes wrote novels and plays, histories and philosophies, dictionaries and encyclopedias, all filled with satire and double meanings to spread their message to the public.

One of the greatest philosophes, the baron de Montesquieu (1689–1755), brilliantly pioneered this approach in *The Persian Letters,* an extremely influential social satire published in 1721. Montesquieu's work consisted of amusing letters supposedly written by Persian travelers, who see European customs in unique ways and thereby cleverly criticize existing practices and beliefs. Having gained fame by using wit as a weapon against cruelty and superstition, Montesquieu settled down on his family estate to study history and politics. He was also inspired by the example of the physical sciences, and he set out to apply the critical method to the problem of government in *The Spirit of Laws* (1748). The result was a complex comparative study of republics, monarchies, and despotisms.

Dismayed by the triumph of royal absolutism under Louis XIV, Montesquieu focused on the conditions that would promote liberty and prevent tyranny. He argued that despotism could be avoided if political power was divided and shared by a variety of classes and legal orders holding unequal rights and privileges. A strong, independent upper class was especially important, according to Montesquieu, because in order to prevent the abuse of power, "it is necessary that by the arrangement of things, power checks power." Admiring greatly the English balance of power among the king, the houses of Parliament, and the independent courts, Montesquieu believed that in France the thirteen high courts—the *parlements*—were front-line defenders of liberty against royal despotism. Apprehensive about the uneducated poor, Montesquieu was clearly no democrat, but his theory of separation of powers had a great impact on France's wealthy, well-educated elite. The constitutions of the young United States in 1789 and of France in 1791 were based in large part on this theory.

The most famous and in many ways most representative philosophe was François Marie Arouet, who was known by the pen name Voltaire (1694–1778). In his long career, this son of a comfortable middle-class family wrote more than seventy witty volumes, hobnobbed with kings and queens, and died a millionaire because of shrewd business speculations. His early career, however, was turbulent. In 1717 Voltaire was imprisoned for eleven months in the Bastille in Paris for insulting the regent of France. In 1726 a barb from his sharp tongue led a great French nobleman to have him beaten and arrested. This experience made a deep impression on Voltaire. All his life he struggled against legal injustice and unequal treatment be-

Madame du Châtelet Fascinated by the new world system of Isaac Newton, this aristocratic woman helped to spread Newton's ideas in France by translating his *Principia* into French and by influencing Voltaire, her companion for fifteen years until her death. (*Source: Private Collection/Photographie Bulloz*)

fore the law. Released from prison after promising to leave the country, Voltaire lived in England for three years and came to share Montesquieu's enthusiasm for English institutions.

Returning to France and soon threatened again with prison in Paris, Voltaire had the great fortune of meeting Gabrielle-Emilie Le Tonnelier de Breteuil, marquise du Châtelet (1706–1749), an intellectually gifted woman from the high aristocracy with a passion for science. Inviting Voltaire to live in her country house at Cirey in Lorraine and becoming his long-time companion (under the eyes of her tolerant husband), Madame du Châtelet studied physics and mathematics and published scientific articles and translations.

Perhaps the finest representative of a small number of elite French women and their scientific accomplishments during the Enlightenment, Madame du Châtelet suffered nonetheless because of her gender. Excluded on principle from the Royal

Academy of Sciences and from stimulating interchange with other scientists because she was a woman, she depended on private tutors for instruction and became uncertain of her ability to make important scientific discoveries. Madame du Châtelet therefore concentrated on spreading the ideas of others, and her translation with an accompanying commentary of Newton's *Principia* into French for the first (and only) time was her greatest work. But she had no doubt that women's limited scientific contributions in the past were due to limited and unequal education. Imagining a scientific experiment that she would make if she were a ruler, Madame du Châtelet wrote, "I would reform an abuse which cuts off, so to speak, half the human race. I would make women participate in all the rights of humankind, and above all in those of the intellect."[8]

While living at Cirey, Voltaire wrote various works praising England and popularizing English scientific progress. Newton, he wrote, was history's greatest man, for he had used his genius for the benefit of humanity. In the true style of the Enlightenment, Voltaire mixed the glorification of science and reason with an appeal for better individuals and institutions. Yet like almost all of the philosophes, Voltaire was a reformer, not a revolutionary, in social and political matters. He was eventually appointed royal historian in 1743, and his *Age of Louis XIV* portrayed Louis as the dignified leader of his age. Voltaire also began a long correspondence with Frederick the Great and, after the death of his beloved Emilie, accepted Frederick's invitation to come brighten up the Prussian court in Berlin. The two men later quarreled, but Voltaire always admired Frederick as a free thinker and an enlightened monarch.

Unlike Montesquieu, Voltaire pessimistically concluded that the best one could hope for in the way of government was a good monarch since human beings "are very rarely worthy to govern themselves." Nor did he believe in social and economic equality in human affairs. The idea of making servants equal to their masters was "absurd and impossible." The only realizable equality, Voltaire thought, was that "by which the citizen only depends on the laws which protect the freedom of the feeble against the ambitions of the strong."[9]

Voltaire's philosophical and religious positions were much more radical. In the tradition of Bayle, Voltaire's voluminous writings challenged, often indirectly, the Catholic church and Christian theology at almost every point. Though he was considered by many devout Christians to be a shallow blasphemer, Voltaire's religious views were influential and quite typical of the mature Enlightenment. Voltaire clearly believed in a God, but his was a distant, deistic God, a great Clockmaker who built an orderly universe and then stepped aside and let it run. Above all, Voltaire and most of the philosophes hated all forms of religious intolerance, which, they believed, often led to fanaticism and savage, inhuman action. Simple piety and human kindness—as embodied in Christ's great commandments to "love God and your neighbor as yourself"—were religion enough, even Christianity enough, as may be seen in Voltaire's famous essay on religion (see Listening to the Past).

The philosophes' greatest and most representative intellectual achievement was, quite fittingly, a group effort—the seventeen-volume *Encyclopedia: The Rational Dictionary of the Sciences, the Arts, and the Crafts,* edited by Denis Diderot (1713–1784) and Jean le Rond d'Alembert. Diderot and d'Alembert set out to teach people how to think critically and objectively about all matters. As Diderot said, he wanted the *Encyclopedia* to "change the general way of thinking."[10]

The editors of the *Encyclopedia* had to conquer innumerable obstacles. After the appearance in 1751 of the first volume, which dealt with such controversial subjects as atheism, the soul, and blind people, the timid publisher watered down some of the articles in the last ten volumes without the editors' consent. Yet Diderot's unwavering belief in the importance of his mission held the encyclopedists together for fifteen years, and the enormous work was completed in 1765. Hundreds of thousands of articles by leading scientists, famous writers, skilled workers, and progressive priests treated every aspect of life and knowledge.

Not every article was daring or original, but the overall effect was little short of revolutionary. Science and the industrial arts were exalted, religion and immortality questioned. Intolerance, legal injustice, and out-of-date social institutions were openly criticized. The encyclopedists were convinced that greater knowledge would result in greater human happiness, for knowledge was useful and made possible economic, social, and political progress. The *Encyclopedia,* widely read and extremely influential throughout western Europe, summed up the new world-view of the Enlightenment.

Canal with Locks Articles on science and the industrial arts in the *Encyclopedia* carried lavish explanatory illustrations. This engraving from the section on water and its uses shows advances in canal building and reflects the encyclopedists' faith in technical progress. *(Source: University of Illinois Library, Champaign)*

The Later Enlightenment

After about 1770, the harmonious unity of the philosophes and their thought began to break down. As the new world-view became increasingly accepted by the educated public, some thinkers sought originality by exaggerating certain Enlightenment ideas to the exclusion of others. These latter-day philosophes often built rigid, dogmatic systems.

In his *System of Nature* (1770) and other works, the wealthy German-born but French-educated Baron Paul d'Holbach (1723–1789) argued that human beings were machines completely determined by outside forces. Free will, God, and immortality of the soul, he claimed, were foolish myths. D'Holbach's aggressive atheism and determinism dealt the unity of the Enlightenment movement a severe blow. Deists such as Voltaire, who believed in God but not in established churches, were repelled by the inflexible atheism they found in the *System of Nature*. They saw in it the same dogmatic intolerance they had been fighting all their lives.

Nevertheless, D'Holbach was a generous patron and witty host of writers and intellectuals. At his twice-weekly dinner parties, an inner circle of regulars exchanged ideas with aspiring philosophes and distinguished visitors. One whose carefully argued skepticism had a powerful long-term influence was the Scottish philosopher David Hume (1711–1776).

Building on Locke's teachings on learning, Hume argued that the human mind is really nothing but a bundle of impressions. These impressions originate only in sense experiences and our habits of joining these experiences together. Reason, therefore, cannot tell us anything about questions that cannot be verified by sense experience (in the form of controlled experiments or mathematics), such as the origin of the universe or the existence of God. Paradoxically, Hume's rationalistic inquiry ended up undermining the Enlightenment's faith in the power of reason.

Another French aristocrat, Marie-Jean Caritat, the marquis de Condorcet (1743–1794), transformed the Enlightenment belief in gradual, hard-won progress into fanciful utopianism. In his *Progress of the Human Mind,* written in 1793 during the French Revolution, Condorcet hypothesized and tracked nine stages of human progress that had already occurred, and he predicted that the tenth would bring perfection. Ironically, Condorcet wrote this work while fleeing for his life. Caught and condemned by revolutionary extremists, he preferred death by his own hand to the blade of the guillotine.

Other thinkers and writers after about 1770 began to attack the Enlightenment's faith in reason, progress, and moderation. The most famous of these was the Swiss Jean-Jacques Rousseau (1712–1778), a brilliant and difficult thinker, an appealing but neurotic individual. Born into a poor family of watchmakers in Geneva, Rousseau went to Paris and was greatly influenced by Diderot and Voltaire. Always extraordinarily sensitive and suspicious, Rousseau came to believe that his philosophe friends and the women of the Parisian salons were plotting against him. In the mid-1750s, he broke with them personally and intellectually, living thereafter as a lonely outsider with his uneducated common-law wife and going in his own highly original direction.

Like other Enlightenment thinkers, Rousseau was passionately committed to individual freedom. Unlike them, however, he attacked rationalism and civilization as destroying, rather than liberating, the individual. Warm, spontaneous feeling had to complement and correct cold intellect, he believed. Moreover, the basic goodness of the individual and the unspoiled child had to be protected from the cruel refinements of civilization. These ideas greatly influenced the early romantic movement (see Chapter 25), which rebelled against the culture of the Enlightenment in the late eighteenth century. They also had a powerful impact on the development of child psychology and modern education (see Chapter 19, Listening to the Past).

Rousseau's contribution to political theory in *The Social Contract* (1762) was equally significant. His contribution was based on two fundamental concepts: the general will and popular sovereignty.

According to Rousseau, the general will is sacred and absolute, reflecting the common interests of all the people, who have displaced the monarch as the holder of sovereign power. The general will is not necessarily the will of the majority, however. At times, the general will may be the authentic, long-term needs of the people as correctly interpreted by a farseeing minority. Little noticed before the French Revolution, Rousseau's concept of the general will appealed greatly to democrats and nationalists after 1789. The concept has also been used since 1789 by many dictators claiming that they, rather than some momentary majority of the voters, represent the general will and thus the true interests of democracy and the sovereign masses.

Urban Culture and Public Opinion

The writings and press campaigns of the philosophes were part of a profound cultural transformation. The object of impressive ongoing research and scholarly debate in recent years, this transformation had several interrelated aspects.

Of great importance, the European market for books grew dramatically in the eighteenth century. In Germany the number of new titles appearing annually grew substantially and at an accelerating rate, from roughly six hundred new titles in 1700 to about eleven hundred in 1764 and about twenty-six hundred in 1780. Well-studied France, which was indicative of general European trends, witnessed an explosive growth in book consumption. The solid and upper middle classes, the clergy, and the aristocracy accounted for most of the change. The number of books in the hands of these privileged groups increased eight- to tenfold between the 1690s and the 1780s. Moreover, the number of religious and devotional books published legally in Paris declined precipitously. History and law held constant, while the proportion of legally published books treating the arts and sciences surged.

In addition, France's unpredictable but pervasive censorship caused many books to be printed abroad and then smuggled back into the country for "under-the-cloak" sale. Experts believe that perhaps the majority of French books produced between 1750 and 1789 came from publishing companies located outside France. These publishers also smuggled forbidden books in French and other languages into the absolutist states of central, southern, and eastern Europe. The recently discovered catalogues of some of these foreign publishers reveal a massive presence of the famous French philosophes, reaffirming the philosophes' central role in the spread of critical secular attitudes.

The illegal book trade in France also featured an astonishing growth of scandalmongering denunciations of high political figures and frankly pornographic works. These literary forms frequently came together in scathing pornographic accounts of the moral and sexual depravity of the French court, allegedly mired in luxury, perversion, and adultery. A favorite theme was the way that some beautiful but immoral aristocratic women used their sexual charms to gain power over weak rulers and high officials, thereby corrupting the process of government. Spurred by repeated royal directives, the French police did its best to stamp out this underground literature, but new slanders kept cropping up, like the wild tabloid fantasies at checkout counters in today's supermarkets.

Reading more books on many more subjects, the educated public in France and throughout Europe increasingly approached reading in a new way. The result was what some German scholars have called a "reading revolution." The old style of reading in Europe had been centered on sacred texts read slowly aloud with the audience reverently savoring each word. Now reading involved many texts, which were constantly changing and commanded no special respect. Reading became individual, silent, and rapid. The well-educated classes were reading insatiably, skeptically, and carelessly. Subtle but profound, the reading revolution was closely linked to the rise of a critical world-view.

As the reading public developed, it joined forces with the philosophes to call for the autonomy of the printed word. Outside Prussia, the Netherlands, and Great Britain, however, censorship was the rule. And the philosophes and the public resorted to discussion and social interchange in order to circumvent censorship and create an autonomous cultural sphere. Indeed, sparkling conversation in private homes spread Enlightenment ideas to Europe's upper middle class and aristocracy. Paris set the example, and other French and European cities followed. In Paris a number of talented and often rich women presided over regular social gatherings in their elegant drawing rooms, or *salons*. There they encouraged the exchange of witty, uncensored observations on literature, science, and philosophy.

Elite women also exercised an unprecedented feminine influence on artistic taste. Soft pastels, ornate interiors, sentimental portraits, and starry-eyed lovers protected by hovering Cupids were all hallmarks of the style they favored. This style, known as the rococo, was popular throughout Europe in the eighteenth century. Some philosophes championed greater rights and expanded education for women, claiming that the position and treatment of women were the best indicators of a society's level of civilization and decency.[11] To be sure, to these male philosophes greater rights for women did not mean equal rights, and the philosophes were not particularly disturbed by the fact that elite women remained legally subordinate to men in economic and political affairs. Elite women lacked many rights, but so did most men.

One of the most famous salons was that of Madame Geoffrin, the unofficial godmother of the *Encyclopedia*. Madame Geoffrin was married by arrangement at fifteen to a rich and boring businessman of forty-eight. After dutifully raising her children, and in spite of her husband's loud protests, she developed a twice-weekly salon that counted Fontenelle and Montesquieu among its regular guests. Inheriting a large fortune after her husband's death, Madame Geoffrin gave the encyclopedists generous financial aid and helped save their enterprise from collapse. Corresponding with the king of Sweden and Catherine the Great of Russia, Madame Geoffrin remained her own woman, a practicing Christian who would not tolerate attacks on the church in her house.

The talented Julie de Lespinasse epitomized the skills of the Enlightenment hostess. Her highly informal salon attracted the keenest minds in France and Europe. As one philosophe wrote:

She could unite the different types, even the most antagonistic, sustaining the conversation by a well-aimed phrase, animating and guiding it at will. . . . Politics, religion, philosophy, news: nothing was excluded. Her circle met daily from five to nine. There one found men of all ranks in the State, the Church, and the Court, soldiers and foreigners, and the leading writers of the day.[12]

As that passage suggests, the salons created an independent cultural realm freed from religious dogma and political censorship. There educated members of the intellectual, economic, and social elites could debate issues and form their own ideas.

✳ **Enlightenment Culture**   The culture of the Enlightenment was elegant, intellectual, and international. This painting shows the seven-year-old Austrian child prodigy, Wolfgang Amadeus Mozart (1756–1791), playing his own composition at an "English tea" given by the Princess de Conti near Paris. Mozart's phenomenal creative powers lasted a lifetime, and he produced a vast range of symphonies, operas, and chamber music. *(Source: Versailles/Photographie Bulloz)*

In this gracious atmosphere, the *public* of philosophes, the French nobility, and the prosperous middle classes intermingled and increasingly influenced one another. Critical thinking about almost any question became fashionable and flourished with hopes for human progress through greater knowledge and enlightened public opinion.

✳ THE ENLIGHTENMENT AND ABSOLUTISM

How did the Enlightenment influence political developments? To this important question there is no easy answer. On the one hand, the French philosophes and kindred spirits in most European countries were primarily interested in converting people to critical, scientific thinking and were not particu-

larly concerned with politics. On the other hand, such thinking naturally led to political criticism and interest in political reform as both possible and desirable.

Some Enlightenment thinkers, led by the nobleman Montesquieu, argued for curbs on monarchial power in order to promote liberty. Until the American Revolution, however, most Enlightenment thinkers outside England and the Netherlands believed that political change could best come from above—from the ruler—rather than from below, especially in central and eastern Europe. Royal absolutism was a fact of life, and the kings and queens of Europe's leading states clearly had no intention of giving up their great powers. Therefore, the philosophes and their sympathizers realistically concluded that a benevolent absolutism offered the best opportunities for improving society. Critical thinking was turning the art of good government into an exact science. It was necessary only to educate and "enlighten" the monarch, who could then make good laws and promote human happiness. Enlightenment thinkers also turned toward rulers because rulers seemed to be listening, treating them with respect, and seeking their advice. Finally, the philosophes distrusted "the people," who they believed were deluded by superstitions and driven by violent passions, little children in need of firm parental guidance.

Encouraged and instructed by the philosophes, many absolutist rulers of the later eighteenth century tried to govern in an "enlightened" manner. Yet the actual programs and accomplishments of these rulers varied greatly. Let us therefore examine the evolution of monarchial absolutism at close range before trying to form any overall judgment about the Enlightenment's effect on it.

Absolutism in Central and Eastern Europe

Enlightenment teachings inspired European rulers in small as well as large states in the second half of the eighteenth century. Yet by far the most influential of the new-style monarchs were in Prussia, Russia, and Austria, and they deserve primary attention.

Frederick the Great of Prussia Frederick II (r. 1740–1786), commonly known as Frederick the Great, built masterfully on the work of his father, Frederick William I (see pages 573–574). This was somewhat surprising, for like many children with tyrannical parents he rebelled against his family's wishes in his early years. Rejecting the crude life of the barracks, Frederick embraced culture and literature, even writing poetry and fine prose in French, a language his father detested. After trying unsuccessfully to run away in 1730 at age eighteen, he was virtually imprisoned and even compelled to watch his companion in flight beheaded at his father's command. Yet like many other rebellious youths, Frederick eventually reached a reconciliation with his father, and by the time he came to the throne ten years later, Frederick was determined to use the splendid army that his father had left him.

Therefore, when the ruler of Austria, Charles VI, also died in 1740 and his young and charismatic daughter, Maria Theresa, inherited the Habsburg dominions, Frederick suddenly and without warning invaded her rich, mainly German province of Silesia. This action defied solemn Prussian promises to respect the Pragmatic Sanction, which guaranteed Maria Theresa's succession. Maria Theresa's ethnically diverse army was no match for Prussian precision. In 1742 as other greedy powers were falling on her lands in the general European War of the Austrian Succession (1740–1748), she was forced to cede almost all of Silesia to Prussia (see Map 17.3). In one stroke Prussia doubled its population to 6 million people. Now Prussia unquestionably towered above all the other German states and stood as a European Great Power.

Though successful in 1742, Frederick had to spend much of his reign fighting against great odds to save Prussia from total destruction. Maria Theresa was determined to regain Silesia, and when the ongoing competition between Britain and France for colonial empire brought renewed conflict in 1756, Austria fashioned an aggressive alliance with France and Russia. During the Seven Years' War (1756–1763), the aim of the alliance was to conquer Prussia and divide up its territory. Frederick led his army brilliantly, striking repeatedly at vastly superior forces invading from all sides. At times he believed all was lost, but he fought on with stoic courage. In the end, he was miraculously saved: Peter III came to the Russian throne in 1762 and called off the attack against Frederick, whom he greatly admired.

In the early years of his reign, Frederick II had kept his enthusiasm for Enlightenment culture strictly separated from a brutal concept of international politics. He wrote:

Of all States, from the smallest to the biggest, one can safely say that the fundamental rule of government is the principle of extending their territories. . . . The passions of rulers have no other curb but the limits of their power. Those are the fixed laws of European politics to which every politician submits.[13]

But the terrible struggle of the Seven Years' War tempered Frederick and brought him to consider how more humane policies for his subjects might also strengthen the state.

Thus Frederick went beyond a superficial commitment to Enlightenment culture for himself and his circle. He tolerantly allowed his subjects to believe as they wished in religious and philosophical matters. He promoted the advancement of knowledge, improving his country's schools and permitting scholars to publish their findings. Moreover, Frederick tried to improve the lives of his subjects more directly. As he wrote his friend Voltaire, "I must enlighten my people, cultivate their manners and morals, and make them as happy as human beings can be, or as happy as the means at my disposal permit." Prussia's laws were simplified, torture of prisoners was abolished, and judges decided cases quickly and impartially. Prussian officials became famous for their hard work and honesty. Frederick himself set a good example. He worked hard and lived modestly, claiming that he was "only the first servant of the state." Thus Frederick justified monarchy in terms of practical results and said nothing of the divine right of kings.

Frederick's dedication to high-minded government went only so far, however. He never tried to

Catherine as Equestrian Catherine took advantage of her intelligence and good looks to overthrow her husband Peter III and become empress of Russia. Strongly influenced by the Enlightenment, she cultivated the French philosophes and instituted moderate reforms only to reverse them in the aftermath of Pugachev's rebellion. Catherine's portrait hangs above her throne. (*Source: Novosti*)

change Prussia's existing social structure. True, he condemned serfdom in the abstract, but he accepted it in practice and did not even free the serfs on his own estates. He accepted and extended the privileges of the nobility, which he saw as his primary ally in the defense and extension of his realm. It became practically impossible for a middle-class person to gain a top position in the government. The Junker nobility remained the backbone of the army and the entire Prussian state.

Catherine the Great of Russia Catherine the Great of Russia (r. 1762–1796) was one of the most remarkable rulers who ever lived, and the French philosophes adored her. Catherine was a German princess from Anhalt-Zerbst, a totally insignificant principality sandwiched between Prussia and Saxony. Her father commanded a regiment of the Prussian army, but her mother was related to the Romanovs of Russia, and that relationship proved to be Catherine's chance.

Peter the Great had abolished the hereditary succession of tsars so that he could name his successor and thus preserve his policies. This move opened a period of palace intrigue and a rapid turnover of rulers until Peter's youngest daughter, Elizabeth, came to the Russian throne in 1741. A shrewd but crude woman—one of her official lovers was an illiterate shepherd boy—Elizabeth named her nephew Peter heir to the throne and chose Catherine to be his wife in 1744. It was a mismatch from the beginning. The fifteen-year-old Catherine was intelligent and attractive; her husband was stupid and ugly, his face badly scarred by smallpox. Ignored by her childish husband, Catherine carefully studied Russian, endlessly read writers such as Bayle and Voltaire, and made friends at court. Soon she knew what she wanted. "I did not care about Peter," she wrote in her *Memoirs,* "but I did care about the crown."[14]

As the old empress Elizabeth approached death, Catherine plotted against her unpopular husband. She selected as her new lover a tall, dashing young officer named Gregory Orlov, who with his four officer brothers commanded considerable support among the soldiers stationed in St. Petersburg. When Peter came to the throne in 1762, his decision to withdraw Russian troops from the coalition against Prussia alienated the army. Nor did Peter III's attempt to gain support from the Russian nobility by freeing it from compulsory state service succeed. At the end of six months, Catherine and her military conspirators deposed Peter III in a palace revolution. Then the Orlov brothers murdered him. The German princess became empress of Russia.

Catherine had drunk deeply at the Enlightenment well. Never questioning the common assumption that absolute monarchy was the best form of government, she set out to rule in an enlightened manner. She had three main goals. First, she worked hard to bring the sophisticated culture of western Europe to backward Russia. To do so, she imported Western architects, sculptors, musicians, and intellectuals. She bought masterpieces of Western art in wholesale lots and patronized the philosophes. An enthusiastic letter writer, she corresponded extensively with Voltaire and praised him as the "champion of the human race." When the French government banned the *Encyclopedia,* she offered to publish it in St. Petersburg. She sent money to Diderot when he needed it. With these and countless similar actions, Catherine won good press in the West for herself and for her country. Moreover, this intellectual ruler, who wrote plays and loved good talk, set the tone for the entire Russian nobility. Peter the Great westernized Russian armies, but it was Catherine who westernized the thinking of the Russian nobility.

Catherine's second goal was domestic reform, and she began her reign with sincere and ambitious projects. Better laws were a major concern. She appointed a special legislative commission to prepare a new law code. No new unified code was ever produced, but Catherine did restrict the practice of torture and allowed limited religious toleration. She also tried to improve education and strengthen local government. The philosophes applauded these measures and hoped more would follow.

Such was not the case. In 1773 a common Cossack soldier named Emelian Pugachev sparked a gigantic uprising of serfs, very much as Stenka Razin had done a century earlier (see page 578). Proclaiming himself the true tsar, Pugachev issued "decrees" abolishing serfdom, taxes, and army service. Thousands joined his cause, slaughtering landlords and officials over a vast area of southwestern Russia. Pugachev's untrained hordes eventually proved no match for Catherine's noble-led regular army. Betrayed by his own company, Pugachev was captured and savagely executed.

Pugachev's rebellion was a decisive turning point in Catherine's domestic policy. On coming to the throne, she had condemned serfdom in theory, but Pugachev's rebellion put an end to any illusions she might have had about attempting reform. The peasants were clearly dangerous, and her empire rested on the support of the nobility. After 1775 Catherine gave the nobles absolute control of their serfs. She extended serfdom into new areas, such as Ukraine. In 1785 she formalized the nobility's privileged position, freeing nobles forever from taxes and state service. She also confiscated the lands of the Russian Orthodox church and gave them to favorite officials. Under Catherine the Russian nobility attained its most exalted position, and serfdom entered its most oppressive phase.

Catherine's third goal was territorial expansion, and in this she was extremely successful. Her armies subjugated the last descendants of the Mongols, the Crimean Tartars, and began the conquest of the Caucasus. Her greatest coup by far was the partitioning of Poland, whose fate in the late eighteenth century demonstrated the dangers of failing to build a strong absolutist state. All important decisions continued to require the unanimous agreement of all nobles elected to the Polish Diet, which meant that nothing could ever be done to strengthen the state. When Frederick of Prussia proposed that Prussia, Austria, and Russia each take a gigantic slice of Polish territory, Catherine jumped at the chance. The first partition of Poland took place in 1772. Two more partitions, in 1793 and 1795, gave all three powers more Polish territory, and the ancient republic of Poland simply vanished from the map.

Expansion helped Catherine keep the nobility happy, for it provided her with vast new lands to give to her faithful servants and her many lovers. On all the official royal favorites she lavished large estates with many serfs, as if to make sure there were no hard feelings when her interest cooled. Until the end this remarkable woman—who always believed that, in spite of her domestic setbacks, she was slowly civilizing Russia—kept her zest for life. Fascinated by a new twenty-two-year-old flame when she was a roly-poly grandmother in her sixties, she happily reported her good fortune to a favorite former lover: "I have come back to life like a frozen fly; I am gay and well."[15]

The Austrian Habsburgs   In Austria, two talented rulers did manage to introduce major reforms, although traditional power politics was more important than Enlightenment teachings. One was Joseph II (r. 1780–1790), a fascinating individual. For an earlier generation of historians he was the "revolutionary emperor," a tragic hero whose lofty reforms were undone by the landowning nobility he challenged. More recent scholarship has revised this romantic interpretation and stressed how Joseph II continued the state-building work of his mother, the empress Maria Theresa (r. 1740–1780), a remarkable but old-fashioned absolutist.

Emerging from the long War of the Austrian Succession in 1748 with only the serious loss of Silesia, Maria Theresa and her closest ministers were determined to introduce reforms that would make the state stronger and more efficient. Three aspects of these reforms were most important. First, Maria Theresa introduced measures aimed at limiting the papacy's political influence in her realm. Second, a whole series of administrative reforms strengthened the central bureaucracy,

Maria Theresa The empress of Austria and her husband pose with eleven of their sixteen children at Schönbrunn palace in this family portrait by court painter Martin Meytens (1695–1770). Joseph, the heir to the throne, stands at the center of the star pattern. Wealthy women often had very large families, in part because they seldom nursed their babies as poor women usually did. *(Source: Kunsthistorisches Museum, Vienna)*

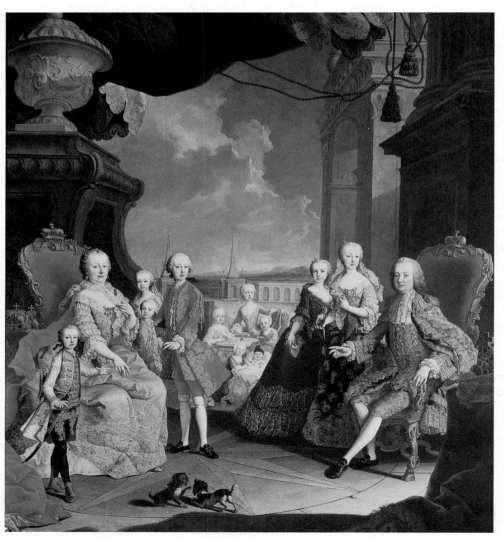

smoothed out some provincial differences, and revamped the tax system, taxing even the lands of nobles without special exemptions. Third, the government sought to improve the lot of the agricultural population, cautiously reducing the power of lords over their hereditary serfs and their partially free peasant tenants.

Coregent with his mother from 1765 onward and a strong supporter of change, Joseph II moved forward rapidly when he came to the throne in 1780. He controlled the established Catholic church even more closely in an attempt to ensure that it produced better citizens. He granted religious toleration and civic rights to Protestants and Jews—a radical innovation that impressed his contemporaries. In even more spectacular peasant reforms, Joseph abolished serfdom in 1781, and in 1789 he decreed that all peasant labor obligations be converted into cash payments. This ill-conceived measure was violently rejected not only by the nobility but also by the peasants it was intended to help, for their primitive barter economy was woefully lacking in money. When a disillusioned Joseph died prematurely at forty-nine, the entire Habsburg Empire was in turmoil. His brother Leopold II (r. 1790–1792) was forced to cancel Joseph's radical edicts in order to re-establish order. Peasants once again were required to do forced labor for their lords.

Absolutism in France

The Enlightenment's influence on political developments in France was complex. The monarchy maintained its absolutist claims, and some philosophes, such as Voltaire, believed that the king was still the best source of needed reform. At the same time, discontented nobles and learned judges drew on thinkers such as Montesquieu for liberal arguments. They sought with some success to limit the king's power, as France diverged from the absolutist states just considered.

When Louis XIV finally died in 1715, to be succeeded by his five-year-old great-grandson, Louis XV (r. 1715–1774), the Sun King's elaborate system of absolutist rule was challenged in a general reaction. Favored by the duke of Orléans (1674–1723), a licentious rake and nephew of Louis XIV who governed as regent until 1723, the nobility made a strong comeback.

Most important, in 1715 the duke restored to the high court of Paris—the Parlement—the an-

cient right to evaluate royal decrees publicly before they were given the force of law. The restoration of this right, which had been suspended under Louis XIV, was a fateful step. The judges of the Parlement of Paris had originally come from the middle class, and their high position reflected the way that Louis XIV (and earlier French monarchs) had chosen to use that class to build the royal bureaucracy so necessary for an absolutist state. By the eighteenth century, however, these middle-class judges had risen to become hereditary nobles. Moreover, although Louis XIV had curbed the political power of the nobility, he had never challenged its enormous social prestige. Thus high position in the government continued to bestow the noble status that middle-class officials wanted. The judges of Paris, like many high-ranking officials, actually owned their government jobs and freely passed them on as private property from father to son. By allowing this well-entrenched and increasingly aristocratic group to evaluate the king's decrees, the duke of Orléans sanctioned a counterweight to absolute power.

These implications became clear when the heavy expenses of the War of the Austrian Succession plunged France into financial crisis. In 1748 Louis XV appointed a finance minister who decreed a 5 percent income tax on every individual regardless of social status. Exemption from most taxation had long been a hallowed privilege of the nobility, and other important groups—the clergy, the large towns, and some wealthy bourgeoisie—had also gained special tax advantages over time. The result was a vigorous protest from many sides, led by the Parlement of Paris. The monarchy retreated; the new tax was dropped.

After the disastrously expensive Seven Years' War, the conflict re-emerged. The government tried to maintain emergency taxes after the war ended. The Parlement of Paris protested and even challenged the basis of royal authority, claiming that the king's power had to be limited to protect liberty. Once again the government caved in and withdrew the wartime taxes in 1764. Emboldened by this striking victory, the judicial opposition asserted that the king could not levy taxes without the consent of the Parlement of Paris acting as the representative of the entire nation.

Indolent and sensual by nature, more interested in his many mistresses than in affairs of state, Louis XV finally roused himself for a determined defense of his absolutist inheritance. "The magistrates," he angrily told the Parlement of Paris in a famous face-to-face confrontation, "are my officers. . . . In my person only does the sovereign power rest."[16] In 1768 Louis appointed a tough career official named René de Maupeou as chancellor and ordered him to crush the judicial opposition.

Maupeou abolished the Parlement of Paris and exiled its members to isolated backwaters in the provinces. He created a new and docile Parlement of royal officials, and he began once again to tax the privileged groups. Most philosophes and educated public opinion as a whole sided with the old Parlement, however, and there was widespread criticism of "royal despotism." The illegal stream of scandalmongering, pornographic attacks on the king and his court became a torrent, and some scholars now believe these lurid denunciations ate away at the foundations of royal authority. Yet the monarchy's power was still great enough for Maupeou simply to ride over the opposition, and Louis XV would probably have prevailed—if he had lived to a very ripe old age.

But Louis XV died in 1774. The new king, Louis XVI (r. 1774–1792), was a shy twenty-year-old with good intentions. Taking the throne, he is reported to have said, "What I should like most is to be loved."[17] The eager-to-please monarch decided to yield in the face of such strong criticism from so much of France's educated elite. He dismissed Maupeou and repudiated the strong-willed minister's work. The old Parlement of Paris was reinstated as enlightened public opinion cheered and anticipated moves toward more representative government. But such moves were not forthcoming. Instead, a weakened but unreformed monarchy faced a judicial opposition that claimed to speak for the entire French nation. Increasingly locked in stalemate, the country was drifting toward renewed financial crisis and political upheaval.

The Overall Influence of the Enlightenment

Having examined the evolution of monarchial absolutism in four leading states, we can begin to look for meaningful generalizations and evaluate the overall influence of Enlightenment thought on politics.

France clearly diverged from its eastern neighbors in its political development in the eighteenth century. The capacity of the French monarch to govern in a truly absolutist manner declined substantially. The political resurgence of the French

nobility after 1715 and the growth of judicial opposition drew crucial support from educated public opinion, which increasingly made the liberal critique of unregulated royal authority its own.

The situation in eastern and east-central Europe was different. The liberal critique of absolute monarchy remained an intellectual curiosity, and proponents of reform from above held sway. Moreover, despite differences, the leading eastern European monarchs of the later eighteenth century all claimed that they were acting on the principles of the Enlightenment. The philosophes generally agreed with this assessment and cheered them on. Beginning in the mid-nineteenth century, historians developed the idea of a common "enlightened despotism" or "enlightened absolutism," and they canonized Frederick, Catherine, and Joseph as its most outstanding examples. More recent research has raised doubts about this old interpretation and has led to a fundamental re-evaluation.

There is general agreement that these absolutists, especially Catherine and Frederick, did encourage and spread the cultural values of the Enlightenment. They were proud of their intellectual accomplishments and good taste, and they supported knowledge, education, and the arts. Historians also agree that the absolutists believed in change from above and tried to enact needed reforms. Yet the results of these efforts brought only very modest improvements, and the life of the peasantry remained very hard in the eighteenth century. Thus some historians have concluded that these monarchs were not really sincere in their reform efforts. Others disagree, arguing that powerful nobilities blocked the absolutists' genuine commitment to reform. (The old interpretation of Joseph II as the tragic revolutionary emperor forms part of this argument.)

The emerging answer to this controversy is that the later eastern absolutists were indeed committed to reform but that humanitarian objectives were of quite secondary importance. Above all, the absolutists wanted reforms that would strengthen the state and allow them to compete militarily with their neighbors. Modern scholarship has therefore stressed how Catherine, Frederick, and Joseph were in many ways simply continuing the state building of their predecessors, reorganizing armies and expanding bureaucracies to raise more taxes and troops. The reason for this continuation was simple. The international political struggle was

THE ENLIGHTENMENT

1686	Fontenelle, *Conversations on the Plurality of Worlds*
1687	Newton, *Principia*
1690	Locke, "Essay Concerning Human Understanding" and "Second Treatise on Civil Government"
1715–1774	Rule of Louis XV in France
1721	Montesquieu, *The Persian Letters*
1740–1748	War of the Austrian Succession
1740–1780	Rule of Maria Theresa in Austria
1740–1786	Rule of Frederick II (the Great) in Prussia
1742	Austria cedes Silesia to Prussia
1743	Voltaire, *Age of Louis XIV*
1748	Montesquieu, *The Spirit of the Laws* Hume, *An Enquiry Concerning Human Understanding*
1751–1765	Publication of the *Encyclopedia,* edited by Diderot and d'Alembert
1756–1763	Seven Years' War
1762	Rousseau, *Social Contract*
1762–1796	Rule of Catherine II (the Great) in Russia
1770	D'Holbach, *The System of Nature*
1771	Maupeou, Louis XV's chancellor, abolishes Parlement of Paris
1772	First partition of Poland among Russia, Prussia, and Austria
1774	Ascension of Louis XVI in France; restoration of Parlement of Paris
1780–1790	Rule of Joseph II in Austria
1781	Abolition of serfdom in Austria
1785	Catherine the Great frees the nobles from taxes and state service
1790–1792	Rule of Leopold II in Austria; serfdom is re-established
1793, 1795	Second and third partitions of Poland, which completes its absorption

brutal, and the stakes were high. First Austria under Maria Theresa and then Prussia under Frederick the Great had to engage in bitter fighting to escape dismemberment. Decentralized Poland was coldly divided and eventually liquidated.

Yet in this drive for more state power, the later absolutists were also innovators, and the idea of an era of enlightened absolutism retains a certain validity. Sharing the Enlightenment faith in critical thinking and believing that knowledge meant power, these absolutists really were more enlightened than their predecessors because they put state-building reforms in a new, broader perspective. Above all, the later absolutists considered how more humane laws and practices could help their populations become more productive and satisfied and thus able to contribute more substantially to the welfare of the state. It was from this perspective that they introduced many of their most progressive reforms, tolerating religious minorities, simplifying legal codes, and promoting practical education. Nevertheless, reforms had to be grafted on to existing political and social structures. Thus each enlightened absolutist sought greater state power, but each believed a different policy would attain it.

The eastern European absolutists of the later eighteenth century combined old-fashioned state building with the culture and critical thinking of the Enlightenment. In doing so, they succeeded in expanding the role of the state in the life of society. Unlike the successors of Louis XIV, they perfected bureaucratic machines that were to prove surprisingly adaptive and capable of enduring into the twentieth century.

SUMMARY

This chapter has focused on the complex development of a new world-view in Western civilization. This new view was essentially critical and secular, drawing its inspiration from the scientific revolution and crystallizing in the Enlightenment.

Decisive breakthroughs in astronomy and physics in the seventeenth century, which demolished the imposing medieval synthesis of Aristotelian philosophy and Christian theology, had only limited practical consequences despite the expectations of scientific enthusiasts. Yet the impact of new scientific knowledge on intellectual life became great. Interpreting scientific findings and Newtonian laws in an antitraditional, antireligious manner, the French philosophes of the Enlightenment extolled the superiority of rational, critical thinking. This new method, they believed, promised not just increased knowledge but even the discovery of the fundamental laws of human society. Although they reached different conclusions when they turned to social and political realities, they did stimulate absolute monarchs to apply reason to statecraft and the search for useful reforms. Above all, the philosophes succeeded in shaping an emerging public opinion and spreading their radically new world-view. These were momentous accomplishments.

NOTES

1. H. Butterfield, *The Origins of Modern Science* (New York: Macmillan, 1951), p. viii.
2. Quoted in A. G. R. Smith, *Science and Society in the Sixteenth and Seventeenth Centuries* (New York: Harcourt Brace Jovanovich, 1972), p. 97.
3. Quoted in Butterfield, *The Origins of Modern Science,* p. 47.
4. Quoted in Smith, *Science and Society in the Sixteenth and Seventeenth Centuries,* p. 120.
5. A. R. Hall, *From Galileo to Newton, 1630–1720* (New York: Harper & Row, 1963), p. 290.
6. Quoted in P. Hazard, *The European Mind, 1680–1715* (Cleveland: Meridian Books, 1963), pp. 304–305.
7. Quoted in R. Chartier, *The Cultural Origins of the French Revolution* (Durham, N.C.: Duke University Press, 1991), p. 27.
8. Quoted in L. Schiebinger, *The Mind Has No Sex?: Women in the Origins of Modern Science* (Cambridge, Mass.: Harvard University Press, 1989), p. 64.
9. Quoted in G. L. Mosse et al., eds., *Europe in Review* (Chicago: Rand McNally, 1964), p. 156.
10. Quoted in P. Gay, "The Unity of the Enlightenment," *History* 3 (1960): 25.
11. See E. Fox-Genovese, "Women in the Enlightenment," in *Becoming Visible: Women in European History,* 2d ed., ed. R. Bridenthal, C. Koonz, and S. Stuard (Boston: Houghton Mifflin, 1987), esp. pp. 252–259 and 263–265.
12. Quoted in G. P. Gooch, *Catherine the Great and Other Studies* (Hamden, Conn.: Archon Books, 1966), p. 149.
13. Quoted in L. Krieger, *Kings and Philosophers, 1689–1789* (New York: Norton, 1970), p. 257.
14. Quoted in Gooch, *Catherine the Great and Other Studies,* p. 15.
15. Ibid., p. 53.
16. Quoted in R. R. Palmer, *The Age of Democratic Revolution,* vol. 1 (Princeton, N.J.: Princeton University Press, 1959), pp. 95–96.
17. Quoted in G. Wright, *France in Modern Times,* 4th ed. (New York: Norton, 1987), p. 34.

SUGGESTED READING

The first three authors cited in the Notes—H. Butterfield, A. G. R. Smith, and A. R. Hall—have written excellent general interpretations of the scientific revolution. These may be compared with an outstanding recent work by M. Jacob, *The Cultural Meaning of the*

Scientific Revolution (1988), which has a useful bibliography. L. Schiebinger, *The Mind Has No Sex?: Women in the Origins of Modern Science* (1989), provides a brilliant analysis of how the new science gradually excluded women interested in science, a question completely neglected in older studies. A. Debus, *Man and Nature in the Renaissance* (1978), is good on the Copernican revolution, whereas M. Boas, *The Scientific Renaissance, 1450–1630* (1966), is especially insightful about the influence of magic on science. S. Drake, *Galileo* (1980), is a good short biography. T. Kuhn, *The Structure of Scientific Revolutions* (1962), is a challenging, much-discussed attempt to understand major breakthroughs in scientific thought over time. E. Andrade, *Sir Isaac Newton* (1958), is a good brief biography, which may be compared with F. Manuel, *The Religion of Isaac Newton* (1974).

The work of P. Hazard listed in the Notes is a classic study of the formative years of Enlightenment thought, and his *European Thought in the Eighteenth Century* (1954) is also recommended. P. Gay has written several major studies on the Enlightenment: *Voltaire's Politics* (1959) and *The Party of Humanity* (1971) are two of the best. J. Sklar, *Montesquieu* (1987), is an engaging biography. I. Wade, *The Structure and Form of the French Enlightenment* (1977), is a major synthesis. F. Baumer, *Religion and the Rise of Skepticism* (1969); H. Payne, *The Philosophes and the People* (1976); and H. Chisick, *The Limits of Reform in the Enlightenment: Attitudes Toward the Education of the Lower Classes in Eighteenth-Century France* (1981), are interesting studies of important aspects of Enlightenment thought. The changing attitudes of the educated public are imaginatively analyzed by R. Chartier in *The Cultural Origins of the French Revolution,* cited in the Notes, and in *French Historical Studies* (Fall 1992). R. Danton, *The Literary Underground of the Old Regime* (1982), provides a fascinating glimpse of low-life publishing. On women, see the stimulating study by E. Fox-Genovese cited in the Notes as well as S. Spencer, ed., *French Women and the Age of Enlightenment* (1984), and K. Rogers, *Feminism in Eighteenth-Century England* (1982). J. Landes, *Women and the Public Sphere in the Age of the French Revolution* (1988), is a fascinating and controversial study of women and politics. Above all, one should read some of the philosophes and let them speak for themselves. Two good anthologies are C. Brinton, ed., *The Portable Age of Reason* (1956), and F. Manuel, ed., *The Enlightenment* (1951). Voltaire's most famous and very amusing novel *Candide* is

highly recommended, as is S. Gendzier, ed., *Denis Diderot: The Encyclopedia: Selections* (1967). A. Wilson's biography, *Diderot* (1972), is long but rewarding.

In addition to the works mentioned in the Suggested Reading for Chapter 17, the monarchies of Europe are carefully analyzed in H. Scott, *Enlightened Absolutism* (1990); in C. Tilly, ed., *The Formation of National States in Western Europe* (1975); and in J. Gagliardo, *Enlightened Despotism* (1967), all of which have useful bibliographies. M. Anderson, *Historians and Eighteenth-Century Europe* (1979), is a valuable introduction to modern scholarship, and C. Behrens, *Society, Government, and the Enlightenment: The Experience of Eighteenth-Century France and Prussia* (1985), is a stimulating comparative study. A recommended study on the struggle for power and reform in France is F. Ford, *Robe and Sword* (1953), which discusses the resurgence of the French nobility after the death of Louis XIV. J. Lynch, *Bourbon Spain, 1700–1808* (1989), and R. Herr, *The Eighteenth-Century Revolution in Spain* (1958), skillfully analyze the impact of Enlightenment thought in Spain. Important works on Austria include C. Macartney, *Maria Theresa and the House of Austria* (1970); P. Bernard, *Joseph II* (1968); and T. Blanning, *Joseph II and Enlightened Absolutism* (1970). There are several fine works on Russia. J. Alexander, *Catherine the Great: Life and Legend* (1989), is the best biography of the famous ruler, which may be compared with the empress's own story, *The Memoirs of Catherine the Great,* edited by D. Maroger (1961). I. de Madariaga, *Russia in the Age of Catherine the Great* (1981); and P. Dukes, *The Making of Russian Absolutism, 1613–1801* (1982), are strongly recommended. The ambitious reader should also look at A. N. Radishchev, *A Journey from St. Petersburg to Moscow* (English trans., 1958), a famous 1790 attack on Russian serfdom and an appeal to Catherine the Great to free the serfs, for which Radishchev was exiled to Siberia.

The culture of the time may be approached through A. Cobban, ed., *The Eighteenth Century* (1969), a richly illustrated work with excellent essays, and C. B. Behrens, *The Ancien Régime* (1967). T. Crow, *Painters and Public Life in Eighteenth-Century Paris* (1985), examines artists and cultural politics. C. Rosen, *The Classical Style: Haydn, Mozart, Beethoven* (1972), brilliantly synthesizes music and society, as did Mozart himself in his great opera *The Marriage of Figaro,* where the count is the buffoon and his servant the hero.

Voltaire on Religion

Voltaire was the most renowned and probably the most influential of the French philosophes. His biting, satirical novel Candide *(1759) is still widely assigned in college courses, and his witty yet serious* Philosophical Dictionary *remains a source of pleasure and stimulation. The* Dictionary *consists of a series of essays on topics ranging from Adam to Zoroaster, from certainty to circumcision. The following passage is taken from the essay on religion.*

Voltaire began writing the Philosophical Dictionary *in 1752, at the age of fifty-eight, after arriving at the Prussian court in Berlin. Frederick the Great applauded Voltaire's efforts, but Voltaire put the project aside after leaving Berlin. The first of several revised editions was published anonymously in 1764. It was an immediate, controversial success. Snapped up by an "enlightened" public, it was denounced by religious leaders as a threat to the Christian community and was burned in Geneva and Paris.*

I meditated last night; I was absorbed in the contemplation of nature; I admired the immensity, the course, the harmony of those infinite globes which the vulgar do not know how to admire.

I admired still more the intelligence which directs these vast forces. I said to myself: "One must be blind not to be dazzled by this spectacle; one must be stupid not to recognize its author; one must be mad not to worship the Supreme Being. What tribute of worship should I render Him? Should not this tribute be the same in the whole of space, since it is the same Supreme Power which reigns equally in all space?

Should not a thinking being who dwells on a star in the Milky Way offer Him the same homage as a thinking being on this little globe of ours? Light is the same for the star Sirius as for us; moral philosophy must also be the same. If a feeling, thinking animal on Sirius is born of a tender father and mother who have been occupied with his happiness, he owes them as much love and care as we owe to our parents. If someone in the Milky Way sees a needy cripple, and if he can aid him and does not do so, then he is guilty toward all the globes.

Everywhere the heart has the same duties: on the steps of the throne of God, if He has a throne; and in the depths of the abyss, if there is an abyss."

I was deep in these ideas when one of those genii who fill the spaces between the worlds came down to me. I recognized the same aerial creature who had appeared to me on another occasion to teach me that the judgments of God are different from our own, and how a good action is preferable to a controversy.

The genii transported me into a desert all covered with piles of bones. . . . He began with the first pile. "These," he said, "are the twenty-three thousand Jews who danced before a calf, together with the twenty-four thousand who were killed while fornicating with Midianitish women. The number of those massacred for such errors and offences amounts to nearly three hundred thousand.

"In the other piles are the bones of the Christians slaughtered by each other because of metaphysical disputes. They are divided into several heaps of four centuries each. One heap would have mounted right to the sky; they had to be divided."

"What!" I cried, "brothers have treated their brothers like this, and I have the misfortune to be of this brotherhood!"

"Here," said the spirit, "are the twelve million native Americans killed in their own land because they had not been baptized."

"My God! . . . Why assemble here all these abominable monuments to barbarism and fanaticism?"

"To instruct you. . . . Follow me now." [The genii takes Voltaire to the "heroes of humanity, who tried to banish violence and plunder from the world," and tells Voltaire to question them.]

[At last] I saw a man with a gentle, simple face, who seemed to me to be about thirty-five years old. From afar he looked with compassion upon those piles of whitened bones, through which I had been led to reach the sage's dwelling place. I was astonished to find his feet swollen and bleeding, his hands likewise, his side pierced, and his ribs laid bare by the cut of the lash. "Good God!" I said to him, "is it possible for a just man, a sage, to be in this state? I have just seen one who was treated in a very hateful way, but there is no comparison between his torture and yours. Wicked priests and wicked judges poisoned him; is it by priests and judges that you were so cruelly assassinated?"

With great courtesy he answered, "Yes."

"And who were these monsters?"

"They were hypocrites."

"Ah! that says everything; I understand by that one word that they would have condemned you to the cruelest punishment. Had you then proved to them, as Socrates did, that the Moon was not a goddess, and that Mercury was not a god?"

"No, it was not a question of planets. My countrymen did not even know what a planet was; they were all arrant ignoramuses. Their superstitions were quite different from those of the Greeks."

"Then you wanted to teach them a new religion?"

"Not at all; I told them simply: 'Love God with all your heart and your neighbor as yourself, for that is the whole of mankind's duty.' Judge yourself if this precept is not as old as the universe; judge yourself if I brought them a new religion." . . .

"But did you say nothing, do nothing that could serve them as a pretext?"

"To the wicked everything serves as pretext."

"Did you not say once that you were come not to bring peace, but a sword?"

"It was a scribe's error; I told them that I brought peace and not a sword. I never wrote anything; what I said can have been changed without evil intention."

"You did not then contribute in any way by your teaching, either badly reported or badly

Voltaire dining at Sans Souci palace.
(*Source: Bildarchiv Preussischer Kulturbesitz*)

interpreted, to those frightful piles of bones which I saw on my way to consult with you?"

"I have only looked with horror upon those who have made themselves guilty of all these murders."

. . . [Finally] I asked him to tell me in what true religion consisted.

"Have I not already told you? Love God and your neighbor as yourself."

"Is it necessary for me to take sides either for the Greek Orthodox Church or the Roman Catholic?"

"When I was in the world I never made any difference between the Jew and the Samaritan."

"Well, if that is so, I take you for my only master." Then he made a sign with his head that filled me with peace. The vision disappeared, and I was left with a clear conscience.

Questions for Analysis

1. Why did Voltaire believe in a Supreme Being? How does this passage reflect the influence of Isaac Newton's scientific system?

2. Was Voltaire trying to entertain or teach or do both? Was he effective? Explain.

3. If Voltaire was trying to convey serious ideas about religion and morality, what were those ideas? What was he attacking?

4. If a person today thought and wrote like Voltaire, would that person be called a defender or a destroyer of Christianity? Why?

Source: F. M. Arouet de Voltaire, *Oeuvres completes* (Paris: Firmin-Didot, 1875), vol. 8, pp. 188–190; translated into English by John McKay.

The Changing Life of
the People in Europe

The Spanish artist Francisco de Goya y Lucientes painted *The Stilts (Los Zacos)* in 1791–1792. *(Source: Museo del Prado, Madrid)*

The world of European absolutism and aristocracy, a combination of raw power and elegant refinement, was a world apart from that of common people. Weakness and uncertainty, poverty and pain—these enduring realities weighed heavily on the vast majority. Yet the common people in Western societies were by no means helpless victims of fate, ignorance, and inequality. With courage and intelligence, with hard work and family loyalties, ordinary men and women struggled and survived. There is a dignity in these efforts that is deeply moving.

This, then, is the story of those ordinary lives at a time when the idea of far-reaching scientific and material progress was only the sweet dream of a privileged elite in fashionable salons.

- How did the common people of Europe wring a living out of the land, and how was cottage industry growing to complement these efforts?
- What changes occurred in marriage and the family in the course of the eighteenth century?
- What was life like for children, and how did attitudes toward children evolve?
- What did people eat, and how did changes in diet and medical care affect their lives?
- What were the patterns of popular religion and culture? How did these patterns come into contact—and conflict—with the critical worldview of the educated public and thereby widen the cultural divide between rich and poor in the era of the Enlightenment?

Such questions help us better understand how the peasant masses and urban poor really lived in western Europe before the age of revolution opened at the end of the eighteenth century. These questions will be the focus of this chapter.

❖ AGRICULTURE AND POPULATION

At the end of the seventeenth century, at least 80 percent of the people of all western European countries, with the possible exception of Holland, drew their livelihood from agriculture. In eastern Europe the percentage was considerably higher. Men and women lavished their attention on the land, and the land repaid their efforts, yielding the food and most of the raw materials for industry that made life possible. But the land was stingy and capricious. Yields were low even in good years, finding enough to eat was an endless challenge, and disease or starvation was the price of failure. As a result, most peasant communities had learned to keep family size under control. If total population grew even modestly, as it did in the eighteenth century, people had to find new sources of food and income.

Working the Land

The greatest accomplishment of medieval agriculture was the open-field system of village agriculture developed by European peasants. That system divided the land to be cultivated by the peasants into a few large fields that in turn were cut up into long narrow strips. The fields and strips were not enclosed. An individual peasant family—if it was fortunate—held a number of strips scattered throughout the large fields. The land of those who owned but did not till—primarily the nobility, the clergy, and wealthy townsmen—was also in scattered strips. The peasants farmed each large field as a community, plowing, sowing, and harvesting in accordance with tradition and the village leaders.

The ever-present problem was exhaustion of the soil. If a community planted wheat year after year in the same field, the nitrogen in the soil was soon depleted, and crop failure and starvation were certain. Since the supply of manure for fertilizer was limited, the only way for land to recover its life-giving fertility was for a field to lie fallow for a period of time. In the early Middle Ages, a year of fallow was alternated with a year of cropping, so that in any given year half of the land stood idle. Eventually, three-year rotations were introduced. This system permitted a year of wheat or rye followed by a year of oats or beans or peas and then a year of fallow. The results of this change were modest, however. In a rich agricultural region like the Po Valley in northern Italy, every bushel of wheat sown yielded on average only five or six bushels of grain at harvest during the seventeenth century. Such yields were no more than those attained in fertile, well-watered areas in the thirteenth century or in ancient Greece. By modern standards, output in 1700 was distressingly low. (Today an American or French farmer with similar land can expect roughly fifty bushels of wheat for each bushel of wheat sown.) Only awareness of the tragic consequences of continuous cropping forced undernourished populations to let a third of their land lie idle at any given time.

Traditional rights reinforced the traditional pattern of farming. In addition to rotating the field crops in a uniform way, villages held open meadows in common to provide animals with hay and natural pasture. After the harvest, the people of the village also pastured their animals on the wheat or rye stubble. In many places such pasturing followed a brief period, also established by tradition, for the gleaning of grain. Poor women would go through the fields picking up the few single grains that had fallen to the ground in the course of the harvest. This backbreaking labor provided the slender margin of survival for some people in the winter months.

In the age of absolutism and nobility, state and landlord levied heavy taxes and high rents as a matter of course. In so doing, they stripped the peasants of much of their meager earnings. Generally speaking, the peasants of eastern Europe were worst off. As discussed in Chapter 18, they were serfs, bound to their lords in hereditary service. Five or six days of unpaid work per week on the lord's land was not uncommon. Well into the nine-

Millet: The Gleaners   Poor French peasant women search for grains and stalks that the harvesters (in the background) have missed. The open-field system seen here could still be found in parts of Europe in 1857, when this picture was painted. Jean-François Millet is known for his great paintings expressing social themes. *(Source: Louvre © Photo R. M. N.)*

teenth century, individual Russian serfs and serf families were regularly sold with and without land. Serfdom was often very close to slavery.

Social conditions were considerably better in western Europe. Peasants were generally free from serfdom. In France and western Germany, they owned land and could pass it on to their children. Yet life was hard and poverty was the great reality for most people. In the Beauvais region of France at the beginning of the eighteenth century, only a tenth of the peasants could live satisfactorily off the fruits of their landholdings. Owning less than half of the land, the peasants had to pay heavy royal taxes, the church's tithe, and dues to the lord, as well as set aside seed for the next season. Left with only half of their crop for their own use, they had to toil for others and seek work far afield in a constant scramble for a meager living.

Technological progress offered a possible way for European peasants to improve their difficult position by producing more. The uncultivated fields were the heart of the matter. If peasants could replace the fallow with crops, they could increase the land under cultivation by 50 percent. The secret was to eliminate the fallow by alternating grain with certain nitrogen-storing crops, such as turnips and potatoes, clovers and grasses, which rejuvenate the soil while still giving produce.

Technological progress, however, did not come easily. To wait for the entire village to agree to a new crop rotation might mean waiting forever. Thus an innovating agriculturalist sought to enclose and consolidate his scattered holdings into a compact, fenced-in field, and he also sought to enclose his share of the natural pasture—known as the common. But because the common rights, like gleaning, were precious to many rural people, only powerful social and political pressures could overcome the traditionalism of rural communities. The old system of open fields held on tenaciously. Indeed, until the end of the eighteenth century, the promise of the new system was extensively realized only in the Low Countries and in England. Across the rest of Europe, technological progress was limited largely to the introduction of a single new but extremely important crop—the potato (see page 614).

The Balance of Numbers

Until 1700 the total population of Europe grew slowly much of the time and by no means con-

FIGURE 19.1 The Growth of Population in England, 1000–1800 England is a good example of both the uneven increase of European population before 1700 and the third great surge of growth, which began in the eighteenth century. (*Source: Data from E. A. Wrigley,* Population and History, *McGraw-Hill, New York, 1969*)

stantly (Figure 19.1). In seventeenth-century Europe, births and deaths were in a crude but effective balance. The birthrate—annual births as a proportion of the population—was fairly high but far lower than it would have been if all women had been having as many children as biologically possible. The death rate in normal years was also high, though somewhat lower than the birthrate. As a result, the population grew modestly in normal years at a rate of perhaps 0.5 to 1 percent. Yet even fairly modest population growth of 1 percent per year produces a large increase over a long period—a fourfold increase in 150 years, for example. Such gigantic increases did not occur in agrarian Europe because in certain tragic periods, many more people died than were born; total population fell sharply, even catastrophically.

The grim reapers of demographic crisis were famine, epidemic disease, and war. Famine, the inevitable result of poor farming methods and periodic crop failures, was particularly murderous because it was accompanied by disease. With a brutal one-two punch, famine stunned and weakened a population, and disease finished it off. Disease, including epidemics of bubonic plague, dysentery, and smallpox, could also ravage independently, even in years of adequate harvests.

War was another scourge. The indirect effects were more harmful than the organized killing. War spread disease. Soldiers and camp followers passed venereal disease throughout the countryside to scar and kill. Armies requisitioned scarce food

Albrecht Dürer: The Four Horsemen of the Apocalypse Dürer combines emotional power and unsurpassed technical skill in this famous 1498 woodcut. Dürer's terrifying vision of Death and his henchmen periodically became reality in Europe well into the eighteenth century. *(Source: Courtesy of Museum of Fine Arts, Boston)*

supplies for their own use and disrupted the agricultural cycle. The Thirty Years' War (see pages 539–540) witnessed all possible combinations of distress. In the German states, the number of inhabitants declined by more than *two-thirds* in some large areas and by at least one-third almost everywhere else. The great sixteenth-century artist Albrecht Dürer captured the horror of demographic crisis in his chilling woodcut *The Four Horsemen of the Apocalypse.* Death, accompanied by his trusty companions War, Famine, and Conflict, takes his merciless ride of destruction. The narrow victory of life over death that prevails in normal times is being undone.

In the eighteenth century, the population of Europe began to grow markedly. This increase in numbers occurred in all areas of Europe: western and eastern, northern and southern, dynamic and stagnant. Growth was especially dramatic after about 1750, as Figure 19.2 shows. Why was this so? In some areas some women did have more babies than before because new opportunities for employment in rural industry allowed them to marry at an earlier age, as we shall see (pages 633–634). But the basic cause for Europe as a whole was a decline in mortality—fewer deaths.

The bubonic plague mysteriously disappeared. After the Black Death in the fourteenth century, plagues had remained a part of the European experience, striking again and again with savage force, particularly in towns. As late as 1720 an epidemic swept southern France, killing one-third, one-half, even three-fourths of those in the larger towns. Once again an awful fear swept across Europe. But the epidemic passed, and that was the last time plague fell on western and central Europe. The final disappearance of plague was due in part to stricter measures of quarantine in plague-prone Mediterranean ports and along the Austrian border with Turkey. Chance and plain good luck were more important, however.

After 1600, for reasons unknown, a new rat of Asiatic origin—the brown, or wander, rat—began to drive out and eventually eliminate the black rat whose flea is the principal carrier of the plague bacillus. Although the brown rat also carries the plague bacillus, another kind of flea is its main parasite. That flea carries the plague poorly and, for good measure, has little taste for human blood.

Advances in medical knowledge did not contribute much to reducing the death rate in the eighteenth century (see pages 642–645). However, improvements in the water supply and sewerage promoted somewhat better public health and helped reduce such diseases as typhoid and typhus in some urban areas of western Europe. These improvements and the drainage of many swamps and marshes reduced the large population of flies and mosquitoes that helped spread serious epidemics and common diseases, especially those striking children and young adults.

Human beings also became more successful in their efforts to safeguard the supply of food and protect against famine. The eighteenth century was a time of considerable canal and road building in western Europe. These advances in transportation, which were among the more positive aspects of strong absolutist states, lessened the impact of local crop failure and famine. Emergency supplies could be brought in. The age-old spectacle of localized starvation became less frequent. Wars became more gentlemanly and less destructive than in the seventeenth century and spread fewer epidemics. New foods, particularly the potato from South America, were introduced. In short, population grew in the eighteenth century primarily because years of abnormal death rates were less catastrophic. Famines, epidemics, and wars continued to occur, but their severity moderated.

The growth of population in the eighteenth century cannot be interpreted as a sign of human progress, however. Serious population pressures on resources were in existence by 1600 and continued throughout the seventeenth and eighteenth cen-

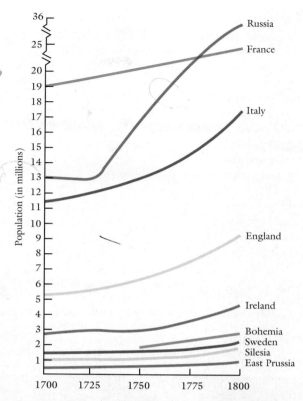

FIGURE 19.2   The Increase of Population in Europe in the Eighteenth Century   France's large population continued to support French political and intellectual leadership. Russia emerged as Europe's most populous state because natural increase was complemented by growth from territorial expansion.

turies. Only so much land was available, and tradition slowed the adoption of better farming methods. Thus agriculture could not provide enough work for the rapidly growing labor force, and poor people in the countryside had to look for new ways to make a living.

The Growth of Cottage Industry

The growth of population increased the number of rural workers with little or no land and this in turn contributed to the development of industry in rural areas. To be sure, peasant communities had always made some clothing, processed some food, and constructed some housing for their own use. But in the Middle Ages, peasants did not produce manufactured goods on a large scale for sale in a market. Instead, industry was dominated and organized by urban craft guilds and urban merchants, who jealously regulated handicraft production and sought to maintain it as an urban monopoly. By the eighteenth century, however, the pressures of rural poverty and the need for employment in the countryside had proved too great, and a new system was expanding lustily.

The new system had many names. It has often been called "cottage industry" or "domestic industry," to distinguish it from the factory industry that came later. In recent years, some scholars have preferred to speak of "protoindustrialization," by which they usually mean a stage of rural industrial development with wage workers and hand tools that necessarily preceded the emergence of large-scale factory industry. This focus has sparked renewed interest in Europe's early industrial development and shown again that the mechanized factories grew out of a vibrant industrial tradition. However, the evolving concept of protoindustrialization has different versions; thus the phrase "putting-out system," widely used by contemporaries to describe the key features of eighteenth-century rural industry, still seems an appropriate term for the new form of industrial production.

The two main participants in the *putting-out system* were the merchant-capitalist and the rural worker. The merchant loaned or "put out" raw materials—raw wool, for example—to several cottage workers. Those workers processed the raw material in their own homes, spinning and weaving the wool into cloth in this case, and returned the finished product to the merchant. The merchant

❅ **The Weaver's Repose**   This painting by Decker Cornelis Gerritz (1594–1637) captures the pleasure of release from long hours of toil in cottage industry. The loom realistically dominates the cramped living space and the family's modest possessions. *(Source: Musées Royaux des Beaux-Arts, Brussels. Copyright A.C.I.)*

then paid the workers by the piece and sold the finished products. There were endless variations on this basic relationship. Sometimes rural workers would buy their own materials and work as independent producers before they delivered finished goods to the merchant. Sometimes several workers toiled together in a workshop to perform a complicated process. The relative importance of earnings from the land and from industry varied greatly for handicraft workers. In all cases, however, the putting-out system was a kind of capitalism. Merchants sold finished goods in distant markets, seeking to make profits and increase their capital in their businesses.

The putting-out system grew because it offered competitive advantages. Underemployed rural labor was abundant, and poor peasants and landless laborers would work for low wages. Since production in the countryside did not need to meet rigid guild standards, which maintained quality but discouraged the development of new methods, workers and merchants could change procedures and experiment as they saw fit. Textiles and all manner of everyday articles such as knives, forks, housewares, buttons and gloves, and clocks and musical instruments could be produced quite satisfactorily in the countryside.

Rural manufacturing did not spread across Europe at an even rate. It appeared first in England and developed most successfully there, particularly for the spinning and weaving of woolen cloth. Continental countries developed rural industry more slowly. In France at the time of Louis XIV, Colbert had revived the urban guilds and used them as a means to control the cities and collect taxes (see page 562). But the pressure of rural poverty proved too great. In 1762 the special privileges of urban manufacturing were severely restricted in France, and the already-developing rural industries were given free rein from then on. Thus in France, as in Germany and other areas, the later part of the eighteenth century witnessed a remarkable expansion of rural industry in certain densely populated regions (Map 19.1). The pattern established in England was spreading to the European continent.

Cottage industry, like peasant agriculture from which it evolved, was based on family enterprise. All the members of the family helped in the work, especially in textiles, the most important cottage industry. Children and aged relatives carded and combed the cotton or wool, women and older

daughters spun the thread, and the man of the house wove the cloth. The availability of work for everyone, even the youngest, encouraged cottage workers to marry early and have large families. After the dirt was beaten out of the raw material, for example, it had to be thoroughly cleaned with strong soap in a tub, where tiny feet took the place of the agitator in a washing machine. A famous English textile inventor recalled that "soon after I was able to walk I was employed in the cotton manufacture. . . . My mother tucked up my petticoats about my waist, and put me into the tub to tread upon the cotton at the bottom."[1] Each family member had a task, and family life overlapped with the work experience.

 MARRIAGE AND THE FAMILY

The family is the basic unit of social organization. It is within the structure of the family that human beings love, mate, and reproduce themselves. It is primarily the family that teaches each child, imparting values and customs that condition an individual's behavior for a lifetime. The family is also an institution woven into the web of history.

Extended and Nuclear Families

In many traditional Asian and African societies, the typical family has often been an extended family. A newly married couple, instead of establishing a home, goes to live with either the bride's or the groom's family. The wife and husband raise their children while living under the same roof with their own brothers and sisters, who may also be married. The extended family is a big, three- or four-generation clan, headed by a patriarch or perhaps a matriarch and encompassing everyone from the youngest infant to the oldest grandparent.

Extended families, it is often said, provide security for adults and children in traditional agrarian peasant economies. Everyone has a place within the extended family, from cradle to grave. Sociologists frequently assume that the extended family gives way to the nuclear family with the advent of industrialization and urbanization. In a society characterized by nuclear families, couples establish their own households when they marry, and they raise their children apart from their parents. A similar process has indeed been occurring in much of

interesting but not pertinant

MAP 19.1 Industry and Population in Eighteenth-Century Europe   The growth of cottage manufacturing in rural areas helped country people to increase their income and contributed to increases in the population. This putting-out system began in England. Most of the work was in the textile industry. Cottage industry was also strong in the Low Countries—modern-day Belgium and Holland.

Asia and Africa today. And since Europe was once agrarian and preindustrial, it has often been believed that the extended family must also have prevailed in Europe before being destroyed by the Industrial Revolution.

In recent years, innovative historians, analyzing previously neglected parish registers of births, deaths, and marriages, have greatly increased knowledge about the details of family life for the great majority of people before the nineteenth century. It seems clear that the extended, three-generation family was a rarity in western and central Europe by 1700. Indeed, the extended family may

never have been common in Europe, although it is hard to know about the early Middle Ages because relatively few records survive. When young European couples married, they normally established their own households and lived apart from their parents. When a three-generation household came into existence, it usually resulted from a parent moving in with a married child rather than a newly married couple moving in with either set of parents.

Most people did not marry young in the seventeenth and early eighteenth centuries. The average person, who was neither rich nor aristocratic, married surprisingly late, many years after reaching adulthood and many more after beginning to work. In one well-studied, apparently typical English village, both men and women married for the first time at an average age of twenty-seven or older in the seventeenth and eighteenth centuries. A similar pattern existed in early-eighteenth-century France. Moreover, a substantial portion of men and women never married at all.

The custom of late marriage in combination with a nuclear-family household was a distinctive characteristic of European society. It seems likely that the aggressiveness and creativity that have characterized European society have been due in part to a pattern of marriage and family that fosters and requires self-reliance and independence. In preindustrial western Europe in the sixteenth through eighteenth centuries, marriage normally joined a mature man and a mature woman—two adults who had already experienced a great deal of life and could transmit self-reliance and real skills to the next generation.

Why was marriage delayed? The main reason was that couples normally could not marry until they could support themselves economically. The land was still the main source of income. The peasant son often needed to wait until his father's death to inherit the family farm and marry his sweetheart. Similarly, the peasant daughter and her family needed to accumulate a small dowry to help her fiancé buy land or build a house.

There were also laws and community controls to temper impetuous love and physical attraction. In some areas, couples needed the legal permission or tacit approval of the local lord or landowner in order to marry, and poor couples had particular difficulty securing the approval of local officials. These officials believed that freedom to marry for the lower classes would mean more landless paupers, more abandoned children, and more money for welfare. Village elders often agreed. Thus prudence, law, and custom combined to postpone the march to the altar. This pattern helped society maintain some kind of balance between the number of people and the available economic resources.

Work Away from Home

Many young people worked within their families until they could start their own households. Boys plowed and wove; girls spun and tended the cows.

Many others left home temporarily to work elsewhere. In the towns, a lad might be apprenticed to a craftsman for seven or fourteen years to learn a trade. During that time, he would not be permitted to marry. In most trades he earned little and worked hard, but if he was lucky, he might eventually be admitted to a guild and establish his economic independence. More often, a young man would drift from one tough job to another: hired hand for a small farmer, wage laborer on a new road, carrier of water in a nearby town. He was always subject to economic fluctuations, and unemployment was a constant threat.

Girls also temporarily left their families to work, at an early age and in large numbers. The range of opportunities open to them was more limited, however. Service in another family's household was

Chardin: The Kitchen Maid   Lost in thought as she pauses in her work, perhaps this young servant is thinking about her village and loved ones there. Jean-Baptiste Chardin was one of eighteenth-century France's greatest painters. His scenes from everyday life provide valuable evidence for the historian. *(Source: National Gallery of Art, Washington, D.C. Samuel H. Kress Collection)*

by far the most common job, and even middle-class families often sent their daughters into service. Thus a few years away from home as a servant were often a normal part of growing up.

The legions of young servant girls worked hard but had little real independence. Sometimes the employer paid the girl's wages directly to her parents. Constantly under the eye of her mistress, the servant girl found her tasks were many—cleaning, shopping, cooking, caring for the baby. Often the work was endless, for there were no laws to limit exploitation. Rarely were girls so brutalized that they snapped under the strain of such treatment like Varka—the Russian servant girl in Anton Chekhov's chilling story "Sleepy"—who, driven beyond exhaustion, finally quieted her mistress's screaming child by strangling it in its cradle. But court records are full of complaints by servant girls of physical mistreatment by their mistresses. There were many others like the fifteen-year-old English girl in the early eighteenth century who told the judge that her mistress had not only called her "very opprobrious names, as Bitch, Whore and the like," but also "beat her without provocation and beyond measure."[2]

There was also the pressure of seducers and sexual attack. In theory, domestic service offered protection and security within a new family for a young girl leaving home. But in practice, she was often the easy prey of a lecherous master or his sons or his friends. Indeed, "the evidence suggests that in all European countries, from Britain to Russia, the upper classes felt perfectly free to exploit sexually girls who were at their mercy."[3] If the girl became pregnant, she was quickly fired and thrown out in disgrace to make her own way. Prostitution and petty thievery were often the harsh consequences of unwanted pregnancy. "What are we?" exclaimed a bitter Parisian prostitute. "Most of us are unfortunate women, without origins, without education, servants and maids for the most part."[4]

Premarital Sex and Community Controls

Did the plight of some former servant girls mean that late marriage in preindustrial Europe went hand in hand with premarital sex and many illegitimate children? For most of western and central Europe until at least 1750, the answer seems to have been no. English parish registers seldom listed more than one bastard out of every twenty children baptized. Some French parishes in the seventeenth century had extraordinarily low rates of illegitimacy: less than 1 percent of all babies were born out of wedlock. Illegitimate babies were apparently a rarity, at least as far as the official church records are concerned.

At the same time, premarital sex was clearly commonplace. In one well-studied English village, 33 percent of all first children were conceived before the couple was married, and many were born within three months of the marriage ceremony. In the mid-eighteenth century, 20 percent of the French women in the village of Auffay, in Normandy, were pregnant when they got married, although only 2 percent of all babies in the village were born to unwed mothers.

The combination of very low rates of illegitimate birth and large numbers of pregnant brides reflected the powerful social controls of the traditional village. The prospect of an unwed (and therefore poor) mother with an illegitimate child was inevitably viewed as a grave threat to the economic, social, and moral stability of the closely knit community. Irate parents and anxious village elders, indignant priests and authoritative landlords, all combined to pressure any young people who wavered about marriage in the face of unexpected pregnancy. In the countryside, premarital sex was not entered into lightly, and it was generally limited to those contemplating marriage.

The concerns of the village and the family weighed heavily on most aspects of a couple's life, both before and after marriage. One leading authority describes the traditional French peasant household in these terms:

The individuality of the couple, or rather, its tendency towards individuality, was crushed by the family institutions, and also by the social pressures exercised by the village community as a whole, and by the neighborhood in particular. Anything that might endanger the [couple's] household might also prejudice the village community, and the community reacted, occasionally violently, to punish those who contravened the rules. The intrusion of the community into every aspect of family life was very noticeable.[5]

Thus whereas uninvolved individuals today are inclined to ignore the domestic disputes and marital scandals of others, the people in peasant communities gave such affairs the loudest and most unfavorable publicity, either at the time of the event or during the Carnival season (see page 000). Re-

David Allan: The Penny Wedding (1775)   The spirited merry-making of a peasant wedding was a popular theme of European artists. In rural Scotland "penny weddings" were common. Guests paid a fee for the food and fun; the money left over went to the newlyweds to help them get started. The dancing, feasting, and drinking that took place at these community parties led the stern elders of the Presbyterian church to oppose them and hastened their decline. (*Source: National Gallery of Scotland*)

lying on degrading public rituals, the young men of the village would typically gang up on the person they wanted to punish and force him or her to sit astride a donkey facing backward and holding up the donkey's tail. They would parade the overly brutal spouse-beating husband (or wife), or the couple whose adultery had been discovered, all around the village, loudly proclaiming the offender's misdeeds with scorn and ridicule. The donkey ride and similar colorful humiliations ranging from rotten vegetables splattered on the doorstep to obscene and insulting midnight serenades were common punishments throughout much of Europe. They epitomized the community's far-reaching effort to police personal behavior and maintain community standards.

Community controls did not extend to family planning, however. Once a man and woman married they generally had several children. Birth con-

trol within marriage was not unknown in western and central Europe before the nineteenth century, but it was primitive and quite undependable. The most common method was *coitus interruptus*—withdrawal by the male before ejaculation. Mechanical and other means of contraception were also used in the eighteenth century, but mainly by certain sectors of the urban population. The "fast set" of London used the "sheath" regularly, though primarily to protect against venereal disease, not pregnancy. Prostitutes used various contraceptive techniques to prevent pregnancy, and such information was available in large towns if a person really sought it.

New Patterns of Marriage and Illegitimacy

In the second half of the eighteenth century, the pattern of late marriage and few births out of wedlock began to change and break down. The number of illegitimate births soared between about 1750 and 1850 as much of Europe experienced an "illegitimacy explosion." In Frankfurt, Germany, for example, illegitimate births rose steadily from about 2 percent of all births in the early 1700s to a peak of about 25 percent around 1850. In Bordeaux, France, 36 percent of all babies were being born out of wedlock by 1840. Small towns and villages experienced less startling climbs, but increases from a range of 1 to 3 percent initially to 10 to 20 percent between 1750 and 1850 were commonplace. Fewer young women were abstaining from premarital intercourse, and, more important, fewer young men were marrying the women they got pregnant. Thus a profound sexual and cultural transformation took place.

Historians are still debating the meaning of this transformation, but two interrelated ideas dominate most interpretations. First, the growth of cottage industry created new opportunities for earning a living, opportunities not tied to the land. Young people attained greater independence and did not have to wait to inherit a farm in order to get married and have children. A scrap of ground for a garden and a cottage for the loom and spinning wheel could be quite enough for a modest living. These circumstances worked against the businesslike, calculating peasant marriage that was often dictated by the needs of the couple's families. After 1750, courtship became more extensive and freer as cottage industry grew. It was easier to yield to the attraction of the opposite sex and fall in love. Sexual activity might follow, and in most cases marriage for love rather than economic considerations also did, as cottage workers blazed a path that factory workers would follow in the nineteenth century.

Second, the needs of a growing population sent many young villagers to towns and cities in search of temporary or permanent employment. Mobility in turn encouraged new sexual and marital relationships, which were less subject to village tradition and resulted in more illegitimate births. Yet most young women in urban areas found work only as servants or textile workers. Poorly paid, insecure, and with little possibility of living truly independent, "liberated" lives, they looked mainly to marriage and family life as an escape from hard work and as the foundation of a satisfying life.

Promises of marriage from a man of the working girl's own class led naturally enough to sex, which was widely viewed as part of serious courtship. In one medium-size French city from 1787 to 1788, the great majority of unwed mothers stated that sexual intimacy had followed promises of marriage. Their sisters in rural Normandy reported again and again that they had been "seduced in anticipation of marriage."[6] Many soldiers, day laborers, and male servants were no doubt sincere in their proposals. But their lives were also insecure, and many hesitated to take on the heavy economic burdens of wife and child.

Thus it became increasingly difficult for a woman to convert pregnancy into marriage, and in a growing number of cases the intended marriage did not take place. The romantic yet practical dreams and aspirations of many young working men and women in towns and villages were frustrated by low wages, inequality, and changing economic and social conditions. Old patterns of marriage and family were breaking down among the common people. Only in the late nineteenth century would more stable patterns reappear.

 ## CHILDREN AND EDUCATION

In the traditional framework of agrarian Europe, women married late but then began bearing children rapidly. If a woman married before she was thirty, and if both she and her husband lived to forty-five, the chances were roughly one in two that she would give birth to six or more children. The newborn child entered a dangerous world. Infant mortality was high. One in five was sure to die, and one in three was quite likely to die in the poorest areas. Newborn children were very likely to catch mysterious infectious diseases of the chest and stomach, and many babies died of dehydration brought about by a bad bout of ordinary diarrhea. Even in rich families little could be done for an ailing child. Childhood itself was dangerous because of adult indifference, neglect, and even abuse.

Schools and formal education played only a modest role in the lives of ordinary children, and many boys and many more girls never learned to read. Nevertheless, basic literacy was growing among the popular classes, whose reading habits have been intensively studied in recent years. Attempting to peer into the collective attitudes of the common people and compare them with those of the book-hungry cultivated public, historians have produced some fascinating insights.

Child Care and Nursing

Women of the lower classes generally breast-fed their infants and for a much longer period than is customary today. Breast-feeding decreases the likelihood of pregnancy for the average woman by delaying the resumption of ovulation. By nursing their babies, women limited their fertility and spaced their children—from two to three years apart. If a newborn baby died, nursing stopped and a new life could be created. Nursing also saved lives: an infant who was breast-fed and received precious immunity-producing substances with its mother's milk was more likely to survive than an infant who was given any other food. In many areas of Russia, where the common practice was to give a new child a sweetened (and germ-laden) rag to suck on for its subsistence, half of the babies did not survive the first year.

In contrast to the laboring poor, the women of the aristocracy and upper middle class seldom nursed their own children. The upper-class woman felt that breast-feeding was crude, common, and undignified. Instead, she hired a wet nurse to suckle her child. The urban mother of more modest means—the wife of a shopkeeper or an artisan—also commonly used a wet nurse in order to facilitate full-time work in the shop.

Wet-nursing was a very widespread and flourishing business in the eighteenth century, a dismal business within the framework of the putting-out system. The traffic was in babies rather than in wool and cloth, and two or three years often passed before the wet-nurse worker finished her task. In the process the poor wet-nurse worker was often exploited and abused. For example, she had little contact with the family that hired her and could be dismissed on a whim by the mother or the family doctor.

Many observers stressed the flaws of wet nurses. It was a common belief that with her milk a nurse passed her bad traits to a baby. When a child turned out poorly, it was assumed that "the nurse had changed it." Many observers charged that nurses were often negligent and greedy. They claimed that there were large numbers of "killing nurses" with whom no child ever survived. Such a

nurse let a child die quickly so that she could take another child and another fee.

Foundlings and Infanticide

In the ancient world it was not uncommon to allow or force newborn babies, particularly girl babies, to die when there were too many mouths to feed. To its great and eternal credit, the early medieval church, strongly influenced by Jewish law, denounced infanticide as a pagan practice and insisted that every human life was sacred. The willful destruction of newborn children became a crime

✳ **Abandoned Children** At this Italian foundlings' home a frightened mother could discreetly deposit her baby on a revolving table, turn the table to move the baby into the home, and hurry away without being seen. (*Source: The Bettmann Archive*)

punishable by death. And yet, as the previous reference to killing nurses suggests, direct and indirect methods of eliminating unwanted babies did not disappear. There were, for example, many cases of "overlaying"—parents rolling over and suffocating the child placed between them in their bed. Such parents claimed they had been drunk and had acted unintentionally. In Austria in 1784, suspicious authorities made it illegal for parents to take children under five into bed with them. Severe poverty, on the one hand, and increasing illegitimacy, on the other, conspired to force the very poor to thin their own ranks.

The young girl—very likely a servant—who could not provide for her child had few choices. If she would not have an abortion or employ the services of a killing nurse, she could bundle up her baby and leave it on the doorstep of a church. In the late seventeenth century, Saint Vincent de Paul was so distressed by the number of babies brought to the steps of Notre Dame in Paris that he established a home for foundlings. Others followed his example. In England the government acted on a petition calling for a foundling hospital "to prevent the frequent murders of poor, miserable infants at birth" and "to suppress the inhuman custom of exposing newborn children to perish in the streets."

In much of Europe in the eighteenth century, foundling homes emerged as a favorite charity of the rich and powerful. Great sums were spent on them. The foundling home in St. Petersburg, perhaps the most elaborate and lavish of its kind, occupied the former palaces of two members of the high nobility. In the early nineteenth century it had twenty-five thousand children in its care and was receiving five thousand new babies a year. At their best, foundling homes in the eighteenth century were a good example of Christian charity and social concern in an age of great poverty and inequality.

Yet the foundling home was no panacea. By the 1770s one-third of all babies born in Paris were immediately abandoned to the foundling home by their mothers. Fully one-third of all those foundlings were abandoned by married couples, a powerful commentary on the standard of living among the working poor, for whom an additional mouth to feed often meant tragedy.

Furthermore, great numbers of babies entered the foundling homes, but few left. Even in the best of these homes, 50 percent of the babies normally died within a year. In the worst, fully 90 percent did not survive. They succumbed to long journeys over rough roads, the intentional and unintentional neglect of their wet nurses, and the customary childhood illnesses. So great was the carnage that some contemporaries called the foundling hospitals "legalized infanticide."

Attitudes Toward Children

What were the typical circumstances of children's lives? Did the treatment of foundlings reflect the attitudes of typical parents? Although some scholars argue otherwise, it seems that the young child was often of little concern to its parents and to society in the eighteenth century. This indifference toward children was found in all classes; rich children were by no means exempt. The practice of using wet nurses, who were casually selected and often negligent, is one example of how even the rich and the prosperous put the child out of sight and out of mind. One French moralist, writing in 1756 about how to improve humanity, observed that "one blushes to think of loving one's children." It has been said that the English gentleman of the period "had more interest in the diseases of his horses than of his children."[7]

Feelings toward children were greatly influenced by the terrible frequency of death among children of all classes. Doctors and clergymen urged parents not to become too emotionally involved with their children, who were so unlikely to survive. Mothers especially did not always heed such warnings, but the risk of emotional devastation was very real for them. The great eighteenth-century English historian Edward Gibbon (1737–1794) wrote that "the death of a new born child before that of its parents may seem unnatural but it is a strictly probable event, since of any given number the greater part are extinguished before the ninth year, before they possess the faculties of the mind and the body." Gibbon's father named all his boys Edward after himself, hoping that at least one of them would survive to carry his name. His prudence was not misplaced. Edward the future historian and eldest survived. Five brothers and sisters who followed him all died in infancy.

The medical establishment was seldom interested in the care of children. One contemporary observer quoted a famous doctor as saying that "he never wished to be called to a young child because he was really at a loss to know what to offer for it." There were "physicians of note who make no scruple to assert that there is nothing to be done for children when they are ill." The best hope for children was often treatment by women healers and midwives, who helped many women deliver their babies and provided advice on child care. Nevertheless, children were still caught in a vicious circle: they were neglected because they were very likely to die, and they were likely to die because they were neglected.

Emotional detachment from children often shaded off into abuse. When parents and other adults did turn toward children, it was normally to discipline and control them. The novelist Daniel Defoe (1660?–1731), who was always delighted when he saw very young children working hard in cottage industry, coined the axiom "Spare the rod and spoil the child." He meant it. So did Susannah Wesley (1669–1742), mother of John Wesley, the founder of Methodism. According to her, the first task of a parent toward her children was "to conquer the will, and bring them to an obedient temper." She reported that her babies were "taught to fear the rod, and to cry softly."[8]

It was hardly surprising that when English parish officials dumped their paupers into the first factories late in the eighteenth century, the children were beaten and brutalized. That was part of the child-rearing pattern—considerable indifference, on the one hand, and strict physical discipline, on the other—that prevailed throughout most of the eighteenth century.

From the middle of the century, this pattern came under increasing attack and began to change. Critics, led by Jean-Jacques Rousseau in his famous treatise *Emile* (see Listening to the Past), called for greater love, tenderness, and understanding toward children. In addition to supporting foundling homes to discourage infanticide and urging wealthy women to nurse their own babies, these new voices ridiculed the practice of swaddling: wrapping youngsters in tight-fitting clothes and blankets was generally believed to form babies properly by "straightening them out." By the end of the eighteenth century, small children were often being dressed in simpler, more comfortable clothing, allowing much greater freedom of movement. More parents expressed a delight in the love and intimacy of the child and found real pleasure in raising their offspring. These changes were part of the general growth of humanitarianism and cautious optimism about human potential that characterized the eighteenth-century Enlightenment.

Schools and Popular Literature

The role of schools and formal education outside the home was also growing more important. The aristocracy and the rich had led the way in the sixteenth century with special colleges, often run by Jesuits. But schools charged specifically with elementary education of the children of the common people usually did not appear until the seventeenth century. Unlike medieval schools, which mingled all age groups, these elementary schools specialized in boys and girls from seven to twelve, who were instructed in basic literacy and religion. The growth of popular education quickened in the eighteenth century, but there was no revolutionary acceleration, and many common people received no formal education.

Prussia led the way in the development of universal education, inspired by the old Protestant idea that every believer should be able to read and study the Bible in the quest for personal salvation and by the new idea of a population capable of effectively serving the state. As early as 1717, Prussia made attendance at elementary schools compulsory, and more Protestant German states, such as Saxony and Württemberg, followed in the eighteenth century. Religious motives were also extremely important elsewhere. From the middle of the seventeenth century, Presbyterian Scotland was convinced that the path to salvation lay in careful study of the Scriptures, and it established an effective network of parish schools for rich and poor alike. The Church of England and the dissenting congregations established "charity schools" to instruct the children of the poor, and in 1682 France began setting up Christian schools to teach the catechism and prayers as well as reading and writing. In 1774 Habsburg empress Maria Theresa established a general system of elementary education that called for compulsory education and a school in every community. Thus some elementary education was becoming a reality for European peoples, and schools were of growing significance in the life of the child.

The result of these efforts was a remarkable growth in basic literacy between 1600 and 1800, especially after 1700. Whereas in 1600 only one male in six was barely literate in France and Scotland, and one in four in England, by 1800 almost nine out of ten Scottish males, two out of three males in France, and more than half of English males were literate. In all three countries the bulk of the jump occurred in the eighteenth century. Women were also increasingly literate, although they lagged behind men in most countries.

The growth in literacy promoted a growth in reading, and historians have carefully examined what the common people read in an attempt to discern what they were thinking. One thing seems certain: the major philosophical works of the Enlightenment had little impact on peasants and workers, who could neither afford nor understand those favorites of the book-hungry educated public.

Although the Bible remained the overwhelming favorite, especially in Protestant countries, the staple of popular literature was short pamphlets known as chapbooks. Printed on the cheapest paper available, many chapbooks dealt with religious subjects. They featured Bible stories, prayers, devotions, and the lives of saints and other exemplary Christians. Promising happiness after death, devotional literature was also intensely practical. It gave the believer moral teachings and a confidence in God that helped in daily living.

Entertaining, often humorous stories formed a second element of popular literature. Fairy tales, medieval romances, fictionalized history, and fantastic adventures—these were some of the delights that filled the peddler's pack as he approached a village. Both heroes and villains possessed superhuman powers in this make-believe world, a world of

A Peasant Family Reading the Bible   Praised by the philosophe Diderot for its moralistic message, this engraving of a painting by Jean-Baptiste Greuze (1725–1805) captures the power of sacred texts and the spoken word. The peasant patriarch reads aloud from the massive family Bible, and the close-knit circle of absorbed listeners concentrates on every word. Only the baby is distracted by the dog. *(Source: Bibliothèque Nationale/Giraudon/Art Resource, NY)*

danger and magic, of fairy godmothers and evil trolls. But the good fairies always triumphed over the evil ones in the story's marvelous resolution. The significance of these entertaining stories for the peasant reader is not clear, however. Many scholars see them reflecting a desire for pure escapism and a temporary flight from harsh everyday reality. Others see these tales reflecting ancient folk wisdom and counseling prudence in a world full of danger and evil, where wolves dress up like grandmothers and eat Little Red Riding Hoods.

Some popular literature was highly practical, dealing with rural crafts, household repairs, useful plants, and similar matters. Much of such lore was stored in almanacs. With calendars listing secular, religious, and astrological events mixed in with agricultural schedules, bizarre bits of information, and jokes, the almanac was universal, noncontroversial, and highly appreciated, even by many in the comfortable classes. "Anyone who could would read an almanac."[9]

In general, however, the reading of the common people had few similarities with that of educated elites. Popular literature was simple and it was practical, both as devotional self-help and as how-to instruction. It was also highly escapist. Yet the common people were apparently content with works that reinforced traditional values and did not foster social or religious criticism. These results fit well with the modest educational objectives of rulers and educated elites. They believed that carefully limited instruction stressing religion and morals was useful to the masses and that too much study would disorient them and foster discontent.

❋ FOOD AND MEDICAL PRACTICE

The European population increased rapidly in the eighteenth century. Plague and starvation gradually disappeared, and Europeans lived longer lives. What were the characteristics of diets and nutrition in this era of improving health and longevity? Although it played only a small part, what was medical practice like in the eighteenth century? What does a comparison of rich and poor reveal?

Diets and Nutrition

At the beginning of the eighteenth century, ordinary men and women depended on grain as fully as they had in the past. Bread was quite literally the staff of life. Peasants in the Beauvais region of France ate two pounds of bread a day, washing it down with water, green wine, beer, or a little skimmed milk. Their dark bread was made from a mixture of roughly ground wheat and rye—the standard flour of the common people. The poor also ate grains in soup and gruel. In rocky northern Scotland, for example, people depended on oatmeal, which they often ate half-cooked so that it would swell in their stomachs and make them feel full.

Not surprisingly, an adequate supply of grain and an affordable price for bread loomed in the popular imagination. Peasants, landless laborers, and urban workers all believed in the old medieval idea of the "just price"—that is, a price that was "fair" to both consumers and producers. But in the later eighteenth century, this traditional, moral view of prices and the economy clashed repeatedly with the emerging free-market philosophy of unregulated supply and demand, which government officials, large landowners, and early economists increasingly favored. In years of poor harvests and soaring prices, this clash often resulted in food riots and popular disturbances. Peasants and workers would try to stop wagons loaded with grain from leaving their region, or they would seize grain held by speculators and big merchants accused of hoarding and rigging the market. (Usually the tumultuous crowd paid what it considered to be a fair price for what it took.) Governments were keenly aware of the problem of adequate grain supplies, and they would sometimes try to control prices to prevent unrest in crisis years.

Although breadstuffs were all-important for the rural and urban poor, they also ate a fair quantity of vegetables. Indeed, vegetables were considered "poor people's food." Peas and beans were probably the most common and were eaten fresh in late spring and summer. Dried, they became the basic ingredients in the soups and stews of the long winter months. In most regions, other vegetables appeared in season on the tables of the poor—primarily cabbages, carrots, and wild greens. Fruit was uncommon and limited to the summer months.

The common people of Europe loved meat and eggs, but they seldom ate their fill. Indeed, as the population surged in the sixteenth century, meat became more expensive, and the poor ate less meat in 1700 than in 1500. Moreover, in most European countries harsh game laws deprived the poor of the right to hunt and eat edible game such as rabbits, deer, and partridges. Only nobles and large landowners could legally kill game. Few laws were more bitterly resented—or more frequently broken—by ordinary people than those governing hunting.

Milk was rarely drunk. Perhaps because some individuals do suffer seriously from dairy allergies, it was widely believed that milk caused sore eyes, headaches, and a variety of ills, except among the very young and very old. Milk was used primarily to make cheese and butter, which the poor liked but could afford only occasionally. Medical and popular opinion considered whey, the watery liquid left after milk was churned, "an excellent temperate drink."

The diet of the rich—aristocrats, officials, and the comfortable bourgeoisie—was traditionally quite different from that of the poor. The men and women of the upper classes were rapacious carnivores. A truly elegant dinner among the great and powerful consisted of one rich meat after another: a chicken pie, a leg of lamb, a grilled steak, for example, perhaps followed by three fish courses, all complemented with sweets, cheeses, and nuts of all kinds. Fruits and vegetables were not often found on the tables of the rich.

There was also an enormous amount of overdrinking among the rich. The English squire who loved to hunt with his hounds loved to drink with a similar passion. With his dinner he drank red wine from France or white wine from the Rhineland, and with his dessert he took sweet but strong port or Madeira from Portugal. Sometimes he ended the evening under the table in a drunken stupor.

The diet of small traders, master craftsmen, minor bureaucrats—the people of the towns and cities—was generally less monotonous than that of the peasantry. The markets, stocked by market gardens on the outskirts, provided a substantial variety of meats, vegetables, and fruits, although bread and beans still formed the bulk of such families' diet.

There were also regional dietary differences in 1700. Generally speaking, northern, Atlantic Europe ate better than southern, Mediterranean Europe. The poor of England probably ate best of all. The Dutch were also considerably better fed than the average European, in large part because of their advanced agriculture and diversified gardens.

The Impact of Diet on Health

How were the poor and the rich served by their quite different diets? At first glance, the diet of the laboring poor, relying as it did on grains and vegetables, might seem low in protein. However, the whole-grain wheat or rye flour used in eighteenth-century bread retained most of the bran—the ground-up husk—and the all-important wheat germ, which contains higher proportions of some minerals, vitamins, and good-quality proteins than does the rest of the grain. In addition, the field peas and beans eaten by poor people since the early Middle Ages contained protein that complemented the proteins in whole-grain bread. The proteins in whey, cheese, and eggs, which the poor ate at least occasionally, also supplemented the bread and vegetables.

The basic bread-and-vegetables diet of the poor *in normal times* was adequate. But a key dietary problem in some seasons, particularly in the late winter and early spring, was probably getting enough green vegetables (or milk) to ensure adequate supplies of vitamins A and C. A severe deficiency of vitamin C produces scurvy, a disease that leads to rotting gums, swelling of the limbs, and great weakness. Before the season's first vegetables, many people had used up their bodily reserves of vitamin C and were suffering from mild cases of scurvy. (Scurvy was an acute problem for sailors on long voyages and by the end of the sixteenth century was being controlled on ships by a daily ration of lime juice for crew members.)

The practice of gorging on meat, sweets, and spirits caused the rich their own nutritional problems. Because of their great disdain for fresh vegetables, they, too, were very often deficient in vitamins A and C. Gout was a common affliction of the overfed and underexercised rich. No wonder they were often caricatured as dragging their flabby limbs and bulging bellies to the table to stuff their swollen cheeks and poison their livers. People of moderate means, who could afford some meat and dairy products with fair regularity but who had not abandoned the bread and vegetables of the poor, were probably best off from a nutritional standpoint.

Patterns of food consumption changed rather markedly as the century progressed. More varied diets associated with new methods of farming were confined largely to the Low Countries and Eng-

Royal Interest in the Potato   Frederick the Great of Prussia, shown here supervising cultivation of the potato, used his influence and position to promote the new food on his estates and throughout Prussia. Peasants could grow potatoes with the simplest hand tools. But doing so was backbreaking labor, as this painting by R. Warthmüller suggests. *(Source: Private Collection, Hamburg/Archiv für Kunst und Geschichte, Berlin)*

land, but a new food—the potato—came to the aid of the poor everywhere. Introduced into Europe from the Americas—along with corn, squash, tomatoes, and many other useful plants—the humble potato is an excellent food. Containing a good supply of carbohydrates, calories, and vitamins A and C (especially if it is not overcooked and the skin is eaten), the potato offset the lack of vitamins from green vegetables in the poor person's winter and early spring diet, and it provided a much higher caloric yield than grain for a given piece of land.

For some desperately poor peasants who needed to get every possible calorie from a tiny plot of land, the potato replaced grain as the primary food in the eighteenth century. This happened first in Ireland, where English (Protestant) repression and exploitation forced large numbers of poor (and Catholic) peasants to live off tiny scraps of rented ground. Elsewhere in Europe, potatoes took hold

more slowly because many people did not like them. Thus potatoes were first fed to pigs and livestock, and there was even debate about whether they were fit for humans. In Germany the severe famines caused by the Seven Years' War settled the matter: potatoes were edible and not just "famine food." By the end of the century, the potato had become an important dietary supplement in much of Europe.

There was also a general growth of market gardening, and a greater variety of vegetables appeared in towns and cities. In the course of the eighteenth century, the large towns and cities of maritime Europe began to receive semitropical fruits, such as oranges and lemons, from Portugal and the West Indies, although they were not cheap.

Not all changes in the eighteenth century were for the better, however. Bread began to change, most noticeably for the English and for the comfortable groups on the European continent. Rising incomes and new tastes led to a shift from whole-grain black or brown bread to "bread as white as snow" and started a decline in bread's nutritional value. The high-roughage bran and some of the dark but high-vitamin germ were increasingly sifted out by millers. This foretold further "improvements" in the nineteenth century, which would leave bread perfectly white and greatly reduced in nutritional value.

Another sign of nutritional decline was the growing consumption of sugar. Initially a luxury, sugar dropped rapidly in price as slave-based production increased in the Americas, and the sweetener was much more widely used in the eighteenth century. This development probably led to an increase in cavities and to other ailments as well, although the greater or lesser poverty of the laboring poor still protected most of them from the sugar-tooth virus of the rich and well-to-do.

Medical Practitioners

Although sickness, pain, and disease—intractable challenges built into the human condition—permeated the European experience in the eighteenth century, medical science played a very small part in improving the health of most people. Yet the Enlightenment's growing focus on discovering the laws of nature and on human problems did give rise to a great deal of research and experimentation. The century also saw a remarkable rise in the number of medical practitioners, and a high value was placed on their services. Therefore, when the great breakthroughs in knowledge came in the middle and late nineteenth century, they could be rapidly evaluated and diffused.

Care of the sick in the eighteenth century was the domain of several competing groups: faith healers, apothecaries (or pharmacists), surgeons, and physicians. Since the great majority of common ailments have a tendency to cure themselves, each group could point to successes and win adherents. When a doctor's treatment made the patient worse, as it often did, the original medical problem could always be blamed.

Faith healers, who had been among the most important kinds of physicians in medieval Europe, remained active. They and their patients believed that demons and evil spirits caused disease by lodging in people and that the proper treatment was to exorcise, or drive out, the offending devil. This demonic view of disease was strongest in the countryside, where popular belief placed great faith in the healing power of religious relics, prayer, and the laying on of hands. Faith healing was particularly effective in the treatment of mental disorders such as hysteria and depression, where the link between attitude and illness is most direct.

Apothecaries sold a vast number of herbs, drugs, and patent medicines for every conceivable "temperament and distemper." Early pharmacists were seldom regulated, and they frequently diagnosed freely. Their prescriptions were incredibly complex—a hundred or more drugs might be included in a single prescription—and often very expensive. Some of the drugs and herbs undoubtedly worked. For example, strong laxatives were given to the rich for their constipated bowels. Indeed, the medical profession continued to believe that regular "purging" of the bowels was essential for good health and the treatment of illness. Much purging was harmful, however, and only bloodletting for the treatment of disease was more effective in speeding patients to their graves.

Surgeons, in contrast, made considerable medical and social progress. Long considered as ordinary artisans comparable to butchers and barbers, surgeons began studying anatomy seriously and improved their art. With endless opportunities to practice, army surgeons on gory battlefields led the way. They learned that a soldier with an extensive wound, such as a shattered leg or arm, could perhaps be saved if the surgeon could obtain above the wound a flat surface that could be cauterized with fire. Thus if a soldier (or a civilian) had a broken limb and the bone stuck out, the surgeon amputated so that the remaining stump could be cauterized and the likelihood of death reduced.

The eighteenth-century surgeon (and patient) labored in the face of incredible difficulties. Almost all operations were performed without any painkiller, for the anesthesias of the day were hard to control and were believed too dangerous for general use. The terrible screams of people whose limbs were being sawed off echoed across battlefields and through hospitals. Many patients died from the agony and shock of such operations. Surgery was also performed in the midst of filth and dirt, for there simply was no knowledge of bacteriology and the nature of infection. The simplest wound treated by a surgeon could fester and lead to death.

Physicians, the fourth major group, were apprenticed in their teens to a practicing physician for several years of on-the-job training. This training was then rounded out with hospital work or some university courses. Because such prolonged training was expensive, physicians continued to come mainly from prosperous families, and they usually concentrated on urban patients from similar social backgrounds. They had little contact with urban workers and even less with peasants.

To their credit, physicians in the eighteenth century were increasingly willing to experiment with new methods, but time-honored practices lay heavily on them. Physicians, like apothecaries, laid great stress on purging. And bloodletting was still considered a medical cure-all. It was the way "bad blood," the cause of illness, was removed and the balance of humors necessary for good health was restored. According to a physician practicing medicine in Philadelphia in 1799, bleeding was proper at the onset of all inflammatory fevers, in all inflammations, and for "asthma, sciatic pains, coughs, head-aches, rheumatisms, the apoplexy, epilepsy, and bloody fluxes."[10] It was also necessary after all falls, blows, and bruises.

While ordinary physicians were bleeding, apothecaries purging, surgeons sawing, and faith healers praying, the leading medical thinkers were attempting to pull together and assimilate all the information and misinformation they had been accumulating. The attempt was ambitious: to systematize medicine around simple, basic principles, as Newton had done in physics. But the schools of thought resulting from such speculation and theorizing did little to improve medical care.

Hospitals and Medical Experiments

Hospitals were terrible places throughout most of the eighteenth century. There was no isolation of patients. Operations were performed in a patient's bed. Nurses were old, ignorant, greedy, and often drunk women. Fresh air was considered harmful, and infections of every kind were rampant. Diderot's article in the *Encyclopedia* on the Hôtel-Dieu in Paris, the "richest and most terrifying of all French hospitals," vividly describes normal conditions of the 1770s:

Imagine a long series of communicating wards filled with sufferers of every kind of disease who are some-times packed three, four, five or even six into a bed, the living alongside the dead and dying, the air polluted by this mass of unhealthy bodies, passing pestilential germs of their afflictions from one to the other, and the spectacle of suffering and agony on every hand. That is the Hôtel-Dieu.[11]

No wonder the poor of Paris hated hospitals and often saw confinement there as a plot to kill paupers.

In the last years of the century, the humanitarian concern already reflected in Diderot's description of the Hôtel-Dieu led to a movement for hospital reform throughout western Europe. Efforts were made to improve ventilation and eliminate filth in the belief that bad air caused disease. The theory was wrong, but the results were beneficial, for the spread of infection was somewhat reduced.

Mental hospitals, too, were incredibly savage institutions. The customary treatment for mental illness was bleeding and cold water, administered more to maintain discipline than to effect a cure. Violent persons were chained to the wall and forgotten. A breakthrough of sorts occurred in the 1790s when William Tuke founded the first humane sanatorium in England. In Paris an innovative warden, Philippe Pinel, took the chains off the mentally disturbed in 1793 and tried to treat them as patients rather than as prisoners.

In the eighteenth century, all sorts of wildly erroneous ideas about mental illness circulated. One was that moonlight caused madness, a belief reflected in the word *lunatic*—someone harmed by lunar light. Another mid-eighteenth-century theory, which lasted until at least 1914, was that masturbation caused madness, not to mention acne, epilepsy, and premature ejaculation. Thus parents, religious institutions, and schools waged relentless war on masturbation by males, although they were curiously uninterested in female masturbation.

In the second half of the eighteenth century, medicine in general turned in a more practical and experimental direction. Some of the experimentation was creative quackery involving the recently discovered phenomenon of electricity. One magnificent quack in London promoted sleep on a cure-all Celestial Bed, which was lavishly decorated with magnets and electrical devices. A single night on the bed cost a small fortune. The rich could buy expensive treatments, but the prevalence of quacks and the general lack of knowledge meant they often got little for their money. Because so

Hospital Life   Patients crowded into hospitals like this one in Hamburg in 1746 had little chance of recovery. A priest by the window administers last rites, while in the center a surgeon coolly saws off the leg of a man who has received no anesthesia. *(Source: Germanisches Nationalmuseum, Nuremberg)*

many treatments were harmful, the common people were probably much less deprived by their reliance on faith healers and folk medicine than one might think.

Experimentation and the intensified search for solutions to human problems led to some real advances in medicine after 1750, however. The eighteenth century's greatest medical triumph was the conquest of smallpox. With the progressive decline of bubonic plague, smallpox became the most terrible of the infectious diseases. In the words of historian Thomas Macaulay, "Smallpox was always present, filling the churchyard with corpses, tormenting with constant fears all whom it had not stricken." It is estimated that 60 million Europeans died of smallpox in the eighteenth century. Fully 80 percent of the population was stricken at some point in life, and 25 percent of the total population was left permanently scarred. If ever a human problem cried out for solution, it was smallpox.

Inoculation against smallpox was already practiced in China and the Muslim lands of western Asia. Something approaching mass inoculation took place in England in the 1760s and the practice spread to the continent of Europe. By the later years of the century, smallpox inoculation was playing some part in the decline of the death rate and the general increase in European population. However, the method of inoculation—using active smallpox to stimulate immunity—could cause a mild, and potentially infectious, case of the disease.

The final breakthrough against smallpox came at the end of the century. Edward Jenner (1749–1823), a talented country doctor, noted that in the English countryside there was a long-standing belief that dairy maids who had contracted cowpox did not get smallpox. Cowpox produces sores on the cow's udder and on the hands of the milker. The sores resemble those of smallpox, but the disease is mild and not contagious. In 1796, using matter taken from a milkmaid with cowpox, Jenner performed his first vaccination on a young boy. In the next two years, he performed twenty-three successful vaccinations and in 1798 published his findings. After Austrian medical authorities replicated Jenner's results, the new method of treatment spread rapidly. Smallpox soon declined to the point of disappearance in Europe and then throughout the world. For his great discovery, Jenner eventually received prizes totaling £30,000 from the British government, a fitting recompense for a man who gave an enormous gift to humanity and helped lay the foundation for the science of immunology in the nineteenth century.

✤ RELIGION AND POPULAR CULTURE

Though the critical spirit of the Enlightenment spread among the educated elite in the eighteenth century, the majority of ordinary men and women remained firmly committed to the Christian religion, especially in rural areas. Religion offered answers to life's mysteries and gave comfort and courage in the face of sorrow and fear. Religion also remained strong because it was usually embedded in local traditions, everyday social experience, and popular culture.

Yet the popular religion of village Europe was everywhere enmeshed in a larger world of church hierarchies and state power. These powerful outside forces sought to regulate religious life at the local level. Their efforts created tensions that helped set the scene for a vigorous religious revival in Germany and England. Similar tensions arose in Catholic countries, where powerful elites criticized and attacked popular religious practices that their increasingly rationalistic minds deemed foolish and superstitious.

The Institutional Church

As in the Middle Ages, the local parish church remained the basic religious unit all across Europe. Still largely coinciding with the agricultural village, the parish fulfilled many needs. Whether Catholic or Protestant, the parish church was the focal point of religious devotion and much more. Villagers came together at services and gossiped and swapped stories afterward, and neighbors joined in church for baptisms, marriages, funerals, and other special events. Thus the parish church was woven into the very fabric of community life.

Moreover, the local church had important administrative tasks. It is because priests and parsons kept such complete parish registers that historians have learned so much about population and family life. Parishes also normally distributed charity to the destitute, looked after orphans, and provided whatever primary education was available for the common people.

The many tasks of the local church were usually the responsibility of a resident priest or pastor, a full-time professional working with assistants and lay volunteers. All clerics—whether Roman Catholic, Protestant, or Orthodox—also shared the fate of middlemen in a complicated institutional system. Charged most often with ministering to poor peasants, the priest or parson was the last link in a powerful church-state hierarchy that was everywhere determined to control religion down to the grassroots. However, the regulatory framework of belief, which went back at least to the fourth century when Christianity became the official religion of the Roman Empire, had undergone important changes since 1500.

The Protestant Reformation had burst forth as a culmination of medieval religiosity and a desire to purify Christian belief. Martin Luther, the greatest of the reformers, preached that all men and women were saved from their sins and God's damnation only by personal faith in Jesus Christ. The individual could reach God directly, without need of priestly intermediaries. This was the revolutionary meaning of Luther's "priesthood of all believers," which broke forever the monopoly of the priestly class over medieval Europe's most priceless treasure—eternal salvation.

As the Reformation gathered force, with peasant upheaval and doctrinal competition, German princes and monarchs in northern Europe put themselves at the head of official churches in their territories. Protestant authorities, with generous assistance from state-certified theologians, then proceeded to regulate their "territorial churches" strictly, selecting personnel and imposing detailed rules. They joined with Catholics to crush the Anabaptists, who, with their belief in freedom of conscience and separation of church and state, had become the real revolutionaries. Thus the Reformation, initially so radical in its rejection of Rome and its stress on individual religious experience, eventually resulted in a bureaucratization of the church and local religious life in Protestant Europe.

The Reformation era also increased the practical power of Catholic rulers over "their" churches, but

❖ **A Religious Festival in Urban France**   This vibrant painting suggests how religious life interacted with powerful institutions in Catholic Europe. Moving past crowds and through the city, this procession is celebrating the Blessed Sacrament on the Feast of Corpus Christi (the Body of Christ). Church dignitaries are grouped in the center; the colorful nobility is on the left; and the middle orders, with their sober black suits, are on the right. Both participation and hierarchical inequality are the rule. (*Source: Bibliothèque des Arts Décoratifs/Jean-Loup Charmet*)

it was only in the eighteenth century that some Catholic monarchs began to impose striking reforms. These reforms, which had their counterparts in Orthodox Russia, had a very "Protestant" aspect. They increased state control over the Catholic church, making it less subject to papal influence. For instance, Spain, a deeply Catholic country with devout rulers, took firm control of ecclesiastical appointments. Papal proclamations could not even be read in Spanish churches without prior approval from the government. Spain also asserted state control over the Spanish Inquisition, which had been ruthlessly pursuing heresy as an independent agency under Rome's direction for two hundred years. In sum, Spain went far toward creating a "national" Catholic church, as France had done earlier.

Some Catholic rulers also turned their reforming efforts on certain religious orders and monasteries and convents. Following the earlier example of

Portugal, the French king ordered the politically influential Jesuits out of France in 1763 and confiscated their property. Believing that the large monastic clergy should make a more practical contribution to social and religious life, Maria Theresa of Austria (see page 000) sharply restricted entry into "unproductive" orders, and her son Joseph II abolished contemplative orders, henceforth permitting only orders that were engaged in teaching, nursing, or other practical work. The state also expropriated the dissolved monasteries and used their great wealth for charitable purposes and higher salaries for ordinary priests.

Protestant Revival

In their attempt to recapture the vital core of the Christian religion, the Protestant reformers had rigorously suppressed all the medieval practices that they considered nonessential or erroneous because they were not founded on Scripture. Relics and crucifixes had been permanently removed from crypt and altar. Stained-glass windows had been smashed, walls and murals covered with whitewash, and processions and pilgrimages eliminated. Such revolutionary changes had often troubled ordinary churchgoers, but by the late seventeenth century the vast reforms of the Reformation had been completed and thoroughly routinized in most Protestant churches.

Indeed, official Protestant churches had generally settled into a smug complacency. In the Reformation heartland, one concerned German minister wrote that the Lutheran church "had become paralyzed in forms of dead doctrinal conformity" and badly needed a return to its original inspiration.[12] This voice was one of many that would prepare and then guide a powerful Protestant revival, which was largely successful because it answered the intense but increasingly unsatisfied needs of common people.

The Protestant revival began in Germany. It was known as Pietism, and three aspects account for its powerful appeal. First, Pietism called for a warm, emotional religion that everyone could experience. Enthusiasm—in prayer, in worship, in preaching, in life itself—was the key concept. "Just as a drunkard becomes full of wine, so must the congregation become filled with spirit," declared one exuberant writer. Another said simply, "The heart must burn."[13]

Second, Pietism reasserted the earlier radical stress on the priesthood of all believers, thereby reducing the wide gulf between the official clergy and the Lutheran laity. Bible reading and study were enthusiastically extended to all classes, and this provided a powerful spur for popular education as well as individual religious development. Third, Pietists believed in the practical power of Christian rebirth in everyday affairs. Reborn Christians were expected to lead good, moral lives and come from all social classes.

Pietism had a major impact on John Wesley (1703–1791), who served as the catalyst for popular religious revival in England. Wesley, who came from a long line of ministers, mapped a fanatically earnest "scheme of religion." As a teaching fellow at Oxford University, he organized a Holy Club for similarly minded students. They were soon known contemptuously as "Methodists" because they were so methodical in their devotion. Yet like the young Luther, Wesley remained intensely troubled about his own salvation, even after his ordination as an Anglican priest in 1728.

Wesley's anxieties related to grave problems of the faith in England. The government shamelessly used the Church of England to provide favorites with high-paying jobs and sinecures. The building of churches practically stopped even though the population was growing and in many parishes there was a grave shortage of pews. Services and sermons had settled into an uninspiring routine, while the skepticism of the Enlightenment was making inroads among the educated classes and deism was becoming popular. Some bishops and church leaders acted as if they believed that doctrines such as the Virgin Birth or the Ascension were little more than elegant superstitions.

Spiritual counseling from a sympathetic Pietist minister from Germany prepared Wesley for a mystical, emotional "conversion" in 1738. He described this critical turning point in his *Journal:*

In the evening I went to a [Christian] society in Aldersgate Street where one was reading Luther's preface to the Epistle to the Romans. About a quarter before nine, while he was describing the change which God works in the heart through faith in Christ, I felt my heart strangely warmed. I felt I did trust in Christ, Christ alone for salvation; and an assurance was given me that he had taken away my sins, even mine, and saved me from the law of sin and death.[14]

Wesley's emotional experience resolved his intellectual doubts. Moreover, he was convinced that any person, no matter how poor or uneducated, might have a similarly heartfelt conversion and gain the same blessed assurance.

Wesley took the good news to the people, traveling some 225,000 miles by horseback and preaching more than forty thousand sermons in fifty years. Since existing churches were often overcrowded and the church-state establishment was hostile, Wesley preached in open fields. People came in large numbers. Of critical importance was Wesley's rejection of Calvinist predestination—the doctrine of salvation granted only to a select few. Expanding on earlier Dutch theologians' views, he preached that *all* men and women who earnestly sought salvation might be saved. It was a message of hope and joy, of free will and universal salvation. Wesley's ministry won converts and eventually resulted in a new denomination.

And as Wesley had been inspired by Pietist revival in Germany, so evangelicals in the Church of

A Midsummer Afternoon with a Methodist Preacher   This detail from a painting by Philippe de Loutherbourg portrays in a humorous manner how John Wesley and his followers took their optimistic Christianity to the people of England. Methodist ministers championed open-air preaching and week-long revivals. *(Source: Royal Ontario Museum)*

England and the old dissenting groups followed his example, giving impetus to an even broader awakening among the lower classes. In Protestant countries religion remained a vital force in the lives of the people.

Catholic Piety

Religion also flourished in Catholic Europe around 1700, but there were important differences with Protestant practice. First of all, the visual contrast was striking. Baroque artists had lavished rich and emotionally exhilarating figures and images on Catholic churches; Protestants excluded such works from their places of worship. Catholics in Europe remained intensely religious. More than 95 percent of the Catholic population probably attended church for Easter Communion, the climax of the Catholic church year.

The tremendous popular strength of religion in Catholic countries reflected religion's integral role in community life and popular culture. Thus although Catholics reluctantly confessed their sins to priests, they enthusiastically joined together in religious festivals to celebrate the passage of the liturgical year. In addition to the great processional days—such as Palm Sunday, the joyful re-enactment of Jesus' triumphal entry into Jerusalem, or Rogations, with its chanted supplications and penances three days before the bodily ascent of Jesus into heaven on Ascension Day—each parish had its own saints' days, processions, and pilgrimages. Led by its priest, a congregation might march around the village or across the countryside to a local shrine or chapel, perhaps closing the event with an enormous picnic. Before each procession or feast day, the priest explained its religious significance to kindle group piety. But processions were also part of folklore and tradition, an escape from work, and a form of recreation. A holiday atmosphere sometimes reigned on longer processions. People drank and danced, and couples disappeared into the woods. — *Woo hoo!*

Indeed, devout Catholics had many religious beliefs that were marginal to the Christian faith, often of obscure or even pagan origin. On the feast of Saint Anthony, for example, priests were expected to bless salt and bread for farm animals to protect them from disease. One saint's relics could help cure a child of fear, and there were healing springs for many ailments. Ordinary people combined a strong Christian faith with a wealth of time-honored superstitions.

Inspired initially by the fervor of the Catholic Counter-Reformation and then to some extent by the critical rationalism of the Enlightenment, parish priests and Catholic hierarchies sought increasingly to "purify" popular religious practice and to detach that purified religion from everyday life in the eighteenth century. Thus one parish priest in France lashed out at his parishioners, claiming that they were "more superstitious than devout . . . and sometimes appear as baptized idolators."[15] French priests particularly denounced the "various remnants of paganism" found in popular bonfire ceremonies during Lent in which young men, "yelling and screaming like madmen," tried to jump over the bonfires in order to help the crops grow and protect themselves from illness. One priest saw rational Christians regressing into pagan animals—"the triumph of Hell and the shame of Christianity."[16]

In contrast with Protestant reformers, who had already used the power of the territorial state to crush such practices, many Catholic priests and bishops preferred a compromise between theological purity and the people's piety, perhaps realizing that the line between divine truth and mere superstition is not easily drawn. Thus the severity of the formal attack on popular Catholicism varied widely by country and region. Where authorities pursued purification vigorously, as in Austria under Joseph II, pious peasants saw only an incomprehensible attack on the true faith and drew back in anger. Their reaction dramatized the growing tension between the educated elites and the common people.

Leisure and Recreation

The combination of religious celebration and popular recreation seen in festivals and processions was most strikingly displayed at Carnival, a time of reveling and excess in Catholic and Mediterranean Europe. Carnival preceded Lent—the forty days of fasting and penitence before Easter—and for a few days in January or February a wild release of drinking, masquerading, and dancing reigned. A combination of plays, processions, and rowdy spectacles turned the established order upside-down. Peasants became nobles, fools turned into philosophers, and the rich were humbled. These once-a-year rituals gave people a much-appreciated chance to release their pent-up frustrations and aggressions before life returned to the usual pattern of leisure and recreation.

That pattern featured socializing in groups, for despite the spread of literacy the culture of the common people was largely oral rather than written. In the cold dark winter months families gathered around the fireplace to talk, sing, tell stories, do craftwork, and keep warm. In some parts of Europe, women gathered together in groups in someone's cottage to chat, sew, spin, and laugh. Sometimes a few young men would be invited so that the daughters (and mothers) could size up potential suitors in a supervised atmosphere. A favorite recreation of men was drinking and talking with buddies in public places. It was a sorry village that had no tavern. In addition to old favorites such as beer and wine, the common people turned with gusto toward cheap and potent hard liquor, which in the eighteenth century fell in price because of the greatly improved techniques for distilling grain.

Towns and cities offered a wide range of amusements. Participants had to pay for many of these because the eighteenth century saw a sharp increase in the commercialization of leisure-time activities—a trend that continues to this day. Urban fairs featured prepared foods, acrobats, freak shows, open-air performances, optical illusions, and the like. Such entertainments attracted a variety of social classes. So did the growing number of commercial, profit-oriented spectator sports. These ranged from traveling circuses and horse races to boxing matches and bullfights. Sports heroes such as hefty heavyweight champions and haughty matadors made their appearance on the historical scene.

"Blood sports," such as bullbaiting and cockfighting, remained popular with the masses. In bullbaiting, a bull, usually chained to a stake in the courtyard of an inn, was attacked by ferocious dogs for the amusement of the innkeeper's guests. Eventually the maimed and tortured animal was slaughtered by a butcher and sold as meat. In a cockfight, two roosters, carefully trained by their owners and armed with razor-sharp steel spurs, slashed and clawed each other in a small ring until the victor won—and the loser died. An added attraction of cockfighting was that the screaming spectators could bet on the lightning-fast combat and its uncertain outcome.

In trying to place the vibrant popular culture of the common people in broad perspective, historians have stressed the growing criticism levied against it by the educated elites in the second half of the eighteenth century. These elites, which had previously shared the popular enthusiasm for religious festivals, Carnival, drinking in taverns, blood sports, and the like, now tended to see only superstition, sin, disorder, and vulgarity.[17] The resulting attack on popular culture, which had its more distant origins in the Protestant clergy's efforts to eliminate frivolity and superstition, was intensified as educated elites embraced the critical world-view of the Enlightenment. This shift in cultural attitudes was yet another aspect of the widening separation between the common people and the educated public. The mutual hostility that this separation engendered played an important role in the emergence of sharp class conflict in the era of the French and the Industrial Revolutions.

Cockfighting in England   This engraving by William Hogarth (1697–1764) satirizes the popular taste for blood sports, which Hogarth despised and lampooned in his famous *Four Stages of Cruelty*. The central figure in the wildly excited gathering is a blind nobleman, who actually existed and seldom missed a fight. Notice the steel spurs on the birds' legs. *(Source: Courtesy of Trustees of the British Museum)*

SUMMARY

In recent years, imaginative research has greatly increased the specialist's understanding of ordinary life and social patterns in the past. The human experience as recounted by historians has become richer and more meaningful, and many mistaken ideas have fallen by the wayside. This has been particularly true of eighteenth-century, predominately agrarian Europe, which combined a fascinating mixture of continuity and change.

The life of the people remained primarily rural and oriented toward the local community. Tradition, routine, and well-established codes of behavior framed much of the everyday experience of the typical villager. Thus just as the three-field agricultural cycle and its pattern of communal rights had determined traditional patterns of grain production, so did community values in the countryside strongly encourage a late age for marriage, a low rate of illegitimate births, and a strict attitude toward children. Patterns of recreation and leisure, from churchgoing and religious festivals to sewing and drinking in groups, also reflected and reinforced community ties and values. Many longstanding ideas and beliefs, ranging from obscure religious customs to support for fair prices, remained strong forces and sustained continuity in popular life.

Yet powerful forces also worked for change. Many of these came from outside and above, from the aggressive capitalists, educated elites, and government officials discussed in the last two chapters. Closely knit villages began to lose control over families and marital practices, as could be seen in the earlier, more romantic marriages of cottage workers and in the beginning of the explosion in illegitimate births. Although the new, less rigorous attitudes toward children that were emerging in elite culture did not reach the common people, the elite belief in the usefulness of some education did result in growing popular literacy. The grain-based diet became more varied with the grudging acceptance of the potato, and the benefits of the spectacular conquest of smallpox began to reach the common people in the late eighteenth century. Finally, the common people found that their beliefs and customs were being increasingly attacked by educated elites, which thought they knew best. The popular reaction to these attacks generally remained muted in the eighteenth century, but the common people and their advocates would offer vigorous responses and counterattacks in the revolutionary era (see Chapter 23).

NOTES

1. Quoted in S. Chapman, *The Lancashire Cotton Industry* (Manchester, Eng.: Manchester University Press, 1903), p. 13.
2. Quoted in J. M. Beattie, "The Criminality of Women in Eighteenth-Century England," *Journal of Social History* 8 (Summer 1975): 86.
3. W. L. Langer, "Infanticide: A Historical Survey," *History of Childhood Quarterly* 1 (Winter 1974): 357.
4. Quoted in R. Cobb, *The Police and the People: French Popular Protest, 1789–1820* (Oxford: Clarendon Press, 1970), p. 238.
5. M. Segalen, *Love and Power in the Peasant Family: Rural France in the Nineteenth Century* (New York: Basil Blackwell, 1983), p. 41. The passage cited here has been edited into the past tense.
6. G. Gullickson, *Spinners and Weavers of Auffay: Rural Industry and the Sexual Division of Labor in a French Village, 1750–1850* (Cambridge: Cambridge University Press, 1986), p. 186. See also L. A. Tilly, J. W. Scott, and M. Cohen, "Women's Work and European Fertility Patterns," *Journal of Interdisciplinary History* 6 (Winter 1976): 447–476.
7. Quoted in B. W. Lorence, "Parents and Children in Eighteenth-Century Europe," *History of Childhood Quarterly* 2 (Summer 1974): 1–2.
8. Quoted ibid., pp. 13, 16.
9. E. Kennedy, *A Cultural History of the French Revolution* (New Haven, Conn.: Yale University Press, 1989), p. 47.
10. Quoted in L. S. King, *The Medical World of the Eighteenth Century* (Chicago: University of Chicago Press, 1958), p. 320.
11. Quoted in R. Sand, *The Advance to Social Medicine* (London: Staples Press, 1952), pp. 86–87.
12. Quoted in K. Pinson, *Pietism as a Factor in the Rise of German Nationalism* (New York: Columbia University Press, 1934), p. 13.
13. Quoted ibid., pp. 43–44.
14. Quoted in S. Andrews, *Methodism and Society* (London: Longmans, Green, 1970), p. 327.
15. Quoted in I. Woloch, *Eighteenth-Century Europe: Tradition and Progress, 1715–1789* (New York: Norton, 1982), p. 292.
16. Quoted in T. Tackett, *Priest and Parish in Eighteenth-Century France* (Princeton, N.J.: Princeton University Press, 1977), p. 214.

17. Woloch, *Eighteenth-Century Europe,* pp. 220–221; see also pp. 214–220.

SUGGESTED READING

Though long ignored in many general histories of the world, social topics of the kind considered in this chapter have come into their own in recent years. The reader is strongly advised to take time to look through recent volumes of journals such as *Journal of Social History, Past and Present, History of Childhood Quarterly,* and *Journal of Interdisciplinary History.* In addition, the number of book-length studies has expanded rapidly and continues to do so.

Two fine books on the growth of population are C. Cipolla's short and lively *The Economic History of World Population* (1962) and T. McKeown's scholarly *The Modern Rise of Population* (1977). W. McNeill, *Plagues and Peoples* (1976), is also noteworthy. B. H. Slicher van Bath, *The Agrarian History of Western Europe, A.D. 500–1850* (1963), is a wide-ranging general introduction to the gradual transformation of European agriculture. J. Blum, *The End of the Old Order in Rural Europe* (1978), is an impressive comparative study. Two recommended and complementary studies on landowning nobilities are R. Forster, *The Nobility of Toulouse in the Eighteenth Century* (1960), and G. E. Mingay, *English Landed Society in the Eighteenth Century* (1963). E. L. R. Ladurie, *The Peasants of Languedoc* (1976), a brilliant and challenging study of rural life in southern France for several centuries, complements J. Goody et al., eds., *Family and Inheritance: Rural Society in Western Europe, 1200–1800* (1976). Life in small-town preindustrial France comes alive in P. Higonnet, *Pont-de-Montvert: Social Structure and Politics in a French Village, 1700–1914* (1971), and O. Hufton deals vividly and sympathetically with rural migration, work, women, and much more in *The Poor in Eighteenth-Century France* (1974). F. Braudel, *Civilization and Capitalism, 15th–18th Century* (1981–1984), is a monumental and highly recommended three-volume synthesis of social and economic development. Another exciting work is J. Nef, *War and Human Progress* (1968), which examines the impact of war on economic and industrial development in European history between about 1500 and 1800 and may be compared with M. Gutmann, *War and Rural Life in the Early Modern Low Countries* (1980).

Among general introductions to the history of the family, women, and children, J. Casey, *The History of the Family* (1989), is recommended. P. Laslett, *The World We Have Lost* (1965), is an exciting, pioneering

investigation of England before the Industrial Revolution, though further research has weakened some of his conclusions. L. Stone, *The Family, Sex and Marriage in England, 1500–1800* (1977), is a provocative general interpretation, and L. Tilly and J. Scott, *Women, Work and Family* (1978), is excellent. Two valuable works on women, both with good bibliographies, are M. Boxer and J. Quataert, eds., *Connecting Spheres: Women in the Western World, 1500 to the Present* (1987), and R. Bridenthal, C. Koonz, and S. Stuard, eds., *Becoming Visible: Women in European History,* 2d ed. (1987). P. Ariès, *Centuries of Childhood: A Social History of Family Life* (1962), is another stimulating study. E. Shorter, *The Making of the Modern Family* (1975), is a lively, controversial interpretation, which should be compared with the excellent study by M. Segalen, *Love and Power in the Peasant Family: Rural France in the Nineteenth Century* (1983). T. Rabb and R. I. Rothberg, eds., *The Family in History* (1973), is a good collection of articles dealing with both Europe and the United States. A. MacFarlane, *The Family Life of Ralph Josselin* (1970), is a brilliant re-creation of the intimate family circle of a seventeenth-century English clergyman who kept a detailed diary; MacFarlane's *Origins of English Individualism: The Family, Property and Social Transition* (1978) is a major work. I. Pinchbeck and M. Hewitt, *Children in English Society* (1973), is a good introduction. B. Lorence-Kot, *Child-Rearing and Reform: A Study of Nobility in Eighteenth-Century Poland* (1985), stresses the harshness of parental discipline.

Various aspects of sexual relationships are treated imaginatively by M. Foucault, *The History of Sexuality* (1981), and R. Wheaton and T. Hareven, eds., *Family and Sexuality in French History* (1980). L. Moch, *Moving Europeans: Migration in Western Europe Since 1650* (1992), offers a rich, human, and highly recommended account of the movements of millions of ordinary people. J. Burnett, *A History of the Cost of Living* (1969), has a great deal of interesting information about what people spent their money on in the past, and complements J. C. Drummond and A. Wilbraham, *The Englishman's Food: A History of Five Centuries of English Diet,* 2d ed. (1958). J. Knyveton, *Diary of a Surgeon in the Year 1751–1752* (1937), gives a contemporary's unforgettable picture of both eighteenth-century medicine and social customs, as do D. Porter and R. Porter, *Patient's Progress: Doctors and Doctoring in Eighteenth-Century England* (1989), and M. Romsey, *Professional and Popular Medicine in France, 1770–1830: The Social World of Medical Practice* (1988). Good introductions to the evolution of medical practices are B. Ingles, *History of Medicine* (1965); O. Bettmann, *A Pictorial History of Medicine* (1956); and L. King, *The Medical World of the Eight-*

eenth Century (1958). W. Boyd, *History of Western Education* (1966), is a standard survey; R. Houston, *Literacy in Early Modern Europe: Culture and Education, 1500–1800* (1988), is brief and engaging.

The study of popular culture is expanding. Among older studies, M. George, *London Life in the Eighteenth Century* (1965), is a delight, and D. Roche, *The People of Paris: An Essay in Popular Culture in the 18th Century* (1987), presents an unforgettable portrait of the Paris poor. I. Woloch, *Eighteenth-Century Europe: Tradition and Progress, 1715–1789* (1982), includes a survey of popular culture and a good bibliography; E. Kennedy, *A Cultural History of the French Revolution* (1989), beautifully captures rural and urban attitudes in France before and during the French Revolution. R. Malcolmson, *Popular Recreation in English Society, 1700–1850* (1973), provides a colorful account of boxers, bettors, bullbaiting, and more. L. Hunt, *The New Cultural History* (1989), provides an engaging discussion of conceptual issues. G. Rude, *The Crowd in History, 1730–1848* (1964), is an influential effort to see politics and popular protest from below. An important series edited by R. Forster and O. Ranuum considers neglected social questions such as diet, abandoned children, and deviants, as does P. Burke's excellent study, *Popular Culture in Early Modern Europe* (1978). J. Gillis, *For Better, for Worse: Marriage in Britain Since 1500* (1985), and R. Philips, *Untying the Knot: A Short History of Divorce* (1991), are good introductions to institutional changes.

Good works on religious life include Tackett, cited in the Notes; J. Delumeau, *Catholicism Between Luther and Voltaire: A New View of the Counter-Reformation* (1977); B. Semmel, *The Methodist Revolution* (1973); and J. Bettey, *Church and Community: The Parish Church in English Life* (1979).

LISTENING TO THE
PAST

A New Way to Educate Children

Emile, by Jean-Jacques Rousseau, is one of history's most original books. Sometimes called a declaration of rights for children, Emile *challenged existing patterns of child rearing and pleaded for humane treatment of children.*

Rousseau's work also had a powerful impact on theories of education. As the following passage suggests, Emile *argued that education must shield the unspoiled child from the corrupting influences of civilization and allow the child to develop naturally and spontaneously. It is eloquent testimony to Rousseau's troubled life that he neglected his own children and placed all five of them in orphanages.*

Rousseau believed that the sexes were by nature intended for different occupations. Thus Emile might eventually tackle difficult academic subjects, but Sophie, his future wife in the book, needed to learn only how to manage the home and be a good mother and an obedient wife. The idea that girls and boys should be educated to operate in "separate spheres" was to gain wide acceptance in the nineteenth century.

A man must know many things which seem useless to a child, but need the child learn, or can he indeed learn, all that the man must know? Try to teach the child what is of use to a child and you will find that it takes all his time. Why urge him to the studies of an age he may never reach, to the neglect of those studies which meet his present needs? "But," you ask, "will it not be too late to learn what he ought to know when the time comes to use it?" I cannot tell; but this I do know, it is impossible to teach it sooner, for our real teachers are experience and emotion, and man will never learn what befits a man except under its own conditions. A child knows he must become a man; all the ideas he may have as to man's place in life are so many opportunities for his instruction, but he should remain in complete ignorance of those ideas which are beyond his grasp. My whole book is one continued argument in support of this fundamental principle of education.

As soon as we have contrived to give our pupil [Emile] an idea of the word "useful," we have got an additional means of controlling him, for this word makes a great impression on him, provided that its meaning for him is a meaning relative to his own age, and provided he clearly sees its relation to his own well-being. . . . "What is the use of that?" In the future this is the sacred formula, the formula by which he and I test every action of our lives. . . .

I do not like verbal explanations. Young people pay little heed to them, nor do they remember them. Things! Things! I cannot repeat it too often. We lay too much stress upon words; we teachers babble, and our students follow our example.

Suppose we are studying the course of the sun and the way to find our bearings, when all at once Emile interrupts me with the question, "What is the use of that?" What a fine lecture I might give [going on and on]! . . . When I have finished I shall have shown myself a regular pedant, I shall have made a great display of learning, and not one single idea has he understood. . . .

But Emile is educated in a simpler fashion. We take so much pains to teach him a difficult idea that he will have heard nothing of all this. At the first word he does not understand, he will run away, he will prance about room, and leave me to speechify by myself. Let us seek a more commonplace explanation; my scientific learning is of no use to him.

We were observing the position of the forest to the north of Montmorency when he interrupted me with the usual question, "What is the use of that?" "You are right," I said. "Let us take time to think it over, and if we find it is no use we will drop it, for we only want useful games." We find something else to do and geography is put aside for the day.

Next morning I suggest a walk; there is nothing he would like better; children are always ready to run about, and he is a good walker. We climb up to the forest, we wander through its clearings and lose ourselves. . . . At last we [are exhausted and] sit down to rest and to consider our position. I assume that Emile has been educated like an ordinary child. He does not think, he begins to cry; he has no idea we are close to Montmorency, which is hidden from our view by a mere thicket. . . .

Jean-Jacques. "My dear Emile, what shall we do to get out?"

Emile. "I am sure I do not know. I am tired, I am hungry, I am thirsty, I cannot go any further."

Jean-Jacques. "Do you suppose I am any better off? I would cry too if I could make my lunch off tears. Crying is no use, we must look about us. What time is it?"

Emile. "It is noon and I am so hungry!"

Jean-Jacques. "I am so hungry too. . . . Unluckily my dinner won't come to find me. It is twelve o'clock. This time yesterday we were observing the position of the forest from Montmorency. If only we could see the position of Montmorency from the forest—"

Emile. "But yesterday we could see the forest, and here we cannot see the town."

Jean-Jacques. "That is just it. If we could only find it without seeing it. . . . Did not we say the forest was—"

Emile. "North of Montmorency."

Jean-Jacques. "Then Montmorency must lie—"

Emile. "South of the forest."

Jean-Jacques. "We know how to find the north at midday."

Emile. "Yes, by the direction of the shadows."

Jean-Jacques. "But the south?"

Emile. "What shall we do?"

Jean-Jacques. "The south is opposite the north."

Emile. "That is true; we need only find the opposite of the shadows. That is the south! That is the south! Montmorency must be over there! Let us look for it there!"

Jean-Jacques. "Perhaps you are right; let us follow this path through the wood."

❋ This illustration depicts children learning about the five senses. (*Source: Caroline Buckler*)

Emile. (Clapping his hands.) "Oh, I can see Montmorency! there it is, quite plain, just in front of us! Come to lunch, come to dinner, make haste! Astronomy is some use after all."

Be sure that he thinks this if he does not say it; no matter which, provided I do not say it myself. He will certainly never forget this day's lesson as long as he lives, while if I had only led him to think of all this at home, my lecture would have been forgotten the next day. Teach by doing whenever you can, and only fall back upon words when doing is out of the question.

Questions for Analysis

1. What criticism did Rousseau direct at the social and educational practices of his time?

2. How did Rousseau propose to educate his pupil?

3. Do you think Rousseau's plan appealed to peasants and urban workers in the eighteenth century? Why or why not?

4. In what ways did Rousseau's plan of education and his assumptions about human nature reflect some major ideas of the Enlightenment?

Source: Slightly adapted from J.-J. Rousseau, *Emile, or Education*, trans. B. Foxley (New York: E. P. Dutton, 1911), pp. 141–144.

This bronze figure of a
hornblower was created
by a royal artisan for the
court of Benin (A.D.
1500–1700). (*Source:
Courtesy of the Trustees of
the British Museum*)

African states and societies of the fifteenth through eighteenth centuries comprised a wide variety of languages, cultures, and kinds of economic and political development. Modern European intrusion into Africa beginning in the fifteenth century led to the transatlantic slave trade, one of the great forced migrations in world history. Africa made a substantial, though involuntary, contribution to the building of the West's industrial civilization. In the seventeenth century, an increasing desire for sugar in Europe resulted in an increasing demand for slave labor in South America and the West Indies. In the eighteenth century, Western technological changes created a demand for cotton and other crops that required extensive human labor. As a result, the West's "need" for slaves from Africa increased dramatically.

Africa's relationship with Asia, the Islamic world, and the West stretches back a very long time, but only recently have anthropologists, economists, and historians begun to ask critical questions about African societies in early modern times.

- What kinds of economic and social structures did African societies have?

- What impact did Islam have on African societies?

- What kinds of literary sources survive?

- What role did slavery play in African societies before European intrusion?

- What were the geographical and societal origins of the slaves involuntarily shipped to America and to Asia?

This chapter explores these questions.

❋ SENEGAMBIA AND BENIN

In Africa in the mid-fifteenth century, there were societies held together by family or kinship ties, and there were kingdoms and states ruled by princes who governed defined areas through bureaucratic hierarchies. Along the 2,000-mile west coast between Senegambia and the northeastern shore of the Gulf of Guinea, a number of kingdoms flourished. Because much of that coastal region is covered by tropical rain forest, in contrast to the western Sudan, it is called the West African Forest Region (Map 20.1). The Senegambian states in the north possessed a homogeneous culture and a common history. For centuries Senegambia—named for the Senegal and Gambia Rivers—had served as an important entrepôt for desert caravan contact with the Islamic civilizations of North Africa and the Middle East. Through the transatlantic slave trade, Senegambia contributed heavily to New World population in the early seventeenth century. That trade brought Senegambia into contact with the Americas and Europe. Thus Senegambia felt the impact of Islamic culture to the north and of European influences from the maritime West.

In the thirteenth century, the kingdoms of Ghana and Mali had incorporated parts of Senegambia. Mali's influence disintegrated after 1450, and successor kingdoms that were independent but connected to one another through family ties emerged. Stronger states rose and temporarily exercised power over weaker ones.

Scholars are still exploring the social and political structures of the various Senegambian states. The peoples of Senegambia spoke Wolof, Serer, and Pulaar, which are all members of the West African language group. Both the Wolof-speakers and the Serer-speakers had clearly defined social classes: royalty, nobility, warriors, peasants, low-caste artisans such as blacksmiths and leatherworkers, and slaves. Slaves were individuals who were pawned for debt, house servants who could not be sold, and people who were acquired through war or purchase. Senegambian slavery varied from society to society but generally was not a benign institution. In some places the treatment of slaves was as harsh as treatment in the Western world later would be. However, many Senegambian slaves were not considered property to be bought and sold, and some served as royal advisers and enjoyed great power and prestige.[1]

The king of the Wolof was elected by the nobility. After his election the king immediately acquired authority and a special religious charisma. He commanded contingents of soldier-slaves and appointed village chiefs. The king gained his revenue from the chiefs, from merchants, and from taxes levied on defeated peoples.[2] The Wolof had a well-defined government hierarchy.

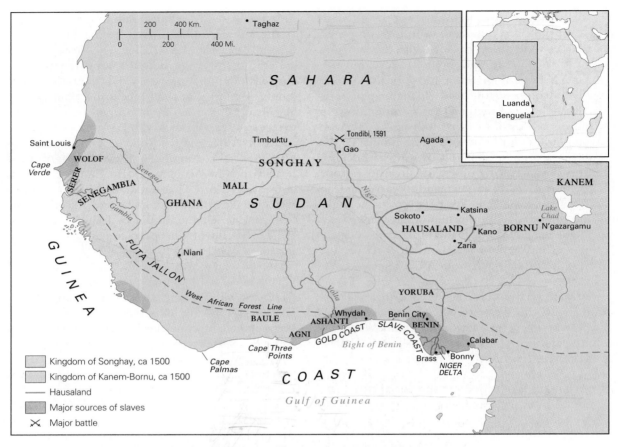

MAP 20.1 West African Kingdoms and the Slave Trade from ca 1500 to 1800
Consider the role that rivers and other geographical factors played in the development of the West African slave trade. Why were Luanda and Benguela the logical Portuguese source for slaves?

Among the stateless societies of Senegambia, where kinship and lineage groups tended to fragment communities, age-grade systems evolved. Age-grades were groups of men and women whom the society initiated into adulthood at the same time. Age-grades cut across family ties, created community-wide loyalties, and provided a means of local law enforcement, because the group was responsible for the behavior of all its members.

The typical Senegambian community was a small self-supporting agricultural village of closely related families. Custom assigned a high value to cultivation of the land—the shared objective of the group. Fields were cut from the surrounding forest, and the average farm of six or eight acres supported a moderate-size family. Often the family worked the land for a common harvest; sometimes individuals had their own private fields. Millet and sorghum were the staple grains in northern Senegambia; farther south, forest dwellers cultivated yams as a staple. Senegambians supplemented their diet with plantains, beans, and bananas, fish, oysters, and small game such as rabbits and monkeys. Along the Guinea coast rice was the basic cereal, and okra, onions, melons, and pepper spiced the regular diet. Frequent fairs in neighboring villages served as markets for the exchange of produce and opportunities for receiving outside news and social diversion. As one scholar has put it, "Life was simple, government largely limited to the settlement

❋ **The Oba of Benin** The walls of the Oba's palace were decorated with bronze plaques that may date to the period from the sixteenth to the eighteenth century. This plaque vividly conveys the Oba's power, majesty, and authority. The necklace (or choker) is his symbol of royalty. Attendants hold up his hands, and warriors raise shields over his head as sunshades. *(Source: The Metropolitan Museum of Art, The Michael C. Rockefeller Memorial Collection, Gift of Nelson A. Rockefeller, 1965)*

of disputes by family heads or elders . . . social life centered on the ceremony accompanying birth, death, and family alliance."[3]

The fifteenth and sixteenth centuries saw the emergence of the great forest kingdom of Benin (see Map 20.1) in what is now southern Nigeria. Although scholars still know little about Benin's origins, its history seems to have been characterized by power struggles between the king and the nobility that neither side ever completely won. An

elaborate court ceremonial exalted the position of the *oba*, or king, and brought stability to the state. In the later fifteenth century, the oba Ewuare played off his palace chiefs against the village chiefs and thereby maintained a balance of power. A great warrior, Ewuare strengthened his army and pushed Benin's borders as far as the Niger River on the east, westward into Yoruba country, and south to the Gulf of Guinea. During the late sixteenth and seventeenth centuries the office of the oba evolved from a warrior kingship to a position of spiritual leadership.

At its height in the late sixteenth century, Benin controlled a vast territory, and European visitors described a sophisticated society. According to a modern historian, the capital, Benin City, "was a stronghold twenty-five miles in circumference, protected by walls and natural defenses, containing an elaborate royal palace and neatly laid-out houses with verandas and balustrades, and divided by broad avenues and smaller intersecting streets."[4] Visitors also noted that Benin City was kept scrupulously clean and had no beggars and that public security was so effective that theft was unknown. The period also witnessed remarkable artistic creativity in ironwork, in carved ivory, and especially in bronze portrait busts. Over nine hundred brass plaques survive, providing important information about Benin court life, military triumphs, and cosmological ideas.

In 1485 the Portuguese and other Europeans in pursuit of trade began to appear in Benin. A small exchange in pepper and slaves developed but never acquired importance in the Benin economy. Nor did the Portuguese have much success in converting the staunchly animistic people to Christianity. Europe's impact on Benin was minimal. In the early eighteenth century, as tributary states and stronger neighbors nibbled at Benin's frontiers, the kingdom underwent a crisis. Benin, however, survived as an independent entity until the British conquered and burned Benin City in 1898.

❀ THE SUDAN: SONGHAY, KANEM-BORNU, AND HAUSALAND

The kingdom of Songhay, a successor state of Ghana and Mali, dominated the whole Niger region of the western and central Sudan (see Map 20.1). Muhammad Toure (1492–1528) completed the expansionist and administrative consolidation begun by his predecessors. Muhammad Toure's power rested on his successful military expeditions. From his capital at Gao he extended his lordship as far north as the salt-mining center at Taghaz in the mid-Sahara and as far east as Agada and Kano. A convert to Islam, Muhammad made a pilgrimage to Mecca. Impressed by what he saw there, he tried to bring about greater centralization in his own territories. In addition to building a strong army and improving taxation procedures, he re-

placed local Songhay officials with more efficient Arab ones in an effort to substitute royal institutions for ancient kinship ties.

What kind of economy existed in the Songhay Empire? What social structures? What role did women play in Songhay society? What is known of Songhay education and culture? The paucity of written records and of surviving artifacts prevent scholars from satisfactorily exploring these questions. Some information is provided by Leo Africanus (ca. 1465–1550), a Moroccan captured by pirates and given as a slave to Pope Leo X. Leo Africanus became a Christian, taught Arabic in Rome, and in 1526 published an account of his many travels, including a stay in the Songhay kingdom.

As a scholar Leo was naturally impressed by Timbuktu, the second city of the empire, which he visited in 1513. "Here [is] a great store of doctors, judges, priests, and other learned men, that are bountifully maintained at the King's court," Leo reported.[5] Many of these Islamic scholars had studied in Cairo and other centers of Muslim learning. They gave Timbuktu a reputation for intellectual sophistication, religious piety, and moral justice.

Songhay under Muhammad Toure seems to have enjoyed economic prosperity. Leo Africanus noted the abundant food supply, which was produced in the southern savanna and carried to Timbuktu by a large fleet of canoes controlled by the king. The Sudanese had large amounts of money to spend, and expensive North African and European luxuries were much in demand: clothes, copperware, glass and stone beads, perfumes, and horses. The existence of many shops and markets implies the development of an urban culture. At Timbuktu, merchants, scholars and judges, and artisans constituted a distinctive bourgeoisie. The presence of many foreign merchants, including Jews and Italians, gave the city a cosmopolitan atmosphere. Jews largely controlled the working of gold.

Slaves played a very important part in the economy of Songhay. On the royal farms scattered throughout the kingdom, slaves produced rice—the staple crop—for the royal granaries. Although slaves could possess their own slaves, land, and cattle, they could not bequeath any of this property; the king inherited all of it. Muhammad Toure greatly increased the number of royal slaves through raids on the pagans (non-Muslims). He

Queen Mother and Attendants As in Ottoman, Chinese, and European societies, so the mothers of rulers in Africa sometimes exercised considerable political power because of their influence on their sons. African kings granted the title "Queen Mother" as a badge of honor. The long beaded cap, called "chicken's beak," symbolizes her rank as do her elaborate neck jewelry and attendants. *(Source: Metropolitan Museum of Art. Gift of Mr. and Mrs. Klaus G. Perls, 1991)*

gave slaves to favorite Muslim scholars, who thus gained a steady source of income. Or the slaves were sold at the large market at Gao. Traders from North Africa bought them for sale in Cairo, Constantinople, Lisbon, Naples, Genoa, and Venice.

The kingdom of Songhay had considerable economic and cultural strengths, but it also had serious internal problems. Islamic institutions never took root in the countryside, and Muslim officials alienated the king from his people. Muhammad Toure's reforms were a failure. He governed a diverse group of peoples—Tuareg, Malinke, Fulani, as well as Songhai—who were often hostile to one another, and no cohesive element united them. Finally, the Songhai never developed an effective method of transferring power. Revolts, conspiracies, and palace intrigues followed the deaths of every king, and only three of the nine rulers in the dynasty begun by Muhammad Toure died natural deaths. Muhammad himself was murdered by one of his sons. His death began a period of political instability that led to the slow disintegration of the kingdom.[6]

In 1582 the sultanate of Morocco began to press southward in search of a greater share of the trans-Saharan trade. The people of Songhay, lacking effective leadership and believing the desert to be a sure protection against invasion, took no defensive precautions. In 1591 a Moroccan army of three thousand soldiers—many of whom were slaves of European origin equipped with European muskets—crossed the Sahara and inflicted a

❄ **"Africa, 1829"** For most of the nineteenth century, what Americans learned of African geography derived from "maps" such as this one, a perfect example of abysmal Western ignorance—or carelessness, since even seventeenth–century Portuguese and British traders knew that Luanda and Benguela are in Angola. Because of its errors, this "map" is now a collector's item. By comparing it to Maps 20.1 and 20.2, you should be able to discover at least ten serious mistakes. *(Source: A private collection)*

crushing defeat on the Songhai at Tondibi. This battle spelled the end of the Songhay Empire. Although a moderate-size kingdom lingered on in the south for a century or so and weak political units arose, not until the eighteenth century did kingdoms able to exercise wide authority emerge again.

To the east of Songhay lay the kingdoms of Kanem-Bornu and Hausaland (see Map 20.1). Under the dynamic military leader Idris Alooma (1571–1603), Kanem-Bornu subdued weaker peoples and gained jurisdiction over an extensive area. Well drilled and equipped with firearms, camel-

mounted cavalry and a standing army decimated warriors fighting with spears and arrows. Idris Alooma perpetuated the feudal pattern of government in which lands were granted to able fighters in return for loyalty and the promise of future military assistance. Meanwhile, agriculture occupied most people, peasants and slaves alike. Kanem-Bornu shared in the trans-Saharan trade, shipping eunuchs and young girls to North Africa in return for horses and firearms. A devout Muslim, Idris Alooma elicited high praise from Ibn Fartura, who wrote a history of his reign called *The Kanem Wars:*

So he made the pilgrimage and visited Medina with delight. . . . Among the benefits which God . . . conferred upon the Sultan Idris Alooma was the acquisition of Turkish musketeers and numerous household slaves who became skilled in firing muskets. . . .

Among the most surprising of his acts was the stand he took against obscenity and adultery, so that no such thing took place openly in his time. Formerly the people had been indifferent to such offences. . . . In fact he was a power among his people and from him came their strength.

The Sultan was intent on the clear path laid down by the Qur'an . . . in all his affairs and actions.[7]

Idris Alooma built mosques at his capital city of N'gazargamu and substituted Muslim courts and Islamic law for African tribunals and ancient customary law. His eighteenth-century successors lacked his vitality and military skills, however, and the empire declined.

Between Songhay and Kanem-Bornu were the lands of the Hausa. An agricultural people living in small villages, the Hausa grew millet, sorghum, barley, rice, cotton, and citrus fruit and raised livestock. Some Hausa merchants carried on a heavy trade in slaves and kola nuts with North African communities across the Sahara. Obscure trading posts evolved into important Hausa city-states like Kano and Katsina, through which Islamic influences entered the region. Kano and Katsina became Muslim intellectual centers and in the fifteenth century attracted scholars from Timbuktu. The Muslim chronicler of the reign of King Muhammad Rimfa of Kano (r. 1463–1499) records that Muhammad introduced the Muslim practices of *purdah,* or seclusion of women, of the *idal-fitr,* or festival after the fast of Ramadan, and of assigning eunuchs to the high offices of state.[8] As in Songhay and Kanem-Bornu, however, Islam made no strong imprint on the mass of the Hausa people until the nineteenth century.

❖ ETHIOPIA

At the beginning of the sixteenth century, the powerful East African Christian kingdom of Ethiopia extended from Massawa in the north to several tributary states in the south (Map 20.2). The ruling Solomonid Dynasty, however, faced serious troubles. Adal, a Muslim state along the southern base of the Red Sea, began incursions into Ethiopia, and in 1529 the Adal general Ahmad ibn-Ghazi inflicted a disastrous defeat on the Ethiopian emperor Lebna Dengel (r. 1508–1540). Ahmad followed up his victory with systematic devastation of the land, destruction of many Ethiopian artistic and literary works, and the forced conversion of thousands to Islam. Lebna Dengel fled to the mountains and appealed to Portugal for assistance. The Portuguese, eager for a share in the wealth of the East African coast and interested in the conversion of Ethiopia to Roman Catholicism, responded with a force of musketeers. In 1541 they decisively defeated the Muslims near Lake Tana.

No sooner had the Muslim threat ended than Ethiopia encountered three more dangers. The Galla, Cushitic-speaking peoples, moved northward in great numbers, occupying portions of Harar, Shoa, and Amhara. The Ethiopians could not defeat them militarily, and the Galla were not interested in assimilation. For the next two centuries the two peoples lived together in an uneasy truce. Simultaneous with the Galla migrations was the Ottoman Turks' seizure of Massawa and other coastal cities. Then the Jesuits arrived, eager to capitalize on earlier Portuguese support, and attempted to force Roman Catholicism on a proud people whose Coptic form of Christianity long antedated the European version. The overzealous Jesuit missionary Alphonse Mendez tried to revamp the Ethiopian liturgy, rebaptize the people, and replace ancient Ethiopian customs and practices with Roman ones. Since Ethiopian national sentiment was closely tied to Coptic Christianity, violent rebellion and anarchy ensued.

In 1633 the Jesuit missionaries were expelled. For the next two centuries hostility to foreigners, weak political leadership, and regionalism characterized Ethiopia. Civil conflicts between the Galla and the Ethiopians erupted continually. The Coptic church, though lacking strong authority, survived as the cornerstone of Ethiopian national identity.

❖ THE SWAHILI CITY-STATES

The word *Swahili,* meaning "People of the Coast," refers to the people living along the East African coast and on the nearby islands. Their history, unlike that of most African peoples, exists in writing. By the eleventh century, the Swahili had accepted

MAP 20.2 East Africa in the Sixteenth Century In early modern times, the Christian kingdom of Ethiopia, first isolated and then subjected to Muslim and European pressures, played an insignificant role in world affairs. But the East African city-states, which stretched from Sofola in the south to Mogadishu in the north, had powerfully important commercial relations with Mughal India, China, the Ottoman world, and southern Europe.

Islam, and "its acceptance was the factor that marked the acquisition of 'Swahili' identity: Islam gave the society coherent cultural form."⁹ The Swahili language is studied today by North Americans who want to identify themselves as having African ancestry, but slaves shipped from East Africa came from inland, not from Swahili-speaking coastal peoples; virtually no Swahili people went to North America. As a people living on the shores of the Indian Ocean, the Swahili felt the influences of Indians, Indonesians, Persians, and especially Arabs.

Swahili civilization was overwhelmingly maritime. A fertile, well-watered, and intensely cultivated stretch of land no more than ten miles wide extends down the coast: it yielded rice, grains, citrus fruit, and cloves. The sea provided fish. But the considerable prosperity of the region rested on trade and commerce. The Swahili acted as middlemen in an Indian Ocean–East African protocapitalism, exchanging ivory, rhinoceros horn, tortoise shells, inlaid ebony chairs, copra (dried coconut meat that yields coconut oil), and inland slaves for Arabian and Persian perfumes and toilet articles, ink and paper, and for Indian textiles, beads, and iron tools. In the fifteenth century, the city-states of Mogadishu, Pate, Lamu, Mombasa, and especially Kilwa enjoyed a worldwide reputation for commercial prosperity.¹⁰ These cities were cosmopolitan, and their standard of living was very high.

The arrival of the Portuguese explorer Vasco da Gama (see Map 16.1, page 517) in 1498 spelled the end of the Swahili cities' independence. Da Gama, lured by the spice trade, wanted to build a Portuguese maritime empire in the Indian Ocean, and between 1502 and 1507 the southern ports of Kilwa, Zanzibar, and Sofala fell before Portuguese guns and became Portuguese tributary states. The better-fortified northern cities, such as Mogadishu, survived as important entrepôts for goods to India.

The Portuguese victory in the south proved hollow, however. Rather than accept Portuguese commercial restrictions, the residents deserted the towns, and the town economies crumbled. Large numbers of Kilwa's people, for example, immigrated to northern cities. The flow of gold from inland mines to Sofala slowed to a trickle. Swahili passive resistance successfully prevented the Portuguese from gaining control of the local coastal trade.

After the intermittent bombardment of several cities, Portugal finally won an administrative

✤ **Saint George in Ethiopian Art**   This image of a black Saint George slaying a dragon from a seventeenth-century Ethiopian manuscript attests to the powerful and pervasive Christian influence in Ethiopian culture. *(Source: The British Library)*

stronghold near Mombasa in 1589. Called Fort Jesus, it remained a Portuguese base for over a century. In the late seventeenth century, pressures from the northern European maritime powers—the Dutch, French, and English—aided greatly by the Arabs of Oman, combined with local African rebellions to bring about the collapse of Portuguese influence in Africa. A Portuguese presence remained only at Mozambique in the far south.

The Portuguese made no religious or cultural impact on the Swahili cities. Their sole effect was the cities' economic decline.

 THE SLAVE TRADE

Slavery had a long history within Africa, and the transatlantic slave trade that began in the late fifteenth century is properly understood against that background. "Slavery was . . . fundamental to the social, political, and economic order of parts of the northern savanna, Ethiopia and the East African coast. . . . Enslavement was an organized activity, sanctioned by law and custom. Slaves were a principal commodity in trade, including the export

❖ **Dutch Colony, Cape of Good Hope** Founded in 1657, by the mid-eighteenth century the Cape Colony had fifteen thousand inhabitants and may have been the largest European settlement on the African continent. Crews took on fresh provisions there, repaired their ships, and awaited favorable winds for crossing the Indian Ocean. *(Source: William Fehr Collection)*

sector, and slaves were important in the domestic sphere" as concubines, servants, soldiers, and ordinary laborers.[11]

Islam had heavily influenced African slavery. African rulers justified enslavement with the Muslim argument that prisoners of war could be sold; and, since captured peoples were considered chattel, they could be used in the same positions that prevailed in the Muslim world. Between 650 and 1600, black as well as white Muslims transported perhaps as many as 4.82 million black slaves across the trans-Saharan trade route.[12] When the transatlantic slave trade began, it represented little that was new.

The African slave trade, extending from the sixteenth to the nineteenth century and involving the forced migration of millions of human beings, represents one of the most inhumane, unjust, and tragic blots on the histories of human societies. The African diaspora immediately provokes a host of questions. What regions of Africa were the sources of slaves? What goods and business procedures were involved in the exchange of slaves? What were the economic, social, political, and demographic effects of the slave trades on African societies? In a period when the enslavement of peoples was dying out in Asian and European societies, when serfdom was declining in western Europe, why were *African* peoples enslaved, when land was so widely available and much of the African continent had a labor *shortage?*

The answer to the last question seems to lie in a technical problem related to African agriculture. Partly because of the tsetse fly, which causes sleeping sickness and other diseases, partly because of easily leached lateritic soils (containing high concentrations of oxides), farmers had great difficulty using draft animals. Tropical soils responded poorly to plowing, and most work had to be done with the hoe. Productivity, therefore, was low. Economists maintain that in most societies the value of a worker's productivity determines the value of his or her labor. In precolonial Africa, the individual's agricultural productivity was low, so his or her economic value to society was less than the economic value of a European peasant in Europe. *Slaves* in the Americas were more productive than free producers in Africa. And European slave dealers were very willing to pay a price higher than the value of an African's productivity in Africa.

The incidence of disease in the Americas also helps to explain the enslavement of Africans. Smallpox took a terrible toll on native Americans (see page 525), and between 30 percent and 50 percent of Europeans exposed to malaria succumbed to that sickness. Africans had developed some immunity to both diseases, and in the New World they experienced the lowest mortality rate of any people. Europeans wanted workers for mines and sugar cane plantations. A coerced (or slave) labor force proved easier to exploit than a wage labor force.[13] As the demand for sugar increased, as the technology for sugar production improved and shipping rates declined, the pressure for slave labor accelerated.

The search for a sea route to India led the Portuguese in the fifteenth century to explore the West African coast. Having "discovered" Brazil in 1500, the Portuguese founded a sugar colony at Bahia in 1551. Between 1551 and 1575, before the traffic to North America had gotten under way, the Portuguese delivered more African slaves to Brazil than would ever reach British North America (Table 20.1). Portugal essentially monopolized the slave trade until 1600 and continued to play a large role in the seventeenth century, though increasingly threatened by the Dutch, French, and English. From 1690 until the House of Commons abolished the slave trade in 1807, England was the leading carrier of African slaves.

Population density and supply conditions along the West African coast and the sailing time to New World markets determined the sources of slaves. As

TABLE 20.1 ESTIMATED SLAVE IMPORTS BY DESTINATION, 1451–1870

Destination	Estimated Total Slave Imports
British North America	399,000
Spanish America	1,552,100
British Caribbean	1,665,000
French Caribbean	1,600,200
Dutch Caribbean	500,000
Danish Caribbean	28,000
Brazil	3,646,800
Old World	175,000
	9,566,100

Source: P. D. Curtin, The Atlantic Slave Trade: A Census *(Madison, Wis.: University of Wisconsin Press, 1969), p. 268. Used with permission.*

the demand for slaves rose, slavers moved down the West African coast from Senegambia to the more densely populated hinterlands of the Bight of Benin and the Bight of Biafra (see Map 16.5, page 545). In the sixteenth and early seventeenth centuries, the Senegambian coast and the area near the mouth of the Congo River yielded the greatest numbers. By the late seventeenth century the British found the Ivory Coast region the most profitable territory. A century later the Bight of Benin and the Gold Coast had become the largest suppliers. The abundant supply of slaves in Angola, the region south of the Congo River, however, and the quick passage from Angola to Brazil and the Caribbean established that region as the major coast for Portuguese slavers.

Transatlantic wind patterns partly determined the routes of exchange. Shippers naturally preferred the swiftest crossing—that is, from the African port nearest the latitude of the intended

American destination. Thus Portuguese shippers carried their cargoes from Angola to Brazil, and British merchants sailed from the Bight of Benin to the Caribbean. The great majority of slaves were intended for the sugar and coffee plantations extending from the Caribbean islands to Brazil.[14]

Angola produced 26 percent of all African slaves and 70 percent of all Portuguese slaves. Trading networks extending deep into the interior culminated at two major ports on the Angolan coast, Luanda and Benguela (see inset to Map 20.1). Between the 1730s and 1770s Luanda shipped between 8,000 and 10,000 slaves each year; at the end of the eighteenth century Benguela's numbers equaled those of Luanda. In 1820, the peak year, 18,957 blacks left Luanda. The Portuguese acquired a few slaves through warfare but secured the vast majority through trade with African dealers. Whites did not participate in the inland markets.

Almost all Portuguese shipments went to satisfy the virtually insatiable Brazilian demand for slaves.[15] The transatlantic slave trade lasted for almost four centuries and involved the brutalization and exploitation of millions of human beings. Here is an excerpt from the report in 1793 of a Portuguese doctor with experience on the Middle Passage between Angola and Brazil:

When the slaves coming from many different parts of the interior reach the maritime ports of Africa, they are there once more traded for goods and merchandise. . . .

Here takes place the second round of hardships that these unlucky people are forced to suffer. . . . They are terribly handled and most scantily provided for . . . their human nature entirely overlooked. The dwelling place of the slave is simply the dirt floor of the compound, and he remains there exposed to harsh conditions and bad weather, and at night there are only a lean-to and some sheds . . . which they are herded into like cattle.

Their food continues scarce as before . . . limited at times to badly cooked beans, at other times to corn. . . . They also add to the diet a small amount of salted fish. . . .

They suffer in other ways. When they are first traded, they are made to bear the brand mark of the backlander who enslaved them, so that they can be recognized in case they run away. And when they reach a port . . . , they are branded on the right breast

with the coat of arms of the king and nation, of whom they have become vassals. . . . This mark is made with a hot silver instrument in the act of paying the king's duties, and this brand mark is called a carimbo.

They are made to bear one more brand mark. This one is ordered by their private master, under whose name they are transported to Brazil. . . .

In this miserable and deprived condition the terrified slaves remain for weeks and months, and the great number of them who die is unspeakable. With some ten or twelve thousand arriving at Luanda each year, it often happens that only six or seven thousand are finally transported to Brazil. . . .

Shackled in the holds of ships, the black slaves . . . are far more deprived than when on land. First of all, with two or three hundred slaves placed under the deck, there is hardly room enough to draw a breath. . . . The captains, aware of their own (financial) interests, recognize the seriousness of the problem, and they try to remedy it to some extent. . . . Each day they order a certain number of slaves brought on deck in chains to get some fresh air, not allowing more because of their fear of rebellion. . . .

Second, the slaves are afflicted with a very short ration of water, of poor quality and lukewarm because of the climate—hardly enough to water their mouths. The suffering that this causes is extraordinary, and their dryness and thirst cause epidemics which, beginning with one person, soon spread to many others. Thus, after only a few days at sea, they start to throw the slaves into the ocean.

Third, they are kept in a state of constant hunger. Their small ration of food, brought over from Brazil on the outward voyage, is spoiled and damaged. . . . They add to each ration a small portion of noxious fish from the Atlantic Ocean, which decays during the voyage.[16]

Unlike Great Britain, France, and the Netherlands, Portugal did not have a strong mercantile class involved in slaving in the eighteenth century. Instead, the Portuguese colony of Brazil provided the ships, capital, and goods for the slave trade. Credit played a major role in the trade: Brazilian-controlled firms in Luanda extended credit to African operators, who had to make payments in slaves six or eight months later. Portuguese ironware and wine, Brazilian tobacco and brandies, European and Asian textiles, firearms, and beads were the main goods exchanged for slaves. All commodities entered Angola from Brazil. The Luandan (or Benguelan) merchants pegged the value of the goods to the value of prime young slaves but then undervalued the worth of the slaves and overpriced the goods. As a result, the African operators frequently ended up in debt to the merchants.

Although the demand was great, Portuguese merchants in Angola and Brazil sought to maintain only a steady trickle of slaves from the African interior to Luanda and across the ocean to Bahia and Rio de Janeiro: a flood of slaves would have depressed the American market. Rio, the port capital through which most slaves passed, commanded the Brazilian trade. Planters and mine operators from the provinces traveled to Rio to buy slaves. Between 1795 and 1808, approximately 10,000 An-golans per year stood in the Rio slave market. In 1810 the figure rose to 18,000; in 1828 it reached 32,000.[17]

The English ports of London, Bristol, and particularly Liverpool dominated the British slave trade. In the eighteenth century Liverpool was the world's greatest slave-trading port. In all three cities, small and cohesive merchant classes exercised great public influence. The cities also had huge stores of industrial products for export, growing shipping industries, and large amounts of ready cash for investment abroad. Merchants generally formed partnerships to raise capital and to share the risks; each voyage was a separate enterprise or venture.

City of Luanda, Angola Founded by the Portuguese in 1575, Luanda was a center of the huge slave trade to Brazil. In this eighteenth-century print, offices and warehouses line the streets, and (right foreground) slaves are dragged to the ships for transportation to America. *(Source: New York Public Library, Astor, Lenox, and Tilden Foundations)*

Ashanti Staff Top In the early eighteenth century, the Ashanti of central Ghana expanded northward, subdued various peoples, and established a powerful successor state to the medieval African kingdoms of Ghana and Mali. The gold trade was the linchpin of its economic and political power. A splendid example of the Ashanti's superb skill in goldworking, this staff top reflects the region's proverbial wealth. (*Source: Lee Boltin Picture Library*)

Slaving ships from Bristol searched the Gold Coast, the Bight of Benin, Bonny, and Calabar. The ships of Liverpool drew slaves from Gambia, the Windward Coast, and the Gold Coast. To Africa, British ships carried textiles, gunpowder and flint, beer and spirits, British and Irish linens, and woolen cloth. A collection of goods was grouped together into what was called the "sorting." An English sorting might include bolts of cloth, firearms, alcohol, tobacco, and hardware; this batch of goods would be traded for an individual slave or a quantity of gold, ivory, or dyewood. When Europeans added a markup for profit, Africans followed suit. Currency was not exchanged; it served as a standard of value and a means of keeping accounts.[18]

European traders had two systems for exchange. First, especially on the Gold Coast, they established factory-forts. These fortified trading posts were expensive to maintain but proved useful for fending off rival Europeans. In the second, or shore, method of trading, European ships sent boats ashore or invited African dealers to bring traders and slaves out to the ships. The English captain John Adams, who made ten voyages to Africa between 1786 and 1800, described the shore method of trading at Bonny:

This place is the wholesale market for slaves, as not fewer than 20,000 are annually sold here; 16,000 of whom are natives of one nation called Ibo. . . . Fairs where the slaves of the Ibo nation are obtained are held every five or six weeks at several villages, which are situated on the banks of the rivers and creeks in the interior, and to which the African traders of Bonny resort to purchase them.

. . . The traders augment the quantity of their merchandise, by obtaining from their friends, the captains of the slave ships, a considerable quantity of goods on credit. . . . Evening is the period chosen for the time of departure, when they proceed in a body, accompanied by the noise of drums, horns, and gongs. At the expiration of the sixth day, they generally return bringing with them 1,500 or 2,000 slaves, who are sold to Europeans the evening after their arrival, and taken on board the ships. . . .

It is expected that every vessel, on her arrival at Bonny, will fire a salute the instant the anchor is let go, as a compliment to the black monarch who soon afterwards makes his appearance in a large canoe, at which time, all those natives who happen to be alongside the vessel are compelled to proceed in their canoes to a respectful distance, and make way for his Majesty's barge. After a few compliments to the captain, he usually enquires after brother George, meaning the King of England, George III, and hopes he and his family are well. He is not pleased unless he is re-

galed with the best the ship affords. . . . His power is absolute; and the surrounding country, to a considerable distance, is subject to his dominion.[19]

The shore method of buying slaves allowed the ship to move easily from market to market. The final prices of the slaves depended on their ethnic origin, their availability when the shipper arrived, and their physical health when offered for sale in the West Indies or the North or South American colonies.

Meanwhile, according to one scholar, the northbound trade in slaves across the Sahara "continued without serious disruption until the late nineteenth century, and in a clandestine way and on a much reduced scale it survived well into the twentieth century."[20] The present scholarly consensus is that the trans-Saharan slave trade in the seventeenth and eighteenth centuries was never as important as the transatlantic trade.

The Savanna and the Horn regions of East Africa experienced a great expansion of the slave trade in the late eighteenth century, and in the first half of the nineteenth century, slave exports from these areas and from the eastern coast amounted to perhaps 30,000 a year. Why this demand? Merchants and planters wanted slaves to work the sugar plantations on the Mascarene Islands, located east of Madagascar, the clove plantations on Zanzibar and Pemba, the food plantations along the Kenya coast. The eastern coast also exported slaves for the Americas, when Brazilian businessmen significantly increased their purchases. Thus, in the late eighteenth and early nineteenth centuries, precisely when the slave trade to North America and the Caribbean declined, the Eastern and Asian markets expanded. Only with colonial conquest by Great Britain, Germany, and Italy after 1870 did suppression begin. Slavery, however, persists. Recent reports (1994) by the United Nations International Labor Organization, the British Anti-Slavery Society, and the U.S. Department of State reveal slavery on an extensive scale in Mauritania (northwestern Africa) and in the Sudan (eastern Africa).[21] The past isn't dead; it's not even past.

Supplying slaves for the foreign market was in the hands of a small wealthy merchant class or was a state monopoly. Gathering a band of raiders and the capital for equipment, guides, tolls, and supplies involved considerable expense. By contemporary standards, slave raiding was a costly operation. Only black entrepreneurs with sizable capital and labor could afford to finance and direct raiding drives. They exported slaves because the profits on exports were greater than the profits to be made from using labor in the domestic economy:

The export price of slaves never rose to the point where it became cheaper for Europeans to turn to alternative sources of supply, and it never fell to the point where it caused more than a temporary check to the trade. . . . The remarkable expansion of the slave trade in the eighteenth century provides a horrific illustration of the rapid response of producers in an underdeveloped economy to price incentives.[22]

Other factors that might result in slavery were kidnapping; judicial enslavement by the state for serious crimes, such as murder or threats to royal authority; state demand for slaves as tribute from subject peoples; destitution following a natural disaster, such as famine or plague, which might force parents to sell "surplus" children; and, as in Russia or China, severe debt, which might lead a person to surrender his or her freedom in return for settlement of the debt. Europeans initiated the Atlantic slave trade, but its continuation was made possible through an alliance between European shippers and African suppliers.

African peoples, captured and forcibly brought to the Americas, played an integral part in the formation of the Atlantic world. They had an enormous impact on the economics of the Portuguese and Spanish colonies of South America and in the Dutch, French, and British colonies of the Caribbean and North America. For example, in the sugar plantations of Mexico and the Caribbean, on the cotton, rice, and tobacco plantations of North America, in the silver and gold mines of Peru and Mexico, slaves of African descent not only worked in the mines and fields, they filled skilled, supervisory, and administrative positions, as well as performing domestic service. African slaves also transmitted their cultures to the Americas. Through language, religion, music, and art they contributed to the cultures of their particular regions and to the development of an Afro-Atlantic civilization.[23]

What economic impact did European trade have on African societies? Africans possessed technology well suited to their environment. Over the

672 CHAPTER 20 AFRICA, 1400–1800

centuries they had cultivated a wide variety of plant foods, developed plant and animal husbandry techniques, and mined, smelted, and otherwise worked a great variety of metals. Apart from firearms, American tobacco and rum, and the cheap brandy brought by the Portuguese, European goods presented no novelty to Africans. What made foreign products desirable to Africans was their price. Traders of hand-woven Indian cotton textiles, Venetian imitations of African beads, and iron bars from European smelters could undersell African manufacturers. Africans exchanged slaves, ivory, gold, pepper, and animal skins for those goods. Their earnings usually did not remain in Africa. African states eager to expand or to control commerce bought European firearms, although the difficulty of maintaining guns often gave gun owners only marginal superiority over skilled bowmen.[24] The kingdom of Dahomey, however, built its power on the effective use of firearms.

The African merchants who controlled the production of exports gained from foreign trade. The king of Dahomey, for example, had a gross income in 1750 of £250,000 from the overseas export of slaves. A portion of his profit was spent on goods that improved the living standards of his people.

Three Traders This sixteenth–century brass plaque shows three traders, probably appointed to deal with Europeans. The one in the center carries his staff of office; the two on the sides hold manillas, an early form of currency. Just as the crocodile holding a fish represents power over the seas, so the traders symbolize royal authority over commerce with outsiders. *(Source: Courtesy of the Trustees of the British Museum)*

[handwritten note in top margin: "3rd time this chapter!"]

Slave-trading entrepôts, which provided opportunities for traders and for farmers who supplied foodstuffs to towns, caravans, and slave ships, prospered. But such economic returns did not spread very far.[25] International trade did not lead to the economic development of Africa. Neither technological growth nor the gradual spread of economic benefits occurred in Africa in early modern times.

The arrival of Europeans did cause basic social changes in some West African societies. In Senegambia, chattel slavery seems to have been unknown before the growth of the transatlantic trade (see page 657). By the late eighteenth century, however, chiefs were using the slave labor of craftsmen, sailors, and farm workers. If the price was right, they were sold off. Those who committed crimes had traditionally paid fines, but because of the urgent demand for slaves, many misdemeanors became punishable by sale to slave dealers. Europeans introduced corn, pineapple, cassava, and sweet potatoes to West Africa, which had important consequences for population growth.

The intermarriage of French traders and Wolof women in Senegambia created a *métis,* or mulatto class. In the emerging urban centers at Saint-Louis, this small class adopted the French language, the Roman Catholic faith, and a French manner of life. The métis exercised considerable political and economic power. When granted French citizenship in the late eighteenth century, its members sent Senegalese grievances to the Estates General of 1789.[26] However, European cultural influences did not penetrate West African society beyond the seacoast.

The political consequences of the slave trade varied from place to place. The trade enhanced the power and wealth of some kings and warlords in the short run but promoted conditions of instability and collapse over the long run. In the kingdom of the Congo the perpetual Portuguese search for slaves undermined the monarchy, destroyed political unity, and led to constant disorder and warfare; power passed to the village chiefs. Likewise in Angola, which became a Portuguese proprietary colony, the slave trade decimated and scattered the population and destroyed the local economy. By contrast, the military kingdom of Dahomey, which entered into the slave trade in the eighteenth century and made it a royal monopoly, prospered enormously from trading in slaves. The economic

TABLE 20.2 THE TRANS-ATLANTIC SLAVE TRADE, 1450–1900

Period	Volume	Percent
1450–1600	367,000	3.1
1601–1700	1,868,000	16.0
1701–1800	6,133,000	52.4
1801–1900	3,330,000	28.5
Total	11,698,000	100.0

Source: P. E. Lovejoy, Transformations in Slavery: A History of Slavery in Africa *(Cambridge: Cambridge University Press, 1983), p. 19. Used with permission.*

strength of the state rested on the slave trade. The royal army raided deep into the interior, and in the late eighteenth century Dahomey became one of the major West African sources of slaves. When slaving expeditions failed to yield sizable catches, and when European demands declined, the resulting depression in the Dahomeyan economy caused serious political unrest. Iboland inland from the Niger Delta, from whose great port cities of Bonny and Brass the British drained tens of thousands of slaves, experienced minimal political effects and suffered no permanent population loss. A high birthrate kept pace with the incursions of the slave trade, and Ibo societies remained demographically and economically strong.

What demographic impact did the slave trade have on Africa? In all, between approximately 1500 and 1900, about 12 million Africans were exported to the Americas, 6 million were exported to Asia, and 8 million were retained within Africa. Tables 20.1 and 20.2 report the somewhat divergent findings of two careful scholars on the number of slaves shipped to the New World. Export figures do not include the approximately 10 to 15 percent who died during procurement or in transit.

Western or American markets wanted young male slaves. The Asian and African markets preferred young females. Women were sought for their reproductive value, as sex objects, and because their economic productivity was not threatened by the possibility of physical rebellion, as might be the case with young men. Consequently, two-thirds of those exported to the Americas were male, one-third female. The population on the western coast of Africa became predominantly female; in the east African Savanna and the Horn regions the population was predominantly male. The slave trade therefore had significant consequences for the institutions of marriage, slavery itself, and the sexual division of labor—topics scholars have yet to explore. Although overall population growth may have shown modest growth from roughly 1650 to 1900, that growth was offset by declines in the Horn and on the eastern and western coasts. While Europe and Asia experienced considerable demographic and economic expansion in the eighteenth century, Africa suffered decline.[27]

SUMMARY

The period between 1400 and 1800 saw the rise of several different African societies. French culture influenced the coastal fringes of Senegambia; the English maintained factories along the Gold Coast; and the Portuguese held Angola as a colony and maintained an insecure grip on Mozambique in East Africa. Yet despite the export of as many as 12 million slaves from Africa to meet the labor needs of South and North America, European influence hardly penetrated the African interior. The overall impact of the slave trade on Africa was devastating for some regions and societies but marginal for others. It appeared around 1810 that Africa's development would be entirely autonomous.

NOTES

1. P. D. Curtin, *Economic Change in Precolonial Africa: Senegambia in the Era of the Slave Trade* (Madison: University of Wisconsin Press, 1975), pp. 34–35; and J. A. Rawley, *The Transatlantic Slave Trade: A History* (New York: Norton, 1981), p. 12.

2. R. W. July, *A History of the African People,* 3d ed. (New York: Scribner's, 1980), pp. 128–129.

3. R. W. July, *Precolonial Africa: An Economic and Social History* (New York: Scribner's, 1975), p. 99.

4. July, *A History of the African People,* p. 141.

5. Quoted in R. Hallett, *Africa to 1875* (Ann Arbor: University of Michigan Press, 1970), p. 151.

6. See *The Cambridge History of Africa,* vol. 3, *ca 1050 to 1600,* ed. R. Oliver (Cambridge: Cambridge University Press, 1977), pp. 427–435.

7. A. ibn-Fartura, "The Kanem Wars," in *Nigerian Perspectives,* ed. T. Hodgkin (London: Oxford University Press, 1966), pp. 111–115.

8. "The Kano Chronicle," quoted in Hodgkin, *Nigerian Perspectives,* pp. 89–90.

9. J. Middleton, *The World of Swahili: An African Mercantile Civilization* (New Haven, Conn.: Yale University Press, 1992), p. 27.

10. Ibid., pp. 35–38.

11. P. E. Lovejoy, *Transformations in Slavery: A History of Slavery in Africa* (Cambridge: Cambridge University Press, 1983), p. 19. This section leans heavily on Lovejoy's work.

12. See Table 2.1, "Trans-Saharan Slave Trade, 650–1600," ibid., p. 25.

13. P. Manning, *Slavery and African Life: Occidental, Oriental, and African Slave Trades* (New York: Cambridge University Press, 1990), pp. 31–37.

14. Rawley, *The Transatlantic Slave Trade,* p. 45.

15. Ibid., pp. 41–47.

16. R. E. Conrad, *Children of God's Fire: A Documentary History of Black Slavery in Brazil* (Princeton, N.J.: Princeton University Press, 1983), pp. 20–23.

17. Rawley, *The Transatlantic Slave Trade,* pp. 45–47.

18. July, *A History of the African People,* p. 208.

19. J. Adams, "Remarks on the Country Extending from Cape Palmas to the River Congo," in Hodgkin, *Nigerian Perspectives,* pp. 178–180.

20. A. G. Hopkins, *An Economic History of West Africa* (New York: Columbia University Press, 1973), p. 83.

21. See Lori Grinker, "Disaster in the Sudan," *New York Times,* February 12, 1993, p. A33; Stanley Miller, "U.N. Agency Assails Mauritania on Slavery," *Los Angeles Times,* March 9, 1993, p. 3; Augustine Lado and Betty Hinds, "Where Slavery Isn't History," *Washington Post,* October 17, 1993, section 3, p. 13; and Charles Jacobs and Mohamed Athie, "Bought and Sold," *New York Times,* July 13, 1994, p. A19.

22. Hopkins, *An Economic History of West Africa,* p. 105.
23. J. Thornton, *Africa and Africans in the Making of the Atlantic World* (New York: Cambridge University Press, 1992), pp. 138–142.
24. July, *Precolonial Africa,* pp. 269–270.
25. Hopkins, *An Economic History of West Africa,* p. 119.
26. July, *A History of the African People,* pp. 201–202.
27. Manning, *Slavery and African Life,* pp. 22–23 and Ch. 3, pp. 38–59.

SUGGESTED READING

Students wishing to explore more fully some of the issues raised in this chapter might begin with *African History: Text and Readings:* vol. 1, *Western African History;* vol. 2, *Eastern African History;* and vol. 3, *Central and Southern African History* (1990), all edited by R. O. Collins. This work gives a useful introduction to the geography and history of the continent and brings together a solid collection of primary documents and scholarly commentaries. *African Civilization Revisited,* ed. B. Davidson (1991), also contains interesting source readings on many facets of African history and cultures from antiquity to the present. K. Shillington, *History of Africa* (1989) provides a soundly researched, highly readable, and well-illustrated survey, while R. Oliver, *The African Experience* (1991) traces African history through particular historical problems. Although many of the articles in *The Cambridge History of Africa,* vol. 4, *From 1600–1790,* ed. R. Gray (1975), are now dated, the following articles are still useful: "The Central Sahara and Sudan," "North-West Africa," and "Southern Africa and Madagascar." V. B. Thompson, *Africa and Unity* (1969), offers an African and African-American response to the traditional Eurocentric interpretation of African history and culture.

J. Thornton, *Africa and Africans in the Making of the Atlantic World, 1400–1680* (1992), places African developments in an Atlantic context. Likewise, both *Atlantic American Societies: From Columbus Through Abolition, 1492–1888,* ed. A. L. Karras and J. R. McNeill (1992), and *Slavery and the Rise of the Atlantic System,* ed. B. Solow (1991), contain important and valuable articles on many of the economic and cultural factors that linked Africa and the Western Hemisphere. For Ethiopia, see H. G. Marcus, *A History of Ethiopia* (1994), a concise but highly readable study. The standard study of the Savanna is probably J. Vansina, *Kingdoms of the Savanna* (1966). For East Africa and the Horn region, see J. Middleton, *The World of Swahili: An African Mercantile Civilization* (1992), which provides an expert synthesis of recent scholarly literature by a social anthropologist; the older study of C. S. Nicholls, *The Swahili Coast* (1971), is still useful. J. Knappert, *Four Centuries of Swahili Verse: A Literary History and Anthology* (1979), is a most interesting celebration of literary manifestations of Swahili culture.

The literature of slavery continues to grow. In addition to the titles by P. Manning and J. Middleton cited in the Notes, see P. Manning, *Slavery, Colonialism and Economic Growth in Dahomey, 1640–1960* (1982), an in-depth study of the kingdom of Dahomey, which, after Angola, was the largest exporter of slaves to the Americas. J. F. Searing, *West African Slavery and Atlantic Commerce, 1700–1860* (1993), explores the effects of the Atlantic slave trade on the societies of the Senegal River Valley. The theme of R. L. Stein's *The French Slave Trade in the Eighteenth Century: An Old Regime Business* (1979) is indicated by its title.

Although the emphasis in *Global Dimensions of African Diaspora,* ed. J. E. Harris (1982), is heavily on the U.S. and the Caribbean, with very little on South America, East or South Asia, some of the articles are very important: see, especially, those by J. E. Harris, L. W. Levine, and S. C. Drake.

PAST

The Abolition of the Slave Trade

Several Western nations outlawed the slave trade in the early nineteenth century. Great Britain took the lead. Laws, however, cannot be enforced if strong sentiment opposes them. And in the nineteenth century the economies of several African kingdoms rested on the slave trade, which thrived because of demands in the Americas for workers on cotton, coffee, and sugar cane plantations and in East Africa for laborers in the spice fields. Just as today the United States subsidizes the development of agricultural products in Colombia and Turkey in order to encourage farmers to stop growing opium and coca (the sources of heroin and cocaine for American users), so in the nineteenth century the British in Africa promoted farming and the production of nonhuman commodities as alternatives to the slave trade.

In 1839, the British government sent Robert Craigie, a naval officer, to discuss the end of the slave trade with King Pepple of Bonny, an area in the Niger Delta now part of Nigeria. Bonny had continued to export thousands of slaves after Britain abolished the trade in 1807. This document reports the negotiations between King Pepple and Captain Craigie.

King Pepple, of Bonny, accompanied by Anna Pepple,[1] by his Juju man or high priest, and Hee Chee, Anna Pepple's secretary, for the first time went on board a man-of-war, for the purpose of paying a visit to Captain Craigie, where he was received with the usual salutes.

When the King and suite had finished breakfast, Captain Craigie presented to His Majesty a box containing presents from the English Government, which the King desired might be opened. As the bales of scarlet and green broad cloth were being lifted out of the case, the King and Anna Pepple especially were struck with the magnificence of the gifts, and Captain Craigie made a request of His Majesty

to allow Anna Pepple to have one piece of cloth and a shawl, which the King at once complied with.

Captain Craigie then proceeded to read to King Pepple and suite the despatch of Lord Palmerston[2] dated 14th April, 1838, relative to Slave abolition, and strongly impressed upon His Majesty that part which states that treaties had already been made between England and other African Princes for the purpose of putting an end to the Slave Trade, and that in those cases the Articles of Treaty had been faithfully maintained.

Captain Craigie assured the King that England . . . . would send out ships in abundance for their palm-oil and other products; and if the Bonny men directed their attention properly to these, he was certain they could easily get rich without exporting slaves. . . .

The King, Anna Pepple, and the Juju man for some time remained silent; their countenances, however, were indicative of their consternation; the idea of making such a proposal seemed to them to be incomprehensible. At length Anna Pepple said—

"If we cease to sell slaves to foreign ships, our principal source of wealth will be gone; the English were our first customers, and the trade has since been our chief means of support."

Captain Craigie: "How much would you lose if you gave up selling slaves for exportation?"

Anna Pepple: "Too much—very much—we gain more by one slave-ship than by five palm-oil ships."

Hee Chee, Anna Pepple's Secretary: "We depend entirely on selling slaves and palm oil for our subsistence; suppose then the Slave Trade done away with, the consumption of palm-oil in England to stop, the crop to fail, or that the English ships did not come to the Bonny, what are we to do? We must starve, as it is contrary to our religion to cultivate the ground."

Captain Craigie: "There need be no apprehension of the demand for palm-oil in England ceasing, or of English ships not coming out to the Bonny to take from you your products in exchange for British merchandise; but if you can show clearly that your losses will be so great by giving up slave exportation, I think it possible that the Queen of England may in some measure remunerate you for such loss. . . . I only wish to know if you are disposed to treat[4] for the abolition of the Slave Trade."

Juju Man: "Suppose a Spanish ship's coming to Bonny with goods to exchange for slaves; are we to send her away? This morning, if the Spanish ship had things which we stood in need of, it would be equally foolish not to take them."

Captain Craigie: "How would the abolition of the slave exportation so materially affect you?"

King Pepple: "It would affect myself and chiefs thus—

"First, by stopping the revenues arising from slaves being exported.

"Secondly, our own profit on slaves, and that arising from piloting slave-ships up and out of Bonny would be lost."

Captain Craigie: ". . . If your requests are within reasonable limits, to make you an annual 'dash,' or remuneration, for a term of years (perhaps five years), how much would you consider to be sufficient?"

After some consultation among themselves, Hee Chee, Anna Pepple's Secretary, said "The King will take 4,000 dollars yearly."

Captain Craigie: . . . I am certain 4,000 would be considered too much; indeed I would not venture to propose more than 2,000 dollars. If you will say that this sum (for the time above specified) will be sufficient, I shall lay the matter before the English Government."

The King, Anna Pepple, the Juju man, and Hee Chee, had a discussion for some time.

Anti-slavery medallion. *(Source: Josiah Wedgwood and Sons, Limited)*

They for a long while insisted on not naming less than 3,000 dollars, till they at last came down to 2,000. . . .

King Pepple and suite then returned to the shore under the same salute as that with which they were received.

Just as today Colombian and Turkish farmers accept American aid for not producing opium and coca but continue to produce them; so (according to a report to the British Parliament in 1849) did King Pepple accept British aid for not selling slaves but continued to sell them to the Spanish and Portuguese.

Questions for Analysis

1. What arguments does Captain Craigie give for the abolition of the slave trade?

2. What is the reaction of King Pepple to Craigie's remarks?

3. Compare efforts to end slave trade in the nineteenth century with recent government efforts to end the drug trade.

Source: A. J. Andrea and J. H. Overfield, eds., *The Human Record: Sources of Global History*, vol. 2 (Boston: Houghton Mifflin, 1990), pp. 316–318.

Notes: 1. A male relative of the king who held some sort of position in directing the family's slaving operations. 2. Palmerston (1789–1865) was British foreign secretary at the time. 3. Negotiate.

21

The Middle East and India, ca 1450–1800

Wedding Celebrations of Prince Dara Shikoh, 1633, from the Padshahnama, Mughal, ca. 1645. The marriage of Shah Jahan's favorite son and intended heir. *(Source: The Royal Collection © Her Majesty Queen Elizabeth II)*

Around 1450, the spiritual descendants of the Prophet Muhammad controlled three vast and powerful empires: the Ottoman Empire centered in Anatolia, the Safavid Empire of Persia, and the Mughal Empire of India. From West Africa to central Asia, from the Balkans to Southeast Asia, Muslim armies pursued policies of territorial expansion. Between 1450 and 1800, these powerful Muslim kingdoms reached the zenith of their territorial extension and of their intellectual and artistic vitality. With the conquest of Constantinople in 1453 the Ottoman Turks gained an impregnable capital and the respect of all Islam. The Ottomans soon overran much of Anatolia, North Africa, and the Balkans. Lasting almost five hundred years (1453–1918), the Ottoman Empire was one of the largest and most enduring political entities in world history. In Persia the Safavid Dynasty created a theocracy and presided over a brilliant culture. A theological dispute between the Ottomans and the Safavids brought bitter division in the Islamic world and weakened both powers. Meanwhile, the Mughal leader Babur and his successors conquered the Indian subcontinent, and Mughal rule inaugurated a period of radical administrative reorganization in India and the flowering of intellectual and architectural creativity.

In 1450 all the great highways of international trade were in Muslim hands, and the wealth of the Muslim states derived largely from commerce. By 1750 the Muslims had lost that control, and the Muslim states were declining economically, politically, and culturally.

- Who were the Ottomans and the Safavids?
- What political and religious factors gave rise to the Ottoman and Safavid Empires, and how were the two empires governed?
- What intellectual developments characterized the Ottoman and Safavid cultures?
- What external and domestic difficulties caused the decline of the Ottoman Empire and Safavid Persia?
- How did Muslim government reform and artistic inspiration affect the dominant Hindu population in India?
- What political and social conditions in India enabled the British to expand their empire?

These are the questions explored in this chapter.

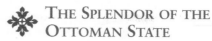 THE SPLENDOR OF THE OTTOMAN STATE

The Ottomans took their name from Osman (1299–1326), the ruler of a Turkish-speaking people in western Anatolia who began expansionist moves in the fourteenth century. The Ottomans gradually absorbed other peoples on the Anatolian peninsula, and the Ottoman state emerged as one of many small Turkish states during the breakup of the empire of the Seljuk Turks. The first Ottoman state thus occupied the border between Islam and Byzantine Christendom. The Ottoman ruler called himself "border chief," or leader of the *gazis,* frontier fighters in the *jihad,* or holy war. The earliest Ottoman historical source, a fourteenth-century saga, describes the gazis as the "instrument of God's religion . . . God's scourge who cleanses the earth from the filth of polytheism . . . God's pure sword."[1]

The principle of jihad was the cornerstone of Ottoman political theory and then of the Ottoman state. Europe was the frontier of the Muslim crusading mission. In 1389 in what is today the former Yugoslavia the Ottomans defeated a combined force of Serbs and Bosnians. In 1396, on the Danube River in modern Bulgaria, they crushed King Sigismund of Hungary, who was supported by French, German, and English knights. The reign of Sultan Mehmet II (r. 1451–1481) saw the end of all Turkish dynasties in Anatolia and the Ottoman conquest of Constantinople, capital of the Byzantine Empire, which had lasted a thousand years.

The six-week siege of Constantinople in 1453 remains one of the dramatic events in world history because Constantinople symbolized the continuation of imperial Rome. The Byzantine emperor Constantine IX Palaeologus (r. 1449–1453), with only about 10,000 men, relied on the magnificent system of circular walls and stone fortifications that had protected the city for a thousand years. Mehmet II had over 100,000 men and a large fleet, but iron chains spanning the harbor kept him out of the Golden Horn, the inlet of the Bosporus Strait that connects the Black and Marmona Seas and forms the harbor of Istanbul.

Western technology eventually decided the battle. A Transylvanian cannon founder who deserted the Byzantines for Ottoman service cast huge bronze cannons on the spot (bringing raw materials to the scene of military action was easier than moving guns long distances).[2] When a cannon shot shattered a city gate, the Turks forced an entry. For three days the city suffered looting and rape. The Muslim historian Oruc described the conquest of Constantinople:

Sultan Mehmet, the son of Sultan Murad, inspired by zeal, said "in the cause of God" and commanded plunder. The gazis, entering by force on every side, found a way in through the breaches in the fortress made by the guns and put the infidels in the fortress to the sword. . . . Mounting on the tower they destroyed the infidels who were inside and entered the city. They looted and plundered. They seized their money and possessions and made their sons and daughters slaves. The Muslims took so much booty that the wealth gathered in Istanbul (Constantinople) since it was built 2400 years before became the portion of the gazis. They plundered for three days, and after three days plunder was forbidden.[3]

The conquest of Constantinople inaugurated the imperial phase of the Ottoman military state. The Ottoman emperors considered themselves successors of the Byzantine emperor, as their title *Sultan-i-Rum* ("Sultan of Rome") attests. They renamed the city Istanbul, "city of Islam," though the name was not officially changed until 1930. Mehmet began the transformation of the city into an Ottoman imperial capital. He ordered Constantinople cleaned up and the walls repaired. He appointed Turkish officials to adapt the city administration to Turkish ways, and he nominated a Greek patriarch over the Greek Orthodox church, giving its members virtual freedom of religion as long as they paid the *jitza,* a tax on non-Muslims. Mehmet's installation of the supreme authority over all Orthodox Christians meant that the patriarch acknowledged Turkish rule; Greek resistance to that rule was rendered virtually impossible.

Because the conquest had severely depopulated the city and many survivors had been sold into slavery, inhabitants of territories later conquered by the Ottomans were transplanted to Constantinople. Jews cruelly oppressed in western Europe found Turkey "a paradise." In 1454, one Jewish resident, Isaac Sarfati, sent a circular letter to his coreligionists in the Rhineland, Swabia, Moravia, and Hungary praising the happy conditions of the Jews under the crescent in contrast to the "great torture chamber" under the cross and urging them to come to Turkey.[4] A massive migration to Ottoman lands followed. When Ferdinand and Isabella of Spain expelled the Jews in 1492 (see page 485), many emigrated to Turkey.

The Ottomans also continued to expand. In 1453, they controlled only the northwest quadrant of Anatolia. Mehmet II completed the conquest of Anatolia. From Constantinople, their new capital, the Ottomans pushed down the Aegean and up the Adriatic. They so severely threatened Italy and southeastern Europe that the aged Pope Pius II himself shouldered the cross of the Crusader in 1464. In 1480 an Ottoman fleet took the Italian port of Otranto, and serious plans were laid for the conquest of all Italy. Only a disputed succession following the death of Mehmet II in 1481 caused the postponement of that conquest and, later, the cancellation of those plans. The Ottoman Turks inspired such fear that even in distant Iceland the Lutheran Book of Common Prayer begged God for protection not only from "the cunning of the Pope" but also from "the terror of the Turk."

Selim the Grim (r. 1512–1520) gained the Ottoman throne by forcing his father's abdication and murdering his brother. A bloodthirsty and inflexible despot, Selim was a superb military commander. Under his leadership, the Ottomans added Syria and Palestine (1516) and Egypt (1517) to their empire and extended their rule across North Africa to Cyrenaica, Tripolitania, Tunisia, and Algeria. Selim's reign marks the beginning of four centuries when most Arabs were under Ottoman rule.

Suleiman (r. 1520–1566), who brought to the throne great experience as a provincial administrator and enormous energy as a soldier, extended Ottoman jurisdiction to its widest geographical extent (Map 21.1). With Greece and the Balkans already under Ottoman domination, Suleiman's army crushed the Hungarians at Mohács in 1526, killing the king and thousands of his nobles. Suleiman seems to have taken this victory entirely as his due. Not long after the battle he recorded laconically in his diary, "The emperor, seated on a

MAP 21.1 The Ottoman Empire at Its Height, 1566   The Ottomans, like their great rivals the Habsburgs, rose to rule a vast dynastic empire encompassing many different peoples and ethnic groups. The army and the bureaucracy served to unite the disparate territories into a single state.

golden throne, receives the homage of the viziers and beys: massacre of 2,000 prisoners: the rains fall in torrents." Three years later the Turks besieged the Habsburg capital at Vienna. Only an accident—the army's insistence on returning home before winter—prevented Muslim control of all central Europe.

In virtually every area, the Ottomans' success was due to the weakness and political disunity of their enemies and to the superiority of Turkish military organization and artillery. Gunpowder, invented by the Chinese and adapted to artillery use by Europeans, played an influential role in the expansion of the Ottoman state.

Though victorious on land, the Ottomans did not enjoy complete dominion on the sea. The middle decades of the sixteenth century witnessed a titanic struggle between the Ottoman and

Habsburg empires for control of the Mediterranean. In September 1538 an Ottoman naval victory at Preveze, the chief Turkish port in Albania, assured Turkish control of the Ionian and Aegean Seas. Meanwhile, attacks from the island of Cyprus by Christian pirates on Ottoman shipping in the eastern Mediterranean provoked the sultan to conquer Cyprus in 1570. He introduced Ottoman administration and settled thousands of Turks from Anatolia there. (Thus began the large Turkish presence on Cyprus that continues to the present day.) In response, Pope Pius V organized the Holy League against the Turks. On October 7, 1571, an armada of over 200 Spanish, Venetian, and papal galleys smashed the Turks at Lepanto at the mouth of the Gulf of Patras in Greece (see Map 21.1). About 15,000 Turks were killed or captured, 10,000 Christian galley slaves were liberated, and the victors lost about 7,000 men. European churches rang with victory celebrations for the first major Ottoman defeat by Christian forces. Lepanto, however, marked no decisive change in Turkish hegemony: the Turks remained supreme on land and quickly rebuilt their entire fleet.

Military organization dominated the Ottoman social and administrative systems, which reached classic form under Suleiman I. The seventeenth-century Ottoman historian Mustafa Naima divided Muslim society into producers of wealth, Muslim and non-Muslim, and the military. In Naima's view there could be no state without the military; wealth was needed to support the military; the state's subjects raised the wealth; subjects could prosper only through justice; and without the state there could be no justice.[5]

The ruling class consisted exclusively of Muslims, theoretically totally loyal to the sultan and fully immersed in the complex Islamic culture. Under Suleiman I, the Ottoman ruling class consisted in part of descendants of Turkish families that had formerly ruled parts of Anatolia. In return for bureaucratic service to the sultan, they held *trimars* (landed estates) on *sipahinek* (property) for the duration of their lifetimes. The ruling class had the usufruct but not the ownership of the land. Since all property belonged to the sultan and reverted to him on the holder's death, Turkish nobles—unlike their European counterparts—could not put down

Procession of Suleiman   In 1533 the Dutch painter and print maker Pieter Coecke van Aelst visited Constantinople, where he sketched the design for this elegant scene. The triumphant procession of the sultan, with his officials and courtiers, through monuments brought from all over the Mediterranean world (notice the column with Egyptian hieroglyphics) captures the power of the Grand Turk. *(Source: The Metropolitan Museum of Art, Harris Brisbane Dick Fund, 1928)*

roots. Because there was no security of landholding and no hereditary nobility, the Ottoman Empire did not develop a feudal structure before 1600.

Slaves who had been purchased from Spain, North Africa, and Venice, captured in battle, and acquired through the system known as *devshirme*—by which the sultan's agents swept the provinces for Christian youths—were recruited for the imperial civil service and the army. Southern Europeans did not shrink from selling people into slavery, and, as the Ottoman jihad advanced in the fifteenth and sixteenth centuries, Albanian, Bosnian, Wallachian, and Hungarian slave boys filled Ottoman imperial needs. Moreover, because devshirme recruitment often meant social advancement, some Christian and Muslim parents bribed government officials to accept their children. All were converted to Islam. (Islamic law forbade the enslavement of Muslims but not of converts.) The brightest 10 percent entered the palace school. There they learned to read and write Arabic, Ottoman Turkish, and Persian, received special religious instruction, and were trained for the civil service. Other boys were sent to Turkish farms, where they acquired physical toughness in preparation for military service. Known as *janissaries* (Turkish for "recruits"), they formed the elite army corps. Thoroughly indoctrinated and absolutely loyal to the sultan, the janissary slave corps eliminated the influence of old Turkish families and played the central role in Ottoman military affairs in the sixteenth century.

All authority theoretically emanated from the sultan and flowed from him to his state servants: police officers, provincial governors, heads of the treasury, generals. The sultan frequently designated these men *pashas*, a title of distinction.

The reign of Suleiman I witnessed an extraordinary artistic flowering and represents the peak of Ottoman influence and culture. In Turkish history Suleiman is known as *Kanuni* ("Lawgiver") because of his profound influence on the civil law. He ordered Lütfi Paşa (d. 1562), a poet of slave origin and juridical scholar, to draw up a new general code of laws. Published in Suleiman's name, this sultanic legal code prescribed penalties for routine criminal acts such as robbery, adultery, and murder. It also sought to reform bureaucratic and financial corruption in areas such as harem intervention in administrative affairs, foreign merchants' payment of bribes to avoid customs duties, imprisonment without trial, and promotion in the provincial administration because of favoritism rather than ability. The legal code also introduced the idea of balanced financial budgets. Suleiman's legal acts influenced many legal codes, including that of the United States. Today, Suleiman's image, along with the images of Solon, Moses, and Thomas Jefferson, and other great lawgivers, appears in the chamber of the U.S. House of Representatives.

Europeans called Suleiman "the Magnificent" because of the grandeur of his court. With annual state revenues of about $80 million (at a time when Elizabeth I of England could expect $150,000 and Francis I of France perhaps $1 million), with thousands of servants to cater to his whims, and with a lifestyle no European monarch could begin to rival, Suleiman was indeed magnificent. He used his fabulous wealth and power to adorn Constantinople with palaces and mosques. Some of his undertakings, such as his reconstruction of the water systems of the great pilgrimage sites at Mecca and Jerusalem, benefited his subjects.

The Ottomans under Suleiman demonstrated splendid creativity in carpet weaving, textiles, ceramics, and, above all, architecture. In the buildings of Pasha Sinan (1491–1588), a Christian slave who rose to become imperial architect, the Ottoman spirit is powerfully expressed. A contemporary of Michelangelo, Sinan designed 312 public buildings—mosques, schools, hospitals, public baths, palaces, and burial chapels. His masterpieces, the Shehzade and Suleimaniye mosques at Constantinople, represented solutions to spatial problems unique to domed buildings and expressed the discipline, power, and devotion to Islam that characterized the Ottoman Empire under Suleiman the Magnificent. With pardonable exaggeration, Suleiman began a letter to the king of France, with whom he was allied against the Habsburgs after 1536, by saying, "I who am the sultan of sultans, the sovereign of sovereigns, the dispenser of crowns to the monarchs on the face of the earth . . . to thee who are Francis, King of the land of France."[6]

The age of Suleiman witnessed a tremendous cultural explosion that may have rivaled the artistic and literary achievements of the European Renaissance. In addition to architecture, Ottoman scholars and artists showed great distinction in poetry, painting, history, mathematics, geographical literature, astronomy, medicine, and the religious sciences.

Poetry, rather than prose, was the main vehicle of Ottoman literary expression. Diwan poetry, so called because it consisted of collections of poems, though written by intellectuals in Turkish, followed classical Islamic (Arabic) forms and rules and addressed the ruling class. Şeyhi of Kütahya (d. 1429) compiled a large Diwan collection and in his *Book of the Donkey* used animals to personify and satirize his political enemies. Modern scholars consider Bursah Ahmet Pasa, an imperial judge and confidential adviser to the sultan Mehmet II, to be the greatest Ottoman poet of the fifteenth century. Bursah Ahmet Pasa's beautiful odes and diversified style won him widespread popularity.

Folk literature, produced by traveling troubadours, described the traditions and wisdom of the people in humorous short stories and anecdotes. The folk collection of Dede Korkut, set down in Turkish prose, includes tribal epics describing the conflicts with the Georgians, Circassians, and Byzantines and serves as a major source for the history of the fourteenth century.

Just as Western historical writing in the early modern period often served to justify the rights of ruling dynasties, so Ottoman historical scholarship under Mehmet II and Suleiman promoted the claims of the family of Osman. Perhaps the greatest historian of the early sixteenth century was Ahmet Semseddin Iba-i Kemal, or Kemalpasazêde (d. 1526), the Muslim judge and administrator whose *History of the House of Osman* gives original source material for the reigns through which he himself lived. Building on the knowledge of earlier Islamic writers and stimulated by Ottoman naval power, the geographer and cartographer Piri Reis produced a map that showed all the known world (1513); another of his maps detailed Columbus's third voyage to the New World. Piri Reis's *Book of the Sea* (1521) contained 129 chapters, each with a map incorporating all Islamic (and Western) knowledge of the seas and navigation and describing harbors, tides, dangerous rocks and shores, and storm areas. Takiyuddin Mehmet (1521–1585), who served as the sultan's chief astronomer, built an observatory at Constantinople. His *Instruments of the Observatory* catalogued astronomical instruments and described an astronomical clock that fixed the location of heavenly bodies with greater precision than ever before.

What medical treatment or health care was available to the sick in the Ottoman world? Muslim medical education was practical, not theoretical: students received their training not in the *madrasas,* or mosque schools, but by apprenticeship to experienced physicians or in the *bimaristans,* the hospitals. Under a senior's supervision, medical students studied the course of various diseases, learned the techniques of surgery, and especially mastered pharmacology—the preparation of drugs from plants. The Muslim knowledge of pharmacology derived from centuries-old traditions, and modern students of the history of medicine believe that pharmacology as an institution is an Islamic invention.

By the fifteenth century, Muslims knew the value of quarantine. Yet when devastating epidemics, such as the bubonic plague, struck the empire during Mehmet II's reign, he and the court fled to the mountains of the Balkans, and the imperial government did little to fight the plague. Under Suleiman, however, the imperial palace itself became a center of medical science, and the large number of hospitals established in Constantinople and throughout the empire testifies to his support for medical research and his concern for the sick. Abi Ahmet Celebi (1436–1523), the chief physician of the empire, produced a study on kidney and bladder stones and supported the research of the Jewish doctor Musa Colinus ul-Israil on the application of drugs. Celebi founded the first Ottoman medical school, which served as a training institution for physicians of the empire.[7] The sultans and the imperial court usually relied on Jewish physicians.

To fight smallpox, the Chinese had successfully practiced inoculation in the sixteenth century, and the procedure spread to Turkey in the seventeenth. Lady Mary Wortley Montague, wife of the British ambassador to Constantinople, had her son inoculated in 1717. Here is her description of the method:

The smallpox, so fatal and so general amongst us (in England), is here entirely harmless by the invention of well, hello madam!

engrafting. . . . Every autumn . . . people send one another to know if any of their family has a mind to have the smallpox (get inoculated). . . . An old woman comes with a nutshell full of the matter of the best sort of smallpox and asks what veins you please (want) to have opened. She immediately rips open what you offer to her with a large needle (which gives you no more pain than a common scratch) and puts into the vein as much venom as can lie upon the head of the needle, and after binds up the little wound. . . . The children or young patients play together all the rest of the day and are in perfect health till the eighth. Then the fever begins to seize 'em and they keep their beds two days, very seldom three. They have very rarely twenty or thirty (pockmarks) in their faces, which never mark (leave a permanent scar), and in eight days' time they are as well as before their illness. . . . Every year thousands undergo this operation, and the French ambassador says pleasantly that they take the smallpox here by way of diversion as they take the waters in other countries (at spas). . . . There is no example of anyone that has died in it.[8]

This was eighty years before the English physician Edward Jenner (see page 644) tried the procedure using cowpox in England.

Lady Mary Wortley Montague marveled at the splendor of Ottoman culture. Remarkably intelligent and fluent in several languages, a pioneer feminist, Lady Mary also had a mind exceptionally open to different cultures. As an aristocrat, the wife of an official foreign representative, and a woman, she had access to people and places (such as the imperial seraglio or harem) off-limits to ordinary tourists. Her many letters to relatives and friends in England provide a wealth of information about upper-class Ottoman society.

On January 19, 1718, Lady Mary gave birth to a daughter and described the experience in a letter to an English friend:

I was brought to bed of a daughter. . . . I must own that it was not half so mortifying here as in England, there being as much difference as there is between a little cold in the head, which sometimes happens here, and the consumptive coughs so common in London.[9]

The naturalness of childbirth in Turkey, Lady Mary suggests, may have been because Turkish women

❁ **Lady Mary Wortley Montague**   Famous in her own time for her letters from Constantinople and, after her return to England, for her efforts to educate the English public about inoculation against smallpox, Lady Mary is praised by twentieth-century scholars as a brilliant and urbane woman struggling for emancipation. *(Source: Boston Athenaeum)*

had much more experience of it than English-women:

in this country 'tis more despicable to be married and not fruitful than 'tis with us to be fruitful before marriage. They have a notion that whenever a woman leaves off bearing children, 'tis because she is too old for that business, whatever her face says to the contrary, and this opinion makes the ladies here so ready to make proofs of their youth. . . . Without any exaggeration, all the women of my acquaintance that have been married ten years have twelve or thirteen children, and the old ones boast of having had five and twenty or thirty apiece and are respected according to the number they have produced.[10]

Turkish women's sense of self-worth seems to have been closely tied to their production of children, as was common in many cultures at the time. As for Turkish morality, "'Tis just as 'tis with you; and the Turkish ladies don't commit one sin the less for not being Christians." In other words, Turkish women are neither better nor worse than European ones. Moreover,

'Tis very easy to see that they have more liberty than we have, . . . and their shapes are wholly concealed by a thing they call a ferigee, which no woman of any sort (class) appears without. . . . You may guess how effectively this disguises them, that there is no distinguishing the great lady from her slave, and 'tis impossible for the most jealous husband to know his wife when he meets her, and no man dare either touch or follow a woman in the street.

This perpetual masquerade gives them entire liberty of following their inclinations without danger of discovery. The most usual method of intrigue is to send an appointment to the lover to meet the lady at a Jew's shop, which are as notoriously convenient as our Indian houses. . . .

You may easily imagine the number of faithful wives very small in a country where they have nothing to fear from their lovers' indiscretion. . . . Neither have they much to apprehend from the resentment of their husbands, those ladies that are rich having all their money in their own hands, which they take with 'em upon a divorce with an addition which he is obliged to give 'em. Upon the whole, I look upon the Turkish woman as the only free people in the empire.[11]

In short, in spite of the legal restrictions of the harem, upper-class ladies found ways to go out and even to have affairs.

In the seventeenth and eighteenth centuries, grave political, social, and economic difficulties afflicted the Ottoman Empire. Ottoman government depended heavily on the sultan, and the matter of the dynastic succession posed a major political problem. In earlier centuries heirs to the throne had gained administrative experience as governors of provinces and military experience on the battlefield as part of their education. After Suleiman's reign, however, this tradition was abandoned. To

prevent threats of usurpation, heirs were brought up in the harem and were denied a role in government. By the time a prince succeeded his father, years of dissipation were likely to have rendered the prince alcoholic, insane, or exhausted from excessive sexual activity. Selim II (r. 1566–1574), whom the Turks called "Selim the Drunkard," left the conduct of public affairs to his vizier while he pursued the pleasures of the harem. Turkish sources attribute his death to a fall in his bath caused by dizziness when he tried to stop drinking. The Ottomans, moreover, abandoned the system whereby the eldest son inherited and instead gave the throne to the member of the dynasty with the greatest political influence at the time of the sultan's death. As the sultan's brothers and sons formed factions, harem coalitions conspired for the throne.

A series of incompetent rulers enabled the janissaries to destroy the influence of the old Turkish families. Members of the elite army corps secured permanent military and administrative offices for their sons through bribery, making their positions hereditary. The janissaries thus became the powerful feudal class in Ottoman Turkey.

Under the very competent vizier Muhammad Kuprili (ca 1570–1661) Ottoman fortunes revived. Kuprili abolished the corruption pervasive throughout the imperial administration, maintained domestic peace, and pursued a vigorous foreign policy. When Kuprili died, his brother-in-law Kara Mustafa directed the empire's military operations. His objective was an attack on the Habsburg capital, Vienna. When battle came on September 12, 1683, the combination of a strong allied Christian force (see page 571) and Habsburg heavy artillery, which the Turks lacked, gave the Europeans the victory. The Ottomans rallied again, but defeat at Vienna and domestic disorders led to the decline of Ottoman power in the Balkans. In the words of one historian, "The Ottoman state was predicated upon, committed to, and organized for conquest. . . . An end to significant and sustained conquest rocked the entire state structure and sent aftershocks through all its institutions."[12]

The peace treaty signed at Karlowitz (1699) marks a watershed in Ottoman history. By its terms the empire lost (to Austria) the major European provinces of Hungary and Transylvania along with the vast tax revenues they had provided. Karlowitz

✦ **Visit to the Lunatic Asylum**   Beginning in the ninth century, Islamic hospitals had special wards for the insane. Therapy consisted of baths, massages, bleeding (for the violently agitated), and drugs given as sedatives, stimulants, or antidepressants. Fear that the violent would harm themselves or others led to shackling. In this scene from an album produced for Sultan Ahmed I (r. 1603–1617) three violent patients are chained; the nearly naked appearance of two of them (which would have shocked Muslim sensibilities) is a sure sign of their insanity. The Jewish doctor (right) is threatened with a knife; his assistant is caught in the stocks from which the third lunatic tries to escape. Two visitors observing the mayhem through the window put their forefingers to their mouths, a common gesture in Muslim society indicating astonishment and a defense against evil. *(Source: Topkapi Saray Museum, Istanbul)*

also shattered Ottoman morale. Eighteenth-century wars against European powers—Venice (1714–1718), Austria and Russia (1736–1739), and Russia (1768–1774 and 1787–1792)—proved indecisive but contributed to general Ottoman internal disintegration.

Rising population caused serious social problems. A long period of peace in the later sixteenth century and again in the mid-eighteenth century—while the War of the Austrian Succession (1740–1748) and the Seven Years' War (1756–1763) were preoccupying the European powers (see page 611)—and a decline in the frequency of visits of

the plague led to a doubling of the population. The land could not sustain so many people, nor could the towns provide jobs for the thousands of agricultural workers who fled to them. The return of demobilized soldiers from the West aggravated the situation. Inflation, famine, and widespread revolts resulted.

Inability to respond to European and worldwide economic changes contributed to Ottoman weakness and decline. The empire did not modernize and thus could not compete effectively with European capitalistic powers. European trade with the Americas, Asia, and Africa by means of the Atlantic

✤ **Polo** Two teams of four on horseback ride back and forth on a grass field 200 by 400 yards trying to hit a 4½-ounce wooden ball with a four-foot mallet through the opponents' goal. Because a typical match involves many high-speed collisions among the horses, each player has to maintain a string of expensive ponies in order to change mounts several times during the game. Students of the history of sports believe the game originated in Persia, as shown in this eighteenth-century miniature, whence it spread to India, China, and Japan. Brought from India to England where it became very popular among the aristocracy in the nineteenth century, polo is a fine example of cross-cultural influences. *(Source: Private Collection)*

Ocean meant that the ancient Middle Eastern trade routes—with their heavy customs duties—were bypassed. The Ottoman state lost vast revenues. Meanwhile, Ottoman guilds set the prices of commodities such as wheat, wool, copper, and precious metals, and European willingness to pay high prices pulled those commodities out of the Ottoman Empire. The result was scarcity, which led to a decline in Turkish industrial production. Likewise in the craft industries, Europeans bought Ottoman raw materials, used them to manufacture textiles and metallurgical goods, and sold them in Turkish lands, thereby destroying Ottoman craft industries in the early nineteenth century. Prices rose; inflation increased; and the government devalued the currency, causing new financial crises.

More than any other single factor, a series of agreements known as capitulations, which the Ottoman government signed with European powers, contributed to the Ottoman decline. A trade compact signed in 1536 and renewed in 1569 virtually exempted French merchants from Ottoman law and allowed them to travel and buy and sell throughout the sultan's dominions and to pay low customs duties on French imports and exports. In 1590, in spite of strong French opposition, a group of English merchants gained the right to trade in Ottoman territory in return for supplying the sultan with iron, steel, brass, and tin for his war with Persia. In 1615, as part of a twenty-year peace treaty, the capitulation rights already given to French and English businessmen were extended to the Habsburgs. These capitulations progressively gave European merchants an economic stranglehold on Ottoman trade and commerce. In the nineteenth century, the Ottoman empire was beset by the loss of territory, the pressures of European capitalistic imperialism, and unresolved internal problems; Tsar Nicholas I of Russia (1825–1855) called it "the sick man of Europe."[13]

✤ THE PERSIAN THEOCRATIC STATE

Describing the Mongol destruction of Persia in the thirteenth century, the Persian historian Juvaini wrote, "With one stroke, a world which billowed with fertility was laid desolate, and the regions thereof became a desert, and the greater part of the living dead, and their skin and bones crumbling dust."[14] Pursuing a scorched-earth policy toward the land and a psychological reign of terror over the people, the Mongols, so modern demographers estimate, reduced the population of Persia, Khurasan, Iraq, and Azerbaijan (Map 21.2) from 2,500,000 to 250,000. Mongol devastation represents the last great sweep of Turkish steppe nomads from central Asia into the European and Islamic heartlands. Turkish tribes in central Asia far outnumbered the ethnic Mongols. The Turks joined Jenghiz Khan partly because he had defeated them, partly because westward expansion with the Mongols offered adventure and rich pasturelands for their herds of sheep and horses.[15]

The rehabilitation of Persia began under Ghazan (r. 1295–1304), the *Ilkhan,* as the Mongol rulers of Persia were called. A descendant of Jenghiz Khan, Ghazan reduced peasants' taxes and thereby encouraged their will to produce. He also worked to improve the fiscal and administrative systems. His declaration of Islam as the state religion had profound political and cultural consequences: native (and Muslim) Persians willingly served the state government; they alone had the literacy needed to run a bureaucracy. Turkish-Mongol soldiers adapted to Persian ways. The court patronized Persian art. Across the central Asian heartlands hundreds of Chinese doctors, engineers, artists, and potterymakers came seeking opportunity in the Persian-Mongol-Turkish capital at Tabriz. Chinese artistic influences left a permanent mark on Persian miniature painting, calligraphy, and pottery design.

But Mongol rule of Persia did not last long. While Mehmet II was extending Ottoman jurisdiction through eastern Anatolia, the Safavid movement advanced in Persia. The Safavid Dynasty, which takes its name from Safi al-Din (1252–1334), a supposed descendant of Ali (the fourth caliph), began as leaders of a contemplative Sufi sect; gradually the dynasty evolved into a militant and heretical Shi'ite regime. The attraction of the masses to Shi'ism perhaps reflects the role of religion as a vehicle for the expression of political feeling—in this case opposition to Mongol domination. In the early sixteenth century, Persia emerged as a powerful Muslim state under the Safavids. (Since 1935 Persia has been known as Iran.)

MAP 21.2 The Safavid Empire In the late sixteenth century, the power of the Safavid kingdom of Persia rested on its strong military force, its Shi'ite Muslim faith, and its extraordinarily rich trade in rugs and pottery. Many of the cities on the map, such as Tabriz, Qum, and Shiraz, were great rug-weaving centers.

Between 1502 and 1510, Ismail (r. 1502–1524) defeated petty Turkish leaders, united Persia under his sovereignty, and proclaimed himself *shah*, or king.

The strength of the Safavid state rested on three crucial features. First, it had the loyalty and military support of Qizilbash nomadic tribesmen. (*Qizilbash*, a Turkish word meaning "redheads," was applied to these people because of the red hats they wore.) The shah secured the loyalty of the Qizilbash by granting them vast grazing lands, especially on the troublesome Ottoman frontier. In return, the Qizilbash supplied him troops. Second, the Safavid state utilized the skills of urban bureaucrats and made them an essential part of the civil machinery of government.

The third source of Safavid strength was the Shi'ite faith. The Shi'ites claimed descent from Ali, Muhammad's cousin and son-in-law, and believed that leadership among Muslims rightfully belonged to the Prophet's descendants. Ismail claimed descent from a line of twelve infallible *imams* (leaders) beginning with Ali and was officially regarded as their representative on earth. When Ismail conquered Tabriz in 1501, he declared Shi'ism the official and compulsory religion of his new empire under penalty of death. Today, in the late twentieth century, Iran remains the only Muslim state in which Shi'ism is the official religion.

Shi'ism gradually shaped the cultural and political identity of Persia (and later Iran). Recent scholarship asserts that Ismail was not "motivated by cynical notions of political manipulation."[16] Shah Ismail imported Shi'ite *ulema* (scholars outstanding in learning and piety) from other Arab lands to instruct and guide his people. With its puritanical emphasis on the holy law and on self-flagellation in penance for any disloyalty to Ali, the Safavid state represented theocracy triumphant throughout the first half century of its existence.

Safavid power reached its height under Shah Abbas (r. 1587–1629), whose military achievements, support for trade and commerce, and endowment of the arts earned him the epithet "the Great." The Persian army had hitherto consisted of tribal units under tribal leadership. Shah Abbas built a national army on the Ottoman model, composed of Armenian and Georgian recruits paid by and loyal to himself. Shah Abbas campaigned against the Turks and captured Baghdad, Mosul, and Diarbakr in Mesopotamia (see Map 21.2).

Military victories account for only part of Shah Abbas's claim to greatness. Determined to improve his country's export trade, he built the small cottage business of carpet weaving into a national industry. In the capital city of Isfahan alone, factories employed over twenty-five thousand weavers who produced woolen carpets, brocades, and silks of brilliant color, design, and quality. Armenians controlled the carpet industry; the Safavids had brought them to Isfahan to protect them from Turkish persecution. Three hundred Chinese potters were imported to make glazed building tiles, which adorned the great Safavid buildings. They captured much of the European tile market.

The jewel of the empire was Isfahan, whose prosperity and beauty rested on trade and industry. A seventeenth-century English visitor described Isfahan's bazaar as "the surprisingest piece of Greatness in Honour of commerce the world can boast of." Besides splendid rugs, stalls displayed pottery and fine china, metalwork of exceptionally high quality, silks and velvets of stunning weave and design. A city of perhaps 750,000 people, Isfahan contained 162 mosques, 48 schools where future members of the ulema learned the sacred Muslim sciences, 273 public baths, and the vast imperial palace. Private houses had their own garden courts; and public gardens, pools, and parks adorned the wide streets. Tales of the beauty of Isfahan circulated worldwide, attracting thousands of tourists annually in the seventeenth and eighteenth centuries.

Shah Abbas was succeeded by inept rulers whose heavy indulgence in wine and the pleasures of the harem weakened the monarchy and fed the slow disintegration of the state. Internal weakness encouraged increased foreign aggression. In the eighteenth century the Turks, Afghans, and Russians invaded and divided Persia among themselves, and political anarchy and social chaos characterized Persian life.

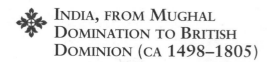

INDIA, FROM MUGHAL DOMINATION TO BRITISH DOMINION (CA 1498–1805)

While powerful Muslim empires developed in Ottoman Turkey and Safavid Persia in the early sixteenth century, the Asian subcontinent of India experienced the intrusion of two vigorous foreign cultures. In 1510 the Portuguese occupied the island of Goa and shortly afterward under Alfonso de Albuquerque (see pages 517–518) extended Portuguese influence on the Indian mainland. The Portuguese soon controlled the trade of the Indian Ocean. On the mainland they used persuasion and force to convert the Indian peoples to Christianity. Fifteen years after the arrival of the Portuguese, an army from Afghanistan and central Asia invaded northern India.

In 1504 Babur (r. 1483–1530), ruler of the small Mughal territory in central Asia, captured Kabul and established a kingdom in Afghanistan. From Kabul he moved southward into India. In 1526 with a force of only twelve thousand men, Babur defeated the decrepit sultan of Delhi at Panipat. Babur's capture of the cities of Agra and Delhi, the key fortresses of the north, paved the way for further conquests in northern India. Thus began Mughal rule, which lasted until the eighteenth century, when domestic disorder and incompetent government opened the door to lengthy European intervention. (*Mughal* refers to the Muslim empire of India. Although the name *Mughal* is a variant of *Mongol,* the founders of the Mughal Empire were mainly Turks and Afghans, not Mongol descendants of Jenghiz Khan.)

The Rule of the Mughals

By the start of the sixteenth century, India had been the object of foreign conquest for almost a millennium. Muslims first invaded India in the seventh century. The Turkish chieftain Mahmud conquered the Punjab in the tenth century, and in the thirteenth century the Turkish Muslim Qutb-ud-din established the sultanate of Delhi, which gained control over most of the subcontinent. In 1398, central Asian armies under Timur the Lame (Tamerlane) swept down through the northwest, looted Delhi, and seized tens of thousands of

Masji-Shah Mosque Just as the Gothic cathedrals manifested the civic pride of medieval European towns, so this mosque with its magnificent tile work and delicate stone tracery celebrated the commercial dynamism of Isfahan and the political power of the Safavid Dynasty of Persia. *(Source: Erwin Böhm, Mainz)*

slaves as booty. Timur, Babur's grandfather, left Delhi completely destroyed with "not a bird moving" and all India politically fragmented. Although the vast majority of the people remained Hindu, Islam had a strong impact on the culture of India, especially in art and architecture.

Babur's son Humayun reigned from 1530 to 1540 and from 1555 to 1556. When the Afghans of northern India rebelled, he lost most of the territories that his father had acquired. Humayun went into temporary exile in Persia, where he developed a deep appreciation for Persian art and literature. This interest led to a remarkable flowering of Mughal art under his son Akbar.

The reign of Akbar (r. 1556–1605) may well have been the greatest in the history of India. Under his dynamic leadership the Mughal state took

definite form. A boy of thirteen when he became *badshah,* or imperial ruler, Akbar was ably assisted during his early years by his father's friend Bairam Khan, a superb military leader. In 1555 Bairam Khan had defeated Hindu forces at Panipat and shortly afterward recaptured Delhi and Agra. Before falling from power in 1560, Bairam Khan took the great fortress of Gwalior, annexed the rich city of Janupur, and prepared for war against Malwa. Akbar continued this expansionist policy throughout this time, gradually adding the territories of Malwa, Gondwana, and Gujarat. Because the Afghan tribesmen put up tremendous resistance, it took Akbar several years to acquire Bengal. The Mughal Empire under Akbar eventually included most of the subcontinent north of the Godavari River (see Map 21.3).

To govern this vast region, Akbar developed an efficient bureaucracy staffed by able and well-trained officials, both Muslim and non-Muslim. As in the early modern nations of Europe, solvency in the Mughal state depended on the establishment of a careful system for recording income and expenditures. Under Akbar's finance minister Raja Todar Mal, a Hindu, a *diwan* (bureau of finance) and royal mint came into existence. Raja Todar Mal devised methods for the assessment and collection of taxes, and those methods were applied throughout the empire. To administer the provinces, Akbar appointed about 800 *mansabdars,* imperial officials who performed a wide variety of financial, military, and judicial functions at the local level. The central government, however, rarely interfered in the life of village communities. Akbar's policies laid the basis for all later Mughal administration in India.

A mark of Akbar's cosmopolitanism was his appointment of the Spanish Jesuit Antonio Monserrate (1536–1600) as tutor to his second son, Prince Murad (see Listening to the Past). The cornerstone of Akbar's policies was religious toleration: he sought the peaceful mutual assimilation of Hindus and Muslims, especially in his government. Although this was not a radical innovation—a few Hindus had long been employed in the imperial army and in the administration—very deep prejudices divided the two peoples. When the refusal of many Hindus to serve under a Muslim ruler or to learn Persian (the court language) thwarted Akbar's goal, he took decisive steps to heal the breach, because, according to his principle of *sulahkul* (universal tolerance), the badshah was responsible for all the people, regardless of their religion.

In 1564 the Muslim ruler ended the pilgrim tax and thus won the gratitude of the many Hindus who traveled to various pilgrimage sites. And by abolishing the *jizya,* a tax imposed on non-Muslim adult males, he immediately earned the support of the Hindu warrior class and the goodwill of the general Hindu population. Twice Akbar married Hindu princesses, one of whom became the mother of his heir Jahangir. Hindus eventually accounted for 30 percent of the imperial bureaucracy.

Scholars have heatedly debated Akbar's own religious beliefs. He considered himself an orthodox Muslim and demonstrated great devotion at the shrine of an Islamic mystic at Ajmer. Yet he supported an eclectic assortment of theological ideas, a policy that caused serious domestic difficulties. Orthodox Muslims became alarmed. After 1579 Akbar invited Jains, Zoroastrians, Hindus, and Jesuits to join the Muslim ulema in debate. From these discussions Akbar created the *Din-i-Ilahi* (literally, "divine discipleship"), which some advisers called a syncretic religion (a religion that reconciles different beliefs).

The Din-i-Ilahi borrowed the concept of great respect for animal life from the Jains and reverence for the sun from the Zoroastrians, but it was primarily based on the rationalistic elements in the Islamic tradition and stressed the emperor as a Perfect Man. Some scholars interpret it as a reflection of Akbar's "cult of personality," intended to serve as a common bond for the court nobility. In any case, the Din-i-Ilahi antagonized all sects and provoked serious Muslim rebellions.

Akbar often sought the spiritual advice of the Sufi mystic Shaykh Salim Chishti. The birth of a long-awaited son, Jahangir, which Akbar interpreted as fulfillment of the shaykh's prophecy, inspired Akbar to build a new city, Fatehpur-Sikri, to symbolize the regime's Islamic foundations. He personally supervised the construction of the new city. It combined the Muslim tradition of domes, arches, and spacious courts with the Hindu tradition of flat stone beams, ornate decoration, and solidity. According to Abu-l-Fazl, the historian of Akbar's reign, "His majesty plans splendid edifices, and dresses the work of his mind and heart in the garment of stone and clay."[17] Completed in 1578, the city included an imperial palace, a mosque, lavish gardens, and a hall of worship, as well as thousands of houses for ordinary people. Akbar placed Shaykh Salim Chishti's tomb inside the great mosque in order to draw on its presumed sanctity. Just as medieval European rulers such as Charlemagne and Phillip the Fair sought to strengthen their political power through association with Christian saints, so Akbar tried to identify Mughal authority with a Muslim saint. Along with the ancient cities of Delhi and Agra, Fatehpur-Sikri served as an imperial capital and the center of Akbar's lavish court.

Akbar was gifted with a creative intellect and imagination. He replaced Barlas Turkish with Persian as the offical language of the Mughal Empire; Persian remained the official language until the

British replaced it with English in 1835. He enthusiastically supported artists who produced magnificent paintings and books in the Indo-Persian style. In Mughal India, as throughout the Muslim world, books were regarded as precious objects. Time, talent, and expensive materials went into their production, and they were highly coveted because they reflected wealth, learning, and power.

Akbar reportedly possessed twenty-four thousand books when he died. Abu-l-Fazl, the historian, described the library and Akbar's love of books:

His Majesty's library is divided into several parts. . . . Prose works, poetical works, Hindi, Persian, Greek, Kashmirian, Arabic, are all separately placed. In this order they are also inspected. Experienced people

City of Fatehpur-Sikri   In 1569 Akbar founded the city of Fatehpur-Sikri to honor the Muslim holy man Shaikh Salim Chishti, who had foretold the birth of Akbar's son and heir, Jahangir. The red sandstone city, probably the finest example of Mughal architecture still intact, was Akbar's capital for fifteen years. *(Source: Nrupen Madhvani/Dinodia Picture Agency, Bombay)*

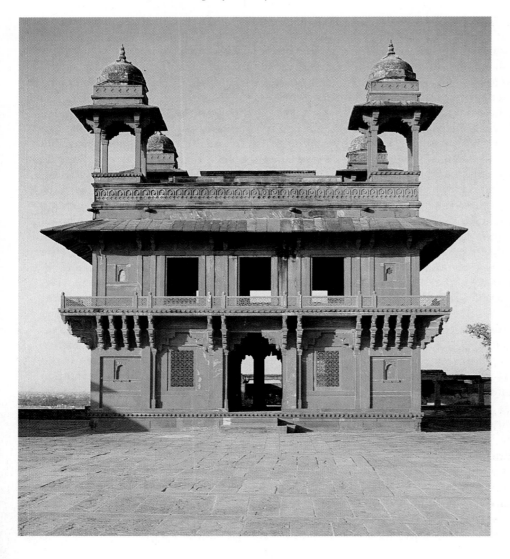

bring them daily and read them before His Majesty, who hears every book from beginning to end . . . and rewards the readers with presents of cash either in gold or silver, according to the number of leaves read out by them. Among books of renown there are few that are not read in His Majesty's assembly hall; and there are no historical facts of past ages, or curiosities of science, or interesting points of philosophy, with which His Majesty, a leader of impartial sages, is unacquainted.[18]

Akbar's son Jahangir (r. 1605–1628) lacked his father's military abilities and administrative genius but did succeed in consolidating Mughal rule in Bengal. His patronage of the arts and lavish court have led scholars to characterize his reign as an "age of splendor."

Jahangir's son Shah Jahan (r. 1628–1658) launched fresh territorial expansion. Faced with dangerous revolts by the Muslims in Ahmadnagar and the resistance of the newly arrived Portuguese in Bengal, Shah Jahan not only crushed them but strengthened his northwestern frontier. He reasserted Mughal authority in the Deccan and Golkunda.

The new capital that Shah Jahan founded at Delhi superseded Agra, Akbar's main capital. Situated on the rich land linking the Indus and Ganges Valleys, Delhi eventually became one of the great cities of the Muslim world. The city boasted one of the finest mosques in Islam, the Juma Masjid, and magnificent boulevards. The Red Fort, named for its red sandstone walls, housed the imperial palace, the headquarters of the imperial administration, the imperial treasury, an arsenal, and a garrison. Subsequent Mughal rulers held their *durbar,* or court, at Delhi.

Shah Jahan ordered the construction of the Peacock Throne. This famous piece, actually a cot resting on golden legs, was encrusted with emeralds, diamonds, pearls, and rubies. It took seven years to fashion and cost the equivalent of $5 million. It served as the imperial throne of India until 1739, when the Persian warrior Nadir Shah seized it as plunder and carried it to Persia.

Shah Jahan's most enduring monument is the Taj Mahal, the supreme example of a garden tomb. The English word *paradise* derives from the old Persian *pairidaeza,* a walled garden. The Mughals sought to bring their vision of paradise alive in the walled garden tombs in which they buried their

Jesuits at the Court of Akbar   Akbar considered the creation of a new faith, synthesizing his Muslim beliefs, Hindu, Parsee, and Christian creeds, but the scheme encountered fierce opposition. The Jesuits' black robes fascinated Mughal artists, and the splendor of the imperial court astounded the Jesuits. *(Source: Reproduced by kind permission of the Trustees of the Chester Beatty Library, Dublin)*

dead. Twenty thousand workers toiled eighteen years to build this memorial in Agra to Shah Jahan's favorite wife, Mumtaz Mahal, who died giving birth to their fifteenth child. One of the most beautiful structures in the world, the Taj Mahal is

Taj Mahal at Agra   This tomb is the finest example of Muslim architecture in India. Its white marble exterior is inlaid with semiprecious stones in Arabic inscriptions and floral designs. The oblong pool reflects the building, which asserts the power of the Mughal Dynasty. *(Source: Ira Kirschenbaum/Stock, Boston)*

both an expression of love and a superb architectural blending of Islamic and Indian culture. It also asserted the power of the Mughal Dynasty.

The Mughal state never developed a formal procedure for the imperial succession, and a crisis occurred toward the end of Shah Jahan's reign. Competition among his sons ended with the victory of Aurangzeb, who executed his elder brother and locked his father away until death in 1666. A puritanically devout and strictly orthodox Muslim, a skillful general and a clever diplomat, Aurangzeb (r. 1658–1707) ruled more of India than did any previous badshah. His reign witnessed the culmination of Mughal power and the beginning of its decline (Map 21.3).

A combination of religious zeal and financial necessity seems to have prompted Aurangzeb to introduce a number of reforms. He appointed cen-

sors of public morals in important cities to enforce Islamic laws against gambling, prostitution, drinking, and the use of narcotics. He forbade *suttee*— the self-immolation of widows on their husbands' funeral pyres—and the castration of boys to be sold as eunuchs. He also abolished all taxes not authorized by Islamic law. This measure led to a serious loss of state revenues. To replace them, Aurangzeb in 1679 reimposed the jizya, the tax on non-Muslims. It fell most on the Hindu majority.

Regulating Indian society according to Islamic law meant modifying the religious toleration and cultural cosmopolitanism instituted by Akbar. Aurangzeb ordered the destruction of some Hindu temples. He required Hindus to pay higher customs duties than Muslims. Out of fidelity to Islamic law, he even criticized his mother's tomb, the Taj Mahal: "The lawfulness of a solid construction

MAP 21.3 India, 1707–1805   In the eighteenth century Mughal power gradually yielded to the Hindu Marathas and to the British East India Company.

over a grave is doubtful, and there can be no doubt about the extravagance involved."[19] Aurangzeb employed more Hindus in the imperial administration than any previous Mughal ruler. But his religious policy proved highly unpopular with the majority of his subjects and created problems that weaker successors could not handle.

Aurangzeb's military ventures also had mixed results. A tireless general, he pushed the conquest of the south and annexed the Golkunda and Bijapur sultanates. The stiffest opposition came from the Marathas, a militant Hindu group centered in the western Deccan. From 1681 until his death in 1707 at the age of ninety, Aurangzeb led repeated sorties through the Deccan. He took many forts and won several battles, but total destruction of the Maratha guerrilla bands eluded him. After his death they played an important role in the collapse of the Mughal Empire.

Aurangzeb's eighteenth-century successors faced formidable problems. Repeated disputes over the succession undermined the stability of the monarchy. Court intrigues replaced the battlefield as the testing ground for the nobility. Mughal provincial governors began to rule independently, giving only minimal allegiance to the badshah at Delhi. The Marathas, who revolted and pressed steadily northward, constituted the gravest threat to Mughal authority. No ruler could defeat them.

In 1739 the Persian adventurer Nadir Shah invaded India, defeated the Mughal army, looted Delhi, and after a savage massacre carried off a huge amount of treasure, including the Peacock Throne. When Nadir Shah withdrew to Afghanistan, he took with him the Mughal government's prestige. Constant skirmishes between the Afghans and the Marathas for control of the Punjab and northern India ended in 1761 at Panipat, where the Marathas were crushingly defeated by the Afghans. At this point, India no longer had any power capable of imposing order on the subcontinent or checking the penetration of the rapacious Europeans.

European Rivalry for the Indian Trade

Shortly before Babur's invasion of India, the Portuguese under the navigator Pedro Alvares Cabral had opened the subcontinent to Portuguese trade. In 1510 they established the port of Goa on the Arabian Sea as their headquarters and through a policy of piracy and terrorism swept the Muslims off the Indian and Arabian Oceans (see Map 21.3). The Portuguese historian Barrões attempted to justify Portugal's seizure of commercial traffic that the Muslims had long dominated:

It is true that there does exist a common right to all to navigate the seas and in Europe we recognize the rights which others hold against us; but the right does not extend beyond Europe and therefore the Portuguese as Lords of the Sea are justified in confiscating the goods of all those who navigate the seas without their permission.[20]

In short, Western principles of international law did not apply in Asia. For almost a century the Portuguese controlled the spice trade over the Indian Ocean.

In 1602 the Dutch formed the Dutch East India Company with the stated goal of wresting the enormously lucrative spice trade from the Portuguese. The scent of fabulous profits also attracted the English. With a charter signed by Queen Elizabeth, eighty London merchants organized the British East India Company. In 1619 Emperor Jahangir granted a British mission important commercial concessions at Surat on the western coast of India. Gifts, medical services, and bribes to Indian rulers enabled the British to set up twenty-seven other coastal forts. Fort St. George on the eastern coast became the modern city of Madras. In 1668 the city of Bombay—given to England when the Portuguese princess Catherine of Braganza married King Charles II—was leased to the company, marking the virtually total British absorption of Portuguese power in India. In 1690 the company founded a fort that became the city of Calcutta. Thus the three places that later became centers of British economic and political imperialism—Madras, Bombay, and Calcutta—existed before 1700. The Dutch concentrated their efforts in Indonesia.

Factory-Fort Societies

The British called their trading post at Surat a "factory," and the word was later used for all European settlements in India. The term did not signify manufacturing; it designated the walled compound containing the residences, gardens, and offices of British East India Company officials and the warehouses where goods were stored before being shipped to Europe. The company president exercised political authority over all residents.

Factory-forts existed to make profits from the Asian-European trade, and they evolved into flourishing centers of economic profit. The British East India Company sold silver, copper, zinc, lead, and fabrics to the Indians and bought cotton goods, silks, pepper and other spices, sugar, and opium from them. By the late seventeenth century the company was earning substantial profits. Profitability increased after 1700 when it began to trade with China. Some Indian merchants in Calcutta and Bombay made gigantic fortunes from trade within Asia.

Because the directors of the British East India Company in London discouraged all unnecessary expenses and financial risks, they opposed any interference in local Indian politics and even missionary activities. Conditions in India, however, brought about a fundamental change in the nature of the company's factories. The violent disorders and political instability that wracked India during Aurangzeb's reign and in the early eighteenth cen- tury caused the factories to evolve into defensive installations manned by small garrisons of native troops. When warlords appeared or an uprising oc- curred, people from the surrounding countryside flocked into the fort, and the company factory- forts gradually came to exercise political authority over the territories around them.

Indian and Chinese wares enjoyed great popu- larity in England and on the European continent in the late seventeenth and early eighteenth cen- turies. The middle classes wanted Indian textiles,

English Factory at Surat   The factory began as a storage place for goods before they were bought and transported abroad; it gradually expanded to include mer- chants' residences and some sort of fortification. By 1650, the English had twenty- three factories in India. Surat, in the Gujarat region on the Gulf of Cambay, was the busiest factory and port until it was sacked by the Marathas in 1664. *(Source: The Mansell Collection)*

which were colorful, durable, cheap, and washable. The upper classes desired Chinese wallpaper and porcelains, Indian silks and brocades. In the European economies, however, Asian goods created serious problems. As early as 1695 English manufacturers called for an embargo on Indian cloth, and silk weavers picketed the House of Commons.

Trade with Asia was one-way: Asians had little interest in European manufactured articles. Finding the Siamese completely uninterested in traditional Dutch goods, the Dutch East India Company tried to interest them in collections of pornography. Europeans had to pay for everything they bought from Asia with precious metals. Thus there was insistent pressure in England, France, and the Netherlands against the importation of Asian goods. As one authority explains it: "The root of the argument from which grew a tree of many branches was the old fear of the drain of gold."[21]

The Rise of the British East India Company

The French were the last to arrive in India. Louis XIV's financial wizard Colbert (see pages 561–562) planned the French East India Company for trade in the Eastern Hemisphere, and in the 1670s the company established factories at Chandernagore in Bengal, Pondicherry, and elsewhere. Joseph Dupleix (1697–1764), who was appointed governor general at Pondicherry in 1742, made allies of Indian princes and built an army of native troops, called *sepoys,* who were trained as infantrymen. The British likewise built an army with Indian surrogates trained in Western military drill and tactics. War broke out at midcentury.

From 1740 to 1763 Britain and France were almost continually engaged in a tremendous global struggle. India, like North America in the Seven Years' War, became a battlefield and a prize. The French won land battles, but English seapower decided the first phase of the war. Then a series of brilliant victories destroyed French power in southern India. By preventing French reinforcements from arriving, British seapower again proved to be the determining factor, and British jurisdiction soon extended over the important northern province of Bengal. The Treaty of Paris of 1763 recognized British control of much of India, and

scholars acknowledge the treaty as the beginning of the British Empire in India.

How was the vast subcontinent to be governed? Parliament believed that the British East India Company had too much power and considered the company responsible for the political disorders in India, which were bad for business. Parliament attempted to solve Indian problems with special legislation. The Regulating Act of 1773 created the office of governor general, with an advisory council, to exercise political authority over the territory controlled by the company. The India Act of 1784 required that the governor general be chosen from outside the company, and it made company directors subject to parliamentary supervision.

Implementation of these reforms fell to Warren Hastings, the governor of Bengal and first governor general (r. 1774–1785) with jurisdiction over Bombay and Madras. Hastings tried to build an effective administrative system and to turn the British East India Company into a government. He laid the foundations for the first Indian civil service, abolished tolls to facilitate internal trade, placed the salt and opium trades under government control, and planned a codification of Muslim and Hindu laws. He sought allies among Indian princes. The biggest problem facing Hastings's administration was a coalition of the rulers of Mysore and the Marathas aimed at the expulsion of the British. Hastings's skillful diplomacy offset this alliance temporarily.

Hastings's successor Lord Charles Cornwallis served as governor general of India from 1786 to 1794. Cornwallis continued the work of building a civil service and the war against Mysore. His introduction of the British style of property relations in effect converted a motley collection of former Mughal officers, tax collectors, and others into English-style landlords. The result was a new system of landholding, in which the rents of tenant farmers supported the landlords.

The third governor general, the marquess Richard Wellesley (r. 1797–1805), defeated Mysore in 1799 and four years later crushed the Marathas at the Battle of Assaye (see Map 21.3). Building on the work of his predecessors, he vastly extended British influence in India. Like most nineteenth-century British governors of India, Wellesley believed that British rule strongly benefited the Indians. With supreme condescension he wrote that

Textile from Kalamkari   Containing a rich variety of Persian, Hindu, Muslim, and Christian motifs, this superb example of seventeenth-century painted cotton suggests the beauty and complexity of Indian textile manufacture as well as the diversity of influences in Indian culture itself. *(Source: The Metropolitan Museum of Art)*

British power should be established over the Indian princes in order

to deprive them of the means of prosecuting any measure or of forming any confederacy hazardous to the security of the British empire, and to enable us to preserve the tranquility of India by exercising a general control over the restless spirit of ambition and violence which is characteristic of every Asiatic government.[22]

By the beginning of the nineteenth century, the authority and power of the British East India Company had yielded to the government in London. Subsequent British rule of India rested on three foundations: the support of puppet Indian princes, who exercised the trappings but not the reality of power; a large army of sepoys of dubious loyalty; and an increasingly effective civil service, staffed largely by Englishmen with Hindus and Muslims in minor positions.

SUMMARY

In the eighteenth century, the Ottoman Turks lived almost entirely within a closed Islamic environment. Very few knew European languages or had firsthand knowledge of Europe. Diplomatic relations with any European power did not exist before 1793. When the Ottomans thought of Europe at all, they believed it inferior to Islamic civilization, despite the plea in 1653 of Katib Chelebi, a renowned Ottoman historian, for greater Muslim knowledge of geography: "Sufficient and compelling proof of the necessity for learning this science is the fact that the unbelievers, by their application to and esteem for those branches of learning, have discovered the New World and have overrun the ports of India and the East Indies."[23] Everyone looked backward to the period of Suleiman the Magnificent, when the empire was at its height. There was little thought of innovation or experimentation. Some scholars believe that Islam's hostility to innovation is traceable to a saying of Muhammad: "The worst things are those that are novelties, every novelty is an innovation, every innovation is an error, and every error leads to Hell-fire." After war with Russia (1736–1739), in which the Turks were largely successful, the Ottomans entered a long period of peace on their western frontier. Not until the reign of Sultan Selim III (r. 1761–1808), during which the imperial administration and the army were restructured, European languages studied, and relations established with European powers, did the Ottoman Empire begin to become a modern state.

In the seventeenth century, the Shi'ite state of Persia enjoyed military success, economic boom, and cultural pre-eminence. The wealth and magnificence of the shah was a legend in sophisticated China and in primitive North America. In the eighteenth century, however, political weakness attracted Russian and Ottoman invasion and led to Persia's dismemberment.

The contemporary Indian writer V. S. Naipaul has called India "a wounded civilization." For centuries the economic prize of European commercial interests, in the 1700s the Indian subcontinent began to experience British political domination. Bitter hostility between Hindus and Muslims persisted as a dominant theme of Indian life.

NOTES

1. Quoted in B. Lewis, *The Muslim Discovery of Europe* (New York: Norton, 1982), p. 29.
2. W. H. McNeill, *The Pursuit of Power: Technology, Armed Force, and Society Since A.D. 1000* (Chicago: University of Chicago Press, 1982), p. 87.
3. Quoted in Lewis, *The Muslim Discovery of Europe,* p. 30.
4. F. Babinger, *Mehmed the Conqueror and His Times,* trans. R. Manheim. (Princeton, N.J.: Princeton University Press, 1978), p. 107.
5. F. Robinson, *Atlas of the Islamic World Since 1500* (New York: Facts on File, 1982), p. 72.
6. Quoted in P. K. Hitti, *The Near East in History* (Princeton, N.J.: Van Nostrand, 1961), p. 336.
7. See S. J. Shaw, *History of the Ottoman Empire and Modern Turkey,* vol. 1, *Empire of the Gazis: The Rise and Decline of the Ottoman Empire, 1208–1808* (Cambridge: Cambridge University Press, 1988), pp. 139–151.
8. *The Selected Letters of Lady Mary Wortley Montagu,* ed. R. Halsband. (London: Longman Group, 1970), pp. 98–99.
9. Ibid., p.106.
10. Ibid., p. 105.
11. Ibid., p. 96–97.
12. N. Itzkowitz, *Ottoman Empire and Islamic Tradition* (Chicago: University of Chicago Press, 1980), p. 95.
13. See Shaw, *Empire of the Gazis,* pp. 171–175, 225, 246–247; V. H. Parry, H. Inalcik, A. N. Kurat, and J. S. Bromley, *A History of the Ottoman Empire to 1715* (New York: Cambridge University Press, 1976), pp. 126, 139–140.
14. Quoted in R. E. Dunn, *The Adventures of Ibn Battuta: A Muslim Traveler of the 14th Century* (Berkeley: University of California Press, 1986), p. 81.
15. Ibid., pp. 83–87.
16. D. Morgan, *Medieval Persia, 1040–1797* (New York: Longman, 1988), pp. 112–113.
17. Quoted in V. A. Smith, *The Oxford History of India* (Oxford: Oxford University Press, 1967), p. 398.
18. Quoted in M. C. Beach, *The Imperial Image: Paintings for the Mughal Court* (Washington, D.C.: Freer Gallery of Art, Smithsonian Institution, 1981), pp. 9–10.
19. Quoted in S. K. Ikram, *Muslim Civilization in India* (New York: Columbia University Press, 1964), p. 202.
20. Quoted in K. M. Panikkar, *Asia and Western*

Domination (London: George Allen & Unwin, 1965), p. 35.

21. Quoted ibid., p. 53.

22. Quoted in W. Bingham, H. Conroy, and F. W. Iklé, *A History of Asia,* vol. 2 (Boston: Allyn and Bacon, 1967), p. 74.

23. Quoted ibid., p. 106.

SUGGESTED READING

The curious student interested in the Ottoman world might begin with A. Wheatcroft, *The Ottomans* (1993), an excitingly written and beautifully illustrated popular account of many facets of Ottoman culture that separates Western myths from Turkish reality; this book also has a helpful bibliography. In addition to the titles by Babinger, Itkowitz, and Shaw cited in the Notes, H. Inalcik, *The Ottoman Empire: the Classical Age, 1300–1600* (1973) and chapters 13, 14, and 15 of A. Hourani, *A History of the Arab Peoples* (1991) should also prove helpful. For Suleiman the Magnificent, E. Atil, *The Age of Sultan Suleyman the Magnificent* (1987) is a splendidly illustrated celebration of the man and his times, while A. Bridge, *Suleiman the Magnificent. Scourge of Heaven* (1972) presents a highly readable, if romantic, view; *Circa 1492. Art in the Age of Exploration,* ed. J. A. Levenson (1991) has several stimulating chapters on the Ottomans and Constantinople. For the later empire, see L. Cassels, *The Struggle for the Ottoman Empire, 1710–1740* (1966) and S. J. Shaw, *Between Old and New: The Ottoman Empire under Sultan Selim III, 1789–1807* (1971).

The literature on women is growing, though still largely restricted to the upper classes. See F. Davis, *The Ottoman Lady: A Social History from 1718 to 1918* (1986); A. L. Croutier, *Harem: The World Behind the Veil* (1989); L. P. Pierce, *The Imperial Harem: Woman and Sovereignty in the Ottoman World* (1993), a fine achievement which treats not only the political roles of Turkish women, but marriage, concubines, and childbirth; and *The Selected Letters of Lady Mary Wortley Montagu,* ed. R. Halsband (1970), which gives the invaluable impressions of a sophisticated Englishwoman.

For slavery in the Ottoman world, see the appropriate pages of B. Lewis, *Race and Slavery in the Middle East* (1990), and E. R. Toledano, *The Ottoman Slave Trade and Its Suppression: 1840–1890* (1982), which although dealing with a period later than this chapter, offers useful references to earlier centuries.

Perhaps the best general introduction to the history and civilization of India is S. Wolpert's elegant appreciation *India* (1990), but see also P. Spears, *A History of India,* vol. II (1986). The titles by V. A. Smith and S. K. Ikram, cited in the Notes, provide broad general treatments, as do P. M. Holt *et al.,* eds., *The Cambridge History of India* 2 vols. (1970), M. Mujeeb, *The Indian Muslims* (1967), and I. Habib, *The Agrarian System of Mughal India, 1556–1707* (1963) whose theme and scope are indicated by the title. Many of the essays in J. F. Richards, *Power, Administration and Finance in Mughal India* (1993) are useful and authoritative. For the decline of imperial authority in eighteenth century India, see the important study of M. Alam, *The Crisis of Empire in Mughal North India: Awadh and the Punjab, 1707–48* (1986). Students wishing to study Indian culture through its architecture, should consult two splendid and recent achievements: C. Tadgell, *The History of Architecture in India: from the Dawn of Civilization to the End of the Raj* (1995) and G. Mitchell, *The Royal Palaces of India* (1995). E. B. Findly, *Nur Jahan. Empress of Mughal India* (1993) provides a vivid picture of one powerful and influential woman. E. Maclagan, *The Jesuits and the Great Mogul* (1932) discusses the Jesuits at the courts of Akbar, Jahangir, and Shah Jahan. B. Gascoigne, *The Great Moghuls* (1971) and G. Hambly, *The Cities of Mughal India: Delhi, Agra, and Fatehpur Sikri* (1968) are well illustrated and highly readable. For the impact of Portuguese, Dutch, and English mercantile activities in India, see M. N. Pearson, *Merchants and Rulers in Gujarat: The Response to the Portuguese in the Sixteenth Century* (1976).

LISTENING TO THE
PAST

Culture Shock

A keen student of comparative religion, the Mughal emperor Akbar invited Jain teachers, Sikh gurus, and Catholic Jesuits to his court. The Jesuits had recently established a mission and college in Goa. One of the Jesuits, Antonio Monserrate, who eventually served as an adviser to the emperor and accompanied him on several military expeditions, had been ordered by the Superior of the Society of Jesus in India to keep a careful record of his experiences at the Mughal court. Monserrate's Commentary *has proved invaluable to scholars for its picture of Akbar's personality and policies and Westerners' reaction to Indian culture in the late sixteenth century.*

The wives of the Brachmans—a famous class of nobly-born Hindus—are accustomed, in accordance with an ancient tradition of their religion, to burn themselves on the same pyres as their dead husbands. The King ordered the priests to be summoned to see an instance of this. They went in ignorance of what was to take place; but when they found out, they plainly indicated by their saddened faces how cruel and savage they felt that crime to be. Finally Rudolf[1] publicly reprimanded the King for showing openly by his presence there that he approved of such a revolting crime, and for supporting it by his weighty judgment and explicit approbation, (for he was heard to say that such fortitude could only come from God). Such was Zelaldinus'[2] kindness and favour towards the priests that he showed no resentment; and a certain chief, a great favourite of his, a Brachman by birth, who held the office of Superintendent of sacred observances, could no longer persuade him to attend such spectacles. The wretched women are rendered quite insensible by means of certain drugs, in order that they may feel no pain. For this purpose opium is used, or a soporific herb named bang, or—more usually—the herb 'duturo,' which is known to the Indians, although entirely unfamiliar alike to modern Europeans and to the ancients. Sometimes they are half-drugged: and, before they lose their resolution, are hurried to the pyre with warnings, prayers and promises of eternal fame. On arriving there they cast themselves into the flames. If they hesitate, the wretched creatures are driven on to the pyre: and if they try to leap off again, are held down with poles and hooks. The nobles who were present were highly incensed at the Fathers' interference. They did not dare to gainsay the King; but they grumbled loudly amongst themselves, saying, 'Away with you, black-clothed Franks.' The whole city was filled with praise and admiration when news was brought that the Franks had dared to rebuke the King regarding this affair.

On one occasion, the Fathers met a crowd of worthless profligates,[3] some of those who dress and adorn themselves like women. The priests were rightly disgusted at this, and took the first opportunity of privately complaining to the King (since he was so favourable to them) about this disgraceful matter. They declared with the greatest emphasis that they were astonished at his permitting such a class of men to live in his kingdom, let alone in his city, and almost under his eyes. They must be banished, as though they were a deadly plague, to his most distant territories; even better, let them be burnt up by devouring flames. They never would have believed that such men could be found in the court itself and in the royal-city, where lived a king of such piety, integrity and prudence. Therefore let him give orders that these libertines should never again be seen in Fattepurum, seeing that his remarkable prophet[4] had guaranteed that good men should never suffer for their good actions. The King laughed at this piece of sarcasm and retired, saying that he would attend to the matter.

Questions for Analysis

1. What does the document reveal about the Jesuits' relations with Akbar?

2. Consider the Jesuits' reactions to the Hindu practice of suttee.[5] Should they have interfered?

3. Contrast the Jesuits' reaction to suttee and to the transvestite prostitutes.

Source: *The Commentary of Father Monserrate, S.J., on His Journey to the Court of Akbar* (London: Oxford University Press, 1922), pp. 61–63.

1. One of the Jesuits.
2. The Jesuits' name for Akbar.
3. Male prostitutes, common in almost all societies.
4. A reference to the Prophet Muhammad. The Jesuits' logic and charity is somewhat faulty here.
5. *Suttee* means "true one" in Sanskrit. The term was used to describe a Hindu widow's self-immolation on the funeral pyre of her dead husband, without whom her life had supposedly lost all meaning. The British abolished suttee in 1829, but even today women whose dowries are not paid are sometimes burned to death.

Antonio at the court of Akbar. (*Source: Reproduced by kind permission of the Trustees of the Chester Beatty Library, Dublin*)

CHAPTER

22

China and Japan,
ca 1400–1800

Toyotomi Hideyoshi (1530–1598) is represented as a knightly archer in this statue in a niche of the Yomei-mon, a gate leading to the Toshogu Shrine at Nikko. *(Source: Photographer, Martin Hürlimann. Courtesy of Reich Verlag, Switzerland.)*

The period from about 1400 to 1800 witnessed growth and dynamic change in East Asia. In China the native Ming Dynasty (1368–1644) had replaced the Yuan (1271–1368) and in 1644 was replaced by the foreign Manchu Dynasty. The early Ming period was a time of remarkable economic reconstruction and of the establishment of new and original social institutions. Over time, however, the bureaucracy prevented the changes necessary to meet new demands on the empire. The Manchus inaugurated a long period of peace, relative prosperity, and population expansion. In the Manchu period the Chinese Empire reached its greatest territorial extent, and literary and artistic creativity reached their apogee.

In the Japanese islands, united by Nobunaga and later the Tokugawa Shogunate (1600–1867), the feudal military aristocracy continued to evolve. Although Japan developed largely in isolation from outside influences, its sociopolitical system bore striking similarities to medieval European feudalism. The period of the Tokugawa Shogunate, like that of the Ming Dynasty in China, was marked by remarkable agricultural productivity and industrial growth.

- What features characterized the governments of the Ming and Manchu Dynasties in China and the Tokugawa Shogunate in Japan?
- How did agricultural and commercial developments affect Chinese and Japanese societies?
- How did Chinese thinkers interpret and explain the shift from the Ming to the Manchus?

This chapter explores these questions.

❖ CHINA, FROM THE MING TO THE MID-MANCHU DYNASTY (CA 1368–1795)

Mongol repression under the Yuan Dynasty, rapid inflation of the currency, disputes over succession among the khans, and the growth of peasant secret societies led to the decay of Mongol government in China. By 1368, Hong Wu, the leader of a secret society called the Red Turbans, had pushed the Mongols out of China. Hong Wu (r. 1368–1398), founder of the Ming Dynasty, and Liu Bang (r. 206–195 B.C.), founder of the Han Dynasty, were the only peasants to found major dy-

nasties in China. The Ming Dynasty (1368–1644) was the only dynasty that originated south of the Yangtze River (see Map 22.1).

Under the Ming, China experienced dynamic change. Agricultural development and commercial reconstruction followed a long period of chaos and disorder. Hong Wu introduced far-reaching social and political institutions. By the middle of the fifteenth century, however, his administrative framework had begun to decay. Externally, defeats in Mongolia in the later fifteenth century led to a long period of Chinese withdrawal. Nevertheless, the Ming period stands out because of its social and cultural achievements.

The Ming Agricultural and Commercial Revolutions

Mongol exploitation and the civil disorders that accompanied the breakdown of Yuan rule left China in economic chaos in the mid-fourteenth century. Vast stretches of farmland were laid waste, some entirely abandoned. Damaged dikes and canals proved unusable, causing trade to decline.

Between 1370 and 1398, a profound economic reconstruction occurred. The agricultural revolution that China underwent in the Ming period was part of a gigantic effort at recovery after the disaster of Mongol rule. At the heart of this revolution was radical improvement in methods of rice production.

More than bread in Europe, rice supplied almost the total nourishment of the population in central and south China. (In north China, wheat, made into steamed or baked bread or into noodles, served as the staple of the diet.) Terracing and irrigation of mountain slopes, introduced in the eleventh century, had increased rice harvests. The introduction of drought-resistant Indochinese, or Champa, rice proved an even greater boon. Although Champa rice was of lower nutritional quality than the native rice, it considerably increased the total output of food. Ming farmers experimented with Champa rice that required only sixty days from planting to harvesting instead of the usual hundred days. Peasants soon reaped two harvests a year, an enormous increase in production.

Other innovations also brought good results. Ming-era peasants introduced irrigation pumps worked by pedals. Farmers began to stock the rice paddies with fish, which continuously fertilized the

Chinese Peasants at Work   The Western artist who sketched this picture in the seventeenth century seems to be telling us that human power in agriculture was as common in China as animal power. Notice that a woman also pulls the plow; she might have been pregnant. Coco palms (left) are not usually found as far north as China. The pigtailed men date the picture from the Manchu period. *(Source: Caroline Buckler)*

rice fields, destroyed malaria-bearing mosquitoes, and enriched the diet. Fish farming in the paddies eventually enabled large, previously uninhabitable parts of southern China to be brought under cultivation. Farmers discovered the possibilities of commercial cropping in cotton, sugar cane, and indigo. And new methods of crop rotation allowed for continuous cultivation and for more than one harvest per year from a single field.

The Ming rulers promoted the repopulation and colonization of devastated regions through massive transfers of people. Immigrants received large plots of land and exemption from taxation for many years. Table 22.1, based on fourteenth-century records of newly reclaimed land, helps tell the story.[1]

Reforestation was a dramatic aspect of the agricultural revolution. In 1391 the Ming government ordered 50 million trees planted in the Nanjing (Nanking) area. Lumber from the trees was intended for the construction of a maritime fleet. In 1392 each family holding colonized land in Anhwei province had to plant 200 each of mulberry, jujube, and persimmon trees. In 1396 peasants in the present-day provinces of Hunan and Hupeh in

the east planted 84 million fruit trees. Historians have estimated that 1 billion trees were planted during Hong Wu's reign.[2]

What were the social consequences of agricultural development? Increased food production led to steady population growth. Demographers date the start of the Chinese population boom at about 1550, as a direct result of improved methods of rice production. Increases in total yields differed fundamentally, however, from comparable agricultural growth in Europe: Chinese grain harvests were improved through intensification of peasant labor. This meant lower income per capita.

Population increase seems to have led to the multiplication of towns and small cities. Urbanization in the Ming era (and, later, in the Manchu period) meant the proliferation of market centers and small towns rather than the growth of "large" cities like those in Europe in the High Middle Ages and China in the Song (Sung) period (960–1279). Most people lived in tiny hamlets or villages that had no markets. What distinguished a village from a town was the existence of a market in a town.

um.. NO!

Towns held markets twice a week; in southern China, where a week was ten days long, markets were held three times a week. Town markets consisted of little open-air shops that sold essential goods—pins, matches, oil for lamps, candles, paper, incense, tobacco—to country people from surrounding hamlets. The market usually included a tearoom or tavern where tea and rice wine were sold, entertainers performed, and moneylenders and pawnshops sometimes did business.

Tradesmen, who carried their wares on their backs, and craftsmen—carpenters, barbers, joiners, locksmiths—moved constantly from market to market. Itinerant salesmen depended on the city market for their wares. In large towns and cities foodstuffs from the countryside and rare and precious goods from distant places were offered for sale. Cities gradually became islands of sophistication in the highly localized Chinese economy. Nanjing, for example, spread out enormously because the presence of the imperial court and bureaucracy generated a great demand for goods. The concentration of people in turn created demand for goods and services. Industrial development was stimulated. Small businesses manufactured textiles, paper, and luxury goods such as silks and porcelains. Nanjing and Shanghai became centers for the production of cotton and silks; Xiangtan specialized in the grain and salt trade and in silver. Small towns remained embedded in peasant culture, but large towns and cities pursued contacts with the wider world.

The Government of Hong Wu

Hong Wu's government reforms rested on a few strong centralizing principles. Hong Wu established China's capital at Nanjing (literally, "southern capital"), his old base on the Yangtze River. He stripped many nobles of their estates and divided the estates among the peasantry. Although Hong Wu had been a monk, he confiscated many of the temples' tax-exempt lands, thereby increasing the proceeds of the state treasury. In the Song period, commercial taxes had fed the treasury. In the Ming and, later, the Manchu periods, imperial revenues came mainly from agriculture: farmers produced the state's resources.

Hong Wu ordered a general survey of all China's land and several censuses of the population. The data gathered were recorded in official

TABLE 22.1 LAND RECLAMATION IN EARLY MING CHINA

Year	Reclaimed Land (in hectares; 1 hectare = 2.5 acres)
1371	576,000
1373	1,912,000
1374	4,974,000
1379	1,486,000

Source: J. Gernet, A History of Chinese Civilization, *trans. J. R. Foster (Cambridge: Cambridge University Press, 1982), p. 391. Used with permission.*

JINGLEHIEMER JUNCTION

registers, which provided valuable information about the taxes that landlords, temples, and peasants owed. According to the registers, the capital was owed 8 million *shih,* or 160,000 tons, of rice per year. Such thorough fiscal information contributed to the efficient operation of the state.

To secure soldiers for the army and personnel for his administration and to generate revenue, Hong Wu adopted the Yuan practice of requiring service to the state. He made all occupations hereditary, classifying the entire Chinese population into three hereditary categories: peasants, artisans, and soldiers. The state ministry that had jurisdiction over a particular category designated an individual's obligations to the state.

The ministry of finance oversaw the peasants, who provided the bulk of the taxes and performed public labor services. The ministry of public works supervised artisans and all people who had special skills and crafts. The ministry of the army controlled the standing army of 2 million men. Each social category prevailed in a particular geographical region. Peasants lived in the countryside. Craftsmen lived mainly in the neighborhoods of the cities for which they produced goods. Army families lived along the coasts and lengthy frontiers that they defended. When a soldier died or proved unable to fight, his family had to provide a replacement.

The Ming emperor wielded absolute and despotic power. Access to his personal favor was the only means of acquiring privilege or some limited derivative power. The complex ceremonial and court ritual surrounding any public appearance by the emperor, the vast imperial palace staffed only by servile women and eunuchs, and the precise procedures of the imperial bureaucracy, which blamed any difficulties on the emperor's advisers— all lent the throne a rarefied aura and exalted the emperor's authority. In addition, Hong Wu demanded that the military nobles (his old rebel comrades-in-arms) live at his court in Nanjing, where he could keep an eye on them. He raised many generals to the nobility, a position that bestowed honor and financial benefits but no political power whatsoever.

Late in his reign Hong Wu executed many nobles and divided China into principalities, putting one of his sons in charge of each. Suspicious even of his sons' loyalty, he carefully limited their power. Positions in the imperial administration were filled in part by means of civil service examinations, which proved to be Hong Wu's most enduring reform. The examination system, which lasted until the twentieth century, later became the exclusive channel for official recruitment. Examinations were given every three years at the district, provincial, and state (imperial) levels; candidates had to pass the lower levels before trying for the imperial level where the success rate in late imperial China was between one and two percent. In the Ming period the examinations required a minute knowledge of the ancient Chinese classics and a formal and precise literary style: they discouraged all originality. In the bureaucrats who passed them, the examinations promoted conservatism and opposition to innovation. To prevent nepotism and corruption, civil service positions were filled according to the "Rule of Avoidance": a candidate could

✳ **An Acrobat Entertains** The hard, dull routine of country or town people could be temporarily lightened by a traveling juggler, gymnast, or comedian who performed skits and then passed the hat for payment. Here an acrobat demonstrates his skill with the lance as spectators watch: at the top, a handicapped person, two beggars, and a boy who calls them; at the left, a group of porters with poles for carrying merchandise on their shoulders; on the right, a group of the well-to-do. *(Source: Art Institute of Chicago/Photo: Wan-go Weng)*

not be appointed to a position in his native province, nor could two members of the same family serve in the same province.

After 1426 the eunuch-dominated secret police controlled the palace guards and the imperial workshops, infiltrated the civil service, and headed all foreign missions. Through blackmail, espionage, and corruption, the secret police exercised enormous domestic power. How did eunuchs acquire such power? Without heirs, they had no immediate family concerns. Drawn from the lowest classes of society, viewed with distaste by respectable people, eunuchs had no hope of gaining status except by satisfying every whim of the emperor. They were indifferent to public opinion. Because of their total submission to the emperor, the emperors believed them absolutely trustworthy. Several eunuchs—Wang Chih in the 1470s, Liu Zhi in the 1500s, and Wei Zhong-xian in the 1620s—gained dictatorial power when their emperors lost interest in affairs of state.

Foreign affairs occupied much of Hong Wu's attention. He sought to control all Chinese contacts with the outside world, and he repeatedly invaded Mongolia. But the strengthening and extension of the Great Wall stands as Hong Wu's and his Ming successors' most visible achievement. According to one record, the defense system of the Great Wall throughout the Ming period formed a protective girdle "10,000 *li* (a *li* is about one-third of a mile) in an unbroken chain from the Yalu River in the east to Jiayuguan in the west."[3] The forts, beacon towers, and garrisons that pierced the wall at militarily strategic spots kept in close contact with the central government. Because of the steady pressure of Mongol attacks in the fifteenth century, Hong Wu's successors continued the work of reinforcing the Great Wall.

Hong Wu forbade free commercial contacts along the coasts between Chinese and foreign merchants. He insisted that foreign states eager to trade with China acknowledge his suzerainty by offering tribute. The early Ming emperors displayed greater military and diplomatic efficiency than had Chinese rulers for centuries. By the mid-fifteenth century, however, Mongol raids by land and Japanese piracy at sea, often with the hidden cooperation of the local Chinese, were commonplace. Along the coasts Koreans, Vietnamese, Malays, Sumatrans, and Japanese entered China disguised as merchants. If they were dissatisfied with the official rates of exchange, they robbed and destroyed. Neither fortresses and the transfer of coastal settlements inland nor precautionary attacks on pirate merchant raiders could suppress the problem. The imperial court came to regard foreigners arriving by ship, including Europeans when they arrived in the sixteenth century, as "barbarians."

Maritime Expansion

Another dramatic development of the Ming period was the series of naval expeditions sent out between 1405 and 1433 under Hong Wu's son Yong Lu and Yong Lu's successor. China had a strong maritime history stretching back to the eleventh century, and these early fifteenth-century voyages were a continuation of that tradition. The Ming expeditions established China as the greatest maritime power in the world—considerably ahead of Portugal, whose major seafaring reconnaissances began a half-century later.

In contrast to Hong Wu, Yong Lu broadened diplomatic and commercial contacts within the tribute system. Yong Lu had two basic motives for launching overseas voyages. First, he sent them in search of Jian Wen, a serious contender for the throne whom he had defeated but who, rumor claimed, had escaped to Southeast Asia. Second, he launched the expeditions to explore, to expand trade, and to provide the imperial court with luxury objects. Led by the Muslim eunuch admiral Zheng He and navigating by compass, seven fleets sailed to East and South Asia. The first expedition (which carried 27,800 men) involved 62 major ships, the largest of which was 440 feet in length and 180 feet in the beam and had 9 masts. The expeditions crossed the Indian Ocean to Ceylon, the Persian Gulf, and the east coast of Africa.

These voyages had important consequences. They extended the prestige of the Ming Dynasty throughout Asia. Trade, in the form of tribute from as far as the west coast of southern India, greatly increased. Diplomatic contacts with the distant Middle East led to the arrival in Nanjing of embassies from Egypt. The maritime expeditions also led to the publication of geographical works such as the *Treatise on the Barbarian Kingdoms on the Western Oceans* (1434) and *The Marvels Discovered by the Boat Bound for the Galaxy* (1436). The information acquired from the voyages served as the basis of Chinese knowledge of the maritime world until the nineteenth century. Finally, these expeditions resulted in Chinese emigration to the countries of Southeast Asia and the ports of southern India. The voyages were terminated because Confucian court intellectuals persuaded the emperor that his quest for strange and exotic things signaled the collapse of the dynasty.[4] After 1435, China returned to a policy of isolation.

Decline of the Ming Dynasty

A bitter struggle for the throne ensued when Hong Wu died. The bloody wars that brought his son Yong Lu to the throne devastated the territory between the Yellow and the Yangtze Rivers. Yong Lu (1403–1424) promoted a policy of resettlement there. He continued his father's policies of requiring civil service examinations, controlling the nobility, and trying to restrain pirates. He also transferred the capital back to Beijing (Peking). A former governor *(wang)* of the north, Yong Lu felt he had greater support there than in the south. Beijing was also closer to the northern frontier and thus was a better place for strategic defense against China's ancient enemies, the Mongols. The move pleased the military faction but hurt the new gentry and mercantile groups, whose economic interests centered around Nanjing.

The extravagance of the imperial court caused economic difficulties. Hong Wu had exercised fiscal restraint, but Yong Lu and his successors tried to outdo the splendor and magnificence of the Mongols. The emperor and his court lived in the Forbidden City, a quarter-mile compound filled with palatial buildings, ceremonial halls, marble terraces, and lengthy galleries; their grandeur surpassed that of Louis XIV's Versailles. Surrounding the Forbidden City and occupying some three square smiles was the Imperial City, where, in the words of a modern historian,

there were also supply depots and material-processing plants. Among them was the court of Imperial Entertainments, which had the capacity to serve banquets for up to 15,000 men on short notice. Next to the bakery, distillery, and confectionery were the emperor's stable, armory, printing-office, and book depository.[5]

A century and a half later, in the reign of the emperor Wan-li, everything required for the maintenance of the Imperial City was manufactured or deposited there. Approximately twenty thousand eunuchs worked there, and some three thousand female domestics performed household tasks. The emperor's immediate court—councilors, bodyguards, relatives, official wives, and concubines—numbered several thousand people. Supporting so many people on a lavish scale placed a great burden on the treasury. Financial difficulties thus played a major role in the decline of the Ming.

Yong Lu's successors lacked his drive and ability. The Mongols continued to press on the northern borders, and the Chinese had to yield some territory. In 1450, during an ill-conceived expedition against the Mongols, the inexperienced young emperor Ying-Zoung (r. 1436–1450 and 1457–1464) was captured and remained a prisoner of the Mongols for seven years. In the south, a Chinese army of 200,000 had pressed into northern Vietnam in 1406. This imperialistic move led to temporary Chinese domination of the Red River basin and of much of central Vietnam. A Vietnamese liberation movement retaliated and by 1427 had driven the occupiers out. In the sixteenth century the Japanese accelerated their coastal raids and even sacked the cities of Ningbo (Ningpo) and Yangzhou (Yangchow). Difficulties in collecting taxes hindered the government's ability to strengthen the army. It was commonplace in the eleven hundred counties of Ming China for people to delay or refuse to pay taxes, aware that no magistrate could prosecute thousands of delinquents. Their taxes were eventually written off.

In spite of these pressures, the empire did not fall apart. In fact, southern China enjoyed considerable prosperity in the late sixteenth and early seventeenth centuries. Japanese, Portuguese, and Dutch merchants paid in silver for the Chinese silks and ceramics they bought. However, because of the steady flow of silver into China from the trade with Japan and, later, from the mines of Mexico and Peru by way of Spain, the value of Chinese paper currency, which had been in circulation since the eleventh century, drastically declined. Unable to control either the state economy or local commercial activity, the imperial government had to acquiesce in foreign trade. The emperor also had to recognize the triumph of silver as a medium of exchange.

By the late sixteenth century China was participating in the emerging global economy. Portuguese ships carried Chinese silks and ceramics to Nagasaki and returned with Japanese silver. The huge Ming merchant marine fleet, built from the trees planted by Hong Wu and technically more

Silkworm Culture   Women traditionally handled silkworm culture, though men helped pick the mulberry leaves that fed the worms. At the left, silkworms are cultivated, graded, and harvested. At the right, the cocoons are boiled in a cauldron before the threads can be drawn, and a boy fans the fire under the pot. *(Source: Library of Congress/Laurie Platt Winfrey, Inc.)*

proficient for long sea voyages than were the Spanish and Portuguese fleets, transported textiles, porcelains, silk, and paper to Manila in the Philippines and brought back sweet potatoes, tobacco, firearms, and silver. From Manila the Spanish fleet carried Chinese goods to the markets of Barcelona, Antwerp, and Venice. The Dutch transported tea by the boatload from Fujian (Fukien) and Zhejiang (Chekiang) for the castles and drawing rooms of Europe.[6] Europeans paid for most of their imports with silver. Scholars argue that between one-third and one-half of all the silver mined in the Americas between 1527 and 1821 wound up in China. Spanish galleons carried it from Acapulco to Manila and from there to Chinese ports[7].

In the middle of the sixteenth century, China showed many signs of developing into an urban mercantile society. Merchants and businessmen had large amounts of capital, and they invested it not in land, as in the past, but in commercial and craft industries. Silk making, cotton weaving, porcelain manufacture, printing, and steel production assumed a definite industrial character. So many peasants seeking employment migrated to the towns that agriculture declined. Some businesses employed several hundred workers, many of them women. According to a French scholar, "Peasant women took jobs at Sung-chiang, southwest of Shanghai in the cotton mills. According to contemporary descriptions, in the big workshops the employees were already the anonymous labor force that we regard as characteristic of the industrial age."[8]

Technical treatises reveal considerable progress in manufacturing procedures. Silk looms had three or four shuttle winders. Printers could produce a sheet of paper with three or four different colors, similar to the page of a modern magazine. Chinese ceramics displayed astonishing technology—which helps explain the huge demand for them. Likewise, agricultural treatises described new machines for working the soil, sowing seed, and irrigation. Population, which stood at roughly 70 million at the start of the Ming period, increased to about 130 million by 1600.

With population, technology, and capital, why did China fail to develop something comparable to what Westerners later called an industrial or commercial revolution? The traditional Chinese value system did not esteem commerce, industry, or social change.

China never experienced a scientific revolution or an Enlightenment, as the European West did in the seventeenth and eighteenth centuries (Ch. 18). Lacking a spirit that criticized existing ideas and institutions, China remained culture bound and conservative. The Chinese practice of partible inheritance in which sons divided parents' estates thwarted, or at least slowed, the accumulation of capital. (The English system of primogeniture by which only the eldest son inherited promoted the accumulation of capital.) Likewise, the extensive pursuit of the Confucian civil service examinations as the path to socio-economic advancement diverted capital from industrial, technical, and even agricultural innovation. The fundamental axiom that China, the Central Kingdom of the universe, was superior to other states and contained within its borders all that was needed for a happy existence likewise discouraged change.

Hostility to the artisan and merchant classes had very deep roots in traditional China. The sixth century B.C. scholar Han Fei had listed merchants and craftsmen among "The Five Vermin of the State," writing:

An enlightened ruler will administer his state in such a way as to decrease the number of merchants, artisans and other men who make their living by wandering from place to place, and will see to it that such men are looked down upon. In this way he lessens the number of people who abandon primary pursuits (agriculture) to take up secondary occupations. . . . When wealth and money, no matter how dishonestly gotten, can buy what is in the market, you may be sure that the number of merchants will not remain small. . . . These are the customs of a disordered state.[9]

Revering such classical Confucian texts, officials in the seventeenth and eighteenth centuries looked on merchants with distrust and distaste.

Wealth was based on agriculture, and from agriculture the state derived its taxes and the ruling class its income. Could trade and manufacturing also be taxed? No, they could not. According to Confucian philosophy, any promotion of trade would encourage people to aspire to a different lifestyle and to a higher social status, and such aspirations would bring change and social disorder. Moreover, Chinese thinkers held that merchants produced nothing: they bought something from its grower or maker and sold it at a higher price than they had paid; thus they were parasites living off the labor of others. In addition, the proliferation of luxury goods, which people did not really need, would lead to extravagance and excessive consumption and in turn to moral decay.

Believing that virtue lies in frugality, vice in extravagance, the Ming emperors issued sumptuary laws restricting or prohibiting certain styles of clothing, tableware, means of conveyance, and articles of household decoration. The effect of these laws, however, was *increased* social stratification: the richer became richer, the poor poorer. Nevertheless, the Confucian ideal remained intact: a "successful merchant" was, by definition, one who had stopped trading and had invested his wealth in agriculture.[10] By contrast, in England, and later in western and central Europe, the upper middle classes gained increasing influence in representative assemblies and passed laws that facilitated commerce, business, and industry.

In 1600 the Ming Dynasty faced grave political and economic problems. The Manchus, a Tungusic people from Manchuria, threatened from the north. Wars against the Japanese and Koreans had depleted the imperial treasury. As rich landowners bought up the lands assigned to farm families, the social structures set up by Hong Wu broke down. The military, considered a disreputable profession, attracted the dregs of society, so the government had to hire mercenaries. According to the Italian Jesuit missionary Matteo Ricci (1552–1610), "All those under arms lead a despicable life, for they have not embraced this profession out of love of their country or devotion to their king or love of honour and glory, but as men in the service of a provider of employment."[11] Maintenance of the army placed a heavy burden on the state.

Meanwhile, the imperial court continued to squander vast sums on an ostentatious lifestyle. Under the emperor Wan-li, forty-five princes of the first rank received annual incomes of 10,000 shih (the money equivalent of 10,000 tons of grain), and 21,000 lesser nobles also received large allowances. The emperors increased domestic sales taxes, established customs posts for export-import duties, and laid ever-more-crushing taxes on the peasants. New taxes provoked violent riots in the large commercial centers of Suzhou (Soochow), Hangzhou (Hangchow), and Beijing.

Finally, the emperors became the victims of the bureaucracy and of Confucian ideology. A Ming emperor was taught that his primary duties were to venerate the heavens, the abode of his ancestors who watched over him; and to follow the precedents set by his ancestors. As long as the emperor performed certain time-honored rituals, he retained the Mandate of Heaven, the traditional legitimization of Chinese rulers. Imperial ritual connected the ordinary person to the state by inspiring awe, respect and loyalty. Thus successive emperors spent a large part of each day in the performance of imperial ceremonies which they began to resent.

The dynastic shift from the Ming to the Qing (Ch-ing) Dynasty established by the Manchus seemed to fulfill the Han Confucian doctrine that history operates in a cyclical fashion. The Ming emperor apparently had forfeited the Mandate of Heaven. According to Han Confucian scholars, a wise ruler satisfies Heaven's mandate by observing the proper Confucian rites of social intercourse. If the emperor is respectful to his parents, attentive to his ministers, and concerned for his subjects, then the empire and the civilized world will flourish. The emperor was supposed to be a model. If he was virtuous, his officials were likely to be so too. If he looked to his own self-interest, his civil servants would probably do likewise, to the cost of the general welfare: corruption would spread, taxes would be oppressive, and peasants would revolt.

The reign of Wan-li (r. 1573–1619), who ruled longer than any other member of the Ming Dynasty, illustrates what happened when the emperor was at odds with the system. An intelligent man with some good ideas, Wan-li felt that the bureaucrats opposed everything he wanted to do. When he tried to increase the size of the army and to improve its effectiveness through drills and maneuvers, civil service officials sent him lengthy petitions calling for an end to such exercises. When he wanted to take personal command of the army at a time of foreign invasion, bureaucrats told him that precedent forbade his leaving the Imperial City. Wan-li gradually reached the conclusion that the monarchy had become no more than a set of stylized performances.

Stymied in whatever he wanted to do, he simply refused to make state decisions. He devoted his time to his horses and, though still a young man, to the construction of his tomb. Imperial decisions were postponed. Factional strife among the court eunuchs and bureaucrats increased. The wheels of government ground to a halt.[12] Between 1619 and 1627, greedy court eunuchs helped precipitate a crisis. The eunuch Wei Zhong-xian (1568–1627) exercised a two-year reign of terror and sent hundreds of honest civil servants to their deaths as conspirators. The bureaucracy, which the eunuchs controlled, was so torn by factions that it could not function.

Meanwhile, the Manchus pressed against China's northeastern border. Under their leader Nurhachi (1559–1626), they built a powerful military and administrative organization and gained the allegiance of the Mongols and other tribes. As the Ming government in Beijing floundered, public anger at bureaucratic corruption mounted. The gentry and business classes, centered in the south around Nanjing, had been alienated by the Ming court's fiscal mismanagement and demands for more taxes. Ming troops, their pay in arrears, turned outlaw. Droughts led to crop failures, which in turn caused widespread famines. Starving peasants turned to banditry, and entire provinces revolted. The general decay paved the way for Manchu conquest.

In the popular understanding of the Mandate of Heaven, the natural and political orders were closely linked. Events such as droughts, famines, earthquakes, floods, and volcanic eruptions were considered signs of Heaven's displeasure and signaled that conditions were ripe for the appearance of a new dynasty. Predictably, when it seemed that the Mandate of Heaven had been withdrawn from the Ming emperor and was about to redescend on someone worthy, ambitious generals, bandit warlords, and popular movements appeared. According to a modern historian, "The prospect of a new mandate feverishly excited rebellions, which seemed in turn to prove that the previous dynastic cycle had reached its term."[13] Such events had accompanied the collapse of the Yuan and the rise of the Ming. Similar developments greeted the fall of the Ming and the emergence of the Manchus.

Manchu Rule

Capitalizing on the internal weaknesses of the Ming, in 1644 the Manchus declared a new dynasty, the Qing. They went on to capture Beijing and slowly gained control of all China. Although various Ming princes and local bandit groups had

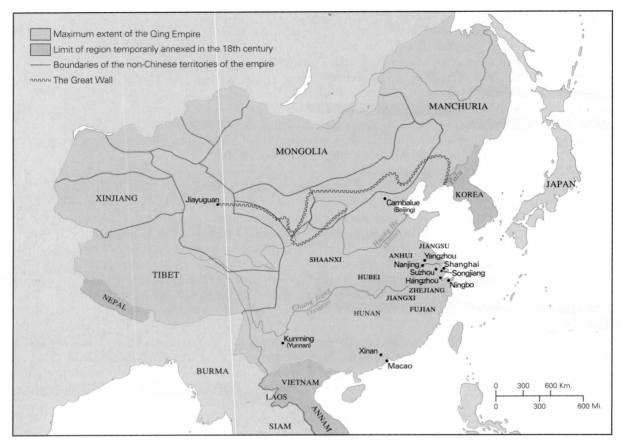

MAP 22.1 The Qing Empire, 1759   The sheer size of the Qing Empire in China almost inevitably led to its profound cultural influence on the rest of Asia. What geographical and political factors limited the extent of the empire?

risen against the Manchus, the army lacked good equipment and staying power and gradually collapsed. The entry of the Manchus' imperial armies into Yunnan in 1681 marked their complete military triumph.

By purging the civil service of the old court eunuchs and troublesome factions, and by offering Chinese intellectuals positions in the bureaucracy, the Manchus gained the support of the influential academic and intellectual classes. Chinese scholars flocked to Beijing. The Manchu government, staffed by able and honest Chinese, became much more efficient than the Ming.

The Qing Dynasty—the name adopted by the Manchus means "pure" or "unsullied"—ruled until 1912. In its heyday in the eighteenth century, the Qing Empire covered much of Asia—China proper, Manchuria, Mongolia, Tibet, and Xinjiang (Sinkiang)—and enjoyed tribute from Burma, Nepal, Laos, Siam, Annam, and Korea (Map 22.1). China had the largest population on earth and achieved an unprecedented degree of prosperity.

How did a million Manchus govern 350 million Chinese? The Qing Dynasty retained the basic structures of Ming and Confucian government. The emperor, possessor of the Mandate of Heaven, governed as a supreme and autocratic ruler. The bureaucracies continued as they had in Ming and earlier times: the imperial household bureaucracy managed the emperor's palaces and households; the central bureaucracy administered his vast empire. Most positions in the empire were assigned on the basis of candidates' performances in the civil service examinations in the Confucian classics. The highest positions in Beijing and in the provinces of China were open to Chinese as well as to Manchus. These measures pacified the Chinese economic and intellectual elites. The Manchus, however, maintained a privileged status in society. They wore distinctive clothes, did not practice footbinding, retained their own language and alphabet, and maintained ethnic separatism by forbidding intermarriage with the Chinese. The Manchus required Chinese males to wear their hair in a pigtail as a sign of subservience.

Along with the agricultural improvements begun in the Ming period, internal peace, relative prosperity, and engineering methods that prevented flooding of the countryside contributed to a population explosion in the eighteenth century, as the statistics in Table 22.2 illustrate. But in the late eighteenth century growth without increased agricultural output led to rebellions and uprisings that eventually weakened the Qing Dynasty.

The reign of the emperor Kang-xi (r. 1662–1722) launched a period of great achievement. A contemporary of the Indian ruler Aurangzeb, the French king Louis XIV, and the Russian tsar Peter the Great, Kang-xi demonstrated exceptional intelligence, energy, and concern for the welfare of his people. He also enjoyed much greater freedom of action than had the Ming emperor Wan-li a century earlier. Whereas Wan-li had been a captive of precedent, incapable of making changes, Kang-xi cut both court expenses and taxes and traveled extensively throughout his domain. On these trips he investigated the conduct of local bureaucrats in an effort to prevent them from oppressing the people. Kang-xi squarely faced and thoroughly crushed a massive rebellion in southern China in 1678. He personally led an army into Mongolia and smashed the forces of the Mongol leader Galdan. This victory permanently eliminated the danger of a reinvigorated Mongolian empire on China's borders.

Kang-xi also cultivated the arts of peace. He invited scholars to his court and subsidized the compilation of a huge encyclopedia and two monumental dictionaries. *The Complete Library of the Four Treasuries,* a collection of all of Chinese literature, required the work of 15,000 calligraphers and 361 editors. It preserved the Chinese literary tradition. Kang-xi's contributions to literature hold a distinguished place in the long history of Chinese culture. Europeans and Americans, however, appreciate this period primarily for its excellent porcelain. An imperial factory at Jiangxi (Kiangsi), directly controlled by Kang-xi's court, produced porcelain masterpieces. Monochrome vases, bowls,

TABLE 22.2 POPULATION OF CHINA, 1578–1989

Year	Government	Population (in millions) Families	Population (in millions) Individuals
1578	Ming Dynasty	10.6	60.7
1662	Qing Dynasty	19.2	100.0
1710		23.3	116.0
1729		25.5	127.0
1741			143.4
1754			184.5
1778			243.0
1796			275.7
1814			374.6
1850			414.5
1953	People's Republic		601.9
1974			800.0
1989			1,064.0

and dishes in oxblood, pale green, and dark blue, and polychromes in blue and white, enjoyed great popularity in Paris, London, and New York in the eighteenth century and ever since.

The long reign of the emperor Qian-long (r. 1736–1795) marked the zenith of the Qing Dynasty. The cultivation of new crops from the Americas—white potatoes, corn, peanuts—on marginal lands helped to support the steadily expanding population. Chinese rule was extended into central Asia. The imperial court continued to support arts and letters. In the last two decades of his reign, however, Qian-long showered titles, gifts, and offices on a handsome young Manchu named He-shen. Contemporaries considered He-shen uncultured, greedy, and ambitious. The corruption of the imperial civil service under He-shen, combined with heavy taxation, sparked revolts that continued to the end of the dynasty in 1912.

The Qianlong Emperor at an Archery Contest Executed by the Italian Jesuit Giuseppe Castiglione, whose portraits and panoramas combine Chinese composition with Western perspective and coloration, this painting—with the elegant garden, stately uniforms of the attendants, and dignified image of the emperor—suggests the formal ritual of the imperial court. Castiglione was a special favorite of the Qianlong emperor, who also supported Jesuit architects and designers. (*Source: A private collection/Photo: Wan-go Weng*)

External Pressures

By the middle years of the eighteenth century, Qianlong also faced increasing foreign pressures. In the north and northwest, the region from which invaders had historically entered China, Mongols, Russians, and ethnic minority peoples pressed the borders. Christian missionaries, notably the Jesuits, wanted greater scope for their proselytizing activities. Nearby Asian countries that had many cultural affinities with China—Korea, Burma, Siam, Vietnam—desired greater trade with China. So, too, did European merchants: the European demand for Chinese silk, porcelain, and tea was enormous. The British East India Company, for example, had by 1740 become an international corporation with

global activities, backed by eager investors in Great Britain. What was the response of the imperial government to these increasing foreign pressures?

The Qing government had no ministry of foreign affairs. Chinese relations with all foreign countries reflected the Chinese belief that China was the "central kingdom" and that all other countries were "peripheral" and removed from the cultural center of the universe. The Office of Border Affairs conducted relations with peoples in the northwest crescent (Mongols and Russians). It took police action when necessary and used the marriages of imperial daughters as the means of making alliance and maintaining peace in the north. Acting on the theory that religious evangelization by foreigners reflected on the prestige of the emperor, the imperial household itself supervised the activities of Jesuit missionaries. The Ministry of Rituals managed commercial relations with the nations of East Asia. Business delegations from Korea, Burma, Siam were termed "tribute missions." As long as they used a language of subservience to the emperor and his ministers and made the ritual prostrations, they were allowed limited amounts of trade with China in precisely defined times and places—in the port of Canton from October to March.[14] As mentioned above, the Chinese value system did not respect business and commerce and distrusted traders.

Sniffing fat profits to be made from expanded trade, the aggressive merchants of London and Liverpool could not comprehend the Chinese attitude. Accordingly, the British East India Company, with the support of King George III's government, resolved on a personal appeal to Qian-long through a delegation headed by an experienced diplomat, Lord George Macartney. Three ships sailed from Portsmouth in September 1792 carrying rich gifts for the emperor: a huge imperial state coach fashioned after George III's own vehicle; a variety of heavily jeweled pocket, wrist, and neck watches; and a planetarium, a working model of the entire solar system. The dazzling array of gifts was intended to show that England was the most scientifically advanced and economically powerful nation on earth. Delivered in a diamond-encrusted gift box, George III's respectful letter to the emperor stated in part:

His Most Sacred Majesty George III . . . to the Supreme Emperor of China Qianlong, worthy to live tens of thousands and tens of thousands thousand years, sendeth

Greeting . . .

We have been still more anxious to inquire into the arts and manners of countries where civilization has been perfected by the wise ordinances and virtuous examples of their Sovereigns thro a long series of ages; and, above all, Our ardent wish had been to become acquainted with those celebrated institutions of Your Majesty's populous and extensive Empire which have carried its prosperity to such a height as to be the admiration of all surrounding nations. . . .

We have the happiness of being at peace with all the World . . . Many of our subjects have also frequented for a long time past a remote part of your

Majesty's dominions for the purpose of Trade. No doubt the interchange of commodities between Nations distantly situated tends to their mutual convenience, industry, and wealth.[15]

The letter went on to ask for the establishment of permanent Chinese-British diplomatic relations; broader trade, including the opening of new ports for international commerce; and a fair system of tariffs or customs duties.

The mission that reached Canton in June 1793 (the long journey is an indication of the time involved in eighteenth-century travel) almost floundered over the issue of ritual and procedure. Court officials agreed that Macartney might see the emperor at his summer palace, if the British emissaries acknowledged that they came as a "tributary nation" and performed the *kowtow*—kneeling and striking their heads on the ground nine times in front of the emperor. Macartney protested that he was not required to show such obeisance even to George III. A compromise was finally reached when Macartney agreed to bow on one knee as he would bow to his English sovereign. Qian-long however, was not pleased. The ruler of China considered himself supreme and all other kings his subordinates. Though thoroughly courteous to his guests, he denied all their requests (see Listening to the Past).

The Macartney mission represented the clash of two different cultures. On the one side was China, "an immobile empire," convinced of its superiority, opposed to all innovation, and convinced that the ancient Confucian texts contained the answers to all problems. On the other side was Great Britain, equally convinced of its superiority "because it was modern: founded on science, the free exchange of ideas, and the mastery of commercial exchange."[16] Understanding and communication proved impossible.

The Life of the People

The family is the fundamental unit of every society. In Ming and Qing China, however, the family exercised greater social influence than it did anywhere else—and far more than in Western societies. The family directed the moral education of the child, the economic advancement and marriage of the young, and religious life through ceremonial rites honoring family ancestors. The Chinese family discharged many of the roles that the Christian church performed in Europe in the Middle Ages and that the state carries out today. It assumed total responsibility for the sick, the indigent, and the aged. The family expected and almost invariably received the full devotion and loyalty of its members. A person without a family had no material or psychological support.

Poor families tended to be nuclear: couples established their own households and raised their own children. The educated, the middle class, and the wealthy frequently resided in extended families: several generations of patrilineal relatives and their wives lived together in one large house or compound, individual families occupying different sections. In both kinds of families, the paternal head of the family held autocratic power over all members of the household. Apart from crimes against the emperor and his family, the worst crimes were those committed by children against their parents. Fathers who harmed their sons received lighter punishment than sons who harmed (or even insulted) their fathers. In one instance the Ministry of Punishments reviewed a local governor's sentence that a father be beaten for burying his son alive. The son had used foul language to his father. The ministry concluded that "although the killing (by the father) was done intentionally, it was the killing of a son who had committed a capital crime by reviling his father. The father was acquitted."[17] When a father died, his authority over the household passed to his eldest son.

The father led the family in the ancient Confucian rites honoring the family ancestors. If these ceremonies were not continued by the next generation, the family suffered social disgrace and, it was believed, the dead endured great misery. Thus marriage and childbearing were extremely important.

Almost everyone married. Reverence for one's parents, maintenance of the family, and perpetuation of the line required that sons marry shortly after reaching puberty. The father and family elders discussed the possibilities and employed a local go-between to negotiate with the prospective bride's family. The go-between drew up a marriage contract specifying the property, furniture, clothing, and gifts that the two young people would bring to the union. As elsewhere, parents wanted to make the most economically and socially advantageous union for their children. The couple had no part in these arrangements. Often they had never met each other until the groom lifted the bride's veil on their wedding day. But they had been brought up to accept this custom.

A Chinese bride became part of her husband's family, subject to him and to her in-laws. Her first duty was to bear sons. If she did not, she might adopt a son. Failure to provide heirs gave her husband grounds for divorce, which brought great disgrace on her family. A woman, however, could not divorce her husband for any reason. Divorce was extremely rare in Chinese society, but a wealthy man with a "nonproductive" wife might bring concubines to live in the house along with his wife.

Men held a much higher position in society than did women. The desperately poor often killed girl babies or sold their daughters as servants or concubines. Young brides came under the direct control of their mothers-in-law, whose severity and cruelty are a common theme in Chinese literature. Once a strong-willed woman had sons, she gained increasing respect as the years went by. The Chinese deeply respected age. Some women of the wealthy classes, with servants to do the household chores, spent their days in semiseclusion nibbling dainties, smoking opium, and gambling. Women who brought large dowries to their marriages could dispose of part of those dowries as they wished. Some invested in profitable business activities. Poor women worked in the fields beside their husbands, in addition to bearing children and managing the household.

The educational system during the Ming and Qing periods had both virtues and weaknesses. Most villages and all towns and cities operated schools that prepared boys for the all-important civil service examinations. Boys learned to write with a brush the approximately three thousand commonly used characters of literary Chinese; and they learned the standard texts of Confucian philosophy, ethics, and history. The curriculum was very limited, and the instructional method stressed memorization and discouraged imagination. The civil service aspirant received no practical training in the work of government. But the system yielded a high percentage of literate men (relative to Europe at the same time) and gave Chinese society cohesion and stability. All educated Chinese shared the same basic ethical and literary culture, much as medieval Europeans were formed by Latin Christian culture.

In China, as in medieval Europe, educational opportunities for girls were severely limited. Rich men occasionally hired tutors for their daughters, and a few women achieved exceptional knowledge. Most women of all classes received training that prepared them for roles as wives and mothers: courteous behavior, submission to their husbands, and the administration of a household.

What of health and medical care in imperial China? Although Egyptian and Babylonian medicine predate Chinese medicine by perhaps a millennium, the Chinese medical tradition is the oldest continuing usage in the world. Chinese medical theory deriving from the Han period (from the third century B.C. to the third century A.D.) attributes all ailments to a lack of harmony in the body; cure, then, rests on restoring harmony. Diagnosis of disease depended on visual observation, studying the case history, auditory symptoms, and taking the pulse. Physicians held that three spots along the wrist gave the pulse readings of different organs, and the experienced physician could diagnose the malfunction of any internal organ by checking the pulse. Two basic forms of therapy (treatment) existed. Medicinal therapy was based on the curative effects of herbs. This treatment entailed taking pills or powders in a boiled broth. The other therapy was acupuncture, the insertion of needles into specific parts of the body.

The theory behind acupuncture was that twelve channels run over the body close to the skin, each channel is related to a specific organ, and the needle stimulates a sluggish or pacifies an overactive organ. The acupuncturist used fine needles and avoided vital organs. Certainly acupuncture was no more dangerous than the widespread European practice of bleeding.

Reliance on acupuncture and the Confucian principle that the body is the sacred gift of parents to child made dissection a terrible violation of filial piety and thus strongly discouraged serious surgery. Another factor militating against surgery was the Chinese culture's disdain for manual work of any kind. A "wise" doctor mastered a body of classical texts, prescribed medicine for treatment, and "did not lower himself to perform manual, surgical operations."[18] Nor should a doctor accept fees for service.

Confucian policy did not allow any experts with specialized knowledge to rise socially as a group: social mobility, it was thought, led to social tensions and demands for restructuring.[19] Thus, while physicians in the Islamic and European worlds enjoyed respect and sometimes modest wealth, the

Ch'en Shu: The White Cockatoo   Like Italy and France in the early modern period, China and Japan can boast of distinguished women artists. This painting in ink and color on a hanging scroll depicts a highly prized species of parrot. The work by Ch'en Shu, a Chinese artist famous in her time, is very much in the Chinese artistic tradition. *(Source: The Metropolitan Museum of Art, 13.220.31)*

position of Chinese doctors was deemed insignificant, and they were considered mere artisans. Rather than consulting medical experts, each person had to acquire sufficient knowledge, including pharmacological knowledge, to help members of his or her family in time of illness.

Several emperors decreed that medical colleges should be established and that annual examinations should test physicians' skills so that the needs of the people, as well as the needs of the imperial court, would be served. But these orders were never implemented. As a result, although the idea of state-supported hospitals was an ancient one in China, the first institutions to provide medical care for the sick of a community were established by Christian medical missionaries in the nineteenth century.

In sharp contrast to Europe, China had few social barriers. The emperors fought the development of a hereditary aristocracy which could have undermined their absolute monarchy, and they granted very few titles of nobility in perpetuity. Though China had no legally defined aristocracy, she did have an "upper class" based on a *combination* of wealth, education, lineage, and bureaucratic position. Agricultural land remained the most highly prized form of wealth, but silver ingots, jade, libraries of classical works, porcelain, and urban real estate also indicated status. Wealth alone, however, did not bring status. Offices in the state bureaucracy provided opportunities and motivation for upward mobility. Family members encouraged intelligent sons to prepare for the civil service examinations, and the work and sacrifice of parents bore fruit in their sons' success. Positions in the bureaucracy brought salaries and gifts which a family invariably invested in land. The competitive examinations with few exceptions were open to all classes, and that accessibility prevented the formation of a ruling caste. China did not develop a politically articulate bourgeoisie. Because everyone accepted the Confucian principle that the learned and civilized should rule the state, scholars ranked highest in the social order. They, along with Heaven, Earth, the emperor, parents deserved special veneration. With the possible exception of the Jewish people, no people has respected learning as much as the Chinese. Merchants tried to marry into the scholar class in order to rise in the world. At the bottom of society were actors, prostitutes, and beggars.

The Chinese found recreation and relaxation in many ways. All classes gambled at cards and simple numbers games. The teahouse served as the local meeting place for exchanging news and gossip and listening to the tales of professional storytellers, who enjoyed great popularity. The affluent indulged in an alcoholic drink made from fermented and distilled rice, and both men and women liked pipes and tobacco. Everyone who could afford to do so went to the theater. The actors, like their ancient Greek counterparts, wore happy and sad masks, and their gestures were formal and stylized. The plays typically dramatized episodes from Chinese history and literature. The Chinese associated athletics, riding, and horse racing with soldiers, at best a necessary evil, and regarded the active life as

Chinese Scholars The civil service examinations, the chief means of access to government positions and social status, inculcated total submission to the autocratic state. The largest number of candidates took the examinations in general knowledge and literary ability. Here candidates stand at writing desks, composing essays. *(Source: Bibliothèque Nationale, Paris)*

Chinese Cookery Everywhere in the world, until very recently, meat was scarce and thus a luxury. In China, the shortage of meat encouraged great sophistication in the preparation of foods, especially vegetables. Although European travelers interpreted the frequent servings of vegetables and fish as a sign of poverty, the Chinese, if we can trust modern nutritionists, probably had a healthier diet than the Europeans. Notice the variety of dishes. Women obviously ate separately from men. *(Source: Roger-Viollet)*

the direct antithesis of the scholarly contemplation they most valued.

JAPAN (CA 1400–1800)

The Ashikaga Shogunate lasted from the middle of the fourteenth to the late sixteenth century. During this period, Japanese society experienced almost continual violence and civil war. Weak central governments could not maintain order. Throughout the islands, local strongmen took charge. Around 1450, 250 *daimyos,* or lords, held power; by 1600, only 12 survivors could claim descent from daimyo families of the earlier date. Successful military leaders carved out large territories and governed them as independent rulers. Political and social conditions in fifteenth- and sixteenth-century Japan strongly resembled conditions in western Europe in the tenth and eleventh centuries. Political power was in the hands of a small group of military leaders. Historians often use the same term—*feudalism*—to describe the Japanese and the European experience. As in medieval Europe, feudalism paved the way for the rise of a strong centralized state in seventeenth-century Japan.

Feudalism in Japan

Feudalism played a powerful role in Japanese culture until the nineteenth century. The similarities

between feudalism in Japan and in medieval Europe have fascinated scholars, as have the very significant differences. In Europe, feudalism emerged out of the fusion of Germanic and Roman social institutions and flowered under the impact of Muslim and Viking invasions. In Japan, feudalism evolved from a combination of the native warrior tradition and Chinese Confucian ethics. Japanese society had adopted the Confucian emphasis on filial respect for the head of the family, for the local civil authorities, and for the supreme authority at the head of the state.

The two constituent elements of Japanese feudalism appeared between the eighth and the twelfth centuries: (1) the *shoen* (private land outside imperial control) with its *shiki* (rights) and (2) the *samurai* (the military warrior clique). Some scholars have equated the shoen with the European manor, but the comparison needs careful qualification. A manor usually corresponded to one composite village; a particular family's shoen was widely scattered. Those who held shoen possessed the shiki there—that is, the right to the income or rice produced by the land. But, just as several persons might hold rights—military, judicial, grazing—on a medieval European manor and all these rights yielded income, so several persons frequently held shiki rights on a Japanese estate.

By the sixteenth century, only a small proportion of samurai had attained the rank of daimyo and possessed a shoen. Most warriors were salaried

Women Husking Rice   Rice was basic to Japanese culture. Farmers paid their taxes to the daimyo's agent in rice, and the daimyo paid the salaries of the samurai in rice. It was the staple of the diet eaten by all classes. Here women husk the rice, separate the grains from the chaff using a primitive machine, and clean and pack the rice in bales made of rice stalks. *(Source: Laurie Platt Winfrey, Inc.)*

fighters with no connection to land. From their daimyos, they received stipends in rice, not in land; and in this respect they resembled European knights, who were supported by cash or money fiefs.

The Japanese samurai warrior resembled the knight of twelfth-century France in other ways as well. Both were armed with expensive weapons, and both fought on horseback. Just as the knight was supposed to live according to the chivalric code, so Japanese samurai were expected to live according to *Bushido,* or "Way of the Warrior," a code that stressed military honor, courage, stoic acceptance of hardship, and, above all, loyalty. Disloyalty brought social disgrace, which the samurai could avoid only through *seppuku,* ritual suicide by slashing his belly. Both samurai and knights were highly conscious of themselves as aristocrats. But knights fought as groups, and samurai fought as individuals.

By the middle of the sixteenth century Japanese feudalism had taken on other distinctive features. As the number of shoen decreased and the powerful daimyos consolidated their territories, the practice of *primogeniture* became common, keeping an estate intact under the eldest or ablest son. Around 1540 the introduction of the musket from Europe made infantrymen effective against mounted samurai, and the use of Western cannon required more elaborately fortified castles. Thus, in addition to armed cavalrymen, daimyos began to employ large numbers of foot soldiers equipped with spears, and they constructed new castles. These military and social developments occurred during a century of turbulence and chronic disorder, out of which emerged a leader who ended the chaos and began the process of unification, laying the foundation of the modern Japanese national state.

Nobunaga and National Unification

Oda Nobunaga (1534–1582), a samurai of the lesser daimyo class, won control of his native province of Owari in 1559. He began immediately to extend his power, defeating a powerful daimyo in 1560 and eight years later seizing Kyoto, the capital city, where the emperor and his court resided. As a result, Nobunaga became the virtual ruler of central Japan.

Scholars have called the years from 1568 to 1600 the period of "national unification." During this time Japan underwent aggressive and dynamic change. Adopting the motto "Rule the empire by force," Nobunaga set out to subdue all real and potential rivals and to replace them with his vassals. With the support of Toyotomi Hideyoshi (1537–1598), a brilliant general, he subdued first western and then eastern and northern Japan.

The great Buddhist temple-fortresses proved to be Nobunaga's biggest problem. Some of these monasteries possessed vast wealth and armed retainers. During the civil wars the Buddhists had supported various daimyos in their private wars, but Nobunaga would tolerate no such interference. The strategically located monastery on Mount Hiei near Kyoto had long provided sanctuary for political factions. Previous daimyos had refused to attack it because it was sacred. Nobunaga, however, used fire to reduce it, and his men slaughtered thousands of its occupants.

Although Nobunaga won control of most of Japan by the sword, he backed up his conquests with government machinery and a policy of conciliation. He gave lands and subordinate positions in the army to his defeated enemies. Trusted daimyos received complete civil jurisdiction over entire provinces. At strategic points, such as Nijo near Kyoto and Azuchi on the shore of Lake Biwa, Nobunaga built castles to serve as key administrative and defensive centers for the surrounding territories. He opened the little fishing village of Nagasaki to foreign commerce; it soon grew into the nation's largest port. He standardized the currency, eliminated customs barriers, and encouraged the development of trade and industry. In 1582, when Nobunaga was murdered by one of his vassals, his general and staunchest adherent, Hideyoshi, carried on his work.

A peasant's son who had risen to power by his military bootstraps, Hideyoshi advanced the unification and centralization of Japan in two important ways. First, in 1582 he attacked the great fortress at Takamatsu. When direct assault failed, his troops flooded the castle and forced its surrender. When Takamatsu fell, so did the large province of Mori. A successful siege of the town of Kagoshima then brought the southern island of Kyushu under his domination. Hideyoshi soothed the vanquished daimyos as Nobunaga had done—

with lands and military positions—but he also required them to swear allegiance and to obey him "down to the smallest particular."[20]

Having reduced his most dangerous adversaries, Hideyoshi ordered a survey of the entire country. The military power of the unified Japanese state depended on a strong agricultural base, and Hideyoshi wanted to exploit the peasantry fully. His agents collected detailed information about the daimyos' lands and about towns, villages, agricultural produce, and industrial output all over Japan. This material enabled Hideyoshi to assess military quotas and taxable property. His surveys tied the peasant population to the land and tightened the collection of the land tax. When Hideyoshi died in 1598, he left a strong centralized state. Brute force had created a unified Japan.

On his deathbed the old soldier had set up a council of regents to govern during the minority of his infant son. The strongest regent was Hideyoshi's long-time supporter Tokugawa Ieyasu (1543–1616), who ruled vast territories around Edo (modern-day Tokyo). Ieyasu quickly eliminated the young ruler and in 1600 at Sekigahara smashed a coalition of daimyo defenders of the heir. This battle was the beginning of the Tokugawa regime.

The Tokugawa Regime

Japanese children are taught that "Ieyasu ate the pie that Nobunaga made and Hideyoshi baked." As the aphorism suggests, Ieyasu took over and completed the work begun by his able predecessors. He took decisive steps to solidify his dynasty and control the feudal nobility and to maintain peace and prosperity in Japan. The Tokugawa regime that Ieyasu fashioned worked remarkably well, lasting until 1867.

Ieyasu obtained from the emperor the title of *shogun,* or general-in-chief. Constitutionally, the emperor exercised sovereign authority. In practice, authority and power—both the legal right and the physical means—were held by the Tokugawa shogun. Ieyasu declared the emperor and his court at Kyoto "very precious and decorative, like gold and silver," and surrounded the imperial court with all the ceremonial trappings but none of the realities of power.

In a scheme resembling the later residency requirements imposed by Louis XIV (see page 560)

Tokugawa Ieyasu A short, stocky man who had spent most of his life on horseback, Ieyasu was sixty-two when he secured appointment as shogun. Having unified Japan and established a peace that lasted 250 years, he ranks with George Washington and Peter the Great of Russia as one of the great nation builders in world history. In this iconic style of Shinto painting, the elderly Ieyasu is depicted as a deity. *(Source: The Tokugawa Foundation)*

and Peter the Great (see page 581), Ieyasu forced the feudal lords to establish "alternate residence" at his capital city of Edo, to spend part of each year there, and to leave their wives and sons there—essentially as hostages. This requirement had obvious advantages: the shogun could keep close tabs on the daimyos, control them through their children, and weaken them financially with the burden of maintaining two residences. Ieyasu justified this course of action by invoking the *Bushido* code, with its emphasis on loyalty. He forbade members of the nobility to marry without his consent, thus preventing the formation of dangerous alliances.

The early Tokugawa shoguns also restricted the construction of castles—symbols, in Japan as in medieval Europe, of feudal independence. Later, the practice of alternate residence led to considerable castle building, castles that represented demands for goods and services and which turned Edo and other cities into huge commercial centers. Members of the aristocratic class exercised full administrative powers within their domains. In effect, the country was governed by martial law in peacetime. Only warriors could hold official positions in the state bureaucracy. A network of spies kept close watch on those lords whose loyalty the shogun suspected.

As in medieval Europe and early modern China, the agricultural class held a respected position because its members provided Japanese society with sustenance. Even so, farmers had to mind their betters, and they bore a disproportionate share of the tax load. According to the survey made by Hideyoshi, taxes were imposed on villages, not on individuals; the tax varied between 30 and 40 percent of the rice crop. Also as in Europe and China, the commercial classes in Japan occupied the lowest rungs on the social ladder because they profited from the toil of others.

The peace that the Tokugawa Shogunate imposed brought a steady rise in population and prosperity. As demand for goods grew, so did the numbers of merchants. To maintain stability, the early Tokugawa shoguns froze the four ancient social categories: imperial court nobility, samurai, peasants, and merchants. Laws rigidly prescribed what each class could and could not do. Nobles, for example, were "strictly forbidden, whether by day or by night, to go sauntering through the streets or lanes in places where they have no business to be." Daimyos were prohibited from moving troops outside their frontiers, making alliances, and coining money. Designated dress and stiff rules of etiquette distinguished one class from another.[21] As intended, this stratification protected the Tokugawa shoguns from daimyo attack and inaugurated a long era of peace.

MAP 22.2 Tokugawa Japan   Consider the cultural and political significance of the fact that Japan is an island. How did the concentration of shogunate lands affect the shogunate's government of Japan?

In the interests of stability and peace, Ieyasu's descendants also imposed measures called *sakoku*. This "closed country policy" sealed Japan's borders around 1636. Japanese were forbidden to leave the country. Foreigners were excluded.

In 1549 the Jesuit missionary Francis Xavier had landed at Kagoshima. He soon made many converts among the poor and even some among the daimyos. By 1600 there were 300,000 baptized Christians in Japan. Most of them lived on Kyushu, the southernmost island (Map 22.2), where the shogun's power was weakest and the loyalty of the daimyos most doubtful. In 1615 bands of Christian samurai supported Ieyasu's enemies at the fierce Battle of Osaka. In 1637, 30,000 peasants in the heavily Catholic area of northern Kyushu revolted. The shoguns thus came to associate Christianity with domestic disorder and feu-

dal rebellion. Accordingly, what had been mild persecution of Christians became ruthless repression after 1639. Foreign priests were expelled or tortured, and thousands of Japanese Christians suffered crucifixion. The "closed country policy" remained in force for almost two centuries. The shogunate kept Japan isolated—but not totally.

Through the Dutch factory on the tiny island of Deshima in Nagasaki harbor (see page 531), a stream of Western ideas and inventions trickled into Japan in the eighteenth century. Western writings, architectural illustrations, calendars, watches, medicine, and paintings deeply impressed the Japanese. Western portraits and other paintings introduced the Japanese to perspective and shading. When the Swedish scientist C. P. Thunberg, physician to the Dutch at Deshima, visited Nagasaki and Edo, the Japanese looked on him as a scientific oracle and plied him with questions. Japanese scholars believed that Western inventions were more efficient than their Japanese equivalents and that these inventions contributed to the prosperity of European nations. Japanese curiosity about things Western gave rise to an intellectual movement known as *rangaku,* foreign studies, which urged that these Western ideas and inventions be adopted by the Japanese.

Japanese understanding of the West was severely limited and often fanciful, as was Western knowledge of Asian civilizations. Like eighteenth-century Europeans who praised Chinese and Persian customs to call attention to shortcomings at home, Japanese scholars idealized Western conditions. Both peoples wanted to create within their countries the desire for reform and progress.[22]

The Life of the People

Two hundred years of peace is no mean achievement in the history of world societies. There is nothing comparable to it in all of medieval and modern times. Moreover, profound social and economic development occurred in spite of Japan's isolation.

The Tokugawa Shogunate subdued the nobility by emasculating it politically. Stripped of power and required to spend part of each year at Edo, the daimyos and samurai passed their lives pursuing pleasure. They spent frantically on fine silks, paintings, concubines, boys, the theater, and the redecoration of their castles. Around 1700 one scholar observed that the entire military class was living "as in an inn, that is, consuming now and pay-

Women Weaving   Often working at home, women made an enormous contribution to the Japanese silk industry: their small, delicate hands (in contrast to the larger and possibly callused hands of men) seemed suited to working with fine silk threads. In an age when public-assisted child care was not dreamed of, working mothers relied on the help of female relatives, or, as here, infants were tied to mothers' backs, an added burden for mothers and probably not ideal for the child. Notice the spinning wheel in the corner and various spindles on the floor. *(Source: By kind permission of the East-West Gallery, New Hope, PA)*

A Male Prostitute He writes a poem as a female prostitute massages their patron's back. Notice the elaborate hairstyles, the rich material of the kimonos, and the boxes of writing instruments. *(Source: The Fine Arts Museums of San Francisco. Achenbach Foundation for Graphic Arts purchase, 1969. 32.20)*

ing later."[23] Eighteenth-century Japanese novels, plays, and histories portray the samurai engrossed in tavern brawls and sexual orgies. These frivolities, plus more sophisticated pleasures and the heavy costs of maintaining an alternate residence at Edo, gradually ruined the warrior class.

In traditional Japanese society, women were subordinate to men, and the civil disorders of the sixteenth century strengthened male domination. Parents in the samurai class arranged their daughters' marriages to advance family interests. Once a woman married, her life centered on her children and domestic chores. The management of a large household with several children and many servants imposed heavy responsibilities on women. An upper-class wife rarely left home unchaperoned. "Middle class" women, however, began to emerge from the home. The development of an urban commercial culture in the cities (see page 732) in the Tokugawa period led to the employment of women in silk and textile manufacture, in publishing, in restaurants and various shops, and especially in entertainment.

All major cities contained places of amusement for men—teahouses, theaters, restaurants, houses of prostitution. Desperately poor parents sometimes sold their daughters to entertainment houses, and the most attractive or talented girls, trained in singing, dancing, and conversational arts, became courtesans called *geishas,* or "accomplished persons," in modern times. The Tokugawa period saw the beginnings for men of the separation of family and business life on the one hand, and leisure and amusement on the other. That separation is still evident in Japanese society.[24]

The samurai spent heavily on kabuki theater. An art form created by townspeople, kabuki consisted of crude, bawdy skits dealing with love and romance or aspects of prostitution, an occupation in which many actors and actresses had professional experience. Performances featured elaborate costumes, song, dance, and poetry. Because actresses were thought to be corrupting the public morals, the Tokugawa government banned them from the stage in 1629. From that time on, men played all the parts. Male actors in female dress and makeup performed as seductively as possible to entice the burly samurai who thronged the theaters. Homosexuality, long accepted in Japan, was widely practiced among the samurai, who pursued the actors and spent profligately on them. According to one seventeenth-century writer:

"Youth's kabuki" began with beautiful youths being made to sing and dance, whereupon droll fools . . . had their hearts captivated and their souls stolen. . . . There were many of these men who soon had run through their fortunes.[25]

Some moralists and bureaucrats complained from time to time, but the Tokugawa government decided to accept kabuki and prostitution as necessary evils. The practices provided employment, gratified the tastes of samurai and townspeople, and diverted former warriors from potential criminal and political mischief.[26] The samurai paid for their costly pleasures in the way their European counterparts did—by fleecing the peasants and borrowing from the merchants.

According to Japanese tradition, farmers deserved respect. In practice, peasants were sometimes severely oppressed and led miserable lives. It was government policy to tax them to the level of bare subsistence, and official legislation repeatedly redefined their duties. In 1649 every village in Japan received these regulations:

Peasants are people without sense or forethought. Therefore they must not give rice to their wives and children at harvest time, but must save food for the future. They should eat millet, vegetables, and other coarse food instead of rice. Even the fallen leaves of plants should be saved as food against famine. . . . During the seasons of planting and harvesting, however, when the labor is arduous, the food taken may be a little better. . . .

They must not buy tea or sake [a fermented liquor made from rice] to drink nor must their wives.

The husband must work in the fields, the wife must work at the loom. Both must do night work. However good-looking a wife may be, if she neglects her household duties by drinking tea or sightseeing or rambling on the hillsides, she must be divorced.

Peasants must wear only cotton or hemp—no silk. They may not smoke tobacco. It is harmful to health, it takes up time, and costs money. It also creates a risk of fire.[27]

The conspicuous consumption of the upper classes led them during the seventeenth and eight-

eenth centuries to increase taxes from 30 or 40 percent of the rice crop to 50 percent. Merchants who bought farm produce fixed the price of rice so low that it seemed to farmers that the more they produced, the less they earned. They found release only by flight or revolt.

After 1704, peasant rebellions were chronic. Oppressive taxation provoked 84,000 farmers in the province of Iwaki to revolt in 1739. After widespread burning and destruction, their demands were met. In other instances the shoguns ordered savage repression.

Natural disasters also added to the peasants' misery. In the 1770s fires, floods, and volcanic eruptions hit all parts of Japan. Drought and torrential rain led to terrible famines between 1783 and 1788 and again between 1832 and 1836. Taxation, disaster, and oppression often combined to make the lot of peasants one of unrelieved wretchedness.

This picture of the Japanese peasantry tells only part of the story, however. Scholarship has demonstrated that in the Tokugawa period peasant society was "a pyramid of wealth and power . . . that rose from the tenant farmer at the bottom through small landholders to wealthy peasants at the top."[28] Agricultural productivity increased substantially, and assessed taxes were fixed, though they remained high. Peasants who improved their lands and increased their yields continued to pay the same assessed tax and could pocket the surplus as profit. Their social situation accordingly improved. By the early nineteenth century there existed a large class of relatively wealthy, educated, and ambitious peasant families who resembled the middle ranks of the warrior class.

Likewise, local economic conditions and family social status shaped the lives of Japanese women. The existence of a rich peasant's wife, daughter, or sister differed considerably from that of poor peasant women. The well-to-do seem to have made few distinctions in the early upbringing of male and female children. Regional prosperity determined the amounts of money spent on the education of both sexes in their early years. In the early nineteenth century the regions around flourishing Edo and Kyoto spent far more than the poor Toh-ku region; and parents in thriving areas devoted considerable sums on their daughters' education. Girls from middle-level peasant families may have had from two to five years of formal schooling. But they were thought incapable of learning the difficult

Kitagawa Utamaro: Ladies at a Tea Shop Famous for his book of insects reflecting remarkable powers of observation, Utamaro (1753–1806) is best known for his portrayal of women in which he accented their sensuous beauty. First of the great masters of the *ukiyo-e* school, "pictures of the floating world," the dominant movement in Japanese art of the Tokugawa period, Utamaro produced wood-block prints such as this with subjects drawn from everyday life. Notice the dress of the ladies and the various activities of the servants. *(Source: Private Collection)*

Chinese characters, so their education focused on moral instruction intended to instill the virtue of obedience. Daughters of wealthy peasant families learned penmanship, the Chinese classics, poetry, and the proper forms of correspondence, and they rounded off their education with travel.[29]

Scholars of the Japanese family, like students of the late medieval and early modern European family (see pages 632–634), have explored the extent of premarital sex, the age at which people married, the frequency with which they married someone from another village, and the level of divorce. For Tokugawa Japan, considerable regional variations make broad generalizations dangerous; research continues. It is clear, however, that marriage linked families of equal status and class; Japanese marriages, therefore, strengthened economic and social divisions. This practice gave Japanese women an advantage over their Chinese counterparts: the Japanese bride had to learn the special ways of her new household, but she was unlikely to be intimidated by her new family. Chinese women married "up" into families of a higher status and thus tended to be overawed by the wealth and status of their in-laws.

On the Japanese bride fell the responsibility of bringing harmony to the household. Harmony

"meant that she had to refrain from quarreling with the members of her new household, do the work expected of her position, and conform to family custom."[30] Both samurai and peasant teaching stressed that "the married couple was the foundation of morality" and that the basis for harmony in the couple rested on good connubial relations. Once the author of *Observations of Agricultural Practices,* a study of rural life, stayed overnight at a farmhouse. Newlyweds in the family went to bed early and, separated from the others by only a screen, began noisy lovemaking. "Outrageous," exclaimed the guest, whereupon the old woman of the family got angry. "Harmony between husband and wife is the basis for prosperity for the descendants. . . . I permit this coupling day and night. People who laugh at their passion are themselves outrageous. Get out!"[31] Domestic harmony and social necessity were closely linked.

A peasant wife shared with her husband responsibility for the family's economic well-being. If of poor or middling status, she worked alongside her husband in the fields, doing the routine work while he did the heavy work. If they were tenant farmers and worked for salaries, the wife invariably earned half or a third less than her husband. Wives of prosperous farmers never worked in the fields, but they spun silk, wove cloth, helped in any family business, and supervised the maids. Whatever their economic status, Japanese women, like women everywhere in the world, tended the children; they were her special responsibility. The production of children, especially sons, strengthened a wife's prestige, but among well-to-do Japanese farm women, the bride's skill in prudent household management was the most desired talent.

How was divorce initiated, and how frequent was it? Customs among the noble class differed considerably from peasant practices. Widows and divorcees of the samurai aristocracy—where female chastity was the core of fidelity—were not expected to remarry. The husband alone could initiate divorce by ordering his wife to leave or by sending her possessions to her natal home. The wife could not prevent divorce or ensure access to her children.

Among the peasant classes, divorce seems to have been fairly common—at least 15 percent in the villages near Osaka in the eighteenth century. Women as well as men could begin the procedure. Wives' reasons were husbands' drunkenness, physical abuse, or failure to support the family. Many women secured divorce from temples whose function was to dissolve marriages: if a married woman entered the temple and performed its rites for three years, her marriage bond was dissolved. Sometimes Buddhist temple priests served as divorce brokers: they went to the village headman and had him force the husband to agree to a divorce. News of the coming of temple officials was usually enough to produce a letter of separation. A poor woman wanting a divorce simply left her husband's home. Opportunities for remarriage were severely limited. Divorce in samurai society carried social stigma; it did not among the peasantry.[32]

The Tokugawa period witnessed a major transformation of agriculture, a great leap in productivity and specialization. The rural population increased, but the agricultural population did not; surplus labor was drawn to other employment and to the cities. In fact, Japan suffered an acute shortage of farm labor from 1720 to 1868. In some villages, industry became almost as important as agriculture. At Hirano near Osaka, for example, 61.7 percent of all arable land was sown in cotton. The peasants had a thriving industry: they ginned the cotton locally before transporting it to wholesalers in Osaka. In many rural places, as many peasants worked in the manufacture of silk, cotton, or veg-

etable oil as in the production of rice.[33] In theory, the urban commercial classes, scorned for benefiting from the misery of the peasants and the appetites of the samurai, occupied the bottom rung of the social ladder. Merchants had no political power, but they accumulated wealth, sometimes great wealth. They also demonstrated the possibility of social mobility and thus the inherent weakness of the regime's system of strict social stratification.

The commercial class grew in response to the phenomenal development of urban life. In the seventeenth century, the surplus rural population, together with underemployed samurai and the ambitious and adventurous, thronged to the cities. All wanted a better way of life than could be found in the dull farming villages. Japan's cities grew tremendously: Kyoto, home to the emperor and his pleasure-loving court; Edo (modern Tokyo), the political capital, with its multitudes of government bureaucrats, daimyos in alternate residence, intellectuals, and police; and Osaka, by this time the greatest commercial city in Japan, with its huge grain exchange and commercial banks. In the eighteenth century, Edo's population of almost a million represented the largest demand for goods and services in the world.

The Tokugawa shoguns turned the samurai into urban consumers by denying them military opportunities. Merchants stood ready to serve them. Towns offered all kinds of luxury goods and catered to every extravagant and exotic taste. By marketing the daimyos' grain, town merchants gave the aristocrats the cash they needed to support their rich establishments. Merchants formed guilds and banks and lent money to the samurai. Those who defaulted on their debts found themselves cut off from further credit.[34]

As the ruling samurai with their fixed stipends became increasingly poorer, the despised merchants grew steadily wealthier. By contemporary standards anywhere in the world, the Japanese "middle" class lived very well. In 1705 the shogunate confiscated the property of a merchant in Osaka "for conduct unbecoming a member of the commercial class." In fact, the confiscation was at the urging of influential daimyos and samurai who owed the merchant gigantic debts. The government seized 50 pairs of gold screens, 360 carpets, several mansions, 48 granaries and warehouses scattered around the country, and hundreds of thousands of gold pieces. This merchant possessed fabulous wealth, but other merchants too enjoyed a rich lifestyle.[35]

SUMMARY

In the eighteenth and early nineteenth centuries China experienced a rapid increase in both prosperity and population. On the basis of highly developed agriculture, the Qing Empire supported a population of 200 million in 1762 and 374 million in 1812, compared with only 193 million in all of Europe in 1800. Qing China was geographically larger than the People's Republic of China today, encompassing some of the present-day Russian federation.

China's political and economic systems began to deteriorate in the late eighteenth and early nineteenth centuries. The country suffered from excessive centralization: all local questions had to be referred to Beijing. The extravagant court was an intolerable drain on the state treasury. Graft and corruption pervaded the imperial bureaucracy, provincial administration, and army. Population explosion led to a severe land shortage, causing tension and revolts in the countryside.

In 1800 Tokugawa Japan was reaping the rewards of two centuries of peace and social order. Steady economic growth and improved agricultural technology had swelled the population. The samurai had been transformed into peaceful city dwellers and civil bureaucrats. The wealth of the business classes grew, and the samurai, dependent on fixed agricultural rents or stipends in rice in a time of rising standards of living, fell into debt. The Tokugawa regime formed submissive citizens whose discipline is apparent even today.

Although the shogunate maintained a policy of national isolation and no foreign power influenced Japan's political or social life, Japan was not really cut off from outside cultural contacts. Through the port of Nagasaki, Western scientific ideas and some Western technology entered Japan in response to the persistent interest of Japanese scholars. The Japanese readily absorbed foreign technological ideas.

NOTES

1. J. Gernet, *A History of Chinese Civilization,* trans. J. R. Foster (New York: Cambridge University Press, 1982), p. 391.
2. Ibid.
3. L. Zewen et al., *The Great Wall* (New York: McGraw-Hill, 1981), p. 140.
4. See E. L. Dreyer, *Early Ming China: A Political History, 1355–1435* (Stanford, Calif.: Stanford University Press, 1982), pp. 194–205.
5. R. Huang, *1587: A Year of No Significance: The Ming Dynasty in Decline* (New Haven, Conn.: Yale University Press, 1981), p. 13.
6. J. E. Wills, Jr., "Maritime China from Wang Chih to Shih Long," in *From Ming to Ch'ing: Conquest, Region, and Continuity in Seventeenth-Century China,* ed. J. D. Spence and J. E. Wills, Jr. (New Haven, Conn.: Yale University Press, 1979), pp. 203–216.
7. F. Braudel, *The Wheels of Commerce: Civilization and Capitalism, 15th–18th Century,* vol. 2, trans. S. Reynolds (New York: Harper & Row, 1982), pp. 198–199.
8. Gernet, *A History of Chinese Civilization,* pp. 425–426.
9. Quoted in C. Clunas, *Superfluous Things: Material Culture and Social Status in Early Modern China* (Urbana: University of Illinois Press, 1991), pp. 141–142.
10. Ibid., pp. 147–165.
11. Quoted in Gernet, *A History of Chinese Civilization,* p. 431.
12. See Huang, *1587,* pp. 120–129.
13. F. Wakeman, Jr., *The Fall of Imperial China* (New York: Free Press, 1975), pp. 58–64.
14. J. D. Spence, *The Search for Modern China* (New York: Norton, 1991), pp. 117–122.
15. Quoted in A. Peyrefitte, *The Immobile Empire,* trans. J. Rothschild (New York: Knopf, 1992), pp. 195–196.
16. Ibid., p. 539.
17. Quoted in Spence, *The Search for Modern China,* p. 125.
18. See R. C. Croizier, *Traditional Medicine in Modern China* (Cambridge, Mass.: Harvard University Press, 1968), pp. 19–27.
19. P. U. Unschuld, *Medicine in China: A History of Pharmaceutics* (Berkeley: University of California Press, 1986), p. 4.
20. See G. B. Sansom, *A History of Japan, 1344–1615,* vol. 2 (Stanford, Calif.: Stanford University Press, 1961), Chs. 20–21.
21. Ibid., Ch. 25.
22. See D. Keene, *The Japanese Discovery of Europe, 1720–1830* (Stanford, Calif.: Stanford University Press, 1969), pp. 24–25, Ch. 4, and passim.
23. Quoted in D. H. Shively, "Bakufu Versus Kabuki," in *Studies in the Institutional History of Early Modern Japan,* ed. J. W. Hall (Princeton, N.J.: Princeton University Press, 1970), p. 236.
24. E. O. Reischauer and A. M. Craig, *Japan: Tradition and Transformation,* rev. ed. (Boston: Houghton Mifflin, 1989), pp. 104–105.
25. Quoted in Shively, "Bakufu Versus Kabuki," pp. 241–242.

The Macartney Mission to China

Lord George Macartney's embassy to China (1792–1794) sought to establish permanent diplomatic relations between China and Great Britain and to expand trade between the two countries. The mission failed when the emperor rejected the British proposals for the reasons that he states in the letter that follows. Although Macartney later wrote, "Nothing could be more fallacious than to judge of China by any European standard," the British refused to recognize the right of Chinese civilization to be different. The Macartney mission thus serves as a parading of the cultural clashes between the West and Asia that marked the next two centuries.

You, O King, from afar have yearned after the blessings of our civilization, and in your eagerness to come into touch with our converting influence have sent an Embassy across the sea bearing a memorial.[1] I have already taken note of your respectful spirit of submission, have treated your mission with extreme favor and loaded it with gifts . . . .

Yesterday your Ambassador petitioned my Ministers to memorialize me regarding your trade with China, but his proposal is not consistent with our dynastic usage and cannot be entertained. Hitherto, all European nations, including your own country's barbarian merchants, have carried on their trade with our Celestial Empire at Canton. Such has been the procedure for many years, although our Celestial Empire possesses all things in prolific abundance and lacks no product within its own borders. There was therefore no need to import the manufactures of outside barbarians in exchange for our own produce. But as the tea, silk and porcelain which the Celestial Empire produces, are absolute necessities to European nations and to yourselves, we have permitted, as a signal mark of favor, that foreign *hongs*[2] should be established at Canton, so that your wants might be supplied and your

country thus participate in our beneficence. But your Ambassador has now put forward new requests which completely fail to recognize the Throne's principle to "treat strangers from afar with indulgence," and to exercise a pacifying control over barbarian tribes, the world over. Moreover, our dynasty, swaying the myriad races of the globe, extends the same benevolence towards all. Your England is not the only nation trading at Canton. If other nations, following your bad example, wrongfully importune my ear with further impossible requests, how will it be possible for me to treat them with easy indulgence? Nevertheless, I do not forget the lonely remoteness of your island, cut off from the world by intervening wastes of sea, nor do I overlook your excusable ignorance of the usages of our Celestial Empire. I have consequently commanded my Ministers to enlighten your Ambassador on the subject, and have ordered the departure of the mission. . . .

Your request for a small island near Chusan,[3] where your merchants may reside and goods be warehoused, arises from your desire to develop trade. As there are neither foreign *hongs* nor interpreters in or near Chusan, where none of your ships have ever called, such an island would be utterly useless for your purposes. Every inch of the territory of our Empire is marked on the map and the strictest vigilance is exercised over it all: even tiny islets and far-lying sand-banks are clearly defined as part of the provinces to which they belong. Consider, moreover, that England is not the only barbarian land which wishes to establish . . . trade with our Empire. . . .

The next request, for a small site in the vicinity of Canton city, where your barbarian merchants may lodge or, alternatively, that there be no longer any restrictions over their movements at Aomen,[4] has arisen from the following causes. Hitherto, the barbarian merchants of Europe have had a definite locality assigned to them at Aomen for residence and trade, and have been forbidden to encroach an inch beyond the limits assigned to that locality.... If these restrictions were withdrawn, friction would inevitably occur between the Chinese and your barbarian subjects, and the results would militate against the benevolent regard that I feel towards you. From every point of view, therefore, it is best that the regulations now in force should continue unchanged....

Regarding your nation's worship of the Lord of Heaven, it is the same religion as that of other European nations. Ever since the beginning of history, sage Emperors and wise rulers have bestowed on China a moral system and inculcated a code, which from time immemorial has been religiously observed by the myriads of my subjects.[5] There has been no hankering after heterodox doctrines. Even the European (missionary) officials in my capital are forbidden to hold intercourse with Chinese subjects; they are restricted within the limits of their appointed residences, and may not go about propagating their religion. The distinction between Chinese and barbarian is most strict, and your Ambassador's request that barbarians shall be given full liberty to disseminate their religion is utterly unreasonable.

It may be, O King, that the above proposals have been wantonly made by your Ambassador on his own responsibility, or peradventure you yourself are ignorant of our dynastic regulations and had no intention of transgressing them when you expressed these wild ideas and hopes.... If, after the receipt of this explicit decree, you lightly give ear to the representations of your subordinates and allow your barbarian merchants to proceed to Chêkiang and Tientsin,[6] with the object of landing and trading there, the ordinances of my Celestial Empire are strict in the extreme, and the local officials, both civil and military, are bound reverently to obey the law of the land. Should your vessels touch the shore, your merchants will assuredly never be permitted to land or to reside there, but will be subject to instant expulsion. In that event your barbarian merchants will have had a long journey for nothing. Do not say that you were not warned in due time! Tremblingly obey and show no negligence! A special mandate!

Lord Macartney tries to impress the emperor Ch'ien-lung with an array of expensive presents. (*Source: National Maritime Museum, London*)

Questions for Analysis

1. Consider the basic premises of eighteenth-century European Enlightenment culture and the premises of Chinese culture.

2. What reasons does the emperor give for denying the British requests? What is the basis for the emperor's position?

3. How does the emperor view China's economic and cultural position in the world?

Source: A. J. Andrea and J. H. Overfield, eds., *The Human Record: Sources of Global History*, vol. 2 (Boston: Houghton Mifflin, 1990), pp. 262–264. Reprinted from E. Backhouse and J. O. P. Brand, *Annals and Memoirs of the Court of Peking* (Boston: Houghton Mifflin, 1914), pp. 325–331.

Notes: **1.** Memorandum. **2.** Groups of merchants. **3.** A group of islands in the East China Sea at the entrance to Hangchow Bay. **4.** A city some 45 miles to the south of Canton, at the lower end of the Pearl (Zhu) River delta. **5.** The reference is to Confucianism. **6.** Two Chinese port cities.

The Macartney Mission to China

Lord George Macartney's embassy to China (1792–1794) sought to establish permanent diplomatic relations between China and Great Britain and to expand trade between the two countries. The mission failed when the emperor rejected the British proposals for the reasons that he states in the letter that follows. Although Macartney later wrote, "Nothing could be more fallacious than to judge of China by any European standard," the British refused to recognize the right of Chinese civilization to be different. The Macartney mission thus serves as a parading of the cultural clashes between the West and Asia that marked the next two centuries.

You, O King, from afar have yearned after the blessings of our civilization, and in your eagerness to come into touch with our converting influence have sent an Embassy across the sea bearing a memorial.[1] I have already taken note of your respectful spirit of submission, have treated your mission with extreme favor and loaded it with gifts . . . .

Yesterday your Ambassador petitioned my Ministers to memorialize me regarding your trade with China, but his proposal is not consistent with our dynastic usage and cannot be entertained. Hitherto, all European nations, including your own country's barbarian merchants, have carried on their trade with our Celestial Empire at Canton. Such has been the procedure for many years, although our Celestial Empire possesses all things in prolific abundance and lacks no product within its own borders. There was therefore no need to import the manufactures of outside barbarians in exchange for our own produce. But as the tea, silk and porcelain which the Celestial Empire produces, are absolute necessities to European nations and to yourselves, we have permitted, as a signal mark of favor, that foreign *hongs*[2] should be established at Canton, so that your wants might be supplied and your

country thus participate in our beneficence. But your Ambassador has now put forward new requests which completely fail to recognize the Throne's principle to "treat strangers from afar with indulgence," and to exercise a pacifying control over barbarian tribes, the world over. Moreover, our dynasty, swaying the myriad races of the globe, extends the same benevolence towards all. Your England is not the only nation trading at Canton. If other nations, following your bad example, wrongfully importune my ear with further impossible requests, how will it be possible for me to treat them with easy indulgence? Nevertheless, I do not forget the lonely remoteness of your island, cut off from the world by intervening wastes of sea, nor do I overlook your excusable ignorance of the usages of our Celestial Empire. I have consequently commanded my Ministers to enlighten your Ambassador on the subject, and have ordered the departure of the mission. . . .

Your request for a small island near Chusan,[3] where your merchants may reside and goods be warehoused, arises from your desire to develop trade. As there are neither foreign *hongs* nor interpreters in or near Chusan, where none of your ships have ever called, such an island would be utterly useless for your purposes. Every inch of the territory of our Empire is marked on the map and the strictest vigilance is exercised over it all: even tiny islets and far-lying sand-banks are clearly defined as part of the provinces to which they belong. Consider, moreover, that England is not the only barbarian land which wishes to establish . . . trade with our Empire. . . .

The next request, for a small site in the vicinity of Canton city, where your barbarian merchants may lodge or, alternatively, that there be no longer any restrictions over their movements at Aomen,[4] has arisen from the following causes. Hitherto, the barbarian

CHAPTER

23

The Revolution in Western Politics, 1775–1815

The mayor of Rouen protects access to the townhall from the onslaught of a crowd rioting over the lack of bread, August 29, 1792. *(Source: Musée des Beaux Arts, Rouen/Laurie Platt Winfrey, Inc.)*

The last years of the eighteenth century were a time of great upheaval in the West. A series of revolutions and revolutionary wars challenged the old order of monarchs and aristocrats. The ideas of freedom and equality, ideas that have not stopped shaping the world since that era, flourished and spread. The revolutionary era began in North America in 1775. Then in 1789 France, the most influential country in Europe, became the leading revolutionary nation. It established first a constitutional monarchy, then a radical republic, and finally a new empire under Napoleon. The armies of France also joined forces with patriots and radicals abroad in an effort to establish throughout much of Europe new governments based on new principles. The world of modern domestic and international politics was born.

- What caused this era of revolution?
- What were the ideas and objectives of the men and women who rose up violently to undo the established system?
- What were the gains and losses for privileged groups and for ordinary people in a generation of war and upheaval?

These are the questions underlying this chapter's examination of the revolutionary era.

❄ LIBERTY AND EQUALITY

Two ideas fueled the revolutionary period in both America and Europe: liberty and equality. What did eighteenth-century politicians and other people mean by liberty and equality, and why were those ideas so radical and revolutionary in their day?

The call for liberty was first of all a call for individual human rights. Even the most enlightened monarchs customarily claimed that it was their duty to regulate what people wrote and believed. Liberals of the revolutionary era protested such controls from on high. They demanded freedom to worship according to the dictates of their consciences, an end to censorship, and freedom from arbitrary laws and from judges who simply obeyed orders from the government. The Declaration of the Rights of Man, issued at the beginning of the French Revolution, proclaimed, "Liberty consists in being able to do anything that does not harm another person." In theory, therefore, a citizen's rights had "no limits except those which assure to the other members of society the enjoyment of these same rights." In the context of the monarchial and absolutist forms of government then dominating Europe, this was a truly radical idea.

The call for liberty was also a call for a new kind of government. Revolutionary liberals believed that the people were sovereign—that is, that the people alone had the authority to make laws limiting an individual's freedom of action. In practice, this system of government meant choosing legislators who represented the people and were accountable to them.

Equality was a more ambiguous idea. Eighteenth-century liberals argued that, in theory, all citizens should have identical rights and civil liberties and that the nobility had no right to special privileges based on the accident of birth. However, liberals accepted some well-established distinctions.

First, most eighteenth-century liberals were *men* of their times, and they generally shared with other men the belief that equality between men and women was neither practical nor desirable. Women played an important political role in the French Revolution at several points, but the men of the French Revolution limited formal political rights—the right to vote, to run for office, to participate in government—to men.

Second, liberals never believed that everyone should be equal economically. Quite the contrary. As Thomas Jefferson wrote in an early draft of the American Declaration of Independence (before he changed "property" to the more noble-sounding "happiness"), everyone was equal in "the pursuit of property." Jefferson and other liberals certainly did not expect equal success in that pursuit. Great differences in wealth and income between rich and poor were perfectly acceptable to liberals. The essential point was that everyone should legally have an equal chance.

In eighteenth-century Europe, however, such equality of opportunity was a truly revolutionary idea. Society was still legally divided into groups with special privileges, such as the nobility and the clergy, and groups with special burdens, such as the peasantry. And in most countries, various middle-class groups—professionals, business people, townspeople, and craftsmen—enjoyed privileges that allowed them to monopolize all sorts of economic activity. Liberals criticized not economic inequality itself but this kind of economic inequality based on artificial legal distinctions.

The ideas of liberty and equality—the central ideas of classical liberalism—had deep roots in Western history. The classical and Judeo-Christian traditions had affirmed for hundreds of years the sanctity and value of the individual human being, as well as personal responsibility on the part of both common folk and exalted rulers. The hounded and persecuted Protestant radicals of the later sixteenth century had died for the revolutionary idea that individuals were entitled to their own religious beliefs.

Although the liberal creed was rooted in the Western tradition, classical liberalism first crystallized at the end of the seventeenth century and during the Enlightenment of the eighteenth century. Liberal ideas reflected the Enlightenment's stress on human dignity and human happiness on earth and its faith in science, rationality, and progress. Almost all the writers of the Enlightenment were passionately committed to greater personal liberty and equal treatment before the law.

Certain English and French thinkers were mainly responsible for joining the Enlightenment's concern for personal freedom and legal equality to a theoretical justification of liberal self-government. The two most important were John Locke and the baron de Montesquieu. Locke maintained that England's long political tradition rested on "the rights of Englishmen" and on representative government through Parliament. He admired especially the great Whig nobles who had deposed James II and made the bloodless revolution of 1688–1689, and he argued that if a government oversteps its proper function of protecting the natural rights of life, liberty, and private property, it becomes a tyranny. Montesquieu was also inspired by English constitutional history. He, too, believed that powerful "intermediary groups"—such as the judicial nobility of which he was a proud member—offered the best defense of liberty against despotism.

The belief that representative institutions could defend their liberty and interests appealed powerfully to well-educated, prosperous groups, which historians have traditionally labeled as the bourgeoisie. Yet liberal ideas about individual rights and political freedom also appealed to much of the hereditary nobility, at least in western Europe and as formulated by Montesquieu. Representative government did not mean democracy, which liberal thinkers tended to equate with mob rule. Rather, they envisioned voting for representatives as being restricted to those who owned property—those with "a stake in society." England had shown the way. After 1688 it had combined a parliamentary system and considerable individual liberty with a restricted franchise and unquestionable aristocratic pre-eminence. In the course of the eighteenth century, many leading French nobles, led by a judicial nobility inspired by the doctrines of Montesquieu, were increasingly eager to follow the English example. Thus eighteenth-century liberalism found broad support among the prosperous, well-educated elites in western Europe.

The Marquis de Lafayette The most famous great noble to embrace the liberal revolution is shown here directing a battle in the American Revolution. He later returned to France to champion liberty and equality there. The elegant black man is Lafayette's servant, a free man in an age of widespread slavery. *(Source: Jean-Loup Charmet)*

What liberalism lacked from the beginning was strong popular support. At least two reasons account for the people's wary attitude. First, for common people, the great questions were not theoretical and political but immediate and economic; getting enough to eat was a crucial challenge. Second, some of the traditional practices and institutions that liberals wanted to abolish were dear to peasants and urban workers. Comfortable elites had already come into conflict with the people in the eighteenth century over the enclosure of common lands and the regulation of food prices. This conflict would sharpen in the revolutionary era as differences in outlook and well-being led to many misunderstandings and disappointments for both groups.

�֎ THE AMERICAN REVOLUTION (1775–1789)

The era of liberal political revolution began in the New World. The thirteen mainland colonies of British North America revolted against their home country and then succeeded in establishing a new unified government.

The American revolutionaries believed that they were demanding only the traditional rights of English men and women. But those traditional rights were liberal rights, and in the American context they had very strong democratic and popular overtones that made them quite radical. In founding a government firmly based on liberal principles, the Americans set an example that had a forceful impact on Europe and sped up political development there.

The Origins of the Revolution

The American Revolution had its immediate origins in a squabble over increased taxes. The British government had fought and decisively won the Seven Years' War on the strength of its professional army and navy. The American colonists had furnished little real aid. The high cost of the war to the British, however, had led to a doubling of the British national debt. Anticipating further expense defending its recently conquered western lands from native American uprisings, the British government in London set about reorganizing the empire with a series of bold, largely unprecedented measures. Breaking with tradition, the British de-

cided to maintain a large army in North America after peace was restored in 1763. Moreover, they sought to exercise strict control over their newly conquered western lands and to tax the colonies directly. In 1765 the government pushed through Parliament the Stamp Act, which levied taxes on a long list of commercial and legal documents, diplomas, pamphlets, newspapers, almanacs, dice, and playing cards. A stamp glued to each article indicated the tax had been paid.

This effort to increase taxes as part of a tightening-up of the empire seemed perfectly reasonable to the British. Americans were being asked to pay only a share of their own defense costs. Moreover, Americans had been paying only very low local taxes. The Stamp Act would have doubled taxes to about 2 shillings per person per year. No other people in the European or colonial world (except the Poles) paid so little. In contrast, the British paid the highest taxes in the Western world—26 shillings per person. The colonists protested the Stamp Act vigorously and violently, however, and after rioting and boycotts against British goods, Parliament reluctantly repealed the new tax.

As the fury over the Stamp Act revealed, much more was involved than taxes. The key questions were political. To what extent could the home government reassert its power while limiting the authority of colonial legislatures and their elected representatives? Who had the right to make laws for Americans? While a troubled majority of Americans searched hard for a compromise, some radicals began to proclaim that "taxation without representation is tyranny." The British government replied that Americans were represented in Parliament, albeit indirectly (like most English people themselves), and that the absolute supremacy of Parliament throughout the empire could not be questioned. Many Americans felt otherwise. As John Adams of Massachusetts put it, "A Parliament of Great Britain can have no more rights to tax the colonies than a Parliament of Paris." At risk were Americans' existing liberties and time-honored institutions.

Americans had long exercised a great deal of independence and gone their own way. The colonial assemblies made the important laws, which were seldom overturned by the home government. The right to vote was much more widespread than in England. In many parts of colonial Massachusetts, for example, as many as 95 percent of the adult males could vote. Moreover, greater political

Toward Revolution in Boston   The Boston Tea Party was one of many angry confrontations between British officials and Boston patriots. On January 27, 1774, a crowd seized and then tarred and feathered a British customs collector. This French engraving from 1784 commemorates the defiant and provocative action. *(Source: The Granger Collection, New York)*

equality was matched by greater social and economic equality. Neither a hereditary nobility nor a hereditary serf population existed, although the slavery of the Americas consigned blacks to a legally oppressed caste. Independent farmers were the largest group in the country and set much of its tone. In short, the colonial experience had slowly formed a people who felt themselves separate and distinct from the home country. The controversies over taxation intensified those feelings of distinctiveness and separation and brought them to the fore.

In 1773 the dispute over taxes and representation flared up again. The British government had permitted the financially hard-pressed East India Company to ship its tea from China directly to its agents in the colonies, rather than through London middlemen who sold to independent colonial

merchants. Thus the company secured a monopoly on the tea trade and colonial merchants were suddenly excluded from a highly profitable business. The colonists were quick to protest.

In Boston men disguised as Indians had a rowdy "tea party" and threw the company's tea into the harbor. This action led to extreme measures. Parliament passed the so-called Coercive Acts, which closed the port of Boston, curtailed local elections and town meetings, and greatly expanded the royal governor's power. County conventions in Massachusetts protested vehemently and urged that the acts be "rejected as the attempts of a wicked administration to enslave America." Other colonial assemblies joined in the denunciations. In September 1774, the First Continental Congress met in Philadelphia, where the more radical members argued successfully against concessions to the Crown. Compromise was also rejected by the British Parliament, and in April 1775 fighting began in Massachusetts, at Lexington and Concord.

Independence

The fighting spread, and the colonists moved slowly but inevitably toward open rebellion and a declaration of independence. The uncompromising attitude of the British government and its use of German mercenaries went a long way toward dissolving long-standing loyalties to the home country and rivalries among the separate colonies. *Common Sense* (1775), a brilliant attack by the recently arrived English radical Thomas Paine (1737–1809), also mobilized public opinion in favor of independence. A runaway bestseller, Paine's tract ridiculed the idea of a small island ruling a great continent. In his call for freedom and republican government, Paine expressed Americans' growing sense of separateness and moral superiority.

On July 4, 1776, the Second Continental Congress adopted the Declaration of Independence, which boldly listed the tyrannical acts committed by King George III (r. 1760–1820) and confidently proclaimed the natural rights of mankind and the sovereignty of the American states. Sometimes called the world's greatest political editorial, the Declaration of Independence in effect universalized the traditional rights of English people and made them the rights of all mankind. It stated "that all men are created equal; that they are endowed by their Creator with certain unalienable rights; that among these are life, liberty, and the pursuit of happiness." No other American political document has ever caused such excitement, either at home or abroad.

Many American families remained loyal to Britain; many others divided bitterly. After the Declaration of Independence, the conflict often took the form of a civil war pitting patriots against those who remained loyal to the King. The loyalists tended to be wealthy and politically moderate. Many patriots, too, were wealthy—individuals such as John Hancock and George Washington—but willingly allied themselves with farmers and artisans in a broad coalition. This coalition harassed the loyalists and confiscated their property to help pay for the American war effort. The broad social base of the revolutionaries tended to make the liberal revolution democratic. State governments extended the right to vote to many more men in the

course of the war and re-established themselves as republics.

On the international scene, the French sympathized with the rebels from the beginning. They wanted revenge for the humiliating defeats of the Seven Years' War. Officially neutral until 1778, they supplied the great bulk of guns and gunpowder used by the American revolutionaries, very much as foreign great powers have supplied weapons for "wars of national liberation" in our time. By 1777 French volunteers were arriving in Virginia, and a dashing young nobleman, the marquis de Lafayette (1757–1834), quickly became one of Washington's most trusted generals. In 1778 the French government offered a formal alliance to the American ambassador in Paris, Benjamin Franklin, and in 1779 and 1780 the Spanish and Dutch declared war on Britain. Catherine the

The Signing of the Declaration, July 4, 1776   John Trumbull's famous painting shows the dignity and determination of America's revolutionary leaders. An extraordinarily talented group, they succeeded in rallying popular support without losing power to more radical forces in the process. *(Source: Yale University Art Gallery)*

Great of Russia helped organize the League of Armed Neutrality in order to protect neutral shipping rights, which Britain refused to recognize.

Thus by 1780 Great Britain was engaged in an imperial war against most of Europe as well as the thirteen colonies. In these circumstances, and in the face of severe reverses in India, the West Indies, and at Yorktown in Virginia, a new British government decided to cut its losses. American negotiators in Paris were receptive. They feared that France wanted a treaty that would bottle up the new United States east of the Allegheny Mountains and give British holdings west of the Alleghenies to France's ally, Spain. Thus the American negotiators separated themselves from their French allies and accepted the extraordinarily favorable terms Britain offered.

By the Treaty of Paris of 1783, Britain recognized the independence of the thirteen colonies and ceded all its territory between the Allegheny Mountains and the Mississippi River to the Americans. Out of the bitter rivalries of the Old World, the Americans snatched dominion over almost half a continent.

Framing the Constitution

The liberal program of the American Revolution was consolidated by the federal Constitution, the Bill of Rights, and the creation of a national republic. Assembling in Philadelphia in the summer of 1787, the delegates to the Constitutional Convention were determined to end the period of economic depression, social uncertainty, and very weak central government that had followed independence. The delegates decided, therefore, to grant the federal, or central, government important powers: regulation of domestic and foreign trade, the right to levy taxes, and the means to enforce its laws.

Strong rule would be placed squarely in the context of representative self-government. Senators and congressmen would be the lawmaking delegates of the voters, and the president of the republic would be an elected official. The central government would operate in Montesquieu's framework of checks and balances. The executive, legislative, and judicial branches would systematically balance one another. The power of the federal government would in turn be checked by the powers of the individual states.

When the results of the secret deliberations of the Constitutional Convention were presented to the states for ratification, a great public debate began. The opponents of the proposed constitution—the Anti-Federalists—charged that the new document took too much power from the individual states and made the federal government too strong. Moreover, many Anti-Federalists feared for the personal liberties and individual freedoms for which they had just fought. In order to overcome these objections, the Federalists solemnly promised to spell out these basic freedoms as soon as the new constitution was adopted. The result was the first ten amendments to the Constitution, which the first Congress passed shortly after it met in New York in March 1789. These amendments formed an effective bill of rights to safeguard the individual. Most of them—trial by jury, due process of law, right to assemble, freedom from unreasonable search—had their origins in English law and the English Bill of Rights of 1689. Others—the freedoms of speech, the press, and religion—reflected natural-law theory and the American experience.

The American Constitution and the Bill of Rights exemplified the great strengths and the limits of what came to be called classical liberalism. Liberty meant individual freedoms and political safeguards. Liberty also meant representative government but did not necessarily mean democracy, with its principle of one person, one vote. Equality—slaves excepted—meant equality before the law, not equality of political participation or economic well-being. Indeed, economic inequality was resolutely defended by the elite that framed the Constitution. The right to own property was guaranteed by the Fifth Amendment, and if the government took private property, the owner was to receive "just compensation." The radicalism of liberal revolution in America was primarily legal and political, *not* economic or social.

❦ THE FRENCH REVOLUTION (1789–1791)

In Europe, hundreds of books, pamphlets, and articles analyzed and romanticized the American upheaval. Thoughtful Europeans noted, first of all, its enormous long-term implications for international politics. A secret report by the Venetian ambassador to Paris in 1783 stated what many felt: if the new nation survived in unity, it might "become the most formidable power in the world."[1] More generally, American independence fired the imaginations of those aristocrats who were uneasy with their hereditary privileges and those commoners who yearned for equality. Many Europeans believed that the world was advancing and that America was leading the way. As one French writer put it in 1789, "This vast continent which the seas surround will soon change Europe and the universe." The Americans had shown how rational beings could assemble together to exercise sovereignty and write a permanent constitution—a new social contract. All this gave greater reality to the concepts of individual liberty and representative government and reinforced one of the primary ideas of the Enlightenment: that a better world was possible.

No country felt the consequences of the American Revolution more directly than France. Hundreds of French officers served in America and were inspired by the experience. The most famous of these, the young and impressionable marquis de Lafayette, left home as a great aristocrat determined to fight only France's traditional foe, England. He returned with a love of liberty and firm republican convictions. French intellectuals and publicists engaged in passionate analysis of the federal and state constitutions. The American Revolution undeniably hastened upheaval in France.

Yet the French Revolution did not mirror the American example. It was more radical and more complex, more influential and more controversial, more loved and more hated. For Europeans and most of the rest of the world, it was the great revolution of the eighteenth century, *the* revolution that opened the modern era in politics.

The Breakdown of the Old Order

Like the American Revolution, the French Revolution had its immediate origins in the financial difficulties of the government. With both the high court of Paris—the Parlement—and public opinion successfully resisting increased taxes, the government was forced to finance all of its enormous expenditures during the American war with borrowed money. As a result, the national debt and the annual budget deficit soared. By the 1780s, fully 50 percent of France's annual budget went for interest on the ever-increasing debt. Another

25 percent went to maintain the military, while 6 percent was absorbed by the costly and extravagant king and his court at Versailles. Less than 20 percent of the entire national budget was available for the productive functions of the state, such as transportation and general administration. This was an impossible financial situation.

One way out would have been for the government to declare partial bankruptcy, forcing its creditors to accept greatly reduced payments on the debt. Both the Spanish and the French monarchies had done this in earlier times. By the 1780s, however, the French debt was being held by an army of aristocratic and bourgeois creditors, and the French monarchy, though absolute in theory, had become far too weak for such a drastic and unpopular action.

Nor could the king and his ministers, unlike modern governments, print money and create inflation to cover their deficits. Unlike England and Holland, which had far larger national debts relative to their populations, France had no central bank, no paper currency, and no means of creating credit. French money was good gold coin. Therefore, when a depressed economy and a lack of public confidence made it increasingly difficult for the government to obtain new gold loans in 1786, it had no alternative but to try increasing taxes. But since France's tax system was unfair and out-of-date, increased revenues were possible only through fundamental reforms. Such reforms, which would affect all groups in France's complex and fragmented society, opened a Pandora's box of social and political demands.

Legal Orders and Social Realities

As in the Middle Ages, France's 25 million inhabitants were still legally divided into three orders, or *estates*—the Roman Catholic clergy, the nobility, and everyone else. As the nation's first estate, the clergy numbered about 100,000 and had important privileges. It owned about 10 percent of the land and paid only a "voluntary gift," rather than regular taxes, to the government every five years. Moreover, the church levied a tax (the tithe) on landowners, which averaged somewhat less than 10 percent. Much of the church's income was actually drained away from local parishes by political appointees and worldly aristocrats at the top of the church hierarchy—to the intense dissatisfaction of the poor parish priests.

The second legally defined estate consisted of some 400,000 noblemen and noblewomen. The nobles owned outright about 25 percent of the land in France, and they, too, were taxed very lightly. Moreover, nobles continued to enjoy certain manorial rights, or privileges of lordship, that dated back to medieval times and allowed them to tax the peasantry for their own profit. They did this by means of exclusive rights to hunt and fish, village monopolies on baking bread and pressing grapes for wine, fees for justice, and a host of other "useful privileges." In addition, nobles had "honorific privileges," such as the right to precedence on public occasions and the right to wear a sword. These rights conspicuously proclaimed the nobility's legal superiority and exalted social position.

Everyone else was a commoner, legally a member of the third estate. A few commoners—prosperous merchants or lawyers and officials—were well educated and rich, and might even buy up manorial rights as profitable investments. Many more commoners were urban artisans and unskilled day laborers. The vast majority of the third estate consisted of the peasants and agricultural workers in the countryside. Thus the third estate was a conglomeration of vastly different social groups united only by their shared legal status as distinct from the nobility and clergy.

In discussing the long-term origins of the French Revolution, historians have long focused on growing tensions between the nobility and the comfortable members of the third estate, usually known as the *bourgeoisie,* or middle class. A dominant historical interpretation, which has held sway for at least two generations, maintains that the bourgeoisie was basically united by economic position and class interest. Aided by a general economic expansion, the middle class grew rapidly in the eighteenth century, tripling to about 2.3 million persons, or about 8 percent of France's population. Increasing in size, wealth, culture, and self-confidence, this rising bourgeoisie became progressively exasperated by archaic "feudal" laws and customs that restrained the economy and their needs and aspirations. As a result, the French bourgeoisie eventually rose up to lead the entire third estate in a great social revolution, a revolution that destroyed feudal privileges and established a capitalist order based on individualism and a market economy.

In recent years, a flood of new research has challenged these accepted views, and once again the French Revolution is a subject of heated scholarly debate. Above all, revisionist historians have questioned the existence of a growing social conflict between a progressive capitalistic bourgeoisie and a reactionary feudal nobility in eighteenth-century France. Instead, these historians see both bourgeoisie and nobility as highly fragmented, riddled with internal rivalries. Rather than standing as unified blocs against each other, nobility and bourgeoisie formed two parallel social ladders increasingly linked together at the top by wealth, marriage, and Enlightenment culture.

Revisionist historians stress three developments in particular. First, the nobility remained a fluid and relatively open order. Throughout the eighteenth century, substantial numbers of successful commoners continued to seek and obtain noble status through government service and purchase of expensive positions conferring nobility. Thus the nobility continued to attract the wealthiest members of the middle class and to permit social mobility. Second, key sections of the nobility and the prosperous bourgeoisie formed together the core of the book-hungry Enlightenment public. Both groups saw themselves as forming part of the educated elite and standing well above the common people—the peasants and the urban poor. Both groups were also equally liberal until revolution actually began, and they generally supported the judicial opposition to the government. Third, the nobility and the bourgeoisie were not really at odds in the economic sphere. Both looked to investment in land and to government service as their preferred activities, and the goal of the merchant capitalist was to gain enough wealth to live nobly as a large landowner. At the same time, wealthy nobles often acted as aggressive capitalists, investing especially in mining, metallurgy, and foreign trade.

The revisionists have clearly shaken the belief that the bourgeoisie and the nobility were inevitably locked in growing conflict before the French Revolution. But in stressing the similarities between the two groups, especially at the top, revisionists have also reinforced the view, long maintained by historians, that the Old Regime had ceased to correspond with social reality by the 1780s. Legally, society was still based on rigid orders inherited from the Middle Ages. But France had moved far toward being a society based on wealth and education, where an emerging elite that included both aristocratic and bourgeois notables was frustrated by a bureaucratic monarchy that continued to claim the right to absolute power.

The Formation of the National Assembly

The Revolution was under way by 1787, though no one could have realized what was to follow. Spurred by a depressed economy and falling tax receipts, Louis XVI's minister of finance convinced the king to call an assembly of notables to gain support for a general tax on all landed property. The assembled notables, who were mainly important noblemen and high-ranking clergy, ultimately responded that such sweeping tax changes required the approval of the Estates General, the representative body of all three estates, which had not met since 1614.

Facing imminent bankruptcy, the king tried to reassert his authority. He dismissed the notables and established new taxes by decree. In stirring language, the Parlement of Paris promptly declared the royal initiative null and void. When the king tried to exile the judges, a tremendous wave of protest swept the country. Frightened investors also refused to advance more loans to the state. Finally in July 1788, a beaten Louis XVI bowed to public opinion and called for a spring session of the Estates General. Absolute monarchy was collapsing.

What would replace it? Throughout the unprecedented election campaign of 1788 and 1789, that question excited France. All across the country, clergy, nobles, and commoners met together in their respective orders to draft petitions for change and to elect their respective delegates to the Estates General. The local assemblies of the clergy chose two-thirds of the delegates from among the poorer parish priests, who were commoners by birth. Among the nobles, already badly split by wealth and education, a conservative majority was drawn from the poorer and more numerous provincial nobility. But fully one-third of the nobility's representatives were liberals committed to major changes.

As for the third estate, there was great popular participation in the elections. Almost all male commoners twenty-five years or older had the right to vote. Still, most of the representatives finally selected were well-educated, prosperous lawyers and government officials. There were no delegates elected from the great mass of laboring poor, an exclusion that would encourage the peasants and also the urban artisans to intervene directly and dramatically at numerous points in the Revolution, as we shall see.

The petitions for change coming from the three estates showed a surprising degree of consensus on most issues. There was general agreement that royal absolutism should give way to constitutional monarchy, in which laws and taxes would require the consent of the Estates General meeting regularly. All agreed that in the future individual liberties would have to be guaranteed by law and that the economic position of the parish clergy would have to be improved. It was generally acknowledged that economic development required reforms, such as the abolition of internal trade barriers. The striking similarities in the grievance petitions of the clergy, nobility, and third estate reflected the broad commitment of France's educated elite to liberalism.

Yet an increasingly bitter quarrel undermined this consensus during the intense electoral campaign. *How* would the Estates General vote, and precisely *who* would lead in the political reorganization that was generally desired? The Estates General of 1614 had sat as three separate houses. Any action had required the agreement of at least two branches, a requirement that had virtually guaranteed control by the nobility and the clergy. The aristocratic Parlement of Paris ruled that the Estates General should once again sit separately. Certain middle-class intellectuals and some liberal nobles demanded instead a single assembly dominated by representatives of the third estate. Amid increased political competition and a growing hostility toward aristocratic aspirations, the government agreed that the third estate should have as many delegates as the clergy and the nobility combined. When it then rendered this act meaningless by upholding voting by separate order, middle-class leaders saw fresh evidence of an aristocratic conspiracy.

The Estates General opened in May 1789 at Versailles with twelve hundred delegates. The estates were almost immediately deadlocked. Delegates of the third estate refused to transact any business until the king ordered the clergy and nobility to sit with them in a single body. Finally, after a six-week war of nerves, the third estate on June 17 voted to call itself the National Assembly. On June 20, the delegates of the third estate, excluded from their hall because of "repairs," moved to a large indoor tennis court. There they swore

The Oath of the Tennis Court   This painting, based on an unfinished work by Jacques-Louis David (1748–1825), enthusiastically celebrates the revolutionary rupture of June 20, 1789. Locked out of their assembly hall at Versailles and joined by some sympathetic priests, the delegates of the third estate have moved to an indoor tennis court and are swearing never to disband until they have written a new constitution and put France on a firm foundation. (*Source: Musée Carnavalet/Photographie Bulloz*)

the Oath of the Tennis Court, pledging not to disband until they had written a new constitution.

The indecisive king's actions were then somewhat contradictory. On June 23 he made a conciliatory speech urging reforms to a joint session and then ordered the three estates to meet together. Then, apparently following the advice of relatives and court nobles that he dissolve the Estates General by force, the king called an army of eighteen thousand troops toward Versailles. On July 11 he dismissed his finance minister and his other more liberal ministers. Having resigned himself to bankruptcy, Louis XVI belatedly sought to reassert his historic "divine right" to rule. The middle-class delegates and their allies from the liberal nobility had done their best, but they were resigned to being disbanded at bayonet point. One third-estate

delegate reassured a worried colleague, "You won't hang—you'll only have to go back home."[2]

The Revolt of the Poor and the Oppressed

While the educated delegates of the third estate pressed for symbolic equality with the nobility and clergy in a single legislative body at Versailles, economic hardship gripped the common people of France in a tightening vise. Grain was the basis of the diet of ordinary people in the eighteenth century, and in 1788 the harvest had been extremely poor. The price of bread, which had been rising gradually since 1785, began to soar. By July 1789 it had climbed as high as 8 sous per pound in the provinces. In Paris, where bread was regularly subsidized by the government in an attempt to prevent popular unrest, the price rose to 4 sous, a price at which a laborer with a wife and three children had to spend most of his wages to buy the family's bread.

Harvest failure and high bread prices unleashed a classic economic depression of the preindustrial age. With food so expensive and with so much uncertainty, the demand for manufactured goods collapsed, resulting in thousands of artisans and small traders being thrown out of work. By the end of 1789, almost half of the French people were in need of relief. In Paris the situation was so desperate in July 1789 that perhaps 150,000 of the city's 600,000 people were without work.

Against this background of dire poverty and excitement generated by the political crisis, the people of Paris entered decisively onto the revolutionary stage. They believed in a general, though ill-defined, way that the economic distress had human causes. They believed that they should have steady work and enough bread at fair prices to survive. Specifically, they feared that the dismissal of the king's moderate finance minister would put them at the mercy of aristocratic landowners and grain speculators. Stories like that quoting the wealthy financier Joseph François Foulon as saying that the poor "should eat grass, like my horses" and rumors that the king's troops would sack the city began to fill the air. Angry crowds formed, and passionate voices urged action. On July 13 the people began to seize arms for the defense of the city, and on July 14 several hundred of the most determined people marched to the Bastille to search for gunpowder.

Storming the Bastille   This representation by an untrained contemporary artist shows civilians and members of the Paris militia—the "conquerors of the Bastille"—on the attack. Their successful action had enormous practical and symbolic significance, and July 14 has long been France's most important national holiday. (*Source: Musée Carnavalet/Photo Hubert Josse*)

The governor of the medieval fortress-prison refused to hand over the powder, panicked, and ordered his men to fire, killing ninety-eight people attempting to enter. Cannons were brought to batter the main gate, and fighting continued until the prison surrendered. The governor of the prison was later hacked to death, and his head was stuck on a pike and paraded through the streets. The next day a committee of citizens appointed the marquis de Lafayette commander of the city's armed forces. Paris was lost to the king, who was forced to recall the finance minister and disperse his troops. The popular uprising had saved the National Assembly.

As the delegates resumed their long-winded and inconclusive debates at Versailles, the people in the countryside sent them a radical and unmistakable message. All across France, peasants began to rise in spontaneous, violent, and effective insurrection against their lords. Neither middle-class landowners nor the larger, more prosperous farmers were spared. In some areas, peasants reinstated traditional village practices, undoing recent enclosures and reoccupying old common lands. Peasants seized forests, and taxes went unpaid. Fear of vagabonds and outlaws—called the Great Fear by contemporaries—seized the countryside and fanned the flames of rebellion.

Faced with chaos yet afraid to call on the king to restore order, some liberal nobles and middle-class delegates at Versailles responded to peasant demands with a surprise maneuver on the night of August 4, 1789. The duke of Aiguillon, one of France's greatest noble landowners, declared that

in several provinces the whole people forms a kind of league for the destruction of the manor houses, the ravaging of the lands, and especially for the seizure of the archives where the title deeds to feudal properties are kept. It seeks to throw off at last a yoke that has for many centuries weighted it down.[3]

He urged equality in taxation and the elimination of feudal dues. In the end, all the old exactions imposed on the peasants—serfdom where it still existed, village monopolies, the right to make peasants work on the roads, and a host of other dues—were abolished. Though a clarifying law passed a week later was less generous, the peasants ignored the "fine print." They never paid feudal dues again. Thus the French peasantry, which already owned about 30 percent of all the land, achieved a great and unprecedented victory in the early days of revolutionary upheaval. Henceforth, the French peasants would seek mainly to protect and consolidate their triumph. As the Great Fear subsided in the countryside, they became a force for order and stability.

A Limited Monarchy

The National Assembly moved forward. On August 27, 1789, it issued the Declaration of the Rights of Man, which stated, "Men are born and remain free and equal in rights." The declaration also maintained that mankind's natural rights are "liberty, property, security, and resistance to oppression" and that "every man is presumed innocent until he is proven guilty." As for law, "it is an expression of the general will; all citizens have the right to concur personally or through their representatives in its formation. . . . Free expression of thoughts and opinions is one of the most precious rights of mankind: every citizen may therefore speak, write, and publish freely." In short, this clarion call of the liberal revolutionary ideal guaranteed equality before the law, representative government for a sovereign people, and individual freedom. This revolutionary credo, only two pages long, was propagandized throughout France and the rest of Europe and around the world.

Moving beyond general principles to draft a constitution proved difficult. The questions of how much power the king should retain led to another deadlock. Once again the decisive answer came from the poor—in this instance, the poor women of Paris.

Women customarily bought the food and managed the poor family's slender resources. In Paris great numbers of women also worked for wages. In the general economic crisis, increasing unemployment and hunger put tremendous pressure on household managers, and the result was another popular explosion.

On October 5 some seven thousand desperate women marched the twelve miles from Paris to Versailles to demand action. This great crowd invaded the National Assembly, "armed with scythes, sticks and pikes." One tough old woman directing a large group of younger women defiantly shouted into the debate, "Who's that talking down there? Make the chatterbox shut up. That's not the point: the point is that we want bread."[4] Hers was the genuine voice of the people, essential to any understanding of the French Revolution.

❋ **"To Versailles"**   This print is one of many commemorating the women's march on Versailles. Notice on the left that the artist has depicted—and criticized—the fashionable lady from the well-to-do as a most reluctant revolutionary. *(Source: Giraudon/Art Resource, NY)*

The women invaded the royal apartments, slaughtered some of the royal bodyguards, and furiously searched for the queen, Marie Antoinette, who was widely despised for her lavish spending and supposedly immoral behavior. "We are going to cut off her head, tear out her heart, fry her liver, and that won't be the end of it," they shouted, surging through the palace in a frenzy. It seems likely that only the intervention of Lafayette and the National Guard saved the royal family. But the only way to calm the disorder was for the king to go and live in Paris, as the crowd demanded. With this victory, the women clearly emerged as a major and enduring element in the Parisian revolutionary crowd.[5]

The National Assembly followed the king to Paris, and the next two years, until September 1791, saw the consolidation of the liberal Revolution. Under middle-class leadership, the National Assembly abolished the French nobility as a legal order and pushed forward with the creation of a constitutional monarchy, which Louis XVI reluctantly agreed to accept in July 1790. In the final constitution, the king remained the head of state, but all lawmaking power was placed in the hands of the National Assembly, elected by the economic upper half of French males.

New laws broadened women's rights to seek divorce, to inherit property, and to obtain financial support from fathers for illegitimate children. But women were not allowed to vote or hold political office. The great majority of comfortable, well-educated males in the National Assembly believed that women should be limited to child raising and domestic duties and should leave politics and most public activities to men. The delegates to the National Assembly also believed that excluding women from politics would free the political system from the harmful effects of the sexual intrigue common at court; and pure, home-focused wives would raise the high-minded sons needed to govern and defend the nation.

The National Assembly replaced the complicated patchwork of historic provinces with eighty-three departments of approximately equal size. It replaced the jumble of weights and measures that varied from province to province with the simple, rational metric system in 1793. It prohibited monopolies, guilds, and workers' combinations, and it abolished barriers to trade within France in the name of economic liberty. Thus the National Assembly applied the critical spirit of the Enlightenment to reform France's laws and institutions completely.

The National Assembly also nationalized the Catholic church's property and abolished monasteries as useless relics of a distant past. The government sold all former church property in an attempt to put the state's finances on a solid footing. Peasants eventually purchased much of this land when it was subdivided. The purchases strengthened their attachment to the revolutionary state. These actions, however, brought the new government into conflict with the Catholic church and with many sincere Christians, especially in the countryside.

Many delegates to the National Assembly, imbued with the rationalism and skepticism of the eighteenth-century philosophes, harbored a deep distrust of popular piety and "superstitious religion." They were interested in the church only to the extent that they could seize its land and use the church to strengthen the new state. Thus they established a national church, with priests chosen by voters. In the face of widespread resistance, the National Assembly then required the clergy to take a loyalty oath to the new government. The Catholic clergy became just so many more employees of the state. The pope formally condemned this attempt to subjugate the church. Only half of the priests of France took the oath of allegiance, and confusion and hostility among French Catholics were pervasive. The attempt to remake the Catholic church, like the National Assembly's abolition of guilds and workers' combinations, sharpened the division between the educated classes and the common people that had been emerging in the eighteenth century. This policy toward the church was the revolutionary government's first important failure.

✤ WORLD WAR AND REPUBLICAN FRANCE (1791–1799)

When Louis XVI accepted the final version of the completed constitution in September 1791, a young and still obscure provincial lawyer and member of the National Assembly named Maximilien Robespierre (1758–1794) evaluated the work of two years and concluded, "The Revolution is over." Robespierre was both right and wrong. He

was right in the sense that the most constructive and lasting reforms were in place. Nothing substantial in the way of liberty and equality would be gained in the next generation. He was wrong in the sense that a much more radical stage lay ahead. New heroes and new ideologies were to emerge in revolutionary wars and international conflict.

Foreign Reactions and the Beginning of War

The outbreak and progress of revolution in France produced great excitement and a sharp division of opinion in Europe and the United States. Liberals and radicals saw a mighty triumph of liberty over despotism. In Great Britain especially, they hoped that the French example would lead to a fundamental reordering of the political system that had placed Parliament in the hands of the aristocracy and a few wealthy merchants, with the great majority of people having very little say in the government. Conservative leaders such as Edmund Burke (1729–1797) were deeply troubled by the aroused spirit of reform. In 1790 Burke published *Reflections on the Revolution in France,* one of the great intellectual defenses of European conservatism. Defending inherited privileges, he glorified the unrepresentative Parliament and predicted that thoroughgoing reform like that occurring in France would lead only to chaos and tyranny. Burke's work sparked vigorous debate.

One passionate rebuttal came from a young writer in London, Mary Wollstonecraft (1759–1797). Born into the middle class, Wollstonecraft was schooled in adversity by a mean-spirited father who beat his wife and squandered his inherited fortune. Determined to be independent in a society that generally expected women of her class to become homebodies and obedient wives, she struggled for years to earn her living as a governess and teacher—practically the only acceptable careers for single, educated women—before attaining success as a translator and author. Interested in politics and believing that "a desperate disease requires a powerful remedy" in Great Britain as well as France, Wollstonecraft was incensed by Burke's book. She immediately wrote a blistering, widely read attack, *A Vindication of the Rights of Man* (1790).

Then, fired up on controversy and commitment, she made a daring intellectual leap. She developed for the first time the logical implications of natural-law philosophy in her masterpiece, *A Vindication of the Rights of Woman* (1792). To fulfill the still-unrealized potential of the French Revolution and to eliminate the many-sided sexual inequality she had felt so keenly, she demanded that

the Rights of Women be respected . . . [and] JUSTICE for one-half of the human race. . . . It is time to effect a revolution in female manners, time to restore to them their lost dignity, and make them, as part of the human species, labor, by reforming themselves, to reform the world.

Setting high standards for women, Wollstonecraft advocated rigorous coeducation, which would make women better wives and mothers, good citizens, and even economically independent people. Women could manage businesses and enter politics if only men would give them the chance. Men themselves would benefit from women's rights, for Wollstonecraft believed that "the two sexes mutually corrupt and improve each other."[6] Wollstonecraft's analysis testified to the power of the Revolution to excite and inspire outside France. Paralleling ideas put forth independently in France by Olympe de Gouges (1748–1793), a self-taught writer and woman of the people (see Listening to the Past), Wollstonecraft's work marked the birth of the modern women's movement for equal rights, and it was ultimately very influential.

The kings and nobles of continental Europe, who had at first welcomed the revolution in France as weakening a competing power, began to feel no less threatened than Burke and his supporters. At their courts they listened to the diatribes of great court nobles who had fled France and were urging intervention in France's affairs. When Louis XVI and Marie Antoinette were arrested and returned to Paris after trying unsuccessfully to slip out of France in June 1791, the monarchs of Austria and Prussia, in the Declaration of Pillnitz, declared their willingness to intervene in France in certain circumstances.

But the crowned heads of Europe did not deter the revolutionary spirit in France. When the National Assembly disbanded, it sought popular support by decreeing that none of its members would be eligible for election to the new Legislative Assembly. This meant that when the new representative body convened in October 1791, it had a different character. The great majority of the legislators were still prosperous, well-educated, middle-class men, but they were younger and less cautious

Mary Wollstonecraft   Painted by an unknown artist when Mary Wollstonecraft was thirty-two and writing her revolutionary *Vindication of the Rights of Woman,* this portrait highlights the remarkable strength of character that energized Wollstonecraft's brilliant intellect. *(Source: The Board of Trustees of the National Museums and Galleries on Merseyside, Walker Art Gallery)*

than their predecessors. Loosely allied and known as Jacobins, after the name of their political club, the representatives to the Legislative Assembly were passionately committed to liberal revolution.

The Jacobins increasingly lumped "useless aristocrats" and "despotic monarchs" together and easily whipped themselves into a patriotic fury with bombastic oratory. If the courts of Europe were attempting to incite a war of kings against France, then "we will incite a war of people against kings. . . . Ten million Frenchmen, kindled by the fire of liberty, armed with the sword, with reason, with eloquence would be able to change the face of the world and make the tyrants tremble on their thrones."[7] Only Robespierre and a very few others argued that people would not welcome liberation at the point of a gun. Such warnings were brushed aside. France would "rise to the full height of her mission," as one deputy urged. In April 1792 France declared war on Francis II, the Habsburg monarch.

France's crusade against tyranny went poorly at first. Prussia joined Austria in the Austrian Netherlands (present-day Belgium), and French forces broke and fled at their first encounter with armies of this First Coalition. The road to Paris lay open, and it is possible that only conflict between the eastern monarchs over the division of Poland saved France from defeat.

Military reversals and Austro-Prussian threats caused a wave of patriotic fervor to sweep France. In this supercharged wartime atmosphere, rumors of treason by the king and queen spread in Paris. Once again, the common people of Paris acted decisively. On August 10, 1792, a revolutionary crowd captured the royal palace at the Tuileries after heavy fighting. The king and his family fled for their lives to the nearby Legislative Assembly, which suspended the king from all his functions, imprisoned him, and called for a new National Convention to be elected by universal male suffrage. Monarchy in France was on its deathbed, mortally wounded by war and popular upheaval.

The Second Revolution

The fall of the monarchy marked a rapid radicalization of the Revolution, a phase that historians often call the "second revolution." Louis's imprisonment was followed by the September Massacres. Wild stories seized the city that imprisoned counter-revolutionary aristocrats and priests were plotting with the allied invaders. As a result, angry crowds invaded the prisons of Paris and summarily slaughtered half of the men and women they found. In late September 1792, the new, popularly elected National Convention proclaimed France a republic.

The republic sought to create a new popular culture to assure its future and fashioned compelling symbols that broke with the past and glorified the new order. It adopted a brand-new revolutionary calendar, which eliminated saints' days and renamed the days and the months after the seasons of the year. Citizens were expected to address each other with the friendly "thou" of the people rather than with the formal "you" of the rich and powerful. The republic energetically promoted broad, open-air, democratic festivals that sought to redirect the people's traditional enthusiasm for Catholic religious celebrations to secular holidays. Instilling republican virtue and a love of nation, these spectacles were less successful in villages than in cities, where popular interest in politics was greater and Catholicism was weaker.

All of the members of the National Convention were Jacobins and republicans, and the great majority continued to come from the well-educated middle class. But the Convention was increasingly divided into two bitterly competitive groups—the Girondists, named after a department in southwestern France, and the Mountain, led by Robespierre and another young lawyer, Georges Jacques Danton. The Mountain was so called because its members sat on the uppermost left-hand benches of the assembly hall.

This division was clearly apparent after the National Convention overwhelmingly convicted Louis XVI of treason. By a single vote, 361 of the 720 members of the Convention then unconditionally sentenced him to death in January 1793. Louis died with tranquil dignity on the newly invented guillotine. One of his last statements was "I am innocent and shall die without fear. I would that my death might bring happiness to the French, and ward off the dangers which I foresee."[8]

Both the Girondists and the Mountain were determined to continue the "war against tyranny." After stopping the Prussians at the indecisive Battle of Valmy on September 20, 1792, Republican armies successfully invaded Savoy and the German Rhineland. To the north, the revolutionary armies won their first major battle at Jemappes and by November 1792 were occupying the entire Austrian Netherlands. Everywhere they went, French armies of occupation chased the princes, "abolished feudalism," and found support among some peasants and middle-class people.

But the French armies also lived off the land, requisitioning food and supplies and plundering local treasures. The liberators looked increasingly like foreign invaders. International tensions mounted. In February 1793 the National Convention, at war with Austria and Prussia, declared war on Britain, Holland, and Spain as well. Republican France was now at war with almost all of Europe, a great war that would last almost without interruption until 1815.

As the forces of the First Coalition drove the French from the Austrian Netherlands, peasants in western France revolted against being drafted into the army. They were supported and encouraged in their resistance by devout Catholics, royalists, and foreign agents.

In Paris the quarrelsome National Convention found itself locked in a life-and-death political struggle between the Girondists and the Mountain. Both groups hated privilege and wanted to temper economic liberalism with social concern. Yet personal hatreds ran deep. The Girondists feared a bloody dictatorship by the Mountain, and the Mountain was no less convinced that the more moderate Girondists would turn to conservatives and even royalists in order to retain power. With the middle-class delegates so bitterly divided, the laboring poor of Paris emerged as the decisive political factor.

The laboring men and women of Paris always constituted—along with the peasantry in the summer of 1789—the elemental force that drove the Revolution forward. It was they who had stormed the Bastille, marched on Versailles, driven the king from the Tuileries, and carried out the September Massacres. The petty traders and laboring poor were often known as the *sans-culottes,* "without breeches," because the men wore trousers instead of the knee breeches of the aristocracy and the solid middle class. The immediate interests of the sans-culottes were mainly economic, and in the spring of 1793 the economic situation was as bad as the military situation. Rapid inflation, unemployment, and food shortages were again weighing heavily on poor families.

By the spring of 1793, sans-culottes men and women, encouraged by the so-called angry men, were demanding radical political action to guarantee them their daily bread. At first the Mountain joined the Girondists in violently rejecting these demands. But in the face of military defeat, peasant revolt, and hatred of the Girondists, Robespierre's group joined with sans-culottes activists in the city government to engineer a popular uprising, which forced the Convention to arrest thirty-one Girondist deputies for treason on June 2. All power passed to the Mountain.

The End of Louis XVI   Some cheered and some wept when the executioner showed the crowd the condemned monarch's severed head. The execution of the king was a victory for the radicals in Paris, but it horrified Europe's monarchs and conservatives, and it strengthened their opposition to the French Revolution. *(Source: Musée Carnavalet/Laurie Platt Winfrey, Inc.)*

Robespierre and others from the Mountain joined the recently formed Committee of Public Safety, to which the Convention had given dictatorial power to deal with the national emergency. These developments in Paris triggered revolt in leading provincial cities, such as Lyons and Marseilles, where moderates denounced Paris and demanded a decentralized government. The peasant revolt spread, and the republic's armies were driven back on all fronts. By July 1793 defeat appeared imminent.

Total War and the Terror

A year later, in July 1794, the Austrian Netherlands and the Rhineland were once again in the hands of conquering French armies, and the First Coalition was falling apart. This remarkable change of fortune was due to the revolutionary government's success in harnessing, for perhaps the first time in history, the explosive forces of a planned economy, revolutionary terror, and modern nationalism in a total war effort.

Robespierre and the Committee of Public Safety advanced with implacable resolution on several fronts in 1793 and 1794. First, in an effort to save revolutionary France, they continued to collaborate with the fiercely patriotic and democratic sansculottes, who retained the common people's traditional faith in fair prices and a moral economic order and who distrusted most wealthy capitalists and all aristocrats. Thus Robespierre and his coworkers established, as best they could, a planned economy with egalitarian social overtones. Rather than let supply and demand determine prices, the government decreed the maximum allowable prices for a host of key products. Though the state was too weak to enforce all its price regulations, it did fix the price of bread in Paris at levels the poor could afford. Bakers were permitted to make only the "bread of equality"—a brown bread made of a mixture of all available flours. White bread and pastries were outlawed as frivolous luxuries. The poor of Paris may not have eaten well, but at least they ate.

They also worked, mainly to produce arms and munitions for the war effort. Craftsmen and small manufacturers were told what to produce and when to deliver. The government nationalized many small workshops and requisitioned raw

 The Last Roll Call Prisoners sentenced to death by revolutionary courts listen to an official solemnly reading the names of those selected for immediate execution. After being bound, the prisoners will ride standing up in a small cart through the streets of Paris to the nearby guillotine. As this painting highlights, both women and men were executed for political crimes under the Terror. *(Source: Mansell Collection)*

THE FRENCH REVOLUTION

May 5, 1789	Estates General convenes at Versailles
June 17, 1789	Third estate declares itself the National Assembly
June 20, 1789	Oath of the Tennis Court
July 14, 1789	Storming of the Bastille
July–Aug. 1789	The Great Fear in the countryside
August 4, 1789	National Assembly abolishes feudal privileges
August 27, 1789	National Assembly issues Declaration of the Rights of Man
October 5, 1789	Women march on Versailles and force royal family to return to Paris
November 1789	National Assembly confiscates lands held by the Catholic church
July 1790	Civil Constitution of the Clergy establishes a national church Louis XVI reluctantly agrees to accept a constitutional monarchy
June 1791	Arrest of the royal family while attempting to flee France
August 1791	Declaration of Pillnitz by Austria and Prussia
April 1792	France declares war on Austria
August 1792	Parisian mob attacks palace and takes Louis XVI prisoner
September 1792	September Massacres National Convention declares France a republic and abolishes monarchy
January 1793	Execution of Louis XVI
February 1793	France declares war on Britain, Holland, and Spain
March 1793	Bitter struggle in the National Convention between Girondists and the Mountain
April–June 1793	Robespierre and the Mountain organize the Committee of Public Safety Revolts in provincial cities
September 1793	Price controls to aid the sans-culottes and mobilize war effort
1793–1794	Reign of Terror in Paris and the provinces
Spring 1794	French armies victorious on all fronts
July 1794	Execution of Robespierre Thermidorian Reaction begins
1795–1799	The Directory
1795	End of economic controls and suppression of the sans-culottes
1797	Napoleon defeats Austrian armies in Italy and returns triumphant to Paris
1798	Austria, Great Britain, and Russia form the Second Coalition against France
1799	Napoleon overthrows the Directory and seizes power

materials and grain from the peasants. Failures to control and coordinate were failures of means and not of desire: seldom if ever before had a government attempted to manage an economy so thoroughly. The second revolution and the ascendancy of the sans-culottes had produced an embryonic emergency socialism, which thoroughly frightened Europe's properties classes and had great influence on the subsequent development of socialist ideology.

Second, while radical economic measures supplied the poor with bread and the armies with weapons, the Reign of Terror (1793–1794) was solidifying the home front. Special revolutionary courts responsible only to Robespierre's Committee of Public Safety tried rebels and "enemies of the nation" for political crimes. Drawing on popular, sans-culottes support, these local courts ignored normal legal procedures and judged severely. Some 40,000 French men and women were executed or died in prison. Another 300,000 suspects crowded the prisons.

Robespierre's Reign of Terror was one of the most controversial phases of the French Revolution. Most historians now believe that the Reign of Terror was not directed against any single class but was a political weapon directed impartially against all who might oppose the revolutionary government. For many Europeans of the time, however, the Reign of Terror represented a terrifying perversion of the generous ideals that had existed in 1789.

The third and perhaps most decisive element in the French republic's victory over the First Coalition was its ability to continue drawing on the explosive power of patriotic dedication to a national state and a national mission. This is the essence of modern nationalism, and it was something new in history. With a common language and a common tradition newly reinforced by the ideas of popular sovereignty and democracy, the French people were stirred by a common loyalty. The shared danger of foreign foes and internal rebels unified all classes in a heroic defense of the nation. Everyone had to participate in the national effort. According to a famous decree of August 23, 1793:

The young men shall go to battle and the married men shall forge arms. The women shall make tents and clothes, and shall serve in the hospitals; children shall tear rags into lint. The old men will be guided to the public places of the cities to kindle the courage of the young warriors and to preach the unity of the Republic and the hatred of kings.

Like the wars of religion, war in 1793 was a crusade, a life-and-death struggle between good and evil. This war, however, was fought for a secular, rather than a religious, ideology.

Because all unmarried young men were subject to the draft, the French armed forces swelled to a million men in fourteen armies. A force of this size was unprecedented in the history of European warfare. The soldiers were led by young, impetuous generals who had often risen rapidly from the ranks and personified the opportunities the Revolution seemed to offer gifted sons of the people. These generals used mass attacks at bayonet point by their highly motivated forces to overwhelm the enemy. By the spring of 1794, French armies were victorious on all fronts. The republic was saved.

The Thermidorian Reaction and the Directory (1794–1799)

The success of the French armies led Robespierre and the Committee of Public Safety to relax the emergency economic controls, but they extended the political Reign of Terror. Their lofty goal was increasingly an ideal democratic republic where justice would reign and there would be neither rich nor poor. Their lowly means were unrestrained despotism and the guillotine, which struck down any who might seriously question the new order. In March 1794, to the horror of many sans-culottes, Robespierre's Terror wiped out many of the angry men, who had been criticizing Robespierre for being soft on the wealthy. Two weeks later, several of Robespierre's long-standing collaborators, led by the famous orator Danton, marched up the steps to the guillotine. A strange assortment of radicals and moderates in the Convention, knowing that they might be next, organized a conspiracy. They howled down Robespierre when he tried to speak to the National Convention on 9 Thermidor (July 27, 1794). On the following day, it was Robespierre's turn to be shaved by the revolutionary razor.

As Robespierre's closest supporters followed their leader, France unexpectedly experienced a thorough reaction to the despotism of the Reign of Terror. In a general way, this "Thermidorian reaction" recalled the early days of the Revolution.

The respectable middle-class lawyers and professionals who had led the liberal revolution of 1789 reasserted their authority, drawing support from their own class, the provincial cities, and the better-off peasants. The National Convention abolished many economic controls, printed more paper currency, and let prices rise sharply. And all the while, wealthy bankers and newly rich speculators celebrated the sudden end of the Terror with an orgy of self-indulgence and ostentatious luxury, an orgy symbolized by the shockingly low-cut gowns that quickly became the rage among their wives and mistresses.

The collapse of economic controls, coupled with runaway inflation, hit the working poor very hard. The gaudy extravagance of the rich wounded their pride. The sans-culottes accepted private property, but they believed passionately in small business, decent wages, and economic justice. Increasingly disorganized after Robespierre purged radical leaders, the common people of Paris finally revolted against the emerging new order in early 1795. The Convention quickly used the army to suppress these insurrections. For the first time since the fall of the Bastille, bread riots and uprisings by Parisians living on the edge of starvation were effectively put down by a government that made no concessions to the poor. In the face of all these catastrophes, the revolutionary fervor of the laboring poor in Paris finally subsided.

In villages and small towns there arose a great cry for peace and a turning toward religion, especially from women, who had seldom experienced the political radicalization of sans-culottes women in the big cities. Instead, these women had frequently and tenaciously defended their culture and religious beliefs. As the frustrated government began to retreat on the religious question from 1796 to 1801, the women of rural France brought back the Catholic church and the open worship of God. In the words of a leading historian, these women worked constructively and effectively for a return to a normal and structured lifestyle:

Peacefully but purposefully, they sought to re-establish a pattern of life punctuated by a peeling bell and one in which the rites of passage—birth, marriage, and death—were respected and hallowed. The state had intruded too far and women entered the public arena to push it back and won. It was one of the most resounding political statements made by the populace in the entire history of the Revolution.[9]

As for the middle-class members of the National Convention, in 1795 they wrote yet another constitution, which they believed would guarantee their economic position and political supremacy. The mass of the population voted only for electors, who were men of means. Electors then elected the members of a reorganized Legislative Assembly, as well as key officials throughout France. The new assembly also chose a five-man executive—the Directory.

The Directory continued to support French military expansion abroad. War was no longer so much a crusade as a means to meet ever-present, ever-unsolved economic problems. Large, victorious French armies reduced unemployment at home and were able to live off the territories they conquered and plundered.

The unprincipled action of the Directory reinforced widespread disgust with war and starvation, and the national elections of 1797 returned a large number of conservative and even monarchist deputies who favored peace at almost any price. The members of the Directory, fearing for their skins, used the army to nullify the elections and began to govern dictatorially. Two years later, Napoleon Bonaparte ended the Directory in a coup d'état and substituted a strong dictatorship for a weak one. The effort to establish stable representative government had failed.

❈ THE NAPOLEONIC ERA (1799–1815)

For almost fifteen years, from 1799 to 1814, France was in the hands of a keen-minded military dictator of exceptional ability. One of history's most fascinating leaders, Napoleon Bonaparte (1769–1821) realized the need to put an end to civil strife in France in order to create unity and consolidate his rule. And he did. But Napoleon saw himself as a man of destiny, and the glory of war and the dream of universal empire proved irresistible.

Napoleon's Rule of France

In 1799 when he seized power, young General Napoleon Bonaparte was a national hero. Born in Corsica into an impoverished noble family in 1769, Napoleon left home and became a lieutenant in the French artillery in 1785. After a brief and unsuccessful adventure fighting for Corsican independence in 1789, he returned to France as a French patriot and a dedicated revolutionary. Rising rapidly in the new army, Napoleon was placed in command of French forces in Italy and won brilliant victories there in 1796 and 1797. His next campaign, in Egypt, was a failure, but Napoleon made his way back to France before the fiasco was generally known. His reputation remained intact.

Napoleon soon learned that some prominent members of the Legislative Assembly were plotting against the Directory. The dissatisfaction of these plotters stemmed not so much from the fact that the Directory was a dictatorship as from the fact that it was a weak dictatorship. Ten years of upheaval and uncertainty had made firm rule much more appealing than liberty and popular politics to these disillusioned revolutionaries. They wanted a strong military ruler, and the flamboyant thirty-year-old Napoleon was ideal. Thus the conspirators and Napoleon organized a takeover. On November 9, 1799, they ousted the Directors, and the following day soldiers disbanded the Legislative Assembly at bayonet point. Napoleon was named first consul of the republic, and a new constitution consolidating his position was overwhelmingly approved in a plebiscite in December 1799. Republican appearances were maintained, but Napoleon was already the real ruler of France.

The essence of Napoleon's domestic policy was to use his great and highly personal powers to maintain order and put an end to civil strife. He did so by working out unwritten agreements with powerful groups in France. Napoleon's bargain with the solid middle class was codified in the Civil Code of 1804, which reasserted two of the fundamental principles of the liberal and essentially moderate revolution of 1789: equality of all male citizens before the law and absolute security of wealth and private property. Napoleon and the leading bankers of Paris established the privately owned Bank of France, which loyally served the interests of both the state and the financial oligarchy. Napoleon's defense of the new economic order also appealed successfully to the peasants, who had gained both land and status from the revolutionary changes.

At the same time, Napoleon accepted and strengthened the position of the French bureaucracy. Building on the solid foundations that revolutionary governments had inherited from the Old Regime, he perfected a thoroughly centralized state. A network of prefects, subprefects, and centrally appointed mayors depended on Napoleon and served him well. Nor were members of the old nobility slighted. Napoleon granted amnesty to émigrés on the condition that they return to France and take a loyalty oath. Members of this returning elite soon ably occupied many high posts in the expanding centralized state. Napoleon also created a new imperial nobility in order to reward his most talented generals and officials.

Napoleon's great skill in gaining support from important and potentially hostile groups is illustrated by his treatment of the Catholic church in France. Personally uninterested in religion, Napoleon wanted to heal the religious division remaining from the Revolution so that a united Catholic church in France could serve as a bulwark of order and social peace. After long and arduous negotiations, Napoleon and Pope Pius VII (r. 1800–1823) signed the Concordat of 1801. The pope gained for French Catholics the precious right to practice their religion freely, but Napoleon gained political power: his government now nominated bishops, paid the clergy, and exerted great influence over the church in France.

The domestic reforms of Napoleon's early years were his greatest achievement. Much of his legal and administrative reorganization has survived in France to this day. More generally, Napoleon's domestic initiatives gave the great majority of French people a welcome sense of order and stability. And when Napoleon added the glory of military victory, he rekindled a spirit of national unity.

Order and unity had their price: Napoleon's authoritarian rule. Women, who had often participated in revolutionary politics without having legal equality, lost many of the gains they had made in the 1790s under the new Napoleonic Code. Under the law, women were dependents of either their fathers or their husbands, and they could not make contracts or even have bank accounts in their own names. Indeed, Napoleon and his advisers aimed at re-establishing a "family monarch," where the power of the husband and father was as absolute over the wife and the children as that of Napoleon was over his subjects.

Free speech and freedom of the press—fundamental rights of the liberal revolution enshrined in the Declaration of the Rights of Man—were continually violated. Napoleon constantly reduced the number of newspapers in Paris. By 1811 only four were left, and they were little more than organs of government propaganda. The occasional elections were a farce. Later laws prescribed harsh penalties for political offenses.

These changes in the law were part of the creation of a police state in France. Since Napoleon was usually busy making war, this task was largely left to Joseph Fouché, an unscrupulous opportunist who had earned a reputation for brutality during the Reign of Terror. As minister of police, Fouché organized a ruthlessly efficient spy system, which kept thousands of citizens under continual police surveillance. People suspected of subversive activities were arbitrarily detained, placed under house arrest, or even consigned to insane asylums. After 1810 political suspects were held in state prisons, as they had been during the Terror. There were about twenty-five hundred such political prisoners in 1814.

Napoleon's Wars and Foreign Policy

Napoleon was above all a military man, and a great one. After coming to power in 1799, he sent peace feelers to Austria and Great Britain, the two remaining members of the Second Coalition, which had been formed against France in 1798. When these overtures were rejected, French armies led by Napoleon decisively defeated the Austrians. Once more, as in 1797, the British were alone—and warweary, like the French. Still seeking to consolidate his regime domestically, Napoleon concluded the Treaty of Amiens with Great Britain in 1802. France remained in control of Holland, the Austrian Netherlands, the west bank of the Rhine, and most of the Italian peninsula. The Treaty of Amiens was clearly a diplomatic triumph for Napoleon, and peace with honor and profit increased his popularity at home.

In 1802 Napoleon was secure but unsatisfied. Ever a romantic gambler as well as a brilliant administrator, he could not contain his power drive. Thus he aggressively threatened British interests in the eastern Mediterranean and tried to restrict British trade with all of Europe. Deciding to renew war with Britain in May 1803, Napoleon began making preparations to invade England. But Great Britain remained dominant on the seas. When Napoleon tried to bring his Mediterranean fleet around Gibraltar to northern France, a combined French and Spanish fleet was, after a series of mishaps, virtually annihilated by Lord Nelson at the Battle of Trafalgar on October 21, 1805. A cross-Channel invasion of England was henceforth impossible. Renewed fighting had its advantages, however, for the first consul used the wartime atmosphere to have himself proclaimed emperor in late 1804.

Austria, Russia, and Sweden joined with Britain to form the Third Coalition against France shortly before the Battle of Trafalgar. Actions such as Napoleon's assumption of the Italian crown had convinced both Alexander I of Russia and Francis II of Austria that Napoleon was a threat to their interests and to the European balance of power. Yet the Austrians and the Russians were no match for Napoleon, who scored a brilliant victory over them at the Battle of Austerlitz in December 1805. Alexander I decided to pull back, and Austria accepted large territorial losses in return for peace as the Third Coalition collapsed.

 David: Napoleon Crossing the Alps Bold and commanding, with flowing cape and surging stallion, the daring young Napoleon Bonaparte leads his army across the Alps from Italy to battle the Austrians in 1797. This painting by the great Jacques-Louis David (1748–1825) is a stirring glorification of Napoleon, a brilliant exercise in mythmaking. (*Source: Louvre © Photo R.M.N.*)

Moscow
Borodino
1812

RUSSIAN EMPIRE

Smolensk

St. Petersburg

Kiev

Black Sea

OTTOMAN EMPIRE

Cyprus

Dnieper

Dniester

Tilsit
Friedland 1807
Königsberg

Warsaw

GRAND DUCHY
OF WARSAW

Danube

Constantinople

Athens

Crete

Danzig

Vistula

PRUSSIA

Oder

Pest
Buda
Pressburg

AUSTRIAN EMPIRE

IONIAN IS.
(Gr. Br.)

Mediterranean

Austerlitz
1805

Stockholm

Baltic
Sea

KINGDOM
OF
SWEDEN

Lübeck
Hamburg

Berlin
SAXONY
Leipzig 1813

Wagram
1809
Vienna

ILLYRIAN PROVINCES

Sea

KINGDOM OF
NORWAY
AND
DENMARK

Copenhagen

Bremen
WESTPHALIA
Auerstädt 1806
Jena 1806

CONFEDERATION
OF THE RHINE

BAVARIA

WÜRTTEMBERG

BADEN

Zürich

KINGDOM
OF
NAPLES

Naples

KINGDOM
OF
SICILY

MALTA
(Gr. Br.)

North
Sea

HELGOLAND
(Gr. Br.)

Brussels
Waterloo
1815

SWITZERLAND

Milan
KINGDOM
OF
ITALY

Marengo
1800
Genoa

Rome

Elba

Corsica

SARDINIA

Antwerp

Amiens
Paris

Lunéville

Rhine

Rhône

Marseilles

Seine

Loire

FRANCE

GREAT BRITAIN

SCOTLAND

ENGLAND

London

Thames

IRELAND

ATLANTIC
OCEAN

SPAIN
Madrid

Tagus

GIBRALTAR
(Gr. Br.)

PORTUGAL

Lisbon

Trafalgar
1805

French empire
Dependent states
Allied with Napoleon
At war with Napoleon
X Major battles

0   150   300 Km.
0   150   300 Mi.

Victorious at Austerlitz, Napoleon proceeded to reorganize the German states to his liking. He established by decree the German Confederation of the Rhine, a union of fifteen German states minus Austria, Prussia, and Saxony. Naming himself "protector" of the confederation, Napoleon firmly controlled western Germany. His intervention in German affairs alarmed the Prussians, who mobilized their armies after more than a decade of peace with France. Napoleon attacked and won two more brilliant victories in October 1806, at Jena and Auerstädt. The war with Prussia, now joined by Russia, continued into the spring. After Napoleon's larger armies won another victory, Alexander I of Russia wanted peace. In the subsequent treaties of Tilsit, Prussia lost half of its population, while Russia accepted Napoleon's reorganization of western and central Europe. Alexander also promised to enforce Napoleon's recently decreed economic blockade against British goods.

After the victory of Austerlitz and even more after the treaties of Tilsit, Napoleon saw himself as the emperor of Europe and not just of France. The so-called Grand Empire he built had three parts. The core, or first part, was an ever-expanding France, which by 1810 included Belgium, Holland, parts of northern Italy, and much German territory on the east bank of the Rhine. Beyond French borders Napoleon established the second part: a number of dependent satellite kingdoms, on the thrones of which he placed (and replaced) the members of his large family. The third part comprised the independent but allied states of Austria, Prussia, and Russia. Both satellites and allies were expected after 1806 to support Napoleon's continental system and cease trade with Britain.

The impact of the Grand Empire on the peoples of Europe was considerable. In the areas incorporated into France and in the satellites (Map 23.1), Napoleon introduced many French laws, abolishing feudal dues and serfdom where French revolutionary armies had not already done so. Some of the peasants and middle class benefited from these reforms. Yet while he extended progressive measures to his cosmopolitan empire, Napoleon had to put the prosperity and special interests of France first in order to safeguard his power base. Levying heavy taxes in money and men for his armies, Napoleon came to be regarded more as a conquering tyrant than as an enlightened liberator.

The first great revolt occurred in Spain. In 1808 a coalition of Catholics, monarchists, and patriots rebelled against Napoleon's attempts to make Spain a French satellite with a Bonaparte as its king. French armies occupied Madrid, but the foes of Napoleon fled to the hills and waged uncompromising guerrilla warfare. Spain was a clear warning: resistance to French imperialism was growing. Yet Napoleon pushed on, determined to hold his complex and far-flung empire together.

In 1810 when the Grand Empire was at its height, Britain still remained at war with France, helping the guerrillas in Spain and Portugal. Napoleon's continental system, organized to exclude British goods from the European continent and force that "nation of shopkeepers" to its knees, was a failure. Instead, it was France that suffered from Britain's counter-blockade, which created hard times for French artisans and the middle class. Perhaps looking for a scapegoat, Napoleon turned on Alexander I of Russia, who had been giving only lukewarm support to Napoleon's war of prohibitions against British goods.

Napoleon's invasion of Russia began in June 1812 with a force that eventually numbered 600,000, probably the largest force yet assembled in a single army. Only one-third of this force was French, however; nationals of all the satellites and allies were drafted into the operation. After the great battle of Borodino, a draw from which the Russians retreated in good order, Alexander ordered the evacuation of Moscow, which then burned, and he refused to negotiate. Finally, after five weeks in the burned-out city, Napoleon ordered a retreat. That retreat was one of the great military disasters in history. The Russian army and the Russian winter cut Napoleon's army to pieces. Only 30,000 men returned to their homelands.

Leaving his troops to their fate, Napoleon raced to Paris to raise yet another army. When he refused to accept a France reduced to its historical size—the proposal offered by Austria's foreign minister, Prince Klemens von Metternich—Austria and Prussia deserted Napoleon and joined Russia and Great Britain in the Fourth Coalition. All across Europe patriots called for a "war of liberation"

Map 23.1 Napoleonic Europe in 1810 Only Great Britain remained at war with Napoleon at the height of the Grand Empire. Many British goods were smuggled through Helgoland, a tiny but strategic British possession off the German coast.

✦ Goya: The Third of May, 1808 This famous painting screams in outrage at the horrors of war, which Goya witnessed in Spain. Spanish rebels, focused around the Christ-like figure at the center, are gunned down by anonymous French soldiers, grim forerunners of modern death squads and their atrocities. *(Source: Museo del Prado, Madrid)*

against Napoleon's oppression, and the well-disciplined regular armies of Napoleon's enemies closed in for the kill. Less than a month later, on April 4, 1814, a defeated, abandoned Napoleon abdicated his throne. After this unconditional abdication, the victorious allies granted Napoleon the island of Elba off the coast of Italy as his own tiny state.

The allies also agreed to the restoration of the Bourbon dynasty. The new monarch, Louis XVIII (r. 1814–1824), issued the Constitutional Charter, which accepted many of France's revolutionary changes and guaranteed civil liberties. Indeed, the Charter gave France a constitutional monarchy roughly similar to that established in 1791, although far fewer people had the right to vote for representatives to the resurrected Chamber of Deputies. Moreover, in an attempt to strengthen popular support for Louis XVIII's new government, France was treated leniently by the allies, who agreed to meet in Vienna to work out a general peace settlement (see pages 805–807).

Louis XVIII—old, ugly, and crippled by gout—totally lacked the glory and magic of Napoleon. Hearing of political unrest in France and diplomatic tensions in Vienna, Napoleon staged a daring escape from Elba in February 1815. Landing in France, he issued appeals for support and marched on Paris with a small band of followers. French officers and soldiers who had fought so

THE NAPOLEONIC ERA

November 1799	Napoleon overthrows the Directory
December 1799	French voters overwhelmingly approve Napoleon's new constitution
1800	Napoleon founds the Bank of France
1801	France defeats Austria and acquires Italian and German territories in the Treaty of Lunéville Napoleon signs a concordat with the pope
1802	Treaty of Amiens with Britain
December 1804	Napoleon crowns himself emperor
October 1805	Battle of Trafalgar: Britain defeats the French and Spanish fleets
December 1805	Battle of Austerlitz: Napoleon defeats Austria and Prussia
1807	Treaties of Tilsit: Napoleon redraws the map of Europe
1810	Height of the Grand Empire
June 1812	Napoleon invades Russia with 600,000 men
Winter 1812	Disastrous retreat from Russia
March 1814	Russia, Prussia, Austria, and Britain form the Quadruple Alliance to defeat France
April 1814	Napoleon abdicates and is exiled to Elba
Feb.–June 1815	Napoleon escapes from Elba and rules France until suffering defeat at Battle of Waterloo

long for their emperor responded to the call. Louis XVIII fled, and once more Napoleon took command. But Napoleon's gamble was a desperate long shot, for the allies were united against him. At the end of a frantic period known as the Hundred Days, they crushed his forces at Waterloo on June 18, 1815, and imprisoned him on the rocky island of St. Helena, far off the western coast of Africa. Old Louis XVIII returned again—this time "in the baggage of the allies," as his detractors scornfully put it—and recommenced his reign. The allies now dealt more harshly with the apparently incorrigible French (see page 807). And Napoleon, doomed to suffer crude insults at the hands of sadistic English jailers on distant St. Helena, could take revenge only by writing his memoirs, skillfully nurturing the myth that he had been Europe's revolutionary liberator, a romantic hero whose lofty work had been undone by oppressive reactionaries. An era had ended.

SUMMARY

The French Revolution left a compelling and many-sided political legacy. This legacy included, most notably, liberalism, assertive nationalism, radical democratic republicanism, embryonic socialism, and self-conscious conservatism. It also left a rich and turbulent history of electoral competition, legislative assemblies, and even mass politics. Thus the French Revolution and conflicting interpretations of its significance presented a whole range of political options and alternative visions of the future. For this reason it was truly *the* revolution in modern European politics.

The revolution that began in America and spread to France was a liberal revolution. Revolutionaries on both sides of the Atlantic wanted to establish civil liberties and equality before the law within the framework of representative government, and they succeeded. In France liberal nobles and an increasingly class-conscious middle class overwhelmed declining monarchial absolutism and feudal privilege, thanks to the intervention of the common people—the sans-culottes and the peasants. France's new political system reflected a social structure based increasingly on wealth and achievement rather than on tradition and legal privileges.

After the establishment of the Republic, the radical phase of the revolution during the Terror, and the fall of Robespierre, the educated elites and the solid middle class reasserted themselves under the Directory. And though Napoleon sharply curtailed representative institutions and individual rights, he effectively promoted the reconciliation of old and new, of centralized bureaucracy and careers open to talent, of noble and bourgeois in a restructured property-owning elite. Louis XVIII had to accept the commanding position of this restructured elite, and in granting representative government and civil liberties to facilitate his restoration to the throne in 1814, he submitted to the rest of the liberal triumph of 1789 to 1791. The liberal core of the French Revolution had successfully survived a generation of war and dictatorship.

The lived experience of the French Revolution and the wars that went with it exercised a pervasive influence on politics and the political imagination in the nineteenth century, not only in France but throughout Europe and even the rest of the world. The radical legacy of the embattled republic of 1793 and 1794, with its sans-culottes democratic republicanism and its egalitarian ideology and embryonic socialism, would inspire republicans, democrats, and early socialists. Indeed, revolutionary upheaval encouraged generations of radicals to believe that political revolution might remake society and even create a new humanity. At the same time, there was a legacy of a powerful and continuing reaction to the French Revolution and to aggressive French nationalism. Monarchists and traditionalists believed that 1789 had been a tragic mistake. They concluded that democratic republicanism and sans-culottes activism led only to war, class conflict, and savage dictatorship. Conservatives and many comfortable moderates were profoundly disillusioned by the revolutionary era. They looked with nostalgia toward the supposedly ordered world of benevolent monarchy, firm government, and respectful common people.

NOTES

1. Quoted in R. R. Palmer, *The Age of the Democratic Revolution,* vol. 1 (Princeton, N.J.: Princeton University Press, 1959), p. 239.
2. G. Lefebvre, *The Coming of the French Revolution* (New York: Vintage Books, 1947), p. 81.
3. P. H. Beik, ed., *The French Revolution* (New York: Walker, 1970), p. 89.
4. G. Pernoud and S. Flaisser, eds., *The French Revolution* (Greenwich, Conn.: Fawcett, 1960), p. 61.
5. O. Hufton, *Women and the Limits of Citizenship in the French Revolution* (Toronto: University of Toronto Press, 1992), pp. 3–22.
6. Quotations from Wollstonecraft are drawn from E. W. Sunstein, *A Different Face: The Life of Mary Wollstonecraft* (New York: Harper & Row, 1975), pp. 208, 211; and H. R . James, *Mary Wollstonecraft: A Sketch* (London: Oxford University Press, 1932), pp. 60, 62, 69.
7. L. Gershoy, *The Era of the French Revolution, 1789–1799* (New York: Van Nostrand, 1957), p. 150.
8. Pernoud and Flaisser, *The French Revolution,* pp. 193–194.
9. Hufton, *Women and the Limits of Citizenship in the French Revolution,* p. 130.

SUGGESTED READING

For fascinating eyewitness reports on the French Revolution, see the edited works by Beik and by Pernoud and Flaisser mentioned in the Notes. In addition, A. Young's *Travels in France During the Years 1787, 1788 and 1789* (1969) offers an engrossing contemporary description of France and Paris on the eve of revolution. E. Burke, *Reflections on the Revolution in France,* first published in 1790, is the classic conservative indictment. The intense passions the French Revolution has generated may be seen in nineteenth-century French historians, notably the enthusiastic J. Michelet, *History of the French Revolution;* the hostile H. Taine; and the judicious A. de Tocqueville, whose masterpiece, *The Old Regime and the French Revolution,* was first published in 1856. Important general studies on the entire period include the work of R. R. Palmer, cited in the Notes, which paints a comparative international picture; E. J. Hobsbawm, *The Age of Revolution, 1789–1848* (1962); C. Breunig, *The Age of Revolution and Reaction, 1789–1850* (1970); O. Connelly, *French Revolution—Napoleonic Era* (1979); and L. Dehio, *The Precarious Balance: Four Centuries of the European Power Struggle* (1962).

Recent years have seen a wealth of new scholarship and interpretation. A. Cobban, *The Social Interpretation of the French Revolution* (1964), and F. Furet, *Interpreting the French Revolution* (1981), are major reassessments of long-dominant ideas, which are admirably presented in N. Hampson, *A Social History of the French Revolution* (1963), and in the volume by Lefebvre listed in the Notes. E. Kennedy, *A Cultural History of the French Revolution* (1989), beautifully written and handsomely illustrated, and W. Doyle, *Origins of the French Revolution,* 3d ed. (1988), are excellent on long-term developments. Among recent studies, which generally are often quite critical of revolutionary developments, several are noteworthy: J. Bosher, *The French Revolution* (1988); S. Schama, *Citizens: A Chronicle of the French Revolution* (1989); W. Doyle, *The Oxford History of the French Revolution* (1989); and D. Sutherland, *France, 1789–1815: Revolution and Counterrevolution* (1986).

Two valuable anthologies concisely presenting a range of interpretations are F. Kafker and J. Laux, eds., *The French Revolutions: Conflicting Interpretations,* 4th ed. (1989), and G. Best, ed., *The Permanent Revolution: The French Revolution and Its Legacy, 1789–1989* (1988). G. Rude makes the men and women of the great days of upheaval come alive in his *The Crowd in the French Revolution* (1959), whereas R. R. Palmer studies sympathetically the leaders of the Terror in *Twelve Who Ruled* (1941). Four other particularly interesting, detailed works are D. Jordan, *The Revolutionary Career of Maximilien Robespierre* (1985); J. P. Bertaud, *The Army of the French Revolution: From Citizen-Soldier to Instrument of Power* (1988); C. L. R. James, *The Black Jacobins* (1938, 1980), on black slave revolt in Haiti; and J. C. Herold, *Mistress to an Age* (1955), on the remarkable writer Madame de Staël. Other significant studies on aspects of revolutionary France include P. Jones's pathbreaking *The Peasantry in the French Revolution*

(1979); W. Sewell, Jr.'s imaginative *Work and Revolution in France: The Language of Labor from the Old Regime to 1848* (1980); and L. Hunt's innovative *Politics, Culture, and Class in the French Revolution* (1984).

An ongoing explosion of studies on women in the French Revolution is increasing knowledge and also raising conflicting interpretations. These developments may be seen by comparing two particularly important works: J. Landes, *Women and the Public Sphere in the Age of the French Revolution* (1988), and O. Hufton, listed in the Notes. D. Outram, *The Body and the French Revolution: Sex, Class and Political Culture* (1989), and L. Hunt, *The Family Romance of the French Revolution* (1992), also provide innovative analyses of the gender-related aspects of revolutionary politics and are highly recommended. D. Levy, H. Applewhite, and M. Johnson, eds., *Women in Revolutionary Paris, 1789–1795* (1979), is a valuable collection of contemporary documents with helpful commentaries. Mary Wollstonecraft's dramatic life is the subject of several good biographies, including those by Sunstein and James cited in the Notes.

Two important works placing political developments in a comparative perspective are P. Higonnet, *Sister Republics: The Origins of French and American Republicanism* (1988), and E. Morgan, *Inventing the People: The Rise of Popular Sovereignty in England and America* (1988). B. Bailyn, *The Ideological Origins of the American Revolution* (1967), is also noteworthy.

The best synthesis on Napoleonic France is L. Bergeron, *France Under Napoleon* (1981). P. Geyl, *Napoleon: For and Against* (1949), is a delightful discussion of changing political interpretations of Napoleon, which may be compared with a more recent treatment by R. Jones, *Napoleon: Man and Myth* (1977). Good biographies are J. Thompson, *Napoleon Bonaparte: His Rise and Fall* (1952); F. Markham, *Napoleon* (1964); and V. Cronin, *Napoleon Bonaparte* (1972). Wonderful novels inspired by the period include Raphael Sabatini's *Scaramouche,* a swashbuckler of revolutionary intrigue with accurate historical details; Charles Dickens's fanciful *Tale of Two Cities;* and Leo Tolstoy's monumental saga of Napoleon's invasion of Russia (and much more), *War and Peace.*

Revolution and Women's Rights

The 1789 Declaration of the Rights of Man was a revolutionary call for legal equality, representative government, and individual freedom. But the new rights were strictly limited to men; Napoleon tightened further the subordination of French women.

Among those who saw the contradiction in granting supposedly universal rights to only half of the population was Marie Gouze (1748–1793), known to history as Olympe de Gouges. The daughter of a provincial butcher and peddler, she pursued a literary career in Paris after the death of her husband. Between 1790 and 1793 she wrote more than two dozen political pamphlets under her new name. De Gouges's great work was her "Declaration of the Rights of Women" (1791). Excerpted here, de Gouges's manifesto went beyond the 1789 Rights of Man. It called on males to end their oppression of women and give women equal rights. A radical on women's issues, de Gouges sympathized with the monarchy and criticized Robespierre in print. Convicted of sedition, she was guillotined in November 1793.

. . . Man, are you capable of being just? . . . Tell me, what gives you sovereign empire to oppress my sex? Your strength? Your talents? Observe the Creator in his wisdom . . . and give me, if you dare, an example of this tyrannical empire. Go back to animals, consult the elements, study plants . . . and distinguish, if you can, the sexes in the administration of nature. Everywhere you will find them mingled; everywhere they cooperate in harmonious togetherness in this immortal masterpiece.

Man alone has raised his exceptional circumstances to a principle. . . . He wants to command as a despot a sex which is in full possession of its intellectual faculties; he pretends to enjoy the Revolution and to claim his rights to equality in order to say nothing more about it.

DECLARATION OF THE RIGHTS OF WOMAN AND THE FEMALE CITIZEN

For the National Assembly to decree in its last session, or in those of the next legislature:

PREAMBLE

Mothers, daughters, sisters and representatives of the nation demand to be constituted into a national assembly. Believing that ignorance, omission, or scorn for the rights of woman are the only causes of public misfortunes and of the corruption of governments, [the women] have resolved to set forth in a solemn declaration the natural, inalienable, and sacred rights of woman. . . .

. . . the sex that is as superior in beauty as it is in courage during the sufferings of maternity recognizes and declares in the presence and under the auspices of the Supreme Being, the following Rights of Woman and of Female Citizens:

I. Woman is born free and lives equal to man in her rights. Social distinctions can be based only on the common utility.

II. The purpose of any political association is the conservation of the natural and imprescriptible rights of woman and man; these rights are liberty, property, security, and especially resistance to oppression.

III. The principle of all sovereignty rests essentially with the nation, which is nothing but the union of woman and man. . . .

IV. Liberty and justice consist of restoring all that belongs to others; thus, the only limits on the exercise of the natural rights of woman are perpetual male tyranny; these limits are to be reformed by the laws of nature and reason.

V. Laws of nature and reason proscribe all acts harmful to society. . . .

VI. The law must be the expression of the general will; all female and male citizens must send representatives to its formation; it must be the same for all: male and female citizens, being equal in the eyes of the law, must be equally admitted to all honors, positions, and public employment according to their capacity and without other distinctions besides those of their virtues and talents.

VII. No woman is an exception; she is accused, arrested, and detained in cases determined by law. Women, like men, obey this rigorous law.

VIII. The law must establish only those penalties that are strictly and obviously necessary. . . .

IX. Once any woman is declared guilty, complete rigor is [to be] exercised by the law.

X. No one is to be disquieted for his very basic opinions; woman has the right to mount the scaffold; she must equally have the right to mount the rostrum, provided that her demonstrations do not disturb the legally established public order.

XI. The free communication of thoughts and opinions is one of the most precious rights of woman, since that liberty assures the recognition of children by their fathers. Any female citizen thus may say freely, I am the mother of a child which belongs to you, without being forced by a barbarous prejudice to hide the truth. . . .

XIII. For the support of the public force and the expenses of administration, the contributions of woman and man are equal; she shares all the duties . . . and all the painful tasks; therefore, she must have the same share in the distribution of positions, employment, offices, honors, and jobs. . . .

XIV. Female and male citizens have the right to verify, either by themselves or through their representatives, the necessity of the public contribution. This can only apply to women if they are granted an equal share, not only of wealth, but also of public administration. . . .

XV. The collectivity of women, joined for tax purposes to the aggregate of men, has the right to demand an accounting of his administration from any public agent.

XVI. No society has a constitution without the guarantee of rights and the separation of powers; the constitution is null if the majority of individuals comprising the nation have not cooperated in drafting it.

XVII. Property belongs to both sexes whether united or separate; for each it is an inviolable and sacred right. . . .

Late-eighteenth-century French painting, *La Liberté*. *(Source: Bibliothèque Nationale/Giraudon/Art Resource, NY)*

POSTSCRIPT

Women, wake up. . . . Discover your rights. . . . Oh women, women! When will you cease to be blind? What advantage have you received from the Revolution? A more pronounced scorn, a more marked disdain. . . . [If men persist in contradicting their revolutionary principles,] courageously oppose the force of reason to the empty pretensions of superiority . . . and you will soon see these haughty men, not groveling at your feet as servile adorers, but proud to share with you the treasure of the Supreme Being. Regardless of what barriers confront you; it is in your power to free yourselves; you have only to want to. . . .

Questions for Analysis

1. On what basis did de Gouges argue for gender equality? Did she believe in natural law?

2. What consequences did "scorn for the rights of women" have for France, according to de Gouges?

3. Did de Gouges stress political rights at the expense of social and economic rights? If so, why?

Source: Olympe de Gouges, "Declaration of the Rights of Woman" in Darline G. Levy, Harriet B. Applewhite, and Mary D. Johnson, eds., *Women in Revolutionary Paris, 1789–1795* (Urbana: University of Illinois Press, 1979), pp. 87–96. Copyright © 1979 by the Board of Trustees, University of Illinois. Used with permission.

24

The Industrial Revolution in Europe

A colored engraving by
J. C. Bourne of the
Great Western Railway
emerging from a tunnel.
*(Source: Science and Pic-
ture Library, London)*

While the Revolution in France was opening a new political era, another revolution was transforming economic and social life. The Industrial Revolution, which began in England around the 1780s, started to influence continental Europe and the rest of the world after 1815. Because the Industrial Revolution was less dramatic than the French Revolution, some historians see industrial development as basically moderate and evolutionary. From a long perspective, however, it was rapid and brought about radical changes. Perhaps only the development of agriculture during Neolithic times had a similar impact and significance.

The Industrial Revolution profoundly modified much of human experience. It changed patterns of work, transformed the social class structure, and even altered the international balance of political and military power, giving added impetus to ongoing Western expansion into non-Western lands. The Industrial Revolution also helped ordinary people gain a higher standard of living as the widespread poverty of the preindustrial world was gradually reduced.

Unfortunately, improvement in the European standard of living was quite limited until about 1850, for at least two reasons. First, even in England only a few key industries experienced a technological revolution. Many more industries continued to use old methods, especially on the European continent, and this held down the increase in total production. Second, the increase in total population, which began in the eighteenth century, continued all across Europe as the era of the Industrial Revolution unfolded. As a result, the rapid growth in population threatened—quite literally—to eat up the growth in production and to leave individuals poorer than ever. Thus rapid population growth formed a somber background for European industrialization and made the wrenching transformation even more difficult.

- What was the Industrial Revolution?
- What were the origins of the Industrial Revolution, and how did it develop?
- How did the changes brought by the Industrial Revolution affect people and society in an era of continued rapid population growth?

These are the questions that this chapter seeks to answer. Chapter 26 examines in detail the emergence of accompanying changes in urban civiliza-

tion, and Chapter 27 probes the consequences of industrialization in Europe for non-Western peoples.

THE INITIAL BREAKTHROUGH IN ENGLAND

The Industrial Revolution began in England. It was something new in history, and it was quite unplanned. With no models to copy and no idea of what to expect, England had to pioneer not only in industrial technology but also in social relations and urban living. Between 1793 and 1815, almost constant war with France complicated these formidable tasks. The trailblazer in economic development, as France was in political change, England must command special attention.

Eighteenth-Century Origins

Although many aspects of the Industrial Revolution are still matters for scholarly debate, it is generally agreed that the industrial changes that did occur grew out of a complex combination of factors. These factors came together in eighteenth-century England and initiated a decisive breakthrough that many place in the 1780s—after the American war for independence and just before the French Revolution.

In analyzing the causes of the late-eighteenth-century acceleration in the English economy, historians have paid particular attention to dramatic changes in agriculture, foreign trade, technology, energy supplies, and transportation. Although this chapter focuses on those issues, one must first understand that England had other, less conspicuous, assets that favored the long process of development that culminated in industrial breakthrough.

Relatively good government was one such asset. The monarchy and the aristocratic oligarchy, which jointly ruled the country after the constitutional settlement of 1688, provided stable and predictable government. Neither civil strife nor invading armies threatened the peace of the realm. Thus the government let the domestic economy operate fairly freely and with few controls, encouraging personal initiative, technological change, and a free market.

A related asset was an experienced business class with very modern characteristics. This business class, which traced its origins to the High Middle Ages, eagerly sought to make profits and to accumulate capital. England also had a large class of hired agricultural laborers. These rural wage earners were relatively mobile—compared with village-bound peasants in France and western Germany, for example—and along with cottage workers they formed a potential labor force for capitalist entrepreneurs.

Several other assets supporting English economic growth stand out. First, unlike France and most other countries, England had an effective central bank and well-developed credit institutions. Second, although England may seem a rather small country today, it undoubtedly enjoyed the largest effective domestic market in eighteenth-century Europe. In an age when shipping goods by water was much cheaper than shipping goods by land, no part of England was more than twenty miles from navigable water. Beginning in the 1770s, a canal-building boom greatly enhanced this natural advantage (Map 24.1). Nor were there any tariffs within the country to hinder trade, as there were in France before 1789 and in politically fragmented Germany and Italy. Finally, only in Holland did the lower classes appear to live as well as in England. The ordinary English family did not have to spend almost everything it earned just to buy bread. It could spend more on other items, thereby adding significantly to the growing demand for manufactured goods that was a critical factor in initiating England's industrial breakthrough.

All these factors combined to bring about the Industrial Revolution, a term that awed contemporaries coined in the 1830s to describe the burst of major inventions and technical changes that they had witnessed in certain industries. This technical revolution went hand in hand with an impressive quickening in the annual rate of industrial growth in England. Thus industry grew at only 0.7 percent per year between 1700 and 1760—before the Industrial Revolution—but it grew at the much higher rate of 3 percent between 1801 and 1831, when industrial transformation was in full swing.[1] The decisive quickening of growth probably came in the 1780s, after the American war of independence and just before the French Revolution.

The great economic and political revolutions that shaped the modern world occurred almost simultaneously. The Industrial Revolution, however, was a longer process. It was not complete in England until 1830 at the earliest, and it had no real impact on continental European countries until after the Congress of Vienna (see page 805) ended the era of revolutionary wars in 1815.

The Agricultural Revolution

Although scholars no longer believe, as did an older generation of historians, that radical agricultural change was a necessary precondition for the industrial breakthrough, a gradual but profound revolution in agricultural methods did promote accelerated economic growth. That revolution mirrored the general economic leadership underpinning England's epoch-making industrial surge. In essence, the agricultural revolution eliminated the traditional pattern of village agriculture found in northern and central Europe. It replaced the medieval open-field system with a new system of continuous rotation that resulted in more food for humans and their animals. The new agricultural system had profound implications, for it eliminated long-standing common rights as well as the fallow. But whereas peasants and rural laborers checked the spread of the new system on the continent of Europe in the eighteenth century, large landowners and powerful market forces overcame such opposition in England.

The new methods of agriculture originated in the Low Countries. The vibrant, dynamic middle-class society of seventeenth-century republican Holland was the most advanced in Europe in many areas of human endeavor, including agriculture. By 1650 intensive farming was well established throughout much of the Low Countries. Enclosed fields, continuous rotation, heavy manuring, and a wide variety of crops—all these innovations were present. Agriculture was highly specialized and commercialized. The same skills that grew turnips produced flax to be spun into linen for clothes, as well as tulip bulbs to lighten the heart with beautiful flowers. The fat cattle of Holland, so beloved by Dutch painters, gave the most milk in Europe. The Low Countries became "the Mecca of foreign agricultural experts who came . . . to see Flemish agriculture with their own eyes, to write about it and to propagate its methods in their home lands."[2]

The English were the best students. They learned about water control from the Dutch, the world's leaders after centuries of effort in the skills of drainage. In the seventeenth century, Dutch experts made a great contribution to draining the extensive marshes, or fens, of wet and rainy England.

On such new land, where traditions and common rights were not established, farmers introduced new crops and new rotations fairly easily.

Dutch experience was also important to Viscount Charles Townsend (1674–1738), one of the pioneers of English agricultural improvement. This lord from the upper reaches of the English aristocracy learned about turnips and clover while serving as English ambassador to Holland. When Lord Charles retired from politics in 1730 and returned to his large estates in Norfolk in eastern England, it was said that he spoke of turnips, turnips, and nothing but turnips. This led some wit to nickname his lordship "Turnip" Townsend. But Townsend had the last laugh. Draining extensively, manuring heavily, and sowing crops in regular rotation without fallowing, the farmers who leased Townsend's lands produced larger crops. They and he earned higher incomes. Those who had scoffed reconsidered. By 1740 agricultural improvement had become a craze among the English aristocracy.

There were also improvements in livestock, inspired in part by the earlier successes of English country gentlemen in breeding ever-faster horses for the races and fox hunts that were their passions. Selective breeding of ordinary livestock was a marked improvement over the old pattern, which has been graphically described as little more than "the haphazard union of nobody's son with everybody's daughter."

By the mid-eighteenth century, English agriculture was in the process of a radical and technologically desirable transformation. The eventual result was that by 1870 English farmers produced 300 percent more food than they had produced in 1700, although the number of people working the land had increased by only 14 percent. This great surge of agricultural production provided food for England's rapidly growing urban population. It was a tremendous achievement.

The Cost of Enclosure

What was the cost of technical progress in England, and to what extent did its payment result in social injustice? Scholars agree that the impetus for enclosing the fields came mainly from the powerful ruling class—the English landowning aristocracy, who benefited directly from higher yields that could support higher rents. Beyond these certainties, there are important differences of interpretation among historians.

MAP 24.1 Cottage Industry and Transportation in Eighteenth-Century England England had an unusually good system of navigable waterways even before river-linking canals made it better.

Many historians assert that the open fields were enclosed fairly and that both large and small owners received their fair share after the strips were surveyed and consolidated. Other historians argue that fairness was more apparent than real. These historians point out that the large landowners controlled Parliament, which made the laws. They had Parliament pass hundreds of "enclosure acts," each of which authorized the fencing of open fields in a given village and the division of the common in proportion to one's property in the open fields. The division of the heavy legal and surveying costs of enclosure among the landowners meant that many peasants who had small holdings had to sell out to pay their share of the expenses. Similarly, landless cottagers lost their age-old access to the common pasture but received no compensation. Landless families were dealt a serious blow, for women were deprived of the means to raise animals for market and to earn vital income. In the spirited words of one critical historian, "Enclosure (when all the sophistications are allowed for) was a plain enough case of class robbery, played according to the fair rules of property and law laid down by a Parliament of property-owners and lawyers."3

In assessing these conflicting interpretations, one needs to put eighteenth-century developments in a longer historical perspective. In the first place, as much as half of English farmland was already enclosed by 1750. A great wave of enclosure of English open fields into sheep pastures had occurred in the sixteenth and early seventeenth centuries, a wave that had dispossessed many English peasants in order to produce wool for the thriving textile industry. In the later seventeenth and early eighteenth centuries, many open fields were enclosed fairly harmoniously by mutual agreement among all classes of landowners in English villages. Thus parliamentary enclosure, the great bulk of which occurred after 1760 and particularly during the

Napoleonic wars, only completed a process that was in full swing.

Indeed, by 1700 a highly distinctive pattern of landownership and production existed in England. At one extreme were a few large landowners, at the other a large mass of landless cottagers who labored mainly for wages and who could graze only a pig or a cow on the village common. In between stood two other groups: small, independent peasant farmers who owned their own land, and substantial tenant farmers who rented land from the big landowners, hired wage laborers, and sold their output on a cash market. Yet the small, independent English farmers had been declining in numbers since the sixteenth-century enclosures (and even before). They could not compete with the profit-minded, market-oriented tenant farmers.

These tenant farmers, many of whom had formerly been independent owners, were the key to mastering the new methods of farming. Well financed by the large landowners, the tenant farmers fenced fields, built drains, and improved the

Enclosing the Fields   This remarkable aerial photograph illustrates key aspects of the agricultural revolution. Though the long ridges and furrows of the old open-field system still stretch across the whole picture, hedgerows now cut through the long strips to divide the land into several enclosed fields. *(Source: Cambridge University Collection)*

soil with fertilizers. Such improvements and new methods of farming actually increased employment opportunities for wage workers. Thus enclosure did not force people off the land by eliminating jobs.

At the same time, by eliminating common rights and greatly reducing the access of poor men and women to the land, the eighteenth-century enclosure movement marked the completion of two major historical developments in England: the rise of market-oriented estate agriculture and the emergence of a landless proletariat. By 1815 a tiny minority of wealthy English (and Scottish) landowners held most of the land and pursued profits aggressively, leasing their holdings through agents at competitive prices to middle-size farmers. These farmers produced mainly for cash markets and relied on landless laborers for their work force. In strictly economic terms, these landless laborers may have lived as well in 1800 as in 1700, but they had lost that bit of independence and self-respect that common rights had provided. They had become completely dependent on cash wages. In no other European country had this proletarianization—this transformation of large numbers of small peasant farmers into landless rural wage earners—gone so far as it had in England by the late eighteenth century. And, as in the earlier English enclosure movement, the village poor found the cost of economic change and technical progress heavy and unjust.

The Growth of Foreign Trade

In addition to leading Europe in agricultural improvement, Great Britain (formed in 1707 by the union of England and Scotland into a single kingdom) gradually became the leading maritime power. In the eighteenth century, British ships and merchants succeeded in dominating long-distance trade, particularly intercontinental trade across the Atlantic. This foreign trade stimulated the economy.

Britain's commercial leadership in the eighteenth century had its origins in the mercantilism of the seventeenth century. European mercantilism was a system of economic regulations aimed at increasing the power of the state. What distinguished English mercantilism was the unusual idea that government economic regulations could and should serve the private interest of individuals and groups as well as the public needs of the state.

The seventeenth-century Navigation Acts reflected the desire of Great Britain to increase both its military power and its private wealth. The initial target of these instruments of economic warfare was the Dutch, who were far ahead of the English in shipping and foreign trade in the mid-seventeenth century. By the later seventeenth century, after three Anglo-Dutch wars, the Netherlands was falling behind England in shipping, trade, and colonies. France then stood clearly as England's most serious rival in the competition for overseas empire. Rich in natural resources and endowed with a population three or four times that of England, continental Europe's leading military power was already building a powerful fleet and a worldwide system of rigidly monopolized colonial trade. Thus from 1701 to 1763, Britain and France were locked in a series of wars to decide, in part, which nation would become the leading maritime power and claim the lion's share of the profits of Europe's overseas expansion (Map 24.2).

The first round was the War of the Spanish Succession, which resulted in major gains for Great Britain in the Peace of Utrecht (1713). France ceded Newfoundland, Nova Scotia, and the Hudson Bay territory to Britain. Spain was compelled to give Britain control of the lucrative West African slave trade—the so-called *asiento*—and to let Britain send one ship of merchandise into the Spanish colonies annually.

The Seven Years' War (1756–1763) was the decisive round in the Franco-British competition for colonial empire. Led by William Pitt, whose grandfather had made a fortune as a trader in India, the British concentrated on using superior sea power to destroy the French fleet and choke off French commerce around the world. With the Treaty of Paris (1763), France lost all its possessions on the mainland of North America and gave up most of its holdings in India as well. By 1763, Britain had realized its goal of monopolizing a vast trade and colonial empire for its benefit.

This interconnected expansion of trade and empire marked a major step toward the Industrial Revolution, although people could not know it at the time. Protected colonial markets provided a great stimulus for many branches of English manufacturing. The value of the sales of manufactured products to the Atlantic economy—primarily the mainland colonies of North America and the West Indian sugar islands, with an important assist from West Africa and Latin America—soared from

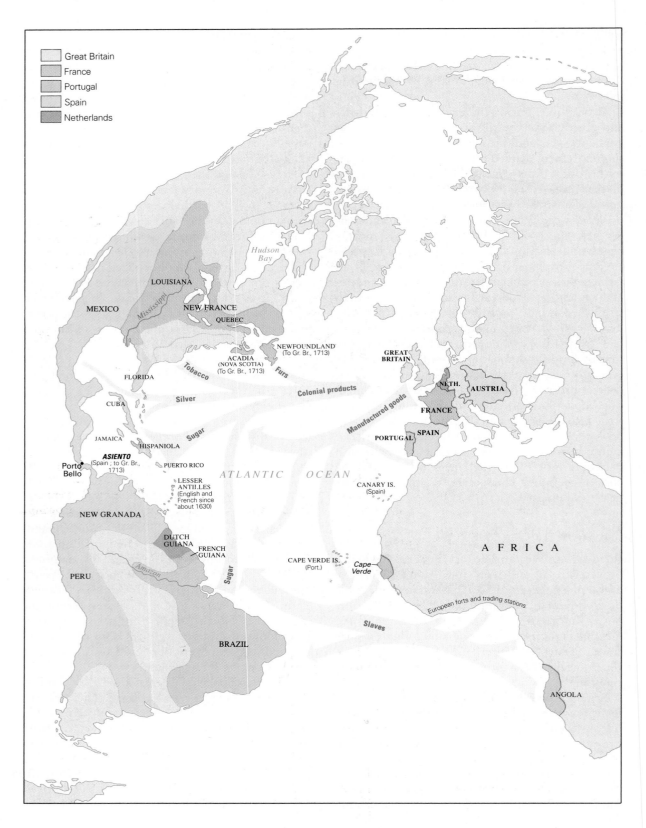

Great Britain
France
Portugal
Spain
Netherlands

Hudson Bay

LOUISIANA

MEXICO

NEW FRANCE

QUEBEC

NEWFOUNDLAND
(To Gr. Br., 1713)

ACADIA
(NOVA SCOTIA)
(To Gr. Br., 1713)

GREAT
BRITAIN

Tobacco

Furs

FLORIDA

Colonial products

NETH.   AUSTRIA

CUBA

Silver

FRANCE

Manufactured goods

Sugar

JAMAICA

HISPANIOLA

PORTUGAL   SPAIN

ASIENTO
(Spain ; to Gr. Br.,
1713)

Porto
Bello

PUERTO RICO

LESSER
ANTILLES
(English and
French since
about 1630)

ATLANTIC   OCEAN

CANARY IS.
(Spain)

NEW GRANADA

DUTCH
GUIANA

FRENCH
GUIANA

Amazon

A F R I C A

PERU

Sugar

CAPE VERDE IS.
(Port.)

*Cape
Verde*

European forts and trading stations

Slaves

BRAZIL

ANGOLA

new highlighter
12·15·99

The East India Dock, London
This painting by Samuel Scott captures the spirit and excitement of British maritime expansion. Great sailing ships line the quay, bringing profit and romance from far-off India. London grew in population from 350,000 in 1650 to 900,000 in 1800, when it was twice as big as Paris, its nearest rival. *(Source: Courtesy of Board of Trustees of the Victoria & Albert Museum)*

£475,000 in 1700 to £3.9 million in 1773 (Figure 24.1). English exports of manufactured goods to continental Europe grew hardly at all in these years, as states there adopted protectionist policies to help develop their own industries.

English exports became much more balanced and diversified. To America and Africa went large quantities of metal items—axes to frontiersmen, firearms, chains for slaveowners. Also exported were clocks and coaches, buttons and saddles, china and furniture, musical instruments and scientific equipment, and a host of other things. Thus the mercantile system established in the seventeenth century continued to shape trade in the eighteenth century, and the English concentrated in their hands much of the demand for manufactured goods from the growing Atlantic economy. Sales to other "colonies"—Ireland and India—also

MAP 24.2 Economy of the Atlantic Basin in 1701   The growth of trade encouraged both economic development and military conflict in the Atlantic basin.

rose substantially in the eighteenth century. Nor was this all. Demand from the well-integrated home market was also rising. The English were relatively well-off, and their population was growing. Moreover, new methods of farming and good weather brought a period of bountiful crops and low food prices, especially before 1760. Ordinary people could buy more manufactured goods. Rising demand from home and abroad put intense pressure on the whole system of production.

Land and Wealth in North America

Britain's colonies on the North American mainland proved particularly valuable in the long run (Map 24.3). Because the settlements along the Atlantic coast provided an important outlet for surplus population, migration abroad limited poverty in England, Scotland, and northern Ireland. The settlers benefited because for most of the eighteenth century they had privileged access to virtually free and unlimited land. The abundance of almost-free land resulted in a rapid increase in the

FIGURE 24.1 Exports of English Manufactured Goods, 1700–1774   Trade between England and Europe stagnated after 1700, but English exports to Africa and the Americas boomed and greatly stimulated English economic development. *(Source: Based on information from R. Davis, "English Foreign Trade, 1700–1774,"* Economic History Review, *2d series, 15 (1962): 302–303. Used with permission of Basil Blackwell Ltd.)*

white population, which multiplied a staggering ten times between 1700 and 1774 as immigrants arrived and colonial couples raised large families. In 1774, 2.2 million whites and 330,000 blacks inhabited what would soon become the independent United States.

Rapid population growth did not reduce the settlers to poverty. On the contrary, agricultural development resulted in fairly high standards of living. It has been estimated that between 1715 and 1775 the real income of the average American was increasing about 1 percent per year per person, almost two-thirds as fast as it increased with massive industrialization between 1840 and 1959.[4] There was also an unusual degree of economic equality, by European standards. Few people were extremely rich, and few were extremely poor. On the eve of the American Revolution, the average white man or woman in the mainland British colonies probably had the highest income and standard of living in the world.

The availability of land made labor expensive. This encouraged the growth of black slavery in the southern colonies and created a wealthy planter class with a taste for luxuries from the home country.

The First Factories

The pressure to produce more goods for a growing market was directly related to the first decisive breakthrough of the Industrial Revolution—the creation of the world's first large factories in the English cotton textile industry. Technological innovations in the manufacture of cloth led to a whole new pattern of production and social relationships. No other industry experienced such a rapid or complete transformation before 1830.

Although the putting-out system of merchant capitalism was expanding all across Europe in the eighteenth century, this pattern of rural industry was most fully developed in England. Thus it was in England, under the pressure of growing demand, that the system's shortcomings first began to outweigh its advantages—especially in the cottage textile industry after about 1760.

There was always a serious imbalance in this family enterprise: the work of four or five spinners was needed to keep one weaver steadily employed. The wife and the husband had constantly to try to find more thread and more spinners. Widows and unmarried women—"spinsters" who spun for their living—were recruited by the wife. Or perhaps the weaver's son went off on horseback to seek thread.

Deep-seated conflict between workers and employers complicated increased production. In "The Clothier's Delight, or the Rich Men's Joy and the Poor Men's Sorrow," an English popular song written about 1700, a merchant boasts of his countless tricks used to "beat down wages":

We heapeth up riches and treasure great store
Which we get by griping and grinding the poor.
And this is a way for to fill up our purse
Although we do get it with many a curse.[5]

There were constant disputes over the weights of materials and the quality of the cloth. Merchants accused workers of stealing raw materials, and weavers complained that merchants delivered underweight bales. Both were right; each tried to cheat the other, even if only in self-defense.

There was another problem, at least from the merchant-capitalist's point of view. Scattered rural labor was cheap, but hard to control. Cottage workers tended to work in spurts. After they got paid on Saturday afternoon, the men in particular tended to drink and carouse for two or three days. By the end of the week the weaver was probably working feverishly to make his quota. But if he did not succeed, there was little the merchant could do. Thus, in spite of its early virtues, the putting-out system in the textile industry revealed growing limitations, and the merchant-capitalist's search for more efficient methods of production intensified.

Attention focused on ways of improving spinning. Many a tinkering worker knew that a better spinning wheel promised rich rewards. It proved hard to spin the traditional raw materials—wool and flax—with improved machines, but cotton was different. Cotton textiles had first been imported into England from India by the East India Company, and by 1760 there was a tiny domestic industry in northern England. After many experiments over a generation, a gifted carpenter and jack-of-all-trades, James Hargreaves, invented his cotton-spinning jenny about 1765. At almost the same moment, a barber-turned-manufacturer named Richard Arkwright invented (or possibly pirated) another kind of spinning machine, the water frame. These breakthroughs produced an explosion in the infant cotton textile industry in the

MAP 24.3 European Claims in North America Before and After the Seven Year's War, 1756–1763   France lost its vast claims in North America, though the British government then prohibited colonists from settling west of a line drawn in 1763. The British wanted to avoid costly wars with native Americans living in the newly conquered territory.

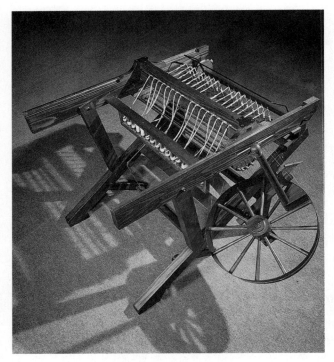

Hargreave's Spinning Jenny The loose cotton strands on the bobbins to the right passed to the sliding carriage and then on to the spindles on the left for fine spinning. The worker, almost always a woman, regulated the sliding carriage with one hand and with the other hand turned the crank on the wheel to supply power. By 1783 one woman could spin by hand a hundred threads at a time on an improved model. *(Source: Science Museum, London/Michael Holford)*

1780s. By 1790 the new machines were producing ten times as much cotton yarn as had been made in 1770.

Hargreaves's jenny was simple and inexpensive. It was also hand operated. In early models, from six to twenty-four spindles were mounted on a sliding carriage, and each spindle spun a fine, slender thread. The woman moved the carriage back and forth with one hand and turned a wheel to supply power with the other. Now it was the male weaver who could not keep up with the vastly more efficient female spinner.

Arkwright's water frame employed a different principle. It quickly acquired a capacity of several hundred spindles and demanded much more power—waterpower. The water frame thus required large specialized mills, factories that employed as many as one thousand workers from the very beginning. The water frame could spin only coarse, strong thread, which was then put out for respinning on hand-powered cottage jennies. After Samuel Crompton invented an alternative technique around 1790, all cotton spinning was gradually concentrated in factories.

The first consequences of these revolutionary developments were more beneficial than is generally believed. Cotton goods became much cheaper, and they were bought and treasured by all classes. In the past, only the wealthy could afford the comfort and cleanliness of underwear, which was called "body linen" because it was made from expensive linen cloth. Now millions of poor people, who had earlier worn nothing underneath their coarse, filthy outer garments, could afford to wear cotton slips and underpants as well as cotton dresses and shirts.

Families using cotton in cottage industry were freed from their constant search for adequate yarn from scattered, part-time spinners, for all the thread needed could be spun in the cottage on the jenny or obtained from a nearby factory. The wages of weavers, now hard pressed to keep up with the spinners, rose markedly until about 1792. Weavers were among the best-paid workers in England. They were known to walk proudly through the streets with £5 notes stuck in their hatbands, and they dressed like the middle class.

One result of this unprecedented prosperity was that large numbers of agricultural laborers became handloom weavers. The growth of handloom cotton weaving was an outstanding example of how breakthroughs in factory production normally stimulated complementary increases in handicraft output. It was also an example of how further mechanization threatened certain groups of handicraft workers, for mechanics and capitalists soon sought to invent a power loom to save on labor costs. This Edmund Cartwright achieved in 1785. But the power looms of the factories worked poorly at first, and handloom weavers continued to receive good wages until at least 1800.

Until the late 1780s, most English factories were in rural areas, where they had access to waterpower. These factories employed a relatively small percentage of all cotton textile workers. Working conditions in the early factories were less satisfactory than the conditions of cottage weavers and spinners, and people were reluctant to work in them. Therefore, factory owners turned to young children who had been abandoned by their parents and put in the care of local parishes. Parish officers often "apprenticed" such unfortunate orphans to factory owners, who gained over them almost the authority of slaveowners.

The creation of the world's first modern factories in the English cotton textile industry in the 1770s and 1780s, which grew out of the putting-out system of cottage production, was a major historical development. Both symbolically and substantially, the big new cotton mills marked the beginning of the Industrial Revolution in England. By 1831 the largely mechanized cotton textile industry towered above all others, accounting for fully 22 percent of the country's entire industrial production.

 ## ENERGY AND TRANSPORTATION

The growth of the cotton textile industry might have been stunted or cut short if water from rivers and streams had remained the primary source of power for the new factories. But this did not occur. Instead, an epoch-making solution was found to the age-old problem of energy and power. It was this solution to the energy problem (a problem that reappeared in recent times) that permitted continued rapid development in cotton textiles, the gradual generalization of the factory system, and the triumph of the Industrial Revolution in England and Scotland.

The Problem of Energy

Human beings, like all living organisms, require energy. Adult men and women need from 2,000 to 4,000 calories (units of energy) daily simply to fuel their bodies, work, and survive. Prehistoric people relied on plants and plant-eating animals as their sources of energy. With the development of agriculture, early civilizations were able to increase the number of useful plants and thus the supply of energy. Some plants could be fed to domesticated animals, such as the horse. Stronger than human beings, these animals converted the energy in the plants into work.

Human beings have used their toolmaking abilities to construct machines that convert one form of energy into another for their own benefit. In the medieval period, people began to develop water mills to grind their grain and windmills to pump water and drain swamps. More efficient use of water and wind in the sixteenth and seventeenth centuries enabled human beings, especially Europeans, to accomplish more; intercontinental sailing ships were a prime example. Nevertheless, even into the eighteenth century, European society continued to rely for energy mainly on plants, and human beings and animals continued to perform most work. This dependence meant that Western civilization remained poor in energy and power.

Lack of power lay at the heart of the poverty that afflicted the large majority of people. The man behind the plow and the woman at the spinning wheel could employ only horsepower and human muscle in their labor. No matter how hard they worked, they could not produce very much. To produce more and live better, people needed new sources of energy and more power at their disposal.

Where was more energy to be found? Almost all energy came directly or indirectly from plants and therefore from the land: grain for people, hay for animals, and wood for heat. The land was also the principal source of raw materials needed for industrial production: wool and flax for clothing; leather for shoes; wood for housing, tools, and ironmaking. And though land could be reclaimed from swamps and marshes and its yield could be increased, as by the elimination of fallow, there were definite limits to such improvements.

The shortage of energy had become particularly severe in England by the eighteenth century. Because of the growth of population, most of the great forests of medieval England had long ago been replaced by fields of grain and hay. Wood was in ever-shorter supply, yet it remained tremendously important. In addition to serving as the primary source of heat for homes and industries and as a basic raw material, processed wood (charcoal) was the fuel that was mixed with iron ore in the blast furnace to produce pig iron. The iron industry's appetite for wood was enormous, and by 1740 the English iron industry was stagnating. Vast forests enabled Russia in the eighteenth century to become the world's leading producer of iron, much of which was exported to England. But Russia's potential for growth was limited, too, and in a few decades Russia would reach the barrier of inadequate energy that was already holding England back.

The Steam Engine Breakthrough

As this early energy crisis grew worse, England looked toward its abundant and widely scattered reserves of coal as an alternative to its vanishing wood. Coal was first used in England in the late Middle Ages as a source of heat. By 1640 most homes in London were heated with it, and it also provided heat for making beer, glass, soap, and other products. Coal, however, was not used to make iron, to produce mechanical energy, or to power machinery. It was there that coal's potential was enormous, as a simple example shows.

A hard-working miner can dig out 500 pounds of coal a day using hand tools. Even an extremely inefficient converter, which transforms only 1 percent of the heat energy in coal into mechanical energy, will produce 27 horsepower-hours of work from that 500 pounds of coal. The miner, by contrast, produces only about 1 horsepower-hour in the course of a day. Early steam engines were just such inefficient converters.

As more coal was produced, mines were dug deeper and deeper and were constantly filling with water. Mechanical pumps, usually powered by animals walking in circles at the surface, had to be installed. At one mine, fully five hundred horses were used in pumping. Such power was expensive and bothersome. In an attempt to overcome these disadvantages, Thomas Savery in 1698 and Thomas Newcomen in 1705 invented the first primitive steam engines. Both engines burned coal to produce steam, which was then used to operate a pump. Both engines were extremely inefficient, but by the early 1770s many of the Savery engines and hundreds of the Newcomen engines were operating successfully in English and Scottish mines.

In the early 1760s, a gifted young Scot named James Watt (1736–1819) was drawn to a critical study of the steam engine. Watt was employed at the time by the University of Glasgow as a skilled craftsman making scientific instruments. The Scottish universities were pioneers in practical technical education, and in 1763 Watt was called on to repair a Newcomen engine being used in a physics course. After a series of observations, Watt saw that the Newcomen engine's great waste of energy could be reduced by adding a separate condenser.

The ENGINE for Raising Water (with a power made) by Fire

The Newcomen Engine
The huge steam-filled cylinder [C] was cooled by injecting water from the tank above [G] through a pipe [M]. Atmospheric pressure then pushed down the piston, raised the beam, and pumped water from the mine. *(Source: Science Museum, London)*

This splendid invention greatly increased the efficiency of the steam engine.

To invent something in a laboratory is one thing; to make it a practical success is quite another. Watt needed skilled workers, precision parts, and capital, and the relatively advanced nature of the English economy proved essential. A partnership with a wealthy, progressive toymaker provided risk capital and a manufacturing plant. In the craft tradition of locksmiths, tinsmiths, and millwrights, Watt found skilled mechanics who could install, regulate, and repair his sophisticated engines. From ingenious manufacturers such as the cannonmaker John Wilkinson, Watt was gradually able to purchase precision parts. This support and more than twenty years of constant effort allowed him to create and regulate a complex engine. By the late 1780s, the steam engine had become a practical and commercial success in England.

The steam engine of Watt and his followers was the Industrial Revolution's most fundamental advance in technology. For the first time in history, humanity had, at least for a few generations, almost unlimited power at its disposal. For the first time, inventors and engineers could devise and implement all kinds of power equipment to aid people in their work. For the first time, abundance was at least a possibility for ordinary men and women.

The steam engine was quickly put to use in several industries in England. It drained mines and made possible the production of ever-more coal to feed steam engines elsewhere. The steampower plant began to replace waterpower in the cotton-spinning mills during the 1780s, contributing greatly to that industry's phenomenal rise. Steam also took the place of waterpower in flour mills, in the malt mills used in breweries, in the flint mills supplying the china industry, and in the mills exported by England to the West Indies to crush sugar cane.

Steampower promoted important breakthroughs in other industries. The English iron industry was radically transformed. The use of powerful, steam-driven bellows in blast furnaces helped ironmakers switch over rapidly from limited charcoal to unlimited coke (which is made from coal) in the smelting of pig iron after 1770. In the 1780s Henry Cort developed the puddling furnace, which allowed pig iron to be refined in turn with coke. Strong, skilled ironworkers—the puddlers—"cooked" molten pig iron in a great vat, raking off globs of refined iron for further processing. Cort also developed heavy-duty, steam-powered rolling mills, which were capable of spewing out finished iron in every shape and form.

The economic consequence of these technical innovations was a great boom in the English iron industry. In 1740 annual British iron production was only 17,000 tons. With the spread of coke smelting and the first impact of Cort's inventions, production reached 68,000 tons in 1788, 125,000 tons in 1796, and 260,000 tons in 1806. In 1844 Britain produced 3 million tons of iron. This was a truly amazing expansion. Once scarce and expensive, iron became the cheap, basic, indispensable building block of the economy.

The Coming of the Railroads

The second half of the eighteenth century saw extensive construction of hard and relatively smooth roads, particularly in France before the Revolution. Yet it was passenger traffic that benefited most from this construction. Overland shipment of freight, relying solely on horsepower, was still quite limited and frightfully expensive. Shippers used rivers and canals for heavy freight whenever possible. It was logical, therefore, that inventors would try to apply steampower to transportation.

As early as 1800, an American ran a "steamer on wheels" through city streets. Other experiments followed. In the 1820s, English engineers created steam cars capable of carrying fourteen passengers at 10 miles an hour—as fast as the mail coach. But the noisy, heavy steam automobiles frightened passing horses and damaged themselves as well as the roads with their vibrations. For the rest of the century, horses continued to reign on highways and city streets.

The coal industry had long been using plank roads and rails to move coal wagons within mines and at the surface. Rails reduced friction and allowed a horse or a human being to pull a heavier load. Thus once a rail capable of supporting a heavy locomotive was developed in 1816, all sorts of experiments with steam engines on rails went forward. In 1825 after ten years of work, George Stephenson built an effective locomotive. In 1830 his *Rocket* sped down the track of the just-completed Liverpool and Manchester Railway at 16 miles per hour. This was the world's first important railroad, fittingly steaming in the heart of industrial England. The line from Liverpool to Manchester was a financial as well as a technical success, and many private

The Third-Class Carriage French artist Honoré Daumier (1808–1879) was fascinated by the railroad and its human significance. This great painting focuses on the peasant grandmother, absorbed in memories. The nursing mother represents love and creativity; the sleeping boy, innocence. *(Source: The Metropolitan Museum of Art. Bequest of Mrs. H. O. Havemeyer, 1929. The H. O. Havemeyer Collection (29.100.129))*

companies were quickly organized to build more rail lines. Within twenty years, these companies had completed the main trunk lines of Great Britain. Other countries were quick to follow.

The significance of the railroad was tremendous. The railroad dramatically reduced the cost and uncertainty of shipping freight overland. This advance had many economic consequences. Previously, markets had tended to be small and local. As the barrier of high transportation costs was lowered, they became larger and even nationwide. Larger markets encouraged larger factories with more sophisticated machinery in a growing number of industries. Such factories could make goods more cheaply, and they gradually subjected most

cottage workers and many urban artisans to severe competitive pressures.

In all countries, the construction of railroads contributed to the growth of a class of urban workers. Cottage workers, farm laborers, and small peasants did not generally leave their jobs and homes to go directly to work in factories. However, the building of railroads created a strong demand for labor, especially unskilled labor, throughout a country. Many landless farm laborers and poor peasants, long accustomed to leaving their villages for temporary employment, went to work on railroad construction gangs. By the time the work was finished, life back home in the village often seemed dull and unappealing, and many men drifted to towns in search of work—with the railroad companies, in construction, in factories. By the time they sent for their wives and sweethearts to join them, they had become urban workers.

The railroad changed the outlook and values of the entire society. The last and culminating invention of the Industrial Revolution, the railroad dramatically revealed the power and increased the speed of the new age. Racing down a track at 16 miles per hour or, by 1850, at a phenomenal 50 miles per hour was a new and awesome experience. As a French economist put it after a ride on the Liverpool and Manchester in 1833, "There are certain impressions that one cannot put into words!"

Some great painters, notably Joseph M. W. Turner (1775–1851) and Claude Monet (1840–1926), succeeded in expressing this sense of power and awe. So did the massive new train stations, the cathedrals of the industrial age. Leading railway engineers such as Isambard Kingdom Brunel and Thomas Brassey, whose tunnels pierced mountains and whose bridges spanned valleys, became public idols—the astronauts of their day. Everyday speech absorbed the images of railroading. After you got up a "full head of steam," you "highballed" along. And if you didn't "go off the track," you might "toot your own whistle." The railroad fired the imagination.

Industry and Population

In 1851 London was the site of a famous industrial fair. This Great Exposition was held in the newly built Crystal Palace, an architectural masterpiece made entirely of glass and iron, both of which were now cheap and abundant. For the millions who visited, one fact stood out: the little island of Britain—England, Wales, and Scotland—was the "workshop of the world." It alone produced two-thirds of the world's coal and more than one-half of its iron and cotton cloth. More generally, it has been carefully estimated that in 1860 Britain produced a truly remarkable 20 percent of the entire world's output of industrial goods, whereas it had produced only about 2 percent of the world total in 1750.[6] Experiencing revolutionary industrial change, Britain became the first industrial nation (Map 24.4).

As the British economy significantly increased its production of manufactured goods, the gross national product (GNP) rose roughly fourfold at constant prices between 1780 and 1851. In other words, the British people as a whole increased their wealth and their national income dramatically. At the same time, the population of Great Britain boomed, growing from about 9 million in 1780 to almost 21 million in 1851. Thus growing numbers consumed much of the increase in total production. According to one important study, average consumption per person increased by only 75 percent between 1780 and 1851, as the growth in the total population ate up a large part of the fourfold increase in GNP in those years.[7]

Although the question is still debated, many economic historians now believe that rapid population growth in Great Britain was not harmful because it facilitated industrial expansion. More people meant a more mobile labor force, with a wealth of young workers in need of employment and

MAP 24.4 The Industrial Revolution in England, ca 1850   Industry concentrated in the rapidly growing cities of the north and the Midlands, where rich coal and iron deposits were in close proximity.

The Crystal Palace   The Great Exhibition of 1851 attracted more than 6 million visitors, many of whom journeyed to London on the newly built railroads. Companies and countries displayed their products and juries awarded prizes in the strikingly modern Crystal Palace. *(Source: GHL 22980 Great Exhibition, 1851: Transept from Dickinson's Comprehensive Pictures (litho). Guildhall Library, Corporation of London/Bridgeman Art Library, London)*

ready to go where the jobs were. Contemporaries were much less optimistic. In his famous and influential *Essay on the Principle of Population* (1798), Thomas Malthus (1766–1834) argued that population would always tend to grow faster than the food supply. In Malthus's opinion, the only hope of warding off such "positive checks" to population growth as war, famine, and disease was "prudential restraint": young men and women had to limit the growth of population by the old tried-and-true means of marrying late in life. But Malthus was not optimistic about this possibility. The powerful attraction of the sexes would cause most people to marry early and have many children.

Wealthy English stockbroker and leading economist David Ricardo (1772–1823) coldly spelled out the pessimistic implications of Malthus's thought. Ricardo's depressing "iron law of wages" posited that because of the pressure of population growth, wages would always sink to subsistence level—that is, wages would be just high enough to keep workers from starving. With Malthus and Ricardo setting the tone, economics was soon dubbed "the dismal science."

Malthus, Ricardo, and their many followers were proved wrong—in the long run. However, as the great economist John Maynard Keynes quipped during the Great Depression of the 1930s, "we are all dead in the long run." Those who lived through the Industrial Revolution could not see the long run in advance. As modern quantitative studies show, until the 1820s, or even the 1840s, contemporary observers might reasonably have concluded that the economy and the total population were racing neck and neck, with the outcome very much in doubt. The closeness of the race added to the difficulties inherent in the unprecedented journey toward industrial civilization.

There was another problem as well. Perhaps workers, farmers, and ordinary people did not get their rightful share of the new wealth. Perhaps only the rich got richer while the poor got poorer or made no progress. We will turn to this great issue after looking at the process of industrialization in continental European countries in the nineteenth century.

INDUSTRIALIZATION IN CONTINENTAL EUROPE

The new technologies developed in the British Industrial Revolution were adopted rather slowly by businesses in continental Europe. Indeed, the process of Western industrialization proceeded gradually, with uneven jerks and national (and regional) variations. Scholars are still struggling to explain these variations, especially since good answers may offer valuable lessons in our own time for poor countries seeking to improve their material condition through industrialization and economic development. The latest findings on the Western experience are encouraging. They suggest that there were alternative paths to the industrial world in the nineteenth century and that there was (and is) no need to follow a rigid, predetermined British model.

National Variations

European industrialization, like most economic developments, requires some statistical analysis as part of the effort to understand it. One set of data, the work of a Swiss scholar, compares the level of industrialization on a per capita basis in several countries from 1750 to 1913. These data are far from perfect because there are gaps in the underlying records. But they reflect basic trends and are presented in Table 24.1 for closer study.

The table is a comparison of how much industrial product was available, on average, to each person in a given country in a given year. Therefore, all the numbers in Table 24.1 are expressed in terms of a single index number of 100, which equals the per capita level of industrial goods in Great Britain (and Ireland) in 1900. Every number is thus a percentage of the 1900 level in Great Britain and is directly comparable. The countries are listed in roughly the order that they began to use large-scale, power-driven technology.

What does this sophisticated quantitative overview of European industrialization tell us? First, it confirms the primacy and relative rapidity of Britain's Industrial Revolution. In 1750 all countries were fairly close together. But by 1800 Britain had opened up a noticeable lead, and that gap progressively widened as the British Industrial Revolution accelerated to full maturity by 1860. The British level of per capita industrialization was twice the French level in 1830, for example, and more than three times the French level in 1860. All other large countries (except the United States) had fallen even farther behind Britain than France had at both dates.

Second, variations in the timing and in the extent of industrialization in the continental powers and the United States are also apparent. Belgium, independent in 1831 and rich in iron and coal, led in adopting Britain's new technology. France developed factory production more gradually, and most historians now detect no burst in French mechanization and industrial output that may accurately be called revolutionary. They stress instead France's relatively good pattern of early industrial growth, which was unjustly tarnished by the spectacular rise of Germany and the United States after 1860. By 1913 Germany was rapidly closing in on Britain, and the United States had already passed Britain in per capita production.

Finally, all European states (as well as the United States, Canada, and Japan) managed to raise per capita industrial levels in the nineteenth century. These continent-wide increases stood in stark contrast to the large and tragic decreases that occurred at the same time in most non-Western countries, most notably in China and India. European countries industrialized to a greater or lesser extent even as most of the non-Western world de-industrialized. Thus differential rates of wealth- and power-creating industrial development, which heightened disparities within Europe, also greatly magnified existing inequalities between Europe and the rest of the world. We shall return to this momentous change in Chapter 27.

TABLE 24.1 PER CAPITA LEVELS OF INDUSTRIALIZATION, 1750–1913

	1750	1800	1830	1860	1880	1900	1913
Great Britain	10	16	25	64	87	100	115
Belgium	9	10	14	28	43	56	88
United States	4	9	14	21	38	69	126
France	9	9	12	20	28	39	59
Germany	8	8	9	15	25	52	85
Austria-Hungary	7	7	8	11	15	23	32
Italy	8	8	8	10	12	17	26
Russia	6	6	7	8	10	15	20
China	8	6	6	4	4	3	3
India	7	6	6	3	2	1	2

Note: All entries are based on an index value of 100, equal to the per capita level of industrialization in Great Britain in 1900.
Source: P. Bairoch, "International Industrialization Levels from 1750 to 1980," Journal of European Economic History *11 (Fall 1982): 294. Data for Great Britain are actually for the United Kingdom, thereby including Ireland with England, Wales, and Scotland.*

The Challenge of Industrialization

The different patterns of industrial development suggest that the process of industrialization was far from automatic. Indeed, building modern industry was an awesome challenge. When the pace of English industry began to accelerate in the 1780s, continental businesses began to adopt the new methods as they proved their profitability. English industry enjoyed clear superiority, but at first continental Europe was close behind. By 1815, however, the situation was quite different. In spite of wartime difficulties, English industry maintained the momentum of the 1780s and continued to grow and improve between 1789 and 1815. On the continent, the unending political and economic upheavals that began with the French Revolution had another effect: they disrupted trade, created runaway inflation, and fostered social anxiety. War severed normal communications between England and the continent, severely handicapping continental efforts to use new British machinery and technology. Moreover, the years from 1789 to 1815 were, even for the privileged French economy, a time of "national catastrophe"—in the graphic words of a leading French scholar.[8] Thus whatever the French Revolution and the Napoleonic era meant politically, economically and industrially they meant that France and the rest of Europe were farther behind Britain in 1815 than in 1789.

This widening gap made it more difficult, if not impossible, for other countries to follow the British pattern in energy and industry after peace was restored in 1815. Above all, in the newly mechanized industries British goods were being produced very economically, and these goods had come to dominate world markets completely while the continental states were absorbed in war between 1792 and 1815. Continental European firms had little hope of competing with mass-produced British goods in foreign markets for a long time. In addition, British technology had become so advanced and complicated that very few engineers or skilled technicians outside England understood it. Moreover, the technology of steampower had grown much more expensive. It involved large investments in the iron and coal industries and, after 1830, required the existence of railroads, which were very costly. Continental business people had great difficulty finding the large sums of money the new methods demanded, and there was a shortage of laborers accustomed to working in factories. Landowners and government officials were often so suspicious of the new form of industry and the changes it brought that they did little

at first to encourage it. All these disadvantages slowed the spread of modern industry (Map 24.5).

After 1815, however, continental countries also had at least three important advantages. First, most had a rich tradition of putting-out enterprise, merchant capitalists, and skilled urban artisans. Such a tradition gave continental firms the ability to adapt and survive in the face of new market conditions. Second, continental capitalists could simply "borrow" the advanced technology already developed in Great Britain, as well as engineers and some of the financial resources these countries lacked. European countries such as France and Russia also had a third asset that many non-Western areas

MAP 24.5 Continental European Industrialization, ca 1850 Although continental European countries were beginning to make progress by 1850, they still lagged far behind England. For example, continental railroad building was still in an early stage, whereas the English rail system was essentially complete.

lacked in the nineteenth century. They had strong independent governments, which did not fall under foreign political control. These governments could fashion economic policies to serve their own interests, and they proceeded to do so. They would eventually use the power of the state to promote the growth of industry and catch up with Britain.

Agents of Industrialization

The British realized the great value of their technical discoveries and tried to keep their secrets to themselves. Until 1825 it was illegal for artisans and skilled mechanics to leave Britain; until 1843 the export of textile machinery and other equipment was forbidden. Many talented, ambitious workers, however, slipped out of the country illegally and introduced the new methods abroad.

One such man was William Cockerill, a Lancashire carpenter. He and his sons began building cotton-spinning equipment in French-occupied Belgium in 1799. In 1817 the most famous son, John Cockerill, purchased the old summer palace of the deposed bishops of Liège in southern Belgium. Cockerill converted the palace into a large industrial enterprise, which produced machinery, steam engines, and then railway locomotives. He also established modern ironworks and coal mines.

Many skilled British workers came illegally to work for Cockerill, and some went on to found their own companies throughout Europe. Newcomers brought the latest plans and secrets, so Cockerill could boast that ten days after an industrial advance occurred in Britain, he knew all about it in Belgium. Thus British technicians and skilled workers were a powerful force in the spread of early industrialization.

A second agent of industrialization was talented entrepreneurs such as Fritz Harkort, a business pioneer in the German machinery industry. Serving in England as a Prussian army officer during the Napoleonic wars, Harkort concluded that Germany had to match English achievements as quickly as possible. Setting up shop in an abandoned castle in the still-tranquil Ruhr Valley, he felt an almost religious calling to build steam engines and become the "Watt of Germany."

Harkort's basic idea was simple but enormously difficult to carry out. Lacking skilled laborers to do the job, Harkort turned to England for experienced, though expensive, mechanics. He had to import from England and at great cost the thick iron boilers that he needed. Moreover, German roads were so bad that steam engines had to be built at the works, completely dismantled, shipped piece by piece to the buyer, and then reassembled by Harkort's technicians. In spite of these problems, Harkort built and sold engines, winning fame and praise. His ambitious efforts over sixteen years also resulted in large financial losses for himself and his partners, and in 1832 his financial backers forced him out of his company and cut back operations to reduce losses. Harkort's career illustrates both the great efforts of a few important business leaders to duplicate the British achievement and the difficulty of the task.

Entrepreneurs like Harkort were obviously exceptional. Most continental businesses adopted factory technology slowly, and handicraft methods lived on. Indeed, as recent research on France has shown, industrialization in continental Europe usually brought substantial but uneven expansion of handicraft industry in both rural and urban areas for a time. Artisan production of luxury items grew in France as the rising income of the international middle class created foreign demand for silk scarfs, embroidered needlework, perfumes, and fine wines.

A third force for industrialization was government, which often helped business people in European countries to overcome some of their difficulties. Tariff protection was one such support. And after 1815 continental governments bore the cost of building roads and canals to improve transportation. They also bore to a significant extent the cost of building railroads, the all-important leading sector in continental industrialization.

The career of German journalist and thinker Friedrich List (1789–1846) reflects government's greater role in industrialization on the European continent than in England. List considered the growth of modern industry of the utmost importance because manufacturing was a primary means of increasing people's well-being and relieving their poverty. Moreover, List was a dedicated nationalist who believed that an agricultural nation was not only poor but also weak, increasingly unable to defend itself and maintain its political independence. To promote industry was to defend the nation.

The practical policies that List focused on were railroad building and the tariff. List supported the formation of a customs union, or *Zollverein,*

A Silesian Ironworks   This plant is using the new British method of smelting iron with coke. Silesia and the Ruhr region emerged as the main centers of German heavy industry in the nineteenth century, but that development was only beginning in 1841, when this picture was painted. *(Source: Deutsches Museum Munich)*

among the separate German states. Such a tariff union came into being in 1834. It allowed goods to move without tariffs between the German member states. A single uniform tariff was erected against all other nations to help infant industries to develop and eventually hold their own against their more advanced British counterparts. List denounced the English doctrine of free trade as little more than England's attempt "to make the rest of the world, like the Hindus, its serfs in all industrial and commercial relations." By the 1840s List's economic nationalism had become increasingly popular in Germany and elsewhere.

Banks, like governments, also played a larger and more creative role in Europe than in England. Previously, almost all banks in Europe had been private, organized as secretive partnerships. All the active partners were liable for all the debts of the firm. This unlimited liability meant that in the event of a disastrous bankruptcy each partner could lose all of his or her personal wealth. Such banks were content to deal with a few rich clients

and a few big merchants. They generally avoided industrial investment as being too risky.

In the 1830s two important Belgian banks pioneered in a new direction, establishing themselves as corporations enjoying limited liability. A stockholder in these two banks could lose only his or her original investment in the bank's common stock. Able to attract many shareholders, large and small, because of the reduced risk, these Belgian banks mobilized impressive resources for investment in big industrial companies. They became industrial banks and successfully promoted industrial development.

Similar corporate banks became important in France and Germany in the 1850s and 1860s. Usually working in collaboration with governments, they established and developed many railroads and many companies working in heavy industry, which were increasingly organized as limited-liability corporations. The most famous such bank was the Crédit Mobilier of Paris, founded by Isaac and Émile Pereire, two young

Jewish journalists from Bordeaux. Using the savings of thousands of small investors as well as the resources of big ones, the Crédit Mobilier built railroads all over France and elsewhere in Europe. As Émile Pereire had said in 1835, "It is not enough to outline gigantic programs on paper. I must write my ideas on the earth."

The combined efforts of skilled workers, entrepreneurs, governments, and industrial banks meshed successfully between 1850 and the financial crash of 1873. In Belgium, Germany, and France, key indicators of modern industrial development—railway mileage, iron and coal production, and steam-engine capacity—increased at average annual rates ranging from 5 to 10 percent compounded. In the early 1870s, Britain was still Europe's most industrial nation, but a select handful of countries was closing the gap that had been opened up by the Industrial Revolution.

❈ CAPITAL AND LABOR

Industrial development brought new social relations and intensified long-standing problems between capital and labor. A new group of factory owners and industrial capitalists arose. These men and women and their families strengthened the wealth and size of the middle class, which had previously been made up mainly of merchants and professional people. The nineteenth century became the golden age of the middle class. Modern industry also created a much larger group: the factory workers. For the first time, large numbers of men, women, and children came together under one roof to work with complicated machinery for a single owner or a few partners in large companies.

The growth of new occupational groups in industry stimulated new thinking about social relations. It was argued, with considerable success, that individuals were members of economically determined classes that had conflicting interests. Accordingly, the comfortable, well-educated "public" of the eighteenth century came increasingly to see itself as the backbone of the middle class (or the middle classes), and the "people" gradually transformed themselves into the modern working class (or working classes). The new class interpretation appealed to many because it seemed to explain what was happening. Thus conflicting classes came

into being, in part, because many individuals came to believe that they existed and developed an appropriate sense of class feeling—what Marxists call "class consciousness."

What, then, was the relationship between capital and labor in the early Industrial Revolution? Did the new industrial middle class ruthlessly exploit the workers, as Karl Marx and others have charged?

The New Class of Factory Owners

Early industrialists operated in a highly competitive economic system in which success and large profits were by no means certain. Manufacturers waged a constant battle to cut their production costs and stay afloat. Much of the profit had to go back into the business for new and better machinery. "Dragged on by the frenzy of this terrible life," according to one of the dismayed critics, the struggling manufacturer had "no time for niceties. He must conquer or die, make a fortune or drown himself."[9]

The early industrialists came from a variety of backgrounds. Many, such as Harkort, were from well-established merchant families, but artisans and skilled workers of exceptional ability had unparalleled opportunities. The ethnic and religious groups that had been discriminated against in the traditional occupations controlled by the landed aristocracy jumped at the new chances. Quakers and Scots were tremendously important in England; Protestants and Jews dominated banking in Catholic France. Many of the industrialists were newly rich and, not surprisingly, very proud and self-satisfied.

As factories grew larger, opportunities declined, at least in well-developed industries. It became considerably harder for a gifted but poor young mechanic to end up as a wealthy manufacturer. Formal education became more important as a means of advancement, and formal education at the advanced level was expensive. In England by 1830 and in France and Germany by 1860, leading industrialists were more likely to have inherited their well-established enterprises, and they were financially much more secure than their fathers and grandfathers had been. They also had a greater sense of class consciousness, fully aware that ongoing industrial development had widened the gap between themselves and their workers.

The New Factory Workers

The social consequences of the Industrial Revolution have long been hotly debated. The condition of English workers during the transformation has always generated the most controversy among historians because England was the first country to industrialize and because the social consequences seemed harshest there. Before 1850 other countries had not proceeded very far with industrialization, and almost everyone agrees that the economic conditions of European workers improved after 1850. The countries that followed England were able to benefit from English experience in social as well as technical matters. Thus the experience of English workers to about 1850 deserves special attention. (Industrial growth also promoted rapid urbanization, with its own awesome problems, as will be shown in Chapter 26.)

From the beginning, the Industrial Revolution in England had its critics. Among the first were the romantic poets. William Blake (1757–1827) called the early factories "satanic mills" and protested against the hard life of the London poor. William Wordsworth (1770–1850) lamented the destruction of the rural way of life and the pollution of the land and water. Some handicraft workers—notably the Luddites, who attacked whole factories in northern England in 1812 and after—smashed the new machines, which they believed were putting them out of work. Doctors and reformers wrote eloquently of problems in the factories and new towns, and Malthus and Ricardo concluded that workers would earn only enough to stay alive.

Friedrich Engels (1820–1895), the future revolutionary and colleague of Karl Marx, accepted and reinforced this pessimistic view. After studying conditions in northern England, this young middle-class German published in 1844 *The Condition of the Working Class in England.* "At the bar of world opinion," he wrote, "I charge the English middle classes with mass murder, wholesale robbery, and all the other crimes in the calendar."[10] The new poverty of industrial workers was worse than the old poverty of cottage workers and agricultural laborers, according to Engels. The culprit was industrial capitalism, with its relentless competition and constant technical change. Engels's extremely influential charge of middle-class exploitation and increasing worker poverty was embellished by Marx and later socialists.

Meanwhile, other observers believed that conditions were improving for the working people. Edwin Chadwick, a great and conscientious government official well acquainted with the problems of the working population, concluded that the "whole mass of the laboring community" was increasingly able "to buy more of the necessities and minor luxuries of life."[11] Nevertheless, if all the contemporary assessments had been counted up, those who thought conditions were getting worse for working people would probably have been the majority.

In an attempt to go beyond the contradictory judgments of contemporaries, some historians have looked at different kinds of sources. Scholarly statistical studies, which continue to multiply rapidly in an age of easy calculations with computer technology, have weakened the idea that the condition of the working class got much worse with industrialization. But the most recent studies also confirm the view that the early years of the Industrial Revolution were hard ones for English and Scottish workers. From about 1780 to about 1820 there was little or no increase in the purchasing power of the average British worker's wages. The years from 1792 to 1815, a period of almost constant warfare with France, were particularly difficult. Food prices rose faster than wages, and the living conditions of the laboring poor declined. Only after 1820, and especially after 1840, did real wages rise substantially. The average worker earned and consumed roughly 50 percent more in real terms in 1850 than in 1770.[12] In short, there was considerable economic improvement for workers throughout Great Britain by 1850, but that improvement was hard won and slow in coming.

This important conclusion must be qualified, however. Increased purchasing power meant more goods but not necessarily greater happiness. More goods may have provided meager compensation for work that was dangerous and monotonous, for example. Also, statistical studies do not say anything about how the level of unemployment may have risen, for the simple reason that there are no good unemployment statistics from this period. Furthermore, the hours in the average workweek increased; to an unknown extent, workers earned more simply because they worked more. Finally, notwithstanding what came afterward, the wartime decline colored the early experience of modern industrial life in somber tones.

Another way to consider the workers' standard of living is to look at the goods they purchased. Again the evidence is somewhat contradictory. Speaking generally, workers ate somewhat more food of higher nutritional quality as the Industrial Revolution progressed, except during wartime, and diets became more varied. Clothing improved, but housing for working people probably deteriorated somewhat. In short, per capita use of specific goods supports the position that the standard of living of the working classes rose, at least moderately, after the long wars with France.

Conditions of Work

What about working conditions? Did workers eventually earn more only at the cost of working longer and harder? Were workers exploited harshly by the new factory owners?

The first factories were cotton mills, which began functioning along rivers and streams in the 1770s. Cottage workers, accustomed to the putting-out system, were reluctant to work in factories even when they received relatively good wages. In the factory, workers had to keep up with the machine and follow its tempo. They had to show up every day and work long, monotonous hours, adjusting their daily lives to the shrill call of the factory whistle.

Cottage workers were not used to that kind of life and discipline. All members of the family worked hard and long, but in spurts, setting their own pace. They could interrupt their work when they wanted to. Women and children could break up their long hours of spinning with other tasks. On Saturday afternoon the head of the family delivered the week's work to the merchant manufacturer and got paid. Saturday night began a time of

A Woolen Mill in 1800   This drawing of a mill near Birmingham highlights the complexity, discipline, and family character of the early factory system. To the right on the top floor, workers turn raw wool into long ropes, which are then drawn out into slivers (lower left) prior to power spinning (center right) and handloom weaving (upper left). The pace and noise are unrelenting. Men, women, and children (often under the supervision of their parents) labor throughout the mill. A giant water wheel provides power to the entire factory by a system of belts and shafts. *(Source: Warwickshire County, Record Office, Warwick, Courtesy of Lord Daventry)*

relaxation and drinking, especially for the men. Recovering from his hangover on Tuesday, the weaver bent to his task on Wednesday and then worked frantically to meet his deadline on Saturday. Like some students today, he might "pull an all-nighter" on Thursday or Friday in order to get his work in.

Also, early factories resembled English poorhouses, where totally destitute people went to live on welfare. Some poorhouses were industrial prisons where the inmates had to work in order to receive their food and lodging. The similarity between large brick factories and large stone poorhouses increased the cottage workers' fear of factories and their hatred of factory discipline.

It was cottage workers' reluctance to work in factories that prompted the early cotton mill owners to turn to abandoned and pauper children for their labor. As we have seen, these owners contracted with local officials to employ large numbers of these children, who had no say in the matter. Apprenticed as young as five or six years of age, boy and girl workers were forced by law to labor for their "master" for as many as fourteen years. Housed, fed, and locked up nightly in factory dormitories, the young workers received little or no pay. Hours were appalling—commonly thirteen or fourteen hours a day, six days a week. Harsh physical punishment maintained brutal discipline. To be sure, poor children typically worked long hours from an early age in the eighteenth century and frequently outside the home for a brutal master. In the eighteenth century, semiforced child labor seemed necessary and was socially accepted. But the wholesale coercion of orphans as factory apprentices constituted exploitation on a truly unprecedented scale. This exploitation ultimately stirred the conscience of reformers and reinforced humanitarian attitudes toward children and their labor.

By 1790 the early pattern was rapidly changing. The use of pauper apprentices was in decline, and in 1802 it was forbidden by Parliament. Many more factories were being built, mainly in urban areas, where they could use steampower rather than waterpower and attract a work force more easily than in the countryside. People came from near and far to work in the cities, both as factory workers and as laborers, builders, and domestic servants. Yet as they took these new jobs, working people did not simply give in to a system of labor that had formerly repelled them. Rather, they

helped modify the system by carrying over old, familiar working traditions.

For one thing, they often came to the mills and the mines as family units. This was how they had worked on farms and in the putting-out system. The mill or mine owner paid the head of the family for the work of the whole family. In the cotton mills, children worked for their mothers or fathers, collecting wastes and "piecing" broken threads together. In the mines, children sorted coal and worked the ventilation equipment. Their mothers hauled coal in the narrow tunnels below the surface, while their fathers hewed with pick and shovel at the face of the seam.

The preservation of the family as an economic unit in the factories from the 1790s on made the new surroundings more tolerable, both in Great Britain and in other countries. Parents disciplined their children and directed their upbringing. The presence of the whole family meant that children and adults worked the same long hours (twelve-hour shifts were normal in cotton mills in 1800). In the early years, some very young children were employed solely to keep the family together. Jedediah Strutt, for example, believed children should be at least ten years old to work in his mills, but he reluctantly employed seven-year-olds to satisfy their parents. Only when technical changes threatened to place control and discipline in the hands of impersonal managers and foremen did adult workers protest against inhuman conditions in the name of their children.

Some enlightened employers and social reformers in Parliament definitely felt otherwise. They argued that more humane standards were necessary, and they used widely circulated parliamentary reports to influence public opinion (see Listening to the Past). For example, Robert Owen (1771–1858), a very successful manufacturer in Scotland, testified in 1816 before an investigating committee on the basis of his experience. He stated that "very strong facts" demonstrated that employing children under ten years of age as factory workers was "injurious to the children, and not beneficial to the proprietors." The parliamentary committee asked him to explain, and the testimony proceeded as follows:

Seventeen years ago, a number of individuals, with myself, purchased the New Lanark establishment from the late Mr Dale, of Glasgow. At that period I find that there were 500 children, who had been taken from poor-houses, chiefly in Edinburgh. . . . The hours of work at that time were thirteen, inclusive of meal times, and an hour and a half was allowed for meals. I very soon discovered that although those children were very well fed, well clothed, well lodged, and very great care taken of them when out of the mills, their growth and their minds were materially injured by being employed at those ages within the cotton mills for eleven and a half hours per day. . . . Their limbs were generally deformed, their growth was stunted, and although one of the best school-masters upon the old plan was engaged to instruct those children every night, in general they made but a very slow progress, even in learning the common alphabet.[13]

Owen had already raised the age of employment in his mills and was promoting education for young children. Workers also provided graphic testimony at such hearings as the reformers pressed Parliament to pass corrective laws. They scored some important successes.

Their first major accomplishment was the Factory Act of 1833. It limited the factory workday for children between nine and thirteen to eight hours and that of adolescents between fourteen and eighteen to twelve hours, although the act made no effort to regulate the hours of work for children at home or in small businesses. The law also prohibited the factory employment of children under nine; they were to be enrolled in the elementary schools that factory owners were required to establish. The employment of children declined rapidly. Thus the Factory Act broke the pattern of whole families working together in the factory.

The Sexual Division of Labor

The era of the Industrial Revolution witnessed major changes in the sexual division of labor. In preindustrial Europe most people generally worked in family units. By tradition, certain jobs were defined by sex—women and girls for milking and spinning, men and boys for plowing and weaving. But many tasks might go to either sex because particular circumstances dictated a family's response in its battle for economic survival. This pattern of family employment carried over into early factories and subcontracting, but it collapsed as child labor was restricted and new attitudes emerged. A different sexual division of labor gradually arose to take its place. The man emerged as the family's primary wage earner, and the woman found only limited job opportunities. Generally denied good jobs at good wages in the growing urban economy, women were expected to concentrate on unpaid housework, child care, and craftwork at home.

This new pattern of "separate spheres" had several aspects. First, all studies agree that married women were much less likely to work full-time for wages outside the house after the first child arrived, although they often earned small amounts doing putting-out handicrafts at home and taking in boarders. Second, married women who did work for wages outside the house usually came from the poorest, most desperate families, where the husbands were poorly paid, sick, unemployed, or missing. Third, these poor married (or widowed) women were joined by legions of young unmarried women, who worked full-time but only in certain jobs. Fourth, all women were generally confined to low-paying, dead-end jobs. Virtually no occupation open to women paid a wage sufficient for a person to live independently. Evolving gradually as family labor declined, but largely in place in the urban sector of the British economy by 1850, the new sexual division of labor constituted a major development in the history of women and of the family.

Although the reorganization of paid work along gender lines is widely recognized, there is as yet no agreement on its causes. One school of scholars sees little connection with industrialization and finds the answer in the deeply ingrained sexist attitudes of a "patriarchal tradition," which predated the economic transformation. These scholars stress the role of male-dominated craft unions in denying women access to good jobs and in reducing them to unpaid maids dependent on their husbands. Other scholars, believing that the gender roles of women and men can vary enormously with time and culture, look more to a combination of economic and biological factors in order to explain the emergence of a sex-segregated division of labor.

Three ideas stand out in this more recent interpretation. First, the new and unfamiliar discipline of the clock and the machine was especially hard on married women. Above all, relentless factory discipline conflicted with child care in a way that labor on the farm or in the cottage had not done. A woman operating ear-splitting spinning machinery could mind a child of seven or eight working beside her (until such work was outlawed), but she could no longer pace herself through pregnancy, even though overwork during pregnancy heightened the already high risks of childbirth. Nor could a woman breast-feed her baby on the job, although breast-feeding saved lives. Thus a working-class woman had strong incentives to concentrate on child care within her home if her family could afford for her to do so.

Second, running a household in conditions of primitive urban poverty was an extremely demanding job in its own right. There were no supermarkets or discount department stores, no running water or public transportation. Everything had to be done on foot. As in the poor sections of many inner cities today, shopping and feeding the family constituted a never-ending challenge. The woman marched from one tiny shop to another, dragging her tired children (for who was to watch them?) and struggling valiantly with heavy sacks, tricky shopkeepers, and walk-up apartments. Yet another brutal job outside the house—a "second shift"—had limited appeal for the average married woman. Thus women might well accept the emerging division of labor as the best available strategy for family survival in the industrializing society.[14]

Third, why were the women who did work for wages outside the home segregated and confined to certain "women's jobs"? No doubt the desire of men to monopolize the best opportunities and hold women down provides part of the answer. But as some feminist scholars have argued, sex-segregated employment was also a collective response to the new industrial system. The growth of factories and mines brought unheard-of opportunities for girls and boys to mix on the job, free of familial supervision. Continuing to mix after work, they were "more likely to form liaisons, initiate courtships, and respond to advances."[15] Such intimacy also led to more unplanned pregnancies and fueled the illegitimacy explosion that had begun in the late eighteenth century and that gathered force until at least 1850. Thus segregation of jobs by gender was partly an effort by older people to help control the sexuality of working-class youths.

Investigations into the British coal industry before 1842 provide a graphic example of this concern (see Listening to the Past). The middle-class men leading the inquiry often failed to appreciate the physical effort of the girls and women who dragged the carts of coal along narrow underground passages. But they professed horror at the sight of girls and women working without shirts, which was a common practice because of the heat, and they quickly assumed the prevalence of licentious sex with the male miners, who also wore very little clothing. In fact, most girls and married

✳ **Girl Dragging a Coal Wagon**   Published by reformers in Parliament as part of a multivolume investigation into child labor in coal mines (see Listening to the Past), this picture was one of several that shocked public opinion and contributed to the Mines Act of 1842. Stripped to the waist and harnessed to the wagon with belt and chain, this underground worker is "hurrying" coal from the face of the seam to the mine shaft. *(Source: The British Library)*

women worked for related males in a family unit that provided considerable protection and restraint. Yet many witnesses from the working class believed that "blackguardism and debauchery" were common and that "they are best out of the pits, the lasses." Some miners stressed particularly the sexual danger of letting girls work past puberty. As one explained: "I consider it a scandal for girls to work in the pits. Till they are 12 or 14 they may work very well but after that it's an abomination. . . . The work of the pit does not hurt them, it is

the effect on their morals that I complain of."[16] The Mines Act of 1842 prohibited underground work for all women as well as for boys under ten.

Some women who had to support themselves protested against being excluded from coal mining, which paid higher wages than most other jobs open to women. But the girls and the women who had worked underground were generally pleased with the law, if they were part of families that could manage economically. In explaining her satisfaction in 1844, one mother of four provided a real insight into why many women accepted the emerging sexual division of labor:

While working in the pit I was worth to my [miner] husband seven shillings a week, out of which we had to pay 2 ½ shillings to a woman for looking after the younger children. I used to take them to her house at 4 o'clock in the morning, out of their own beds, to put them into hers. Then there was one shilling a week for washing; besides, there was mending to pay for, and other things. The house was not guided. The other children broke things; they did not go to school when they were sent; they would be playing about, and get ill-used by other children, and their clothes torn. Then when I came home in the evening, everything was to do after the day's labor, and I was so tired I had no heart for it; no fire lit, nothing cooked, no water fetched, the house dirty, and nothing comfortable for my husband. It is all far better now, and I wouldn't go down again.[17]

The Early Labor Movement

Many kinds of employment changed slowly during and after the Industrial Revolution in Great Britain. In 1850 more British people still worked on farms than in any other occupation. The second largest occupation was domestic service, with more than a million household servants, 90 percent of whom were women. Thus many old, familiar jobs outside industry lived on and provided alternatives for individual workers. This helped ease the transition to industrial civilization.

Within industry itself, the pattern of small-scale production with handicraft skills remained unchanged in many trades even as technological change revolutionized some others. For example, as in the case of cotton and coal, large-scale capitalist firms completely dominated the British iron industry by 1850, employing more than one thousand people. Yet the firms that fashioned iron into

Union Membership Issued in Glasgow in 1833, this card testifies that the bearer is a member of the West of Scotland Power Loom Female Workers. Unions were legalized in Great Britain in 1824 and 1825, and they played an important part in British industrial life. (*Source: Mansell Collection*)

small metal goods—such as tools, tableware, and toys—employed on average fewer than ten wage workers, who used time-honored handicraft skills. The survival of small workshops in some handicraft industries gave many workers an alternative to factory employment.

In Great Britain and in other countries later on, workers gradually built a labor movement to improve working conditions and to serve their needs. In 1799, partly in panicked reaction to the French Revolution, Parliament had passed the Combination Acts outlawing unions and strikes. These acts were widely disregarded by workers. Societies of skilled factory workers organized unions, as printers, papermakers, carpenters, and other such craftsmen had long since done. The unions sought to control the number of skilled workers, limit apprenticeship to members' own children, and bargain with owners over wages. They were not afraid to strike; there was, for example, a general strike of adult cotton spinners in Manchester in 1810. In the face of widespread union activity, Parliament repealed the Combination Acts in 1824, and unions were tolerated though not fully accepted after 1825.

The next stage in the development of the British trade-union movement was the attempt to create a single large national union. This effort was led not so much by working people as by social reformers such as Robert Owen. Owen, the self-made cotton manufacturer quoted earlier, had pioneered in industrial relations by combining firm discipline with concern for the health, safety, and hours of his workers. After 1815 he experimented with cooperative and socialist communities, including one at New Harmony, Indiana. Then in 1834 Owen organized one of the largest and most visionary of the early national unions, the Grand National Consolidated Trades Union. When this and other gradiose schemes collapsed, the British labor movement moved once again after 1851 in the direction of craft unions. The most famous of these "new model unions" was the Amalgamated Society of Engineers. These unions won real benefits for members by fairly conservative means and thus became an accepted part of the industrial scene.

British workers also engaged in direct political activity in defense of their own interests. After the collapse of Owen's national trade union, a great deal of the energy of working people went into the Chartist movement, whose goal was political democracy. The key Chartist demand—that all men

be given the right to vote—became the great hope of millions of aroused people. Workers were also active in campaigns to limit the workday in factories to ten hours and to permit duty-free importation of wheat into Great Britain to secure cheap bread. Thus working people developed a sense of their own identity and played an active role in shaping the new industrial system. Clearly, they were neither helpless victims nor passive beneficiaries.

SUMMARY

Western society's industrial breakthrough grew out of a long process of economic and social change in which the rise of capitalism, overseas expansion, and the growth of rural industry stood out as critical preparatory developments. Eventually taking the lead in all of these developments, and also profiting from stable government, abundant natural resources, and a flexible labor force, England experienced between the 1780s and the 1850s an epoch-making transformation, one that is still aptly termed the Industrial Revolution. Building on technical breakthroughs, power-driven equipment, and large-scale enterprise, Great Britain became the first industrial nation. By 1850 the level of British per capita industrial production was surpassing levels on the European continent by a growing margin, and Britain savored a near monopoly in world markets for mass-produced goods.

Continental European countries inevitably took rather different paths to the urban industrial society. They relied more on handicraft production in both towns and villages. Only in the 1840s did railroad construction begin to create the strong demand for iron, coal, and railway equipment that speeded up the process of industrialization in the 1850s and 1860s.

The rise of modern industry had a profound impact on people and their lives. In the early stages Britain again led the way, experiencing in a striking manner the long-term social changes accompanying the economic transformation. Factory discipline and Britain's stern capitalist economy weighed heavily on working people, who, however, actively fashioned their destinies and refused to be passive victims. Improvements in the standard of living came slowly, although they were substantial by 1850. The era of industrialization fostered new attitudes toward child labor, encouraged protective factory legislation, and called forth a new sense of class feeling and an assertive labor movement. It also promoted within the family a more rigid division of roles and responsibilities that severely restricted women socially and economically, another gradual but profound change of revolutionary proportions.

NOTES

1. N. F. R. Crafts, *British Economic Growth During the Industrial Revolution* (Oxford: Oxford University Press, 1985), p. 32. These estimates are for Great Britain as a whole.
2. B. H. Slicher van Bath, *The Agrarian History of Western Europe, A.D. 500–1850* (New York: St. Martin's Press, 1963), p. 240.
3. E. P. Thompson, *The Making of the English Working Class* (New York: Vintage Books, 1966), p. 218.
4. G. Taylor, "America's Growth Before 1840," *Journal of Economic History* 24 (December 1970): 427–444.
5. Quoted in P. Mantoux, *The Industrial Revolution in the Eighteenth Century* (New York: Harper & Row, 1961), p. 75.
6. P. Bairoch, "International Industrialization Levels from 1750 to 1980," *Journal of European Economic History* 11 (Spring 1982): 269–333.
7. Crafts, *British Economic Growth During the Industrial Revolution,* pp. 45, 95–102.
8. M. Lévy-Leboyer, *Les banques européennes et l'industrialisation dans la première moitié du XIXe siècle* (Paris: Presses Universitaires de France, 1964), p. 29.
9. J. Michelet, *The People,* trans. with an introduction by J. P. McKay (Urbana: University of Illinois Press, 1973; original publication, 1846), p. 64.
10. F. Engels, *The Condition of the Working Class in England,* trans. and ed. W. O. Henderson and W. H. Chaloner (Stanford, Calif.: Stanford University Press, 1968), p. xxiii.
11. Quoted in W. A. Hayek, ed., *Capitalism and the Historians* (Chicago: University of Chicago Press, 1954), p. 126.
12. Crafts, *British Economic Growth During the Industrial Revolution,* p. 95.
13. Quoted in E. R. Pike, *"Hard Times": Human Documents of the Industrial Revolution* (New York: Praeger, 1966), p. 109.
14. See especially J. Brenner and M. Rama, "Rethinking Women's Oppression," *New Left Review* 144 (March–April 1984): 33–71, and sources cited there.
15. J. Humphries, ". . . 'The Most Free from Objection' . . . : The Sexual Division of Labor and Women's Work in Nineteenth-Century England," *Journal of Economic History* 47 (December 1987): 948.
16. Ibid., p. 941; Pike, *"Hard Times,"* p. 266.
17. Quoted in Pike, *"Hard Times,"* p. 208.

SUGGESTED READING

There is a vast and exciting literature on the Industrial Revolution. R. Cameron, *A Concise Economic History of the World* (1989), provides an introduction to the issues and has a carefully annotated bibliography. J. Goodman and K. Honeyman, *Gainful Pursuits: The Making of Industrial Europe, 1600–1914* (1988); D. S. Landes, *The Unbound Prometheus: Technological Change and Industrial Development in Western Europe from 1750 to the Present* (1969); and S. Pollard, *Peaceful Conquest: The Industrialization of Europe* (1981), are excellent general treatments of European industrial growth. These studies also suggest the range of issues and interpretations. T. Kemp, *Industrialization in Europe,* 2d ed. (1985), is also useful. M. Berg, *The Age of Manufactures: Industry, Innovation and Work in Britain, 1700–1820* (1985); P. Mathias, *The First Industrial Nation: An Economic History of Britain, 1700–1914* (1969); and P. Mantoux, *The Industrial Revolution in the Eighteenth Century* (1961), admirably discuss the various aspects of the English breakthrough and offer good bibliographies, as does the work by Crafts mentioned in the Notes. W. Rostow, *The Stages of Economic Growth: A Non-Communist Manifesto* (1960), is a popular, provocative study.

H. Kirsh, *From Domestic Manufacturing to Industrial Revolution: The Case of the Rhineland Textile Districts* (1989), and M. Neufield, *The Skilled Metalworkers of Nuremberg: Craft and Class in the Industrial Revolution* (1985), examine the persistence and gradual transformation of handicraft techniques. R. Cameron traces the spread of railroads and industry across Europe in *France and the Economic Development of Europe, 1800–1914* (1961). The works of A. S. Milward and S. B. Saul, *The Economic Development of Continental Europe, 1780–1870* (1973), and *The Development of the Economies of Continental Europe, 1850–1914* (1977), may be compared with J. Clapham's old-fashioned classic, *Economic Development of France and Germany* (1963). C. Kindleberger,

Economic Growth in France and Britain, 1851–1950 (1964), is a stimulating study, especially for those with some background in economics. Other important works in recent years on industrial developments are C. Tilly and E. Shorter, *Strikes in France, 1830–1848* (1974); D. Ringrose, *Transportation and Economic Stagnation in Spain, 1750–1850* (1970); and W. Blackwell, *The Industrialization of Russia,* 2d ed. (1982). L. Moch, *Paths to the City: Regional Migration in Nineteenth-Century France* (1983), and W. Schivelbusch, *Disenchanted Night: The Industrialization of Light in the Nineteenth Century* (1983), imaginatively analyze quite different aspects of industrialization's many consequences.

The debate between "optimists" and "pessimists" about the consequences of industrialization in England goes on. P. Taylor, ed., *The Industrial Revolution: Triumph or Disaster?* (1970), is a useful introduction to different viewpoints; Hayek's collection of essays, cited in the Notes, stresses positive aspects. It is also fascinating to compare F. Engels's classic condemnation, cited in the Notes, with Andrew Ure's optimistic defense, *The Philosophy of Manufactures,* first published in 1835 and reprinted recently. J. Rule, *The Labouring Classes in Early Industrial England, 1750–1850* (1987), is a recommended synthesis, whereas E. P. Thompson continues and enriches the Engels tradition in *The Making of the English Working Class* (1963), an exciting book rich in detail and early working-class lore. E. R. Pike's documentary collection, cited in the Notes, provides fascinating insights into the lives of working people. An unorthodox but moving account of a doomed group is D. Bythell, *The Handloom Weavers* (1969). F. Klingender, *Art and the Industrial Revolution,* rev. ed. (1968), is justly famous, and M. Ignatieff, *A Just Measure of Pain* (1980), is an engrossing study of prisons during English industrialization. D. S. Landes, *Revolution in Time: Clocks and the Making of the Modern World* (1983), is a brilliant integration of industrial and cultural history.

Among general studies, G. S. R. Kitson Clark, *The Making of Victorian England* (1967), is particularly imaginative. A. Briggs, *Victorian People* (1955), provides an engrossing series of brief biographies. H. Ausubel discusses a major reformer in *John Bright* (1966), and B. Harrison skillfully illuminates the problem of heavy drinking in *Drink and the Victorians* (1971). The most famous contemporary novel dealing with the new industrial society is Charles Dickens's *Hard Times,* an entertaining but exaggerated story. *Mary Barton* and *North and South* by Elizabeth Gaskell are more realistic portrayals, and both are highly recommended.

The Testimony of Young Mining Workers

The use of child labor in British industrialization quickly attracted the attention of humanitarians and social reformers. This interest led to investigations by parliamentary commissions, which resulted in laws limiting the hours and the ages of children working in large factories. Designed to build a case for remedial legislation, parliamentary inquiries gave large numbers of workers a rare chance to speak directly to contemporaries and to historians.

The moving passages that follow are taken from testimony gathered in 1841 and 1842 by the Ashley Mines Commission. Interviewing employers and many male and female workers, the commissioners focused on the physical condition of the youth and on the sexual behavior of workers far underground. The subsequent Mines Act of 1842 sought to reduce immoral behavior and sexual bullying by prohibiting underground work for all women (and for boys younger than ten).

Mr. Payne, coal master:

That children are employed generally at nine years old in the coal pits and sometimes at eight. In fact, the smaller the vein of coal is in height, the younger and smaller are the children required; the work occupies from six to seven hours per day in the pits; they are not ill-used or worked beyond their strength; a good deal of depravity exists but they are certainly not worse in morals than in other branches of the Sheffield trade, but upon the whole superior; the morals of this district are materially improving; Mr. Bruce, the clergyman, has been zealous and active in endeavoring to ameliorate their moral and religious education. . . .

Ann Eggley, hurrier, 18 years old:

I'm sure I don't know how to spell my name. We go at four in the morning, and sometimes at half-past four. We begin to work as soon as we get down. We get out after four,

sometimes at five, in the evening. We work the whole time except an hour for dinner, and sometimes we haven't time to eat. I hurry [move coal wagons underground] by myself, and have done so for long. I know the corves [small coal wagons] are very heavy, they are the biggest corves anywhere about. The work is far too hard for me; the sweat runs off me all over sometimes. I am very tired at night. Sometimes when we get home at night we have not power to wash us, and then we go to bed. Sometimes we fall asleep in the chair. Father said last night it was both a shame and a disgrace for girls to work as we do, but there was naught else for us to do. I began to hurry when I was seven and I have been hurrying ever since. I have been 11 years in the pits. The girls are always tired. I was poorly twice this winter; it was with headache. I hurry for Robert Wiggins; he is not akin to me. . . . We don't always get enough to eat and drink, but we get a good supper. I have known my father go at two in the morning to work . . . and he didn't come out till four. I am quite sure that we work constantly 12 hours except on Saturdays. We wear trousers and our shifts in the pit and great big shoes clinkered and nailed. The girls never work naked to the waist in our pit. The men don't insult us in the pit. The conduct of the girls in the pit is good enough sometimes and sometimes bad enough. I never went to a day-school. I went a little to a Sunday-school, but I soon gave it over. I thought it too bad to be confined both Sundays and week-days. I walk about and get the fresh air on Sundays. I have not learnt to read. I don't know my letters. I never learnt naught. I never go to church or chapel; there is no church or chapel at Gawber, there is none nearer than a mile. . . . I have never heard that a good man came into the world who was God's son to save sinners. I never heard of Christ at all. Nobody has ever told me about him, nor have my father and mother ever taught me to pray. I know no prayer; I never pray.

Patience Kershaw, aged 17:

My father has been dead about a year; my mother is living and has ten children, five lads and five lasses; the oldest is about thirty, the youngest is four; three lasses go to mill; all the lads are colliers, two getters and three hurriers; one lives at home and does nothing; mother does nought but look after home.

All my sisters have been hurriers, but three went to the mill. Alice went because her legs swelled from hurrying in cold water when she was hot. I never went to day-school; I go to Sunday-school, but I cannot read or write; I go to pit at five o'clock in the morning and come out at five in the evening; I get my breakfast of porridge and milk first; I take my dinner with me, a cake, and eat it as I go; I do not stop or rest any time for the purpose; I get nothing else until I get home, and then have potatoes and meat, not every day meat. I hurry in the clothes I have now got on, trousers and ragged jacked; the bald place upon my head is made by thrusting the corves; my legs have never swelled, but sisters' did when they went to mill; I hurry the corves a mile and more under ground and back; they weigh 300; I hurry 11 a day; I wear a belt and chain at the workings to get the corves out; the putters [miners] that I work for are *naked* except their caps; they pull off all their clothes; I see them at work when I go up; sometimes they beat me, if I am not quick enough, with their hands; they strike me upon my back; the boys take liberties with me, sometimes, they pull me about; I am the only girl in the pit; there are about 20 boys and 15 men; all the men are naked; I would rather work in mill than in coal-pit.

Isabel Wilson, 38 years old, coal putter:

When women have children thick [fast] they are compelled to take them down early. I have been married 19 years and have had 10 bairns [children]; seven are in life. When on Sir John's work was a carrier of coals, which caused me to miscarry five times from the strains, and was gai [very] ill after each. Putting is no so oppressive; last child was born on Saturday morning, and I was at work on the Friday night.

❄ Female mine worker, from a parliamentary report, 1842. (*Source: Mary Evans Picture Library/Photo Researchers, Inc.*)

Once met with an accident; a coal brake my cheek-bone, which kept me idle some weeks.

I have wrought below 30 years, and so has the guid man; he is getting touched in the breath now.

None of the children read, as the work is no regular. I did read once, but no able to attend to it now; when I go below lassie 10 years of age keeps house and makes the broth or stir-about.

Questions for Analysis

1. To what extent are the testimonies of Ann Eggley and Patience Kershaw in harmony with that of Mr. Payne?

2. Describe the work of Eggley and Kershaw. What do you think of their work? Why?

3. What strikes you most about the lives of these workers?

4. The witnesses were responding to questions from middle-class commissioners. What did the commissioners seem interested in? Why?

Source: J. Bowditch and C. Ramsland, eds., *Voices of the Industrial Revolution.* Copyright © 1961, 1989 by the University of Michigan. Reprinted by permission.

Ideologies and Upheavals, 1815–1871

A painting by Champin of revolutionary up-heaval in Paris in 1848. *(Source: Ville de Paris/Pho-tographie Bulloz)*

The momentous economic and political transformation of modern times began in the late eighteenth century with the Industrial Revolution in England and then the French Revolution. Until about 1815, these economic and political revolutions were separate, involving different countries and activities and proceeding at very different paces. The Industrial Revolution created the factory system and new groups of capitalists and industrial workers in northern England, but almost continual warfare with France checked the spread of that revolution to continental Europe. Meanwhile, England's ruling aristocracy suppressed all forms of political radicalism at home and joined with crowned heads abroad to oppose and eventually defeat revolutionary and Napoleonic France. The economic and political revolutions worked at cross-purposes and even neutralized each other.

After peace returned in 1815, the situation changed. Economic and political changes tended to fuse, reinforcing each other and bringing about what historian Eric Hobsbawm has incisively called the "dual revolution." For instance, the growth of the industrial middle class encouraged the drive for representative government, and the demands of the French sans-culottes in 1793 and 1794 inspired many socialist thinkers. Gathering strength, the dual revolution rushed on to alter completely first Europe and then the rest of the world. Much of world history in the last two centuries can be seen as the progressive unfolding of the dual revolution.

In Europe in the nineteenth century, as in Asia and Africa in more recent times, the interrelated economic and political transformation was built on complicated histories, strong traditions, and highly diverse cultures. Radical change was eventually a constant, but the particular results varied enormously. In central and eastern Europe especially, the traditional elites—the monarchs, noble landowners, and bureaucrats—proved capable of defending their privileges and eventually using the nationalism of the dual revolution to serve their interests.

The dual revolution posed a tremendous intellectual challenge. The meanings of the economic, political, and social changes that were occurring as well as the ways they would be shaped by human action were anything but clear. These changes fascinated observers and stimulated the growth of new ideas and powerful ideologies. The most important of these were conservatism, liberalism, nationalism, and socialism.

- How did thinkers develop these ideas to describe and shape the transformation going on before their eyes?

- How did the artists and writers of the romantic movement reflect and influence changes in this era?

- How after 1815 did popular political revolution well up again against established governments, and why did the revolutionary surge fail almost completely in 1848 after a fleeting moment of victory?

- How did strong leaders and the power of nationalism combine to redraw the map of Europe in the 1860s and provide a fateful answer to the challenge of the dual revolution?

These are the questions this chapter will explore.

THE PEACE SETTLEMENT

The eventual triumph of revolutionary economic and political forces was by no means certain as the Napoleonic era ended. Quite the contrary. The conservative, aristocratic monarchies of Russia, Prussia, Austria, and Great Britain had finally defeated France and reaffirmed their determination to hold France in line. But many other international questions were outstanding, and the allies agreed to meet at the Congress of Vienna to fashion a general peace settlement.

Most people felt a profound longing for peace. The great challenge for political leaders in 1814 was to construct a settlement that would last and not sow the seeds of another war. Their efforts were largely successful and contributed to a century unmarred by destructive, generalized war (Map 25.1).

The European Balance of Power

The allied powers were concerned first and foremost with the defeated enemy, France. Agreeing to the restoration of the Bourbon dynasty (see page 764), the allies were quite lenient toward France after Napoleon's abdication. France was given the boundaries it possessed in 1792, which were larger

805

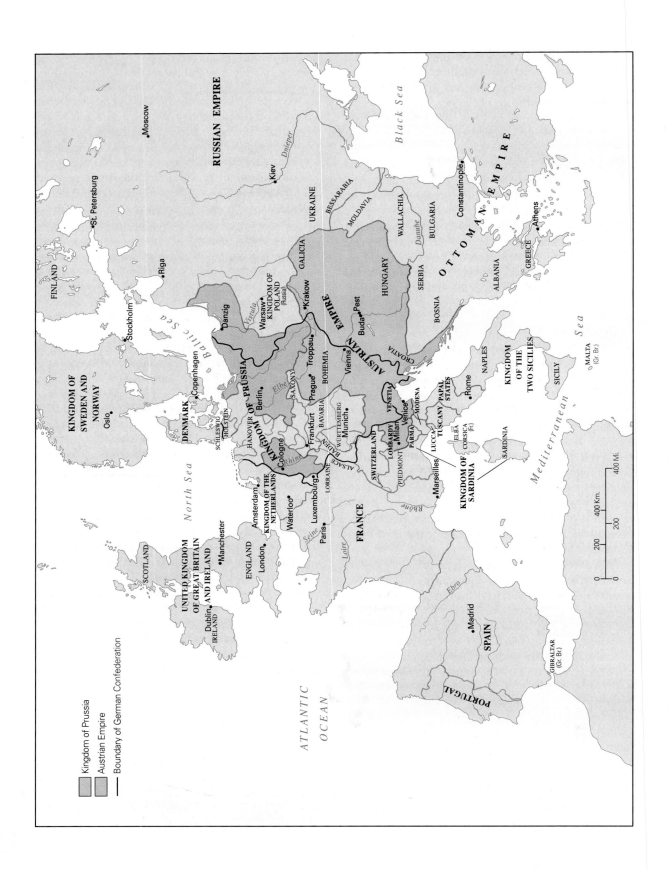

Kingdom of Prussia

Austrian Empire

Boundary of German Confederation

RUSSIAN EMPIRE

Moscow

St. Petersburg

FINLAND

Riga

Kiev

Dnieper

BESSARABIA

UKRAINE

MOLDAVIA

WALLACHIA

Danube

BULGARIA

Constantinople

OTTOMAN EMPIRE

Athens

GREECE

ALBANIA

SERBIA

BOSNIA

Black Sea

GALICIA

HUNGARY

KINGDOM OF POLAND (Russia)

Warsaw

Krakow

Vistula

Danzig

Stockholm

Baltic Sea

KINGDOM OF SWEDEN AND NORWAY

Oslo

Copenhagen

DENMARK

SCHLESWIG

HOLSTEIN

North Sea

UNITED KINGDOM OF GREAT BRITAIN AND IRELAND

SCOTLAND

Manchester

ENGLAND

London

Dublin

IRELAND

ATLANTIC OCEAN

Amsterdam

KINGDOM OF THE NETHERLANDS

Waterloo

Luxembourg

Paris

Seine

Loire

FRANCE

Rhône

Marseilles

ALSACE

LORRAINE

Cologne

Rhine

HANOVER

KINGDOM OF PRUSSIA

Berlin

SAXONY

Elbe

Frankfurt

Prague

BOHEMIA

Troppau

Vienna

AUSTRIAN EMPIRE

Buda Pest

CROATIA

BAVARIA

Munich

WÜRTTEMBERG

BADEN

SWITZERLAND

PIEDMONT

LOMBARDY

Milan

Venice

VENETIA

PARMA

MODENA

LUCCA

TUSCANY

PAPAL STATES

Rome

KINGDOM OF SARDINIA

ELBA

CORSICA (Fr.)

SARDINIA

Mediterranean Sea

NAPLES

KINGDOM OF THE TWO SICILIES

SICILY

MALTA (Gr. Br.)

Madrid

SPAIN

PORTUGAL

Ebro

GIBRALTAR (Gr. Br.)

400 Mi.

200

0

400 Km.

200

0

than those of 1789, and France did not have to pay any war reparations. Thus the victorious powers did not foment a spirit of injustice and revenge in the defeated country.

When the four allies of the Quadruple Alliance met together at the Congress of Vienna, assisted in a minor way by a host of delegates from the smaller European states, they also agreed to raise a number of formidable barriers against renewed French aggression. The Low Countries—Belgium and Holland—were united under an enlarged Dutch monarchy capable of opposing France more effectively. Moreover, Prussia received considerably more territory on France's eastern border so as to stand as the "sentinel on the Rhine" against France. In these ways the Quadruple Alliance combined leniency toward France with strong defensive measures.

In their moderation toward France, the allies were motivated by self-interest and traditional ideas about the balance of power. To Klemens von Metternich and Robert Castlereagh, the foreign ministers of Austria and Great Britain, respectively, as well as their French counterpart, Charles Talleyrand, the balance of power meant an international equilibrium of political and military forces that would discourage aggression by any combination of states or, worse, the domination of Europe by any single state.

The Great Powers—Austria, Britain, Prussia, Russia, and France—used the balance of power to settle their own dangerous disputes at the Congress of Vienna. There was general agreement among the victors that each of them should receive compensation in the form of territory for their successful struggle against the French. Great Britain had already won colonies and strategic outposts during the long wars. Metternich's Austria gave up territories in Belgium and southern Germany but expanded greatly elsewhere, taking the rich provinces of Venetia and Lombardy in northern Italy as well as former Polish possessions and new lands on the eastern coast of the Adriatic (see Map 25.1). There was also agreement that Prussia and Russia should be compensated. But where and to

what extent? That was the ticklish question that almost led to renewed war in January 1815.

The vaguely progressive, impetuous Tsar Alexander I of Russia wanted to restore the ancient kingdom of Poland, on which he expected to bestow the benefits of his rule. The Prussians agreed, provided they could swallow up the large and wealthy kingdom of Saxony, their German neighbor to the south. These demands were too much for Castlereagh and Metternich, who feared an unbalancing of forces in central Europe. In an astonishing about-face, they turned for diplomatic support to the wily Talleyrand and the defeated France he represented, signing a secret alliance directed against Russia and Prussia. War seemed imminent.

But the threat of war caused the rulers of Russia and Prussia to moderate their demands. Russia accepted a small Polish kingdom, and Prussia took only part of Saxony (see Map 25.1). This compromise was very much within the framework of balance-of-power ideology. And it enabled France to regain its Great Power status and end its diplomatic isolation.

Unfortunately for France, Napoleon suddenly escaped from his "comic kingdom" on the island of Elba. Yet the peace concluded after Napoleon's final defeat at Waterloo was still relatively moderate toward France. Fat old Louis XVIII was restored to his throne for a second time. France lost some territory, had to pay an indemnity of 700 million francs, and had to support a large army of occupation for five years.

The rest of the settlement already concluded at the Congress of Vienna was left intact. The members of the Quadruple Alliance, however, did agree to meet periodically to discuss their common interests and to consider appropriate measures for the maintenance of peace in Europe. This agreement marked the beginning of the European "congress system," which lasted long into the nineteenth century and settled many international crises through international conferences and balance-of-power diplomacy.

Intervention and Repression

There was also a domestic political side to the re-establishment of peace. Within their own countries, the leaders of the victorious states were much less flexible. In 1815 under Metternich's leadership, Austria, Prussia, and Russia embarked on a

❋ **MAP 25.1 Europe in 1815** Europe's leaders re-established a balance of political power after the defeat of Napoleon. Prussia gained territory on the Rhine and in Saxony and consolidated its power as a Great Power.

crusade against the ideas and politics of the dual revolution. This crusade lasted until 1848. The first step was the Holy Alliance, formed by Austria, Prussia, and Russia in September 1815. First proposed by Russia's Alexander I, the alliance soon became a symbol of the repression of liberal and revolutionary movements all over Europe.

In 1820 revolutionaries succeeded in forcing the monarchs of Spain and the southern Italian kingdom of the Two Sicilies to grant liberal constitutions against their wills. Metternich was horrified: revolution was rising once again. Calling a conference at Troppau in Austria under the provisions of the Quadruple Alliance, he and Alexander I proclaimed the principle of active intervention to maintain all autocratic regimes whenever they were threatened. Austrian forces then marched into Naples in 1821 and restored Ferdinand I to the

Metternich This portrait by Sir Thomas Lawrence (1769–1830) reveals much about Metternich the man. Handsome, refined, and intelligent, Metternich was a great aristocrat who was passionately devoted to his class and the defense of its interests. *(Source: Copyright reserved to Her Majesty Queen Elizabeth II)*

throne of the Two Sicilies, while French armies likewise restored the Spanish regime.

In the following years Metternich continued to battle against liberal political change. Sometimes he could do little, as in the case of the new Latin American republics that broke away from Spain. Nor could he undo the dynastic changes of 1830 and 1831 in France and Belgium. Nonetheless, until 1848 Metternich's system proved quite effective in central Europe, where his power was the greatest.

Metternich's policies dominated not only Austria and the Italian peninsula but also the entire German Confederation, which the peace settlement of Vienna had called into being. The confederation was composed of thirty-eight independent German states, including Prussia and Austria. These states met in complicated assemblies dominated by Austria, with Prussia a willing junior partner in the planning and execution of repressive measures.

It was through the German Confederation that Metternich had the infamous Carlsbad Decrees issued in 1819. These decrees required the thirty-eight German member states to root out subversive ideas in their universities and newspapers. The decrees also established a permanent committee with spies and informers to investigate and punish any liberal or radical organizations. Metternich's ruthless imposition of repressive internal policies on the governments of central Europe contrasted with the intelligent moderation he had displayed in the general peace settlement of 1815.

Metternich and Conservatism

Metternich's determined defense of the status quo made him a villain in the eyes of most progressive, optimistic historians of the nineteenth century. Yet rather than denounce the man, we can try to understand him and the general conservatism he represented.

Born into the middle ranks of the landed nobility of the Rhineland, Prince Klemens von Metternich (1773–1859) was an internationally oriented aristocrat who made a brilliant diplomatic career in Austria. Austrian foreign minister from 1809 to 1848, the cosmopolitan Metternich always remained loyal to his class and jealously defended its rights and privileges to the day he died. Like most other conservatives of his time, he did so with a clear conscience. The nobility was one of Europe's most ancient institutions, and conservatives regarded tradition as the basic source of human institutions. In their view, the proper state and society remained those of pre-1789 Europe, which rested on a judicious blend of monarchy, bureaucracy, aristocracy, and respectful commoners.

Metternich firmly believed that liberalism, as embodied in revolutionary America and France, had been responsible for a generation of war with untold bloodshed and suffering. Liberal demands for representative government and civil liberties had unfortunately captured the imaginations of some middle-class lawyers, business people, and intellectuals, who were engaged in a vast conspiracy to impose their beliefs on society and destroy the existing order. Like many other conservatives then and since, Metternich blamed liberal revolutionaries for stirring up the lower classes, which he believed desired nothing more than peace and quiet.

The threat of liberalism appeared doubly dangerous to Metternich because it generally went with national aspirations. Liberals believed that each people, each national group, had a right to establish its own independent government and seek to fulfill its own destiny. The idea of national self-determination was repellent to Metternich. It not only threatened the existence of the aristocracy but also threatened to destroy the Austrian Empire and revolutionize central Europe.

The vast Austrian Empire of the Habsburgs was a great dynastic state. Formed over centuries by war, marriage, and luck, it was made up of many peoples (Map 25.2). The Germans had long dominated the empire, yet they accounted for only one-fourth of the population. The Magyars (Hungarians), a substantially smaller group, dominated the kingdom of Hungary though even they did not account for a majority of the population in that part of the Austrian Empire.

The Czechs, the third major group, were concentrated in Bohemia and Moravia. There were also large numbers of Italians, Poles, and Ukrainians as well as smaller groups of Slovenes, Croats, Serbs, Ruthenians, and Rumanians. The various Slavic peoples, together with the Italians and the Rumanians, represented a widely scattered and completely divided majority in an empire dominated by Germans and Hungarians. Different ethnic groups often lived in the same provinces and even in the same villages. Thus the different parts and provinces of the empire differed in languages, customs, and institutions.

The multinational state that Metternich served was both strong and weak. It was strong because of its large population and vast territories; it was weak because of its many and potentially dissatisfied nationalities. In these circumstances, Metternich virtually had to oppose liberalism and nationalism, for Austria was simply unable to accommodate those ideologies of the dual revolution. Other conservatives supported Austria because they could imagine no better fate for the jumble of small nationalities wedged precariously between masses of Germans and hordes of Russians in east-central Europe. Metternich's repressive conservatism had understandable roots in the dilemma of a multinational state in an age of rising nationalism.

RADICAL IDEAS AND EARLY SOCIALISM

The years following the peace settlement of 1815 were years of profound intellectual activity. Intellectuals and social observers were seeking to understand the revolutionary changes that were taking place. These efforts led to ideas that still motivate the world.

Almost all of these basic ideas were radical. In one way or another they rejected the old, deeply felt conservatism, with its stress on tradition, a hereditary monarchy, a strong and privileged landowning aristocracy, and an official church. Instead, radicals developed and refined alternative visions—alternative ideologies—and tried to convince society to act on them. With time, they were very successful.

Liberalism

The principal ideas of liberalism—liberty and equality—were by no means defeated in 1815. First realized successfully in the American Revolution and then achieved in part in the French Revolution, liberalism demanded representative government as opposed to autocratic monarchy, equality before the law as opposed to legally separate classes. The idea of liberty also continued to mean specific individual freedoms: freedom of the press, freedom of speech, freedom of assembly, and freedom from arbitrary arrest. In Europe only France with Louis XVIII's Constitutional Charter and Great Britain with its Parliament and historic rights of English men and women had realized much of

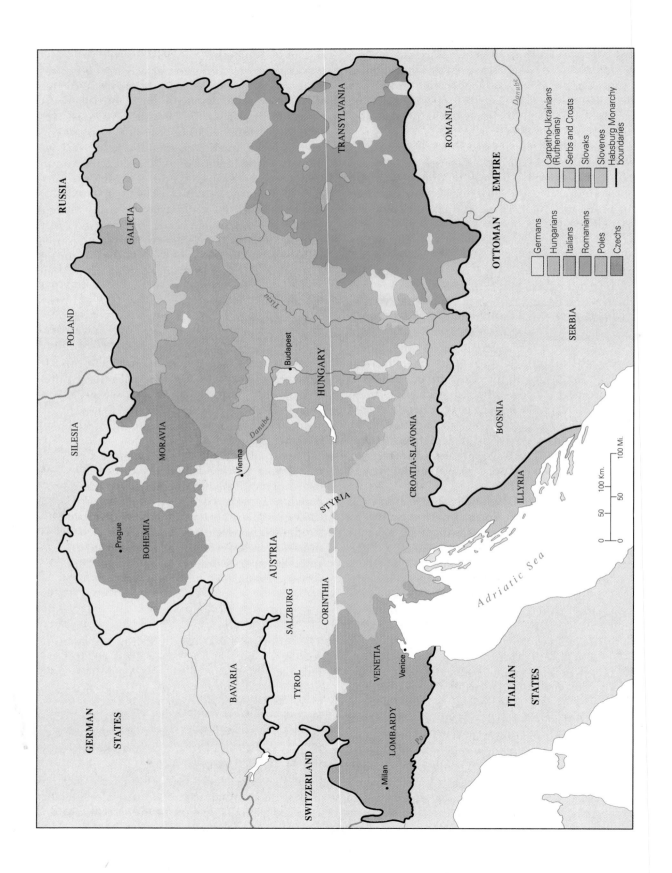

the liberal program in 1815. Even in those countries, liberalism had not fully succeeded.

Although liberalism retained its cutting edge, many considered it a somewhat duller tool than it had been. The reasons for this opinion were that liberalism faced more radical ideological competitors in the early nineteenth century. Opponents of classical liberalism especially criticized its economic principles, which called for unrestricted private enterprise and no government interference in the economy. This philosophy was popularly known as the doctrine of *laissez faire.* (This form of liberalism is often called "classical" liberalism in the United States to distinguish it sharply from modern American liberalism, which usually favors more government programs to meet social needs and to regulate the economy.)

The idea of a free economy had first been persuasively formulated by Scottish philosophy professor Adam Smith, whose *Inquiry into the Nature and Causes of the Wealth of Nations* (1776) founded modern economics. Smith was highly critical of eighteenth-century mercantilism and its attempt to regulate trade and economic activity. Far preferable, he believed, were free competition and the "invisible hand" of the self-regulating market, which would give all citizens a fair and equal opportunity to do what they did best. Smith argued effectively that freely competitive private enterprise would result in greater income for everyone, not just the rich.

In the early nineteenth century in Britain, this economic liberalism, which promoted economic growth in the Industrial Revolution, was embraced most enthusiastically by business groups and became a doctrine associated with business interests. Businessmen used the doctrine to defend their right to do as they wished in their factories. Labor unions were outlawed because they supposedly restricted free competition and the individual's "right to work."

In the early nineteenth century, liberal political ideals also became more closely associated with narrow class interests. Early-nineteenth-century liberals favored representative government, but

MAP 25.2 **Peoples of the Habsburg Monarchy, 1815**   The old dynastic state was a patchwork of nationalities. Notice the widely scattered pockets of Germans and Hungarians.

they generally wanted property qualifications attached to the right to vote. In practice, this meant limiting the vote to well-to-do aristocratic landowners, substantial businessmen, and successful members of the professions. Workers and peasants as well as the lower middle class of shopkeepers, clerks, and artisans did not own the necessary property and so could not vote.

Thus liberalism became increasingly identified with the middle class after 1815, and some intellectuals and foes of conservatism felt that liberalism did not go nearly far enough. Inspired by memories of the French Revolution and the young American republic, they called for universal voting rights, at least for males, and for democracy. These democrats and republicans were more radical than the liberals. They detested the power of the monarchy, the privileges of the aristocracy, and the great wealth of the upper middle class. Democrats and republicans were also more willing than most liberals to endorse violent upheaval to achieve goals. All of this meant that liberals and radical, democratic republicans could join forces against conservatives only up to a point.

Nationalism

Nationalism was a second radical idea in the years after 1815, an idea destined to have an enormous influence in the modern world. Nationalism has normally evolved from a real or imagined *cultural* unity, manifesting itself especially in a common language, history, and territory. And nationalists have usually sought to turn this cultural unity into *political* reality so that the territory of each people coincides with its state boundaries. It was this goal that made nationalism so potentially explosive in central and eastern Europe after 1815, when there were either too few states (Austria, Russia, and the Ottoman Empire) or too many (the Italian peninsula and the German Confederation) and when different peoples overlapped and intermingled. First harnessed by the French republic, nationalism had been preached by some patriots in the war against Napoleon. By 1815 there were already hints of nationalism's remarkable ability to spread and develop.

Between 1815 and 1850, most people who believed in nationalism also believed in either liberalism or radical, democratic republicanism. In more recent times, however, many governments have been very nationalistic without favoring liberty and democracy. Why, then, was love of liberty almost synonymous with love of nation in the early nineteenth century?

A common faith in the creativity and nobility of the people was perhaps the single most important reason for the linking of these two concepts. Liberals and especially democrats saw the people as the ultimate source of all good government. Yet the benefits of self-government were possible only if the people were united by common traditions, loyalties, and language that transcended local interests and even class differences.

Early nationalists usually believed that every nation, like every citizen, had the right to exist in freedom and to develop its character and spirit. They were confident that a symphony of free nations would promote the harmony and ultimate unity of all peoples. As French historian Jules Michelet put it in *The People* in 1846, each citizen "learns to recognize his country . . . as a note in the grand concert; through it he himself participates and loves the world." Similarly, the great Italian patriot Giuseppe Mazzini (see Listening to the Past) believed that "in laboring according to the true principles of our country we are laboring for Humanity." Thus the liberty of the individual and the love of a free nation overlapped greatly in the early nineteenth century.

Yet even as early nationalists talked of serving the cause of humanity, they stressed the differences among peoples. German pastor and philosopher Johann Herder (1744–1803) had argued that every people has its own particular spirit and genius, which it expresses through culture and language. Herder (and others after him), however, could not define the uniqueness of the French, German, and Slavic peoples without comparing and contrasting one people with another. Thus even early nationalism developed a strong sense of "we" and "they."

To this "we-they" outlook, it was all too easy for nationalists to add two other highly volatile ingredients: a sense of national mission and a sense of national superiority. As Mazzini characteristically wrote, "Peoples never stop before they have achieved the ultimate aim of their existence, before having fulfilled their mission." In 1845 American journalist and strident nationalist John Louis O'Sullivan wrote that taking land from an "imbecile and distracted Mexico" was a laudable step in the "fulfillment of our manifest destiny to over-

spread the continent."[1] Even Michelet, so alive to the aspirations of other peoples, could not help speaking in 1846 of the "superiority of France"; the principles espoused in the French Revolution had made France the "salvation of mankind."

German and Spanish nationalists had a very different opinion of France. To them, the French often seemed oppressive, as the Germans did to the Czechs, as the Russians did to the Poles. Thus "they" were often the enemy.

Early nationalism was ambiguous. Its main thrust was liberal and democratic. But below the surface lurked ideas of national superiority and national mission that could lead to aggression and conflict.

French Utopian Socialism

Socialism was the new radical doctrine after 1815, and to understand it one must begin with France. Despite the fact that France trailed Great Britain in developing modern industry, most early socialists were French. These French thinkers were acutely aware that the political revolution in France, the rise of laissez faire, and the emergence of factory industry in England were transforming society. They were disturbed by what they saw. Liberal practices in politics, such as competition for votes, and in economics, such as free markets and the end of guild regulation, appeared to be fomenting selfish individualism and splitting the community into isolated fragments. There was, they believed, an urgent need for a further reorganization of society to establish cooperation and a new sense of community. Starting from this shared outlook, individual French thinkers searched the past, analyzed existing conditions, and fashioned luxurious utopias.

Early French socialists believed in economic planning. Inspired by the emergency measures of 1793 and 1794 in France, they argued that the government should rationally organize the economy and not depend on destructive competition to do the job. Early socialists also shared an intense desire to help the poor, and they preached that the rich and the poor should be more nearly equal economically. Finally, socialists believed that private property should be strictly regulated by the government or that it should be abolished and replaced by state or community ownership. Planning, greater economic equality, and state control of property—these were the key ideas of early French socialism and of all socialism since.

❋ **Fourier's Utopia**   The vision of a harmonious planned community freed from capitalism and selfish individualism radiates from this 1847 illustration of Charles Fourier's principles. *(Source: Mary Evans Picture Library/Photo Researchers)*

Baba

One of the most influential early socialist thinkers was a nobleman, Count Henri de Saint-Simon (1760–1825). Saint-Simon optimistically proclaimed the tremendous possibilities of industrial development: "The age of gold is before us!" The key to progress was proper social organization. Such an arrangement of society required the "parasites"—the court, the aristocracy, lawyers, churchmen—to give way, once and for all, to the "doers"—the leading scientists, engineers, and industrialists. The doers would carefully plan the economy and guide it forward by undertaking vast public works projects and establishing investment banks. Saint-Simon also stressed in highly moralistic terms that every social institution ought to have as its main goal improved conditions for the poor.

After 1830 the socialist critique of capitalism became sharper. Charles Fourier (1772–1837), a lonely, saintly man with a tenuous hold on reality, envisaged a socialist utopia of mathematically pre-

cise, self-sufficient communities, each made up of 1,620 people. Each day at noon Fourier stayed in his apartment, expecting a wealthy philanthropist who would endow his visionary schemes. He waited in vain, but several Fourier communities were founded, mainly in the United States.

Fourier was also an early proponent of the total emancipation of women. Extremely critical of middle-class family life, Fourier believed that most marriages were only another kind of prostitution. According to Fourier, young single women were shamelessly "sold" to their future husbands for dowries and other financial considerations. Fourier called for the abolition of marriage, free unions based only on love, and sexual freedom. To many middle-class men and women, these ideas were shocking and immoral. The suggested liberation of women as well as workers made the socialist program appear to them as doubly dangerous and revolutionary.

Louis Blanc (1811–1882), an intelligent journalist, was much more practical. In his *Organization of Work* (1839), he urged workers to agitate for universal voting rights and to take control of the state peacefully. Blanc believed that the state should guarantee full employment. The right to work had to become as sacred as any other right.

Finally, there was Pierre Joseph Proudhon (1809–1865), a self-educated printer who wrote a pamphlet in 1840 entitled *What Is Property?* His answer was that it was nothing but theft. Property was profit that was stolen from the worker, who was the source of all wealth. Unlike most socialists, Proudhon feared the power of the state and was often considered an anarchist.

Of great importance, the message of French utopian socialists interacted with the experiences of French urban workers. In Paris especially, workers cherished the memory of the radical phase of the French Revolution and its efforts to regulate economic life and protect the poor. Skilled artisans, with a long tradition of exercising some control of their trades and conditions of work through guilds, became violently opposed to laissez-faire laws that denied workers the right to organize and instead promoted brutal, unrestrained competition. Developing a sense of class in the process, workers favored collective action and government intervention in economic life. Thus the aspirations of workers and utopian theorists reinforced each other, and a genuine socialist movement emerged in Paris in the 1830s and 1840s.

The French utopians had some influence outside France, but their specific programs often seemed too fanciful to be taken seriously. To Karl Marx was left the task of establishing firm foundations for modern socialism.

The Birth of Marxian Socialism

In 1848 the thirty-year-old Karl Marx (1818–1883) and the twenty-eight-year-old Friedrich Engels (1820–1895) published the *Communist Manifesto,* which became the bible of socialism. The son of a Jewish lawyer who had converted to Christianity, the atheistic young Marx had studied philosophy at the University of Berlin before turning to journalism and economics. He read widely in French socialist thought and like Fourier looked forward to the emancipation of women and the abolition of the family. By the time Marx was twenty-five, he was developing his own socialist ideas.

Early French socialists often appealed to the middle class and the state to help the poor. Marx ridiculed such appeals as naive. He argued that the interests of the middle class and those of the industrial working class were inevitably opposed to each other. Indeed, according to the *Manifesto,* the "history of all previously existing society is the history of class struggles." In Marx's view, one class had always exploited the other, and with the advent of modern industry, society was split more clearly than ever before: between the middle class (the bourgeoisie) and the modern working class (the proletariat). Moreover, the bourgeoisie had reduced everything to a matter of money and "naked self-interest." "In a word, for exploitation, veiled by religious and political illusions, the bourgeoisie had substituted naked, shameless, direct brutal exploitation."

Just as the bourgeoisie had triumphed over the feudal aristocracy, the proletariat, Marx predicted, would conquer the bourgeoisie in a violent revolution. While a tiny minority owned the means of production and grew richer, the ever-poorer proletariat was constantly growing in size and in class consciousness. The critical moment, Marx thought, was very near. "Let the ruling classes tremble at a Communist revolution. The proletarians have nothing to lose but their chains. They have a world to win. WORKING MEN OF ALL COUNTRIES, UNITE!" So ends the *Communist Manifesto.*

Marx's ideas united sociology, economics, and all human history in a vast and imposing edifice. He synthesized in his socialism not only French utopian schemes but also English classical economics and German philosophy—the major intellectual currents of his day.

Marx's debt to England was great. He was the last of the classical economists. Following David Ricardo, who had taught that labor was the source of all value, Marx went on to argue that profits were really wages stolen from the workers. Moreover, Marx incorporated Engels's account of the terrible oppression of the new class of factory workers in England; thus Marx's doctrines seemed to be based on hard facts.

Marx's theory of historical evolution was built on the philosophy of the German Georg Hegel (1770–1831). Hegel believed that each age in history is characterized by a dominant set of ideas, which produces opposing ideas and eventually a new synthesis. Thus history has pattern and purpose. Marx retained Hegel's view of history as a dialectic process of change but made economic relationships between classes the driving force. This dialectic explained the decline of agrarian feudalism and the rise of industrial capitalism. And Marx stressed again and again that the "bourgeoisie, historically, has played a most revolutionary part. . . . During its rule of scarcely one hundred years the bourgeoisie has created more massive and more colossal productive forces than have all preceding generations together." Marx's next idea, that it was now the bourgeoisie's turn to give way to the socialism of revolutionary workers, appeared to many the irrefutable capstone of a brilliant interpretation of humanity's long development. Thus Marx pulled together powerful insights to create one of the great secular religions of modern times.

 ## THE ROMANTIC MOVEMENT

Radical concepts of politics and society were accompanied by comparable changes in literature and other arts during the dual revolution. The early nineteenth century marked the acme of the romantic movement, which profoundly influenced the arts and enriched European culture immeasurably.

The romantic movement was in part a revolt against classicism and the Enlightenment. The classicists believed that the ancient Greeks and Romans had discovered eternally valid aesthetic rules, that these rules fit with the Enlightenment's belief in rationality, order, and restraint, and that playwrights and painters should continue to follow them. Classicists could enforce these rules in the eighteenth century because they dominated the courts and academies for which artists worked.

Forerunners of the romantic movement appeared from about 1750 on. Of these, Rousseau—the passionate advocate of feeling, freedom, and natural goodness—was the most influential. Romanticism then crystallized fully in the 1790s, primarily in England and Germany. The French Revolution kindled the belief that radical reconstruction was also possible in cultural and artistic life (even though many early English and German romantics became disillusioned with events in France and turned from liberalism to conservatism in politics). Romanticism gained strength until the 1840s.

Karl Marx Active in the revolution of 1848, Marx fled from Germany in 1849 and settled in London. There he wrote *Capital,* the weighty exposition of his socialist theories, and worked to organize the working class. Marx earned a modest living as a journalist, supplemented by financial support from his coauthor, Friedrich Engels. *(Source: Istar-Tass/Sovfoto)*

Romanticism's Tenets

Romanticism was characterized by a belief in emotional exuberance, unrestrained imagination, and spontaneity in both art and personal life. In Germany early romantics of the 1770s and 1780s called themselves the "Storm and Stress" (*Sturm und Drang*) group, and many romantic artists of the early nineteenth century lived lives of tremendous emotional intensity. Suicide, duels to the death, madness, and strange illnesses were not uncommon among leading romantics. Romantics rejected materialism and sought to escape to lofty spiritual heights through their art. Great individualists, they believed the full development of one's unique human potential to be the supreme purpose in life. The romantics were driven by a sense of an unlimited universe and by a yearning for the unattained, the unknown, the unknowable.

Nowhere was the break with classicism more apparent than in romanticism's general conception of nature. Classicism was not particularly interested in nature. In the words of eighteenth-century English author Samuel Johnson, "A blade of grass is always a blade of grass; men and women are my subjects of inquiry." The romantics, in contrast, were enchanted by nature. Sometimes fascinated by its awesome and tempestuous side, at other times they saw nature as a source of spiritual inspiration. As the great English landscape artist John Constable declared, "Nature is Spirit visible."

Most romantics saw the growth of modern industry as an ugly, brutal attack on their beloved nature and on the human personality. They sought escape—in the unspoiled Lake District of northern England, in exotic North Africa, in an idealized Middle Ages. Yet some romantics found a vast, awesome, terribly moving power in the new industrial landscape. One of John Martin's greatest paintings, vividly depicting the Last Judgment foretold in Revelation 6, was inspired directly by a journey through the "Black country" of the industrial Midlands in the dead of night. According to Martin's son: "The glow of the furnaces, the red blaze of light, together with the liquid fire, seemed to him truly sublime and awful. He could not imagine anything more terrible even in the regions of everlasting punishment."[2]

Fascinated by color and diversity, the romantic imagination turned toward history with a passion. For romantics, history was beautiful and exciting. And it was the art of change over time—the key to a universe that was now perceived to be organic and dynamic. Historical studies supported the development of national aspirations and encouraged entire peoples to seek in the past their special destinies. This trend was especially strong in Germany and other eastern European countries.

Literature

Britain was the first country where romanticism flowered fully in poetry and prose, and the British romantic writers were among the most prominent in Europe. Wordsworth, Coleridge, and Scott were all active by 1800, to be followed shortly by Byron, Shelley, and Keats. All were poets: romanticism found its distinctive voice in poetry, as the Enlightenment had in prose.

A towering leader of English romanticism, William Wordsworth (1770–1850) traveled in France after his graduation from Cambridge University. There he fell passionately in love with a French woman, who bore him a daughter. He was deeply influenced by the philosophy of Rousseau and the spirit of the early French Revolution. Back in England, prevented by war and the Terror from returning to France, Wordsworth settled in the countryside with his sister, Dorothy, and Samuel Taylor Coleridge (1772–1834).

In 1798 the two poets published their *Lyrical Ballads,* one of the most influential literary works in the history of the English language. In defiance of classical rules, Wordsworth and Coleridge abandoned flowery poetic conventions for the language of ordinary speech, simultaneously endowing simple subjects with the loftiest majesty. One of Wordsworth's poems gracefully celebrates "a crowd,/A host, of golden daffodils; . . . /Fluttering and dancing in the breeze," and confides that "A poet could not but be gay,/In such a jocund company." Sharing the romantic conviction that nature has the power to elevate and instruct, Wordsworth also believed that nature could be appreciated, very democratically, by everyone and not just by an intellectual elite.

Born in Edinburgh, Walter Scott (1771–1832) personified the romantic movement's fascination with history. Raised on his grandfather's farm, Scott fell under the spell of the old ballads and tales of the Scottish border. He was also deeply influenced by German romanticism, particularly by the immortal poet and dramatist Johann Wolfgang von Goethe (1749–1832). A natural storyteller, Scott composed long narrative poems and a series of historical novels. He excelled in faithfully recreating the spirit of bygone ages and great historical events, especially those of Scotland.

At first, the strength of classicism in France inhibited the growth of romanticism there. Then between 1820 and 1850, the romantic impulse broke through in the poetry and prose of Lamartine, de Vigny, Hugo, Dumas, and Sand. Of these, Victor Hugo (1802–1885) was the greatest in both poetry and prose.

Son of a Napoleonic general, Hugo achieved an amazing range of rhythm, language, and image in his lyric poetry. His powerful novels exemplified the romantic fascination with fantastic characters,

John Martin: The Great Day of His Wrath   The combination of the terrible and the sublime fascinated English romantic artist John Martin (1789–1854). He painted wild visions of hell for a popular illustrated edition of John Milton's great epic poem *Paradise Lost*. But the reality of ironworks blazing in the night seemed to him even more awesome, and it inspired this image of the Last Judgment and the end of human history. *(Source: Tate Gallery, London/Art Resource, NY)*

strange settings, and human emotions. The hero of Hugo's famous *Hunchback of Notre Dame* (1831) is the great cathedral's deformed bellringer, a "human gargoyle" overlooking the teeming life of fifteenth-century Paris. Hugo also championed romanticism in drama. His play *Hernani* (1830) consciously broke all the old rules as Hugo renounced his early conservatism and equated freedom in literature with liberty in politics and society. Hugo's political evolution was thus exactly the opposite of Wordsworth's. In the English poet youthful radicalism gave way to middle-aged caution. As the contrast between the two artists suggests, romanticism was a cultural movement compatible with many political beliefs.

Amandine Aurore Lucie Dupin (1804–1876), a strong-willed and gifted woman generally known by her pen name, George Sand, defied the narrow conventions of her time in an unending search for self-fulfillment. After eight years of unhappy marriage in the provinces, she abandoned her dullard of a husband and took her two children to Paris to pursue a career as a writer. There Sand soon achieved fame and wealth, eventually writing over eighty novels on a variety of romantic and social themes. Her striking individualism went far beyond her flamboyant preference for men's clothing and cigars and her notorious love affairs. Her semi-autobiographical novel *Lélia* was shockingly modern, delving deeply into her tortuous quest for sexual and personal freedom.

In central and eastern Europe, literary romanticism and early nationalism often reinforced each other. Seeking a unique greatness in every people, well-educated romantics plumbed their own histories and cultures. Like modern anthropologists, they turned their attention to peasant life and transcribed the folk songs, tales, and proverbs that the cosmopolitan Enlightenment had disdained. The brothers Jacob and Wilhelm Grimm were particularly successful at rescuing German fairy tales from oblivion. In the Slavic lands, romantics played a decisive role in converting spoken peasant languages into modern written languages. The greatest of all Russian poets, Aleksander Pushkin (1799–1837), used his lyric genius to mold the modern literary language of Russia.

Art and Music

The greatest and most moving romantic painter in France was Eugène Delacroix (1798–1863), probably the illegitimate son of French foreign minister Talleyrand. Delacroix was a master of dramatic, colorful scenes that stirred the emotions. He was fascinated with remote and exotic subjects, whether lion hunts in Morocco or the languishing, sensuous women of a sultan's harem. He was also a passionate spokesman for freedom. His master-

Heroes of Romanticism   Observed by a portrait of Byron and a bust of Beethoven, Franz Liszt plays for friends in this painting by Josef Danhauser (1805–1845). From left to right sit Alexandre Dumas, George Sand (characteristically wearing men's garb), and Marie d'Agoult, Liszt's mistress. Standing are Victor Hugo, Nicolo Paganini, and Gioacchino Rossini. This gathering of geniuses was purely imaginary, part of an advertising campaign by a German piano manufacturer to sell pianos to the comfortable middle class. *(Source: Bildarchiv Preussischer Kulturbesitz)*

piece, *Liberty Leading the People,* celebrated the nobility of popular revolution in general and revolution in France in particular.

In England the most notable romantic painters were Joseph M. W. Turner (1775–1851) and John Constable (1776–1837). Both were fascinated by nature, but their interpretations of it contrasted sharply, aptly symbolizing the tremendous emotional range of the romantic movement. Turner depicted nature's power and terror; wild storms and sinking ships were favorite subjects. Constable painted gentle Wordsworthian landscapes in which human beings were at one with their environment, the comforting countryside of unspoiled rural England.

It was in music that romanticism realized most fully and permanently its goals of free expression and emotional intensity. Whereas the composers of the eighteenth century had remained true to well-defined structures, such as the classical symphony, the great romantics used a great range of forms. Romantic composers also transformed the small classical orchestra, tripling its size by adding wind instruments, percussion, and more brass and strings. The crashing chords evoking the surge of the masses in Frédéric Chopin's "Revolutionary" etude, the bottomless despair of the funeral march in Beethoven's Third Symphony—such were the musical paintings that plumbed the depths of human feeling.

This range and intensity gave music and musicians much greater prestige than in the past. Music no longer simply complemented a church service or helped a nobleman digest his dinner. It became for many the greatest of the arts, worthy of great concert halls and the most dedicated sacrifice. The one-in-a-million performer—the great virtuoso who could transport the listener to ecstasy and hysteria—became a cultural hero. People swooned for the composer Franz Liszt (1811–1886), lionized as the greatest pianist of his age, as they scream for rock stars today.

Though romanticism dominated music until late in the nineteenth century, no composer ever surpassed its first great master, Ludwig van Beethoven (1770–1827). As the contemporary German novelist Ernst Hoffmann (1776–1822) wrote, "Beethoven's music sets in motion the lever of fear, of awe, of horror, of suffering, and awakens just that infinite longing which is the essence of Romanticism." Beethoven's range was tremendous. He continued to pour out immortal music—

symphonies, chamber music, sonatas for violin and piano, masses, an opera, and a great many songs—until his death. But he never heard much of his later work, including the unforgettable choral finale to the Ninth Symphony, for his last years were spent in total deafness.

REFORMS AND REVOLUTIONS (1815–1850)

While the romantic movement was developing, liberal, national, and socialist forces battered against the conservatism of 1815. In a few countries, change occurred gradually and peacefully. Elsewhere, pressure built up like steam in a pressure cooker without a safety valve. Then in 1848 revolutionary political and social ideologies combined with economic crisis and the romantic impulse to produce a vast upheaval. National independence, liberal-democratic constitutions, and social reform: the lofty aspirations of a generation seemed at hand. Yet in the end the revolutions failed, and the lofty aspirations were shattered.

National Liberation in Greece

National, liberal revolution, frustrated in Italy and Spain by conservative statesmen, succeeded first after 1815 in Greece. Since the fifteenth century, the Greeks had been living under the domination of the Ottoman Turks. In spite of centuries of foreign rule, the Greeks had survived as a people, united by their language and the Greek Orthodox religion. It was perfectly natural that the general growth of national aspirations and a desire for independence would inspire some Greeks in the early nineteenth century. This rising national movement led to revolt in 1821.

The Great Powers, particularly Metternich, were opposed to all revolution, even revolution against the Islamic Turks, and they supported the Ottoman Empire. Yet for many Europeans, the Greek cause became a holy one. Educated Americans and Europeans were in love with the culture of classical Greece; Russians were stirred by the piety of their Orthodox brethren. Writers and artists, moved by the romantic impulse, responded enthusiastically to the Greek struggle. The flamboyant, radical poet Lord Byron went to Greece and died there in the struggle "that Greece might still be free."

Turkish atrocities toward the rebels fanned the fires of European outrage and Greek determination. One of Delacroix's romantic masterpieces memorialized the massacre at Chios, where the Turks had slaughtered nearly a hundred thousand Greeks.

In 1827 Great Britain, France, and Russia responded to popular demands at home and directed Turkey to accept an armistice. When the Turks refused, the navies of these three powers trapped the Turkish fleet at Navarino and destroyed it. Russia then declared another of its periodic wars of expansion against the Turks. This led to the establishment of a Russian protectorate over much of present-day Rumania, which had also been under Turkish rule. Great Britain, France, and Russia finally declared Greece independent in 1830. In the end the Greeks had won: a small nation had gained its independence in a heroic war against a foreign empire.

Liberal Reform in Great Britain

Eighteenth-century British society had been both flexible and remarkably stable. It was dominated by the landowning aristocracy, but that class was neither closed nor rigidly defined. Successful business and professional people could buy land and become gentlefolk, while the common people had more than the usual opportunities of the preindustrial world. Basic civil rights for all were balanced by a tradition of deference to one's social superiors. Parliament was manipulated by the king and was thoroughly undemocratic. Only about 6 percent of the population could vote for representatives to Parliament, and by the 1780s there was growing interest in some kind of political reform. But the French Revolution threw the British aristocracy into a panic for a generation. The Tory party, completely controlled by the landed aristocracy, was particularly fearful of radical movements at home and abroad. After 1815 the aristocracy energetically defended its ruling position.

The first step in this direction began in 1815 with revival of the Corn Laws restricting foreign grain imports. During a generation of war with France the British had been unable to import cheap grain from eastern Europe. As shortages occurred and agricultural prices skyrocketed, a great deal of marginal land had been brought under cultivation, fattening the landed aristocracy's rent rolls. Peace meant that grain could be imported again and that the price of wheat and bread would go down, benefiting almost everyone except the aristocracy. The aristocracy, however, rammed through Parliament a new law that prohibited the importation of foreign grain unless the price at home rose to improbable levels. Seldom has a class legislated more selfishly for its own narrow economic advantage or done more to promote a class-based interpretation of political action.

The change in the Corn Laws, coming at a time of widespread unemployment and postwar adjustment, led to protests and demonstrations by urban laborers, supported by radical intellectuals. In 1817 the Tory government responded by temporarily suspending the traditional rights of peaceable assembly and habeas corpus. Two years later, an enormous but orderly protest, at Saint Peter's Fields in Manchester, was savagely broken up by armed cavalry. Nicknamed the "Battle of Peterloo," in scornful reference to the British victory at Waterloo, this incident expressed the government's determination to repress and stand fast.

Strengthened by ongoing industrial development, the new manufacturing and commercial groups insisted on a place for their new wealth alongside the landed wealth of the aristocracy in the framework of political power and social prestige. They called for many kinds of liberal reform and pressed especially for reform of Parliament. The Whig party, though led like the Tories by great aristocrats, had by tradition been more responsive to commercial and manufacturing interests. In 1830 a Whig ministry introduced "an act to amend the representation of the people of England and Wales." The House of Lords successfully blocked this reform bill until 1832, when a mighty surge of popular protest helped convince the king and lords to give in.

The Reform Bill of 1832 had profound significance. First, the House of Commons had emerged as the all-important legislative body. Second, the new industrial areas of the country gained representation in the Commons, and many old "rotten boroughs"—electoral districts with very few voters that the landed aristocracy had bought and sold—were eliminated so that representation better reflected the shift in population to the northern manufacturing counties. Third, the number of voters increased by about 50 percent. Comfortable middle-class groups in the urban population, as well as some substantial farmers who leased their land, received the vote. Thus the pressures build-

✳ **Evictions of Irish Peasants**   Surrounded by their few meager possessions, this family was turned out of their cottage in the 1880s. The door was nailed shut to prevent their return. The eviction of peasants who could not pay their rent continued for decades after the Great Famine. *(Source: Lawrence Collection, National Library of Ireland, Dublin)*

ing in Great Britain were temporarily released without revolution or civil war. More radical reforms within the system appeared difficult but not impossible.

The principal radical program was embodied in the "People's Charter" of 1838 and the Chartist movement (see page 799), with its core demand for universal male (but not female) suffrage. In three separate campaigns hundreds of thousands of people signed gigantic petitions calling on Parliament to grant all men the right to vote. Parliament rejected the petitions, but the working poor learned a valuable lesson in mass politics.

While calling for universal male suffrage, many working-class people joined with middle-class manufacturers in the Anti–Corn Law League, founded in Manchester in 1839. Mass participation made possible a popular crusade led by fighting liberals who argued that lower food prices and

more jobs in industry depended on repeal of the Corn Laws, which in the 1820s had been revised to allow grain imports subject to high tariffs. When Ireland's potato crop failed in 1845, famine prices for food and even famine itself also seemed likely in England. To avert the impending catastrophe, Tory prime minister Robert Peel joined with the Whigs and a minority of his own party to repeal the Corn Laws in 1846 and allow free imports of grain. England escaped famine. Thereafter, the liberal doctrine of free trade became almost sacred dogma in Great Britain.

The following year, the Tories passed a bill designed to help the working classes, but in a different way. The Ten Hours Act of 1847 limited the workday for women and young people in factories to ten hours. Tory aristocrats continued to champion legislation regulating factory conditions. They were competing vigorously with the middle class for the support of the working class. This healthy competition between a still-vigorous aristocracy and a strong middle class was a crucial factor in Great Britain's peaceful evolution. The working classes could make temporary alliances with either competitor to better their own conditions.

The people of Ireland did not benefit from this political competition. Long ruled as a conquered people, the great mass of the population (outside the northern counties of Ulster, which were partly Presbyterian) were Irish Catholic peasants who rented their land from a tiny minority of Church of England Protestants, many of whom lived in England. Ruthlessly exploited and growing rapidly in numbers, Irish peasants had come to depend on the potato crop.

The potato crop failed in 1845, 1846, 1848, and 1851 in Ireland and throughout much of Europe. Blight attacked the young plants, and the tubers rotted. The general result was high food prices, widespread suffering, and, frequently, social upheaval. In Ireland the result was unmitigated disaster—the Great Famine. Widespread starvation and mass fever epidemics occurred. Total losses of population were staggering. Fully 1 million emigrants fled the famine between 1845 and 1851, going primarily to the United States and Great Britain, and at least 1.5 million people died or went unborn because of the disaster. At the same time, the British government energetically supported heartless landowner demands with armed force. Tenants who could not pay their rents were evicted and their homes broken up or burned. Famine or not, Ireland remained a conquered province.

Revolutions in France

Louis XVIII's Constitutional Charter of 1814—theoretically a gift from the king but actually a response to political pressures—was basically a liberal constitution (see page 764). The economic and social gains made by sections of the middle class and the peasantry in the French Revolution were fully protected, great intellectual and artistic freedom was permitted, and a real parliament with upper and lower houses was created. The worldly and politically expedient Louis appointed as his ministers moderate royalists. These ministers obtained the support of a majority of the representatives elected to the lower Chamber of Deputies between 1816 and Louis's death in 1824.

Louis XVIII's charter was anything but democratic. Only about 100,000 of the wealthiest people out of a total population of 30 million had the right to vote for the deputies who, with the king and his ministers, made the laws of the nation. Nonetheless, the "notable people" who did vote came from very different backgrounds. There were wealthy businessmen, war profiteers, successful professionals, former revolutionaries, large landowners from the old aristocracy and the middle class, Bourbons, and Bonapartists.

The old aristocracy, with its pre-1789 mentality, was a minority within the voting population. It was this situation that Louis's successor, his brother Charles X (r. 1824–1830), could not abide. Crowned in a lavish, utterly medieval ceremony in 1824, Charles was a true reactionary who wanted to re-establish the old order in France. Finally repudiating the Constitutional Charter in an attempted coup in July 1830, Charles issued decrees stripping much of the wealthy middle class of its voting rights, and he censored the press. The immediate reaction, encouraged by journalists and lawyers, was an insurrection in the capital by printers, other artisans, and small traders. In "three glorious days" the revolution of 1830 brought down the government. Charles fled. Then the upper middle class, which had encouraged the revolt, skillfully seated Charles's cousin, Louis Philippe, duke of Orléans, on the vacant throne.

Louis Philippe (r. 1830–1848) accepted the Constitutional Charter of 1814; adopted the red, white, and blue flag of the French Revolution; and admitted that he was merely the "king of the French people." In spite of such symbolic actions, the situation in France remained fundamentally unchanged. The vote was extended only from 100,000 to 170,000 citizens. The wealthy notable elite actually tightened its control as the old aristocracy retreated to the provinces to sulk harmlessly. For the upper middle class, there had been a change in dynasty in order to protect the status quo and the narrowly liberal institutions of 1815. Republicans, democrats, social reformers, and the poor of Paris were bitterly disappointed.

These disappointments in France grew in the 1840s, which were economically hard and politically tense throughout Europe. Echoes of the potato famine in Ireland, bad harvests in France and other countries jacked up food prices and caused misery and unemployment in the cities. "Prerevolutionary" outbreaks occurred all across

Europe. Revolution was widely expected, but it took revolution in Paris—once again—to turn expectations into realities.

Louis Philippe's "bourgeois monarchy" had been characterized by stubborn inaction and complacency. There was a glaring lack of social legislation, and politics was dominated by corruption and selfish special interests. With only the rich voting for deputies, many of the deputies were docile government bureaucrats.

The government's stubborn refusal to consider electoral reform heightened a sense of class injus-

tice among shopkeepers and urban working people, and it eventually touched off a popular revolt in Paris. Barricades went up on the night of February 22, 1848, and by February 24 Louis Philippe had abdicated in favor of his grandson. But the common people in arms would tolerate no more monarchy. This refusal led to the proclamation of a provisional republic, headed by a ten-man executive committee and certified by cries of approval from the revolutionary crowd.

A generation of historians and journalists had praised the First French Republic, and their work

Delacroix: Liberty Leading the People   This romantic painting glorifies the July revolution in Paris in 1830. Raising high the revolutionary tricolor, Liberty unites the worker, the bourgeois, and the street child in a righteous crusade against privilege and oppression. The revolution of 1848 began as a similar crusade, but class warfare in Paris soon shattered the hope of rich and poor joining together for freedom. (*Source: Louvre © Photo R.M.N*)

had borne fruit: the revolutionaries were firmly committed to a republic (as opposed to any form of constitutional monarchy), and they immediately set about drafting a constitution for France's Second Republic. Moreover, they wanted a truly popular and democratic republic so that the healthy, life-giving forces of the common people—the peasants and the workers—could reform society with wise legislation. In practice, building such a republic meant giving the right to vote to every adult male, and this was quickly done. Revolutionary compassion and sympathy for freedom were expressed in the freeing of all slaves in French colonies, the abolition of the death penalty, and the establishment of a ten-hour workday for Paris.

Yet there were profound differences within the revolutionary coalition in Paris. On the one hand, there were the moderate, liberal republicans of the middle class. They viewed universal male suffrage as the ultimate concession to be made to popular forces, and they strongly opposed any further radical social measures. On the other hand, there were the radical republicans. Influenced by a generation of utopian socialists, and appalled by the poverty and misery of the urban poor, the radical republicans were committed to some kind of socialism.

Worsening depression and rising unemployment brought these conflicting goals to the fore. Louis Blanc, who along with a worker named Albert represented the republican socialists in the provisional government, pressed for recognition of a socialist right to work. Blanc asserted that permanent government-sponsored cooperative workshops should be established for workers. Such workshops would be an alternative to capitalist employment and a decisive step toward a new, noncompetitive social order.

The moderate republicans wanted no such thing. They were willing to provide only temporary relief. The resulting compromise set up national workshops—soon to become little more than a vast program of pick-and-shovel public works—and established a special commission under Blanc to "study the question." This satisfied no one. The national workshops were, however, better than nothing. An army of desperate poor from the French provinces and even from foreign countries streamed into Paris to sign up. The number enrolled in the workshops soared from 10,000 in March to 120,000 by June, and another 80,000 were trying unsuccessfully to join.

While the workshops in Paris grew, the French masses went to the election polls in late April. Voting in most cases for the first time, the people elected a majority of moderate republicans to the new Constituent Assembly. The socialism that seemed the most characteristic aspect of the revolution in Paris was evoking a violent reaction not only among the frightened middle and upper classes but also among the bulk of the population—the peasants. Many French peasants owned land and they had been seized with a universal hatred of radical Paris. A majority of the Constituent Assembly members were thus firmly committed to the republic and strongly opposed to the socialists.

This clash of ideologies—of liberal capitalism and socialism—became a clash of classes and arms after the elections. As the workshops continued to fill and grow more radical, the fearful but powerful propertied classes in the Assembly took the offensive. On June 22 the government dissolved the national workshops in Paris, giving the workers the choice of joining the army or going to workshops in the provinces.

The result was a spontaneous and violent uprising. Frustrated in attempts to create a socialist society, masses of desperate people were now losing even their life-sustaining relief. When the famous astronomer François Arago counseled patience, a voice from the crowd cried out, "Ah, Monsieur Arago, you have never been hungry!"[3] Barricades sprang up in the narrow streets of Paris, and a terrible class war began. Working people fought with the courage of utter desperation, but the government had the army and the support of peasant France. After three terrible "June Days" and the death or injury of more than ten thousand people, the republican army under General Louis Cavaignac stood triumphant in a sea of working-class blood and hatred.

The revolution in France thus ended in spectacular failure. The February coalition of the middle and working classes had in four short months become locked in mortal combat. In place of a generous democratic republic, the Constituent Assembly completed a constitution featuring a strong executive. This allowed Louis Napoleon, nephew of Napoleon Bonaparte, to win a landslide victory in the election of December 1848.

The Austrian Empire in 1848

Throughout central Europe, news of the upheaval in France evoked feverish excitement and eventually revolution. Liberals demanded written consti-

THE REVOLUTIONS OF 1848

February	Revolt in Paris against Louis Philippe's "bourgeois monarchy" Louis Philippe abdicates Proclamation of a provisional republic
February–June	Establishment and rapid growth of government-sponsored workshops in France
March 3	Nationalistic Hungarians demand autonomy from Austrian Empire
March 13	Uprising of students and workers in Vienna; Metternich flees to London
March 20	Ferdinand I of Austria abolishes serfdom and promises reforms
March 21	Frederick William IV of Prussia agrees to a liberal constitution and to the merger of Prussia into a new German state
March 26	Workers in Berlin issue a series of democratic and vaguely socialist demands
April 22	French voters favor moderate republicans over radicals
May 18	Frankfurt Assembly begins writing a new German constitution
June 17	Austrian army crushes working-class revolt in Prague
June 22–26	French government abolishes the national workshops, provoking an uprising June Days: republican army defeats rebellious Parisian working class
October	Austrian army besieges and retakes Vienna from students and working-class radicals
December	Conservatives force Ferdinand I of Austria to abdicate in favor of young Francis Joseph Frederick William IV disbands Prussian Constituent Assembly and grants Prussia a conservative constitution Louis Napoleon wins a landslide victory in French presidential elections
March 1849	Frankfurt Assembly elects Frederick William IV of Prussia emperor of the new German state; Frederick William refuses and reasserts royal authority in Prussia
June–August 1849	Habsburg and Russian forces defeat the Hungarian independence movement

tutions, representative government, and greater civil liberties from authoritarian regimes. When governments hesitated, popular revolts followed. Urban workers and students served as the shock troops, but they were allied with middle-class lib-

erals and peasants. In the face of this united front, monarchs collapsed and granted almost everything. The popular revolutionary coalition, having secured great and easy victories, then broke down as it had in France. The traditional forces—the monarchy, the aristocracy, and the regular army—recovered their nerve, reasserted their authority, and took back many, though not all, of the concessions. Reaction was everywhere victorious.

The revolution in the Austrian Empire began in Hungary, where nationalistic Hungarians demanded national autonomy, full civil liberties, and universal suffrage. When the monarchy in Vienna hesitated, Viennese students and workers took to the streets, and peasant disorders broke out in parts of the empire. The Habsburg emperor Ferdinand I (r. 1835–1848) capitulated and promised reforms and a liberal constitution. Metternich fled in disguise toward London. The old absolutist order seemed to be collapsing with unbelievable rapidity.

The coalition of revolutionaries was not stable, however. The Austrian Empire was overwhelmingly agricultural, and serfdom still existed. On March 20, as part of its capitulation before upheaval, the monarchy abolished serfdom, with its degrading forced labor and feudal services. Feeling they had won a victory reminiscent of that in France in 1789, newly free men and women of the land then lost interest in the political and social questions agitating the cities. Meanwhile, the coalition of urban revolutionaries also broke down. When the urban poor rose in arms and presented its own demands for socialist workshops and universal voting rights for men, the prosperous middle classes recoiled in alarm.

The coalition of March was also weakened, and ultimately destroyed, by conflicting national aspirations. In March the Hungarian revolutionary leaders pushed through an extremely liberal, almost democratic, constitution. But the Hungarian revolutionaries also sought to transform the mosaic of provinces and peoples that was the kingdom of Hungary into a unified, centralized, Hungarian nation. To the minority groups that formed half of the population—the Croats, Serbs, and Rumanians—such unification was completely unacceptable. Each felt entitled to political autonomy and cultural independence. The Habsburg monarchy in Vienna exploited the fears of the minority groups, and they were soon locked in armed combat with the new Hungarian government. In a somewhat similar way, Czech nationalists based in Bohemia and the city of Prague came into conflict with German nationalists. Thus the national aspirations within the Austrian Empire enabled the monarchy to play off one group against the other.

Finally, the conservative aristocratic forces gathered around Emperor Ferdinand I regained their nerve and reasserted their great strength. The archduchess Sophia, a conservative but intelligent and courageous Bavarian princess married to the emperor's brother, provided a rallying point. Deeply ashamed of the emperor's collapse before a "mess of students," she insisted that Ferdinand, who had no heir, abdicate in favor of her son, Francis Joseph.[4] Powerful nobles who held high positions in the government, the army, and the church agreed completely. They organized around Sophia in a secret conspiracy to reverse and crush the revolution.

Their first breakthrough came when the army bombarded Prague and savagely crushed a working-class revolt there on June 17. Other Austrian officials and nobles began to lead the minority nationalities of Hungary against the revolutionary government proclaimed by the Hungarian patriots. At the end of October, the well-equipped, predominantly peasant troops of the regular Austrian army attacked the student and working-class radicals in Vienna and retook the city at the cost of more than four thousand casualties. Thus the determination of the Austrian aristocracy and the loyalty of its army were the final ingredients in the triumph of reaction and the defeat of revolution.

When Francis Joseph (r. 1848–1916) was crowned emperor of Austria immediately after his eighteenth birthday in December 1848, only Hungary had yet to be brought under control. But another determined conservative, Nicholas I of Russia (r. 1825–1855), obligingly lent his iron hand. On June 6, 1849, 130,000 Russian troops poured into Hungary and subdued the country after bitter fighting. For a number of years, the Habsburgs ruled Hungary as a conquered territory.

Prussia and the Frankfurt Assembly

After Austria, Prussia was the largest and most influential German kingdom. Prior to 1848, the goal of middle-class Prussian liberals had been to transform absolutist Prussia into a liberal constitutional monarchy, which would lead the thirty-eight states of the German Confederation into the liberal, unified nation desired by liberals throughout the German states. The agitation following the fall of Louis Philippe encouraged Prussian liberals to press their demands. When the artisans and factory

Revolutionary Justice in Vienna As part of the conservative resurgence, in October 1848 the Austrian minister of war ordered up reinforcements for an army that was marching on Hungary. In a last defiant gesture the outraged revolutionaries in Vienna seized the minister and hung him from a lamppost for treason. The army then reconquered the city in a week of bitter fighting. *(Source: Mary Evans Picture Library/Photo Researchers)*

workers in Berlin exploded in March and joined temporarily with the middle-class liberals in the struggle against the monarchy, the autocratic yet paternalistic Frederick William IV (r. 1840–1861) vacillated and finally caved in. On March 21 he promised to grant Prussia a liberal constitution and to merge Prussia into a new national German state that was to be created. But urban workers wanted much more and the Prussian aristocracy wanted

much less than the moderate constitutional liberalism the king conceded. The workers issued a series of democratic and vaguely socialist demands that troubled their middle-class allies, and the conservative clique gathered around the king to urge counter-revolution.

As an elected Prussian Constituent Assembly met in Berlin to write a constitution for the Prussian state, a self-appointed committee of liberals from various German states successfully called for a national assembly to begin writing a federal constitution for a unified German state. Meeting in Frankfurt in May, the National Assembly was a curious revolutionary body. It was really a serious middle-class body of lawyers, professors, doctors, officials, and businessmen.

Convened to write a constitution, the learned body was soon absorbed in a battle with Denmark over the provinces of Schleswig and Holstein, an extremely complicated issue from a legal point of view. The provinces were inhabited primarily by Germans but were ruled by the king of Denmark, although Holstein was a member of the German Confederation. When Frederick VII, the new nationalistic king of Denmark, tried to integrate both provinces into the rest of his state, the Germans in these provinces revolted. Hypnotized by this conflict, the National Assembly at Frankfurt debated ponderously and finally called on the Prussian army to oppose Denmark in the name of the German nation. Prussia responded and began war with Denmark. As the Schleswig-Holstein issue demonstrated, the national ideal was a crucial factor motivating the German middle classes in 1848.

In March 1849 the National Assembly finally completed its drafting of a liberal constitution and elected King Frederick William of Prussia emperor of the new German national state (minus Austria and Schleswig-Holstein). By early 1849, however, reaction had been successful almost everywhere. Frederick William had reasserted his royal authority, disbanded the Prussian Constituent Assembly, and granted his subjects a limited, essentially conservative constitution. Reasserting that he ruled by divine right, Frederick William contemptuously refused to accept the "crown from the gutter." Bogged down by their preoccupation with nationalist issues, the reluctant revolutionaries in Frankfurt had waited too long and acted too timidly.

When Frederick William, who really wanted to be emperor but only on his own authoritarian terms, tried to get the small monarchs of Germany to elect him emperor, Austria balked. Supported by Russia, Austria forced Prussia to renounce all its schemes of unification in late 1850. The German Confederation was re-established. Attempts to unite the Germans—first in a liberal national state and then in a conservative Prussian empire—had failed completely.

NATION BUILDING IN FRANCE, ITALY, AND GERMANY

Political, economic, and social pressures building up after 1815 exploded dramatically in 1848. But the upheavals were abortive, and very few revolutionary goals were realized. The moderate, nationalistic middle classes were unable to consolidate their initial victories in France or elsewhere in Europe. Instead, they drew back when artisans, factory workers, and radical socialists rose up to present their own much more revolutionary demands. This retreat made possible the crushing of Parisian workers by a coalition of solid bourgeoisie and landowning peasantry in France, and it facilitated the efforts of dedicated aristocrats in central Europe. A sea of blood and disillusion had washed away the lofty ideals and utopian visions of a generation. Thus the revolutions of 1848 closed one era in the West and opened another.

In thought and culture, exuberant romanticism gave way to hardheaded realism. In the Atlantic economy, the hard years of the 1840s were followed by good times and prosperity throughout most of the 1850s and 1860s. In international politics, the repressive peace and diplomatic stability of Metternich's time were replaced by a period of war and rapid change. Perhaps most important of all, Western society progressively found, for better or worse, a new and effective organizing principle capable of coping with the many-sided challenges of the dual revolution and the emerging urban civilization. That principle was nationalism—dedication to and identification with the nation-state.

The triumph of modern nationalism was an enormously significant historical development. A powerful force since at least 1789, after 1850 nationalism became an almost universal faith in Western society, evolving away from a narrow appeal to predominately middle-class liberals to an intoxicating creed moving the broad masses. Leaders of the entire world eventually embraced large parts of the doctrine of nationalism and the nation-state.

Louis Napoleon in France

France was representative of the general trend. Early nationalism in France was at least liberal and idealistic and often democratic and radical as well. The ideas of nationhood and popular sovereignty, so seductive in France, posed an awesome threat to conservatives like Metternich. Yet from the vantage point of the twentieth century, it is clear that nationalism can flourish in dictatorial states that are conservative, fascist, or communist. In France, Napoleon I had already combined national devotion with authoritarian rule. Significantly, it was Napoleon's nephew, Louis Napoleon, who revived and extended this merger. He showed how governments could reconcile popular and conservative forces in an authoritarian nationalism. In doing so, he provided a model for political leaders elsewhere.

Although Louis Napoleon Bonaparte had played no part in French politics before 1848, universal male suffrage gave him three times as many votes as the four other presidential candidates combined in the French presidential election of December 1848. This outcome occurred for several reasons. First, Louis Napoleon had the great name of his uncle, whom romantics had transformed from a dictator into a demigod as they created a Napoleonic legend after 1820. Second, as Karl Marx stressed at the time, middle-class and peasant property owners feared the socialist challenge of urban workers, and they wanted a tough ruler to provide protection. Third, in late 1848 Louis Napoleon had a positive "program" for France, which was to guide him throughout most of his long reign. This program had been elaborated earlier in pamphlets he had written while imprisoned for an attempt to overthrow Louis Philippe's government. Prior to the presidential election, these pamphlets had been widely circulated.

Above all, Louis Napoleon believed that the government should represent the people and that it should try hard to help them economically. But how were these tasks to be done? Parliaments and political parties were not the answer, according to Louis Napoleon. French politicians represented special-interest groups, particularly middle-class ones. When they ran a parliamentary government, they stirred up class hatred because they were not interested in helping the poor. The answer was a strong, even authoritarian, national leader, like the first Napoleon, who would serve all the people, rich and poor. This leader would be linked to the people by direct democracy, his sovereignty uncorrupted by politicians and legislative bodies. These political ideas went hand in hand with Louis Napoleon's vision of national unity and social progress. Rather than doing nothing or providing only temporary relief for the awful poverty of the poor, the state and its leader had a sacred duty to provide jobs and stimulate the economy. All classes would benefit by such action.

Louis Napoleon's political and social ideas were at least vaguely understood by large numbers of French peasants and workers in December 1848. To many common people he appeared to be a strong man *and* a forward-looking champion of their interests, and that is why they voted for him.

Elected to a four-year term, President Louis Napoleon at first shared power with a conservative National Assembly. But in 1851, after the Assembly failed to change the constitution so he could run for a second term, Louis Napoleon began to organize a conspiracy with key army officers. On December 2, 1851, he illegally dismissed the Assembly and seized power in a coup d'état. Armed resistance in Paris and widespread insurrection in the countryside in southern France were quickly crushed by the army. Louis Napoleon called on the French, as his uncle had done, to legalize his actions. They did: 92 percent voted to make him a strong president for ten years. A year later, 97 percent agreed in a national plebiscite to make him hereditary emperor; for the third time, and by the greatest margin yet, the authoritarian Louis Napoleon was overwhelmingly elected to lead France.

Louis Napoleon—now proclaimed Emperor Napoleon III—experienced both success and failure between 1852 and 1870. His greatest success was with the economy, particularly in the 1850s. His government encouraged the new investment banks and massive railroad construction that were at the heart of the Industrial Revolution in Europe. The government also fostered general economic expansion through an ambitious program of public works, which included the rebuilding of Paris to improve the urban environment. The profits of business people soared with prosperity, and unemployment declined greatly.

Louis Napoleon always hoped that economic progress would reduce social and political tensions. This hope was at least partially realized. Until the mid-1860s, there was considerable support for his government from France's most dissatisfied group, the urban workers. In the 1860s, Napoleon III granted workers the right to form unions and the right to strike—important economic rights denied by earlier governments.

At first, political power remained in the hands of the emperor. He alone chose his ministers, and they had great freedom of action. At the same time, Napoleon III restricted but did not abolish the Assembly. Members were elected by universal male suffrage every six years, and Louis Napoleon and his government took the parliamentary elections very seriously. They tried to entice notable people, even those who had opposed the regime, to stand as government candidates in order to expand the government's base of support. Moreover, the government used its officials and appointed mayors to spread the word that the election of the government's candidates—and the defeat of the opposition—were the key to roads, schools, tax rebates, and a thousand other local concerns.

In 1857 and again in 1863, Louis Napoleon's system worked brilliantly and produced overwhelming electoral victories. Yet in the 1860s, Napoleon III's electoral system gradually disintegrated. France's problems in Italy and the rising power of Prussia led to increasing criticism at home from his Catholic and nationalist supporters. With growing effectiveness, the middle-class liberals who had always wanted a less authoritarian regime continued to denounce his rule.

Napoleon was always sensitive to the public mood. Public opinion, he once said, always wins the last victory. Thus in the 1860s, he progressively liberalized his empire. He gave the Assembly greater powers and the opposition candidates greater freedom, which they used to good advantage. In 1869 the opposition, consisting of republicans, monarchists, and liberals, polled almost 45 percent of the vote.

The next year, a sick and weary Louis Napoleon again granted France a new constitution, which combined a basically parliamentary regime with a hereditary emperor as chief of state. In a final great plebiscite on the eve of a disastrous war with Prussia, 7.5 million Frenchmen voted in favor of the new constitution, and only 1.5 million opposed it. Napoleon III's attempt to reconcile a strong national state with universal male suffrage was still evolving and was doing so in a democratic direction.

Cavour, Garibaldi, and the Unification of Italy

Italy had never been a united nation prior to 1860. Part of Rome's great empire in ancient times, the Italian peninsula was divided in the Middle Ages into competing city-states, and it became a battleground for great powers after 1494. Italy was reor-

ganized in 1815 at the Congress of Vienna. The rich northern provinces of Lombardy and Venetia were taken by Metternich's Austria. Sardinia and Piedmont were under the rule of an Italian monarch, and Tuscany, with its famous capital of Florence, shared north-central Italy with several smaller states. Central Italy and Rome were ruled by the papacy. Naples and Sicily were ruled by a branch of the Bourbons. Metternich was not wrong in dismissing Italy as "a geographical expression" (Map 25.3).

Between 1815 and 1848, the goal of a unified Italian nation captured the imaginations of increasing numbers of Italians. There were three basic approaches. The first was the radical program of the idealistic patriot Giuseppe Mazzini, who preached a centralized democratic republic based on universal suffrage and the will of the people (see pages 840–841). The second was that of Vincenzo Gioberti, a Catholic priest who called for a federation of existing states under the presidency of a progressive pope. The third was the program of those who looked for leadership toward the autocratic kingdom of Sardinia-Piedmont, much as many Germans looked toward Prussia.

The third alternative was strengthened by the failures of 1848, when an Austrian army smashed Italian revolutionaries in Austria's possessions in northern Italy and discredited Mazzini's republicanism. Almost by accident, independent Sardinia's monarch, Victor Emmanuel, retained the moderate liberal constitution granted under duress in March 1848. To the Italian middle classes, Sardinia appeared to be a liberal, progressive state ideally suited to achieve the goal of national unification. By contrast, Mazzini's brand of democratic republicanism seemed quixotic and too radical. As for the papacy, the initial cautious support by Pope Pius IX (r. 1846–1878) for unification had given way to fear and hostility after he was temporarily driven from Rome during the upheavals of 1848. For a long generation, the papacy would stand resolutely opposed not only to national unification but also to most modern trends. In 1864 in the *Syllabus of Errors,* Pius IX strongly denounced rationalism, socialism, separation of church and state, and religious liberty, denying that "the Roman pontiff can and ought to reconcile and align himself with progress, liberalism, and modern civilization."

Sardinia had the good fortune of being led by a brilliant statesman, Count Camillo Benso di

MAP 25.3 Unification of Italy, 1859–1870   The leadership of Sardinia-Piedmont and nationalist fervor were decisive factors in the unification of Italy.

Cavour, the dominant figure in the Sardinian government from 1850 until his death in 1861. Indicative of the coming tacit alliance between the aristocracy and the solid middle class under the banner of the strong nation-state, Cavour came

from a noble family and embraced the economic doctrines and business activities associated with the prosperous middle class. Before entering politics, he made a substantial fortune in sugar mills, steamships, banks, and railroads. Cavour's national goals were limited and realistic. Until 1859 he sought unity only for the states of northern and perhaps central Italy in a greatly expanded kingdom of Sardinia. He did not seek to incorporate the Papal States or the kingdom of the Two Sicilies, with their very different cultures and governments, into an Italy of all the Italians.

In the 1850s, Cavour worked to consolidate Sardinia as a liberal constitutional state capable of leading northern Italy. His program of highways and railroads, of civil liberties and opposition to clerical privilege, increased support for Sardinia throughout northern Italy. Yet Cavour realized that Sardinia could not drive Austria out of Lom-

bardy and Venetia and unify northern Italy under Victor Emmanuel without the help of a powerful ally. Accordingly, he worked for a secret diplomatic alliance with Napoleon III against Austria. Finally, in July 1858 he succeeded and goaded Austria into attacking Sardinia. Napoleon III came to Sardinia's defense. Then after the victory of the combined Franco-Sardinian forces, Napoleon III did a complete about-face. Nauseated by the gore of war and criticized by French Catholics for supporting the pope's declared enemy, Napoleon III abandoned Cavour. He made a compromise peace with the Austrians in July 1859. Sardinia would receive only Lombardy, the area around Milan. The rest of the

 Garibaldi and Victor Emmanuel The historic meeting in Naples between the leader of Italy's revolutionary nationalists and the king of Sardinia sealed the unification of northern and southern Italy in a unitary state. With only the sleeve of his red shirt showing, Garibaldi offers his hand—and his conquests—to the uniformed king and his moderate monarchial government. *(Source: Fabio Lensini/Madeline Grimoldi)*

map of Italy would remain essentially unchanged. Cavour resigned in a rage.

Popular revolts and Italian nationalism salvaged Cavour's plans. While the war against Austria had raged in the north, dedicated nationalists in central Italy had risen and driven out their rulers. Nationalist fervor seized the urban masses, and the leaders of the nationalist movement called for fusion with Sardinia. This was not at all what France and the other Great Powers wanted, but the nationalists held firm and eventually had their way. Cavour returned to power in early 1860, and the people of central Italy voted overwhelmingly to join a greatly enlarged kingdom of Sardinia. Cavour had achieved his original goal of a north Italian state (see Map 25.3).

For superpatriots such as Giuseppe Garibaldi (1807–1882), the job of unification was still only half done. The son of a poor sailor, Garibaldi personified the romantic, revolutionary nationalism of Mazzini and 1848. Sentenced to death in 1834 for his part in an uprising in Genoa, Garibaldi escaped to South America. For twelve years, he led a guerrilla band in Uruguay's struggle for independence. Along the way, he found in a tough young woman, Anna da Silva, a mate and companion-in-arms. Their first children nearly starved in the jungle while Garibaldi, clad in his long red shirt, fashioned a revolutionary legend for himself. Returning to Italy to fight in 1848 and leading a corps of volunteers against Austria in 1859, Garibaldi emerged in 1860 as a powerful independent force in Italian politics.

Partly to use him and partly to get rid of him, Cavour secretly supported Garibaldi's bold plan to "liberate" the kingdom of the Two Sicilies. Landing on the shores of Sicily in May 1860, Garibaldi's guerrilla band of a thousand "Red Shirts" captured the imagination of the Sicilian peasantry. Outwitting the twenty-thousand-man royal army, the guerrilla leader took Palermo. Then he and his men crossed to the mainland, marched triumphantly toward Naples, and prepared to attack Rome and the pope. But the wily Cavour quickly sent Sardinian forces to occupy most of the Papal States (but not Rome) and to intercept Garibaldi.

Cavour realized that an attack on Rome would bring about war with France, and he also feared Garibaldi's popular appeal. Thus he immediately organized a plebiscite in the conquered territories.

Despite the urging of some more radical supporters, the patriotic Garibaldi did not oppose Cavour, and the people of the south voted to join Sardinia. When Garibaldi and Victor Emmanuel rode through Naples to cheering crowds, they symbolically sealed the union of north and south, of monarch and people.

Cavour had succeeded. He had controlled Garibaldi and had turned popular nationalism in a conservative direction. The new kingdom of Italy, which did not include Venice until 1866 or Rome until 1870, was a parliamentary monarchy under Victor Emmanuel, neither radical nor democratic. Only a small minority of Italian males had the right to vote. Despite political unity, the propertied classes and the common people were divided. A great and growing social and cultural gap separated the progressive, industrializing north from the stagnant, agrarian south.

Bismarck and German Unification

In the aftermath of 1848 the German states were locked in a political stalemate. After Austria and Russia had blocked Frederick William's attempt to unify Germany "from above," tension grew between Austria and Prussia as each power sought to block the other within the German Confederation. Stalemate and reaction also prevailed in the domestic politics of the individual German states in the 1850s.

At the same time, powerful economic forces were undermining the political status quo. Modern industry grew rapidly within the German customs union (*Zollverein*), founded officially in 1834 to stimulate trade and increase the revenues of member states. By the end of 1853 all the German states except Austria had joined the customs union, and a new Germany excluding Austria was becoming an economic reality. Prussia's leading role in the Zollverein gave it a valuable advantage in its struggle against Austria's supremacy in German political affairs.

The national uprising in Italy in 1859 made a profound impression in Prussia. Great political change and war—perhaps with Austria, perhaps with France—seemed quite possible. Along with his top military advisers, the tough-minded William I of Prussia (r. 1861–1888), who had replaced the unstable Frederick William IV as regent in

Otto von Bismarck   The commanding presence and the fierce pride of the Prussian statesman are evident in this photo taken shortly before he came to power. Dressed in formal diplomatic attire as Prussia's ambassador in Paris, Bismarck is perhaps on his way to see Emperor Louis Napoleon and size up his future adversary. *(Source: Archiv für Kunst und Geschichte, Berlin)*

parliament, not the king, had the ultimate political power. They also wanted to ensure that the army was responsible to Prussia's elected representatives and was not a "state within a state." These demands were popular. The parliament rejected the military budget in 1862, and the liberals triumphed completely. King William then called on Count Otto von Bismarck to head a new ministry and defy the parliament. This was a momentous choice.

The most important figure in German history between Luther and Hitler, Otto von Bismarck (1815–1898) has been the object of enormous interest and debate. A great hero to some, a great villain to others, Bismarck was above all a master of politics. Born into the Prussian landowning aristocracy, the young Bismarck was a wild and tempestuous student given to duels and drinking. Proud of his Junker heritage and always devoted to his Prussian sovereign, Bismarck had a strong personality and an unbounded desire for power. Yet in his drive to secure power for himself and for Prussia, Bismarck was extraordinarily flexible and pragmatic. "One must always have two irons in the fire," he once said. He kept his options open, pursuing one policy and then another as he moved with skill and cunning toward his goal.

Bismarck first honed his political skills as a diplomat. Acquiring a reputation as an ultraconservative in the Prussian Assembly in 1848, he fought against Austria as the Prussian ambassador to the German Confederation from 1851 to 1859. Transferred next to St. Petersburg and then to Paris, he worked to build up Prussia's strength and consolidate Prussia's precarious Great Power status.

When Bismarck took office as chief minister in 1862, his appointment made a strong but unfavorable impression. His speeches were a sensation and a scandal. Declaring that the government would rule without parliamentary consent, Bismarck lashed out at the middle-class opposition: "The great questions of the day will not be decided by speeches and resolutions—that was the blunder of 1848 and 1849—but by blood and iron." Denounced for this view that "might makes right," Bismarck had the Prussian bureaucracy go right on collecting taxes even though the parliament refused to approve the budget. Bismarck reorganized the army. And for four years, from 1862 to 1866, the voters of Prussia continued to express their opposition by sending large liberal majorities to the parliament.

1858 and become king himself in 1861, was convinced of the need for major army reforms and wanted to double the size of the regular army. Army reforms meant a bigger defense budget and higher taxes.

Prussia had emerged from 1848 with a parliament of sorts, the Prussian Assembly, which was in the hands of the liberal middle class by 1859. The wealthy middle class wanted society to be less, not more, militaristic. Above all, middle-class representatives wanted to establish once and for all that the

THE ERA OF NATION BUILDING IN EUROPE, 1850–1871

1851	Louis Napoleon dismisses French National Assembly in coup d'état
1852–1870	Second Empire in France
1853–1856	Crimean War
1859–1870	Unification of Italy
1861	Abolition of serfdom in Russia
1862–1890	Bismarck's reign of power in German affairs
1864–1871	First Socialist International
1866	Prussia wins decisive victory in Austro-Prussian War
1866–1871	Unification of the German Empire
1867	Magyar nobility increases its power by restoring the constitution of 1848 in Hungary, thereby further dividing the Austro-Hungarian Empire Marx, *Capital* Second Reform Bill passed by British Parliament
1870–1871	Prussia wins decisive victory in Franco-Prussian War; William I proclaimed emperor of a united Germany
1871	Paris Commune

Opposition at home spurred the search for success abroad. The ever-knotty question of Schleswig-Holstein provided a welcome opportunity. When the Danish king tried again, as in 1848, to bring the provinces into a centralized Danish state, Prussia joined Austria in a short and successful war against Denmark in 1864. However, Bismarck was convinced that Prussia had to control completely the northern, predominantly Protestant part of the German Confederation, which meant expelling Austria from German affairs. After the victory over Denmark, Bismarck's skillful maneuvering had Prussia in position to force Austria out by war, if necessary. Bismarck knew that a war with Austria would have to be a localized one that would not provoke a mighty alliance against Prussia. Russia was no problem because Bismarck had gained Alexander II's gratitude by supporting Russia's repression of a Polish uprising in 1863. Napoleon III—the "sphinx without a riddle," according to Bismarck—was charmed into neutrality with vague promises of more territory along the Rhine. Thus when Austria proved unwilling to give up its historic role in German affairs, Bismarck was in a position to engage in a war of his own making.

The Austro-Prussian War of 1866 lasted only seven weeks. Utilizing railroads to mass troops and the new breechloading needle gun to achieve maximum firepower, the reorganized Prussian army overran northern Germany and defeated Austria decisively at the Battle of Sadowa in Bohemia. Anticipating Prussia's future needs, Bismarck offered Austria realistic, even generous, peace terms. Austria paid no reparations and lost no territory to Prussia, although Venice was ceded to Italy. But the German Confederation was dissolved, and Austria agreed to withdraw from German affairs. The states north of the Main River were grouped in the new North German Confederation, led by an expanded Prussia. The mainly Catholic states of the south remained independent while forming alliances with Prussia. Bismarck's fundamental goal of Prussian expansion was being realized (Map 25.4).

Bismarck had long been convinced that the old order he so ardently defended should make peace,

MAP 25.4 Unification of Germany, 1866–1871   Prussian expansion, Austrian expulsion from the old German Confederation, and the creation of a new German Empire went hand in hand. Austria lost no territory, but Prussia's neighbors in the north suffered grievously or simply disappeared. The annexation of Alsace-Lorraine turned France into an enemy of Germany before 1914.

on its own conservative terms, with the liberal middle class and the nationalist movement. Moreover, Bismarck believed that because of the events of 1848, the German middle class could eventually be led to prefer the reality of national unity under conservative leadership to a long, uncertain battle for truly liberal institutions. Thus during the attack on Austria in 1866, he increasingly identified Prussia's fate with the "national development of Germany."

In the aftermath of victory, Bismarck fashioned a federal constitution for the new North German Confederation. Each state retained its own local government, but the king of Prussia became president of the Confederation and the chancellor—Bismarck—was responsible only to the president. The federal government—William I and Bismarck—controlled the army and foreign affairs. There was also a legislature consisting of two houses that shared equally in the making of laws. Delegates to the upper house were appointed by the different states, but members of the lower house were elected by universal, single category, male suffrage. With this radical innovation, Bismarck opened the door to popular participation and the possibility of going over the head of the middle class directly to the people, much as Napoleon III had done in France. All the while, however, ultimate power rested as securely as ever in the hands of Prussia and its king and army.

In Prussia itself Bismarck held out an olive branch to the parliamentary opposition. Marshaling all his diplomatic skill, he asked the parliament to pass a special indemnity bill to approve after the fact all of the government's spending between 1862 and 1866. Most of the liberals snatched at the chance to cooperate. For four long years, they had opposed and criticized Bismarck's "illegal" measures. Yet Bismarck, the king, and the army with its aristocratic leadership had in the end succeeded beyond the wildest dreams of the liberal middle class. In 1866 German unity was in sight, and the people were going to be allowed to participate actively in the new state.

Many liberals repented their "sins," and none more ardently than Hermann Baumgarten, a thoroughly decent history professor and member of the liberal opposition. In his essay "A Self-Criticism of German Liberalism," he confessed in 1866: "We thought by agitation we could transform Germany. . . . Yet we have experienced a mir-

acle almost without parallel. The victory of our principles would have brought us misery, whereas the defeat of our principles has brought boundless salvation."[5] The constitutional struggle was over. The German middle class was bowing respectfully before Bismarck and the monarchial authority and aristocratic superiority he represented.

The final act in the drama of German unification followed quickly. Bismarck realized that a patriotic war with France would drive the south German states into his arms. The French obligingly played their part. The apparent issue—whether a distant relative of Prussia's William I (and France's Napoleon III) might become king of Spain—was only a diplomatic pretext. By 1870 the French leaders of the Second Empire, alarmed by their powerful new neighbor on the Rhine, had decided on a war to teach Prussia a lesson.

As soon as war against France began in 1870, Bismarck had the wholehearted support of the south German states. With other governments standing still—Bismarck's generosity to Austria in 1866 was paying big dividends—German forces under Prussian leadership decisively defeated Louis Napoleon's armies at Sedan on September 1, 1870. Three days later, French patriots in Paris proclaimed yet another French republic (the third) and vowed to continue fighting. But after five months, in January 1871, a starving Paris surrendered, and France went on to accept Bismarck's harsh peace terms. By this time, the south German states had agreed to join a new German empire. The victorious William I was proclaimed emperor of Germany in the Hall of Mirrors in the palace of Versailles. Europe had a nineteenth-century German "sun king." As in the 1866 constitution, the king of Prussia and his ministers had ultimate power in the new German Empire, and the lower house of the legislature was elected by universal male suffrage.

The Franco-Prussian War, which Europeans generally saw as a test of nations in a pitiless Darwinian struggle for existence, released an enormous surge of patriotic feeling in Germany. Bismarck's genius, the invincible Prussian army, the solidarity of king and people in a unified nation—these and similar themes were trumpeted endlessly during and after the war. The weakest of the Great Powers in 1862 (after Austria, Britain, France, and Russia), Prussia had become the most powerful state in Europe in less than a decade. Most

Germans were enormously proud, blissfully imagining themselves the fittest and best of the European species. Semi-authoritarian nationalism and a "new conservatism," which was based on an alliance of the properted classes and sought the active support of the working classes, had triumphed in Germany.

Summary

In 1814 the victorious allied powers sought to restore peace and stability in Europe. Dealing moderately with France and wisely settling their own differences, the allies laid the foundations for beneficial international cooperation throughout much of the nineteenth century. Led by Metternich, the conservative powers also sought to prevent the spread of subversive ideas and radical changes in domestic politics. Yet European thought has seldom been more powerfully creative than after 1815, and ideologies of liberalism, nationalism, and socialism all developed to challenge the existing order. The romantic movement, breaking decisively with the dictates of classicism, reinforced the spirit of change and revolutionary anticipation.

All of these forces culminated in the liberal and nationalistic revolutions of 1848. Political, economic, and social pressures that had been building since 1815 exploded dramatically. Yet the failed upheavals of 1848 realized very few revolutionary goals. The moderate middle classes were unable to consolidate their initial victories. Instead, they drew back in fear when artisans, factory workers, and radical socialists rose up to present their own much more revolutionary demands.

This retreat facilitated a resurgence of conservative forces that crushed revolution all across Europe. These conservative forces then took the lead in refashioning politics after 1850, relying on strong rule that was fortified by popular nationalism at critical moments. Thus larger, more unified, and more popular states emerged in the West, and support for the nation appeared to provide the basis for a stabilizing response to the profoundly unsettling challenges of the dual revolution.

Notes

1. Quoted in H. Kohn, *Nationalism* (New York: Van Nostrand, 1955), pp. 141–142.

2. Quoted in F. D. Klingender, *Art and the Industrial Revolution* (St. Albans, Eng.: Paladin, 1972), p. 117.
3. M. Agulhon, *1848* (Paris: Éditions du Seuil, 1973), pp. 68–69.
4. Quoted in W. L. Langer, *Political and Social Upheaval, 1832–1852* (New York: Harper & Row, 1969), p. 361.
5. Quoted in H. Kohn, *The Mind of Germany: The Education of a Nation* (New York: Charles Scribner's Sons/Macmillan, 1960), p. 159.

Suggested Reading

All of the works cited in the Notes are highly recommended. Kohn has written perceptively on nationalism in many books, and Langer's book is a balanced synthesis with an excellent bibliography. Among general studies, C. Morazé, *The Triumph of the Middle Classes* (1968), a wide-ranging procapitalist interpretation, may be compared with E. J. Hobsbawm's flexible Marxism in *The Age of Revolution, 1789–1848* (1962). Two important reconsiderations of nationalism are B. Anderson, *Imagined Communities,* 2d ed. (1991), and E. Hobsbawm and T. Ranger, *The Invention of Tradition* (1990). E. Kedourie, *Nationalism* (1960), is an influential historical critique of the new faith. H. Kissinger, *A World Restored* (1957), offers not only a provocative interpretation of the Congress of Vienna but also insights into the mind of Richard Nixon's famous secretary of state. Compare that volume with H. Nicolson's entertaining *The Congress of Vienna* (1946). On 1848, P. Robertson, *Revolutions of 1848: A Social History* (1960), is outstanding, and I. Deak, *The Lawful Revolution: Louis Kossuth and the Hungarians, 1848–49* (1979), is a noteworthy study of an interesting figure.

On early socialism and Marxism, there are A. Lindemann's stimulating survey, *A History of European Socialism* (1983), and W. Sewell, Jr.'s *Work and Revolution in France: The Language of Labor from the Old Regime to 1848* (1980) as well as G. Lichtheim's high-powered *Marxism* (1961) and his *Short History of Socialism* (1970). J. Seigel, *Marx's Fate: The Shape of a Life* (1978), is an outstanding biography. Fourier is treated sympathetically in J. Beecher, *Charles Fourier* (1986). J. Schumpeter, *Capitalism, Socialism and Democracy* (1947), is important but challenging, a real mind-stretcher. Also highly recommended is B. Taylor, *Eve and the New Jerusalem: Socialism and Feminism in the Nineteenth Century* (1983), which explores fascinating English attempts to emancipate workers and women at the same time. On liberalism, there are R. Heilbroner's entertaining *The Worldly Philosophers* (1967) and G. de Ruggiero's classic *History of Euro-*

pean Liberalism (1959). J. Barzun, *Classic, Romantic and Modern* (1961), skillfully discusses the emergence of romanticism, and J. Seigel, *Bohemian Paris: Culture, Politics, and the Boundaries of Bourgeois Life* (1986), imaginatively places romantic aspirations in a broad cultural framework. R. Stromberg, *An Intellectual History of Modern Europe,* 3d ed. (1981), is a valuable survey. The important place of religion in nineteenth-century thought is considered from different perspectives in H. McLeod, *Religion and the People of Western Europe* (1981), and O. Chadwick, *The Secularization of the European Mind in the Nineteenth Century* (1976). Two good church histories with useful bibliographies are J. Altholz, *The Churches in the Nineteenth Century* (1967), and A. Vidler, *The Church in an Age of Revolution: 1789 to the Present Day* (1961).

For English history, A. Briggs's socially oriented *The Making of Modern England, 1784–1867* (1967) and D. Thomson's *England in the Nineteenth Century, 1815–1914* (1951), are excellent. Restoration France is sympathetically portrayed by G. de Bertier de Sauvigny in *The Bourbon Restoration* (1967), whereas R. Price, *A Social History of Nineteenth-Century France* (1987), is a fine synthesis incorporating recent research. D. Harvey, *Napoleon III and His Comic Empire* (1988), brings the world of Napoleon III vibrantly alive. Émile Zola's novel *The Debacle* treats the Franco-Prussian War realistically. D. M. Smith has written widely on Italy, and his *Garibaldi* (1956) and *Italy: A Modern History,* rev. ed. (1969), are recommended. Two stimulating general histories of Germany that skillfully incorporate recent research are H. James, *A German Identity, 1770–1990* (1989), and J. Sheehan, *Germany, 1770–1866* (1989), which may be compared with H. Treitschke's bombastic, pro-Prussian *History of Germany in the Nineteenth Century* (1915–1919), a classic of nationalistic history. O.

Pflanze, *Bismarck and the Development of Germany,* (1963), and E. Eyck, *Bismarck and the German Empire* (1964), are excellent biographies. H. Glasser, ed., *The German Mind in the Nineteenth Century* (1981), is an outstanding anthology, as are R. E. Joeres and M. Maynes, eds., *German Women in the Eighteenth and Nineteenth Centuries* (1986), and P. Mendes-Flohr, ed., *The Jew in the Modern World: A Documentary History* (1980). A. Sked, *The Decline and Fall of the Habsburg Empire, 1815–1918* (1989), and R. Kann, *The Multinational Empire,* 2 vols. (1950, 1964), probe the intricacies of the nationality problem in Austria-Hungary.

The thoughtful reader is strongly advised to delve into the rich writing of contemporaries. J. Bowditch and C. Ramsland, eds., *Voices of the Industrial Revolution* (1961), is an excellent starting point, with well-chosen selections from leading economic thinkers and early socialists. H. Hugo, ed., *The Romantic Reader,* is another fine anthology. Mary Shelley's *Frankenstein,* a great romantic novel, draws an almost lovable picture of the famous monster and is highly recommended. Jules Michelet's compassionate masterpiece *The People* is a famous historian's anguished examination of French social divisions on the eve of 1848. Alexis de Tocqueville covers some of the same ground less romantically in his *Recollections,* which may be compared with Karl Marx's white-hot "instant history," *Class Struggles in France, 1848–1850* (1850). Great novels that accurately portray aspects of the times are Victor Hugo, *Les Misérables,* an exciting story of crime and passion among France's poor; Honoré de Balzac, *La Cousine Bette* and *Le Père Goriot*; and Thomas Mann, *Buddenbrooks,* a wonderful historical novel that traces the rise and fall of a prosperous German family over three generations during the nineteenth century.

LISTENING TO THE
PAST

Faith in Democratic Nationalism

Early advocates of the national ideal usually believed that progress for one people would contribute to the progress of all humanity. They believed that a Europe of independent nation-states would provide the proper framework for securing freedom, democracy, social justice, and even international peace.

This optimistic faith guided Giuseppe Mazzini (1805–1872), the leading prophet of Italian nationalism and unification. Banished from Italy in 1830, the exiled Mazzini founded a secret society called Young Italy to fight for Italian unification and a democratic republic. Mazzini's group inspired numerous local insurrections and then led Italy's radicals in the unsuccessful revolutions of 1848. Italy was united a decade later, but by other means.

Mazzini's best known work was The Duties of Man, *a collection of essays. The following selection, entitled "Duties Towards Your Country," was written in 1858 and addressed to Italian working men.*

Your first Duties . . . are to Humanity. . . . But what can each of you, with his isolated powers, do for the moral improvement, for the progress of Humanity? . . .

God gave you the means of multiplying your forces and your powers of action indefinitely when he gave you a Country, when, like a wise overseer of labor, who distributes the different parts of the work according to the capacity of the workmen, he divided Humanity into distinct groups upon the face of our globe, and thus planted the seeds of nations. Evil governments have disfigured the design of God, which you may see clearly marked out, as far, at least, as regards Europe, by the courses of the great rivers, by the lines of the lofty mountains, and by other geographical conditions; they have disfigured it by conquest, by greed, by jealousy of the just sover-

eignty of others; disfigured it so much that today there is perhaps no nation except England and France whose confines correspond to this design.

[These evil governments] did not, and they do not, recognize any country except their own families and dynasties, the egoism of caste. But the divine design will infallibly be fulfilled. Natural divisions, the innate spontaneous tendencies of the peoples will replace the arbitrary divisions sanctioned by evil governments. The map of Europe will be remade. The Countries of the People will rise, defined by the voice of the free, upon the ruins of the Countries of Kings and privileged castes. Between these Countries there will be harmony and brotherhood. And then the work of Humanity for the general amelioration, for the discovery and application of the real law of life, carried on in association and distributed according to local capacities, will be accomplished by peaceful and progressive development.

Then each of you, strong in the affections and in the aid of many millions of men speaking the same language, endowed with the same tendencies, and educated by the same historic tradition, may hope by your personal effort to benefit the whole of Humanity.

Without Country you have neither name, voice, nor rights, no admission as brothers into the fellowship of the Peoples. You are the bastards of Humanity. Soldiers without a banner, . . . you will find neither faith nor protection. . . . Do not beguile yourselves with the hope of emancipation from unjust social conditions if you do not first conquer a Country for yourselves; where there is no Country there is no common agreement to which you can appeal; the egoism of self-interest rules alone, and he who has the upper hand keeps it, since there is no common safeguard for the interests of all. . . .

O my Brothers! love your Country. Our Country is our home, the home which God has given us, placing therein a numerous family which we love and are loved by. . . . In labouring according to true principles for our Country we are labouring for Humanity; our Country is the fulcrum of the lever which we have to wield for the common good. If we give up this fulcrum we run the risk of becoming useless to our Country and to Humanity. . . .

There is no true Country without a uniform law. There is no true Country where the uniformity of that law is violated by the existence of caste, privilege, and inequality, where the powers and faculties of a large number of individuals are suppressed or dormant, where there is no common principle accepted, recognized, and developed by all. In such a state of things there can be no Nation, no People, but only a multitude, a fortuitous agglomeration of men whom circumstances have brought together and different circumstances will separate. In the name of your love for your Country you must combat without truce the existence of every privilege, every inequality, upon the soil which has given you birth. . . .

Your Country should be your Temple. God at the summit, a People of equals at the base. Do not accept any other formula, any other moral law, if you do not want to dishonour your Country and yourselves. Let the secondary laws for the gradual regulation of your existence be the progressive application of this supreme law.

And in order that they should be so, it is necessary that *all* should contribute to the making of them. The laws made by one fraction of the citizens only can never by the nature of things and men do otherwise than reflect the thoughts and aspirations and desires of that fraction; they represent, not the whole country, but a third, a fourth part, a class, a zone of the country. The law must express the general aspiration, promote the good of all, respond to a beat of the nation's heart. The whole nation therefore should be, directly or indirectly, the legislator. By yielding this mission to a few men, you put the egoism of one class in the place of the Country, which is the union of *all* the classes.

A Country is not a mere territory; the particular territory is only its foundation. The Country is the idea which rises upon that

✦ Portrait of Giuseppe Mazzini *(Source: Museo del Risorgimento, Scala/Art Resource, NY)*

foundation; it is the sentiment of love, the sense of fellowship which binds together all the sons of that territory.

So long as a single one of your brothers is not represented by his own vote in the development of the national life—so long as a single one vegetates uneducated among the educated—so long as a single one able and willing to work languishes in poverty for want of work—you have not got a Country such as it ought to be, the Country of all and for all.

Votes, education, work are the three main pillars of the nation; do not rest until your hands have solidly erected them.

Questions for Analysis

1. What did Mazzini mean by "evil governments"? Why are they evil?

2. What are the characteristics of "the true country"?

3. What form of government is best? Why?

4. Why, according to Mazzini, should poor working men have been interested in the political unification of Italy?

5. How might a woman today criticize Mazzini's program? Debate how Mazzini might respond to such criticism.

Source: Slightly adapted from J. Mazzini, *The Duties of Man and Other Essays* (London: J. M. Dent and Sons, 1907), pp. 51–57.

CHAPTER

26

European Life in the
Age of Nationalism

A painting by Gustav Klimt (1862–1918) of the old Burgtheater in Vienna. *(Source: Museen der Stadt Wien)*

fter 1848, as identification with the nation-state was becoming one of the basic organizing principles of Western society, the growth of towns and cities rushed forward with undiminished force. In 1900 Western society was urban and industrial as surely as it had been rural and agrarian in 1800. This rapid urbanization, both a result of the Industrial Revolution and a key element in its enormous long-term impact, posed pressing practical problems that governments had to deal with. Eventual success with urban problems encouraged people to look to government as a problem solver and put their faith in a responsive national state. Even socialists forming international alliances were not exempt from the trend.

- How did life in cities change?
- What did the emergence of urban industrial society mean for rich and poor and those in between?
- How did families change as they coped with the developing urban civilization?
- What changes in science and culture reflected and influenced this new civilization?
- How did governments respond to problems and try to win the support of politically active citizens?

These are the questions this chapter will investigate.

❊ CITIES AND SOCIAL CLASSES

The growth of industry posed enormous challenges for all elements of Western society, from young factory workers confronting relentless discipline to aristocratic elites maneuvering to retain political power. As we saw in Chapter 23, the early consequences of economic transformation were mixed and far-reaching and by no means wholly negative. By 1850 at the latest, working conditions were improving and real wages were rising for the mass of the population, and they continued to do so until 1914. Given the poverty and uncertainty of preindustrial life, some historians maintain that the history of European industrialization in the nineteenth century is probably better written in terms of increasing opportunities than of greater

hardships. Critics of this relatively optimistic view of industrialization claim that it neglects the quality of life in urban areas, where poor people especially suffered from bad housing, lack of sanitation, and a sense of hopelessness. Did not these drawbacks more than cancel out higher wages and greater opportunity? An examination of cities in the nineteenth century provides some answers to this complex question.

Industry and the Growth of Cities

Since the Middle Ages, European cities had been centers of government, culture, and large-scale commerce. They had also been congested, dirty, and unhealthy. People were packed together almost as tightly as possible within the city limits. The typical city was a "walking city": for all but the wealthiest classes, walking was the only available form of transportation. Infectious disease spread with deadly speed in cities, and people were always more likely to die in the city than in the countryside.

Clearly, deplorable urban conditions did not originate with the Industrial Revolution. What the Industrial Revolution did was to reveal those conditions more nakedly than ever before. The steam engine freed industrialists from dependence on the energy of fast-flowing streams and rivers, so by 1800 there was every incentive to build new factories in urban areas. Cities had better shipping facilities than the countryside and thus better supplies of coal and raw materials. There were also many hands wanting work in the cities, for cities drew people like a magnet. Therefore, as industry grew, there was also a rapid expansion of already overcrowded and unhealthy cities.

The challenge of the urban environment was felt first and most acutely in Great Britain. The number of people living in cities of 20,000 or more in England and Wales jumped from 1.5 million in 1801 to 6.3 million in 1851 and reached 15.6 million in 1891. Such cities accounted for 17 percent of the total English population in 1801, 35 percent as early as 1851, and fully 54 percent in 1891. Other countries duplicated the English pattern as they industrialized. An American observer was hardly exaggerating when he wrote in 1899 that "the most remarkable social phenomenon of the present century is the concentration of population in cities" (Map 26.1).[1]

✳ **MAP 26.1 European Cities of 100,000 or More in 1800 and 1900** There were more large cities in Great Britain in 1900 than in all of Europe in 1800. Northwestern Europe was the most urbanized area.

In the 1820s and 1830s, people in Britain and France began to worry about the condition of their cities. With urban areas expanding at such previously undreamed-of rates, people's fatalistic acceptance of overcrowded, unsanitary urban living conditions began to give way to active concern.

On one point everyone could agree: except on the outskirts, each town or city was using every scrap of land to the fullest extent. Parks and open areas for exercise and recreation were almost nonexistent. Buildings were erected on the smallest possible lots in order to pack the maximum number of people into a given space. Narrow houses were built wall to wall in long rows. These row houses had neither front nor back yards, and only a narrow alley in back separated one row from the next. Or buildings were built around tiny courtyards completely enclosed on all four sides. Many people lived in extremely small, often overcrowded cellars or attics. "Six, eight, and even ten occupying one room is anything but uncommon," wrote a doctor from Aberdeen in Scotland for a government investigation in 1842.

These highly concentrated urban populations lived in extremely unsanitary and unhealthy conditions. Open drains and sewers flowed alongside or down the middle of unpaved streets. Toilet facilities were primitive in the extreme. In parts of Man-chester, as many as two hundred people shared a single outhouse. Such privies filled up rapidly, and sewage often overflowed and seeped into cellar dwellings. Moreover, some courtyards in the poorest neighborhoods became dunghills, collecting excrement that was sometimes sold as fertilizer. By the 1840s there was among the better-off classes a growing, shocking "realization that, to put it as mildly as possible, millions of English men, women, and children were living in shit."[2]

Who or what was responsible for these awful conditions? The crucial factors were the tremendous pressure of more people and the total absence of public transportation. People simply had to jam themselves together if they were to be able to walk to shops and factories. Another factor was that government, often uncertain how best to approach the problems, was slow to provide sanitary facilities and establish adequate building codes. Even many continental cities with strong traditions of municipal regulation were beset by overcrowded and unhealthy conditions. Also responsible was the sad legacy of rural housing conditions in preindustrial society. As one authority concludes, "the decent cottage was the exception, the hovel the rule."[3] Thus housing was far down on the newcomer's list of priorities, and ordinary people generally took dirt and dung for granted.

Public Health and the Bacterial Revolution

Although cleanliness was not next to godliness in most people's eyes, it was becoming so for some reformers. The most famous of these was Edwin Chadwick, one of the commissioners charged with the administration of relief to paupers under Britain's revised Poor Law of 1834. Chadwick was a good *Benthamite*—that is, a follower of radical philosopher Jeremy Bentham (1748–1832). Bentham had taught that public problems ought to be dealt with on a rational, scientific basis and according to the "greatest good for the greatest number." Applying these principles, Chadwick soon became convinced that disease and death actually caused poverty simply because a sick worker was an unemployed worker and orphaned children were poor children. Most important, Chadwick believed that disease could be prevented by cleaning up the urban environment. That was his "sanitary idea."

Building on a growing number of medical and sociological studies, Chadwick collected detailed reports from local Poor Law officials on the "sanitary conditions of the laboring population" and published his hard-hitting findings in 1842. This mass of widely publicized evidence proved that disease was related to filthy environmental conditions, which were in turn caused largely by lack of drainage, sewers, and garbage collection. Putrefying, smelly excrement was worse than just revolting. It polluted the atmosphere and caused disease.

Chadwick correctly believed that the stinking excrement of communal outhouses could be dependably carried off by water through sewers at less than one-twentieth the cost of removing it by hand. The cheap iron pipes and tile drains of the industrial age would provide running water and sewerage for all sections of town, not just the wealthy ones. In 1848, with the cause strengthened by the cholera epidemic of 1846, Chadwick's

 Filth and Disease This 1852 drawing from *Punch* tells volumes about the unhealthy living conditions of the urban poor. In the foreground, children play with a dead rat, and a woman scavenges a dungheap. Cheap rooming houses provide shelter for the frightfully overcrowded population. *(Source: The British Library)*

A COURT FOR KING CHOLERA.

report became the basis of Great Britain's first public health law, which created a national health board and gave cities broad authority to build modern sanitary systems.

The public health movement won dedicated supporters in the United States, France, and Germany from the 1840s on. Governments accepted at least limited responsibility for the health of all citizens, and their programs broke decisively with the age-old fatalism of urban populations in the face of shockingly high mortality. By the 1860s and 1870s European cities were making real progress toward adequate water supplies and sewerage systems, and city dwellers were beginning to reap the reward of better health.

Still, effective control of communicable disease required a great leap forward in medical knowledge and biological theory. Early reformers such as Chadwick were seriously handicapped by the prevailing *miasmatic theory* of disease—the belief that people contract disease when they breathe the bad

Louis Pasteur   Shown here working in his laboratory, Pasteur made fundamental discoveries in biology and chemistry. A symbol of scientific achievement, he was—and is—greatly revered by all classes in France. *(Source: Institut Pasteur)*

odors of decay and putrefying excrement—in short, the theory that smells cause disease. The miasmatic theory was a reasonable deduction from empirical observations: cleaning up filth did produce laudable results. Yet the theory was very incomplete. Keen observation by doctors and public health officials in the 1840s and 1850s pinpointed the role of bad drinking water in the transmission of disease and suggested that contagion was *spread through* filth and not caused by it, thus weakening the miasmatic idea.

The breakthrough was the development of the *germ theory* of disease by Louis Pasteur (1822–1895), a French chemist who began studying fermentation in 1854 at the request of brewers. Using his microscope to develop a simple test that brewers could use to monitor the fermentation process and avoid spoilage, Pasteur found that fermentation depended on the growth of living organisms and that the activity of these organisms could be suppressed by heating the beverage—by "pasteurizing" it. The breathtaking implication was that specific diseases were caused by specific living organisms—germs—and that those organisms could be controlled in people as well as in beer, wine, and milk.

By 1870 the work of Pasteur and others had demonstrated the general connection between germs and disease. When, in the middle of the 1870s, German country doctor Robert Koch and his coworkers developed pure cultures of harmful bacteria and described their life cycles, the dam broke. Over the next twenty years, researchers—mainly Germans—identified the organisms responsible for disease after disease. These discoveries led to the development of a number of effective vaccines.

Acceptance of the germ theory brought about dramatic improvements in the deadly environment of hospitals and surgery. In 1865 when Pasteur showed that the air was full of bacteria, English surgeon Joseph Lister (1827–1912) immediately grasped the connection between aerial bacteria and the problem of wound infection. He reasoned that a chemical disinfectant applied to a wound dressing would "destroy the life of the floating particles." Lister's "antiseptic principle" worked wonders. In the 1880s, German surgeons developed the more sophisticated practice of sterilizing not only the wound but also everything—hands, instruments, clothing—that entered the operating room.

The achievements of the bacterial revolution coupled with the ever-more-sophisticated public health movement saved millions of lives, particularly after about 1890. Mortality rates began to decline dramatically in European countries (Figure 26.1) as the awful death sentences of the past—diphtheria, typhoid, typhus, cholera, yellow fever—became vanishing diseases. City dwellers benefited especially from these developments. By 1910 a great silent revolution had occurred: the death rates for people of all ages in urban areas were generally no greater than in rural areas, and sometimes they were less.

Urban Planning and Public Transportation

More effective urban planning also improved the quality of urban life. Urban planning was in decline by the early nineteenth century, but after 1850 its practice was revived and extended. France took the lead during the rule of Napoleon III (r. 1848–1870), who sought to stand above class conflict and believed that rebuilding much of Paris would provide employment, improve living conditions, and glorify his empire. In the baron Georges Haussmann (1809–1884), an aggressive, impatient Alsatian whom he placed in charge of Paris, Napoleon III found an authoritarian planner capable of bulldozing both buildings and opposition. In twenty years Paris was transformed (Map 26.2).

The Paris of 1850 was a labyrinth of narrow, dark streets, the results of desperate overcrowding. Terrible slum conditions and extremely high death rates were facts of life. There were few open spaces and only two public parks for the entire metropolis of 1 million. Public transportation played a very small role in this enormous walking city.

Haussmann and his fellow planners proceeded on many interrelated fronts. With a bold energy that often shocked their contemporaries, they razed old buildings in order to cut broad, straight, tree-lined boulevards through the center of the city as well as in new quarters on the outskirts. These boulevards, designed in part to prevent the easy construction and defense of barricades by revolutionary crowds, permitted traffic to flow freely and also afforded impressive vistas. Their creation also demolished some of the worst slums. New streets stimulated the construction of better housing, especially for the middle classes. Small neighborhood parks and open spaces were created

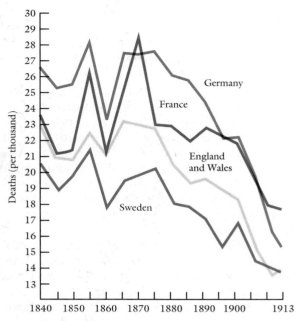

FIGURE 26.1 **The Decline of Death Rates in England and Wales, Germany, France, and Sweden, 1840–1913**   A rising standard of living, improvements in public health, and better medical knowledge all contributed to the dramatic decline of death rates in the nineteenth century.

throughout the city, and two very large parks suitable for all kinds of holiday activities were developed—one on the wealthy west side and one on the poor east side of the city. The city also improved its sewers and doubled the supply of good fresh water.

Rebuilding Paris provided a new model for urban planning and stimulated modern urbanism throughout Europe, particularly after 1870. In city after city, public authorities mounted a coordinated attack on many of the interrelated problems of the urban environment. As in Paris, improvements in public health through better water supply and waste disposal often went hand in hand with new boulevard construction, as did office buildings, town halls, theaters, opera houses, and museums. New boulevards also radiated out toward the outskirts, easing movement and encouraging urban expansion (see Map 26.2).

The development of mass public transportation was also of great importance in the improvement of urban living conditions. In the 1870s, many European cities authorized private companies to operate horse-drawn streetcars, which had been

❋ **MAP 26.2 Modernization of Paris, ca 1850–1870** Broad boulevards, large parks, and grandiose train stations transformed Paris. The cutting of the new north-south axis—known as the Boulevard Saint-Michel—was one of Haussmann's most controversial projects. It razed much of Paris's medieval core and filled the Île de la Cité with massive government buildings.

developed in the United States. Then in the 1890s the real revolution occurred: European countries adopted another American transit innovation, the electric streetcar.

Electric streetcars were cheaper, faster, more dependable, and more comfortable than their horse-drawn counterparts. Service improved dramatically. Millions of Europeans—workers, shoppers, school-children—hopped on board during the workweek. And on weekends and holidays, streetcars carried millions on happy outings to parks and the countryside, racetracks and music halls. In 1886 the horse-drawn streetcars of Austria-Hungary, France, Germany, and Great Britain were carrying about 900 million riders. By 1910 electric streetcars in the four countries were carrying 6.7 billion riders.[4] Each person was using public transportation four times as often in 1910 as in 1886.

Good mass transit helped greatly in the struggle for decent housing. The new boulevards and horse-drawn streetcars had facilitated a middle-class move to better housing in the 1860s and 1870s; similarly, after 1890 electric streetcars gave people of modest means access to new, improved housing. The still-crowded city was able to expand and become less congested. In England in 1901, only 9 percent of the urban population was "over-crowded" in terms of the official definition of more than two persons per room. On the European continent, many city governments in the early twentieth century were building electric streetcar systems that provided transportation for the working classes to new public and private housing developments in outlying areas of the city. Poor, overcrowded housing, long one of the blackest blots on the urban landscape, was in retreat—another example of the gradual taming of the urban environment.

Urbanization and Social Structure

With general improvements in health and in the urban environment, the almost-completed journey to an urban industrialized world was bringing beneficial consequences for all kinds of people. The first great change was a substantial and undeniable increase in the standard of living for the average person. The real wages of British workers, for example, which had already risen by 1850, almost doubled between 1850 and 1906. Similar increases occurred in continental European countries as industrial development quickened after 1850. Ordinary people took a major step forward in the centuries-old battle against poverty, reinforcing efforts to improve many aspects of human existence.

There is another side to the income coin, however. Greater economic rewards for the average person did *not* eliminate hardship and poverty, nor did they make the wealth and income of the rich and the poor significantly more equal. In almost every advanced country around 1900, the richest 20 percent of households received anywhere from 50 to 60 percent of all national income, and the bottom 30 percent of households received 10 percent or less of all income (Figure 26.2). The middle classes, which were smaller than they are today, accounted for less than 20 percent of the population; thus the statistics show that the upper and middle classes alone received more than 50 percent of all income. The poorest 80 percent—the working classes, including peasants and agricultural laborers—received less altogether than the two richest classes. Moreover, income taxes on the wealthy were light or nonexistent. Thus the gap between rich and poor remained enormous. It was probably almost as great in 1900 as it had been in the age of agriculture and aristocracy before the Industrial Revolution.

The great gap between rich and poor endured, in part, because industrial and urban development

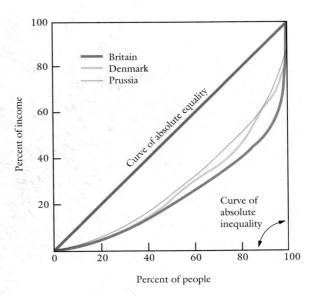

DISTRIBUTION OF INCOME

Country	Richest 5%	Richest 10%	Richest 20%	Poorest 60%
Britain	43%		59%	
Denmark	30	39%	55	31%
Prussia	30		50	33

 FIGURE 26.2 The Distribution of Income in Britain, Denmark, and Prussia in 1913 The Lorenz curve is useful for showing the degree of economic inequality in a given society. The closer the actual distribution of income lies to the (theoretical) curve of absolute equality, where each 20 percent of the population receives 20 percent of all income, the more nearly equal are incomes. European society was very far from any such equality before the First World War. Notice that incomes in Prussia were somewhat more equal than those in Britain. (*Source: Based on information from S. Kuznets,* Modern Economic Growth, *Yale University Press, New Haven, 1966, pp. 208–209. Copyright © 1966 by Yale University Press. Used with permission.*)

Apartment Living in Paris As this drawing shows, different social classes lived close together in European cities about 1850. A middle-class family lives on the first (American second) floor, and the economic condition of the tenants declines at each higher floor. Residents of the garret live in abject poverty. *(Source: Bibliothèque Nationale, Paris)*

made society more diverse and less unified. By no means did society split into two sharply defined opposing classes, as Marx had predicted. Instead, economic specialization created more new social groups than it destroyed. There developed an almost unlimited range of jobs, skills, and earnings; one group or subclass shaded off into another in a complex, confusing hierarchy. The tiny elite of the very rich and the sizable mass of the dreadfully poor were separated from each other by a range of subclasses, each filled with individuals struggling to rise or at least to hold their own in the social order. In this atmosphere of competition and hierarchy, neither the middle classes nor the working classes acted as a unified force. This social and occupational hierarchy developed enormous variations, but the age-old pattern of great economic inequality remained firmly intact.

The Middle Classes

By the beginning of the twentieth century, the diversity and range within the urban middle class were striking. Indeed, it is more meaningful to think of a confederation of middle classes loosely united by occupations requiring primarily mental, rather than physical, skill. At the top stood the upper middle class, composed mainly of the most successful business families from banking, industry, and large-scale commerce. These families were the prime beneficiaries of modern industry and scientific progress. As people in the upper middle class gained in income and progressively lost all traces of radicalism after the trauma of 1848, they were almost irresistibly drawn toward the aristocratic lifestyle. And although the genuine hereditary aristocracy constituted only a tiny minority in every European country, it retained imposing wealth, unrivaled social prestige, and substantial political influence. This was especially true in central and eastern Europe, where the monarch—the highest-ranking noble of them all—continued to hold great political power.

As the aristocracy had long divided the year between palatial country estates and lavish townhouses during "the season," so the upper middle class purchased country places or built beach houses for weekend and summer use. The number of servants was an important indicator of wealth and standing for the middle class, as it had always been for the aristocracy. Private coaches and carriages, ever expensive items in the city, were also

signs of rising social status. More generally, the rich businessman and certainly his son devoted less time to business and more to "culture" and easy living than was the case in less wealthy or well-established commercial families.

The topmost reaches of the upper middle class tended to shade off into the old aristocracy to form a new upper class of at most 5 percent of the population. Much of the aristocracy welcomed this development. Having experienced a sharp decline in its relative income in the course of industrialization, the landed aristocracy had met big business coming up the staircase and was often delighted to trade titles, country homes, and snobbish elegance for good hard cash. Some of the best bargains were made through marriages to American heiresses. Correspondingly, wealthy aristocrats tended increasingly to exploit their agricultural and mineral resources as if they were business people. Bismarck was not the only proud nobleman to make a fortune distilling brandy on his estates.

Below the wealthy upper middle class were much larger, much less wealthy, and increasingly diversified middle-class groups. Here one found the moderately successful industrialists and merchants as well as professionals in law and medicine. This was the middle middle class, solid and quite comfortable but lacking great wealth. Below it were independent shopkeepers, small traders, and tiny manufacturers—the lower middle class. Both of these traditional elements of the middle class expanded modestly in size with economic development.

Meanwhile, the traditional middle class was gaining two particularly important additions. The expansion of industry and technology created a growing demand for experts with specialized knowledge. The most valuable of the specialties became solid middle-class professions. Engineering, for example, emerged from the world of skilled labor as a full-fledged profession of great importance, considerable prestige, and many branches. Architects, chemists, accountants, and surveyors, to name only a few, first achieved professional standing in this period. They established criteria for advanced training and certification and banded together in organizations to promote and defend their interests.

Management of large public and private institutions also emerged as a kind of profession as governments provided more services and as very large corporations such as railroads came into being.

Government officials and many private executives were not capitalists in the sense that they owned business enterprises. But public and private managers had specialized knowledge and good salaries. And they shared most of the values of the business-owning entrepreneurs and the older professionals.

Industrialization and urbanization also expanded and diversified the lower middle class. The number of shopkeepers and small business people grew, and so did the number of white-collar employees—a mixed group of traveling salesmen, bookkeepers, store managers, and clerks who staffed the offices and branch stores of large corporations. White-collar employees were propertyless and often earned no more than the better-paid workers. Yet white-collar workers were fiercely committed to the middle class and to the ideal of moving up in society. In the Balkans, for example, clerks let their fingernails grow very long to distinguish themselves from people who worked with their hands. The tie, the suit, and soft, clean hands were no-less-subtle marks of class distinction than wages.

Relatively well educated but without complex technical skills, many white-collar groups aimed at achieving professional standing and the accompanying middle-class status. Elementary school teachers largely succeeded in this effort. From being miserably paid part-time workers in the early nineteenth century, teachers rode the wave of mass education to respectable middle-class status and income.

In spite of growing occupational diversity and conflicting interests, the middle classes were loosely united by a certain style of life. Food was the largest item in the household budget, for middle-class people liked to eat very well. In France and Italy, the middle classes' love of good eating meant that even in large cities, activity ground almost to a halt between half past twelve and half past two on weekdays as husbands and school-children returned home for the midday meal. The European middle classes consumed meat in abundance, and a well-off family might spend 10 percent of its substantial earnings on meat and fully 25 percent of its income on food and drink.

Spending on food was also great because the dinner party was this class's favored social occasion. A wealthy family might give a lavish party for eight to twelve almost every week, whereas more modest households would settle for once a month. Throughout middle-class Europe, such dinners were served in the "French manner": eight or nine separate courses, from appetizers at the beginning to coffee and liqueurs at the end. An ordinary family meal normally consisted of only four courses—soup, fish, meat, and dessert.

The middle-class wife could cope with this endless procession of meals, courses, and dishes because she had both servants and money at her disposal. Indeed, the employment of at least one enormously helpful full-time maid to cook and clean was the best single sign that a family had crossed the cultural divide separating the working classes from what some contemporary observers called the "servant-keeping classes." The greater a family's income, the greater the number of servants it employed. A really prosperous English family in 1900 might employ a hierarchy of ten servants: a manservant, a cook, a kitchen maid, two housemaids, a serving maid, a governess, a gardener, a coachman, and a stable boy. Food and servants together absorbed about 50 percent of income at all levels of the middle classes.

Well fed and well served, the middle classes were also well housed by 1900. Many quite prosperous families rented, rather than owned, their homes. Apartment living, complete with tiny rooms for servants under the eaves of the top floor, was commonplace, and wealthy investors and speculative builders found good profits in middle-class housing. By 1900 the middle classes were also quite clothes conscious. The factory, the sewing machine, and the department store had all helped reduce the cost and expand the variety of clothing. Middle-class women were particularly attentive to the fickle dictates of fashion.

Education was another growing expense, as middle-class parents tried to provide their children with ever-more-crucial advanced education. The keystones of culture and leisure were books, music, and travel. The long realistic novel, the heroics of composers Wagner and Verdi, the diligent striving of the dutiful daughter at the piano, and the packaged tour to a foreign country were all sources of middle-class pleasure.

Finally, the middle classes were loosely united by a shared code of expected behavior and morality. This code was strict and demanding. It laid great stress on hard work, self-discipline, and personal achievement. Men and women who fell into crime or poverty were generally assumed to be responsible for their own circumstances. Traditional Christian morality was reaffirmed by this code and was

Chabas: A Corner of the Table (1904) In this oil painting French academic artist Paul-Émile Chabas (1867–1937) skillfully idealizes the elegance and intimacy of a sumptuous dinner party with photographic precision. *(Source: Bibliothèque des Arts Décoratifs/Jean-Loup Charmet)*

preached tirelessly by middle-class people. Drinking and gambling were denounced as vices; sexual purity and fidelity were celebrated as virtues. In short, the middle-class person was supposed to know right from wrong and was expected to act accordingly.

The Working Classes

About four out of five people belonged to the working classes at the turn of the century. Many members of the working classes—that is, people whose livelihoods depended on physical labor and who did not employ domestic servants—were still small landowning peasants and hired farm hands. This was especially true in eastern Europe. In western and central Europe, however, the typical

worker had left the land. In Great Britain, less than 8 percent of the people worked in agriculture, and in rapidly industrializing Germany only 25 percent were employed in agriculture and forestry. Even in less industrialized France, less than 50 percent of the people depended on the land in 1900.

The urban working classes were even less unified and homogeneous than the middle classes. In the first place, economic development and increased specialization expanded the traditional range of working-class skills, earnings, and experiences. Meanwhile, the old sharp distinction between highly skilled artisans and unskilled manual workers gradually broke down. To be sure, highly skilled printers and masons as well as unskilled dockworkers and common laborers continued to exist. But between these extremes there appeared ever-more semiskilled groups, many of which were

FIGURE 26.3 The Urban Social Hierarchy

composed of factory workers and machine tenders (Figure 26.3).

In the second place, skilled, semiskilled, and unskilled workers developed widely divergent lifestyles and cultural values, and their differences contributed to a keen sense of social status and hierarchy within the working classes. The result was great variety and limited class unity.

Highly skilled workers, who made up about 15 percent of the working classes, became a real "labor aristocracy." These workers earned only about two-thirds of the income of the bottom ranks of the servant-keeping classes, but that was fully twice as much as the earnings of unskilled workers. The most "aristocratic" of the highly skilled workers were construction bosses and factory foremen, men who had often risen from the ranks and were fiercely proud of their achievement. The labor aristocracy also included members of the traditional highly skilled handicraft trades that had not been mechanized or placed in factories, like cabinetmakers, jewelers, and printers. This group as a whole was under constant long-term pressure. Irregularly but inexorably, factory methods were being extended to more crafts, and many skilled artisans were being replaced by lower-paid semiskilled factory workers. In the later nineteenth century, traditional woodcarvers and watchmakers virtually disappeared, for example, as the making of furniture and timepieces was put into the factory.

At the same time, the labor aristocracy was consistently being enlarged by new kinds of skilled workers such as shipbuilders and railway locomotive engineers. Thus the labor elite remained in a state of flux as individuals and whole crafts moved in and out of it.

To maintain this precarious standing, the upper working class adopted distinctive values and straitlaced, almost puritanical behavior. Like the middle classes, the labor aristocracy was strongly committed to the family and to economic improvement. Families in the upper working class saved money regularly, worried about their children's education, and valued good housing. Yet skilled workers viewed themselves primarily not as aspirants to the middle class but as the pacesetters and natural leaders of all the working classes. Well aware of the degradation not so far below them, they practiced self-discipline and generally frowned on heavy drinking and sexual permissiveness.

Men and women of the labor aristocracy were quick to find fault with those below them who failed to meet their standards. In 1868 William Lovett, an English labor aristocrat if ever there was one, denounced "this ignorant recklessness and improvidence that produce the swarms of half-starved, neglected, and ignorant children we see in all directions; who mostly grow up to become the burdens and often the pests of society, which the industrious and frugal have to support."[5] Finally, many members of the labor aristocracy had definite political and philosophical beliefs, whether Christian or socialist or both. Such beliefs further strengthened the firm moral code of the upper working class.

Below the labor aristocracy stood semiskilled and unskilled urban workers. The enormous complexity of this sector of the world of labor is not easily summarized. Workers in the established crafts—carpenters, bricklayers, pipefitters—stood near the top of the semiskilled hierarchy, often flirting with (or sliding back from) the labor elite. A large number of the semiskilled were factory workers who earned highly variable but relatively good wages and whose relative importance in the labor force was increasing.

Below the semiskilled workers was a larger group of unskilled workers that included day laborers such as longshoremen, wagon-driving teamsters, teenagers, and every kind of "helper." Many of these people had real skills and performed valuable services, but they were unorganized and divided, united only by the common fate of meager earnings. The same lack of unity characterized street vendors and market people—self-employed workers who competed savagely with each other and with the established shopkeepers of the lower middle class.

One of the largest components of the unskilled group was domestic servants, whose numbers grew steadily in the nineteenth century. In advanced Great Britain, for example, one out of every seven employed persons was a domestic servant in 1911. The great majority were women; indeed, one out of every three girls in Britain between the ages of fifteen and twenty was a domestic servant. Throughout Europe and America, a great many female domestics in the cities were recent migrants from rural areas. As in earlier times, domestic service was still hard work at low pay with limited personal independence. For the full-time general maid in a lower-middle-class family, there was an unending routine of baby-sitting, shopping, cooking, and cleaning. In the great households, the girl was at the bottom of a rigid hierarchy of status-conscious butlers and housekeepers.

Nonetheless, domestic service had real attractions for "rough country girls" with strong hands and few specialized skills. Marriage prospects were better, or at least more varied, in the city. And though wages were low, they were higher and more regular than in hard agricultural work. Finally, as one London observer noted, young girls and other migrants were drawn to the city by

the contagion of numbers, the sense of something going on, the theaters and the music halls, the brightly lighted streets and busy crowds—all, in short, that makes the difference between the Mile End fair on a Saturday night, and a dark and muddy country lane, with no glimmer of gas and with nothing to do.[6]

Many young domestics from the countryside made a successful transition to working-class wife and mother. Yet with an unskilled or unemployed husband and a growing family, such a woman often had to join the broad ranks of working women in the "sweated industries." These industries flowered after 1850 and resembled the old putting-out and cottage industries of earlier times. The women

A School for Servants   Although domestic service was poorly paid, there was always plenty of competition for the available jobs. Schools sprang up to teach young women the manners and the household skills that employers in the servant-keeping classes demanded. *(Source: Greater London Council Photograph Library)*

normally worked at home, paid by the piece and not by the hour. They and their young daughters, for whom organization and collective action were virtually impossible, earned pitiful wages and lacked any job security.

Some women did hand-decorating of every conceivable kind of object; the majority, however, made clothing, especially after the advent of the foot-powered sewing machine. By 1900 only a few highly skilled male tailors lingered on in high-priced "tailor-made" shops. An army of poor women accounted for the bulk of the inexpensive "ready-made" clothes displayed on department store racks and in tiny shops.

Notwithstanding the rise and fall of groups and individuals, the urban working classes sought fun and recreation, and they found both. Across the face of Europe, drinking remained unquestionably the favorite leisure-time activity of working people. For many middle-class moralists as well as moralizing historians since, love of drink has been a curse of the modern age—a sign of social dislocation and popular suffering. Certainly, drinking was deadly serious business. One English slum dweller recalled that "drunkenness was by far the commonest cause of dispute and misery in working class homes. On account of it one saw many a decent family drift down through poverty into total want."[7]

Generally, however, heavy "problem" drinking declined in the late nineteenth century as it became less and less socially acceptable. This decline reflected in part the moral leadership of the upper working class. At the same time, drinking became more public and social. Cafés and pubs became increasingly bright, friendly places. Working-class political activities, both moderate and radical, were also concentrated in taverns and pubs. Moreover, social drinking in public places by married couples and sweethearts became an accepted and widespread practice for the first time. This greater participation by women undoubtedly helped civilize the world of drink and hard liquor.

The two other leisure-time passions of the working classes were sports and music halls. A great decline in "cruel sports," such as bullbaiting and cockfighting, had occurred throughout Europe by the late nineteenth century. Their place was filled by modern spectator sports, of which racing and soccer were the most popular. There was a great deal of gambling on sports events, and for many a working person a desire to decipher racing forms

provided a powerful incentive toward literacy. Music halls and vaudeville theaters, the working-class counterparts of middle-class opera and classical theater, were enormously popular throughout Europe. In 1900 there were more than fifty such halls and theaters in London alone. Music hall audiences were thoroughly mixed, which may account for the fact that drunkenness, sexual intercourse and pregnancy before marriage, marital difficulties, and problems with mothers-in-law were favorite themes of broad jokes and bittersweet songs.

Did religion and Christian churches continue to provide working people with solace and meaning? Although many historians see the early nineteenth century as an age of religious revival, historians also recognize that in the late nineteenth century a considerable decline in both church attendance and church donations was occurring in most European countries. And it seems clear that this decline was greater for the urban working classes than for their rural counterparts or for the middle classes. Yet most working-class families still baptized their children and considered themselves Christians.

Although more research is necessary, it appears that the urban working classes in Europe did become more secular and less religious in the late nineteenth and early twentieth centuries. They rarely repudiated the Christian religion, but it tended to play a diminishing role in their daily lives. Part of the reason for this change was that the construction of churches failed to keep up with the rapid growth of urban population, especially in new working-class neighborhoods. Thus in the vibrant, materialistic urban environment, popular religious impulses were poorly served.

Equally important, however, was the fact that throughout the nineteenth century both Catholic and Protestant churches were normally seen as they saw themselves—as conservative institutions defending social order and custom. Therefore, as the European working classes became more politically conscious, they tended to see the established (or quasi-established) "territorial church" as the defender of what they wished to change and as the ally of their political opponents. Especially the men of the urban working classes developed vaguely antichurch attitudes, even though they remained neutral or positive toward religion. They tended to regard regular church attendance as "not our kind of thing"—not part of urban working-class culture.

Renoir: Le Moulin de la Galette à Montmartre   In this 1876 masterpiece impressionist painter Auguste Renoir (1841–1919) has transformed a popular outdoor dance hall enjoyed by the Parisian masses into an enchanted fairyland. Renoir was a joyous artist, and his work optimistically affirmed the beauty and value of modern life. *(Source: Musée d'Orsay © Photo R.M.N)*

The pattern was different in the United States. There, most churches also preached social conservatism in the nineteenth century. But church and state had always been separate, and there was always a host of competing denominations and even different religions. So working people in the United States identified churches much less with the political and social status quo and more often with an ethnic group, and churches thrived, in part, as an assertion of ethnic identity. This same process occurred in Europe if the church or synagogue had never been linked to the state and served as a focus for ethnic cohesion. Irish Catholic churches in Protestant Britain and Jewish synagogues in Russia were outstanding examples.

THE CHANGING FAMILY

Urban life wrought many fundamental changes in the family. Although much is still unknown, it seems clear that in the second half of the nineteenth century the family had stabilized considerably after the disruption of the late eighteenth and early nineteenth centuries. The home became more important for both men and women. The role of women and attitudes toward children underwent substantial change, and the concept of adolescence as a distinct stage of life emerged. These are but a few of the transformations that affected all social classes in varying degrees.

Premarital Sex and Marriage

By 1850 the preindustrial pattern of lengthy courtship and mercenary marriage was pretty well dead among the working classes. In its place, the ideal of romantic love had triumphed. Couples were ever-more likely to come from different, even distant, towns and to be more nearly the same age, as romantic sentiment replaced tradition and financial considerations.

Economic considerations in marriage remained more important to the middle classes after 1850. In France dowries and elaborate legal marriage contracts were common practice among the middle classes in the later nineteenth century, and marriage was for many families one of life's most crucial financial transactions. A popular author advised young Frenchmen that "marriage is in general a means of increasing one's credit and one's fortune and of insuring one's success in the world."[8] This preoccupation with money led many middle-class men in France and elsewhere to marry late, after they had become established economically, and to choose women considerably younger and less sexually experienced than themselves. These differences between husband and wife became a source of tension in many middle-class marriages.

A young woman of the middle class found her romantic life carefully supervised by her well-meaning mother, who schemed for a proper marriage and guarded her daughter's virginity like the family's credit. After marriage, middle-class morality sternly demanded fidelity.

Middle-class boys were watched too, but not as vigilantly. By the time they reached late adolescence, they had usually attained considerable sexual experience with maids or prostitutes. With marriage a distant, uncertain possibility, it was all too easy for the young man of the middle classes to turn to the urban underworld of prostitution and sexual exploitation to satisfy his desires.

In the early nineteenth century among the working classes, sexual experimentation before marriage also triumphed, as did illegitimacy. By the 1840s, as many as one birth in three was occurring outside of wedlock in many large cities. In the second half of the century, however, the rising rate of illegitimacy was reversed: more babies were born to married mothers. Some have argued that this shift reflected the growth of puritanism and a lessening of sexual permissiveness among the unmarried. This explanation, however, is unconvincing.

The percentage of brides who were pregnant continued to be high and showed little or no tendency to decline after 1850. In many parts of urban Europe around 1900, as many as one woman in three was going to the altar an expectant mother. Moreover, unmarried people almost certainly used the cheap condoms and diaphragms the industrial age had made available to prevent pregnancy, at least in predominately Protestant countries. Unmarried young people were probably engaging in just as much sexual activity as their parents and grandparents who had created the illegitimacy explosion of 1750 to 1850. But in the later nineteenth century, pregnancy for a young single woman led increasingly to marriage and the establishment of a two-parent household. This important development reflected the growing respectability of the working classes as well as their gradual economic improvement. Skipping out was less acceptable, and marriage was less of an economic challenge. Thus the urban working-class couple became more stable, and that stability strengthened the family as an institution.

Prostitution

In Paris alone, 155,000 women were registered as prostitutes between 1871 and 1903, and 750,000 others were suspected of prostitution in the same years. Men of all classes visited prostitutes, but the middle and upper classes supplied much of the motivating cash. Although many middle-class men abided by the publicly professed code of stern puritanical morality, others indulged their appetites for prostitutes and sexual promiscuity.

My Secret Life, the anonymous eleven-volume autobiography of an English sexual adventurer from the servant-keeping classes, provides a remarkable picture of such a man. Beginning at an early age with a maid, the author becomes progressively obsessed with sex and devotes his life to living his sexual fantasies. In almost every one of his innumerable encounters all across Europe, this man of wealth simply buys his pleasure. Usually meetings are arranged in a businesslike manner: regular and part-time prostitutes quote their prices; working-class girls are corrupted by hot meals and baths.

At one point, he offers a young girl a sixpence for a kiss and gets it. Learning that the pretty, unskilled working girl earns nine pence a day, he offers her the equivalent of a week's salary for a few moments of fondling. When she finally agrees, he savagely exults that "*her* want was my opportunity." Later he offers more money for more gratification, and when she refuses, he tries unsuccessfully to rape her in a hackney cab. On another occasion he takes a farm worker by force: "Her tears ran down. If I had not committed a rape, it looked uncommonly like one." He then forces his victim to take money to prevent a threatened lawsuit, while the foreman advises the girl to keep quiet and realize that "you be in luck if he likes you."[9]

Obviously atypical in its excesses, *My Secret Life,* in its encyclopedic thoroughness, does reveal the dark side of sex and class in urban society. Frequently thinking of their wives largely in terms of money, family, and social position, the men of the comfortable classes often purchased sex and even affection from poor girls both before and after marriage. Moreover, the great continuing differences between rich and poor made for every kind of debauchery and sexual exploitation, including the brisk trade in poor virgins that the author of *My Secret Life* particularly relishes. Brutal sexist behavior was part of life—a part the sternly moral women (and men) of the upper working class detested and tried to shield their daughters from. For many poor young women, prostitution, like domestic service, was a stage of life and not a permanent employment. Having chosen it for two or three years in their twenties, they went on to marry (or live with) men of their own class and establish homes and families.

Sex Roles and Family Life

Industrialization and the growth of modern cities brought great changes to the lives of European women. These changes were particularly consequential for married women, and most women did marry in the nineteenth century.

After 1850 the work of most wives continued to become increasingly distinct and separate from that of their husbands (see pages 796–798). Husbands became wage earners in factories and offices; wives tended to stay home and manage households and care for children. As economic conditions improved, only married women in poor families tended more and more to work outside the home. One old English worker recalled that "the boy wanted to get into a position that would enable him to keep a wife and family, as it was considered

a thoroughly unsatisfactory state of affairs if the wife had to work to help maintain the home."[10] The ideal became a strict division of labor by sex: the wife as mother and homemaker, the husband as wage earner.

This rigid division of labor meant that married women faced great injustice if they tried to move into the man's world of employment outside the home. Husbands were unsympathetic or hostile. Well-paying jobs were off-limits to women, and a woman's wage was almost always less than a man's, even for the same work. Moreover, married women were subordinated to their husbands by law and lacked many basic legal rights. In France, for example, the Napoleonic Code enshrined the principle of female subordination and gave the wife few legal rights regarding property, divorce, and custody of the children.

With middle-class women suffering, sometimes severely, from a lack of legal rights and with all women facing discrimination in education and employment, there is little wonder that some women rebelled and began the long-continuing fight for equality of the sexes and the rights of women. Their struggle proceeded on two main fronts. First, following in the steps of women such as Mary Wollstonecraft (see page 752), organizations founded by middle-class feminists campaigned for equal legal rights for women as well as access to higher education and professional employment. In the later nineteenth century, these organizations scored some significant victories, such as the 1882 law giving English married women full property rights. In the years before 1914, middle-class feminists increasingly shifted their attention to securing the right to vote for women.

Women inspired by utopian and especially Marxian socialism blazed a second path. Often scorning the programs of middle-class feminists, socialist women leaders argued that the liberation of (working-class) women would come only with the liberation of the entire working class through revolution. In the meantime, they championed the cause of working women and won some practical improvements, especially in Germany, where the socialist movement was most effectively organized. In a general way, these different approaches to women's issues reflected the diversity of classes in urban society.

If the ideology and practice of rigidly separate roles undoubtedly narrowed women's horizons and caused some women to rebel, there was a brighter side to the same coin. As home and children became the typical wife's main concerns in the later nineteenth century, her control and influence there apparently became increasingly strong throughout Europe. Among the English working classes, it was the wife who generally determined how the family's money was spent. In many families the husband gave all his earnings to his wife to manage, whatever the law might read. She returned to him only a small allowance for carfare, beer, tobacco, and union dues. All the major domestic decisions, from the children's schooling and religious instruction to the selection of new furniture or a new apartment, were hers. In France women had even greater power in their assigned domain. One English feminist noted in 1908 that "though legally women occupy a much inferior status than men [in France], in practice they constitute the superior sex. They are the power behind the throne."[11]

Women ruled at home partly because running the urban household was a complicated, demanding, and valuable task. Twice-a-day food shopping, penny-pinching, economizing, and the growing crusade against dirt—not to mention child rearing—were a full-time occupation. Nor were there

any laborsaving appliances to help. Working yet another job for wages outside the home had limited appeal for most married women unless such earnings were essential for family survival. Many married women in the working classes did make a monetary contribution to family income by taking in boarders or doing piecework at home in the sweated industries (see page 855).

The woman's guidance of the household went hand in hand with the increased emotional importance of home and family. The home she ran was idealized as a warm shelter in a hard and impersonal urban world. For a child of the English slums in the early 1900s, home, however poor, was the focus of all love and interests, a sure fortress against a hostile world. Songs about its beauties were ever on people's lips. "Home, Sweet Home," first heard in the 1870s, had become "almost a second national anthem." Wall hangings like "HOME IS THE NEST WHERE ALL IS BEST" attested to domestic joys.[12] By 1900 home and family were what life was all about for millions of people of all classes.

Married couples also developed stronger emotional ties to each other. Even in the comfortable classes, marriages in the late nineteenth century

A Working-Class Home, 1875 Emotional ties within ordinary families grew stronger in the nineteenth century. Parents gave their children more love and better care. *(Source: Illustrated London News, LXVI, 1875. Photo courtesy of Boston Public Library)*

were increasingly based on sentiment and sexual attraction as money and financial calculation gradually declined in importance. Affection and eroticism became more central to the couple after marriage. Gustave Droz, whose bestseller *Mr., Mrs., and Baby* went through 121 editions between 1866 and 1884, saw love within marriage as the key to human happiness. He urged women to follow their hearts and marry a man of nearly their own age:

A husband who is stately and a little bald is all right, but a young husband who loves you and who drinks out of your glass without ceremony, is better. Let him, if he ruffles your dress a little and places a kiss on your neck as he passes. Let him, if he undresses you after the ball, laughing like a fool. You have fine spiritual qualities, it is true, but your little body is not bad either and when one loves, one loves completely. Behind these follies lies happiness.[13]

Many French marriage manuals of the late 1800s stressed that women had legitimate sexual needs, such as the "right to orgasm." The rise of public socializing by couples in cafés and music halls as well as franker affection within the family suggests a more erotic, pleasurable intimate life for women throughout Western society. This, too, helped make the woman's role as mother and homemaker acceptable and even satisfying.

Child Rearing

One of the most striking signs of deepening emotional ties within the family was the growing love and concern that mothers gave their tiny infants. This was a sharp break with the past. Although it may seem hard to believe today, the typical mother in preindustrial Western society was frequently indifferent toward her baby. This indifference—an unwillingness to make real sacrifices for the welfare of the infant—was beginning to give way among the comfortable classes by the end of the eighteenth century, but the ordinary mother of modest means adopted new attitudes only as the nineteenth century progressed. The baby became more important, and women became better mothers.

Mothers increasingly breast-fed their infants, for example, rather than paying wet nurses to do so. Breast-feeding involved sacrifice—a temporary loss of freedom, if nothing else. Yet in an age when there was no good alternative to mother's milk, it saved lives. The surge of maternal feeling also gave rise to a wave of specialized books on child rearing and infant hygiene. Swaddling disappeared completely, as ordinary mothers allowed their babies freedom of movement and delighted in their spontaneity.

The loving care lavished on infants was matched by greater concern for older children and adolescents. They, too, were wrapped in the strong emotional ties of a more intimate and protective family. For one thing, European women began to limit the number of children they bore in order to care adequately for those they had. By the end of the century the birthrate was declining across Europe, and it continued to do so until after World War II (Figure 26.4). The Englishwoman who married in the 1860s, for example, had an average of about

FIGURE 26.4 The Decline of Birthrates in England and Wales, France, Germany, and Sweden, 1840–1913 Women had fewer babies for a variety of reasons, including the fact that their children were increasingly less likely to die before reaching adulthood. Compare with Figure 26.1.

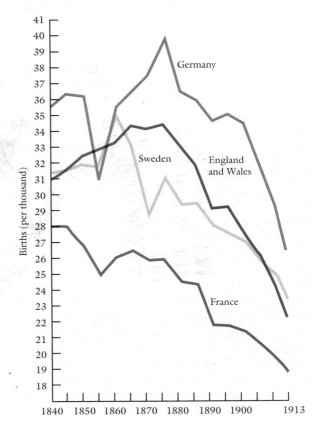

six children; her daughter marrying in the 1890s had only four; and her granddaughter marrying in the 1920s had only two or possibly three.

The most important reason for this revolutionary reduction in family size, in which the comfortable and well-educated classes took the lead, was parents' desire to improve their economic and social position and that of their children by having fewer youngsters. Thus the growing tendency of couples in the late nineteenth century to use a variety of contraceptive methods—rhythm, withdrawal, and mechanical devices—certainly reflected increased concern for children. Indeed, many parents, especially in the middle classes, probably became *too* concerned about their children, unwittingly subjecting them to an emotional pressure cooker of almost unbearable intensity. The result was that many children and especially adolescents came to feel trapped and in desperate need of greater independence.

Prevailing biological and medical theories led parents to believe in the possibility that their own emotional characteristics were passed on to their offspring and that they were thus directly responsible for any abnormality in a child. The rigid determinism of such views left little scope for the child's individual development. Another area of excessive parental concern was the sexual behavior of the child. Masturbation was viewed with horror, for it represented an act of independence and even defiance. Diet, clothing, games, and sleeping were carefully regulated. Girls were discouraged from riding horses and bicycling because rhythmic friction simulated masturbation. Boys were dressed in trousers with shallow and widely separated pockets. Between 1850 and 1880, there were surgical operations for children who persisted in masturbating. These and less blatant attempts to repress the child's sexuality were a source of unhealthy tension, often made worse by the rigid division of sexual roles within the family.

Sigmund Freud (1856–1939), the Viennese founder of psychoanalysis, formulated the most striking analysis of the explosive dynamics of the family, particularly the middle-class family in the late nineteenth century. A physician by training, Freud began his career treating mentally ill patients. He noted that the hysteria of his patients appeared to originate in bitter early childhood experiences wherein the child had been obliged to repress strong feelings. When these painful experiences were recalled and reproduced under hypno-

sis or through the patient's free association of ideas, the patient could be brought to understand his or her unhappiness and eventually deal with it.

One of Freud's most influential ideas concerned the Oedipal tensions resulting from the son's instinctive competition with the father for the mother's love and affection. More generally, Freud postulated that much of human behavior is motivated by unconscious emotional needs whose nature and origins are kept from conscious awareness by various mental devices he called "defense mechanisms." Freud concluded that much unconscious psychological energy is sexual energy, which is repressed and precariously controlled by rational thinking and moral rules. If Freud exaggerated the sexual and familial roots of adult behavior, that exaggeration was itself a reflection of the tremendous emotional intensity of family life in the late nineteenth century.

The working classes probably had more avenues of escape from such tensions than did the middle classes. Unlike their middle-class counterparts, who remained economically dependent on their families until a long education was finished or a proper marriage secured, working-class boys and girls went to work when they reached adolescence. Earning wages on their own, they could bargain with their parents for greater independence within the household by the time they were sixteen or seventeen. If they were unsuccessful, they could and did leave home to live cheaply as paying lodgers in other working-class homes. Thus the young person from the working classes broke away from the family more easily when emotional ties became oppressive. In the twentieth century, middle-class youths would follow this lead.

❖ SCIENCE AND CULTURE

Major changes in Western thought and culture accompanied the emergence of urban society. Two aspects of these complex developments stand out as especially significant. Scientific knowledge expanded rapidly and came to influence the Western world-view even more profoundly than it had since the scientific revolution and the early Enlightenment. And between about the 1840s and the 1890s, European literature underwent a shift from soaring romanticism to tough-minded realism.

The Triumph of Science

The intellectual achievements of the scientific revolution had resulted in few practical benefits, and theoretical knowledge had also played a relatively small role in the Industrial Revolution in England. But breakthroughs in industrial technology enormously stimulated basic scientific inquiry, as researchers sought to explain theoretically how such things as steam engines and blast furnaces actually worked. The result was an explosive growth of fundamental scientific discoveries from the 1830s onward, which were increasingly transformed into material improvements for the general population.

A perfect example of the translation of better scientific knowledge into practical human benefits was the work of Pasteur and his followers in biology and the medical sciences. Another was the development of the branch of physics known as *thermodynamics.* Building on Isaac Newton's laws of mechanics and on studies of steam engines, thermodynamics investigated the relationship between heat and mechanical energy. By midcentury, physicists had formulated the fundamental laws of thermodynamics, which were then applied to mechanical engineering, chemical processes, and many other fields.

Chemistry and electricity were two other fields characterized by extremely rapid scientific progress. Chemists devised ways of measuring the atomic weight of different elements, and in 1869 the Russian chemist Dmitri Mendeleev (1834–1907) codified the rules of chemistry in the periodic law and the periodic table. Chemistry was subdivided into many specialized branches, such as *organic chemistry*—the study of the compounds of carbon. Applying theoretical insights gleaned from this new field, researchers in large German chemical companies discovered ways of transforming the dirty, useless coal tar that accumulated in coke ovens into beautiful, expensive synthetic dyes for the world of fashion. The basic discoveries of Michael Faraday (1791–1867) on electromagnetism in the 1830s and 1840s resulted in the first dynamo (generator) and opened the way for the subsequent development of electric motors, electric lights, and electric streetcars. The rapid development of the electrical and organic chemical industries spurred European economic growth between 1880 and 1913.

The triumph of science and technology had at least three significant consequences. First, though ordinary citizens continued to lack detailed scientific knowledge, everyday experience and innumerable popularizers impressed the importance of science on the popular mind.

Second, as science became more prominent in popular thinking, the philosophical implications of science formulated in the Enlightenment spread to broad sections of the population. Natural processes appeared to be determined by rigid laws, leaving little room for either divine intervention or human will. Yet scientific and technical advances had also fed the Enlightenment's optimistic faith in human progress.

Third, the methods of science acquired unrivaled prestige after 1850. For many, the union of careful experiment and abstract theory was the only reliable route to truth and objective reality. Thus many thinkers tried to apply the objective methods of science to the study of society from the 1830s onward.

The new "social scientists" had access to the massive sets of numerical data that governments had begun to collect on everything from children to crime, from population to prostitution. In response, social scientists developed new statistical methods to analyze these facts "scientifically" and supposedly to test their theories. Leading nineteenth-century social scientists resembled the eighteenth-century philosophes, but their systems were more all-encompassing and dogmatic. Marx was a prime example (see pages 814–815).

Another extremely influential system builder was French philosopher Auguste Comte (1798–1857). Initially a disciple of the utopian socialist Saint-Simon (see page 813), Comte wrote the six-volume *System of Positive Philosophy* (1830–1842), which came into its own after 1850. Comte postulated that all intellectual activity progresses through predictable stages:

The great fundamental law . . . is this:—that each of our leading conceptions—each branch of our knowledge—passes successively through three different theoretical conditions: the Theological, or fictitious; the Metaphysical, or abstract; and the Scientific, or positive. . . . The first is the necessary point of departure of human understanding, and the third is the fixed and definitive state. The second is merely a transition.[14]

By way of example, Comte noted that the prevailing explanation of cosmic patterns had shifted, as knowledge of astronomy developed, from the will of God (the theological) to the will of an orderly nature (the metaphysical) to the rule of unchanging laws (the scientific). Later, this same intellectual progression took place in increasingly complex fields—physics, chemistry, and, finally, the study of society. By applying the scientific or *positivist* method, Comte believed, his new discipline of sociology would soon discover the eternal laws of human relations, which would enable expert social scientists to impose a disciplined harmony and well-being on less enlightened citizens.

Comte's stages of knowledge exemplify the nineteenth-century fascination with the idea of evolution and dynamic development. Thinkers in many fields, such as the romantic historians and "scientific" Marxists, shared and applied this basic

concept. In geology, Charles Lyell (1797–1875) effectively discredited the long-standing view that the earth's surface had been formed by short-lived cataclysms, such as biblical floods and earthquakes. Instead, according to Lyell's principle of uniformitarianism, the same geological processes that are at work today slowly formed the earth's surface over an immensely long time. CONTINENTAL DRIFT!!

The most influential of all nineteenth-century evolutionary thinkers was Charles Darwin (1809–1882). As the official naturalist on a five-year scientific cruise to Latin America and the South Pacific beginning in 1831, Darwin carefully collected specimens of the different animal species he encountered on the voyage. Back in England, from fossil evidence, Darwin came to doubt the general belief in a special divine creation of each species of animals. Instead, he concluded, all life had gradually evolved from a common ancestral origin in an unending "struggle for survival." After long hesitation, Darwin published his research, which immediately attracted wide attention.

Darwin's theory is summarized in the title of his work *On the Origin of Species by the Means of Natural Selection* (1859). Darwin argued that chance differences among the members of a given species help some survive while others die. Thus the variations that prove useful in the struggle for survival are selected naturally and spread gradually to the entire species through reproduction.

As the capstone of already widespread evolutionary thinking, Darwin's theory had a powerful and many-sided influence on European thought and the European middle classes. Darwin was hailed as the great scientist par excellence, the "Newton of biology," who had revealed once again the powers of objective science. Darwin's findings also reinforced the teachings of secularists such as Comte and Marx, who scornfully dismissed religious belief in favor of agnostic or atheistic materialism. In the great cities especially, religion was on the defensive. Finally, many writers applied the theory of biological evolution to human affairs. Herbert Spencer (1820–1903), an English disciple of Auguste Comte, saw the human race as driven forward to ever-greater specialization and progress by the brutal economic struggle that efficiently determined the "survival of the fittest." The poor were the ill-fated weak; the prosperous, the chosen strong. Understandably, Spencer and other Social Darwinists were especially popular with the upper middle class.

Attracting Females   Darwin theorized that those males who were most attractive to females would have the most offspring, like this type of monkey, which had developed ornamental hair, giving him devastating sex appeal. Darwin used this illustration in *The Descent of Man* (1871). *(Source: Library of Congress)*

Realism in Literature

In 1868 Émile Zola (1840–1902), the giant of the realist movement in literature, defended his violently criticized first novel against charges of pornography and corruption of morals. Such accusations were meaningless, Zola claimed: he was only a purely objective scientist using

the modern method, the universal instrument of inquiry of which this age makes such ardent use to open up the future. . . . I chose characters completely dominated by their nerves and their blood, deprived of free-will, pushed to each action of their lives by the fatality of their flesh. . . . I have simply done on living bodies the work of analysis which surgeons perform on corpses.[15]

Zola's literary manifesto articulated the key themes of realism, which had emerged in the 1840s and continued to dominate Western culture and style until the 1890s. Realist writers believed that literature should depict life exactly as it was. Forsaking poetry for prose and the personal, emotional viewpoint of the romantics for strict, scientific objectivity, the realists simply observed and recorded—content to let the facts speak for themselves.

The major realist writers focused their extraordinary powers of observation on contemporary everyday life. Emphatically rejecting the romantic search for the exotic and the sublime, they energetically pursued the typical and the commonplace. Beginning with a dissection of the middle classes, from which most of them sprang, many realists eventually focused on the working classes, especially the urban working classes, which had been neglected in imaginative literature before this time. The realists put a microscope to many unexplored and taboo subjects—sex, strikes, violence, alcoholism—and hastened to report that slums and factories teemed with savage behavior. Many shocked middle-class critics denounced realism as ugly sensationalism wrapped provocatively in pseudoscientific declarations and crude language.

The realists' claims of objectivity did not prevent the elaboration of a definite world-view. Unlike the romantics, who had gloried in individual freedom and an unlimited universe, realists such as Zola were strict determinists. Human beings, like atoms, were components of the physical world, and all human actions were caused by unalterable natural laws. Heredity and environment determined human behavior; good and evil were merely social conventions.

The realist movement began in France, where romanticism had never been completely dominant, and three of its greatest practitioners—Balzac, Flaubert, and Zola—were French. Honoré de Balzac (1799–1850) spent thirty years writing a vastly ambitious panorama of postrevolutionary French life. Known collectively as *The Human Comedy,* this series of nearly one hundred books vividly portrays more than two thousand characters from virtually all sectors of French society. Balzac pictures urban society as grasping, amoral, and brutal, characterized by a Darwinian struggle for wealth and power.

Madame Bovary (1857), the masterpiece of Gustave Flaubert (1821–1880), strove for depth and accuracy of psychological insight. Unsuccessfully prosecuted as an outrage against public morality and religion, Flaubert's carefully crafted novel tells the ordinary story of a frustrated middle-class housewife who has an adulterous love affair and is betrayed by her lover. Without moralizing, Flaubert portrays the provincial middle class as petty, smug, and hypocritical.

Zola was most famous for his seamy, animalistic view of working-class life. But he also wrote gripping, carefully researched stories featuring the stock exchange, the big department store, and the army as well as urban slums and bloody coal strikes. Like many later realists, Zola sympathized with socialism, a sympathy evident in his overpowering *Germinal* (1885).

Realism quickly spread beyond France. In England, Mary Ann Evans (1819–1880), who wrote under the pen name George Eliot, brilliantly achieved a more deeply felt, less sensational kind of realism. "It is the habit of my imagination," George Eliot wrote, "to strive after as full a vision of the medium in which a character moves" as of the character itself. Her great novel *Middlemarch: A Study of Provincial Life* examines the ways in which people are shaped by their social medium as well as their own inner strivings, conflicts, and moral choices. Thomas Hardy (1840–1928) was more in the Zola tradition. His novels, such as *Tess of the D'Urbervilles* and *Return of the Native,* depict men and women frustrated and crushed by fate and bad luck.

The greatest Russian realist, Count Leo Tolstoy (1828–1910), combined realism in description and character development with an atypical moralizing, which came to dominate his later work. Tolstoy's greatest work was *War and Peace,* a monumental novel set against the historical background of Napoleon's invasion of Russia in 1812. Tolstoy went to great pains to develop his fatalistic theory of history, which regards free will as an illusion and the achievements of even the greatest leaders as only the channeling of historical necessity. Yet Tolstoy's central message was one that most of the people discussed in this chapter would have readily accepted: human love, trust, and everyday family ties are life's enduring values.

THE RESPONSIVE NATIONAL STATE (1871–1914)

After 1871 the heartland of Europe was organized into strong national states, and the common themes within that framework were the emergence of mass politics and growing mass loyalty toward the national state. On the borders of Europe—in Ireland and Russia, in Austria-Hungary and the Balkans—the dynamics were different. Subject peoples there were still striving for political unity and independence. National aspirations created tensions, and mass politics often undermined existing states.

There were good reasons why ordinary people—the masses of an industrializing, urbanizing society—felt increasing loyalty to their governments in central and western Europe. More people could vote. By 1914 universal male suffrage had become the rule rather than the exception. This development had as much psychological as political significance. Ordinary men were no longer denied the right to vote because they lacked wealth or education. They felt that they were becoming "part of the system."

Women also began to demand the right to vote. The women's suffrage movement achieved its first success in the western United States, and by 1913 women could vote in twelve states. Europe, too, moved slowly in this direction. In 1914 Norway gave the vote to most women. Elsewhere, women such as the English Emmeline Pankhurst were militant in their demands. They heckled politicians and held public demonstrations. These efforts generally failed before 1914, but they prepared the way for the triumph of the women's suffrage movement in many countries immediately after World War I.

As the right to vote spread, politicians and parties in national parliaments represented the people more responsively. The multiparty system prevailing in most countries meant that parliamentary majorities were built on shifting coalitions, which gave parties leverage to obtain benefits for their supporters. Governments also passed laws to alleviate general problems, thereby acquiring greater legitimacy and appearing more worthy of support.

Less positively, governments found that they could manipulate national feeling to create a sense of unity and to divert attention away from underlying class conflicts. For example, in Germany conservative and moderate leaders who despised socialism found that workers who voted socialist would still rally around the flag in a diplomatic crisis or that they would cheer enthusiastically when distant territory of doubtful value was seized in Africa or Asia (see Chapter 27). In Austria-Hungary and Russia conflicting ethnic groups would also close ranks when faced with a foreign foe. Therefore, governing elites frequently channeled national sentiment in an antiliberal and militaristic direction after 1871. This policy helped manage domestic conflicts, but only at the expense of increasing the international tensions that erupted in 1914 in cataclysmic war and revolution (see Chapter 29).

The German Empire

Politics in Germany after 1871 reflected many of the general developments. The new German Empire was a federal union of Prussia and twenty-four smaller states. Much of the everyday business of government was conducted by the separate states, but there was a strong national government with a chancellor—until 1890, Bismarck—and a popularly elected parliament, called the *Reichstag.* Although Bismarck refused to be bound by a parliamentary majority, he tried nonetheless to maintain one. This situation gave the political parties opportunities. Until 1878 Bismarck relied mainly on the National Liberals, who had rallied to him after 1866. They supported legislation useful for further economic and legal unification of the country.

Less wisely, they backed Bismarck's attack on the Catholic church, the so-called *Kulturkampf,* or "struggle for civilization." Like Bismarck, the middle-class National Liberals were particularly alarmed by Pius IX's declaration of papal infallibility in 1870. That dogma seemed to ask German

Catholics to put loyalty to their church above loyalty to their nation. Only in Protestant Prussia did the Kulturkampf have even limited success. Catholics throughout the country generally voted for the Catholic Center party, which blocked passage of national laws hostile to the church. Finally, in 1878 Bismarck abandoned his attack. Indeed, he and the Catholic Center party entered into an uneasy but mutually advantageous alliance. Their reasons for doing so were largely economic.

As cheap grain poured in from new lands in the United States, Canada, and Russia, European peasants, with their smaller, less efficient farms, could not compete in cereal production. In western and southern Germany, the peasantry was largely Catholic, and the Catholic Center party was thus converted to higher tariffs to protect the economic interests of its supporters.

The same competitive pressures caused the Protestant Junkers, who owned large estates in eastern Germany, to embrace the cause of higher tariffs. They were joined by some iron and steel magnates. Thus in going along with a new protective tariff in 1879, Bismarck won new Catholic and conservative supporters in the Reichstag, and he held on to most of the National Liberals.

Many other governments turned to higher tariffs in the 1880s and 1890s to protect agriculture and industry from foreign competition. Thus the German government and other governments responded to a major economic problem and won greater loyalty. The general rise of protectionism in the late nineteenth century was also an outstanding example of the dangers of self-centered nationalism: high tariffs led to international name calling and nasty trade wars.

As for socialism, Bismarck tried to stop its growth in Germany because he genuinely feared its revolutionary language and allegiance to a movement transcending the nation-state. In 1878, after two attempts on the life of William I by radicals (though not socialists), Bismarck used a carefully orchestrated national outcry to ram through the Reichstag a law that strictly controlled socialist meetings and publications and outlawed the Social Democratic party, which was thereby driven underground. German socialists, however, displayed a discipline and organization worthy of the Prussian army itself, so Bismarck decided to try another tack.

Bismarck's essentially conservative nation-state pioneered with social measures designed to win the support of working-class people. In 1883 he pushed through the Reichstag the first of several modern social security laws to help wage earners. Henceforth sick, injured, and retired workers could look forward to some regular benefits from the state. This national social security system, paid for through compulsory contributions by wage earners and employers as well as grants from the state, was the first of its kind anywhere. (The United States would not take similar measures for fifty years.) This enormously significant development was a product of political competition and government efforts to win popular support.

Increasingly, the great issues in German domestic politics were socialism and the Marxian Social Democratic party. In 1890 the new emperor, the young, idealistic, and unstable William II (r. 1888–1918), opposed Bismarck's attempt to renew the law outlawing the Social Democratic party. Eager to rule in his own right and to earn the support of the workers, William II forced Bismarck to resign. After this "dropping of the pilot," German foreign policy changed profoundly and mostly for the worse, but the government did pass new laws to aid workers and to legalize socialist political activity.

Yet William II was no more successful than Bismarck in getting workers to renounce socialism. Indeed, socialist ideas spread rapidly, and more and more Social Democrats were elected to the Reichstag in the 1890s. In the elections of 1912 the German Social Democratic party became the largest single party in the Reichstag. This victory shocked aristocrats and their wealthy conservative middle-class allies, heightening their fears of an impending socialist upheaval. Yet the "revolutionary" socialists were actually becoming less and less revolutionary in Germany. In the years before World War I, as the Social Democratic party broadened its base and adopted a more patriotic tone, German socialists identified increasingly with the German state, and they concentrated on gradual social and political reform.

Republican France

Although Napoleon III's reign made some progress in reducing antagonisms between classes, the war with Prussia undid these efforts, and in 1871 France seemed hopelessly divided once again. The patriotic republicans who proclaimed the Third Republic in Paris after the military disaster at

Sedan refused to admit defeat. They defended Paris with great heroism for weeks, living off rats and zoo animals until they were starved into submission by German armies in January 1871. When national elections then sent a large majority of conservatives and monarchists to the National Assembly, the traumatized Parisians exploded in patriotic frustration and proclaimed the Paris Commune in March 1871. Vaguely radical, the leaders of the Commune wanted to govern Paris without interference by the conservative French countryside. The National Assembly, led by aging politician Adolphe Thiers, would hear none of it. The Assembly ordered the French army into Paris and brutally crushed the Commune. Twenty thousand people died in the fighting. As in June 1848, it was Paris against the provinces, French against French.

Out of this tragedy France slowly formed a new national unity, achieving considerable stability before 1914. How is one to account for this? Luck played a part. Until 1875 the monarchists in the "republican" National Assembly had a majority but could not agree about who should be king. The compromise Bourbon candidate refused to rule except under the white flag of his ancestors—a completely unacceptable condition. In the meantime, Thiers's destruction of the radical Commune and his other firm measures showed the fearful provinces and the middle class that the Third Republic might be moderate and socially conservative. France therefore retained the republic, though reluctantly. As President Thiers cautiously said, this was "the government which divides us least."

Another stabilizing factor was the skill and determination of the moderate republican leaders in the early years. The most famous of these was Léon Gambetta, the son of an Italian grocer, a warm, easygoing lawyer who had turned professional politician. A master of emerging mass politics, Gambetta combined eloquence with the personal touch as he preached a republic of truly equal opportunity. Gambetta was also instrumental in establishing absolute parliamentary supremacy between 1877 and 1879, when the deputies forced the somewhat autocratic president of the republic to resign. By 1879 the great majority of members of both the upper and the lower houses of the National Assembly were republicans, and the Third Republic had firm foundations after almost a decade.

The moderate republicans sought to preserve their creation by winning the hearts and minds of the next generation. Trade unions were fully legalized, and France acquired a colonial empire. More important, a series of laws between 1879 and 1886 established free compulsory elementary education for both girls and boys. At the same time, the state system of public tax-supported schools was expanded. In France and elsewhere the general expansion of public education served as a critical nation-building tool in the late nineteenth century.

In France most elementary and much secondary education had traditionally been in the parochial schools of the Catholic church, which had long been hostile to republics and to much of secular life. Free compulsory elementary education in France became secular republican education. The pledge of allegiance and the national anthem replaced the catechism and the "Ave Maria." Militant young male and female teachers carried the ideology of patriotic republicanism into every corner of France. In their classes, these women and men sought to win the loyalty of the young citizens to the republic so that France would never again vote en masse for dictators like the two Napoleons.

Unlike most Western countries (including the United States), which insisted on the total "purity" of their female elementary teachers and would not hire a married woman, the Third Republic actively encouraged young teachers to marry and guaranteed that both partners would teach in the same location. There were three main reasons for this unusual policy. First, married female (and male) teachers with their own children provided a vivid contrast to celibate nuns (and priests), who had for generations stood for most primary education in the popular mind. Second, the republican leaders believed that married women (and men) would better cope with the potential loneliness and social isolation of unfamiliar towns and villages, especially where the local Catholic school was strong. Third, French politicians and opinion leaders worried continually about France's very low birthrate after 1870, and they believed that women combining teaching careers and motherhood would provide the country with a good example. The hiring of married schoolteachers was part of an effort to create a whole new culture of universal, secular, and republican education. This illustrates a larger truth—that truly lasting political change must usually be supported by changes in the underlying culture.

Although the educational reforms of the 1880s disturbed French Catholics, many of them rallied to the republic in the 1890s, and tensions between church and state eased. Unfortunately, the Dreyfus affair changed all that. Alfred Dreyfus, a Jewish captain in the French army, was falsely accused and convicted of treason. His family never doubted his innocence and fought to reopen the case, enlisting the support of prominent republicans and intellectuals such as novelist Émile Zola. In 1898 and 1899, the case split France apart. On one side was the army, which had manufactured evidence against Dreyfus, joined by anti-Semites and most of the Catholic establishment. On the other side stood the civil libertarians and most of the more radical republicans.

This battle, which eventually led to Dreyfus's being declared innocent, revived republican feeling against the church. Between 1901 and 1905, the government severed all ties between the state and the Catholic church after centuries of close relations. The salaries of priests and bishops were no longer paid by the government. Catholic schools were put completely on their own financially, and in a short time they lost a third of their students. The state school system's power of indoctrination was greatly strengthened. In France only the growing socialist movement, with its very different but thoroughly secular ideology, stood in opposition to patriotic, republican nationalism.

Captain Alfred Dreyfus   Leaving an 1899 reconsideration of his original court-martial, Dreyfus receives an insulting "guard of dishonor" from soldiers who turn their backs to him. Top army leaders were determined to brand Dreyfus as a traitor. (*Source: Bibliothèque Nationale, Paris*)

Great Britain and Ireland

Britain in the late nineteenth century has often been seen as a shining example of peaceful and successful political evolution, where an effective two-party parliament skillfully guided the country from classical liberalism to full-fledged democracy with hardly a misstep. This view of Great Britain is not so much wrong as incomplete. After the right to vote was granted to males of the solid middle class in 1832, opinion leaders and politicians wrestled with the uncertainties of a further extension of the franchise. In 1867 Benjamin Disraeli and the Conservatives extended the vote to all middle-class males and the best-paid workers in the Second Reform bill. The son of a Jewish stockbroker and himself a novelist and urban dandy, the ever-fascinating Disraeli (1804–1881) was willing to risk

this "leap in the dark" in order to broaden the Conservative party's traditional base of aristocratic and landed support. After 1867 English political parties and electoral campaigns became more modern, and the "lower orders" appeared to vote as responsibly as their "betters." Hence the Third Reform Bill of 1884 gave the vote to almost every adult male.

While the House of Commons was drifting toward democracy, the House of Lords, between 1901 and 1910, tried and ultimately failed to reassert itself. Aristocratic conservatism yielded to popular democracy once and for all. The result was that extensive social welfare measures, slow to come to Great Britain, were passed in a spectacular rush between 1906 and 1914. During those years, the Liberal party, inspired by the fiery Welshman David Lloyd George (1863–1945), substantially raised taxes on the rich as part of the so-called People's Budget. This income helped the government pay for national health insurance, unemployment benefits, old-age pensions, and a host of other social measures. The state was integrating the urban masses socially as well as politically.

This record of accomplishment was only part of the story, however. On the eve of World War I, the question of Ireland brought Great Britain to the brink of civil war. The Irish famine in the 1840s (see page 822) fueled an Irish revolutionary movement. Thereafter, the English slowly granted concessions, such as the abolition of the privileges of the Anglican church and rights for Irish peasants. Liberal prime minister William Gladstone (1809–1898) introduced bills to give Ireland self-government in 1886 and in 1893, but they failed to pass. After two decades of relative quiet, Irish nationalists in the British Parliament saw their chance. They supported the Liberals in their battle for the People's Budget and in 1913 received a home-rule bill for Ireland in return.

Ireland, however, was composed of two peoples. As much as the Irish Catholic majority in the southern counties wanted home rule, precisely that much did the Irish Protestants in the northern counties of Ulster come to oppose it. Motivated by the accumulated fears and hostilities of generations, the Ulsterites vowed to resist home rule in northern Ireland. By December 1913 they had raised a hundred thousand armed volunteers, and they were supported by much of English public opinion. Thus in 1914 the Liberals in the House of Lords introduced a compromise home-rule bill that did not apply to the northern counties. This bill, which openly betrayed promises made to Irish nationalists, was rejected, and in September the original home-rule bill was passed but simultaneously suspended for the duration of the hostilities. The momentous Irish question was overtaken by an earth-shattering world war in August 1914.

Irish developments illustrated once again that governments could not elicit greater loyalty unless they could capture and control that elemental current of national feeling. Though Great Britain had much going for it—power, Parliament, prosperity—none of these availed in the face of the conflicting nationalisms espoused by Catholics and Protestants in northern Ireland. Similarly, progressive Sweden was powerless to stop the growth of the Norwegian national movement, which culminated in Norway's breaking away from Sweden and becoming a fully independent nation in 1905. In this light, one can also see how hopeless was the case of the Ottoman Empire in Europe in the later nineteenth century. It was only a matter of time before the Serbs, Bulgarians, and Rumanians would break away, and they did.

The Austro-Hungarian Empire

The dilemma of conflicting nationalisms in Ireland also helps one appreciate how desperate the situation in the Austro-Hungarian Empire had become by the early twentieth century. In 1849 Magyar nationalism had driven Hungarian patriots to declare an independent Hungarian republic, which was savagely crushed by Russian and Austrian armies (see pages 824–826). Throughout the 1850s, Hungary was ruled as a conquered territory, and Emperor Francis Joseph and his bureaucracy tried hard to centralize the state and Germanize the language and culture of the different nationalities.

Then in the wake of defeat by Prussia in 1866, a weakened Austria was forced to strike a compromise and establish the so-called dual monarchy. The empire was divided in two, and the nationalistic Magyars gained virtual independence for Hungary. The two states were joined only by a shared monarch and common ministries for finance, defense, and foreign affairs. After 1867 the disintegrating force of competing nationalisms continued unabated, for both Austria and Hungary had several "Irelands" within their borders.

In Austria ethnic Germans were only one-third of the population, and by 1895 many Germans saw their traditional dominance threatened by Czechs, Poles, and other Slavs. A particularly emotional issue in the Austrian parliament was the language used in government and elementary education at the local level. From 1900 to 1914, the parliament was so divided that ministries generally could not obtain a majority and ruled instead by decree. Efforts by both conservatives and socialists to defuse national antagonisms by stressing economic issues that cut across ethnic lines—endeavors that led to the introduction of universal male suffrage in 1907—proved largely unsuccessful.

One aspect of such national antagonisms was anti-Semitism, which was particularly virulent in Austria. The Jewish populations of Austrian cities grew very rapidly after Jews obtained full legal equality in 1867, and by 1900 Jews constituted 10 percent of the population of Vienna. Many Jewish

THE AGE OF NATIONALISM IN EUROPE, 1871–1914

1871–1914	Third Republic in France
1878	Suppression of Social Democrats in Germany
1881	Assassination of Tsar Alexander II
1883–1889	Enactment of social security laws in Germany
1884	Third Reform Bill passed by British Parliament
1889–1914	Second Socialist International
1890	Repeal of anti–Social Democrat law in Germany
1892–1903	Witte directs modernization of Russian economy
1904–1905	Japan wins decisive victory in Russo-Japanese War
1905	Revolution in Russia: Tsar Nicholas II forced to issue the October Manifesto promising a popularly elected Duma
1906–1914	Liberal reform in Great Britain
1907–1912	Stolypin's agrarian reforms in Russia
1912	German Social Democratic party becomes largest party in the German Reichstag
1914	Irish Home Rule bill passed by British Parliament but immediately suspended with outbreak of First World War

business people were quite successful in banking and retail trade, and Jewish artists, intellectuals, and scientists, such as the world-famous Sigmund Freud, played a major role in making Vienna a leading center of European culture and modern thought. When extremists charged the Jews with controlling the economy and corrupting German culture with alien ideas and ultramodern art, anxious Germans of all classes tended to listen—including an unsuccessful young artist named Adolf Hitler. ← penis, evil

In Hungary the Magyar nobility in 1867 restored the constitution of 1848 and used it to dominate both the Magyar peasantry and the minority populations until 1914. Only the wealthiest one-fourth of adult males had the right to vote, making the parliament the creature of the Magyar elite. Laws promoting use of the Magyar (Hungarian) language in schools and government were rammed through and bitterly resented, especially

by the Croatians and Rumanians. While Magyar extremists campaigned loudly for total separation from Austria, the radical leaders of the subject nationalities dreamed in turn of independence from Hungary. Unlike most major countries, which harnessed nationalism to strengthen the state after 1871, the Austro-Hungarian Empire was progressively weakened and destroyed by nationalism.

The Modernization of Russia

The Russian Empire was also an enormous multinational state, containing all the ethnic Russians and many other nationalities as well. Thus Russia's rulers saw national self-determination as a subversive ideology in the early nineteenth century, and they tried with some success to limit its development among their non-Russian subjects. Then after 1853 old autocratic Russia found itself in serious trouble. It became clear to Russia's leaders that the country had to embrace the process of modernization. A vague and often overworked term, *modernization* can be a useful concept if it is defined narrowly as the changes that enable a country to compete effectively with the leading countries at a given time. This concept of modernization fits Russia after the Crimean War particularly well.

In the 1850s Russia was a poor agrarian society. Industry was little developed, and almost 90 percent of the population lived on the land. Agricultural techniques were backward: the ancient openfield system reigned supreme. Serfdom was still the basic social institution, but it had become the great moral and political issue for the government by the 1840s. Then the Crimean War of 1853 to 1856, arising out of a dispute with France over who should protect certain Christian shrines in the Ottoman Empire, brought crisis. Because the fighting was concentrated in the Crimean peninsula on the Black Sea, Russia's transportation network of rivers and wagons failed to supply the distant Russian armies adequately. France and Great Britain, aided by Sardinia and the Ottoman Empire, inflicted a humiliating defeat on Russia.

Military defeat marked a turning point in Russian history because it clearly demonstrated that Russia had fallen behind the rapidly industrializing nations of western Europe in many areas. At the very least, Russia needed railroads, better armaments, and reorganization of the army if it was to maintain its international position. Moreover, the disastrous war had caused hardship and raised the specter of massive peasant rebellion. Reform of serfdom was imperative. Military disaster thus forced the new tsar, Alexander II (r. 1855–1881), and his ministers along the path of rapid social change and general modernization.

The first and greatest of the reforms was the freeing of the serfs in 1861. Human bondage was abolished forever, and the emancipated peasants received, on average, about half of the land. Yet they had to pay fairly high prices for their land, and because the land was owned collectively, each peasant village was jointly responsible for the payments of all the families in the village. The government hoped that collective responsibility would strengthen the peasant village as a social unit and prevent the development of a class of landless peasants. In practice, collective ownership and responsibility made it very difficult for individual peasants

to improve agricultural methods or leave their villages. Thus the effects of the reform were limited.

Most of the later reforms were also halfway measures. In 1864 the government established a new institution of local government, the *zemstvo,* but the local zemstvo remained subordinate to the traditional bureaucracy and the local nobility. More successful was reform of the legal system, which established independent courts and equality before the law. Education was also liberalized somewhat, and censorship was relaxed but not removed.

Until 1905 Russia's greatest strides toward modernization were economic rather than political. Industry and transport, both so vital to the military, were transformed in two industrial surges. After 1860 the government subsidized private railway companies, and construction boomed. In 1860 the empire had only about 1,250 miles of railroads; by 1880 it had about 15,500 miles. The railroads enabled agricultural Russia to export grain and thus earn money for further industrialization. Industrial suburbs grew up around Moscow and St. Petersburg, and a class of modern factory workers began to take shape.

Industrial development strengthened Russia's military forces and gave rise to territorial expansion to the south and east. Imperial expansion greatly excited many ardent Russian nationalists and superpatriots, who became some of the government's most enthusiastic supporters. Industrial development also contributed mightily to the spread of Marxian thought and the transformation of the Russian revolutionary movement after 1890.

In 1881 a small group of terrorists assassinated Alexander II. The era of reform came to an abrupt end, for the new tsar, Alexander III (r. 1881–1894), was a determined reactionary. Political modernization remained frozen until 1905, but economic modernization sped forward in the massive industrial surge of the 1890s. Nationalism played a decisive role, as it had after the Crimean War. The key leader was Sergei Witte, the tough, competent minister of finance from 1892 to 1903. Inspired by the writings of Friedrich List (see page 790), Witte believed that industrial backwardness was threatening Russia's power and greatness. Therefore, under Witte's leadership the government built state-owned railroads rapidly, doubling the network to 35,000 miles by the end of the century. The gigantic trans-Siberian line connecting Moscow with Vladivostok on the Pacific Ocean

5,000 miles away was Witte's pride. Following List's advice, Witte established high protective tariffs to build Russian industry, and he put the country on the gold standard of the "civilized world" to strengthen Russian finances.

Witte's greatest innovation, however, was to use the West to catch up with the West. He aggressively encouraged foreigners to use their abundant capital and advanced technology to build great factories in backward Russia. As he told the tsar, "The inflow of foreign capital is . . . the only way by which our industry will be able to supply our country quickly with abundant and cheap products."[16] This policy was brilliantly successful, especially in southern Russia. There, in eastern Ukraine, foreign capitalists and their engineers built an enormous and very modern steel and coal industry almost from scratch in little more than a decade. By 1900 only the United States, Germany, and Great Britain were producing more steel than Russia. The Russian petroleum industry had even pulled up alongside that of the United States and was producing and refining half of the world's output of oil. A fiercely autocratic and independent Russia was catching up with the advanced nations of the West.

Catching up partly meant vigorous territorial expansion, for this was the age of Western imperialism. By 1903 Russia had established a sphere of influence in Chinese Manchuria and was casting greedy eyes on northern Korea. When the diplomatic protests of equally imperialistic Japan were ignored, the Japanese launched a surprise attack in February 1904. To the amazement of self-confident Europeans, Asian Japan scored repeated victories, and Russia was forced in August 1905 to accept a humiliating defeat.

As is often the case, military disaster abroad brought political upheaval at home. The business and professional classes had long wanted to match economic with political modernization and a representative regime. Factory workers, strategically concentrated in the large cities, had all the grievances of early industrialization and were organized in a radical and still illegal labor movement. Peasants suffered from poverty and overpopulation. At the same time, nationalist sentiment was emerging among the empire's minorities. The politically and culturally dominant ethnic Russians were only about 45 percent of the population, and by 1900 some intellectuals among the subject nationalities,

especially the Poles and Ukrainians, were calling for self-rule and autonomy. With the army pinned down in Manchuria, all these currents of discontent converged in the revolution of 1905.

The beginning of the revolution pointed up the incompetence of the government. On a Sunday in January 1905, a massive crowd of workers and their families converged peacefully on the Winter Palace in St. Petersburg to present a petition to the tsar. Led by a trade-unionist priest, carrying icons, and respectfully singing, "God save the tsar," the workers did not know that Tsar Nicholas II (r. 1894–1917) had fled the city. Suddenly troops opened fire, killing and wounding hundreds. The "Bloody Sunday" massacre turned ordinary workers against the tsar and produced a wave of general indignation.

 The Limits of Russian Modernization   The business and professional classes grew stronger and became more prosperous in the era of reform, but the hard life of Russian peasants changed slowly. The striking contrast between the rugged old peasant and the elegant middle-class women in this photo aptly symbolizes the widening gap between the two sections of the population. (*Source: Sovfoto/Eastfoto*)

Outlawed political parties came out into the open, and by the summer of 1905 strikes, peasant uprisings, revolts among minority nationalities, and troop mutinies were sweeping the country. The revolutionary surge culminated in October 1905 in a great paralyzing general strike, which forced the government to capitulate. The tsar issued the October Manifesto, which granted full civil rights and promised a popularly elected *Duma* (parliament) with real legislative power.

On the eve of the opening of the first Duma in May 1906, the government issued the new constitution, the Fundamental Laws. The tsar retained great powers. The Duma, elected indirectly by universal male suffrage, and a largely appointive upper house could debate and pass laws, but the tsar had an absolute veto. As in Bismarck's Germany, the emperor appointed his ministers, who did not need to command a majority in the Duma.

The disappointed, predominately middle-class liberals, the largest group in the newly elected Duma, saw the Fundamental Laws as a step backward. Efforts to cooperate with the tsar's ministers soon broke down. The tsar then dismissed the Duma, only to see a more hostile and radical opposition elected in 1907. After three months of deadlock, the tsar dismissed the second Duma. Thereupon he and his reactionary advisers unilaterally rewrote the electoral law to increase greatly the weight of the propertied classes at the expense of workers, peasants, and national minorities.

The new law had the intended effect. With landowners assured half of the seats in the Duma, the government secured a loyal majority in 1907. Thus armed, the tough, energetic chief minister, Peter Stolypin, pursued a policy seeking to broaden support for the state. He pushed through important agrarian reforms designed to break down collective village ownership of land and to encourage the more enterprising peasants—a strategy known as the "wager on the strong." On the eve of World War I, Russia was partially modernized, a conservative constitutional monarchy with a peasant-based but industrializing economy.

❉ MARXISM AND THE SOCIALIST MOVEMENT

Nationalism served, for better or worse, as a new unifying principle. But what about socialism? Did the rapid growth of socialist parties, which were generally Marxian parties dedicated to an international proletarian revolution, mean that national states had failed to gain the support of workers? This question requires close examination.

The Socialist International

Certainly socialism appealed to large numbers of working men and women in the late nineteenth century (see Listening to the Past), and the growth of socialist parties after 1871 was phenomenal. Neither Bismarck's antisocialist laws nor his extensive social security system checked the growth of the German Social Democratic party, which espoused the Marxian ideology. By 1912 it had millions of followers and was the largest party in the Reichstag. Socialist parties also grew in other countries, though nowhere else with such success. In France various socialist parties were unified in 1905 in an increasingly powerful Marxian party called the French Section of the Workers International.

As the name of the French party suggests, Marxian socialist parties were eventually linked together in an international organization. As early as 1848, Marx had laid out his intellectual system in the *Communist Manifesto* (see pages 814–815). He had declared that "the working men have no country," and he had urged proletarians of all nations to unite against their governments. Joining the flood of radicals and republicans who fled continental Europe for England and America after the unsuccessful revolutions of 1848, Marx settled in London. Poor and depressed, he lived on his meager earnings as a journalist and on the gifts of his friend Engels. Marx never stopped thinking of revolution. Digging deeply into economics and history, he concluded that revolution follows economic crisis and tried to prove this position in *Critique of Political Economy* (1859) and in his greatest theoretical work, *Capital* (1867).

The bookish Marx also showed a rare flair for combining theorization with both lively popular writing and organizational ability. In 1864 he played an important role in founding the First International of socialists—the International Working Men's Association. In the following years, he battled successfully to control the organization, and he used its annual meetings as a means of spreading his realistic, "scientific" doctrines of inevitable socialist revolution. Then Marx enthusiastically embraced the passionate, vaguely radical patriotism of the Paris Commune and its terrible conflict with the French National Assembly as a giant step toward socialist revolution. This impetuous action frightened many of his early supporters, especially the more moderate British labor leaders. The First International collapsed.

Yet international proletarian solidarity remained an important objective for Marxists. In 1889, as the individual parties in different countries grew stronger, socialist leaders came together to form the Second International, which lasted until 1914. The International was only a federation of national socialist parties, but it had great psychological impact. Every three years, delegates from the different parties met to interpret Marxian doctrines and plan coordinated action. May 1 (May Day) was declared an annual international one-day strike, a day of marches and demonstrations. A permanent executive for the International was established. Many feared and many others rejoiced in the growing power of socialism and the Second International.

Unions and Revisionism

Was socialism really radical and revolutionary in these years? On the whole, it was not. Indeed, as socialist parties grew and attracted large numbers of members, they looked more and more toward gradual change and steady improvement for the working class and less and less toward revolution.

Workers themselves were progressively less inclined to follow radical programs. There were several reasons for this. As workers gained the right to vote and won real, tangible benefits, their attention focused more on elections than on revolutions. Workers were also not immune to patriotic education and indoctrination during military service, and many responded positively to drum-beating parades and aggressive foreign policy as they loyally voted for socialists. Nor were workers a unified social group.

Perhaps most important of all, workers' standard of living rose gradually but substantially after 1850 as the promise of the Industrial Revolution was at least partially realized. In Great Britain, for example, workers could buy almost twice as much with their wages in 1906 as in 1850, and most of the increase came after 1870. The quality of life also improved dramatically in urban areas. For all these reasons, workers tended more and more to become militantly moderate: they demanded gains, but they were less likely to take to the barricades in pursuit of them.

The growth of labor unions reinforced this trend toward moderation. In the early stages of industrialization, modern unions were considered subversive bodies and were generally prohibited by law. From this sad position workers struggled to escape. Great Britain led the way in 1824 and 1825 when unions won the right to exist but (generally) not the right to strike. After the collapse of Robert Owen's attempt to form one big union in the 1830s (see page 799), new and more practical kinds of unions appeared. Limited primarily to highly skilled workers such as machinists and carpenters, the "new model unions" avoided both radical politics and costly strikes. Instead, their sober, respectable leaders concentrated on winning better wages and hours for their members through collective bargaining and compromise. This approach helped pave the way to full acceptance in Britain in the 1870s, when unions won the right to strike without being held legally liable for the financial damage inflicted on employers. After 1890 unions for unskilled workers developed, and between 1901 and 1906 the legal position of British unions was further strengthened.

Germany was the most industrialized, socialized, and unionized country in continental Europe by 1914. German unions were not granted important rights until 1869, and until the antisocialist law was repealed in 1890, the government frequently harassed them as socialist fronts. The result was that as late as 1895, there were only about 270,000 union members in a male industrial work force of nearly 8 million. Then with German industrialization still storming ahead and almost all legal harassment eliminated, union membership skyrocketed, reaching roughly 3 million in 1912. Genuine collective bargaining, long opposed by socialist intellectuals as a "sellout," was officially recognized as desirable by the German Trade Union Congress in 1899. When employers proved unwilling to bargain, a series of strikes forced them to change their minds. Between 1906 and 1913, successful collective bargaining gained a prominent place in German industrial relations. Gradual improvement, not revolution, was becoming the primary goal of the German trade-union movement.

The German trade unions and their leaders were in fact, if not in name, thoroughgoing revisionists. *Revisionism* was an effort by various socialists to update Marxian doctrines to reflect the realities of the time. The socialist Edward Bernstein (1850–1932) argued in 1899 in his *Evolutionary Socialism*

May Day in Dresden, 1890 As this print from a German newspaper suggests, workers participated enthusiastically in the one-day strike honoring international socialist solidarity. But May Day was also a happy holiday, a celebration of working-class respectability and an independent working-class culture. *(Source: Archiv für Kunst und Geschichte, Berlin)*

that Marx's predictions of ever-greater poverty for workers had been proved false. Therefore, Bernstein suggested, socialists should reform their doctrines and tactics. They should combine with other progressive forces to win gradual evolutionary gains for workers through legislation, unions, and further economic development. The German Social Democratic party and later the entire Second International denounced these views as heresy. Yet the revisionist, gradualist approach continued to gain the tacit acceptance of many German socialists, particularly in the trade unions.

Moderation found followers elsewhere. In France the great socialist leader Jean Jaurès (1859–1914) formally repudiated revisionist doctrines in order to establish a unified socialist party, but he remained at heart a gradualist. Questions of revolutionary versus gradualist policies split Russian Marxists.

Socialist parties before 1914 had clear-cut national characteristics. Russians and socialists in the Austro-Hungarian Empire tended to be the most radical. The German party talked revolution and practiced reformism, greatly influenced by its enormous trade-union movement. The French party talked revolution and tried to practice it, unrestrained by a trade-union movement that was both very weak and very radical. In England the socialist but non-Marxian Labour party, reflecting the well-established union movement, was formally committed to gradual reform. In Spain and Italy Marxian socialism was very weak. There anarchism, seeking to smash the state rather than the bourgeoisie, dominated radical thought and action.

In short, socialist policies and doctrines varied from country to country. Socialism itself was to a large extent "nationalized" behind the imposing façade of international unity. This helps explain why almost all socialist leaders supported their governments when war came in 1914.

SUMMARY

The Industrial Revolution had a decisive influence on the urban environment. As the populations of towns and cities grew rapidly, long-standing over-crowding and unhealthy living conditions worsened alarmingly. Eventually government leaders, city planners, reformers, scientists, and ordinary citizens responded to this frightening challenge. They took effective action in public health, developed badly needed urban services, and gradually tamed the savagery of the traditional city.

As urban civilization came to prevail, there were major changes in family life. Especially among the working classes, family life became more stable, more loving, and less mercenary. These improvements exacted a price, however. Sex roles for men and women became sharply defined and rigidly separate. Women tended to be locked into a subordinate and stereotypical role. Nonetheless, on balance, the quality of family life improved. Better, more stable family relations reinforced the benefits for the masses of higher real wages, increased social security, political participation, and education.

While the quality of urban and family life improved, the class structure became more complex and diversified than before. Urban society featured many distinct social groups, and the gap between rich and poor remained enormous. Large numbers of poor women in particular continued to labor as workers in sweated industries and as domestic servants and prostitutes, meeting the demands of the servant-keeping classes. Small wonder then that inequality was a favorite theme of realist novelists such as Balzac and Zola. More generally, literary realism reflected Western society's growing faith in science, material progress, and evolutionary thinking. The emergence of urban, industrial civilization accelerated the secularization of the Western world-view.

Finally, Western society became increasingly nationalistic as well as urban and industrial. Nation-states enlisted widespread support and gave men and women a greater sense of belonging. Even socialism became increasingly national in orientation, gathering strength as a champion of working-class interests in domestic politics. Yet even though nationalism served to unite peoples, it also drove them apart—not only in Austria-Hungary and Ireland but throughout Europe and the rest of the world. The national faith, which reduced social tensions within states, promoted a bitter, almost Darwinian competition between states and thus threatened the progress and unity it had helped to build, as we shall see in Chapter 32.

NOTES

1. A. Weber, *The Growth of Cities in the Nineteenth Century* (New York: Columbia University Press, 1899), p. 1.
2. S. Marcus, "Reading the Illegible," in *The Victorian City: Images and Realities,* ed. H. J. Dyos and Michael Wolff, vol. 1 (London: Routledge & Kegan Paul, 1973), p. 266.
3. E. Gauldie, *Cruel Habitations: A History of Working-Class Housing, 1780–1918* (London: George Allen & Unwin, 1974), p. 21.
4. J. P. McKay, *Tramways and Trolleys: The Rise of Urban Mass Transport in Europe* (Princeton, N.J.: Princeton University Press, 1976), p. 81.
5. Quoted in B. Harrison, "Underneath the Victorians," *Victorian Studies* 10 (March 1967): 260.
6. Quoted in J. A. Banks, "The Contagion of Numbers," in Dyos and Wolff, *The Victorian City,* p. 112.
7. Quoted in R. Roberts, *The Classic Slum: Salford Life in the First Quarter of the Century* (Manchester, Eng.: University of Manchester Press, 1971), p. 95.
8. Quoted in T. Zeldin, *France, 1848–1945,* vol. 1 (Oxford: Clarendon Press, 1973), p. 288.
9. Quoted in S. Marcus, *The Other Victorians: A Study of Sexuality and Pornography in Mid-Nineteenth-Century England* (New York: Basic Books, 1966), p. 142.
10. Quoted in G. S. Jones, "Working-Class Culture and Working-Class Politics in London, 1870–1900: Notes on the Remaking of a Working Class," *Journal of Social History* 7 (Summer 1974): 486.
11. Quoted in Zeldin, *France, 1848–1945,* p. 346.

12. Roberts, *The Classic Slum,* p. 35.

13. Quoted in Zeldin, *France, 1848–1945,* p. 295.

14. A. Comte, *The Positive Philosophy of Auguste Comte,* trans. H. Martineau, vol. 1 (London: J. Chapman, 1853), pp. 1–2.

15. Quoted in G. J. Becker, ed., *Documents of Modern Literary Realism* (Princeton, N.J.: Princeton University Press, 1963), p. 159.

16. Quoted in J. P. McKay, *Pioneers for Profit: Foreign Entrepreneurship and Russian Industrialization, 1885–1913* (Chicago: University of Chicago Press, 1970), p. 11.

SUGGESTED READING

All of the books and articles cited in the Notes are highly recommended. T. Zeldin, *France, 1848–1945,* is a pioneering social history. T. Hamerow, *The Birth of a New Europe: State and Society in the Nineteenth Century* (1983) is an ambitious synthesis, and P. Pillbeam, *The Middle Classes in Europe, 1789–1914: France, Germany, Italy, and Russia* (1990), is a stimulating introduction. Aristocratic strength and survival is the theme of A. Mayer's *Persistence of the Old Regime: Europe to the Great War* (1981).

On the European city, D. Harvey, *Consciousness and the Urban Experience* (1985), is provocative. D. Silverman's, *Art Nouveau in Fin-de-Siècle France: Politics, Psychology, and Style* (1989) and N. Evenson's beautifully illustrated *Paris: A Century of Change, 1878–1978* (1979), are fascinating, as are G. Masur's, *Imperial Berlin* (1970), M. Hamm, ed., *The City in Russian History* (1976), and D. Grew's authoritative *Town in the Ruhr: A Social History of Bochum, 1860–1914* (1979). J. Merriman, *Margins of City Life: Explorations on the French Urban Frontier* (1991), is an important work on France. The outstanding study by J. Schmiechen, *Sweated Industries and Sweated Labor: The London Clothing Trades* (1984), complements H. Mayhew's wonderful contemporary study, *London Labour and the Labouring Poor* (1861), reprinted recently. Michael Crichton's realistic historical novel on organized crime, *The Great Train Robbery* (1976), is excellent. J. P. Goubert, *The Conquest of Water: The Advent of Health in the Industrial Age* (1989), and G. Rosen, *History of Public Health* (1958), offer a fine introduction to sanitary and medical developments.

For society as a whole, J. Burnett, *History of the Cost of Living* (1969), cleverly shows how different classes spent their money, and B. Tuchman, *The Proud Tower* (1966), draws an unforgettable portrait of people and classes before 1914. J. Laver's handsomely illustrated *Manners and Morals in the Age of Optimism, 1848–1914* (1966) investigates the urban underworld and relations between the sexes. Sexual attitudes are also examined by J. Walkowitz, *Prostitution and Victorian Society: Women, Class and State* (1890); J. Phayer, *Sexual Liberation and Religion in Nineteenth-Century Europe* (1977); and L. Engelstein, *The Key to Happiness: Sex and the Search for Modernity in Fin-de-Siècle Russia* (1992). G. Alter, *Family and Female Life Course: The Women of Verviers, Belgium, 1849–1880* (1988), and A. McLaren, *Sexuality and Social Order: Birth Control in Nineteenth-Century France* (1982), explore attitudes toward family planning.

Women have come into their own in historical studies. Among general works L. Tilly and J. Scott, *Women, Work and Family* (1978), is especially recommended. There are a growing number of eye-opening specialized investigations. These include L. Davidoff, *The Best Circles* (1973), and P. Jalland, *Women, Marriage and Politics, 1860–1914* (1986), on upper-class society types; and P. Branca, *Women in Europe Since 1750* (1978). M. J. Peterson, *Love and Work in the Lives of Victorian Gentlewomen* (1989), L. Holcombe, *Victorian Ladies at Work* (1973), and M. Vicinus, *Independent Women: Work and Community for Single Women, 1850–1920* (1985), examine women at work. M. Vicinus, ed., *Suffer and Be Still* (1972), and *A Widening Sphere* (1981), are far-ranging collections of essays on women's history, as is R. Bridenthal, C. Koonz, and S. Stuard, eds., *Becoming Visible: Women in European History,* 2d ed. (1987). Feminism is treated perceptively in R. Evans, *The Feminists: Women's Emancipation in Europe, America, and Australia* (1979), and in C. Moses, *French Feminism in the Nineteenth Century* (1984). L. Tickner, *The Spectacle of Women: Imagery of the Suffrage Campaign, 1907–1914* (1988), perceptively discusses Britain. J. Gillis, *Youth and History* (1974), is a good introduction. D. Ransel, ed., *The Family in Imperial Russia* (1978), is an important work on the subject.

Among studies of special groups, J. R. Wegs, *Growing Up Working Class: Continuity and Change Among Viennese Youth, 1890–1938* (1989), is recommended. Two fine studies on universities and their professors are S. Rothblatt, *Revolution of the Dons: Cambridge and Society in Victorian England* (1968), and F. Ringer, *The Decline of the German Mandarins* (1969). Servants and their employers receive excellent treatment in T. McBride, *The Domestic Revolution: The Modernization of Household Service in England and France, 1820–1920* (1976), and B. Smith, *Ladies of the Leisure Class: The Bourgeoises of Northern France in the Nineteenth Century* (1981), which may be compared with the innovative study by M. Miller, *The Bon Marché: Bourgeois Culture and the Department Store, 1869–1920* (1981).

On Darwin, M. Ruse, *The Darwinian Revolution* (1979), and P. Bowler, *Evolution: The History of an Idea,* rev. ed. (1989), are good starting points. O. Chadwick, *The Secularization of the European Mind in the Nineteenth Century* (1976), analyzes the impact of science (and other factors) on religious belief. The masterpieces of the great realist social novelists remain one of the best and most memorable introductions to nineteenth-century culture and thought. In addition to the novels discussed in this chapter and those cited in the Suggested Reading for Chapters 24 and 25, Ivan Turgenev's *Fathers and Sons* and Émile Zola's *The Dram-Shop* are especially recommended.

For individual countries, in addition to the general works mentioned in the Suggested Reading for Chapter 25, G. Craig, *Germany, 1866–1945* (1980), and B. Moore, *Social Origins of Dictatorship and Democracy* (1966), are outstanding. R. Anderson, *France, 1870–1914* (1977), provides a good introduction and has a useful bibliography. E. Weber, *France, Fin de Siècle* (1986), captures the spirit of Paris at the end of the century. G. Chapman, *The Dreyfus Case: A Reassessment* (1955), and D. Johnson, *France and the Dreyfus Affair* (1967), are careful examinations of the famous case. In *Jean Barois,* Nobel Prize winner Roger Du Gard accurately recreates in novel form the Dreyfus affair. D. M. Smith has written widely on Italy, and his *Garibaldi* (1956) and *Italy: A Modern History,* rev. ed. (1969), are recommended.

H. Wehler, *The German Empire, 1871–1918* (1985), stresses the strength of the landed nobility and the weakness of the middle class in an influential synthesis, which is challenged by D. Blackbourn and G. Eley, *The Peculiarities of German History: Bourgeois Society and Politics in 19th-Century Germany* (1984). F. Stern, *Gold and Iron* (1977), is a fascinating examination of relations between Bismarck and his financial adviser, the Jewish banker Bleichröder. L. Cecil, *Wilhelm II: Prince and Emperor, 1859–1900* (1989), probes the character and politics of Germany's ruler. G. Iggers, *The German Conception of History* (1968), and E. Spencer, *Management and Labor in Imperial Germany: Ruhr Industrialists as Employers* (1984), are valuable in-depth investigations. C. Schorske, *Fin de Siècle Vienna: Politics and Culture* (1980), is brilliant on aspects of modern culture.

On Russia, in addition to McKay cited in the Notes, see T. von Laue, *Sergei Witte and the Industrialization of Russia* (1970); A. Rieber, *Merchants and Entrepreneurs in Imperial Russia* (1982); and H. Rogger, *Russia in the Age of Modernization and Revolution, 1881–1917* (1983), which has an excellent bibliography. H. Troyat, *Daily Life in Russia Under the Last Tsar* (1962), is lively and recommended. T. Friedgut, *Iuzovka and Revolution: Life and Work in Russia's Donbass, 1869–1924* (1989); R. Zelnik, *Labor and Society in Tsarist Russia, 1855–1870* (1971); and R. Johnson, *Peasant and Proletarian: The Working Class of Moscow at the End of the Nineteenth Century* (1979), skillfully treat different aspects of working-class life and politics. W. E. Mosse, *Alexander II and the Modernization of Russia* (1958), discusses midcentury reforms, whereas C. Black, ed., *The Transformation of Russian Society* (1960), offers a collection of essays on Russian modernization.

G. Dangerfield, *The Strange Death of Liberal England* (1961), brilliantly examines social tensions in Ireland as well as English women's struggle for the vote before 1914. D. Boyce, *Nationalism in Ireland,* 2d ed. (1991), provides an excellent account of the Irish struggle for nationhood.

J. Seigel, *Marx's Fate: The Shape of a Life* (1978), is an outstanding biography. C. Schorske, *German Social Democracy, 1905–1917* (1955), is a modern classic. V. Lidtke, *The Alternative Culture: Socialist Labor in Imperial Germany* (1985), and J. Quataert, *Reluctant Feminists in German Social Democracy, 1885–1917* (1979), are also recommended for the study of the German socialists. H. Goldberg, *The Life of Jean Jaurès* (1962), is a sympathetic account of the great French socialist leader. D. Geary, ed., *Labour and Socialist Movements in Europe Before 1914* (1989), contains excellent studies on different countries and has up-to-date references.

LISTENING TO THE
PAST

The Making of a Socialist

Nationalism and socialism appeared locked in bitter competition in Europe before 1914, but they actually complemented each other in many ways. Both faiths were secular as opposed to religious, and both fostered political awareness. A working person who became interested in politics and developed nationalist beliefs might well convert to socialism at a later date.

This was the case for Adelheid Popp (1869–1939), a self-taught working woman who became an influential socialist leader. Born into a desperately poor working-class family in Vienna and remembering only a "hard and gloomy childhood," she was forced by her parents to quit school at age ten to begin full-time work. She struggled with low-paying piecework for years before she landed a solid factory job, as she recounts in the following selection from her widely read autobiography.

Always an avid reader, Popp became the editor of a major socialist newspaper for German working women. She then told her life story so that all working women might share her truth: "Socialism could change and strengthen others, at it did me."

[Finally] I found work again; I took everything that was offered me in order to show my willingness to work, and I passed through much. But at last things became better. [At age fifteen] I was recommended to a great factory which stood in the best repute. Three hundred girls and about fifty men were employed. I was put in a big room where sixty women and girls were at work. Against the windows stood twelve tables, and at each sat four girls. We had to sort the goods which had been manufactured, others had to count them, and a third set had to brand on them the mark of the firm. We worked from 7 A.M. to 7 P.M. We had an hour's rest at noon, half-an-hour in the afternoon. . . . I had never yet been paid so much. . . .

I seemed to myself to be almost rich. . . . [Yet] from the women of this factory one can judge how sad and full of deprivation is the lot of a factory worker. In none of the neighbouring factories were the wages so high; we were envied everywhere. Parents considered themselves fortunate if they could get their daughters of fourteen in there on leaving school. . . . And even here, in this paradise, all were badly nourished. Those who stayed at the factory for the dinner hour would buy themselves for a few pennies a sausage or the leavings of a cheese shop. . . . In spite of all the diligence and economy, every one was poor, and trembled at the thought of losing her work. All humbled themselves, and suffered the worst injustice from the foremen, not to risk losing this good work, not to be without food. . . .

I did not only read novels and tales; I had begun . . . to read the classics and other good books. I also began to take an interest in public events. . . . I was not democratically inclined. I was full of enthusiasm then for emperors, and kings and highly placed personages played no small part in my fancies. . . . I bought myself a strict Catholic paper, that criticized very adversely the workers' movement, which was attracting notice. Its aim was to educate in a patriotic and religious direction. . . . I took the warmest interest in the events that occurred in the royal families, and I took the death of the Crown Prince of Austria so much to heart that I wept a whole day. . . . Political events [also] held me in suspense. The possibility of a war with Russia roused my patriotic enthusiasm. I saw my brother already returning from the battlefield covered with glory. . . .

When a particularly strong anti-Semitic feeling was noticeable in political life, I sympathised with it for a time. A broad sheet, "How Israel Attained Power and Sovereignty over all the Nations of the Earth," fascinated me. . . .

About this time an Anarchist group was active. Some mysterious murders which had taken place were ascribed to the Anarchists, and the police made use of them to oppress the rising workmen's movement. . . . I followed the trial of the Anarchists with passionate sympathy. I read all the speeches, and because, as always happens, Social Democrats, whom the authorities really wanted to attack, were among the accused, I learned their views. I became full of enthusiasm. Every single Social Democrat . . . seemed to me a hero. . . .

There was unrest among the workers . . . and demonstrations of protest followed. When these were repeated the military entered the "threatened" streets. . . . In the evenings I rushed in the greatest excitement from the factory to the scene of the disturbance. The military did not frighten me; I only left the place when it was "cleared."

Later on my mother and I lived with one of my brothers who had married. Friends came to him, among them some intelligent workmen. One of these workmen was particularly intelligent, and . . . could talk on many subjects. He was the first Social Democrat I knew. He brought me many books, and explained to me the difference between Anarchism and Socialism. I heard from him, also for the first time, what a republic was, and in spite of my former enthusiasm for royal dynasties, I also declared myself in favour of a republican form of government. I saw everything so near and so clearly, that I actually counted the weeks which must still elapse before the revolution of state and society would take place.

From this workman I received the first Social Democratic party organ. . . . I first learned from it to understand and judge of my own lot. I learned to see that all I had suffered was the result not of a divine ordinance, but of an unjust organization of society. . . .

In the factory I became another woman. . . . I told my [female] comrades all that I had read of the workers' movement. Formerly I had often told stories when they had begged me for them. But instead of narrating . . . the fate of some queen, I now held forth on oppression and exploitation. I told of accumu-

Engraving (1890) of a meeting of workers in Berlin. (*Source: Bildarchiv Preussischer Kulturbesitz*)

lated wealth in the hands of a few, and introduced as a contrast the shoemakers who had no shoes and the tailors who had no clothes. On breaks I read aloud the articles in the Social Democratic paper and explained what Socialism was as far as I understood it. . . . [While I was reading] it often happened that one of the clerks passing by shook his head and said to another clerk: "The girl speaks like a man."

Questions for Analysis

1. How did Popp describe and interpret work in the factory?

2. To what extent did Popp's socialist interpretation of factory life fit the facts she described?

3. What were Popp's political interests before she became a socialist?

4. How and why did Popp become a Social Democrat?

5. Was this account likely to lead other working women to socialism? Why or why not?

Source: Slightly adapted from A. Popp, *The Autobiography of a Working Woman*, trans. E. C. Harvey (Chicago: F. G. Browne, 1913), pp. 29, 34–35, 39, 66–69, 71, 74, 82–90.

The World and the West

The Emigrant Ship
(1898) by British painter
Charles J. Staniland.
*(Source: Bridgeman Art
Library, London)*

While industrialization and nationalism were transforming urban life and Western society, Western society itself was reshaping the world. At the peak of its power and pride, the West entered the third and most dynamic phase of the aggressive expansion that had begun with the Crusades and continued with the great discoveries and the rise of seaborne colonial empires. An ever-growing stream of products, people, and ideas flowed out of Europe in the nineteenth century. Hardly any corner of the globe was left untouched. The most spectacular manifestations of Western expansion came in the late nineteenth century when the leading European nations established or enlarged their far-flung political empires. The political annexation of territory in the 1880s—the "new imperialism," as it is often called by historians—was the capstone of a profound underlying economic and technological process.

- How and why did this many-sided, epoch-making expansion occur in the nineteenth century?
- What were some of its consequences for the West and the rest of the world?

These are the questions this chapter will examine.

❖ INDUSTRIALIZATION AND THE WORLD ECONOMY

The Industrial Revolution created, first in Great Britain and then in continental Europe and North America, a growing and tremendously dynamic economic system. In the course of the nineteenth century, that system was extended across the face of the earth. Some of this extension into non-Western areas was peaceful and beneficial for all concerned, for the West had many products and techniques that the rest of the world desired. If peaceful methods failed, however, Europeans used their superior military power to force non-Western nations to open their doors to Western economic interests. In general, Westerners fashioned the global economic system so that the largest share of the ever-increasing gains from trade, technology, and migration flowed to the West and its propertied classes.

The Rise of Global Inequality

The Industrial Revolution in Europe marked a momentous turning point in human history. Indeed, only by placing Europe's economic breakthrough in a global perspective can one truly appreciate its revolutionary implications and consequences.

From such a global perspective, the ultimate significance of the Industrial Revolution was that it allowed those regions of the world that industrialized in the nineteenth century to increase their wealth and power enormously in comparison to those that did not. As a result, a gap between the industrializing regions (mainly Europe and North America) and the nonindustrializing ones (mainly Africa, Asia, and Latin America) opened up and grew steadily throughout the nineteenth century. Moreover, this pattern of uneven global development became institutionalized, or built into the structure of the world economy, and the "lopsided world"—a world of rich lands and poor—evolved.

Historians have long been aware of this gap, but only recently have historical economists begun to chart its long-term evolution with some precision. Their findings are extremely revealing, although they contain a margin of error and other limitations as well. Figure 27.1 summarizes the findings of one such study. It compares the long-term evolution of average income per person in today's "developed" (or industrialized) regions with average income per person in the "Third World" (or developing regions) (see page 1173). To get these individual income figures, researchers estimate a country's gross national product (GNP) at different points in time, convert those estimates to some common currency, and divide by the total population.

Figure 27.1 highlights three main points. First, in 1750 the average standard of living was no higher in Europe as a whole than in the rest of the world. In 1750 Europe as a whole was still a poor agricultural society. By 1970, however, the average person in the wealthiest countries had an income fully twenty-five times as great as the income received by the average person in the poorest Third World countries of Africa and Asia.

Second, it was industrialization that opened the gaps in average wealth and well-being among countries and regions. Great Britain had jumped

883

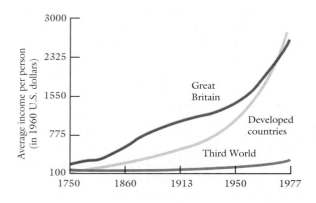

Note: The Third World includes Africa, Asia, Latin America, and Oceania. Developed countries include all European countries, Canada, the United States, and Japan.

FIGURE 27.1 The Growth of Average Income per Person in the Third World, Developed Countries, and Great Britain, 1750–1970 (*Source: Data from P. Bairoch and M. Lévy-Leboyer, eds.,* Disparities in Economic Development Since the Industrial Revolution. *St. Martin's Press, New York, 1981, pp. 7–8, 10)*

well above the developed countries' average by 1830. But as the developed countries successfully industrialized in the course of the nineteenth century, Great Britain's lead gradually narrowed.

Third, income per person stagnated in the Third World before 1913, in striking contrast to the industrializing regions. Only after 1945, in the era of political independence and decolonization, did Third World countries finally make some real economic progress, beginning the critical process of industrialization.

The rise of these enormous income disparities, which are poignant indicators of disparities in food and clothing, health and education, life expectancy and general material well-being, has generated a great deal of debate. One school of interpretation stresses that the West used science, technology, capitalist organization, and even its critical worldview to create its wealth and greater physical well-being. Another school argues that the West used its political and economic power to steal much of its riches, continuing in the nineteenth (and twentieth) century the ~~rapacious~~ colonialism born of the era of expansion.

These issues are complex, and there are few simple answers. As noted in Chapter 24, the wealth-creating potential of technological improvement

and more intensive capitalist organization was indeed great. At the same time, those breakthroughs rested, in part, on Great Britain's having already used political force to dominate the world economy in the nineteenth century. Wealth—unprecedented wealth—was indeed created, but the lion's share of that new wealth flowed to the West and its propertied classes and to a tiny non-Western elite of cooperative rulers, landowners, and merchants.

The World Market

Commerce between nations has always been a powerful stimulus to economic development. Never was this more true than in the nineteenth century. World trade grew modestly until about 1840 and then took off. After a slowdown in the last years of the century, another surge lasted until World War I. In 1913 the value of world trade was roughly $38 billion, or about *twenty-five* times what it had been in 1800, even though prices of manufactured goods and raw materials were lower in 1913 than in 1800. In a general way, the enormous increase in international commerce summed up the growth of an interlocking world economy centered in and directed by Europe.

Great Britain played a key role in using trade to tie the world together economically. In 1815 Britain already had a colonial empire, for India, Canada, Australia, and other scattered areas remained British possessions after American independence. The technological breakthroughs of the Industrial Revolution allowed Britain to manufacture cotton textiles, iron, and other goods more cheaply and to far outstrip domestic demand for such products. Thus British manufacturers sought export markets first in Europe and then around the world.

Take the case of cotton textiles. By 1820 Britain was exporting 50 percent of its production. Europe bought 50 percent of these cotton textile exports, and India, the world's largest producer of cotton textiles in the seventeenth century, bought 6 percent. When European nations and the United States erected protective tariff barriers and promoted domestic industry, British cotton textile manufacturers aggressively sought and found new foreign markets in non-Western areas. By 1850 India was buying 25 percent and Europe only 16 percent of a much larger total of exported British cotton textiles. As a British colony, India could not raise tariffs to protect its ancient cotton textile industry, so thousands of Indian weavers lost their livelihoods.

After the repeal of the Corn Laws in 1846 (see page 820), Britain became the world's single best market, and it remained the world's emporium until 1914. Free access to Britain's enormous market stimulated the development of mines and plantations in many non-Western areas.

The growth of trade was facilitated by the conquest of distance. The earliest railroad construction occurred in Europe (including Russia) and in America north of the Rio Grande; other parts of the globe saw the building of rail lines after 1860. By 1920 more than a quarter of the world's railroads were in Latin America, Asia, Africa, and Australia. Wherever railroads were built, they drastically reduced transportation costs, opened new economic opportunities, and called forth new skills and attitudes.

The power of steam revolutionized transportation by sea as well as by land. Steampower, long used to drive paddle-wheelers on rivers, particularly in Russia and North America, finally began to supplant sails on the oceans of the world in the late 1860s. Lighter, stronger, cheaper steel replaced iron, which had replaced wood. Screw propellers superseded paddle wheels, and mighty compound steam engines cut fuel consumption by half. Passenger and freight rates tumbled, and the shipment of low-priced raw materials from one continent to another became feasible.

An account of an actual voyage by a typical tramp freighter highlights nineteenth-century developments in global trade. The ship left England in 1910 carrying rails and general freight to western Australia. From there it carried lumber to Melbourne in southeastern Australia, where it took on harvester combines for Argentina. In Buenos Aires it loaded wheat for Calcutta, and in Calcutta it took on jute for New York. From New York it carried a variety of industrial products to Australia before returning to England with lead, wool, and wheat after a voyage of approximately 72,000 miles to six continents in seventeen months.

The revolution in land and sea transportation helped European pioneers open vast new territories and produce agricultural products and raw materials there for sale in Europe. Moreover, the development of refrigerated railway cars and, from the 1880s, refrigerator ships enabled first Argentina and then the United States, Australia, and New Zealand to ship mountains of chilled or frozen beef and mutton to European (mainly British) consumers. From Asia, Africa, and Latin America came not only the traditional tropical products—spices, tea, sugar, coffee—but also new raw materials for industry, such as jute, rubber, cotton, and coconut oil.

Intercontinental trade was enormously facilitated by the Suez and Panama canals. Of great importance, too, was large and continual investment in modern port facilities, which made loading and unloading cheaper, faster, and more dependable. Finally, transoceanic telegraph cables inaugurated rapid communications among the financial centers of the world. While a British tramp freighter steamed from Calcutta to New York, a broker in London was arranging by telegram for it to carry an American cargo to Australia. World commodity prices were also instantaneously conveyed by the same network of communications.

The growth of trade and the conquest of distance encouraged the expanding European economy to make massive foreign investments, beginning about 1840. By the outbreak of the First World War in 1914, Europeans had invested more than $40 billion abroad. Great Britain, France, and Germany were the principal investing countries, although by 1913 the United States was emerging as a substantial foreign investor. The sums involved were enormous. In the decade before 1914, Great Britain was investing 7 percent of its annual national income abroad, or slightly more than it was investing in its entire domestic economy. The great gap between rich and poor within Europe meant that the wealthy and moderately well-to-do could and did send great sums abroad in search of interest and dividends.

Most of the capital exported did not go to European colonies or protectorates in Asia and Africa. About three-quarters of total European investment went to other European countries, the United States and Canada, Australia and New Zealand, and Latin America. Europe found its most profitable opportunities for investment in construction of the railroads, ports, and utilities that were necessary to settle and develop the almost-vacant lands. Much of this investment was peaceful and mutually beneficial for lenders and borrowers. The victims were native American Indians and Australian aborigines, who were displaced and decimated by the diseases, liquor, and weapons of an aggressively expanding Western society.

The Opening of China and Japan

Europe's relatively peaceful development of robust offshoots in sparsely populated North America, Australia, and much of Latin America absorbed huge quantities of goods, investments, and migrants. From a Western point of view, that was the most important aspect of Europe's global thrust. Yet Europe's economic and cultural penetration of old, densely populated civilizations was also profoundly significant, especially for the non-European peoples affected by it. With such civilizations Europeans also increased their trade and profit. Moreover, as had been the case ever since Vasco da Gama and Christopher Columbus, the expanding Western society was prepared to use force, if necessary, to attain its desires. This was what happened in China and Japan, two crucial examples of the general pattern of intrusion into non-Western lands.

Traditional Chinese civilization was self-sufficient. For centuries China had sent more goods and inventions to Europe than it had received, and this was still the case in the eighteenth century. Europeans and the English in particular had developed a taste for Chinese tea, but they had to pay for it with hard silver since China was supremely uninterested in European wares. Trade with Europe was carefully regulated by the Chinese imperial government—the Manchu Dynasty—which was more interested in isolating and controlling the strange "sea barbarians" than in pursuing commercial exchange. The imperial government refused to establish diplomatic relations with the "inferior" European states, and it required all foreign merchants to live in the southern city of Gwangzhou (Canton) and to buy from and sell to only the local merchant monopoly. Practices considered harmful to Chinese interests, such as the sale of opium and the export of silver from China, were strictly forbidden.

For years the little community of foreign merchants in Gwangzhou had to accept the Chinese system. By the 1820s, however, the dominant group, the British, were flexing their muscles. Moreover, in the smoking of opium—that "destructive and ensnaring vice" denounced by patriotic Chinese decrees—they had found something the Chinese really wanted. Grown legally in British-occupied India, opium was smuggled into China by means of fast ships and bribed officials. The more this rich trade developed, the greedier British merchants became. By 1836 the aggressive goal of the British merchants in Gwangzhou was an independent British colony in China and "safe and unrestricted liberty" in trade. Spurred on by economic motives, they pressured the British government to take decisive action and enlisted the support of British manufacturers with visions of vast Chinese markets to be opened.

At the same time, the Manchu government decided that the opium trade had to be stamped out. The tide of drug addiction was ruining the people and stripping the empire of its silver, which was going to British merchants to pay for the opium. The government began to prosecute Chinese drug dealers vigorously and in 1839 sent special envoy Lin Tse-hsü to Gwangzhou. Lin Tse-hsü ordered the foreign merchants to obey China's laws, "for our great unified Manchu Empire regards itself as responsible for the habits and morals of its subjects and cannot rest content to see any of them become victims of a deadly poison."[1] The British merchants refused and were expelled, whereupon war soon broke out.

Using troops from India and being in control of the seas, the British occupied several coastal cities and forced China to surrender. In the Treaty of Nanjing (Nanking) in 1842, the imperial government was forced to cede the island of Hong Kong to Britain forever, pay an indemnity of $100 million, and open four large cities to foreign trade with low tariffs.

Thereafter the opium trade flourished, and Hong Kong developed rapidly as an Anglo-Chinese enclave. China continued, however, to refuse to accept foreign diplomats in Beijing (Peking), the imperial capital. Finally, there was a second round of foreign attack between 1856 and 1860, culminating in the occupation of Beijing by seventeen thousand British and French troops and the intentional burning of the emperor's summer palace. Another round of harsh treaties gave European merchants and missionaries greater privileges and protection and forced the Chinese to accept trade and investment on unfavorable terms for the foreseeable future. Thus did Europeans use military aggression to blow a hole in the wall of Chinese seclusion and sovereignty.

China's neighbor Japan had its own highly distinctive civilization and even less use for Westerners. European traders and missionaries first arrived in Japan in the sixteenth century. By 1640 Japan had reacted quite negatively to their presence. The

Britain and China at War, 1841   Britain capitalized on its overwhelming naval superiority, and this British aquatint celebrates a dramatic moment in a crucial battle near Gwangzhou. Having received a direct hit from a steam-powered British ironclad, a Chinese sailing ship explodes into a wall of flame. The Chinese lost eleven ships and 500 men in the two-hour engagement; the British suffered only minor damage. (*Source: National Maritime Museum, London*)

government decided to seal off the country from all European influences in order to preserve traditional Japanese culture and society. When American and British whaling ships began to appear off Japanese coasts almost two hundred years later, the policy of exclusion was still in effect. An order of 1825 commanded Japanese officials to "drive away foreign vessels without second thought."[2]

Japan's unbending isolation seemed hostile and barbaric to the West, particularly to the United States. Americans shared the self-confidence and dynamism of expanding Western society and felt destined to play a great role in the Pacific. To Americans, therefore, it seemed their duty to force the Japanese to share their ports and behave as a "civilized" nation.

After several unsuccessful American attempts to establish commercial relations with Japan, Commodore Matthew Perry steamed into Edo (now Tokyo) Bay in 1853 and demanded diplomatic negotiations with the emperor. Japan entered a grave crisis. Some Japanese warriors urged resistance, but

senior officials realized how defenseless their cities were against naval bombardment. Shocked and humiliated, they reluctantly signed a treaty with the United States that opened two ports and permitted trade. Japan was "opened." What the British had done in China with war, the Americans had done in Japan with the threat of war.

Western Penetration of Egypt

Egypt's experience illustrates not only the explosive power of the expanding European economy and society but also their seductive appeal in non-Western lands. European involvement in Egypt also led to a new model of formal political control, which European powers applied widely in Africa and Asia after 1882.

Of great importance in African and Middle Eastern history, since 525 B.C. the ancient land of the pharaohs had been ruled by a succession of foreigners, most recently by the Ottoman Turks. In

avaclous

1798 French armies under young General Napoleon Bonaparte invaded the Egyptian part of the Ottoman Empire and occupied the territory for three years. Into the power vacuum left by the French withdrawal stepped an extraordinary Albanian-born Turkish general, Muhammad Ali (1769–1849).

First appointed governor of Egypt by the Turkish sultan, Muhammad Ali soon disposed of his political rivals and set out to build his own state on the strength of a large, powerful army organized along European lines and trained by hired French and Italian army officers. The government was also reformed, new lands were cultivated, and communications were improved. By the time of his death in 1849, Muhammad Ali had established a strong and virtually independent Egyptian state, to be ruled by his family on a hereditary basis within the Turkish empire.

Muhammad Ali's policies of modernization attracted large numbers of Europeans to the banks of the Nile. As one Arab sheik of the Ottoman Empire remarked in the 1830s, "Englishmen are like ants; if one finds a bit of meat, hundreds follow."[3] The port city of Alexandria had more than fifty thousand Europeans by 1864. Europeans served not only as army officers but also as engineers, doctors, high government officials, and police officers. Others found their "meat" in trade, finance, and shipping.

To pay for a modern army as well as for European services and manufactured goods, Muhammad Ali encouraged the development of commercial agriculture geared to the European market. This development had profound implications. Egyptian peasants had been poor but largely self-sufficient, growing food for their own consumption on state-owned lands allotted to them by tradition. Faced with the possibility of export agriculture, high-ranking officials and members of Muhammad Ali's family began carving large private landholdings out of the state domain. The new landlords made the peasants their tenants and forced them to grow cash crops for European markets. Borrowing money from European lenders at high rates and still making good profits, Egyptian landowners "modernized" agriculture, but to the detriment of peasant well-being.

These trends continued under Muhammad Ali's grandson Ismail, who in 1863 began his sixteen-

East Meets West This painting gives a Japanese view of the first audience of the American consul and his staff with the shogun, Japan's hereditary military governor, in 1859. The Americans appear strange and ill at ease. *(Source: Laurie Platt Winfrey, Inc.)*

A Western Hotel in Cairo This photo suggests both the reality and the limits of modernization in Ismail's Egypt. An expensive hotel, complete with terrace café and gas lighting, adorns the Egyptian capital. But the hotel is for foreigners, and the native Egyptians are servants and outsiders. *(Source: Popperfoto)*

year rule as Egypt's khedive, or prince. Educated at France's leading military academy, Ismail was a westernizing autocrat. He dreamed of using European technology and capital to modernize Egypt quickly and build a vast empire in northeast Africa. The large irrigation networks he promoted caused cotton production and exports to Europe to boom. Ismail also borrowed large sums to install modern communications, and with his support the Suez Canal was completed by a French company in 1869. The Arabic of the masses, rather than the Turkish of the conquerors, became the official language, and young Egyptians educated in Europe helped spread new skills and new ideas in the bureaucracy. Cairo acquired modern boulevards, Western hotels, and an opera house. As Ismail proudly declared, "My country is no longer in Africa, we now form part of Europe."[4]

But Ismail was impatient and reckless. His projects were enormously expensive, and by 1876

Egypt owed foreign bondholders a colossal $450 million and could not pay the interest on its debt. Rather than let Egypt go bankrupt and repudiate its loans, as some Latin American countries and U.S. state governments had done in the early nineteenth century, the governments of France and Great Britain intervened politically to protect the European bankers who held the Egyptian bonds. They forced Ismail to appoint French and British commissioners to oversee Egyptian finances so that the Egyptian debt would be paid in full. This was a momentous decision. It implied direct European political control: Europeans were going to determine the state budget and in effect rule Egypt.

Foreign financial control evoked a violent nationalistic reaction among Egyptian religious leaders, young intellectuals, and army officers. In 1879, under the leadership of Colonel Ahmed Arabi, they formed the Egyptian Nationalist party. Continuing diplomatic pressure, which forced

Ismail to abdicate in favor of his weak son, Tewfiq (r. 1879–1892), resulted in bloody anti-European riots in Alexandria in 1882. A number of Europeans were killed, and Tewfiq and his court had to flee to British ships for safety. When the British fleet bombarded Alexandria, more riots swept the country, and Colonel Arabi declared that "an irreconcilable war existed between the Egyptians and the English." But a British expeditionary force decimated Arabi's forces and occupied all of Egypt.

The British said their occupation was temporary, but British armies remained in Egypt until 1956. They maintained the façade of the khedive's government as an autonomous province of the Ottoman Empire, but the khedive was a mere puppet. The able British consul, General Evelyn Baring, later Lord Cromer, ruled the country after 1883. Once a vocal opponent of involvement in Egypt, Baring was a paternalistic reformer who had come to believe that "without European interference and initiative reform is impossible here." Baring's rule did result in tax reforms and better conditions for peasants, while foreign bondholders tranquilly clipped their coupons and Egyptian nationalists nursed their injured pride.

In Egypt Baring and the British reluctantly but spectacularly provided a new model for European expansion in densely populated lands. Such expansion was based on military force, political domination, and a self-justifying ideology of beneficial reform. This model was to predominate until 1914. Thus did Europe's Industrial Revolution lead to tremendous political as well as economic expansion throughout the world.

 ## THE GREAT MIGRATION

A poignant human drama was interwoven with economic expansion: millions of people pulled up stakes and left their ancestral lands in the course of history's greatest migration. To millions of ordinary people, for whom the opening of China and the interest on the Egyptian debt had not the slightest significance, this great movement was the central experience in the saga of Western expansion.

The Pressure of Population

In the early eighteenth century, the growth of European population entered its third and decisive stage, which continued unabated until the twentieth century. Birthrates eventually declined in the nineteenth century, but so did death rates, mainly because of the rising standard of living and secondarily because of the medical revolution. Thus the population of Europe (including Asiatic Russia) more than doubled, from approximately 188 million in 1800 to roughly 432 million in 1900.

These figures actually understate Europe's population explosion, for between 1815 and 1932 more than 60 million people left Europe. These migrants went primarily to "areas of European settlement"—North and South America, Australia, New Zealand, and Siberia—where they contributed to a rapid growth in numbers. The population of North America (the United States and Canada) alone grew from 6 million to 81 million between 1800 and 1900 because of continual immigration and high fertility rates. Since population grew more slowly in Africa and Asia than in Europe, Europeans and people of European origin

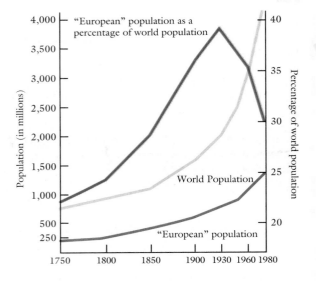

FIGURE 27.2 The Increase of European and World Populations, 1750–1980 *(Source: Data from W. Woodruff,* Impact of Western Man: A Study of Europe's Role in the World Economy. *St. Martin's Press, New York, 1967, p. 103; United Nations, Statistical Yearbook, 1982, 1985, pp. 2–3)*

Note: "European" population includes Europe and also areas of predominately European settlement—Asiatic Russia, North America, South America, and Australia/New Zealand.

jumped from about 22 percent of the world's total to about 38 percent on the eve of World War I, as Figure 27.2 shows.

The growing number of Europeans was a driving force behind emigration and Western expansion. As in the eighteenth century, the rapid increase in numbers led to relative overpopulation in area after area. Children of these baby booms grew up, saw little available land and few opportunities, and migrated, especially where rapid population increase predated extensive industrial development. Thus millions of country folk went abroad as well as to nearby cities in search of work and economic opportunity.

Before looking at the people who migrated, let us consider three facts. First, as Figure 27.3 shows, more than 11 million men and women left Europe in the first decade of the twentieth century, over five times the number departing in the 1850s. The outflow of migrants was clearly an enduring characteristic of European society for the entire period.

Second, different countries had very different patterns of movement. As Figure 27.3 also shows, people left Britain and Ireland (which are not distinguished in the British figures) in large numbers from the 1840s on. This emigration reflected not only rural poverty but also the movement of skilled, industrial technicians and the preferences shown to British migrants in the British Empire. Ultimately, about one-third of all European migrants between 1840 and 1920 came from the British Isles. German migration was quite different. It grew irregularly after about 1830, reaching a first peak in the early 1850s and another in the early 1880s. Thereafter it declined rapidly, for Germany's rapid industrialization was providing adequate jobs at home. This pattern contrasted sharply with that of Italy. More and more Italians left the country right up to 1914, reflecting severe problems in Italian villages and relatively slow industrial growth. Thus migration patterns mirrored social and economic conditions in the various European countries and provinces.

Third, although the United States absorbed the largest number of European migrants, less than half of all migrants went to the United States. Asiatic Russia, Canada, Argentina, Brazil, and Australia also attracted large numbers, as Figure 27.4 shows. Moreover, migrants accounted for a larger proportion of the total population in Argentina, Brazil, and Canada than in the United States. The common American assumption that European mi-

FIGURE 27.3 Emigration from Europe by Decades, 1851–1940 *(Source: Data from W. Woodruff,* Impact of Western Man: A Study of Europe's Role in the World Economy. *St. Martin's Press, New York, 1967, pp. 106–107 and references cited therein)*

gration meant migration to the United States is quite inaccurate.

European Migrants

What kind of people left Europe, and what were their reasons for leaving? The European migrant was most often a small peasant landowner or a village craftsman whose traditional way of life was threatened by too little land, estate agriculture, and cheap, factory-made goods. German peasants who left the Rhineland and southwestern Germany between 1830 and 1854, for example, felt trapped by what Friedrich List called the "dwarf economy," with its tiny landholdings and declining craft industries. Selling out and moving to buy much cheaper land in the American Midwest became a common response.

Contrary to what is often said, the European migrant was generally an energetic small farmer or skilled artisan trying hard to stay ahead of poverty,

ORIGINS

DESTINATIONS

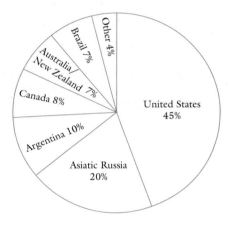

* Not including migrants to Asiatic Russia.

 FIGURE 27.4 Origin and Destination of European Emigrants, 1851–1960 *(Source: Data from W. Woodruff,* Impact of Western Man: A Study of Europe's Role in the World Economy. *St. Martin's Press, New York, 1967, pp. 108–109 and references cited therein)*

not a desperately impoverished landless peasant or urban proletarian. Determined to maintain or improve their status, migrants were a great asset to the countries that received them. This was doubly so because the vast majority were young and very often unmarried. Fully 67 percent of those admitted to the United States were under thirty-one years of age, and 90 percent were under forty. They came in the prime of life and were ready to

work hard in the new land, at least for a time. Many Europeans, especially by the end of the nineteenth century, were truly migrants as opposed to immigrants—that is, they returned home after some time abroad. One in two migrants to Argentina and probably one in three to the United States eventually returned to their native land.

The likelihood of repatriation varied greatly by nationality. People who migrated from the Balkans, for instance, were far more likely to return to their countries than were people from Ireland and eastern European Jews. Once again, the possibility of buying land in the old country was of central importance. In Ireland (as well as in England and Scotland) land was tightly held by large, often absentee landowners, and little land was available for purchase. In Russia most land was held by non-Jews. Russia's 5 million Jews were already confined to the market towns and small cities of the so-called Pale of Settlement, where they worked as artisans and petty traders. They lived in relative peace until the assassination of Alexander II by non-Jewish terrorists in 1881 brought a new tsar and an official policy of pogroms and savage discrimination. Therefore, when Russian Jewish artisans began in the 1880s to escape both oppression and factory competition by migrating—a migration that eventually totaled 2 million people—this was basically a once-and-for-all departure.

In contrast, most Italian migrants were not landless laborers from areas dominated by large estates; such people tended to stay in Italy and turned increasingly toward radical politics. Instead, most Italian migrants were small landowning peasants whose standard of living was falling because of rural overpopulation and agricultural depression. Migration provided them with an escape valve and possible income to buy more land. Many Italians had no intention of settling abroad permanently. Some called themselves "swallows." After harvesting their own wheat and flax in Italy, they "flew" to Argentina to harvest wheat between December and April. Returning to Italy for the spring planting, they repeated this exhausting process. This was a very hard life, but a frugal worker could save from $250 to $300 in the course of a season.

Ties of family and friendship played a crucial role in the movement of peoples. Many people from a given province or village settled together in rural enclaves or tightly knit urban neighborhoods thousands of miles away. Very often a strong individual—a businessman, a religious leader—would

❋ **The Drama of Migration**   These Italian migrants are passing through the port of
Naples around 1900, heading for temporary work and permanent settlement in
North and South America. Naples was the principal outlet for large-scale migration
from southern Italy. It handled more passengers than all other Italian ports combined. (*Source: Touring Club Italiano, Milan*)

blaze the way and others would follow, forming a
"migration chain."

Many landless young European men and women
were spurred to leave by a spirit of revolt and independence. In Sweden and in Norway, in Jewish
Russia and in Italy, these young people felt frustrated by the small privileged classes, which often
controlled both church and government and
resisted demands for change and greater opportunity. Many a young Norwegian seconded the passionate cry of Norway's national poet, Bjørn-
stjerne Bjørnson (1832–1910): "Forth will I! Forth!
I will be crushed and consumed if I stay."[5]

Many young Jews wholeheartedly agreed with a
spokesman of Kiev's Jewish community who declared in 1882, "Our human dignity is being trampled upon, our wives and daughters are being dis-
honored, we are looted and pillaged: either we get
decent human rights or else let us go wherever our
eyes may lead us."[6] Thus for many, migration was
a radical way to "get out from under." Migration
slowed when the people won basic political and social reforms, such as the right to vote and social security.

Asian Migrants

Not all migration was from Europe. A substantial
number of Chinese, Japanese, Indians, and Filipinos—to name only four key groups—responded
to rural hardship with temporary or permanent migration. At least 3 million Asians (as opposed to
more than 60 million Europeans) moved abroad
before 1920. Most went as indentured laborers to
work under incredibly difficult conditions on the
plantations or in the gold mines of Latin America,
southern Asia, Africa, California, Hawaii, and Australia.

The Jewish Market Located on New York's Lower East Side, this market was a
bustling center of economic and social life in 1900. Jewish immigrants could usually
find work with Jewish employers, and New York's Jewish population soared from
73,000 in 1880 to 1.1 million in 1910. (*Source: The Granger Collection*)

White estate owners very often used Asians to
replace or supplement blacks after the suppression
of the slave trade. In the 1840s, for example, there
was a strong demand for field hands in Cuba, and
the Spanish government actively recruited Chinese
laborers. They came under eight-year contracts,
were paid about 25 cents a day, and were fed potatoes and salted beef. Between 1853 and 1873,
more than 130,000 Chinese laborers went to
Cuba. The majority spent their lives as virtual
slaves. Such migration was stopped in 1873. The
great landlords of Peru also brought in more than
100,000 workers from China in the nineteenth
century, and there were similar movements of
Asians elsewhere.

Such migration from Asia would undoubtedly have grown to much greater proportions if

planters and mine owners in search of cheap labor
had had their way. But they did not. Asians fled the
plantations and gold mines as soon as possible,
seeking greater opportunities in trade and towns,
where they came into conflict with brown-skinned
peoples—as in Malaya and East Africa—and with
white settlers in areas of European settlement.
These settlers demanded a halt to Asian migration.
One Australian brutally summed up the typical
view: "The Chinaman knows nothing about Caucasian civilization. . . . It would be less objection-
able to drive a flock of sheep to the poll than to allow Chinamen to vote. The sheep at all events
would be harmless."[7] By the 1880s Americans and
Australians were building "great white walls"—discriminatory laws designed to keep Asians out.
Thus a final, crucial factor in the migrations before

1914 was the general policy of "whites only" in the open lands of possible permanent settlement. This, too, was part of Western dominance in the increasingly lopsided world.

Largely successful in monopolizing the best overseas opportunities, Europeans and people of European ancestry reaped the main benefits from the great migration. By 1913 people in Australia, Canada, and the United States all had higher average incomes than people in Great Britain, still Europe's wealthiest nation.

 ## WESTERN IMPERIALISM

The expansion of Western society reached its apex between about 1880 and 1914. In those years, the leading European nations continued to send massive streams of migrants, money, and manufactured goods around the world, and they rushed to create or enlarge vast *political* empires abroad. This fran-

tic political empire building contrasted sharply with the economic penetration of non-Western territories between 1816 and 1880, which, albeit by naked military force, had left a China or a Japan "opened" but politically independent. By contrast, the empires of the late nineteenth century recalled the old European colonial empires of the seventeenth and eighteenth centuries and led contemporaries to speak of the "new imperialism."

The new imperialism had momentous consequences. It resulted in new tensions among competing European states, and it led to wars and rumors of war with non-European powers. The new imperialism was aimed primarily at Africa and Asia. It put millions of black, brown, and yellow peoples directly under the rule of whites. How and why did whites come to rule these peoples?

The Scramble for Africa

The most spectacular manifestation of the new imperialism was the seizure of Africa, which broke

"Is She Hardworking?" Entering the United States in their colorful kimonos, these Japanese women are "picture brides." Their marriages to Japanese men in the United States have already been arranged by friends and marriage brokers, who have used pictures and references to strike bargains with prospective husbands. About six hundred Japanese picture brides entered annually until the U.S. government outlawed the practice in 1921. *(Source: California Department of Parks and Recreation)*

sharply with previous patterns and fascinated contemporary Europeans and Americans. As late as 1880, European nations controlled only 10 percent of the African continent, and their possessions were hardly increasing.

The French had begun conquering Algeria in 1830, and within fifty years substantial numbers of French, Italian, and Spanish colonists had settled among the overwhelming Arab majority. At the other end of the continent, in South Africa, the British had taken possession of the Dutch settlements at Cape Town during the wars with Napoleon I. This takeover had led disgruntled Dutch cattle ranchers and farmers in 1835 to make their so-called Great Trek into the interior, where they fought the Zulu and Xhosa peoples for land. After 1853, the Boers, or Afrikaners (as the descendants of the Dutch in the Cape Colony were beginning to call themselves), proclaimed their political independence and defended it against British armies. By 1880 Afrikaner and British settlers, who detested each other, had wrested control of much of South Africa from the Zulu, Xhosa, and other African peoples.

European trading posts and forts dating back to the Age of Discovery and the slave trade dotted the coast of West Africa. The Portuguese proudly but ineffectively held their old possessions in Angola and Mozambique. Elsewhere over the great mass of the continent, Europeans did not rule.

Between 1880 and 1900, the situation changed drastically. Britain, France, Germany, and Italy scrambled for African possessions as if their national livelihoods were at stake. By 1900 nearly the whole continent had been carved up and placed under European rule. Only Ethiopia in northeast Africa and Liberia on the West African coast remained independent. Even the Dutch settler republics of southern Africa were conquered by the British in the bloody Boer War (1899–1902). In the years before 1914, the European powers tightened their control and established colonial governments to rule their gigantic empires (Map 27.1).

In the complexity of the European seizure of Africa, certain events and individuals stand out. Of enormous importance was the British occupation of Egypt, which established the new model of formal political control. There was also the role of Leopold II of Belgium (r. 1865–1909), an energetic, strong-willed monarch with a lust for distant territory. "The sea bathes our coast, the world lies

before us," he had exclaimed in 1861. "Steam and electricity have annihilated distance, and all the non-appropriated lands on the surface of the globe can become the field of our operations and of our success."[8] By 1876 Leopold was focusing on central Africa. Subsequently, he formed a financial syndicate under his personal control to send Henry M. Stanley, a sensation-seeking journalist and part-time explorer, to the Congo basin. Stanley was able to establish trading stations, sign "treaties" with African chiefs, and plant Leopold's flag. Leopold's actions alarmed the French, who quickly sent out an expedition under Pierre de Brazza. In 1880 de Brazza signed a treaty of protection with the chief of the large Teke tribe and began to establish a French protectorate on the north bank of the Congo River.

Leopold's buccaneering intrusion into the Congo area raised the question of the political fate of black Africa—Africa south of the Sahara. By 1882 when the British successfully invaded and occupied Egypt, Europe had caught "African fever." There was a gold-rush mentality, and the race for territory was on.

To lay down some basic rules for this new and dangerous game of imperialist competition, Premier Jules Ferry of France and Chancellor Otto von Bismarck of Germany arranged an international conference on Africa in Berlin in 1884 and 1885. The conference established the principle that European claims to African territory had to rest on "effective occupation" in order to be recognized by other states. This principle was very important. It meant that Europeans would push relentlessly into interior regions from all sides and that no single European power would be able to claim the entire continent. The conference recognized Leopold's personal rule over a neutral Congo free state and declared all of the Congo basin a free-trade zone. The conference also agreed to work to stop slavery and the slave trade in Africa.

The Berlin conference coincided with Germany's sudden emergence as an imperial power. Prior to about 1880, Bismarck, like many other

MAP 27.1 The Partition of Africa European nations carved up Africa after 1880 and built vast political empires. What African states remained independent?

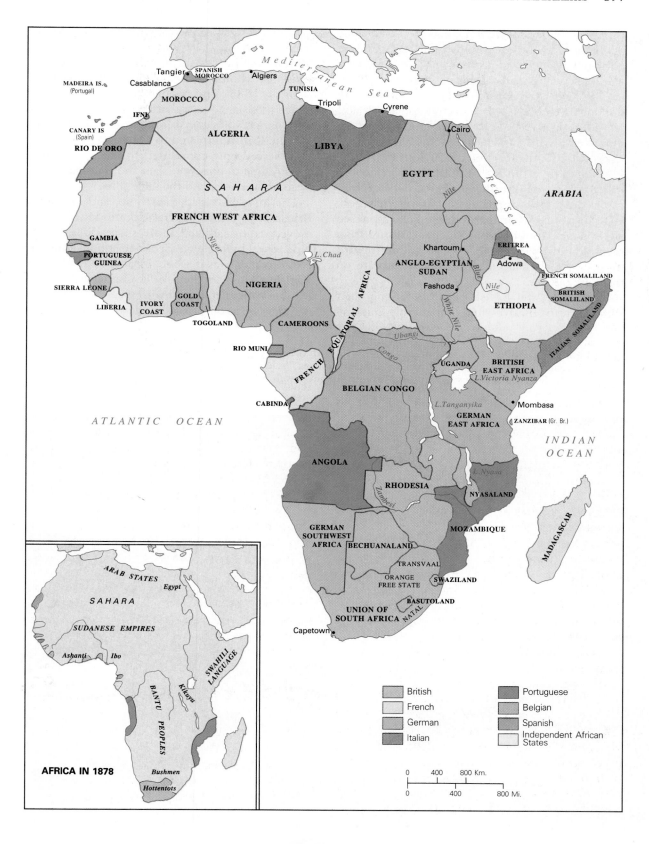

Tangier
MADEIRA IS.
(Portugal)
Casablanca
SPANISH MOROCCO
Algiers
Mediterranean Sea
TUNISIA
Tripoli
Cyrene
MOROCCO
IFNI
CANARY IS
(Spain)
Cairo
RIO DE ORO
ALGERIA
LIBYA
EGYPT
ARABIA
S A H A R A
Nile
Red Sea
FRENCH WEST AFRICA
GAMBIA
Niger
L. Chad
Khartoum
ERITREA
PORTUGUESE GUINEA
ANGLO-EGYPTIAN SUDAN
Adowa
FRENCH SOMALILAND
SIERRA LEONE
NIGERIA
Blue Nile
Fashoda
BRITISH SOMALILAND
LIBERIA
IVORY COAST
GOLD COAST
White Nile
ETHIOPIA
TOGOLAND
CAMEROONS
FRENCH EQUATORIAL AFRICA
ITALIAN SOMALILAND
RIO MUNI
Ubangi
UGANDA
BRITISH EAST AFRICA
Congo
L. Victoria Nyanza
ATLANTIC OCEAN
BELGIAN CONGO
L. Tanganyika
Mombasa
CABINDA
GERMAN EAST AFRICA
ZANZIBAR (Gr. Br.)
INDIAN OCEAN
ANGOLA
RHODESIA
L. Nyasa
Zambesi
NYASALAND
GERMAN SOUTHWEST AFRICA
BECHUANALAND
MOZAMBIQUE
MADAGASCAR
TRANSVAAL
ORANGE FREE STATE
SWAZILAND
BASUTOLAND
UNION OF SOUTH AFRICA
NATAL
Capetown

ARAB STATES
Egypt
SAHARA
SUDANESE EMPIRES
SWAHILI LANGUAGE
Ashanti
Ibo
Kikuyu
BANTU PEOPLES
Bushmen
Hottentots

AFRICA IN 1878

British
French
German
Italian
Portuguese
Belgian
Spanish
Independent African States

0   400   800 Km.
0   400   800 Mi.

European leaders at the time, had seen little value in colonies. Colonies reminded him, he said, of a poor but proud nobleman who wore a fur coat when he could not afford a shirt underneath. Then in 1884 and 1885 as political agitation for expansion increased, Bismarck did an abrupt about-face, and Germany established protectorates over a number of small African kingdoms and tribes in Togo, Cameroon, Southwest Africa, and, later, East Africa. In acquiring colonies, Bismarck cooperated against the British with France's Ferry, who was as ardent for empire as he was for education. With Bismarck's tacit approval, the French pressed vigorously southward from Algeria, eastward from their old forts on the Senegal coast, and northward from de Brazza's newly formed protectorate on the Congo River.

Meanwhile, the British began enlarging their West African enclaves and impatiently pushing northward from the Cape Colony and westward from Zanzibar. Their thrust southward from Egypt was blocked in the Sudan by fiercely independent Muslims, who massacred a British force at Khartoum in 1885. The peoples of the Sudan maintained the Islamic state that they had established in 1881 in a revolt against foreign control of Egypt, and the British retreated to Cairo. Sudanese Muslims were deeply committed to Islam. For them the struggle to preserve Islam and the struggle for freedom were one and the same thing.

The invaders bided their time, and in 1896 a British force under General Horatio H. Kitchener moved cautiously and more successfully up the Nile River, building a railroad to supply arms and reinforcements as it went. Finally, in 1898 these British troops met their foe at Omdurman, where Muslim tribesmen armed with spears charged time and time again only to be cut down by the recently

Omdurman, 1898 European machine guns cut down the charging Muslim tribesmen again and again. "It was not a battle but an execution," said one witness. Thus the Sudan was conquered, and a million square miles were added to the British Empire. *(Source: E. T. Archive)*

invented machine gun. For one smug participant, the young British officer Winston Churchill, it was "like a pantomime scene" in a play. "These extraordinary foreign figures . . . march up one by one from the darkness of Barbarism to the footlights of civilization . . . and their conquerors, taking their possessions, forget even their names. Nor will history record such trash." For another, more somber English observer, "It was not a battle but an execution. The bodies were not in heaps . . . but they spread evenly over acres and acres."[9] In the end, eleven thousand brave but poorly armed Muslim tribesmen lay dead. Only twenty-eight Britons had been killed.

The British conquest of the Sudan exemplifies the general process of empire building in Africa. The fate of the Muslim force at Omdurman was eventually inflicted on all native peoples who resisted European rule: they were blown away by vastly superior military force. But however much the European powers squabbled for territory and privilege around the world, they always had the sense to stop short of actually fighting each other. Imperial ambitions were not worth a great European war.

Imperialism in Asia

Although the sudden division of Africa was more spectacular, Europeans also extended their political control in Asia. In 1815 the Dutch ruled little more than the island of Java in the East Indies. Thereafter they gradually brought almost all of the 3,000-mile archipelago under their political authority, though—in good imperialist fashion—they had to share some of the spoils with Britain and Germany. In the critical decade of the 1880s, the French under the leadership of Ferry took Indochina. India, Japan, and China also experienced a profound imperialist impact (Map 27.2).

Two other great imperialist powers, Russia and the United States, also acquired rich territories in Asia. Russia, whose history since the later Middle Ages had been marked by almost continual expansion, moved steadily forward on two fronts throughout the nineteenth century. Russians conquered Muslim areas to the south in the Caucasus and in central Asia and also proceeded to nibble greedily on China's outlying provinces in the Far East, especially in the 1890s.

The United States' great conquest was the Philippines, taken from Spain in 1898 after the Spanish-American War. When it quickly became clear that the United States had no intention of granting independence, Philippine patriots rose in revolt and were suppressed only after long, bitter fighting.

Causes of the New Imperialism

Many factors contributed to the late-nineteenth-century rush for territory and empire, which was in turn one aspect of Western society's generalized expansion in the age of industry and nationalism. It is little wonder that controversies have raged over interpretation of the new imperialism. But despite complexity and controversy, basic causes are clearly identifiable.

Economic motives played an important role in the extension of political empires, especially the British Empire. By the late 1870s, France, Germany, and the United States were industrializing rapidly behind rising tariff barriers. Great Britain was losing its early lead and facing increasingly tough competition in foreign markets. In this new economic situation, Britain came to value old possessions, such as India and Canada, more highly. But when European continental powers began to grab any and all unclaimed territory in the 1880s, the British followed suit immediately. They feared that France and Germany would seal off their empires with high tariffs and restrictions and that future economic opportunities would be lost forever.

Actually, the overall economic gains of the new imperialism proved quite limited before 1914. The new colonies were simply too poor to buy much, and they offered few immediately profitable investments. Nonetheless, even the poorest, most barren desert was jealously prized, and no territory was ever abandoned. Colonies became important for political and diplomatic reasons. Each leading country saw colonies as crucial to national security, military power, and international prestige. For instance, safeguarding the Suez Canal played a key role in the British occupation of Egypt, and protecting Egypt in turn led to the bloody conquest of the Sudan. National security was a major factor in the U.S. decision to establish firm control over the Panama Canal Zone in 1903. Far-flung possessions guaranteed ever-growing navies the safe havens and the dependable coaling stations they needed in time of crisis or war.

Many people were convinced that colonies were essential to great nations. "There has never been a

Sea of
Okhotsk

Sakhalin

KARAFUTO
(Jap. 1905)

JAPANESE EMPIRE

PACIFIC OCEAN

RUSSIAN EMPIRE

•Khabarovsk
(1858)

AMUR DISTRICT
(1858)

•Vladivostok
(1860)

Sea of
Japan

•Tokyo

•Harbin

MANCHURIA

Shenyang•
(Mukden)

KOREA
(1905, 1910)

Lüshun (Port Arthur)
(Rus. 1898, Jap. 1905)

Weihai•
(Gr. Br. 1898)

East
China
Sea

Ryukyu Is. (Jap.)

New Guinea

INNER
MONGOLIA

•Beijing

•Tianjin

Jiaozhou
(Ger. 1898)

•Nanjing

Shanghai•
(Gr. Br. 1842)

Penghu Ch'üntao
(Pescadores)
(Jap. 1895)

Taiwan (Formosa)
(Jap. 1895)

Timor
(Port. 1859)
(Neth.)

DUTCH EAST INDIES

OUTER MONGOLIA
(Autonomous, Russian sphere 1912)

•Chita

L.Baikal

•Irkutsk

SIBERIA

Lena

Amur

Yenisei

Huang He
(Yangtze)

CHINA

•Chongqing

Wuhan•
(Hankow)

Fuzhou•

Xiamen•

Guangzhou•
(Gr. Br. 1842)

Macao•
(Port. 1557)

Hong Kong•
(Gr. Br. 1842)

Zhanjiang
(Fr. 1898)

•Manila

PHILIPPINE IS.
(U.S.; from Spain 1898)

South
China
Sea

Celebes

BRITISH
NORTH BORNEO
(1888)

SARAWAK
(1888)

Borneo

SINKIANG

Tobolsk•

•Omsk

Trans-Siberian Railway

Tashkent•
(1864)

L.Balkhash
(1854)

Ob

Irtysh

•Lhasa

TIBET

BHUTAN

HIMALAYAS

NEPAL

BURMA
(1852, 1885)

Rangoon•

Bay
of
Bengal

Andaman Is.
(Gr. Br.)

SIAM

•Bangkok

Hanoi•

FRENCH
INDOCHINA
(1884, 1907)

•Saigon

MALAY STATES
(1800, 1824)

Singapore•
(Gr. Br. 1819)

Sumatra

Java

Aral
Sea
(1873)

Mery•
(1884)

AFGHANISTAN

KASHMIR
(1846)

PUNJAB

BALUCHISTAN
(1883)

BRITISH
SPHERE
(1907)

Indus

Karachi•

Delhi•

BRITISH INDIA

INDIA

Calcutta•

Ganges

Bombay•

Diu
(Port.)

Goa
(Port.)

Madras•

Yanaon
(Fr.)

Pondichéry
(Fr.)

Karikal
(Fr.)

Ceylon

INDIAN OCEAN

Caspian Sea

Teheran•

PERSIA

RUSSIAN SPHERE
(1907)

Arabian
Sea

Territories held by:

Great Britain
Netherlands
France
United States
Russia
Japan
Railroads

1000 Mi.

1000 Km.

500

500

0

0

great power without great colonies," wrote one French publicist in 1877. "Every virile people has established colonial power," echoed the famous nationalist historian of Germany, Heinrich von Treitschke. "All great nations in the fullness of their strength have desired to set their mark upon barbarian lands and those who fail to participate in this great rivalry will play a pitiable role in time to come."[10]

Treitschke's harsh statement reflects not only the increasing aggressiveness of European nationalism after Bismarck's wars of German unification but also Social Darwinian theories of brutal competition among races. Thus European nations, which were seen as racially distinct parts of the dominant white race, had to seize colonies to show they were strong and virile. Moreover, the conquest of inferior peoples was just. "The path of progress is strewn with the wreck . . . of inferior races," wrote one professor in 1900. "Yet these dead peoples are, in very truth, the stepping stones on which mankind has risen to the higher intellectual and deeper emotional life of today."[11] Social Darwinism and harsh racial doctrines fostered imperialist expansion.

So did the industrial world's unprecedented technological and military superiority. Three aspects were crucial. First, the rapidly firing machine gun, so lethal at Omdurman in the Sudan, was an ultimate weapon in many another unequal battle. Second, newly discovered quinine proved effective in controlling attacks of malaria, which had previously decimated whites in the tropics whenever they left breezy coastal enclaves and dared to venture into mosquito-infested interiors. Third, the combination of the steamship and the international telegraph permitted Western powers to quickly concentrate their firepower in a given area when it was needed. Never before—and never again after 1914—would the technological gap between the West and non-Western regions of the world be so great.

Social tensions and domestic political conflicts also contributed mightily to overseas expansion,

according to a prominent interpretation of recent years. In Germany, in Russia, and in other countries to a lesser extent, conservative political leaders were charged with manipulating colonial issues in order to divert popular attention from the class struggle at home and to create a false sense of national unity. Therefore, imperial propagandists relentlessly stressed that colonies benefited workers as well as capitalists, providing jobs and cheap raw materials that raised workers' standard of living. Government leaders and their allies in the tabloid press successfully encouraged the masses to savor foreign triumphs and glory in the supposed increase in national prestige.

Finally, certain special-interest groups in each country were powerful agents of expansion. Shipping companies wanted lucrative subsidies. White settlers on dangerous, turbulent frontiers constantly demanded more land and greater protection. Missionaries and humanitarians wanted to spread religion and stop the slave trade. Explorers and adventurers sought knowledge and excitement. Military men and colonial officials, whose role has often been overlooked by those who write on imperialism, foresaw rapid advancement and high-paid positions in growing empires. The actions of such groups and the determined individuals who led them thrust the course of empire forward.

Western society did not rest the case for empire solely on naked conquest and a Darwinian racial struggle or on power politics and the need for naval bases on every ocean. Imperialists developed additional arguments in order to satisfy their consciences and answer their critics. A favorite idea was that Europeans and Americans could and should "civilize" supposedly primitive, nonwhite peoples (see Listening to the Past). According to this view, nonwhites would receive the benefits of modern economies, cities, advanced medicine, and higher standards of living and eventually might be ready for self-government and Western democracy.

Another argument was that imperial government protected natives from tribal warfare as well as from cruder forms of exploitation by white settlers and business people. Thus the French spoke of their sacred "civilizing mission." Rudyard Kipling (1865–1936), who wrote masterfully of Anglo-Indian life and was perhaps the most influential British writer of the 1890s, exhorted Europeans to unselfish service in distant lands:

✳ **MAP 27.2 Asia in 1914** India remained under British rule while China precariously preserved its political independence. The Dutch empire in modern-day Indonesia was old, but French control of Indochina was a product of the new imperialism.

A Missionary School A Swahili schoolboy leads his classmates in a reading lesson in Dar es Salaam in German East Africa before 1914, as portraits of Emperor William II and his wife look down on the classroom. Europeans argued that they were spreading the benefits of a superior civilization with schools like this one, which is unusually solid because of its strategic location in the capital city. *(Source: Ullstein Bilderdienst)*

Take up the White Man's Burden—
Send forth the best ye breed—
Go bind your sons to exile
To serve your captives' need,
To wait in heavy harness,
On fluttered folk and wild—
Your new-caught, sullen peoples
Half-devil and half-child.[12]

Another rationalization for the new imperialism was that peace and stability under European control would permit the spread of Christianity. In Africa Catholic and Protestant missionaries competed with Islam south of the Sahara, seeking converts and building schools to spread the Gospel. Many Africans' first real contact with whites was in mission schools. Some peoples, such as the Ibo in Nigeria, became highly Christianized.

Such occasional successes in black Africa contrasted with the general failure of missionary efforts in India, China, and the Islamic world. There Christians often preached in vain to peoples with ancient, complex religious beliefs. Yet the number of Christian believers around the world did increase substantially in the nineteenth century, and missionary groups kept trying. Unfortunately, "many missionaries had drunk at the well of European racism," and this probably prevented them from doing better.[13]

Critics of Imperialism

The expansion of empire aroused sharp, even bitter, critics. A forceful attack was delivered in 1902, after the unpopular Boer War, by radical English economist J. A. Hobson (1858–1940) in his *Imperialism,* a work that influenced Lenin and others. Hobson contended that the rush to acquire colonies was due to the economic needs of unregulated capitalism, particularly the need of the rich to find outlets for their surplus capital. Yet, Hobson argued, imperial possessions did not pay off economically for the home country as a whole. Only unscrupulous special-interest groups profited from them, at the expense of both the European taxpayer and the natives. Moreover, Hobson argued that the quest for empire diverted popular attention away from domestic reform and the need to reduce the great gap between rich and poor. These and similar arguments were not very persuasive, however. Most people then (and now) were sold on the idea that imperialism was economically profitable for the homeland, and a broad and genuine enthusiasm for empire developed among the masses.

Hobson and many other critics struck home, however, with their moral condemnation of whites imperiously ruling nonwhites. They rebelled against crude Social Darwinian thought. "O Evolution, what crimes are committed in thy name!" cried one foe. Another sardonically coined a new beatitude: "Blessed are the strong, for they shall prey on the weak."[14] Kipling and his kind were lampooned as racist bullies whose rule rested on brutality, racial contempt, and the Maxim machine gun. Polish-born novelist Joseph Conrad (1857–1924), in *Heart of Darkness,* castigated the "pure selfishness" of Europeans in "civilizing" Africa. The main character in the novel, once a liberal scholar, turns into a savage brute.

Critics charged Europeans with applying a degrading double standard and failing to live up to their own noble ideals. At home Europeans had won or were winning representative government, individual liberties, and a certain equality of opportunity. In their empires Europeans imposed military dictatorships on Africans and Asians; forced them to work involuntarily, almost like slaves; and discriminated against them shamelessly. Only by renouncing imperialism, critics insisted, and giving captive peoples the freedoms idealized in Western society would Europeans be worthy of their traditions. Europeans who denounced the imperialist tide provided colonial peoples with a Western ideology of liberation.

✤ RESPONSES TO WESTERN IMPERIALISM

To peoples in Africa and Asia, Western expansion represented a profoundly disruptive assault. Everywhere it threatened traditional ruling classes, economies, and ways of life. Christian missionaries and European secular ideologies challenged established beliefs and values. Non-Western peoples experienced a crisis of identity, one made all the more painful by the power and arrogance of the white intruders.

Often the initial response of African and Asian rulers was to try driving the unwelcome foreigners away, as in China, Japan, and the upper Sudan. Violent antiforeign reactions exploded elsewhere again and again, but the superior military technology of the industrialized West almost invariably prevailed. Beaten in battle, many Africans and Asians concentrated on preserving their cultural traditions at all costs. Others found themselves forced to reconsider their initial hostility. Some (such as Ismail of Egypt) concluded that the West was indeed superior in some ways and that it was therefore necessary to reform their societies and copy European achievements. Thus it is possible to think of responses to the Western impact as a spectrum, with "traditionalists" at one end, "westernizers" or "modernizers" at the other, and many shades of opinion in between. The struggle among these groups was often intense. With time, however, the modernizers tended to gain the upper hand.

When resistance to European domination was thoroughly shattered by superior force, the great majority of Asians and Africans accepted imperial rule. Political participation in non-Western lands was historically limited to small elites, and the masses were used to doing what their rulers told them. In these circumstances Europeans, clothed in power and convinced of their righteousness, governed smoothly and effectively. They received considerable support from both traditionalists (local chiefs, landowners, religious leaders) and modernizers (Western-educated professional classes and civil servants).

Nevertheless, imperial rule was in many ways an imposing edifice built on sand. Support for European rule among the conforming and accepting millions was shallow and weak. Thus the conforming masses followed with greater or lesser enthusiasm a few determined personalities who came to oppose the Europeans. Such leaders always arose, both when Europeans ruled directly and when they manipulated native governments, for at least two basic reasons.

First, the nonconformists—the eventual antiimperialist leaders—developed a burning desire for human dignity. They came to feel that such dignity was incompatible with foreign rule, with its smirks and smiles, its paternalism and condescension.

Second, potential leaders found in the Western world the ideologies and justification for their protest. They discovered liberalism, with its credo of civil liberty and political self-determination. They echoed the demands of anti-imperialists in Europe and America that the West live up to its own ideals.

More important, they found themselves attracted to modern nationalism, which asserted that every people had the right to control its own destiny. After 1917 anti-imperialist revolt would find another weapon in Lenin's version of Marxian socialism. Thus the anti-imperialist search for dignity drew strength from Western culture, as is apparent in the development of three major Asian countries—India, Japan, and China.

Empire in India

India was the jewel of the British Empire, and no colonial area experienced a more profound British impact. Unlike Japan and China, which maintained a real or precarious independence, and unlike African territories, which were annexed by Europeans only at the end of the nineteenth century, India was ruled more or less absolutely by Britain for a very long time.

Arriving in India on the heels of the Portuguese in the seventeenth century, the British East India Company had conquered the last independent native state by 1848. The last "traditional" response to European rule—the attempt by the established ruling classes to drive the white man out by military force—was broken in India in 1857 and 1858. Those were the years of the Great Rebellion (which the British called a "mutiny"), when an insurrection by Muslim and Hindu mercenaries in the British army spread throughout northern and central India before it was finally crushed, primarily by loyal native troops from southern India. Thereafter Britain ruled India directly. India illustrates, therefore, for better and for worse, what generations of European domination might produce.

 The British in India This photo suggests not only the power and luxury of the British ruling class in India but also its confidence and self-satisfaction. As one British viceroy said, "We are all British gentlemen engaged in the magnificent work of governing an inferior race." *(Source: Hulton Deutsch Collection)*

After 1858 India was ruled by the British Parliament in London and administered by a tiny, all-white civil service in India. In 1900 this elite consisted of fewer than 3,500 top officials, for a population of 300 million. The white elite, backed by white officers and native troops, was competent and generally well disposed toward the welfare of the Indian peasant masses. Yet it practiced strict job discrimination and social segregation, and most of its members quite frankly considered the jumble of Indian peoples and castes to be racially inferior. As Lord Kitchener, one of the most distinguished top military commanders of India, stated:

It is this consciousness of the inherent superiority of the European which has won for us India. However well educated and clever a native may be, and however brave he may prove himself, I believe that no rank we can bestow on him would cause him to be considered an equal of the British officer.[15]

When, for example, the British Parliament in 1883 was considering a major bill to allow Indian judges to try white Europeans in India, the British community rose in protest and defeated the measure. The idea of being judged by Indians was inconceivable to the Europeans, for it was clear to them that the empire in India rested squarely on racial inequality.

In spite of (or perhaps even because of) their strong feelings of racial and cultural superiority, the British acted energetically and introduced many desirable changes to India. Realizing that they needed well-educated Indians to serve as skilled subordinates in the government and army, the British established a modern system of progressive secondary education in which all instruction was in English. Thus through education and government service, the British offered some Indians excellent opportunities for both economic and social advancement. High-caste Hindus formed a new elite profoundly influenced by Western thought and culture.

This new bureaucratic elite played a crucial role in modern economic development, which was a second result of British rule. Irrigation projects for agriculture, the world's third largest railroad network for good communications, and large tea and jute plantations geared to the world economy were all developed. Unfortunately, the lot of the Indian masses improved little, for the increase in production was eaten up by an increase in population.

Finally, with a well-educated, English-speaking Indian bureaucracy and modern communications, the British created a unified, powerful state. They placed under the same general system of law and administration the different Hindu and Muslim peoples of the subcontinent that had fought each other for centuries during the Middle Ages and had been repeatedly conquered by Muslim and Mongol invaders. It was as if Europe, with its many states and varieties of Christianity, had been conquered and united in a single great empire.

In spite of these achievements, the decisive reaction to European rule was the rise of nationalism among the Indian elite. No matter how anglicized and necessary a member of the educated classes became, he or she could never become the white ruler's equal. The top jobs, the best clubs, the modern hotels, and even certain railroad compartments were sealed off to brown-skinned men and women. The peasant masses might accept such inequality as the latest version of age-old oppression, but the well-educated, English-speaking elite eventually could not. For the elite, racial discrimination meant not only injured pride but also bitter injustice. And it was based on dictatorship, no matter how benign.

By 1885 when educated Indians came together to found the predominately Hindu Indian National Congress, demands were increasing for the equality and self-government that Britain enjoyed and had already granted white-settler colonies, such as Canada and Australia. By 1907, emboldened in part by Japan's success (see the next section), the radicals in the Indian National Congress were calling for complete independence. Even the moderates were demanding home rule for India through an elected parliament. Although there were sharp divisions between Hindus and Muslims, the common heritage of British rule and Western ideals, along with the reform and revitalization of the Hindu religion, had created a genuine movement for national independence.

The Example of Japan

When Commodore Perry arrived in Japan in 1853 with his crude but effective gunboat diplomacy, Japan was a complex feudal society. At the top stood a figurehead emperor, but for more than two hundred years real power had been in the hands of the *shogun,* general-in-chief. With the help of the warrior nobility *samurai,* the shogun governed a country of hard-working, productive peasants and city dwellers. Often poor and restless, the intensely proud samurai were humiliated by the sudden American intrusion and the unequal treaties with Western countries.

When foreign diplomats and merchants began to settle in Yokohama, radical samurai reacted with a wave of antiforeign terrorism and antigovernment assassinations between 1858 and 1863. The

A Japanese View of America   Japanese publishers memorialized the opening of Japan to foreign trade with popular woodblock prints. An 1860 American newspaper illustration showing the visit of the Japanese embassy to the sewing and laundry rooms of the Willard Hotel in Washington, D.C., inspired this print. The Americans hold symbols of their technology—a pocket watch and a sewing machine. The Japanese text celebrates American wealth, power, and technological superiority, which the Japanese admired and soon imitated. *(Source: Private Collection)*

imperialist response was swift and unambiguous. An allied fleet of American, British, Dutch, and French warships demolished key forts, further weakening the power and prestige of the shogun's government. Then in 1867, a coalition led by patriotic samurai seized control of the government with hardly any bloodshed and restored the political power of the emperor. This was the Meiji Restoration, a great turning point in Japanese development.

The immediate, all-important goal of the new government was to meet the foreign threat. The battle cry of the Meiji reformers was "Enrich the state and strengthen the armed forces." But how were these tasks to be done? In an about-face that was one of history's most remarkable chapters, the young but well-trained, idealistic but flexible leaders of Meiji Japan dropped their antiforeign attacks. Convinced that Western civilization was indeed superior in its military and industrial aspects, they initiated from above a series of measures to reform Japan along modern, Western lines. They were convinced that "Japan must be reborn with America its mother and France its father."[16]

In 1871 the new leaders abolished the old feudal structure of aristocratic, decentralized government and formed a strong unified state. Following the example of the French Revolution, they dismantled the four-class legal system and declared social equality. They decreed freedom of movement in a country where traveling abroad had been a most serious crime. They created a free, competitive, government-stimulated economy. Japan began to build railroads and modern factories. Thus the new generation adopted many principles of a free, liberal society. As in Europe, such freedom resulted in a tremendously creative release of human energy.

The overriding concern of Japan's political leadership, however, was always a powerful state, and to achieve this, the new leaders borrowed more than liberalism from the West. A powerful modern navy was created, and the army was completely reorganized along French and German lines, with three-year military service for all males and a professional officer corps. In 1877, this army of draftees crushed a major rebellion by feudal elements protesting the loss of their privileges. Japan also borrowed rapidly and adapted skillfully the West's science and modern technology, particularly in industry, medicine, and education. Many Japanese were encouraged to study abroad, and the

THE SPREAD OF WESTERN IMPERIALISM

1800–1913	World trade increases 25-fold
1816–1880	European economic penetration of non-Western countries
1835	Great Trek: Boers proclaim independence from Great Britain in the South African hinterland
1840s	European capitalists begin large-scale foreign investment
1842	Treaty of Nanjing: Manchu government of China cedes Hong Kong to Great Britain
1846	Repeal of Corn Laws: Great Britain declares its strong support of free trade
1848	British defeat of last independent native state in India
1853	Perry's arrival in Tokyo: Japan opened to European influence
1857–1858	Great Rebellion in India
1858–1863	Anti-foreign reaction in Japan
1867	Meiji Restoration in Japan: adoption of Western reforms
1869	Completion of Suez Canal
1871	Abolition of feudal domains in Japan
1876	Ismail, khedive of Egypt, appoints British and French commissioners to oversee government finances
1880	Establishment of French protectorate on the northern bank of the Congo
1880–1900	European powers intensify their "scramble for Africa"
1882	British occupation of Egypt
1884–1885	International conference on Africa in Berlin: European powers require "effective occupation"; Germany acquires protectorates in Togo, Cameroon, Southwest Africa, and East Africa; Belgium acquires the Congo free state
1885	Formation of the Indian National Congress
1890	Establishment of an authoritarian constitution in Japan
1893	France completes its acquisition of Indochina
1894	Sino-Japanese War: Japan acquires Formosa
1898	Battle of Omdurman: under Kitchener, British forces reconquer the Sudan Spanish-American War: United States acquires the Philippines "Hundred Days of Reform" in China
1899–1902	Boer War: British defeat Dutch settlers in South Africa
1900	The Boxer Rebellion in China
1903	American occupation of the Panama Canal Zone
1904–1905	Russo-Japanese War: Japan wins protectorate over Port Arthur in China
1910	Japanese annexation of Korea
1912	Fall of Manchu Dynasty in China

government paid large salaries to attract foreign experts. These experts were always carefully controlled, however, and were replaced by trained Japanese as soon as possible.

By 1890, when the new state was firmly established, the wholesale borrowing of the early restoration had given way to more selective emphasis on those things foreign that were in keeping with Japanese tradition. Following the model of the German Empire, Japan established an authoritarian constitution and rejected democracy. The power of the emperor and his ministers was vast; that of the legislature, limited.

Japan successfully copied the imperialism of Western society. Expansion not only proved that Japan was strong; it also cemented the nation together in a great mission. Having "opened" Korea with the gunboat diplomacy of imperialism in 1876, Japan decisively defeated China in a war over Korea in 1894 to 1895 and took Formosa (modern-day Taiwan). In the next years, Japan competed aggressively with the leading European powers for influence and territory in China, particularly Manchuria. There Japanese and Russian imperialism met and collided. In 1904 Japan attacked Russia without warning, and after a bloody war Japan emerged with a valuable foothold in China—Russia's former protectorate over Port Arthur (see Map 27.2). By 1910, with the annexation of Korea, Japan had become a major imperialist power.

Japan became the first non-Western country to use an ancient love of country to transform itself and thereby meet the many-sided challenge of Western expansion. Moreover, Japan demonstrated convincingly that a modern Asian nation could defeat and humble a great Western power. Japan provided patriots in Asia and Africa with an inspiring example of national recovery and liberation.

Toward Revolution in China

In 1860 the two-hundred-year-old Manchu Dynasty in China appeared on the verge of collapse. Efforts to repel foreigners had failed, and rebellion and chaos wracked the country. Yet two factors helped the government achieve a surprising comeback that lasted more than thirty years. First, the traditional ruling groups temporarily produced new and effective leadership. Loyal scholar-statesmen and generals quelled disturbances such as the great Tai Ping Rebellion. The empress dowager Tzu Hsi, a truly remarkable woman, governed in the name of her young son and combined shrewd insight with vigorous action to revitalize the bureaucracy. Second, destructive foreign aggression lessened, for the Europeans had obtained their primary goal of commercial and diplomatic relations. Indeed, some Europeans assisted in the dynasty's efforts to adopt some aspects of Western government and technology while maintaining traditional Chinese values and beliefs.

The parallel movement toward domestic reform and limited cooperation with the West collapsed under the blows of Japanese imperialism. The Sino-Japanese War of 1894 to 1895 and the subsequent harsh peace treaty revealed China's helplessness in the face of aggression, triggering a rush for foreign concessions and protectorates in China. At the high point of this rush in 1898, it appeared that the European powers might actually divide China among themselves, as they had recently divided Africa. Probably only the jealousy each nation felt toward its imperialist competitors saved China from partition, although the U.S. Open Door policy, which opposed formal annexation of Chinese territory, may have helped tip the balance. In any event, the tempo and impact of foreign penetration greatly accelerated after 1894.

So, too, did the intensity and radicalism of the Chinese reaction. Like the leaders of the Meiji Restoration, some modernizers saw salvation in Western institutions. In 1898 the government launched a desperate "hundred days of reform" in an attempt to meet the foreign challenge. Radical reformers, such as the revolutionary Sun Yat-sen (1866–1925), who came from the peasantry and was educated in Hawaii by Christian missionaries, sought to overthrow the Manchu Dynasty altogether and establish a republic.

On the other side, some traditionalists turned back toward ancient practices, political conservatism, and fanatical hatred of the "foreign devils." "Protect the country, destroy the foreigner" was their simple motto. Such conservative, antiforeign patriots had often clashed with foreign missionaries, whom they charged with undermining reverence for ancestors and thereby threatening the Chinese family and the entire society. In the agony of defeat and unwanted reforms, secret societies such as the Boxers rebelled. In northeastern China, more than two hundred foreign missionaries and several thousand Chinese Christians were killed.

The Empress Dowager Tzu Hsi   To maintain her power, the empress drew on conservative forces such as the court eunuchs surrounding her here. Three years after her death in 1908, a revolution broke out and forced the last Chinese emperor, a boy of six, to abdicate. *(Source: Courtesy of the Freer Gallery of Art, Smithsonian Institution, Washington, D.C.)*

Once again the imperialist response was swift and harsh. Foreign armies occupied and plundered Beijing. A heavy indemnity was imposed.

The years after the Boxer Rebellion in 1900 were ever more troubled. Anarchy and foreign influence spread as the power and prestige of the Manchu Dynasty declined still further. Antiforeign, antigovernment revolutionary groups agitated and plotted. Finally in 1912, a spontaneous uprising toppled the Manchu Dynasty. After thousands of years of emperors and empires, a loose coalition of revolutionaries proclaimed a Western-style republic and called for an elected parliament. The transformation of China under the impact of expanding Western society entered a new phase, and the end was not in sight.

SUMMARY

In the nineteenth century, the industrializing West entered the third and most dynamic phase of its centuries-old expansion into non-Western lands. In so doing, Western nations profitably subordinated those lands to their economic interests, sent forth millions of emigrants, and established political influence in Asia and vast political empires in Africa. The reasons for this culminating surge were many, but the economic thrust of robust industrial capitalism, an ever-growing lead in technology, and the competitive pressures of European nationalism were particularly important.

Western expansion had far-reaching consequences. For the first time in human history, the world became in many ways a single unit. Moreover, European expansion diffused the ideas and techniques of a highly developed civilization. Yet the West relied on force to conquer and rule, and it treated non-Western peoples as racial inferiors. Thus non-Western elites, often armed with Western doctrines, gradually responded to the Western challenge. They launched a national, anti-imperialist struggle for dignity, genuine independence, and modernization. This struggle would emerge as a central drama of world history after the great European civil war of 1914 to 1918, which reduced the West's technological advantage and shattered its self-confidence and complacent moral superiority.

NOTES

1. Quoted in A. Waley, *The Opium War Through Chinese Eyes* (New York: Macmillan, 1958), p. 29.

2. Quoted in J. W. Hall, *Japan, from Prehistory to Modern Times* (New York: Delacorte Press, 1970), p. 250.

3. Quoted in R. Hallett, *Africa to 1875* (Ann Arbor: University of Michigan Press, 1970), p. 109.

4. Quoted in Earl of Cromer, *Modern Egypt* (London, 1911), p. 48.

5. Quoted in T. Blegen, *Norwegian Migration to America*, vol. 2 (Northfield, Minn.: Norwegian-American Historical Association, 1940), p. 468.

6. Quoted in I. Howe, *World of Our Fathers* (New York: Harcourt Brace Jovanovich, 1976), p. 25.

7. Quoted in C. A. Price, *The Great White Walls Are Built: Restrictive Immigration to North America and Australia, 1836–1888* (Canberra: Australian National University Press, 1974), p. 175.

8. Quoted in W. L. Langer, *European Alliances and Alignments, 1871–1890* (New York: Vintage Books, 1931), p. 290.

9. Quoted in J. Ellis, *The Social History of the Machine Gun* (New York: Pantheon Books, 1975), pp. 86, 101.

10. Quoted in G. H. Nadel and P. Curtis, eds., *Imperialism and Colonialism* (New York: Macmillan, 1964), p. 94.

11. Quoted in W. L. Langer, *The Diplomacy of Imperialism*, 2d ed. (New York: Knopf, 1951), pp. 86, 88.

12. Rudyard Kipling, *The Five Nations* (London, 1903), quoted by the permission of Mrs. George Bambridge, Methuen & Company, and Doubleday & Company, Inc.

13. E. H. Berman, "African Responses to Christian Mission Education," *African Studies Review* 17 (1974): 530.

14. Quoted in Langer, *The Diplomacy of Imperialism*, p. 88.

15. Quoted in K. M. Panikkar, *Asia and Western Dominance: A Survey of the Vasco da Gama Epoch of Asian History* (London: George Allen & Unwin, 1959), p. 116.

16. Quoted in Hall, *Japan, from Prehistory to Modern Times*, p. 289.

SUGGESTED READING

General surveys of European expansion in a broad perspective include R. Betts, *Europe Overseas* (1968); A. Thornton, *Imperialism in the Twentieth Century* (1977); T. Smith, *The Patterns of Imperialism* (1981); and W. Woodruff, *Impact of Western Man* (1967), which has an extensive bibliography. D. K. Fieldhouse has written two fine surveys, *Economics and Empire, 1830–1914* (1970), and *Colonialism, 1870–1945* (1981). G. Barraclough, *An Introduction to Contemporary History* (1964), argues powerfully that Western imperialism and the non-Western reaction to it have been crucial in world history since about 1890. J. A. Hobson's classic *Imperialism* (1902) is readily available, and the Marxist-Leninist case is effectively presented in V. G. Kieran, *Marxism and Imperialism* (1975). Two excellent anthologies on the problem of European expansion are the volume by Nadel and Curtis cited in the Notes, and H. Wright, ed., *The "New Imperialism,"* rev. ed. (1975).

Britain's leading position in European imperialism is examined in a lively way by B. Porter, *The Lion's Share* (1976); J. Morris, *Pax Britannica* (1968); and D. Judd, *The Victorian Empire* (1970), a stunning pictorial history. G. Stocking, *Victorian Anthropology* (1987), is a brilliant analysis of the cultural and racial implications of Western expansion. B. Semmel has written widely on the intellectual foundations of English expansion, as in *The Rise of Free Trade Imperialism* (1970). J. Gallagher and R. Robinson, *Africa and the Victorians: The Climax of Imperialism* (1961), is an influential reassessment. H. Brunschwig, *French Colonialism, 1871–1914* (1966), and W. Baumgart, *Imperialism: The Idea and Reality of British and French Colonial Expansion* (1982), are well-balanced studies. A. Moorehead, *The White Nile* (1971), tells the fascinating story of the European exploration of the mysterious Upper Nile. Volumes 5 and 6 of K. Latourette, *History of the Expansion of Christianity, 7* vols. (1937–1945), examine the powerful impulse for missionary work in non-European areas. D. Headrick stresses Western technological superiority in *Tools of Empire* (1981). C. Erikson, *Emigration from Europe, 1815–1914* (1976), and R. Vecoli and S. Sinke, eds., *A Century of European Migrations, 1830–1930* (1991), are valuable general studies.

Howe and Blegen, cited in the Notes, provide dramatic accounts of Jewish and Norwegian migration to the United States. Most other migrant groups have also found their historians: M. Walker, *Germany and the Emigration, 1816–1885* (1964), and W. Adams, *Ireland and Irish Emigration to the New World* (reissued 1967), are outstanding. Langer's volumes consider the diplomatic aspects of imperialism in exhaustive detail. Ellis's well-illustrated study of the machine gun is fascinating, as is Price on the restriction of Asian migration to Australia. All these works are cited in the Notes.

E. Wolf, *Europe and the People Without History* (1982), considers, with skill and compassion, the impact of imperialism on non-Western peoples. Two unusual and provocative studies on personal relations between European rulers and non-European subjects are D. Mannoni, *Prospero and Caliban: The Psychology of Colonialization* (1964), and F. Fanon, *Wretched of the Earth* (1965), a bitter attack on white racism by a black psychologist active in the Algerian revolution. V. Ware, *Beyond the Pale: White Women, Racism and History* (1992), examines the complex role of European women in imperialism. Novels also bring the psychological and human dimensions of imperialism alive. H. Rider Haggard, *King Solomon's Mines,* portrays the powerful appeal of adventure in exotic lands; Rudyard Kipling, the greatest writer of European expansion, is at his stirring best in *Kim* and *Soldiers Three.* Joseph Conrad unforgettably probes European motives in *Heart of Darkness,* and André Gide, *The Immoralist,* closely examines European moral corruption in North Africa. William Boyd, *An Ice-Cream War,* a good story of British and Germans fighting each other in Africa during the First World War, is a favorite with students.

Hall, cited in the Notes, is an excellent introduction to the history of Japan. Waley, also cited in the Notes, has written extensively and well on China. I. Hsü, *The Rise of Modern China,* 2d ed. (1975), and K. Latourette, *The Chinese: Their History and Culture,* rev. ed. (1964), are fine histories with many suggestions for further reading. E. Reischauer's topical survey, *Japan: The Story of a Nation* (1981), is recommended, as are T. Huber, *The Revolutionary Origins of Modern Japan* (1981), and Y. Fukuzawa, *Autobiography* (1966), the personal account of a leading intellectual who witnessed the emergence of modern Japan.

G. Perry, *The Middle East: Fourteen Islamic Centuries* (1983), concisely surveys nineteenth-century developments and provides an up-to-date bibliography. B. Lewis, *The Middle East and the West* (1963), is a penetrating analysis of the impact of Western ideas on Middle Eastern thought. Hallett, cited in the Notes, and R. July, *A History of the African People* (1970), contain excellent introductions to Africa in the age of imperialism. J. D. Fage, *A History of Africa* (1978), is also recommended. A classic study of Western expansion from an Indian viewpoint is Panikkar's volume mentioned in the Notes. S. Wolpert, *A New History of India,* 2d ed. (1982), incorporates recent scholarship in a wide-ranging study that is highly recommended.

A Scholar's Defense of Imperialism

Western expansion in the nineteenth century offered opportunities not only to soldiers and foreign investors but also to those spurred by non-economic motives. For example, some scholars plunged into the study of the different non-Western cultures and became experts on their languages and customs. Such scholars also provided general interpretations that usually supported at least some aspects of Western imperialism.

One such scholar was Arminius Vambery (1832–1913), an influential professor of Asian languages at the University of Budapest in Hungary. Living in Constantinople in his twenties and learning several Asian languages and dialects, Vambery wrote many books on his travels and on the peoples and languages of central and western Asia. The following defense of Western expansion is taken from his introductory overview to Western Culture in Eastern Lands *(1906), a comparison on English and Russian imperialism in action.*

There are, perhaps, no subjects of human knowledge and research in which such progress has been made during the past century as in those of the geography and ethnography of Asia. . . . For instance, on the subject of Central Asia . . . we now have elaborate and exhaustive narratives and descriptions upon all possible subjects connected with those countries. In the regions where some decades ago the traveller's life was in constant danger, and where the struggle with the elements and with the natives made his progress necessarily slow and tedious, we now find a well-organised railway system, and in the place of the grunting camel the fiery steam-horse ploughs its way through endless vistas of sandy steppes. . . .

And great changes similar to those which have taken place in Central Asia may also be

noticed in greater or less degree in other parts and regions of the Eastern world, [where] . . . we now find that the supreme power of the Western world is gradually making itself felt. The walls of seclusion are ruthlessly pulled down, and the resistance caused by the favoured superstitions, prejudices, and the ignorance of the sleepy and apathetic man in the East, is slowly being overcome. . . . Our present-day Europe, in its restless, bustling activity will take good care not to let the East relapse again into its former indolence. We forcibly tear its eyes open; we push, jolt, toss, and shake it, and we compel it to exchange its world-worn, hereditary ideas and customs for our modern views of life; nay, we have even succeeded to some extent in convincing our Eastern neighbours that our civilisation, our faith, our customs, our philosophy, are the only means whereby the well-being, the progress, and the happiness, of the human race can be secured.

For well-nigh 300 years we have been carrying on this struggle with the Eastern world, and persist in our unsolicited interference, following in the wake of ancient Rome, which began the work with marked perseverance, but naturally never met with much success because of the inadequate means at its disposal. . . . Compared with the real earnest work done in our days by Western Powers, the efforts of Rome are as the flickering of an oil-lamp in comparison with the radiance of the sun in its full glory. It may be said without exaggeration that never in the world's history has any one continent exercised such influence over another as has the Europe of our days over Asia: never were two such diametrically opposed elements engaged in so deadly a strife as is now to be seen in all parts of the Old World. This being so, it appears to me most important that we should realise what is the extent and the purpose of our civilising influence over Asia. We have to consider not only its historical growth and the means employed in its development, but also the results so far obtained, and the ultimate ends to be accomplished. . . . In the first place, then, we must ask ourselves the question: Have we a right thus to interfere in the concerns of the ancient world; and in the second place, What do the Asiatics think of it?

If we start with the assumption that every man has a right to his own opinion and to the views which best correspond with his ideas of morality and material comfort, our pretended crusade in the name of civilisation must look like an unwarrantable interference. But the correctness of this assumption has so far been contradicted by historical events, for no community can remain in absolute isolation. Even China, the prototype of a seclusion extending over thousands of years, has before now migrated far into neighbouring lands. . . . If Western nations had checked their passion for migration the aspect of things in Asia would now be even worse than it actually is. Of course the Asiatics themselves do not view the matter in this light. Many of them look upon our enforced reforms as hostile attacks upon their liberty, and as means to bring their people under our yoke. But the better-informed amongst them, who know what the East now is and what it used to be, will hardly share this view. Humanity in Asia has never known culture and liberty in the sense in which we understand it, and has therefore never known true happiness, which is unavoidably dependent upon these two chief factors of mental and physical well-being.

During the much-extolled golden era of the history of Asia, tyranny and despotism were the ruling elements, justice a vain chimera, everything depended on the arbitrary will of the Sovereign, and a prolonged period of rest and peace was quite the exception. Asiatics, from motives of vanity or inborn laziness, may condone these abnormal conditions, but still it remains our duty to recognise the true state of affairs, and to take pity upon our oppressed fellow-men. Without our help Asia will never rise above its low level, and even granted that

❋ Oil painting (on glass) of Western factories in Canton. (*Source: Courtesy Peabody Essex Museum, Salem, Mass.*)

the politics of European Powers are not purely unselfish, we must nevertheless, keeping the ultimate object in view, approve of the interference of Europe in the affairs of the East, and give the undertaking our hearty support.

Viewed in this light, we may be thankful that the Christian West for 300 years has been unceasing in its interference in Asiatic affairs.

Questions for Analysis

1. What changes did Vambery see occurring in Asia?

2. Why, according to Vambery, did Western nations have a right to "interfere" in Asia?

3. How did Asians react to Western interference? Did all Asians react the same way? Why or why not?

4. Did Vambery believe in progress? What lessons did he draw from history?

Source: A. Vambery, *Western Culture in Eastern Lands: A Comparison of the Methods Adopted by England and Russia in the Middle East* (New York: E. P. Dutton, 1906), pp. 1–6.

28

Nation Building in the Western Hemisphere and in Australia

An allegorical painting of 1825 honoring Simón Bolívar, center, as the Liberator of Peru. Other portraits on the shield include that of Antonio Sucre, Bolívar's favorite general, top right, and William Miller, a British general who volunteered to serve under Bolívar, bottom right. *(Source: Instituto Nacional De Cultura Tesoreria General, Peru. Courtesy the Haywood Gallery, London)*

In the Western Hemisphere and in Australia, as in Europe, the nineteenth century was a period of nation building, geographic expansion, and industrial and commercial growth. Waves of emigrants moved from Europe and Asia to the Americas and to Australia. The millions who braved the oceans populated and built new nations and linked the Western Hemisphere and Australia with the rest of the globe.

The countries of North and South America became highly diverse ethnically and culturally, and the issue of race created serious tensions throughout the hemisphere. In the United States it helped to bring on the Civil War. In the late nineteenth and early twentieth centuries, European immigration directly affected the ways with which the United States and the Latin American nations coped with racial situations.

At the end of the eighteenth century, Canada and the countries of South America remained colonies. Their European mother countries looked on the democratic experiment of the infant United States with suspicion and scorn. The island continent of Australia, remote from Europe and economically undeveloped, served as a dumping ground for English criminals. By 1914 the Latin American states, Canada, and Australia were enjoying political independence and playing a crucial role in the world economy. The United States had become a colossus on which the Old World depended in the First World War.

- Why and how did the Spanish colonies of Latin America shake off European domination and develop into national states?
- What role did the concept of manifest destiny play in the evolution of the United States?
- How did slavery affect blacks in the United States?
- How did the Americas and Australia absorb new peoples, and what was the social impact of the immigrants?
- What geographical, economic, and political conditions shaped the development of Canada?
- What factors aided the economic growth of Australia?

These are among the questions that this chapter addresses.

LATIN AMERICA (1800–1929)

In 1800 the Spanish Empire in the Western Hemisphere stretched from the headwaters of the Mississippi River in present-day Minnesota to the tip of Cape Horn in the Antarctic (see Map 28.1). According to the Kentucky statesman Henry Clay (1777–1852), "Within this vast region, we behold the most sublime and interesting objects of creation: the loftiest mountains, the most majestic rivers in the world; the richest mines of precious metals, the choicest productions of the earth."[1] Spain believed that this great wealth existed for its benefit, and Spanish policies fostered bitterness and the desire for independence in the colonies. Between 1806 and 1825 the Spanish colonies in Latin America were convulsed by upheavals that ultimately resulted in their separation from Spain.

The Latin American wars were *revolutions* because the colonists were revolting against the domination of Spain and fighting for direct self-government. They were *wars of independence* because the colonies were seeking economic liberation and management of their own commercial affairs. They were *civil wars* because social and racial groups were fighting one another. The *Creoles*—people of Spanish descent born in America—resented the economic and political dominance of the *peninsulares,* as natives of Spain or Portugal were called. Peninsulares controlled the rich export-import trade, intercolonial trade, and the mining industries. At the same time, *mestizos* of mixed Spanish and Indian background and *mulattos* of mixed Spanish and African heritage sought an end to their systematic subordination.

Between 1850 and the worldwide depression of 1929, the countries of Latin America developed into national states. The predominant factors in this evolution were the heritage of colonial exploitation, a neocolonial economic structure, massive immigration from Europe and Asia, and the fusion of Amerindian, Caucasian, African, and Asian peoples.

The Origins of the Revolutions

Because of regional, geographic, and racial differences, the Latin American movements for independence took different forms in different places. Everywhere, however, they grew out of recent

915

colonial economic grievances. By the late seventeenth century the Spanish colonies had achieved a high degree of economic diversity and independence. The mercantilist imperialism of the days of Hernando Cortés (1485–1547) and Francisco Pizarro (1470–1541), which held that the colonies existed for Spain's financial benefit and should be economically dependent on Spain, had faded away. The colonies had become self-sufficient producers of foodstuffs, wine, textiles, and consumer goods. What was not produced domestically was secured through a healthy intercolonial trade that had developed independently of Spain, despite formidable geographic obstacles and colonial policies designed to restrict it.

In Peru, for example, domestic agriculture supported the large mining settlements, and the colony did not have to import food. Craft workshops owned by the state or by private individuals produced consumer goods for the working class; what was not manufactured locally was bought from Mexico and transported by the Peruvian merchant marine. By 1700 Mexico and Peru were sending shrinking percentages of their revenues to Spain and retaining more for public works, defense, and administration. The colonies lived for themselves, not for Spain.

The reforms of the Spanish Bourbons radically reversed this economic independence. Spain's humiliating defeat in the War of the Spanish Succession (1701–1713) prompted demands for sweeping reform of all of Spain's institutions, including colonial policies and practices. To improve administrative efficiency, the enlightened monarch Charles III (r. 1759–1788) carved the region of modern Colombia, Venezuela, and Ecuador out of the vast viceroyalty of Peru; it became the new viceroyalty of New Granada with its capital at Bogotá. The Crown also created the viceroyalty of Rio de la Plata (present-day Argentina) with its capital at Buenos Aires (Map 28.1).

Far more momentous was Charles III's radical overhaul of colonial trade policies, to enable Spain to compete with Great Britain and Holland in the great eighteenth-century struggle for empire. The Spanish crown intended the colonies to serve as sources of raw materials and as markets for Spanish manufactured goods. Charles III's free-trade policies cut duties and restrictions drastically for Spanish merchants. In Latin America these actions stimulated the production of crops in demand in

Europe: coffee in Venezuela; sugar in Cuba and throughout the Caribbean; hides, leather, and salted beef in the Rio de la Plata viceroyalty. In Mexico and Peru, production of silver climbed steadily in the last quarter of the century. The volume of Spain's trade with the colonies soared, possibly as much as 700 percent between 1778 and 1788.[2]

Colonial manufacturing, which had been growing steadily, suffered severely. Better-made and cheaper European goods drove colonial goods out of the marketplace. Colonial textiles, china, and wine, for example, could not compete with cheap Spanish products. For one thing, Latin American free laborers were paid more than European workers in the eighteenth century; this disparity helps explain the great numbers of immigrants to the colonies. Also, intercolonial transportation costs were higher than transatlantic costs. In the Rio de la Plata region, for example, heavy export taxes and light import duties shattered the wine industry. Geographic obstacles—mountains, deserts, jungles, and inadequate natural harbors—also frustrated colonial efforts to promote economic integration.

Having made the colonies dependent on essential Spanish goods, however, Spain found that it could not keep the sea routes open. After 1789 the French Revolution and Napoleonic wars isolated Spain from Latin America. Foreign traders, especially from the United States, swarmed into Spanish-American ports. In 1796 the Madrid government lifted the restrictions against neutrals trading with the colonies, thus acknowledging Spain's inability to supply the colonies with needed goods and markets.[3] All these difficulties spelled disaster for colonial trade and industry.

At the end of the eighteenth century colonists also complained bitterly that only peninsulares were appointed to the *audiencias*—the colonies' highest judicial bodies, which also served as councils to the viceroys—and to other positions in the colonial governments. According to the nineteenth-century Mexican statesman and historian Lucas Alamán (1792–1853),

 MAP 28.1 Latin America Before Independence Consider the factors that led to the boundaries of the various Spanish and Portuguese colonies in North and South America.

Disputed by Great Britain,
Spain, and Russia

Effective frontier of
Spanish settlement

*ATLANTIC
OCEAN*

COAHUILA

**VICEROYALTY
OF
NEW SPAIN**

BAJIO LEÓN

Mexico City• •Veracruz

Havana•

CUBA

SAINT DOMINGUE (HAITI)

JAMAICA

SANTO
DOMINGO

PUERTO
RICO

Caribbean Sea

Guatemala•

Caracas•

Suarez

Magdalena

Bogotá•

**VICEROYALTY OF
NEW GRANADA**

GUIANA

Amazon

*PACIFIC

OCEAN*

*A
N
D
E
S*

**VICEROYALTY
OF PERU**

Lima•

VICEROYALTY OF BRAZIL

•Bahia

*A
N
D
E
S*

Paraná

São Paulo•

•Rio de Janeiro

**VICEROYALTY OF
RIO DE LA PLATA**

Santiago•

Buenos Aires• •Montevideo

**AUDIENCIA
OF CHILE**

Spanish colonies

- Viceroyalty of New Spain
- Viceroyalty of New Granada
- Viceroyalty of Peru
- Audiencia of Chile
- Viceroyalty of Rio de la Plata

Portuguese colony

- Viceroyalty of Brazil

Disputed territory

- Disputed by Great Britain, Spain, and Russia

| 0 | 500 | 1000 Km. |
| 0 | 500 | 1000 Mi. |

ISLAS MALVINAS
(FALKLAND ISLANDS)

Cape Horn

this preference shown to Spaniards in political offices and ecclesiastical benefices has been the principal cause of the rivalry between the two classes; add to this the fact that Europeans possessed great wealth, which although it may have been the just reward of effort and industry, excited the envy of Americans and was considered as so much usurpation from them; consider that for all these reasons the Spaniards had obtained a decided preponderance over those born in the country; and it will not be difficult to explain the increasing jealousy and rivalry between the two groups which culminated in hatred and enmity.[4]

From 1751 to 1775, only 13 percent of appointees to the audiencias were Creoles.[5] To the Creole elite of Spanish America, the world seemed "upside down."[6] Creoles hungered for political office and resented their successful Spanish rivals.

Madrid's tax reforms also aggravated discontent. In the 1770s and 1780s the Spanish crown needed income to finance imperial defense. Colonial ports had to be fortified and standing armies built. Like Great Britain, Spain believed its colonies should bear some of the costs of their own defense. Accordingly, Madrid raised the prices of tobacco and liquor and increased the *alcabala* (a sales tax of Arabic origin) on many items. Improved government administration made tax collection more efficient. Creole business and agricultural interests resented the Crown's monopoly of the tobacco industry and opposed new taxes.

As in the thirteen North American colonies a decade earlier, protest movements in Latin America claimed that the colonies were being taxed unconstitutionally. Merchants in Boston and Philadelphia had protested taxation without representation; the Spanish colonies, however, had no tradition of legislative approval of taxes. Creole mercantile leaders argued instead that relations between imperial authorities and colonial interests stayed on an even keel through consultation and compromise and that when the Crown imposed taxes without consultation, it violated ancient constitutional practice.

The imperial government recognized the potential danger of the North American example. Although Spain had joined France on the side of the rebel colonies against Great Britain during the American Revolution, the Madrid government refused in 1783 to grant diplomatic recognition to the new United States. North American ships calling at South American ports had introduced the

subversive writings of Thomas Paine and Thomas Jefferson. For decades the ideas of Voltaire, Rousseau, and Montesquieu had been trickling into Latin America. In 1794 the Colombian Antonio Nariño translated and published the French *Declaration of the Rights of Man and the Citizen* (Spanish authorities sentenced him to ten years in an African prison, but he lived to become the father of Colombian independence). By 1800 the Creole elite throughout Latin America was familiar with liberal Enlightenment political thought.[7] The Creoles assumed, however, that the "rights of man" were limited, and they did not share such rights with Indians and blacks.

Race in the Colonial Period

The racial complexion of Latin American societies is one of the most complicated in the world. Because few European women emigrated to the colonies, Spanish men had relations with Indian and African women. African men deprived of black women sought Indian women. The result was a population composed of every possible combination of Indian, Spanish, and African blood.

Spanish theories of racial purity rejected people of mixed blood, particularly those of African descent. A person's social status depended on the degree of European blood he or she possessed or appeared to possess. Peninsulares and Creoles reinforced their privileged status by showing contempt for people who were not white. As the great nineteenth-century German scientist Alexander von Humboldt put it, having spent five years traveling throughout South America, "Any white person, although he rides his horse barefoot, imagines himself to be of the nobility of the country."[8] Coupled with the Spaniard's aristocratic disdain for manual labor, a three-hundred-year tradition had instilled in the minds of Latin Americans the notion that dark skin and manual labor went together. Owners of mines, plantations, and factories had a vested interest in keeping blacks and Indians in servile positions. Racism and discrimination pervaded all the Latin American colonies.

Demographers estimate that Indians still accounted for between three-fifths and three-fourths of the total population of Latin America at the end of the colonial period, in spite of the tremendous population losses caused by the introduction of diseases in the sixteenth and seventeenth centuries. The colonies that became Peru and Bolivia had Indian majorities; the regions that became Argentina and Chile had European majorities. Indians and black slaves toiled in the silver and gold mines of Mexico, Colombia, and Peru, in the wheat fields of Chile, in the humid, mosquito-ridden cane brakes of Mexico and the Caribbean, and in the diamond mines and coffee and sugar plantations of Brazil.

Nevertheless, nonwhites in Latin America did experience some social mobility in the colonial period, certainly more than nonwhites in North America experienced. In Mexico, decreasing reliance on slaves led to a great increase in manumissions. Once freed, however, Negroes (the Spanish term for "black persons" coined in 1555) immediately became subject to the payment of a money tribute, as were the Indians. Freedmen also incurred the obligation of military service. A few mulattos rose in the army, some as high as the rank of colonel. The army and the church seem to have offered the greatest opportunities for social mobility. Many black slaves gained their freedom by fleeing to the jungles or mountains, where they established self-governing communities. Around the year 1800 Venezuela counted 24,000 fugitive slaves in a total population of 87,000.

Many Indians were still subject to the mita and repartimiento. The *mita,* a system of forced labor requiring all adult Indian males to work for part of each year in the silver mines, was thinly disguised slave labor; the silver mines were deathtraps. The law of *repartimiento* required Indians to buy goods solely from local *corregidores,* officials who collected taxes. The new taxes of the 1770s and 1780s fell particularly heavily on the Indians. When Indian opposition to these taxes and to oppressive conditions exploded into violence, Creoles organized the protest movements and assumed leadership of them.

The Comunero Revolution

In Peru in November 1779 the wealthy, well-educated mestizo Tupac Amaru (1742–1781), a descendant of the Inca kings, captured, tried, and executed the local corregidor. Tupac Amaru and his mostly Indian followers demanded the abolition of both the alcabala tax and the mita and replacement of the corregidores with Indian governors. Proclaiming himself liberator of the people, Tupac Amaru waged a costly war of blood and fire against the Spanish governors. Poor communication among the rebel forces and the superior organiza-

Diamond Mining in Brazil   The discovery of gold and diamonds in Brazil in the seventeenth century increased the demand for slave labor. The English geologist John Mawe made this dramatic engraving of slaves washing for diamonds in the early nineteenth century. *(Source: Courtesy, Oliveira Lima Library, The Catholic University of America. Photo: Paul McKane, OSB)*

tion of the imperial armies enabled the Spanish to crush the revolt. Tupac Amaru, his family, and his captains were captured and savagely executed. Frightened colonial administrators did grant some reforms. The Crown repealed the repartimiento, reduced the mita, and replaced the corregidores with a lighter system of intendants. The condition of the Indians temporarily improved.

News of the rebellion of Tupac Amaru trickled northward, where it helped stimulate revolution in the New Granada viceroyalty. Disorders occurred first at Socorro in modern Colombia (Map 28.2). Throughout the eighteenth century Socorro had prospered. Sugar cane, corn, and cattle flourished because of its exceptionally fertile soil. Large cotton crops stimulated the production of textiles,

mostly in a primitive cottage industry worked by women. Socorro's location on the Suarez River made it an agricultural and manufacturing center and an entrepôt for trade with the hinterland. Hard-working Spanish immigrants had prospered and often intermarried with the Indians.

When the viceroy published new taxes on tobacco and liquor and reorganized the alcabala, riots broke out in Socorro in March 1781 and spread to other towns. Representatives of peasants and artisan groups from many towns elected a *comun,* or central committee, to lead the insurrection. Each town elected its local comun and the captain of its militia. Known as the Comunero Revolution, the insurrection in New Granada enjoyed broad-based support and good organization and appeared far more threatening to government authorities than had the uprising in Peru.

An Indian peasant army commanded by Creole captains marched on Bogotá. Government officials, lacking adequate military resources, sent a commission to play for time by negotiating with the comuneros. On June 4 the commission agreed to the rebels' terms: reduction of the alcabala and of the Indians' forced tribute, abolition of the new taxes on tobacco, and preference for Creoles over peninsulares in government positions. The joyful Indian army disbanded and went home. What the Indians did not know was that the commission had already secretly disclaimed the agreement with the rebels on the grounds that it had been achieved by force. Having succeeded in dispersing the Indians, the government at Bogotá won over the Creole leaders with promise of pardons and then moved in reserve troops who captured large numbers of rebels. When the last rebel base—that of José Antonio Galan—had been captured, a kangaroo court tried Galan and condemned him

to be taken out of jail, dragged and taken to the place of execution where he will be hung until dead, that his head be removed from his dead body, that the rest of his body be quartered, that his torso be committed to flames for which purpose a fire shall be lit in front of the platform. . . . All his descendants shall be declared infamous, all his property shall be confiscated by the

royal treasury, his home shall be burnt, and the ground salted, so that in this fashion his infamous name may be forgotten.[9]

Thus ended the revolt of the comuneros in New Granada. They failed to win self-rule, but they forced the authorities to act in accordance with the spirit of the "unwritten constitution," whose guiding principle was consultation and compromise.

Independence

In 1808, as part of his effort to rule Europe, Napoleon Bonaparte deposed the Spanish king Ferdinand VII and placed his own brother on the Spanish throne (see page 763). In Latin America the Creoles subsequently seized the opportunity. Since everything in Spanish America was done in the name of the king, the Creoles argued that the removal of the legitimate king shifted sovereignty to the people—that is, to themselves. In 1810 the small, wealthy Creole aristocracy used the removal of the Spanish king as justification for their seizure of political power and their preservation of that power.

The Creoles who led the various movements for independence did not intend a radical redistribution of property or reconstruction of society. They merely rejected the authority of the Spanish crown. An able scholar has described the war for independence as

a prolonged, confused, and in many ways contradictory movement. In Mexico it began as a popular social movement and ended many years later as a conservative uprising against a liberal Spanish constitution. In Venezuela it came to be a war unto the death; in other places it was a war between a small Creole minority and the Spanish authorities. It was not an organized movement with a central revolutionary directorate. It had no Continental Congress. . . . If there was no central direction, no centrally recognized leadership, likewise there was no formally accepted political doctrine. . . .

In Latin America each separate area went its own way. Central America broke way from Mexico and then splintered into five separate nations. Uruguay, Paraguay, and Bolivia separated themselves from Argentina, Chile from Peru, and [Simón] Bolívar's attempt to federate the state of Greater Colombia (Venezuela, Colombia, and Ecuador) with Peru and Bolivia under a centralized government broke down.[10]

※ **MAP 28.2 Latin America in 1830** What geographical factors have led to the relative political power of the United States and the Latin American nations?

❋ **Fernando Leal: Epic of Bolívar**   Often hated in his lifetime, Simón Bolívar is today revered as the greatest Latin American hero, and a rich body of legend surrounds him. This huge three-paneled watercolor mural showing "Bolívar as a Child," "Bolívar as Liberator," and "The Death of Bolívar" contributes to the Bolívar legend. (*Source: ARCHIVO CENIDIAP-INBA, Mexico City. Collection Fernando Leal Audirac*)

The great hero of the movement for independence was Simón Bolívar (1783–1830), a very able general who is considered the Latin American George Washington. Bolívar's victories over the royalist armies won him the presidency of Greater Colombia in 1819. He dreamed of a continental union and in 1826 summoned a conference of the American republics at Panama. The meeting achieved little. Bolívar organized the government of Bolivia and became the head of the new state of Peru. The territories of Greater Colombia splintered apart, however, and a sadly disillusioned Bolívar went into exile, saying, "America is ungovernable. Those who served the revolution plowed the seas." The failure of Pan-Americanism isolated individual countries, prevented collective action, and later paved the way for the political and economic intrusion of the United States and other powers.

Brazil's quest for independence from Portugal was unique: Brazil won its independence without violent upheaval. When Napoleon's troops entered Portugal, the royal family fled to Brazil and made Rio de Janeiro the capital of the Portuguese Empire. The new government immediately lifted the old mercantilist restrictions and opened Brazilian ports to the ships of all friendly nations. Under popular pressure, King Pedro I (r. 1822–1831)

proclaimed Brazil's independence in 1822 and published a constitution. Pedro's administration was wracked by factional disputes between Portuguese courtiers and Brazilian Creoles, a separatist movement in the Rio Grande do Sul region, and provincial revolts. His successor, Pedro II (r. 1831–1889), restored order and laid the foundations of the modern Brazilian state. The reign of Pedro II witnessed the expansion of the coffee industry, the beginnings of the rubber industry, and massive immigration.

The Consequences of Independence

The wars of independence ended around 1825. What effects did they have on Latin American societies, governments, and national development? Because the movements for independence differed in character and course in different regions and countries, generalizations are likely to be misleading. Significant changes did occur, however, throughout Latin America.

The newly independent nations did not achieve immediate political stability when the wars of independence ended. The Spanish crown had served as a unifying symbol, and its disappearance left a power vacuum. Civil disorder typically followed. The Creole leaders of the revolutions had no experience in government, and the wars left a legacy of military, not civilian, leadership. Throughout the continent, idealistic but impractical leaders proclaimed republics governed by representative assemblies. In practice, the generals ruled.

In Argentina, Juan Manuel de Rosas (r. 1835–1852) assumed power amid widespread public disorder and ruled as dictator. In Mexico, liberals declared a federal republic, but incessant civil strife led to the rise of the dictator Antonio López de Santa Anna in the mid-nineteenth century. Likewise in Venezuela, strongmen, dictators, and petty aristocratic oligarchs governed from 1830 to 1892. Some countries suffered constant revolutions. In the course of the century Bolivia had sixty and Venezuela fifty-two. The rule of force prevailed almost everywhere. Enlightened dictatorship was the typical form of government.

Although isolated territories such as Paraguay and much of Central America suffered little damage, the wars of liberation disrupted the economic life of most Latin American countries. The prosperity that many areas had achieved toward the end of the colonial period was destroyed. Mexico and Venezuela in particular lost large percentages of their populations and suffered great destruction of farmland and animals. Even areas that saw relatively little violence, such as Chile and New Granada, experienced a weakening of economic life. Armies were frequently recruited by force; and when the men were demobilized, many did not return home. The consequent population dislocation hurt agriculture and mining. Guerrilla warfare disrupted trade and communications. Forced loans and the seizure of private property for military use ruined many people.

Brazil, which had a large slave population, did not free the slaves until 1888. Spain abolished slavery in its Cuban colony in a series of measures between 1870 and 1886; Cuba itself became independent in 1903, a consequence of the Spanish-American War. Elsewhere, however, independence accelerated the abolition of slavery. The destruction of agriculture in countries such as Mexico and Venezuela caused the collapse of the plantation system, and fugitive slaves could not be recaptured. Also, the royalists and patriot generals such as Bolívar offered slaves their freedom in exchange for military service. Most of the new independent states adopted republican constitutions declaring the legal equality of all men. For Indians and blacks, however, these noble words were meaning-

less, for the revolution brought about no redistribution of property. Nor could long-standing racist attitudes be eliminated by the stroke of a pen.

Although the edifice of racism persisted in the nineteenth century, Latin America experienced much more assimilation and offered Negroes greater economic and social mobility than did the United States. As a direct result of their heroic military service in the wars of independence, a substantial number of Negroes improved their social

Diego Rivera: Orgy Night of the Rich Depicting upper-class Mexican society as rife with drunkenness, bribery, and corruption and backed by the military, while the church feigns shock, Rivera (1886–1957) painted this enormous fresco, part of a series, as a condemnation of capitalism and a glorification of ordinary people. Although the artist was familiar with artistic movements in Europe, his work paintings are rooted in the Mexican tradition. *(Source: ARCHIVO CENIDIAP-INBA, Mexico City)*

status. Some even attained the political heights: the Mexican revolutionary Vicente Guerrero, served as president of his country in 1829; Antonio Guzmán governed Venezuela as a benevolent dictator (r. 1870–1888); Ramón Castilla served as president of Peru (r. 1845–1851 and 1855–1862) and made great improvements in state financing.

What accounts for the relative racial permeability of Latin America in contrast with the severe segregation in the United States? As the Dutch scholar H. Hoetink points out, Latin American countries evolved a three-tiered sociocial structure, in contrast to the two-tiered racial edifice in the United States. Legally and socially, Latin American societies classified people as white, colored, or black, and marriages between whites and light-skinned colored people were commonly accepted. Legislative discrimination against colored people proved unenforceable. Thus light skin allowed for gradual assimilation into the middle and upper social echelons. In the United States, by contrast, anyone who was not "pure" white was classified as black (see page 940).

Hoetink explains the problem partly in terms of the large population of poor whites in the United States: "Nowhere, but in the North American mainland, did the number of extremely poor whites always exceed the number of slaves. Nowhere, but in the U.S. South, were special police forces predominantly manned by poor whites."[11] Also, Latin American elites' definition of *whiteness* and perception of physical beauty seem to have been broader than the definition and perception of the white majority in the United States.

Nevertheless, the advantages of assimilation did not (and do not) apply to dark-skinned people in Latin America. Substantial numbers of light-skinned colored people rose economically and socially, but the great mass of dark-skinned blacks continued to experience all the consequences of systematic and insistent racism.

Neocolonialism

At first, political instability and the preoccupation of European and North American financiers with industrial expansion in their own countries discouraged foreign investment in Latin America's newly independent nations. The advent of stable dictatorships, however, eventually paved the way for economic growth. After 1870 capital began to flow south and across the Atlantic. In Mexico,

North American capital supported the production of hemp (used in the United States for grain harvesting), sugar, bananas, and rubber, frequently on American-owned plantations. British and American interests backed the development of tin, copper, and gold mining in Mexico. By 1911 Mexico had taken third place among the world's oil producers. British financiers built Argentina's railroads, meatpacking industry, and utilities. British businessmen in Chile developed the copper and nitrate industries (nitrate is used in the production of pharmaceuticals and fertilizers). Likewise in Brazil, foreign capital—primarily British—flowed into coffee, cotton, and sugar production and manufacturing. By 1904, Brazil produced 76 percent of the world's coffee. When massive overproduction of coffee led to a sharp drop in prices in 1906, a commission of British, American, German, and French bankers rescued the Brazilian government from near disaster.

The price that Latin America paid for economic development at the end of the nineteenth century was a new form of economic domination. Foreign investors acquired control of the railroads, mineral resources, and banking, and they made heavy inroads into real estate. British investments led all others. But beginning in 1898, the United States flexed its imperialistic muscles and sent gunboats and troops to defend its dollars in the Caribbean and Central America. By the turn of the century the Latin American nations were active participants in the international economic order, but foreigners controlled most of their industries. Between 1904 and 1929, for example, the United States intervened in Latin American affairs whenever it felt its economic interests threatened. Americans secured control of the Panama Canal in 1904 on their own terms; in 1912 and 1926 U.S. Marines interfered in Nicaragua to bolster conservative governments; and the Marines that were sent to Haiti in 1915 to protect American property stayed until 1934. The result has been a bitter legacy of anti-American feeling throughout Latin America. Only with the launching of President Franklin Roosevelt's Good Neighbor Policy did relations between the United States and Latin America begin to improve.

Another distinctive feature of the neocolonial order was that each country's economy revolved around only one or two products: sugar in Cuba, nitrates and copper in Chile, meat in Argentina, coffee in Brazil. A sharp drop in the world market demand for a product could destroy the industry

LATIN AMERICA, CA 1760–1900

1764–1780	Charles III of Spain's administrative and economic reforms
1781	Comunero Revolution in New Granada
1810–1825	Latin American wars of independence against Spain
1822	Proclamation by Portugal of Brazil's independence
1826	Call by Simón Bolívar for Panama Conference on Latin American union
1825–ca 1870	Political instability in most Latin American nations
ca 1870–1919	Latin American neocolonialism
1876–1911	Porfirio Díaz's control of Mexico
1888	Emancipation of slaves in Brazil Final abolition of slavery in Western Hemisphere
1880–1914	Massive immigration from Europe and Asia to Latin America
1898	Spanish American War End of Spanish control over Cuba Transfer of Puerto Rico and the Philippines to United States

and with it the nation's economic structure. The outbreak of the First World War in 1914 drastically reduced exports of Latin American raw materials and imports of European manufactured goods, provoking general economic crisis.[12]

Throughout the eighteenth century the Spanish-owned *haciendas*—large landed estates—and plantations had continued to expand to meet the needs of commercial agriculture: wheat for the cities, corn for the Indians' consumption, sugar for export to Europe and North America. By means of purchase, forced removal of Indians, and outright seizure, the Spanish continued to take Indian land, as they had done in the seventeenth century. Some land was acquired merely to eliminate competition by depriving Indians of their fields, which were then left fallow.

The late nineteenth century witnessed ever greater concentrations of land in ever fewer hands. In places like the Valley of Mexico in southern Mexico, a few large haciendas controlled all the land. Under the dictatorship of General Porfirio Díaz, the Mexican government in 1883 passed a law allowing real estate companies (controlled by Díaz's political cronies) to survey public and "vacant" lands and to retain one-third of the land they surveyed. An 1894 law provided that land could be declared vacant if legal title to it could not be produced. Since few Indians had deeds to the land that their ancestors had worked for centuries, the door swung open to wholesale expropriation of small landowners and entire villages. Shrewd speculators tricked illiterate Indians into selling their lands for trifling sums. Thousands of litigants clogged the courts. Indians who dared armed resistance were crushed by government troops and carried off to virtual slave labor. Vast stretches of land came into the hands of private individuals—in one case, 12 million acres. Stripped of their lands, the Indians were a ready labor supply. They were mercilessly exploited. Debt peonage became common: landowners paid their laborers not in cash but in vouchers redeemable only at the company store, whose high prices and tricky bookkeeping kept the peons permanently in debt.

Some scholars maintain that the hacienda owners usually let their land lie fallow until it rose in value or attracted American investors. The lack of cultivation, they assert, kept the prices of corn and other crops artificially high. The owners themselves, supported by rents, passed indolent lives in extravagant luxury in Mexico City and other cities.

Other scholars argue that the haciendas were efficient enterprises whose owners sought to maximize profits on invested capital. The Sanchez Navarro family of northwestern Mexico, for instance, engaged in a wide variety of agricultural and commercial pursuits, exploiting their lands and resources as fully as possible. Ultimately, their *latifundio*—a large landed estate—was about the size of West Virginia. Along with vast cattle ranches and sheep runs containing as many as 250,000 sheep, the Sanchez Navarros cultivated maize, wheat, and cotton. They invested heavily and profitably in silver mining and manufacturing and lent sizable sums at high interest. Although they brutally exploited their peons and practiced debt peonage, the Sanchez Navarros lived very modestly on their own estates rather than luxuriating in Mexico City.[13] A final determination of whether the Sanchez Navarros were unique or representative of Mexican agricultural and business communities must await further investigation.

The Impact of Immigration

In 1852 the Argentine political philosopher Juan Bautista Alberdi published *Bases and Points of Departure for Argentine Political Organization,* arguing that "to govern is to populate." Alberdi meant that the development of his country—and, by extension, all of Latin America—depended on immigration. Argentina had an adequate labor supply, but it was unevenly distributed throughout the country. Moreover, Alberdi maintained, Indians and blacks lacked basic skills, and it would take too long to train them. Thus he pressed for massive immigration from the "advanced" countries of northern Europe and the United States. Alberdi's ideas won immediate acceptance and were even incorporated into the Argentine constitution, which declared that "the Federal government will encourage European immigration." Other Latin American countries adopted similar policies promoting immigration.[14]

European needs coincided perfectly with those of Latin America. After 1880, Ireland, Great Britain, Germany, Italy, Spain, and the central European nations experienced greater population growth than their labor markets could absorb. Meanwhile, the growing industries of Europe needed South American raw materials and markets for their finished goods, and South American countries wanted European markets for their minerals, coffee, sugar, beef, and manufactured goods. Italian, Spanish, and Portuguese peoples poured into Latin America.

Immigration led to rapid urbanization, which meant Europeanization and industrialization. By 1900, Buenos Aires and Rio de Janeiro had populations of more than 500,000 people; Mexico City, Montevideo, Santiago, and Havana also experienced spectacular growth. Portuguese, Italian, French, Chinese, and Japanese immigrants gave an international flavor to the cities, and a more vigorous tempo replaced the somnolent Spanish atmosphere.

By 1914 Buenos Aires had emerged as one of the most cosmopolitan cities in the world. In less than a half-century, the population of the city and its province had grown from 500,000 to 3.6 million. As Argentina's political capital, the city housed all its government bureaucracies and agencies. The meatpacking, food-processing, flourmilling, and wool industries were concentrated in Buenos Aires. Half of all overseas tonnage passed through the city, which was also the heart of the nation's railroad network. The University of Buenos Aires was the intellectual hub of the nation. Elegant shops near the Plaza de Mayo catered to the expensive tastes of the elite upper classes, who constituted about 5 percent of the population. But the thousands of immigrants who toiled twelve hours a day, six days a week, on docks and construction sites and in meatpacking plants crowded into the city's *conventillos,* or tenements:

The one-room dwelling . . . served a family with two to five children or a group of four or five single men. At the door to each room stood a pile of wooden boxes. One generally held a basin for washing; another a charcoal brazier on which to cook the daily watery stew, or puchero; and garbage accumulated in a third. Two or three iron cots, a pine table, a few wooden chairs, an old trunk, perhaps a sewing machine, and more boxes completed the furnishings. Light came from the open door and one window, from an oil or gas lamp, or occasionally from a bare electric light bulb. On the once-whitewashed walls were tacked pictures of popular heroes, generals, or kings torn from magazines, an image of the Madonna and a couple of saints, perhaps a faded photograph of fam-

ily members in Europe. The women often eked out miserable incomes by taking in laundry and washing and drying it in the patios. Others ironed or sewed on a piecework basis. Some men worked here: in one corner a shoemaker might ply his trade, in another a man might bend over a small table repairing watches.[15]

Immigrants dreamed of rapid economic success in the New World, and there was in fact plenty of upward social mobility. The first generation almost always did manual labor, but its sons often advanced to upper blue-collar or to white-collar jobs. The rare Genoese or Neapolitan immigrant whose labor and thrift made his son a millionaire quickly learned the meaning of assimilation: the son typically imitated the dress, style, and values of the Spanish elite. Hispanic attitudes toward class, manual labor, and egalitarianism prevailed.[16]

Europeans gave an enormous boost to the development of industry and commerce. Italian and Spanish settlers in Argentina stimulated the expansion of the cattle industry and the development of the wheat and shoe industries. In Brazil, Swiss immigrants built the cheese business; Italians gained a leading role in the coffee industry; and the Japanese pioneered the development of the cotton industry. In Peru, the British controlled railroad construction, Italians became influential in banking and the restaurant business, and the French dominated jewelry, dressmaking, and pharmaceuticals. The arrival of millions of migrants changed the entire commercial structure of South America.

Immigration promoted further ethnic integration. The vast majority of migrants were unmarried males; seven out of ten people who landed in Argentina between 1857 and 1924 were single males between thirteen and forty years old. There, as in other South American countries, many of those who stayed sought out Indian or other low-status women. Male settlers from eastern Europe and women of all nationalities preferred to marry within their own ethnic groups. But men greatly outnumbered women, and a man who chose to marry usually had to marry an Indian.[17] Immigration, then, furthered the racial mixture of Europeans, Asians, and native South Americans.

For Latin America's sizable black population, immigration proved a calamity. The abolition of slavery in Spanish America had scarcely changed the economic and social status of the Negro population. Accustomed to working the rural coffee plantations and the mines, blacks sometimes had little preparation for urban living. Many former slaves had skills, even for factory work, but racism explains the greater presence of white immigrants in factories. In 1893, 71.2 percent of the working population of São Paulo was foreign-born. Anxious to adapt to America and to climb the economic ladder, immigrants quickly learned the traditional racial prejudices. Negro women usually found work as domestics, but employers excluded black males from good jobs. Racial prejudice kept the vast bulk of the South American black population in a wretched socioeconomic position until the Second World War.

Independence did little to change the basic social, economic, and political structure of Latin American countries. Although republican constitutions declared all men (but not women) equal under law, the elite continued to control status, wealth, and power almost everywhere as Creoles moved into positions formerly held by peninsulares. Neocolonialism's modernizing influence on commerce and industry strengthened the position of the elite and allowed it to use capitalistic values and ideals as a shield against demands for fundamental socioeconomic reforms. European styles in art, clothing, housing, and literature became highly popular, particularly among members of the elite as they sought acceptance and approval by their economic masters. Meaningful structural change would await the revolutions and violent confrontations of the twentieth century.

❖ THE UNITED STATES (1789–1929)

The victory of the North American colonies and the founding of the United States seemed to validate the Enlightenment idea that a better life on earth was possible. Americans carried over into the nineteenth and twentieth centuries an unbounded optimism about the future. Although most eastern states retained a property or tax-paying qualification for the vote down to 1860, the suffrage was gradually expanded to include most adult white males; New Jersey alone gave (propertied) women the vote for a time. The movement toward popular democracy accelerated as the young nation, confident of its "manifest destiny," pushed relentlessly across the continent. Westward movement, however, threatened to extend black slavery, which

Christian Mayr, Kitchen Ball at White Sulphur Springs, 1838   The German artist who painted this picture shortly after his arrival in the U.S. apparently had no preconceived racial views; he portrayed blacks without the insulting caricatures, marginalized situations, or political formulas typical of many mid-century representations. Rather, African Americans are shown here as graceful, dignified, and in a social scene of their own creation. Light-skinned and dark-skinned, old and young, plain and beautiful celebrate and reveal an individual and a group dignity. White Sulphur Springs was (and is) a fashionable resort. *(Source: North Carolina Museum of Art, Raleigh. Purchased with funds from the state of North Carolina)*

generated increasing disagreement between the industrialized North and the agricultural South. The ensuing Civil War cost more American lives than any other war the nation was to fight. The victory of the North did not resolve the racial issue that had led to war, but it did preserve the federal system.

The years between 1865 and 1917 witnessed the building of a new industrialized nation. Immigrants settled much of the West, provided the labor to exploit the country's mineral resources, turned small provincial towns into sophisticated centers of ethnic and cultural diversity, and built the railroads that tied the country together. The ideology of manifest destiny lived on after the frontier closed and considerably affected relations between the United States and Latin America. In the First World War, American aid and American troops were the deciding factor in the Allied victory. After the war, "normalcy" and the façade of prosperity supported a persistent optimism.

Manifest Destiny

In an 1845 issue of the *United States Magazine and Democratic Review,* editor John L. O'Sullivan boldly declared that foreign powers were trying to prevent American annexation of Texas in order to impede "the fulfillment of our manifest destiny to overspread the continent allotted by Providence for the free development of our yearly multiplying millions." O'Sullivan was articulating a sentiment prevalent in the United States since early in its history: that God had foreordained the nation to cover the entire continent. After a large-circulation newspaper picked up the phrase "manifest destiny," it was used on the floor of Congress and soon entered the language as a catchword for and justification of expansion. The concept of manifest destiny played an important role in some basic developments in American history: the settlement of peoples of diverse nationalities, the issue of slavery, the conflict over whether the United States was to remain agrarian or become a commercial and industrial society.

Two other concepts also played a powerful role in the formation of the young republic: social equality, by which was meant equality of opportunity, and optimism about the future. After a visit to the United States in 1831, the French nobleman Alexis de Tocqueville wrote in *Democracy in America,* a classic analysis of American civilization, "No novelty in the United States struck me more visibly during my stay there than the equality of conditions." By equality Tocqueville meant the relative fluidity of American society, and he attributed this to Americans' mobility. Unlike Europe, where family and inherited wealth meant a great deal and people typically lived all their lives in the regions where they were born, geographic mobility in America provided enormous opportunity. A deeply rooted work ethic taught that everyone could advance through thrift and hard work. Americans also had an unbounded faith in the future. This belief that America offered golden and limitless opportunities is epitomized in the letter an immigrant Englishman wrote home to his wife:

I do not repent coming, for you know that there was nothing but poverty before me, and to see you and the dear children want was more than I could bear. I would rather cross the Atlantic ten times than hear my children cry for victuals. . . . There is plenty of room yet, and will be for a thousand years to come.[18]

When George Washington took office in 1789, fewer than 4 million people inhabited the thirteen states on the eastern seaboard. By the time Abraham Lincoln became the sixteenth president in 1861, the United States stretched across the continent and had 31 million inhabitants.

During the colonial period, pioneers had pushed westward to the Appalachian Mountains. After independence, westward movement accelerated. The eastern states claimed all the land from the Atlantic Ocean to the Mississippi River, but two forces blocked immediate expansion. The Indians, trying to save their lands, allied with the British in Canada to prevent further American encroachment. In 1794, however, Britain agreed to evacuate border forts in the Northwest Territory, roughly the area north of the Ohio River and east of the Mississippi, and thereby end British support for the Indians. A similar treaty with Spain paved the way for southeastern expansion (Map 28.3).

Events in Europe and the Caribbean led to a massive increase in American territory. In 1800 Spain ceded the Louisiana Territory—the land between the Mississippi River and the Rocky Mountains—to France. Napoleon intended to use the Louisiana Territory to make France an imperial power in America, but a black revolution on the island of Hispaniola (present-day Haiti and Dominican Republic) upset his plans. Led by Toussaint L'Ouverture, Haiti's 500,000 slaves revolted against their 40,000 white owners. Napoleon quickly dispatched troops with orders to crush the revolt, seize New Orleans, and take possession of the Louisiana Territory. Alarmed, President Thomas Jefferson ordered the American minister in Paris, Robert Livingston, to negotiate to buy the Louisiana Territory.

When yellow fever and Haitian bullets carried off most of the French troops in Haiti, Napoleon relinquished his grandiose plans. He was planning war with Great Britain, and on the day he opened hostilities with England, his foreign minister Talleyrand casually asked Livingston, "What would you give us for the whole of Louisiana?" The astonished American proposed $4 million. "Too low!" said Talleyrand. "Reflect and see me tomorrow." Less than three weeks later the deed of sale was signed. The United States paid only $12 million for millions of acres of some of the world's richest farmland.

Scarcely was the ink dry on the agreement when pressure rose for war with England. Repeated British attacks on American vessels on the high seas and British interference in American trade provided diplomatic justification for the War of 1812. Western "war hawks" wanted further expansion and believed that a war with Britain would yield Canada, permanently end Indian troubles, and open up vast forest lands for settlement. The Treaty of Ghent (1814) ended the conflict but left the prewar boundaries unchanged.

After the restoration of peace, settlers poured into the Northwest Territory and the Gulf Plains (the region of Georgia, Alabama, and Mississippi). Congress sold land in lots of 160 acres at $2 an acre; only $80 was needed as down payment. Irish and German immigrants rapidly put the black earth of Indiana and Illinois under cultivation. Pioneers of American stock planted cotton in the lush delta of the Gulf Plains. Scandinavian and German settlers found the softly rolling hills of the Wisconsin country ideal for cattle.

United States 1783
Louisiana Purchase 1803
Ceded by Great Britain 1818
Treaty with Spain 1819
Annexation of Texas 1845
Oregon Country 1846
Ceded by Mexico 1848
Gadsden Purchase 1853

Boston
New York
Philadelphia
Baltimore
Washington
Charleston
Savannah
Pittsburgh
Columbus
Chattanooga
Indianapolis
St. Louis
New Orleans
Duluth
Council Bluffs
St. Joseph
Kansas City
Topeka
Omaha
Dodge City
Houston
San Antonio
Fargo
Bismarck
Denver
Albuquerque
El Paso
Cheyenne
Salt Lake City
Butte
Spokane
Seattle
Portland
Virginia City
Sacramento
San Francisco
Los Angeles

NORTHWEST TERRITORY

Erie Canal
BOSTON POST ROAD
CUMBERLAND ROAD
GREAT VALLEY ROAD
NATCHEZ TRACE
OREGON TRAIL
NORTHERN PACIFIC RAILROAD
UNION PACIFIC RAILROAD
CENTRAL PACIFIC RAILROAD

400 Mi.
400 Km.
200
0

Spain, preoccupied with rebellions in South America, sold the Florida Territory to the U.S. government; and beginning in 1821, American settlers poured into the Mexican territory of Texas, whose soil proved excellent for the production of cotton and sugar. Contemptuous of the government of the Mexican president Santa Anna, Texans rebelled and proclaimed Texas an independent republic in 1836. Southern politicians, fearing that Texas would become a refuge for fugitive slaves, pressured President John Tyler to admit Texas to the United States. A joint resolution of Congress, hastily signed by Tyler, did so in 1845.

The absorption of Texas's 267,339 square miles (France, by comparison, covers 211,200 square miles) whetted American appetites for the rest of the old Spanish Empire in North America. Some expansionists even dreamed of taking Cuba and Central America.

Exploiting Mexico's political instability, President James Polk goaded Mexico into war. Mexico suffered total defeat and in the Treaty of Guadalupe Hidalgo (1848) surrendered its remaining claims to Texas, yielded New Mexico and California, and recognized the Rio Grande as the international border. A treaty with Great Britain in 1846 had already recognized the American settlement in the Oregon Territory. The continent had been acquired. Then, in 1898, a revolt in Cuba against incompetent Spanish administration had consequences beyond "manifest destiny." Inflamed by press reports of Spanish atrocities, public opinion swept the United States into war. The Spanish-American War—the "splendid little war," as Secretary of State John Hay called it—lasted just ten weeks and brought U.S. control over Cuba, the Philippine Islands, and Puerto Rico. Denying imperialistic ambitions, President William McKinley justified the U.S. acquisition of Cuba and the Philippines with a classic imperialistic argument: the nation wanted only "to take them all and educate the Filipinos and uplift and civilize and Chris-

Richard Caton Woodville: War News from Mexico (1848)   In this scene of everyday life, the front porch of the "American Hotel" represents a microcosm of American society. The man reading the newspaper bursts with excitement, as the well-dressed white men (and woman, partly hidden) eagerly listen to the news from the front. In showing the black child in a tattered dress while the seated black man drinks whiskey (a jug is half hidden under his hat) from a silver cup, Woodville makes a stereotypically racist statement. The American artist, however, did not witness such a scene: he painted this in Dusseldorf, Germany. (Source: Manoogian Foundation)

tianize them." McKinley, like most other Americans, did not know that the Filipinos had an old, sophisticated culture and that they had been Christians for three centuries. The nation's "manifest destiny" had evolved into worldwide imperialism.

The Fate of the Indians

How did the only people who were native to this vast continent fare under manifest destiny? The Indians faithfully observed their treaties with the United States, but "white pioneers in the Northwest committed the most wanton and cruel murders of them, for which it was almost impossible to

MAP 28.3 Territorial Growth of the United States   The Cumberland Road between Cumberland, Maryland, and—by 1833—Columbus, Ohio, and the Erie Canal, which linked New York City and the Great Lakes region, carried thousands of easterners and immigrants to the Old Northwest and the frontier beyond. Transcontinental railroads subsequently made all the difference.

obtain a conviction from a pioneer jury."[19] Government officials sometimes manipulated the Indians by gathering a few chiefs, plying them with cheap whiskey, then inducing them to hand over the tribes' hunting grounds. Sometimes officials exploited rivlaries among tribes, or used bribes. By these methods, William Henry Harrison, superintendent of the Indians of the Northwest Territory and a future president, got some native Americans to cede 48 million acres. He had the full backing of President Jefferson.

The policy of pushing the Indians westward across the Mississippi, which President James Mon-

✳ **Jackson as the "Great Father"**   This cartoon satirizes Andrew Jackson, who as president (1829–1837) pushed a policy forcing the relocation of eastern Indian tribes to the west of the Mississippi. The cartoon also insults native Americans by depicting them as diminutive, doll-like, and dependent on the "Great Father," who stands for the power of the federal government. *(Source: William L. Clements Library, The University of Michigan, Ann Arbor)*

roe's administration had adopted early in the century, accelerated during Andrew Jackson's presidency (1829–1837). Thousands of Delawares, Shawnees, and Wyandots, tricked into moving from the Northwest Territory to reservations west of Missouri, died of cholera and measles during the journey. The survivors found themselves hopelessly in debt for supplies and farming equipment. The state of Georgia, meanwhile, was nibbling away at Cherokee lands, which were theoretically protected by treaty with the U.S. government. Then gold was discovered on the Cherokee lands, and a gold rush took place. A Vermont missionary, the Reverend Samuel C. Worcester, carried the Indians' case to the Supreme Court. Chief Justice John Marshall ruled that the laws of Georgia had no force within the Cherokee territory and that white settlers and gold rustlers had to leave. President Jackson retorted, "John Marshall has made his decision. Now let him enforce it." The Creek, Cherokee, and other tribes were rounded up, expelled, and sent beyond the western boundaries of Missouri and Arkansas.[20] Later in the century, Indians in the West were forced onto government-designated reservations. The shameful price of westward expansion was the dislocation and extermination of millions of native Americans (Map 28.4).

Black Slavery in the South

Dutch traders brought the first black people as prisoners to Virginia in 1619 as one solution to the chronic shortage of labor in North America (white indentured servants who worked for a term of years was another solution). The first black arrivals, however, were not slaves. In the seventeenth century, a system of racial servitude and discrimination did not exist. Some blacks themselves acquired property and indentured servants.

In the early eighteenth century, as rice cultivation expanded in the Carolinas and tobacco in the Chesapeake Bay colonies of Virginia and Maryland, planters demanded more laborers. Between 1720 and 1770, black prisoners poured into the southern colonies. In South Carolina they came to outnumber whites by almost two to one. In the decades 1730 through 1760 white fears of black revolts pushed colonial legislatures to pass laws that established tight white control and blacks' legal position as slaves, enshrining the slave system in law. Economic demands led to the legal and social institutionalization of black slavery in North Amer-

John Antrobus: Plantation Burial   Apart from the detached figure (far left) and the couple strolling under the trees—presumably the plantation owner and his wife (far right)—all the figures in this painting are black. English art historian Hugh Honour described the painting as a "rare surviving visual record of the independent culture of Afro-Americans under slavery." The preacher raises his hands in blessing and consigns the dead to the grave. Some listen; some mourn; some seem indifferent or preoccupied. (*Source: The Historic New Orleans Collection, Accession no. 1760.46*)

ica. Racist arguments of blacks' supposed inferiority were used to justify that institutionalization.

Slavery and race relations have posed a serious dilemma for the American majority for more than two centuries. Powerful moral, legal, political, and sociological arguments have characterized slavery as a great evil, a violation of the central principle of the Declaration of Independence that all men are created equal. Eighteenth- and nineteenth-century Americans, however, could not decide whether the ringing words of the Declaration applied to blacks. One scholar posed the question in this way:

How did the slave-holding class, which was molded by the same forces that shaped the nation, which fought America's wars and helped inspire its Revolution, a class which boasted of its patriotism, its devotion to freedom, its adherence to the major tenets of liberalism—how did such a class justify its continuing commitment to slavery?[21]

The answer can be given in two words: *profit* and *status*.

The system of slavery involved many factors—the size of a plantation or farm and the number of slaves working it, the arability of the soil and the quantity of rainfall, the efficiency of plantation management, and individual initiative. Many slaveowners realized reasonable, sometimes handsome, profits in the decades before the Civil War. For white planters and farmers, slavery proved lucrative, and ownership of slaves was a status symbol as well as a means of social control. Slavery "was at the center of a well-established way of life to which

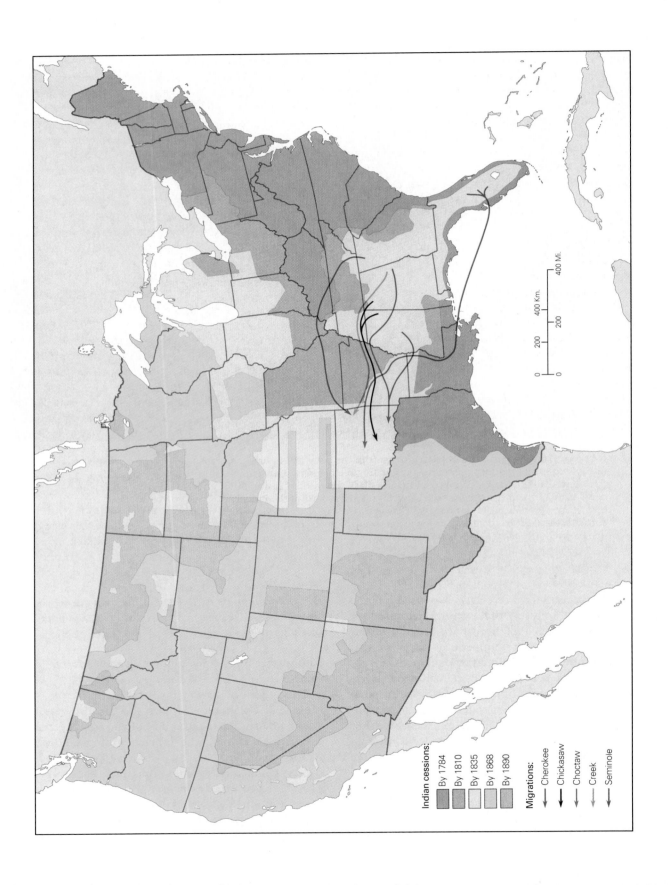

Indian cessions:

By 1784
By 1810
By 1835
By 1868
By 1890

Migrations:

→ Cherokee
→ Chickasaw
→ Choctaw
→ Creek
→ Seminole

400 Km.

400 Mi.

0   200   400

0   200

[slaveowners] were accustomed and attached, and the disruption or demise of which they feared above all else."[22] Millions of whites, whether or not they owned many slaves, would have agreed with the South Carolina planter who wrote, "Slavery informs all our modes of life, all our habits of thought, lies at the basis of our social existence, and of our political faith." Since the possession of slaves brought financial profit *and* conferred social status and prestige, struggling small farmers had a material and psychological interest in maintaining black bondage. Slavery provided the means by which they might rise, and the floor beneath which they could not fall.

American society subsequently paid a high price in guilt and psychological conflict. Some slaveholders, like President George Washington, found the subject of slavery too uncomfortable even to talk about: "I shall frankly declare to you that I do not like even to think, much less talk of it."[23] In the half-century before the Civil War, most slaveowners were deeply religious. On the one hand, they taught their children to get rich by the accumulation of land and slaves; on the other hand, they taught that God would punish the greedy with eternal damnation. Slaveholders justified slavery by dismissing blacks as inferior, but religion preached that in the eyes of God black and white were equal and would ultimately be judged on that basis.

Some slaveowners felt completely trapped by the system. One master wrote, "I cannot just take them up and sell them though that would be clearly the best I could do for myself. I cannot free them. I cannot keep them with comfort. . . . What would I not give to be freed from responsibility for these poor creatures." Perhaps to an even greater extent than men, women of the planter class felt troubled by slavery. The South Carolina aristocrat Mary Boykin Chesnut confided to her diary in 1861:

I wonder if it be a sin to think slavery a curse to any land. . . . God forgive us, but ours is a monstrous system and wrong and iniquity. Perhaps the rest of the world is as bad—this only I see. Like the patriarchs of old our men live all in one house with their wives and their concubines, and the mulattoes one sees in every family exactly resemble the white children—and every lady tells you who is the father of all the mulatto children in everybody's household, but those in her own she seems to think drop from the clouds, or pretends so to think.[24]

Mary Chesnut believed that most white women of the South were abolitionists in their hearts. She enjoyed the attentions and services of her slaves, but when Lincoln issued the Emancipation Proclamation, she welcomed it with "an unholy joy."[25]

What impact did slavery have on the black family? Herbert G. Gutman's authoritative *The Black Family in Slavery and Freedom, 1750–1925,* has demonstrated that, in spite of the destructive effects of slavery, African-Americans established strong family units.[26] Most slave couples had long marriages. A study of the entire adult slave population of North Carolina in 1860 has shown that 25 percent of slave marriages lasted between ten and nineteen years, 20 percent lasted at least twenty years, and almost 10 percent endured thirty years or more. Most slave women spent their entire adult lives in settled unions with the same husband. Planters encouraged slave marriages, because, as one owner put it, "marriage adds to the comfort, happiness, and health of those entering upon it, besides insuring a greater increase."[27] Large slave families advanced owners' economic interests, and planters rewarded slave women who had many children. Forcible separation due to the sale of one partner proved the greatest threat to the permanence of slave marriages. Evidence from all parts of the South reveals that, in spite of illiteracy, separated spouses tried to remain in touch with one another and, once slavery had been abolished, went to enormous lengths to reunite their families.

Women often had to resist the attentions of the slaveowners. In addition, owners not infrequently supplied slave women with black men who had reputations for sexual prowess. Slave women, however, made choices: they tried to select their own husbands, rejecting—up to the point of risking being sold—mates chosen by their owners.

Typically, slave women had their first child around the age of nineteen. On the Good Hope

❋ **MAP 28.4 Indian Cession of Lands to the United States**   Forced removal of the Creek, Cherokee, and Chickasaw Indians led to the deaths of thousands on the Trail of Tears to reservations in Oklahoma, and to the destruction of their cultures.

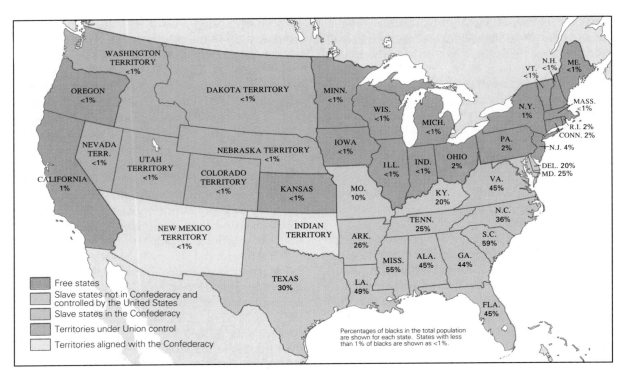

MAP 28.5 Slavery in the United States, 1860 The Confederacy waged a heroic struggle, but the North's industrial might and the waves of immigrants who fought in the Union army decided the outcome of the war. Note the slave populations of such states as South Carolina and Mississippi, and consider how they influenced the later social and economic history of those regions.

plantation in South Carolina, 80 percent of slave couples had at least four children. Almost all women had all their children by one husband, and most children grew to their teens in households with both parents present. Although premarital intercourse was common among slaves—though not as common as among young American adults during the 1970s—the weight of the evidence shows that women rarely engaged in extramarital sexual activity. The pattern of stable black marriages lasted into the present century.

Westward Expansion and Civil War

Cotton was king in the mid-nineteenth century, and cotton carried slavery westward. It was westward expansion, not moral outrage, that brought the controversy over slavery to a head. As Congress created new territories, the question of whether slavery would be extended arose again and again (Map 28.5). For years elaborate com-

promises were worked out, but the North increasingly feared that the South was intent on controlling the nation. The South was afraid that free territories would harbor fugitive slaves. Issues of sectional political power became more and more heated.

In the 1850s the question of the further expansion of slavery agitated the nation. Perhaps no statesman better summarized the dilemma than Abraham Lincoln in a speech in 1854:

Slavery is founded in the selfishness of man's nature—opposition to it, in his love of justice. These principles are in eternal antagonism; and when brought into collision so fiercely, as slavery extension brings them, shocks, and throes, and convulsions must ceaselessly follow.[28]

Accepting the Republican party nomination for a seat in the U.S. Senate in 1858, Lincoln predicted the tragic events ahead:

A house divided against itself cannot stand.

I believe this government cannot endure, permanently half slave *and half free.*

I do not expect the Union to be dissolved—*I do not expect the house to fall—but I* do *expect it will cease to be divided.*

It will become all one thing, or all the other.

Either the opponents of slavery will arrest the further spread of it, and place it where the public mind shall rest in the belief that it is in the course of ultimate extinction; or its advocates will push it forward, till it shall become alike lawful in all *the States, old as well as new—North as well as South.*[29]

In this and every other speech that Lincoln made between 1854 and his election to the presidency in 1860, he argued against slavery less on moral or legal grounds and more in terms of free labor's self-interest.

If slavery continued to expand, Lincoln insisted, it would become a nationwide institution. He appealed to both immigrants and native-born whites when he declared that slavery should be excluded from new territories so that they could be "an outlet for free white people everywhere, the world over—in which Hans, and Baptiste, and Patrick, and all other men from all the world, may find new homes and better their condition in life."[30] Free white workers, in other words, could not compete in the labor market against blacks; therefore, the territories should be kept open.

To protest Lincoln's victory in the election of 1860, South Carolina seceded from the Union in December 1860. Ten southern states soon followed South Carolina's example and formed the Confederacy. Its capital was at Richmond, Virginia.

The Civil War began in 1861. Lincoln fought it to preserve the Union and to maintain the free labor system; the abolition of slavery was a secondary outcome, which he in fact tried to avoid. When a Union general in the field declared the slaves of South Carolina and Georgia free, Lincoln overruled the order. He wanted to bring the seceding states back into the Union with their institutions intact. To many people it seemed absurd to fight the Confederacy, which depended on slavery to wage the war, without abolishing slavery. In the words of one historian, Lincoln wanted "to conduct the war for the preservation of *status quo,* which had produced the war."[31] Only after the war had dragged on and the slaughter had become frightful on both sides, and only when it had been

proved that the southern war effort benefited considerably from slave labor, did Lincoln, reluctantly, resolve on emancipation.

The Emancipation Proclamation became effective on January 1, 1863. It expressed no moral indignation. It freed slaves only in states and areas that were in rebellion against the United States. It preserved slavery in states that were loyal to the United States or under military jurisdiction. The London *Spectator* sneered, "The principle is not that a human being cannot justly own another, but that he cannot own him unless he is loyal to the United States."[32] The Emancipation Proclamation nevertheless spelled the doom of North American slavery. It transformed the Civil War from a political struggle to preserve the Union into a moral crusade for the liberty of more Americans.

European and English liberals greeted the proclamation with joy. A gathering of working people in Manchester, England, wrote President Lincoln: "The erasure of that foul blot upon civilization and Christianity—chattel slavery—during your Presidency will cause the name of Abraham Lincoln to be honoured and revered by posterity."[33] As Lincoln acknowledged, this was a magnanimous statement, for the Civil War hurt working people in Manchester. In fact, it had a worldwide impact socially and economically.

By 1862, deprived of cotton from the American South because of the Union blockade of Confederate ports, the mills of Lancashire in England had closed. Tens of thousands of workers were thrown out of work and nearly starved. Many emigrated to the United States. Between 1862 and 1864, efforts to alleviate the terrible suffering severely taxed the resources of the British government. English manufacturers looked for new suppliers and found them in Egypt, India, and Brazil, where cotton production had been stimulated by the Union blockade. The demands of English industry for Egyptian and Indian cotton played a significant role in the expansion of the English merchant marine fleet. Although England initially opposed construction of the Suez Canal, it later became a major shareholder. The canal was the swiftest route to Indian cotton.

The war also had important political consequences in Europe. In 1861 British and European opinion had divided along class lines. The upper classes sympathized with the American South; the commercial classes and working people sided with the North. The English people interpreted the northern victory as a triumph of the democratic experiment over aristocratic oligarchy. Thus the United States gave a powerful stimulus to those in Britain and elsewhere who supported the cause of political democracy. When parliaments debated the extension of suffrage, the American example was frequently cited.

Military historians describe the American Civil War as the first modern war:

It was the first conflict in which the massive productive capacities of the Industrial Revolution were placed at the disposal of the military machine. It witnessed the first prominent use of mass production of goods to sustain mass armies, mass transportation on railroads, and telegraphic communication between different theaters and on the battlefield. It saw also the first use of such devices of the future as armored warships, breech-loading and repeating rifles, rifled artillery, land and sea mines, submarines, balloons, precursors of the machine gun, and trench warfare. . . . In its material manifestations alone, in its application of the resources of technology to the business of killing, the Civil War presaged the later world wars.[34]

In April 1865, the Confederate general Robert E. Lee surrendered his army at Appomattox Court House in Virginia, ending the war. Lincoln had called for "malice toward none and charity for all" in his second inaugural address in 1864 and

❋ **The Battle of Gettysburg, July 1–3, 1863**   This battle marked the high point of the Confederate advance and was the greatest battle of the American Civil War. This painting commemorates the climax on the third day, when Confederate General Robert E. Lee commanded Pickett's division to charge the Union center. Coming toward the viewer in the face of terrible fire, the brave southerners have reached the first Union line. But General Hancock, shown with arm extended in the left foreground, is ordering the northern counterattack that will decimate Pickett's troops and force the Confederates back into Virginia. *(Source: Photograph by Al Freni © 1985 Time-Life Books, Inc. Courtesy, The Seventh Regiment Fund, Inc.)*

planned a generous policy toward the defeated South. The bullet that killed him brought on a different kind of reconstruction, the central figure in which was the Negro.

During the period called Reconstruction (1865–1877), the vanquished South adjusted to a new social and economic order without slavery, and the eleven Confederate states rejoined the Union. For former slaves, Reconstruction meant the reunion of black families separated before emancipation. Reconstruction also represented an opportunity for blacks to exercise their new freedom, though southerners detested the very notion of social equality and northerners were ambivalent on the subject.

Blacks wanted land to farm; but, lacking cash, they soon accepted the sharecropping system: farmers paid landowners about half of a year's crops at harvest time in return for a cabin, food, mules, seed, and tools the rest of the year. Believing that education was the key to economic advancement, blacks flocked to country schools and to colleges supported by northern religious groups. Although the Fifteenth Amendment to the U.S. Constitution forbade states to deny anyone the vote "on account of race, color, or previous condition of servitude," whites used violence, terror, and, between 1880 and 1920, so-called Jim Crow laws to prevent blacks from voting and to enforce rigid racial segregation. Lacking strong northern support, blacks did not gain legal equality or suffrage in many parts of the old Confederacy until the 1960s. Racist assumptions and attitudes thwarted their legal, social, and economic advance.

In the construction of a black community, no institution played a larger role than the black Protestant churches. Local black churches provided hope, education, and a forum for the spread of political ideas and platforms. During Reconstruction, black preachers esteemed for their oratorical skill, organizational ability, and practical judgment held important positions in black politics. In a racist and exploitative society, the black church gave support, security, and a sense of solidarity.

Who Is Black? The Racial Debate

In the summer of 1925, Abraham Lincoln's aging son, Robert Todd Lincoln, visited a resort in Manchester, Vermont. Lincoln hated blacks and refused to allow them to wait on him, and if a black man touched his luggage, car, or possessions, he whacked him with his cane. Lincoln selected the fair, blue-eyed, blond-haired Adam Clayton Powell (1908–1972) as his servant. Powell was an undergraduate at Colgate University working as a bellhop for the summer. The other bellhops were very amused because Powell, by the peculiarity of American society, was "black." Powell went on to represent Harlem in the U.S. Congress, 1945–1970.

Millions of other biracial Americans could tell a similar tale. From the seventeenth century to the present, the issue of race has permeated virtually every aspect of American life and culture. Although Americans rarely explore the terms they use when discussing race, a critical analysis of racial concepts is as important to the study of U.S. history as analyses of concept of gender and class.[35] Who is black? How have Americans come to make racial classifications? Why are millions of people whose genetic origins are more European than African defined by custom, by law, and by even themselves as black? Why is there a tremendous disparity between the scientific definition of who is black and the socio-cultural one?

Words can mean anything a community wants them to mean. The use of "black" as a racial category in the United States is actually of recent origin. Until the 1960s, persons with some African ancestry were described in the United States as "negro" or sometimes "colored"; neither the federal government nor people of some African ancestry described themselves as "black." In the late 1960s, leaders of the Black Power movement (see page 1117), which emphasized racial pride and insisted on self-definition, demanded the substitution of the Old English word *black* for the traditional Spanish or Portuguese term *negro*. The broader American society accepted the word. The recent adoption of the expression *African American* suggests blacks' conscious desire to preserve a link with Africa. Some research shows that in the nineteenth century, however, no one tried to preserve an African culture in the United States and free people of color strongly rejected any hint of an African connection.

Since the arrival of the first Africans in Jamestown, Virginia, in 1619, sexual contacts have taken place between whites and blacks. The colonists and later the young American republic, with some hesitations and variation, defined all children born of such unions, regardless of their personal appearances, as negro. In the American South this manner of definition became known as the "one drop rule," meaning a single drop of "African blood" made a person "black." Anthropologists call this the "hypo descent rule": racially mixed persons are arbitrarily assigned the status of the subordinate group.

During the long period of slavery (1619–1865), when white planters sexually exploited slave women and when some free blacks and whites intermingled, the number of mixed-race children multiplied. The U.S. census of 1850 showed that 11.2 percent of the population classed as negro were of mixed race; the 1910 census put the figure at 20.9 percent. Because these counts were based solely on the census taker's perception of racial visibility, the estimates were probably gross undercounts of all Negroes with some white ancestry. Today, according to reliable estimates, between 75 and 90 percent of all American blacks have some white ancestry, and millions of white Americans have at least small amounts of black genetic heritage. A central theme in *Light in August* and other novels by Mississippi writer William Faulkner is the anxiety that thousands of white southerners have felt about their racial purity.

Before the Civil War many parts of the South, but especially Charleston and New Orleans, had sizable populations of mulattos (persons with one negro parent), quadroons (one negro grandparent), and octoroons (one negro great-grandparent). These persons were the results of liaisons (some of long, sometimes lifelong duration) between whites and women of some African ancestry. Louisiana and South Carolina did not apply the "one drop rule" to these mixed-race people, and in 1835 Judge William Harper of South Carolina ruled that a person's acceptance as white, not the proportion of white and black "blood," determined a person's race. In short, the local community determined an individual's race. But as the South came under increasing abolitionist pressure to defend slavery, and as fears of slave revolts increased, attitudes hardened. Custom became law that defined as negro all persons with any perceptible African ancestry (see Listening to the Past).

Southerners encouraged the "one drop rule" as a way of enlarging the slave population. Likewise, after 1865 when native-born whites feared and resented blacks' economic and political potential; and when, between 1880 and 1910 floods of poor immigrants from southern and eastern Europe

competed with former slaves for jobs, the physical contrast between blacks and whites (skin pigmentation) proved useful to whites in justifying and legitimating their economic interests. After 1920, because there were so many mixed-race persons, and because so many Americans with some black ancestry appeared white, the U.S. census stopped counting mixed-race peoples, and the "one drop rule" became the national legal standard. Scorned and rejected by whites, biracial persons allied with "pure" blacks and in the twentieth century began to lead the struggle for racial equality.[36] The great advocate of nonviolent social action and perhaps the greatest leader of the civil rights movement, Martin Luther King, Jr. (see page 1117), had an Irish grandmother.

Racial categories rest on socially constructed beliefs and on custom backed by law, not on any biological or anthropological classification. Race and culture are not the same thing. Anthropologists define *race* as a grouping of human beings on the basis of average differences in biological characteristics; biological characteristics of race cannot be equated with mental characteristics, such as intelligence, personality, character. *Culture,* in contrast, is patterns of behavior, life, and beliefs. Peoples of the same race often have vastly different cultures, as, for example, Chinese culture differs from Japanese culture though both the Chinese and the Japanese are Asian, or as Italian culture differs from Russian culture though both peoples are Caucasian. So with African-Americans among whom different cultures also exist.

The accelerated immigration of huge numbers of Latin Americans and Asians to the United States since 1975 has complicated these issues. In preparation for the federal census of the year 2000, government agencies are considering modifications of customary racial categories and questioning whether it is even proper for the national government to classify people according to the arbitrary and nonscientific criteria of race. The federal Office of Management and Budget, which sets racial and ethnic standards on all governmental forms on the basis of census results, will provide rules that will influence the size and shape of congressional districts, college and business affirmative action programs, university scholarships, loans and mortgages. As one congressman puts it, "The numbers drive the dollars."

More native Americans marry outside their group than within it. In the 1980s black men mar-

Harlem Hellfighters   Returning to New York in 1919 aboard the U.S.S. *Stockholm*, these black men of the famed U.S. 369th Division had fought in the bloody battle of the Meuse-Argonne during the First World War. The French government awarded 150 of them the coveted Croix de Guerre. (*Source: Springer/ Bettmann Film Archive*)

ried white women at the rate of 10 percent (black women married whites at half that rate). Immigration also means cultural change. Large numbers of Asian women are today marrying white, Hispanic, and black men. Hispanic people pose the greatest complexity. According to the Latin American concept of race, skin color is an individual variable, not a group marker; thus within a given family, one child might be considered white, another black.

The 1960 census listed all people from Latin America as white—blacks from the Dominican Republic, European whites from Argentina, and Mexicans who resembled native Americans (Indians). In neither the State of Hawaii nor the Commonwealth of Puerto Rico does the term *race* carry the connotation it has on the U.S. mainland.

As the millennial year 2000 approaches, three broad currents of opinion about racial classification are emerging. One group urges doing away with all racial classifications because they are meaningless and unscientific and have been the historical means of exploiting persons perceived as "inferior." Other thinkers, primarily African-American scholars, agree that the notion of race is a cruel hoax but insist that the racial idea of "black" makes an important political statement. They argue that racial categories are needed to correct injustices and that the U.S. relinquishing of the racial idea of "black" would amount to the abandonment of a poor underclass. These writers have not so far addressed the situations of Hispanics, Asians, and native Americans. The third group consists of increasing numbers of biracial and multiracial persons who resent being assigned to any single category—persons who feel strong ethnic and cultural ties to two or more groups.[37] Should their feelings and pain be ignored? What do racial categories mean, anyway? Should people be discriminated against, or rewarded, on the basis of others' perceptions of who they are? Should the federal government continue its pattern of defining race in order to support the dominant race's economic goals? What if the dominant race is Hispanic? Should "the numbers drive the dollars"?

Industrialization and Immigration

After the Civil War the United States underwent an industrial boom powered by exploitation of the country's natural resources. The federal government turned over vast amounts of land and mineral resources to industry for development. In particular, the railroads—the foundation of industrial expansion—received 130 million acres. By 1900 the American railroad system was 193,000 miles long, connected every part of the nation, and represented 40 percent of the railroad mileage of the entire world. Immigrant workers built it.

The late nineteenth and early twentieth centuries witnessed the immigration of unprecedented numbers of Europeans and Asians to the United States (see page 892). Between 1860 and 1900, 14 million immigrants came, and during the peak years between 1900 and 1914, another 14 million passed through the U.S. customs inspection station at Ellis Island in New York City. All sought a better life and higher standard of living.

The immigrants' ambitions precisely matched the labor needs of the times. Chinese, Scandinavian, and Irish immigrants laid 30,000 miles of railroad tracks between 1867 and 1873 and another 73,000 miles in the 1880s. Poles, Hungarians, Bohemians, and Italians poured into the coal and iron mines of western Pennsylvania and Appalachia. At the Carnegie Steel Corporation (later USX), Slavs and Italians produced one-third of the world's total steel supply in 1900. Thousands of Czechs, Poles, and other Slavs worked in oil fields around the country. Lithuanians, Poles, Croats, Scandinavians, Irish, and Negroes entered the Chicago stockyards and built the meatpacking industry. Irish immigrants continued to operate the spinning frames and knitting machines of New England's textile mills. Industrial America developed on the sweat and brawn—the cheap labor—of its immigrant millions.

As industrial expansion transformed the eastern half of the United States, thousands of land-hungry farmers moved westward, where land was still only $1.25 an acre. In the final third of the nineteenth century, pioneers put 225 million acres under cultivation.

The West also held precious metals. The discovery of gold and silver in California, Colorado, Arizona, and Montana, and on the reservations of the Sioux Indians of South Dakota, precipitated huge rushes. Even before 1900, miners had extracted $1.24 billion in gold and $901 million in silver from western mines. Many miners settled down to farm and help their territories toward statehood. By 1912 the West had been won.

Generally speaking, the settler's life blurred sex roles. Women commonly did the same dawn-to-dusk backbreaking agricultural work as men.[38] In addition, it fell to women to make a home out of crude log cabins that had no windows or doors or out of tarpaper shacks that had mud floors. One "gently reared" bride of seventeen took one look at her mud roof and dirt floor and indignantly announced, "My father had a much better house for his hogs!" Lacking cookstoves, they prepared food over open fireplaces, using all kinds of substitutes for ingredients easily available back east. Before they could wash clothes, women had to make soap out of lye and carefully saved household ashes.

Considered the carriers of "high culture," women organized whatever educational, religious, musical, and recreational activities the settlers' society possessed. Women also had to defend their homes against prairie fires and Indian attacks. These burdens were accompanied by frequent pregnancies and, often, the need to give birth without medical help or even the support of other women. Many women settlers used such contraceptive devices as spermicides, condoms, and, after 1864, vaginal diaphragms. The death rate for infants and young children ran as high as 30 percent in the mid-nineteenth century. Even so, these women had large families.

As in South America, immigration led to rapid urbanization. In 1790 only 5.1 percent of Americans were living in centers of 2,500 or more people. By 1860 this figure had risen to 19.9 percent, and by 1900 almost 40 percent were living in cities. The overwhelming majority of the southern and eastern Europeans who came to North America at the turn of the century became urban industrial workers, their entire existence framed by the factory and the tenement. Newly uprooted from rural Europe, Italians, Greeks, Croats, Hungarians, Czechs, Poles, Russians, and Jews contrasted sharply with their urban neighbors and with each other. Older residents saw only "a sea of strange faces, babbling in alien tongues and framed by freakish clothes. Walking through these multitudes now was really like a voyage round the globe."[39]

Between 1880 and 1920 industrial production soared. New inventions such as the steam engine, the dynamo (generator), and the electric light were given industrial and agricultural applications. Large factories replaced small ones. Large factories could buy large machines, operate them at full capacity, and take advantage of railroad discount rates. In the automobile industry, Henry Ford of Detroit set up assembly lines. Each worker working on the line performed only one task instead of assembling an entire car. In 1910 Ford sold 10,000 cars; in 1914, a year after he inaugurated the first moving assembly line, he sold 248,000 cars. Such developments changed the face of American society. Sewing machines made cheap, varied, mass-produced clothing available to city people in department stores and to country people through mail-order catalogues. The automobile increased opportunities for travel, general mobility, and change.

As elsewhere, by the 1890s U.S. factory managers were stressing industrial efficiency and the importance of time. Management engineers wanted to produce more at lower cost. They aimed to reduce labor costs by eliminating unnecessary workers. As quantity rather than quality became the measure of acceptability, workers' skills were less valued. Assembly-line workers more and more performed only monotonous and time-determined work; in effect they became interchangeable parts of the machines they operated.

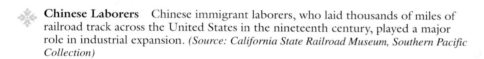

Chinese Laborers   Chinese immigrant laborers, who laid thousands of miles of railroad track across the United States in the nineteenth century, played a major role in industrial expansion. *(Source: California State Railroad Museum, Southern Pacific Collection)*

Despite accelerated production, and perhaps because of overproduction, the national economy experienced repeated cycles of boom and bust in the late nineteenth century. Serious depressions in 1873, 1884, and 1893 slashed prices and threw many people out of work. Leading industrialists responded by establishing larger corporations and consolidated companies into huge conglomerates. As a result of the merger of several small oil companies, John D. Rockefeller's Standard Oil Company controlled 84 percent of the nation's oil and most American pipelines in 1898. J. P. Morgan's United States Steel monopolized the iron and steel industries; and Swift & Co. of Chicago, the meat-processing industry.

Industrialization led to the creation of a vast class of wage workers who depended totally on their employers for work. Corporate managers, however, were always preoccupied with cutting labor costs. Thus employers paid workers piecemeal for the number of articles produced, to encourage the use of the new machines; and managers hired more women and children and paid them much less than they paid men. Most women worked in the textile industry. Some earned as little as $1.56 for seventy hours of work, while men received from $7 to $9 for the same work. Employers reduced wages, forcing workers to toil longer and harder to maintain a certain level of income. Owners fought in legislatures and courts against the installation of safety devices, so working conditions in mines and mills were frightful. In 1913, even after some safety measures had been taken, 25,000 people died in industrial accidents. Between 1900 and 1917, 72,000 railroad worker deaths occurred. Workers responded with strikes, violence, and, gradually, unionization.

Urbanization brought serious problems. In *How the Other Half Lives* (1890), Jacob Riis, a newspaper reporter and recent immigrant from Denmark, drew national attention to what he called "the foul core of New York's slums." Riis estimated that 300,000 people inhabited a single square mile on New York's Lower East Side. Overcrowding, poor sanitation, and lack of health services caused frequent epidemics. The blight of slums increased crime, prostitution, alcoholism, and other drug-related addictions. Riis attacked the vicious economic exploitation of the poor.

New York City was not unique; slums and the social problems resulting from them existed in all large American cities. Reformers fought for slum clearance, but public apathy and vested economic interests delayed massive urban renewal until after the Second World War. In spite of all these industrial and urban difficulties, immigrants continued to come: the United States offered opportunity, upward social mobility, and a better life.

European and Asian immigrants aroused nativist sentiments—that is, intense hostility to foreign and "un-American" looks, behavior, and loyalties—in native-born Americans. Some of this antagonism sprang from the deep-rooted Anglo-Saxon racism of many Americans. Some grew out of old Protestant suspicions of Roman Catholicism, the faith of most of the new arrivals. A great deal of the dislike of the foreign-born sprang from fear of economic competition. To most Americans, the Chinese with their exotic looks and willingness to work for very little seemed the most dangerous. Increasingly violent agitation against Asians led to race riots in California and finally culminated in the Chinese Exclusion Act of 1882, which denied Chinese laborers entrance to the country.

Immigrants from Europe seized on white racism as a way to compensate for their immigrant status by claiming superiority to former slaves and their descendants. The arrival of thousands of Irish immigrants in the 1850s, followed by millions of Italians and Slavs between 1880 and 1914, aggravated an already bad situation. What the German scientist Alexander von Humboldt wrote about the attitude of peninsulares toward Creoles in Latin America in the early nineteenth century—"the lowest, least educated, and uncultivated European believes himself superior to the white born in the New World"[40]—precisely applies to the outlook of Irish, Italian, or Slavic immigrants to the United States at the turn of this century if one merely substitutes *black* for *white*. In the eyes of all ethnic groups, the social status of blacks remained the lowest, while that of immigrants rose. As the United States underwent expansion and industrialization during the nineteenth century, blacks remained the worst off *because of immigration.*[41]

In the 1890s the nation experienced a severe economic depression. Faced with overproduction, the rich and politically powerful owners of mines, mills, and factories fought the organization of labor unions, laid off thousands, slashed wages, and ruthlessly exploited their workers. Workers in turn feared that immigrant labor would drive salaries lower. The frustrations provoked during the depression boiled over into savage attacks on the foreign-born. One of the bloodiest incidents took place in western Pennsylvania in 1897, when about 150 unarmed Polish and Hungarian coal miners tried to persuade others to join their walkout. The mine owners convinced the local sheriff that the strike was illegal. As the strikers approached, the sheriff panicked and ordered his deputies to shoot. Twenty-one immigrants died, and forty were wounded. The sheriff declared that the miners were only "infuriated foreigners . . . like wild beasts." Local people agreed that if the strikers had been American-born, no blood would have been shed.[42]

After the First World War, labor leaders lobbied Congress for restrictions because they feared losing the wage gains achieved during the war. Some intellectuals argued that immigrants from southern and eastern Europe, with their unfamiliar cultural traditions, threatened to destroy American society. Italians were feared because of possible Cosa Nostra connections. Eastern Europeans were thought to have communist connections. In the 1920s Congress responded with laws that set severe quotas—2 percent of resident nationals as of the 1890 census—on immigration from southern and eastern Europe. The Japanese were completely excluded. These racist laws remained on the books until 1965.

�֎ CANADA, FROM FRENCH COLONY TO NATION

In 1608 the French explorer Samuel de Champlain (1567–1635) sailed down the St. Lawrence River and established a trading post on the site of present-day Quebec. Thus began the permanent colony of New France. The fur-trading monopolies subsequently granted to Champlain by the French crown attracted settlers, and Jesuit missionaries to the Indians further increased the French population. The British, however, vigorously challenged French control of the lucrative fur trade, and the long mid-eighteenth-century global struggle for empire between the British and the French, known in North America as the French and Indian Wars because of Indian border warfare, tested French control. In 1759, on the Plains of Abraham, a field next to the city of Quebec, the English under General James Wolfe defeated the French under General Louis Montcalm. This battle ended the French Empire in North America. By the Treaty of Paris of 1763, France ceded Canada to Great Britain.

British Colony (1763–1839)

For the French Canadians, who in 1763 numbered about 90,000, the British conquest was a tragedy and the central event in their history. British governors replaced the French; English-speaking merchants from Britain and the thirteen American colonies to the south took over the colony's economic affairs. The Roman Catholic church remained and until about 1960 played a powerful role in the political and cultural, as well as religious, life of French Canadians. Most of the French Canadians engaged in agriculture, though a small merchant class sold furs and imported manufactured goods.

Intending to establish a permanent administration for Canada, in 1774 the British Parliament passed the Quebec Act. This law granted religious freedom to French Canadians and recognized French law in civil matters, but it denied Canadians a legislative assembly, a traditional feature of British colonial government. Parliament placed power in the hands of an appointed governor and an appointed council; the latter, however, was composed of French Canadians as well as English-speaking members. English Canadian businessmen protested that they were being denied a basic right of Englishmen—representation.

During the American Revolution, about forty thousand Americans demonstrated their loyalty to Great Britain and its empire by emigrating to Canada. These "loyalists" not only altered the French-English ratio in the population but also pressed for a representative assembly. In 1791 Parliament responded with the Constitution Act, which divided the province of Quebec at the Ottawa River into Lower Canada (present-day Quebec, predominantly French and Catholic) and Upper Canada (present-day Ontario, primarily English and Protestant). The act also provided for an elective assembly in each of the two provinces. Because the assemblies' decisions could be vetoed by an appointed upper house or by the governor and his council, general discontent continued. Finally, in 1837, disputes over control of revenue, the judiciary, and the established churches erupted into open rebellion in both Upper and Lower Canada. The British government, fearful of a repetition of the American events of 1776, decided on a full investigation and appointed Lord Durham, a prominent liberal reformer, to make recommendations for reform. Lord Durham published his

Report on the Affairs of British North America, later called the "Magna Carta" of British colonial administration, in 1839.

The Age of Confederation (1840–1905)

Acting on Lord Durham's recommendations, Parliament in 1840 passed the Union Act, which united Ontario and Quebec under one government composed of a governor, an appointed legislative council, and an elective assembly in which the two provinces had equal representation. The imperial government in London was to retain control over trade, foreign affairs, public lands, and the colonial constitution. The Union Act marks an important milestone toward confederation. When Lord Durham's son-in-law, Lord Elgin, was appointed governor in 1847, he made it clear that his cabinet (council) would be chosen from the party with the majority in the elected assembly; and, following the British model, the cabinet had to retain the support of that majority in order to stay in office.

The idea of a union or confederation of the other Canadian provinces persisted in the 1860s. During the American Civil War, English-American relations were severely strained, and according to one historian, "Canada found herself in the centre of the storm. The resulting fear of American aggression was a powerful factor in bringing confederation to completion."[43] Parliament's passage of the British North America Act in 1867 brought the Canadian constitution to its modern form. By the act the traditional British parliamentary system was adapted to the needs of the new North American nation. The provinces of New Brunswick and Nova Scotia joined Ontario and Quebec to form the Dominion of Canada. A governor general, who represented the British crown and fulfilled ceremonial functions, governed through the Dominion Cabinet, which, like the British Cabinet, was composed of members selected from the lower house of the legislature, to which it was responsible.

Legislative power rested in a Parliament of two houses: a Senate, whose members were appointed for life by the governor general, and a House of Commons, whose members were elected by adult males. (Canadian women won the right to vote in national elections in 1917, shortly before women in the United States and Great Britain but after women in Australia.) In theory, the two houses had equal power, though money bills had to originate in the House of Commons; in practice, the Senate came to serve only as a deliberative check on hasty legislation and as a means of rewarding elder statesmen for their party services.

The Dominion Cabinet received complete jurisdiction over internal affairs. Britain retained control over foreign policy. (In 1931 the British Statute of Westminster officially recognized Canadian autonomy in foreign affairs.)

Believing that the American system of the division of powers between the states and the federal government left the states too strong and helped to bring on the Civil War, the framers of the Canadian constitution intended to create a powerful central government. Thus provincial legislatures were assigned powers explicitly stated and applicable only to local conditions. With the implementation of the British North America Act, John A. Macdonald (1815–1891), the strongest advocate of confederation, became the Dominion's first prime minister.

Macdonald vigorously pushed Canada's "manifest destiny" to absorb all the northern part of the continent. In 1869 his government purchased for $1,500,000 the vast Northwest Territories of the Hudson Bay Company. From this territory the province of Manitoba emerged to become part of the Dominion in 1870. Fearful that the sparsely settled colony of British Columbia would join the United States, Macdonald lured British Columbia into the confederation with a subsidy to pay its debts and the promise of a transcontinental railroad. Likewise, the debt-ridden little maritime province of Prince Edward Island was drawn into confederation with a large subsidy. In five short years, between 1868 and 1873, through Macdonald's imagination and drive, Canadian sovereignty stretched from coast to coast.

Believing that a transcontinental railroad was essential to Canada's survival as a nation, Macdonald declared that "until this great work is completed our Dominion is little more than a 'geographical expression.' We have as much interest in British Columbia as in Australia, and no more. The railroad, once finished, we become a great united country with a large interprovincial trade and a common interest."[44] On November 7, 1885, Macdonald received a telegram announcing that the first train from Montreal in Quebec was approaching the Pacific; traveling at 24 miles per hour, the train had made the coast-to-coast trip in a little

Russian Immigrant Women in Saskatchewan   These women were Duokhobors, a religious sect that came to Canada seeking religious freedom from tsarist persecution. Because most of the men took railroad jobs, the women planted the vast plains with rye, wheat, oats, and flax. Their farms and orchards flourished, and the Duokhobors played an important part in the development of western Canada. *(Source: Saskatchewan Archives, University of Saskatchewan)*

over five days. The completion of the railroad led to the formation of two new prairie provinces, Alberta and Saskatchewan, which in 1905 entered the Dominion. (Only in 1949 did the island of Newfoundland renounce colonial status and join the Dominion.) The Canadian Pacific Railroad was Macdonald's greatest achievement.

Growth, Development, and National Maturity

Macdonald's hopes for large numbers of immigrants to people the thinly populated country did not immediately materialize. Between 1897 and 1912, however, 961,000 entered Canada from the British Isles, 594,000 from Europe, and 784,000 from the United States. Some immigrants went to work in the urban factories of Hamilton, Toronto, and Montreal. Most immigrants from continental Europe—Poles, Germans, Scandinavians, and Russians—flooded the midwestern plains and soon

transformed the prairies into one of the world's greatest grain-growing regions.

Because of Canada's small population, most of which in the early twentieth century was concentrated in Ontario and Quebec, the assimilation of the immigrants to the older English-Canadian culture occurred more slowly than in the "melting pot" of the United States. French Canadians remained the largest minority in the population. Distinctively different in language, law, and religion, and fiercely proud of their culture, they resisted assimilation. Since the 1950s, Italian and Hungarian immigration has contributed to the evolution of a more cosmopolitan culture.

Supported by population growth, Canada experienced an agricultural and industrial boom between 1891 and 1914. In those years wheat production rocketed from 2 million bushels per year to 150 million bushels. The discovery of gold, silver, copper, and nickel in northern Ontario led to the full exploitation of those mineral resources.

British Columbia, Ontario, and Quebec produced large quantities of wood pulp, much of it sold to the United States. Canada's great rivers were harnessed to supply hydroelectric power for industrial and domestic use. Meanwhile, the government erected tariffs to protect industry, established a national civil service, and built a sound banking system.

Canada's powerful support of the Allied cause in the First World War demonstrated its full maturity as a nation. In 1914 the British government still controlled the foreign policy of all parts of the empire. When Britain declared war on Germany, Canada unhesitatingly followed. More than 600,000 Canadian soldiers served with distinction in the army, some of them in the bloodiest battles in France. The 60,661 Canadians killed represent a greater loss than that experienced by the more populous United States. Canadian grain and foodstuffs supplied much of the food of the Allied troops, and Canadian metals were in demand for guns and shells. Canadian resentment, therefore, over lack of voice in the formulation of Allied war policies was understandable.

In 1917 the British government established the Imperial War Cabinet, a body composed of the chief British ministers and the prime ministers of the Dominions (Australia, Canada, New Zealand, and South Africa) to set policy. In 1918 Canada demanded and received—over the initial opposition of Britain, France, and the United States—the right to participate in the Versailles Peace Conference and in the League of Nations. Canada had become a respected and independent nation. Since 1939, Canada has been a member of the British Commonwealth of Nations. The constitution of 1982 abolished the power of the London Parliament to amend Canada's constitution and ended all appeals from the provinces to London. Quebec did not sign the 1982 document, and the strong separatist movement within Quebec continues to articulate the desire of French-speaking Canadians for independence from English Canada and sovereignty as a separate nation.

�֍ AUSTRALIA, FROM PENAL COLONY TO NATION

In April 1770, James Cook, the English explorer, navigator, and captain of H.M.S. *Endeavor,* dropped anchor in a wide bay about ten miles south of the present city of Sydney on the coast of eastern Australia. Because the young botanist on board the ship, Joseph Banks, subsequently discovered 30,000 specimens of plant life in the bay, 1,600 of them unknown to European science, Captain Cook called the place Botany Bay. Totally unimpressed by the flat landscape and its few naked inhabitants—the Aborigines, or native people—Cook sailed north along the coast. Finally, the ship rounded Cape York Peninsula, the northernmost point of Australia (Map 28.6). On August 21, on a rock later named Possession Island, Cook formally claimed the entire land south of where he stood for King George III, 16,000 miles away. Cook called the land "New South Wales." In accepting possession, the British crown acted on the legal fiction that Australia was *Terra Nullius,* completely unoccupied, thus entirely ignoring the native people.

The world's smallest continent, Australia is located southeast of Asia between the Pacific and Indian Oceans. It is about half the size of Europe and almost as large as the United States (excluding Alaska and Hawaii). Three topographical zones roughly divide the continent. The Western Plateau, a vast desert and semidesert region, covers almost two-thirds. The Central Eastern Lowlands extend from the Gulf of Carpentaria in the north to western Victoria in the south. The Eastern Highlands are a complex belt of tablelands. Australia is one of the world's driest continents. It has a temperate climate and little intense cold.

When Cook arrived in Australia, about 300,000 Aborigines inhabited the continent. A peaceful and nomadic people who had emigrated from southern Asia millennia before, the Aborigines lived entirely by food gathering, fishing, and hunting. They had no domestic agriculture. Tribal customs governed their lives. Although they used spears and bows and arrows in hunting, they never practiced warfare as it was understood by more technologically advanced peoples such as the Aztecs of Mexico or the Mandinke of West Africa. When white settlers arrived, they occupied the Aborigines' lands unopposed. According to one Australian scholar, from 1788 to the present "Australian governments have been much more concerned with protecting the Aborigines than with fighting them."[45] Nevertheless, like the Indians of Central and South America, the Aborigines fell victim to the white peoples' diseases and to a spiritual malaise caused by the breakdown of their tribal life. Today, only about 45,000 pureblood Aborigines survive.

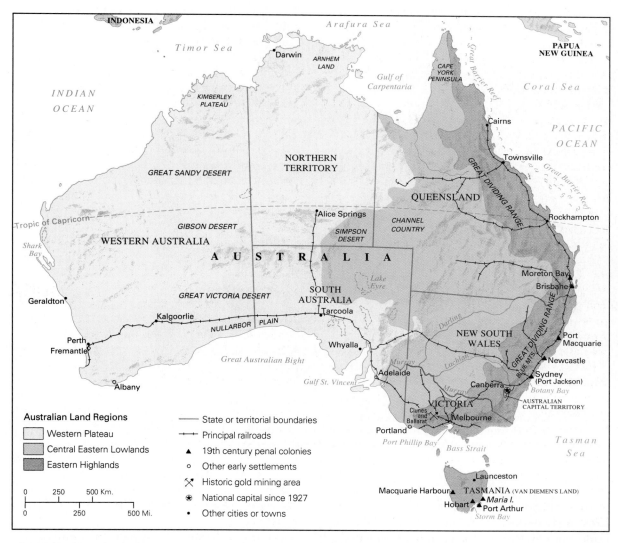

MAP 28.6 Australia   The vast deserts in western Australia meant that cities and industries would develop mainly in the east. Australia's early geographical and cultural isolation bred a sense of inferiority. Air travel, the communications revolution, and the massive importation of Japanese products and American popular culture have changed that.

Penal Colony

The victory of the thirteen North American colonies in 1783 inadvertently contributed to the establishment of a colony in Australia five years later. Before 1775, the British government had shipped about one thousand convicts annually to Georgia. Crime in England was increasing in the 1770s and 1780s, and the transportation of felons "beyond the seas" seemed the answer to the problem of overcrowded prisons. Moreover, the estab-lishment of a colony in Australia would provide a home for dispossessed loyalists who had fled America during the American Revolution.

In England, the prisons were so full that old transport ships in southern naval ports were being used to house criminals, and pressure on the government to do something was intense. Finally, in August 1786, the British Cabinet approved the establishment of a penal colony at Botany Bay to serve as "a remedy for the evils likely to result from the late alarming and numerous increase of felons

✤ **Convicts Embarking for Botany Bay**   The English printmaker and caricaturist Thomas Rowlandson (1756–1827) sketched this scene with ink and watercolor wash. In the background the gibbet with hanging felons shows the legal alternative to transportation to Australia. *(Source: National Library of Australia)*

in this country, and more particularly in the metropolis (London)."[46] The name "Botany Bay" became a byword for the forced and permanent exile of criminals. In May 1787 a fleet of eleven ships packed with one thousand felons and their jailers sailed for Australia. After an eight-month voyage it landed in Sydney Cove on January 28, 1788.

Mere survival in an alien world was the first challenge. Because the land at Botany Bay proved completely unsuited for agriculture and lacked decent water, the first governor, Arthur Phillip, moved the colony ten miles north to Port Jackson, later called Sydney. Announcing that those who did not work would not eat, Phillip set the prisoners to planting seeds. Coming from the slums of London, the convicts knew nothing of agriculture, and some were too ill or old to work. The colony lacked draft animals and plows. The troop detachments sent to guard the prisoners considered it below their dignity to work the land. For years the

colony of New South Wales tottered on the brink of starvation.

For the first thirty years, men far outnumbered women. Because the British government refused to allow wives to accompany their convict-husbands, prostitution flourished. Many women convicts, if not professional prostitutes when they left England, became such during the long voyage south. Army officers, government officials, and free immigrants chose favorite convicts as mistresses.

Recent research provides useful information about the official attitude toward women. On May 3, 1791, Lieutenant Ralph Clark recorded in his diary that he had ordered three women convicts flogged. Catherine White fainted after the first 15 lashes, Mary Teut after 22. When Mary Higgins had received 26 lashes, Lieutenant Clark "forgave her the remainder [he had ordered 50] because she was an old woman." From other sources we know that another woman convict was six months pregnant at the time with Clark's child.[47] This incident shows the brutality of power and the hypocrisy of an administration that simultaneously savagely punished and sexually exploited women. The vast majority of children born in the colony were illegitimate.

Officers and jailers, though descended from the middle and lower middle classes, tried to establish a colonial gentry and to impose the rigid class distinctions that they had known in England. Known as *exclusionists,* this self-appointed colonial gentry tried to exclude from polite society all freed or emancipated persons, called *emancipists.* Deep and bitter class feeling took root.

Economic Development

For eighty long years after 1787, Britain continued to transport convicts to New South Wales. Transportation rested on two premises: that criminals should be punished and that they should not be a financial burden on the state. Convicts became free when their sentences expired or were remitted. Few returned to England.

Governor Phillip and his successors urged the Colonial Office to send free settlers. The Napoleonic war slowed emigration before 1815, but thereafter a steady stream of people relocated. The end of the European wars also released capital for potential investment. But investment in what? What commodity could be developed and exported to England?

Immigrants explored several economic enterprises. In the last decade of the eighteenth century, for example, sealing seemed a likely possibility. Sealing merchants hired Aborigine women to swim out to the seal rocks, lie down among the seals until their suspicions were dulled, and then at a signal rise up and club the seals to death. In 1815, a single ship carried 60,000 seal skins to London (a normal cargo contained at least 10,000 skins). Such destruction rapidly depleted the seals.

Credit for the development of the product that was to be Australia's staple commodity for export—wool—goes to John Macarthur (1767–1834). Granted a large tract of crown lands and assigned thirty convicts to work for him, Macarthur conducted experiments in the production of fine merino wool. In 1800 he sent sample fleeces to England to determine their quality. He also worked to change the government's penal view of New South Wales to a commercial one and to attract the financial support of British manufacturers.

The report of J. T. Bigge, an able lawyer sent out in 1819 to evaluate the colony, proved decisive. Persuaded by large landowners like Macarthur, Bigge reported that wool was the country's future staple. He recommended that convicts be removed from the temptations of towns and seaports and dispersed to work on the estates of men of capital. He also urged that British duties on colonial wool be suspended. The Colonial Office accepted this advice, and the pastoral economy of Australia, as the continent was beginning to be called, began.

Australia's temperate though capricious climate is ideally suited to sheep farming. Moreover, wool production requires much land and little labor—precisely the situation in Australia. In 1820 the sheep population was 120,000; by 1830 it reached a half-million. After 1820 the commercial importance of Australia exceeded its significance as a penal colony, and wool export steadily increased: from 75,400 pounds in 1821, to 2 million pounds in 1830, to 24 million pounds in 1845.

Settlers also experimented with wheat farming. Soil deficiencies and the dry climate slowed early production, but farmers eventually developed a successful white-grained winter variety. By 1900 wheat proved Australia's second most valuable crop.

Population shortage remained a problem. In this area, the development of Australia owes something to the vision of Edward Gibbon Wakefield (1769–1862), a theorist of colonization. Between 1825 and 1850, 3 million people emigrated from Great Britain. In the quest for immigrants, Australia could not really compete with North America. The 12,000-mile journey to Australia cost between £20 and £25 and could take five weary months. By contrast, the trip to Canada or the United States cost only £5 and lasted just ten weeks. Wakefield proposed that Australian land be sold relatively cheaply and that proceeds from the sale be used to pay the passages of free laborers and mechanics. That eliminated the disadvantage of cost. Although over 2,500,000 British immigrants went to North America, 223,000 industrious English and Irish people chose Australia.

Population in the early nineteenth century concentrated on the eastern coast of the continent. The growth of sheep farming stimulated exploration and led to the opening of the interior. In 1813 explorers discovered a route over the Blue Mountains. New settlements were made in Hobart, Tasmania, in 1813; in Queensland on the

Brisbane River in 1824; and on the Swan River in Western Australia in 1829. Melbourne was established on Port Phillip Bay in 1835 and Adelaide on Gulf St. Vincent in 1836. These settlements served as the bases for further exploration and settlement. Population continued to grow with the arrival of more convicts (a total of 161,000 when the system was finally abolished in 1868). The Ripon Land Regulation Act of 1831, which provided land grants, attracted free settlers. By 1850 Australia had 500,000 inhabitants. The discovery of gold in Victoria in 1851 quadrupled that number in a few years.

From Colony to Nation

On February 12, 1851, Edward Hargraves, an Australian-born prospector who had returned to Australia after unsuccessful digging in the California gold rush of 1849, discovered gold in a creek on the western slopes of the Blue Mountains. Hargraves gave the district the biblical name Ophir (Job 22:24), and the newspapers said the region was "one vast gold field." In July a miner found gold at Clunes, 100 miles west of Melbourne, and in September gold was found in what proved to be the richest field of all, Ballarat, just 75 miles west of Melbourne. Gold fever convulsed Australia. Although the government charged prospectors a very high license fee, men and women from all parts of the globe flocked to Australia to share in the fabulous wealth.

Contemporaries agreed with explorer and politician W. C. Wentworth, who said that the gold rush opened in Australia a new era "which must in a very few years precipitate us from a colony to a nation."[48] Although recent scholars have disputed Wentworth, there is much truth to his viewpoint. The gold rush led to an enormous improvement in transportation within Australia. People customarily traveled by horseback or on foot and used two-wheel ox-drawn carts to bring wool from inland ranches to coastal cities. Then two newly arrived Americans, Freeman Cobb and James Rutherford, built sturdy four-wheel coaches capable of carrying heavy cargo and of negotiating the bush tracks. Carrying passengers and mail up to 80 miles a day, a week's work for ox-drawn vehicles, by 1870 Cobb and Co. coaches covered 28,000 miles per week. Railroad construction began in the 1870s, and by 1890 9,000 miles of track were laid. Rail-road construction, financed by British investors, stimulated agricultural growth.

The gold rush also provided the financial means for the promotion of education and culture. The 1850s witnessed the establishment of universities at Sydney and Melbourne and later at Adelaide and Hobart. Public libraries, museums, art galleries, and schools opened in the thirty years after 1851. In keeping with the overwhelmingly British ethnic origin of most immigrants to Australia, these institutions dispensed a distinctly British culture, though a remote and provincial version.

On the negative side, the large numbers of Asians in the gold fields—in Victoria in 1857 one adult male in seven was Chinese—sparked bitter racial prejudice. Scholars date the "white Australia policy" to the hostility, resentment, and fear that whites showed the Chinese.

Although Americans numbered only about 5,000 in Victoria and Asians 40,000, Americans with their California gold-rush experience, aggressive ways, and "democratic" frontier outlook, exercised an influence on Australian society far out of proportion to their numbers. "There was evidence to suggest that some Americans, bringing with them their pre–Civil War racist attitudes, had an appreciable influence on the growth of color prejudice in Australia."[49] On the Fourth of July in 1852, 1854, and 1857 (anniversaries of the American Declaration of Independence), anti-Chinese riots occurred in the gold fields of Victoria. After the gold-rush decade, public pressure for the exclusion of all colored peoples increased. Nevertheless, Asian peoples continued to arrive. Chinese and Japanese built the railroads and ran the market gardens near, and the shops in, the towns. Filipinos and Pacific Islanders did the hard work in the sugar-cane fields. Afghanis and their camels controlled the carrying trade in some areas.

"Colored peoples" (as all nonwhites were called in Australia) adapted more easily than the British to the warm climate and worked for lower wages. Thus they proved essential to the country's economic development in the nineteenth century. But fear that colored labor would lower living standards and undermine Australia's distinctly British culture triumphed. The Commonwealth Immigration Restriction Act of 1901 closed immigration to Asians and established the "white Australia policy." Australia achieved racial and cultural unity only at the price of Asian resentment at discrimination and

Ladies Embarking for Australia   When the blockade of southern ports during the American Civil War halted the flow of cotton to England, the mills of Lancashire were forced to lay off thousands who emigrated to the United States, Canada, and Australia. *The Illustrated London News* referred to these emigrants as "Distressed Needlewomen." *(Source: The Illustrated London News Picture Library)*

retarded economic development in the northern colonies, which desperately needed labor. The laws of 1901 remained on the books until the 1970s.

The gold rush had a considerable political impact. In 1850 the British Parliament had passed the Australian Colonies Government Act, which allowed the four most populous colonies—New South Wales, Tasmania, Victoria, and South Australia—to establish colonial legislatures, determine the franchise, and frame their own constitutions. The gold rush, vastly increasing population, accelerated the movement for self-government. Acknowledging this demand, the Colonial Secretary in London wrote that the gold discoveries "imparted new and unforeseen features to (Australia's) political and social condition." Western Australia's

decision to remain a penal colony delayed responsible government there, but by 1859 all other colonies were self-governing. The provincial parliament of South Australia was probably the most democratic in the world, since it was elected by universal manhood suffrage and by secret ballot. Other colonies soon adopted the secret ballot. In 1909 Australia became the first country in the world to adopt woman suffrage.

The government of Australia combines features of the British and American systems. In the later nineteenth century, pressure for continental federation culminated in meetings of the premiers (governors) of the colonies. They drafted a constitution that the British Parliament approved in 1900. The Commonwealth of Australia came into existence on January 1, 1901. From the British model, Australia adopted the parliamentary form of government in which a cabinet is responsible to the House of Commons. From the American system, Australia took the concept of decentralized government whereby the states and the federal government share power. The states in Australia, as in the United States, retain considerable power, especially in local or domestic affairs.

Deep loyalty to the mother country led Australia to send 329,000 men and vast economic aid to Britain in the First World War. The issue of conscription, however, bitterly divided the country, partly along religious lines. About one-fourth of Australia's population was (and is) Irish and Roman Catholic. Although the Catholic population, like the dominant Anglican one, split over conscription, the powerful, influential, and long-lived Catholic archbishop of Melbourne, Daniel Mannix (r. 1917–1963) publicly supported the Sinn Fein, the Irish nationalist (and later terrorist) movement. Mannix also denounced the English and the European war.

Twice submitted to public referendum, conscription twice failed. When the Australian poet Frank Wilmot (1881–1942) wrote, "The fumes of ancient hells have invaded your spirit," he meant that English wrongs in Ireland had become part of Australian culture.

Australian troops fought valiantly in the Dardanelles campaign, where more than 10,000 died. During the long nightmare of trench warfare on the western front, Australian soldiers were brilliantly led by Sir John Monash, a Jewish Australian whose planning led to the Allied breakthrough and the ultimate defeat of Germany. Australia's staggering 213,850 casualties, however, exerted a traumatic effect on Australian life and society. With the young men died the illusion that remote Australia could escape the problems and sins of the Old World. But the experience of the Great War forged a sense of national identity among the states of Australia.

At the Paris Peace Conference in 1919, Australian delegates succeeded in excluding recognition of the principle of racial equality in the League of Nations Covenant. Australians did not want Asian immigrants. The treaties that followed the war allowed Australia a mandate over German New Guinea and the equatorial island of Nauru. Nauru had vast quantities of phosphates that Australian wheatfields needed as fertilizer. The former penal colony had become a colonial power.

SUMMARY

Between 1788 and 1931, the United States, Canada, and Australia developed from weak, agricultural colonies of Great Britain into powerful industrial and commercial nations, and the countries of Latin America first secured independence from Spain and then began the process of nation building. Inspired by notions of social equality and manifest destiny, galvanized by the optimism of millions of immigrants who came seeking a better life, Americans subdued the continent, linked it with railroads, and built gigantic steel, oil, textile, food-processing, and automobile industries. The North's victory in the bloody Civil War, fought largely over the issue of black slavery, proved the permanence of the Union, but the unresolved ideal of equality remains the American dilemma. Industrialization and the assimilation of foreign peoples also preoccupied the nations of Latin America, but political instability and economies often dominated by the United States or Great Britain slowed growth.

Canada and Australia followed the path of the United States, though at a slower pace. Adopting the British model of cabinet government under John A. Macdonald, and utilizing rich natural resources, the provinces of Canada formed a strong federation with close economic ties to the United States; each is the other's major trading partner. French separatism, centered in Quebec, remains the Canadian dilemma. Australia utilized political features of both the British and the American systems. Immigrant production of wool, wheat, and now wine has transformed Australia from a remote penal colony into the great democratic nation of the Pacific.

NOTES

1. Quoted in W. S. Robertson, *Rise of the Spanish American Republics* (New York: Free Press, 1965), p. 19.
2. See B. Keen and M. Wasserman, *A Short History of Latin America* (Boston: Houghton Mifflin, 1980), pp. 109–115.

3. J. Lynch, *The Spanish-American Revolutions, 1808–1826* (New York: Norton, 1973), pp. 13–14; Keen and Wasserman, *A Short History of Latin America,* pp. 145–146.

4. Quoted in Lynch, *The Spanish-American Revolutions, 1808–1826,* p. 18.

5. M. Burkholder and D. S. Chandler, *From Impotence to Authority: The Spanish Crown and the American Audiencias, 1687–1808* (Columbia: University of Missouri Press, 1977), p. 145.

6. Ibid., p. 141.

7. Keen and Wasserman, *A Short History of Latin America,* p. 146.

8. Quoted in J. L. Phelan, *The People and the King: The Comunero Revolution in Colombia, 1781* (Madison: University of Wisconsin Press, 1978), p. 62; see also L. B. Rout, *The African Experience in Spanish America* (New York: Cambridge University Press, 1977), p. 165.

9. Quoted in Phelan, *The People and the King,* pp. 206–207.

10. F. Tannenbaum, *Ten Keys to Latin America* (New York: Random House, 1962), pp. 69–71.

11. H. Hoetink, *Slavery and Race Relations in the Americas* (New York: Harper & Row, 1973), p. 14.

12. Keen and Wasserman, *A Short History of Latin America,* pp. 201–204.

13. See C. H. Harris, *A Mexican Family Empire: The Latifundio of the Sanchez Navarros, 1765–1867* (Austin: University of Texas Press, 1975).

14. N. Sanchez-Albornoz, *The Population of Latin America: A History,* trans. W. A. R. Richardson (Berkeley: University of California Press, 1974), pp. 151–152.

15. J. R. Scobie, "Buenos Aires as a Commercial-Bureaucratic City, 1880–1910: Characteristics of a City's Orientation," *American Historical Review* 77 (October 1972): 1046.

16. Ibid., p. 1064.

17. See M. Morner, ed., *Race and Class in Latin America. Part II: Immigration, Stratification, and Race Relations* (New York: Columbia University Press, 1971), pp. 73–122; Sanchez-Albornoz, *The Population of Latin America,* pp. 160–167.

18. Quoted in M. B. Norton et al., *A People and a Nation: A History of the United States,* 4th ed. (Boston: Houghton Mifflin, 1994), p. 351.

19. S. E. Morison, *The Oxford History of the American People* (New York: Oxford University Press, 1965), pp. 380–381.

20. Ibid., pp. 446–452.

21. J. Oakes, *The Ruling Race: A History of American Slaveholders* (New York: Knopf, 1982), pp. x–xi.

22. See P. J. Parish, *Slavery: History and Historians* (New York: Harper & Row, 1989), pp. 45–46.

23. Quoted in Oakes, *The Ruling Race,* p. 120.

24. C. V. Woodward, ed., *Mary Chesnut's Civil War* (New Haven, Conn.: Yale University Press, 1981), p. 29.

25. Ibid., pp. xlix–l.

26. H. G. Gutman, *The Black Family in Slavery and Freedom, 1750–1925* (New York: Random House, 1977).

27. Quoted in R. W. Fogel and S. L. Engerman, *Time on the Cross: The Economics of American Negro Slavery* (Boston: Little, Brown, 1974), p. 84.

28. R. P. Basler, ed., *The Collected Works of Abraham Lincoln,* vol. 2 (New Brunswick, N.J.: Rutgers University Press, 1953), pp. 255–256, 271.

29. Ibid., pp. 461–462.

30. Quoted in R. Hofstadter, *The American Political Tradition* (New York: Random House, 1948), p. 114.

31. T. H. Williams, quoted ibid., pp. 128–129.

32. Quoted in ibid., p. 132.

33. Quoted in Morison, *The Oxford History of the American People,* p. 654.

34. T. H. Williams, *The History of American Wars: From Colonial Times to World War I* (New York: Knopf, 1981), p. 202.

35. Report of the University Committee on Diversity and Liberal Education to President Harold Shapiro of Princeton University as cited in *Princeton Today,* vol. 7, no. 2 (Summer 1994): 7.

36. F. James Davis, *Who Is Black? One Nation's Definition* (University Park: Pennsylvania State University Press, 1991), passim, but esp. Chs. 2 and 3, pp. 31–80.

37. See Lawrence Wright, "One Drop of Blood," *The New Yorker,* July 25, 1994, pp. 46–55.

38. S. L. Myres, *Westering Women and the Frontier Experience, 1800–1915* (Albuquerque: University of New Mexico Press, 1982), Chs. 6 and 7.

39. G. Barth, *City People: The Rise of Modern City Culture in the Nineteenth Century* (New York: Oxford University Press, 1980), p. 15.

40. Quoted in Lynch, *The Spanish-American Revolutions, 1808–1826,* p. 18.

41. Hoetink, *Slavery and Race Relations in the Americas,* p. 18.

42. Quoted in J. Higham, *Strangers in the Land: Patterns of American Nativism, 1860–1925* (New York: Atheneum, 1971), pp. 89–90.

43. Quoted in R. Cook, *Canada: A Modern Study* (Toronto: Clarke, Irwin, 1971), p. 89.

44. Quoted ibid., p. 127.

45. R. Ward, *Australia* (Englewood Cliffs, N.J.: Prentice-Hall, 1965), p. 21.

46. Quoted in R. Hughes, *The Fatal Shore* (New York: Knopf, 1987), p. 66.

47. J. Kociumbas, *The Oxford History of Australia,* Vol. 2, *Colonial Australia, 1770–1860* (New York: Oxford University Press, 1992), p. 1.

48. Quoted in Ward, *Australia,* p. 60.

49. Ibid., p. 59.

SUGGESTED READING

Perhaps the best introduction to the independence movements in Latin America is J. Lynch, *The Spanish-American Revolutions, 1808–1826* (1973), which is soundly researched and includes a good bibliography. The most useful biographies of Simón Bolívar are those of G. Masur, *Simón Bolívar,* 2d ed. (1969), and J. J. Johnson and D. M. Ladd, *Simón Bolívar and Spanish American Independence, 1783–1830* (1968); the latter contains good selections of Bolívar's writings. For Brazil, see K. R. Maxwell, *Conflicts and Conspiracies: Brazil and Portugal, 1750–1808* (1973), and A. J. R. Russell-Wood, ed., *From Colony to Nation: Essays in the Independence of Brazil* (1975). A. P. Whitaker, *The United States and the Independence of Latin America, 1800–1830* (1941), remains the standard study of the role of the United States. The essays in E. Viotti da Costa, *The Brazilian Empire: Myths and Histories* (1985), are sound and penetrating.

J. Bazant, *A Concise History of Mexico* (1978), is a good starting point for the study of Mexican history, but M. C. Meyer and W. L. Sherman, *The Course of Mexican History* (1979), is the most thorough treatment. T. Halperin-Donghi, *The Aftermath of Revolution in Latin America* (1973), and C. C. Griffin, "Economic and Social Aspects of the Era of Spanish-American Independence," *Hispanic American Historical Review* 29 (1949), provide important interpretations of the consequences of the revolutions.

The following studies offer good treatments of society and politics in Latin America in the nineteenth century: R. Graham and P. H. Smith, eds., *New Approaches to Latin American History* (1974); R. Roeder, *Juarez and His Mexico,* 2 vols. (1947), perhaps the best available work in English; H. S. Ferns, *Argentina* (1969); J. Kinsbruner, *Chile: A Historical Interpretation* (1973); A. J. Bauer, *Chilean Rural Society from the Spanish Conquest to 1930* (1975); E. B. Burns, *A History of Brazil* (1970); Robert Conrad, *The Destruction of Brazilian Slavery, 1850–1888* (1973).

J. C. Miller, *Slavery and Slaving in World History: A Bibliography, 1900–1901* (1993) is a useful reference tool with material comparing slavery in North and in South America. Some important comparative studies are I. Berlin and P. Morgan, eds. *Cultivation and Culture: Labor and the Shaping of Slave Life in the Americas* (1991); H. Klein, *Slavery in the Americas: A Comparative Study of Virginia and Cuba* (1967); C. Degler, *Neither Black Nor White: Slavery and Race Relations in Brazil and the United States* (1971). For South American labor and conditions of slavery, see S. Schwartz, *Sugar Plantations in the Formation of Brazilian Society* (1985) and the same author's *Slaves, Peasants, and Rebels: Reconsidering Brazilian Society* (1992); F. P. Bowser, *African Slavery in Colonial Peru* (1974); C. E. Martin, *Rural Society in Colonial Morelos* (1985); P. J. Carroll, *Blacks in Colonial Veracruz* (1991); and for North America, see S. Innes, *Work and Labor in Early America* (1988); J. F. Smith, *Slavery and Rice Culture in Colonial Georgia, 1750–1860* (1985); R. L. Lewis, *Coal, Iron, and Slaves: Industrial Slavery in Maryland and Virginia, 1715–1865* (1979) and S. Mintz, *Sweetness and Power: The Place of Sugar in Modern History* (1985). The elegant study by P. J. Parish cited in the Notes surveys a large body of scholarship. W. Jordan, *White Over Black: American Attitudes Towards the Negro, 1550–1812* (1969) remains a solid treatment of the relationship of racism to slavery. E. D. Genovese, *Roll, Jordan, Roll: The World the Slaves Made* (1974) gives a Marxist interpretation.

For social and economic developments and the triumph of neocolonialism, the following titles are useful: R. C. Conde, *The First Stages of Modernization in Spanish America* (1967); J. Bazant, *A Concise History of Mexico from Hidalgo to Cardenas, 1805–1940* (1978); R. Knowlton, *Church Property and the Mexican Reform, 1856–1910* (1976); R. D. Anderson, *Outcasts in Their Own Land: Mexican Industrial Workers, 1906–1911* (1976); J. Scobie, *Argentina: A City and a Nation,* 2d ed. (1971); M. J. Mamalakis, *The Growth and Structure of the Chilean Economy from Independence to Allende* (1976), which provides an excellent economic overview; A. G. Frank, *Capitalism and Underdevelopment in Latin America: Historical Studies of Chile and Brazil* (1969); D. Rock, *Politics in Argentina, 1890–1930: The Rise and Fall of Radicalism* (1975); and R. Graham, *Britain and the Onset of Modernization in Brazil, 1850–1914* (1968).

The major themes in U.S. history have been extensively treated by many able scholars, and students will have no difficulty finding a wealth of material. J. M. Burns, *The Vineyard of Liberty* (1982), traces the origins and development of American society, politics, and culture, from the 1780s to 1863, emphasizing the growth of liberty; this work is a classic achievement. The standard study of manifest destiny remains F. Merk, *Manifest Destiny and Mission in American History: A Reinterpretation* (1963), but see also K.

Jack Bauer, *The Mexican-American War, 1846–1848* (1976). In *The Only Land They Knew: The Tragic Story of the American Indians in the Old South* (1981), J. Leitch Wright recounts the interaction of native Americans, Africans, and Europeans in the American South.

On black culture and black women and the family, see, in addition to Gutman's work cited in the Notes, J. Jones, *Labor of Love, Labor of Sorrow: Black Women, Work, and the Family from Slavery to the Present* (1985); C. Neverdon-Morton, *Afro-American Women of the South and the Advancement of the Race, 1895–1925* (1989); and M. R. Malson et al., *Black Women in America: Social Science Perspectives* (1988), which offers useful essays for classroom discussion. See also W. S. McFeely, *Frederick Douglass* (1991), and I. Berlin et al., eds., *Freedom: A Documentary History of Emancipation* (1990). For the powerful influence of the black church see E. Lincoln and C. H. Mamiya, *The Black Church in the African American Experience* (1990).

The literature on the Civil War and Reconstruction is mammoth. The best comprehensive treatment of the pre-Civil War years is K. M. Stampp, *America in 1857: A Nation on the Brink* (1990). The following titles should also prove useful to students: J. M. McPherson, *Battle Cry of Freedom: The Era of the Civil War* (1988); D. M. Potter, *The Impending Crisis, 1848–1861* (1976); D. Donald, ed., *Why the North Won the Civil War* (1977); and E. Foner, *Reconstruction: America's Unfinished Revolution, 1863–1877* (1988).

T. C. Cochrane, *Business in American Life* (1977); A. D. Chandler, *Strategy and Structure: Chapters in the History of American Industrial Enterprise* (1966); H.

C. Livesay, *Andrew Carnegie and the Rise of Big Business* (1975); and D. F. Hawkes, *John D.: The Founding Father of the Rockefellers* (1980), are fine studies of industrialism and corporate growth in the late nineteenth century.

On the lives of Jews and other immigrants in American cities, see I. Howe's brilliant achievement, *World of Our Fathers* (1976), which is splendidly illustrated and contains a good bibliography, and S. S. Weinberg, *The World of Our Mothers: The Lives of Jewish Immigrant Women* (1988).

For developments in Canada, see, in addition to the highly readable sketch by R. Cook cited in the Notes, K. McNaught, *The Pelican History of Canada* (1976), a sound survey that emphasizes those cultural traits that are distinctly Canadian. For the Age of Confederation, J. M. S. Careless, *The Union of the Canadas, 1841–1857* (1967), offers a solid treatment by a distinguished scholar. D. G. Creighton, *John A. Macdonald,* 2 vols. (1952, 1955), is probably the best study of the great prime minister. The critical years of expansion and development are discussed in the full accounts of R. C. Brown and G. R. Cook, *Canada, 1896–1921* (1974), and R. Graham, *Canada, 1922–1939* (1979).

Perhaps the best starting point for the study of Australian history is the title by R. Hughes, cited in the Notes. M. Clark, *A Short History of Australia* (1987), is a highly readable general sketch. C. M. H. Clark, *A History of Australia,* 6 vols. (1962–1987), is the standard political history. R. Terrill, *The Australians* (1987), offers an attractive appreciation of the Australian people and the society they made, from the first settlers to the present.

Separate but Equal

"We hold these truths to be self-evident that all men are created equal," Thomas Jefferson wrote in the Declaration of Independence. But how could the rich merchants and slaveholders of the Second Continental Congress believe in equality? Jefferson recognized the contradiction and laid the blame on George III: the draft of the Declaration charged that the English king had "waged a cruel war . . . by assaulting distant people and captivating and carrying them into slavery in another hemisphere." Southern delegates rejected the notion that slavery violated "the most sacred rights of life and liberty" and, as a condition for endorsing the entire document, insisted that the slavery passage be deleted. Jefferson acquiesced, but the term equality remained. So did the contradiction.

The Thirteenth Amendment to the U.S. Constitution abolished slavery (1865), the Fourteenth granted civil rights to freed persons (1868), and the Fifteenth gave blacks the right to vote (1869). Between 1880 and 1910, southern legislatures responded with a flood of legislation designed to reduce blacks to a servile position and to create a system of rigid racial segregation. Laws required separate schools; separate public accommodations on trains and buses and in libraries, restaurants, parks, prisons, and institutions for the blind and deaf; separate telephone booths, water fountains, rest rooms, and even cemeteries. The State of Louisiana in 1890 adopted a law providing for "equal but separate" accommodations for the white and colored races on its railroads, with the interesting proviso that "nothing in this act shall be construed as applying to (black) nurses attending children of the other race." In 1892, Homer Plessy, seven of whose eight great-grandparents had been white, a passenger between two train stations in Louisiana, refused to sit in the railcar marked for blacks only. He was taken before Judge John H. Ferguson of the New Orleans Criminal Court. Ferguson upheld the Louisiana law, and the case

was appealed to the U.S. Supreme Court. Refusing to rule on who is a Negro, the Court took "judicial notice" of Mr. Plessy's background, based its decision on sociocultural, not genetic, factors, and held that being known in the community as Negro is evidence of Negro ancestry.

The object of the Fourteenth Amendment was undoubtedly to enforce the absolute equality of the two races before the law, but in the nature of things it could not have been intended to abolish distinctions based upon color or to enforce social, as distinguished from political, equality or a commingling of the races upon terms unsatisfactory to either. . . . The case reduces itself to the question whether the statute of Louisiana is a reasonable regulation, and . . . it is at liberty to act with reference to established usages, customs, and traditions of the people, and with a view to the promotion of their comfort, and the preservation of public peace and good order. Gauged by this standard, we cannot say that a law which authorizes or even requires the separation of the two races in public conveyances is unreasonable or more obnoxious to the Fourteenth Amendment than the acts of Congress requiring separate schools for colored children in the District of Columbia, the constitutionality of which does not seem to have been questioned. . . . If the two races are to meet on terms of social equality, it must be the result of natural affinities, a mutual appreciation of each other's merits. . . . If one race be inferior to the other socially, the Constitution of the United States cannot put them upon the same plane.

Mr. Justice John Marshall Harlan dissented:

Our Constitution is color blind, and neither knows nor tolerates classes among citizens. In respect of civil rights, all citizens are equal before the law. . . . The arbitrary separation of citizens, on the basis of race, while they are on a public highway, is a badge of servitude wholly inconsistent with the civil freedom and the equality before the law established by the Constitution. It cannot be justified upon any legal grounds.

Harlan was the sole dissenter. The majority opinion in Plessy v. Ferguson *(1896) remained the law of the land until the 1950s, when a school girl in Topeka, Kansas, appealed to the courts claiming that separate schools were unequal. The case that came before the U.S. Supreme Court in 1954,* Brown v. Board of Education of Topeka *combined a series of cases designed to challenge segregation in Kansas, Delaware, South Carolina, and Virginia. Delivering the unanimous opinion of the Court, Chief Justice Earl Warren declared:*

We come to the question presented: Does segregation of children in public schools solely on the basis of race, even though the facilities may be equal and other "tangible" factors may be equal, deprive the children of the minority group of equal educational opportunities? We believe that it does. . . . To separate them from others of similar age and qualifications solely because of their race generates a feeling of inferiority as to their status in the community that may affect their hearts and minds in a way unlikely ever to be undone. . . . We conclude that in the field of public education the doctrine of "separate but equal" has no place. Separate educational facilities are inherently unequal. . . . We have now announced that segregation is a denial of the equal protection of the laws.

The Georgetown Election. In 1866, as the United States Congress prepared to enfranchise negroes in D.C., the city's mayor took a vote to ascertain public opinion. The results: 6,591 against black suffrage, 35 in favor; in Georgetown the vote was 712 against, 1 in favor. President Johnson vetoed the enfranchisement bill and Congress immediately overrode it. The strongly Republican cartoonist Thomas Nast drew this scene prior to Congress's passage of the XVth Amendment (1867) granting blacks the right to vote. *(Source: Private Collection)*

Questions for Analysis

1. What was Homer Plessy's race? Why?

2. How would you evaluate the Supreme Court's comments in *Plessy v. Ferguson* on general race relations?

3. How does the decision in the *Brown* case sound the death knell for all segregation?

4. The 1954 Supreme Court has been accused of "social engineering." What does that phrase mean? Is it proper for the Supreme Court to attempt to reform society?

959

29

The Great Break:
War and Revolution

Gassed, a World War I
painting by John Singer
Sargent (1856–1925).
*(Source: By courtesy of the
Trustees of the Imperial
War Museum)*

In the summer of 1914 the nations of Europe went willingly to war. They believed they had no other choice. Moreover, both peoples and governments confidently expected a short war leading to a decisive victory. Such a war, they believed, would "clear the air," and then European society would be able to go on as before.

These expectations were almost totally mistaken. The First World War was long, indecisive, and tremendously destructive. To the shell-shocked generation of survivors, it was known simply as the Great War: the war of unprecedented scope and intensity. From today's perspective it is clear that the First World War marked a great break in the course of world historical development. The war accelerated the growth of nationalism in Asia (see Chapter 30), and it consolidated the position of the United States as a global power. Yet the war's greatest impact was on Europe, the focus of this chapter. A noted British political scientist has gone so far as to say that even in victorious and relatively fortunate Great Britain, the First World War was *the* great turning point in government and society "as in everything else in modern British history. . . . There's a much greater difference between the Britain of 1914 and, say, 1920, than between the Britain of 1920 and today."[1] This strong statement contains a great amount of truth, for all Europe as well as for Britain.

- What caused the Great War?
- How did the war lead to revolution and the fall of empires?
- How and why did war and revolution have such enormous and destructive consequences?
- How did the years of trauma and bloodshed form elements of today's world, many of which people now accept and even cherish?

These are the questions this chapter will try to answer.

❄ THE FIRST WORLD WAR

The First World War was so long and destructive because it involved all the Great Powers and because it quickly degenerated into a senseless military stalemate. Like evenly matched boxers in a championship bout, the two sides tried to wear each other down. But there was no referee to call a draw, only the blind hammering of a life-or-death struggle.

The Bismarckian System of Alliances

The defeat of France in 1871 (see page 868) and the founding of the German Empire opened a new era in international relations. In ten short years, from 1862 to 1871, Bismarck had made Prussia-Germany—traditionally the weakest of the Great Powers—the most powerful nation in Europe. Yet, as Bismarck never tired of repeating after 1871, Germany was a "satisfied" power. Within Europe, Germany had no territorial ambitions and wanted only peace.

But how was peace to be preserved? Bismarck's first concern was to keep an embittered France diplomatically isolated and without military allies. His second concern was the threat to peace posed by Austria-Hungary and Russia. Those two enormous multinational empires had many conflicting interests, particularly in the Balkans, where the Ottoman Empire—the "sick man of Europe"—was ebbing fast. There was a real threat that Germany might be dragged into a great war between the two rival empires. Bismarck's solution was a system of alliances (Figure 29.1) to restrain both Russia and Austria-Hungary, to prevent conflict between them, and to isolate a hostile France.

A first step was the creation in 1873 of the conservative Three Emperors' League, which linked the monarchs of Austria-Hungary, Germany, and Russia in an alliance against radical movements. In 1877 and 1878, when Russia's victories over the Ottoman Empire threatened the balance of Austrian and Russian interests in the Balkans and the balance of British and Russian interests in the Middle East, Bismarck played the role of sincere peacemaker at the Congress of Berlin in 1878 (see page 965). But his balancing efforts at the congress infuriated Russian nationalists, and their anger led Bismarck to conclude a defensive military alliance with Austria against Russia in 1879. Motivated by tensions with France, Italy joined Germany and Austria in 1882, thereby forming what became known as the Triple Alliance.

Bismarck continued to work for peace in eastern Europe, seeking to neutralize tensions between Austria-Hungary and Russia. In 1881 he cajoled them both into a secret alliance with Germany.

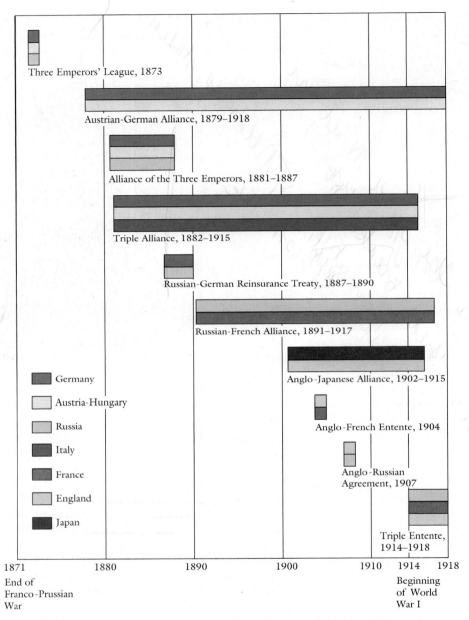

FIGURE 29.1 The Alliance System After 1871   Bismarck's subtle diplomacy maintained reasonably good relations among the eastern monarchies—Germany, Russia, and Austria-Hungary—and kept France isolated. The situation changed dramatically in 1891, when the Russian-French Alliance divided the Great Powers into two fairly equal military blocs.

This Alliance of the Three Emperors lasted until 1887.

Bismarck also maintained good relations with Britain and Italy while encouraging France in Africa but keeping France isolated in Europe. In 1887 Russia declined to renew the Alliance of the Three Emperors because of new tensions in the Balkans. Bismarck craftily substituted the Russian-German Reinsurance Treaty, by which both states promised neutrality if the other was attacked.

✦ **The Congress of Berlin, 1878**   With the Austrian representative on his right and with other participants looking on, Bismarck the mediator symbolically seals the hard-won agreement by shaking hands with the chief Russian negotiator. In the nineteenth century the Great Powers often relied on such special conferences to settle their international disputes. *(Source: The Bettmann Archive)*

Bismarck's accomplishments in foreign policy after 1871 were great. For almost a generation, he maintained German leadership in international affairs, and he worked successfully for peace by managing conflicts and by restraining Austria-Hungary and Russia with defensive alliances.

The Rival Blocs

In 1890 the young, impetuous German emperor William II dismissed Bismarck, in part because of the chancellor's friendly policy toward Russia since the 1870s. William then adamantly refused to renew the Russian-German Reinsurance Treaty, in spite of Russian willingness to do so. This fateful departure in foreign affairs prompted long-isolated republican France to court absolutist Russia, offering loans, arms, and friendship. In both countries there were enthusiastic public demonstrations, and in St. Petersburg Harbor the autocratic tsar Alexander III stood bareheaded on a French battleship while a band played the "Marseillaise," the hymn of the French Revolution. After a preliminary agreement was reached in 1891, France and Russia became military allies in 1894, pledging to remain so as long as the Triple Alliance of Austria, Germany, and Italy existed (see Figure 29.1). As a result, continental Europe was dangerously divided into two rival blocs.

Great Britain's foreign policy became increasingly crucial. Long content with "splendid isolation" and no permanent alliances, Britain after 1891 was the only uncommitted Great Power. Could Britain afford to remain isolated, or would it feel compelled to take sides? Alliance with France or Russia certainly seemed highly unlikely. With a vast and rapidly expanding empire, Britain was often in serious conflict with these countries around the world.

Britain also squabbled with Germany, but many Germans and some Britons felt that a "natural alliance" united the advanced, racially related Germanic and Anglo-Saxon peoples. However, the generally good relations that had prevailed between Prussia and Great Britain ever since the mid-eighteenth century, and certainly under Bismarck, gave way to a bitter Anglo-German rivalry.

There were several reasons for this tragic development. Commercial rivalry in world markets between Germany and Great Britain increased sharply in the 1890s. Above all, Germany's decision in 1900 to expand greatly its battle fleet posed a challenge to Britain's long-standing naval supremacy. This decision coincided with the hard-fought Boer War (1899–1902) between the British and the tiny Dutch republics of South Africa, a conflict that had a major impact on British policy. British political leaders saw that Britain was overextended around the world. The Boer War also brought into the open widespread anti-British feeling as editorial writers in many nations denounced this latest manifestation of British imperialism. There was even talk of Germany, Austria, France, and Russia forming a grand alliance against the bloated but insatiable British Empire. Thus British leaders prudently set about shoring up their exposed position with alliances and agreements.

Britain improved its often-strained relations with the United States and in 1902 concluded a formal alliance with Japan (see Figure 29.1). Britain then responded favorably to the advances of France's skillful foreign minister Théophile Delcassé, who wanted better relations with Britain and was willing to accept British rule in Egypt in return for British support of French plans to dominate Morocco. The resulting Anglo-French Entente of 1904 settled all outstanding colonial disputes between Britain and France.

Frustrated by Britain's turn toward France in 1904 and wanting a diplomatic victory to gain greater popularity at home, Germany's leaders decided to test the strength of the entente. Rather than accept the typical territorial payoff of imperial competition—a slice of French jungle somewhere in Africa or a port in Morocco—in return for French primacy in Morocco, the Germans foolishly rattled their swords by insisting in 1905 on an international conference on the whole Moroccan question; nor did the Germans present precise or reasonable demands. Germany's crude bullying forced France and Britain closer together, and Ger-

many left the resulting Algeciras Conference of 1906 empty-handed and isolated (except for Austria-Hungary).

The result of the Moroccan crisis and the Algeciras Conference was something of a diplomatic revolution. Britain, France, Russia, and even the United States began to see Germany as a potential threat, a would-be intimidator that might seek to dominate all Europe. At the same time, German leaders began to see sinister plots to "encircle" Germany and block its development as a world power. In 1907 Russia, battered by its disastrous war with Japan and the revolution of 1905, agreed to settle its quarrels with Great Britain in Persia and central Asia with a special Anglo-Russian Agreement (see Figure 29.1). As a result of that agreement, Germany's blustering paranoia increased, as did Britain's thinly disguised hostility.

Germany's decision to add a large, enormously expensive fleet of big-gun battleships to its already expanding navy also heightened tensions after 1907. German nationalists saw a large navy as the legitimate mark of a great world power and as a source of pride and patriotic unity. But British leaders such as David Lloyd George saw it as a detestable military challenge that forced them to spend the "People's Budget" on battleships rather than social welfare. Ongoing economic rivalry also contributed to distrust and hostility between the two nations, while proud nationalists in both countries simultaneously admired and feared the power and accomplishments of their nearly equal rival. In 1909 the mass-circulation London *Daily Mail* hysterically informed its readers in a series of reports that "Germany is deliberately preparing to destroy the British Empire."[2] By then Britain was psychologically, if not officially, in the Franco-Russian camp. The leading nations of Europe were divided into two hostile blocs, both ill prepared to deal with upheaval on Europe's southeastern frontier.

The Outbreak of War

In the early years of the twentieth century, war in the Balkans was as inevitable as anything can be in human history. The reason was simple: nationalism was destroying the Ottoman Empire and threatening to break up the Austro-Hungarian Empire. The only questions were what kinds of wars would occur and where would they lead.

German Warships Under Full Steam   As these impressive ships engaged in battle exercises in 1907 suggest, Germany did succeed in building a large modern navy. But Britain was determined to maintain its naval superiority, and the spiraling arms race helped poison relations between the two countries. *(Source: Bibliothèque des Arts Décoratifs/Jean-Loup Charmet)*

Greece had long before led the struggle for national liberation, winning its independence in 1832. In 1875 widespread nationalist rebellion in the Ottoman Empire had resulted in Turkish repression, Russian intervention, and Great Power tensions. Bismarck had helped resolve this crisis at the 1878 Congress of Berlin, which worked out the partial division of Turkish possessions in Europe. Austria-Hungary obtained the right to "occupy and administer" Bosnia and Herzegovina. Serbia and Romania won independence, and a part of Bulgaria won local autonomy. The Ottoman Empire retained important Balkan holdings, for Austria-Hungary and Russia each feared the other's domination of totally independent states in the area (Map 29.1).

By 1903 Balkan nationalism was asserting itself once again. Serbia led the way, becoming openly hostile toward both Austria-Hungary and the Ottoman Empire. The Serbs, a Slavic people, looked to Slavic Russia for support of their national aspirations. To block Serbian expansion and to take advantage of Russia's weakness after the revolution of 1905, Austria in 1908 formally annexed Bosnia and Herzegovina, with their large Serbian, Croatian, and Muslim populations. The kingdom of Serbia erupted in rage but could do nothing without Russian support.

Then in 1912, in the First Balkan War, Serbia turned southward. With Greece and Bulgaria it took Macedonia from the Ottoman Empire and then quarreled with Bulgaria over the spoils of victory—a dispute that led in 1913 to the Second Balkan War. Austria intervened in 1913 and forced Serbia to give up Albania. After centuries, nationalism had finally destroyed the Ottoman Empire in Europe (Map 29.2). This sudden but long-awaited event elated the Balkan nationalists and dismayed

❄ **MAP 29.1 The Balkans After the Congress of Berlin, 1878**   The Ottoman Empire suffered large territorial losses but remained a power in the Balkans.

❄ **MAP 29.2 The Balkans in 1914**   Ethnic boundaries did not follow political boundaries, and Serbian national aspirations threatened Austria-Hungry.

the leaders of multinational Austria-Hungary. The former hoped and the latter feared that Austria might be next to be broken apart.

Within this tense context, Archduke Francis Ferdinand, heir to the Austrian and Hungarian thrones, and his wife, Sophie, were assassinated by ultranationalist Serbian revolutionaries on June 28, 1914, during a state visit to the Bosnian capital of Sarajevo. Although the leaders of Austria-Hungary did not and could not know all the details of Serbia's involvement in the assassination plot, they concluded after some hesitation that Serbia had to be severely punished once and for all. On July 23 Austria-Hungary presented Serbia with an unconditional ultimatum. The Serbian government had just forty-eight hours in which to agree to de-

mands that would amount to Austrian control of the Serbian state. When Serbia replied moderately but evasively, Austria began to mobilize and then declared war on Serbia on July 28. Thus a desperate multinational Austria-Hungary deliberately chose war in a last-ditch attempt to stem the rising tide of hostile nationalism within its borders and save the existing state. The "Third Balkan War" had begun.

Of prime importance in Austria-Hungary's fateful decision was Germany's unconditional support. Emperor William II and his chancellor, Theobald von Bethmann-Hollweg, gave Austria-Hungary a "blank check" and urged aggressive measures in early July, even though they realized that war between Austria and Russia was the most probable result. A resurgent Russia could not stand by, as in the Bosnian crisis, and simply watch the Serbs be crushed. Yet Bethmann-Hollweg apparently hoped that while Russia (and therefore France) would go to war, Great Britain would remain neutral, unwilling to fight for "Russian aggression" in the distant Balkans.

In fact, the diplomatic situation was already out of control. Military plans and timetables began to dictate policy. On July 28 as Austrian armies bombarded Belgrade, Tsar Nicholas II ordered a partial mobilization against Austria-Hungary. Almost immediately he found that this was impossible. All the complicated mobilization plans of the Russian general staff had assumed a war with both Austria and Germany: Russia could not mobilize against one without mobilizing against the other. Therefore, on July 29 Russia ordered full mobilization and in effect declared general war.

The same tragic subordination of political considerations to military strategy shaped events in Germany. The German general staff had also thought only in terms of a two-front war. The staff's plan for war called for knocking out France first with a lightning attack through neutral Belgium before turning on Russia. So on August 2, 1914, General Helmuth von Moltke, "acting under a dictate of self-preservation," demanded that Belgium permit German armies to pass through its territory. Belgium, whose neutrality had been solemnly guaranteed in 1839 by all the great states including Prussia, refused. Germany attacked. Thus Germany's terrible, politically disastrous response to a war in the Balkans was an all-out invasion of France by way of the plains of neutral Belgium on August 3. In the face of this act of aggression, Great Britain joined France and declared war on Germany the following day. The First World War had begun.

In reflecting on the origins of the First World War, it seems clear that Austria-Hungary deliberately started the conflict. A war for the right to survive was Austria-Hungary's desperate response to the aggressive, revolutionary drive of Serbian nationalists to unify their people in a single state. Moreover, in spite of Russian intervention in the quarrel, it is also clear that Germany was most responsible for turning a third war in the Balkans into the Great War by means of a sledgehammer attack on Belgium and France. Why Germany was so aggressive in 1914 is less certain.

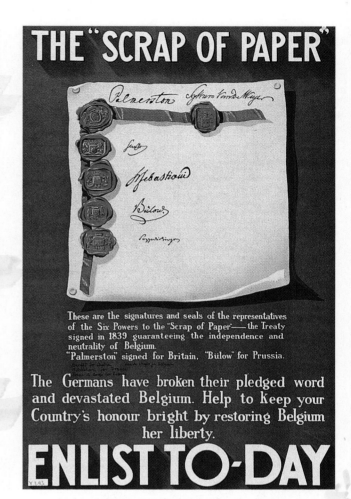

Anti-German Propaganda This British poster shows the signature page of the 1839 treaty guaranteeing the neutrality of Belgium. When German armies invaded Belgium in 1914, Chancellor Bethmann-Hollweg cynically dismissed the treaty as a "scrap of paper"—a perfect line for anti-German propaganda. (*Source: By courtesy of the Trustees of the Imperial War Museum*)

Diplomatic historians stress that German leaders lost control of the international system after Bismarck's resignation in 1890. They felt increasingly that Germany's status as a world power was declining while the status of Britain, France, Russia, and the United States was growing. Indeed, the powers of what officially became in August 1914 the Triple Entente—Great Britain, France, and Russia—were checking Germany's vague but real aspirations as well as working to strangle Austria-Hungary, Germany's only real ally. Germany's

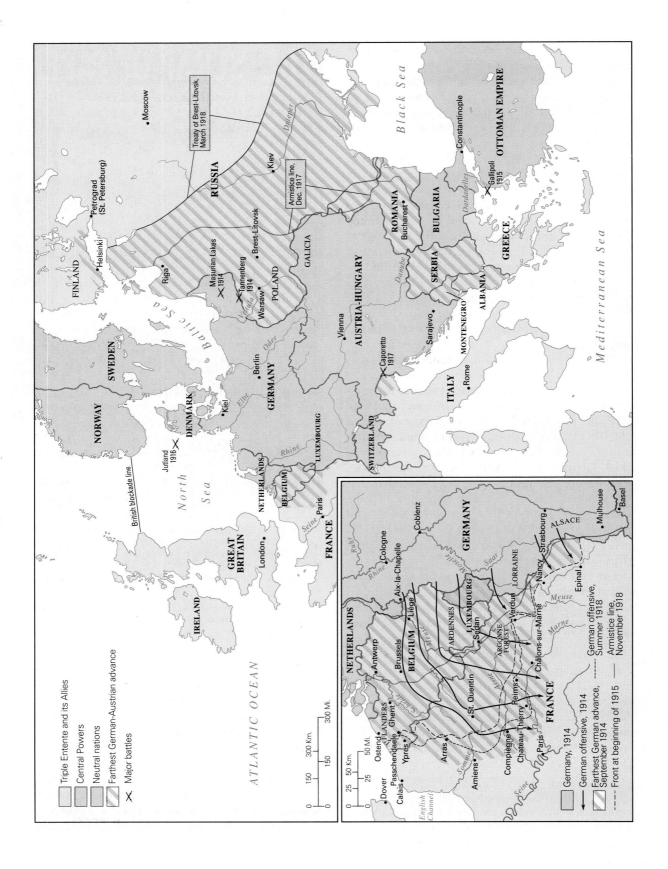

Moscow

Treaty of Brest-Litovsk, March 1918

Black Sea

Petrograd (St. Petersburg)

RUSSIA

Kiev

Armistice line, Dec. 1917

Constantinople

OTTOMAN EMPIRE

Helsinki

FINLAND

ROMANIA

Bucharest

BULGARIA

Dardanelles

Gallipoli 1915

Riga

Masurian Lakes 1914

Tannenberg 1914

Brest-Litovsk

GALICIA

Dnieper

Vistula

Oder

Warsaw

POLAND

AUSTRIA-HUNGARY

Danube

SERBIA

GREECE

ALBANIA

MONTENEGRO

Sarajevo

SWEDEN

NORWAY

Baltic Sea

Berlin

Elbe

Kiel

DENMARK

GERMANY

Vienna

Caporetto 1917

ITALY

Rome

Mediterranean Sea

Jutland 1916

North Sea

British blockade line

LUXEMBOURG

Rhine

SWITZERLAND

NETHERLANDS

BELGIUM

Seine

Paris

FRANCE

GREAT BRITAIN

London

IRELAND

ATLANTIC OCEAN

Triple Entente and its Allies
Central Powers
Neutral nations
Farthest German-Austrian advance
Major battles

300 Km.
150
0

300 Mi.
150
0

Ruhr

Rhine

Coblenz

GERMANY

Basel

Mulhouse

Cologne

Aix-la-Chapelle

Liège

Meuse

ARDENNES

LUXEMBOURG

Sedan

ARGONNE FOREST

Verdun

LORRAINE

Moselle

Saar

Nancy

Strasbourg

ALSACE

Meuse

Epinal

NETHERLANDS

Antwerp

Brussels

BELGIUM

St. Quentin

Oise

Reims

Châlons-sur-Marne

Marne

Château-Thierry

FRANCE

Ostend

FLANDERS

Ghent

Passchendaele

Ypres

Arras

Somme

Amiens

Compiègne

Paris

Seine

Aisne

Dover

Calais

English Channel

Scheldt

German offensive, Summer 1918
Armistice line, November 1918

Germany, 1914
German offensive, 1914
Farthest German advance, September 1914
Front at beginning of 1915

50 Km.
25
0

50 Mi.
25
0

aggression in 1914 reflected the failure of all European leaders, not just those in Germany, to incorporate Bismarck's mighty empire permanently and peacefully into the international system.

Growing tensions between European states correctly suggest that the triumph of nationalism was a crucial underlying precondition of the Great War. Nationalism was at the heart of the Balkan wars, and it drove the spiraling international arms race. Broad popular commitment to "my country right or wrong" weakened groups that thought in terms of international communities and consequences. Thus the big international bankers, who were frightened by the prospect of war in July 1914, and the extreme-left socialists, who believed that the enemy was at home and not abroad, were equally out of step with national feeling. In each country the great majority of the population enthusiastically embraced the outbreak of war in August 1914. They rallied to defend the nation, and patriotic nationalism brought unity in the short run.

In all of this, Europe's governing classes underestimated the risk of war to themselves in 1914. They had forgotten that great wars and great social revolutions very often go hand in hand. Metternich's alliance of conservative forces in support of international peace and the social status quo had become a distant memory.

Stalemate and Slaughter

When the Germans invaded Belgium in August 1914, they and everyone else believed that the war would be short, for urban society rested on the food and raw materials of the world economy: "The boys will be home by Christmas." The Belgian army heroically defended its homeland, however, and fell back in good order to join a rapidly landed British army corps near the Franco-Belgian border. Instead of quickly capturing Paris in a vast encircling movement, by the end of August deadtired German soldiers were advancing along an enormous front in the scorching summer heat. On

September 6, the French attacked a gap in the German line at the Battle of the Marne. For three days, France threw everything into the attack. At one point, the French government desperately requisitioned all the taxis of Paris to rush reserves to the troops at the front. Finally, the Germans fell back. Paris and France had been miraculously saved (Map 29.3).

Soon, with the armies stalled, both sides began to dig trenches to protect themselves from machine-gun fire. By November 1914 an unbroken line of trenches extended from the Belgian ports through northern France past the fortress of Verdun and on to the Swiss frontier. In the face of this unexpected stalemate, slaughter on the western front began in earnest. The defenders on both sides dug in behind rows of trenches, mines, and barbed wire. For days and even weeks, ceaseless shelling by heavy artillery supposedly "softened up" the enemy in a given area (and also signaled the coming attack). Then young draftees and their junior officers went "over the top" of the trenches in frontal attacks on the enemy's line.

The cost in lives was staggering; the gains in territory, minuscule. The massive French and British offensives during 1915 never gained more than three miles of blood-soaked earth from the enemy. In the Battle of the Somme in the summer of 1916, the British and French gained an insignificant 125 square miles at the cost of 600,000 dead or wounded, and the Germans lost 500,000 men. In that same year, the unsuccessful German campaign against Verdun cost 700,000 lives on both sides. British poet Siegfried Sassoon (1886–1967) wrote of the Somme offensive, "I am staring at a sunlit picture of Hell."

The year 1917 was equally terrible. The hero of Erich Remarque's great novel *All Quiet on the Western Front* (1929) describes a typical attack:

We see men living with their skulls blown open; we see soldiers run with their two feet cut off. . . . Still the little piece of convulsed earth in which we lie is held. We have yielded no more than a few hundred yards of it as a prize to the enemy. But on every yard there lies a dead man.

Such was war on the western front.

The war of the trenches shattered an entire generation of young men. Millions who could have provided political creativity and leadership after the

MAP 29.3 The First World War in Europe
Trench warfare on the western front was concentrated in Belgium and northern France. The war in the east encompassed an enormous territory.

The Fruits of War   The extent of the carnage, the emotional damage, and the physical destruction on the western front were all unprecedented. Once-great cathedrals standing in ruin symbolized the disaster. *(Source: UPI/Bettmann Newsphotos)*

war were forever missing. Moreover, those who lived through the holocaust were maimed, shell-shocked, embittered, and profoundly disillusioned. The young soldiers went to war believing in the world of their leaders and elders—the pre-1914 world of order, progress, and patriotism. Then, in Remarque's words, the "first bombardment showed us our mistake, and under it the world as they had taught it to us broke in pieces."

The Widening War

On the eastern front, slaughter did not degenerate into suicidal trench warfare. With the outbreak of

the war, the "Russian steamroller" immediately moved into eastern Germany. Very badly damaged by the Germans under General Paul von Hindenburg and General Erich Ludendorff at the Battle of Tannenberg and the Battle of the Masurian Lakes in August and September 1914, Russia never threatened Germany again (see Map 29.3). On the Austrian front, enormous armies seesawed back and forth, suffering enormous losses. Austro-Hungarian armies were repulsed twice by little Serbia in bitter fighting. But with the help of German forces, they reversed the Russian advances of 1914 and forced the Russians to retreat deep into their own territory in the eastern campaign of 1915.

A staggering 2.5 million Russians were killed, wounded, or taken prisoner that year.

These changing tides of victory and hopes of territorial gains brought neutral countries into the war. Italy, a member of the Triple Alliance since 1882, had declared its neutrality in 1914 on the grounds that Austria had launched a war of aggression. Then, in May 1915, Italy joined the Triple Entente of Great Britain, France, and Russia in return for promises of Austrian territory. Bulgaria also declared its neutrality in 1914. But after the Ottoman Empire joined in October 1914 with Austria and Germany, by then known as the Central Powers, Bulgaria weighed enticing promises from all sides. In September 1915 it decided to follow the Ottoman Empire's lead in order to settle old scores with Serbia. Bulgarian and German armies were successful, and the Central Powers occupied all of the Balkans, with the exception of Greece (see Map 29.3).

The entry of the Ottoman Turks carried the war into the Middle East, a momentous development. Heavy fighting with Russia saw bloody battle lines seesawing back and forth. In 1915 British forces tried to take the Dardanelles and Constantinople from Turkey but were badly defeated. The British were more successful at inciting Arab nationalists against their Turkish overlords. An enigmatic British colonel, soon known to millions as Lawrence of Arabia, helped lead the Arab revolt in early 1917. In 1918 British armies totally smashed the old Ottoman state, drawing primarily on imperial forces from Egypt, India, Australia, and New Zealand. Thus war brought revolutionary change to the Middle East (see pages 996, 999).

War also spread to some parts of East Asia and Africa. Instead of revolting as the Germans hoped, the colonial subjects of the British and French supported their foreign masters, providing critical supplies and fighting in armies in Europe and in the Ottoman Empire. They also helped local British and French commanders seize Germany's colonies around the globe. The Japanese, allied in Asia with the British since 1902, similarly used the war to grab German outposts in the Pacific Ocean and on the Chinese mainland, infuriating Chinese patriots and heightening long-standing tensions between China and Japan.

Another crucial development in the expanding conflict came in April 1917 when the United States declared war on Germany. American intervention grew out of the war at sea, sympathy for the Triple Entente, and the increasing desperation of total war. At the beginning of the war, Britain and France had established a total naval blockade to strangle the Central Powers. No neutral ship was permitted to sail to Germany with any cargo. The blockade annoyed Americans, but effective propaganda about German atrocities in occupied Belgium as well as lush profits from selling war supplies to Britain and France blunted American indignation.

Moreover, in early 1915 Germany launched a counter-blockade using the murderously effective submarine, a new weapon that sank ships without traditional niceties of fair warning under international law. In May 1915, a German submarine sank the British passenger liner *Lusitania,* which was also carrying arms and munitions. More than a thousand lives, among them 139 Americans, were lost. President Woodrow Wilson protested vigorously. Germany was forced to relax its submarine warfare for almost two years; the alternative was almost certain war with the United States.

Early in 1917, the German military command—confident that improved submarines could starve Britain into submission before the United States could come to its rescue—resumed unrestricted submarine warfare. Like the invasion of Belgium, this was a reckless gamble. "German submarine warfare against commerce," President Wilson told a sympathetic Congress and people, "is a warfare against mankind." Thus the last uncommitted great nation, as fresh and enthusiastic as Europe had been in 1914, entered the world war in April 1917, almost three years after it began. Eventually the United States was to tip the balance in favor of the Triple Entente and its allies.

�֍ THE HOME FRONT

Before looking at the last year of the Great War, let us turn our attention to the people on the home front. They were tremendously involved in the titanic struggle. War's impact on them was no less massive than on the men crouched in the trenches.

Mobilizing for Total War

In August 1914 most people had greeted the outbreak of hostilities enthusiastically. In every country the masses believed that their nation was in the right and was defending itself from aggression. With the exception of a few extreme left-wingers, even socialists supported the war. A German socialist volunteered for the front, explaining to fellow members of the Reichstag that "to shed one's blood for the fatherland is not difficult: it is enveloped in romantic heroism."[3] Everywhere the support of the masses and working class contributed to national unity and an energetic war effort.

By mid-October generals and politicians had begun to realize that more than patriotism would be needed to win the war, whose end was not in sight. Each country experienced a relentless, desperate demand for men and weapons. And each quickly faced countless shortages, for prewar Europe had depended on foreign trade and a great international division of labor. In each country economic life and organization had to change and change fast to keep the war machine from sputtering to a stop. And change they did.

In each country a government of national unity began to plan and control economic and social life in order to wage "total war." Free-market capitalism was abandoned, at least "for the duration." Instead, government planning boards established priorities and decided what was to be produced and consumed. Rationing, price and wage controls, and even restrictions on workers' freedom of movement were imposed by government. Only through such regimentation could a country make the greatest possible military effort. Thus, though there were national variations, the great nations all moved toward planned economies commanded by the established political leadership.

The economy of total war blurred the old distinction between soldiers on the battlefield and civilians at home. The war was a war of whole peoples and entire populations. Based on tremendously productive industrial economies not confined to a single nation, total war yielded an effective—and therefore destructive—war effort on all sides.

However awful the war was, the ability of governments to manage and control highly complicated economies strengthened the cause of socialism. With the First World War, socialism became for the first time a realistic economic blueprint rather than a utopian program. Germany illustrates the general trend. It also went furthest in developing a planned economy to wage total war.

As soon as war began, the talented, foresighted, Jewish industrialist Walter Rathenau convinced the German government to set up the War Raw Materials Board to ration and distribute raw materials. Under Rathenau's direction, every useful material from foreign oil to barnyard manure was inventoried and rationed. Moreover, the board launched successful attempts to produce substitutes, such as synthetic rubber and synthetic nitrates, needed to make explosives and essential to the blockaded German war machine. Food was also rationed in accordance with physical need. Men and women doing hard manual work were given extra rations. During the last two years of the war, only children and expectant mothers received milk rations. At the same time, Germany failed to tax the war profits of private firms heavily enough. This failure contributed to massive deficit financing, inflation, the growth of a black market, and the eventual reemergence of class conflict.

Following the terrible battles of Verdun and the Somme in 1916, Chancellor Bethmann-Hollweg was driven from office in 1917 by military leaders Hindenburg and Ludendorff, who became the real rulers of Germany. They decreed the ultimate mobilization for total war: all agriculture, industry, and labor must be "used exclusively for the conduct of War."[4] Thus in December 1916, military leaders rammed through the Reichstag the Auxiliary Service Law, which required all males between seventeen and sixty to work only at jobs considered critical to the war effort.

Although women and children were not specifically mentioned, this forced-labor law was also aimed at them. Many women already worked in war factories, mines, and steel mills, where they labored, like men, at the heaviest and most dangerous jobs. With the passage of the Auxiliary Service Law, many more women followed. Children were organized by their teachers into garbage brigades to collect every scrap of useful materials: grease strained from dishwater, coffee grounds, waste paper, tin cans, metal door knockers, bottles, rags, hair, bones, and so forth, as well as acorns, chestnuts, pine cones, and rotting leaves. Potatoes gave way to turnips, and people averaged little more than 1,000 calories a day. Thus in Germany total war led to the establishment of history's first "totalitarian" society, and war production increased while some people starved to death.

Waging Total War A British war plant strains to meet the insatiable demand for trench-smashing heavy artillery shells. Quite typically, many of these defense workers are women. *(Source: By courtesy of the Trustees of the Imperial War Museum)*

Great Britain mobilized for total war less rapidly and less completely than Germany, for it could import materials from its empire and from the United States. By 1915, however, a serious shortage of shells had led to the establishment of the Ministry of Munitions under David Lloyd George. The ministry organized private industry to produce for the war, controlled profits, allocated labor, fixed wage rates, and settled labor disputes. By December 1916 the British economy was largely planned and regulated directly by the state. Subsequently, even food was strictly rationed, while war production continued to soar. Great Britain had followed successfully in Germany's footsteps.

The Social Impact

The social impact of total war was no less profound than the economic impact, though again there were important national variations. The insatiable needs of the military created a tremendous de-mand for workers. Jobs were available for everyone. This situation—seldom, if ever, seen before 1914, when unemployment and poverty had been facts of urban life—brought about momentous changes.

One such change was greater power and prestige for labor unions. Having proved their loyalty in August 1914, labor unions cooperated with war governments on work rules, wages, and production schedules in return for real participation in important decisions. This entry of labor leaders into policy-making councils paralleled the entry of socialist leaders into the war governments.

The role of women changed dramatically. In every country large numbers of women left home and domestic service to work in industry, transportation, and offices. Moreover, women became highly visible—not only as munitions workers but as bank tellers, mail carriers, even police officers. Women also served as nurses and doctors at the front. In general, the war greatly expanded the range of women's activities and changed attitudes toward women. As a direct result of women's many-sided war effort, Britain, Germany, and Austria granted women the right to vote immediately after the war. Women also showed a growing spirit of independence during the war, as they started to bob their hair, shorten their skirts, and smoke in public.

War promoted greater social equality, blurring class distinctions and lessening the gap between rich and poor. This blurring was most apparent in Great Britain, where wartime hardship was never extreme. In fact, the bottom third of the population generally lived better than they ever had, for the poorest gained most from the severe shortage of labor. English writer Robert Roberts recalled

how his parents' tiny grocery store in the slums of Manchester thrived during the war as never before when people who had scrimped to buy bread and soup bones were able to afford fancy cakes and thick steaks. In continental European countries greater equality was reflected in full employment, rationing according to physical needs, and a sharing of hardships. There, too, society became more uniform and more egalitarian, in spite of some war profiteering.

Finally, death itself had no respect for traditional social distinctions. It savagely decimated both the young aristocratic officers who led the charge and the mass of drafted peasants and unskilled workers who followed. Death, however, often spared the aristocrats of labor—the skilled workers and fore-

Wartime Propaganda The poster on the left celebrates African Army Day and tells French civilians that loyal troops from Africa and the colonies will help turn the tide against Germany. The German poster on the right draws upon a rich historical image, linking the brave German knight who slew the dragon with an appeal to patriotic citizens to buy yet another series of war bonds. *(Source: By courtesy of the Trustees of the Imperial War Museum)*

men. Their lives were too valuable to squander at the front, for they were needed to train the newly recruited women and older unskilled men laboring valiantly in war plants at home.

Growing Political Tensions

During the first two years of war, most soldiers and civilians supported their governments. Even in Austria-Hungary—the most vulnerable of the belligerents, with its competing nationalities—loyalty to the state and monarchy remained astonishingly strong through 1916. Belief in a just cause, patriotic nationalism, the planned economy, and a sharing of burdens united peoples behind their various national leaders.

Each government employed rigorous censorship to control public opinion and to bolster morale. And each used both crude and subtle propaganda to maintain popular support. German propaganda hysterically pictured black soldiers from France's African empire raping German women. The French and British ceaselessly recounted and exaggerated German atrocities in Belgium and elsewhere. Patriotic posters and slogans, slanted news, and biased editorials inflamed national hatreds and helped sustain superhuman efforts.

By the spring of 1916, however, people were beginning to crack under the strain of total war. In April 1916 Irish nationalists in Dublin tried to take advantage of this situation and rose up against British rule in their great Easter Rebellion. A week of bitter fighting passed before the rebels were crushed and their leaders executed. Strikes and protest marches over inadequate food began to flare up on every home front. Soldiers' morale began to decline. Italian troops mutinied. Numerous French units refused to fight for a time after General Robert Nivelle's disastrous offensive of May 1917. A rising tide of war-weariness and defeatism also swept France's civilian population before Georges Clemenceau emerged as a ruthless and effective wartime leader in November 1917. Clemenceau (1841–1929) established a virtual dictatorship, pouncing on strikers and jailing without trial journalists and politicians who dared to suggest a compromise peace with Germany.

The strains were worse for the Central Powers. In October 1916 the chief minister of Austria was assassinated by a young socialist crying, "Down with Absolutism! We want peace!"[5] The following month, when feeble old Emperor Francis Joseph died, a symbol of unity disappeared. In spite of absolute censorship, political dissatisfaction and conflicts among nationalities grew. Both Czech and Yugoslav leaders demanded autonomous democratic states for their peoples. In April 1917 Austria's chief minister summed up the situation in the gloomiest possible terms. The country and army were exhausted. Another winter of war would bring revolution and disintegration.

The strain of total war and of the Auxiliary Service Law was also evident in Germany. By 1917 the national political unity of the first two years of war was collapsing as the social conflict of prewar Germany re-emerged. A growing minority of socialists in the Reichstag began to vote against war credits. In July 1917 a coalition of socialists and Catholics passed a resolution in the Reichstag calling for a compromise "peace without annexations or reparations." Such a peace was unthinkable for conservatives and military leaders. So also was the surge in revolutionary agitation and strikes by war-weary workers that occurred in early 1917. When the bread ration was further reduced in April, more than 200,000 workers struck and demonstrated for a week in Berlin, returning to work only under the threat of prison and military discipline. Thus militaristic Germany, like its ally Austria-Hungary (and its enemy France), was beginning to crack in 1917. But it was Russia that collapsed first and saved the Central Powers—for a time.

❈ THE RUSSIAN REVOLUTION

The Russian Revolution of 1917, directly related to the growing tensions of World War I, had a significance far beyond the wartime agonies of a single European nation. The Russian Revolution opened a new era. For some, it was Marx's socialist vision come true; for others, it was the triumph of dictatorship. To all, it presented a radically new prototype of state and society.

The Fall of Imperial Russia

Like its allies and its enemies, Russia embraced war with patriotic enthusiasm in 1914. At the Winter Palace, while throngs of people knelt and sang "God Save the Tsar," Tsar Nicholas II (r. 1894–1917) repeated the oath Alexander I had sworn in 1812 and vowed never to make peace as long as the enemy stood on Russian soil. Russia's lower

Family Portrait With husband Nicholas II standing behind, the beautiful but tense Alexandra shows one of her daughters, who could not inherit the throne, to her grandmother, Queen Victoria of Britain, and Victoria's son, the future Edward VII. European monarchs were closely related by blood and breeding before 1914. (*Source: Nicholas A. de Basily Collection, Hoover Institution*)

house, the Duma, voted war credits. Conservatives anticipated expansion in the Balkans. Liberals and most socialists believed alliance with Britain and France would bring democratic reforms. For a moment, Russia was united. But soon the strains of war began to take their toll.

Unprecedented artillery barrages used up Russia's supplies of shells and ammunition, and better-equipped German armies inflicted terrible losses. In 1915, substantial numbers of Russian soldiers were sent to the front without rifles; they were told to find their arms among the dead. There were 2 million Russian casualties in 1915 alone. Nevertheless, Russia's battered peasant army continued to fight courageously, and Russia moved toward full mobilization on the home front. The Duma and organs of local government took the lead, setting

up special committees to coordinate defense, industry, transportation, and agriculture. These efforts improved the military situation, and Russian factories produced more than twice as many shells in 1916 as in 1915. Yet there were many failures, and Russia mobilized less effectively for total war than the other warring nations.

The great problem was leadership. Under the constitution resulting from the revolution of 1905 (see pages 873–874), the tsar had retained complete control over the bureaucracy and the army. Legislation proposed by the Duma, which was weighted in favor of the wealthy and conservative classes, was subject to the tsar's veto. Moreover, Nicholas II fervently wished to maintain the sacred inheritance of supreme royal power, which, with the Orthodox church, was for him the key to Russia's greatness. A kindly, slightly stupid man, of whom a friend said he "would have been an ideal country gentleman, devoting his life to wife and children, his farms and his sport," Nicholas failed to form a close partnership with his citizens in order to fight the war more effectively. He relied instead on the old bureaucratic apparatus, distrusting the moderate Duma, rejecting popular involvement, and resisting calls to share power.

As a result, the Duma, the educated middle classes, and the masses became increasingly critical of the tsar's leadership. Following Nicholas's belated dismissal of the incompetent minister of war, demands for more democratic and responsive government exploded in the Duma in the summer of 1915. In September parties ranging from conservative to moderate socialist formed the Progressive Bloc, which called for a completely new government responsible to the Duma instead of to the tsar. In answer, Nicholas temporarily adjourned the Duma and announced that he was traveling to the front in order to lead and rally Russia's armies.

His departure was a fatal turning point. With the tsar in the field with the troops, control of the government was taken over by the hysterical empress, Tsarina Alexandra, and a debauched adventurer, the monk Rasputin. A minor German princess and granddaughter of England's Queen Victoria, Nicholas's wife was a devoted mother with a sick child, a strong-willed woman with a hatred of parliaments. Having constantly urged her husband to rule absolutely, Alexandra herself tried to do so in his absence. She seated and unseated the top ministers. Her most trusted adviser was "our Friend Grigori," an uneducated Siberian preacher who was appropriately nicknamed "Rasputin"—the "Degenerate."

Rasputin began his career with a sect noted for mixing sexual orgies with religious ecstasies, and his influence rested on mysterious healing powers. Alexis, Alexandra's fifth child and heir to the throne, suffered from a rare disease, hemophilia. The tiniest cut meant uncontrollable bleeding, terrible pain, and possible death. Medical science could do nothing. Only Rasputin could miraculously stop the bleeding, perhaps through hypnosis. The empress's faith in Rasputin was limitless. "Believe more in our Friend," she wrote her husband in 1916. "He lives for you and Russia." In this atmosphere of unreality, the government slid steadily toward revolution.

In a desperate attempt to right the situation and end unfounded rumors that Rasputin was the empress's lover, three members of the high aristocracy murdered Rasputin in December 1916. The empress went into semipermanent shock, her mind haunted by the dead man's prophecy: "If I die or you desert me, in six months you will lose your son and your throne."[6] Food shortages in the cities worsened; morale declined. On March 8 women calling for bread in Petrograd (formerly St. Petersburg) started riots, which spontaneously spread throughout the city. From the front the tsar ordered troops to restore order, but discipline broke down, and the soldiers joined the revolutionary crowd. The Duma responded by declaring a provisional government on March 12, 1917. Three days later, Nicholas abdicated.

The Provisional Government

The March revolution was joyfully accepted throughout the country. The patriotic upper and middle classes rejoiced at the prospect of a more determined and effective war effort. Workers happily anticipated better wages and more food. All classes and political parties called for liberty and democracy. They were not disappointed. After generations of arbitrary authoritarianism, the provisional government quickly established equality before the law; freedom of religion, speech, and assembly; the right of unions to organize and strike; and the rest of the classic liberal program.

But both the liberal and the moderate socialist leaders of the provisional government rejected social revolution. The reorganized government formed in May 1917, which included the fiery agrarian socialist Alexander Kerensky, who became prime minister in July, refused to confiscate large landholdings and give them to peasants, fearing that such drastic action in the countryside would only complete the disintegration of Russia's peasant army. For the patriotic Kerensky as for other moderate socialists, the continuation of war was still the all-important national duty. There would be plenty of time for land reform later, and thus all the government's efforts were directed toward a last offensive in July. Human suffering and war-weariness grew, sapping the limited strength of the provisional government.

From its first day, the provisional government had to share power with a formidable rival—the Petrograd Soviet (or council) of Workers' and Soldiers' Deputies. Modeled on the revolutionary soviets of 1905, the Petrograd Soviet was a huge, fluctuating mass meeting of from two to three thousand workers, soldiers, and socialist intellectuals. This counter- or half-government issued its own radical orders, further weakening the provisional government. Most famous of these was Army Order No. 1, which stripped officers of their authority and placed power in the hands of elected committees of common soldiers.

Army Order No. 1 led to a total collapse of army discipline. Many an officer was hanged for his sins. Meanwhile, following the foolhardy summer offensive, masses of peasant soldiers began "voting with their feet," to use Lenin's graphic phrase. They began returning to their villages to help their families get a share of the land, which peasants were simply seizing as they settled old scores in a great agrarian upheaval. All across the country, liberty was turning into anarchy in the summer of 1917. It was an unparalleled opportunity for the most radical and most talented of Russia's many socialist leaders, Vladimir Ilyich Lenin (1870–1924).

Lenin and the Bolshevik Revolution

From his youth, Lenin's whole life had been dedicated to the cause of revolution. Born into the middle class, Lenin became an implacable enemy of imperial Russia when his older brother was executed for plotting to kill the tsar in 1887. As a law student Lenin began searching for a revolutionary faith. He found it in Marxian socialism. Exiled to Siberia for three years because of socialist agitation, Lenin studied Marxian doctrines with religious intensity. After his release, this young priest of socialism joined fellow believers in western Europe. There he lived for seventeen years and developed his own revolutionary interpretations of the body of Marxian thought.

Three interrelated ideas were central for Lenin. First, turning to the early fire-breathing Marx of 1848 and the *Communist Manifesto* for inspiration, Lenin stressed that capitalism could be destroyed only by violent revolution. He tirelessly denounced all revisionist theories of a peaceful evolution to socialism as betraying Marx's message of unending class conflict. Lenin's second, more original, idea was that a socialist revolution was possible even in a country like Russia, where capitalism was not fully developed. There the industrial working class was small, but the peasants were poor and thus potential revolutionaries.

Lenin believed that at a given moment revolution was determined more by human leadership than by vast historical laws. Thus was born his third basic idea: the necessity of a highly disciplined workers' party, strictly controlled by a dedicated elite of intellectuals and full-time revolutionaries like Lenin himself. Unlike ordinary workers and trade-union officials, this elite would never be seduced by short-term gains. It would not stop until revolution brought it to power.

Lenin's theories and methods did not go unchallenged by other Russian Marxists. At meetings of the Russian Social Democratic Labor party in London in 1903, matters came to a head. Lenin demanded a small, disciplined, elitist party; his opponents wanted a more democratic party with mass membership. The Russian party of Marxian socialism promptly split into two rival factions.

 Mass Demonstrations in Petrograd in June 1917 In this surge of working-class support for the Bolsheviks, the few banners of the Mensheviks and other moderate socialists are drowned in a sea of Bolshevik slogans. *(Source: Sovfoto)*

Lenin's camp was called *Bolsheviks,* or "majority group"; his opponents were *Mensheviks,* or "minority group." Lenin's majority did not last, but Lenin did not care. He kept the fine-sounding name Bolshevik and developed the party he wanted: tough, disciplined, revolutionary.

Lenin, from neutral Switzerland, saw the war as a product of imperialistic rivalries and as a marvelous opportunity for class war and socialist upheaval. After the March revolution, the German government provided the impatient Lenin, his wife, and about twenty trusted colleagues with safe passage across Germany and back into Russia in April 1917. The Germans hoped that Lenin would undermine Russia's sagging war effort. They were not disappointed.

Arriving triumphantly at Petrograd's Finland Station on April 3, Lenin attacked at once. To the great astonishment of the local Bolsheviks, he rejected all cooperation with the "bourgeois" provisional government of the liberals and moderate socialists. His slogans were radical in the extreme: "All power to the soviets"; "All land to the peasants"; "Stop the war now." Never a slave to Marxian determinism, the brilliant but not unduly intellectual Lenin was a superb tactician. The moment was now.

Yet Lenin almost overplayed his hand. An attempt by the Bolsheviks to seize power in July collapsed, and Lenin fled and went into hiding. He was charged with being a German agent, and indeed he and the Bolsheviks were getting money from Germany.[7] But no matter. In September commander-in-chief General Lavr Kornilov, a popular war hero "with the heart of a lion and the brains of a sheep," led a feeble attack against the provisional government. In the face of this rightist "counter-revolutionary" threat, the Bolsheviks were rearmed and redeemed. Kornilov's forces disintegrated, but Kerensky lost all credit with the army, the only force that might have saved him and democratic government in Russia.

Throughout the summer, the Bolsheviks markedly increased their popular support, and in October they gained a fragile majority in the Petrograd Soviet. It was now Lenin's supporter Leon Trotsky (1879–1940), a spellbinding revolutionary orator and independent radical Marxist, who brilliantly executed the Bolshevik seizure of power.

Painting a vivid but untruthful picture of German and counter-revolutionary plots, Trotsky first convinced the Petrograd Soviet to form a special military-revolutionary committee in October and make him its leader. Military power in the capital passed into Bolshevik hands. Trotsky then insisted that the Bolsheviks take power in the name not of the Bolsheviks but of the more popular and democratic soviets, which were meeting in Petrograd from all over Russia in early November. On the night of November 6, militants from Trotsky's committee joined with trusty Bolshevik soldiers to seize government buildings and pounce on members of the provisional government. Then they went on to the congress of soviets. There a Bolshevik majority—roughly 390 of 650 turbulent delegates—declared that all power had passed to the soviets and named Lenin head of the new government, which was soon named the Union of Soviet Socialist Republics, or Soviet Union for short.

The Bolsheviks came to power for three key reasons. First, by late 1917 democracy had given way to anarchy: power was there for those who would take it. Second, in Lenin and Trotsky the Bolsheviks had an utterly determined and truly superior leadership. Third, in 1917 the Bolsheviks succeeded in appealing to many soldiers and urban workers, people who were exhausted by war and eager for socialism. With time, many workers would become bitterly disappointed, but for the moment they had good reason to believe that they had won what they wanted.

Dictatorship and Civil War

History is full of short-lived coups and unsuccessful revolutions. The truly monumental accomplishment of Lenin, Trotsky, and the rest of the Bolsheviks was not taking power but keeping it and conquering the chaos they had helped create. How was this done?

Lenin had the genius to profit from developments over which he and the Bolsheviks had no control. Since summer, a peasant revolution had been sweeping across Russia as the tillers of the soil invaded and divided among themselves the estates of the landlords and the church. Peasant seizure of the land was not very Marxian, but it was unstoppable in 1917. Thus Lenin's first law, which supposedly gave land to the peasants, actually merely approved what peasants were already doing. Urban workers' great demand in November was direct control of individual factories by local workers' committees. This, too, Lenin rectified with a decree in November.

✤ **Vladimir Lenin**   Displaying his determination and skill as a revolutionary orator, Lenin in 1920 exhorts soldiers in the Red Army to defend the revolution in the last stage of the civil war. These units departing from Moscow will help retake Kiev and establish unshakable Bolshevik power in Ukraine and Belorussia. *(Source: Novosti)*

Lenin also acknowledged that Russia had lost the war with Germany and that the only realistic goal was peace at any price. That price was very high. Germany demanded in December 1917 that the Soviet government give up all its western territories. These areas were inhabited by Poles, Finns, Lithuanians, and other non-Russians—all those people who had been conquered by the tsars over three centuries and put into the "prisonhouse of nationalities," as Lenin had earlier called the Russian Empire.

At first, Lenin's fellow Bolsheviks would not accept such great territorial losses. But when German armies resumed their unopposed march into Russia in February 1918, Lenin had his way in a very close vote in the Central Committee of the party. A third of old Russia's population was sliced away by the German meat ax in the Treaty of Brest-Litovsk in March 1918. With peace, Lenin had escaped the certain disaster of continued war and could pursue his goal of absolute political power for the Bolsheviks—now renamed Communists—within Russia.

In November 1917 the Bolsheviks had cleverly proclaimed their regime only a "provisional workers' and peasants' government," promising that a freely elected Constituent Assembly would draw up a new constitution. But after the Bolsheviks won less than one-fourth of the elected delegates, the Constituent Assembly met for only one day, on January 18, 1918. It was then permanently disbanded by Bolshevik soldiers acting under Lenin's orders.

With the destruction of the democratically elected Constituent Assembly, people who had risen up for self-rule in November saw that once again they were getting dictatorship from the capital. For the next three years, "Long live the [democratic] soviets; down with the Bolsheviks" was to be a popular slogan. The officers of the old army took the lead in organizing the so-called White opposition to the Bolsheviks in southern Russia, Ukraine, Siberia, and west of Petrograd. The Whites came from many social groups and were united only by their hatred of the Bolsheviks—the Reds. By the end of 1918, White armies were on the attack. In October 1919 it appeared they might triumph, as they closed in on Lenin's government from three sides. Yet they did not. By the spring of 1920, the White armies had been almost completely defeated, and by the following year the civil war was over. Lenin had won.

Lenin and the Bolsheviks won for several reasons. Strategically, they controlled the center, while the Whites were always on the fringes and disunited. Moreover, the poorly defined political program of the Whites was vaguely conservative, and it did not unite all the foes of the Bolsheviks under a progressive, democratic banner. Most important, the Communists quickly developed a better army, an army for which the divided Whites were no match.

Once again, Trotsky's leadership was decisive. As war commissar Trotsky re-established the draft and the most drastic discipline for the newly formed Red Army. Soldiers deserting or disobeying an order were summarily shot. Moreover, Trotsky effectively recruited former tsarist army officers. In short, he formed a disciplined and effective fighting force.

The Bolsheviks also mobilized the home front. Establishing "war communism"—the application of the total-war concept to a civil conflict—they seized grain from peasants, introduced rationing, nationalized all banks and industry, and required everyone to work. Although these measures contributed to a breakdown of normal economic activity, they also served to maintain labor discipline and to keep the Red Army supplied.

"Revolutionary terror" also contributed to the Communist victory. The old tsarist secret police was re-established as the Cheka, which hunted down and executed thousands of real or supposed foes, such as the tsar and his family and other "class enemies." Moreover, people were shot or threatened with being shot for minor nonpolitical failures. The terror caused by the secret police became a tool of the government. The Cheka sowed fear, and fear silenced opposition.

Finally, foreign military intervention in the civil war ended up helping the Communists. The Allies (the Americans, British, and Japanese) sent troops to Archangel and Vladivostok to prevent war material that they had sent to the provisional government from being captured by the Germans. After the Soviet government nationalized all foreign-owned factories without compensation and refused to pay all of Russia's foreign debts, Western governments, particularly that of France, began to support White armies. Yet these efforts were small and halfhearted. Allied intervention in the civil war did not aid the Whites effectively, though it did permit the Communists to appeal to the patriotic nationalism of ethnic Russians, in particular former tsarist army officers.

Together, the Russian Revolution and the Bolshevik triumph were one of the reasons why the First World War was such a great turning point in modern history. A radically new government, based on socialism and one-party dictatorship, came to power in a great European state, maintained power, and eagerly encouraged worldwide revolution. Although Russia was undoubtedly headed for some kind of political crisis before 1914, it is hard to imagine the triumph of the most radical proponents of change and reform except in a situation of total collapse. That was precisely what happened to Russia in the First World War.

THE RUSSIAN REVOLUTION

1914	Russia enthusiastically enters the First World War
1915	Two million Russian casualties Progressive Bloc calls for a new government responsible to the Duma rather than to the tsar Tsar Nicholas adjourns the Duma and departs for the front Strong influence of Alexandra and Rasputin on the government
December 1916	Murder of Rasputin
March 8, 1917	Bread riots in Petrograd (St. Petersburg)
March 12, 1917	Duma declares a provisional government
March 15, 1917	Tsar Nicholas abdicates without protest
April 3, 1917	Lenin returns from exile and denounces the provisional government
May 1917	Reorganized provisional government, including Kerensky, continues the war Petrograd Soviet issues Army Order no. 1, granting military power to committees of common soldiers
Summer 1917	Agrarian upheavals: peasants seize estates, peasant soldiers desert the army to participate
October 1917	Bolsheviks gain a majority in the Petrograd Soviet
November 6, 1917	Bolsheviks seize power Lenin heads the new "provisional workers' and peasants' government"
November 1917	Lenin accepts peasant seizure of land and worker control of factories All banks nationalized
January 1918	Lenin permanently disbands the Constituent Assembly
February 1918	Lenin convinces the Bolshevik Central Committee to accept a humiliating peace with Germany in order to safeguard the revolution
March 1918	Treaty of Brest-Litovsk: Russia loses one-third of its population Trotsky as war commissioner begins to rebuild the Russian army
1918–1920	Civil war between the Whites and the Reds
1919	White armies on the offensive but divided politically They receive little benefit from Allied intervention
1920	Lenin and Red armies victorious

�֎ THE PEACE SETTLEMENT

Victory over revolutionary Russia boosted sagging German morale, and in the spring of 1918 the Germans launched their last major attack against France. This offensive, just like those before it, failed. With breathtaking rapidity, the United States, Great Britain, and France decisively defeated Germany militarily. Austria-Hungary and the Ottoman Empire broke apart and ceased to exist. The guns of world war finally fell silent. Then as civil war spread in Russia and as chaos engulfed much of eastern Europe, the victorious Western Allies came together in Paris to establish a lasting peace.

Expectations were high; optimism was almost unlimited. The Allies labored intensively and soon worked out terms for peace with Germany and for the creation of the peacekeeping League of Nations. Nevertheless, the hopes of peoples and politicians were soon disappointed, for the peace settlement of 1919 turned out to be a failure. Rather than creating conditions for peace, it sowed the seeds of another war. Surely this was the ultimate tragedy of the Great War, a war that directly and indirectly cost $332 billion and left 10 million people dead and another 20 million wounded. How did this tragedy happen? Why was the peace settlement unsuccessful?

The End of the War

In early 1917 the strain of total war was showing everywhere. After the Russian Revolution in March, there were major strikes in Germany. In July a coalition of moderates passed a "peace resolution" in the Reichstag, calling for peace without territorial annexations. To counter this moderation born of war-weariness, the German military established a virtual dictatorship. The military also aggressively exploited the collapse of Russian armies, winning great concessions in the Treaty of Brest-Litovsk.

With victory in the east quieting German moderates, General Ludendorff and company fell on France once more in the great spring offensive of 1918. For a time, German armies pushed forward, coming within thirty-five miles of Paris. But Ludendorff's exhausted, overextended forces never broke through. They were decisively stopped in July at the second Battle of the Marne, where

140,000 fresh American soldiers saw action. Adding 2 million men in arms to the war effort by August, the late but massive American intervention decisively tipped the scales in favor of Allied victory.

By September, British, French, and American armies were advancing steadily on all fronts, and on October 4 the emperor formed a new, more liberal German government to sue for peace. As negotiations over an armistice dragged on, an angry and frustrated German people finally rose up. On November 3 sailors in Kiel mutinied, and throughout northern Germany soldiers and workers began to establish revolutionary councils on the Russian soviet model. The same day Austria-Hungary surrendered to the Allies and began breaking apart. With army discipline collapsing, the German emperor abdicated and fled to Holland. Socialist leaders in Berlin proclaimed a German republic on November 9 and simultaneously agreed to tough Allied terms of surrender. The armistice went into effect on November 11, 1918. The war was over.

Military defeat brought political revolution to Austria-Hungary, as it had to Germany, Russia, and the Ottoman Empire (see pages 999–1000). In Austria-Hungary the revolution was primarily nationalistic and republican in character. Independent Austrian, Hungarian, and Czechoslovak republics were proclaimed, and a greatly expanded Serbian monarchy united the south Slavs and took the name Yugoslavia. The prospect of firmly establishing the new national states overrode class considerations for most people in east-central Europe.

The Treaty of Versailles

The peace conference opened in Paris in January 1919 with seventy delegates representing twenty-seven victorious nations. There were great expectations. A young British diplomat later wrote that the victors "believed in nationalism, we believed in the self-determination of peoples." Indeed, "we were journeying to Paris . . . to found a new order in Europe. We were preparing not Peace only, but Eternal Peace."[8] This general optimism and idealism had been greatly strengthened by President Wilson's January 1918 peace proposal, the Fourteen Points, which stressed national self-determination and the rights of small countries.

The real powers at the conference were the United States, Great Britain, and France, for Germany was not allowed to participate and Russia was locked in civil war and did not attend. Italy was considered one of the Big Four, but its role was quite limited. Almost immediately the three great Allies began to quarrel. President Wilson, who was wildly cheered by European crowds as the spokesman for a new idealistic and democratic international cooperation, was almost obsessed with creating the League of Nations. Wilson insisted that this question come first, for he passionately believed that only a permanent international organization could protect member states from aggression and avert future wars. Wilson had his way, although Lloyd George of Great Britain and especially Clemenceau of France were unenthusiastic. They were primarily concerned with punishing Germany.

Playing on British nationalism, Lloyd George had already won a smashing electoral victory in December on the popular platform of making Germany pay for the war. "We shall," the British prime minister promised, "squeeze the orange until the pips squeak." Personally inclined to make a somewhat moderate peace with Germany, Lloyd George was to a considerable extent a captive of demands for a total victory worthy of the sacrifices of total war against a totally depraved enemy. As Rudyard Kipling summed up the general British feeling at the end of the war, the Germans were "a people with the heart of beasts."[9]

France's Georges Clemenceau, "the Tiger" who had broken wartime defeatism and led his country to victory, wholeheartedly agreed. Like most French people, Clemenceau wanted old-fashioned revenge. He also wanted lasting security for France. This, he believed, required the creation of a buffer state between France and Germany, the permanent demilitarization of Germany, and vast German reparations. He feared that sooner or later Germany with its 60 million people would attack France with its 40 million, unless the Germans were permanently weakened. Moreover, France had no English Channel (or Atlantic Ocean) as a reassuring barrier against German aggression. Wilson, supported by Lloyd George, would hear none of this. Clemenceau's demands seemed vindictive, violating morality and the principle of national self-determination. By April the conference was deadlocked on the German question, and Wilson packed his bags to go home.

In the end, convinced that France should not break with its allies because France could not af-

ford to face Germany alone in the future, Clemenceau agreed to a compromise. He gave up the French demand for a Rhineland buffer state in return for a formal defensive alliance with the United States and Great Britain. Under the terms of this alliance, both Wilson and Lloyd George promised that their countries would come to France's aid in the event of a German attack. Thus Clemenceau appeared to win his goal of French security, as Wilson had won his of a permanent international organization. The Allies moved quickly to finish the settlement, believing that any adjustments would later be possible within the dual framework of a strong Western alliance and the League of Nations (Map 29.4).

The Treaty of Versailles between the Allies and Germany was the key to the settlement, and the terms were not unreasonable as a first step toward re-establishing international order (see Listening to the Past). (Had Germany won, it seems certain that France and Belgium would have been treated with greater severity, as Russia had been at Brest-Litovsk.) Germany's colonies were given to France, Britain, and Japan as League of Nations mandates. Germany's territorial losses within Europe were minor, thanks to Wilson. Alsace-Lorraine was returned to France. Parts of Germany inhabited primarily by Poles were ceded to the new Polish state, in keeping with the principle of national self-determination. Germany had to limit its army to 100,000 men and agree to build no military fortifications in the Rhineland.

More harshly, the Allies declared that Germany (with Austria) was responsible for the war and had therefore to pay reparations equal to all civilian damages caused by the war. This unfortunate and much-criticized clause expressed inescapable popular demands for German blood, but the actual figure was not set, and there was the clear possibility that reparations might be set at a reasonable level in the future when tempers had cooled.

When presented with the treaty, the German government protested vigorously. But there was no alternative, especially considering that Germany was still starving because the Allies had not yet lifted their naval blockade. On June 28, 1919, German representatives of the ruling moderate Social Democrats and the Catholic party signed the treaty in the Sun King's Hall of Mirrors at Versailles, where Bismarck's empire had been joyously proclaimed almost fifty years before.

MAP 29.4 Shattered Empires and Territorial Changes After the First World War   The Great War brought tremendous changes in eastern Europe. New nations were established, and a dangerous power vacuum was created between Germany and Soviet Russia.

Separate peace treaties were concluded with the other defeated powers—Austria, Hungary, Bulgaria, and Turkey. For the most part, these treaties merely ratified the existing situation in east-central Europe following the breakup of the Austro-Hungarian Empire. Like Austria, Hungary was a particularly big loser, as its "captive" nationalities (and some interspersed Hungarians) were ceded to

✳ **Versailles, June 28, 1919**   This group portrait by William Orpen features the three principal Allied leaders, seated in the center, who have finally reached an agreement. The scholarly Wilson is third from the left, next to the old tiger, Clemenceau of France, who is turned toward the strong-willed Lloyd George of Britain. *(Source: By courtesy of the Trustees of the Imperial War Museum)*

Romania, Czechoslovakia, Poland, and Yugoslavia. Italy got some Austrian territory. The Turkish empire was broken up. France received Lebanon and Syria. Britain took Iraq and Palestine, which was to include a Jewish national homeland first promised by Britain in 1917. Officially League of Nations mandates, these acquisitions of the Western powers were one of the most imperialistic elements of the peace settlement. Another was mandating Germany's holdings in China to Japan (see pages

1010–1012). The age of Western imperialism lived on. National self-determination remained a reality only for Europeans and their offspring.

American Rejection of the Versailles Treaty

The rapidly concluded peace settlement of early 1919 was not perfect, but within the context of war-shattered Europe it was an acceptable beginning. The principle of national self-determination, which had played such a large role in starting the war, was accepted and served as an organizing framework. Germany had been punished but not dismembered. A new world organization complemented a traditional defensive alliance of satisfied powers. The serious remaining problems could be worked out in the future. Moreover, Allied leaders had seen speed as essential for another reason: they detested Lenin and feared that his Bolshevik Revolution might spread. They realized that their best answer to Lenin's unending calls for worldwide upheaval was peace and tranquility for war-weary peoples.

There were, however, two great interrelated obstacles to such peace: Germany and the United States. Plagued by communist uprisings, reactionary plots, and popular disillusionment with losing the war at the last minute, Germany's moderate socialists and their liberal and Catholic supporters faced an enormous challenge. Like French republicans after 1871, they needed time (and luck) if they were to establish firmly a peaceful and democratic republic. Progress in this direction required understanding yet firm treatment of Germany by the victorious Western Allies, particularly by the United States.

However, the U.S. Senate and, to a lesser extent, the American people rejected Wilson's handiwork. Republican senators led by Henry Cabot Lodge refused to ratify the Treaty of Versailles without changes in the articles creating the League of Nations. The key issue was the League's power—more apparent than real—to require member states to take collective action against aggression. Lodge and others believed that this requirement gave away Congress's constitutional right to declare war. In failing health, Wilson, with narrow-minded self-righteousness, rejected all attempts at compromise. In doing so, he assured that the treaty would never be ratified by the United States in any form and that the United States would

never join the League of Nations. Moreover, the Senate refused to ratify Wilson's defensive alliance with France and Great Britain. America turned its back on Europe.

The Wilson-Lodge fiasco and the new-found gospel of isolationism represented a tragic and cowardly renunciation of America's responsibility. Using America's action as an excuse, Great Britain, too, refused to ratify its defensive alliance with France. Bitterly betrayed by its allies, France stood alone. Very shortly France was to take actions against Germany that would feed the fires of German resentment and seriously undermine democratic forces in the new German republic. The great hopes of early 1919 had turned to ashes by the end of the year. The Western alliance had collapsed, and a grandiose plan for permanent peace had given way to a fragile truce. For this and for what came later, the United States must share a large part of the guilt.

SUMMARY

Why did World War I have such revolutionary consequences? Why was it such a great break with the past? World War I was, first of all, a war of committed peoples. In France, Britain, and Germany in particular, governments drew on genuine popular support. This support reflected not only the diplomatic origins of the war but also the way western European society had been unified under the nationalist banner in the later nineteenth century, despite the fears that the growing socialist movement aroused in conservatives. The relentlessness of total war helps explain why so many died, why so many were crippled physically and psychologically, and why Western civilization would in so many ways never be the same again. More concretely, the war swept away monarchs and multinational empires. National self-determination apparently triumphed, not only in Austria-Hungary but also in many of Russia's western borderlands. Except in Ireland and parts of Soviet Russia, the revolutionary dream of national unity, born of the French Revolution, had finally come true.

Two other revolutions were products of the war. In Russia the Bolsheviks established a radical regime, smashed existing capitalist institutions, and stayed in power with a new kind of authoritarian rule. Whether the new Russian regime was truly rule. Whether the new Russian regime was truly Marxian or socialist was questionable, but it indisputably posed a powerful, ongoing revolutionary challenge to Europe and its colonial empires.

More subtle but quite universal in its impact was an administrative revolution. This revolution, born of the need to mobilize entire societies and economies for total war, greatly increased the power of government in the West. And after the guns grew still, government planning and wholesale involvement in economic and social life did not disappear in Europe. Liberal market capitalism and a well-integrated world economy were among the many casualties of the administrative revolution, and greater social equality was everywhere one of its results. Thus even in European countries where a communist takeover never came close to occurring, society still experienced a great revolution.

Finally, the "war to end war" brought not peace but only a fragile truce. In the West the Allies failed to maintain their wartime solidarity. Germany remained unrepentant and would soon have more grievances to nurse. Moreover, the victory of national self-determination in eastern Europe created a power vacuum between a still-powerful Germany and a potentially mighty communist Russia. A vast area lay open to military aggression from two sides.

NOTES

1. M. Beloff, quoted in *U.S. News & World Report,* March 8, 1976, p. 53.
2. Quoted in J. Remak, *The Origins of World War I* (New York: Holt, Rinehart and Winston, 1967), p. 84.
3. Quoted in J. E. Rodes, *The Quest for Unity: Modern Germany, 1848–1970* (New York: Holt, Rinehart and Winston, 1971), p. 178.
4. Quoted in F. P. Chambers, *The War Behind the War, 1914–1918* (London: Faber & Faber, 1939), p. 168.
5. Quoted in R. O. Paxton, *Europe in the Twentieth Century* (New York: Harcourt Brace Jovanovich, 1975), p. 109.
6. Quoted in Chambers, *The War Behind the War, 1914–1918,* pp. 302, 304.
7. A. B. Ulam, *The Bolsheviks* (New York: Collier Books, 1968), p. 349.
8. H. Nicolson, *Peacemaking 1919* (New York: Grosset & Dunlap Universal Library, 1965), pp. 8, 31–32.
9. Quoted ibid., p. 24.

SUGGESTED READING

O. Hale, *The Great Illusion, 1900–1914* (1971), is a thorough account of the prewar era. Remak's volume cited in the Notes; J. Joll, *The Origins of the First World War* (1992); and L. Lafore, *The Long Fuse* (1971), are recommended studies of the causes of the First World War. A. J. P. Taylor, *The Struggle for Mastery in Europe, 1848–1919* (1954), is an outstanding survey of diplomatic developments, with an exhaustive bibliography. V. Steiner, *Britain and the Origins of the First World War* (1978), and G. Kennan, *The Decline of Bismarck's European Order: Franco-Russian Relations, 1875–1890* (1979), are also major contributions. K. Jarausch's *The Enigmatic Chancellor* (1973) is an important recent study on Bethmann-Hollweg and German policy in 1914. C. Falls, *The Great War* (1961), is the best brief introduction to military aspects of the war. B. Tuchman, *The Guns of August* (1962), is a marvelous account of the dramatic first month of the war and the beginning of military stalemate. G. Ritter provides an able study in *The Schlieffen Plan* (1958). J. Winter, *The Experience of World War I* (1988), is a strikingly illustrated history of the war, and A. Horne, *The Price of Glory: Verdun 1916* (1979), is a moving account of the famous siege. J. Ellis, *Eye-Deep in Hell* (1976), is a vivid account of trench warfare, whereas J. Keegan's fascinating *Face of Battle* (1976) examines soldiers and warfare in a long-term perspective. V. Brittain's *Testament of Youth,* the moving autobiography of an English nurse in wartime, shows lives buffeted by new ideas and personal tragedies. A. Marwick, *War and Change in Twentieth-Century Europe* (1990), is a useful synthesis.

F. L. Carsten, *War Against War* (1982), considers radical movements in Britain and Germany. The best single volume on the home fronts is still the one by Chambers mentioned in the Notes. Chambers draws heavily on the many fine books on the social and economic impact of the war in different countries published by the Carnegie Endowment for International Peace under the general editorship of J. T. Shotwell. M. Higonnet, J. Jensen, and M. Weitz, eds., *Behind the Lines: Gender and the Two World Wars* (1987), examines the changes that the war brought for women and for relations between the sexes. A. Marwick, *The Deluge* (1970), is a lively account of war and society in Britain; G. Feldman, *Army, Industry, and Labor in Germany, 1914–1918* (1966), shows the impact of total war and military dictatorship on Germany. Three excellent collections of essays—R. Wall and J. Winter, eds., *The Upheaval of War: Family, Work, and Welfare* in Europe, 1914–1918 (1988); J. Roth, ed., *World War I* (1967); and R. Albrecht-Carrié, ed., *The Meaning of the First World War* (1965)—probe the enormous consequences of the war for people and society. The debate over Germany's guilt and aggression, which has been reopened in recent years, may be best approached through G. Feldman, ed., *German Imperialism, 1914–1918* (1972), and A. Hillgruber, *Germany and the Two World Wars* (1981). M. Fainsod, *International Socialism and the World War* (1935), ably discusses the splits between radical and moderate socialists during the conflict. In addition to Erich Maria Remarque's great novel *All Quiet on the Western Front,* Henri Barbusse, *Under Fire* (1917), and Jules Romains, *Verdun* (1939), are highly recommended for their fictional yet realistic re-creations of the war. P. Fussell, *The Great War and Modern Memory* (1975), probes all the powerful literature inspired by the war. M. Ecksteins, *Rites of Spring: The Great War and the Birth of the Modern Age* (1989), is an imaginative cultural investigation that has won critical acclaim.

R. Suny and A. Adams, eds., *The Russian Revolution and Bolshevik Victory* (1990), presents a wide range of old and new interpretations. A. Ulam's work cited in the Notes, which focuses on Lenin, is a masterful introduction to the Russian Revolution, whereas S. Fitzpatrick, *The Russian Revolution* (1982), provides a provocative reconsideration. B. Wolfe, *Three Who Made a Revolution* (1955), a collective biography of

Lenin, Trotsky, and Stalin, and R. Conquest, *V. I. Lenin* (1972), are recommended. L. Trotsky himself wrote the colorful and exciting *History of the Russian Revolution* (1932), which may be compared with the classic eyewitness account of the young, pro-Bolshevik American J. Reed, *Ten Days That Shook the World* (1919). R. Daniels, *Red October* (1969), provides a clear account of the Bolshevik seizure of power, and R. Pipes, *The Formation of the Soviet Union* (1968), is recommended for its excellent treatment of the nationality problem during the revolution. D. Koenker, W. Rosenberg, and R. Suny, eds., *Party, State and Society in the Russian Civil War* (1989), probes the social foundations of Bolshevik victory. A. Wildman, *The End of the Russian Imperial Army* (1980), is a fine account of the soldiers' revolt, and G. Leggett, *The Cheka: Lenin's Secret Police* (1981), shows revolutionary terror in action. Boris Pasternak's justly celebrated *Doctor Zhivago* is a great historical novel of the revolutionary era. R. Massie, *Nicholas and Alexandra* (1971), is a moving popular biography of Russia's last royal family and the terrible health problem of the heir to the throne. H. Nicolson's study listed in the Notes captures the spirit of the Versailles settlement. T. Bailey, *Woodrow Wilson and the Lost Peace* (1963), and W. Widenor, *Henry Cabot Lodge and the Search for an American Foreign Policy* (1981), are also highly recommended. A. Mayer provocatively stresses the influence of domestic social tensions and widespread

German War Aims and the Treaty of Versailles

Was Germany treated too harshly by the Allies in the Treaty of Versailles? Or before and during the First World War, was Germany pursuing reckless and aggressive policies that justified the victors' attempt to restrain Germany in 1919? Politicians and historians have long debated these questions.

Fresh controversies arose in the 1960s when young German historians argued that Germany not only was especially responsible for the outbreak of the First World War but also planned to impose brutal terms on its foes after they were defeated. A newly discovered memorandum, which was prepared on September 9, 1914, by German chancellor Bethmann-Hollweg after consulting with powerful business leaders, supported the young historians and attracted great interest. Bethmann-Hollweg's memorandum, which follows first (1), may be compared with key provisions from the June 28, 1919, Treaty of Versailles, excerpted second (2).

(1)

[The general aim is security] for the German Reich in west and east for all imaginable time. For this purpose France must be so weakened as to make her revival as a great power impossible for all time. Russia must be thrust back as far as possible from Germany's eastern frontier and her domination over the non-Russian vassal peoples [of the Russian empire] broken. . . .

1. *France.* . . . The [French iron] ore-field of Briey, which is necessary for the supply of ore for our industry, to be ceded [to Germany].

Further, a war indemnity, to be paid in installments; it must be high enough to prevent France from spending any considerable sums on armaments in the next 15–20 years.

Furthermore: a commercial treaty which makes France economically dependent on Germany, secures the French market for our exports and makes it possible to exclude British commerce from France. . . .

2. *Belgium.* . . . At any rate Belgium, even if allowed to continue to exist as a state, must be reduced to a vassal state, must allow us to occupy any militarily important ports, must place her coast at our disposal in military aspects, must become economically a German province. . . .

3. *Luxemburg.* [This country] will become a German federal state and will receive a strip of the present Belgian province of Luxemburg and perhaps the corner of Longwy [in France]. . . .

4. We must create a *central European economic association* through common custom treaties, to include France, Belgium, Holland, Denmark, Austria-Hungary, Poland, and perhaps Italy, Sweden and Norway. This association will not have any common constitutional supreme authority and all its members will be formally equal, but in practice will be under German leadership and must stabilize Germany's economic dominance over Mitteleuropa [central Europe].

5. *The question of colonial acquisitions,* where the first aim is the creation of a continuous Central African colonial empire, will be considered later . . . .

7. *Holland.* . . . [This country] must be left independent in externals, but be made internally dependent on us.

(2)

ARTICLE 42. Germany is forbidden to maintain or construct any fortifications either on the left bank of the Rhine or on the right bank to the west of a line drawn 50 kilometers to the East of the Rhine. . . .

ARTICLE 45. As compensation for the destruction of the coal mines in the north of France and as part payment towards the total reparation due from Germany for the damage resulting from the war, Germany cedes to France in full and absolute possession, with exclusive right of exploitation, unencumbered and free from all debts and charges of any kind, the coal mines situated in the Saar Basin. . . .

ARTICLE 49. Germany renounces in favor of the League of Nations, in the capacity of trustee, the government of the territory defined above [Saar Basin].

At the end of fifteen years . . . the inhabitants of the said territory shall be called upon to indicate the sovereignty under which they desire to be placed. . . .

ARTICLE 51. The territories [of Alsace and Lorraine] which were ceded to Germany [in 1871] . . . are restored to French sovereignty. . . .

ARTICLES 80, 81, AND 87. Germany acknowledges and will strictly respect the independence of Austria . . . [and] recognizes the complete independence of the Czecho-Slovak state . . . and of Poland. . . .

ARTICLE 116. Germany acknowledges and agrees to respect as permanent and inalienable the independence of all the territories which were part of the former Russian empire on August 1, 1914. . . .

ARTICLE 159. The German military forces shall be demobilized and reduced as prescribed hereinafter.

ARTICLE 160. . . . After that date [March 31, 1920] the total number of effectives in the Army of the States constituting Germany must not exceed 100,000 men, including officers and establishments of depots. The Army shall be devoted exclusively to the maintenance of order within the territory and to the control of the frontiers. . . .

ARTICLE 231. The Allied and Associated Governments affirm and Germany accepts the responsibility of Germany and her allies for causing all the loss and damage to which the Allied and Associated Governments and their nationals have been subjected as a consequence of the war imposed upon them by the aggression of Germany and her allies.

ARTICLE 232. The Allied and Associated Governments recognize that the resources of Germany are not adequate . . . to make complete reparation for all such loss and damage.

The Allied and Associated Governments, however, require, and Germany undertakes, that she will make compensation for all damage done to the civilian population of the Allied and Associated Power and to their property. . . .

ARTICLE 233. The amount of the above damage for which compensation is to be made

 The last two pages of the Treaty of Versailles, with seals and signatures of participants. (*Source: Courtesy of the Trustees of the Imperial War Museum*)

by Germany shall be determined by an Inter-Allied Commission. . . . The findings of the commission as to the amount of damage defined as above shall be concluded and notified to the German Government on or before May 1, 1921. . . .

ARTICLE 428. As a guarantee for the execution of the present Treaty by Germany, the German territory situated to the west of the Rhine, together with the bridgeheads, will be occupied by Allied and Associated troops for a period of fifteen years from the coming into force of the present Treaty.

Questions for Analysis

1. How did Bethmann-Hollweg believe Germany should treat a defeated France? A defeated Belgium?

2. How would you characterize Bethmann-Hollweg's proposals in general?

3. Locate on Map 29.4 the territories discussed in the Treaty of Versailles. (The Saar is on Map 32.1.) Were the territorial changes imposed on Germany harsh or fair? Why or why not?

4. What measures were the Allies taking to enforce the treaty?

5. Imagine you are a lawyer. Prepare a defense of Germany's actions before and during World War I.

Source: F. Fischer, *Germany's Aims in the First World War* (New York: Norton, 1967) pp. 103–104; United States, Foreign Relations, *Treaty of Versailles, Paris Peace Conference, 1919* (Washington, D.C.: Government Printing Office, 1947).

30 Nationalism in Asia, 1914–1939

Turks celebrating victory at Smyrna, October 1922. *(Source: Bettmann/Hulton)*

From Asia's perspective the First World War was largely a European civil war that shattered the united front of Western imperialism and convulsed prewar relationships throughout Asia. Most crucially, the war speeded the development of modern nationalism in Asia. Before 1914, the nationalist gospel of anti-imperialist political freedom and racial equality had already won converts among Asia's westernized, educated elites. In the 1920s and 1930s it increasingly won the allegiance of the masses. As in Europe in the nineteenth century, nationalism in Asia between 1914 and 1939 became a mass movement with potentially awesome power.

There were at least three reasons for the upsurge of nationalism in Asia. First and foremost, nationalism provided the most effective means of organizing the anti-imperialist resistance both to direct foreign rule and to indirect Western domination. Second, nationalism called for fundamental changes and challenged old political and social practices and beliefs. Thus modernizers used it as a weapon in their ongoing contest for influence and power with conservative traditionalists. Third, nationalism spread because it gave both leaders and followers a vision of a shining future for a rejuvenated people. Thus nationalism provided an ideology to ennoble the sacrifices that the struggle for rejuvenation would require.

The spread of nationalism also had its dark side. As in Europe (see page 812), nationalists in Asia developed a strong sense of "we" and "they." "They" were often the enemy—the oppressor. White-skinned European imperialists were just such a "they," and nationalist feeling generated the power to destroy European empires and challenge foreign economic domination. But, as in Europe, nationalism in Asia also stimulated bitter conflicts and wars between peoples, in two different ways.

First, it stimulated conflicts between relatively homogeneous peoples in large states, rallying, for example, Chinese against Japanese and vice versa. Second, nationalism often heightened tensions between ethnic (or religious) groups within states, especially states with a variety of peoples, like British India or the Ottoman Empire. Such states had been formed by authoritarian rulers and their armies and bureaucracies, very much like the Austrian or Russian empires before 1914. When their rigid rule declined or snapped, increasingly self-conscious and nationalistic peoples might easily quarrel, seeking to divide the existing state or to dominate the enemy "they" within its borders.

Although modern nationalism has everywhere exhibited certain shared characteristics, it has never been monolithic. In Asia especially, the range of historical experience has been enormous, and the new and often narrow ideology of nationalism was grafted onto old, rich, and complex civilizations. Between the outbreak of the First and Second World Wars each Asian country developed a distinctive national movement, rooted in its unique culture and history. Each nation's people created its own national reawakening, which renovated thought and culture as well as politics and economics.

- How did modern nationalism—the dominant force in most of the world in the twentieth century—develop in Asia between the First and Second World Wars?

- How did national movements arise in different countries, and how did some of these parallel movements come into brutal conflict?

These are the questions that this chapter seeks to answer.

✦ THE FIRST WORLD WAR AND WESTERN IMPERIALISM

Every Asian national movement shared in a burning desire for genuine freedom from foreign imperialism. The First World War had a profound effect on these aspirations by altering relations between Asia and Europe.

In the words of a distinguished Indian historian, "the Great War of 1914–1918 was from the Asian point of view a civil war within the European community of nations."[1] For four years Asians watched the haughty bearers of what Kipling had called "the White Man's Burden" (see page 901) vilifying and destroying each other. Far from standing united and supremely self-confident, the Western nations were clawing at each other in total disarray. The impact of this spectacle was enormous. Japan's defeat of imperial Russia in 1904 (see page 908) had shown that an Asian power could beat a European Great Power; now for the first time Asians saw the entire West as divided and vulnerable.

In the East Asian countries of China and Japan few people particularly cared who won the vicious family quarrel in distant Europe. In India and French Indochina enthusiasm was also limited, but the impact of the war was unavoidably greater. The British and the French were driven by the harsh logic of total war to draft their colonial subjects into the conflict. They uprooted hundreds of thousands of Asians to fight the Germans and the Ottoman Turks. This too had major consequences. An Indian or Vietnamese soldier who fought in France and came in contact there with democratic and republican ideas was likely to be less willing to accept foreign rule when he returned home.

The British and the French also made rash promises to gain the support of colonial peoples during the war. British leaders promised Jewish nationalists in Europe a homeland in Palestine even as they promised Arab nationalists independence from the Ottoman Empire. In India the British were forced in 1917 to announce a new policy of self-governing institutions in order to counteract Indian popular unrest fanned by wartime inflation and heavy taxation. After the war the nationalist genie that the colonial powers had called on refused to slip meekly back into the bottle.

The war aims of President Wilson also raised the hopes of peoples under imperial rule. In January 1918 Wilson proposed to make peace on the basis of his Fourteen Points (see page 983), whose key idea was national self-determination for the peoples of Europe and of the Ottoman Empire. Wilson also proposed that in all colonial questions "the interests of native populations be given equal weight with the desires of European governments," and he seemed to call for national self-rule. This subversive message had enormous appeal for educated Asians, fueling their hopes of freedom and dignity.

Military service and Wilsonian self-determination also fired the hopes of some Africans and some visionary American black supporters of African freedom. The First World War, however, had less impact on European imperialism in sub-Saharan Africa than in Asia and the Arab world. For sub-Saharan Africa, the Great Depression and the Second World War were to prove much more influential in the growth of nationalist movements (see pages 1156, 1157).

Once the Allies had won the war, they tried to shift gears and re-establish or increase their political and economic domination in Asia and Africa. Although fatally weakened, Western imperialism remained very much alive in 1918. Part of the reason for its survival was that President Wilson was certainly no revolutionary. At the Versailles Peace Conference he proved willing to compromise on colonial questions in order to achieve some of his European goals and the creation of the League of Nations. Also, Allied statesmen and ordinary French and British citizens quite rightly believed that their colonial empires had contributed to their ultimate victory over the Central Powers. They were in no mood to give up such valuable possessions voluntarily. Finally, the victors remained convinced of the superiority of their civilization. They believed that their rule was best for colonial peoples. A few "discontented" Asian or African intellectuals might agitate for self-rule, but Europeans generally believed that the "humble masses" were grateful for the law and order brought by the white man's administration. If pressed, Europeans said that such administration was preparing colonial subjects for eventual self-rule, but only in the distant future.

The compromise at Versailles between Wilson's vague, moralistic idealism and the European preoccupation with "good administration" was the establishment of a system of League of Nations mandates over Germany's former colonies and the old Ottoman Empire. Article 22 of the League of Nations Covenant, which was part of the Treaty of Versailles, assigned territories "inhabited by peoples incapable of governing themselves" to various "developed nations." "The well-being and development of such peoples" was declared "a sacred trust of civilization." A Permanent Mandates Commission was created to oversee the developed nations' fulfillment of their international responsibility; most of the members of the Permanent Mandates Commission came from European countries that had colonies. Thus the League elaborated a new principle—development toward the eventual goal of self-government—but left its implementation to the colonial powers themselves.

The mandates system demonstrated that Europe was determined to maintain its imperial power and influence. It is no wonder that patriots throughout Asia were bitterly disappointed after the First World War. They saw France, Great Britain, and other nations—industrialized Japan was the only Asian state to obtain mandates—grabbing Ger-

❊ **Delegates to the Peace Conference of 1919** Standing in the foreground is Prince Faisal, third son of King Hussein of Hejaz and frustrated spokesman for the Arab cause at Versailles. The British officer T. E. Lawrence—popularly known as Lawrence of Arabia because of his daring campaign against the Turks in World War I—is second from the right in the middle row. *(Source: By courtesy of the Trustees of the Imperial War Museum)*

many's colonies as spoils of war and extending the existing system of colonial protectorates in Muslim North Africa into the territories of the old Ottoman Empire. Yet Asian patriots were not about to give up. They preached national self-determination and struggled to build mass movements capable of achieving freedom and independence.

In this struggle they were encouraged and sometimes inspired by Soviet communism. Immediately after seizing power in 1917, Lenin and his fellow Bolsheviks declared that the Asian peoples conquered by the tsars, now inhabitants of the new Soviet Union, were complete equals of the Russians with a right to their own development. (In actuality this equality hardly existed, but the propaganda was effective nonetheless.) The Communists also denounced European and American imperialism and pledged to support revolutionary movements in all colonial countries, even when they were primarily movements of national independence led by "middle-class" intellectuals instead of by revolutionary workers. Foreign political and economic exploitation was the immediate enemy, they said, and socialist revolution could wait until after Western imperialism had been defeated.

The example, ideology, and support of Russian Communists exerted a powerful influence in the

1920s and 1930s, particularly in China and French Indochina. A nationalistic young Vietnamese man who had pleaded the cause of Vietnamese independence unsuccessfully at the Versailles Peace Conference described his feelings when he read Lenin's statement on national self-determination for colonial peoples, adopted by the Communist Third International in 1920:

These resolutions filled me with great emotion, enthusiasm, and faith. They helped me see the problem clearly. My joy was so great I began to cry. Alone in my room I wrote the following words, as if I were addressing a great crowd: "My dear compatriots, so miserable and oppressed, here is what we need. Here is the path to our liberation." [2]

The young nationalist was Ho Chi Minh (1890–1969), who was to fight a lifetime to create an independent, communist Vietnam.

The appeal of nationalism in Asia was not confined to territories under direct European rule. The extraordinary growth of international trade after 1850 had drawn millions of peasants and shopkeepers throughout Asia into the Western-dominated world economy, disrupting local markets and often creating hostility toward European businessmen. Moreover, Europe and the United States had forced even the most solid Asian states, China and Japan, to accept unequal treaties and humiliating limitations on their sovereignty. Thus the nationalist promise of genuine economic independence and true political equality with the West appealed as powerfully in old but weak states like China as in colonial territories like British India.

Finally, as in Russia after the Crimean War or in Japan after the Meiji Restoration, the nationalist creed went hand in hand with acceptance of modernization by the educated elites. Modernization promised changes that would enable old societies to compete effectively with the world's leading nations.

❖ THE MIDDLE EAST

The most flagrant attempt to expand the scope of Western imperialism occurred in what is usually called the Middle East but is perhaps more accurately termed West Asia—that vast expanse that stretches eastward from the Suez Canal and Turkey's Mediterranean shores across the Tigris-Euphrates Valley and the Iranian Plateau to the Arabian Sea and the Indus Valley. There the British and the French successfully encouraged an Arab revolt in 1916 and destroyed the Ottoman Empire. The conquering Europeans then sought to replace the Turks as principal rulers throughout the region, even in Turkey itself. Turkish, Arab, and Iranian nationalists, as well as Jewish nationalists arriving from Europe, reacted violently. They struggled to win dignity and nationhood, and as the Europeans were forced to make concessions, they sometimes came into sharp conflict with each other, most notably in Palestine.

The First World War and the Arab Revolt

The Ottoman Empire, like neighboring Egypt (see pages 887–880), had long been subject to European pressure and had also adopted European military and educational reforms in the 1820s and 1830s. In the late nineteenth century, however, the Ottoman Empire became increasingly weak and autocratic. The combination of declining international stature and domestic tyranny eventually led to an upsurge of revolutionary activity among idealistic exiles and young army officers who wanted to seize power and save the Ottoman state. These fervent patriots, the so-called Young Turks, succeeded in the revolution of 1908, and subsequently they were determined to hold together the remnants of the vast multiethnic empire. Defeated by Bulgaria, Serbia, and Greece in the Balkan War of 1912, stripped of practically all territory in Europe, the Young Turks redoubled their efforts in Asia. The most important of their Asian possessions were Syria—consisting of modern-day Lebanon, Syria, Israel, and Jordan—and Iraq. The Ottoman Turks also claimed the Arabian peninsula but exercised only a loose control there.

For centuries the largely Arabic populations of Syria and Iraq had been tied to their Ottoman rulers by their common faith in Islam (though there were Christian Arabs as well). Yet beneath the surface, ethnic and linguistic tensions simmered between Turks and Arabs, who were as different as Chinese and Japanese or French and Germans. As early as 1883, a Frenchman who had traveled widely in the Arab provinces claimed:

Everywhere I came upon the same abiding and universal sentiment: hatred of the Turks. The notion of concerted action to throw off the detested yoke is gradually shaping itself. . . . An Arab movement, newly-risen, is looming in the distance; a race hitherto downtrodden will presently claim its due place in the destinies of Islam.[3]

The actions of the Young Turks after 1908 made the embryonic "Arab movement" a reality. Although some Turkish reformers argued for an Ottoman federalism that would give equal political rights to all ethnic and religious groups within the empire, the majority successfully insisted on a narrow Turkish nationalism. They further centralized the Ottoman Empire and extended the sway of the Turkish language, culture, and race. In 1909 the Turkish government brutally slaughtered thousands of Armenian Christians, a prelude to the wholesale destruction of more than a million Armenians during the heavy fighting with Russia in the First World War. Meanwhile, the Arab revolt gathered strength. By 1914 a large majority of Arab leaders believed that armed conflict with their Turkish masters was inevitable.

In close contact with Europeans for centuries, the Turks willingly joined forces with Germany and Austria-Hungary in late 1914. The Young Turks were pro-German because Germans had helped reform Ottoman armies before the war and had built important railroads, like the one to Baghdad. Alliance with Germany permitted the Turks to renounce immediately the limitations on Ottoman sovereignty that the Europeans had imposed in the nineteenth century, and it offered the prospect of settling old scores with Russia, the historic enemy.

The Young Turks' fatal decision to side with the Central Powers pulled the entire Middle East into the European civil war and made it truly a world conflict. While Russia attacked the Ottomans in the Caucasus, the British had to protect Egypt and the Suez Canal, the life line to India. Thus Arab leaders opposed to Ottoman rule suddenly found an unexpected ally in Great Britain. The foremost Arab leader was Hussein ibn-Ali (1856–1931), a direct descendant of the prophet Muhammad through the house of Quraysh. As the *sharif*, or chief magistrate of Mecca, the most holy city in the Muslim world, Hussein governed much of the Ottoman Empire's territory along the Red Sea, an area known as the Hejaz (Map 30.1). Basically anti-Turkish, Hussein refused to second the Turkish sultan's call for a holy war against the Triple Entente. His refusal pleased the British, who feared that such calls would trigger a Muslim revolt in India.

In 1915 Hussein managed to win vague British commitments for an independent Arab kingdom. The British attempt to take the Dardanelles and capture Constantinople in 1915 failed miserably, and Britain (and Russia) badly needed a new ally on the Ottoman front. Thus in 1916 Hussein revolted against the Turks, proclaiming himself king of the Arabs. Hussein joined forces with the British under T. E. Lawrence, who in 1917 led Arab tribesmen and Indian soldiers in a highly successful guerrilla war against the Turks on the Arabian peninsula. In September 1918, British armies and their Arab allies smashed into Syria. This offensive culminated in the triumphal entry of Hussein's son Faisal into Damascus.

Similar victories were eventually scored in the Ottoman province of Iraq. Britain occupied the southern Iraqi city of Basra in 1914 and captured Baghdad in 1917. Throughout Syria and Iraq there was wild Arab rejoicing. Many patriots expected a large, unified Arab state to rise from the dust of the Ottoman collapse. Within two years, however, many Arab nationalists felt bitterly betrayed by Great Britain and its allies. The issues involved are complex and controversial, but it is undeniable that this bitterness left a legacy of hatred toward the West.

Part of the reason for the Arabs' bitterness was that Britain and France had signed secret wartime treaties to divide and rule the old Ottoman Empire. In the Sykes-Picot Agreement of 1916, Britain and France had secretly agreed that France would receive modern-day Lebanon, Syria, and much of southern Turkey, and Britain would receive Palestine, Jordan, and Iraq. The Sykes-Picot treaties contradicted British (and later Wilsonian) promises concerning Arab independence after the war. When Britain and France set about implementing these secret plans, Arab nationalists felt cheated and betrayed.

A related source of Arab bitterness was Britain's wartime commitment to a Jewish homeland in Palestine. The Balfour Declaration of November

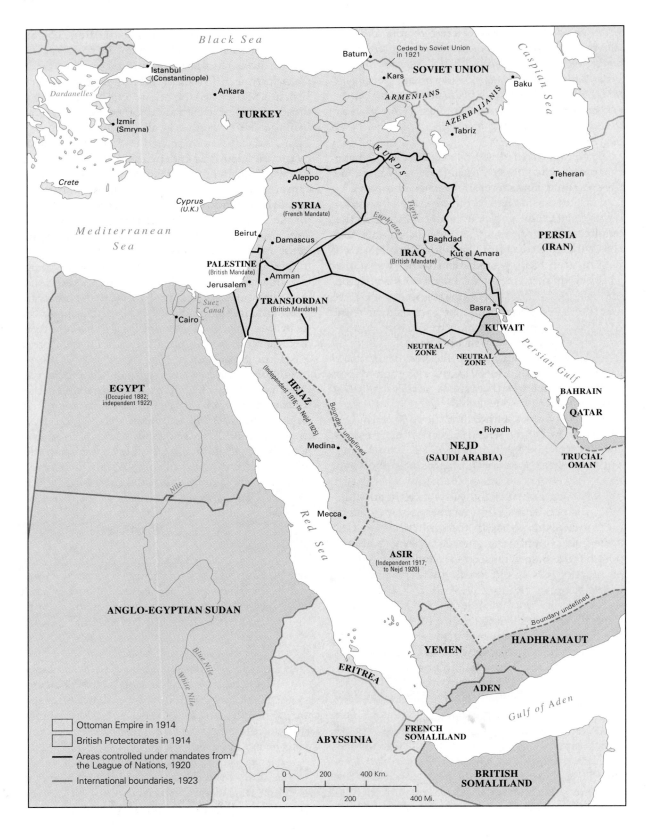

Black Sea

Istanbul
(Constantinople)

Dardanelles

Izmir
(Smryna)

Ankara

TURKEY

Crete

Cyprus
(U.K.)

Aleppo

SYRIA
(French Mandate)

Beirut

Damascus

Mediterranean
Sea

PALESTINE
(British Mandate)

Jerusalem

Amman

TRANSJORDAN
(British Mandate)

Suez
Canal

Cairo

EGYPT
(Occupied 1882;
independent 1922)

HEJAZ
(Independent 1916; to Nejd 1925)

Boundary undefined

Medina

Red Sea

Mecca

ANGLO-EGYPTIAN SUDAN

Nile

Blue Nile

White Nile

ERITREA

ABYSSINIA

FRENCH
SOMALILAND

Batum

Ceded by Soviet Union
in 1921

Kars

SOVIET UNION

ARMENIANS

Baku

Caspian Sea

AZERBAIJANIS

Tabriz

K U R D S

Tigris

Euphrates

Baghdad

IRAQ
(British Mandate)

Kut el Amara

Teheran

PERSIA
(IRAN)

Basra

KUWAIT

NEUTRAL
ZONE

NEUTRAL
ZONE

Persian Gulf

BAHRAIN

QATAR

Riyadh

NEJD
(SAUDI ARABIA)

TRUCIAL
OMAN

ASIR
(Independent 1917;
to Nejd 1920)

Boundary undefined

HADHRAMAUT

YEMEN

ADEN

Gulf of Aden

BRITISH
SOMALILAND

☐ Ottoman Empire in 1914

☐ British Protectorates in 1914

▬ Areas controlled under mandates from
the League of Nations, 1920

▬ International boundaries, 1923

0   200   400 Km.

0   200   400 Mi.

1917, made by the Britsh foreign secretary Arthur Balfour, declared:

His Majesty's Government views with favor the establishment in Palestine of a National Home for the Jewish People, and will use their best endeavors to facilitate the achievement of this object, it being clearly understood that nothing shall be done which may prejudice the civil and religious rights of existing non-Jewish communities in Palestine, or the rights and political status enjoyed by Jews in any other country.

As careful reading reveals, the Balfour Declaration made contradictory promises to European Jews and Middle Eastern Arabs. It has been a subject of passionate debate ever since 1917.

Some British Cabinet members apparently believed such a declaration would appeal to German, Austrian, and American Jews and thus help the British war effort. Others sincerely supported the Zionist vision of a Jewish homeland. These supporters also believed that such a homeland would be grateful to Britain and help maintain British control of the Suez Canal. In any event, Arabs were dismayed.

In 1914 Jews accounted for about 11 percent of the predominantly Arab population in the three Ottoman administrative units that would subsequently be lumped together by the British to form Palestine. The "National Home for the Jewish People" mentioned in the Balfour Declaration implied to the Arabs—and to the Zionist Jews as well—the establishment of some kind of Jewish state that would be incompatible with majority rule. But a state founded on religious and ethnic exclusivity was out of keeping with both Islamic and Ottoman tradition, which had historically been more tolerant of religious diversity and minorities than had the Christian monarchs or nation-states in Europe.

Despite strong French objections, Hussein's son Faisal (1885–1933) was allowed to attend the Paris Peace Conference, but his effort to secure an independent state embracing all Arabs came to nothing. The independence of the kingdom of Hejaz was confirmed, but in return Faisal was forced to accept Franco-British demands for mandates in Syria, Iraq, and Palestine. (The Saudis had attacked Hussein in 1916, and they conquered his kingdom of Hejaz in 1924–1925, incorporating it with the Nejd in 1932 to form Saudi Arabia.) The British mandate in Palestine formally incorporated the Balfour Declaration and its commitment to a Jewish national home. On his return to Syria, Faisal's followers repudiated the agreement he had reluctantly accepted. In March 1920 they met as the Syrian National Congress and proclaimed Syria independent with Faisal as king. A similar congress declared Iraq an independent kingdom.

Western reaction to events in Syria and Iraq was swift and decisive. A French army stationed in Lebanon attacked Syria, taking Damascus in July 1920. Faisal fled and the French took over. Meanwhile, the British put down an uprising in Iraq with bloody fighting and established military rule there. Western imperialism appeared to have replaced Turkish rule in the Middle East (see Map 30.1).

The Turkish Revolution

In November 1918 the Allied fleet entered Constantinople, the Ottoman capital. A young English official vividly described the strange and pathetic situation he encountered:

I found the Ottoman Empire utterly smashed, her vast territories stripped into pieces, and her conquered populations blinded and bewildered by their sudden release. The Turks were worn out, dead-tired, and without bitterness awaited their fate. . . . The debris of the old order waited to be constructed into a new system.[4]

The Allies' "new system" was blatant imperialism, and it proved harsher for the defeated Turks than for the "liberated" Arabs. A treaty forced on

MAP 30.1 The Partition of the Ottoman Empire, 1914–1923 The decline of the mighty Ottoman Empire began in 1699, when the Habsburgs conquered Hungary, and it accelerated after 1805, when Egypt became virtually independent. By 1914 the Ottoman Turks had been pushed out of the Balkans, and their Arab provinces were on the edge of revolt; that revolt erupted in the First World War and contributed greatly to the Ottomans' defeat. When the Allies then attempted to implement their plans, including independence for the Armenian people, Mustafa Kemal arose to forge in battle the modern Turkish state.

the helpless sultan dismembered Turkey and reduced it to a puppet state. Great Britain and France occupied parts of Turkey, and Italy and Greece claimed shares as well. There was a sizable Greek minority in western Turkey, and Greek nationalists cherished the "Great Idea" of incorporating this territory into a modern Greek empire modeled on long-dead Christian Byzantium. In 1919 Greek armies carried by British ships landed on the Turkish coast at Smyrna. The sultan ordered his exhausted troops not to resist, and Greek armies advanced into the interior. Turkey seemed finished.

But Turkey produced a great leader and revived to become an inspiration to the entire Middle East. Mustafa Kemal (1881–1938), the father of modern Turkey, was a military man. The son of a petty government official and sympathetic to the Young Turk movement, Kemal had distinguished himself in the Great War by directing the successful defense of the Dardanelles against British attack. After the armistice, Mustafa Kemal watched with anguish the Allies' aggression and the sultan's cowardice. In early 1919 he moved from Constantinople to central Turkey and began working to unify the Turkish resistance.

Greek Exodus In the port city of Smyrna in 1922, Greeks are evacuated after Turkish victory over the Greek and British invaders. After three years of fighting, Mustafa Kemal ended the Greek idea of establishing a modern empire that would include part of Turkey. (*Source: Hulton Deutsch Collection Ltd.*)

The sultan, bowing to Allied pressure, initially denounced Kemal, but the cause of national liberation proved more powerful. The catalyst was the Greek invasion and attempted annexation of much of western Turkey. A young woman who was to play a major role in the Turkish revolution described feelings she shared with countless others:

After I learned about the details of the Smyrna occupation by Greek armies, I hardly opened my mouth on any subject except when it concerned the sacred struggle. . . . I suddenly ceased to exist as an individual. I worked, wrote and lived as a unit of that magnificent national madness.[5]

Refusing to acknowledge the Allied dismemberment of their country, the Turks battled on through 1920 despite staggering defeats. The next year the Greeks, egged on by the British, advanced almost to Ankara, the nationalist stronghold in central Turkey. There Mustafa Kemal's forces took the offensive and won a great victory. The Greeks and their British allies sued for peace. After long negotiations, the resulting Treaty of Lausanne (1923) solemnly abolished the hated Capitulations, which the European powers had imposed in the nineteenth century to give their citizens special privileges in the Ottoman Empire, and recognized the territorial integrity of a truly independent Turkey. Turkey lost only its former Arab provinces.

Mustafa Kemal, a nationalist without religious faith, believed that Turkey should modernize and secularize along Western lines. His first moves were political. Drawing on his prestige as a war hero, Kemal called on the somewhat reluctant National Assembly to depose the sultan and establish a republic. He had himself elected president and moved the capital from cosmopolitan Constantinople (soon to be renamed Istanbul) to Ankara in the Turkish heartland. Kemal savagely crushed the demands for independence of ethnic minorities like the Armenians and the Kurds, but he realistically abandoned all thought of winning back lost Arab territories. He focused instead on internal affairs, creating a one-party system—partly inspired by the Bolshevik example—in order to work his will.

The most radical of Kemal's changes pertained to religion and culture. For centuries, most of the intellectual and social activities of believers had been sternly regulated by Islamic religious authori-

Mustafa Kemal The father of modern Turkey explains his radical reform of the written Turkish language. Impeccably elegant European dress symbolizes Kemal's conception of a modernized Turkey. *(Source: Stock Montage)*

ties, in keeping with the Sacred Law. Profoundly influenced by the example of western Europe, Mustafa Kemal set out, like the philosophes of the Enlightenment, to limit the place of religion and religious leaders in daily affairs. Like Russia's Peter the Great, he employed dictatorial measures rather than reason to reach his goal. Kemal and his followers simply decreed a revolutionary separation of church and state. Religious courts were abolished, replaced by a completely new legal system based on European law codes. Religious schools gave way to state schools that taught such secular subjects as science, mathematics, and social sciences.

To dramatize the break with the past, Mustafa Kemal struck down many entrenched patterns of behavior. Women, traditionally secluded and inferior to males in Islamic society, received the right to vote. Marriage was now governed by civil law on a European model, rather than by the Islamic code. Women were allowed to seek divorces, and no man could have more than one wife at a time. Men were forbidden to wear the tall red fez as headgear; government employees were ordered to wear business suits and felt hats, erasing the visible differences between Muslims and "infidel" Europeans. The old Arabic script was replaced with a new Turkish alphabet based on Roman letters, which moved the written language closer to the spoken vernacular and facilitated massive government efforts to spread literacy after 1928. Finally, in 1935, family names on the European model were introduced. The National Assembly granted Mustafa Kemal the surname Atatürk, which means "father of the Turks."

By the time of his death in 1938, Atatürk and his supporters had consolidated their revolution. Government-sponsored industrialization was fostering urban growth and new attitudes, encouraging Turks to embrace business and science. Poverty persisted in rural areas, as did some religious discontent among devout Muslims. But like the Japanese after the Meiji Restoration, the Turkish people had rallied around the nationalist banner to repulse European imperialism and were building a modern secular nation-state.

Iran and Afghanistan

In Persia (renamed Iran in 1935), strong-arm efforts to build a unified modern nation ultimately proved less successful than in Turkey.

The late nineteenth century had been a sorry period in Iran's long and sometimes glorious history. Iran was subject to extreme foreign pressure: the Russians were pressing relentlessly from the north, and the British were pushing upward from India and the Persian Gulf. Like China in a similar predicament at the same time, Iran managed to play the Great Powers against each other to maintain a precarious independence. However, the spectacle of the shah granting economic privileges to foreigners alienated native merchants. An inspired religious leader, Jamal al-Din al-Afghani (1838–

1897), began to preach government reform as a means of reviving Islamic civilization. In 1906 a nationalistic coalition of merchants, religious leaders, and intellectuals revolted. The despotic shah was forced to grant a constitution and establish a national assembly, the *Majlis*. Nationalist hopes ran high.

Yet the Iranian revolution of 1906 was doomed to failure, largely because of European imperialism. Without consulting Iran, Britain and Russia in 1907 simply divided the country into spheres of influence. Britain's sphere ran along the Persian Gulf; the Russian sphere encompassed the whole northern half of Iran (see Map 30.1). Thereafter Russia intervened constantly. It blocked reforms, occupied cities, and completely dominated the country by 1912. When Russian power temporarily collapsed in the Bolshevik Revolution, British armies rushed into the power vacuum. By bribing corrupt Iranians liberally, Great Britain in 1919 negotiated a treaty allowing the installation of British "advisers" in every department of the government.

The Majlis refused to ratify the treaty, and the blatant attempt to make Iran a British satellite aroused the national spirit. In 1921 reaction against the British brought to power a military dictator, Reza Shah Pahlavi (1877–1944), who proclaimed himself shah in 1925 and ruled until 1941.

Inspired throughout his reign by the example of Turkey's Mustafa Kemal, the patriotic, religiously indifferent Reza Shah had three basic goals: to build a modern nation, to free Iran from foreign domination, and to rule with an iron fist. The challenge was enormous. Iran was a vast, backward country of deserts, mountain barriers, and rudimentary communications. Most of the rural population was poor and illiterate, and among the Persian majority were sizable ethnic minorities with their own aspirations. Furthermore, Iran's powerful religious leaders hated Western (Christian) domination but were no less opposed to a more secular, less Islamic society.

To realize his vision of a strong Iran, the energetic shah created a modern army, built railroads, and encouraged commerce and industry. He won control over ethnic minorities such as the Kurds in the north and Arab tribesmen on the border with Iraq. He withdrew many of the privileges granted to foreigners and raised taxes on the powerful Anglo-Persian Oil Company, which had been founded in 1909 to exploit the first great oil strike in the Middle East. Yet Reza Shah was less successful than Atatürk.

Because the European-educated elite in Iran was smaller than the comparable group in Turkey, the idea of re-creating Persian greatness on the basis of a secularized society attracted relatively few determined supporters. Many powerful religious leaders turned against Reza Shah, and he became increasingly brutal, greedy, and tyrannical, murdering his enemies and lining his pockets. His support of Hitler's Nazi Germany also exposed Iran's tenuous and fragile independence to the impact of European conflicts.

Afghanistan, meanwhile, was nominally independent in the nineteenth century, but the British imposed political restrictions and constantly meddled in the country. In 1919 the new, violently anti-British amir Amanullah (1892–1960) declared a holy war on the British government in India and won complete independence for the first time. Amanullah then decreed revolutionary reforms designed to hurl his primitive country into the twentieth century. The result was tribal and religious revolt, civil war, and retreat from reform. Islam remained both religion and law. A powerful but primitive patriotism had enabled Afghanistan to win political independence from the West, but modest efforts to build a modern society met with little success.

The Arab States and Palestine

The establishment of French and British mandates at gunpoint forced Arab nationalists to seek independence by gradual means after 1920. Arab nationalists were indirectly aided by Western taxpayers, who wanted cheap—that is, peaceful—empires. As a result, Arabs won considerable control over local affairs in the mandated states, except Palestine, though the mandates remained European satellites in international and economic affairs.

The wily British chose Faisal, whom the French had so recently deposed in Syria, as king of Iraq. Faisal obligingly signed an alliance giving British advisers broad behind-the-scenes control. The king also accepted British ownership of Iraq's oil fields, thereby giving the West a stranglehold on the Iraqi economy. Given the limitations imposed on him, Faisal (r. 1921–1933) proved an able

ruler, gaining the support of his people and encouraging moderate reforms. In 1932 he secured Iraqi independence at the price of a long-term military alliance with Great Britain.

Egypt, occupied by Great Britain ever since 1882 (see page 890) and a British protectorate since 1914, pursued a similar path. Following intense nationalist agitation after the Great War, Great Britain in 1922 proclaimed Egypt formally independent but continued to occupy the country militarily. In 1936, the British agreed to a treaty restricting their troops to their big bases in the Suez Canal Zone.

The French were less compromising in Syria. They practiced a policy of divide-and-rule, carving out a second mandate in Lebanon and generally playing off ethnic and religious minorities against each other. Lebanon eventually became a republic, dominated by a very slender Christian majority and under French protection. Arab nationalists in Syria finally won promises of Syrian independence in 1936 in return for a treaty of friendship with France.

In short, the Arab states gradually freed themselves from Western political mandates but not from the Western military threat or from pervasive Western influence. Of great importance, large Arab landowners and urban merchants increased their wealth and political power after 1918, and they often supported the Western hegemony, from which they benefited greatly. Western control over the newly discovered oil fields by foreign companies helped to convince radical nationalists that economic independence and genuine freedom had not yet been achieved.

Relations between the Arabs and the West were complicated by the tense situation in the British mandate of Palestine, and that situation deteriorated in the interwar years. Both Arabs and Jews denounced the British, who tried unsuccessfully to compromise with both sides. The anger of Arab nationalists, however, was aimed primarily at Jewish settlers. The key issue was Jewish migration from Europe to Palestine.

A small Jewish community had survived in Palestine ever since the destruction of Jerusalem and the dispersal of the Jews in Roman times. But Jewish nationalism, known as Zionism, was a recent phenomenon of European origin. The Dreyfus affair (see page 869) and anti-Jewish riots in Russia had convinced a cultured Austrian

→ anti-semitism in France military officer

✳ **Home to Zion**   Chaim Weizmann carries sacred Torahs of the Jewish people toward a synagogue in Tel-Aviv, a new city founded in 1909. Born in Russia and educated as a chemist in Berlin, Weizmann became a British citizen and in 1917 helped secure the Balfour Declaration. In the 1920s Weizmann led the Zionist movement. In 1948 he became the first president of Israel. *(Source: Central Zionist Archives, Jerusalem)*

journalist named Theodore Herzl (1860–1904) that even nonreligious Jews would never be fully accepted in Europe. He believed that only the recreation of a Jewish state could guarantee Jews dignity and security. Under Herzl's leadership, the Zionist movement encouraged Jews from all over the world to settle in the Palestine region, but until 1921 the great majority of Jewish emigrants preferred the United States.

After 1921 the situation changed radically. An isolationist United States drastically limited immigration from eastern Europe, where war and revolution had caused chaos and kindled anti-Semitism. Moreover, the British began honoring the Balfour Declaration despite Arab protests. Thus the number of Jewish immigrants to Palestine from turbulent Europe grew rapidly. In the 1930s German and Polish persecution created a mass of Jewish refugees. By 1939 the Jewish population of Palestine had increased almost fivefold since 1914 and accounted for about 30 percent of all inhabitants.

Jewish settlers in Palestine faced formidable economic and political difficulties. Much of the land purchased by the Jewish National Fund was productive. But many of the sellers of such land were wealthy absentee Arab landowners who had little interest in the welfare of their Arab tenants (see page 888). When the new Jewish owners subsequently replaced those age-old Arab tenants with Jewish settlers, Arab farmers and intellectuals burned with a sense of injustice. Moreover, most Jewish immigrants came from urban backgrounds and preferred to establish new cities like Tel Aviv

THE MIDDLE EAST, 1914–1939

1914	Ottoman Empire enters First World War on Germany's side
1916	Allies agree secretly to partition Ottoman Empire
1916–1917	Arab revolt against Turkish rule grows
November 1917	Balfour Declaration pledges British support for a Jewish homeland in Palestine
October 1918	Arabs and British triumph as Ottoman Empire collapses
1919	Treaty of Versailles divides old Ottoman Empire into League of Nations mandates
1919	Mustafa Kemal mounts nationalist struggle against foreign occupation
1920	Faisal proclaimed king of Syria but quickly deposed by the French, who establish their mandate in Syria
Early 1920s	Tide of Jewish immigration surges into British mandate of Palestine
1923	Treaty of Lausanne recognizes independent Turkey Mustafa Kemal begins to secularize Turkish society
1925	Reza Shah takes power in Iran and rules to 1941
1932	Iraq gains independence in return for military alliance with Great Britain
1936	Syrian nationalists sign treaty with France in return for promises of independence
late 1930s	Tensions mount between Arabs and Jews in Palestine

or to live in existing towns, where they competed with the Arabs. The land issue combined with economic and cultural friction to harden Arab protest into hatred. Anti-Jewish riots and even massacres ensued.

The British gradually responded to Arab pressure and tried to slow Jewish immigration. This effort satisfied neither Jews nor Arabs, and by 1938 the two communities were engaged in an undeclared civil war. On the eve of the Second World War, the frustrated British proposed an independent Palestine as well as a cap of seventy-five thousand additional Jewish immigrants. The reason for this low number was to permanently limit the Jews

to being only about one-third of Palestine's total population. Zionists felt themselves in grave danger.

In the face of adversity, Jewish settlers from many different countries gradually succeeded in forging a cohesive community. Hebrew, which for centuries had been used only in religious worship, was revived as a living language to bind the Jews in Palestine together. Despite its slow beginnings, rural development achieved often spectacular results. The key unit of agricultural organization was the *kibbutz,* a collective farm on which each member shared equally in the work, rewards, and defense of the farm. Men and women labored side by side; a nursery cared for the children, and a common dining hall served meals. Some cooperative farms turned arid grazing land into citrus groves and irrigated gardens. An egalitarian socialist ideology also characterized industry, which grew rapidly and was owned largely by the Jewish trade unions. By 1939 a new but old nation was emerging in the Middle East.

✹ TOWARD SELF-RULE IN INDIA

The national movement in British India grew out of two interconnected cultures, Hindu and Muslim, which came to see themselves as fundamentally different in rising to challenge British rule. Nowhere has the power of modern nationalism, both to unify and to divide, been more strikingly demonstrated than in India.

Promises and Repression (1914–1919)

Indian nationalism had emerged in the late nineteenth century (see page 905), and when the First World War began, the British feared revolt. Instead, somewhat like Europe's equally mistrusted socialist workers, Indians supported the war effort. About 1.2 million Indian soldiers and laborers volunteered for duty and served in Europe, Africa, and the Middle East. The British government in India and the native Indian princes sent large supplies of food, money, and ammunition. In return, the British opened more good government jobs to Indians and made other minor concessions.

As the war in distant Europe ground on, however, inflation, high taxes, food shortages, and a terrible influenza epidemic created widespread suffering and discontent. The prewar nationalist movement revived, stronger than ever, and the moderate and radical wings of the Indian National Congress joined forces. Moreover, in 1916 the Hindus leading the Congress party hammered out an alliance—the Lucknow Pact—with India's Muslim League. Founded in 1906 to uphold Muslim interests, the league had grown out of fears arising from the fact that under British rule the once-dominant Muslim minority had fallen behind the Hindu majority, especially in the Western education necessary to secure good jobs in the government. The Lucknow Pact forged a powerful united front of Hindus and Muslims and called for putting India on equal footing with self-governing white British dominions like Canada, Australia, and New Zealand.

The British response was contradictory. On the one hand, the secretary of state for India made the unprecedented announcement in August 1917 that British policy in India called for the "gradual development of self-governing institutions and the progressive realization of responsible government." The means of achieving this great step forward were spelled out in late 1919 in the Government of India Act, which established a dual administration: part Indian and elected, part British and authoritarian. Such noncontroversial activities as agriculture, health, and education were transferred from British to Indian officials who were accountable to elected provincial assemblies. More sensitive matters like taxes, police, and the courts remained solely in British hands.

The positive impact of this reform, so typical of the British tradition of gradual political change, was seriously undermined by old-fashioned authoritarian rule. Despite the unanimous opposition of the elected Indian members, the British in 1919 rammed the repressive Rowlatt Acts through India's Imperial Legislative Council. These acts indefinitely extended wartime "emergency measures" designed to curb unrest and root out "conspiracy." The result was a wave of rioting across India.

Under these tense conditions an unsuspecting crowd of some ten thousand gathered to celebrate a Hindu religious festival in an enclosed square in Amritsar, a city in the northern province of Punjab. Without the knowledge of the crowd, the local English commander, General Reginald Dyer, had banned all public meetings that very day. Dyer marched his native Gurkha troops onto the field and, without warning, ordered them to fire into the unarmed mass at point-blank range until the ammunition ran out. The Amritsar Massacre, killing 379 and wounding 1,137, shattered wartime hopes in a frenzy of postwar reaction. India seemed to stand on the verge of more violence and repression and, sooner or later, terrorism and guerrilla war. That India took a different path to national liberation was due largely to Mohandas "Mahatma" Gandhi (1869–1948), who became the most fascinating and influential Indian of modern times.

Hindu Society and Mahatma Gandhi

By the time of Gandhi's birth in 1869, the Indian subcontinent was firmly controlled by the British. Part of the country was directly ruled by British (and subordinate Indian) officials, ultimately answerable to the British Parliament in London. These areas included Bengal and its teeming capital Calcutta in eastern India, Bombay and its hinterland in western India, the Punjab in the northwest, and Madras on the southeast coast (see Map 34.1, page 1142). So-called protected states were more sheltered from European ideas and from the world economy. There many of the old ways remained intact. The native prince—usually known as the *maharaja*—remained the titular ruler, though he was bound to the British by unequal treaties and had to accept the "advice" of the British resident assigned to his court.

It was in just such a tiny backwater protected state that Gandhi grew up. His father was a member of the merchant caste. But the Indian caste system has always been more flexible and dynamic than unsympathetic Westerners have wanted to believe, and for six generations the heads of Gandhi's family had served as hereditary prime ministers in various minuscule realms on the Kathiawar peninsula, north of Bombay on the Arabian Sea.

British Repression   After the Amritsar massacre of 1919 British repression in northern India was harsh and sadistic. Assisted by obedient native policemen wielding heavy clubs, these British officers are inflicting the kind of pain and humiliation that would soon fuel Gandhi's nationalist movement. *(Source: J. C. Allen)*

The extended (or joint) family, which had for generations been the most important unit of Indian society, powerfully influenced young Gandhi. Gandhi's father was the well-to-do head of the clan, which included five brothers and their wives, children, and children's children. The big three-story ancestral home swarmed with relatives. A whole community crowded into the labyrinth of tiny rooms and spilled out into the open courtyards. In such a communal atmosphere, patience, kindness, and a good-natured love of people were essential virtues. The aggressive, solitary individualism so prized in Europe and North America would have threatened group harmony. So it was for Gandhi.

In the Hindu family the woman was subordinate but respected. She was "worshipped as a mother, venerated as a wife, loved as a sister, but not much regarded as a woman." Her duty was "to worship her husband, to bear and rear her children."[6] Every Hindu girl married young, often before puberty; her husband was chosen by her parents. The young bride moved into her father-in-law's house. Marriage was a sacrament that could not be dissolved by divorce or even by death. Widows were forbidden by custom to remarry. More generally, a woman's fate was linked to that of the family, in which she was the trusted guardian of orthodox Hindu values.

Gandhi's mother was the ideal Hindu housewife. Married as a young illiterate girl to a forty-two-year-old man whose first wives had died without male children, Putali Ba bore three boys and a girl. According to Gandhi, his ever-cheerful mother was "the first to rise and the last to go to bed . . . and she never made any distinction between her own children and other children in the family."[7] Very devoted but undogmatic in religious matters, Putali Ba fasted regularly and exercised a strong influence on her precocious son. Gandhi was married at thirteen to a local girl who became his lifelong companion.

After his father's death, Gandhi decided to study law in England. No member of his subcaste had ever done so, and the local elders declared Gandhi an outcaste, claiming that Hindu practices would not be possible in alien England. Gandhi disagreed. To win over his wife and anxious mother, he swore that he would not touch meat, women, or wine in the foreign land. Gandhi kept his word.

After passing the English bar, he returned to India. But his practice in Bombay failed, and in 1893 he decided to try his luck as a lawyer for wealthy Indian merchants in South Africa. It was a momentous decision.

The Roots of Militant Nonviolence

Soon after arriving in South Africa, the elegant young lawyer in Western dress took a business trip by train. A white man entered the first-class compartment in which Gandhi was riding, took one look at him, and called the conductor. Gandhi was ordered to ride in the baggage car. When he protested, a policeman threw him off the train. Years later Gandhi recalled this experience as a critical turning point in his life. He had refused to bow to naked racial injustice.

As Gandhi's law practice flourished, he began to examine the plight of Indians in South Africa. After the British abolished black slavery in the empire, plantation owners in South Africa and elsewhere had developed a "new system of slavery."[8] They imported desperately poor Indians as indentured laborers on five-year renewable contracts. When some thrifty, hard-working Indians completed their terms and remained in South Africa as free persons and economic competitors, the Dutch and British settlers passed brutally discriminatory laws. Poor Indians had to work on white-owned plantations or return to India; rich Indians lost the vote. Gandhi undertook the legal defense of his countrymen, infuriating the whites. In 1896 a hysterical mob almost lynched the "coolie lawyer."

Meanwhile, Gandhi was searching for a spiritual theory of social action. Identifying with South Africa's black majority as well as with his own countrymen, he meditated on the Hindu pursuit of spiritual strength through fasting, sexual abstinence, devotion to duty, and reincarnation. He also studied Christian teachings. Gradually Gandhi developed and articulated a weapon for the weak that he called *Satyagraha*. Gandhi conceived of Satyagraha, loosely translated as "Soul Force," as a means of striving for truth and social justice through love, suffering, and conversion of the oppressor. Its tactic is courageous nonviolent resistance. Satyagraha owed a good deal to the Christian Gospels, for Christ's call to "love your enemies" touched Gandhi to the core.

As the undisputed leader of South Africa's Indians before the First World War, Gandhi put his philosophy into action. When the white government of South Africa severely restricted Asians' immigration and internal freedom of movement, he led a campaign of mass resistance. Thousands of Indian men and women marched across forbidden borders and peacefully withstood beatings, arrest, and imprisonment.

In 1914, South Africa's exasperated whites agreed to many of the Indians' demands. A law was passed abolishing discriminatory taxes on Indian traders, recognizing the legality of non-Christian marriages, and permitting the continued immigration of free Indians. Satyagraha—militant nonviolence in pursuit of social justice—had proved itself a powerful force in Gandhi's hands.

Gandhi Leads the Way

In 1915 Gandhi returned to India. His reputation had preceded him: the masses hailed him as a *Mahatma,* or "Great Soul"—a Hindu title of veneration for a man of great knowledge and humanity—and the name stuck. Feeling his way into Indian affairs, Gandhi, dressed in peasant garb, crisscrossed India on third-class trains, listening to common folk and talking to Congress party leaders. Moved by the wretched misery of the very poor, he led some sharecroppers against British landowners and organized a strike of textile workers in his native Gujarat. But it was the aftermath of the Amritsar Massacre that catapulted Gandhi to leadership of the national movement in India.

Drawing on his South African experience, Gandhi in 1920 launched a national campaign of nonviolent resistance to British rule. Denouncing British injustice, he urged his countrymen to boycott British goods and jobs and honors. He told peasants not to pay taxes or buy heavily taxed liquor. Gandhi electrified the people. The result was nothing less than a revolution in Indian politics.

The nationalist movement had previously touched only the tiny, prosperous, Western-educated elite. Now both the illiterate masses of village India and the educated classes heard a voice that seemed to be in harmony with their profoundest values. Even Gandhi's renunciation of sex—with his wife's consent—accorded with a popular

Hindu belief attributing special power to those who do not squander their life force in sexual intercourse. Gandhi's call for militant nonviolence was particularly appealing to the masses of Hindus who were not members of the warrior caste or the so-called military races and who were traditionally passive and nonviolent. The British had regarded ordinary Hindus as cowards. Gandhi told them that they could be courageous and even morally superior:

What do you think? Wherein is courage required—in blowing others to pieces from behind a cannon, or with a smiling face to approach a cannon and be blown to pieces? Who is the true warrior—he who keeps death always as a bosom-friend, or he who controls the death of others? Believe me that a man devoid of courage and manhood can never be a passive resister.[9]

Gandhi made Congress into a mass political party, welcoming members from every ethnic group and cooperating closely with the Muslim minority.

In 1922, some Indian resisters turned to violence. A mob murdered twenty-two policemen, and savage riots broke out. Gandhi abruptly called off his campaign. Arrested for fomenting rebellion, Gandhi told the British judge that he had committed "a Himalayan blunder to believe that India had accepted nonviolence."[10] Released from prison after two years, Gandhi set up a commune, established a national newspaper, and set out to reform Indian society and improve the lot of the poor. He welcomed the outcaste untouchables into his fellowship. He worked to help child widows, promote cottage industry, and end the use of alcohol. For Gandhi, moral improvement, social progress, and the national movement went hand in hand.

The resistance campaign of 1920–1922 left the British severely shaken. Although moderate Indians had participated effectively in the system of dual government, the commission formed by the British in 1927 to consider further steps toward self-rule included no Indian members. Indian resentment was intense. In 1929, the radical nationalists, led by the able and aristocratic Jawaharlal Nehru (1889–1964), pushed through the National Congress a resolution calling for virtual independence within a year. The British stiffened, and Indian radicals talked of a bloody showdown.

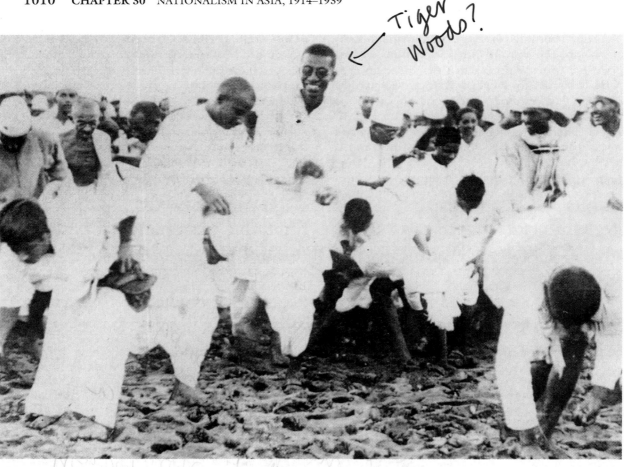

Tiger Woods?

The March to the Sea   Gandhi repeatedly used nonviolent confrontation to challenge British rule and mobilize the Indian masses. These marchers are picking up salt-encrusted sand in defiance of British law. Gandhi is on the left and wearing eyeglasses. He was arrested but the march continued (see Listening to the Past). *(Source: The Bettmann Archive)*

In this tense situation Gandhi masterfully reasserted his leadership. To satisfy the extremists, he took a hard line toward the British, but he controlled the extremists by insisting on nonviolent methods. He then organized another massive resistance campaign, this time against the hated salt tax, which affected every Indian family. Gandhi himself led fifty thousand people in a spectacular march to the sea to make salt without paying a tax, in defiance of the law. Gandhi was arrested but his followers continued the march to the sea. Demonstrating peacefully at the salt pans and disregarding orders to disperse, they were then beaten senseless by policemen in a brutal and well-publicized encounter (see Listening to the Past). The marchers did not even raise their arms to protect themselves. "They went down like ten-pins. . . . The survivors, without breaking ranks, silently and doggedly marched on until struck down."[11]

Over the next few months sixty thousand protesters followed Gandhi to jail. But this time there was very little rioting. Finally, in 1931, the frustrated, unnerved British released Gandhi from jail and sat down to negotiate with him, as an equal, over self-rule for India. There were many complications, including the determined opposition of diehard imperialists like Winston Churchill. But in 1935 the negotiations resulted in a new constitution, which greatly strengthened India's parliamentary representative institutions. It was virtually a blueprint for independence, which would come quickly after World War Two.

Gandhi inspired people far beyond India's borders. Martin Luther King, Jr., was later to be deeply influenced by his tactic and philosophy of nonviolent social action. Gandhi did much to transform the elitist nationalism of Indian intellectuals into a mighty mass movement with social as well as political concerns. Above all, Gandhi nurtured national identity and self-respect. As Nehru summed it up, Gandhi "instilled courage and man-hood in India's people; . . . courage is the one sure foundation of character, he had said; without courage there is no morality, no religion, no love."[12]

Despite his best efforts, Gandhi failed to heal a widening split between Hindus and Muslims. The development of an Indian nationalism based largely on Hindu symbols and customs increasingly disturbed the Muslim minority. Tempers mounted, and atrocities were committed by both sides. By the late 1930s the leaders of the Muslim

Textile Workers in Lancashire When Gandhi came to Britain for negotiations in 1931, these textile workers cheered him. The Great Depression had sent unemployment soaring, but many British workers told Gandhi that they could understand why he had organized an effective boycott against the sale of British cloth in India. *(Source: The Bettman Archive)*

League were calling for the creation of a Muslim nation in British India, a "Pakistan" or "land of the pure." As in Palestine, the rise of conflicting nationalisms in India was to lead to tragedy (see page 0000).

✤ TURMOIL IN EAST ASIA

Because of the efforts of the Meiji reformers, nationalism and modernization were well developed in Japan by 1914. Not only was Japan capable of competing politically and economically with the world's leading nations, but it had already begun building its own empire and proclaiming its special mission in Asia. China lagged far behind, but after 1912 the pace of nationalist development there began to quicken.

In the 1920s the Chinese nationalist movement managed to win a large measure of political independence from the imperialist West and promoted extensive modernization. But these achievements were soon undermined by internal conflict and war with an expanding Japan. Nationalism also flourished elsewhere in Asia, scoring a major victory in the Philippine Islands.

The Rise of Nationalist China

The revolution of 1911–1912, which overthrew the Manchu Dynasty (see page 909), opened an era of unprecedented change for Chinese society. Before the revolution, many progressive Chinese had realized that fundamental technological and political reforms were necessary to save the Chinese state and to meet the many-sided Western challenge. Most had hoped, however, to preserve the traditional core of Chinese civilization and culture. The fall of the two-thousand-year-old dynastic system shattered such hopes. If the emperor himself was no longer sacred, what was? Everything was open to question and to alteration.

The central figure in the revolution was a crafty old military man, Yuan Shigai (Yüan Shih-k'ai). Called out of retirement to save the dynasty, Yuan (1859–1916) betrayed the Manchus and convinced the revolutionaries that he was a strong man who could unite the country peacefully and prevent foreign intervention. Once elected president of the republic, however, Yuan concentrated on building his own power. In 1913, he used military force to dissolve China's parliament and ruled as a dictator. China's first modern revolution had failed.

The extent of the failure became apparent only after Yuan's death in 1916. The central government in Beijing (Peking) almost disintegrated. For more than a decade power resided in a multitude of local military leaders, the so-called warlords. Most warlords were men of strong, flamboyant personality, capable of building armies by preying on the peasantry and of winning legal recognition from Beijing. None of them proved able to establish either a new dynasty or a modern state. Their wars, taxes, and corruption created only terrible suffering.

Foreign imperialism intensified the agony of warlordism. Although China declared its neutrality in 1914, Japan used the Great War in Europe as an opportunity to seize Germany's holdings on the Shandong (Shantung) Peninsula and in 1915 forced China to accept Japanese control of Shandong and southern Manchuria (see Map 29.4, page 000). Japan's expansion angered China's growing middle class and enraged China's young patriots. On May 4, 1919, five thousand students in Beijing exploded against the decision of the Versailles Peace Conference to leave the Shandong Peninsula in Japanese hands. This famous incident launched the May Fourth Movement, which opposed both foreign domination and warlord government.

The May Fourth Movement and the anti-imperialism of Bolshevik Russia renewed the hopes of Chinese nationalists. Struggling for a foothold in southern China, Sun Yat-sen (1866–1925) decided in 1923 to ally his Nationalist party, or Guomindang (Kuomintang), with the Communist Third International and the newly formed Chinese Communist party. The result was the first of many so-called national liberation fronts, in keeping with Lenin's blueprint for (temporarily) uniting all anti-conservative, anti-imperialist forces in a common revolutionary struggle. In an effort to develop a disciplined party apparatus and a well-indoctrinated party army, Sun reorganized the Nationalist party along Bolshevik lines.

Sun, however, was no Communist. In his *Three Principles of the People,* elaborating on the official Nationalist party ideology—nationalism, democ-

EAST ASIA, 1911–1939

1911–1912	Revolution in China overthrows Manchu Dynasty and establishes republic
1915	Japan seizes German holdings in China and expands into southern Manchuria
May 4, 1919	Demonstration by Chinese students against Versailles Peace Conference and Japan sparks broad nationalist movement
1920s	New Cultural Movement challenges traditional Chinese values
1922	Japan signs naval agreement with Western powers
1923	Sun Yat-sen allies the Nationalist party with Chinese Communists Kita Ikki advocates ultranationalism in Japan
1925–1928	Chiang Kai-shek, leader of the Nationalist Party, attacks warlord government and seeks to unify China
1927	Chiang Kai-shek purges his Communist allies Mao Tse-tung recognizes the revolutionary potential of the Chinese peasantry
1930–1934	Nationalists campaign continually against the Chinese Communists
1931	Mukden Incident leads to Japanese occupation of Manchuria
1932	Japan proclaims Manchuria an independent state
1934	Mao leads Communists on Long March to new base in northwestern China The Philippines gain self-governing commonwealth status from United States
1936	Japan allies with Germany in anti-Communist pact
1937	Japanese militarists launch general attack on China

racy, and people's livelihood—nationalism remained of prime importance:

Compared to the other peoples of the world we have the greatest population and our civilization is four thousand years old; we should be advancing in the front rank with the nations of Europe and America. But the Chinese people have only family and clan solidarity, they do not have national spirit. Therefore even though we have four hundred million people gathered together in one China, in reality they are just a heap of loose sand. Today we are the poorest and weakest nation in the world, and occupy the lowest position in international affairs. . . . If we do not earnestly espouse nationalism and weld together our four hundred million people into a strong nation, there is a danger of China's being lost and our people being destroyed. If we wish to avert this catastrophe, we must espouse nationalism and bring this national spirit to the salvation of the country.[13]

Democracy, in contrast, had a less exalted meaning. Sun equated it with firm rule by the Nationalists, who would promote the people's livelihood through land reform and welfare measures. Sun was in some ways a traditional Chinese rebel and reformer who wanted to re-establish order and protect the peasants.

Sun's plan was to use the Nationalist party's revolutionary army to crush the warlords and reunite China under a strong central government. When Sun unexpectedly died in 1925, this task was assumed by Jiang Jieshi (Chiang Kai-shek), the young Japanese-educated director of the party's army training school. In 1926 and 1927, Jiang (1887–1975) led enthusiastic Nationalist armies in a highly successful attack on warlord governments in central and northern China. Preceded by teams of party propagandists, the well-disciplined Nationalist armies were welcomed by the people. In a series of complicated moves, the Nationalists consolidated their rule in 1928 and established a new capital at Nanjing (Nanking). Foreign states recognized the Nanjing government, and superficial observers believed China to be truly reunified.

In fact, national unification was only skin deep. China remained a vast agricultural country plagued by foreign concessions, regional differences, and a lack of modern communications. Moreover, Japan was opposed to a China strong enough to challenge Japan's stranglehold on Manchuria. And the uneasy alliance between the Nationalist party and the Chinese Communist party had turned into a bitter, deadly rivalry. Justifiably fearful of Communist subversion of the Nationalist government and encouraged by his military success and by wealthy Chinese capitalists, Jiang decided in April 1927 to liquidate his left-wing "allies" in a bloody purge. Secret agents raided Communist cells without warning, and soldiers gunned down suspects on sight. Chinese Communists went into hiding and vowed revenge.

China's Intellectual Revolution

Nationalism was the most powerful idea in China between 1911 and 1929, but it was only one aspect of a complex intellectual revolution that hammered at traditional Chinese thought and custom, advocated cultural renaissance, and pushed China into the modern world. Two other currents in that intellectual revolution, generally known as the New Culture Movement, were significant.

The New Culture Movement was founded by young Western-oriented intellectuals in Beijing during the May Fourth era. These intellectuals fiercely attacked China's ancient Confucian ethics, which subordinated subjects to rulers, sons to fathers, and wives to husbands. Confucius had lived in a distant feudal age, they said; his teachings were totally inappropriate to modern life. In such widely read magazines as *New Youth* and *New Tide,* the modernists provocatively advocated new and anti-Confucian virtues: individualism, democratic equality, and the critical scientific method. They also promoted the use of simple, understandable written language, a language freed from classical scholarship and literary conventions, as a means to clear thinking and mass education. China, they said, needed a whole new culture, a radically different world-view.

The most influential of these intellectuals championing liberalism was Hu Shi (1891–1962). Educated on a scholarship in the United States, the mature Hu Shi envisioned a vague and uninspiring future. The liberation and reconstruction of China was possible, he said, but it would have to occur gradually, "bit by bit, drop by drop." Hu personified the limitations of the Western liberal tradition in China.

The other major current growing out of the New Culture Movement was Marxian socialism. It too was Western in origin, "scientific" in approach, and materialist in its denial of religious belief and Confucian family ethics. But while liberalism and individualism reflected the bewildering range of Western thought since the Enlightenment, Marxian socialism offered Chinese intellectuals the certainty of a single all-encompassing creed. As one young Communist exclaimed: "I am now able to impose order on all the ideas which I could not reconcile; I have found the key to all the problems which appeared to me self-contradictory and insoluble."[14]

Marxism was undeniably Western and therefore modern. But it also provided a means of criticizing Western dominance, thereby salving Chinese pride. Chinese Communists could blame China's pitiful weakness on rapacious foreign capitalistic imperialism. Thus Marxism, as modified by Lenin and applied by the Bolsheviks in the Soviet Union, appeared as a means of catching up with the hated but envied West. For Chinese believers, it promised salvation soon.

Chinese Communists could and did interpret Marxism-Leninism to appeal to the masses—the peasants. Mao Zedong (Mao Tse-tung) in particular recognized quickly the enormous revolutionary potential of the Chinese peasantry, impoverished and oppressed by parasitic landlords. A member of a prosperous, hard-working peasant family, Mao (1893–1976) converted to Marxian socialism in 1918 while employed as an assistant librarian at Beijing University. He began his revolutionary career as an urban labor organizer. In 1925 protest strikes by Chinese textile workers against their Japanese employers unexpectedly spread from the big coastal cities to rural China, prompting Mao to reconsider the peasants. Investigating the rapid growth of radical peasant associations in Hunan province, Mao argued passionately in a 1927 report that

the force of the peasantry is like that of the raging winds and driving rain. It is rapidly increasing in violence. No force can stand in its way. The peasantry will tear apart all nets which bind it and hasten along the road to liberation. They will bury beneath them all forces of imperialism, militarism, corrupt officialdom, village bosses and evil gentry. Every revolutionary party, every revolutionary comrade will be subjected to their scrutiny and be accepted or rejected by them.[15]

The task of Communists was to harness the peasant hurricane and use its elemental force to destroy the existing order and take power. Mao's first experiment in peasant revolt—the Autumn Harvest Uprising of September 1927—was no more successful than the abortive insurrections of urban workers launched by his more orthodox comrades. But Mao learned quickly. He advocated equal distribution of land and broke up his forces into small guerrilla groups. After 1928 he and his supporters built up a self-governing Communist soviet, centered at Ruijin (Juichin) in southeastern China, and dug in against Nationalist attacks.

The Changing Chinese Family

For many generations, Confucian reverence for the family and family ties had helped to stabilize traditional Chinese society and had given life meaning. The Confucian principle of subordination had suffused family life—subordination of the individual to the group, of the young to the old, of the wife to the husband.

A Daughter of Han, a rare autobiography of a Chinese woman, as told to an American friend, of-

Mao Zedong Adapting Marxian theory to Chinese reality, Mao concentrated on the revolutionary potential of the peasantry. Here the forty-year-old Mao is preaching his gospel to representatives of poor peasants in southern China in 1933. *(Source: Wide World Photos)*

fers an unforgettable glimpse of traditional Chinese family life. Born in 1867 to poor parents in a northern city, Lao Tai Tai lived it all. Her footbinding was delayed to age nine, "since I loved so much to run and play." When the bandages were finally drawn tight, "my feet hurt so much that for two years I had to crawl on my knees."[16] Her arranged marriage at fourteen was a disaster: her husband was a drug addict—"in those days everyone took opium to some extent"—who grabbed everything to pay for his habit. "There was no freedom then for women," and she endured her situation until her husband sold their four-year-old daughter to buy opium. Taking her remaining baby daughter, Lao Tai Tai fled. She became a beggar, a cook in wealthy households, and a peddler of luxury goods to wealthy cooped-up women.

The two unshakable values that buoyed her were a tough, fatalistic acceptance—"Only fortune that comes of itself will come. There is no use to seek for it"—and devotion to her family. Lao Tai Tai eventually returned home to her husband, who was "good" in those years, "but I did not miss him when he died. I had my newborn son and I was happy. My house was established. . . . Truly all my life I spent thinking of my family." Her lifelong devotion was reciprocated by her faithful son and granddaughter, who cared for her well in old age.

Lao Tai Tai's remarkable life history encompasses both old and new Chinese attitudes toward the family. Her son moved to the city, prospered, and had only one wife. Her granddaughter eventually became a college teacher, an anti-Japanese patriot, and a determined foe of arranged marriages, admirably personifying the trend toward greater freedom and equality for Chinese women after 1911. Foot-binding was outlawed and gradually

died out unlamented. Marriage for love became increasingly common, and unprecedented educational and economic opportunities opened up for women. Polygamy declined. In the short space of three generations, rising nationalism and the intellectual revolution accomplished monumental changes in Chinese family life.

From Liberalism to Ultranationalism in Japan

The efforts of the Meiji reformers (see page 906) to build a powerful nationalistic state and resist Western imperialism were spectacularly successful and deeply impressive to Japan's fellow Asians. The Japanese, alone among the peoples of Asia, had mastered modern industrial technology by 1910 and fought victorious wars against both China and Russia. The First World War brought more triumphs. Japan easily seized Germany's Asian holdings and held on to most of them as League of Nations mandates. The Japanese economy expanded

❀ **Lao Tai Tai** Seated beside her American friend Ida Pruitt, a tough and resilient Lao Tai Tai shares her remarkable story and reflects on the meaning of her life. *(Source: From Ida Pruitt,* A Daughter of Han, *Yale University Press. Reproduced with permission)*

Japanese Suffragettes   In the 1920s Japanese women pressed for political emancipation in demonstrations like this one, but they did not receive the right to vote until 1946. Like these suffragettes, some young women adopted Western fashions. Most workers in modern Japanese textile factories were also women. *(Source: Mansell Collection)*

enormously. Profits soared as Japan won new markets that wartime Europe could no longer supply.

In the early 1920s Japan seemed to make further progress on all fronts. Most Japanese nationalists believed that Japan had a semidivine mission to enlighten and protect Asia, but some were convinced that they could achieve their goal peacefully. In 1922, Japan signed a naval arms limitation treaty with the Western powers and returned some of its control over the Shandong Peninsula to China. These conciliatory moves reduced tensions in East Asia. At home, Japan seemed headed toward genuine democracy. The electorate expanded twelve-fold between 1918 and 1925 as all males over twenty-five won the vote. Two-party competition was intense, and cabinet ministers were made responsible to the lower house. Japanese living standards were the highest in Asia. Literacy was universal.

Japan's remarkable rise, however, was accompanied by serious problems. Japan had a rapidly growing population, but natural resources were scarce. As early as the 1920s Japan was exporting manufactured goods in order to pay for imports of food and essential raw materials. Deeply enmeshed in world trade, Japan was vulnerable to every boom and bust. These conditions reinforced the widespread belief that colonies and foreign expansion were matters of life and death for Japan.

Also, rapid industrial development had created an imbalanced "dualistic" economy. The modern sector consisted of a handful of giant conglomerate

Farewell, my concubine...

firms, the *zaibatsu,* or "financial combine." A zaibatsu firm like Mitsubishi employed thousands of workers and owned banks, mines, steel mills, cotton factories, shipyards, and trading companies, all of which were closely interrelated. Zaibatsu firms had enormous economic power and dominated the other sector of the economy, which consisted of an unorganized multitude of peasant farmers and craftsmen. The result was financial oligarchy, corruption of government officials, and a weak middle class.

Behind the façade of party politics, the old and new elites—the emperor, high government officials, big businessmen, and military leaders—were jockeying savagely for the real power. Cohesive leadership, which had played such an important role in Japan's modernization by the Meiji reformers, had ceased to exist. By far the most serious challenge to peaceful progress, however, was fanatical nationalism. As in Europe, ultranationalism first emerged in Japan in the late nineteenth century but did not flower fully until the First World War and the 1930s.

Though often vague, Japan's ultranationalists shared several fundamental beliefs. They were violently anti-Western. They rejected democracy, big business, and Marxian socialism, which they blamed for destroying the older, superior Japanese practices that they wanted to restore. Reviving old myths, they stressed the emperor's godlike qualities and the samurai warrior's code of honor and obedience. Despising party politics, they assassinated moderate leaders and plotted armed uprisings to achieve their goals. Above all else, the ultranationalists preached foreign expansion. Like Western imperialists shouldering "the White Man's Burden," Japanese ultranationalists thought their mission was a noble one. "Asia for the Asians" was their self-satisfied rallying cry. As the famous ultranationalist Kita Ikki wrote in 1923:

Our seven hundred million brothers in China and India have no other path to independence than that offered by our guidance and protection. . . . The noble Greece of Asian culture [Japan] must complete her national reorganization on the basis of her own national polity. At the same time, let her lift the virtuous banner of an Asian league and take the leadership in a world federation which must come.[17]

The ultranationalists were noisy and violent in the 1920s, but it took the Great Depression of the 1930s to tip the scales decisively in their favor. The worldwide depression hit Japan like a tidal wave in 1930. Exports and wages collapsed; unemployment and raw suffering soared. Starving peasants ate the bark off trees and sold their daughters to brothels. The ultranationalists blamed the system, and people listened.

Japan Against China

Among those who listened with particular care were young Japanese army officers in Manchuria, the underpopulated, resource-rich province of northeastern China, controlled by the Japanese army since its victory over Russia in 1905. Many junior Japanese officers in Manchuria came from the peasantry and were distressed by the stories of rural suffering they heard from home. They also knew that the budget and prestige of the Japanese army had declined in the prosperous 1920s.

Most worrisome of all to the young officers was the rise of Chinese nationalism. This new political force challenged the control that Japan exercised over Manchuria through Chinese warlords that they controlled. In response, junior Japanese officers in Manchuria, in cooperation with top generals in Tokyo, secretly manufactured an excuse for aggression in late 1931. They blew up some tracks on a Japanese-owned railroad near the city of Mukden and then quickly occupied all of Manchuria in "self-defense."

In 1932 Japan proclaimed Manchuria an independent state and installed a member of the old Manchu dynasty as puppet emperor. When the League of Nations condemned its aggression in Manchuria, Japan resigned in protest. Politics in Japan became increasingly chaotic. The army, though reporting directly to the emperor of Japan, was clearly an independent force subject to no outside control.

For China, the Japanese conquest of Manchuria was disastrous. Japanese aggression in Manchuria drew attention away from modernizing efforts, which in any event had been none too vigorous. The Nationalist government promoted a massive boycott of Japanese goods but lost interest in social reform. Above all, the Nationalist government after 1931 completely neglected land reform and the grinding poverty of the Chinese peasants. As in many poor agricultural societies throughout history, Chinese peasants paid roughly half of their crops to their landlords as rent. Ownership of land was very unequal. One careful study estimated that fully half of the land was owned by a mere 4 percent of the families, usually absentee landlords living in cities. Poor peasants and farm laborers—70 percent of the rural population—owned only one-sixth of the land.

As a result, peasants were heavily in debt and chronically underfed. Eggs and meat accounted for only 2 percent of the food consumed by poor and middle-income peasants. A contemporary Chinese economist spelled out the revolutionary implications: "It seems clear that the land problem in China today is as acute as that of eighteenth-century France or nineteenth-century Russia."[18] Mao Zedong certainly agreed.

Having abandoned land reform, partly because they themselves were often landowners, the Nationalists under Jiang Jieshi devoted their energies between 1930 and 1934 to five great campaigns of encirclement and extermination against the Communists' rural power base in southeastern China. In 1934 they closed in for the kill, only to miss again. In one of the most incredible sagas of modern times, the main Communist army broke out of the Nationalist encirclement, beat off attacks, and marched 6,000 miles in twelve months to a remote region on the northwestern border (Map 30.2). Of the estimated 100,000 men and women who began the Long March, only from 8,000 to 10,000 reached the final destination. There Mao built up his forces once again, established a new territorial base, and won the support of local peasants by undertaking land reform.

In 1937, the Japanese military and the ultranationalists were in command and decided to use a minor incident near Beijing as a pretext for a general attack. The Nationalist government, which had just formed a united front with the Communists in response to the demands of Chinese patriots, fought hard but could not halt the Japanese. By late 1938, Japanese armies occupied sizable portions of coastal China (see Map 30.2). The Nationalists and the Communists had retreated to the interior, both refusing to accept defeat. The determination of the Communist guerrillas equaled that of the Nationalists, and their political skill proved superior. In 1939, as Europe (and the United States) edged toward another great war, the undeclared war between China and Japan bogged down in a savage stalemate. The bloody clash on the mainland provided a spectacular example of conflicting nationalisms, convulsing China and prepar-

The Fall of Nanjing   In December 1937 Japanese armies crossed into the fallen Chinese city and disgraced themselves in a frenzy of destruction known as the Rape of Nanjing. Japanese soldiers' reputation for brutality lasted until the end of World War II. *(Source: Robert Hunt Library)*

ing for Communist victory (see pages 1133, 1134).

Southeast Asia

The tide of nationalism was also rising in Southeast Asia. Like their counterparts in India, China, and Japan, nationalists in Southeast Asia urgently

U.S.S.R.

MANCHURIA

Qiqihar

Jiamusi

OUTER MONGOLIA
(Independent 1924)

Harbin

Baotou

Zhangjiakou
(Kalgan)

Jinzhou

Shenyang
(Mukden)

KOREA
(Japanese 1910–1945)

Beijing

Tianjin

Lanzhou

Taiyuan

Lüshun
(Port Arthur)

Yan'an

SHAANXI

Xi'an

Jinan

Qingdao

Luoyang

Zhengzhou

Huang He (Yellow)

Xuzhou

CHINA

Nanjing

Chengdu

Chang Jiang
(Yangtze)

SICHUAN

Wuhan

Hangzhou

Shanghai

Chongqing

Nanchang

Zunyi

Changsha

Kiangsi Soviet under
Mao Zedong and
Chu Teh, 1929–1934

HUNAN

Guiyang

Ji'an

Kunming

Canton uprising
Dec. 1927

Shantou

Xiamen
(Amoy)

TAIWAN
(Japanese
1895–1945)

*PACIFIC
OCEAN*

BURMA

Guangzhou
(Canton)

Hong Kong
(British)

Hailufeng Soviet,
1927–1928

FRENCH
INDO-CHINA

Amur

Ussuri

Areas under Communist control before Nov. 1934

Areas under Communist control, 1929–1938

Areas occupied by Japan by end of 1938

Route of the Long March, Oct. 1934–Oct. 1935: Main forces from Ji'an

Other forces

wanted genuine political independence and freedom from foreign rule. In both French Indochina and the Dutch East Indies, local nationalists, inspired by events elsewhere in Asia, pressed their own demands. In both cases they ran up against an imperialist stone wall.

In the words of one historian, "Indochina was governed by Frenchmen for Frenchmen, and the great liberal slogans of liberty, equality, and fraternity were not considered to be export goods for overseas dominions."[19] This uncompromising attitude stimulated the growth of an equally stubborn Communist opposition, which despite ruthless repression emerged as the dominant anti-French force.

In the East Indies—modern Indonesia—the Dutch made some concessions after the First World War, establishing a people's council with very limited lawmaking power. But in the 1930s the Dutch cracked down hard, jailing all the important nationalist leaders. Like the French, the Dutch were determined to hold on.

In the Philippines, however, a well-established nationalist movement achieved greater success. As in colonial Latin America, the Spanish in the Philippines had been indefatigable missionaries. By the late nineteenth century 80 percent of the Filipino population was Catholic. Filipinos shared a common cultural heritage as well as a common racial origin. Education, especially for girls, was quite advanced for Southeast Asia, and in 1843 a higher percentage of people could read in the Philippines than in Spain itself. Economic development helped to create a westernized elite, which turned first to reform and then to revolution in the 1890s. As in Egypt or Turkey, long-standing intimate contact with Western civilization created a strong nationalist movement at an early date.

Filipino nationalists were bitterly disillusioned when the United States, having taken the Philippines from Spain in the Spanish-American War of 1898, ruthlessly beat down a patriotic revolt and denied the universal Filipino desire for independence. The Americans claimed that the Philippines were not ready and might be seized by Germany or Britain. As the imperialist power in the Philippines, the United States encouraged education and promoted capitalistic economic development. As in British India, an elected legislature was given some real powers. In 1919 President Wilson even promised eventual independence, though subsequent Republican administrations saw it as a distant goal.

As in India and French Indochina, demands for independence grew. One important contributing factor was American racial attitudes. Americans treated Filipinos as inferiors and introduced segregationist practices borrowed from the American South. American racism made passionate nationalists of many Filipinos. However, it was the Great Depression that had the most radical impact on the Philippines.

As the United States collapsed economically, the Philippines suddenly appeared to be a liability rather than an asset. American farm groups lobbied for protection from cheap Filipino sugar. To protect American jobs, labor unions demanded an end to Filipino immigration. In 1934 Congress made the Philippines a self-governing commonwealth and scheduled independence for 1944. Sugar imports were reduced, and immigration was limited to only fifty Filipinos per year.

Like Britain and France in the Middle East, the United States was determined to hold on to its big military bases in the Philippines as it permitted increased local self-government and promised eventual political independence. Some Filipino nationalists denounced the continued presence of U.S. fleets and armies. Others were less certain that the American presence was the immediate problem. Japan was fighting in China and expanding economically into the Philippines and throughout Southeast Asia. By 1939, a new threat to Filipino independence appeared to come from Asia itself.

MAP 30.2 The Chinese Communist Movement and the War with Japan, 1927–1938
After urban uprisings ordered by Stalin failed in 1927, Mao Zedong succeeded in forming a self-governing Communist soviet in mountainous southern China. Relentless Nationalist attacks between 1930 and 1934 finally forced the Long March to Yenan, where the Communists were well positioned for guerrilla war against the Japanese.

SUMMARY

The Asian revolt against the West began before the First World War. But only after 1914 did Asian nationalist movements broaden their bases and become capable of challenging Western domination effectively. These mass movements sought human dignity as well as political freedom. Generally speaking, Asian nationalists favored modernization and adopted Western techniques and ideas even as they rejected Western rule. Everywhere Asian nationalists had to fight long and hard, though their struggle gained momentum from growing popular support and the encouragement of the Soviet Union.

Asia's nationalist movements arose out of separate historical experiences and distinct cultures. Variations on the common theme of nationalism were evident in Turkey, the Arab world, India, China, Japan, and the Philippines. This diversity helps explain why Asian peoples became defensive in their relations with one another while rising against Western rule. Like earlier nationalists in Europe, Asian nationalists developed a strong sense of "we" and "they"; "they" included other Asians as well as Europeans. Nationalism meant freedom, modernization, and cultural renaissance, but it nonetheless proved a mixed blessing.

NOTES

1. K. M. Panikkar, *Asia and Western Dominance: A Survey of the Vasco da Gama Epoch of Asian History* (London: George Allen & Unwin, 1959), p. 197.
2. Quoted in H. Grimal, *La Décolonisation, 1919–1965* (Paris: Armand Colin, 1965), p. 100.
3. Quoted in P. Mansfield, *The Ottoman Empire and Its Successors* (New York: St. Martin's Press, 1973), p. 18.
4. H. Armstrong, *Turkey in Travail: The Birth of a New Nation* (London: John Lane, 1925), p. 75.
5. Quoted in Lord Kinross, *Atatürk: A Biography of Mustafa Kemal, Father of Modern Turkey* (New York: Morrow, 1965), p. 181.
6. P. Spear, *India, Pakistan, and the West,* 3d ed. (Oxford: Oxford University Press, 1958), p. 67.
7. Quoted in E. Erikson, *Gandhi's Truth: On the Origins of Militant Nonviolence* (New York: Norton, 1969), p. 105.
8. H. Tinker, *A New System of Slavery: The Export of Indian Labour Overseas, 1830–1920* (London: Oxford University Press, 1974).
9. Quoted in Erikson, *Gandhi's Truth,* p. 225.
10. Quoted in W. Bingham, H. Conroy, and F. Iklé, *A History of Asia,* vol. 1, 2d ed. (Boston: Allyn and Bacon, 1974), p. 447.
11. W. Miller, *I Found No Peace: The Journal of a Foreign Correspondent* (New York: Simon and Schuster, 1936), p. 193.
12. Quoted in L. Rudolph and S. Rudolph, *The Modernity of Tradition: Political Development in India* (Chicago: University of Chicago Press, 1967), p. 248.
13. Quoted in W. T. deBary, W. Chan, and B. Watson, *Sources of Chinese Tradition* (New York: Columbia University Press, 1964), pp. 768–769.
14. Quoted in J. F. Fairbank, E. O. Reischauer, and A. M. Craig, *East Asia: Tradition and Transformation* (Boston: Houghton Mifflin, 1973), p. 774.
15. Quoted in B. I. Schwartz, *Chinese Communism and the Rise of Mao* (Cambridge, Mass.: Harvard University Press, 1951), p. 74.
16. I. Pruitt, *A Daughter of Han: The Autobiography of a Chinese Working Woman* (New Haven, Conn.: Yale University Press, 1945), p. 22. Other quotations are taken, in order, from pages 83, 71, 182, 166, and 235.
17. Quoted in W. T. deBary, R. Tsunoda, and D. Keene, *Sources of Japanese Tradition,* vol. 2 (New York: Columbia University Press, 1958), p. 269.
18. Quoted in O. Lang, *Chinese Family and Society* (New Haven, Conn.: Yale University Press, 1946), p. 70.
19. Quoted in W. Bingham, H. Conroy, and F. Iklé, *A History of Asia,* vol. 2, 2d ed. (Boston: Allyn and Bacon, 1974), p. 480.

SUGGESTED READING

All of the works cited in the Notes are highly recommended. Two important general interpretations of nationalism and independence movements are P. Chatterjee, *Nationalist Thought and the Colonial World: A Derivative Discourse* (1986), and R. Emerson, *From Empire to Nation: The Rise to Self-Assertion of Asian and African Peoples* (1960). These may be compared with the provocative works of E. Kedourie, including *Nationalism in Asia and Africa* (1970), and with an influential global history of the twentieth century by G. Barraclough, *An Introduction to Contemporary History* (1975). B. Lewis, *The Shaping of the Modern Middle East* (1993), is a reflective work by a leading historian, which complements A. Hourani,

History of the Arab Peoples (1991). On Turkey, in addition to Lord Kinross's *Atatürk* (1965), see B. Lewis, *The Emergence of Modern Turkey* (1961), and D. Kushner, *The Rise of Turkish Nationalism, 1876–1908* (1977). Peter Mansfield, *The Arab World: A Comprehensive History* (1976), and S. G. Haim, ed., *Arab Nationalism: An Anthology* (1964), provide engaging general coverage and important source materials. W. Lacqueur, *A History of Zionism* (1972), and A. Eban, *My People* (1968), discuss the Jewish homeland in Palestine. The Arab viewpoint is presented by G. Antonius, *The Arab Awakening: The Story of the Arab National Movement* (1946). R. Cottam, *Nationalism in Iran,* rev. ed. (1979), complements the classic study of D. Wilbur, *Iran: Past and Present,* 9th ed. (1981).

The historical literature on modern India is very rich. S. Wolpert, *A New History of India,* 4th ed. (1993), is an excellent introduction, with up-to-date scholarship and detailed suggestions for further reading. Also see the handsomely illustrated volume by F. Watson, *A Concise History of India* (1975). In addition to the biography by Erikson cited in the Notes, L. Fischer, *Gandhi: His Life and Message for the World* (1954), is fascinating. J. Brown, *Gandhi's Rise to Power: Indian Politics, 1915–1922* (1972), and V. Mehta, *Mahatma Gandhi and His Apostles* (1977), are major studies. Developments in the Muslim community are considered by P. Hardy, *The Muslims of British India* (1972); B. Metcalf, *Islamic Revival in British India: Deoband, 1860–1900* (1982); and F. Robinson, *Atlas of the Islamic World Since 1500* (1982), a beautifully illustrated survey encompassing far more than India.

Studies of China in the twentieth century are also very numerous. J. Spence, *The Search for Modern China* (1990), and I. Hsü, *The Rise of Modern China,* 4th ed. (1990), are comprehensive studies with extensive bibliographies, which may be supplemented by the documentary collection of F. Schurmann and O. Schell, eds., *Republican China: Nationalism, War and the Rise of Communism, 1911–1949* (1967). J. Spence, *The Gate of Heavenly Peace: The Chinese and Their Revolution, 1895–1980* (1981), skillfully focuses on leading literary figures. T. Chow, *The May Fourth Movement: Intellectual Revolution in Modern China* (1960), examines a critical time period. Other important studies of China in this period include R. Hofheinz, Jr., *The Broken Wave: The Chinese Communist Peasant Movement, 1922–1928* (1977); S. Schram, *Mao Tse-tung* (1966); and H. Schriffrin, *Sun Yat-sen and the Origins of the Chinese Revolution* (1970). L. Eastman, *Family, Consistency and Change in China's Social and Economic History, 1550–1949* (1974), is a masterful synthesis. P. Ebrey, ed., *Chinese Civilization and Society: A Sourcebook* (1981), complements the classic studies of the Chinese family by Lang and Pruitt, which may be compared with M. J. Levy, *The Family Revolution in Modern China* (1949).

E. Reischauer, *Japan: The Story of a Nation,* rev. ed. (1970), and P. Duus, *The Rise of Modern Japan* (1976), are excellent interpretations of the recent history of the island nation. W. Lockwood, *The Economic Development of Japan, 1868–1938* (1954), and R. Storry, *The Double Patriots: A Story of Japanese Nationalism* (1973), are valuable specialized works. M. Hane, *Peasants, Rebels, and Outcasts: The Underside of Modern Japan* (1982), sees few benefits for the poor before 1945. S. Garon, *The State and Labor in Modern Japan* (1988), skillfully analyzes the history of Japanese labor relations. Two edited collections, J. Morley, *The China Quagmire* (1983), and R. Myers and M. Peattie, *The Japanese Colonial Expansion, 1895–1945* (1984), probe Japan's imperial expansion.

For Southeast Asia, see D. G. E. Hall, *A History of South-East Asia,* 4th ed. (1981); J. Pluvier, *South-East Asia from Colonialism to Independence* (1974); and the Suggested Reading for Chapter 34. Two more recommended works are M. Osborne, *Southeast Asia: An Illustrated History,* expanded ed. (1988), and D. R. Sardesa, *Southeast Past and Present,* 2d ed. (1989).

Nonviolent Resistance in India

Mahatma Gandhi developed a powerful spiritual theory of social action. Drawing on both Hindu and Christian morality, Gandhi taught that the weak and unarmed could combine love and courage to overcome oppression and injustice. Gandhi's chosen tactic was nonviolent resistance, which challenged British rule in India with illegal protest marches and mass civil disobedience. Nonviolent resistance demanded tremendous self-discipline from protesters because they had to "turn the other cheek" and accept great pain and suffering.

The first protest campaign, in 1920–1922, ended in violence, and Gandhi felt compelled to call it off. In 1930 Gandhi launched a new round of nonviolent disobedience, which focused on the hated salt tax. Gandhi was jailed, but his army of peaceful resisters continued the struggle and did not give in to violence.

One eyewitness was Webb Miller, an American correspondent dispatched from London to cover the story in India. Arriving in India by air on the weekly passenger service after fifteen days and 16,000 miles, Miller met with Congress party leaders and caught up with the protesters near the sea. There he saw the dramatic climax of the salt-tax demonstrations, foiled the British censorship, and got the story out to the world's newspapers. The following account comes from Webb's 1936 autobiography.

After plodding about six miles across country [from the nearest railroad station] . . . I reached the assembling place of the Gandhi followers. Several long, open, thatched sheds . . . buzzed like a beehive with some 2,500 Congress or Gandhi men dressed in the regulation uniform of rough homespun cotton dhotis and triangular Gandhi caps. . . . I was warmly welcomed by young college-educated, English-speaking men and escorted to Mme. Naidu. The famous Indian poetess . . . explained that she was busy martialing her forces for the demonstration against the salt pans.

. . . She was educated in England and spoke English fluently.

Mme. Naidu called for prayer before the march started and the entire assemblage knelt. She exhorted them: "Gandhi's body is in jail but his soul is with you. India's prestige is in your hands. You must not use any violence under any circumstances. You will be beaten but you must not resist; you must not even raise a hand to ward off blows." Wild, shrill cheers terminated her speech.

Slowly and in silence the throng commenced the half-mile march to the salt deposits. . . .

The salt deposits were surrounded by ditches filled with water and guarded by four hundred native Surat police in khaki shorts and brown turbans. Half a dozen British officials commanded them. The police carried *lathis*—five-foot clubs tipped with steel. Inside the stockade twenty-five native riflemen were drawn up.

In complete silence the Gandhi men drew up and halted a hundred yards from the stockade. A picked column advanced from the crowd, waded the ditches, and approached the barbed-wire stockade, which the Surat police surrounded, holding their clubs at the ready. Police officials ordered the marchers to disperse. . . . The column silently ignored the warning and slowly walked forward.

Suddenly, at a word of command, scores of native policemen rushed upon the advancing marchers and rained blows on their heads with their steel-shod *lathis*. Not one of the marchers even raised an arm to fend off the blows. They went down like ten-pins. From where I stood I heard the sickening whacks of the clubs on unprotected skulls. The waiting crowd of watchers groaned and sucked in their breaths in sympathetic pain at every blow.

Those struck down fell sprawling, unconscious or writhing in pain with fractured skulls or broken shoulders. In two or three minutes the ground was quilted with bodies. Great patches of blood widened on their white clothes. The survivors, without breaking ranks, silently and doggedly marched on until struck down. When every one of the first column had been knocked down stretcher-bearers rushed up unmolested by the police and carried off the injured to a thatched hut which had been arranged as a temporary hospital.

Then another column formed while the leaders pleaded with them to retain their self-control. They marched slowly toward the police. Although every one knew that within a few minutes he would be beaten, perhaps killed, I could detect no signs of wavering or fear. They marched steadily with heads up, without the encouragement of music or cheering or any possibility that they might escape serious injury or death. The police rushed out and methodically and mechanically beat down the second column. There was no fight, no struggle; the marchers simply walked forward until struck down. There were no outcries, only groans after they fell. . . .

At times the spectacle of unresisting men being methodically bashed into a bloody pulp sickened me so much that I had to turn away. The Western mind finds it difficult to grasp the idea of nonresistance. I felt an indefinable sense of helpless rage and loathing, almost as much against the men who were submitting unresistingly to being beaten as against the police wielding the clubs, and this despite the fact that when I came to India I sympathized with the Gandhi cause.

Several times the leaders nearly lost control of the waiting crowd. They rushed up and down, frantically pleading with and exhorting the intensely excited men to remember Gandhi's instructions. It seemed that the unarmed throng was on the verge of launching a mass attack upon the police. . . . [But this did not happen.] Group after group walked forward, sat down, and submitted to being beaten into insensibility without raising an arm to fend off the blows. . . .

Hour after hour stretcher-bearers carried back a stream of inert, bleeding bodies . . . back to the temporary hospital. . . . I counted 320 injured, many still insensible with fractured skulls, others writing in agony from kicks in the testicles and stomach. . . .

I was the only foreign correspondent who had witnessed the amazing scene—a classic

Gandhi chose the Indian spinning wheel as a symbol of national rejuvenation. (*Source: Wide World Photos*)

example of "Satyagraha" or nonviolent civil disobedience. . . . My story of the beatings at Dharasana caused a sensation when it appeared in the 1,350 newspapers served by the United Press throughout the world. . . . Representatives of the Gandhi movement in the United States printed it as a leaflet and distributed more than a quarter of a million copies.

Questions for Analysis

1. What happened at this demonstration against the salt tax in India? What seems most important to you?

2. How did Miller react to what he saw? Do you share his reaction? Why or why not?

3. Gandhi believed that nonviolent resistance required great courage. Do you agree or disagree? Why?

4. What are the strengths and weaknesses of nonviolent resistance as a strategy of social action?

Source: Webb Miller, *I Found No Peace: The Journal of a Foreign Correspondent* (New York: Simon and Schuster, 1925), pp. 192–96, 198–99.

1025

31

The Age of Anxiety
in the West

Dust, a painting of the Great Depression by the Russian-born American painter Ben Shahn (1898–1969). *(Source: Courtesy, Kennedy Galleries, New York)*

When Allied diplomats met in Paris in early 1919 with their optimistic plans for building a lasting peace, most looked forward to happier times. They hoped that life would return to normal after the terrible trauma of total war. They hoped that once again life would make sense in the familiar prewar terms of peace, prosperity, and progress. These hopes were in vain. The Great Break—the First World War and the Russian Revolution—had mangled too many things beyond repair. Life would no longer fit neatly into the old molds.

Instead, great numbers of men and women in the West felt themselves increasingly adrift in a strange, uncertain, and uncontrollable world. They saw themselves living in an age of anxiety, an age of continual crisis (this age lasted until at least the early 1950s). In almost every area of human experience, people went searching for ways to put meaning back into life.

- What did such doubts and searching mean for Western thought, art, and culture?
- How did leaders deal with the political dimensions of uncertainty and try to re-establish real peace and prosperity between 1919 and 1939?
- Why did those leaders fail?

These are the questions this chapter will explore.

✤ UNCERTAINTY IN MODERN THOUGHT

A complex revolution in thought and ideas was under way in Western society before the First World War, but only small, unusual groups were aware of it. After the war, new and upsetting ideas began to spread through the entire population. Western society began to question and even abandon many cherished values and beliefs that had guided it since the eighteenth-century Enlightenment and the nineteenth-century triumph of industrial development, scientific advances, and evolutionary thought.

Before 1914 most people in the West still believed in progress, reason, and the rights of the individual. Progress was a daily reality, apparent in the rising standard of living, the taming of the city, and the steady increase in popular education. Such developments also encouraged the comforting be-lief in the logical universe of Newtonian physics as well as faith in the ability of a rational human mind to understand that universe through intellectual investigation. And just as there were laws of science, so were there laws of society that rational human beings could discover and then wisely act on. At the same time, the rights of the individual were not just taken for granted; they were actually increasing. Well-established rights were gradually spreading to women and workers, and new "social rights," such as old-age pensions, were emerging. In short, before World War I most Europeans and North Americans had a moderately optimistic view of the world, and with good reason.

Nevertheless, since the 1880s, a small band of serious thinkers and creative writers had been attacking these well-worn optimistic ideas. These critics rejected the general faith in progress and the power of the rational human mind. An expanding chorus of thinkers echoed and enlarged their views after the experience of history's most destructive war—a war that suggested to many that human beings were a pack of violent, irrational animals quite capable of tearing the individual and his or her rights to shreds. Disorientation and pessimism were particularly acute in the 1930s, when the rapid rise of harsh dictatorships and the Great Depression transformed old certainties into bitter illusions.

No one expressed this state of uncertainty better than French poet and critic Paul Valéry (1871–1945) in the early 1920s. Speaking of the "crisis of the mind," Valéry noted that Europe was looking at its future with dark foreboding:

The storm has died away, and still we are restless, uneasy, as if the storm were about to break. Almost all the affairs of men remain in a terrible uncertainty. We think of what has disappeared, and we are almost destroyed by what has been destroyed; we do not know what will be born, and we fear the future, not without reason. . . . Doubt and disorder are in us and with us. There is no thinking man, however shrewd or learned he may be, who can hope to dominate this anxiety, to escape from this impression of darkness.[1]

In the midst of economic, political, and social disruptions, Valéry saw the "cruelly injured mind," besieged by doubts and suffering from anxieties. In this general intellectual crisis of the twentieth

❋ **"The War, as I Saw It"**
This was the title of a series of grotesque drawings that appeared in 1920 in *Simplicissimus,* Germany's leading satirical magazine. Nothing shows better the terrible impact of the First World War than this profoundly disturbing example of expressionist art. *(Source: Caroline Buckler)*

century, the implications of new ideas and discoveries in philosophy, physics, psychology, and literature played a central role.

Modern Philosophy

Among those thinkers in the late nineteenth century who challenged the belief in progress and the general faith in the rational human mind, German philosopher Friedrich Nietzsche (1844–1900) was particularly influential. The son of a Lutheran minister, Nietzsche utterly rejected Christianity. In

1872 in his first great work he argued that ever since classical Athens the West had overemphasized rationality and stifled the passion and animal instinct that drive human activity and true creativity. Nietzsche went on to question all values. He claimed that Christianity embodied a "slave morality" that glorified weakness, envy, and mediocrity. In Nietzsche's most famous line, a wise fool proclaims that "God is dead," murdered by lackadaisical modern Christians who no longer really believe in Him. Nietzsche viewed the pillars of conventional morality—reason, democracy, progress, respectability—as outworn social and psychological constructs whose influence was suffocating self-realization and excellence.

Nietzsche painted a dark world, foreshadowing perhaps his loss of sanity in 1889. The West was in decline; false values had triumphed. The only hope for the individual was to accept the meaninglessness of human existence and then make that very meaninglessness a source of self-defined personal integrity and hence liberation. This would at least be possible for a few superior individuals, who could free themselves from the humdrum thinking of the masses and become true heroes. Little read during his active years, Nietzsche attracted growing attention in the early twentieth century, and his influence remains enormous to this day.

Growing dissatisfaction with established ideas before 1914 was apparent in other important thinkers. In the 1890s, French philosophy professor Henri Bergson (1859–1941) convinced many young people through his writing that immediate experience and intuition were as important as rational and scientific thinking for understanding reality. Indeed, according to Bergson, a religious experience or a mystical poem was often more accessible to human comprehension than was a scientific law or a mathematical equation.

Another thinker who agreed about the limits of rational thinking was French socialist Georges Sorel (1847–1922). Sorel frankly characterized Marxian socialism as an inspiring but unprovable religion rather than a rational scientific truth. Socialism would come to power, he believed, through a great, violent strike of all working people, which would miraculously shatter capitalist society. Sorel rejected democracy and believed that the masses of the new socialist society would have to be tightly controlled by a small revolutionary elite.

The First World War accelerated the revolt against established certainties in philosophy, but that revolt went in two very different directions. In English-speaking countries, the main development was the acceptance of logical empiricism (or logical positivism) in university circles. In continental Europe, where esoteric and remote logical empiricism did not win many converts, the primary development in philosophy was existentialism.

Logical empiricism was truly revolutionary. It rejected most of the concerns of traditional philosophy, from the existence of God to the meaning of happiness, as nonsense and hot air. This outlook began primarily with Austrian philosopher Ludwig Wittgenstein (1889–1951), who later emigrated to England, where he trained numerous disciples.

Wittgenstein argued in his pugnacious *Tractatus Logico-Philosophicus* (*Essay on Logical Philosophy*) in 1922 that philosophy is only the logical clarification of thoughts and that it therefore becomes the study of language, which expresses thoughts. In Wittgenstein's opinion, the great philosophical issues of the ages—God, freedom, morality, and so on—are quite literally senseless, a great waste of time, for statements about them can neither be

Friedrich Nietzsche   This colored photograph of the German philosopher was taken in 1882, when he was at the height of his creative powers. A brilliant iconoclast, Nietzsche debunked European values and challenged the optimistic faith in human rationality before the World War I. (*Source: Archiv für Kunst and Geschichte, Berlin*)

tested by scientific experiments nor demonstrated by the logic of mathematics. Instead, statements about such matters reflect only the personal preferences of a given individual. As Wittgenstein put it in the famous last sentence of his work, "Of what one cannot speak, of that one must keep silent." Logical empiricism drastically reduced the scope of philosophical inquiry. Anxious people could find few, if any, answers in this direction.

Some looked for answers in *existentialism*. Highly diverse and even contradictory, existential thinkers were loosely united in a courageous search for moral values in a world of terror and uncertainty. Theirs were true voices of the age of anxiety.

Most existential thinkers in the twentieth century were atheists. Often inspired by Nietzsche, they did not believe a supreme being had established humanity's fundamental nature and given life its meaning. In the words of the famous French existentialist Jean-Paul Sartre (1905–1980), human beings simply exist: "They turn up, appear on the scene." Only after they "turn up" do they seek to define themselves. Honest human beings are terribly alone, for there is no God to help them. They are hounded by despair and the meaninglessness of life. The crisis of the existential thinker epitomized the modern intellectual crisis—the shattering of traditional beliefs in God, reason, and progress.

Existentialists did recognize that human beings, unless they kill themselves, must act. Indeed, in the words of Sartre, "man is condemned to be free." There is therefore the possibility—indeed, the necessity—of giving meaning to life through actions, of defining oneself through choices. To do so, individuals must become "engaged" and choose their own actions courageously and consistently and in full awareness of their inescapable responsibility for their own behavior. In the end, existentialists argued, human beings can overcome life's absurdity.

It was in France during and immediately after World War II that existentialism came of age. The terrible conditions of the war reinforced the existential view of and approach to life. With the German dictator Hitler's hideous reign of barbarism, men and women had more than ever to define themselves by their actions. Specifically, each individual had to choose whether to join the resistance against Hitler or accept and even abet tyranny. Sartre himself was active in the French Resistance, and he and his colleagues offered a powerful answer to profound moral issues and the contemporary crisis.

The Revival of Christianity

The loss of faith in human reason and in continual progress also led to a renewed interest in the Christian view of the world. Christianity and religion in general had been on the defensive in intellectual circles since the Enlightenment. In the years before 1914, some theologians, especially Protestant ones, had felt the need to interpret Christian doctrine and the Bible so that they did not seem to contradict science, evolution, and common sense. Christ was therefore seen primarily as the greatest moral teacher, and the "supernatural" aspects of his divinity were strenuously played down. Indeed, some modern theologians were embarrassed by the miraculous, unscientific aspects of Christianity and turned away from them.

Especially after World War I, a number of thinkers and theologians began to revitalize the fundamentals of Christianity. Sometimes described as Christian existentialists because they shared the loneliness and despair of atheistic existentialists, they stressed human beings' sinful nature, the need for faith, and the mystery of God's forgiveness. The revival of fundamental Christian belief after World War I was fed by rediscovery of the work of nineteenth-century Danish religious philosopher Søren Kierkegaard (1813–1855), whose ideas became extremely influential. Having rejected formalistic religion, Kierkegaard had eventually resolved his personal anguish over his imperfect nature by making a total religious commitment to a remote and majestic God.

Similar ideas were brilliantly developed by Swiss Protestant theologian Karl Barth (1886–1968). Barth maintained that religious truth is made known to human beings only through God's grace. Sinful creatures whose reason and will are hopelessly flawed, people have to accept God's word and the supernatural revelation of Jesus Christ with awe, trust, and obedience. Lowly mortals should not expect to "reason out" God and his ways.

Among Catholics, the leading existential Christian thinker was Gabriel Marcel (1887–1973), who found in the Catholic church an answer to what he called the postwar "broken world." Catholicism and religious belief provided the hope, humanity, honesty, and piety for which he hungered. Flexible

alliteration! clever!

and gentle, Marcel and his countryman Jacques Maritain (1882–1973) denounced anti-Semitism and supported closer ties with non-Catholics.

After 1914 religion became much more relevant and meaningful to thinking people than it had been before the Great War. In addition to Marcel and Maritain, many other illustrious individuals turned to religion between about 1920 and 1950. Poets T. S. Eliot and W. H. Auden, novelists Evelyn Waugh and Aldous Huxley, historian Arnold Toynbee, Oxford professor C. S. Lewis, psychoanalyst Karl Stern, physicist Max Planck, and philosopher Cyril Joad were all either converted to religion or attracted to it for the first time (see Listening to the Past). Religion, often of a despairing, existential variety, was one meaningful answer to terror and anxiety. In the words of another famous Roman Catholic convert, English novelist Graham Greene, "One began to believe in heaven because one believed in hell."[2]

The New Physics

Ever since the scientific revolution of the seventeenth century, scientific advances and their implications had greatly influenced the beliefs of thinking people. By the late nineteenth century, science was one of the main pillars supporting Western society's optimistic and rationalistic view of the world. Progressive minds believed that science, unlike religion and philosophical speculation, was based on hard facts and controlled experiments. Science seemed to have achieved an unerring and almost completed picture of reality. Unchanging natural laws seemed to determine physical processes and permit useful solutions to more and more problems. All this was comforting, especially to people who were no longer committed to traditional religious beliefs. And all this was challenged by the new physics.

An important first step toward the new physics was the discovery at the end of the nineteenth century that atoms were not like hard, permanent little billiard balls. They were actually composed of many far-smaller, fast-moving particles, such as electrons and protons. Polish-born physicist Marie Curie (1867–1934) and her French husband discovered that radium constantly emits subatomic particles and thus does not have a constant atomic weight. Building on this and other work in radiation, German physicist Max Planck (1858–1947) showed in 1900 that subatomic energy is emit-

ted in uneven little spurts, which Planck called "quanta," and not in a steady stream, as previously believed. Planck's discovery called into question the old sharp distinction between matter and energy and challenged the old view of atoms as the stable, basic building blocks of nature.

In 1905 German-born Jewish genius Albert Einstein (1879–1955) went further than the Curies and Planck in challenging Newtonian physics. His famous theory of special relativity postulated that time and space are relative to the viewpoint of the observer and that only the speed of light is constant for all frames of reference in the universe. In order to make his revolutionary and paradoxical idea somewhat comprehensible to the nonmathematical lay person, Einstein later used analogies involving moving trains. For example, if a woman in the middle of a moving car gets up and walks forward to the door, she has gone, relative to the train, a half car length. But relative to an observer on the embankment, she has gone farther. The closed framework of Newtonian physics was quite limited compared to that of Einsteinian physics, which unified an apparently infinite universe with the incredibly small, fast-moving subatomic world. Moreover, Einstein's theory stated clearly that matter and energy are interchangeable and that even a particle of matter contains enormous levels of potential energy.

The 1920s opened the "heroic age of physics," in the apt words of one of its leading pioneers, Ernest Rutherford (1871–1937). Breakthrough followed breakthrough. In 1919 Rutherford showed that the atom could be split. By 1944 seven subatomic particles had been identified, of which the most important was the neutron. The neutron's capacity to pass through other atoms allowed for even more intense experimental bombardment of matter, leading to chain reactions of unbelievable force. This was the road to the atomic bomb.

Although few nonscientists understood this revolution in physics, the implications of the new theories and discoveries, as presented by newspapers and popular writers, were disturbing to millions of men and women in the 1920s and 1930s. The new universe was strange and troubling. It seemed to lack any absolute objective reality. Everything was said to be "relative"—that is, dependent on the observer's frame of reference. Moreover, in 1927 German physicist Werner Heisenberg (1901–1976) formulated the "principle of uncertainty," which postulates that because it is impossible to know the position and speed of an individual electron, it is therefore impossible to predict its behavior. Instead of Newton's dependable, rational laws, there seemed to be only tendencies and probabilities in an extraordinarily complex and uncertain universe that was described by abstract mathematical symbols and seemed to have little to do with human experience and human problems. When, for example, Planck was asked what science could contribute to resolving conflicts of values, his response was simple: "Science is not qualified to speak to this question."

Freudian Psychology

With physics presenting an uncertain universe so unrelated to ordinary human experience, questions about the power and potential of the human mind assumed special significance. The findings and speculations of leading psychologist Sigmund Freud (see page 862) were particularly disturbing.

Before Freud, poets and mystics had probed the unconscious and irrational aspects of human behavior. But most professional, "scientific" psychologists assumed that human behavior was the result of rational calculation—of "thinking"—by the single, unified conscious mind. Basing his insights on the analysis of dreams and of hysteria, Freud developed a very different view of the human psyche, beginning in the late 1880s.

According to Freud, human behavior is basically irrational. The key to understanding the mind is the primitive, irrational unconscious, which he called the *id.* The unconscious is driven by sexual, aggressive, and pleasure-seeking desires and is locked in a constant battle with the other parts of the mind: the rationalizing conscious (the *ego*), which mediates what a person *can* do, and ingrained moral values (the *superego*), which specify what a person *should* do. Human behavior is a product of a fragile compromise between instinctual drives and the controls of rational thinking and moral values. Since the instinctual drives are extremely powerful, the ever-present danger for individuals and whole societies is that unacknowledged drives will overwhelm the control mechanisms in a violent, distorted way. Yet Freud also agreed with Nietzsche that the mechanisms of rational thinking and traditional moral values can be too strong. They can repress sexual desires too effectively, crippling individuals and entire peoples with guilt and neurotic fears.

Freudian psychology and clinical psychiatry had become an international movement by 1910, but only after 1918 did they receive popular attention, especially in the Protestant countries of northern Europe and in the United States. Many interpreted

Lord Rutherford The great physicist Ernest Rutherford split the atom in 1919 with a small device that he could hold in his hands. Here he stands with a colleague in Cambridge University's renowned Cavendish Laboratory in 1932, when scientific laboratories engaging in pure research were still relatively small. *(Source: Cavendish Laboratory, Cambridge University/C. E. Wynn-Williams)*

Edvard Munch: The Dance of Life (1899–1900)   Like his contemporary Sigmund Freud, the expressionist Norwegian painter Edvard Munch (1863–1944) studied the turmoil and fragility of human thought and action. Solitary figures struggling with fear and uncertainty dominate his work. Here the girl in white represents innocence, the tense woman in black stands for mourning and rejection, and the woman in red evokes the joy of passing pleasure. *(Source: Nasjonalgalleriet, Oslo. Photo: Jacques Lathion)*

Freud as saying that the first requirement for mental health is an uninhibited sex life. This popular interpretation reflected and encouraged growing sexual experimentation, particularly among middle-class women. For more serious students, the psychology of Freud and his followers drastically undermined the old, easy optimism about the rational and progressive nature of the human mind.

Twentieth-Century Literature

The general intellectual climate of pessimism, relativism, and alienation was also articulated in literature. Novelists developed new techniques to express new realities. The great nineteenth-century novelists had typically written as all-knowing narrators, describing realistic characters and their relationship to an understandable, if sometimes harsh, society. In the twentieth century, most major writers adopted the limited, often confused viewpoint of a single individual. Like Freud, these novelists focused their attention on the complexity and irrationality of the human mind, where feelings, memories, and desires are forever scrambled. The great French novelist Marcel Proust (1871–1922), in his semiautobiographical *Remembrance of Things Past* (1913–1927), recalled bittersweet memories of childhood and youthful love and tried to discover their innermost meaning. To do so, Proust lived like a hermit in a soundproof Paris apartment for ten years, withdrawing from the present to dwell on the past.

Virginia Woolf Her novels captured sensations like impressionist paintings, and her home attracted a circle of artists and writers known as the Bloomsbury Group. Many of Woolf's essays dealt with women's issues and urged greater opportunity for women's creativity. *(Source: Gisèle Freund/Photo Researchers)*

Serious novelists also used the stream-of-consciousness technique to explore the psyche. In *Jacob's Room* (1922), Virginia Woolf (1882–1941) created a novel made up of a series of internal monologues, in which ideas and emotions from different periods of time bubble up as randomly as from a patient on a psychoanalyst's couch. William Faulkner (1897–1962), perhaps America's greatest twentieth-century novelist, used the same technique in *The Sound and the Fury* (1922), much of whose intense drama is confusedly seen through the eyes of an idiot. The most famous stream-of-consciousness novel—and surely the most disturb-ing novel of its generation—is *Ulysses,* which Irish novelist James Joyce (1882–1941) published in 1922. Into an account of an ordinary day in the life of an ordinary man, Joyce weaves an extended ironic parallel between his hero's aimless wanderings through the streets and pubs of Dublin and the adventures of Homer's hero Ulysses on his way home from Troy. Abandoning conventional grammar and blending foreign words, puns, bits of knowledge, and scraps of memory together in bewildering confusion, the language of *Ulysses* is intended to mirror modern life itself: a gigantic riddle waiting to be unraveled.

As creative writers turned their attention from society to the individual and from realism to psychological relativity, they rejected the idea of progress. Some even described "anti-utopias," nightmare visions of things to come. In 1918 an obscure German high school teacher named Oswald Spengler (1880–1936) published *The Decline of the West,* which quickly became an international sensation. According to Spengler, every culture experiences a life cycle of growth and decline. Western civilization, in Spengler's opinion, was in its old age, and death was approaching in the form of conquest by the yellow race. T. S. Eliot (1888–1965), in his famous poem *The Waste Land* (1922), depicted a world of growing desolation, although after his conversion to Anglo-Catholicism in 1927, Eliot came to hope cautiously for humanity's salvation. No such hope appeared in the work of Franz Kafka (1883–1924), whose novels *The Trial* (1925) and *The Castle* (1926) as well as several of his greatest short stories portray helpless individuals crushed by inexplicably hostile forces.

Englishman George Orwell (1903–1950) had seen the nightmarish reality of the Nazi state and its Stalinist counterpart by 1949 when he wrote perhaps the ultimate in anti-utopian literature: *1984.* Orwell set the action in the future, in 1984. Big Brother—the dictator—and his totalitarian state use a new kind of language, sophisticated technology, and psychological terror to strip a weak individual of his last shred of human dignity. The supremely self-confident chief of the Thought Police tells the tortured, broken, and framed Winston Smith, "If you want a picture of the future, imagine a boot stamping on a human face—forever."[3] A phenomenal bestseller, *1984* spoke to millions of people in the closing years of the age of anxiety.

❖ MODERN ART AND MUSIC

Throughout the twentieth century, there has been considerable unity in the arts. The "modernism" of the immediate prewar years and the 1920s is still strikingly modern. Like the scientists and creative artists who were partaking of the same culture, creative artists rejected old forms and old values. Modernism in art and music meant constant experimentation and a search for new kinds of expression. And though many people find the many and varied modern visions of the arts strange, disturbing, and even ugly, the twentieth century, so dismal in many respects, will probably stand as one of Western civilization's great artistic eras.

Architecture and Design

Modernism in the arts was loosely unified by a revolution in architecture. This revolution intended nothing less than a transformation of the physical framework of urban society according to a new principle: *functionalism.* Buildings, like industrial products, should be useful and "functional"—that is, they should serve, as well as possible, the purpose for which they were made. Thus architects and designers had to work with engineers, town planners, and even sanitation experts. Moreover, they had to throw away useless ornamentation and find beauty and aesthetic pleasure in the clean lines of practical constructions and efficient machinery. Franco-Swiss genius Le Corbusier (1887–1965) insisted that "a house is a machine for living in."[4]

The United States, with its rapid urban growth and lack of rigid building traditions, pioneered in the new architecture. In the 1890s the Chicago school of architects, led by Louis H. Sullivan (1856–1924), used cheap steel, reinforced concrete, and electric elevators to build skyscrapers and office buildings lacking almost any exterior ornamentation. In the first decade of the twentieth century, Sullivan's student Frank Lloyd Wright (1869–1959) built a series of radically new and truly modern houses featuring low lines, open interiors, and mass-produced building materials. Europeans were inspired by these and other American examples of functional construction, like the massive, unadorned grain elevators of the Midwest.

In Europe, architectural leadership centered in German-speaking countries until Hitler took

power in 1933. In 1911 twenty-eight-year-old Walter Gropius (1883–1969) broke sharply with the past in his design of the Fagus shoe factory at Alfeld, Germany, a clean, light, elegant building of glass and iron. After the First World War, Gropius merged the schools of fine and applied arts at Weimar into a single, interdisciplinary school, the Bauhaus. The Bauhaus brought together many leading modern architects, artists, designers, and theatrical innovators. Working as an effective, inspired team, they combined the study of fine art, such as painting and sculpture, with the study of applied art in the crafts of printing, weaving, and furniture making. Throughout the 1920s, the Bauhaus, with its stress on functionalism and good design for everyday life, attracted enthusiastic students from all over the world. It had a great and continuing impact.

Another leader in the "international" style, Ludwig Mies van der Rohe (1886–1969), followed Gropius as director of the Bauhaus in 1930 and immigrated to the United States in 1937. His classic Lake Shore Apartments in Chicago, built between 1948 and 1951, symbolized the triumph of steel-frame and glass-wall modern architecture in the great building boom after the Second World War.

Modern Painting and Music

Modern painting grew out of a revolt against French impressionism. The *impressionism* of such French painters as Claude Monet (1840–1926), Pierre Auguste Renoir (1841–1919), and Camille Pissarro (1830–1903) was, in part, a kind of "superrealism." Leaving exact copying of objects to photography, these artists sought to capture the momentary overall feeling, or impression, of light falling on a real-life scene before their eyes. By 1890, when impressionism was finally established, a few artists known as *postimpressionists,* or sometimes as *expressionists,* were already striking out in new directions. After 1905 art increasingly took on a nonrepresentational, abstract character, a development that reached its high point after World War II.

Though individualistic in their styles, postimpressionists were united in their desire to know and depict unseen, inner worlds of emotion and imagination. Like modern novelists, they wanted to express a complicated psychological view of

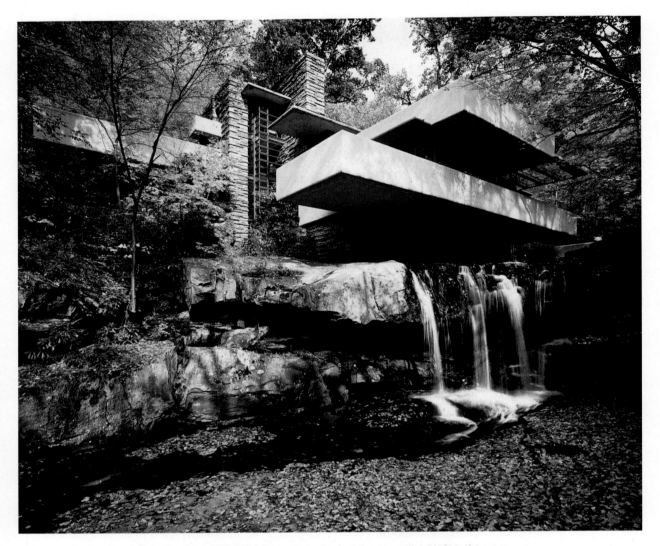

✳ **Frank Lloyd Wright: The "Falling Water" House**   Often considered Wright's masterpiece, Falling Water combines modern architectural concepts with close attention to a spectacular site. Anchored to a high rock ledge by means of reinforced concrete, the house soars out over a cascading waterfall at Bear Run in western Pennsylvania. Built in 1937 for a Pittsburgh businessman, Falling Water is now open to the public and attracts seventy thousand visitors each year. *(Source: Western Pennsylvania Conservancy/Art Resource, NY)*

reality as well as an overwhelming emotional intensity. In *The Starry Night* (1889), for example, the great Dutch expressionist Vincent van Gogh (1853–1890) painted the vision of his mind's eye. Flaming cypress trees, exploding stars, and a cometlike Milky Way swirl together in one great cosmic rhythm. Paul Gauguin (1848–1903), the French stockbroker-turned-painter, pioneered in expressionist techniques, though he used them to infuse his work with tranquillity and mysticism. In 1891 he fled to the South Pacific in search of unspoiled beauty and a primitive way of life. Gauguin believed that the form and design of a picture were important in themselves and that the painter need not try to represent objects on canvas as the eye actually saw them.

Fascination with form, as opposed to light, was characteristic of postimpressionism and expressionism. Paul Cézanne (1839–1906), who had a profound influence on twentieth-century painting, was particularly committed to form and ordered design. He told a young painter, "You must see in nature the cylinder, the sphere, and the cone."[5] As Cézanne's later work became increasingly abstract and nonrepresentational, it also moved away from the traditional three-dimensional perspective toward the two-dimensional plane, which has characterized much of modern art. The expressionism of a group of painters led by Henri Matisse (1869–1954) was so extreme that an exhibition of their work in Paris in 1905 prompted shocked critics to call them *les fauves*—"the wild beasts." Matisse and his followers still painted real objects, but their primary concern was the arrangement of color, line, and form as an end in itself.

In 1907 a young Spaniard in Paris, Pablo Picasso (1881–1973), founded another movement—*cubism.* Cubism concentrated on a complex geometry of zigzagging lines and sharply angled, overlapping planes. About three years later came the ultimate stage in the development of abstract, nonrepresentational art. Artists such as the Russianborn Wassily Kandinsky (1866–1944) turned away from nature completely. "The observer," said Kandinsky, "must learn to look at [my] pictures . . . as form and color combinations . . . as a representation of mood and not as a representation of *objects.*"[6]

In the 1920s and 1930s, the artistic movements of the prewar years were extended and consolidated. The most notable new developments were *dadaism* and *surrealism.* Dadaism attacked all accepted standards of art and behavior, delighting in outrageous conduct. Its name, from the French word *dada,* meaning "hobbyhorse," is deliberately nonsensical. A famous example of dadaism was a reproduction of Leonardo da Vinci's *Mona Lisa* in which the famous woman with the mysterious smile sports a mustache and is ridiculed with an obscene inscription. After 1924 many dadaists were attracted to surrealism, which became very influential in art in the late 1920s and 1930s. Surrealists painted a fantastic world of wild dreams and complex symbols, where watches melted and giant metronomes beat time in precisely drawn but impossible alien landscapes.

Refusing to depict ordinary visual reality, surrealist painters made powerful statements about the age of anxiety. Picasso's 26-foot-long mural *Guernica* (1937) masterfully unites several powerful

Picasso: Guernica (1937)   In this rich, complex work a shrieking woman falls from a burning house on the far right. On the left a woman holds a dead child. Toward the center are fragments of a warrior and a screaming horse pierced by a spear. Picasso used only the mournful colors of black, white, and gray. *(Source: Museo del Prado, Madrid. Pablo Picasso, Guernica [1937, May–early June]. Oil on canvas. © SPADEM, Paris/VAGA, New York, 1982)*

strands in twentieth-century art. Inspired by the Spanish civil war (see page 1076), the painting commemorates the bombing of the ancient Spanish town of Guernica by fascist planes, an attack that took the lives of a thousand people—one out of every eight inhabitants—in a single night of terror. Combining the free distortion of expressionism, the overlapping planes of cubism, and the surrealist fascination with grotesque subject matter, *Guernica* is what Picasso meant it to be: an unforgettable attack on "brutality and darkness."

Developments in modern music were strikingly parallel to those in painting. Composers, too, were attracted by the emotional intensity of expressionism. The ballet *The Rite of Spring* by composer Igor Stravinsky (1882–1971) practically caused a riot when it was first performed in Paris in 1913 by Sergei Diaghilev's famous Russian dance company. The combination of pulsating, dissonant rhythms from the orchestra pit and an earthy representation of lovemaking by the dancers on the stage seemed a shocking, almost pornographic enactment of a primitive fertility rite.

After the experience of the First World War, when irrationality and violence seemed to pervade the human experience, expressionism in opera and ballet flourished. Some composers turned their backs on long-established musical conventions. As abstract painters arranged lines and color but did not draw identifiable objects, so modern composers arranged sounds without creating recognizable harmonies. Led by Viennese composer Arnold Schönberg (1874–1951), they abandoned traditional harmony and tonality. The musical notes in a given piece were no longer united and organized by a key; instead they were independent and unrelated. Schönberg's twelve-tone music of the 1920s arranged all twelve notes of the scale in an abstract, mathematical pattern, or "tone row." This pattern sounded like no pattern at all to the ordinary listener. Accustomed to the harmonies of classical and romantic music, audiences generally resisted modern atonal music.

❖ MOVIES AND RADIO

Until after World War II at the earliest, these revolutionary changes in art and music appealed mainly to a minority of "highbrows" and not to the general public. That public was primarily and enthusi-astically wrapped up in movies and radio. The long-declining traditional arts and amusements of people in villages and small towns almost vanished, replaced by standardized, commercial entertainment.

Moving pictures were first shown as a popular novelty in naughty peepshows—"What the Butler Saw"—and penny arcades in the 1890s, especially in Paris. The first movie houses date from an experiment in Los Angeles in 1902. They quickly attracted large audiences and led to the production of short, silent action films such as the eight-minute *Great Train Robbery* of 1903. American directors and business people then set up "movie factories," at first in the New York area and then after 1910 in Los Angeles. These factories churned out two short films each week. On the eve of the First World War, full-length feature films such as the Italian *Quo Vadis* and the American *Birth of a Nation,* coupled with improvements in the quality of pictures, suggested the screen's vast possibilities.

During the First World War, the United States became the dominant force in the rapidly expanding silent-film industry. In the 1920s, Mack Sennett (1884–1960) and his zany Keystone Cops specialized in short, slapstick comedies noted for frantic automobile chases, custard-pie battles, and gorgeous bathing beauties. Screen stars such as Mary Pickford and Lillian Gish, Douglas Fairbanks and Rudolph Valentino, had their own "fan clubs" and became household names. But in the 1920s Charlie Chaplin (1889–1978), a funny little Englishman working in Hollywood, was unquestionably the king of the "silver screen." In his enormously popular role as a lonely tramp, complete with baggy trousers, battered derby, and an awkward, shuffling walk, Chaplin symbolized the "gay spirit of laughter in a cruel, crazy world."[7] Chaplin also demonstrated that in the hands of a genius the new medium could combine mass entertainment and artistic accomplishment.

The early 1920s was also the great age of German films. Protected and developed during the war, the large German studios excelled in bizarre expressionist dramas, beginning with *The Cabinet of Dr. Caligari* in 1919. Unfortunately, their period of creativity was short-lived. By 1926 American money was drawing the leading German talents to Hollywood and consolidating America's international domination. Film making was big business, and European theater owners were forced to book whole blocks of American films to get the few pictures they really wanted. This system put European producers at a great disadvantage until "talkies" permitted a revival of national film industries in the 1930s, particularly in France.

Whether foreign or domestic, motion pictures became the main entertainment of the masses until after the Second World War. In Great Britain one in every four adults went to the movies twice a week in the late 1930s, and two in five went at least once a week. Continental European countries had similar figures. The greatest appeal of motion pictures was that they offered ordinary people a temporary escape from the hard realities of international tensions, uncertainty, unemployment, and personal frustrations. The appeal of escapist entertainment was especially strong during the Great Depression. Millions flocked to musical comedies featuring glittering stars such as Ginger Rogers and Fred Astaire and to the fanciful cartoons of Mickey Mouse and his friends.

Radio became possible with the transatlantic "wireless" communication of Guglielmo Marconi (1874–1937) in 1901 and the development of the vacuum tube in 1904, which permitted the transmission of speech and music. But only in 1920 were the first major public broadcasts of special events made in Great Britain and the United States. Singing from London in English, Italian, and French, "the world's very best, the soprano Nellie Melba,"[8] was heard simultaneously all over Europe on June 16, 1920. This historic event captured the public's imagination. The meteoric career of radio was launched.

Every major country quickly established national broadcasting networks. In the United States, such networks were privately owned and were financed by advertising. In Great Britain, Parliament set up an independent, public corporation, the British Broadcasting Corporation (BBC), supported by licensing fees. Elsewhere in Europe, the typical pattern was direct control by the government. Whatever the institutional framework, radio became popular and influential. By the late 1930s, more than three out of every four households in both democratic Great Britain and dictatorial Germany had at least one cheap, mass-produced radio. In other European countries, radio ownership was not quite so widespread, but the new medium was no less important.

Radio was particularly well suited for political propaganda. Dictators such as Mussolini and Hitler controlled the airwaves and could reach enormous national audiences with their frequent, dramatic speeches. In democratic countries, politicians such as President Franklin Roosevelt and Prime Minister Stanley Baldwin effectively used informal "fireside chats" to bolster their support.

Motion pictures also became powerful tools of indoctrination, especially in countries with dictatorial regimes. Lenin himself encouraged the development of Soviet film making, believing that the new medium was essential to the social and ideological transformation of the country. Beginning in the mid-1920s, a series of epic films, the most famous of which were directed by Sergei Eisenstein (1898–1948), brilliantly dramatized the communist view of Russian history.

In Germany Hitler turned to a young and immensely talented woman film maker, Leni

 The Great Dictator   In 1940 Charlie Chaplin, the renowned actor and director, abandoned his popular characterization of little tramp to satirize the great dictator, Adolf Hitler. Chaplin (1889–1977) had strong political views and made a number of films with political themes as the escapist fare of the Great Depression gave way to the reality of the Second World War. *(Source: The Museum of Modern Art/Still Film Archives)*

Riefenstahl (b. 1902), for a masterpiece of documentary propaganda, *The Triumph of the Will,* based on the Nazi party rally at Nuremberg in 1934. Riefenstahl combined stunning aerial photography, joyful crowds welcoming Hitler, and mass processions of young Nazi fanatics. Her film was a brilliant and all-too-powerful documentary of Germany's "Nazi rebirth." The new media of mass culture were potentially dangerous instruments of political manipulation.

❈ THE SEARCH FOR PEACE AND POLITICAL STABILITY

As established patterns of thought and culture were challenged and mangled by the ferocious impact of World War I, so also was the political fabric stretched and torn by the consequences of the great conflict. The Versailles settlement had established a shaky truce, not a solid peace. Thus national leaders faced a gigantic task as they struggled with uncertainty and sought to create a stable international order within the general context of intellectual crisis and revolutionary artistic experimentation.

The pursuit of real and lasting peace proved difficult for many reasons. Germany hated the Treaty of Versailles. France was fearful and isolated. Britain was undependable, and the United States had turned its back on European problems. Eastern Europe was in ferment, and no one could predict the future of communist Russia. In addition, the international economic situation was poor and greatly complicated by war debts and disrupted patterns of trade. Yet for a time, from 1925 to late 1929, it appeared that peace and stability were within reach. When the subsequent collapse of the 1930s mocked these hopes, the disillusionment of liberals in the democracies was intensified.

Germany and the Western Powers

Germany was the key to lasting peace. Yet to Germans of all political parties, the Treaty of Versailles represented a harsh, dictated peace, to be revised or repudiated as soon as possible. The treaty had neither broken nor reduced Germany, which was potentially still the strongest country in Europe. Thus the treaty had fallen between two stools: too harsh for a peace of reconciliation, too soft for a peace of conquest.

Moreover, with ominous implications for the future, France and Great Britain did not see eye to eye on Germany. By the end of 1919, France wanted to stress the harsh elements in the Treaty of Versailles. Most of the war in the West had been fought on French soil, and the expected costs of reconstruction, as well as repaying war debts to the United States, were staggering. Thus French politicians believed that massive reparations from Germany were a vital economic necessity. Also, having compromised with President Wilson only to be betrayed by America's failure to ratify the treaty, many French leaders saw strict implementation of all provisions of the Treaty of Versailles as France's last best hope. Large reparation payments could hold Germany down indefinitely, and France would realize its goal of security.

The British soon felt differently. Prewar Germany had been Great Britain's second-best market in the entire world, and after the war a healthy, prosperous Germany appeared to be essential to the British economy. Indeed, many English people agreed with the analysis of the young English economist John Maynard Keynes (1883–1946). In his famous *Economic Consequences of the Peace* (1919), Keynes argued that astronomical reparations and harsh economic measures would indeed reduce Germany to the position of an impoverished second-rate power but such impoverishment would increase economic hardship in all countries. Only a complete revision of the foolish treaty could save Germany—and Europe. Keynes's attack stirred deep guilt feelings about Germany in the English-speaking world, feelings that often paralyzed English and American leaders in their relations with Germany and its leaders between the First and the Second World Wars.

The British were also suspicious of France's army—momentarily the largest in Europe—and France's foreign policy. Ever since 1890, France had looked to Russia as a powerful ally against Germany. But with Russia hostile and socialist, and with Britain and the United States unwilling to make any firm commitments, France associated itself closely with the newly formed states of eastern Europe and their alliance against defeated and bitter Hungary. The British and the French were also on cool terms because of conflicts relating to their League of Nations mandates in the Middle East (see page 994).

While French and British leaders drifted in different directions, the Allied reparations commission completed its work. In April 1921 it announced that Germany had to pay the enormous sum of 132 billion gold marks ($33 billion) in annual installments of 2.5 billion gold marks. Facing possible occupation of more of its territory, the young German republic, which had been founded in Weimar but moved back to Berlin, made its first payment in 1921. Then in 1922, wracked by rapid inflation and political assassinations and motivated by hostility and arrogance as well, the Weimar Republic announced its inability to pay more. It proposed a moratorium on reparations for three years, and the implication was that thereafter reparations would either be drastically reduced or eliminated entirely.

The British were willing to accept a moratorium on reparations, but the French were not. Led by their tough-minded, legalistic prime minister, Raymond Poincaré (1860–1934), they decided they either had to call Germany's bluff or see the entire peace settlement dissolve to France's great disadvantage. So, despite strong British protests, in early January 1923, armies of France and its ally Belgium began to occupy the Ruhr district, the heartland of industrial Germany, creating the most serious international crisis of the 1920s. If forcible collection proved impossible, France would use occupation to paralyze Germany and force it to accept the Treaty of Versailles.

Strengthened by a wave of patriotism, the German government ordered the people of the Ruhr to stop working and start passively resisting the French occupation. The coal mines and steel mills of the Ruhr grew silent, leaving 10 percent of Germany's total population in need of relief. The French answer to passive resistance was to seal off not only the Ruhr but also the entire Rhineland from the rest of Germany, letting in only enough food to prevent starvation. The French also revived plans for a separate state in the Rhineland.

By the summer of 1923, France and Germany were engaged in a great test of wills. French armies could not collect reparations from striking workers at gunpoint. But French occupation was indeed paralyzing Germany and its economy and had turned rapid German inflation into runaway inflation. Faced with the need to support the striking Ruhr workers and their employers, the German government began to print money to pay its bills. Prices soared. People went to the store with a big bag of paper money; they returned home with a handful of groceries. German money rapidly lost

"Hands Off the Ruhr" The French occupation of the Ruhr to collect reparations payments raised a storm of patriotic protest in Germany. This anti-French poster of 1923 turns Marianne, the symbol of French republican virtue, into a vicious harpy. *(Source: Internationaal Instituut voor Sociale Geschiedenis)*

all value, and so did anything else with a stated fixed value.

Runaway inflation brought about a social revolution. The accumulated savings of many retired and middle-class people were wiped out. Catastrophic inflation cruelly mocked the old middle-class virtues of thrift, caution, and self-reliance. Many Germans felt betrayed. They hated and blamed the Western governments, their own government, big business, the Jews, the workers, and the communists for their misfortune. They were psychologically prepared to follow radical leaders in a crisis.

In August 1923, as the mark fell and political unrest grew throughout Germany, Gustav Stresemann (1878–1929) assumed leadership of the government. Stresemann adopted a compromising attitude. He called off passive resistance in the Ruhr and in October agreed in principle to pay reparations but asked for a re-examination of Germany's ability to pay. Poincaré accepted. His hard line was becoming increasingly unpopular with French citizens, and it was hated in Britain and the United States.

More generally, in both Germany and France power was finally passing to the moderates, who realized that continued confrontation was a destructive, no-win situation. Thus after five long years of hostility and tension, culminating in a kind of undeclared war in the Ruhr in 1923, Germany and France decided to give compromise and cooperation a try. The British, and even the Americans, were willing to help. The first step was a reasonable compromise on the reparations question.

Hope in Foreign Affairs (1924–1929)

The reparations commission appointed an international committee of financial experts headed by American banker Charles G. Dawes to re-examine reparations from a broad perspective. The resulting Dawes Plan (1924) was accepted by France, Germany, and Britain. Germany's yearly reparations were reduced and depended on the level of German economic prosperity. Germany would also receive large loans from the United States to promote German recovery. In short, Germany would get private loans from the United States and pay reparations to France and Britain, thus enabling those countries to repay the large sums they owed the United States.

This circular flow of international payments was complicated and risky. But for a while it worked. The German republic experienced a spectacular economic recovery. By 1929 Germany's wealth and income were 50 percent greater than in 1913. With prosperity and large, continual inflows of American capital, Germany easily paid about $1.3 billion in reparations in 1927 and 1928, enabling France and Britain to pay the United States. In this way the Americans, who did not have armies but who did have money, belatedly played a part in the

general economic settlement that, though far from ideal, facilitated the worldwide recovery of the late 1920s.

This economic settlement was matched by a political settlement. In 1925 the leaders of Europe signed a number of agreements at Locarno, Switzerland. Germany and France solemnly pledged to accept their common border, and both Britain and Italy agreed to fight either France or Germany if one invaded the other. Stresemann also agreed to settle boundary disputes with Poland and Czechoslovakia by peaceful means, and France promised those countries military aid if Germany attacked them. For years, a "spirit of Locarno" gave Europeans a sense of growing security and stability in international affairs.

Other developments also strengthened hopes. In 1926 Germany joined the League of Nations, where Stresemann continued his "peace offensive." In 1928 fifteen countries signed the Kellogg-Briand Pact, initiated by French Prime Minister Aristide Briand and U.S. Secretary of State Frank B. Kellogg. This multinational pact "condemned and renounced war as an instrument of national policy." The signing states agreed to settle international disputes peacefully. Often seen as idealistic nonsense because it made no provisions for action in case war actually occurred, the pact was still a positive step. It fostered the cautious optimism of the late 1920s and also encouraged the hope that the United States would accept its responsibilities as a great world power and contribute to European stability.

Domestic politics also offered reason to hope. During the occupation of the Ruhr and the great inflation, republican government in Germany had appeared on the verge of collapse. In 1923 communists momentarily entered provincial governments, and in November an obscure nobody named Adolf Hitler leaped on to a table in a beer hall in Munich and proclaimed a "national socialist revolution." But Hitler's plot to seize control of the government was poorly organized and easily crushed, and Hitler was sentenced to prison, where he outlined his theories and program in his book *Mein Kampf (My Struggle)*. Throughout the 1920s, Hitler's National Socialist party attracted support only from a few fanatical anti-Semites, ultranationalists, and disgruntled former servicemen.

The moderate businessmen who tended to dominate the various German coalition governments believed that economic prosperity demanded good relations with the Western powers, and they supported parliamentary government at home. Stresemann himself was a man of this class, and he was the key figure in every government until his death in 1929. Elections were held regularly, and as the economy boomed, republican democracy appeared to have growing support among a majority of the Germans.

There were, however, sharp political divisions in the country. Many unrepentant nationalists and monarchists populated the right and the army. Germany's Communists were noisy and active on the left. The Communists, directed from Moscow, reserved their greatest hatred and sharpest barbs for their cousins the Social Democrats, whom they endlessly accused of betraying the revolution. The working classes were divided politically, but most

supported the nonrevolutionary but socialist Social Democrats.

The situation in France had numerous similarities to that in Germany. Communists and Socialists battled for the support of the workers. After 1924 the democratically elected government rested mainly in the hands of coalitions of moderates, and business interests were well represented. France's great accomplishment was rapid rebuilding of its war-torn northern region. The expense of this undertaking, however, led to a large deficit and substantial inflation by 1926. The government proceeded to slash spending and raise taxes, restoring confidence in the economy. Good times prevailed until 1930.

Despite political shortcomings, France attracted artists and writers from all over the world in the

An American in Paris The young Josephine Baker (1906–1975) suddenly became a star when she brought an exotic African eroticism to French music halls in 1925. American blacks and Africans had a powerful impact on entertainment in Europe in the 1920s and 1930s. *(Source: Hulton Deutsch Collection)*

1920s. Much of the intellectual and artistic ferment of the times flourished in Paris. As writer Gertrude Stein (1874–1946), a leader of the large colony of American expatriates living in Paris, later recalled, "Paris was where the twentieth century was."[9] More generally, France appealed to foreigners and to the French as a harmonious combination of small businesses and family farms, of bold innovation and solid traditions.

Britain, too, faced challenges after 1920. The wartime trend toward greater social equality continued, however, helping maintain social harmony. The great problem was unemployment. Many of Britain's best markets had been lost during the war, and throughout the 1920s unemployment hovered around 12 percent. The state provided unemployment benefits of equal size to all those without jobs and supplemented those payments with subsidized housing, medical aid, and increased old-age pensions. These and other measures kept living standards from seriously declining, defused class tensions, and pointed the way toward the welfare state that Britain established after World War II.

Relative social harmony was accompanied by the rise of the Labour party as a determined champion of the working classes and of greater social equality. Committed to the kind of moderate, "revisionist" socialism that had emerged before World War I (see page 878), the Labour party replaced the Liberal party as the main opposition to the Conservatives. The new prominence of the Labour party reflected the decline of old liberal ideals of competitive capitalism, limited government control, and individual responsibility. In 1924 and 1929, the Labour party under Ramsay MacDonald (1866–1937) governed the country with the support of the smaller Liberal party. Yet Labour moved toward socialism gradually and democratically, so that the middle classes were not overly frightened as the working classes won new benefits.

The Conservatives under Stanley Baldwin (1867–1947) showed the same compromising spirit on social issues. The last line of Baldwin's greatest speech in March 1925 summarized his international and domestic programs: "Give us peace in our time, O Lord." In spite of such conflicts as the 1926 strike by hard-pressed coal miners, which ended in an unsuccessful general strike, social unrest in Britain was limited in the 1920s and in the 1930s as well. In 1922 Britain granted southern, Catholic Ireland full autonomy after a bitter guerrilla war, thereby removing another source of prewar friction. Thus developments in both international relations and in the domestic politics of the leading democracies gave cause for cautious optimism in the late 1920s.

THE GREAT DEPRESSION (1929–1939)

Like the Great War, the Great Depression must be spelled with capital letters. Economic depression was nothing new. Depressions occurred throughout the nineteenth century with predictable regularity, as they recur in the form of recessions and slumps to this day. What was new about this depression was its severity and duration. It struck the entire world with ever-greater intensity from 1929 to 1933, and recovery was uneven and slow. Only with the Second World War did the depression disappear in much of the world.

The social and political consequences of prolonged economic collapse were enormous all around the world. Subsequent military expansion in Japan has already been described (see page 908), and later chapters examine a similarly powerful impact on Latin America and Africa. In Europe and the United States the depression shattered the fragile optimism of political leaders in the late 1920s. Mass unemployment made insecurity a reality for millions of ordinary people, who had paid little attention to the intellectual crisis or to new directions in art and ideas. In desperation, people looked for leaders who would "do something." They were willing to support radical attempts to deal with the crisis by both democratic leaders and dictators.

The Economic Crisis

Though economic activity was already declining moderately in many countries by early 1929, the crash of the stock market in the United States in October of that year really started the Great Depression. The American stock market boom, which had seen stock prices double between early 1928 and September 1929, was built on borrowed money. Many wealthy investors, speculators, and people of modest means had bought stocks by paying only a small fraction of the total purchase price and borrowing the remainder from their stockbrokers. Such buying "on margin" was extremely dangerous. When prices started falling, the hardpressed margin buyers started selling all at once. The result was a financial panic. Countless investors and speculators were wiped out in a matter of days or weeks.

The general economic consequences were swift and severe. Stripped of wealth and confidence, battered investors and their fellow citizens reduced their purchases of goods. Production began to slow down, and unemployment began to rise. Soon the entire American economy was caught in a vicious, spiraling decline.

The financial panic in the United States triggered a worldwide financial crisis, and that crisis resulted in a drastic decline in production in country after country. Throughout the 1920s, American bankers and investors had lent large amounts of capital not only to Germany but also to many other countries. Many of these loans were shortterm, and once panic broke, New York bankers began recalling them. It became very hard for European business people to borrow money, and the panicky public began to withdraw its savings from the banks. These banking problems eventually led to the crash of the largest bank in Austria in 1931 and then to general financial chaos. The recall of private loans by American bankers also accelerated the collapse in world prices, as business people around the world dumped industrial goods and agricultural commodities in a frantic attempt to get cash to pay what they owed.

The financial crisis led to a general crisis of production. Between 1929 and 1933, world output of goods fell by an estimated 38 percent. As this happened, each country turned inward and tried to go it alone. Country after country followed the example of the United States when it raised protective tariffs to their highest levels ever in 1930 and tried to seal off shrinking national markets for American producers only. Within this context of fragmented and destructive economic nationalism, recovery finally began in 1933.

Although opinions differ, two factors probably best explain the relentless slide to the bottom from 1929 to early 1933. First, the international economy lacked a leadership able to maintain stability when the crisis came. Specifically, as a noted American economic historian concludes, the seriously weakened British, the traditional leaders of the world economy, "couldn't and the United States

wouldn't" stabilize the international economic system in 1929.[10] The United States, which had momentarily played a positive role after the occupation of the Ruhr, cut back its international lending and erected high tariffs.

The second factor was poor national economic policy in almost every country. Governments generally cut their budgets and reduced spending when they should have run large deficits in an attempt to stimulate their economies. Since World War II, such a "counter-cyclical policy," advocated by John Maynard Keynes, has become a wellestablished weapon against depression. But in the 1930s, orthodox economists generally regarded Keynes's prescription with horror.

Mass Unemployment

The need for large-scale government spending was tied to mass unemployment (Map 31.1). As the financial crisis led to cuts in production, workers lost their jobs and had little money to buy goods. This led to still more cuts in production and still more unemployment, until millions were out of work. In Britain unemployment had averaged 12 percent in the 1920s; between 1930 and 1935, it averaged more than 18 percent. Far worse was the case of the United States. In the 1920s, unemployment there had averaged only 5 percent; in 1932, unemployment soared to about 33 percent of the entire labor force: 14 million people were out of work. Only by pumping new money into the economy could the government increase demand and break the vicious cycle of decline.

Along with economic effects, mass unemployment posed a great social problem that mere numbers cannot adequately express. Millions of people lost their spirit and dignity in an apparently hopeless search for work. Homes and ways of life were disrupted in millions of personal tragedies. In 1932 the workers of Manchester, England, appealed to their city officials—a typical appeal echoed throughout the Western world:

We tell you that thousands of people . . . are in desperate straits. We tell you that men, women, and children are going hungry. . . . We tell you that great numbers are being rendered distraught through the stress and worry of trying to exist without work. . . .

If you do not do this—if you do not provide useful work for the unemployed—what, we ask, is your alternative? Do not imagine that this colossal tragedy of

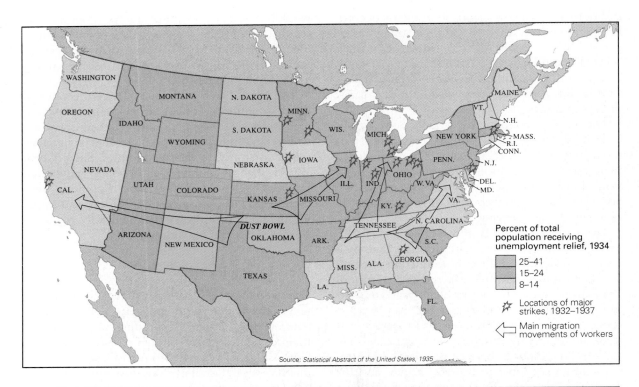

Percent of total population receiving unemployment relief, 1934

25–41
15–24
8–14

Locations of major strikes, 1932–1937

Main migration movements of workers

Source: *Statistical Abstract of the United States, 1935*

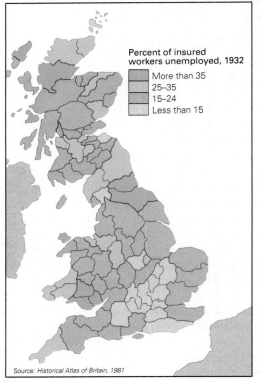

Percent of insured workers unemployed, 1932

More than 35
25–35
15–24
Less than 15

Source: *Historical Atlas of Britain, 1981*

Percent of workers unemployed, 1932

25–32
15–24

No comparable data available

Sources: *European Historical Statistics, 1790–1970*
Monthly Labor Review, U.S. Dept. of Labor, 1934, vol. 39

MAP 31.1 The Great Depression in the United States, Britain, and Europe
National and regional differences were substantial. Germany, industrial northern Britain, and the American Middle West were particularly hard hit.

✳ **Isaac Soyer: Employment Agency (1937)** The frustration and agony of looking for work against long odds are painfully evident in this American masterpiece. The time-killing, the resignation, and the dejection seen in the four figures are only as- pects of the larger problem. One of three talented brothers born in Russia and trained as artists in New York, Isaac Soyer worked in the tradition of American real- ism and concentrated on people and the influence of their environment. *(Source: Col- lection of Whitney Museum of American Art)*

unemployment is going on endlessly without some fateful catastrophe. Hungry men are angry men.[11]

Mass unemployment was a terrible time bomb preparing to explode.

The New Deal in the United States

Of all the major industrial countries, only Germany was harder hit by the Great Depression, or reacted more radically to it, than the United States. De- pression was so traumatic in the United States be- cause the 1920s had been a period of complacent prosperity. The Great Depression and the response

to it marked a major turning point in American history.

President Herbert Hoover (1895–1972) and his administration initially reacted to the stock market crash and economic decline with dogged optimism and limited action. But when the full force of the financial crisis struck Europe in the summer of 1931 and boomeranged back to the United States, people's worst fears became reality. Banks failed; unemployment soared. In 1932 industrial produc- tion fell to about 50 percent of its 1929 level. In these tragic circumstances Franklin Delano Roosevelt (1882–1945), an inspiring wheelchair- bound aristocrat previously crippled by polio, won a landslide electoral victory with grand but vague promises of a "New Deal for the forgotten man."

Roosevelt's basic goal was to reform capitalism in order to preserve it. In his words, "A frank examination of the profit system in the spring of 1933 showed it to be in collapse; but substantially everybody in the United States, in public office and out of public office, from the very rich to the very poor, was as determined as was my Administration to save it."[12] Roosevelt rejected socialism and government ownership of industry in 1933. To right the situation, he chose forceful government intervention in the economy.

In this choice, Roosevelt was flexible, pragmatic, and willing to experiment. Roosevelt and his "brain trust" of advisers adopted policies echoing the American experience in World War I, when the American economy had been thoroughly planned and regulated.

The first and most ambitious attempt to control and plan the economy was the National Recovery Administration (NRA). Intended to reduce competition and fix prices and wages for everyone's benefit, the NRA broke with the cherished American tradition of free competition and aroused conflicts among business people, consumers, and bureaucrats. It did not work well and was declared unconstitutional in 1935.

Roosevelt and his advisers then attacked the key problem of mass unemployment directly. The federal government accepted the responsibility of employing directly as many people as financially possible. New agencies were created to undertake a vast range of public works projects. The most famous of these was the Works Progress Administration (WPA), set up in 1935. One-fifth of the entire labor force worked for the WPA at some point in the 1930s, building public buildings, bridges, and highways. The WPA was enormously popular, and the hope of a job with the government helped check the threat of social revolution in the United States.

Other social measures aimed in the same direction. Following the path blazed by Germany's Bismarck in the 1880s (see page 867), the U.S. government in 1935 established a national social security system, with old-age pensions and unemployment benefits, to protect many workers against some of life's uncertainties. The National Labor Relations Act of 1935 gave union organizers the green light by declaring collective bargaining to be the policy of the United States. Follow-

ing some bitter strikes, such as a sit-down strike at General Motors in early 1937, union membership more than doubled, from 4 million in 1935 to 9 million in 1940. In general, between 1935 and 1938, government rulings and social reforms chipped away at the privileges of the wealthy and tried to help ordinary people.

Yet despite undeniable accomplishments in social reform, the New Deal was only partly successful as a response to the Great Depression. At the height of the recovery in May 1937, 7 million workers were still unemployed. The economic situation then worsened seriously in the recession of 1937 and 1938. Production fell sharply, and although unemployment never again reached the 15 million mark of 1933, it hit 11 million in 1938 and was still a staggering 10 million when war broke out in Europe in September 1939. The New Deal brought fundamental reform, but it never did pull the United States out of the depression.

The Scandinavian Response to the Depression

Of all the Western democracies, the Scandinavian countries under Socialist leadership responded most successfully to the challenge of the Great Depression. Having grown steadily in number in the late nineteenth century, the Socialists became the largest political party in Sweden and then in Norway after the First World War. In the 1920s they passed important social reform legislation for both peasants and workers, gained practical administrative experience, and developed a unique kind of socialism. Flexible and nonrevolutionary, Scandinavian socialism grew out of a strong tradition of cooperative community action. Even before 1900, Scandinavian agricultural cooperatives had shown how individual peasant families could join together for everyone's benefit. Labor leaders and capitalists were also inclined to work together.

When the economic crisis struck in 1929, Socialist governments in Scandinavia built on this pattern of cooperative social action. Sweden in particular pioneered in the use of large-scale deficits to finance public works and thereby maintain production and employment. Scandinavian governments also increased social welfare benefits, from old-age pensions and unemployment insurance to subsidized housing and maternity allowances. All this spending required a large bureaucracy and high taxes, first on the rich and then on practically everyone. Yet both private and cooperative enterprise thrived, as did democracy. Some observers saw Scandinavia's welfare socialism as an appealing "middle way" between sick capitalism and cruel communism or fascism.

Recovery and Reform in Britain and France

In Britain MacDonald's Labour government and then, after 1931, the Conservative-dominated coalition government followed orthodox economic theory. The budget was balanced, but unemployed workers received barely enough welfare to live. Despite government lethargy, the economy recovered considerably after 1932. By 1937 total production was about 20 percent higher than in 1929. In fact, for Britain the years after 1932 were actually somewhat better than the 1920s had been, quite the opposite of the situation in the United States and France.

This good but by no means brilliant performance reflected the gradual reorientation of the British economy. After going off the gold standard in 1931 and establishing protective tariffs in 1932, Britain concentrated increasingly on the national, rather than the international, market. The old export industries of the Industrial Revolution, such as textiles and coal, continued to decline, but new industries, such as automobiles and electrical appliances, grew in response to British home demand. Moreover, low interest rates encouraged a housing boom. These developments encouraged Britain to look inward and avoid unpleasant foreign questions.

Because France was relatively less industrialized and more isolated from the world economy, the Great Depression came there late. But once the depression hit France, it stayed and stayed. Decline was steady until 1935, and a short-lived recovery never brought production or employment back up to predepression levels. Economic stagnation both reflected and heightened an ongoing political crisis. There was no stability in government. As before 1914, the French parliament was made up of many political parties, which could never cooperate for very long. In 1933, for example, five coalition cabinets formed and fell in rapid succession.

The French lost the underlying unity that had made government instability bearable before 1914. Fascist-type organizations agitated against parliamentary democracy and looked to Mussolini's Italy and Hitler's Germany for inspiration. In Feb-

ruary 1934 French fascists and semifascists rioted and threatened to overturn the republic. At the same time, the Communist party and many workers opposed to the existing system were looking to Stalin's Russia for guidance. The vital center of moderate republicanism was sapped from both sides.

Frightened by the growing strength of the fascists at home and abroad, the Communists, the Socialists, and the Radicals formed an alliance—the Popular Front—for the national elections of May 1936. Their clear victory reflected the trend toward polarization. The number of Communists in the parliament jumped dramatically from 10 to 72, and the Socialists, led by Léon Blum, became the strongest party in France, with 146 seats. The really quite moderate Radicals slipped badly, and the conservatives lost ground to the semifascists.

In the next few months, Blum's Popular Front government made the first and only real attempt to deal with the social and economic problems of the 1930s in France. Inspired by Roosevelt's New Deal, the Popular Front encouraged the union movement and launched a far-reaching program of social reform, complete with paid vacations and a forty-hour workweek. Popular with workers and the lower middle class, these measures were quickly sabotaged by rapid inflation and cries of revolution from fascists and frightened conservatives. Wealthy people sneaked their money out of the country, labor unrest grew, and France entered a severe financial crisis. Blum was forced to announce a "breathing spell" in social reform.

The fires of political dissension were also fanned by civil war in Spain. Communists demanded that France support the Spanish republicans, while many French conservatives would gladly have joined Hitler and Mussolini in aiding the attack of Spanish fascists. Extremism grew, and France itself was within sight of civil war. Blum was forced to resign in June 1937, and the Popular Front quickly collapsed. An anxious and divided France drifted aimlessly once again, preoccupied by Hitler and German rearmament.

SUMMARY

After the First World War, Western society entered a complex and difficult era—truly an age of anxiety. Intellectual life underwent a crisis marked by pessimism, uncertainty, and fascination with irrational forces. Ceaseless experimentation and rejection of old forms characterized art and music, while motion pictures and radio provided a new, standardized entertainment for the masses. Intellectual and artistic developments that before 1914 had been confined to small avant-garde groups gained wider currency, as did the insecure state of mind they expressed.

Politics and economics were similarly disrupted. In the 1920s political leaders groped to create an enduring peace and rebuild the prewar prosperity, and for a brief period late in the decade they seemed to have succeeded. Then the Great Depression shattered that fragile stability. Uncertainty returned with redoubled force in the 1930s. The international economy collapsed, and unemployment struck millions worldwide. The democracies turned inward as they sought to cope with massive domestic problems and widespread disillusionment. Generally speaking, they were not very successful. The old liberal ideals of individual rights and responsibilities, elected government, and economic freedom, even when they managed to survive, seemed ineffective and outmoded to many. And in many countries these ideals were abandoned completely.

NOTES

1. P. Valéry, *Variety,* trans. M. Cowley (New York: Harcourt Brace, 1927), pp. 27–28.

2. G. Greene, *Another Mexico* (New York: Viking Press, 1939), p. 3.

3. G. Orwell, *1984* (New York: New American Library, 1950), p. 220.

4. C. E. Jeanneret-Gris (Le Corbusier), *Towards a New Architecture* (London: J. Rodker, 1931), p. 15.

5. Quoted in A. H. Barr, Jr., *What Is Modern Painting?* 9th ed. (New York: Museum of Modern Art, 1966), p. 27.

6. Quoted ibid., p. 25.

7. R. Graves and A. Hodge, *The Long Week End: A Social History of Great Britain, 1918–1939* (New York: Macmillan, 1941), p. 131.

8. Quoted in A. Briggs, *The Birth of Broadcasting,* vol. 1 (London: Oxford University Press, 1961), p. 47.

9. Quoted in R. J. Sontag, *A Broken World, 1919–1939* (New York: Harper & Row, 1971), p. 129.

10. C. P. Kindleberger, *The World in Depression, 1929–1939* (Berkeley: University of California Press, 1973), p. 292.

11. Quoted in S. B. Clough et al., eds., *Economic History of Europe: Twentieth Century* (New York: Harper & Row, 1968), pp. 243–245.

12. Quoted in D. Dillard, *Economic Development of the North Atlantic Community* (Englewood Cliffs, N.J.: Prentice-Hall, 1967), p. 591.

SUGGESTED READING

Among general works, E. Wiskemann's *Europe of the Dictators, 1919–1945* (1966), and Sontag's study cited in the Notes are particularly recommended. The latter has an excellent bibliography. A. Bullock, ed., *The Twentieth Century* (1971), is a lavish visual feast combined with penetrating essays on major developments since 1900. Two excellent accounts of contemporary history—one with a liberal and the other with a conservative point of view—are R. Paxton, *Europe in the Twentieth Century* (1975), and P. Johnson, *Modern Times: The World from the Twenties to the Eighties* (1983). Crucial changes in thought before and after World War I are discussed in three rewarding intellectual histories: G. Masur, *Prophets of Yesterday* (1961); H. S. Hughes, *Consciousness and Society* (1956); and M. Biddiss, *Age of the Masses: Ideas and Society Since 1870* (1977). R. Stromberg, *European Intellectual History Since 1789* (1986), and F. Baumer, *Modern European Thought: Continuity and Change in Ideas, 1600–1950* (1970), are recommended general surveys. W. Kaufmann, *Nietzsche* (1974), is a sympathetic and justly famous study, and S. Aschheim, *The Nietzsche Legacy in Germany, 1890–1990* (1992), considers the range of responses to the pioneering philosopher. W. Barrett, *Irrational Man: A Study in Existential Philosophy* (1958), is still useful.

N. Cantor, *Twentieth-Century Culture: Modernism to Deconstruction* (1988), is a pugnacious and stimulating survey. J. Rewald's *The History of Impressionism* (1961) and *Post-Impressionism* (1956) are excellent, as is the work by Barr cited in the Notes. P. Collaer, *A History of Modern Music* (1961), and H. R. Hitchcock, *Architecture: Nineteenth and Twentieth Centuries* (1958), are good introductions. T. Wolfe, *From Bauhaus to My House* (1981), is a lively critique of modern architecture. L. Barnett, *The Universe and Dr. Einstein* (1952), is a fascinating study of the new physics. A. Storr, *Freud* (1989), and P. Rieff, *Freud* (1956), consider the man and how his theories have stood the test of time. In *Civilization and Its Discontents* (1930), which is highly recommended, S. Freud explores his theory of instinct and repression, arguing that society's necessary repression of instinctual drives will always leave people unhappy. M. White, ed., *The Age of Analysis* (1955), opens up basic questions of twentieth-century psychology and philosophy. H. Liebersohn, *Fate and Utopia in German Sociology* (1988), analyzes developments in German social science. J. Willett, *The New Sobriety: Art and Politics in the Weimar Period, 1917–1933* (1978), and P. Gay, *Weimar Culture* (1970), consider the artistic renaissance and the political culture in Germany in the 1920s. M. Marrus, ed., *Emergence of Leisure* (1974), is a pioneering inquiry into an important aspect of mass culture. H. Daniels-Rops, *A Fight for God*, 2 vols. (1966), is a sympathetic history of the Catholic church between 1870 and 1939.

G. Ambrosius and W. Hibbard, *A Social and Economic History of Twentieth-Century Europe* (1989), provides a good survey; C. Maier, *Recasting Bourgeois Europe* (1975), is an ambitious comparative study of social classes and conflicts in France, Germany, and Italy after World War I. P. Fritzsche, *Rehearsals for Fascism: Populism and Political Mobilization in Weimar Germany* (1990); R. Wohl, *The Generation of 1914* (1979); R. Kuisel, *Capital and State in Modern France: Renovation and Economic Management* (1982); and W. McDougall, *France's Rhineland Diplomacy, 1914–1924* (1978), are four more important studies on aspects of the postwar challenge. H. James, *The German Slump: Politics and Economics, 1924–1936* (1986), is an excellent analysis of economic recovery and subsequent collapse. M. Childs, *Sweden: The Middle Way* (1961), applauds Sweden's efforts at social reform. W. Neuman, *The Balance of Power in the Interwar Years, 1919–1939* (1968), perceptively examines international politics after the Locarno treaties of 1925. In addition to the contemporary works discussed in the text, the crisis of the interwar period comes alive in R. Crossman, ed., *The God That Failed* (1950), in which famous Western writers tell why they were attracted to and later repelled by communism; J. Ortega y Gasset's renowned *The Revolt of the Masses* (1932); and F. A. Hayek's *The Road to Serfdom* (1944), a famous warning of the dangers to democratic freedoms.

In addition to Kindleberger's excellent study of the Great Depression cited in the Notes, there is J. Galbraith's very lively and understandable account of the stock market collapse, *The Great Crash* (1955). J. Garraty, *Unemployment in History* (1978), is noteworthy, though novels best portray the human tragedy of economic decline. Winifred Holtby, *South Riding* (1936), and Walter Greenwood, *Love on the Dole* (1933), are moving stories of the Great Depression in England; Hans Fallada, *Little Man, What Now?* (1932), is the classic counterpart for Germany. Also highly recommended as commentaries on English life between the wars are Robert Graves, *Goodbye to All That* (1957), and George Orwell, *The Road to Wigan Pier* (1972). Among French novelists, André Gide painstakingly examines the French middle class and its values in *The Counterfeiters;* and the great existentialist Albert Camus is at his unforgettable best in *The Stranger* (1942) and *The Plague* (1947).

A Christian View of Evil

The English philosopher C. E. M. Joad (1891–1953) stands out among intellectuals who turned toward religion in the age of anxiety. As a university student he shed his faith and became a militant rationalist who was "frequently in demand for lectures and articles which adopted an attitude hostile to revealed religion in general, and to the Christian Church in particular." Only after intense reflection did Joad retrace his steps and come to reaccept Christianity. Ever the serious intellectual, he described and analyzed his "spiritual odyssey" in closely reasoned and influential writings.

The following selection is taken from God and Evil, *published in 1942 when Hitler's empire posed the problem of human depravity in the starkest terms. Reconsidering the modern secular faith in the primacy of environmental influences and in the perfectibility of humankind, Joad found these beliefs wanting. He reaffirmed the Christian focus on sin and the need for God's grace to escape from evil and find salvation.*

There is, we are told, a revival of interest in religious matters. . . . In this revival of interest I have shared. . . . As a young man at Oxford, I participated, as was natural to my age and generation, in prolonged and frequent discussions of religion which, finding me a Christian, left me as they did many of my generation, an agnostic, an agnostic who entertained a deep-seated suspicion of all dogmatic creeds. . . .

As an agnostic, I felt convinced of two things: first, . . . within the sphere of religion that we did not and probably could not know the truth; secondly, in regard to the so-called religious truths that I had been taught, as, for example, that God created the world as stated in Genesis [and] . . . sent His Son into it to redeem mankind, that it was improbable that they were true and certain that they could not

be *known* to be true. In the confidence of this conviction I proceeded, to all intents and purposes, to turn my back upon the whole subject. . . .

It was only after the coming of the Nazis that my mind began again to turn in the direction of religion. . . . [With] the outbreak of [the Second World] war the subject leapt straight into the forefront of my consciousness where it has remained ever since. . . .

I take it [my spiritual odyssey] to be not untypical. From conversations and discussions, especially with students, I surmise that the revival of interest in religion is widespread. . . . This topical relevance of religion derives from two sources. [First, there is] the relation between religion and politics. This connection . . . subsists at all times, but in quiet times of peace it usually remains implicit. The peculiar circumstances of the last twenty-five years have, however, combined to thrust it into the foreground of men's consciousness. . . . Thus times of revolutionary political change are also times of religious questioning and discussion.

The other source of the specifically topical interest in religion is . . . the obtrusiveness of evil. [Perhaps] there is no more evil abroad in Western civilization than there was at the end of the last century, but it cannot be denied that what there is of it is more obtrusive. I am not referring to evils arising from the relation between the sexes upon which the Church has laid such exclusive stress. . . . I mean the evils of cruelty, savagery, oppression, violence, egotism, aggrandisement, and lust for power. So pervasive and insistent have these evils become that it is at times difficult to avoid concluding that the Devil has been given a longer rope than usual, . . . [and] it becomes correspondingly more difficult to explain it away by the various methods which have been fashionable during the last twenty years.

There was, for example, the explanation of evil in terms of economic inequality and injustice. Socialist writers had taught my generation that bad conditions were the cause of human wretchedness . . . and also of human wickedness. Poverty . . . was the supreme sin; supreme if only because it was the source of all the others. . . .

And the moral [of this teaching]? That evil is due to bad social conditions. Now you can reform bad social conditions by Act of Parliament, substituting comfort, cleanliness, security, and financial competence for discomfort, dirt, insecurity, and want. Therefore, presumably, you can make men virtuous . . . by Act of Parliament.

There was a later explanation of evil in terms of early psychological maltreatment and consequent psychological maladjustment. Evil, then, according to this view, was the result not of bad social, but of bad psychological conditions; not so much of an imperfect society, as of an imperfect family, an ill-directed nursery, and a wrongly run school. Reform society, said the Socialist, and evil will disappear. Reform the school and the family, the psychoanalysts added, and society will reform itself and, once again, evil will disappear. . . .

The contemporary view of evil is untenable. . . . Evil is not *merely* a by-product of unfavourable circumstances; it is too widespread and too deep-seated to admit of any such explanation; so widespread, so deep-seated that one can only conclude that what the religions have always taught is true, and that evil is endemic in the heart of man. . . . The intellectual blunder [of the comfortable and secure late-nineteenth century was] . . . denying what we had traditionally been taught, the doctrine of original sin. . . .

For the simple truth is that one cannot help oneself. . . . For one cannot help but know that one's character is *not* strong enough, one's efforts *not* efficacious, at least, that they are not, if unaided. . . . There are two alternatives [to giving in to evil].

The first, since the world is evil, is to escape from it and to find, first in withdrawal, and, as an ultimate hope, in Nirvana, the true way of life. The second is to face evil and to seek to overcome it. . . . The first is the way of the East, the second of Christianity. My temperament and disposition incline me to the second, but the second I know to be impossible

The British philosopher Cyril Edwin Mitchinson Joad (1891–1953). *(Source: Hulton-Deutsch Collection)*

unless I am assisted from without. By the grace of God we are assured, such assistance may be obtained and evil may be overcome; otherwise, there is no resource and no resistance.

Questions for Analysis

1. How did Joad account for a renewed interest in religious matters?

2. Joad concentrated on the problem of evil in human affairs. What did he mean by "evil"? Was it becoming more powerful in his time?

3. What, according to Joad, were the usual explanations for the existence of evil? What was his view of these explanations?

4. In Joad's view, how did the Christian doctrine of original sin relate to the problem of evil? How could the Christian overcome sin and evil?

Source: C. E. M. Joad, *God and Evil* (New York: Harper and Brothers, 1943), pp. 9–20, 103–104.

32

Dictatorships and the Second World War

Hugo Jager's photograph of a crowd of enthusiastic Hitler supporters *(Source: Hugo Jager, Life Magazine, © Time Warner, Inc.)*

The era of anxiety and economic depression was also a time of growing strength for political dictatorship. In Europe, as in Japan and China in the 1930s, popularly elected governments and basic civil liberties declined drastically. On the eve of the Second World War, liberal democratic governments were surviving only in Great Britain, France, the Low Countries, the Scandinavian nations, and neutral Switzerland. Elsewhere in Europe, various kinds of strongmen ruled. Dictatorship seemed the wave of the future. Thus the decline in liberal political institutions and the intellectual crisis were related elements in the general crisis of European civilization.

The West's era of dictatorship is a highly disturbing chapter in the history of civilization. The key development was not only the resurgence of authoritarian rule but also the rise of a particularly ruthless and dynamic tyranny. This new kind of tyranny reached its fullest realization in the Soviet Union and Nazi Germany in the 1930s. Stalin and Hitler mobilized their peoples for enormous undertakings and ruled with unprecedented severity. Hitler's mobilization was ultimately directed toward racial aggression and territorial expansion, and his sudden attack on Poland in 1939 started World War II.

Nazi armies were defeated by a great coalition, and today we want to believe that the era of totalitarian dictatorship was a terrible accident, that Stalin's slave labor camps and Hitler's gas chambers "can't happen again." But the cruel truth is that horrible atrocities continue to plague the world in our time. The Khmer Rouge inflicted genocide on its people in Kampuchea (Cambodia), and civil war in Bosnia led to ethnically motivated atrocities recalling the horrors of the Second World War. And there are other examples. Thus it is vital that we understand Europe's era of brutal dictatorship in order to guard against the possibility of its recurrence.

- What was the nature of twentieth-century dictatorship and authoritarian rule?
- How did people live in the most extreme states: the Soviet Union and Nazi Germany?
- How did the rise of aggressive dictatorships result in another world war?

These are the questions this chapter will seek to answer.

AUTHORITARIAN STATES

Both conservative and radical dictatorships swept through Europe in the 1920s and the 1930s. Although these two types of dictatorship shared some characteristics and sometimes overlapped in practice, they were in essence profoundly different. Conservative authoritarian regimes were an old story in Europe. Radical dictatorships were a new and frightening development.

Conservative Authoritarianism

The traditional form of antidemocratic government in European history was conservative authoritarianism. Like Catherine the Great in Russia and Metternich in Austria, the leaders of such governments tried to prevent major changes that would undermine the existing social order. To do so, they relied on obedient bureaucracies, vigilant police departments, and trustworthy armies. They forbade popular participation in government or else severely limited it to natural allies such as landlords, bureaucrats, and high church officials. They persecuted liberals, democrats, and socialists as subversive radicals, often consigning them to jail or exile.

Yet old-fashioned authoritarian governments were limited in their power and in their objectives. They had neither the ability nor the desire to control many aspects of their subjects' lives. Preoccupied with the goal of mere survival, these governments largely limited their demands to taxes, army recruits, and passive acceptance. As long as the people did not try to change the system, they often had considerable personal independence.

After the First World War, this kind of authoritarian government revived, especially in the less developed eastern part of Europe. There the parliamentary regimes that had been founded on the wreckage of empires in 1918 fell one by one. There were several reasons for this development. These lands lacked a strong tradition of self-government, with its necessary restraint and compromise, and many of these new states, such as Yugoslavia, were torn by ethnic conflicts. Dictatorship appealed to nationalists and military leaders as a way to repress such tensions and preserve national unity. Large landowners and the church were still powerful forces in these largely agrarian areas, and they often looked to dictators to save them from progressive land reform or communist agrarian upheaval. So did some members of the middle class, which was small and weak in eastern Europe. Finally, though some kind of democracy managed to stagger through the 1920s in Austria, Bulgaria, Romania, Greece, Estonia, and Latvia, the Great Depression delivered the final blow to those countries in 1936. By early 1938 in eastern Europe only economically and socially advanced Czechoslovakia remained true to liberal political ideals. Conservative dictators also took over in Spain and Portugal.

Although some of the conservative authoritarian regimes adopted certain Hitlerian and fascist characteristics in the 1930s, their general aims were limited. They were concerned more with maintaining the status quo than with mobilizing the masses or forcing society into rapid change or war. This tradition continued into our own time, especially in some of the military dictatorships that ruled in Latin America until quite recently.

Hungary was a good example of conservative authoritarianism. In the chaos of collapse in 1919, Béla Kun formed a Lenin-style government, but foreign troops, large landowners, and hostile peasants soon crushed communism in Hungary. Thereafter, a combination of great and medium-size landowners instituted a semi-authoritarian regime, which maintained the status quo in the 1920s. Hungary had a parliament, but elections were carefully controlled. The peasants did not have the right to vote, and an upper house representing the landed aristocracy was re-established. There was no land reform or major social change. The Hungarian government remained conservative and nationalistic throughout the 1930s.

Radical Dictatorships

While conservative authoritarianism predominated in the smaller states of central and eastern Europe by the mid-1930s, radical dictatorships emerged in the Soviet Union, in Germany, and to a lesser extent in Italy. Almost all scholars agree that the leaders of these radical dictatorships violently rejected parliamentary restraint and liberal values. Scholars also agree that these dictatorships exercised unprecedented control over the masses and sought to mobilize them for constant action. But beyond

these certainties, there has always been controversy and debate over how best to interpret and explain these regimes.

Three leading interpretations of radical dictatorships will concern us here. The first interpretation relates the radical dictatorships to the rise of modern totalitarianism. The second interpretation focuses on the idea of fascism as the unifying impulse. The third stresses the limitations of such broad generalizations and the uniqueness of each regime. Each school of interpretation has strengths and weaknesses.

The concept of *totalitarianism* as an explanation of radical twentieth-century dictatorships emerged in the 1920s and the 1930s, although it is frequently and mistakenly seen as developing only after 1945 during the cold war.[1] In 1924 Mussolini spoke of the "fierce totalitarian will" of his movement in Italy. In the 1930s many British, American, and German writers-in-exile used the concept of totalitarianism to link Italian and German fascism with Soviet communism under a common antiliberal umbrella. The alliance between Hitler and Stalin in 1939 reinforced this explanation.

Early writers believed that modern totalitarianism burst on the scene with the revolutionary total-war effort of 1914 to 1918. The war called forth a tendency to subordinate all institutions and all classes to one supreme objective: victory. As French thinker Elie Halévy put it in 1936, the varieties of modern totalitarian tyranny—fascism, Nazism, and communism—could be thought of as "feuding brothers" with a common father: the nature of modern war.[2]

Writers such as Halévy believed that the crucial experience of World War I was carried further by Lenin and the Bolsheviks during the Russian civil war. Lenin showed that a dedicated minority could make a total effort and achieve victory over a less determined majority. Lenin also demonstrated how institutions and human rights might be subordinated to the needs of a single group—the Communist party—and its leader, Lenin. Thus he provided a model for single-party dictatorship, and he inspired imitators, including Adolf Hitler. According to this school of interpretation, modern totalitarianism reached maturity in the 1930s in the Stalinist Soviet Union and in Nazi Germany.

As numerous Western political scientists and historians argued in the 1950s and the 1960s, the totalitarian state used modern technology and communications to exercise complete political power. But it did not stop there. Increasingly, the state took over and tried to control just as completely the economic, social, intellectual, and cultural aspects of people's lives. Deviation from the norm even in art or family behavior could become a crime. In theory, nothing was politically neutral; nothing was outside the scope of the state.

This grandiose vision of total state control broke decisively not only with conservative authoritarianism but also with nineteenth-century liberalism and democracy. Indeed, totalitarianism was a radical revolt against liberalism. Classical liberalism (see page 811) sought to limit the power of the state and protect the sacred rights of the individual. Liberals stood for rationality, peaceful progress, economic freedom, and a strong middle class. All of that disgusted totalitarians as sentimental slop. They believed in willpower, preached conflict, and worshiped violence. They believed that the individual was infinitely less valuable than the state and that there were no lasting rights, only temporary rewards for loyal and effective service. Only a single powerful leader and a single party, both unrestrained by law or tradition, determined the destiny of the totalitarian state.

Unlike old-fashioned authoritarianism, modern totalitarianism was based not on an elite but on mass movements led by committed individuals. Totalitarian societies were fully mobilized societies moving toward some goal and possessing boundless dynamism. As soon as one goal was achieved at

 Nazi Mass Rally in 1936   This picture captures the essence of the totalitarian interpretation of dynamic modern dictatorship. The uniformed members of the Nazi party have willingly merged themselves into a single force and await the command of the godlike leader. *(Source: Wide World Photos)*

the cost of enormous sacrifice, another arose at the leader's command to take its place. Thus totalitarianism was in the end a *permanent* revolution, an *unfinished* revolution, in which rapid, profound change imposed from on high went on forever.

A second group of writers developed the concept of *fascism* to explain the rise of radical dictatorships outside the Soviet Union. A term of pride for Mussolini and Hitler, who used it to describe the supposedly "total" and revolutionary character of their movements, fascism was severely criticized by these writers. They linked it to reactionary forces, decaying capitalism, and domestic class conflict. Orthodox Marxists first argued that fascism was the way powerful capitalists sought to create a mass nationalist movement capable of destroying the revolutionary working class, thereby protecting the enormous profits that capitalists reaped through war and territorial expansion. Both orthodox Marxists and less doctrinaire socialists usually rejected the totalitarian interpretation, discerning in communist regimes such as that of Stalin at least some elements of the genuine socialism they desired.

Recent comparative studies of fascist movements all across Europe have shown that they shared many characteristics, including extreme, often expansionist nationalism; antipathy to socialism and a desire to destroy working-class movements; alliances with powerful capitalists and landowners; mass parties that appealed especially to the middle class and the peasantry; a dynamic and violent leader; and glorification of war and the military. European fascism remains a product of class conflict, capitalist crisis, and postwar upheaval in these recent studies, but the basic interpretation has become less dogmatic and more convincing.

Historians today often adopt a third interpretive approach, which emphasizes the uniqueness of developments in each country. This approach has been both reflected and encouraged in recent years by an outpouring of specialized historical studies that challenge parts of the overarching totalitarian and fascist interpretations. This is especially true for Hitler's Germany, and a similar re-evaluation of Stalin's Soviet Union may be expected now that the fall of communism has opened Soviet archives to new research. To this third school of historians, differences in historical patterns are often more important than striking but frequently superficial similarities.

Four tentative judgments concerning these debates about radical dictatorships in the twentieth century seem appropriate. First, as is often the case in history, the leading interpretations are rather closely linked to the political passions and the ideological commitments of the age. Thus in the 1930s and in the early cold war, modern Western "bourgeois-liberal" observers, worried by the dual challenge of the Nazi and Soviet dictatorships, often found the totalitarian explanation convincing. At the same time, Marxist, socialist, and New Left writers easily saw profound structural differences between the continued capitalism in fascist countries and the socialism established in the Soviet Union.

Second, as a noted scholar has recently concluded, the concept of totalitarianism retains real value. It correctly highlights that both Hitler's Germany and Stalin's Soviet Union made an unprecedented "total claim" on the belief and behavior of their respective citizens.[3] Third, antidemocratic, antisocialist movements sprang up all over Europe, but only in Italy and Germany (and some would say Spain) were they able to take power. Studies of fascist movements seeking power locate common elements, but they do not explain what fascist governments actually did. Fourth, the problem of Europe's radical dictatorships is complex, and there are few easy answers.

✤ STALIN'S SOVIET UNION

Lenin's harshest critics claim that he established the basic outlines of a modern totalitarian dictatorship after the Bolshevik Revolution and during the Russian civil war. If this is so, then Joseph Stalin (1879–1953) certainly finished the job. A master of political infighting, Stalin cautiously consolidated his power and eliminated his enemies in the mid-1920s. Then in 1928, as undisputed leader of the ruling Communist party, he launched the first five-year plan—the "revolution from above," as he so aptly termed it.

The five-year plans were extremely ambitious. Often incorrectly considered a mere set of economic measures to speed the Soviet Union's industrial development, the five-year plans marked the beginning of a renewed attempt to mobilize and transform Soviet society along socialist lines.

Their ultimate goal was to generate new attitudes, new loyalties, and a new socialist humanity. The means Stalin and the small Communist party elite chose in order to do so were constant propaganda, enormous sacrifice, and unlimited violence and state control. Thus many historians argue that the Soviet Union in the 1930s became a dynamic, modern totalitarian state.

From Lenin to Stalin

By spring 1921 Lenin and the Bolsheviks had won the civil war, but they ruled a shattered and devastated land. Many farms were in ruins, and food supplies were exhausted. In southern Russia drought combined with the ravages of war to produce the worst famine in generations. By 1920, according to the government, from 50 to 90 percent of the population in seventeen provinces was starving. Industrial production also broke down completely. In 1921, for example, output of steel and cotton textiles was only about 4 percent of what it had been in 1913. Leon Trotsky later wrote that the "collapse of the productive forces surpassed anything of the kind history had ever seen. The country, and the government with it, were at the very edge of the abyss."[4] The Bolsheviks had destroyed the economy as well as their foes.

In the face of economic disintegration, riots by peasants and workers, and an open rebellion by

Lenin and Stalin in 1922   Lenin re-established limited economic freedom throughout Russia in 1921, but he ran the country and the Communist party in an increasingly authoritarian way. Stalin carried the process much further and eventually built a regime based on harsh dictatorship. *(Source: Sovfoto)*

previously pro-Bolshevik sailors at Kronstadt, the tough but ever-flexible Lenin changed course. In March 1921 he announced the New Economic Policy (NEP), which re-established limited economic freedom in an attempt to rebuild agriculture and industry. During the civil war, the communists had simply seized grain without payment. With the NEP, Lenin substituted a grain tax on the country's peasant producers, who were permitted to sell their surpluses in free markets. Peasants were also encouraged to buy as many goods as they could afford from private traders and small handicraft manufacturers, groups that were now allowed to reappear. Heavy industry, railroads, and banks, however, remained wholly nationalized.

The NEP was shrewd and successful both politically and economically. Politically, it was a necessary but temporary compromise with the Soviet Union's overwhelming peasant majority. Flushed with victory after the revolutionary gains of 1917, the peasants would have fought to hold onto their land. Realizing that his government was not strong enough to take land from the peasants, Lenin made a deal with the only force capable of overturning his government. Economically, the NEP brought rapid recovery. In 1926 industrial output surpassed the level of 1913, and Soviet peasants were producing almost as much grain as before the war. Counting shorter hours and increased social benefits, workers were living somewhat better than they had in the past.

As the economy recovered and the government partially relaxed its censorship and repression, an intense struggle for power began in the inner circles of the Communist party, for Lenin had left no chosen successor when he died in 1924. The principal contenders were the stolid Stalin and the flamboyant Trotsky.

The son of a shoemaker, Joseph Dzhugashvili—later known as Stalin—studied for the priesthood but was expelled from his theological seminary, probably for rude rebelliousness. By 1903 he had joined the Bolsheviks. In the years before the First World War, he engaged in many revolutionary activities in the southern Transcaucasian area of the multinational Russian Empire, including a daring bank robbery to get money for the Bolsheviks. This raid gained Lenin's attention and approval.

Stalin was a good organizer but a poor speaker and writer, with no experience outside Russia. Trotsky, a great and inspiring leader who had planned the 1917 takeover (see page 000) and then created the victorious Red Army, appeared to have all the advantages. Yet it was Stalin who succeeded Lenin. Stalin won because he was more effective at gaining the all-important support of the party, the only genuine source of power in the one-party state. Rising to general secretary of the party's Central Committee just before Lenin's first stroke in 1922, Stalin used his office to win friends and allies with jobs and promises.

The practical Stalin also won because he appeared better able than the brilliant Trotsky to relate Marxian teaching to Soviet realities in the 1920s. Stalin developed a theory of "socialism in one country" that was more appealing to the majority of communists than Trotsky's doctrine of "permanent revolution." Stalin argued that the Russian-dominated Soviet Union had the ability to build socialism on its own. Trotsky maintained that socialism in the Soviet Union could succeed only if revolution occurred quickly throughout Europe. To many communists, especially Soviet communists, Trotsky's views seemed to sell their country short and to promise risky conflicts with capitalist countries by recklessly encouraging revolutionary movements around the world. Stalin's willingness to break with the NEP and push socialism at home appealed to many in the party who had come to detest the capitalist-appearing NEP.

With cunning skill Stalin gradually achieved absolute power between 1922 and 1927. First, he allied with Trotsky's personal enemies to crush Trotsky, who was expelled from the Soviet Union in 1929 and eventually was murdered in Mexico in 1940, undoubtedly on Stalin's order. Second, Stalin aligned with the moderates, who wanted to go slow at home, to suppress Trotsky's radical followers. Third, having defeated all the radicals, he turned against his allies, the moderates, and destroyed them as well. Stalin's final triumph came at the party congress of December 1927, which condemned all "deviation from the general party line" formulated by Stalin. The dictator was then ready to launch his revolution from above—the real revolution for millions of ordinary citizens.

The Five-Year Plans

The party congress of 1927, which ratified Stalin's seizure of power, marked the end of the NEP and the beginning of the era of socialist five-year plans.

The first five-year plan had staggering economic objectives. In just five years, total industrial output was to increase by 250 percent. Heavy industry, the preferred sector, was to grow even faster; steel production, for example, was to jump almost 300 percent. Agricultural production was slated to increase by 150 percent, and one-fifth of the peasants in the Soviet Union were scheduled to give up their private plots and join socialist collective farms. In spite of warnings from moderate communists that these goals were unrealistic, Stalin raised them higher as the plan got under way. By 1930 economic and social change was sweeping the country.

Stalin unleashed his "second revolution" for a variety of interrelated reasons. There were, first of all, ideological considerations. Like Lenin, Stalin and his militant supporters were deeply committed to socialism as they understood it. Purely economic motivations were also important. Although the economy had recovered, it seemed to have stalled in 1927 and 1928. A new socialist offensive seemed necessary if industry and agriculture were to grow rapidly.

Political considerations were most important. Internationally, there was the old problem, remaining from prerevolutionary times, of catching up with the advanced and presumably hostile capitalist nations of the West. Stalin said in 1931, when he pressed for ever-greater speed and sacrifice, "We are fifty or a hundred years behind the advanced countries. We must make good this distance in ten years. Either we do it, or we shall go under."[5]

Domestically, there was what communist writers of the 1920s called the "cursed problem"—the problem of the peasants. For centuries, the peasants had wanted to own the land, and finally they had it. Sooner or later, the communists reasoned, the peasants would become conservative little capitalists and pose a threat to the regime. Therefore, Stalin decided on a preventive war against the peasantry in order to bring it under the absolute control of the state.

That war was *collectivization*—the forcible consolidation of individual peasant farms into large, state-controlled enterprises. Beginning in 1929, peasants all over the Soviet Union were ordered to give up their land and animals and become members of collective farms, although they continued to live in their own homes. As for the *kulaks*, the better-off peasants, Stalin instructed party workers

to "liquidate them as a class." Stripped of land and livestock, the kulaks were generally not even permitted to join the collective farms. Many starved or were deported to forced-labor camps for "re-education."

Since almost all peasants were in fact poor, the term *kulak* soon meant any peasant who opposed the new system. Whole villages were often attacked. One conscience-stricken colonel in the secret police confessed to a foreign journalist, "I am an old Bolshevik. I worked in the underground against the Tsar and then I fought in the Civil War. Did I do all that in order that I should now surround villages with machine guns and order my men to fire indiscriminately into crowds of peasants? Oh, no, no!"[6]

Forced collectivization of the peasants led to economic and human disaster. Large numbers of peasants slaughtered their animals and burned their crops in sullen, hopeless protest. Between 1929 and 1933, the number of horses, cattle, sheep, and goats in the Soviet Union fell by at least half. Nor were the state-controlled collective farms more productive. The output of grain barely increased between 1928 and 1938, when it was almost identical to the output of 1913. Collectivized agriculture was unable to make any substantial financial contribution to Soviet industrial development during the first five-year plan. And the human dimension of the tragedy was shocking. Collectivization created human-made famine in 1932 and 1933, and many perished. Indeed, Stalin confided to British prime minister Winston Churchill at Yalta in 1945 (see page 1092) that 10 million people had died in the course of collectivization.

Nevertheless, collectivization was a political victory of sorts. By the end of 1932, fully 60 percent of peasant families had been herded onto collective farms; by 1938, 93 percent. Regimented and indoctrinated as employees of an all-powerful state, the peasants were no longer even a potential political threat to Stalin and the Communist party. Moreover, the state was assured of grain for bread for urban workers, who were much more important politically than the peasants. Collective farmers had to meet their grain quotas first and worry about feeding themselves second. Many collectivized peasants drew much of their own food from tiny, grudgingly tolerated garden plots that they worked in their off hours.

✳ **Decorative Art in Soviet Russia**   Russia had a rich tradition of icon-painting and decorative religious art, which was expected to glorify Soviet life and socialist achievements after the Russian Revolution. This beautiful lacquered lid of a wooden box was produced in the old icon-painting center of Palekh, 200 miles east of Moscow. The painter skillfully combines modern motifs, such as tractors and factories, with traditional themes of peasant life. Historians usually find considerable continuity in the midst of revolutionary change. *(Source: Novosti)*

The industrial side of the five-year plans was more successful—indeed, quite spectacular. Soviet industry produced about four times as much in 1937 as it had in 1928. No other major country had ever achieved such rapid industrial growth. Heavy industry led the way; consumer industry grew quite slowly. Steel production—a near-obsession with Stalin, whose name fittingly meant "man of steel" in Russian—increased roughly 500 percent between 1928 and 1937. A new heavy industrial complex was built almost from scratch in western Siberia. Industrial growth also went hand in hand with urban development. Cities rose where nomadic tribes had grazed their flocks. More than 25 million people migrated to cities during the 1930s.

The great industrialization drive, concentrated between 1928 and 1937, was an awe-inspiring achievement purchased at enormous sacrifice. The sudden creation of dozens of new factories (*and* the increasingly voracious military) demanded tremendous resources. The money was collected from the people by means of heavy, hidden sales taxes. There was therefore no improvement in the average standard of living. Indeed, the most careful studies show that the average nonfarm wage apparently purchased only about *half* as many goods in 1932 as in 1928. After 1932 real wages rose slowly, so that in 1937 workers could buy about 60 percent of what they had bought in 1928.

Two other factors contributed importantly to rapid industrialization: firm labor discipline and foreign engineers. Between 1930 and 1932, trade unions lost most of their power. The government could assign workers to any job anywhere in the country, and individuals could not move without the permission of the police. When factory managers needed more hands, they called on their counterparts on the collective farms, who sent them millions of "unneeded" peasants over the years.

Foreign engineers were hired to plan and construct many of the new factories. Highly skilled American engineers, hungry for work in the depression years, were particularly important until newly trained Soviet experts began to replace them after 1932. The gigantic mills of the new Siberian steel industry were modeled on America's best.

Stalin's planners harnessed even the skill and technology of capitalist countries to promote the surge of socialist industry.

Life in Stalinist Society

The aim of Stalin's five-year plans was to create a new kind of society and human personality as well as a strong industrial economy and a powerful army. Stalin and his helpers were Marxian economic determinists. Once everything was owned by the state, they believed, a socialist society and a new kind of human being would inevitably emerge. They were by no means totally successful, but they did build a new society, whose broad outlines existed through the early 1980s. For the people, life in Stalinist society had both good and bad aspects.

The most frightening aspect of Stalinist society was brutal, unrestrained police terrorism. First directed primarily against the peasants after 1929, terror was increasingly turned on leading Communists, powerful administrators, and ordinary people for no apparent reason. As one Soviet woman later recalled, "We all trembled because there was no way of getting out of it. Even a Communist himself can be caught. To avoid trouble became an exception."[7] A climate of fear swept over the land.

In the early 1930s, the top members of the party and government were Stalin's obedient servants, but there was some grumbling in the party. At a small gathering in November 1932, even Stalin's wife complained bitterly about the misery of the people. Stalin showered her with insults, and she died that same night, apparently by her own hand. In late 1934 Stalin's number-two man, Sergei Kirov, was suddenly and mysteriously murdered. Although Stalin himself probably ordered Kirov's murder, he used the incident to launch a reign of terror.

In August 1936 sixteen prominent old Bolsheviks confessed to all manner of plots against Stalin in spectacular public trials in Moscow. Then in 1937 lesser party officials and newer henchmen were arrested. Some prisoners were cruelly tortured and warned that their loved ones would also die if they did not confess. In addition to party members, union officials, managers, intellectuals, army officers, and countless ordinary citizens were struck down. Local units of the secret police were even ordered to arrest a certain percentage of the people in their districts. In all, at least 8 million people were probably arrested, and millions never returned from prisons and forced-labor camps.

Stalin's mass purges were truly baffling, and many explanations have been given for them. Possibly Stalin believed that the old Communists, like the peasants under NEP, were a potential threat to be wiped out in a preventive attack. There are many other interpretations. Some scholars argue that the purges demonstrated that Stalin was sadistic or insane, for his bloodbath greatly weakened the government and the army. Others see the terror as an aspect of the fully developed totalitarian state, which must by its nature always be fighting real or imaginary enemies. At the least, the mass purges were a message to the people: no one was secure; everyone had to serve the party and its leader with redoubled devotion.

Another aspect of life in the 1930s was constant propaganda and indoctrination. Party activists lectured workers in factories and peasants on collective farms. Newspapers, films, and radio broadcasts endlessly recounted socialist achievements and capitalist plots. Art and literature became highly political. Intellectuals were ordered by Stalin to become "engineers of human minds." Writers and artists who could effectively combine genuine creativity and political propaganda became the darlings of the regime. They often lived better than top members of the political elite. It became increasingly important for the successful writer and artist to glorify Russian nationalism. Russian history was rewritten so that early tsars such as Ivan the Terrible and Peter the Great became worthy forerunners of the greatest Russian leader of all—Stalin.

Stalin seldom appeared in public, but his presence was everywhere—in portraits, statues, books, and quotations from his "sacred" writings. Although the government persecuted religion and turned churches into "museums of atheism," the state had both an earthly religion and a high priest—Marxism-Leninism and Joseph Stalin.

Life was hard in Stalin's Soviet Union. The masses of people lived primarily on black bread and wore old, shabby clothing. There were constant shortages in the stores, although very heavily taxed vodka was always readily available. A shortage of housing was a particularly serious problem. Millions were moving into the cities, but the government built few new apartments. In 1940 there were approximately 4 people per room in every urban dwelling, as opposed to 2.7 per room in 1926. A relatively lucky family received one room for all its members and shared both a kitchen and a toilet with others on the floor. Less fortunate workers, kulaks, and class enemies built scrap-lumber shacks or underground dugouts in shantytowns.

Life was hard but by no means hopeless. Idealism and ideology had real appeal for many communists, who saw themselves heroically building the world's first socialist society while capitalism crumbled and degenerated into fascism in the West. This optimistic belief in the future of the Soviet Union also attracted many disillusioned Westerners to communism in the 1930s.

On a more practical level, Soviet workers did receive some important social benefits, such as old-age pensions, free medical services, free education,

and day-care centers for children. Unemployment was almost unknown. And there was the possibility of personal advancement.

The keys to improving one's position were specialized skills and technical education. Rapid industrialization required massive numbers of trained experts, such as skilled workers, engineers, and plant managers. Thus the state provided tremendous incentives to those who could serve its needs. It paid the mass of unskilled workers and collective farmers very low wages, but it dangled high salaries and many special privileges before its growing technical and managerial elite. This elite joined with the political and artistic elites in a new upper class, whose members were rich, powerful, and insecure, especially during the purges. Yet the possible gains of moving up outweighed the risks. Millions struggled bravely in universities, institutes, and night schools for the all-important spe-

Adult Education Illiteracy, especially among women, was a serious problem after the Russian Revolution. This early photo shows how adults successfully learned to read and write throughout the Soviet Union. *(Source: Sovfoto)*

cialized education. One young man summed it up: "In Soviet Russia there is no capital except education. If a person does not want to become a collective farmer or just a cleaning woman, the only means you have to get something is through education."[8]

Mobilizing Women in the Soviet Union

The radical transformation of Soviet society had a profound impact on women's lives. Marxists had traditionally believed that both capitalism and the middle-class husband exploited women. The Russian Revolution of 1917 immediately proclaimed complete equality of rights for women. In the 1920s divorce and abortion were made easily available, and women were urged to work outside the home and liberate themselves sexually. After Stalin came to power, sexual and familial liberation was played down, and the most lasting changes for women involved work and education.

These changes were truly revolutionary. Young women were constantly told that they had to be fully equal to men, that they could and should do anything men could do. Peasant women in Russia had long experienced the equality of backbreaking physical labor in the countryside, and they continued to enjoy that equality on collective farms. With the advent of the five-year plans, millions of women also began to toil in factories and in heavy construction, building dams, roads, and steel mills in summer heat and winter frost. Most of the opportunities open to men through education were also open to women. Determined women pursued their studies and entered the ranks of the better-paid specialists in industry and science. Medicine practically became a woman's profession. By 1950, 75 percent of all doctors in the Soviet Union were women.

Thus Stalinist society gave women great opportunities but demanded great sacrifices as well. The vast majority of women simply *had* to work outside the home. Wages were so low that it was almost impossible for a family or couple to live only on the husband's earnings. Moreover, the full-time working woman had a heavy burden of household tasks in her off hours, for most Soviet men in the 1930s still considered the home and the children the woman's responsibility. Men continued to monopolize the best jobs. Finally, rapid change and economic hardship led to many broken families, creat-

ing further physical, emotional, and mental strains for women. In any event, the often-neglected human resource of women was ruthlessly mobilized in Stalinist society. This, too, was an aspect of the Soviet totalitarian state.

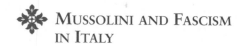

MUSSOLINI AND FASCISM IN ITALY

Mussolini's movement and his seizure of power in 1922 were important steps in the rise of dictatorships in Europe between the two world wars. Like all the future dictators, the young Mussolini hated liberalism and wanted to destroy it in Italy. At the same time, he and his supporters were the first to call themselves "fascists"—revolutionaries determined to create a certain kind of totalitarian state. Few scholars today would argue that Mussolini succeeded. His dictatorship was brutal and theatrical, but it remained a halfway house between conservative authoritarianism and modern totalitarianism.

The Seizure of Power

In the early twentieth century Italy was a liberal state with civil rights and a constitutional monarchy. On the eve of the First World War, the parliamentary regime finally granted universal male suffrage. But there were serious problems. Much of the Italian population was still poor, and many peasants were more attached to their villages and local interests than to the national state. Moreover, the papacy, many devout Catholics, conservatives, and landowners remained strongly opposed to the middle-class lawyers and politicians who ran the country largely for their own benefit. Relations between church and state were often tense. Class differences were also extreme, and a powerful revolutionary socialist movement had developed. The radical left wing of the Socialist party gained the leadership as early as 1912, and the party unanimously opposed the war from the very beginning.[9]

The war worsened the political situation. Having fought on the side of the Allies almost exclusively for purposes of territorial expansion, the parliamentary government bitterly disappointed Italian nationalists with Italy's modest gains at Versailles. Workers and peasants also felt cheated: to win their support during the war, the government had promised social and land reform, which it did not deliver after the war.

The Russian Revolution inspired and energized Italy's revolutionary socialist movement, and radical workers and peasants began occupying factories and seizing land in 1920. These actions scared and mobilized the property-owning classes. Moreover, after the war the pope lifted his ban on participation by Catholics in Italian politics, and a strong Catholic party quickly emerged. Thus by 1921 revolutionary socialists, antiliberal conservatives, and frightened property owners were all opposed—though for different reasons—to the liberal parliamentary government.

Into these crosscurrents of unrest and fear stepped the blustering, bullying Benito Mussolini (1883–1945). Son of a village schoolteacher and a poor blacksmith, Mussolini began his political career as a Socialist leader and radical newspaper editor before World War I. In 1914, powerfully influenced by antidemocratic cults of violent action, the young Mussolini urged that Italy join the Allies, a stand for which he was expelled from the Italian Socialist party. Later Mussolini fought at the front and was wounded in 1917. Returning home, he began organizing bitter war veterans like himself into a band of fascists—from the Italian word for "a union of forces."

At first Mussolini's program was a radical combination of nationalist and socialist demands, including territorial expansion, benefits for workers, and land reform for peasants. It competed directly with the well-organized Socialist party and failed to get off the ground. When Mussolini saw that his violent verbal assaults on rival Socialists won him growing support from conservatives and the frightened middle classes, he shifted gears in 1920. In thought and action, Mussolini was a striking example of the turbulent uncertainty of the age of anxiety.

Mussolini and his growing private army of Black Shirts began to grow violent. Typically, a band of fascist toughs would roar off in trucks at night and swoop down on a few isolated Socialist organizers, beating them up and force-feeding them almost deadly doses of castor oil. Few people were killed, but socialist newspapers, union halls, and local Socialist party headquarters were destroyed. Mussolini's toughs pushed Socialists out of the city governments of northern Italy.

A skillful politician, Mussolini allowed his followers to convince themselves that they were not just opposing the "Reds" but also making a real revolution of their own, forging a strong, dynamic movement that would help the little people against the established interests. With the government breaking down in 1922, largely because of the chaos created by his direct-action bands, Mussolini stepped forward as the savior of order and property. Striking a conservative note in his speeches and gaining the sympathetic neutrality of army leaders, Mussolini demanded the resignation of the existing government and his own appointment by the king. In October 1922, to force matters, a large group of Fascists marched on Rome to threaten the king and force him to call on Mussolini. The threat worked. Victor Emmanuel III (r. 1900–1946), who had no love for the old liberal politicians, asked Mussolini to form a new cabinet. Thus after widespread violence and a threat of armed uprising, Mussolini seized power "legally." He was immediately granted dictatorial authority for one year by the king and the parliament.

The Regime in Action

Mussolini became dictator on the strength of Italians' rejection of parliamentary government coupled with fears of Soviet-style revolution. Yet what he intended to do with his power was by no means clear until 1924. Some of his dedicated supporters pressed for a "second revolution." Mussolini's ministers, however, included old conservatives, moderates, and even two reform-minded Socialists. A new electoral law was passed giving two-thirds of the representatives in the parliament to the party that won the most votes. That change allowed the Fascists and their allies to win an overwhelming majority in 1924. Shortly thereafter five of Mussolini's fascist thugs kidnapped and murdered Giacomo Matteotti, the leader of the Socialists in the parliament. In the face of this outrage, the opposition demanded that Mussolini's armed squads be dissolved and all violence be banned.

Although Mussolini may or may not have ordered Matteotti's murder, he stood at the crossroads of a severe political crisis. After some hesitation, he charged forward. Declaring his desire to "make the nation Fascist," he imposed a series of repressive measures. Freedom of the press was abolished, elections were fixed, and the government ruled by decree. Mussolini arrested his political opponents, disbanded all independent labor unions, and put dedicated fascists in control of Italy's schools. He created a fascist youth movement, fascist labor unions, and many other fascist organizations. He trumpeted his goal in a famous slogan of 1926, "Everything in the state, nothing outside the state, nothing against the state." By the end of that year, Italy was a one-party dictatorship under Mussolini's unquestioned leadership.

Mussolini, however, did not complete the establishment of a modern totalitarian state. His Fascist party never became all-powerful. It never destroyed the old power structure, as the communists did in the Soviet Union; nor did it succeed in dominating the old power structure, as the Nazis did in Germany. Membership in the Fascist party was more a sign of an Italian's respectability than a commitment to radical change. Interested primarily in personal power, Mussolini was content to compromise with the old conservative classes that controlled the army, the economy, and the state. He never tried to purge these classes or even move very vigorously against them. He controlled and propagandized labor but left big business to regulate itself, profitably and securely. There was no land reform.

Mussolini also drew increasing support from the Catholic church. In the Lateran Agreement of 1929, he recognized the Vatican as a tiny independent state, and he agreed to give the church heavy financial support. The pope expressed his satisfaction and urged Italians to support Mussolini's government.

Nothing better illustrates Mussolini's unwillingness to harness everyone and everything for dynamic action than his treatment of women. He abolished divorce and told women to stay at home and produce children. To promote that goal, he decreed a special tax on bachelors in 1934. In 1938 women were limited by law to a maximum of 10 percent of the better-paying jobs in industry and government. Italian women appear not to have changed their attitudes or behavior in any important way under fascist rule.

Mussolini's government did not pass racial laws until 1938 and did not persecute Jews savagely until late in the Second World War, when Italy was under Nazi control. Nor did Mussolini establish a truly ruthless police state. Only twenty-three political prisoners were condemned to death between

Mussolini A charismatic orator with a sure touch for emotional propaganda, Mussolini loved settings that linked fascist Italy to the glories of imperial Rome. Poised to address a mass rally in Rome at the time of Matteotti's murder, Mussolini then called for ninety thousand more volunteers to join his gun-toting fascist militia. Members of the militia stand as an honor guard in front of the podium. *(Source: Popperfoto)*

1926 and 1944. In spite of much pompous posing by the chauvinist leader and in spite of mass meetings, salutes, and a certain copying of Hitler's aggression in foreign policy after 1933, Mussolini's fascist Italy, though repressive and undemocratic, was never really totalitarian.

�֎ HITLER AND NAZISM IN GERMANY

The most frightening dictatorship developed in Nazi Germany. A product of Hitler's evil genius as well as of Germany's social and political situation and the general attack on liberalism and rationality in the age of anxiety, the Nazi movement shared some of the characteristics of Mussolini's Italian model and was a form of fascism. The Nazi dictatorship smashed or took over most independent organizations, mobilized the economy, and began brutally persecuting the Jewish population. Thus Nazism asserted an unlimited claim over German society and put all final power in the hands of its endlessly aggressive leader—Adolf Hitler. In this regard Nazism was truly totalitarian.

The Roots of Nazism

Nazism grew out of many complex developments, of which the most influential were extreme nationalism and racism. These two ideas captured the mind of the young Hitler, and it was he who dominated Nazism for as long as it lasted.

Born the fourth child of a successful Austrian customs official and an indulgent mother, Adolf Hitler (1889–1945) spent his childhood in small towns in Austria. A good student in grade school, Hitler did poorly in high school and dropped out at age fourteen after the death of his father. After four years of unfocused loafing, Hitler finally left for Vienna to become an artist. Denied admission to the Imperial Academy of Fine Arts because he lacked talent, the dejected Hitler stayed in Vienna. There he lived a comfortable, lazy life on his generous orphan's pension and found most of the perverted beliefs that guided his life.

In Vienna Hitler soaked up extreme German nationalism, which was particularly strong there. Austro-German nationalists, as if to compensate for their declining position in the Austro-Hungarian Empire, believed Germans to be a superior people and the natural rulers of central Europe. They often advocated union with Germany and violent expulsion of "inferior" peoples as the means of maintaining German domination of the Austro-Hungarian Empire.

Hitler was deeply impressed by Vienna's mayor, Karl Lueger (1844–1910). With the help of the Catholic trade unions, Lueger had succeeded in winning the support of the little people of Vienna for an attack on capitalism and liberalism. A master of mass politics in the urban world, Lueger showed Hitler the enormous potential of anticapitalist and antiliberal propaganda.

From Lueger and others, Hitler eagerly absorbed virulent anti-Semitism, racism, and hatred of Slavs, along with an unshakable belief in the crudest, most exaggerated distortions of the Darwinian theory of survival, the superiority of Germanic races, and the inevitability of racial conflict. Anti-Semitism and racism became Hitler's most passionate convictions, his explanation for everything. The Jews, he claimed, directed an international conspiracy of finance capitalism and Marxian socialism against German culture, German unity, and the German race. Hitler's belief was totally irrational, but he never doubted it.

Although he moved to Munich in 1913 to avoid being drafted into the Austrian army, the lonely Hitler greeted the outbreak of the First World War as a salvation. He later wrote in his autobiography, *Mein Kampf,* that, "overcome by passionate enthusiasm, I fell to my knees and thanked heaven out of an overflowing heart." The struggle and discipline of war gave life meaning, and Hitler served bravely as a dispatch carrier on the western front.

When Germany was suddenly defeated in 1918, Hitler's world was shattered. Not only was he a fanatical nationalist, but war was his reason for living. Convinced that Jews and Marxists had "stabbed Germany in the back," he vowed to fight on. And in the bitterness and uncertainty of postwar Germany, his wild speeches began to attract attention.

In late 1919 Hitler joined a tiny extremist group in Munich called the German Workers' party. In addition to denouncing Jews, Marxists, and democrats, the German Workers' party promised unity under a uniquely German "national socialism," which would abolish the injustices of capitalism and create a mighty "people's community." By 1921 Hitler had gained absolute control of this small but growing party. He was already a master of mass propaganda and political showmanship. His most effective tool was the mass rally, a kind of political revival meeting, where he often worked his audience into a frenzy with wild, demagogic attacks on the Versailles treaty, the Jews, war profiteers, and Germany's Weimar Republic.

Party membership multiplied tenfold after early 1922. In late 1923, when the Weimar Republic seemed on the verge of collapse, Hitler decided on an armed uprising in Munich, inspired by Mussolini's recent easy victory. Despite the failure of the poorly organized plot and the arrest of Hitler, Nazism had been born.

Hitler's Road to Power

At his trial, Hitler violently denounced the Weimar Republic and skillfully presented his own program. In doing so, he gained enormous publicity and attention. Moreover, he learned from his unsuccessful revolt. Hitler concluded that he had to undermine, rather than overthrow, the government, that he had to use its tolerant democratic framework to intimidate the opposition and come to power through electoral competition. He forced his more violent supporters to accept his new strategy. He also used his brief prison term—he was released in less than a year—to dictate *Mein Kampf* (1924). There he expounded on his basic themes: "race," with a stress on anti-Semitism; "living space," with a sweeping vision of war and conquered territory; and the leader-dictator (*Führer*), with unlimited, arbitrary power. Hitler's followers had their bible.

In the years of prosperity and relative stability between 1924 and 1929, Hitler concentrated on building his National Socialist German Workers' party, or Nazi party. By 1928 the party had a hundred thousand highly disciplined members under Hitler's absolute control. To appeal to the middle classes, Hitler de-emphasized the anticapitalist elements of national socialism and vowed to fight Bolshevism.

The Nazis were still a small splinter group in 1928, when they received only 2.6 percent of the vote in the general elections and twelve seats in the Reichstag. There the Nazi deputies pursued the legal strategy of using democracy to destroy democracy. As Hitler's talented future minister of propaganda, Joseph Goebbels (1897–1945), explained in 1928 in the party newspaper, "We become Reichstag deputies in order to paralyze the spirit of Weimar with its own aid. . . . We come as enemies! As the wolf breaks into the sheepfold, so we come."[10]

In 1929 the Great Depression began striking down economic prosperity, one of the barriers that

had kept the wolf at bay. In 1930 Germany had almost as many unemployed as all the other countries of Europe combined. By the end of 1932, an incredible 43 percent of the labor force was unemployed, and it was estimated that only one in every three union members was working full-time. No factor contributed more to Hitler's success than the economic crisis. Never very interested in economics before, Hitler began promising German

Hitler in Opposition Hitler returns the salute of his Brown Shirts in this photograph from the third party day rally in Nuremberg in 1927. The Brown Shirts formed a private army within the Nazi movement, and their uniforms, marches, salutes, and vandalism helped keep Hitler in the public eye in the 1920s. (*Source: Courtesy, Bison Books, London*)

voters economic as well as political and military salvation. He pitched his speeches especially to the middle and lower middle classes—small business people, office workers, artisans, and peasants. Already disillusioned by the great inflation of 1923, these people were seized by panic as bankruptcies increased, unemployment soared, and the dreaded Communists made dramatic election gains. The middle and lower middle classes deserted the conservative and moderate parties for the Nazis in great numbers.

Simultaneously, Hitler worked hard behind the scenes to win the support of two key elite groups. First, he promised big business leaders that he would restore their depression-shattered profits, by breaking Germany's strong labor movement and reducing workers' wages if need be. Second, he assured top army leaders that the Nazis would overturn the Versailles settlement and rearm Germany. Thus Hitler successfully followed Mussolini's fascist recipe. He won at least the tacit approval of powerful conservatives who could have blocked his bid for power.

The Nazis also appealed strongly to German youth. Indeed, in some ways the Nazi movement was a mass movement of young Germans. "National Socialism is the organized will of the youth," proclaimed the official Nazi slogan, and the battle cry of Gregor Strasser, a leading Nazi organizer, was "Make way, you old ones."[11] In 1931 almost 40 percent of Nazi party members were under thirty, compared with 20 percent of Social Democrats. National recovery, exciting and rapid change, and personal advancement: these were the appeals of Nazism to millions of German youths.

As the economic and political situation continued to deteriorate, Hitler and the Nazis kept promising that they would bring economic recovery and national unity. In the election of 1932 the Nazis won 14.5 million votes and became the largest party in the Reichstag.

Another reason why Hitler came to power was the breakdown of democratic government as early as May 1930. Unable to gain the support of a majority in the Reichstag, Chancellor Heinrich Brüning convinced the president, the aging war hero General Hindenburg, to authorize rule by decree, which the Weimar Republic's constitution permitted in emergency situations. Brüning was determined to overcome the economic crisis by cutting back government spending and ruthlessly forcing down prices and wages. These failed policies convinced the lower middle classes that the country's republican leaders were stupid and corrupt. These classes were pleased, rather than dismayed, by Hitler's attacks on the republican system. After President Hindenburg forced Brüning to resign in May 1932, the new government continued to rule by decree.

Meanwhile, the struggle between the Social Democrats and Communists persisted right up until the moment Hitler took power. Even after the elections of 1932, the Communists refused to cooperate with the Social Democrats, despite the fact that the two parties together outnumbered the Nazis in the Reichstag. German Communists (and the still-complacent Stalin) were blinded by hatred of Socialists and by ideology. Socialist leaders pleaded, even at the Soviet Embassy, for at least a temporary alliance with the Communists to block Hitler, but to no avail.

Finally, there was Hitler's skill as a politician. A master of mass propaganda and psychology, he had written in *Mein Kampf* that the masses were the "driving force of the most important changes in this world" and were themselves driven by hysterical fanaticism and not by knowledge. To arouse such hysterical fanaticism, he believed, all propaganda had to be limited to a few simple, endlessly repeated slogans. Thus in the terrible economic and political crisis, he harangued vast audiences with passionate, irrational oratory. Men moaned and women cried, seized by emotion. And many uncertain individuals, surrounded by thousands of entranced listeners, found security and a sense of belonging.

At the same time, Hitler continued to excel at dirty, back-room politics. That, in fact, brought him to power. Through complicated infighting in 1932 he cleverly succeeded in gaining additional support from key people in the army and big business. These people thought they could use Hitler for their own advantage to get increased military spending, fat contracts, and tough measures against workers. Many conservative and nationalistic politicians thought similarly. They thus accepted Hitler's demand to join the government only if he became chancellor. There would be only two other National Socialists and nine staunch conservatives as ministers, and in such a coalition government, they reasoned, Hitler could be used and controlled. On January 30, 1933, Hitler was legally appointed chancellor by President Hindenburg.

The Nazi State and Society

Hitler moved rapidly and skillfully to establish an unshakable dictatorship. Continuing to maintain legal appearances, he immediately called for new elections. In the midst of a violent electoral campaign, the Reichstag building was partly destroyed by fire. Although the Nazis themselves may have set the fire, Hitler screamed that the Communist party was responsible. On the strength of this accusation, he convinced President Hindenburg to sign dictatorial emergency acts that practically abolished freedom of speech and assembly as well as most personal liberties.

When the Nazis won only 44 percent of the vote in the elections, Hitler immediately outlawed the Communist party and arrested its parliamentary representatives. Then on March 23, 1933, the Nazis used threats and blackmail to help push through the Reichstag the so-called Enabling Act, which gave Hitler absolute dictatorial power for four years. Armed with the Enabling Act, Hitler and the Nazis moved to smash or control all independent organizations. Their deceitful stress on legality, coupled with divide-and-conquer techniques, disarmed the opposition until it was too late for effective resistance. Germany soon became a one-party state. Only the Nazi party was legal. Elections were farces. The Reichstag was jokingly referred to as the most expensive glee club in the country, for its only function was to sing hymns of praise to the Führer. Hitler and the Nazis took over the government bureaucracy intact, installing many Nazis in top positions. At the same time, they created a series of overlapping Nazi party organizations responsible solely to Hitler.

As recent research shows, the resulting system of dual government was riddled with rivalries, contradictions, and inefficiencies. The Nazi state lacked the all-compassing unity that its propagandists claimed and was sloppy and often disorganized, but this fractured system suited Hitler and his purposes. He could play the established bureaucracy against his private, personal "party government" and maintain his freedom of action. Hitler could concentrate on general principles and the big decisions, which he always made.

In the economic sphere, one big decision outlawed strikes and abolished independent labor unions, which were replaced by the Nazi Labor Front. Professional people—doctors and lawyers, teachers and engineers—also saw their previously

The Mobilization of Young People A prime objective of the Nazi leadership was to appeal to young Germans. Here boys in a Nazi youth group—some of them are only children—are disciplined and conditioned to devote themselves to the regime. (*Source: Hulton Deutsch Collection*)

independent organizations swallowed up in Nazi associations. Nor did the Nazis neglect cultural and intellectual life. Publishing houses and universities were put under Nazi control. Democratic, socialist, and Jewish literature was put on ever-growing blacklists. Passionate students and pitiful professors burned forbidden books in public squares. Modern art and architecture were ruthlessly prohibited. Life became violently anti-intellectual. As the cynical Goebbels put it, "When I hear the word 'culture' I reach for my gun."[12] By 1934 a brutal dictatorship characterized by frightening dynamism and obedience to Hitler was already largely in place.

That's the 3rd time its mentioned!

Only the army retained independence, and Hitler moved ruthlessly and skillfully to establish his control there, too. The Nazi storm troopers (the SA), the quasi-military band of 3 million toughs in brown shirts who had fought communists and beaten up Jews before the Nazis took power, expected top positions in the army and even talked of a "second revolution" against capitalism. Needing to preserve good relations with the army and with big business, Hitler decided that the SA leaders had to be eliminated. On the night of June 30, 1934, he struck. Hitler's elite personal guard—the SS—arrested and shot without trial roughly a thousand SA leaders and assorted political enemies. Shortly thereafter army leaders swore a binding oath of "unquestioning obedience . . . to the Leader of the German State and People, Adolf Hitler." The SS grew rapidly. Under its methodical, inhuman leader, Heinrich Himmler (1900–1945), the SS joined with the political police, the Gestapo, to expand its network of special courts and concentration camps. Nobody was safe.

From the beginning, Jews were a special object of Nazi persecution. By the end of 1934, most Jewish lawyers, doctors, professors, civil servants, and musicians had lost their jobs and the right to practice their professions. In 1935 the infamous Nuremberg Laws classified as Jewish anyone having one or more Jewish grandparents and deprived Jews of all rights of citizenship. By 1938 roughly one-quarter of Germany's half-million Jews had emigrated, sacrificing almost all their property in order to leave Germany.

In late 1938 the attack on the Jews accelerated. A well-organized wave of violence destroyed homes, synagogues, and businesses, after which German Jews were rounded up and made to pay for the damage. It became very difficult for Jews to leave Germany. Some Germans privately opposed these outrages, but most went along or looked the other way. Although this lack of response reflected the individual's helplessness in a totalitarian state, it was more certainly a sign of the strong popular support Hitler's government enjoyed.

Hitler's Popularity

Hitler had promised the masses economic recovery—"work and bread"—and he delivered. Breaking with Brüning's do-nothing policies, Hitler immediately launched a large public works program to pull Germany out of the depression. Work began on superhighways, offices, gigantic sports stadiums, and public housing. In 1936 Germany turned decisively toward rearmament, and government spending began to concentrate on the military. The result was that unemployment dropped steadily, from 6 million in January 1933 to about 1 million in late 1936. By 1938 there was a shortage of workers, and women eventually took many jobs previously denied them by the antifeminist Nazis. Thus everyone had work, and between 1932 and 1938 the standard of living for the average employed worker increased moderately. The profits of business rose sharply. For millions of people, economic recovery was tangible evidence that Nazi promises were more than show and propaganda.

For the masses of ordinary German citizens who were not Jews, Slavs, Gypsies, Jehovah's Witnesses, communists, or homosexuals, Hitler's government meant greater equality and more opportunities. In 1933 barriers between classes in Germany were generally high. Hitler's rule introduced changes that lowered these barriers. For example, stiff educational requirements, which favored the well-to-do, were relaxed. The new Nazi elite included many young and poorly educated dropouts, rootless lower-middle-class people like Hitler who rose to the top with breathtaking speed. More generally, the Nazis tolerated privilege and wealth only as long as they served the needs of the party. Even big business was constantly ordered around.

Yet few historians today believe that Hitler and the Nazis brought about a real social revolution, as an earlier generation of scholars often argued. Quantitative studies show that the well-educated classes held on to most of their advantages and that only a modest social leveling occurred in the Nazi years. It is significant that the Nazis shared with

EVENTS LEADING TO WORLD WAR II

1919	Treaty of Versailles; J. M. Keynes, *Economic Consequences of the Peace*
1919–1920	U.S. Senate rejects the Treaty of Versailles
1922	Mussolini seizes power in Italy; Germany stops paying reparations
January 1923	France and Belgium occupy the Ruhr; Germany orders passive resistance
October 1923	Stresemann agrees to reparations with re-examination of Germany's ability to pay
1924	Dawes Plan: German reparations reduced; occupation of the Ruhr ends Adolf Hitler, *Mein Kampf*
1924–1929	Spectacular German economic recovery; international flow of capital
1925	Treaties of Locarno promote European security and stability
1928	Kellogg-Briand Pact renounces war as an instrument of international policy
1929	Crash of U.S. stock market
1930–1933	Depths of the Great Depression
1931	Japan invades Manchuria
1932	Nazis become the largest party in the Reichstag
January 1933	Hitler appointed chancellor
March 1933	Reichstag passes the Enabling Act, granting Hitler absolute dictatorial power
March 1935	Hitler establishes military draft and begins German rearmament
June 1935	Anglo-German naval agreement
September 1935	Nuremberg Laws deprive Jews of all rights of citizenship
October 1935	Mussolini invades Ethiopia and receives Hitler's support
March 1936	German armies move unopposed into the demilitarized Rhineland
July 1936	Outbreak of civil war in Spain
October 1936	Rome-Berlin Axis
1937	Japan invades China
March 1938	Germany annexes Austria
September 1938	Munich Conference: Britain and France agree to German seizure of the Sudetenland from Czechoslovakia
March 1939	Germany occupies the rest of Czechoslovakia; the end of appeasement in Britain
August 1939	Nazi-Soviet nonaggression pact
September 1939	Germany invades Poland; Britain and France then declare war on Germany

the Italian fascists the stereotypic view of women as housewives and mothers. Only under the relentless pressure of war did they reluctantly mobilize large numbers of German women for work in offices and factories.

Hitler's rabid nationalism, which had helped him gain power, continued to appeal to Germans after 1933. Thus in later years when Hitler went from one foreign triumph to another and a great German empire seemed within reach, the majority of the population was delighted and kept praising the Führer's actions well into the war.

Not all Germans supported Hitler, however, and a number of German groups actively resisted him after 1933. Tens of thousands of political enemies were imprisoned, and thousands were executed. In the first years of Hitler's rule, the principal resisters were the communists and the social democrats in the trade unions. But the expansion of the SS sys-tem of terror after 1935 smashed most of these leftists. A second group of opponents arose in the Catholic and Protestant churches. However, their efforts were directed primarily at preserving gen-uine religious life, not at overthrowing Hitler. Fi-nally in 1938 (and again from 1942 to 1944), some high-ranking army officers, who feared the consequences of Hitler's reckless aggression, plot-ted against him, unsuccessfully.

NAZI EXPANSION AND THE SECOND WORLD WAR

Although economic recovery and somewhat greater opportunity for social advancement won Hitler support, they were only byproducts of the Nazi regime. The guiding and unique concepts of Nazism remained space and race—the territorial

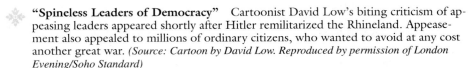

"Spineless Leaders of Democracy"   Cartoonist David Low's biting criticism of ap-peasing leaders appeared shortly after Hitler remilitarized the Rhineland. Appease-ment also appealed to millions of ordinary citizens, who wanted to avoid at any cost another great war. *(Source: Cartoon by David Low. Reproduced by permission of London Evening/Soho Standard)*

expansion of the superior German race. As Germany regained its economic strength and as independent organizations were brought under control, Hitler formed alliances with other dictators and began expanding. German expansion was facilitated by the uncertain, divided, pacific Western democracies, which tried to buy off Hitler to avoid war.

Yet war inevitably broke out, in both the West and the East, for Hitler's ambitions were essentially unlimited. On both war fronts Nazi soldiers scored enormous successes until late 1942, establishing a horrifyingly vast empire of death and destruction. Hitler's reckless aggression also raised a mighty coalition determined to smash the Nazi order. Led by Britain, the United States, and the Soviet Union, the Grand Alliance—to use Winston Churchill's favorite term—functioned quite effectively in military terms. Thus the terrible Nazi empire proved short-lived.

Aggression and Appeasement (1933–1939)

Hitler realized that his aggressive policies had to be carefully camouflaged at first, for Germany's army was limited by the Treaty of Versailles to only a hundred thousand men. As he told a group of army commanders in February 1933, the early stages of his policy of "conquest of new living space in the East and its ruthless Germanization" had serious dangers. If France had real leaders, Hitler said, it would "not give us time but attack us, presumably with its eastern satellites."[13] To avoid such threats to his plans, Hitler loudly proclaimed his peaceful intentions to all the world. Nevertheless, he felt strong enough to walk out of a sixty-nation disarmament conference and withdraw from the League of Nations in October 1933. The Nazi determination to rearm was out in the open.

Following this action, which met with widespread approval at home, Hitler moved to incorporate independent Austria into a greater Germany. Austrian Nazis climaxed an attempted overthrow by murdering the Austrian chancellor in July 1934. They were unable to take power, however, because a worried Mussolini, who had initially greeted Hitler as a fascist little brother, massed his troops on the Brenner Pass and threatened to fight. When in March 1935 Hitler established a general military draft and declared the "unequal" disarmament

clauses of the Treaty of Versailles null and void, other countries appeared to understand the danger. With France taking the lead, Italy and Great Britain protested strongly and warned against future aggressive actions.

But the emerging united front against Hitler quickly collapsed. Britain adopted a policy of appeasement, granting Hitler everything he could reasonably want (and more) in order to avoid war. The first step was an Anglo-German naval agreement in June 1935 that broke Germany's isolation. The second step came in March 1936 when Hitler suddenly marched his armies into the demilitarized Rhineland, brazenly violating the treaties of Versailles and Locarno. This was the last good chance to stop the Nazis, for Hitler had ordered his troops to retreat if France resisted militarily. But an uncertain France would not move without British support, and the occupation of German soil by German armies seemed right and just to Britain (Map 32.1). With a greatly improved strategic position, Germany handed France a tremendous psychological defeat.

British appeasement, which practically dictated French policy, lasted far into 1939. It was motivated by British feelings of guilt toward Germany and the pacifism of a population still horrified by the memory of the First World War. As in Germany, many powerful conservatives in Britain underestimated Hitler. They also believed that Soviet communism was the real danger and that Hitler could be used to stop it. A leading member of Britain's government personally told Hitler in November 1937 that it was his conviction that Hitler "not only had accomplished great things in Germany itself, but that through the total destruction of Communism in his own country . . . Germany rightly had to be considered as a Western bulwark against Communism."[14] Such rigid anticommunist feelings made an alliance between the Western powers and Stalin unlikely.

As Britain and France opted for appeasement and the Soviet Union watched all developments suspiciously, Hitler found powerful allies. In 1935 the bombastic Mussolini decided that imperial expansion was needed to revitalize Italian fascism. From Italian colonies on the east coast of Africa, he attacked the independent African kingdom of Ethiopia. The Western powers and the League of Nations piously condemned Italian aggression—a posture that angered Mussolini—without saving

⚜ MAP 32.1 The Growth of Nazi Germany, 1933–1939 Until March 1939
Hitler brought ethnic Germans into the Nazi state; then he turned on the Slavic peoples, whom he had always hated. He stripped Czechoslovakia of its independence and prepared for an attack on Poland in September 1939.

Ethiopia from defeat. Hitler, who had secretly supplied Ethiopia with arms to heat up the conflict, supported Italy energetically and thereby overcame Mussolini's lingering doubts about the Nazis. The result in 1936 was an agreement on close cooperation between Italy and Germany, the so-called Rome-Berlin Axis. Japan, which had been expanding into Manchuria since 1931, soon joined the Axis alliance.

At the same time, Germany and Italy intervened in the Spanish civil war (1936–1939). Their support eventually helped General Francisco Franco's fascist movement defeat republican Spain. Spain's only official aid came from the Soviet Union, for public opinion in Britain and especially in France was hopelessly divided on the Spanish question.

In late 1937, while proclaiming peaceful intentions to the British and their gullible prime minister Neville Chamberlain, Hitler moved forward with his plans to crush Austria and Czechoslovakia as the first step in his long-contemplated drive to the east for living space. By threatening Austria with invasion, Hitler forced the Austrian chancellor in March 1938 to put local Nazis in control of the government. The next day German armies moved in unopposed, and Austria became two provinces of Greater Germany (see Map 32.1).

Simultaneously, Hitler began demanding that the pro-Nazi, German-speaking minority of western Czechoslovakia—the Sudetenland—be turned over to Germany. Democratic Czechoslovakia, however, was prepared to defend itself. Moreover, France had been Czechoslovakia's ally since 1924; and if France fought, the Soviet Union was pledged to help. War appeared inevitable, for Hitler had already told the leader of the Sudeten Germans that "we must always ask so much we cannot be satisfied." But appeasement triumphed again. In September 1938 Prime Minister Chamberlain flew to Germany three times in fourteen days. In these negotiations, to which the Soviet Union was deliberately not invited, Chamberlain and the French agreed with Hitler that the Sudetenland should be ceded to Germany immediately. Returning to London from the Munich Conference, Chamberlain told cheering crowds that he had secured "peace with honor . . . peace for our time." Sold out by the Western powers, Czechoslovakia gave in.

Confirmed once again in his opinion of the Western democracies as weak and racially degenerate, Hitler accelerated his aggression. In a shocking violation of his solemn assurances that the Sudetenland was his last territorial demand, Hitler sent his armies to occupy the remainder of Czechoslovakia in March 1939. The effect on Western public opinion was electrifying. For the first time, there was no possible rationale of self-determination for Nazi aggression, because Hitler was treating the Czechs and Slovaks as captive peoples. Thus when Hitler used the question of German minorities in Danzig as a pretext to confront Poland, a suddenly militant Chamberlain declared that Britain and France would fight if Hitler attacked his eastern neighbor.

Hitler did not take these warnings seriously and decided to press on.

In an about-face that stunned the world, Hitler offered and Stalin signed a ten-year Nazi-Soviet nonaggression pact in August 1939. Each dictator promised to remain neutral if the other became involved in war. An attached secret protocol, which became known only after the war, ruthlessly divided eastern Europe into German and Soviet zones "in the event of a political territorial reorganization." The nonaggression pact itself was enough to make Britain and France cry treachery, for they, too, had been negotiating with Stalin. But Stalin had remained distrustful of Western intentions, and Hitler had offered territorial gain.

For Hitler, everything was set. He told his generals on the day of the nonaggression pact, "My only fear is that at the last moment some dirty dog will come up with a mediation plan." On September 1, 1939, German armies and warplanes smashed into Poland from three sides. Two days later Britain and France, finally true to their word, declared war on Germany. The Second World War had begun.

Hitler's Empire (1939–1942)

Using planes, tanks, and trucks in the first example of a *blitzkrieg,* or "lightning war," Hitler's armies crushed Poland in four weeks. The Soviet Union quickly took its part of the booty—the eastern half of Poland and the Baltic states of Lithuania, Estonia, and Latvia. French and British armies dug in in the west; they expected another war of attrition and economic blockade.

In spring 1940 the lightning war struck again. After occupying Denmark, Norway, and Holland, German motorized columns broke through southern Belgium, split the Franco-British forces, and trapped the entire British army on the beaches of Dunkirk. By heroic efforts the British were able to withdraw their troops but not their equipment.

France was taken by the Nazis. Aging marshal Henri-Philippe Pétain formed a new French government—the so-called Vichy government—to accept defeat, and German armies occupied most of France. By July 1940 Hitler ruled practically all of western continental Europe; Italy was an ally, the Soviet Union a friendly neutral (Map 32.2). Only Britain, led by the uncompromising Winston Churchill (1874–1965), remained unconquered.

Hitler's Greater Germany
Allied with Germany
Occupied by Germany and its allies
Grand Alliance
Neutral nations
X **Major battles**

ATLANTIC
OCEAN

North
Sea

GREAT
BRITAIN

NORTHERN
IRELAND

IRELAND

London•
Dunkirk•

Battle of Britain
Fall 1940

Invasion of Normandy
June 6, 1944

Paris•
FRANCE

Vichy•
VICHY FRANCE
(occupied Nov. 1942)

PORTUGAL
Lisbon•

Madrid•
SPAIN

GIBRALTAR (Gr. Br.)
SP. MOROCCO

Casablanca
Nov. 1942

FRENCH
MOROCCO

Ebro

NORWAY
Oslo•

SWEDEN
Stockholm•

DENMARK
Copenhagen•

Berlin•
GERMANY

NETHERLANDS
BELGIUM
Battle of
the Bulge
Dec. 1944

Western front, Feb. 1945

SWITZERLAND

Rhine

Elbe

FINLAND
Helsinki•

Riga•
Leningrad•

Baltic Sea

Vistula

Posen•
Warsaw•
•Krakow

Russian front, Feb. 1945

SLOVAKIA

Danube

Vienna•
HUNGARY
Budapest•

CROATIA

Po

Bologna•

ITALY
•Rome   Monte Casino
•May 1944

Salerno•
Sept. 1943

Italian front,
Feb. 1945

MALTA
(Gr. Br.)

Sicily
July 1943

Rommel defeated
in Tunisia
(May 1943)

ALGERIA
(Vichy France)

TUNISIA

LIBYA

Mediterranean Sea

SOVIET UNION

Volga

Stalingrad•

Russian front, Nov. 1942

Don

Russian front,
Dec. 1941

Moscow•
Smolensk•
•Tula

Russian front,
Spring 1944

Pinsk•
Kiev•
UKRAINE

Dniester

Yalta•

Black Sea

ROMANIA
Bucharest•

Danube

BULGARIA
Sofia•

SERBIA
YUGOSLAVIA
ALBANIA

GREECE
Athens•

Crete

TURKEY
Ankara•

CYPRUS

SYRIA

PALESTINE
(Br. Mandate)

TRANS-
JORDAN
(Br. Mandate)

Suez
Canal
Cairo•

EGYPT

El Alamein
Summer 1942

Nile

400 Mi.

400 Km.

200

200

0

0

Prelude to Murder This photo conveys the inhumanity of Nazi racism. Frightened and bewildered families from the soon-to-be-destroyed Warsaw ghetto are being forced out of their homes by German soldiers for deportation to concentration camps. There they face murder in the gas chambers. *(Source: Roger-Viollet)*

Germany sought to gain control of the air, the necessary first step for an amphibious invasion of Britain. In the Battle of Britain, up to a thousand German planes attacked British airfields and key factories in a single day, dueling with British defenders high in the skies. Losses were heavy on both sides. Then in September Hitler angrily and foolishly changed his strategy, turning from military objectives to indiscriminate bombing of British cities in an attempt to break British morale.

MAP 32.2 The Second World War in Europe This map shows the extent of Hitler's empire at its height, before the Battle of Stalingrad in late 1942, and the subsequent advances of the Allies until Germany surrendered on May 7, 1945.

British factories increased production of their excellent fighter planes, anti-aircraft defense improved with the help of radar, and the heavily bombed people of London defiantly dug in. In September and October 1940, Britain was beating Germany three to one in the air war. There was no possibility of immediate German invasion of Britain.

In these circumstances, the most reasonable German strategy would have been to attack Britain through the eastern Mediterranean, taking Egypt and the Suez Canal and pinching off Britain's supply of oil. By April 1941 Germany had already moved to the southeast, conquering Greece and Yugoslavia and forcing Hungary, Romania, and Bulgaria into alliances. But Hitler was not a reasonable person. His lifetime obsession with a vast eastern European empire for the "master race" dictated policy. So in June 1941 German armies suddenly attacked the Soviet Union along a vast front. By October Leningrad was practically surrounded, Moscow was besieged, and most of Ukraine had been conquered. But with Britain still unconquered, Hitler's decision to strike at Stalin was a wild, irrational gamble epitomizing the violent, unlimited, and ultimately self-destructive ambitions of Nazism. The Soviets did not collapse, and when a severe winter struck German armies that were outfitted in summer uniforms, the invaders were stopped.

While Hitler's armies dramatically expanded the war in Europe, his Japanese allies did the same in Asia. Engaged in an undeclared war against China since 1937, Japan's rulers had increasingly come into diplomatic conflict with the Pacific basin's other great power, the United States. When the Japanese occupied French Indochina in July 1941, the United States retaliated by cutting off sales of vital rubber, scrap iron, oil, and aviation fuel. Tension mounted, and on December 7, 1941, Japan attacked the U.S. naval base at Pearl Harbor in Hawaii. Hitler immediately declared war on the United States, and Japanese forces advanced swiftly into Southeast Asia (Map 32.3).

Meanwhile, though stalled in Russia, Hitler had come to rule a vast European empire stretching from the outskirts of Moscow to the English Channel. He and the top Nazi leadership began building their "New Order," and they continued their efforts until their final collapse in 1945. In doing so, they showed what Nazi victory would have meant.

Hitler's New Order was based firmly on the guiding principle of Nazi totalitarianism: racial imperialism. Within this New Order, the Nordic peoples—the Dutch, Norwegians, and Danes—received preferential treatment, for they were racially related to the Germans. The French, an "inferior" Latin people, occupied the middle position. They were heavily taxed to support the Nazi war effort but were tolerated as a race. All the occupied territories of western and northern Europe, however, were to be exploited with increasing intensity. Material shortages and both mental and physical suffering afflicted millions of people.

Slavs in the conquered territories to the east were treated with harsh hatred as "subhumans."

Hitler painted for his intimate circle the fantastic details of a vast eastern colonial empire where Poles, Ukrainians, and Russians would be enslaved and forced to die out while Germanic peasants resettled the resulting abandoned lands. Himmler and the elite corps of SS volunteers struggled loyally, sometimes against the German army, to implement part of this general program. In parts of Poland, the SS arrested and evacuated Polish peasants to create a German "mass settlement space." Polish workers and Soviet prisoners of war were transported to Germany, where they did most of the heavy labor and were systematically worked to death. The conditions of Soviet slave labor in Germany were so harsh that four out of five Soviet prisoners did not survive the war.

Jews were condemned to extermination, along with Gypsies, Jehovah's Witnesses, and captured communists. By 1939 German Jews had lost all their civil rights, and after the fall of Warsaw the Nazis began deporting them to Poland. There they and Jews from all over Europe were concentrated in ghettos, compelled to wear the Jewish star, and turned into slave laborers. But by late 1941 Himmler's SS was beginning to carry out the "final solution of the Jewish question"—the murder of every Jew. All over Hitler's empire, Jews were systematically arrested, packed like cattle onto freight trains, and dispatched to extermination camps. Many Jews in small towns could hardly imagine the enormity of the crime that lay before them (see Listening to the Past).

At the camps the victims were taken by force or deception to "shower rooms," which were actually gas chambers. These gas chambers, first perfected in the quiet, efficient execution of seventy thousand mentally ill Germans between 1938 and 1941, permitted rapid, hideous, and thoroughly bureaucratized mass murder. For fifteen to twenty minutes came the terrible screams and gasping sobs of men, women, and children choking to death on poison gas. Then, only silence. Special camp workers quickly yanked the victims' gold teeth from their jaws and cut off their hair for use as chair stuffing. The bodies were then cremated or sometimes boiled for oil to make soap. The bones were crushed to produce fertilizer. At Auschwitz-Birkenau, the most infamous of the Nazi death factories, as many as twelve thousand human beings were slaughtered each day. On the

❀ **MAP 32.3 The Second World War in the Pacific** In 1942 Japanese forces overran an enormous territory, which the Allies slowly recaptured in a long, bitter struggle. As this map shows, Japan still held a large Asian empire in August 1945, when the unprecedented devastation of atomic warfare suddenly forced it to surrender.

turbulent Russian front, the SS death squads forced the Jewish population to dig giant pits, which became mass graves when the victims were lined up on the edge and cut down by machine guns. The extermination of European Jews was the ultimate monstrosity of Nazi racism and racial imperialism. By 1945 6 million Jews had been murdered.

The Grand Alliance

While the Nazis built their savage empire, the Allies faced the hard fact that chance, rather than choice, had brought them together. Stalin had been cooperating fully with Hitler between August 1939 and June 1941, and only the Japanese attack on Pearl Harbor in December 1941 and Hitler's immediate declaration of war had overwhelmed powerful isolationism in the United States. The Allies' first task was to overcome their mutual suspicions and build an unshakable alliance on the quicksand of accident. By means of three interrelated policies they succeeded.

First, U.S. president Franklin D. Roosevelt accepted the contention of Winston Churchill (Chamberlain's successor as British prime minister) that the United States should concentrate first on defeating Hitler. Only after victory in Europe was achieved would the United States turn toward the Pacific for an all-out attack on Japan, the lesser

"For the Motherland's Sake, Go Forward, Heroes" Joining the historic Russian warrior and the young Soviet soldier in the common cause, this poster portrays the defense of the nation as a sacred mission and illustrates the way Soviet leaders successfully appealed to Russian nationalism during the war. *(Source: Library of Congress)*

threat. The promise of huge military aid under America's policy of "Europe first" helped solidify the anti-Hitler coalition.

Second, within the European framework the Americans and the British put immediate military needs first. They consistently postponed until after the war tough political questions relating to the eventual peace settlement and thereby avoided conflicts that might have split the alliance.

Third, to further encourage mutual trust, the Allies adopted the principle of the "unconditional surrender" of Germany and Japan. This policy cemented the Grand Alliance because it denied Hitler any hope of dividing his foes. Of great importance for the postwar shape of Europe, it meant that Soviet and Anglo-American armies would almost certainly come together to divide all of Germany, and most of the European continent, among the victorious allies.

The military resources of the Grand Alliance were awesome. The strengths of the United States were its mighty industry, its large population, and its national unity. Even before the attack on Pearl Harbor, President Roosevelt had called America the "arsenal of democracy" and had given military aid to Britain and the Soviet Union. Now the United States geared up rapidly for all-out war production and drew heavily on a generally cooperative Latin America for resources. It not only equipped its own armies but also eventually gave its allies about $50 billion in arms and equipment.

Too strong to lose and too weak to win standing alone, Britain continued to make a great contribution as well. The British economy was totally and effectively mobilized, and the sharing of burdens through rationing and heavy taxes on war profits maintained social harmony. Moreover, by early 1943 the Americans and the British were combining small aircraft carriers with radar-guided bombers to rid the Atlantic of German submarines. Britain, the impregnable floating fortress, became a gigantic front-line staging area for the decisive blow to the heart of Germany.

As for the Soviet Union, so great was its strength that it might well have defeated Germany without Western help. In the face of the German advance, whole factories and populations were successfully evacuated to eastern Russia and Siberia. There war production was reorganized and expanded, and the Red Army was increasingly well supplied. The Red Army was also well led, for a new generation of talented military leaders quickly arose to replace those so recently purged. Most important of all, Stalin drew on the massive support and heroic determination of the Soviet people, especially those in the central Russian heartland. Broad-based Russian nationalism, as opposed to narrow communist ideology, became the powerful unifying force in what the Soviet people appropriately called the "Great Patriotic War of the Fatherland."

Finally, the United States, Britain, and the Soviet Union were not alone. They had the resources of much of the world at their command. And, to a greater or lesser extent, they were aided by a growing resistance movement against the Nazis throughout Europe, even in Germany. Thus although Ukrainian peasants often welcomed the Germans as liberators, the barbaric occupation policies of the Nazis quickly drove them to join and support behind-the-lines guerrilla forces. More generally, after the Soviet Union was invaded in June 1941, communists throughout Europe took the lead in the underground resistance, joined by a growing number of patriots and Christians. Anti-Nazi leaders from occupied countries established governments-in-exile in London, like that of the Free French under the intensely proud General Charles de Gaulle. These governments gathered valuable secret information from resistance fighters and even organized armies to help defeat Hitler.

The Tide of Battle

Barely halted at the gates of Moscow and Leningrad in 1941, the Germans renewed their offensive against the Soviet Union in July 1942, driving toward the southern city of Stalingrad and occupying most of the city in a month of incredibly savage house-to-house fighting.

Then in November 1942, Soviet armies counterattacked. They quickly rolled over Romanian and Italian troops to close a trap surrounding the entire German Sixth Army of 300,000 men. The surrounded Germans were systematically destroyed, until by the end of January 1943 only 123,000 soldiers were left to surrender. Hitler, who had refused to allow a retreat, had suffered a catastrophic defeat. In the summer of 1943, the larger, better-equipped Soviet armies took the offensive and began moving forward (see Map 32.2).

In late 1942 the tide also turned in the Pacific and in North Africa. By late spring 1942, Japan had established a great empire in East Asia (Map 32.3). Unlike the Nazis, the Japanese made clever appeals to local nationalists, who hated European imperial domination and preferred Japan's so-called Greater Asian Co-prosperity Sphere.

Then in the Battle of the Coral Sea in May 1942, Allied naval and air power stopped the Japanese advance and also relieved Australia from the threat of invasion. This victory was followed by the Battle of Midway Island, in which American pilots sank all four of the attacking Japanese aircraft carriers and established American naval superiority in the Pacific. In August 1942 American marines attacked Guadalcanal in the Solomon Islands. Badly hampered by the policy of "Europe first"— only 15 percent of Allied resources were going to fight the war in the Pacific in early 1943—the Americans and the Australians nevertheless began "island hopping" toward Japan. Japanese forces were on the defensive.

In North Africa the war had been seesawing back and forth since 1940 (see Map 32.2). In the summer of 1942 combined German and Italian armies were finally defeated by British forces at the Battle of El Alamein, only seventy miles from Alexandria. In October the British counterattacked in Egypt, and almost immediately thereafter an Anglo-American force landed in Morocco and Algeria. These French possessions, which were under the control of Pétain's Vichy French government, quickly went over to the side of the Allies.

Having driven the Axis powers from North Africa by the spring of 1943, Allied forces maintained the initiative by invading Sicily and then mainland Italy. Mussolini was deposed by a war-weary people, and the new Italian government publicly accepted unconditional surrender in September 1943. Italy, it seemed, was liberated. But then German commandos in a daring raid rescued Mussolini and put him at the head of a puppet government. German armies seized Rome and all of northern Italy. Fighting continued in Italy.

Indeed, bitter fighting continued in Europe for almost two years. Germany, less fully mobilized for war than Britain in 1941, applied itself to total war in 1942 and enlisted millions of German women and millions of prisoners of war and slave laborers from all across occupied Europe in that effort. Between early 1942 and July 1944, German war production actually tripled. Although British and American bombing raids killed many German civilians, these raids were surprisingly ineffective from a military point of view. Also, German resistance against Hitler failed. After an unsuccessful attempt on Hitler's life in July 1944, SS fanatics brutally liquidated thousands of Germans. Terrorized at home and frightened by the prospect of unconditional surrender, the Germans fought on with suicidal stoicism.

On June 6, 1944, American and British forces under General Dwight Eisenhower landed on the beaches of Normandy, France, in history's greatest naval invasion. In a hundred dramatic days, more than 2 million men and almost a half-million vehicles pushed inland and broke through German lines. Rejecting proposals to strike straight at Berlin in a massive attack, Eisenhower moved for-

ward cautiously on a broad front. Not until March 1945 did American troops cross the Rhine and enter Germany.

The Soviets, who had been advancing steadily since July 1943, reached the outskirts of Warsaw by August 1944. For the next six months they moved southward into Romania, Hungary, and Yugoslavia. In January 1945 Red armies again moved westward through Poland, and on April 26 they met American forces on the Elbe River. The Allies had closed their vise on Nazi Germany and overrun Europe. As Soviet forces fought their way into Berlin, Hitler committed suicide in his bunker, and on May 7 the remaining German commanders capitulated.

Three months later, the United States dropped atomic bombs on Hiroshima and Nagasaki in Japan. Mass bombing of cities and civilians, one of

The City of Nagasaki   An atomic bomb struck Nagasaki on August 9, 1945, three days after an atomic blast incinerated Hiroshima. Approximately seventy-five thousand Japanese were killed or injured at Nagasaki. In this grim photo, taken about a month after the attack, a Japanese survivor pushes his bicycle along a path cleared through the ruins. *(Source: UPI/Bettmann Newsphotos)*

the terrible new practices of World War II, had ended in the final nightmare—unprecedented human destruction in a single blinding flash. On August 14, 1945, the Japanese announced their surrender. The Second World War, which had claimed the lives of more than 50 million soldiers and civilians, was over.

SUMMARY

The Second World War marked the climax of the tremendous practical and spiritual maladies of the age of anxiety, maladies which led in many lands to the rise of dictatorships. Many of these dictatorships were variations on conservative authoritarianism, but there was also a fateful innovation—a new kind of radical dictatorship that was exceptionally dynamic and theoretically unlimited in its actions.

When apprehensive middle-class liberals in the West faced the rise of these new dictatorships, they often focused on their perceived similarities. Liberals fastened on the violent, profoundly antiliberal, and apparently totalitarian character of these brutal challengers, linking the one-party socialism of Lenin and Stalin with the one-party fascism of Mussolini and Hitler. In contrast, the political left usually insisted on the differences between the revolutionary socialist tradition—triumphing, however imperfectly, in the Bolsheviks' Soviet Union —and the reactionary and capitalist nature of European fascist movements and fascist governments in Italy and Germany. As the dramatic struggles of the 1930s and the Second World War (and early cold war) fall into a longer historical perspective and as more research adds new insights, a growing number of historians are stressing the limitations of both the totalitarian and the fascist interpretations and are concentrating instead on the uniqueness of developments in each regime.

Hitler's Nazism appears increasingly as a uniquely evil and nihilistic system. Nazism had fascist origins, but German fascism in power ultimately presented only superficial similarities with fascism in Italy. As for Hitler's Germany and Stalin's Soviet Union, both asserted a total claim on the lives of their citizens, posed ambitious goals, and demanded popular support. This combination gave both dictatorships their awesome power and dynamism. That dynamism, however, was channeled in quite different directions. Stalin and the Communist party aimed at building their kind of socialism and the new socialist personality at home. Hitler and the Nazi elite aimed at unlimited territorial and racial aggression on behalf of a "master race"; domestic recovery was only a means to that end.

Nazi racism and unlimited aggression made war inevitable, first with the western European democracies, then with hated eastern neighbors, and finally with the United States. Plunging Europe into the ultimate nightmare, unlimited aggression unwittingly forged a mighty coalition that smashed the racist Nazi empire and its leader. In the words of the ancient Greeks, he whom the gods would destroy, they first make mad.

NOTES

1. I. Kershaw, *The Nazi Dictatorship: Problems and Perspectives of Interpretation,* 2d ed. (London: Edward Arnold, 1989), pp. 20–23.
2. E. Halévy, *The Era of Tyrannies* (Garden City, N.Y.: Doubleday, 1965), pp. 265–316, esp. p. 300.
3. Kershaw, *The Nazi Dictatorship,* p. 34.
4. Quoted in P. C. Roberts, " 'War Communism': A Re-examination," *Slavic Review* 29 (June 1970): 257.
5. Quoted in A. G. Mazour, *Soviet Economic Development: Operation Outstrip, 1921–1965* (Princeton, N.J.: Van Nostrand, 1967), p. 130.
6. Quoted in I. Deutscher, *Stalin: A Political Biography,* 2d ed. (New York: Oxford University Press, 1967), p. 325.
7. Quoted in H. K. Geiger, *The Family in Soviet Russia* (Cambridge, Mass.: Harvard University Press, 1968), p. 123.
8. Quoted ibid., p. 156.
9. R. Vivarelli, "Interpretations on the Origins of Fascism," *Journal of Modern History* 63 (March 1991): 41.
10. Quoted in K. D. Bracher, "The Technique of the National Socialist Seizure of Power," in *The Path to Dictatorship, 1918–1933,* ed. T. Eschenburg et al. (Garden City, N.Y.: Doubleday, 1966), p. 117.
11. Quoted in K. D. Bracher, *The German Dictatorship: The Origins, Structure and Effects of National Socialism* (New York: Praeger, 1970), pp. 146–147.
12. Quoted in R. Stromberg, *An Intellectual History of Modern Europe* (New York: Appleton-Century-Crofts, 1966), p. 393.

13. Quoted in Bracher, *The German Dictatorship*, p. 289.

14. Quoted ibid., p. 306.

SUGGESTED READING

The historical literature on fascist and totalitarian dictatorships is rich and fascinating. Kershaw's work cited in the Notes provides an excellent recent survey of this literature, includes extensive bibliographical references, and is highly recommended. H. Arendt, *The Origins of Totalitarianism* (1951), and D. Schoenbaum, *Hitler's Social Revolution: Class and Status in Nazi Germany, 1933–1939* (1967), are classic, influential interpretations. E. Weber, *Varieties of Fascism* (1964), stresses the radical social aspirations of fascist movements all across Europe. F. L. Carsten, *The Rise of Fascism* (1982), and W. Laqueur, ed., *Fascism* (1976), are also recommended. Z. Sternhell, *Neither Right nor Left: Fascist Ideology in France* (1986), is important and stimulating, stressing the antiliberal and antisocialist origins of fascist thinking in France.

R. Stites, *The Women's Liberation Movement in Russia: Feminism, Nihilism, and Bolshevism, 1860–1930* (1978); S. Fitzpatrick, *Cultural Revolution in Russia, 1928–1931* (1978); and the works by Geiger and Deutscher cited in the Notes are all highly recommended, as is Deutscher's sympathetic three-volume study of Trotsky. R. McNeal, *Stalin: Man and Ruler* (1988), is useful. S. Cohen, *Bukharin and the Bolshevik Revolution* (1973), examines the leading spokesman of moderate communism, who was destroyed by Stalin. R. Conquest, *The Great Terror* (1968), is an excellent account of Stalin's purges of the 1930s. A. Solzhenitsyn, *The Gulag Archipelago* (1964), passionately condemns Soviet police terror, which Solzhenitsyn tracks back to Lenin. Arthur Koestler, *Darkness at Noon* (1956), is a famous fictional account of Stalin's trials of the Old Bolsheviks. R. Medvedev, *Let History Judge* (1972), is a penetrating and highly recommended history of Stalinism by a Russian dissident. It may be compared with the excellent synthesis by M. Lewin, *The Making of the Soviet System* (1985). R. Conquest, *The Harvest of Sorrow* (1986), authoritatively recounts Soviet collectivization and the human-made famine. Three other remarkable books are J. Scott, *Behind the Urals* (1973), an eyewitness account of an American steelworker in the Soviet Union in the 1930s; S. Alliluyeva, *Twenty Letters to a Friend* (1967), the amazing reflections of Stalin's daughter, who chose twice to live in the United States before returning home; and M. Fainsod, *Smolensk Under Soviet Rule* (1958), a unique study based on communist records captured first by the Germans and then by the Americans.

A. De Grand, *Italian Fascism: Its Origins and Development* (1989); A. Lyttelton, *The Seizure of Power* (1987); and E. R. Tannebaum, *The Fascist Experience* (1972), are excellent studies of Italy under Mussolini. D. Mack Smith, *Mussolini* (1982), is authoritative. Ignazio Silone, *Bread and Wine* (1937), is a moving novel by a famous opponent of dictatorship in Italy. Elsa Morante, *History: A Novel* (1978), a fictional account of one family's divergent reactions to Mussolini's rule, is recommended. Two excellent books on Spain are H. Thomas, *The Spanish Civil War* (1977), and E. Malefakis, *Agrarian Reform and Peasant Revolution in Spain* (1970).

In the area of foreign relations, G. Kennan, *Russia and the West Under Lenin and Stalin* (1961), is justly famous; A. L. Rowse, *Appeasement* (1961), powerfully denounces the policies of the appeasers. R. Paxton, *Vichy France* (1973), tells a controversial story extremely well, and J. Lukac, *The Last European War* (1976), argues provocatively that victory by Hitler could have saved Europe from both Soviet and American domination.

On Germany, F. Stern, *The Politics of Cultural Despair* (1963), and W. Smith, *The Ideological Origins of Nazi Imperialism* (1986), are fine complementary studies on the origins of Nazism. Bracher's *The German Dictatorship*, cited in the Notes, remains the best single work on Hitler's Germany. It may be compared with the important work by M. Brozat, *The Nazi State* (1981), and with W. Shirer, *The Rise and Fall of the Third Reich* (1960), a gripping account of an American journalist who experienced Nazi Germany firsthand. J. Fest, *Hitler* (1974), and A. Bullock, *Hitler: A Study in Tyranny* (1964), are engrossing biographies of the Führer. In addition to *Mein Kampf*, *Hitler's Secret Conversations, 1941–1944* (1953) reveals the dictator's wild dreams and beliefs. I. Kershaw, *The "Hitler Myth": Image and Reality in the Third Reich* (1987), is a provocative reassessment of the limits of Hitler's power. M. Mayer, *They Thought They Were Free* (1955), probes the minds of ten ordinary Nazis and why they believed Hitler was their liberator. A. Speer, *Inside the Third Reich* (1970), contains the fascinating recollections of Hitler's wizard of the armaments industry. C. Koonz, *Mothers in the Fatherland: Women, the Family, and Nazi Politics* (1987), and D. Peukert, *Inside Nazi Germany: Conformity, Opposition, and Racism in Everyday Life* (1987), are pioneering forays into the social history of the Nazi era. G. Mosse, *Toward the Final Solution* (1978), is a powerful history of European racism.

Moving accounts of the Holocaust include A. Mayer, *Why Did the Heavens Not Darken? The "Final*

Solution" in History (1989); M. Gilbert, *The Holocaust: The History of the Jews During the Second World War* (1985); and L. Dawidowicz, *The War Against the Jews, 1933–1945* (1975). M. Marrus, *The Holocaust in History* (1987), is an excellent interpretive survey by a leading authority. Especially recommended is E. Weisel, *Night* (1961), a brief and very compelling autobiographical account of a young Jew in a Nazi concentration camp. J. Haestrup, *Europe Ablaze* (1978), is a monumental account of wartime resistance movements throughout Europe, and A. Frank, *The Diary of a Young Girl* (1947, reissued 1995) is a remarkable personal account of a young Jewish girl in hiding during the Nazi occupation of Holland.

J. Campbell's *The Experience of World War II* (1989) is attractively illustrated and captures the drama of global conflict, as does G. Keegan, *The Second World War* (1990). G. Wright, *The Ordeal of Total War, 1939–1945* (1990), and C. Emsley, *World War II and Its Consequences* (1990), are also recommended. B. H. Liddell Hart, *The History of the Second World War* (1971), is an overview of military developments. G. Weinberg, *The Foreign Policy of Hitler,* 2 vols. (1970, 1980), is an excellent detailed account of the diplomatic origins and course of World War II from the German perspective. Three dramatic studies of special aspects of the war are A. Dallin, *German Rule in Russia, 1941–1945* (1981), which analyzes the effects of Nazi occupation policies on the Soviet population; L. Collins and D. La Pierre, *Is Paris Burning?* (1965), a best-selling account of the liberation of Paris and Hitler's plans to destroy the city; and J. Toland, *The Last Hundred Days* (1966), a lively account of the end of the war.

LISTENING TO THE
PAST

Witness to the Holocaust

The Second World War brought mass murder to the innocent. The Nazis and their allies slaughtered 6 million Jews in addition to about 5 million Slavs, Gypsies, Jehovah's Witnesses, homosexuals, and mentally ill. On the Russian front some Jews were simply mowed down with machine guns, but most Jews were arrested in their homelands and taken in freight cars to unknown destinations, which were in fact extermination camps. The most infamous camp—really two camps on different sides of a railroad track—was Auschwitz-Birkenau in eastern Poland. There 2 million people were murdered in gas chambers.

The testimony of camp survivors helps us comprehend the unspeakable crime known to history as the Holocaust. One eyewitness was Marco Nahon, a Greek Jew and physician who escaped extermination at Auschwitz-Birkenau along with several thousand other slave laborers in the camp. The following passage is taken from Birkenau: The Camp of Death, *which Nahon wrote in 1945 after his liberation. Conquered by Germany in 1941, Greece was divided into German, Italian, and Bulgarian zones of occupation. The Nahon family lived in Dimotika in the Bulgarian zone.*

Early in March 1943, disturbing news arrives from Salonika [in the German occupation zone]: the Germans are deporting the Jews [of Salonika]. They lock them up in railway cattlecars . . . and send them to an unknown destination—to Poland, it is said. . . . Relatives and friends deliberate. What can be done in the face of this imminent threat? . . . My friend Vitalis Djivré speaks with conviction: "We must flee, cross over into Turkey at once, go to Palestine, Egypt—anywhere at all—but leave immediately." . . . A few friends and I held a completely different opinion. . . . [I say that] I am not going to emigrate. They are going to take us away to Germany or Poland

[to work]? If so, I'll work. . . . It is certain that the Allies will be the victors, and once the war is over, we'll go back home. . . .

Until the end we were deaf to all the warnings. . . . [None of the warnings] would be regarded as indicating the seriousness of the drama in preparation. But does not the human mind find inconceivable the total extermination of an innocent population? In this tragic error lay the main cause, the sole cause, of our perdition. . . .

On Monday May 10, 1943, the bugles awaken us at a very early hour. We [have already been arrested and] today we are leaving for Poland. . . . As soon as a freight car has been packed to capacity with people, it is quickly locked up, and immediately the remaining passengers are pushed into the next one. . . .

Every two days the train stops in some meadow in open country. The car doors are flung open, and the whole transport spreads out in the fields. Men and women attend to their natural needs, side by side, without any embarrassment. Necessity and common misfortune have made them part of one and the same family. . . .

We are now in a small station in Austria. Our car door half opens; a Schupo [German police officer] is asking for the doctor. . . . He leads me to the rear of the convoy and shuts me inside the car where the woman is in labor. She is very young; this is her first child. The car, like all the others, is overcrowded. The delivery takes place in deplorable conditions, in front of everybody—men, women, and children. Fortunately, everything turns out well, and a few hours later a baby boy comes into the world. The new mother's family is very happy and passes candy around. Surely no one realizes that two days later the mother and her baby and more than half of the company will pass through the chimney of a crematorium at Birkenau.

It is May 16, 1943. We have reached the end of our journey [and arrived at Auschwitz-Birkenau]. The train stops along a wooden platform. Through the openings of the cars we can see people wearing strange costumes of blue and white stripes [the prisoners who work in the camp]. We immediately notice that they are doing nothing voluntarily but are moving and acting on command. . . . The people in stripes . . . line us up five by five, the women on one side, the men on the other. I lose sight of my wife and little girl in the crowd. I will never see them again.

They make us march, swiftly as always, before a group of [German] officers. One of them, without uttering a word and with the tip of his forefinger, makes a rapid selection. He is, as we know later on, the Lagerarzt, the SS medical doctor of the camp [the notorious Dr. Mengele]. They call him here the "Angel of Death." [Mengele divides the men into two groups; those who are young and sturdy for work in the camp, and those who are old, sick, and children. The women are also divided and only healthy young women without children are assigned to work. All those not selected for work] are immediately loaded on trucks and driven off somewhere. Where? Nobody knows yet. . . .

[After being assigned to a crude windowless barrack,] we must file before the . . . scribes, who are responsible for receiving and registering the transport. Each prisoner must fill out a form in which he relinquishes his identity and becomes a mere number. . . . I am given the number 122274. My son, who is next, gets 122275. This tattoo alarms us terribly. . . . Each one of us now comes to realize in the deepest part of his conscious being, and with a bitter sense of affliction, that from this moment on he is no more than an animal. . . .

After our meal [of watery soup] Léon Yahiel, a veteran among the Lager inmates, . . . gives us this little speech: "My friends, here you must . . . forget your families, your wives, your children. You must live only for yourselves and try to last as long as possible." At these words our spirits plunge into grief and despair. Forget about our families? The hint is

Deportees getting off the coaches at Auschwitz. *(Source: Hulton Deutsch Collection Limited)*

unmistakable. Our minds are confused. . . . Our families taken away from us forever? No, it is humanly not conceivable that we should pay such a penalty without having done anything to deserve it, without any provocation.

What miserable wretches we prisoners are! We have no idea that while we entertain these thoughts, our wives, our children, our mothers and our fathers have already ceased to exist. They have arrived at Auschwitz this morning, healthy and full of life. They have now been reduced to smoke and ashes.

Questions for Analysis

1. How did the Jews of Dimotika react in early 1943 to the news of Jews being deported? Why?

2. Describe the journey to Auschwitz-Birkenau. Did those on the train know what was awaiting them there?

3. How did the Nazis divide the Jews at Auschwitz-Birkenau? Why?

4. What did you learn from Nahon's account? What parts of his testimony made the greatest impression on you?

Source: Slightly adapted from M. Nahon, *Birkenau: The Camp of Death,* trans. J. Bowers (Tuscaloosa: University of Alabama Press, 1989), pp. 21, 23, 33–39.

33
Recovery and Crisis in Europe and the Americas

The reality of the Berlin Wall, grim symbol of postwar division in Europe. *(Source: Sahm Doherty/Liaison)*

The total defeat of the Nazis and their allies laid the basis for one of Western civilization's most remarkable recoveries. A battered western Europe dug itself out from under the rubble and fashioned a great renaissance. The Western Hemisphere, with its strong European heritage, also made exemplary progress. And the Soviet Union became more humane and less totalitarian after Stalin's death. Yet there was also a tragic setback. Dictatorship settled over eastern Europe, and the Grand Alliance against Hitler gave way to an apparently endless cold war, in which tension between East and West threatened world peace.

As cold war competition originating in Europe became a factor in the lives of peoples the world over, the global economic boom of the 1950s and 1960s finally came to an end in the early 1970s. In Europe and the Americas postwar certainties like domestic political stability and social harmony evaporated, and several countries experienced major crises. Subsequently, serious economic difficulties returned with distressing regularity to Europe and the Americas in the 1980s and 1990s, and these difficulties encompassed much of the globe, as the next two chapters will show. This similarity of world economic trends accelerated the knitting together of the world's peoples and regions in recent times. The spectacular collapse of communism in eastern Europe in 1989 and the end of the cold war reinforced the trend toward global integration.

- What were the causes of the cold war?

- How and why, in spite of the cold war, did western Europe recover so successfully from the ravages of war and Nazism?

- To what extent did communist eastern Europe and the Americas experience a similar recovery?

- Why, after a generation, did the economy shift into reverse gear, and what were some of the social consequences of the reversal?

- How did political crisis strike many countries from the late 1960s onward?

- Why did a reform movement eventually triumph in eastern Europe in 1989 and bring an end to the cold war?

These are the questions that this chapter seeks to answer.

✵ THE COLD WAR (1942–1953)

In 1945 triumphant American and Russian soldiers came together and embraced on the banks of the Elbe River in the heart of vanquished Germany. At home, in the United States and in the Soviet Union, the soldiers' loved ones erupted in joyous celebration. Yet victory was flawed. The Allies could not cooperate politically in peacemaking. Motivated by different goals and hounded by misunderstandings, the United States and the Soviet Union soon found themselves at loggerheads. By the end of 1947, Europe was rigidly divided. It was West versus East in a cold war that eventually was waged around the world.

The Origins of the Cold War

The most powerful allies in the wartime coalition—the Soviet Union and the United States—began to quarrel almost as soon as the unifying threat of Nazi Germany disappeared. A tragic disappointment for millions of people, the hostility between the Eastern and Western superpowers was the sad but logical outgrowth of military developments, wartime agreements, and long-standing political and ideological differences.

In the early phases of the Second World War, the Americans and the British made military victory their highest priority. They consistently avoided discussion of Stalin's war aims and the shape of the eventual peace settlement. For example, when Stalin asked the United States and Britain to agree to the Soviet Union's moving its western border of 1938 farther west at the expense of Poland, in effect ratifying the gains that Stalin had made from his deal with Hitler in 1939, the British and Americans declined. Stalin received only a military alliance and no postwar commitments. Yet the United States and Britain did not try to take advantage of the Soviet Union's precarious position in 1942, because they feared that hard bargaining would encourage Stalin to consider making a separate peace with Hitler. They focused instead on the policy of unconditional surrender to solidify the alliance.

By late 1943 decisions that would affect the shape of the postwar world could no longer be postponed. The conference that Stalin, Roosevelt, and Churchill held in the Iranian capital of

Teheran in November 1943 thus proved of crucial importance in determining subsequent events. There, the "Big Three" jovially reaffirmed their determination to crush Germany and searched for the appropriate military strategy. Churchill, fearful of the military dangers of a direct attack, argued that American and British forces should follow up their Italian campaign with an indirect attack on Germany through the Balkans. Roosevelt, however, agreed with Stalin that an American-British frontal assault through France would be better. This agreement was part of Roosevelt's general effort to meet Stalin's wartime demands whenever possible, and it had momentous political implications. It meant that Soviet armies, on their own, would liberate eastern Europe.

When the Big Three met again in February 1945 at Yalta on the Black Sea in southern Russia, advancing Soviet armies were within a hundred miles of Berlin. The Red Army had occupied not only Poland but also Bulgaria, Romania, Hungary, part of Yugoslavia, and much of Czechoslovakia. The temporarily stalled American-British forces had yet to cross the Rhine into Germany. Moreover, the United States was far from defeating Japan. In short, the Soviet Union's position was strong and America's weak.

There was little the increasingly sick and apprehensive Roosevelt could do but double his bet on Stalin's peaceful intentions. It was agreed at Yalta that Germany would be divided into zones of occupation and would pay heavy reparations to the Soviet Union. At American insistence, Stalin agreed to declare war on Japan after Germany was defeated. As for Poland and eastern Europe—"that Pandora's Box of infinite troubles," according to American Secretary of State Cordell Hull—the Big Three struggled to reach an ambiguous compromise at Yalta: eastern European governments were to be freely elected but pro-Russian. As Churchill put it at the time, "The Poles will have their future in their own hands, with the single limitation that they must honestly follow, in harmony with their allies, a policy friendly to Russia."[1]

The Yalta compromise over eastern Europe broke down almost immediately. Even before the Yalta Conference, Bulgaria and Poland were controlled by communists who arrived home with the Red Army. Elsewhere in eastern Europe, pro-Soviet "coalition" governments of several parties were formed, but the key ministerial posts were reserved for Moscow-trained communists.

At the postwar Potsdam Conference of July 1945, the long-avoided differences over eastern Europe finally surged to the fore. The compromising Roosevelt had died and been succeeded by the more determined President Harry Truman, who demanded immediate free elections throughout eastern Europe. Stalin refused point-blank. "A freely elected government in any of these East European countries would be anti-Soviet," he admitted simply, "and that we cannot allow."[2]

Here, then, is the key to the much-debated origins of the cold war. American ideals, pumped up by the crusade against Hitler, and American politics, heavily influenced by millions of U.S. voters of eastern European heritage, demanded free elections in Soviet-occupied eastern Europe. Stalin, who had lived through two enormously destructive German invasions, wanted absolute military security from Germany and its potential eastern European allies, once and for all. Suspicious by nature, he believed that only communist states could be truly dependable allies, and he realized that free elections would result in independent and possibly hostile governments on his western border. Moreover, by the middle of 1945 there was no way short of war that the United States could determine political developments in eastern Europe, and war was out of the question. Stalin was bound to have his way.

West Versus East

The American response to Stalin's exaggerated conception of security was to "get tough." In May 1945 Truman abruptly cut off all aid to Russia. In October he declared that the United States would never recognize any government established by force against the free will of its people. In March 1946 former British prime minister Churchill ominously informed an American audience that an "iron curtain" had fallen across the European continent, dividing Germany and all of Europe into two antagonistic camps. Emotional, moralistic denunciations of Stalin and communist Russia emerged as part of American political life. Yet the United States also responded to the popular desire to "bring the boys home" and demobilized with great speed. When the war against Japan ended in

❋ **The Big Three**   In 1945 a triumphant Winston Churchill, an ailing Franklin Roosevelt, and a determined Joseph Stalin met at Yalta in southern Russia to plan for peace. Cooperation soon gave way to bitter hostility. *(Source: F. D. R. Library)*

September 1945, there were 12 million Americans in the armed forces; by 1947 there were only 1.5 million, as opposed to 6 million for the Soviet Union. Some historians have argued that American leaders believed that the atomic bomb gave the United States all the power it needed, but "getting tough" really meant "talking tough."

Stalin's agents quickly reheated what they viewed as the "ideological struggle against capitalist imperialism." The large, well-organized Communist parties of France and Italy obediently started to uncover American plots to take over Europe and challenged their own governments with violent criticisms and large strikes. The Soviet Union also put pressure on Iran, Turkey, and Greece, while a bitter civil war raged in China. By the spring of 1947, it appeared to many Americans that Stalin was determined to export communism by subversion throughout Europe and around the world.

The United States responded to this challenge with the Truman Doctrine, which was aimed at "containing" communism in areas already occupied by the Red Army. Truman told Congress in March 1947: "I believe it must be the policy of the United States to support free people who are resisting attempted subjugation by armed minorities or by outside pressure." To begin, Truman asked Congress for military aid to Greece and Turkey. Then, in June, Secretary of State George C. Marshall offered Europe economic aid—the Marshall Plan—to help it rebuild (see Listening to the Past).

Stalin refused Marshall Plan assistance for all of eastern Europe. He purged the last remaining noncommunist elements from the coalition governments of eastern Europe and established Soviet-style, one-party communist dictatorships. The seizure of power in Czechoslovakia in February 1948 was particularly brutal and antidemocratic, and it greatly strengthened Western fears of limitless communist expansion, beginning with Germany. Thus, when Stalin blocked all traffic through the Soviet zone of Germany to Berlin, the former capital, which the occupying powers had also divided into sectors at the end of the war, the Western Allies acted firmly but not provocatively.

Hundreds of planes began flying over the Soviet roadblocks around the clock, supplying provisions to thwart Soviet efforts to swallow up the West Berliners. After 324 days the Soviets backed down: containment seemed to work. In 1949, therefore, the United States formed an anti-Soviet military alliance of Western governments: the North Atlantic Treaty Organization (NATO). Stalin countered by tightening his hold on his satellites, later united in the Warsaw Pact. Europe was divided into two hostile blocs.

In late 1949 the communists triumphed in China (see page 1133), frightening and angering many Americans, who saw new evidence of a pow-

The Berlin Airlift Standing in the rubble of their bombed-out city, Germans in the American sector await the arrival of a U.S. transport plane flying in over the Soviet blockade in 1948. The crisis over Berlin was a dramatic indication of growing tensions among the Allies, which resulted in the division of Europe into two hostile camps. *(Source: Walter Sanders, Life Magazine, © Time Warner, Inc.)*

erful worldwide communist conspiracy. When the Russian-backed communist forces of northern Korea invaded southern Korea in 1950, President Truman acted swiftly. American-led United Nations armies intervened. The cold war had spread around the world and had become very hot.

The rapid descent from victorious Grand Alliance to bitter cold war was intimately connected with the tragic fate of eastern Europe. After having appeased Nazi racist imperialism in eastern Europe, the Western democracies during the war chose to ignore the question of Stalin's aims on his western borders and hope for the best. But when Stalin later began to claim the spoils of victory, the United States began to protest and professed outrage. This belated opposition quite possibly encouraged even more aggressive measures by the always-suspicious Stalin, and it helped explode the quarrel over eastern Europe into a global confrontation. This Soviet-American confrontation became institutionalized, and it lasted until the Soviet Union's policy toward eastern Europe changed dramatically in the 1980s (see pages 1114, 1115).

THE WESTERN EUROPEAN RENAISSANCE

As the cold war divided Europe into two blocs, the future appeared bleak on both sides of the iron curtain. Economic conditions were the worst in generations. Politically, Europe was weak and divided, a battleground for cold war ambitions. Moreover, European empires were crumbling in the face of nationalism in Asia and Africa. Yet Europe recovered, and the Western nations led the way. In less than a generation, western Europe achieved unprecedented economic prosperity and peaceful social transformation. It was an amazing rebirth—a true renaissance.

The Postwar Challenge

After the war, economic conditions in western Europe were terrible. Runaway inflation and black markets testified to severe shortages and hardship. Many believed that Europe was simply finished.

Suffering was most intense in defeated Germany. The major territorial change of the war had moved the Soviet Union's border far to the west. Poland was in turn compensated for this loss to the Soviets with land taken from Germany (Map 33.1). To solidify these changes in boundaries, 13 million people were driven from their homes in eastern Germany (and other countries in eastern Europe) and forced to resettle in a greatly reduced Germany. The Russians were also seizing factories and equipment as reparations, even tearing up railroad tracks and sending the rails to the Soviet Union.

In 1945 and 1946, conditions were not much better in the Western zones, for the Western Allies also treated the German population with great severity at first. Countless Germans sold prized possessions to American soldiers to buy food. By the spring of 1947, refugee-clogged, hungry, prostrate Germany was on the verge of total collapse and threatening to drag down the rest of Europe. Yet western Europe was not finished. The Nazi occupation and the war had discredited old ideas and old leaders. All over Europe, many people were willing to change and experiment, and new groups and new leaders were coming to the fore to guide these aspirations. Progressive Catholics and revitalized Catholic political parties—the Christian Democrats—were particularly influential.

In Italy, the Christian Democrats emerged as the leading party, and in early 1948 they won an absolute majority in the parliament in a landslide victory. Their very able leader was Alcide De Gasperi, a courageous antifascist firmly committed to political democracy, economic reconstruction, and moderate social reform. In France, too, the Catholic party also provided some of the best postwar leaders after January 1946, when General Charles de Gaulle, the inspiring wartime leader of the Free French, resigned after having re-established the free and democratic Fourth Republic. As Germany was partitioned by the cold war, a radically purified Federal Republic of Germany (as West Germany was officially known) found new and able leadership among its Catholics. In 1949 Konrad Adenauer, the former mayor of Cologne and a long-time anti-Nazi, began his long, highly successful democratic rule; the Christian Democrats became West Germany's majority party for a generation. In providing effective leadership for their respective countries, the Christian Democrats were inspired and united by a common Christian and European heritage. They steadfastly rejected totalitarianism

MAP 33.1 Europe After the Second World War Both the Soviet Union and Poland took land from Germany, which the Allies partitioned into four occupation zones. Those zones subsequently formed the basis of the east and the west German states, as the iron curtain fell to divide both Germany and Europe. Austria was detached from Germany and also divided into four occupation zones, but the Soviets later permitted Austria to be unified as a neutral state.

and narrow nationalism and placed their faith in democracy and cooperation.

The Socialists and the Communists, active in the Resistance against Hitler, also emerged from the war with increased power and prestige, especially in France and Italy. They, too, provided fresh leadership and pushed for social change and economic reform with considerable success. In the immediate postwar years, welfare measures such as family allowances, health insurance, and increased public housing were enacted throughout much of continental Europe. Britain followed the same trend. The voters threw out Churchill and the Conservatives in 1945, and the victorious socialist Labour party moved toward establishment of a "welfare state." Many industries were nationalized, and the government provided free medical service. Thus all across Europe, social reform complemented political transformation, creating solid foundations for a great European renaissance.

The United States also supplied strong and creative leadership, providing western Europe with both massive economic aid and ongoing military protection. Economic aid was channeled through the Marshall Plan and military security was provided through NATO, which featured American troops stationed permanently in Europe and the American nuclear umbrella. Thus the United States assumed its international responsibilities after the Second World War, exercising the leadership it had shunned after 1919.

As Marshall Plan aid poured in, the battered economies of western Europe began to turn the corner in 1948, and Europe entered a period of unprecedented economic progress that lasted into the late 1960s. There were many reasons for this brilliant economic performance. American aid helped the process get off to a fast start. Moreover, economic growth became a basic objective of all western European governments, for leaders and voters were determined to avoid a return to the dangerous and demoralizing stagnation of the 1930s. Thus governments generally accepted Keynesian economics (see page 1045) and sought to stimulate their economies. They also adopted a variety of imaginative and successful strategies.

In postwar West Germany, Minister of Economy Ludwig Erhard, a roly-poly, cigar-smoking former professor, broke decisively with the straitjacketed Nazi economy. Erhard bet on the free-market economy while maintaining the extensive social welfare network inherited from the Hitler era. He and his teachers believed not only that capitalism was more efficient but also that political and social freedom could thrive only if there were real economic freedom. Erhard's first step was to reform the currency and abolish rationing and price controls in 1948. He boldly declared, "The only ration coupon is the Mark."[3] West German success renewed respect for free-market capitalism.

The French innovation was a new kind of planning. A planning commission set ambitious but flexible goals for the French economy and used the nationalized banks to funnel money into key industries. Thus France combined flexible planning and a "mixed" state and private economy to achieve the most rapid economic development in its long history.

In most countries there were many people ready to work hard for low wages and the hope of a better future. Moreover, although many consumer products had been invented or perfected since the late 1920s, during the Great Depression and war few Europeans had been able to buy them. In 1945 the electric refrigerator, the washing machine, and the automobile were rare luxuries. There was great potential demand, which the economic system moved to satisfy. Finally, West European nations abandoned protectionism and gradually created a large, unified market known as the Common Market. This historic action, which certainly stimulated the economy, was part of a larger search for European unity.

Toward European Unity

Western Europe's political recovery was spectacular in the generation after 1945. Republics were reestablished in France, West Germany, and Italy. Constitutional monarchs were restored in Belgium, the Netherlands, and Norway. Democratic governments, often within the framework of multiparty politics and shifting parliamentary coalitions, took root again and thrived in an atmosphere of civil liberties and individual freedom.

A similarly extraordinary achievement was the march toward a united Europe. The Christian Democrats with their common Catholic heritage were particularly committed to "building Europe," and other groups shared their dedication. Many Europeans believed that only unity could forestall European conflict in the future and that only a new

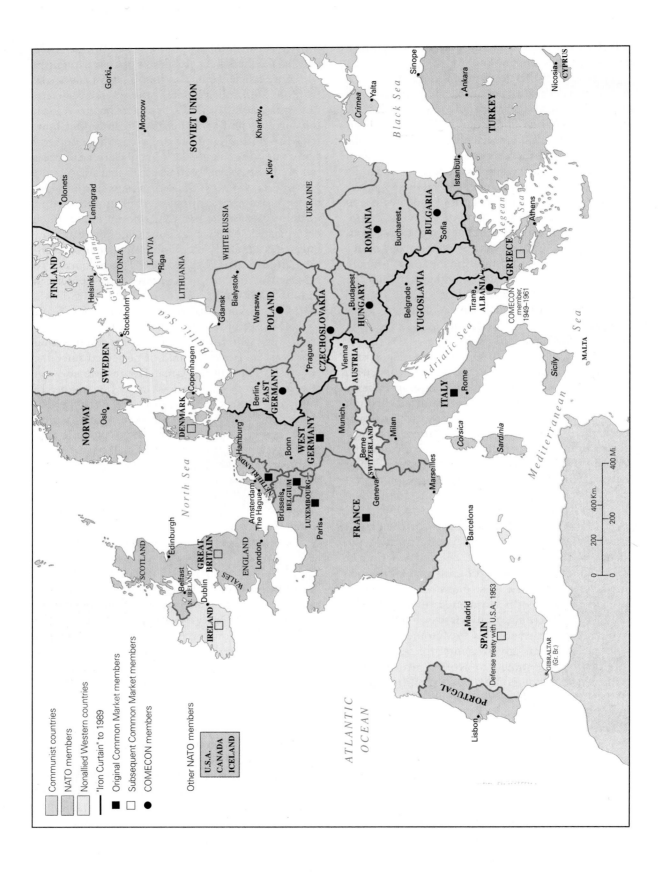

Communist countries
NATO members
Nonallied Western countries
"Iron Curtain" to 1989

Original Common Market members
Subsequent Common Market members
COMECON members

Other NATO members

U.S.A.
CANADA
ICELAND

SOVIET UNION

FINLAND

Gorki

Olonets
Leningrad

Moscow

Kharkov

Kiev

UKRAINE

Crimea
Yalta

Black Sea

Sinope

Ankara

TURKEY

Nicosia
CYPRUS

Helsinki

Gulf of Finland

ESTONIA

LATVIA

Riga

LITHUANIA

WHITE RUSSIA

Bialystok

Gdansk

Warsaw

POLAND

Stockholm

SWEDEN

Copenhagen

DENMARK

Baltic Sea

NORWAY

Oslo

Berlin

EAST GERMANY

Hamburg

Bonn

WEST GERMANY

Munich

Prague

CZECHOSLOVAKIA

Vienna

AUSTRIA

Budapest

HUNGARY

ROMANIA

Bucharest

BULGARIA

Sofia

Belgrade

YUGOSLAVIA

Tirane
ALBANIA

GREECE

Athens

Aegean Sea

Istanbul

COMECON member, 1949–1961

Adriatic Sea

ITALY

Rome

Milan

Berne

SWITZERLAND

Geneva

Marseilles

Corsica

Sardinia

Sicily

MALTA

Mediterranean Sea

North Sea

NETHERLANDS

Amsterdam
The Hague

Brussels
BELGIUM

LUXEMBOURG

Paris

FRANCE

SCOTLAND

Edinburgh

GREAT BRITAIN

ENGLAND

WALES

London

Belfast
N. IRELAND

Dublin

IRELAND

ATLANTIC OCEAN

Barcelona

Madrid

SPAIN

Defense treaty with U.S.A., 1953

GIBRALTAR
(Gr. Br.)

PORTUGAL

Lisbon

0   200   400 Km.
0   200   400 Mi.

"European nation" could reassert western Europe's influence in world affairs dominated by the United States and the Soviet Union.

The close cooperation among European states required by the Americans for Marshall Plan aid led to the creation of both the Organization of European Economic Cooperation (OEEC) and the Council of Europe in 1948. European federalists hoped that the Council of Europe would quickly evolve into a true European parliament with sovereign rights, but this did not happen. Britain, with its empire and its "special relationship" with the United States, consistently opposed giving any real political power—any sovereignty—to the council. Many old-fashioned continental nationalists and communists felt similarly.

Frustrated in the direct political approach, European federalists turned toward economics as a way of working toward genuine unity. French statesmen took the lead in 1950 and called for a special international organization to control and integrate all European steel and coal production. West Germany, Italy, Belgium, the Netherlands, and Luxembourg accepted the French idea in 1952; the British would have none of it. The immediate economic goal—a single steel and coal market without national tariffs or quotas—was rapidly realized. The more far-reaching political goal was to bind the six member nations so closely together economically that war among them would become unthinkable and virtually impossible.

In 1957 the six nations of the Coal and Steel Community signed the Treaty of Rome, which created the European Economic Community, generally known as the Common Market (Map 33.2). The first goal of the treaty was a gradual reduction of all tariffs among the Six in order to create a single market almost as large as that of the United States. Other goals included the free movement of capital and labor and common economic policies and institutions. The Common Market was a great success, encouraging companies and regions to specialize in what they did best.

MAP 33.2 European Alliance Systems After the cold war divided Europe into two hostile military alliances, six western European countries formed the Common Market in 1957. The Common Market grew later to include most of western Europe. The Communist states organized their own economic association—COMECON.

The development of the Common Market fired imaginations and encouraged hopes of rapid progress toward political as well as economic union. In the 1960s, however, these hopes were frustrated by a resurgence of more traditional nationalism. France took the lead. Mired in a bitter colonial war in Algeria, the French turned in 1958 to General de Gaulle, who established the Fifth French Republic and ruled as its president until 1969. De Gaulle was at heart a romantic nationalist, and he labored to re-create a powerful, truly independent France. Viewing the United States as the main threat to genuine French (and European) independence, he withdrew all French military forces from the "American-controlled" NATO command as France developed its own nuclear weapons. Within the Common Market, de Gaulle refused to permit the scheduled advent of majority rule. Thus throughout the 1960s the Common Market thrived economically but remained a union of sovereign states.

Decolonization

In the postwar era Europe's long overseas expansion was dramatically reversed. Between 1947 and 1962 almost every colonial territory gained formal independence. Future generations will almost certainly see this rolling back of Western expansion as one of world history's truly great turning points (Map 33.3).

The basic cause of imperial collapse—what Europeans called *decolonization*—was the rising demand of Asian and African peoples for national self-determination, racial equality, and personal dignity. This demand spread from intellectuals to the masses in virtually every colonial territory after the First World War. As a result, colonial empires had already been shaken by 1939, and the way was prepared for the eventual triumph of independence movements (see pages 1040–1058). Yet decolonization also involved the imperial powers, and looking at the process from their perspective helps explain why independence came so quickly and why a kind of neocolonialism subsequently took its place in some areas.

European empires had been based on an enormous power differential between the rulers and the ruled, a difference that had declined almost to the vanishing point by 1945. Not only was western

JAPAN

NORTH KOREA 1948
SOUTH KOREA 1948
From Japan

PHILIPPINES 1946

BRUNEI 1984
From Great Britain

NORTH VIETNAM 1954
Unified 1974
SOUTH VIETNAM 1954

CAMBODIA 1954

MALAYSIA 1963
SINGAPORE 1965

INDONESIA 1949

LAOS 1949

MYANMAR (BURMA) 1947

PAKISTAN 1947, BANGLADESH 1973

INDIA 1947

SRI LANKA (CEYLON) 1948

PACIFIC OCEAN

PAKISTAN 1947

INDIAN OCEAN

P.D.R. OF YEMEN 1967 Unified with Yemen 1990

SOMALIA 1960

MAURITIUS 1968 From Great Britain

MADAGASCAR 1960

KUWAIT 1961

BAHRAIN 1971
QATAR 1971
UNITED ARAB EMIRATES 1971

YEMEN

DJIBOUTI 1977

KENYA 1963

UGANDA 1962
TANZANIA 1964

MALAWI 1964

MOZAMBIQUE 1974

SWAZILAND 1968

LESOTHO 1966

JORDAN 1946

CYPRUS 1960
ISRAEL 1948

MALTA 1964 From Great Britain

SUDAN 1956

ZAIRE 1960

RWANDA 1962
BURUNDI 1962

ZAMBIA 1964

ZIMBABWE 1980

BOTSWANA 1966

SOUTH AFRICA (Republic 1961)

LIBYA 1951

CHAD 1960

CENTRAL AFRICAN REPUBLIC 1960

ANGOLA 1975

NAMIBIA 1990

GREAT BRITAIN

NETHERLANDS
BELGIUM

FRANCE

ITALY

SPAIN

PORTUGAL

TUNISIA 1957

ALGERIA 1962

NIGER 1960

NIGERIA 1960

BENIN 1960

CAMEROON 1960

GABON 1960

CONGO 1960

MOROCCO 1956

MALI 1960

BURKINA FASO 1960

TOGO 1960

GHANA 1957

EQUATORIAL GUINEA 1968 From Spain

WESTERN SAHARA (MOROCCO) 1975 From Spain

MAURITANIA 1960

SENEGAL 1960
GAMBIA 1965
GUINEA-BISSAU 1974
GUINEA 1958
SIERRA LEONE 1961
LIBERIA 1820s
CÔTE D'IVOIRE 1960

ATLANTIC OCEAN

Date is year independence was achieved.
Shading indicates former ruler.

	Great Britain		Belgium
	France		Portugal
	Netherlands		United States
	Italy		

| 0 | 500 | 1000 | 1500 Km. |
| 0 | 500 | 1000 | 1500 Mi. |

Europe poor and battered, but most Europeans regarded their empires very differently after 1945 than before 1914, or even before 1939. Empire had rested on self-confidence and self-righteousness; Europeans had believed their superiority to be not only technical and military but spiritual and moral as well. The horrors of the Second World War destroyed such complacent arrogance and gave opponents of imperialism much greater influence in Europe. With its political power and moral authority in tatters, Europe could either submit to decolonization or enter into risky wars of reconquest. After 1945 many Europeans were willing to let go of their colonies more or less voluntarily and to concentrate on rebuilding at home.

Indian independence played a key role in decolonization. When the Labour party came to power in Great Britain in 1945, it was determined to leave India. British socialists had always opposed imperialism, and the heavy cost of governing India had become an intolerable burden. Empire in India ended in 1947, and most Asian colonies achieved independence shortly thereafter. Although the French obstinately tried to re-establish colonial rule in Indochina, they were defeated in 1954, and two independent Vietnamese states came into being. The French also fought a long, dirty war to keep Algeria French, but Algeria won its independence in 1962 (see Map 33.3).

In much of Africa south of the Sahara, decolonization proceeded much more smoothly. Beginning in 1957, Britain's colonies achieved independence with little or no bloodshed and then entered a very loose association with Britain as members of the British Commonwealth of Nations. In 1958 the clever de Gaulle offered the leaders of French black Africa the choice of a total break with France or immediate independence within a kind of French commonwealth. All but one of the new states chose association with France (see page 1160). As in the past, the French and their Common Market partners saw themselves as continuing their civilizing mission in black Africa. More im-

portant, they saw in Africa untapped markets for their industrial goods, raw materials for their factories, outlets for profitable investment, and good temporary jobs for their engineers and teachers. The British acted somewhat similarly.

As a result, western European countries actually managed to increase their economic and cultural ties with their former African colonies in the 1960s and 1970s. Above all, they used the lure of special trading privileges with the Common Market and heavy investment in French- and English-language education to enhance a powerful Western presence in the new African states. This situation led a variety of leaders and scholars to charge that western Europe (and the United States) had imposed a system of neocolonialism on the former colonies. According to this view, *neocolonialism* was a system designed to perpetuate Western economic domination and undermine the promise of political independence, thereby extending to Africa (and much of Asia) the neocolonial subordination that the United States had established in Latin America after the political revolutions of the early nineteenth century. At the very least, enduring influence in black Africa testified to western Europe's resurgent economic and political power in international relations.

The Changing Class Structure

Rapid economic growth went a long way toward creating a new society in Europe after the Second World War. European society became more mobile and more democratic. Old class barriers relaxed, and class distinctions became fuzzier.

Changes in the structure of the middle class were particularly influential in the general drift toward a less rigid class structure. In the nineteenth and early twentieth centuries, the model for the middle class had been the independent, self-employed property owner who owned a business or practiced a liberal profession like law or medicine. After 1945, a new breed of managers and experts replaced traditional property owners as the leaders of the middle class. Ability to serve the needs of a big organization largely replaced inherited property and family connections in determining an individual's social position in the middle and upper middle class. At the same time, the middle class grew massively and became harder to define.

❧ **MAP 33.3 New States in Africa and Asia**
Divided primarily along religious lines into two states, British India led the way to political independence in 1947. Most African territories achieved statehood by the mid-1960s, as European empires passed away, unlamented.

There were several reasons for these developments. Rapid industrial and technological expansion created in large corporations and government agencies a powerful demand for technologists and managers. Moreover, the old propertied middle class lost control of many family-owned businesses (including family farms) and joined the ranks of salaried employees.

Top managers and ranking civil servants therefore represented the model for a new middle class of salaried specialists. Well paid and highly trained, pragmatic and realistic, these experts increasingly came from all social classes, even the working class. Everywhere successful managers and technocrats passed on the opportunity for all-important advanced education to their children, but only in rare instances could they pass on the positions they had attained. Thus the new middle class, which was based largely on specialized skills and high levels of education, was more open, democratic, and insecure than the old propertied middle class.

The structure of the lower classes also became more flexible and open. There was a mass exodus from farms and the countryside, as one of the most traditional and least mobile groups in European society drastically declined. Meanwhile, because of rapid technological change, the industrial working class ceased to expand, and job opportunities for white-collar and service employees grew rapidly. Such employees bore a greater resemblance to the new middle class of salaried specialists than to industrial workers, who were also better educated and more specialized.

European governments were reducing class tensions with a series of social security reforms. Many of these reforms—like increased unemployment benefits and more extensive old-age pensions—simply strengthened social security measures first pioneered in Bismarck's Germany before the First World War. Other programs were new, like comprehensive national health systems directed by the state. Most countries also introduced family allowances—direct government grants to parents to help them raise their children. These allowances helped many poor families make ends meet. Most European governments also gave maternity grants and built inexpensive public housing for low-income families and individuals. These and other social reforms provided a humane floor of well-being. Reforms also promoted greater equality be-

cause they were expensive and were paid for in part by higher taxes on the rich.

The rising standard of living and the spread of standardized consumer goods also worked to level Western society, as the percentage of income spent on food and drink declined substantially. For example, in 1948 there were only 5 million cars in western Europe, but in 1965 there were 44 million. Car ownership was democratized and came within the range of better-paid workers.

Europeans took great pleasure in the products of the "gadget revolution" as well. Like Americans, Europeans filled their houses and apartments with washing machines, vacuum cleaners, refrigerators, dishwashers, radios, TVs, and stereos. The purchase of consumer goods was greatly facilitated by installment purchasing. Before the Second World War, Europeans had rarely bought on credit. But with the expansion of social security safeguards, reducing the need to accumulate savings for hard times, ordinary people were increasingly willing to take on debt. This change had far-reaching consequences.

The most astonishing leisure-time development in the consumer society was the blossoming of mass travel and tourism. With month-long paid vacations required by law in most European countries, and widespread automobile ownership, beaches and ski resorts came within the reach of the middle class and many workers. By the late 1960s packaged tours with cheap group flights and bargain hotel accommodations had made even distant lands easily accessible. A French company grew rich building imitation Tahitian paradises around the world. At Swedish nudist colonies on secluded West African beaches, office workers from Stockholm fleetingly worshiped the sun in the middle of the long northern winter. Truly, consumerism had come of age.

The Troubled Economy in Recent Times

For twenty years after 1945, most Europeans were preoccupied with the possibilities of economic progress and consumerism. The more democratic class structure also helped to reduce social tension, and ideological conflict went out of style. In the late 1960s, however, sharp criticism and social conflicts re-emerged, heralding a new era of uncertainty and crisis.

A Modern Manager   Despite considerable discrimination, women were increasingly found in the expanding middle class of salaried experts after World War II, working in business, science, and technology. *(Source: Niépce-Rapho/Photo Researchers)*

Much of the criticism in western Europe came from radical students, who formed part of an international counterculture that came to oppose the Vietnam War as immoral and imperialistic (see pages 1120–1121). But student protests in western Europe also highlighted more general problems of education in a society of specialists. Higher education expanded rapidly in western Europe after World War II, and this expansion created problems as well as opportunities for students. Classes were badly overcrowded, and competition for grades was intense. "Practical" areas of study were added to the curriculum, but they were added less quickly than some students wanted. Thus many students felt that Western governments were evil and imperialistic or that governments were not providing the kind of education that young people needed for jobs in the modern economy. They concluded that universities as well as society needed fundamental, even revolutionary reforms.

Tensions came to a head in the late 1960s and early 1970s. Following in the footsteps of their American counterparts, European university students rose to challenge their university administrations and even their governments. The most far-reaching of these revolts occurred in France in 1968. Students occupied university buildings, clashed violently with police, and appealed to France's industrial workers for help. A general strike then spread across France in May 1968, and it seemed certain that President de Gaulle's Fifth Republic would collapse. De Gaulle, however, stiffened, moving troops toward Paris and calling for new elections. Thoroughly frightened and fearful that a successful revolution could lead only to an eventual communist takeover, the masses of France voted for a return to law and order. De Gaulle and his party scored the biggest electoral victory in modern French history, and the mini-revolution collapsed. But the proud de Gaulle and the confident though old-fashioned nationalism that he represented had been cruelly mocked. In 1969, tired and discouraged, he resigned over a minor issue, and within a year he was dead.

The international student revolution of the late 1960s announced the passing of postwar social

✳ **Student Rebellion in Paris**   These rock-throwing students in the Latin Quarter of Paris are trying to force education reforms and even to topple de Gaulle's government. Throughout May 1968 students clashed repeatedly with France's tough riot police in bloody street fighting. De Gaulle remained in power, but a major reform of French education did follow. *(Source: Bruno Barbey/Magnum)*

stability, but it was the reappearance of economic crisis in the 1970s that brought the most serious challenges for the average person. The postwar international monetary system was based on the American dollar. Foreign governments could exchange dollars for gold at $35 an ounce and considered dollars "as good as gold." Giving foreign aid and fighting foreign wars, the United States sent billions of dollars abroad. By early 1971, it had only $11 billion in gold left, and Europe had accumulated 50 billion American dollars. Foreigners then panicked and raced to exchange their dollars for gold. President Richard Nixon responded

by stopping the sale of American gold; the value of the dollar fell sharply, and inflation accelerated worldwide. Fixed rates of exchange were abandoned, and great uncertainty replaced postwar predictability in international trade and finance.

Even more damaging was the dramatic reversal in the price and availability of energy. The great postwar boom was fueled by cheap oil, especially in western Europe. By 1971, the Arab-led Organization of Petroleum Exporting Countries (OPEC) had watched the price of crude oil decline consistently compared with the rising price of manufactured goods. OPEC decided to reverse that trend by presenting a united front against the oil companies. After the fourth Arab-Israeli war in October 1973 (see page 0000), crude oil prices quadrupled in the course of a year. It was widely realized that the rapid price rise was economically destructive, but the world's big powers did nothing. The Soviet Union was a great oil exporter and benefited directly; the United States was immobilized, its attention absorbed by the Watergate crisis in politics (see page 0000). Thus governments, companies, and individuals had no choice other than to deal piecemeal with the so-called oil shock—a "shock" that really turned out to be an earthquake.

Coming on the heels of upheaval in the international monetary system, the revolution in energy prices plunged the world into its worst economic decline since the 1930s. Unemployment rose. Productivity and living standards declined. By 1976 a modest recovery was in progress, but when Iranian oil production collapsed during Iran's fundamentalist Islamic revolution (see page 1152), the price of crude oil doubled again in 1979, and the world economy succumbed to its second oil shock. Unemployment and inflation rose dramatically before another uneven recovery began in 1982. But in the summer of 1985 the unemployment rate in western Europe rose again, to its highest levels since the Great Depression. Although unemployment declined somewhat in the late 1980s, the 1990s opened with renewed recession in the United States and in Europe, where it was especially severe. Global recovery was painfully slow until late 1993.

One telling measure of the troubled economy was the "misery index," first used with considerable effect by candidate Jimmy Carter in the 1976 U.S. presidential debates. The misery index combined rates of inflation and unemployment in a single, powerfully emotional number. Figure 33.1 presents a comparison of misery indexes for the United States, Japan, and the European Economic Community (the Common Market) between 1970 and 1986. "Misery" increased on both sides of the Atlantic, but the increase was substantially greater in western Europe—where these hard times are often referred to simply as "the crisis"—and it remained so in the early 1990s.

Throughout the 1970s and 1980s anxious observers, recalling the disastrous consequences of the Great Depression, worried that the Common Market might disintegrate in the face of severe

 FIGURE 33.1 The Misery Index, 1970–1986 Combining rates of unemployment and inflation provided a simple but effective measure of economic hardship. This particular index represents the sum of two times the unemployment rate plus the inflation rate, reflecting the widespread belief that joblessness causes more suffering than higher prices. EEC = European Economic Community, or Common Market countries. (*Source: OECD data, as given in* The Economist, *June 15, 1985, p. 69.*)

economic dislocation and that economic nationalism would halt steps toward European unity. Yet the Common Market continued to exert a powerful attraction on nonmembers. In 1973, Denmark and Iceland, in addition to Britain, finally joined. Greece joined in 1981, and Portugal and Spain entered in 1986.

After de Gaulle's death, the nations of the Common Market cooperated more closely in many international undertakings, and the movement toward European unity stayed alive. The Common Market countries eventually set 1992 as the year for the attainment of total economic and social integration, which was achieved, at least on paper, in the Maastricht treaty of 1992. The European Community was renamed the European Union, and 1997 was ambitiously set as the date for full monetary union with a single European currency. Western Europe had weathered the storms of the 1970s and 1980s, which contrasted so sharply with the clear sailing of the 1950s and 1960s.

Saudi Riches   Enormous oil reserves make Saudi Arabia one of the most influential members of the Organization of Petroleum Exporting Countries (OPEC) and give it one of the world's highest per capita incomes. Oil has also made rich men of Prince Fahd and King Khalid, shown here considering plans for a new urban development. *(Source: Robert Azzi/Woodfin Camp & Associates)*

Society in a Time of Economic Uncertainty

The most pervasive consequences of this recent economic stagnation were probably psychological and attitudinal. Optimism gave way to pessimism; romantic utopianism yielded to sober realism. This drastic change in mood—a complete surprise only to those who had never studied history—affected states, institutions, and individuals in countless ways.

To be sure, there were heartbreaking human tragedies—lost jobs, bankruptcies, homelessness, and mental breakdowns. But on the whole, the welfare system fashioned in the postwar era prevented mass suffering and degradation through extended benefits for the unemployed, free medical care and special allowances for the needy, and a host of lesser supports. The responsive, socially concerned national state undoubtedly contributed to the preservation of political stability and democracy in the face of economic difficulties that might have brought revolution and dictatorship in earlier times.

The energetic response of governments to social needs helps explain the sharp increase in total government spending in most countries during the 1970s and 1980s. In 1982 western European governments spent an average of more than 50 percent of gross national income, as compared to only 37 percent fifteen years earlier. In all countries, people were much more willing to see their governments increase spending than raise taxes. This imbalance contributed to the rapid growth of budget deficits, national debts, and inflation. By the late 1970s, a powerful reaction against government's ever-increasing role had set in, however, and Western governments were gradually forced to introduce austerity measures to slow the seemingly inexorable growth of public spending and the welfare state.

Part of a broad cultural shift toward greater conservatism, growing voter dissatisfaction with government and government spending helped bring Margaret Thatcher (b. 1925) to power in Britain in 1979. Thatcher had some success in slowing government spending and in privatizing industry—that is, in selling off state-owned companies to private investors. Of great social significance, Thatcher's Conservative government encouraged low- and moderate-income renters in state-owned housing projects to buy their apartments at rock-bottom prices. This privatization initiative created a whole new class of property owners, thereby eroding the electoral base of Britain's socialist Labour party.

The striking but temporary exception to the trend toward greater frugality was François Mitterrand (b. 1916) of France. After his election as president in 1981, Mitterrand led his Socialist party and Communist allies on a lurch to the left, launching a vast program of nationalization and public investment designed to spend France out of economic stagnation. By 1983 this attempt had clearly failed. Mitterrand's Socialist government was then compelled to impose a wide variety of austerity measures, but the French economy continued to limp and sputter through the decade.

In early 1993 frustrated French voters gave a coalition of conservatives and moderates an overwhelming victory, as the Socialist party suffered total defeat and the once-powerful Communists were reduced almost to fringe party status. With industrial production and national income declining in France (and in Germany, Italy, and Spain, among others), and with unemployment climbing to a new high of 10.7 percent in the European Union in October 1993, the hard times that began in the West in 1973 were continuing.

When governments were forced to restrain spending, large scientific projects were often singled out for cuts. These reductions reinforced the ongoing computer revolution. That revolution thrived on the diffusion of ever-cheaper computa-tional and informational capacity to small research groups and private businesses, which were both cause and effect of the revolution itself. Big organizations lost some of their advantages as small firms and even individuals became able to link electronically with their region and most of the world. By the 1990s a student with an inexpensive personal computer had the power of a 1950s mainframe that had filled a room and cost hundreds of thousands of dollars. From fax machines to new cars, computer technology was everywhere.

Despite the advantages offered by electronic gadgetry, individuals felt the impact of austerity at an early date, for, unlike governments, they could not pay their bills by printing money and going ever further into debt. The energy crisis of the 1970s forced them to re-examine not only their fuel bills but also the whole pattern of self-indulgent materialism in the postwar era. The result in both Europe and North America was a leaner, tougher lifestyle, featuring more attention to nutrition and a passion for exercise. Correspondingly, there was less blind reliance on medical science for good health and a growing awareness that individuals had to accept a large portion of the responsibility for illness and disease. More people began to realize that they could substantially increase their life spans simply by eating regular meals, sleeping seven or eight hours each night, exercising two or three times a week, maintaining moderate weight, foregoing smoking, and using alcohol only in moderation. For example, a forty-five-year-old American male who practiced three or fewer of these habits in the late 1970s could expect to live to be sixty-seven, but one who adhered to five or six could expect to live eleven more years, to age seventy-eight.

Economic troubles also strengthened existing trends within the family. Men and women were encouraged to postpone marriage until they had put their careers on a firm foundation, so the age of marriage rose sharply for both sexes in many Western countries. Indeed, the very real threat of unemployment—or "underemployment" in a dead-end job—seemed to shape the outlook of a whole generation. The students of the 1980s were serious, practical, and often conservative. As one young woman at a French university told a reporter in 1985, "Jobs are the big worry now, so everyone wants to learn something practical."[4] In France as elsewhere, the shift away from the romantic visions and the political activism of the late 1960s was astonishing.

Harder times also meant that ever-more women entered or remained in the work force after they married. Although attitudes related to personal fulfillment were one reason for the continuing increase—especially for well-educated, upper-middle-class women—many wives in poor and middle-class families simply had to work outside the home because of economic necessity. As in preindustrial Europe, the wife's earnings provided the margin of survival for millions of hard-pressed families.

 ## SOVIET EASTERN EUROPE

While western Europe surged ahead economically after the Second World War and regained political independence as American influence gradually waned, eastern Europe followed a different path. The Soviet Union under Stalin first tightened its grip on the "liberated" nations of eastern Europe and then refused to let go. Thus postwar economic recovery in eastern Europe proceeded along Soviet lines, and changes in the Soviet Union strongly influenced political and social developments. These changes went forward at a slow and uneven pace, and they appeared to almost halt after Leonid Brezhnev came to power and crushed a socialist reform movement in Czechoslovakia in 1968.

Yet beneath the apparent stagnation of the Brezhnev years Soviet society experienced a major transformation. This transformation encouraged new political thinking in the Soviet Union and in turn enabled the long-frustrated reform movement to triumph spectacularly in eastern Europe in the unexpected revolution of 1989. Thus one must look primarily at the Soviet Union in order to understand the history of eastern European peoples since 1945.

Stalin's Last Years

Americans were not the only ones who felt betrayed by Stalin's postwar actions. The Great Patriotic War of the Fatherland had fostered Russian nationalism and a relaxation of totalitarian terror. It also produced a rare but real unity between Soviet rulers and most Russian people. Having made a heroic war effort, the vast majority of the Soviet people hoped in 1945 that a grateful party and government would grant greater freedom and democracy. Such hopes were soon crushed.

Even before the war ended, Stalin was moving his country back toward rigid dictatorship. As early as 1944, the leading members of the Communist party were being given a new motivating slogan: "The war on Fascism ends, the war on capitalism begins."[5] By early 1946, Stalin was publicly singing the old tune that war was inevitable as long as capitalism existed. Stalin's new foreign foe in the West provided an excuse for re-establishing a harsh dictatorship. Thousands of returning soldiers and ordinary civilians were purged in 1945 and 1946, as Stalin revived the terrible forced-labor camps of the 1930s.

Culture and art were also purged in violent campaigns that reimposed rigid anti-Western ideological conformity. Many artists were denounced, including the composers Sergei Prokofiev and Dimitri Shostakovich and the outstanding film director Sergei Eisenstein. In 1949 Stalin launched a savage verbal attack on Soviet Jews, accusing them of being pro-Western and antisocialist.

In the political realm, Stalin reasserted the Communist party's complete control of the government and his absolute mastery of the party. Five-year plans were reintroduced to cope with the enormous task of economic reconstruction. Once again, heavy and military industry were given top priority, and consumer goods, housing, and collectivized agriculture were neglected. Everyday life was very hard. In short, it was the 1930s all over again in the Soviet Union, although police terror was less intense.

Stalin's prime postwar innovation was to export the Stalinist system to the countries of eastern Europe. The Communist parties of eastern Europe had established one-party states by 1948, thanks to the help of the Red Army and the Russian secret police. Rigid ideological indoctrination, attacks on religion, and a lack of civil liberties were soon facts of life. Industry was nationalized, and the middle class was stripped of its possessions. Economic life was then faithfully recast in the Stalinist mold. Forced industrialization, with five-year plans and a stress on heavy industry, lurched forward without regard for human costs. The collectivization of agriculture began.

Only Josip Tito (1892–1980), the popular resistance leader and Communist chief of Yugoslavia, was able to resist Soviet domination successfully. Tito openly broke with Stalin in 1948, and since

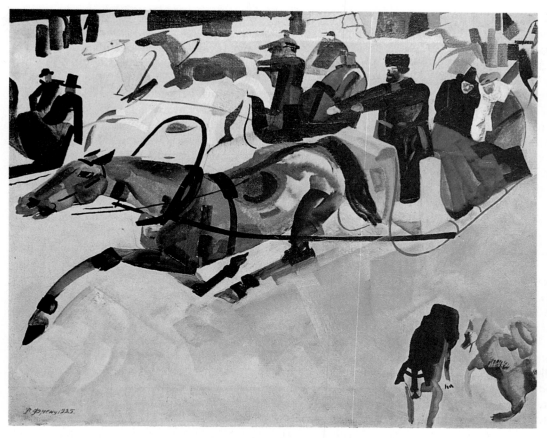

Frenz: Pink Snow   This lighthearted rendition of traditional Russian themes hardly seems a threat to the Stalinist state. Yet it failed to conform to the official style of socialist realism and thus was suppressed along with a host of other works during Zhdanov's brutal cultural purge. *(Source: Sovfoto)*

there was no Russian army in Yugoslavia, he got away with it. Yugoslavia thrived until it began to break apart in the late 1980s (see pages 1209–1210). Tito's successful proclamation of Communist independence led the infuriated and humiliated Stalin to re-enact the great show trials of the 1930s (see page 1063). Popular Communist leaders in eastern Europe who, like Tito, had led the resistance against Germany were thus purged as Stalin sought to create absolutely obedient instruments of domination in eastern Europe.

Reform and De-Stalinization

In 1953 the aging Stalin finally died, and the dictatorship that he had built began to change. Even as Stalin's heirs struggled for power, they realized that reforms were necessary because of the widespread fear and hatred of Stalin's political terrorism. The power of the secret police was curbed, and gradually many of the forced-labor camps were closed. Change was also necessary for economic reasons. Agriculture was in bad shape, and shortages of consumer goods were discouraging hard work and initiative. Moreover, Stalin's belligerent foreign policy had led directly to a strong Western alliance, which isolated the Soviet Union.

On the question of just how much change should be permitted, the Communist leadership was badly split. Conservatives wanted to make as few changes as possible. Reformers, who were led by Nikita Khrushchev, argued for major innovations. Khrushchev (1894–1971) had joined the party as an uneducated coal miner in 1918 at twenty-four and had risen steadily to a high-level position in the 1930s. By 1955 he was emerging as the new ruler.

To strengthen his position and that of his fellow reformers within the party, Khrushchev launched an all-out attack on Stalin and his crimes at a closed session of the Twentieth Party Congress in 1956. In gory detail he described to the startled Communist delegates how Stalin had tortured and murdered thousands of loyal Communists, how he had trusted Hitler completely and bungled the country's defense, and how he had "supported the glorification of his own person with all conceivable methods." Khrushchev's "secret speech" was read to Communist party meetings throughout the country, and it strengthened the reform movement.

The liberalization—or *de-Stalinization,* as it was called in the West—of the Soviet Union was genuine. The Communist party jealously maintained its monopoly on political power, but Khrushchev shook up the party and brought in new members. Some resources were shifted from heavy industry and the military toward consumer goods and agriculture, and Stalinist controls over workers were relaxed. The Soviet Union's very low standard of living finally began to improve and continued to rise substantially throughout the booming 1960s.

De-Stalinization created great ferment among writers and intellectuals who hungered for cultural freedom. The poet Boris Pasternak (1890–1960) finished his great novel *Doctor Zhivago* in 1956. Published in the West but not in Russia, *Doctor Zhivago* is both a literary masterpiece and a powerful challenge to communism. It tells the story of a prerevolutionary intellectual who rejects the violence and brutality of the revolution of 1917 and the Stalinist years. Even as he is destroyed, he triumphs because of his humanity and Christian spirit. Pasternak was denounced—but he was not shot. Other talented writers followed Pasternak's lead, and courageous editors let the sparks fly.

The writer Alexander Solzhenitsyn (b. 1918) created a sensation when his *One Day in the Life of Ivan Denisovich* was published in the Soviet Union in 1962. Solzhenitsyn's novel portrays in grim detail life in a Stalinist concentration camp—a life to which Solzhenitsyn himself had been unjustly condemned—and is a damning indictment of the Stalinist past.

Khrushchev also de-Stalinized Soviet foreign policy. "Peaceful coexistence" with capitalism was

possible, he argued, and great wars were not inevitable. Khrushchev even made concessions, agreeing in 1955 to real independence for a neutral Austria after ten long years of Allied occupation. Thus there was considerable relaxation of cold war tensions between 1955 and 1957. At the same time, Khrushchev began wooing the new nations of Asia and Africa—even if they were not communist—with promises and aid.

De-Stalinization stimulated rebelliousness in the eastern European satellites. Having suffered in silence under Stalin, Communist reformers and the masses were quickly emboldened to seek much greater liberty and national independence. Poland took the lead in 1956, when extensive rioting brought a new government that managed to win greater autonomy.

Hungary experienced a real and tragic revolution. Led by students and workers—the classic urban revolutionaries—the people of Budapest installed a liberal Communist reformer as their new chief in October 1956. Soviet troops were forced to leave the country. But after the new government promised free elections and renounced Hungary's military alliance with Moscow, the Russian leaders ordered an invasion and crushed the national and democratic revolution. Fighting was bitter until the end, for the Hungarians hoped that the United States would come to their aid. When this did not occur, most people in eastern Europe concluded that their only hope was to strive for small domestic gains while following Russia obediently in foreign affairs.

Brezhnev and Stagnation

By late 1962, opposition in party circles to Khrushchev's policies was strong, and within two years Khrushchev fell in a bloodless palace revolution. Under Leonid Brezhnev (1906–1982), the Soviet Union began a period of stagnation and limited *re-Stalinization.* The basic reason for this development was that Khrushchev's Communist colleagues saw de-Stalinization as a dangerous, two-sided threat. How could Khrushchev denounce the dead dictator without eventually denouncing and perhaps even arresting his still-powerful henchmen? Moreover, the widening campaign of de-Stalinization posed a clear threat to the dictatorial authority of the party. It was producing growing, perhaps uncontrollable, criticism of the whole communist system. The party had to tighten up while there was still time. Khrushchev had to go.

Another reason for conservative opposition was that Khrushchev's policy toward the West was erratic and ultimately unsuccessful. In 1958 he ordered the Western allies to evacuate West Berlin within six months. In response, the allies reaffirmed their unity, and Khrushchev backed down. Then in 1961, as relations with communist China deteriorated dramatically, Khrushchev ordered the East Germans to build a wall between East and West Berlin. After the recently elected U.S. president, John F. Kennedy, acquiesced to the construction of the Berlin Wall, an emboldened Khrushchev ordered missiles with nuclear warheads installed in Fidel Castro's communist Cuba in 1962. President Kennedy countered with a naval blockade of Cuba. After a tense diplomatic crisis, Khrushchev agreed to remove the Soviet missiles in return for American pledges not to disturb Castro's regime. Khrushchev looked like a bumbling buffoon; his influence, already slipping, declined rapidly after the Cuban fiasco.

After Brezhnev and his supporters took over in 1964, they started talking quietly of Stalin's "good points" and ignoring his crimes. This change informed Soviet citizens that further liberalization could not be expected at home. Soviet leaders, determined never to suffer Khrushchev's humiliation in the face of American nuclear superiority, also launched a massive arms buildup. Yet Brezhnev and company proceeded cautiously in the mid-1960s.

In the wake of Khrushchev's reforms, the 1960s brought modest liberalization and more consumer goods to eastern Europe, as well as somewhat greater national autonomy, especially in Poland and Romania. In January 1968, the reform elements in the Czechoslovak Communist party gained a majority and voted out the long-time Stalinist leader in favor of Alexander Dubček (b. 1921), whose new government launched dramatic reforms.

Educated in Moscow, Dubček was a dedicated Communist. But he and his allies believed that they could reconcile genuine socialism with personal freedom and internal party democracy. Thus local decision making by trade unions, managers, and consumers replaced rigid bureaucratic planning. Censorship was relaxed, and the reform program proved enormously popular.

Although Dubček remembered the lesson of the Hungarian revolution and constantly proclaimed his loyalty to the Warsaw Pact, the determination of the Czech reformers to build what they called "socialism with a human face" frightened hard-line Communists. These fears were particularly strong in Poland and East Germany, where leaders knew full well that they lacked popular support. Moreover, the Soviet Union feared that a liberalized Czechoslovakia would eventually be drawn to neutralism or even to the democratic West. Thus in August 1968, 500,000 Russian and allied eastern European troops suddenly occupied Czechoslovakia. The Czechs made no attempt to resist militarily, and the arrested Czech leaders surrendered to Soviet demands. The reform program was abandoned, and the Czechoslovak experiment in humanizing communism came to an end. Shortly afterward, Brezhnev declared the so-called Brezhnev Doctrine, according to which the Soviet Union and its allies had the right to intervene in any socialist country whenever they saw the need.

The 1968 invasion of Czechoslovakia was the crucial event of the Brezhnev era, which really lasted beyond the aging leader's death in 1982 until the emergence in 1985 of Mikhail Gorbachev. The invasion demonstrated the determination of the Soviet Union's ruling elite to maintain the status quo in the Soviet bloc. In the U.S.S.R. that determination resulted in further repression, but the Soviet Union appeared quite stable in the 1970s and early 1980s.

A rising standard of living for ordinary people contributed to stability, although the economic crisis of the 1970s greatly slowed the rate of improvement, and long lines and innumerable shortages persisted. The enduring advantages of the elite also reinforced the system. Ambitious individuals still had tremendous incentive to do as the state wished in order to gain access to special, well-stocked stores, attend superior schools, and travel abroad.

Another source of stability was the enduring nationalism of ordinary Russians. Party leaders successfully identified themselves with Russian patriotism, stressing their role in saving the motherland during the Second World War and protecting it now from foreign foes, including eastern European "counter-revolutionaries." Moreover, the politically dominant Great Russians, who constituted only half of the total Soviet population, held through the Communist party the commanding leadership positions in the Soviet Union's non-Russian republics. The Great Russian leaders generally feared that greater freedom might result in demands for autonomy and even independence by non-Russian nationalities. Thus liberalism and democracy appeared as alien and divisive political philosophies that would undermine the U.S.S.R.'s power and achievements.

The strength of the government was expressed in the re-Stalinization of culture and art. Free expression and open protest disappeared. Modest acts of open nonconformity and protest were severely punished—but sophisticated, cunning methods of coercion replaced the uncontrolled terror of the Stalin era. Most frequently, dissidents were blacklisted and thus rendered unable to find a decent job. The most determined but least well known protesters were quietly imprisoned in jails or mental institutions. Celebrated nonconformists such as Solzhenitsyn were permanently expelled from the country. Overall, rule by a self-perpetuating Communist elite apeared to be quite solid in the 1970s and early 1980s.

Beneath the immobility of political life in the Brezhnev era, however, the Soviet Union was experiencing profound changes. As a perceptive British journalist put it in 1986, "The country went through a social revolution while Brezhnev slept."[6] Three aspects of this revolution, which was appreciated by few Western observers at the time, were particularly significant.

First, the growth of the urban population continued rapidly in the 1960s and 1970s. In 1985 two-thirds of all Soviet citizens lived in cities, and one-fourth lived in big cities. This expanding urban population lost its old peasant ways, exchanging them for more education, better job skills, and greater sophistication.

Second, the number of highly trained scientists, managers, and specialists expanded prodigiously, jumping fourfold between 1960 and 1985. Thus the class of well-educated, pragmatic, and self-confident experts, which played such an important role in restructuring industrial societies after the Second World War (see pages 1101–1102), developed rapidly in the Soviet Union.

Third, the education that created expertise also helped foster the growth of Soviet public opinion. Educated people read, discussed, and formed definite ideas about social questions, from environmental pollution to urban transportation. Thus educated urban people increasingly saw themselves as

worthy of having a voice in society's decisions, even its political decisions. This change was also part of the quiet transformation that set the stage for the dramatic reforms of the Gorbachev era.

The Gorbachev Era

Fundamental change in Russian history has often come in short, intensive spurts, which contrast vividly with long periods of immobility. So it was with the era of fundamental reforms launched by Mikhail Gorbachev in 1985. Gorbachev's initiatives brought liberalization in the Soviet Union, and they then permitted democracy and national self-determination to triumph spectacularly in the old satellite empire and eventually in the Soviet Union itself.

The Soviet Union's Communist elite seemed safe in the early 1980s from any challenge from below. The Communist party's long-established system of centralized administrative controls stretched downward to provincial cities and from there to factories, neighborhoods, and villages. The party hierarchy continued to manipulate every aspect of national life. Organized opposition was impossible, and average people simply left politics to the bosses.

The massive state and party bureaucracy safeguarded the elite, but it discouraged personal initiative and promoted economic inefficiency and apathy among the masses and the rapidly growing class of well-educated urban experts. Therefore, when the ailing Brezhnev finally died in 1982, efforts were made to improve economic performance and to combat worker absenteeism and high-level corruption. These efforts set the stage for the emergence in 1985 of Mikhail Gorbachev (b. 1931), the most vigorous Soviet leader since Stalin.

Smart, charming, and tough, Gorbachev was also an idealist who believed in communism, though he realized it was failing. He (and his intelligent, influential wife, Raisa, a dedicated professor of Marxist-Leninist thought) wanted to save the Soviet system by improving it with fundamental reforms. And Gorbachev realized full well that success at home required better relations with the West, for the endless waste of the arms race had had a disastrous impact on living standards in the Soviet Union.

In his first year in office, Gorbachev attacked corruption and incompetence in the upper reaches of the bureaucracy, and he consolidated his power by packing the top level of the party with his supporters. He also attacked alcoholism and drunkenness, which were deadly scourges of Soviet society. More basically, he elaborated a series of reform policies designed to revive and even remake the vast Soviet Union.

The first set of reform policies was designed to transform and restructure the economy, which was falling ever further behind the economy of the West and failing to provide for the very real needs of the Soviet population. To accomplish this economic restructuring—this *perestroika*—Gorbachev and his supporters permitted freer prices, more independence for state enterprises, and the setting up of some profit-seeking private cooperatives. But the reforms were rather timid and left the economy stalled between central planning and free-market mechanisms. This lack of success gradually eroded Gorbachev's popular support and that of the Communist party.

Gorbachev's bold and far-reaching campaign "to tell it like it is" was much more successful. Very popular in a country where censorship, dull uniformity, and outright lies had long characterized public discourse, the newfound openness—the *glasnost*—of the government and the media marked an astonishing break with the past. A disaster like the Chernobyl nuclear-reactor accident, which devastated part of the Ukraine and showered Europe with radioactive fallout, was investigated and reported with honesty and painstaking thoroughness. The works of long-banned and vilified Russian émigré writers sold millions of copies in new editions, and denunciations of Stalin and his terror became standard fare in plays and movies. Openness in government pronouncements led rather quickly to something approaching free speech and free expression, a veritable cultural revolution.

Democratization was the third element of Gorbachev's reform. Beginning as an attack on corruption in the Communist party and as an attempt to bring the class of educated experts into the decision-making process, it led to the first free elections in the Soviet Union since 1917. Gorbachev and the party remained in control, but a minority of critical independents were elected in April 1989 to a revitalized Congress of People's Deputies. Many top-ranking Communists who ran unopposed saw themselves defeated as a majority of angry voters struck their names from the ballot.

Democratization also encouraged demands for greater autonomy by non-Russian minorities, especially in the Baltic region and in the Caucasus.

Newly Elected President Mikhail Gorbachev In his acceptance speech before the Supreme Soviet, Gorbachev vowed to assume "all responsibility" for the success or failure of *perestroika*. Previous Soviet parliaments were no more than tools of the Communist party, but this one actively debated and even opposed government programs. *(Source: Vlastimir Shone/Liaison)*

These demands certainly went beyond what Gorbachev had envisaged. In April 1989 troops with sharpened shovels charged into a rally of Georgian separatists in Tbilisi and left twenty dead. But whereas China's Communist leaders brutally massacred similar prodemocracy demonstrators in Beijing (Peking) in June 1989 (see page 1136), Gorbachev drew back from repression. Thus nationalist demands continued to grow in the non-Russian Soviet republics.

Finally, the Soviet leader brought "new political thinking" to the field of foreign affairs—and he acted on it. He withdrew Soviet troops from Afghanistan, encouraged reform movements in Poland and Hungary, and sought to reduce East-West tensions. Of enormous historical importance, Gorbachev pledged to respect the political choices of the peoples of eastern Europe, and he thereby repudiated the Brezhnev Doctrine. By 1989 it seemed that if Gorbachev held to his word, the tragic Soviet occupation of eastern Europe might gradually wither away, taking the long cold war with it.

The Revolutions of 1989

Instead, history accelerated, and 1989 brought a series of largely peaceful revolutions throughout eastern Europe. These revolutions overturned existing communist regimes and led to the formation of provisional governments dedicated to democratic elections, human rights, and national rejuvenation. The face of eastern Europe changed dramatically, almost overnight.

The Polish people led the way. Poland had been an unruly satellite from the beginning, and Stalin said that introducing communism to Poland was like putting a saddle on a cow. Efforts to saddle the cow—really a spirited stallion—had led to widespread riots in 1956. As a result, the Polish Communists dropped efforts to impose Soviet-style collectivization on the peasants and to break the Roman Catholic church. With an independent agriculture and a vigorous church, the Communists failed to monopolize society.

They also failed to manage the economy effectively, and bureaucratic incompetence coupled with worldwide recession had put the economy of Poland into a nosedive by the mid-1970s. Then the "Polish miracle" occurred: Cardinal Karol Wojtyla, archbishop of Cracow, was elected pope, and in

June 1979 he returned to his native land to preach the love of Christ and country and the "inalienable rights of man." Pope John Paul II electrified the Polish nation, and the economic crisis became a spiritual crisis as well.

In August 1980, scattered strikes snowballed into a working-class revolt. Led by a feisty electrician and devout Catholic named Lech Walesa, the workers organized a free and democratic trade union that they called "Solidarity." Solidarity became the union of the nation, and cultural and intellectual freedom blossomed in Poland. As economic hardship increased, grassroots radicalism and frustration mounted: a hunger-march banner proclaimed that "A hungry nation can eat its rulers."[7] In response the Communist leader General Wojciech Jaruzelski proclaimed martial law in December 1981 and arrested Solidarity's leaders.

Although outlawed and driven underground, Solidarity maintained its organization, and popular support remained strong and deep under martial law in the 1980s. By 1988 widespread labor unrest, raging inflation, and the refusal of outlawed Solidarity to cooperate with the military government had brought Poland to the brink of economic collapse. Profiting from Gorbachev's tolerant attitude and skillfully mobilizing its forces, Solidarity pressured Poland's frustrated Communist leaders into another round of negotiations that might work out a sharing of power. The subsequent agreement legalized Solidarity again and announced free elections for some seats in the Polish parliament for June 1989. Solidarity won every single contested seat in an overwhelming victory. A month later the editor of Solidarity's weekly newspaper was sworn in as the first noncommunist leader in eastern Europe in a generation. Communism also died in Czechoslovakia in 1989. In December an almost good-humored ousting of Communist bosses occurred in ten short days.

Hungary followed Poland and Czechoslovakia when growing popular resistance forced the Hungarian Communist party to renounce one-party rule and schedule free elections for early 1990. Hungarians gleefully tore down the barbed-wire "iron curtain" that separated Hungary and Austria and opened their border to refugees from East Germany.

As thousands of dissatisfied East Germans began pouring through Hungary on their way to thriving West Germany, growing economic dislocation and huge candlelight demonstrations brought revolution in East Berlin. The Berlin Wall was opened, and people danced for joy atop that grim symbol of the prison state. East Germany's aging Communist leaders were swept aside and in some cases arrested. In general elections in March 1990, a conservative-liberal "Alliance for Germany" defeated the East German Social Democrats and quickly negotiated an economic union on favorable terms with West Germany. In July 1990 a historic agreement between West German Chancellor Helmut Kohl and Gorbachev removed the last obstacles to German unification, which came in October 1990.

Only in Romania was revolution violent and bloody. There the iron-fisted Communist dictator Nicolae Ceausescu, alone among eastern European bosses, ordered his ruthless security forces to slaughter thousands, thereby sparking a classic armed uprising. After Ceausescu's forces were defeated, the tyrant and his wife were captured and executed by a military court. A coalition government emerged to govern the troubled country.

As the 1990s began, the great question then became whether the Soviet Union would follow its former satellites in a popular anticommunist revolution. Near civil war between Armenians and Azerbaijanis in the Caucasus, assertions of independence in the Baltic states, and growing dissatisfaction among the Great Russian masses were all parts of a fluid, unstable political situation. Increasingly, the reform-minded Gorbachev stood as a moderate, besieged by those who wanted revolutionary changes and by hard-line Communists who longed to reverse course and clamp down.

East Germans Escaping to the West   After Hungary allowed more than thirty thousand "vacationing" East Germans to pass into Austria and on to a tumultuous welcome in West Germany, Czechoslovakia followed suit. Hordes of East Germans, like those shown here, converged on the West German embassy in Prague. Then the East German government gave up, opening the Berlin Wall and scheduling free elections. *(Source: BUU/Saussier/Liaison)*

✳ **MAP 33.4 The End of the Soviet Union** After the attempt in August 1991 to depose Gorbachev failed, an anticommunist revolution swept the Soviet Union. Led by Russia and Boris Yeltsin, the republics that formed the Soviet Union declared their sovereignty and independence. Most of the fifteen republics then formed a loose confederation with an uncertain future, the Commonwealth of Independent States.

In August 1991 a gang of hard-liners kidnapped Gorbachev and his family and tried to seize the Soviet government. The attempted coup collapsed in the face of massive popular resistance, which rallied in Moscow around Boris Yeltsin, the popularly elected president of the Russian Federation. Gorbachev was rescued and returned to power as head of the Soviet Union.

The leaders of the coup wanted to preserve communist power and the multinational Soviet Union, but they succeeded only in destroying both. An anticommunist revolution swept the Russian Federation as the Communist party was outlawed and its property confiscated. Locked in a personal and political duel with Gorbachev, Yeltsin and his liberal allies declared Russia independent and withdrew from the Soviet Union. All the other Soviet republics followed suit; the Soviet Union—and Gorbachev's job—ceased to exist on December 25, 1991 (Map 33.4). A loose but indispensable confederation of former Soviet republics, named the Commonwealth of Independent States, was established in 1992.

The early 1990s remained turbulent, for three reasons. First, ethnic tensions abounded in the Commonwealth of Independent States. Localized civil war broke out in newly independent Georgia and Armenia. In 1995 civil war spread to Russia itself as Yeltsin ordered the Russian army to attack secessionist Chechnya and destroy the city of Grosny. Second, the Russian economy continued to decline. The result was rapid inflation and intense hardship for millions of ordinary people. Third, ethnic conflict, economic collapse, and political stalemate encouraged millions of dissatisfied Russians to vote against the democratic reforms in the general elections of December 1993. The old communists made a strong comeback, and a flamboyant ultranationalist named Vladimir Zhirinovsky captured a surprisingly large share of the vote. Communist dictatorship was gone, but the ultimate fate of Russia and the states of the old Soviet Union remained uncertain.

✹ THE WESTERN HEMISPHERE

One way to think of what historians used to call the "New World" is as a vigorous offshoot of Western civilization, an offshoot that has gradually developed its own characteristics while retaining European roots. From this perspective can be seen many illuminating parallels and divergences in the histories of Europe and the Americas. After the Second World War, the Western Hemisphere experienced a many-faceted recovery, somewhat similar to that of Europe though it began earlier, especially in Latin America. And after a generation the countries of the New World experienced their own period of turbulence and crisis.

America's Civil Rights Revolution

The Second World War ended the Great Depression in the United States and brought about a great economic boom. Unemployment practically vanished, and the well-being of Americans increased dramatically. Despite fears that peace would bring renewed depression, conversion to a peacetime economy went smoothly. Then, as in western Europe, the U.S. economy proceeded to advance fairly steadily for a long generation.

Prosperity helps explain why postwar domestic politics consisted largely of modest adjustments to the status quo until the 1960s. Truman's upset victory in 1948 demonstrated that Americans had no interest in undoing Roosevelt's social and economic reforms. The Congress proceeded to increase social security benefits, subsidize middle- and lower-class housing, and raise the minimum wage. These and other liberal measures consoli-

dated the New Deal. In 1952 the Republican party and the voters turned to General Dwight D. Eisenhower (1890–1969), a national hero and self-described moderate.

The federal government's only major new undertaking during the Eisenhower years (1952–1960) was the interstate highway system, a suitable symbol of the basic satisfaction of the vast majority. Some Americans feared that the United States was becoming a "blocked society," obsessed with stability and incapable of wholesome change. This feeling contributed in 1960 to the election of the young John F. Kennedy (1917–1963), who promised to "get the country moving again." President Kennedy captured the popular imagination, revitalized the old Roosevelt coalition, and modestly expanded existing liberal legislation before he was struck down by an assassin's bullet in 1963.

Belatedly and reluctantly, complacent postwar America did experience a genuine social revolution: after a long struggle, African Americans (and their white supporters) threw off a deeply entrenched system of segregation, discrimination, and repression. This civil rights movement advanced on several fronts. Eloquent lawyers from the National Association for the Advancement of Colored People (NAACP) challenged school segregation in the courts. In 1954 they won a landmark decision in the Supreme Court, which ruled in *Brown v. Board of Education* that "separate educational facilities are inherently unequal." Blacks effectively challenged institutionalized inequality with bus boycotts, sit-ins, and demonstrations. As civil rights leader Martin Luther King, Jr. (1929–1968), told the white power structure, "We will not hate you, but we will not obey your evil laws."[8]

In key northern states African Americans used their growing political power to gain the support of the liberal wing of the Democratic party. In a liberal landslide, Lyndon Johnson (1908–1973) won the presidential election in 1964. The Civil Rights Act of 1964 categorically prohibited discrimination in public services and on the job. In the follow-up Voting Rights Act of 1965, the federal government firmly guaranteed all blacks the right to vote. By the 1970s, substantial numbers of blacks had been elected to public and private office throughout the southern states, proof positive that dramatic changes had occurred in American race relations.

African Americans enthusiastically supported new social legislation in the mid-1960s. President Johnson solemnly declared "unconditional war on poverty." Congress and the administration created a host of antipoverty projects, such as a domestic peace corps, free preschools for poor children, and community-action programs. Although these programs were directed to all poor Americans—the majority of whom were white—they were also intended to increase economic equality for blacks. Thus the United States promoted in the mid-1960s the kind of fundamental social reform that western Europe had embraced immediately after the Second World War. The United States became more of a welfare state, as government spending for social benefits rose dramatically and approached European levels.

Youth and the Counterculture

Economic prosperity and a more democratic class structure had a powerful impact on youth throughout the Western world. The bulging cohort of youth born after World War II developed a distinctive and very international youth culture. Self-consciously different in the late 1950s, this youth culture became increasingly oppositional in the 1960s, interacting with a revival of leftist thought to create a counterculture that rebelled against parents, authority figures, and the status quo.

Young people in the United States took the lead. American college students in the 1950s were docile and often dismissed as the "Silent Generation," but some young people did revolt against

"**I Have a Dream**" August 1963 marked a dramatic climax in the civil rights struggle in the United States. More than 200,000 people gathered at the Lincoln Memorial in Washington, D.C., to hear Martin Luther King, Jr., deliver his greatest address. *(Source: Francis Miller, Life Magazine, © Time Warner, Inc.)*

The Beatles in Concert   The older generation often saw sexual license and immorality in the group's frank lyrics and suggestive style. But in comparison with all that came after them in the world of pop music, the Beatles were sentimental and wholesome, as this concert scene suggests. *(Source: Fred Ward/Black Star)*

the conformity and boredom of middle-class suburbs. These "young rebels" wore tightly pegged pants and idolized singer Elvis Presley and actor James Dean. The "beat" movement of the late 1950s expanded on the theme of revolt, and Jack Kerouac vividly captured the restless motion of the beatniks in his autobiographical novel *On the Road.* People like Kerouac clustered together in certain urban areas, such as the Haight-Ashbury district of San Francisco or the Near North Side of Chicago. There the young (and the not-so-young) fashioned a highly publicized subculture that blended radical politics, unbridled personal experimentation (with drugs and communal living, for example), and new artistic styles. This subculture quickly spread to major American and western European cities.

Rock music helped tie this international subculture together. Rock grew out of the black music culture of rhythm and blues, which was flavored with country and western to make it more accessible to white teenagers. The mid-1950s signaled a breakthrough: Bill Haley called on record buyers to "Rock Around the Clock," and Elvis Presley

warned them not to step on his "Blue Suede Shoes." In the 1960s the Beatles thrilled millions of young people, often to their parents' dismay. Like Elvis, the Beatles suggested personal and sexual freedom that many older people found disturbing.

It was Bob Dylan, a young folk singer turned rock poet with an electric guitar, who best expressed the radical political as well as cultural aspirations of the "younger generation." In a song that became a rallying cry, Dylan sang that "the times they are a'changing."[9] The song captured the spirit of growing alienation between the generation whose defining experience had been World War II and the generation ready to reject the complacency of the 1950s. Increasing discontent with middle-class conformity and the injustices of racism and imperialism fueled the young leaders of social protest and reflected a growing spirit of rebellion.

Certainly the sexual behavior of young people, or at least some young people, appeared to change dramatically in the 1960s and into the 1970s. More young people engaged in intercourse, and they did so at an earlier age. Perhaps even more significant was the growing tendency of young unmarried people to live together in a separate household on a semipermanent basis, with little thought of getting married or having children. Thus many youths, especially middle-class youths, defied social custom, claiming in effect that the long-standing monopoly of married couples on legitimate sexual unions was dead.

Several factors contributed to the emergence of the international youth culture in the 1960s. First, mass communications and youth travel linked countries and continents together. Second, the postwar baby boom meant that young people became an unusually large part of the population and could therefore exercise exceptional influence on society as a whole. Third, postwar prosperity and greater equality gave young people more purchasing power than ever before. This enabled them to set their own trends and fads in everything from music to chemical stimulants. Common patterns of consumption and behavior fostered generational loyalty. Finally, prosperity meant that good jobs were readily available. Students and young job seekers had little need to fear punishment from strait-laced employers for unconventional behavior.

The youth culture practically fused with the counterculture in opposition to the established order in the late 1960s. Student protesters embraced romanticism and revolutionary idealism, dreaming of complete freedom and simpler, purer societies. The materialistic West was hopelessly rotten, but better societies were being built in the newly independent countries of Asia and Africa, or so many young radicals believed. Thus the Vietnam War took on special significance. Many politically active students in the United States and Europe believed that the older generation in general and American leaders in particular were fighting an immoral and imperialistic war against a small and heroic people that wanted only national unity and human dignity. As the war in Vietnam intensified, so did worldwide student opposition to it.

The Vietnam Trauma and Beyond

President Johnson wanted to go down in history as a master reformer and a healer of old wounds. Instead he opened new ones with the Vietnam War.

Although many student radicals believed that imperialism was the main cause, American involvement in Vietnam was more clearly a product of the cold war and the ideology of containment (see page 0000). From the late 1940s on, most Americans and their leaders viewed the world in terms of a constant struggle to stop the spread of communism. As Europe began to revive and China established a communist government in 1949, efforts to contain communism shifted to Asia. The bloody Korean War (1950–1953) ended in stalemate, but the United States did succeed in preventing a communist government in South Korea. After the defeat of the French in Indochina in 1954 (see page 1148), the Eisenhower administration refused to sign the Geneva accords that temporarily divided the country into two zones pending national unification by means of free elections. President Eisenhower then acquiesced in the refusal of the anticommunist South Vietnamese government to accept the verdict of elections and provided it with military aid. President Kennedy greatly increased the number of American "military advisers" to sixteen thousand.

After successfully depicting his opponent, Barry Goldwater, as a trigger-happy extremist in a nuclear age and resoundingly winning the 1964 election in large part on a peace platform, President Johnson greatly expanded the American role in the Vietnam conflict. As Johnson explained to his ambassador in Saigon, "I am not going to lose Vietnam. I am not going to be the President who saw Southeast Asia go the way China went."[10] American strategy was to "escalate" the war sufficiently to break the will of the North Vietnamese and their southern allies without resorting to "overkill" that might risk war with the entire communist bloc. Thus South Vietnam received massive military aid; American forces in the South gradually grew to a half-million men; and the United States bombed North Vietnam with ever-greater intensity. But there was no invasion of the North or naval blockade. In the end, the American strategy of limited warfare backfired. It was the Americans themselves who grew weary and the American leadership that cracked.

The undeclared war in Vietnam, fought nightly on American television, eventually divided the nation. Initial support was strong. The politicians, the media, and the population as a whole saw the war as part of a legitimate defense against communist totalitarianism in all poor countries. But an antiwar movement quickly emerged on college campuses, where the prospect of being drafted to fight savage battles in Asian jungles made male stomachs churn. In October 1965 student protesters joined forces with old-line socialists, New Left intellectuals, and pacifists in antiwar demonstrations in fifty American cities. By 1967 a growing number of critics denounced the war as a criminal intrusion into a complex and distant civil war.

Criticism reached a crescendo after the Vietcong Tet Offensive against major cities in South Vietnam in January 1968. The attack was a military failure, but it resulted in heavy losses on both sides, and it belied Washington's claims that victory in South Vietnam was in sight. The U.S. critics of the Vietnam War quickly interpreted the bloody combat as a decisive American defeat. America's leaders lost heart, and in 1968 President Johnson called for negotiations with North Vietnam and announced that he would not stand for re-election.

Elected by a razor-slim margin in 1968, Richard Nixon (1913–1994) sought to disengage America gradually from Vietnam and the accompanying national crisis. Intensifying the continuous bombardment of the enemy while simultaneously pursuing peace talks with the North Vietnamese, President Nixon suspended the draft, so hated on college campuses, and cut American forces in Vietnam from 550,000 to 24,000 in four years. Moreover, he launched a flank attack in diplomacy. He journeyed to China in 1972 and reached a spectacular if limited reconciliation with the People's Republic of China. In doing so, Nixon took advantage of China's growing fears of the Soviet Union and undermined North Vietnam's position.

Fortified by the overwhelming endorsement of the voters in his 1972 electoral triumph, President Nixon and Secretary of State Henry Kissinger finally reached a peace agreement with North Vietnam in 1973. The agreement allowed remaining American forces to complete their withdrawal, and the United States reserved the right to resume bombing if the accords were broken. Fighting declined markedly in South Vietnam. The storm of crisis in the United States seemed past.

On the contrary, the country reaped the Watergate whirlwind. Like some other recent American presidents, Nixon authorized domestic spying activities that went beyond the law. Going further than his predecessors, Nixon authorized special units to use various illegal means to stop the leaking of government documents to the press. One such group broke into the Democratic party headquarters in Washington's Watergate complex in June 1972 and was promptly arrested. Nixon and many of his assistants then tried to hush up the bungled job, but the media and the machinery of congressional investigation eventually exposed the administration's web of lies and lawbreaking. In 1974 a beleaguered Nixon was forced to resign in disgrace.

The consequences of renewed political crisis flowing from the Watergate affair were profound. First, Watergate resulted in a major shift of power away from the presidency toward Congress, especially in foreign affairs. Therefore, as American aid to South Vietnam diminished in 1973 and as an emboldened North Vietnam launched a general invasion against South Vietnamese armies in early 1974, Congress refused to permit any American military response. After more than thirty-five years of battle, the Vietnamese communists unified their country in 1975 as a harsh dictatorial state—a second consequence of the U.S. crisis. Third, the belated fall of South Vietnam in the wake of Watergate shook America's postwar confidence and left the country divided and uncertain about its proper role in world affairs.

One alternative to the badly damaged policy of containing communism was the policy of *détente*, or progressive relaxation of cold war tensions. Nixon's phased withdrawal from Vietnam was sold as part of détente. Détente reached its high point when all European nations (except isolationist Albania), the United States, and Canada signed the Final Act of the Helsinki Conference in 1975. Thirty-five nations agreed that Europe's existing political frontiers could not be changed by force, and they solemnly accepted numerous provisions guaranteeing the human rights and political freedoms of their citizens.

Optimistic hopes for détente in international relations gradually faded in the later 1970s. Brezhnev's Soviet Union ignored the human rights provisions of the Helsinki agreement, and East-West political competition remained very much alive outside Europe. Many Americans became convinced that the Soviet Union was taking advantage of détente, steadily building up its military might and pushing for political gains and revolutions in Africa, Asia, and Latin America. The Soviet invasion of Afghanistan in December 1979, which was designed to save an increasingly unpopular Marxist regime, was especially alarming. Many Americans feared that the oil-rich states of the Persian Gulf would be next, and once again they looked to the

Margaret Thatcher and Ronald Reagan   The British prime minister and American president, seen here in the White House garden, worked well together, united by a fierce determination to oppose communism abroad and to reduce spending on social programs at home. *(Source: Brad Markel/Liaison)*

Atlantic alliance and military might to thwart communist expansion.

Jimmy Carter (b. 1924), elected president in 1976, tried to lead the Atlantic alliance beyond verbal condemnation, but among the European allies only Great Britain supported the American policy of economic sanctions. The alliance showed the same lack of concerted action when Solidarity rose in Poland. Some observers concluded that the alliance had lost the will to think and act decisively in dealings with the Soviet bloc.

The Atlantic alliance endured, however. The U.S. military buildup launched by Jimmy Carter in his last years in office was greatly accelerated by Ronald Reagan (b. 1911), who was swept into office in 1980 by a wave of patriotism and economic discontent. The new American leadership acted as if the military balance had tipped in favor of the Soviet Union, which President Reagan anathema-

tized as the "evil empire." Increasing defense spending enormously, the Reagan administration concentrated especially on nuclear arms and an expanded navy as keys to American power in the post-Vietnam age.

The broad swing of the historical pendulum toward greater conservatism in the 1980s gave Reagan invaluable allies in western Europe. In Great Britain a strong-willed Margaret Thatcher (see page 1109) worked well with Reagan and was a strong advocate for a revitalized Atlantic alliance. After a distinctly pro-American Helmut Kohl (b. 1930) came to power with the conservative Christian Democrats in 1982, West Germany and the United States once again effectively coordinated military and political policy toward the Soviet bloc.

Passing from détente to confusion to regeneration, the Atlantic alliance bent but did not break. In maintaining the alliance, the Western nations gave indirect support to ongoing efforts to liberalize authoritarian communist eastern Europe and probably helped convince Mikhail Gorbachev that endless cold war conflict was foolish and dangerous.

Economic Nationalism in Latin America

Although the countries of Latin America exhibit striking differences, the growth of economic nationalism has been a major development throughout the region in the twentieth century. As the early nineteenth century saw Spanish and Portuguese colonies win wars of political independence, so has much of recent history been a quest for genuine economic independence through local control and industrialization.

To understand the rise of economic nationalism, one must remember that Latin American countries developed as producers of foodstuffs and raw materials that were exported to Europe and the United States in return for manufactured goods and capital investment. This exchange brought considerable economic development but exacted a heavy price: neocolonialism (see pages 924–926). Latin America became very dependent on foreign markets, products, and investments. Industry did not develop, and large landowners tied to production for the world market profited most from economic development and thus enhanced their social and political power.

The old international division of labor, badly shaken by World War I, was destroyed by the Great Depression. Prices and exports of Latin American commodities collapsed as Europe and the United States drastically reduced their purchases and raised tariffs to protect domestic products. With their foreign sales plummeting, Latin American countries could not buy the industrial goods that they needed from abroad.

Latin America suffered the full force of the global depression. Especially in the largest Latin American countries—Argentina, Brazil, Chile, and Mexico—the result was a profound shift toward economic nationalism after 1930. The most popularly based governments worked to reduce foreign influence and gain control of their own economies and natural resources. They energetically promoted national industry by means of high tariffs, government grants, and even state enterprise. They favored the lower middle and urban working classes with social benefits and higher wages in order to increase their purchasing power and gain their support. These efforts at recovery gathered speed during the Second World War and were fairly successful. By the late 1940s, the factories of Argentina, Brazil, and Chile could generally satisfy domestic consumer demand for the products of light industry. In the 1950s, some countries began moving into heavy industry.

Economic nationalism and the rise of industry are particularly striking in the two largest and most influential countries, Mexico and Brazil. These countries account for half of the population of Latin America.

The spasmodic, often-chaotic Mexican Revolution of 1910 overthrew the elitist, upper-class rule of the tyrant Porfirio Díaz and culminated in 1917 in a new constitution. This radical nationalistic document called for universal suffrage, massive land reform, benefits for labor, and strict control of foreign capital. Actual progress was quite modest until 1934, when a charismatic young Indian from a poor family, Lázaro Cárdenas, became president and dramatically revived the languishing revolution. Under Cárdenas, many large estates were divided up among small farmers or returned undivided to Indian communities.

Meanwhile, state-supported Mexican businessmen built many small factories to meet domestic needs. The government also championed the cause of industrial workers. In 1938, when Mexican workers became locked in a bitter dispute with British and American oil companies, Cárdenas nationalized the petroleum industry—to the amazement of a world unaccustomed to such bold action. Finally, the 1930s saw the flowering of a distinctive Mexican culture, which proudly embraced its long-despised Indian past and gloried in the modern national revolution.

In 1940 the official, semi-authoritarian party that has governed Mexico continuously since the revolution selected the first of a series of more moderate presidents. These presidents used the full power of the state to promote industrialization through a judicious mixture of public, private, and even foreign enterprise. Following the postwar trend in Europe and the United States, the Mexican economy grew rapidly, at about 6 percent per year from the early 1940s to the late 1960s. However, in Mexico, unlike Europe and the United States, the upper and middle classes reaped the lion's share of the benefits.

In Brazil, politics was dominated by the coffee barons and by regional rivalries after the fall of Brazil's monarchy in 1889 (see page 922). Regional rivalries and deteriorating economic conditions allowed a military revolt led by Getúlio Vargas to seize control of the federal government in 1930. Vargas, who proved to be a consummate politician, fragmented the opposition and established a mild dictatorship that lasted until 1945. His rule was generally popular, combining effective economic nationalism and moderate social reform.

Vargas and his allies set out to industrialize Brazil and gain economic independence. While the national coffee board used mountains of surplus coffee beans to fire railroad locomotives, the government supported Brazilian manufacturers with high tariffs, generous loans, and labor peace encouraged by new social legislation: workers received shorter hours, pensions, health and accident insurance, paid vacations, and other benefits. Finally, Vargas shrewdly upheld the nationalist cause in his relations with the giant to the north. Brazil was modernizing rapidly.

Modernization continued for the next fifteen years. The economy boomed. Presidential politics was re-established, though the military kept a watchful eye for extremism among the civilian politicians. Economic nationalism was especially vigorous under the flamboyant President Juscelino Kubitschek. Between 1956 and 1960, the government borrowed heavily from international bankers to promote industry and built the new capital of Brasília in the midst of a wilderness. Kubitschek's slogan was "Fifty Years' Progress in Five," and he meant it.

The Brazilian and Mexican formula of national economic development, varying degrees of electoral competition, and social reform was shared by some other Latin American countries, notably Argentina and Chile. By the late 1950s, optimism was widespread though cautious. Economic and social progress seemed to be bringing less violent, more democratic politics to the region. These expectations were shaken by the Cuban Revolution.

The Cuban Revolution

Achieving nominal independence in 1898 as a result of the Spanish-American War, Cuba was for many years virtually an American protectorate. The Cuban constitution gave the United States the legal right to intervene in Cuban affairs, a right that was frequently exercised until President Franklin Roosevelt renounced it in 1934. Partly because the American army had often been the real power on the island, Cuba's political institutions were weak and Cuban politicians were corrupt. Nevertheless, Cuba was one of Latin America's most prosperous countries by the 1950s, although its sugar-and-tourist economy was completely dependent on the United States and it displayed the enormous differences between rich and poor that were typical of Latin America.

Fidel Castro (b. 1927), a magnetic leader with the gift of oratory, managed to unify all opposition elements in a revolutionary front, and his guerrilla forces triumphed in late 1958. Castro had promised a "real" revolution, and it soon became clear that "real" meant "communist." Wealthy Cubans fled to Miami, and the middle class began to follow. Cuban relations with the Eisenhower administration deteriorated rapidly. Thus in April 1961 the newly elected U.S. president, John Kennedy, went ahead with a pre-existing CIA plan to use Cuban exiles to topple Castro. But the Kennedy administration abandoned the exiles as soon as they were put ashore at the Bay of Pigs, and the invaders were quickly captured.

The Bay of Pigs invasion—a triumph for Castro and a humiliating fiasco for the United States—freed Castro to build his version of a communist society. Political life in Cuba featured "anti-imperialism," an alliance with the Soviet bloc, the dictatorship of the party, and a Castro cult. Revolutionary enthusiasm was genuine among party activists, much of Cuba's youth, and some of the masses some of the time. Prisons and emigration silenced opposition. The economy was characterized by state ownership, collective farms, and Soviet trade and aid. Early efforts to industrialize ran aground, and sugar production continued to dominate the economy. Socially, the Castro regime pursued equality and the creation of a new socialist personality. In short, the communism of eastern Europe came to the Americas.

The failure of the United States to derail Castro probably encouraged Khrushchev to start putting nuclear missiles in Cuba and in turn led directly to the most serious East-West crisis since the Korean War. The Soviets backed down (see page 0000), but Castro's survival heightened both hopes and fears that similar revolutions could spread throughout Latin America. In the United States, such cold war fears led in 1961 to a pledge of $10 billion in aid over ten years to a new hemispheric "Alliance for Progress." The Alliance was intended to promote long-term economic development and social reform, which American liberals assumed would immunize the rest of Latin America from the Cuban disease.

Authoritarianism and Democracy in Latin America

U.S. aid contributed modestly to continued Latin American economic development in the 1960s, although population growth canceled out two-thirds of the increase on a per capita basis. Democratic social reforms—the other half of the Alliance for Progress formula—proceeded slowly, however. Instead, the era following the Cuban Revolution saw increasing conflict between leftist movements and ruling elites contending for power. In most countries the elites and their military allies won the struggle, but at the cost of imposing a new kind of conservative authoritarianism as their collective response to the social and economic crisis. By the late 1970s, only four Latin American countries—Costa Rica, Venezuela, Colombia, and Mexico—retained some measure of democratic government. Brazil, Argentina, and Chile represented the general trend.

Influential Brazil led the way. Intense political competition in the early 1960s prompted President João Goulart to swing to the left to gain fresh support. Castroism appeared to spread in the impoverished northeast, and mass meetings of leftists were answered by huge demonstrations of conservatives. Meanwhile, Goulart called for radical change, proposing that the great landed estates be broken up and that Brazil's many illiterates receive the right to vote. When Goulart and his followers appeared ready to use force to implement their program, army leaders took over in 1964. The right-wing military government banned political parties and ruled by decree. Industrialization and urbanization went forward under military rule, but the gap between rich and poor widened as well.

In Argentina, the military had intervened in 1955 to oust the dictatorial populist and economic nationalist Juan Perón, but it had restored elected government. Then, worried by a Peronist revival and heartened by the Brazilian example, the army

took control in 1966 and again in 1976 after a brief civilian interlude. Each military takeover was followed by an escalation of repression. Culturally and economically advanced Argentina became a brutal military dictatorship.

Events in Chile were truly tragic. Chile has a population of predominantly European origin and a long tradition of democracy and moderate reform. Thus when Salvador Allende, a doctor and the Marxist head of a coalition of Communists, Socialists, and Radicals, won a plurality of 36 percent of the vote in fair elections in 1970, he was duly elected president by the Congress. Allende completed the nationalization of the American-owned copper companies—the great majority of Chileans had already embraced economic nationalism—and proceeded to socialize private industry, accelerate the breakup of landed estates, and radicalize the poor.

Marxism in action evoked a powerful backlash in Chile. The middle class struck back, and by 1973 Chile seemed headed for civil war. Then, with widespread conservative support and strong U.S. backing, the traditionally impartial army struck in a well-organized coup. Allende died, probably murdered, and thousands of his supporters were arrested, or worse. As in Argentina, the military imposed a harsh despotism.

The military governments that revived antidemocratic authoritarianism in Latin America, with Washington's support, blocked not only the Marxist and socialist program but most liberal and moderate reform as well. Yet the new military governments grew out of political crises that threatened national unity as well as the upper classes and big business. In such circumstances, the politically conscious officer corps saw the military as the only institution capable of preventing chaos. Moreover, the new authoritarians were determined modernizers. Eager to catch up with the more advanced countries, they were often deeply committed to nationalism, industrialization, technology, and some modest social progress. They even promised free elections in the future.

That time came in the 1980s, when another democratic wave gained momentum throughout Latin America. The three Andean nations—Peru, Bolivia, and Ecuador—led the way with the reestablishment of elected governments, all of which were committed in varying degrees to genuine social reform. In Argentina, the military government gradually lost almost all popular support because of its "dirty war" against its own citizens, in which it imprisoned, tortured, and murdered thousands whom it arbitrarily accused of opposing the regime. In 1982, in a desperate gamble to rally the people around the nationalist flag, Argentina's military rulers sent nine thousand troops to seize the Falkland (or Malvinas) Islands (see Map 28.2, page 920) from Great Britain. But the British retook the islands in a brief war, routing Argentina's poorly led troops and forcing its humiliated generals to schedule national elections. The democratically elected government prosecuted the former military rulers for their crimes, reformed the currency, and laid solid foundations for liberty and political democracy.

In 1985, the Brazilian military also turned over power to an elected government. Relatively successful in its industrialization effort, Brazil's military government had proved unable (or unwilling) to improve the social and economic position of the masses. After twenty-one years of rule the military leaders were ready to let civilian politicians have a try. Chile also turned from right-wing military dictatorship to elected government. Thus by the second half of the 1980s 94 percent of Latin America's population lived under regimes that guaranteed elections and civil liberties.

The most dramatic developments in Central America occurred in Nicaragua. In 1979, a broad coalition of liberals, socialists, and Marxist revolutionaries drove long-time dictator Anastasio So-

Return to Democracy in Argentina Elected president in 1983 after seven years of brutal military rule, Raul Alfonsín stands with sash and rod—the symbols of authority—to swear the presidential oath of office in Buenos Aires. Alfonsín's inauguration gave rise to great popular rejoicing. *(Source: Urraca/Sygma)*

moza from power. The Somoza family had relied on solid U.S. support in its four-decade dictatorship. The new leaders, known as the Sandinistas, wanted genuine political and economic independence from the United States, as well as thoroughgoing land reform, some state ownership of industry, and friendly ties with communist countries. These policies infuriated the Reagan administration, which tried to undermine the Sandinista government. The Nicaraguan economy collapsed, and the popularity of the Sandinista government eventually declined. Then, after a decade of rule, the Sandinistas accepted free elections and stepped down when they were defeated by a coalition of opposition parties. In 1994 Haiti, one of the last repressive dictatorships in the Americas, also established democratic rule, with the help of U.S. military intervention.

As the 1990s progressed, Latin America's popularly elected governments boldly extended greater liberty from the political to the economic sphere. Beginning with Argentina in 1989 and followed by Chile, Mexico, and Brazil, governments moved from tariff protection and economic nationalism toward free markets and international trade, revitalizing their economies and registering solid gains. Mexico, for example, turned from high tariffs to free trade with its powerful northern neighbors, as in 1994 it joined with the United States and Canada in the North American Free Trade Agreement, commonly known as NAFTA. Building on NAFTA and the Southern Common Market, which already linked Brazil, Argentina, Paraguay, and Uruguay, a summit meeting of thirty-four governments agreed in Miami in December 1994 to forge a vast free-trade area incorporating every country of the Americas by 2005. Latin Americans were eager to trade freely with the United States, confident they could prosper by competing successfully with the hemisphere's largest economic power.

SUMMARY

The postwar recovery of western Europe and the Americas was a memorable achievement in the long, uneven course of Western civilization. The transition from imperialism to decolonization proceeded rapidly and without serious damage to western Europe. Genuine political democracy gained unprecedented strength in the West, and economic progress and social reforms improved the lives of ordinary citizens.

Postwar developments in eastern Europe displayed both similarities to and differences from developments in western Europe and the Americas. Perhaps the biggest difference was that Stalin imposed harsh one-party rule in the lands occupied by his armies, which led to the long and bitter cold war. Nevertheless, the Soviet Union became more liberal and less dictatorial under Khrushchev, and in the 1950s and 1960s the standard of living in the Soviet Union improved markedly.

In the late 1960s and early 1970s, Europe and the Americas entered a new and turbulent time of crisis. Many nations, from France to Czechoslovakia and from Argentina to the United States, experienced major political difficulties, as social conflicts and ideological battles divided peoples and shook governments. Beginning with the oil shocks of the 1970s, severe economic problems added to the turmoil. Yet in western Europe and North America the welfare system held firm, and both democracy and the movement toward European unity successfully passed through the storm.

Elsewhere the response to political and economic crisis sent many countries veering off toward repression. The communist system in eastern Europe was tightened up in the Brezhnev years, and a new kind of conservative authoritarianism arose in most of Latin America. Then, in the 1980s, both regions turned toward free elections and civil liberties, most spectacularly so in the east European revolutions of 1989. Like eastern Europe, Latin America also moved toward freer markets and embraced international trade and foreign investment, thereby abandoning its long-standing commitment to economic nationalism. The remarkable result of all these parallel developments was that differences in political organization, human rights, and economic philosophy were less pronounced in the reuniting Western civilization of the 1990s than at any time since the guns of 1914 had opened a new era.

NOTES

1. Quoted in N. Graebner, *Cold War Diplomacy, 1945–1960* (Princeton, N.J.: Van Nostrand, 1962), p. 17.
2. Ibid.

3. Quoted in J. Hennessy, *Economic "Miracles"* (London: André Deutsch, 1964), p. 5.

4. *Wall Street Journal,* June 25, 1985, p. 1.

5. Quoted in D. Treadgold, *Twentieth Century Russia,* 5th ed. (Boston: Houghton Mifflin, 1981), p. 442.

6. M. Walker, *The Waking Giant: Gorbachev's Russia* (New York: Pantheon Books, 1987), p. 175.

7. T. G. Ash, *The Polish Revolution: Solidarity* (New York: Scribner's, 1983), p. 186.

8. Quoted in S. E. Morison et al., *A Concise History of the American Republic* (New York: Oxford University Press, 1977), p. 697.

9. Quoted in N. Cantor, *Twentieth Century Culture: Modernism to Deconstruction* (New York: Peter Lang, 1988), p. 252.

10. Quoted in Morison et al., *A Concise History of the American Republic,* p. 735.

Suggested Reading

A good introduction to international politics is provided by W. Keylor, *The Twentieth Century: An International History* (1984), which has extensive, up-to-date bibliographies. An excellent way to approach wartime diplomacy is through the accounts of the statesmen involved. Great leaders and matchless stylists, both Winston Churchill and Charles de Gaulle have written histories of the war in the form of memoirs. Other interesting memoirs are those of Harry Truman (1958); Dwight Eisenhower, *Crusade in Europe* (1948); and Dean Acheson, *Present at the Creation* (1969), a beautifully written defense of American foreign policy in the early cold war. W. A. Williams, *The Tragedy of American Diplomacy* (1962), and W. La Feber, *America, Russia, and the Cold War* (1967), claim, on the contrary, that the United States was primarily responsible for the conflict with the Soviet Union. Two other important studies focusing on American policy are J. Gaddis, *The United States and the Origins of the Cold War* (1972), and D. Yergin, *Shattered Peace: The Origins of the Cold War and the National Security Council* (1977). V. Mastny's thorough investigation of Stalin's war aims, *Russia's Road to the Cold War* (1979), is recommended.

Three important general studies with extensive bibliographies are W. Laqueur, *Europe in Our Time: A History, 1945–1992* (1992); P. Johnson, *Modern Times: The World from the Twenties to the Eighties* (1983); and C. Black, *Rebirth: A History of Europe Since World War II* (1992). P. Lane, *Europe Since 1945: An Introduction* (1985), is an interesting combination of text and political documents. I. Unger and D. Unger, *Postwar America: The United States Since 1945*

(1989), and W. Leuchtenberg, *In the Shadow of FDR: From Harry Truman to Ronald Reagan* (1989), ably discuss developments in the United States. Postwar economic and social developments are analyzed in G. Ambrosius and W. Hibbard, *A Social and Economic History of Twentieth-Century Europe* (1989), and F. Tipton and R. Aldrich, *An Economic and Social History of Europe from 1939 to the Present* (1986).

The culture and politics of protest are provocatively analyzed in H. Hughes, *Sophisticated Rebels: The Political Culture of European Dissent, 1968–1987* (1988), and W. Hampton, *Guerrilla Minstrels: John Lennon, Joe Hill, Woody Guthrie, Bob Dylan* (1986). The work by N. Cantor, cited in the Notes is stimulating general cultural history. Two outstanding works on France are J. Ardagh, *The New French Revolution* (1969), which puts the momentous social changes after 1945 in human terms, and S. Bernstein, *The Republic of de Gaulle, 1958–1969* (1993). On Germany, H. Turner, *The Two Germanies Since 1945: East and West* (1987), and R. Dahrendorf, *Society and Democracy in Germany* (1971), are recommended. The spiritual dimension of West German recovery is probed by Gunter Grass in his world-famous novel *The Tin Drum* (1963). W. Laqueur, *The Germans* (1985), is a recent journalistic report by a well-known historian. A. Marwick, *British Society Since 1945* (1982), is good on postwar developments; P. Jenkins, *Mrs. Thatcher's Revolution: The End of the Socialist Era* (1988), is a provocative critique. Two outstanding books on the Vietnam War are N. Sheehan, *A Bright and Shining Lie: John Paul Vann and America in Vietnam* (1988), and A. Short, *The Origins of the Vietnam War* (1989). On feminism and the women's movement, see N. Cott, *The Grounding of Modern Feminism* (1987). J. Lovenduski, *Women and European Politics: Contemporary Feminism and Public Policy* (1986), provides an extremely useful comparative study of similar developments in different countries.

Z. Brzezinski, *The Grand Failure: The Birth and Death of Communism in the Twentieth Century* (1989), is a readable overview by a leading American scholar. H. Seton-Watson, *The East European Revolution* (1965), is a good history of the communization of eastern Europe, and S. Fischer-Galati, ed., *Eastern Europe in the Sixties* (1963), discusses early developments. P. Zinner, *Revolution in Hungary* (1962), is excellent on the tragic events of 1956. I. Svitak, *The Czechoslovak Experiment, 1968–1969* (1971), and Z. Zeman, *Prague Spring* (1969), are good on Czechoslovakia. T. Ash, cited in the Notes, is the best book on Solidarity, and M. Kaufman, *Mad Dreams, Saving Graces: Poland, a Nation in Conspiracy* (1989), is recommended. J. Hough and M. Fainsod, *How the Soviet Union Is Governed* (1978), is an important general study. A. Amalrik, *Will the Soviet Union Survive*

Until 1984? (1970), is a fascinating interpretation of Soviet society and politics in the 1960s by a Russian who paid for his criticism with prison and exile. A. Lee, *Russian Journal* (1981), is a moving personal account of a young American woman. H. Smith has written two outstanding journalistic reports on the Soviet Union under Brezhnev and Gorbachev, *The Russians* (1976) and *The New Russians* (1990). Gorbachev's reforms are perceptively examined by M. Walker, cited in the Notes, and M. Lewin, *The Gorbachev Phenomenon: A Historical Interpretation* (1988). G. Stokes, *The Walls Came Tumbling Down: The Collapse of Communism in Eastern Europe* (1993), is wide ranging and recommended.

R. von Albertini, *Decolonialization* (1971), is a good history of the decline and fall of European empires; T. von Laue, *The World Revolution of Westernization: The Twentieth Century in Global Perspective* (1987), is a stimulating interpretation. Related economic developments are considered in T. Vadney, *The World Since 1945* (1988), and H. van der Wee, *Prosperity and Upheaval: The World Economy, 1945–1980* (1986). Two excellent general studies on Latin America are J. E. Fagg, *Latin America: A General History,* 3d ed. (1977), and R. J. Shafer, *A History of Latin America* (1978). Both contain detailed suggestions for further reading. A. Lowenthal and G. Treverton, eds., *Latin America in a New World* (1994), analyzes the move toward regional cooperation and market economies. E. Burns, *A History of Brazil* (1970); M. Meyer and W. Sherman, *The Course of Mexican History* (1979); and B. Loveman, *Chile: The Legacy of Hispanic Capitalism* (1979), are recommended studies of developments in three leading nations. W. La Feber, *Inevitable Revolutions: The United States in Central America* (1983), is an important, quite critical assessment of U.S. support of neocolonial patterns in Central America. F. Fukuyama, *The End of History and the Last Man* (1992), sees the collapse of communism as the victory of democratic capitalism over all its competitors.

George Marshall's Plan for European Recovery, 1947

Although commencement speeches are usually quickly forgotten, the following address by Secretary of State George C. Marshall at the Harvard University graduation ceremonies on June 5, 1947, was a famous exception. Signaling a historic U.S. initiative, Marshall analyzed Europe's desperate economic conditions and proposed a program of American aid—the Marshall Plan.

Marshall offered U.S. aid to all European governments willing to cooperate, and the Soviet Union joined in early European efforts to draw up a collective response to the American proposal. But Joseph Stalin, probably fearing American domination and wanting to conceal the Soviet Union's terrible economic position, refused to provide the detailed data that western Europeans (and Americans) deemed essential for effective coordination. Marshall Plan aid went only to western Europe, accelerating the division of Europe and the onset of the cold war.

I need not tell you gentlemen that the world situation is very serious. That must be apparent to all intelligent people. . . .

In considering the requirements for the rehabilitation of Europe, the physical loss of life, the visible destruction of cities, factories, mines, and railroads was correctly estimated, but it has become obvious during recent months that this visible destruction was probably less serious than the dislocation of the entire fabric of the European economy. For the past ten years conditions have been highly abnormal. The feverish preparation for war and more feverish maintenance of the war effort engulfed all aspects of national economies. Machinery has fallen into disrepair or is entirely obsolete. . . . In many countries, confidence in the local currency has been severely shaken. The breakdown of the business structure of Europe during the war was complete. Recovery has been seriously retarded by the fact that two years after the close of hostilities a peace settlement with Germany and Austria has not been agreed upon. But even given a more prompt solution of these difficult problems, the rehabilitation of the economic structure of Europe quite evidently will require a much longer time and a greater effort than had been foreseen.

[One aspect of the situation in Europe is that] the farmer has always produced the foodstuffs to exchange with the city dweller for the other necessities of life. [But now] the town and city industries are not producing adequate goods to exchange with the food-producing farmer. [Thus farmers and peasants keep the food they produce, and] meanwhile people in the cities are short of food and fuel. So the governments are forced to use their foreign money and [dollar] credits to procure these necessities abroad. This process exhausts the funds which are urgently needed for reconstruction. [Thus a very serious situation is rapidly developing, and the modern exchange economy is in danger of breaking down.]

The truth of the matter is that Europe's requirements for the next three or four years of foreign food and other essential products —principally from America—are so much greater than her present ability to pay that she must have substantial additional help or face economic, social, and political deterioration of a very grave character.

The remedy lies in breaking the vicious circle and restoring the confidence of the European people in the economic future of their own countries and of Europe as a whole. The manufacturer and the farmer throughout wide areas must be able and willing to exchange their products for currencies the continuing value of which is not open to question.

Aside from the demoralizing effect on the world at large and possibilities of disturbances arising as a result of the desperation of the people concerned, the consequences to the economy of the United States should be apparent to all. It is logical that the United States should do whatever it is able to do to assist in the return of normal economic health in the world, without which there can be no political stability and no assured peace. Our policy is directed not against any country or doctrine but against hunger, poverty, desperation, and chaos. Its purpose should be the revival of a working economy in the world so as to permit the emergence of political and social conditions in which free institutions can exist. Such assistance, I am convinced, must not be on a piecemeal basis as various crises develop. Any assistance that this Government may render in the future should provide a cure rather than a mere palliative. Any government that is willing to assist in the task of recovery will find full cooperation, I am sure, on the part of the United States Government. Any government which maneuvers to block the recovery of other countries cannot expect help from us. Furthermore, governments, political parties, or groups which seek to perpetuate human misery in order to profit therefrom politically or otherwise will encounter the opposition of the United States.

It is already evident that, before the United States Government can proceed much further in its efforts to alleviate the situation and help start the European world on its way to recovery, there must be some agreement among the countries of Europe as to the requirements of the situation and the part those countries will take in order to give proper effect to whatever action might be taken by this Government. It would be neither fitting nor efficacious for this Government to undertake to draw up unilaterally a program designed to place Europe on its feet economically. This is the business of the Europeans. The initiative, I think, must come from Europe. The role of this country should consist of friendly aid in the drafting of a European program and of later support of such a program so far as it may be practical for us to do so. The program should be a joint one, agreed by a number of, if not all, European nations.

An essential part of any successful action on the part of the United States is an understanding on the part of the people of America of the character of the problem and remedies to be applied. Political passion and prejudice should have no part. With foresight, and a

German poster promoting Marshall Plan aid. *(Source: Bundesarchiv, Koblenz)*

willingness on the part of our people to face up to the vast responsibility which history has clearly placed upon our country, the difficulties I have outlined can and will be overcome.

Questions for Analysis

1. Why, according to Marshall, was the European economy on the verge of a breakdown? What was the specific financial problem?

2. What kind of responses did Marshall want Americans and Europeans to make? Why?

3. Do you find any evidence of tensions between the United States and the Soviet Union in Marshall's speech? What evidence?

4. What assumptions did Marshall make about the relationship between economics and politics? What caused upheaval and instability, according to Marshall?

Source: Slightly adapted from G. Marshall, "Address at Harvard University, June 5, 1947," *A Decade of American Foreign Policy: Basic Documents, 1941–1949,* U.S. Senate Document 123, 81st Cong., 1st sess., (Washington, D.C.: Government Printing Office, 1950), pp. 1268–1270.

34

Asia and Africa in the Contemporary World

Shinto priests perform a ceremony of purification in front of a reactor pressure chamber, Japan. *(Source: Yoshitaka Nakatani/PLUS ONE, Inc., Tokyo)*

When future historians look back at our era, they are likely to be particularly struck by the epoch-making resurgence of Asia and Africa after the Second World War. They will try to explain the astonishingly rapid rise of new or radically reorganized Asian and African countries and their increasingly prominent role in world affairs. And they will try to understand the continued development of these countries as they sought to realize the promise of independence and build strong nations and societies.

- How did Asian and African countries reassert or establish their political independence in the postwar era?
- How in the postindependence world did leading states face up to the enormous challenges of nation building, challenges that were all the more difficult after the 1960s?

These are the questions that this chapter seeks to answer.

THE RESURGENCE OF EAST ASIA

In 1945 Japan and China, the two great powers of East Asia, lay exhausted and devastated. Japanese aggression had sown extreme misery in China and reaped an atomic whirlwind at Hiroshima and Nagasaki. The future looked bleak. Yet both nations recovered even more spectacularly than western Europe. In the course of recovery the two countries, closely linked since the 1890s, went their separate ways. China under Mao Zedong (Mao Tsetung) transformed itself into a strong, one-party communist state. Japan under American occupation turned from military expansion to democracy and extraordinarily successful economic development. Not until the 1970s did the reborn giants begin moving somewhat closer together.

The Communist Victory in China

There were many reasons for the triumph of communism in China. As a noted historian has forcefully argued, however, "Japanese aggression was . . . the most important single factor in Mao's rise to power."[1] When Japanese armies advanced rapidly in 1938, the Nationalist government of Jiang Jieshi (Chiang Kai-shek) moved its capital to Chongqing (Chungking), deep in the Chinese interior (see page 1019). As the Communists, aided by their uneasy "united front" alliance with the Nationalists, built up their strength in guerrilla bases in the countryside behind Japanese lines, Mao, at the peak of his creative powers, avoided pitched battles and concentrated on winning peasant support and forming a broad anti-Japanese coalition. By reducing rents, promising land redistribution, enticing intellectuals, and spreading propaganda, Mao and the Communists emerged in peasant eyes as the true patriots, the genuine nationalists.

Meanwhile, the long war with Japan was exhausting the established government and its supporters. Half of Japan's overseas armies were pinned down in China in 1945. Jiang Jieshi's Nationalists had mobilized 14 million men, and a staggering 3 million Chinese soldiers had been killed or wounded. The war created massive Chinese deficits and runaway inflation, hurting morale and ruining lives.

When Japan suddenly collapsed in August 1945, Communists and Nationalists both rushed to seize evacuated territory. Heavy fighting broke out in Manchuria. The United States, which had steadfastly supported the Nationalists during the Second World War, tried unsuccessfully to work out a political compromise, but civil war resumed in earnest in April 1946. At first Jiang Jieshi's more numerous Nationalists had the upper hand. Soon the better-led, more determined Communists rallied, and by 1948 the demoralized Nationalist forces were disintegrating. The following year Jiang Jieshi and a million mainland Chinese fled to the island of Taiwan, and in October 1949 Mao Zedong proclaimed the People's Republic of China.

Within three years the Communists had succeeded in consolidating their rule. The Communist government seized the holdings of landlords and rich peasants—10 percent of the farm population had owned between 70 and 80 percent of the land—and distributed it to 300 million poor peasants and landless laborers. This revolutionary land reform was extremely popular. Although the Chinese Communists soon began pushing the development of socialist collectives, they did so less brutally than had the Soviets in the 1930s, and they retained genuine support in the countryside.

Meanwhile, the Communists were dealing harshly with their foes. Mao admitted in 1957 that 800,000 "class enemies" had been summarily liquidated between 1949 and 1954; the true figure is probably much higher. By means of mass arrests, forced-labor camps, and re-education through relentless propaganda and self-criticism sessions, all visible opposition from the old ruling groups was destroyed.

Finally, Mao and the Communists reunited China's 550 million inhabitants in a strong centralized state. They laid claim to a new Mandate of Heaven and demonstrated that China was once again a great power. This was the real significance of China's participation in the Korean War. In 1950, when the American-led United Nations forces in Korea crossed the 38th parallel and appeared to threaten China's industrial base in Manchuria, the Chinese attacked, advanced swiftly, and fought the Americans to a bloody standstill on the Korean peninsula. This struggle against "American imperialism" mobilized the masses, and military success increased Chinese self-confidence.

Mao's China

Asserting Chinese power and prestige in world affairs, Mao and the party looked to the Soviet Union for inspiration in the early 1950s. Along with the gradual collectivization of agriculture, China adopted a typical Soviet five-year plan to develop large factories and heavy industry rapidly. Russian specialists built many Chinese plants. Soviet economic aid was also considerable. The first five-year plan was successful, as were associated efforts to redirect higher education away from the liberal arts toward science and engineering. People were very poor, but undeniable economic growth followed the Communists' social revolution.

In the cultural and intellectual realms too, the Chinese followed the Soviet example. Basic civil and political rights, which had been seriously cur-

✳ **A People's Court** The man on his knees is accused in a people's court of selling a young girl living in his household, an old practice that became a serious crime in revolutionary China. Local villagers follow the proceedings intently. *(Source: Popperfoto/ Archive Photos)*

tailed by the Nationalists, were simply abolished. Temples and churches were closed; all religion was persecuted. Freedom of the press died, and the government went to incredible lengths to control information. A Soviet-style puritanism took hold. To the astonishment of "old China hands," the Communists quickly eradicated the long-standing scourges of prostitution and drug abuse, which they had long regarded as humiliating marks of exploitation and national decline. The Communists enthusiastically promoted Soviet-Marxian ideas concerning women and the family. Full equality, work outside the home, and state-supported child care became primary goals.

By the mid-1950s, the People's Republic of China seemed to be firmly set on the Marxist-Leninist course of development previously perfected in the Soviet Union. In 1958, however, China began to go its own way. Mao had always stressed revolutionary free will and peasant equality. Now he proclaimed a spectacular acceleration of development, a "Great Leap Forward" in which soaring industrial growth was to be based on small-scale backyard workshops run by peasants living in gigantic self-contained communes. Creating an authentic new socialist personality that rejected individualism and traditional family values was a second goal. In extreme cases, commune members ate in common dining halls, nurseries cared for children, and fiery crusaders preached the evils of family ties.

The intended great leap past the Soviets to socialist utopia—true communism—produced an economic disaster in the countryside, for frantic efforts with primitive technology often resulted only in chaos. By 1960, only China's efficient rationing system was preventing starvation. But when Soviet premier Nikita Khrushchev criticized Chinese policy, Mao condemned Khrushchev and his Russian colleagues as detestable "modern revisionists"— capitalists and cowards unwilling to risk a world war that would bring communist revolution in the United States. The Russians abruptly cut off economic and military aid. A mood of fear and hostility developed in both China and the Soviet Union in the 1960s as the communist world split apart.

Mao lost influence in the party after the fiasco of the Great Leap Forward and the Sino-Soviet split, but in 1965 the old revolutionary staged a dramatic comeback. Fearing that China was becoming bureaucratic, capitalistic, and "revisionist" like the

Soviet Union, Mao launched what he called the "Great Proletarian Cultural Revolution." Its objective was to purge the party of time-serving bureaucrats and to recapture the revolutionary fervor of his guerrilla struggle (see page 1019). The army and the nation's young people, especially students, responded enthusiastically. Encouraged by Mao to organize themselves into radical cadres called Red Guards, young people denounced their teachers and practiced rebellion in the name of revolution. One Red Guard manifesto, "Long Live the Revolutionary Rebel Spirit of the Proletariat," exulted:

Revolution is rebellion, and rebellion is the soul of Mao Tse-tung's thought. Daring to think, to speak, to act, to break through, and to make revolution—in a word, daring to rebel—is the most fundamental and most precious quality of proletarian revolutionaries; it is fundamental to the Party spirit of the Party of the proletariat! . . .

You say we are too arrogant? "Arrogant" is just what we want to be. Chairman Mao says, "And those in high positions we counted as no more than the dust." We are bent on striking down not only the reactionaries in our school, but the reactionaries all over the world. Revolutionaries take it as their task to transform the world. How can we not be "arrogant"?[2]

The Red Guards sought to purge China of all traces of "feudal" and "bourgeois" culture and thought. Some ancient monuments and works of art were destroyed. Party officials, professors, and intellectuals were exiled to remote villages to purify themselves with heavy labor. The Red Guards attracted enormous worldwide attention and served as an extreme model for the student rebellions in the West in the late 1960s (see page 1120).

The Limits of Reform

Mao and the Red Guards succeeded in mobilizing the masses, shaking up the party, and creating greater social equality. But the Cultural Revolution also created growing chaos and a general crisis of confidence, especially in the cities. Persecuted intellectuals, technicians, and purged party officials launched a counterattack on the radicals and regained much of their influence by 1969. Thus China shifted to the right at the same time that Europe and the United States did. This shift in

China, coupled with actual fighting between China and the Soviet Union on the northern border in 1969, opened the door to a limited but lasting reconciliation between China and the United States in 1972.

The moderates were led by Deng Xiaoping (b. 1904), a long-time member of the Communist elite who had been branded a dangerous agent of capitalism during the Cultural Revolution. After Mao's death in 1976, Deng and his supporters initiated a series of new policies, embodied in the ongoing campaign of the "Four Modernizations"—agriculture, industry, science and technology, and national defense. The campaign to modernize had a profound effect on China's people, and Deng proudly called it China's "second revolution."

China's 800 million peasants experienced the greatest and most beneficial change from this "second revolution"—a fact that at first glance may seem surprising. The support of the peasantry had played a major role in the Communist victory. After 1949, land reform and rationing undoubtedly improved the diet of poor peasants. Subsequently, literacy campaigns taught rural people how to read, and "barefoot doctors"—local peasants trained to do simple diagnosis and treatment—brought modern medicine to the countryside. Handicraft industries grew to provide rural employment. But rigid collectivized agriculture failed to provide either the peasants or the country with adequate food, as Chinese documents published in the 1980s made clear. Levels of agricultural production and per capita food consumption were no higher in the mid-1970s than in the mid-1950s, and only slightly higher than in 1937, before the war with Japan.

Determined to prevent a return to Maoist extremism as well as to modernize the economy, Deng and the reformers looked to the peasants as natural allies. Their answer to the stalemate in agricultural production was to let China's peasants farm the land in small family units rather than in large collectives. Peasants were encouraged to produce what they could produce best and "dare to be rich." Peasants responded enthusiastically, increasing food production by more than 50 percent in just six years after 1978. Thus most Chinese finally gained enough calories and protein for normal life and growth.

The successful use of free markets and family responsibility in agriculture encouraged further economic experimentation. Foreign capitalists were allowed to open factories in southern China, and they successfully exported Chinese products around the world. The private enterprise of Chinese citizens was also permitted in cities. Snack shops, beauty parlors, and a host of small businesses sprang up. As signs of liberalization abounded, the Chinese economy bucked the world trend and grew rapidly between 1978 and 1987. The level of per capita income doubled in these years.

Change, however, was also circumscribed. As in the Soviet Union under Mikhail Gorbachev (see page 1113), most large-scale industry remained state owned and state subsidized. Cultural change proceeded slowly, and the party maintained its strict control of the media. Above all, under Deng's leadership the Communist party zealously preserved its monopoly of political power.

When the worldwide movement for greater democracy and political freedom in the late 1980s also took root in China, the government responded by banning all demonstrations and slowing the trend toward a freer economy. Inflation then soared to more than 30 percent a year, and in 1988 consumers cleared the shelves in a buying panic. The economic reversal, the continued lack of political freedom, and the conviction that Chinese society was becoming more corrupt led China's idealistic university students to spearhead demonstrations in April 1989.

The students evoked tremendous popular support, and more than a million people streamed into Beijing's central Tiananmen Square on May 17 in support of their demands. The government then declared martial law and ordered the army to clear the students. Incredibly, masses of courageous Chinese citizens using only their bodies and voices as weapons peacefully blocked the soldiers' entry into the city for two weeks. But the hesitant army finally struck. In the early hours of June 4, 1989, tanks rolled into Tiananmen Square. At least seven hundred students died as a wave of repression, arrests, and executions descended on China. China's Communist leaders claimed that they had saved the country from plots to destroy socialism and national unity. Advocates of democracy were outraged around the world.

In the months after Tiananmen Square, communism fell in eastern Europe, the Soviet Union broke apart, and China's rulers felt vindicated.

Chinese Students in 1989   These exuberant demonstrators in Tiananmen Square personify the idealism and the optimism of China's pro-democracy movement. After some hesitation the Communist government crushed the student leaders and their supporters with tanks and executions, reaffirming its harsh, authoritarian character. *(Source: Erika Lansner/Black Star)*

They believed that their strong action had preserved Communist power, prevented chaos, and showed the limits of permissible reform. After some hesitation Deng reaffirmed economic liberalization. Private enterprise and foreign investment boomed. Consumerism was encouraged, and the regime permitted ever more products. But the rulers tortured and jailed critics of Communist rule, and they made every effort to ensure that the People's Army would again crush the people if called to do so. Thus the 1990s coupled growing economic freedom with rigid political repression, a contradictory and unstable combination in the eyes of many foreign observers.

Japan's American Revolution

After Japan's surrender in August 1945, American occupation forces began landing in the Tokyo-Yokohama area. Riding through what had been the heart of industrial Japan, where mighty mills and factories had once hummed with activity, they found only smokestacks and giant steel safes standing amid miles of rubble and debris. The bleak landscape manifested Japan's state of mind as the nation lay helpless before its conqueror.

Japan, like Nazi Germany, was formally occupied by all the Allies, but real power resided in American hands. The commander was General Douglas MacArthur (1880–1964), the five-star hero of the Pacific, who with his advisers exercised almost absolute authority.

MacArthur and the Americans had a revolutionary plan for defeated Japan. Convinced that militaristic, antidemocratic forces were responsible for Japanese aggression and had to be destroyed, they introduced fundamental reforms designed to make Japan a free, democratic society along American lines. The exhausted, demoralized Japanese, who had feared a worse fate, accepted passively. Long-suppressed liberal leaders emerged to offer crucial support and help carry the reforms forward.

Japan's sweeping American revolution began with demilitarization and a systematic purge. A special international tribunal tried and convicted as war criminals twenty-five top government leaders and army officers. Other courts sentenced hundreds to death and sent thousands to prison. Over 220,000 politicians, businessmen, and army officers were declared ineligible for office.

Although the American-dictated constitution of 1946 allowed the emperor to remain "the symbol of the State," the new constitution made the government fully responsible to the Diet, whose members were popularly elected by all adults. A bill of rights granted basic civil liberties and freed all political prisoners, including Communists. The constitution also abolished all Japanese armed forces. Japan's resurrected liberals enthusiastically supported this American move to destroy militarism.

The American occupation left Japan's powerful bureaucracy largely intact and used it to implement the fundamental social and economic reforms that were rammed through the Japanese Diet. Many had a New Deal flavor. The occupation promoted the Japanese labor movement and introduced American-style antitrust laws. The gigantic zaibatsu firms were broken up into many separate companies in order to encourage competition and economic democracy. The American reformers proudly "emancipated" Japanese women, granting them equality before the law.

The occupation also imposed revolutionary land reform. MacArthur pressured the Japanese Diet into buying up the land owned by absentee landlords and selling it to peasants on very generous terms. This reform strengthened the small, independent peasant, who became a staunch defender of postwar democracy.

The United States' efforts to remake Japan in its own image were powerful but short-lived. By 1948, when the United States began to look at the world through a cold war lens, occupation policy shifted gears. The Japanese later referred to this about-face as "the reverse course." As China went decisively communist, American leaders began to see Japan as a potential ally, not as an object of social reform. The American command began purging leftists and rehabilitating prewar nationalists, many of whom joined the Liberal Democratic party, which became increasingly conservative and emerged as the dominant political organization in postwar Japan. The United States ended the occupation in 1952. Under the treaty terms, Japan regained independence, and the United States retained its vast military complex in Japan.

"Japan, Inc."

Restricted to satellite status in world politics, the Japanese people applied their exceptional creative powers to rebuilding their country. Japan's economic recovery, like Germany's, proceeded painfully slowly immediately after the war. At the time of the Korean War, however, the economy took off and grew with spectacular speed for a whole generation. Between 1950 and 1970 the real growth rate of Japan's economy—adjusted for inflation—averaged a breathtaking 10 percent a year—almost three times that of the United States. Even after the shock of much higher energy prices in 1973, the petroleum-poor Japanese did considerably better than most other peoples. In 1986 average per capita income in Japan exceeded that in the United States for the first time. As recently as 1965, the average Japanese had earned only one-fourth of the average American's income.

Japan's emergence as an economic superpower fascinated some outsiders and troubled others. Many Asians and Africans looked to Japan for the secrets of successful modernization, but some of Japan's Asian neighbors again feared Japanese exploitation. And in the 1970s and 1980s, some Americans and Europeans bitterly accused "Japan, Inc.," of an unholy alliance between government and business and urged their governments to retaliate.

Many of the ingredients in western Europe's recovery also operated in Japan. American aid, cheap labor, and freer international trade all helped spark the process. Japan's astonishing economic surge also seems to have had deep roots in Japanese history, culture, and national character. By the time American and European pressure forced open its gates in the mid-nineteenth century, Japanese agriculture, education, and material well-being were advanced even by European standards. Moreover, a culturally homogeneous Japanese society put the needs of the group before those of the individual. When the Meiji reformers redefined Japan's primary task as catching up with the West, they had the support of a sophisticated and disciplined people (see pages 906–908). Japan's modernization, even including a full share of aggressive imperialism, was extremely rapid.

Building Team Spirit   Shouting company slogans in unison, these young managers and salespeople are hiking near snowcapped Mount Fuji as part of a two-week training course teaching business skills and company loyalty. Many customs encourage group solidarity in Japan, where the success of the group is placed above the success of the individual. *(Source: M. MacIntyre/The Hutchinson Library)*

By the end of the American occupation, this tight-knit, group-centered society had reassessed its future and worked out a new national consensus. Japan's new task was to build its economy and compete efficiently in world markets. Improved living standards emerged as a related goal after the initial successes of the 1950s. The ambitious "double-your-income" target for the 1960s was ultimately surpassed by 50 percent.

Government and big business shared leading roles in the drama of economic growth. As during the Meiji Restoration, capable, respected bureaucrats directed and aided the efforts of cooperative business leaders. The government decided which industries were important, then made loans and encouraged mergers to create powerful firms in those industries. The antitrust policy introduced by the American occupation was scrapped, and the home market was protected from foreign competition by various measures.

Big business was valued and respected because it served the national goal and mirrored Japanese society. Big companies, and to a lesser extent small ones, traditionally hired workers for life immediately after they finished school, and in return workers were loyal and obedient. The business firm in Japan was a big, well-disciplined family. The workday began with the company song. Employees' social lives revolved around the company. Wages were based on age. (Discrimination against women remained severe: their wages and job security were strikingly inferior to men's.) Most unions became moderate, agreeable company unions. The social and economic distance between salaried managers and workers was slight and often breached. *Efficiency, quality,* and *quantity* were the watchwords. Management was quick to retrain employees, who would not take their valuable new skills elsewhere. These factors were most important in accounting for Japan's economic success. Japan's stubborn protection of its home market, which foreigners frequently decried as "unfair" competition, played only a supporting role.

Japanese society, with its inescapable stress on discipline, cooperation, and national self-interest, has proved well adapted to the unending challenges of modern industrial urban civilization. Japan alone among industrial nations has experienced a marked decrease in crime over the last generation. In the 1970s and 1980s the Japanese ad-dressed themselves effectively to such previously neglected problems as serious industrial pollution and their limited energy resources. Highly dependent on imported resources and foreign sales, Japan groped for a new role in world politics. Closer relations with China, increased loans to Southeast Asia, and tough trade negotiations with the United States were all features of that ongoing effort.

NEW NATIONS IN SOUTH ASIA AND THE MUSLIM WORLD

South Asia and the Muslim world have transformed themselves no less spectacularly than China and Japan. The national independence movements, which had been powerful mass campaigns since the 1930s, triumphed decisively over weakened and demoralized European imperialism after the Second World War. Between 1947 and 1962, as decolonization gathered irresistible strength, virtually every colonial territory won its political freedom. The complete reversal of the long process of European expansion was a turning point in world history.

The newly independent nations of South Asia and the revitalized states of the Muslim world exhibited many variations on the dominant themes of national renaissance and modernization, especially as the struggle for political independence receded into the past. Both ethnic rivalries and cold war conflict complicated the process of renewal and development.

The Indian Subcontinent

After the First World War, Mahatma Gandhi and the Indian Congress party developed the philosophy of militant nonviolence to oppose British rule of India and to lessen oppression of the Indian poor by the Indian rich (see pages 1009–1011). By 1929 Gandhi had succeeded in transforming the Congress party from a narrow, middle-class party into a mass independence movement. Gradually and grudgingly, Britain's rulers introduced reforms culminating in limited self-government in 1937.

The Second World War accelerated the drive toward independence but also pointed it in a new direction. Congress party leaders, humiliated that

Great Britain had declared war against Germany on India's behalf without consulting them, resigned their posts in the Indian government and demanded self-rule as the immediate price of political cooperation. In 1942, Gandhi called on the British to "Quit India" and threatened another civil disobedience campaign. He and the other Congress leaders were quickly arrested and jailed for most of the war. As a result, India's wartime support for hard-pressed Britain was substantial but not always enthusiastic. Meanwhile, the Congress party's prime political rival skillfully seized the opportunity to increase its influence.

That rival was the Muslim League, led by the brilliant, elegant, English-educated lawyer Muhammad Ali Jinnah (1876–1948). Jinnah and the other leaders of the Muslim League feared Hindu domination of an independent Indian state led by the Congress party. Asserting in nationalist terms the right of Muslim areas to separate from the Hindu majority, Jinnah described the Muslims of India as "a nation with our distinct culture and civilization, . . . our own distinctive outlook on life and of life."[3] Thus Jinnah told a hundred thousand listeners at the Muslim League's Lahore Conference in March 1940,

If the British Government is really in earnest and sincere to secure the peace and happiness of the people of the subcontinent, the only course open to us all is to allow the major nations separate homelands by dividing India into autonomous national states.[4]

The Muslim League's insistence on the division of India appalled Gandhi. He regarded Jinnah's two-nation theory as simply untrue and as promising the victory of hate over love. The passionate debate continued unabated during the war as millions argued whether India was one nation or two. By 1945 the subcontinent was intellectually and emotionally divided, though still momentarily held together by British rule.

When Britain's Labour government agreed to speedy independence for India after 1945, conflicting Hindu and Muslim nationalisms and religious hatred became obstacles leading to murderous clashes between the two communities in 1946. In a last attempt to preserve the subcontinent's political unity, the British proposed a federal constitution providing for extensive provincial—and thus

religious and cultural—autonomy. When after some hesitation Jinnah and the Muslim League would accept nothing less than an independent Pakistan, India's last viceroy—war hero Lord Louis Mountbatten (1900–1979), Queen Victoria's great-grandson—proposed partition. Both sides accepted. At the stroke of midnight on August 14, 1947, one-fifth of humanity gained political independence.

Yet independence through partition also brought tragedy. In the weeks after independence, communal strife exploded into an orgy of massacres and mass expulsions. Perhaps a hundred thousand Hindus and Muslims were slaughtered, and an estimated 5 million refugees from both communities fled in opposite directions to escape being hacked to death by frenzied mobs.

This wave of violence was a bitter potion for Congress leaders, who were completely powerless to stop it. "What is there to celebrate?" exclaimed Gandhi. "I see nothing but rivers of blood."[5]

In January 1948, announcing yet another fast to protest Hindu persecution of Muslims in the Indian capital of New Delhi and to restore "heart friendship" between the two communities, Gandhi was gunned down by a Hindu fanatic. As the Mahatma's death tragically testifies, the constructive and liberating forces of modern nationalism have frequently deteriorated into blind hatred.

After the ordeal of independence, relations between India and Pakistan—both members of the British Commonwealth—remained tense. Fighting over the disputed area of Kashmir continued until 1949 and broke out again in 1965–1966 and 1971. Mutual hostility remains deeply ingrained to this day (Map 34.1).

Pakistan Like many newly independent states, Pakistan eventually adopted an authoritarian government in 1958. Unlike most, Pakistan failed to preserve its exceptionally fragile unity, which proved to be the unworkable dream of the intellectuals leading the Muslim League.

Pakistan's western and eastern provinces were separated by more than a thousand miles of Indian territory, as well as by language, ethnic background, and social custom. They shared only the Muslim faith that had temporarily brought them together against the Hindus. The Bengalis of East Pakistan constituted a majority of the population

MAP 34.1 The Partition of British India, 1947 Violence and fighting were most intense where there were large Hindu and Muslim minorities—in Kashmir, Punjab, and Bengal. The tragic result of partition, which has occurred repeatedly throughout the world in the twentieth century, was a forced exchange of populations and greater homogeneity on both sides of the border.

of Pakistan as a whole but were neglected by the central government, which remained in the hands of West Pakistan's elite after Jinnah's death. In essence, East Pakistan remained a colony of West Pakistan.

Tensions gradually came to a head in the late 1960s. Bengali leaders calling for virtual independence were charged with treason, and martial law was proclaimed in East Pakistan. In 1971 the Bengalis revolted. Despite savage repression—10 million Muslim Bengalis fled temporarily to India, which provided some military aid—the Bengalis won their independence as the new nation of Bangladesh in 1973. The world's eighth most populous country, Bangladesh was also one of its poorest.

India   India was ruled for a generation after 1947 by Jawaharlal Nehru (1889–1964) and the Con-

gress party, which introduced major social reforms. Hindu women and even young girls were granted legal equality, which included the right to vote, to seek a divorce, and to marry outside their caste. The constitution abolished the untouchable caste and, in an effort to compensate for centuries of the most profound discrimination, established "ex-untouchable" quotas for university scholarships and government jobs. In practice, attitudes toward

Indian Refugees   Independence and partition brought a wave of bloodshed that sent millions of Hindus and Muslims fleeing for their lives in opposite directions. Here desperate Muslims seek precious space atop a train that will carry them to safety in Pakistan. *(Source: Wide World Photos)*

women and untouchables evolved slowly—especially in the villages, where 85 percent of the people lived.

The Congress leadership tried with modest success to develop the country economically by means of democratic socialism. But population growth of about 2.4 percent per year ate up much of the increase in output, and halfhearted government efforts to promote birth control met with in difference or hostility. Intense poverty remained the lot of most people and encouraged widespread corruption within the bureaucracy.

The Congress party maintained a moralizing neutrality in the cold war and sought to group India and other newly independent states in Asia and Africa into a "third force" of "nonaligned" nations. This effort culminated in the Afro-Asian Conference in Bandung, Indonesia, in 1955.

Nehru's daughter, Indira Gandhi (1917–1984), became prime minister in 1966. Mrs. Gandhi (whose deceased husband was no relation to Mahatma Gandhi) dominated Indian political life for a generation with a combination of charm, tact, and toughness. As it became clear that population growth was frustrating efforts to improve living standards, Mrs. Gandhi's government stepped up measures to promote family planning and birth control measures, including vasectomy for both psychological and religious reasons. As a doctor in a market town explained to a Western journalist:

They have mostly heard of family planning around here by now, but they are afraid. They are afraid that the sterilizing operation will destroy their male power and make them docile, like castrated animals. Mostly, they are afraid of interfering with God's will.[6]

In the face of such reluctance—and in an effort to clamp down on widespread corruption at all levels of government—Mrs. Gandhi in 1975 subverted parliamentary democracy and proclaimed a state of emergency. Attacking dishonest officials, black-marketeers, and tax evaders, she also threw the weight of the government behind a heavy-handed campaign of mass sterilization to reduce population growth. In some areas, poor men with large families were made to accept a few cents' payment to submit to a simple, almost painless irreversible vasectomy. More than 7 million men were sterilized in 1976.

Many Indian and foreign observers believed that Mrs. Gandhi's emergency measures marked the end of the parliamentary democracy and Western liberties introduced in the last phase of British rule. But Mrs. Gandhi—true to the British tradition—called for free elections. She suffered a spectacular electoral defeat, largely because of the vastly unpopular sterilization campaign and her subversion of democracy. Her successors, however, fell to fighting among themselves, and in 1980 Mrs. Gandhi won an equally stunning electoral victory. Her defeat and re-election undoubtedly strengthened India's democratic tradition.

Mrs. Gandhi's last years in office were plagued by another old political problem, one that cost her her life. Democratic India remained a patchwork of religions, languages, and peoples. This enduring diversity threatened to further divide the country along ethnic or religious lines, as several peoples began to make political demands—most notably the 15 million Sikhs of the Punjab in northern India (see Map 34.1).

The Sikhs have their own religion—a blend of Islam and Hinduism—and a distinctive culture, including a warrior tradition and the wearing of elegantly coiled turbans. Industrious and cohesive, most Sikhs wanted greater autonomy for the Punjab. By 1984, some radicals were fighting for an independent homeland—a Sikh national state. In retaliation, Mrs. Gandhi tightened control in the Punjab and ordered the army to storm the Sikhs' sacred Golden Temple at Amritsar. Six hundred died in the assault. Five months later, two of Mrs. Gandhi's Sikh bodyguards—she prided herself on their loyalty—cut her down with machine-gun fire in her own garden. Violence followed as Hindu mobs slaughtered over a thousand Sikhs throughout India.

Elected prime minister by a landslide sympathy vote, one of Mrs. Gandhi's sons, Rajiv Gandhi (1944–1991), showed considerable skill at effecting a limited reconciliation with a majority of the Sikh population. But slow economic growth, government corruption, and Rajiv Gandhi's lack of warmth gradually undermined his support. In 1989, he was voted out of office, and a fragile coalition of opposition took power. Despite poverty and ethnic tensions, India remained committed to free elections and representative government.

✻ **Sikh Patriots** With the domes of the majestic Golden Temple rising behind them, a mass of Sikhs gather to protest the Indian army's bloody assault on their most holy shrine. The vast majority of Sikhs want greater autonomy at the least. Sikh radicals seek an independent state. *(Source: Bartholomew/Liaison)*

Southeast Asia

The rest of southeast Asia gained independence quickly after 1945, but the attainment of stable political democracy proved a more difficult goal. Ethnic conflicts and cold war battles could easily divide countries. Thus leaders frequently turned to authoritarian rule and military power in an effort to impose order and unity.

Malaysia and Singapore Malaya encountered serious problems not unlike those of British India. The native Malays, an Islamic agricultural people, feared and disliked the Chinese, who had come to the Malay Peninsula as poor migrant workers in the nineteenth century and stayed on to dominate the urban economy. The Malays pressured the British into giving them the dominant voice in a multiethnic federation of Malayan territories. In 1948 local Chinese communists launched an all-out guerrilla war. They were eventually defeated by the British and the Malays, and Malaya became self-governing in 1957 and independent in 1961. Yet two peoples soon meant two nations. In 1965, the largely Chinese city of Singapore was pushed out of the Malayan-dominated Federation of Malaysia. The independent city-state of Singapore prospered on the hard work and inventiveness of its largely Chinese population.

The Philippine Islands The Philippine Islands suffered greatly under Japanese occupation during the

ASIA SINCE 1945

1945	Japan surrenders Civil war begins in China
1946	Japan receives democratic constitution Philippines gain independence
1947	Communal strife follows independence for India and Pakistan
1948	Civil war between Arabs and Jews in Palestine
1949	Mao Zedong proclaims the People's Republic of China Indonesia under Sukarno wins independence from the Dutch
1950	Korean War begins Japan begins long period of rapid economic growth
1952	U.S. occupation of Japan officially ends
1954	Vietnamese nationalists defeat the French at Dien Bien Phu
1955	First Afro-Asian Conference of nonaligned nations meets at Bandung, Indonesia
1958	Mao announces the "Great Leap Forward"
1960	Open split between China and the Soviet Union emerges
1965	The "Great Proletarian Cultural Revolution" begins in China Growing U.S. involvement in the Vietnamese civil war
1966	Indira Gandhi becomes prime minister of India
1967	Arab-Israeli conflict: Six-Day War
1972	President Nixon's visit to China signals improved Sino-American relations
1973	Arab-Israeli conflict: Yom Kippur War
1975	War in Vietnam ends with Communist victory
1976	China pursues modernization after Mao's death
1979	Revolution topples the shah of Iran
1980–1988	War between Iran and Iraq
1984	Growth of Sikh nationalism in India
1986	Democratic movement in the Philippines brings Corazón Aquino to power
1989	Chinese government uses the army to crush student demonstrations
1991	U.S.-led United Nations–sanctioned military coalition forces Iraq out of Kuwait
1993	Unexpected agreement between Israel and the Palestinian Liberation Organization

Second World War. After the war the United States retained its large military bases but followed through on its earlier promises by granting the Philippines independence in 1946. As in Malaya, communist guerrillas tried unsuccessfully to seize power. The Philippines pursued American-style two-party competition until 1965, when President Ferdinand Marcos (1917–1989) subverted the constitution and ruled as a dictator. Abolishing martial law in 1981 but retaining most of his power, Marcos faced growing opposition as the economy crumbled and land-hungry communist guerrillas made striking gains in the countryside. Led by a courageous Corazón Aquino (b. 1933), whose politician husband had been murdered, probably by Marcos supporters, the opposition won a spectacular electoral victory in 1986 and forced Marcos to take refuge in Hawaii, where he subsequently died.

As president, Mrs. Aquino negotiated a cease-fire with the communist rebels, beat off several attempted takeovers by dissident army officers, and pursued a policy of national reconciliation. She eventually sided with nationalists who argued that U.S. military bases in the Philippines should be closed in order for the nation to achieve complete independence. When the lease on the bases was not renewed in 1991, the American military left. Yet a tiny elite continued to dominate the country, and years of mismanagement had led to decline in the standard of living. The Filipino people still faced an enormous challenge.

Indonesia   The Netherlands East Indies emerged in 1949 as independent Indonesia under the nationalist leader Achmed Sukarno (1901–1970),

President Corazón Aquino   Shown here with her infectious smile and dignity, Corazón Aquino led the democratic movement to power in the Philippines and enjoyed tremendous popular support. For millions of Filipinos she was simply "Cory"—their trusted friend. (*Source: Wide World Photos*)

after successfully resisting stubborn Dutch efforts at reconquest. Like the Philippines, the populous new nation encompassed a variety of peoples, islands, and religions (Islam was predominant; see Map 34.2). Beginning in 1957, Sukarno tried to forge unity by means of his so-called guided democracy. He rejected parliamentary democracy as politically divisive and claimed to replicate at the national level the traditional deliberation and consensus of the Indonesian village. For a time the authoritarian, anti-Western Sukarno seemed to be under the sway of well-organized Indonesian communists, who murdered and mutilated seven leading army generals as part of an unsuccessful uprising in 1965. The army immediately retaliated, systematically slaughtering a half-million or more Indonesian communists, radicals, and noncommunist Chinese. Sukarno was forced to resign.

The Muslim military leaders, led by General Suharto, established their own form of authoritarian rule and concentrated on economic development. Blessed with large oil revenues, Suharto's New Order welcomed foreign capital, expanded the Indonesian middle classes, and achieved solid economic growth in the 1970s and 1980s. Combining controlled elections with government-party majorities, the government promoted an official ideology stressing belief in one God, nationalism, humanitarianism, democracy, and social justice. Largely secular in inspiration, this ideology appeared to strengthen the modernizing effort, although it was questioned by some devout Muslims.

Vietnam, Laos, and Cambodia The most bitter struggle for independence in Southeast Asia occurred in French Indochina. The French tried to reimpose imperial rule there after the communist and nationalist guerrilla leader Ho Chi Minh (1890–1969) declared an independent republic in 1945, but they were decisively defeated in 1954 in the Battle of Dien Bien Phu. At the subsequent international peace conference, French Indochina gained independence. Laos and Cambodia (later known as Kampuchea) became separate states; Vietnam was "temporarily" divided into two hostile sections at the 17th parallel pending elections to select a single unified government within two years (see Map 33.3, page 000).

The elections were never held, and the civil war that soon broke out between the two Vietnamese governments, one communist and one anticommunist, became the hottest cold war conflict in the 1960s. The United States invested tremendous military effort but fought its Vietnam War as a deeply divided country (see pages 0000–0000). The tough, dedicated communists eventually proved victorious in 1975. Thus events in Vietnam roughly recapitulated those in China, but in a long, drawn-out fashion: after a bitter civil war worsened by cold war hatreds, the communists succeeded in creating a unified Marxist nation. And after another generation the Vietnamese communists also began to turn from central planning toward freer markets and private initiative, even as they zealously guarded their political power.

The Muslim World

Throughout the vast arc of predominantly Islamic lands that stretches from Indonesia in Southeast Asia to Senegal in West Africa (Map 34.2), nationalism remained the predominant political force after 1945. Anti-Western and anticommunist in most instances, nationalism in the Muslim world generally combined a strong secular state with a basic loyalty to Islam. Cold war conflicts and enormous oil resources enhanced the region's global standing.

In the Arab countries of North Africa and the Middle East, with their shared but highly differentiated language and culture, nationalism wore two faces. The idealistic side focused on the Pan-Arab dream of uniting all Arabs in a single nation that would be strong enough to resist the West and achieve genuine independence. This Pan-Arab vision contributed to political and economic alliances like the Arab League; but no Arab Bismarck appeared, and the vision foundered on intense regional, ideological, and personal rivalries. Thus the practical, down-to-earth side of Arab nationalism focused largely on nation building within the particular states that supplanted former League of Nations mandates and European colonies.

This effort eventually seemed to some to result in one-party dictatorship, corruption, and continued daily hardship. Beginning in the 1970s, some Islamic preachers and devoted lay people charged that the model of modernizing, Western-inspired nationalism had failed. These critics, known in the West as fundamentalists, urged a return to Islamic principles and traditional morality. They evoked a

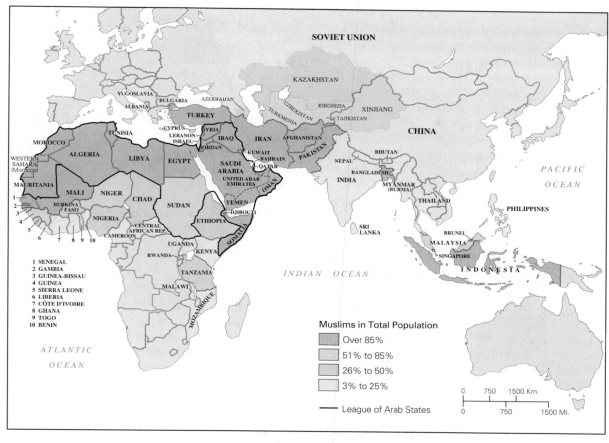

MAP 34.2 **Modern Islam, ca 1990** Although the Islamic heartland remains the Middle East and North Africa, Islam is growing steadily in Africa south of the Sahara and is the faith of heavily populated Indonesia.

sympathetic response among many educated Muslims as well as among villagers and city dwellers.

Israel and the Palestinian Question Before the Second World War, Arab nationalists were loosely united in their opposition to the colonial powers and to Jewish migration to Palestine. The French gave up their League of Nations mandates in Syria and Lebanon in 1945, having been forced by popular uprisings to follow the British example. Attention then focused even more sharply on British-mandated Palestine. The situation was volatile. The Jews' demand that the British permit all survivors of Hitler's death camps to settle in Palestine was strenuously opposed by the Palestinian Arabs and the seven independent states of the newly founded Arab League (Egypt, Iraq, Jordan, Lebanon, Saudi Arabia, Syria, and Yemen). Murder and terrorism flourished, nurtured by bitterly conflicting Arab and Jewish nationalisms.

The British—their occupation policies in Palestine condemned by Arabs and Jews, by Russians and Americans—announced in 1947 their intention to withdraw from Palestine in 1948. The insoluble problem was dumped in the lap of the United Nations. In November 1947 the United Nations General Assembly passed a nonbinding resolution supporting a plan to partition Palestine into two separate states—one Arab and one Jewish (Map 34.3). The Jews accepted, but the Arabs rejected partition of Palestine.

By early 1948 an undeclared civil war was raging in Palestine. When the British mandate officially ended on May 14, 1948, the Jews proclaimed the

Israel after Arab invasion and War of Independence, 1948
Occupied by Israel in Six-Day War, 1967
Maximum occupation by Israel, 1982
Arab nations
Oil fields
Suez Canal

MAP 34.3 Palestine, Israel, and the Middle East, 1947–1993 Since the British mandate expired on May 14, 1948, there have been five major wars and innumerable armed clashes in what was formerly Palestine. After winning the War of Independence in 1948, Israel achieved spectacular victories in 1967 in the Six-Day War, occupying the Sinai Peninsula, the Golan Heights, and the West Bank. The Yom Kippur War of 1973 eventually led to the Israeli evacuation of the Sinai and peace with Egypt. In 1993 Israel and the Palestinian Liberation Organization agreed to self-rule for Palestinian Arabs in the West Bank in five years.

state of Israel. Arab countries immediately launched an attack on the new Jewish state. Fighting for their lives, the Israelis drove off the invaders and conquered more territory. Roughly 900,000 Arab refugees—the exact number is disputed—fled or were expelled from old Palestine. This war left an enormous legacy of Arab bitterness toward Israel and its political allies, Great Britain and the United States, and it led to the creation of the Palestine Liberation Organization, a loose union of Palestinian refugee groups opposed to Israel.

Egypt In Egypt the humiliation of Arab defeat triggered a nationalist revolution. A young army colonel named Gamal Abdel Nasser (1918–1970)

drove out the corrupt and pro-Western king Farouk in 1952. A gifted politician and the unchallenged leader of the largest Arab state, Nasser enjoyed powerful influence in the Middle East and throughout Asia and Africa. Perhaps his most successful and widely imitated move was radical land reform: large estates along the Nile were nationalized and divided up among peasants without violence or drastic declines in production.

Nasser preached the gospel of neutralism in the cold war, jailed Egyptian communists, and turned for aid to the Soviet Union to demonstrate Egypt's independence of the West. Relations with Israel and the West worsened, and in 1956 the United States abruptly canceled its offer to finance a giant

Freedom for Palestinians Jubilant friends and relatives embrace the first political prisoners released by Israel from the grim central prison in Gaza city. Israel freed a thousand Palestinian political prisoners to show its willingness to implement the interim peace agreement with the Palestinian Liberation Movement. *(Source: Larry Towell/Magnum Photos)*

new dam on the Nile, intended to promote economic development. Nasser retaliated by immediately nationalizing the European-owned Suez Canal Company, the last remaining vestige and symbol of European power in the Middle East. Outraged, the British and French joined forces with the Israelis and successfully invaded Egypt. The Americans, suddenly moralistic, reversed course and sided with the Soviets—who were at that very moment crushing the Hungarian revolution (see page1110)—to force the British, French, and Israelis to withdraw from Egypt.

This great victory for Nasser encouraged anti-Western radicalism, hopes of Pan-Arab political unity, and a vague "Arab socialism." Yet the Arab world remained deeply divided. The only shared goals were bitter opposition to Israel—war recurred in 1967 and in 1973—and support for the right of Palestinian refugees to return to their homeland. In late 1977 President Anwar Sadat of Egypt tried another tack: a stunningly unexpected official visit to Israel.

Sadat's visit led to direct negotiations between Israel and Egypt, which were effectively mediated by U.S. president Jimmy Carter, and a historic though limited peace settlement. Each country gained: Egypt got back the Sinai Peninsula, which Israel had taken in the 1967 Six-Day War (see Map 34.3), and Israel obtained peace and normal relations with Egypt. Other Arab leaders denounced Sadat's initiative as treason and continued to support the Palestine Liberation Organization against Israel.

After Sadat's assassination by Islamic radicals in 1981, Egypt's relations with Israel deteriorated badly over the question of ever-increasing Israeli settlement on the West Bank—the area west of the Jordan River inhabited by Palestinian Arabs but taken by Israel from Jordan during the 1967 war. Yet Egypt and Israel maintained their fragile peace.

In 1988 young Palestins in the occupied territories began a prolonged campaign of rock throwing and civil disobedience against Israeli soldiers. Inspired increasingly by Islamic fundamentalists, the Palestinian uprising eventually posed a serious challenge not only to Israel but to the secular Palestinian liberation movement, long led from abroad by Yasir Arafat. The result was a totally unexpected agreement in 1993 between Israel and the Palestinian Liberation Organization. The agreement granted Palestinian self-rule in Gaza and Jericho and called for self-rule throughout the West Bank in five years. Almost miraculously, peace between Israel and its neighbors seemed possible in the foreseeable future.

Nationalism, Fundamentalism, and Competition The recent history of the non-Arab states of Turkey and Iran and of the Arab states of Iraq and Algeria (see Map 34.2) testifies to the diversity of national development in the Muslim world. That history also dramatically illustrates the intense competition between rival states and the growing strength of Islamic revival.

Turkey remained basically true to Atatürk's vision of a thoroughly modernized, secularized, Europeanized state (see page 1001). Islam continued to exert less influence in daily life and thought there than it did in other Middle Eastern countries. Turkey still looked toward the West, joining NATO in 1952 and becoming an associate member of the European Community.

Iran tried again to follow Turkey's example, as it had before 1939 (see page 1002). Once again, its success was limited. The new shah—Muhammad Reza Pahlavi (r. 1941–1979), the son of Reza Shah Pahlavi—angered Iranian nationalists by courting Western powers and Western oil companies in the course of freeing his country from Soviet influence after the Second World War. In 1953, after leading the effort to nationalize the British-owned Anglo-Iranian Oil Company, the Iranian Majlis and the fiery Prime Minister Muhammad Mossaddeq forced the shah to flee to Europe. But Mossaddeq's victory was short-lived. Loyal army officers, with the help of the American CIA, quickly restored the shah to his throne.

The shah set out to build a powerful modern nation to ensure his rule. Iran's gigantic oil revenues provided the necessary cash. The shah undermined the power bases of the traditional politicians—large landowners and religious leaders—by means of land reform, secular education, and increased power for the central government. Modernization surged forward, but at the price of ancient values, widespread corruption, and harsh dictatorship. The result was a violent reaction against modernization and secular values: an Islamic revolution in 1978 that aimed at infusing strict Islamic principles into all aspects of personal and public life. Led by religious leaders grouped around the spellbinding Ayatollah Ruholla Khomeini, the radicals deposed the shah and tried to build their vision of a true Islamic state.

Iran's Islamic republic frightened its neighbors. Iraq, especially, feared that Iran—a nation of Shi'ite Muslims—would succeed in getting Iraq's Shi'ite majority to revolt against its Sunnite leaders. Thus in September 1980, Iraq's president Saddam Hussein (b. 1937) launched a surprise attack, expecting his well-equipped armies to defeat an increasingly chaotic Iran. Instead, Iraqi aggression galvanized the Iranian revolutionaries in a fanatical determination to defend their homeland and punish Iraq's leader. Iranians and Iraqis—Persians and Arabs—clashed in one of the bloodiest wars in modern times, a savage stalemate that killed hundreds of thousands of soldiers before finally grinding to a halt in 1988.

Emerging from the eight-year war with a big tough army equipped by Western countries and the Soviet bloc, Iraq's strongman set out to make himself the leader of the entire Arab world. Eyeing the great oil wealth of his tiny southern neighbor, Saddam Hussein suddenly ordered his forces to overrun Kuwait in August 1990, and he proclaimed its annexation to Iraq. To Saddam's surprise, his aggression brought a vigorous international response (see page 1205).

In early 1991 his troops were chased out of Kuwait by an American-led, United Nations–sanctioned military coalition, after American planes had first destroyed most of Iraq's infrastructure with the heaviest bombing since the Second World War. American troops, accompanied by small British, French, and Italian forces, were joined in ground operations against Iraq by some Arab forces from Egypt, Syria, and Saudia Arabia. Thus the Arab peoples, long wracked by bitter rivalries between nation-building states, came to fight a kind of bloody civil war. Disillusionment with existing Arab governments increased in the early 1990s.

The important north African country of Algeria highlighted the development of first nationalism and then fundamentalism. Nationalism in the French colony of Algeria was emboldened by Nasser's great triumph—and by the defeat of the French in Indochina. But Algeria's large European population of more than a million considered Algeria home and were determined to keep it an integral part of France. It was this determination that made the ensuing Algerian war so bitter and bloody.

In 1958 a military coup in Algeria, resulting from the fears of the European settlers that a disillusioned, anticolonial majority of French voters would sell them out, brought General Charles de Gaulle back to power in France. Contrary to expectations, de Gaulle accepted the principle of self-determination for Algeria in 1959, and French voters agreed in a national referendum. In 1962, after more than a century of French conquest, Algeria became an independent Arab state. The European population quickly fled.

The victorious anticolonial movement, known as the National Liberation Front, or FLN, used the revenues of Algeria's nationalized oil fields to promote state-owned industries, urban growth, and technical education. But the FLN also imposed a one-party state, which crushed dissent and favored a self-serving party elite. In the 1980s increasing numbers of dissatisfied Algerians looked toward Islam for moral and social revival, and in the early 1990s the Islamic opposition swept municipal and national elections. The FLN called on the army to preserve its power, claiming that the fundamentalists would "hijack" democracy and create an Islamic dictatorship. Military rule then led to growing violence and armed struggle between the government and the radical minority in the fundamentalist opposition, placing in bold relief the cultural and ideological divisions simmering just below the surface in the Muslim world.

IMPERIALISM AND NATIONALISM IN BLACK AFRICA

Most of sub-Saharan Africa won political independence fairly rapidly after the Second World War. Only Portugal's old but relatively underdeveloped African territories and white-dominated southern Africa remained beyond the reach of African nationalists by 1964. The rise of independent states in black Africa—a major development in world history—resulted directly from both a reaction against Western imperialism and the growth of African nationalism.

The Imperial System (1900–1930)

After 1880 the Great Powers scrambled for territory and pushed into the interior, using overwhelming military force to mow down or intimidate

African opposition and establish firm rule (see pages 000–000). By 1900, most of black Africa had been conquered—or, as Europeans preferred to say, "pacified"—and a system of imperial administration was taking shape.

Gradually but relentlessly, this imperial system transformed Africa. Generally, its effect was to weaken or shatter the traditional social order and challenge accepted values. Yet this generalization must be qualified. For one thing, sub-Saharan Africa consisted of an astonishing diversity of peoples and cultures prior to the European invasion. There were, for example, over eight hundred distinct languages and literally thousands of independent political units, ranging from tiny kinship groups to large and powerful kingdoms like Ashanti of central Ghana and Ethiopia. The effects of imperialism varied accordingly.

European powers also took rather different approaches to colonial rule. The British tended to exercise indirect rule through existing chiefs. The French believed in direct rule by appointed officials, both black and white. Moreover, the number of white settlers varied greatly from region to region, and their presence had important consequences. In light of these qualifications, how did imperial systems generally operate in black Africa?

The self-proclaimed political goal of the French and the British—the principal foreign powers in black Africa—was to provide good government for their African subjects, especially after 1919. "Good government" meant, above all, law and order. It meant strong, authoritarian government, which maintained a small army, and building up an African police force to put down rebellion, suppress tribal warfare, and protect life and property. Good government required a modern bureaucracy capable of taxing and governing the population. Many African leaders and their peoples had chosen not to resist the invaders' superior force, and most others had stopped fighting after experiencing crushing military defeat. Thus the goal of law and order was widely achieved.

Colonial governments demonstrated much less interest in providing basic social services. Expenditures on education, public health, hospitals, and other social services increased after the First World War but still remained small. Europeans feared the political implications of mass education and typically relied instead on the modest efforts of state-subsidized mission schools. Moreover, they tried to make even their poorest colonies pay for themselves. Thus salaries for government workers normally absorbed nearly all tax revenues.

Economically, the imperialist goal was to draw the African interior into the world economy on terms favorable to the dominant Europeans. The key was railroads linking coastal trading centers to outposts hundreds of miles into the interior. Cheap, dependable transportation facilitated easy shipment of raw materials out and manufactured goods in. Most African railroads were built after 1900; fifty-two hundred miles were in operation by 1926, when attention turned to road building for trucks. Railroads and roads had two other important outcomes. They allowed the quick movement of troops to put down any local unrest, and they allowed many African peasants to earn wages for the first time.

Efforts to force Africa into the world economy on European terms went hand in hand with the advent of plantations and mines. The Europeans often imposed head taxes, payable in money or labor, to compel Africans to work for their white overlords. No aspect of imperialism was more disruptive and more despised by Africans than forced labor, widespread until about 1920. In some regions, however, particularly in West Africa, African peasants responded freely to the new economic opportunities by voluntarily shifting to export crops on their own farms. Overall, the result was increased production geared to the world market and a gradual decline in both traditional self-sufficient farming and nomadic herding.

In sum, the imposition of bureaucratic Western rule and the gradual growth of a world-oriented cash economy between 1900 and 1930 had a revolutionary impact on large parts of Africa. The experiences of Ghana and Kenya, two very different African countries, dramatically illustrate variations on the general pattern.

Present-day Ghana (see Map 34.4), which takes its name from one of West Africa's famous early kingdoms, had a fairly complex economy well before British armies smashed the powerful Ashanti kingdom in 1873 and established the Crown colony that they called the Gold Coast. Precolonial local trade was vigorous and varied. Into this sophisticated economy the British introduced production of cocoa beans for the world's chocolate bars. Output rose spectacularly, from a few hundred tons in the 1890s to 305,000 tons in 1936.

British imperialists loved to brag about the railroads to the interior, but recent studies clearly show that independent peasants and energetic African business people—many of the traders were women—were mainly responsible for the spectacular success of cocoa-bean production. Creative African entrepreneurs even went so far as to build their own roads, and they sometimes reaped big profits. During the boom of 1920, "motor cars were purchased right and left, champagne flowed freely, and expensive cigars scented the air."[7] As neighboring West African territories followed the Gold Coast's entrepreneurial example, West Africa took its place in the world economy.

The Gold Coast also showed the way politically and culturally. The westernized elite—relatively prosperous and well-educated lawyers, professionals, and journalists—and business people took full advantage of opportunities provided by the fairly enlightened colonial regime. The black elite was the main presence in the limited local elections permitted by the British, for few permanent white settlers had ventured to hot and densely populated West Africa.

Across the continent in the British East African colony of Kenya, events unfolded differently. The East African peoples were more self-sufficient, less numerous, and less advanced commercially and politically than Africans in the Gold Coast. Once the British had built a strategic railroad from the Indian Ocean coast across Kenya to Uganda, foreigners from Great Britain and India moved in to exploit the situation. Indian settlers became shopkeepers, clerks, and laborers in the towns. The British settlers dreamed of turning the cool, beautiful, and fertile Kenya highlands into a "white man's country" like Southern Rhodesia or the Union of South Africa. They dismissed the local population of peasant farmers as "barbarians," fit only to toil as cheap labor on their large estates and plantations. By 1929, two thousand white settlers were producing a variety of crops for export. The white settlers in Kenya manipulated the colonial government for their own interests and imposed rigorous segregation on the black and Indian populations. Kenya's Africans thus experienced much harsher colonial rule than did their fellow Africans in the Gold Coast.

African Traders This colorful display of produce suggests the competition and the dynamism of a West African market. African traders and peasants have played a key role in the economic development of West Africa since the 1920s. *(Source: Cynthia Johnson/Liaison)*

The Growth of African Nationalism

Western intrusion was the critical factor in the development of African nationalism, as it had been in Asia and the Middle East. But two things were different about Africa. Because the imperial system and Western education did not solidify in Africa until after 1900, national movements did not come of age there until after 1945. And, too, Africa's multiplicity of ethnic groups, coupled with imperial boundaries that often bore no resemblance to existing ethnic boundaries, greatly complicated the development of political—as distinct from cultural—nationalism. Was a modern national state to be based on ethnic tribal loyalties (as it had been in France and Germany, in China and Japan)? Was it to be founded on an all-African union of all black peoples? Or would such a state have to be built on the multitribal territories arbitrarily carved out by competing European empires? Only after 1945 did a tentative answer emerge.

A few educated West Africans in British colonies had articulated a kind of black nationalism before 1914. But the first real impetus came from the United States and the British West Indies. American blacks struggling for racial justice and black self-confidence took a keen interest in their African origins and in the common problems of all black people. Their influence on educated Africans was great.

Of the many persons who participated in this "black nationalism" and in the "Renaissance" of American black literature in the 1920s, the most renowned was W. E. B. Du Bois (1868–1963). The first black to receive a Ph.D. from Harvard, this brilliant writer and historian organized Pan-African congresses in Paris during the Versailles Peace Conference and in Brussels in 1921. The goals of Pan-Africanists were solidarity among blacks everywhere and, eventually, a vast self-governing union of all African peoples.

The European powers were hostile, of course, but so was the tiny minority of educated blacks in French Africa. As the influential Blaise Daigne, a black politician elected to the French parliament by the privileged African "citizens" of Senegal, told Du Bois:

We Frenchmen of Africa wish to remain French, for France has given us every liberty and accepted us without reservation along with her European children. None of us aspire to see French Africa delivered exclusively to the Africans as is demanded, though without any authority, by the American Negroes.[8]

Many educated French and British Africans, however, experienced a strong surge of pride and cultural nationalism in the 1920s and 1930s, inspired in part by American and West Indian blacks. The Senegalese poet and political leader Léopold Senghor (b. 1906) is an outstanding example. A gifted interpreter of Catholicism and of the French language in his native Senegal, Senghor discovered his African heritage in the cafés and lecture halls of Paris. He and other black and white students and intellectuals marveled at the accomplishments of American blacks in art, literature, African history, and anthropology. They listened to black musicians—jazz swept Europe by storm—and concluded that "in music American Negroes have acquired since the War a place which one can call pre-eminent; for they have impressed the entire world with their vibrating or melancholy rhythms."[9]

Senghor and his circle formulated and articulated the rich idea of *négritude,* or blackness: racial pride, self-confidence, and joy in black creativity and the black spirit. The powerful cultural nationalism that grew out of the cross-fertilization of African intellectuals and blacks from the United States and the West Indies was an unexpected byproduct of European imperialism.

Black consciousness also emerged in the British colonies between the world wars—especially in West Africa. The westernized elite pressed for more equal access to government jobs, modest steps toward self-government, and an end to humiliating discrimination. This elite began to claim the right to speak for ordinary Africans and to denounce the government-supported chiefs as "Uncle Toms." Yet the great majority of well-educated British and French Africans remained moderate in their demands.

The Great Depression was the decisive turning point in the development of African nationalism. For the first time, unemployment was widespread among educated Africans. Hostility toward well-paid white officials rose sharply. The Western-educated elite became more vocal, and some real radicals appeared.

Educated Africans ventured into new activities, often out of necessity. Especially in the towns, they supplied the leadership for many new organizations, including not only political parties and trade unions but also social clubs, native churches, and agricultural cooperatives. Radical journalists published uncompromising attacks on colonial governments in easy-to-read mass-circulation newspapers. The most spectacular of these journalists was the Nigerian Nnamdi Azikiwe, who had attended black colleges in the United States and learned his trade on an African-American weekly in Baltimore. The popular, flamboyant "Zik" was demanding independence for Nigeria as early as the late 1930s.

The Great Depression also produced extreme hardship and profound discontent among the African masses. African peasants and small business people who had been drawn into world trade, and who sometimes profited from booms, felt the agony of the decade-long bust, as did urban workers. In some areas the result was unprecedented mass protest. The Gold Coast "cocoa holdups" of 1930–1931 and 1937–1938 are the most famous example.

Cocoa completely dominated the Gold Coast's economy. As prices plummeted after 1929, cocoa farmers refused to sell their beans to the large British firms that fixed prices and monopolized the export trade. Instead, the farmers organized cooperatives to cut back production and sell their crops directly to European and American chocolate manufacturers. Small African traders and traditional tribal leaders largely supported the movement, which succeeded in mobilizing much of the population against the foreign companies. Many Africans saw the economic conflict in racial terms.

The holdups were only partially successful, but they did force the government to establish an independent cocoa marketing board. They also demonstrated that mass organization and mass protest had come to advanced West Africa. Powerful mass movements for national independence would not be far behind.

Achieving Independence with New Leaders

The repercussions of the Second World War in black Africa greatly accelerated the changes begun in the 1930s. Mines and plantations strained to meet wartime demands. Towns mushroomed into cities whose tin-can housing, inflation, and shortages of consumer goods created discontent and

hardship. Africans had such eye-opening experiences as the curious spectacle of the British denouncing the racism of the Germans. Many African soldiers who served in India were powerfully impressed by Indian nationalism.

The attitudes of Western imperialists changed also. Both the British and the French acknowledged the need for rapid social and economic improvement in their colonies; both began sending money and aid on a large scale for the first time. The French funneled more money into their West African colonies between 1947 and 1957 than during the entire previous half-century. The principle of self-government was written into the United Nations charter and was supported by Great Britain's postwar Labour government. As one top British official stated in 1948:

The central purpose of British colonial policy is simple. It is to guide the colonial territories to responsible government within the commonwealth in conditions that ensure to the people concerned both a fair standard of living and freedom from oppression from any quarter.[10]

Thus the key question for Great Britain's various African colonies was their rate of progress toward self-government. The British and the French were in no rush. But a new breed of African leader was emerging. Impatient and insistent, these spokesmen for modern African nationalism were remarkably successful: by 1964 almost all of western, eastern, and central Africa had achieved statehood, usually without much bloodshed.

The new postwar African leaders shared common characteristics. They formed an elite by virtue of advanced European or American education, and they were profoundly influenced by Western thought. But compared with the interwar generation of educated Africans, they were more radical and humbler in social origin. Among them were former schoolteachers, union leaders, government clerks, and unemployed students, as well as lawyers and prize-winning poets.

Furthermore, the postwar African leaders expressed their nationalism in terms of the existing territorial governments. They accepted prevailing boundaries to avoid border disputes and to achieve freedom as soon as possible. Sometimes tribal chiefs became their worst political enemies. Skillfully, the new leaders channeled postwar hope and

NATIONALISM IN BLACK AFRICA

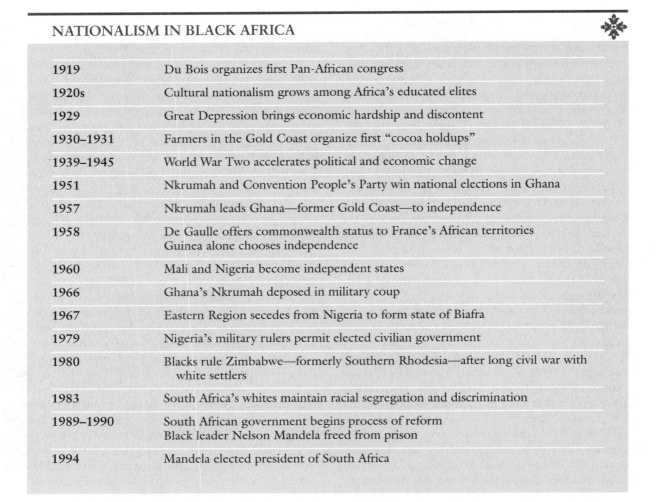

1919	Du Bois organizes first Pan-African congress
1920s	Cultural nationalism grows among Africa's educated elites
1929	Great Depression brings economic hardship and discontent
1930–1931	Farmers in the Gold Coast organize first "cocoa holdups"
1939–1945	World War Two accelerates political and economic change
1951	Nkrumah and Convention People's Party win national elections in Ghana
1957	Nkrumah leads Ghana—former Gold Coast—to independence
1958	De Gaulle offers commonwealth status to France's African territories Guinea alone chooses independence
1960	Mali and Nigeria become independent states
1966	Ghana's Nkrumah deposed in military coup
1967	Eastern Region secedes from Nigeria to form state of Biafra
1979	Nigeria's military rulers permit elected civilian government
1980	Blacks rule Zimbabwe—formerly Southern Rhodesia—after long civil war with white settlers
1983	South Africa's whites maintain racial segregation and discrimination
1989–1990	South African government begins process of reform Black leader Nelson Mandela freed from prison
1994	Mandela elected president of South Africa

discontent into support for mass political organizations. These organizations staged gigantic protests and became political parties. Eventually they came to power by winning the general elections that the colonial government belatedly called to choose its successor.

Ghana Shows the Way

Perhaps the most charismatic of this generation of African leaders was Kwame Nkrumah (1909–1972). Under his leadership the Gold Coast—which he rechristened "Ghana"—became the first independent African state to emerge from colonialism. Having begun his career as a schoolteacher in the Gold Coast, Nkrumah spent ten years studying in the United States, where he was deeply influ-

enced by European socialists and by the Jamaican-born black leader Marcus Garvey (1887–1940). Convinced that blacks could never win justice in countries with white majorities, Garvey had organized a massive "Back to Africa" movement in the 1920s. He also preached "Africa for the Africans," calling for independence. Nkrumah returned to the Gold Coast immediately after the Second World War and entered politics.

The time was ripe. Economic discontent erupted in rioting in February 1948; angry crowds looted European and Lebanese stores. The British, embarking on their new course, invited African proposals for constitutional reform. These proposals became the basis of the new constitution, which gave more power to Africans within the framework of (eventual) parliamentary democracy. Mean-

✦ **The Opening of Parliament in Ghana**   As part of an ancient ritual, two medicine men pour out sacred oil and call on the gods to bless the work of the Second Parliament and President Kwame Nkrumah, standing on the right. The combination of time-honored customs and modern political institutions has been characteristic of African states since independence. *(Source: Wide World Photos)*

while, Nkrumah was building a radical mass party appealing particularly to modern elements—former servicemen, market women, union members, urban toughs, and cocoa farmers. He and his party injected the joy and enthusiasm of religious revivals into their rallies and propaganda: "Self-Government Now" was their credo, secular salvation the promise.

Rejecting halfway measures—"We prefer self-government with danger to servitude in tranquillity"—Nkrumah and his Convention People's party staged strikes and riots. Arrested, the "Deliv-

erer of Ghana" campaigned from jail and saw his party win a smashing victory in the national elections of 1951. Called from prison to head the transitional government, Nkrumah and his nationalist party defeated both westernized moderates and more traditional "tribal" rivals in free elections. By 1957 Nkrumah had achieved worldwide fame and influence as Ghana became the first African state to emerge from colonial control.

After Ghana's breakthrough, independence for other African colonies followed rapidly. As in Algeria, the main problem was the permanent white settlers, as distinguished from the colonial officials. Wherever white settlers were at all numerous, as in Kenya, they sought to preserve their privileged position. But only in Southern Rhodesia were whites numerous enough to prevail long. Southern Rhodesian whites declared independence illegally in 1965 and held out until 1980, when black nationalists won a long guerrilla war and renamed the country Zimbabwe. In Zambia (formerly Northern Rhodesia) and East Africa, white settlers simply lacked the numbers to challenge black nationalists or the British colonial office for long.

French-speaking Regions

Decolonization took a somewhat different course in French-speaking Africa. France tried hard to hold on to Indochina and Algeria after 1945. Thus although France upped its aid to its African colonies, independence remained a dirty word until de Gaulle came to power in 1958. Seeking to head off radical nationalists, and receiving the crucial support of moderate black leaders, de Gaulle chose a divide-and-rule strategy. He divided the federations of French West Africa and French Equatorial Africa into thirteen separate governments, thus creating a "French commonwealth." Plebiscites were called in each territory to ratify the new arrangement. An affirmative vote meant continued ties with France; a negative vote signified immediate independence and a complete break with France.

De Gaulle's gamble was shrewd. The educated black elite—as personified by the poet Senghor, who now led the government of Senegal (see Map 34.4)—loved France and dreaded a sudden divorce. They also wanted French aid to continue. France, in keeping with its ideology of assimilation, had given the vote to the educated elite in its colonies after the Second World War, and about forty Africans held seats in the French parliament after 1946. Some of these impressive African politicians exercised real power and influence in metropolitan France. The Ivory Coast's Félix Houphouét-Boigny, for instance, served for a time as France's minister of health. For both cultural and practical reasons, therefore, French Africa's leaders tended to be moderate and in no rush for independence.

Yet political nationalism was not totally submerged. In Guinea, an inspiring young radical named Sekou Touré (1922–1984) led his people in overwhelming rejection of the new constitution in 1958. Inspired by Ghana's Nkrumah, Touré laid it out to de Gaulle, face to face:

We have to tell you bluntly, Mr. President, what the demands of the people are. . . . We have one prime and essential need: our dignity. But there is no dignity without freedom. . . . We prefer freedom in poverty to opulence in slavery.[11]

De Gaulle punished Guinea as best he could. French officials and equipment were withdrawn, literally overnight, down to the last man and pencil. Guinea's total collapse was widely predicted—and devoutly hoped for in France. But Guinea's new government survived. Following Guinea's lead, Mali asked for independence in 1960. The other French territories quickly followed suit, though the new states retained close ties with France.

Belgium tried belatedly to imitate de Gaulle in its enormous Congo colony, but without success. Long-time practitioners of paternalism, coupled with harsh, selfish rule, the Belgians had discouraged the development of an educated elite. In 1959, therefore, when after wild riots they suddenly decided to grant independence, the fabric of government simply broke down. Independence was soon followed by violent tribal conflict, civil war, and foreign intervention. The Belgian Congo was the great exception to black Africa's generally peaceful and successful transition to independence between 1957 and 1964.

❖ BLACK AFRICA SINCE 1960

The facility with which most of black Africa achieved independence stimulated buoyant optimism in the early 1960s. As Europeans congratulated themselves on having fulfilled their "civilizing mission," Africans anticipated even more rapid progress. But in the course of a generation the outlook changed. In most former colonies, democratic government and civil liberties gave way to one-party rule or military dictatorship. In many countries it became common for the winners in a political power struggle to imprison, exile, or murder the losers. Corruption was widespread; politicians, army officers, and even lowly government clerks used their positions to line their pockets and reward their relatives.

Nevertheless, conditions should be viewed in historical perspective. Given the tremendous scope of their challenges, the new African countries did rather well after achieving political independence. Nationalism, first harnessed to throw off imperialism, served to promote some degree of unity and ongoing modernization. Divisive ethnic conflicts arose, but fragile states survived.

Striving for National Unity

The course of African history after independence was complex and often confusing, but the common legacy of imperialism resulted in certain basic patterns and problems. The legacy of imperialism in Africa was not all bad. One positive outcome was the creation of about forty well-defined states (see Map 33.3, page 1110). These new states inherited functioning bureaucracies, some elected political leaders, and some modern infrastructure—that is, transportation, schools, hospitals, and the like.

The new African states inherited relatively modern, diversified social structures. Traditional tribal and religious rulers had generally lost out to a dynamic westernized elite whose moderate and radical wings faithfully reproduced the twentieth-century political spectrum. Each new state had the beginnings of an industrial working class and a volatile urban poor. Each country inherited the cornerstone of imperial power—a tough, well-equipped army to maintain order.

Other features of the imperialist legacy, however, served to torment independent Africa. The disruption of traditional life caused real suffering and resulted in postindependence expectations that could not be met. The prevailing export economies were weak, lopsided, and concentrated in foreign hands. Technical, managerial, and medical skills were in acutely short supply. Above all, the legacy of political boundaries imposed by foreigners without regard to ethnic and cultural groupings weighed heavily on postindependence Africa. Almost all of the new states encompassed a variety of peoples, with different languages, religions, and cultures. As in the Austrian Empire in the nineteenth century or in British India before independence, different peoples might easily develop conflicting national aspirations.

Great Britain and France had granted their African colonies democratic government as they prepared to depart. Yet belated, Western-style democracy served the new multiethnic states poorly. After freedom from imperialism no longer provided a unifying common objective, political parties often coalesced along regional and ethnic lines. Open political competition often encouraged regional and ethnic conflict, complicated nation building, and promoted political crisis. Many African leaders concluded that democracy threatened to destroy the existing states, which they deemed essential for social and economic progress in spite of their less-than-perfect boundaries. Thus these leaders did not abandon the authoritarian tradition they inherited from the imperialists. They imposed tough measures to hold their countries together, and free elections often gave way to dictators and one-party rule.

After Ghana won its independence, for instance, Nkrumah jailed without trial his main opponents—chiefs, lawyers, and intellectuals—and outlawed opposition parties. Embracing the authoritarian model, Nkrumah worked to build a dynamic "revolutionary" one-party state. His personality, his calls for African unity, and his bitter attacks on "Western imperialists" aroused both strong support and growing opposition. By the mid-1960s Nkrumah's grandiose economic projects had almost bankrupted Ghana, and in 1966 the army suddenly seized power while Nkrumah was visiting China. Across the continent in East Africa, Kenya and Tanzania likewise became one-party states with strong leaders.

The French-speaking countries also shifted toward one-party government to promote state unity and develop distinctive characteristics that could serve as the basis for statewide nationalism. Mali followed Guinea into fiery radicalism. Senegal and the Ivory Coast stressed moderation and close economic and cultural ties with France.

Like Nkrumah, many of the politicians at the helm of one-party states were eventually overthrown by military leaders. Between 1952, when Egypt's King Farouk was overthrown by Colonel Nasser, and 1968, Africa experienced at least seventy attempted military takeovers. Twenty of them succeeded. The trend continued after 1968. The rise of would-be Napoleons was lamented by many

Western liberals and African intellectuals, who often failed to note that military rule was also widespread in Latin America, Asia, and the Near East.

As elsewhere, military rule in Africa was authoritarian and undemocratic. Sometimes it placed a terrible burden on Africans. In Uganda, for instance, Idi Amin (b. 1925?), a brutal former sergeant, seized power in 1971, packed the army with his tribal supporters, and terrorized the population for a decade. Yet military government often had redeeming qualities. African military leaders generally managed to hold their countries together, and they worked to build existing states into viable nations.

Equally important, many military regimes, like their counterparts in Latin America (see pages 1125–1126), were committed to social and economic modernization. Drawing on an educated, well-organized, and highly motivated elite, they sometimes accomplished a good deal. African military leaders often believed in the ultimate goal of free, representative civilian government, which they sometimes restored after surmounting a grave national crisis. It was a question of priorities: unity came first, democracy second.

Nigeria, Africa's Giant

The history of Nigeria illustrates just how difficult nation building could be when state and ethnic boundaries were at odds with each other. "Nigeria" was a name coined by the British to designate their conquests in the Niger River basin (Map 34.4). The peoples of Nigeria encompassed many ancient kingdoms and hundreds of smaller groupings. The northern region was part of a great open plain, devoted to grazing and intensive farming. The much smaller southern region was a combination of coastal swamp and inland forest belt. Most of the peoples of the north were Muslims; most southerners were Christians or animists. The south was dominated by two very different peoples: in the west the proud Yorubas, with a military tradition and strong, well-defined kingdom; in the east the Ibos, with a tradition of business enterprise and independent villages.

Modern Nigeria came into being in 1914, when the British arbitrarily consolidated the northern and southern territories for administrative convenience. At least one British governor, who described Nigeria in 1920 as a "collection of self-contained and mutually independent Native States,"[12] believed such a land could never be welded into a single nation. However, in spite of its internal divisions, by 1945 Nigeria had spawned a powerful independence movement. The British responded receptively, and Nigeria entered into a period of intense but peaceful negotiation. In 1954, the third constitution in seven years set up the framework within which independence was achieved in 1960.

The key constitutional question was the relationship between the central government and the various regions. Some Nigerians, like the fiery Ibo journalist Azikiwe, wanted a strong centralized state, but the Yorubas in the west and the Muslim Hausa-Fulani leaders in the north wanted real power concentrated in large regions. Ultimately Nigeria adopted a federal system, whereby the national government at Lagos shared power with three regional or state governments in the north, west, and east. Each region had a dominant tribe and a corresponding political party. The parties were expected to cooperate in the national parliament, and the rights of minorities were protected by law.

With a population of 55 million in 1963, "Africa's Giant" towered over the other new African nations. But after independence, Nigerians' bright hopes gradually dimmed because of ethnic rivalries. In 1964, minorities in the Western Region began forming their own Midwestern Region in an attempt to escape Yoruba domination (see Map 34.4), and tribal battles followed in the Western Region. At this point a group of young army officers seized power in the capital city of Lagos, executing leading politicians and all officers above the rank of major. In an attempt to end the national crisis, the new military council imposed martial law and abolished the regional governments.

At first the young officers were popular, for the murdered politicians had been widely considered weak, corrupt, and too pro-Western. However,

 MAP 34.4 Nationalism and Independence in West Africa   Most of West Africa achieved independence by 1960. Borders inherited from the colonial era were generally accepted, although the Ibo people tried unsuccessfully to break away from Nigeria in the bitter Nigerian civil war.

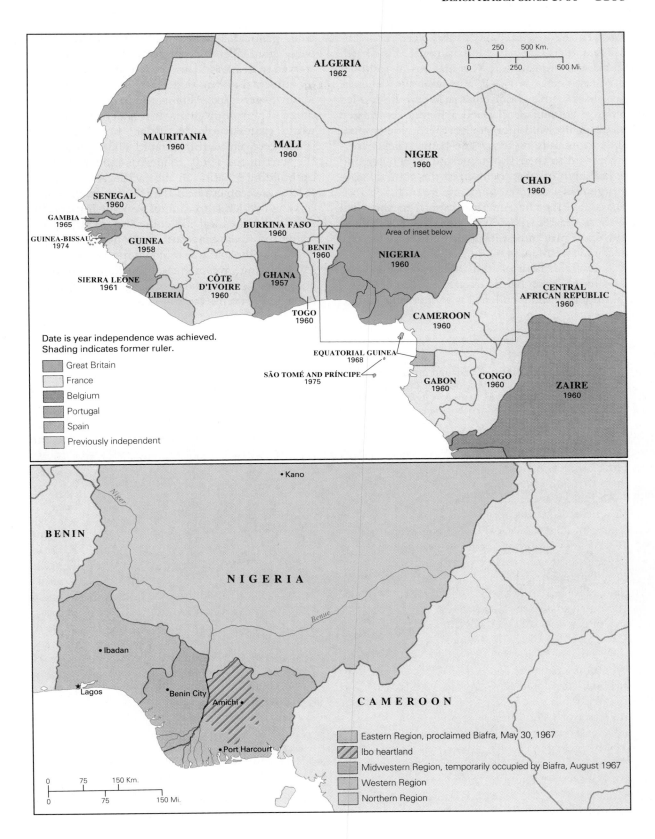

Date is year independence was achieved.
Shading indicates former ruler.

- Great Britain
- France
- Belgium
- Portugal
- Spain
- Previously independent

ALGERIA
1962

MAURITANIA
1960

MALI
1960

NIGER
1960

CHAD
1960

SENEGAL
1960

GAMBIA
1965

GUINEA-BISSAU
1974

GUINEA
1958

BURKINA FASO
1960

BENIN
1960

NIGERIA
1960

CENTRAL
AFRICAN REPUBLIC
1960

SIERRA LEONE
1961

CÔTE
D'IVOIRE
1960

GHANA
1957

LIBERIA

TOGO
1960

CAMEROON
1960

EQUATORIAL GUINEA
1968

SÃO TOMÉ AND PRÍNCIPE
1975

GABON
1960

CONGO
1960

ZAIRE
1960

Area of inset below

0   250   500 Km.
0   250   500 Mi.

Kano

BENIN

NIGERIA

Niger

Benue

CAMEROON

Ibadan

Lagos

Benin City

Amichi

Port Harcourt

- Eastern Region, proclaimed Biafra, May 30, 1967
- Ibo heartland
- Midwestern Region, temporarily occupied by Biafra, August 1967
- Western Region
- Northern Region

0   75   150 Km.
0   75   150 Mi.

many of the new military leaders were Ibos. The Muslim northerners had long distrusted the hardworking, clannish, non-Muslim Ibos, who under the British had come to dominate business and the professions throughout Nigeria. When the Ibo-led military council proclaimed a highly centralized dictatorship, wild mobs in northern cities massacred thousands of Ibos. The panic-stricken survivors fled to their Ibo homeland. When a group of northern officers then seized the national government in a counter-coup, the traumatized Ibos revolted. Like the American South in the Civil War, the Eastern Region seceded from Nigeria in 1967 and proclaimed itself the independent state of Biafra (see Map 34.4).

The war in Biafra lasted three long years. The Ibos fought with heroic determination, believing that political independence was their only refuge from genocide. Heavily outnumbered, the Ibos were gradually surrounded. Perhaps millions starved to death as Biafra became another name for monumental human tragedy.

But Nigeria, like Abraham Lincoln's Union, endured. The bloody civil war in Nigeria showed the world that Africa's "artificial" boundaries and states were remarkably durable. Having preserved the state in the 1960s, Nigeria's military focused on building a nation in the 1970s. Although the federal government held the real power, the country was divided into nineteen small, manageable units to handle local and cultural matters. The defeated Ibos were generously pardoned, not slaughtered, and Iboland was rebuilt with federal money. Modernizing investments of this kind were made possible by soaring oil revenues; Nigeria became the world's seventh largest oil producer.

Mobilizing in Biafra   A Biafran officer, himself only nine years old, drills a column of fresh recruits in 1969 during the Nigerian civil war. The boy soldiers were used for spying and sabotage, as Biafra struggled desperately against encirclement and starvation to win its independence. *(Source: Pictorial Parade)*

In 1979, after thirteen years of military rule, Nigeria's army leaders were confident enough to return power to an elected civilian government. But four years later the army again seized control, arresting the civilian politicians who had mismanaged the economy and demanded bribes and kickbacks. The military rulers soon imposed a harsh dictatorship, which was dominated by Hausa-Fulani Muslims. These northerners practiced a tribal favoritism that threatened to re-ignite regional and ethnic tensions that were never far beneath the surface. Thus a group of reforming officers engineered another coup in 1985, promising more liberty and less favoritism. The new generals did show greater respect for basic rights, but they repeatedly postponed or nullified national elections. Elected government remained an enduring goal in Nigeria, but military rule to preserve unity has been the reality.

The Struggle in Southern Africa

After the great rush toward political independence, decolonization stalled. Southern Africa remained under white rule, largely because of the numerical strength and determination of its white settlers. In Portuguese Angola and Mozambique, the white population actually increased from 70,000 to 380,000 between 1940 and the mid-1960s as white settlers using forced native labor established large coffee farms.

As economic exploitation grew, so did resentment. Nationalist liberation movements arose to wage unrelenting guerrilla warfare. After a coup overturned the long-established dictatorship in Portugal, African guerrillas managed to take control in Angola and Mozambique in 1975. Shortly thereafter, a coalition of nationalist groups also won in Zimbabwe after a long struggle.

This second round of decolonization in black Africa was bloodier than the first, and a third round in South Africa threatened to be still worse. The racial conflict in the white-ruled Republic of South Africa could be traced back in part to the outcome of the Boer War (see page 896). Although the British finally conquered the inland Afrikaner republics, they had to compromise to avoid a long guerrilla war. Specifically, the British agreed to grant all of South Africa self-government as soon as possible and to let its government decide which nonwhites, if any, should vote. It was to be a tragic compromise.

Defeated on the battlefield, the embittered Afrikaners elaborated a potently racist nationalism. Between 1910—when South Africa became basically a self-governing dominion, like Canada and Australia—and 1948, the Afrikaners gradually won political power from their English-speaking settler rivals. After their decisive electoral victory in 1948, Afrikaner nationalists spoke increasingly for a large majority of South African whites, who supported the political leadership with varying degrees of enthusiasm.

The goals of Afrikaner nationalism in the twentieth century were remarkably consistent: white supremacy and racial segregation. In 1913, the new South African legislature passed the Native Land Act, which limited black ownership of land to native reserves encompassing a mere one-seventh of the country. Poor, overpopulated, and too small to feed themselves, the native reserves in the countryside served as a pool of cheap, temporary black labor for white farms, gold mines, and urban factories. A black worker—typically a young single person—could leave the reserve only with special permission. In the eyes of the law, he or she was only a temporary migrant who could be returned at will by the employer or the government. The native reserves system, combining racial segregation and indirect forced labor, formed the foundation of white supremacy in South Africa.

After 1948, successive Afrikaner governments wove the somewhat haphazard early racist measures into an authoritarian fabric of racial discrimination and inequality. This system was officially known as *apartheid,* meaning "separation" or "segregation." The population was divided into four legally unequal racial groups: whites, blacks, Asians, and racially mixed "coloureds." Afrikaner propagandists claimed to serve the interests of all racial groups by preserving separate cultures and racial purity; marriage and sexual relations between races became criminal offenses. Most observers saw apartheid as a way of maintaining the lavish privileges of the white minority, which accounted for only one-sixth of the total population.

After 1940, South Africa's cities grew rapidly in conjunction with its emergence as the most highly industrialized country in Africa. Urbanization changed the face of the country, but good jobs in the cities were reserved for whites. Whites lived in luxurious modern central cities. Blacks, legally classified as temporary migrants, were restricted to outlying black townships plagued by poverty, crime, and white policemen. In spite of segregation, the growing cities produced a vibrant urban black culture, largely distinct from that of the tribal reserves. As a black journalist in Johannesburg explained in 1966:

I am supposed to be a Pondo, but I don't even know the language of that tribe. . . . I am just not a tribesman, whether I like it or not. I am, inescapably, a part of the city slums, the factory machines and our beloved shebeens [illegal bars].[13]

South Africa's harsh white supremacy elicited many black nationalist protests from the 1920s onward. Black nationalists began as moderates, seeking gradual reforms. By the 1950s, blacks—and their coloured, white, and Asian allies—were staging large-scale peaceful protests. A high point came in 1960, when police at Sharpeville fired into a crowd of demonstrators and killed sixty-nine blacks. The main black nationalist organization— the African National Congress (ANC)—was outlawed but sent some of its leaders abroad to establish new headquarters. Other members, led by a young black lawyer named Nelson Mandela (b. 1918), stayed in South Africa to set up an underground army to oppose the government. Captured after seventeen months, Mandela was tried for treason and sentenced to life imprisonment (see Listening to the Past). With harsh laws, a powerful police force, and an army of spies, the South African government defended and strengthened the apartheid system.

By the late 1970s, the white government had apparently destroyed the moderate black opposition within South Africa. Operating out of the sympathetic black states of Zimbabwe and Mozambique to the north, the militant ANC turned increasingly to armed struggle. South Africa struck back hard. It supported separatist movements that destabilized its neighbors, and it forced Marxist Mozambique in particular to curtail the ANC's guerrilla activities. Fortified by these successes, South Africa's white leaders launched in 1984 a program of "reforms"—changes designed to preserve white domination by means of a few strategic concessions.

For the first time, the 3 million coloureds and the 1 million South Africans of Asian descent were granted limited parliamentary representation. But no provision was made for any representation of the country's 22 million blacks. The government also made minor adjustments to apartheid, permitting marriage between races, for example. But laws controlling black movement and settlement were maintained.

The government's self-serving reforms provoked black indignation and triggered a massive reaction. In the segregated townships young black militants took to the streets, attacking in particular black civil servants and policemen as agents of white oppression. Heavily armed white security forces clashed repeatedly with black protesters, who turned funerals for fallen comrades into mass demonstrations. In 1985 the white government declared a state of emergency, and in 1986 it imposed unlimited press censorship and took a gigantic step toward dictatorship for all, regardless of race. Between 1985 and 1989, 5,000 died and 50,000 were jailed without charges because of the political unrest.

By 1989, the white government and the black opposition had reached an impasse. Black protesters had been bloodied but not beaten, and their movement for democracy had gathered worldwide support. The U.S. Congress had applied strong sanctions against South Africa in October 1986, and the Common Market had followed. The white government still held power, but the white population was increasingly divided. Being rejected as outcasts by the world community wounded the pride of some whites, and, more important, harsh repression of the black resistance had obviously failed.

A major step toward breaking the political stalemate came in September 1989 with the election of a new state president, Frederik W. de Klerk, an Afrikaner lawyer and politician. A late-blooming reformer, de Klerk moved cautiously toward reducing tensions and opening a dialogue with the ANC leaders. Negotiating with Nelson Mandela, whose reputation had soared among urban blacks during his long years in prison, de Klerk lifted the state of emergency in most of the country, legalized the ANC, and freed Mandela in February 1990. Emerging from prison as a proud and impressive leader, Mandela received a hero's welcome in South Africa and then in the United States and Europe.

In August 1990, Mandela showed again his courage and statesmanship. Overriding the doubts

✶ **Men of Destiny** Nelson Mandela shakes hands with Frederik de Klerk following a televised presidential debate in the 1994 electoral campaign. Mandela won and replaced de Klerk as president of South Africa after 350 years of white supremacy. De Klerk became vice president. Both leaders vowed to build a multiracial democratic society. *(Source: Mark Peters/Sipa Press)*

of some militant supporters, he suspended the ANC's armed struggle, thereby meeting de Klerk's condition for serious talks on South Africa's political future. Negotiations were long and difficult, greatly complicated by bitter opposition from right-wing whites and by violent clashes between some Zulus and some supporters of the ANC. But Mandela and de Klerk persevered. They reached an agreement calling for universal suffrage, which meant black majority rule, and they also guaranteed the civil rights of minorities.

Elected president of South Africa by an overwhelming majority in May 1994, Mandela told his jubilant supporters of his "deep pride and joy— pride in the ordinary, humble people of this country. . . . And joy that we can loudly proclaim from the roof tops—free at last!"[14] Heading the new "government of national unity," which included de Klerk as vice president, Mandela and the peoples of South Africa set about building a democratic, multiracial nation. It was a stunning climax to the long struggle for African liberation.

SUMMARY

Asian and African peoples experienced a remarkable resurgence after the Second World War, a resurgence that will almost certainly stand as a decisive turning point in world history. The long-developing nationalist movement in China culminated in a social revolution led by communists who went on to pursue innovative and fiercely independent policies that redeemed China as a great power in world affairs. Japan, defeated, demilitarized, and democratized, took a completely different path to the rank of economic superpower in a no less spectacular renaissance. Elsewhere—in India, Indonesia, and the Philippines—Asian peoples won their freedom and self-confidently charted independent courses. The Muslim world was also rejuvenated, most notably under Nasser in Egypt. In black Africa, a generation of nationalist leaders successfully guided colonial territories to self-rule by the middle of the 1960s, although liberation did not come in South Africa until the 1990s.

The resurgence and political self-assertion of Asian and African peoples in revitalized or developing nation-states did not proceed without conflict. Serious regional and ethnic confrontations erupted, notably between Hindus and Muslims in India and between Arabs and Israelis in the Middle East, and similar conflicts continued after independence was won. The vestiges of Western colonialism and cold war struggles resulted in atypical but highly destructive conflicts in Algeria, Vietnam, and Zimbabwe. The revitalized peoples of Asia and Africa continued to face tremendous economic and social challenges, which had to be met if the emerging nations were to realize fully the promise of self-assertion and independence.

NOTES

1. S. Schram, *Mao Tse-tung* (New York: Simon and Schuster, 1966), p. 151.
2. Quoted in P. B. Ebrey, ed., *Chinese Civilization and Society: A Source Book* (New York: Free Press, 1981), p. 393.
3. Quoted in W. Bingham, H. Conroy, and F. Iklé, *A History of Asia*, vol. 2, 2d ed. (Boston: Allyn and Bacon, 1974), p. 459.
4. Quoted in S. Wolpert, *A New History of India*, 2d ed. (New York: Oxford University Press, 1982), p. 330.
5. Quoted in K. Bhata, *The Ordeal of Nationhood: A Social Study of India Since Independence, 1947–1970* (New York: Atheneum, 1971), p. 9.
6. Quoted in B. D. Nossiter, *Soft State: A Newspaperman's Chronicle of India* (New York: Harper & Row, 1970), p. 52.
7. G. B. Kay, ed., *The Political Economy of Colonialism in Ghana: A Collection of Documents and Statistics* (Cambridge: Cambridge University Press, 1972), p. 48.
8. Quoted in R. W. July, *A History of the African People*, 3d ed. (New York: Scribner's, 1980), pp. 519–520.
9. Quoted in J. L. Hymans, *Léopold Sédar Senghor: An Intellectual Biography* (Edinburgh: University of Edinburgh Press, 1971), p. 58.
10. Quoted in L. H. Gann and P. Duignan, *Colonialism in Africa*, vol. 2 (Cambridge: Cambridge University Press, 1970), p. 512.
11. Quoted in R. Hallett, *Africa Since 1875: A Modern History* (Ann Arbor: University of Michigan Press, 1974), pp. 378–379.
12. Ibid., p. 345.
13. Ibid., p. 657.
14. Quoted in *Chicago Tribune*, May 3, 1994, section 1, p. 5.

SUGGESTED READING

Many of the works mentioned in the Suggested Reading for Chapter 30 are also valuable for considering postwar developments in Asia and the Middle East. Three other important studies on developments in China are E. Friedman, *Chinese Village, Socialist State* (1991); C. Johnson, *Peasant Nationalism and Communist Power: The Emergence of Revolutionary China, 1937–1945* (1962); and W. L. Parish and M. K. Whyte, *Village and Family in Contemporary China* (1978). M. Meisner, *Mao's China: A History of the People's Republic* (1977), is an excellent comprehensive study, and C. P. FitzGerald, *Communism Takes China: How the Revolution Went Red* (1971), is a lively, illustrated account by a scholar who spent many years in China. Recent developments are ably analyzed by J. Spence, *The Search for Modern China* (1990), and Lin Binyan, *China's Crisis, China's Hope* (1990). T. Yueh and C. Wakeman, *To the Storm: The Odyssey of a Revolutionary Chinese Woman* (1985), is the poignant drama of a participant. R. Lardy, *Agriculture in China's Economic Development* (1983), carefully studies the poor performance that led to Deng's reforms, which are fully examined in R. Evans, *Deng Xiaoping and the Making of Modern China* (1994).

K. Kawai, *Japan's American Interlude* (1960), and R. P. Dore, *Land Reform in Japan* (1959), consider key problems of occupation policy. A. Gordon, ed., *Postwar Japan as History* (1993), contains essays by leading scholars and has an extensive bibliography. Three excellent and thought-provoking studies of contemporary Japanese society are E. Reischauer, *The Japanese Today, Change and Continuity* (1989); F. Gibney, *Japan, the Fragile Superpower* (1977); and E. Vogel, *Japan as Number One: Lessons for America* (1979). G. Bernstein, *Haruko's World: A Japanese Farm Woman and Her Community* (1983), probes changing patterns of rural life. Akira Iriye, *The Cold*

War in Asia: A Historical Introduction (1974), and M. Schaller, *The United States and China in the Twentieth Century* (1979), analyze international conflicts in the postwar Pacific basin.

S. Wolpert, *India* (1991), a wise and beautifully written introduction, is highly recommended. G. Hutchins, *India's Revolution: Gandhi and the Quit India Movement* (1973), is an excellent account of wartime developments in India, which may be compared with J. Nehru, *An Autobiography* (1962), the appealing testimony of a principal architect of Indian freedom. F. Frankel, *India's Political Economy, 1947–1977* (1978), intelligently discusses the economic policies of independent India. There is a good biography of Indira Gandhi by D. Moraes (1980). J. Novak, *Bangladesh: Reflections of the Water* (1993), is a moving introduction. H. Tinker, *South Asia: A Short History*, 2d ed. (1990), is a good guide to the states of the Indian subcontinent.

For Southeast Asia there are solid general accounts by C. Dubois, *Social Forces in Southeast Asia* (1967), and R. N. Kearney, *Politics and Modernization in South and Southeast Asia* (1974). C. Cooper, *The Lost Crusade: America in Vietnam* (1972), and F. FitzGerald, *Fire in the Lake* (1973), probe the tragic war in Vietnam. Two valuable works on other Asian countries are B. Dahm, *Sukarno and the Struggle for Indonesian Independence* (1969), and T. Friend, *Between Two Empires: The Ordeal of the Philippines, 1929–1946* (1965).

Recommended studies of the Middle East and Israel include a cultural investigation by R. Patai, *The Arab Mind* (1973); a balanced account by C. Smith, *Palestine and the Arab-Israeli Conflict* (1988); an excellent biography of Israel's inspiring leader during its war for independence by A. Avi-Hai, *Ben Gurion, State Builder* (1974); and B. Kimmerling and J. Migdal, *The Palestinians: The Making of a People* (1992). A. Goldschmidt, Jr., *Modern Egypt: The Formation of a Nation-State* (1988), treats the post-Nasser years extensively. Religious fundamentalism is sympathetically analyzed in J. Esposito, *The Islamic Threat:*

Myth or Reality? (1992). H. Munson, Jr., *Islam and Revolution in the Middle East* (1988), is an earlier comparison of Iran and Arab countries.

The studies by July and Hallett cited in the Notes are outstanding interpretations of modern Africa's rich and complex history. Both have extensive bibliographies. Important works on the colonial era include A. Boahen, *African Perspectives on Colonialism* (1989); J. A. Langley, *Pan-Africanism and Nationalism in West Africa, 1900–1945: A Study in Ideology and Social Classes* (1973); and R. O. Collins, *Problems in the History of Colonial Africa, 1860–1960* (1970). B. Davidson, *The Black Man's Burden: Africa and the Curse of the Nation State* (1993), is a thought-provoking reconsideration by a noted historian. W. E. B. Du Bois, *The World and Africa* (1947), and J. Kenyatta, *Facing Mount Kenya* (1953), are powerful comments on African nationalism by, respectively, the distinguished American black thinker and Kenya's foremost revolutionary and political leader. R. July, *The African Voice: The Role of the Humanities in African Independence* (1987), focuses on intellectuals and artists struggling against cultural imperialism. A. Hopkins, *An Economic History of West Africa* (1973), is a pioneering synthesis. C. Dewey and A. Hopkins, eds., *The Imperial Impact: Studies in the Economic History of Africa and India* (1978), is an innovative comparative study. R. Olaniyan, ed., *African History and Culture* (1982), is a valuable recent collection. M. Crowder, ed., *The Cambridge History of Africa,* vol. 8, examines the struggle for independence and nationhood between 1940 and 1975 in broad perspective. Major works on specific countries include M. Crowder, *The Story of Nigeria,* 4th ed. (1978); P. Hill, *Migrant Cocoa Farmers in Ghana* (1963); and R. W. Johnson, *How Long Will South Africa Survive?* (1977). P. C. Lloyd, *Africa in Social Change* (1972), is a useful study on the contemporary era, and F. Willett, *African Art* (1971), is a good introduction. Nelson Mandela tells his story in his autobiography, *Long Walk to Freedom* (1994).

LISTENING TO THE
PAST

The Struggle for Freedom in South Africa

Many African territories won political freedom in the mid-1960s, but in South Africa the struggle was long and extremely difficult. Only in 1990 did the white government release Nelson Mandela from prison and begin negotiations with the famous black leader and the African National Congress (ANC). Only in 1994 did Mandela and the ANC finally come to power and establish a new system based on majority rule and racial equality.

Born in 1918 into the royal family of the Transkei, Nelson Mandela received an education befitting the son of a tribal chief. But he ran away to escape an arranged tribal marriage, experienced the harsh realities of black life in Johannesburg, studied law, and became an attorney. A born leader with a natural air of authority, Mandela was drawn to politics and the ANC. In the 1950s the white government responded to the growing popularity of Mandela and the ANC with tear gas and repression.

In 1960 the ANC called a general strike to protest the shooting of peaceful protesters at Sharpeville. Acts of sabotage then shook South Africa, and Mandela led the underground opposition. Betrayed by an informer, he was convicted of treason in 1964 and sentenced to life imprisonment. Mandela defended all of the accused in the 1964 treason trial. The following selection is taken from Mandela's opening statement.

At the outset, I want to say that the suggestion made by the State in its opening that the struggle in South Africa is under the influence of foreigners or communists is wholly incorrect. I have done whatever I did, both as an individual and as a leader of my people, because of my experience in South Africa and my own proudly felt African background, and not because of what any outsider might have said.

In my youth in the Transkei I listened to the elders of my tribe telling stories of the old days. Amongst the tales they related to me were those of wars fought by our ancestors in defence of the fatherland. . . . I hoped then that life might offer me the opportunity to serve my people and make my own humble contribution to their freedom struggle. . . .

It is true that there has often been close cooperation between the ANC [African National Congress] and the Communist Party. But cooperation is merely proof of a common goal—in this case the removal of White supremacy—and is not proof of a complete community of interests. . . . What is more, for many decades communists were the only political group in South Africa who were prepared to treat Africans as human beings and their equals; who were prepared to eat with us, talk with us, live with us, and work with us. . . . Because of this, there are many Africans who today tend to equate freedom with communism. . . .

I turn now to my own position. I have denied that I am a communist. . . . [But] I am attracted by the idea of a classless society, an attraction which springs in part from Marxist reading and, in part, from my admiration of the structure and organization of early African societies in this country. The land, then the main means of production, belonged to the tribe. There were no rich or poor and there was no exploitation. . . .

[Unlike communists] I am an admirer of the parliamentary system of the West. . . . [Thus] I have been influenced in my thinking by both West and East. . . . [I believe] I should be absolutely impartial and objective. I should tie myself to no particular system of society other than of socialism. I must leave myself free to borrow the best from the West and from the East. . . .

Our fight is against real, and not imaginary, hardships or, to use the language of the State

Prosecutor, "so-called hardships".... Basically, we fight against two features which are the hallmarks of African life in South Africa and which are entrenched by legislation which we seek to have repealed. These features are poverty and lack of human dignity, and we do not need communists or so-called "agitators" to teach us about these things.

South Africa is the richest country in Africa, and could be one of the richest countries in the world. But it is a land of extremes and remarkable contrasts. The Whites enjoy what may well be the highest standard of living in the world, while Africans live in poverty and misery.... Poverty goes hand in hand with malnutrition and disease....

The lack of human dignity experienced by Africans is the direct result of the policy of White supremacy. White supremacy implies Black inferiority. Legislation designed to preserve White supremacy entrenches this notion.... Because of this sort of attitude, Whites tend to regard Africans as a separate breed. They do not look upon them as people with families of their own; they do not realize that they have emotions....

Africans want to be paid a living wage. Africans want to perform work which they are capable of doing, and not work which the Government declares them to be capable of. ... Africans want a just share in the whole of South Africa; they want security and a stake in society.

Above all, we want equal political rights, because without them our disabilities will be permanent. I know this sounds revolutionary to the Whites in this country, because the majority of voters will be Africans. This makes the White man fear democracy.

But this fear cannot be allowed to stand in the way of the only solution which will guarantee racial harmony and freedom for all. It is not true that the enfranchisement of all will result in racial domination. Political division, based on color, is entirely artificial and, when it disappears, so will the domination of one color group by another. The ANC has spent half a century fighting against racialism. When it triumphs it will not change that policy.

This then is what the ANC is fighting. Their struggle is a truly national one. It is a struggle of the African people, inspired by their own suffering and their own experience. It is a struggle for the right to live.

✳ Nelson Mandela at the time of his imprisonment in 1964. (*Source: Mohamed Lounes/Liaison*)

During my lifetime I have dedicated myself to this struggle of the African people. I have fought against White domination, and I have fought against Black domination. I have cherished the ideal of a democratic and free society in which all persons live together in harmony and with equal opportunities. It is an ideal which I hope to live for and to achieve. But if needs be, it is an ideal for which I am prepared to die.

Questions for Analysis

1. How does Nelson Mandela respond to the charge that he and the ANC are controlled by communists?

2. What factors influenced Mandela's thinking? In what ways has he been influenced by "both East and West" and by his African background?

3. According to Mandela, what is wrong with South Africa? What needs to be done?

4. What are Mandela's goals for South Africa? Are his goals realistic or idealistic? Or both?

Source: Slightly adapted from Nelson Mandela, *No Easy Walk to Freedom: Articles, Speeches and Trial Addresses* (London: Heinemann, 1973), pp. 163, 179–185, 187–189.

35

The Changing Lives of
Third World Peoples

Women in the west African country of Burkina Faso handle industrial waste as part of their work. *(Source: Sipa Press)*

After the Second World War everyday life in the emerging nations of Asia and Africa changed dramatically as many peoples struggled to overcome the legacy of imperialism and build effective nation-states. Some of the changes paralleled the experiences of Europe and North America: science and modern technology altered individuals' lives in countless ways, and efforts to raise the standard of living by means of industrialization profoundly affected relations among social classes. Most observers, however, stressed the differences in development between the emerging nations and the industrialized nations. The new nations—along with the older states of Latin America—suffered widespread poverty and had a heritage of foreign domination, and life there remained very hard. Many observers discerned a widening economic gap between the industrialized nations of Europe and North America on the one hand and most of the emerging nations on the other. Some writers even argued that the gap between North and South—that is, between rich nations and poor nations—had replaced the cold war between East and West and its immediate aftermath as humankind's most explosive division.

This chapter concentrates on shared problems of development and everyday life in Asia, Africa, and Latin America—a vast geographical expanse commonly known as the Third World.

- How have the emerging nations of the Third World sought to escape from poverty, and what have been the results of their efforts?
- What has caused the prodigious growth of cities in the Third World, and what does their growth mean for their inhabitants?
- How have thinkers and artists from the Third World interpreted the modern world and the experiences of their peoples before, during, and after foreign domination?

These three questions guide the investigation.

 ## DEFINING THE THIRD WORLD

Since the late 1950s many scholars, journalists, and politicians have viewed Africa, Asia, and Latin America as a single entity—the "Third World." Is this label valid and useful? Some experts prefer to speak of these regions as containing the "emerging nations" or the "less-developed countries"—deliberately vague terms suggesting a spectrum of conditions ranging from near-hopeless poverty to moderate well-being. Other experts increasingly add a "Fourth" and even a "Fifth World" in recognition of the growing diversity among the less-developed nations in recent years. Nevertheless, for a long generation the countries commonly termed "Third World" have shared characteristics that have joined them together and created a Third World consciousness and ideology. There are several reasons for this important development.

First, virtually all the countries of Africa, Asia, and even Latin America experienced political or economic domination, nationalist reaction, and a struggle for genuine independence. This shared past gave rise to a common consciousness and a widespread feeling of having been oppressed and victimized in dealings with Europe and North America. A variety of nationalists, Marxists, and anti-imperialist intellectuals has nurtured this outlook arguing forcibly that the Third World's problems are the result of past and present exploitation the wealthy capitalist nations. Precisely because of their shared sense of past injustice, many influential Latin Americans have identified with the Third World, despite their countries' greater affluence. The term also came into global use in the cold war era as a handy way of distinguishing Africa, Asia, and Latin America from the "First" and "Second Worlds"—the capitalist and communist industrialized nations, respectively.

Second, in the 1950s and 1960s a large majority of men and women in most Third World countries lived in the countryside and depended on agriculture for a living. Agricultural goods and raw materials are still the primary exports of many Third World countries. In Europe, North America, and Japan, by contrast, most people live in cities and depend mainly on industry and urban services for employment.

Finally, the agricultural countries of Asia, Africa, and most of Latin America were united by awareness of their common poverty. By no means was everyone in the Third World poor; some people were quite wealthy. The average standard of living, however, was low, especially compared with that of people in the wealthy industrial nations, and massive poverty was ever present.

Coal Miner Families in India   With their tools and many of their possessions loaded on their rickety carts, these workers struggle with steep grades and grinding poverty. The hardships of life in the Third World weigh heavily on these people. *(Source: Sebastiao Salgado/Magnum Photos)*

ECONOMIC AND SOCIAL CHALLENGES IN THE THIRD WORLD

As the Third World confronted the tough postindependence task of preserving political unity and building cohesive nation-states, the enormous challenges of poverty, malnutrition, and disease weighed especially heavily on rural people. In the 1950s and 1960s most Third World leaders and their advisers saw rapid industrialization and "modernization" as the answer to rural poverty and disease. Industrialization and modernization also kindled popular enthusiasm and thus served nation building, which in turn promised economic self-sufficiency and cultural renewal. For these reasons, the leaders and peoples of the Third World in the 1950s and 1960s set themselves the massive task of building modern factories, roads, and public health services like those of Europe and North America. Their considerable success fueled rapid economic progress.

Yet social problems, complicated by surging population growth, almost dwarfed the accomplishment. Disappointments multiplied. By and large, the poorest rural people in the poorest countries gained the least from industrialization, and industrial expansion provided jobs for only a small segment even of the urban population. By the late 1960s, widespread dissatisfaction with policies of all-out industrialization prompted a greater emphasis on rural development.

Poverty

It was easy to lose sight of the true dimensions of poverty in the Third World in a fog of economic statistics. In the 1950s and 1960s the United Nations and the emerging nations began collecting national income statistics. Dividing those estimates by total population yields a nation's average per capita income. These figures received enormous attention because they were stunningly low compared with those of wealthy nations. In 1960, for example, average annual income per person in all of Africa and Southeast Asia was about $100. In North America it was $2,500—twenty-five times more. Journalists, politicians, and scholars using such figures often concluded that Third World people were unspeakably poor and verging on mass starvation.

Such comparisons, however, exaggerated the economic gap between the North and the South because income data on poor countries were incomplete and usually did not include some productive activities. Simplistic comparisons also failed to adjust for the fact that basic necessities cost considerably less in poor countries than in rich countries. Still, the gap in *real income*—income adjusted for differences in prices—between the industrialized world and the former colonies and dependencies of Africa, Asia, and Latin America was truly enormous. According to a leading historian, in 1950, when war-scarred Europe was in the early phase of postwar reconstruction,

the real income per capita of the Third World was five or six times lower than that of the developed countries. . . . In the developed countries, a century and a half of Industrial Revolution had resulted in a multiplication by more than five of the average standard of living in 1950. . . . For the average Third World countries the 1950s level was practically that of 1800 or, at best, only 10–20 percent above.[1]

A deeper understanding arises from considering Third World poverty not just in statistical terms but also in human terms, as did the postwar generation of nationalist leaders. To them, poverty meant, above all, not having enough to eat. For millions, hunger and malnutrition were harsh facts of life. In India, Ethiopia, Bolivia, and other extremely poor countries, the average adult ate fewer than 2,000 calories a day—only 85 percent of the minimal requirement. Although many poor countries fared better, in the 1960s none but Argentina could match the 3,000 or more calories consumed in the more fortunate North. Even Third World people who consumed enough calories often suffered from the effects of unbalanced high-starch diets and inadequate protein. Severe protein deficiency stunts the brain as well as the body, and

many of the poorest children grew up mentally retarded.

Poor housing—crowded, often damp, and exposed to the elements—also contributed significantly to the less-developed world's high incidence of chronic ill health. So too did scanty education and lack of the fundamentals of modern public health: adequate and safe water, sewage disposal, immunizations, prenatal care, and control of communicable diseases. Village women around the world spent much of each day carrying water and searching for firewood or dung to use as fuel, as they must still do in many countries. Infant mortality was savage, and chronic illness weakened and demoralized many adults, making them unfit for the hard labor that their lives required.

Generally speaking, health status in Asia and Latin America was better than in the new states of sub-Saharan Africa. As one authority described the situation in the early 1960s:

In the African social drama, sickness has a strong claim to being archvillain. . . . In tropical Africa, most men, women, and children are habitually unwell. Many are unwell from the day of their birth to the day of their death. . . . Most of the sick are sick of more than one disease.[2]

The people of poor countries were overwhelmingly concentrated in the countryside as small farmers and landless laborers. Mass poverty represented an awesome challenge to the postwar leaders of the newly emerging nations. Having raised peoples' hopes in the struggle for freedom, they had to start delivering on their promises if they were to maintain trust and stay in power. A strong commitment to modern economic and social development, already present in parts of Latin America in the 1930s, took hold in Asia and Africa in the postwar era.

The Medical Revolution and the Population Explosion

The most thoroughgoing success achieved by the Third World after the Second World War was a spectacular medical revolution. Immediately after winning independence, the governments of emerging nations began adopting modern methods of immunology and public health. These methods were often simple and inexpensive but extremely effective. One famous measure was spraying DDT in Southeast Asia to control mosquitoes bearing malaria, one of the deadliest and most debilitating tropical diseases. In Sri Lanka (formerly Ceylon), DDT spraying halved the yearly toll of deaths in the very first postwar decade—at a modest cost of $2 per person. According to the United Nations' World Health Organization, which helped provide medical expertise to the new states, deaths from smallpox, cholera, and plague declined by more than 95 percent worldwide between 1951 and 1966.

Asian and African countries increased the small numbers of hospitals, doctors, and nurses that they had inherited from the colonial past. Sophisticated medical facilities became symbols of the commitment to a better life. Some critics, however, maintained that expensive medical technology was an indulgence that Third World countries could not afford, for it was ill suited to the pressing health problems of most of the population. Such criticism eventually prompted greater emphasis on delivering medical services to the countryside. Local people were successfully trained as paramedics to staff rural outpatient clinics that offered medical treatment, health education, and prenatal and postnatal care. Many paramedics were women: many health problems involved childbirth and infancy, and villagers the world over considered it improper for a male to examine a woman's body.

The medical revolution significantly lowered death rates and lengthened life expectancy. In particular, children became increasingly likely to survive their early years, though infant and juvenile mortality remained far higher in the Third World

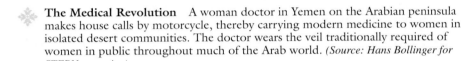 **The Medical Revolution**   A woman doctor in Yemen on the Arabian peninsula makes house calls by motorcycle, thereby carrying modern medicine to women in isolated desert communities. The doctor wears the veil traditionally required of women in public throughout much of the Arab world. *(Source: Hans Bollinger for STERN magazine)*

Improving Public Health This poster from the early 1970s urges Chinese children to kill as many flies as possible in order to help the authorities prevent the spread of infectious diseases. Mass campaigns to improve public health played a major role in reducing mortality in the Third World. *(Source: From Eileen Hsü-Balzer, Richard Balzer, Francis L. K. Hsü,* China Day by Day. *Reproduced with permission.)*

than in rich countries. By 1980 the average inhabitant of the Third World could expect at birth to live about 54 years; life expectancy varied from 40 to 64 years depending on the country. In developed countries, by contrast, life expectancy at birth averaged 71 years.

A less favorable consequence of the medical revolution was the acceleration of population growth. As in Europe during the nineteenth century, a rapid decline in the death rate was not immediately accompanied by a similar decline in the birthrate. Third World women continued to bear from five to seven children, as their mothers and grandmothers had done. The combined populations of Asia, Africa, and Latin America, which had grown relatively modestly from 1925 to 1950, increased between 1950 and 1975 from 1,750 million to 3,000 million (Map 35.1). Barring catastrophe, experts predicted that the population of the three continents would surge to 5,200 million in the year 2000—an unprecedented explosion.

The population explosion aroused fears of approaching famine and starvation. Thomas Malthus's gloomy late-eighteenth-century conclusion that population always tends to grow faster than the food supply (see page 786) was revived and updated by "neo-Malthusian" social scientists. Such fears were exaggerated, but they did produce uneasiness in the Third World, where leaders saw that their countries had to run fast just to maintain already low standards of living.

Some governments began pushing family planning and birth control to slow population growth. These measures were not very successful in the 1950s and 1960s. In many countries, Islamic and Catholic religious teachings were hostile to birth control. Moreover, widespread cultural attitudes dictated that a real man keep his wife pregnant. There were also economic reasons for preferring large families. Farmers needed the help of plenty of children at planting and harvest times. And sons and daughters were a sort of social security system for their elders; thus a prudent couple wanted several children because some would surely die young.

The Race to Industrialize (1950–1970)

Throughout the 1950s and most of the 1960s, many key Third World leaders, pressed on by their European, American, and Soviet advisers, were convinced that all-out industrialization was the only answer to poverty and population growth. The masses, they concluded, were poor because they were imprisoned in a primitive, inefficient agricultural economy. Only modern factory industry appeared capable of creating wealth quickly enough to outrace the growth of numbers.

The two-century experience of the West, Japan, and the Soviet Union seemed to validate this faith in industrialization. To Third World elites economic history taught the encouraging lesson that the wealthy countries had also been agricultural and "underdeveloped" until the Industrial Revolution had lifted them out of poverty, one by one. According to this view, the uneven progress of industrialization was primarily responsible for the great income gap that existed between the rich

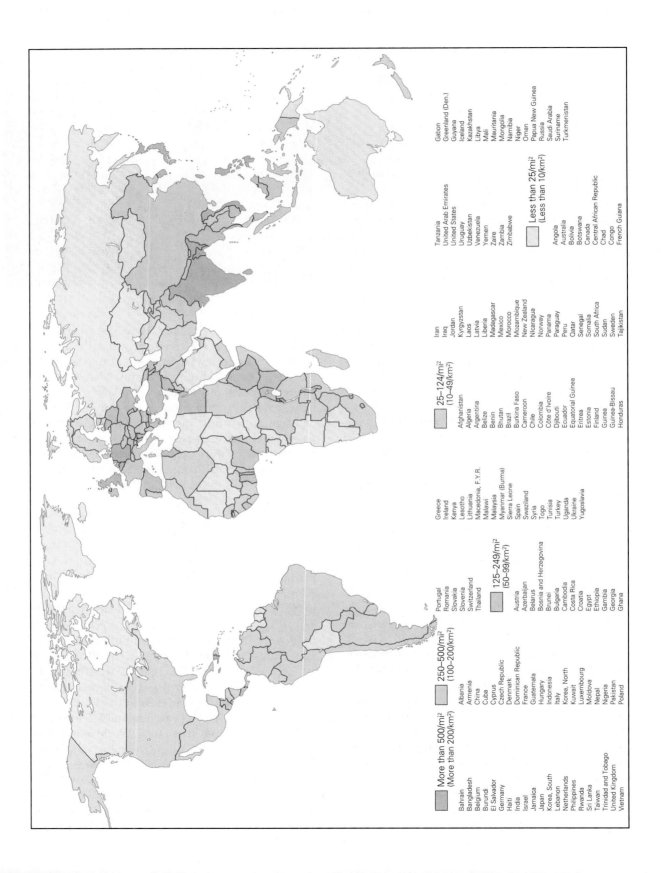

Population density (people per square mile / square kilometer)

More than 500/mi² (More than 200/km²)
Bahrain, Bangladesh, Belgium, Burundi, El Salvador, Germany, Haiti, India, Jamaica, Japan, Korea, South, Lebanon, Netherlands, Philippines, Rwanda, Sri Lanka, Taiwan, Trinidad and Tobago, United Kingdom, Vietnam

250–500/mi² (100–200/km²)
Albania, Armenia, China, Cuba, Cyprus, Czech Republic, Denmark, Dominican Republic, France, Guatemala, Hungary, Indonesia, Italy, Korea, North, Kuwait, Luxembourg, Moldova, Nepal, Nigeria, Pakistan, Poland, Portugal, Romania, Slovakia, Slovenia, Switzerland, Thailand

125–249/mi² (50–99/km²)
Austria, Azerbaijan, Belarus, Bosnia and Herzegovina, Brunei, Bulgaria, Cambodia, Costa Rica, Croatia, Egypt, Ethiopia, Gambia, Georgia, Ghana, Greece, Ireland, Kenya, Lesotho, Lithuania, Macedonia, F. Y. R., Malawi, Malaysia, Myanmar (Burma), Sierra Leone, Spain, Swaziland, Syria, Togo, Tunisia, Turkey, Uganda, Ukraine, Yugoslavia

25–124/mi² (10–49/km²)
Afghanistan, Algeria, Argentina, Belize, Benin, Bhutan, Brazil, Burkina Faso, Cameroon, Chile, Colombia, Côte d'Ivoire, Djibouti, Ecuador, Equatorial Guinea, Eritrea, Estonia, Finland, Guinea, Guinea-Bissau, Honduras, Iran, Iraq, Jordan, Kyrgyzstan, Laos, Latvia, Liberia, Madagascar, Mexico, Morocco, Mozambique, Nicaragua, New Zealand, Norway, Panama, Paraguay, Peru, Qatar, Senegal, Somalia, South Africa, Sudan, Sweden, Tajikistan, Tanzania, United Arab Emirates, United States, Uruguay, Uzbekistan, Venezuela, Yemen, Zaire, Zambia, Zimbabwe

Less than 25/mi² (Less than 10/km²)
Angola, Australia, Bolivia, Botswana, Canada, Central African Republic, Chad, Congo, French Guiana, Gabon, Greenland (Den.), Guyana, Iceland, Kazakhstan, Libya, Mali, Mauritania, Mongolia, Namibia, Niger, Oman, Papua New Guinea, Russia, Saudi Arabia, Suriname, Turkmenistan

countries and the poor countries of the postindependence Third World.

Theories of modernization, which were particularly popular in the 1960s, also assumed that all countries were following the path already taken by the industrialized nations and that the task of the elite was to speed the trip. Marxism, with its industrial and urban bias, preached a similar gospel. These ideas reinforced the Third World's desire to industrialize.

Nationalist leaders believed that successful industrialization required state action and enterprise. Many were impressed by socialism in general and by Stalin's forced industrialization in particular, which they saw as having won the Soviet Union international power and prominence, whatever its social costs. In Asia and Africa, furthermore, capitalists and private enterprise were often equated with the old rulers and colonial servitude. The reasoning was practical as well as ideological: socialism meant an expansion of steady government jobs for political and ethnic allies, and modern industry meant ports, roads, schools, and hospitals, as well as factories. Only the state could afford such expensive investments. With the exception of the People's Republic of China, however, the new governments recognized private property and also tolerated native (and foreign) businessmen. The "mixed economy"—part socialist, part capitalist—became the general rule in the Third World.

Political leaders concentrated state investment in big, highly visible projects that proclaimed the country's independence and stimulated national pride. Enormous dams for irrigation and hydroelectric power were favored undertakings. Nasser's stupendous Aswan Dam harnessed the Nile, demonstrating that modern Egyptians could surpass even the pyramids of their ancient ancestors. The gigantic state-owned steel mill was another favorite project. These big projects testified to the prevailing faith in expensive advanced technology and modernization along European lines.

Nationalist leaders and their economic experts measured overall success by how fast national income grew, and they tended to assume that social problems and income distribution would take care of themselves. India, the world's most popu-

lous noncommunist country, exemplified the general trends. After India achieved independence in 1947, Mahatma Gandhi's special brand of nationalism was redirected toward economic and social rebirth through state enterprise and planning. Jawaharlal Nehru and many Congress party leaders believed that unregulated capitalism and free trade under British rule had deepened Indian poverty. Considering themselves democratic socialists, they introduced five-year plans, built state-owned factories and steel mills, and raised tariffs to protect Indian manufacturers. Quite typically, they neglected agriculture, land reform, and village life.

The Third World's first great industrialization drive was in many ways a success. Industry grew faster than ever before, though from an admittedly low base in Africa and most of Asia. According to the United Nations, industry in the noncommunist developing nations grew at more than 7 percent per year between 1950 and 1970, which meant a per capita rate of about 4.5 percent per year. This was very solid industrial growth by historical standards. It matched the fastest rates of industrialization in the United States before 1914 and was double the rate of Britain and France in the same years.

Industrial expansion stimulated the other sectors of Third World economies. National income per capita grew about 2.5 percent per year in the booming world economy of the 1950s and 1960s. This pace was far superior to the very modest increases that had occurred under colonial domination between 1900 and 1950. Future historians may well see the era after political emancipation as the era of industrial revolution in Asia and Africa. This was certainly the case for a few small Asian countries that downgraded government control and emphasized private enterprise and the export of manufactured goods. South Korea, Taiwan, the city-state of Singapore, and the British colony of Hong Kong were genuine "economic miracles," rapidly industrializing and remarkably improving the living standards of ordinary people.

Nevertheless, by the late 1960s, disillusionment with the Third World's relatively rapid industrialization was spreading, for several reasons. In the first place, the experience of a few small states like South Korea and Taiwan was the exception. The countries of Asia, Africa, and Latin America did not as a whole match the "miraculous" concurrent advances of western Europe and Japan, and the

MAP 35.1 World Population Density

Building the Aswan Dam   Financed and engineered by the Soviet Union, the massive high dam at Aswan was Nasser's dream for Egypt's economic future. Here an army of workers lay the stones that will harness the Nile for irrigation and hydro-electric power. (*Source: Popperfoto*)

great economic gap between the rich and the poor nations continued to widen.

Also, most Third World leaders had genuinely believed that rapid industrial development would help the rural masses. Yet careful studies were showing that the main beneficiaries of industrialization were businessmen, bureaucrats, skilled workers, and urban professionals. Peasants and agricultural laborers gained little or nothing. It was estimated that about 40 percent of the population in fast-growing, dynamic Mexico, for instance, was completely excluded from the benefits of industrialization. Moreover, the very poorest countries—such as India and Indonesia in Asia, and Ethiopia

and the Sudan in Africa—were growing most slowly in per capita terms. The industrialization prescription appeared least effective where poverty was most intense. Economic dislocations after 1973, and especially the worldwide economic crisis of the early 1980s, accentuated this trend, visiting particularly devastating effects on the poorest countries.

Perhaps most serious, industrialization failed to provide the sheer number of jobs needed for the sons and daughters of the population explosion. Statisticians estimated that the growth of Third World manufacturing between 1950 and 1970 provided jobs for only about one-fifth of the 200 million young men and women who entered the exploding labor force in the same period. For the foreseeable future, most Third World people would have to remain on the farm or work in traditional handicrafts and service occupations. All-out modern industrialization had failed as a panacea.

Agriculture and Village Life

From the late 1960s onward, the limitations of industrial development forced Third World governments to take a renewed interest in rural people and village life. At best, this attention meant giving agriculture its due and coordinating rural development with industrialization and urbanization. At worst, especially in the very poorest countries, it deflated the optimistic vision of living standards approaching those of the wealthy North and led to the pessimistic conclusion that it was possible to ease only modestly the great hardships.

Nationalist elites had neglected agriculture in the 1950s and the 1960s for various reasons. They regarded an agricultural economy as a mark of colonial servitude, which they were symbolically repudiating by embracing industrialization. They wanted to squeeze agriculture and peasant producers in order to provide capital for industry. Thus governments often established artificially low food prices, which also subsidized their volatile urban supporters at the expense of the farmers.

In addition, the obstacles to more productive farming seemed overwhelming to unsympathetic urban elites and condescending foreign experts:

Peasants Farming in Ecuador Cultivating the land with simple hand tools, these peasant women in Latin America appear doomed to poverty despite backbreaking labor. In many cases, a high rent to an absentee landlord reduces the peasants' income still further. *(Source: Bernard Pierre Wolff/Photo Researchers)*

farms were too small and fragmented for mechanization, peasants were too stubborn and ignorant to change their ways, and so on. Little wonder that only big farmers and some plantations received much government support. Wherever large estates and absentee landlords predominated—in large parts of Asia and in most of Latin America, excluding Mexico, though not in sub-Saharan Africa—landless laborers and poor peasants who had no other choice than to rent land simply lacked the incentive to work harder. Any increased profits from larger crops went mainly to the absentee landowners.

Most honest observers were convinced that improved farm performance required land reform. Yet ever since the French Revolution, genuine land reform has been a profoundly radical measure, frequently bringing violence and civil war. Powerful landowners and their allies generally succeeded in blocking or subverting redistribution of land to benefit the poor. Land reform, unlike industrialization, was generally too hot for most politicians to handle.

Third World governments also neglected agriculture because feeding the masses was deceptively easy in the 1950s and early 1960s. Very poor countries received food from the United States at giveaway prices as part of a U.S. effort to dispose of enormous grain surpluses and help American farmers. Before 1939, the countries of Asia, Africa, and Latin America had collectively produced more grain than they consumed. But after 1945, as their populations soared, they began importing ever-increasing quantities.

Crops might fail in poor countries, but starvation seemed a thing of the past. In 1965, when India was urged to build up its food reserves, one top Indian official expressed a widespread attitude: "Why should we bother? Our reserves are the wheat fields of Kansas."[3] In the short run, the Indian official was right. In 1966 and again in 1967, when the monsoon failed to deliver its life-giving rains to the Indo-Pakistan subcontinent and famine gripped the land, the United States gave India one-fifth of the U.S. wheat crop. More than 60 million Indians lived exclusively on American grain. The effort required a food armada of six hundred ships, the largest fleet assembled since the Normandy invasion of 1944. The famine was ultimately contained, and instead of millions of deaths there were only a few thousand.

That close brush with mass starvation sent a shiver down the world's spine. Complacency dissolved in the Third World, and prophecies of disaster multiplied in wealthy nations. Paul Ehrlich, an American scientist, envisioned a grisly future in his polemical 1968 bestseller *The Population Bomb:*

The battle to feed all of humanity is over. In the 1970s the world will undergo famines—hundreds of millions of people are going to starve to death in spite of any crash programs embarked upon now. At this stage nothing can prevent a substantial increase in the world death rate.[4]

Other Western commentators outdid each other with nightmare visions. One portrayed the earth as a crowded lifeboat in a sea of hungry poor who would have to drown in order not to swamp the lifeboat. Another vision compared truly poor countries like Bangladesh, Ethiopia, and Haiti to hopelessly wounded soldiers on a gory battlefield. Such victims were best left to die so that scarce resources could be concentrated on the "walking wounded" who might yet be saved. Such crude and brutal Social Darwinism made it easy for Third World intellectuals to believe the worst about the rich industrialized nations and their economies.

Countering such visions was technology. Plant scientists and agricultural research stations had already set out to develop new hybrid seeds genetically engineered to suit the growing conditions of tropical agriculture. Their model was extraordinarily productive hybrid corn developed for the American Midwest in the 1940s. The first breakthrough came in Mexico in the 1950s, when an American-led team developed new high-yielding dwarf wheats. These varieties enabled farmers to double their yields, though they demanded greater amounts of fertilizer and water for irrigation. Mexican wheat production soared. Thus began the transformation of Third World agriculture—the so-called Green Revolution.

In the 1960s an American-backed team of scientists in the Philippines turned their attention to rice, the Asian staff of life; they quickly developed a "miracle rice." The new hybrid required more fertilizer and water but yielded more and grew much faster. It permitted the revolutionary advent of year-round farming on irrigated land, making possible two, three, or even four crops a year. The brutal tropical sun of the hot dry season became an

Old and New   A fetish statue designed to frighten off evil spirits stands by as the proud owner of a two-acre plot in southern India shows a visiting expert his crop of miracle rice. As this picture suggests, the acceptance of modern technology does not necessarily require the repudiation of cultural traditions. *(Source: Marc and Evelyne Bernheim/Woodfin Camp & Associates)*

agricultural blessing for the first time. Asian scientists, financed by their governments, developed similar hybrids to meet local conditions.

Increases in grain production were rapid and dramatic in some Asian countries. In gigantic India, for example, farmers upped production more than 60 percent in fifteen years. By 1980, thousands of new grain bins dotted the countryside, symbols of the agricultural revolution in India and the country's new-found ability to feed all its people. China followed with its own highly successful version of the Green Revolution under Deng Xiaoping.

The Green Revolution offered new hope to the Third World but was no cure-all. At first most of its benefits seemed to flow to large landowners and substantial peasant farmers who could afford the necessary investments in irrigation and fertilizer. Subsequent experience in China and other Asian countries showed, however, that even peasant families with tiny farms could gain substantially. Indeed, the Green Revolution's greatest successes occurred in Asian countries with broad-based peasant ownership of land.

The technical revolution shared relatively few of its benefits with the poorest classes—landless laborers, tenant farmers, and tiny landholders. Lacking even the two or three acres necessary to feed themselves with intensive effort, the very poorest groups gained only slightly more regular employment from the Green Revolution's demand for more labor. Pakistan, the Philippines, and other countries with large numbers of landless peasants and insecure tenant farmers experienced less improvement than did countries like South Korea and Taiwan, where land was generally owned by peasants. This helps to explain why the Green Revolution failed to spread from Mexico throughout Latin America: as long as 3 or 4 percent of the rural population owned 60 to 80 percent of the land, as was still the case in many Latin American countries, the Green Revolution usually remained stillborn.

The same fatal equation of property ownership has prevailed in Bangladesh. There an elite tenth of the population owned half of the land, and the poorest half owned nothing at all. People ate less in the 1970s and 1980s, yet land reform remained a political and social minefield. One member of a big (fifty-acre) landowning family in Bangladesh told an American reporter in 1981: "They talk of removing property markers. It cannot happen. I will kill you if you move my property markers one inch."[5]

Sub-Saharan Africa benefited little from the new agricultural techniques, even though land reform was a serious problem only in white-ruled South Africa. Poor transportation, inadequate storage facilities, and low government-imposed agricultural prices must bear much of the blame. More generally, the climatic conditions of black Africa encouraged continued adherence to dry farming and root crops, whereas the Green Revolution has been almost synonymous with intensive irrigation and grain production.

The Green Revolution, like the medical revolution and industrialization, represented a large but uneven step forward for the Third World. Relatively few of its benefits flowed to the poorest groups. These poor, who lacked political influence and had no clear idea about what needed to be done, increasingly longed to escape from ill-paid, irregular work in somebody else's fields. For many of the bravest and most enterprising, life in a nearby town or city seemed a way out.

� THE GROWTH OF CITIES

The changing lives of Third World people were marked by violent contrasts, which were most striking in urban areas. Shiny airports, international hotels, and massive government buildings were built next to tar-paper slums. Like their counterparts in the North, these rapidly growing cities were monuments to political independence and ongoing industrial development. They were also testimonials to increasing population, limited opportunities in the countryside, and neocolonial influence. Runaway urban growth became a distinctive feature of the Third World.

Urbanization in the Third World

The cities of the Third World expanded at an astonishing pace after the Second World War. Many doubled and some even tripled in size in a single decade. The Algerian city of Algiers jumped from 300,000 to 900,000 between 1950 and 1960; Accra in Ghana, Lima in Peru, and Nairobi in Kenya grew just as fast. Moreover, rapid urban growth continued. The less-developed countries became far more thoroughly urbanized in recent times than most people realize. In Latin America, three out of four people lived in towns and cities by 1975; in Asia and Africa, as Table 35.1 shows, one in four lived in an urban area by the same year.

The urban explosion continued in the 1980s, so that by 1990 fully 60 percent of the planet's city dwellers lived in the cities of the Third World, according to United Nations estimates. Rapid Third World urbanization represented a tremendous historical change. As recently as 1920, three out of every four of the world's urban inhabitants were concentrated in Europe and North America.

In most Third World countries the largest cities grew fastest. Gigantic "super cities" of from 2 million to 10 million persons arose. The capital typically emerged as the all-powerful urban center, encompassing all the important elite groups and dwarfing smaller cities as well as villages. Mexico City, for example, grew from 3 million to 12 million people between 1950 and 1975, and it will probably reach 20 million in the year 2000. The pattern of a dominant megalopolis has continued to spread from Latin America to Africa and Asia (though not to Asia's giants, China and India).

In the truly poor countries of Africa and Asia, the process of urbanization is still in the early stages. However populous the cities, the countryside still holds the majority of the people. But if present trends continue, a city like Jakarta, the capital of Indonesia, will have about 15 million people by the end of this century. Calcutta and Bombay will be equally large. In the year 2000, the world will have twenty-six megalopolises with more than 10 million people, and twenty of them will be in Asia, Latin America, and Africa, according to World Bank estimates. Such rapid urbanization has posed enormous challenges for peoples and governments.

What caused this urban explosion? First, the general growth of population in the Third World was critical. Urban residents gained substantially

TABLE 35.1   URBAN POPULATION AS A PERCENTAGE OF TOTAL POPULATION IN THE WORLD AND IN EIGHT MAJOR AREAS, 1925–2025

Area	1925	1950	1975	2000 (est.)	2025 (est.)
World total	21	28	39	50	63
North America	54	64	77	86	93
Europe	48	55	67	79	88
Soviet Union	18	39	61	76	87
East Asia	10	15	30	46	63
Latin America	25	41	60	74	85
Africa	8	13	24	37	54
South Asia	9	15	23	35	51
Oceania	54	65	71	77	87

Little more than one-fifth of the world's population was urban in 1925. In 1990 the urban proportion in the world total was about 45 percent and, according to United Nations experts, it should reach one-half by the century's end and two-thirds by about 2025. The most rapid urban growth will come in Africa and Asia, where the move to cities is still in its early stages. (*Source: United Nations,* Concise Report on the World Population Situation in 1970–1975 and Its Long-Range Implications, *New York, 1974, p. 63.*)

from the medical revolution but only gradually began to reduce the size of their families. At the same time, the pressure of numbers in the countryside encouraged millions to set out for the nearest city. More than half of all urban growth has been due to rural migration.

Second, in the less-developed countries even more than in Europe and North America in the nineteenth century, great cities became the undisputed centers of industry. Half of all the industrial jobs in Mexico were concentrated in Mexico City in 1980. The same kind of extreme concentration of industry occurred in many Third World countries. Yet careful study leads scholars to play down industrialization as a cause of urban explosion. In the words of a leading authority:

After about 1930 a new phenomenon which might be termed "urbanization without industrialization" began to appear in the Third World. This phenomenon very rapidly acquired an inflationary character and in the early 1960s began to present most serious problems of urban employment and underemployment.[6]

In short, urban population grew much faster than industrial employment. It was a lucky migrant who found a real factory job.

Third, newcomers also streamed to the cities for nonindustrial employment. Many were pushed: they simply lacked enough land to survive. Large landowners found it more profitable to produce export crops, like sugar or coffee, for wealthy industrialized countries, and their increasingly mechanized operations provided few jobs for agricultural laborers. The push factor was particularly strong in Latin America, with its neocolonial pattern of large landowners and foreign companies exporting food and raw materials. More generally, much migration was seasonal or temporary. Many a young person left home for the city to work in construction or serve as a maid, expecting higher wages and steadier work in the city and planning to return shortly with a modest nest egg.

Finally, the magnetic attraction of Third World cities was more than economic. Their attraction rested on the services and opportunities they offered, as well as on changing attitudes and the urge to escape from the traditional restraints of village life. Most of the modern hospitals, secondary schools, and transportation systems in less-developed countries were in the cities. So were most banks, libraries, movie houses, and basic conveniences. Safe piped water and processed food were rare in rural areas, for instance, and village women by necessity spent much of their time carrying water and grinding grain.

The city held a special appeal for rural people who had been exposed to the seductive influence of modern education. In Africa, a European economist concluded that "the number of people who are prepared to go back to the land after more than three or four years in the classroom is infinitesimal."[7] One survey from the 1960s in the Ivory Coast found two out of three rural high school graduates planning to move to the city; only one in ten of the illiterates expressed the same intention. Africa was not unique in this. For the young and the ambitious, the allure of the city was the excitement and opportunity of modern life. The village took on the curse of boredom and failure.

Overcrowding and Shantytowns

Rapid population growth placed great pressure on existing urban social services, and in many Third World cities the local authorities could not keep up with demand. New neighborhoods often lacked running water, paved streets, electricity, and police and fire protection. As in the early days of Europe's industrialization, sanitation was minimal in poor sections of town. Outdoor toilets were shared by many. Raw sewage often ran in streets and streams.

Faced with a rising human tide, government officials and their well-to-do urban allies sometimes tried to restrict internal migration to preserve the cities. Particularly in Africa, politicians talked of sending newcomers "back to the land" in order to reduce urban unemployment, crime rates, conges-

tion, and environmental decline. In Africa as elsewhere, these antimigration efforts proved unsuccessful, and frustrated officials often threw up their hands in despair.

Surging population growth had particularly severe consequences for housing. As in western Europe in the early nineteenth century, overcrowding reached staggering proportions in a great many Third World cities. Old buildings were often divided and redivided until population density reached the absolute saturation point. Take, for example, this vivid description of an old inner-city area, Singapore's Chinatown, in the late 1950s:

Chinatown . . . consists almost entirely of two or three story shop-houses. These shop-houses, originally intended to house one or two families, have been divided by a maze of interior partitions into cubicles, the majority of which are without windows and in permanent semi-darkness. Most of these cubicles are about the size of two double beds, placed side by side. In one such cubicle—dark, confined, unsanitary, and without comfort—may live a family of seven or more persons. Many of them sleep on the floor, often under the bed. Their possessions are in boxes, placed on shelves to leave the floor free for sleeping. Their food . . . is kept in tiny cupboards, which hang from the rafters. Their clothes hang on the walls, or from racks.[8]

Makeshift squatter settlements were another manifestation of the urban housing problem. These shantytowns sprang up continuously, almost overnight, on the worst possible urban land—dismal mudflats, garbage dumps, railroad sidings, steep hills on the outskirts, even polluted waterfronts. Typically, a group of urban poor "invaded" unoccupied land and quickly threw up tents or huts. Often beaten off by the police, they invaded again and again until the authorities gave up and a new squatter beachhead had been secured.

Squatter shantytowns grew much faster than more conventional urban areas in most Third World cities. In the giant Brazilian city of Rio de Janeiro, for example, the population of the shantytowns grew four times faster than the population of the rest of the city in the 1950s and 1960s. As a result, the Third World's squatter settlements came to house up to two-fifths of the urban population. The proportion was particularly high in Asia. Such settlements had occasionally grown up in American

Shacks and Skyscrapers   This striking view of Bombay, India, has many counterparts in the Third World. Makeshift dwellings coexist with luxurious high-rise apartments, and the urban landscape expands rapidly as newcomers pour into the swollen city from rural areas. *(Source: Camera Press London/Globe Photos; Photographer, Alan Whicker)*

mining towns and in Europe, but never to the same extent as in Latin America, Asia, and Africa. The Third World created a new urban form.

The meaning of squatter housing has been hotly debated. For a long time "pessimists" stressed the miseries of squatter settlements—the lack of the most basic services, the pitiful one-room shacks, the hopelessness of disoriented migrants in a strange environment, the revolutionary discontent. Recently, in detailed case studies, "optimists" have stressed the vitality of what are seen as real neighborhoods whose resourceful residents often share common ethnic origins and kinship ties.

Moreover, the shantytowns themselves evolved, most notably in Latin America, where they have existed longest. There poor but enterprising inhabitants relied on self-help to improve their living conditions. With much sweat labor and a little

hard-earned cash, a family replaced its mud walls with concrete blocks and gradually built a real home. Or the community pressured the city to install a central water pump or build a school. Low-paid office workers in search of cheap housing sometimes moved in and continued the upgrading process.

Few members of squatter communities were particularly attracted to revolutionary doctrines, despite widespread fears (and hopes) to the contrary. Indeed, one observer described squatters' beliefs as resembling those of the classic small businessman:

These beliefs can be summed up in the familiar and accepted maxims: Work hard, save your money, trust only family members (and them not too much), outwit the state, vote conservatively if possible, but always in your own economic self-interest; educate your children for their future and as old-age insurance for yourself.[9]

Thus the optimists counseled politicians to abandon their hostility to squatter settlements and help them to help themselves. The rush to the city could not be stopped, they said. However bad life in the city was, it appeared relatively desirable to the millions of rural people who "voted with their feet." Since hard-pressed Third World governments could provide only a fraction of the urban masses with subsidized housing, they were urged to support the creativity of the "spontaneous settlement." However squalid such settlements appear, they are preferable to sleeping on sidewalks.

Rich and Poor

After the less-developed countries achieved political independence, massive inequality continued, with few exceptions, to be the reality of life. A monumental gap separated rich and poor. In about 1975 in most developing countries, the top 20 percent took more than 50 percent of all national income. At the other end of the scale, the poorest 60 percent received on average less than 30 percent of all income, and the poorest fifth got about 5 percent. Thus the average household in the top fifth of the population received about ten times as much monetary income as the average household in the bottom fifth in the 1970s. This situation did not change significantly in the 1980s.

Such differences have been the rule in human history. The distribution of income in the Third World strongly resembled that of Europe prior to the First World War, before the movement toward greater equality accelerated sharply (see page 849). It is noteworthy that types of economy—rightist or leftist, capitalist or socialist—have had limited effect on shares of income. For example, in the 1970s income inequality was almost as pronounced in Mexico with its progressive, even revolutionary, tradition as in Brazil with its rightist military rule.

Differences in wealth and well-being were most pronounced in the exploding towns and cities of the Third World. Few rich or even middle-class people lived in the countryside. Urban squatters may have been better off than landless rural laborers, but they were light-years away from the luxury of the urban elite. In Asia and Africa, the rich often moved into the luxurious sections previously reserved for colonial administrators and white businessmen. Particularly in Latin America, upper-class and upper-middle-class people built fine mansions in exclusive suburbs, where they lived behind high walls, with many servants, protected from intruders by armed guards and fierce dogs.

A lifestyle in the "modern" mold was almost the byword of the Third World's urban elite. From French perfume and Scotch whiskey to electronic gadgets and the latest rock music, imported luxuries, especially automobiles, became the unmistakable signs of wealth and privilege. In Swahili-speaking East Africa, the common folk called the elite *wa Benzi,* "those who ride in a Mercedes-Benz." Even in Mao Zedong's relatively egalitarian China, the urban masses saved to buy bicycles while government officials rode in chauffeur-driven state-owned limousines.

Education also distinguished the wealthy from the masses. Young people from the elite often studied abroad at leading European and North American universities, or they monopolized openings in local universities. While absorbing the latest knowledge in a prestigious field like civil engineering or economics, they also absorbed foreign customs and values. They mastered the fluent English or French that is indispensable for many top-paying jobs, especially with international agencies and giant multinational corporations. Thus Third World elites often had more in common with the power brokers of the industrialized nations than with their own people, and they seemed willing tools of neocolonial penetration.

The middle classes of the Third World generally remained small relative to the total population. White-collar workers and government bureaucrats joined the traditional ranks of merchants and professionals in the urban middle class. Their salaries, though modest, were wonderfully secure and usually carried valuable fringe benefits. Unlike recent migrants and the rural poor, white-collar workers often received ration cards entitling them to cheap subsidized food.

An unexpected component of the urban middle classes was the modern factory proletariat, a privileged segment of the population in many poor countries. Few in number because sophisticated machines require few workers relative to agriculture or traditional crafts, they received high wages for their skilled work. On the Caribbean island of Jamaica in the late 1960s, for example, aluminum workers in big, modern American-owned plants earned from $60 to $65 a week. Meanwhile, cane cutters on sugar plantations earned $3 a week, and many laborers on small farms earned only $1 a week. Little wonder that modern factory workers tended to be self-satisfied in the Third World.

The great majority, the urban poor, earned precarious livings in a modern yet traditional "bazaar economy"—an economy of petty trades and unskilled labor. Here regular salaried jobs were rare and highly prized, and a complex world of tiny, unregulated businesses and service occupations predominated.

As in industrializing countries a century ago, irregular armies of peddlers and pushcart operators hawked their wares and squeezed a living from commerce. West African market women, with their colorful dresses and overflowing baskets, provided a classic example of this pattern. Sweatshops and home-based workers manufactured cheap goods for popular consumption. Maids, prostitutes, small-time crooks, and unemployed former students sold all kinds of services. This old-yet-new bazaar economy continued to grow prodigiously as migrants streamed to the cities, as modern industry provided few jobs, and as the wide gap between rich and poor persisted.

Migration and the Family

Large-scale urban migration had a massive impact on traditional family patterns in the Third World. Particularly in Africa and Asia, the great majority of migrants to the city were young men, married and unmarried; women tended to stay in the villages. The result was a sexual imbalance in both places. There were several reasons for this pattern. Much of the movement to cities (and mines) remained

A Sleek Automobile The most ambitious of these four boys in an African village may already dream of acquiring power and wealth in the city. (*Source: Marc and Evelyne Bernheim/Woodfin Camp & Associates*)

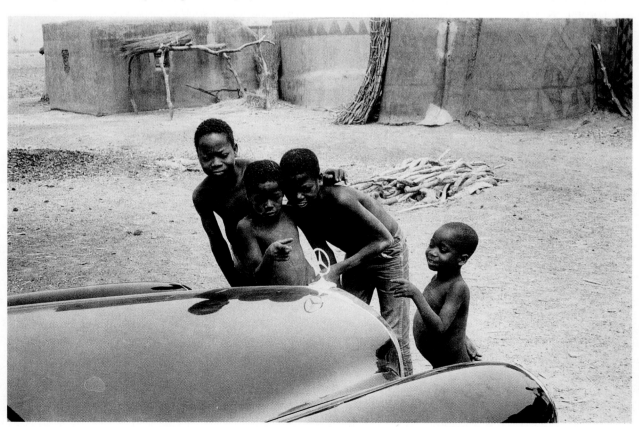

temporary or seasonal. At least at first, young men left home to earn hard cash to bring back to their villages. Moreover, the cities were expensive, and prospects there were uncertain. Only after a man secured a genuine foothold did he become married or send for his wife and children.

Kinship and village ties helped ease the rigors of temporary migration. Often a young man could go to the city rather easily because his family had close ties with friends and relatives there. Many city neighborhoods were urban versions of their residents' original villages. Networks of friendship and mutual aid helped young men (and some women, especially brides) move back and forth without being overwhelmed.

For rural women, the consequences of male out-migration were mixed. Asian and African women had long been treated as subordinates, if not inferiors, by their fathers and husbands (see Listening to the Past). Rather suddenly, such women found themselves heads of households, faced with managing the farm, feeding the children, and running their own lives. In the east African country of Kenya, for instance, one-third of all rural households were headed by women in the late 1970s.

African and Asian village women had to become unprecedentedly self-reliant and independent. The real beginnings of more equal rights and opportunities, of women's liberation, became readily visible in Africa and Asia. But the price was high and progress uneven. Rural women often had only their children to help in the endless, backbreaking labor. And their husbands, when they returned, often expected their wives to revert to the old subordination.

In economically more advanced Latin America, the pattern of migration was different. Whole families migrated, very often to squatter settlements, much more commonly than in Asia and Africa. These families frequently belonged to the class of landless laborers, which was generally larger in Latin America than in Africa or even Asia. Migration was also more likely to be once-and-for-all. Another difference was that single women were as likely as single men to move to the city. The situation in Mexico in the late 1970s was typical:

They [women] leave the village seeking employment, often as domestic servants. When they do not find work in the cities, they have few alternatives. If they are young, they frequently turn to prostitution; if not, they often resort to begging in the streets. Homeless peasant women, often carrying small children, roam every quarter of Mexico City.[10]

Some women also left to escape the narrow, male-dominated villages. Even so, in Latin America urban migration seemed to have less impact on traditional family patterns and on women's attitudes than it did in Asia and Africa. This helps explain why the women's movement lagged in Latin America.

Developments Since 1980

The urban explosion promoted diversity within the Third World. This growing diversity had several aspects. First, in addition to the uneven impact of urban migration on women, the transformation of modest cities into gigantic agglomerations sharpened the contrast between life in urban and rural areas. This difference in life experiences made individual Third World countries and their citizens less homogeneous. Second, ongoing urbanization diversified further the class structure in those countries achieving solid economic growth, expanding especially the middle classes. Third, the growth of middle-income people was itself very uneven in the Third World. It depended primarily on economic performance, which has varied greatly by country and region since the world recession of the early 1980s.

Momentous economic changes occurred in East Asia. The breathtaking industrial progress that characterized first Japan and then the "Four Dragons"—Taiwan, Hong Kong, Singapore, and South Korea—was replicated in China in the 1980s and the early 1990s. After Deng Xiaoping took over in 1978 and launched economic reforms (see page 1136), the Chinese economy grew through 1993 at an average annual rate of about 9 percent. Per capita income in China was doubling every ten years, a rate three to five times faster than the rate in successfully industrializing countries like the United States and Britain before 1914. According to the World Bank, the number of very poor people in China declined by 60 percent after 1978. The spectacular economic surge of almost one-fourth of the human race helped to vitalize all of East Asia. Among big countries, first Indonesia and then India did fairly well; Malaysia and Thai-

✳ **The World's Largest McDonald's**   The remarkable success of the Beijing McDonald's, shown here, illustrates how rapidly China has been urbanizing and industrializing since 1980. China is moving swiftly in the direction of a consumer society. *(Source: Mu Zhou/Sipa Press)*

land led the smaller countries. A vibrant, independent East Asia emerged as the world's economic pacesetter, an event of enormous significance in long-term historical perspective.

One key to China's success was the example of South Korea and Taiwan, which showed the way in the postwar years. Both South Korea and Taiwan were typical underdeveloped countries after the Second World War—poor, small, agricultural, densely populated, and lacking in natural resources. They had also suffered from Japanese imperialism, yet they managed to make good. How was this possible?

Radical land reform drew the mass of small farmers into a competitive market economy, which proved an excellent school of self-reliance and initiative. As in Japan, probusiness governments in South Korea and Taiwan cooperated with capitalists and helped keep wages low. These governments protected their own farmers and industrialists from foreign competition while also securing almost free access to the large American market.

And like Japan, both countries succeeded in preserving many fundamentals of their interrelated Korean and Chinese cultures even as they accepted and mastered Western technology. Tough nationalist leaders maintained political stability at the expense of genuine political democracy.

When China turned toward the market in 1979, it could also build on the national unity and radical land distribution inherited from Mao. Introducing economic reforms gradually, China also drew on the business talent of wealthy "overseas" Chinese in Hong Kong and Taiwan. They knew the world, needed cheap labor, and played a key role in the emerging "Greater China." Harsh authoritarian political rule encouraged China's people to focus on "daring to be rich," as Deng advised them.

No other region of the Third World (or Europe or North America) came close to matching East Asia after 1980. Latin America revealed some bright spots, most notably in Brazil and Argentina. But West Asia and North Africa, wracked by war, political instability, and low oil prices, experienced spiraling urbanization without much new industrialization or economic development. The situation in sub-Saharan Africa was particularly grave. Severe famines, bitter ethnic conflicts, and low prices for African exports weighed heavily on the vast region, vivid testimony to growing diversity in the Third World.

✦ MASS CULTURE AND CONTEMPORARY THOUGHT

Ideas and beliefs continued to change dramatically in the Third World after independence. Education fostered new attitudes, and mass communications relentlessly spread the sounds and viewpoints of modern life. Third World intellectuals, in their search for the meanings of their countries' experiences, articulated a wide spectrum of independent opinion in keeping with growing regional and national diversity.

Education and Mass Communications

In their efforts to modernize and better their societies, Third World leaders became increasingly convinced of the critical importance of education. They realized that "human capital"—skilled and educated workers, managers, and citizens—played a critical role in the development process. Faith in education and "book learning" spread surprisingly rapidly to the Third World's masses, for whom education principally meant jobs (see Listening to the Past). Thus young people in the Third World headed for schools and universities in unprecedented numbers. There still remained, however, a wide education gap with the rich countries, where more than 90 percent of both sexes attended school through age seventeen.

Moreover, the quality of education in the Third World was often mediocre. African and Asian universities tended to retain the old colonial values, stressing law and liberal arts at the expense of technical and vocational training. As a result, many poor countries found themselves with large numbers of unemployed or underemployed liberal-arts graduates. These "generalists" competed for scarce jobs in the already bloated government bureaucracies while less prestigious technical jobs went begging.

A related problem was the Third World's "brain drain": many gifted students in vital fields like engineering and medicine ended up pursuing their careers in the rich countries of the developed world. For example, in the early 1980s, as many Indian-trained doctors practiced abroad, mainly in advanced countries, as served India's entire rural population of 480 million. The threat represented by the brain drain helped explain why the Third World's professional elite received high salaries even in very poor countries.

In recent years many observers have concluded that the education drive, like its forerunner the industrialization drive, served the rural masses poorly. It sometimes seemed that its greatest beneficiaries were schoolteachers, who profited from the elite status provided by a permanent government job. Instruction was often impractical and mind numbing. The children of farmers generally learned little about agriculture, animal raising, or practical mechanics. Instead, students often memorized passages from ancient literary works and religious texts and spewed back cut-and-dried answers. No wonder children stayed away from school in droves. Village schools succeeded best at identifying the exceptional pupils, who were then siphoned off to the city for further study and were lost forever to the village.

Whatever its shortcomings, formal education spread with another influential agent of popular instruction: mass communications. The transistor radio penetrated the most isolated hamlets of the Third World. Governments universally embraced radio broadcasting as a means of power, propaganda, and education. Relentlessly, the transistor radio propagated the outlook and attitudes of urban elites and in the process challenged old values.

The second communications revolution—the visual one—is now in the process of reaching rural people everywhere. Television is bringing the whole planet into the bars and meetinghouses of the world's villages. Experience elsewhere—in remote French villages, in Eskimo communities above the Arctic Circle—shows that television is having a profound, even revolutionary impact. At the very least the lure of the city continues to grow.

Interpreting the Experiences of the Emerging World

Popular education and mass communications compounded the influence of the Third World's writers and thinkers—its purveyors of explanations.

Some intellectuals meekly obeyed their employers, whether the ministry of information or a large newspaper. Others simply embellished or reiterated some received ideology like Marxism or free-market capitalism. But some Third World intellectuals led in the search for meanings and direction that has accompanied rapid social change and economic struggle.

Having come of age during and after the struggle for political emancipation, some Third World intellectuals argued that genuine independence and freedom from outside control required a total break with the former colonial powers and a total rejection of Western values. This was the message of Frantz Fanon (1925–1961) in his powerful study of colonial peoples, *The Wretched of the Earth* (1968).

Fanon, a French-trained black psychiatrist from the Caribbean island of Martinique, was assigned to a hospital in Algeria during the bloody war for Algerian independence. He quickly came to sympathize with the guerrillas and probed deeply into the psychology of colonial revolt. According to Fanon, decolonization is always a violent and totally consuming process whereby one "species" of men, the colonizers, is completely replaced by an absolutely different species—the colonized, the wretched of the earth. During decolonization the colonized masses mock colonial values, "insult them, and vomit them up," in a psychic purge.

Fanon believed that the battle for formal independence was only the first step. The former imperialists and their local collaborators—the "white men with black faces"—remained the enemy:

Education in an African Village   An instructor at an open-air school in Kenya teaches blue-shirted children from the Masai tribe to tell time. Basic literacy has risen substantially in Third World countries since they achieved independence. *(Source: Peter Carmichael/Aspect Picture Library)*

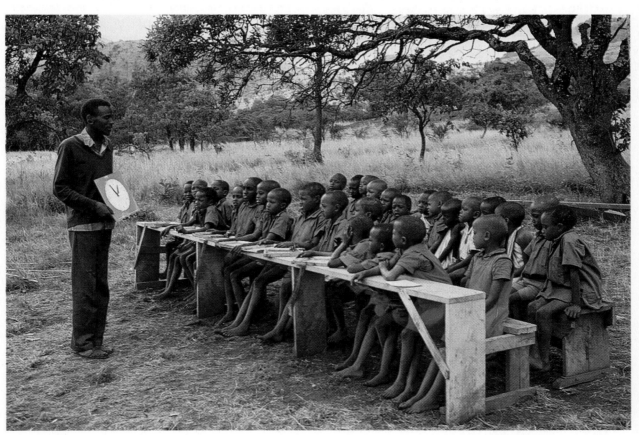

During the colonial period the people are called upon to fight against oppression; after national liberation, they are called upon to fight against poverty, illiteracy, and underdevelopment. The struggle, they say, goes on. The people realize that life is an unending contest.

. . . The apotheosis of independence is transformed into the curse of independence, and the colonial power through its immense resources of coercion condemns the young nation to regression. In plain words, the colonial power says: "Since you want independence, take it and starve."

. . . We are not blinded by the moral reparation of national independence; nor are we fed by it. The wealth of the imperial countries is our wealth too. . . . Europe is literally the creation of the Third World. The wealth which smothers her is that which was stolen from the underdeveloped peoples.[11]

For Fanon, independence and national solidarity went hand in hand with outrage at the misdeeds

❋ **A Proud Warrior of the Samburu tribe** This man personifies the precolonial values and dignified self-confidence that African writers like Chinua Achebe have celebrated in the postindependence era. One great political leader who was inspired by his African heritage was Nelson Mandela, the son of a chief. *(Source: From* Samburu: The Proud Warriors/*photo by Mohamed Amin. Reproduced by permission.)*

and moral posturings of the former colonial powers. Fanon's passionate, angry work became a sacred text for radicals attacking imperialism and struggling for liberation.

As independence was gained and nationalist governments were established, some later writers looked beyond wholesale rejection of the industrialized powers. They too were "anti-imperialist," but they saw colonial domination as only one chapter in the life of their people. Many of these writers were cultural nationalists who applied their talents to celebrating the rich histories and cultures of their people. At the same time, they did not hesitate to criticize their own leaders and fellow citizens, with whom they often disagreed.

The Nigerian writer Chinua Achebe (b. 1930) rendered these themes with acute insight and vivid specificity in his short, moving novels. Achebe wrote in English rather than his native Ibo tongue, but he wrote primarily for Africans, seeking to restore his people's self-confidence by reinterpreting the past. For Achebe, the "writer in a new nation" had first to embrace the "fundamental theme":

This theme—quite simply—is that the African people did not hear of culture for the first time from Europeans; that their societies were not mindless but frequently had a philosophy of great depth and volume and beauty, that they had poetry and above all, they had dignity. It is this dignity that many African peoples all but lost in the colonial period, and it is this that they must now regain. The worst thing that can happen to any people is the loss of their dignity and self-respect. The writer's duty is to help them regain it by showing what happened to them, what they lost.[12]

In *Things Fall Apart* (1959) Achebe achieves his goal by bringing vividly to life the men and women of an Ibo village at the beginning of the twentieth century, with all their virtues and frailties. The hero, Okonkwo, is a mighty wrestler and a hardworking, prosperous farmer, but he is stern and easily angered. Enraged at the failure of his people to reject newcomers, and especially at the white missionaries who convert his son to Christianity and provoke the slaying of the sacred python, Okonkwo kills a colonial messenger. When his act fails to spark a tribal revolt, he commits suicide. Okonkwo is destroyed by the general breakdown of tribal authority and his own intransigent recklessness. Woven into the story are the proverbs and

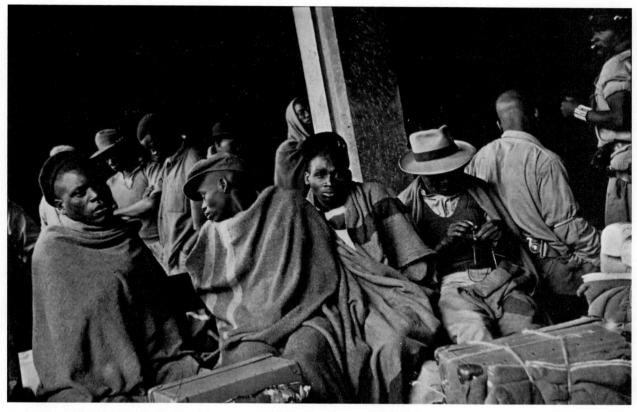

Nyassa Miners Going Home Photographed in 1952 as they waited patiently at a railway station near Johannesburg, these migrant workers have completed a year's contract in a South African gold mine and are returning home. Laden with presents for their families, these Africans are living through an era of enormous change. *(Source: David Goldblatt)*

wisdom of a sophisticated people and the beauty of a vanishing world.

In later novels, especially *A Man of the People* (1966), Achebe portrays the postindependence disillusionment of many Third World intellectuals. The villain is Chief The Honorable Nanga, a politician with the popular touch. This "man of the people" lives in luxury, takes bribes to build expensive apartment buildings for foreigners, and flimflams the voters with celebrations and empty words. The hero, an idealistic young schoolteacher, tries to unseat Chief Nanga, with disastrous results. Beaten up and hospitalized, the hero broods that the people "had become even more cynical than their leaders and were apathetic into the bargain."[13] Achebe's harsh but considered judgment reflected trends in many Third World nations in the 1960s

and 1970s: the rulers seemed increasingly corrupted by Western luxury and estranged from the rural masses, and idealistic intellectuals could only gnash their teeth in frustration.

The celebrated novelist V. S. Naipaul, born in Trinidad in 1932 of Indian parents, has also castigated Third World governments for corruption, ineptitude, and self-deception. Another of Naipaul's recurring themes is the poignant loneliness and homelessness of uprooted people. In *The Mimic Men* (1967), the blacks and whites and the Hindus and Chinese who populate the tiny Caribbean islands are all aliens, thrown together by "shipwreck." As one of the characters says:

It was my hope in writing to give expression to the restlessness, the deep disorder, which the great

*exploration, the overthrow in three continents of es-
tablished social organizations, the unnatural bringing
together of peoples who could achieve fulfillment only
within the security of their own societies and the landscapes hymned by their ancestors . . . has brought
about. The empires of our time were short-lived, but
they altered the world for ever; their passing away is
their least significant feature.*[14]

Naipaul and Achebe, like many other talented
Third World writers and intellectuals, probed
Third World experiences in pursuit of understanding and identity. A similar soul searching went on
in other creative fields, from art and dance to architecture and social science, and seemed to reflect
the intellectual maturity of genuine independence.

SUMMARY

As Third World leaders and peoples threw off foreign domination after 1945 and reasserted themselves in new or revitalized states, they turned increasingly inward to attack poverty and limited
economic development. The collective response
was an unparalleled medical revolution and the
Third World's first great industrialization drive.
Long-neglected agriculture also made progress,
and some countries experienced a veritable Green
Revolution. Moreover, rapid urbanization, expanding educational opportunities, and greater
rights for women were striking evidence of modernization and fundamental human progress. The
achievement was great.

But so was the challenge, and results fell far
short of aspirations. Deep and enduring rural
poverty, overcrowded cities, enormous class differences, and the sharp criticisms of leading Third
World writers mocked early hopes of quick solutions. Since the late 1960s there has been growing
dissatisfaction and frustration in Third World nations, lessened only slightly by the emergence of
China and East Asia as an economic powerhouse.
Thus, as the next chapter will examine, the belief
has grown that the Third World can meet the challenge only by reordering the global system and
dissolving the unequal ties that bind it to the rich
nations.

NOTES

1. P. Bairoch, *Economics and World History: Myths
   and Paradoxes* (Chicago: University of Chicago
   Press, 1993), p. 95.
2. P. J. McEwan and R. B. Sutcliffe, eds., *Modern
   Africa* (New York: Thomas Y. Crowell, 1965),
   p. 349.
3. Quoted in L. R. Brown, *Seeds of Change: The
   Green Revolution and Development in the 1970s*
   (New York: Praeger, 1970), p. 16.
4. P. Ehrlich, *The Population Bomb* (New York:
   Ballantine, 1968), p. 11.
5. *Wall Street Journal*, April 16, 1981, p. 17.
6. P. Bairoch, *The Economic Development of the
   Third World Since 1900* (London: Methuen,
   1975), p. 144.
7. R. Dumont, *False Start in Africa* (London: André Deutsch, 1966), p. 88.
8. B. Kaye, *Upper Nankin Street, Singapore: A Sociological Study of Households Living in a Densely
   Populated Area* (Singapore: University of Malaya
   Press, 1960), p. 2.
9. W. Mangin, "Latin American Squatter Settlements," *Latin American Research Review* 2
   (1967): 84–85.
10. P. Hudson, *Third World Women Speak Out: Inter-
    views in Six Countries on Change, Development,
    and Basic Needs* (New York: Praeger, 1979), p.
    11.
11. F. Fanon, *The Wretched of the Earth* (New York:
    Grove Press, 1968), pp. 43, 93–94, 97, 102.
12. C. Achebe, *Morning Yet on Creation Day* (Lon-
    don: Heinemann, 1975), p. 81.
13. C. Achebe, *A Man of the People* (London:
    Heinemann, 1966), p. 161.
14. V. S. Naipaul, *The Mimic Men* (New York:
    Macmillan, 1967), p. 38.

SUGGESTED READING

Many of the suggested readings for Chapter 34 dis-
cuss themes considered in this chapter. P. Bairoch,
Economics and World History: Myths and Paradoxes
(1993), is a concise summatiom of a leading special-
ist's many valuable studies. T. von Laue, *The World
Revolution of Westernization: The 20th Century in
Global Perspective* (1988), and L. Harrison, *Who
Prospers? How Cultural Values Shape Economic and
Polical Success* (1992), are stimulating recent inter-
pretations of development problems in the Third
World. A. B. Mountjoy, ed., *The Third World: Prob-
lems and Perspectives* (1978), and A. MacBean and V.

N. Balasubramanyam, *Meeting the Third World Challenge* (1976), are reliable, evenhanded introductions to postindependence trends and policies. R. Gamer, *The Developing Nations: A Comparative Perspective,* 2d ed. (1986), is a useful synthesis. Two excellent works from a truly Third World perspective are especially recommended: E. Hermassi, *The Third World Reassessed* (1980), and M. ul-Haq, *The Poverty Curtain: Choices for the Third World* (1976). B. Ward, *The Lopsided World* (1968), and G. Myrdal: *Asian Drama: An Inquiry into the Poverty of Nations,* 3 vols. (1968), movingly convey the hopes and frustrations of sympathetic Western economists in the 1960s. Valuable introductions to world agriculture and population are found in various works by L. R. Brown, notably the work cited in the Notes and in *In the Human Interest: A Strategy to Stabilize World Population* (1974). R. King, *Land Reform: A World Survey* (1977), is a good introduction to key problems.

Three valuable studies on African questions are R. Austen, *African Economic History: Internal Development and External Dependency* (1987); B. Turner et al., eds., *Population Growth and Agricultural Change in Africa* (1993); and P. Lloyd, ed., *The New Elites of Tropical Africa* (1966). C. Turnbull, *The Lonely African* (1962), provides intimate portraits of Africans caught up in decolonization and rapid social change; J. Iliffe, *The African Poor: A History* (1987), is an original and important work that is highly recommended. Critical aspects of contemporary Indian economic development are carefully considered by M. Franda, *India's Rural Development: An Assessment of Alternatives* (1980), and A. G. Noble and A. K. Dutt, eds., *Indian Urbanization and Planning: Vehicles of Modernization* (1977). China's economic and social challenges in the early 1980s are skillfully placed in a broad and somewhat somber perspective by two Chinese-speaking journalists, F. Butterfield, *China: Alive in the Bitter Sea* (1982), and R. Bernstein, *From the Center of the Earth: The Search for the Truth About China* (1982). W. Overholt, *The Rise of China: How Economic Reform Is Creating a Modern Superpower* (1993), is an enthusiastic account of recent success.

For the prodigious growth of Third World cities, J. Abu-Lughod and R. Hay, Jr., eds., *Third World Urbanization* (1977); P. Bairoch, *Cities and Economic Development* (1988); and D. J. Dwyer, *People and Housing in Third World Cities: Perspectives on the Problem of Spontaneous Settlements* (1975), are highly recommended. Similarly recommended is a fascinating investigation of enduring urban-rural differences by M. Lipton, *Why Poor People Stay Poor: Urban Bias in World Development* (1977).

A good introduction to changes within families is Hudson, cited in the Notes, a truly remarkable study. C. Johnson-Odim and M. Stroebel, eds., *Expanding the Boundaries of Women's History: Essays on Women in the Third World* (1992), is an important recent study. Other useful works on Third World women and the changes they are experiencing include L. Iglitzen and R. Ross, *Women in the World: A Comparative Study* (1976); N. Keddie and B. Baron, eds., *Women in Middle Eastern History: Shifting Boundaries in Sex and Gender* (1992); A. de Souza, *Women in Contemporary India and South Asia* (1980); N. J. Hafkin and E. Bay, eds., *Women in Africa* (1977); and M. Wolf, *Revolution Postponed: Women in Contemporary China* (1985). K. Kakar, *The Inner World: A Psychoanalytic Study of Childhood and Society in India* (1978), is a stimulating interpretation of Indian dependence on family and personal relations, which is provocatively compared with the compulsive individualism of Western society.

The reader is especially encouraged to enter into the contemporary Third World with the aid of the gifted writers discussed in this chapter. F. Fanon, *The Wretched of the Earth* (1968), is a particularly strong indictment of colonialism from the 1960s. Chinua Achebe illuminates the proud search for a viable past in his classic novel of precolonial Africa, *Things Fall Apart* (1959), and the disillusionment with unprincipled postindependence leaders in *A Man of the People* (1966). G. Moore and U. Beier, eds., *Modern Poetry from Africa* (1963), is a recommended anthology. In addition to his rich and introspective novels like *The Mimic Men* (1967), V. S. Naipaul has reported extensively on life in Third World countries. His *India: A Wounded Civilization* (1978), impressions gleaned from a trip to his family's land of origin, and *A Bend in the River* (1980), an investigation of the high price that postcolonial Africa is paying for modernization, are especially original and thought provoking. E. Burke III, ed., *Struggle and Survival in the Modern Middle East, 1700 to the Present* (1993), contains colorful brief biographies of a wide variety of ordinary people and is outstanding. L. Heng and J. Shapiro, *Son of the Revolution* (1983), brilliantly captures the drama of Mao's China through the turbulent real-life story of a young Red Guard.

LISTENING TO THE
PAST

Voices from the Village

How has social and economic development been changing women's lives and family relations in the villages of the Third World? How have women and families been coping with enormous changes, and how can governments and international agencies better respond to the real needs of rural people? These questions have fascinated the American writer Perdita Huston ever since she worked as a medical-social worker in rural North Africa in the early 1960s. The only literate woman in the area, she served as "nurse, letter-writer, marriage counselor, and midwife." And she learned to respect the wisdom and courage of poor peasant women "who searched ceaselessly for food, firewood, dung, water, and hope."

In the mid-1970s, as the critical importance of women in both development and population control was increasingly recognized, Huston received a grant from the United Nations to study the needs of village women in Tunisia, Egypt, Sudan, Kenya, Sri Lanka, and Mexico. Assisted by interpreters and using unstructured interviews, Huston talked first with women in groups and then with volunteers in private, "heart-to-heart" exchanges. In each village she began with a simple but profound question: "How does your life differ from that of your mother or grandmother?" This question brought many answers and opened up further discussion of key issues, such as housing, education, jobs, male-female relationships, and children. The following women were representative.

A young, high-school educated woman in Sri Lanka, the eldest of nine children:

"My mother's generation did not have all the opportunities we have. They did not have education, health services, or the transportation systems that exist now. But economically, they were better off. The income they got was sufficient to meet all their needs. At the moment, the high cost of living makes life diffi-

cult. They find it difficult to have a happy life.

Today young people have the opportunity to show their capabilities in sports and cultural activities—even in social and public affairs. Earlier generations did not allow girls to leave the home and attend public meetings. Now we have that opportunity. Even without the consent of our parents, we take part in social and public affairs or in political matters.

That is why I wanted to come and join this [agricultural] cooperative. When I live at home, I have no freedom. Wherever I go, I have to be accompanied by a brother and I have to return home early. I am questioned all the time. . . . But here I can earn my living and have some freedom to move about and make choices about participation in after-work activities.

Of course, my parents didn't want me to come here. They refused at first. They were concerned about letting a daughter come to a place like this, but the second time I asked—or rather, insisted—they gave their consent.

You see, my father is a farmer. My parents lived from the land, but when my grandfather died, the land was distributed among his sons. Now my parents' portion is very small. It is not sufficient for them to exist on. They continue to work the land and to search for other jobs.

I want my children to have a firmer footing—not to have this type of life. They must learn a profession and have a better job than mine. Women in Sri Lanka need employment. They should all have jobs. They must be taught skills so that they can earn a bit for their families.

I will have only two children: When you have more than two, you have all sorts of problems and expenses to worry about."

A nomadic Bedouin woman in Tunisia:

"I was given in marriage at age thirteen. I hadn't even reached puberty. My father was

1198

dead, so my uncle arranged the marriage with a neighbor. Now it is better; there is a law that says girls mustn't marry before the age of seventeen. That is good. You know, I hadn't had my period when I married. A month later it came—and a month after that I was pregnant. I had five children—three girls and two boys—but one daughter was stillborn.

My children go to school, and I want them, both sons and daughters, to go as far as their ability lets them. I want them to have a good future, a profession, a happy life. I don't want them working in the fields, picking up straws and leftovers as I do. I would like so much to have gone to school. I would like to have opened my mind. I would have taught other people about things. I want to know everything—everything you can learn if you have an education. I won't let my daughters marry earlier than seventeen.

Men are much better these days than they were before. They respect women more. . . . Before, a woman could be divorced, beaten, and poorly treated. That kind of thing doesn't exist anymore, thanks to President Bourguiba. Thanks to him and the laws, women are much better off today.

We have family planning now, and you can take better care of your children. That, too, is different. You can't imagine how many things I tried to swallow to prevent myself from having more children. I even used to eat mothballs, thinking that would help. I am only thirty-six years old, and I have planned my family now for five years. I have a loop. I don't want any more children. Life is too difficult." [She paused.] "Before the new laws, all women lived the lives of beasts."

A young Muslim woman in Sudan:

"Mother's life was, and is, very different from my own. She couldn't go out or talk to any men other than her husband. She never even went out into the street with him. She just stays home all the time; that is her life. But I go to market; I go out with my husband; we may even go to a movie. My husband does not mind. Sometimes I don't even put on my tow [veil]. Mother would never go outside without a full veil covering her face and hair.

These changes are all due to education. Before, women did not go to school. They did not know their husbands. They never saw them until the wedding night, once they were already married. But here in Sudan, women

Village women and their daughters in a hut in southern Mexico. (*Source: Cindy Karp/ Black Star*)

don't have as much access to education as men. It is better for boys, much better. I want my children to have more education than I did; then they will be different from me, just as I am different from my mother. The main thing is education. Schools are very important for girls.

A girl and a boy must be equal. A woman must work in all areas—doctor, teacher, anything. Any work a man can do, a woman can do also."

Questions for Analysis

1. In what ways do these women think their lives are different from their mothers'?

2. What common themes emerge in these responses?

3. What do these women think about education and jobs? About marriage and children?

4. Huston found many women who spoke openly in private but who did not want their names used or their neighbors or husbands informed of their views. How do you explain this?

Source: Perdita Huston, *Third World Women Speak Out: Interviews in Six Countries on Change, Development, and Basic Needs* (New York: Praeger, 1979), pp. 25, 27–28.

36

One Small Planet

Thousands of women from various countries and cultures gathered in the Beijing Olympic Stadium for the United Nations Fourth World Conference on Women in September 1995. *(Source: Forrest Anderson/Gamma Liaison)*

The idea of visitors from elsewhere in the universe has kindled the modern imagination. Motorists swear that they have seen unidentified flying objects; the alchemy of imagination even lands the crew of the starship *Enterprise* on our earth in our era. A best-selling author spins preposterous theories about "ancient astronauts" who landed on earth and built everything from the pyramids at Giza to the temples of the Aztecs. It is as if we earthlings, believers in the power of technology but weighed down by apparently insoluble human conflicts, yearn for some superior intelligence to decipher our little world and set it straight.

Perhaps our yearning for enlightened interstellar guidance can be put to good use. We can imagine how superior intelligences, easily able to grasp our world and its complex history, would view the planet and its talented but quarrelsome human race. Surely interstellar observers would take a genuinely global perspective, free from our customary biases of creed and nation. If we try to do the same, perhaps we too can gain insight into our world's ongoing development and its prospects.

- How has the planet organized itself politically, and will competing nation-states continue to dominate world politics?

- How has the human race been using its resources to meet its material needs?

- What key ideas are guiding human behavior as our planet moves toward an uncertain future?

From a global perspective, these questions might seem particularly important.

❋ WORLD POLITICS

Although many earthlings are deeply impressed by our recent scientific and technological achievements, highly advanced space travelers might be less so. They might instead be astonished that accelerated technological achievement has not been matched by any corresponding change in the way the human race governs—or fails to govern—itself. Sovereign nation-states reign supreme, as assertive and as competitive as ever, and are reinforced by enormously destructive weapons. The embryonic growth of an effective global political organization, of a government that could protect the world's nations from themselves, appears permanently arrested. The tension generated by powerful, warlike states in a fragile and interdependent world remains one of the most striking—and dangerous—characteristics of this small planet.

Nation-States and the United Nations

The rise of the nation-state and the global triumph of nationalism have been a grand theme of modern world history. The independent territorial nation-state—sometimes containing separatist ethnic groups striving for nationhood in their own right—is clearly the fundamental principle of political organization in our times. Yet from a global perspective we must surely question what we take for granted.

Has the nation-state system, with its apparently inevitable conflicts, become a threat to life on the planet? Some have thought so. It is one of history's ironies that nationalism has been widely condemned in the twentieth century, especially in Europe, just as it has triumphed decisively in world politics. In *Mankind and Mother Earth* (1976), his last work, the renowned British historian Arnold Toynbee (1889–1975) poignantly expressed the post-1914 disillusionment of many European and American intellectuals. At the time of his birth, Toynbee wrote, his middle-class countrymen "supposed Earthly Paradise was just around the corner." They also assumed that the national state was "the natural, normal, rightful political unit." Toynbee's generation of Europeans, however, lived through an era of "self-inflicted tribulation," war and genocide, largely due to their "explosive, subversive" faith in national self-determination.

Toynbee borrowed a term from the ancient Greeks to explain that the spread of the western European political idea of the national state, first to eastern Europe and then to Asia and Africa, had created a fatal discrepancy—

the discrepancy between the political partition of the Oikoumené [the habitat of the human race] into local sovereign states and the global unification of the Oikoumené on technological and economic planes. This misfit is the crux of mankind's present plight. Some form of global government is now needed for keeping the peace . . . and for reestablishing the balance between Man and the rest of the biosphere.[1]

A small but articulate group of intellectuals and political scientists has continued to advocate similar views. Thus we should probably take the "unrealistic" question of world government seriously. Let us look more closely than usual at the United Nations for signs of the emergence of a global authority transcending sovereign states.

When the United Nations was founded in San Francisco in 1945, the United States was the driving force behind its creation. President Franklin D. Roosevelt and Democrats in the Wilsonian tradition believed that the failure of the United States to join the League of Nations had contributed to the tragic breakdown of "collective security" in the 1930s. A resurrected League, they believed, would facilitate Allied cooperation in the postwar era.

The prime purpose of the new organization was to be "to maintain international peace and security." Primary responsibility for this awesome task was assigned to the twelve-nation Security Council. According to the United Nations charter, the Security Council had the authority to examine any international conflict, impose economic and political penalties on an aggressor, and even "take such action by air, sea, or land forces as may be necessary to restore international peace and security." In short, the Security Council had the power to police the world.

In practice, however, this theoretical power was severely restricted. China, Great Britain, France, the Soviet Union, and the United States were all made permanent members of the Security Council,

The United Nations in Action   These soldiers are part of a French battalion serving in a United Nations peacekeeping operation in Cambodia (Kampuchea), a country wracked by war and civil conflict since 1970. United Nations forces usually provide humanitarian aid as they try to preserve fragile cease-fires after warring armies agree to stop fighting. *(Source: J. F. Roussier/Sipa Press)*

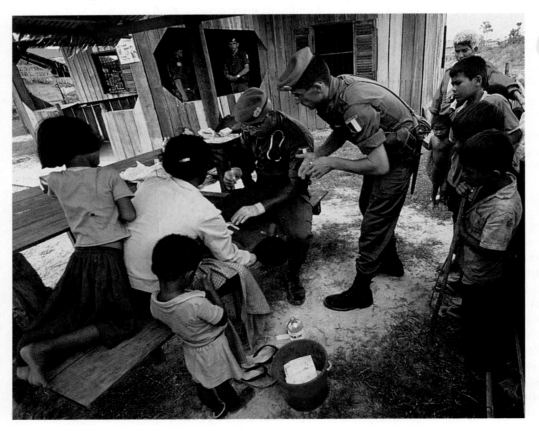

and all five had to agree on any peacekeeping action. The veto power of the Big Five has been criticized for preventing the United Nations from ever regulating its most powerful members. But that was precisely the point: none of the Big Five, and certainly not the United States, was willing to surrender sovereign power to a potential world government.

Indeed, a second principle of the United Nations affirmed and reinforced the primacy of the national state in world politics. The charter directed the United Nations to pursue "friendly relations between nations based on the principle of equal rights and self-determination of peoples." Every "peace-loving" state was eligible to join and to participate in the General Assembly, the United Nations' second main body. Founded with 50 members, the General Assembly reached 122 members in 1965 and 159 in 1990. Each member state, whatever its size, always had one voice and one vote on all resolutions, but the resolutions of the General Assembly became legally binding on states only if all five of the Security Council's permanent members agreed. The General Assembly was a world debating society for nation-states, not a lawmaking body for the peoples of the planet.

The third express purpose of the United Nations testified to the expanded scope of government tasks since the late nineteenth century, as well as to global interdependence. According to its charter, the United Nations was "to achieve international cooperation in solving international problems of an economic, social, cultural, or humanitarian character, and in promoting and encouraging respect for human rights and for fundamental freedom for all without distinction as to race, sex, language, or religion." This open-ended assignment was the province of a Social and Economic Council, whose eighteen members were to be elected periodically by the General Assembly. The council was also to work with specialized affiliated agencies such as the World Health Organization in Geneva and the Food and Agriculture Organization in Rome.

The scope of its original purposes helps explain the evolution of the United Nations. Hopes of effective Allied cooperation in the Security Council faded as cold war rhetoric and vetoes by the outnumbered Soviet Union began to paralyze that body. The Security Council proved somewhat more successful at quieting bloody conflicts between smaller states where the interests of the superpowers were not directly involved, such as the dispute between India and Pakistan over Kashmir and that between Greece and Turkey over Cyprus. In 1960, it even sent military forces to re-establish order in the former Belgian Congo. This ambitious undertaking, criticized from all sides and ultimately unsuccessful, marked an early high point of Security Council peacekeeping.

With the Security Council often deadlocked, the rapidly changing General Assembly claimed ever greater authority. As decolonization picked up speed and the number of member states more than doubled by the early 1960s, a nonaligned, anticolonial Afro-Asian bloc emerged. Reinforced by sympathetic Latin American countries, the bloc succeeded in organizing a coherent Third World majority in the General Assembly by the mid-1960s. This majority concentrated on economic and social issues, passing many fiery and fine-sounding resolutions often directed against the former colonial powers, the United States, Israel, imperialist Portugal, and the white government of South Africa.

The long-term significance of these developments at the United Nations was by no means clear. The Third World majority, predominantly composed of small and poor countries, clearly mistook the illusion of power at the United Nations for the substance of power in world affairs. By the late 1970s, many of the General Assembly's resolutions were simply ignored. Meanwhile, many critical international issues, such as the Arab-Israeli conflict, were increasingly resolved by resort to traditional diplomacy or war. From the mid-1980s onward, the United Nations experienced a serious financial crisis as the United States and other Western countries cut their contributions in order to retaliate against United Nations policies that they opposed.

Nor did the United Nations generate much popular support around the world. Most people continued to identify with their national states, which may even provide adults with a psychological substitute for the family bonds that nurtured them in childhood. Thus nation-states have continued to weave the powerful social bonds necessary for group action. As two American political scientists put it, "The nation-state may all too seldom speak the voice of reason. But it remains the only serious alternative to chaos."[2]

Famine Relief These desperate Ethiopians, fleeing from drought and starvation in 1985, hope to find enough food to escape death in makeshift refugee camps. The recent arrivals in the foreground are completely exhausted by hunger, fatigue, and a cold night in the desert. The United Nations has coordinated most famine relief in recent years. *(Source: Sebastiao Salgado/Magnum Photos)*

Despite these limitations the United Nations also proved to be a remarkably hardy institution. Particularly significant was the Third World majority's successful expansion of the scope of the organization's economic, social, and cultural mission. By the 1970s, an alphabet soup of United Nations committees, specialized agencies, and affiliated international organizations was studying and promoting health, labor, agriculture, industrial development, and world trade, not to mention disarmament, control of narcotics, and preservation of the great whales. These agencies and affiliated organizations derived their initial authority from treaties and agreements between sovereign states, but once in operation they took on a life of their own.

Staffed by a talented international bureaucracy, United Nations agencies worked tenaciously to consolidate their power and to serve their main constituency—the overwhelming Third World majority in both the General Assembly and the world's total population. Without directly challenging national sovereignty, they exerted a steady pressure for more "international cooperation" in dealing with specific global issues, and the world's big powers sometimes went along. The United Nations also emerged as the central forum for the debate on the world economic order and the relations between rich and poor countries, issues of fundamental importance in the late twentieth century. Thus sharp-eyed observers detected a gradual, many-sided enlargement of United Nations involvement in the planet's social and economic affairs.

Throughout the 1970s and 1980s the United Nations also continued to play a role in establishing peace in conflicts that did not directly involve the superpowers. Typically, United Nations negotiators helped weary foes to work out a cease-fire agreement, which was then monitored by a United Nations command drawing its troops mainly from small neutral countries. Then, as the 1990s opened, the United Nations again acted on a grand scale to stop aggression and police the world. In response to Iraq's invasion and annexation of the small state of Kuwait, the five permanent members of the Security Council agreed in August 1990 to impose a strict naval blockade on Iraq. Naval forces, led by the United States but augmented by ships from several nations, then enforced the blockade and halted all trade between Saddam Hussein's country and the rest of the world. Receiving the support of ground units from some Arab states as well as from Great Britain and France, the United States also landed first 200,000 and then a total of 500,000 American soldiers in Saudia Arabia near the border of Kuwait. When a defiant Saddam Hussein refused to withdraw from Kuwait and pay reparations, the Security Council authorized the U.S.-led military coalition to attack Iraq.

The subsequent war (Map 36.1) and the defeat of Iraqi armies received saturation coverage in the world's media. It was clear that this spectacular military operation could not have occurred—at least under United Nations auspices—without the approval of China and the Soviet Union. Once before, in the Korean War, the United States and its Western allies had fought with United Nations authorization. But that was only because an angry Soviet Union had walked out of the Security Council and was not present to cast its veto—a tactical error that none of the five permanent members ever repeated when their far-flung interests appeared threatened or even challenged. In the flush of victory over Iraqi armies, some leaders and observers believed that a "new world order" might

be at hand. Perhaps Great Power cooperation on the Security Council would enable the United Nations to fulfill its original purpose and impose peace and security throughout the world.

One such attempt came in December 1992, when armed forces from the United States landed on the east African beaches of Somalia in order to stop a savage civil war and allow United Nations soldiers to maintain peace thereafter. But the operation failed, as some Somali fighters attacked, killed, and drove out their would-be benefactors. United Nations negotiators and miliary observers (as well as NATO) were also unable to stop the equally savage civil war in Bosnia. These setbacks discredited United Nations efforts to impose peace on unwilling warring factions and forced a scaling back of United Nations peacekeeping ambitions. As a result the United Nations again concentrated on helping warring factions that wanted peace and did not try to impose peace. Even this was an awesome task: in early 1995 more than sixty-seven thousand United Nations soldiers were stationed in hot spots—such as Cyprus, the Gaza strip, Kashmir, Lebanon, and Haiti—all around the world. United Nations peacekeeping efforts were imperfect, but they were also indispensable. These efforts, combined with the United Nations' ambitious range of social and economic activities, suggest that the first historic steps toward some kind of world government have been taken.

Complexity and Violence

In between territorial nation-states and international organizations that focus on specific problems stretches a vast middle ground of alliances, blocs, partnerships, and ongoing conflicts and rivalries. It is often difficult to make sense of this tangle of associations, for four fundamental developments have structured a complexity sometimes bordering on chaos.

First, East-West competition and the mutual hostility of the bloc leaders, the Soviet Union and the United States, was until recently one of the planet's most enduring realities. The cold war raged in the 1980s, when Soviet armies decimated Afghanistan and the United States modernized its military might. To be sure, neither bloc by then was as solid as it had been a generation earlier. China had long since broken with the Soviet

MAP 36.1 The Persian Gulf War   The United States' most valuable ally in the
Gulf War was the kingdom of Saudi Arabia, which feared it might be next on the list
after Iraq suddenly seized Kuwait. Providing U.S. commanders with both bases and
troops, Saudi Arabia emerged from the war with increased regional influence and
unique superpower status in the world oil industry.

Union, and Poland's effort to chart its own course testified eloquently to tensions within the East bloc. As for the West, serious differences on military matters surfaced within NATO (which France had long since quit), and economic quarrels flared between the Common Market and the United States. In short, during the cold war the hostile superpowers both dominated their allies and were restrained by them. The sudden end of the cold war shattered these interlocking restraints, removing a basic principle of global organization and signaling a new era in world politics.

The long cold war contributed to the ideology of Third World solidarity, a second significant factor in planetary affairs. A critical step was taken in 1955, when Asian and African nations came together in Bandung, Indonesia, to form a "third force" of nonaligned nations. The neutralist leaders of Asia and Africa believed that genuine independence and social justice were the real challenges before them, and they considered the cold war a wasteful and irrelevant diversion. African, Asian, and Latin American countries learned to work together at the United Nations, and they called for a restructuring of the world economic system. These efforts brought mixed results (see below), but a loose majority of Third World countries did coalesce around some global issues.

A striking third development was the increasingly "multipolar" nature of world politics. Regional conflict and a fluid, complicated jockeying for regional influence were the keynotes. During the cold war, while the two superpowers struggled to control their allies and competed for global power and influence, a number of increasingly assertive "middle powers" arose around the world. Often showing by their actions only limited commitment to Third World solidarity, these middle powers strove to be capable of leading or dominating their neighbors and of standing up to the world's superpowers on regional questions. The rise of middle powers reflected the fact that most of the world's countries were small and weak, with fewer than 20 million people. Only a few countries had the large populations, natural resources, and industrial bases necessary for real power on a regional or global scale.

Latin America presented two striking examples of rising middle powers. Brazil, with more than 140 million people, vast territory and resources, and one of the world's most rapidly industrializing economies, emerged rather suddenly as South America's dominant nation-state. Equally impressive was the emergence of Mexico, with its population of over 80 million, its substantial industrial base and oil wealth, and its tradition of revolution and proud nationalism. By the early 1980s, Mexico clearly saw itself as the natural leader of the Spanish-speaking Americas.

Strong regional powers like France and West Germany had re-emerged in western Europe by the early 1960s. The unification of Germany in 1990 created a dominant economic power in Europe, with far-reaching implications for the Common Market and Europe's role in world affairs. Resurgent Nigeria was unquestionably the leading power in sub-Saharan Africa. Heavily populated Egypt and much smaller Israel were also regional powerhouses. Iran sought under the shah to dominate the Persian Gulf but came out of the long, bitter war with Iraq in the 1980s a bloodied loser. This defeat encouraged Saddam Hussein to launch his surprise attack on tiny Kuwait as part of Iraq's unsuccessful bid to become the dominant power in the region. China, India, and Japan were all leading regional powers, and several other Asian countries—notably Indonesia, Vietnam, Pakistan, and the Philippines—were determined to join them.

A fourth development is the high degree of conflict and violence that has characterized the emerging multipolar political system. Conflict in Europe remained mainly verbal during the cold war, but in Africa, Asia, and Central America blood flowed freely. Of the 145 wars that occurred worldwide between 1945 and 1979, 117 were in the Third World. Some countries were literally torn apart. Lebanon, which had long been considered the most advanced state in the Arab world, was practically destroyed by endless war, civil conflict, and foreign occupation. Cambodia (Kampuchea), invaded by American armies in 1970, then ravaged by the savage Pol Pot regime and finally occupied by Vietnamese armies, became another terrible tragedy.

The ongoing plague of local wars and civil conflicts caused great suffering. Millions of refugees, like Vietnam's "boat people," fled for their lives. The war for independence in Bangladesh temporarily created over 10 million refugees, who fled into India toward Calcutta. Hungry, homeless

✳ **Beirut: The Fruits of Civil War** Savage conflict between rival militias divided and decimated the Lebanese capitol in the 1980s. This Muslim family is walking along the previously fortified "green line," which separated the city's warring Muslim and Christian quarters for fifteen years before it was dismantled by a resurgent national government in 1990. (*Source: Wide World Photos*)

people overwhelmed the Indian relief centers, sleeping in trees, huddling in the rain, starving to death. After the Soviet invasion of Afghanistan, fully one-tenth of that country's population of 1.7 million people fled. In 1981, the United Nations' commission for emergency relief counted 10 million refugees in Asia and Africa. It was an appalling commentary on organized violence in our time.

Regional competition and local hot wars brought military questions once again to the forefront of world attention. During the cold war nearly every country in the world joined the superpowers in an ever-intensifying arms race. In garrison states like Israel, South Africa, and Vietnam, defense expenditures assumed truly fantastic proportions. For example, in the early 1980s Vietnam was spending half of its national income on the military; its standing army of a million men was the world's third largest, after the Soviet Union and China, and one of the best.

The end of the cold war did not reduce the level of local strife and violence. In many African states local politicians and ethnic rivalries had sometimes been restrained by superpower patrons and their aid. Now Africans found themselves neglected by the superpowers and without much outside financial support. Competition for power and resources increased in Africa, leading to still more ethnic battles and civil wars.

The most brutal, destructive, and long-lasting conflict has been occurring not in the Third World but in supposedly advanced Europe, in Bosnia-

Herzegovina and Croatia in the former Yugoslavia. Long-standing tensions between the country's three main ethnic groups—the Catholic Croats, the Orthodox Serbs, and the Muslim Bosnians—was rekindled by civil war and Nazi occupation in the Second World War. After the liberation the communist war leader Tito, who broke with Stalin in 1948 (see page 1108), established a federated Yugoslavia consisting of six separate republics. Tito then ruled his independent communist state with a firm hand. After his death in 1980, economic difficulties and large foreign debts weakened Yugoslavia. In 1989 the complex ethnic quota system that Tito had established finally fell apart as communist power withered away. Ethnic conflicts reignited. Politicians and peoples could not agree on whether Yugoslavia should remain united, though

under Serb domination, or whether the six republics should become independent sovereign states.

The Serbs insisted that Serbian minorities living in Croatia and Bosnia-Herzegovina had to be included in a new and expanded "Greater Serbia." When the Croats refused to accept this demand, Serbs in Croatia declared their autonomy. Fighting began in 1991, and Serbian forces occupied roughly one-third of Croatian territory. Fighting then spread to Bosnia-Herzegovina, where the Serbs seized about two-thirds of the territory and inflicted heavy losses on Croats and Bosnian Muslims. Serbian forces repeatedly expelled Croats and Bosnian Muslims from their homes and villages, terrorizing the women and imprisoning the men in concentration camps. These acts of barbarism,

A Victim in Bosnia   This child lives in an orphanage in Sarajevo, the capital of Bosnia-Herzegovina. The orphanage has no food and has sent the orphans out to scavenge in dumpsters for scraps of garbage. For many Europeans the terrible Bosnian tragedy recalls the Nazi nightmare. (*Source: Roger Richards/Liaison*)

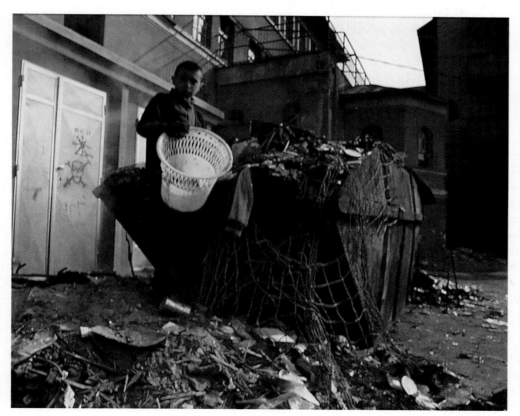

known as "ethnic cleansing," shocked world public opinion and led to many United Nations–sponsored cease-fires and efforts to restore peace. As of May 1995, all of these efforts had failed. The Serbs, the Croats, and the Bosnian Muslims were all rebuilding their armies, and renewed heavy fighting was much more likely than a negotiated peace.

In summary, regional competition, local hot wars, and brutal civil conflicts brought military matters once again to the forefront of the world's attention. In an effort to deal with insecurity and violence almost every country in the world joined the superpowers in a global arms race.

Nuclear Arms and Nuclear Proliferation

A particularly ominous aspect of the global arms race was the threat of nuclear war and nuclear proliferation. For a generation after 1945, nuclear weapons were concentrated mainly in the hands of the two superpowers, who learned a grudging respect for each other. But other states also developed nuclear weapons, and by the 1970s many more were capable of doing so. Some experts then feared that as many as twenty countries might have their own atomic bombs in a few brief years. By the early 1990s these fears had not come true. Moreover, the end of the cold war reduced the logic of superpower arsenals, encouraging widespread hopes that the nightmare vision of the mushroom cloud would be permanently lifted. In fact, the specter of nuclear proliferation still loomed, and the threat of nuclear war remained. How, a superior intelligence would surely ask, had this frightening situation arisen? And what was being done to find a solution?

Having let the atomic genie out of the bottle at Hiroshima and Nagasaki in 1945, a troubled United States immediately proposed that it be recaptured through effective international control of all atomic weapons. As American representative Bernard Baruch told the first meeting of the United Nations Atomic Energy Commission in 1946:

We are here to make a choice between the quick and the dead. . . . We must elect World Peace or World Destruction. . . . Therefore the United States proposes the creation of an International Atomic Development

Authority, to which should be entrusted all phases of the development and use of atomic energy.

The Soviets, suspicious that the United States was really trying to preserve its atomic monopoly through its proposal for international control and inspection, rejected the American idea and continued their crash program to catch up with the United States. The Soviet Union exploded its first atomic bomb in 1949. As the cold war raged on in the 1950s, the two superpowers pressed forward with nuclear development. The United States exploded its first hydrogen bomb in 1952; within ten months the Soviet Union did the same. Further American, Soviet, and then British tests aroused intense worldwide concern about nuclear fallout. There was well-founded fear that radioactive fallout entering the food chain would cause leukemia, bone cancer, and genetic damage. Concerned scientists called for an international agreement to stop all testing of atomic bombs.

Partly in response to worldwide public pressure, the United States, the Soviet Union, and Great Britain agreed in 1958 to stop testing for three years. In 1963 these three powers signed an agreement, later signed by more than one hundred countries, banning nuclear tests in the atmosphere. A second step toward control was the 1968 Treaty on the Non-Proliferation of Nuclear Weapons, designed to halt their spread to other states and to reduce stockpiles of existing bombs. It seemed that the nuclear arms race might yet be reversed.

This outcome did not come to pass. De Gaulle's France and Mao's China, seeing themselves as great world powers, simply disregarded the test ban and refused to sign the nonproliferation treaty. By 1968, they too had hydrogen bombs. Reversing its previous commitment to nuclear arms limitations, India also refused to sign the treaty. In 1974, India exploded an atomic device.

India's reversal was partly due to the failure of the Soviet Union and the United States to abide by the terms of the 1968 treaty on nuclear nonproliferation. According to the terms of the treaty, the nuclear powers agreed "to pursue negotiations in good faith on effective measures relating to cessation of the nuclear arms race at an early date and to nuclear disarmament, and on a treaty on general and complete disarmament under strict and effective international control." The non-nuclear states, which had seen serious efforts at disarmament by the superpowers as their payoff for promising not to go nuclear, had offered a series of proposals ranging from a complete test ban to a freeze or reduction on nuclear weapons before agreeing to sign the treaty.

In fact, the nuclear arms race between the Soviet Union and the United States surged ahead after 1968. According to American officials, the United States was capable in 1974 of dropping 36 bombs on each of the 218 Soviet cities with populations of 100,000 or more. The Soviet Union had 11 nuclear weapons for each American city of comparable size. The much-discussed SALT talks confined themselves to limiting the rate at which the Soviet Union and the United States produced more nuclear warheads. After 1980, when the second Strategic Arms Limitation Treaty failed to be ratified by the U.S. Senate, the superpowers appeared once again to be locked into a nuclear arms race.

Partly out of fear for their own security, many near-nuclear powers appeared poised to go nuclear in the 1980s. The worldwide energy crisis of the 1970s had played a part: peaceful use of the atom to generate electric power had created as a byproduct large quantities of plutonium, the raw material for bombs. Ominously, some countries began to regard nuclear bombs as just another weapon in the struggle for power and survival.

India developed its atomic capability partly out of fear of China, which had manhandled India in a savage border war in 1962. India's nuclear blast in 1974 in turn frightened Pakistan, which regarded India as a bitter enemy after 1947 and lost Bangladesh because of Indian armies. Pakistan's President Zulfikar Ali Bhutto (1928–1979) was reported to have said that Pakistan must have the bomb even if its people had to eat grass. In the 1980s, Pakistan was clearly on the verge of producing nuclear weapons.

It was also generally believed that both Israel and South Africa had arsenals of nuclear bombs. Israel's apparent nuclear superiority was profoundly distasteful to the Arabs. Hence Iraq pushed hard, with help from France, to develop nuclear capability. In June 1981, Israel responded suddenly, attacking and destroying the Iraqi nuclear reactor. When Iraq subsequently used deadly chemical weapons in its war against Iran and against its own dissatisfied minorities, the terrible

The Nuclear Arms Buildup As this 1972 cartoon suggests, during the cold war each side added ever more weapons and probed for advantage in a stalemated situation. Would someone make a rash move that would end the "game"? *(Source: Bruce Shanks © 1972 Buffalo Evening News)*

dangers of nuclear proliferation were driven home to all.

If countries like Iraq developed nuclear arms, and if regional conflicts remained so intense, would not some nation use the dreadful weapons sooner or later? And what about nuclear terrorism and blackmail? In a world full of nuclear weapons and nuclear potential, might not fanatical political groups and desperate states resort to nuclear blackmail to gain their demands? None of these menacing possibilities came to pass in the 1980s, but in a world of bitter political rivalries they made the hard-headed observer grimly apprehensive. Was the human race, as one expert on nuclear arms warned, "an endangered species"?[3]

The end of the cold war offered new hope. The likelihood of nuclear war between the United States and the Soviet Union declined greatly. In addition, effective Soviet-American cooperation presented the possibility of a great reduction in existing nuclear arsenals along with a continued renunciation of such weapons by non-nuclear countries, as already spelled out in the 1968 Treaty on the Non-Proliferation of Nuclear Weapons. One important step in this direction was taken in July 1990, when the Soviet Union, no doubt with U.S. support, required West Germany to renounce forever the manufacture of nuclear arms in return for Soviet agreement to German reunification. After the breakup of the Soviet Union, the United States and Russia agreed to big cuts in their respective nuclear arsenals, so that in a few years the United States would have thirty-five hundred nuclear warheads and Russia would have three thousand.

Apparently planning to maintain such enormous nuclear power, the United States and Russia, as well as the other nuclear powers, showed little interest in realizing the 1968 goal of *complete* nuclear disarmament. Thus when negotiations opened on a permanent extension of the 1968 Treaty on the Non-Proliferation of Nuclear Weapons, which was scheduled to expire in 1995, a large number of non-nuclear countries voiced objections. These countries charged that the treaty had created an exclusive club of nuclear powers and had condemned the non-nuclear powers signing the treaty to permanent inferiority. They pressed the five declared nuclear powers to move meaningfully toward total nuclear disarmament. Regional conflicts also undermined support for a permanent extension of the treaty. In particular, Arab nations wanted Israel to sign the treaty and renounce nuclear arms, which Israel was not prepared to do. The difficult negotiations over the renewal of the Non-Proliferation Treaty poignantly illustrated the tremendous difficulty of effective international cooperation in a world of proud and suspicious nation-states.

❋ GLOBAL INTERDEPENDENCE

Alongside political competition, war, and violence, a contradictory phenomenon unfolded: as Toynbee suggested, the nations of our small world became increasingly interdependent both economically and technologically. Even the great continental states with the largest landmasses and populations and the richest natural resources found that they could not depend only on themselves. The United States required foreign oil, and Russia needed foreign grain. All countries and peoples had need of each other.

Mutual dependence in economic affairs was often interpreted as a promising sign for the human race. Dependence promoted peaceful cooperation and limited the scope of violence. Yet the existing framework of global interdependence also came under intense attack. The poor countries of the South—the Third World—charged that the North continued to receive far more than its rightful share from existing economic relationships—relationships that had been forged to the South's disadvantage in the era of European expansion and political domination. The South demanded a new international economic order (see Listening to the Past). Critics also saw strong evidence of neocolonialism in the growing importance of the North's huge global business corporations—the so-called multinationals—in world economic development. Thus global interdependence was widely acknowledged in principle and hotly debated in practice.

Pressure on Vital Resources

During the postwar economic boom of the 1950s and the 1960s, the nations of the world became more dependent on each other for vital resources. Yet resources also seemed abundant, and rapid industrialization was a worldwide article of faith. Only those alarmed by the population explosion predicted grave shortages, and they spoke almost exclusively about food shortages in the Third World.

The situation changed suddenly in the early 1970s. Fear that the world was running out of resources was widely voiced. In a famous study aptly titled *The Limits to Growth* (1972), a group of American and European scholars argued that unlimited growth is impossible on a finite planet. By the early twenty-first century, they predicted, the ever-increasing demands of too many people and factories would exhaust the world's mineral resources and destroy the fragile biosphere with pollution.

Meanwhile, Japan was importing 99 percent of its petroleum, western Europe 96 percent. When the Organization of Petroleum Exporting Countries (OPEC) increased the price of crude oil fourfold in 1973 (see page 0000), there was panic in many industrial countries. Skyrocketing prices for oil and other raw materials seemed to confirm grim predictions that the world was exhausting its vital resources.

In much of the Third World, the pressure to grow more food for more people led to piecemeal destruction of forests and increased soil erosion. Much of the Third World suffered from what has been called "the other energy crisis"—a severe lack of firewood for cooking and heat. A striking case was the southern edge of the Sahara. Population growth caused the hard-pressed peoples of this region to overgraze the land and denude the forests. As a result, the sterile sand of the Sahara advanced southward as much as thirty miles a year along a 3,000-mile front. Thus land available for cultivation decreased, leaving Africa all the more exposed to terrible droughts. In the 1980s, crops shriveled up, and famine stalked the land; but an interdependent world mobilized, and international relief prevented mass starvation.

Recognition of interdependence was also reinforced by a common dependence on the air and the sea. Just as radioactive fallout has no respect for national boundaries, so pollution may sully the whole globe. Deadly chemicals, including mercury, lead, and arsenic, accumulated in the biosphere. Some feared that pollution of the oceans would lead to the contamination of fish, one of the world's main sources of protein. Others, worried that the oceans had been overfished, feared that the significant decline in the worldwide fish catch in the 1970s indicated abuse of the sea, the common heritage of humankind.

Of all the long-term pressures on global resources, many observers believed that the growth of population was the most serious. Here recent experience offered room for cautious optimism. Population growth in the industrialized countries slowed markedly or even stopped. Of much greater importance from a global perspective, the world's poor women began to bear fewer children. Small countries like Barbados, Chile, Costa Rica, South Korea, Taiwan, Tunisia, and the British colony of Hong Kong led the way. Between 1970 and 1975 China followed, registering the fastest five-year decline in the birthrate in recorded history. Then other big countries, especially in Latin America

and East Asia, also experienced large declines in fertility. In 1970, the average Brazilian woman had close to six children; by 1994, she had slightly more more than two. In 1970, the average woman in Bangladesh had more than seven children; in 1994, she had 4.5. Overall, the average Third World woman had 6.2 children in 1950 and 3.6 in 1994.

There were several reasons for the decline of fertility among Third World women. Fewer babies were dying of disease or malnutrition; thus couples needed fewer births to guarantee the survival of the number of children they wanted. As had happened earlier in the industrialized nations, better living conditions, urbanization, and more education encouraged women to have fewer children. No wonder that the most rapidly industrializing countries, like Taiwan or South Korea, led the way in birthrate declines. On the other hand, state-run birth control programs proved most successful in authoritarian China. The birth control pill, borrowed from the West but manufactured locally, was widely used in conjunction with heavy financial penalties for couples who exceeded the birth quota, increasingly fixed at one child per couple. As in most communist countries, abortion was free and available on demand.

Outside East Asia, contraception and especially abortion remained controversial. This helps explain why birthrates and population growth remained much higher in Africa and in the Muslim world than in East Asia. In 1985, Africa led the world with a population growth of 3.2 percent per year—enough to double the continent's numbers in only twenty-two years. Yet even in fast-growing Africa the rate of growth began to fall, with the average woman having about six children in 1994 as opposed to eight a few years earlier.

Indira Gandhi's fiasco with compulsory sterilization (see page 1144) and recent experience suggest that, barring catastrophe, worldwide population growth will continue to decline primarily as the result of billions of private decisions, decisions supplemented by government policies supporting contraception. These decisions are being made. Half of the world's couples now practice birth control, up from one in eight 40 years ago. Nonetheless, as the Third World's current huge population of young adults form their own families, the world's population will grow for a long time even if the use of contraception continues to increase.

The One-Child Family   China's continued moderate rate of population increase resulted in the early 1980s in drastic laws that generally prohibit Chinese families from having more than one child. The happy grandmother and the government posters behind preach the joys of the one-child family, which is at odds with Chinese tradition. *(Source: Jin Xuqi/Picture Group)*

Thus the world's population—5.6 billion in 1994, as opposed to 1.6 billion in 1900—will probably not stabilize until the mid-twenty-first century at the earliest, when it is estimated to reach between 10 billion and 11 billion people. Such continued growth will put tremendous pressure on global resources.

Gloom, however, is not the proper perspective. Even with 11 billion people, the earth would be less densely populated than Europe is today, and only one-fourth as densely populated as small, prosperous countries like Belgium and the Netherlands, which largely feed themselves (see Map 35.1, page 1178). Such countries, often overlooked in world politics, are promising models for life on a crowded planet. Moreover, the human race has exhibited considerable skill throughout its history at finding new resources and inventing new technologies. A striking example was the way that conservation, alternative energy sources, and world recession in the early 1980s at least temporarily belied gloomy prophecies about dwindling energy resources. An optimist could conclude that, at least from a quantitative and technical point of view, the adequacy of resources is a serious but by no means insoluble problem.

North-South Relations

The real key to adequate resources is probably global cooperation. Will the world's peoples work together, or will they eventually fight over resources like wild dogs over meat?

After the late 1960s there was dissatisfaction in Asia, Africa, and Latin America not only with the fruits of the industrialization drive but also with the world's economic system. Scholars imbued with a Third World perspective and spokesmen for the United Nations majority declared that the international system was unjust and in need of radicals change. A brilliant Pakistani, World Bank official and member of the international bureaucratic elite, sympathetically articulated this position in 1976:

The vastly unequal relationship between the rich and the poor nations is fast becoming the central issue of our time. The poor nations are beginning to question the basic premises of an international order which leads to ever-widening disparities between the rich and the poor countries and to a persistent denial of equality of opportunity to many poor nations. They are, in fact, arguing that in international order—just as much as within national orders—all distribution of benefits, credit, services, and decision-making becomes warped in favor of a privileged minority and that this situation cannot be changed except through fundamental institutional reforms.[4]

The subsequent Third World demand for a "new international economic order" had many causes, both distant and immediate. Critics of imperialism like J. A. Hobson (see page 902) and Third World writers on decolonization like Frantz Fanon (see page 1193) had long charged that the colonial powers grew rich exploiting Asia, Africa, and Latin America. Beginning in the 1950s, a number of writers, many of them Latin American Marxists, breathed new life into these ideas with their "theory of dependency."

The poverty and so-called underdevelopment of the South, they argued, were not the starting points but the deliberate and permanent results of exploitation by the capitalist industrialized nations in the modern era. Third World countries produced cheap raw materials for wealthy, industrialized countries and were conditioned to buy their expensive manufactured goods. As in the case of Latin America since the nineteenth century, the industrialized nations perpetuated this neocolonial pattern after Third World countries gained political independence. Thus the prevailing economic interdependence was the unequal, unjust interdependence of dominant and subordinate, of master and peon. Declining economic aid, smug pro-

nouncements about the overpopulation of the Third World, and the natural resentment of the poor toward the rich also fostered calls for radical restructuring of the international order.

It was the highly successful OPEC oil coup of 1973–1974 that ignited Third World hopes of actually achieving a new system of economic interdependence. From the industrialized North's point of view, OPEC's action in quadrupling the price of oil was a dangerous attack. It brought an end to the postwar economic boom and created serious social problems. From a global perspective, however, the sudden price rise brought a massive global transfer of wealth unprecedented since the looting of Mexico and Peru by the Spanish conquistadors. Perhaps 2 percent of all the income of the rich nations was suddenly forwarded to the OPEC countries (Map 36.2). Third World critics of dependence and neocolonialism were euphoric. For years the developed countries had gradually been reducing their economic aid. They had never seriously tried to meet the goal suggested by the United Nations General Assembly of earmarking 1 percent of their income each year for foreign aid. OPEC's success suggested that radical change was possible.

In 1974, a special session of the General Assembly rammed through two landmark resolutions calling for a "new international economic order" and a "program of action" to attain it. Among the specific demands were firm control by each country of its own natural resources, higher and more stable prices for raw materials, and equal tariff treatment for manufactured goods from the Third World. These demands were subject to "collective bargaining," but the Third World vigorously insisted on new terms. As one sympathetic scholar observed in 1980:

There has taken place a unionization of the Third World that has marked a profound shift in international relations. It looks as if the confrontation between unions and employers that stirred capitalist societies in the nineteenth century is being reenacted, but this time on a world scale between developed and developing nations. The question this time is whether the new nations command as many assets and opportunities as did the laboring classes of capitalist nations.[5]

That profound question remained unanswered in the late twentieth century. The developing

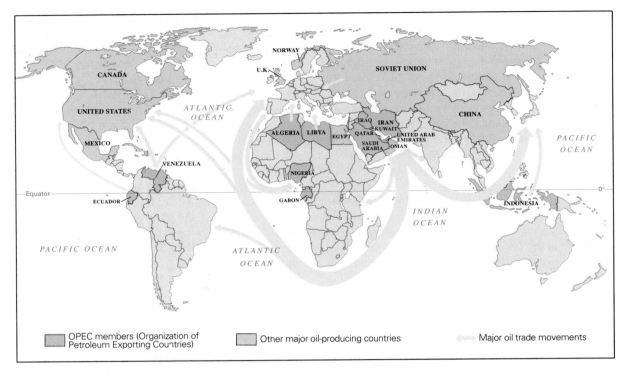

MAP 36.2 OPEC and the World Oil Trade   Though much of the world depends on imported oil, western Europe and Japan are OPEC's biggest customers. What major oil exporters remain outside of OPEC?

countries did negotiate some victories, notably a Common Fund under United Nations auspices to support the prices of raw materials and a scaling down of their enormous debts to the industrial nations (see below). Moderate socialists and some liberal economists in the North also supported some of the demands of the developing countries (see Listening to the Past). But generally the North, deeply troubled by inflation and by its own economic problems, proved a very tough bargainer when it came to basic changes.

For example, in the late 1970s the South laid great hopes on a long, complicated conference to formulate a new Law of the Sea. The proposed new law was based on the principle that the world's oceans are "a common heritage of mankind" and should be exploited only for the benefit of all nations. In practice, this was to mean that a United Nations–sponsored authority would regulate and tax use of the sea and that a global organization would even mine the ocean floor.

Some wealthy countries and their business firms were reluctant to accept such an infringement of their economic sovereignty and scope of action. The United States withdrew from the negotiations in 1981, and in 1982 the administration of U.S. president Ronald Reagan and the governments of several other developed nations refused to sign the final draft of the new Law of the Sea.

Increasingly frustrated in their desire to fashion a new international economic order quickly, some Third World leaders predicted more confrontation and perhaps military conflict between North and South. Some alarmists in the North voiced similar concerns. For example, these alarmists charged that many Third World governments secretly condoned the production of illegal drugs for sale in the industrialized nations, and they predicted that this behavior would dangerously increase the tensions existing between the rich and the poor countries (Map 36.3).

In considering these frightening predictions, an impartial observer was initially struck by the great gap between the richest and poorest nations. That gap was built on the coercive power of Western imperialism as well as on the wealth-creating achievements of continuous technological improvement since the Industrial Revolution. In the face of bitter poverty, unbalanced economies, and local elites that often cater to Western interests, Third World peoples had reason for anger.

But close examination of our small planet hardly suggested two sharply defined economic camps, a "North" and a "South." Rather, by the early 1980s there were several distinct classes of nations in terms of wealth and income, as may be seen in Map 36.4. The communist countries of eastern Europe formed something of a middle-income group, as did the major oil-exporting states, which still lagged behind the wealthier countries of western Europe and North America. Latin America was much better off than sub-Saharan Africa, having a number of middle-range countries to match their counterparts in highly diverse Asia.

When one added global differences in culture, religion, politics, and historical development, the supposed clear-cut split between the rich North and the poor South broke down further. Moreover, the solidarity of the Third World was fragile, resting largely on the ideas of some Third World intellectuals and their supporters. As one writer put it,

in the advocacy of growth and equalization at the international level . . . Third World states have astonished everybody, their enemies and their friends alike, for no one has ever believed that such a diverse congress of countries, separated by geography, geopolitics, cultural traditions, size, ideology, and a host of other factors, could ever manage to build a cohesive alliance.[6]

The oil cartel's achievement rested in large part on regional (and perhaps temporary) Arab solidarity, for example, and duplicating its success with less vital raw materials and more complicated issues proved impossible. Thus a continuation of the global collective bargaining that emerged in the 1970s seems more likely than an international class (and race) war. The poorer nations will press to reduce international economic differences through trade preferences, redistribution measures, and

special aid to the most unfortunate countries. And because global interdependence has become a reality, they will gradually win concessions, as the working classes have won gains within the wealthy nations since the late nineteenth century.

The international debt crisis of recent times illustrated the process of global bargaining. The economic dislocations of the 1970s and early 1980s worsened the problems of many Third World countries, especially those that had to import the oil they needed. Growing unemployment, unbalanced budgets, and large trade deficits forced many Third World countries to borrow rapidly from the wealthy industrialized nations. By the middle of 1982, Third World nations—led by Mexico, Brazil, and Argentina—owed foreign banks and governments about $600 billion. Much of this staggering debt was short-term and could not possibly be repaid as it fell due.

In 1982, when Mexico was unable to keep up with the payments on $80 billion of foreign debts, default and financial chaos in Mexico seemed at hand. Yet the Reagan administration, consistently opposed to Third World calls for a new international system, quickly organized a gigantic rescue operation to pump new money into Mexico and prevent default. The reason was simple: Mexico's failure to service its foreign debt would cripple large American banks that had lent Mexico money and possibly cause a financial panic that would plunge the whole world into depression and turmoil. Thus a series of international negotiations in the 1980s reduced the debts of Third World countries, granted desperately needed new loans, and encouraged economic liberalization. Lenders and borrowers, rich and poor, North and South, realized that they were bound together in mutual dependence by the international debt crisis. In 1995 Mexico again could not pay its debts, and the administration of U.S. president Bill Clinton granted another round of emergency loans, convinced that it was rescuing the United States as well as Mexico.

The Multinational Corporations

One of the most striking features of global economic interdependence since the early 1950s has been the rapid emergence of *multinational corporations,* business firms that operate in a number of different countries and tend to adopt a global rather than a national perspective. Multinational

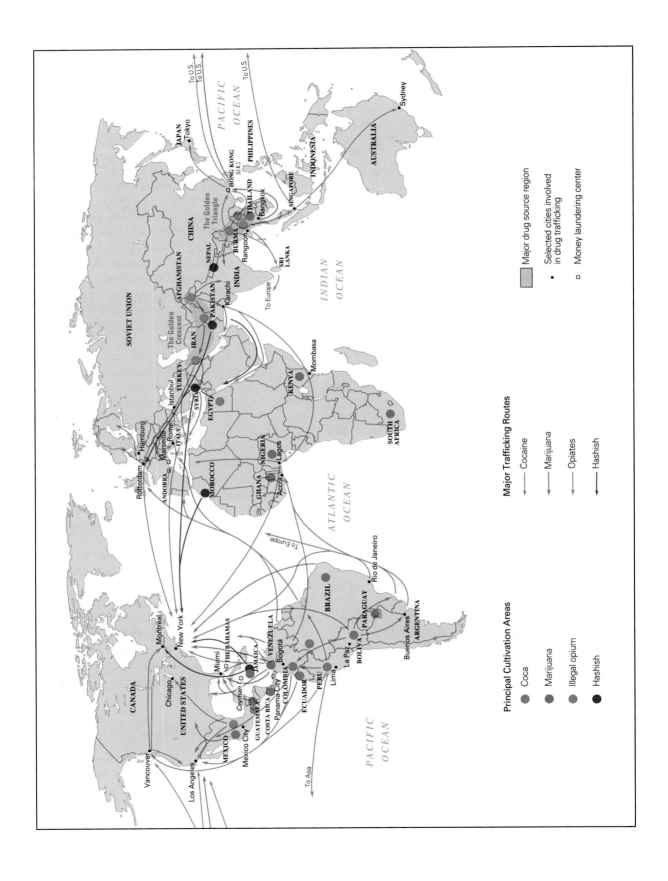

Principal Cultivation Areas

● Coca
● Marijuana
● Illegal opium
● Hashish

Major Trafficking Routes

→ Cocaine
→ Marijuana
→ Opiates
→ Hashish

▨ Major drug source region
● Selected cities involved in drug trafficking
□ Money laundering center

PACIFIC OCEAN

JAPAN
Tokyo
To U.S.
To U.S.
To U.S.

HONG KONG (U.K.)
PHILIPPINES
THAILAND
Bangkok
SINGAPORE
INDONESIA
AUSTRALIA
Sydney

CHINA
The Golden Triangle
BURMA
Rangoon
NEPAL
AFGHANISTAN
The Golden Crescent
PAKISTAN
Karachi
INDIA
SRI LANKA
To Europe

SOVIET UNION

IRAN
TURKEY
Istanbul
SYRIA
EGYPT
Marseille
Rome
ITALY
Hamburg
Rotterdam
ANDORRA
MOROCCO

INDIAN OCEAN

KENYA
Mombasa

NIGERIA
Lagos
GHANA
Accra

SOUTH AFRICA

ATLANTIC OCEAN

To Europe

CANADA
Vancouver
Chicago
UNITED STATES
Montréal
New York
Los Angeles
Miami
THE BAHAMAS
Cayman I.
MEXICO
Mexico City
GUATEMALA
COSTA RICA
Panama City
JAMAICA
VENEZUELA
Bogotá
COLOMBIA
ECUADOR
PERU
Lima
BOLIVIA
La Paz
BRAZIL
Rio de Janeiro
PARAGUAY
ARGENTINA
Buenos Aires

PACIFIC OCEAN

To Asia

corporations themselves were not new, but their great importance was. By 1971, each of the ten largest multinational corporations—the IBMs, the Royal Dutch Shells, the General Motors—was selling more than $3 billion worth of goods annually, more than the total national incomes of four-fifths of the world's countries. Multinational corporations accounted for fully a fifth of the noncommunist world's annual income, and they have grown even more important in the last two decades.

The rise of multinationals aroused a great deal of heated discussion around the world. Defenders saw the multinational corporations as building an efficient world economic system and transcending narrow national ties. In the words of a top manager of Royal Dutch Shell, the multinational corporation was

a new form of social architecture, matching the world-girding potential inherent in modern technology. . . .

In an age when modern technology has shrunk the world, and brought us all closer together, the multinational corporation and the nation state must get used to living with each other.[7]

Critics worried precisely that the nation-state was getting the worst of the new arrangement. Provocative book titles portrayed *Frightening Angels* holding *Sovereignty at Bay* while building *Invisible Empires* and extending their nefarious *Global Reach*. As usual whenever a major development attracted widespread attention, exaggerations and unreasonable predictions abounded on both sides.

The rise of the multinationals was partly due to the general revival of capitalism after the Second World War, relatively free international economic relations, and the worldwide drive for rapid industrialization. The multinationals also had three specific assets, which they used to their advantage.

First, "pure" scientific knowledge unrelated to the military was freely available, but its highly profitable industrial applications remained in the hands of the world's largest business firms. These firms

MAP 36.3 World Drug Trade As the drug trade has grown, the area of production has greatly expanded from the traditional Asian centers—the Golden Crescent and the Golden Triangle—to include many Third World countries. Poverty provides the drug lords with an army of drug runners.

held advanced, fast-changing technology as a kind of property and hurried to make profitable use of it wherever they could. Second, the multinationals knew how to sell, as well as how to innovate and produce. They used modern advertising and marketing skills to push their products relentlessly, especially the ever-expanding range of consumer products, around the world. Third, the multinationals developed new techniques to escape from political controls and national policies. Managers found ways to treat the world as one big market, coordinating complex activities across many political boundaries so as to reap the greatest profits.

Multinational industrial corporations began in the last quarter of the nineteenth century. U.S. businessmen took the lead, for reasons rooted in the nature of the American economy and society. Above all, the United States had a vast, unified market and the world's highest standard of living by 1890, so U.S. businessmen were positioned to pioneer in the mass production of standardized consumer goods. Many of the most famous examples—such as kerosene (John D. Rockefeller and Standard Oil), sewing machines (Singer), and farm machinery (Cyrus McCormick and International Harvester)—date from the 1880s. Others—like the cheap automobile (Henry Ford), the mass retailer (Sears), and standardized food (Coca-Cola, Wrigley's chewing gum)—were thriving by 1914.

Having developed mass-marketing techniques as well as new products, the biggest, most monopolistic American corporations quickly expanded abroad. Before 1914 they had created wholly owned subsidiaries to produce and sell American-style consumer goods in foreign lands, and they continued to do so between the world wars. With ever more products and the attractions of the European Common Market, there followed a mighty surge of American investment in Europe after 1945. Nor were other parts of the world neglected by the giant American manufacturing firms: there was continued multinational investment in raw-material production in Latin America (particularly copper, sugar, and bananas) as well as in the Middle East and Africa (primarily oil and gold). By 1967, American corporations—mainly the largest, most familiar household names—had sunk $60 billion into their foreign operations (Figure 36.1).

A few European companies, notably German chemical and electrical firms, also became

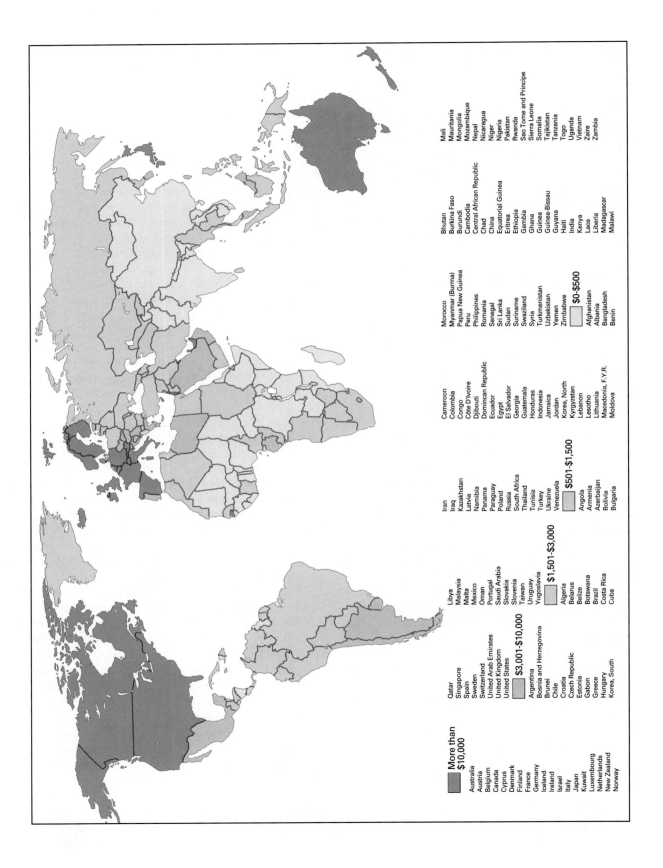

More than
$10,000

Australia
Austria
Belgium
Canada
Cyprus
Denmark
Finland
France
Germany
Iceland
Ireland
Israel
Italy
Japan
Kuwait
Luxembourg
Netherlands
New Zealand
Norway

Qatar
Singapore
Spain
Sweden
Switzerland
United Arab Emirates
United Kingdom
United States

$3,001–$10,000

Argentina
Bosnia and Herzegovina
Brunei
Chile
Croatia
Czech Republic
Estonia
Gabon
Greece
Hungary
Korea, South

Libya
Malaysia
Malta
Mexico
Oman
Portugal
Saudi Arabia
Slovakia
Slovenia
Taiwan
Uruguay
Yugoslavia

$1,501–$3,000

Algeria
Belarus
Belize
Botswana
Brazil
Costa Rica
Cuba

Iran
Iraq
Kazakhstan
Latvia
Namibia
Panama
Paraguay
Poland
Russia
South Africa
Thailand
Tunisia
Turkey
Ukraine
Venezuela

$501–$1,500

Angola
Armenia
Azerbaijan
Bolivia
Bulgaria

Cameroon
Colombia
Congo
Côte D'Ivoire
Djibouti
Dominican Republic
Ecuador
Egypt
El Salvador
Georgia
Guatemala
Honduras
Indonesia
Jamaica
Jordan
Korea, North
Lebanon
Lithuania
Macedonia, F.Y.R.
Moldova

Morocco
Myanmar (Burma)
Papua New Guinea
Peru
Philippines
Romania
Senegal
Sri Lanka
Sudan
Suriname
Swaziland
Syria
Turkmenistan
Uzbekistan
Yemen
Zimbabwe

$0–$500

Afghanistan
Albania
Bangladesh
Benin

Bhutan
Burkina Faso
Burundi
Cambodia
Central African Republic
Chad
China
Equatorial Guinea
Eritrea
Ethiopia
Gambia
Ghana
Guinea
Guinea-Bissau
Guyana
Haiti
India
Kenya
Laos
Liberia
Madagascar
Malawi

Mali
Mauritania
Mongolia
Mozambique
Nepal
Nicaragua
Niger
Nigeria
Pakistan
Rwanda
Sao Tome and Principe
Sierra Leone
Somalia
Tajikistan
Tanzania
Togo
Uganda
Vietnam
Zaire
Zambia

multinationals before 1900. Others emerged in the twentieth century. By the 1970s these European multinationals were in hot pursuit. Some, like Volkswagen, pushed directly into the American heartland and also into the Third World. Big Japanese firms like Sony also rushed to catch up and go multinational in the 1960s and 1970s. Whereas American investment had been heavily concentrated in Europe, Canada, and the Middle East, Japanese firms turned at first to Asia for raw materials and cheap, high-quality factory labor. By the 1970s Japanese subsidiaries in Taiwan, Thailand, Hong Kong, and Malaysia were pouring out a torrent of transistor radios, televisions, cameras, and pocket calculators.

Fearful of a growing protectionist reaction in their largest foreign market, the United States (where unemployed autoworkers symbolically demolished a Japanese automobile with sledgehammers in 1979), a host of Japanese firms followed Sony's example and began manufacturing in the United States in the 1980s. The Japanese inflow was so great that by 1989 Japanese multinationals had invested $70 billion in their subsidiaries in the United States, far surpassing the $19 billion that American multinationals had invested in Japan. In 1989 investment by European multinationals in the United States was also about 50 percent greater than American multinational investment in Europe. The emergence of European and Japanese multinational corporations alongside their American forerunners marked the coming of age of global business in an interdependent world.

The impact of multinational corporations, especially on Third World countries, has been heatedly debated. From an economic point of view, the effects were mixed. The giant firms provided advanced technology, but the technology was expensive and often inappropriate for poor countries with widespread unemployment.

The social consequences were quite striking. The multinationals helped spread the products and values of consumer society to the elites of the Third World. They fostered the creation of growing islands of Western wealth, management, and consumer culture around the world. After buying

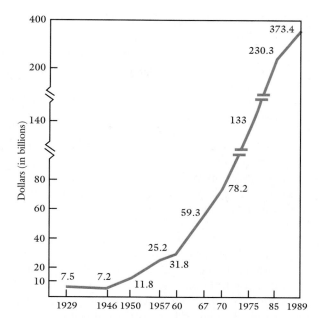

FIGURE 36.1 Total Investment by American Corporations in Foreign Subsidiaries (*Source: Data from U.S. Department of Commerce. Survey of Current Business*)

up local companies with offers that local business people did not dare to refuse, multinational corporations often hired Third World business leaders to manage their operations abroad. Critics considered this practice an integral part of the process of neocolonialism, whereby local elites abandoned the national interest and made themselves willing tools of continued foreign domination.

Some global corporations used aggressive techniques of modern marketing to sell products that are not well suited to Third World conditions. For example, Third World mothers were urged to abandon "old-fashioned, primitive" breast-feeding (which was, ironically, making a strong comeback in rich countries) and to buy powdered milk formulas for their babies. But the use of unsanitary bottles and contaminated water and the dilution of the expensive formula to make it last longer resulted in additional infant deaths. On this and many other issues, the multinationals came into sharp conflict with host countries.

Far from acting helpless in such conflicts, some poor countries found ways to assert their sovereign rights over the foreign multinationals. Many foreign

MAP 36.4 Estimated GNP per Capita in the Early 1990s

mining companies, like the fabulously profitable U.S. oil companies in the Middle East, were simply nationalized by the host countries. More important, Third World governments began to learn how to make foreign manufacturing companies conform to some of their plans and desires. Increasingly, multinationals had to share ownership with local investors, hire more local managers, provide technology on better terms, and accept a variety of controls.

Host governments learned to play Americans, Europeans, and Japanese off against each other. Frustrated by such treatment, one American managing director in Malaysia pounded his desk in 1979 and sputtered, "This little country and her little people need help, but they must be reasonable, otherwise we will get out of here." A Japanese manager in the same country expressed a more cooperative view: "We came here as guests, and our nation is small and needs natural resources, as well as foreign trade and investment to survive."[8] A growing proliferation of multinationals opened up new opportunities for Third World countries that wanted to use these powerful foreign corporations without being dominated by them.

❖ PATTERNS OF THOUGHT

The renowned economist John Maynard Keynes often said that we live by our ideas and by very little else. True or not, a global perspective surely requires keen attention to patterns of collective thinking. As Keynes saw, we need to be aware of the ideas that are shaping the uncertain destiny of this small, politically fragmented, economically interdependent planet.

To be sure, human thought can be baffling in its rich profusion. Nevertheless, in the late twentieth century, three distinct patterns on a global scale can be identified: the enduring strength of the modern world's secular ideologies, a vigorous revival of the world's great religions, and a search for mystical experience.

Secular Ideologies

Almost all of the modern world's great secular ideologies—liberalism, nationalism, Marxian socialism, as well as faith in scientific and technical progress, industrialism, and democratic republi-

canism—took form in Europe between the eighteenth-century Enlightenment and the revolutions of 1848. These ideologies continued to evolve with the coming of mass society in the late nineteenth century and were carried by imperialism to the highly diverse societies of Asia and Africa. There they won converts among the local elites, who eventually conquered their imperialist masters in the twentieth century. European ideologies became worldwide ideologies, gradually outgrowing their early, specifically European character.

All this can be seen as a fundamental aspect of global interdependence. The world came to live, in part, by shared ideas. These ideas continued to develop in a complex global dialogue, and champions of competing views arose from all regions. This was certainly true of nationalist ideology and also of Marxism. Europe, the birthplace of Marxism, made few original intellectual contributions to Marxism after Stalin transformed it into a totalitarian ideology of forced industrialization. After 1945, it was Marxists from the Third World who injected new meanings into the old ideology, notably with Mao's brand of peasant-based revolution and the Marxist theory of Third World dependency. Leftist intellectuals in Europe cheered and said "me too."

It was primarily as critics that Europeans contributed to world Marxism. Yugoslavs were particularly influential. After breaking with Stalin in 1948, they revived and expanded the ideas of Stalin's vanquished rival, Leon Trotsky. Trotsky claimed that Stalin perverted socialism by introducing "state capitalism" and reactionary bureaucratic dictatorship. According to the influential Yugoslav Milovan Djilas (b. 1911), Lenin's dedicated elite of full-time revolutionaries became Stalin's ruthless bureaucrats, "a new class" that was unprecedented in history. Djilas's powerful impact stemmed from his mastery of the Marxian theory of history and the Marxian dialectic:

The social origin of the new class lies in the proletariat just as the aristocracy arose in peasant society, and the bourgeoisie in a commercial and artisans' society....

Former sons of the working class are the most steadfast members of the new class. It has always been the fate of slaves to provide for their masters the most clever and gifted representatives. In this case a new exploiting and governing class is born from the exploited class....

The communists are . . . a new class.

As in other owning classes, the proof that it is a special class lies in its ownership and in its special relations to other classes. In the same way, the class to which a member belongs is indicated by the material and other privileges which ownership brings him. . . . The communist political bureaucracy uses, enjoys, and disposes of nationalized property.[9]

Non-Marxian criticism of communism also continued to develop, as in Jean François Revel's provocative *The Totalitarian Temptation* (1977). According to Revel, the application of the Marxist-Leninist-Maoist model brought about phony revolution. Under the guise of supposedly progressive socialism, it built reactionary totalitarian states of the Stalinist variety. Critics of Marxism-Leninism like Revel and Djilas undermined the intellectual appeal of communism and thereby contributed to its being overthrown in eastern Europe in 1989.

As the varieties of Marxism lost luster, old-fashioned, long-battered liberalism and democracy survived and flourished as a global ideology. In every communist country small, persecuted human rights movements bravely demanded the basic liberties first set into law in the American and French Revolutions, preparing the way against all odds for the renewed triumph of liberal revolution in eastern Europe in 1989. And there were always some African and Asian intellectuals, often in exile, calling for similar rights even in the most authoritarian states. The call for human rights and representative government coincided with a renewed faith in market forces and economic liberalism as effective tools of economic and social development. That countries as highly diverse as Brazil, China, Ghana, and the Soviet Union all moved in this direction in recent times was little short of astonishing.

Efforts to combine the best elements of socialism and liberalism in a superior hybrid were also important. The physicist Andrei Sakharov (1921–1990), the father of the Russian atomic bomb, who in the 1960s became a fearless leader of the human rights movement in the Soviet Union, was an eloquent spokesman for what might be called the "convergence school." According to Sakharov, humanity's best hope lay in the accelerated convergence of liberal capitalism and dictatorial communism on some middle ground of welfare capitalism and democratic socialism, like that which has flourished in the small, close-knit societies of Scandinavia, Iceland, and New Zealand. This outlook

✦ **Solzhenitsyn Returns to Russia** In 1994, after living in exile in the United States for twenty years, the great novelist and implacable foe of communism moved back to Russia, taking a train trip home to Moscow across Siberia. Shown here with his son, Solzhenitsyn preached rebirth for Russia to crowds along the way. *(Source: Sichov/Sipa Press)*

waned somewhat in the 1980s, but it had deep historical roots in Western society and remained a potent force in world thought.

Finally, there was a many-sided global reaction to the dominant faith in industrialization, consumerism, and unrestrained "modernization." The disillusionment of the Third World was matched by disillusionment in the developed countries and a search for alternative secular visions of the future. The student revolt of the 1960s (see page 1120), with its vague ideology of broad participation in community decisions, coincided with widespread nostalgia for simple, close-knit rural societies. The great Russian novelist Alexander Solzhenitsyn, caught up in the vanishing-resources doctrine of the 1970s, called on Soviet leaders to renounce Western technology and return to the earth:

Herein lies Russia's hope for winning time and winning salvation: In our vast northeastern spaces, which over four centuries our sluggishness has prevented us from mutilating by our mistakes, we can build anew: not the senseless, voracious civilization of "progress"—no; we can set up a stable economy without pain or delay and settle people there for the first time according to the needs and principles of that economy. These spaces allow us to hope that we shall not destroy Russia in the general crisis of Western civilization.[10]

Communes sprang up in the United States and Europe in the late 1960s. There were many advocates of alternative lifestyles and technologies friendly to the environment. E. F. Schumacher, an English disciple of Mahatma Gandhi, in *Small Is Beautiful* (1973) urged the building of solar-heated houses to conserve nonrenewable oil. Africa and Asia increasingly stressed "appropriate technologies" tailored to village life rather than borrowed from large-scale urban industrialized society—such as small, rugged, three-wheeled motorized carts suited to existing country lanes, rather than large trucks requiring expensive modern highways and imported fuel.

A striking aspect of the worldwide reappraisal of industrialization was the heretical revival of Jean-Jacques Rousseau's belief in the superiority of the simple, frugal "noble savage." As Robert Heilbroner poignantly put it in 1974 in his otherwise gloomy *An Inquiry into the Human Prospect*:

One element [of hope] . . . is our knowledge that some human societies have existed for millennia, and that others can probably exist for future millennia, in a continuous rhythm of birth and coming of age and death, without pressing toward those dangerous ecological limits, or engendering those dangerous social tensions, that threaten present-day "advanced" societies. In our discovery of "primitive" cultures, living out their timeless histories, we may have found the single most important object lesson for future man.[11]

Other writers from the industrialized countries reassessed traditional cultures and found nobility and value similar to that championed by the Nigerian novelist Chinua Achebe (see page 1194). Opponents of modern industrial society and defenders of the environment remained only a vocal minority, but their worldwide presence was a vivid example of the globalization of intellectual life.

✤ **The Revolution in Communications** Although this young man must carry his motorbike up a rocky path to reach his home, he has gained access to speed and excitement, to roads and cities. The messages of the modern world easily reach remote villages by transistor radio. *(Source: S. Pern/The Hutchinson Library)*

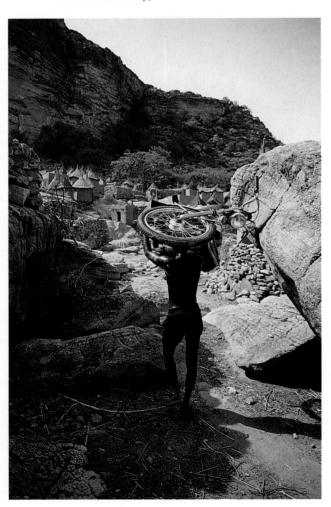

Religious Belief: Christianity and Islam

The reaction to industrialism and consumerism was part of a broader religious response to the dominance of secular ideologies in general. The revival of Christianity among intellectuals after the

Pope John Paul II   Nuns radiant with joy welcome the man of peace and goodwill in 1993 as he arrives in West Africa. John Paul, determined to minister to Catholics in all lands, has drawn large and enthusiastic crowds on repeated visits to Africa. *(Source: Paul Yao/Liaison)*

First World War (see pages 1030–1031) was matched in the 1970s and 1980s by a surge of popular, often fundamentalist, Christianity in many countries. Judaism and Islam also experienced resurgence, and Buddhism and Hinduism stopped losing ground. The continuing importance of religion in contemporary human thought—an importance that has often escaped those fascinated by secular ideology and secular history—must impress the unbiased observer.

Pope John Paul II (r. 1978–) exemplified several aspects of the worldwide Christian revival. A jet-age global evangelist, John Paul journeyed to Africa, Asia, and North and South America, inspiring enthusiastic multitudes with his warm sincerity and unfailing popular touch. John Paul's melding of a liberal social gospel with conservatism in doctrinal matters often seemed to reflect the spirit of the age. Thus the pope boldly urged a more equitable distribution of wealth in plutocratic Brazil

and more civil liberties in Marcos's authoritarian Philippines while reaffirming the church's long-standing opposition to mechanical contraception and women in the priesthood. Many of Christianity's most rapidly growing Protestant churches also espoused theological fundamentalism, based on a literal reading of the Bible.

It was also emblematic that the "Polish Pope" came from an officially atheist communist country. Yet after thirty-five years of communist rule, Poland was more intensely Catholic than ever before. Lech Walesa, the courageous leader of Poland's trade union Solidarity, said that he never could be a communist because he was a devout Roman Catholic. Poland illustrated the enduring strength of spiritual life in the face of materialistic culture and secular ideologies, of which communism was only the most openly hostile.

Islam, the religion of one-seventh of the earth's people, also experienced a powerful resurgence

❖ **Ayatollah Khomeini** The apostle of Islamic regeneration and the unwavering critic of the shah returned in triumph to Teheran from exile in February 1979. The shah had visions of making Iran a major military power, but all his military might crumbled before the emotional appeal of Islamic revolution. *(Source: Setboun/Sipa Press)*

from the 1970s onward. Like orthodox Christianity, Islam had been challenged by the self-confident secular ideologies of the West since the early nineteenth century. And although the acids of modern thought did not eat as deeply as in Europe and North America, they etched a seductive alternative to Islam. Moderate Muslim intellectuals advocated religious reforms; radicals wanted drastic surgery. The most famous and successful of the radicals was the twentieth-century Turkish nationalist Kemal Atatürk (see pages 0000–0000), who reflected and

accelerated the impact of secularism on the Muslim world.

The generation of Muslim intellectual and political leaders born in the interwar years, who reached maturity after the Second World War, agreed that Islam required at least some modernizing. They accepted the attractively simple Muslim creed "There is no god but Allah, and Muhammad is his Prophet," but they did not think that the laws of the Qur'an should be taken literally. The prohibition on lending money at interest, the social inferiority of women, even cutting off the hands of thieves and public beheading of murderers, had made sense for the Arabian peninsula in the Middle Ages. But, they argued, such practices did not suit the modern age. It was necessary for Islam to adapt.

These views were still common among educated elites in the 1970s, and they remained dominant in Turkey and probably in Egypt. But throughout much of the Middle East they had to bow before a revival of Islamic fundamentalism, the critical development of recent years. Like some of their Christian and Jewish counterparts, orthodox Muslim believers wanted to return to unalterable fundamentals. In taking the Qur'an literally, they demanded that the modern world adapt to the Prophet's teachings, not vice versa. And because the masses remained deeply religious and profoundly disturbed by rapid change, Islamic fundamentalism aroused a heartfelt popular response.

Iran provided a spectacular manifestation of resurgent Islamic fundamentalism. In the 1970s, Iran's religious leaders, notably the charismatic Ayatollah Khomeini, catalyzed intense popular dissatisfaction with the shah's all-out industrialization and heavy-handed religious reform into a successful revolution. An "Islamic Republic" was established to govern according to the sacred laws of the Qur'an. State and church were tightly bound together. The holy men and their followers sanctioned the stoning to death of prostitutes and adulterers and revised the legal code along strictly Qur'anic lines.

Iran's fundamentalism was exceptionally rigid and antimodern, partly because the country adhered to the minority Shi'ite version of Islam. But similar movements developed in every Muslim country. In Algeria in the early 1990s only harsh military rule prevented the fundamentalists from forming a popularly elected government (see page

1153). Even where the fundamentalists seemed unlikely to take power, as in Indonesia or Pakistan, and where they were co-opted and neutralized, as in Saudi Arabia, they found enthusiastic support among the masses and revitalized the Muslim faith. Islamic missionary activity also remained extremely vigorous and continued to win converts, especially in black Africa.

Searching for Mystical Experience

Alongside secular ideologies and a revival of the world's great religions, the third powerful current of intellectual attraction was an enormous variety of religious sects, cults, and spiritual yearnings. Some of these new outpourings welled up within one or another of the great religions; many more did not. Though widely divergent, these movements seemed to share a common urge toward nonrational experiences such as meditation, spiritual mysteries, and direct communication with supernatural forces.

Not that this was new. So-called primitive peoples have always embraced myths, visions, and continuous revelation. So too have the world's main religions, especially those of the ancient East—Taoism, Hinduism, and the Zen form of Buddhism. What was new was the receptiveness of many people in the rationalistic, scientific industrialized countries (and their disciples, the Third World elite) to ancient modes of mystical experience. Some of this interest stems from the doubt about the power of the rational human mind that blossomed after the First World War. By the 1960s, it had struck deep roots in the mass culture of Europe and North America.

In this sense, the late twentieth century is reminiscent of the initial encounter of West and East in the Hellenistic Age. Then, the rationalistic, humanistic Greeks encountered the Eastern mystery religions and were profoundly influenced by them. Now, various strains of mystical thought are again appearing from the East and from "primitive" peoples. It can be said that the non-Western world is providing intellectual repayment for the powerful secular ideologies that it borrowed in the nineteenth century.

Reflecting on this ongoing encounter, the American social scientist Robert Heilbroner was not alone in suggesting startling implications for the future:

It is therefore possible that a post-industrial society would also turn in the direction of many preindustrial societies—toward the exploration of inner states of experience rather than the outer world of fact and material accomplishment. Tradition and ritual, the pillars of life in virtually all societies other than those of an industrial character, would probably once again assert their ancient claims as the guide to and solace for life.[12]

Some observers saw the onrush of science and technology as actually reinforcing the search for

 Buddhism in the West Americans from different backgrounds come together for worship in this Buddhist temple in Santa Fe, New Mexico. This temple adheres to the Tibetan form of Buddhism, which combines mysticism and colorful ceremony. *(Source: Mimi Forsyth/Monkmeyer Press)*

spiritual experience. Electronic communications are demolishing time and distance; information itself is becoming the new global environment. According to the philosopher William Thompson:

Culture is full of many surprises, because culture is full of the play of opposites. And so there will be scientists and mystics in the New Age. . . . To look at the American counterculture today, one would guess . . . that the East was about to engulf the West. But in fact . . . America is swallowing up and absorbing the traditional Eastern techniques of transformation, because only these are strong enough to humanize its technology. In the days before planetization, when civilization was split between East and West, there were basically two cultural directions. The Westerner went outward to level forests, conquer nations, and walk on the moon; the Easterner went inward and away from the physical into the astral and causal planes. Now . . . we can glimpse the beginnings of a new level of religious experience, neither Eastern nor Western, but planetary.[13]

Many people may have doubts about the significance of such views. But it seems quite possible that the upsurge of mysticism and religious searching will exert a growing influence in the coming era, especially if political conflict and economic problems continue to undermine the old secular faith in endless progress.

SUMMARY

Whatever does or does not happen, the study of world history puts the future in perspective. Future developments on this small planet will surely build on the many-layered foundations hammered out in the past. Moreover, the study of world history, of mighty struggles and fearsome challenges, of shining achievements and tragic failures, imparts a strong sense of life's essence: the process of change over time. Again and again we have seen how peoples and societies evolve, influenced by ideas, human passions, and material conditions. Armed with the ability to think historically, students of history are prepared to comprehend this inexorable process of change in their own lifetimes, as the world races forward toward an uncertain destiny.

NOTES

1. A. Toynbee, *Mankind and Mother Earth* (New York: Oxford University Press, 1976), pp. 576–577.
2. D. Calleo and B. Rowland, *America and the World Political Economy* (Bloomington: Indiana University Press, 1973), p. 191.
3. W. Epstein, *The Last Chance: Nuclear Proliferation and Arms Control* (New York: Free Press, 1976), p. 274.
4. M. ul-Haq, *The Poverty Curtain: Choices for the Third World* (New York: Columbia University Press, 1976), p. 152.
5. E. Hermassi, *The Third World Reassessed* (Berkeley: University of California Press, 1980), p. 76.
6. Ibid., p. 185.
7. Quoted in H. Stephenson, *The Coming Clash: The Impact of Multinational Corporations on National States* (New York: Saturday Review Press, 1973), p. 60.
8. Quoted in A. R. Negandhi, *The Functioning of the Multinational Corporation: A Global Comparative Study* (New York: Pergamon Press, 1980), p. 142.
9. M. Djilas, *The New Class* (New York: Praeger, 1957), pp. 41–42, 44.
10. A. I. Solzhenitsyn, *Letter to the Soviet Leaders* (New York: Harper & Row, 1974), p. 33.
11. R. L. Heilbroner, *An Inquiry into the Human Prospect* (New York: Norton, 1974), p. 141.
12. Ibid., p. 140.
13. W. I. Thompson, *Evil and World Order* (New York: Harper & Row, 1980), p. 53.

SUGGESTED READING

Many of the books cited in the Suggested Reading for Chapter 35 pertain to the themes of this chapter. Three helpful and stimulating studies on global politics from different viewpoints are R. Barnet, *The Lean Years: The Politics of the Age of Scarcity* (1980); F. M. Lappé and J. Collins, *Food First: Beyond the Myth of Scarcity* (1977); and S. Hoffman, *Primacy or World Order: American Foreign Policy Since the Cold War* (1978). Two wide-ranging appraisals of current trends are found in Z. Brzezinski, *Out of Control: Global Turmoil on the Eve of the 21st Century* (1993), and D. Snow, *The Shape of the Future: The Post–Cold War World* (1991).

An excellent introduction to international negotiations for the control of nuclear arms is W. Epstein,

The Last Chance: Nuclear Proliferation and Arms Control (1976). Other recommended studies are D. Holloway, *The Soviet Union and the Arms Race* (1983), and L. Freedman, *The Evolution of Nuclear Strategy* (1982), a history of American thinking about nuclear weapons and nuclear war. Stimulating recent works include K. Bailey, *Doomsday in the Hands of Many: The Arms Control Challenge of the '90s* (1991), and M. van Creveld, *Nuclear Proliferation and the Future of Conflict* (1993).

M. ul Haq's book cited in the Notes is an excellent presentation of Third World demands for a new economic order. This position is expanded in J. Tinbergen and A. J. Dolman, eds., *RIO, Reshaping the International Order: A Report to the Club of Rome* (1977), and *North-South: A Program for Survival* (1980), a report calling for increased help for the South by the blue-ribbon Independent Commission on International Development Issues, under the chairmanship of Willy Brandt. Such views do not go unchallenged, and P. T. Bauer, *Equality, the Third World, and Economic Delusion* (1981), is a vigorous defense of the industrialized nations and their wealth. J. K. Galbraith, the witty economist and former U.S. ambassador to India, argues simply and effectively in *The Voice of the Poor* (1983) that poor countries have important lessons to teach rich countries. Common problems and aspirations are also the focus of E. Laszlo et al., *Goals for Mankind* (1977). The important study by R. Ayres, *Banking on the Poor: The World Bank and World Poverty* (1983), shows how this international financial organization has emerged as a standard-bearer for the poorest countries. *World Development Report,* which the World Bank publishes annually, is an outstanding source of information about current trends. Valuable studies on multinational corporations and global indebtedness include L. Solomon, *Multinational Corporations and the Emerging World Order* (1978); the work by A. R. Negandhi, cited in the Notes; R. Barnet and R. Muller, *Global Reach: The Power of the Multinational Corporations* (1975); and A. Sampson, *The Money Lenders: The People and Politics of the World Banking Crisis* (1983).

Contemporary thought is so rich and diverse that any selection must be highly arbitrary. Among works not mentioned elsewhere, G. Blainey, *The Great Seesaw: A New View of the Western World, 1750–2000* (1988), uncovers a cyclical pattern of optimism and pessimism and is recommended as an introduction to the history of ideas. E. Banfield, *The Unheavenly City Revisited* (1974), is a provocative and influential reassessment of urban problems and solutions in the United States. D. H. Meadows and D. L. Meadows, *The Limits of Growth* (1974), argue that the world will soon exhaust its natural resources. E. F. Schumacher, *Small Is Beautiful: Economics as If People Mattered* (1973), advocates conservation and a scaling-down of technology to avoid disaster. R. M. Pirsig, *Zen and the Art of Motorcycle Maintenance: An Inquiry into Values* (1976), is a stimulating exploration of the tie between modern technology and personal development.

E. Rice, *Wars of the Third Kind: Conflict in Underdeveloped Countries* (1988), is a thoughtful inquiry into the dynamics of guerrilla movements. T. R. Gurr, *Why Men Rebel* (1970), skillfully reworks the idea that revolutions occur when rising expectations are frustrated. M. Djilas, in the work cited in the Notes, criticizes the ruling Communist bureaucracies from a Marxist point of view. J. Revel, *The Totalitarian Temptation* (1977), claims that many Western intellectuals have been seduced into seeing Communist dictatorships as progressive socialist societies. A. Sakharov, *Progress, Coexistence, and Intellectual Freedom,* rev. ed. (1970), soberly assesses the prospects for improved relations between the Soviet Union and the United States.

The Islamic revival may be approached through the sympathetic work of E. Gellner, *Muslim Society* (1981); and the reservations of V. S. Naipaul, *Among the Believers: An Islamic Journey* (1981); H. Algar, ed., *Islam and Revolution: Writings and Declarations of Imam Khomeini* (1982); and J. Stempel, *Inside the Iranian Revolution* (1981). Muslim writers address issues in the Islamic world in J. Donohue and J. Esposito, eds., *Islam in Transition: Muslim Perspectives* (1982).

Studies of the future are so numerous that M. Marien, *Societal Directions and Alternatives: A Critical Guide to the Literature* (1977), is a useful aid with its annotated bibliography. P. Kennedy, *Preparing for the Twenty-first Century* (1993), is the work of a well-known historian. Also recommended is J. Lukacs, *The End of the Twentieth Century and the End of the Modern Age* (1993).

The many future-oriented works of the members of the Hudson Institute usually combine optimism and conservatism, as in H. Kahn et al., *The Next Two Hundred Years* (1976), and H. Kahn, *The Coming Boom* (1982). J. Lorraine's *Global Signposts to the 21st Century* (1979) and R. L. Heilbroner's work cited in the Notes are stimulating and intelligent studies.

One World and a Plan for Survival

In the 1970s Third World countries of the South called on the industrialized countries of the North to join with them in establishing a "new international order." Using the United Nations General Assembly as a platform, Third World countries argued that the world economy worked to their disadvantage and that the ominous gap between the wealthy North and the poor South was widening.

Third World countries found only limited support from politicians and voters in the North, which was wracked by a deep recession caused in part by an explosion in oil prices. Yet the South did find some sympathy in the North, especially among journalists, professors, and moderate west European socialists.

An outstanding example of such support came from the Brandt Commission, an independent, self-appointed international study group chaired by Willy Brandt, the former chancellor of West Germany, a moderate socialist and a renowned world leader. Brandt's blue-ribbon commission presented its findings and proposals in 1980 as North-South Relations: A Program for Survival. *The following selection is taken from this influential and widely publicized call to action.*

The crisis through which international relations and the world economy are now passing presents great dangers, and they appear to be growing more serious. We believe that the gap which separates rich and poor countries—a gap so wide that at the extremes people seem to live in different worlds—has not been sufficiently recognized as a major factor in this crisis. It is a great contradiction of our age that these disparities exist—and are in some respects widening—just when human society is beginning to have a clearer perception of how it is interrelated and of how North and South depend on each other in a single world economy. . . .

The nations of the South see themselves as sharing a common predicament. Their solidarity in global negotiations stems from the awareness of being dependent on the North, and unequal to it; and a great many of them are bound together by their common colonial experience. The North including Eastern Europe has a quarter of the world's population and four-fifths of its income; the South including China has three billion people—three-quarters of the world's population but living on one-fifth of the world's income. . . .

Behind these differences lies the fundamental inequality of economic strength. . . . Because of this economic power northern countries dominate the international economic system—its rules and regulations, and international institutions of trade, money and finance. Some developing nations have swum against this tide . . . but most of them find the currents too strong for them. In the world as in nations, economic forces left entirely to themselves tend to produce growing inequality. Within nations public policy has to protect the weaker partners. The time has come to apply this precept to relations between nations within the world community. . . .

The North-South debate is often described as if the rich were being asked to make sacrifices in response to the demands of the poor. We reject this view. The world is now a fragile and interlocking system, whether for its people, its ecology or its resources. Many individual societies have settled their inner conflicts by accommodation, to protect the weak and to promote principles of justice, becoming stronger as a result. The world too can become stronger by becoming a just and humane society. If it fails in this, it will move towards its own destruction. . . .

[In conclusion] mankind already faces basic problems which cannot be solved purely at the national or even regional levels, such as security, protection of the environment, energy, and the control of space and ocean resources. The international community has begun to tackle these problems, though inadequately.

At the beginning of the 1980s the world community faces much greater dangers than at any time since the Second World War. It is clear that the world economy is now functioning so badly that it damages both the immediate and the longer-run interests of all nations. . . . A new international order will take time to achieve. . . . But the present world crisis is so acute that we also feel compelled to draw up an emergency program . . . [and lay out the] tasks for the 80s and 90s. . . .

Priority must be given to the needs of the poorest countries and regions. We call for a major initiative in favor of the poverty belts of Africa and Asia. We recognize that the removal of poverty requires both substantial resource transfers from the developed countries and an increased determination of the developing countries to improve economic management and deal with social and economic inequalities.

The world must aim to abolish hunger and malnutrition by the end of the century through the elimination of absolute poverty. Greater food production, intensified agricultural development, and measures for international food security are essential. These too require both major additional external assistance and revised priorities in many developing countries. . . .

The North should reverse the present trend towards protecting its industries against competition from the Third World. . . .

The objectives we have defined . . . will call for a transfer of funds [from North to South] on a very considerable scale . . . [and] will require sums equal to more than a doubling of the current $20 billion of annual official development assistance, together with substantial additional lending on market terms. . . . The large-scale transfer of resources we call for should be organized in partnership between developed and developing countries. . . .

The global agreement we envisage, with the understanding that must lie behind it, will call for a joint effort of political will and a high degree of trust between the partners, with a common conviction in their mutual interest. . . . [And indeed] whatever their differences and however profound, there is a mutuality of in-

Earth Summit in Rio de Janeiro, 1992
(Source: Claus Meyer/Black Star)

terest between North and South. The fate of both is intimately connected. The search for solutions is not an act of benevolence but a condition of mutual survival. We believe it is dramatically urgent today to start taking concrete steps, without which the world situation can only deteriorate still further, even leading to conflict and catastrophe.

Questions for Analysis

1. Why do the nations of the South "see themselves sharing a common predicament"?

2. Why, according to the Brandt Commission, should the North aid the South?

3. What does the Brandt Commission propose. What are the most urgent priorities?

4. "Resolved: the North must help the South to avoid conflict and global catastrophe." What are the arguments for and against this proposition? Take sides, and debate this proposition.

5. Do you think the members of this commission would support steps toward world government? Why or why not?

Source: Independent Commission on International Development Issues [Brandt Commission], *North-South Relations: A Program for Survival* (Cambridge, Mass.: MIT Press, 1980), pp. 30–33, 267, 270–273, 280–282.

A History of World Societies: A Brief Overview

Period (CA 10,000–CA 400 B.C.)	Africa and the Middle East	The Americas
10,000 B.C.	New Stone Age culture, ca 10,000–3500	Migration into Americas begins, ca 11,000
5000 B.C.	"Agricultural revolution" originates in Tigris-Euphrates and Nile River Valleys, ca 6000 First writing in Sumeria; Sumerian city-states emerge, ca 3500 Egypt unified under Narmer, 3100–2660 Metalworking in Caucasus, 3000	Maize domesticated in Mexico, ca 5000
2500 B.C.	Old Kingdom in Egypt; construction of the pyramids, 2660–2180 Akkadian Empire, 2370–2150 Middle Kingdom in Egypt, 2080–1640 Hyksos "invade" Egypt, 1640–1570 Hammurabi, 1792–1750 Hebrew monotheism, ca 1700	First pottery in Americas, Ecuador, ca 3000 First metalworking in Peru, ca 2000
1500 B.C.	Hittite Empire, ca 1450–1200 Akhenaten institutes worship of Aton, ca 1360 New Kingdom in Egypt; creation of Egyptian Empire, ca 1570–1075 Moses leads Hebrews out of Egypt, ca 1300–1200	Olmec civilization, Mexico, ca 1500 B.C.–A.D. 300
1000 B.C.	Political fragmentation of Egypt; rise of small kingdoms, ca 1100–700 United Hebrew kingdom, 1020–922: Saul, David, Solomon Ironworking spreads throughout Africa, ca 1000 B.C.–A.D. 300 Divided Hebrew kingdom: Israel (922–721), Judah (922–586) Assyrian Empire, 745–612 Zoroaster, ca 600	Olmec center at San Lorenzo destroyed, ca 900; power passes to La Venta in Tabasco Chavin civilization in Andes, ca 1000–200 B.C.
500 B.C.	Babylonian captivity of the Hebrews, 586–539 Cyrus the Great founds Persian Empire, 550 Persians conquer Egypt, 525 Darius and Xerxes complete Persian conquest of Middle East, 521–464	Olmec civilization, ca 1500 B.C.–A.D. 300 Fall of La Venta; Tres Zapotes becomes leading Olmec site
400 B.C.	Spartan Hegemony in Greece 399–371 B.C. Theban Hegemony in Greece 371–362 B.C. Philip of Macedon's Conquest of Greece, 338 B.C.	

East Asia	India and Southeast Asia	Europe
"Agricultural revolution" originates in Yellow River Valley, ca 4000		
Horse domesticated in China, ca 2500	Indus River Valley civilization, ca 2500–1500; capitals at Mohenjo-daro and Harappa	Greek Bronze Age, 2000–1100 Arrival of Greeks in peninsular Greece
Shang Dynasty, first writing in China, ca 1523–ca 1027	Aryans arrive in India; Early Vedic Age, ca 1500–1000 Vedas, oldest Hindu sacred texts	Height of Minoan culture, 1700–1450 Mycenaeans conquer Minoan Crete, ca 1450 Mycenaean Age, 1450–1200
Zhou Dynasty, promulgation of the Mandate of Heaven, ca 1027–221	Later Vedic Age; solidification of caste system, ca 1000–500 Upanishads; foundation of Hinduism, 800–600	Trojan War, ca 1180 Fall of the Mycenaean kingdom, 1100 Greek Dark Age, ca 1100–800 Roman Republic founded, 509 Origin of Greek polis, ca 700 Greek Lyric Age; rise of Sparta and Athens, 800–500
Confucius, 551–479 First written reference to iron, ca 521	Siddhartha Gautama (Buddha), 563–483	Persian Wars, 499–479 Growth of Athenian Empire; flowering of Greek drama, philosophy, and history, 5th century Peloponnesian War, 431–404 Plato, 426–347

Period (CA 300 B.C.–AD 500)	Africa and the Middle East	The Americas
300 B.C.	Alexander the Great extends empire, 334–331 Death of Alexander (323): Ptolemy conquers Egypt, Seleucus rules Asia	
200 B.C.	Scipio Africanus defeats Hannibal at Zama, 202	
100 B.C.	Dead Sea Scrolls Pompey conquers Syria and Palestine, 63	
A.D 100	Jesus Christ, ca 4 B.C.–A.D. 30 Paul, d. ca 65 Bantu migrations begin Jews revolt from Rome, Romans destroy Hebrew temple in Jerusalem: end of the ancient Hebrew state, 70	
A.D 200	Camel first used for trans-Saharan transport, ca 200 Expansion of Bantu peoples, ca 200–900 Axum (Ethiopia) controls Red Sea trade, ca 250	Classic Age of the Maya, ca 300–900 Olmec civilization, ca 1500 B.C.–A.D. 300
A.D 300	Axum accepts Christianity, ca 4th century	Maya civilization in Central America, ca 300–1500 Classic period of Teotihuacán civilization in Mexico, ca 300–900
A.D 500	Political and commercial ascendancy of Axum, ca 6th–7th centuries Muhammad, 570–632; the *hijra,* 622 Extensive slave trade from sub-Saharan Africa to Mediterranean, ca 600–1500 Umayyad Dynasty, 661–750, with capital at Damascus; continued expansion of Islam	Tiahuanaco civilization in South America, ca 600–1000

East Asia	India and Southeast Asia	Europe
Lao-tzu and development of Taoism, 4th century	Alexander invades India, 327–326	Peloponnesian War, 431–404
Han Fei-tzu and Li Ssu and development of Legalism, ca 250–208	Chandragupta founds Mauryan Dynasty, 322–ca 185	Plato, 426–347
	Ashoka, 273–232	Gauls sack Rome, ca 390
	King Arsaces of Parthia defeats Seleucid monarchy and begins conquest of Persia, ca 250–137	Roman expansion, 390–146
		Sparton Hegemony in Greece, 399–371 B.C.
		Theban Hegemony in Greece, 371–362 B.C.
		Philip of Macedon's Conquest of Greece, 338 B.C.
		Conquests of Alexander the Great, 334–323
		Punic Wars, destruction of Carthage, 264–146
Qin Dynasty and unification of China; construction of the Great Wall, destruction of Confucian literature, 221–210	Greeks invade India, ca 183–145	Late Roman Republic, 133–27
	Mithridates creates Parthian Empire, ca 171–131	
Han Dynasty, 202 B.C.–A.D. 220		
Chinese expansion to South China Sea and Vietnam, ca 111	First Chinese ambassadors to India and Parthia, ca 140	Formation of First Triumvirate (Caesar, Crassus, Pompey), 60
Silk Road opens to Parthian and Roman Empires; Buddhism enters China, ca 104	Bhagavad Gita, ca 100 B.C.–A.D. 100	Julius Caesar killed, 44
		Formation of Second Triumvirate, (Octavian, Antony, Lepidus), 43
		Octavian seizes power, 31
First written reference (Chinese) to Japan, A.D. 45	Shakas and Kushans invade eastern Parthia and India, 1st century A.D.	Octavian rules imperial Rome as Augustus, 27 B.C.–A.D. 14
Chinese invent paper, 105	Roman attacks on Parthian Empire, 115–211	Roman Empire at greatest extent, 117
Emperor Wu, 140–186		
Creation of Yamato state in Japan, ca 3d century	Kushan rule in northwestern India, A.D. 2d–3d centuries	Breakdown of the pax Romana, ca 180–284; civil wars, economic decline, invasions
Buddhism gains popularity in China and Japan, ca 220–590	Fall of the Parthian Empire, rise of the Sassanids, ca 225	Reforms by Diocletian, 284–305
Fall of Han Dynasty, 220		
Three Kingdoms era in China, 221–280		
Barbarian invasions, 4th–5th centuries	Chandragupta I founds Gupta Dynasty in India, ca 320–500	Reign of Constantine, 306–337; Edict of Milan, 313; founding of Constantinople, 324; Council of Nicaea, 325
	Chandragupta II conquers western India, establishes trade with Middle East and China, ca 400	Theodosius recognizes Christianity as official state religion, 380
	Huns invade India, ca 450	Germanic raids of western Europe, 5th century
		Clovis unites Franks and rules Gauls, 481–511
Sui Dynasty in China, 580–618; restoration of public order	Sanskrit drama, ca 600–1000	Saint Benedict publishes his *Rule,* 529
"Constitution" of Shotoku in Japan, 604	Muslim invasions of India, ca 636–1206	Law Code of Justinian, 529
Tang Dynasty, 618–907; cultural flowering		Synod of Whitby, 664

Period (CA 700–1500)	Africa and the Middle East	The Americas
700	Abbasid Dynasty, 750–1258; Islamic capital moved to Baghdad Decline of Ethiopia, ca 9th century Golden age of Muslim learning, ca 900–1100 Kingdom of Ghana, ca 900–1100 Mahmud of Ghazna, 998–1030	"Time of Troubles" in Mesoamerica, 800–1000
1000	Islam penetrates sub-Saharan Africa, ca 11th century Kingdom of Benin, ca 1100–1897 Kingdom of Mali, middle Niger region, ca 1200–1450 Mongol invasion of Middle East, ca 1220	Inca civilization in South America, ca 1000–1500 Toltec hegemony, ca 1000–1300 Aztecs arrive in Valley of Mexica, ca 1325
1200	Kingdom of Mali, ca 1200–1450 Mongols conquer Baghdad, 1258; fall of Abbasid Dynasty	Maya civilization in Central America, ca 300–1500 Inca civilization in South America, ca 1000–1500 Toltec hegemony, ca 1000–1300
1300	Rise of Yoruba states, West Africa, ca 1300 Height of Swahili (East African) city-states, ca 1300–1500 Mansa Musa rules Mali, 1312–1337	Tenochtitlán (Mexico City) founded by Aztecs, 1325
1400	Zara Yakob rules Ethiopia, 1434–1468 Arrival of Portugese in Benin, ca 1440 Songhay Empire, West Africa, ca 1450–1591 Atlantic slave trade, ca 1450–1850 Ottoman Empire, 1453–1918 Vasco da Gama arrives on East African coast, 1498	Height of Inca Empire, 1438–1493 Reign of Montezuma I, 1440–1468; height of Aztec culture Columbus reaches the Americas, 1492
1500	Portugal dominates East Africa, ca 1500–1650 Safavid Empire in Persia, 1501–1722 Peak of Ottoman power under Suleiman the Magnificent, 1520–1566 Height of Kanem-Bornu under Idris Alooma, 1571–1603 Portuguese found Angola, 1571 Battle of Lepanto, 1571, signals Ottoman naval weakness in the eastern Mediterranean Height of Safavid power under Shah Abbas, 1587–1629	South American holocaust, ca 1500–1600 First African slaves, ca 1510 Cortés arrives in Mexico, 1519; Aztec Empire falls, 1521 Pizarro reaches Peru, 1531; conquers Incas Spanish conquer the Philippines, 1571

East Asia	India and Southeast Asia	Europe
Taika Reform Edict in Japan, 655 Nara era, creation of Japan's first capital, 710–784 Heian era in Japan, 794–1185; literary flowering Era of the Five Dynasties in China, 907–960; warfare, revolt Song Dynasty, 960–1279	Khmer Empire (Kampuchea) founded, 802	Charles Martel defeats Muslims at Tours, 733 Charles the Great (Charlemagne), 768–814 Invasions of Carolingian Empire, 9th–10th centuries Treaty of Verdun divides Carolingian Empire, 843 Cluny monastery founded, 910
Vietnam gains independence from China, ca 1000 China divided between empires of Song (south) and Jin (north), 1127 Kamakura Shogunate, 1185–1333 Mongol conquest of China, 1215–1368	Construction of Angkor Wat, ca 1100–1150 Muslim conquerors end Buddhism in India, 1192 Peak of Khmer Empire in southeast Asia, ca 1200 Turkish sultanate at Delhi, 1206–1526; Indian culture divided into Hindu and Muslim	Yaroslav the Wise, 1019–1054; peak of Kievan Russia Schism between Latin and Greek churches, 1054 Norman Conquest of England, 1066 Investiture struggle, 1073–1122 The Crusades, 1096–1270 Growth of trade and towns, 12th–13th centuries Frederick Barbarossa invades Italy, 1154–1158
Kamakura Shogunate, 1185–1333 Unsuccessful Mongol invasions of Japan, 1274, 1281 Yuan (Mongol) Dynasty, 1279–1368	Peak of Khmer Empire in southeast Asia, ca 1200 Turkish sultanate at Delhi, 1206–1526; Indian culture divided into Hindu and Muslim	Magna Carta, 1215 Thomas Aquinas, *Summa Theologica*, 1253 Prince Alexander Nevsky recognizes Mongol overlordship of Moscow, 1252
Marco Polo arrives at Kublai Khan's court, ca 1275 Ashikaga Shogunate, 1336–1408 Hung Wu drives Mongols from China, 1368; founds Ming Dynasty, 1368–1644	Mongol chieftain Timur the Lame (Tamerlame) conquers the Punjab, 1398	Babylonian Captivity of the papacy, 1309–1376 Tver revolt in Russia, 1327–1328 Hundred Years' War, 1337–1453 Bubonic plague, 1347–1700 Ottoman Turks invade Europe, 1356 Peasants' Revolt in England, 1381
Early Ming policy encourages foreign trade, ca 15th century Ming maritime expeditions to India, Middle East, Africa, 1405–1433	Sultan Mehmed II, 1451–1481 Pasha Sinon, Ottoman architect, 1491–1588 Vasco da Gama reaches India, 1498	Beginnings of representative government, ca 1350–1500 Italian Renaissance, ca 1400–1530 Voyages of discovery, ca 1450–1600 Ottomans capture Constantinople, 1453; end of Byzantine Empire War of the Roses in England, 1455–1485 Unification of Spain completed, 1492
Portuguese trade monopoly in East Asia, ca 16th century Christian missionaries active in China and Japan, ca 1550–1650 Unification of Japan, 1568–1600	Barbur defeats Delhi sultanate, 1526–1527; founds Mughal Empire Akbar expands Mughal Empire, 1556–1605	Martin Luther, Ninety-five Theses, 1517 Charles V elected Holy Roman emperor, 1519 Henry VIII leads English Reformation, 1534 Council of Trent, 1545–1563 Dutch United Provinces declare independence, 1581 Spanish Armada, 1588

Period (CA 1600–1900)	Africa and the Middle East	The Americas
1600	Dutch West India Co. supplants Portuguese in West Africa, ca 1630 Dutch settle Cape Town, 1651 Rise of Ashanti Empire, founded on Gold Coast trade, ca 1700–1750	British settle Jamestown, 1607 Champlain founds Quebec, 1608 Dutch found New Amsterdam, 1624 Black labor allows tenfold increase in production of Carolinian rice and Virginian tobacco, ca 1730–1760 Silver production quadruples in Mexico and Peru, ca 1700–1800
1700	Approximately 11 million slaves shipped from Africa, ca 1450–1850 Dutch found Cape Colony, 1657 Rise of the Ashanti, West Africa, ca 1700 Decline of the Safavid Empire under Nadir Shah, 1737–1747	Spain's defeat in War of the Spanish Succession, 1701–1714, prompts trade reform, leading to colonial dependence on Spanish goods, 18th century
1750	Sultan Selim III introduces administrative and military reforms, 1761–1808 British seize Cape Town, 1795 Napoleon's campaign in Egypt, 1798	"French and Indian Wars," 1756–1763 Quebec Act, 1774 American Revolution, 1775–1783 Comunero revolution, New Granada, 1781
1800	Muhammad Ali founds dynasty in Egypt, 1805–1848 Slavery abolished in British Empire, 1807 Peak year of African transatlantic slave trade, 1820	Latin American wars of independence from Spain, 1806–1825 Brazil wins independence from Portugal, 1822 Monroe Doctrine, 1823 Political instability in most Latin American countries, 1825–1870 Mexican War, 1846–1848
1850	Crimean War, 1853–1856 Suez Canal opens, 1869 Europeans intensify "scramble for Africa," 1880–1900 Battle of Omdurman, 1898 Boer War, 1899–1902	American Civil War, 1861–1865 British North America Act, 1867, for Canada Porfirio Diaz controls Mexico, 1876–1911 United States practices "dollar diplomacy" in Latin America, 1890–1920s Spanish-American War, 1898; United States gains Philippines
1900	Union of South Africa formed, 1910 French annex Morocco, 1912 Ottoman Empire enters World War One on Germany's side Treaty of Sèvres dissolves Ottoman Empire, 1919; Mustafa Kemal mounts nationalist struggle in Turkey	Massive immigration from Europe and Asia to the Americas, 1880–1914 Mexican Revolution, 1910 Panama Canal opens, 1914 United States enters World War One, 1917 Mexico adopts constitution, 1917

East Asia	India and Southeast Asia	Europe
Tokugawa Shogunate, 1600–1867 Japan expels all Europeans, 1637 Manchus establish Qing Dynasty, 1644 Height of Qing Dynasty under K'ang-hsi, 1662–1722 Height of Edo urban culture in Japan, ca 1700	Height of Mughal Empire under Shah Jahan, 1628–1658 British found Calcutta, 1690 Decline of Mughal Empire, ca 1700–1800 Persian invaders sack Delhi, 1739	Romanov Dynasty in Russia, 1613 Thirty Years' War, 1618–1648 Brandenburg-Prussia unified, 1640–1688 English Civil War, 1642–1646 Louis XIV, king of France, 1643–1715 Ottoman Turks besiege Vienna, 1683 Revocation of Edict of Nantes, 1685 The Glorious Revolution in England, 1688 War of Spanish Succession, 1701–1713 Treaty of Utrecht, 1713
Tokugawa regime in Japan, characterized by political stability and economic growth, 1600–1867 Manchus establish Qing Dynasty, 1644–1911 Height of Qing Dynasty under Emperor Ch'ien-lung, 1736–1799	Mughal power contested by Hindus and Muslims, 18th century Persian invaders defeat Mughal army, loot Delhi, 1739 French and British fight for control of India, 1740–1763	Growth of absolutism in central and eastern Europe, ca 1680–1790 The Enlightenment, ca 1680–1800 Development of Cabinet system in England, 1714–1742 Height of land enclosure in England, ca 1760–1810
Maximum extent of Qing Empire, 1759	Battle of Plassey, 1757 Treaty of Paris, 1763; French colonies to Britain Cook in Australia, 1768–1771; first British prisoners to Australia, 1788 East India Act, 1784	Englishman James Watt produces first steam engine, 1769 Louis XVI of France, 1774–1792 Outbreak of French Revolution, 1789 National Convention declares France a republic, 1792
Java War, 1825–1830 Anglo-Chinese Opium War, 1839–1842 Treaty of Nanjing, 1842: Manchus surrender Hong Kong to British	British found Singapore, 1819 British defeat last independent native state in India, 1848	Napoleonic Empire, 1804–1814 Congress of Vienna, 1814–1815 European economic penetration of non-Western countries, ca 1816–1880 Greece wins independence from Ottoman Empire, 1829 Revolutions in France, Prussia, Italy, and Austria, 1848–1849
Taiping Rebellion, 1850–1864 Perry's arrival opens Japan to United States and Europe, 1853 Meiji Restoration in Japan, 1867 Adoption of constitution in Japan, 1890 Sino-Japanese War, 1894–1895 "Hundred Days of Reform" in China, 1898	Great Rebellion in India, 1857–1858 French seize Saigon, 1859 Indian National Congress formed, 1885 French acquire Indochina, 1893	Second Empire and Third Republic in France, 1852–1914 Unification of Italy, 1859–1870 Otto von Bismarck's reign of power in German affairs, 1862–1890 Franco-Prussian War, 1870–1871; foundation of the German Empire Parliamentary Reform Bill, Great Britain, 1867 Second Socialist International, 1889–1914
Boxer Rebellion in China, 1900–1903 Russo-Japanese War, 1904–1905 Chinese Revolution; fall of Qing Dynasty, 1911 Chinese Republic, 1912–1949	Commonwealth of Australia, 1900 Muslim League formed, 1906 Radicals make first calls for Indian independence, 1907 Amritsar massacre in India, 1919 Intensification of Indian nationalism, 1919–1947	Revolution in Russia; Tsar Nicholas II forced to issue October Manifesto, 1905 Triple Entente (Britain, Russia, France), 1914–1918 World War One, 1914–1918 Treaty of Versailles, 1919

Period (CA 1920–1990)	Africa and the Middle East	The Americas
1920	Cultural nationalism in Africa, 1920s Treaty of Lausanne recognizes Turkish Republic, 1923 Reza Shah leads Iran, 1925–1941	U.S. "consumer revolution," 1920s Stock market crash in United States; Great Depression begins, 1929
1930	African farmers organize first "cocoa holdups," 1930–1931 Iraq gains independence, 1932 Syrian-French friendship treaty, 1936	Revolutions in six South American countries, 1930 New Deal begins in United States, 1933
1940	Civil war between Arabs and Jews in Palestine; state of Israel is created, 1948 Apartheid system in South Africa, 1948–1991 Libya gains independence, 1949	Surprise attack by Japan on Pearl Harbor, 1941 United Nations established, 1945 Perón regime in Argentina, 1946–1953
1950	Egypt declared a republic; Nasser named premier, 1954 Morocco, Tunisia, Sudan, and Ghana gain independence, 1956–1957 French-British Suez invasion, 1956	Fidel Castro takes power in Cuba, 1959
1960	Mali, Nigeria, and the Congo gain independence, 1960 Biafra declares independence from Nigeria, 1967 Arab-Israeli Six-Day War, 1967	Cuban missile crisis, 1962 Military dictatorship in Brazil, 1964–1985 United States escalates war in Vietnam, 1964
1970	"Yom Kippur War," 1973 Islamic revolution in Iran, 1979 Camp David Accords, 1979	Military coup in Chile, 1973 U.S. Watergate scandal, 1974 Revolutions in Nicaragua and El Salvador, 1979
1980	Iran-Iraq War, 1980–1988 Reforms in South Africa, 1989 to present	U.S. military buildup, 1980–1988 Argentina restores civilian rule, 1983
1990	Growth of Islamic fundamentalism, 1990 to present Iraq driven from Kuwait by United States and allies, 1991 Israel and Palestinians sign peace agreement, 1993 Nelson Mandela elected president of South Africa, 1994	Canada, Mexico, and United States form free-trade area (NAFTA), 1994 Haiti establishes democratic government, 1994 Permanent extension of Treaty on the Non-Proliferation of Nuclear Weapons, 1995

East Asia	India and Southeast Asia	Europe
Kita Ikki advocates ultranationalism in Japan, 1923 Jiang Jieshi unites China, 1928	Mohandas "Mahatma" Gandhi launches nonviolent resistance campaign, 1920	Mussolini seizes power in Italy, 1922 Stalin takes power in U.S.S.R., 1927 Depths of Great Depression, 1929–1933
Japan invades China, 1931 Mao Zedong's Long March, 1934 Sino-Japanese War, 1937–1945	Mahatma Gandhi's Salt March, 1930 Japanese conquer empire in southeast Asia, 1939–1942	Hitler gains dictatorial power, 1933 Civil War in Spain, 1936–1939 Germany invades Poland, 1939 World War Two, 1939–1945
United States drops atomic bombs on Hiroshima and Nagasaki, 1945 Chinese civil war, 1945–1949; Communists win	Philippines gain independence, 1946 India (Hindu) and Pakistan (Muslim) gain independence, 1947	Yalta Conference, 1945 Marshall Plan, 1947 NATO alliance, 1949 Soviet Union and Red China sign 30-year alliance treaty, 1949
Korean War, 1950–1953 Japan begins long period of rapid economic growth, 1950 Mao Zedong announces Great Leap Forward, 1958	Vietnamese nationalists defeat French; Vietnam divided, 1954 Islamic Republic of Pakistan declared, 1956	Death of Stalin, 1953 Warsaw Pact, 1955 Revolution in Hungary, 1956 Creation of the Common Market, 1957
Sino-Soviet split becomes apparent, 1960 Great Proletarian Cultural Revolution in China, 1965–1969	Indira Gandhi prime minister of India, 1966–1977, 1980–1984	Student revolution in France, 1968 Soviet invasion of Czechoslovakia, 1968
Communist victory in Vietnam War, 1975 China pursues modernization, 1976 to present	India-Pakistan war, 1971 Chinese invade Vietnam, 1979	German Chancellor Willy Brandt's Ostpolitik, 1969–1973 Soviet invasion of Afghanistan, 1979
Japanese foreign investment surge, 1980–1992 China crushes democracy movement, 1989	Sikh nationalism in India, 1984 to present Corazón Aquino takes power in Philippines, 1986	Soviet reform under Mikhail Gorbachev, 1985–1991 Anticommunist revolutions sweep eastern Europe, 1989
Birthrates keep falling Economic growth and political repression in China, 1990 to present Japan and United States reach auto agreement, 1995	Vietnam embraces foreign investment, 1990 to present U.S. military bases closed in Philippines, 1991	Continued high unemployment, 1990 to present Soviet Union ceases to exist, 1991 Civil war in Bosnia, 1991 to present

Index

Muslim world, 1148–1153; Israel and, 1149–1153

Mussolini, Benito, 1049, 1056, 1067 (illus.); seizure of power by, 1065–1066; and fascism in Italy, 1065–1067; as Nazi ally, 1075–1076; deposed by Allies, 1083

Mustafa, Kara (Ottoman Empire), 686

al-Mustakfi, 262

Mutapa region, gold in, 303

Mycenae, Greece, 117, 120

Myoshu, 338

My Secret Life, prostitution and, 858–859

Mysore, India, 700

Mystery religions, 1227; in Greece, 138; in Hellenistic Greece, 159, 160–161; Christianity and, 196–197, 209; Jesus and, 215

Mystics and mysticism: Sufism and, 276; Hildegard of Bingen, 416 (illus.); searching for, 1227–1228

Mythology: celestial globe in, 165 (illus.); Indian, 318. *See also* Gods and goddesses; Greece, ancient; Religion(s)

Myths, Mesopotamian, 17

N

NAACP, *see* National Association for the Advancement of Colored People

Nabataean Petra (Arabia), as caravan state, 157

Nadir Shah, invasion of India by, 698

NAFTA, *see* North American Free Trade Agreement

Nagasaki, 531, 1210; Nobunaga and, 725; Dutch in, 727–728; atomic bombing of, 1084 and *illus.*

Nahon, Marco, 1088–1089

Nahuatl language, of Aztecs, 449, 453 (illus.)

Nahum (prophet), 51

Naima, Mustafa, 682

Naipaul, V. S., 1195–1196

Nairobi, Kenya, 1184

Nalanda, university at, 320

Namib Desert, 285

Nammu (goddess), 17

Nanjing (Nanking), China, 1014; reforestation in, 708; as capital, 709; commerce in, 709; Treaty of, 886; Japanese conquest of, 1019 (illus.)

Naples: kingdom of, 468, 469; Holy Roman Empire claims on, 486; Austrian intervention in, 808

Napoleon I, 759–765; French economy and, 760; Roman Catholic Church and, 760; government by, 760–761; defeat at Trafalgar, 761; crossing

Alps, 761 (illus.); wars and foreign policy of, 761–765; Grand Empire of, 762 (map); as Emperor, 763; German Confederation of, 763; invasion of Russia by, 763; war of liberation against, 763–764; revolts against, 763–765; granted Elba after defeat, 764; defeat at Waterloo, 765; Hundred Days of, 765; abdication of, 805; Egyptian invasion by, 888; Spanish throne and, 921; Portuguese Empire and, 922; Louisiana Purchase and, 929. *See also* Louis Napoleon

Napoleonic Code, 760; women's roles and, 859

Napoleonic Era, 765; Congress of Vienna after, 805. *See also* Napoleon I

Napoleon III, *see* Louis Napoleon

Nara, Japan, 336

Naramsin (god), 17 (illus.)

Nariño, Antonio, 918

Narmer (pharaoh), 26 (illus.)

Nasser, Gamal Abdel, 1151, 1161

National Assembly (France), 426, 747–748; Declaration of the Rights of Man and, 750; abolition of nobility by, 751; national reorganization by, 751–752; in Prussia, 828; Louis Napoleon and, 829; Paris Commune and, 868

National Association for the Advancement of Colored People (NAACP), 1117

National Congress, in India, 1009

National Convention (France), 754; war declaration by, 754; Directory and, 759

National debts, 1107

Nationalism, 811–812; and Hundred Years' War, 426–427; in language and literature, 432; economic, 790–791; democratic, 840–841; in Europe, 843, 871 (illus.); organization of society during period of, 843–857; national state and, 866–874; in Asia, 904, 992, 993; in India, 905, 1006–1012; in Latin America, 915–927; in United States, 927–945; in Canada, 945–946; in Australia, 948–954; in Balkans, 964–967; First World War and, 969; in Africa, 994; in Ottoman Empire, 996–999; Turkish, 997; in Middle East, 997–999; Turkish revolution and, 999–1002; in Afghanistan, 1002–1003; in Iran, 1002–1003; in China, 1012–1014; in Japan, 1016–1018; in Southeast Asia, 1019–1021; in Philippines, 1021; German, 1068; of Hitler, 1074; of Soviet citizens, 1111; economic, in Latin America, 1123–1124; in South Asia, 1140–1148; in Arab world,

1152–1153; in black Africa, 1153–1160; cultural, 1156; African, 1156–1160; in West Africa, 1163 (map); in Third World, 1173. *See also* National state; Nations

Nationalist China, 1012–1014, 1019, 1133

National Labor Relations Act, 1048

National Liberal party, in Germany, 866, 867

National liberation: wars of, 743; in Greece, 819–820

National Liberation Front (FLN), 1153

National Recovery Administration (NRA), 1048

National self-determination, 984

National Socialism: Hitler and, 1042, 1068; youth movement of, 1070

National state, 866–874; loyalty to, 866–867

National unification, in Japan, 725

National unity, in Africa, 1161–1162

National workshops, in Paris, 824

Nations: France as, 828–830; in Europe (1850–1871), 835

Nation-states, and United Nations, 1201–1205

Native Americans: Columbus and, 522; South American slaughter by Europeans, 524–526; gold and, 525 (illus.); as slave labor, 545; in Latin America, 918–919; as Latin American labor, 919; revolt by, 925; American expansion and, 929; fate of, 931–932; cession of lands to U.S., 934 (map); race in U.S. and, 941; in Canada, 945; Mexican, 1123. *See also* Amerindians

Native Land Act (South Africa), 1165

Nativism, in U.S., 944

NATO, *see* North Atlantic Treaty Organization

Natural laws, 178

Natural resources, *see* Resources

Natural science, botany and, 165. *See also* Science

Natural selection, 864

Naval agreement, Anglo-German, 1075

Naval arms limitation treaty (1922), 1017

Naval battles, over Mediterranean, 682. *See also* Battles; battles by name

Navarino, Battle at, 820

Navarre, 484

Navarro, Sanchez, family of, 926

Navigation: developments in, 518–519; and scientific revolution, 600

Navigation act, of England, 584; British trade and, 775

Navy: Roman, 201; Turkish, 536 (illus.); Spanish vs. English, 537; German, 964, 964 (illus.)

80°N
GREENLAND
(DENMARK)

ICELAND

ALASKA
(U.S.)

60°N

CANADA

UNIT
KING
IRELAND

40°N

SPA

UNITED STATES

PORTUGAL

Azores

ATLANTIC OCEAN

MOROCC

Bermuda

Midway Is.

BAHAMAS

WESTERN
SAHARA
(MOROCCO)

Hawaiian Is.

MEXICO

CUBA
JAMAICA
BELIZE
HONDURAS

DOMINICAN REP.
Virgin Is.
HAITI
Puerto Rico

20°N

MAURITANIA

M

ST. CHRISTOPHER AND NEVIS
ANTIGUA AND BARBUDA
DOMINICA
BARBADOS

CAPE
VERDE

SENEGAL

BOU

GUATEMALA
EL SALVADOR

NICARAGUA

ST. LUCIA
GRENADA

ST. VINCENT AND
THE GRENADINES

GAMBIA

GUINEA

GUINEA-BISSAU

PACIFIC OCEAN

COSTA RICA

TRINIDAD AND TOBAGO

SIERRA
LEONE

IVORY
COAST

PANAMA

VENEZUELA

GUYANA

LIBERIA

GHAN
EQUATOR

COLOMBIA

FR. GUIANA

Equator

Galapagos Is.

ECUADOR

SURINAM

0°

SAO TOME AN

PERU

BRAZIL

WESTERN
SAMOA

BOLIVIA

TONGA

20°S

PARAGUAY

Easter Is.

CHILE

URUGUAY

ARGENTINA

40°S

160°W   140°W   120°W   100°W   80°W   60°W   40°W   20°W

Falkland Is.

60°S

80°S